THIS

HOLY BIBLE

IS PRESENTED TO

____

BY

____

____

ON

____

____

YOUR WORD IS A LAMP TO MY FEET
AND A LIGHT TO MY PATH.

PSALM 119:105

NEW KING JAMES VERSION

PERSONAL SIZE GIANT PRINT BIBLE

www.ThomasNelsonBibles.com

NKJV Personal Size Giant Print Bible

Published in Nashville, TN, by Thomas Nelson. Thomas Nelson is a registered trademark of HarperCollins Christian Publishing, Inc.

Library of Congress Control Number: 2024943746

Printed in India

25 26 27 28 29 30 31 32 33 / BPI / 14 13 12 11 10 9 8 7 6 5 4 3 2 1

CONTENTS

OLD TESTAMENT

NEW TESTAMENT

PREFACE

TO THE NEW KING JAMES VERSION®

To understand the heart behind the New King James Version, one need look no further than the stated intentions of the original King James scholars: "Not to make a new translation . . . but to make a good one better." The New King James Version is a continuation of the labors of the King James translators, unlocking for today's readers the spiritual treasures found especially in the Authorized Version of the Holy Bible.

While seeking to maintain the excellent *form* of the traditional English Bible, special care has also been taken to preserve the work of *precision* that is the legacy of the King James translators.

Where new translation has been necessary, the most complete representation of the original has been rendered by considering the definition and usage of the Hebrew, Aramaic, and Greek words in their contexts. This translation principle, known as *complete equivalence*, seeks to preserve accurately all of the information in the text while presenting it in good literary form.

In addition to accuracy, the translators have also sought to maintain those lyrical and devotional qualities that are so highly regarded in the King James Version. The thought flow and selection of phrases from the King James Version have been preserved wherever possible without sacrificing clarity.

The format of the New King James Version is designed to enhance the vividness, devotional quality, and usefulness of the Bible. Words or phrases in italics indicate expressions in the original language that require clarification by additional English words, as was done in the King James Version. Poetry is structured as verse to reflect the form and beauty of the passage in the original language. The covenant name of God was usually translated from the Hebrew as LORD or GOD, *using* capital letters as shown, as in the King James Version. This convention is also maintained in the New King James Version when the Old Testament is quoted in the New.

The Hebrew text used for the Old Testament is the 1967/1977 Stuttgart edition of the *Biblia Hebraica*, with frequent comparisons to the Bomberg edition of 1524–1525. Ancient versions and the Dead Sea Scrolls were consulted, but the Hebrew is followed wherever possible.

The Greek text used for the New Testament is the one that was followed by the King James translators: the traditional text of the Greek-speaking churches, called the Received Text or Textus Receptus, first published in 1516.

THE
OLD TESTAMENT

THE FIRST BOOK OF MOSES CALLED

GENESIS

THE HISTORY OF CREATION

1 In the beginning God created the heavens and the earth. 2 The earth was without form, and void; and darkness *was*[a] on the face of the deep. And the Spirit of God was hovering over the face of the waters.

3 Then God said, "Let there be light"; and there was light. 4 And God saw the light, that *it was* good; and God divided the light from the darkness. 5 God called the light Day, and the darkness He called Night. So the evening and the morning were the first day.

6 Then God said, "Let there be a firmament in the midst of the waters, and let it divide the waters from the waters." 7 Thus God made the firmament, and divided the waters which *were* under the firmament from the waters which *were* above the firmament; and it was so. 8 And God called the firmament Heaven. So the evening and the morning were the second day.

9 Then God said, "Let the waters under the heavens be gathered together into one place, and let the dry *land* appear"; and it was so. 10 And God called the dry *land* Earth, and the gathering together of the waters He called Seas. And God saw that *it was* good.

11 Then God said, "Let the earth bring forth grass, the herb *that* yields seed, *and* the fruit tree *that* yields fruit according to its kind, whose seed *is* in itself, on the earth"; and it was so. 12 And the earth brought forth grass, the herb *that* yields seed according to its kind, and the tree *that* yields fruit, whose seed *is* in itself according to its kind. And God saw that *it was* good. 13 So the evening and the morning were the third day.

14 Then God said, "Let there be lights in the firmament of the heavens to divide the day from the night; and let them be for signs and seasons, and for days and years; 15 and let them be for lights in the firmament of the heavens to give light on the earth"; and it was so. 16 Then God made two great lights: the greater light to rule the day, and the lesser light to rule the night. *He made* the stars also. 17 God set them in the firmament of the

1:2 [a] Words in italic type have been added for clarity. They are not found in the original Hebrew or Aramaic.

heavens to give light on the
earth, 18and to rule over the
day and over the night, and to
divide the light from the darkness. And God saw that *it was*
good. 19So the evening and the
morning were the fourth day.

20Then God said, "Let the
waters abound with an abundance of living creatures, and
let birds fly above the earth
across the face of the firmament of the heavens." 21So
God created great sea creatures and every living thing
that moves, with which the
waters abounded, accord-
ing to their kind, and every
winged bird according to its
kind. And God saw that *it
was* good. 22And God blessed
them, saying, "Be fruitful and
multiply, and fill the waters in
the seas, and let birds multiply
on the earth." 23So the evening and the morning were
the fifth day.

24Then God said, "Let the
earth bring forth the living
creature according to its kind:
cattle and creeping thing
and beast of the earth, *each*
according to its kind"; and it
was so. 25And God made the
beast of the earth according
to its kind, cattle according to
its kind, and everything that
creeps on the earth according
to its kind. And God saw that
it was good.

26Then God said, "Let Us
make man in Our image, according to Our likeness; let
them have dominion over
the fish of the sea, over the
birds of the air, and over the
cattle, over all[a] the earth and
over every creeping thing
that creeps on the earth." 27So
God created man in His *own*
image; in the image of God He
created him; male and female
He created them. 28Then God
blessed them, and God said to
them, "Be fruitful and multiply; fill the earth and subdue
it; have dominion over the fish
of the sea, over the birds of the
air, and over every living thing
that moves on the earth."

29And God said, "See, I
have given you every herb
that yields seed which *is* on
the face of all the earth, and
every tree whose fruit yields
seed; to you it shall be for
food. 30Also, to every beast
of the earth, to every bird of
the air, and to everything that
creeps on the earth, in which
there is life, *I have given* every
green herb for food"; and it
was so. 31Then God saw everything that He had made, and
indeed *it was* very good. So
the evening and the morning
were the sixth day.

2 Thus the heavens and the
earth, and all the host of
them, were finished. 2And on
the seventh day God ended
His work which He had done,
and He rested on the seventh
day from all His work which

1:26 [a] Syriac reads *all the wild animals of.*

He had done. 3 Then God blessed the seventh day and sanctified it, because in it He rested from all His work which God had created and made.

4 This *is* the history[a] of the heavens and the earth when they were created, in the day that the LORD God made the earth and the heavens, 5 before any plant of the field was in the earth and before any herb of the field had grown. For the LORD God had not caused it to rain on the earth, and *there was* no man to till the ground; 6 but a mist went up from the earth and watered the whole face of the ground.

7 And the LORD God formed man *of* the dust of the ground, and breathed into his nostrils the breath of life; and man became a living being.

LIFE IN GOD'S GARDEN

8 The LORD God planted a garden eastward in Eden, and there He put the man whom He had formed. 9 And out of the ground the LORD God made every tree grow that is pleasant to the sight and good for food. The tree of life *was* also in the midst of the garden, and the tree of the knowledge of good and evil.

10 Now a river went out of Eden to water the garden, and from there it parted and became four riverheads. 11 The name of the first *is* Pishon; it *is* the one which skirts the whole land of Havilah, where *there is* gold. 12 And the gold of that land *is* good. Bdellium and the onyx stone *are* there. 13 The name of the second river *is* Gihon; it *is* the one which goes around the whole land of Cush. 14 The name of the third river *is* Hiddekel;[a] it *is* the one which goes toward the east of Assyria. The fourth river *is* the Euphrates.

15 Then the LORD God took the man and put him in the garden of Eden to tend and keep it. 16 And the LORD God commanded the man, saying, "Of every tree of the garden you may freely eat; 17 but of the tree of the knowledge of good and evil you shall not eat, for in the day that you eat of it you shall surely die."

18 And the LORD God said, "*It is* not good that man should be alone; I will make him a helper comparable to him." 19 Out of the ground the LORD God formed every beast of the field and every bird of the air, and brought *them* to Adam to see what he would call them. And whatever Adam called each living creature, that *was* its name. 20 So Adam gave names to all cattle, to the birds of the air, and to every beast of the field. But for Adam there was not found a helper comparable to him.

2:4 [a] Hebrew *toledoth,* literally *generations*   2:14 [a] Or *Tigris*

21 And the LORD God caused
a deep sleep to fall on Adam,
and he slept; and He took one
of his ribs, and closed up the
flesh in its place. 22 Then the
rib which the LORD God had
taken from man He made into
a woman, and He brought her
to the man.
23 And Adam said:

"This *is* now bone
of my bones
And flesh of my flesh;
She shall be called
Woman,
Because she was taken
out of Man."

24 Therefore a man shall leave
his father and mother and be
joined to his wife, and they
shall become one flesh.
25 And they were both
naked, the man and his wife,
and were not ashamed.

THE TEMPTATION AND FALL OF MAN

3 Now the serpent was more
cunning than any beast of
the field which the LORD God
had made. And he said to the
woman, "Has God indeed said,
'You shall not eat of every tree
of the garden'?"
2 And the woman said to the
serpent, "We may eat the fruit
of the trees of the garden; 3 but
of the fruit of the tree which
is in the midst of the garden,
God has said, 'You shall not
eat it, nor shall you touch it,
lest you die.'"
4 Then the serpent said
to the woman, "You will not
surely die. 5 For God knows
that in the day you eat of it
your eyes will be opened, and
you will be like God, knowing
good and evil."
6 So when the woman saw
that the tree *was* good for
food, that it *was* pleasant to
the eyes, and a tree desirable
to make *one* wise, she took
of its fruit and ate. She also
gave to her husband with her,
and he ate. 7 Then the eyes of
both of them were opened,
and they knew that they
were naked; and they sewed
fig leaves together and made
themselves coverings.
8 And they heard the sound
of the LORD God walking in
the garden in the cool of the
day, and Adam and his wife
hid themselves from the presence of the LORD God among
the trees of the garden.
9 Then the LORD God called
to Adam and said to him,
"Where *are* you?"
10 So he said, "I heard Your
voice in the garden, and I was
afraid because I was naked;
and I hid myself."
11 And He said, "Who told
you that you *were* naked?
Have you eaten from the tree
of which I commanded you
that you should not eat?"
12 Then the man said, "The
woman whom You gave *to be*
with me, she gave me of the
tree, and I ate."
13 And the LORD God said to

the woman, "What *is* this you
have done?"

The woman said, "The ser-
pent deceived me, and I ate."

14So the LORD God said to
the serpent:

"Because you have
done this,
You *are* cursed more
than all cattle,
And more than every
beast of the field;
On your belly you
shall go,
And you shall eat dust
All the days of your life.
15 And I will put enmity
Between you and
the woman,
And between your
seed and her Seed;
He shall bruise your head,
And you shall bruise
His heel."

16To the woman He said:

"I will greatly multiply
your sorrow and
your conception;
In pain you shall bring
forth children;
Your desire *shall be*
for your husband,
And he shall rule
over you."

17Then to Adam He said,
"Because you have heeded the
voice of your wife, and have
eaten from the tree of which I
commanded you, saying, 'You
shall not eat of it':

"Cursed *is* the ground
for your sake;
In toil you shall eat
of it
All the days of your
life.
18 Both thorns and
thistles it shall bring
forth for you,
And you shall eat the
herb of the field.
19 In the sweat of your face
you shall eat bread
Till you return to
the ground,
For out of it you
were taken;
For dust you *are,*
And to dust you
shall return."

20And Adam called his
wife's name Eve, because she
was the mother of all living.

21Also for Adam and his
wife the LORD God made tunics of skin, and clothed them.

22Then the LORD God said,
"Behold, the man has become
like one of Us, to know good
and evil. And now, lest he put
out his hand and take also of
the tree of life, and eat, and
live forever"— 23therefore
the LORD God sent him out
of the garden of Eden to till
the ground from which he was
taken. 24So He drove out the
man; and He placed cheru-
bim at the east of the garden
of Eden, and a flaming sword
which turned every way, to
guard the way to the tree of
life.

CAIN MURDERS ABEL

4 Now Adam knew Eve his
wife, and she conceived
and bore Cain, and said, "I
have acquired a man from
the LORD." 2Then she bore
again, this time his brother
Abel. Now Abel was a keeper
of sheep, but Cain was a tiller
of the ground. 3And in the
process of time it came to pass
that Cain brought an offering
of the fruit of the ground to
the LORD. 4Abel also brought
of the firstborn of his flock
and of their fat. And the LORD
respected Abel and his offering, 5but He did not respect
Cain and his offering. And
Cain was very angry, and his
countenance fell.

6So the LORD said to Cain,
"Why are you angry? And why
has your countenance fallen?
7If you do well, will you not be
accepted? And if you do not do
well, sin lies at the door. And
its desire *is* for you, but you
should rule over it."

8Now Cain talked with Abel
his brother;[a] and it came to
pass, when they were in the
field, that Cain rose up against
Abel his brother and killed
him.

9Then the LORD said to
Cain, "Where *is* Abel your
brother?"

He said, "I do not know. *Am*
I my brother's keeper?"

10And He said, "What have
you done? The voice of your
brother's blood cries out to
Me from the ground. 11So now
you *are* cursed from the earth,
which has opened its mouth
to receive your brother's blood
from your hand. 12When you
till the ground, it shall no longer yield its strength to you. A
fugitive and a vagabond you
shall be on the earth."

13And Cain said to the LORD,
"My punishment *is* greater
than I can bear! 14Surely You
have driven me out this day
from the face of the ground;
I shall be hidden from Your
face; I shall be a fugitive and a
vagabond on the earth, and it
will happen *that* anyone who
finds me will kill me."

15And the LORD said to him,
"Therefore,[a] whoever kills
Cain, vengeance shall be taken
on him sevenfold." And the
LORD set a mark on Cain, lest
anyone finding him should
kill him.

THE FAMILY OF CAIN

16Then Cain went out from
the presence of the LORD and
dwelt in the land of Nod on the
east of Eden. 17And Cain knew
his wife, and she conceived
and bore Enoch. And he built
a city, and called the name of
the city after the name of his
son—Enoch. 18To Enoch was

4:8 [a] Samaritan Pentateuch, Septuagint, Syriac, and Vulgate add *"Let us go out to the field."* 4:15 [a] Following Masoretic Text and Targum; Septuagint, Syriac, and Vulgate read *Not so.*

born Irad; and Irad begot Mehujael, and Mehujael begot
Methushael, and Methushael
begot Lamech.
19Then Lamech took for
himself two wives: the name
of one *was* Adah, and the
name of the second *was* Zillah. 20And Adah bore Jabal.
He was the father of those who
dwell in tents and have livestock. 21His brother's name
was Jubal. He was the father
of all those who play the harp
and flute. 22And as for Zillah,
she also bore Tubal-Cain, an
instructor of every craftsman
in bronze and iron. And the
sister of Tubal-Cain *was* Naamah.
23Then Lamech said to his
wives:

"Adah and Zillah,
hear my voice;
Wives of Lamech, listen
to my speech!
For I have killed a man
for wounding me,
Even a young man
for hurting me.
24 If Cain shall be
avenged sevenfold,
Then Lamech
seventy-sevenfold."

A NEW SON

25And Adam knew his wife
again, and she bore a son and
named him Seth, "For God has
appointed another seed for
me instead of Abel, whom
Cain killed." 26And as for Seth,
to him also a son was born;
and he named him Enosh.[a]
Then *men* began to call on the
name of the LORD.

THE FAMILY OF ADAM

5 This is the book of the genealogy of Adam. In the
day that God created man, He
made him in the likeness of
God. 2He created them male
and female, and blessed them
and called them Mankind in
the day they were created.
3And Adam lived one hundred
and thirty years, and begot *a*
son in his own likeness, after
his image, and named him
Seth. 4After he begot Seth, the
days of Adam were eight hundred years; and he had sons
and daughters. 5So all the days
that Adam lived were nine
hundred and thirty years; and
he died.
6Seth lived one hundred
and five years, and begot
Enosh. 7After he begot Enosh,
Seth lived eight hundred and
seven years, and had sons and
daughters. 8So all the days of
Seth were nine hundred and
twelve years; and he died.
9Enosh lived ninety years,
and begot Cainan.[a] 10After he
begot Cainan, Enosh lived eight
hundred and fifteen years, and
had sons and daughters. 11So
all the days of Enosh were nine
hundred and five years; and
he died.

4:26 [a] Greek *Enos* 5:9 [a] Hebrew *Qenan*

12 Cainan lived seventy
years, and begot Mahalalel.
13 After he begot Mahalalel, Cainan lived eight hundred and
forty years, and had sons and
daughters. 14 So all the days
of Cainan were nine hundred
and ten years; and he died.

15 Mahalalel lived sixty-
five years, and begot Jared.
16 After he begot Jared, Mahalalel lived eight hundred and
thirty years, and had sons and
daughters. 17 So all the days of
Mahalalel were eight hundred
and ninety-five years; and he
died.

18 Jared lived one hun-
dred and sixty-two years, and
begot Enoch. 19 After he begot
Enoch, Jared lived eight hundred years, and had sons and
daughters. 20 So all the days of
Jared were nine hundred and
sixty-two years; and he died.

21 Enoch lived sixty-five
years, and begot Methuse-
lah. 22 After he begot Methuselah, Enoch walked with God
three hundred years, and had
sons and daughters. 23 So all
the days of Enoch were three
hundred and sixty-five years.
24 And Enoch walked with God;
and he *was* not, for God took
him.

25 Methuselah lived one
hundred and eighty-seven
years, and begot Lamech.
26 After he begot Lamech, Methuselah lived seven hundred
and eighty-two years, and had
sons and daughters. 27 So all
the days of Methuselah were
nine hundred and sixty-nine
years; and he died.

28 Lamech lived one hun-
dred and eighty-two years, and
had a son. 29 And he called his
name Noah, saying, "This *one*
will comfort us concerning
our work and the toil of our
hands, because of the ground
which the LORD has cursed."
30 After he begot Noah, Lamech lived five hundred and
ninety-five years, and had
sons and daughters. 31 So
all the days of Lamech were
seven hundred and seventy-
seven years; and he died.

32 And Noah was five hun-
dred years old, and Noah begot
Shem, Ham, and Japheth.

THE WICKEDNESS AND JUDGMENT OF MAN

6 Now it came to pass, when
men began to multiply
on the face of the earth, and
daughters were born to them,
2 that the sons of God saw the
daughters of men, that they
were beautiful; and they took
wives for themselves of all
whom they chose.

3 And the LORD said, "My
Spirit shall not strive[a] with
man forever, for he *is* indeed
flesh; yet his days shall be one
hundred and twenty years."
4 There were giants on the
earth in those days, and also
afterward, when the sons of

6:3 [a] Septuagint, Syriac, Targum, and Vulgate read *abide*.

God came in to the daughters
of men and they bore *children* to them. Those *were* the
mighty men who *were* of old,
men of renown.
5Then the LORD[a] saw that
the wickedness of man *was*
great in the earth, and *that*
every intent of the thoughts
of his heart *was* only evil
continually. 6And the LORD
was sorry that He had made
man on the earth, and He was
grieved in His heart. 7So the
LORD said, "I will destroy man
whom I have created from the
face of the earth, both man
and beast, creeping thing and
birds of the air, for I am sorry
that I have made them." 8But
Noah found grace in the eyes
of the LORD.

NOAH PLEASES GOD

9This is the genealogy of
Noah. Noah was a just man,
perfect in his generations.
Noah walked with God. 10And
Noah begot three sons: Shem,
Ham, and Japheth.
11The earth also was cor-
rupt before God, and the earth
was filled with violence. 12So
God looked upon the earth,
and indeed it was corrupt; for
all flesh had corrupted their
way on the earth.

THE ARK PREPARED

13And God said to Noah,
"The end of all flesh has come
before Me, for the earth is
filled with violence through
them; and behold, I will destroy them with the earth.
14Make yourself an ark of
gopherwood; make rooms in
the ark, and cover it inside and
outside with pitch. 15And this
is how you shall make it: The
length of the ark *shall be* three
hundred cubits, its width fifty
cubits, and its height thirty
cubits. 16You shall make a
window for the ark, and you
shall finish it to a cubit from
above; and set the door of
the ark in its side. You shall
make it *with* lower, second,
and third *decks.* 17And behold,
I Myself am bringing floodwaters on the earth, to destroy
from under heaven all flesh
in which *is* the breath of life;
everything that *is* on the earth
shall die. 18But I will establish
My covenant with you; and
you shall go into the ark—you,
your sons, your wife, and your
sons' wives with you. 19And of
every living thing of all flesh
you shall bring two of every
sort into the ark, to keep *them*
alive with you; they shall be
male and female. 20Of the
birds after their kind, of animals after their kind, and of
every creeping thing of the
earth after its kind, two of
every *kind* will come to you
to keep *them* alive. 21And you
shall take for yourself of all

6:5 [a] Following Masoretic Text and Targum; Vulgate reads *God;* Septuagint reads *LORD God.*

food that is eaten, and you
shall gather *it* to yourself; and
it shall be food for you and
for them."
22Thus Noah did; according
to all that God commanded
him, so he did.

THE GREAT FLOOD

7 Then the LORD said to
Noah, "Come into the ark,
you and all your household,
because I have seen *that* you
are righteous before Me in
this generation. 2You shall
take with you seven each of
every clean animal, a male
and his female; two each of
animals that *are* unclean, a
male and his female; 3also
seven each of birds of the air,
male and female, to keep the
species alive on the face of
all the earth. 4For after seven
more days I will cause it to
rain on the earth forty days
and forty nights, and I will
destroy from the face of the
earth all living things that I
have made." 5And Noah did
according to all that the LORD
commanded him. 6Noah *was*
six hundred years old when
the floodwaters were on the
earth.
7So Noah, with his sons,
his wife, and his sons' wives,
went into the ark because of
the waters of the flood. 8Of
clean animals, of animals that
are unclean, of birds, and of
everything that creeps on the
earth, 9two by two they went
into the ark to Noah, male
and female, as God had commanded Noah. 10And it came
to pass after seven days that
the waters of the flood were
on the earth. 11In the six hundredth year of Noah's life, in
the second month, the seventeenth day of the month,
on that day all the fountains
of the great deep were broken up, and the windows of
heaven were opened. 12And
the rain was on the earth forty
days and forty nights.
13On the very same day
Noah and Noah's sons, Shem,
Ham, and Japheth, and Noah's
wife and the three wives of
his sons with them, entered
the ark— 14they and every
beast after its kind, all cattle
after their kind, every creeping thing that creeps on the
earth after its kind, and every
bird after its kind, every bird
of every sort. 15And they went
into the ark to Noah, two by
two, of all flesh in which *is* the
breath of life. 16So those that
entered, male and female of
all flesh, went in as God had
commanded him; and the
LORD shut him in.
17Now the flood was on the
earth forty days. The waters
increased and lifted up the
ark, and it rose high above
the earth. 18The waters prevailed and greatly increased
on the earth, and the ark
moved about on the surface
of the waters. 19And the waters
prevailed exceedingly on the
earth, and all the high hills

under the whole heaven were
covered. 20The waters prevailed fifteen cubits upward,
and the mountains were covered. 21And all flesh died that
moved on the earth: birds and
cattle and beasts and every
creeping thing that creeps
on the earth, and every man.
22All in whose nostrils *was* the
breath of the spirit[a] of life, all
that *was* on the dry *land,* died.
23So He destroyed all living
things which were on the face
of the ground: both man and
cattle, creeping thing and bird
of the air. They were destroyed
from the earth. Only Noah and
those who *were* with him in
the ark remained *alive.* 24And
the waters prevailed on the
earth one hundred and fifty
days.

NOAH'S DELIVERANCE

8 Then God remembered
Noah, and every living
thing, and all the animals
that *were* with him in the
ark. And God made a wind to
pass over the earth, and the
waters subsided. 2The fountains of the deep and the
windows of heaven were also
stopped, and the rain from
heaven was restrained. 3And
the waters receded continually from the earth. At the end
of the hundred and fifty days
the waters decreased. 4Then
the ark rested in the seventh
month, the seventeenth day
of the month, on the mountains of Ararat. 5And the waters decreased continually
until the tenth month. In the
tenth *month,* on the first *day*
of the month, the tops of the
mountains were seen.

6So it came to pass, at the
end of forty days, that Noah
opened the window of the ark
which he had made. 7Then he
sent out a raven, which kept
going to and fro until the waters had dried up from the
earth. 8He also sent out from
himself a dove, to see if the
waters had receded from the
face of the ground. 9But the
dove found no resting place
for the sole of her foot, and
she returned into the ark to
him, for the waters *were* on
the face of the whole earth.
So he put out his hand and
took her, and drew her into
the ark to himself. 10And he
waited yet another seven days,
and again he sent the dove
out from the ark. 11Then the
dove came to him in the evening, and behold, a freshly
plucked olive leaf *was* in her
mouth; and Noah knew that
the waters had receded from
the earth. 12So he waited yet
another seven days and sent
out the dove, which did not
return again to him anymore.

13And it came to pass in the
six hundred and first year, in
the first *month,* the first *day*
of the month, that the waters

7:22 [a] Septuagint and Vulgate omit *of the spirit.*

were dried up from the earth;
and Noah removed the cov-
ering of the ark and looked,
and indeed the surface of the
ground was dry. 14And in the
second month, on the twenty-
seventh day of the month, the
earth was dried.

15Then God spoke to Noah,
saying, 16"Go out of the ark,
you and your wife, and your
sons and your sons' wives
with you. 17Bring out with you
every living thing of all flesh
that *is* with you: birds and cattle and every creeping thing
that creeps on the earth, so
that they may abound on the
earth, and be fruitful and multiply on the earth." 18So Noah
went out, and his sons and
his wife and his sons' wives
with him. 19Every animal,
every creeping thing, every
bird, *and* whatever creeps on
the earth, according to their
families, went out of the ark.

GOD'S COVENANT WITH CREATION

20Then Noah built an altar
to the LORD, and took of every
clean animal and of every
clean bird, and offered burnt
offerings on the altar. 21And
the LORD smelled a soothing
aroma. Then the LORD said in
His heart, "I will never again
curse the ground for man's
sake, although the imagination of man's heart *is* evil from
his youth; nor will I again destroy every living thing as I
have done.

22"While the earth
remains,
Seedtime and harvest,
Cold and heat,
Winter and summer,
And day and night
Shall not cease."

9

So God blessed Noah and
his sons, and said to them:
"Be fruitful and multiply, and
fill the earth.[a] 2And the fear
of you and the dread of you
shall be on every beast of the
earth, on every bird of the air,
on all that move *on* the earth,
and on all the fish of the sea.
They are given into your hand.
3Every moving thing that lives
shall be food for you. I have
given you all things, even as
the green herbs. 4But you shall
not eat flesh with its life, *that*
is, its blood. 5Surely for your
lifeblood I will demand *a reck-*
oning; from the hand of every
beast I will require it, and from
the hand of man. From the
hand of every man's brother
I will require the life of man.

6 "Whoever sheds
man's blood,
By man his blood
shall be shed;
For in the image of God
He made man.
7 And as for you, be
fruitful and multiply;

9:1 [a] Compare Genesis 1:28

Bring forth abundantly
  in the earth
And multiply in it."

8Then God spoke to Noah
and to his sons with him, saying: 9"And as for Me, behold,
I establish My covenant with
you and with your descen-
dants[a] after you, 10and with
every living creature that *is*
with you: the birds, the cattle, and every beast of the
earth with you, of all that go
out of the ark, every beast of
the earth. 11Thus I establish
My covenant with you: Never
again shall all flesh be cut off
by the waters of the flood;
never again shall there be a
flood to destroy the earth."

12And God said: "This *is* the
sign of the covenant which I
make between Me and you,
and every living creature that
is with you, for perpetual generations: 13I set My rainbow
in the cloud, and it shall be
for the sign of the covenant
between Me and the earth.
14It shall be, when I bring a
cloud over the earth, that the
rainbow shall be seen in the
cloud; 15and I will remember
My covenant which *is* between
Me and you and every living
creature of all flesh; the waters
shall never again become a
flood to destroy all flesh. 16The
rainbow shall be in the cloud,
and I will look on it to remember the everlasting covenant
between God and every living creature of all flesh that *is*
on the earth." 17And God said
to Noah, "This *is* the sign of
the covenant which I have
established between Me and
all flesh that *is* on the earth."

NOAH AND HIS SONS

18Now the sons of Noah
who went out of the ark were
Shem, Ham, and Japheth.
And Ham *was* the father of
Canaan. 19These three *were*
the sons of Noah, and from
these the whole earth was
populated.

20And Noah began *to be*
a farmer, and he planted a
vineyard. 21Then he drank of
the wine and was drunk, and
became uncovered in his tent.
22And Ham, the father of Canaan, saw the nakedness of
his father, and told his two
brothers outside. 23But Shem
and Japheth took a garment,
laid *it* on both their shoulders,
and went backward and covered the nakedness of their
father. Their faces *were* turned
away, and they did not see
their father's nakedness.

24So Noah awoke from
his wine, and knew what his
younger son had done to him.
25Then he said:

"Cursed *be* Canaan;
A servant of servants
He shall be to his
  brethren."

9:9 [a] Literally *seed*

26And he said:

"Blessed *be* the LORD,
The God of Shem,
And may Canaan
be his servant.
27 May God enlarge
Japheth,
And may he dwell in
the tents of Shem;
And may Canaan be
his servant."

28And Noah lived after
the flood three hundred and
fifty years. 29So all the days of
Noah were nine hundred and
fifty years; and he died.

NATIONS DESCENDED FROM NOAH

10 Now this *is* the genealogy of the sons of Noah:
Shem, Ham, and Japheth. And
sons were born to them after
the flood.
2The sons of Japheth *were*
Gomer, Magog, Madai, Javan,
Tubal, Meshech, and Tiras.
3The sons of Gomer *were*
Ashkenaz, Riphath,[a] and Togarmah. 4The sons of Javan
were Elishah, Tarshish, Kittim,
and Dodanim.[a] 5From these
the coastland *peoples* of the
Gentiles were separated into
their lands, everyone according to his language, according
to their families, into their nations.
6The sons of Ham *were*
Cush, Mizraim, Put,[a] and Canaan. 7The sons of Cush *were*
Seba, Havilah, Sabtah, Raamah, and Sabtechah; and the
sons of Raamah *were* Sheba
and Dedan.
8Cush begot Nimrod; he
began to be a mighty one on
the earth. 9He was a mighty
hunter before the LORD; therefore it is said, "Like Nimrod
the mighty hunter before the
LORD." 10And the beginning
of his kingdom was Babel,
Erech, Accad, and Calneh, in
the land of Shinar. 11From that
land he went to Assyria and
built Nineveh, Rehoboth Ir,
Calah, 12and Resen between
Nineveh and Calah (that *is* the
principal city).
13Mizraim begot Ludim,
Anamim, Lehabim, Naph-
tuhim, 14Pathrusim, and
Casluhim (from whom came
the Philistines and Caph-
torim).
15Canaan begot Sidon his
firstborn, and Heth; 16the Jebusite, the Amorite, and the
Girgashite; 17the Hivite, the
Arkite, and the Sinite; 18the
Arvadite, the Zemarite, and
the Hamathite. Afterward
the families of the Canaanites were dispersed. 19And the
border of the Canaanites was
from Sidon as you go toward
Gerar, as far as Gaza; then as
you go toward Sodom, Go-
morrah, Admah, and Zeboiim,

10:3 [a] Spelled *Diphath* in 1 Chronicles 1:6 **10:4** [a] Spelled *Rodanim* in Samaritan Pentateuch and 1 Chronicles 1:7 **10:6** [a] Or *Phut*

as far as Lasha. 20These *were* the sons of Ham, according to their families, according to their languages, in their lands *and* in their nations.

21And *children* were born also to Shem, the father of all the children of Eber, the brother of Japheth the elder. 22The sons of Shem *were* Elam, Asshur, Arphaxad, Lud, and Aram. 23The sons of Aram *were* Uz, Hul, Gether, and Mash.[a] 24Arphaxad begot Salah,[a] and Salah begot Eber. 25To Eber were born two sons: the name of one *was* Peleg, for in his days the earth was divided; and his brother's name *was* Joktan. 26Joktan begot Almodad, Sheleph, Hazarmaveth, Jerah, 27Hadoram, Uzal, Diklah, 28Obal,[a] Abimael, Sheba, 29Ophir, Havilah, and Jobab. All these *were* the sons of Joktan. 30And their dwelling place was from Mesha as you go toward Sephar, the mountain of the east. 31These *were* the sons of Shem, according to their families, according to their languages, in their lands, according to their nations.

32These *were* the families of the sons of Noah, according to their generations, in their nations; and from these the nations were divided on the earth after the flood.

THE TOWER OF BABEL

11 Now the whole earth had one language and one speech. 2And it came to pass, as they journeyed from the east, that they found a plain in the land of Shinar, and they dwelt there. 3Then they said to one another, "Come, let us make bricks and bake *them* thoroughly." They had brick for stone, and they had asphalt for mortar. 4And they said, "Come, let us build ourselves a city, and a tower whose top *is* in the heavens; let us make a name for ourselves, lest we be scattered abroad over the face of the whole earth."

5But the LORD came down to see the city and the tower which the sons of men had built. 6And the LORD said, "Indeed the people *are* one and they all have one language, and this is what they begin to do; now nothing that they propose to do will be withheld from them. 7Come, let Us go down and there confuse their language, that they may not understand one another's speech." 8So the LORD scattered them abroad from there over the face of all the earth, and they ceased building the city. 9Therefore its name is called Babel, because there the LORD confused the language of all the earth; and

10:23 [a] Called *Meshech* in Septuagint and 1 Chronicles 1:17
10:24 [a] Following Masoretic Text, Vulgate, and Targum; Septuagint reads *Arphaxad begot Cainan, and Cainan begot Salah* (compare Luke 3:35, 36). **10:28** [a] Spelled *Ebal* in 1 Chronicles 1:22

from there the LORD scattered
them abroad over the face of
all the earth.

SHEM'S DESCENDANTS

10This *is* the genealogy of
Shem: Shem *was* one hundred
years old, and begot Arphaxad
two years after the flood.
11After he begot Arphaxad,
Shem lived five hundred
years, and begot sons and
daughters.
12Arphaxad lived thirty-five
years, and begot Salah. 13After
he begot Salah, Arphaxad
lived four hundred and three
years, and begot sons and
daughters.
14Salah lived thirty years,
and begot Eber. 15After he
begot Eber, Salah lived four
hundred and three years, and
begot sons and daughters.
16Eber lived thirty-four
years, and begot Peleg. 17After
he begot Peleg, Eber lived four
hundred and thirty years, and
begot sons and daughters.
18Peleg lived thirty years,
and begot Reu. 19After he
begot Reu, Peleg lived two
hundred and nine years, and
begot sons and daughters.
20Reu lived thirty-two years,
and begot Serug. 21After he
begot Serug, Reu lived two
hundred and seven years, and
begot sons and daughters.
22Serug lived thirty years,
and begot Nahor. 23After he
begot Nahor, Serug lived two
hundred years, and begot
sons and daughters.
24Nahor lived twenty-nine
years, and begot Terah. 25After
he begot Terah, Nahor lived
one hundred and nineteen
years, and begot sons and
daughters.
26Now Terah lived seventy
years, and begot Abram,
Nahor, and Haran.

TERAH'S DESCENDANTS

27This *is* the genealogy of
Terah: Terah begot Abram,
Nahor, and Haran. Haran
begot Lot. 28And Haran died
before his father Terah in
his native land, in Ur of the
Chaldeans. 29Then Abram and
Nahor took wives: the name of
Abram's wife *was* Sarai, and
the name of Nahor's wife, Milcah, the daughter of Haran
the father of Milcah and the
father of Iscah. 30But Sarai
was barren; she had no child.
31And Terah took his son
Abram and his grandson Lot,
the son of Haran, and his
daughter-in-law Sarai, his son
Abram's wife, and they went
out with them from Ur of the
Chaldeans to go to the land
of Canaan; and they came to
Haran and dwelt there. 32So
the days of Terah were two
hundred and five years, and
Terah died in Haran.

PROMISES TO ABRAM

12 Now the LORD had said
to Abram:

"Get out of your country,
From your family

And from your
father's house,
To a land that I will
show you.
2 I will make you a
great nation;
I will bless you
And make your
name great;
And you shall be
a blessing.
3 I will bless those
who bless you,
And I will curse him
who curses you;
And in you all the
families of the earth
shall be blessed."

4So Abram departed as
the LORD had spoken to him,
and Lot went with him. And
Abram *was* seventy-five years
old when he departed from
Haran. 5Then Abram took
Sarai his wife and Lot his
brother's son, and all their
possessions that they had
gathered, and the people
whom they had acquired in
Haran, and they departed to
go to the land of Canaan. So
they came to the land of Canaan. 6Abram passed through
the land to the place of Shechem, as far as the terebinth
tree of Moreh.[a] And the Canaanites *were* then in the
land.
7Then the LORD appeared
to Abram and said, "To your
descendants I will give this
land." And there he built an
altar to the LORD, who had
appeared to him. 8And he
moved from there to the
mountain east of Bethel, and
he pitched his tent *with* Bethel
on the west and Ai on the east;
there he built an altar to the
LORD and called on the name
of the LORD. 9So Abram journeyed, going on still toward
the South.[a]

ABRAM IN EGYPT

10Now there was a famine
in the land, and Abram went
down to Egypt to dwell there,
for the famine *was* severe in
the land. 11And it came to pass,
when he was close to entering
Egypt, that he said to Sarai
his wife, "Indeed I know that
you *are* a woman of beautiful
countenance. 12Therefore it
will happen, when the Egyptians see you, that they will
say, 'This *is* his wife'; and they
will kill me, but they will let
you live. 13Please say you *are*
my sister, that it may be well
with me for your sake, and
that I[a] may live because of
you."
14So it was, when Abram
came into Egypt, that the
Egyptians saw the woman,
that she *was* very beautiful.
15The princes of Pharaoh also
saw her and commended her
to Pharaoh. And the woman

12:6 [a] Hebrew *Alon Moreh* 12:9 [a] Hebrew *Negev* 12:13 [a] Literally *my soul*

was taken to Pharaoh's house. [16]He treated Abram well for her sake. He had sheep, oxen, male donkeys, male and female servants, female donkeys, and camels.

[17]But the LORD plagued Pharaoh and his house with great plagues because of Sarai, Abram's wife. [18]And Pharaoh called Abram and said, "What *is* this you have done to me? Why did you not tell me that she *was* your wife? [19]Why did you say, 'She *is* my sister'? I might have taken her as my wife. Now therefore, here is your wife; take *her* and go your way." [20]So Pharaoh commanded *his* men concerning him; and they sent him away, with his wife and all that he had.

ABRAM INHERITS CANAAN

13 Then Abram went up from Egypt, he and his wife and all that he had, and Lot with him, to the South.[a] [2]Abram *was* very rich in livestock, in silver, and in gold. [3]And he went on his journey from the South as far as Bethel, to the place where his tent had been at the beginning, between Bethel and Ai, [4]to the place of the altar which he had made there at first. And there Abram called on the name of the LORD.

[5]Lot also, who went with Abram, had flocks and herds and tents. [6]Now the land was not able to support them, that they might dwell together, for their possessions were so great that they could not dwell together. [7]And there was strife between the herdsmen of Abram's livestock and the herdsmen of Lot's livestock. The Canaanites and the Perizzites then dwelt in the land.

[8]So Abram said to Lot, "Please let there be no strife between you and me, and between my herdsmen and your herdsmen; for we *are* brethren. [9]*Is* not the whole land before you? Please separate from me. If *you take* the left, then I will go to the right; or, if *you go* to the right, then I will go to the left."

[10]And Lot lifted his eyes and saw all the plain of Jordan, that it *was* well watered everywhere (before the LORD destroyed Sodom and Gomorrah) like the garden of the LORD, like the land of Egypt as you go toward Zoar. [11]Then Lot chose for himself all the plain of Jordan, and Lot journeyed east. And they separated from each other. [12]Abram dwelt in the land of Canaan, and Lot dwelt in the cities of the plain and pitched *his* tent even as far as Sodom. [13]But the men of Sodom *were* exceedingly wicked and sinful against the LORD.

[14]And the LORD said to Abram, after Lot had sepa-

13:1 [a] Hebrew *Negev*

rated from him: "Lift your eyes now and look from the place where you are—northward, southward, eastward, and westward; 15for all the land which you see I give to you and your descendants[a] forever. 16And I will make your descendants as the dust of the earth; so that if a man could number the dust of the earth, *then* your descendants also could be numbered. 17Arise, walk in the land through its length and its width, for I give it to you."

18Then Abram moved *his* tent, and went and dwelt by the terebinth trees of Mamre,[a] which *are* in Hebron, and built an altar there to the LORD.

LOT'S CAPTIVITY AND RESCUE

14 And it came to pass in the days of Amraphel king of Shinar, Arioch king of Ellasar, Chedorlaomer king of Elam, and Tidal king of nations,[a] 2*that* they made war with Bera king of Sodom, Birsha king of Gomorrah, Shinab king of Admah, Shemeber king of Zeboiim, and the king of Bela (that is, Zoar). 3All these joined together in the Valley of Siddim (that is, the Salt Sea). 4Twelve years they served Chedorlaomer, and in the thirteenth year they rebelled.

5In the fourteenth year Chedorlaomer and the kings that *were* with him came and attacked the Rephaim in Ashteroth Karnaim, the Zuzim in Ham, the Emim in Shaveh Kiriathaim, 6and the Horites in their mountain of Seir, as far as El Paran, which *is* by the wilderness. 7Then they turned back and came to En Mishpat (that *is,* Kadesh), and attacked all the country of the Amalekites, and also the Amorites who dwelt in Hazezon Tamar.

8And the king of Sodom, the king of Gomorrah, the king of Admah, the king of Zeboiim, and the king of Bela (that *is,* Zoar) went out and joined together in battle in the Valley of Siddim 9against Chedorlaomer king of Elam, Tidal king of nations,[a] Amraphel king of Shinar, and Arioch king of Ellasar—four kings against five. 10Now the Valley of Siddim *was full of* asphalt pits; and the kings of Sodom and Gomorrah fled; *some* fell there, and the remainder fled to the mountains. 11Then they took all the goods of Sodom and Gomorrah, and all their provisions, and went their way. 12They also took Lot, Abram's brother's son who dwelt in Sodom, and his goods, and departed.

13Then one who had escaped came and told Abram the Hebrew, for he dwelt by

13:15 [a] Literally *seed,* and so throughout the book 13:18 [a] Hebrew *Alon Mamre* 14:1 [a] Hebrew *goyim* 14:9 [a] Hebrew *goyim*

the terebinth trees of Mamre[a]
the Amorite, brother of Eshcol
and brother of Aner; and they
were allies with Abram. 14Now
when Abram heard that his
brother was taken captive, he
armed his three hundred and
eighteen trained *servants* who
were born in his own house,
and went in pursuit as far as
Dan. 15He divided his forces
against them by night, and
he and his servants attacked
them and pursued them as
far as Hobah, which *is* north
of Damascus. 16So he brought
back all the goods, and also
brought back his brother Lot
and his goods, as well as the
women and the people.

17And the king of Sodom
went out to meet him at the
Valley of Shaveh (that *is,* the
King's Valley), after his return
from the defeat of Chedorlaomer and the kings who *were*
with him.

ABRAM AND MELCHIZEDEK

18Then Melchizedek king of
Salem brought out bread and
wine; he *was* the priest of God
Most High. 19And he blessed
him and said:

"Blessed be Abram of
God Most High,
Possessor of heaven
and earth;
20 And blessed be God
Most High,
Who has delivered
your enemies into
your hand."

And he gave him a tithe of all.

21Now the king of Sodom
said to Abram, "Give me the
persons, and take the goods
for yourself."

22But Abram said to the
king of Sodom, "I have raised
my hand to the LORD, God
Most High, the Possessor of
heaven and earth, 23that I *will*
take nothing, from a thread
to a sandal strap, and that I
will not take anything that
is yours, lest you should say,
'I have made Abram rich'—
24except only what the young
men have eaten, and the portion of the men who went with
me: Aner, Eshcol, and Mamre;
let them take their portion."

GOD'S COVENANT WITH ABRAM

15 After these things the
word of the LORD came
to Abram in a vision, saying,
"Do not be afraid, Abram. I *am*
your shield, your exceedingly
great reward."

2But Abram said, "Lord
GOD, what will You give me,
seeing I go childless, and the
heir of my house *is* Eliezer of
Damascus?" 3Then Abram
said, "Look, You have given
me no offspring; indeed one
born in my house is my heir!"

4And behold, the word of
the LORD *came* to him, saying,

14:13 [a] Hebrew *Alon Mamre*

"This one shall not be your
heir, but one who will come
from your own body shall be
your heir." 5Then He brought
him outside and said, "Look
now toward heaven, and
count the stars if you are able
to number them." And He said
to him, "So shall your descendants be."

6And he believed in the
LORD, and He accounted it to
him for righteousness.

7Then He said to him, "I
am the LORD, who brought
you out of Ur of the Chaldeans, to give you this land to
inherit it."

8And he said, "Lord GOD,
how shall I know that I will
inherit it?"

9So He said to him, "Bring
Me a three-year-old heifer, a
three-year-old female goat, a
three-year-old ram, a turtledove, and a young pigeon."
10Then he brought all these
to Him and cut them in two,
down the middle, and placed
each piece opposite the other;
but he did not cut the birds in
two. 11And when the vultures
came down on the carcasses,
Abram drove them away.

12Now when the sun was
going down, a deep sleep fell
upon Abram; and behold,
horror *and* great darkness fell
upon him. 13Then He said to
Abram: "Know certainly that
your descendants will be
strangers in a land *that is* not
theirs, and will serve them,
and they will afflict them four
hundred years. 14And also the
nation whom they serve I will
judge; afterward they shall
come out with great possessions. 15Now as for you, you
shall go to your fathers in
peace; you shall be buried at
a good old age. 16But in the
fourth generation they shall
return here, for the iniquity of
the Amorites *is* not yet complete."

17And it came to pass, when
the sun went down and it was
dark, that behold, there appeared a smoking oven and a
burning torch that passed between those pieces. 18On the
same day the LORD made a
covenant with Abram, saying:

"To your descendants I
have given this land, from the
river of Egypt to the great river,
the River Euphrates— 19the
Kenites, the Kenezzites, the
Kadmonites, 20the Hittites,
the Perizzites, the Rephaim,
21the Amorites, the Canaanites, the Girgashites, and the
Jebusites."

HAGAR AND ISHMAEL

16 Now Sarai, Abram's wife,
had borne him no *chil-
dren.* And she had an Egyptian maidservant whose name
was Hagar. 2So Sarai said to
Abram, "See now, the LORD
has restrained me from bearing *children.* Please, go in to
my maid; perhaps I shall
obtain children by her." And
Abram heeded the voice of
Sarai. 3Then Sarai, Abram's

wife, took Hagar her maid, the
Egyptian, and gave her to her
husband Abram to be his wife,
after Abram had dwelt ten
years in the land of Canaan.
4So he went in to Hagar, and
she conceived. And when she
saw that she had conceived,
her mistress became despised
in her eyes.
5Then Sarai said to Abram,
"My wrong *be* upon you! I gave
my maid into your embrace;
and when she saw that she
had conceived, I became despised in her eyes. The LORD
judge between you and me."
6So Abram said to Sarai,
"Indeed your maid *is* in your
hand; do to her as you please."
And when Sarai dealt harshly
with her, she fled from her
presence.
7Now the Angel of the
LORD found her by a spring
of water in the wilderness,
by the spring on the way to
Shur. 8And He said, "Hagar,
Sarai's maid, where have you
come from, and where are you
going?"
She said, "I am fleeing from
the presence of my mistress
Sarai."
9The Angel of the LORD
said to her, "Return to your
mistress, and submit yourself under her hand." 10Then
the Angel of the LORD said to
her, "I will multiply your descendants exceedingly, so that
they shall not be counted for
multitude." 11And the Angel of
the LORD said to her:

"Behold, you *are*
with child,
And you shall bear a son.
You shall call his
name Ishmael,
Because the LORD has
heard your affliction.
12 He shall be a wild man;
His hand *shall be*
against every man,
And every man's hand
against him.
And he shall dwell
in the presence of
all his brethren."

13Then she called the name
of the LORD who spoke to her,
You-Are-the-God-Who-Sees;
for she said, "Have I also here
seen Him who sees me?"
14Therefore the well was called
Beer Lahai Roi;[a] observe, *it is*
between Kadesh and Bered.
15So Hagar bore Abram a
son; and Abram named his
son, whom Hagar bore, Ishmael. 16Abram *was* eighty-six
years old when Hagar bore
Ishmael to Abram.

THE SIGN OF THE COVENANT

17 When Abram was ninety-
nine years old, the LORD
appeared to Abram and said
to him, "I *am* Almighty God;
walk before Me and be blameless. 2And I will make My cov-

16:14 [a] Literally *Well of the One Who Lives and Sees Me*

enant between Me and you,
and will multiply you exceedingly." 3Then Abram fell on his
face, and God talked with him,
saying: 4"As for Me, behold,
My covenant is with you, and
you shall be a father of many
nations. 5No longer shall your
name be called Abram, but
your name shall be Abraham;
for I have made you a father of
many nations. 6I will make you
exceedingly fruitful; and I will
make nations of you, and kings
shall come from you. 7And
I will establish My covenant
between Me and you and your
descendants after you in their
generations, for an everlasting
covenant, to be God to you and
your descendants after you.
8Also I give to you and your
descendants after you the land
in which you are a stranger,
all the land of Canaan, as an
everlasting possession; and I
will be their God."

9And God said to Abra-
ham: "As for you, you shall
keep My covenant, you and
your descendants after you
throughout their generations.
10This *is* My covenant which
you shall keep, between Me
and you and your descen-
dants after you: Every male
child among you shall be
circumcised; 11and you shall
be circumcised in the flesh
of your foreskins, and it shall
be a sign of the covenant between Me and you. 12He who
is eight days old among you
shall be circumcised, every
male child in your generations, he who is born in your
house or bought with money
from any foreigner who is not
your descendant. 13He who
is born in your house and
he who is bought with your
money must be circumcised,
and My covenant shall be in
your flesh for an everlasting
covenant. 14And the uncircumcised male child, who is
not circumcised in the flesh of
his foreskin, that person shall
be cut off from his people; he
has broken My covenant."

15Then God said to Abra-
ham, "As for Sarai your wife,
you shall not call her name
Sarai, but Sarah *shall be* her
name. 16And I will bless her
and also give you a son by her;
then I will bless her, and she
shall be *a mother of* nations;
kings of peoples shall be from
her."

17Then Abraham fell on his
face and laughed, and said in
his heart, "Shall *a child* be
born to a man who is one
hundred years old? And shall
Sarah, who is ninety years old,
bear *a child?*" 18And Abraham
said to God, "Oh, that Ishmael
might live before You!"

19Then God said: "No, Sarah
your wife shall bear you a son,
and you shall call his name
Isaac; I will establish My covenant with him for an everlasting covenant, *and* with
his descendants after him.
20And as for Ishmael, I have
heard you. Behold, I have

blessed him, and will make him fruitful, and will multiply him exceedingly. He shall beget twelve princes, and I will make him a great nation. 21But My covenant I will establish with Isaac, whom Sarah shall bear to you at this set time next year." 22Then He finished talking with him, and God went up from Abraham.

23So Abraham took Ishmael his son, all who were born in his house and all who were bought with his money, every male among the men of Abraham's house, and circumcised the flesh of their foreskins that very same day, as God had said to him. 24Abraham *was* ninety-nine years old when he was circumcised in the flesh of his foreskin. 25And Ishmael his son *was* thirteen years old when he was circumcised in the flesh of his foreskin. 26That very same day Abraham was circumcised, and his son Ishmael; 27and all the men of his house, born in the house or bought with money from a foreigner, were circumcised with him.

THE SON OF PROMISE

18 Then the LORD appeared to him by the terebinth trees of Mamre,[a] as he was sitting in the tent door in the heat of the day. 2So he lifted his eyes and looked, and behold, three men were standing by him; and when he saw *them,* he ran from the tent door to meet them, and bowed himself to the ground, 3and said, "My Lord, if I have now found favor in Your sight, do not pass on by Your servant. 4Please let a little water be brought, and wash your feet, and rest yourselves under the tree. 5And I will bring a morsel of bread, that you may refresh your hearts. After that you may pass by, inasmuch as you have come to your servant."

They said, "Do as you have said."

6So Abraham hurried into the tent to Sarah and said, "Quickly, make ready three measures of fine meal; knead *it* and make cakes." 7And Abraham ran to the herd, took a tender and good calf, gave *it* to a young man, and he hastened to prepare it. 8So he took butter and milk and the calf which he had prepared, and set *it* before them; and he stood by them under the tree as they ate.

9Then they said to him, "Where *is* Sarah your wife?"

So he said, "Here, in the tent."

10And He said, "I will certainly return to you according to the time of life, and behold, Sarah your wife shall have a son."

(Sarah was listening in the tent door which *was* behind him.) 11Now Abraham

18:1 [a] Hebrew *Alon Mamre*

and Sarah were old, well
advanced in age; *and* Sarah
had passed the age of childbearing.[a] 12Therefore Sarah
laughed within herself, saying, "After I have grown old,
shall I have pleasure, my lord
being old also?"

13And the LORD said to
Abraham, "Why did Sarah
laugh, saying, 'Shall I surely
bear *a child,* since I am old?'
14Is anything too hard for the
LORD? At the appointed time
I will return to you, according
to the time of life, and Sarah
shall have a son."

15But Sarah denied *it,* saying, "I did not laugh," for she
was afraid.

And He said, "No, but you
did laugh!"

ABRAHAM INTERCEDES FOR SODOM

16Then the men rose from
there and looked toward
Sodom, and Abraham went
with them to send them on
the way. 17And the LORD said,
"Shall I hide from Abraham
what I am doing, 18since Abraham shall surely become a
great and mighty nation, and
all the nations of the earth
shall be blessed in him? 19For I
have known him, in order that
he may command his children
and his household after him,
that they keep the way of the
LORD, to do righteousness
and justice, that the LORD
may bring to Abraham what
He has spoken to him." 20And
the LORD said, "Because the
outcry against Sodom and Gomorrah is great, and because
their sin is very grave, 21I will
go down now and see whether
they have done altogether according to the outcry against
it that has come to Me; and if
not, I will know."

22Then the men turned
away from there and went toward Sodom, but Abraham still
stood before the LORD. 23And
Abraham came near and said,
"Would You also destroy the
righteous with the wicked?
24Suppose there were fifty righteous within the city; would
You also destroy the place and
not spare *it* for the fifty righteous that were in it? 25Far be it
from You to do such a thing as
this, to slay the righteous with
the wicked, so that the righteous should be as the wicked;
far be it from You! Shall not the
Judge of all the earth do right?"

26So the LORD said, "If I
find in Sodom fifty righteous
within the city, then I will
spare all the place for their
sakes."

27Then Abraham answered
and said, "Indeed now, I who
am but dust and ashes have
taken it upon myself to speak
to the Lord: 28Suppose there
were five less than the fifty
righteous; would You destroy
all of the city for *lack of* five?"

18:11 [a] Literally *the manner of women had ceased to be with Sarah*

So He said, "If I find there
forty-five, I will not destroy *it.*"
29And he spoke to Him yet
again and said, "Suppose there
should be forty found there?"
So He said, "I will not do *it*
for the sake of forty."
30Then he said, "Let not
the Lord be angry, and I will
speak: Suppose thirty should
be found there?"
So He said, "I will not do *it*
if I find thirty there."
31And he said, "Indeed now,
I have taken it upon myself
to speak to the Lord: Suppose twenty should be found
there?"
So He said, "I will not destroy *it* for the sake of twenty."
32Then he said, "Let not the
Lord be angry, and I will speak
but once more: Suppose ten
should be found there?"
And He said, "I will not destroy *it* for the sake of ten."
33So the LORD went His way
as soon as He had finished
speaking with Abraham; and
Abraham returned to his
place.

SODOM'S DEPRAVITY

19 Now the two angels
came to Sodom in the
evening, and Lot was sitting
in the gate of Sodom. When
Lot saw *them,* he rose to meet
them, and he bowed him-
self with his face toward the
ground. 2And he said, "Here
now, my lords, please turn in
to your servant's house and
spend the night, and wash
your feet; then you may rise
early and go on your way."
And they said, "No, but we
will spend the night in the
open square."
3But he insisted strongly; so
they turned in to him and entered his house. Then he made
them a feast, and baked unleavened bread, and they ate.
4Now before they lay down,
the men of the city, the men of
Sodom, both old and young, all
the people from every quarter,
surrounded the house. 5And
they called to Lot and said to
him, "Where are the men who
came to you tonight? Bring
them out to us that we may
know them *carnally.*"
6So Lot went out to them
through the doorway, shut the
door behind him, 7and said,
"Please, my brethren, do not
do so wickedly! 8See now, I
have two daughters who have
not known a man; please, let
me bring them out to you,
and you may do to them as
you wish; only do nothing to
these men, since this is the
reason they have come under
the shadow of my roof."
9And they said, "Stand
back!" Then they said, "This
one came in to stay *here,* and
he keeps acting as a judge;
now we will deal worse with
you than with them." So they
pressed hard against the man
Lot, and came near to break
down the door. 10But the men
reached out their hands and
pulled Lot into the house with

them, and shut the door. 11And
they struck the men who *were*
at the doorway of the house
with blindness, both small
and great, so that they became
weary *trying* to find the door.

SODOM AND GOMORRAH DESTROYED

12Then the men said to Lot,
"Have you anyone else here?
Son-in-law, your sons, your
daughters, and whomever you
have in the city—take *them*
out of this place! 13For we will
destroy this place, because
the outcry against them has
grown great before the face
of the LORD, and the LORD has
sent us to destroy it."

14So Lot went out and spoke
to his sons-in-law, who had
married his daughters, and
said, "Get up, get out of this
place; for the LORD will destroy
this city!" But to his sons-in-
law he seemed to be joking.

15When the morning
dawned, the angels urged Lot
to hurry, saying, "Arise, take
your wife and your two daughters who are here, lest you be
consumed in the punishment
of the city." 16And while he lingered, the men took hold of
his hand, his wife's hand, and
the hands of his two daughters, the LORD being merciful
to him, and they brought him
out and set him outside the
city. 17So it came to pass, when
they had brought them outside, that he[a] said, "Escape for
your life! Do not look behind
you nor stay anywhere in the
plain. Escape to the mountains, lest you be destroyed."

18Then Lot said to them,
"Please, no, my lords! 19Indeed
now, your servant has found
favor in your sight, and you
have increased your mercy
which you have shown me by
saving my life; but I cannot
escape to the mountains, lest
some evil overtake me and
I die. 20See now, this city *is*
near *enough* to flee to, and it
is a little one; please let me
escape there (*is* it not a little
one?) and my soul shall live."

21And he said to him, "See,
I have favored you concerning this thing also, in that I
will not overthrow this city
for which you have spoken.
22Hurry, escape there. For I
cannot do anything until you
arrive there."

Therefore the name of the
city was called Zoar.

23The sun had risen upon
the earth when Lot entered
Zoar. 24Then the LORD rained
brimstone and fire on Sodom
and Gomorrah, from the LORD
out of the heavens. 25So He
overthrew those cities, all the
plain, all the inhabitants of
the cities, and what grew on
the ground.

26But his wife looked back
behind him, and she became
a pillar of salt.

19:17 [a] Septuagint, Syriac, and Vulgate read *they*.

27And Abraham went early in the morning to the place where he had stood before the Lord. 28Then he looked toward Sodom and Gomorrah, and toward all the land of the plain; and he saw, and behold, the smoke of the land which went up like the smoke of a furnace. 29And it came to pass, when God destroyed the cities of the plain, that God remembered Abraham, and sent Lot out of the midst of the overthrow, when He overthrew the cities in which Lot had dwelt.

THE DESCENDANTS OF LOT

30Then Lot went up out of Zoar and dwelt in the mountains, and his two daughters were with him; for he was afraid to dwell in Zoar. And he and his two daughters dwelt in a cave. 31Now the firstborn said to the younger, "Our father *is* old, and *there is* no man on the earth to come in to us as is the custom of all the earth. 32Come, let us make our father drink wine, and we will lie with him, that we may preserve the lineage of our father." 33So they made their father drink wine that night. And the firstborn went in and lay with her father, and he did not know when she lay down or when she arose.

34It happened on the next day that the firstborn said to the younger, "Indeed I lay with my father last night; let us make him drink wine tonight also, and you go in *and* lie with him, that we may preserve the lineage of our father." 35Then they made their father drink wine that night also. And the younger arose and lay with him, and he did not know when she lay down or when she arose.

36Thus both the daughters of Lot were with child by their father. 37The firstborn bore a son and called his name Moab; he *is* the father of the Moabites to this day. 38And the younger, she also bore a son and called his name Ben-Ammi; he *is* the father of the people of Ammon to this day.

ABRAHAM AND ABIMELECH

20 And Abraham journeyed from there to the South, and dwelt between Kadesh and Shur, and stayed in Gerar. 2Now Abraham said of Sarah his wife, "She *is* my sister." And Abimelech king of Gerar sent and took Sarah.

3But God came to Abimelech in a dream by night, and said to him, "Indeed you *are* a dead man because of the woman whom you have taken, for she *is* a man's wife."

4But Abimelech had not come near her; and he said, "Lord, will You slay a righteous nation also? 5Did he not say to me, 'She *is* my sister'? And she, even she herself said, 'He *is* my brother.' In the integrity

of my heart and innocence of
my hands I have done this."
6And God said to him in
a dream, "Yes, I know that
you did this in the integrity
of your heart. For I also withheld you from sinning against
Me; therefore I did not let you
touch her. 7Now therefore, restore the man's wife; for he *is*
a prophet, and he will pray for
you and you shall live. But if
you do not restore *her,* know
that you shall surely die, you
and all who *are* yours."

8So Abimelech rose early in
the morning, called all his servants, and told all these things
in their hearing; and the men
were very much afraid. 9And
Abimelech called Abraham
and said to him, "What have
you done to us? How have I
offended you, that you have
brought on me and on my
kingdom a great sin? You have
done deeds to me that ought
not to be done." 10Then Abimelech said to Abraham, "What
did you have in view, that you
have done this thing?"

11And Abraham said, "Be-
cause I thought, surely the
fear of God *is* not in this place;
and they will kill me on account of my wife. 12But indeed
she is truly my sister. She *is*
the daughter of my father,
but not the daughter of my
mother; and she became my
wife. 13And it came to pass,
when God caused me to wander from my father's house,
that I said to her, 'This *is* your
kindness that you should do
for me: in every place, wherever we go, say of me, "He *is*
my brother."'"

14Then Abimelech took
sheep, oxen, and male and
female servants, and gave
them to Abraham; and he restored Sarah his wife to him.
15And Abimelech said, "See,
my land *is* before you; dwell
where it pleases you." 16Then
to Sarah he said, "Behold, I
have given your brother a
thousand *pieces* of silver; indeed this vindicates you[a] before all who *are* with you and
before everybody." Thus she
was rebuked.

17So Abraham prayed to
God; and God healed Abimelech, his wife, and his female
servants. Then they bore
children; 18for the LORD had
closed up all the wombs of the
house of Abimelech because
of Sarah, Abraham's wife.

ISAAC IS BORN

21 And the LORD visited
Sarah as He had said, and
the LORD did for Sarah as He
had spoken. 2For Sarah conceived and bore Abraham a son
in his old age, at the set time
of which God had spoken to
him. 3And Abraham called the
name of his son who was born
to him—whom Sarah bore to
him—Isaac. 4Then Abraham

20:16 [a] Literally *it is a covering of the eyes for you*

circumcised his son Isaac
when he was eight days old,
as God had commanded him.
5Now Abraham was one hun-
dred years old when his son
Isaac was born to him. 6And
Sarah said, "God has made me
laugh, *and* all who hear will
laugh with me." 7She also said,
"Who would have said to Abraham that Sarah would nurse
children? For I have borne *him*
a son in his old age."

HAGAR AND ISHMAEL DEPART

8So the child grew and was
weaned. And Abraham made
a great feast on the same day
that Isaac was weaned.

9And Sarah saw the son of
Hagar the Egyptian, whom
she had borne to Abraham,
scoffing. 10Therefore she said
to Abraham, "Cast out this
bondwoman and her son; for
the son of this bondwoman
shall not be heir with my son,
namely with Isaac." 11And the
matter was very displeasing
in Abraham's sight because
of his son.

12But God said to Abraham,
"Do not let it be displeasing in
your sight because of the lad or
because of your bondwoman.
Whatever Sarah has said to
you, listen to her voice; for in
Isaac your seed shall be called.
13Yet I will also make a nation
of the son of the bondwoman,
because he *is* your seed."

14So Abraham rose early in
the morning, and took bread
and a skin of water; and putting *it* on her shoulder, he
gave *it* and the boy to Hagar,
and sent her away. Then she
departed and wandered in
the Wilderness of Beersheba.
15And the water in the skin was
used up, and she placed the
boy under one of the shrubs.
16Then she went and sat down
across from *him* at a distance
of about a bowshot; for she
said to herself, "Let me not see
the death of the boy." So she
sat opposite *him,* and lifted
her voice and wept.

17And God heard the voice
of the lad. Then the angel of
God called to Hagar out of
heaven, and said to her, "What
ails you, Hagar? Fear not, for
God has heard the voice of
the lad where he *is.* 18Arise,
lift up the lad and hold him
with your hand, for I will make
him a great nation."

19Then God opened her
eyes, and she saw a well of
water. And she went and filled
the skin with water, and gave
the lad a drink. 20So God was
with the lad; and he grew and
dwelt in the wilderness, and
became an archer. 21He dwelt
in the Wilderness of Paran;
and his mother took a wife for
him from the land of Egypt.

A COVENANT WITH ABIMELECH

22And it came to pass at
that time that Abimelech and
Phichol, the commander of
his army, spoke to Abraham,

saying, "God *is* with you in all that you do. [23]Now therefore, swear to me by God that you will not deal falsely with me, with my offspring, or with my posterity; but that according to the kindness that I have done to you, you will do to me and to the land in which you have dwelt."

[24]And Abraham said, "I will swear."

[25]Then Abraham rebuked Abimelech because of a well of water which Abimelech's servants had seized. [26]And Abimelech said, "I do not know who has done this thing; you did not tell me, nor had I heard *of it* until today." [27]So Abraham took sheep and oxen and gave them to Abimelech, and the two of them made a covenant. [28]And Abraham set seven ewe lambs of the flock by themselves.

[29]Then Abimelech asked Abraham, "What *is the meaning of* these seven ewe lambs which you have set by themselves?"

[30]And he said, "You will take *these* seven ewe lambs from my hand, that they may be my witness that I have dug this well." [31]Therefore he called that place Beersheba,[a] because the two of them swore an oath there.

[32]Thus they made a covenant at Beersheba. So Abimelech rose with Phichol, the commander of his army, and they returned to the land of the Philistines. [33]Then *Abraham* planted a tamarisk tree in Beersheba, and there called on the name of the LORD, the Everlasting God. [34]And Abraham stayed in the land of the Philistines many days.

ABRAHAM'S FAITH CONFIRMED

22 Now it came to pass after these things that God tested Abraham, and said to him, "Abraham!"

And he said, "Here I am."

[2]Then He said, "Take now your son, your only *son* Isaac, whom you love, and go to the land of Moriah, and offer him there as a burnt offering on one of the mountains of which I shall tell you."

[3]So Abraham rose early in the morning and saddled his donkey, and took two of his young men with him, and Isaac his son; and he split the wood for the burnt offering, and arose and went to the place of which God had told him. [4]Then on the third day Abraham lifted his eyes and saw the place afar off. [5]And Abraham said to his young men, "Stay here with the donkey; the lad[a] and I will go yonder and worship, and we will come back to you."

21:31 [a] Literally *Well of the Oath* or *Well of the Seven* **22:5** [a] Or *young man*

6So Abraham took the
wood of the burnt offering
and laid *it* on Isaac his son;
and he took the fire in his
hand, and a knife, and the two
of them went together. 7But
Isaac spoke to Abraham his
father and said, "My father!"

And he said, "Here I am,
my son."

Then he said, "Look, the
fire and the wood, but where *is*
the lamb for a burnt offering?"

8And Abraham said, "My
son, God will provide for Himself the lamb for a burnt offering." So the two of them went
together.

9Then they came to the
place of which God had told
him. And Abraham built an
altar there and placed the
wood in order; and he bound
Isaac his son and laid him
on the altar, upon the wood.
10And Abraham stretched out
his hand and took the knife to
slay his son.

11But the Angel of the LORD
called to him from heaven and
said, "Abraham, Abraham!"

So he said, "Here I am."

12And He said, "Do not lay
your hand on the lad, or do
anything to him; for now I
know that you fear God, since
you have not withheld your
son, your only *son,* from Me."

13Then Abraham lifted his
eyes and looked, and there behind *him was* a ram caught
in a thicket by its horns. So
Abraham went and took the
ram, and offered it up for a
burnt offering instead of his
son. 14And Abraham called the
name of the place, The-LORD-
Will-Provide;[a] as it is said *to*
this day, "In the Mount of the
LORD it shall be provided."

15Then the Angel of the
LORD called to Abraham a
second time out of heaven,
16and said: "By Myself I have
sworn, says the LORD, because
you have done this thing, and
have not withheld your son,
your only *son*— 17blessing I
will bless you, and multiplying I will multiply your descendants as the stars of the
heaven and as the sand which
is on the seashore; and your
descendants shall possess
the gate of their enemies.
18In your seed all the nations
of the earth shall be blessed,
because you have obeyed My
voice." 19So Abraham returned
to his young men, and they
rose and went together to Beersheba; and Abraham dwelt
at Beersheba.

THE FAMILY OF NAHOR

20Now it came to pass after
these things that it was told
Abraham, saying, "Indeed
Milcah also has borne children to your brother Nahor:
21Huz his firstborn, Buz his
brother, Kemuel the father
of Aram, 22Chesed, Hazo, Pil-
dash, Jidlaph, and Bethuel."

22:14 [a] Hebrew *YHWH Yireh*

23And Bethuel begot Rebekah.[a] These eight Milcah bore to Nahor, Abraham's brother. 24His concubine, whose name was Reumah, also bore Tebah, Gaham, Thahash, and Maachah.

SARAH'S DEATH AND BURIAL

23 Sarah lived one hundred and twenty-seven years; *these were* the years of the life of Sarah. 2So Sarah died in Kirjath Arba (that *is,* Hebron) in the land of Canaan, and Abraham came to mourn for Sarah and to weep for her.

3Then Abraham stood up from before his dead, and spoke to the sons of Heth, saying, 4"I *am* a foreigner and a visitor among you. Give me property for a burial place among you, that I may bury my dead out of my sight."

5And the sons of Heth answered Abraham, saying to him, 6"Hear us, my lord: You *are* a mighty prince among us; bury your dead in the choicest of our burial places. None of us will withhold from you his burial place, that you may bury your dead."

7Then Abraham stood up and bowed himself to the people of the land, the sons of Heth. 8And he spoke with them, saying, "If it is your wish that I bury my dead out of my sight, hear me, and meet with Ephron the son of Zohar for me, 9that he may give me the cave of Machpelah which he has, which *is* at the end of his field. Let him give it to me at the full price, as property for a burial place among you."

10Now Ephron dwelt among the sons of Heth; and Ephron the Hittite answered Abraham in the presence of the sons of Heth, all who entered at the gate of his city, saying, 11"No, my lord, hear me: I give you the field and the cave that *is* in it; I give it to you in the presence of the sons of my people. I give it to you. Bury your dead!"

12Then Abraham bowed himself down before the people of the land; 13and he spoke to Ephron in the hearing of the people of the land, saying, "If you *will give it,* please hear me. I will give you money for the field; take *it* from me and I will bury my dead there."

14And Ephron answered Abraham, saying to him, 15"My lord, listen to me; the land *is worth* four hundred shekels of silver. What *is* that between you and me? So bury your dead." 16And Abraham listened to Ephron; and Abraham weighed out the silver for Ephron which he had named in the hearing of the sons of Heth, four hundred shekels of silver, currency of the merchants.

22:23 [a] Spelled *Rebecca* in Romans 9:10

17So the field of Ephron
which *was* in Machpelah,
which *was* before Mamre, the
field and the cave which *was*
in it, and all the trees that *were*
in the field, which *were* within
all the surrounding borders,
were deeded 18to Abraham as
a possession in the presence of
the sons of Heth, before all who
went in at the gate of his city.
19And after this, Abraham
buried Sarah his wife in the
cave of the field of Machpelah, before Mamre (that *is*, Hebron) in the land of Canaan.
20So the field and the cave
that *is* in it were deeded to
Abraham by the sons of Heth
as property for a burial place.

A BRIDE FOR ISAAC

24 Now Abraham was old,
well advanced in age;
and the LORD had blessed
Abraham in all things. 2So
Abraham said to the oldest
servant of his house, who
ruled over all that he had,
"Please, put your hand under
my thigh, 3and I will make you
swear by the LORD, the God
of heaven and the God of the
earth, that you will not take
a wife for my son from the
daughters of the Canaanites,
among whom I dwell; 4but you
shall go to my country and to
my family, and take a wife for
my son Isaac."
5And the servant said to
him, "Perhaps the woman will
not be willing to follow me to
this land. Must I take your son
back to the land from which
you came?"
6But Abraham said to him,
"Beware that you do not take
my son back there. 7The LORD
God of heaven, who took me
from my father's house and
from the land of my family,
and who spoke to me and
swore to me, saying, 'To your
descendants[a] I give this land,'
He will send His angel before
you, and you shall take a wife
for my son from there. 8And
if the woman is not willing to
follow you, then you will be released from this oath; only do
not take my son back there."
9So the servant put his hand
under the thigh of Abraham
his master, and swore to him
concerning this matter.
10Then the servant took
ten of his master's camels and
departed, for all his master's
goods *were in* his hand. And
he arose and went to Mesopotamia, to the city of Nahor.
11And he made his camels
kneel down outside the city
by a well of water at evening
time, the time when women
go out to draw *water*. 12Then
he said, "O LORD God of my
master Abraham, please give
me success this day, and show
kindness to my master Abraham. 13Behold, *here* I stand
by the well of water, and the
daughters of the men of the

24:7 [a] Literally *seed*

city are coming out to draw
water. 14Now let it be that the
young woman to whom I say,
'Please let down your pitcher
that I may drink,' and she says,
'Drink, and I will also give your
camels a drink'—*let* her *be the*
one You have appointed for
Your servant Isaac. And by
this I will know that You have
shown kindness to my master."

15And it happened, before
he had finished speaking, that
behold, Rebekah, who was
born to Bethuel, son of Milcah, the wife of Nahor, Abraham's brother, came out with
her pitcher on her shoulder.
16Now the young woman *was*
very beautiful to behold, a
virgin; no man had known
her. And she went down to
the well, filled her pitcher,
and came up. 17And the servant ran to meet her and said,
"Please let me drink a little
water from your pitcher."

18So she said, "Drink, my
lord." Then she quickly let
her pitcher down to her hand,
and gave him a drink. 19And
when she had finished giving
him a drink, she said, "I will
draw *water* for your camels
also, until they have finished
drinking." 20Then she quickly
emptied her pitcher into the
trough, ran back to the well
to draw *water,* and drew for
all his camels. 21And the man,
wondering at her, remained
silent so as to know whether
the LORD had made his journey prosperous or not.

22So it was, when the camels had finished drinking, that
the man took a golden nose
ring weighing half a shekel, and two bracelets for her
wrists weighing ten *shekels*
of gold, 23and said, "Whose
daughter *are* you? Tell me,
please, is there room *in* your
father's house for us to lodge?"

24So she said to him, "I *am*
the daughter of Bethuel, Milcah's son, whom she bore to
Nahor." 25Moreover she said
to him, "We have both straw
and feed enough, and room
to lodge."

26Then the man bowed
down his head and worshiped
the LORD. 27And he said,
"Blessed *be* the LORD God of
my master Abraham, who has
not forsaken His mercy and
His truth toward my master.
As for me, being on the way,
the LORD led me to the house
of my master's brethren." 28So
the young woman ran and
told her mother's household
these things.

29Now Rebekah had a
brother whose name *was*
Laban, and Laban ran out to
the man by the well. 30So it
came to pass, when he saw the
nose ring, and the bracelets on
his sister's wrists, and when he
heard the words of his sister
Rebekah, saying, "Thus the
man spoke to me," that he
went to the man. And there
he stood by the camels at the
well. 31And he said, "Come in,
O blessed of the LORD! Why

do you stand outside? For I
have prepared the house, and
a place for the camels."
32 Then the man came to
the house. And he unloaded
the camels, and provided
straw and feed for the camels, and water to wash his feet
and the feet of the men who
were with him. 33 *Food* was set
before him to eat, but he said,
"I will not eat until I have told
about my errand."
And he said, "Speak on."
34 So he said, "I *am* Abraham's servant. 35 The LORD
has blessed my master greatly,
and he has become great; and
He has given him flocks and
herds, silver and gold, male
and female servants, and camels and donkeys. 36 And Sarah
my master's wife bore a son to
my master when she was old;
and to him he has given all
that he has. 37 Now my master
made me swear, saying, 'You
shall not take a wife for my
son from the daughters of the
Canaanites, in whose land I
dwell; 38 but you shall go to
my father's house and to my
family, and take a wife for my
son.' 39 And I said to my master, 'Perhaps the woman will
not follow me.' 40 But he said to
me, 'The LORD, before whom I
walk, will send His angel with
you and prosper your way;
and you shall take a wife for
my son from my family and
from my father's house. 41 You
will be clear from this oath
when you arrive among my
family; for if they will not give
her to you, then you will be
released from my oath.'
42 "And this day I came to
the well and said, 'O LORD
God of my master Abraham,
if You will now prosper the
way in which I go, 43 behold,
I stand by the well of water;
and it shall come to pass
that when the virgin comes
out to draw *water,* and I say
to her, "Please give me a little water from your pitcher
to drink," 44 and she says to
me, "Drink, and I will draw
for your camels also,"—*let* her
be the woman whom the LORD
has appointed for my master's
son.'
45 "But before I had finished
speaking in my heart, there
was Rebekah, coming out with
her pitcher on her shoulder;
and she went down to the well
and drew *water.* And I said
to her, 'Please let me drink.'
46 And she made haste and
let her pitcher down from
her *shoulder,* and said, 'Drink,
and I will give your camels a
drink also.' So I drank, and she
gave the camels a drink also.
47 Then I asked her, and said,
'Whose daughter *are* you?'
And she said, 'The daugh-
ter of Bethuel, Nahor's son,
whom Milcah bore to him.'
So I put the nose ring on her
nose and the bracelets on her
wrists. 48 And I bowed my head
and worshiped the LORD, and
blessed the LORD God of my
master Abraham, who had led

me in the way of truth to take
the daughter of my master's
brother for his son. [49]Now if
you will deal kindly and truly
with my master, tell me. And if
not, tell me, that I may turn to
the right hand or to the left."
[50]Then Laban and Bethuel
answered and said, "The thing
comes from the LORD; we cannot speak to you either bad or
good. [51]Here *is* Rebekah before you; take *her* and go, and
let her be your master's son's
wife, as the LORD has spoken."
[52]And it came to pass, when
Abraham's servant heard their
words, that he worshiped the
LORD, *bowing himself* to the
earth. [53]Then the servant
brought out jewelry of silver,
jewelry of gold, and clothing,
and gave *them* to Rebekah. He
also gave precious things to
her brother and to her mother.
[54]And he and the men who
were with him ate and drank
and stayed all night. Then they
arose in the morning, and he
said, "Send me away to my
master."
[55]But her brother and her
mother said, "Let the young
woman stay with us *a few*
days, at least ten; after that
she may go."
[56]And he said to them, "Do
not hinder me, since the LORD
has prospered my way; send
me away so that I may go to
my master."
[57]So they said, "We will call
the young woman and ask her
personally." [58]Then they called
Rebekah and said to her, "Will
you go with this man?"

And she said, "I will go."

[59]So they sent away Re-
bekah their sister and her
nurse, and Abraham's ser-
vant and his men. [60]And they
blessed Rebekah and said to
her:

"Our sister, *may*
you *become*
The mother of thousands
of ten thousands;
And may your
descendants possess
The gates of those
who hate them."

[61]Then Rebekah and her
maids arose, and they rode
on the camels and followed
the man. So the servant took
Rebekah and departed.
[62]Now Isaac came from
the way of Beer Lahai Roi, for
he dwelt in the South. [63]And
Isaac went out to meditate in
the field in the evening; and
he lifted his eyes and looked,
and there, the camels *were*
coming. [64]Then Rebekah
lifted her eyes, and when she
saw Isaac she dismounted
from her camel; [65]for she had
said to the servant, "Who *is*
this man walking in the field
to meet us?"

The servant said, "It *is* my
master." So she took a veil and
covered herself.

[66]And the servant told
Isaac all the things that he had
done. [67]Then Isaac brought

her into his mother Sarah's
tent; and he took Rebekah
and she became his wife, and
he loved her. So Isaac was
comforted after his mother's
death.

ABRAHAM AND KETURAH

25 Abraham again took a
wife, and her name *was*
Keturah. 2And she bore him
Zimran, Jokshan, Medan, Mid-
ian, Ishbak, and Shuah. 3Jok-
shan begot Sheba and Dedan.
And the sons of Dedan were
Asshurim, Letushim, and
Leummim. 4And the sons of
Midian *were* Ephah, Epher,
Hanoch, Abidah, and Eldaah.
All these *were* the children of
Keturah.

5And Abraham gave all that
he had to Isaac. 6But Abraham
gave gifts to the sons of the
concubines which Abraham
had; and while he was still living he sent them eastward,
away from Isaac his son, to
the country of the east.

ABRAHAM'S DEATH AND BURIAL

7This *is* the sum of the
years of Abraham's life which
he lived: one hundred and
seventy-five years. 8Then
Abraham breathed his last
and died in a good old age,
an old man and full *of years,*
and was gathered to his people. 9And his sons Isaac and
Ishmael buried him in the
cave of Machpelah, which *is*
before Mamre, in the field of
Ephron the son of Zohar the
Hittite, 10the field which Abraham purchased from the sons
of Heth. There Abraham was
buried, and Sarah his wife.
11And it came to pass, after
the death of Abraham, that
God blessed his son Isaac. And
Isaac dwelt at Beer Lahai Roi.

THE FAMILIES OF ISHMAEL AND ISAAC

12Now this *is* the genealogy
of Ishmael, Abraham's son,
whom Hagar the Egyptian,
Sarah's maidservant, bore
to Abraham. 13And these
were the names of the sons
of Ishmael, by their names,
according to their generations: The firstborn of Ishmael, Nebajoth; then Kedar,
Adbeel, Mibsam, 14Mishma,
Dumah, Massa, 15Hadar,[a]
Tema, Jetur, Naphish, and
Kedemah. 16These *were* the
sons of Ishmael and these
were their names, by their
towns and their settlements,
twelve princes according to
their nations. 17These *were* the
years of the life of Ishmael:
one hundred and thirty-seven
years; and he breathed his last
and died, and was gathered to
his people. 18(They dwelt from
Havilah as far as Shur, which
is east of Egypt as you go toward Assyria.) He died in the
presence of all his brethren.

25:15 [a] Masoretic Text reads *Hadad.*

19This *is* the genealogy of
Isaac, Abraham's son. Abraham begot Isaac. 20Isaac was
forty years old when he took
Rebekah as wife, the daughter
of Bethuel the Syrian of Padan
Aram, the sister of Laban the
Syrian. 21Now Isaac pleaded
with the LORD for his wife,
because she *was* barren; and
the LORD granted his plea, and
Rebekah his wife conceived.
22But the children struggled
together within her; and she
said, "If *all is* well, why *am I
like* this?" So she went to inquire of the LORD.
23And the LORD said to her:

"Two nations *are*
in your womb,
Two peoples shall
be separated from
your body;
One people shall be
stronger than the other,
And the older shall
serve the younger."

24So when her days were
fulfilled *for her* to give birth,
indeed *there were* twins in
her womb. 25And the first
came out red. *He was* like a
hairy garment all over; so
they called his name Esau.[a]
26Afterward his brother came
out, and his hand took hold of
Esau's heel; so his name was
called Jacob.[a] Isaac *was* sixty
years old when she bore them.
27So the boys grew. And
Esau was a skillful hunter, a
man of the field; but Jacob
was a mild man, dwelling in
tents. 28And Isaac loved Esau
because he ate *of his* game, but
Rebekah loved Jacob.

ESAU SELLS HIS BIRTHRIGHT

29Now Jacob cooked a stew;
and Esau came in from the
field, and he *was* weary. 30And
Esau said to Jacob, "Please
feed me with that same red
stew, for I *am* weary." Therefore his name was called
Edom.[a]
31But Jacob said, "Sell me
your birthright as of this day."
32And Esau said, "Look, I
am about to die; so what *is* this
birthright to me?"
33Then Jacob said, "Swear
to me as of this day."
So he swore to him, and
sold his birthright to Jacob.
34And Jacob gave Esau bread
and stew of lentils; then he ate
and drank, arose, and went
his way. Thus Esau despised
his birthright.

ISAAC AND ABIMELECH

26 There was a famine in
the land, besides the
first famine that was in the
days of Abraham. And Isaac
went to Abimelech king of the
Philistines, in Gerar.
2Then the LORD appeared

25:25 [a] Literally *Hairy* 25:26 [a] Literally *Supplanter* 25:30 [a] Literally *Red*

to him and said: "Do not go
down to Egypt; live in the
land of which I shall tell you.
[3]Dwell in this land, and I will
be with you and bless you; for
to you and your descendants
I give all these lands, and I
will perform the oath which I
swore to Abraham your father.
[4]And I will make your descendants multiply as the stars of
heaven; I will give to your descendants all these lands; and
in your seed all the nations
of the earth shall be blessed;
[5]because Abraham obeyed My
voice and kept My charge, My
commandments, My statutes,
and My laws."

[6]So Isaac dwelt in Gerar.
[7]And the men of the place
asked about his wife. And he
said, "She *is* my sister"; for he
was afraid to say, "*She is* my
wife," *because he thought,* "lest
the men of the place kill me
for Rebekah, because she *is*
beautiful to behold." [8]Now it
came to pass, when he had
been there a long time, that
Abimelech king of the Philistines looked through a window, and saw, and there was
Isaac, showing endearment
to Rebekah his wife. [9]Then
Abimelech called Isaac and
said, "Quite obviously she *is*
your wife; so how could you
say, 'She *is* my sister'?"

Isaac said to him, "Because
I said, 'Lest I die on account
of her.'"

[10]And Abimelech said,
"What *is* this you have done
to us? One of the people might
soon have lain with your wife,
and you would have brought
guilt on us." [11]So Abimelech
charged all *his* people, saying,
"He who touches this man or
his wife shall surely be put to
death."

[12]Then Isaac sowed in that
land, and reaped in the same
year a hundredfold; and the
LORD blessed him. [13]The man
began to prosper, and continued prospering until he became very prosperous; [14]for
he had possessions of flocks
and possessions of herds and
a great number of servants.
So the Philistines envied him.
[15]Now the Philistines had
stopped up all the wells which
his father's servants had dug
in the days of Abraham his father, and they had filled them
with earth. [16]And Abimelech
said to Isaac, "Go away from
us, for you are much mightier
than we."

[17]Then Isaac departed from
there and pitched his tent in
the Valley of Gerar, and dwelt
there. [18]And Isaac dug again
the wells of water which they
had dug in the days of Abraham his father, for the Philistines had stopped them up
after the death of Abraham.
He called them by the names
which his father had called
them.

[19]Also Isaac's servants dug
in the valley, and found a well
of running water there. [20]But
the herdsmen of Gerar quar-

reled with Isaac's herdsmen,
saying, "The water *is* ours." So
he called the name of the well
Esek,[a] because they quarreled
with him. 21Then they dug another well, and they quarreled
over that *one* also. So he called
its name Sitnah.[a] 22And he
moved from there and dug
another well, and they did not
quarrel over it. So he called
its name Rehoboth,[a] because
he said, "For now the LORD
has made room for us, and we
shall be fruitful in the land."

23Then he went up from
there to Beersheba. 24And
the LORD appeared to him the
same night and said, "I *am* the
God of your father Abraham;
do not fear, for I *am* with you.
I will bless you and multiply
your descendants for My servant Abraham's sake." 25So he
built an altar there and called
on the name of the LORD, and
he pitched his tent there; and
there Isaac's servants dug a
well.

26Then Abimelech came to
him from Gerar with Ahuz-
zath, one of his friends, and
Phichol the commander of
his army. 27And Isaac said to
them, "Why have you come
to me, since you hate me and
have sent me away from you?"

28But they said, "We have
certainly seen that the LORD is
with you. So we said, 'Let there
now be an oath between us,
between you and us; and let
us make a covenant with you,
29that you will do us no harm,
since we have not touched
you, and since we have done
nothing to you but good and
have sent you away in peace.
You *are* now the blessed of the
LORD.'"

30So he made them a feast,
and they ate and drank. 31Then
they arose early in the morning and swore an oath with
one another; and Isaac sent
them away, and they departed
from him in peace.

32It came to pass the same
day that Isaac's servants came
and told him about the well
which they had dug, and said
to him, "We have found water."
33So he called it Shebah.[a]
Therefore the name of the
city *is* Beersheba[b] to this day.

34When Esau was forty
years old, he took as wives
Judith the daughter of Beeri
the Hittite, and Basemath the
daughter of Elon the Hittite.
35And they were a grief of
mind to Isaac and Rebekah.

ISAAC BLESSES JACOB

27 Now it came to pass,
when Isaac was old and
his eyes were so dim that he
could not see, that he called
Esau his older son and said
to him, "My son."

26:20 [a] Literally *Quarrel* 26:21 [a] Literally *Enmity*
26:22 [a] Literally *Spaciousness* 26:33 [a] Literally *Oath* or
Seven [b] Literally *Well of the Oath* or *Well of the Seven*

And he answered him, "Here I am."

[2]Then he said, "Behold now, I am old. I do not know the day of my death. [3]Now therefore, please take your weapons, your quiver and your bow, and go out to the field and hunt game for me. [4]And make me savory food, such as I love, and bring *it* to me that I may eat, that my soul may bless you before I die."

[5]Now Rebekah was listening when Isaac spoke to Esau his son. And Esau went to the field to hunt game and to bring *it*. [6]So Rebekah spoke to Jacob her son, saying, "Indeed I heard your father speak to Esau your brother, saying, [7]'Bring me game and make savory food for me, that I may eat it and bless you in the presence of the LORD before my death.' [8]Now therefore, my son, obey my voice according to what I command you. [9]Go now to the flock and bring me from there two choice kids of the goats, and I will make savory food from them for your father, such as he loves. [10]Then you shall take *it* to your father, that he may eat *it*, and that he may bless you before his death."

[11]And Jacob said to Rebekah his mother, "Look, Esau my brother *is* a hairy man, and I *am* a smooth-*skinned* man. [12]Perhaps my father will feel me, and I shall seem to be a deceiver to him; and I shall bring a curse on myself and not a blessing."

[13]But his mother said to him, "*Let* your curse *be* on me, my son; only obey my voice, and go, get *them* for me." [14]And he went and got *them* and brought *them* to his mother, and his mother made savory food, such as his father loved. [15]Then Rebekah took the choice clothes of her elder son Esau, which *were* with her in the house, and put them on Jacob her younger son. [16]And she put the skins of the kids of the goats on his hands and on the smooth part of his neck. [17]Then she gave the savory food and the bread, which she had prepared, into the hand of her son Jacob.

[18]So he went to his father and said, "My father."

And he said, "Here I am. Who *are* you, my son?"

[19]Jacob said to his father, "I *am* Esau your firstborn; I have done just as you told me; please arise, sit and eat of my game, that your soul may bless me."

[20]But Isaac said to his son, "How *is it* that you have found *it* so quickly, my son?"

And he said, "Because the LORD your God brought *it* to me."

[21]Isaac said to Jacob, "Please come near, that I may feel you, my son, whether you *are* really my son Esau or not." [22]So Jacob went near to Isaac

his father, and he felt him and
said, "The voice *is* Jacob's
voice, but the hands *are* the
hands of Esau." 23And he did
not recognize him, because
his hands were hairy like his
brother Esau's hands; so he
blessed him.
24Then he said, "*Are* you
really my son Esau?"
He said, "I *am.*"
25He said, "Bring *it* near to
me, and I will eat of my son's
game, so that my soul may
bless you." So he brought *it*
near to him, and he ate; and
he brought him wine, and he
drank. 26Then his father Isaac
said to him, "Come near now
and kiss me, my son." 27And
he came near and kissed him;
and he smelled the smell of
his clothing, and blessed him
and said:

"Surely, the smell
 of my son
Is like the smell of a field
Which the LORD
 has blessed.
28 Therefore may
 God give you
Of the dew of heaven,
Of the fatness of
 the earth,
And plenty of grain
 and wine.
29 Let peoples serve you,
And nations bow
 down to you.
Be master over
 your brethren,
And let your mother's
 sons bow down to you.
Cursed *be* everyone
 who curses you,
And blessed *be* those
 who bless you!"

ESAU'S LOST HOPE

30Now it happened, as soon
as Isaac had finished blessing
Jacob, and Jacob had scarcely
gone out from the presence
of Isaac his father, that Esau
his brother came in from his
hunting. 31He also had made
savory food, and brought it
to his father, and said to his
father, "Let my father arise
and eat of his son's game, that
your soul may bless me."
32And his father Isaac said
to him, "Who *are* you?"
So he said, "I *am* your son,
your firstborn, Esau."
33Then Isaac trembled ex-
ceedingly, and said, "Who?
Where *is* the one who hunted
game and brought *it* to me? I
ate all *of it* before you came,
and I have blessed him—*and*
indeed he shall be blessed."
34When Esau heard the
words of his father, he cried
with an exceedingly great
and bitter cry, and said to his
father, "Bless me—me also,
O my father!"
35But he said, "Your brother
came with deceit and has
taken away your blessing."
36And *Esau* said, "Is he not
rightly named Jacob? For he
has supplanted me these
two times. He took away my
birthright, and now look, he
has taken away my blessing!"

And he said, "Have you not
reserved a blessing for me?"
37 Then Isaac answered and
said to Esau, "Indeed I have
made him your master, and
all his brethren I have given
to him as servants; with grain
and wine I have sustained
him. What shall I do now for
you, my son?"
38 And Esau said to his father, "Have you only one blessing, my father? Bless me—me
also, O my father!" And Esau
lifted up his voice and wept.
39 Then Isaac his father answered and said to him:

"Behold, your dwelling
shall be of the fatness
of the earth,
And of the dew of
heaven from above.
40 By your sword you
shall live,
And you shall serve
your brother;
And it shall come
to pass, when you
become restless,
That you shall break his
yoke from your neck."

JACOB ESCAPES FROM ESAU

41 So Esau hated Jacob because of the blessing with
which his father blessed him,
and Esau said in his heart,
"The days of mourning for
my father are at hand; then
I will kill my brother Jacob."
42 And the words of Esau
her older son were told to
Rebekah. So she sent and
called Jacob her younger
son, and said to him, "Surely
your brother Esau comforts
himself concerning you *by*
intending to kill you.
43 Now
therefore, my son, obey my
voice: arise, flee to my brother
Laban in Haran.
44 And stay
with him a few days, until your
brother's fury turns away,
45 until your brother's anger
turns away from you, and he
forgets what you have done
to him; then I will send and
bring you from there. Why
should I be bereaved also of
you both in one day?"
46 And Rebekah said to
Isaac, "I am weary of my life
because of the daughters of
Heth; if Jacob takes a wife of
the daughters of Heth, like
these *who are* the daughters
of the land, what good will my
life be to me?"

28 Then Isaac called Jacob and blessed him,
and charged him, and said
to him: "You shall not take
a wife from the daughters of
Canaan.
2 Arise, go to Padan
Aram, to the house of Bethuel
your mother's father; and take
yourself a wife from there of
the daughters of Laban your
mother's brother.

3 "May God Almighty
bless you,
And make you fruitful
and multiply you,
That you may be an
assembly of peoples;

4 And give you the
blessing of Abraham,
To you and your
descendants with you,
That you may
inherit the land
In which you are
a stranger,
Which God gave to
Abraham."

5So Isaac sent Jacob away,
and he went to Padan Aram,
to Laban the son of Bethuel
the Syrian, the brother of Rebekah, the mother of Jacob
and Esau.

ESAU MARRIES MAHALATH

6Esau saw that Isaac had
blessed Jacob and sent him
away to Padan Aram to take
himself a wife from there, *and*
that as he blessed him he gave
him a charge, saying, "You
shall not take a wife from the
daughters of Canaan," 7and
that Jacob had obeyed his father and his mother and had
gone to Padan Aram. 8Also
Esau saw that the daughters
of Canaan did not please his
father Isaac. 9So Esau went
to Ishmael and took Maha-
lath the daughter of Ishmael,
Abraham's son, the sister of
Nebajoth, to be his wife in
addition to the wives he had.

JACOB'S VOW AT BETHEL

10Now Jacob went out from
Beersheba and went toward
Haran. 11So he came to a certain place and stayed there
all night, because the sun had
set. And he took one of the
stones of that place and put it
at his head, and he lay down in
that place to sleep. 12Then he
dreamed, and behold, a ladder
was set up on the earth, and
its top reached to heaven; and
there the angels of God were
ascending and descending
on it.

13And behold, the LORD
stood above it and said: "I
am the LORD God of Abraham your father and the God
of Isaac; the land on which
you lie I will give to you and
your descendants. 14Also your
descendants shall be as the
dust of the earth; you shall
spread abroad to the west
and the east, to the north and
the south; and in you and in
your seed all the families of
the earth shall be blessed.
15Behold, I *am* with you and
will keep you wherever you
go, and will bring you back to
this land; for I will not leave
you until I have done what I
have spoken to you."

16Then Jacob awoke from
his sleep and said, "Surely
the LORD is in this place, and
I did not know *it*." 17And he
was afraid and said, "How
awesome *is* this place! This
is none other than the house
of God, and this *is* the gate of
heaven!"

18Then Jacob rose early in
the morning, and took the
stone that he had put at his
head, set it up as a pillar, and

poured oil on top of it. 19And he
called the name of that place
Bethel;[a] but the name of that
city had been Luz previously.
20Then Jacob made a vow, saying, "If God will be with me,
and keep me in this way that I
am going, and give me bread
to eat and clothing to put on,
21so that I come back to my father's house in peace, then the
LORD shall be my God. 22And
this stone which I have set as
a pillar shall be God's house,
and of all that You give me I
will surely give a tenth to You."

JACOB MEETS RACHEL

29 So Jacob went on his
journey and came to
the land of the people of the
East. 2And he looked, and saw
a well in the field; and behold, there *were* three flocks
of sheep lying by it; for out
of that well they watered the
flocks. A large stone *was* on
the well's mouth. 3Now all
the flocks would be gathered
there; and they would roll the
stone from the well's mouth,
water the sheep, and put the
stone back in its place on the
well's mouth.

4And Jacob said to them,
"My brethren, where *are* you
from?"

And they said, "We *are*
from Haran."

5Then he said to them, "Do
you know Laban the son of
Nahor?"

And they said, "We know
him."

6So he said to them, "Is he
well?"

And they said, "*He is* well.
And look, his daughter Rachel
is coming with the sheep."

7Then he said, "Look, *it is*
still high day; *it is* not time
for the cattle to be gathered
together. Water the sheep, and
go and feed *them*."

8But they said, "We cannot
until all the flocks are gathered together, and they have
rolled the stone from the
well's mouth; then we water
the sheep."

9Now while he was still
speaking with them, Rachel
came with her father's sheep,
for she was a shepherdess.
10And it came to pass, when
Jacob saw Rachel the daughter
of Laban his mother's brother,
and the sheep of Laban his
mother's brother, that Jacob
went near and rolled the stone
from the well's mouth, and
watered the flock of Laban his
mother's brother. 11Then Jacob kissed Rachel, and lifted
up his voice and wept. 12And
Jacob told Rachel that he *was*
her father's relative and that
he *was* Rebekah's son. So she
ran and told her father.

13Then it came to pass,
when Laban heard the report
about Jacob his sister's son,
that he ran to meet him, and
embraced him and kissed

28:19 [a] Literally *House of God*

him, and brought him to his
house. So he told Laban all
these things. 14And Laban
said to him, "Surely you *are*
my bone and my flesh." And
he stayed with him for a
month.

JACOB MARRIES LEAH AND RACHEL

15Then Laban said to Jacob,
"Because you *are* my relative,
should you therefore serve
me for nothing? Tell me, what
should your wages *be?*" 16Now
Laban had two daughters: the
name of the elder *was* Leah,
and the name of the younger
was Rachel. 17Leah's eyes *were*
delicate, but Rachel was beautiful of form and appearance.

18Now Jacob loved Rachel;
so he said, "I will serve you
seven years for Rachel your
younger daughter."

19And Laban said, "*It is* better that I give her to you than
that I should give her to another man. Stay with me." 20So
Jacob served seven years for
Rachel, and they seemed *only*
a few days to him because of
the love he had for her.

21Then Jacob said to Laban,
"Give *me* my wife, for my days
are fulfilled, that I may go in
to her." 22And Laban gathered
together all the men of the
place and made a feast. 23Now
it came to pass in the evening,
that he took Leah his daughter
and brought her to Jacob; and
he went in to her. 24And Laban
gave his maid Zilpah to his
daughter Leah *as* a maid. 25So
it came to pass in the morning, that behold, it *was* Leah.
And he said to Laban, "What
is this you have done to me?
Was it not for Rachel that I
served you? Why then have
you deceived me?"

26And Laban said, "It must
not be done so in our country,
to give the younger before the
firstborn. 27Fulfill her week,
and we will give you this one
also for the service which
you will serve with me still
another seven years."

28Then Jacob did so and
fulfilled her week. So he gave
him his daughter Rachel as
wife also. 29And Laban gave
his maid Bilhah to his daughter Rachel as a maid. 30Then
Jacob also went in to Rachel,
and he also loved Rachel more
than Leah. And he served with
Laban still another seven
years.

THE CHILDREN OF JACOB

31When the LORD saw that
Leah *was* unloved, He opened
her womb; but Rachel *was*
barren. 32So Leah conceived
and bore a son, and she called
his name Reuben;[a] for she
said, "The LORD has surely
looked on my affliction. Now
therefore, my husband will
love me." 33Then she con-
ceived again and bore a son,

29:32 [a] Literally *See, a Son*

and said, "Because the LORD
has heard that I *am* unloved,
He has therefore given me
this *son* also." And she called
his name Simeon.[a] 34She conceived again and bore a son,
and said, "Now this time my
husband will become attached
to me, because I have borne
him three sons." Therefore his
name was called Levi.[a] 35And
she conceived again and bore
a son, and said, "Now I will
praise the LORD." Therefore
she called his name Judah.[a]
Then she stopped bearing.

30 Now when Rachel saw
that she bore Jacob no
children, Rachel envied her
sister, and said to Jacob, "Give
me children, or else I die!"

2And Jacob's anger was
aroused against Rachel, and
he said, "*Am* I in the place of
God, who has withheld from
you the fruit of the womb?"

3So she said, "Here is my
maid Bilhah; go in to her, and
she will bear *a child* on my
knees, that I also may have
children by her." 4Then she
gave him Bilhah her maid as
wife, and Jacob went in to her.
5And Bilhah conceived and
bore Jacob a son. 6Then Rachel said, "God has judged my
case; and He has also heard
my voice and given me a son."
Therefore she called his name
Dan.[a] 7And Rachel's maid Bilhah conceived again and bore
Jacob a second son. 8Then Rachel said, "With great wres-
tlings I have wrestled with
my sister, *and* indeed I have
prevailed." So she called his
name Naphtali.[a]

9When Leah saw that she
had stopped bearing, she took
Zilpah her maid and gave her
to Jacob as wife. 10And Leah's
maid Zilpah bore Jacob a son.
11Then Leah said, "A troop
comes!"[a] So she called his
name Gad.[b] 12And Leah's maid
Zilpah bore Jacob a second
son. 13Then Leah said, "I am
happy, for the daughters will
call me blessed." So she called
his name Asher.[a]

14Now Reuben went in
the days of wheat harvest
and found mandrakes in the
field, and brought them to
his mother Leah. Then Ra-
chel said to Leah, "Please give
me *some* of your son's mandrakes."

15But she said to her, "*Is it*
a small matter that you have
taken away my husband?
Would you take away my son's
mandrakes also?"

And Rachel said, "Therefore
he will lie with you tonight for
your son's mandrakes."

16When Jacob came out of
the field in the evening, Leah

29:33 [a] Literally *Heard* 29:34 [a] Literally Attached
29:35 [a] Literally *Praise* 30:6 [a] Literally *Judge* 30:8 [a] Literally
My Wrestling 30:11 [a] Following Qere, Syriac, and
Targum; Kethib, Septuagint, and Vulgate read *in fortune.*
[b] Literally *Troop* or *Fortune* 30:13 [a] Literally *Happy*

went out to meet him and said, "You must come in to me, for I have surely hired you with my son's mandrakes." And he lay with her that night.

17And God listened to Leah, and she conceived and bore Jacob a fifth son. 18Leah said, "God has given me my wages, because I have given my maid to my husband." So she called his name Issachar.[a] 19Then Leah conceived again and bore Jacob a sixth son. 20And Leah said, "God has endowed me *with* a good endowment; now my husband will dwell with me, because I have borne him six sons." So she called his name Zebulun.[a] 21Afterward she bore a daughter, and called her name Dinah.

22Then God remembered Rachel, and God listened to her and opened her womb. 23And she conceived and bore a son, and said, "God has taken away my reproach." 24So she called his name Joseph,[a] and said, "The LORD shall add to me another son."

JACOB'S AGREEMENT WITH LABAN

25And it came to pass, when Rachel had borne Joseph, that *Jacob said* to Laban, "Send me away, that I may go to my own place and to my country. 26Give *me* my wives and my children for whom I have served you, and let me go; for you know my service which I have done for you."

27And Laban said to him, "Please *stay,* if I have found favor in your eyes, *for* I have learned by experience that the LORD has blessed me for your sake." 28Then he said, "Name me your wages, and I will give *it.*"

29So *Jacob* said to him, "You know how I have served you and how your livestock has been with me. 30For what you had before I *came was* little, and it has increased to a great amount; the LORD has blessed you since my coming. And now, when shall I also provide for my own house?"

31So he said, "What shall I give you?"

And Jacob said, "You shall not give me anything. If you will do this thing for me, I will again feed and keep your flocks: 32Let me pass through all your flock today, removing from there all the speckled and spotted sheep, and all the brown ones among the lambs, and the spotted and speckled among the goats; and *these* shall be my wages. 33So my righteousness will answer for me in time to come, when the subject of my wages comes before you: every one that *is* not speckled and spotted among the goats, and brown among

30:18 [a] Literally *Wages* 30:20 [a] Literally *Dwelling* 30:24 [a] Literally *He Will Add*

the lambs, will be considered
stolen, if *it is* with me."
34And Laban said, "Oh,
that it were according to your
word!" 35So he removed that
day the male goats that were
speckled and spotted, all the
female goats that were speckled and spotted, every one that
had *some* white in it, and all the
brown ones among the lambs,
and gave *them* into the hand of
his sons. 36Then he put three
days' journey between himself
and Jacob, and Jacob fed the
rest of Laban's flocks.
37Now Jacob took for him-
self rods of green poplar and
of the almond and chestnut
trees, peeled white strips in
them, and exposed the white
which *was* in the rods. 38And
the rods which he had peeled,
he set before the flocks in
the gutters, in the watering
troughs where the flocks came
to drink, so that they should
conceive when they came to
drink. 39So the flocks conceived before the rods, and the
flocks brought forth streaked,
speckled, and spotted. 40Then
Jacob separated the lambs,
and made the flocks face toward the streaked and all the
brown in the flock of Laban;
but he put his own flocks by
themselves and did not put
them with Laban's flock.
41And it came to pass,
whenever the stronger livestock conceived, that Jacob
placed the rods before the
eyes of the livestock in the gutters, that they might conceive
among the rods. 42But when
the flocks were feeble, he did
not put *them* in; so the feebler
were Laban's and the stronger
Jacob's. 43Thus the man became exceedingly prosperous,
and had large flocks, female
and male servants, and camels and donkeys.

JACOB FLEES FROM LABAN

31 Now *Jacob* heard the
words of Laban's sons,
saying, "Jacob has taken away
all that was our father's, and
from what was our father's he
has acquired all this wealth."
2And Jacob saw the countenance of Laban, and indeed it
was not *favorable* toward him
as before. 3Then the LORD said
to Jacob, "Return to the land
of your fathers and to your
family, and I will be with you."
4So Jacob sent and called
Rachel and Leah to the field, to
his flock, 5and said to them, "I
see your father's countenance,
that it *is* not *favorable* toward
me as before; but the God of
my father has been with me.
6And you know that with all
my might I have served your
father. 7Yet your father has deceived me and changed my
wages ten times, but God did
not allow him to hurt me. 8If
he said thus: 'The speckled
shall be your wages,' then all
the flocks bore speckled. And
if he said thus: 'The streaked
shall be your wages,' then all
the flocks bore streaked. 9So

God has taken away the livestock of your father and given
them to me.
10“And it happened, at the
time when the flocks con-
ceived, that I lifted my eyes and
saw in a dream, and behold, the
rams which leaped upon the
flocks *were* streaked, speckled,
and gray-spotted. 11Then the
Angel of God spoke to me in a
dream, saying, ‘Jacob.’ And I
said, ‘Here I am.’ 12And He said,
‘Lift your eyes now and see,
all the rams which leap on the
flocks *are* streaked, speckled,
and gray-spotted; for I have
seen all that Laban is doing to
you. 13I *am* the God of Bethel,
where you anointed the pillar
and where you made a vow to
Me. Now arise, get out of this
land, and return to the land of
your family.’ ”
14Then Rachel and Leah
answered and said to him,
“Is there still any portion or
inheritance for us in our father’s house? 15Are we not
considered strangers by him?
For he has sold us, and also
completely consumed our
money. 16For all these riches
which God has taken from our
father are *really* ours and our
children’s; now then, whatever
God has said to you, do it.”
17Then Jacob rose and
set his sons and his wives
on camels. 18And he carried
away all his livestock and all
his possessions which he had
gained, his acquired livestock
which he had gained in Padan
Aram, to go to his father Isaac
in the land of Canaan. 19Now
Laban had gone to shear his
sheep, and Rachel had stolen
the household idols that were
her father’s. 20And Jacob stole
away, unknown to Laban the
Syrian, in that he did not tell
him that he intended to flee.
21So he fled with all that he
had. He arose and crossed the
river, and headed toward the
mountains of Gilead.

LABAN PURSUES JACOB

22And Laban was told on
the third day that Jacob had
fled. 23Then he took his brethren with him and pursued
him for seven days’ journey,
and he overtook him in the
mountains of Gilead. 24But
God had come to Laban the
Syrian in a dream by night,
and said to him, “Be careful
that you speak to Jacob neither good nor bad.”
25So Laban overtook Jacob.
Now Jacob had pitched his tent
in the mountains, and Laban
with his brethren pitched in
the mountains of Gilead.
26And Laban said to Jacob:
“What have you done, that you
have stolen away unknown
to me, and carried away my
daughters like captives *taken*
with the sword? 27Why did you
flee away secretly, and steal
away from me, and not tell
me; for I might have sent you
away with joy and songs, with
timbrel and harp? 28And you
did not allow me to kiss my

sons and my daughters. Now
you have done foolishly in *so*
doing. 29It is in my power to
do you harm, but the God of
your father spoke to me last
night, saying, 'Be careful that
you speak to Jacob neither
good nor bad.' 30And now you
have surely gone because you
greatly long for your father's
house, *but* why did you steal
my gods?"

31Then Jacob answered
and said to Laban, "Because I
was afraid, for I said, 'Perhaps
you would take your daughters from me by force.' 32With
whomever you find your gods,
do not let him live. In the presence of our brethren, identify
what I have of yours and take
it with you." For Jacob did not
know that Rachel had stolen
them.

33And Laban went into Ja-
cob's tent, into Leah's tent, and
into the two maids' tents, but
he did not find *them.* Then he
went out of Leah's tent and entered Rachel's tent. 34Now Rachel had taken the household
idols, put them in the camel's
saddle, and sat on them. And
Laban searched all about the
tent but did not find *them.*
35And she said to her father,
"Let it not displease my lord
that I cannot rise before you,
for the manner of women *is*
with me." And he searched but
did not find the household
idols.

36Then Jacob was angry
and rebuked Laban, and Jacob
answered and said to Laban:
"What *is* my trespass? What *is*
my sin, that you have so hotly
pursued me? 37Although you
have searched all my things,
what part of your household
things have you found? Set
it here before my brethren
and your brethren, that they
may judge between us both!
38These twenty years I *have*
been with you; your ewes and
your female goats have not
miscarried their young, and
I have not eaten the rams of
your flock. 39That which was
torn *by beasts* I did not bring
to you; I bore the loss of it.
You required it from my hand,
whether stolen by day or stolen
by night. 40*There* I was! In the
day the drought consumed me,
and the frost by night, and my
sleep departed from my eyes.
41Thus I have been in your
house twenty years; I served
you fourteen years for your
two daughters, and six years
for your flock, and you have
changed my wages ten times.
42Unless the God of my father,
the God of Abraham and the
Fear of Isaac, had been with
me, surely now you would have
sent me away empty-handed.
God has seen my affliction and
the labor of my hands, and rebuked *you* last night."

LABAN'S COVENANT WITH JACOB

43And Laban answered and
said to Jacob, "*These* daughters
are my daughters, and *these*

children *are* my children, and
this flock *is* my flock; all that
you see *is* mine. But what can I
do this day to these my daughters or to their children whom
they have borne? [44]Now therefore, come, let us make a covenant, you and I, and let it be a
witness between you and me."
[45]So Jacob took a stone and
set it up *as* a pillar. [46]Then
Jacob said to his brethren,
"Gather stones." And they took
stones and made a heap, and
they ate there on the heap.
[47]Laban called it Jegar Saha-
dutha,[a] but Jacob called it Galeed.[b] [48]And Laban said, "This
heap *is* a witness between you
and me this day." Therefore
its name was called Galeed,
[49]also Mizpah,[a] because he
said, "May the LORD watch
between you and me when we
are absent one from another.
[50]If you afflict my daughters,
or if you take *other* wives besides my daughters, *although*
no man *is* with us—see, God *is*
witness between you and me!"
[51]Then Laban said to Jacob,
"Here is this heap and here is
this pillar, which I have placed
between you and me. [52]This
heap *is* a witness, and *this* pillar
is a witness, that I will not pass
beyond this heap to you, and
you will not pass beyond this
heap and this pillar to me, for
harm. [53]The God of Abraham,
the God of Nahor, and the God
of their father judge between
us." And Jacob swore by the
Fear of his father Isaac. [54]Then
Jacob offered a sacrifice on
the mountain, and called his
brethren to eat bread. And
they ate bread and stayed all
night on the mountain. [55]And
early in the morning Laban
arose, and kissed his sons and
daughters and blessed them.
Then Laban departed and returned to his place.

ESAU COMES TO MEET JACOB

32 So Jacob went on his
way, and the angels of
God met him. [2]When Jacob saw
them, he said, "This *is* God's
camp." And he called the name
of that place Mahanaim.[a]
[3]Then Jacob sent messengers before him to Esau his
brother in the land of Seir,
the country of Edom. [4]And
he commanded them, saying,
"Speak thus to my lord Esau,
'Thus your servant Jacob says:
"I have dwelt with Laban and
stayed there until now. [5]I have
oxen, donkeys, flocks, and
male and female servants; and
I have sent to tell my lord, that I
may find favor in your sight." ' "
[6]Then the messengers returned to Jacob, saying, "We
came to your brother Esau,
and he also is coming to meet

31:47 [a] Literally, in Aramaic, *Heap of Witness* [b] Literally, in Hebrew, *Heap of Witness* 31:49 [a] Literally *Watch* 32:2 [a] Literally *Double Camp*

you, and four hundred men
are with him." 7So Jacob was
greatly afraid and distressed;
and he divided the people
that *were* with him, and the
flocks and herds and camels,
into two companies. 8And he
said, "If Esau comes to the one
company and attacks it, then
the other company which is
left will escape."

9Then Jacob said, "O God
of my father Abraham and
God of my father Isaac, the
LORD who said to me, 'Return
to your country and to your
family, and I will deal well
with you': 10I am not worthy
of the least of all the mercies
and of all the truth which You
have shown Your servant; for I
crossed over this Jordan with
my staff, and now I have become two companies. 11De-
liver me, I pray, from the hand
of my brother, from the hand
of Esau; for I fear him, lest he
come and attack me *and* the
mother with the children.
12For You said, 'I will surely
treat you well, and make your
descendants as the sand of the
sea, which cannot be num-
bered for multitude.'"

13So he lodged there that
same night, and took what
came to his hand as a present
for Esau his brother: 14two
hundred female goats and
twenty male goats, two hundred ewes and twenty rams,
15thirty milk camels with their
colts, forty cows and ten bulls,
twenty female donkeys and
ten foals. 16Then he delivered
them to the hand of his servants, every drove by itself,
and said to his servants, "Pass
over before me, and put some
distance between successive
droves." 17And he commanded
the first one, saying, "When
Esau my brother meets you
and asks you, saying, 'To whom
do you belong, and where are
you going? Whose *are* these
in front of you?' 18then you
shall say, 'They *are* your servant Jacob's. It *is* a present sent
to my lord Esau; and behold,
he also *is* behind us.'" 19So he
commanded the second, the
third, and all who followed the
droves, saying, "In this manner
you shall speak to Esau when
you find him; 20and also say,
'Behold, your servant Jacob
is behind us.'" For he said, "I
will appease him with the present that goes before me, and
afterward I will see his face;
perhaps he will accept me."
21So the present went on over
before him, but he himself
lodged that night in the camp.

WRESTLING WITH GOD

22And he arose that night
and took his two wives, his
two female servants, and his
eleven sons, and crossed over
the ford of Jabbok. 23He took
them, sent them over the
brook, and sent over what
he had. 24Then Jacob was left
alone; and a Man wrestled
with him until the breaking of
day. 25Now when He saw that

He did not prevail against him, He touched the socket of his hip; and the socket of Jacob's hip was out of joint as He wrestled with him. 26And He said, "Let Me go, for the day breaks."

But he said, "I will not let You go unless You bless me!"

27So He said to him, "What *is* your name?"

He said, "Jacob."

28And He said, "Your name shall no longer be called Jacob, but Israel;[a] for you have struggled with God and with men, and have prevailed."

29Then Jacob asked, saying, "Tell *me* Your name, I pray."

And He said, "Why *is* it *that* you ask about My name?" And He blessed him there.

30So Jacob called the name of the place Peniel:[a] "For I have seen God face to face, and my life is preserved." 31Just as he crossed over Penuel[a] the sun rose on him, and he limped on his hip. 32Therefore to this day the children of Israel do not eat the muscle that shrank, which *is* on the hip socket, because He touched the socket of Jacob's hip in the muscle that shrank.

JACOB AND ESAU MEET

33 Now Jacob lifted his eyes and looked, and there, Esau was coming, and with him were four hundred men. So he divided the children among Leah, Rachel, and the two maidservants. 2And he put the maidservants and their children in front, Leah and her children behind, and Rachel and Joseph last. 3Then he crossed over before them and bowed himself to the ground seven times, until he came near to his brother.

4But Esau ran to meet him, and embraced him, and fell on his neck and kissed him, and they wept. 5And he lifted his eyes and saw the women and children, and said, "Who *are* these with you?"

So he said, "The children whom God has graciously given your servant." 6Then the maidservants came near, they and their children, and bowed down. 7And Leah also came near with her children, and they bowed down. Afterward Joseph and Rachel came near, and they bowed down.

8Then Esau said, "What *do* you *mean by* all this company which I met?"

And he said, "*These are* to find favor in the sight of my lord."

9But Esau said, "I have enough, my brother; keep what you have for yourself."

10And Jacob said, "No, please, if I have now found favor in your sight, then receive my present from my hand, inasmuch as I have seen

32:28 [a] Literally *Prince with God* 32:30 [a] Literally *Face of God* 32:31 [a] Same as *Peniel,* verse 30

your face as though I had seen
the face of God, and you were
pleased with me. 11Please, take
my blessing that is brought to
you, because God has dealt
graciously with me, and because I have enough." So he
urged him, and he took *it*.
12Then Esau said, "Let us
take our journey; let us go,
and I will go before you."
13But Jacob said to him,
"My lord knows that the
children *are* weak, and the
flocks and herds which are
nursing *are* with me. And if
the men should drive them
hard one day, all the flock will
die. 14Please let my lord go on
ahead before his servant. I will
lead on slowly at a pace which
the livestock that go before
me, and the children, are able
to endure, until I come to my
lord in Seir."
15And Esau said, "Now let
me leave with you *some* of the
people who *are* with me."
But he said, "What need is
there? Let me find favor in the
sight of my lord." 16So Esau
returned that day on his way
to Seir. 17And Jacob journeyed
to Succoth, built himself a
house, and made booths for
his livestock. Therefore the
name of the place is called
Succoth.[a]

JACOB COMES TO CANAAN

18Then Jacob came safely
to the city of Shechem, which
is in the land of Canaan, when
he came from Padan Aram;
and he pitched his tent before the city. 19And he bought
the parcel of land, where he
had pitched his tent, from the
children of Hamor, Shechem's
father, for one hundred pieces
of money. 20Then he erected
an altar there and called it El
Elohe Israel.[a]

THE DINAH INCIDENT

34 Now Dinah the daugh-
ter of Leah, whom she
had borne to Jacob, went out
to see the daughters of the
land. 2And when Shechem
the son of Hamor the Hivite,
prince of the country, saw her,
he took her and lay with her,
and violated her. 3His soul was
strongly attracted to Dinah
the daughter of Jacob, and
he loved the young woman
and spoke kindly to the young
woman. 4So Shechem spoke
to his father Hamor, saying,
"Get me this young woman
as a wife."
5And Jacob heard that he
had defiled Dinah his daughter. Now his sons were with his
livestock in the field; so Jacob held his peace until they
came. 6Then Hamor the father
of Shechem went out to Jacob
to speak with him. 7And the
sons of Jacob came in from
the field when they heard *it*;
and the men were grieved and
very angry, because he had

33:17 [a] Literally *Booths* **33:20** [a] Literally *God, the God of Israel*

done a disgraceful thing in
Israel by lying with Jacob's
daughter, a thing which ought
not to be done. [8]But Hamor
spoke with them, saying, "The
soul of my son Shechem longs
for your daughter. Please give
her to him as a wife. [9]And
make marriages with us; give
your daughters to us, and take
our daughters to yourselves.
[10]So you shall dwell with us,
and the land shall be before
you. Dwell and trade in it, and
acquire possessions for yourselves in it."

[11]Then Shechem said to her
father and her brothers, "Let
me find favor in your eyes,
and whatever you say to me
I will give. [12]Ask me ever so
much dowry and gift, and I
will give according to what
you say to me; but give me
the young woman as a wife."

[13]But the sons of Jacob answered Shechem and Hamor
his father, and spoke deceitfully, because he had defiled
Dinah their sister. [14]And they
said to them, "We cannot do
this thing, to give our sister
to one who is uncircumcised,
for that *would be* a reproach
to us. [15]But on this *condition*
we will consent to you: If you
will become as we *are*, if every
male of you is circumcised,
[16]then we will give our daughters to you, and we will take
your daughters to us; and we
will dwell with you, and we
will become one people. [17]But
if you will not heed us and be
circumcised, then we will take
our daughter and be gone."

[18]And their words pleased
Hamor and Shechem, Ha-
mor's son. [19]So the young
man did not delay to do the
thing, because he delighted
in Jacob's daughter. He *was*
more honorable than all the
household of his father.

[20]And Hamor and She-
chem his son came to the gate
of their city, and spoke with
the men of their city, saying:
[21]"These men *are* at peace
with us. Therefore let them
dwell in the land and trade
in it. For indeed the land *is*
large enough for them. Let
us take their daughters to us
as wives, and let us give them
our daughters. [22]Only on this
condition will the men consent to dwell with us, to be one
people: if every male among
us is circumcised as they *are*
circumcised. [23]*Will* not their
livestock, their property, and
every animal of theirs *be*
ours? Only let us consent to
them, and they will dwell with
us." [24]And all who went out
of the gate of his city heeded
Hamor and Shechem his son;
every male was circumcised,
all who went out of the gate
of his city.

[25]Now it came to pass on
the third day, when they were
in pain, that two of the sons
of Jacob, Simeon and Levi,
Dinah's brothers, each took
his sword and came boldly
upon the city and killed all

the males. 26And they killed
Hamor and Shechem his son
with the edge of the sword,
and took Dinah from She-
chem's house, and went out.
27The sons of Jacob came
upon the slain, and plundered
the city, because their sister
had been defiled. 28They took
their sheep, their oxen, and
their donkeys, what *was* in
the city and what *was* in the
field, 29and all their wealth.
All their little ones and their
wives they took captive; and
they plundered even all that
was in the houses.

30Then Jacob said to Sim-
eon and Levi, "You have
troubled me by making me
obnoxious among the inhabitants of the land, among the
Canaanites and the Perizzites;
and since I *am* few in number,
they will gather themselves
together against me and kill
me. I shall be destroyed, my
household and I."

31But they said, "Should he
treat our sister like a harlot?"

JACOB'S RETURN TO BETHEL

35 Then God said to Ja-
cob, "Arise, go up to
Bethel and dwell there; and
make an altar there to God,
who appeared to you when
you fled from the face of Esau
your brother."

2And Jacob said to his
household and to all who *were*
with him, "Put away the foreign gods that *are* among you,
purify yourselves, and change
your garments. 3Then let us
arise and go up to Bethel; and
I will make an altar there to
God, who answered me in
the day of my distress and
has been with me in the way
which I have gone." 4So they
gave Jacob all the foreign gods
which *were* in their hands,
and the earrings which *were*
in their ears; and Jacob hid
them under the terebinth tree
which *was* by Shechem.

5And they journeyed, and
the terror of God was upon
the cities that *were* all around
them, and they did not pursue
the sons of Jacob. 6So Jacob
came to Luz (that *is,* Bethel),
which *is* in the land of Canaan, he and all the people
who *were* with him. 7And he
built an altar there and called
the place El Bethel,[a] because
there God appeared to him
when he fled from the face of
his brother.

8Now Deborah, Rebekah's
nurse, died, and she was buried below Bethel under the
terebinth tree. So the name of
it was called Allon Bachuth.[a]

9Then God appeared to Ja-
cob again, when he came from
Padan Aram, and blessed him.
10And God said to him, "Your
name *is* Jacob; your name

35:7 [a] Literally *God of the House of God*
35:8 [a] Literally *Terebinth of Weeping*

shall not be called Jacob anymore, but Israel shall be your
name." So He called his name
Israel. 11 Also God said to him:
"I *am* God Almighty. Be fruitful and multiply; a nation and
a company of nations shall
proceed from you, and kings
shall come from your body.
12 The land which I gave Abraham and Isaac I give to you;
and to your descendants after
you I give this land." 13 Then
God went up from him in the
place where He talked with
him. 14 So Jacob set up a pillar
in the place where He talked
with him, a pillar of stone; and
he poured a drink offering
on it, and he poured oil on it.
15 And Jacob called the name
of the place where God spoke
with him, Bethel.

DEATH OF RACHEL

16 Then they journeyed
from Bethel. And when there
was but a little distance to go
to Ephrath, Rachel labored *in
childbirth,* and she had hard
labor. 17 Now it came to pass,
when she was in hard labor,
that the midwife said to her,
"Do not fear; you will have this
son also." 18 And so it was, as
her soul was departing (for
she died), that she called his
name Ben-Oni;[a] but his father
called him Benjamin.[b] 19 So
Rachel died and was buried
on the way to Ephrath (that *is,*
Bethlehem). 20 And Jacob set
a pillar on her grave, which *is*
the pillar of Rachel's grave to
this day.

21 Then Israel journeyed
and pitched his tent beyond
the tower of Eder. 22 And it
happened, when Israel dwelt
in that land, that Reuben
went and lay with Bilhah his
father's concubine; and Israel
heard *about it.*

JACOB'S TWELVE SONS

Now the sons of Jacob
were twelve: 23 the sons of
Leah *were* Reuben, Jacob's
firstborn, and Simeon, Levi,
Judah, Issachar, and Zebulun; 24 the sons of Rachel *were*
Joseph and Benjamin; 25 the
sons of Bilhah, Rachel's maidservant, *were* Dan and Naphtali; 26 and the sons of Zilpah,
Leah's maidservant, *were* Gad
and Asher. These *were* the
sons of Jacob who were born
to him in Padan Aram.

DEATH OF ISAAC

27 Then Jacob came to his
father Isaac at Mamre, or Kirjath Arba[a] (that *is,* Hebron),
where Abraham and Isaac had
dwelt. 28 Now the days of Isaac
were one hundred and eighty
years. 29 So Isaac breathed his
last and died, and was gathered to his people, *being* old
and full of days. And his sons
Esau and Jacob buried him.

35:18 [a] Literally *Son of My Sorrow* [b] Literally *Son of the Right Hand* 35:27 [a] Literally *Town of Arba*

THE FAMILY OF ESAU

36 Now this *is* the genealogy of Esau, who is
Edom. 2Esau took his wives
from the daughters of Canaan:
Adah the daughter of Elon
the Hittite; Aholibamah the
daughter of Anah, the daughter of Zibeon the Hivite; 3and
Basemath, Ishmael's daughter,
sister of Nebajoth. 4Now Adah
bore Eliphaz to Esau, and Basemath bore Reuel. 5And Aholibamah bore Jeush, Jaalam,
and Korah. These *were* the
sons of Esau who were born
to him in the land of Canaan.
6Then Esau took his wives,
his sons, his daughters, and
all the persons of his household, his cattle and all his
animals, and all his goods
which he had gained in the
land of Canaan, and went
to a country away from the
presence of his brother Jacob.
7For their possessions were
too great for them to dwell
together, and the land where
they were strangers could not
support them because of their
livestock. 8So Esau dwelt in
Mount Seir. Esau *is* Edom.
9And this *is* the genealogy of Esau the father of
the Edomites in Mount Seir.
10These *were* the names of
Esau's sons: Eliphaz the son
of Adah the wife of Esau, and
Reuel the son of Basemath the
wife of Esau. 11And the sons of
Eliphaz were Teman, Omar,
Zepho,[a] Gatam, and Kenaz.
12Now Timna was the con-
cubine of Eliphaz, Esau's son,
and she bore Amalek to Eliphaz. These *were* the sons of
Adah, Esau's wife.
13These *were* the sons of
Reuel: Nahath, Zerah, Shammah, and Mizzah. These were
the sons of Basemath, Esau's
wife.
14These were the sons of
Aholibamah, Esau's wife, the
daughter of Anah, the daughter of Zibeon. And she bore
to Esau: Jeush, Jaalam, and
Korah.

THE CHIEFS OF EDOM

15These *were* the chiefs of
the sons of Esau. The sons
of Eliphaz, the firstborn *son*
of Esau, were Chief Teman,
Chief Omar, Chief Zepho, Chief
Kenaz, 16Chief Korah,[a] Chief
Gatam, *and* Chief Amalek.
These *were* the chiefs of Eliphaz in the land of Edom. They
were the sons of Adah.
17These *were* the sons of
Reuel, Esau's son: Chief Nahath, Chief Zerah, Chief Shammah, and Chief Mizzah. These
were the chiefs of Reuel in the
land of Edom. These *were* the
sons of Basemath, Esau's wife.
18And these *were* the sons of
Aholibamah, Esau's wife: Chief
Jeush, Chief Jaalam, and Chief
Korah. These *were* the chiefs

36:11 [a] Spelled *Zephi* in 1 Chronicles 1:36 36:16 [a] Samaritan Pentateuch omits *Chief Korah*.

who descended from Aholibamah, Esau's wife, the daughter of Anah. 19These *were* the sons of Esau, who is Edom, and these *were* their chiefs.

THE SONS OF SEIR

20These *were* the sons of Seir the Horite who inhabited the land: Lotan, Shobal, Zibeon, Anah, 21Dishon, Ezer, and Dishan. These *were* the chiefs of the Horites, the sons of Seir, in the land of Edom.

22And the sons of Lotan were Hori and Hemam.[a] Lotan's sister *was* Timna.

23These *were* the sons of Shobal: Alvan,[a] Manahath, Ebal, Shepho,[b] and Onam.

24These *were* the sons of Zibeon: both Ajah and Anah. This *was the* Anah who found the water[a] in the wilderness as he pastured the donkeys of his father Zibeon. 25These *were* the children of Anah: Dishon and Aholibamah the daughter of Anah.

26These *were* the sons of Dishon:[a] Hemdan,[b] Eshban, Ithran, and Cheran. 27These *were* the sons of Ezer: Bilhan, Zaavan, and Akan.[a] 28These *were* the sons of Dishan: Uz and Aran.

29These *were* the chiefs of the Horites: Chief Lotan, Chief Shobal, Chief Zibeon, Chief Anah, 30Chief Dishon, Chief Ezer, and Chief Dishan. These *were* the chiefs of the Horites, according to their chiefs in the land of Seir.

THE KINGS OF EDOM

31Now these *were* the kings who reigned in the land of Edom before any king reigned over the children of Israel: 32Bela the son of Beor reigned in Edom, and the name of his city *was* Dinhabah. 33And when Bela died, Jobab the son of Zerah of Bozrah reigned in his place. 34When Jobab died, Husham of the land of the Temanites reigned in his place. 35And when Husham died, Hadad the son of Bedad, who attacked Midian in the field of Moab, reigned in his place. And the name of his city *was* Avith. 36When Hadad died, Samlah of Masrekah reigned in his place. 37And when Samlah died, Saul of Rehoboth-*by*-the-River reigned in his place. 38When Saul died, Baal-Hanan the son of Achbor reigned in his place. 39And when Baal-Hanan the son of Achbor died, Hadar[a] reigned in his place; and the name of his city *was*

36:22 [a] Spelled *Homam* in 1 Chronicles 1:39 36:23 [a] Spelled *Alian* in 1 Chronicles 1:40 [b] Spelled *Shephi* in 1 Chronicles 1:40 36:24 [a] Following Masoretic Text and Vulgate (*hot springs*); Septuagint reads *Jamin;* Targum reads *mighty men;* Talmud interprets as *mules.* 36:26 [a] Hebrew *Dishan* [b] Spelled *Hamran* in 1 Chronicles 1:41 36:27 [a] Spelled *Jaakan* in 1 Chronicles 1:42 36:39 [a] Spelled *Hadad* in Samaritan Pentateuch, Syriac, and 1 Chronicles 1:50

Pau.[b] His wife's name *was* Mehetabel, the daughter of Matred, the daughter of Mezahab.

THE CHIEFS OF ESAU

40 And these *were* the names of the chiefs of Esau, according to their families and their places, by their names: Chief Timnah, Chief Alvah,[a] Chief Jetheth, 41 Chief Aholibamah, Chief Elah, Chief Pinon, 42 Chief Kenaz, Chief Teman, Chief Mibzar, 43 Chief Magdiel, and Chief Iram. These *were* the chiefs of Edom, according to their dwelling places in the land of their possession. Esau *was* the father of the Edomites.

JOSEPH DREAMS OF GREATNESS

37 Now Jacob dwelt in the land where his father was a stranger, in the land of Canaan. 2 This *is* the history of Jacob.

Joseph, *being* seventeen years old, was feeding the flock with his brothers. And the lad *was* with the sons of Bilhah and the sons of Zilpah, his father's wives; and Joseph brought a bad report of them to his father.

3 Now Israel loved Joseph more than all his children, because he *was* the son of his old age. Also he made him a tunic of *many* colors. 4 But when his brothers saw that their father loved him more than all his brothers, they hated him and could not speak peaceably to him.

5 Now Joseph had a dream, and he told *it* to his brothers; and they hated him even more. 6 So he said to them, "Please hear this dream which I have dreamed: 7 There we were, binding sheaves in the field. Then behold, my sheaf arose and also stood upright; and indeed your sheaves stood all around and bowed down to my sheaf."

8 And his brothers said to him, "Shall you indeed reign over us? Or shall you indeed have dominion over us?" So they hated him even more for his dreams and for his words.

9 Then he dreamed still another dream and told it to his brothers, and said, "Look, I have dreamed another dream. And this time, the sun, the moon, and the eleven stars bowed down to me."

10 So he told *it* to his father and his brothers; and his father rebuked him and said to him, "What *is* this dream that you have dreamed? Shall your mother and I and your brothers indeed come to bow down to the earth before you?" 11 And his brothers envied him, but his father kept the matter *in mind.*

36:39 [b] Spelled *Pai* in 1 Chronicles 1:50
36:40 [a] Spelled *Aliah* in 1 Chronicles 1:51

JOSEPH SOLD BY HIS BROTHERS

12 Then his brothers went to feed their father's flock in Shechem. 13 And Israel said to Joseph, "Are not your brothers feeding *the flock* in Shechem? Come, I will send you to them."

So he said to him, "Here I am."

14 Then he said to him, "Please go and see if it is well with your brothers and well with the flocks, and bring back word to me." So he sent him out of the Valley of Hebron, and he went to Shechem.

15 Now a certain man found him, and there he was, wandering in the field. And the man asked him, saying, "What are you seeking?"

16 So he said, "I am seeking my brothers. Please tell me where they are feeding *their flocks.*"

17 And the man said, "They have departed from here, for I heard them say, 'Let us go to Dothan.'" So Joseph went after his brothers and found them in Dothan.

18 Now when they saw him afar off, even before he came near them, they conspired against him to kill him. 19 Then *they said* to one another, "Look, this dreamer is coming! 20 Come therefore, let us now kill him and cast him into some pit; and we shall say, 'Some wild beast has devoured him.' We shall see what will become of his dreams!"

21 But Reuben heard *it,* and he delivered him out of their hands, and said, "Let us not kill him." 22 And Reuben said to them, "Shed no blood, *but* cast him into this pit which *is* in the wilderness, and do not lay a hand on him"—that he might deliver him out of their hands, and bring him back to his father.

23 So it came to pass, when Joseph had come to his brothers, that they stripped Joseph *of* his tunic, the tunic of *many* colors that *was* on him. 24 Then they took him and cast him into a pit. And the pit *was* empty; *there was* no water in it.

25 And they sat down to eat a meal. Then they lifted their eyes and looked, and there was a company of Ishmaelites, coming from Gilead with their camels, bearing spices, balm, and myrrh, on their way to carry *them* down to Egypt. 26 So Judah said to his brothers, "What profit *is there* if we kill our brother and conceal his blood? 27 Come and let us sell him to the Ishmaelites, and let not our hand be upon him, for he *is* our brother *and* our flesh." And his brothers listened. 28 Then Midianite traders passed by; so *the brothers* pulled Joseph up and lifted him out of the pit, and sold him to the Ishmaelites for twenty *shekels* of silver. And they took Joseph to Egypt.

29 Then Reuben returned
to the pit, and indeed Joseph
was not in the pit; and he tore
his clothes. 30 And he returned
to his brothers and said, "The
lad *is* no *more;* and I, where
shall I go?"

31 So they took Joseph's
tunic, killed a kid of the goats,
and dipped the tunic in the
blood. 32 Then they sent the
tunic of *many* colors, and they
brought *it* to their father and
said, "We have found this. Do
you know whether it *is* your
son's tunic or not?"

33 And he recognized it and
said, "*It is* my son's tunic. A
wild beast has devoured him.
Without doubt Joseph is torn
to pieces." 34 Then Jacob tore
his clothes, put sackcloth
on his waist, and mourned for
his son many days. 35 And all
his sons and all his daughters
arose to comfort him; but he
refused to be comforted, and
he said, "For I shall go down
into the grave to my son in
mourning." Thus his father
wept for him.

36 Now the Midianites[a] had
sold him in Egypt to Potiphar,
an officer of Pharaoh *and* captain of the guard.

JUDAH AND TAMAR

38 It came to pass at that
time that Judah de-
parted from his brothers, and
visited a certain Adullamite
whose name *was* Hirah. 2 And
Judah saw there a daughter
of a certain Canaanite whose
name *was* Shua, and he married her and went in to her.
3 So she conceived and bore a
son, and he called his name
Er. 4 She conceived again and
bore a son, and she called his
name Onan. 5 And she con-
ceived yet again and bore a
son, and called his name Shelah. He was at Chezib when
she bore him.

6 Then Judah took a wife
for Er his firstborn, and her
name *was* Tamar. 7 But Er, Judah's firstborn, was wicked in
the sight of the LORD, and the
LORD killed him. 8 And Judah
said to Onan, "Go in to your
brother's wife and marry her,
and raise up an heir to your
brother." 9 But Onan knew that
the heir would not be his; and
it came to pass, when he went
in to his brother's wife, that
he emitted on the ground,
lest he should give an heir to
his brother. 10 And the thing
which he did displeased the
LORD; therefore He killed him
also.

11 Then Judah said to Tamar
his daughter-in-law, "Remain
a widow in your father's house
till my son Shelah is grown."
For he said, "Lest he also die
like his brothers." And Tamar
went and dwelt in her father's
house.

12 Now in the process of
time the daughter of Shua,

37:36 [a] Masoretic Text reads *Medanites.*

Judah's wife, died; and Judah was comforted, and went up to his sheepshearers at Timnah, he and his friend Hirah the Adullamite. 13And it was told Tamar, saying, "Look, your father-in-law is going up to Timnah to shear his sheep." 14So she took off her widow's garments, covered *herself* with a veil and wrapped herself, and sat in an open place which *was* on the way to Timnah; for she saw that Shelah was grown, and she was not given to him as a wife. 15When Judah saw her, he thought she *was* a harlot, because she had covered her face. 16Then he turned to her by the way, and said, "Please let me come in to you"; for he did not know that she *was* his daughter-in-law.

So she said, "What will you give me, that you may come in to me?"

17And he said, "I will send a young goat from the flock."

So she said, "Will you give *me* a pledge till you send *it?*"

18Then he said, "What pledge shall I give you?"

So she said, "Your signet and cord, and your staff that *is* in your hand." Then he gave *them* to her, and went in to her, and she conceived by him. 19So she arose and went away, and laid aside her veil and put on the garments of her widowhood.

20And Judah sent the young goat by the hand of his friend the Adullamite, to receive *his* pledge from the woman's hand, but he did not find her. 21Then he asked the men of that place, saying, "Where is the harlot who *was* openly by the roadside?"

And they said, "There was no harlot in this *place.*"

22So he returned to Judah and said, "I cannot find her. Also, the men of the place said there was no harlot in this *place.*"

23Then Judah said, "Let her take *them* for herself, lest we be shamed; for I sent this young goat and you have not found her."

24And it came to pass, about three months after, that Judah was told, saying, "Tamar your daughter-in-law has played the harlot; furthermore she *is* with child by harlotry."

So Judah said, "Bring her out and let her be burned!"

25When she *was* brought out, she sent to her father-in-law, saying, "By the man to whom these belong, I *am* with child." And she said, "Please determine whose these *are*—the signet and cord, and staff."

26So Judah acknowledged *them* and said, "She has been more righteous than I, because I did not give her to Shelah my son." And he never knew her again.

27Now it came to pass, at the time for giving birth, that behold, twins *were* in her womb. 28And so it was, when she was giving birth, that *the*

one put out *his* hand; and the midwife took a scarlet *thread* and bound it on his hand, saying, "This one came out first." 29Then it happened, as he drew back his hand, that his brother came out unexpectedly; and she said, "How did you break through? *This* breach *be* upon you!" Therefore his name was called Perez.[a] 30Afterward his brother came out who had the scarlet *thread* on his hand. And his name was called Zerah.

JOSEPH A SLAVE IN EGYPT

39 Now Joseph had been taken down to Egypt. And Potiphar, an officer of Pharaoh, captain of the guard, an Egyptian, bought him from the Ishmaelites who had taken him down there. 2The LORD was with Joseph, and he was a successful man; and he was in the house of his master the Egyptian. 3And his master saw that the LORD *was* with him and that the LORD made all he did to prosper in his hand. 4So Joseph found favor in his sight, and served him. Then he made him overseer of his house, and all *that* he had he put under his authority. 5So it was, from the time *that* he had made him overseer of his house and all that he had, that the LORD blessed the Egyptian's house for Joseph's sake; and the blessing of the LORD was on all that he had in the house and in the field. 6Thus he left all that he had in Joseph's hand, and he did not know what he had except for the bread which he ate.

Now Joseph was handsome in form and appearance.

7And it came to pass after these things that his master's wife cast longing eyes on Joseph, and she said, "Lie with me."

8But he refused and said to his master's wife, "Look, my master does not know what *is* with me in the house, and he has committed all that he has to my hand. 9*There is* no one greater in this house than I, nor has he kept back anything from me but you, because you *are* his wife. How then can I do this great wickedness, and sin against God?"

10So it was, as she spoke to Joseph day by day, that he did not heed her, to lie with her *or* to be with her.

11But it happened about this time, when Joseph went into the house to do his work, and none of the men of the house *was* inside, 12that she caught him by his garment, saying, "Lie with me." But he left his garment in her hand, and fled and ran outside. 13And so it was, when she saw that he had left his garment in her hand and fled outside, 14that she called to the men of

38:29 [a] Literally *Breach* or *Breakthrough*

her house and spoke to them,
saying, "See, he has brought
in to us a Hebrew to mock
us. He came in to me to lie
with me, and I cried out with a
loud voice. 15And it happened,
when he heard that I lifted my
voice and cried out, that he
left his garment with me, and
fled and went outside."

16So she kept his garment
with her until his master came
home. 17Then she spoke to
him with words like these,
saying, "The Hebrew servant
whom you brought to us came
in to me to mock me; 18so it
happened, as I lifted my voice
and cried out, that he left his
garment with me and fled
outside."

19So it was, when his master heard the words which
his wife spoke to him, saying, "Your servant did to me
after this manner," that his
anger was aroused. 20Then
Joseph's master took him
and put him into the prison,
a place where the king's prisoners *were* confined. And he
was there in the prison. 21But
the LORD was with Joseph and
showed him mercy, and He
gave him favor in the sight
of the keeper of the prison.
22And the keeper of the prison
committed to Joseph's hand
all the prisoners who *were* in
the prison; whatever they did
there, it was his doing. 23The
keeper of the prison did not
look into anything *that was*
under *Joseph's* authority,[a] because the LORD was with him;
and whatever he did, the LORD
made *it* prosper.

THE PRISONERS' DREAMS

40 It came to pass after
these things *that* the
butler and the baker of the
king of Egypt offended their
lord, the king of Egypt. 2And
Pharaoh was angry with his
two officers, the chief butler
and the chief baker. 3So he put
them in custody in the house
of the captain of the guard, in
the prison, the place where Joseph *was* confined. 4And the
captain of the guard charged
Joseph with them, and he
served them; so they were in
custody for a while.

5Then the butler and the
baker of the king of Egypt,
who *were* confined in the
prison, had a dream, both
of them, each man's dream
in one night *and* each man's
dream with its *own* interpretation. 6And Joseph came in
to them in the morning and
looked at them, and saw that
they *were* sad. 7So he asked
Pharaoh's officers who *were*
with him in the custody of his
lord's house, saying, "Why do
you look *so* sad today?"

8And they said to him, "We
each have had a dream, and
there is no interpreter of it."

So Joseph said to them, "Do

39:23 [a] Literally *his hand*

not interpretations belong to
God? Tell *them* to me, please."
9Then the chief butler told
his dream to Joseph, and said
to him, "Behold, in my dream
a vine *was* before me, 10and in
the vine *were* three branches;
it *was* as though it budded,
its blossoms shot forth, and
its clusters brought forth ripe
grapes. 11Then Pharaoh's cup
was in my hand; and I took the
grapes and pressed them into
Pharaoh's cup, and placed the
cup in Pharaoh's hand."
12And Joseph said to him,
"This *is* the interpretation of it:
The three branches *are* three
days. 13Now within three days
Pharaoh will lift up your head
and restore you to your place,
and you will put Pharaoh's
cup in his hand according to
the former manner, when you
were his butler. 14But remember me when it is well with you,
and please show kindness to
me; make mention of me to
Pharaoh, and get me out of this
house. 15For indeed I was stolen away from the land of the
Hebrews; and also I have done
nothing here that they should
put me into the dungeon."
16When the chief baker
saw that the interpretation
was good, he said to Joseph,
"I also *was* in my dream, and
there *were* three white baskets
on my head. 17In the uppermost basket *were* all kinds of
baked goods for Pharaoh, and
the birds ate them out of the
basket on my head."
18So Joseph answered and
said, "This *is* the interpretation of it: The three baskets
are three days. 19Within three
days Pharaoh will lift off your
head from you and hang you
on a tree; and the birds will eat
your flesh from you."
20Now it came to pass on
the third day, *which was* Pharaoh's birthday, that he made a
feast for all his servants; and
he lifted up the head of the
chief butler and of the chief
baker among his servants.
21Then he restored the chief
butler to his butlership again,
and he placed the cup in Pharaoh's hand. 22But he hanged
the chief baker, as Joseph had
interpreted to them. 23Yet the
chief butler did not remember
Joseph, but forgot him.

PHARAOH'S DREAMS

41 Then it came to pass, at
the end of two full years,
that Pharaoh had a dream;
and behold, he stood by the
river. 2Suddenly there came
up out of the river seven cows,
fine looking and fat; and they
fed in the meadow. 3Then behold, seven other cows came
up after them out of the river,
ugly and gaunt, and stood by
the *other* cows on the bank of
the river. 4And the ugly and
gaunt cows ate up the seven
fine looking and fat cows. So
Pharaoh awoke. 5He slept and
dreamed a second time; and
suddenly seven heads of grain
came up on one stalk, plump

and good. 6Then behold,
seven thin heads, blighted by
the east wind, sprang up after
them. 7And the seven thin
heads devoured the seven
plump and full heads. So
Pharaoh awoke, and indeed,
it was a dream. 8Now it came
to pass in the morning that
his spirit was troubled, and
he sent and called for all the
magicians of Egypt and all its
wise men. And Pharaoh told
them his dreams, but *there
was* no one who could interpret them for Pharaoh.

9Then the chief butler
spoke to Pharaoh, saying: "I
remember my faults this day.
10When Pharaoh was angry
with his servants, and put me
in custody in the house of the
captain of the guard, *both* me
and the chief baker, 11we each
had a dream in one night, he
and I. Each of us dreamed according to the interpretation
of his *own* dream. 12Now there
was a young Hebrew man with
us there, a servant of the captain of the guard. And we told
him, and he interpreted our
dreams for us; to each man
he interpreted according to
his *own* dream. 13And it came
to pass, just as he interpreted
for us, so it happened. He restored me to my office, and
he hanged him."

14Then Pharaoh sent and
called Joseph, and they
brought him quickly out of
the dungeon; and he shaved,
changed his clothing, and
came to Pharaoh. 15And Pharaoh said to Joseph, "I have
had a dream, and *there is* no
one who can interpret it. But I
have heard it said of you *that*
you can understand a dream,
to interpret it."

16So Joseph answered
Pharaoh, saying, "*It is* not in
me; God will give Pharaoh an
answer of peace."

17Then Pharaoh said to Joseph: "Behold, in my dream I
stood on the bank of the river.
18Suddenly seven cows came
up out of the river, fine looking and fat; and they fed in
the meadow. 19Then behold,
seven other cows came up
after them, poor and very ugly
and gaunt, such ugliness as
I have never seen in all the
land of Egypt. 20And the gaunt
and ugly cows ate up the first
seven, the fat cows. 21When
they had eaten them up, no
one would have known that
they had eaten them, for they
were just as ugly as at the beginning. So I awoke. 22Also I
saw in my dream, and sud-
denly seven heads came up
on one stalk, full and good.
23Then behold, seven heads,
withered, thin, *and* blighted
by the east wind, sprang up
after them. 24And the thin
heads devoured the seven
good heads. So I told *this* to
the magicians, but *there was*
no one who could explain *it*
to me."

25Then Joseph said to Pharaoh, "The dreams of Pharaoh

are one; God has shown Pharaoh what He *is* about to do:
26The seven good cows *are*
seven years, and the seven
good heads *are* seven years;
the dreams *are* one. 27And
the seven thin and ugly cows
which came up after them *are*
seven years, and the seven
empty heads blighted by the
east wind are seven years of
famine. 28This *is* the thing
which I have spoken to Pharaoh. God has shown Phar-
aoh what He *is* about to do.
29Indeed seven years of great
plenty will come throughout
all the land of Egypt; 30but
after them seven years of
famine will arise, and all the
plenty will be forgotten in the
land of Egypt; and the famine
will deplete the land. 31So the
plenty will not be known in
the land because of the famine following, for it *will be* very
severe. 32And the dream was
repeated to Pharaoh twice because the thing *is* established
by God, and God will shortly
bring it to pass.

33"Now therefore, let Pharaoh select a discerning and
wise man, and set him over the
land of Egypt. 34Let Pharaoh
do *this,* and let him appoint
officers over the land, to collect one-fifth *of the produce* of
the land of Egypt in the seven
plentiful years. 35And let them
gather all the food of those
good years that are coming,
and store up grain under the
authority of Pharaoh, and let
them keep food in the cities.
36Then that food shall be as
a reserve for the land for the
seven years of famine which
shall be in the land of Egypt,
that the land may not perish
during the famine."

JOSEPH'S RISE TO POWER

37So the advice was good in
the eyes of Pharaoh and in the
eyes of all his servants. 38And
Pharaoh said to his servants,
"Can we find *such a one* as this,
a man in whom *is* the Spirit
of God?"

39Then Pharaoh said to Joseph, "Inasmuch as God has
shown you all this, *there is* no
one as discerning and wise as
you. 40You shall be over my
house, and all my people shall
be ruled according to your
word; only in regard to the
throne will I be greater than
you." 41And Pharaoh said to
Joseph, "See, I have set you
over all the land of Egypt."

42Then Pharaoh took his
signet ring off his hand and
put it on Joseph's hand; and
he clothed him in garments
of fine linen and put a gold
chain around his neck. 43And
he had him ride in the second chariot which he had;
and they cried out before
him, "Bow the knee!" So he
set him over all the land of
Egypt. 44Pharaoh also said to
Joseph, "I *am* Pharaoh, and
without your consent no man
may lift his hand or foot in
all the land of Egypt." 45And

Pharaoh called Joseph's name
Zaphnath-Paaneah. And he
gave him as a wife Asenath,
the daughter of Poti-Pherah
priest of On. So Joseph went
out over *all* the land of Egypt.
46 Joseph was thirty years
old when he stood before
Pharaoh king of Egypt. And
Joseph went out from the
presence of Pharaoh, and
went throughout all the land
of Egypt. 47 Now in the seven
plentiful years the ground
brought forth abundantly.
48 So he gathered up all the
food of the seven years which
were in the land of Egypt,
and laid up the food in the
cities; he laid up in every city
the food of the fields which
surrounded them. 49 Joseph
gathered very much grain, as
the sand of the sea, until he
stopped counting, for *it was*
immeasurable.
50 And to Joseph were born
two sons before the years of
famine came, whom Asenath,
the daughter of Poti-Pherah
priest of On, bore to him. 51 Joseph called the name of the
firstborn Manasseh:[a] "For God
has made me forget all my toil
and all my father's house."
52 And the name of the second
he called Ephraim:[a] "For God
has caused me to be fruitful
in the land of my affliction."
53 Then the seven years
of plenty which were in the
land of Egypt ended, 54 and the
seven years of famine began to
come, as Joseph had said. The
famine was in all lands, but
in all the land of Egypt there
was bread. 55 So when all the
land of Egypt was famished,
the people cried to Pharaoh
for bread. Then Pharaoh said
to all the Egyptians, "Go to Joseph; whatever he says to you,
do." 56 The famine was over
all the face of the earth, and
Joseph opened all the storehouses[a] and sold to the Egyptians. And the famine became
severe in the land of Egypt.
57 So all countries came to Joseph in Egypt to buy *grain,* because the famine was severe
in all lands.

JOSEPH'S BROTHERS GO TO EGYPT

42 When Jacob saw that
there was grain in
Egypt, Jacob said to his sons,
"Why do you look at one another?" 2 And he said, "Indeed I have heard that there
is grain in Egypt; go down
to that place and buy for us
there, that we may live and
not die."
3 So Joseph's ten brothers
went down to buy grain in
Egypt. 4 But Jacob did not send
Joseph's brother Benjamin
with his brothers, for he said,
"Lest some calamity befall
him." 5 And the sons of Israel

41:51 [a] Literally *Making Forgetful* 41:52 [a] Literally *Fruitfulness* 41:56 [a] Literally *all that was in them*

went to buy *grain* among those
who journeyed, for the famine
was in the land of Canaan.
[6]Now Joseph *was* governor over the land; and it was
he who sold to all the people of the land. And Joseph's
brothers came and bowed
down before him with *their*
faces to the earth. [7]Joseph
saw his brothers and recognized them, but he acted as a
stranger to them and spoke
roughly to them. Then he said
to them, "Where do you come
from?"

And they said, "From the
land of Canaan to buy food."

[8]So Joseph recognized his
brothers, but they did not recognize him. [9]Then Joseph remembered the dreams which
he had dreamed about them,
and said to them, "You *are*
spies! You have come to see
the nakedness of the land!"

[10]And they said to him, "No,
my lord, but your servants
have come to buy food. [11]We
are all one man's sons; we *are*
honest *men;* your servants are
not spies."

[12]But he said to them, "No,
but you have come to see the
nakedness of the land."

[13]And they said, "Your servants *are* twelve brothers, the
sons of one man in the land of
Canaan; and in fact, the youngest *is* with our father today,
and one *is* no more."

[14]But Joseph said to them,
"It *is* as I spoke to you, saying,
'You *are* spies!' [15]In this *man-*
ner you shall be tested: By the
life of Pharaoh, you shall not
leave this place unless your
youngest brother comes here.
[16]Send one of you, and let him
bring your brother; and you
shall be kept in prison, that
your words may be tested
to see whether *there is* any
truth in you; or else, by the
life of Pharaoh, surely you *are*
spies!" [17]So he put them all
together in prison three days.

[18]Then Joseph said to them
the third day, "Do this and
live, *for* I fear God: [19]If you *are*
honest *men,* let one of your
brothers be confined to your
prison house; but you, go and
carry grain for the famine of
your houses. [20]And bring your
youngest brother to me; so
your words will be verified,
and you shall not die."

And they did so. [21]Then
they said to one another, "We
are truly guilty concerning
our brother, for we saw the
anguish of his soul when he
pleaded with us, and we would
not hear; therefore this distress has come upon us."

[22]And Reuben answered
them, saying, "Did I not
speak to you, saying, 'Do not
sin against the boy'; and you
would not listen? Therefore
behold, his blood is now required of us." [23]But they did
not know that Joseph understood *them,* for he spoke to
them through an interpreter.
[24]And he turned himself away
from them and wept. Then he

returned to them again, and
talked with them. And he took
Simeon from them and bound
him before their eyes.

THE BROTHERS RETURN TO CANAAN

25Then Joseph gave a com-
mand to fill their sacks with
grain, to restore every man's
money to his sack, and to give
them provisions for the journey. Thus he did for them. 26So
they loaded their donkeys with
the grain and departed from
there. 27But as one *of them*
opened his sack to give his
donkey feed at the encampment, he saw his money; and
there it was, in the mouth of
his sack. 28So he said to his
brothers, "My money has been
restored, and there it is, in my
sack!" Then their hearts failed
them and they were afraid, saying to one another, "What *is*
this *that* God has done to us?"

29Then they went to Jacob
their father in the land of Canaan and told him all that
had happened to them, saying: 30"The man *who is* lord
of the land spoke roughly to
us, and took us for spies of
the country. 31But we said to
him, 'We *are* honest *men;* we
are not spies. 32We *are* twelve
brothers, sons of our father;
one *is* no *more,* and the youngest *is* with our father this day
in the land of Canaan.' 33Then
the man, the lord of the country, said to us, 'By this I will
know that you *are* honest *men:*
Leave one of your brothers
here with me, take *food for* the
famine of your households,
and be gone. 34And bring your
youngest brother to me; so I
shall know that you *are* not
spies, but *that* you *are* honest
men. I will grant your brother
to you, and you may trade in
the land.'"

35Then it happened as they
emptied their sacks, that surprisingly each man's bundle
of money *was* in his sack; and
when they and their father
saw the bundles of money,
they were afraid. 36And Jacob their father said to them,
"You have bereaved me: Joseph is no *more,* Simeon is no
more, and you want to take
Benjamin. All these things are
against me."

37Then Reuben spoke to his
father, saying, "Kill my two
sons if I do not bring him *back*
to you; put him in my hands,
and I will bring him back to
you."

38But he said, "My son shall
not go down with you, for his
brother is dead, and he is left
alone. If any calamity should
befall him along the way in
which you go, then you would
bring down my gray hair with
sorrow to the grave."

JOSEPH'S BROTHERS RETURN WITH BENJAMIN

43 Now the famine *was* severe in the land. 2And it
came to pass, when they had
eaten up the grain which they

had brought from Egypt, that
their father said to them, "Go
back, buy us a little food."
3But Judah spoke to him,
saying, "The man solemnly
warned us, saying, 'You shall
not see my face unless your
brother *is* with you.' 4If you
send our brother with us, we
will go down and buy you
food. 5But if you will not send
him, we will not go down; for
the man said to us, 'You shall
not see my face unless your
brother *is* with you.'"
6And Israel said, "Why did
you deal *so* wrongfully with
me *as* to tell the man whether
you had still *another* brother?"
7But they said, "The man
asked us pointedly about ourselves and our family, saying,
'*Is* your father still alive? Have
you *another* brother?' And we
told him according to these
words. Could we possibly have
known that he would say,
'Bring your brother down'?"
8Then Judah said to Israel
his father, "Send the lad with
me, and we will arise and go,
that we may live and not die,
both we and you *and* also our
little ones. 9I myself will be
surety for him; from my hand
you shall require him. If I do
not bring him *back* to you and
set him before you, then let
me bear the blame forever.
10For if we had not lingered,
surely by now we would have
returned this second time."
11And their father Israel
said to them, "If *it must be* so,
then do this: Take some of the
best fruits of the land in your
vessels and carry down a present for the man—a little balm
and a little honey, spices and
myrrh, pistachio nuts and almonds. 12Take double money
in your hand, and take back in
your hand the money that was
returned in the mouth of your
sacks; perhaps it was an oversight. 13Take your brother also,
and arise, go back to the man.
14And may God Almighty give
you mercy before the man,
that he may release your other
brother and Benjamin. If I am
bereaved, I am bereaved!"
15So the men took that
present and Benjamin, and
they took double money in
their hand, and arose and
went down to Egypt; and they
stood before Joseph. 16When
Joseph saw Benjamin with
them, he said to the steward
of his house, "Take *these* men
to my home, and slaughter an
animal and make ready; for
these men will dine with me at
noon." 17Then the man did as
Joseph ordered, and the man
brought the men into Joseph's
house.
18Now the men were afraid
because they were brought
into Joseph's house; and
they said, "*It is* because of the
money, which was returned in
our sacks the first time, that
we are brought in, so that he
may make a case against us
and seize us, to take us as
slaves with our donkeys."

19When they drew near to
the steward of Joseph's house,
they talked with him at the
door of the house, 20and said,
"O sir, we indeed came down
the first time to buy food; 21but
it happened, when we came
to the encampment, that we
opened our sacks, and there,
each man's money *was* in the
mouth of his sack, our money
in full weight; so we have
brought it back in our hand.
22And we have brought down
other money in our hands to
buy food. We do not know who
put our money in our sacks."

23But he said, "Peace *be* with
you, do not be afraid. Your
God and the God of your father has given you treasure in
your sacks; I had your money."
Then he brought Simeon out
to them.

24So the man brought the
men into Joseph's house and
gave *them* water, and they
washed their feet; and he gave
their donkeys feed. 25Then
they made the present ready
for Joseph's coming at noon,
for they heard that they would
eat bread there.

26And when Joseph came
home, they brought him the
present which *was* in their
hand into the house, and
bowed down before him to the
earth. 27Then he asked them
about *their* well-being, and
said, "*Is* your father well, the
old man of whom you spoke?
Is he still alive?"

28And they answered, "Your
servant our father *is* in good
health; he *is* still alive." And
they bowed their heads down
and prostrated themselves.

29Then he lifted his eyes
and saw his brother Benjamin,
his mother's son, and said, "*Is*
this your younger brother of
whom you spoke to me?" And
he said, "God be gracious to
you, my son." 30Now his heart
yearned for his brother; so Joseph made haste and sought
somewhere to weep. And he
went into *his* chamber and
wept there. 31Then he washed
his face and came out; and he
restrained himself, and said,
"Serve the bread."

32So they set him a place by
himself, and them by themselves, and the Egyptians who
ate with him by themselves;
because the Egyptians could
not eat food with the Hebrews,
for that *is* an abomination to
the Egyptians. 33And they sat
before him, the firstborn according to his birthright and
the youngest according to his
youth; and the men looked
in astonishment at one another. 34Then he took serv-
ings to them from before him,
but Benjamin's serving was
five times as much as any of
theirs. So they drank and were
merry with him.

JOSEPH'S CUP

44 And he commanded the
steward of his house,
saying, "Fill the men's sacks
with food, as much as they

can carry, and put each man's money in the mouth of his sack. 2Also put my cup, the silver cup, in the mouth of the sack of the youngest, and his grain money." So he did according to the word that Joseph had spoken. 3As soon as the morning dawned, the men were sent away, they and their donkeys. 4When they had gone out of the city, *and* were not *yet* far off, Joseph said to his steward, "Get up, follow the men; and when you overtake them, say to them, 'Why have you repaid evil for good? 5*Is* not this *the one* from which my lord drinks, and with which he indeed practices divination? You have done evil in so doing.'"

6So he overtook them, and he spoke to them these same words. 7And they said to him, "Why does my lord say these words? Far be it from us that your servants should do such a thing. 8Look, we brought back to you from the land of Canaan the money which we found in the mouth of our sacks. How then could we steal silver or gold from your lord's house? 9With whomever of your servants it is found, let him die, and we also will be my lord's slaves."

10And he said, "Now also *let* it *be* according to your words; he with whom it is found shall be my slave, and you shall be blameless." 11Then each man speedily let down his sack to the ground, and each opened his sack. 12So he searched. He began with the oldest and left off with the youngest; and the cup was found in Benjamin's sack. 13Then they tore their clothes, and each man loaded his donkey and returned to the city.

14So Judah and his brothers came to Joseph's house, and he *was* still there; and they fell before him on the ground. 15And Joseph said to them, "What deed *is* this you have done? Did you not know that such a man as I can certainly practice divination?"

16Then Judah said, "What shall we say to my lord? What shall we speak? Or how shall we clear ourselves? God has found out the iniquity of your servants; here we are, my lord's slaves, both we and *he* also with whom the cup was found."

17But he said, "Far be it from me that I should do so; the man in whose hand the cup was found, he shall be my slave. And as for you, go up in peace to your father."

JUDAH INTERCEDES FOR BENJAMIN

18Then Judah came near to him and said: "O my lord, please let your servant speak a word in my lord's hearing, and do not let your anger burn *against* your servant; for you *are* even like Pharaoh. 19My lord asked his servants, saying, 'Have you a father or a

brother?' 20And we said to my lord, 'We have a father, an old man, and a child of *his* old age, *who is* young; his brother is dead, and he alone is left of his mother's children, and his father loves him.' 21Then you said to your servants, 'Bring him down to me, that I may set my eyes on him.' 22And we said to my lord, 'The lad cannot leave his father, for *if* he should leave his father, *his father* would die.' 23But you said to your servants, 'Unless your youngest brother comes down with you, you shall see my face no more.'

24"So it was, when we went up to your servant my father, that we told him the words of my lord. 25And our father said, 'Go back *and* buy us a little food.' 26But we said, 'We cannot go down; if our youngest brother is with us, then we will go down; for we may not see the man's face unless our youngest brother *is* with us.' 27Then your servant my father said to us, 'You know that my wife bore me two sons; 28and the one went out from me, and I said, "Surely he is torn to pieces"; and I have not seen him since. 29But if you take this one also from me, and calamity befalls him, you shall bring down my gray hair with sorrow to the grave.'

30"Now therefore, when I come to your servant my father, and the lad *is* not with us, since his life is bound up in the lad's life, 31it will happen, when he sees that the lad *is* not *with us,* that he will die. So your servants will bring down the gray hair of your servant our father with sorrow to the grave. 32For your servant became surety for the lad to my father, saying, 'If I do not bring him *back* to you, then I shall bear the blame before my father forever.' 33Now therefore, please let your servant remain instead of the lad as a slave to my lord, and let the lad go up with his brothers. 34For how shall I go up to my father if the lad *is* not with me, lest perhaps I see the evil that would come upon my father?"

JOSEPH REVEALED TO HIS BROTHERS

45 Then Joseph could not restrain himself before all those who stood by him, and he cried out, "Make everyone go out from me!" So no one stood with him while Joseph made himself known to his brothers. 2And he wept aloud, and the Egyptians and the house of Pharaoh heard *it.*

3Then Joseph said to his brothers, "I *am* Joseph; does my father still live?" But his brothers could not answer him, for they were dismayed in his presence. 4And Joseph said to his brothers, "Please come near to me." So they came near. Then he said: "I *am* Joseph your brother, whom you sold

into Egypt. 5But now, do not
therefore be grieved or angry
with yourselves because you
sold me here; for God sent me
before you to preserve life. 6For
these two years the famine *has*
been in the land, and *there are*
still five years in which *there*
will be neither plowing nor
harvesting. 7And God sent me
before you to preserve a posterity for you in the earth, and
to save your lives by a great
deliverance. 8So now *it was* not
you *who* sent me here, but God;
and He has made me a father
to Pharaoh, and lord of all his
house, and a ruler throughout
all the land of Egypt.

9"Hurry and go up to my
father, and say to him, 'Thus
says your son Joseph: "God
has made me lord of all Egypt;
come down to me, do not tarry.
10You shall dwell in the land of
Goshen, and you shall be near
to me, you and your children,
your children's children, your
flocks and your herds, and all
that you have. 11There I will
provide for you, lest you and
your household, and all that
you have, come to poverty;
for *there are* still five years of
famine."'

12"And behold, your eyes
and the eyes of my brother
Benjamin see that *it is* my
mouth that speaks to you.
13So you shall tell my father
of all my glory in Egypt, and
of all that you have seen; and
you shall hurry and bring my
father down here."

14Then he fell on his
brother Benjamin's neck and
wept, and Benjamin wept on
his neck. 15Moreover he kissed
all his brothers and wept
over them, and after that his
brothers talked with him.

16Now the report of it was
heard in Pharaoh's house, saying, "Joseph's brothers have
come." So it pleased Pharaoh
and his servants well. 17And
Pharaoh said to Joseph, "Say
to your brothers, 'Do this:
Load your animals and de-
part; go to the land of Canaan.
18Bring your father and your
households and come to me;
I will give you the best of the
land of Egypt, and you will
eat the fat of the land. 19Now
you are commanded—do this:
Take carts out of the land of
Egypt for your little ones and
your wives; bring your father
and come. 20Also do not be
concerned about your goods,
for the best of all the land of
Egypt *is* yours.'"

21Then the sons of Israel
did so; and Joseph gave them
carts, according to the command of Pharaoh, and he
gave them provisions for the
journey. 22He gave to all of
them, to each man, changes
of garments; but to Benjamin
he gave three hundred *pieces*
of silver and five changes of
garments. 23And he sent to
his father these *things:* ten
donkeys loaded with the good
things of Egypt, and ten female donkeys loaded with

grain, bread, and food for his
father for the journey. 24So he
sent his brothers away, and
they departed; and he said to
them, "See that you do not become troubled along the way."
25Then they went up out of
Egypt, and came to the land of
Canaan to Jacob their father.
26And they told him, saying,
"Joseph *is* still alive, and he
is governor over all the land
of Egypt." And Jacob's heart
stood still, because he did not
believe them. 27But when they
told him all the words which
Joseph had said to them, and
when he saw the carts which
Joseph had sent to carry him,
the spirit of Jacob their father
revived. 28Then Israel said, "*It
is* enough. Joseph my son *is*
still alive. I will go and see him
before I die."

JACOB'S JOURNEY TO EGYPT

46 So Israel took his journey with all that he had,
and came to Beersheba, and
offered sacrifices to the God
of his father Isaac. 2Then God
spoke to Israel in the visions
of the night, and said, "Jacob,
Jacob!"
And he said, "Here I am."
3*So He said,* "*I am* God, the
God of your father; do not fear
to go down to Egypt, for I will
make of you a great nation
there. 4I will go down with you
to Egypt, and I will also surely
bring you up *again;* and Joseph
will put his hand on your eyes."
5Then Jacob arose from Beersheba; and the sons of Israel
carried their father Jacob, their
little ones, and their wives, in
the carts which Pharaoh had
sent to carry him. 6So they took
their livestock and their goods,
which they had acquired in the
land of Canaan, and went to
Egypt, Jacob and all his descendants with him. 7His sons and
his sons' sons, his daughters
and his sons' daughters, and
all his descendants he brought
with him to Egypt.
8Now these *were* the names
of the children of Israel, Jacob and his sons, who went
to Egypt: Reuben *was* Jacob's
firstborn. 9The sons of Reuben *were* Hanoch, Pallu, Hezron, and Carmi. 10The sons of
Simeon *were* Jemuel,[a] Jamin,
Ohad, Jachin,[b] Zohar,[c] and
Shaul, the son of a Canaanite woman. 11The sons of Levi
were Gershon, Kohath, and
Merari. 12The sons of Judah
were Er, Onan, Shelah, Perez,
and Zerah (but Er and Onan
died in the land of Canaan).
The sons of Perez were Hezron and Hamul. 13The sons of
Issachar *were* Tola, Puvah,[a]
Job,[b] and Shimron. 14The sons
of Zebulun *were* Sered, Elon,

46:10 [a] Spelled *Nemuel* in 1 Chronicles 4:24 [b] Called *Jarib* in 1 Chronicles 4:24 [c] Called *Zerah* in 1 Chronicles 4:24 46:13 [a] Spelled *Puah* in 1 Chronicles 7:1 [b] Same as *Jashub* in Numbers 26:24 and 1 Chronicles 7:1

and Jahleel. 15These *were* the
sons of Leah, whom she bore
to Jacob in Padan Aram, with
his daughter Dinah. All the
persons, his sons and his
daughters, *were* thirty-three.
16The sons of Gad *were*
Ziphion,[a] Haggi, Shuni, Ezbon,[b]
Eri, Arodi,[c] and Areli. 17The
sons of Asher *were* Jimnah,
Ishuah, Isui, Beriah, and Serah,
their sister. And the sons of Beriah *were* Heber and Malchiel.
18These *were* the sons of Zilpah, whom Laban gave to Leah
his daughter; and these she
bore to Jacob: sixteen persons.
19The sons of Rachel, Ja-
cob's wife, *were* Joseph and
Benjamin. 20And to Joseph
in the land of Egypt were
born Manasseh and Ephraim,
whom Asenath, the daughter
of Poti-Pherah priest of On,
bore to him. 21The sons of
Benjamin *were* Belah, Becher,
Ashbel, Gera, Naaman, Ehi,
Rosh, Muppim, Huppim,[a] and
Ard. 22These *were* the sons of
Rachel, who were born to Jacob: fourteen persons in all.
23The son of Dan *was* Hushim.[a] 24The sons of Naphtali
were Jahzeel,[a] Guni, Jezer, and
Shillem.[b] 25These *were* the
sons of Bilhah, whom Laban
gave to Rachel his daughter,
and she bore these to Jacob:
seven persons in all.
26All the persons who went
with Jacob to Egypt, who came
from his body, besides Jacob's
sons' wives, *were* sixty-six persons in all. 27And the sons of
Joseph who were born to him
in Egypt *were* two persons.
All the persons of the house
of Jacob who went to Egypt
were seventy.

JACOB SETTLES IN GOSHEN

28Then he sent Judah be-
fore him to Joseph, to point
out before him *the way* to Goshen. And they came to the
land of Goshen. 29So Joseph
made ready his chariot and
went up to Goshen to meet
his father Israel; and he presented himself to him, and
fell on his neck and wept on
his neck a good while.
30And Israel said to Joseph,
"Now let me die, since I have
seen your face, because you
are still alive."
31Then Joseph said to his
brothers and to his father's
household, "I will go up and
tell Pharaoh, and say to him,
'My brothers and those of my
father's house, who *were* in the
land of Canaan, have come to
me. 32And the men *are* shepherds, for their occupation has
been to feed livestock; and they
have brought their flocks, their
herds, and all that they have.'

46:16 [a] Spelled *Zephon* in Samaritan Pentateuch, Septuagint, and Numbers 26:15 [b] Called *Ozni* in Numbers 26:16 [c] Spelled *Arod* in Numbers 26:17 **46:21** [a] Called *Hupham* in Numbers 26:39 **46:23** [a] Called *Shuham* in Numbers 26:42 **46:24** [a] Spelled *Jahziel* in 1 Chronicles 7:13 [b] Spelled *Shallum* in 1 Chronicles 7:13

33So it shall be, when Pharaoh calls you and says, 'What
is your occupation?' 34that you
shall say, 'Your servants' occupation has been with livestock
from our youth even till now,
both we *and* also our fathers,'
that you may dwell in the land
of Goshen; for every shepherd
is an abomination to the Egyptians."

47 Then Joseph went and
told Pharaoh, and said,
"My father and my brothers,
their flocks and their herds
and all that they possess, have
come from the land of Ca-
naan; and indeed they *are* in
the land of Goshen." 2And he
took five men from among his
brothers and presented them
to Pharaoh. 3Then Pharaoh
said to his brothers, "What *is*
your occupation?"

And they said to Pharaoh,
"Your servants *are* shepherds,
both we *and* also our fathers."
4And they said to Pharaoh,
"We have come to dwell in
the land, because your servants have no pasture for
their flocks, for the famine *is*
severe in the land of Canaan.
Now therefore, please let your
servants dwell in the land of
Goshen."

5Then Pharaoh spoke to
Joseph, saying, "Your father
and your brothers have come
to you. 6The land of Egypt *is*
before you. Have your father
and brothers dwell in the best
of the land; let them dwell
in the land of Goshen. And
if you know *any* competent
men among them, then make
them chief herdsmen over my
livestock."

7Then Joseph brought in his
father Jacob and set him before
Pharaoh; and Jacob blessed
Pharaoh. 8Pharaoh said to Jacob, "How old *are* you?"

9And Jacob said to Pharaoh,
"The days of the years of my
pilgrimage *are* one hundred
and thirty years; few and evil
have been the days of the years
of my life, and they have not attained to the days of the years
of the life of my fathers in the
days of their pilgrimage." 10So
Jacob blessed Pharaoh, and
went out from before Pharaoh.

11And Joseph situated his
father and his brothers, and
gave them a possession in the
land of Egypt, in the best of the
land, in the land of Rameses,
as Pharaoh had commanded.
12Then Joseph provided his
father, his brothers, and all his
father's household with bread,
according to the number in
their families.

JOSEPH DEALS WITH THE FAMINE

13Now *there was* no bread
in all the land; for the famine
was very severe, so that the
land of Egypt and the land of
Canaan languished because of
the famine. 14And Joseph gathered up all the money that was
found in the land of Egypt and
in the land of Canaan, for the
grain which they bought; and

Joseph brought the money
into Pharaoh's house.
15So when the money failed
in the land of Egypt and in the
land of Canaan, all the Egyptians came to Joseph and said,
"Give us bread, for why should
we die in your presence? For
the money has failed."
16Then Joseph said, "Give
your livestock, and I will give
you *bread* for your livestock,
if the money is gone." 17So
they brought their livestock
to Joseph, and Joseph gave
them bread *in exchange* for
the horses, the flocks, the cattle of the herds, and for the
donkeys. Thus he fed them
with bread *in exchange* for all
their livestock that year.
18When that year had
ended, they came to him the
next year and said to him, "We
will not hide from my lord that
our money is gone; my lord
also has our herds of livestock.
There is nothing left in the
sight of my lord but our bodies
and our lands. 19Why should
we die before your eyes, both
we and our land? Buy us and
our land for bread, and we and
our land will be servants of
Pharaoh; give *us* seed, that we
may live and not die, that the
land may not be desolate."
20Then Joseph bought all
the land of Egypt for Pharaoh;
for every man of the Egyptians sold his field, because
the famine was severe upon
them. So the land became
Pharaoh's. 21And as for the
people, he moved them into
the cities,[a] from *one* end of
the borders of Egypt to the
other end. 22Only the land of
the priests he did not buy; for
the priests had rations *allotted
to them* by Pharaoh, and they
ate their rations which Pharaoh gave them; therefore they
did not sell their lands.
23Then Joseph said to the
people, "Indeed I have bought
you and your land this day for
Pharaoh. Look, *here is* seed
for you, and you shall sow the
land. 24And it shall come to
pass in the harvest that you
shall give one-fifth to Pharaoh. Four-fifths shall be your
own, as seed for the field and
for your food, for those of
your households and as food
for your little ones."
25So they said, "You have
saved our lives; let us find
favor in the sight of my lord,
and we will be Pharaoh's servants." 26And Joseph made it
a law over the land of Egypt to
this day, *that* Pharaoh should
have one-fifth, except for the
land of the priests only, *which*
did not become Pharaoh's.

JOSEPH'S VOW TO JACOB

27So Israel dwelt in the
land of Egypt, in the country
of Goshen; and they had pos-

47:21 [a] Following Masoretic Text and Targum; Samaritan Pentateuch, Septuagint, and Vulgate read *made the people virtual slaves*.

sessions there and grew and multiplied exceedingly. 28And Jacob lived in the land of Egypt seventeen years. So the length of Jacob's life was one hundred and forty-seven years. 29When the time drew near that Israel must die, he called his son Joseph and said to him, "Now if I have found favor in your sight, please put your hand under my thigh, and deal kindly and truly with me. Please do not bury me in Egypt, 30but let me lie with my fathers; you shall carry me out of Egypt and bury me in their burial place."

And he said, "I will do as you have said."

31Then he said, "Swear to me." And he swore to him. So Israel bowed himself on the head of the bed.

JACOB BLESSES JOSEPH'S SONS

48 Now it came to pass after these things that Joseph was told, "Indeed your father *is* sick"; and he took with him his two sons, Manasseh and Ephraim. 2And Jacob was told, "Look, your son Joseph is coming to you"; and Israel strengthened himself and sat up on the bed. 3Then Jacob said to Joseph: "God Almighty appeared to me at Luz in the land of Canaan and blessed me, 4and said to me, 'Behold, I will make you fruitful and multiply you, and I will make of you a multitude of people, and give this land to your descendants after you *as* an everlasting possession.' 5And now your two sons, Ephraim and Manasseh, who were born to you in the land of Egypt before I came to you in Egypt, *are* mine; as Reuben and Simeon, they shall be mine. 6Your offspring whom you beget after them shall be yours; they will be called by the name of their brothers in their inheritance. 7But as for me, when I came from Padan, Rachel died beside me in the land of Canaan on the way, when *there was* but a little distance to go to Ephrath; and I buried her there on the way to Ephrath (that is, Bethlehem)."

8Then Israel saw Joseph's sons, and said, "Who *are* these?"

9Joseph said to his father, "They *are* my sons, whom God has given me in this *place*."

And he said, "Please bring them to me, and I will bless them." 10Now the eyes of Israel were dim with age, *so that* he could not see. Then Joseph brought them near him, and he kissed them and embraced them. 11And Israel said to Joseph, "I had not thought to see your face; but in fact, God has also shown me your offspring!"

12So Joseph brought them from beside his knees, and he bowed down with his face to the earth. 13And Joseph took them both, Ephraim with his right hand toward Israel's left hand, and Manasseh with his

left hand toward Israel's right
hand, and brought *them* near
him. 14 Then Israel stretched
out his right hand and laid *it*
on Ephraim's head, who *was*
the younger, and his left hand
on Manasseh's head, guiding
his hands knowingly, for Manasseh *was* the firstborn. 15 And
he blessed Joseph, and said:

"God, before whom my
fathers Abraham
and Isaac walked,
The God who has
fed me all my life
long to this day,
16 The Angel who has
redeemed me
from all evil,
Bless the lads;
Let my name be named
upon them,
And the name of my
fathers Abraham
and Isaac;
And let them grow into
a multitude in the
midst of the earth."

17 Now when Joseph saw
that his father laid his right
hand on the head of Ephraim,
it displeased him; so he took
hold of his father's hand to remove it from Ephraim's head
to Manasseh's head. 18 And Joseph said to his father, "Not
so, my father, for this *one is*
the firstborn; put your right
hand on his head."

19 But his father refused and
said, "I know, my son, I know.
He also shall become a people, and he also shall be great;
but truly his younger brother
shall be greater than he, and
his descendants shall become
a multitude of nations."

20 So he blessed them that
day, saying, "By you Israel
will bless, saying, 'May God
make you as Ephraim and as
Manasseh!'" And thus he set
Ephraim before Manasseh.

21 Then Israel said to Joseph, "Behold, I am dying, but
God will be with you and bring
you back to the land of your fathers. 22 Moreover I have given
to you one portion above your
brothers, which I took from
the hand of the Amorite with
my sword and my bow."

JACOB'S LAST WORDS TO HIS SONS

49 And Jacob called his
sons and said, "Gather
together, that I may tell you
what shall befall you in the
last days:

2 "Gather together and hear,
you sons of Jacob,
And listen to Israel
your father.

3 "Reuben, you are
my firstborn,
My might and the
beginning of
my strength,
The excellency of
dignity and the
excellency of power.
4 Unstable as water, you
shall not excel,

Because you went up
to your father's bed;
Then you defiled *it*—
He went up to my couch.

5 "Simeon and Levi
are brothers;
Instruments of cruelty *are*
in their dwelling place.
6 Let not my soul enter
their council;
Let not my honor
be united to their
assembly;
For in their anger
they slew a man,
And in their self-will they
hamstrung an ox.
7 Cursed *be* their anger,
for *it is* fierce;
And their wrath,
for it is cruel!
I will divide them in Jacob
And scatter them in Israel.

8 "Judah, you *are he*
whom your brothers
shall praise;
Your hand *shall be* on the
neck of your enemies;
Your father's children
shall bow down
before you.
9 Judah *is* a lion's whelp;
From the prey, my son,
you have gone up.
He bows down, he lies
down as a lion;
And as a lion, who
shall rouse him?
10 The scepter shall not
depart from Judah,
Nor a lawgiver from
between his feet,
Until Shiloh comes;
And to Him *shall be* the
obedience of the people.
11 Binding his donkey
to the vine,
And his donkey's colt
to the choice vine,
He washed his
garments in wine,
And his clothes in the
blood of grapes.
12 His eyes *are* darker
than wine,
And his teeth whiter
than milk.

13 "Zebulun shall dwell by
the haven of the sea;
He *shall become* a
haven for ships,
And his border shall
adjoin Sidon.

14 "Issachar is a strong
donkey,
Lying down between
two burdens;
15 He saw that rest *was* good,
And that the land
was pleasant;
He bowed his shoulder
to bear *a burden,*
And became a band
of slaves.

16 "Dan shall judge his people
As one of the tribes
of Israel.
17 Dan shall be a serpent
by the way,
A viper by the path,
That bites the horse's heels
So that its rider shall
fall backward.

18 I have waited for your
salvation, O LORD!

19 "Gad, a troop shall
tramp upon him,
But he shall triumph
at last.

20 "Bread from Asher
shall be rich,
And he shall yield
royal dainties.

21 "Naphtali *is* a deer
let loose;
He uses beautiful words.

22 "Joseph *is* a
fruitful bough,
A fruitful bough by a well;
His branches run
over the wall.
23 The archers have
bitterly grieved him,
Shot *at him* and
hated him.
24 But his bow remained
in strength,
And the arms of
his hands were
made strong
By the hands of the
Mighty *God* of Jacob
(From there *is* the
Shepherd, the
Stone of Israel),
25 By the God of your father
who will help you,
And by the Almighty
who will bless you
With blessings of
heaven above,
Blessings of the deep
that lies beneath,
Blessings of the breasts
and of the womb.
26 The blessings of
your father
Have excelled the
blessings of my
ancestors,
Up to the utmost bound
of the everlasting hills.
They shall be on the
head of Joseph,
And on the crown
of the head of him
who was separate
from his brothers.

27 "Benjamin is a
ravenous wolf;
In the morning he shall
devour the prey,
And at night he shall
divide the spoil."

28 All these *are* the twelve
tribes of Israel, and this *is*
what their father spoke to
them. And he blessed them;
he blessed each one according
to his own blessing.

JACOB'S DEATH AND BURIAL

29 Then he charged them
and said to them: "I am to be
gathered to my people; bury
me with my fathers in the cave
that *is* in the field of Ephron
the Hittite, 30 in the cave that
is in the field of Machpelah,
which *is* before Mamre in the
land of Canaan, which Abraham bought with the field of
Ephron the Hittite as a possession for a burial place.

31There they buried Abraham
and Sarah his wife, there they
buried Isaac and Rebekah his
wife, and there I buried Leah.
32The field and the cave that
is there *were* purchased from
the sons of Heth." 33And when
Jacob had finished commanding his sons, he drew his feet
up into the bed and breathed
his last, and was gathered to
his people.

50 Then Joseph fell on his
father's face and wept
over him, and kissed him.
2And Joseph commanded his
servants the physicians to em-
balm his father. So the physicians embalmed Israel. 3Forty
days were required for him,
for such are the days required
for those who are embalmed;
and the Egyptians mourned
for him seventy days.

4Now when the days of his
mourning were past, Joseph
spoke to the household of
Pharaoh, saying, "If now I have
found favor in your eyes, please
speak in the hearing of Pharaoh, saying, 5'My father made
me swear, saying, "Behold, I
am dying; in my grave which
I dug for myself in the land of
Canaan, there you shall bury
me." Now therefore, please let
me go up and bury my father,
and I will come back.'"

6And Pharaoh said, "Go up
and bury your father, as he
made you swear."

7So Joseph went up to bury
his father; and with him went
up all the servants of Pharaoh,
the elders of his house, and all
the elders of the land of Egypt,
8as well as all the house of Joseph, his brothers, and his father's house. Only their little
ones, their flocks, and their
herds they left in the land of
Goshen. 9And there went up
with him both chariots and
horsemen, and it was a very
great gathering.

10Then they came to the
threshing floor of Atad, which
is beyond the Jordan, and they
mourned there with a great
and very solemn lamenta-
tion. He observed seven days
of mourning for his father.
11And when the inhabitants of
the land, the Canaanites, saw
the mourning at the threshing
floor of Atad, they said, "This *is*
a deep mourning of the Egyptians." Therefore its name was
called Abel Mizraim,[a] which *is*
beyond the Jordan.

12So his sons did for him
just as he had commanded
them. 13For his sons carried
him to the land of Canaan,
and buried him in the cave
of the field of Machpelah, before Mamre, which Abraham
bought with the field from
Ephron the Hittite as property
for a burial place. 14And after
he had buried his father, Joseph returned to Egypt, he and
his brothers and all who went
up with him to bury his father.

50:11 [a] Literally *Mourning of Egypt*

JOSEPH REASSURES HIS BROTHERS

15When Joseph's brothers
saw that their father was dead,
they said, "Perhaps Joseph
will hate us, and may actually
repay us for all the evil which
we did to him." 16So they sent
messengers to Joseph, saying,
"Before your father died he
commanded, saying, 17'Thus
you shall say to Joseph: "I beg
you, please forgive the trespass of your brothers and their
sin; for they did evil to you."'
Now, please, forgive the trespass of the servants of the God
of your father." And Joseph
wept when they spoke to him.
18Then his brothers also
went and fell down before his
face, and they said, "Behold,
we *are* your servants."
19Joseph said to them, "Do
not be afraid, for *am* I in the
place of God? 20But as for you,
you meant evil against me;
but God meant it for good, in
order to bring it about as *it is*
this day, to save many people
alive. 21Now therefore, do not
be afraid; I will provide for
you and your little ones." And
he comforted them and spoke
kindly to them.

DEATH OF JOSEPH

22So Joseph dwelt in Egypt,
he and his father's household.
And Joseph lived one hun-
dred and ten years. 23Joseph
saw Ephraim's children to the
third *generation.* The children
of Machir, the son of Manasseh, were also brought up on
Joseph's knees.
24And Joseph said to his
brethren, "I am dying; but God
will surely visit you, and bring
you out of this land to the land
of which He swore to Abraham,
to Isaac, and to Jacob." 25Then
Joseph took an oath from the
children of Israel, saying, "God
will surely visit you, and you
shall carry up my bones from
here." 26So Joseph died, *being*
one hundred and ten years old;
and they embalmed him, and
he was put in a coffin in Egypt.

THE SECOND BOOK OF MOSES CALLED EXODUS

ISRAEL'S SUFFERING IN EGYPT

1 Now these *are* the names of
the children of Israel who
came to Egypt; each man and
his household came with Jacob: 2Reuben, Simeon, Levi,
and Judah; 3Issachar, Zebulun,
and Benjamin; 4Dan, Naphtali,
Gad, and Asher. 5All those who

were descendants[a] of Jacob
were seventy[b] persons (for
Joseph was in Egypt *already*).
6And Joseph died, all his
brothers, and all that generation. 7But the children of Israel
were fruitful and increased
abundantly, multiplied and
grew exceedingly mighty; and
the land was filled with them.

8Now there arose a new
king over Egypt, who did not
know Joseph. 9And he said to
his people, "Look, the people
of the children of Israel *are*
more and mightier than we;
10come, let us deal shrewdly
with them, lest they multiply,
and it happen, in the event
of war, that they also join our
enemies and fight against us,
and *so* go up out of the land."
11Therefore they set taskmasters over them to afflict
them with their burdens. And
they built for Pharaoh supply
cities, Pithom and Raamses.
12But the more they afflicted
them, the more they multiplied and grew. And they were
in dread of the children of Israel. 13So the Egyptians made
the children of Israel serve
with rigor. 14And they made
their lives bitter with hard
bondage—in mortar, in brick,
and in all manner of service
in the field. All their service in
which they made them serve
was with rigor.

15Then the king of Egypt
spoke to the Hebrew midwives,
of whom the name of one *was*
Shiphrah and the name of
the other Puah; 16and he said,
"When you do the duties of a
midwife for the Hebrew women,
and see *them* on the birthstools,
if it *is* a son, then you shall kill
him; but if it *is* a daughter, then
she shall live." 17But the midwives feared God, and did not
do as the king of Egypt commanded them, but saved the
male children alive. 18So the
king of Egypt called for the midwives and said to them, "Why
have you done this thing, and
saved the male children alive?"

19And the midwives said
to Pharaoh, "Because the Hebrew women *are* not like the
Egyptian women; for they *are*
lively and give birth before the
midwives come to them."

20Therefore God dealt well
with the midwives, and the
people multiplied and grew
very mighty. 21And so it was,
because the midwives feared
God, that He provided households for them.

22So Pharaoh commanded
all his people, saying, "Every
son who is born[a] you shall
cast into the river, and every
daughter you shall save alive."

MOSES IS BORN

2 And a man of the house
of Levi went and took *as
wife* a daughter of Levi. 2So the

1:5 [a] Literally *who came from the loins of* [b] Dead Sea Scrolls and Septuagint read *seventy-five* (compare Acts 7:14). 1:22 [a] Samaritan Pentateuch, Septuagint, and Targum add *to the Hebrews.*

woman conceived and bore a
son. And when she saw that he
was a beautiful *child,* she hid
him three months. 3But when
she could no longer hide him,
she took an ark of bulrushes
for him, daubed it with asphalt
and pitch, put the child in it,
and laid *it* in the reeds by the
river's bank. 4And his sister
stood afar off, to know what
would be done to him.

5Then the daughter of
Pharaoh came down to bathe
at the river. And her maidens
walked along the riverside;
and when she saw the ark
among the reeds, she sent her
maid to get it. 6And when she
opened *it,* she saw the child,
and behold, the baby wept. So
she had compassion on him,
and said, "This is one of the
Hebrews' children."

7Then his sister said to
Pharaoh's daughter, "Shall I go
and call a nurse for you from
the Hebrew women, that she
may nurse the child for you?"

8And Pharaoh's daughter
said to her, "Go." So the maiden
went and called the child's
mother. 9Then Pharaoh's
daughter said to her, "Take this
child away and nurse him for
me, and I will give *you* your
wages." So the woman took the
child and nursed him. 10And
the child grew, and she brought
him to Pharaoh's daughter,
and he became her son. So
she called his name Moses,[a]
saying, "Because I drew him
out of the water."

MOSES FLEES TO MIDIAN

11Now it came to pass in
those days, when Moses was
grown, that he went out to his
brethren and looked at their
burdens. And he saw an Egyptian beating a Hebrew, one of
his brethren. 12So he looked
this way and that way, and
when he saw no one, he killed
the Egyptian and hid him in
the sand. 13And when he went
out the second day, behold,
two Hebrew men were fighting, and he said to the one who
did the wrong, "Why are you
striking your companion?"

14Then he said, "Who made
you a prince and a judge over
us? Do you intend to kill me
as you killed the Egyptian?"

So Moses feared and said,
"Surely this thing is known!"
15When Pharaoh heard of
this matter, he sought to kill
Moses. But Moses fled from
the face of Pharaoh and dwelt
in the land of Midian; and he
sat down by a well.

16Now the priest of Midian
had seven daughters. And
they came and drew water,
and they filled the troughs
to water their father's flock.
17Then the shepherds came
and drove them away; but
Moses stood up and helped
them, and watered their flock.

18When they came to Reuel

2:10 [a] Literally *Drawn Out*

their father, he said, "How *is*
it that you have come so soon
today?"
19 And they said, "An Egyptian delivered us from the
hand of the shepherds, and
he also drew enough water for
us and watered the flock."
20 So he said to his daughters, "And where *is* he? Why
is it *that* you have left the
man? Call him, that he may
eat bread."
21 Then Moses was content
to live with the man, and he
gave Zipporah his daughter to
Moses. 22 And she bore *him* a
son. He called his name Gershom,[a] for he said, "I have been
a stranger in a foreign land."
23 Now it happened in the
process of time that the king
of Egypt died. Then the children of Israel groaned because of the bondage, and
they cried out; and their cry
came up to God because of
the bondage. 24 So God heard
their groaning, and God remembered His covenant with
Abraham, with Isaac, and with
Jacob. 25 And God looked upon
the children of Israel, and God
acknowledged *them.*

MOSES AT THE BURNING *BUSH*

3 Now Moses was tending
the flock of Jethro his
father-in-law, the priest of
Midian. And he led the flock
to the back of the desert, and
came to Horeb, the mountain
of God. 2 And the Angel of the
LORD appeared to him in a
flame of fire from the midst
of a bush. So he looked, and
behold, the bush was burning
with fire, but the bush *was* not
consumed. 3 Then Moses said,
"I will now turn aside and see
this great sight, why the bush
does not burn."
4 So when the LORD saw that
he turned aside to look, God
called to him from the midst
of the bush and said, "Moses,
Moses!"
And he said, "Here I am."
5 Then He said, "Do not
draw near this place. Take your
sandals off your feet, for the
place where you stand *is* holy
ground." 6 Moreover He said,
"I *am* the God of your father—
the God of Abraham, the God
of Isaac, and the God of Jacob."
And Moses hid his face, for he
was afraid to look upon God.
7 And the LORD said: "I have
surely seen the oppression of
My people who *are* in Egypt,
and have heard their cry because of their taskmasters,
for I know their sorrows. 8 So
I have come down to deliver
them out of the hand of the
Egyptians, and to bring them
up from that land to a good
and large land, to a land flowing with milk and honey, to
the place of the Canaanites
and the Hittites and the Amorites and the Perizzites and

2:22 [a] Literally *Stranger There*

the Hivites and the Jebusites. 9 Now therefore, behold, the cry of the children of Israel has come to Me, and I have also seen the oppression with which the Egyptians oppress them. 10 Come now, therefore, and I will send you to Pharaoh that you may bring My people, the children of Israel, out of Egypt."

11 But Moses said to God, "Who *am* I that I should go to Pharaoh, and that I should bring the children of Israel out of Egypt?"

12 So He said, "I will certainly be with you. And this *shall be* a sign to you that I have sent you: When you have brought the people out of Egypt, you shall serve God on this mountain."

13 Then Moses said to God, "Indeed, *when* I come to the children of Israel and say to them, 'The God of your fathers has sent me to you,' and they say to me, 'What *is* His name?' what shall I say to them?"

14 And God said to Moses, "I AM WHO I AM." And He said, "Thus you shall say to the children of Israel, 'I AM has sent me to you.'" 15 Moreover God said to Moses, "Thus you shall say to the children of Israel: 'The LORD God of your fathers, the God of Abraham, the God of Isaac, and the God of Jacob, has sent me to you. This *is* My name forever, and this *is* My memorial to all generations.' 16 Go and gather the elders of Israel together, and say to them, 'The LORD God of your fathers, the God of Abraham, of Isaac, and of Jacob, appeared to me, saying, "I have surely visited you and *seen* what is done to you in Egypt; 17 and I have said I will bring you up out of the affliction of Egypt to the land of the Canaanites and the Hittites and the Amorites and the Perizzites and the Hivites and the Jebusites, to a land flowing with milk and honey."' 18 Then they will heed your voice; and you shall come, you and the elders of Israel, to the king of Egypt; and you shall say to him, 'The LORD God of the Hebrews has met with us; and now, please, let us go three days' journey into the wilderness, that we may sacrifice to the LORD our God.' 19 But I am sure that the king of Egypt will not let you go, no, not even by a mighty hand. 20 So I will stretch out My hand and strike Egypt with all My wonders which I will do in its midst; and after that he will let you go. 21 And I will give this people favor in the sight of the Egyptians; and it shall be, when you go, that you shall not go empty-handed. 22 But every woman shall ask of her neighbor, namely, of her who dwells near her house, articles of silver, articles of gold, and clothing; and you shall put *them* on your sons and on your daughters. So you shall plunder the Egyptians."

MIRACULOUS SIGNS FOR PHARAOH

4 Then Moses answered and said, "But suppose they will not believe me or listen to my voice; suppose they say, 'The LORD has not appeared to you.'"

2So the LORD said to him, "What *is* that in your hand?"

He said, "A rod."

3And He said, "Cast it on the ground." So he cast it on the ground, and it became a serpent; and Moses fled from it. 4Then the LORD said to Moses, "Reach out your hand and take *it* by the tail" (and he reached out his hand and caught it, and it became a rod in his hand), 5"that they may believe that the LORD God of their fathers, the God of Abraham, the God of Isaac, and the God of Jacob, has appeared to you."

6Furthermore the LORD said to him, "Now put your hand in your bosom." And he put his hand in his bosom, and when he took it out, behold, his hand *was* leprous, like snow. 7And He said, "Put your hand in your bosom again." So he put his hand in his bosom again, and drew it out of his bosom, and behold, it was restored like his *other* flesh. 8"Then it will be, if they do not believe you, nor heed the message of the first sign, that they may believe the message of the latter sign. 9And it shall be, if they do not believe even these two signs, or listen to your voice, that you shall take water from the river[a] and pour *it* on the dry *land.* The water which you take from the river will become blood on the dry *land.*"

10Then Moses said to the LORD, "O my Lord, I *am* not eloquent, neither before nor since You have spoken to Your servant; but I *am* slow of speech and slow of tongue."

11So the LORD said to him, "Who has made man's mouth? Or who makes the mute, the deaf, the seeing, or the blind? *Have* not I, the LORD? 12Now therefore, go, and I will be with your mouth and teach you what you shall say."

13But he said, "O my Lord, please send by the hand of whomever *else* You may send."

14So the anger of the LORD was kindled against Moses, and He said: "Is not Aaron the Levite your brother? I know that he can speak well. And look, he is also coming out to meet you. When he sees you, he will be glad in his heart. 15Now you shall speak to him and put the words in his mouth. And I will be with your mouth and with his mouth, and I will teach you what you shall do. 16So he shall be your spokesman to the people. And he himself shall be as a mouth

4:9 [a] That is, the Nile

for you, and you shall be to
him as God. 17And you shall
take this rod in your hand,
with which you shall do the
signs."

MOSES GOES TO EGYPT

18So Moses went and re-
turned to Jethro his father-in-
law, and said to him, "Please
let me go and return to my
brethren who *are* in Egypt,
and see whether they are still
alive."

And Jethro said to Moses,
"Go in peace."

19Now the LORD said to
Moses in Midian, "Go, return
to Egypt; for all the men who
sought your life are dead."
20Then Moses took his wife
and his sons and set them on a
donkey, and he returned to the
land of Egypt. And Moses took
the rod of God in his hand.

21And the LORD said to
Moses, "When you go back
to Egypt, see that you do all
those wonders before Pharaoh which I have put in your
hand. But I will harden his
heart, so that he will not let
the people go. 22Then you
shall say to Pharaoh, 'Thus
says the LORD: "Israel *is* My
son, My firstborn. 23So I say to
you, let My son go that he may
serve Me. But if you refuse to
let him go, indeed I will kill
your son, your firstborn."'"

24And it came to pass on
the way, at the encampment,
that the LORD met him and
sought to kill him. 25Then Zipporah took a sharp stone and
cut off the foreskin of her son
and cast *it* at *Moses'*[a] feet, and
said, "Surely you *are* a husband of blood to me!" 26So He
let him go. Then she said, "*You
are* a husband of blood!"—
because of the circumcision.

27And the LORD said to
Aaron, "Go into the wilderness
to meet Moses." So he went
and met him on the moun-
tain of God, and kissed him.
28So Moses told Aaron all the
words of the LORD who had
sent him, and all the signs
which He had commanded
him. 29Then Moses and Aaron
went and gathered together
all the elders of the children
of Israel. 30And Aaron spoke
all the words which the LORD
had spoken to Moses. Then
he did the signs in the sight
of the people. 31So the people
believed; and when they heard
that the LORD had visited the
children of Israel and that He
had looked on their affliction,
then they bowed their heads
and worshiped.

FIRST ENCOUNTER WITH PHARAOH

5 Afterward Moses and
Aaron went in and told
Pharaoh, "Thus says the LORD
God of Israel: 'Let My people
go, that they may hold a feast
to Me in the wilderness.'"

4:25 [a] Literally *his*

2And Pharaoh said, "Who *is*
the LORD, that I should obey
His voice to let Israel go? I do
not know the LORD, nor will I
let Israel go."

3So they said, "The God of
the Hebrews has met with us.
Please, let us go three days'
journey into the desert and
sacrifice to the LORD our God,
lest He fall upon us with pestilence or with the sword."

4Then the king of Egypt
said to them, "Moses and
Aaron, why do you take the
people from their work? Get
back to your labor." 5And
Pharaoh said, "Look, the people of the land *are* many now,
and you make them rest from
their labor!"

6So the same day Pharaoh
commanded the taskmasters
of the people and their officers, saying, 7"You shall no
longer give the people straw
to make brick as before. Let
them go and gather straw for
themselves. 8And you shall lay
on them the quota of bricks
which they made before. You
shall not reduce it. For they
are idle; therefore they cry
out, saying, 'Let us go *and* sacrifice to our God.' 9Let more
work be laid on the men, that
they may labor in it, and let
them not regard false words."

10And the taskmasters of
the people and their officers
went out and spoke to the
people, saying, "Thus says
Pharaoh: 'I will not give you
straw. 11Go, get yourselves
straw where you can find it; yet
none of your work will be reduced.'" 12So the people were
scattered abroad throughout
all the land of Egypt to gather
stubble instead of straw. 13And
the taskmasters forced *them*
to hurry, saying, "Fulfill your
work, *your* daily quota, as
when there was straw." 14Also
the officers of the children of
Israel, whom Pharaoh's taskmasters had set over them,
were beaten *and* were asked,
"Why have you not fulfilled
your task in making brick
both yesterday and today, as
before?"

15Then the officers of the
children of Israel came and
cried out to Pharaoh, saying,
"Why are you dealing thus
with your servants? 16There
is no straw given to your
servants, and they say to us,
'Make brick!' And indeed your
servants *are* beaten, but the
fault *is* in your *own* people."

17But he said, "You *are* idle!
Idle! Therefore you say, 'Let us
go *and* sacrifice to the LORD.'
18Therefore go now *and* work;
for no straw shall be given
you, yet you shall deliver the
quota of bricks." 19And the officers of the children of Israel
saw *that* they *were* in trouble
after it was said, "You shall not
reduce *any* bricks from your
daily quota."

20Then, as they came out
from Pharaoh, they met Moses
and Aaron who stood there to
meet them. 21And they said to

them, "Let the LORD look on
you and judge, because you
have made us abhorrent in
the sight of Pharaoh and in
the sight of his servants, to
put a sword in their hand to
kill us."

ISRAEL'S DELIVERANCE ASSURED

22So Moses returned to the
LORD and said, "Lord, why
have You brought trouble on
this people? Why *is* it You have
sent me? 23For since I came
to Pharaoh to speak in Your
name, he has done evil to this
people; neither have You delivered Your people at all."

6 Then the LORD said to
Moses, "Now you shall see
what I will do to Pharaoh. For
with a strong hand he will let
them go, and with a strong
hand he will drive them out
of his land."

2And God spoke to Moses
and said to him: "I *am* the
LORD. 3I appeared to Abraham, to Isaac, and to Jacob,
as God Almighty, but *by* My
name LORD[a] I was not known
to them. 4I have also established My covenant with
them, to give them the land
of Canaan, the land of their
pilgrimage, in which they
were strangers. 5And I have
also heard the groaning of the
children of Israel whom the
Egyptians keep in bondage,
and I have remembered My
covenant. 6Therefore say to
the children of Israel: 'I *am*
the LORD; I will bring you out
from under the burdens of
the Egyptians, I will rescue
you from their bondage, and
I will redeem you with an outstretched arm and with great
judgments. 7I will take you as
My people, and I will be your
God. Then you shall know that
I *am* the LORD your God who
brings you out from under
the burdens of the Egyptians.
8And I will bring you into the
land which I swore to give to
Abraham, Isaac, and Jacob;
and I will give it to you *as* a
heritage: I *am* the LORD.'" 9So
Moses spoke thus to the children of Israel; but they did
not heed Moses, because of
anguish of spirit and cruel
bondage.

10And the LORD spoke to
Moses, saying, 11"Go in, tell
Pharaoh king of Egypt to let
the children of Israel go out
of his land."

12And Moses spoke before
the LORD, saying, "The children of Israel have not heeded
me. How then shall Pharaoh
heed me, for I *am* of uncircumcised lips?"

13Then the LORD spoke to
Moses and Aaron, and gave
them a command for the children of Israel and for Pharaoh king of Egypt, to bring the
children of Israel out of the
land of Egypt.

6:3 [a] Hebrew *YHWH,* traditionally *Jehovah*

THE FAMILY OF MOSES AND AARON

14These *are* the heads of
their fathers' houses: The sons
of Reuben, the firstborn of Israel, *were* Hanoch, Pallu, Hezron, and Carmi. These are the
families of Reuben. 15And the
sons of Simeon *were* Jemuel,[a]
Jamin, Ohad, Jachin, Zohar,
and Shaul the son of a Canaanite woman. These *are* the
families of Simeon. 16These
are the names of the sons of
Levi according to their generations: Gershon, Kohath, and
Merari. And the years of the
life of Levi *were* one hundred
and thirty-seven. 17The sons of
Gershon *were* Libni and Shimi
according to their families.
18And the sons of Kohath *were*
Amram, Izhar, Hebron, and
Uzziel. And the years of the life
of Kohath *were* one hundred
and thirty-three. 19The sons of
Merari *were* Mahli and Mushi.
These *are* the families of Levi
according to their generations.

20Now Amram took for
himself Jochebed, his father's
sister, as wife; and she bore
him Aaron and Moses. And
the years of the life of Amram
were one hundred and thirty-
seven. 21The sons of Izhar *were*
Korah, Nepheg, and Zichri.
22And the sons of Uzziel *were*
Mishael, Elzaphan, and Zithri.
23Aaron took to himself Elish-
eba, daughter of Amminadab,
sister of Nahshon, as wife; and
she bore him Nadab, Abihu, Eleazar, and Ithamar. 24And the
sons of Korah *were* Assir, Elkanah, and Abiasaph. These are
the families of the Korahites.
25Eleazar, Aaron's son, took for
himself one of the daughters
of Putiel as wife; and she bore
him Phinehas. These *are* the
heads of the fathers' houses of
the Levites according to their
families.

26These *are the same* Aaron
and Moses to whom the LORD
said, "Bring out the children of
Israel from the land of Egypt
according to their armies."
27These *are* the ones who spoke
to Pharaoh king of Egypt, to
bring out the children of Israel
from Egypt. These *are the same*
Moses and Aaron.

AARON IS MOSES' SPOKESMAN

28And it came to pass, on
the day the LORD spoke to
Moses in the land of Egypt,
29that the LORD spoke to
Moses, saying, "I *am* the
LORD. Speak to Pharaoh king
of Egypt all that I say to you."

30But Moses said before the
LORD, "Behold, I *am* of uncir-
cumcised lips, and how shall
Pharaoh heed me?"

7 So the LORD said to Moses:
"See, I have made you *as*
God to Pharaoh, and Aaron
your brother shall be your
prophet. 2You shall speak
all that I command you. And

6:15 [a] Spelled *Nemuel* in Numbers 26:12

Aaron your brother shall tell
Pharaoh to send the children
of Israel out of his land. [3]And
I will harden Pharaoh's heart,
and multiply My signs and My
wonders in the land of Egypt.
[4]But Pharaoh will not heed
you, so that I may lay My hand
on Egypt and bring My armies
and My people, the children of
Israel, out of the land of Egypt
by great judgments. [5]And the
Egyptians shall know that I
am the LORD, when I stretch
out My hand on Egypt and
bring out the children of Israel from among them."

[6]Then Moses and Aaron
did *so;* just as the LORD commanded them, so they did.
[7]And Moses *was* eighty years
old and Aaron eighty-three
years old when they spoke to
Pharaoh.

AARON'S MIRACULOUS ROD

[8]Then the LORD spoke to
Moses and Aaron, saying,
[9]"When Pharaoh speaks to
you, saying, 'Show a miracle
for yourselves,' then you shall
say to Aaron, 'Take your rod
and cast *it* before Pharaoh,
and let it become a serpent.'"
[10]So Moses and Aaron went in
to Pharaoh, and they did so,
just as the LORD commanded.
And Aaron cast down his rod
before Pharaoh and before
his servants, and it became
a serpent.

[11]But Pharaoh also called
the wise men and the sorcerers; so the magicians of Egypt,
they also did in like manner
with their enchantments.
[12]For every man threw down
his rod, and they became serpents. But Aaron's rod swallowed up their rods. [13]And
Pharaoh's heart grew hard,
and he did not heed them, as
the LORD had said.

THE FIRST PLAGUE: WATERS BECOME BLOOD

[14]So the LORD said to Moses:
"Pharaoh's heart *is* hard; he
refuses to let the people go.
[15]Go to Pharaoh in the morning, when he goes out to the
water, and you shall stand by
the river's bank to meet him;
and the rod which was turned
to a serpent you shall take in
your hand. [16]And you shall
say to him, 'The LORD God of
the Hebrews has sent me to
you, saying, "Let My people
go, that they may serve Me in
the wilderness"; but indeed,
until now you would not hear!
[17]Thus says the LORD: "By this
you shall know that I *am* the
LORD. Behold, I will strike
the waters which *are* in the
river with the rod that *is* in
my hand, and they shall be
turned to blood. [18]And the fish
that *are* in the river shall die,
the river shall stink, and the
Egyptians will loathe to drink
the water of the river."'"

[19]Then the LORD spoke to
Moses, "Say to Aaron, 'Take
your rod and stretch out your
hand over the waters of Egypt,
over their streams, over their

rivers, over their ponds, and over all their pools of water, that they may become blood. And there shall be blood throughout all the land of Egypt, both in *buckets of* wood and *pitchers of* stone.'" 20And Moses and Aaron did so, just as the LORD commanded. So he lifted up the rod and struck the waters that *were* in the river, in the sight of Pharaoh and in the sight of his servants. And all the waters that *were* in the river were turned to blood. 21The fish that *were* in the river died, the river stank, and the Egyptians could not drink the water of the river. So there was blood throughout all the land of Egypt.

22Then the magicians of Egypt did so with their enchantments; and Pharaoh's heart grew hard, and he did not heed them, as the LORD had said. 23And Pharaoh turned and went into his house. Neither was his heart moved by this. 24So all the Egyptians dug all around the river for water to drink, because they could not drink the water of the river. 25And seven days passed after the LORD had struck the river.

THE SECOND PLAGUE: FROGS

8 And the LORD spoke to Moses, "Go to Pharaoh and say to him, 'Thus says the LORD: "Let My people go, that they may serve Me. 2But if you refuse to let *them* go, behold, I will smite all your territory with frogs. 3So the river shall bring forth frogs abundantly, which shall go up and come into your house, into your bedroom, on your bed, into the houses of your servants, on your people, into your ovens, and into your kneading bowls. 4And the frogs shall come up on you, on your people, and on all your servants."'"

5Then the LORD spoke to Moses, "Say to Aaron, 'Stretch out your hand with your rod over the streams, over the rivers, and over the ponds, and cause frogs to come up on the land of Egypt.'" 6So Aaron stretched out his hand over the waters of Egypt, and the frogs came up and covered the land of Egypt. 7And the magicians did so with their enchantments, and brought up frogs on the land of Egypt.

8Then Pharaoh called for Moses and Aaron, and said, "Entreat the LORD that He may take away the frogs from me and from my people; and I will let the people go, that they may sacrifice to the LORD."

9And Moses said to Pharaoh, "Accept the honor of saying when I shall intercede for you, for your servants, and for your people, to destroy the frogs from you and your houses, *that* they may remain in the river only."

10So he said, "Tomorrow."

And he said, "*Let it be* according to your word, that you may know that *there is* no one like the LORD our God. 11And the frogs shall depart from you, from your houses, from your servants, and from your people. They shall remain in the river only."

12Then Moses and Aaron went out from Pharaoh. And Moses cried out to the LORD concerning the frogs which He had brought against Pharaoh. 13So the LORD did according to the word of Moses. And the frogs died out of the houses, out of the courtyards, and out of the fields. 14They gathered them together in heaps, and the land stank. 15But when Pharaoh saw that there was relief, he hardened his heart and did not heed them, as the LORD had said.

The Third Plague: Lice

16So the LORD said to Moses, "Say to Aaron, 'Stretch out your rod, and strike the dust of the land, so that it may become lice throughout all the land of Egypt.'" 17And they did so. For Aaron stretched out his hand with his rod and struck the dust of the earth, and it became lice on man and beast. All the dust of the land became lice throughout all the land of Egypt.

18Now the magicians so worked with their enchantments to bring forth lice, but they could not. So there were lice on man and beast. 19Then the magicians said to Pharaoh, "This *is* the finger of God." But Pharaoh's heart grew hard, and he did not heed them, just as the LORD had said.

The Fourth Plague: Flies

20And the LORD said to Moses, "Rise early in the morning and stand before Pharaoh as he comes out to the water. Then say to him, 'Thus says the LORD: "Let My people go, that they may serve Me. 21Or else, if you will not let My people go, behold, I will send swarms *of flies* on you and your servants, on your people and into your houses. The houses of the Egyptians shall be full of swarms *of flies,* and also the ground on which they *stand.* 22And in that day I will set apart the land of Goshen, in which My people dwell, that no swarms *of flies* shall be there, in order that you may know that I *am* the LORD in the midst of the land. 23I will make a difference[a] between My people and your people. Tomorrow this sign shall be."'" 24And the LORD did so. Thick swarms *of flies* came into the house of Pharaoh, *into* his servants' houses, and

8:23 [a] Literally *set a ransom* (compare Exodus 9:4 and 11:7)

into all the land of Egypt. The
land was corrupted because
of the swarms *of flies.*

25Then Pharaoh called for
Moses and Aaron, and said,
"Go, sacrifice to your God in
the land."

26And Moses said, "It is not
right to do so, for we would be
sacrificing the abomination
of the Egyptians to the LORD
our God. If we sacrifice the
abomination of the Egyptians
before their eyes, then will
they not stone us? 27We will
go three days' journey into
the wilderness and sacrifice
to the LORD our God as He will
command us."

28So Pharaoh said, "I will
let you go, that you may sacrifice to the LORD your God in
the wilderness; only you shall
not go very far away. Intercede
for me."

29Then Moses said, "Indeed
I am going out from you, and
I will entreat the LORD, that
the swarms *of flies* may depart tomorrow from Pharaoh,
from his servants, and from
his people. But let Pharaoh
not deal deceitfully anymore
in not letting the people go to
sacrifice to the LORD."

30So Moses went out from
Pharaoh and entreated the
LORD. 31And the LORD did according to the word of Moses;
He removed the swarms *of
flies* from Pharaoh, from his
servants, and from his people. Not one remained. 32But
Pharaoh hardened his heart at
this time also; neither would
he let the people go.

THE FIFTH PLAGUE: LIVESTOCK DISEASED

9 Then the LORD said to
Moses, "Go in to Pharaoh
and tell him, 'Thus says the
LORD God of the Hebrews: "Let
My people go, that they may
serve Me. 2For if you refuse
to let *them* go, and still hold
them, 3behold, the hand of the
LORD will be on your cattle in
the field, on the horses, on the
donkeys, on the camels, on
the oxen, and on the sheep—a
very severe pestilence. 4And
the LORD will make a difference between the livestock
of Israel and the livestock of
Egypt. So nothing shall die of
all *that* belongs to the children
of Israel."'" 5Then the LORD
appointed a set time, saying,
"Tomorrow the LORD will do
this thing in the land."

6So the LORD did this thing
on the next day, and all the
livestock of Egypt died; but of
the livestock of the children
of Israel, not one died. 7Then
Pharaoh sent, and indeed, not
even one of the livestock of
the Israelites was dead. But
the heart of Pharaoh became
hard, and he did not let the
people go.

THE SIXTH PLAGUE: BOILS

8So the LORD said to
Moses and Aaron, "Take for
yourselves handfuls of ashes
from a furnace, and let Moses

scatter it toward the heavens
in the sight of Pharaoh. 9And it
will become fine dust in all the
land of Egypt, and it will cause
boils that break out in sores on
man and beast throughout all
the land of Egypt." 10Then they
took ashes from the furnace
and stood before Pharaoh, and
Moses scattered *them* toward
heaven. And *they* caused boils
that break out in sores on man
and beast. 11And the magicians
could not stand before Moses
because of the boils, for the
boils were on the magicians
and on all the Egyptians. 12But
the LORD hardened the heart
of Pharaoh; and he did not
heed them, just as the LORD
had spoken to Moses.

THE SEVENTH PLAGUE: HAIL

13Then the LORD said to
Moses, "Rise early in the
morning and stand before
Pharaoh, and say to him, 'Thus
says the LORD God of the Hebrews: "Let My people go, that
they may serve Me, 14for at this
time I will send all My plagues
to your very heart, and on your
servants and on your people,
that you may know that *there*
is none like Me in all the earth.
15Now if I had stretched out
My hand and struck you and
your people with pestilence,
then you would have been cut
off from the earth. 16But indeed for this *purpose* I have
raised you up, that I may show
My power *in* you, and that My
name may be declared in all
the earth. 17As yet you exalt
yourself against My people in
that you will not let them go.
18Behold, tomorrow about this
time I will cause very heavy
hail to rain down, such as has
not been in Egypt since its
founding until now. 19There-
fore send now *and* gather your
livestock and all that you have
in the field, for the hail shall
come down on every man and
every animal which is found
in the field and is not brought
home; and they shall die."'"

20He who feared the word
of the LORD among the servants of Pharaoh made his
servants and his livestock flee
to the houses. 21But he who
did not regard the word of the
LORD left his servants and his
livestock in the field.

22Then the LORD said to
Moses, "Stretch out your hand
toward heaven, that there
may be hail in all the land of
Egypt—on man, on beast,
and on every herb of the field,
throughout the land of Egypt."
23And Moses stretched out his
rod toward heaven; and the
LORD sent thunder and hail,
and fire darted to the ground.
And the LORD rained hail on
the land of Egypt. 24So there
was hail, and fire mingled
with the hail, so very heavy
that there was none like it in
all the land of Egypt since it
became a nation. 25And the *hail*
struck throughout the whole
land of Egypt, all that *was* in

the field, both man and beast; and the hail struck every herb of the field and broke every tree of the field. [26]Only in the land of Goshen, where the children of Israel *were,* there was no hail.

[27]And Pharaoh sent and called for Moses and Aaron, and said to them, "I have sinned this time. The LORD *is* righteous, and my people and I *are* wicked. [28]Entreat the LORD, that there may be no *more* mighty thundering and hail, for *it is* enough. I will let you go, and you shall stay no longer."

[29]So Moses said to him, "As soon as I have gone out of the city, I will spread out my hands to the LORD; the thunder will cease, and there will be no more hail, that you may know that the earth *is* the LORD's. [30]But as for you and your servants, I know that you will not yet fear the LORD God."

[31]Now the flax and the barley were struck, for the barley *was* in the head and the flax *was* in bud. [32]But the wheat and the spelt were not struck, for they *are* late crops.

[33]So Moses went out of the city from Pharaoh and spread out his hands to the LORD; *then the* thunder and the hail ceased, and the rain was not poured on the earth. [34]And when Pharaoh saw that the rain, the hail, and the thunder had ceased, he sinned yet more; and he hardened his heart, he and his servants. [35]So the heart of Pharaoh was hard; neither would he let the children of Israel go, as the LORD had spoken by Moses.

THE EIGHTH PLAGUE: LOCUSTS

10 Now the LORD said to Moses, "Go in to Pharaoh; for I have hardened his heart and the hearts of his servants, that I may show these signs of Mine before him, [2]and that you may tell in the hearing of your son and your son's son the mighty things I have done in Egypt, and My signs which I have done among them, that you may know that I *am* the LORD."

[3]So Moses and Aaron came in to Pharaoh and said to him, "Thus says the LORD God of the Hebrews: 'How long will you refuse to humble yourself before Me? Let My people go, that they may serve Me. [4]Or else, if you refuse to let My people go, behold, tomorrow I will bring locusts into your territory. [5]And they shall cover the face of the earth, so that no one will be able to see the earth; and they shall eat the residue of what is left, which remains to you from the hail, and they shall eat every tree which grows up for you out of the field. [6]They shall fill your houses, the houses of all your servants, and the houses of all the Egyptians—which neither your fathers nor your fathers' fathers have seen, since the

day that they were on the earth
to this day.'" And he turned
and went out from Pharaoh.
7Then Pharaoh's servants
said to him, "How long shall
this man be a snare to us? Let
the men go, that they may
serve the LORD their God. Do
you not yet know that Egypt
is destroyed?"
8So Moses and Aaron were
brought again to Pharaoh, and
he said to them, "Go, serve the
LORD your God. Who *are* the
ones that are going?"
9And Moses said, "We will
go with our young and our
old; with our sons and our
daughters, with our flocks and
our herds we will go, for we
must hold a feast to the LORD."
10Then he said to them,
"The LORD had better be with
you when I let you and your little ones go! Beware, for evil is
ahead of you. 11Not so! Go now,
you *who are* men, and serve
the LORD, for that is what you
desired." And they were driven
out from Pharaoh's presence.
12Then the LORD said to
Moses, "Stretch out your hand
over the land of Egypt for the
locusts, that they may come
upon the land of Egypt, and
eat every herb of the land—
all that the hail has left." 13So
Moses stretched out his rod
over the land of Egypt, and the
LORD brought an east wind on
the land all that day and all
that night. When it was morning, the east wind brought
the locusts. 14And the locusts
went up over all the land of
Egypt and rested on all the
territory of Egypt. *They were*
very severe; previously there
had been no such locusts as
they, nor shall there be such
after them. 15For they covered
the face of the whole earth, so
that the land was darkened;
and they ate every herb of the
land and all the fruit of the
trees which the hail had left.
So there remained nothing
green on the trees or on the
plants of the field throughout
all the land of Egypt.
16Then Pharaoh called for
Moses and Aaron in haste, and
said, "I have sinned against
the LORD your God and
against you. 17Now therefore,
please forgive my sin only this
once, and entreat the LORD
your God, that He may take
away from me this death only."
18So he went out from Pharaoh and entreated the LORD.
19And the LORD turned a very
strong west wind, which took
the locusts away and blew
them into the Red Sea. There
remained not one locust in all
the territory of Egypt. 20But
the LORD hardened Pharaoh's
heart, and he did not let the
children of Israel go.

THE NINTH PLAGUE: DARKNESS

21Then the LORD said to
Moses, "Stretch out your
hand toward heaven, that
there may be darkness over
the land of Egypt, darkness

which may even be felt." 22So
Moses stretched out his hand
toward heaven, and there was
thick darkness in all the land
of Egypt three days. 23They
did not see one another; nor
did anyone rise from his
place for three days. But all
the children of Israel had light
in their dwellings.

24Then Pharaoh called to
Moses and said, "Go, serve
the LORD; only let your flocks
and your herds be kept back.
Let your little ones also go
with you."

25But Moses said, "You must
also give us sacrifices and
burnt offerings, that we may
sacrifice to the LORD our God.
26Our livestock also shall go
with us; not a hoof shall be left
behind. For we must take some
of them to serve the LORD our
God, and even we do not know
with what we must serve the
LORD until we arrive there."

27But the LORD hardened
Pharaoh's heart, and he would
not let them go. 28Then Pharaoh said to him, "Get away
from me! Take heed to yourself and see my face no more!
For in the day you see my face
you shall die!"

29So Moses said, "You have
spoken well. I will never see
your face again."

DEATH OF THE FIRSTBORN ANNOUNCED

11 And the LORD said to
Moses, "I will bring one
more plague on Pharaoh and
on Egypt. Afterward he will let
you go from here. When he
lets *you* go, he will surely drive
you out of here altogether.
2Speak now in the hearing
of the people, and let every
man ask from his neighbor
and every woman from her
neighbor, articles of silver
and articles of gold." 3And the
LORD gave the people favor
in the sight of the Egyptians.
Moreover the man Moses *was*
very great in the land of Egypt,
in the sight of Pharaoh's servants and in the sight of the
people.

4Then Moses said, "Thus
says the LORD: 'About midnight I will go out into the
midst of Egypt; 5and all the
firstborn in the land of Egypt
shall die, from the firstborn
of Pharaoh who sits on his
throne, even to the firstborn
of the female servant who *is*
behind the handmill, and all
the firstborn of the animals.
6Then there shall be a great
cry throughout all the land
of Egypt, such as was not like
it *before,* nor shall be like it
again. 7But against none of
the children of Israel shall a
dog move its tongue, against
man or beast, that you may
know that the LORD does
make a difference between
the Egyptians and Israel.'
8And all these your servants
shall come down to me and
bow down to me, saying, 'Get
out, and all the people who
follow you!' After that I will go

out." Then he went out from
Pharaoh in great anger.
9But the LORD said to
Moses, "Pharaoh will not heed
you, so that My wonders may
be multiplied in the land of
Egypt." 10So Moses and Aaron
did all these wonders before
Pharaoh; and the LORD hardened Pharaoh's heart, and he
did not let the children of Israel go out of his land.

THE PASSOVER INSTITUTED

12 Now the LORD spoke to
Moses and Aaron in the
land of Egypt, saying, 2"This
month *shall be* your beginning
of months; it *shall be* the first
month of the year to you.
3Speak to all the congregation of Israel, saying: 'On the
tenth of this month every man
shall take for himself a lamb,
according to the house of *his*
father, a lamb for a household. 4And if the household
is too small for the lamb, let
him and his neighbor next to
his house take *it* according to
the number of the persons;
according to each man's need
you shall make your count for
the lamb. 5Your lamb shall be
without blemish, a male of
the first year. You may take
it from the sheep or from the
goats. 6Now you shall keep it
until the fourteenth day of the
same month. Then the whole
assembly of the congregation
of Israel shall kill it at twilight.
7And they shall take *some* of
the blood and put *it* on the two
doorposts and on the lintel of
the houses where they eat it.
8Then they shall eat the flesh
on that night; roasted in fire,
with unleavened bread *and*
with bitter *herbs* they shall
eat it. 9Do not eat it raw, nor
boiled at all with water, but
roasted in fire—its head with
its legs and its entrails. 10You
shall let none of it remain
until morning, and what remains of it until morning you
shall burn with fire. 11And thus
you shall eat it: *with* a belt on
your waist, your sandals on
your feet, and your staff in
your hand. So you shall eat it
in haste. It *is* the LORD's Passover.
12'For I will pass through
the land of Egypt on that
night, and will strike all the
firstborn in the land of Egypt,
both man and beast; and
against all the gods of Egypt
I will execute judgment: I *am*
the LORD. 13Now the blood
shall be a sign for you on the
houses where you *are*. And
when I see the blood, I will
pass over you; and the plague
shall not be on you to destroy
you when I strike the land of
Egypt.
14'So this day shall be to
you a memorial; and you
shall keep it as a feast to the
LORD throughout your gen-
erations. You shall keep it as
a feast by an everlasting ordinance. 15Seven days you shall
eat unleavened bread. On the

first day you shall remove
leaven from your houses.
For whoever eats leavened
bread from the first day until
the seventh day, that person
shall be cut off from Israel.
16On the first day *there shall*
be a holy convocation, and on
the seventh day there shall be
a holy convocation for you.
No manner of work shall be
done on them; but *that* which
everyone must eat—that only
may be prepared by you. 17So
you shall observe *the Feast of*
Unleavened Bread, for on this
same day I will have brought
your armies out of the land
of Egypt. Therefore you shall
observe this day throughout
your generations as an everlasting ordinance. 18In the first
month, on the fourteenth day
of the month at evening, you
shall eat unleavened bread,
until the twenty-first day of
the month at evening. 19For
seven days no leaven shall be
found in your houses, since
whoever eats what is leavened,
that same person shall be cut
off from the congregation of
Israel, whether *he is* a stranger
or a native of the land. 20You
shall eat nothing leavened; in
all your dwellings you shall
eat unleavened bread.'"

21Then Moses called for all
the elders of Israel and said
to them, "Pick out and take
lambs for yourselves according to your families, and kill
the Passover *lamb.* 22And you
shall take a bunch of hyssop,
dip *it* in the blood that *is* in
the basin, and strike the lintel
and the two doorposts with
the blood that *is* in the basin.
And none of you shall go out
of the door of his house until
morning. 23For the LORD will
pass through to strike the
Egyptians; and when He sees
the blood on the lintel and on
the two doorposts, the LORD
will pass over the door and not
allow the destroyer to come
into your houses to strike
you. 24And you shall observe
this thing as an ordinance for
you and your sons forever. 25It
will come to pass when you
come to the land which the
LORD will give you, just as He
promised, that you shall keep
this service. 26And it shall be,
when your children say to
you, 'What do you mean by
this service?' 27that you shall
say, 'It *is* the Passover sacrifice of the LORD, who passed
over the houses of the children of Israel in Egypt when
He struck the Egyptians and
delivered our households.'" So
the people bowed their heads
and worshiped. 28Then the
children of Israel went away
and did *so;* just as the LORD
had commanded Moses and
Aaron, so they did.

THE TENTH PLAGUE: DEATH OF THE FIRSTBORN

29And it came to pass at
midnight that the LORD struck
all the firstborn in the land of
Egypt, from the firstborn of

Pharaoh who sat on his throne
to the firstborn of the captive
who *was* in the dungeon, and
all the firstborn of livestock.
30So Pharaoh rose in the
night, he, all his servants, and
all the Egyptians; and there
was a great cry in Egypt, for
there was not a house where
there was not one dead.

THE EXODUS

31Then he called for Moses
and Aaron by night, and said,
"Rise, go out from among my
people, both you and the children of Israel. And go, serve
the LORD as you have said.
32Also take your flocks and
your herds, as you have said,
and be gone; and bless me
also."

33And the Egyptians urged
the people, that they might
send them out of the land in
haste. For they said, "We *shall*
all *be* dead." 34So the people
took their dough before it was
leavened, having their kneading bowls bound up in their
clothes on their shoulders.
35Now the children of Israel
had done according to the
word of Moses, and they had
asked from the Egyptians articles of silver, articles of gold,
and clothing. 36And the LORD
had given the people favor in
the sight of the Egyptians, so
that they granted them *what*
they requested. Thus they
plundered the Egyptians.

37Then the children of Israel journeyed from Rameses
to Succoth, about six hundred thousand men on foot,
besides children. 38A mixed
multitude went up with them
also, and flocks and herds—a
great deal of livestock. 39And
they baked unleavened cakes
of the dough which they had
brought out of Egypt; for it
was not leavened, because
they were driven out of Egypt
and could not wait, nor had
they prepared provisions for
themselves.

40Now the sojourn of the
children of Israel who lived
in Egypt[a] *was* four hundred
and thirty years. 41And it came
to pass at the end of the four
hundred and thirty years—on
that very same day—it came
to pass that all the armies of
the LORD went out from the
land of Egypt. 42It *is* a night
of solemn observance to the
LORD for bringing them out
of the land of Egypt. This *is*
that night of the LORD, a solemn observance for all the
children of Israel throughout
their generations.

PASSOVER REGULATIONS

43And the LORD said to
Moses and Aaron, "This *is* the
ordinance of the Passover: No
foreigner shall eat it. 44But
every man's servant who is
bought for money, when you
have circumcised him, then

12:40 [a] Samaritan Pentateuch and Septuagint read *Egypt and Canaan.*

he may eat it. 45A sojourner
and a hired servant shall not
eat it. 46In one house it shall
be eaten; you shall not carry
any of the flesh outside the
house, nor shall you break one
of its bones. 47All the congregation of Israel shall keep it.
48And when a stranger dwells
with you *and wants* to keep
the Passover to the LORD, let
all his males be circumcised,
and then let him come near
and keep it; and he shall be
as a native of the land. For no
uncircumcised person shall
eat it. 49One law shall be for
the native-born and for the
stranger who dwells among
you."

50Thus all the children of
Israel did; as the LORD commanded Moses and Aaron, so
they did. 51And it came to pass,
on that very same day, that the
LORD brought the children of
Israel out of the land of Egypt
according to their armies.

THE FIRSTBORN CONSECRATED

13 Then the LORD spoke to
Moses, saying, 2"Conse-
crate to Me all the firstborn,
whatever opens the womb
among the children of Israel,
both of man and beast; it is
Mine."

THE FEAST OF UNLEAVENED BREAD

3And Moses said to the
people: "Remember this
day in which you went out
of Egypt, out of the house of
bondage; for by strength of
hand the LORD brought you
out of this *place.* No leavened
bread shall be eaten. 4On this
day you are going out, in the
month Abib. 5And it shall be,
when the LORD brings you
into the land of the Canaanites and the Hittites and the
Amorites and the Hivites and
the Jebusites, which He swore
to your fathers to give you, a
land flowing with milk and
honey, that you shall keep this
service in this month. 6Seven
days you shall eat unleavened
bread, and on the seventh day
there shall be a feast to the
LORD. 7Unleavened bread
shall be eaten seven days.
And no leavened bread shall
be seen among you, nor shall
leaven be seen among you in
all your quarters. 8And you
shall tell your son in that day,
saying, '*This is done* because
of what the LORD did for me
when I came up from Egypt.'
9It shall be as a sign to you on
your hand and as a memorial
between your eyes, that the
LORD's law may be in your
mouth; for with a strong hand
the LORD has brought you out
of Egypt. 10You shall therefore
keep this ordinance in its season from year to year.

THE LAW OF THE FIRSTBORN

11"And it shall be, when the
LORD brings you into the land
of the Canaanites, as He swore

to you and your fathers, and
gives it to you, 12that you shall
set apart to the LORD all that
open the womb, that is, every
firstborn that comes from an
animal which you have; the
males *shall be* the LORD's.
13But every firstborn of a donkey you shall redeem with a
lamb; and if you will not redeem *it,* then you shall break
its neck. And all the firstborn
of man among your sons you
shall redeem. 14So it shall be,
when your son asks you in
time to come, saying, 'What *is*
this?' that you shall say to him,
'By strength of hand the LORD
brought us out of Egypt, out of
the house of bondage. 15And it
came to pass, when Pharaoh
was stubborn about letting
us go, that the LORD killed
all the firstborn in the land
of Egypt, both the firstborn
of man and the firstborn of
beast. Therefore I sacrifice to
the LORD all males that open
the womb, but all the firstborn of my sons I redeem.'
16It shall be as a sign on your
hand and as frontlets between
your eyes, for by strength of
hand the LORD brought us out
of Egypt."

THE WILDERNESS WAY

17Then it came to pass,
when Pharaoh had let the people go, that God did not lead
them *by* way of the land of the
Philistines, although that *was*
near; for God said, "Lest perhaps the people change their
minds when they see war, and
return to Egypt." 18So God led
the people around *by* way of
the wilderness of the Red Sea.
And the children of Israel
went up in orderly ranks out
of the land of Egypt.

19And Moses took the bones
of Joseph with him, for he had
placed the children of Israel
under solemn oath, saying,
"God will surely visit you, and
you shall carry up my bones
from here with you."[a]

20So they took their journey from Succoth and camped
in Etham at the edge of the
wilderness. 21And the LORD
went before them by day in a
pillar of cloud to lead the way,
and by night in a pillar of fire
to give them light, so as to go
by day and night. 22He did not
take away the pillar of cloud
by day or the pillar of fire by
night *from* before the people.

THE RED SEA CROSSING

14 Now the LORD spoke to
Moses, saying: 2"Speak
to the children of Israel, that
they turn and camp before
Pi Hahiroth, between Migdol
and the sea, opposite Baal Zephon; you shall camp before
it by the sea. 3For Pharaoh
will say of the children of Israel, 'They *are* bewildered by
the land; the wilderness has
closed them in.' 4Then I will

13:19 [a] Genesis 50:25

harden Pharaoh's heart, so
that he will pursue them; and
I will gain honor over Pharaoh
and over all his army, that the
Egyptians may know that I *am*
the LORD." And they did so.
5Now it was told the king
of Egypt that the people had
fled, and the heart of Pharaoh
and his servants was turned
against the people; and they
said, "Why have we done this,
that we have let Israel go from
serving us?" 6So he made
ready his chariot and took
his people with him. 7Also,
he took six hundred choice
chariots, and all the chariots
of Egypt with captains over
every one of them. 8And the
LORD hardened the heart of
Pharaoh king of Egypt, and
he pursued the children of Israel; and the children of Israel
went out with boldness. 9So
the Egyptians pursued them,
all the horses *and* chariots of
Pharaoh, his horsemen and
his army, and overtook them
camping by the sea beside Pi
Hahiroth, before Baal Zephon.
10And when Pharaoh drew
near, the children of Israel
lifted their eyes, and behold,
the Egyptians marched after
them. So they were very
afraid, and the children of
Israel cried out to the LORD.
11Then they said to Moses, "Because *there were* no graves in
Egypt, have you taken us away
to die in the wilderness? Why
have you so dealt with us, to
bring us up out of Egypt? 12*Is*
this not the word that we told
you in Egypt, saying, 'Let us
alone that we may serve the
Egyptians'? For *it would have*
been better for us to serve the
Egyptians than that we should
die in the wilderness."
13And Moses said to the
people, "Do not be afraid.
Stand still, and see the salvation of the LORD, which He
will accomplish for you today.
For the Egyptians whom you
see today, you shall see again
no more forever. 14The LORD
will fight for you, and you
shall hold your peace."
15And the LORD said to
Moses, "Why do you cry to
Me? Tell the children of Israel to go forward. 16But lift
up your rod, and stretch out
your hand over the sea and
divide it. And the children of
Israel shall go on dry *ground*
through the midst of the sea.
17And I indeed will harden the
hearts of the Egyptians, and
they shall follow them. So I
will gain honor over Pharaoh
and over all his army, his chariots, and his horsemen. 18Then
the Egyptians shall know that
I *am* the LORD, when I have
gained honor for Myself over
Pharaoh, his chariots, and his
horsemen."
19And the Angel of God,
who went before the camp of
Israel, moved and went behind them; and the pillar of
cloud went from before them
and stood behind them. 20So
it came between the camp of

the Egyptians and the camp
of Israel. Thus it was a cloud
and darkness *to the one,* and it
gave light by night *to the other,*
so that the one did not come
near the other all that night.
21 Then Moses stretched out
his hand over the sea; and the
LORD caused the sea to go *back*
by a strong east wind all that
night, and made the sea into
dry *land,* and the waters were
divided. 22 So the children of
Israel went into the midst of
the sea on the dry *ground,* and
the waters *were* a wall to them
on their right hand and on
their left. 23 And the Egyptians
pursued and went after them
into the midst of the sea, all
Pharaoh's horses, his chariots,
and his horsemen.
24 Now it came to pass, in the
morning watch, that the LORD
looked down upon the army
of the Egyptians through the
pillar of fire and cloud, and
He troubled the army of the
Egyptians. 25 And He took off[a]
their chariot wheels, so that
they drove them with difficulty; and the Egyptians said,
"Let us flee from the face of
Israel, for the LORD fights for
them against the Egyptians."
26 Then the LORD said to
Moses, "Stretch out your hand
over the sea, that the waters
may come back upon the Egyptians, on their chariots, and on
their horsemen." 27 And Moses
stretched out his hand over the
sea; and when the morning
appeared, the sea returned to
its full depth, while the Egyptians were fleeing into it. So
the LORD overthrew the Egyptians in the midst of the sea.
28 Then the waters returned
and covered the chariots, the
horsemen, *and* all the army of
Pharaoh that came into the sea
after them. Not so much as one
of them remained. 29 But the
children of Israel had walked
on dry *land* in the midst of the
sea, and the waters *were* a wall
to them on their right hand
and on their left.
30 So the LORD saved Is-
rael that day out of the hand
of the Egyptians, and Israel
saw the Egyptians dead on
the seashore. 31 Thus Israel
saw the great work which the
LORD had done in Egypt; so
the people feared the LORD,
and believed the LORD and
His servant Moses.

THE SONG OF MOSES

15 Then Moses and the children of Israel sang this
song to the LORD, and spoke,
saying:

"I will sing to the LORD,
For He has triumphed
gloriously!
The horse and its rider
He has thrown
into the sea!
2 The LORD is my
strength and song,

14:25 [a] Samaritan Pentateuch, Septuagint, and Syriac read *bound.*

And He has become
my salvation;
He *is* my God, and I
will praise Him;
My father's God, and
I will exalt Him.
3 The LORD *is* a man of war;
The LORD *is* His name.
4 Pharaoh's chariots
and his army He has
cast into the sea;
His chosen captains
also are drowned
in the Red Sea.
5 The depths have
covered them;
They sank to the
bottom like a stone.

6 "Your right hand,
O LORD, has become
glorious in power;
Your right hand,
O LORD, has dashed
the enemy in pieces.
7 And in the greatness
of Your excellence
You have overthrown
those who rose
against You;
You sent forth
Your wrath;
It consumed them
like stubble.
8 And with the blast
of Your nostrils
The waters were
gathered together;
The floods stood
upright like a heap;
The depths congealed in
the heart of the sea.
9 The enemy said, 'I
will pursue,
I will overtake,
I will divide the spoil;
My desire shall be
satisfied on them.
I will draw my sword,
My hand shall
destroy them.'
10 You blew with Your wind,
The sea covered them;
They sank like lead in
the mighty waters.

11 "Who *is* like You, O LORD,
among the gods?
Who *is* like You,
glorious in holiness,
Fearful in praises,
doing wonders?
12 You stretched out
Your right hand;
The earth swallowed
them.
13 You in Your mercy
have led forth
The people whom You
have redeemed;
You have guided *them*
in Your strength
To Your holy habitation.

14 "The people will hear
and be afraid;
Sorrow will take hold
of the inhabitants
of Philistia.
15 Then the chiefs of Edom
will be dismayed;
The mighty men of Moab,
Trembling will take
hold of them;
All the inhabitants of
Canaan will melt away.
16 Fear and dread will
fall on them;

By the greatness
of Your arm
They will be *as* still
as a stone,
Till Your people pass
over, O LORD,
Till the people pass over
Whom You have
purchased.
17 You will bring them
in and plant them
In the mountain of
Your inheritance,
In the place, O LORD,
which You have made
For Your own dwelling,
The sanctuary, O Lord,
which Your hands
have established.

18 "The LORD shall reign
forever and ever."

19 For the horses of Pharaoh
went with his chariots and his
horsemen into the sea, and the
LORD brought back the waters
of the sea upon them. But the
children of Israel went on dry
land in the midst of the sea.

THE SONG OF MIRIAM

20 Then Miriam the proph-
etess, the sister of Aaron, took
the timbrel in her hand; and all
the women went out after her
with timbrels and with dances.
21 And Miriam answered them:

"Sing to the LORD,
For He has triumphed
gloriously!
The horse and its rider
He has thrown
into the sea!"

BITTER WATERS MADE SWEET

22 So Moses brought Israel
from the Red Sea; then they
went out into the Wilderness
of Shur. And they went three
days in the wilderness and
found no water. 23 Now when
they came to Marah, they
could not drink the waters
of Marah, for they *were* bitter. Therefore the name of it
was called Marah.[a] 24 And the
people complained against
Moses, saying, "What shall
we drink?" 25 So he cried out
to the LORD, and the LORD
showed him a tree. When he
cast *it* into the waters, the waters were made sweet.

There He made a statute
and an ordinance for them,
and there He tested them,
26 and said, "If you diligently
heed the voice of the LORD
your God and do what is right
in His sight, give ear to His
commandments and keep all
His statutes, I will put none
of the diseases on you which
I have brought on the Egyptians. For I *am* the LORD who
heals you."

27 Then they came to Elim,
where there *were* twelve wells
of water and seventy palm
trees; so they camped there
by the waters.

15:23 [a] Literally *Bitter*

BREAD FROM HEAVEN

16 And they journeyed
from Elim, and all the
congregation of the children
of Israel came to the Wilderness of Sin, which is between Elim and Sinai, on the
fifteenth day of the second
month after they departed
from the land of Egypt. 2 Then
the whole congregation of the
children of Israel complained
against Moses and Aaron in
the wilderness. 3 And the children of Israel said to them,
"Oh, that we had died by the
hand of the LORD in the land
of Egypt, when we sat by the
pots of meat *and* when we
ate bread to the full! For you
have brought us out into this
wilderness to kill this whole
assembly with hunger."

4 Then the LORD said to
Moses, "Behold, I will rain
bread from heaven for you.
And the people shall go out
and gather a certain quota
every day, that I may test
them, whether they will walk
in My law or not. 5 And it shall
be on the sixth day that they
shall prepare what they bring
in, and it shall be twice as
much as they gather daily."

6 Then Moses and Aaron
said to all the children of Israel, "At evening you shall
know that the LORD has
brought you out of the land
of Egypt. 7 And in the morning you shall see the glory
of the LORD; for He hears
your complaints against the
LORD. But what *are* we, that
you complain against us?"
8 Also Moses said, "*This shall be
seen* when the LORD gives you
meat to eat in the evening,
and in the morning bread to
the full; for the LORD hears
your complaints which you
make against Him. And what
are we? Your complaints *are*
not against us but against the
LORD."

9 Then Moses spoke to
Aaron, "Say to all the congregation of the children of
Israel, 'Come near before the
LORD, for He has heard your
complaints.'" 10 Now it came
to pass, as Aaron spoke to the
whole congregation of the
children of Israel, that they
looked toward the wilderness,
and behold, the glory of the
LORD appeared in the cloud.

11 And the LORD spoke to
Moses, saying, 12 "I have heard
the complaints of the children
of Israel. Speak to them, saying, 'At twilight you shall eat
meat, and in the morning you
shall be filled with bread. And
you shall know that I *am* the
LORD your God.'"

13 So it was that quail came
up at evening and covered the
camp, and in the morning the
dew lay all around the camp.
14 And when the layer of dew
lifted, there, on the surface of
the wilderness, was a small
round substance, *as* fine as
frost on the ground. 15 So when
the children of Israel saw *it,*
they said to one another,

"What is it?" For they did not
know what it *was.*
And Moses said to them,
"This *is* the bread which the
LORD has given you to eat.
16This is the thing which the
LORD has commanded: 'Let
every man gather it according
to each one's need, one omer
for each person, *according to
the* number of persons; let
every man take for *those* who
are in his tent.'"
17Then the children of Israel did so and gathered, some
more, some less. 18So when
they measured *it* by omers,
he who gathered much had
nothing left over, and he who
gathered little had no lack.
Every man had gathered according to each one's need.
19And Moses said, "Let no one
leave any of it till morning."
20Notwithstanding they did
not heed Moses. But some of
them left part of it until morning, and it bred worms and
stank. And Moses was angry
with them. 21So they gathered
it every morning, every man
according to his need. And
when the sun became hot, it
melted.
22And so it was, on the sixth
day, *that* they gathered twice
as much bread, two omers for
each one. And all the rulers of
the congregation came and
told Moses. 23Then he said to
them, "This *is what* the LORD
has said: 'Tomorrow *is* a Sabbath rest, a holy Sabbath to
the LORD. Bake what you will
bake *today,* and boil what you
will boil; and lay up for yourselves all that remains, to be
kept until morning.'" 24So
they laid it up till morning,
as Moses commanded; and it
did not stink, nor were there
any worms in it. 25Then Moses
said, "Eat that today, for today
is a Sabbath to the LORD; today
you will not find it in the field.
26Six days you shall gather it,
but on the seventh day, the
Sabbath, there will be none."
27Now it happened *that
some* of the people went out
on the seventh day to gather,
but they found none. 28And
the LORD said to Moses, "How
long do you refuse to keep My
commandments and My laws?
29See! For the LORD has given
you the Sabbath; therefore He
gives you on the sixth day
bread for two days. Let every
man remain in his place; let
no man go out of his place on
the seventh day." 30So the people rested on the seventh day.
31And the house of Israel
called its name Manna.[a] And
it *was* like white coriander
seed, and the taste of it *was*
like wafers *made* with honey.
32Then Moses said, "This
is the thing which the LORD
has commanded: 'Fill an omer
with it, to be kept for your generations, that they may see
the bread with which I fed

16:31 [a] Literally *What?* (compare Exodus 16:15)

you in the wilderness, when I
brought you out of the land of
Egypt.'" 33And Moses said to
Aaron, "Take a pot and put an
omer of manna in it, and lay it
up before the LORD, to be kept
for your generations." 34As the
LORD commanded Moses, so
Aaron laid it up before the Testimony, to be kept. 35And the
children of Israel ate manna
forty years, until they came
to an inhabited land; they ate
manna until they came to the
border of the land of Canaan.
36Now an omer *is* one-tenth of
an ephah.

WATER FROM THE ROCK

17 Then all the congrega-
tion of the children of Israel set out on their journey
from the Wilderness of Sin, according to the commandment
of the LORD, and camped in
Rephidim; but *there was* no
water for the people to drink.
2Therefore the people contended with Moses, and said,
"Give us water, that we may
drink."

So Moses said to them,
"Why do you contend with me?
Why do you tempt the LORD?"

3And the people thirsted
there for water, and the people
complained against Moses,
and said, "Why *is* it you have
brought us up out of Egypt, to
kill us and our children and
our livestock with thirst?"

4So Moses cried out to the
LORD, saying, "What shall I
do with this people? They are
almost ready to stone me!"

5And the LORD said to
Moses, "Go on before the people, and take with you some of
the elders of Israel. Also take
in your hand your rod with
which you struck the river,
and go. 6Behold, I will stand
before you there on the rock
in Horeb; and you shall strike
the rock, and water will come
out of it, that the people may
drink."

And Moses did so in the
sight of the elders of Israel.
7So he called the name of the
place Massah[a] and Meribah,[b]
because of the contention of
the children of Israel, and because they tempted the LORD,
saying, "Is the LORD among
us or not?"

VICTORY OVER THE AMALEKITES

8Now Amalek came and
fought with Israel in Rephidim. 9And Moses said to
Joshua, "Choose us some men
and go out, fight with Amalek.
Tomorrow I will stand on the
top of the hill with the rod of
God in my hand." 10So Joshua
did as Moses said to him, and
fought with Amalek. And
Moses, Aaron, and Hur went
up to the top of the hill. 11And
so it was, when Moses held
up his hand, that Israel prevailed; and when he let down

17:7 [a] Literally *Tempted* [b] Literally *Contention*

his hand, Amalek prevailed. [12]But Moses' hands *became* heavy; so they took a stone and put *it* under him, and he sat on it. And Aaron and Hur supported his hands, one on one side, and the other on the other side; and his hands were steady until the going down of the sun. [13]So Joshua defeated Amalek and his people with the edge of the sword.

[14]Then the LORD said to Moses, "Write this *for* a memorial in the book and recount *it* in the hearing of Joshua, that I will utterly blot out the remembrance of Amalek from under heaven." [15]And Moses built an altar and called its name, The-LORD-Is-My-Banner;[a] [16]for he said, "Because the LORD has sworn: the LORD *will have* war with Amalek from generation to generation."

JETHRO'S ADVICE

18 And Jethro, the priest of Midian, Moses' father-in-law, heard of all that God had done for Moses and for Israel His people—that the LORD had brought Israel out of Egypt. [2]Then Jethro, Moses' father-in-law, took Zipporah, Moses' wife, after he had sent her back, [3]with her two sons, of whom the name of one *was* Gershom (for he said, "I have been a stranger in a foreign land")[a] [4]and *the name of the* other *was* Eliezer[a] (for *he said*, "The God of my father *was* my help, and delivered me from the sword of Pharaoh"); [5]and Jethro, Moses' father-in-law, came with his sons and his wife to Moses in the wilderness, where he was encamped at the mountain of God. [6]Now he had said to Moses, "I, your father-in-law Jethro, am coming to you with your wife and her two sons with her."

[7]So Moses went out to meet his father-in-law, bowed down, and kissed him. And they asked each other about *their* well-being, and they went into the tent. [8]And Moses told his father-in-law all that the LORD had done to Pharaoh and to the Egyptians for Israel's sake, all the hardship that had come upon them on the way, and *how* the LORD had delivered them. [9]Then Jethro rejoiced for all the good which the LORD had done for Israel, whom He had delivered out of the hand of the Egyptians. [10]And Jethro said, "Blessed *be* the LORD, who has delivered you out of the hand of the Egyptians and out of the hand of Pharaoh, *and* who has delivered the people from under the hand of the Egyptians. [11]Now I know that the LORD *is* greater than all the gods; for in the very thing in which they behaved proudly,

17:15 [a] Hebrew *YHWH Nissi* 18:3 [a] Compare Exodus 2:22 18:4 [a] Literally *My God Is Help*

He was above them." [12]Then Jethro, Moses' father-in-law, took[a] a burnt offering and *other* sacrifices *to offer* to God. And Aaron came with all the elders of Israel to eat bread with Moses' father-in-law before God.

[13]And so it was, on the next day, that Moses sat to judge the people; and the people stood before Moses from morning until evening. [14]So when Moses' father-in-law saw all that he did for the people, he said, "What *is* this thing that you are doing for the people? Why do you alone sit, and all the people stand before you from morning until evening?"

[15]And Moses said to his father-in-law, "Because the people come to me to inquire of God. [16]When they have a difficulty, they come to me, and I judge between one and another; and I make known the statutes of God and His laws."

[17]So Moses' father-in-law said to him, "The thing that you do *is* not good. [18]Both you and these people who *are* with you will surely wear yourselves out. For this thing *is* too much for you; you are not able to perform it by yourself. [19]Listen now to my voice; I will give you counsel, and God will be with you: Stand before God for the people, so that you may bring the difficulties to God. [20]And you shall teach them the statutes and the laws, and show them the way in which they must walk and the work they must do. [21]Moreover you shall select from all the people able men, such as fear God, men of truth, hating covetousness; and place *such* over them *to be* rulers of thousands, rulers of hundreds, rulers of fifties, and rulers of tens. [22]And let them judge the people at all times. Then it will be *that* every great matter they shall bring to you, but every small matter they themselves shall judge. So it will be easier for you, for they will bear *the burden* with you. [23]If you do this thing, and God *so* commands you, then you will be able to endure, and all this people will also go to their place in peace."

[24]So Moses heeded the voice of his father-in-law and did all that he had said. [25]And Moses chose able men out of all Israel, and made them heads over the people: rulers of thousands, rulers of hundreds, rulers of fifties, and rulers of tens. [26]So they judged the people at all times; the hard cases they brought to Moses, but they judged every small case themselves.

[27]Then Moses let his father-in-law depart, and he went his way to his own land.

18:12 [a] Following Masoretic Text and Septuagint; Syriac, Targum, and Vulgate read *offered.*

ISRAEL AT MOUNT SINAI

19 In the third month after
the children of Israel
had gone out of the land of
Egypt, on the same day, they
came *to* the Wilderness of
Sinai. 2For they had departed
from Rephidim, had come *to*
the Wilderness of Sinai, and
camped in the wilderness. So
Israel camped there before
the mountain.

3And Moses went up to
God, and the LORD called to
him from the mountain, saying, "Thus you shall say to the
house of Jacob, and tell the
children of Israel: 4'You have
seen what I did to the Egyptians, and *how* I bore you on
eagles' wings and brought you
to Myself. 5Now therefore, if
you will indeed obey My voice
and keep My covenant, then
you shall be a special treasure to Me above all people;
for all the earth *is* Mine. 6And
you shall be to Me a kingdom
of priests and a holy nation.'
These *are* the words which
you shall speak to the children of Israel."

7So Moses came and called
for the elders of the people,
and laid before them all these
words which the LORD com-
manded him. 8Then all the
people answered together and
said, "All that the LORD has
spoken we will do." So Moses
brought back the words of the
people to the LORD. 9And the
LORD said to Moses, "Behold,
I come to you in the thick
cloud, that the people may
hear when I speak with you,
and believe you forever."

So Moses told the words of
the people to the LORD.

10Then the LORD said to
Moses, "Go to the people and
consecrate them today and
tomorrow, and let them wash
their clothes. 11And let them
be ready for the third day. For
on the third day the LORD will
come down upon Mount Sinai
in the sight of all the people.
12You shall set bounds for the
people all around, saying,
'Take heed to yourselves *that*
you do *not* go up to the mountain or touch its base. Whoever
touches the mountain shall
surely be put to death. 13Not a
hand shall touch him, but he
shall surely be stoned or shot
with an arrow; whether man or
beast, he shall not live.' When
the trumpet sounds long, they
shall come near the mountain."

14So Moses went down from
the mountain to the people
and sanctified the people, and
they washed their clothes.
15And he said to the people,
"Be ready for the third day;
do not come near *your* wives."

16Then it came to pass on
the third day, in the morning,
that there were thunderings
and lightnings, and a thick
cloud on the mountain; and
the sound of the trumpet was
very loud, so that all the people
who *were* in the camp trembled. 17And Moses brought
the people out of the camp to

meet with God, and they stood
at the foot of the mountain.
18Now Mount Sinai *was* completely in smoke, because the
LORD descended upon it in
fire. Its smoke ascended like
the smoke of a furnace, and
the whole mountain[a] quaked
greatly. 19And when the blast
of the trumpet sounded long
and became louder and louder,
Moses spoke, and God an-
swered him by voice. 20Then
the LORD came down upon
Mount Sinai, on the top of
the mountain. And the LORD
called Moses to the top of the
mountain, and Moses went up.
21And the LORD said to
Moses, "Go down and warn
the people, lest they break
through to gaze at the LORD,
and many of them perish.
22Also let the priests who
come near the LORD con-
secrate themselves, lest the
LORD break out against them."
23But Moses said to the
LORD, "The people cannot
come up to Mount Sinai; for
You warned us, saying, 'Set
bounds around the mountain
and consecrate it.'"
24Then the LORD said to
him, "Away! Get down and then
come up, you and Aaron with
you. But do not let the priests
and the people break through
to come up to the LORD, lest
He break out against them."
25So Moses went down to the
people and spoke to them.

THE TEN COMMANDMENTS

20 And God spoke all
these words, saying:

2 "I *am* the LORD your God,
who brought you out of
the land of Egypt, out of
the house of bondage.
3 "You shall have no other
gods before Me.
4 "You shall not make for
yourself a carved image—
any likeness *of anything*
that *is* in heaven above,
or that *is* in the earth beneath, or that *is* in the
water under the earth;
5you shall not bow down
to them nor serve them.
For I, the LORD your God,
am a jealous God, visiting
the iniquity of the fathers
upon the children to the
third and fourth *genera-
tions* of those who hate
Me, 6but showing mercy
to thousands, to those
who love Me and keep
My commandments.
7 "You shall not take the
name of the LORD your
God in vain, for the LORD
will not hold *him* guiltless who takes His name
in vain.
8 "Remember the Sabbath day,
to keep it holy. 9Six days
you shall labor and do all
your work, 10but the sev-
enth day *is* the Sabbath
of the LORD your God. *In
it* you shall do no work:

19:18 [a] Septuagint reads *all the people.*

you, nor your son, nor
your daughter, nor your
male servant, nor your
female servant, nor your
cattle, nor your stranger
who *is* within your gates.
11For *in* six days the LORD
made the heavens and
the earth, the sea, and all
that *is* in them, and rested
the seventh day. There-
fore the LORD blessed
the Sabbath day and hal-
lowed it.
12"Honor your father and
your mother, that your
days may be long upon
the land which the LORD
your God is giving you.
13"You shall not murder.
14"You shall not commit
adultery.
15"You shall not steal.
16"You shall not bear false
witness against your
neighbor.
17"You shall not covet your
neighbor's house; you
shall not covet your
neighbor's wife, nor his
male servant, nor his fe-
male servant, nor his ox,
nor his donkey, nor any-
thing that *is* your neighbor's."

THE PEOPLE AFRAID OF GOD'S PRESENCE

18Now all the people wit-
nessed the thunderings, the
lightning flashes, the sound
of the trumpet, and the mountain smoking; and when the
people saw *it,* they trembled
and stood afar off. 19Then they
said to Moses, "You speak with
us, and we will hear; but let not
God speak with us, lest we die."
20And Moses said to the
people, "Do not fear; for God
has come to test you, and that
His fear may be before you,
so that you may not sin." 21So
the people stood afar off, but
Moses drew near the thick
darkness where God *was.*

THE LAW OF THE ALTAR

22Then the LORD said to
Moses, "Thus you shall say
to the children of Israel: 'You
have seen that I have talked
with you from heaven. 23You
shall not make *anything to*
be with Me—gods of silver
or gods of gold you shall not
make for yourselves. 24An
altar of earth you shall make
for Me, and you shall sacrifice on it your burnt offerings
and your peace offerings, your
sheep and your oxen. In every
place where I record My name
I will come to you, and I will
bless you. 25And if you make
Me an altar of stone, you shall
not build it of hewn stone; for
if you use your tool on it, you
have profaned it. 26Nor shall
you go up by steps to My altar,
that your nakedness may not
be exposed on it.'

THE LAW CONCERNING SERVANTS

21 "Now these *are* the judgments which you shall
set before them: 2If you buy a

Hebrew servant, he shall serve
six years; and in the seventh
he shall go out free and pay
nothing. [3]If he comes in by
himself, he shall go out by
himself; if he *comes in* married, then his wife shall go out
with him. [4]If his master has
given him a wife, and she has
borne him sons or daughters,
the wife and her children shall
be her master's, and he shall
go out by himself. [5]But if the
servant plainly says, 'I love
my master, my wife, and my
children; I will not go out free,'
[6]then his master shall bring
him to the judges. He shall
also bring him to the door, or
to the doorpost, and his master shall pierce his ear with an
awl; and he shall serve him
forever.

[7]"And if a man sells his
daughter to be a female slave,
she shall not go out as the
male slaves do. [8]If she does
not please her master, who
has betrothed her to him-
self, then he shall let her be
redeemed. He shall have no
right to sell her to a foreign
people, since he has dealt
deceitfully with her. [9]And if
he has betrothed her to his
son, he shall deal with her
according to the custom of
daughters. [10]If he takes another *wife,* he shall not diminish her food, her clothing, and
her marriage rights. [11]And if
he does not do these three
for her, then she shall go out
free, without *paying* money.

THE LAW CONCERNING VIOLENCE

[12]"He who strikes a man so
that he dies shall surely be put
to death. [13]However, if he did
not lie in wait, but God delivered *him* into his hand, then
I will appoint for you a place
where he may flee.

[14]"But if a man acts with
premeditation against his
neighbor, to kill him by treachery, you shall take him from
My altar, that he may die.

[15]"And he who strikes his
father or his mother shall
surely be put to death.

[16]"He who kidnaps a man
and sells him, or if he is found
in his hand, shall surely be put
to death.

[17]"And he who curses his father or his mother shall surely
be put to death.

[18]"If men contend with
each other, and one strikes the
other with a stone or with *his*
fist, and he does not die but is
confined to *his* bed, [19]if he rises
again and walks about outside
with his staff, then he who
struck *him* shall be acquitted.
He shall only pay *for* the loss of
his time, and shall provide *for*
him to be thoroughly healed.

[20]"And if a man beats his
male or female servant with
a rod, so that he dies under
his hand, he shall surely be
punished. [21]Notwithstanding,
if he remains alive a day or
two, he shall not be punished;
for he *is* his property.

[22]"If men fight, and hurt

a woman with child, so that
she gives birth prematurely,
yet no harm follows, he shall
surely be punished accordingly as the woman's husband
imposes on him; and he shall
pay as the judges *determine.*
23But if *any* harm follows,
then you shall give life for life,
24eye for eye, tooth for tooth,
hand for hand, foot for foot,
25burn for burn, wound for
wound, stripe for stripe.
26"If a man strikes the eye
of his male or female servant,
and destroys it, he shall let
him go free for the sake of his
eye. 27And if he knocks out the
tooth of his male or female
servant, he shall let him go
free for the sake of his tooth.

ANIMAL CONTROL LAWS

28"If an ox gores a man or
a woman to death, then the
ox shall surely be stoned, and
its flesh shall not be eaten;
but the owner of the ox *shall
be* acquitted. 29But if the ox
tended to thrust with its horn
in times past, and it has been
made known to his owner, and
he has not kept it confined, so
that it has killed a man or a
woman, the ox shall be stoned
and its owner also shall be put
to death. 30If there is imposed
on him a sum of money, then
he shall pay to redeem his life,
whatever is imposed on him.
31Whether it has gored a son
or gored a daughter, according to this judgment it shall be
done to him. 32If the ox gores
a male or female servant, he
shall give to their master
thirty shekels of silver, and
the ox shall be stoned.
33"And if a man opens a pit,
or if a man digs a pit and does
not cover it, and an ox or a donkey falls in it, 34the owner of the
pit shall make *it* good; he shall
give money to their owner, but
the dead *animal* shall be his.
35"If one man's ox hurts another's, so that it dies, then
they shall sell the live ox and
divide the money from it; and
the dead *ox* they shall also
divide. 36Or if it was known
that the ox tended to thrust in
time past, and its owner has
not kept it confined, he shall
surely pay ox for ox, and the
dead animal shall be his own.

RESPONSIBILITY FOR PROPERTY

22 "If a man steals an ox
or a sheep, and slaugh-
ters it or sells it, he shall restore
five oxen for an ox and four
sheep for a sheep. 2If the thief
is found breaking in, and he
is struck so that he dies, *there
shall be* no guilt for his bloodshed. 3If the sun has risen on
him, *there shall be* guilt for his
bloodshed. He should make
full restitution; if he has nothing, then he shall be sold for
his theft. 4If the theft is certainly found alive in his hand,
whether it is an ox or donkey or
sheep, he shall restore double.
5"If a man causes a field
or vineyard to be grazed, and

lets loose his animal, and it
feeds in another man's field,
he shall make restitution from
the best of his own field and
the best of his own vineyard.
6"If fire breaks out and
catches in thorns, so that
stacked grain, standing grain,
or the field is consumed, he
who kindled the fire shall
surely make restitution.
7"If a man delivers to his
neighbor money or articles
to keep, and it is stolen out of
the man's house, if the thief is
found, he shall pay double. 8If
the thief is not found, then the
master of the house shall be
brought to the judges *to see*
whether he has put his hand
into his neighbor's goods.
9"For any kind of trespass,
whether it concerns an ox, a
donkey, a sheep, or clothing,
or for any kind of lost thing
which *another* claims to be
his, the cause of both parties
shall come before the judges;
and whomever the judges
condemn shall pay double to
his neighbor. 10If a man delivers to his neighbor a donkey,
an ox, a sheep, or any animal
to keep, and it dies, is hurt, or
driven away, no one seeing
it, 11*then* an oath of the LORD
shall be between them both,
that he has not put his hand
into his neighbor's goods; and
the owner of it shall accept
that, and he shall not make *it*
good. 12But if, in fact, it is stolen from him, he shall make
restitution to the owner of
it. 13If it is torn to pieces *by
a beast, then* he shall bring it
as evidence, *and* he shall not
make good what was torn.
14"And if a man borrows
anything from his neighbor,
and it becomes injured or
dies, the owner of it not *being*
with it, he shall surely make *it*
good. 15If its owner *was* with it,
he shall not make *it* good; if it
was hired, it came for its hire.

MORAL AND CEREMONIAL PRINCIPLES

16"If a man entices a virgin
who is not betrothed, and lies
with her, he shall surely pay
the bride-price for her *to be*
his wife. 17If her father utterly
refuses to give her to him, he
shall pay money according to
the bride-price of virgins.
18"You shall not permit a
sorceress to live.
19"Whoever lies with an
animal shall surely be put to
death.
20"He who sacrifices to *any*
god, except to the LORD only,
he shall be utterly destroyed.
21"You shall neither mis-
treat a stranger nor oppress
him, for you were strangers
in the land of Egypt.
22"You shall not afflict any
widow or fatherless child. 23If
you afflict them in any way,
and they cry at all to Me, I will
surely hear their cry; 24and My
wrath will become hot, and I
will kill you with the sword;
your wives shall be widows,
and your children fatherless.

25“If you lend money to
any of My people *who are* poor
among you, you shall not be
like a moneylender to him; you
shall not charge him interest.
26If you ever take your neighbor’s garment as a pledge, you
shall return it to him before
the sun goes down. 27For that
is his only covering, it *is* his
garment for his skin. What will
he sleep in? And it will be that
when he cries to Me, I will hear,
for I *am* gracious.

28“You shall not revile God,
nor curse a ruler of your people.

29“You shall not delay *to*
offer the first of your ripe
produce and your juices. The
firstborn of your sons you
shall give to Me. 30Likewise
you shall do with your oxen
and your sheep. It shall be
with its mother seven days;
on the eighth day you shall
give it to Me.

31“And you shall be holy
men to Me: you shall not eat
meat torn *by beasts* in the
field; you shall throw it to the
dogs.

JUSTICE FOR ALL

23 “You shall not circulate
a false report. Do not
put your hand with the wicked
to be an unrighteous witness.
2You shall not follow a crowd
to do evil; nor shall you testify
in a dispute so as to turn aside
after many to pervert *justice*.
3You shall not show partiality
to a poor man in his dispute.

4“If you meet your enemy’s
ox or his donkey going astray,
you shall surely bring it back
to him again. 5If you see the
donkey of one who hates you
lying under its burden, and
you would refrain from helping it, you shall surely help
him with it.

6“You shall not pervert the
judgment of your poor in his
dispute. 7Keep yourself far
from a false matter; do not
kill the innocent and righteous. For I will not justify the
wicked. 8And you shall take no
bribe, for a bribe blinds the
discerning and perverts the
words of the righteous.

9“Also you shall not op-
press a stranger, for you know
the heart of a stranger, because you were strangers in
the land of Egypt.

THE LAW OF SABBATHS

10“Six years you shall sow
your land and gather in its
produce, 11but the seventh
year you shall let it rest and
lie fallow, that the poor of your
people may eat; and what they
leave, the beasts of the field
may eat. In like manner you
shall do with your vineyard
and your olive grove. 12Six
days you shall do your work,
and on the seventh day you
shall rest, that your ox and
your donkey may rest, and
the son of your female servant and the stranger may be
refreshed.

13“And in all that I have

said to you, be circumspect
and make no mention of the
name of other gods, nor let it
be heard from your mouth.

THREE ANNUAL FEASTS

14“Three times you shall
keep a feast to Me in the year:
15You shall keep the Feast of
Unleavened Bread (you shall
eat unleavened bread seven
days, as I commanded you,
at the time appointed in the
month of Abib, for in it you
came out of Egypt; none shall
appear before Me empty);
16and the Feast of Harvest, the
firstfruits of your labors which
you have sown in the field;
and the Feast of Ingathering
at the end of the year, when
you have gathered in *the fruit
of* your labors from the field.

17“Three times in the year
all your males shall appear
before the Lord GOD.[a]

18“You shall not offer the
blood of My sacrifice with
leavened bread; nor shall the
fat of My sacrifice remain
until morning. 19The first of
the firstfruits of your land you
shall bring into the house of
the LORD your God. You shall
not boil a young goat in its
mother’s milk.

THE ANGEL AND THE PROMISES

20“Behold, I send an Angel
before you to keep you in the
way and to bring you into the
place which I have prepared.
21Beware of Him and obey His
voice; do not provoke Him,
for He will not pardon your
transgressions; for My name
is in Him. 22But if you indeed
obey His voice and do all that I
speak, then I will be an enemy
to your enemies and an adversary to your adversaries. 23For
My Angel will go before you
and bring you in to the Amorites and the Hittites and the
Perizzites and the Canaanites
and the Hivites and the Jebusites; and I will cut them off.
24You shall not bow down to
their gods, nor serve them, nor
do according to their works;
but you shall utterly overthrow
them and completely break
down their *sacred* pillars.

25“So you shall serve the
LORD your God, and He will
bless your bread and your
water. And I will take sickness away from the midst of
you. 26No one shall suffer miscarriage or be barren in your
land; I will fulfill the number
of your days.

27“I will send My fear before you, I will cause confusion among all the people
to whom you come, and will
make all your enemies turn
their backs to you. 28And I
will send hornets before you,
which shall drive out the Hivite, the Canaanite, and the
Hittite from before you. 29I
will not drive them out from

23:17 [a] Hebrew *YHWH,* usually translated *LORD*

before you in one year, lest
the land become desolate and
the beasts of the field become
too numerous for you. 30Little
by little I will drive them out
from before you, until you
have increased, and you inherit the land. 31And I will set
your bounds from the Red Sea
to the sea, Philistia, and from
the desert to the River.[a] For I
will deliver the inhabitants of
the land into your hand, and
you shall drive them out before you. 32You shall make no
covenant with them, nor with
their gods. 33They shall not
dwell in your land, lest they
make you sin against Me. For
if you serve their gods, it will
surely be a snare to you."

ISRAEL AFFIRMS THE COVENANT

24 Now He said to Moses,
"Come up to the LORD,
you and Aaron, Nadab and
Abihu, and seventy of the
elders of Israel, and worship
from afar. 2And Moses alone
shall come near the LORD, but
they shall not come near; nor
shall the people go up with
him."
3So Moses came and told
the people all the words of the
LORD and all the judgments.
And all the people answered
with one voice and said, "All
the words which the LORD has
said we will do." 4And Moses
wrote all the words of the
LORD. And he rose early in the
morning, and built an altar
at the foot of the mountain,
and twelve pillars according
to the twelve tribes of Israel.
5Then he sent young men of
the children of Israel, who offered burnt offerings and sacrificed peace offerings of oxen
to the LORD. 6And Moses took
half the blood and put *it* in
basins, and half the blood he
sprinkled on the altar. 7Then
he took the Book of the Covenant and read in the hearing
of the people. And they said,
"All that the LORD has said
we will do, and be obedient."
8And Moses took the blood,
sprinkled *it* on the people, and
said, "This is the blood of the
covenant which the LORD has
made with you according to
all these words."

ON THE MOUNTAIN WITH GOD

9Then Moses went up, also
Aaron, Nadab, and Abihu, and
seventy of the elders of Israel,
10and they saw the God of Israel. And *there was* under His
feet as it were a paved work
of sapphire stone, and it was
like the very heavens in *its*
clarity. 11But on the nobles of
the children of Israel He did
not lay His hand. So they saw
God, and they ate and drank.
12Then the LORD said to
Moses, "Come up to Me on the
mountain and be there; and I

23:31 [a] Hebrew *Nahar,* the Euphrates

will give you tablets of stone,
and the law and command-
ments which I have written,
that you may teach them."
13So Moses arose with his
assistant Joshua, and Moses
went up to the mountain of
God. 14And he said to the elders, "Wait here for us until
we come back to you. Indeed,
Aaron and Hur *are* with you.
If any man has a difficulty,
let him go to them." 15Then
Moses went up into the mountain, and a cloud covered the
mountain.
16Now the glory of the LORD
rested on Mount Sinai, and the
cloud covered it six days. And
on the seventh day He called
to Moses out of the midst of
the cloud. 17The sight of the
glory of the LORD *was* like a
consuming fire on the top of
the mountain in the eyes of
the children of Israel. 18So
Moses went into the midst of
the cloud and went up into the
mountain. And Moses was on
the mountain forty days and
forty nights.

OFFERINGS FOR THE SANCTUARY

25 Then the LORD spoke to
Moses, saying: 2"Speak
to the children of Israel, that
they bring Me an offering.
From everyone who gives it
willingly with his heart you
shall take My offering. 3And
this *is* the offering which you
shall take from them: gold,
silver, and bronze; 4blue, purple, and scarlet *thread,* fine
linen, and goats' *hair;* 5ram
skins dyed red, badger skins,
and acacia wood; 6oil for
the light, and spices for the
anointing oil and for the sweet
incense; 7onyx stones, and
stones to be set in the ephod
and in the breastplate. 8And
let them make Me a sanctuary,
that I may dwell among them.
9According to all that I show
you, *that is,* the pattern of the
tabernacle and the pattern of
all its furnishings, just so you
shall make *it.*

THE ARK OF THE TESTIMONY

10"And they shall make an
ark of acacia wood; two and a
half cubits *shall be* its length, a
cubit and a half its width, and
a cubit and a half its height.
11And you shall overlay it with
pure gold, inside and out you
shall overlay it, and shall make
on it a molding of gold all
around. 12You shall cast four
rings of gold for it, and put
them in its four corners; two
rings *shall be* on one side, and
two rings on the other side.
13And you shall make poles
of acacia wood, and overlay
them with gold. 14You shall put
the poles into the rings on the
sides of the ark, that the ark
may be carried by them. 15The
poles shall be in the rings of
the ark; they shall not be taken
from it. 16And you shall put
into the ark the Testimony
which I will give you.

17“You shall make a mercy seat of pure gold; two and a half cubits *shall be* its length and a cubit and a half its width. 18And you shall make two cherubim of gold; of hammered work you shall make them at the two ends of the mercy seat. 19Make one cherub at one end, and the other cherub at the other end; you shall make the cherubim at the two ends of it *of one piece* with the mercy seat. 20And the cherubim shall stretch out *their* wings above, covering the mercy seat with their wings, and they shall face one another; the faces of the cherubim *shall be* toward the mercy seat. 21You shall put the mercy seat on top of the ark, and in the ark you shall put the Testimony that I will give you. 22And there I will meet with you, and I will speak with you from above the mercy seat, from between the two cherubim which *are* on the ark of the Testimony, about everything which I will give you in commandment to the children of Israel.

THE TABLE FOR THE SHOWBREAD

23“You shall also make a table of acacia wood; two cubits *shall be* its length, a cubit its width, and a cubit and a half its height. 24And you shall overlay it with pure gold, and make a molding of gold all around. 25You shall make for it a frame of a handbreadth all around, and you shall make a gold molding for the frame all around. 26And you shall make for it four rings of gold, and put the rings on the four corners that *are* at its four legs. 27The rings shall be close to the frame, as holders for the poles to bear the table. 28And you shall make the poles of acacia wood, and overlay them with gold, that the table may be carried with them. 29You shall make its dishes, its pans, its pitchers, and its bowls for pouring. You shall make them of pure gold. 30And you shall set the showbread on the table before Me always.

THE GOLD LAMPSTAND

31“You shall also make a lampstand of pure gold; the lampstand shall be of hammered work. Its shaft, its branches, its bowls, its *ornamental* knobs, and flowers shall be *of one piece.* 32And six branches shall come out of its sides: three branches of the lampstand out of one side, and three branches of the lampstand out of the other side. 33Three bowls *shall be* made like almond *blossoms* on one branch, *with* an *ornamental* knob and a flower, and three bowls made like almond *blossoms* on the other branch, *with* an *ornamental* knob and a flower—and so for the six branches that come out of the lampstand. 34On the

lampstand itself four bowls
shall be made like almond
blossoms, each with its *orna-*
mental knob and flower. 35And
there shall be a knob under
the *first* two branches of the
same, a knob under the *sec-*
ond two branches of the same,
and a knob under the *third*
two branches of the same, according to the six branches
that extend from the lampstand. 36Their knobs and their
branches *shall be of one piece;*
all of it *shall be* one hammered
piece of pure gold. 37You shall
make seven lamps for it, and
they shall arrange its lamps
so that they give light in front
of it. 38And its wick-trimmers
and their trays *shall be* of pure
gold. 39It shall be made of a
talent of pure gold, with all
these utensils. 40And see to
it that you make *them* according to the pattern which was
shown you on the mountain.

THE TABERNACLE

26 "Moreover you shall
make the taberna-
cle *with* ten curtains *of* fine
woven linen and blue, purple, and scarlet *thread;* with
artistic designs of cherubim
you shall weave them. 2The
length of each curtain *shall be*
twenty-eight cubits, and the
width of each curtain four
cubits. And every one of the
curtains shall have the same
measurements. 3Five curtains
shall be coupled to one another, and *the other* five curtains *shall be* coupled to one
another. 4And you shall make
loops of blue *yarn* on the edge
of the curtain on the selvedge
of *one* set, and likewise you
shall do on the outer edge of
the other curtain of the second set. 5Fifty loops you shall
make in the one curtain, and
fifty loops you shall make on
the edge of the curtain that *is*
on the end of the second set,
that the loops may be clasped
to one another. 6And you shall
make fifty clasps of gold, and
couple the curtains together
with the clasps, so that it may
be one tabernacle.

7"You shall also make curtains of goats' *hair,* to be a tent
over the tabernacle. You shall
make eleven curtains. 8The
length of each curtain *shall be*
thirty cubits, and the width of
each curtain four cubits; and
the eleven curtains shall all
have the same measurements.
9And you shall couple five
curtains by themselves and
six curtains by themselves,
and you shall double over the
sixth curtain at the forefront
of the tent. 10You shall make
fifty loops on the edge of the
curtain that is outermost in
one set, and fifty loops on
the edge of the curtain of the
second set. 11And you shall
make fifty bronze clasps, put
the clasps into the loops, and
couple the tent together, that
it may be one. 12The remnant
that remains of the curtains of
the tent, the half curtain that

remains, shall hang over the
back of the tabernacle. 13And
a cubit on one side and a cubit
on the other side, of what remains of the length of the curtains of the tent, shall hang
over the sides of the tabernacle, on this side and on that
side, to cover it.

14"You shall also make a
covering of ram skins dyed
red for the tent, and a covering of badger skins above
that.

15"And for the tabernacle
you shall make the boards
of acacia wood, standing upright. 16Ten cubits *shall be* the
length of a board, and a cubit
and a half *shall be* the width of
each board. 17Two tenons *shall
be* in each board for binding
one to another. Thus you shall
make for all the boards of the
tabernacle. 18And you shall
make the boards for the tabernacle, twenty boards for the
south side. 19You shall make
forty sockets of silver under
the twenty boards: two sockets under each of the boards
for its two tenons. 20And for
the second side of the tabernacle, the north side, *there
shall be* twenty boards 21and
their forty sockets of silver:
two sockets under each of
the boards. 22For the far side
of the tabernacle, westward,
you shall make six boards.
23And you shall also make two
boards for the two back corners of the tabernacle. 24They
shall be coupled together at
the bottom and they shall be
coupled together at the top
by one ring. Thus it shall be
for both of them. They shall
be for the two corners. 25So
there shall be eight boards
with their sockets of silver—
sixteen sockets—two sockets
under each of the boards.

26"And you shall make
bars of acacia wood: five for
the boards on one side of the
tabernacle, 27five bars for the
boards on the other side of
the tabernacle, and five bars
for the boards of the side of
the tabernacle, for the far side
westward. 28The middle bar
shall pass through the midst
of the boards from end to end.
29You shall overlay the boards
with gold, make their rings of
gold *as* holders for the bars,
and overlay the bars with gold.
30And you shall raise up the
tabernacle according to its
pattern which you were shown
on the mountain.

31"You shall make a veil
woven of blue, purple, and
scarlet *thread,* and fine woven
linen. It shall be woven with
an artistic design of cherubim. 32You shall hang it upon
the four pillars of acacia *wood*
overlaid with gold. Their
hooks *shall be* gold, upon four
sockets of silver. 33And you
shall hang the veil from the
clasps. Then you shall bring
the ark of the Testimony in
there, behind the veil. The
veil shall be a divider for you
between the holy *place* and

the Most Holy. 34You shall put
the mercy seat upon the ark
of the Testimony in the Most
Holy. 35You shall set the table
outside the veil, and the lampstand across from the table
on the side of the tabernacle
toward the south; and you
shall put the table on the
north side.

36"You shall make a screen
for the door of the tabernacle, *woven of* blue, purple, and
scarlet *thread,* and fine woven
linen, made by a weaver. 37And
you shall make for the screen
five pillars of acacia *wood,*
and overlay them with gold;
their hooks *shall be* gold, and
you shall cast five sockets of
bronze for them.

THE ALTAR OF BURNT OFFERING

27 "You shall make an
altar of acacia wood,
five cubits long and five cubits wide—the altar shall be
square—and its height *shall
be* three cubits. 2You shall
make its horns on its four corners; its horns shall be of one
piece with it. And you shall
overlay it with bronze. 3Also
you shall make its pans to receive its ashes, and its shovels
and its basins and its forks
and its firepans; you shall
make all its utensils of bronze.
4You shall make a grate for it,
a network of bronze; and on
the network you shall make
four bronze rings at its four
corners. 5You shall put it
under the rim of the altar beneath, that the network may
be midway up the altar. 6And
you shall make poles for the
altar, poles of acacia wood,
and overlay them with bronze.
7The poles shall be put in the
rings, and the poles shall be
on the two sides of the altar
to bear it. 8You shall make it
hollow with boards; as it was
shown you on the mountain,
so shall they make *it.*

THE COURT OF THE TABERNACLE

9"You shall also make the
court of the tabernacle. For
the south side *there shall be*
hangings for the court *made
of* fine woven linen, one hundred cubits long for one side.
10And its twenty pillars and
their twenty sockets *shall be*
bronze. The hooks of the pillars and their bands *shall be*
silver. 11Likewise along the
length of the north side *there
shall be* hangings one hundred
cubits long, with its twenty pillars and their twenty sockets
of bronze, and the hooks of
the pillars and their bands of
silver.

12"And along the width of
the court on the west side *shall
be* hangings of fifty cubits,
with their ten pillars and their
ten sockets. 13The width of the
court on the east side *shall be*
fifty cubits. 14The hangings on
one side *of the gate shall be* fifteen cubits, *with* their three
pillars and their three sockets.

[15]And on the other side *shall*
be hangings of fifteen *cubits,*
with their three pillars and
their three sockets.
[16]"For the gate of the court
there shall be a screen twenty
cubits long, *woven of* blue,
purple, and scarlet *thread,*
and fine woven linen, made
by a weaver. It *shall have* four
pillars and four sockets. [17]All
the pillars around the court
shall have bands of silver;
their hooks *shall be* of silver
and their sockets of bronze.
[18]The length of the court *shall*
be one hundred cubits, the
width fifty throughout, and
the height five cubits, *made*
of fine woven linen, and its
sockets of bronze. [19]All the
utensils of the tabernacle for
all its service, all its pegs, and
all the pegs of the court, *shall*
be of bronze.

THE CARE OF THE LAMPSTAND

[20]"And you shall command
the children of Israel that they
bring you pure oil of pressed
olives for the light, to cause
the lamp to burn continually.
[21]In the tabernacle of meeting, outside the veil which *is*
before the Testimony, Aaron
and his sons shall tend it from
evening until morning before
the LORD. *It shall be* a statute
forever to their generations
on behalf of the children of
Israel.

GARMENTS FOR THE PRIESTHOOD

28 "Now take Aaron your
brother, and his sons
with him, from among the
children of Israel, that he may
minister to Me as priest, Aaron
and Aaron's sons: Nadab,
Abihu, Eleazar, and Ithamar.
[2]And you shall make holy garments for Aaron your brother,
for glory and for beauty. [3]So
you shall speak to all *who are*
gifted artisans, whom I have
filled with the spirit of wisdom, that they may make Aaron's garments, to consecrate
him, that he may minister
to Me as priest. [4]And these
are the garments which they
shall make: a breastplate, an
ephod,[a] a robe, a skillfully
woven tunic, a turban, and a
sash. So they shall make holy
garments for Aaron your
brother and his sons, that he
may minister to Me as priest.

THE EPHOD

[5]"They shall take the gold,
blue, purple, and scarlet
thread, and the fine linen, [6]and
they shall make the ephod of
gold, blue, purple, *and* scarlet
thread, and fine woven linen,
artistically worked. [7]It shall
have two shoulder straps
joined at its two edges, and
so it shall be joined together.
[8]And the intricately woven
band of the ephod, which *is* on
it, shall be of the same work-

28:4 [a] That is, an ornamented vest

manship, *made of* gold, blue,
purple, and scarlet *thread,* and
fine woven linen.
9"Then you shall take two
onyx stones and engrave on
them the names of the sons
of Israel: 10six of their names
on one stone and six names
on the other stone, in order of
their birth. 11With the work of
an engraver in stone, *like* the
engravings of a signet, you
shall engrave the two stones
with the names of the sons
of Israel. You shall set them
in settings of gold. 12And you
shall put the two stones on
the shoulders of the ephod
as memorial stones for the
sons of Israel. So Aaron shall
bear their names before the
LORD on his two shoulders as
a memorial. 13You shall also
make settings of gold, 14and
you shall make two chains of
pure gold like braided cords,
and fasten the braided chains
to the settings.

THE BREASTPLATE

15"You shall make the
breastplate of judgment. Artistically woven according
to the workmanship of the
ephod you shall make it: of
gold, blue, purple, and scarlet
thread, and fine woven linen,
you shall make it. 16It shall
be doubled into a square: a
span *shall be* its length, and a
span *shall be* its width. 17And
you shall put settings of stones
in it, four rows of stones: *The
first* row *shall be* a sardius, a
topaz, and an emerald; *this
shall be* the first row; 18the second row *shall be* a turquoise,
a sapphire, and a diamond;
19the third row, a jacinth,
an agate, and an amethyst;
20and the fourth row, a beryl,
an onyx, and a jasper. They
shall be set in gold settings.
21And the stones shall have
the names of the sons of Israel, twelve according to their
names, *like* the engravings of
a signet, each one with its own
name; they shall be according
to the twelve tribes.

22"You shall make chains
for the breastplate at the end,
like braided cords of pure
gold. 23And you shall make
two rings of gold for the
breastplate, and put the two
rings on the two ends of the
breastplate. 24Then you shall
put the two braided *chains* of
gold in the two rings which
are on the ends of the breastplate; 25and the *other* two ends
of the two braided *chains* you
shall fasten to the two settings, and put them on the
shoulder straps of the ephod
in the front.

26"You shall make two rings
of gold, and put them on the
two ends of the breastplate, on
the edge of it, which is on the
inner side of the ephod. 27And
two *other* rings of gold you
shall make, and put them on
the two shoulder straps, underneath the ephod toward its
front, right at the seam above
the intricately woven band of

the ephod. 28They shall bind the breastplate by means of its rings to the rings of the ephod, using a blue cord, so that it is above the intricately woven band of the ephod, and so that the breastplate does not come loose from the ephod.

29"So Aaron shall bear the names of the sons of Israel on the breastplate of judgment over his heart, when he goes into the holy *place,* as a memorial before the LORD continually. 30And you shall put in the breastplate of judgment the Urim and the Thummim,[a] and they shall be over Aaron's heart when he goes in before the LORD. So Aaron shall bear the judgment of the children of Israel over his heart before the LORD continually.

OTHER PRIESTLY GARMENTS

31"You shall make the robe of the ephod all of blue. 32There shall be an opening for his head in the middle of it; it shall have a woven binding all around its opening, like the opening in a coat of mail, so that it does not tear. 33And upon its hem you shall make pomegranates of blue, purple, and scarlet, all around its hem, and bells of gold between them all around: 34a golden bell and a pomegranate, a golden bell and a pomegranate, upon the hem of the robe all around. 35And it shall be upon Aaron when he ministers, and its sound will be heard when he goes into the holy *place* before the LORD and when he comes out, that he may not die.

36"You shall also make a plate of pure gold and engrave on it, *like* the engraving of a signet:

HOLINESS TO THE LORD.

37And you shall put it on a blue cord, that it may be on the turban; it shall be on the front of the turban. 38So it shall be on Aaron's forehead, that Aaron may bear the iniquity of the holy things which the children of Israel hallow in all their holy gifts; and it shall always be on his forehead, that they may be accepted before the LORD.

39"You shall skillfully weave the tunic of fine linen *thread,* you shall make the turban of fine linen, and you shall make the sash of woven work.

40"For Aaron's sons you shall make tunics, and you shall make sashes for them. And you shall make hats for them, for glory and beauty. 41So you shall put them on Aaron your brother and on his sons with him. You shall anoint them, consecrate them, and sanctify them, that they may minister to Me as

28:30 [a] Literally *the Lights and the Perfections* (compare Leviticus 8:8)

priests. 42And you shall make
for them linen trousers to
cover their nakedness; they
shall reach from the waist to
the thighs. 43They shall be on
Aaron and on his sons when
they come into the tabernacle of meeting, or when they
come near the altar to minister in the holy *place,* that they
do not incur iniquity and die.
It shall be a statute forever to
him and his descendants after
him.

AARON AND HIS SONS CONSECRATED

29 "And this is what you
shall do to them to hal-
low them for ministering to Me
as priests: Take one young bull
and two rams without blemish, 2and unleavened bread,
unleavened cakes mixed with
oil, and unleavened wafers
anointed with oil (you shall
make them of wheat flour).
3You shall put them in one
basket and bring them in the
basket, with the bull and the
two rams.

4"And Aaron and his sons
you shall bring to the door
of the tabernacle of meeting,
and you shall wash them with
water. 5Then you shall take
the garments, put the tunic
on Aaron, and the robe of
the ephod, the ephod, and
the breastplate, and gird him
with the intricately woven
band of the ephod. 6You shall
put the turban on his head,
and put the holy crown on
the turban. 7And you shall
take the anointing oil, pour
it on his head, and anoint
him. 8Then you shall bring
his sons and put tunics on
them. 9And you shall gird
them with sashes, Aaron and
his sons, and put the hats on
them. The priesthood shall be
theirs for a perpetual statute.
So you shall consecrate Aaron
and his sons.

10"You shall also have the
bull brought before the tabernacle of meeting, and Aaron
and his sons shall put their
hands on the head of the bull.
11Then you shall kill the bull
before the LORD, *by* the door
of the tabernacle of meeting.
12You shall take *some* of the
blood of the bull and put *it*
on the horns of the altar with
your finger, and pour all the
blood beside the base of the
altar. 13And you shall take all
the fat that covers the entrails,
the fatty lobe *attached* to the
liver, and the two kidneys and
the fat that *is* on them, and
burn *them* on the altar. 14But
the flesh of the bull, with its
skin and its offal, you shall
burn with fire outside the
camp. It *is* a sin offering.

15"You shall also take one
ram, and Aaron and his sons
shall put their hands on the
head of the ram; 16and you
shall kill the ram, and you
shall take its blood and sprinkle *it* all around on the altar.
17Then you shall cut the ram
in pieces, wash its entrails and

its legs, and put *them* with its
pieces and with its head. 18And
you shall burn the whole ram
on the altar. It *is* a burnt offering to the LORD; it *is* a sweet
aroma, an offering made by
fire to the LORD.

19"You shall also take the
other ram, and Aaron and his
sons shall put their hands on
the head of the ram. 20Then
you shall kill the ram, and take
some of its blood and put *it*
on the tip of the right ear of
Aaron and on the tip of the
right ear of his sons, on the
thumb of their right hand
and on the big toe of their
right foot, and sprinkle the
blood all around on the altar.
21And you shall take some of
the blood that is on the altar,
and some of the anointing oil,
and sprinkle *it* on Aaron and
on his garments, on his sons
and on the garments of his
sons with him; and he and his
garments shall be hallowed,
and his sons and his sons' garments with him.

22"Also you shall take the fat
of the ram, the fat tail, the fat
that covers the entrails, the
fatty lobe *attached to* the liver,
the two kidneys and the fat on
them, the right thigh (for it *is*
a ram of consecration), 23one
loaf of bread, one cake *made
with* oil, and one wafer from
the basket of the unleavened
bread that *is* before the LORD;
24and you shall put all these
in the hands of Aaron and in
the hands of his sons, and you
shall wave them *as* a wave offering before the LORD. 25You
shall receive them back from
their hands and burn *them* on
the altar as a burnt offering,
as a sweet aroma before the
LORD. It *is* an offering made
by fire to the LORD.

26"Then you shall take the
breast of the ram of Aaron's
consecration and wave it *as*
a wave offering before the
LORD; and it shall be your
portion. 27And from the ram
of the consecration you shall
consecrate the breast of the
wave offering which is waved,
and the thigh of the heave offering which is raised, of *that*
which *is* for Aaron and of *that*
which is for his sons. 28It shall
be from the children of Israel *for* Aaron and his sons
by a statute forever. For it is
a heave offering; it shall be a
heave offering from the children of Israel from the sacrifices of their peace offerings,
that is, their heave offering to
the LORD.

29"And the holy garments
of Aaron shall be his sons'
after him, to be anointed in
them and to be consecrated
in them. 30That son who becomes priest in his place shall
put them on for seven days,
when he enters the tabernacle
of meeting to minister in the
holy *place.*

31"And you shall take the
ram of the consecration
and boil its flesh in the holy
place. 32Then Aaron and his

sons shall eat the flesh of the ram, and the bread that *is* in the basket, *by* the door of the tabernacle of meeting. 33They shall eat those things with which the atonement was made, to consecrate *and* to sanctify them; but an outsider shall not eat *them,* because they *are* holy. 34And if any of the flesh of the consecration offerings, or of the bread, remains until the morning, then you shall burn the remainder with fire. It shall not be eaten, because it *is* holy.

35“Thus you shall do to Aaron and his sons, according to all that I have commanded you. Seven days you shall consecrate them. 36And you shall offer a bull every day *as* a sin offering for atonement. You shall cleanse the altar when you make atonement for it, and you shall anoint it to sanctify it. 37Seven days you shall make atonement for the altar and sanctify it. And the altar shall be most holy. Whatever touches the altar must be holy.[a]

THE DAILY OFFERINGS

38“Now this *is* what you shall offer on the altar: two lambs of the first year, day by day continually. 39One lamb you shall offer in the morning, and the other lamb you shall offer at twilight. 40With the one lamb shall be one-tenth *of an ephah* of flour mixed with one-fourth of a hin of pressed oil, and one-fourth of a hin of wine *as* a drink offering. 41And the other lamb you shall offer at twilight; and you shall offer with it the grain offering and the drink offering, as in the morning, for a sweet aroma, an offering made by fire to the LORD. 42*This shall be* a continual burnt offering throughout your generations *at* the door of the tabernacle of meeting before the LORD, where I will meet you to speak with you. 43And there I will meet with the children of Israel, and *the tabernacle* shall be sanctified by My glory. 44So I will consecrate the tabernacle of meeting and the altar. I will also consecrate both Aaron and his sons to minister to Me as priests. 45I will dwell among the children of Israel and will be their God. 46And they shall know that I *am* the LORD their God, who brought them up out of the land of Egypt, that I may dwell among them. I *am* the LORD their God.

THE ALTAR OF INCENSE

30 “You shall make an altar to burn incense on; you shall make it of acacia wood. 2A cubit *shall be* its length and a cubit its width—it shall be square—and two cubits *shall be* its height. Its horns *shall be* of one piece with it. 3And

29:37 [a] Compare Numbers 4:15 and Haggai 2:11–13

you shall overlay its top, its
sides all around, and its horns
with pure gold; and you shall
make for it a molding of gold
all around. 4Two gold rings
you shall make for it, under
the molding on both its sides.
You shall place *them* on its two
sides, and they will be holders for the poles with which
to bear it. 5You shall make
the poles of acacia wood,
and overlay them with gold.
6And you shall put it before
the veil that *is* before the ark
of the Testimony, before the
mercy seat that *is* over the
Testimony, where I will meet
with you.

7"Aaron shall burn on it
sweet incense every morn-
ing; when he tends the lamps,
he shall burn incense on it.
8And when Aaron lights the
lamps at twilight, he shall
burn incense on it, a perpetual incense before the LORD
throughout your generations.
9You shall not offer strange
incense on it, or a burnt offering, or a grain offering;
nor shall you pour a drink
offering on it. 10And Aaron
shall make atonement upon
its horns once a year with the
blood of the sin offering of
atonement; once a year he
shall make atonement upon it
throughout your generations.
It *is* most holy to the LORD."

THE RANSOM MONEY

11Then the LORD spoke to
Moses, saying: 12"When you
take the census of the children of Israel for their number, then every man shall
give a ransom for himself to
the LORD, when you number
them, that there may be no
plague among them when
you number them. 13This is
what everyone among those
who are numbered shall give:
half a shekel according to the
shekel of the sanctuary (a
shekel *is* twenty gerahs). The
half-shekel *shall be* an offering to the LORD. 14Everyone
included among those who
are numbered, from twenty
years old and above, shall give
an offering to the LORD. 15The
rich shall not give more and
the poor shall not give less
than half a shekel, when *you*
give an offering to the LORD,
to make atonement for yourselves. 16And you shall take
the atonement money of the
children of Israel, and shall
appoint it for the service of
the tabernacle of meeting,
that it may be a memorial for
the children of Israel before
the LORD, to make atonement
for yourselves."

THE BRONZE LAVER

17Then the LORD spoke to
Moses, saying: 18"You shall
also make a laver of bronze,
with its base also of bronze,
for washing. You shall put it
between the tabernacle of
meeting and the altar. And
you shall put water in it, 19for
Aaron and his sons shall wash

their hands and their feet in
water from it. 20When they go
into the tabernacle of meeting, or when they come near
the altar to minister, to burn
an offering made by fire to
the LORD, they shall wash with
water, lest they die. 21So they
shall wash their hands and
their feet, lest they die. And
it shall be a statute forever
to them—to him and his descendants throughout their
generations."

THE HOLY ANOINTING OIL

22Moreover the LORD spoke
to Moses, saying: 23"Also take
for yourself quality spices—
five hundred *shekels* of liquid
myrrh, half as much sweet-
smelling cinnamon (two hundred and fifty *shekels*), two
hundred and fifty *shekels* of
sweet-smelling cane, 24five
hundred *shekels* of cassia, according to the shekel of the
sanctuary, and a hin of olive
oil. 25And you shall make
from these a holy anointing
oil, an ointment compounded
according to the art of the
perfumer. It shall be a holy
anointing oil. 26With it you
shall anoint the tabernacle
of meeting and the ark of the
Testimony; 27the table and all
its utensils, the lampstand and
its utensils, and the altar of incense; 28the altar of burnt offering with all its utensils, and
the laver and its base. 29You
shall consecrate them, that
they may be most holy; whatever touches them must be
holy.[a] 30And you shall anoint
Aaron and his sons, and consecrate them, that *they* may
minister to Me as priests.

31"And you shall speak to
the children of Israel, saying:
'This shall be a holy anointing oil to Me throughout your
generations. 32It shall not be
poured on man's flesh; nor
shall you make *any other* like
it, according to its composition. It *is* holy, *and* it shall be
holy to you. 33Whoever com-
pounds *any* like it, or whoever
puts *any* of it on an outsider,
shall be cut off from his people.'"

THE INCENSE

34And the LORD said to
Moses: "Take sweet spices,
stacte and onycha and gal-
banum, and pure frankin-
cense with *these* sweet spices;
there shall be equal amounts
of each. 35You shall make of
these an incense, a compound
according to the art of the perfumer, salted, pure, *and* holy.
36And you shall beat *some* of
it very fine, and put some of
it before the Testimony in the
tabernacle of meeting where I
will meet with you. It shall be
most holy to you. 37But *as for*
the incense which you shall
make, you shall not make any
for yourselves, according to

30:29 [a] Compare Numbers 4:15 and Haggai 2:11–13

its composition. It shall be to you holy for the LORD. 38Whoever makes *any* like it, to smell it, he shall be cut off from his people."

ARTISANS FOR BUILDING THE TABERNACLE

31 Then the LORD spoke to Moses, saying: 2"See, I have called by name Bezalel the son of Uri, the son of Hur, of the tribe of Judah. 3And I have filled him with the Spirit of God, in wisdom, in understanding, in knowledge, and in all *manner of* workmanship, 4to design artistic works, to work in gold, in silver, in bronze, 5in cutting jewels for setting, in carving wood, and to work in all *manner of* workmanship.

6"And I, indeed I, have appointed with him Aholiab the son of Ahisamach, of the tribe of Dan; and I have put wisdom in the hearts of all the gifted artisans, that they may make all that I have commanded you: 7the tabernacle of meeting, the ark of the Testimony and the mercy seat that *is* on it, and all the furniture of the tabernacle— 8the table and its utensils, the pure *gold* lampstand with all its utensils, the altar of incense, 9the altar of burnt offering with all its utensils, and the laver and its base— 10the garments of ministry,[a] the holy garments for Aaron the priest and the garments of his sons, to minister as priests, 11and the anointing oil and sweet incense for the holy *place*. According to all that I have commanded you they shall do."

THE SABBATH LAW

12And the LORD spoke to Moses, saying, 13"Speak also to the children of Israel, saying: 'Surely My Sabbaths you shall keep, for it *is* a sign between Me and you throughout your generations, that *you* may know that I *am* the LORD who sanctifies you. 14You shall keep the Sabbath, therefore, for *it is* holy to you. Everyone who profanes it shall surely be put to death; for whoever does *any* work on it, that person shall be cut off from among his people. 15Work shall be done for six days, but the seventh *is* the Sabbath of rest, holy to the LORD. Whoever does *any* work on the Sabbath day, he shall surely be put to death. 16Therefore the children of Israel shall keep the Sabbath, to observe the Sabbath throughout their generations *as* a perpetual covenant. 17It *is* a sign between Me and the children of Israel forever; for *in* six days the LORD made the heavens and the earth, and on the seventh day He rested and was refreshed.'"

18And when He had made

31:10 [a] Or *woven garments*

an end of speaking with him
on Mount Sinai, He gave
Moses two tablets of the Testimony, tablets of stone, written
with the finger of God.

THE GOLD CALF

32 Now when the people
saw that Moses delayed
coming down from the mountain, the people gathered together to Aaron, and said to
him, “Come, make us gods
that shall go before us; for *as*
for this Moses, the man who
brought us up out of the land
of Egypt, we do not know what
has become of him.”

2And Aaron said to them,
“Break off the golden earrings
which *are* in the ears of your
wives, your sons, and your
daughters, and bring *them*
to me.” 3So all the people
broke off the golden earrings
which *were* in their ears, and
brought *them* to Aaron. 4And
he received *the gold* from their
hand, and he fashioned it with
an engraving tool, and made
a molded calf.

Then they said, “This *is* your
god, O Israel, that brought you
out of the land of Egypt!”

5So when Aaron saw *it,* he
built an altar before it. And
Aaron made a proclamation
and said, “Tomorrow *is* a feast
to the LORD.” 6Then they rose
early on the next day, offered
burnt offerings, and brought
peace offerings; and the people sat down to eat and drink,
and rose up to play.

7And the LORD said to
Moses, “Go, get down! For your
people whom you brought out
of the land of Egypt have corrupted *themselves.* 8They have
turned aside quickly out of
the way which I commanded
them. They have made themselves a molded calf, and worshiped it and sacrificed to it,
and said, ‘This *is* your god,
O Israel, that brought you out
of the land of Egypt!’ ” 9And
the LORD said to Moses, “I
have seen this people, and
indeed it *is* a stiff-necked
people! 10Now therefore, let
Me alone, that My wrath may
burn hot against them and I
may consume them. And I will
make of you a great nation.”

11Then Moses pleaded with
the LORD his God, and said:
“LORD, why does Your wrath
burn hot against Your people whom You have brought
out of the land of Egypt
with great power and with a
mighty hand? 12Why should
the Egyptians speak, and
say, ‘He brought them out to
harm them, to kill them in the
mountains, and to consume
them from the face of the
earth’? Turn from Your fierce
wrath, and relent from this
harm to Your people. 13Re-
member Abraham, Isaac, and
Israel, Your servants, to whom
You swore by Your own self,
and said to them, ‘I will multiply your descendants as the
stars of heaven; and all this
land that I have spoken of I

give to your descendants, and
they shall inherit *it* forever.' "[a]
14So the LORD relented from
the harm which He said He
would do to His people.

15And Moses turned and
went down from the moun-
tain, and the two tablets of the
Testimony *were* in his hand.
The tablets *were* written on
both sides; on the one *side*
and on the other they were
written. 16Now the tablets *were*
the work of God, and the writing *was* the writing of God engraved on the tablets.

17And when Joshua heard
the noise of the people as they
shouted, he said to Moses,
"*There is* a noise of war in the
camp."

18But he said:

"*It is* not the noise of
the shout of victory,
Nor the noise of the
cry of defeat,
But the sound of
singing I hear."

19So it was, as soon as he
came near the camp, that he
saw the calf *and* the dancing.
So Moses' anger became hot,
and he cast the tablets out of
his hands and broke them
at the foot of the mountain.
20Then he took the calf which
they had made, burned *it* in
the fire, and ground *it* to powder; and he scattered *it* on the
water and made the children
of Israel drink *it*. 21And Moses
said to Aaron, "What did this
people do to you that you have
brought *so* great a sin upon
them?"

22So Aaron said, "Do not let
the anger of my lord become
hot. You know the people, that
they *are set* on evil. 23For they
said to me, 'Make us gods that
shall go before us; *as for* this
Moses, the man who brought
us out of the land of Egypt, we
do not know what has become
of him.' 24And I said to them,
'Whoever has any gold, let
them break *it* off.' So they gave
it to me, and I cast it into the
fire, and this calf came out."

25Now when Moses saw that
the people *were* unrestrained
(for Aaron had not restrained
them, to *their* shame among
their enemies), 26then Moses
stood in the entrance of the
camp, and said, "Whoever
is on the LORD's side—*come*
to me!" And all the sons of
Levi gathered themselves together to him. 27And he said
to them, "Thus says the LORD
God of Israel: 'Let every man
put his sword on his side, and
go in and out from entrance
to entrance throughout the
camp, and let every man kill
his brother, every man his
companion, and every man
his neighbor.' " 28So the sons of
Levi did according to the word
of Moses. And about three
thousand men of the people

32:13 [a] Genesis 13:15 and 22:17

fell that day. 29Then Moses
said, "Consecrate yourselves
today to the LORD, that He may
bestow on you a blessing this
day, for every man has opposed his son and his brother."
30Now it came to pass on
the next day that Moses said
to the people, "You have committed a great sin. So now I
will go up to the LORD; perhaps I can make atonement
for your sin." 31Then Moses
returned to the LORD and said,
"Oh, these people have committed a great sin, and have
made for themselves a god
of gold! 32Yet now, if You will
forgive their sin—but if not, I
pray, blot me out of Your book
which You have written."
33And the LORD said to
Moses, "Whoever has sinned
against Me, I will blot him out
of My book. 34Now therefore,
go, lead the people to *the place*
of which I have spoken to you.
Behold, My Angel shall go before you. Nevertheless, in the
day when I visit for punishment, I will visit punishment
upon them for their sin."
35So the LORD plagued the
people because of what they
did with the calf which Aaron
made.

THE COMMAND TO LEAVE SINAI

33 Then the LORD said to
Moses, "Depart *and* go
up from here, you and the people whom you have brought
out of the land of Egypt, to
the land of which I swore to
Abraham, Isaac, and Jacob,
saying, 'To your descendants
I will give it.' 2And I will send
My Angel before you, and I
will drive out the Canaanite
and the Amorite and the Hittite and the Perizzite and the
Hivite and the Jebusite. 3*Go*
up to a land flowing with milk
and honey; for I will not go up
in your midst, lest I consume
you on the way, for you *are* a
stiff-necked people."
4And when the people heard
this bad news, they mourned,
and no one put on his ornaments. 5For the LORD had said
to Moses, "Say to the children
of Israel, 'You *are* a stiff-necked
people. I could come up into
your midst in one moment
and consume you. Now therefore, take off your ornaments,
that I may know what to do to
you.'" 6So the children of Israel
stripped themselves of their
ornaments by Mount Horeb.

MOSES MEETS WITH THE LORD

7Moses took his tent and
pitched it outside the camp,
far from the camp, and called
it the tabernacle of meeting.
And it came to pass *that* everyone who sought the LORD
went out to the tabernacle of
meeting which *was* outside
the camp. 8So it was, whenever Moses went out to the
tabernacle, *that* all the people rose, and each man stood
at his tent door and watched

Moses until he had gone into
the tabernacle. 9And it came
to pass, when Moses entered
the tabernacle, that the pillar
of cloud descended and stood
at the door of the tabernacle, and *the LORD* talked with
Moses. 10All the people saw
the pillar of cloud standing
at the tabernacle door, and
all the people rose and worshiped, each man *in* his tent
door. 11So the LORD spoke to
Moses face to face, as a man
speaks to his friend. And he
would return to the camp, but
his servant Joshua the son of
Nun, a young man, did not
depart from the tabernacle.

THE PROMISE OF GOD'S PRESENCE

12Then Moses said to the
LORD, "See, You say to me,
'Bring up this people.' But
You have not let me know
whom You will send with
me. Yet You have said, 'I
know you by name, and you
have also found grace in My
sight.' 13Now therefore, I pray,
if I have found grace in Your
sight, show me now Your way,
that I may know You and that
I may find grace in Your sight.
And consider that this nation
is Your people."

14And He said, "My Pres-
ence will go *with you,* and I
will give you rest."

15Then he said to Him, "If
Your Presence does not go
with us, do not bring us up
from here. 16For how then will
it be known that Your people
and I have found grace in Your
sight, except You go with us?
So we shall be separate, Your
people and I, from all the people who *are* upon the face of
the earth."

17So the LORD said to Moses,
"I will also do this thing that
you have spoken; for you have
found grace in My sight, and
I know you by name."

18And he said, "Please,
show me Your glory."

19Then He said, "I will make
all My goodness pass before
you, and I will proclaim the
name of the LORD before you.
I will be gracious to whom I
will be gracious, and I will
have compassion on whom I
will have compassion." 20But
He said, "You cannot see My
face; for no man shall see Me,
and live." 21And the LORD said,
"Here is a place by Me, and
you shall stand on the rock.
22So it shall be, while My glory
passes by, that I will put you
in the cleft of the rock, and
will cover you with My hand
while I pass by. 23Then I will
take away My hand, and you
shall see My back; but My face
shall not be seen."

MOSES MAKES NEW TABLETS

34 And the LORD said to
Moses, "Cut two tablets
of stone like the first *ones,* and
I will write on *these* tablets
the words that were on the
first tablets which you broke.

2So be ready in the morning,
and come up in the morning
to Mount Sinai, and present
yourself to Me there on the
top of the mountain. 3And
no man shall come up with
you, and let no man be seen
throughout all the mountain;
let neither flocks nor herds
feed before that mountain."
4So he cut two tablets of
stone like the first *ones.* Then
Moses rose early in the morning and went up Mount Sinai,
as the LORD had commanded
him; and he took in his hand
the two tablets of stone.
5Now the LORD descended
in the cloud and stood with
him there, and proclaimed
the name of the LORD. 6And
the LORD passed before him
and proclaimed, "The LORD,
the LORD God, merciful and
gracious, longsuffering, and
abounding in goodness and
truth, 7keeping mercy for thousands, forgiving iniquity and
transgression and sin, by no
means clearing *the guilty,* visiting the iniquity of the fathers
upon the children and the children's children to the third and
the fourth generation."
8So Moses made haste and
bowed his head toward the
earth, and worshiped. 9Then
he said, "If now I have found
grace in Your sight, O Lord,
let my Lord, I pray, go among
us, even though we *are* a stiff-
necked people; and pardon
our iniquity and our sin, and
take us as Your inheritance."

THE COVENANT RENEWED

10And He said: "Behold, I
make a covenant. Before all
your people I will do mar-
vels such as have not been
done in all the earth, nor in
any nation; and all the people
among whom you *are* shall see
the work of the LORD. For it *is*
an awesome thing that I will
do with you. 11Observe what I
command you this day. Behold,
I am driving out from before
you the Amorite and the Canaanite and the Hittite and the
Perizzite and the Hivite and the
Jebusite. 12Take heed to yourself, lest you make a covenant
with the inhabitants of the land
where you are going, lest it be
a snare in your midst. 13But
you shall destroy their altars,
break their *sacred* pillars, and
cut down their wooden im-
ages 14(for you shall worship
no other god, for the LORD,
whose name *is* Jealous, *is* a
jealous God), 15lest you make
a covenant with the inhabitants
of the land, and they play the
harlot with their gods and
make sacrifice to their gods,
and *one of them* invites you and
you eat of his sacrifice, 16and
you take of his daughters for
your sons, and his daughters
play the harlot with their gods
and make your sons play the
harlot with their gods.
17"You shall make no
molded gods for yourselves.
18"The Feast of Unleavened
Bread you shall keep. Seven
days you shall eat unleavened

bread, as I commanded you,
in the appointed time of the
month of Abib; for in the
month of Abib you came out
from Egypt.

19"All that open the womb
are Mine, and every male firstborn among your livestock,
whether ox or sheep. 20But the
firstborn of a donkey you shall
redeem with a lamb. And if
you will not redeem *him,* then
you shall break his neck. All
the firstborn of your sons you
shall redeem.

"And none shall appear before Me empty-handed.

21"Six days you shall work,
but on the seventh day you
shall rest; in plowing time and
in harvest you shall rest.

22"And you shall observe
the Feast of Weeks, of the firstfruits of wheat harvest, and
the Feast of Ingathering at the
year's end.

23"Three times in the year
all your men shall appear before the Lord, the LORD God
of Israel. 24For I will cast out
the nations before you and
enlarge your borders; neither
will any man covet your land
when you go up to appear before the LORD your God three
times in the year.

25"You shall not offer the
blood of My sacrifice with
leaven, nor shall the sacrifice
of the Feast of the Passover be
left until morning.

26"The first of the firstfruits
of your land you shall bring to
the house of the LORD your
God. You shall not boil a young
goat in its mother's milk."

27Then the LORD said to
Moses, "Write these words, for
according to the tenor of these
words I have made a covenant
with you and with Israel." 28So
he was there with the LORD
forty days and forty nights; he
neither ate bread nor drank
water. And He wrote on the tablets the words of the covenant,
the Ten Commandments.[a]

THE SHINING FACE OF MOSES

29Now it was so, when Moses
came down from Mount Sinai
(and the two tablets of the Testimony *were* in Moses' hand
when he came down from
the mountain), that Moses
did not know that the skin of
his face shone while he talked
with Him. 30So when Aaron
and all the children of Israel
saw Moses, behold, the skin
of his face shone, and they
were afraid to come near him.
31Then Moses called to them,
and Aaron and all the rulers
of the congregation returned
to him; and Moses talked with
them. 32Afterward all the children of Israel came near, and
he gave them as command-
ments all that the LORD had
spoken with him on Mount
Sinai. 33And when Moses had
finished speaking with them,

34:28 [a] Literally *Ten Words*

he put a veil on his face. 34But
whenever Moses went in before the LORD to speak with
Him, he would take the veil
off until he came out; and he
would come out and speak to
the children of Israel whatever
he had been commanded.
35And whenever the children
of Israel saw the face of Moses,
that the skin of Moses' face
shone, then Moses would put
the veil on his face again, until
he went in to speak with Him.

SABBATH REGULATIONS

35 Then Moses gathered
all the congregation of
the children of Israel together,
and said to them, "These *are*
the words which the LORD has
commanded *you* to do: 2Work
shall be done for six days, but
the seventh day shall be a holy
day for you, a Sabbath of rest
to the LORD. Whoever does
any work on it shall be put to
death. 3You shall kindle no
fire throughout your dwellings on the Sabbath day."

OFFERINGS FOR THE TABERNACLE

4And Moses spoke to all the
congregation of the children of
Israel, saying, "This *is* the thing
which the LORD commanded,
saying: 5'Take from among
you an offering to the LORD.
Whoever *is* of a willing heart,
let him bring it as an offering
to the LORD: gold, silver, and
bronze; 6blue, purple, and scarlet *thread,* fine linen, and goats'
hair; 7ram skins dyed red, badger skins, and acacia wood; 8oil
for the light, and spices for the
anointing oil and for the sweet
incense; 9onyx stones, and
stones to be set in the ephod
and in the breastplate.

ARTICLES OF THE TABERNACLE

10'All *who are* gifted artisans among you shall come
and make all that the LORD has
commanded: 11the tabernacle,
its tent, its covering, its clasps,
its boards, its bars, its pillars,
and its sockets; 12the ark and
its poles, *with* the mercy seat,
and the veil of the covering;
13the table and its poles, all
its utensils, and the showbread; 14also the lampstand
for the light, its utensils, its
lamps, and the oil for the light;
15the incense altar, its poles,
the anointing oil, the sweet
incense, and the screen for
the door at the entrance of
the tabernacle; 16the altar of
burnt offering with its bronze
grating, its poles, all its utensils, *and* the laver and its base;
17the hangings of the court,
its pillars, their sockets, and
the screen for the gate of the
court; 18the pegs of the tabernacle, the pegs of the court,
and their cords; 19the garments of ministry,[a] for ministering in the holy *place*—the

35:19 [a] Or *woven garments*

holy garments for Aaron the
priest and the garments of his
sons, to minister as priests.'"

THE TABERNACLE OFFERINGS PRESENTED

20And all the congregation
of the children of Israel departed from the presence of
Moses. 21Then everyone came
whose heart was stirred, and
everyone whose spirit was
willing, *and* they brought the
LORD's offering for the work
of the tabernacle of meeting,
for all its service, and for the
holy garments. 22They came,
both men and women, as
many as had a willing heart,
and brought earrings and
nose rings, rings and necklaces, all jewelry of gold, that
is, every man who *made* an
offering of gold to the LORD.
23And every man, with whom
was found blue, purple, and
scarlet *thread,* fine linen, and
goats' *hair,* red skins of rams,
and badger skins, brought
them. 24Everyone who offered
an offering of silver or bronze
brought the LORD's offering.
And everyone with whom was
found acacia wood for any
work of the service, brought
it. 25All the women *who were*
gifted artisans spun yarn with
their hands, and brought what
they had spun, of blue, purple, *and* scarlet, and fine linen.
26And all the women whose
hearts stirred with wisdom
spun yarn of goats' *hair.* 27The
rulers brought onyx stones,
and the stones to be set in the
ephod and in the breastplate,
28and spices and oil for the
light, for the anointing oil, and
for the sweet incense. 29The
children of Israel brought a
freewill offering to the LORD,
all the men and women whose
hearts were willing to bring
material for all kinds of work
which the LORD, by the hand
of Moses, had commanded to
be done.

THE ARTISANS CALLED BY GOD

30And Moses said to the
children of Israel, "See, the
LORD has called by name Bezalel the son of Uri, the son of
Hur, of the tribe of Judah;
31and He has filled him with
the Spirit of God, in wisdom
and understanding, in knowledge and all manner of workmanship, 32to design artistic
works, to work in gold and silver and bronze, 33in cutting
jewels for setting, in carving
wood, and to work in all manner of artistic workmanship.

34"And He has put in his
heart the ability to teach, *in*
him and Aholiab the son of
Ahisamach, of the tribe of
Dan. 35He has filled them
with skill to do all manner
of work of the engraver and
the designer and the tapestry
maker, in blue, purple, and
scarlet *thread,* and fine linen,
and of the weaver—those who
do every work and those who
design artistic works.

36 "And Bezalel and Aho-
liab, and every gifted
artisan in whom the LORD
has put wisdom and under-
standing, to know how to do
all manner of work for the service of the sanctuary, shall do
according to all that the LORD
has commanded."

THE PEOPLE GIVE MORE THAN ENOUGH

2Then Moses called Bez-
alel and Aholiab, and every
gifted artisan in whose heart
the LORD had put wisdom,
everyone whose heart was
stirred, to come and do the
work. 3And they received from
Moses all the offering which
the children of Israel had
brought for the work of the
service of making the sanctuary. So they continued bringing to him freewill offerings
every morning. 4Then all the
craftsmen who were doing
all the work of the sanctuary
came, each from the work he
was doing, 5and they spoke
to Moses, saying, "The people bring much more than
enough for the service of the
work which the LORD com-
manded *us* to do."

6So Moses gave a com-
mandment, and they caused it
to be proclaimed throughout
the camp, saying, "Let neither
man nor woman do any more
work for the offering of the
sanctuary." And the people
were restrained from bringing, 7for the material they had
was sufficient for all the work
to be done—indeed too much.

BUILDING THE TABERNACLE

8Then all the gifted artisans
among them who worked on
the tabernacle made ten curtains woven of fine linen, and
of blue, purple, and scarlet
thread; with artistic designs
of cherubim they made them.
9The length of each curtain
was twenty-eight cubits, and
the width of each curtain four
cubits; the curtains *were* all the
same size. 10And he coupled
five curtains to one another,
and *the other* five curtains he
coupled to one another. 11He
made loops of blue *yarn* on
the edge of the curtain on the
selvedge of one set; likewise
he did on the outer edge of
the other curtain of the second
set. 12Fifty loops he made on
one curtain, and fifty loops
he made on the edge of the
curtain on the end of the second set; the loops held one
curtain to another. 13And he
made fifty clasps of gold, and
coupled the curtains to one
another with the clasps, that
it might be one tabernacle.

14He made curtains of
goats' *hair* for the tent over
the tabernacle; he made
eleven curtains. 15The length
of each curtain *was* thirty
cubits, and the width of each
curtain four cubits; the eleven
curtains *were* the same size.
16He coupled five curtains by

themselves and six curtains by themselves. 17And he made fifty loops on the edge of the curtain that is outermost in one set, and fifty loops he made on the edge of the curtain of the second set. 18He also made fifty bronze clasps to couple the tent together, that it might be one. 19Then he made a covering for the tent of ram skins dyed red, and a covering of badger skins above *that.*

20For the tabernacle he made boards of acacia wood, standing upright. 21The length of each board *was* ten cubits, and the width of each board a cubit and a half. 22Each board had two tenons for binding one to another. Thus he made for all the boards of the tabernacle. 23And he made boards for the tabernacle, twenty boards for the south side. 24Forty sockets of silver he made to go under the twenty boards: two sockets under each of the boards for its two tenons. 25And for the other side of the tabernacle, the north side, he made twenty boards 26and their forty sockets of silver: two sockets under each of the boards. 27For the west side of the tabernacle he made six boards. 28He also made two boards for the two back corners of the tabernacle. 29And they were coupled at the bottom and coupled together at the top by one ring. Thus he made both of them for the two corners. 30So there were eight boards and their sockets—sixteen sockets of silver—two sockets under each of the boards.

31And he made bars of acacia wood: five for the boards on one side of the tabernacle, 32five bars for the boards on the other side of the tabernacle, and five bars for the boards of the tabernacle on the far side westward. 33And he made the middle bar to pass through the boards from one end to the other. 34He overlaid the boards with gold, made their rings of gold *to be* holders for the bars, and overlaid the bars with gold.

35And he made a veil of blue, purple, and scarlet *thread,* and fine woven linen; it was worked *with* an artistic design of cherubim. 36He made for it four pillars of acacia *wood,* and overlaid them with gold, with their hooks of gold; and he cast four sockets of silver for them.

37He also made a screen for the tabernacle door, of blue, purple, and scarlet *thread,* and fine woven linen, made by a weaver, 38and its five pillars with their hooks. And he overlaid their capitals and their rings with gold, but their five sockets *were* bronze.

MAKING THE ARK OF THE TESTIMONY

37 Then Bezalel made the ark of acacia wood; two and a half cubits *was* its length, a cubit and a half its width, and

a cubit and a half its height.
2He overlaid it with pure gold
inside and outside, and made
a molding of gold all around it.
3And he cast for it four rings of
gold *to be set* in its four corners:
two rings on one side, and two
rings on the other side of it.
4He made poles of acacia wood,
and overlaid them with gold.
5And he put the poles into the
rings at the sides of the ark, to
bear the ark. 6He also made
the mercy seat of pure gold;
two and a half cubits *was* its
length and a cubit and a half its
width. 7He made two cherubim
of beaten gold; he made them
of one piece at the two ends of
the mercy seat: 8one cherub
at one end on this side, and
the other cherub at the *other*
end on that side. He made the
cherubim at the two ends *of
one piece* with the mercy seat.
9The cherubim spread out *their*
wings above, *and* covered the
mercy seat with their wings.
They faced one another; the
faces of the cherubim were toward the mercy seat.

MAKING THE TABLE FOR THE SHOWBREAD

10He made the table of acacia wood; two cubits *was* its
length, a cubit its width, and
a cubit and a half its height.
11And he overlaid it with pure
gold, and made a molding
of gold all around it. 12Also
he made a frame of a handbreadth all around it, and
made a molding of gold for
the frame all around it. 13And
he cast for it four rings of gold,
and put the rings on the four
corners that *were* at its four
legs. 14The rings were close to
the frame, as holders for the
poles to bear the table. 15And
he made the poles of acacia
wood to bear the table, and
overlaid them with gold. 16He
made of pure gold the utensils
which were on the table: its
dishes, its cups, its bowls, and
its pitchers for pouring.

MAKING THE GOLD LAMPSTAND

17He also made the lamp-
stand of pure gold; of hammered work he made the
lampstand. Its shaft, its
branches, its bowls, its *ornamental* knobs, and its flowers
were of the same piece. 18And
six branches came out of its
sides: three branches of the
lampstand out of one side,
and three branches of the
lampstand out of the other
side. 19There were three bowls
made like almond *blossoms*
on one branch, with an *ornamental* knob and a flower,
and three bowls made like almond *blossoms* on the other
branch, with an *ornamental*
knob and a flower—and so for
the six branches coming out
of the lampstand. 20And on
the lampstand itself *were* four
bowls made like almond *blossoms, each with* its *ornamental* knob and flower. 21*There
was* a knob under the *first*

two branches of the same, a
knob under the *second* two
branches of the same, and
a knob under the *third* two
branches of the same, ac-
cording to the six branches
extending from it. 22Their
knobs and their branches
were of one piece; all of it *was*
one hammered piece of pure
gold. 23And he made its seven
lamps, its wick-trimmers, and
its trays of pure gold. 24Of a
talent of pure gold he made
it, with all its utensils.

MAKING THE ALTAR OF INCENSE

25He made the incense
altar of acacia wood. Its length
was a cubit and its width a
cubit—*it was* square—and
two cubits *was* its height. Its
horns were *of one piece* with
it. 26And he overlaid it with
pure gold: its top, its sides all
around, and its horns. He also
made for it a molding of gold
all around it. 27He made two
rings of gold for it under its
molding, by its two corners
on both sides, as holders for
the poles with which to bear
it. 28And he made the poles
of acacia wood, and overlaid
them with gold.

MAKING THE ANOINTING OIL AND THE INCENSE

29He also made the holy
anointing oil and the pure
incense of sweet spices, according to the work of the
perfumer.

MAKING THE ALTAR OF BURNT OFFERING

38 He made the altar of
burnt offering of acacia
wood; five cubits *was* its length
and five cubits its width—*it
was* square—and its height
was three cubits. 2He made its
horns on its four corners; the
horns were *of one piece* with it.
And he overlaid it with bronze.
3He made all the utensils for
the altar: the pans, the shovels, the basins, the forks, and
the firepans; all its utensils
he made of bronze. 4And he
made a grate of bronze network for the altar, under its
rim, midway from the bottom.
5He cast four rings for the four
corners of the bronze grating,
as holders for the poles. 6And
he made the poles of acacia
wood, and overlaid them with
bronze. 7Then he put the poles
into the rings on the sides of
the altar, with which to bear
it. He made the altar hollow
with boards.

MAKING THE BRONZE LAVER

8He made the laver of
bronze and its base of bronze,
from the bronze mirrors of
the serving women who as-
sembled at the door of the
tabernacle of meeting.

MAKING THE COURT OF THE TABERNACLE

9Then he made the court
on the south side; the hangings of the court *were of* fine

woven linen, one hundred cubits long. [10]There *were* twenty
pillars for them, with twenty
bronze sockets. The hooks of
the pillars and their bands
were silver. [11]On the north side
the hangings were one hundred cubits *long,* with twenty
pillars and their twenty bronze
sockets. The hooks of the pillars and their bands *were* silver. [12]And on the west side
there were hangings of fifty
cubits, with ten pillars and
their ten sockets. The hooks
of the pillars and their bands
were silver. [13]For the east side
the hangings were fifty cubits.
[14]The hangings of one side *of
the gate were* fifteen cubits
long, with their three pillars
and their three sockets, [15]and
the same for the other side of
the court gate; on this side and
that *were* hangings of fifteen
cubits, *with* their three pillars
and their three sockets. [16]All
the hangings of the court all
around *were of* fine woven
linen. [17]The sockets for the
pillars *were* bronze, the hooks
of the pillars and their bands
were silver, and the overlay of
their capitals *was* silver; and
all the pillars of the court had
bands of silver. [18]The screen
for the gate of the court *was*
woven of blue, purple, and
scarlet *thread,* and of fine
woven linen. The length *was*
twenty cubits, and the height
along its width *was* five cubits,
corresponding to the hangings of the court. [19]And *there
were* four pillars *with* their four
sockets of bronze; their hooks
were silver, and the overlay of
their capitals and their bands
was silver. [20]All the pegs of the
tabernacle, and of the court all
around, *were* bronze.

MATERIALS OF THE TABERNACLE

[21]This is the inventory of
the tabernacle, the tabernacle of the Testimony, which
was counted according to the
commandment of Moses, for
the service of the Levites, by
the hand of Ithamar, son of
Aaron the priest.

[22]Bezalel the son of Uri,
the son of Hur, of the tribe of
Judah, made all that the LORD
had commanded Moses. [23]And
with him *was* Aholiab the son
of Ahisamach, of the tribe of
Dan, an engraver and designer,
a weaver of blue, purple, and
scarlet *thread,* and of fine linen.

[24]All the gold that was used
in all the work of the holy *place,*
that is, the gold of the offering,
was twenty-nine talents and
seven hundred and thirty shekels, according to the shekel of
the sanctuary. [25]And the silver
from those who were num-
bered of the congregation *was*
one hundred talents and one
thousand seven hundred and
seventy-five shekels, according
to the shekel of the sanctuary:
[26]a bekah for each man (*that
is,* half a shekel, according to
the shekel of the sanctuary),
for everyone included in the

numbering from twenty years old and above, for six hundred and three thousand, five hundred and fifty *men.* 27And from the hundred talents of silver were cast the sockets of the sanctuary and the bases of the veil: one hundred sockets from the hundred talents, one talent for each socket. 28Then from the one thousand seven hundred and seventy-five *shekels* he made hooks for the pillars, overlaid their capitals, and made bands for them.

29The offering of bronze *was* seventy talents and two thousand four hundred shekels. 30And with it he made the sockets for the door of the tabernacle of meeting, the bronze altar, the bronze grating for it, and all the utensils for the altar, 31the sockets for the court all around, the bases for the court gate, all the pegs for the tabernacle, and all the pegs for the court all around.

MAKING THE GARMENTS OF THE PRIESTHOOD

39 Of the blue, purple, and scarlet *thread* they made garments of ministry,[a] for ministering in the holy *place,* and made the holy garments for Aaron, as the LORD had commanded Moses.

MAKING THE EPHOD

2He made the ephod of gold, blue, purple, and scarlet *thread,* and of fine woven linen. 3And they beat the gold into thin sheets and cut *it into* threads, to work *it* in *with* the blue, purple, and scarlet *thread,* and the fine linen, *into* artistic designs. 4They made shoulder straps for it to couple *it* together; it was coupled together at its two edges. 5And the intricately woven band of his ephod that *was* on it *was* of the same workmanship, *woven of* gold, blue, purple, and scarlet *thread,* and *of* fine woven linen, as the LORD had commanded Moses.

6And they set onyx stones, enclosed in settings of gold; they were engraved, as signets are engraved, with the names of the sons of Israel. 7He put them on the shoulders of the ephod *as* memorial stones for the sons of Israel, as the LORD had commanded Moses.

MAKING THE BREASTPLATE

8And he made the breastplate, artistically woven like the workmanship of the ephod, of gold, blue, purple, and scarlet *thread,* and of fine woven linen. 9They made the breastplate square by doubling it; a span *was* its length and a span its width when doubled. 10And they set in it four rows of stones: a row with a sardius, a topaz, and an emerald was the first row; 11the second row, a turquoise, a sapphire, and

39:1 [a] Or *woven garments*

a diamond; 12the third row,
a jacinth, an agate, and an
amethyst; 13the fourth row, a
beryl, an onyx, and a jasper.
They were enclosed in settings
of gold in their mountings.
14*There were* twelve stones according to the names of the
sons of Israel: according to
their names, *engraved like* a
signet, each one with its own
name according to the twelve
tribes. 15And they made chains
for the breastplate at the ends,
like braided cords of pure
gold. 16They also made two
settings of gold and two gold
rings, and put the two rings
on the two ends of the breastplate. 17And they put the two
braided *chains* of gold in the
two rings on the ends of the
breastplate. 18The two ends of
the two braided *chains* they
fastened in the two settings,
and put them on the shoulder straps of the ephod in the
front. 19And they made two
rings of gold and put *them* on
the two ends of the breastplate, on the edge of it, which
was on the inward side of the
ephod. 20They made two *other*
gold rings and put them on
the two shoulder straps, underneath the ephod toward
its front, right at the seam
above the intricately woven
band of the ephod. 21And
they bound the breastplate by
means of its rings to the rings
of the ephod with a blue cord,
so that it would be above the
intricately woven band of the
ephod, and that the breastplate would not come loose
from the ephod, as the LORD
had commanded Moses.

MAKING THE OTHER PRIESTLY GARMENTS

22He made the robe of
the ephod of woven work, all
of blue. 23And *there was* an
opening in the middle of the
robe, like the opening in a coat
of mail, *with* a woven binding all around the opening, so
that it would not tear. 24They
made on the hem of the robe
pomegranates of blue, purple,
and scarlet, and of fine woven
linen. 25And they made bells
of pure gold, and put the bells
between the pomegranates on
the hem of the robe all around
between the pomegranates:
26a bell and a pomegranate,
a bell and a pomegranate, all
around the hem of the robe to
minister in, as the LORD had
commanded Moses.

27They made tunics, artistically woven of fine linen, for
Aaron and his sons, 28a turban
of fine linen, exquisite hats of
fine linen, short trousers of
fine woven linen, 29and a sash
of fine woven linen with blue,
purple, and scarlet *thread,*
made by a weaver, as the LORD
had commanded Moses.

30Then they made the plate
of the holy crown of pure gold,
and wrote on it an inscription
like the engraving of a signet:

HOLINESS TO THE LORD.

31 And they tied to it a blue
cord, to fasten *it* above on
the turban, as the LORD had
commanded Moses.

THE WORK COMPLETED

32 Thus all the work of the
tabernacle of the tent of meeting was finished. And the children of Israel did according
to all that the LORD had commanded Moses; so they did.
33 And they brought the tabernacle to Moses, the tent and
all its furnishings: its clasps,
its boards, its bars, its pillars,
and its sockets; 34 the covering of ram skins dyed red, the
covering of badger skins, and
the veil of the covering; 35 the
ark of the Testimony with its
poles, and the mercy seat;
36 the table, all its utensils,
and the showbread; 37 the pure
gold lampstand with its lamps
(the lamps set in order), all its
utensils, and the oil for light;
38 the gold altar, the anointing oil, and the sweet incense;
the screen for the tabernacle
door; 39 the bronze altar, its
grate of bronze, its poles, and
all its utensils; the laver with
its base; 40 the hangings of the
court, its pillars and its sockets, the screen for the court
gate, its cords, and its pegs; all
the utensils for the service of
the tabernacle, for the tent of
meeting; 41 and the garments
of ministry,[a] to minister in the
holy *place:* the holy garments
for Aaron the priest, and his
sons' garments, to minister
as priests.
42 According to all that the
LORD had commanded Moses,
so the children of Israel did
all the work. 43 Then Moses
looked over all the work, and
indeed they had done it; as
the LORD had commanded,
just so they had done it. And
Moses blessed them.

THE TABERNACLE ERECTED AND ARRANGED

40 Then the LORD spoke
to Moses, saying: 2 "On
the first day of the first month
you shall set up the tabernacle
of the tent of meeting. 3 You
shall put in it the ark of the
Testimony, and partition off
the ark with the veil. 4 You shall
bring in the table and arrange
the things that are to be set in
order on it; and you shall bring
in the lampstand and light its
lamps. 5 You shall also set the
altar of gold for the incense
before the ark of the Testimony, and put up the screen
for the door of the tabernacle.
6 Then you shall set the altar
of the burnt offering before
the door of the tabernacle
of the tent of meeting. 7 And
you shall set the laver between
the tabernacle of meeting and
the altar, and put water in it.
8 You shall set up the court
all around, and hang up the
screen at the court gate.

39:41 [a] Or *woven garments*

9“And you shall take the
anointing oil, and anoint the
tabernacle and all that *is* in
it; and you shall hallow it and
all its utensils, and it shall be
holy. 10You shall anoint the
altar of the burnt offering and
all its utensils, and consecrate
the altar. The altar shall be
most holy. 11And you shall
anoint the laver and its base,
and consecrate it.

12“Then you shall bring
Aaron and his sons to the door
of the tabernacle of meeting
and wash them with water.
13You shall put the holy garments on Aaron, and anoint
him and consecrate him,
that he may minister to Me
as priest. 14And you shall
bring his sons and clothe
them with tunics. 15You shall
anoint them, as you anointed
their father, that they may
minister to Me as priests; for
their anointing shall surely
be an everlasting priesthood
throughout their genera-
tions.”

16Thus Moses did; accord-
ing to all that the LORD had
commanded him, so he did.

17And it came to pass in the
first month of the second year,
on the first *day* of the month,
that the tabernacle was raised
up. 18So Moses raised up the
tabernacle, fastened its sockets, set up its boards, put in
its bars, and raised up its pillars. 19And he spread out the
tent over the tabernacle and
put the covering of the tent
on top of it, as the LORD had
commanded Moses. 20He took
the Testimony and put *it* into
the ark, inserted the poles
through the rings of the ark,
and put the mercy seat on top
of the ark. 21And he brought
the ark into the tabernacle,
hung up the veil of the covering, and partitioned off the
ark of the Testimony, as the
LORD had commanded Moses.

22He put the table in the
tabernacle of meeting, on the
north side of the tabernacle,
outside the veil; 23and he set
the bread in order upon it before the LORD, as the LORD had
commanded Moses. 24He put
the lampstand in the tabernacle of meeting, across from
the table, on the south side of
the tabernacle; 25and he lit the
lamps before the LORD, as the
LORD had commanded Moses.
26He put the gold altar in the
tabernacle of meeting in front
of the veil; 27and he burned
sweet incense on it, as the
LORD had commanded Moses.
28He hung up the screen *at* the
door of the tabernacle. 29And
he put the altar of burnt offering *before* the door of the tabernacle of the tent of meeting,
and offered upon it the burnt
offering and the grain offering, as the LORD had com-
manded Moses. 30He set the
laver between the tabernacle
of meeting and the altar, and
put water there for washing;
31and Moses, Aaron, and his
sons would wash their hands

and their feet *with water* from it. 32 Whenever they went into the tabernacle of meeting, and when they came near the altar, they washed, as the LORD had commanded Moses. 33 And he raised up the court all around the tabernacle and the altar, and hung up the screen of the court gate. So Moses finished the work.

THE CLOUD AND THE GLORY

34 Then the cloud covered the tabernacle of meeting, and the glory of the LORD filled the tabernacle. 35 And Moses was not able to enter the tabernacle of meeting, because the cloud rested above it, and the glory of the LORD filled the tabernacle. 36 Whenever the cloud was taken up from above the tabernacle, the children of Israel would go onward in all their journeys. 37 But if the cloud was not taken up, then they did not journey till the day that it was taken up. 38 For the cloud of the LORD *was* above the tabernacle by day, and fire was over it by night, in the sight of all the house of Israel, throughout all their journeys.

THE THIRD BOOK OF MOSES CALLED LEVITICUS

THE BURNT OFFERING

1 Now the LORD called to Moses, and spoke to him from the tabernacle of meeting, saying, 2 "Speak to the children of Israel, and say to them: 'When any one of you brings an offering to the LORD, you shall bring your offering of the livestock—of the herd and of the flock.

3 'If his offering *is* a burnt sacrifice of the herd, let him offer a male without blemish; he shall offer it of his own free will at the door of the tabernacle of meeting before the LORD. 4 Then he shall put his hand on the head of the burnt offering, and it will be accepted on his behalf to make atonement for him. 5 He shall kill the bull before the LORD; and the priests, Aaron's sons, shall bring the blood and sprinkle the blood all around on the altar that *is by* the door of the tabernacle of meeting. 6 And he shall skin the burnt offering and cut it into its pieces. 7 The sons of Aaron the priest shall put fire on the altar, and lay the wood in order on the fire. 8 Then the priests, Aaron's sons, shall lay

the parts, the head, and the fat
in order on the wood that *is* on
the fire upon the altar; 9but he
shall wash its entrails and its
legs with water. And the priest
shall burn all on the altar as
a burnt sacrifice, an offering
made by fire, a sweet aroma
to the LORD.

10'If his offering *is* of the
flocks—of the sheep or of the
goats—as a burnt sacrifice,
he shall bring a male without
blemish. 11He shall kill it on
the north side of the altar before the LORD; and the priests,
Aaron's sons, shall sprinkle its
blood all around on the altar.
12And he shall cut it into its
pieces, with its head and its fat;
and the priest shall lay them
in order on the wood that *is* on
the fire upon the altar; 13but he
shall wash the entrails and the
legs with water. Then the priest
shall bring *it* all and burn *it* on
the altar; it *is* a burnt sacrifice, an offering made by fire,
a sweet aroma to the LORD.

14'And if the burnt sacrifice
of his offering to the LORD *is*
of birds, then he shall bring
his offering of turtledoves or
young pigeons. 15The priest
shall bring it to the altar,
wring off its head, and burn *it*
on the altar; its blood shall be
drained out at the side of the
altar. 16And he shall remove
its crop with its feathers and
cast it beside the altar on the
east side, into the place for
ashes. 17Then he shall split it at
its wings, *but* shall not divide
it completely; and the priest
shall burn it on the altar, on
the wood that *is* on the fire. It
is a burnt sacrifice, an offering
made by fire, a sweet aroma
to the LORD.

THE GRAIN OFFERING

2 'When anyone offers a
grain offering to the LORD,
his offering shall be *of* fine
flour. And he shall pour oil
on it, and put frankincense on
it. 2He shall bring it to Aaron's
sons, the priests, one of whom
shall take from it his handful of fine flour and oil with
all the frankincense. And the
priest shall burn *it as* a memorial on the altar, an offering
made by fire, a sweet aroma
to the LORD. 3The rest of the
grain offering *shall be* Aaron's
and his sons'. *It is* most holy
of the offerings to the LORD
made by fire.

4'And if you bring as an offering a grain offering baked
in the oven, *it shall be* unleavened cakes of fine flour mixed
with oil, or unleavened wafers
anointed with oil. 5But if your
offering *is* a grain offering
baked in a pan, *it shall be of*
fine flour, unleavened, mixed
with oil. 6You shall break it in
pieces and pour oil on it; it *is*
a grain offering.

7'If your offering *is* a grain
offering *baked* in a covered
pan, it shall be made *of* fine
flour with oil. 8You shall bring
the grain offering that is made
of these things to the LORD.

And when it is presented to
the priest, he shall bring it to
the altar. 9Then the priest shall
take from the grain offering a
memorial portion, and burn
it on the altar. *It is* an offering
made by fire, a sweet aroma
to the LORD. 10And what is
left of the grain offering *shall*
be Aaron's and his sons'. *It is*
most holy of the offerings to
the LORD made by fire.

11'No grain offering which
you bring to the LORD shall
be made with leaven, for you
shall burn no leaven nor any
honey in any offering to the
LORD made by fire. 12As for the
offering of the firstfruits, you
shall offer them to the LORD,
but they shall not be burned
on the altar for a sweet aroma.
13And every offering of your
grain offering you shall season
with salt; you shall not allow
the salt of the covenant of your
God to be lacking from your
grain offering. With all your
offerings you shall offer salt.

14'If you offer a grain offering of your firstfruits to the
LORD, you shall offer for the
grain offering of your firstfruits green heads of grain
roasted on the fire, grain
beaten from full heads. 15And
you shall put oil on it, and lay
frankincense on it. It *is* a grain
offering. 16Then the priest
shall burn the memorial portion: *part* of its beaten grain
and *part* of its oil, with all the
frankincense, as an offering
made by fire to the LORD.

THE PEACE OFFERING

3 'When his offering *is* a
sacrifice of a peace offering, if he offers *it* of the herd,
whether male or female, he
shall offer it without blemish
before the LORD. 2And he shall
lay his hand on the head of his
offering, and kill it *at* the door
of the tabernacle of meeting;
and Aaron's sons, the priests,
shall sprinkle the blood all
around on the altar. 3Then he
shall offer from the sacrifice of
the peace offering an offering
made by fire to the LORD. The
fat that covers the entrails and
all the fat that *is* on the entrails,
4the two kidneys and the fat
that *is* on them by the flanks,
and the fatty lobe *attached* to
the liver above the kidneys,
he shall remove; 5and Aaron's
sons shall burn it on the altar
upon the burnt sacrifice, which
is on the wood that *is* on the
fire, *as* an offering made by
fire, a sweet aroma to the LORD.

6'If his offering as a sacrifice of a peace offering to the
LORD *is* of the flock, *whether*
male or female, he shall offer
it without blemish. 7If he offers a lamb as his offering,
then he shall offer it before
the LORD. 8And he shall lay
his hand on the head of his
offering, and kill it before the
tabernacle of meeting; and
Aaron's sons shall sprinkle its
blood all around on the altar.

9'Then he shall offer from
the sacrifice of the peace offering, as an offering made by

fire to the LORD, its fat *and* the
whole fat tail which he shall
remove close to the backbone.
And the fat that covers the entrails and all the fat that *is* on
the entrails, 10the two kidneys
and the fat that *is* on them by
the flanks, and the fatty lobe
attached to the liver above the
kidneys, he shall remove; 11and
the priest shall burn *them* on
the altar *as* food, an offering
made by fire to the LORD.
12'And if his offering *is* a
goat, then he shall offer it before the LORD. 13He shall lay his
hand on its head and kill it before the tabernacle of meeting;
and the sons of Aaron shall
sprinkle its blood all around
on the altar. 14Then he shall
offer from it his offering, as
an offering made by fire to the
LORD. The fat that covers the
entrails and all the fat that *is* on
the entrails, 15the two kidneys
and the fat that *is* on them by
the flanks, and the fatty lobe
attached to the liver above the
kidneys, he shall remove; 16and
the priest shall burn them on
the altar *as* food, an offering
made by fire for a sweet aroma;
all the fat *is* the LORD's.
17'*This shall be* a perpetual
statute throughout your generations in all your dwellings:
you shall eat neither fat nor
blood.'"

THE SIN OFFERING

4 Now the LORD spoke to
Moses, saying, 2"Speak to
the children of Israel, saying:
'If a person sins unintentionally against any of the commandments of the LORD *in
anything* which ought not
to be done, and does any of
them, 3if the anointed priest
sins, bringing guilt on the
people, then let him offer to
the LORD for his sin which
he has sinned a young bull
without blemish as a sin offering. 4He shall bring the bull
to the door of the tabernacle
of meeting before the LORD,
lay his hand on the bull's
head, and kill the bull before
the LORD. 5Then the anointed
priest shall take some of the
bull's blood and bring it to the
tabernacle of meeting. 6The
priest shall dip his finger in
the blood and sprinkle some
of the blood seven times before the LORD, in front of the
veil of the sanctuary. 7And
the priest shall put some
of the blood on the horns of
the altar of sweet incense before the LORD, which is in the
tabernacle of meeting; and
he shall pour the remaining
blood of the bull at the base of
the altar of the burnt offering,
which is at the door of the tabernacle of meeting. 8He shall
take from it all the fat of the
bull as the sin offering. The fat
that covers the entrails and all
the fat which *is* on the entrails,
9the two kidneys and the fat
that *is* on them by the flanks,
and the fatty lobe *attached* to
the liver above the kidneys,
he shall remove, 10as it was

taken from the bull of the
sacrifice of the peace offering; and the priest shall burn
them on the altar of the burnt
offering. 11But the bull's hide
and all its flesh, with its head
and legs, its entrails and offal— 12the whole bull he shall
carry outside the camp to a
clean place, where the ashes
are poured out, and burn it
on wood with fire; where the
ashes are poured out it shall
be burned.

13'Now if the whole con-
gregation of Israel sins unintentionally, and the thing
is hidden from the eyes of the
assembly, and they have done
something against any of the
commandments of the LORD
in anything which should
not be done, and are guilty;
14when the sin which they
have committed becomes
known, then the assembly
shall offer a young bull for
the sin, and bring it before the
tabernacle of meeting. 15And
the elders of the congregation shall lay their hands on
the head of the bull before the
LORD. Then the bull shall be
killed before the LORD. 16The
anointed priest shall bring
some of the bull's blood to the
tabernacle of meeting. 17Then
the priest shall dip his finger
in the blood and sprinkle *it*
seven times before the LORD,
in front of the veil. 18And he
shall put *some* of the blood on
the horns of the altar which
is before the LORD, which *is*
in the tabernacle of meeting;
and he shall pour the remaining blood at the base of the
altar of burnt offering, which
is at the door of the tabernacle of meeting. 19He shall
take all the fat from it and
burn *it* on the altar. 20And he
shall do with the bull as he
did with the bull as a sin offering; thus he shall do with
it. So the priest shall make
atonement for them, and it
shall be forgiven them. 21Then
he shall carry the bull outside
the camp, and burn it as he
burned the first bull. It *is* a
sin offering for the assembly.

22'When a ruler has sinned,
and done *something* unintentionally *against* any of the
commandments of the LORD
his God *in anything* which
should not be done, and is
guilty, 23or if his sin which
he has committed comes to
his knowledge, he shall bring
as his offering a kid of the
goats, a male without blemish.
24And he shall lay his hand
on the head of the goat, and
kill it at the place where they
kill the burnt offering before
the LORD. It *is* a sin offering.
25The priest shall take some of
the blood of the sin offering
with his finger, put *it* on the
horns of the altar of burnt offering, and pour its blood at
the base of the altar of burnt
offering. 26And he shall burn
all its fat on the altar, like the
fat of the sacrifice of the peace
offering. So the priest shall

make atonement for him concerning his sin, and it shall be forgiven him.

27 'If anyone of the common people sins unintentionally by doing *something against* any of the commandments of the LORD *in anything* which ought not to be done, and is guilty, 28 or if his sin which he has committed comes to his knowledge, then he shall bring as his offering a kid of the goats, a female without blemish, for his sin which he has committed. 29 And he shall lay his hand on the head of the sin offering, and kill the sin offering at the place of the burnt offering. 30 Then the priest shall take *some* of its blood with his finger, put *it* on the horns of the altar of burnt offering, and pour all *the remaining* blood at the base of the altar. 31 He shall remove all its fat, as fat is removed from the sacrifice of the peace offering; and the priest shall burn it on the altar for a sweet aroma to the LORD. So the priest shall make atonement for him, and it shall be forgiven him.

32 'If he brings a lamb as his sin offering, he shall bring a female without blemish. 33 Then he shall lay his hand on the head of the sin offering, and kill it as a sin offering at the place where they kill the burnt offering. 34 The priest shall take *some* of the blood of the sin offering with his finger, put *it* on the horns of the altar of burnt offering, and pour all *the remaining* blood at the base of the altar. 35 He shall remove all its fat, as the fat of the lamb is removed from the sacrifice of the peace offering. Then the priest shall burn it on the altar, according to the offerings made by fire to the LORD. So the priest shall make atonement for his sin that he has committed, and it shall be forgiven him.

THE TRESPASS OFFERING

5 'If a person sins in hearing the utterance of an oath, and *is* a witness, whether he has seen or known *of the matter*—if he does not tell *it*, he bears guilt.

2 'Or if a person touches any unclean thing, whether *it is* the carcass of an unclean beast, or the carcass of unclean livestock, or the carcass of unclean creeping things, and he is unaware of it, he also shall be unclean and guilty. 3 Or if he touches human uncleanness—whatever uncleanness with which a man may be defiled, and he is unaware of it—when he realizes *it*, then he shall be guilty.

4 'Or if a person swears, speaking thoughtlessly with *his* lips to do evil or to do good, whatever *it is* that a man may pronounce by an oath, and he is unaware of it—when he realizes *it*, then he shall be guilty in any of these *matters*.

5'And it shall be, when he is guilty in any of these *matters*, that he shall confess that he has sinned in that *thing;* 6and he shall bring his trespass offering to the LORD for his sin which he has committed, a female from the flock, a lamb or a kid of the goats as a sin offering. So the priest shall make atonement for him concerning his sin.

7'If he is not able to bring a lamb, then he shall bring to the LORD, for his trespass which he has committed, two turtledoves or two young pigeons: one as a sin offering and the other as a burnt offering. 8And he shall bring them to the priest, who shall offer *that* which *is* for the sin offering first, and wring off its head from its neck, but shall not divide *it* completely. 9Then he shall sprinkle *some* of the blood of the sin offering on the side of the altar, and the rest of the blood shall be drained out at the base of the altar. It *is* a sin offering. 10And he shall offer the second *as* a burnt offering according to the prescribed manner. So the priest shall make atonement on his behalf for his sin which he has committed, and it shall be forgiven him.

11'But if he is not able to *bring* two turtledoves or two young pigeons, then he who sinned shall bring for his offering one-tenth of an ephah of fine flour as a sin offering. He shall put no oil on it, nor shall he put frankincense on it, for it *is* a sin offering. 12Then he shall bring it to the priest, and the priest shall take his handful of it as a memorial portion, and burn *it* on the altar according to the offerings made by fire to the LORD. It *is* a sin offering. 13The priest shall make atonement for him, for his sin that he has committed in any of these matters; and it shall be forgiven him. *The rest* shall be the priest's as a grain offering.'"

OFFERINGS WITH RESTITUTION

14Then the LORD spoke to Moses, saying: 15"If a person commits a trespass, and sins unintentionally in regard to the holy things of the LORD, then he shall bring to the LORD as his trespass offering a ram without blemish from the flocks, with your valuation in shekels of silver according to the shekel of the sanctuary, as a trespass offering. 16And he shall make restitution for the harm that he has done in regard to the holy thing, and shall add one-fifth to it and give it to the priest. So the priest shall make atonement for him with the ram of the trespass offering, and it shall be forgiven him.

17"If a person sins, and commits any of these things which are forbidden to be done by the commandments

of the LORD, though he does
not know *it,* yet he is guilty
and shall bear his iniquity.
18And he shall bring to the
priest a ram without blemish from the flock, with your
valuation, as a trespass offering. So the priest shall make
atonement for him regard-
ing his ignorance in which he
erred and did not know *it,* and
it shall be forgiven him. 19It
is a trespass offering; he has
certainly trespassed against
the LORD."

6 And the LORD spoke
to Moses, saying: 2"If a
person sins and commits a
trespass against the LORD by
lying to his neighbor about
what was delivered to him
for safekeeping, or about a
pledge, or about a robbery,
or if he has extorted from his
neighbor, 3or if he has found
what was lost and lies concerning it, and swears falsely—in any one of these things
that a man may do in which
he sins: 4then it shall be, because he has sinned and is
guilty, that he shall restore
what he has stolen, or the
thing which he has extorted,
or what was delivered to him
for safekeeping, or the lost
thing which he found, 5or all
that about which he has sworn
falsely. He shall restore its full
value, add one-fifth more to
it, *and* give it to whomever it
belongs, on the day of his trespass offering. 6And he shall
bring his trespass offering
to the LORD, a ram without
blemish from the flock, with
your valuation, as a trespass
offering, to the priest. 7So the
priest shall make atonement
for him before the LORD, and
he shall be forgiven for any
one of these things that he
may have done in which he
trespasses."

THE LAW OF THE BURNT OFFERING

8Then the LORD spoke to
Moses, saying, 9"Command
Aaron and his sons, saying,
'This *is* the law of the burnt
offering: The burnt offering
shall be on the hearth upon
the altar all night until morning, and the fire of the altar
shall be kept burning on it.
10And the priest shall put on
his linen garment, and his
linen trousers he shall put
on his body, and take up the
ashes of the burnt offering
which the fire has consumed
on the altar, and he shall put
them beside the altar. 11Then
he shall take off his garments,
put on other garments, and
carry the ashes outside the
camp to a clean place. 12And
the fire on the altar shall be
kept burning on it; it shall
not be put out. And the priest
shall burn wood on it every
morning, and lay the burnt
offering in order on it; and
he shall burn on it the fat of
the peace offerings. 13A fire
shall always be burning on the
altar; it shall never go out.

THE LAW OF THE GRAIN OFFERING

14‘This *is* the law of the
grain offering: The sons of
Aaron shall offer it on the
altar before the LORD. 15He
shall take from it his handful
of the fine flour of the grain
offering, with its oil, and all
the frankincense which *is* on
the grain offering, and shall
burn *it* on the altar *for* a sweet
aroma, as a memorial to the
LORD. 16And the remainder
of it Aaron and his sons shall
eat; with unleavened bread it
shall be eaten in a holy place;
in the court of the tabernacle
of meeting they shall eat it. 17It
shall not be baked with leaven.
I have given it *as* their portion of My offerings made by
fire; it *is* most holy, like the sin
offering and the trespass offering. 18All the males among
the children of Aaron may eat
it. *It shall be* a statute forever
in your generations concerning the offerings made by fire
to the LORD. Everyone who
touches them must be holy.’”[a]

19And the LORD spoke to
Moses, saying, 20“This *is* the
offering of Aaron and his
sons, which they shall offer
to the LORD, *beginning* on
the day when he is anointed:
one-tenth of an ephah of fine
flour as a daily grain offering,
half of it in the morning and
half of it at night. 21It shall be
made in a pan with oil. *When
it is* mixed, you shall bring it
in. The baked pieces of the
grain offering you shall offer
for a sweet aroma to the LORD.
22The priest from among his
sons, who is anointed in his
place, shall offer it. *It is* a statute forever to the LORD. It
shall be wholly burned. 23For
every grain offering for the
priest shall be wholly burned.
It shall not be eaten.”

THE LAW OF THE SIN OFFERING

24Also the LORD spoke to
Moses, saying, 25“Speak to
Aaron and to his sons, saying, ‘This *is* the law of the sin
offering: In the place where
the burnt offering is killed, the
sin offering shall be killed before the LORD. It *is* most holy.
26The priest who offers it for
sin shall eat it. In a holy place
it shall be eaten, in the court
of the tabernacle of meeting. 27Everyone who touches
its flesh must be holy.[a] And
when its blood is sprinkled on
any garment, you shall wash
that on which it was sprinkled, in a holy place. 28But
the earthen vessel in which
it is boiled shall be broken.
And if it is boiled in a bronze
pot, it shall be both scoured
and rinsed in water. 29All the
males among the priests may
eat it. It *is* most holy. 30But no

6:18 [a] Compare Numbers 4:15 and Haggai 2:11–13
6:27 [a] Compare Numbers 4:15 and Haggai 2:11–13

sin offering from which *any* of the blood is brought into the tabernacle of meeting, to make atonement in the holy *place*,[a] shall be eaten. It shall be burned in the fire.

THE LAW OF THE TRESPASS OFFERING

7 'Likewise this *is* the law of the trespass offering (it *is* most holy): 2In the place where they kill the burnt offering they shall kill the trespass offering. And its blood he shall sprinkle all around on the altar. 3And he shall offer from it all its fat. The fat tail and the fat that covers the entrails, 4the two kidneys and the fat that *is* on them by the flanks, and the fatty lobe *attached* to the liver above the kidneys, he shall remove; 5and the priest shall burn them on the altar *as* an offering made by fire to the LORD. It *is* a trespass offering. 6Every male among the priests may eat it. It shall be eaten in a holy place. It *is* most holy. 7The trespass offering *is* like the sin offering; *there is* one law for them both: the priest who makes atonement with it shall have *it*. 8And the priest who offers anyone's burnt offering, that priest shall have for himself the skin of the burnt offering which he has offered. 9Also every grain offering that is baked in the oven and all that is prepared in the covered pan, or in a pan, shall be the priest's who offers it. 10Every grain offering, *whether* mixed with oil or dry, shall belong to all the sons of Aaron, to one *as much* as the other.

THE LAW OF PEACE OFFERINGS

11'This *is* the law of the sacrifice of peace offerings which he shall offer to the LORD: 12If he offers it for a thanksgiving, then he shall offer, with the sacrifice of thanksgiving, unleavened cakes mixed with oil, unleavened wafers anointed with oil, or cakes of blended flour mixed with oil. 13Besides the cakes, *as* his offering he shall offer leavened bread with the sacrifice of thanksgiving of his peace offering. 14And from it he shall offer one cake from each offering *as* a heave offering to the LORD. It shall belong to the priest who sprinkles the blood of the peace offering.

15'The flesh of the sacrifice of his peace offering for thanksgiving shall be eaten the same day it is offered. He shall not leave any of it until morning. 16But if the sacrifice of his offering *is* a vow or a voluntary offering, it shall be eaten the same day that he offers his sacrifice; but on the next day the remainder of it also may be eaten; 17the

6:30 [a] The Most Holy Place when capitalized

remainder of the flesh of the
sacrifice on the third day must
be burned with fire. 18And if
any of the flesh of the sacrifice
of his peace offering is eaten
at all on the third day, it shall
not be accepted, nor shall it
be imputed to him; it shall be
an abomination *to* him who
offers it, and the person who
eats of it shall bear guilt.
19'The flesh that touches
any unclean thing shall not
be eaten. It shall be burned
with fire. And as for the *clean*
flesh, all who are clean may
eat of it. 20But the person who
eats the flesh of the sacrifice
of the peace offering that *belongs* to the LORD, while he
is unclean, that person shall
be cut off from his people.
21Moreover the person who
touches any unclean thing,
such as human uncleanness,
an unclean animal, or any
abominable unclean thing,[a]
and who eats the flesh of the
sacrifice of the peace offering
that *belongs* to the LORD, that
person shall be cut off from
his people.'"

FAT AND BLOOD MAY NOT BE EATEN

22And the LORD spoke to
Moses, saying, 23"Speak to the
children of Israel, saying: 'You
shall not eat any fat, of ox or
sheep or goat. 24And the fat
of an animal that dies *naturally*, and the fat of what is
torn by wild beasts, may be
used in any other way; but
you shall by no means eat
it. 25For whoever eats the fat
of the animal of which men
offer an offering made by fire
to the LORD, the person who
eats *it* shall be cut off from
his people. 26Moreover you
shall not eat any blood in any
of your dwellings, *whether* of
bird or beast. 27Whoever eats
any blood, that person shall
be cut off from his people.'"

THE PORTION OF AARON AND HIS SONS

28Then the LORD spoke to
Moses, saying, 29"Speak to
the children of Israel, saying:
'He who offers the sacrifice
of his peace offering to the
LORD shall bring his offering
to the LORD from the sacrifice
of his peace offering. 30His
own hands shall bring the
offerings made by fire to the
LORD. The fat with the breast
he shall bring, that the breast
may be waved *as* a wave offering before the LORD. 31And the
priest shall burn the fat on the
altar, but the breast shall be
Aaron's and his sons'. 32Also
the right thigh you shall give
to the priest *as* a heave offering from the sacrifices of your
peace offerings. 33He among
the sons of Aaron, who offers
the blood of the peace offer-

7:21 [a] Following Masoretic Text, Septuagint, and Vulgate; Samaritan Pentateuch, Syriac, and Targum read *swarming thing* (compare 5:2).

ing and the fat, shall have the
right thigh for *his* part. 34For
the breast of the wave offering and the thigh of the heave
offering I have taken from the
children of Israel, from the
sacrifices of their peace offerings, and I have given them
to Aaron the priest and to his
sons from the children of Israel by a statute forever.'"

35This *is* the consecrated
portion for Aaron and his
sons, from the offerings made
by fire to the LORD, on the day
when *Moses* presented them
to minister to the LORD as
priests. 36The LORD com-
manded this to be given to
them by the children of Israel,
on the day that He anointed
them, *by* a statute forever
throughout their generations.

37This *is* the law of the
burnt offering, the grain offering, the sin offering, the
trespass offering, the conse-
crations, and the sacrifice of
the peace offering, 38which
the LORD commanded Moses
on Mount Sinai, on the day
when He commanded the
children of Israel to offer their
offerings to the LORD in the
Wilderness of Sinai.

AARON AND HIS SONS CONSECRATED

8 And the LORD spoke to
Moses, saying: 2"Take
Aaron and his sons with him,
and the garments, the anointing oil, a bull as the sin offering, two rams, and a basket
of unleavened bread; 3and
gather all the congregation
together at the door of the
tabernacle of meeting."

4So Moses did as the LORD
commanded him. And the
congregation was gathered
together at the door of the
tabernacle of meeting. 5And
Moses said to the congregation, "This *is* what the LORD
commanded to be done."

6Then Moses brought Aaron
and his sons and washed them
with water. 7And he put the
tunic on him, girded him with
the sash, clothed him with the
robe, and put the ephod on
him; and he girded him with
the intricately woven band
of the ephod, and with it tied
the ephod on him. 8Then he
put the breastplate on him,
and he put the Urim and the
Thummim[a] in the breastplate.
9And he put the turban on his
head. Also on the turban, on
its front, he put the golden
plate, the holy crown, as the
LORD had commanded Moses.

10Also Moses took the
anointing oil, and anointed
the tabernacle and all that
was in it, and consecrated
them. 11He sprinkled some
of it on the altar seven times,
anointed the altar and all its
utensils, and the laver and
its base, to consecrate them.
12And he poured some of the

8:8 [a] Literally *the Lights and the Perfections* (compare Exodus 28:30)

anointing oil on Aaron's head
and anointed him, to consecrate him.

13Then Moses brought
Aaron's sons and put tunics
on them, girded them with
sashes, and put hats on them,
as the LORD had commanded
Moses.

14And he brought the bull
for the sin offering. Then
Aaron and his sons laid their
hands on the head of the bull
for the sin offering, 15and
Moses killed *it*. Then he took
the blood, and put *some* on the
horns of the altar all around
with his finger, and purified
the altar. And he poured the
blood at the base of the altar,
and consecrated it, to make
atonement for it. 16Then he
took all the fat that *was* on the
entrails, the fatty lobe *attached*
to the liver, and the two kidneys with their fat, and Moses
burned *them* on the altar. 17But
the bull, its hide, its flesh, and
its offal, he burned with fire
outside the camp, as the LORD
had commanded Moses.

18Then he brought the ram
as the burnt offering. And
Aaron and his sons laid their
hands on the head of the ram,
19and Moses killed *it*. Then he
sprinkled the blood all around
on the altar. 20And he cut the
ram into pieces; and Moses
burned the head, the pieces,
and the fat. 21Then he washed
the entrails and the legs in
water. And Moses burned the
whole ram on the altar. It *was*
a burnt sacrifice for a sweet
aroma, an offering made by
fire to the LORD, as the LORD
had commanded Moses.

22And he brought the sec-
ond ram, the ram of consecration. Then Aaron and his
sons laid their hands on the
head of the ram, 23and Moses
killed *it*. Also he took *some* of
its blood and put it on the tip
of Aaron's right ear, on the
thumb of his right hand, and
on the big toe of his right foot.
24Then he brought Aaron's
sons. And Moses put *some* of
the blood on the tips of their
right ears, on the thumbs of
their right hands, and on the
big toes of their right feet. And
Moses sprinkled the blood all
around on the altar. 25Then
he took the fat and the fat
tail, all the fat that *was* on
the entrails, the fatty lobe
attached to the liver, the two
kidneys and their fat, and the
right thigh; 26and from the
basket of unleavened bread
that was before the LORD he
took one unleavened cake, a
cake of bread *anointed with*
oil, and one wafer, and put
them on the fat and on the
right thigh; 27and he put all
these in Aaron's hands and in
his sons' hands, and waved
them *as* a wave offering before the LORD. 28Then Moses
took them from their hands
and burned *them* on the altar,
on the burnt offering. They
were consecration offerings
for a sweet aroma. That *was*

an offering made by fire to the
LORD. 29And Moses took the
breast and waved it *as* a wave
offering before the LORD. It
was Moses' part of the ram of
consecration, as the LORD had
commanded Moses.
30Then Moses took some
of the anointing oil and some
of the blood which *was* on
the altar, and sprinkled *it* on
Aaron, on his garments, on
his sons, and on the garments
of his sons with him; and he
consecrated Aaron, his garments, his sons, and the garments of his sons with him.
31And Moses said to Aaron
and his sons, "Boil the flesh
at the door of the tabernacle
of meeting, and eat it there
with the bread that *is* in the
basket of consecration offerings, as I commanded, saying, 'Aaron and his sons shall
eat it.' 32What remains of the
flesh and of the bread you
shall burn with fire. 33And you
shall not go outside the door
of the tabernacle of meeting *for* seven days, until the
days of your consecration are
ended. For seven days he shall
consecrate you. 34As he has
done this day, *so* the LORD has
commanded to do, to make
atonement for you. 35There-
fore you shall stay *at* the door
of the tabernacle of meeting
day and night for seven days,
and keep the charge of the
LORD, so that you may not
die; for so I have been commanded." 36So Aaron and his
sons did all the things that the
LORD had commanded by the
hand of Moses.

THE PRIESTLY MINISTRY BEGINS

9 It came to pass on the
eighth day that Moses
called Aaron and his sons and
the elders of Israel. 2And he
said to Aaron, "Take for yourself a young bull as a sin offering and a ram as a burnt
offering, without blemish, and
offer *them* before the LORD.
3And to the children of Israel
you shall speak, saying, 'Take
a kid of the goats as a sin offering, and a calf and a lamb,
both of the first year, without
blemish, as a burnt offering,
4also a bull and a ram as peace
offerings, to sacrifice before
the LORD, and a grain offering
mixed with oil; for today the
LORD will appear to you.'"
5So they brought what
Moses commanded before the
tabernacle of meeting. And all
the congregation drew near
and stood before the LORD.
6Then Moses said, "This *is* the
thing which the LORD com-
manded you to do, and the
glory of the LORD will appear
to you." 7And Moses said to
Aaron, "Go to the altar, offer
your sin offering and your
burnt offering, and make
atonement for yourself and
for the people. Offer the offering of the people, and make
atonement for them, as the
LORD commanded."

8Aaron therefore went to the altar and killed the calf of the sin offering, which *was* for himself. 9Then the sons of Aaron brought the blood to him. And he dipped his finger in the blood, put *it* on the horns of the altar, and poured the blood at the base of the altar. 10But the fat, the kidneys, and the fatty lobe from the liver of the sin offering he burned on the altar, as the LORD had commanded Moses. 11The flesh and the hide he burned with fire outside the camp.

12And he killed the burnt offering; and Aaron's sons presented to him the blood, which he sprinkled all around on the altar. 13Then they presented the burnt offering to him, with its pieces and head, and he burned *them* on the altar. 14And he washed the entrails and the legs, and burned *them* with the burnt offering on the altar.

15Then he brought the people's offering, and took the goat, which *was* the sin offering for the people, and killed it and offered it for sin, like the first one. 16And he brought the burnt offering and offered it according to the prescribed manner. 17Then he brought the grain offering, took a handful *of it, and burned it* on the altar, besides the burnt sacrifice of the morning.

18He also killed the bull and the ram *as* sacrifices of peace offerings, which *were* for the people. And Aaron's sons presented to him the blood, which he sprinkled all around on the altar, 19and the fat from the bull and the ram—the fatty tail, what covers *the entrails* and the kidneys, and the fatty lobe *attached to* the liver; 20and they put the fat on the breasts. Then he burned the fat on the altar; 21but the breasts and the right thigh Aaron waved *as* a wave offering before the LORD, as Moses had commanded.

22Then Aaron lifted his hand toward the people, blessed them, and came down from offering the sin offering, the burnt offering, and peace offerings. 23And Moses and Aaron went into the tabernacle of meeting, and came out and blessed the people. Then the glory of the LORD appeared to all the people, 24and fire came out from before the LORD and consumed the burnt offering and the fat on the altar. When all the people saw *it*, they shouted and fell on their faces.

THE PROFANE FIRE OF NADAB AND ABIHU

10 Then Nadab and Abihu, the sons of Aaron, each took his censer and put fire in it, put incense on it, and offered profane fire before the LORD, which He had not commanded them. 2So fire went out from the LORD and

devoured them, and they died before the LORD. 3And Moses said to Aaron, "This is what the LORD spoke, saying:

'By those who come
near Me
I must be regarded
as holy;
And before all the people
I must be glorified.'"

So Aaron held his peace.

4Then Moses called Mishael and Elzaphan, the sons of Uzziel the uncle of Aaron, and said to them, "Come near, carry your brethren from before the sanctuary out of the camp." 5So they went near and carried them by their tunics out of the camp, as Moses had said.

6And Moses said to Aaron, and to Eleazar and Ithamar, his sons, "Do not uncover your heads nor tear your clothes, lest you die, and wrath come upon all the people. But let your brethren, the whole house of Israel, bewail the burning which the LORD has kindled. 7You shall not go out from the door of the tabernacle of meeting, lest you die, for the anointing oil of the LORD *is* upon you." And they did according to the word of Moses.

CONDUCT PRESCRIBED FOR PRIESTS

8Then the LORD spoke to Aaron, saying: 9"Do not drink wine or intoxicating drink, you, nor your sons with you, when you go into the tabernacle of meeting, lest you die. *It shall be* a statute forever throughout your generations, 10that you may distinguish between holy and unholy, and between unclean and clean, 11and that you may teach the children of Israel all the statutes which the LORD has spoken to them by the hand of Moses."

12And Moses spoke to Aaron, and to Eleazar and Ithamar, his sons who were left: "Take the grain offering that remains of the offerings made by fire to the LORD, and eat it without leaven beside the altar; for it *is* most holy. 13You shall eat it in a holy place, because it *is* your due and your sons' due, of the sacrifices made by fire to the LORD; for so I have been commanded. 14The breast of the wave offering and the thigh of the heave offering you shall eat in a clean place, you, your sons, and your daughters with you; for *they are* your due and your sons' due, *which* are given from the sacrifices of peace offerings of the children of Israel. 15The thigh of the heave offering and the breast of the wave offering they shall bring with the offerings of fat made by fire, to offer *as* a wave offering before the LORD. And it shall be yours and your sons' with you, by a statute forever, as the LORD has commanded."

16Then Moses made careful inquiry about the goat of the sin offering, and there it was—burned up. And he was angry with Eleazar and Ithamar, the sons of Aaron *who were* left, saying, 17"Why have you not eaten the sin offering in a holy place, since it *is* most holy, and *God* has given it to you to bear the guilt of the congregation, to make atonement for them before the LORD? 18See! Its blood was not brought inside the holy *place;*[a] indeed you should have eaten it in a holy *place,* as I commanded."

19And Aaron said to Moses, "Look, this day they have offered their sin offering and their burnt offering before the LORD, and such things have befallen me! *If* I had eaten the sin offering today, would it have been accepted in the sight of the LORD?" 20So when Moses heard *that,* he was content.

FOODS PERMITTED AND FORBIDDEN

11 Now the LORD spoke to Moses and Aaron, saying to them, 2"Speak to the children of Israel, saying, 'These *are* the animals which you may eat among all the animals that *are* on the earth: 3Among the animals, whatever divides the hoof, having cloven hooves *and* chewing the cud—that you may eat. 4Nevertheless these you shall not eat among those that chew the cud or those that have cloven hooves: the camel, because it chews the cud but does not have cloven hooves, is unclean to you; 5the rock hyrax, because it chews the cud but does not have cloven hooves, *is* unclean to you; 6the hare, because it chews the cud but does not have cloven hooves, *is* unclean to you; 7and the swine, though it divides the hoof, having cloven hooves, yet does not chew the cud, *is* unclean to you. 8Their flesh you shall not eat, and their carcasses you shall not touch. They *are* unclean to you.

9'These you may eat of all that *are* in the water: whatever in the water has fins and scales, whether in the seas or in the rivers—that you may eat. 10But all in the seas or in the rivers that do not have fins and scales, all that move in the water or any living thing which *is* in the water, they *are* an abomination to you. 11They shall be an abomination to you; you shall not eat their flesh, but you shall regard their carcasses as an abomination. 12Whatever in the water does not have fins or scales—that *shall be* an abomination to you.

13'And these you shall

10:18 [a] The Most Holy Place when capitalized

regard as an abomination
among the birds; they shall
not be eaten, they *are* an
abomination: the eagle, the
vulture, the buzzard, [14]the
kite, and the falcon after its
kind; [15]every raven after its
kind, [16]the ostrich, the short-
eared owl, the sea gull, and the
hawk after its kind; [17]the little
owl, the fisher owl, and the
screech owl; [18]the white owl,
the jackdaw, and the carrion
vulture; [19]the stork, the heron
after its kind, the hoopoe, and
the bat.

[20]'All flying insects that
creep on *all* fours *shall be* an
abomination to you. [21]Yet
these you may eat of every
flying insect that creeps on
all fours: those which have
jointed legs above their feet
with which to leap on the
earth. [22]These you may eat:
the locust after its kind, the
destroying locust after its
kind, the cricket after its kind,
and the grasshopper after its
kind. [23]But all *other* flying
insects which have four feet
shall be an abomination to
you.

UNCLEAN ANIMALS

[24]'By these you shall become unclean; whoever
touches the carcass of any of
them shall be unclean until
evening; [25]whoever carries
part of the carcass of any of
them shall wash his clothes
and be unclean until evening:
[26]*The carcass* of any animal
which divides the foot, but is
not cloven-hoofed or does not
chew the cud, *is* unclean to
you. Everyone who touches it
shall be unclean. [27]And whatever goes on its paws, among
all kinds of animals that go on
all fours, those *are* unclean
to you. Whoever touches any
such carcass shall be unclean
until evening. [28]Whoever carries *any such* carcass shall
wash his clothes and be unclean until evening. It *is* unclean to you.

[29]'These also *shall be* unclean to you among the creeping things that creep on the
earth: the mole, the mouse,
and the large lizard after its
kind; [30]the gecko, the mon-
itor lizard, the sand reptile,
the sand lizard, and the cha-
meleon. [31]These *are* unclean
to you among all that creep.
Whoever touches them when
they are dead shall be unclean
until evening. [32]Anything on
which *any* of them falls, when
they are dead shall be unclean,
whether *it is* any item of wood
or clothing or skin or sack,
whatever item *it is*, in which
any work is done, it must be
put in water. And it shall be
unclean until evening; then it
shall be clean. [33]Any earthen
vessel into which *any* of them
falls you shall break; and whatever *is* in it shall be unclean:
[34]in such a vessel, any ed-
ible food upon which water
falls becomes unclean, and
any drink that may be drunk

from it becomes unclean.
35And everything on which *a*
part of *any such* carcass falls
shall be unclean; *whether it*
is an oven or cooking stove,
it shall be broken down; *for*
they *are* unclean, and shall be
unclean to you. 36Nevertheless
a spring or a cistern, *in which*
there is plenty of water, shall
be clean, but whatever touches
any such carcass becomes unclean. 37And if a part of *any*
such carcass falls on any planting seed which is to be sown,
it *remains* clean. 38But if water
is put on the seed, and if *a part*
of *any such* carcass falls on it,
it *becomes* unclean to you.

39'And if any animal which
you may eat dies, he who
touches its carcass shall be
unclean until evening. 40He
who eats of its carcass shall
wash his clothes and be unclean until evening. He also
who carries its carcass shall
wash his clothes and be unclean until evening.

41'And every creeping thing
that creeps on the earth *shall*
be an abomination. It shall not
be eaten. 42Whatever crawls
on its belly, whatever goes
on *all* fours, or whatever has
many feet among all creeping things that creep on the
earth—these you shall not eat,
for they *are* an abomination.
43You shall not make yourselves abominable with any
creeping thing that creeps;
nor shall you make yourselves
unclean with them, lest you
be defiled by them. 44For I *am*
the LORD your God. You shall
therefore consecrate yourselves, and you shall be holy;
for I *am* holy. Neither shall
you defile yourselves with any
creeping thing that creeps on
the earth. 45For I *am* the LORD
who brings you up out of the
land of Egypt, to be your God.
You shall therefore be holy, for
I *am* holy.

46'This *is* the law of the animals and the birds and every
living creature that moves in
the waters, and of every creature that creeps on the earth,
47to distinguish between the
unclean and the clean, and
between the animal that may
be eaten and the animal that
may not be eaten.' "

THE RITUAL AFTER CHILDBIRTH

12 Then the LORD spoke to
Moses, saying, 2"Speak
to the children of Israel, saying: 'If a woman has con-
ceived, and borne a male
child, then she shall be unclean seven days; as in the
days of her customary im-
purity she shall be unclean.
3And on the eighth day the
flesh of his foreskin shall be
circumcised. 4She shall then
continue in the blood of *her*
purification thirty-three days.
She shall not touch any hallowed thing, nor come into
the sanctuary until the days of
her purification are fulfilled.

5'But if she bears a female

child, then she shall be unclean two weeks, as in her
customary impurity, and she
shall continue in the blood of
her purification sixty-six days.
6‘When the days of her purification are fulfilled, whether
for a son or a daughter, she
shall bring to the priest a lamb
of the first year as a burnt offering, and a young pigeon or
a turtledove as a sin offering,
to the door of the tabernacle
of meeting. 7Then he shall
offer it before the LORD, and
make atonement for her. And
she shall be clean from the
flow of her blood. This *is* the
law for her who has borne a
male or a female.
8‘And if she is not able to
bring a lamb, then she may
bring two turtledoves or two
young pigeons—one as a
burnt offering and the other
as a sin offering. So the priest
shall make atonement for her,
and she will be clean.’”

THE LAW CONCERNING LEPROSY

13 And the LORD spoke to
Moses and Aaron, say-
ing: 2“When a man has on the
skin of his body a swelling, a
scab, or a bright spot, and it
becomes on the skin of his
body *like* a leprous[a] sore, then
he shall be brought to Aaron
the priest or to one of his sons
the priests. 3The priest shall
examine the sore on the skin
of the body; and if the hair on
the sore has turned white, and
the sore appears *to be* deeper
than the skin of his body, it *is*
a leprous sore. Then the priest
shall examine him, and pronounce him unclean. 4But if
the bright spot *is* white on
the skin of his body, and does
not appear *to be* deeper than
the skin, and its hair has not
turned white, then the priest
shall isolate *the one who has*
the sore seven days. 5And the
priest shall examine him on
the seventh day; and indeed
if the sore appears to be as
it was, *and* the sore has not
spread on the skin, then the
priest shall isolate him another seven days. 6Then the
priest shall examine him
again on the seventh day; and
indeed *if* the sore has faded,
and the sore has not spread
on the skin, then the priest
shall pronounce him clean;
it *is only* a scab, and he shall
wash his clothes and be clean.
7But if the scab should at all
spread over the skin, after he
has been seen by the priest
for his cleansing, he shall
be seen by the priest again.
8And *if* the priest sees that
the scab has indeed spread
on the skin, then the priest
shall pronounce him unclean.
It *is* leprosy.
9“When the leprous sore is

13:2 [a] Hebrew *saraath,* disfiguring skin diseases, including leprosy, and so in verses 2–46 and 14:2–32

on a person, then he shall be
brought to the priest. 10And
the priest shall examine *him;*
and indeed *if* the swelling on
the skin *is* white, and it has
turned the hair white, and
there is a spot of raw flesh in
the swelling, 11it *is* an old leprosy on the skin of his body.
The priest shall pronounce
him unclean, and shall not
isolate him, for he *is* unclean.

12"And if leprosy breaks out
all over the skin, and the leprosy covers all the skin of *the*
one who has the sore, from his
head to his foot, wherever the
priest looks, 13then the priest
shall consider; and indeed *if*
the leprosy has covered all his
body, he shall pronounce *him*
clean *who has* the sore. It has
all turned white. He *is* clean.
14But when raw flesh appears
on him, he shall be unclean.
15And the priest shall examine
the raw flesh and pronounce
him to be unclean; *for* the raw
flesh *is* unclean. It *is* leprosy.
16Or if the raw flesh changes
and turns white again, he shall
come to the priest. 17And the
priest shall examine him; and
indeed *if* the sore has turned
white, then the priest shall
pronounce *him* clean *who has*
the sore. He *is* clean.

18"If the body develops
a boil in the skin, and it is
healed, 19and in the place of
the boil there comes a white
swelling or a bright spot,
reddish-white, then it shall
be shown to the priest; 20and
if, when the priest sees it, it
indeed appears deeper than
the skin, and its hair has
turned white, the priest shall
pronounce him unclean. It *is*
a leprous sore which has broken out of the boil. 21But if the
priest examines it, and indeed
there are no white hairs in it,
and it *is* not deeper than the
skin, but has faded, then the
priest shall isolate him seven
days; 22and if it should at all
spread over the skin, then the
priest shall pronounce him
unclean. It *is* a leprous sore.
23But if the bright spot stays in
one place, *and* has not spread,
it *is* the scar of the boil; and
the priest shall pronounce
him clean.

24"Or if the body receives
a burn on its skin by fire, and
the raw *flesh* of the burn becomes a bright spot, reddish-
white or white, 25then the
priest shall examine it; and
indeed *if* the hair of the bright
spot has turned white, and it
appears deeper than the skin,
it *is* leprosy broken out in the
burn. Therefore the priest
shall pronounce him unclean.
It *is* a leprous sore. 26But if
the priest examines it, and indeed *there are* no white hairs
in the bright spot, and it *is* not
deeper than the skin, but has
faded, then the priest shall
isolate him seven days. 27And
the priest shall examine him
on the seventh day. If it has at
all spread over the skin, then
the priest shall pronounce

him unclean. It *is* a leprous sore. 28But if the bright spot stays in one place, *and* has not spread on the skin, but has faded, it *is* a swelling from the burn. The priest shall pronounce him clean, for it *is* the scar from the burn.

29"If a man or woman has a sore on the head or the beard, 30then the priest shall examine the sore; and indeed if it appears deeper than the skin, *and there is* in it thin yellow hair, then the priest shall pronounce him unclean. It *is* a scaly leprosy of the head or beard. 31But if the priest examines the scaly sore, and indeed it does not appear deeper than the skin, and *there is* no black hair in it, then the priest shall isolate *the one who has* the scale seven days. 32And on the seventh day the priest shall examine the sore; and indeed *if* the scale has not spread, and there is no yellow hair in it, and the scale does not appear deeper than the skin, 33he shall shave himself, but the scale he shall not shave. And the priest shall isolate *the one who has* the scale another seven days. 34On the seventh day the priest shall examine the scale; and indeed *if* the scale has not spread over the skin, and does not appear deeper than the skin, then the priest shall pronounce him clean. He shall wash his clothes and be clean. 35But if the scale should at all spread over the skin after his cleansing, 36then the priest shall examine him; and indeed *if* the scale has spread over the skin, the priest need not seek for yellow hair. He *is* unclean. 37But if the scale appears to be at a standstill, and there is black hair grown up in it, the scale has healed. He *is* clean, and the priest shall pronounce him clean.

38"If a man or a woman has bright spots on the skin of the body, *specifically* white bright spots, 39then the priest shall look; and indeed *if* the bright spots on the skin of the body *are* dull white, it *is* a white spot *that* grows on the skin. He *is* clean.

40"As for the man whose hair has fallen from his head, he *is* bald, *but* he *is* clean. 41He whose hair has fallen from his forehead, he *is* bald on the forehead, *but* he *is* clean. 42And if there is on the bald head or bald forehead a reddish-white sore, it *is* leprosy breaking out on his bald head or his bald forehead. 43Then the priest shall examine it; and indeed *if* the swelling of the sore *is* reddish-white on his bald head or on his bald forehead, as the appearance of leprosy on the skin of the body, 44he is a leprous man. He *is* unclean. The priest shall surely pronounce him unclean; his sore *is* on his head.

45"Now the leper on whom the sore *is*, his clothes shall be

torn and his head bare; and
he shall cover his mustache,
and cry, 'Unclean! Unclean!'
46He shall be unclean. All the
days he has the sore he shall
be unclean. He *is* unclean, and
he shall dwell alone; his dwelling *shall be* outside the camp.

THE LAW CONCERNING LEPROUS GARMENTS

47"Also, if a garment has a
leprous plague[a] in it, *whether
it is* a woolen garment or a
linen garment, 48whether *it
is* in the warp or woof of linen
or wool, whether in leather or
in anything made of leather,
49and if the plague is greenish or reddish in the garment
or in the leather, whether in
the warp or in the woof, or
in anything made of leather,
it *is* a leprous plague and
shall be shown to the priest.
50The priest shall examine
the plague and isolate *that
which has* the plague seven
days. 51And he shall examine
the plague on the seventh day.
If the plague has spread in the
garment, either in the warp or
in the woof, in the leather *or* in
anything made of leather, the
plague *is* an active leprosy. It *is*
unclean. 52He shall therefore
burn that garment in which
is the plague, whether warp
or woof, in wool or in linen,
or anything of leather, for it *is*
an active leprosy; *the garment*
shall be burned in the fire.

53"But if the priest examines *it*, and indeed the plague
has not spread in the garment,
either in the warp or in the
woof, or in anything made of
leather, 54then the priest shall
command that they wash *the
thing* in which *is* the plague;
and he shall isolate it another
seven days. 55Then the priest
shall examine the plague
after it has been washed; and
indeed *if* the plague has not
changed its color, though
the plague has not spread,
it *is* unclean, and you shall
burn it in the fire; it continues eating away, *whether* the
damage *is* outside or inside.
56If the priest examines *it*,
and indeed the plague has
faded after washing it, then
he shall tear it out of the garment, whether out of the warp
or out of the woof, or out of
the leather. 57But if it appears
again in the garment, either in
the warp or in the woof, or in
anything made of leather, it *is*
a spreading *plague;* you shall
burn with fire that in which is
the plague. 58And if you wash
the garment, either warp or
woof, or whatever is made of
leather, if the plague has dis-
appeared from it, then it shall
be washed a second time, and
shall be clean.

59"This *is* the law of the
leprous plague in a garment
of wool or linen, either in the
warp or woof, or in anything

13:47 [a] A mold, fungus, or similar infestation, and so in verses 47–59

made of leather, to pronounce
it clean or to pronounce it unclean."

THE RITUAL FOR CLEANSING HEALED LEPERS

14 Then the LORD spoke
to Moses, saying, 2"This
shall be the law of the leper for
the day of his cleansing: He
shall be brought to the priest.
3And the priest shall go out of
the camp, and the priest shall
examine *him;* and indeed, *if*
the leprosy is healed in the
leper, 4then the priest shall
command to take for him who
is to be cleansed two living
and clean birds, cedar wood,
scarlet, and hyssop. 5And the
priest shall command that
one of the birds be killed in
an earthen vessel over running water. 6As for the living
bird, he shall take it, the cedar
wood and the scarlet and the
hyssop, and dip them and
the living bird in the blood
of the bird *that was* killed over
the running water. 7And he
shall sprinkle it seven times
on him who is to be cleansed
from the leprosy, and shall
pronounce him clean, and
shall let the living bird loose
in the open field. 8He who is
to be cleansed shall wash his
clothes, shave off all his hair,
and wash himself in water,
that he may be clean. After
that he shall come into the
camp, and shall stay outside
his tent seven days. 9But on
the seventh day he shall shave
all the hair off his head and
his beard and his eyebrows—
all his hair he shall shave off.
He shall wash his clothes and
wash his body in water, and he
shall be clean.

10"And on the eighth day
he shall take two male lambs
without blemish, one ewe
lamb of the first year without blemish, three-tenths *of*
an ephah of fine flour mixed
with oil as a grain offering,
and one log of oil. 11Then the
priest who makes *him* clean
shall present the man who is
to be made clean, and those
things, before the LORD, *at*
the door of the tabernacle of
meeting. 12And the priest shall
take one male lamb and offer
it as a trespass offering, and
the log of oil, and wave them
as a wave offering before the
LORD. 13Then he shall kill the
lamb in the place where he
kills the sin offering and the
burnt offering, in a holy place;
for as the sin offering *is* the
priest's, so *is* the trespass offering. It *is* most holy. 14The
priest shall take *some* of the
blood of the trespass offering,
and the priest shall put *it* on
the tip of the right ear of him
who is to be cleansed, on the
thumb of his right hand, and
on the big toe of his right foot.
15And the priest shall take
some of the log of oil, and pour
it into the palm of his own left
hand. 16Then the priest shall
dip his right finger in the oil

that *is* in his left hand, and
shall sprinkle some of the oil
with his finger seven times
before the LORD. 17 And of the
rest of the oil in his hand, the
priest shall put *some* on the tip
of the right ear of him who is
to be cleansed, on the thumb
of his right hand, and on the
big toe of his right foot, on the
blood of the trespass offering.
18 The rest of the oil that *is* in
the priest's hand he shall put
on the head of him who is to
be cleansed. So the priest shall
make atonement for him before the LORD.

19 "Then the priest shall
offer the sin offering, and
make atonement for him who
is to be cleansed from his uncleanness. Afterward he shall
kill the burnt offering. 20 And
the priest shall offer the burnt
offering and the grain offering
on the altar. So the priest shall
make atonement for him, and
he shall be clean.

21 "But if he *is* poor and cannot afford it, then he shall take
one male lamb *as* a trespass
offering to be waved, to make
atonement for him, one-tenth
of an ephah of fine flour mixed
with oil as a grain offering,
a log of oil, 22 and two turtledoves or two young pigeons,
such as he is able to afford:
one shall be a sin offering
and the other a burnt offering. 23 He shall bring them to
the priest on the eighth day
for his cleansing, to the door
of the tabernacle of meeting,
before the LORD. 24 And the
priest shall take the lamb
of the trespass offering and
the log of oil, and the priest
shall wave them *as* a wave
offering before the LORD.
25 Then he shall kill the lamb
of the trespass offering, and
the priest shall take *some* of
the blood of the trespass offering and put *it* on the tip of
the right ear of him who is to
be cleansed, on the thumb of
his right hand, and on the big
toe of his right foot. 26 And the
priest shall pour some of the
oil into the palm of his own
left hand. 27 Then the priest
shall sprinkle with his right
finger *some* of the oil that *is*
in his left hand seven times
before the LORD. 28 And the
priest shall put *some* of the oil
that *is* in his hand on the tip
of the right ear of him who is
to be cleansed, on the thumb
of the right hand, and on the
big toe of his right foot, on
the place of the blood of the
trespass offering. 29 The rest
of the oil that *is* in the priest's
hand he shall put on the head
of him who is to be cleansed,
to make atonement for him
before the LORD. 30 And he
shall offer one of the turtledoves or young pigeons, such
as he can afford— 31 such as
he is able to afford, the one
as a sin offering and the other
as a burnt offering, with the
grain offering. So the priest
shall make atonement for him
who is to be cleansed before

the LORD. 32 This *is* the law *for one* who had a leprous sore, who cannot afford the usual cleansing."

THE LAW CONCERNING LEPROUS HOUSES

33 And the LORD spoke to Moses and Aaron, saying: 34 "When you have come into the land of Canaan, which I give you as a possession, and I put the leprous plague[a] in a house in the land of your possession, 35 and he who owns the house comes and tells the priest, saying, 'It seems to me that *there is* some plague in the house,' 36 then the priest shall command that they empty the house, before the priest goes *into it* to examine the plague, that all that *is* in the house may not be made unclean; and afterward the priest shall go in to examine the house. 37 And he shall examine the plague; and indeed *if* the plague *is* on the walls of the house with ingrained streaks, greenish or reddish, which appear to be deep in the wall, 38 then the priest shall go out of the house, to the door of the house, and shut up the house seven days. 39 And the priest shall come again on the seventh day and look; and indeed *if* the plague has spread on the walls of the house, 40 then the priest shall command that they take away the stones in which *is* the plague, and they shall cast them into an unclean place outside the city. 41 And he shall cause the house to be scraped inside, all around, and the dust that they scrape off they shall pour out in an unclean place outside the city. 42 Then they shall take other stones and put *them* in the place of *those* stones, and he shall take other mortar and plaster the house.

43 "Now if the plague comes back and breaks out in the house, after he has taken away the stones, after he has scraped the house, and after it is plastered, 44 then the priest shall come and look; and indeed *if* the plague has spread in the house, it *is* an active leprosy in the house. It *is* unclean. 45 And he shall break down the house, its stones, its timber, and all the plaster of the house, and he shall carry *them* outside the city to an unclean place. 46 Moreover he who goes into the house at all while it is shut up shall be unclean until evening. 47 And he who lies down in the house shall wash his clothes, and he who eats in the house shall wash his clothes.

48 "But if the priest comes in and examines *it,* and indeed the plague has not spread in the house after the house was

14:34 [a] Decomposition by mildew, mold, dry rot, etc., and so in verses 34–53

plastered, then the priest shall
pronounce the house clean,
because the plague is healed.
49And he shall take, to cleanse
the house, two birds, cedar
wood, scarlet, and hyssop.
50Then he shall kill one of the
birds in an earthen vessel over
running water; 51and he shall
take the cedar wood, the hyssop, the scarlet, and the living bird, and dip them in the
blood of the slain bird and in
the running water, and sprinkle the house seven times.
52And he shall cleanse the
house with the blood of the
bird and the running water
and the living bird, with the
cedar wood, the hyssop, and
the scarlet. 53Then he shall
let the living bird loose outside the city in the open field,
and make atonement for the
house, and it shall be clean.

54"This *is* the law for any
leprous sore and scale, 55for
the leprosy of a garment and
of a house, 56for a swelling
and a scab and a bright spot,
57to teach when *it is* unclean
and when *it is* clean. This *is*
the law of leprosy."

THE LAW CONCERNING BODILY DISCHARGES

15 And the LORD spoke to
Moses and Aaron, say-
ing, 2"Speak to the children of
Israel, and say to them: 'When
any man has a discharge from
his body, his discharge *is* unclean. 3And this shall be his
uncleanness in regard to his
discharge—whether his body
runs with his discharge, or
his body is stopped up by his
discharge, it *is* his uncleanness. 4Every bed is unclean
on which he who has the discharge lies, and everything
on which he sits shall be unclean. 5And whoever touches
his bed shall wash his clothes
and bathe in water, and be unclean until evening. 6He who
sits on anything on which he
who has the discharge sat
shall wash his clothes and
bathe in water, and be unclean until evening. 7And he
who touches the body of him
who has the discharge shall
wash his clothes and bathe
in water, and be unclean until
evening. 8If he who has the
discharge spits on him who
is clean, then he shall wash
his clothes and bathe in water,
and be unclean until evening.
9Any saddle on which he
who has the discharge rides
shall be unclean. 10Whoever
touches anything that was
under him shall be unclean
until evening. He who carries *any of* those things shall
wash his clothes and bathe in
water, and be unclean until
evening. 11And whomever the
one who has the discharge
touches, and has not rinsed
his hands in water, he shall
wash his clothes and bathe
in water, and be unclean until
evening. 12The vessel of earth
that he who has the discharge
touches shall be broken, and

every vessel of wood shall be rinsed in water.

13'And when he who has a discharge is cleansed of his discharge, then he shall count for himself seven days for his cleansing, wash his clothes, and bathe his body in running water; then he shall be clean. 14On the eighth day he shall take for himself two turtledoves or two young pigeons, and come before the LORD, to the door of the tabernacle of meeting, and give them to the priest. 15Then the priest shall offer them, the one *as* a sin offering and the other *as* a burnt offering. So the priest shall make atonement for him before the LORD because of his discharge.

16'If any man has an emission of semen, then he shall wash all his body in water, and be unclean until evening. 17And any garment and any leather on which there is semen, it shall be washed with water, and be unclean until evening. 18Also, when a woman lies with a man, and *there is* an emission of semen, they shall bathe in water, and be unclean until evening.

19'If a woman has a discharge, *and* the discharge from her body is blood, she shall be set apart seven days; and whoever touches her shall be unclean until evening. 20Everything that she lies on during her impurity shall be unclean; also everything that she sits on shall be unclean. 21Whoever touches her bed shall wash his clothes and bathe in water, and be unclean until evening. 22And whoever touches anything that she sat on shall wash his clothes and bathe in water, and be unclean until evening. 23If *anything* is on *her* bed or on anything on which she sits, when he touches it, he shall be unclean until evening. 24And if any man lies with her at all, so that her impurity is on him, he shall be unclean seven days; and every bed on which he lies shall be unclean.

25'If a woman has a discharge of blood for many days, other than at the time of her *customary* impurity, or if it runs beyond her *usual time of* impurity, all the days of her unclean discharge shall be as the days of her *customary* impurity. She *shall be* unclean. 26Every bed on which she lies all the days of her discharge shall be to her as the bed of her impurity; and whatever she sits on shall be unclean, as the uncleanness of her impurity. 27Whoever touches those things shall be unclean; he shall wash his clothes and bathe in water, and be unclean until evening.

28'But if she is cleansed of her discharge, then she shall count for herself seven days, and after that she shall be clean. 29And on the eighth day she shall take for herself

two turtledoves or two young
pigeons, and bring them to
the priest, to the door of the
tabernacle of meeting. 30Then
the priest shall offer the one
as a sin offering and the other
as a burnt offering, and the
priest shall make atonement
for her before the LORD for the
discharge of her uncleanness.
31'Thus you shall separate
the children of Israel from
their uncleanness, lest they
die in their uncleanness when
they defile My tabernacle
that *is* among them. 32This
is the law for one who has a
discharge, and *for him* who
emits semen and is unclean
thereby, 33and for her who
is indisposed because of her
customary impurity, and for
one who has a discharge, either man or woman, and for
him who lies with her who is
unclean.'"

THE DAY OF ATONEMENT

16 Now the LORD spoke to
Moses after the death of
the two sons of Aaron, when
they offered *profane fire* before the LORD, and died; 2and
the LORD said to Moses: "Tell
Aaron your brother not to
come at *just* any time into the
Holy *Place* inside the veil, before the mercy seat which *is*
on the ark, lest he die; for I
will appear in the cloud above
the mercy seat.
3"Thus Aaron shall come
into the Holy *Place:* with *the
blood of* a young bull as a sin
offering, and *of* a ram as a
burnt offering. 4He shall put
the holy linen tunic and the
linen trousers on his body;
he shall be girded with a linen
sash, and with the linen turban he shall be attired. These
are holy garments. Therefore he shall wash his body
in water, and put them on.
5And he shall take from the
congregation of the children
of Israel two kids of the goats
as a sin offering, and one ram
as a burnt offering.
6"Aaron shall offer the bull
as a sin offering, which *is* for
himself, and make atone-
ment for himself and for his
house. 7He shall take the two
goats and present them before the LORD *at* the door of
the tabernacle of meeting.
8Then Aaron shall cast lots
for the two goats: one lot for
the LORD and the other lot for
the scapegoat. 9And Aaron
shall bring the goat on which
the LORD's lot fell, and offer
it *as* a sin offering. 10But the
goat on which the lot fell to
be the scapegoat shall be presented alive before the LORD,
to make atonement upon it,
and to let it go as the scapegoat into the wilderness.
11"And Aaron shall bring
the bull of the sin offering,
which is for himself, and make
atonement for himself and
for his house, and shall kill
the bull as the sin offering
which *is* for himself. 12Then
he shall take a censer full of

burning coals of fire from the
altar before the LORD, with his
hands full of sweet incense
beaten fine, and bring *it* inside the veil. 13And he shall
put the incense on the fire
before the LORD, that the
cloud of incense may cover
the mercy seat that *is* on the
Testimony, lest he die. 14He
shall take some of the blood
of the bull and sprinkle *it* with
his finger on the mercy seat
on the east *side;* and before
the mercy seat he shall sprinkle some of the blood with his
finger seven times.

15"Then he shall kill the
goat of the sin offering, which
is for the people, bring its
blood inside the veil, do with
that blood as he did with the
blood of the bull, and sprinkle it on the mercy seat and
before the mercy seat. 16So
he shall make atonement for
the Holy *Place*, because of the
uncleanness of the children
of Israel, and because of their
transgressions, for all their
sins; and so he shall do for the
tabernacle of meeting which
remains among them in the
midst of their uncleanness.
17There shall be no man in the
tabernacle of meeting when
he goes in to make atone-
ment in the Holy *Place*, until
he comes out, that he may
make atonement for himself,
for his household, and for all
the assembly of Israel. 18And
he shall go out to the altar
that *is* before the LORD, and
make atonement for it, and
shall take some of the blood
of the bull and some of the
blood of the goat, and put it
on the horns of the altar all
around. 19Then he shall sprinkle some of the blood on it
with his finger seven times,
cleanse it, and consecrate it
from the uncleanness of the
children of Israel.

20"And when he has made
an end of atoning for the Holy
Place, the tabernacle of meeting, and the altar, he shall
bring the live goat. 21Aaron
shall lay both his hands on
the head of the live goat, confess over it all the iniquities
of the children of Israel, and
all their transgressions, concerning all their sins, putting
them on the head of the goat,
and shall send *it* away into the
wilderness by the hand of a
suitable man. 22The goat shall
bear on itself all their iniquities to an uninhabited land;
and he shall release the goat
in the wilderness.

23"Then Aaron shall come
into the tabernacle of meeting, shall take off the linen
garments which he put on
when he went into the Holy
Place, and shall leave them
there. 24And he shall wash
his body with water in a holy
place, put on his garments,
come out and offer his burnt
offering and the burnt offering of the people, and make
atonement for himself and for
the people. 25The fat of the sin

offering he shall burn on the altar. 26And he who released the goat as the scapegoat shall wash his clothes and bathe his body in water, and afterward he may come into the camp. 27The bull *for* the sin offering and the goat *for* the sin offering, whose blood was brought in to make atonement in the Holy *Place*, shall be carried outside the camp. And they shall burn in the fire their skins, their flesh, and their offal. 28Then he who burns them shall wash his clothes and bathe his body in water, and afterward he may come into the camp.

29"*This* shall be a statute forever for you: In the seventh month, on the tenth *day* of the month, you shall afflict your souls, and do no work at all, *whether* a native of your own country or a stranger who dwells among you. 30For on that day *the priest* shall make atonement for you, to cleanse you, *that* you may be clean from all your sins before the LORD. 31It *is* a sabbath of solemn rest for you, and you shall afflict your souls. *It is* a statute forever. 32And the priest, who is anointed and consecrated to minister as priest in his father's place, shall make atonement, and put on the linen clothes, the holy garments; 33then he shall make atonement for the Holy Sanctuary,[a] and he shall make atonement for the tabernacle of meeting and for the altar, and he shall make atonement for the priests and for all the people of the assembly. 34This shall be an everlasting statute for you, to make atonement for the children of Israel, for all their sins, once a year." And he did as the LORD commanded Moses.

THE SANCTITY OF BLOOD

17 And the LORD spoke to Moses, saying, 2"Speak to Aaron, to his sons, and to all the children of Israel, and say to them, 'This *is* the thing which the LORD has commanded, saying: 3"Whatever man of the house of Israel who kills an ox or lamb or goat in the camp, or who kills *it* outside the camp, 4and does not bring it to the door of the tabernacle of meeting to offer an offering to the LORD before the tabernacle of the LORD, the guilt of bloodshed shall be imputed to that man. He has shed blood; and that man shall be cut off from among his people, 5to the end that the children of Israel may bring their sacrifices which they offer in the open field, that they may bring them to the LORD at the door of the tabernacle of meeting, to the priest, and offer them *as* peace offerings to the LORD.

16:33 [a] That is, *the Most Holy Place*

6And the priest shall sprinkle the blood on the altar of
the LORD *at* the door of the
tabernacle of meeting, and
burn the fat for a sweet aroma
to the LORD. 7They shall no
more offer their sacrifices
to demons, after whom they
have played the harlot. This
shall be a statute forever for
them throughout their generations."'
8"Also you shall say to
them: 'Whatever man of the
house of Israel, or of the
strangers who dwell among
you, who offers a burnt offering or sacrifice, 9and does
not bring it to the door of the
tabernacle of meeting, to offer
it to the LORD, that man shall
be cut off from among his
people.
10'And whatever man of
the house of Israel, or of the
strangers who dwell among
you, who eats any blood, I
will set My face against that
person who eats blood, and
will cut him off from among
his people. 11For the life of
the flesh *is* in the blood, and
I have given it to you upon the
altar to make atonement for
your souls; for it *is* the blood
that makes atonement for the
soul.' 12Therefore I said to the
children of Israel, 'No one
among you shall eat blood,
nor shall any stranger who
dwells among you eat blood.'
13"Whatever man of the
children of Israel, or of the
strangers who dwell among
you, who hunts and catches
any animal or bird that may
be eaten, he shall pour out its
blood and cover it with dust;
14for *it is* the life of all flesh. Its
blood sustains its life. Therefore I said to the children of
Israel, 'You shall not eat the
blood of any flesh, for the life
of all flesh is its blood. Whoever eats it shall be cut off.'
15"And every person who
eats what died *naturally*
or what was torn *by beasts*,
whether he is a native of your
own country or a stranger, he
shall both wash his clothes and
bathe in water, and be unclean
until evening. Then he shall
be clean. 16But if he does not
wash *them* or bathe his body,
then he shall bear his guilt."

LAWS OF SEXUAL MORALITY

18 Then the LORD spoke to
Moses, saying, 2"Speak
to the children of Israel, and
say to them: 'I am the LORD
your God. 3According to the
doings of the land of Egypt,
where you dwelt, you shall
not do; and according to the
doings of the land of Canaan,
where I am bringing you, you
shall not do; nor shall you walk
in their ordinances. 4You shall
observe My judgments and
keep My ordinances, to walk in
them: I *am* the LORD your God.
5You shall therefore keep My
statutes and My judgments,
which if a man does, he shall
live by them: I *am* the LORD.

6'None of you shall approach anyone who is near of kin to him, to uncover his nakedness: I *am* the LORD. 7The nakedness of your father or the nakedness of your mother you shall not uncover. She *is* your mother; you shall not uncover her nakedness. 8The nakedness of your father's wife you shall not uncover; it *is* your father's nakedness. 9The nakedness of your sister, the daughter of your father, or the daughter of your mother, *whether* born at home or elsewhere, their nakedness you shall not uncover. 10The nakedness of your son's daughter or your daughter's daughter, their nakedness you shall not uncover; for theirs *is* your own nakedness. 11The nakedness of your father's wife's daughter, begotten by your father—she *is* your sister—you shall not uncover her nakedness. 12You shall not uncover the nakedness of your father's sister; she *is* near of kin to your father. 13You shall not uncover the nakedness of your mother's sister, for she *is* near of kin to your mother. 14You shall not uncover the nakedness of your father's brother. You shall not approach his wife; she *is* your aunt. 15You shall not uncover the nakedness of your daughter-in-law—she *is* your son's wife—you shall not uncover her nakedness. 16You shall not uncover the nakedness of your brother's wife; it *is* your brother's nakedness. 17You shall not uncover the nakedness of a woman and her daughter, nor shall you take her son's daughter or her daughter's daughter, to uncover her nakedness. They *are* near of kin to her. It *is* wickedness. 18Nor shall you take a woman as a rival to her sister, to uncover her nakedness while the other is alive.

19'Also you shall not approach a woman to uncover her nakedness as long as she is in her *customary* impurity. 20Moreover you shall not lie carnally with your neighbor's wife, to defile yourself with her. 21And you shall not let any of your descendants pass through *the fire* to Molech, nor shall you profane the name of your God: I *am* the LORD. 22You shall not lie with a male as with a woman. It *is* an abomination. 23Nor shall you mate with any animal, to defile yourself with it. Nor shall any woman stand before an animal to mate with it. It *is* perversion.

24'Do not defile yourselves with any of these things; for by all these the nations are defiled, which I am casting out before you. 25For the land is defiled; therefore I visit the punishment of its iniquity upon it, and the land vomits out its inhabitants. 26You shall therefore keep My statutes and My judgments, and shall not

commit *any* of these abominations, *either* any of your
own nation or any stranger
who dwells among you 27(for
all these abominations the
men of the land have done,
who *were* before you, and thus
the land is defiled), 28lest the
land vomit you out also when
you defile it, as it vomited out
the nations that *were* before
you. 29For whoever commits
any of these abominations,
the persons who commit *them*
shall be cut off from among
their people.
30'Therefore you shall keep
My ordinance, so that *you*
do not commit *any* of these
abominable customs which
were committed before you,
and that you do not defile
yourselves by them: I *am* the
LORD your God.'"

MORAL AND CEREMONIAL LAWS

19 And the LORD spoke to
Moses, saying, 2"Speak
to all the congregation of the
children of Israel, and say to
them: 'You shall be holy, for I
the LORD your God *am* holy.
3'Every one of you shall
revere his mother and his father, and keep My Sabbaths: I
am the LORD your God.
4'Do not turn to idols, nor
make for yourselves molded
gods: I *am* the LORD your God.
5'And if you offer a sac-
rifice of a peace offering to
the LORD, you shall offer it of
your own free will. 6It shall
be eaten the same day you
offer *it*, and on the next day.
And if any remains until the
third day, it shall be burned
in the fire. 7And if it is eaten
at all on the third day, it *is* an
abomination. It shall not be
accepted. 8Therefore *everyone*
who eats it shall bear his iniquity, because he has profaned
the hallowed *offering* of the
LORD; and that person shall
be cut off from his people.
9'When you reap the har-
vest of your land, you shall
not wholly reap the corners
of your field, nor shall you
gather the gleanings of your
harvest. 10And you shall not
glean your vineyard, nor shall
you gather *every* grape of your
vineyard; you shall leave them
for the poor and the stranger:
I *am* the LORD your God.
11'You shall not steal, nor
deal falsely, nor lie to one
another. 12And you shall not
swear by My name falsely, nor
shall you profane the name of
your God: I *am* the LORD.
13'You shall not cheat your
neighbor, nor rob *him*. The
wages of him who is hired
shall not remain with you all
night until morning. 14You
shall not curse the deaf, nor
put a stumbling block before
the blind, but shall fear your
God: I *am* the LORD.
15'You shall do no injustice
in judgment. You shall not be
partial to the poor, nor honor
the person of the mighty. In
righteousness you shall judge

your neighbor. 16You shall not go about *as* a talebearer among your people; nor shall you take a stand against the life of your neighbor: I *am* the LORD.

17'You shall not hate your brother in your heart. You shall surely rebuke your neighbor, and not bear sin because of him. 18You shall not take vengeance, nor bear any grudge against the children of your people, but you shall love your neighbor as yourself: I *am* the LORD.

19'You shall keep My statutes. You shall not let your livestock breed with another kind. You shall not sow your field with mixed seed. Nor shall a garment of mixed linen and wool come upon you.

20'Whoever lies carnally with a woman who *is* betrothed to a man as a concubine, and who has not at all been redeemed nor given her freedom, for this there shall be scourging; *but* they shall not be put to death, because she was not free. 21And he shall bring his trespass offering to the LORD, to the door of the tabernacle of meeting, a ram as a trespass offering. 22The priest shall make atonement for him with the ram of the trespass offering before the LORD for his sin which he has committed. And the sin which he has committed shall be forgiven him.

23'When you come into the land, and have planted all kinds of trees for food, then you shall count their fruit as uncircumcised. Three years it shall be as uncircumcised to you. *It* shall not be eaten. 24But in the fourth year all its fruit shall be holy, a praise to the LORD. 25And in the fifth year you may eat its fruit, that it may yield to you its increase: I *am* the LORD your God.

26'You shall not eat *anything* with the blood, nor shall you practice divination or soothsaying. 27You shall not shave around the sides of your head, nor shall you disfigure the edges of your beard. 28You shall not make any cuttings in your flesh for the dead, nor tattoo any marks on you: I *am* the LORD.

29'Do not prostitute your daughter, to cause her to be a harlot, lest the land fall into harlotry, and the land become full of wickedness.

30'You shall keep My Sabbaths and reverence My sanctuary: I *am* the LORD.

31'Give no regard to mediums and familiar spirits; do not seek after them, to be defiled by them: I *am* the LORD your God.

32'You shall rise before the gray headed and honor the presence of an old man, and fear your God: I *am* the LORD.

33'And if a stranger dwells with you in your land, you shall not mistreat him. 34The stranger who dwells among you shall be to you as one born

among you, and you shall love
him as yourself; for you were
strangers in the land of Egypt:
I *am* the LORD your God.

35'You shall do no injustice
in judgment, in measurement
of length, weight, or volume.
36You shall have honest scales,
honest weights, an honest
ephah, and an honest hin: I
am the LORD your God, who
brought you out of the land
of Egypt.

37'Therefore you shall observe all My statutes and all
My judgments, and perform
them: I *am* the LORD.'"

PENALTIES FOR BREAKING THE LAW

20 Then the LORD spoke to
Moses, saying, 2"Again,
you shall say to the children of
Israel: 'Whoever of the children of Israel, or of the strangers who dwell in Israel, who
gives *any* of his descendants
to Molech, he shall surely be
put to death. The people of
the land shall stone him with
stones. 3I will set My face
against that man, and will
cut him off from his people,
because he has given *some* of
his descendants to Molech, to
defile My sanctuary and profane My holy name. 4And if the
people of the land should in
any way hide their eyes from
the man, when he gives *some*
of his descendants to Molech,
and they do not kill him, 5then
I will set My face against that
man and against his family;
and I will cut him off from his
people, and all who prostitute
themselves with him to commit harlotry with Molech.

6'And the person who turns
to mediums and familiar spirits, to prostitute himself with
them, I will set My face against
that person and cut him off
from his people. 7Consecrate
yourselves therefore, and be
holy, for I *am* the LORD your
God. 8And you shall keep My
statutes, and perform them:
I *am* the LORD who sanctifies
you.

9'For everyone who curses
his father or his mother shall
surely be put to death. He
has cursed his father or his
mother. His blood *shall be*
upon him.

10'The man who commits
adultery with *another* man's
wife, *he* who commits adultery
with his neighbor's wife, the
adulterer and the adulteress,
shall surely be put to death.
11The man who lies with his
father's wife has uncovered
his father's nakedness; both
of them shall surely be put
to death. Their blood *shall be*
upon them. 12If a man lies
with his daughter-in-law, both
of them shall surely be put to
death. They have committed
perversion. Their blood *shall be*
upon them. 13If a man lies with
a male as he lies with a woman,
both of them have committed
an abomination. They shall
surely be put to death. Their
blood *shall be* upon them. 14If a

man marries a woman and her
mother, it *is* wickedness. They
shall be burned with fire, both
he and they, that there may be
no wickedness among you. 15If
a man mates with an animal,
he shall surely be put to death,
and you shall kill the animal.
16If a woman approaches any
animal and mates with it, you
shall kill the woman and the
animal. They shall surely be
put to death. Their blood *is*
upon them.

17'If a man takes his sister,
his father's daughter or his
mother's daughter, and sees
her nakedness and she sees
his nakedness, it *is* a wicked
thing. And they shall be cut
off in the sight of their people.
He has uncovered his sister's
nakedness. He shall bear his
guilt. 18If a man lies with a
woman during her sickness
and uncovers her nakedness,
he has exposed her flow, and
she has uncovered the flow of
her blood. Both of them shall
be cut off from their people.

19'You shall not uncover the
nakedness of your mother's
sister nor of your father's sister, for that would uncover his
near of kin. They shall bear
their guilt. 20If a man lies with
his uncle's wife, he has uncovered his uncle's nakedness.
They shall bear their sin; they
shall die childless. 21If a man
takes his brother's wife, it *is* an
unclean thing. He has uncovered his brother's nakedness.
They shall be childless.

22'You shall therefore
keep all My statutes and all
My judgments, and perform
them, that the land where I am
bringing you to dwell may not
vomit you out. 23And you shall
not walk in the statutes of the
nation which I am casting out
before you; for they commit
all these things, and therefore
I abhor them. 24But I have said
to you, "You shall inherit their
land, and I will give it to you
to possess, a land flowing with
milk and honey." I *am* the
LORD your God, who has separated you from the peoples.
25You shall therefore distinguish between clean animals
and unclean, between unclean
birds and clean, and you shall
not make yourselves abominable by beast or by bird, or
by any kind of living thing that
creeps on the ground, which
I have separated from you as
unclean. 26And you shall be
holy to Me, for I the LORD *am*
holy, and have separated you
from the peoples, that you
should be Mine.

27'A man or a woman who is
a medium, or who has familiar
spirits, shall surely be put to
death; they shall stone them
with stones. Their blood *shall
be* upon them.' "

REGULATIONS FOR CONDUCT OF PRIESTS

21 And the LORD said to
Moses, "Speak to the
priests, the sons of Aaron, and
say to them: 'None shall defile

himself for the dead among
his people, 2except for his relatives who are nearest to him:
his mother, his father, his son,
his daughter, and his brother;
3also his virgin sister who is
near to him, who has had no
husband, for her he may defile
himself. 4*Otherwise* he shall
not defile himself, *being* a
chief man among his people,
to profane himself.

5'They shall not make any
bald *place* on their heads, nor
shall they shave the edges of
their beards nor make any
cuttings in their flesh. 6They
shall be holy to their God
and not profane the name of
their God, for they offer the
offerings of the LORD made
by fire, *and* the bread of their
God; therefore they shall be
holy. 7They shall not take a
wife *who is* a harlot or a defiled woman, nor shall they
take a woman divorced from
her husband; for *the priest*[a]
is holy to his God. 8Therefore
you shall consecrate him, for
he offers the bread of your
God. He shall be holy to you,
for I the LORD, who sanctify
you, *am* holy. 9The daughter
of any priest, if she profanes
herself by playing the harlot,
she profanes her father. She
shall be burned with fire.

10'*He who is* the high priest
among his brethren, on whose
head the anointing oil was
poured and who is conse-
crated to wear the garments,
shall not uncover his head nor
tear his clothes; 11nor shall he
go near any dead body, nor
defile himself for his father
or his mother; 12nor shall he
go out of the sanctuary, nor
profane the sanctuary of his
God; for the consecration of
the anointing oil of his God
is upon him: I *am* the LORD.
13And he shall take a wife in
her virginity. 14A widow or a
divorced woman or a defiled
woman *or* a harlot—these he
shall not marry; but he shall
take a virgin of his own people
as wife. 15Nor shall he profane
his posterity among his people, for I the LORD sanctify
him.'"

16And the LORD spoke to
Moses, saying, 17"Speak to
Aaron, saying: 'No man of
your descendants in *succeed-
ing* generations, who has *any*
defect, may approach to offer
the bread of his God. 18For any
man who has a defect shall
not approach: a man blind or
lame, who has a marred *face*
or any *limb* too long, 19a man
who has a broken foot or broken hand, 20or is a hunchback
or a dwarf, or *a man* who has a
defect in his eye, or eczema or
scab, or is a eunuch. 21No man
of the descendants of Aaron
the priest, who has a defect,
shall come near to offer the
offerings made by fire to the
LORD. He has a defect; he shall

21:7 [a] Literally *he*

not come near to offer the
bread of his God. 22He may
eat the bread of his God, *both*
the most holy and the holy;
23only he shall not go near the
veil or approach the altar, because he has a defect, lest he
profane My sanctuaries; for I
the LORD sanctify them.'"

24And Moses told *it* to
Aaron and his sons, and to
all the children of Israel.

22 Then the LORD spoke to
Moses, saying, 2"Speak
to Aaron and his sons, that
they separate themselves
from the holy things of the
children of Israel, and that
they do not profane My holy
name *by* what they dedicate
to Me: I *am* the LORD. 3Say to
them: 'Whoever of all your descendants throughout your
generations, who goes near
the holy things which the children of Israel dedicate to the
LORD, while he has uncleanness upon him, that person
shall be cut off from My presence: I *am* the LORD.

4'Whatever man of the
descendants of Aaron, who
is a leper or has a discharge,
shall not eat the holy offerings
until he is clean. And whoever
touches anything made un-
clean *by* a corpse, or a man
who has had an emission of
semen, 5or whoever touches
any creeping thing by which
he would be made unclean, or
any person by whom he would
become unclean, whatever his
uncleanness may be— 6the
person who has touched any
such thing shall be unclean
until evening, and shall not
eat the holy *offerings* unless
he washes his body with water.
7And when the sun goes down
he shall be clean; and afterward he may eat the holy *offerings*, because it *is* his food.
8Whatever dies *naturally* or
is torn *by beasts* he shall not
eat, to defile himself with it:
I *am* the LORD.

9'They shall therefore keep
My ordinance, lest they bear
sin for it and die thereby, if
they profane it: I the LORD
sanctify them.

10'No outsider shall eat
the holy *offering;* one who
dwells with the priest, or a
hired servant, shall not eat
the holy thing. 11But if the
priest buys a person with his
money, he may eat it; and one
who is born in his house may
eat his food. 12If the priest's
daughter is married to an
outsider, she may not eat of
the holy offerings. 13But if the
priest's daughter is a widow
or divorced, and has no child,
and has returned to her father's house as in her youth,
she may eat her father's food;
but no outsider shall eat it.

14'And if a man eats the
holy *offering* unintentionally,
then he shall restore a holy
offering to the priest, and add
one-fifth to it. 15They shall not
profane the holy *offerings* of
the children of Israel, which
they offer to the LORD, 16or

allow them to bear the guilt
of trespass when they eat their
holy *offerings;* for I the LORD
sanctify them.'"

OFFERINGS ACCEPTED AND NOT ACCEPTED

17And the LORD spoke to
Moses, saying, 18"Speak to
Aaron and his sons, and to all
the children of Israel, and
say to them: 'Whatever man
of the house of Israel, or of
the strangers in Israel, who
offers his sacrifice for any of
his vows or for any of his freewill offerings, which they offer
to the LORD as a burnt offering— 19*you shall offer* of your
own free will a male without
blemish from the cattle, from
the sheep, or from the goats.
20Whatever has a defect, you
shall not offer, for it shall not
be acceptable on your behalf.
21And whoever offers a sacrifice of a peace offering to
the LORD, to fulfill *his* vow, or
a freewill offering from the
cattle or the sheep, it must
be perfect to be accepted;
there shall be no defect in it.
22Those *that are* blind or broken or maimed, or have an
ulcer or eczema or scabs, you
shall not offer to the LORD,
nor make an offering by fire of
them on the altar to the LORD.
23Either a bull or a lamb that
has any limb too long or too
short you may offer *as* a freewill offering, but for a vow it
shall not be accepted.
24'You shall not offer to
the LORD what is bruised or
crushed, or torn or cut; nor
shall you make *any offering
of them* in your land. 25Nor
from a foreigner's hand shall
you offer any of these as the
bread of your God, because
their corruption *is* in them,
and defects *are* in them. They
shall not be accepted on your
behalf.'"

26And the LORD spoke to
Moses, saying: 27"When a bull
or a sheep or a goat is born,
it shall be seven days with its
mother; and from the eighth
day and thereafter it shall be
accepted as an offering made
by fire to the LORD. 28*Whether
it is* a cow or ewe, do not kill
both her and her young on
the same day. 29And when
you offer a sacrifice of thanksgiving to the LORD, offer *it* of
your own free will. 30On the
same day it shall be eaten;
you shall leave none of it until
morning: I *am* the LORD.

31"Therefore you shall keep
My commandments, and per-
form them: I *am* the LORD.
32You shall not profane My
holy name, but I will be hallowed among the children
of Israel. I *am* the LORD who
sanctifies you, 33who brought
you out of the land of Egypt, to
be your God: I *am* the LORD."

FEASTS OF THE LORD

23 And the LORD spoke to
Moses, saying, 2"Speak
to the children of Israel, and
say to them: 'The feasts of the

LORD, which you shall proclaim *to be* holy convocations,
these *are* My feasts.

THE SABBATH

3‘Six days shall work be
done, but the seventh day *is* a
Sabbath of solemn rest, a holy
convocation. You shall do no
work *on it;* it *is* the Sabbath of
the LORD in all your dwellings.

THE PASSOVER AND UNLEAVENED BREAD

4‘These *are* the feasts of
the LORD, holy convocations
which you shall proclaim at
their appointed times. 5On
the fourteenth *day* of the
first month at twilight *is* the
LORD's Passover. 6And on
the fifteenth day of the same
month *is* the Feast of Unleavened Bread to the LORD; seven
days you must eat unleavened
bread. 7On the first day you
shall have a holy convocation;
you shall do no customary
work on it. 8But you shall offer
an offering made by fire to
the LORD for seven days. The
seventh day *shall be* a holy
convocation; you shall do no
customary work *on it.*’”

THE FEAST OF FIRSTFRUITS

9And the LORD spoke to
Moses, saying, 10“Speak to the
children of Israel, and say to
them: ‘When you come into
the land which I give to you,
and reap its harvest, then
you shall bring a sheaf of the
firstfruits of your harvest to
the priest. 11He shall wave the
sheaf before the LORD, to be
accepted on your behalf; on
the day after the Sabbath the
priest shall wave it. 12And you
shall offer on that day, when
you wave the sheaf, a male
lamb of the first year, without
blemish, as a burnt offering to
the LORD. 13Its grain offering
shall be two-tenths *of an ephah*
of fine flour mixed with oil,
an offering made by fire to
the LORD, for a sweet aroma;
and its drink offering *shall be*
of wine, one-fourth of a hin.
14You shall eat neither bread
nor parched grain nor fresh
grain until the same day that
you have brought an offering to your God; *it shall be* a
statute forever throughout
your generations in all your
dwellings.

THE FEAST OF WEEKS

15‘And you shall count for
yourselves from the day after
the Sabbath, from the day that
you brought the sheaf of the
wave offering: seven Sabbaths
shall be completed. 16Count
fifty days to the day after the
seventh Sabbath; then you
shall offer a new grain offering to the LORD. 17You shall
bring from your dwellings two
wave *loaves* of two-tenths *of*
an ephah. They shall be of fine
flour; they shall be baked with
leaven. *They are* the firstfruits
to the LORD. 18And you shall
offer with the bread seven
lambs of the first year, with-

out blemish, one young bull,
and two rams. They shall be *as*
a burnt offering to the LORD,
with their grain offering and
their drink offerings, an offering made by fire for a sweet
aroma to the LORD. 19Then
you shall sacrifice one kid of
the goats as a sin offering, and
two male lambs of the first
year as a sacrifice of a peace
offering. 20The priest shall
wave them with the bread of
the firstfruits *as* a wave offering before the LORD, with
the two lambs. They shall be
holy to the LORD for the priest.
21And you shall proclaim on
the same day *that* it is a holy
convocation to you. You shall
do no customary work *on it*.
It shall be a statute forever in
all your dwellings throughout
your generations.

22'When you reap the har-
vest of your land, you shall
not wholly reap the corners of
your field when you reap, nor
shall you gather any gleaning from your harvest. You
shall leave them for the poor
and for the stranger: I *am* the
LORD your God.'"

THE FEAST OF TRUMPETS

23Then the LORD spoke to
Moses, saying, 24"Speak to
the children of Israel, saying: 'In the seventh month,
on the first *day* of the month,
you shall have a sabbath-*rest*,
a memorial of blowing of
trumpets, a holy convocation.
25You shall do no customary
work *on it;* and you shall offer
an offering made by fire to
the LORD.'"

THE DAY OF ATONEMENT

26And the LORD spoke to
Moses, saying: 27"Also the
tenth *day* of this seventh
month *shall be* the Day of
Atonement. It shall be a holy
convocation for you; you shall
afflict your souls, and offer
an offering made by fire to
the LORD. 28And you shall do
no work on that same day, for
it *is* the Day of Atonement,
to make atonement for you
before the LORD your God.
29For any person who is not
afflicted *in soul* on that same
day shall be cut off from his
people. 30And any person
who does any work on that
same day, that person I will
destroy from among his people. 31You shall do no manner
of work; *it shall be* a statute
forever throughout your generations in all your dwellings.
32It *shall be* to you a sabbath
of *solemn* rest, and you shall
afflict your souls; on the ninth
day of the month at evening,
from evening to evening, you
shall celebrate your sabbath."

THE FEAST OF TABERNACLES

33Then the LORD spoke to
Moses, saying, 34"Speak to the
children of Israel, saying: 'The
fifteenth day of this seventh
month *shall be* the Feast of
Tabernacles *for* seven days to

the LORD. [35]On the first day
there shall be a holy convocation. You shall do no customary work *on it.* [36]*For* seven
days you shall offer an offering
made by fire to the LORD. On
the eighth day you shall have
a holy convocation, and you
shall offer an offering made by
fire to the LORD. It *is* a sacred
assembly, *and* you shall do no
customary work *on it.*

[37]'These *are* the feasts of
the LORD which you shall
proclaim *to be* holy convocations, to offer an offering
made by fire to the LORD, a
burnt offering and a grain offering, a sacrifice and drink
offerings, everything on its
day— [38]besides the Sabbaths
of the LORD, besides your gifts,
besides all your vows, and besides all your freewill offerings
which you give to the LORD.

[39]'Also on the fifteenth day
of the seventh month, when
you have gathered in the fruit
of the land, you shall keep the
feast of the LORD *for* seven
days; on the first day *there
shall be* a sabbath-*rest*, and on
the eighth day a sabbath-*rest*.
[40]And you shall take for yourselves on the first day the fruit
of beautiful trees, branches
of palm trees, the boughs of
leafy trees, and willows of the
brook; and you shall rejoice
before the LORD your God for
seven days. [41]You shall keep
it as a feast to the LORD for
seven days in the year. *It shall
be* a statute forever in your
generations. You shall celebrate it in the seventh month.
[42]You shall dwell in booths
for seven days. All who are
native Israelites shall dwell
in booths, [43]that your generations may know that I made
the children of Israel dwell in
booths when I brought them
out of the land of Egypt: I *am*
the LORD your God.' "

[44]So Moses declared to the
children of Israel the feasts of
the LORD.

CARE OF THE TABERNACLE LAMPS

24 Then the LORD spoke to
Moses, saying: [2]"Com-
mand the children of Israel
that they bring to you pure
oil of pressed olives for the
light, to make the lamps burn
continually. [3]Outside the veil
of the Testimony, in the tabernacle of meeting, Aaron
shall be in charge of it from
evening until morning before
the LORD continually; *it shall
be* a statute forever in your
generations. [4]He shall be in
charge of the lamps on the
pure *gold* lampstand before
the LORD continually.

THE BREAD OF THE TABERNACLE

[5]"And you shall take fine
flour and bake twelve cakes
with it. Two-tenths *of an ephah*
shall be in each cake. [6]You
shall set them in two rows, six
in a row, on the pure *gold* table
before the LORD. [7]And you

shall put pure frankincense
on *each* row, that it may be
on the bread for a memorial,
an offering made by fire to
the LORD. 8Every Sabbath he
shall set it in order before the
LORD continually, *being taken*
from the children of Israel by
an everlasting covenant. 9And
it shall be for Aaron and his
sons, and they shall eat it in a
holy place; for it *is* most holy
to him from the offerings of
the LORD made by fire, by a
perpetual statute."

THE PENALTY FOR BLASPHEMY

10Now the son of an Israelite
woman, whose father *was* an
Egyptian, went out among the
children of Israel; and this Israelite *woman's* son and a man
of Israel fought each other in
the camp. 11And the Israelite
woman's son blasphemed the
name *of the LORD* and cursed;
and so they brought him to
Moses. (His mother's name
was Shelomith the daughter
of Dibri, of the tribe of Dan.)
12Then they put him in custody, that the mind of the LORD
might be shown to them.

13And the LORD spoke to
Moses, saying, 14"Take outside
the camp him who has cursed;
then let all who heard *him* lay
their hands on his head, and
let all the congregation stone
him.

15"Then you shall speak to
the children of Israel, saying:
'Whoever curses his God shall
bear his sin. 16And whoever
blasphemes the name of the
LORD shall surely be put to
death. All the congregation
shall certainly stone him, the
stranger as well as him who
is born in the land. When he
blasphemes the name *of the
LORD*, he shall be put to death.

17'Whoever kills any man
shall surely be put to death.
18Whoever kills an animal
shall make it good, animal
for animal.

19'If a man causes disfigurement of his neighbor, as he
has done, so shall it be done to
him— 20fracture for fracture,
eye for eye, tooth for tooth; as
he has caused disfigurement
of a man, so shall it be done
to him. 21And whoever kills
an animal shall restore it; but
whoever kills a man shall be
put to death. 22You shall have
the same law for the stranger
and for one from your own
country; for I *am* the LORD
your God.'"

23Then Moses spoke to the
children of Israel; and they
took outside the camp him
who had cursed, and stoned
him with stones. So the children of Israel did as the LORD
commanded Moses.

THE SABBATH OF THE SEVENTH YEAR

25 And the LORD spoke to
Moses on Mount Sinai,
saying, 2"Speak to the children
of Israel, and say to them:
'When you come into the land

which I give you, then the land shall keep a sabbath to the LORD. 3Six years you shall sow your field, and six years you shall prune your vineyard, and gather its fruit; 4but in the seventh year there shall be a sabbath of solemn rest for the land, a sabbath to the LORD. You shall neither sow your field nor prune your vineyard. 5What grows of its own accord of your harvest you shall not reap, nor gather the grapes of your untended vine, *for* it is a year of rest for the land. 6And the sabbath *produce* of the land shall be food for you: for you, your male and female servants, your hired man, and the stranger who dwells with you, 7for your livestock and the beasts that *are* in your land—all its produce shall be for food.

THE YEAR OF JUBILEE

8'And you shall count seven sabbaths of years for yourself, seven times seven years; and the time of the seven sabbaths of years shall be to you forty-nine years. 9Then you shall cause the trumpet of the Jubilee to sound on the tenth *day* of the seventh month; on the Day of Atonement you shall make the trumpet to sound throughout all your land. 10And you shall consecrate the fiftieth year, and proclaim liberty throughout *all* the land to all its inhabitants. It shall be a Jubilee for you; and each of you shall return to his possession, and each of you shall return to his family. 11That fiftieth year shall be a Jubilee to you; in it you shall neither sow nor reap what grows of its own accord, nor gather *the grapes* of your untended vine. 12For it *is* the Jubilee; it shall be holy to you; you shall eat its produce from the field.

13'In this Year of Jubilee, each of you shall return to his possession. 14And if you sell anything to your neighbor or buy from your neighbor's hand, you shall not oppress one another. 15According to the number of years after the Jubilee you shall buy from your neighbor, and according to the number of years of crops he shall sell to you. 16According to the multitude of years you shall increase its price, and according to the fewer number of years you shall diminish its price; for he sells to you *according* to the number *of the years* of the crops. 17Therefore you shall not oppress one another, but you shall fear your God; for I *am* the LORD your God.

PROVISIONS FOR THE SEVENTH YEAR

18'So you shall observe My statutes and keep My judgments, and perform them; and you will dwell in the land in safety. 19Then the land will yield its fruit, and you will eat your fill, and dwell there in safety.

[20]'And if you say, "What
shall we eat in the seventh
year, since we shall not sow
nor gather in our produce?"
[21]Then I will command My
blessing on you in the sixth
year, and it will bring forth
produce enough for three
years. [22]And you shall sow in
the eighth year, and eat old
produce until the ninth year;
until its produce comes in,
you shall eat *of* the old *harvest*.

REDEMPTION OF PROPERTY

[23]'The land shall not be
sold permanently, for the land
is Mine; for you *are* strangers and sojourners with Me.
[24]And in all the land of your
possession you shall grant redemption of the land.

[25]'If one of your brethren
becomes poor, and has sold
some of his possession, and if
his redeeming relative comes
to redeem it, then he may redeem what his brother sold.
[26]Or if the man has no one
to redeem it, but he himself
becomes able to redeem it,
[27]then let him count the years
since its sale, and restore the
remainder to the man to
whom he sold it, that he may
return to his possession. [28]But
if he is not able to have *it* restored to himself, then what
was sold shall remain in the
hand of him who bought it
until the Year of Jubilee; and
in the Jubilee it shall be released, and he shall return to
his possession.

[29]'If a man sells a house in
a walled city, then he may redeem it within a whole year
after it is sold; *within* a full year
he may redeem it. [30]But if it
is not redeemed within the
space of a full year, then the
house in the walled city shall
belong permanently to him
who bought it, throughout his
generations. It shall not be released in the Jubilee. [31]How-
ever the houses of villages
which have no wall around
them shall be counted as the
fields of the country. They may
be redeemed, and they shall be
released in the Jubilee. [32]Nev-
ertheless the cities of the Levites, *and* the houses in the
cities of their possession, the
Levites may redeem at any
time. [33]And if a man purchases
a house from the Levites, then
the house that was sold in the
city of his possession shall be
released in the Jubilee; for
the houses in the cities of the
Levites *are* their possession
among the children of Israel.
[34]But the field of the common-
land of their cities may not be
sold, for it *is* their perpetual
possession.

LENDING TO THE POOR

[35]'If one of your brethren
becomes poor, and falls into
poverty among you, then you
shall help him, like a stranger
or a sojourner, that he may
live with you. [36]Take no usury
or interest from him; but fear
your God, that your brother

may live with you. 37You shall not lend him your money for usury, nor lend him your food at a profit. 38I *am* the LORD your God, who brought you out of the land of Egypt, to give you the land of Canaan *and* to be your God.

THE LAW CONCERNING SLAVERY

39'And if *one of* your brethren *who dwells* by you becomes poor, and sells himself to you, you shall not compel him to serve as a slave. 40As a hired servant *and* a sojourner he shall be with you, *and* shall serve you until the Year of Jubilee. 41And *then* he shall depart from you—he and his children with him—and shall return to his own family. He shall return to the possession of his fathers. 42For they *are* My servants, whom I brought out of the land of Egypt; they shall not be sold as slaves. 43You shall not rule over him with rigor, but you shall fear your God. 44And as for your male and female slaves whom you may have—from the nations that are around you, from them you may buy male and female slaves. 45Moreover you may buy the children of the strangers who dwell among you, and their families who are with you, which they beget in your land; and they shall become your property. 46And you may take them as an inheritance for your children after you, to inherit *them as* a possession; they shall be your permanent slaves. But regarding your brethren, the children of Israel, you shall not rule over one another with rigor.

47'Now if a sojourner or stranger close to you becomes rich, and *one of* your brethren *who dwells* by him becomes poor, and sells himself to the stranger *or* sojourner close to you, or to a member of the stranger's family, 48after he is sold he may be redeemed again. One of his brothers may redeem him; 49or his uncle or his uncle's son may redeem him; or *anyone* who is near of kin to him in his family may redeem him; or if he is able he may redeem himself. 50Thus he shall reckon with him who bought him: The price of his release shall be according to the number of years, from the year that he was sold to him until the Year of Jubilee; *it shall be* according to the time of a hired servant for him. 51If *there are* still many years *remaining*, according to them he shall repay the price of his redemption from the money with which he was bought. 52And if there remain but a few years until the Year of Jubilee, then he shall reckon with him, *and* according to his years he shall repay him the price of his redemption. 53He shall be with him as a yearly hired servant, and he shall not rule with rigor over him in your sight. 54And

if he is not redeemed in these
years, then he shall be released
in the Year of Jubilee—he and
his children with him. 55For
the children of Israel *are* servants to Me; they *are* My servants whom I brought out of
the land of Egypt: I *am* the
LORD your God.

PROMISE OF BLESSING AND RETRIBUTION

26 'You shall not make idols for yourselves;
neither a carved image nor a *sacred* pillar shall you rear up for yourselves;
nor shall you set up an engraved stone in your land, to bow down to it;
for I *am* the LORD your God.
2 You shall keep My Sabbaths and reverence My sanctuary:
I *am* the LORD.

3 'If you walk in My statutes and keep My commandments, and perform them,
4 then I will give you rain in its season, the land shall yield its produce, and the trees of the field shall yield their fruit.
5 Your threshing shall last till the time of vintage, and the vintage shall last till the time of sowing;
you shall eat your bread to the full, and dwell in your land safely.
6 I will give peace in the land, and you shall lie down, and none will make *you* afraid;
I will rid the land of evil beasts,
and the sword will not go through your land.
7 You will chase your enemies, and they shall fall by the sword before you.
8 Five of you shall chase a hundred, and a hundred of you shall put ten thousand to flight;
your enemies shall fall by the sword before you.

9 'For I will look on you favorably and make you fruitful, multiply you and confirm My covenant with you.
10 You shall eat the old harvest, and clear out the old because of the new.
11 I will set My tabernacle among you, and My soul shall not abhor you.
12 I will walk among you and be your God, and you shall be My people.
13 I *am* the LORD your God, who brought you out of the land of Egypt, that *you* should not be their slaves;
I have broken the bands of your yoke and made you walk upright.

14 'But if you do not obey Me, and do not observe all these commandments,
15 and if you despise My statutes, or if your soul abhors My judgments, so

that you do not perform
all My commandments,
but break My covenant,
16 I also will do this to you:
I will even appoint terror
over you, wasting disease
and fever which shall
consume the eyes and
cause sorrow of heart.
And you shall sow your
seed in vain, for your
enemies shall eat it.
17 I will set My face against
you, and you shall be defeated by your enemies.
Those who hate you shall
reign over you, and you
shall flee when no one
pursues you.

18 'And after all this, if you do
not obey Me, then I will
punish you seven times
more for your sins.
19 I will break the pride of
your power;
I will make your heavens
like iron and your earth
like bronze.
20 And your strength shall be
spent in vain;
for your land shall not yield
its produce, nor shall the
trees of the land yield
their fruit.

21 'Then, if you walk contrary to Me, and are not
willing to obey Me, I will
bring on you seven times
more plagues, according
to your sins.
22 I will also send wild beasts
among you, which shall
rob you of your children,
destroy your livestock,
and make you few in
number;
and your highways shall be
desolate.

23 'And if by these things you
are not reformed by Me,
but walk contrary to Me,
24 then I also will walk contrary to you, and I will
punish you yet seven
times for your sins.
25 And I will bring a sword
against you that will execute the vengeance of
the covenant;
when you are gathered together within your cities I will send pestilence
among you;
and you shall be delivered
into the hand of the
enemy.
26 When I have cut off your
supply of bread, ten
women shall bake your
bread in one oven, and
they shall bring back
your bread by weight,
and you shall eat and not
be satisfied.

27 'And after all this, if you do
not obey Me, but walk
contrary to Me,
28 then I also will walk contrary to you in fury;
and I, even I, will chastise
you seven times for your
sins.
29 You shall eat the flesh of
your sons, and you shall

eat the flesh of your daughters.
30 I will destroy your high places, cut down your incense altars, and cast your carcasses on the lifeless forms of your idols;
and My soul shall abhor you.
31 I will lay your cities waste and bring your sanctuaries to desolation, and I will not smell the fragrance of your sweet aromas.
32 I will bring the land to desolation, and your enemies who dwell in it shall be astonished at it.
33 I will scatter you among the nations and draw out a sword after you;
your land shall be desolate and your cities waste.
34 Then the land shall enjoy its sabbaths as long as it lies desolate and you *are* in your enemies' land;
then the land shall rest and enjoy its sabbaths.
35 As long as *it* lies desolate it shall rest—
for the time it did not rest on your sabbaths when you dwelt in it.

36 'And as for those of you who are left, I will send faintness into their hearts in the lands of their enemies;
the sound of a shaken leaf shall cause them to flee;
they shall flee as though fleeing from a sword, and they shall fall when no one pursues.
37 They shall stumble over one another, as it were before a sword, when no one pursues;
and you shall have no *power* to stand before your enemies.
38 You shall perish among the nations, and the land of your enemies shall eat you up.
39 And those of you who are left shall waste away in their iniquity in your enemies' lands;
also in their fathers' iniquities, which are with them, they shall waste away.

40 '*But* if they confess their iniquity and the iniquity of their fathers, with their unfaithfulness in which they were unfaithful to Me, and that they also have walked contrary to Me,
41 and *that* I also have walked contrary to them and have brought them into the land of their enemies;
if their uncircumcised hearts are humbled, and they accept their guilt—
42 then I will remember My covenant with Jacob, and My covenant with Isaac and My covenant with Abraham I will remember;

I will remember the land.
43 The land also shall be left
empty by them, and will
enjoy its sabbaths while
it lies desolate without
them;
they will accept their guilt,
because they despised
My judgments and be-
cause their soul abhorred
My statutes.
44 Yet for all that, when they
are in the land of their
enemies, I will not cast
them away, nor shall I
abhor them, to utterly
destroy them and break
My covenant with them;
for I *am* the LORD their God.
45 But for their sake I will remember the covenant of
their ancestors, whom I
brought out of the land
of Egypt in the sight of
the nations, that I might
be their God:
I *am* the LORD.'"

46These *are* the statutes and
judgments and laws which the
LORD made between Himself
and the children of Israel on
Mount Sinai by the hand of
Moses.

REDEEMING PERSONS AND PROPERTY DEDICATED TO GOD

27 Now the LORD spoke to
Moses, saying, 2"Speak
to the children of Israel, and
say to them: 'When a man consecrates by a vow certain persons to the LORD, according to
your valuation, 3if your valuation is of a male from twenty
years old up to sixty years old,
then your valuation shall be
fifty shekels of silver, according to the shekel of the sanctuary. 4If it *is* a female, then
your valuation shall be thirty
shekels; 5and if from five years
old up to twenty years old,
then your valuation for a male
shall be twenty shekels, and
for a female ten shekels; 6and
if from a month old up to five
years old, then your valuation
for a male shall be five shekels of silver, and for a female
your valuation shall be three
shekels of silver; 7and if from
sixty years old and above, if *it*
is a male, then your valuation
shall be fifteen shekels, and for
a female ten shekels.

8'But if he is too poor to pay
your valuation, then he shall
present himself before the
priest, and the priest shall set
a value for him; according to
the ability of him who vowed,
the priest shall value him.

9'If *it is* an animal that men
may bring as an offering to
the LORD, all that *anyone* gives
to the LORD shall be holy. 10He
shall not substitute it or exchange it, good for bad or bad
for good; and if he at all exchanges animal for animal,
then both it and the one exchanged for it shall be holy.
11If *it is* an unclean animal
which they do not offer as a
sacrifice to the LORD, then
he shall present the animal

before the priest; 12and the
priest shall set a value for it,
whether it is good or bad; as
you, the priest, value it, so it
shall be. 13But if he *wants* at all
to redeem it, then he must add
one-fifth to your valuation.

14'And when a man dedi-
cates his house *to be* holy to
the LORD, then the priest shall
set a value for it, whether it is
good or bad; as the priest val-
ues it, so it shall stand. 15If he
who dedicated it *wants to* redeem his house, then he must
add one-fifth of the money
of your valuation to it, and it
shall be his.

16'If a man dedicates to the
LORD *part* of a field of his possession, then your valuation
shall be according to the seed
for it. A homer of barley seed
shall be valued at fifty shekels
of silver. 17If he dedicates his
field from the Year of Jubilee,
according to your valuation it
shall stand. 18But if he dedicates his field after the Jubilee,
then the priest shall reckon to
him the money due according
to the years that remain till the
Year of Jubilee, and it shall be
deducted from your valuation.
19And if he who dedicates the
field ever wishes to redeem
it, then he must add one-fifth
of the money of your valuation to it, and it shall belong
to him. 20But if he does not
want to redeem the field, or if
he has sold the field to another
man, it shall not be redeemed
anymore; 21but the field, when
it is released in the Jubilee,
shall be holy to the LORD, as
a devoted field; it shall be the
possession of the priest.

22'And if a man dedicates to
the LORD a field which he has
bought, which is not the field
of his possession, 23then the
priest shall reckon to him the
worth of your valuation, up
to the Year of Jubilee, and he
shall give your valuation on
that day *as* a holy *offering* to
the LORD. 24In the Year of Jubilee the field shall return to
him from whom it was bought,
to the one who *owned* the land
as a possession. 25And all your
valuations shall be according
to the shekel of the sanctuary:
twenty gerahs to the shekel.

26'But the firstborn of the
animals, which should be the
LORD's firstborn, no man shall
dedicate; whether *it is* an ox or
sheep, it *is* the LORD's. 27And if
it is an unclean animal, then
he shall redeem *it* according
to your valuation, and shall
add one-fifth to it; or if it is not
redeemed, then it shall be sold
according to your valuation.

28'Nevertheless no devoted
offering that a man may devote
to the LORD of all that he has,
both man and beast, or the
field of his possession, shall
be sold or redeemed; every devoted *offering is* most holy to
the LORD. 29No person under
the ban, who may become
doomed to destruction among
men, shall be redeemed, *but*
shall surely be put to death.

30And all the tithe of the land,
whether of the seed of the land
or of the fruit of the tree, *is*
the LORD's. It *is* holy to the
LORD. 31If a man wants at all
to redeem *any* of his tithes,
he shall add one-fifth to it.
32And concerning the tithe of
the herd or the flock, of whatever passes under the rod, the
tenth one shall be holy to the
LORD. 33He shall not inquire
whether it is good or bad, nor
shall he exchange it; and if he
exchanges it at all, then both
it and the one exchanged for
it shall be holy; it shall not be
redeemed.'"

34These *are* the commandments which the LORD commanded Moses for the children
of Israel on Mount Sinai.

THE FOURTH BOOK OF MOSES CALLED NUMBERS

THE FIRST CENSUS OF ISRAEL

1 Now the LORD spoke to
Moses in the Wilderness
of Sinai, in the tabernacle of
meeting, on the first *day* of
the second month, in the second year after they had come
out of the land of Egypt, saying: 2"Take a census of all the
congregation of the children
of Israel, by their families, by
their fathers' houses, according to the number of names,
every male individually, 3from
twenty years old and above—
all who *are able to* go to war
in Israel. You and Aaron shall
number them by their armies.
4And with you there shall be a
man from every tribe, each one
the head of his father's house.

5"These are the names of
the men who shall stand with
you: from Reuben, Elizur the
son of Shedeur; 6from Simeon, Shelumiel the son of
Zurishaddai; 7from Judah,
Nahshon the son of Amminadab; 8from Issachar, Nethanel
the son of Zuar; 9from Zebulun, Eliab the son of Helon;
10from the sons of Joseph:
from Ephraim, Elishama the
son of Ammihud; from Manasseh, Gamaliel the son of
Pedahzur; 11from Benjamin,
Abidan the son of Gideoni;
12from Dan, Ahiezer the son
of Ammishaddai; 13from
Asher, Pagiel the son of Ocran;
14from Gad, Eliasaph the
son of Deuel;[a] 15from Naphtali, Ahira the son of Enan."

1:14 [a] Spelled *Reuel* in 2:14

16These *were* chosen from the
congregation, leaders of their
fathers' tribes, heads of the
divisions in Israel.

17Then Moses and Aaron
took these men who had
been mentioned by name,
18and they assembled all the
congregation together on
the first *day* of the second
month; and they recited their
ancestry by families, by their
fathers' houses, according to
the number of names, from
twenty years old and above,
each one individually. 19As the
LORD commanded Moses, so
he numbered them in the Wilderness of Sinai.

20Now the children of Reuben, Israel's oldest son, their
genealogies by their families, by their fathers' house,
according to the number of
names, every male individually, from twenty years old
and above, all who *were able
to* go to war: 21those who were
numbered of the tribe of Reuben *were* forty-six thousand
five hundred.

22From the children of
Simeon, their genealogies by
their families, by their fathers'
house, of those who were
numbered, according to the
number of names, every male
individually, from twenty
years old and above, all who
were able to go to war: 23those
who were numbered of the
tribe of Simeon *were* fifty-
nine thousand three hundred.

24From the children of Gad,
their genealogies by their families, by their fathers' house,
according to the number of
names, from twenty years old
and above, all who *were able
to* go to war: 25those who were
numbered of the tribe of Gad
were forty-five thousand six
hundred and fifty.

26From the children of
Judah, their genealogies by
their families, by their fathers'
house, according to the number of names, from twenty
years old and above, all who
were able to go to war: 27those
who were numbered of the
tribe of Judah *were* seventy-
four thousand six hundred.

28From the children of Issachar, their genealogies by
their families, by their fathers'
house, according to the number of names, from twenty
years old and above, all who
were able to go to war: 29those
who were numbered of the
tribe of Issachar *were* fifty-
four thousand four hundred.

30From the children of
Zebulun, their genealogies by
their families, by their fathers'
house, according to the number of names, from twenty
years old and above, all who
were able to go to war: 31those
who were numbered of the
tribe of Zebulun *were* fifty-
seven thousand four hundred.

32From the sons of Joseph,
the children of Ephraim, their
genealogies by their families, by their fathers' house,
according to the number of

names, from twenty years old and above, all who *were able to* go to war: 33those who were numbered of the tribe of Ephraim *were* forty thousand five hundred.

34From the children of Manasseh, their genealogies by their families, by their fathers' house, according to the number of names, from twenty years old and above, all who *were able to* go to war: 35those who were numbered of the tribe of Manasseh *were* thirty-two thousand two hundred.

36From the children of Benjamin, their genealogies by their families, by their fathers' house, according to the number of names, from twenty years old and above, all who *were able to* go to war: 37those who were numbered of the tribe of Benjamin *were* thirty-five thousand four hundred.

38From the children of Dan, their genealogies by their families, by their fathers' house, according to the number of names, from twenty years old and above, all who *were able to* go to war: 39those who were numbered of the tribe of Dan *were* sixty-two thousand seven hundred.

40From the children of Asher, their genealogies by their families, by their fathers' house, according to the number of names, from twenty years old and above, all who *were able to* go to war: 41those who were numbered of the tribe of Asher *were* forty-one thousand five hundred.

42From the children of Naphtali, their genealogies by their families, by their fathers' house, according to the number of names, from twenty years old and above, all who *were able to* go to war: 43those who were numbered of the tribe of Naphtali *were* fifty-three thousand four hundred.

44These are the ones who were numbered, whom Moses and Aaron numbered, with the leaders of Israel, twelve men, each one representing his father's house. 45So all who were numbered of the children of Israel, by their fathers' houses, from twenty years old and above, all who *were able to* go to war in Israel— 46all who were numbered were six hundred and three thousand five hundred and fifty.

47But the Levites were not numbered among them by their fathers' tribe; 48for the LORD had spoken to Moses, saying: 49"Only the tribe of Levi you shall not number, nor take a census of them among the children of Israel; 50but you shall appoint the Levites over the tabernacle of the Testimony, over all its furnishings, and over all things that belong to it; they shall carry the tabernacle and all its furnishings; they shall attend to it and camp around the tab-

ernacle. 51And when the tabernacle is to go forward, the
Levites shall take it down; and
when the tabernacle is to be
set up, the Levites shall set it
up. The outsider who comes
near shall be put to death.
52The children of Israel shall
pitch their tents, everyone by
his own camp, everyone by his
own standard, according to
their armies; 53but the Levites
shall camp around the tabernacle of the Testimony, that
there may be no wrath on the
congregation of the children
of Israel; and the Levites shall
keep charge of the tabernacle
of the Testimony."

54Thus the children of Israel did; according to all that
the LORD commanded Moses,
so they did.

THE TRIBES AND LEADERS BY ARMIES

2 And the LORD spoke to
Moses and Aaron, saying:
2"Everyone of the children of
Israel shall camp by his own
standard, beside the emblems
of his father's house; they
shall camp some distance
from the tabernacle of meeting. 3On the east side, toward
the rising of the sun, those of
the standard of the forces with
Judah shall camp according
to their armies; and Nahshon
the son of Amminadab *shall
be* the leader of the children
of Judah." 4And his army was
numbered at seventy-four
thousand six hundred.

5"Those who camp next to
him *shall be* the tribe of Issachar, and Nethanel the son of
Zuar *shall be* the leader of the
children of Issachar." 6And his
army was numbered at fifty-
four thousand four hundred.

7"Then *comes* the tribe of
Zebulun, and Eliab the son of
Helon *shall be* the leader of the
children of Zebulun." 8And his
army was numbered at fifty-
seven thousand four hundred.
9"All who were numbered according to their armies of the
forces with Judah, one hundred and eighty-six thousand
four hundred—these shall
break camp first.

10"On the south side *shall
be* the standard of the forces
with Reuben according to
their armies, and the leader
of the children of Reuben *shall
be* Elizur the son of Shedeur."
11And his army was numbered
at forty-six thousand five hundred.

12"Those who camp next
to him *shall be* the tribe of
Simeon, and the leader of
the children of Simeon *shall
be* Shelumiel the son of Zurishaddai." 13And his army was
numbered at fifty-nine thousand three hundred.

14"Then *comes* the tribe
of Gad, and the leader of the
children of Gad *shall be* Eliasaph the son of Reuel."[a] 15And

2:14 [a] Spelled *Deuel* in 1:14 and 7:42

his army was numbered at forty-five thousand six hundred and fifty. 16“All who were numbered according to their armies of the forces with Reuben, one hundred and fifty-one thousand four hundred and fifty—they shall be the second to break camp.

17“And the tabernacle of meeting shall move out with the camp of the Levites in the middle of the camps; as they camp, so they shall move out, everyone in his place, by their standards.

18“On the west side *shall be* the standard of the forces with Ephraim according to their armies, and the leader of the children of Ephraim *shall be* Elishama the son of Ammihud.” 19And his army was numbered at forty thousand five hundred.

20“Next to him *comes* the tribe of Manasseh, and the leader of the children of Manasseh *shall be* Gamaliel the son of Pedahzur.” 21And his army was numbered at thirty-two thousand two hundred.

22“Then *comes* the tribe of Benjamin, and the leader of the children of Benjamin *shall be* Abidan the son of Gideoni.” 23And his army was numbered at thirty-five thousand four hundred. 24“All who were numbered according to their armies of the forces with Ephraim, one hundred and eight thousand one hundred—they shall be the third to break camp.

25“The standard of the forces with Dan *shall be* on the north side according to their armies, and the leader of the children of Dan *shall be* Ahiezer the son of Ammishaddai.” 26And his army was numbered at sixty-two thousand seven hundred.

27“Those who camp next to him *shall be* the tribe of Asher, and the leader of the children of Asher *shall be* Pagiel the son of Ocran.” 28And his army was numbered at forty-one thousand five hundred.

29“Then *comes* the tribe of Naphtali, and the leader of the children of Naphtali *shall be* Ahira the son of Enan.” 30And his army was numbered at fifty-three thousand four hundred. 31“All who were numbered of the forces with Dan, one hundred and fifty-seven thousand six hundred—they shall break camp last, with their standards.”

32These *are* the ones who were numbered of the children of Israel by their fathers’ houses. All who were numbered according to their armies of the forces *were* six hundred and three thousand five hundred and fifty. 33But the Levites were not numbered among the children of Israel, just as the LORD commanded Moses.

34Thus the children of Israel did according to all that the LORD commanded Moses; so they camped by their stan-

dards and so they broke camp, each one by his family, according to their fathers' houses.

THE SONS OF AARON

3 Now these *are* the records of Aaron and Moses when the LORD spoke with Moses on Mount Sinai. 2And these *are* the names of the sons of Aaron: Nadab, the firstborn, and Abihu, Eleazar, and Ithamar. 3These *are* the names of the sons of Aaron, the anointed priests, whom he consecrated to minister as priests. 4Nadab and Abihu had died before the LORD when they offered profane fire before the LORD in the Wilderness of Sinai; and they had no children. So Eleazar and Ithamar ministered as priests in the presence of Aaron their father.

THE LEVITES SERVE IN THE TABERNACLE

5And the LORD spoke to Moses, saying: 6"Bring the tribe of Levi near, and present them before Aaron the priest, that they may serve him. 7And they shall attend to his needs and the needs of the whole congregation before the tabernacle of meeting, to do the work of the tabernacle. 8Also they shall attend to all the furnishings of the tabernacle of meeting, and to the needs of the children of Israel, to do the work of the tabernacle. 9And you shall give the Levites to Aaron and his sons; they *are* given entirely to him[a] from among the children of Israel. 10So you shall appoint Aaron and his sons, and they shall attend to their priesthood; but the outsider who comes near shall be put to death."

11Then the LORD spoke to Moses, saying: 12"Now behold, I Myself have taken the Levites from among the children of Israel instead of every firstborn who opens the womb among the children of Israel. Therefore the Levites shall be Mine, 13because all the firstborn *are* Mine. On the day that I struck all the firstborn in the land of Egypt, I sanctified to Myself all the firstborn in Israel, both man and beast. They shall be Mine: I *am* the LORD."

CENSUS OF THE LEVITES COMMANDED

14Then the LORD spoke to Moses in the Wilderness of Sinai, saying: 15"Number the children of Levi by their fathers' houses, by their families; you shall number every male from a month old and above."

16So Moses numbered them according to the word of the LORD, as he was commanded. 17These were the sons of Levi by their names:

3:9 [a] Samaritan Pentateuch and Septuagint read *Me.*

Gershon, Kohath, and Merari.
18And these *are* the names of
the sons of Gershon by their
families: Libni and Shimei.
19And the sons of Kohath by
their families: Amram, Izehar,
Hebron, and Uzziel. 20And the
sons of Merari by their families: Mahli and Mushi. These
are the families of the Levites
by their fathers' houses.

21From Gershon *came* the
family of the Libnites and the
family of the Shimites; these
were the families of the Gershonites. 22Those who were
numbered, according to the
number of all the males from
a month old and above—of
those who were numbered
there were seven thousand
five hundred. 23The families
of the Gershonites were to
camp behind the tabernacle
westward. 24And the leader
of the father's house of the
Gershonites *was* Eliasaph the
son of Lael. 25The duties of
the children of Gershon in
the tabernacle of meeting *included* the tabernacle, the tent
with its covering, the screen
for the door of the tabernacle of meeting, 26the screen
for the door of the court, the
hangings of the court which
are around the tabernacle and
the altar, and their cords, according to all the work relating to them.

27From Kohath *came* the
family of the Amramites, the
family of the Izharites, the
family of the Hebronites, and
the family of the Uzzielites;
these *were* the families of the
Kohathites. 28According to the
number of all the males, from
a month old and above, *there
were* eight thousand six[a] hundred keeping charge of the
sanctuary. 29The families of
the children of Kohath were to
camp on the south side of the
tabernacle. 30And the leader
of the fathers' house of the
families of the Kohathites *was*
Elizaphan the son of Uzziel.
31Their duty *included* the ark,
the table, the lampstand, the
altars, the utensils of the sanctuary with which they ministered, the screen, and all the
work relating to them.

32And Eleazar the son of
Aaron the priest *was to be*
chief over the leaders of the
Levites, *with* oversight of
those who kept charge of the
sanctuary.

33From Merari *came* the
family of the Mahlites and
the family of the Mushites;
these *were* the families of Merari. 34And those who were
numbered, according to the
number of all the males from
a month old and above, *were*
six thousand two hundred.
35The leader of the fathers'
house of the families of Merari *was* Zuriel the son of Abihail. These *were* to camp on
the north side of the taber-

3:28 [a] Some manuscripts of the Septuagint read *three*.

nacle. 36And the appointed
duty of the children of Merari *included* the boards of
the tabernacle, its bars, its
pillars, its sockets, its utensils,
all the work relating to them,
37and the pillars of the court
all around, with their sockets,
their pegs, and their cords.

38Moreover those who were
to camp before the tabernacle
on the east, before the tabernacle of meeting, *were* Moses,
Aaron, and his sons, keeping
charge of the sanctuary, to
meet the needs of the children of Israel; but the outsider
who came near was to be put
to death. 39All who were numbered of the Levites, whom
Moses and Aaron numbered
at the commandment of the
LORD, by their families, all
the males from a month old
and above, *were* twenty-two
thousand.

LEVITES DEDICATED INSTEAD OF THE FIRSTBORN

40Then the LORD said to
Moses: "Number all the firstborn males of the children of
Israel from a month old and
above, and take the number of
their names. 41And you shall
take the Levites for Me—I *am*
the LORD—instead of all the
firstborn among the children
of Israel, and the livestock
of the Levites instead of all
the firstborn among the livestock of the children of Israel." 42So Moses numbered
all the firstborn among the
children of Israel, as the LORD
commanded him. 43And all
the firstborn males, according to the number of names
from a month old and above,
of those who were numbered
of them, were twenty-two
thousand two hundred and
seventy-three.

44Then the LORD spoke to
Moses, saying: 45"Take the Levites instead of all the firstborn among the children of
Israel, and the livestock of
the Levites instead of their
livestock. The Levites shall be
Mine: I *am* the LORD. 46And
for the redemption of the two
hundred and seventy-three of
the firstborn of the children of
Israel, who are more than the
number of the Levites, 47you
shall take five shekels for each
one individually; you shall
take *them* in the currency
of the shekel of the sanctuary, the shekel of twenty gerahs. 48And you shall give the
money, with which the excess
number of them is redeemed,
to Aaron and his sons."

49So Moses took the re-
demption money from those
who were over and above
those who were redeemed
by the Levites. 50From the
firstborn of the children of
Israel he took the money, one
thousand three hundred and
sixty-five *shekels*, according
to the shekel of the sanctuary. 51And Moses gave their
redemption money to Aaron

and his sons, according to the word of the LORD, as the LORD commanded Moses.

DUTIES OF THE SONS OF KOHATH

4 Then the LORD spoke to Moses and Aaron, saying: 2"Take a census of the sons of Kohath from among the children of Levi, by their families, by their fathers' house, 3from thirty years old and above, even to fifty years old, all who enter the service to do the work in the tabernacle of meeting.

4"This *is* the service of the sons of Kohath in the tabernacle of meeting, *relating to* the most holy things: 5When the camp prepares to journey, Aaron and his sons shall come, and they shall take down the covering veil and cover the ark of the Testimony with it. 6Then they shall put on it a covering of badger skins, and spread over *that* a cloth entirely of blue; and they shall insert its poles.

7"On the table of showbread they shall spread a blue cloth, and put on it the dishes, the pans, the bowls, and the pitchers for pouring; and the showbread[a] shall be on it. 8They shall spread over them a scarlet cloth, and cover the same with a covering of badger skins; and they shall insert its poles. 9And they shall take a blue cloth and cover the lampstand of the light, with its lamps, its wick-trimmers, its trays, and all its oil vessels, with which they service it. 10Then they shall put it with all its utensils in a covering of badger skins, and put *it* on a carrying beam.

11"Over the golden altar they shall spread a blue cloth, and cover it with a covering of badger skins; and they shall insert its poles. 12Then they shall take all the utensils of service with which they minister in the sanctuary, put *them* in a blue cloth, cover them with a covering of badger skins, and put *them* on a carrying beam. 13Also they shall take away the ashes from the altar, and spread a purple cloth over it. 14They shall put on it all its implements with which they minister there—the firepans, the forks, the shovels, the basins, and all the utensils of the altar—and they shall spread on it a covering of badger skins, and insert its poles. 15And when Aaron and his sons have finished covering the sanctuary and all the furnishings of the sanctuary, when the camp is set to go, then the sons of Kohath shall come to carry *them;* but they shall not touch any holy thing, lest they die.

"These *are* the things in the tabernacle of meeting

4:7 [a] Literally *the continual bread*

which the sons of Kohath are
to carry.
16“The appointed duty of
Eleazar the son of Aaron the
priest *is* the oil for the light,
the sweet incense, the daily
grain offering, the anointing
oil, the oversight of all the
tabernacle, of all that *is* in it,
with the sanctuary and its furnishings.”
17Then the LORD spoke to
Moses and Aaron, saying:
18“Do not cut off the tribe of
the families of the Kohathites
from among the Levites; 19but
do this in regard to them, that
they may live and not die
when they approach the most
holy things: Aaron and his
sons shall go in and appoint
each of them to his service
and his task. 20But they shall
not go in to watch while the
holy things are being covered,
lest they die.”

DUTIES OF THE SONS OF GERSHON

21Then the LORD spoke to
Moses, saying: 22“Also take
a census of the sons of Gershon, by their fathers' house,
by their families. 23From
thirty years old and above,
even to fifty years old, you
shall number them, all who
enter to perform the service,
to do the work in the tabernacle of meeting. 24This *is* the
service of the families of the
Gershonites, in serving and
carrying: 25They shall carry
the curtains of the tabernacle
and the tabernacle of meeting
with its covering, the covering
of badger skins that *is* on it,
the screen for the door of the
tabernacle of meeting, 26the
screen for the door of the gate
of the court, the hangings of
the court which *are* around
the tabernacle and altar, and
their cords, all the furnishings
for their service and all that is
made for these things: so shall
they serve.
27“Aaron and his sons shall
assign all the service of the
sons of the Gershonites, all
their tasks and all their service. And you shall appoint
to them all their tasks as their
duty. 28This *is* the service of
the families of the sons of
Gershon in the tabernacle
of meeting. And their duties
shall be under the authority[a]
of Ithamar the son of Aaron
the priest.

DUTIES OF THE SONS OF MERARI

29“*As for* the sons of Merari, you shall number them
by their families and by their
fathers' house. 30From thirty
years old and above, even to
fifty years old, you shall number them, everyone who enters the service to do the work
of the tabernacle of meeting.
31And this *is* what they must
carry as all their service for

4:28 [a] Literally *hand*

the tabernacle of meeting: the boards of the tabernacle, its bars, its pillars, its sockets, [32]and the pillars around the court with their sockets, pegs, and cords, with all their furnishings and all their service; and you shall assign *to each man* by name the items he must carry. [33]This *is* the service of the families of the sons of Merari, as all their service for the tabernacle of meeting, under the authority[a] of Ithamar the son of Aaron the priest."

CENSUS OF THE LEVITES

[34]And Moses, Aaron, and the leaders of the congregation numbered the sons of the Kohathites by their families and by their fathers' house, [35]from thirty years old and above, even to fifty years old, everyone who entered the service for work in the tabernacle of meeting; [36]and those who were numbered by their families were two thousand seven hundred and fifty. [37]These *were* the ones who were numbered of the families of the Kohathites, all who might serve in the tabernacle of meeting, whom Moses and Aaron numbered according to the commandment of the LORD by the hand of Moses.

[38]And those who were numbered of the sons of Gershon, by their families and by their fathers' house, [39]from thirty years old and above, even to fifty years old, everyone who entered the service for work in the tabernacle of meeting— [40]those who were numbered by their families, by their fathers' house, were two thousand six hundred and thirty. [41]These *are* the ones who were numbered of the families of the sons of Gershon, of all who might serve in the tabernacle of meeting, whom Moses and Aaron numbered according to the commandment of the LORD.

[42]Those of the families of the sons of Merari who were numbered, by their families, by their fathers' house, [43]from thirty years old and above, even to fifty years old, everyone who entered the service for work in the tabernacle of meeting— [44]those who were numbered by their families were three thousand two hundred. [45]These *are* the ones who were numbered of the families of the sons of Merari, whom Moses and Aaron numbered according to the word of the LORD by the hand of Moses.

[46]All who were numbered of the Levites, whom Moses, Aaron, and the leaders of Israel numbered, by their families and by their fathers' houses, [47]from thirty years old and above, even to fifty years

4:33 [a] Literally *hand*

old, everyone who came to do
the work of service and the
work of bearing burdens in
the tabernacle of meeting—
48those who were numbered
were eight thousand five hundred and eighty.

49According to the com-
mandment of the LORD they
were numbered by the hand
of Moses, each according to
his service and according to
his task; thus were they numbered by him, as the LORD
commanded Moses.

CEREMONIALLY UNCLEAN PERSONS ISOLATED

5 And the LORD spoke to
Moses, saying: 2"Com-
mand the children of Israel
that they put out of the camp
every leper, everyone who has
a discharge, and whoever becomes defiled by a corpse.
3You shall put out both male
and female; you shall put
them outside the camp, that
they may not defile their
camps in the midst of which
I dwell." 4And the children of
Israel did so, and put them
outside the camp; as the LORD
spoke to Moses, so the children of Israel did.

CONFESSION AND RESTITUTION

5Then the LORD spoke to
Moses, saying, 6"Speak to the
children of Israel: 'When a
man or woman commits any
sin that men commit in unfaithfulness against the LORD,
and that person is guilty, 7then
he shall confess the sin which
he has committed. He shall
make restitution for his trespass in full, plus one-fifth of
it, and give *it* to the one he
has wronged. 8But if the man
has no relative to whom restitution may be made for the
wrong, the restitution for the
wrong *must go* to the LORD for
the priest, in addition to the
ram of the atonement with
which atonement is made for
him. 9Every offering of all the
holy things of the children of
Israel, which they bring to
the priest, shall be his. 10And
every man's holy things shall
be his; whatever any man
gives the priest shall be his.'"

CONCERNING UNFAITHFUL WIVES

11And the LORD spoke to
Moses, saying, 12"Speak to the
children of Israel, and say to
them: 'If any man's wife goes
astray and behaves unfaithfully toward him, 13and a man
lies with her carnally, and it
is hidden from the eyes of
her husband, and it is concealed that she has defiled
herself, and *there was* no witness against her, nor was she
caught— 14if the spirit of jealousy comes upon him and he
becomes jealous of his wife,
who has defiled herself; or if
the spirit of jealousy comes
upon him and he becomes
jealous of his wife, although
she has not defiled herself—

15then the man shall bring his wife to the priest. He shall bring the offering required for her, one-tenth of an ephah of barley meal; he shall pour no oil on it and put no frankincense on it, because it *is* a grain offering of jealousy, an offering for remembering, for bringing iniquity to remembrance.

16'And the priest shall bring her near, and set her before the LORD. 17The priest shall take holy water in an earthen vessel, and take some of the dust that is on the floor of the tabernacle and put *it* into the water. 18Then the priest shall stand the woman before the LORD, uncover the woman's head, and put the offering for remembering in her hands, which *is* the grain offering of jealousy. And the priest shall have in his hand the bitter water that brings a curse. 19And the priest shall put her under oath, and say to the woman, "If no man has lain with you, and if you have not gone astray to uncleanness *while* under your husband's *authority,* be free from this bitter water that brings a curse. 20But if you have gone astray *while* under your husband's *authority,* and if you have defiled yourself and some man other than your husband has lain with you"— 21then the priest shall put the woman under the oath of the curse, and he shall say to the woman—"the LORD make you a curse and an oath among your people, when the LORD makes your thigh rot and your belly swell; 22and may this water that causes the curse go into your stomach, and make *your* belly swell and *your* thigh rot."

'Then the woman shall say, "Amen, so be it."

23'Then the priest shall write these curses in a book, and he shall scrape *them* off into the bitter water. 24And he shall make the woman drink the bitter water that brings a curse, and the water that brings the curse shall enter her *to become* bitter. 25Then the priest shall take the grain offering of jealousy from the woman's hand, shall wave the offering before the LORD, and bring it to the altar; 26and the priest shall take a handful of the offering, as its memorial portion, burn *it* on the altar, and afterward make the woman drink the water. 27When he has made her drink the water, then it shall be, if she has defiled herself and behaved unfaithfully toward her husband, that the water that brings a curse will enter her *and become* bitter, and her belly will swell, her thigh will rot, and the woman will become a curse among her people. 28But if the woman has not defiled herself, and is clean, then she shall be free and may conceive children.

29‘This *is* the law of jealousy, when a wife, *while* under
her husband’s *authority,* goes
astray and defiles herself, 30or
when the spirit of jealousy
comes upon a man, and he becomes jealous of his wife; then
he shall stand the woman before the LORD, and the priest
shall execute all this law upon
her. 31Then the man shall be
free from iniquity, but that
woman shall bear her guilt.’”

THE LAW OF THE NAZIRITE

6 Then the LORD spoke to
Moses, saying, 2“Speak
to the children of Israel, and
say to them: ‘When either a
man or woman consecrates
an offering to take the vow of
a Nazirite, to separate himself
to the LORD, 3he shall separate
himself from wine and *similar*
drink; he shall drink neither
vinegar made from wine nor
vinegar made from *similar*
drink; neither shall he drink
any grape juice, nor eat fresh
grapes or raisins. 4All the days
of his separation he shall eat
nothing that is produced by
the grapevine, from seed to
skin.

5‘All the days of the vow of
his separation no razor shall
come upon his head; until the
days are fulfilled for which he
separated himself to the LORD,
he shall be holy. *Then* he shall
let the locks of the hair of his
head grow. 6All the days that
he separates himself to the
LORD he shall not go near a
dead body. 7He shall not make
himself unclean even for his
father or his mother, for his
brother or his sister, when
they die, because his separation to God *is* on his head. 8All
the days of his separation he
shall be holy to the LORD.

9‘And if anyone dies very
suddenly beside him, and he
defiles his consecrated head,
then he shall shave his head
on the day of his cleansing;
on the seventh day he shall
shave it. 10Then on the eighth
day he shall bring two turtledoves or two young pigeons to
the priest, to the door of the
tabernacle of meeting; 11and
the priest shall offer one as a
sin offering and *the* other as
a burnt offering, and make
atonement for him, because
he sinned in regard to the
corpse; and he shall sanctify
his head that same day. 12He
shall consecrate to the LORD
the days of his separation, and
bring a male lamb in its first
year as a trespass offering; but
the former days shall be lost,
because his separation was
defiled.

13‘Now this *is* the law of the
Nazirite: When the days of his
separation are fulfilled, he shall
be brought to the door of the
tabernacle of meeting. 14And
he shall present his offering to
the LORD: one male lamb in its
first year without blemish as a
burnt offering, one ewe lamb
in its first year without blemish as a sin offering, one ram

without blemish as a peace
offering, [15]a basket of unleavened bread, cakes of fine flour
mixed with oil, unleavened
wafers anointed with oil, and
their grain offering with their
drink offerings.
[16]'Then the priest shall
bring *them* before the LORD
and offer his sin offering and
his burnt offering; [17]and he
shall offer the ram as a sacrifice of a peace offering to
the LORD, with the basket of
unleavened bread; the priest
shall also offer its grain offering and its drink offering. [18]Then the Nazirite shall
shave his consecrated head
at the door of the tabernacle
of meeting, and shall take the
hair from his consecrated
head and put *it* on the fire
which is under the sacrifice
of the peace offering.
[19]'And the priest shall take
the boiled shoulder of the
ram, one unleavened cake
from the basket, and one unleavened wafer, and put *them*
upon the hands of the Nazirite
after he has shaved his consecrated *hair,* [20]and the priest
shall wave them as a wave
offering before the LORD;
they *are* holy for the priest,
together with the breast of the
wave offering and the thigh of
the heave offering. After that
the Nazirite may drink wine.'
[21]"This is the law of the
Nazirite who vows to the LORD
the offering for his separation, and besides that, whatever else his hand is able to
provide; according to the vow
which he takes, so he must
do according to the law of his
separation."

THE PRIESTLY BLESSING

[22]And the LORD spoke to
Moses, saying: [23]"Speak to
Aaron and his sons, saying,
'This is the way you shall bless
the children of Israel. Say to
them:

[24]"The LORD bless you
    and keep you;
[25] The LORD make His
    face shine upon you,
  And be gracious to you;
[26] The LORD lift up His
    countenance upon you,
  And give you peace."'

[27]"So they shall put My
name on the children of Israel, and I will bless them."

OFFERINGS OF THE LEADERS

7 Now it came to pass, when
Moses had finished setting
up the tabernacle, that he
anointed it and consecrated
it and all its furnishings, and
the altar and all its utensils; so
he anointed them and consecrated them. [2]Then the leaders of Israel, the heads of their
fathers' houses, who *were* the
leaders of the tribes and over
those who were numbered,
made an offering. [3]And they
brought their offering before
the LORD, six covered carts

and twelve oxen, a cart for
every two of the leaders, and
for each one an ox; and they
presented them before the
tabernacle.

4Then the LORD spoke to
Moses, saying, 5"Accept *these*
from them, that they may be
used in doing the work of the
tabernacle of meeting; and
you shall give them to the Levites, *to* every man according
to his service." 6So Moses took
the carts and the oxen, and
gave them to the Levites. 7Two
carts and four oxen he gave to
the sons of Gershon, according to their service; 8and four
carts and eight oxen he gave
to the sons of Merari, according to their service, under the
authority[a] of Ithamar the son
of Aaron the priest. 9But to the
sons of Kohath he gave none,
because theirs *was* the service
of the holy things, *which* they
carried on their shoulders.

10Now the leaders offered
the dedication *offering* for the
altar when it was anointed;
so the leaders offered their
offering before the altar. 11For
the LORD said to Moses, "They
shall offer their offering, one
leader each day, for the dedication of the altar."

12And the one who offered
his offering on the first day
was Nahshon the son of Amminadab, from the tribe of
Judah. 13His offering *was* one
silver platter, the weight of
which *was* one hundred and
thirty *shekels,* and one silver
bowl of seventy shekels, according to the shekel of the
sanctuary, both of them full
of fine flour mixed with oil
as a grain offering; 14one gold
pan of ten *shekels,* full of incense; 15one young bull, one
ram, and one male lamb in
its first year, as a burnt offering; 16one kid of the goats as
a sin offering; 17and for the
sacrifice of peace offerings:
two oxen, five rams, five male
goats, and five male lambs in
their first year. This *was* the
offering of Nahshon the son
of Amminadab.

18On the second day Ne-
thanel the son of Zuar, leader of
Issachar, presented *an offering.*
19*For* his offering he offered
one silver platter, the weight
of which *was* one hundred and
thirty *shekels,* and one silver
bowl of seventy shekels, according to the shekel of the
sanctuary, both of them full of
fine flour mixed with oil as a
grain offering; 20one gold pan
of ten *shekels,* full of incense;
21one young bull, one ram, and
one male lamb in its first year,
as a burnt offering; 22one kid
of the goats as a sin offering;
23and as the sacrifice of peace
offerings: two oxen, five rams,
five male goats, and five male
lambs in their first year. This
was the offering of Nethanel
the son of Zuar.

7:8 [a] Literally *hand*

24 On the third day Eliab the
son of Helon, leader of the
children of Zebulun, *presented
an offering.* 25 His offering *was*
one silver platter, the weight of
which *was* one hundred and
thirty *shekels,* and one silver
bowl of seventy shekels, according to the shekel of the
sanctuary, both of them full of
fine flour mixed with oil as a
grain offering; 26 one gold pan
of ten *shekels,* full of incense;
27 one young bull, one ram,
and one male lamb in its first
year, as a burnt offering; 28 one
kid of the goats as a sin offering; 29 and for the sacrifice of
peace offerings: two oxen, five
rams, five male goats, and five
male lambs in their first year.
This *was* the offering of Eliab
the son of Helon.

30 On the fourth day Elizur
the son of Shedeur, leader of
the children of Reuben, *presented an offering.* 31 His offering *was* one silver platter,
the weight of which *was* one
hundred and thirty *shekels,*
and one silver bowl of seventy shekels, according to
the shekel of the sanctuary,
both of them full of fine flour
mixed with oil as a grain offering; 32 one gold pan of ten
shekels, full of incense; 33 one
young bull, one ram, and one
male lamb in its first year, as
a burnt offering; 34 one kid of
the goats as a sin offering;
35 and as the sacrifice of peace
offerings: two oxen, five rams,
five male goats, and five male
lambs in their first year. This
was the offering of Elizur the
son of Shedeur.

36 On the fifth day Shelumiel the son of Zurishaddai,
leader of the children of Simeon, *presented an offering.*
37 His offering *was* one silver
platter, the weight of which
was one hundred and thirty
shekels, and one silver bowl
of seventy shekels, according
to the shekel of the sanctuary,
both of them full of fine flour
mixed with oil as a grain offering; 38 one gold pan of ten
shekels, full of incense; 39 one
young bull, one ram, and one
male lamb in its first year, as
a burnt offering; 40 one kid
of the goats as a sin offering;
41 and as the sacrifice of peace
offerings: two oxen, five rams,
five male goats, and five male
lambs in their first year. This
was the offering of Shelumiel
the son of Zurishaddai.

42 On the sixth day Eliasaph
the son of Deuel,[a] leader of
the children of Gad, *presented
an offering.* 43 His offering *was*
one silver platter, the weight
of which *was* one hundred
and thirty *shekels,* and one
silver bowl of seventy shekels, according to the shekel of
the sanctuary, both of them
full of fine flour mixed with
oil as a grain offering; 44 one
gold pan of ten *shekels,* full of

7:42 [a] Spelled *Reuel* in 2:14

incense; 45one young bull, one
ram, and one male lamb in its
first year, as a burnt offering;
46one kid of the goats as a sin
offering; 47and as the sacrifice
of peace offerings: two oxen,
five rams, five male goats, and
five male lambs in their first
year. This *was* the offering of
Eliasaph the son of Deuel.

48On the seventh day
Elishama the son of Ammi-
hud, leader of the children of
Ephraim, *presented an offering.* 49His offering *was* one
silver platter, the weight of
which *was* one hundred and
thirty *shekels,* and one silver
bowl of seventy shekels, according to the shekel of the
sanctuary, both of them full of
fine flour mixed with oil as a
grain offering; 50one gold pan
of ten *shekels,* full of incense;
51one young bull, one ram, and
one male lamb in its first year,
as a burnt offering; 52one kid
of the goats as a sin offering;
53and as the sacrifice of peace
offerings: two oxen, five rams,
five male goats, and five male
lambs in their first year. This
was the offering of Elishama
the son of Ammihud.

54On the eighth day Ga-
maliel the son of Pedahzur,
leader of the children of Manasseh, *presented an offering.*
55His offering *was* one silver
platter, the weight of which
was one hundred and thirty
shekels, and one silver bowl
of seventy shekels, according
to the shekel of the sanctuary,
both of them full of fine flour
mixed with oil as a grain offering; 56one gold pan of ten
shekels, full of incense; 57one
young bull, one ram, and one
male lamb in its first year, as
a burnt offering; 58one kid of
the goats as a sin offering;
59and as the sacrifice of peace
offerings: two oxen, five rams,
five male goats, and five male
lambs in their first year. This
was the offering of Gamaliel
the son of Pedahzur.

60On the ninth day Abidan
the son of Gideoni, leader of
the children of Benjamin, *presented an offering.* 61His offering *was* one silver platter, the
weight of which *was* one hundred and thirty *shekels,* and one
silver bowl of seventy shekels,
according to the shekel of the
sanctuary, both of them full of
fine flour mixed with oil as a
grain offering; 62one gold pan
of ten *shekels,* full of incense;
63one young bull, one ram, and
one male lamb in its first year,
as a burnt offering; 64one kid
of the goats as a sin offering;
65and as the sacrifice of peace
offerings: two oxen, five rams,
five male goats, and five male
lambs in their first year. This
was the offering of Abidan the
son of Gideoni.

66On the tenth day Ahi-
ezer the son of Ammishad-
dai, leader of the children of
Dan, *presented an offering.*
67His offering *was* one silver
platter, the weight of which
was one hundred and thirty

shekels, and one silver bowl
of seventy shekels, according
to the shekel of the sanctuary,
both of them full of fine flour
mixed with oil as a grain offering; 68one gold pan of ten
shekels, full of incense; 69one
young bull, one ram, and one
male lamb in its first year, as
a burnt offering; 70one kid of
the goats as a sin offering;
71and as the sacrifice of peace
offerings: two oxen, five rams,
five male goats, and five male
lambs in their first year. This
was the offering of Ahiezer
the son of Ammishaddai.

72On the eleventh day Pagiel
the son of Ocran, leader of the
children of Asher, *presented*
an offering. 73His offering *was*
one silver platter, the weight of
which *was* one hundred and
thirty *shekels,* and one silver
bowl of seventy shekels, according to the shekel of the
sanctuary, both of them full of
fine flour mixed with oil as a
grain offering; 74one gold pan
of ten *shekels,* full of incense;
75one young bull, one ram, and
one male lamb in its first year,
as a burnt offering; 76one kid
of the goats as a sin offering;
77and as the sacrifice of peace
offerings: two oxen, five rams,
five male goats, and five male
lambs in their first year. This
was the offering of Pagiel the
son of Ocran.

78On the twelfth day Ahira
the son of Enan, leader of the
children of Naphtali, *presented*
an offering. 79His offering *was*
one silver platter, the weight
of which *was* one hundred
and thirty *shekels,* and one
silver bowl of seventy shekels, according to the shekel of
the sanctuary, both of them
full of fine flour mixed with
oil as a grain offering; 80one
gold pan of ten *shekels,* full of
incense; 81one young bull, one
ram, and one male lamb in its
first year, as a burnt offering;
82one kid of the goats as a sin
offering; 83and as the sacrifice
of peace offerings: two oxen,
five rams, five male goats, and
five male lambs in their first
year. This *was* the offering of
Ahira the son of Enan.

84This *was* the dedication
offering for the altar from the
leaders of Israel, when it was
anointed: twelve silver platters, twelve silver bowls, and
twelve gold pans. 85Each silver platter *weighed* one hundred and thirty *shekels* and
each bowl seventy *shekels.*
All the silver of the vessels
weighed two thousand four
hundred *shekels,* according to
the shekel of the sanctuary.
86The twelve gold pans full of
incense *weighed* ten *shekels*
apiece, according to the shekel
of the sanctuary; all the gold
of the pans *weighed* one hundred and twenty *shekels.* 87All
the oxen for the burnt offering
were twelve young bulls, the
rams twelve, the male lambs
in their first year twelve, with
their grain offering, and the
kids of the goats as a sin offer-

ing twelve. 88And all the oxen for the sacrifice of peace offerings were twenty-four bulls, the rams sixty, the male goats sixty, and the lambs in their first year sixty. This *was* the dedication *offering* for the altar after it was anointed.

89Now when Moses went into the tabernacle of meeting to speak with Him, he heard the voice of One speaking to him from above the mercy seat that *was* on the ark of the Testimony, from between the two cherubim; thus He spoke to him.

ARRANGEMENT OF THE LAMPS

8 And the LORD spoke to Moses, saying: 2"Speak to Aaron, and say to him, 'When you arrange the lamps, the seven lamps shall give light in front of the lampstand.'" 3And Aaron did so; he arranged the lamps to face toward the front of the lampstand, as the LORD commanded Moses. 4Now this workmanship of the lampstand *was* hammered gold; from its shaft to its flowers it *was* hammered work. According to the pattern which the LORD had shown Moses, so he made the lampstand.

CLEANSING AND DEDICATION OF THE LEVITES

5Then the LORD spoke to Moses, saying: 6"Take the Levites from among the children of Israel and cleanse them *ceremonially.* 7Thus you shall do to them to cleanse them: Sprinkle water of purification on them, and let them shave all their body, and let them wash their clothes, and *so* make themselves clean. 8Then let them take a young bull with its grain offering of fine flour mixed with oil, and you shall take another young bull as a sin offering. 9And you shall bring the Levites before the tabernacle of meeting, and you shall gather together the whole congregation of the children of Israel. 10So you shall bring the Levites before the LORD, and the children of Israel shall lay their hands on the Levites; 11and Aaron shall offer the Levites before the LORD *like* a wave offering from the children of Israel, that they may perform the work of the LORD. 12Then the Levites shall lay their hands on the heads of the young bulls, and you shall offer one as a sin offering and the other as a burnt offering to the LORD, to make atonement for the Levites.

13"And you shall stand the Levites before Aaron and his sons, and then offer them *like* a wave offering to the LORD. 14Thus you shall separate the Levites from among the children of Israel, and the Levites shall be Mine. 15After that the Levites shall go in to service the tabernacle of meeting. So you shall cleanse them and

offer them *like* a wave offering. 16For they *are* wholly
given to Me from among the
children of Israel; I have taken
them for Myself instead of
all who open the womb, the
firstborn of all the children of
Israel. 17For all the firstborn
among the children of Israel
are Mine, *both* man and beast;
on the day that I struck all the
firstborn in the land of Egypt
I sanctified them to Myself.
18I have taken the Levites instead of all the firstborn of
the children of Israel. 19And
I have given the Levites as
a gift to Aaron and his sons
from among the children of
Israel, to do the work for the
children of Israel in the tabernacle of meeting, and to make
atonement for the children of
Israel, that there be no plague
among the children of Israel
when the children of Israel
come near the sanctuary."

20Thus Moses and Aaron
and all the congregation of
the children of Israel did to
the Levites; according to all
that the LORD commanded
Moses concerning the Levites,
so the children of Israel did to
them. 21And the Levites purified themselves and washed
their clothes; then Aaron
presented them *like* a wave
offering before the LORD, and
Aaron made atonement for
them to cleanse them. 22After
that the Levites went in to do
their work in the tabernacle of
meeting before Aaron and his
sons; as the LORD commanded
Moses concerning the Levites,
so they did to them.

23Then the LORD spoke
to Moses, saying, 24"This *is*
what *pertains* to the Levites:
From twenty-five years old
and above one may enter to
perform service in the work
of the tabernacle of meeting;
25and at the age of fifty years
they must cease performing
this work, and shall work no
more. 26They may minister
with their brethren in the tabernacle of meeting, to attend
to needs, but they *themselves*
shall do no work. Thus you
shall do to the Levites regarding their duties."

THE SECOND PASSOVER

9 Now the LORD spoke to
Moses in the Wilderness
of Sinai, in the first month of
the second year after they had
come out of the land of Egypt,
saying: 2"Let the children of
Israel keep the Passover at
its appointed time. 3On the
fourteenth day of this month,
at twilight, you shall keep it at
its appointed time. According
to all its rites and ceremonies
you shall keep it." 4So Moses
told the children of Israel that
they should keep the Passover. 5And they kept the Passover on the fourteenth day of
the first month, at twilight, in
the Wilderness of Sinai; according to all that the LORD
commanded Moses, so the
children of Israel did.

[6]Now there were *certain*
men who were defiled by a
human corpse, so that they
could not keep the Passover
on that day; and they came
before Moses and Aaron that
day. [7]And those men said to
him, "We *became* defiled by
a human corpse. Why are
we kept from presenting the
offering of the LORD at its
appointed time among the
children of Israel?"

[8]And Moses said to them,
"Stand still, that I may hear
what the LORD will command
concerning you."

[9]Then the LORD spoke to
Moses, saying, [10]"Speak to
the children of Israel, saying: 'If anyone of you or your
posterity is unclean because
of a corpse, or *is* far away on
a journey, he may still keep
the LORD's Passover. [11]On the
fourteenth day of the second
month, at twilight, they may
keep it. They shall eat it with
unleavened bread and bitter
herbs. [12]They shall leave none
of it until morning, nor break
one of its bones. According to
all the ordinances of the Passover they shall keep it. [13]But
the man who *is* clean and is
not on a journey, and ceases to
keep the Passover, that same
person shall be cut off from
among his people, because he
did not bring the offering of
the LORD at its appointed time;
that man shall bear his sin.

[14]'And if a stranger dwells
among you, and would keep
the LORD's Passover, he must
do so according to the rite of
the Passover and according to
its ceremony; you shall have
one ordinance, both for the
stranger and the native of the
land.'"

THE CLOUD AND THE FIRE

[15]Now on the day that the
tabernacle was raised up, the
cloud covered the tabernacle,
the tent of the Testimony;
from evening until morning it
was above the tabernacle like
the appearance of fire. [16]So it
was always: the cloud covered
it *by day,* and the appearance
of fire by night. [17]Whenever
the cloud was taken up from
above the tabernacle, after
that the children of Israel
would journey; and in the
place where the cloud settled,
there the children of Israel
would pitch their tents. [18]At
the command of the LORD the
children of Israel would journey, and at the command of
the LORD they would camp; as
long as the cloud stayed above
the tabernacle they remained
encamped. [19]Even when the
cloud continued long, many
days above the tabernacle,
the children of Israel kept the
charge of the LORD and did
not journey. [20]So it was, when
the cloud was above the tabernacle a few days: according
to the command of the LORD
they would remain encamped,
and according to the com-
mand of the LORD they would

journey. 21So it was, when the cloud remained only from evening until morning: when the cloud was taken up in the morning, then they would journey; whether by day or by night, whenever the cloud was taken up, they would journey. 22*Whether it was* two days, a month, or a year that the cloud remained above the tabernacle, the children of Israel would remain encamped and not journey; but when it was taken up, they would journey. 23At the command of the LORD they remained encamped, and at the command of the LORD they journeyed; they kept the charge of the LORD, at the command of the LORD by the hand of Moses.

TWO SILVER TRUMPETS

10 And the LORD spoke to Moses, saying: 2"Make two silver trumpets for yourself; you shall make them of hammered work; you shall use them for calling the congregation and for directing the movement of the camps. 3When they blow both of them, all the congregation shall gather before you at the door of the tabernacle of meeting. 4But if they blow *only* one, then the leaders, the heads of the divisions of Israel, shall gather to you. 5When you sound the advance, the camps that lie on the east side shall then begin their journey. 6When you sound the advance the second time, then the camps that lie on the south side shall begin their journey; they shall sound the call for them to begin their journeys. 7And when the assembly is to be gathered together, you shall blow, but not sound the advance. 8The sons of Aaron, the priests, shall blow the trumpets; and these shall be to you as an ordinance forever throughout your generations.

9"When you go to war in your land against the enemy who oppresses you, then you shall sound an alarm with the trumpets, and you will be remembered before the LORD your God, and you will be saved from your enemies. 10Also in the day of your gladness, in your appointed feasts, and at the beginning of your months, you shall blow the trumpets over your burnt offerings and over the sacrifices of your peace offerings; and they shall be a memorial for you before your God: I *am* the LORD your God."

DEPARTURE FROM SINAI

11Now it came to pass on the twentieth *day* of the second month, in the second year, that the cloud was taken up from above the tabernacle of the Testimony. 12And the children of Israel set out from the Wilderness of Sinai on their journeys; then the cloud settled down in the Wilderness of Paran. 13So they started out

for the first time according to
the command of the LORD by
the hand of Moses.

14The standard of the camp
of the children of Judah set out
first according to their armies;
over their army was Nahshon
the son of Amminadab. 15Over
the army of the tribe of the
children of Issachar *was* Nethanel the son of Zuar. 16And
over the army of the tribe of
the children of Zebulun *was*
Eliab the son of Helon.

17Then the tabernacle was
taken down; and the sons of
Gershon and the sons of Merari set out, carrying the tabernacle.

18And the standard of the
camp of Reuben set out according to their armies; over
their army *was* Elizur the son
of Shedeur. 19Over the army
of the tribe of the children of
Simeon *was* Shelumiel the
son of Zurishaddai. 20And
over the army of the tribe of
the children of Gad *was* Eliasaph the son of Deuel.

21Then the Kohathites set
out, carrying the holy things.
(The tabernacle would be prepared for their arrival.)

22And the standard of
the camp of the children of
Ephraim set out according to
their armies; over their army
was Elishama the son of Ammihud. 23Over the army of the
tribe of the children of Manasseh *was* Gamaliel the son
of Pedahzur. 24And over the
army of the tribe of the children of Benjamin *was* Abidan
the son of Gideoni.

25Then the standard of
the camp of the children of
Dan (the rear guard of all the
camps) set out according to
their armies; over their army
was Ahiezer the son of Ammishaddai. 26Over the army
of the tribe of the children of
Asher *was* Pagiel the son of
Ocran. 27And over the army
of the tribe of the children of
Naphtali *was* Ahira the son
of Enan.

28Thus *was* the order of
march of the children of Israel, according to their armies,
when they began their journey.

29Now Moses said to Hobab
the son of Reuel[a] the Midianite, Moses' father-in-law, "We
are setting out for the place
of which the LORD said, 'I will
give it to you.' Come with us,
and we will treat you well; for
the LORD has promised good
things to Israel."

30And he said to him, "I will
not go, but I will depart to my
own land and to my relatives."

31So *Moses* said, "Please do
not leave, inasmuch as you
know how we are to camp in
the wilderness, and you can
be our eyes. 32And it shall be,
if you go with us—indeed it
shall be—that whatever good
the LORD will do to us, the
same we will do to you."

10:29 [a] Septuagint reads *Raguel* (compare Exodus 2:18).

33So they departed from
the mountain of the LORD on
a journey of three days; and
the ark of the covenant of the
LORD went before them for the
three days' journey, to search
out a resting place for them.
34And the cloud of the LORD
was above them by day when
they went out from the camp.
35So it was, whenever the
ark set out, that Moses said:

"Rise up, O LORD!
Let Your enemies
be scattered,
And let those who hate
You flee before You."

36And when it rested, he said:

"Return, O LORD,
To the many thousands
of Israel."

THE PEOPLE COMPLAIN

11 Now *when* the people complained, it displeased the
LORD; for the LORD heard *it,*
and His anger was aroused. So
the fire of the LORD burned
among them, and consumed
some in the outskirts of the
camp. 2Then the people cried
out to Moses, and when Moses
prayed to the LORD, the fire was
quenched. 3So he called the
name of the place Taberah,[a]
because the fire of the LORD
had burned among them.
4Now the mixed multitude
who were among them yielded
to intense craving; so the children of Israel also wept again
and said: "Who will give us
meat to eat? 5We remember
the fish which we ate freely
in Egypt, the cucumbers, the
melons, the leeks, the onions,
and the garlic; 6but now our
whole being *is* dried up; *there
is* nothing at all except this
manna *before* our eyes!"
7Now the manna *was* like
coriander seed, and its color
like the color of bdellium.
8The people went about and
gathered *it,* ground *it* on millstones or beat *it* in the mortar,
cooked *it* in pans, and made
cakes of it; and its taste was
like the taste of pastry prepared with oil. 9And when the
dew fell on the camp in the
night, the manna fell on it.
10Then Moses heard the
people weeping throughout
their families, everyone at
the door of his tent; and the
anger of the LORD was greatly
aroused; Moses also was displeased. 11So Moses said to
the LORD, "Why have You afflicted Your servant? And why
have I not found favor in Your
sight, that You have laid the
burden of all these people on
me? 12Did I conceive all these
people? Did I beget them,
that You should say to me,
'Carry them in your bosom,
as a guardian carries a nursing child,' to the land which
You swore to their fathers?

11:3 [a] Literally *Burning*

13Where am I to get meat to
give to all these people? For
they weep all over me, saying, 'Give us meat, that we may
eat.' 14I am not able to bear all
these people alone, because
the burden *is* too heavy for
me. 15If You treat me like
this, please kill me here and
now—if I have found favor in
Your sight—and do not let me
see my wretchedness!"

THE SEVENTY ELDERS

16So the LORD said to Moses:
"Gather to Me seventy men of
the elders of Israel, whom you
know to be the elders of the
people and officers over them;
bring them to the tabernacle
of meeting, that they may
stand there with you. 17Then
I will come down and talk with
you there. I will take of the
Spirit that *is* upon you and
will put *the same* upon them;
and they shall bear the burden
of the people with you, that
you may not bear *it* yourself
alone. 18Then you shall say to
the people, 'Consecrate yourselves for tomorrow, and you
shall eat meat; for you have
wept in the hearing of the
LORD, saying, "Who will give
us meat to eat? For *it was* well
with us in Egypt." Therefore
the LORD will give you meat,
and you shall eat. 19You shall
eat, not one day, nor two days,
nor five days, nor ten days,
nor twenty days, 20but *for* a
whole month, until it comes
out of your nostrils and becomes loathsome to you, because you have despised the
LORD who is among you, and
have wept before Him, saying,
"Why did we ever come up out
of Egypt?"'"

21And Moses said, "The
people whom I *am* among *are*
six hundred thousand men on
foot; yet You have said, 'I will
give them meat, that they may
eat *for* a whole month.' 22Shall
flocks and herds be slaughtered for them, to provide
enough for them? Or shall all
the fish of the sea be gathered
together for them, to provide
enough for them?"

23And the LORD said to
Moses, "Has the LORD's arm
been shortened? Now you
shall see whether what I say
will happen to you or not."

24So Moses went out and
told the people the words of
the LORD, and he gathered the
seventy men of the elders of
the people and placed them
around the tabernacle. 25Then
the LORD came down in the
cloud, and spoke to him, and
took of the Spirit that *was*
upon him, and placed *the
same* upon the seventy elders;
and it happened, when the
Spirit rested upon them, that
they prophesied, although
they never did *so* again.[a]

26But two men had re-
mained in the camp: the

11:25 [a] Targum and Vulgate read *did not cease*.

name of one *was* Eldad, and
the name of the other Medad.
And the Spirit rested upon
them. Now they *were* among
those listed, but who had not
gone out to the tabernacle; yet
they prophesied in the camp.
27And a young man ran and
told Moses, and said, "Eldad
and Medad are prophesying
in the camp."

28So Joshua the son of Nun,
Moses' assistant, *one* of his
choice men, answered and
said, "Moses my lord, forbid
them!"

29Then Moses said to him,
"Are you zealous for my sake?
Oh, that all the LORD's people
were prophets *and* that the
LORD would put His Spirit
upon them!" 30And Moses
returned to the camp, he and
the elders of Israel.

THE LORD SENDS QUAIL

31Now a wind went out
from the LORD, and it brought
quail from the sea and left
them fluttering near the
camp, about a day's jour-
ney on this side and about
a day's journey on the other
side, all around the camp, and
about two cubits above the
surface of the ground. 32And
the people stayed up all that
day, all night, and all the next
day, and gathered the quail
(he who gathered least gathered ten homers); and they
spread *them* out for themselves all around the camp.
33But while the meat *was* still
between their teeth, before it
was chewed, the wrath of the
LORD was aroused against the
people, and the LORD struck
the people with a very great
plague. 34So he called the
name of that place Kibroth
Hattaavah,[a] because there
they buried the people who
had yielded to craving.

35From Kibroth Hattaavah
the people moved to Haze-
roth, and camped at Hazeroth.

DISSENSION OF AARON AND MIRIAM

12 Then Miriam and Aaron
spoke against Moses be-
cause of the Ethiopian woman
whom he had married; for
he had married an Ethiopian
woman. 2So they said, "Has
the LORD indeed spoken only
through Moses? Has He not
spoken through us also?" And
the LORD heard *it*. 3(Now the
man Moses *was* very humble,
more than all men who *were*
on the face of the earth.)

4Suddenly the LORD said
to Moses, Aaron, and Miriam,
"Come out, you three, to the
tabernacle of meeting!" So
the three came out. 5Then the
LORD came down in the pillar
of cloud and stood *in* the door
of the tabernacle, and called
Aaron and Miriam. And they
both went forward. 6Then He
said,

11:34 [a] Literally *Graves of Craving*

“Hear now My words:
If there is a prophet
among you,
I, the LORD, make
Myself known to
him in a vision;
I speak to him in a dream.
7 Not so with My
servant Moses;
He *is* faithful in all
My house.
8 I speak with him
face to face,
Even plainly, and not
in dark sayings;
And he sees the form
of the LORD.
Why then were you
not afraid
To speak against My
servant Moses?”

9So the anger of the LORD
was aroused against them, and
He departed. 10And when the
cloud departed from above
the tabernacle, suddenly Miriam *became* leprous, as *white*
as snow. Then Aaron turned
toward Miriam, and there she
was, a leper. 11So Aaron said to
Moses, “Oh, my lord! Please
do not lay *this* sin on us, in
which we have done foolishly
and in which we have sinned.
12Please do not let her be as
one dead, whose flesh is half
consumed when he comes out
of his mother’s womb!”
13So Moses cried out to the
LORD, saying, “Please heal her,
O God, I pray!”
14Then the LORD said to
Moses, “If her father had but
spit in her face, would she not
be shamed seven days? Let
her be shut out of the camp
seven days, and afterward she
may be received *again*.” 15So
Miriam was shut out of the
camp seven days, and the people did not journey till Miriam
was brought in *again*. 16And
afterward the people moved
from Hazeroth and camped
in the Wilderness of Paran.

SPIES SENT INTO CANAAN

13 And the LORD spoke to
Moses, saying, 2“Send
men to spy out the land of
Canaan, which I am giving to
the children of Israel; from
each tribe of their fathers you
shall send a man, every one a
leader among them.”
3So Moses sent them from
the Wilderness of Paran according to the command of
the LORD, all of them men
who *were* heads of the children of Israel. 4Now these
were their names: from the
tribe of Reuben, Shammua
the son of Zaccur; 5from the
tribe of Simeon, Shaphat the
son of Hori; 6from the tribe
of Judah, Caleb the son of
Jephunneh; 7from the tribe
of Issachar, Igal the son
of Joseph; 8from the tribe of
Ephraim, Hoshea[a] the son of
Nun; 9from the tribe of Benjamin, Palti the son of Raphu;

13:8 [a] Septuagint and Vulgate read *Oshea*.

10from the tribe of Zebulun,
Gaddiel the son of Sodi; 11from
the tribe of Joseph, *that is,*
from the tribe of Manasseh,
Gaddi the son of Susi; 12from
the tribe of Dan, Ammiel the
son of Gemalli; 13from the
tribe of Asher, Sethur the son
of Michael; 14from the tribe of
Naphtali, Nahbi the son of Vo-
phsi; 15from the tribe of Gad,
Geuel the son of Machi.

16These *are* the names of
the men whom Moses sent to
spy out the land. And Moses
called Hoshea[a] the son of
Nun, Joshua.

17Then Moses sent them
to spy out the land of Canaan, and said to them, "Go
up this *way* into the South,
and go up to the mountains,
18and see what the land is like:
whether the people who dwell
in it *are* strong or weak, few
or many; 19whether the land
they dwell in *is* good or bad;
whether the cities they inhabit
are like camps or strongholds;
20whether the land *is* rich
or poor; and whether there
are forests there or not. Be
of good courage. And bring
some of the fruit of the land."
Now the time *was* the season
of the first ripe grapes.

21So they went up and spied
out the land from the Wilderness of Zin as far as Rehob,
near the entrance of Hamath.
22And they went up through
the South and came to He-
bron; Ahiman, Sheshai, and
Talmai, the descendants of
Anak, *were* there. (Now Hebron was built seven years before Zoan in Egypt.) 23Then
they came to the Valley of
Eshcol, and there cut down
a branch with one cluster of
grapes; they carried it between two of them on a pole.
They also *brought* some of the
pomegranates and figs. 24The
place was called the Valley of
Eshcol,[a] because of the cluster which the men of Israel
cut down there. 25And they
returned from spying out the
land after forty days.

26Now they departed and
came back to Moses and
Aaron and all the congregation of the children of Israel
in the Wilderness of Paran,
at Kadesh; they brought back
word to them and to all the
congregation, and showed
them the fruit of the land.
27Then they told him, and
said: "We went to the land
where you sent us. It truly
flows with milk and honey,
and this *is* its fruit. 28Never-
theless the people who dwell
in the land *are* strong; the
cities *are* fortified *and* very
large; moreover we saw the
descendants of Anak there.
29The Amalekites dwell in the
land of the South; the Hittites,
the Jebusites, and the Amorites dwell in the mountains;
and the Canaanites dwell by

13:16 [a] Septuagint and Vulgate read *Oshea.* 13:24 [a] Literally *Cluster*

the sea and along the banks
of the Jordan."
30Then Caleb quieted the
people before Moses, and said,
"Let us go up at once and take
possession, for we are well
able to overcome it."
31But the men who had
gone up with him said, "We
are not able to go up against
the people, for they *are* stronger than we." 32And they gave
the children of Israel a bad
report of the land which they
had spied out, saying, "The
land through which we have
gone as spies *is* a land that
devours its inhabitants, and
all the people whom we saw
in it *are* men of *great* stature.
33There we saw the giants[a]
(the descendants of Anak
came from the giants); and
we were like grasshoppers in
our own sight, and so we were
in their sight."

ISRAEL REFUSES TO ENTER CANAAN

14 So all the congregation
lifted up their voices
and cried, and the people
wept that night. 2And all the
children of Israel complained
against Moses and Aaron, and
the whole congregation said
to them, "If only we had died
in the land of Egypt! Or if
only we had died in this wilderness! 3Why has the LORD
brought us to this land to fall
by the sword, that our wives
and children should become
victims? Would it not be better
for us to return to Egypt?" 4So
they said to one another, "Let
us select a leader and return
to Egypt."
5Then Moses and Aaron fell
on their faces before all the
assembly of the congregation
of the children of Israel.
6But Joshua the son of Nun
and Caleb the son of Jephunneh, *who were* among those
who had spied out the land,
tore their clothes; 7and they
spoke to all the congregation of the children of Israel,
saying: "The land we passed
through to spy out *is* an exceedingly good land. 8If the
LORD delights in us, then He
will bring us into this land and
give it to us, 'a land which flows
with milk and honey.'[a] 9Only
do not rebel against the LORD,
nor fear the people of the land,
for they *are* our bread; their
protection has departed from
them, and the LORD *is* with us.
Do not fear them."
10And all the congrega-
tion said to stone them with
stones. Now the glory of the
LORD appeared in the tabernacle of meeting before all the
children of Israel.

MOSES INTERCEDES FOR THE PEOPLE

11Then the LORD said to
Moses: "How long will these
people reject Me? And how

13:33 [a] Hebrew *nephilim* 14:8 [a] Exodus 3:8

long will they not believe Me,
with all the signs which I have
performed among them? 12I
will strike them with the pestilence and disinherit them,
and I will make of you a nation greater and mightier than
they."
13And Moses said to the
LORD: "Then the Egyptians
will hear *it,* for by Your might
You brought these people up
from among them, 14and they
will tell *it* to the inhabitants
of this land. They have heard
that You, LORD, *are* among
these people; that You, LORD,
are seen face to face and Your
cloud stands above them, and
You go before them in a pillar
of cloud by day and in a pillar
of fire by night. 15Now *if* You kill
these people as one man, then
the nations which have heard
of Your fame will speak, saying, 16'Because the LORD was
not able to bring this people
to the land which He swore to
give them, therefore He killed
them in the wilderness.' 17And
now, I pray, let the power of my
Lord be great, just as You have
spoken, saying, 18'The LORD is
longsuffering and abundant
in mercy, forgiving iniquity
and transgression; but He by
no means clears *the guilty,*
visiting the iniquity of the fathers on the children to the
third and fourth *generation.*'[a]
19Pardon the iniquity of this
people, I pray, according to
the greatness of Your mercy,
just as You have forgiven this
people, from Egypt even until
now."
20Then the LORD said: "I
have pardoned, according to
your word; 21but truly, as I live,
all the earth shall be filled with
the glory of the LORD— 22be-
cause all these men who have
seen My glory and the signs
which I did in Egypt and in the
wilderness, and have put Me to
the test now these ten times,
and have not heeded My voice,
23they certainly shall not see
the land of which I swore to
their fathers, nor shall any of
those who rejected Me see it.
24But My servant Caleb, because he has a different spirit
in him and has followed Me
fully, I will bring into the
land where he went, and his
descendants shall inherit it.
25Now the Amalekites and the
Canaanites dwell in the valley;
tomorrow turn and move out
into the wilderness by the Way
of the Red Sea."

DEATH SENTENCE ON THE REBELS

26And the LORD spoke to
Moses and Aaron, saying,
27"How long *shall I bear with*
this evil congregation who
complain against Me? I have
heard the complaints which
the children of Israel make
against Me. 28Say to them, 'As
I live,' says the LORD, 'just as

14:18 [a] Exodus 34:6, 7

you have spoken in My hearing, so I will do to you: [29]The
carcasses of you who have
complained against Me shall
fall in this wilderness, all of
you who were numbered, according to your entire number, from twenty years old and
above. [30]Except for Caleb the
son of Jephunneh and Joshua
the son of Nun, you shall by no
means enter the land which
I swore I would make you
dwell in. [31]But your little ones,
whom you said would be victims, I will bring in, and they
shall know the land which you
have despised. [32]But *as for*
you, your carcasses shall fall
in this wilderness. [33]And your
sons shall be shepherds in the
wilderness forty years, and
bear the brunt of your infi-
delity, until your carcasses are
consumed in the wilderness.
[34]According to the number of
the days in which you spied
out the land, forty days, for
each day you shall bear your
guilt one year, *namely* forty
years, and you shall know My
rejection. [35]I the LORD have
spoken this. I will surely do
so to all this evil congregation
who are gathered together
against Me. In this wilderness
they shall be consumed, and
there they shall die.'"

[36]Now the men whom
Moses sent to spy out the land,
who returned and made all
the congregation complain
against him by bringing a bad
report of the land, [37]those
very men who brought the
evil report about the land,
died by the plague before the
LORD. [38]But Joshua the son
of Nun and Caleb the son of
Jephunneh remained alive,
of the men who went to spy
out the land.

A FUTILE INVASION ATTEMPT

[39]Then Moses told these
words to all the children of Israel, and the people mourned
greatly. [40]And they rose early
in the morning and went up
to the top of the mountain,
saying, "Here we are, and we
will go up to the place which
the LORD has promised, for
we have sinned!"

[41]And Moses said, "Now
why do you transgress the
command of the LORD? For
this will not succeed. [42]Do not
go up, lest you be defeated by
your enemies, for the LORD
is not among you. [43]For the
Amalekites and the Canaanites *are* there before you, and
you shall fall by the sword;
because you have turned away
from the LORD, the LORD will
not be with you."

[44]But they presumed to
go up to the mountaintop.
Nevertheless, neither the ark
of the covenant of the LORD
nor Moses departed from the
camp. [45]Then the Amalekites
and the Canaanites who dwelt
in that mountain came down
and attacked them, and drove
them back as far as Hormah.

LAWS OF GRAIN AND DRINK OFFERINGS

15 And the LORD spoke to Moses, saying, 2“Speak to the children of Israel, and say to them: ‘When you have come into the land you are to inhabit, which I am giving to you, 3and you make an offering by fire to the LORD, a burnt offering or a sacrifice, to fulfill a vow or as a freewill offering or in your appointed feasts, to make a sweet aroma to the LORD, from the herd or the flock, 4then he who presents his offering to the LORD shall bring a grain offering of one-tenth *of an ephah* of fine flour mixed with one-fourth of a hin of oil; 5and one-fourth of a hin of wine as a drink offering you shall prepare with the burnt offering or the sacrifice, for each lamb. 6Or for a ram you shall prepare as a grain offering two-tenths *of an ephah* of fine flour mixed with one-third of a hin of oil; 7and as a drink offering you shall offer one-third of a hin of wine as a sweet aroma to the LORD. 8And when you prepare a young bull as a burnt offering, or as a sacrifice to fulfill a vow, or as a peace offering to the LORD, 9then shall be offered with the young bull a grain offering of three-tenths *of an ephah* of fine flour mixed with half a hin of oil; 10and you shall bring as the drink offering half a hin of wine as an offering made by fire, a sweet aroma to the LORD.

11“Thus it shall be done for each young bull, for each ram, or for each lamb or young goat. 12According to the number that you prepare, so you shall do with everyone according to their number. 13All who are native-born shall do these things in this manner, in presenting an offering made by fire, a sweet aroma to the LORD. 14And if a stranger dwells with you, or whoever *is* among you throughout your generations, and would present an offering made by fire, a sweet aroma to the LORD, just as you do, so shall he do. 15One ordinance *shall be* for you of the assembly and for the stranger who dwells *with you*, an ordinance forever throughout your generations; as you are, so shall the stranger be before the LORD. 16One law and one custom shall be for you and for the stranger who dwells with you.’”[a]

17Again the LORD spoke to Moses, saying, 18“Speak to the children of Israel, and say to them: ‘When you come into the land to which I bring you, 19then it will be, when you eat of the bread of the land, that you shall offer up a heave offering to the LORD. 20You shall offer up a cake of the first of your ground meal *as* a heave

15:16 [a] Compare Exodus 12:49

offering; as a heave offering
of the threshing floor, so shall
you offer it up. 21Of the first of
your ground meal you shall
give to the LORD a heave offering throughout your generations.

LAWS CONCERNING UNINTENTIONAL SIN

22'If you sin unintentionally,
and do not observe all these
commandments which the
LORD has spoken to Moses—
23all that the LORD has commanded you by the hand of
Moses, from the day the LORD
gave commandment and on-
ward throughout your gen-
erations— 24then it will be,
if it is unintentionally committed, without the knowledge of the congregation,
that the whole congregation
shall offer one young bull as
a burnt offering, as a sweet
aroma to the LORD, with its
grain offering and its drink
offering, according to the ordinance, and one kid of the
goats as a sin offering. 25So
the priest shall make atonement for the whole congregation of the children of Israel,
and it shall be forgiven them,
for it was unintentional; they
shall bring their offering, an
offering made by fire to the
LORD, and their sin offering
before the LORD, for their
unintended sin. 26It shall be
forgiven the whole congregation of the children of Israel
and the stranger who dwells
among them, because all the
people *did it* unintentionally.

27'And if a person sins unintentionally, then he shall
bring a female goat in its first
year as a sin offering. 28So the
priest shall make atonement
for the person who sins unintentionally, when he sins unintentionally before the LORD,
to make atonement for him;
and it shall be forgiven him.
29You shall have one law for
him who sins unintentionally,
for him who is native-born
among the children of Is-
rael and for the stranger who
dwells among them.

LAW CONCERNING PRESUMPTUOUS SIN

30'But the person who
does *anything* presumptuously, *whether he is* native-
born or a stranger, that one
brings reproach on the LORD,
and he shall be cut off from
among his people. 31Because
he has despised the word of
the LORD, and has broken His
commandment, that person
shall be completely cut off;
his guilt *shall be* upon him.'"

PENALTY FOR VIOLATING THE SABBATH

32Now while the children of
Israel were in the wilderness,
they found a man gathering
sticks on the Sabbath day.
33And those who found him
gathering sticks brought him
to Moses and Aaron, and to all
the congregation. 34They put

him under guard, because it
had not been explained what
should be done to him.
35Then the LORD said to
Moses, "The man must surely
be put to death; all the congregation shall stone him with
stones outside the camp."
36So, as the LORD commanded
Moses, all the congregation
brought him outside the camp
and stoned him with stones,
and he died.

TASSELS ON GARMENTS

37Again the LORD spoke to
Moses, saying, 38"Speak to the
children of Israel: Tell them to
make tassels on the corners
of their garments throughout
their generations, and to put
a blue thread in the tassels of
the corners. 39And you shall
have the tassel, that you may
look upon it and remember
all the commandments of
the LORD and do them, and
that you *may* not follow the
harlotry to which your own
heart and your own eyes are
inclined, 40and that you may
remember and do all My commandments, and be holy for
your God. 41I *am* the LORD
your God, who brought you
out of the land of Egypt, to
be your God: I *am* the LORD
your God."

REBELLION AGAINST MOSES AND AARON

16 Now Korah the son of
Izhar, the son of Kohath,
the son of Levi, with Dathan
and Abiram the sons of Eliab,
and On the son of Peleth, sons
of Reuben, took *men;* 2and
they rose up before Moses
with some of the children of
Israel, two hundred and fifty
leaders of the congregation,
representatives of the congregation, men of renown. 3They
gathered together against
Moses and Aaron, and said
to them, "*You take* too much
upon yourselves, for all the
congregation *is* holy, every
one of them, and the LORD
is among them. Why then do
you exalt yourselves above
the assembly of the LORD?"
4So when Moses heard *it,*
he fell on his face; 5and he
spoke to Korah and all his
company, saying, "Tomorrow
morning the LORD will show
who *is* His and *who is* holy, and
will cause *him* to come near
to Him. That one whom He
chooses He will cause to come
near to Him. 6Do this: Take
censers, Korah and all your
company; 7put fire in them
and put incense in them before the LORD tomorrow, and
it shall be *that* the man whom
the LORD chooses *is* the holy
one. *You take* too much upon
yourselves, you sons of Levi!"
8Then Moses said to Korah,
"Hear now, you sons of Levi:
9*Is it* a small thing to you that
the God of Israel has separated
you from the congregation
of Israel, to bring you near to
Himself, to do the work of the
tabernacle of the LORD, and to

stand before the congregation
to serve them; 10and that He
has brought you near *to Himself,* you and all your brethren, the sons of Levi, with
you? And are you seeking the
priesthood also? 11Therefore
you and all your company *are*
gathered together against the
LORD. And what *is* Aaron that
you complain against him?"

12And Moses sent to call
Dathan and Abiram the
sons of Eliab, but they said,
"We will not come up! 13*Is it*
a small thing that you have
brought us up out of a land
flowing with milk and honey,
to kill us in the wilderness,
that you should keep acting
like a prince over us? 14More-
over you have not brought
us into a land flowing with
milk and honey, nor given
us inheritance of fields and
vineyards. Will you put out
the eyes of these men? We will
not come up!"

15Then Moses was very
angry, and said to the LORD,
"Do not respect their offering.
I have not taken one donkey
from them, nor have I hurt
one of them."

16And Moses said to Korah,
"Tomorrow, you and all your
company be present before
the LORD—you and they, as
well as Aaron. 17Let each take
his censer and put incense in
it, and each of you bring his
censer before the LORD, two
hundred and fifty censers;
both you and Aaron, each *with*
his censer." 18So every man
took his censer, put fire in it,
laid incense on it, and stood
at the door of the tabernacle
of meeting with Moses and
Aaron. 19And Korah gathered
all the congregation against
them at the door of the tabernacle of meeting. Then the
glory of the LORD appeared to
all the congregation.

20And the LORD spoke to
Moses and Aaron, saying,
21"Separate yourselves from
among this congregation,
that I may consume them in
a moment."

22Then they fell on their
faces, and said, "O God, the
God of the spirits of all flesh,
shall one man sin, and You
be angry with all the congregation?"

23So the LORD spoke to
Moses, saying, 24"Speak to
the congregation, saying, 'Get
away from the tents of Korah,
Dathan, and Abiram.'"

25Then Moses rose and
went to Dathan and Abiram,
and the elders of Israel followed him. 26And he spoke
to the congregation, saying,
"Depart now from the tents
of these wicked men! Touch
nothing of theirs, lest you be
consumed in all their sins."
27So they got away from
around the tents of Korah,
Dathan, and Abiram; and Dathan and Abiram came out
and stood at the door of their
tents, with their wives, their
sons, and their little children.

[28]And Moses said: "By this
you shall know that the LORD
has sent me to do all these
works, for *I have* not *done them*
of my own will. [29]If these men
die naturally like all men, or
if they are visited by the common fate of all men, *then* the
LORD has not sent me. [30]But if
the LORD creates a new thing,
and the earth opens its mouth
and swallows them up with
all that belongs to them, and
they go down alive into the
pit, then you will understand
that these men have rejected
the LORD."

[31]Now it came to pass, as
he finished speaking all these
words, that the ground split
apart under them, [32]and the
earth opened its mouth and
swallowed them up, with
their households and all the
men with Korah, with all *their*
goods. [33]So they and all those
with them went down alive
into the pit; the earth closed
over them, and they perished
from among the assembly.
[34]Then all Israel who *were*
around them fled at their cry,
for they said, "Lest the earth
swallow us up *also!*"

[35]And a fire came out from
the LORD and consumed the
two hundred and fifty men
who were offering incense.

[36]Then the LORD spoke to
Moses, saying: [37]"Tell Eleazar,
the son of Aaron the priest, to
pick up the censers out of the
blaze, for they are holy, and
scatter the fire some distance
away. [38]The censers of these
men who sinned against their
own souls, let them be made
into hammered plates as a
covering for the altar. Because
they presented them before
the LORD, therefore they are
holy; and they shall be a sign
to the children of Israel." [39]So
Eleazar the priest took the
bronze censers, which those
who were burned up had presented, and they were hammered out as a covering on
the altar, [40]*to be* a memorial
to the children of Israel that
no outsider, who *is* not a descendant of Aaron, should
come near to offer incense before the LORD, that he might
not become like Korah and
his companions, just as the
LORD had said to him through
Moses.

COMPLAINTS OF THE PEOPLE

[41]On the next day all the
congregation of the children
of Israel complained against
Moses and Aaron, saying,
"You have killed the people of
the LORD." [42]Now it happened,
when the congregation had
gathered against Moses and
Aaron, that they turned toward the tabernacle of meeting; and suddenly the cloud
covered it, and the glory of the
LORD appeared. [43]Then Moses
and Aaron came before the
tabernacle of meeting.

[44]And the LORD spoke to
Moses, saying, [45]"Get away

from among this congre-
gation, that I may consume
them in a moment."

And they fell on their faces.
46 So Moses said to Aaron,
"Take a censer and put fire in
it from the altar, put incense
on it, and take it quickly to
the congregation and make
atonement for them; for wrath
has gone out from the LORD.
The plague has begun." 47 Then
Aaron took *it* as Moses commanded, and ran into the
midst of the assembly; and
already the plague had begun
among the people. So he put in
the incense and made atonement for the people. 48 And he
stood between the dead and
the living; so the plague was
stopped. 49 Now those who
died in the plague were fourteen thousand seven hundred,
besides those who died in the
Korah incident. 50 So Aaron returned to Moses at the door of
the tabernacle of meeting, for
the plague had stopped.

THE BUDDING OF AARON'S ROD

17 And the LORD spoke to
Moses, saying: 2 "Speak
to the children of Israel, and
get from them a rod from each
father's house, all their leaders according to their fathers'
houses—twelve rods. Write
each man's name on his rod.
3 And you shall write Aaron's
name on the rod of Levi. For
there shall be one rod for the
head of *each* father's house.
4 Then you shall place them
in the tabernacle of meeting
before the Testimony, where I
meet with you. 5 And it shall be
that the rod of the man whom
I choose will blossom; thus
I will rid Myself of the complaints of the children of Israel, which they make against
you."

6 So Moses spoke to the
children of Israel, and each
of their leaders gave him a rod
apiece, for each leader according to their fathers' houses,
twelve rods; and the rod of
Aaron *was* among their rods.
7 And Moses placed the rods
before the LORD in the tabernacle of witness.

8 Now it came to pass on the
next day that Moses went into
the tabernacle of witness, and
behold, the rod of Aaron, of the
house of Levi, had sprouted
and put forth buds, had produced blossoms and yielded
ripe almonds. 9 Then Moses
brought out all the rods from
before the LORD to all the children of Israel; and they looked,
and each man took his rod.

10 And the LORD said to
Moses, "Bring Aaron's rod
back before the Testimony,
to be kept as a sign against
the rebels, that you may put
their complaints away from
Me, lest they die." 11 Thus did
Moses; just as the LORD had
commanded him, so he did.

12 So the children of Is-
rael spoke to Moses, saying,
"Surely we die, we perish, we

all perish! 13Whoever even
comes near the tabernacle of
the LORD must die. Shall we
all utterly die?"

DUTIES OF PRIESTS AND LEVITES

18 Then the LORD said to
Aaron: "You and your
sons and your father's house
with you shall bear the iniquity *related to* the sanctuary,
and you and your sons with
you shall bear the iniquity
associated with your priesthood. 2Also bring with you
your brethren of the tribe of
Levi, the tribe of your father,
that they may be joined with
you and serve you while you
and your sons *are* with you before the tabernacle of witness.
3They shall attend to your
needs and all the needs of the
tabernacle; but they shall not
come near the articles of the
sanctuary and the altar, lest
they die—they and you also.
4They shall be joined with
you and attend to the needs
of the tabernacle of meeting,
for all the work of the tabernacle; but an outsider shall
not come near you. 5And you
shall attend to the duties of
the sanctuary and the duties
of the altar, that there *may* be
no more wrath on the children of Israel. 6Behold, I Myself have taken your brethren
the Levites from among the
children of Israel; *they are* a
gift to you, given by the LORD,
to do the work of the tabernacle of meeting. 7Therefore you
and your sons with you shall
attend to your priesthood for
everything at the altar and behind the veil; and you shall
serve. I give your priesthood
to you as a gift for service, but
the outsider who comes near
shall be put to death."

OFFERINGS FOR SUPPORT OF THE PRIESTS

8And the LORD spoke to
Aaron: "Here, I Myself have
also given you charge of My
heave offerings, all the holy
gifts of the children of Israel;
I have given them as a portion
to you and your sons, as an ordinance forever. 9This shall be
yours of the most holy things
reserved from the fire: every
offering of theirs, every grain
offering and every sin offering
and every trespass offering
which they render to Me, *shall
be* most holy for you and your
sons. 10In a most holy *place*
you shall eat it; every male
shall eat it. It shall be holy to
you.

11"This also *is* yours: the
heave offering of their gift,
with all the wave offerings
of the children of Israel; I
have given them to you, and
your sons and daughters with
you, as an ordinance forever.
Everyone who is clean in your
house may eat it.

12"All the best of the oil,
all the best of the new wine
and the grain, their firstfruits
which they offer to the LORD,

I have given them to you.
13 Whatever first ripe fruit is
in their land, which they bring
to the LORD, shall be yours.
Everyone who is clean in your
house may eat it.

14 "Every devoted thing in
Israel shall be yours.

15 "Everything that first
opens the womb of all flesh,
which they bring to the LORD,
whether man or beast, shall be
yours; nevertheless the firstborn of man you shall surely
redeem, and the firstborn of
unclean animals you shall redeem. 16 And those redeemed
of the devoted things you shall
redeem when one month old,
according to your valuation,
for five shekels of silver, according to the shekel of the
sanctuary, which *is* twenty gerahs. 17 But the firstborn of a
cow, the firstborn of a sheep,
or the firstborn of a goat you
shall not redeem; they *are*
holy. You shall sprinkle their
blood on the altar, and burn
their fat *as* an offering made
by fire for a sweet aroma to
the LORD. 18 And their flesh
shall be yours, just as the wave
breast and the right thigh are
yours.

19 "All the heave offerings
of the holy things, which the
children of Israel offer to the
LORD, I have given to you and
your sons and daughters with
you as an ordinance forever;
it *is* a covenant of salt forever
before the LORD with you and
your descendants with you."

20 Then the LORD said to
Aaron: "You shall have no
inheritance in their land,
nor shall you have any portion among them; I *am* your
portion and your inheritance
among the children of Israel.

TITHES FOR SUPPORT OF THE LEVITES

21 "Behold, I have given
the children of Levi all the
tithes in Israel as an inheritance in return for the work
which they perform, the work
of the tabernacle of meeting.
22 Hereafter the children of Israel shall not come near the
tabernacle of meeting, lest
they bear sin and die. 23 But
the Levites shall perform
the work of the tabernacle of
meeting, and they shall bear
their iniquity; *it shall be* a statute forever, throughout your
generations, that among the
children of Israel they shall
have no inheritance. 24 For the
tithes of the children of Israel, which they offer up *as* a
heave offering to the LORD, I
have given to the Levites as an
inheritance; therefore I have
said to them, 'Among the children of Israel they shall have
no inheritance.'"

THE TITHE OF THE LEVITES

25 Then the LORD spoke to
Moses, saying, 26 "Speak thus
to the Levites, and say to them:
'When you take from the chil-
dren of Israel the tithes which
I have given you from them

as your inheritance, then you
shall offer up a heave offering
of it to the LORD, a tenth of the
tithe. 27And your heave offering shall be reckoned to you
as though *it were* the grain
of the threshing floor and as
the fullness of the winepress.
28Thus you shall also offer a
heave offering to the LORD
from all your tithes which you
receive from the children of
Israel, and you shall give the
LORD's heave offering from
it to Aaron the priest. 29Of all
your gifts you shall offer up
every heave offering due to
the LORD, from all the best of
them, the consecrated part of
them.' 30Therefore you shall
say to them: 'When you have
lifted up the best of it, then
the rest shall be accounted
to the Levites as the produce
of the threshing floor and as
the produce of the winepress.
31You may eat it in any place,
you and your households, for
it *is* your reward for your work
in the tabernacle of meeting.
32And you shall bear no sin
because of it, when you have
lifted up the best of it. But you
shall not profane the holy gifts
of the children of Israel, lest
you die.'"

LAWS OF PURIFICATION

19 Now the LORD spoke to
Moses and Aaron, say-
ing, 2"This *is* the ordinance
of the law which the LORD has
commanded, saying: 'Speak
to the children of Israel, that
they bring you a red heifer
without blemish, in which
there *is* no defect *and* on
which a yoke has never come.
3You shall give it to Eleazar
the priest, that he may take
it outside the camp, and it
shall be slaughtered before
him; 4and Eleazar the priest
shall take some of its blood
with his finger, and sprinkle some of its blood seven
times directly in front of the
tabernacle of meeting. 5Then
the heifer shall be burned in
his sight: its hide, its flesh, its
blood, and its offal shall be
burned. 6And the priest shall
take cedar wood and hyssop
and scarlet, and cast *them* into
the midst of the fire burning
the heifer. 7Then the priest
shall wash his clothes, he shall
bathe in water, and afterward
he shall come into the camp;
the priest shall be unclean
until evening. 8And the one
who burns it shall wash his
clothes in water, bathe in
water, and shall be unclean
until evening. 9Then a man
who is clean shall gather up
the ashes of the heifer, and
store *them* outside the camp
in a clean place; and they shall
be kept for the congregation
of the children of Israel for
the water of purification;[a] it *is*
for purifying from sin. 10And
the one who gathers the ashes

19:9 [a] Literally *impurity*

of the heifer shall wash his clothes, and be unclean until evening. It shall be a statute forever to the children of Israel and to the stranger who dwells among them.

11'He who touches the dead body of anyone shall be unclean seven days. 12He shall purify himself with the water on the third day and on the seventh day; *then* he will be clean. But if he does not purify himself on the third day and on the seventh day, he will not be clean. 13Whoever touches the body of anyone who has died, and does not purify himself, defiles the tabernacle of the LORD. That person shall be cut off from Israel. He shall be unclean, because the water of purification was not sprinkled on him; his uncleanness *is* still on him.

14'This *is* the law when a man dies in a tent: All who come into the tent and all who *are* in the tent shall be unclean seven days; 15and every open vessel, which has no cover fastened on it, *is* unclean. 16Whoever in the open field touches one who is slain by a sword or who has died, or a bone of a man, or a grave, shall be unclean seven days.

17'And for an unclean *person* they shall take some of the ashes of the heifer burnt for purification from sin, and running water shall be put on them in a vessel. 18A clean person shall take hyssop and dip *it* in the water, sprinkle *it* on the tent, on all the vessels, on the persons who were there, or on the one who touched a bone, the slain, the dead, or a grave. 19The clean *person* shall sprinkle the unclean on the third day and on the seventh day; and on the seventh day he shall purify himself, wash his clothes, and bathe in water; and at evening he shall be clean.

20'But the man who is unclean and does not purify himself, that person shall be cut off from among the assembly, because he has defiled the sanctuary of the LORD. The water of purification has not been sprinkled on him; he *is* unclean. 21It shall be a perpetual statute for them. He who sprinkles the water of purification shall wash his clothes; and he who touches the water of purification shall be unclean until evening. 22Whatever the unclean *person* touches shall be unclean; and the person who touches *it* shall be unclean until evening.' "

MOSES' ERROR AT KADESH

20 Then the children of Israel, the whole congregation, came into the Wilderness of Zin in the first month, and the people stayed in Kadesh; and Miriam died there and was buried there.

2Now there was no water for the congregation; so they

gathered together against
Moses and Aaron. 3And the
people contended with Moses
and spoke, saying: "If only we
had died when our brethren
died before the LORD! 4Why
have you brought up the assembly of the LORD into this
wilderness, that we and our
animals should die here?
5And why have you made
us come up out of Egypt, to
bring us to this evil place? It *is*
not a place of grain or figs or
vines or pomegranates; nor *is*
there any water to drink." 6So
Moses and Aaron went from
the presence of the assembly
to the door of the tabernacle
of meeting, and they fell on
their faces. And the glory of
the LORD appeared to them.

7Then the LORD spoke to
Moses, saying, 8"Take the rod;
you and your brother Aaron
gather the congregation together. Speak to the rock
before their eyes, and it will
yield its water; thus you shall
bring water for them out of
the rock, and give drink to
the congregation and their
animals." 9So Moses took the
rod from before the LORD as
He commanded him.

10And Moses and Aaron
gathered the assembly to-
gether before the rock; and
he said to them, "Hear now,
you rebels! Must we bring
water for you out of this rock?"
11Then Moses lifted his hand
and struck the rock twice
with his rod; and water came
out abundantly, and the congregation and their animals
drank.

12Then the LORD spoke to
Moses and Aaron, "Because
you did not believe Me, to
hallow Me in the eyes of the
children of Israel, therefore
you shall not bring this assembly into the land which I
have given them."

13This *was* the water of Meribah,[a] because the children
of Israel contended with the
LORD, and He was hallowed
among them.

PASSAGE THROUGH EDOM REFUSED

14Now Moses sent mes-
sengers from Kadesh to the
king of Edom. "Thus says your
brother Israel: 'You know all
the hardship that has be-
fallen us, 15how our fathers
went down to Egypt, and we
dwelt in Egypt a long time,
and the Egyptians afflicted
us and our fathers. 16When
we cried out to the LORD, He
heard our voice and sent the
Angel and brought us up out
of Egypt; now here we are in
Kadesh, a city on the edge of
your border. 17Please let us
pass through your country. We
will not pass through fields or
vineyards, nor will we drink
water from wells; we will go
along the King's Highway;

20:13 [a] Literally *Contention*

we will not turn aside to the
right hand or to the left until
we have passed through your
territory.'"
18Then Edom said to him,
"You shall not pass through
my *land,* lest I come out
against you with the sword."
19So the children of Israel
said to him, "We will go by the
Highway, and if I or my livestock drink any of your water,
then I will pay for it; let me
only pass through on foot,
nothing *more.*"
20Then he said, "You shall
not pass through." So Edom
came out against them with
many men and with a strong
hand. 21Thus Edom refused to
give Israel passage through
his territory; so Israel turned
away from him.

DEATH OF AARON

22Now the children of Is-
rael, the whole congregation,
journeyed from Kadesh and
came to Mount Hor. 23And
the LORD spoke to Moses and
Aaron in Mount Hor by the
border of the land of Edom,
saying: 24"Aaron shall be gathered to his people, for he shall
not enter the land which I have
given to the children of Israel,
because you rebelled against
My word at the water of Meribah. 25Take Aaron and Eleazar
his son, and bring them up to
Mount Hor; 26and strip Aaron
of his garments and put them
on Eleazar his son; for Aaron
shall be gathered *to his people*
and die there." 27So Moses did
just as the LORD commanded,
and they went up to Mount
Hor in the sight of all the congregation. 28Moses stripped
Aaron of his garments and put
them on Eleazar his son; and
Aaron died there on the top
of the mountain. Then Moses
and Eleazar came down from
the mountain. 29Now when
all the congregation saw that
Aaron was dead, all the house
of Israel mourned for Aaron
thirty days.

CANAANITES DEFEATED AT HORMAH

21 The king of Arad, the Canaanite, who dwelt in the
South, heard that Israel was
coming on the road to Atha-
rim. Then he fought against
Israel and took *some* of them
prisoners. 2So Israel made a
vow to the LORD, and said, "If
You will indeed deliver this
people into my hand, then I
will utterly destroy their cities."
3And the LORD listened to the
voice of Israel and delivered
up the Canaanites, and they
utterly destroyed them and
their cities. So the name of
that place was called Hormah.[a]

THE BRONZE SERPENT

4Then they journeyed
from Mount Hor by the Way
of the Red Sea, to go around

21:3 [a] Literally *Utter Destruction*

the land of Edom; and the
soul of the people became
very discouraged on the way.
5And the people spoke against
God and against Moses: "Why
have you brought us up out of
Egypt to die in the wilderness?
For *there is* no food and no
water, and our soul loathes
this worthless bread." 6So
the LORD sent fiery serpents
among the people, and they
bit the people; and many of
the people of Israel died.

7Therefore the people came
to Moses, and said, "We have
sinned, for we have spoken
against the LORD and against
you; pray to the LORD that He
take away the serpents from
us." So Moses prayed for the
people.

8Then the LORD said to
Moses, "Make a fiery *serpent,*
and set it on a pole; and it
shall be that everyone who
is bitten, when he looks at it,
shall live." 9So Moses made a
bronze serpent, and put it on a
pole; and so it was, if a serpent
had bitten anyone, when he
looked at the bronze serpent,
he lived.

FROM MOUNT HOR TO MOAB

10Now the children of Is-
rael moved on and camped
in Oboth. 11And they journeyed
from Oboth and camped at
Ije Abarim, in the wilderness
which *is* east of Moab, toward
the sunrise. 12From there they
moved and camped in the
Valley of Zered. 13From there
they moved and camped on
the other side of the Arnon,
which *is* in the wilderness that
extends from the border of the
Amorites; for the Arnon *is* the
border of Moab, between Moab
and the Amorites. 14Therefore
it is said in the Book of the
Wars of the LORD:

"Waheb in Suphah,[a]
The brooks of the Arnon,
15 And the slope of
the brooks
That reaches to the
dwelling of Ar,
And lies on the
border of Moab."

16From there *they went* to
Beer, which *is* the well where
the LORD said to Moses,
"Gather the people together,
and I will give them water."
17Then Israel sang this song:

"Spring up, O well!
All of you sing to it—
18 The well the leaders sank,
Dug by the nation's
nobles,
By the lawgiver, with
their staves."

And from the wilderness
they went to Mattanah, 19from
Mattanah to Nahaliel, from

21:14 [a] Ancient unknown places; Vulgate reads *What He did in the Red Sea.*

Nahaliel to Bamoth, [20]and
from Bamoth, *in* the valley
that *is* in the country of Moab,
to the top of Pisgah which
looks down on the wasteland.[a]

KING SIHON DEFEATED

[21]Then Israel sent mes-
sengers to Sihon king of the
Amorites, saying, [22]"Let me
pass through your land. We
will not turn aside into fields
or vineyards; we will not drink
water from wells. We will go by
the King's Highway until we
have passed through your territory." [23]But Sihon would not
allow Israel to pass through
his territory. So Sihon gathered all his people together
and went out against Israel in
the wilderness, and he came
to Jahaz and fought against
Israel. [24]Then Israel defeated
him with the edge of the
sword, and took possession of
his land from the Arnon to the
Jabbok, as far as the people of
Ammon; for the border of the
people of Ammon *was* fortified. [25]So Israel took all these
cities, and Israel dwelt in all
the cities of the Amorites, in
Heshbon and in all its villages.
[26]For Heshbon *was* the city of
Sihon king of the Amorites,
who had fought against the
former king of Moab, and
had taken all his land from
his hand as far as the Arnon.
[27]Therefore those who speak
in proverbs say:

"Come to Heshbon,
let it be built;
Let the city of Sihon
be repaired.

[28]"For fire went out
from Heshbon,
A flame from the
city of Sihon;
It consumed Ar of Moab,
The lords of the heights
of the Arnon.
[29] Woe to you, Moab!
You have perished,
O people of Chemosh!
He has given his sons
as fugitives,
And his daughters
into captivity,
To Sihon king of
the Amorites.

[30]"But we have shot at them;
Heshbon has perished
as far as Dibon.
Then we laid waste
as far as Nophah,
Which *reaches* to
Medeba."

[31]Thus Israel dwelt in the
land of the Amorites. [32]Then
Moses sent to spy out Jazer;
and they took its villages and
drove out the Amorites who
were there.

KING OG DEFEATED

[33]And they turned and
went up by the way to Ba-
shan. So Og king of Bashan
went out against them, he

21:20 [a] Hebrew *Jeshimon*

and all his people, to battle at Edrei. 34 Then the LORD said to Moses, "Do not fear him, for I have delivered him into your hand, with all his people and his land; and you shall do to him as you did to Sihon king of the Amorites, who dwelt at Heshbon." 35 So they defeated him, his sons, and all his people, until there was no survivor left him; and they took possession of his land.

BALAK SENDS FOR BALAAM

22 Then the children of Israel moved, and camped in the plains of Moab on the side of the Jordan *across from* Jericho.

2 Now Balak the son of Zippor saw all that Israel had done to the Amorites. 3 And Moab was exceedingly afraid of the people because they *were* many, and Moab was sick with dread because of the children of Israel. 4 So Moab said to the elders of Midian, "Now this company will lick up everything around us, as an ox licks up the grass of the field." And Balak the son of Zippor *was* king of the Moabites at that time. 5 Then he sent messengers to Balaam the son of Beor at Pethor, which *is* near the River[a] in the land of the sons of his people,[b] to call him, saying: "Look, a people has come from Egypt. See, they cover the face of the earth, and are settling next to me! 6 Therefore please come at once, curse this people for me, for they *are* too mighty for me. Perhaps I shall be able to defeat them and drive them out of the land, for I know that he whom you bless *is* blessed, and he whom you curse is cursed."

7 So the elders of Moab and the elders of Midian departed with the diviner's fee in their hand, and they came to Balaam and spoke to him the words of Balak. 8 And he said to them, "Lodge here tonight, and I will bring back word to you, as the LORD speaks to me." So the princes of Moab stayed with Balaam.

9 Then God came to Balaam and said, "Who *are* these men with you?"

10 So Balaam said to God, "Balak the son of Zippor, king of Moab, has sent to me, *saying,* 11 'Look, a people has come out of Egypt, and they cover the face of the earth. Come now, curse them for me; perhaps I shall be able to overpower them and drive them out.'"

12 And God said to Balaam, "You shall not go with them; you shall not curse the people, for they *are* blessed."

13 So Balaam rose in the morning and said to the princes of Balak, "Go back to your land, for the LORD has refused to give me permission to go with you."

22:5 [a] That is, the Euphrates [b] Or *the people of Amau*

14And the princes of Moab
rose and went to Balak, and
said, "Balaam refuses to come
with us."

15Then Balak again sent
princes, more numerous
and more honorable than
they. 16And they came to Balaam and said to him, "Thus
says Balak the son of Zippor:
'Please let nothing hinder you
from coming to me; 17for I will
certainly honor you greatly,
and I will do whatever you say
to me. Therefore please come,
curse this people for me.'"

18Then Balaam answered
and said to the servants of
Balak, "Though Balak were
to give me his house full of
silver and gold, I could not go
beyond the word of the LORD
my God, to do less or more.
19Now therefore, please, you
also stay here tonight, that
I may know what more the
LORD will say to me."

20And God came to Balaam
at night and said to him, "If
the men come to call you, rise
and go with them; but only the
word which I speak to you—
that you shall do." 21So Balaam
rose in the morning, saddled
his donkey, and went with the
princes of Moab.

BALAAM, THE DONKEY, AND THE ANGEL

22Then God's anger was
aroused because he went, and
the Angel of the LORD took
His stand in the way as an
adversary against him. And
he was riding on his donkey,
and his two servants *were*
with him. 23Now the donkey
saw the Angel of the LORD
standing in the way with His
drawn sword in His hand, and
the donkey turned aside out
of the way and went into the
field. So Balaam struck the
donkey to turn her back onto
the road. 24Then the Angel of
the LORD stood in a narrow
path between the vineyards,
with a wall on this side and a
wall on that side. 25And when
the donkey saw the Angel of
the LORD, she pushed herself
against the wall and crushed
Balaam's foot against the wall;
so he struck her again. 26Then
the Angel of the LORD went
further, and stood in a narrow
place where there *was* no way
to turn either to the right hand
or to the left. 27And when the
donkey saw the Angel of the
LORD, she lay down under Balaam; so Balaam's anger was
aroused, and he struck the
donkey with his staff.

28Then the LORD opened
the mouth of the donkey, and
she said to Balaam, "What have
I done to you, that you have
struck me these three times?"

29And Balaam said to the
donkey, "Because you have
abused me. I wish there were
a sword in my hand, for now
I would kill you!"

30So the donkey said to Balaam, "*Am* I not your donkey
on which you have ridden,
ever since *I became* yours, to

this day? Was I ever disposed
to do this to you?"
And he said, "No."
31Then the LORD opened
Balaam's eyes, and he saw the
Angel of the LORD standing in
the way with His drawn sword
in His hand; and he bowed
his head and fell flat on his
face. 32And the Angel of the
LORD said to him, "Why have
you struck your donkey these
three times? Behold, I have
come out to stand against you,
because *your* way is perverse
before Me. 33The donkey saw
Me and turned aside from Me
these three times. If she had
not turned aside from Me,
surely I would also have killed
you by now, and let her live."
34And Balaam said to the
Angel of the LORD, "I have
sinned, for I did not know You
stood in the way against me.
Now therefore, if it displeases
You, I will turn back."
35Then the Angel of the
LORD said to Balaam, "Go with
the men, but only the word
that I speak to you, that you
shall speak." So Balaam went
with the princes of Balak.
36Now when Balak heard
that Balaam was coming,
he went out to meet him at
the city of Moab, which *is* on
the border at the Arnon, the
boundary of the territory.
37Then Balak said to Balaam,
"Did I not earnestly send to
you, calling for you? Why did
you not come to me? Am I not
able to honor you?"
38And Balaam said to Balak,
"Look, I have come to you!
Now, have I any power at all
to say anything? The word that
God puts in my mouth, that I
must speak." 39So Balaam went
with Balak, and they came to
Kirjath Huzoth. 40Then Balak
offered oxen and sheep, and
he sent *some* to Balaam and to
the princes who *were* with him.

BALAAM'S FIRST PROPHECY

41So it was, the next day,
that Balak took Balaam and
brought him up to the high
places of Baal, that from there
he might observe the extent
of the people.

23 Then Balaam said to
Balak, "Build seven al-
tars for me here, and prepare
for me here seven bulls and
seven rams."
2And Balak did just as Balaam had spoken, and Balak
and Balaam offered a bull and
a ram on *each* altar. 3Then
Balaam said to Balak, "Stand
by your burnt offering, and I
will go; perhaps the LORD will
come to meet me, and whatever He shows me I will tell
you." So he went to a desolate
height. 4And God met Balaam,
and he said to Him, "I have
prepared the seven altars, and
I have offered on *each* altar a
bull and a ram."
5Then the LORD put a word
in Balaam's mouth, and said,
"Return to Balak, and thus
you shall speak." 6So he returned to him, and there he

was, standing by his burnt offering, he and all the princes
of Moab.
7And he took up his oracle
and said:

"Balak the king of
Moab has brought
me from Aram,
From the mountains
of the east.
'Come, curse Jacob for me,
And come, denounce
Israel!'

8 "How shall I curse whom
God has not cursed?
And how shall I denounce
whom the LORD has
not denounced?
9 For from the top of the
rocks I see him,
And from the hills
I behold him;
There! A people
dwelling alone,
Not reckoning itself
among the nations.

10 "Who can count the
dust[a] of Jacob,
Or number one-fourth
of Israel?
Let me die the death
of the righteous,
And let my end
be like his!"

11Then Balak said to Ba-
laam, "What have you done
to me? I took you to curse my
enemies, and look, you have
blessed *them* bountifully!"
12So he answered and said,
"Must I not take heed to speak
what the LORD has put in my
mouth?"

BALAAM'S SECOND PROPHECY

13Then Balak said to him,
"Please come with me to another place from which you
may see them; you shall see
only the outer part of them,
and shall not see them all;
curse them for me from there."
14So he brought him to the
field of Zophim, to the top of
Pisgah, and built seven altars,
and offered a bull and a ram
on *each* altar.
15And he said to Balak,
"Stand here by your burnt offering while I meet[a] *the LORD*
over there."
16Then the LORD met Ba-
laam, and put a word in his
mouth, and said, "Go back
to Balak, and thus you shall
speak." 17So he came to him,
and there he was, standing
by his burnt offering, and
the princes of Moab were with
him. And Balak said to him,
"What has the LORD spoken?"
18Then he took up his oracle and said:

"Rise up, Balak, and hear!
Listen to me, son
of Zippor!

23:10 [a] Or *dust cloud* **23:15** [a] Following Masoretic Text, Targum, and Vulgate; Syriac reads *call;* Septuagint reads *go and ask God.*

19"God *is* not a man, that
He should lie,
Nor a son of man, that
He should repent.
Has He said, and
will He not do?
Or has He spoken, and will
He not make it good?
20 Behold, I have received
a command to bless;
He has blessed, and I
cannot reverse it.

21"He has not observed
iniquity in Jacob,
Nor has He seen
wickedness in Israel.
The LORD his God
is with him,
And the shout of a King
is among them.
22 God brings them
out of Egypt;
He has strength
like a wild ox.

23"For *there is* no sorcery
against Jacob,
Nor any divination
against Israel.
It now must be
said of Jacob
And of Israel, 'Oh, what
God has done!'
24 Look, a people rises
like a lioness,
And lifts itself up
like a lion;
It shall not lie down until
it devours the prey,
And drinks the blood
of the slain."

25Then Balak said to Ba-
laam, "Neither curse them at
all, nor bless them at all!"
26So Balaam answered and
said to Balak, "Did I not tell
you, saying, 'All that the LORD
speaks, that I must do'?"

BALAAM'S THIRD PROPHECY

27Then Balak said to Ba-
laam, "Please come, I will take
you to another place; perhaps
it will please God that you
may curse them for me from
there." 28So Balak took Balaam
to the top of Peor, that overlooks the wasteland.[a] 29Then
Balaam said to Balak, "Build
for me here seven altars, and
prepare for me here seven
bulls and seven rams." 30And
Balak did as Balaam had said,
and offered a bull and a ram
on *every* altar.

24 Now when Balaam saw
that it pleased the LORD
to bless Israel, he did not go as
at other times, to seek to use
sorcery, but he set his face toward the wilderness. 2And Balaam raised his eyes, and saw
Israel encamped according to
their tribes; and the Spirit of
God came upon him.
3Then he took up his oracle
and said:

"The utterance of Balaam
the son of Beor,
The utterance of the man
whose eyes are opened,

23:28 [a] Hebrew *Jeshimon*

4 The utterance of him
who hears the
words of God,
Who sees the vision
of the Almighty,
Who falls down, with
eyes wide open:

5 "How lovely are your
tents, O Jacob!
Your dwellings, O Israel!
6 Like valleys that
stretch out,
Like gardens by
the riverside,
Like aloes planted
by the LORD,
Like cedars beside
the waters.
7 He shall pour water
from his buckets,
And his seed *shall be*
in many waters.

"His king shall be
higher than Agag,
And his kingdom
shall be exalted.

8 "God brings him
out of Egypt;
He has strength
like a wild ox;
He shall consume the
nations, his enemies;
He shall break their bones
And pierce *them*
with his arrows.
9 'He bows down, he lies
down as a lion;
And as a lion, who
shall rouse him?'[a]

"Blessed *is* he who
blesses you,
And cursed *is* he
who curses you."

10Then Balak's anger was
aroused against Balaam, and
he struck his hands together;
and Balak said to Balaam, "I
called you to curse my enemies, and look, you have
bountifully blessed *them*
these three times! 11Now
therefore, flee to your place.
I said I would greatly honor
you, but in fact, the LORD has
kept you back from honor."
12So Balaam said to Balak,
"Did I not also speak to your
messengers whom you sent
to me, saying, 13'If Balak were
to give me his house full of
silver and gold, I could not go
beyond the word of the LORD,
to do good or bad of my own
will. What the LORD says, that
I must speak'? 14And now, indeed, I am going to my people.
Come, I will advise you what
this people will do to your
people in the latter days."

BALAAM'S FOURTH PROPHECY

15So he took up his oracle
and said:

"The utterance of Balaam
the son of Beor,
And the utterance
of the man whose
eyes are opened;

24:9 [a] Genesis 49:9

16 The utterance of him
who hears the
words of God,
And has the knowledge
of the Most High,
Who sees the vision
of the Almighty,
Who falls down, with
eyes wide open:

17 "I see Him, but not now;
I behold Him, but
not near;
A Star shall come
out of Jacob;
A Scepter shall rise
out of Israel,
And batter the
brow of Moab,
And destroy all the
sons of tumult.[a]

18 "And Edom shall
be a possession;
Seir also, his enemies,
shall be a possession,
While Israel does
valiantly.
19 Out of Jacob One shall
have dominion,
And destroy the
remains of the city."

20Then he looked on Ama-
lek, and he took up his oracle
and said:

"Amalek *was* first
among the nations,
But *shall be* last until
he perishes."

21Then he looked on the
Kenites, and he took up his
oracle and said:

"Firm is your
dwelling place,
And your nest is set
in the rock;
22 Nevertheless Kain
shall be burned.
How long until
Asshur carries you
away captive?"

23Then he took up his oracle and said:

"Alas! Who shall live
when God does this?
24 But ships *shall come* from
the coasts of Cyprus,[a]
And they shall afflict
Asshur and afflict Eber,
And so shall *Amalek*,[b]
until he perishes."

25So Balaam rose and de-
parted and returned to his
place; Balak also went his way.

ISRAEL'S HARLOTRY IN MOAB

25 Now Israel remained
in Acacia Grove,[a] and
the people began to commit
harlotry with the women of
Moab. 2They invited the people to the sacrifices of their
gods, and the people ate and
bowed down to their gods.
3So Israel was joined to Baal

24:17 [a] Hebrew *Sheth* (compare Jeremiah 48:45) 24:24 [a] Hebrew *Kittim* [b] Literally *he* or *that one* 25:1 [a] Hebrew *Shittim*

of Peor, and the anger of the LORD was aroused against Israel.

4 Then the LORD said to Moses, "Take all the leaders of the people and hang the offenders before the LORD, out in the sun, that the fierce anger of the LORD may turn away from Israel."

5 So Moses said to the judges of Israel, "Every one of you kill his men who were joined to Baal of Peor."

6 And indeed, one of the children of Israel came and presented to his brethren a Midianite woman in the sight of Moses and in the sight of all the congregation of the children of Israel, who *were* weeping at the door of the tabernacle of meeting. 7 Now when Phinehas the son of Eleazar, the son of Aaron the priest, saw *it,* he rose from among the congregation and took a javelin in his hand; 8 and he went after the man of Israel into the tent and thrust both of them through, the man of Israel, and the woman through her body. So the plague was stopped among the children of Israel. 9 And those who died in the plague were twenty-four thousand.

10 Then the LORD spoke to Moses, saying: 11 "Phinehas the son of Eleazar, the son of Aaron the priest, has turned back My wrath from the children of Israel, because he was zealous with My zeal among them, so that I did not consume the children of Israel in My zeal. 12 Therefore say, 'Behold, I give to him My covenant of peace; 13 and it shall be to him and his descendants after him a covenant of an everlasting priesthood, because he was zealous for his God, and made atonement for the children of Israel.' "

14 Now the name of the Israelite who was killed, who was killed with the Midianite woman, *was* Zimri the son of Salu, a leader of a father's house among the Simeonites. 15 And the name of the Midianite woman who was killed *was* Cozbi the daughter of Zur; he *was* head of the people of a father's house in Midian.

16 Then the LORD spoke to Moses, saying: 17 "Harass the Midianites, and attack them; 18 for they harassed you with their schemes by which they seduced you in the matter of Peor and in the matter of Cozbi, the daughter of a leader of Midian, their sister, who was killed in the day of the plague because of Peor."

THE SECOND CENSUS OF ISRAEL

26 And it came to pass, after the plague, that the LORD spoke to Moses and Eleazar the son of Aaron the priest, saying: 2 "Take a census of all the congregation of the children of Israel from twenty years old and above, by their

fathers' houses, all who are able to go to war in Israel." 3So Moses and Eleazar the priest spoke with them in the plains of Moab by the Jordan, *across from* Jericho, saying: 4"*Take a census of the people* from twenty years old and above, just as the LORD commanded Moses and the children of Israel who came out of the land of Egypt."

5Reuben *was* the firstborn of Israel. The children of Reuben *were: of* Hanoch, the family of the Hanochites; *of* Pallu, the family of the Palluites; 6*of* Hezron, the family of the Hezronites; *of* Carmi, the family of the Carmites. 7These *are* the families of the Reubenites: those who were numbered of them were forty-three thousand seven hundred and thirty. 8And the son of Pallu *was* Eliab. 9The sons of Eliab *were* Nemuel, Dathan, and Abiram. These *are* the Dathan and Abiram, representatives of the congregation, who contended against Moses and Aaron in the company of Korah, when they contended against the LORD; 10and the earth opened its mouth and swallowed them up together with Korah when that company died, when the fire devoured two hundred and fifty men; and they became a sign. 11Nevertheless the children of Korah did not die.

12The sons of Simeon according to their families *were: of* Nemuel,[a] the family of the Nemuelites; *of* Jamin, the family of the Jaminites; *of* Jachin,[b] the family of the Jachinites; 13*of* Zerah,[a] the family of the Zarhites; *of* Shaul, the family of the Shaulites. 14These *are* the families of the Simeonites: twenty-two thousand two hundred.

15The sons of Gad according to their families *were: of* Zephon,[a] the family of the Zephonites; *of* Haggi, the family of the Haggites; *of* Shuni, the family of the Shunites; 16*of* Ozni,[a] the family of the Oznites; *of* Eri, the family of the Erites; 17*of* Arod,[a] the family of the Arodites; *of* Areli, the family of the Arelites. 18These *are* the families of the sons of Gad according to those who were numbered of them: forty thousand five hundred.

19The sons of Judah *were* Er and Onan; and Er and Onan died in the land of Canaan. 20And the sons of Judah according to their families were: *of* Shelah, the family of the Shelanites; *of* Perez, the family of the Parzites; *of* Zerah, the family of the Zarhites. 21And

26:12 [a] Spelled *Jemuel* in Genesis 46:10 and Exodus 6:15 [b] Called *Jarib* in 1 Chronicles 4:24 **26:13** [a] Called *Zohar* in Genesis 46:10 **26:15** [a] Called *Ziphion* in Genesis 46:16 **26:16** [a] Called *Ezbon* in Genesis 46:16 **26:17** [a] Spelled *Arodi* in Samaritan Pentateuch, Syriac, and Genesis 46:16

the sons of Perez were: *of* Hezron, the family of the Hezronites; *of* Hamul, the family of the Hamulites. 22 These *are* the families of Judah according to those who were numbered of them: seventy-six thousand five hundred.

23 The sons of Issachar according to their families *were*: *of* Tola, the family of the Tolaites; of Puah,[a] the family of the Punites;[b] 24 of Jashub, the family of the Jashubites; of Shimron, the family of the Shimronites. 25 These *are* the families of Issachar according to those who were numbered of them: sixty-four thousand three hundred.

26 The sons of Zebulun according to their families *were*: of Sered, the family of the Sardites; of Elon, the family of the Elonites; of Jahleel, the family of the Jahleelites. 27 These *are* the families of the Zebulunites according to those who were numbered of them: sixty thousand five hundred.

28 The sons of Joseph according to their families, by Manasseh and Ephraim, *were*: 29 The sons of Manasseh: of Machir, the family of the Machirites; and Machir begot Gilead; of Gilead, the family of the Gileadites. 30 These *are* the sons of Gilead: *of* Jeezer,[a] the family of the Jeezerites; of Helek, the family of the Helekites; 31 *of* Asriel, the family of the Asrielites; *of* Shechem, the family of the Shechemites; 32 *of* Shemida, the family of the Shemidaites; *of* Hepher, the family of the Hepherites. 33 Now Zelophehad the son of Hepher had no sons, but daughters; and the names of the daughters of Zelophehad *were* Mahlah, Noah, Hoglah, Milcah, and Tirzah. 34 These *are* the families of Manasseh; and those who were numbered of them *were* fifty-two thousand seven hundred.

35 These *are* the sons of Ephraim according to their families: of Shuthelah, the family of the Shuthalhites; of Becher,[a] the family of the Bachrites; of Tahan, the family of the Tahanites. 36 And these *are* the sons of Shuthelah: of Eran, the family of the Eranites. 37 These *are* the families of the sons of Ephraim according to those who were numbered of them: thirty-two thousand five hundred.

These *are* the sons of Joseph according to their families.

38 The sons of Benjamin according to their families were: of Bela, the family of the Belaites; of Ashbel, the family of

26:23 [a] Hebrew *Puvah* (compare Genesis 46:13 and 1 Chronicles 7:1); Samaritan Pentateuch, Septuagint, Syriac, and Vulgate read *Puah.* [b] Samaritan Pentateuch, Septuagint, Syriac, and Vulgate read *Puaites.* **26:30** [a] Called *Abiezer* in Joshua 17:2 **26:35** [a] Called *Bered* in 1 Chronicles 7:20

the Ashbelites; of Ahiram, the
family of the Ahiramites; 39of
Shupham,[a] the family of the
Shuphamites; of Hupham,[b]
the family of the Huphamites.
40And the sons of Bela were
Ard[a] and Naaman: *of Ard,* the
family of the Ardites; of Naaman, the family of the Naa-
mites. 41These *are* the sons of
Benjamin according to their
families; and those who were
numbered of them *were* forty-
five thousand six hundred.

42These *are* the sons of
Dan according to their families: of Shuham,[a] the family
of the Shuhamites. These *are*
the families of Dan according to their families. 43All the
families of the Shuhamites,
according to those who were
numbered of them, *were* sixty-
four thousand four hundred.

44The sons of Asher according to their families *were:* of
Jimna, the family of the Jim-
nites; of Jesui, the family of
the Jesuites; of Beriah, the
family of the Beriites. 45Of
the sons of Beriah: of Heber,
the family of the Heberites;
of Malchiel, the family of the
Malchielites. 46And the name
of the daughter of Asher *was*
Serah. 47These *are* the families
of the sons of Asher according
to those who were numbered
of them: fifty-three thousand
four hundred.

48The sons of Naphtali according to their families *were:*
of Jahzeel,[a] the family of the
Jahzeelites; of Guni, the family of the Gunites; 49of Jezer,
the family of the Jezerites;
of Shillem, the family of the
Shillemites. 50These *are* the
families of Naphtali according
to their families; and those
who were numbered of them
were forty-five thousand four
hundred.

51These *are* those who were
numbered of the children of
Israel: six hundred and one
thousand seven hundred and
thirty.

52Then the LORD spoke to
Moses, saying: 53"To these
the land shall be divided as
an inheritance, according to
the number of names. 54To
a large *tribe* you shall give a
larger inheritance, and to
a small *tribe* you shall give
a smaller inheritance. Each
shall be given its inheritance
according to those who were
numbered of them. 55But the
land shall be divided by lot;
they shall inherit according
to the names of the tribes of
their fathers. 56According to
the lot their inheritance shall
be divided between the larger
and the smaller."

57And these *are* those who
were numbered of the Levites
according to their families:

26:39 [a] Masoretic Text reads *Shephupham,* spelled *Shephuphan* in 1 Chronicles 8:5. [b] Called *Huppim* in Genesis 46:21 **26:40** [a] Called *Addar* in 1 Chronicles 8:3 **26:42** [a] Called *Hushim* in Genesis 46:23 **26:48** [a] Spelled *Jahziel* in 1 Chronicles 7:13

of Gershon, the family of the
Gershonites; of Kohath, the
family of the Kohathites; of
Merari, the family of the Me-
rarites. 58These *are* the families of the Levites: the family
of the Libnites, the family of
the Hebronites, the family of
the Mahlites, the family of the
Mushites, and the family of
the Korathites. And Kohath
begot Amram. 59The name of
Amram's wife *was* Jochebed
the daughter of Levi, who was
born to Levi in Egypt; and to
Amram she bore Aaron and
Moses and their sister Miriam.
60To Aaron were born Nadab
and Abihu, Eleazar and Ithamar. 61And Nadab and Abihu
died when they offered profane fire before the LORD.

62Now those who were num-
bered of them were twenty-
three thousand, every male
from a month old and above;
for they were not numbered
among the other children of
Israel, because there was no
inheritance given to them
among the children of Israel.

63These *are* those who were
numbered by Moses and Eleazar the priest, who numbered
the children of Israel in the
plains of Moab by the Jordan, *across from* Jericho. 64But
among these there was not a
man of those who were numbered by Moses and Aaron the
priest when they numbered
the children of Israel in the
Wilderness of Sinai. 65For the
LORD had said of them, "They
shall surely die in the wilderness." So there was not left a
man of them, except Caleb the
son of Jephunneh and Joshua
the son of Nun.

INHERITANCE LAWS

27 Then came the daugh-
ters of Zelophehad the
son of Hepher, the son of Gilead, the son of Machir, the son
of Manasseh, from the families of Manasseh the son of
Joseph; and these *were* the
names of his daughters: Mahlah, Noah, Hoglah, Milcah, and
Tirzah. 2And they stood before Moses, before Eleazar the
priest, and before the leaders
and all the congregation, *by*
the doorway of the tabernacle of meeting, saying: 3"Our
father died in the wilderness;
but he was not in the company of those who gathered
together against the LORD,
in company with Korah, but
he died in his own sin; and
he had no sons. 4Why should
the name of our father be removed from among his family
because he had no son? Give
us a possession among our
father's brothers."

5So Moses brought their
case before the LORD.

6And the LORD spoke to
Moses, saying: 7"The daughters of Zelophehad speak *what
is* right; you shall surely give
them a possession of inheritance among their father's
brothers, and cause the inheritance of their father to pass to

them. 8And you shall speak to
the children of Israel, saying:
'If a man dies and has no son,
then you shall cause his inheritance to pass to his daughter.
9If he has no daughter, then
you shall give his inheritance
to his brothers. 10If he has no
brothers, then you shall give
his inheritance to his father's
brothers. 11And if his father has
no brothers, then you shall give
his inheritance to the relative
closest to him in his family, and
he shall possess it.'" And it shall
be to the children of Israel a
statute of judgment, just as the
LORD commanded Moses.

JOSHUA THE NEXT LEADER OF ISRAEL

12Now the LORD said to
Moses: "Go up into this Mount
Abarim, and see the land which
I have given to the children of
Israel. 13And when you have
seen it, you also shall be gathered to your people, as Aaron
your brother was gathered.
14For in the Wilderness of Zin,
during the strife of the congregation, you rebelled against
My command to hallow Me at
the waters before their eyes."
(These *are* the waters of Meribah, at Kadesh in the Wilderness of Zin.)

15Then Moses spoke to the
LORD, saying: 16"Let the LORD,
the God of the spirits of all
flesh, set a man over the congregation, 17who may go out
before them and go in before
them, who may lead them out
and bring them in, that the
congregation of the LORD may
not be like sheep which have
no shepherd."

18And the LORD said to
Moses: "Take Joshua the son
of Nun with you, a man in
whom *is* the Spirit, and lay
your hand on him; 19set him
before Eleazar the priest and
before all the congregation,
and inaugurate him in their
sight. 20And you shall give
some of your authority to him,
that all the congregation of
the children of Israel may be
obedient. 21He shall stand before Eleazar the priest, who
shall inquire before the LORD
for him by the judgment of
the Urim. At his word they
shall go out, and at his word
they shall come in, he and
all the children of Israel with
him—all the congregation."

22So Moses did as the LORD
commanded him. He took
Joshua and set him before
Eleazar the priest and before
all the congregation. 23And
he laid his hands on him and
inaugurated him, just as the
LORD commanded by the
hand of Moses.

DAILY OFFERINGS

28 Now the LORD spoke to
Moses, saying, 2"Com-
mand the children of Israel,
and say to them, 'My offering,
My food for My offerings made
by fire as a sweet aroma to Me,
you shall be careful to offer to
Me at their appointed time.'

3"And you shall say to them,
'This *is* the offering made by
fire which you shall offer to
the LORD: two male lambs in
their first year without blemish, day by day, as a regular
burnt offering. 4The one lamb
you shall offer in the morning,
the other lamb you shall offer
in the evening, 5and one-tenth
of an ephah of fine flour as a
grain offering mixed with one-
fourth of a hin of pressed oil.
6*It is* a regular burnt offering
which was ordained at Mount
Sinai for a sweet aroma, an
offering made by fire to the
LORD. 7And its drink offering
shall be one-fourth of a hin
for each lamb; in a holy *place*
you shall pour out the drink to
the LORD as an offering. 8The
other lamb you shall offer in
the evening; as the morning
grain offering and its drink offering, you shall offer *it* as an
offering made by fire, a sweet
aroma to the LORD.

SABBATH OFFERINGS

9'And on the Sabbath day
two lambs in their first year,
without blemish, and two-
tenths *of an ephah* of fine flour
as a grain offering, mixed with
oil, with its drink offering—
10*this is* the burnt offering for
every Sabbath, besides the
regular burnt offering with
its drink offering.

MONTHLY OFFERINGS

11'At the beginnings of your
months you shall present a
burnt offering to the LORD:
two young bulls, one ram,
and seven lambs in their first
year, without blemish; 12three-
tenths *of an ephah* of fine flour
as a grain offering, mixed with
oil, for each bull; two-tenths *of
an ephah* of fine flour as a grain
offering, mixed with oil, for
the one ram; 13and one-tenth
of an ephah of fine flour, mixed
with oil, as a grain offering for
each lamb, as a burnt offering of sweet aroma, an offering made by fire to the LORD.
14Their drink offering shall be
half a hin of wine for a bull,
one-third of a hin for a ram,
and one-fourth of a hin for a
lamb; this *is* the burnt offering
for each month throughout
the months of the year. 15Also
one kid of the goats as a sin
offering to the LORD shall be
offered, besides the regular
burnt offering and its drink
offering.

OFFERINGS AT PASSOVER

16'On the fourteenth day of
the first month *is* the Passover
of the LORD. 17And on the fifteenth day of this month *is* the
feast; unleavened bread shall
be eaten for seven days. 18On
the first day *you shall have* a
holy convocation. You shall
do no customary work. 19And
you shall present an offering
made by fire as a burnt offering to the LORD: two young
bulls, one ram, and seven
lambs in their first year. Be
sure they are without blemish.

20Their grain offering shall be
of fine flour mixed with oil:
three-tenths *of an ephah* you
shall offer for a bull, and two-
tenths for a ram; 21you shall
offer one-tenth *of an ephah*
for each of the seven lambs;
22also one goat *as* a sin offering, to make atonement for
you. 23You shall offer these
besides the burnt offering of
the morning, which *is* for a
regular burnt offering. 24In
this manner you shall offer
the food of the offering made
by fire daily for seven days, as
a sweet aroma to the LORD; it
shall be offered besides the
regular burnt offering and its
drink offering. 25And on the
seventh day you shall have a
holy convocation. You shall
do no customary work.

OFFERINGS AT THE FEAST OF WEEKS

26'Also on the day of the
firstfruits, when you bring
a new grain offering to the
LORD at your *Feast of* Weeks,
you shall have a holy convocation. You shall do no
customary work. 27You shall
present a burnt offering as
a sweet aroma to the LORD:
two young bulls, one ram,
and seven lambs in their first
year, 28with their grain offering of fine flour mixed with
oil: three-tenths *of an ephah*
for each bull, two-tenths for
the one ram, 29and one-tenth
for each of the seven lambs;
30*also* one kid of the goats, to
make atonement for you. 31Be
sure they are without blemish.
You shall present *them* with
their drink offerings, besides
the regular burnt offering
with its grain offering.

OFFERINGS AT THE FEAST OF TRUMPETS

29 'And in the seventh
month, on the first *day*
of the month, you shall have a
holy convocation. You shall do
no customary work. For you it
is a day of blowing the trumpets. 2You shall offer a burnt
offering as a sweet aroma to
the LORD: one young bull,
one ram, *and* seven lambs in
their first year, without blemish. 3Their grain offering *shall
be* fine flour mixed with oil:
three-tenths *of an ephah* for
the bull, two-tenths for the
ram, 4and one-tenth for each of
the seven lambs; 5also one kid
of the goats *as* a sin offering,
to make atonement for you;
6besides the burnt offering
with its grain offering for the
New Moon, the regular burnt
offering with its grain offering, and their drink offerings,
according to their ordinance,
as a sweet aroma, an offering
made by fire to the LORD.

OFFERINGS ON THE DAY OF ATONEMENT

7'On the tenth *day* of this
seventh month you shall
have a holy convocation.
You shall afflict your souls;
you shall not do any work.

[8]You shall present a burnt
offering to the LORD *as* a
sweet aroma: one young bull,
one ram, *and* seven lambs
in their first year. Be sure
they are without blemish.
[9]Their grain offering *shall*
be of fine flour mixed with
oil: three-tenths *of an ephah*
for the bull, two-tenths for
the one ram, [10]and one-tenth
for each of the seven lambs;
[11]also one kid of the goats *as*
a sin offering, besides the sin
offering for atonement, the
regular burnt offering with
its grain offering, and their
drink offerings.

OFFERINGS AT THE FEAST OF TABERNACLES

[12]'On the fifteenth day of
the seventh month you shall
have a holy convocation. You
shall do no customary work,
and you shall keep a feast to
the LORD seven days. [13]You
shall present a burnt offering, an offering made by fire
as a sweet aroma to the LORD:
thirteen young bulls, two rams,
and fourteen lambs in their
first year. They shall be without
blemish. [14]Their grain offering
shall be of fine flour mixed with
oil: three-tenths *of an ephah*
for each of the thirteen bulls,
two-tenths for each of the two
rams, [15]and one-tenth for each
of the fourteen lambs; [16]also
one kid of the goats *as* a sin
offering, besides the regular
burnt offering, its grain offering, and its drink offering.

[17]'On the second day *pres-*
ent twelve young bulls, two
rams, fourteen lambs in their
first year without blemish,
[18]and their grain offering and
their drink offerings for the
bulls, for the rams, and for
the lambs, by their number,
according to the ordinance;
[19]also one kid of the goats
as a sin offering, besides the
regular burnt offering with its
grain offering, and their drink
offerings.

[20]'On the third day *present*
eleven bulls, two rams, fourteen lambs in their first year
without blemish, [21]and their
grain offering and their drink
offerings for the bulls, for the
rams, and for the lambs, by
their number, according to
the ordinance; [22]also one
goat *as* a sin offering, besides
the regular burnt offering, its
grain offering, and its drink
offering.

[23]'On the fourth day *present*
ten bulls, two rams, *and* fourteen lambs in their first year,
without blemish, [24]and their
grain offering and their drink
offerings for the bulls, for the
rams, and for the lambs, by
their number, according to
the ordinance; [25]also one kid
of the goats *as* a sin offering,
besides the regular burnt offering, its grain offering, and
its drink offering.

[26]'On the fifth day *present*
nine bulls, two rams, *and* fourteen lambs in their first year
without blemish, [27]and their

grain offering and their drink
offerings for the bulls, for the
rams, and for the lambs, by
their number, according to the
ordinance; 28also one goat *as* a
sin offering, besides the regular burnt offering, its grain offering, and its drink offering.
29'On the sixth day *pre-
sent* eight bulls, two rams,
and fourteen lambs in their
first year without blemish,
30and their grain offering and
their drink offerings for the
bulls, for the rams, and for
the lambs, by their number,
according to the ordinance;
31also one goat *as* a sin offering, besides the regular burnt
offering, its grain offering,
and its drink offering.
32'On the seventh day *present* seven bulls, two rams,
and fourteen lambs in their
first year without blemish,
33and their grain offering and
their drink offerings for the
bulls, for the rams, and for
the lambs, by their number,
according to the ordinance;
34also one goat *as* a sin offering, besides the regular burnt
offering, its grain offering,
and its drink offering.
35'On the eighth day you
shall have a sacred assembly.
You shall do no customary
work. 36You shall present a
burnt offering, an offering
made by fire as a sweet aroma
to the LORD: one bull, one ram,
seven lambs in their first year
without blemish, 37and their
grain offering and their drink
offerings for the bull, for the
ram, and for the lambs, by
their number, according to the
ordinance; 38also one goat *as*
a sin offering, besides the regular burnt offering, its grain
offering, and its drink offering.
39'These you shall present
to the LORD at your appointed
feasts (besides your vowed
offerings and your freewill
offerings) as your burnt offerings and your grain offerings,
as your drink offerings and
your peace offerings.'"
40So Moses told the chil-
dren of Israel everything,
just as the LORD commanded
Moses.

THE LAW CONCERNING VOWS

30 Then Moses spoke to
the heads of the tribes
concerning the children of Israel, saying, "This *is* the thing
which the LORD has com-
manded: 2If a man makes a
vow to the LORD, or swears an
oath to bind himself by some
agreement, he shall not break
his word; he shall do according to all that proceeds out of
his mouth.
3"Or if a woman makes a
vow to the LORD, and binds
herself by some agreement
while in her father's house
in her youth, 4and her father hears her vow and the
agreement by which she has
bound herself, and her father
holds his peace, then all her
vows shall stand, and every

agreement with which she has bound herself shall stand. 5But if her father overrules her on the day that he hears, then none of her vows nor her agreements by which she has bound herself shall stand; and the LORD will release her, because her father overruled her.

6"If indeed she takes a husband, while bound by her vows or by a rash utterance from her lips by which she bound herself, 7and her husband hears *it,* and makes no response to her on the day that he hears, then her vows shall stand, and her agreements by which she bound herself shall stand. 8But if her husband overrules her on the day that he hears *it,* he shall make void her vow which she took and what she uttered with her lips, by which she bound herself, and the LORD will release her.

9"Also any vow of a widow or a divorced woman, by which she has bound herself, shall stand against her.

10"If she vowed in her husband's house, or bound herself by an agreement with an oath, 11and her husband heard *it,* and made no response to her *and* did not overrule her, then all her vows shall stand, and every agreement by which she bound herself shall stand. 12But if her husband truly made them void on the day he heard *them,* then whatever proceeded from her lips concerning her vows or concerning the agreement binding her, it shall not stand; her husband has made them void, and the LORD will release her. 13Every vow and every binding oath to afflict her soul, her husband may confirm it, or her husband may make it void. 14Now if her husband makes no response whatever to her from day to day, then he confirms all her vows or all the agreements that bind her; he confirms them, because he made no response to her on the day that he heard *them.* 15But if he does make them void after he has heard *them,* then he shall bear her guilt."

16These *are* the statutes which the LORD commanded Moses, between a man and his wife, and between a father and his daughter in her youth in her father's house.

VENGEANCE ON THE MIDIANITES

31 And the LORD spoke to Moses, saying: 2"Take vengeance on the Midianites for the children of Israel. Afterward you shall be gathered to your people."

3So Moses spoke to the people, saying, "Arm some of yourselves for war, and let them go against the Midianites to take vengeance for the LORD on Midian. 4A thousand from each tribe of all the tribes of Israel you shall send to the war."

[5]So there were recruited
from the divisions of Israel
one thousand from *each* tribe,
twelve thousand armed for
war. [6]Then Moses sent them
to the war, one thousand
from *each* tribe; he sent
them to the war with Phinehas the son of Eleazar the
priest, with the holy articles
and the signal trumpets in
his hand. [7]And they warred
against the Midianites, just as
the LORD commanded Moses,
and they killed all the males.
[8]They killed the kings of Midian with *the rest of* those who
were killed—Evi, Rekem, Zur,
Hur, and Reba, the five kings
of Midian. Balaam the son of
Beor they also killed with the
sword.

[9]And the children of Israel took the women of Midian captive, with their little
ones, and took as spoil all
their cattle, all their flocks,
and all their goods. [10]They
also burned with fire all the
cities where they dwelt, and all
their forts. [11]And they took all
the spoil and all the booty—of
man and beast.

RETURN FROM THE WAR

[12]Then they brought the
captives, the booty, and the
spoil to Moses, to Eleazar
the priest, and to the congregation of the children of Israel, to the camp in the plains
of Moab by the Jordan, *across
from* Jericho. [13]And Moses, Eleazar the priest, and all the
leaders of the congregation,
went to meet them outside the
camp. [14]But Moses was angry
with the officers of the army,
with the captains over thousands and captains over hundreds, who had come from the
battle.

[15]And Moses said to them:
"Have you kept all the women
alive? [16]Look, these *women*
caused the children of Israel, through the counsel of
Balaam, to trespass against
the LORD in the incident of
Peor, and there was a plague
among the congregation of
the LORD. [17]Now therefore, kill
every male among the little
ones, and kill every woman
who has known a man inti-
mately. [18]But keep alive for
yourselves all the young girls
who have not known a man
intimately. [19]And as for you,
remain outside the camp
seven days; whoever has killed
any person, and whoever has
touched any slain, purify
yourselves and your captives
on the third day and on the
seventh day. [20]Purify every
garment, everything made
of leather, everything woven
of goats' *hair,* and everything
made of wood."

[21]Then Eleazar the priest
said to the men of war who
had gone to the battle, "This
is the ordinance of the law
which the LORD commanded
Moses: [22]Only the gold, the
silver, the bronze, the iron, the
tin, and the lead, [23]everything

that can endure fire, you shall
put through the fire, and it
shall be clean; and it shall
be purified with the water
of purification. But all that
cannot endure fire you shall
put through water. [24]And you
shall wash your clothes on the
seventh day and be clean, and
afterward you may come into
the camp."

DIVISION OF THE PLUNDER

[25]Now the LORD spoke
to Moses, saying: [26]"Count
up the plunder that was
taken—of man and beast—
you and Eleazar the priest
and the chief fathers of the
congregation; [27]and divide
the plunder into two parts,
between those who took part
in the war, who went out to
battle, and all the congregation. [28]And levy a tribute for
the LORD on the men of war
who went out to battle: one
of every five hundred of the
persons, the cattle, the donkeys, and the sheep; [29]take *it*
from their half, and give *it* to
Eleazar the priest as a heave
offering to the LORD. [30]And
from the children of Israel's half you shall take one of
every fifty, drawn from the
persons, the cattle, the donkeys, and the sheep, from all
the livestock, and give them to
the Levites who keep charge
of the tabernacle of the LORD."
[31]So Moses and Eleazar the
priest did as the LORD commanded Moses.

[32]The booty remaining
from the plunder, which the
men of war had taken, was
six hundred and seventy-five
thousand sheep, [33]seventy-
two thousand cattle, [34]sixty-
one thousand donkeys, [35]and
thirty-two thousand persons
in all, of women who had
not known a man intimately.
[36]And the half, the portion
for those who had gone out
to war, was in number three
hundred and thirty-seven
thousand five hundred sheep;
[37]and the LORD's tribute of
the sheep was six hundred
and seventy-five. [38]The cattle *were* thirty-six thousand,
of which the LORD's tribute
was seventy-two. [39]The donkeys *were* thirty thousand five
hundred, of which the LORD's
tribute *was* sixty-one. [40]The
persons *were* sixteen thousand, of which the LORD's tribute *was* thirty-two persons.
[41]So Moses gave the tribute
which was the LORD's heave
offering to Eleazar the priest,
as the LORD commanded
Moses.

[42]And from the children
of Israel's half, which Moses
separated from the men who
fought— [43]now the half belonging to the congregation
was three hundred and thirty-
seven thousand five hundred
sheep, [44]thirty-six thousand
cattle, [45]thirty thousand five
hundred donkeys, [46]and sixteen thousand persons—
[47]and from the children of

Israel's half Moses took one
of every fifty, drawn from man
and beast, and gave them to
the Levites, who kept charge
of the tabernacle of the LORD,
as the LORD commanded
Moses.
48Then the officers who
were over thousands of the
army, the captains of thousands and captains of hundreds, came near to Moses;
49and they said to Moses,
"Your servants have taken a
count of the men of war who
are under our command, and
not a man of us is missing.
50Therefore we have brought
an offering for the LORD, what
every man found of orna-
ments of gold: armlets and
bracelets and signet rings
and earrings and necklaces,
to make atonement for ourselves before the LORD." 51So
Moses and Eleazar the priest
received the gold from them,
all the fashioned ornaments.
52And all the gold of the offering that they offered to
the LORD, from the captains
of thousands and captains of
hundreds, was sixteen thousand seven hundred and fifty
shekels. 53(The men of war
had taken spoil, every man
for himself.) 54And Moses and
Eleazar the priest received
the gold from the captains of
thousands and of hundreds,
and brought it into the tabernacle of meeting as a memorial for the children of Israel
before the LORD.

THE TRIBES SETTLING EAST OF THE JORDAN

32 Now the children of
Reuben and the chil-
dren of Gad had a very great
multitude of livestock; and
when they saw the land of
Jazer and the land of Gilead,
that indeed the region *was* a
place for livestock, 2the children of Gad and the children
of Reuben came and spoke to
Moses, to Eleazar the priest,
and to the leaders of the
congregation, saying, 3"Ataroth, Dibon, Jazer, Nimrah,
Heshbon, Elealeh, Shebam,
Nebo, and Beon, 4the country which the LORD defeated
before the congregation of Israel, *is* a land for livestock, and
your servants have livestock."
5Therefore they said, "If we
have found favor in your sight,
let this land be given to your
servants as a possession. Do
not take us over the Jordan."
6And Moses said to the children of Gad and to the children of Reuben: "Shall your
brethren go to war while you
sit here? 7Now why will you
discourage the heart of the
children of Israel from going
over into the land which the
LORD has given them? 8Thus
your fathers did when I sent
them away from Kadesh Barnea to see the land. 9For when
they went up to the Valley of
Eshcol and saw the land, they
discouraged the heart of the
children of Israel, so that they
did not go into the land which

the LORD had given them. 10So
the LORD's anger was aroused
on that day, and He swore an
oath, saying, 11'Surely none of
the men who came up from
Egypt, from twenty years old
and above, shall see the land
of which I swore to Abraham,
Isaac, and Jacob, because they
have not wholly followed Me,
12except Caleb the son of Jephunneh, the Kenizzite, and
Joshua the son of Nun, for
they have wholly followed the
LORD.' 13So the LORD's anger
was aroused against Israel,
and He made them wander
in the wilderness forty years,
until all the generation that
had done evil in the sight of
the LORD was gone. 14And
look! You have risen in your
fathers' place, a brood of sinful men, to increase still more
the fierce anger of the LORD
against Israel. 15For if you turn
away from following Him, He
will once again leave them in
the wilderness, and you will
destroy all these people."

16Then they came near to
him and said: "We will build
sheepfolds here for our livestock, and cities for our little
ones, 17but we ourselves will
be armed, ready *to go* before
the children of Israel until we
have brought them to their
place; and our little ones will
dwell in the fortified cities
because of the inhabitants
of the land. 18We will not return to our homes until every
one of the children of Israel
has received his inheritance.
19For we will not inherit with
them on the other side of the
Jordan and beyond, because
our inheritance has fallen to
us on this eastern side of the
Jordan."

20Then Moses said to them:
"If you do this thing, if you
arm yourselves before the
LORD for the war, 21and all
your armed men cross over
the Jordan before the LORD
until He has driven out His
enemies from before Him,
22and the land is subdued
before the LORD, then afterward you may return and be
blameless before the LORD
and before Israel; and this
land shall be your possession
before the LORD. 23But if you
do not do so, then take note,
you have sinned against the
LORD; and be sure your sin
will find you out. 24Build cities
for your little ones and folds
for your sheep, and do what
has proceeded out of your
mouth."

25And the children of Gad
and the children of Reuben
spoke to Moses, saying: "Your
servants will do as my lord
commands. 26Our little ones,
our wives, our flocks, and all
our livestock will be there in
the cities of Gilead; 27but your
servants will cross over, every
man armed for war, before the
LORD to battle, just as my lord
says."

28So Moses gave command
concerning them to Eleazar

the priest, to Joshua the son of
Nun, and to the chief fathers
of the tribes of the children
of Israel. 29And Moses said
to them: "If the children of
Gad and the children of Reuben cross over the Jordan with
you, every man armed for battle before the LORD, and the
land is subdued before you,
then you shall give them the
land of Gilead as a possession.
30But if they do not cross over
armed with you, they shall
have possessions among you
in the land of Canaan."

31Then the children of Gad
and the children of Reuben
answered, saying: "As the
LORD has said to your servants, so we will do. 32We will
cross over armed before the
LORD into the land of Canaan,
but the possession of our inheritance *shall remain* with
us on this side of the Jordan."

33So Moses gave to the children of Gad, to the children of
Reuben, and to half the tribe
of Manasseh the son of Joseph, the kingdom of Sihon
king of the Amorites and the
kingdom of Og king of Ba-
shan, the land with its cities
within the borders, the cities
of the surrounding country.
34And the children of Gad built
Dibon and Ataroth and Aroer,
35Atroth and Shophan and
Jazer and Jogbehah, 36Beth
Nimrah and Beth Haran, fortified cities, and folds for sheep.
37And the children of Reuben
built Heshbon and Elealeh
and Kirjathaim, 38Nebo and
Baal Meon (*their* names being
changed) and Shibmah; and
they gave *other* names to the
cities which they built.

39And the children of
Machir the son of Manas-
seh went to Gilead and took
it, and dispossessed the Amorites who *were* in it. 40So
Moses gave Gilead to Machir
the son of Manasseh, and he
dwelt in it. 41Also Jair the son
of Manasseh went and took its
small towns, and called them
Havoth Jair.[a] 42Then Nobah
went and took Kenath and
its villages, and he called it
Nobah, after his own name.

ISRAEL'S JOURNEY FROM EGYPT REVIEWED

33 These *are* the journeys
of the children of Is-
rael, who went out of the land
of Egypt by their armies under
the hand of Moses and Aaron.
2Now Moses wrote down the
starting points of their journeys at the command of the
LORD. And these *are* their
journeys according to their
starting points:

3They departed from Ram-
eses in the first month, on
the fifteenth day of the first
month; on the day after the
Passover the children of Israel
went out with boldness in the
sight of all the Egyptians. 4For

32:41 [a] Literally *Towns of Jair*

the Egyptians were burying
all *their* firstborn, whom the
LORD had killed among them.
Also on their gods the LORD
had executed judgments.
5Then the children of Is-
rael moved from Rameses
and camped at Succoth. 6They
departed from Succoth and
camped at Etham, which *is*
on the edge of the wilderness.
7They moved from Etham and
turned back to Pi Hahiroth,
which *is* east of Baal Zephon;
and they camped near Migdol.
8They departed from before
Hahiroth[a] and passed through
the midst of the sea into the
wilderness, went three days'
journey in the Wilderness of
Etham, and camped at Marah.
9They moved from Marah and
came to Elim. At Elim *were*
twelve springs of water and
seventy palm trees; so they
camped there.
10They moved from Elim
and camped by the Red Sea.
11They moved from the Red
Sea and camped in the Wilderness of Sin. 12They journeyed from the Wilderness of
Sin and camped at Dophkah.
13They departed from Dophkah and camped at Alush.
14They moved from Alush and
camped at Rephidim, where
there was no water for the
people to drink.
15They departed from
Rephidim and camped in the
Wilderness of Sinai. 16They
moved from the Wilderness of
Sinai and camped at Kibroth
Hattaavah. 17They departed
from Kibroth Hattaavah and
camped at Hazeroth. 18They
departed from Hazeroth and
camped at Rithmah. 19They
departed from Rithmah and
camped at Rimmon Perez.
20They departed from Rim-
mon Perez and camped at
Libnah. 21They moved from
Libnah and camped at Rissah.
22They journeyed from Rissah
and camped at Kehelathah.
23They went from Kehela-
thah and camped at Mount
Shepher. 24They moved from
Mount Shepher and camped at
Haradah. 25They moved from
Haradah and camped at Makheloth. 26They moved from
Makheloth and camped at Tahath. 27They departed from
Tahath and camped at Terah.
28They moved from Terah
and camped at Mithkah.
29They went from Mithkah
and camped at Hashmonah.
30They departed from Hashmonah and camped at Mo-
seroth. 31They departed from
Moseroth and camped at Bene
Jaakan. 32They moved from
Bene Jaakan and camped at
Hor Hagidgad. 33They went
from Hor Hagidgad and
camped at Jotbathah. 34They
moved from Jotbathah and
camped at Abronah. 35They

33:8 [a] Many Hebrew manuscripts, Samaritan Pentateuch, Syriac, Targum, and Vulgate read *from Pi Hahiroth* (compare verse 7).

departed from Abronah and camped at Ezion Geber. 36They moved from Ezion Geber and camped in the Wilderness of Zin, which *is* Kadesh. 37They moved from Kadesh and camped at Mount Hor, on the boundary of the land of Edom.

38Then Aaron the priest went up to Mount Hor at the command of the LORD, and died there in the fortieth year after the children of Israel had come out of the land of Egypt, on the first *day* of the fifth month. 39Aaron *was* one hundred and twenty-three years old when he died on Mount Hor.

40Now the king of Arad, the Canaanite, who dwelt in the South in the land of Canaan, heard of the coming of the children of Israel.

41So they departed from Mount Hor and camped at Zalmonah. 42They departed from Zalmonah and camped at Punon. 43They departed from Punon and camped at Oboth. 44They departed from Oboth and camped at Ije Abarim, at the border of Moab. 45They departed from Ijim[a] and camped at Dibon Gad. 46They moved from Dibon Gad and camped at Almon Diblathaim. 47They moved from Almon Diblathaim and camped in the mountains of Abarim, before Nebo. 48They departed from the mountains of Abarim and camped in the plains of Moab by the Jordan, *across from* Jericho. 49They camped by the Jordan, from Beth Jesimoth as far as the Abel Acacia Grove[a] in the plains of Moab.

INSTRUCTIONS FOR THE CONQUEST OF CANAAN

50Now the LORD spoke to Moses in the plains of Moab by the Jordan, *across from* Jericho, saying, 51"Speak to the children of Israel, and say to them: 'When you have crossed the Jordan into the land of Canaan, 52then you shall drive out all the inhabitants of the land from before you, destroy all their engraved stones, destroy all their molded images, and demolish all their high places; 53you shall dispossess *the inhabitants of* the land and dwell in it, for I have given you the land to possess. 54And you shall divide the land by lot as an inheritance among your families; to the larger you shall give a larger inheritance, and to the smaller you shall give a smaller inheritance; there everyone's *inheritance* shall be whatever falls to him by lot. You shall inherit according to the tribes of your fathers. 55But if you do not drive out the inhabitants of the land from before you, then it shall be that those whom you let remain *shall be* irri-

33:45 [a] Same as *Ije Abarim*, verse 44 **33:49** [a] Hebrew *Abel Shittim*

tants in your eyes and thorns
in your sides, and they shall
harass you in the land where
you dwell. 56Moreover it shall
be *that* I will do to you as I
thought to do to them.'"

THE APPOINTED BOUNDARIES OF CANAAN

34 Then the LORD spoke to
Moses, saying, 2"Com-
mand the children of Israel,
and say to them: 'When you
come into the land of Canaan,
this *is* the land that shall fall
to you as an inheritance—the
land of Canaan to its boundaries. 3Your southern border
shall be from the Wilderness
of Zin along the border of
Edom; then your southern
border shall extend east-
ward to the end of the Salt
Sea; 4your border shall turn
from the southern side of the
Ascent of Akrabbim, continue
to Zin, and be on the south
of Kadesh Barnea; then it
shall go on to Hazar Addar,
and continue to Azmon; 5the
border shall turn from Azmon
to the Brook of Egypt, and it
shall end at the Sea.

6'As for the western border,
you shall have the Great Sea
for a border; this shall be your
western border.

7'And this shall be your
northern border: From the
Great Sea you shall mark out
your *border* line to Mount Hor;
8from Mount Hor you shall
mark out *your border* to the
entrance of Hamath; then the
direction of the border shall
be toward Zedad; 9the border
shall proceed to Ziphron, and
it shall end at Hazar Enan. This
shall be your northern border.

10'You shall mark out your
eastern border from Hazar
Enan to Shepham; 11the border shall go down from Shepham to Riblah on the east
side of Ain; the border shall
go down and reach to the eastern side of the Sea of Chinnereth; 12the border shall go
down along the Jordan, and it
shall end at the Salt Sea. This
shall be your land with its surrounding boundaries.'"

13Then Moses commanded
the children of Israel, saying:
"This *is* the land which you
shall inherit by lot, which the
LORD has commanded to give
to the nine tribes and to the
half-tribe. 14For the tribe of the
children of Reuben according
to the house of their fathers,
and the tribe of the children of Gad according to the
house of their fathers, have
received *their inheritance;* and
the half-tribe of Manasseh
has received its inheritance.
15The two tribes and the half-
tribe have received their inheritance on this side of the
Jordan, *across from* Jericho
eastward, toward the sunrise."

THE LEADERS APPOINTED TO DIVIDE THE LAND

16And the LORD spoke to
Moses, saying, 17"These *are* the
names of the men who shall

divide the land among you
as an inheritance: Eleazar the
priest and Joshua the son of
Nun. 18And you shall take one
leader of every tribe to divide
the land for the inheritance.
19These *are* the names of the
men: from the tribe of Judah,
Caleb the son of Jephunneh;
20from the tribe of the children of Simeon, Shemuel the
son of Ammihud; 21from the
tribe of Benjamin, Elidad the
son of Chislon; 22a leader from
the tribe of the children of
Dan, Bukki the son of Jogli;
23from the sons of Joseph: a
leader from the tribe of the
children of Manasseh, Han-
niel the son of Ephod, 24and
a leader from the tribe of the
children of Ephraim, Kemuel
the son of Shiphtan; 25a leader
from the tribe of the children
of Zebulun, Elizaphan the son
of Parnach; 26a leader from the
tribe of the children of Issachar, Paltiel the son of Azzan;
27a leader from the tribe of the
children of Asher, Ahihud the
son of Shelomi; 28and a leader
from the tribe of the children
of Naphtali, Pedahel the son
of Ammihud."

29These *are* the ones the
LORD commanded to divide
the inheritance among the
children of Israel in the land
of Canaan.

CITIES FOR THE LEVITES

35 And the LORD spoke
to Moses in the plains
of Moab by the Jordan *across*
from Jericho, saying: 2"Command the children of Israel
that they give the Levites
cities to dwell in from the
inheritance of their possession, and you shall *also* give
the Levites common-land
around the cities. 3They shall
have the cities to dwell in; and
their common-land shall be
for their cattle, for their herds,
and for all their animals. 4The
common-land of the cities
which you will give the Levites
shall extend from the wall of
the city outward a thousand
cubits all around. 5And you
shall measure outside the city
on the east side two thousand
cubits, on the south side two
thousand cubits, on the west
side two thousand cubits, and
on the north side two thousand cubits. The city *shall be* in
the middle. This shall belong
to them as common-land for
the cities.

6"Now among the cities
which you will give to the
Levites *you shall appoint* six
cities of refuge, to which a
manslayer may flee. And to
these you shall add forty-two
cities. 7So all the cities you
will give to the Levites *shall*
be forty-eight; these *you shall*
give with their common-land.
8And the cities which you will
give *shall be* from the possession of the children of Israel;
from the larger *tribe* you shall
give many, from the smaller
you shall give few. Each shall
give some of its cities to the

Levites, in proportion to the
inheritance that each re-
ceives."

CITIES OF REFUGE

[9]Then the LORD spoke to
Moses, saying, [10]"Speak to the
children of Israel, and say to
them: 'When you cross the
Jordan into the land of Canaan, [11]then you shall appoint
cities to be cities of refuge for
you, that the manslayer who
kills any person accidentally
may flee there. [12]They shall
be cities of refuge for you
from the avenger, that the
manslayer may not die until
he stands before the congregation in judgment. [13]And of
the cities which you give, you
shall have six cities of refuge.
[14]You shall appoint three cities on this side of the Jordan,
and three cities you shall appoint in the land of Canaan,
which will be cities of refuge.
[15]These six cities shall be for
refuge for the children of Israel, for the stranger, and for
the sojourner among them,
that anyone who kills a person accidentally may flee
there.

[16]'But if he strikes him with
an iron implement, so that
he dies, he *is* a murderer; the
murderer shall surely be put
to death. [17]And if he strikes
him with a stone in the hand,
by which one could die, and he
does die, he *is* a murderer; the
murderer shall surely be put
to death. [18]Or *if* he strikes him
with a wooden hand weapon,
by which one could die, and
he does die, he *is* a murderer;
the murderer shall surely be
put to death. [19]The avenger
of blood himself shall put the
murderer to death; when he
meets him, he shall put him
to death. [20]If he pushes him
out of hatred or, while lying in
wait, hurls something at him
so that he dies, [21]or in enmity
he strikes him with his hand
so that he dies, the one who
struck *him* shall surely be put
to death. He *is* a murderer. The
avenger of blood shall put the
murderer to death when he
meets him.

[22]'However, if he pushes
him suddenly without en-
mity, or throws anything at
him without lying in wait, [23]or
uses a stone, by which a man
could die, throwing *it* at him
without seeing *him,* so that
he dies, while he was not his
enemy or seeking his harm,
[24]then the congregation shall
judge between the manslayer
and the avenger of blood according to these judgments.
[25]So the congregation shall
deliver the manslayer from
the hand of the avenger of
blood, and the congregation
shall return him to the city of
refuge where he had fled, and
he shall remain there until
the death of the high priest
who was anointed with the
holy oil. [26]But if the manslayer at any time goes outside the limits of the city of

refuge where he fled, [27]and
the avenger of blood finds
him outside the limits of his
city of refuge, and the avenger
of blood kills the manslayer,
he shall not be guilty of blood,
[28]because he should have remained in his city of refuge
until the death of the high
priest. But after the death of
the high priest the manslayer
may return to the land of his
possession.

[29]'And these *things* shall be
a statute of judgment to you
throughout your generations
in all your dwellings. [30]Who-
ever kills a person, the murderer shall be put to death on
the testimony of witnesses;
but one witness is not *sufficient* testimony against a
person for the death *penalty.*
[31]Moreover you shall take no
ransom for the life of a murderer who *is* guilty of death,
but he shall surely be put to
death. [32]And you shall take
no ransom for him who has
fled to his city of refuge, that
he may return to dwell in the
land before the death of the
priest. [33]So you shall not pollute the land where you *are;*
for blood defiles the land, and
no atonement can be made
for the land, for the blood
that is shed on it, except by
the blood of him who shed
it. [34]Therefore do not defile
the land which you inhabit,
in the midst of which I dwell;
for I the LORD dwell among
the children of Israel.'"

MARRIAGE OF FEMALE HEIRS

36 Now the chief fathers
of the families of the
children of Gilead the son of
Machir, the son of Manasseh,
of the families of the sons of
Joseph, came near and spoke
before Moses and before the
leaders, the chief fathers of
the children of Israel. [2]And
they said: "The LORD com-
manded my lord *Moses* to give
the land as an inheritance by
lot to the children of Israel,
and my lord was commanded
by the LORD to give the inheritance of our brother Zelophehad to his daughters. [3]Now
if they are married to any of
the sons of the *other* tribes of
the children of Israel, then
their inheritance will be taken
from the inheritance of our
fathers, and it will be added
to the inheritance of the tribe
into which they marry; so it
will be taken from the lot of
our inheritance. [4]And when
the Jubilee of the children of
Israel comes, then their inheritance will be added to the
inheritance of the tribe into
which they marry; so their inheritance will be taken away
from the inheritance of the
tribe of our fathers."

[5]Then Moses commanded
the children of Israel according to the word of the LORD,
saying: "What the tribe of
the sons of Joseph speaks is
right. [6]This *is* what the LORD
commands concerning the

daughters of Zelophehad, saying, 'Let them marry whom
they think best, but they may
marry only within the family
of their father's tribe.' 7So the
inheritance of the children of
Israel shall not change hands
from tribe to tribe, for every
one of the children of Israel
shall keep the inheritance of
the tribe of his fathers. 8And
every daughter who possesses
an inheritance in any tribe of
the children of Israel shall be
the wife of one of the family
of her father's tribe, so that
the children of Israel each
may possess the inheritance
of his fathers. 9Thus no inheritance shall change hands
from *one* tribe to another, but
every tribe of the children of
Israel shall keep its own inheritance."

10Just as the LORD com-
manded Moses, so did the
daughters of Zelophehad; 11for
Mahlah, Tirzah, Hoglah, Milcah, and Noah, the daughters
of Zelophehad, were married
to the sons of their father's
brothers. 12They were married
into the families of the children of Manasseh the son of
Joseph, and their inheritance
remained in the tribe of their
father's family.

13These *are* the commandments and the judgments
which the LORD commanded
the children of Israel by the
hand of Moses in the plains
of Moab by the Jordan, *across
from* Jericho.

THE FIFTH BOOK OF MOSES CALLED

DEUTERONOMY

THE PREVIOUS COMMAND TO ENTER CANAAN

1 These *are* the words which
Moses spoke to all Israel on
this side of the Jordan in the
wilderness, in the plain[a] opposite Suph,[b] between Paran,
Tophel, Laban, Hazeroth, and
Dizahab. 2*It is* eleven days'
journey from Horeb by way of
Mount Seir to Kadesh Barnea.
3Now it came to pass in the
fortieth year, in the eleventh
month, on the first *day* of the
month, *that* Moses spoke to
the children of Israel according to all that the LORD had
given him as commandments
to them, 4after he had killed
Sihon king of the Amorites,

1:1 [a] Hebrew *arabah* [b] One manuscript of the Septuagint, also Targum and Vulgate, read *Red Sea*.

who dwelt in Heshbon, and
Og king of Bashan, who dwelt
at Ashtaroth in[a] Edrei.
5On this side of the Jordan
in the land of Moab, Moses
began to explain this law,
saying, 6"The LORD our God
spoke to us in Horeb, saying:
'You have dwelt long enough
at this mountain. 7Turn and
take your journey, and go to
the mountains of the Amo-
rites, to all the neighboring
places in the plain,[a] in the
mountains and in the low-
land, in the South and on the
seacoast, to the land of the
Canaanites and to Lebanon,
as far as the great river, the
River Euphrates. 8See, I have
set the land before you; go in
and possess the land which
the LORD swore to your fathers—to Abraham, Isaac, and
Jacob—to give to them and
their descendants after them.'

TRIBAL LEADERS APPOINTED

9"And I spoke to you at that
time, saying: 'I alone am not
able to bear you. 10The LORD
your God has multiplied you,
and here you *are* today, as the
stars of heaven in multitude.
11May the LORD God of your
fathers make you a thousand
times more numerous than
you are, and bless you as He
has promised you! 12How can
I alone bear your problems
and your burdens and your
complaints? 13Choose wise,
understanding, and knowl-
edgeable men from among
your tribes, and I will make
them heads over you.' 14And
you answered me and said,
'The thing which you have told
us to do *is* good.' 15So I took
the heads of your tribes, wise
and knowledgeable men, and
made them heads over you,
leaders of thousands, leaders
of hundreds, leaders of fifties,
leaders of tens, and officers
for your tribes.
16"Then I commanded your
judges at that time, saying,
'Hear *the cases* between your
brethren, and judge righ-
teously between a man and
his brother or the stranger
who is with him. 17You shall
not show partiality in judgment; you shall hear the small
as well as the great; you shall
not be afraid in any man's
presence, for the judgment *is*
God's. The case that is too hard
for you, bring to me, and I will
hear it.' 18And I commanded
you at that time all the things
which you should do.

ISRAEL'S REFUSAL TO ENTER THE LAND

19"So we departed from
Horeb, and went through all
that great and terrible wilderness which you saw on the way
to the mountains of the Am-

1:4 [a] Septuagint, Syriac, and Vulgate read *and* (compare Joshua 12:4). 1:7 [a] Hebrew *arabah*

orites, as the LORD our God
had commanded us. Then we
came to Kadesh Barnea. 20And
I said to you, 'You have come
to the mountains of the Amorites, which the LORD our God
is giving us. 21Look, the LORD
your God has set the land before you; go up *and* possess
it, as the LORD God of your
fathers has spoken to you; do
not fear or be discouraged.'

22"And every one of you
came near to me and said, 'Let
us send men before us, and let
them search out the land for
us, and bring back word to us
of the way by which we should
go up, and of the cities into
which we shall come.'

23"The plan pleased me
well; so I took twelve of your
men, one man from *each*
tribe. 24And they departed and
went up into the mountains,
and came to the Valley of Eshcol, and spied it out. 25They
also took *some* of the fruit of
the land in their hands and
brought *it* down to us; and
they brought back word to us,
saying, '*It is* a good land which
the LORD our God is giving us.'

26"Nevertheless you would
not go up, but rebelled against
the command of the LORD
your God; 27and you com-
plained in your tents, and
said, 'Because the LORD hates
us, He has brought us out of
the land of Egypt to deliver us
into the hand of the Amorites,
to destroy us. 28Where can
we go up? Our brethren have
discouraged our hearts, saying, "The people *are* greater
and taller than we; the cities
are great and fortified up to
heaven; moreover we have
seen the sons of the Anakim
there."'

29"Then I said to you, 'Do
not be terrified, or afraid of
them. 30The LORD your God,
who goes before you, He will
fight for you, according to all
He did for you in Egypt before
your eyes, 31and in the wilderness where you saw how the
LORD your God carried you,
as a man carries his son, in
all the way that you went until
you came to this place.' 32Yet,
for all that, you did not believe
the LORD your God, 33who
went in the way before you
to search out a place for you
to pitch your tents, to show
you the way you should go,
in the fire by night and in the
cloud by day.

THE PENALTY FOR ISRAEL'S REBELLION

34"And the LORD heard the
sound of your words, and was
angry, and took an oath, saying, 35'Surely not one of these
men of this evil generation
shall see that good land of
which I swore to give to your
fathers, 36except Caleb the
son of Jephunneh; he shall
see it, and to him and his children I am giving the land on
which he walked, because he
wholly followed the LORD.'
37The LORD was also angry

with me for your sakes, saying, 'Even you shall not go
in there. 38 Joshua the son of
Nun, who stands before you,
he shall go in there. Encourage him, for he shall cause Israel to inherit it.
39 'Moreover your little ones
and your children, who you
say will be victims, who today
have no knowledge of good
and evil, they shall go in there;
to them I will give it, and they
shall possess it. 40 But *as for*
you, turn and take your journey into the wilderness by the
Way of the Red Sea.'
41 "Then you answered and
said to me, 'We have sinned
against the LORD; we will go
up and fight, just as the LORD
our God commanded us.' And
when everyone of you had
girded on his weapons of war,
you were ready to go up into
the mountain.
42 "And the LORD said to me,
'Tell them, "Do not go up nor
fight, for I *am* not among you;
lest you be defeated before
your enemies."' 43 So I spoke
to you; yet you would not listen, but rebelled against the
command of the LORD, and
presumptuously went up into
the mountain. 44 And the Amorites who dwelt in that mountain came out against you and
chased you as bees do, and
drove you back from Seir to
Hormah. 45 Then you returned
and wept before the LORD, but
the LORD would not listen to
your voice nor give ear to you.
46 "So you remained in Kadesh many days, according to
the days that you spent *there.*

THE DESERT YEARS

2 "Then we turned and journeyed into the wilderness
of the Way of the Red Sea, as
the LORD spoke to me, and we
skirted Mount Seir for many
days.
2 "And the LORD spoke to
me, saying: 3 'You have skirted
this mountain long enough;
turn northward. 4 And command the people, saying, "You
are about to pass through the
territory of your brethren, the
descendants of Esau, who live
in Seir; and they will be afraid
of you. Therefore watch yourselves carefully. 5 Do not meddle with them, for I will not
give you *any* of their land, no,
not so much as one footstep,
because I have given Mount
Seir to Esau *as* a possession.
6 You shall buy food from them
with money, that you may eat;
and you shall also buy water
from them with money, that
you may drink.
7 "For the LORD your God
has blessed you in all the work
of your hand. He knows your
trudging through this great
wilderness. These forty years
the LORD your God *has been*
with you; you have lacked
nothing."'
8 "And when we passed be-
yond our brethren, the descendants of Esau who dwell
in Seir, away from the road

of the plain, away from Elath
and Ezion Geber, we turned
and passed by way of the Wilderness of Moab. 9Then the
LORD said to me, 'Do not harass Moab, nor contend with
them in battle, for I will not
give you *any* of their land *as*
a possession, because I have
given Ar to the descendants
of Lot *as* a possession.'"

10(The Emim had dwelt
there in times past, a people
as great and numerous and
tall as the Anakim. 11They were
also regarded as giants,[a] like
the Anakim, but the Moabites
call them Emim. 12The Horites
formerly dwelt in Seir, but the
descendants of Esau dispossessed them and destroyed
them from before them, and
dwelt in their place, just as Israel did to the land of their
possession which the LORD
gave them.)

13"'Now rise and cross over
the Valley of the Zered.' So we
crossed over the Valley of
the Zered. 14And the time we
took to come from Kadesh
Barnea until we crossed over
the Valley of the Zered *was*
thirty-eight years, until all the
generation of the men of war
was consumed from the midst
of the camp, just as the LORD
had sworn to them. 15For indeed the hand of the LORD was
against them, to destroy them
from the midst of the camp
until they were consumed.

16"So it was, when all the
men of war had finally perished from among the people,
17that the LORD spoke to me,
saying: 18'This day you are to
cross over at Ar, the boundary of Moab. 19And *when*
you come near the people of
Ammon, do not harass them
or meddle with them, for I will
not give you *any* of the land
of the people of Ammon *as*
a possession, because I have
given it to the descendants of
Lot *as* a possession.'"

20(That was also regarded
as a land of giants;[a] giants
formerly dwelt there. But
the Ammonites call them
Zamzummim, 21a people as
great and numerous and tall
as the Anakim. But the LORD
destroyed them before them,
and they dispossessed them
and dwelt in their place, 22just
as He had done for the descendants of Esau, who dwelt
in Seir, when He destroyed the
Horites from before them.
They dispossessed them and
dwelt in their place, even to
this day. 23And the Avim,
who dwelt in villages as far
as Gaza—the Caphtorim, who
came from Caphtor, destroyed
them and dwelt in their place.)

24"'Rise, take your jour-
ney, and cross over the River
Arnon. Look, I have given into
your hand Sihon the Amorite,
king of Heshbon, and his land.
Begin to possess *it,* and engage

2:11 [a] Hebrew *rephaim*

2:20 [a] Hebrew *rephaim*

him in battle. 25This day I will
begin to put the dread and
fear of you upon the nations
under the whole heaven, who
shall hear the report of you,
and shall tremble and be in
anguish because of you.'

KING SIHON DEFEATED

26"And I sent messen-
gers from the Wilderness
of Kedemoth to Sihon king
of Heshbon, with words of
peace, saying, 27'Let me pass
through your land; I will keep
strictly to the road, and I will
turn neither to the right nor
to the left. 28You shall sell me
food for money, that I may eat,
and give me water for money,
that I may drink; only let me
pass through on foot, 29just as
the descendants of Esau who
dwell in Seir and the Moabites
who dwell in Ar did for me,
until I cross the Jordan to the
land which the LORD our God
is giving us.'

30"But Sihon king of Heshbon would not let us pass
through, for the LORD your
God hardened his spirit and
made his heart obstinate, that
He might deliver him into
your hand, as *it is* this day.

31"And the LORD said to
me, 'See, I have begun to give
Sihon and his land over to you.
Begin to possess *it,* that you
may inherit his land.' 32Then
Sihon and all his people came
out against us to fight at Jahaz.
33And the LORD our God delivered him over to us; so we
defeated him, his sons, and all
his people. 34We took all his cities at that time, and we utterly
destroyed the men, women,
and little ones of every city; we
left none remaining. 35We took
only the livestock as plunder
for ourselves, with the spoil
of the cities which we took.
36From Aroer, which *is* on the
bank of the River Arnon, and
from the city that *is* in the ravine, as far as Gilead, there was
not one city too strong for us;
the LORD our God delivered
all to us. 37Only you did not go
near the land of the people of
Ammon—anywhere along the
River Jabbok, or to the cities of
the mountains, or wherever
the LORD our God had forbidden us.

KING OG DEFEATED

3 "Then we turned and went
up the road to Bashan; and
Og king of Bashan came out
against us, he and all his people, to battle at Edrei. 2And the
LORD said to me, 'Do not fear
him, for I have delivered him
and all his people and his land
into your hand; you shall do to
him as you did to Sihon king
of the Amorites, who dwelt at
Heshbon.'

3"So the LORD our God also
delivered into our hands Og
king of Bashan, with all his
people, and we attacked him
until he had no survivors remaining. 4And we took all his
cities at that time; there was
not a city which we did not

take from them: sixty cities,
all the region of Argob, the
kingdom of Og in Bashan.
5All these cities *were* fortified with high walls, gates,
and bars, besides a great
many rural towns. 6And we
utterly destroyed them, as we
did to Sihon king of Heshbon,
utterly destroying the men,
women, and children of every
city. 7But all the livestock and
the spoil of the cities we took
as booty for ourselves.
8"And at that time we took
the land from the hand of the
two kings of the Amorites who
were on this side of the Jordan, from the River Arnon to
Mount Hermon 9(the Sidonians call Hermon Sirion, and
the Amorites call it Senir), 10all
the cities of the plain, all Gilead, and all Bashan, as far as
Salcah and Edrei, cities of the
kingdom of Og in Bashan.
11"For only Og king of Bashan remained of the rem-
nant of the giants.[a] Indeed
his bedstead *was* an iron bedstead. (*Is* it not in Rabbah of
the people of Ammon?) Nine
cubits *is* its length and four
cubits its width, according to
the standard cubit.

THE LAND EAST OF THE JORDAN DIVIDED

12"And this land, *which* we
possessed at that time, from
Aroer, which *is* by the River
Arnon, and half the moun-
tains of Gilead and its cities, I
gave to the Reubenites and the
Gadites. 13The rest of Gilead,
and all Bashan, the kingdom
of Og, I gave to half the tribe of
Manasseh. (All the region of
Argob, with all Bashan, was
called the land of the giants.[a]
14Jair the son of Manasseh
took all the region of Argob, as
far as the border of the Geshurites and the Maachathites,
and called Bashan after his
own name, Havoth Jair,[a] to
this day.)
15"Also I gave Gilead to
Machir. 16And to the Reu-
benites and the Gadites I gave
from Gilead as far as the River
Arnon, the middle of the river
as *the* border, as far as the
River Jabbok, the border of
the people of Ammon; 17the
plain also, with the Jordan as
the border, from Chinnereth
as far as the east side of the
Sea of the Arabah (the Salt
Sea), below the slopes of Pisgah.
18"Then I commanded
you at that time, saying: 'The
LORD your God has given you
this land to possess. All you
men of valor shall cross over
armed before your brethren,
the children of Israel. 19But
your wives, your little ones,
and your livestock (I know
that you have much livestock)
shall stay in your cities which

3:11 [a] Hebrew *rephaim* 3:13 [a] Hebrew *rephaim* 3:14 [a] Literally *Towns of Jair*

I have given you, 20until the
LORD has given rest to your
brethren as to you, and they
also possess the land which
the LORD your God is giving
them beyond the Jordan.
Then each of you may return
to his possession which I have
given you.'
21"And I commanded
Joshua at that time, saying,
'Your eyes have seen all that
the LORD your God has done
to these two kings; so will
the LORD do to all the kingdoms through which you pass.
22You must not fear them, for
the LORD your God Himself
fights for you.'

MOSES FORBIDDEN TO ENTER THE LAND

23"Then I pleaded with
the LORD at that time, saying: 24'O Lord GOD, You have
begun to show Your servant
Your greatness and Your
mighty hand, for what god *is*
there in heaven or on earth
who can do *anything* like Your
works and Your mighty *deeds?*
25I pray, let me cross over and
see the good land beyond the
Jordan, those pleasant mountains, and Lebanon.'
26"But the LORD was angry
with me on your account, and
would not listen to me. So the
LORD said to me: 'Enough
of that! Speak no more to
Me of this matter. 27Go up
to the top of Pisgah, and lift
your eyes toward the west,
the north, the south, and the
east; behold *it* with your eyes,
for you shall not cross over
this Jordan. 28But command
Joshua, and encourage him
and strengthen him; for he
shall go over before this people, and he shall cause them
to inherit the land which you
will see.'
29"So we stayed in the valley opposite Beth Peor.

MOSES COMMANDS OBEDIENCE

4 "Now, O Israel, listen to
the statutes and the judgments which I teach you to
observe, that you may live,
and go in and possess the land
which the LORD God of your fathers is giving you. 2You shall
not add to the word which I
command you, nor take from
it, that you may keep the commandments of the LORD your
God which I command you.
3Your eyes have seen what the
LORD did at Baal Peor; for the
LORD your God has destroyed
from among you all the men
who followed Baal of Peor.
4But you who held fast to the
LORD your God *are* alive today,
every one of you.
5"Surely I have taught you
statutes and judgments, just
as the LORD my God com-
manded me, that you should
act according *to them* in the
land which you go to possess.
6Therefore be careful to observe *them;* for this *is* your
wisdom and your understanding in the sight of the peoples

who will hear all these statutes, and say, ‘Surely this great
nation *is* a wise and understanding people.’
7“For what great nation *is*
there that has God *so* near to
it, as the LORD our God *is* to us,
for whatever *reason* we may
call upon Him? 8And what
great nation *is there* that has
such statutes and righteous
judgments as are in all this
law which I set before you
this day? 9Only take heed to
yourself, and diligently keep
yourself, lest you forget the
things your eyes have seen,
and lest they depart from your
heart all the days of your life.
And teach them to your children and your grandchildren,
10*especially concerning* the day
you stood before the LORD
your God in Horeb, when the
LORD said to me, ‘Gather the
people to Me, and I will let
them hear My words, that they
may learn to fear Me all the
days they live on the earth,
and *that* they may teach their
children.’
11“Then you came near
and stood at the foot of the
mountain, and the mountain
burned with fire to the midst
of heaven, with darkness,
cloud, and thick darkness.
12And the LORD spoke to you
out of the midst of the fire.
You heard the sound of the
words, but saw no form; *you*
only *heard* a voice. 13So He
declared to you His covenant
which He commanded you to
perform, the Ten Command-
ments; and He wrote them on
two tablets of stone. 14And the
LORD commanded me at that
time to teach you statutes and
judgments, that you might observe them in the land which
you cross over to possess.

BEWARE OF IDOLATRY

15“Take careful heed to
yourselves, for you saw no
form when the LORD spoke
to you at Horeb out of the
midst of the fire, 16lest you
act corruptly and make for
yourselves a carved image
in the form of any figure: the
likeness of male or female,
17the likeness of any animal
that *is* on the earth or the likeness of any winged bird that
flies in the air, 18the likeness
of anything that creeps on
the ground or the likeness of
any fish that *is* in the water
beneath the earth. 19And *take*
heed, lest you lift your eyes
to heaven, and *when* you see
the sun, the moon, and the
stars, all the host of heaven,
you feel driven to worship
them and serve them, which
the LORD your God has given
to all the peoples under the
whole heaven as a heritage.
20But the LORD has taken you
and brought you out of the
iron furnace, out of Egypt, to
be His people, an inheritance,
as you are this day. 21Further-
more the LORD was angry with
me for your sakes, and swore
that I would not cross over the

Jordan, and that I would not
enter the good land which the
LORD your God is giving you
as an inheritance. 22But I must
die in this land, I must not
cross over the Jordan; but you
shall cross over and possess
that good land. 23Take heed
to yourselves, lest you forget the covenant of the LORD
your God which He made with
you, and make for yourselves
a carved image in the form
of anything which the LORD
your God has forbidden you.
24For the LORD your God *is* a
consuming fire, a jealous God.

25"When you beget chil-
dren and grandchildren and
have grown old in the land,
and act corruptly and make a
carved image in the form of
anything, and do evil in the
sight of the LORD your God to
provoke Him to anger, 26I call
heaven and earth to witness
against you this day, that you
will soon utterly perish from
the land which you cross over
the Jordan to possess; you will
not prolong *your* days in it,
but will be utterly destroyed.
27And the LORD will scatter
you among the peoples, and
you will be left few in number among the nations where
the LORD will drive you. 28And
there you will serve gods, the
work of men's hands, wood
and stone, which neither see
nor hear nor eat nor smell.
29But from there you will seek
the LORD your God, and you
will find *Him* if you seek Him
with all your heart and with all
your soul. 30When you are in
distress, and all these things
come upon you in the latter
days, when you turn to the
LORD your God and obey His
voice 31(for the LORD your God
is a merciful God), He will not
forsake you nor destroy you,
nor forget the covenant of
your fathers which He swore
to them.

32"For ask now concerning
the days that are past, which
were before you, since the
day that God created man on
the earth, and *ask* from one
end of heaven to the other,
whether *any* great *thing* like
this has happened, or *anything* like it has been heard.
33Did *any* people *ever* hear
the voice of God speaking out
of the midst of the fire, as you
have heard, and live? 34Or did
God *ever* try to go *and* take
for Himself a nation from the
midst of *another* nation, by
trials, by signs, by wonders,
by war, by a mighty hand and
an outstretched arm, and by
great terrors, according to all
that the LORD your God did
for you in Egypt before your
eyes? 35To you it was shown,
that you might know that the
LORD Himself *is* God; *there is*
none other besides Him. 36Out
of heaven He let you hear His
voice, that He might instruct
you; on earth He showed you
His great fire, and you heard
His words out of the midst
of the fire. 37And because He

loved your fathers, therefore
He chose their descendants
after them; and He brought
you out of Egypt with His
Presence, with His mighty
power, 38driving out from before you nations greater and
mightier than you, to bring
you in, to give you their land
as an inheritance, as *it is* this
day. 39Therefore know this
day, and consider *it* in your
heart, that the LORD Himself
is God in heaven above and
on the earth beneath; *there*
is no other. 40You shall therefore keep His statutes and
His commandments which
I command you today, that
it may go well with you and
with your children after you,
and that you may prolong
your days in the land which
the LORD your God is giving
you for all time."

CITIES OF REFUGE EAST OF THE JORDAN

41Then Moses set apart
three cities on this side of the
Jordan, toward the rising of
the sun, 42that the manslayer
might flee there, who kills his
neighbor unintentionally,
without having hated him in
time past, and that by fleeing
to one of these cities he might
live: 43Bezer in the wilderness
on the plateau for the Reubenites, Ramoth in Gilead for the
Gadites, and Golan in Bashan
for the Manassites.

INTRODUCTION TO GOD'S LAW

44Now this *is* the law which
Moses set before the children
of Israel. 45These *are* the testimonies, the statutes, and the
judgments which Moses spoke
to the children of Israel after
they came out of Egypt, 46on
this side of the Jordan, in the
valley opposite Beth Peor, in
the land of Sihon king of the
Amorites, who dwelt at Heshbon, whom Moses and the children of Israel defeated after
they came out of Egypt. 47And
they took possession of his
land and the land of Og king of
Bashan, two kings of the Amorites, who *were* on this side of
the Jordan, toward the rising of
the sun, 48from Aroer, which *is*
on the bank of the River Arnon,
even to Mount Sion[a] (that is,
Hermon), 49and all the plain
on the east side of the Jordan
as far as the Sea of the Arabah,
below the slopes of Pisgah.

THE TEN COMMANDMENTS REVIEWED

5 And Moses called all Israel,
and said to them: "Hear,
O Israel, the statutes and judgments which I speak in your
hearing today, that you may
learn them and be careful to
observe them. 2The LORD our
God made a covenant with us
in Horeb. 3The LORD did not
make this covenant with our
fathers, but with us, those who

4:48 [a] Syriac reads *Sirion* (compare 3:9).

are here today, all of us who *are*
alive. 4The LORD talked with
you face to face on the mountain from the midst of the fire.
5I stood between the LORD and
you at that time, to declare
to you the word of the LORD;
for you were afraid because of
the fire, and you did not go up
the mountain. *He* said:
6 'I *am* the LORD your God
who brought you out of
the land of Egypt, out of
the house of bondage.
7 'You shall have no other
gods before Me.
8 'You shall not make for
yourself a carved image—
any likeness *of anything*
that *is* in heaven above,
or that *is* in the earth beneath, or that *is* in the
water under the earth;
9you shall not bow down
to them nor serve them.
For I, the LORD your God,
am a jealous God, visiting
the iniquity of the fathers
upon the children to the
third and fourth *genera-
tions* of those who hate
Me, 10but showing mercy
to thousands, to those
who love Me and keep
My commandments.
11 'You shall not take the
name of the LORD your
God in vain, for the LORD
will not hold *him* guiltless who takes His name
in vain.
12 'Observe the Sabbath day, to
keep it holy, as the LORD
your God commanded
you. 13Six days you shall
labor and do all your
work, 14but the seventh
day *is* the Sabbath of the
LORD your God. *In it* you
shall do no work: you,
nor your son, nor your
daughter, nor your male
servant, nor your female
servant, nor your ox, nor
your donkey, nor any
of your cattle, nor your
stranger who *is* within
your gates, that your male
servant and your female
servant may rest as well
as you. 15And remember
that you were a slave in
the land of Egypt, and the
LORD your God brought
you out from there by a
mighty hand and by an
outstretched arm; there-
fore the LORD your God
commanded you to keep
the Sabbath day.
16 'Honor your father and your
mother, as the LORD your
God has commanded
you, that your days may
be long, and that it may
be well with you in the
land which the LORD
your God is giving you.
17 'You shall not murder.
18 'You shall not commit
adultery.
19 'You shall not steal.
20 'You shall not bear false
witness against your
neighbor.
21 'You shall not covet your
neighbor's wife; and you
shall not desire your

neighbor’s house, his
field, his male servant,
his female servant, his ox,
his donkey, or anything
that *is* your neighbor’s.’
22“These words the LORD
spoke to all your assembly,
in the mountain from the
midst of the fire, the cloud,
and the thick darkness, with
a loud voice; and He added no
more. And He wrote them on
two tablets of stone and gave
them to me.

THE PEOPLE AFRAID OF GOD’S PRESENCE

23“So it was, when you heard
the voice from the midst of the
darkness, while the mountain
was burning with fire, that you
came near to me, all the heads
of your tribes and your elders.
24And you said: ‘Surely the
LORD our God has shown us
His glory and His greatness,
and we have heard His voice
from the midst of the fire. We
have seen this day that God
speaks with man; yet he *still*
lives. 25Now therefore, why
should we die? For this great
fire will consume us; if we hear
the voice of the LORD our God
anymore, then we shall die.
26For who *is there* of all flesh
who has heard the voice of the
living God speaking from the
midst of the fire, as we *have,*
and lived? 27You go near and
hear all that the LORD our God
may say, and tell us all that the
LORD our God says to you, and
we will hear and do *it.*’
28“Then the LORD heard the
voice of your words when you
spoke to me, and the LORD said
to me: ‘I have heard the voice
of the words of this people
which they have spoken to you.
They are right *in* all that they
have spoken. 29Oh, that they
had such a heart in them that
they would fear Me and always
keep all My commandments,
that it might be well with them
and with their children forever! 30Go and say to them,
“Return to your tents.” 31But
as for you, stand here by Me,
and I will speak to you all the
commandments, the statutes,
and the judgments which you
shall teach them, that they may
observe *them* in the land which
I am giving them to possess.’
32“Therefore you shall be
careful to do as the LORD your
God has commanded you;
you shall not turn aside to
the right hand or to the left.
33You shall walk in all the ways
which the LORD your God has
commanded you, that you
may live and *that it may be*
well with you, and *that* you
may prolong *your* days in the
land which you shall possess.

THE GREATEST COMMANDMENT

6 “Now this *is* the com-
mandment, *and these are*
the statutes and judgments
which the LORD your God has
commanded to teach you, that
you may observe *them* in the
land which you are crossing

over to possess, 2 that you may fear the LORD your God, to keep all His statutes and His commandments which I command you, you and your son and your grandson, all the days of your life, and that your days may be prolonged. 3 Therefore hear, O Israel, and be careful to observe *it,* that it may be well with you, and that you may multiply greatly as the LORD God of your fathers has promised you—'a land flowing with milk and honey.'[a]

4 "Hear, O Israel: The LORD our God, the LORD *is* one![a] 5 You shall love the LORD your God with all your heart, with all your soul, and with all your strength.

6 "And these words which I command you today shall be in your heart. 7 You shall teach them diligently to your children, and shall talk of them when you sit in your house, when you walk by the way, when you lie down, and when you rise up. 8 You shall bind them as a sign on your hand, and they shall be as frontlets between your eyes. 9 You shall write them on the doorposts of your house and on your gates.

CAUTION AGAINST DISOBEDIENCE

10 "So it shall be, when the LORD your God brings you into the land of which He swore to your fathers, to Abraham, Isaac, and Jacob, to give you large and beautiful cities which you did not build, 11 houses full of all good things, which you did not fill, hewn-out wells which you did not dig, vineyards and olive trees which you did not plant—when you have eaten and are full— 12 *then* beware, lest you forget the LORD who brought you out of the land of Egypt, from the house of bondage. 13 You shall fear the LORD your God and serve Him, and shall take oaths in His name. 14 You shall not go after other gods, the gods of the peoples who *are* all around you 15 (for the LORD your God *is* a jealous God among you), lest the anger of the LORD your God be aroused against you and destroy you from the face of the earth.

16 "You shall not tempt the LORD your God as you tempted *Him* in Massah. 17 You shall diligently keep the commandments of the LORD your God, His testimonies, and His statutes which He has commanded you. 18 And you shall do *what is* right and good in the sight of the LORD, that it may be well with you, and that you may go in and possess the good land of which the LORD swore to your fathers, 19 to cast out all your enemies

6:3 [a] Exodus 3:8 **6:4** [a] Or *The LORD is our God, the LORD alone* (that is, the only one)

from before you, as the LORD
has spoken.
20“When your son asks you
in time to come, saying, ‘What *is*
the meaning of the testimonies,
the statutes, and the judgments
which the LORD our God has
commanded you?’ 21then you
shall say to your son: ‘We were
slaves of Pharaoh in Egypt,
and the LORD brought us out
of Egypt with a mighty hand;
22and the LORD showed signs
and wonders before our eyes,
great and severe, against Egypt,
Pharaoh, and all his household.
23Then He brought us out from
there, that He might bring us
in, to give us the land of which
He swore to our fathers. 24And
the LORD commanded us to observe all these statutes, to fear
the LORD our God, for our good
always, that He might preserve
us alive, as *it is* this day. 25Then
it will be righteousness for us,
if we are careful to observe all
these commandments before
the LORD our God, as He has
commanded us.’

A CHOSEN PEOPLE

7 “When the LORD your God
brings you into the land
which you go to possess, and
has cast out many nations before you, the Hittites and the
Girgashites and the Amorites
and the Canaanites and the
Perizzites and the Hivites and
the Jebusites, seven nations
greater and mightier than you,
2and when the LORD your God
delivers them over to you, you
shall conquer them *and* utterly destroy them. You shall
make no covenant with them
nor show mercy to them. 3Nor
shall you make marriages with
them. You shall not give your
daughter to their son, nor take
their daughter for your son.
4For they will turn your sons
away from following Me, to
serve other gods; so the anger
of the LORD will be aroused
against you and destroy you
suddenly. 5But thus you shall
deal with them: you shall destroy their altars, and break
down their *sacred* pillars, and
cut down their wooden im-
ages,[a] and burn their carved
images with fire.
6“For you *are* a holy people to the LORD your God; the
LORD your God has chosen
you to be a people for Himself, a special treasure above
all the peoples on the face of
the earth. 7The LORD did not
set His love on you nor choose
you because you were more in
number than any other people, for you were the least of
all peoples; 8but because the
LORD loves you, and because
He would keep the oath which
He swore to your fathers, the
LORD has brought you out
with a mighty hand, and redeemed you from the house
of bondage, from the hand of
Pharaoh king of Egypt.

7:5 [a] Hebrew *Asherim,* Canaanite deities

9"Therefore know that the LORD your God, He *is* God, the faithful God who keeps covenant and mercy for a thousand generations with those who love Him and keep His commandments; 10and He repays those who hate Him to their face, to destroy them. He will not be slack with him who hates Him; He will repay him to his face. 11Therefore you shall keep the commandment, the statutes, and the judgments which I command you today, to observe them.

BLESSINGS OF OBEDIENCE

12"Then it shall come to pass, because you listen to these judgments, and keep and do them, that the LORD your God will keep with you the covenant and the mercy which He swore to your fathers. 13And He will love you and bless you and multiply you; He will also bless the fruit of your womb and the fruit of your land, your grain and your new wine and your oil, the increase of your cattle and the offspring of your flock, in the land of which He swore to your fathers to give you. 14You shall be blessed above all peoples; there shall not be a male or female barren among you or among your livestock. 15And the LORD will take away from you all sickness, and will afflict you with none of the terrible diseases of Egypt which you have known, but will lay *them* on all those who hate you. 16Also you shall destroy all the peoples whom the LORD your God delivers over to you; your eye shall have no pity on them; nor shall you serve their gods, for that *will be* a snare to you.

17"If you should say in your heart, 'These nations are greater than I; how can I dispossess them?'— 18you shall not be afraid of them, *but* you shall remember well what the LORD your God did to Pharaoh and to all Egypt: 19the great trials which your eyes saw, the signs and the wonders, the mighty hand and the outstretched arm, by which the LORD your God brought you out. So shall the LORD your God do to all the peoples of whom you are afraid. 20Moreover the LORD your God will send the hornet among them until those who are left, who hide themselves from you, are destroyed. 21You shall not be terrified of them; for the LORD your God, the great and awesome God, *is* among you. 22And the LORD your God will drive out those nations before you little by little; you will be unable to destroy them at once, lest the beasts of the field become *too* numerous for you. 23But the LORD your God will deliver them over to you, and will inflict defeat upon them until they are destroyed. 24And He will deliver their kings into your hand,

and you will destroy their
name from under heaven;
no one shall be able to stand
against you until you have
destroyed them. 25You shall
burn the carved images of
their gods with fire; you shall
not covet the silver or gold
that is on them, nor take *it* for
yourselves, lest you be snared
by it; for it *is* an abomination
to the LORD your God. 26Nor
shall you bring an abomination into your house, lest you
be doomed to destruction like
it. You shall utterly detest it
and utterly abhor it, for it *is*
an accursed thing.

REMEMBER THE LORD YOUR GOD

8 "Every commandment
which I command you
today you must be careful to
observe, that you may live
and multiply, and go in and
possess the land of which the
LORD swore to your fathers.
2And you shall remember
that the LORD your God led
you all the way these forty
years in the wilderness, to
humble you *and* test you, to
know what *was* in your heart,
whether you would keep His
commandments or not. 3So
He humbled you, allowed you
to hunger, and fed you with
manna which you did not
know nor did your fathers
know, that He might make
you know that man shall not
live by bread alone; but man
lives by every *word* that proceeds from the mouth of the
LORD. 4Your garments did not
wear out on you, nor did your
foot swell these forty years.
5You should know in your
heart that as a man chastens
his son, *so* the LORD your God
chastens you.

6"Therefore you shall keep
the commandments of the
LORD your God, to walk in
His ways and to fear Him. 7For
the LORD your God is bringing
you into a good land, a land of
brooks of water, of fountains
and springs, that flow out of
valleys and hills; 8a land of
wheat and barley, of vines and
fig trees and pomegranates,
a land of olive oil and honey;
9a land in which you will eat
bread without scarcity, in
which you will lack nothing;
a land whose stones *are* iron
and out of whose hills you can
dig copper. 10When you have
eaten and are full, then you
shall bless the LORD your God
for the good land which He
has given you.

11"Beware that you do not
forget the LORD your God by
not keeping His command-
ments, His judgments, and
His statutes which I command
you today, 12lest—*when* you
have eaten and are full, and
have built beautiful houses
and dwell *in them;* 13and *when*
your herds and your flocks
multiply, and your silver and
your gold are multiplied, and
all that you have is multiplied;
14when your heart is lifted up,

and you forget the LORD your
God who brought you out of
the land of Egypt, from the
house of bondage; 15who led
you through that great and
terrible wilderness, *in which
were* fiery serpents and scorpions and thirsty land where
there was no water; who
brought water for you out of
the flinty rock; 16who fed you
in the wilderness with manna,
which your fathers did not
know, that He might hum-
ble you and that He might
test you, to do you good in
the end— 17then you say in
your heart, 'My power and the
might of my hand have gained
me this wealth.'

18"And you shall remember
the LORD your God, for *it is*
He who gives you power to
get wealth, that He may establish His covenant which
He swore to your fathers, as
it is this day. 19Then it shall
be, if you by any means forget
the LORD your God, and follow
other gods, and serve them
and worship them, I testify
against you this day that you
shall surely perish. 20As the
nations which the LORD destroys before you, so you shall
perish, because you would not
be obedient to the voice of the
LORD your God.

ISRAEL'S REBELLIONS REVIEWED

9 "Hear, O Israel: You *are*
to cross over the Jordan
today, and go in to dispossess
nations greater and mightier than yourself, cities great
and fortified up to heaven,
2a people great and tall, the
descendants of the Anakim,
whom you know, and *of whom*
you heard *it said,* 'Who can
stand before the descendants
of Anak?' 3Therefore understand today that the LORD
your God *is* He who goes over
before you *as* a consuming
fire. He will destroy them and
bring them down before you;
so you shall drive them out
and destroy them quickly, as
the LORD has said to you.

4"Do not think in your
heart, after the LORD your
God has cast them out before
you, saying, 'Because of my
righteousness the LORD has
brought me in to possess this
land'; but *it is* because of the
wickedness of these nations
that the LORD is driving them
out from before you. 5*It is* not
because of your righteousness
or the uprightness of your
heart *that* you go in to possess
their land, but because of the
wickedness of these nations
that the LORD your God drives
them out from before you,
and that He may fulfill the
word which the LORD swore
to your fathers, to Abraham,
Isaac, and Jacob. 6Therefore
understand that the LORD
your God is not giving you this
good land to possess because
of your righteousness, for you
are a stiff-necked people.

7"Remember! Do not for-

get how you provoked the
LORD your God to wrath in
the wilderness. From the day
that you departed from the
land of Egypt until you came
to this place, you have been
rebellious against the LORD.
8Also in Horeb you provoked
the LORD to wrath, so that
the LORD was angry *enough*
with you to have destroyed
you. 9When I went up into
the mountain to receive the
tablets of stone, the tablets of
the covenant which the LORD
made with you, then I stayed
on the mountain forty days
and forty nights. I neither ate
bread nor drank water. 10Then
the LORD delivered to me two
tablets of stone written with
the finger of God, and on them
were all the words which the
LORD had spoken to you on
the mountain from the midst
of the fire in the day of the assembly. 11And it came to pass,
at the end of forty days and
forty nights, *that* the LORD
gave me the two tablets of
stone, the tablets of the covenant.

12"Then the LORD said to
me, 'Arise, go down quickly
from here, for your people
whom you brought out of
Egypt have acted corruptly;
they have quickly turned
aside from the way which I
commanded them; they have
made themselves a molded
image.'

13"Furthermore the LORD
spoke to me, saying, 'I have
seen this people, and indeed
they are a stiff-necked people.
14Let Me alone, that I may destroy them and blot out their
name from under heaven; and
I will make of you a nation
mightier and greater than
they.'

15"So I turned and came
down from the mountain,
and the mountain burned
with fire; and the two tablets
of the covenant *were* in my
two hands. 16And I looked,
and behold, you had sinned
against the LORD your God—
had made for yourselves a
molded calf! You had turned
aside quickly from the way
which the LORD had com-
manded you. 17Then I took
the two tablets and threw
them out of my two hands and
broke them before your eyes.
18And I fell down before the
LORD, as at the first, forty days
and forty nights; I neither ate
bread nor drank water, because of all your sin which you
committed in doing wickedly
in the sight of the LORD, to
provoke Him to anger. 19For
I was afraid of the anger and
hot displeasure with which
the LORD was angry with
you, to destroy you. But the
LORD listened to me at that
time also. 20And the LORD was
very angry with Aaron *and*
would have destroyed him;
so I prayed for Aaron also at
the same time. 21Then I took
your sin, the calf which you
had made, and burned it with

fire and crushed it *and* ground
it very small, until it was as
fine as dust; and I threw its
dust into the brook that descended from the mountain.
22“Also at Taberah and
Massah and Kibroth Hattaavah you provoked the LORD
to wrath. 23Likewise, when the
LORD sent you from Kadesh
Barnea, saying, ‘Go up and
possess the land which I have
given you,’ then you rebelled
against the commandment of
the LORD your God, and you
did not believe Him nor obey
His voice. 24You have been
rebellious against the LORD
from the day that I knew you.
25“Thus I prostrated my-
self before the LORD; forty
days and forty nights I kept
prostrating myself, because
the LORD had said He would
destroy you. 26Therefore
I prayed to the LORD, and
said: ‘O Lord GOD, do not destroy Your people and Your
inheritance whom You have
redeemed through Your
greatness, whom You have
brought out of Egypt with a
mighty hand. 27Remember
Your servants, Abraham,
Isaac, and Jacob; do not look
on the stubbornness of this
people, or on their wickedness
or their sin, 28lest the land
from which You brought us
should say, “Because the LORD
was not able to bring them
to the land which He promised them, and because He
hated them, He has brought
them out to kill them in the
wilderness.” 29Yet they *are*
Your people and Your inheritance, whom You brought out
by Your mighty power and by
Your outstretched arm.’

THE SECOND PAIR OF TABLETS

10 “At that time the LORD
said to me, ‘Hew for
yourself two tablets of stone
like the first, and come up to
Me on the mountain and make
yourself an ark of wood. 2And
I will write on the tablets the
words that were on the first
tablets, which you broke; and
you shall put them in the ark.’
3“So I made an ark of acacia
wood, hewed two tablets of
stone like the first, and went
up the mountain, having the
two tablets in my hand. 4And
He wrote on the tablets according to the first writing,
the Ten Commandments,
which the LORD had spoken
to you in the mountain from
the midst of the fire in the
day of the assembly; and the
LORD gave them to me. 5Then
I turned and came down from
the mountain, and put the
tablets in the ark which I had
made; and there they are, just
as the LORD commanded me.”
6(Now the children of Is-
rael journeyed from the wells
of Bene Jaakan to Moserah,
where Aaron died, and where
he was buried; and Eleazar
his son ministered as priest
in his stead. 7From there

they journeyed to Gudgo-
dah, and from Gudgodah to
Jotbathah, a land of rivers of
water. 8At that time the LORD
separated the tribe of Levi to
bear the ark of the covenant of
the LORD, to stand before the
LORD to minister to Him and
to bless in His name, to this
day. 9Therefore Levi has no
portion nor inheritance with
his brethren; the LORD *is* his
inheritance, just as the LORD
your God promised him.)
10"As at the first time, I
stayed in the mountain forty
days and forty nights; the
LORD also heard me at that
time, *and* the LORD chose
not to destroy you. 11Then the
LORD said to me, 'Arise, begin
your journey before the people, that they may go in and
possess the land which I swore
to their fathers to give them.'

THE ESSENCE OF THE LAW

12"And now, Israel, what
does the LORD your God require of you, but to fear the
LORD your God, to walk in all
His ways and to love Him, to
serve the LORD your God with
all your heart and with all your
soul, 13*and* to keep the commandments of the LORD and
His statutes which I command
you today for your good? 14In-
deed heaven and the highest
heavens belong to the LORD
your God, *also* the earth with
all that *is* in it. 15The LORD delighted only in your fathers, to
love them; and He chose their
descendants after them, you
above all peoples, as *it is* this
day. 16Therefore circumcise
the foreskin of your heart, and
be stiff-necked no longer. 17For
the LORD your God *is* God of
gods and Lord of lords, the
great God, mighty and awesome, who shows no partiality
nor takes a bribe. 18He admin-
isters justice for the fatherless
and the widow, and loves the
stranger, giving him food and
clothing. 19Therefore love the
stranger, for you were strangers in the land of Egypt. 20You
shall fear the LORD your God;
you shall serve Him, and to
Him you shall hold fast, and
take oaths in His name. 21He
is your praise, and He *is* your
God, who has done for you
these great and awesome
things which your eyes have
seen. 22Your fathers went
down to Egypt with seventy
persons, and now the LORD
your God has made you as the
stars of heaven in multitude.

LOVE AND OBEDIENCE REWARDED

11 "Therefore you shall love
the LORD your God, and
keep His charge, His statutes,
His judgments, and His commandments always. 2Know
today that *I do* not *speak* with
your children, who have not
known and who have not seen
the chastening of the LORD
your God, His greatness and
His mighty hand and His outstretched arm— 3His signs

and His acts which He did in
the midst of Egypt, to Pharaoh
king of Egypt, and to all his
land; 4what He did to the army
of Egypt, to their horses and
their chariots: how He made
the waters of the Red Sea
overflow them as they pursued you, and *how* the LORD
has destroyed them to this
day; 5what He did for you in
the wilderness until you came
to this place; 6and what He
did to Dathan and Abiram the
sons of Eliab, the son of Reuben: how the earth opened its
mouth and swallowed them
up, their households, their
tents, and all the substance
that *was* in their possession,
in the midst of all Israel—
7but your eyes have seen every
great act of the LORD which
He did.

8"Therefore you shall keep
every commandment which
I command you today, that
you may be strong, and go in
and possess the land which
you cross over to possess,
9and that you may prolong
your days in the land which
the LORD swore to give your
fathers, to them and their
descendants, 'a land flowing
with milk and honey.'[a] 10For
the land which you go to
possess *is* not like the land of
Egypt from which you have
come, where you sowed your
seed and watered *it* by foot, as
a vegetable garden; 11but the
land which you cross over to
possess *is* a land of hills and
valleys, which drinks water
from the rain of heaven,
12a land for which the LORD
your God cares; the eyes of
the LORD your God *are* always
on it, from the beginning of
the year to the very end of the
year.

13'And it shall be that if you
earnestly obey My commandments which I command you
today, to love the LORD your
God and serve Him with all
your heart and with all your
soul, 14then I[a] will give *you* the
rain for your land in its season, the early rain and the latter rain, that you may gather
in your grain, your new wine,
and your oil. 15And I will send
grass in your fields for your
livestock, that you may eat
and be filled.' 16Take heed to
yourselves, lest your heart be
deceived, and you turn aside
and serve other gods and worship them, 17lest the LORD's
anger be aroused against you,
and He shut up the heavens
so that there be no rain, and
the land yield no produce, and
you perish quickly from the
good land which the LORD is
giving you.

18"Therefore you shall lay
up these words of mine in
your heart and in your soul,
and bind them as a sign on

11:9 [a] Exodus 3:8 11:14 [a] Following Masoretic Text and Targum; Samaritan Pentateuch, Septuagint, and Vulgate read *He*.

your hand, and they shall
be as frontlets between your
eyes. [19]You shall teach them
to your children, speaking
of them when you sit in your
house, when you walk by the
way, when you lie down, and
when you rise up. [20]And you
shall write them on the doorposts of your house and on
your gates, [21]that your days
and the days of your children
may be multiplied in the land
of which the LORD swore to
your fathers to give them, like
the days of the heavens above
the earth.

[22]"For if you carefully keep
all these commandments
which I command you to do—
to love the LORD your God, to
walk in all His ways, and to
hold fast to Him— [23]then the
LORD will drive out all these
nations from before you, and
you will dispossess greater
and mightier nations than
yourselves. [24]Every place on
which the sole of your foot
treads shall be yours: from
the wilderness and Lebanon,
from the river, the River Euphrates, even to the Western
Sea,[a] shall be your territory.
[25]No man shall be able to
stand against you; the LORD
your God will put the dread of
you and the fear of you upon
all the land where you tread,
just as He has said to you.

[26]"Behold, I set before you
today a blessing and a curse:
[27]the blessing, if you obey the
commandments of the LORD
your God which I command
you today; [28]and the curse,
if you do not obey the commandments of the LORD your
God, but turn aside from the
way which I command you
today, to go after other gods
which you have not known.
[29]Now it shall be, when the
LORD your God has brought
you into the land which you
go to possess, that you shall
put the blessing on Mount Gerizim and the curse on Mount
Ebal. [30]*Are* they not on the
other side of the Jordan, toward the setting sun, in the
land of the Canaanites who
dwell in the plain opposite
Gilgal, beside the terebinth
trees of Moreh? [31]For you will
cross over the Jordan and go
in to possess the land which
the LORD your God is giving
you, and you will possess it
and dwell in it. [32]And you shall
be careful to observe all the
statutes and judgments which
I set before you today.

A PRESCRIBED PLACE OF WORSHIP

12 "These *are* the statutes
and judgments which
you shall be careful to observe in the land which the
LORD God of your fathers is
giving you to possess, all the
days that you live on the earth.
[2]You shall utterly destroy all

11:24 [a] That is, the Mediterranean

the places where the nations
which you shall dispossess
served their gods, on the high
mountains and on the hills
and under every green tree.
3And you shall destroy their
altars, break their *sacred* pillars, and burn their wooden
images with fire; you shall cut
down the carved images of
their gods and destroy their
names from that place. 4You
shall not worship the LORD
your God *with* such *things*.

5"But you shall seek the
place where the LORD your
God chooses, out of all your
tribes, to put His name for His
dwelling place; and there you
shall go. 6There you shall take
your burnt offerings, your sacrifices, your tithes, the heave
offerings of your hand, your
vowed offerings, your freewill
offerings, and the firstborn of
your herds and flocks. 7And
there you shall eat before the
LORD your God, and you shall
rejoice in all to which you
have put your hand, you and
your households, in which the
LORD your God has blessed
you.

8"You shall not at all do as
we are doing here today—
every man doing whatever *is*
right in his own eyes— 9for as
yet you have not come to the
rest and the inheritance which
the LORD your God is giving
you. 10But *when* you cross
over the Jordan and dwell in
the land which the LORD your
God is giving you to inherit,
and He gives you rest from all
your enemies round about, so
that you dwell in safety, 11then
there will be the place where
the LORD your God chooses
to make His name abide.
There you shall bring all that
I command you: your burnt
offerings, your sacrifices, your
tithes, the heave offerings of
your hand, and all your choice
offerings which you vow to the
LORD. 12And you shall rejoice
before the LORD your God,
you and your sons and your
daughters, your male and female servants, and the Levite
who *is* within your gates, since
he has no portion nor inheritance with you. 13Take heed to
yourself that you do not offer
your burnt offerings in every
place that you see; 14but in the
place which the LORD chooses,
in one of your tribes, there you
shall offer your burnt offerings, and there you shall do
all that I command you.

15"However, you may
slaughter and eat meat within
all your gates, whatever your
heart desires, according to the
blessing of the LORD your God
which He has given you; the
unclean and the clean may
eat of it, of the gazelle and the
deer alike. 16Only you shall not
eat the blood; you shall pour it
on the earth like water. 17You
may not eat within your gates
the tithe of your grain or your
new wine or your oil, of the
firstborn of your herd or your
flock, of any of your offerings

which you vow, of your freewill offerings, or of the heave
offering of your hand. 18But
you must eat them before the
LORD your God in the place
which the LORD your God
chooses, you and your son
and your daughter, your male
servant and your female servant, and the Levite who *is*
within your gates; and you
shall rejoice before the LORD
your God in all to which you
put your hands. 19Take heed
to yourself that you do not
forsake the Levite as long as
you live in your land.

20"When the LORD your
God enlarges your border as
He has promised you, and you
say, 'Let me eat meat,' because
you long to eat meat, you may
eat as much meat as your heart
desires. 21If the place where
the LORD your God chooses to
put His name is too far from
you, then you may slaugh-
ter from your herd and from
your flock which the LORD has
given you, just as I have commanded you, and you may eat
within your gates as much as
your heart desires. 22Just as
the gazelle and the deer are
eaten, so you may eat them;
the unclean and the clean
alike may eat them. 23Only
be sure that you do not eat
the blood, for the blood *is* the
life; you may not eat the life
with the meat. 24You shall not
eat it; you shall pour it on the
earth like water. 25You shall
not eat it, that it may go well
with you and your children
after you, when you do *what is*
right in the sight of the LORD.
26Only the holy things which
you have, and your vowed offerings, you shall take and go
to the place which the LORD
chooses. 27And you shall offer
your burnt offerings, the meat
and the blood, on the altar
of the LORD your God; and
the blood of your sacrifices
shall be poured out on the
altar of the LORD your God,
and you shall eat the meat.
28Observe and obey all these
words which I command you,
that it may go well with you
and your children after you
forever, when you do *what is*
good and right in the sight of
the LORD your God.

BEWARE OF FALSE GODS

29"When the LORD your
God cuts off from before you
the nations which you go to
dispossess, and you displace
them and dwell in their land,
30take heed to yourself that
you are not ensnared to follow
them, after they are destroyed
from before you, and that you
do not inquire after their gods,
saying, 'How did these nations
serve their gods? I also will
do likewise.' 31You shall not
worship the LORD your God
in that way; for every abomination to the LORD which He
hates they have done to their
gods; for they burn even their
sons and daughters in the fire
to their gods.

32“Whatever I command
you, be careful to observe it;
you shall not add to it nor take
away from it.

PUNISHMENT OF APOSTATES

13 “If there arises among
you a prophet or a
dreamer of dreams, and he
gives you a sign or a wonder,
2and the sign or the wonder
comes to pass, of which he
spoke to you, saying, ‘Let us
go after other gods’—which
you have not known—‘and
let us serve them,’ 3you shall
not listen to the words of that
prophet or that dreamer of
dreams, for the LORD your God
is testing you to know whether
you love the LORD your God
with all your heart and with all
your soul. 4You shall walk after
the LORD your God and fear
Him, and keep His commandments and obey His voice; you
shall serve Him and hold fast
to Him. 5But that prophet or
that dreamer of dreams shall
be put to death, because he
has spoken in order to turn
you away from the LORD your
God, who brought you out
of the land of Egypt and redeemed you from the house
of bondage, to entice you from
the way in which the LORD
your God commanded you to
walk. So you shall put away the
evil from your midst.

6“If your brother, the son
of your mother, your son or
your daughter, the wife of your
bosom, or your friend who is
as your own soul, secretly entices you, saying, ‘Let us go and
serve other gods,’ which you
have not known, neither you
nor your fathers, 7of the gods
of the people which *are* all
around you, near to you or far
off from you, from *one* end of
the earth to the *other* end of the
earth, 8you shall not consent to
him or listen to him, nor shall
your eye pity him, nor shall
you spare him or conceal him;
9but you shall surely kill him;
your hand shall be first against
him to put him to death, and
afterward the hand of all the
people. 10And you shall stone
him with stones until he dies,
because he sought to entice
you away from the LORD your
God, who brought you out of
the land of Egypt, from the
house of bondage. 11So all Israel shall hear and fear, and
not again do such wickedness
as this among you.

12“If you hear someone in
one of your cities, which the
LORD your God gives you to
dwell in, saying, 13‘Corrupt men
have gone out from among you
and enticed the inhabitants of
their city, saying, “Let us go and
serve other gods”’—which you
have not known— 14then you
shall inquire, search out, and
ask diligently. And *if it is* indeed
true *and* certain *that* such an
abomination was committed
among you, 15you shall surely
strike the inhabitants of that
city with the edge of the sword,

utterly destroying it, all that is in it and its livestock—with the edge of the sword. 16And you shall gather all its plunder into the middle of the street, and completely burn with fire the city and all its plunder, for the LORD your God. It shall be a heap forever; it shall not be built again. 17So none of the accursed things shall remain in your hand, that the LORD may turn from the fierceness of His anger and show you mercy, have compassion on you and multiply you, just as He swore to your fathers, 18because you have listened to the voice of the LORD your God, to keep all His commandments which I command you today, to do *what is* right in the eyes of the LORD your God.

IMPROPER MOURNING

14 "You *are* the children of the LORD your God; you shall not cut yourselves nor shave the front of your head for the dead. 2For you *are* a holy people to the LORD your God, and the LORD has chosen you to be a people for Himself, a special treasure above all the peoples who *are* on the face of the earth.

CLEAN AND UNCLEAN MEAT

3"You shall not eat any detestable thing. 4These *are* the animals which you may eat: the ox, the sheep, the goat, 5the deer, the gazelle, the roe deer, the wild goat, the mountain goat,[a] the antelope, and the mountain sheep. 6And you may eat every animal with cloven hooves, having the hoof split into two parts, *and that* chews the cud, among the animals. 7Nevertheless, of those that chew the cud or have cloven hooves, you shall not eat, *such as* these: the camel, the hare, and the rock hyrax; for they chew the cud but do not have cloven hooves; they *are* unclean for you. 8Also the swine is unclean for you, because it has cloven hooves, yet *does* not *chew* the cud; you shall not eat their flesh or touch their dead carcasses.

9"These you may eat of all that *are* in the waters: you may eat all that have fins and scales. 10And whatever does not have fins and scales you shall not eat; it *is* unclean for you.

11"All clean birds you may eat. 12But these you shall not eat: the eagle, the vulture, the buzzard, 13the red kite, the falcon, and the kite after their kinds; 14every raven after its kind; 15the ostrich, the short-eared owl, the sea gull, and the hawk after their kinds; 16the little owl, the screech owl, the white owl, 17the jackdaw, the carrion vulture, the

14:5 [a] Or *addax*

fisher owl, 18the stork, the heron after its kind, and the hoopoe and the bat.

19"Also every creeping thing that flies is unclean for you; they shall not be eaten.

20"You may eat all clean birds.

21"You shall not eat anything that dies *of itself;* you may give it to the alien who *is* within your gates, that he may eat it, or you may sell it to a foreigner; for you *are* a holy people to the LORD your God.

"You shall not boil a young goat in its mother's milk.

TITHING PRINCIPLES

22"You shall truly tithe all the increase of your grain that the field produces year by year. 23And you shall eat before the LORD your God, in the place where He chooses to make His name abide, the tithe of your grain and your new wine and your oil, of the firstborn of your herds and your flocks, that you may learn to fear the LORD your God always. 24But if the journey is too long for you, so that you are not able to carry *the tithe, or* if the place where the LORD your God chooses to put His name is too far from you, when the LORD your God has blessed you, 25then you shall exchange *it* for money, take the money in your hand, and go to the place which the LORD your God chooses. 26And you shall spend that money for whatever your heart desires: for oxen or sheep, for wine or similar drink, for whatever your heart desires; you shall eat there before the LORD your God, and you shall rejoice, you and your household. 27You shall not forsake the Levite who *is* within your gates, for he has no part nor inheritance with you.

28"At the end of *every* third year you shall bring out the tithe of your produce of that year and store *it* up within your gates. 29And the Levite, because he has no portion nor inheritance with you, and the stranger and the fatherless and the widow who *are* within your gates, may come and eat and be satisfied, that the LORD your God may bless you in all the work of your hand which you do.

DEBTS CANCELED EVERY SEVEN YEARS

15 "At the end of *every* seven years you shall grant a release *of debts.* 2And this *is* the form of the release: Every creditor who has lent *anything* to his neighbor shall release *it;* he shall not require *it* of his neighbor or his brother, because it is called the LORD's release. 3Of a foreigner you may require *it;* but you shall give up your claim to what is owed by your brother, 4except when there may be no poor among you; for the LORD will greatly bless you in the land

which the LORD your God is
giving you to possess *as* an
inheritance— 5only if you
carefully obey the voice of
the LORD your God, to observe
with care all these commandments which I command you
today. 6For the LORD your
God will bless you just as He
promised you; you shall lend
to many nations, but you shall
not borrow; you shall reign
over many nations, but they
shall not reign over you.

GENEROSITY TO THE POOR

7"If there is among you a
poor man of your brethren,
within any of the gates in
your land which the LORD
your God is giving you, you
shall not harden your heart
nor shut your hand from your
poor brother, 8but you shall
open your hand wide to him
and willingly lend him sufficient for his need, whatever
he needs. 9Beware lest there
be a wicked thought in your
heart, saying, 'The seventh
year, the year of release, is at
hand,' and your eye be evil
against your poor brother and
you give him nothing, and he
cry out to the LORD against
you, and it become sin among
you. 10You shall surely give to
him, and your heart should
not be grieved when you give
to him, because for this thing
the LORD your God will bless
you in all your works and
in all to which you put your
hand. 11For the poor will never
cease from the land; therefore
I command you, saying, 'You
shall open your hand wide to
your brother, to your poor and
your needy, in your land.'

THE LAW CONCERNING BONDSERVANTS

12"If your brother, a Hebrew
man, or a Hebrew woman, is
sold to you and serves you six
years, then in the seventh year
you shall let him go free from
you. 13And when you send him
away free from you, you shall
not let him go away empty-
handed; 14you shall supply him
liberally from your flock, from
your threshing floor, and from
your winepress. *From what* the
LORD your God has blessed
you with, you shall give to him.
15You shall remember that
you were a slave in the land
of Egypt, and the LORD your
God redeemed you; therefore I
command you this thing today.
16And if it happens that he says
to you, 'I will not go away from
you,' because he loves you and
your house, since he prospers
with you, 17then you shall take
an awl and thrust *it* through
his ear to the door, and he shall
be your servant forever. Also to
your female servant you shall
do likewise. 18It shall not seem
hard to you when you send
him away free from you; for
he has been worth a double
hired servant in serving you
six years. Then the LORD your
God will bless you in all that
you do.

THE LAW CONCERNING FIRSTBORN ANIMALS

19“All the firstborn males
that come from your herd and
your flock you shall sanctify to
the LORD your God; you shall
do no work with the firstborn
of your herd, nor shear the
firstborn of your flock. 20You
and your household shall
eat *it* before the LORD your
God year by year in the place
which the LORD chooses. 21But
if there is a defect in it, *if it*
is lame or blind *or has* any
serious defect, you shall not
sacrifice it to the LORD your
God. 22You may eat it within
your gates; the unclean and
the clean *person* alike *may eat*
it, as *if it were* a gazelle or a
deer. 23Only you shall not eat
its blood; you shall pour it on
the ground like water.

THE PASSOVER REVIEWED

16 “Observe the month of
Abib, and keep the Pass-
over to the LORD your God, for
in the month of Abib the LORD
your God brought you out of
Egypt by night. 2Therefore
you shall sacrifice the Passover to the LORD your God,
from the flock and the herd,
in the place where the LORD
chooses to put His name. 3You
shall eat no leavened bread
with it; seven days you shall
eat unleavened bread with
it, *that is,* the bread of affliction (for you came out of the
land of Egypt in haste), that
you may remember the day
in which you came out of the
land of Egypt all the days of
your life. 4And no leaven shall
be seen among you in all your
territory for seven days, nor
shall *any* of the meat which
you sacrifice the first day at
twilight remain overnight
until morning.

5“You may not sacrifice the
Passover within any of your
gates which the LORD your
God gives you; 6but at the
place where the LORD your
God chooses to make His
name abide, there you shall
sacrifice the Passover at twilight, at the going down of the
sun, at the time you came out
of Egypt. 7And you shall roast
and eat *it* in the place which
the LORD your God chooses,
and in the morning you shall
turn and go to your tents. 8Six
days you shall eat unleavened
bread, and on the seventh day
there *shall be* a sacred assembly to the LORD your God. You
shall do no work *on it.*

THE FEAST OF WEEKS REVIEWED

9“You shall count seven
weeks for yourself; begin to
count the seven weeks from
the time you begin *to put* the
sickle to the grain. 10Then you
shall keep the Feast of Weeks
to the LORD your God with the
tribute of a freewill offering
from your hand, which you
shall give as the LORD your
God blesses you. 11You shall
rejoice before the LORD your

God, you and your son and
your daughter, your male servant and your female servant,
the Levite who *is* within your
gates, the stranger and the fatherless and the widow who
are among you, at the place
where the LORD your God
chooses to make His name
abide. 12And you shall remember that you were a slave in
Egypt, and you shall be careful
to observe these statutes.

THE FEAST OF TABERNACLES REVIEWED

13"You shall observe the
Feast of Tabernacles seven
days, when you have gathered
from your threshing floor and
from your winepress. 14And
you shall rejoice in your feast,
you and your son and your
daughter, your male servant
and your female servant and
the Levite, the stranger and
the fatherless and the widow,
who *are* within your gates.
15Seven days you shall keep
a sacred feast to the LORD
your God in the place which
the LORD chooses, because
the LORD your God will bless
you in all your produce and in
all the work of your hands, so
that you surely rejoice.

16"Three times a year all
your males shall appear before the LORD your God in the
place which He chooses: at the
Feast of Unleavened Bread, at
the Feast of Weeks, and at the
Feast of Tabernacles; and they
shall not appear before the
LORD empty-handed. 17Every
man *shall give* as he is able,
according to the blessing of
the LORD your God which He
has given you.

JUSTICE MUST BE ADMINISTERED

18"You shall appoint judges
and officers in all your gates,
which the LORD your God
gives you, according to your
tribes, and they shall judge
the people with just judgment.
19You shall not pervert justice;
you shall not show partiality,
nor take a bribe, for a bribe
blinds the eyes of the wise
and twists the words of the
righteous. 20You shall follow
what is altogether just, that
you may live and inherit the
land which the LORD your God
is giving you.

21"You shall not plant for
yourself any tree, as a wooden
image, near the altar which
you build for yourself to the
LORD your God. 22You shall
not set up a *sacred* pillar,
which the LORD your God
hates.

17 "You shall not sacrifice
to the LORD your God a
bull or sheep which has any
blemish *or* defect, for that *is*
an abomination to the LORD
your God.

2"If there is found among
you, within any of your gates
which the LORD your God
gives you, a man or a woman
who has been wicked in the

sight of the LORD your God, in transgressing His covenant, 3who has gone and served other gods and worshiped them, either the sun or moon or any of the host of heaven, which I have not commanded, 4and it is told you, and you hear *of it,* then you shall inquire diligently. And if *it is* indeed true *and* certain that such an abomination has been committed in Israel, 5then you shall bring out to your gates that man or woman who has committed that wicked thing, and shall stone to death that man or woman with stones. 6Whoever is deserving of death shall be put to death on the testimony of two or three witnesses; he shall not be put to death on the testimony of one witness. 7The hands of the witnesses shall be the first against him to put him to death, and afterward the hands of all the people. So you shall put away the evil from among you.

8"If a matter arises which is too hard for you to judge, between degrees of guilt for bloodshed, between one judgment or another, or between one punishment or another, matters of controversy within your gates, then you shall arise and go up to the place which the LORD your God chooses. 9And you shall come to the priests, the Levites, and to the judge *there* in those days, and inquire *of them;* they shall pronounce upon you the sentence of judgment. 10You shall do according to the sentence which they pronounce upon you in that place which the LORD chooses. And you shall be careful to do according to all that they order you. 11According to the sentence of the law in which they instruct you, according to the judgment which they tell you, you shall do; you shall not turn aside *to* the right hand or *to* the left from the sentence which they pronounce upon you. 12Now the man who acts presumptuously and will not heed the priest who stands to minister there before the LORD your God, or the judge, that man shall die. So you shall put away the evil from Israel. 13And all the people shall hear and fear, and no longer act presumptuously.

PRINCIPLES GOVERNING KINGS

14"When you come to the land which the LORD your God is giving you, and possess it and dwell in it, and say, 'I will set a king over me like all the nations that *are* around me,' 15you shall surely set a king over you whom the LORD your God chooses; *one* from among your brethren you shall set as king over you; you may not set a foreigner over you, who *is* not your brother. 16But he shall not multiply horses for himself, nor cause the people

to return to Egypt to multiply
horses, for the LORD has said
to you, 'You shall not return
that way again.' 17Neither shall
he multiply wives for himself,
lest his heart turn away; nor
shall he greatly multiply silver
and gold for himself.

18"Also it shall be, when he
sits on the throne of his kingdom, that he shall write for
himself a copy of this law in a
book, from *the one* before the
priests, the Levites. 19And it
shall be with him, and he shall
read it all the days of his life,
that he may learn to fear the
LORD his God and be careful
to observe all the words of this
law and these statutes, 20that
his heart may not be lifted
above his brethren, that he
may not turn aside from the
commandment *to* the right
hand or *to* the left, and that
he may prolong *his* days in his
kingdom, he and his children
in the midst of Israel.

THE PORTION OF THE PRIESTS AND LEVITES

18 "The priests, the Le-
vites—all the tribe of
Levi—shall have no part nor
inheritance with Israel; they
shall eat the offerings of the
LORD made by fire, and His
portion. 2Therefore they shall
have no inheritance among
their brethren; the LORD is
their inheritance, as He said
to them.

3"And this shall be the
priest's due from the people, from those who offer a
sacrifice, whether *it is* bull
or sheep: they shall give to
the priest the shoulder, the
cheeks, and the stomach.
4The firstfruits of your grain
and your new wine and your
oil, and the first of the fleece
of your sheep, you shall give
him. 5For the LORD your God
has chosen him out of all your
tribes to stand to minister in
the name of the LORD, him
and his sons forever.

6"So if a Levite comes from
any of your gates, from where
he dwells among all Israel,
and comes with all the desire
of his mind to the place which
the LORD chooses, 7then he
may serve in the name of the
LORD his God as all his brethren the Levites *do*, who stand
there before the LORD. 8They
shall have equal portions to
eat, besides what comes from
the sale of his inheritance.

AVOID WICKED CUSTOMS

9"When you come into the
land which the LORD your God
is giving you, you shall not
learn to follow the abominations of those nations. 10There
shall not be found among you
anyone who makes his son
or his daughter pass through
the fire, *or one* who practices
witchcraft, *or* a soothsayer, or
one who interprets omens, or
a sorcerer, 11or one who con-
jures spells, or a medium, or
a spiritist, or one who calls

up the dead. 12For all who do
these things *are* an abomination to the LORD, and because
of these abominations the
LORD your God drives them
out from before you. 13You
shall be blameless before the
LORD your God. 14For these
nations which you will dispossess listened to soothsayers
and diviners; but as for you,
the LORD your God has not
appointed such for you.

A NEW PROPHET LIKE MOSES

15"The LORD your God will
raise up for you a Prophet like
me from your midst, from
your brethren. Him you shall
hear, 16according to all you desired of the LORD your God in
Horeb in the day of the assembly, saying, 'Let me not hear
again the voice of the LORD
my God, nor let me see this
great fire anymore, lest I die.'

17"And the LORD said to
me: 'What they have spo-
ken is good. 18I will raise up
for them a Prophet like you
from among their brethren,
and will put My words in His
mouth, and He shall speak
to them all that I command
Him. 19And it shall be *that*
whoever will not hear My
words, which He speaks in
My name, I will require *it* of
him. 20But the prophet who
presumes to speak a word in
My name, which I have not
commanded him to speak, or
who speaks in the name of
other gods, that prophet shall
die.' 21And if you say in your
heart, 'How shall we know the
word which the LORD has not
spoken?'— 22when a prophet
speaks in the name of the
LORD, if the thing does not
happen or come to pass, that
is the thing which the LORD
has not spoken; the prophet
has spoken it presumptu-
ously; you shall not be afraid
of him.

THREE CITIES OF REFUGE

19 "When the LORD your
God has cut off the na-
tions whose land the LORD
your God is giving you, and
you dispossess them and
dwell in their cities and in
their houses, 2you shall separate three cities for yourself in
the midst of your land which
the LORD your God is giving
you to possess. 3You shall prepare roads for yourself, and
divide into three parts the territory of your land which the
LORD your God is giving you
to inherit, that any manslayer
may flee there.

4"And this *is* the case of the
manslayer who flees there,
that he may live: Whoever kills
his neighbor unintentionally,
not having hated him in time
past— 5as when *a man* goes to
the woods with his neighbor
to cut timber, and his hand
swings a stroke with the ax
to cut down the tree, and the
head slips from the handle
and strikes his neighbor so

that he dies—he shall flee to
one of these cities and live;
6lest the avenger of blood,
while his anger is hot, pursue
the manslayer and overtake
him, because the way is long,
and kill him, though he *was*
not deserving of death, since
he had not hated the victim
in time past. 7Therefore I
command you, saying, 'You
shall separate three cities for
yourself.'

8"Now if the LORD your
God enlarges your territory,
as He swore to your fathers,
and gives you the land which
He promised to give to your
fathers, 9and if you keep all
these commandments and
do them, which I command
you today, to love the LORD
your God and to walk always
in His ways, then you shall add
three more cities for yourself
besides these three, 10lest innocent blood be shed in the
midst of your land which the
LORD your God is giving you
as an inheritance, and *thus*
guilt of bloodshed be upon
you.

11"But if anyone hates his
neighbor, lies in wait for him,
rises against him and strikes
him mortally, so that he dies,
and he flees to one of these
cities, 12then the elders of
his city shall send and bring
him from there, and deliver
him over to the hand of the
avenger of blood, that he may
die. 13Your eye shall not pity
him, but you shall put away
the guilt of innocent blood
from Israel, that it may go
well with you.

PROPERTY BOUNDARIES

14"You shall not remove
your neighbor's landmark,
which the men of old have set,
in your inheritance which you
will inherit in the land that the
LORD your God is giving you
to possess.

THE LAW CONCERNING WITNESSES

15"One witness shall not
rise against a man concerning
any iniquity or any sin that he
commits; by the mouth of two
or three witnesses the matter shall be established. 16If a
false witness rises against any
man to testify against him of
wrongdoing, 17then both men
in the controversy shall stand
before the LORD, before the
priests and the judges who
serve in those days. 18And
the judges shall make careful inquiry, and indeed, *if* the
witness *is* a false witness, who
has testified falsely against
his brother, 19then you shall
do to him as he thought to
have done to his brother; so
you shall put away the evil
from among you. 20And those
who remain shall hear and
fear, and hereafter they shall
not again commit such evil
among you. 21Your eye shall
not pity: life *shall be* for life,
eye for eye, tooth for tooth,
hand for hand, foot for foot.

PRINCIPLES GOVERNING WARFARE

20 "When you go out to
battle against your
enemies, and see horses and
chariots *and* people more
numerous than you, do not
be afraid of them; for the
LORD your God *is* with you,
who brought you up from the
land of Egypt. 2So it shall be,
when you are on the verge
of battle, that the priest shall
approach and speak to the
people. 3And he shall say to
them, 'Hear, O Israel: Today
you are on the verge of battle
with your enemies. Do not
let your heart faint, do not be
afraid, and do not tremble or
be terrified because of them;
4for the LORD your God *is* He
who goes with you, to fight for
you against your enemies, to
save you.'

5"Then the officers shall
speak to the people, saying:
'What man *is there* who has
built a new house and has not
dedicated it? Let him go and
return to his house, lest he
die in the battle and another
man dedicate it. 6Also what
man *is there* who has planted
a vineyard and has not eaten
of it? Let him go and return
to his house, lest he die in the
battle and another man eat of
it. 7And what man *is there* who
is betrothed to a woman and
has not married her? Let him
go and return to his house,
lest he die in the battle and
another man marry her.'

8"The officers shall speak
further to the people, and say,
'What man *is there who is* fearful and fainthearted? Let him
go and return to his house,
lest the heart of his brethren
faint[a] like his heart.' 9And so
it shall be, when the officers
have finished speaking to the
people, that they shall make
captains of the armies to lead
the people.

10"When you go near a city
to fight against it, then proclaim an offer of peace to it.
11And it shall be that if they
accept your offer of peace, and
open to you, then all the people *who are* found in it shall be
placed under tribute to you,
and serve you. 12Now if *the city*
will not make peace with you,
but war against you, then you
shall besiege it. 13And when
the LORD your God delivers
it into your hands, you shall
strike every male in it with
the edge of the sword. 14But
the women, the little ones,
the livestock, and all that is in
the city, all its spoil, you shall
plunder for yourself; and you
shall eat the enemies' plunder which the LORD your God
gives you. 15Thus you shall do
to all the cities *which are* very

20:8 [a] Following Masoretic Text and Targum; Samaritan Pentateuch, Septuagint, Syriac, and Vulgate read *lest he make his brother's heart faint.*

far from you, which *are* not
of the cities of these nations.
16"But of the cities of these
peoples which the LORD your
God gives you *as* an inheritance, you shall let nothing
that breathes remain alive,
17but you shall utterly destroy them: the Hittite and
the Amorite and the Canaanite and the Perizzite and the
Hivite and the Jebusite, just
as the LORD your God has
commanded you, 18lest they
teach you to do according to
all their abominations which
they have done for their gods,
and you sin against the LORD
your God.
19"When you besiege a city
for a long time, while making
war against it to take it, you
shall not destroy its trees by
wielding an ax against them;
if you can eat of them, do not
cut them down to use in the
siege, for the tree of the field
is man's *food.* 20Only the trees
which you know *are* not trees
for food you may destroy and
cut down, to build siegeworks
against the city that makes
war with you, until it is subdued.

THE LAW CONCERNING UNSOLVED MURDER

21 "If *anyone* is found slain,
lying in the field in the
land which the LORD your
God is giving you to possess,
and it is not known who killed
him, 2then your elders and
your judges shall go out and
measure *the distance* from the
slain man to the surrounding
cities. 3And it shall be *that* the
elders of the city nearest to
the slain man will take a heifer
which has not been worked
and which has not pulled with
a yoke. 4The elders of that city
shall bring the heifer down to
a valley with flowing water,
which is neither plowed nor
sown, and they shall break the
heifer's neck there in the valley. 5Then the priests, the sons
of Levi, shall come near, for
the LORD your God has chosen them to minister to Him
and to bless in the name of
the LORD; by their word every
controversy and every assault
shall be *settled.* 6And all the
elders of that city nearest to
the slain *man* shall wash their
hands over the heifer whose
neck was broken in the valley.
7Then they shall answer and
say, 'Our hands have not shed
this blood, nor have our eyes
seen *it.* 8Provide atonement,
O LORD, for Your people Israel,
whom You have redeemed,
and do not lay innocent blood
to the charge of Your people
Israel.' And atonement shall
be provided on their behalf
for the blood. 9So you shall
put away the *guilt of* innocent
blood from among you when
you do *what is* right in the
sight of the LORD.

FEMALE CAPTIVES

10"When you go out to war
against your enemies, and the

LORD your God delivers them
into your hand, and you take
them captive, 11and you see
among the captives a beautiful woman, and desire her
and would take her for your
wife, 12then you shall bring
her home to your house, and
she shall shave her head and
trim her nails. 13She shall put
off the clothes of her captivity, remain in your house, and
mourn her father and her
mother a full month; after
that you may go in to her and
be her husband, and she shall
be your wife. 14And it shall be,
if you have no delight in her,
then you shall set her free, but
you certainly shall not sell her
for money; you shall not treat
her brutally, because you have
humbled her.

FIRSTBORN INHERITANCE RIGHTS

15"If a man has two wives,
one loved and the other unloved, and they have borne
him children, *both* the loved
and the unloved, and *if* the
firstborn son is of her who
is unloved, 16then it shall be,
on the day he bequeaths his
possessions to his sons, *that*
he must not bestow firstborn
status on the son of the loved
wife in preference to the son
of the unloved, the *true* firstborn. 17But he shall acknowledge the son of the unloved
wife *as* the firstborn by giving
him a double portion of all
that he has, for he *is* the beginning of his strength; the
right of the firstborn *is* his.

THE REBELLIOUS SON

18"If a man has a stubborn
and rebellious son who will
not obey the voice of his father or the voice of his mother,
and *who,* when they have
chastened him, will not heed
them, 19then his father and
his mother shall take hold of
him and bring him out to the
elders of his city, to the gate of
his city. 20And they shall say
to the elders of his city, 'This
son of ours is stubborn and
rebellious; he will not obey
our voice; he is a glutton and a
drunkard.' 21Then all the men
of his city shall stone him to
death with stones; so you shall
put away the evil from among
you, and all Israel shall hear
and fear.

MISCELLANEOUS LAWS

22"If a man has committed a
sin deserving of death, and he
is put to death, and you hang
him on a tree, 23his body shall
not remain overnight on the
tree, but you shall surely bury
him that day, so that you do
not defile the land which the
LORD your God is giving you
as an inheritance; for he who
is hanged *is* accursed of God.

22 "You shall not see your
brother's ox or his
sheep going astray, and hide
yourself from them; you shall
certainly bring them back to
your brother. 2And if your

brother *is* not near you, or if you do not know him, then you shall bring it to your own house, and it shall remain with you until your brother seeks it; then you shall restore it to him. 3You shall do the same with his donkey, and so shall you do with his garment; with any lost thing of your brother's, which he has lost and you have found, you shall do likewise; you must not hide yourself.

4"You shall not see your brother's donkey or his ox fall down along the road, and hide yourself from them; you shall surely help him lift *them* up again.

5"A woman shall not wear anything that pertains to a man, nor shall a man put on a woman's garment, for all who do so *are* an abomination to the LORD your God.

6"If a bird's nest happens to be before you along the way, in any tree or on the ground, with young ones or eggs, with the mother sitting on the young or on the eggs, you shall not take the mother with the young; 7you shall surely let the mother go, and take the young for yourself, that it may be well with you and *that* you may prolong *your* days.

8"When you build a new house, then you shall make a parapet for your roof, that you may not bring guilt of bloodshed on your household if anyone falls from it.

9"You shall not sow your vineyard with different kinds of seed, lest the yield of the seed which you have sown and the fruit of your vineyard be defiled.

10"You shall not plow with an ox and a donkey together.

11"You shall not wear a garment of different sorts, *such as* wool and linen mixed together.

12"You shall make tassels on the four corners of the clothing with which you cover *yourself*.

LAWS OF SEXUAL MORALITY

13"If any man takes a wife, and goes in to her, and detests her, 14and charges her with shameful conduct, and brings a bad name on her, and says, 'I took this woman, and when I came to her I found she *was* not a virgin,' 15then the father and mother of the young woman shall take and bring out *the evidence of* the young woman's virginity to the elders of the city at the gate. 16And the young woman's father shall say to the elders, 'I gave my daughter to this man as wife, and he detests her. 17Now he has charged her with shameful conduct, saying, "I found your daughter *was* not a virgin," and yet these *are the evidences of* my daughter's virginity.' And they shall spread the cloth before the elders of the city. 18Then

the elders of that city shall take that man and punish him; 19and they shall fine him one hundred *shekels* of silver and give *them* to the father of the young woman, because he has brought a bad name on a virgin of Israel. And she shall be his wife; he cannot divorce her all his days.

20"But if the thing is true, *and evidences of* virginity are not found for the young woman, 21then they shall bring out the young woman to the door of her father's house, and the men of her city shall stone her to death with stones, because she has done a disgraceful thing in Israel, to play the harlot in her father's house. So you shall put away the evil from among you.

22"If a man is found lying with a woman married to a husband, then both of them shall die—the man that lay with the woman, and the woman; so you shall put away the evil from Israel.

23"If a young woman *who is* a virgin is betrothed to a husband, and a man finds her in the city and lies with her, 24then you shall bring them both out to the gate of that city, and you shall stone them to death with stones, the young woman because she did not cry out in the city, and the man because he humbled his neighbor's wife; so you shall put away the evil from among you.

25"But if a man finds a betrothed young woman in the countryside, and the man forces her and lies with her, then only the man who lay with her shall die. 26But you shall do nothing to the young woman; *there is* in the young woman no sin *deserving* of death, for just as when a man rises against his neighbor and kills him, even so *is* this matter. 27For he found her in the countryside, *and* the betrothed young woman cried out, but *there was* no one to save her.

28"If a man finds a young woman *who is* a virgin, who is not betrothed, and he seizes her and lies with her, and they are found out, 29then the man who lay with her shall give to the young woman's father fifty *shekels* of silver, and she shall be his wife because he has humbled her; he shall not be permitted to divorce her all his days.

30"A man shall not take his father's wife, nor uncover his father's bed.

THOSE EXCLUDED FROM THE CONGREGATION

23 "He who is emasculated by crushing or mutilation shall not enter the assembly of the LORD.

2"One of illegitimate birth shall not enter the assembly of the LORD; even to the tenth generation none of his *descendants* shall enter the assembly of the LORD.

3"An Ammonite or Moabite shall not enter the assembly of the LORD; even to the tenth generation none of his *descendants* shall enter the assembly of the LORD forever, 4because they did not meet you with bread and water on the road when you came out of Egypt, and because they hired against you Balaam the son of Beor from Pethor of Mesopotamia,[a] to curse you. 5Nevertheless the LORD your God would not listen to Balaam, but the LORD your God turned the curse into a blessing for you, because the LORD your God loves you. 6You shall not seek their peace nor their prosperity all your days forever.

7"You shall not abhor an Edomite, for he *is* your brother. You shall not abhor an Egyptian, because you were an alien in his land. 8The children of the third generation born to them may enter the assembly of the LORD.

CLEANLINESS OF THE CAMPSITE

9"When the army goes out against your enemies, then keep yourself from every wicked thing. 10If there is any man among you who becomes unclean by some occurrence in the night, then he shall go outside the camp; he shall not come inside the camp. 11But it shall be, when evening comes, that he shall wash with water; and when the sun sets, he may come into the camp.

12"Also you shall have a place outside the camp, where you may go out; 13and you shall have an implement among your equipment, and when you sit down outside, you shall dig with it and turn and cover your refuse. 14For the LORD your God walks in the midst of your camp, to deliver you and give your enemies over to you; therefore your camp shall be holy, that He may see no unclean thing among you, and turn away from you.

MISCELLANEOUS LAWS

15"You shall not give back to his master the slave who has escaped from his master to you. 16He may dwell with you in your midst, in the place which he chooses within one of your gates, where it seems best to him; you shall not oppress him.

17"There shall be no *ritual* harlot[a] of the daughters of Israel, or a perverted[b] one of the sons of Israel. 18You shall not bring the wages of a harlot or the price of a dog to the house of the LORD your God for any

23:4 [a] Hebrew *Aram Naharaim* 23:17 [a] Hebrew *qedeshah,* feminine of *qadesh* (see next note) [b] Hebrew *qadesh,* that is, one practicing sodomy and prostitution in religious rituals

vowed offering, for both of
these *are* an abomination to
the LORD your God.
19“You shall not charge interest to your brother—interest
on money *or* food *or* anything
that is lent out at interest. 20To
a foreigner you may charge interest, but to your brother you
shall not charge interest, that
the LORD your God may bless
you in all to which you set your
hand in the land which you are
entering to possess.
21“When you make a vow
to the LORD your God, you
shall not delay to pay it; for
the LORD your God will surely
require it of you, and it would
be sin to you. 22But if you abstain from vowing, it shall not
be sin to you. 23That which
has gone from your lips you
shall keep and perform, for
you voluntarily vowed to the
LORD your God what you have
promised with your mouth.
24“When you come into
your neighbor's vineyard, you
may eat your fill of grapes at
your pleasure, but you shall
not put *any* in your container.
25When you come into your
neighbor's standing grain, you
may pluck the heads with your
hand, but you shall not use
a sickle on your neighbor's
standing grain.

LAW CONCERNING DIVORCE

24 “When a man takes a
wife and marries her,
and it happens that she finds
no favor in his eyes because
he has found some uncleanness in her, and he writes her
a certificate of divorce, puts
it in her hand, and sends her
out of his house, 2when she
has departed from his house,
and goes and becomes an-
other man's *wife,* 3*if* the latter husband detests her and
writes her a certificate of divorce, puts *it* in her hand, and
sends her out of his house,
or if the latter husband dies
who took her as his wife, 4*then*
her former husband who divorced her must not take her
back to be his wife after she
has been defiled; for that *is* an
abomination before the LORD,
and you shall not bring sin
on the land which the LORD
your God is giving you *as* an
inheritance.

MISCELLANEOUS LAWS

5“When a man has taken
a new wife, he shall not go
out to war or be charged with
any business; he shall be free
at home one year, and bring
happiness to his wife whom
he has taken.
6“No man shall take the
lower or the upper millstone
in pledge, for he takes *one's*
living in pledge.
7“If a man is found kid-
napping any of his brethren
of the children of Israel, and
mistreats him or sells him,
then that kidnapper shall die;
and you shall put away the evil
from among you.

8"Take heed in an outbreak
of leprosy, that you carefully
observe and do according to
all that the priests, the Levites,
shall teach you; just as I commanded them, *so* you shall
be careful to do. 9Remember
what the LORD your God did
to Miriam on the way when
you came out of Egypt!

10"When you lend your
brother anything, you shall
not go into his house to get
his pledge. 11You shall stand
outside, and the man to
whom you lend shall bring
the pledge out to you. 12And
if the man *is* poor, you shall
not keep his pledge overnight.
13You shall in any case return
the pledge to him again when
the sun goes down, that he
may sleep in his own garment
and bless you; and it shall be
righteousness to you before
the LORD your God.

14"You shall not oppress a
hired servant *who is* poor and
needy, *whether* one of your
brethren or one of the aliens
who *is* in your land within
your gates. 15Each day you
shall give *him* his wages, and
not let the sun go down on
it, for he *is* poor and has set
his heart on it; lest he cry out
against you to the LORD, and
it be sin to you.

16"Fathers shall not be put
to death for *their* children, nor
shall children be put to death
for *their* fathers; a person shall
be put to death for his own
sin.

17"You shall not pervert justice due the stranger or the
fatherless, nor take a widow's
garment as a pledge. 18But you
shall remember that you were
a slave in Egypt, and the LORD
your God redeemed you from
there; therefore I command
you to do this thing.

19"When you reap your harvest in your field, and forget
a sheaf in the field, you shall
not go back to get it; it shall
be for the stranger, the fatherless, and the widow, that the
LORD your God may bless you
in all the work of your hands.
20When you beat your olive
trees, you shall not go over
the boughs again; it shall be
for the stranger, the fatherless, and the widow. 21When
you gather the grapes of your
vineyard, you shall not glean
it afterward; it shall be for the
stranger, the fatherless, and
the widow. 22And you shall
remember that you were a
slave in the land of Egypt;
therefore I command you to
do this thing.

25 "If there is a dispute
between men, and
they come to court, that *the
judges* may judge them, and
they justify the righteous and
condemn the wicked, 2then
it shall be, if the wicked man
deserves to be beaten, that
the judge will cause him to
lie down and be beaten in his
presence, according to his
guilt, with a certain number
of blows. 3Forty blows he may

give him *and* no more, lest he
should exceed this and beat
him with many blows above
these, and your brother be
humiliated in your sight.

4“You shall not muzzle an
ox while it treads out *the grain.*

MARRIAGE DUTY OF THE SURVIVING BROTHER

5“If brothers dwell together,
and one of them dies and has
no son, the widow of the dead
man shall not be *married* to
a stranger outside *the family;*
her husband’s brother shall go
in to her, take her as his wife,
and perform the duty of a husband’s brother to her. 6And
it shall be *that* the firstborn
son which she bears will succeed to the name of his dead
brother, that his name may
not be blotted out of Israel.
7But if the man does not want
to take his brother’s wife, then
let his brother’s wife go up to
the gate to the elders, and
say, ‘My husband’s brother
refuses to raise up a name to
his brother in Israel; he will
not perform the duty of my
husband’s brother.’ 8Then the
elders of his city shall call him
and speak to him. But *if* he
stands firm and says, ‘I do not
want to take her,’ 9then his
brother’s wife shall come to
him in the presence of the elders, remove his sandal from
his foot, spit in his face, and
answer and say, ‘So shall it be
done to the man who will not
build up his brother’s house.’
10And his name shall be called
in Israel, ‘The house of him
who had his sandal removed.’

MISCELLANEOUS LAWS

11“If *two* men fight together,
and the wife of one draws near
to rescue her husband from
the hand of the one attacking
him, and puts out her hand
and seizes him by the geni-
tals, 12then you shall cut off
her hand; your eye shall not
pity *her.*

13“You shall not have in
your bag differing weights, a
heavy and a light. 14You shall
not have in your house differing measures, a large and a
small. 15You shall have a perfect and just weight, a perfect
and just measure, that your
days may be lengthened in the
land which the LORD your God
is giving you. 16For all who do
such things, all who behave
unrighteously, *are* an abomination to the LORD your God.

DESTROY THE AMALEKITES

17“Remember what Am-
alek did to you on the way
as you were coming out of
Egypt, 18how he met you on
the way and attacked your
rear ranks, all the stragglers
at your rear, when you *were*
tired and weary; and he did
not fear God. 19Therefore it
shall be, when the LORD your
God has given you rest from
your enemies all around, in
the land which the LORD your

God is giving you to possess
as an inheritance, *that* you will
blot out the remembrance of
Amalek from under heaven.
You shall not forget.

OFFERINGS OF FIRSTFRUITS AND TITHES

26 “And it shall be, when
you come into the land
which the LORD your God is
giving you *as* an inheritance,
and you possess it and dwell
in it, 2that you shall take some
of the first of all the produce
of the ground, which you shall
bring from your land that the
LORD your God is giving you,
and put *it* in a basket and go
to the place where the LORD
your God chooses to make His
name abide. 3And you shall
go to the one who is priest in
those days, and say to him,
‘I declare today to the LORD
your[a] God that I have come
to the country which the
LORD swore to our fathers to
give us.’
4“Then the priest shall take
the basket out of your hand
and set it down before the
altar of the LORD your God.
5And you shall answer and say
before the LORD your God: ‘My
father *was* a Syrian,[a] about
to perish, and he went down
to Egypt and dwelt there, few
in number; and there he became a nation, great, mighty,
and populous. 6But the Egyptians mistreated us, afflicted
us, and laid hard bondage on
us. 7Then we cried out to the
LORD God of our fathers, and
the LORD heard our voice
and looked on our affliction
and our labor and our oppression. 8So the LORD brought
us out of Egypt with a mighty
hand and with an outstretched
arm, with great terror and
with signs and wonders. 9He
has brought us to this place
and has given us this land, “a
land flowing with milk and
honey”;[a] 10and now, behold,
I have brought the firstfruits
of the land which you, O LORD,
have given me.’
“Then you shall set it before the LORD your God, and
worship before the LORD your
God. 11So you shall rejoice in
every good *thing* which the
LORD your God has given to
you and your house, you and
the Levite and the stranger
who *is* among you.
12“When you have finished
laying aside all the tithe of
your increase in the third
year—the year of tithing—
and have given *it* to the Levite,
the stranger, the fatherless,
and the widow, so that they
may eat within your gates and
be filled, 13then you shall say
before the LORD your God: ‘I
have removed the holy *tithe*
from *my* house, and also have
given them to the Levite, the
stranger, the fatherless, and
the widow, according to all

26:3 [a] Septuagint reads *my*. 26:5 [a] Or *Aramean* 26:9 [a] Exodus 3:8

Your commandments which
You have commanded me; I
have not transgressed Your
commandments, nor have I
forgotten *them.* 14I have not
eaten any of it when in mourning, nor have I removed *any*
of it for an unclean *use,* nor
given *any* of it for the dead. I
have obeyed the voice of the
LORD my God, and have done
according to all that You have
commanded me. 15Look down
from Your holy habitation,
from heaven, and bless Your
people Israel and the land
which You have given us, just
as You swore to our fathers,
"a land flowing with milk and
honey."'[a]

A SPECIAL PEOPLE OF GOD

16"This day the LORD your
God commands you to ob-
serve these statutes and judgments; therefore you shall be
careful to observe them with
all your heart and with all
your soul. 17Today you have
proclaimed the LORD to be
your God, and that you will
walk in His ways and keep
His statutes, His commandments, and His judgments,
and that you will obey His
voice. 18Also today the LORD
has proclaimed you to be
His special people, just as He
promised you, that *you* should
keep all His commandments,
19and that He will set you high
above all nations which He
has made, in praise, in name,
and in honor, and that you
may be a holy people to the
LORD your God, just as He has
spoken."

THE LAW INSCRIBED ON STONES

27 Now Moses, with the
elders of Israel, com-
manded the people, saying:
"Keep all the commandments
which I command you today.
2And it shall be, on the day
when you cross over the Jordan to the land which the
LORD your God is giving you,
that you shall set up for yourselves large stones, and whitewash them with lime. 3You
shall write on them all the
words of this law, when you
have crossed over, that you
may enter the land which the
LORD your God is giving you,
'a land flowing with milk and
honey,'[a] just as the LORD God
of your fathers promised you.
4Therefore it shall be, when
you have crossed over the
Jordan, *that* on Mount Ebal
you shall set up these stones,
which I command you today,
and you shall whitewash
them with lime. 5And there
you shall build an altar to the
LORD your God, an altar of
stones; you shall not use an
iron *tool* on them. 6You shall
build with whole stones the
altar of the LORD your God,
and offer burnt offerings on

26:15 [a] Exodus 3:8 27:3 [a] Exodus 3:8

it to the LORD your God. 7You
shall offer peace offerings,
and shall eat there, and rejoice before the LORD your
God. 8And you shall write very
plainly on the stones all the
words of this law."
9Then Moses and the
priests, the Levites, spoke to
all Israel, saying, "Take heed
and listen, O Israel: This day
you have become the peo-
ple of the LORD your God.
10Therefore you shall obey the
voice of the LORD your God,
and observe His command-
ments and His statutes which
I command you today."

CURSES PRONOUNCED FROM MOUNT EBAL

11And Moses commanded
the people on the same day,
saying, 12"These shall stand
on Mount Gerizim to bless the
people, when you have crossed
over the Jordan: Simeon, Levi,
Judah, Issachar, Joseph, and
Benjamin; 13and these shall
stand on Mount Ebal to curse:
Reuben, Gad, Asher, Zebulun,
Dan, and Naphtali.
14"And the Levites shall
speak with a loud voice and
say to all the men of Israel:
15'Cursed *is* the one who
makes a carved or molded
image, an abomination to the
LORD, the work of the hands
of the craftsman, and sets *it*
up in secret.'
"And all the people shall
answer and say, 'Amen!'
16'Cursed *is* the one who
treats his father or his mother
with contempt.'
"And all the people shall
say, 'Amen!'
17'Cursed *is* the one who
moves his neighbor's landmark.'
"And all the people shall
say, 'Amen!'
18'Cursed *is* the one who
makes the blind to wander
off the road.'
"And all the people shall
say, 'Amen!'
19'Cursed *is* the one who
perverts the justice due the
stranger, the fatherless, and
widow.'
"And all the people shall
say, 'Amen!'
20'Cursed *is* the one who
lies with his father's wife, because he has uncovered his
father's bed.'
"And all the people shall
say, 'Amen!'
21'Cursed *is* the one who lies
with any kind of animal.'
"And all the people shall
say, 'Amen!'
22'Cursed *is* the one who
lies with his sister, the daughter of his father or the daughter of his mother.'
"And all the people shall
say, 'Amen!'
23'Cursed *is* the one who
lies with his mother-in-law.'
"And all the people shall
say, 'Amen!'
24'Cursed *is* the one who
attacks his neighbor secretly.'
"And all the people shall
say, 'Amen!'

25‘Cursed *is* the one who
takes a bribe to slay an innocent person.’

“And all the people shall
say, ‘Amen!’

26‘Cursed *is* the one who
does not confirm *all* the words
of this law by observing them.’

“And all the people shall
say, ‘Amen!’”

BLESSINGS ON OBEDIENCE

28 “Now it shall come to
pass, if you diligently
obey the voice of the LORD
your God, to observe carefully
all His commandments which
I command you today, that the
LORD your God will set you
high above all nations of the
earth. 2And all these blessings
shall come upon you and overtake you, because you obey the
voice of the LORD your God:

3“Blessed *shall* you *be* in the
city, and blessed *shall* you *be*
in the country.

4“Blessed *shall be* the fruit
of your body, the produce of
your ground and the increase
of your herds, the increase of
your cattle and the offspring
of your flocks.

5“Blessed *shall be* your basket and your kneading bowl.

6“Blessed *shall* you *be* when
you come in, and blessed *shall*
you *be* when you go out.

7“The LORD will cause your
enemies who rise against you
to be defeated before your
face; they shall come out
against you one way and flee
before you seven ways.

8“The LORD will command
the blessing on you in your
storehouses and in all to
which you set your hand, and
He will bless you in the land
which the LORD your God is
giving you.

9“The LORD will establish
you as a holy people to Himself, just as He has sworn to
you, if you keep the commandments of the LORD your God
and walk in His ways. 10Then
all peoples of the earth shall
see that you are called by the
name of the LORD, and they
shall be afraid of you. 11And
the LORD will grant you plenty
of goods, in the fruit of your
body, in the increase of your
livestock, and in the produce
of your ground, in the land
of which the LORD swore to
your fathers to give you. 12The
LORD will open to you His
good treasure, the heavens,
to give the rain to your land
in its season, and to bless all
the work of your hand. You
shall lend to many nations,
but you shall not borrow.
13And the LORD will make you
the head and not the tail; you
shall be above only, and not
be beneath, if you heed the
commandments of the LORD
your God, which I command
you today, and are careful to
observe *them.* 14So you shall
not turn aside from any of the
words which I command you
this day, *to* the right or the left,
to go after other gods to serve
them.

CURSES ON DISOBEDIENCE

15“But it shall come to pass,
if you do not obey the voice of
the LORD your God, to observe
carefully all His commandments and His statutes which
I command you today, that all
these curses will come upon
you and overtake you:

16“Cursed *shall* you *be* in the
city, and cursed *shall* you *be* in
the country.

17“Cursed *shall be* your basket and your kneading bowl.

18“Cursed *shall be* the fruit
of your body and the produce
of your land, the increase of
your cattle and the offspring
of your flocks.

19“Cursed *shall* you *be* when
you come in, and cursed *shall*
you *be* when you go out.

20“The LORD will send on
you cursing, confusion, and
rebuke in all that you set
your hand to do, until you
are destroyed and until you
perish quickly, because of the
wickedness of your doings
in which you have forsaken
Me. 21The LORD will make the
plague cling to you until He
has consumed you from the
land which you are going to
possess. 22The LORD will strike
you with consumption, with
fever, with inflammation, with
severe burning fever, with the
sword, with scorching, and
with mildew; they shall pursue
you until you perish. 23And
your heavens which *are* over
your head shall be bronze, and
the earth which is under you
shall be iron. 24The LORD will
change the rain of your land
to powder and dust; from the
heaven it shall come down on
you until you are destroyed.

25“The LORD will cause you
to be defeated before your enemies; you shall go out one way
against them and flee seven
ways before them; and you
shall become troublesome to
all the kingdoms of the earth.
26Your carcasses shall be food
for all the birds of the air and
the beasts of the earth, and no
one shall frighten *them* away.
27The LORD will strike you
with the boils of Egypt, with
tumors, with the scab, and
with the itch, from which you
cannot be healed. 28The LORD
will strike you with madness
and blindness and confusion
of heart. 29And you shall grope
at noonday, as a blind man
gropes in darkness; you shall
not prosper in your ways; you
shall be only oppressed and
plundered continually, and no
one shall save *you*.

30“You shall betroth a wife,
but another man shall lie with
her; you shall build a house,
but you shall not dwell in it;
you shall plant a vineyard,
but shall not gather its grapes.
31Your ox *shall be* slaughtered
before your eyes, but you shall
not eat of it; your donkey *shall*
be violently taken away from
before you, and shall not be
restored to you; your sheep
shall be given to your enemies,
and you shall have no one to

rescue *them.* 32Your sons and
your daughters *shall be* given
to another people, and your
eyes shall look and fail *with
longing* for them all day long;
and *there shall be* no strength
in your hand. 33A nation whom
you have not known shall eat
the fruit of your land and the
produce of your labor, and you
shall be only oppressed and
crushed continually. 34So you
shall be driven mad because of
the sight which your eyes see.
35The LORD will strike you in
the knees and on the legs with
severe boils which cannot be
healed, and from the sole of
your foot to the top of your
head.

36"The LORD will bring you
and the king whom you set
over you to a nation which
neither you nor your fathers
have known, and there you
shall serve other gods—wood
and stone. 37And you shall
become an astonishment, a
proverb, and a byword among
all nations where the LORD
will drive you.

38"You shall carry much
seed out to the field but gather
little in, for the locust shall
consume it. 39You shall plant
vineyards and tend *them,* but
you shall neither drink *of* the
wine nor gather the *grapes;*
for the worms shall eat them.
40You shall have olive trees
throughout all your territory,
but you shall not anoint *yourself* with the oil; for your olives shall drop off. 41You shall
beget sons and daughters, but
they shall not be yours; for
they shall go into captivity.
42Locusts shall consume all
your trees and the produce
of your land.

43"The alien who *is* among
you shall rise higher and
higher above you, and you
shall come down lower and
lower. 44He shall lend to you,
but you shall not lend to him;
he shall be the head, and you
shall be the tail.

45"Moreover all these
curses shall come upon you
and pursue and overtake you,
until you are destroyed, because you did not obey the
voice of the LORD your God,
to keep His commandments
and His statutes which He
commanded you. 46And they
shall be upon you for a sign
and a wonder, and on your
descendants forever.

47"Because you did not
serve the LORD your God with
joy and gladness of heart,
for the abundance of everything, 48therefore you shall
serve your enemies, whom
the LORD will send against
you, in hunger, in thirst, in
nakedness, and in need of
everything; and He will put
a yoke of iron on your neck
until He has destroyed you.
49The LORD will bring a nation
against you from afar, from
the end of the earth, *as swift* as
the eagle flies, a nation whose
language you will not understand, 50a nation of fierce

countenance, which does not
respect the elderly nor show
favor to the young. 51And they
shall eat the increase of your
livestock and the produce of
your land, until you are destroyed; they shall not leave
you grain or new wine or oil,
or the increase of your cattle
or the offspring of your flocks,
until they have destroyed you.
52"They shall besiege you
at all your gates until your
high and fortified walls, in
which you trust, come down
throughout all your land; and
they shall besiege you at all
your gates throughout all your
land which the LORD your God
has given you. 53You shall eat
the fruit of your own body, the
flesh of your sons and your
daughters whom the LORD
your God has given you, in
the siege and desperate straits
in which your enemy shall
distress you. 54The sensitive
and very refined man among
you will be hostile toward his
brother, toward the wife of his
bosom, and toward the rest of
his children whom he leaves
behind, 55so that he will not
give any of them the flesh of
his children whom he will eat,
because he has nothing left
in the siege and desperate
straits in which your enemy
shall distress you at all your
gates. 56The tender and delicate woman among you, who
would not venture to set the
sole of her foot on the ground
because of her delicateness
and sensitivity, will refuse[a] to
the husband of her bosom, and
to her son and her daughter,
57her placenta which comes
out from between her feet and
her children whom she bears;
for she will eat them secretly
for lack of everything in the
siege and desperate straits in
which your enemy shall distress you at all your gates.
58"If you do not carefully observe all the words of this law
that are written in this book,
that you may fear this glorious and awesome name, THE
LORD YOUR GOD, 59then the
LORD will bring upon you and
your descendants extraordi-
nary plagues—great and prolonged plagues—and serious
and prolonged sicknesses.
60Moreover He will bring
back on you all the diseases
of Egypt, of which you were
afraid, and they shall cling
to you. 61Also every sickness
and every plague, which *is* not
written in this Book of the Law,
will the LORD bring upon you
until you are destroyed. 62You
shall be left few in number,
whereas you were as the stars
of heaven in multitude, because you would not obey the
voice of the LORD your God.
63And it shall be, *that* just as
the LORD rejoiced over you to
do you good and multiply you,
so the LORD will rejoice over

28:56 [a] Literally *her eye shall be evil toward*

you to destroy you and bring
you to nothing; and you shall
be plucked from off the land
which you go to possess.
64"Then the LORD will scatter you among all peoples,
from one end of the earth to
the other, and there you shall
serve other gods, which neither you nor your fathers have
known—wood and stone.
65And among those nations
you shall find no rest, nor
shall the sole of your foot have
a resting place; but there the
LORD will give you a trembling
heart, failing eyes, and anguish of soul. 66Your life shall
hang in doubt before you; you
shall fear day and night, and
have no assurance of life. 67In
the morning you shall say, 'Oh,
that it were evening!' And at
evening you shall say, 'Oh, that
it were morning!' because of
the fear which terrifies your
heart, and because of the sight
which your eyes see.
68"And the LORD will take
you back to Egypt in ships, by
the way of which I said to you,
'You shall never see it again.'
And there you shall be offered
for sale to your enemies as
male and female slaves, but
no one will buy *you*."

THE COVENANT RENEWED IN MOAB

29 These *are* the words
of the covenant which
the LORD commanded Moses
to make with the children of
Israel in the land of Moab, besides the covenant which He
made with them in Horeb.
2Now Moses called all Is-
rael and said to them: "You
have seen all that the LORD did
before your eyes in the land of
Egypt, to Pharaoh and to all his
servants and to all his land—
3the great trials which your
eyes have seen, the signs, and
those great wonders. 4Yet the
LORD has not given you a heart
to perceive and eyes to see and
ears to hear, to this *very* day.
5And I have led you forty years
in the wilderness. Your clothes
have not worn out on you, and
your sandals have not worn
out on your feet. 6You have
not eaten bread, nor have you
drunk wine or *similar* drink,
that you may know that I *am*
the LORD your God. 7And when
you came to this place, Sihon
king of Heshbon and Og king
of Bashan came out against
us to battle, and we conquered
them. 8We took their land and
gave it as an inheritance to the
Reubenites, to the Gadites, and
to half the tribe of Manasseh.
9Therefore keep the words of
this covenant, and do them,
that you may prosper in all
that you do.
10"All of you stand today
before the LORD your God:
your leaders and your tribes
and your elders and your officers, all the men of Israel,
11your little ones and your
wives—also the stranger who
is in your camp, from the one
who cuts your wood to the

one who draws your water—
[12]that you may enter into covenant with the LORD your God,
and into His oath, which the
LORD your God makes with
you today, [13]that He may establish you today as a people
for Himself, and *that* He may
be God to you, just as He has
spoken to you, and just as He
has sworn to your fathers, to
Abraham, Isaac, and Jacob.

[14]"I make this covenant and
this oath, not with you alone,
[15]but with *him* who stands here
with us today before the LORD
our God, as well as with *him*
who *is* not here with us today
[16](for you know that we dwelt
in the land of Egypt and that
we came through the nations
which you passed by, [17]and you
saw their abominations and
their idols which *were* among
them—wood and stone and
silver and gold); [18]so that there
may not be among you man
or woman or family or tribe,
whose heart turns away today
from the LORD our God, to go
and serve the gods of these nations, and that there may not
be among you a root bearing
bitterness or wormwood; [19]and
so it may not happen, when he
hears the words of this curse,
that he blesses himself in his
heart, saying, 'I shall have
peace, even though I follow
the dictates[a] of my heart'—as
though the drunkard could be
included with the sober.

[20]"The LORD would not
spare him; for then the anger
of the LORD and His jealousy
would burn against that man,
and every curse that is written in this book would settle
on him, and the LORD would
blot out his name from under
heaven. [21]And the LORD would
separate him from all the
tribes of Israel for adversity,
according to all the curses of
the covenant that are written
in this Book of the Law, [22]so
that the coming generation
of your children who rise up
after you, and the foreigner
who comes from a far land,
would say, when they see the
plagues of that land and the
sicknesses which the LORD
has laid on it:

[23]'The whole land *is* brimstone, salt, and burning; it is
not sown, nor does it bear, nor
does any grass grow there, like
the overthrow of Sodom and
Gomorrah, Admah, and Ze-
boiim, which the LORD overthrew in His anger and His
wrath.' [24]All nations would
say, 'Why has the LORD done
so to this land? What does
the heat of this great anger
mean?' [25]Then *people* would
say: 'Because they have forsaken the covenant of the
LORD God of their fathers,
which He made with them
when He brought them out
of the land of Egypt; [26]for they
went and served other gods

29:19 [a] Or *stubbornness*

and worshiped them, gods
that they did not know and
that He had not given to them.
27Then the anger of the LORD
was aroused against this land,
to bring on it every curse that
is written in this book. 28And
the LORD uprooted them from
their land in anger, in wrath,
and in great indignation, and
cast them into another land,
as *it is* this day.'

29"The secret *things belong*
to the LORD our God, but those
things which are revealed *be-*
long to us and to our children
forever, that *we* may do all the
words of this law.

THE BLESSING OF RETURNING TO GOD

30 "Now it shall come to
pass, when all these
things come upon you, the
blessing and the curse which
I have set before you, and you
call *them* to mind among all the
nations where the LORD your
God drives you, 2and you return to the LORD your God and
obey His voice, according to
all that I command you today,
you and your children, with all
your heart and with all your
soul, 3that the LORD your God
will bring you back from captivity, and have compassion
on you, and gather you again
from all the nations where the
LORD your God has scattered
you. 4If *any* of you are driven
out to the farthest *parts* under
heaven, from there the LORD
your God will gather you, and
from there He will bring you.
5Then the LORD your God will
bring you to the land which
your fathers possessed, and
you shall possess it. He will
prosper you and multiply
you more than your fathers.
6And the LORD your God will
circumcise your heart and the
heart of your descendants, to
love the LORD your God with
all your heart and with all your
soul, that you may live.

7"Also the LORD your God
will put all these curses on
your enemies and on those
who hate you, who persecuted
you. 8And you will again obey
the voice of the LORD and do
all His commandments which
I command you today. 9The
LORD your God will make you
abound in all the work of your
hand, in the fruit of your body,
in the increase of your livestock, and in the produce of
your land for good. For the
LORD will again rejoice over
you for good as He rejoiced
over your fathers, 10if you obey
the voice of the LORD your
God, to keep His command-
ments and His statutes which
are written in this Book of the
Law, *and* if you turn to the
LORD your God with all your
heart and with all your soul.

THE CHOICE OF LIFE OR DEATH

11"For this commandment
which I command you today *is*
not *too* mysterious for you, nor
is it far off. 12It *is* not in heaven,

that you should say, 'Who will ascend into heaven for us and bring it to us, that we may hear it and do it?' 13 Nor *is* it beyond the sea, that you should say, 'Who will go over the sea for us and bring it to us, that we may hear it and do it?' 14 But the word *is* very near you, in your mouth and in your heart, that you may do it.

15 "See, I have set before you today life and good, death and evil, 16 in that I command you today to love the LORD your God, to walk in His ways, and to keep His commandments, His statutes, and His judgments, that you may live and multiply; and the LORD your God will bless you in the land which you go to possess. 17 But if your heart turns away so that you do not hear, and are drawn away, and worship other gods and serve them, 18 I announce to you today that you shall surely perish; you shall not prolong *your* days in the land which you cross over the Jordan to go in and possess. 19 I call heaven and earth as witnesses today against you, *that* I have set before you life and death, blessing and cursing; therefore choose life, that both you and your descendants may live; 20 that you may love the LORD your God, that you may obey His voice, and that you may cling to Him, for He *is* your life and the length of your days; and that you may dwell in the land which the LORD swore to your fathers, to Abraham, Isaac, and Jacob, to give them."

JOSHUA THE NEW LEADER OF ISRAEL

31 Then Moses went and spoke these words to all Israel. 2 And he said to them: "I *am* one hundred and twenty years old today. I can no longer go out and come in. Also the LORD has said to me, 'You shall not cross over this Jordan.' 3 The LORD your God Himself crosses over before you; He will destroy these nations from before you, and you shall dispossess them. Joshua himself crosses over before you, just as the LORD has said. 4 And the LORD will do to them as He did to Sihon and Og, the kings of the Amorites and their land, when He destroyed them. 5 The LORD will give them over to you, that you may do to them according to every commandment which I have commanded you. 6 Be strong and of good courage, do not fear nor be afraid of them; for the LORD your God, He *is* the One who goes with you. He will not leave you nor forsake you."

7 Then Moses called Joshua and said to him in the sight of all Israel, "Be strong and of good courage, for you must go with this people to the land which the LORD has sworn to their fathers to give them, and you shall cause them to

inherit it. 8And the LORD, He *is*
the One who goes before you.
He will be with you, He will
not leave you nor forsake you;
do not fear nor be dismayed."

THE LAW TO BE READ EVERY SEVEN YEARS

9So Moses wrote this law
and delivered it to the priests,
the sons of Levi, who bore
the ark of the covenant of the
LORD, and to all the elders
of Israel. 10And Moses commanded them, saying: "At the
end of *every* seven years, at the
appointed time in the year of
release, at the Feast of Tabernacles, 11when all Israel comes
to appear before the LORD
your God in the place which
He chooses, you shall read this
law before all Israel in their
hearing. 12Gather the people
together, men and women and
little ones, and the stranger
who *is* within your gates, that
they may hear and that they
may learn to fear the LORD
your God and carefully observe all the words of this law,
13and *that* their children, who
have not known it, may hear
and learn to fear the LORD
your God as long as you live
in the land which you cross
the Jordan to possess."

PREDICTION OF ISRAEL'S REBELLION

14Then the LORD said to
Moses, "Behold, the days
approach when you must
die; call Joshua, and present
yourselves in the tabernacle
of meeting, that I may inaugurate him."

So Moses and Joshua went
and presented themselves in
the tabernacle of meeting.
15Now the LORD appeared at
the tabernacle in a pillar of
cloud, and the pillar of cloud
stood above the door of the
tabernacle.

16And the LORD said to
Moses: "Behold, you will rest
with your fathers; and this
people will rise and play the
harlot with the gods of the foreigners of the land, where they
go *to be* among them, and they
will forsake Me and break My
covenant which I have made
with them. 17Then My anger
shall be aroused against them
in that day, and I will forsake
them, and I will hide My face
from them, and they shall be
devoured. And many evils and
troubles shall befall them, so
that they will say in that day,
'Have not these evils come
upon us because our God *is*
not among us?' 18And I will
surely hide My face in that day
because of all the evil which
they have done, in that they
have turned to other gods.

19"Now therefore, write
down this song for your-
selves, and teach it to the children of Israel; put it in their
mouths, that this song may
be a witness for Me against
the children of Israel. 20When
I have brought them to the
land flowing with milk and

honey, of which I swore to
their fathers, and they have
eaten and filled themselves
and grown fat, then they will
turn to other gods and serve
them; and they will provoke
Me and break My covenant.
21 Then it shall be, when many
evils and troubles have come
upon them, that this song
will testify against them as a
witness; for it will not be forgotten in the mouths of their
descendants, for I know the
inclination of their behavior today, even before I have
brought them to the land of
which I swore *to give them.*"

22 Therefore Moses wrote
this song the same day, and
taught it to the children of Israel. 23 Then He inaugurated
Joshua the son of Nun, and
said, "Be strong and of good
courage; for you shall bring
the children of Israel into the
land of which I swore to them,
and I will be with you."

24 So it was, when Moses had
completed writing the words
of this law in a book, when they
were finished, 25 that Moses
commanded the Levites, who
bore the ark of the covenant
of the LORD, saying: 26 "Take
this Book of the Law, and put
it beside the ark of the covenant of the LORD your God,
that it may be there as a witness against you; 27 for I know
your rebellion and your stiff
neck. *If* today, while I am yet
alive with you, you have been
rebellious against the LORD,
then how much more after
my death? 28 Gather to me all
the elders of your tribes, and
your officers, that I may speak
these words in their hearing
and call heaven and earth to
witness against them. 29 For I
know that after my death you
will become utterly corrupt,
and turn aside from the way
which I have commanded
you. And evil will befall you
in the latter days, because
you will do evil in the sight
of the LORD, to provoke Him
to anger through the work of
your hands."

THE SONG OF MOSES

30 Then Moses spoke in the
hearing of all the assembly of
Israel the words of this song
until they were ended:

32 "Give ear, O heavens,
and I will speak;
And hear, O earth, the
words of my mouth.
2 Let my teaching
drop as the rain,
My speech distill
as the dew,
As raindrops on the
tender herb,
And as showers
on the grass.
3 For I proclaim the
name of the LORD:
Ascribe greatness
to our God.
4 *He is* the Rock, His
work *is* perfect;
For all His ways
are justice,

A God of truth and
without injustice;
Righteous and
upright *is* He.

5 "They have corrupted
themselves;
They are not His
children,
Because of their blemish:
A perverse and crooked
generation.
6 Do you thus deal
with the LORD,
O foolish and
unwise people?
Is He not your Father,
who bought you?
Has He not made you
and established you?

7 "Remember the
days of old,
Consider the years of
many generations.
Ask your father, and
he will show you;
Your elders, and they
will tell you:
8 When the Most
High divided their
inheritance to
the nations,
When He separated
the sons of Adam,
He set the boundaries
of the peoples
According to the
number of the
children of Israel.
9 For the LORD's portion
is His people;
Jacob *is* the place of
His inheritance.

10 "He found him in
a desert land
And in the wasteland, a
howling wilderness;
He encircled him, He
instructed him,
He kept him as the
apple of His eye.
11 As an eagle stirs
up its nest,
Hovers over its young,
Spreading out its wings,
taking them up,
Carrying them on
its wings,
12 *So* the LORD alone
led him,
And *there was* no foreign
god with him.

13 "He made him ride in the
heights of the earth,
That he might eat the
produce of the fields;
He made him draw
honey from the rock,
And oil from the
flinty rock;
14 Curds from the cattle,
and milk of the flock,
With fat of lambs;
And rams of the breed
of Bashan, and goats,
With the choicest wheat;
And you drank wine, the
blood of the grapes.

15 "But Jeshurun grew
fat and kicked;
You grew fat, you
grew thick,
You are obese!
Then he forsook God
who made him,

And scornfully
esteemed the Rock
of his salvation.
16 They provoked Him
to jealousy with
foreign *gods;*
With abominations they
provoked Him to anger.
17 They sacrificed to
demons, not to God,
To gods they did
not know,
To new *gods,* new arrivals
That your fathers
did not fear.
18 Of the Rock *who* begot
you, you are unmindful,
And have forgotten the
God who fathered you.

19 "And when the LORD saw
it, He spurned *them,*
Because of the
provocation of His sons
and His daughters.
20 And He said: 'I will hide
My face from them,
I will see what their
end *will be,*
For they *are* a perverse
generation,
Children in whom
is no faith.
21 They have provoked
Me to jealousy by
what is not God;
They have moved Me
to anger by their
foolish idols.
But I will provoke them
to jealousy by *those*
who are not a nation;
I will move them to anger
by a foolish nation.
22 For a fire is kindled
in My anger,
And shall burn to
the lowest hell;
It shall consume the
earth with her increase,
And set on fire the
foundations of
the mountains.

23 'I will heap disasters
on them;
I will spend My
arrows on them.
24 *They shall be* wasted
with hunger,
Devoured by pestilence
and bitter destruction;
I will also send
against them the
teeth of beasts,
With the poison of
serpents of the dust.
25 The sword shall
destroy outside;
There shall be
terror within
For the young man
and virgin,
The nursing child with
the man of gray hairs.
26 I would have said, "I will
dash them in pieces,
I will make the memory
of them to cease
from among men,"
27 Had I not feared the
wrath of the enemy,
Lest their adversaries
should misunderstand,
Lest they should say,
"Our hand *is* high;
And it is not the LORD
who has done all this."'

28 "For they *are* a nation
void of counsel,
Nor *is there any*
understanding in them.
29 Oh, that they were
wise, *that* they
understood this,
That they would consider
their latter end!
30 How could one chase
a thousand,
And two put ten
thousand to flight,
Unless their Rock
had sold them,
And the LORD had
surrendered them?
31 For their rock *is* not
like our Rock,
Even our enemies
themselves
being judges.
32 For their vine *is* of the
vine of Sodom
And of the fields
of Gomorrah;
Their grapes *are*
grapes of gall,
Their clusters *are* bitter.
33 Their wine *is* the
poison of serpents,
And the cruel venom
of cobras.

34 '*Is* this not laid up in
store with Me,
Sealed up among
My treasures?
35 Vengeance is Mine,
and recompense;
Their foot shall slip
in *due* time;
For the day of their
calamity *is* at hand,
And the things to come
hasten upon them.'

36 "For the LORD will
judge His people
And have compassion
on His servants,
When He sees that
their power is gone,
And *there is* no one
remaining, bond or free.
37 He will say: 'Where
are their gods,
The rock in which they
sought refuge?
38 Who ate the fat of
their sacrifices,
And drank the wine of
their drink offering?
Let them rise and
help you,
And be your refuge.

39 'Now see that I,
even I, *am* He,
And *there is* no God
besides Me;
I kill and I make alive;
I wound and I heal;
Nor *is there any* who can
deliver from My hand.
40 For I raise My hand
to heaven,
And say, "*As* I live forever,
41 If I whet My glittering
sword,
And My hand takes
hold on judgment,
I will render vengeance
to My enemies,
And repay those
who hate Me.
42 I will make My arrows
drunk with blood,

And My sword shall
devour flesh,
With the blood of the
slain and the captives,
From the heads of the
leaders of the enemy."'

43"Rejoice, O Gentiles,
with His people;[a]
For He will avenge the
blood of His servants,
And render vengeance
to His adversaries;
He will provide
atonement for His
land *and* His people."

44So Moses came with
Joshua[a] the son of Nun and
spoke all the words of this
song in the hearing of the people. 45Moses finished speaking
all these words to all Israel,
46and he said to them: "Set
your hearts on all the words
which I testify among you
today, which you shall command your children to be
careful to observe—all the
words of this law. 47For it *is* not
a futile thing for you, because
it *is* your life, and by this word
you shall prolong *your* days in
the land which you cross over
the Jordan to possess."

MOSES TO DIE ON MOUNT NEBO

48Then the LORD spoke to
Moses that very same day, saying: 49"Go up this mountain
of the Abarim, Mount Nebo,
which *is* in the land of Moab,
across from Jericho; view the
land of Canaan, which I give
to the children of Israel as a
possession; 50and die on the
mountain which you ascend,
and be gathered to your people, just as Aaron your brother
died on Mount Hor and was
gathered to his people; 51be-
cause you trespassed against
Me among the children of Israel at the waters of Meribah
Kadesh, in the Wilderness
of Zin, because you did not
hallow Me in the midst of the
children of Israel. 52Yet you
shall see the land before *you,*
though you shall not go there,
into the land which I am giving to the children of Israel."

MOSES' FINAL BLESSING ON ISRAEL

33 Now this *is* the blessing with which Moses
the man of God blessed the
children of Israel before his
death. 2And he said:

"The LORD came
from Sinai,
And dawned on
them from Seir;
He shone forth from
Mount Paran,
And He came with ten
thousands of saints;

32:43 [a] A Dead Sea Scroll fragment adds *And let all the gods (angels) worship Him* (compare Septuagint and Hebrews 1:6). 32:44 [a] Hebrew *Hoshea* (compare Numbers 13:8, 16)

From His right hand
Came a fiery law for them.
3 Yes, He loves the people;
All His saints *are*
in Your hand;
They sit down at Your feet;
Everyone receives
Your words.
4 Moses commanded
a law for us,
A heritage of the
congregation of Jacob.
5 And He was King
in Jeshurun,
When the leaders of the
people were gathered,
All the tribes of
Israel together.

6 "Let Reuben live,
and not die,
Nor let his men be few."

7 And this he said of Judah:

"Hear, LORD, the
voice of Judah,
And bring him to
his people;
Let his hands be
sufficient for him,
And may You be a help
against his enemies."

8 And of Levi he said:

"*Let* Your Thummim
and Your Urim *be*
with Your holy one,
Whom You tested
at Massah,
And with whom You
contended at the
waters of Meribah,
9 Who says of his father
and mother,
'I have not seen them';
Nor did he acknowledge
his brothers,
Or know his own children;
For they have observed
Your word
And kept Your covenant.
10 They shall teach Jacob
Your judgments,
And Israel Your law.
They shall put incense
before You,
And a whole burnt
sacrifice on Your altar.
11 Bless his substance,
LORD,
And accept the work
of his hands;
Strike the loins of those
who rise against him,
And of those who
hate him, that they
rise not again."

12 Of Benjamin he said:

"The beloved of the
LORD shall dwell in
safety by Him,
Who shelters him all
the day long;
And he shall dwell
between His shoulders."

13 And of Joseph he said:

"Blessed of the LORD
is his land,
With the precious things
of heaven, with the dew,
And the deep lying
beneath,

14 With the precious
fruits of the sun,
With the precious
produce of the months,
15 With the best things
of the ancient
mountains,
With the precious things
of the everlasting hills,
16 With the precious
things of the earth
and its fullness,
And the favor of Him
who dwelt in the bush.
Let *the blessing* come 'on
the head of Joseph,
And on the crown of
the head of him *who*
was separate from
his brothers.'[a]
17 His glory *is like* a
firstborn bull,
And his horns *like* the
horns of the wild ox;
Together with them
He shall push the peoples
To the ends of the earth;
They *are* the ten
thousands of Ephraim,
And they *are* the
thousands of
Manasseh."

18 And of Zebulun he said:

"Rejoice, Zebulun, in
your going out,
And Issachar in
your tents!
19 They shall call the
peoples *to* the
mountain;
There they shall
offer sacrifices of
righteousness;
For they shall partake
of the abundance
of the seas
And *of* treasures hidden
in the sand."

20 And of Gad he said:

"Blessed *is* he who
enlarges Gad;
He dwells as a lion,
And tears the arm and
the crown of his head.
21 He provided the first
part for himself,
Because a lawgiver's
portion was
reserved there.
He came *with* the heads
of the people;
He administered the
justice of the LORD,
And His judgments
with Israel."

22 And of Dan he said:

"Dan *is* a lion's whelp;
He shall leap from
Bashan."

23 And of Naphtali he said:

"O Naphtali, satisfied
with favor,
And full of the blessing
of the LORD,
Possess the west
and the south."

33:16 [a] Genesis 49:26

24And of Asher he said:

"Asher *is* most
blessed of sons;
Let him be favored
by his brothers,
And let him dip
his foot in oil.
25 Your sandals *shall be*
iron and bronze;
As your days, *so shall*
your strength *be.*

26"*There is* no one like the
God of Jeshurun,
Who rides the heavens
to help you,
And in His excellency
on the clouds.
27 The eternal God *is*
your refuge,
And underneath *are* the
everlasting arms;
He will thrust out the
enemy from before you,
And will say, 'Destroy!'
28 Then Israel shall
dwell in safety,
The fountain of
Jacob alone,
In a land of grain
and new wine;
His heavens shall
also drop dew.
29 Happy *are* you, O Israel!
Who *is* like you, a people
saved by the LORD,
The shield of your help
And the sword of
your majesty!
Your enemies shall
submit to you,
And you shall tread down
their high places."

MOSES DIES ON MOUNT NEBO

34 Then Moses went up
from the plains of Moab
to Mount Nebo, to the top of
Pisgah, which is across from
Jericho. And the LORD showed
him all the land of Gilead as far
as Dan, 2all Naphtali and the
land of Ephraim and Manasseh, all the land of Judah as
far as the Western Sea,[a] 3the
South, and the plain of the Valley of Jericho, the city of palm
trees, as far as Zoar. 4Then the
LORD said to him, "This *is* the
land of which I swore to give
Abraham, Isaac, and Jacob,
saying, 'I will give it to your
descendants.' I have caused
you to see *it* with your eyes, but
you shall not cross over there."
5So Moses the servant of
the LORD died there in the
land of Moab, according to
the word of the LORD. 6And
He buried him in a valley in
the land of Moab, opposite
Beth Peor; but no one knows
his grave to this day. 7Moses
was one hundred and twenty
years old when he died. His
eyes were not dim nor his natural vigor diminished. 8And
the children of Israel wept for
Moses in the plains of Moab
thirty days. So the days of
weeping *and* mourning for
Moses ended.

34:2 [a] That is, the Mediterranean

9Now Joshua the son of
Nun was full of the spirit of
wisdom, for Moses had laid his
hands on him; so the children
of Israel heeded him, and did
as the LORD had commanded
Moses.
10But since then there has
not arisen in Israel a prophet
like Moses, whom the LORD
knew face to face, 11in all the
signs and wonders which the
LORD sent him to do in the
land of Egypt, before Pharaoh, before all his servants,
and in all his land, 12and by
all that mighty power and all
the great terror which Moses
performed in the sight of all
Israel.

THE BOOK OF JOSHUA

GOD'S COMMISSION TO JOSHUA

1 After the death of Moses
the servant of the LORD, it
came to pass that the LORD
spoke to Joshua the son of
Nun, Moses' assistant, saying:
2"Moses My servant is dead.
Now therefore, arise, go over
this Jordan, you and all this
people, to the land which I am
giving to them—the children
of Israel. 3Every place that the
sole of your foot will tread
upon I have given you, as I
said to Moses. 4From the wilderness and this Lebanon as
far as the great river, the River
Euphrates, all the land of the
Hittites, and to the Great Sea
toward the going down of the
sun, shall be your territory.
5No man shall *be able to* stand
before you all the days of your
life; as I was with Moses, *so*
I will be with you. I will not
leave you nor forsake you. 6Be
strong and of good courage,
for to this people you shall divide as an inheritance the land
which I swore to their fathers
to give them. 7Only be strong
and very courageous, that you
may observe to do according
to all the law which Moses My
servant commanded you; do
not turn from it to the right
hand or to the left, that you
may prosper wherever you go.
8This Book of the Law shall
not depart from your mouth,
but you shall meditate in it
day and night, that you may
observe to do according to all
that is written in it. For then
you will make your way prosperous, and then you will have
good success. 9Have I not
commanded you? Be strong
and of good courage; do not

be afraid, nor be dismayed, for
the LORD your God *is* with you
wherever you go."

THE ORDER TO CROSS THE JORDAN

10 Then Joshua commanded
the officers of the people, saying, 11 "Pass through the camp
and command the people,
saying, 'Prepare provisions
for yourselves, for within
three days you will cross over
this Jordan, to go in to possess
the land which the LORD your
God is giving you to possess.'"
12 And to the Reubenites,
the Gadites, and half the tribe
of Manasseh Joshua spoke,
saying, 13 "Remember the word
which Moses the servant of the
LORD commanded you, say-
ing, 'The LORD your God is giving you rest and is giving you
this land.' 14 Your wives, your
little ones, and your livestock
shall remain in the land which
Moses gave you on this side of
the Jordan. But you shall pass
before your brethren armed,
all your mighty men of valor,
and help them, 15 until the
LORD has given your brethren
rest, as He *gave* you, and they
also have taken possession of
the land which the LORD your
God is giving them. Then you
shall return to the land of your
possession and enjoy it, which
Moses the LORD's servant gave
you on this side of the Jordan
toward the sunrise."
16 So they answered Joshua,
saying, "All that you command us we will do, and wherever you send us we will go.
17 Just as we heeded Moses
in all things, so we will heed
you. Only the LORD your God
be with you, as He was with
Moses. 18 Whoever rebels
against your command and
does not heed your words, in
all that you command him,
shall be put to death. Only be
strong and of good courage."

RAHAB HIDES THE SPIES

2 Now Joshua the son of
Nun sent out two men
from Acacia Grove[a] to spy secretly, saying, "Go, view the
land, especially Jericho."
So they went, and came to
the house of a harlot named
Rahab, and lodged there. 2 And
it was told the king of Jericho,
saying, "Behold, men have
come here tonight from the
children of Israel to search
out the country."
3 So the king of Jericho sent
to Rahab, saying, "Bring out
the men who have come to
you, who have entered your
house, for they have come to
search out all the country."
4 Then the woman took the
two men and hid them. So she
said, "Yes, the men came to
me, but I did not know where
they *were* from. 5 And it happened as the gate was being
shut, when it was dark, that

2:1 [a] Hebrew *Shittim*

the men went out. Where
the men went I do not know;
pursue them quickly, for you
may overtake them." 6(But she
had brought them up to the
roof and hidden them with
the stalks of flax, which she
had laid in order on the roof.)
7Then the men pursued them
by the road to the Jordan,
to the fords. And as soon as
those who pursued them had
gone out, they shut the gate.

8Now before they lay down,
she came up to them on the
roof, 9and said to the men: "I
know that the LORD has given
you the land, that the terror of
you has fallen on us, and that
all the inhabitants of the land
are fainthearted because of
you. 10For we have heard how
the LORD dried up the water
of the Red Sea for you when
you came out of Egypt, and
what you did to the two kings
of the Amorites who *were* on
the other side of the Jordan,
Sihon and Og, whom you utterly destroyed. 11And as soon
as we heard *these things,* our
hearts melted; neither did
there remain any more courage in anyone because of you,
for the LORD your God, He *is*
God in heaven above and on
earth beneath. 12Now therefore, I beg you, swear to me
by the LORD, since I have
shown you kindness, that
you also will show kindness
to my father's house, and give
me a true token, 13and spare
my father, my mother, my
brothers, my sisters, and all
that they have, and deliver our
lives from death."

14So the men answered her,
"Our lives for yours, if none of
you tell this business of ours.
And it shall be, when the LORD
has given us the land, that we
will deal kindly and truly with
you."

15Then she let them down
by a rope through the window,
for her house *was* on the city
wall; she dwelt on the wall.
16And she said to them, "Get to
the mountain, lest the pursuers meet you. Hide there three
days, until the pursuers have
returned. Afterward you may
go your way."

17So the men said to her:
"We *will be* blameless of this
oath of yours which you have
made us swear, 18unless, *when*
we come into the land, you
bind this line of scarlet cord
in the window through which
you let us down, and unless
you bring your father, your
mother, your brothers, and
all your father's household to
your own home. 19So it shall
be *that* whoever goes outside
the doors of your house into
the street, his blood *shall be* on
his own head, and we *will be*
guiltless. And whoever is with
you in the house, his blood
shall be on our head if a hand
is laid on him. 20And if you
tell this business of ours, then
we will be free from your oath
which you made us swear."

21Then she said, "According

to your words, so *be* it." And
she sent them away, and they
departed. And she bound the
scarlet cord in the window.

22They departed and went
to the mountain, and stayed
there three days until the
pursuers returned. The pursuers sought *them* all along
the way, but did not find *them.*
23So the two men returned,
descended from the moun-
tain, and crossed over; and
they came to Joshua the son
of Nun, and told him all that
had befallen them. 24And
they said to Joshua, "Truly
the LORD has delivered all
the land into our hands, for
indeed all the inhabitants of
the country are fainthearted
because of us."

ISRAEL CROSSES THE JORDAN

3 Then Joshua rose early in
the morning; and they set
out from Acacia Grove[a] and
came to the Jordan, he and
all the children of Israel, and
lodged there before they
crossed over. 2So it was, after
three days, that the officers
went through the camp; 3and
they commanded the people,
saying, "When you see the ark
of the covenant of the LORD
your God, and the priests, the
Levites, bearing it, then you
shall set out from your place
and go after it. 4Yet there shall
be a space between you and it,
about two thousand cubits by
measure. Do not come near
it, that you may know the way
by which you must go, for you
have not passed *this* way before."

5And Joshua said to the
people, "Sanctify yourselves,
for tomorrow the LORD will do
wonders among you." 6Then
Joshua spoke to the priests,
saying, "Take up the ark of
the covenant and cross over
before the people."

So they took up the ark of
the covenant and went before
the people.

7And the LORD said to
Joshua, "This day I will begin
to exalt you in the sight of all
Israel, that they may know
that, as I was with Moses, *so*
I will be with you. 8You shall
command the priests who
bear the ark of the covenant,
saying, 'When you have come
to the edge of the water of the
Jordan, you shall stand in the
Jordan.'"

9So Joshua said to the children of Israel, "Come here,
and hear the words of the
LORD your God." 10And Joshua
said, "By this you shall know
that the living God *is* among
you, and *that* He will without
fail drive out from before you
the Canaanites and the Hittites and the Hivites and the
Perizzites and the Girgashites
and the Amorites and the Jebusites: 11Behold, the ark of the

3:1 [a] Hebrew *Shittim*

covenant of the Lord of all the earth is crossing over before you into the Jordan. 12Now therefore, take for yourselves twelve men from the tribes of Israel, one man from every tribe. 13And it shall come to pass, as soon as the soles of the feet of the priests who bear the ark of the LORD, the Lord of all the earth, shall rest in the waters of the Jordan, *that* the waters of the Jordan shall be cut off, the waters that come down from upstream, and they shall stand as a heap."

14So it was, when the people set out from their camp to cross over the Jordan, with the priests bearing the ark of the covenant before the people, 15and as those who bore the ark came to the Jordan, and the feet of the priests who bore the ark dipped in the edge of the water (for the Jordan overflows all its banks during the whole time of harvest), 16that the waters which came down from upstream stood *still, and* rose in a heap very far away at Adam, the city that *is* beside Zaretan. So the waters that went down into the Sea of the Arabah, the *Salt Sea, failed, and* were cut off; and the people crossed over opposite Jericho. 17Then the priests who bore the ark of the covenant of the LORD stood firm on dry ground in the midst of the Jordan; and all Israel crossed over on dry ground, until all the people had crossed completely over the Jordan.

THE MEMORIAL STONES

4 And it came to pass, when all the people had completely crossed over the Jordan, that the LORD spoke to Joshua, saying: 2"Take for yourselves twelve men from the people, one man from every tribe, 3and command them, saying, 'Take for yourselves twelve stones from here, out of the midst of the Jordan, from the place where the priests' feet stood firm. You shall carry them over with you and leave them in the lodging place where you lodge tonight.'"

4Then Joshua called the twelve men whom he had appointed from the children of Israel, one man from every tribe; 5and Joshua said to them: "Cross over before the ark of the LORD your God into the midst of the Jordan, and each one of you take up a stone on his shoulder, according to the number of the tribes of the children of Israel, 6that this may be a sign among you when your children ask in time to come, saying, 'What do these stones *mean* to you?' 7Then you shall answer them that the waters of the Jordan were cut off before the ark of the covenant of the LORD; when it crossed over the Jordan, the waters of the Jordan

were cut off. And these stones
shall be for a memorial to the
children of Israel forever."

8And the children of Israel
did so, just as Joshua commanded, and took up twelve
stones from the midst of the
Jordan, as the LORD had spoken to Joshua, according to
the number of the tribes of the
children of Israel, and carried
them over with them to the
place where they lodged, and
laid them down there. 9Then
Joshua set up twelve stones
in the midst of the Jordan, in
the place where the feet of the
priests who bore the ark of the
covenant stood; and they are
there to this day.

10So the priests who bore
the ark stood in the midst of
the Jordan until everything
was finished that the LORD
had commanded Joshua to
speak to the people, according to all that Moses had
commanded Joshua; and the
people hurried and crossed
over. 11Then it came to pass,
when all the people had completely crossed over, that the
ark of the LORD and the priests
crossed over in the presence
of the people. 12And the men
of Reuben, the men of Gad,
and half the tribe of Manasseh
crossed over armed before the
children of Israel, as Moses
had spoken to them. 13About
forty thousand prepared for
war crossed over before the
LORD for battle, to the plains
of Jericho. 14On that day the
LORD exalted Joshua in the
sight of all Israel; and they
feared him, as they had feared
Moses, all the days of his life.

15Then the LORD spoke to
Joshua, saying, 16"Command
the priests who bear the ark
of the Testimony to come up
from the Jordan." 17Joshua
therefore commanded the
priests, saying, "Come up from
the Jordan." 18And it came to
pass, when the priests who
bore the ark of the covenant
of the LORD had come from
the midst of the Jordan, *and*
the soles of the priests' feet
touched the dry land, that the
waters of the Jordan returned
to their place and overflowed
all its banks as before.

19Now the people came up
from the Jordan on the tenth
day of the first month, and
they camped in Gilgal on the
east border of Jericho. 20And
those twelve stones which
they took out of the Jordan,
Joshua set up in Gilgal. 21Then
he spoke to the children of
Israel, saying: "When your
children ask their fathers in
time to come, saying, 'What
are these stones?' 22then you
shall let your children know,
saying, 'Israel crossed over
this Jordan on dry land'; 23for
the LORD your God dried up
the waters of the Jordan before you until you had crossed
over, as the LORD your God
did to the Red Sea, which He
dried up before us until we
had crossed over, 24that all

the peoples of the earth may
know the hand of the LORD,
that it *is* mighty, that you may
fear the LORD your God forever."

THE SECOND GENERATION CIRCUMCISED

5 So it was, when all the
kings of the Amorites who
were on the west side of the
Jordan, and all the kings of
the Canaanites who *were* by
the sea, heard that the LORD
had dried up the waters of the
Jordan from before the children of Israel until we[a] had
crossed over, that their heart
melted; and there was no spirit
in them any longer because of
the children of Israel.
2At that time the LORD said
to Joshua, "Make flint knives
for yourself, and circumcise
the sons of Israel again the
second time." 3So Joshua
made flint knives for himself,
and circumcised the sons of
Israel at the hill of the foreskins.[a] 4And this *is* the reason why Joshua circumcised
them: All the people who
came out of Egypt *who were*
males, all the men of war, had
died in the wilderness on the
way, after they had come out
of Egypt. 5For all the people
who came out had been circumcised, but all the people
born in the wilderness, on the
way as they came out of Egypt,
had not been circumcised.
6For the children of Israel
walked forty years in the wilderness, till all the people *who*
were men of war, who came
out of Egypt, were consumed,
because they did not obey the
voice of the LORD—to whom
the LORD swore that He would
not show them the land which
the LORD had sworn to their
fathers that He would give
us, "a land flowing with milk
and honey."[a] 7Then Joshua
circumcised their sons *whom*
He raised up in their place;
for they were uncircumcised,
because they had not been circumcised on the way.
8So it was, when they had
finished circumcising all the
people, that they stayed in
their places in the camp till
they were healed. 9Then the
LORD said to Joshua, "This
day I have rolled away the
reproach of Egypt from you."
Therefore the name of the
place is called Gilgal[a] to this
day.
10Now the children of Israel
camped in Gilgal, and kept the
Passover on the fourteenth
day of the month at twilight
on the plains of Jericho. 11And
they ate of the produce of the
land on the day after the Passover, unleavened bread and
parched grain, on the very

5:1 [a] Following Kethib; Qere, some Hebrew manuscripts and editions, Septuagint, Syriac, Targum, and Vulgate read *they.* 5:3 [a] Hebrew *Gibeath Haaraloth* 5:6 [a] Exodus 3:8 5:9 [a] Literally *Rolling*

same day. 12Then the manna
ceased on the day after they
had eaten the produce of the
land; and the children of Israel no longer had manna, but
they ate the food of the land
of Canaan that year.

THE COMMANDER OF THE ARMY OF THE LORD

13And it came to pass, when
Joshua was by Jericho, that he
lifted his eyes and looked, and
behold, a Man stood opposite
him with His sword drawn in
His hand. And Joshua went to
Him and said to Him, "*Are* You
for us or for our adversaries?"

14So He said, "No, but *as*
Commander of the army of
the LORD I have now come."

And Joshua fell on his face
to the earth and worshiped,
and said to Him, "What does
my Lord say to His servant?"

15Then the Commander
of the LORD's army said to
Joshua, "Take your sandal off
your foot, for the place where
you stand *is* holy." And Joshua
did so.

THE DESTRUCTION OF JERICHO

6 Now Jericho was securely
shut up because of the
children of Israel; none went
out, and none came in. 2And
the LORD said to Joshua: "See!
I have given Jericho into your
hand, its king, *and* the mighty
men of valor. 3You shall march
around the city, all *you* men of
war; you shall go all around
the city once. This you shall do
six days. 4And seven priests
shall bear seven trumpets of
rams' horns before the ark.
But the seventh day you shall
march around the city seven
times, and the priests shall
blow the trumpets. 5It shall
come to pass, when they make
a long *blast* with the ram's
horn, *and* when you hear the
sound of the trumpet, that all
the people shall shout with a
great shout; then the wall of
the city will fall down flat. And
the people shall go up every
man straight before him."

6Then Joshua the son of
Nun called the priests and
said to them, "Take up the ark
of the covenant, and let seven
priests bear seven trumpets of
rams' horns before the ark of
the LORD." 7And he said to the
people, "Proceed, and march
around the city, and let him
who is armed advance before
the ark of the LORD."

8So it was, when Joshua
had spoken to the people,
that the seven priests bearing the seven trumpets of
rams' horns before the LORD
advanced and blew the trumpets, and the ark of the covenant of the LORD followed
them. 9The armed men went
before the priests who blew
the trumpets, and the rear
guard came after the ark, while
the priests continued blowing
the trumpets. 10Now Joshua
had commanded the people,
saying, "You shall not shout

or make any noise with your voice, nor shall a word proceed out of your mouth, until the day I say to you, 'Shout!' Then you shall shout." [11]So he had the ark of the LORD circle the city, going around *it* once. Then they came into the camp and lodged in the camp.

[12]And Joshua rose early in the morning, and the priests took up the ark of the LORD. [13]Then seven priests bearing seven trumpets of rams' horns before the ark of the LORD went on continually and blew with the trumpets. And the armed men went before them. But the rear guard came after the ark of the LORD, while *the priests* continued blowing the trumpets. [14]And the second day they marched around the city once and returned to the camp. So they did six days.

[15]But it came to pass on the seventh day that they rose early, about the dawning of the day, and marched around the city seven times in the same manner. On that day only they marched around the city seven times. [16]And the seventh time it happened, when the priests blew the trumpets, that Joshua said to the people: "Shout, for the LORD has given you the city! [17]Now the city shall be doomed by the LORD to destruction, it and all who *are* in it. Only Rahab the harlot shall live, she and all who *are* with her in the house, because she hid the messengers that we sent. [18]And you, by all means abstain from the accursed things, lest you become accursed when you take of the accursed things, and make the camp of Israel a curse, and trouble it. [19]But all the silver and gold, and vessels of bronze and iron, *are* consecrated to the LORD; they shall come into the treasury of the LORD."

[20]So the people shouted when *the priests* blew the trumpets. And it happened when the people heard the sound of the trumpet, and the people shouted with a great shout, that the wall fell down flat. Then the people went up into the city, every man straight before him, and they took the city. [21]And they utterly destroyed all that *was* in the city, both man and woman, young and old, ox and sheep and donkey, with the edge of the sword.

[22]But Joshua had said to the two men who had spied out the country, "Go into the harlot's house, and from there bring out the woman and all that she has, as you swore to her." [23]And the young men who had been spies went in and brought out Rahab, her father, her mother, her brothers, and all that she had. So they brought out all her relatives and left them outside the camp of Israel. [24]But they burned the city and all that *was* in it with fire. Only

the silver and gold, and the
vessels of bronze and iron,
they put into the treasury of
the house of the LORD. 25And
Joshua spared Rahab the harlot, her father's household,
and all that she had. So she
dwells in Israel to this day, because she hid the messengers
whom Joshua sent to spy out
Jericho.

26Then Joshua charged
them at that time, saying,
"Cursed *be* the man before the
LORD who rises up and builds
this city Jericho; he shall lay
its foundation with his firstborn, and with his youngest
he shall set up its gates."

27So the LORD was with
Joshua, and his fame spread
throughout all the country.

DEFEAT AT AI

7 But the children of Israel
committed a trespass re-
garding the accursed things,
for Achan the son of Carmi,
the son of Zabdi,[a] the son of
Zerah, of the tribe of Judah,
took of the accursed things; so
the anger of the LORD burned
against the children of Israel.

2Now Joshua sent men
from Jericho to Ai, which *is*
beside Beth Aven, on the east
side of Bethel, and spoke to
them, saying, "Go up and spy
out the country." So the men
went up and spied out Ai.
3And they returned to Joshua
and said to him, "Do not let
all the people go up, but let
about two or three thousand
men go up and attack Ai. Do
not weary all the people there,
for *the people of Ai are* few."
4So about three thousand men
went up there from the people, but they fled before the
men of Ai. 5And the men of
Ai struck down about thirty-
six men, for they chased them
from before the gate as far as
Shebarim, and struck them
down on the descent; therefore the hearts of the people
melted and became like water.

6Then Joshua tore his
clothes, and fell to the earth
on his face before the ark of
the LORD until evening, he
and the elders of Israel; and
they put dust on their heads.
7And Joshua said, "Alas, Lord
GOD, why have You brought
this people over the Jordan
at all—to deliver us into the
hand of the Amorites, to
destroy us? Oh, that we had
been content, and dwelt on
the other side of the Jordan!
8O Lord, what shall I say when
Israel turns its back before its
enemies? 9For the Canaanites
and all the inhabitants of the
land will hear *it*, and surround
us, and cut off our name from
the earth. Then what will You
do for Your great name?"

THE SIN OF ACHAN

10So the LORD said to
Joshua: "Get up! Why do you

7:1 [a] Called *Zimri* in 1 Chronicles 2:6

lie thus on your face? [11]Israel
has sinned, and they have
also transgressed My cov-
enant which I commanded
them. For they have even
taken some of the accursed
things, and have both stolen
and deceived; and they have
also put *it* among their own
stuff. [12]Therefore the children
of Israel could not stand before their enemies, *but* turned
their backs before their enemies, because they have become doomed to destruction.
Neither will I be with you anymore, unless you destroy the
accursed from among you.
[13]Get up, sanctify the people,
and say, 'Sanctify yourselves
for tomorrow, because thus
says the LORD God of Israel:
"*There is* an accursed thing
in your midst, O Israel; you
cannot stand before your enemies until you take away the
accursed thing from among
you." [14]In the morning therefore you shall be brought according to your tribes. And it
shall be *that* the tribe which
the LORD takes shall come according to families; and the
family which the LORD takes
shall come by households;
and the household which
the LORD takes shall come
man by man. [15]Then it shall
be *that* he who is taken with
the accursed thing shall be
burned with fire, he and all
that he has, because he has
transgressed the covenant of
the LORD, and because he has
done a disgraceful thing in
Israel.'"

[16]So Joshua rose early in
the morning and brought Israel by their tribes, and the
tribe of Judah was taken. [17]He
brought the clan of Judah,
and he took the family of the
Zarhites; and he brought the
family of the Zarhites man
by man, and Zabdi was taken.
[18]Then he brought his household man by man, and Achan
the son of Carmi, the son of
Zabdi, the son of Zerah, of the
tribe of Judah, was taken.

[19]Now Joshua said to
Achan, "My son, I beg you,
give glory to the LORD God
of Israel, and make confession
to Him, and tell me now what
you have done; do not hide *it*
from me."

[20]And Achan answered
Joshua and said, "Indeed
I have sinned against the
LORD God of Israel, and this
is what I have done: [21]When I
saw among the spoils a beautiful Babylonian garment, two
hundred shekels of silver, and
a wedge of gold weighing fifty
shekels, I coveted them and
took them. And there they
are, hidden in the earth in the
midst of my tent, with the silver under it."

[22]So Joshua sent messengers, and they ran to the tent;
and there it was, hidden in his
tent, with the silver under it.
[23]And they took them from
the midst of the tent, brought
them to Joshua and to all the

children of Israel, and laid
them out before the LORD.
24Then Joshua, and all Israel
with him, took Achan the
son of Zerah, the silver, the
garment, the wedge of gold,
his sons, his daughters, his
oxen, his donkeys, his sheep,
his tent, and all that he had,
and they brought them to the
Valley of Achor. 25And Joshua
said, "Why have you troubled
us? The LORD will trouble you
this day." So all Israel stoned
him with stones; and they
burned them with fire after
they had stoned them with
stones.

26Then they raised over
him a great heap of stones,
still there to this day. So the
LORD turned from the fierceness of His anger. Therefore
the name of that place has
been called the Valley of
Achor[a] to this day.

THE FALL OF AI

8 Now the LORD said to
Joshua: "Do not be afraid,
nor be dismayed; take all the
people of war with you, and
arise, go up to Ai. See, I have
given into your hand the king
of Ai, his people, his city, and
his land. 2And you shall do to
Ai and its king as you did to
Jericho and its king. Only its
spoil and its cattle you shall
take as booty for yourselves.
Lay an ambush for the city
behind it."

3So Joshua arose, and all
the people of war, to go up
against Ai; and Joshua chose
thirty thousand mighty men
of valor and sent them away
by night. 4And he commanded
them, saying: "Behold, you
shall lie in ambush against the
city, behind the city. Do not go
very far from the city, but all
of you be ready. 5Then I and
all the people who *are* with
me will approach the city;
and it will come about, when
they come out against us as
at the first, that we shall flee
before them. 6For they will
come out after us till we have
drawn them from the city, for
they will say, '*They are* fleeing
before us as at the first.' Therefore we will flee before them.
7Then you shall rise from the
ambush and seize the city, for
the LORD your God will deliver it into your hand. 8And it
will be, when you have taken
the city, *that* you shall set the
city on fire. According to the
commandment of the LORD
you shall do. See, I have commanded you."

9Joshua therefore sent
them out; and they went to
lie in ambush, and stayed between Bethel and Ai, on the
west side of Ai; but Joshua
lodged that night among the
people. 10Then Joshua rose
up early in the morning and
mustered the people, and
went up, he and the elders of

7:26 [a] Literally *Trouble*

Israel, before the people to
Ai. 11And all the people of war
who *were* with him went up
and drew near; and they came
before the city and camped on
the north side of Ai. Now a valley *lay* between them and Ai.
12So he took about five thousand men and set them in
ambush between Bethel and
Ai, on the west side of the city.
13And when they had set the
people, all the army that *was*
on the north of the city, and its
rear guard on the west of the
city, Joshua went that night
into the midst of the valley.

14Now it happened, when
the king of Ai saw *it,* that
the men of the city hurried
and rose early and went out
against Israel to battle, he and
all his people, at an appointed
place before the plain. But he
did not know that *there was* an
ambush against him behind
the city. 15And Joshua and all
Israel made as if they were
beaten before them, and fled
by the way of the wilderness.
16So all the people who *were* in
Ai were called together to pursue them. And they pursued
Joshua and were drawn away
from the city. 17There was not
a man left in Ai or Bethel who
did not go out after Israel. So
they left the city open and
pursued Israel.

18Then the LORD said to
Joshua, "Stretch out the spear
that *is* in your hand toward
Ai, for I will give it into your
hand." And Joshua stretched
out the spear that *was* in his
hand toward the city. 19So
those in ambush arose quickly
out of their place; they ran as
soon as he had stretched out
his hand, and they entered the
city and took it, and hurried
to set the city on fire. 20And
when the men of Ai looked
behind them, they saw, and
behold, the smoke of the city
ascended to heaven. So they
had no power to flee this way
or that way, and the people
who had fled to the wilderness
turned back on the pursuers.

21Now when Joshua and all
Israel saw that the ambush
had taken the city and that the
smoke of the city ascended,
they turned back and struck
down the men of Ai. 22Then
the others came out of the city
against them; so they were
caught in the midst of Israel,
some on this side and some
on that side. And they struck
them down, so that they let
none of them remain or escape. 23But the king of Ai they
took alive, and brought him
to Joshua.

24And it came to pass when
Israel had made an end of
slaying all the inhabitants
of Ai in the field, in the wilderness where they pursued
them, and when they all had
fallen by the edge of the sword
until they were consumed,
that all the Israelites returned
to Ai and struck it with the
edge of the sword. 25So it was
that all who fell that day, both

men and women, *were* twelve
thousand—all the people of
Ai. 26For Joshua did not draw
back his hand, with which he
stretched out the spear, until
he had utterly destroyed all
the inhabitants of Ai. 27Only
the livestock and the spoil of
that city Israel took as booty
for themselves, according to
the word of the LORD which
He had commanded Joshua.
28So Joshua burned Ai and
made it a heap forever, a desolation to this day. 29And the
king of Ai he hanged on a tree
until evening. And as soon
as the sun was down, Joshua
commanded that they should
take his corpse down from the
tree, cast it at the entrance of
the gate of the city, and raise
over it a great heap of stones
that remains to this day.

JOSHUA RENEWS THE COVENANT

30Now Joshua built an altar
to the LORD God of Israel in
Mount Ebal, 31as Moses the
servant of the LORD had commanded the children of Israel,
as it is written in the Book of
the Law of Moses: "an altar
of whole stones over which
no man has wielded an iron
tool."[a] And they offered on it
burnt offerings to the LORD,
and sacrificed peace offerings.
32And there, in the presence
of the children of Israel, he
wrote on the stones a copy of
the law of Moses, which he had
written. 33Then all Israel, with
their elders and officers and
judges, stood on either side
of the ark before the priests,
the Levites, who bore the ark
of the covenant of the LORD,
the stranger as well as he who
was born among them. Half of
them *were* in front of Mount
Gerizim and half of them in
front of Mount Ebal, as Moses
the servant of the LORD had
commanded before, that they
should bless the people of Israel. 34And afterward he read
all the words of the law, the
blessings and the cursings,
according to all that is written in the Book of the Law.
35There was not a word of all
that Moses had commanded
which Joshua did not read
before all the assembly of Israel, with the women, the little
ones, and the strangers who
were living among them.

THE TREATY WITH THE GIBEONITES

9 And it came to pass when
all the kings who *were* on
this side of the Jordan, in the
hills and in the lowland and
in all the coasts of the Great
Sea toward Lebanon—the
Hittite, the Amorite, the Canaanite, the Perizzite, the Hivite, and the Jebusite—heard
about it, 2that they gathered
together to fight with Joshua
and Israel with one accord.

8:31 [a] Deuteronomy 27:5, 6

3But when the inhabitants
of Gibeon heard what Joshua
had done to Jericho and Ai,
4they worked craftily, and
went and pretended to be ambassadors. And they took old
sacks on their donkeys, old
wineskins torn and mended,
5old and patched sandals on
their feet, and old garments
on themselves; and all the
bread of their provision was
dry *and* moldy. 6And they
went to Joshua, to the camp
at Gilgal, and said to him and
to the men of Israel, "We have
come from a far country; now
therefore, make a covenant
with us."

7Then the men of Israel
said to the Hivites, "Perhaps
you dwell among us; so how
can we make a covenant with
you?"

8But they said to Joshua,
"We *are* your servants."

And Joshua said to them,
"Who *are* you, and where do
you come from?"

9So they said to him: "From
a very far country your servants have come, because of
the name of the LORD your
God; for we have heard of His
fame, and all that He did in
Egypt, 10and all that He did
to the two kings of the Amorites who *were* beyond the
Jordan—to Sihon king of
Heshbon, and Og king of Bashan, who was at Ashtaroth.
11Therefore our elders and
all the inhabitants of our
country spoke to us, saying,
'Take provisions with you for
the journey, and go to meet
them, and say to them, "We
are your servants; now therefore, make a covenant with
us."' 12This bread of ours we
took hot *for* our provision
from our houses on the day
we departed to come to you.
But now look, it is dry and
moldy. 13And these wineskins
which we filled *were* new, and
see, they are torn; and these
our garments and our sandals
have become old because of
the very long journey."

14Then the men of Israel
took some of their provisions;
but they did not ask counsel
of the LORD. 15So Joshua made
peace with them, and made
a covenant with them to let
them live; and the rulers of
the congregation swore to
them.

16And it happened at the
end of three days, after they
had made a covenant with
them, that they heard that
they *were* their neighbors who
dwelt near them. 17Then the
children of Israel journeyed
and came to their cities on
the third day. Now their cities *were* Gibeon, Chephirah,
Beeroth, and Kirjath Jearim.
18But the children of Israel did
not attack them, because the
rulers of the congregation had
sworn to them by the LORD
God of Israel. And all the congregation complained against
the rulers.

19Then all the rulers said

to all the congregation, "We have sworn to them by the LORD God of Israel; now therefore, we may not touch them. 20This we will do to them: We will let them live, lest wrath be upon us because of the oath which we swore to them." 21And the rulers said to them, "Let them live, but let them be woodcutters and water carriers for all the congregation, as the rulers had promised them."

22Then Joshua called for them, and he spoke to them, saying, "Why have you deceived us, saying, 'We *are* very far from you,' when you dwell near us? 23Now therefore, you *are* cursed, and none of you shall be freed from being slaves—woodcutters and water carriers for the house of my God."

24So they answered Joshua and said, "Because your servants were clearly told that the LORD your God commanded His servant Moses to give you all the land, and to destroy all the inhabitants of the land from before you; therefore we were very much afraid for our lives because of you, and have done this thing. 25And now, here we are, in your hands; do with us as it seems good and right to do to us." 26So he did to them, and delivered them out of the hand of the children of Israel, so that they did not kill them. 27And that day Joshua made them woodcutters and water carriers for the congregation and for the altar of the LORD, in the place which He would choose, even to this day.

THE SUN STANDS STILL

10 Now it came to pass when Adoni-Zedek king of Jerusalem heard how Joshua had taken Ai and had utterly destroyed it—as he had done to Jericho and its king, so he had done to Ai and its king—and how the inhabitants of Gibeon had made peace with Israel and were among them, 2that they feared greatly, because Gibeon *was* a great city, like one of the royal cities, and because it *was* greater than Ai, and all its men *were* mighty. 3Therefore Adoni-Zedek king of Jerusalem sent to Hoham king of Hebron, Piram king of Jarmuth, Japhia king of Lachish, and Debir king of Eglon, saying, 4"Come up to me and help me, that we may attack Gibeon, for it has made peace with Joshua and with the children of Israel." 5Therefore the five kings of the Amorites, the king of Jerusalem, the king of Hebron, the king of Jarmuth, the king of Lachish, *and* the king of Eglon, gathered together and went up, they and all their armies, and camped before Gibeon and made war against it.

6And the men of Gibeon sent to Joshua at the camp at Gilgal, saying, "Do not forsake

your servants; come up to us
quickly, save us and help us,
for all the kings of the Amorites who dwell in the mountains have gathered together
against us."
7So Joshua ascended from
Gilgal, he and all the people
of war with him, and all the
mighty men of valor. 8And
the LORD said to Joshua, "Do
not fear them, for I have delivered them into your hand;
not a man of them shall stand
before you." 9Joshua therefore
came upon them suddenly,
having marched all night from
Gilgal. 10So the LORD routed
them before Israel, killed them
with a great slaughter at Gibeon, chased them along the
road that goes to Beth Horon,
and struck them down as far as
Azekah and Makkedah. 11And it
happened, as they fled before
Israel *and* were on the descent
of Beth Horon, that the LORD
cast down large hailstones
from heaven on them as far
as Azekah, and they died. *There
were* more who died from the
hailstones than the children
of Israel killed with the sword.
12Then Joshua spoke to
the LORD in the day when the
LORD delivered up the Am-
orites before the children of
Israel, and he said in the sight
of Israel:

"Sun, stand still
over Gibeon;
And Moon, in the
Valley of Aijalon."

13 So the sun stood still,
And the moon stopped,
Till the people
had revenge
Upon their enemies.

Is this not written in the Book
of Jasher? So the sun stood still
in the midst of heaven, and
did not hasten to go *down* for
about a whole day. 14And there
has been no day like that, before it or after it, that the LORD
heeded the voice of a man; for
the LORD fought for Israel.
15Then Joshua returned,
and all Israel with him, to the
camp at Gilgal.

THE AMORITE KINGS EXECUTED

16But these five kings had
fled and hidden themselves in
a cave at Makkedah. 17And it
was told Joshua, saying, "The
five kings have been found hidden in the cave at Makkedah."
18So Joshua said, "Roll large
stones against the mouth of
the cave, and set men by it to
guard them. 19And do not stay
there yourselves, *but* pursue
your enemies, and attack their
rear *guard.* Do not allow them
to enter their cities, for the
LORD your God has delivered
them into your hand." 20Then
it happened, while Joshua and
the children of Israel made
an end of slaying them with
a very great slaughter, till
they had finished, that those
who escaped entered fortified
cities. 21And all the people

returned to the camp, to
Joshua at Makkedah, in peace.
No one moved his tongue
against any of the children of
Israel.
22Then Joshua said, "Open
the mouth of the cave, and
bring out those five kings to
me from the cave." 23And they
did so, and brought out those
five kings to him from the
cave: the king of Jerusalem,
the king of Hebron, the king of
Jarmuth, the king of Lachish,
and the king of Eglon.
24So it was, when they
brought out those kings to
Joshua, that Joshua called for
all the men of Israel, and said
to the captains of the men
of war who went with him,
"Come near, put your feet on
the necks of these kings." And
they drew near and put their
feet on their necks. 25Then
Joshua said to them, "Do not
be afraid, nor be dismayed; be
strong and of good courage,
for thus the LORD will do to all
your enemies against whom
you fight." 26And afterward
Joshua struck them and killed
them, and hanged them on
five trees; and they were hanging on the trees until evening.
27So it was at the time of the
going down of the sun *that*
Joshua commanded, and they
took them down from the
trees, cast them into the cave
where they had been hidden,
and laid large stones against
the cave's mouth, *which re-*
main until this very day.

CONQUEST OF THE SOUTHLAND

28On that day Joshua took
Makkedah, and struck it and
its king with the edge of the
sword. He utterly destroyed
them[a]—all the people who
were in it. He let none remain.
He also did to the king of Makkedah as he had done to the
king of Jericho.
29Then Joshua passed
from Makkedah, and all Israel with him, to Libnah; and
they fought against Libnah.
30And the LORD also delivered
it and its king into the hand
of Israel; he struck it and all
the people who *were* in it with
the edge of the sword. He let
none remain in it, but did to
its king as he had done to the
king of Jericho.
31Then Joshua passed from
Libnah, and all Israel with
him, to Lachish; and they encamped against it and fought
against it. 32And the LORD delivered Lachish into the hand
of Israel, who took it on the
second day, and struck it and
all the people who *were* in it
with the edge of the sword, according to all that he had done
to Libnah. 33Then Horam king

10:28 [a] Following Masoretic Text and most authorities; many Hebrew manuscripts, some manuscripts of the Septuagint, and some manuscripts of the Targum read *it*.

of Gezer came up to help Lachish; and Joshua struck him
and his people, until he left
him none remaining.
[34]From Lachish Joshua
passed to Eglon, and all Israel
with him; and they encamped
against it and fought against
it. [35]They took it on that day
and struck it with the edge of
the sword; all the people who
were in it he utterly destroyed
that day, according to all that
he had done to Lachish.
[36]So Joshua went up from
Eglon, and all Israel with him,
to Hebron; and they fought
against it. [37]And they took it
and struck it with the edge
of the sword—its king, all
its cities, and all the people
who *were* in it; he left none
remaining, according to all
that he had done to Eglon, but
utterly destroyed it and all the
people who *were* in it.
[38]Then Joshua returned,
and all Israel with him, to
Debir; and they fought against
it. [39]And he took it and its king
and all its cities; they struck
them with the edge of the
sword and utterly destroyed
all the people who *were* in it.
He left none remaining; as he
had done to Hebron, so he did
to Debir and its king, as he
had done also to Libnah and
its king.
[40]So Joshua conquered
all the land: the mountain
country and the South[a] and
the lowland and the wilderness slopes, and all their kings;
he left none remaining, but
utterly destroyed all that
breathed, as the LORD God of
Israel had commanded. [41]And
Joshua conquered them from
Kadesh Barnea as far as Gaza,
and all the country of Goshen, even as far as Gibeon.
[42]All these kings and their
land Joshua took at one time,
because the LORD God of Israel fought for Israel. [43]Then
Joshua returned, and all Israel
with him, to the camp at Gilgal.

THE NORTHERN CONQUEST

11 And it came to pass, when
Jabin king of Hazor heard
these things, that he sent to
Jobab king of Madon, to the
king of Shimron, to the king
of Achshaph, [2]and to the kings
who *were* from the north, in
the mountains, in the plain
south of Chinneroth, in the
lowland, and in the heights
of Dor on the west, [3]to the
Canaanites in the east and
in the west, the Amorite, the
Hittite, the Perizzite, the Jebusite in the mountains, and
the Hivite below Hermon in
the land of Mizpah. [4]So they
went out, they and all their
armies with them, *as* many
people *as* the sand that *is* on
the seashore in multitude,
with very many horses and
chariots. [5]And when all these

10:40 [a] Hebrew *Negev*, and so throughout this book

kings had met together, they
came and camped together at
the waters of Merom to fight
against Israel.
6But the LORD said to
Joshua, "Do not be afraid because of them, for tomorrow
about this time I will deliver
all of them slain before Israel. You shall hamstring their
horses and burn their chariots
with fire." 7So Joshua and all
the people of war with him
came against them suddenly
by the waters of Merom, and
they attacked them. 8And the
LORD delivered them into the
hand of Israel, who defeated
them and chased them to
Greater Sidon, to the Brook
Misrephoth,[a] and to the Valley of Mizpah eastward; they
attacked them until they left
none of them remaining.
9So Joshua did to them as
the LORD had told him: he
hamstrung their horses and
burned their chariots with
fire.
10Joshua turned back at
that time and took Hazor, and
struck its king with the sword;
for Hazor was formerly the
head of all those kingdoms.
11And they struck all the people who *were* in it with the
edge of the sword, utterly
destroying *them.* There was
none left breathing. Then he
burned Hazor with fire.
12So all the cities of those
kings, and all their kings,
Joshua took and struck with
the edge of the sword. He utterly destroyed them, as Moses
the servant of the LORD had
commanded. 13But *as for*
the cities that stood on their
mounds,[a] Israel burned none
of them, except Hazor only,
which Joshua burned. 14And all
the spoil of these cities and the
livestock, the children of Israel
took as booty for themselves;
but they struck every man with
the edge of the sword until they
had destroyed them, and they
left none breathing. 15As the
LORD had commanded Moses
His servant, so Moses commanded Joshua, and so Joshua
did. He left nothing undone
of all that the LORD had commanded Moses.

SUMMARY OF JOSHUA'S CONQUESTS

16Thus Joshua took all this
land: the mountain country,
all the South, all the land of
Goshen, the lowland, and the
Jordan plain[a]—the moun-
tains of Israel and its lowlands, 17from Mount Halak
and the ascent to Seir, even
as far as Baal Gad in the Valley of Lebanon below Mount
Hermon. He captured all their
kings, and struck them down
and killed them. 18Joshua
made war a long time with
all those kings. 19There was

11:8 [a] Hebrew *Misrephoth Maim* 11:13 [a] Hebrew *tel,* a heap of successive city ruins 11:16 [a] Hebrew *arabah*

not a city that made peace
with the children of Israel,
except the Hivites, the inhabitants of Gibeon. All *the others* they took in battle. 20For
it was of the LORD to harden
their hearts, that they should
come against Israel in battle,
that He might utterly destroy
them, *and* that they might
receive no mercy, but that
He might destroy them, as
the LORD had commanded
Moses.

21And at that time Joshua
came and cut off the Anakim
from the mountains: from
Hebron, from Debir, from
Anab, from all the mountains
of Judah, and from all the
mountains of Israel; Joshua
utterly destroyed them with
their cities. 22None of the
Anakim were left in the land
of the children of Israel; they
remained only in Gaza, in
Gath, and in Ashdod.

23So Joshua took the whole
land, according to all that the
LORD had said to Moses; and
Joshua gave it as an inheritance to Israel according to
their divisions by their tribes.
Then the land rested from
war.

THE KINGS CONQUERED BY MOSES

12 These *are* the kings of
the land whom the chil-
dren of Israel defeated, and
whose land they possessed
on the other side of the Jordan toward the rising of the
sun, from the River Arnon
to Mount Hermon, and all
the eastern Jordan plain:
2*One king was* Sihon king of
the Amorites, who dwelt in
Heshbon *and* ruled half of Gilead, from Aroer, which is on
the bank of the River Arnon,
from the middle of that river,
even as far as the River Jabbok, *which is* the border of the
Ammonites, 3and the eastern
Jordan plain from the Sea of
Chinneroth as far as the Sea
of the Arabah (the Salt Sea),
the road to Beth Jeshimoth,
and southward below the
slopes of Pisgah. 4*The other
king was* Og king of Bashan
and his territory, *who was* of
the remnant of the giants,
who dwelt at Ashtaroth and
at Edrei, 5and reigned over
Mount Hermon, over Salcah,
over all Bashan, as far as the
border of the Geshurites and
the Maachathites, and over
half of Gilead *to* the border of
Sihon king of Heshbon.

6These Moses the servant
of the LORD and the children
of Israel had conquered; and
Moses the servant of the LORD
had given it *as* a possession to
the Reubenites, the Gadites,
and half the tribe of Manasseh.

THE KINGS CONQUERED BY JOSHUA

7And these *are* the kings
of the country which Joshua
and the children of Israel
conquered on this side of the

Jordan, on the west, from Baal
Gad in the Valley of Lebanon
as far as Mount Halak and the
ascent to Seir, which Joshua
gave to the tribes of Israel *as* a
possession according to their
divisions, [8]in the mountain
country, in the lowlands, in
the *Jordan* plain, in the slopes,
in the wilderness, and in the
South—the Hittites, the Amorites, the Canaanites, the Perizzites, the Hivites, and the
Jebusites: [9]the king of Jericho,
one; the king of Ai, which *is*
beside Bethel, one; [10]the king
of Jerusalem, one; the king
of Hebron, one; [11]the king of
Jarmuth, one; the king of Lachish, one; [12]the king of Eglon,
one; the king of Gezer, one;
[13]the king of Debir, one; the
king of Geder, one; [14]the king
of Hormah, one; the king of
Arad, one; [15]the king of Libnah, one; the king of Adullam,
one; [16]the king of Makkedah,
one; the king of Bethel, one;
[17]the king of Tappuah, one;
the king of Hepher, one;
[18]the king of Aphek, one; the
king of Lasharon, one; [19]the
king of Madon, one; the king
of Hazor, one; [20]the king of
Shimron Meron, one; the king
of Achshaph, one; [21]the king
of Taanach, one; the king of
Megiddo, one; [22]the king of
Kedesh, one; the king of Jokneam in Carmel, one; [23]the
king of Dor in the heights
of Dor, one; the king of the
people of Gilgal, one; [24]the
king of Tirzah, one—all the
kings, thirty-one.

REMAINING LAND TO BE CONQUERED

13 Now Joshua was old, advanced in years. And the
LORD said to him: "You are
old, advanced in years, and
there remains very much land
yet to be possessed. [2]This is
the land that yet remains: all
the territory of the Philistines
and all *that of* the Geshurites,
[3]from Sihor, which *is* east of
Egypt, as far as the border of
Ekron northward (*which* is
counted as Canaanite); the
five lords of the Philistines—
the Gazites, the Ashdodites,
the Ashkelonites, the Gittites,
and the Ekronites; also the
Avites; [4]from the south, all the
land of the Canaanites, and
Mearah that belongs to the
Sidonians as far as Aphek, to
the border of the Amorites;
[5]the land of the Gebalites,[a]
and all Lebanon, toward the
sunrise, from Baal Gad below
Mount Hermon as far as the
entrance to Hamath; [6]all the
inhabitants of the mountains
from Lebanon as far as the
Brook Misrephoth,[a] *and* all
the Sidonians—them I will
drive out from before the children of Israel; only divide it
by lot to Israel as an inheritance, as I have commanded
you. [7]Now therefore, divide

13:5 [a] Or *Giblites* 13:6 [a] Hebrew *Misrephoth Maim*

this land as an inheritance to
the nine tribes and half the
tribe of Manasseh."

THE LAND DIVIDED EAST OF THE JORDAN

8With the other half-tribe
the Reubenites and the Gadites received their inheritance,
which Moses had given them,
beyond the Jordan eastward, as
Moses the servant of the LORD
had given them: 9from Aroer
which *is* on the bank of the
River Arnon, and the town that
is in the midst of the ravine,
and all the plain of Medeba as
far as Dibon; 10all the cities of
Sihon king of the Amorites,
who reigned in Heshbon, as far
as the border of the children
of Ammon; 11Gilead, and the
border of the Geshurites and
Maachathites, all Mount Hermon, and all Bashan as far as
Salcah; 12all the kingdom of
Og in Bashan, who reigned in
Ashtaroth and Edrei, who remained of the remnant of the
giants; for Moses had defeated
and cast out these.

13Nevertheless the children
of Israel did not drive out
the Geshurites or the Maachathites, but the Geshurites
and the Maachathites dwell
among the Israelites until this
day.

14Only to the tribe of Levi
he had given no inheritance;
the sacrifices of the LORD
God of Israel made by fire *are*
their inheritance, as He said
to them.

THE LAND OF REUBEN

15And Moses had given to
the tribe of the children of
Reuben *an inheritance* according to their families. 16Their
territory was from Aroer,
which *is* on the bank of the
River Arnon, and the city that
is in the midst of the ravine,
and all the plain by Medeba;
17Heshbon and all its cities
that *are* in the plain: Dibon,
Bamoth Baal, Beth Baal Meon,
18Jahaza, Kedemoth, Meph-
aath, 19Kirjathaim, Sibmah,
Zereth Shahar on the mountain of the valley, 20Beth Peor,
the slopes of Pisgah, and Beth
Jeshimoth— 21all the cities of
the plain and all the kingdom
of Sihon king of the Amorites,
who reigned in Heshbon,
whom Moses had struck with
the princes of Midian: Evi,
Rekem, Zur, Hur, and Reba,
who *were* princes of Sihon
dwelling in the country. 22The
children of Israel also killed
with the sword Balaam the
son of Beor, the soothsayer,
among those who were killed
by them. 23And the border of
the children of Reuben was
the bank of the Jordan. This
was the inheritance of the
children of Reuben according
to their families, the cities and
their villages.

THE LAND OF GAD

24Moses also had given *an
inheritance* to the tribe of Gad,
to the children of Gad according to their families. 25Their

territory was Jazer, and all the cities of Gilead, and half the land of the Ammonites as far as Aroer, which *is* before Rabbah, 26and from Heshbon to Ramath Mizpah and Betonim, and from Mahanaim to the border of Debir, 27and in the valley Beth Haram, Beth Nimrah, Succoth, and Zaphon, the rest of the kingdom of Sihon king of Heshbon, with the Jordan as *its* border, as far as the edge of the Sea of Chinnereth, on the other side of the Jordan eastward. 28This *is* the inheritance of the children of Gad according to their families, the cities and their villages.

HALF THE TRIBE OF MANASSEH (EAST)

29Moses also had given *an inheritance* to half the tribe of Manasseh; it was for half the tribe of the children of Manasseh according to their families: 30Their territory was from Mahanaim, all Bashan, all the kingdom of Og king of Bashan, and all the towns of Jair which are in Bashan, sixty cities; 31half of Gilead, and Ashtaroth and Edrei, cities of the kingdom of Og in Bashan, *were* for the children of Machir the son of Manasseh, for half of the children of Machir according to their families.

32These *are the areas* which Moses had distributed as an inheritance in the plains of Moab on the other side of the Jordan, by Jericho eastward. 33But to the tribe of Levi Moses had given no inheritance; the LORD God of Israel *was* their inheritance, as He had said to them.

THE LAND DIVIDED WEST OF THE JORDAN

14 These *are the areas* which the children of Israel inherited in the land of Canaan, which Eleazar the priest, Joshua the son of Nun, and the heads of the fathers of the tribes of the children of Israel distributed as an inheritance to them. 2Their inheritance *was* by lot, as the LORD had commanded by the hand of Moses, for the nine tribes and the half-tribe. 3For Moses had given the inheritance of the two tribes and the half-tribe on the other side of the Jordan; but to the Levites he had given no inheritance among them. 4For the children of Joseph were two tribes: Manasseh and Ephraim. And they gave no part to the Levites in the land, except cities to dwell *in,* with their commonlands for their livestock and their property. 5As the LORD had commanded Moses, so the children of Israel did; and they divided the land.

CALEB INHERITS HEBRON

6Then the children of Judah came to Joshua in Gilgal. And Caleb the son of Jephunneh the Kenizzite said

to him: "You know the word which the LORD said to Moses the man of God concerning you and me in Kadesh Barnea. 7I *was* forty years old when Moses the servant of the LORD sent me from Kadesh Barnea to spy out the land, and I brought back word to him as *it was* in my heart. 8Nevertheless my brethren who went up with me made the heart of the people melt, but I wholly followed the LORD my God. 9So Moses swore on that day, saying, 'Surely the land where your foot has trodden shall be your inheritance and your children's forever, because you have wholly followed the LORD my God.' 10And now, behold, the LORD has kept me alive, as He said, these forty-five years, ever since the LORD spoke this word to Moses while Israel wandered in the wilderness; and now, here I am this day, eighty-five years old. 11As yet I *am as* strong this day as on the day that Moses sent me; just as my strength *was* then, so now *is* my strength for war, both for going out and for coming in. 12Now therefore, give me this mountain of *which the* LORD spoke in that day; for you heard in that day how the Anakim *were* there, and *that* the cities *were* great *and* fortified. It may be that the LORD *will be* with me, and I shall be able to drive them out as the LORD said."

13And Joshua blessed him, and gave Hebron to Caleb the son of Jephunneh as an inheritance. 14Hebron therefore became the inheritance of Caleb the son of Jephunneh the Kenizzite to this day, because he wholly followed the LORD God of Israel. 15And the name of Hebron formerly was Kirjath Arba (*Arba was* the greatest man among the Anakim).

Then the land had rest from war.

THE LAND OF JUDAH

15 So *this* was the lot of the tribe of the children of Judah according to their families:

The border of Edom at the Wilderness of Zin southward *was* the extreme southern boundary. 2And their southern border began at the shore of the Salt Sea, from the bay that faces southward. 3Then it went out to the southern side of the Ascent of Akrabbim, passed along to Zin, ascended on the south side of Kadesh Barnea, passed along to Hezron, went up to Adar, and went around to Karkaa. 4*From there* it passed toward Azmon and went out to the Brook of Egypt; and the border ended at the sea. This shall be your southern border.

5The east border *was* the Salt Sea as far as the mouth of the Jordan.

And the border on the northern quarter *began* at the

bay of the sea at the mouth of
the Jordan. [6]The border went
up to Beth Hoglah and passed
north of Beth Arabah; and the
border went up to the stone
of Bohan the son of Reuben.
[7]Then the border went up toward Debir from the Valley of
Achor, and it turned northward toward Gilgal, which *is*
before the Ascent of Adummim, which *is* on the south
side of the valley. The border
continued toward the waters
of En Shemesh and ended at
En Rogel. [8]And the border
went up by the Valley of the
Son of Hinnom to the southern slope of the Jebusite *city*
(which *is* Jerusalem). The
border went up to the top of
the mountain that *lies* before
the Valley of Hinnom westward, which *is* at the end of
the Valley of Rephaim[a] northward. [9]Then the border went
around from the top of the hill
to the fountain of the water of
Nephtoah, and extended to
the cities of Mount Ephron.
And the border went around
to Baalah (which *is* Kirjath
Jearim). [10]Then the border
turned westward from Baalah
to Mount Seir, passed along to
the side of Mount Jearim on
the north (which *is* Chesalon),
went down to Beth Shemesh,
and passed on to Timnah.
[11]And the border went out to
the side of Ekron northward.
Then the border went around
to Shicron, passed along to
Mount Baalah, and extended
to Jabneel; and the border
ended at the sea.

[12]The west border *was* the
coastline of the Great Sea.
This *is* the boundary of the
children of Judah all around
according to their families.

CALEB OCCUPIES HEBRON AND DEBIR

[13]Now to Caleb the son of
Jephunneh he gave a share
among the children of Judah,
according to the command-
ment of the LORD to Joshua,
namely, Kirjath Arba, which *is*
Hebron (*Arba was* the father
of Anak). [14]Caleb drove out the
three sons of Anak from there:
Sheshai, Ahiman, and Talmai,
the children of Anak. [15]Then
he went up from there to the
inhabitants of Debir (formerly
the name of Debir *was* Kirjath
Sepher).

[16]And Caleb said, "He who
attacks Kirjath Sepher and
takes it, to him I will give
Achsah my daughter as wife."
[17]So Othniel the son of Kenaz,
the brother of Caleb, took it;
and he gave him Achsah his
daughter as wife. [18]Now it was
so, when she came *to him,* that
she persuaded him to ask her
father for a field. So she dismounted from *her* donkey,
and Caleb said to her, "What
do you wish?" [19]She answered,
"Give me a blessing; since you

15:8 [a] Literally *Giants*

have given me land in the
South, give me also springs
of water." So he gave her the
upper springs and the lower
springs.

THE CITIES OF JUDAH

20This *was* the inheritance
of the tribe of the children of
Judah according to their families:
21The cities at the limits
of the tribe of the children
of Judah, toward the border
of Edom in the South, were
Kabzeel, Eder, Jagur, 22Kinah,
Dimonah, Adadah, 23Kedesh,
Hazor, Ithnan, 24Ziph, Telem,
Bealoth, 25Hazor, Hadattah, Kerioth, Hezron (which *is* Hazor),
26Amam, Shema, Moladah,
27Hazar Gaddah, Heshmon,
Beth Pelet, 28Hazar Shual, Beersheba, Bizjothjah, 29Baalah,
Ijim, Ezem, 30Eltolad, Chesil,
Hormah, 31Ziklag, Madman-
nah, Sansannah, 32Lebaoth,
Shilhim, Ain, and Rimmon:
all the cities *are* twenty-nine,
with their villages.
33In the lowland: Eshtaol,
Zorah, Ashnah, 34Zanoah, En
Gannim, Tappuah, Enam,
35Jarmuth, Adullam, Socoh,
Azekah, 36Sharaim, Adithaim,
Gederah, and Gederothaim:
fourteen cities with their villages; 37Zenan, Hadashah,
Migdal Gad, 38Dilean, Mizpah, Joktheel, 39Lachish,
Bozkath, Eglon, 40Cabbon,
Lahmas,[a] Kithlish, 41Gede-
roth, Beth Dagon, Naamah,
and Makkedah: sixteen cities
with their villages; 42Libnah,
Ether, Ashan, 43Jiphtah, Ashnah, Nezib, 44Keilah, Achzib,
and Mareshah: nine cities
with their villages; 45Ekron,
with its towns and villages;
46from Ekron to the sea, all
that *lay* near Ashdod, with
their villages; 47Ashdod with
its towns and villages, Gaza
with its towns and villages—as
far as the Brook of Egypt and
the Great Sea with *its* coastline.
48And in the mountain
country: Shamir, Jattir, Sochoh, 49Dannah, Kirjath San-
nah (which *is* Debir), 50Anab,
Eshtemoh, Anim, 51Goshen,
Holon, and Giloh: eleven cities with their villages; 52Arab,
Dumah, Eshean, 53Janum, Beth
Tappuah, Aphekah, 54Humtah,
Kirjath Arba (which *is* Hebron),
and Zior: nine cities with their
villages; 55Maon, Carmel, Ziph,
Juttah, 56Jezreel, Jokdeam,
Zanoah, 57Kain, Gibeah, and
Timnah: ten cities with their
villages; 58Halhul, Beth Zur,
Gedor, 59Maarath, Beth Anoth,
and Eltekon: six cities with
their villages; 60Kirjath Baal
(which *is* Kirjath Jearim) and
Rabbah: two cities with their
villages.
61In the wilderness: Beth
Arabah, Middin, Secacah,
62Nibshan, the City of Salt,
and En Gedi: six cities with
their villages.

15:40 [a] Or *Lahmam*

63As for the Jebusites, the
inhabitants of Jerusalem, the
children of Judah could not
drive them out; but the Jebusites dwell with the children
of Judah at Jerusalem to this
day.

EPHRAIM AND WEST MANASSEH

16 The lot fell to the children of Joseph from
the Jordan, by Jericho, to the
waters of Jericho on the east,
to the wilderness that goes
up from Jericho through the
mountains to Bethel, 2then
went out from Bethel to Luz,[a]
passed along to the border of
the Archites at Ataroth, 3and
went down westward to the
boundary of the Japhletites,
as far as the boundary of
Lower Beth Horon to Gezer;
and it ended at the sea.
4So the children of Joseph,
Manasseh and Ephraim, took
their inheritance.

THE LAND OF EPHRAIM

5The border of the children
of Ephraim, according to their
families, was *thus:* The border of their inheritance on the
east side was Ataroth Addar
as far as Upper Beth Horon.
6And the border went out
toward the sea on the north
side of Michmethath; then the
border went around eastward
to Taanath Shiloh, and passed
by it on the east of Janohah.
7Then it went down from
Janohah to Ataroth and Naarah,[a] reached to Jericho, and
came out at the Jordan.
8The border went out from
Tappuah westward to the
Brook Kanah, and it ended
at the sea. This *was* the inheritance of the tribe of the
children of Ephraim according to their families. 9The separate cities for the children
of Ephraim *were* among the
inheritance of the children of
Manasseh, all the cities with
their villages.
10And they did not drive
out the Canaanites who dwelt
in Gezer; but the Canaanites
dwell among the Ephraimites
to this day and have become
forced laborers.

THE OTHER HALF-TRIBE OF MANASSEH (WEST)

17 There was also a lot for
the tribe of Manasseh,
for he *was* the firstborn of
Joseph: *namely* for Machir
the firstborn of Manasseh,
the father of Gilead, because
he was a man of war; therefore he was given Gilead and
Bashan. 2And there was *a lot*
for the rest of the children of
Manasseh according to their
families: for the children
of Abiezer,[a] the children of
Helek, the children of Asriel,
the children of Shechem, the

16:2 [a] Septuagint reads *Bethel* (that is, Luz). 16:7 [a] Or *Naaran* (compare 1 Chronicles 7:28) 17:2 [a] Called *Jeezer* in Numbers 26:30

children of Hepher, and the
children of Shemida; these
were the male children of
Manasseh the son of Joseph
according to their families.
3But Zelophehad the son of
Hepher, the son of Gilead, the
son of Machir, the son of Manasseh, had no sons, but only
daughters. And these *are* the
names of his daughters: Mahlah, Noah, Hoglah, Milcah, and
Tirzah. 4And they came near
before Eleazar the priest, before Joshua the son of Nun,
and before the rulers, saying, "The LORD commanded
Moses to give us an inheritance among our brothers."
Therefore, according to the
commandment of the LORD,
he gave them an inheritance
among their father's brothers.
5Ten shares fell to Manasseh,
besides the land of Gilead and
Bashan, which *were* on the
other side of the Jordan, 6be-
cause the daughters of Manasseh received an inheritance
among his sons; and the rest
of Manasseh's sons had the
land of Gilead.
7And the territory of Ma-
nasseh was from Asher to
Michmethath, that *lies* east of
Shechem; and the border went
along south to the inhabitants
of En Tappuah. 8Manasseh had
the land of Tappuah, but Tappuah on the border of Manasseh *belonged* to the children of
Ephraim. 9And the border descended to the Brook Kanah,
southward to the brook. These
cities of Ephraim *are* among
the cities of Manasseh. The
border of Manasseh *was* on
the north side of the brook;
and it ended at the sea.
10Southward *it was* Ephraim's, northward *it was* Manasseh's, and the sea was its
border. Manasseh's territory
was adjoining Asher on the
north and Issachar on the
east. 11And in Issachar and
in Asher, Manasseh had Beth
Shean and its towns, Ibleam
and its towns, the inhab-
itants of Dor and its towns,
the inhabitants of En Dor and
its towns, the inhabitants of
Taanach and its towns, and
the inhabitants of Megiddo
and its towns—three hilly
regions. 12Yet the children of
Manasseh could not drive out
the inhabitants of those cities,
but the Canaanites were determined to dwell in that land.
13And it happened, when the
children of Israel grew strong,
that they put the Canaanites
to forced labor, but did not
utterly drive them out.

MORE LAND FOR EPHRAIM AND MANASSEH

14Then the children of Joseph spoke to Joshua, saying,
"Why have you given us *only*
one lot and one share to inherit, since we *are* a great people, inasmuch as the LORD has
blessed us until now?"
15So Joshua answered them,
"If you *are* a great people, *then*
go up to the forest *country*

and clear a place for yourself
there in the land of the Perizzites and the giants, since the
mountains of Ephraim are too
confined for you."
16But the children of Jo-
seph said, "The mountain
country is not enough for us;
and all the Canaanites who
dwell in the land of the valley have chariots of iron, *both*
those who *are* of Beth Shean
and its towns and *those* who
are of the Valley of Jezreel."
17And Joshua spoke to the
house of Joseph—to Ephraim
and Manasseh—saying, "You
are a great people and have
great power; you shall not
have *only* one lot, 18but the
mountain country shall be
yours. Although it *is* wooded,
you shall cut it down, and its
farthest extent shall be yours;
for you shall drive out the Canaanites, though they have
iron chariots *and* are strong."

THE REMAINDER OF THE LAND DIVIDED

18 Now the whole congre-
gation of the children of
Israel assembled together at
Shiloh, and set up the tabernacle of meeting there. And
the land was subdued before
them. 2But there remained
among the children of Israel
seven tribes which had not
yet received their inheritance.
3Then Joshua said to the
children of Israel: "How long
will you neglect to go and possess the land which the LORD
God of your fathers has given
you? 4Pick out from among
you three men for *each* tribe,
and I will send them; they shall
rise and go through the land,
survey it according to their inheritance, and come *back* to
me. 5And they shall divide it
into seven parts. Judah shall
remain in their territory on the
south, and the house of Joseph
shall remain in their territory
on the north. 6You shall therefore survey the land in seven
parts and bring *the survey* here
to me, that I may cast lots for
you here before the LORD our
God. 7But the Levites have no
part among you, for the priesthood of the LORD *is* their inheritance. And Gad, Reuben,
and half the tribe of Manasseh
have received their inheritance
beyond the Jordan on the east,
which Moses the servant of the
LORD gave them."
8Then the men arose to
go away; and Joshua charged
those who went to survey
the land, saying, "Go, walk
through the land, survey it,
and come back to me, that I
may cast lots for you here before the LORD in Shiloh." 9So
the men went, passed through
the land, and wrote the survey
in a book in seven parts by cities; and they came to Joshua
at the camp in Shiloh. 10Then
Joshua cast lots for them in
Shiloh before the LORD, and
there Joshua divided the land
to the children of Israel according to their divisions.

THE LAND OF BENJAMIN

11Now the lot of the tribe of
the children of Benjamin came
up according to their families,
and the territory of their lot
came out between the children
of Judah and the children of
Joseph. 12Their border on the
north side began at the Jordan, and the border went up
to the side of Jericho on the
north, and went up through
the mountains westward; it
ended at the Wilderness of
Beth Aven. 13The border went
over from there toward Luz, to
the side of Luz (which *is* Bethel)
southward; and the border descended to Ataroth Addar, near
the hill that *lies* on the south
side of Lower Beth Horon.

14Then the border extended
around the west side to the
south, from the hill that *lies*
before Beth Horon south-
ward; and it ended at Kirjath
Baal (which *is* Kirjath Jearim),
a city of the children of Judah.
This *was* the west side.

15The south side *began* at
the end of Kirjath Jearim,
and the border extended on
the west and went out to the
spring of the waters of Nephtoah. 16Then the border came
down to the end of the moun-
tain that lies before the Valley
of the Son of Hinnom, which
is in the Valley of the Rephaim[a] on the north, descended
to the Valley of Hinnom, to the
side of the Jebusite *city* on the
south, and descended to En
Rogel. 17And it went around
from the north, went out to
En Shemesh, and extended
toward Geliloth, which is before the Ascent of Adummim,
and descended to the stone
of Bohan the son of Reuben.
18Then it passed along toward
the north side of Arabah,[a] and
went down to Arabah. 19And
the border passed along to the
north side of Beth Hoglah;
then the border ended at the
north bay at the Salt Sea, at the
south end of the Jordan. This
was the southern boundary.

20The Jordan was its bor-
der on the east side. This *was*
the inheritance of the children of Benjamin, according
to its boundaries all around,
according to their families.

21Now the cities of the tribe
of the children of Benjamin,
according to their families,
were Jericho, Beth Hoglah,
Emek Keziz, 22Beth Arabah,
Zemaraim, Bethel, 23Avim,
Parah, Ophrah, 24Chephar
Haammoni, Ophni, and Gaba:
twelve cities with their villages; 25Gibeon, Ramah, Beeroth, 26Mizpah, Chephirah,
Mozah, 27Rekem, Irpeel, Tar-
alah, 28Zelah, Eleph, Jebus
(which *is* Jerusalem), Gibeath,
and Kirjath: fourteen cities
with their villages. This was
the inheritance of the children
of Benjamin according to their
families.

18:16 [a] Literally *Giants* 18:18 [a] Or *Beth Arabah* (compare 15:6 and 18:22)

SIMEON'S INHERITANCE WITH JUDAH

19 The second lot came out
for Simeon, for the tribe
of the children of Simeon according to their families. And
their inheritance was within
the inheritance of the children
of Judah. 2They had in their inheritance Beersheba (Sheba),
Moladah, 3Hazar Shual, Balah,
Ezem, 4Eltolad, Bethul, Hormah, 5Ziklag, Beth Marcaboth,
Hazar Susah, 6Beth Lebaoth,
and Sharuhen: thirteen cities
and their villages; 7Ain, Rimmon, Ether, and Ashan: four
cities and their villages; 8and
all the villages that *were* all
around these cities as far as
Baalath Beer, Ramah of the
South. This *was* the inheritance of the tribe of the children of Simeon according to
their families.

9The inheritance of the
children of Simeon *was included* in the share of the children of Judah, for the share of
the children of Judah was too
much for them. Therefore the
children of Simeon had *their*
inheritance within the inheritance of that people.

THE LAND OF ZEBULUN

10The third lot came out
for the children of Zebulun
according to their families,
and the border of their inheritance was as far as Sarid.
11Their border went toward
the west and to Maralah,
went to Dabbasheth, and extended along the brook that
is east of Jokneam. 12Then
from Sarid it went eastward
toward the sunrise along the
border of Chisloth Tabor, and
went out toward Daberath, bypassing Japhia. 13And from
there it passed along on the
east of Gath Hepher, toward
Eth Kazin, and extended to
Rimmon, which borders on
Neah. 14Then the border went
around it on the north side
of Hannathon, and it ended
in the Valley of Jiphthah El.
15Included were Kattath, Na-
hallal, Shimron, Idalah, and
Bethlehem: twelve cities with
their villages. 16This *was* the
inheritance of the children
of Zebulun according to their
families, these cities with their
villages.

THE LAND OF ISSACHAR

17The fourth lot came out
to Issachar, for the children
of Issachar according to their
families. 18And their territory went to Jezreel, and *included* Chesulloth, Shunem,
19Haphraim, Shion, Anaha-
rath, 20Rabbith, Kishion,
Abez, 21Remeth, En Gannim,
En Haddah, and Beth Pazzez.
22And the border reached to
Tabor, Shahazimah, and Beth
Shemesh; their border ended
at the Jordan: sixteen cities
with their villages. 23This *was*
the inheritance of the tribe of
the children of Issachar according to their families, the
cities and their villages.

THE LAND OF ASHER

24The fifth lot came out
for the tribe of the children
of Asher according to their
families. 25And their territory
included Helkath, Hali, Beten,
Achshaph, 26Alammelech,
Amad, and Mishal; it reached
to Mount Carmel westward,
along *the Brook* Shihor Libnath.
27It turned toward the sunrise
to Beth Dagon; and it reached
to Zebulun and to the Valley of
Jiphthah El, then northward
beyond Beth Emek and Neiel,
bypassing Cabul *which was* on
the left, 28including Ebron,[a]
Rehob, Hammon, and Kanah,
as far as Greater Sidon. 29And
the border turned to Ramah
and to the fortified city of
Tyre; then the border turned
to Hosah, and ended at the sea
by the region of Achzib. 30Also
Ummah, Aphek, and Rehob
were included: twenty-two cities with their villages. 31This
was the inheritance of the
tribe of the children of Asher
according to their families,
these cities with their villages.

THE LAND OF NAPHTALI

32The sixth lot came out
to the children of Naphtali,
for the children of Naphtali
according to their families.
33And their border began at
Heleph, enclosing the territory from the terebinth tree
in Zaanannim, Adami Nekeb,
and Jabneel, as far as Lak-
kum; it ended at the Jordan.
34From Heleph the border extended westward to Aznoth
Tabor, and went out from
there toward Hukkok; it ad-
joined Zebulun on the south
side and Asher on the west
side, and ended at Judah by
the Jordan toward the sunrise. 35And the fortified cities
are Ziddim, Zer, Hammath,
Rakkath, Chinnereth, 36Ada-
mah, Ramah, Hazor, 37Kedesh,
Edrei, En Hazor, 38Iron, Migdal
El, Horem, Beth Anath, and
Beth Shemesh: nineteen cities
with their villages. 39This *was*
the inheritance of the tribe of
the children of Naphtali according to their families, the
cities and their villages.

THE LAND OF DAN

40The seventh lot came out
for the tribe of the children of
Dan according to their families. 41And the territory of their
inheritance was Zorah, Eshtaol, Ir Shemesh, 42Shaalab-
bin, Aijalon, Jethlah, 43Elon,
Timnah, Ekron, 44Eltekeh, Gibbethon, Baalath, 45Jehud, Bene
Berak, Gath Rimmon, 46Me
Jarkon, and Rakkon, with the
region near Joppa. 47And the
border of the children of Dan
went beyond these, because
the children of Dan went up to
fight against Leshem and took
it; and they struck it with the

19:28 [a] Following Masoretic Text, Targum, and Vulgate; a few Hebrew manuscripts read *Abdon* (compare 21:30 and 1 Chronicles 6:74).

edge of the sword, took possession of it, and dwelt in it.
They called Leshem, Dan, after
the name of Dan their father.
48This *is* the inheritance of the
tribe of the children of Dan
according to their families,
these cities with their villages.

JOSHUA'S INHERITANCE

49When they had made an
end of dividing the land as an
inheritance according to their
borders, the children of Israel
gave an inheritance among
them to Joshua the son of
Nun. 50According to the word
of the LORD they gave him the
city which he asked for, Timnath Serah in the mountains
of Ephraim; and he built the
city and dwelt in it.

51These *were* the inheri-
tances which Eleazar the priest,
Joshua the son of Nun, and
the heads of the fathers of the
tribes of the children of Israel
divided as an inheritance by
lot in Shiloh before the LORD,
at the door of the tabernacle of
meeting. So they made an end
of dividing the country.

THE CITIES OF REFUGE

20 The LORD also spoke to
Joshua, saying, 2"Speak
to the children of Israel, saying: 'Appoint for yourselves cities of refuge, of which I spoke
to you through Moses, 3that
the slayer who kills a person
accidentally *or* unintentionally may flee there; and they
shall be your refuge from the
avenger of blood. 4And when
he flees to one of those cities,
and stands at the entrance of
the gate of the city, and declares his case in the hearing
of the elders of that city, they
shall take him into the city as
one of them, and give him a
place, that he may dwell among
them. 5Then if the avenger of
blood pursues him, they shall
not deliver the slayer into his
hand, because he struck his
neighbor unintentionally, but
did not hate him beforehand.
6And he shall dwell in that city
until he stands before the congregation for judgment, *and*
until the death of the one who
is high priest in those days.
Then the slayer may return
and come to his own city and
his own house, to the city from
which he fled.'"

7So they appointed Kedesh
in Galilee, in the mountains
of Naphtali, Shechem in the
mountains of Ephraim, and
Kirjath Arba (which *is* Hebron)
in the mountains of Judah.
8And on the other side of the
Jordan, by Jericho eastward,
they assigned Bezer in the
wilderness on the plain, from
the tribe of Reuben, Ramoth in
Gilead, from the tribe of Gad,
and Golan in Bashan, from the
tribe of Manasseh. 9These were
the cities appointed for all the
children of Israel and for the
stranger who dwelt among
them, that whoever killed a
person accidentally might flee
there, and not die by the hand

of the avenger of blood until he stood before the congregation.

CITIES OF THE LEVITES

21 Then the heads of the fathers' *houses* of the Levites came near to Eleazar the priest, to Joshua the son of Nun, and to the heads of the fathers' *houses* of the tribes of the children of Israel. [2]And they spoke to them at Shiloh in the land of Canaan, saying, "The LORD commanded through Moses to give us cities to dwell in, with their common-lands for our livestock." [3]So the children of Israel gave to the Levites from their inheritance, at the commandment of the LORD, these cities and their common-lands:

[4]Now the lot came out for the families of the Kohathites. And the children of Aaron the priest, *who were* of the Levites, had thirteen cities by lot from the tribe of Judah, from the tribe of Simeon, and from the tribe of Benjamin. [5]The rest of the children of Kohath had ten cities by lot from the families of the tribe of Ephraim, from the tribe of Dan, and from the half-tribe of Manasseh.

[6]And the children of Gershon had thirteen cities by lot from the families of the tribe of Issachar, from the tribe of Asher, from the tribe of Naphtali, and from the half-tribe of Manasseh in Bashan.

[7]The children of Merari according to their families had twelve cities from the tribe of Reuben, from the tribe of Gad, and from the tribe of Zebulun.

[8]And the children of Israel gave these cities with their common-lands by lot to the Levites, as the LORD had commanded by the hand of Moses.

[9]So they gave from the tribe of the children of Judah and from the tribe of the children of Simeon these cities which are designated by name, [10]which were for the children of Aaron, one of the families of the Kohathites, *who were* of the children of Levi; for the lot was theirs first. [11]And they gave them Kirjath Arba (*Arba was* the father of Anak), which *is* Hebron, in the mountains of Judah, with the common-land surrounding it. [12]But the fields of the city and its villages they gave to Caleb the son of Jephunneh as his possession.

[13]Thus to the children of Aaron the priest they gave Hebron with its common-land (a city of refuge for the slayer), Libnah with its common-land, [14]Jattir with its common-land, Eshtemoa with its common-land, [15]Holon with its common-land, Debir with its common-land, [16]Ain with its common-land, Juttah with its common-land, and Beth Shemesh with its common-land: nine cities from those two tribes; [17]and from the tribe of Benjamin, Gibeon with its common-land,

Geba with its common-land, [18]Anathoth with its common-land, and Almon with its common-land: four cities. [19]All the cities of the children of Aaron, the priests, *were* thirteen cities with their common-lands.

[20]And the families of the children of Kohath, the Levites, the rest of the children of Kohath, even they had the cities of their lot from the tribe of Ephraim. [21]For they gave them Shechem with its common-land in the mountains of Ephraim (a city of refuge for the slayer), Gezer with its common-land, [22]Kibzaim with its common-land, and Beth Horon with its common-land: four cities; [23]and from the tribe of Dan, Eltekeh with its common-land, Gibbethon with its common-land, [24]Aijalon with its common-land, *and* Gath Rimmon with its common-land: four cities; [25]and from the half-tribe of Manasseh, Tanach with its common-land and Gath Rimmon with its common-land: two cities. [26]All the ten cities with their common-lands were for the rest of the families of the children of Kohath.

[27]Also to the children of Gershon, of the families of the Levites, from the *other* half-tribe of Manasseh, *they gave* Golan in Bashan with its common-land (a city of refuge for the slayer), and Be Eshterah with its common-land: two cities; [28]and from the tribe of Issachar, Kishion with its common-land, Daberath with its common-land, [29]Jarmuth with its common-land, *and* En Gannim with its common-land: four cities; [30]and from the tribe of Asher, Mishal with its common-land, Abdon with its common-land, [31]Helkath with its common-land, and Rehob with its common-land: four cities; [32]and from the tribe of Naphtali, Kedesh in Galilee with its common-land (a city of refuge for the slayer), Hammoth Dor with its common-land, and Kartan with its common-land: three cities. [33]All the cities of the Gershonites according to their families *were* thirteen cities with their common-lands.

[34]And to the families of the children of Merari, the rest of the Levites, from the tribe of Zebulun, Jokneam with its common-land, Kartah with its common-land, [35]Dimnah with its common-land, *and* Nahalal with its common-land: four cities; [36]and from the tribe of Reuben, Bezer with its common-land, Jahaz with its common-land, [37]Kedemoth with its common-land, and Mephaath with its common-land: four cities;[a] [38]and from

21:37 [a] Following Septuagint and Vulgate (compare 1 Chronicles 6:78, 79); Masoretic Text, Bomberg, and Targum omit verses 36 and 37.

the tribe of Gad, Ramoth in Gilead with its common-land (a city of refuge for the slayer), Mahanaim with its common-land, 39Heshbon with its common-land, *and* Jazer with its common-land: four cities in all. 40So all the cities for the children of Merari according to their families, the rest of the families of the Levites, were *by* their lot twelve cities.

41All the cities of the Levites within the possession of the children of Israel *were* forty-eight cities with their common-lands. 42Every one of these cities had its common-land surrounding it; thus *were* all these cities.

THE PROMISE FULFILLED

43So the LORD gave to Israel all the land of which He had sworn to give to their fathers, and they took possession of it and dwelt in it. 44The LORD gave them rest all around, according to all that He had sworn to their fathers. And not a man of all their enemies stood against them; the LORD delivered all their enemies into their hand. 45Not a word failed of any good thing which the LORD had spoken to the house of Israel. All came to pass.

EASTERN TRIBES RETURN TO THEIR LANDS

22 Then Joshua called the Reubenites, the Gadites, and half the tribe of Manasseh, 2and said to them: "You have kept all that Moses the servant of the LORD commanded you, and have obeyed my voice in all that I commanded you. 3You have not left your brethren these many days, up to this day, but have kept the charge of the commandment of the LORD your God. 4And now the LORD your God has given rest to your brethren, as He promised them; now therefore, return and go to your tents *and* to the land of your possession, which Moses the servant of the LORD gave you on the other side of the Jordan. 5But take careful heed to do the commandment and the law which Moses the servant of the LORD commanded you, to love the LORD your God, to walk in all His ways, to keep His commandments, to hold fast to Him, and to serve Him with all your heart and with all your soul." 6So Joshua blessed them and sent them away, and they went to their tents.

7Now to half the tribe of Manasseh Moses had given a possession in Bashan, but to the *other* half of it Joshua gave *a possession* among their brethren on this side of the Jordan, westward. And indeed, when Joshua sent them away to their tents, he blessed them, 8and spoke to them, saying, "Return with much riches to your tents, with very much livestock,

with silver, with gold, with
bronze, with iron, and with
very much clothing. Divide
the spoil of your enemies with
your brethren."
9So the children of Reu-
ben, the children of Gad, and
half the tribe of Manasseh returned, and departed from the
children of Israel at Shiloh,
which *is* in the land of Canaan,
to go to the country of Gilead,
to the land of their possession, which they had obtained
according to the word of the
LORD by the hand of Moses.

AN ALTAR BY THE JORDAN

10And when they came
to the region of the Jordan
which *is* in the land of Canaan,
the children of Reuben, the
children of Gad, and half the
tribe of Manasseh built an
altar there by the Jordan—a
great, impressive altar. 11Now
the children of Israel heard
someone say, "Behold, the children of Reuben, the children
of Gad, and half the tribe of
Manasseh have built an altar
on the frontier of the land of
Canaan, in the region of the
Jordan—on the children of
Israel's side." 12And when the
children of Israel heard *of it,*
the whole congregation of the
children of Israel gathered together at Shiloh to go to war
against them.
13Then the children of Israel sent Phinehas the son
of Eleazar the priest to the
children of Reuben, to the
children of Gad, and to half
the tribe of Manasseh, into
the land of Gilead, 14and with
him ten rulers, one ruler each
from the chief house of every
tribe of Israel; and each one
was the head of the house of
his father among the divisions[a] of Israel. 15Then they
came to the children of Reuben, to the children of Gad,
and to half the tribe of Manasseh, to the land of Gilead, and
they spoke with them, saying,
16"Thus says the whole congregation of the LORD: 'What
treachery *is* this that you have
committed against the God of
Israel, to turn away this day
from following the LORD,
in that you have built for
yourselves an altar, that you
might rebel this day against
the LORD? 17*Is* the iniquity of
Peor not enough for us, from
which we are not cleansed till
this day, although there was
a plague in the congregation
of the LORD, 18but that you
must turn away this day from
following the LORD? And it
shall be, if you rebel today
against the LORD, that tomorrow He will be angry with the
whole congregation of Israel.
19Nevertheless, if the land of
your possession *is* unclean,
then cross over to the land of
the possession of the LORD,
where the LORD's tabernacle

22:14 [a] Literally *thousands*

stands, and take possession
among us; but do not rebel
against the LORD, nor rebel
against us, by building yourselves an altar besides the
altar of the LORD our God.
20Did not Achan the son of
Zerah commit a trespass in
the accursed thing, and wrath
fell on all the congregation of
Israel? And that man did not
perish alone in his iniquity.'"
21Then the children of
Reuben, the children of Gad,
and half the tribe of Manasseh answered and said to
the heads of the divisions[a]
of Israel: 22"The LORD God of
gods, the LORD God of gods,
He knows, and let Israel itself
know—if *it is* in rebellion, or if
in treachery against the LORD,
do not save us this day. 23If we
have built ourselves an altar
to turn from following the
LORD, or if to offer on it burnt
offerings or grain offerings,
or if to offer peace offerings
on it, let the LORD Himself require *an account*. 24But in fact
we have done it for fear, for
a reason, saying, 'In time to
come your descendants may
speak to our descendants,
saying, "What have you to
do with the LORD God of Israel? 25For the LORD has made
the Jordan a border between
you and us, *you* children of
Reuben and children of Gad.
You have no part in the LORD."
So your descendants would
make our descendants cease
fearing the LORD.' 26Therefore
we said, 'Let us now prepare
to build ourselves an altar,
not for burnt offering nor for
sacrifice, 27but *that* it *may be*
a witness between you and
us and our generations after
us, that we may perform the
service of the LORD before
Him with our burnt offerings,
with our sacrifices, and with
our peace offerings; that your
descendants may not say to
our descendants in time to
come, "You have no part in
the LORD."' 28Therefore we
said that it will be, when they
say *this* to us or to our generations in time to come, that we
may say, 'Here is the replica
of the altar of the LORD which
our fathers made, though not
for burnt offerings nor for
sacrifices; but it *is* a witness
between you and us.' 29Far
be it from us that we should
rebel against the LORD, and
turn from following the LORD
this day, to build an altar for
burnt offerings, for grain offerings, or for sacrifices, besides the altar of the LORD
our God which *is* before His
tabernacle."
30Now when Phinehas the
priest and the rulers of the
congregation, the heads of
the divisions[a] of Israel who
were with him, heard the
words that the children of
Reuben, the children of Gad,

22:21 [a] Literally *thousands*

22:30 [a] Literally *thousands*

and the children of Manasseh
spoke, it pleased them. 31Then
Phinehas the son of Eleazar
the priest said to the children
of Reuben, the children of
Gad, and the children of Manasseh, "This day we perceive
that the LORD *is* among us,
because you have not com-
mitted this treachery against
the LORD. Now you have delivered the children of Israel
out of the hand of the LORD."

32And Phinehas the son
of Eleazar the priest, and the
rulers, returned from the children of Reuben and the children of Gad, from the land of
Gilead to the land of Canaan,
to the children of Israel, and
brought back word to them.
33So the thing pleased the
children of Israel, and the
children of Israel blessed
God; they spoke no more of
going against them in battle,
to destroy the land where the
children of Reuben and Gad
dwelt.

34The children of Reu-
ben and the children of Gad[a]
called the altar, *Witness,* "For
it is a witness between us that
the LORD *is* God."

JOSHUA'S FAREWELL ADDRESS

23 Now it came to pass,
a long time after the
LORD had given rest to Israel
from all their enemies round
about, that Joshua was old,
advanced in age. 2And Joshua
called for all Israel, for their
elders, for their heads, for
their judges, and for their officers, and said to them:

"I am old, advanced in
age. 3You have seen all that
the LORD your God has done
to all these nations because
of you, for the LORD your
God *is* He who has fought
for you. 4See, I have divided
to you by lot these nations
that remain, to be an inheritance for your tribes, from
the Jordan, with all the nations that I have cut off, as
far as the Great Sea westward.
5And the LORD your God will
expel them from before you
and drive them out of your
sight. So you shall possess
their land, as the LORD your
God promised you. 6There-
fore be very courageous to
keep and to do all that is written in the Book of the Law of
Moses, lest you turn aside
from it to the right hand or
to the left, 7*and* lest you go
among these nations, these
who remain among you. You
shall not make mention of the
name of their gods, nor cause
anyone to swear *by them;*
you shall not serve them nor
bow down to them, 8but you
shall hold fast to the LORD
your God, as you have done
to this day. 9For the LORD has
driven out from before you
great and strong nations; but

22:34 [a] Septuagint adds *and half the tribe of Manasseh.*

as for you, no one has been
able to stand against you to
this day. 10One man of you
shall chase a thousand, for
the LORD your God *is* He who
fights for you, as He promised
you. 11Therefore take careful
heed to yourselves, that you
love the LORD your God. 12Or
else, if indeed you do go back,
and cling to the remnant of
these nations—these that remain among you—and make
marriages with them, and go
in to them and they to you,
13know for certain that the
LORD your God will no longer
drive out these nations from
before you. But they shall be
snares and traps to you, and
scourges on your sides and
thorns in your eyes, until you
perish from this good land
which the LORD your God has
given you.

14"Behold, this day I *am*
going the way of all the earth.
And you know in all your
hearts and in all your souls
that not one thing has failed
of all the good things which
the LORD your God spoke concerning you. All have come to
pass for you; not one word of
them has failed. 15Therefore
it shall come to pass, that as
all the good things have come
upon you which the LORD
your God promised you, so the
LORD will bring upon you all
harmful things, until He has
destroyed you from this good
land which the LORD your God
has given you. 16When you
have transgressed the covenant of the LORD your God,
which He commanded you,
and have gone and served
other gods, and bowed down
to them, then the anger of the
LORD will burn against you,
and you shall perish quickly
from the good land which He
has given you."

THE COVENANT AT SHECHEM

24 Then Joshua gathered
all the tribes of Israel to
Shechem and called for the elders of Israel, for their heads,
for their judges, and for their
officers; and they presented
themselves before God. 2And
Joshua said to all the people,
"Thus says the LORD God of
Israel: 'Your fathers, *including*
Terah, the father of Abraham
and the father of Nahor, dwelt
on the other side of the River[a]
in old times; and they served
other gods. 3Then I took your
father Abraham from the
other side of the River, led
him throughout all the land
of Canaan, and multiplied his
descendants and gave him
Isaac. 4To Isaac I gave Jacob
and Esau. To Esau I gave the
mountains of Seir to possess,
but Jacob and his children
went down to Egypt. 5Also I
sent Moses and Aaron, and I
plagued Egypt, according to

24:2 [a] Hebrew *Nahar,* the Euphrates, and so in verses 3, 14, and 15

what I did among them. Afterward I brought you out.
[6]'Then I brought your fathers out of Egypt, and you
came to the sea; and the
Egyptians pursued your fathers with chariots and horsemen to the Red Sea. [7]So they
cried out to the LORD; and He
put darkness between you
and the Egyptians, brought
the sea upon them, and covered them. And your eyes saw
what I did in Egypt. Then you
dwelt in the wilderness a long
time. [8]And I brought you into
the land of the Amorites, who
dwelt on the other side of the
Jordan, and they fought with
you. But I gave them into your
hand, that you might possess
their land, and I destroyed
them from before you. [9]Then
Balak the son of Zippor, king
of Moab, arose to make war
against Israel, and sent and
called Balaam the son of Beor
to curse you. [10]But I would not
listen to Balaam; therefore
he continued to bless you.
So I delivered you out of his
hand. [11]Then you went over
the Jordan and came to Jericho. And the men of Jericho
fought against you—*also* the
Amorites, the Perizzites, the
Canaanites, the Hittites, the
Girgashites, the Hivites, and
the Jebusites. But I delivered
them into your hand. [12]I sent
the hornet before you which
drove them out from before
you, *also* the two kings of the
Amorites, *but* not with your
sword or with your bow. [13]I
have given you a land for
which you did not labor,
and cities which you did not
build, and you dwell in them;
you eat of the vineyards and
olive groves which you did
not plant.'
[14]"Now therefore, fear the
LORD, serve Him in sincerity
and in truth, and put away
the gods which your fathers
served on the other side of
the River and in Egypt. Serve
the LORD! [15]And if it seems
evil to you to serve the LORD,
choose for yourselves this day
whom you will serve, whether
the gods which your fathers
served that *were* on the other
side of the River, or the gods
of the Amorites, in whose land
you dwell. But as for me and
my house, we will serve the
LORD."
[16]So the people answered
and said: "Far be it from us
that we should forsake the
LORD to serve other gods; [17]for
the LORD our God *is* He who
brought us and our fathers
up out of the land of Egypt,
from the house of bondage,
who did those great signs in
our sight, and preserved us in
all the way that we went and
among all the people through
whom we passed. [18]And the
LORD drove out from before
us all the people, including
the Amorites who dwelt in the
land. We also will serve the
LORD, for He *is* our God."
[19]But Joshua said to the

people, "You cannot serve the
LORD, for He *is* a holy God. He
is a jealous God; He will not
forgive your transgressions
nor your sins. 20If you forsake
the LORD and serve foreign
gods, then He will turn and do
you harm and consume you,
after He has done you good."

21And the people said to
Joshua, "No, but we will serve
the LORD!"

22So Joshua said to the people, "You *are* witnesses against
yourselves that you have chosen the LORD for yourselves,
to serve Him."

And they said, "*We are* witnesses!"

23"Now therefore," *he said,*
"put away the foreign gods
which *are* among you, and incline your heart to the LORD
God of Israel."

24And the people said to
Joshua, "The LORD our God
we will serve, and His voice
we will obey!"

25So Joshua made a cov-
enant with the people that
day, and made for them a
statute and an ordinance in
Shechem.

26Then Joshua wrote these
words in the Book of the Law
of God. And he took a large
stone, and set it up there
under the oak that *was* by the
sanctuary of the LORD. 27And
Joshua said to all the people,
"Behold, this stone shall be a
witness to us, for it has heard
all the words of the LORD
which He spoke to us. It shall
therefore be a witness to you,
lest you deny your God." 28So
Joshua let the people depart,
each to his own inheritance.

DEATH OF JOSHUA AND ELEAZAR

29Now it came to pass after
these things that Joshua the
son of Nun, the servant of the
LORD, died, *being* one hundred and ten years old. 30And
they buried him within the
border of his inheritance at
Timnath Serah, which *is* in the
mountains of Ephraim, on the
north side of Mount Gaash.

31Israel served the LORD all
the days of Joshua, and all the
days of the elders who outlived Joshua, who had known
all the works of the LORD
which He had done for Israel.

32The bones of Joseph,
which the children of Israel
had brought up out of Egypt,
they buried at Shechem, in the
plot of ground which Jacob
had bought from the sons of
Hamor the father of Shechem
for one hundred pieces of silver, and which had become an
inheritance of the children of
Joseph.

33And Eleazar the son of
Aaron died. They buried him
in a hill *belonging to* Phinehas his son, which was given
to him in the mountains of
Ephraim.

THE BOOK OF
JUDGES

THE CONTINUING CONQUEST OF CANAAN

1 Now after the death of
Joshua it came to pass that
the children of Israel asked
the LORD, saying, "Who shall
be first to go up for us against
the Canaanites to fight against
them?"
2And the LORD said, "Judah
shall go up. Indeed I have delivered the land into his hand."
3So Judah said to Simeon
his brother, "Come up with me
to my allotted territory, that we
may fight against the Canaanites; and I will likewise go with
you to your allotted territory."
And Simeon went with him.
4Then Judah went up, and the
LORD delivered the Canaanites
and the Perizzites into their
hand; and they killed ten thousand men at Bezek. 5And they
found Adoni-Bezek in Bezek,
and fought against him; and
they defeated the Canaan-
ites and the Perizzites. 6Then
Adoni-Bezek fled, and they
pursued him and caught him
and cut off his thumbs and
big toes. 7And Adoni-Bezek
said, "Seventy kings with their
thumbs and big toes cut off
used to gather *scraps* under
my table; as I have done, so
God has repaid me." Then they
brought him to Jerusalem,
and there he died.
8Now the children of Judah
fought against Jerusalem and
took it; they struck it with the
edge of the sword and set
the city on fire. 9And afterward the children of Judah
went down to fight against the
Canaanites who dwelt in the
mountains, in the South,[a] and
in the lowland. 10Then Judah
went against the Canaanites
who dwelt in Hebron. (Now the
name of Hebron *was* formerly
Kirjath Arba.) And they killed
Sheshai, Ahiman, and Talmai.
11From there they went
against the inhabitants of
Debir. (The name of Debir *was*
formerly Kirjath Sepher.)
12Then Caleb said, "Who-
ever attacks Kirjath Sepher
and takes it, to him I will
give my daughter Achsah as
wife." 13And Othniel the son
of Kenaz, Caleb's younger
brother, took it; so he gave
him his daughter Achsah
as wife. 14Now it happened,
when she came *to him,* that
she urged him[a] to ask her father for a field. And she dis-

1:9 [a] Hebrew *Negev,* and so throughout this book
1:14 [a] Septuagint and Vulgate read *he urged her.*

mounted from *her* donkey,
and Caleb said to her, "What
do you wish?" 15So she said
to him, "Give me a blessing;
since you have given me land
in the South, give me also
springs of water."
And Caleb gave her the
upper springs and the lower
springs.
16Now the children of the
Kenite, Moses' father-in-law,
went up from the City of Palms
with the children of Judah
into the Wilderness of Judah,
which *lies* in the South *near*
Arad; and they went and dwelt
among the people. 17And
Judah went with his brother
Simeon, and they attacked the
Canaanites who inhabited Ze-
phath, and utterly destroyed
it. So the name of the city was
called Hormah. 18Also Judah
took Gaza with its territory,
Ashkelon with its territory, and
Ekron with its territory. 19So
the LORD was with Judah. And
they drove out the mountain-
eers, but they could not drive
out the inhabitants of the lowland, because they had chariots of iron. 20And they gave
Hebron to Caleb, as Moses had
said. Then he expelled from
there the three sons of Anak.
21But the children of Benjamin
did not drive out the Jebusites
who inhabited Jerusalem; so
the Jebusites dwell with the
children of Benjamin in Jerusalem to this day.
22And the house of Joseph
also went up against Bethel,
and the LORD *was* with them.
23So the house of Joseph sent
men to spy out Bethel. (The
name of the city *was* formerly
Luz.) 24And when the spies
saw a man coming out of the
city, they said to him, "Please
show us the entrance to the
city, and we will show you
mercy." 25So he showed them
the entrance to the city, and
they struck the city with the
edge of the sword; but they
let the man and all his family
go. 26And the man went to the
land of the Hittites, built a city,
and called its name Luz, which
is its name to this day.

INCOMPLETE CONQUEST OF THE LAND

27However, Manasseh did
not drive out *the inhabitants*
of Beth Shean and its villages,
or Taanach and its villages, or
the inhabitants of Dor and its
villages, or the inhabitants of
Ibleam and its villages, or the
inhabitants of Megiddo and
its villages; for the Canaanites were determined to dwell
in that land. 28And it came to
pass, when Israel was strong,
that they put the Canaanites
under tribute, but did not
completely drive them out.
29Nor did Ephraim drive
out the Canaanites who dwelt
in Gezer; so the Canaanites
dwelt in Gezer among them.
30Nor did Zebulun drive
out the inhabitants of Kitron
or the inhabitants of Naha-
lol; so the Canaanites dwelt

among them, and were put under tribute.

31Nor did Asher drive out the inhabitants of Acco or the inhabitants of Sidon, or of Ahlab, Achzib, Helbah, Aphik, or Rehob. 32So the Asherites dwelt among the Canaanites, the inhabitants of the land; for they did not drive them out.

33Nor did Naphtali drive out the inhabitants of Beth Shemesh or the inhabitants of Beth Anath; but they dwelt among the Canaanites, the inhabitants of the land. Nevertheless the inhabitants of Beth Shemesh and Beth Anath were put under tribute to them.

34And the Amorites forced the children of Dan into the mountains, for they would not allow them to come down to the valley; 35and the Amorites were determined to dwell in Mount Heres, in Aijalon, and in Shaalbim;[a] yet when the strength of the house of Joseph became greater, they were put under tribute.

36Now the boundary of the Amorites *was* from the Ascent of Akrabbim, from Sela, and upward.

ISRAEL'S DISOBEDIENCE

2 Then the Angel of the LORD came up from Gilgal to Bochim, and said: "I led you up from Egypt and brought you to the land of which I swore to your fathers; and I said, 'I will never break My covenant with you. 2And you shall make no covenant with the inhabitants of this land; you shall tear down their altars.' But you have not obeyed My voice. Why have you done this? 3Therefore I also said, 'I will not drive them out before you; but they shall be *thorns* in your side,[a] and their gods shall be a snare to you.'" 4So it was, when the Angel of the LORD spoke these words to all the children of Israel, that the people lifted up their voices and wept.

5Then they called the name of that place Bochim;[a] and they sacrificed there to the LORD. 6And when Joshua had dismissed the people, the children of Israel went each to his own inheritance to possess the land.

DEATH OF JOSHUA

7So the people served the LORD all the days of Joshua, and all the days of the elders who outlived Joshua, who had seen all the great works of the LORD which He had done for Israel. 8Now Joshua the son of Nun, the servant of the LORD, died *when he was* one hundred and ten years old. 9And they buried him within the border of his inheritance at Timnath Heres, in the mountains of Ephraim, on the north

1:35 [a] Spelled *Shaalabbin* in Joshua 19:42 2:3 [a] Septuagint, Targum, and Vulgate read *enemies to you.* 2:5 [a] Literally *Weeping*

side of Mount Gaash. 10When
all that generation had been
gathered to their fathers, another generation arose after
them who did not know the
LORD nor the work which He
had done for Israel.

ISRAEL'S UNFAITHFULNESS

11Then the children of Israel did evil in the sight of the
LORD, and served the Baals;
12and they forsook the LORD
God of their fathers, who had
brought them out of the land
of Egypt; and they followed
other gods from *among* the
gods of the people who *were*
all around them, and they
bowed down to them; and
they provoked the LORD to
anger. 13They forsook the
LORD and served Baal and the
Ashtoreths.[a] 14And the anger
of the LORD was hot against
Israel. So He delivered them
into the hands of plunderers
who despoiled them; and He
sold them into the hands of
their enemies all around, so
that they could no longer
stand before their enemies.
15Wherever they went out, the
hand of the LORD was against
them for calamity, as the LORD
had said, and as the LORD had
sworn to them. And they were
greatly distressed.

16Nevertheless, the LORD
raised up judges who delivered them out of the hand of
those who plundered them.
17Yet they would not listen to
their judges, but they played
the harlot with other gods,
and bowed down to them.
They turned quickly from
the way in which their fathers walked, in obeying the
commandments of the LORD;
they did not do so. 18And when
the LORD raised up judges for
them, the LORD was with the
judge and delivered them out
of the hand of their enemies
all the days of the judge; for
the LORD was moved to pity
by their groaning because of
those who oppressed them
and harassed them. 19And it
came to pass, when the judge
was dead, that they reverted
and behaved more corruptly
than their fathers, by following other gods, to serve them
and bow down to them. They
did not cease from their own
doings nor from their stubborn way.

20Then the anger of the
LORD was hot against Israel;
and He said, "Because this
nation has transgressed My
covenant which I commanded
their fathers, and has not
heeded My voice, 21I also will
no longer drive out before
them any of the nations which
Joshua left when he died, 22so
that through them I may test
Israel, whether they will keep
the ways of the LORD, to walk
in them as their fathers kept
them, or not." 23Therefore the

2:13 [a] Canaanite goddesses

LORD left those nations, without driving them out immediately; nor did He deliver them into the hand of Joshua.

THE NATIONS REMAINING IN THE LAND

3 Now these *are* the nations which the LORD left, that He might test Israel by them, *that is,* all who had not known any of the wars in Canaan 2(*this was* only so that the generations of the children of Israel might be taught to know war, at least those who had not formerly known it), 3*namely,* five lords of the Philistines, all the Canaanites, the Sidonians, and the Hivites who dwelt in Mount Lebanon, from Mount Baal Hermon to the entrance of Hamath. 4And they were *left, that He might* test Israel by them, to know whether they would obey the commandments of the LORD, which He had commanded their fathers by the hand of Moses.

5Thus the children of Israel dwelt among the Canaanites, the Hittites, the Amorites, the Perizzites, the Hivites, and the Jebusites. 6And they took their daughters to be their wives, and gave their daughters to their sons; and they served their gods.

OTHNIEL

7So the children of Israel did evil in the sight of the LORD. They forgot the LORD their God, and served the Baals and Asherahs.[a] 8Therefore the anger of the LORD was hot against Israel, and He sold them into the hand of Cushan-Rishathaim king of Mesopotamia; and the children of Israel served Cushan-Rishathaim eight years. 9When the children of Israel cried out to the LORD, the LORD raised up a deliverer for the children of Israel, who delivered them: Othniel the son of Kenaz, Caleb's younger brother. 10The Spirit of the LORD came upon him, and he judged Israel. He went out to war, and the LORD delivered Cushan-Rishathaim king of Mesopotamia into his hand; and his hand prevailed over Cushan-Rishathaim. 11So the land had rest for forty years. Then Othniel the son of Kenaz died.

EHUD

12And the children of Israel again did evil in the sight of the LORD. So the LORD strengthened Eglon king of Moab against Israel, because they had done evil in the sight of the LORD. 13Then he gathered to himself the people of Ammon and Amalek, went and defeated Israel, and took possession of the City of Palms. 14So the children of Israel served Eglon king of Moab eighteen years.

3:7 [a] Name or symbol for Canaanite goddesses

[15]But when the children of Israel cried out to the LORD, the LORD raised up a deliverer for them: Ehud the son of Gera, the Benjamite, a left-handed man. By him the children of Israel sent tribute to Eglon king of Moab. [16]Now Ehud made himself a dagger (it was double-edged and a cubit in length) and fastened it under his clothes on his right thigh. [17]So he brought the tribute to Eglon king of Moab. (Now Eglon *was* a very fat man.) [18]And when he had finished presenting the tribute, he sent away the people who had carried the tribute. [19]But he himself turned back from the stone images that *were* at Gilgal, and said, "I have a secret message for you, O king."

He said, "Keep silence!" And all who attended him went out from him.

[20]So Ehud came to him (now he was sitting upstairs in his cool private chamber). Then Ehud said, "I have a message from God for you." So he arose from *his* seat. [21]Then Ehud reached with his left hand, took the dagger from his right thigh, and thrust it into his belly. [22]Even the hilt went in after the blade, and the fat closed over the blade, for he did not draw the dagger out of his belly; and his entrails came out. [23]Then Ehud went out through the porch and shut the doors of the upper room behind him and locked them.

[24]When he had gone out, *Eglon's*[a] servants came to look, and *to their* surprise, the doors of the upper room were locked. So they said, "He is probably attending to his needs in the cool chamber." [25]So they waited till they were embarrassed, and still he had not opened the doors of the upper room. Therefore they took the key and opened *them*. And there was their master, fallen dead on the floor.

[26]But Ehud had escaped while they delayed, and passed beyond the stone images and escaped to Seirah. [27]And it happened, when he arrived, that he blew the trumpet in the mountains of Ephraim, and the children of Israel went down with him from the mountains; and he led them. [28]Then he said to them, "Follow *me*, for the LORD has delivered your enemies the Moabites into your hand." So they went down after him, seized the fords of the Jordan leading to Moab, and did not allow anyone to cross over. [29]And at that time they killed about ten thousand men of Moab, all stout men of valor; not a man escaped. [30]So Moab was subdued that day under the hand of Israel. And the land had rest for eighty years.

3:24 [a] Literally *his*

SHAMGAR

31After him was Shamgar the son of Anath, who killed six hundred men of the Philistines with an ox goad; and he also delivered Israel.

DEBORAH

4 When Ehud was dead, the children of Israel again did evil in the sight of the LORD. 2So the LORD sold them into the hand of Jabin king of Canaan, who reigned in Hazor. The commander of his army *was* Sisera, who dwelt in Harosheth Hagoyim. 3And the children of Israel cried out to the LORD; for Jabin had nine hundred chariots of iron, and for twenty years he had harshly oppressed the children of Israel.

4Now Deborah, a prophetess, the wife of Lapidoth, was judging Israel at that time. 5And she would sit under the palm tree of Deborah between Ramah and Bethel in the mountains of Ephraim. And the children of Israel came up to her for judgment. 6Then she sent and called for Barak the son of Abinoam from Kedesh in Naphtali, and said to him, "Has not the LORD God of Israel commanded, 'Go and deploy *troops* at Mount Tabor; take with you ten thousand men of the sons of Naphtali and of the sons of Zebulun; 7and against you I will deploy Sisera, the commander of Jabin's army, with his chariots and his multitude at the River Kishon; and I will deliver him into your hand'?"

8And Barak said to her, "If you will go with me, then I will go; but if you will not go with me, I will not go!"

9So she said, "I will surely go with you; nevertheless there will be no glory for you in the journey you are taking, for the LORD will sell Sisera into the hand of a woman." Then Deborah arose and went with Barak to Kedesh. 10And Barak called Zebulun and Naphtali to Kedesh; he went up with ten thousand men under his command,[a] and Deborah went up with him.

11Now Heber the Kenite, of the children of Hobab the father-in-law of Moses, had separated himself from the Kenites and pitched his tent near the terebinth tree at Zaanaim, which *is* beside Kedesh.

12And they reported to Sisera that Barak the son of Abinoam had gone up to Mount Tabor. 13So Sisera gathered together all his chariots, nine hundred chariots of iron, and all the people who *were* with him, from Harosheth Hagoyim to the River Kishon.

14Then Deborah said to Barak, "Up! For this *is* the day in which the LORD has delivered Sisera into your hand. Has not the LORD gone out

4:10 [a] Literally *at his feet*

before you?" So Barak went
down from Mount Tabor with
ten thousand men following
him. 15And the LORD routed
Sisera and all *his* chariots and
all *his* army with the edge of the
sword before Barak; and Sisera
alighted from *his* chariot and
fled away on foot. 16But Barak
pursued the chariots and the
army as far as Harosheth Hagoyim, and all the army of
Sisera fell by the edge of the
sword; not a man was left.

17However, Sisera had fled
away on foot to the tent of Jael,
the wife of Heber the Kenite;
for *there was* peace between
Jabin king of Hazor and the
house of Heber the Kenite.
18And Jael went out to meet
Sisera, and said to him, "Turn
aside, my lord, turn aside to
me; do not fear." And when
he had turned aside with her
into the tent, she covered him
with a blanket.

19Then he said to her,
"Please give me a little water
to drink, for I am thirsty." So
she opened a jug of milk, gave
him a drink, and covered him.
20And he said to her, "Stand
at the door of the tent, and if
any man comes and inquires
of you, and says, 'Is there any
man here?' you shall say, 'No.'"

21Then Jael, Heber's wife,
took a tent peg and took a
hammer in her hand, and
went softly to him and drove
the peg into his temple, and
it went down into the ground;
for he was fast asleep and
weary. So he died. 22And then,
as Barak pursued Sisera, Jael
came out to meet him, and
said to him, "Come, I will show
you the man whom you seek."
And when he went into her
tent, there lay Sisera, dead
with the peg in his temple.

23So on that day God sub-
dued Jabin king of Canaan in
the presence of the children
of Israel. 24And the hand of
the children of Israel grew
stronger and stronger against
Jabin king of Canaan, until
they had destroyed Jabin king
of Canaan.

THE SONG OF DEBORAH

5 Then Deborah and Barak
the son of Abinoam sang
on that day, saying:

2 "When leaders
lead in Israel,
When the people willingly
offer themselves,
Bless the LORD!

3 "Hear, O kings! Give
ear, O princes!
I, *even* I, will sing
to the LORD;
I will sing praise to the
LORD God of Israel.

4 "LORD, when You went
out from Seir,
When You marched from
the field of Edom,
The earth trembled and
the heavens poured,
The clouds also
poured water;

5 The mountains gushed
before the LORD,
This Sinai, before the
LORD God of Israel.

6 "In the days of Shamgar,
son of Anath,
In the days of Jael,
The highways were
deserted,
And the travelers walked
along the byways.
7 Village life ceased, it
ceased in Israel,
Until I, Deborah, arose,
Arose a mother in
Israel.
8 They chose new gods;
Then *there was* war
in the gates;
Not a shield or spear
was seen among forty
thousand in Israel.
9 My heart *is* with the
rulers of Israel
Who offered themselves
willingly with
the people.
Bless the LORD!

10 "Speak, you who ride
on white donkeys,
Who sit in judges' attire,
And who walk along
the road.
11 Far from the noise of
the archers, among
the watering places,
There they shall recount
the righteous acts
of the LORD,
The righteous acts *for*
His villagers in Israel;
Then the people of
the LORD shall go
down to the gates.

12 "Awake, awake, Deborah!
Awake, awake,
sing a song!
Arise, Barak, and lead
your captives away,
O son of Abinoam!

13 "Then the survivors
came down, the people
against the nobles;
The LORD came down
for me against
the mighty.
14 From Ephraim *were*
those whose roots
were in Amalek.
After you, Benjamin,
with your peoples,
From Machir rulers
came down,
And from Zebulun
those who bear the
recruiter's staff.
15 And the princes of
Issachar[a] *were*
with Deborah;
As Issachar, so *was* Barak
Sent into the valley
under his command;[b]
Among the divisions
of Reuben
There were great
resolves of heart.
16 Why did you sit among
the sheepfolds,

5:15 [a] Following Septuagint, Syriac, Targum, and Vulgate; Masoretic Text reads *And my princes in Issachar.* [b] Literally *at his feet*

To hear the pipings
for the flocks?
The divisions of
Reuben have great
searchings of heart.
17 Gilead stayed beyond
the Jordan,
And why did Dan
remain on ships?[a]
Asher continued at
the seashore,
And stayed by his inlets.
18 Zebulun *is* a people *who*
jeopardized their lives
to the point of death,
Naphtali also, on
the heights of the
battlefield.

19 "The kings came
and fought,
Then the kings of
Canaan fought
In Taanach, by the
waters of Megiddo;
They took no spoils
of silver.
20 They fought from
the heavens;
The stars from their
courses fought
against Sisera.
21 The torrent of Kishon
swept them away,
That ancient torrent, the
torrent of Kishon.
O my soul, march
on in strength!
22 Then the horses'
hooves pounded,
The galloping, galloping
of his steeds.

23 'Curse Meroz,' said the
angel[a] of the LORD,
'Curse its inhabitants
bitterly,
Because they did not
come to the help
of the LORD,
To the help of the LORD
against the mighty.'

24 "Most blessed among
women is Jael,
The wife of Heber
the Kenite;
Blessed is she among
women in tents.
25 He asked for water,
she gave milk;
She brought out cream
in a lordly bowl.
26 She stretched her hand
to the tent peg,
Her right hand to the
workmen's hammer;
She pounded Sisera, she
pierced his head,
She split and struck
through his temple.
27 At her feet he sank,
he fell, he lay still;
At her feet he
sank, he fell;
Where he sank, there
he fell dead.

28 "The mother of Sisera
looked through
the window,
And cried out through
the lattice,
'Why is his chariot *so*
long in coming?

5:17 [a] Or *at ease*   5:23 [a] Or *Angel*

Why tarries the clatter
of his chariots?'
29 Her wisest ladies
answered her,
Yes, she answered herself,
30 'Are they not finding and
dividing the spoil:
To every man a girl *or* two;
For Sisera, plunder of
dyed garments,
Plunder of garments
embroidered and dyed,
Two pieces of dyed
embroidery for the
neck of the looter?'

31 "Thus let all Your
enemies perish,
O LORD!
But *let* those who love
Him *be* like the sun
When it comes out
in full strength."

So the land had rest for forty years.

MIDIANITES OPPRESS ISRAEL

6 Then the children of Israel
did evil in the sight of the
LORD. So the LORD delivered
them into the hand of Midian
for seven years, 2and the hand
of Midian prevailed against
Israel. Because of the Midianites, the children of Israel
made for themselves the dens,
the caves, and the strongholds
which *are* in the mountains.
3So it was, whenever Israel
had sown, Midianites would
come up; also Amalekites and
the people of the East would
come up against them. 4Then
they would encamp against
them and destroy the produce
of the earth as far as Gaza, and
leave no sustenance for Israel,
neither sheep nor ox nor donkey. 5For they would come up
with their livestock and their
tents, coming in as numerous
as locusts; both they and their
camels were without number;
and they would enter the land
to destroy it. 6So Israel was
greatly impoverished because
of the Midianites, and the children of Israel cried out to the
LORD.

7And it came to pass, when
the children of Israel cried out
to the LORD because of the
Midianites, 8that the LORD
sent a prophet to the children
of Israel, who said to them,
"Thus says the LORD God of
Israel: 'I brought you up from
Egypt and brought you out of
the house of bondage; 9and I
delivered you out of the hand
of the Egyptians and out of the
hand of all who oppressed you,
and drove them out before
you and gave you their land.
10Also I said to you, "I *am* the
LORD your God; do not fear the
gods of the Amorites, in whose
land you dwell." But you have
not obeyed My voice.'"

GIDEON

11Now the Angel of the
LORD came and sat under
the terebinth tree which *was*
in Ophrah, which *belonged* to
Joash the Abiezrite, while his

son Gideon threshed wheat
in the winepress, in order to
hide *it* from the Midianites.
12And the Angel of the LORD
appeared to him, and said to
him, "The LORD *is* with you,
you mighty man of valor!"
13Gideon said to Him, "O my
lord,[a] if the LORD is with us,
why then has all this happened
to us? And where *are* all His
miracles which our fathers
told us about, saying, 'Did not
the LORD bring us up from
Egypt?' But now the LORD has
forsaken us and delivered us
into the hands of the Midianites."
14Then the LORD turned
to him and said, "Go in this
might of yours, and you shall
save Israel from the hand of
the Midianites. Have I not
sent you?"
15So he said to Him, "O my
Lord,[a] how can I save Israel?
Indeed my clan *is* the weak-
est in Manasseh, and I *am* the
least in my father's house."
16And the LORD said to him,
"Surely I will be with you, and
you shall defeat the Midianites as one man."
17Then he said to Him, "If
now I have found favor in
Your sight, then show me a
sign that it is You who talk
with me. 18Do not depart from
here, I pray, until I come to
You and bring out my offering
and set *it* before You."
And He said, "I will wait
until you come back."
19So Gideon went in and
prepared a young goat, and
unleavened bread from an
ephah of flour. The meat he
put in a basket, and he put the
broth in a pot; and he brought
them out to Him under the
terebinth tree and presented
them. 20The Angel of God said
to him, "Take the meat and
the unleavened bread and lay
them on this rock, and pour
out the broth." And he did so.
21Then the Angel of the
LORD put out the end of the
staff that *was* in His hand, and
touched the meat and the unleavened bread; and fire rose
out of the rock and consumed
the meat and the unleavened
bread. And the Angel of the
LORD departed out of his sight.
22Now Gideon perceived
that He *was* the Angel of the
LORD. So Gideon said, "Alas,
O Lord GOD! For I have seen the
Angel of the LORD face to face."
23Then the LORD said to
him, "Peace *be* with you; do
not fear, you shall not die."
24So Gideon built an altar
there to the LORD, and called
it The-LORD-*Is*-Peace.[a] To this
day it *is* still in Ophrah of the
Abiezrites.
25Now it came to pass the
same night that the LORD said
to him, "Take your father's
young bull, the second bull

6:13 [a] Hebrew *adoni,* used of man 6:15 [a] Hebrew *Adonai,* used of God 6:24 [a] Hebrew *YHWH Shalom*

of seven years old, and tear down the altar of Baal that your father has, and cut down the wooden image[a] that *is* beside it; [26]and build an altar to the LORD your God on top of this rock in the proper arrangement, and take the second bull and offer a burnt sacrifice with the wood of the image which you shall cut down." [27]So Gideon took ten men from among his servants and did as the LORD had said to him. But because he feared his father's household and the men of the city too much to do *it* by day, he did *it* by night.

GIDEON DESTROYS THE ALTAR OF BAAL

[28]And when the men of the city arose early in the morning, there was the altar of Baal, torn down; and the wooden image that *was* beside it was cut down, and the second bull was being offered on the altar *which had been* built. [29]So they said to one another, "Who has done this thing?" And when they had inquired and asked, they said, "Gideon the son of Joash has done this thing." [30]Then the men of the city said to Joash, "Bring out your son, that he may die, because he has torn down the altar of Baal, and because he has cut down the wooden image that *was* beside it."

[31]But Joash said to all who stood against him, "Would you plead for Baal? Would you save him? Let the one who would plead for him be put to death by morning! If he *is* a god, let him plead for himself, because his altar has been torn down!" [32]Therefore on that day he called him Jerubbaal,[a] saying, "Let Baal plead against him, because he has torn down his altar."

[33]Then all the Midianites and Amalekites, the people of the East, gathered together; and they crossed over and encamped in the Valley of Jezreel. [34]But the Spirit of the LORD came upon Gideon; then he blew the trumpet, and the Abiezrites gathered behind him. [35]And he sent messengers throughout all Manasseh, who also gathered behind him. He also sent messengers to Asher, Zebulun, and Naphtali; and they came up to meet them.

THE SIGN OF THE FLEECE

[36]So Gideon said to God, "If You will save Israel by my hand as You have said— [37]look, I shall put a fleece of wool on the threshing floor; if there is dew on the fleece only, and *it is* dry on all the ground, then I shall know that You will save Israel by my hand, as You have said." [38]And it was so.

6:25 [a] Hebrew *Asherah,* a Canaanite goddess
6:32 [a] Literally *Let Baal Plead*

When he rose early the next
morning and squeezed the
fleece together, he wrung the
dew out of the fleece, a bowl-
ful of water. 39Then Gideon
said to God, "Do not be angry
with me, but let me speak just
once more: Let me test, I pray,
just once more with the fleece;
let it now be dry only on the
fleece, but on all the ground
let there be dew." 40And God
did so that night. It was dry on
the fleece only, but there was
dew on all the ground.

GIDEON'S VALIANT THREE HUNDRED

7 Then Jerubbaal (that *is,*
Gideon) and all the people
who *were* with him rose early
and encamped beside the well
of Harod, so that the camp
of the Midianites was on the
north side of them by the hill
of Moreh in the valley.

2And the LORD said to Gideon, "The people who *are* with
you *are* too many for Me to
give the Midianites into their
hands, lest Israel claim glory
for itself against Me, saying,
'My own hand has saved me.'
3Now therefore, proclaim in
the hearing of the people, saying, 'Whoever *is* fearful and
afraid, let him turn and depart
at once from Mount Gilead.'"
And twenty-two thousand of
the people returned, and ten
thousand remained.

4But the LORD said to Gideon, "The people *are* still
too many; bring them down
to the water, and I will test
them for you there. Then it
will be, *that* of whom I say
to you, 'This one shall go
with you,' the same shall go
with you; and of whomever
I say to you, 'This one shall
not go with you,' the same
shall not go." 5So he brought
the people down to the water.
And the LORD said to Gideon,
"Everyone who laps from the
water with his tongue, as a
dog laps, you shall set apart
by himself; likewise everyone
who gets down on his knees
to drink." 6And the number
of those who lapped, *putting*
their hand to their mouth,
was three hundred men; but
all the rest of the people got
down on their knees to drink
water. 7Then the LORD said to
Gideon, "By the three hundred
men who lapped I will save
you, and deliver the Midianites into your hand. Let all the
other people go, every man to
his place." 8So the people took
provisions and their trumpets
in their hands. And he sent
away all *the rest of* Israel, every
man to his tent, and retained
those three hundred men.
Now the camp of Midian was
below him in the valley.

9It happened on the same
night that the LORD said to
him, "Arise, go down against
the camp, for I have delivered
it into your hand. 10But if you
are afraid to go down, go down
to the camp with Purah your
servant, 11and you shall hear

what they say; and afterward
your hands shall be strengthened to go down against the
camp." Then he went down
with Purah his servant to the
outpost of the armed men
who *were* in the camp. 12 Now
the Midianites and Amalekites, all the people of the East,
were lying in the valley as numerous as locusts; and their
camels *were* without number,
as the sand by the seashore in
multitude.

13 And when Gideon had
come, there was a man telling
a dream to his companion. He
said, "I have had a dream: *To
my* surprise, a loaf of barley
bread tumbled into the camp
of Midian; it came to a tent and
struck it so that it fell and overturned, and the tent collapsed."

14 Then his companion
answered and said, "This *is*
nothing else but the sword
of Gideon the son of Joash, a
man of Israel! Into his hand
God has delivered Midian and
the whole camp."

15 And so it was, when Gideon heard the telling of the
dream and its interpreta-
tion, that he worshiped. He
returned to the camp of Israel, and said, "Arise, for the
LORD has delivered the camp
of Midian into your hand."
16 Then he divided the three
hundred men into three companies, and he put a trumpet
into every man's hand, with
empty pitchers, and torches
inside the pitchers. 17 And he
said to them, "Look at me
and do likewise; watch, and
when I come to the edge of
the camp you shall do as I do:
18 When I blow the trumpet, I
and all who *are* with me, then
you also blow the trumpets
on every side of the whole
camp, and say, '*The sword of*
the LORD and of Gideon!'"

19 So Gideon and the hun-
dred men who *were* with him
came to the outpost of the
camp at the beginning of the
middle watch, just as they had
posted the watch; and they
blew the trumpets and broke
the pitchers that *were* in their
hands. 20 Then the three companies blew the trumpets and
broke the pitchers—they held
the torches in their left hands
and the trumpets in their
right hands for blowing—
and they cried, "The sword
of the LORD and of Gideon!"
21 And every man stood in his
place all around the camp;
and the whole army ran and
cried out and fled. 22 When the
three hundred blew the trumpets, the LORD set every man's
sword against his companion
throughout the whole camp;
and the army fled to Beth Acacia,[a] toward Zererah, as far as
the border of Abel Meholah,
by Tabbath.

23 And the men of Israel
gathered together from Naph-

7:22 [a] Hebrew *Beth Shittah*

tali, Asher, and all Manasseh,
and pursued the Midianites.
24Then Gideon sent mes-
sengers throughout all the
mountains of Ephraim, saying, "Come down against the
Midianites, and seize from
them the watering places as
far as Beth Barah and the
Jordan." Then all the men of
Ephraim gathered together
and seized the watering places
as far as Beth Barah and the
Jordan. 25And they captured
two princes of the Midianites,
Oreb and Zeeb. They killed
Oreb at the rock of Oreb, and
Zeeb they killed at the winepress of Zeeb. They pursued
Midian and brought the heads
of Oreb and Zeeb to Gideon on
the other side of the Jordan.

GIDEON SUBDUES THE MIDIANITES

8 Now the men of Ephraim
said to him, "Why have you
done this to us by not calling
us when you went to fight with
the Midianites?" And they rep-
rimanded him sharply.
2So he said to them, "What
have I done now in comparison with you? *Is* not the gleaning *of the grapes* of Ephraim
better than the vintage of
Abiezer? 3God has delivered
into your hands the princes
of Midian, Oreb and Zeeb. And
what was I able to do in comparison with you?" Then their
anger toward him subsided
when he said that.
4When Gideon came to
the Jordan, he and the three
hundred men who *were* with
him crossed over, exhausted
but still in pursuit. 5Then he
said to the men of Succoth,
"Please give loaves of bread
to the people who follow me,
for they are exhausted, and I
am pursuing Zebah and Zalmunna, kings of Midian."
6And the leaders of Suc-
coth said, "*Are* the hands of
Zebah and Zalmunna now in
your hand, that we should give
bread to your army?"
7So Gideon said, "For this
cause, when the LORD has delivered Zebah and Zalmunna
into my hand, then I will tear
your flesh with the thorns of
the wilderness and with briers!" 8Then he went up from
there to Penuel and spoke to
them in the same way. And the
men of Penuel answered him
as the men of Succoth had
answered. 9So he also spoke
to the men of Penuel, saying,
"When I come back in peace,
I will tear down this tower!"
10Now Zebah and Zalmunna
were at Karkor, and their armies
with them, about fifteen thousand, all who were left of all the
army of the people of the East;
for one hundred and twenty
thousand men who drew the
sword had fallen. 11Then Gideon went up by the road of
those who dwell in tents on the
east of Nobah and Jogbehah;
and he attacked the army while
the camp felt secure. 12When
Zebah and Zalmunna fled, he

pursued them; and he took
the two kings of Midian, Zebah
and Zalmunna, and routed the
whole army.
13Then Gideon the son of
Joash returned from battle,
from the Ascent of Heres.
14And he caught a young
man of the men of Succoth
and interrogated him; and he
wrote down for him the leaders of Succoth and its elders,
seventy-seven men. 15Then
he came to the men of Succoth and said, "Here are Zebah
and Zalmunna, about whom
you ridiculed me, saying, '*Are*
the hands of Zebah and Zalmunna now in your hand, that
we should give bread to your
weary men?'" 16And he took the
elders of the city, and thorns
of the wilderness and briers,
and with them he taught the
men of Succoth. 17Then he tore
down the tower of Penuel and
killed the men of the city.
18And he said to Zebah and
Zalmunna, "What kind of men
were they whom you killed at
Tabor?"

So they answered, "As you
are, so *were* they; each one
resembled the son of a king."
19Then he said, "They *were*
my brothers, the sons of my
mother. *As* the LORD lives, if
you had let them live, I would
not kill you." 20And he said to
Jether his firstborn, "Rise, kill
them!" But the youth would
not draw his sword; for he was
afraid, because he *was* still a
youth.
21So Zebah and Zalmunna
said, "Rise yourself, and kill
us; for as a man *is, so is* his
strength." So Gideon arose
and killed Zebah and Zal-
munna, and took the crescent
ornaments that *were* on their
camels' necks.

GIDEON'S EPHOD

22Then the men of Israel
said to Gideon, "Rule over us,
both you and your son, and
your grandson also; for you
have delivered us from the
hand of Midian."
23But Gideon said to them,
"I will not rule over you, nor
shall my son rule over you;
the LORD shall rule over you."
24Then Gideon said to them, "I
would like to make a request
of you, that each of you would
give me the earrings from his
plunder." For they had golden
earrings, because they *were*
Ishmaelites.
25So they answered, "We
will gladly give *them.*" And
they spread out a garment,
and each man threw into it
the earrings from his plunder.
26Now the weight of the gold
earrings that he requested
was one thousand seven hundred *shekels* of gold, besides
the crescent ornaments, pendants, and purple robes which
were on the kings of Midian,
and besides the chains that
were around their camels'
necks. 27Then Gideon made it
into an ephod and set it up in
his city, Ophrah. And all Israel

played the harlot with it there.
It became a snare to Gideon
and to his house.
28Thus Midian was sub-
dued before the children of
Israel, so that they lifted their
heads no more. And the country was quiet for forty years in
the days of Gideon.

DEATH OF GIDEON

29Then Jerubbaal the son
of Joash went and dwelt in his
own house. 30Gideon had seventy sons who were his own
offspring, for he had many
wives. 31And his concubine
who *was* in Shechem also
bore him a son, whose name
he called Abimelech. 32Now
Gideon the son of Joash died
at a good old age, and was
buried in the tomb of Joash
his father, in Ophrah of the
Abiezrites.
33So it was, as soon as Gideon was dead, that the children of Israel again played
the harlot with the Baals, and
made Baal-Berith their god.
34Thus the children of Israel
did not remember the LORD
their God, who had delivered
them from the hands of all
their enemies on every side;
35nor did they show kindness
to the house of Jerubbaal (Gideon) in accordance with the
good he had done for Israel.

ABIMELECH'S CONSPIRACY

9 Then Abimelech the
son of Jerubbaal went
to Shechem, to his mother's
brothers, and spoke with them
and with all the family of the
house of his mother's father,
saying, 2"Please speak in the
hearing of all the men of Shechem: 'Which is better for you,
that all seventy of the sons of
Jerubbaal reign over you, or
that one reign over you?' Remember that I *am* your own
flesh and bone."
3And his mother's brothers
spoke all these words concerning him in the hearing
of all the men of Shechem;
and their heart was inclined
to follow Abimelech, for they
said, "He is our brother." 4So
they gave him seventy *shekels* of silver from the temple
of Baal-Berith, with which
Abimelech hired worthless
and reckless men; and they
followed him. 5Then he went
to his father's house at Ophrah and killed his brothers,
the seventy sons of Jerubbaal,
on one stone. But Jotham the
youngest son of Jerubbaal
was left, because he hid himself. 6And all the men of Shechem gathered together, all of
Beth Millo, and they went and
made Abimelech king beside
the terebinth tree at the pillar
that *was* in Shechem.

THE PARABLE OF THE TREES

7Now when they told Jo-
tham, he went and stood on
top of Mount Gerizim, and
lifted his voice and cried out.
And he said to them:

"Listen to me, you
men of Shechem,
That God may
listen to you!

8 "The trees once went
forth to anoint a
king over them.
And they said to
the olive tree,
'Reign over us!'
9 But the olive tree
said to them,
'Should I cease
giving my oil,
With which they honor
God and men,
And go to sway
over trees?'

10 "Then the trees said
to the fig tree,
'You come *and*
reign over us!'
11 But the fig tree
said to them,
'Should I cease my
sweetness and
my good fruit,
And go to sway
over trees?'

12 "Then the trees
said to the vine,
'You come *and*
reign over us!'
13 But the vine said to
them,
'Should I cease my
new wine,
Which cheers *both*
God and men,
And go to sway
over trees?'

14 "Then all the trees
said to the bramble,
'You come *and*
reign over us!'
15 And the bramble
said to the trees,
'If in truth you anoint
me as king over you,
Then come *and* take
shelter in my shade;
But if not, let fire come
out of the bramble
And devour the cedars
of Lebanon!'

16 "Now therefore, if you
have acted in truth and sincerity in making Abimelech
king, and if you have dealt
well with Jerubbaal and his
house, and have done to him
as he deserves— 17 for my father fought for you, risked
his life, and delivered you out
of the hand of Midian; 18 but
you have risen up against my
father's house this day, and
killed his seventy sons on
one stone, and made Abim-
elech, the son of his female
servant, king over the men of
Shechem, because he is your
brother— 19 if then you have
acted in truth and sincerity
with Jerubbaal and with his
house this day, *then* rejoice in
Abimelech, and let him also
rejoice in you. 20 But if not,
let fire come from Abime-
lech and devour the men of
Shechem and Beth Millo; and
let fire come from the men
of Shechem and from Beth
Millo and devour Abimelech!"

21And Jotham ran away and fled; and he went to Beer and dwelt there, for fear of Abimelech his brother.

DOWNFALL OF ABIMELECH

22After Abimelech had reigned over Israel three years, 23God sent a spirit of ill will between Abimelech and the men of Shechem; and the men of Shechem dealt treacherously with Abimelech, 24that the crime *done* to the seventy sons of Jerubbaal might be settled and their blood be laid on Abimelech their brother, who killed them, and on the men of Shechem, who aided him in the killing of his brothers. 25And the men of Shechem set men in ambush against him on the tops of the mountains, and they robbed all who passed by them along that way; and it was told Abimelech.

26Now Gaal the son of Ebed came with his brothers and went over to Shechem; and the men of Shechem put their confidence in him. 27So they went out into the fields, and gathered *grapes* from their vineyards and trod *them,* and made merry. And they went into the house of their god, and ate and drank, and cursed Abimelech. 28Then Gaal the son of Ebed said, "Who *is* Abimelech, and who *is* Shechem, that we should serve him? *Is he* not the son of Jerubbaal, and *is not* Zebul his officer? Serve the men of Hamor the father of Shechem; but why should we serve him? 29If only this people were under my authority![a] Then I would remove Abimelech." So he[b] said to Abimelech, "Increase your army and come out!"

30When Zebul, the ruler of the city, heard the words of Gaal the son of Ebed, his anger was aroused. 31And he sent messengers to Abimelech secretly, saying, "Take note! Gaal the son of Ebed and his brothers have come to Shechem; and here they are, fortifying the city against you. 32Now therefore, get up by night, you and the people who *are* with you, and lie in wait in the field. 33And it shall be, as soon as the sun is up in the morning, *that* you shall rise early and rush upon the city; and *when* he and the people who are with him come out against you, you may then do to them as you find opportunity."

34So Abimelech and all the people who *were* with him rose by night, and lay in wait against Shechem in four companies. 35When Gaal the son of Ebed went out and stood in the entrance to the city gate, Abimelech and the

9:29 [a] Literally *hand* [b] Following Masoretic Text and Targum; Dead Sea Scrolls read *they;* Septuagint reads *I.*

people who *were* with him
rose from lying in wait. 36And
when Gaal saw the people, he
said to Zebul, "Look, people
are coming down from the
tops of the mountains!"

But Zebul said to him, "You
see the shadows of the mountains as *if they were* men."

37So Gaal spoke again and
said, "See, people are coming
down from the center of the
land, and another company
is coming from the Diviners'[a]
Terebinth Tree."

38Then Zebul said to him,
"Where indeed *is* your mouth
now, with which you said,
'Who is Abimelech, that we
should serve him?' *Are* not
these the people whom you
despised? Go out, if you will,
and fight with them now."

39So Gaal went out, lead-
ing the men of Shechem, and
fought with Abimelech. 40And
Abimelech chased him, and
he fled from him; and many
fell wounded, to the *very* entrance of the gate. 41Then
Abimelech dwelt at Arumah,
and Zebul drove out Gaal and
his brothers, so that they
would not dwell in Shechem.

42And it came about on
the next day that the people
went out into the field, and
they told Abimelech. 43So he
took his people, divided them
into three companies, and
lay in wait in the field. And
he looked, and there were the
people, coming out of the city;
and he rose against them and
attacked them. 44Then Abimelech and the company that
was with him rushed forward
and stood at the entrance of
the gate of the city; and the
other two companies rushed
upon all who *were* in the fields
and killed them. 45So Abimelech fought against the city all
that day; he took the city and
killed the people who *were* in
it; and he demolished the city
and sowed it with salt.

46Now when all the men
of the tower of Shechem had
heard *that,* they entered the
stronghold of the temple of
the god Berith. 47And it was
told Abimelech that all the
men of the tower of Shechem
were gathered together. 48Then
Abimelech went up to Mount
Zalmon, he and all the people who *were* with him. And
Abimelech took an ax in his
hand and cut down a bough
from the trees, and took it and
laid *it* on his shoulder; then he
said to the people who were
with him, "What you have
seen me do, make haste *and*
do as I *have done.*" 49So each of
the people likewise cut down
his own bough and followed
Abimelech, put *them* against
the stronghold, and set the
stronghold on fire above them,
so that all the people of the
tower of Shechem died, about
a thousand men and women.

9:37 [a] Hebrew *Meonenim*

50Then Abimelech went to Thebez, and he encamped against Thebez and took it. 51But there was a strong tower in the city, and all the men and women—all the people of the city—fled there and shut themselves in; then they went up to the top of the tower. 52So Abimelech came as far as the tower and fought against it; and he drew near the door of the tower to burn it with fire. 53But a certain woman dropped an upper millstone on Abimelech's head and crushed his skull. 54Then he called quickly to the young man, his armorbearer, and said to him, "Draw your sword and kill me, lest men say of me, 'A woman killed him.'" So his young man thrust him through, and he died. 55And when the men of Israel saw that Abimelech was dead, they departed, every man to his place.

56Thus God repaid the wickedness of Abimelech, which he had done to his father by killing his seventy brothers. 57And all the evil of the men of Shechem God returned on their own heads, and on them came the curse of Jotham the son of Jerubbaal.

TOLA

10 After Abimelech there arose to save Israel Tola the son of Puah, the son of Dodo, a man of Issachar; and he dwelt in Shamir in the mountains of Ephraim. 2He judged Israel twenty-three years; and he died and was buried in Shamir.

JAIR

3After him arose Jair, a Gileadite; and he judged Israel twenty-two years. 4Now he had thirty sons who rode on thirty donkeys; they also had thirty towns, which are called "Havoth Jair"[a] to this day, which *are* in the land of Gilead. 5And Jair died and was buried in Camon.

ISRAEL OPPRESSED AGAIN

6Then the children of Israel again did evil in the sight of the LORD, and served the Baals and the Ashtoreths, the gods of Syria, the gods of Sidon, the gods of Moab, the gods of the people of Ammon, and the gods of the Philistines; and they forsook the LORD and did not serve Him. 7So the anger of the LORD was hot against Israel; and He sold them into the hands of the Philistines and into the hands of the people of Ammon. 8From that year they harassed and oppressed the children of Israel for eighteen years—all the children of Israel who *were* on the other side of the Jordan in the land of the Amorites, in Gilead. 9Moreover

10:4 [a] Literally *Towns of Jair* (compare Numbers 32:41 and Deuteronomy 3:14)

the people of Ammon crossed
over the Jordan to fight against
Judah also, against Benjamin, and against the house
of Ephraim, so that Israel was
severely distressed.
10And the children of Is-
rael cried out to the LORD, saying, "We have sinned against
You, because we have both
forsaken our God and served
the Baals!"
11So the LORD said to the
children of Israel, "*Did I* not
deliver you from the Egyptians
and from the Amorites and
from the people of Ammon
and from the Philistines?
12Also the Sidonians and
Amalekites and Maonites[a]
oppressed you; and you cried
out to Me, and I delivered you
from their hand. 13Yet you
have forsaken Me and served
other gods. Therefore I will
deliver you no more. 14Go and
cry out to the gods which you
have chosen; let them deliver
you in your time of distress."
15And the children of Israel
said to the LORD, "We have
sinned! Do to us whatever
seems best to You; only deliver us this day, we pray." 16So
they put away the foreign gods
from among them and served
the LORD. And His soul could
no longer endure the misery
of Israel.
17Then the people of
Ammon gathered together
and encamped in Gilead. And
the children of Israel assembled together and encamped
in Mizpah. 18And the people,
the leaders of Gilead, said
to one another, "Who *is* the
man who will begin the fight
against the people of Ammon?
He shall be head over all the
inhabitants of Gilead."

JEPHTHAH

11 Now Jephthah the Gileadite was a mighty man of
valor, but he *was* the son of a
harlot; and Gilead begot Jephthah. 2Gilead's wife bore sons;
and when his wife's sons grew
up, they drove Jephthah out,
and said to him, "You shall have
no inheritance in our father's
house, for you *are* the son of
another woman." 3Then Jephthah fled from his brothers
and dwelt in the land of Tob;
and worthless men banded together with Jephthah and went
out *raiding* with him.
4It came to pass after a time
that the people of Ammon
made war against Israel. 5And
so it was, when the people of
Ammon made war against Israel, that the elders of Gilead
went to get Jephthah from the
land of Tob. 6Then they said to
Jephthah, "Come and be our
commander, that we may fight
against the people of Ammon."
7So Jephthah said to the elders of Gilead, "Did you not
hate me, and expel me from
my father's house? Why have

10:12 [a] Some Septuagint manuscripts read *Midianites*.

you come to me now when
you are in distress?"
8And the elders of Gilead
said to Jephthah, "That is why
we have turned again to you
now, that you may go with us
and fight against the people of
Ammon, and be our head over
all the inhabitants of Gilead."
9So Jephthah said to the
elders of Gilead, "If you take
me back home to fight against
the people of Ammon, and the
LORD delivers them to me,
shall I be your head?"
10And the elders of Gilead
said to Jephthah, "The LORD
will be a witness between us,
if we do not do according to
your words." 11Then Jephthah
went with the elders of Gilead, and the people made him
head and commander over
them; and Jephthah spoke all
his words before the LORD in
Mizpah.
12Now Jephthah sent mes-
sengers to the king of the people of Ammon, saying, "What
do you have against me, that
you have come to fight against
me in my land?"
13And the king of the people of Ammon answered the
messengers of Jephthah, "Because Israel took away my
land when they came up out
of Egypt, from the Arnon as
far as the Jabbok, and to the
Jordan. Now therefore, restore those *lands* peaceably."
14So Jephthah again sent
messengers to the king of the
people of Ammon, 15and said
to him, "Thus says Jephthah:
'Israel did not take away the
land of Moab, nor the land of
the people of Ammon; 16for
when Israel came up from
Egypt, they walked through
the wilderness as far as the
Red Sea and came to Kadesh.
17Then Israel sent messengers
to the king of Edom, saying,
"Please let me pass through
your land." But the king of
Edom would not heed. And
in like manner they sent to the
king of Moab, but he would not
consent. So Israel remained in
Kadesh. 18And they went along
through the wilderness and
bypassed the land of Edom
and the land of Moab, came
to the east side of the land of
Moab, and encamped on the
other side of the Arnon. But
they did not enter the border
of Moab, for the Arnon *was* the
border of Moab. 19Then Israel
sent messengers to Sihon king
of the Amorites, king of Heshbon; and Israel said to him,
"Please let us pass through
your land into our place."
20But Sihon did not trust Israel to pass through his territory. So Sihon gathered all his
people together, encamped
in Jahaz, and fought against
Israel. 21And the LORD God of
Israel delivered Sihon and all
his people into the hand of Israel, and they defeated them.
Thus Israel gained possession
of all the land of the Amorites,
who inhabited that country.
22They took possession of all

the territory of the Amorites, from the Arnon to the Jabbok and from the wilderness to the Jordan.

23'And now the LORD God of Israel has dispossessed the Amorites from before His people Israel; should you then possess it? 24Will you not possess whatever Chemosh your god gives you to possess? So whatever the LORD our God takes possession of before us, we will possess. 25And now, *are* you any better than Balak the son of Zippor, king of Moab? Did he ever strive against Israel? Did he ever fight against them? 26While Israel dwelt in Heshbon and its villages, in Aroer and its villages, and in all the cities along the banks of the Arnon, for three hundred years, why did you not recover *them* within that time? 27Therefore I have not sinned against you, but you wronged me by fighting against me. May the LORD, the Judge, render judgment this day between the children of Israel and the people of Ammon.'" 28However, the king of the people of Ammon did not heed the words which Jephthah sent him.

JEPHTHAH'S VOW AND VICTORY

29Then the Spirit of the LORD came upon Jephthah, and he passed through Gilead and Manasseh, and passed through Mizpah of Gilead; and from Mizpah of Gilead he advanced *toward* the people of Ammon. 30And Jephthah made a vow to the LORD, and said, "If You will indeed deliver the people of Ammon into my hands, 31then it will be that whatever comes out of the doors of my house to meet me, when I return in peace from the people of Ammon, shall surely be the LORD's, and I will offer it up as a burnt offering."

32So Jephthah advanced toward the people of Ammon to fight against them, and the LORD delivered them into his hands. 33And he defeated them from Aroer as far as Minnith—twenty cities—and to Abel Keramim,[a] with a very great slaughter. Thus the people of Ammon were subdued before the children of Israel.

JEPHTHAH'S DAUGHTER

34When Jephthah came to his house at Mizpah, there was his daughter, coming out to meet him with timbrels and dancing; and she *was his* only child. Besides her he had neither son nor daughter. 35And it came to pass, when he saw her, that he tore his clothes, and said, "Alas, my daughter! You have brought me very low! You are among those who trouble me! For I have given my word to the LORD, and I cannot go back on it."

11:33 [a] Literally *Plain of Vineyards*

36So she said to him, "My
father, *if* you have given your
word to the LORD, do to me according to what has gone out of
your mouth, because the LORD
has avenged you of your enemies, the people of Ammon."
37Then she said to her father,
"Let this thing be done for me:
let me alone for two months,
that I may go and wander on
the mountains and bewail my
virginity, my friends and I."
38So he said, "Go." And he
sent her away *for* two months;
and she went with her friends,
and bewailed her virginity on
the mountains. 39And it was
so at the end of two months
that she returned to her father, and he carried out his
vow with her which he had
vowed. She knew no man.

And it became a custom
in Israel 40*that* the daughters
of Israel went four days each
year to lament the daughter of
Jephthah the Gileadite.

JEPHTHAH'S CONFLICT WITH EPHRAIM

12 Then the men of
Ephraim gathered to-
gether, crossed over toward
Zaphon, and said to Jephthah,
"Why did you cross over to
fight against the people of
Ammon, and did not call us
to go with you? We will burn
your house down on you with
fire!"
2And Jephthah said to
them, "My people and I were
in a great struggle with the
people of Ammon; and when
I called you, you did not deliver me out of their hands.
3So when I saw that you would
not deliver *me,* I took my life
in my hands and crossed over
against the people of Ammon;
and the LORD delivered them
into my hand. Why then have
you come up to me this day to
fight against me?" 4Now Jephthah gathered together all
the men of Gilead and fought
against Ephraim. And the men
of Gilead defeated Ephraim,
because they said, "You Gileadites *are* fugitives of Ephraim
among the Ephraimites *and*
among the Manassites." 5The
Gileadites seized the fords of
the Jordan before the Ephraimites *arrived.* And when *any*
Ephraimite who escaped said,
"Let me cross over," the men of
Gilead would say to him, "*Are*
you an Ephraimite?" If he said,
"No," 6then they would say to
him, "Then say, 'Shibboleth'!"
And he would say, "Sibboleth,"
for he could not pronounce
it right. Then they would take
him and kill him at the fords
of the Jordan. There fell at
that time forty-two thousand
Ephraimites.

7And Jephthah judged Is-
rael six years. Then Jephthah
the Gileadite died and was buried among the cities of Gilead.

IBZAN, ELON, AND ABDON

8After him, Ibzan of Bethlehem judged Israel. 9He had
thirty sons. And he gave away

thirty daughters in marriage,
and brought in thirty daughters from elsewhere for his
sons. He judged Israel seven
years. 10Then Ibzan died and
was buried at Bethlehem.

11After him, Elon the Zebulunite judged Israel. He
judged Israel ten years. 12And
Elon the Zebulunite died and
was buried at Aijalon in the
country of Zebulun.

13After him, Abdon the son
of Hillel the Pirathonite judged
Israel. 14He had forty sons and
thirty grandsons, who rode
on seventy young donkeys.
He judged Israel eight years.
15Then Abdon the son of Hillel
the Pirathonite died and was
buried in Pirathon in the land
of Ephraim, in the mountains
of the Amalekites.

THE BIRTH OF SAMSON

13 Again the children of Israel did evil in the sight
of the LORD, and the LORD delivered them into the hand of
the Philistines for forty years.

2Now there was a certain
man from Zorah, of the family
of the Danites, whose name
was Manoah; and his wife *was*
barren and had no children.
3And the Angel of the LORD
appeared to the woman and
said to her, "Indeed now, you
are barren and have borne no
children, but you shall conceive and bear a son. 4Now
therefore, please be careful
not to drink wine or *similar*
drink, and not to eat anything
unclean. 5For behold, you
shall conceive and bear a son.
And no razor shall come upon
his head, for the child shall
be a Nazirite to God from the
womb; and he shall begin to
deliver Israel out of the hand
of the Philistines."

6So the woman came and
told her husband, saying, "A
Man of God came to me, and
His countenance *was* like the
countenance of the Angel of
God, very awesome; but I did
not ask Him where He *was*
from, and He did not tell me
His name. 7And He said to me,
'Behold, you shall conceive
and bear a son. Now drink
no wine or *similar* drink, nor
eat anything unclean, for the
child shall be a Nazirite to God
from the womb to the day of
his death.'"

8Then Manoah prayed to
the LORD, and said, "O my
Lord, please let the Man of
God whom You sent come to
us again and teach us what we
shall do for the child who will
be born."

9And God listened to the
voice of Manoah, and the Angel
of God came to the woman
again as she was sitting in the
field; but Manoah her husband
was not with her. 10Then the
woman ran in haste and told
her husband, and said to him,
"Look, the Man who came to
me the *other* day has just now
appeared to me!"

11So Manoah arose and followed his wife. When he came

to the Man, he said to Him, "Are You the Man who spoke to this woman?"

And He said, "I *am.*"

12Manoah said, "Now let Your words come *to pass!* What will be the boy's rule of life, and his work?"

13So the Angel of the LORD said to Manoah, "Of all that I said to the woman let her be careful. 14She may not eat anything that comes from the vine, nor may she drink wine or *similar* drink, nor eat anything unclean. All that I commanded her let her observe."

15Then Manoah said to the Angel of the LORD, "Please let us detain You, and we will prepare a young goat for You."

16And the Angel of the LORD said to Manoah, "Though you detain Me, I will not eat your food. But if you offer a burnt offering, you must offer it to the LORD." (For Manoah did not know He *was* the Angel of the LORD.)

17Then Manoah said to the Angel of the LORD, "What *is* Your name, that when Your words come *to pass* we may honor You?"

18And the Angel of the LORD said to him, "Why do you ask My name, seeing it *is* wonderful?"

19So Manoah took the young goat with the grain offering, and offered it upon the rock to the LORD. And He did a wondrous thing while Manoah and his wife looked on— 20it happened as the flame went up toward heaven from the altar—the Angel of the LORD ascended in the flame of the altar! When Manoah and his wife saw *this,* they fell on their faces to the ground. 21When the Angel of the LORD appeared no more to Manoah and his wife, then Manoah knew that He *was* the Angel of the LORD.

22And Manoah said to his wife, "We shall surely die, because we have seen God!"

23But his wife said to him, "If the LORD had desired to kill us, He would not have accepted a burnt offering and a grain offering from our hands, nor would He have shown us all these *things,* nor would He have told us *such things* as these at this time."

24So the woman bore a son and called his name Samson; and the child grew, and the LORD blessed him. 25And the Spirit of the LORD began to move upon him at Mahaneh Dan[a] between Zorah and Eshtaol.

SAMSON'S PHILISTINE WIFE

14 Now Samson went down to Timnah, and saw a woman in Timnah of the daughters of the Philistines. 2So he went up and told his father and mother, saying, "I have seen a woman in Timnah

13:25 [a] Literally *Camp of Dan* (compare 18:12)

of the daughters of the Philistines; now therefore, get her
for me as a wife."

3Then his father and mother
said to him, "*Is there* no woman
among the daughters of your
brethren, or among all my people, that you must go and get a
wife from the uncircumcised
Philistines?"

And Samson said to his father, "Get her for me, for she
pleases me well."

4But his father and mother
did not know that it was of the
LORD—that He was seeking
an occasion to move against
the Philistines. For at that
time the Philistines had dominion over Israel.

5So Samson went down to
Timnah with his father and
mother, and came to the vineyards of Timnah.

Now *to his* surprise, a young
lion *came* roaring against him.
6And the Spirit of the LORD
came mightily upon him, and
he tore the lion apart as one
would have torn apart a young
goat, though *he had* nothing
in his hand. But he did not tell
his father or his mother what
he had done.

7Then he went down and
talked with the woman; and she
pleased Samson well. 8After
some time, when he returned
to get her, he turned aside to
see the carcass of the lion. And
behold, a swarm of bees and
honey *were* in the carcass of
the lion. 9He took some of it
in his hands and went along,
eating. When he came to his
father and mother, he gave
some to them, and they also
ate. But he did not tell them
that he had taken the honey
out of the carcass of the lion.

10So his father went down
to the woman. And Samson
gave a feast there, for young
men used to do so. 11And it
happened, when they saw
him, that they brought thirty
companions to be with him.

12Then Samson said to
them, "Let me pose a riddle to
you. If you can correctly solve
and explain it to me within the
seven days of the feast, then I
will give you thirty linen garments and thirty changes of
clothing. 13But if you cannot
explain *it* to me, then you shall
give me thirty linen garments
and thirty changes of clothing."

And they said to him, "Pose
your riddle, that we may
hear it."

14So he said to them:

"Out of the eater came
something to eat,
And out of the strong
came something sweet."

Now for three days they could
not explain the riddle.

15But it came to pass on the
seventh[a] day that they said to

14:15 [a] Following Masoretic Text, Targum, and Vulgate; Septuagint and Syriac read *fourth*.

Samson's wife, "Entice your
husband, that he may explain
the riddle to us, or else we will
burn you and your father's
house with fire. Have you invited us in order to take what
is ours? *Is that* not *so?*"
16 Then Samson's wife wept
on him, and said, "You only
hate me! You do not love me!
You have posed a riddle to the
sons of my people, but you
have not explained *it* to me."
And he said to her, "Look, I
have not explained *it* to my father or my mother; so should
I explain *it* to you?" 17 Now she
had wept on him the seven
days while their feast lasted.
And it happened on the seventh day that he told her,
because she pressed him so
much. Then she explained
the riddle to the sons of her
people. 18 So the men of the
city said to him on the seventh
day before the sun went down:

"What *is* sweeter
than honey?
And what *is* stronger
than a lion?"

And he said to them:

"If you had not plowed
with my heifer,
You would not have
solved my riddle!"

19 Then the Spirit of the
LORD came upon him mightily,
and he went down to Ashkelon
and killed thirty of their men,
took their apparel, and gave
the changes *of clothing* to those
who had explained the riddle.
So his anger was aroused, and
he went back up to his father's
house. 20 And Samson's wife
was *given* to his companion,
who had been his best man.

SAMSON DEFEATS THE PHILISTINES

15 After a while, in the time
of wheat harvest, it hap-
pened that Samson visited his
wife with a young goat. And he
said, "Let me go in to my wife,
into *her* room." But her father
would not permit him to go in.
2 Her father said, "I really
thought that you thoroughly
hated her; therefore I gave
her to your companion. *Is* not
her younger sister better than
she? Please, take her instead."
3 And Samson said to them,
"This time I shall be blameless regarding the Philistines
if I harm them!" 4 Then Samson went and caught three
hundred foxes; and he took
torches, turned *the foxes* tail to
tail, and put a torch between
each pair of tails. 5 When he
had set the torches on fire, he
let *the foxes* go into the standing grain of the Philistines, and
burned up both the shocks and
the standing grain, as well as
the vineyards *and* olive groves.
6 Then the Philistines said,
"Who has done this?"
And they answered, "Sam-
son, the son-in-law of the Tim-
nite, because he has taken his

wife and given her to his companion." So the Philistines
came up and burned her and
her father with fire.
7 Samson said to them,
"Since you would do a thing
like this, I will surely take revenge on you, and after that
I will cease." 8 So he attacked
them hip and thigh with a
great slaughter; then he went
down and dwelt in the cleft of
the rock of Etam.
9 Now the Philistines went
up, encamped in Judah, and
deployed themselves against
Lehi. 10 And the men of Judah
said, "Why have you come up
against us?"
So they answered, "We have
come up to arrest Samson, to
do to him as he has done to us."
11 Then three thousand men
of Judah went down to the
cleft of the rock of Etam, and
said to Samson, "Do you not
know that the Philistines rule
over us? What *is* this you have
done to us?"
And he said to them, "As
they did to me, so I have done
to them."
12 But they said to him, "We
have come down to arrest you,
that we may deliver you into
the hand of the Philistines."
Then Samson said to them,
"Swear to me that you will not
kill me yourselves."
13 So they spoke to him, saying, "No, but we will tie you
securely and deliver you into
their hand; but we will surely
not kill you." And they bound
him with two new ropes and
brought him up from the rock.
14 When he came to Lehi,
the Philistines came shouting
against him. Then the Spirit of
the LORD came mightily upon
him; and the ropes that *were*
on his arms became like flax
that is burned with fire, and
his bonds broke loose from
his hands. 15 He found a fresh
jawbone of a donkey, reached
out his hand and took it, and
killed a thousand men with it.
16 Then Samson said:

"With the jawbone
  of a donkey,
Heaps upon heaps,
With the jawbone
  of a donkey
I have slain a
  thousand men!"

17 And so it was, when he had
finished speaking, that he
threw the jawbone from his
hand, and called that place
Ramath Lehi.[a]
18 Then he became very
thirsty; so he cried out to the
LORD and said, "You have
given this great deliverance by
the hand of Your servant; and
now shall I die of thirst and
fall into the hand of the uncircumcised?" 19 So God split the
hollow place that *is* in Lehi,[a]

15:17 [a] Literally *Jawbone Height* 15:19 [a] Literally *Jawbone* (compare verse 14)

and water came out, and he drank; and his spirit returned, and he revived. Therefore he called its name En Hakkore,[b] which is in Lehi to this day. 20 And he judged Israel twenty years in the days of the Philistines.

SAMSON AND DELILAH

16 Now Samson went to Gaza and saw a harlot there, and went in to her. 2 *When* the Gazites *were told,* "Samson has come here!" they surrounded *the place* and lay in wait for him all night at the gate of the city. They were quiet all night, saying, "In the morning, when it is daylight, we will kill him." 3 And Samson lay *low* till midnight; then he arose at midnight, took hold of the doors of the gate of the city and the two gateposts, pulled them up, bar and all, put *them* on his shoulders, and carried them to the top of the hill that faces Hebron.

4 Afterward it happened that he loved a woman in the Valley of Sorek, whose name *was* Delilah. 5 And the lords of the Philistines came up to her and said to her, "Entice him, and find out where his great strength *lies,* and by what *means* we may overpower him, that we may bind him to afflict him; and every one of us will give you eleven hundred *pieces* of silver."

6 So Delilah said to Samson, "Please tell me where your great strength *lies,* and with what you may be bound to afflict you."

7 And Samson said to her, "If they bind me with seven fresh bowstrings, not yet dried, then I shall become weak, and be like any *other* man."

8 So the lords of the Philistines brought up to her seven fresh bowstrings, not yet dried, and she bound him with them. 9 Now *men were* lying in wait, staying with her in the room. And she said to him, "The Philistines *are* upon you, Samson!" But he broke the bowstrings as a strand of yarn breaks when it touches fire. So the secret of his strength was not known.

10 Then Delilah said to Samson, "Look, you have mocked me and told me lies. Now, please tell me what you may be bound with."

11 So he said to her, "If they bind me securely with new ropes that have never been used, then I shall become weak, and be like any *other* man."

12 Therefore Delilah took new ropes and bound him with them, and said to him, "The Philistines *are* upon you, Samson!" And *men were* lying in wait, staying in the room. But he broke them off his arms like a thread.

15:19 [b] Literally *Spring of the Caller*

13Delilah said to Samson,
"Until now you have mocked
me and told me lies. Tell me
what you may be bound with."
And he said to her, "If
you weave the seven locks of
my head into the web of the
loom"—
14So she wove *it* tightly with
the batten of the loom, and
said to him, "The Philistines
are upon you, Samson!" But
he awoke from his sleep, and
pulled out the batten and the
web from the loom.
15Then she said to him,
"How can you say, 'I love you,'
when your heart *is* not with
me? You have mocked me
these three times, and have
not told me where your great
strength *lies*." 16And it came
to pass, when she pestered
him daily with her words
and pressed him, *so* that his
soul was vexed to death, 17that
he told her all his heart, and
said to her, "No razor has ever
come upon my head, for I
have been a Nazirite to God
from my mother's womb. If I
am shaven, then my strength
will leave me, and I shall become weak, and be like any
other man."
18When Delilah saw that he
had told her all his heart, she
sent and called for the lords of
the Philistines, saying, "Come
up once more, for he has told
me all his heart." So the lords
of the Philistines came up to
her and brought the money in
their hand. 19Then she lulled
him to sleep on her knees, and
called for a man and had him
shave off the seven locks of his
head. Then she began to torment him,[a] and his strength
left him. 20And she said, "The
Philistines *are* upon you, Samson!" So he awoke from his
sleep, and said, "I will go out
as before, at other times, and
shake myself free!" But he did
not know that the LORD had
departed from him.
21Then the Philistines took
him and put out his eyes, and
brought him down to Gaza.
They bound him with bronze
fetters, and he became a
grinder in the prison. 22How-
ever, the hair of his head
began to grow again after it
had been shaven.

SAMSON DIES WITH THE PHILISTINES

23Now the lords of the Philistines gathered together to
offer a great sacrifice to Dagon
their god, and to rejoice. And
they said:

"Our god has delivered
into our hands
Samson our enemy!"

24When the people saw him,
they praised their god; for
they said:

16:19 [a] Following Masoretic Text, Targum, and Vulgate; Septuagint reads *he began to be weak*.

"Our god has delivered
into our hands
our enemy,
The destroyer of our
land,
And the one who
multiplied our dead."

25So it happened, when their
hearts were merry, that they
said, "Call for Samson, that he
may perform for us." So they
called for Samson from the
prison, and he performed for
them. And they stationed him
between the pillars. 26Then
Samson said to the lad who
held him by the hand, "Let me
feel the pillars which support
the temple, so that I can lean
on them." 27Now the temple
was full of men and women.
All the lords of the Philistines
were there—about three thousand men and women on the
roof watching while Samson
performed.

28Then Samson called to
the LORD, saying, "O Lord
GOD, remember me, I pray!
Strengthen me, I pray, just
this once, O God, that I may
with one *blow* take vengeance
on the Philistines for my two
eyes!" 29And Samson took
hold of the two middle pillars
which supported the temple,
and he braced himself against
them, one on his right and the
other on his left. 30Then Samson said, "Let me die with the
Philistines!" And he pushed
with *all his* might, and the
temple fell on the lords and
all the people who *were* in it.
So the dead that he killed at
his death were more than he
had killed in his life.

31And his brothers and all
his father's household came
down and took him, and
brought *him* up and buried
him between Zorah and Eshtaol in the tomb of his father
Manoah. He had judged Israel
twenty years.

MICAH'S IDOLATRY

17 Now there was a man
from the mountains of
Ephraim, whose name *was*
Micah. 2And he said to his
mother, "The eleven hun-
dred *shekels* of silver that were
taken from you, and on which
you put a curse, even saying it
in my ears—here *is* the silver
with me; I took it."

And his mother said, "*May
you be* blessed by the LORD,
my son!" 3So when he had
returned the eleven hundred
shekels of silver to his mother,
his mother said, "I had wholly
dedicated the silver from my
hand to the LORD for my son,
to make a carved image and a
molded image; now therefore,
I will return it to you." 4Thus
he returned the silver to his
mother. Then his mother took
two hundred *shekels* of silver
and gave them to the silversmith, and he made it into a
carved image and a molded
image; and they were in the
house of Micah.

5The man Micah had a

shrine, and made an ephod
and household idols;[a] and he
consecrated one of his sons,
who became his priest. 6In
those days *there was* no king
in Israel; everyone did *what*
was right in his own eyes.

7Now there was a young
man from Bethlehem in
Judah, of the family of Judah;
he *was* a Levite, and was staying there. 8The man departed
from the city of Bethlehem
in Judah to stay wherever
he could find *a place.* Then
he came to the mountains
of Ephraim, to the house of
Micah, as he journeyed. 9And
Micah said to him, "Where do
you come from?"

So he said to him, "I *am*
a Levite from Bethlehem in
Judah, and I am on my way
to find *a place* to stay."

10Micah said to him, "Dwell
with me, and be a father and
a priest to me, and I will give
you ten *shekels* of silver per
year, a suit of clothes, and
your sustenance." So the Levite went in. 11Then the Levite
was content to dwell with the
man; and the young man became like one of his sons to
him. 12So Micah consecrated
the Levite, and the young
man became his priest, and
lived in the house of Micah.
13Then Micah said, "Now I
know that the LORD will be
good to me, since I have a Levite as priest!"

THE DANITES ADOPT MICAH'S IDOLATRY

18 In those days *there was*
no king in Israel. And
in those days the tribe of the
Danites was seeking an inheritance for itself to dwell
in; for until that day *their* inheritance among the tribes of
Israel had not fallen to them.
2So the children of Dan sent
five men of their family from
their territory, men of valor
from Zorah and Eshtaol, to
spy out the land and search it.
They said to them, "Go, search
the land." So they went to the
mountains of Ephraim, to the
house of Micah, and lodged
there. 3While they *were* at the
house of Micah, they recognized the voice of the young
Levite. They turned aside and
said to him, "Who brought you
here? What are you doing in
this *place?* What do you have
here?"

4He said to them, "Thus
and so Micah did for me. He
has hired me, and I have become his priest."

5So they said to him,
"Please inquire of God, that
we may know whether the
journey on which we go will
be prosperous."

6And the priest said to
them, "Go in peace. The presence of the LORD *be* with you
on your way."

7So the five men departed
and went to Laish. They saw

17:5 [a] Hebrew *teraphim*

the people who *were* there, how they dwelt safely, in the manner of the Sidonians, quiet and secure. *There were* no rulers in the land who might put *them* to shame for anything. They *were* far from the Sidonians, and they had no ties with anyone.[a]

8 Then *the spies* came back to their brethren at Zorah and Eshtaol, and their brethren said to them, "What *is* your *report?*"

9 So they said, "Arise, let us go up against them. For we have seen the land, and indeed it *is* very good. *Would* you *do* nothing? Do not hesitate to go, *and* enter to possess the land. 10 When you go, you will come to a secure people and a large land. For God has given it into your hands, a place where *there is* no lack of anything that *is* on the earth."

11 And six hundred men of the family of the Danites went from there, from Zorah and Eshtaol, armed with weapons of war. 12 Then they went up and encamped in Kirjath Jearim in Judah. (Therefore they call that place Mahaneh Dan[a] to this day. There *it is,* west of Kirjath Jearim.) 13 And they passed from there to the mountains of Ephraim, and came to the house of Micah.

14 Then the five men who had gone to spy out the country of Laish answered and said to their brethren, "Do you know that there are in these houses an ephod, household idols, a carved image, and a molded image? Now therefore, consider what you should do." 15 So they turned aside there, and came to the house of the young Levite man—to the house of Micah—and greeted him. 16 The six hundred men armed with their weapons of war, who *were* of the children of Dan, stood by the entrance of the gate. 17 Then the five men who had gone to spy out the land went up. Entering there, they took the carved image, the ephod, the household idols, and the molded image. The priest stood at the entrance of the gate with the six hundred men *who were* armed with weapons of war.

18 When these went into Micah's house and took the carved image, the ephod, the household idols, and the molded image, the priest said to them, "What are you doing?"

19 And they said to him, "Be quiet, put your hand over your mouth, and come with us; be a father and a priest to us. *Is it* better for you to be a priest to the household of one man, or that you be a priest to a tribe and a family in Israel?" 20 So the priest's heart was

18:7 [a] Following Masoretic Text, Targum, and Vulgate; Septuagint reads *with Syria*. 18:12 [a] Literally *Camp of Dan*

glad; and he took the ephod, the household idols, and the carved image, and took his place among the people.

21Then they turned and
departed, and put the little ones, the livestock, and
the goods in front of them.
22When they were a good way
from the house of Micah, the men who *were* in the houses near Micah's house gathered together and overtook the
children of Dan. 23And they
called out to the children of Dan. So they turned around and said to Micah, "What ails you, that you have gathered such a company?"

24So he said, "You have
taken away my gods which I made, and the priest, and you have gone away. Now what more do I have? How can you say to me, 'What ails you?'"

25And the children of Dan
said to him, "Do not let your voice be heard among us, lest angry men fall upon you, and you lose your life, with the lives of your household!"
26Then the children of Dan
went their way. And when Micah saw that they *were* too strong for him, he turned and went back to his house.

DANITES SETTLE IN LAISH

27So they took *the things*
Micah had made, and the priest who had belonged to him, and went to Laish, to a people quiet and secure; and they struck them with the edge of the sword and burned
the city with fire. 28*There was*
no deliverer, because it *was* far from Sidon, and they had no ties with anyone. It was in the valley that belongs to Beth Rehob. So they rebuilt the city
and dwelt there. 29And they
called the name of the city Dan, after the name of Dan their father, who was born to Israel. However, the name of the city formerly *was* Laish.

30Then the children of Dan
set up for themselves the carved image; and Jonathan the son of Gershom, the son of Manasseh,[a] and his sons were priests to the tribe of Dan until the day of the captivity
of the land. 31So they set up
for themselves Micah's carved image which he made, all the time that the house of God was in Shiloh.

THE LEVITE'S CONCUBINE

19 And it came to pass in those days, when *there was* no king in Israel, that there was a certain Levite staying in the remote mountains of Ephraim. He took for himself a concubine from
Bethlehem in Judah. 2But his
concubine played the harlot against him, and went away from him to her father's house at Bethlehem in Judah, and was there four whole months.

18:30 [a] Septuagint and Vulgate read *Moses*.

3Then her husband arose and
went after her, to speak kindly
to her *and* bring her back, having his servant and a couple
of donkeys with him. So she
brought him into her father's
house; and when the father of
the young woman saw him, he
was glad to meet him. 4Now
his father-in-law, the young
woman's father, detained him;
and he stayed with him three
days. So they ate and drank
and lodged there.

5Then it came to pass on
the fourth day that they arose
early in the morning, and
he stood to depart; but the
young woman's father said to
his son-in-law, "Refresh your
heart with a morsel of bread,
and afterward go your way."

6So they sat down, and the
two of them ate and drank
together. Then the young
woman's father said to the
man, "Please be content to
stay all night, and let your
heart be merry." 7And when
the man stood to depart, his
father-in-law urged him; so he
lodged there again. 8Then he
arose early in the morning on
the fifth day to depart, but the
young woman's father said,
"Please refresh your heart." So
they delayed until afternoon;
and both of them ate.

9And when the man stood
to depart—he and his con-
cubine and his servant—
his father-in-law, the young
woman's father, said to him,
"Look, the day is now drawing
toward evening; please spend
the night. See, the day is coming to an end; lodge here, that
your heart may be merry. Tomorrow go your way early, so
that you may get home."

10However, the man was
not willing to spend that night;
so he rose and departed, and
came opposite Jebus (that *is,*
Jerusalem). With him were
the two saddled donkeys; his
concubine *was* also with him.
11They *were* near Jebus, and
the day was far spent; and
the servant said to his master, "Come, please, and let us
turn aside into this city of the
Jebusites and lodge in it."

12But his master said to
him, "We will not turn aside
here into a city of foreigners,
who *are* not of the children
of Israel; we will go on to Gibeah." 13So he said to his servant, "Come, let us draw near
to one of these places, and
spend the night in Gibeah or
in Ramah." 14And they passed
by and went their way; and
the sun went down on them
near Gibeah, which belongs to
Benjamin. 15They turned aside
there to go in to lodge in Gibeah. And when he went in, he
sat down in the open square
of the city, for no one would
take them into *his* house to
spend the night.

16Just then an old man
came in from his work in the
field at evening, who also
was from the mountains of
Ephraim; he was staying in

Gibeah, whereas the men of the place *were* Benjamites. 17 And when he raised his eyes, he saw the traveler in the open square of the city; and the old man said, "Where are you going, and where do you come from?"

18 So he said to him, "We *are* passing from Bethlehem in Judah toward the remote mountains of Ephraim; I *am* from there. I went to Bethlehem in Judah; *now* I am going to the house of the LORD. But there *is* no one who will take me into his house, 19 although we have both straw and fodder for our donkeys, and bread and wine for myself, for your female servant, and for the young man *who is* with your servant; *there is* no lack of anything."

20 And the old man said, "Peace *be* with you! However, *let* all your needs *be* my responsibility; only do not spend the night in the open square." 21 So he brought him into his house, and gave fodder to the donkeys. And they washed their feet, and ate and drank.

GIBEAH'S CRIME

22 As they were enjoying themselves, suddenly certain men of the city, perverted men,[a] surrounded the house *and* beat on the door. They spoke to the master of the house, the old man, saying, "Bring out the man who came to your house, that we may know him *carnally!*"

23 But the man, the master of the house, went out to them and said to them, "No, my brethren! I beg you, do not act *so* wickedly! Seeing this man has come into my house, do not commit this outrage. 24 Look, *here is* my virgin daughter and *the man's*[a] concubine; let me bring them out now. Humble them, and do with them as you please; but to this man do not do such a vile thing!" 25 But the men would not heed him. So the man took his concubine and brought *her* out to them. And they knew her and abused her all night until morning; and when the day began to break, they let her go.

26 Then the woman came as the day was dawning, and fell down at the door of the man's house where her master *was,* till it was light.

27 When her master arose in the morning, and opened the doors of the house and went out to go his way, there was his concubine, fallen *at* the door of the house with her hands on the threshold. 28 And he said to her, "Get up and let us be going." But there was no answer. So the man lifted her onto the donkey; and the man got up and went to his place.

19:22 [a] Literally *sons of Belial* 19:24 [a] Literally *his*

29When he entered his house he took a knife, laid hold of his concubine, and divided her into twelve pieces, limb by limb,[a] and sent her throughout all the territory of Israel. 30And so it was that all who saw it said, "No such deed has been done or seen from the day that the children of Israel came up from the land of Egypt until this day. Consider it, confer, and speak up!"

ISRAEL'S WAR WITH THE BENJAMITES

20 So all the children of Israel came out, from Dan to Beersheba, as well as from the land of Gilead, and the congregation gathered together as one man before the LORD at Mizpah. 2And the leaders of all the people, all the tribes of Israel, presented themselves in the assembly of the people of God, four hundred thousand foot soldiers who drew the sword. 3(Now the children of Benjamin heard that the children of Israel had gone up to Mizpah.)

Then the children of Israel said, "Tell *us,* how did this wicked deed happen?"

4So the Levite, the husband of the woman who was murdered, answered and said, "My concubine and I went into Gibeah, which belongs to Benjamin, to spend the night. 5And the men of Gibeah rose against me, and surrounded the house at night because of me. They intended to kill me, but instead they ravished my concubine so that she died. 6So I took hold of my concubine, cut her in pieces, and sent her throughout all the territory of the inheritance of Israel, because they committed lewdness and outrage in Israel. 7Look! All of you *are* children of Israel; give your advice and counsel here and now!"

8So all the people arose as one man, saying, "None *of us* will go to his tent, nor will any turn back to his house; 9but now this *is* the thing which we will do to Gibeah: *We will go up* against it by lot. 10We will take ten men out of *every* hundred throughout all the tribes of Israel, a hundred out of *every* thousand, and a thousand out of *every* ten thousand, to make provisions for the people, that when they come to Gibeah in Benjamin, they may repay all the vileness that they have done in Israel." 11So all the men of Israel were gathered against the city, united together as one man.

12Then the tribes of Israel sent men through all the tribe of Benjamin, saying, "What *is* this wickedness that has occurred among you? 13Now therefore, deliver up the men, the perverted men[a] who *are* in

19:29 [a] Literally *with her bones*

20:13 [a] Literally *sons of Belial*

Gibeah, that we may put them
to death and remove the evil
from Israel!" But the children
of Benjamin would not listen
to the voice of their brethren,
the children of Israel. 14In-
stead, the children of Benjamin gathered together from
their cities to Gibeah, to go to
battle against the children of
Israel. 15And from their cities
at that time the children of
Benjamin numbered twenty-
six thousand men who drew
the sword, besides the inhabitants of Gibeah, who numbered seven hundred select
men. 16Among all this people *were* seven hundred select
men *who were* left-handed;
every one could sling a stone
at a hair's *breadth* and not
miss. 17Now besides Benjamin,
the men of Israel numbered
four hundred thousand men
who drew the sword; all of
these *were* men of war.

18Then the children of Israel arose and went up to the
house of God[a] to inquire of
God. They said, "Which of
us shall go up first to battle
against the children of Benjamin?"

The LORD said, "Judah first!"

19So the children of Is-
rael rose in the morning and
encamped against Gibeah.
20And the men of Israel went
out to battle against Benjamin, and the men of Israel put
themselves in battle array to
fight against them at Gibeah.
21Then the children of Benjamin came out of Gibeah, and
on that day cut down to the
ground twenty-two thousand
men of the Israelites. 22And
the people, that is, the men
of Israel, encouraged themselves and again formed the
battle line at the place where
they had put themselves in
array on the first day. 23Then
the children of Israel went
up and wept before the LORD
until evening, and asked
counsel of the LORD, saying,
"Shall I again draw near for
battle against the children of
my brother Benjamin?"

And the LORD said, "Go up
against him."

24So the children of Israel
approached the children of
Benjamin on the second day.
25And Benjamin went out
against them from Gibeah on
the second day, and cut down
to the ground eighteen thousand more of the children
of Israel; all these drew the
sword.

26Then all the children
of Israel, that is, all the people, went up and came to the
house of God[a] and wept. They
sat there before the LORD and
fasted that day until evening;
and they offered burnt offerings and peace offerings
before the LORD. 27So the
children of Israel inquired
of the LORD (the ark of the

20:18 [a] Or *Bethel*

20:26 [a] Or *Bethel*

covenant of God *was* there in
those days, 28and Phinehas
the son of Eleazar, the son of
Aaron, stood before it in those
days), saying, "Shall I yet again
go out to battle against the
children of my brother Benjamin, or shall I cease?"

And the LORD said, "Go up,
for tomorrow I will deliver
them into your hand."

29Then Israel set men in
ambush all around Gibeah.
30And the children of Israel
went up against the children
of Benjamin on the third day,
and put themselves in battle
array against Gibeah as at the
other times. 31So the children
of Benjamin went out against
the people, *and* were drawn
away from the city. They began
to strike down *and* kill some
of the people, as at the other
times, in the highways (one of
which goes up to Bethel and
the other to Gibeah) and in
the field, about thirty men of
Israel. 32And the children of
Benjamin said, "They *are* defeated before us, as at first."

But the children of Israel
said, "Let us flee and draw
them away from the city to the
highways." 33So all the men of
Israel rose from their place
and put themselves in battle
array at Baal Tamar. Then Israel's men in ambush burst
forth from their position in
the plain of Geba. 34And ten
thousand select men from all
Israel came against Gibeah,
and the battle was fierce. But
the Benjamites[a] did not know
that disaster *was* upon them.
35The LORD defeated Benjamin before Israel. And the
children of Israel destroyed
that day twenty-five thousand
one hundred Benjamites; all
these drew the sword.

36So the children of Ben-
jamin saw that they were
defeated. The men of Israel
had given ground to the Benjamites, because they relied
on the men in ambush whom
they had set against Gibeah.
37And the men in ambush
quickly rushed upon Gibeah;
the men in ambush spread
out and struck the whole city
with the edge of the sword.
38Now the appointed sig-
nal between the men of Israel and the men in ambush
was that they would make a
great cloud of smoke rise up
from the city, 39whereupon
the men of Israel would turn
in battle. Now Benjamin had
begun to strike *and* kill about
thirty of the men of Israel. For
they said, "Surely they are defeated before us, as *in* the first
battle." 40But when the cloud
began to rise from the city in
a column of smoke, the Benjamites looked behind them,
and there was the whole city
going up *in smoke* to heaven.
41And when the men of Is-
rael turned back, the men of

20:34 [a] Literally *they*

Benjamin panicked, for they
saw that disaster had come
upon them. 42Therefore they
turned *their backs* before the
men of Israel in the direction
of the wilderness; but the battle overtook them, and whoever *came* out of the cities
they destroyed in their midst.
43They surrounded the Benjamites, chased them, *and* easily
trampled them down as far
as the front of Gibeah toward
the east. 44And eighteen thousand men of Benjamin fell;
all these *were* men of valor.
45Then they[a] turned and fled
toward the wilderness to the
rock of Rimmon; and they cut
down five thousand of them
on the highways. Then they
pursued them relentlessly up
to Gidom, and killed two thousand of them. 46So all who fell
of Benjamin that day were
twenty-five thousand men
who drew the sword; all these
were men of valor.

47But six hundred men
turned and fled toward the
wilderness to the rock of
Rimmon, and they stayed at
the rock of Rimmon for four
months. 48And the men of
Israel turned back against
the children of Benjamin,
and struck them down with
the edge of the sword—from
every city, men and beasts, all
who were found. They also
set fire to all the cities they
came to.

WIVES PROVIDED FOR THE BENJAMITES

21 Now the men of Israel
had sworn an oath at
Mizpah, saying, "None of us
shall give his daughter to
Benjamin as a wife." 2Then
the people came to the house
of God,[a] and remained there
before God till evening. They
lifted up their voices and wept
bitterly, 3and said, "O LORD
God of Israel, why has this
come to pass in Israel, that
today there should be one
tribe *missing* in Israel?"

4So it was, on the next
morning, that the people rose
early and built an altar there,
and offered burnt offerings
and peace offerings. 5The
children of Israel said, "Who
is there among all the tribes
of Israel who did not come
up with the assembly to the
LORD?" For they had made a
great oath concerning anyone
who had not come up to the
LORD at Mizpah, saying, "He
shall surely be put to death."
6And the children of Israel
grieved for Benjamin their
brother, and said, "One tribe
is cut off from Israel today.
7What shall we do for wives
for those who remain, seeing
we have sworn by the LORD
that we will not give them our
daughters as wives?"

8And they said, "What one
is there from the tribes of Israel who did not come up to

20:45 [a] Septuagint reads *the rest.* 21:2 [a] Or *Bethel*

Mizpah to the LORD?" And, in
fact, no one had come to the
camp from Jabesh Gilead to
the assembly. 9For when the
people were counted, indeed,
not one of the inhabitants
of Jabesh Gilead *was* there.
10So the congregation sent
out there twelve thousand of
their most valiant men, and
commanded them, saying,
"Go and strike the inhab-
itants of Jabesh Gilead with
the edge of the sword, including the women and children.
11And this *is* the thing that you
shall do: You shall utterly destroy every male, and every
woman who has known a man
intimately." 12So they found
among the inhabitants of
Jabesh Gilead four hundred
young virgins who had not
known a man intimately;
and they brought them to the
camp at Shiloh, which is in the
land of Canaan.

13Then the whole congre-
gation sent *word* to the children of Benjamin who *were* at
the rock of Rimmon, and announced peace to them. 14So
Benjamin came back at that
time, and they gave them the
women whom they had saved
alive of the women of Jabesh
Gilead; and yet they had not
found enough for them.

15And the people grieved
for Benjamin, because the
LORD had made a void in the
tribes of Israel.

16Then the elders of the
congregation said, "What
shall we do for wives for those
who remain, since the women
of Benjamin have been de-
stroyed?" 17And they said,
"*There must be* an inheritance
for the survivors of Benjamin, that a tribe may not be
destroyed from Israel. 18How-
ever, we cannot give them
wives from our daughters,
for the children of Israel have
sworn an oath, saying, 'Cursed
be the one who gives a wife to
Benjamin.'" 19Then they said,
"In fact, *there is* a yearly feast
of the LORD in Shiloh, which
is north of Bethel, on the east
side of the highway that goes
up from Bethel to Shechem,
and south of Lebonah."

20Therefore they instructed
the children of Benjamin,
saying, "Go, lie in wait in the
vineyards, 21and watch; and
just when the daughters of
Shiloh come out to perform
their dances, then come out
from the vineyards, and every
man catch a wife for himself
from the daughters of Shiloh;
then go to the land of Benjamin. 22Then it shall be, when
their fathers or their brothers
come to us to complain, that
we will say to them, 'Be kind
to them for our sakes, because
we did not take a wife for any
of them in the war; for *it is* not
as though you have given the
women to them at this time,
making yourselves guilty of
your oath.'"

23And the children of
Benjamin did so; they took

enough wives for their number from those who danced,
whom they caught. Then they
went and returned to their
inheritance, and they rebuilt
the cities and dwelt in them.
24So the children of Israel
departed from there at that
time, every man to his tribe
and family; they went out
from there, every man to his
inheritance.
25In those days *there was*
no king in Israel; everyone
did *what was* right in his own
eyes.

THE BOOK OF RUTH

ELIMELECH'S FAMILY GOES TO MOAB

1 Now it came to pass, in the
days when the judges ruled,
that there was a famine in
the land. And a certain man
of Bethlehem, Judah, went to
dwell in the country of Moab,
he and his wife and his two
sons. 2The name of the man
was Elimelech, the name of
his wife *was* Naomi, and the
names of his two sons *were*
Mahlon and Chilion—Eph-
rathites of Bethlehem, Judah.
And they went to the country
of Moab and remained there.
3Then Elimelech, Naomi's
husband, died; and she was
left, and her two sons. 4Now
they took wives of the women
of Moab: the name of the one
was Orpah, and the name
of the other Ruth. And they
dwelt there about ten years.
5Then both Mahlon and Chilion also died; so the woman
survived her two sons and her
husband.

NAOMI RETURNS WITH RUTH

6Then she arose with her
daughters-in-law that she
might return from the country
of Moab, for she had heard in
the country of Moab that the
LORD had visited His people by
giving them bread. 7Therefore
she went out from the place
where she was, and her two
daughters-in-law with her;
and they went on the way to
return to the land of Judah.
8And Naomi said to her two
daughters-in-law, "Go, return
each to her mother's house.
The LORD deal kindly with you,
as you have dealt with the dead
and with me. 9The LORD grant
that you may find rest, each
in the house of her husband."

So she kissed them, and
they lifted up their voices and

wept. 10And they said to her,
"Surely we will return with
you to your people."
11But Naomi said, "Turn
back, my daughters; why will
you go with me? *Are* there still
sons in my womb, that they
may be your husbands? 12Turn
back, my daughters, go—for
I am too old to have a husband. If I should say I have
hope, *if* I should have a husband tonight and should also
bear sons, 13would you wait
for them till they were grown?
Would you restrain yourselves
from having husbands? No,
my daughters; for it grieves
me very much for your sakes
that the hand of the LORD has
gone out against me!"
14Then they lifted up their
voices and wept again; and
Orpah kissed her mother-in-law,
but Ruth clung to her.
15And she said, "Look, your
sister-in-law has gone back to
her people and to her gods; return after your sister-in-law."
16But Ruth said:

"Entreat me not to
leave you,
Or to turn back from
following after you;
For wherever you
go, I will go;
And wherever you
lodge, I will lodge;
Your people *shall*
be my people,
And your God, my God.
17 Where you die, I will die,
And there will I be buried.
The LORD do so to me,
and more also,
If *anything but* death
parts you and me."

18When she saw that she was
determined to go with her, she
stopped speaking to her.
19Now the two of them went
until they came to Bethlehem.
And it happened, when they
had come to Bethlehem, that
all the city was excited because
of them; and the women said,
"*Is* this Naomi?"
20But she said to them, "Do
not call me Naomi;[a] call me
Mara,[b] for the Almighty has
dealt very bitterly with me. 21I
went out full, and the LORD
has brought me home again
empty. Why do you call me
Naomi, since the LORD has
testified against me, and the
Almighty has afflicted me?"
22So Naomi returned,
and Ruth the Moabitess her
daughter-in-law with her, who
returned from the country
of Moab. Now they came to
Bethlehem at the beginning
of barley harvest.

RUTH MEETS BOAZ

2 There was a relative of
Naomi's husband, a man
of great wealth, of the family
of Elimelech. His name *was*
Boaz. 2So Ruth the Moabitess said to Naomi, "Please let

1:20 [a] Literally *Pleasant* [b] Literally *Bitter*

me go to the field, and glean heads of grain after *him* in whose sight I may find favor."

And she said to her, "Go, my daughter."

3 Then she left, and went and gleaned in the field after the reapers. And she happened to come to the part of the field *belonging* to Boaz, who *was* of the family of Elimelech.

4 Now behold, Boaz came from Bethlehem, and said to the reapers, "The LORD *be* with you!"

And they answered him, "The LORD bless you!"

5 Then Boaz said to his servant who was in charge of the reapers, "Whose young woman *is* this?"

6 So the servant who was in charge of the reapers answered and said, "It *is* the young Moabite woman who came back with Naomi from the country of Moab. 7 And she said, 'Please let me glean and gather after the reapers among the sheaves.' So she came and has continued from morning until now, though she rested a little in the house."

8 Then Boaz said to Ruth, "You will listen, my daughter, will you not? Do not go to glean in another field, nor go from here, but stay close by my young women. 9 *Let* your eyes *be* on the field which they reap, and go after them. Have I not commanded the young men not to touch you? And when you are thirsty, go to the vessels and drink from what the young men have drawn."

10 So she fell on her face, bowed down to the ground, and said to him, "Why have I found favor in your eyes, that you should take notice of me, since I *am* a foreigner?"

11 And Boaz answered and said to her, "It has been fully reported to me, all that you have done for your mother-in-law since the death of your husband, and *how* you have left your father and your mother and the land of your birth, and have come to a people whom you did not know before. 12 The LORD repay your work, and a full reward be given you by the LORD God of Israel, under whose wings you have come for refuge."

13 Then she said, "Let me find favor in your sight, my lord; for you have comforted me, and have spoken kindly to your maidservant, though I am not like one of your maidservants."

14 Now Boaz said to her at mealtime, "Come here, and eat of the bread, and dip your piece of bread in the vinegar." So she sat beside the reapers, and he passed parched *grain* to her; and she ate and was satisfied, and kept some back. 15 And when she rose up to glean, Boaz commanded his young men, saying, "Let her glean even among the sheaves, and do not reproach

her. 16Also let *grain* from the
bundles fall purposely for her;
leave *it* that she may glean,
and do not rebuke her."

17So she gleaned in the field
until evening, and beat out
what she had gleaned, and it
was about an ephah of barley. 18Then she took *it* up and
went into the city, and her
mother-in-law saw what she
had gleaned. So she brought
out and gave to her what she
had kept back after she had
been satisfied.

19And her mother-in-law
said to her, "Where have you
gleaned today? And where did
you work? Blessed be the one
who took notice of you."

So she told her mother-in-law
with whom she had worked,
and said, "The man's name with
whom I worked today *is* Boaz."

20Then Naomi said to her
daughter-in-law, "Blessed *be*
he of the LORD, who has not
forsaken His kindness to the
living and the dead!" And
Naomi said to her, "This man
is a relation of ours, one of our
close relatives."

21Ruth the Moabitess said,
"He also said to me, 'You shall
stay close by my young men
until they have finished all my
harvest.'"

22And Naomi said to Ruth
her daughter-in-law, "*It is*
good, my daughter, that you
go out with his young women,
and that people do not meet
you in any other field." 23So
she stayed close by the young
women of Boaz, to glean until
the end of barley harvest and
wheat harvest; and she dwelt
with her mother-in-law.

RUTH'S REDEMPTION ASSURED

3 Then Naomi her
mother-in-law said to her,
"My daughter, shall I not seek
security for you, that it may
be well with you? 2Now Boaz,
whose young women you were
with, *is he* not our relative? In
fact, he is winnowing barley
tonight at the threshing floor.
3Therefore wash yourself and
anoint yourself, put on your
best garment and go down
to the threshing floor; *but* do
not make yourself known to
the man until he has finished
eating and drinking. 4Then it
shall be, when he lies down,
that you shall notice the place
where he lies; and you shall
go in, uncover his feet, and
lie down; and he will tell you
what you should do."

5And she said to her, "All
that you say to me I will do."

6So she went down to
the threshing floor and did
according to all that her
mother-in-law instructed her.
7And after Boaz had eaten
and drunk, and his heart was
cheerful, he went to lie down
at the end of the heap of grain;
and she came softly, uncovered his feet, and lay down.

8Now it happened at mid-
night that the man was startled, and turned himself; and

there, a woman was lying at his feet. 9And he said, "Who *are* you?"

So she answered, "I *am* Ruth, your maidservant. Take your maidservant under your wing,[a] for you are a close relative."

10Then he said, "Blessed *are* you of the LORD, my daughter! For you have shown more kindness at the end than at the beginning, in that you did not go after young men, whether poor or rich. 11And now, my daughter, do not fear. I will do for you all that you request, for all the people of my town know that you *are* a virtuous woman. 12Now it is true that I *am* a close relative; however, there is a relative closer than I. 13Stay this night, and in the morning it shall be *that* if he will perform the duty of a close relative for you—good; let him do it. But if he does not want to perform the duty for you, then I will perform the duty for you, *as* the LORD lives! Lie down until morning."

14So she lay at his feet until morning, and she arose before one could recognize another. Then he said, "Do not let it be known that the woman came to the threshing floor." 15Also he said, "Bring the shawl that *is* on you and hold it." And when she held it, he measured six *ephahs* of barley, and laid *it* on her. Then she[a] went into the city.

16When she came to her mother-in-law, she said, "*Is* that you, my daughter?"

Then she told her all that the man had done for her. 17And she said, "These six *ephahs* of barley he gave me; for he said to me, 'Do not go empty-handed to your mother-in-law.'"

18Then she said, "Sit still, my daughter, until you know how the matter will turn out; for the man will not rest until he has concluded the matter this day."

BOAZ REDEEMS RUTH

4 Now Boaz went up to the gate and sat down there; and behold, the close relative of whom Boaz had spoken came by. So Boaz said, "Come aside, friend,[a] sit down here." So he came aside and sat down. 2And he took ten men of the elders of the city, and said, "Sit down here." So they sat down. 3Then he said to the close relative, "Naomi, who has come back from the country of Moab, sold the piece of land which *belonged* to our brother Elimelech. 4And I thought to inform you, saying, 'Buy *it* back in the presence of the inhabitants and the elders

3:9 [a] Or *Spread the corner of your garment over your maidservant*
3:15 [a] Many Hebrew manuscripts, Syriac, and Vulgate read *she;* Masoretic Text, Septuagint, and Targum read *he.*
4:1 [a] Hebrew *peloni almoni;* literally *so and so*

of my people. If you will redeem *it,* redeem *it;* but if you[a] will not redeem *it, then* tell me, that I may know; for *there is* no one but you to redeem *it,* and I *am* next after you.'"

And he said, "I will redeem *it.*"

5Then Boaz said, "On the day you buy the field from the hand of Naomi, you must also buy *it* from Ruth the Moabitess, the wife of the dead, to perpetuate[a] the name of the dead through his inheritance."

6And the close relative said, "I cannot redeem *it* for myself, lest I ruin my own inheritance. You redeem my right of redemption for yourself, for I cannot redeem *it.*"

7Now this *was the custom* in former times in Israel concerning redeeming and exchanging, to confirm anything: one man took off his sandal and gave *it* to the other, and this *was* a confirmation in Israel.

8Therefore the close relative said to Boaz, "Buy *it* for yourself." So he took off his sandal. 9And Boaz said to the elders and all the people, "You *are* witnesses this day that I have bought all that was Elimelech's, and all that *was* Chilion's and Mahlon's, from the hand of Naomi. 10Moreover, Ruth the Moabitess, the widow of Mahlon, I have acquired as my wife, to perpetuate the name of the dead through his inheritance, that the name of the dead may not be cut off from among his brethren and from his position at the gate.[a] You *are* witnesses this day."

11And all the people who *were* at the gate, and the elders, said, "*We are* witnesses. The LORD make the woman who is coming to your house like Rachel and Leah, the two who built the house of Israel; and may you prosper in Ephrathah and be famous in Bethlehem. 12May your house be like the house of Perez, whom Tamar bore to Judah, because of the offspring which the LORD will give you from this young woman."

DESCENDANTS OF BOAZ AND RUTH

13So Boaz took Ruth and she became his wife; and when he went in to her, the LORD gave her conception, and she bore a son. 14Then the women said to Naomi, "Blessed *be* the LORD, who has not left you this day without a close relative; and may his name be famous in Israel! 15And may he be to you a restorer of life and a nourisher of your old age; for your daughter-in-law, who loves you, who is better

4:4 [a] Following many Hebrew manuscripts, Septuagint, Syriac, Targum, and Vulgate; Masoretic Text reads *he.* 4:5 [a] Literally *raise up* 4:10 [a] Probably his civic office

to you than seven sons, has borne him." 16Then Naomi took the child and laid him on her bosom, and became a nurse to him. 17Also the neighbor women gave him a name, saying, "There is a son born to Naomi." And they called his name Obed. He *is* the father of Jesse, the father of David.

18Now this *is* the genealogy of Perez: Perez begot Hezron; 19Hezron begot Ram, and Ram begot Amminadab; 20Amminadab begot Nahshon, and Nahshon begot Salmon;[a] 21Salmon begot Boaz, and Boaz begot Obed; 22Obed begot Jesse, and Jesse begot David.

THE FIRST BOOK OF SAMUEL

THE FAMILY OF ELKANAH

1 Now there was a certain man of Ramathaim Zophim, of the mountains of Ephraim, and his name *was* Elkanah the son of Jeroham, the son of Elihu,[a] the son of Tohu,[b] the son of Zuph, an Ephraimite. 2And he had two wives: the name of one *was* Hannah, and the name of the other Peninnah. Peninnah had children, but Hannah had no children. 3This man went up from his city yearly to worship and sacrifice to the LORD of hosts in Shiloh. Also the two sons of Eli, Hophni and Phinehas, the priests of the LORD, *were* there. 4And whenever the time *came for* Elkanah to make an offering, he would give portions to Peninnah his wife and to all her sons and daughters. 5But to Hannah he would give a double portion, for he loved Hannah, although the LORD had closed her womb. 6And her rival also provoked her severely, to make her miserable, because the LORD had closed her womb. 7So it was, year by year, when she went up to the house of the LORD, that she provoked her; therefore she wept and did not eat.

HANNAH'S VOW

8Then Elkanah her husband said to her, "Hannah, why do you weep? Why do you not eat? And why is your heart grieved? *Am* I not better to you than ten sons?"

4:20 [a] Hebrew *Salmah* 1:1 [a] Spelled *Eliel* in 1 Chronicles 6:34 [b] Spelled *Toah* in 1 Chronicles 6:34

9So Hannah arose after
they had finished eating and
drinking in Shiloh. Now Eli the
priest was sitting on the seat
by the doorpost of the tabernacle[a] of the LORD. 10And she
was in bitterness of soul, and
prayed to the LORD and wept
in anguish. 11Then she made a
vow and said, "O LORD of hosts,
if You will indeed look on the
affliction of Your maidservant
and remember me, and not
forget Your maidservant, but
will give Your maidservant a
male child, then I will give him
to the LORD all the days of his
life, and no razor shall come
upon his head."

12And it happened, as she
continued praying before the
LORD, that Eli watched her
mouth. 13Now Hannah spoke in
her heart; only her lips moved,
but her voice was not heard.
Therefore Eli thought she was
drunk. 14So Eli said to her, "How
long will you be drunk? Put
your wine away from you!"

15But Hannah answered
and said, "No, my lord, I *am*
a woman of sorrowful spirit.
I have drunk neither wine nor
intoxicating drink, but have
poured out my soul before
the LORD. 16Do not consider
your maidservant a wicked
woman,[a] for out of the abundance of my complaint and
grief I have spoken until now."

17Then Eli answered and
said, "Go in peace, and the God
of Israel grant your petition
which you have asked of Him."

18And she said, "Let your
maidservant find favor in
your sight." So the woman
went her way and ate, and her
face was no longer *sad.*

SAMUEL IS BORN AND DEDICATED

19Then they rose early in
the morning and worshiped
before the LORD, and returned
and came to their house at
Ramah. And Elkanah knew
Hannah his wife, and the
LORD remembered her. 20So it
came to pass in the process of
time that Hannah conceived
and bore a son, and called his
name Samuel,[a] *saying,* "Because I have asked for him
from the LORD."

21Now the man Elkanah
and all his house went up to
offer to the LORD the yearly
sacrifice and his vow. 22But
Hannah did not go up, for she
said to her husband, "*Not* until
the child is weaned; then I will
take him, that he may appear
before the LORD and remain
there forever."

23So Elkanah her husband
said to her, "Do what seems
best to you; wait until you
have weaned him. Only let
the LORD establish His[a] word."

1:9 [a] Hebrew *heykal,* palace or temple 1:16 [a] Literally *daughter of Belial*
1:20 [a] Literally *Heard by God* 1:23 [a] Following Masoretic Text, Targum, and Vulgate; Dead Sea Scrolls, Septuagint, and Syriac read *your.*

Then the woman stayed and
nursed her son until she had
weaned him.
24Now when she had
weaned him, she took him
up with her, with three bulls,[a]
one ephah of flour, and a skin
of wine, and brought him to
the house of the LORD in Shiloh. And the child *was* young.
25Then they slaughtered a
bull, and brought the child to
Eli. 26And she said, "O my lord!
As your soul lives, my lord, I
am the woman who stood by
you here, praying to the LORD.
27For this child I prayed, and
the LORD has granted me my
petition which I asked of Him.
28Therefore I also have lent
him to the LORD; as long as
he lives he shall be lent to the
LORD." So they worshiped the
LORD there.

HANNAH'S PRAYER

2 And Hannah prayed and said:

"My heart rejoices
in the LORD;
My horn[a] is exalted
in the LORD.
I smile at my enemies,
Because I rejoice in
Your salvation.

2 "No one is holy like
the LORD,
For *there is* none
besides You,
Nor *is there* any rock
like our God.

3 "Talk no more so
very proudly;
Let no arrogance come
from your mouth,
For the LORD *is* the
God of knowledge;
And by Him actions
are weighed.

4 "The bows of the mighty
men *are* broken,
And those who
stumbled are girded
with strength.
5 *Those who were* full
have hired themselves
out for bread,
And the hungry have
ceased *to hunger.*
Even the barren has
borne seven,
And she who has
many children has
become feeble.

6 "The LORD kills and
makes alive;
He brings down to the
grave and brings up.
7 The LORD makes poor
and makes rich;
He brings low and lifts up.
8 He raises the poor
from the dust
And lifts the beggar
from the ash heap,
To set *them* among
princes

1:24 [a] Dead Sea Scrolls, Septuagint, and Syriac read *a three-year-old bull.* 2:1 [a] That is, strength

And make them inherit
the throne of glory.

"For the pillars of the
earth *are* the LORD's,
And He has set the
world upon them.
9 He will guard the feet
of His saints,
But the wicked shall be
silent in darkness.

"For by strength no
man shall prevail.
10 The adversaries of
the LORD shall be
broken in pieces;
From heaven He will
thunder against them.
The LORD will judge the
ends of the earth.

"He will give strength
to His king,
And exalt the horn
of His anointed."

11 Then Elkanah went to his
house at Ramah. But the child
ministered to the LORD before
Eli the priest.

THE WICKED SONS OF ELI

12 Now the sons of Eli *were*
corrupt;[a] they did not know
the LORD. 13 And the priests'
custom with the people *was*
that when any man offered a
sacrifice, the priest's servant
would come with a three-
pronged fleshhook in his hand
while the meat was boiling.
14 Then he would thrust *it* into
the pan, or kettle, or caldron,
or pot; and the priest would
take for himself all that the
fleshhook brought up. So they
did in Shiloh to all the Israelites who came there. 15 Also,
before they burned the fat, the
priest's servant would come
and say to the man who sacrificed, "Give meat for roasting
to the priest, for he will not
take boiled meat from you,
but raw."

16 And *if* the man said to
him, "They should really burn
the fat first; *then* you may take
as much as your heart desires," he would then answer
him, "*No,* but you must give
it now; and if not, I will take
it by force."

17 Therefore the sin of the
young men was very great
before the LORD, for men
abhorred the offering of the
LORD.

SAMUEL'S CHILDHOOD MINISTRY

18 But Samuel ministered
before the LORD, *even as* a
child, wearing a linen ephod.
19 Moreover his mother used
to make him a little robe, and
bring *it* to him year by year
when she came up with her
husband to offer the yearly
sacrifice. 20 And Eli would
bless Elkanah and his wife,
and say, "The LORD give you
descendants from this woman

2:12 [a] Literally *sons of Belial*

for the loan that was given to
the LORD." Then they would
go to their own home.
21And the LORD visited
Hannah, so that she con-
ceived and bore three sons
and two daughters. Mean-
while the child Samuel grew
before the LORD.

PROPHECY AGAINST ELI'S HOUSEHOLD

22Now Eli was very old; and
he heard everything his sons
did to all Israel,[a] and how they
lay with the women who assembled at the door of the
tabernacle of meeting. 23So
he said to them, "Why do you
do such things? For I hear of
your evil dealings from all the
people. 24No, my sons! For *it is*
not a good report that I hear.
You make the LORD's peo-
ple transgress. 25If one man
sins against another, God will
judge him. But if a man sins
against the LORD, who will
intercede for him?" Nevertheless they did not heed the
voice of their father, because
the LORD desired to kill them.
26And the child Samuel
grew in stature, and in favor
both with the LORD and men.
27Then a man of God came
to Eli and said to him, "Thus
says the LORD: 'Did I not clearly
reveal Myself to the house of
your father when they were
in Egypt in Pharaoh's house?
28Did I not choose him out of
all the tribes of Israel *to be* My
priest, to offer upon My altar,
to burn incense, and to wear
an ephod before Me? And
did I not give to the house of
your father all the offerings
of the children of Israel made
by fire? 29Why do you kick at
My sacrifice and My offering
which I have commanded *in
My* dwelling place, and honor
your sons more than Me, to
make yourselves fat with the
best of all the offerings of Israel My people?' 30Therefore
the LORD God of Israel says:
'I said indeed *that* your house
and the house of your father
would walk before Me forever.'
But now the LORD says: 'Far
be it from Me; for those who
honor Me I will honor, and
those who despise Me shall
be lightly esteemed. 31Behold,
the days are coming that I will
cut off your arm and the arm
of your father's house, so that
there will not be an old man
in your house. 32And you will
see an enemy *in My* dwelling
place, *despite* all the good
which God does for Israel.
And there shall not be an old
man in your house forever.
33But any of your men *whom*
I do not cut off from My altar
shall consume your eyes and
grieve your heart. And all the
descendants of your house
shall die in the flower of their

2:22 [a] Following Masoretic Text, Targum, and Vulgate; Dead Sea Scrolls and Septuagint omit the rest of this verse.

age. 34Now this *shall be* a sign
to you that will come upon
your two sons, on Hophni
and Phinehas: in one day
they shall die, both of them.
35Then I will raise up for Myself a faithful priest *who* shall
do according to what *is* in My
heart and in My mind. I will
build him a sure house, and he
shall walk before My anointed
forever. 36And it shall come to
pass that everyone who is left
in your house will come *and*
bow down to him for a piece of
silver and a morsel of bread,
and say, "Please, put me in one
of the priestly positions, that
I may eat a piece of bread." ' "

SAMUEL'S FIRST PROPHECY

3 Now the boy Samuel min-
istered to the LORD before
Eli. And the word of the LORD
was rare in those days; *there*
was no widespread revelation.
2And it came to pass at that
time, while Eli *was* lying down
in his place, and when his eyes
had begun to grow so dim that
he could not see, 3and before
the lamp of God went out in
the tabernacle[a] of the LORD
where the ark of God *was*, and
while Samuel was lying down,
4that the LORD called Samuel. And he answered, "Here I
am!" 5So he ran to Eli and said,
"Here I am, for you called me."

And he said, "I did not call;
lie down again." And he went
and lay down.

6Then the LORD called yet
again, "Samuel!"

So Samuel arose and went
to Eli, and said, "Here I am, for
you called me." He answered,
"I did not call, my son; lie
down again." 7(Now Samuel
did not yet know the LORD,
nor was the word of the LORD
yet revealed to him.)

8And the LORD called Sam-
uel again the third time. So
he arose and went to Eli, and
said, "Here I am, for you did
call me."

Then Eli perceived that
the LORD had called the boy.
9Therefore Eli said to Samuel,
"Go, lie down; and it shall be,
if He calls you, that you must
say, 'Speak, LORD, for Your servant hears.' " So Samuel went
and lay down in his place.

10Now the LORD came and
stood and called as at other
times, "Samuel! Samuel!"

And Samuel answered,
"Speak, for Your servant
hears."

11Then the LORD said to
Samuel: "Behold, I will do
something in Israel at which
both ears of everyone who
hears it will tingle. 12In that
day I will perform against Eli
all that I have spoken concerning his house, from beginning to end. 13For I have
told him that I will judge his
house forever for the iniquity
which he knows, because his
sons made themselves vile,

3:3 [a] Hebrew *heykal*, palace or temple

and he did not restrain them. 14And therefore I have sworn to the house of Eli that the iniquity of Eli's house shall not be atoned for by sacrifice or offering forever."

15So Samuel lay down until morning,[a] and opened the doors of the house of the LORD. And Samuel was afraid to tell Eli the vision. 16Then Eli called Samuel and said, "Samuel, my son!"

He answered, "Here I am."

17And he said, "What *is* the word that *the LORD* spoke to you? Please do not hide *it* from me. God do so to you, and more also, if you hide anything from me of all the things that He said to you." 18Then Samuel told him everything, and hid nothing from him. And he said, "It *is* the LORD. Let Him do what seems good to Him."

19So Samuel grew, and the LORD was with him and let none of his words fall to the ground. 20And all Israel from Dan to Beersheba knew that Samuel *had been* established as a prophet of the LORD. 21Then the LORD appeared again in Shiloh. For the LORD revealed Himself to Samuel in Shiloh by the word of the LORD.

4 And the word of Samuel came to all Israel.[a]

THE ARK OF GOD CAPTURED

Now Israel went out to battle against the Philistines, and encamped beside Ebenezer; and the Philistines encamped in Aphek. 2Then the Philistines put themselves in battle array against Israel. And when they joined battle, Israel was defeated by the Philistines, who killed about four thousand men of the army in the field. 3And when the people had come into the camp, the elders of Israel said, "Why has the LORD defeated us today before the Philistines? Let us bring the ark of the covenant of the LORD from Shiloh to us, that when it comes among us it may save us from the hand of our enemies." 4So the people sent to Shiloh, that they might bring from there the ark of the covenant of the LORD of hosts, who dwells *between* the cherubim. And the two sons of Eli, Hophni and Phinehas, *were* there with the ark of the covenant of God.

5And when the ark of the covenant of the LORD came into the camp, all Israel shouted so loudly that the earth shook. 6Now when the Philistines heard the noise of the shout, they said, "What *does* the sound of this great

3:15 [a] Following Masoretic Text, Targum, and Vulgate; Septuagint adds *and he arose in the morning.* 4:1 [a] Following Masoretic Text and Targum; Septuagint and Vulgate add *And it came to pass in those days that the Philistines gathered themselves together to fight;* Septuagint adds further *against Israel.*

shout in the camp of the
Hebrews *mean?*" Then they
understood that the ark of
the LORD had come into the
camp. 7So the Philistines were
afraid, for they said, "God has
come into the camp!" And
they said, "Woe to us! For such
a thing has never happened
before. 8Woe to us! Who will
deliver us from the hand of
these mighty gods? These *are*
the gods who struck the Egyptians with all the plagues in
the wilderness. 9Be strong and
conduct yourselves like men,
you Philistines, that you do
not become servants of the
Hebrews, as they have been to
you. Conduct yourselves like
men, and fight!"

10So the Philistines fought,
and Israel was defeated, and
every man fled to his tent.
There was a very great slaughter, and there fell of Israel
thirty thousand foot soldiers.
11Also the ark of God was captured; and the two sons of Eli,
Hophni and Phinehas, died.

DEATH OF ELI

12Then a man of Benjamin
ran from the battle line the
same day, and came to Shiloh
with his clothes torn and dirt
on his head. 13Now when he
came, there was Eli, sitting on
a seat by the wayside watching,[a] for his heart trembled for
the ark of God. And when the
man came into the city and
told *it,* all the city cried out.
14When Eli heard the noise
of the outcry, he said, "What
does the sound of this tumult
mean?" And the man came
quickly and told Eli. 15Eli was
ninety-eight years old, and his
eyes were so dim that he could
not see.

16Then the man said to Eli,
"I *am* he who came from the
battle. And I fled today from
the battle line."

And he said, "What hap-
pened, my son?"

17So the messenger an-
swered and said, "Israel has
fled before the Philistines, and
there has been a great slaughter among the people. Also
your two sons, Hophni and
Phinehas, are dead; and the
ark of God has been captured."

18Then it happened, when
he made mention of the ark
of God, that Eli fell off the seat
backward by the side of the
gate; and his neck was broken and he died, for the man
was old and heavy. And he had
judged Israel forty years.

ICHABOD

19Now his daughter-in-law,
Phinehas' wife, was with child,
due to be delivered; and when
she heard the news that the
ark of God was captured, and
that her father-in-law and
her husband were dead, she

4:13 [a] Following Masoretic Text and Vulgate; Septuagint reads *beside the gate watching the road.*

bowed herself and gave birth,
for her labor pains came upon
her. 20 And about the time of
her death the women who
stood by her said to her, "Do
not fear, for you have borne
a son." But she did not answer, nor did she regard *it.*
21 Then she named the child
Ichabod,[a] saying, "The glory
has departed from Israel!"
because the ark of God had
been captured and because
of her father-in-law and her
husband. 22 And she said, "The
glory has departed from Israel, for the ark of God has
been captured."

THE PHILISTINES AND THE ARK

5 Then the Philistines took
the ark of God and brought
it from Ebenezer to Ashdod.
2 When the Philistines took
the ark of God, they brought it
into the house of Dagon[a] and
set it by Dagon. 3 And when
the people of Ashdod arose
early in the morning, there
was Dagon, fallen on its face
to the earth before the ark of
the LORD. So they took Dagon
and set it in its place again.
4 And when they arose early
the next morning, there was
Dagon, fallen on its face to the
ground before the ark of the
LORD. The head of Dagon and
both the palms of its hands
were broken off on the threshold; only Dagon's *torso*[a] was
left of it. 5 Therefore neither
the priests of Dagon nor any
who come into Dagon's house
tread on the threshold of
Dagon in Ashdod to this day.

6 But the hand of the LORD
was heavy on the people of
Ashdod, and He ravaged them
and struck them with tumors,[a]
both Ashdod and its territory.
7 And when the men of Ashdod saw how *it was,* they said,
"The ark of the God of Israel
must not remain with us, for
His hand is harsh toward us
and Dagon our god." 8 Therefore they sent and gathered to
themselves all the lords of the
Philistines, and said, "What
shall we do with the ark of the
God of Israel?"

And they answered, "Let
the ark of the God of Israel
be carried away to Gath." So
they carried the ark of the
God of Israel away. 9 So it
was, after they had carried
it away, that the hand of the
LORD was against the city with
a very great destruction; and
He struck the men of the city,
both small and great, and tumors broke out on them.

10 Therefore they sent the
ark of God to Ekron. So it
was, as the ark of God came

4:21 [a] Literally *Inglorious* 5:2 [a] A Philistine idol 5:4 [a] Following Septuagint, Syriac, Targum, and Vulgate; Masoretic Text reads *Dagon.* 5:6 [a] Probably bubonic plague. Septuagint and Vulgate add here *And in the midst of their land rats sprang up, and there was a great death panic in the city.*

to Ekron, that the Ekronites cried out, saying, "They have brought the ark of the God of Israel to us, to kill us and our people!" [11]So they sent and gathered together all the lords of the Philistines, and said, "Send away the ark of the God of Israel, and let it go back to its own place, so that it does not kill us and our people." For there was a deadly destruction throughout all the city; the hand of God was very heavy there. [12]And the men who did not die were stricken with the tumors, and the cry of the city went up to heaven.

THE ARK RETURNED TO ISRAEL

6 Now the ark of the LORD was in the country of the Philistines seven months. [2]And the Philistines called for the priests and the diviners, saying, "What shall we do with the ark of the LORD? Tell us how we should send it to its place."

[3]So they said, "If you send away the ark of the God of Israel, do not send it empty; but by all means return *it* to Him *with* a trespass offering. Then you will be healed, and it will be known to you why His hand is not removed from you."

[4]Then they said, "What *is* the trespass offering which we shall return to Him?"

They answered, "Five golden tumors and five golden rats, *according to* the number of the lords of the Philistines. For the same plague *was* on all of you and on your lords. [5]Therefore you shall make images of your tumors and images of your rats that ravage the land, and you shall give glory to the God of Israel; perhaps He will lighten His hand from you, from your gods, and from your land. [6]Why then do you harden your hearts as the Egyptians and Pharaoh hardened their hearts? When He did mighty things among them, did they not let the people go, that they might depart? [7]Now therefore, make a new cart, take two milk cows which have never been yoked, and hitch the cows to the cart; and take their calves home, away from them. [8]Then take the ark of the LORD and set it on the cart; and put the articles of gold which you are returning to Him *as* a trespass offering in a chest by its side. Then send it away, and let it go. [9]And watch: if it goes up the road to its own territory, to Beth Shemesh, *then* He has done us this great evil. But if not, then we shall know that *it is* not His hand *that* struck us—it happened to us by chance."

[10]Then the men did so; they took two milk cows and hitched them to the cart, and shut up their calves at home. [11]And they set the ark of the LORD on the cart, and the chest with the gold rats and the images of their tumors.

12Then the cows headed
straight for the road to Beth
Shemesh, *and* went along the
highway, lowing as they went,
and did not turn aside to the
right hand or the left. And the
lords of the Philistines went
after them to the border of
Beth Shemesh.
13Now *the people of* Beth
Shemesh *were* reaping their
wheat harvest in the valley;
and they lifted their eyes and
saw the ark, and rejoiced to see
it. 14Then the cart came into
the field of Joshua of Beth Shemesh, and stood there; a large
stone *was* there. So they split
the wood of the cart and offered the cows as a burnt offering to the LORD. 15The Levites
took down the ark of the LORD
and the chest that *was* with
it, in which *were* the articles
of gold, and put *them* on the
large stone. Then the men of
Beth Shemesh offered burnt
offerings and made sacrifices
the same day to the LORD. 16So
when the five lords of the Philistines had seen *it,* they returned to Ekron the same day.
17These *are* the golden tumors which the Philistines returned *as* a trespass offering to
the LORD: one for Ashdod, one
for Gaza, one for Ashkelon, one
for Gath, one for Ekron; 18and
the golden rats, *according to*
the number of all the cities of
the Philistines *belonging* to the
five lords, *both* fortified cities
and country villages, even as
far as the large *stone of* Abel on
which they set the ark of the
LORD, *which stone remains* to
this day in the field of Joshua
of Beth Shemesh.
19Then He struck the men
of Beth Shemesh, because
they had looked into the ark
of the LORD. He struck fifty
thousand and seventy men[a]
of the people, and the people
lamented because the LORD
had struck the people with a
great slaughter.

THE ARK AT KIRJATH JEARIM

20And the men of Beth
Shemesh said, "Who is able
to stand before this holy LORD
God? And to whom shall it go
up from us?" 21So they sent
messengers to the inhabitants
of Kirjath Jearim, saying, "The
Philistines have brought back
the ark of the LORD; come
down *and* take it up with you."
7 Then the men of Kirjath
Jearim came and took the
ark of the LORD, and brought
it into the house of Abinadab
on the hill, and consecrated
Eleazar his son to keep the ark
of the LORD.

SAMUEL JUDGES ISRAEL

2So it was that the ark remained in Kirjath Jearim a
long time; it was there twenty
years. And all the house of Israel lamented after the LORD.

6:19 [a] *Or He struck seventy men of the people and fifty oxen of a man*

3Then Samuel spoke to all
the house of Israel, saying, "If
you return to the LORD with
all your hearts, *then* put away
the foreign gods and the Ashtoreths[a] from among you, and
prepare your hearts for the
LORD, and serve Him only;
and He will deliver you from
the hand of the Philistines."
4So the children of Israel put
away the Baals and the Ashtoreths,[a] and served the LORD
only.

5And Samuel said, "Gather
all Israel to Mizpah, and I will
pray to the LORD for you." 6So
they gathered together at Mizpah, drew water, and poured *it*
out before the LORD. And they
fasted that day, and said there,
"We have sinned against the
LORD." And Samuel judged the
children of Israel at Mizpah.

7Now when the Philistines
heard that the children of Israel had gathered together at
Mizpah, the lords of the Philistines went up against Israel. And when the children
of Israel heard *of it,* they were
afraid of the Philistines. 8So
the children of Israel said to
Samuel, "Do not cease to cry
out to the LORD our God for
us, that He may save us from
the hand of the Philistines."

9And Samuel took a suck-
ling lamb and offered *it as* a
whole burnt offering to the
LORD. Then Samuel cried out
to the LORD for Israel, and the
LORD answered him. 10Now as
Samuel was offering up the
burnt offering, the Philistines
drew near to battle against Israel. But the LORD thundered
with a loud thunder upon the
Philistines that day, and so
confused them that they were
overcome before Israel. 11And
the men of Israel went out
of Mizpah and pursued the
Philistines, and drove them
back as far as below Beth Car.
12Then Samuel took a stone
and set *it* up between Mizpah
and Shen, and called its name
Ebenezer,[a] saying, "Thus far
the LORD has helped us."

13So the Philistines were
subdued, and they did not
come anymore into the territory of Israel. And the hand of
the LORD was against the Philistines all the days of Samuel.
14Then the cities which the
Philistines had taken from Israel were restored to Israel,
from Ekron to Gath; and Israel recovered its territory
from the hands of the Philistines. Also there was peace
between Israel and the Amorites.

15And Samuel judged Israel
all the days of his life. 16He
went from year to year on a
circuit to Bethel, Gilgal, and
Mizpah, and judged Israel in
all those places. 17But he always returned to Ramah, for

7:3 [a] Canaanite goddesses **7:4** [a] Canaanite goddesses **7:12** [a] Literally *Stone of Help*

his home *was* there. There he judged Israel, and there he built an altar to the LORD.

ISRAEL DEMANDS A KING

8 Now it came to pass when Samuel was old that he made his sons judges over
Israel. [2]The name of his first-born was Joel, and the name of his second, Abijah; *they were* judges in Beersheba.
[3]But his sons did not walk in his ways; they turned aside after dishonest gain, took bribes, and perverted justice.
[4]Then all the elders of Israel gathered together and came to Samuel at Ramah,
[5]and said to him, "Look, you are old, and your sons do not walk in your ways. Now make us a king to judge us like all the nations."
[6]But the thing displeased Samuel when they said, "Give us a king to judge us." So Samuel prayed to the LORD. [7]And the LORD said to Samuel, "Heed the voice of the people in all that they say to you; for they have not rejected you, but they have rejected Me, that I should not reign over
them. [8]According to all the works which they have done since the day that I brought them up out of Egypt, even to this day—with which they have forsaken Me and served other gods—so they are doing
to you also. [9]Now therefore, heed their voice. However, you shall solemnly forewarn them, and show them the behavior of the king who will reign over them."
[10]So Samuel told all the words of the LORD to the people who asked him for a king.
[11]And he said, "This will be the behavior of the king who will reign over you: He will take your sons and appoint *them* for his own chariots and *to be* his horsemen, and *some* will run before his chariots. [12]He will appoint captains over his thousands and captains over his fifties, *will set some* to plow his ground and reap his harvest, and *some* to make his weapons of war and equipment for his chariots. [13]He will take your daughters *to be* perfumers, cooks, and bakers.
[14]And he will take the best of your fields, your vineyards, and your olive groves, and give *them* to his servants. [15]He will take a tenth of your grain and your vintage, and give it to his officers and servants. [16]And he will take your male servants, your female servants, your finest young men,[a] and your donkeys, and put *them* to his
work. [17]He will take a tenth of your sheep. And you will be
his servants. [18]And you will cry out in that day because of your king whom you have chosen for yourselves, and the LORD will not hear you in that day."

8:16 [a] Septuagint reads *cattle*.

19Nevertheless the people
refused to obey the voice of
Samuel; and they said, "No,
but we will have a king over us,
20that we also may be like all
the nations, and that our king
may judge us and go out before us and fight our battles."
21And Samuel heard all the
words of the people, and he
repeated them in the hearing
of the LORD. 22So the LORD
said to Samuel, "Heed their
voice, and make them a king."
And Samuel said to the
men of Israel, "Every man go
to his city."

SAUL CHOSEN TO BE KING

9 There was a man of Ben-
jamin whose name *was*
Kish the son of Abiel, the son
of Zeror, the son of Bechorath,
the son of Aphiah, a Benjamite,
a mighty man of power. 2And
he had a choice and handsome
son whose name *was* Saul.
There was not a more handsome person than he among
the children of Israel. From
his shoulders upward *he was*
taller than any of the people.
3Now the donkeys of Kish,
Saul's father, were lost. And
Kish said to his son Saul,
"Please take one of the servants with you, and arise, go
and look for the donkeys." 4So
he passed through the mountains of Ephraim and through
the land of Shalisha, but they
did not find *them*. Then they
passed through the land of
Shaalim, and *they were* not
there. Then he passed through
the land of the Benjamites,
but they did not find *them*.
5When they had come to
the land of Zuph, Saul said to
his servant who *was* with him,
"Come, let us return, lest my
father cease *caring* about the
donkeys and become worried
about us."
6And he said to him, "Look
now, *there is* in this city a man
of God, and *he is* an honorable
man; all that he says surely
comes to pass. So let us go
there; perhaps he can show
us the way that we should go."
7Then Saul said to his servant, "But look, *if* we go, what
shall we bring the man? For
the bread in our vessels is all
gone, and *there is* no present
to bring to the man of God.
What do we have?"
8And the servant answered
Saul again and said, "Look, I
have here at hand one-fourth
of a shekel of silver. I will give
that to the man of God, to tell us
our way." 9(Formerly in Israel,
when a man went to inquire of
God, he spoke thus: "Come, let
us go to the seer"; for *he who is*
now *called* a prophet was formerly called a seer.)
10Then Saul said to his servant, "Well said; come, let us
go." So they went to the city
where the man of God *was*.
11As they went up the hill
to the city, they met some
young women going out to
draw water, and said to them,
"Is the seer here?"

[12]And they answered them
and said, "Yes, there he is, just
ahead of you. Hurry now; for
today he came to this city, because there is a sacrifice of
the people today on the high
place. [13]As soon as you come
into the city, you will surely
find him before he goes up to
the high place to eat. For the
people will not eat until he
comes, because he must bless
the sacrifice; afterward those
who are invited will eat. Now
therefore, go up, for about
this time you will find him."
[14]So they went up to the city.
As they were coming into the
city, there was Samuel, coming out toward them on his
way up to the high place.

[15]Now the LORD had told
Samuel in his ear the day
before Saul came, saying,
[16]"Tomorrow about this time
I will send you a man from
the land of Benjamin, and you
shall anoint him commander
over My people Israel, that he
may save My people from the
hand of the Philistines; for I
have looked upon My people,
because their cry has come
to Me."

[17]So when Samuel saw Saul,
the LORD said to him, "There
he is, the man of whom I
spoke to you. This one shall
reign over My people." [18]Then
Saul drew near to Samuel in
the gate, and said, "Please tell
me, where *is* the seer's house?"

[19]Samuel answered Saul
and said, "I *am* the seer. Go
up before me to the high
place, for you shall eat with
me today; and tomorrow I will
let you go and will tell you all
that *is* in your heart. [20]But as
for your donkeys that were
lost three days ago, do not
be anxious about them, for
they have been found. And
on whom *is* all the desire of
Israel? *Is it* not on you and on
all your father's house?"

[21]And Saul answered and
said, "*Am* I not a Benjamite,
of the smallest of the tribes
of Israel, and my family the
least of all the families of the
tribe[a] of Benjamin? Why then
do you speak like this to me?"

[22]Now Samuel took Saul
and his servant and brought
them into the hall, and had
them sit in the place of honor
among those who were in-
vited; there *were* about thirty
persons. [23]And Samuel said to
the cook, "Bring the portion
which I gave you, of which I
said to you, 'Set it apart.'" [24]So
the cook took up the thigh
with its upper part and set *it*
before Saul. And *Samuel* said,
"Here it is, what was kept back.
It was set apart for you. Eat;
for until this time it has been
kept for you, since I said I invited the people." So Saul ate
with Samuel that day.

[25]When they had come
down from the high place into

9:21 [a] Literally *tribes*

the city, *Samuel* spoke with
Saul on the top of the house.[a]
26 They arose early; and it was
about the dawning of the day
that Samuel called to Saul on
the top of the house, saying,
"Get up, that I may send you
on your way." And Saul arose,
and both of them went outside, he and Samuel.

SAUL ANOINTED KING

27 As they were going down
to the outskirts of the city,
Samuel said to Saul, "Tell
the servant to go on ahead
of us." And he went on. "But
you stand here awhile, that
I may announce to you the
word of God."

10 Then Samuel took a
flask of oil and poured
it on his head, and kissed
him and said: "*Is it* not because the LORD has anointed
you commander over His inheritance?[a] 2 When you have
departed from me today, you
will find two men by Rachel's
tomb in the territory of Benjamin at Zelzah; and they
will say to you, 'The donkeys
which you went to look for
have been found. And now
your father has ceased caring about the donkeys and is
worrying about you, saying,
"What shall I do about my
son?"' 3 Then you shall go on
forward from there and come
to the terebinth tree of Tabor.
There three men going up to
God at Bethel will meet you,
one carrying three young
goats, another carrying three
loaves of bread, and another
carrying a skin of wine. 4 And
they will greet you and give
you two *loaves* of bread, which
you shall receive from their
hands. 5 After that you shall
come to the hill of God where
the Philistine garrison *is.* And
it will happen, when you have
come there to the city, that you
will meet a group of prophets
coming down from the high
place with a stringed instrument, a tambourine, a flute,
and a harp before them; and
they will be prophesying.
6 Then the Spirit of the LORD
will come upon you, and you
will prophesy with them and
be turned into another man.
7 And let it be, when these signs
come to you, *that* you do as the
occasion demands; for God *is*
with you. 8 You shall go down
before me to Gilgal; and surely
I will come down to you to
offer burnt offerings *and* make

9:25 [a] Following Masoretic Text and Targum; Septuagint omits *He spoke with Saul on the top of the house;* Septuagint and Vulgate add *And he prepared a bed for Saul on the top of the house, and he slept.*
10:1 [a] Following Masoretic Text, Targum, and Vulgate; Septuagint reads *His people Israel; and you shall rule the people of the Lord;* Septuagint and Vulgate add *And you shall deliver His people from the hands of their enemies all around them. And this shall be a sign to you, that God has anointed you to be a prince.*

sacrifices of peace offerings. Seven days you shall wait, till I come to you and show you what you should do."

9So it was, when he had turned his back to go from Samuel, that God gave him another heart; and all those signs came to pass that day. 10When they came there to the hill, there was a group of prophets to meet him; then the Spirit of God came upon him, and he prophesied among them. 11And it happened, when all who knew him formerly saw that he indeed prophesied among the prophets, that the people said to one another, "What *is* this *that* has come upon the son of Kish? *Is* Saul also among the prophets?" 12Then a man from there answered and said, "But who *is* their father?" Therefore it became a proverb: "*Is* Saul also among the prophets?" 13And when he had finished prophesying, he went to the high place.

14Then Saul's uncle said to him and his servant, "Where did you go?"

So he said, "To look for the donkeys. When we saw that *they were* nowhere *to be found,* we went to Samuel."

15And Saul's uncle said, "Tell me, please, what Samuel said to you."

16So Saul said to his uncle, "He told us plainly that the donkeys had been found." But about the matter of the kingdom, he did not tell him what Samuel had said.

SAUL PROCLAIMED KING

17Then Samuel called the people together to the LORD at Mizpah, 18and said to the children of Israel, "Thus says the LORD God of Israel: 'I brought up Israel out of Egypt, and delivered you from the hand of the Egyptians *and* from the hand of all kingdoms and from those who oppressed you.' 19But you have today rejected your God, who Himself saved you from all your adversities and your tribulations; and you have said to Him, 'No, set a king over us!' Now therefore, present yourselves before the LORD by your tribes and by your clans."[a]

20And when Samuel had caused all the tribes of Israel to come near, the tribe of Benjamin was chosen. 21When he had caused the tribe of Benjamin to come near by their families, the family of Matri was chosen. And Saul the son of Kish was chosen. But when they sought him, he could not be found. 22Therefore they inquired of the LORD further, "Has the man come here yet?"

And the LORD answered, "There he is, hidden among the equipment."

23So they ran and brought him from there; and when

10:19 [a] Literally *thousands*

he stood among the people,
he was taller than any of the
people from his shoulders upward. 24And Samuel said to all
the people, "Do you see him
whom the LORD has chosen,
that *there is* no one like him
among all the people?"

So all the people shouted
and said, "Long live the king!"

25Then Samuel explained
to the people the behavior
of royalty, and wrote *it* in a
book and laid *it* up before the
LORD. And Samuel sent all the
people away, every man to his
house. 26And Saul also went
home to Gibeah; and valiant
men went with him, whose
hearts God had touched. 27But
some rebels said, "How can
this man save us?" So they
despised him, and brought
him no presents. But he held
his peace.

SAUL SAVES JABESH GILEAD

11 Then Nahash the Am-
monite came up and
encamped against Jabesh
Gilead; and all the men of Jabesh said to Nahash, "Make a
covenant with us, and we will
serve you."

2And Nahash the Ammon-
ite answered them, "On this
condition I will make *a covenant* with you, that I may put
out all your right eyes, and
bring reproach on all Israel."

3Then the elders of Ja-
besh said to him, "Hold off
for seven days, that we may
send messengers to all the
territory of Israel. And then,
if *there is* no one to save us, we
will come out to you."

4So the messengers came
to Gibeah of Saul and told
the news in the hearing of
the people. And all the people lifted up their voices and
wept. 5Now there was Saul,
coming behind the herd from
the field; and Saul said, "What
troubles the people, that they
weep?" And they told him the
words of the men of Jabesh.
6Then the Spirit of God came
upon Saul when he heard
this news, and his anger was
greatly aroused. 7So he took a
yoke of oxen and cut them in
pieces, and sent *them* throughout all the territory of Israel
by the hands of messengers,
saying, "Whoever does not go
out with Saul and Samuel to
battle, so it shall be done to
his oxen."

And the fear of the LORD
fell on the people, and they
came out with one consent.
8When he numbered them in
Bezek, the children of Israel
were three hundred thou-
sand, and the men of Judah
thirty thousand. 9And they
said to the messengers who
came, "Thus you shall say to
the men of Jabesh Gilead: 'Tomorrow, by *the time* the sun is
hot, you shall have help.'" Then
the messengers came and reported *it* to the men of Jabesh,
and they were glad. 10There-
fore the men of Jabesh said,
"Tomorrow we will come out

to you, and you may do with us
whatever seems good to you."
11 So it was, on the next
day, that Saul put the people
in three companies; and they
came into the midst of the
camp in the morning watch,
and killed Ammonites until
the heat of the day. And it happened that those who survived
were scattered, so that no two
of them were left together.
12 Then the people said to
Samuel, "Who *is* he who said,
'Shall Saul reign over us?'
Bring the men, that we may
put them to death."
13 But Saul said, "Not a man
shall be put to death this day,
for today the LORD has accomplished salvation in Israel."
14 Then Samuel said to the
people, "Come, let us go to Gilgal and renew the kingdom
there." 15 So all the people went
to Gilgal, and there they made
Saul king before the LORD in
Gilgal. There they made sacrifices of peace offerings before
the LORD, and there Saul and
all the men of Israel rejoiced
greatly.

SAMUEL'S ADDRESS AT SAUL'S CORONATION

12 Now Samuel said to all
Israel: "Indeed I have
heeded your voice in all that
you said to me, and have made
a king over you. 2 And now here
is the king, walking before you;
and I am old and grayheaded,
and look, my sons *are* with
you. I have walked before you
from my childhood to this day.
3 Here I am. Witness against
me before the LORD and before His anointed: Whose ox
have I taken, or whose donkey
have I taken, or whom have
I cheated? Whom have I oppressed, or from whose hand
have I received *any* bribe with
which to blind my eyes? I will
restore *it* to you."
4 And they said, "You have
not cheated us or oppressed
us, nor have you taken anything from any man's hand."
5 Then he said to them, "The
LORD *is* witness against you,
and His anointed *is* witness
this day, that you have not
found anything in my hand."
And they answered, "*He is*
witness."
6 Then Samuel said to the
people, "*It is* the LORD who
raised up Moses and Aaron,
and who brought your fathers
up from the land of Egypt.
7 Now therefore, stand still, that
I may reason with you before
the LORD concerning all the
righteous acts of the LORD
which He did to you and your
fathers: 8 When Jacob had gone
into Egypt,[a] and your fathers
cried out to the LORD, then the
LORD sent Moses and Aaron,
who brought your fathers out
of Egypt and made them dwell

12:8 [a] Following Masoretic Text, Targum, and Vulgate; Septuagint adds *and the Egyptians afflicted them.*

in this place. 9And when they
forgot the LORD their God, He
sold them into the hand of Sisera, commander of the army
of Hazor, into the hand of the
Philistines, and into the hand
of the king of Moab; and they
fought against them. 10Then
they cried out to the LORD, and
said, 'We have sinned, because
we have forsaken the LORD
and served the Baals and Ashtoreths;[a] but now deliver us
from the hand of our enemies,
and we will serve You.' 11And
the LORD sent Jerubbaal,[a]
Bedan,[b] Jephthah, and Samuel,[c] and delivered you out of
the hand of your enemies on
every side; and you dwelt in
safety. 12And when you saw
that Nahash king of the Ammonites came against you, you
said to me, 'No, but a king shall
reign over us,' when the LORD
your God *was* your king.

13"Now therefore, here is
the king whom you have chosen *and* whom you have desired. And take note, the LORD
has set a king over you. 14If you
fear the LORD and serve Him
and obey His voice, and do not
rebel against the commandment of the LORD, then both
you and the king who reigns
over you will continue following the LORD your God. 15How-
ever, if you do not obey the
voice of the LORD, but rebel
against the commandment
of the LORD, then the hand of
the LORD will be against you,
as *it was* against your fathers.

16"Now therefore, stand
and see this great thing which
the LORD will do before your
eyes: 17*Is* today not the wheat
harvest? I will call to the LORD,
and He will send thunder and
rain, that you may perceive
and see that your wickedness
is great, which you have done
in the sight of the LORD, in
asking a king for yourselves."

18So Samuel called to the
LORD, and the LORD sent
thunder and rain that day;
and all the people greatly
feared the LORD and Samuel.

19And all the people said
to Samuel, "Pray for your servants to the LORD your God,
that we may not die; for we
have added to all our sins the
evil of asking a king for ourselves."

20Then Samuel said to the
people, "Do not fear. You have
done all this wickedness; yet
do not turn aside from following the LORD, but serve
the LORD with all your heart.
21And do not turn aside; for
then you would go after empty
things which cannot profit or
deliver, for they *are* nothing.
22For the LORD will not forsake His people, for His great
name's sake, because it has

12:10 [a] Canaanite goddesses 12:11 [a] Syriac reads *Deborah;* Targum reads *Gideon.* [b] Septuagint and Syriac read *Barak;* Targum reads *Simson.* [c] Syriac reads *Simson.*

pleased the LORD to make you His people. [23]Moreover, as for me, far be it from me that I should sin against the LORD in ceasing to pray for you; but I will teach you the good and the right way. [24]Only fear the LORD, and serve Him in truth with all your heart; for consider what great things He has done for you. [25]But if you still do wickedly, you shall be swept away, both you and your king."

SAUL'S UNLAWFUL SACRIFICE

13 Saul reigned one year; and when he had reigned two years over Israel,[a] [2]Saul chose for himself three thousand *men* of Israel. Two thousand were with Saul in Michmash and in the mountains of Bethel, and a thousand were with Jonathan in Gibeah of Benjamin. The rest of the people he sent away, every man to his tent.

[3]And Jonathan attacked the garrison of the Philistines that *was* in Geba, and the Philistines heard *of it.* Then Saul blew the trumpet throughout all the land, saying, "Let the Hebrews hear!" [4]Now all Israel heard it said *that* Saul had attacked a garrison of the Philistines, and *that* Israel had also become an abomination to the Philistines. And the people were called together to Saul at Gilgal.

[5]Then the Philistines gathered together to fight with Israel, thirty[a] thousand chariots and six thousand horsemen, and people as the sand which *is* on the seashore in multitude. And they came up and encamped in Michmash, to the east of Beth Aven. [6]When the men of Israel saw that they were in danger (for the people were distressed), then the people hid in caves, in thickets, in rocks, in holes, and in pits. [7]And *some of* the Hebrews crossed over the Jordan to the land of Gad and Gilead.

As for Saul, he *was* still in Gilgal, and all the people followed him trembling. [8]Then he waited seven days, according to the time set by Samuel. But Samuel did not come to Gilgal; and the people were scattered from him. [9]So Saul said, "Bring a burnt offering and peace offerings here to me." And he offered the burnt offering. [10]Now it happened, as soon as he had finished presenting the burnt offering, that Samuel came; and Saul went out to meet him, that he might greet him.

[11]And Samuel said, "What have you done?"

Saul said, "When I saw that the people were scattered from

13:1 [a] The Hebrew is difficult (compare 2 Samuel 5:4; 2 Kings 14:2; see also 2 Samuel 2:10; Acts 13:21). 13:5 [a] Following Masoretic Text, Septuagint, Targum, and Vulgate; Syriac and some manuscripts of the Septuagint read *three.*

me, and *that* you did not come
within the days appointed, and
that the Philistines gathered
together at Michmash, 12then I
said, 'The Philistines will now
come down on me at Gilgal,
and I have not made supplication to the LORD.' Therefore
I felt compelled, and offered
a burnt offering."

13And Samuel said to Saul,
"You have done foolishly. You
have not kept the commandment of the LORD your God,
which He commanded you.
For now the LORD would have
established your kingdom
over Israel forever. 14But now
your kingdom shall not continue. The LORD has sought
for Himself a man after His
own heart, and the LORD has
commanded him *to be* commander over His people, because you have not kept what
the LORD commanded you."

15Then Samuel arose and
went up from Gilgal to Gibeah
of Benjamin.[a] And Saul numbered the people present with
him, about six hundred men.

NO WEAPONS FOR THE ARMY

16Saul, Jonathan his son,
and the people present with
them remained in Gibeah
of Benjamin. But the Philistines encamped in Michmash.
17Then raiders came out of
the camp of the Philistines
in three companies. One company turned onto the road to
Ophrah, to the land of Shual,
18another company turned to
the road *to* Beth Horon, and
another company turned *to*
the road of the border that
overlooks the Valley of Zeboim toward the wilderness.

19Now there was no black-
smith to be found throughout
all the land of Israel, for the
Philistines said, "Lest the Hebrews make swords or spears."
20But all the Israelites would
go down to the Philistines to
sharpen each man's plow-
share, his mattock, his ax, and
his sickle; 21and the charge for
a sharpening was a pim[a] for
the plowshares, the mattocks,
the forks, and the axes, and
to set the points of the goads.
22So it came about, on the day
of battle, that there was neither sword nor spear found in
the hand of any of the people
who *were* with Saul and Jonathan. But they were found with
Saul and Jonathan his son.

23And the garrison of the
Philistines went out to the
pass of Michmash.

JONATHAN DEFEATS THE PHILISTINES

14 Now it happened one day
that Jonathan the son of
Saul said to the young man

13:15 [a] Following Masoretic Text and Targum; Septuagint and Vulgate add *And the rest of the people went up after Saul to meet the people who fought against them, going from Gilgal to Gibeah in the hill of Benjamin.* 13:21 [a] About two-thirds shekel weight

who bore his armor, "Come, let
us go over to the Philistines'
garrison that *is* on the other
side." But he did not tell his father. 2And Saul was sitting in
the outskirts of Gibeah under
a pomegranate tree which *is*
in Migron. The people who
were with him *were* about six
hundred men. 3Ahijah the son
of Ahitub, Ichabod's brother,
the son of Phinehas, the son of
Eli, the LORD's priest in Shiloh,
was wearing an ephod. But
the people did not know that
Jonathan had gone.

4Between the passes, by
which Jonathan sought to go
over to the Philistines' garrison, *there was* a sharp rock
on one side and a sharp rock
on the other side. And the
name of one *was* Bozez, and
the name of the other Seneh.
5The front of one faced northward opposite Michmash, and
the other southward opposite
Gibeah.

6Then Jonathan said to
the young man who bore his
armor, "Come, let us go over
to the garrison of these uncircumcised; it may be that
the LORD will work for us. For
nothing restrains the LORD
from saving by many or by
few."

7So his armorbearer said
to him, "Do all that is in your
heart. Go then; here I am with
you, according to your heart."

8Then Jonathan said, "Very
well, let us cross over to *these*
men, and we will show ourselves to them. 9If they say
thus to us, 'Wait until we come
to you,' then we will stand still
in our place and not go up to
them. 10But if they say thus,
'Come up to us,' then we will
go up. For the LORD has delivered them into our hand, and
this *will be* a sign to us."

11So both of them showed
themselves to the garrison of
the Philistines. And the Philistines said, "Look, the Hebrews
are coming out of the holes
where they have hidden."
12Then the men of the garrison called to Jonathan and his
armorbearer, and said, "Come
up to us, and we will show you
something."

Jonathan said to his armorbearer, "Come up after me, for
the LORD has delivered them
into the hand of Israel." 13And
Jonathan climbed up on his
hands and knees with his
armorbearer after him; and
they fell before Jonathan.
And as he came after him,
his armorbearer killed them.
14That first slaughter which
Jonathan and his armor-
bearer made was about twenty
men within about half an acre
of land.[a]

15And there was trembling
in the camp, in the field,
and among all the people.
The garrison and the raiders also trembled; and the

14:14 [a] Literally *half the area plowed by a yoke* (of oxen in a day)

earth quaked, so that it was
a very great trembling. 16Now
the watchmen of Saul in Gibeah of Benjamin looked, and
there was the multitude, melt-
ing away; and they went here
and there. 17Then Saul said
to the people who *were* with
him, "Now call the roll and see
who has gone from us." And
when they had called the roll,
surprisingly, Jonathan and his
armorbearer *were* not *there.*
18And Saul said to Ahijah,
"Bring the ark[a] of God here"
(for at that time the ark[b] of
God was with the children of
Israel). 19Now it happened,
while Saul talked to the priest,
that the noise which *was* in the
camp of the Philistines continued to increase; so Saul said
to the priest, "Withdraw your
hand." 20Then Saul and all the
people who *were* with him assembled, and they went to the
battle; and indeed every man's
sword was against his neighbor, *and there was* very great
confusion. 21Moreover the
Hebrews *who* were with the
Philistines before that time,
who went up with them into
the camp *from the* surrounding *country,* they also joined
the Israelites who *were* with
Saul and Jonathan. 22Likewise
all the men of Israel who had
hidden in the mountains of
Ephraim, *when* they heard
that the Philistines fled, they
also followed hard after them
in the battle. 23So the LORD
saved Israel that day, and the
battle shifted to Beth Aven.

SAUL'S RASH OATH

24And the men of Israel
were distressed that day, for
Saul had placed the people
under oath, saying, "Cursed
is the man who eats *any* food
until evening, before I have
taken vengeance on my en-
emies." So none of the people tasted food. 25Now all *the*
people of the land came to a
forest; and there was honey
on the ground. 26And when
the people had come into the
woods, there was the honey,
dripping; but no one put his
hand to his mouth, for the people feared the oath. 27But Jonathan had not heard his father
charge the people with the
oath; therefore he stretched
out the end of the rod that
was in his hand and dipped
it in a honeycomb, and put
his hand to his mouth; and
his countenance brightened.
28Then one of the people said,
"Your father strictly charged
the people with an oath, saying, 'Cursed *is* the man who
eats food this day.'" And the
people were faint.

29But Jonathan said, "My
father has troubled the land.

14:18 [a] Following Masoretic Text, Targum, and Vulgate; Septuagint reads *ephod.* [b] Following Masoretic Text, Targum, and Vulgate; Septuagint reads *ephod.*

Look now, how my counte-
nance has brightened be-
cause I tasted a little of this
honey. 30How much better if
the people had eaten freely
today of the spoil of their enemies which they found! For
now would there not have
been a much greater slaughter
among the Philistines?"
31Now they had driven back
the Philistines that day from
Michmash to Aijalon. So the
people were very faint. 32And
the people rushed on the
spoil, and took sheep, oxen,
and calves, and slaughtered
them on the ground; and
the people ate *them* with the
blood. 33Then they told Saul,
saying, "Look, the people are
sinning against the LORD by
eating with the blood!"

So he said, "You have
dealt treacherously; roll a
large stone to me this day."
34Then Saul said, "Disperse
yourselves among the peo-
ple, and say to them, 'Bring
me here every man's ox and
every man's sheep, slaughter
them here, and eat; and do not
sin against the LORD by eating with the blood.'" So every
one of the people brought his
ox with him that night, and
slaughtered *it* there. 35Then
Saul built an altar to the LORD.
This was the first altar that he
built to the LORD.

36Now Saul said, "Let us go
down after the Philistines by
night, and plunder them until
the morning light; and let us
not leave a man of them."

And they said, "Do what-
ever seems good to you."

Then the priest said, "Let us
draw near to God here."

37So Saul asked counsel of
God, "Shall I go down after
the Philistines? Will You deliver them into the hand of
Israel?" But He did not answer him that day. 38And
Saul said, "Come over here,
all you chiefs of the people,
and know and see what this
sin was today. 39For *as* the
LORD lives, who saves Israel,
though it be in Jonathan my
son, he shall surely die." But
not a man among all the people answered him. 40Then he
said to all Israel, "You be on
one side, and my son Jonathan and I will be on the other
side."

And the people said to Saul,
"Do what seems good to you."
41Therefore Saul said to
the LORD God of Israel, "Give
a perfect *lot.*"[a] So Saul and
Jonathan were taken, but the
people escaped. 42And Saul
said, "Cast *lots* between my
son Jonathan and me." So
Jonathan was taken. 43Then
Saul said to Jonathan, "Tell
me what you have done."

14:41 [a] Following Masoretic Text and Targum; Septuagint and Vulgate read *Why do You not answer Your servant today? If the injustice is with me or Jonathan my son, O LORD God of Israel, give proof; and if You say it is with Your people Israel, give holiness.*

And Jonathan told him, and said, "I only tasted a little honey with the end of the rod that *was* in my hand. So now I must die!"

[44]Saul answered, "God do so and more also; for you shall surely die, Jonathan."

[45]But the people said to Saul, "Shall Jonathan die, who has accomplished this great deliverance in Israel? Certainly not! *As* the LORD lives, not one hair of his head shall fall to the ground, for he has worked with God this day." So the people rescued Jonathan, and he did not die.

[46]Then Saul returned from pursuing the Philistines, and the Philistines went to their own place.

SAUL'S CONTINUING WARS

[47]So Saul established his sovereignty over Israel, and fought against all his enemies on every side, against Moab, against the people of Ammon, against Edom, against the kings of Zobah, and against the Philistines. Wherever he turned, he harassed *them.*[a] [48]And he gathered an army and attacked the Amalekites, and delivered Israel from the hands of those who plundered them.

[49]The sons of Saul were Jonathan, Jishui,[a] and Malchishua. And the names of his two daughters *were these:* the name of the firstborn Merab, and the name of the younger Michal. [50]The name of Saul's wife *was* Ahinoam the daughter of Ahimaaz. And the name of the commander of his army *was* Abner the son of Ner, Saul's uncle. [51]Kish *was* the father of Saul, and Ner the father of Abner *was* the son of Abiel.

[52]Now there was fierce war with the Philistines all the days of Saul. And when Saul saw any strong man or any valiant man, he took him for himself.

SAUL SPARES KING AGAG

15 Samuel also said to Saul, "The LORD sent me to anoint you king over His people, over Israel. Now therefore, heed the voice of the words of the LORD. [2]Thus says the LORD of hosts: 'I will punish Amalek *for* what he did to Israel, how he ambushed him on the way when he came up from Egypt. [3]Now go and attack Amalek, and utterly destroy all that they have, and do not spare them. But kill both man and woman, infant and nursing child, ox and sheep, camel and donkey.'"

[4]So Saul gathered the people together and numbered them in Telaim, two hundred thousand foot soldiers and

14:47 [a] Septuagint and Vulgate read *prospered.* 14:49 [a] Called *Abinadab* in 1 Chronicles 8:33 and 9:39

ten thousand men of Judah.
5And Saul came to a city of
Amalek, and lay in wait in the
valley.
6Then Saul said to the Kenites, "Go, depart, get down
from among the Amalekites,
lest I destroy you with them.
For you showed kindness to
all the children of Israel when
they came up out of Egypt."
So the Kenites departed from
among the Amalekites. 7And
Saul attacked the Amalekites,
from Havilah all the way to
Shur, which is east of Egypt.
8He also took Agag king of
the Amalekites alive, and utterly destroyed all the people
with the edge of the sword.
9But Saul and the people
spared Agag and the best of
the sheep, the oxen, the fatlings, the lambs, and all *that*
was good, and were unwilling to utterly destroy them.
But everything despised and
worthless, that they utterly
destroyed.

SAUL REJECTED AS KING

10Now the word of the LORD
came to Samuel, saying, 11"I
greatly regret that I have set
up Saul *as* king, for he has
turned back from following
Me, and has not performed
My commandments." And it
grieved Samuel, and he cried
out to the LORD all night. 12So
when Samuel rose early in the
morning to meet Saul, it was
told Samuel, saying, "Saul
went to Carmel, and indeed,
he set up a monument for
himself; and he has gone on
around, passed by, and gone
down to Gilgal." 13Then Samuel went to Saul, and Saul said
to him, "Blessed *are* you of the
LORD! I have performed the
commandment of the LORD."
14But Samuel said, "What
then *is* this bleating of the
sheep in my ears, and the lowing of the oxen which I hear?"
15And Saul said, "They have
brought them from the Amalekites; for the people spared
the best of the sheep and the
oxen, to sacrifice to the LORD
your God; and the rest we have
utterly destroyed."
16Then Samuel said to Saul,
"Be quiet! And I will tell you
what the LORD said to me last
night."

And he said to him,
"Speak on."
17So Samuel said, "When
you *were* little in your own
eyes, *were* you not head of the
tribes of Israel? And did not
the LORD anoint you king over
Israel? 18Now the LORD sent
you on a mission, and said,
'Go, and utterly destroy the
sinners, the Amalekites, and
fight against them until they
are consumed.' 19Why then
did you not obey the voice of
the LORD? Why did you swoop
down on the spoil, and do evil
in the sight of the LORD?"
20And Saul said to Samuel,
"But I have obeyed the voice
of the LORD, and gone on the
mission on which the LORD

sent me, and brought back
Agag king of Amalek; I have
utterly destroyed the Amalekites. 21But the people took of
the plunder, sheep and oxen,
the best of the things which
should have been utterly destroyed, to sacrifice to the
LORD your God in Gilgal."
22So Samuel said:

"Has the LORD *as great*
delight in burnt
offerings and sacrifices,
As in obeying the
voice of the LORD?
Behold, to obey is better
than sacrifice,
And to heed than
the fat of rams.
23 For rebellion *is as* the
sin of witchcraft,
And stubbornness *is as*
iniquity and idolatry.
Because you have
rejected the word
of the LORD,
He also has rejected you
from *being* king."

24Then Saul said to Sam-
uel, "I have sinned, for I have
transgressed the command-
ment of the LORD and your
words, because I feared the
people and obeyed their voice.
25Now therefore, please pardon my sin, and return with
me, that I may worship the
LORD."
26But Samuel said to Saul,
"I will not return with you, for
you have rejected the word of
the LORD, and the LORD has
rejected you from being king
over Israel."
27And as Samuel turned
around to go away, *Saul* seized
the edge of his robe, and it
tore. 28So Samuel said to him,
"The LORD has torn the kingdom of Israel from you today,
and has given it to a neighbor
of yours, *who is* better than
you. 29And also the Strength
of Israel will not lie nor relent.
For He *is* not a man, that He
should relent."
30Then he said, "I have
sinned; *yet* honor me now,
please, before the elders of
my people and before Israel,
and return with me, that I may
worship the LORD your God."
31So Samuel turned back after
Saul, and Saul worshiped the
LORD.
32Then Samuel said, "Bring
Agag king of the Amalekites
here to me." So Agag came to
him cautiously.
And Agag said, "Surely the
bitterness of death is past."
33But Samuel said, "As your
sword has made women childless, so shall your mother be
childless among women." And
Samuel hacked Agag in pieces
before the LORD in Gilgal.
34Then Samuel went to
Ramah, and Saul went up to
his house at Gibeah of Saul.
35And Samuel went no more
to see Saul until the day of his
death. Nevertheless Samuel
mourned for Saul, and the
LORD regretted that He had
made Saul king over Israel.

DAVID ANOINTED KING

16 Now the LORD said to
Samuel, "How long will
you mourn for Saul, seeing I
have rejected him from reigning over Israel? Fill your horn
with oil, and go; I am sending
you to Jesse the Bethlehemite.
For I have provided Myself a
king among his sons."
2And Samuel said, "How
can I go? If Saul hears *it,* he
will kill me."
But the LORD said, "Take
a heifer with you, and say, 'I
have come to sacrifice to the
LORD.' 3Then invite Jesse to
the sacrifice, and I will show
you what you shall do; you
shall anoint for Me the one I
name to you."
4So Samuel did what the
LORD said, and went to Bethlehem. And the elders of the
town trembled at his coming,
and said, "Do you come peaceably?"
5And he said, "Peaceably; I
have come to sacrifice to the
LORD. Sanctify yourselves,
and come with me to the sacrifice." Then he consecrated
Jesse and his sons, and invited
them to the sacrifice.
6So it was, when they
came, that he looked at Eliab
and said, "Surely the LORD's
anointed *is* before Him!"
7But the LORD said to Samuel, "Do not look at his appearance or at his physical stature,
because I have refused him.
For *the LORD does* not *see* as
man sees;[a] for man looks at
the outward appearance, but
the LORD looks at the heart."
8So Jesse called Abinadab,
and made him pass before
Samuel. And he said, "Neither has the LORD chosen
this one." 9Then Jesse made
Shammah pass by. And he
said, "Neither has the LORD
chosen this one." 10Thus Jesse
made seven of his sons pass
before Samuel. And Samuel
said to Jesse, "The LORD has
not chosen these." 11And Samuel said to Jesse, "Are all the
young men here?" Then he
said, "There remains yet the
youngest, and there he is,
keeping the sheep."
And Samuel said to Jesse,
"Send and bring him. For we
will not sit down[a] till he comes
here." 12So he sent and brought
him in. Now he *was* ruddy, with
bright eyes, and good-looking.
And the LORD said, "Arise,
anoint him; for this *is* the one!"
13Then Samuel took the horn
of oil and anointed him in the
midst of his brothers; and the
Spirit of the LORD came upon
David from that day forward.
So Samuel arose and went to
Ramah.

16:7 [a] Septuagint reads *For God does not see as man sees;* Targum reads *It is not by the appearance of a man;* Vulgate reads *Nor do I judge according to the looks of a man.* 16:11 [a] Following Septuagint and Vulgate; Masoretic Text reads *turn around;* Targum and Syriac read *turn away.*

A DISTRESSING SPIRIT TROUBLES SAUL

14But the Spirit of the LORD departed from Saul, and a distressing spirit from the LORD troubled him. 15And Saul's servants said to him, "Surely, a distressing spirit from God is troubling you. 16Let our master now command your servants, *who are* before you, to seek out a man *who is* a skillful player on the harp. And it shall be that he will play it with his hand when the distressing spirit from God is upon you, and you shall be well."

17So Saul said to his servants, "Provide me now a man who can play well, and bring *him* to me."

18Then one of the servants answered and said, "Look, I have seen a son of Jesse the Bethlehemite, *who is* skillful in playing, a mighty man of valor, a man of war, prudent in speech, and a handsome person; and the LORD *is* with him."

19Therefore Saul sent messengers to Jesse, and said, "Send me your son David, who *is* with the sheep." 20And Jesse took a donkey *loaded with* bread, a skin of wine, and a young goat, and sent *them* by his son David to Saul. 21So David came to Saul and stood before him. And he loved him greatly, and he became his armorbearer. 22Then Saul sent to Jesse, saying, "Please let David stand before me, for he has found favor in my sight." 23And so it was, whenever the spirit from God was upon Saul, that David would take a harp and play *it* with his hand. Then Saul would become refreshed and well, and the distressing spirit would depart from him.

DAVID AND GOLIATH

17 Now the Philistines gathered their armies together to battle, and were gathered at Sochoh, which *belongs* to Judah; they encamped between Sochoh and Azekah, in Ephes Dammim. 2And Saul and the men of Israel were gathered together, and they encamped in the Valley of Elah, and drew up in battle array against the Philistines. 3The Philistines stood on a mountain on one side, and Israel stood on a mountain on the other side, with a valley between them.

4And a champion went out from the camp of the Philistines, named Goliath, from Gath, whose height *was* six cubits and a span. 5*He had* a bronze helmet on his head, and he *was* armed with a coat of mail, and the weight of the coat *was* five thousand shekels of bronze. 6And *he had* bronze armor on his legs and a bronze javelin between his shoulders. 7Now the staff of his spear *was* like a weaver's beam, and his iron spearhead *weighed* six hundred shekels;

and a shield-bearer went before him. 8Then he stood and
cried out to the armies of Israel, and said to them, "Why
have you come out to line up
for battle? *Am* I not a Philistine, and you the servants of
Saul? Choose a man for yourselves, and let him come down
to me. 9If he is able to fight
with me and kill me, then we
will be your servants. But if I
prevail against him and kill
him, then you shall be our
servants and serve us." 10And
the Philistine said, "I defy the
armies of Israel this day; give
me a man, that we may fight
together." 11When Saul and all
Israel heard these words of
the Philistine, they were dismayed and greatly afraid.

12Now David *was* the son of
that Ephrathite of Bethlehem
Judah, whose name *was* Jesse,
and who had eight sons. And
the man was old, advanced
in years, in the days of Saul.
13The three oldest sons of
Jesse had gone to follow Saul
to the battle. The names of his
three sons who went to the
battle *were* Eliab the firstborn,
next to him Abinadab, and the
third Shammah. 14David *was*
the youngest. And the three
oldest followed Saul. 15But
David occasionally went and
returned from Saul to feed his
father's sheep at Bethlehem.

16And the Philistine drew
near and presented himself
forty days, morning and evening.

17Then Jesse said to his son
David, "Take now for your
brothers an ephah of this dried
grain and these ten loaves, and
run to your brothers at the
camp. 18And carry these ten
cheeses to the captain of *their*
thousand, and see how your
brothers fare, and bring back
news of them." 19Now Saul and
they and all the men of Israel
were in the Valley of Elah,
fighting with the Philistines.

20So David rose early in the
morning, left the sheep with a
keeper, and took *the things* and
went as Jesse had commanded
him. And he came to the camp
as the army was going out to
the fight and shouting for the
battle. 21For Israel and the Philistines had drawn up in battle array, army against army.
22And David left his supplies in
the hand of the supply keeper,
ran to the army, and came and
greeted his brothers. 23Then
as he talked with them, there
was the champion, the Philistine of Gath, Goliath by name,
coming up from the armies of
the Philistines; and he spoke
according to the same words.
So David heard *them.* 24And all
the men of Israel, when they
saw the man, fled from him
and were dreadfully afraid.
25So the men of Israel said,
"Have you seen this man who
has come up? Surely he has
come up to defy Israel; and it
shall be *that* the man who kills
him the king will enrich with
great riches, will give him his

daughter, and give his father's
house exemption *from taxes*
in Israel."
26Then David spoke to the
men who stood by him, saying, "What shall be done for
the man who kills this Philistine and takes away the reproach from Israel? For who *is*
this uncircumcised Philistine,
that he should defy the armies
of the living God?"
27And the people answered
him in this manner, saying,
"So shall it be done for the
man who kills him."
28Now Eliab his oldest
brother heard when he spoke
to the men; and Eliab's anger
was aroused against David,
and he said, "Why did you
come down here? And with
whom have you left those
few sheep in the wilderness?
I know your pride and the insolence of your heart, for you
have come down to see the
battle."
29And David said, "What
have I done now? *Is there* not
a cause?" 30Then he turned
from him toward another and
said the same thing; and these
people answered him as the
first ones *did*.
31Now when the words
which David spoke were
heard, they reported *them*
to Saul; and he sent for him.
32Then David said to Saul, "Let
no man's heart fail because of
him; your servant will go and
fight with this Philistine."
33And Saul said to David,
"You are not able to go against
this Philistine to fight with
him; for you *are* a youth, and
he a man of war from his
youth."
34But David said to Saul,
"Your servant used to keep
his father's sheep, and when a
lion or a bear came and took a
lamb out of the flock, 35I went
out after it and struck it, and
delivered *the lamb* from its
mouth; and when it arose
against me, I caught *it* by its
beard, and struck and killed
it. 36Your servant has killed
both lion and bear; and this
uncircumcised Philistine will
be like one of them, seeing he
has defied the armies of the
living God." 37Moreover David
said, "The LORD, who delivered me from the paw of the
lion and from the paw of the
bear, He will deliver me from
the hand of this Philistine."
And Saul said to David, "Go,
and the LORD be with you!"
38So Saul clothed David
with his armor, and he put a
bronze helmet on his head; he
also clothed him with a coat
of mail. 39David fastened his
sword to his armor and tried
to walk, for he had not tested
them. And David said to Saul,
"I cannot walk with these, for
I have not tested *them*." So
David took them off.
40Then he took his staff in
his hand; and he chose for
himself five smooth stones
from the brook, and put them
in a shepherd's bag, in a pouch

which he had, and his sling was
in his hand. And he drew near
to the Philistine. 41So the Philistine came, and began drawing
near to David, and the man who
bore the shield *went* before
him. 42And when the Philistine
looked about and saw David,
he disdained him; for he was
only a youth, ruddy and good-
looking. 43So the Philistine said
to David, "*Am* I a dog, that you
come to me with sticks?" And
the Philistine cursed David by
his gods. 44And the Philistine
said to David, "Come to me,
and I will give your flesh to the
birds of the air and the beasts
of the field!"

45Then David said to the
Philistine, "You come to me
with a sword, with a spear, and
with a javelin. But I come to
you in the name of the LORD
of hosts, the God of the armies
of Israel, whom you have defied. 46This day the LORD will
deliver you into my hand, and
I will strike you and take your
head from you. And this day I
will give the carcasses of the
camp of the Philistines to the
birds of the air and the wild
beasts of the earth, that all
the earth may know that there
is a God in Israel. 47Then all
this assembly shall know that
the LORD does not save with
sword and spear; for the battle
is the LORD's, and He will give
you into our hands."

48So it was, when the Philistine arose and came and drew
near to meet David, that David
hurried and ran toward the
army to meet the Philistine.
49Then David put his hand in
his bag and took out a stone;
and he slung *it* and struck the
Philistine in his forehead, so
that the stone sank into his
forehead, and he fell on his
face to the earth. 50So David
prevailed over the Philistine
with a sling and a stone, and
struck the Philistine and killed
him. But *there was* no sword
in the hand of David. 51There-
fore David ran and stood over
the Philistine, took his sword
and drew it out of its sheath
and killed him, and cut off his
head with it.

And when the Philistines
saw that their champion was
dead, they fled. 52Now the men
of Israel and Judah arose and
shouted, and pursued the Philistines as far as the entrance
of the valley[a] and to the gates
of Ekron. And the wounded of
the Philistines fell along the
road to Shaaraim, even as far
as Gath and Ekron. 53Then the
children of Israel returned
from chasing the Philistines,
and they plundered their
tents. 54And David took the
head of the Philistine and
brought it to Jerusalem, but
he put his armor in his tent.

55When Saul saw David

17:52 [a] Following Masoretic Text, Syriac, Targum, and Vulgate; Septuagint reads *Gath*.

going out against the Philistine, he said to Abner, the commander of the army, "Abner, whose son *is* this youth?"

And Abner said, "As your soul lives, O king, I do not know."

56 So the king said, "Inquire whose son this young man *is.*"

57 Then, as David returned from the slaughter of the Philistine, Abner took him and brought him before Saul with the head of the Philistine in his hand. 58 And Saul said to him, "Whose son *are* you, young man?"

So David answered, "*I am* the son of your servant Jesse the Bethlehemite."

SAUL RESENTS DAVID

18 Now when he had finished speaking to Saul, the soul of Jonathan was knit to the soul of David, and Jonathan loved him as his own soul. 2 Saul took him that day, and would not let him go home to his father's house anymore. 3 Then Jonathan and David made a covenant, because he loved him as his own soul. 4 And Jonathan took off the robe that *was* on him and gave it to David, with his armor, even to his sword and his bow and his belt.

5 So David went out wherever Saul sent him, *and* behaved wisely. And Saul set him over the men of war, and he was accepted in the sight of all the people and also in the sight of Saul's servants. 6 Now it had happened as they were coming *home,* when David was returning from the slaughter of the Philistine, that the women had come out of all the cities of Israel, singing and dancing, to meet King Saul, with tambourines, with joy, and with musical instruments. 7 So the women sang as they danced, and said:

"Saul has slain his
thousands,
And David his ten
thousands."

8 Then Saul was very angry, and the saying displeased him; and he said, "They have ascribed to David ten thousands, and to me they have ascribed *only* thousands. Now *what* more can he have but the kingdom?" 9 So Saul eyed David from that day forward.

10 And it happened on the next day that the distressing spirit from God came upon Saul, and he prophesied inside the house. So David played *music* with his hand, as at other times; but *there was* a spear in Saul's hand. 11 And Saul cast the spear, for he said, "I will pin David to the wall!" But David escaped his presence twice.

12 Now Saul was afraid of David, because the LORD was with him, but had departed from Saul. 13 Therefore Saul removed him from his presence,

and made him his captain over
a thousand; and he went out
and came in before the people.
14And David behaved wisely in
all his ways, and the LORD *was*
with him. 15Therefore, when
Saul saw that he behaved very
wisely, he was afraid of him.
16But all Israel and Judah loved
David, because he went out and
came in before them.

DAVID MARRIES MICHAL

17Then Saul said to David,
"Here is my older daughter
Merab; I will give her to you
as a wife. Only be valiant for
me, and fight the LORD's battles." For Saul thought, "Let
my hand not be against him,
but let the hand of the Philistines be against him."

18So David said to Saul,
"Who *am* I, and what *is* my life
or my father's family in Israel,
that I should be son-in-law to
the king?" 19But it happened
at the time when Merab, Saul's
daughter, should have been
given to David, that she was
given to Adriel the Meholathite as a wife.

20Now Michal, Saul's daughter, loved David. And they told
Saul, and the thing pleased
him. 21So Saul said, "I will give
her to him, that she may be
a snare to him, and that the
hand of the Philistines may be
against him." Therefore Saul
said to David a second time,
"You shall be my son-in-law
today."

22And Saul commanded
his servants, "Communicate
with David secretly, and say,
'Look, the king has delight in
you, and all his servants love
you. Now therefore, become
the king's son-in-law.'"

23So Saul's servants spoke
those words in the hearing of
David. And David said, "Does
it seem to you *a* light *thing* to
be a king's son-in-law, seeing
I *am* a poor and lightly esteemed man?" 24And the servants of Saul told him, saying,
"In this manner David spoke."

25Then Saul said, "Thus you
shall say to David: 'The king
does not desire any dowry but
one hundred foreskins of the
Philistines, to take vengeance
on the king's enemies.'" But
Saul thought to make David
fall by the hand of the Philistines. 26So when his servants
told David these words, it
pleased David well to become
the king's son-in-law. Now the
days had not expired; 27there-
fore David arose and went, he
and his men, and killed two
hundred men of the Philistines. And David brought their
foreskins, and they gave them
in full count to the king, that
he might become the king's
son-in-law. Then Saul gave him
Michal his daughter as a wife.

28Thus Saul saw and knew
that the LORD *was* with
David, and *that* Michal, Saul's
daughter, loved him; 29and
Saul was still more afraid of
David. So Saul became David's
enemy continually. 30Then

the princes of the Philistines
went out *to war.* And so it was,
whenever they went out, *that*
David behaved more wisely
than all the servants of Saul,
so that his name became
highly esteemed.

SAUL PERSECUTES DAVID

19 Now Saul spoke to Jon-
athan his son and to
all his servants, that they
should kill David; but Jonathan, Saul's son, delighted
greatly in David. 2So Jonathan
told David, saying, "My father
Saul seeks to kill you. Therefore please be on your guard
until morning, and stay in a
secret *place* and hide. 3And I
will go out and stand beside
my father in the field where
you *are,* and I will speak with
my father about you. Then
what I observe, I will tell you."

4Thus Jonathan spoke well
of David to Saul his father,
and said to him, "Let not the
king sin against his servant,
against David, because he has
not sinned against you, and
because his works *have been*
very good toward you. 5For he
took his life in his hands and
killed the Philistine, and the
LORD brought about a great
deliverance for all Israel. You
saw *it* and rejoiced. Why then
will you sin against innocent
blood, to kill David without a
cause?"

6So Saul heeded the voice
of Jonathan, and Saul swore,
"*As* the LORD lives, he shall
not be killed." 7Then Jonathan
called David, and Jonathan
told him all these things. So
Jonathan brought David to
Saul, and he was in his presence as in times past.

8And there was war again;
and David went out and
fought with the Philistines,
and struck them with a mighty
blow, and they fled from him.

9Now the distressing spirit
from the LORD came upon
Saul as he sat in his house
with his spear in his hand. And
David was playing *music* with
his hand. 10Then Saul sought
to pin David to the wall with
the spear, but he slipped away
from Saul's presence; and he
drove the spear into the wall.
So David fled and escaped that
night.

11Saul also sent messengers
to David's house to watch him
and to kill him in the morning. And Michal, David's wife,
told him, saying, "If you do
not save your life tonight, tomorrow you will be killed."
12So Michal let David down
through a window. And he
went and fled and escaped.
13And Michal took an image
and laid *it* in the bed, put a
cover of goats' *hair* for his
head, and covered *it* with
clothes. 14So when Saul sent
messengers to take David, she
said, "He *is* sick."

15Then Saul sent the mes-
sengers *back* to see David, saying, "Bring him up to me in
the bed, that I may kill him."

16 And when the messengers
had come in, there was the
image in the bed, with a cover
of goats' *hair* for his head.
17 Then Saul said to Michal,
"Why have you deceived me
like this, and sent my enemy
away, so that he has escaped?"
And Michal answered Saul,
"He said to me, 'Let me go!
Why should I kill you?'"
18 So David fled and es-
caped, and went to Samuel at
Ramah, and told him all that
Saul had done to him. And he
and Samuel went and stayed
in Naioth. 19 Now it was told
Saul, saying, "Take note, David
is at Naioth in Ramah!" 20 Then
Saul sent messengers to take
David. And when they saw the
group of prophets prophesying, and Samuel standing *as*
leader over them, the Spirit
of God came upon the mes-
sengers of Saul, and they also
prophesied. 21 And when Saul
was told, he sent other messengers, and they prophe-
sied likewise. Then Saul sent
messengers again the third
time, and they prophesied
also. 22 Then he also went to
Ramah, and came to the great
well that *is* at Sechu. So he
asked, and said, "Where *are*
Samuel and David?"
And *someone* said, "Indeed
they are at Naioth in Ramah."
23 So he went there to Naioth in
Ramah. Then the Spirit of God
was upon him also, and he
went on and prophesied until
he came to Naioth in Ramah.
24 And he also stripped off his
clothes and prophesied before
Samuel in like manner, and
lay down naked all that day
and all that night. Therefore
they say, "*Is* Saul also among
the prophets?"[a]

JONATHAN'S LOYALTY TO DAVID

20 Then David fled from
Naioth in Ramah, and
went and said to Jonathan,
"What have I done? What *is*
my iniquity, and what *is* my
sin before your father, that he
seeks my life?"
2 So Jonathan said to him,
"By no means! You shall not
die! Indeed, my father will do
nothing either great or small
without first telling me. And
why should my father hide this
thing from me? It *is* not *so!*"
3 Then David took an oath
again, and said, "Your father
certainly knows that I have
found favor in your eyes, and
he has said, 'Do not let Jonathan know this, lest he be
grieved.' But truly, *as* the LORD
lives and *as* your soul lives,
there is but a step between me
and death."
4 So Jonathan said to David,
"Whatever you yourself desire, I will do *it* for you."
5 And David said to Jona-
than, "Indeed tomorrow *is*
the New Moon, and I should

19:24 [a] Compare 1 Samuel 10:12

not fail to sit with the king to
eat. But let me go, that I may
hide in the field until the third
day at evening. 6If your father
misses me at all, then say,
'David earnestly asked *permis-*
sion of me that he might run
over to Bethlehem, his city, for
there is a yearly sacrifice there
for all the family.' 7If he says
thus: '*It is* well,' your servant
will be safe. But if he is very
angry, be sure that evil is determined by him. 8Therefore
you shall deal kindly with your
servant, for you have brought
your servant into a covenant
of the LORD with you. Nevertheless, if there is iniquity in
me, kill me yourself, for why
should you bring me to your
father?"

9But Jonathan said, "Far
be it from you! For if I knew
certainly that evil was determined by my father to come
upon you, then would I not
tell you?"

10Then David said to Jon-
athan, "Who will tell me, or
what *if* your father answers
you roughly?"

11And Jonathan said to
David, "Come, let us go out
into the field." So both of them
went out into the field. 12Then
Jonathan said to David: "The
LORD God of Israel *is witness!*
When I have sounded out my
father sometime tomorrow,
or the third *day,* and indeed
there is good toward David,
and I do not send to you and
tell you, 13may the LORD do
so and much more to Jon-
athan. But if it pleases my
father *to do* you evil, then I
will report it to you and send
you away, that you may go in
safety. And the LORD be with
you as He has been with my
father. 14And you shall not
only show me the kindness
of the LORD while I still live,
that I may not die; 15but you
shall not cut off your kindness
from my house forever, no,
not when the LORD has cut
off every one of the enemies
of David from the face of the
earth." 16So Jonathan made
a covenant with the house of
David, *saying,* "Let the LORD
require *it* at the hand of David's enemies."

17Now Jonathan again
caused David to vow, be-
cause he loved him; for he
loved him as he loved his own
soul. 18Then Jonathan said to
David, "Tomorrow *is* the New
Moon; and you will be missed,
because your seat will be
empty. 19And *when* you have
stayed three days, go down
quickly and come to the place
where you hid on the day of
the deed; and remain by the
stone Ezel. 20Then I will shoot
three arrows to the side, as
though I shot at a target; 21and
there I will send a lad, *saying,*
'Go, find the arrows.' If I expressly say to the lad, 'Look,
the arrows *are* on this side of
you; get them and come'—
then, as the LORD lives, *there*
is safety for you and no harm.

22 But if I say thus to the young
man, 'Look, the arrows *are* beyond you'—go your way, for
the LORD has sent you away.
23 And as for the matter which
you and I have spoken of, indeed the LORD *be* between you
and me forever."

24 Then David hid in the
field. And when the New
Moon had come, the king sat
down to eat the feast. 25 Now
the king sat on his seat, as at
other times, on a seat by the
wall. And Jonathan arose,[a]
and Abner sat by Saul's side,
but David's place was empty.
26 Nevertheless Saul did not
say anything that day, for he
thought, "Something has happened to him; he *is* unclean,
surely he *is* unclean." 27 And
it happened the next day, the
second *day* of the month, that
David's place was empty. And
Saul said to Jonathan his son,
"Why has the son of Jesse not
come to eat, either yesterday
or today?"

28 So Jonathan answered
Saul, "David earnestly asked
permission of me *to go* to Bethlehem. 29 And he said, 'Please
let me go, for our family has
a sacrifice in the city, and my
brother has commanded me
to be there. And now, if I have
found favor in your eyes,
please let me get away and see
my brothers.' Therefore he has
not come to the king's table."

30 Then Saul's anger was
aroused against Jonathan,
and he said to him, "You
son of a perverse, rebellious
woman! Do I not know that
you have chosen the son of
Jesse to your own shame and
to the shame of your mother's
nakedness? 31 For as long as
the son of Jesse lives on the
earth, you shall not be established, nor your kingdom.
Now therefore, send and bring
him to me, for he shall surely
die."

32 And Jonathan answered
Saul his father, and said to
him, "Why should he be killed?
What has he done?" 33 Then
Saul cast a spear at him to kill
him, by which Jonathan knew
that it was determined by his
father to kill David.

34 So Jonathan arose from
the table in fierce anger, and
ate no food the second day of
the month, for he was grieved
for David, because his father
had treated him shamefully.

35 And so it was, in the
morning, that Jonathan went
out into the field at the time
appointed with David, and a
little lad *was* with him. 36 Then
he said to his lad, "Now run,
find the arrows which I shoot."
As the lad ran, he shot an
arrow beyond him. 37 When
the lad had come to the place
where the arrow was which
Jonathan had shot, Jona-

20:25 [a] Following Masoretic Text, Syriac, Targum, and Vulgate; Septuagint reads *he sat across from Jonathan.*

than cried out after the lad
and said, "*Is* not the arrow beyond you?" 38And Jonathan
cried out after the lad, "Make
haste, hurry, do not delay!" So
Jonathan's lad gathered up
the arrows and came back to
his master. 39But the lad did
not know anything. Only Jonathan and David knew of the
matter. 40Then Jonathan gave
his weapons to his lad, and
said to him, "Go, carry *them*
to the city."

41As soon as the lad had
gone, David arose from *a place*
toward the south, fell on his
face to the ground, and bowed
down three times. And they
kissed one another; and they
wept together, but David more
so. 42Then Jonathan said to
David, "Go in peace, since we
have both sworn in the name
of the LORD, saying, 'May the
LORD be between you and me,
and between your descen-
dants and my descendants,
forever.'" So he arose and departed, and Jonathan went
into the city.

DAVID AND THE HOLY BREAD

21 Now David came to Nob,
to Ahimelech the priest.
And Ahimelech was afraid
when he met David, and said
to him, "Why *are* you alone,
and no one is with you?"

2So David said to Ahim-
elech the priest, "The king
has ordered me on some
business, and said to me, 'Do
not let anyone know any-
thing about the business on
which I send you, or what I
have commanded you.' And I
have directed *my* young men
to such and such a place. 3Now
therefore, what have you on
hand? Give *me* five *loaves of*
bread in my hand, or whatever
can be found."

4And the priest answered
David and said, "*There is* no
common bread on hand; but
there is holy bread, if the
young men have at least kept
themselves from women."

5Then David answered the
priest, and said to him, "Truly,
women *have been* kept from
us about three days since I
came out. And the vessels of
the young men are holy, and
the bread is in effect common,
even though it was conse-
crated in the vessel this day."

6So the priest gave him
holy *bread;* for there was no
bread there but the show-
bread which had been taken
from before the LORD, in
order to put hot bread *in its*
place on the day when it was
taken away.

7Now a certain man of the
servants of Saul *was* there
that day, detained before
the LORD. And his name *was*
Doeg, an Edomite, the chief of
the herdsmen who *belonged*
to Saul.

8And David said to Ahim-
elech, "Is there not here on
hand a spear or a sword? For
I have brought neither my

sword nor my weapons with
me, because the king's business required haste."
9So the priest said, "The
sword of Goliath the Philistine, whom you killed in the
Valley of Elah, there it is,
wrapped in a cloth behind the
ephod. If you will take that,
take *it.* For *there is* no other
except that one here."
And David said, "*There is*
none like it; give it to me."

DAVID FLEES TO GATH

10Then David arose and
fled that day from before Saul,
and went to Achish the king
of Gath. 11And the servants of
Achish said to him, "*Is* this not
David the king of the land?
Did they not sing of him to
one another in dances, saying:

'Saul has slain his
thousands,
And David his ten
thousands'?"[a]

12Now David took these
words to heart, and was very
much afraid of Achish the king
of Gath. 13So he changed his behavior before them, pretended
madness in their hands,
scratched on the doors of the
gate, and let his saliva fall down
on his beard. 14Then Achish
said to his servants, "Look,
you see the man is insane. Why
have you brought him to me?
15Have I need of madmen, that
you have brought this *fellow* to
play the madman in my presence? Shall this *fellow* come
into my house?"

DAVID'S FOUR HUNDRED MEN

22 David therefore de-
parted from there and
escaped to the cave of Adullam. So when his brothers and
all his father's house heard *it,*
they went down there to him.
2And everyone *who was* in
distress, everyone who *was*
in debt, and everyone *who was*
discontented gathered to him.
So he became captain over
them. And there were about
four hundred men with him.
3Then David went from
there to Mizpah of Moab; and
he said to the king of Moab,
"Please let my father and
mother come here with you,
till I know what God will do
for me." 4So he brought them
before the king of Moab, and
they dwelt with him all the
time that David was in the
stronghold.
5Now the prophet Gad said
to David, "Do not stay in the
stronghold; depart, and go to
the land of Judah." So David
departed and went into the
forest of Hereth.

SAUL MURDERS THE PRIESTS

6When Saul heard that
David and the men who

21:11 [a] Compare 1 Samuel 18:7

were with him had been
discovered—now Saul was
staying in Gibeah under a
tamarisk tree in Ramah, with
his spear in his hand, and all
his servants standing about
him— [7]then Saul said to his
servants who stood about
him, "Hear now, you Benjamites! Will the son of Jesse
give every one of you fields
and vineyards, *and* make you
all captains of thousands and
captains of hundreds? [8]All of
you have conspired against
me, and *there is* no one who
reveals to me that my son has
made a covenant with the son
of Jesse; and *there is* not one
of you who is sorry for me or
reveals to me that my son has
stirred up my servant against
me, to lie in wait, as *it is* this
day."

[9]Then answered Doeg the
Edomite, who was set over the
servants of Saul, and said, "I
saw the son of Jesse going to
Nob, to Ahimelech the son of
Ahitub. [10]And he inquired of
the LORD for him, gave him
provisions, and gave him the
sword of Goliath the Philistine."

[11]So the king sent to call
Ahimelech the priest, the son
of Ahitub, and all his father's
house, the priests who *were* in
Nob. And they all came to the
king. [12]And Saul said, "Hear
now, son of Ahitub!"

He answered, "Here I am,
my lord."

[13]Then Saul said to him,
"Why have you conspired
against me, you and the son of
Jesse, in that you have given
him bread and a sword, and
have inquired of God for him,
that he should rise against
me, to lie in wait, as it is this
day?"

[14]So Ahimelech answered
the king and said, "And who
among all your servants *is as*
faithful as David, who is the
king's son-in-law, who goes
at your bidding, and is honorable in your house? [15]Did I
then begin to inquire of God
for him? Far be it from me! Let
not the king impute anything
to his servant, *or* to any in the
house of my father. For your
servant knew nothing of all
this, little or much."

[16]And the king said, "You
shall surely die, Ahimelech,
you and all your father's
house!" [17]Then the king said
to the guards who stood about
him, "Turn and kill the priests
of the LORD, because their
hand also *is* with David, and
because they knew when he
fled and did not tell it to me."
But the servants of the king
would not lift their hands to
strike the priests of the LORD.
[18]And the king said to Doeg,
"You turn and kill the priests!"
So Doeg the Edomite turned
and struck the priests, and
killed on that day eighty-
five men who wore a linen
ephod. [19]Also Nob, the city
of the priests, he struck with
the edge of the sword, both

men and women, children
and nursing infants, oxen and
donkeys and sheep—with the
edge of the sword.
20Now one of the sons of
Ahimelech the son of Ahitub,
named Abiathar, escaped and
fled after David. 21And Abiathar told David that Saul
had killed the LORD's priests.
22So David said to Abiathar,
"I knew that day, when Doeg
the Edomite *was* there, that
he would surely tell Saul. I
have caused *the death* of all
the persons of your father's
house. 23Stay with me; do not
fear. For he who seeks my life
seeks your life, but with me
you *shall be* safe."

DAVID SAVES THE CITY OF KEILAH

23 Then they told David,
saying, "Look, the Phi-
listines are fighting against
Keilah, and they are robbing
the threshing floors."
2Therefore David inquired
of the LORD, saying, "Shall I go
and attack these Philistines?"
And the LORD said to David,
"Go and attack the Philistines,
and save Keilah."
3But David's men said to
him, "Look, we are afraid here
in Judah. How much more
then if we go to Keilah against
the armies of the Philistines?"
4Then David inquired of the
LORD once again.
And the LORD answered
him and said, "Arise, go down
to Keilah. For I will deliver the
Philistines into your hand."
5And David and his men went
to Keilah and fought with the
Philistines, struck them with
a mighty blow, and took away
their livestock. So David saved
the inhabitants of Keilah.
6Now it happened, when
Abiathar the son of Ahimelech fled to David at Keilah,
that he went down *with* an
ephod in his hand.
7And Saul was told that
David had gone to Keilah. So
Saul said, "God has delivered
him into my hand, for he has
shut himself in by entering
a town that has gates and
bars." 8Then Saul called all
the people together for war, to
go down to Keilah to besiege
David and his men.
9When David knew that
Saul plotted evil against
him, he said to Abiathar the
priest, "Bring the ephod here."
10Then David said, "O LORD
God of Israel, Your servant has
certainly heard that Saul seeks
to come to Keilah to destroy
the city for my sake. 11Will
the men of Keilah deliver me
into his hand? Will Saul come
down, as Your servant has
heard? O LORD God of Israel,
I pray, tell Your servant."
And the LORD said, "He will
come down."
12Then David said, "Will
the men of Keilah deliver me
and my men into the hand of
Saul?"
And the LORD said, "They
will deliver *you*."

13So David and his men,
about six hundred, arose and
departed from Keilah and
went wherever they could
go. Then it was told Saul that
David had escaped from Keilah; so he halted the expe-
dition.

DAVID IN WILDERNESS STRONGHOLDS

14And David stayed in
strongholds in the wilderness,
and remained in the moun-
tains in the Wilderness of Ziph.
Saul sought him every day, but
God did not deliver him into
his hand. 15So David saw that
Saul had come out to seek his
life. And David *was* in the Wilderness of Ziph in a forest.[a]
16Then Jonathan, Saul's son,
arose and went to David in
the woods and strengthened
his hand in God. 17And he said
to him, "Do not fear, for the
hand of Saul my father shall
not find you. You shall be king
over Israel, and I shall be next
to you. Even my father Saul
knows that." 18So the two of
them made a covenant before
the LORD. And David stayed in
the woods, and Jonathan went
to his own house.

19Then the Ziphites came
up to Saul at Gibeah, saying,
"Is David not hiding with us
in strongholds in the woods,
in the hill of Hachilah, which
is on the south of Jeshimon?
20Now therefore, O king, come
down according to all the
desire of your soul to come
down; and our part *shall be*
to deliver him into the king's
hand."

21And Saul said, "Blessed
are you of the LORD, for you
have compassion on me.
22Please go and find out for
sure, and see the place where
his hideout is, *and* who has
seen him there. For I am told
he is very crafty. 23See therefore, and take knowledge of
all the lurking places where
he hides; and come back to
me with certainty, and I will
go with you. And it shall be,
if he is in the land, that I will
search for him throughout all
the clans[a] of Judah."

24So they arose and went
to Ziph before Saul. But
David and his men *were* in
the Wilderness of Maon, in
the plain on the south of Jeshimon. 25When Saul and his
men went to seek *him,* they
told David. Therefore he
went down to the rock, and
stayed in the Wilderness of
Maon. And when Saul heard
that, he pursued David in the
Wilderness of Maon. 26Then
Saul went on one side of the
mountain, and David and his
men on the other side of the
mountain. So David made
haste to get away from Saul,
for Saul and his men were encircling David and his men to
take them.

23:15 [a] Or *in Horesh* 23:23 [a] Literally *thousands*

27But a messenger came
to Saul, saying, "Hurry and
come, for the Philistines have
invaded the land!" 28There-
fore Saul returned from pursuing David, and went against
the Philistines; so they called
that place the Rock of Escape.[a]
29Then David went up from
there and dwelt in strongholds at En Gedi.

DAVID SPARES SAUL

24 Now it happened, when
Saul had returned from
following the Philistines, that
it was told him, saying, "Take
note! David *is* in the Wilderness of En Gedi." 2Then Saul
took three thousand chosen
men from all Israel, and went
to seek David and his men on
the Rocks of the Wild Goats.
3So he came to the sheepfolds
by the road, where there *was*
a cave; and Saul went in to attend to his needs. (David and
his men were staying in the
recesses of the cave.) 4Then
the men of David said to him,
"This is the day of which the
LORD said to you, 'Behold, I
will deliver your enemy into
your hand, that you may do to
him as it seems good to you.'"
And David arose and secretly
cut off a corner of Saul's robe.
5Now it happened afterward
that David's heart troubled
him because he had cut Saul's
robe. 6And he said to his men,
"The LORD forbid that I should
do this thing to my master, the
LORD's anointed, to stretch out
my hand against him, seeing
he *is* the anointed of the LORD."
7So David restrained his servants with *these* words, and did
not allow them to rise against
Saul. And Saul got up from the
cave and went on *his* way.

8David also arose after-
ward, went out of the cave,
and called out to Saul, saying, "My lord the king!" And
when Saul looked behind him,
David stooped with his face to
the earth, and bowed down.
9And David said to Saul: "Why
do you listen to the words of
men who say, 'Indeed David
seeks your harm'? 10Look, this
day your eyes have seen that
the LORD delivered you today
into my hand in the cave, and
someone urged *me* to kill you.
But *my eye* spared you, and I
said, 'I will not stretch out my
hand against my lord, for he *is*
the LORD's anointed.' 11More-
over, my father, see! Yes, see
the corner of your robe in my
hand! For in that I cut off the
corner of your robe, and did
not kill you, know and see
that *there is* neither evil nor
rebellion in my hand, and I
have not sinned against you.
Yet you hunt my life to take
it. 12Let the LORD judge between you and me, and let the
LORD avenge me on you. But
my hand shall not be against
you. 13As the proverb of the

23:28 [a] Hebrew *Sela Hammahlekoth*

ancients says, 'Wickedness
proceeds from the wicked.'
But my hand shall not be
against you. 14After whom has
the king of Israel come out?
Whom do you pursue? A dead
dog? A flea? 15Therefore let the
LORD be judge, and judge between you and me, and see
and plead my case, and deliver
me out of your hand."
16So it was, when David had
finished speaking these words
to Saul, that Saul said, "*Is* this
your voice, my son David?"
And Saul lifted up his voice
and wept. 17Then he said to
David: "You *are* more righteous than I; for you have rewarded me with good, whereas
I have rewarded you with evil.
18And you have shown this
day how you have dealt well
with me; for when the LORD
delivered me into your hand,
you did not kill me. 19For if a
man finds his enemy, will he
let him get away safely? Therefore may the LORD reward you
with good for what you have
done to me this day. 20And
now I know indeed that you
shall surely be king, and that
the kingdom of Israel shall
be established in your hand.
21Therefore swear now to me
by the LORD that you will not
cut off my descendants after
me, and that you will not destroy my name from my fa-
ther's house."
22So David swore to Saul.
And Saul went home, but
David and his men went up
to the stronghold.

DEATH OF SAMUEL

25 Then Samuel died; and
the Israelites gathered
together and lamented for
him, and buried him at his
home in Ramah. And David
arose and went down to the
Wilderness of Paran.[a]

DAVID AND THE WIFE OF NABAL

2Now *there was* a man in
Maon whose business *was*
in Carmel, and the man *was*
very rich. He had three thousand sheep and a thousand
goats. And he was shearing his
sheep in Carmel. 3The name
of the man *was* Nabal, and
the name of his wife Abigail.
And *she was* a woman of good
understanding and beautiful
appearance; but the man *was*
harsh and evil in *his* doings.
He *was of the house of* Caleb.
4When David heard in the
wilderness that Nabal was
shearing his sheep, 5David
sent ten young men; and
David said to the young men,
"Go up to Carmel, go to Nabal,
and greet him in my name.
6And thus you shall say to
him who lives *in prosperity:*
'Peace *be* to you, peace to your
house, and peace to all that

25:1 [a] Following Masoretic Text, Syriac, Targum, and Vulgate; Septuagint reads *Maon*.

you have! 7Now I have heard
that you have shearers. Your
shepherds were with us, and
we did not hurt them, nor was
there anything missing from
them all the while they were
in Carmel. 8Ask your young
men, and they will tell you.
Therefore let *my* young men
find favor in your eyes, for we
come on a feast day. Please
give whatever comes to your
hand to your servants and to
your son David.'"

9So when David's young
men came, they spoke to Nabal
according to all these words in
the name of David, and waited.

10Then Nabal answered
David's servants, and said,
"Who *is* David, and who *is*
the son of Jesse? There are
many servants nowadays who
break away each one from his
master. 11Shall I then take my
bread and my water and my
meat that I have killed for my
shearers, and give *it* to men
when I do not know where
they *are* from?"

12So David's young men
turned on their heels and
went back; and they came
and told him all these words.
13Then David said to his
men, "Every man gird on his
sword." So every man girded
on his sword, and David also
girded on his sword. And
about four hundred men went
with David, and two hundred
stayed with the supplies.

14Now one of the young
men told Abigail, Nabal's
wife, saying, "Look, David
sent messengers from the wilderness to greet our master;
and he reviled them. 15But the
men *were* very good to us, and
we were not hurt, nor did we
miss anything as long as we
accompanied them, when
we were in the fields. 16They
were a wall to us both by night
and day, all the time we were
with them keeping the sheep.
17Now therefore, know and
consider what you will do, for
harm is determined against
our master and against all his
household. For he *is such* a
scoundrel[a] that *one* cannot
speak to him."

18Then Abigail made haste
and took two hundred *loaves*
of bread, two skins of wine,
five sheep already dressed,
five seahs of roasted *grain,*
one hundred clusters of raisins, and two hundred cakes
of figs, and loaded *them* on
donkeys. 19And she said to her
servants, "Go on before me;
see, I am coming after you."
But she did not tell her husband Nabal.

20So it was, *as* she rode
on the donkey, that she went
down under cover of the hill;
and there were David and his
men, coming down toward
her, and she met them. 21Now
David had said, "Surely in vain
I have protected all that this

25:17 [a] Literally *son of Belial*

fellow has in the wilderness, so that nothing was missed of all that *belongs* to him. And he has repaid me evil for good. 22May God do so, and more also, to the enemies of David, if I leave one male of all who *belong* to him by morning light."

23Now when Abigail saw David, she dismounted quickly from the donkey, fell on her face before David, and bowed down to the ground. 24So she fell at his feet and said: "On me, my lord, *on* me *let* this iniquity *be!* And please let your maidservant speak in your ears, and hear the words of your maidservant. 25Please, let not my lord regard this scoundrel Nabal. For as his name *is,* so *is* he: Nabal[a] *is* his name, and folly *is* with him! But I, your maidservant, did not see the young men of my lord whom you sent. 26Now therefore, my lord, *as* the LORD lives and *as* your soul lives, since the LORD has held you back from coming to bloodshed and from avenging yourself with your own hand, now then, let your enemies and those who seek harm for my lord be as Nabal. 27And now this present which your maidservant has brought to my lord, let it be given to the young men who follow my lord. 28Please forgive the trespass of your maidservant. For the LORD will certainly make for my lord an enduring house, because my lord fights the battles of the LORD, and evil is not found in you throughout your days. 29Yet a man has risen to pursue you and seek your life, but the life of my lord shall be bound in the bundle of the living with the LORD your God; and the lives of your enemies He shall sling out, *as from* the pocket of a sling. 30And it shall come to pass, when the LORD has done for my lord according to all the good that He has spoken concerning you, and has appointed you ruler over Israel, 31that this will be no grief to you, nor offense of heart to my lord, either that you have shed blood without cause, or that my lord has avenged himself. But when the LORD has dealt well with my lord, then remember your maidservant."

32Then David said to Abigail: "Blessed *is* the LORD God of Israel, who sent you this day to meet me! 33And blessed *is* your advice and blessed *are* you, because you have kept me this day from coming to bloodshed and from avenging myself with my own hand. 34For indeed, *as* the LORD God of Israel lives, who has kept me back from hurting you, unless you had hurried and come to meet me, surely by morning light no males would

25:25 [a] Literally *Fool*

have been left to Nabal!" 35 So David received from her hand what she had brought him, and said to her, "Go up in peace to your house. See, I have heeded your voice and respected your person."

36 Now Abigail went to Nabal, and there he was, holding a feast in his house, like the feast of a king. And Nabal's heart *was* merry within him, for he *was* very drunk; therefore she told him nothing, little or much, until morning light. 37 So it was, in the morning, when the wine had gone from Nabal, and his wife had told him these things, that his heart died within him, and he became *like* a stone. 38 Then it happened, *after* about ten days, that the LORD struck Nabal, and he died.

39 So when David heard that Nabal was dead, he said, "Blessed *be* the LORD, who has pleaded the cause of my reproach from the hand of Nabal, and has kept His servant from evil! For the LORD has returned the wickedness of Nabal on his own head."

And David sent and proposed to Abigail, to take her as his wife. 40 When the servants of David had come to Abigail at Carmel, they spoke to her saying, "David sent us to you, to ask you to become his wife."

41 Then she arose, bowed her face to the earth, and said, "Here is your maidservant, a servant to wash the feet of the servants of my lord." 42 So Abigail rose in haste and rode on a donkey, attended by five of her maidens; and she followed the messengers of David, and became his wife. 43 David also took Ahinoam of Jezreel, and so both of them were his wives.

44 But Saul had given Michal his daughter, David's wife, to Palti[a] the son of Laish, who *was* from Gallim.

DAVID SPARES SAUL A SECOND TIME

26 Now the Ziphites came to Saul at Gibeah, saying, "Is David not hiding in the hill of Hachilah, opposite Jeshimon?" 2 Then Saul arose and went down to the Wilderness of Ziph, having three thousand chosen men of Israel with him, to seek David in the Wilderness of Ziph. 3 And Saul encamped in the hill of Hachilah, which *is* opposite Jeshimon, by the road. But David stayed in the wilderness, and he saw that Saul came after him into the wilderness. 4 David therefore sent out spies, and understood that Saul had indeed come.

5 So David arose and came to the place where Saul had encamped. And David saw the place where Saul lay, and Abner the son of Ner, the com-

25:44 [a] Spelled *Paltiel* in 2 Samuel 3:15

mander of his army. Now Saul lay within the camp, with the people encamped all around him. 6Then David answered, and said to Ahimelech the Hittite and to Abishai the son of Zeruiah, brother of Joab, saying, "Who will go down with me to Saul in the camp?"

And Abishai said, "I will go down with you."

7So David and Abishai came to the people by night; and there Saul lay sleeping within the camp, with his spear stuck in the ground by his head. And Abner and the people lay all around him. 8Then Abishai said to David, "God has delivered your enemy into your hand this day. Now therefore, please, let me strike him at once with the spear, right to the earth; and I will not *have to strike* him a second time!"

9But David said to Abishai, "Do not destroy him; for who can stretch out his hand against the LORD's anointed, and be guiltless?" 10David said furthermore, "*As* the LORD lives, the LORD shall strike him, or his day shall come to die, or he shall go out to battle and perish. 11The LORD forbid that I should stretch out my hand against the LORD's anointed. But please, take now the spear and the jug of water that *are* by his head, and let us go." 12So David took the spear and the jug of water *by* Saul's head, and they got away; and no man saw or knew *it* or awoke. For they *were* all asleep, because a deep sleep from the LORD had fallen on them.

13Now David went over to the other side, and stood on the top of a hill afar off, a great distance *being* between them. 14And David called out to the people and to Abner the son of Ner, saying, "Do you not answer, Abner?"

Then Abner answered and said, "Who *are* you, calling out to the king?"

15So David said to Abner, "*Are* you not a man? And who *is* like you in Israel? Why then have you not guarded your lord the king? For one of the people came in to destroy your lord the king. 16This thing that you have done *is* not good. *As* the LORD lives, you deserve to die, because you have not guarded your master, the LORD's anointed. And now see where the king's spear *is,* and the jug of water that *was* by his head."

17Then Saul knew David's voice, and said, "*Is* that your voice, my son David?"

David said, "*It is* my voice, my lord, O king." 18And he said, "Why does my lord thus pursue his servant? For what have I done, or what evil *is* in my hand? 19Now therefore, please, let my lord the king hear the words of his servant: If the LORD has stirred you up against me, let Him accept an offering. But if *it is*

the children of men, *may* they
be cursed before the LORD, for
they have driven me out this
day from sharing in the inheritance of the LORD, saying, 'Go,
serve other gods.' 20So now,
do not let my blood fall to the
earth before the face of the
LORD. For the king of Israel
has come out to seek a flea, as
when one hunts a partridge in
the mountains."
21Then Saul said, "I have
sinned. Return, my son David.
For I will harm you no more,
because my life was precious
in your eyes this day. Indeed I
have played the fool and erred
exceedingly."
22And David answered
and said, "Here is the king's
spear. Let one of the young
men come over and get it.
23May the LORD repay every
man *for* his righteousness
and his faithfulness; for the
LORD delivered you into *my*
hand today, but I would not
stretch out my hand against
the LORD's anointed. 24And
indeed, as your life was valued much this day in my eyes,
so let my life be valued much
in the eyes of the LORD, and
let Him deliver me out of all
tribulation."
25Then Saul said to David,
"*May* you *be* blessed, my son
David! You shall both do great
things and also still prevail."
So David went on his way,
and Saul returned to his place.

DAVID ALLIED WITH THE PHILISTINES

27 And David said in his
heart, "Now I shall per-
ish someday by the hand of
Saul. *There is* nothing better for
me than that I should speedily escape to the land of the
Philistines; and Saul will despair of me, to seek me anymore in any part of Israel. So
I shall escape out of his hand."
2Then David arose and went
over with the six hundred men
who *were* with him to Achish
the son of Maoch, king of Gath.
3So David dwelt with Achish
at Gath, he and his men, each
man with his household, *and*
David with his two wives, Ahinoam the Jezreelitess, and Abigail the Carmelitess, Nabal's
widow. 4And it was told Saul
that David had fled to Gath; so
he sought him no more.
5Then David said to Achish,
"If I have now found favor in
your eyes, let them give me
a place in some town in the
country, that I may dwell there.
For why should your servant
dwell in the royal city with
you?" 6So Achish gave him Ziklag that day. Therefore Ziklag
has belonged to the kings of
Judah to this day. 7Now the
time that David dwelt in the
country of the Philistines was
one full year and four months.
8And David and his men
went up and raided the Geshurites, the Girzites,[a] and the

27:8 [a] Or *Gezrites*

Amalekites. For those *nations*
were the inhabitants of the
land from of old, as you go to
Shur, even as far as the land
of Egypt. 9Whenever David
attacked the land, he left neither man nor woman alive,
but took away the sheep, the
oxen, the donkeys, the camels,
and the apparel, and returned
and came to Achish. 10Then
Achish would say, "Where
have you made a raid today?"
And David would say, "Against
the southern *area* of Judah, or
against the southern *area* of
the Jerahmeelites, or against
the southern *area* of the Kenites." 11David would save neither man nor woman alive,
to bring *news* to Gath, saying,
"Lest they should inform on
us, saying, 'Thus David did.'"
And thus *was* his behavior
all the time he dwelt in the
country of the Philistines.
12So Achish believed David,
saying, "He has made his people Israel utterly abhor him;
therefore he will be my servant forever."

28 Now it happened in
those days that the
Philistines gathered their
armies together for war, to
fight with Israel. And Achish
said to David, "You assuredly
know that you will go out with
me to battle, you and your
men."

2So David said to Achish,
"Surely you know what your
servant can do."

And Achish said to David,
"Therefore I will make you
one of my chief guardians
forever."

SAUL CONSULTS A MEDIUM

3Now Samuel had died,
and all Israel had lamented
for him and buried him in
Ramah, in his own city. And
Saul had put the mediums
and the spiritists out of the
land.

4Then the Philistines gathered together, and came and
encamped at Shunem. So
Saul gathered all Israel together, and they encamped
at Gilboa. 5When Saul saw the
army of the Philistines, he was
afraid, and his heart trembled
greatly. 6And when Saul inquired of the LORD, the LORD
did not answer him, either by
dreams or by Urim or by the
prophets.

7Then Saul said to his servants, "Find me a woman who
is a medium, that I may go to
her and inquire of her."

And his servants said to
him, "In fact, *there is* a woman
who is a medium at En Dor."

8So Saul disguised himself
and put on other clothes, and
he went, and two men with
him; and they came to the
woman by night. And he said,
"Please conduct a séance for
me, and bring up for me the
one I shall name to you."

9Then the woman said to
him, "Look, you know what
Saul has done, how he has
cut off the mediums and the

spiritists from the land. Why
then do you lay a snare for my
life, to cause me to die?"
10 And Saul swore to her
by the LORD, saying, "*As* the
LORD lives, no punishment
shall come upon you for this
thing."
11 Then the woman said,
"Whom shall I bring up for
you?"

And he said, "Bring up
Samuel for me."
12 When the woman saw
Samuel, she cried out with a
loud voice. And the woman
spoke to Saul, saying, "Why
have you deceived me? For
you *are* Saul!"
13 And the king said to her,
"Do not be afraid. What did
you see?"

And the woman said to
Saul, "I saw a spirit[a] ascending out of the earth."
14 So he said to her, "What
is his form?"

And she said, "An old man
is coming up, and he *is* covered with a mantle." And Saul
perceived that it *was* Samuel,
and he stooped with *his* face to
the ground and bowed down.
15 Now Samuel said to Saul,
"Why have you disturbed me
by bringing me up?"

And Saul answered, "I am
deeply distressed; for the Philistines make war against me,
and God has departed from
me and does not answer me
anymore, neither by prophets nor by dreams. There-
fore I have called you, that
you may reveal to me what I
should do."
16 Then Samuel said: "So
why do you ask me, seeing
the LORD has departed from
you and has become your
enemy? 17 And the LORD has
done for Himself[a] as He spoke
by me. For the LORD has torn
the kingdom out of your hand
and given it to your neighbor,
David. 18 Because you did not
obey the voice of the LORD
nor execute His fierce wrath
upon Amalek, therefore the
LORD has done this thing to
you this day. 19 Moreover the
LORD will also deliver Israel
with you into the hand of the
Philistines. And tomorrow
you and your sons *will be*
with me. The LORD will also
deliver the army of Israel into
the hand of the Philistines."
20 Immediately Saul fell full
length on the ground, and was
dreadfully afraid because of
the words of Samuel. And
there was no strength in him,
for he had eaten no food all
day or all night.
21 And the woman came to
Saul and saw that he was severely troubled, and said to
him, "Look, your maidservant
has obeyed your voice, and I
have put my life in my hands
and heeded the words which
you spoke to me. 22 Now therefore, please, heed also the

28:13 [a] Hebrew *elohim* **28:17** [a] Or *him,* that is, David

voice of your maidservant,
and let me set a piece of bread
before you; and eat, that you
may have strength when you
go on *your* way."
[23]But he refused and said,
"I will not eat."
So his servants, together
with the woman, urged him;
and he heeded their voice.
Then he arose from the
ground and sat on the bed.
[24]Now the woman had a fatted calf in the house, and she
hastened to kill it. And she
took flour and kneaded *it,*
and baked unleavened bread
from it. [25]So she brought *it*
before Saul and his servants,
and they ate. Then they rose
and went away that night.

THE PHILISTINES REJECT DAVID

29 Then the Philistines
gathered together all
their armies at Aphek, and
the Israelites encamped by a
fountain which *is* in Jezreel.
[2]And the lords of the Philistines passed in review by hundreds and by thousands, but
David and his men passed in
review at the rear with Achish.
[3]Then the princes of the Philistines said, "What *are* these
Hebrews *doing here?*"
And Achish said to the
princes of the Philistines, "*Is*
this not David, the servant of
Saul king of Israel, who has
been with me these days, or
these years? And to this day
I have found no fault in him
since he defected *to me.*"
[4]But the princes of the Philistines were angry with him;
so the princes of the Philistines said to him, "Make this
fellow return, that he may go
back to the place which you
have appointed for him, and
do not let him go down with
us to battle, lest in the battle
he become our adversary. For
with what could he reconcile
himself to his master, if not
with the heads of these men?
[5]*Is* this not David, of whom
they sang to one another in
dances, saying:

'Saul has slain his
thousands,
And David his ten
thousands'?"[a]

[6]Then Achish called David
and said to him, "Surely, *as* the
LORD lives, you have been upright, and your going out and
your coming in with me in the
army *is* good in my sight. For
to this day I have not found
evil in you since the day of
your coming to me. Never-
theless the lords do not favor
you. [7]Therefore return now,
and go in peace, that you may
not displease the lords of the
Philistines."
[8]So David said to Achish,
"But what have I done? And to
this day what have you found

29:5 [a] Compare 1 Samuel 18:7

in your servant as long as I
have been with you, that I may
not go and fight against the
enemies of my lord the king?"
9 Then Achish answered
and said to David, "I know that
you *are* as good in my sight as
an angel of God; nevertheless
the princes of the Philistines
have said, 'He shall not go up
with us to the battle.' 10 Now
therefore, rise early in the
morning with your master's
servants who have come with
you.[a] And as soon as you are
up early in the morning and
have light, depart."
11 So David and his men
rose early to depart in the
morning, to return to the land
of the Philistines. And the Philistines went up to Jezreel.

DAVID'S CONFLICT WITH THE AMALEKITES

30 Now it happened, when
David and his men
came to Ziklag, on the third
day, that the Amalekites had
invaded the South and Ziklag,
attacked Ziklag and burned
it with fire, 2 and had taken
captive the women and those
who *were* there, from small to
great; they did not kill anyone,
but carried *them* away and
went their way. 3 So David and
his men came to the city, and
there it was, burned with fire;
and their wives, their sons,
and their daughters had been
taken captive. 4 Then David
and the people who *were* with
him lifted up their voices and
wept, until they had no more
power to weep. 5 And David's
two wives, Ahinoam the Jezreelitess, and Abigail the
widow of Nabal the Carmelite,
had been taken captive. 6 Now
David was greatly distressed,
for the people spoke of stoning
him, because the soul of all the
people was grieved, every man
for his sons and his daughters.
But David strengthened himself in the LORD his God.
7 Then David said to Abiathar the priest, Ahimelech's
son, "Please bring the ephod
here to me." And Abiathar
brought the ephod to David.
8 So David inquired of the
LORD, saying, "Shall I pursue
this troop? Shall I overtake
them?"
And He answered him,
"Pursue, for you shall surely
overtake *them* and without fail
recover *all.*"
9 So David went, he and the
six hundred men who *were*
with him, and came to the
Brook Besor, where those
stayed who were left behind.
10 But David pursued, he and
four hundred men; for two
hundred stayed *behind,* who
were so weary that they could
not cross the Brook Besor.

29:10 [a] Following Masoretic Text, Targum, and Vulgate; Septuagint adds *and go to the place which I have selected for you there; and set no bothersome word in your heart, for you are good before me. And rise on your way.*

11Then they found an Egyptian in the field, and brought
him to David; and they gave
him bread and he ate, and
they let him drink water.
12And they gave him a piece
of a cake of figs and two clusters of raisins. So when he
had eaten, his strength came
back to him; for he had eaten
no bread nor drunk water for
three days and three nights.
13Then David said to him,
"To whom do you *belong,* and
where *are* you from?"

And he said, "I *am* a young
man from Egypt, servant of
an Amalekite; and my master
left me behind, because three
days ago I fell sick. 14We made
an invasion of the southern
area of the Cherethites, in
the *territory* which *belongs* to
Judah, and of the southern
area of Caleb; and we burned
Ziklag with fire."

15And David said to him,
"Can you take me down to this
troop?"

So he said, "Swear to me by
God that you will neither kill
me nor deliver me into the
hands of my master, and I will
take you down to this troop."

16And when he had brought
him down, there they were,
spread out over all the land,
eating and drinking and dancing, because of all the great
spoil which they had taken
from the land of the Philistines and from the land of
Judah. 17Then David attacked
them from twilight until the
evening of the next day. Not
a man of them escaped, except four hundred young men
who rode on camels and fled.
18So David recovered all that
the Amalekites had carried
away, and David rescued his
two wives. 19And nothing
of theirs was lacking, either
small or great, sons or daughters, spoil or anything which
they had taken from them;
David recovered all. 20Then
David took all the flocks and
herds they had driven before
those *other* livestock, and said,
"This *is* David's spoil."

21Now David came to the
two hundred men who had
been so weary that they could
not follow David, whom they
also had made to stay at the
Brook Besor. So they went out
to meet David and to meet the
people who *were* with him.
And when David came near
the people, he greeted them.
22Then all the wicked and
worthless men[a] of those who
went with David answered and
said, "Because they did not go
with us, we will not give them
any of the spoil that we have
recovered, except for every
man's wife and children, that
they may lead *them* away and
depart."

23But David said, "My
brethren, you shall not do so
with what the LORD has given

30:22 [a] Literally *men of Belial*

us, who has preserved us and
delivered into our hand the
troop that came against us.
24For who will heed you in
this matter? But as his part *is*
who goes down to the battle,
so *shall* his part *be* who stays
by the supplies; they shall
share alike." 25So it was, from
that day forward; he made it
a statute and an ordinance for
Israel to this day.

26Now when David came
to Ziklag, he sent *some* of the
spoil to the elders of Judah, to
his friends, saying, "Here is a
present for you from the spoil
of the enemies of the LORD"—
27to *those* who *were* in Bethel,
those who *were* in Ramoth of
the South, *those* who *were*
in Jattir, 28*those* who *were*
in Aroer, *those* who *were* in
Siphmoth, *those* who *were* in
Eshtemoa, 29*those* who *were*
in Rachal, *those* who *were* in
the cities of the Jerahmeelites,
those who *were* in the cities of
the Kenites, 30*those* who *were*
in Hormah, *those* who *were* in
Chorashan,[a] *those* who *were*
in Athach, 31*those* who *were* in
Hebron, and to all the places
where David himself and his
men were accustomed to rove.

THE TRAGIC END OF SAUL AND HIS SONS

31 Now the Philistines
fought against Israel;
and the men of Israel fled
from before the Philistines,
and fell slain on Mount Gilboa.
2Then the Philistines followed
hard after Saul and his sons.
And the Philistines killed Jonathan, Abinadab, and Malchishua, Saul's sons. 3The battle
became fierce against Saul.
The archers hit him, and he
was severely wounded by the
archers.

4Then Saul said to his
armorbearer, "Draw your
sword, and thrust me through
with it, lest these uncircumcised men come and thrust
me through and abuse me."

But his armorbearer would
not, for he was greatly afraid.
Therefore Saul took a sword
and fell on it. 5And when his
armorbearer saw that Saul
was dead, he also fell on his
sword, and died with him.
6So Saul, his three sons, his
armorbearer, and all his men
died together that same day.

7And when the men of Is-
rael who *were* on the other
side of the valley, and *those*
who *were* on the other side
of the Jordan, saw that the
men of Israel had fled and
that Saul and his sons were
dead, they forsook the cities
and fled; and the Philistines
came and dwelt in them. 8So
it happened the next day,
when the Philistines came to
strip the slain, that they found
Saul and his three sons fallen
on Mount Gilboa. 9And they
cut off his head and stripped

30:30 [a] Or *Borashan*

off his armor, and sent *word*
throughout the land of the
Philistines, to proclaim *it in*
the temple of their idols and
among the people. 10Then
they put his armor in the temple of the Ashtoreths, and they
fastened his body to the wall
of Beth Shan.[a]
11Now when the inhabitants
of Jabesh Gilead heard what
the Philistines had done to
Saul, 12all the valiant men
arose and traveled all night,
and took the body of Saul and
the bodies of his sons from the
wall of Beth Shan; and they
came to Jabesh and burned
them there. 13Then they took
their bones and buried *them*
under the tamarisk tree at Jabesh, and fasted seven days.

THE SECOND BOOK OF SAMUEL

THE REPORT OF SAUL'S DEATH

1 Now it came to pass after
the death of Saul, when
David had returned from the
slaughter of the Amalekites,
and David had stayed two
days in Ziklag, 2on the third
day, behold, it happened that
a man came from Saul's camp
with his clothes torn and dust
on his head. So it was, when
he came to David, that he fell
to the ground and prostrated
himself.
3And David said to him,
"Where have you come from?"
So he said to him, "I have escaped from the camp of Israel."
4Then David said to him,
"How did the matter go?
Please tell me."
And he answered, "The people have fled from the battle,
many of the people are fallen
and dead, and Saul and Jonathan his son are dead also."
5So David said to the young
man who told him, "How do
you know that Saul and Jonathan his son are dead?"
6Then the young man who
told him said, "As I happened
by chance *to be* on Mount Gilboa, there was Saul, leaning
on his spear; and indeed the
chariots and horsemen followed hard after him. 7Now
when he looked behind him,
he saw me and called to me.
And I answered, 'Here I am.'
8And he said to me, 'Who *are*
you?' So I answered him, 'I
am an Amalekite.' 9He said to

31:10 [a] Spelled *Beth Shean* in Joshua 17:11 and elsewhere

me again, 'Please stand over
me and kill me, for anguish
has come upon me, but my
life still *remains* in me.' 10So
I stood over him and killed
him, because I was sure that
he could not live after he had
fallen. And I took the crown
that *was* on his head and the
bracelet that *was* on his arm,
and have brought them here
to my lord."
11Therefore David took hold
of his own clothes and tore
them, and *so did* all the men
who *were* with him. 12And
they mourned and wept and
fasted until evening for Saul
and for Jonathan his son, for
the people of the LORD and for
the house of Israel, because
they had fallen by the sword.
13Then David said to the
young man who told him,
"Where *are* you from?"
And he answered, "I *am* the
son of an alien, an Amalekite."
14So David said to him, "How
was it you were not afraid to
put forth your hand to destroy
the LORD's anointed?" 15Then
David called one of the young
men and said, "Go near, *and*
execute him!" And he struck
him so that he died. 16So David
said to him, "Your blood *is* on
your own head, for your own
mouth has testified against
you, saying, 'I have killed the
LORD's anointed.'"

THE SONG OF THE BOW

17Then David lamented
with this lamentation over
Saul and over Jonathan his
son, 18and he told *them* to
teach the children of Judah
the Song of the Bow; indeed
it is written in the Book of
Jasher:

19"The beauty of Israel
is slain on your
high places!
How the mighty
have fallen!
20 Tell *it* not in Gath,
Proclaim *it* not in the
streets of Ashkelon—
Lest the daughters of the
Philistines rejoice,
Lest the daughters of
the uncircumcised
triumph.

21"O mountains of Gilboa,
Let there be no dew
nor rain upon you,
Nor fields of offerings.
For the shield of
the mighty is cast
away there!
The shield of Saul, not
anointed with oil.
22 From the blood
of the slain,
From the fat of
the mighty,
The bow of Jonathan
did not turn back,
And the sword of Saul
did not return empty.

23"Saul and Jonathan *were*
beloved and pleasant
in their lives,
And in their death they
were not divided;

They were swifter
than eagles,
They were stronger
than lions.

24 "O daughters of Israel,
weep over Saul,
Who clothed you in
scarlet, with luxury;
Who put ornaments of
gold on your apparel.

25 "How the mighty have
fallen in the midst
of the battle!
Jonathan *was* slain in
your high places.
26 I am distressed for you,
my brother Jonathan;
You have been very
pleasant to me;
Your love to me was
wonderful,
Surpassing the love
of women.

27 "How the mighty
have fallen,
And the weapons of
war perished!"

DAVID ANOINTED KING OF JUDAH

2 It happened after this
that David inquired of the
LORD, saying, "Shall I go up
to any of the cities of Judah?"
And the LORD said to him,
"Go up."
David said, "Where shall I
go up?"
And He said, "To Hebron."
2 So David went up there,
and his two wives also, Ahinoam the Jezreelitess, and
Abigail the widow of Nabal
the Carmelite. 3 And David
brought up the men who *were*
with him, every man with his
household. So they dwelt in
the cities of Hebron.
4 Then the men of Judah
came, and there they anointed
David king over the house of
Judah. And they told David,
saying, "The men of Jabesh
Gilead *were the ones* who buried Saul." 5 So David sent messengers to the men of Jabesh
Gilead, and said to them, "You
are blessed of the LORD, for
you have shown this kindness
to your lord, to Saul, and have
buried him. 6 And now may
the LORD show kindness and
truth to you. I also will repay
you this kindness, because
you have done this thing.
7 Now therefore, let your hands
be strengthened, and be valiant; for your master Saul is
dead, and also the house of
Judah has anointed me king
over them."

ISHBOSHETH MADE KING OF ISRAEL

8 But Abner the son of Ner,
commander of Saul's army,
took Ishbosheth[a] the son of
Saul and brought him over
to Mahanaim; 9 and he made
him king over Gilead, over the
Ashurites, over Jezreel, over

2:8 [a] Called *Esh-Baal* in 1 Chronicles 8:33 and 9:39

Ephraim, over Benjamin, and over all Israel. 10Ishbosheth, Saul's son, *was* forty years old when he began to reign over Israel, and he reigned two years. Only the house of Judah followed David. 11And the time that David was king in Hebron over the house of Judah was seven years and six months.

ISRAEL AND JUDAH AT WAR

12Now Abner the son of Ner, and the servants of Ishbosheth the son of Saul, went out from Mahanaim to Gibeon. 13And Joab the son of Zeruiah, and the servants of David, went out and met them by the pool of Gibeon. So they sat down, one on one side of the pool and the other on the other side of the pool. 14Then Abner said to Joab, "Let the young men now arise and compete before us."

And Joab said, "Let them arise."

15So they arose and went over by number, twelve from Benjamin, *followers* of Ishbosheth the son of Saul, and twelve from the servants of David. 16And each one grasped his opponent by the head and *thrust* his sword in his opponent's side; so they fell down together. Therefore that place was called the Field of Sharp Swords,[a] which *is* in Gibeon. 17So there was a very fierce battle that day, and Abner and the men of Israel were beaten before the servants of David.

18Now the three sons of Zeruiah were there: Joab and Abishai and Asahel. And Asahel *was as* fleet of foot as a wild gazelle. 19So Asahel pursued Abner, and in going he did not turn to the right hand or to the left from following Abner.

20Then Abner looked behind him and said, "*Are* you Asahel?"

He answered, "I *am*."

21And Abner said to him, "Turn aside to your right hand or to your left, and lay hold on one of the young men and take his armor for yourself." But Asahel would not turn aside from following him. 22So Abner said again to Asahel, "Turn aside from following me. Why should I strike you to the ground? How then could I face your brother Joab?" 23However, he refused to turn aside. Therefore Abner struck him in the stomach with the blunt end of the spear, so that the spear came out of his back; and he fell down there and died on the spot. So it was *that* as many as came to the place where Asahel fell down and died, stood still.

24Joab and Abishai also pursued Abner. And the sun

2:16 [a] Hebrew *Helkath Hazzurim*

was going down when they
came to the hill of Ammah,
which *is* before Giah by the
road to the Wilderness of Gibeon. 25Now the children of
Benjamin gathered together
behind Abner and became
a unit, and took their stand
on top of a hill. 26Then Abner
called to Joab and said, "Shall
the sword devour forever? Do
you not know that it will be
bitter in the latter end? How
long will it be then until you
tell the people to return from
pursuing their brethren?"

27And Joab said, "*As* God
lives, unless you had spoken,
surely then by morning all the
people would have given up
pursuing their brethren." 28So
Joab blew a trumpet; and all
the people stood still and did
not pursue Israel anymore,
nor did they fight anymore.
29Then Abner and his men
went on all that night through
the plain, crossed over the
Jordan, and went through all
Bithron; and they came to Mahanaim.

30So Joab returned from
pursuing Abner. And when he
had gathered all the people
together, there were missing
of David's servants nineteen
men and Asahel. 31But the
servants of David had struck
down, of Benjamin and Ab-
ner's men, three hundred and
sixty men who died. 32Then
they took up Asahel and buried him in his father's tomb,
which *was in* Bethlehem. And
Joab and his men went all
night, and they came to Hebron at daybreak.

3 Now there was a long war
between the house of
Saul and the house of David.
But David grew stronger and
stronger, and the house of
Saul grew weaker and weaker.

SONS OF DAVID

2Sons were born to David
in Hebron: His firstborn was
Amnon by Ahinoam the Jez-
reelitess; 3his second, Chileab,
by Abigail the widow of Nabal
the Carmelite; the third, Absalom the son of Maacah, the
daughter of Talmai, king of
Geshur; 4the fourth, Adonijah
the son of Haggith; the fifth,
Shephatiah the son of Abital;
5and the sixth, Ithream, by David's wife Eglah. These were
born to David in Hebron.

ABNER JOINS FORCES WITH DAVID

6Now it was so, while there
was war between the house of
Saul and the house of David,
that Abner was strengthening
his hold on the house of Saul.

7And Saul had a concu-
bine, whose name *was* Rizpah, the daughter of Aiah.
So *Ishbosheth* said to Abner,
"Why have you gone in to my
father's concubine?"

8Then Abner became very
angry at the words of Ishbosheth, and said, "*Am* I a
dog's head that belongs to
Judah? Today I show loyalty

to the house of Saul your
father, to his brothers, and
to his friends, and have not
delivered you into the hand
of David; and you charge me
today with a fault concerning
this woman? 9May God do so
to Abner, and more also, if
I do not do for David as the
LORD has sworn to him— 10to
transfer the kingdom from
the house of Saul, and set up
the throne of David over Israel
and over Judah, from Dan to
Beersheba." 11And he could
not answer Abner another
word, because he feared him.
12Then Abner sent messen-
gers on his behalf to David,
saying, "Whose *is* the land?"
saying *also,* "Make your covenant with me, and indeed my
hand *shall be* with you to bring
all Israel to you."
13And *David* said, "Good,
I will make a covenant with
you. But one thing I require
of you: you shall not see my
face unless you first bring Michal, Saul's daughter, when
you come to see my face."
14So David sent messengers
to Ishbosheth, Saul's son, saying, "Give *me* my wife Michal,
whom I betrothed to myself
for a hundred foreskins of the
Philistines." 15And Ishbosheth
sent and took her from *her*
husband, from Paltiel[a] the son
of Laish. 16Then her husband
went along with her to Bahurim, weeping behind her. So
Abner said to him, "Go, return!" And he returned.
17Now Abner had commu-
nicated with the elders of Israel, saying, "In time past you
were seeking for David *to be*
king over you. 18Now then, do
it! For the LORD has spoken of
David, saying, 'By the hand
of My servant David, I[a] will
save My people Israel from
the hand of the Philistines
and the hand of all their enemies.'" 19And Abner also spoke
in the hearing of Benjamin.
Then Abner also went to speak
in the hearing of David in Hebron all that seemed good to
Israel and the whole house of
Benjamin.
20So Abner and twenty men
with him came to David at Hebron. And David made a feast
for Abner and the men who
were with him. 21Then Abner
said to David, "I will arise and
go, and gather all Israel to my
lord the king, that they may
make a covenant with you,
and that you may reign over
all that your heart desires." So
David sent Abner away, and he
went in peace.

JOAB MURDERS ABNER

22At that moment the
servants of David and Joab
came from a raid and brought
much spoil with them. But
Abner *was* not with David

3:15 [a] Spelled *Palti* in 1 Samuel 25:44 3:18 [a] Following many Hebrew manuscripts, Septuagint, Syriac, and Targum; Masoretic Text reads *he*.

in Hebron, for he had sent
him away, and he had gone
in peace. 23When Joab and
all the troops that *were* with
him had come, they told Joab,
saying, "Abner the son of Ner
came to the king, and he sent
him away, and he has gone in
peace." 24Then Joab came to
the king and said, "What have
you done? Look, Abner came
to you; why *is* it *that* you sent
him away, and he has already
gone? 25Surely you realize that
Abner the son of Ner came
to deceive you, to know your
going out and your coming
in, and to know all that you
are doing."

26And when Joab had gone
from David's presence, he
sent messengers after Abner,
who brought him back from
the well of Sirah. But David
did not know *it*. 27Now when
Abner had returned to Hebron,
Joab took him aside in
the gate to speak with him
privately, and there stabbed
him in the stomach, so that
he died for the blood of Asahel
his brother.

28Afterward, when David
heard *it*, he said, "My kingdom
and I *are* guiltless before the
LORD forever of the blood of
Abner the son of Ner. 29Let it
rest on the head of Joab and
on all his father's house; and
let there never fail to be in the
house of Joab one who has a
discharge or is a leper, who
leans on a staff or falls by the
sword, or who lacks bread."
30So Joab and Abishai his
brother killed Abner, because
he had killed their brother Asahel
at Gibeon in the battle.

DAVID'S MOURNING FOR ABNER

31Then David said to Joab
and to all the people who were
with him, "Tear your clothes,
gird yourselves with sackcloth,
and mourn for Abner."
And King David followed the
coffin. 32So they buried Abner
in Hebron; and the king lifted
up his voice and wept at the
grave of Abner, and all the
people wept. 33And the king
sang *a lament* over Abner and
said:

"Should Abner die
as a fool dies?
34 Your hands were
not bound
Nor your feet put
into fetters;
As a man falls before
wicked men, *so*
you fell."

Then all the people wept over
him again.

35And when all the people
came to persuade David to
eat food while it was still day,
David took an oath, saying,
"God do so to me, and more
also, if I taste bread or anything
else till the sun goes
down!" 36Now all the people
took note *of it*, and it pleased
them, since whatever the king
did pleased all the people.

37For all the people and all
Israel understood that day
that it had not been the king's
intent to kill Abner the son
of Ner. 38Then the king said
to his servants, "Do you not
know that a prince and a great
man has fallen this day in Israel? 39And I *am* weak today,
though anointed king; and
these men, the sons of Zeruiah, *are* too harsh for me. The
LORD shall repay the evildoer
according to his wickedness."

ISHBOSHETH IS MURDERED

4 When Saul's son[a] heard
that Abner had died in
Hebron, he lost heart, and
all Israel was troubled. 2Now
Saul's son *had* two men *who*
were captains of troops. The
name of one *was* Baanah and
the name of the other Rechab,
the sons of Rimmon the Beerothite, of the children of
Benjamin. (For Beeroth also
was *part* of Benjamin, 3be-
cause the Beerothites fled to
Gittaim and have been so-
journers there until this day.)
4Jonathan, Saul's son, had a
son *who was* lame in *his* feet.
He was five years old when the
news about Saul and Jonathan
came from Jezreel; and his
nurse took him up and fled.
And it happened, as she made
haste to flee, that he fell and
became lame. His name *was*
Mephibosheth.[a]

5Then the sons of Rimmon
the Beerothite, Rechab and
Baanah, set out and came
at about the heat of the day
to the house of Ishbosheth,
who was lying on his bed at
noon. 6And they came there,
all the way into the house, *as*
though to get wheat, and they
stabbed him in the stomach.
Then Rechab and Baanah his
brother escaped. 7For when
they came into the house, he
was lying on his bed in his bedroom; then they struck him
and killed him, beheaded him
and took his head, and were
all night escaping through the
plain. 8And they brought the
head of Ishbosheth to David
at Hebron, and said to the
king, "Here is the head of Ishbosheth, the son of Saul your
enemy, who sought your life;
and the LORD has avenged my
lord the king this day of Saul
and his descendants."
9But David answered
Rechab and Baanah his
brother, the sons of Rimmon
the Beerothite, and said to
them, "*As* the LORD lives, who
has redeemed my life from
all adversity, 10when someone told me, saying, 'Look,
Saul is dead,' thinking to have
brought good news, I arrested
him and had him executed in
Ziklag—the one who *thought*
I would give him a reward for
his news. 11How much more,

4:1 [a] That is, Ishbosheth 4:4 [a] Called *Merib-Baal* in 1 Chronicles 8:34 and 9:40

when wicked men have killed
a righteous person in his own
house on his bed? Therefore,
shall I not now require his
blood at your hand and remove you from the earth?"
[12]So David commanded his
young men, and they executed
them, cut off their hands and
feet, and hanged *them* by the
pool in Hebron. But they took
the head of Ishbosheth and
buried *it* in the tomb of Abner
in Hebron.

DAVID REIGNS OVER ALL ISRAEL

5 Then all the tribes of Israel
came to David at Hebron
and spoke, saying, "Indeed
we *are* your bone and your
flesh. [2]Also, in time past,
when Saul was king over us,
you were the one who led Israel out and brought them in;
and the LORD said to you, 'You
shall shepherd My people Israel, and be ruler over Israel.'"
[3]Therefore all the elders of Israel came to the king at Hebron, and King David made
a covenant with them at Hebron before the LORD. And
they anointed David king over
Israel. [4]David *was* thirty years
old when he began to reign,
and he reigned forty years. [5]In
Hebron he reigned over Judah
seven years and six months,
and in Jerusalem he reigned
thirty-three years over all Israel and Judah.

THE CONQUEST OF JERUSALEM

[6]And the king and his men
went to Jerusalem against the
Jebusites, the inhabitants of
the land, who spoke to David,
saying, "You shall not come
in here; but the blind and the
lame will repel you," thinking,
"David cannot come in here."
[7]Nevertheless David took the
stronghold of Zion (that *is,* the
City of David).

[8]Now David said on that
day, "Whoever climbs up by
way of the water shaft and de-
feats the Jebusites (the lame
and the blind, *who are* hated
by David's soul), *he shall be
chief and captain.*"[a] Therefore
they say, "The blind and the
lame shall not come into the
house."

[9]Then David dwelt in the
stronghold, and called it the
City of David. And David built
all around from the Millo[a] and
inward. [10]So David went on
and became great, and the
LORD God of hosts *was* with
him.

[11]Then Hiram king of Tyre
sent messengers to David, and
cedar trees, and carpenters
and masons. And they built
David a house. [12]So David
knew that the LORD had established him as king over Israel, and that He had exalted
His kingdom for the sake of
His people Israel.

[13]And David took more

5:8 [a] Compare 1 Chronicles 11:6 5:9 [a] Literally *The Landfill*

concubines and wives from
Jerusalem, after he had come
from Hebron. Also more sons
and daughters were born to
David. 14Now these *are* the
names of those who were
born to him in Jerusalem:
Shammua,[a] Shobab, Nathan,
Solomon, 15Ibhar, Elishua,[a]
Nepheg, Japhia, 16Elishama,
Eliada, and Eliphelet.

THE PHILISTINES DEFEATED

17Now when the Philistines
heard that they had anointed
David king over Israel, all the
Philistines went up to search
for David. And David heard
of it and went down to the
stronghold. 18The Philistines
also went and deployed themselves in the Valley of Rephaim. 19So David inquired of
the LORD, saying, "Shall I go
up against the Philistines?
Will You deliver them into
my hand?"

And the LORD said to David,
"Go up, for I will doubtless deliver the Philistines into your
hand."

20So David went to Baal
Perazim, and David defeated
them there; and he said, "The
LORD has broken through
my enemies before me, like
a breakthrough of water."
Therefore he called the name
of that place Baal Perazim.[a]
21And they left their images
there, and David and his men
carried them away.

22Then the Philistines went
up once again and deployed
themselves in the Valley of
Rephaim. 23Therefore David
inquired of the LORD, and He
said, "You shall not go up; circle around behind them, and
come upon them in front of
the mulberry trees. 24And it
shall be, when you hear the
sound of marching in the tops
of the mulberry trees, then
you shall advance quickly. For
then the LORD will go out before you to strike the camp of
the Philistines." 25And David
did so, as the LORD com-
manded him; and he drove
back the Philistines from
Geba[a] as far as Gezer.

THE ARK BROUGHT TO JERUSALEM

6 Again David gathered all
the choice *men* of Israel,
thirty thousand. 2And David
arose and went with all the
people who *were* with him
from Baale Judah to bring
up from there the ark of God,
whose name is called by the
Name,[a] the LORD of Hosts, who
dwells *between* the cherubim.
3So they set the ark of God on a
new cart, and brought it out of

5:14 [a] Spelled *Shimea* in 1 Chronicles 3:5 5:15 [a] Spelled *Elishama* in 1 Chronicles 3:6 5:20 [a] Literally *Master of Breakthroughs* 5:25 [a] Following Masoretic Text, Targum, and Vulgate; Septuagint reads *Gibeon.* 6:2 [a] Septuagint, Targum, and Vulgate omit *by the Name;* many Hebrew manuscripts and Syriac read *there.*

the house of Abinadab, which
was on the hill; and Uzzah and
Ahio, the sons of Abinadab,
drove the new cart.[a] 4And they
brought it out of the house of
Abinadab, which *was* on the
hill, accompanying the ark of
God; and Ahio went before the
ark. 5Then David and all the
house of Israel played *music*
before the LORD on all kinds
of *instruments of* fir wood,
on harps, on stringed instruments, on tambourines, on
sistrums, and on cymbals.

6And when they came to
Nachon's threshing floor,
Uzzah put out *his hand* to
the ark of God and took hold
of it, for the oxen stumbled.
7Then the anger of the LORD
was aroused against Uzzah,
and God struck him there for
his error; and he died there
by the ark of God. 8And David
became angry because of
the LORD's outbreak against
Uzzah; and he called the name
of the place Perez Uzzah[a] to
this day.

9David was afraid of the
LORD that day; and he said,
"How can the ark of the LORD
come to me?" 10So David
would not move the ark of
the LORD with him into the
City of David; but David took
it aside into the house of
Obed-Edom the Gittite. 11The
ark of the LORD remained in
the house of Obed-Edom the
Gittite three months. And the
LORD blessed Obed-Edom and
all his household.

12Now it was told King
David, saying, "The LORD has
blessed the house of Obed-
Edom and all that *belongs*
to him, because of the ark
of God." So David went and
brought up the ark of God
from the house of Obed-Edom
to the City of David with gladness. 13And so it was, when
those bearing the ark of the
LORD had gone six paces, that
he sacrificed oxen and fatted
sheep. 14Then David danced
before the LORD with all *his*
might; and David *was* wearing
a linen ephod. 15So David and
all the house of Israel brought
up the ark of the LORD with
shouting and with the sound
of the trumpet.

16Now as the ark of the
LORD came into the City of
David, Michal, Saul's daughter,
looked through a window and
saw King David leaping and
whirling before the LORD; and
she despised him in her heart.
17So they brought the ark of
the LORD, and set it in its place
in the midst of the tabernacle
that David had erected for it.
Then David offered burnt offerings and peace offerings
before the LORD. 18And when
David had finished offering
burnt offerings and peace offerings, he blessed the people

6:3 [a] Septuagint adds *with the ark.* 6:8 [a] Literally *Outburst Against Uzzah*

in the name of the LORD of
hosts. 19Then he distributed
among all the people, among
the whole multitude of Israel,
both the women and the men,
to everyone a loaf of bread, a
piece *of meat,* and a cake of
raisins. So all the people departed, everyone to his house.
20Then David returned
to bless his household. And
Michal the daughter of Saul
came out to meet David, and
said, "How glorious was the
king of Israel today, uncover-
ing himself today in the eyes
of the maids of his servants, as
one of the base fellows shame-
lessly uncovers himself!"
21So David said to Michal,
"*It was* before the LORD, who
chose me instead of your
father and all his house, to
appoint me ruler over the people of the LORD, over Israel.
Therefore I will play *music* before the LORD. 22And I will be
even more undignified than
this, and will be humble in my
own sight. But as for the maidservants of whom you have
spoken, by them I will be held
in honor."
23Therefore Michal the
daughter of Saul had no children to the day of her death.

GOD'S COVENANT WITH DAVID

7 Now it came to pass when
the king was dwelling in his
house, and the LORD had given
him rest from all his enemies
all around, 2that the king
said to Nathan the prophet,
"See now, I dwell in a house
of cedar, but the ark of God
dwells inside tent curtains."
3Then Nathan said to the
king, "Go, do all that *is* in your
heart, for the LORD *is* with
you."
4But it happened that night
that the word of the LORD
came to Nathan, saying, 5"Go
and tell My servant David,
'Thus says the LORD: "Would
you build a house for Me to
dwell in? 6For I have not dwelt
in a house since the time that I
brought the children of Israel
up from Egypt, even to this
day, but have moved about
in a tent and in a tabernacle. 7Wherever I have moved
about with all the children
of Israel, have I ever spoken
a word to anyone from the
tribes of Israel, whom I commanded to shepherd My people Israel, saying, 'Why have
you not built Me a house of
cedar?'"' 8Now therefore, thus
shall you say to My servant
David, 'Thus says the LORD
of hosts: "I took you from
the sheepfold, from following the sheep, to be ruler over
My people, over Israel. 9And I
have been with you wherever
you have gone, and have cut
off all your enemies from before you, and have made you a
great name, like the name of
the great men who *are* on the
earth. 10Moreover I will appoint a place for My people Israel, and will plant them, that

they may dwell in a place of
their own and move no more;
nor shall the sons of wickedness oppress them anymore,
as previously, 11since the time
that I commanded judges *to
be* over My people Israel, and
have caused you to rest from
all your enemies. Also the
LORD tells you that He will
make you a house.[a]

12"When your days are fulfilled and you rest with your
fathers, I will set up your seed
after you, who will come from
your body, and I will establish
his kingdom. 13He shall build
a house for My name, and I
will establish the throne of his
kingdom forever. 14I will be his
Father, and he shall be My son.
If he commits iniquity, I will
chasten him with the rod of
men and with the blows of the
sons of men. 15But My mercy
shall not depart from him, as
I took *it* from Saul, whom I removed from before you. 16And
your house and your kingdom
shall be established forever
before you.[a] Your throne shall
be established forever." ' "

17According to all these
words and according to all
this vision, so Nathan spoke
to David.

DAVID'S THANKSGIVING TO GOD

18Then King David went in
and sat before the LORD; and
he said: "Who *am* I, O Lord
GOD? And what is my house,
that You have brought me this
far? 19And yet this was a small
thing in Your sight, O Lord
GOD; and You have also spoken of Your servant's house
for a great while to come.
Is this the manner of man,
O Lord GOD? 20Now what more
can David say to You? For You,
Lord GOD, know Your servant.
21For Your word's sake, and
according to Your own heart,
You have done all these great
things, to make Your servant
know *them*. 22Therefore You
are great, O Lord GOD.[a] For
there is none like You, nor *is
there any* God besides You,
according to all that we have
heard with our ears. 23And
who *is* like Your people, like
Israel, the one nation on the
earth whom God went to redeem for Himself as a people, to make for Himself a
name—and to do for Your-
self great and awesome deeds
for Your land—before Your
people whom You redeemed
for Yourself from Egypt, the
nations, and their gods? 24For
You have made Your people
Israel Your very own people
forever; and You, LORD, have
become their God.

25"Now, O LORD God, the
word which You have spo-
ken concerning Your servant
and concerning his house,

7:11 [a] That is, a royal dynasty 7:16 [a] Septuagint reads *Me.* 7:22 [a] Targum and Syriac read *O LORD God.*

establish *it* forever and do as
You have said. 26So let Your
name be magnified forever,
saying, 'The LORD of hosts *is*
the God over Israel.' And let
the house of Your servant
David be established before
You. 27For You, O LORD of
hosts, God of Israel, have revealed *this* to Your servant,
saying, 'I will build you a
house.' Therefore Your servant has found it in his heart
to pray this prayer to You.

28"And now, O Lord GOD,
You are God, and Your words
are true, and You have promised this goodness to Your servant. 29Now therefore, let it
please You to bless the house
of Your servant, that it may
continue before You forever;
for You, O Lord GOD, have spoken *it*, and with Your blessing
let the house of Your servant
be blessed forever."

DAVID'S FURTHER CONQUESTS

8 After this it came to pass
that David attacked the
Philistines and subdued
them. And David took Metheg
Ammah from the hand of the
Philistines.

2Then he defeated Moab.
Forcing them down to the
ground, he measured them
off with a line. With two lines
he measured off those to be
put to death, and with one full
line those to be kept alive. So
the Moabites became David's
servants, *and* brought tribute.

3David also defeated Had-
adezer the son of Rehob, king
of Zobah, as he went to recover his territory at the River
Euphrates. 4David took from
him one thousand *chariots*,
seven hundred[a] horsemen,
and twenty thousand foot soldiers. Also David hamstrung
all the chariot *horses*, except
that he spared *enough* of them
for one hundred chariots.

5When the Syrians of Da-
mascus came to help Had-
adezer king of Zobah, David
killed twenty-two thousand
of the Syrians. 6Then David
put garrisons in Syria of Damascus; and the Syrians became David's servants, *and*
brought tribute. So the LORD
preserved David wherever
he went. 7And David took the
shields of gold that had belonged to the servants of Hadadezer, and brought them to
Jerusalem. 8Also from Betah[a]
and from Berothai, cities of
Hadadezer, King David took
a large amount of bronze.

9When Toi[a] king of Hamath
heard that David had defeated
all the army of Hadadezer,
10then Toi sent Joram[a] his son
to King David, to greet him
and bless him, because he had

8:4 [a] Or *seven thousand* (compare 1 Chronicles 18:4) 8:8 [a] Spelled *Tibhath* in 1 Chronicles 18:8 8:9 [a] Spelled *Tou* in 1 Chronicles 18:9 8:10 [a] Spelled *Hadoram* in 1 Chronicles 18:10

fought against Hadadezer and
defeated him (for Hadadezer
had been at war with Toi); and
Joram brought with him articles of silver, articles of gold,
and articles of bronze. 11King
David also dedicated these to
the LORD, along with the silver
and gold that he had dedicated
from all the nations which he
had subdued— 12from Syria,[a]
from Moab, from the people
of Ammon, from the Philistines, from Amalek, and from
the spoil of Hadadezer the son
of Rehob, king of Zobah.
13And David made *himself* a
name when he returned from
killing eighteen thousand Syrians[a] in the Valley of Salt. 14He
also put garrisons in Edom;
throughout all Edom he put
garrisons, and all the Edomites became David's servants.
And the LORD preserved
David wherever he went.

DAVID'S ADMINISTRATION

15So David reigned over
all Israel; and David administered judgment and justice
to all his people. 16Joab the
son of Zeruiah *was* over the
army; Jehoshaphat the son of
Ahilud *was* recorder; 17Zadok
the son of Ahitub and Ahimelech the son of Abiathar *were*
the priests; Seraiah[a] *was* the
scribe; 18Benaiah the son of
Jehoiada *was over* both the
Cherethites and the Pele-
thites; and David's sons were
chief ministers.

DAVID'S KINDNESS TO MEPHIBOSHETH

9 Now David said, "Is there
still anyone who is left of
the house of Saul, that I may
show him kindness for Jonathan's sake?"
2And *there was* a servant of
the house of Saul whose name
was Ziba. So when they had
called him to David, the king
said to him, "*Are* you Ziba?"
He said, "At your service!"
3Then the king said, "*Is*
there not still someone of the
house of Saul, to whom I may
show the kindness of God?"
And Ziba said to the king,
"There is still a son of Jonathan *who is* lame in *his* feet."
4So the king said to him,
"Where *is* he?"
And Ziba said to the king,
"Indeed he *is* in the house of
Machir the son of Ammiel, in
Lo Debar."
5Then King David sent and
brought him out of the house
of Machir the son of Ammiel,
from Lo Debar.
6Now when Mephibosheth
the son of Jonathan, the son
of Saul, had come to David, he
fell on his face and prostrated

8:12 [a] Septuagint, Syriac, and some Hebrew manuscripts read *Edom*. **8:13** [a] Septuagint, Syriac, and some Hebrew manuscripts read *Edomites* (compare 1 Chronicles 18:12). **8:17** [a] Spelled *Shavsha* in 1 Chronicles 18:16

himself. Then David said, "Mephibosheth?"
And he answered, "Here is
your servant!"
7So David said to him, "Do
not fear, for I will surely show
you kindness for Jonathan
your father's sake, and will
restore to you all the land of
Saul your grandfather; and
you shall eat bread at my table
continually."
8Then he bowed himself,
and said, "What *is* your servant, that you should look
upon such a dead dog as I?"
9And the king called to
Ziba, Saul's servant, and said
to him, "I have given to your
master's son all that belonged
to Saul and to all his house.
10You therefore, and your sons
and your servants, shall work
the land for him, and you shall
bring in *the harvest,* that your
master's son may have food to
eat. But Mephibosheth your
master's son shall eat bread
at my table always." Now Ziba
had fifteen sons and twenty
servants.
11Then Ziba said to the king,
"According to all that my lord
the king has commanded
his servant, so will your servant do."
"As for Mephibosheth," *said
the king,* "he shall eat at my
table[a] like one of the king's
sons." 12Mephibosheth had a
young son whose name *was*
Micha. And all who dwelt in
the house of Ziba *were* servants of Mephibosheth. 13So
Mephibosheth dwelt in Jerusalem, for he ate continually
at the king's table. And he was
lame in both his feet.

THE AMMONITES AND SYRIANS DEFEATED

10 It happened after this
that the king of the
people of Ammon died, and
Hanun his son reigned in his
place. 2Then David said, "I will
show kindness to Hanun the
son of Nahash, as his father
showed kindness to me."
So David sent by the hand
of his servants to comfort him
concerning his father. And
David's servants came into the
land of the people of Ammon.
3And the princes of the people of Ammon said to Hanun
their lord, "Do you think that
David really honors your father because he has sent comforters to you? Has David not
rather sent his servants to you
to search the city, to spy it out,
and to overthrow it?"
4Therefore Hanun took Da-
vid's servants, shaved off half
of their beards, cut off their
garments in the middle, at
their buttocks, and sent them
away. 5When they told David,
he sent to meet them, because
the men were greatly ashamed.
And the king said, "Wait at Jericho until your beards have
grown, and *then* return."

9:11 [a] Septuagint reads *David's table.*

6When the people of
Ammon saw that they had
made themselves repulsive to
David, the people of Ammon
sent and hired the Syrians of
Beth Rehob and the Syrians
of Zoba, twenty thousand foot
soldiers; and from the king of
Maacah one thousand men,
and from Ish-Tob twelve thousand men. 7Now when David
heard *of it,* he sent Joab and all
the army of the mighty men.
8Then the people of Ammon
came out and put themselves
in battle array at the entrance
of the gate. And the Syrians
of Zoba, Beth Rehob, Ish-Tob,
and Maacah *were* by themselves in the field.

9When Joab saw that the
battle line was against him
before and behind, he chose
some of Israel's best and put
them in battle array against
the Syrians. 10And the rest
of the people he put under
the command of Abishai his
brother, that he might set
them in battle array against
the people of Ammon. 11Then
he said, "If the Syrians are too
strong for me, then you shall
help me; but if the people of
Ammon are too strong for
you, then I will come and help
you. 12Be of good courage, and
let us be strong for our people
and for the cities of our God.
And may the LORD do *what is*
good in His sight."
13So Joab and the people
who *were* with him drew near
for the battle against the Syrians, and they fled before him.
14When the people of Ammon
saw that the Syrians were
fleeing, they also fled before
Abishai, and entered the city.
So Joab returned from the
people of Ammon and went
to Jerusalem.

15When the Syrians saw
that they had been defeated
by Israel, they gathered together. 16Then Hadadezer[a]
sent and brought out the
Syrians who *were* beyond
the River,[b] and they came to
Helam. And Shobach the commander of Hadadezer's army
went before them. 17When it
was told David, he gathered
all Israel, crossed over the Jordan, and came to Helam. And
the Syrians set themselves in
battle array against David and
fought with him. 18Then the
Syrians fled before Israel; and
David killed seven hundred
charioteers and forty thousand horsemen of the Syrians,
and struck Shobach the commander of their army, who
died there. 19And when all
the kings *who were* servants
to Hadadezer[a] saw that they
were defeated by Israel, they
made peace with Israel and
served them. So the Syrians
were afraid to help the people
of Ammon anymore.

10:16 [a] Hebrew *Hadarezer* [b] That is, the Euphrates **10:19** [a] Hebrew *Hadarezer*

DAVID, BATHSHEBA, AND URIAH

11 It happened in the spring
of the year, at the time
when kings go out *to battle,*
that David sent Joab and his
servants with him, and all
Israel; and they destroyed
the people of Ammon and
besieged Rabbah. But David
remained at Jerusalem.

2 Then it happened one evening that David arose from
his bed and walked on the
roof of the king's house. And
from the roof he saw a woman
bathing, and the woman *was*
very beautiful to behold. 3 So
David sent and inquired about
the woman. And *someone* said,
"*Is* this not Bathsheba, the
daughter of Eliam, the wife
of Uriah the Hittite?" 4 Then
David sent messengers, and
took her; and she came to
him, and he lay with her, for
she was cleansed from her impurity; and she returned to
her house. 5 And the woman
conceived; so she sent and
told David, and said, "I *am*
with child."

6 Then David sent to Joab,
saying, "Send me Uriah the
Hittite." And Joab sent Uriah
to David. 7 When Uriah had
come to him, David asked
how Joab was doing, and how
the people were doing, and
how the *war prospered.* 8 And
David said to Uriah, "Go down
to your house and wash your
feet." So Uriah departed from
the king's house, and a gift *of*
food from the king followed
him. 9 But Uriah slept at the
door of the king's house with
all the servants of his lord, and
did not go down to his house.
10 So when they told David, saying, "Uriah did not go down
to his house," David said to
Uriah, "Did you not come
from a journey? Why did you
not go down to your house?"

11 And Uriah said to David,
"The ark and Israel and Judah
are dwelling in tents, and my
lord Joab and the servants of
my lord are encamped in the
open fields. Shall I then go to
my house to eat and drink,
and to lie with my wife? *As* you
live, and *as* your soul lives, I
will not do this thing."

12 Then David said to Uriah,
"Wait here today also, and tomorrow I will let you depart."
So Uriah remained in Jerusalem that day and the next.
13 Now when David called him,
he ate and drank before him;
and he made him drunk. And
at evening he went out to lie
on his bed with the servants
of his lord, but he did not go
down to his house.

14 In the morning it hap-
pened that David wrote a
letter to Joab and sent *it* by
the hand of Uriah. 15 And he
wrote in the letter, saying,
"Set Uriah in the forefront
of the hottest battle, and re-
treat from him, that he may
be struck down and die." 16 So
it was, while Joab besieged the
city, that he assigned Uriah to

a place where he knew there
were valiant men. 17Then the
men of the city came out and
fought with Joab. And *some*
of the people of the servants
of David fell; and Uriah the
Hittite died also.

18Then Joab sent and told
David all the things concerning the war, 19and charged the
messenger, saying, "When
you have finished telling the
matters of the war to the king,
20if it happens that the king's
wrath rises, and he says to
you: 'Why did you approach
so near to the city when you
fought? Did you not know that
they would shoot from the
wall? 21Who struck Abimelech
the son of Jerubbesheth?[a]
Was it not a woman who cast
a piece of a millstone on him
from the wall, so that he died
in Thebez? Why did you go
near the wall?'—then you shall
say, 'Your servant Uriah the
Hittite is dead also.'"

22So the messenger went,
and came and told David all
that Joab had sent by him.
23And the messenger said to
David, "Surely the men prevailed against us and came
out to us in the field; then we
drove them back as far as the
entrance of the gate. 24The
archers shot from the wall at
your servants; and *some* of the
king's servants are dead, and
your servant Uriah the Hittite
is dead also."

25Then David said to the
messenger, "Thus you shall
say to Joab: 'Do not let this
thing displease you, for the
sword devours one as well as
another. Strengthen your attack against the city, and overthrow it.' So encourage him."

26When the wife of Uriah
heard that Uriah her husband
was dead, she mourned for
her husband. 27And when her
mourning was over, David
sent and brought her to his
house, and she became his
wife and bore him a son. But
the thing that David had done
displeased the LORD.

NATHAN'S PARABLE AND DAVID'S CONFESSION

12 Then the LORD sent Na-
than to David. And he
came to him, and said to him:
"There were two men in one
city, one rich and the other
poor. 2The rich *man* had exceedingly many flocks and
herds. 3But the poor *man* had
nothing, except one little ewe
lamb which he had bought
and nourished; and it grew
up together with him and with
his children. It ate of his own
food and drank from his own
cup and lay in his bosom; and
it was like a daughter to him.
4And a traveler came to the
rich man, who refused to take
from his own flock and from
his own herd to prepare one
for the wayfaring man who

11:21 [a] Same as *Jerubbaal* (Gideon), Judges 6:32ff

had come to him; but he took
the poor man's lamb and prepared it for the man who had
come to him."
5So David's anger was
greatly aroused against the
man, and he said to Nathan,
"*As* the LORD lives, the man
who has done this shall surely
die! 6And he shall restore
fourfold for the lamb, because
he did this thing and because
he had no pity."
7Then Nathan said to
David, "You *are* the man!
Thus says the LORD God of
Israel: 'I anointed you king
over Israel, and I delivered
you from the hand of Saul. 8I
gave you your master's house
and your master's wives into
your keeping, and gave you
the house of Israel and Judah.
And if *that had been* too little,
I also would have given you
much more! 9Why have you
despised the commandment
of the LORD, to do evil in His
sight? You have killed Uriah
the Hittite with the sword;
you have taken his wife *to be*
your wife, and have killed him
with the sword of the people
of Ammon. 10Now therefore,
the sword shall never depart
from your house, because you
have despised Me, and have
taken the wife of Uriah the
Hittite to be your wife.' 11Thus
says the LORD: 'Behold, *I will*
raise up adversity against you
from your own house; and I
will take your wives before
your eyes and give *them* to
your neighbor, and he shall
lie with your wives in the sight
of this sun. 12For you did *it* secretly, but I will do this thing
before all Israel, before the
sun.'"
13So David said to Nathan,
"I have sinned against the
LORD."
And Nathan said to David,
"The LORD also has put away
your sin; you shall not die.
14However, because by this
deed you have given great
occasion to the enemies of
the LORD to blaspheme, the
child also *who is* born to you
shall surely die." 15Then Nathan departed to his house.

THE DEATH OF DAVID'S SON

And the LORD struck the
child that Uriah's wife bore
to David, and it became ill.
16David therefore pleaded
with God for the child, and
David fasted and went in and
lay all night on the ground.
17So the elders of his house
arose *and went* to him, to raise
him up from the ground. But
he would not, nor did he eat
food with them. 18Then on the
seventh day it came to pass
that the child died. And the
servants of David were afraid
to tell him that the child was
dead. For they said, "Indeed,
while the child was alive, we
spoke to him, and he would
not heed our voice. How can
we tell him that the child is
dead? He may do some harm!"

[19]When David saw that his
servants were whispering,
David perceived that the child
was dead. Therefore David
said to his servants, "Is the
child dead?"

And they said, "He is dead."
[20]So David arose from the
ground, washed and anointed
himself, and changed his
clothes; and he went into the
house of the LORD and worshiped. Then he went to his
own house; and when he requested, they set food before
him, and he ate. [21]Then his
servants said to him, "What *is*
this that you have done? You
fasted and wept for the child
while he was alive, but when
the child died, you arose and
ate food."

[22]And he said, "While the
child was alive, I fasted and
wept; for I said, 'Who can
tell *whether* the LORD[a] will
be gracious to me, that the
child may live?' [23]But now
he is dead; why should I fast?
Can I bring him back again?
I shall go to him, but he shall
not return to me."

SOLOMON IS BORN

[24]Then David comforted
Bathsheba his wife, and went
in to her and lay with her. So
she bore a son, and he[a] called
his name Solomon. Now the
LORD loved him, [25]and He sent
word by the hand of Nathan
the prophet: So he[a] called his
name Jedidiah,[b] because of
the LORD.

RABBAH IS CAPTURED

[26]Now Joab fought against
Rabbah of the people of
Ammon, and took the royal
city. [27]And Joab sent messengers to David, and said, "I
have fought against Rabbah,
and I have taken the city's
water *supply*. [28]Now therefore,
gather the rest of the people
together and encamp against
the city and take it, lest I take
the city and it be called after
my name." [29]So David gathered all the people together
and went to Rabbah, fought
against it, and took it. [30]Then
he took their king's crown
from his head. Its weight *was*
a talent of gold, with precious
stones. And it was *set* on David's head. Also he brought
out the spoil of the city in
great abundance. [31]And he
brought out the people who
were in it, and put *them to
work* with saws and iron picks
and iron axes, and made them
cross over to the brick works.
So he did to all the cities of
the people of Ammon. Then
David and all the people returned to Jerusalem.

12:22 [a] A few Hebrew manuscripts and Syriac read *God*.
12:24 [a] Following Kethib, Septuagint, and Vulgate; Qere, a few Hebrew manuscripts, Syriac, and Targum read *she*.
12:25 [a] Qere, some Hebrew manuscripts, Syriac, and Targum read *she*. [b] Literally *Beloved of the LORD*

AMNON AND TAMAR

13 After this Absalom
the son of David had a
lovely sister, whose name *was*
Tamar; and Amnon the son of
David loved her. 2Amnon was
so distressed over his sister
Tamar that he became sick;
for she *was* a virgin. And it was
improper for Amnon to do
anything to her. 3But Amnon
had a friend whose name *was*
Jonadab the son of Shimeah,
David's brother. Now Jonadab
was a very crafty man. 4And
he said to him, "Why *are* you,
the king's son, becoming thin-
ner day after day? Will you not
tell me?"

Amnon said to him, "I love
Tamar, my brother Absalom's
sister."

5So Jonadab said to him,
"Lie down on your bed and
pretend to be ill. And when
your father comes to see you,
say to him, 'Please let my sister Tamar come and give me
food, and prepare the food in
my sight, that I may see *it* and
eat it from her hand.'" 6Then
Amnon lay down and pre-
tended to be ill; and when the
king came to see him, Amnon
said to the king, "Please let
Tamar my sister come and
make a couple of cakes for
me in my sight, that I may eat
from her hand."

7And David sent home *to
Tamar, saying,* "Now go to
your brother Amnon's house,
and prepare food for him." 8So
Tamar went to her brother
Amnon's house; and he was
lying down. Then she took
flour and kneaded *it,* made
cakes in his sight, and baked
the cakes. 9And she took the
pan and placed *them* out before him, but he refused to
eat. Then Amnon said, "Have
everyone go out from me."
And they all went out from
him. 10Then Amnon said to
Tamar, "Bring the food into
the bedroom, that I may eat
from your hand." And Tamar
took the cakes which she had
made, and brought *them* to
Amnon her brother in the
bedroom. 11Now when she had
brought *them* to him to eat,
he took hold of her and said
to her, "Come, lie with me, my
sister."

12But she answered him,
"No, my brother, do not force
me, for no such thing should
be done in Israel. Do not do
this disgraceful thing! 13And I,
where could I take my shame?
And as for you, you would be
like one of the fools in Israel. Now therefore, please
speak to the king; for he will
not withhold me from you."
14However, he would not heed
her voice; and being stronger
than she, he forced her and
lay with her.

15Then Amnon hated her
exceedingly, so that the ha-
tred with which he hated her
was greater than the love with
which he had loved her. And
Amnon said to her, "Arise, be
gone!"

16So she said to him, "No,
indeed! This evil of sending
me away *is* worse than the
other that you did to me."
But he would not listen to
her. 17Then he called his servant who attended him, and
said, "Here! Put this *woman*
out, away from me, and bolt
the door behind her." 18Now
she had on a robe of many
colors, for the king's virgin
daughters wore such apparel.
And his servant put her out
and bolted the door behind
her.
19Then Tamar put ashes on
her head, and tore her robe of
many colors that *was* on her,
and laid her hand on her head
and went away crying bitterly.
20And Absalom her brother
said to her, "Has Amnon your
brother been with you? But
now hold your peace, my sister. He *is* your brother; do not
take this thing to heart." So
Tamar remained desolate in
her brother Absalom's house.
21But when King David
heard of all these things, he
was very angry. 22And Ab-
salom spoke to his brother
Amnon neither good nor bad.
For Absalom hated Amnon,
because he had forced his sister Tamar.

ABSALOM MURDERS AMNON

23And it came to pass, after
two full years, that Absalom
had sheepshearers in Baal
Hazor, which *is* near Ephraim;
so Absalom invited all the
king's sons. 24Then Absalom
came to the king and said,
"Kindly note, your servant has
sheepshearers; please, let the
king and his servants go with
your servant."
25But the king said to Absalom, "No, my son, let us not
all go now, lest we be a burden
to you." Then he urged him,
but he would not go; and he
blessed him.
26Then Absalom said, "If
not, please let my brother
Amnon go with us."
And the king said to him,
"Why should he go with you?"
27But Absalom urged him;
so he let Amnon and all the
king's sons go with him.
28Now Absalom had com-
manded his servants, saying,
"Watch now, when Amnon's
heart is merry with wine,
and when I say to you, 'Strike
Amnon!' then kill him. Do not
be afraid. Have I not commanded you? Be courageous
and valiant." 29So the servants
of Absalom did to Amnon as
Absalom had commanded.
Then all the king's sons arose,
and each one got on his mule
and fled.
30And it came to pass,
while they were on the way,
that news came to David, saying, "Absalom has killed all
the king's sons, and not one
of them is left!" 31So the king
arose and tore his garments
and lay on the ground, and
all his servants stood by with

their clothes torn. 32Then Jonadab the son of Shimeah, David's brother, answered and said, "Let not my lord suppose they have killed all the young men, the king's sons, for only Amnon is dead. For by the command of Absalom this has been determined from the day that he forced his sister Tamar. 33Now therefore, let not my lord the king take the thing to his heart, to think that all the king's sons are dead. For only Amnon is dead."

ABSALOM FLEES TO GESHUR

34Then Absalom fled. And the young man who was keeping watch lifted his eyes and looked, and there, many people were coming from the road on the hillside behind him.[a] 35And Jonadab said to the king, "Look, the king's sons are coming; as your servant said, so it is." 36So it was, as soon as he had finished speaking, that the king's sons indeed came, and they lifted up their voice and wept. Also the king and all his servants wept very bitterly.

37But Absalom fled and went to Talmai the son of Ammihud, king of Geshur. And *David* mourned for his son every day. 38So Absalom fled and went to Geshur, and was there three years. 39And King David[a] longed to go to[b] Absalom. For he had been comforted concerning Amnon, because he was dead.

ABSALOM RETURNS TO JERUSALEM

14 So Joab the son of Zeruiah perceived that the king's heart *was* concerned about Absalom. 2And Joab sent to Tekoa and brought from there a wise woman, and said to her, "Please pretend to be a mourner, and put on mourning apparel; do not anoint yourself with oil, but act like a woman who has been mourning a long time for the dead. 3Go to the king and speak to him in this manner." So Joab put the words in her mouth.

4And when the woman of Tekoa spoke[a] to the king, she fell on her face to the ground and prostrated herself, and said, "Help, O king!"

5Then the king said to her, "What troubles you?"

And she answered, "Indeed I *am* a widow, my husband is dead. 6Now your maidservant

13:34 [a] Septuagint adds *And the watchman went and told the king, and said, "I see men from the way of Horonaim, from the regions of the mountains."* 13:39 [a] Following Masoretic Text, Syriac, and Vulgate; Septuagint reads *the spirit of the king;* Targum reads *the soul of King David.* [b] Following Masoretic Text and Targum; Septuagint and Vulgate read *ceased to pursue after.* 14:4 [a] Many Hebrew manuscripts, Septuagint, Syriac, and Vulgate read *came.*

had two sons; and the two
fought with each other in the
field, and *there was* no one
to part them, but the one
struck the other and killed
him. 7And now the whole
family has risen up against
your maidservant, and they
said, 'Deliver him who struck
his brother, that we may execute him for the life of his
brother whom he killed; and
we will destroy the heir also.'
So they would extinguish my
ember that is left, and leave to
my husband *neither* name nor
remnant on the earth."

8Then the king said to the
woman, "Go to your house,
and I will give orders concerning you."

9And the woman of Tekoa
said to the king, "My lord,
O king, *let* the iniquity *be* on
me and on my father's house,
and the king and his throne
be guiltless."

10So the king said, "Who-
ever says *anything* to you,
bring him to me, and he shall
not touch you anymore."

11Then she said, "Please let
the king remember the LORD
your God, and do not permit
the avenger of blood to destroy anymore, lest they destroy my son."

And he said, "*As* the LORD
lives, not one hair of your son
shall fall to the ground."

12Therefore the woman
said, "Please, let your maidservant speak *another* word
to my lord the king."

And he said, "Say on."

13So the woman said: "Why
then have you schemed such
a thing against the people of
God? For the king speaks this
thing as one who is guilty, *in
that* the king does not bring
his banished one home again.
14For we will surely die and
become like water spilled on
the ground, which cannot be
gathered up again. Yet God
does not take away a life; but
He devises means, so that His
banished ones are not ex-
pelled from Him. 15Now therefore, I have come to speak of
this thing to my lord the king
because the people have made
me afraid. And your maid-
servant said, 'I will now speak
to the king; it may be that the
king will perform the request
of his maidservant. 16For the
king will hear and deliver his
maidservant from the hand
of the man *who would* destroy
me and my son together from
the inheritance of God.' 17Your
maidservant said, 'The word
of my lord the king will now be
comforting; for as the angel
of God, so *is* my lord the king
in discerning good and evil.
And may the LORD your God
be with you.'"

18Then the king answered
and said to the woman,
"Please do not hide from me
anything that I ask you."

And the woman said,
"Please, let my lord the king
speak."

19So the king said, "*Is* the

hand of Joab with you in all
this?" And the woman an-
swered and said, "*As* you live,
my lord the king, no one can
turn to the right hand or to
the left from anything that
my lord the king has spoken.
For your servant Joab commanded me, and he put all
these words in the mouth
of your maidservant. 20To
bring about this change of
affairs your servant Joab has
done this thing; but my lord
is wise, according to the wisdom of the angel of God, to
know everything that *is* in the
earth."

21And the king said to Joab,
"All right, I have granted this
thing. Go therefore, bring back
the young man Absalom."

22Then Joab fell to the
ground on his face and bowed
himself, and thanked the king.
And Joab said, "Today your
servant knows that I have
found favor in your sight, my
lord, O king, in that the king
has fulfilled the request of his
servant." 23So Joab arose and
went to Geshur, and brought
Absalom to Jerusalem. 24And
the king said, "Let him return
to his own house, but do not
let him see my face." So Absalom returned to his own
house, but did not see the
king's face.

DAVID FORGIVES ABSALOM

25Now in all Israel there
was no one who was praised
as much as Absalom for his
good looks. From the sole of
his foot to the crown of his
head there was no blemish in
him. 26And when he cut the
hair of his head—at the end
of every year he cut *it* because
it was heavy on him—when
he cut it, he weighed the hair
of his head at two hundred
shekels according to the king's
standard. 27To Absalom were
born three sons, and one
daughter whose name *was*
Tamar. She was a woman of
beautiful appearance.

28And Absalom dwelt two
full years in Jerusalem, but
did not see the king's face.
29Therefore Absalom sent for
Joab, to send him to the king,
but he would not come to him.
And when he sent again the
second time, he would not
come. 30So he said to his servants, "See, Joab's field is near
mine, and he has barley there;
go and set it on fire." And Absalom's servants set the field
on fire.

31Then Joab arose and
came to Absalom's house, and
said to him, "Why have your
servants set my field on fire?"

32And Absalom answered
Joab, "Look, I sent to you, saying, 'Come here, so that I may
send you to the king, to say,
"Why have I come from Ge-
shur? *It would be* better for me
to be there still."' Now therefore, let me see the king's face;
but if there is iniquity in me,
let him execute me."

33So Joab went to the king

and told him. And when he
had called for Absalom, he
came to the king and bowed
himself on his face to the
ground before the king. Then
the king kissed Absalom.

ABSALOM'S TREASON

15 After this it happened
that Absalom provided
himself with chariots and
horses, and fifty men to run
before him. 2Now Absalom
would rise early and stand
beside the way to the gate.
So it was, whenever anyone
who had a lawsuit came to the
king for a decision, that Absalom would call to him and
say, "What city *are* you from?"
And he would say, "Your servant *is* from such and such a
tribe of Israel." 3Then Absalom would say to him, "Look,
your case *is* good and right;
but *there is* no deputy of the
king to hear you." 4Moreover
Absalom would say, "Oh,
that I were made judge in
the land, and everyone who
has any suit or cause would
come to me; then I would give
him justice." 5And *so* it was,
whenever anyone came near
to bow down to him, that he
would put out his hand and
take him and kiss him. 6In
this manner Absalom acted
toward all Israel who came
to the king for judgment. So
Absalom stole the hearts of
the men of Israel.

7Now it came to pass after
forty[a] years that Absalom
said to the king, "Please, let
me go to Hebron and pay
the vow which I made to the
LORD. 8For your servant took
a vow while I dwelt at Geshur
in Syria, saying, 'If the LORD
indeed brings me back to Jerusalem, then I will serve the
LORD.'"

9And the king said to him,
"Go in peace." So he arose and
went to Hebron.

10Then Absalom sent spies
throughout all the tribes of
Israel, saying, "As soon as
you hear the sound of the
trumpet, then you shall say,
'Absalom reigns in Hebron!'"
11And with Absalom went two
hundred men invited from Jerusalem, and they went along
innocently and did not know
anything. 12Then Absalom
sent for Ahithophel the Gilonite, David's counselor, from
his city—from Giloh—while
he offered sacrifices. And the
conspiracy grew strong, for
the people with Absalom continually increased in number.

DAVID ESCAPES FROM JERUSALEM

13Now a messenger came
to David, saying, "The hearts
of the men of Israel are with
Absalom."

14So David said to all his
servants who *were* with him
at Jerusalem, "Arise, and let

15:7 [a] Septuagint manuscripts, Syriac, and Josephus read *four*.

us flee, or we shall not escape
from Absalom. Make haste
to depart, lest he overtake us
suddenly and bring disaster
upon us, and strike the city
with the edge of the sword."

15And the king's servants
said to the king, "We *are* your
servants, *ready to do* whatever
my lord the king commands."
16Then the king went out with
all his household after him.
But the king left ten women,
concubines, to keep the house.
17And the king went out with
all the people after him, and
stopped at the outskirts.
18Then all his servants passed
before him; and all the Cherethites, all the Pelethites, and
all the Gittites, six hundred
men who had followed him
from Gath, passed before the
king.

19Then the king said to
Ittai the Gittite, "Why are you
also going with us? Return
and remain with the king.
For you *are* a foreigner and
also an exile from your own
place. 20In fact, you came *only*
yesterday. Should I make you
wander up and down with us
today, since I go I know not
where? Return, and take your
brethren back. Mercy and
truth *be* with you."

21But Ittai answered the
king and said, "*As* the LORD
lives, and as my lord the king
lives, surely in whatever place
my lord the king shall be,
whether in death or life, even
there also your servant will be."

22So David said to Ittai, "Go,
and cross over." Then Ittai the
Gittite and all his men and all
the little ones who *were* with
him crossed over. 23And all
the country wept with a loud
voice, and all the people
crossed over. The king himself
also crossed over the Brook
Kidron, and all the people
crossed over toward the way
of the wilderness.

24There was Zadok also,
and all the Levites with him,
bearing the ark of the covenant of God. And they set
down the ark of God, and
Abiathar went up until all the
people had finished crossing
over from the city. 25Then the
king said to Zadok, "Carry the
ark of God back into the city.
If I find favor in the eyes of
the LORD, He will bring me
back and show me *both* it and
His dwelling place. 26But if He
says thus: 'I have no delight
in you,' here I am, let Him do
to me as seems good to Him."
27The king also said to Zadok
the priest, "*Are* you *not* a seer?
Return to the city in peace,
and your two sons with you,
Ahimaaz your son, and Jonathan the son of Abiathar.
28See, I will wait in the plains
of the wilderness until word
comes from you to inform
me." 29Therefore Zadok and
Abiathar carried the ark of
God back to Jerusalem. And
they remained there.

30So David went up by the
Ascent of the *Mount of* Olives,

and wept as he went up; and
he had his head covered and
went barefoot. And all the
people who *were* with him
covered their heads and went
up, weeping as they went up.
31Then *someone* told David,
saying, "Ahithophel *is* among
the conspirators with Absalom." And David said, "O LORD,
I pray, turn the counsel of
Ahithophel into foolishness!"

32Now it happened when
David had come to the top *of
the mountain,* where he worshiped God—there was Hu-
shai the Archite coming to
meet him with his robe torn
and dust on his head. 33David
said to him, "If you go on with
me, then you will become a
burden to me. 34But if you return to the city, and say to Absalom, 'I will be your servant,
O king; *as* I *was* your father's
servant previously, so I *will*
now also *be* your servant,' then
you may defeat the counsel
of Ahithophel for me. 35And
do you not *have* Zadok and
Abiathar the priests with you
there? Therefore it will be *that*
whatever you hear from the
king's house, you shall tell
to Zadok and Abiathar the
priests. 36Indeed *they have*
there with them their two
sons, Ahimaaz, Zadok's *son,*
and Jonathan, Abiathar's *son;*
and by them you shall send
me everything you hear."

37So Hushai, David's friend,
went into the city. And Absalom came into Jerusalem.

MEPHIBOSHETH'S SERVANT

16 When David was a lit-
tle past the top *of the
mountain,* there was Ziba the
servant of Mephibosheth, who
met him with a couple of saddled donkeys, and on them
two hundred *loaves* of bread,
one hundred clusters of raisins, one hundred summer
fruits, and a skin of wine. 2And
the king said to Ziba, "What do
you mean to do with these?"

So Ziba said, "The donkeys
are for the king's household to
ride on, the bread and summer fruit for the young men
to eat, and the wine for those
who are faint in the wilderness to drink."

3Then the king said, "And
where *is* your master's son?"

And Ziba said to the king,
"Indeed he is staying in Jerusalem, for he said, 'Today the
house of Israel will restore the
kingdom of my father to me.'"

4So the king said to Ziba,
"Here, all that *belongs* to Mephibosheth *is* yours."

And Ziba said, "I humbly
bow before you, *that* I may
find favor in your sight, my
lord, O king!"

SHIMEI CURSES DAVID

5Now when King David
came to Bahurim, there was
a man from the family of the
house of Saul, whose name
was Shimei the son of Gera,
coming from there. He came
out, cursing continuously as

he came. 6And he threw stones
at David and at all the servants
of King David. And all the people and all the mighty men
were on his right hand and on
his left. 7Also Shimei said thus
when he cursed: "Come out!
Come out! You bloodthirsty
man, you rogue! 8The LORD
has brought upon you all the
blood of the house of Saul, in
whose place you have reigned;
and the LORD has delivered
the kingdom into the hand
of Absalom your son. So now
you *are caught* in your own
evil, because you are a bloodthirsty man!"

9Then Abishai the son of
Zeruiah said to the king, "Why
should this dead dog curse my
lord the king? Please, let me
go over and take off his head!"

10But the king said, "What
have I to do with you, you sons
of Zeruiah? So let him curse,
because the LORD has said
to him, 'Curse David.' Who
then shall say, 'Why have you
done so?'"

11And David said to Abishai
and all his servants, "See how
my son who came from my
own body seeks my life. How
much more now *may this* Benjamite? Let him alone, and let
him curse; for so the LORD has
ordered him. 12It may be that
the LORD will look on my affliction,[a] and that the LORD
will repay me with good for
his cursing this day." 13And as
David and his men went along
the road, Shimei went along
the hillside opposite him
and cursed as he went, threw
stones at him and kicked up
dust. 14Now the king and all
the people who *were* with
him became weary; so they
refreshed themselves there.

THE ADVICE OF AHITHOPHEL

15Meanwhile Absalom and
all the people, the men of Israel, came to Jerusalem; and
Ahithophel *was* with him.
16And so it was, when Hushai
the Archite, David's friend,
came to Absalom, that Hushai
said to Absalom, "*Long* live
the king! *Long* live the king!"

17So Absalom said to Hu-
shai, "*Is* this your loyalty to
your friend? Why did you not
go with your friend?"

18And Hushai said to Ab-
salom, "No, but whom the
LORD and this people and all
the men of Israel choose, his I
will be, and with him I will remain. 19Furthermore, whom
should I serve? *Should I* not
serve in the presence of his
son? As I have served in your
father's presence, so will I be
in your presence."

20Then Absalom said to
Ahithophel, "Give advice as
to what we should do."

21And Ahithophel said to

16:12 [a] Following Kethib, Septuagint, Syriac, and Vulgate; Qere reads *my eyes;* Targum reads *tears of my eyes*.

Absalom, "Go in to your father's concubines, whom he has left to keep the house; and all Israel will hear that you are abhorred by your father. Then the hands of all who are with you will be strong." 22So they pitched a tent for Absalom on the top of the house, and Absalom went in to his father's concubines in the sight of all Israel.

23Now the advice of Ahithophel, which he gave in those days, *was* as if one had inquired at the oracle of God. So *was* all the advice of Ahithophel both with David and with Absalom.

17 Moreover Ahithophel said to Absalom, "Now let me choose twelve thousand men, and I will arise and pursue David tonight. 2I will come upon him while he *is* weary and weak, and make him afraid. And all the people who *are* with him will flee, and I will strike only the king. 3Then I will bring back all the people to you. When all return except the man whom you seek, all the people will be at peace." 4And the saying pleased Absalom and all the elders of Israel.

THE ADVICE OF HUSHAI

5Then Absalom said, "Now call Hushai the Archite also, and let us hear what he says too." 6And when Hushai came to Absalom, Absalom spoke to him, saying, "Ahithophel has spoken in this manner. Shall we do as he says? If not, speak up."

7So Hushai said to Absalom: "The advice that Ahithophel has given *is* not good at this time. 8For," said Hushai, "you know your father and his men, that they *are* mighty men, and they *are* enraged in their minds, like a bear robbed of her cubs in the field; and your father *is* a man of war, and will not camp with the people. 9Surely by now he is hidden in some pit, or in some *other* place. And it will be, when some of them are overthrown at the first, that whoever hears *it* will say, 'There is a slaughter among the people who follow Absalom.' 10And even he *who is* valiant, whose heart *is* like the heart of a lion, will melt completely. For all Israel knows that your father *is* a mighty man, and *those* who *are* with him *are* valiant men. 11Therefore I advise that all Israel be fully gathered to you, from Dan to Beersheba, like the sand that *is* by the sea for multitude, and that you go to battle in person. 12So we will come upon him in some place where he may be found, and we will fall on him as the dew falls on the ground. And of him and all the men who *are* with him there shall not be left so much as one. 13Moreover, if he has withdrawn into a city, then all Israel shall bring ropes to that city; and we will pull it into the river,

until there is not one small
stone found there."
[14]So Absalom and all the
men of Israel said, "The advice of Hushai the Archite
is better than the advice of
Ahithophel." For the LORD had
purposed to defeat the good
advice of Ahithophel, to the
intent that the LORD might
bring disaster on Absalom.

HUSHAI WARNS DAVID TO ESCAPE

[15]Then Hushai said to Zadok
and Abiathar the priests, "Thus
and so Ahithophel advised Absalom and the elders of Israel,
and thus and so I have advised.
[16]Now therefore, send quickly
and tell David, saying, 'Do not
spend this night in the plains
of the wilderness, but speedily
cross over, lest the king and all
the people who *are* with him
be swallowed up.'" [17]Now Jonathan and Ahimaaz stayed at
En Rogel, for they dared not
be seen coming into the city;
so a female servant would
come and tell them, and
they would go and tell King
David. [18]Nevertheless a lad
saw them, and told Absalom.
But both of them went away
quickly and came to a man's
house in Bahurim, who had
a well in his court; and they
went down into it. [19]Then the
woman took and spread a covering over the well's mouth,
and spread ground grain on it;
and the thing was not known.
[20]And when Absalom's servants came to the woman at
the house, they said, "Where
are Ahimaaz and Jonathan?"

So the woman said to them,
"They have gone over the
water brook."

And when they had
searched and could not find
them, they returned to Jerusalem. [21]Now it came to pass,
after they had departed, that
they came up out of the well
and went and told King David,
and said to David, "Arise and
cross over the water quickly.
For thus has Ahithophel advised against you." [22]So David
and all the people who *were*
with him arose and crossed
over the Jordan. By morning
light not one of them was left
who had not gone over the
Jordan.

[23]Now when Ahithophel
saw that his advice was not
followed, he saddled a donkey,
and arose and went home to
his house, to his city. Then he
put his household in order,
and hanged himself, and died;
and he was buried in his father's tomb.

[24]Then David went to Mahanaim. And Absalom crossed
over the Jordan, he and all the
men of Israel with him. [25]And
Absalom made Amasa captain
of the army instead of Joab.
This Amasa *was* the son of a
man whose name *was* Jithra,[a]

17:25 [a] Spelled *Jether* in 1 Chronicles 2:17 and elsewhere

an Israelite,[b] who had gone in to Abigail the daughter of Nahash, sister of Zeruiah, Joab's mother. 26So Israel and Absalom encamped in the land of Gilead.

27Now it happened, when David had come to Mahanaim, that Shobi the son of Nahash from Rabbah of the people of Ammon, Machir the son of Ammiel from Lo Debar, and Barzillai the Gileadite from Rogelim, 28brought beds and basins, earthen vessels and wheat, barley and flour, parched *grain* and beans, lentils and parched *seeds,* 29honey and curds, sheep and cheese of the herd, for David and the people who *were* with him to eat. For they said, "The people are hungry and weary and thirsty in the wilderness."

ABSALOM'S DEFEAT AND DEATH

18 And David numbered the people who *were* with him, and set captains of thousands and captains of hundreds over them. 2Then David sent out one third of the people under the hand of Joab, one third under the hand of Abishai the son of Zeruiah, Joab's brother, and one third under the hand of Ittai the Gittite. And the king said to the people, "I also will surely go out with you myself."

3But the people answered, "You shall not go out! For if we flee away, they will not care about us; nor if half of us die, will they care about us. But *you are* worth ten thousand of us now. For you are now more help to us in the city."

4Then the king said to them, "Whatever seems best to you I will do." So the king stood beside the gate, and all the people went out by hundreds and by thousands. 5Now the king had commanded Joab, Abishai, and Ittai, saying, "*Deal* gently for my sake with the young man Absalom." And all the people heard when the king gave all the captains orders concerning Absalom.

6So the people went out into the field of battle against Israel. And the battle was in the woods of Ephraim. 7The people of Israel were overthrown there before the servants of David, and a great slaughter of twenty thousand took place there that day. 8For the battle there was scattered over the face of the whole countryside, and the woods devoured more people that day than the sword devoured.

9Then Absalom met the servants of David. Absalom rode on a mule. The mule went

17:25 [b] Following Masoretic Text, some manuscripts of the Septuagint, and Targum; some manuscripts of the Septuagint read *Ishmaelite* (compare 1 Chronicles 2:17); Vulgate reads *of Jezrael.*

under the thick boughs of a great terebinth tree, and his head caught in the terebinth; so he was left hanging between heaven and earth. And the mule which *was* under him went on.
[10]Now a certain man saw *it* and told Joab, and said, "I just saw Absalom hanging in a terebinth tree!"

[11]So Joab said to the man who told him, "You just saw *him!* And why did you not strike him there to the ground? I would have given you ten *shekels* of silver and a belt."

[12]But the man said to Joab, "Though I were to receive a thousand *shekels* of silver in my hand, I would not raise my hand against the king's son. For in our hearing the king commanded you and Abishai and Ittai, saying, 'Beware lest anyone *touch* the young man Absalom!'[a]
[13]Otherwise I would have dealt falsely against my own life. For there is nothing hidden from the king, and you yourself would have set yourself against *me.*"

[14]Then Joab said, "I cannot linger with you." And he took three spears in his hand and thrust them through Absalom's heart, while he was *still* alive in the midst of the terebinth tree.
[15]And ten young men who bore Joab's armor *surrounded Absalom, and* struck and killed him.

[16]So Joab blew the trumpet, and the people returned from pursuing Israel. For Joab held back the people.
[17]And they took Absalom and cast him into a large pit in the woods, and laid a very large heap of stones over him. Then all Israel fled, everyone to his tent.

[18]Now Absalom in his lifetime had taken and set up a pillar for himself, which *is* in the King's Valley. For he said, "I have no son to keep my name in remembrance." He called the pillar after his own name. And to this day it is called Absalom's Monument.

DAVID HEARS OF ABSALOM'S DEATH

[19]Then Ahimaaz the son of Zadok said, "Let me run now and take the news to the king, how the LORD has avenged him of his enemies."

[20]And Joab said to him, "You shall not take the news this day, for you shall take the news another day. But today you shall take no news, because the king's son is dead."
[21]Then Joab said to the Cushite, "Go, tell the king what you have seen." So the Cushite bowed himself to Joab and ran.

[22]And Ahimaaz the son of Zadok said again to Joab, "But whatever happens, please let me also run after the Cushite."

So Joab said, "Why will you

18:12 [a] The ancient versions read *'Protect the young man Absalom for me!'*

run, my son, since you have
no news ready?”
23“But whatever happens,”
he said, “let me run.”
So he said to him, “Run.”
Then Ahimaaz ran by way
of the plain, and outran the
Cushite.
24Now David was sitting between the two gates. And the
watchman went up to the roof
over the gate, to the wall, lifted
his eyes and looked, and there
was a man, running alone.
25Then the watchman cried
out and told the king. And the
king said, “If he *is* alone, *there*
is news in his mouth.” And he
came rapidly and drew near.
26Then the watchman saw
another man running, and
the watchman called to the
gatekeeper and said, “There is
another man, running alone!”
And the king said, “He also
brings news.”
27So the watchman said, “I
think the running of the first
is like the running of Ahimaaz
the son of Zadok.”
And the king said, “He *is*
a good man, and comes with
good news.”
28So Ahimaaz called out
and said to the king, “All is
well!” Then he bowed down
with his face to the earth
before the king, and said,
“Blessed *be* the LORD your
God, who has delivered up the
men who raised their hand
against my lord the king!”
29The king said, “Is the
young man Absalom safe?”
Ahimaaz answered, “When
Joab sent the king’s servant
and *me* your servant, I saw
a great tumult, but I did not
know what *it was about.*”
30And the king said, “Turn
aside *and* stand here.” So he
turned aside and stood still.
31Just then the Cushite
came, and the Cushite said,
“There is good news, my lord
the king! For the LORD has
avenged you this day of all
those who rose against you.”
32And the king said to the
Cushite, “Is the young man
Absalom safe?”
So the Cushite answered,
“May the enemies of my lord
the king, and all who rise
against you to do harm, be
like *that* young man!”

DAVID’S MOURNING FOR ABSALOM

33Then the king was deeply
moved, and went up to the
chamber over the gate, and
wept. And as he went, he said
thus: “O my son Absalom—my
son, my son Absalom—if only
I had died in your place! O Absalom my son, my son!”
19 And Joab was told,
“Behold, the king is
weeping and mourning for
Absalom.” 2So the victory that
day was *turned* into mourning for all the people. For the
people heard it said that day,
“The king is grieved for his
son.” 3And the people stole
back into the city that day, as
people who are ashamed steal

away when they flee in battle. 4But the king covered his face, and the king cried out with a loud voice, "O my son Absalom! O Absalom, my son, my son!"

5Then Joab came into the house to the king, and said, "Today you have disgraced all your servants who today have saved your life, the lives of your sons and daughters, the lives of your wives and the lives of your concubines, 6in that you love your enemies and hate your friends. For you have declared today that you regard neither princes nor servants; for today I perceive that if Absalom had lived and all of us had died today, then it would have pleased you well. 7Now therefore, arise, go out and speak comfort to your servants. For I swear by the LORD, if you do not go out, not one will stay with you this night. And that will be worse for you than all the evil that has befallen you from your youth until now." 8Then the king arose and sat in the gate. And they told all the people, saying, "There is the king, sitting in the gate." So all the people came before the king.

For everyone of Israel had fled to his tent.

DAVID RETURNS TO JERUSALEM

9Now all the people were in a dispute throughout all the tribes of Israel, saying, "The king saved us from the hand of our enemies, he delivered us from the hand of the Philistines, and now he has fled from the land because of Absalom. 10But Absalom, whom we anointed over us, has died in battle. Now therefore, why do you say nothing about bringing back the king?"

11So King David sent to Zadok and Abiathar the priests, saying, "Speak to the elders of Judah, saying, 'Why are you the last to bring the king back to his house, since the words of all Israel have come to the king, to his *very* house? 12You *are* my brethren, you *are* my bone and my flesh. Why then are you the last to bring back the king?' 13And say to Amasa, '*Are* you not my bone and my flesh? God do so to me, and more also, if you are not commander of the army before me continually in place of Joab.'" 14So he swayed the hearts of all the men of Judah, just as *the heart of* one man, so that they sent *this word* to the king: "Return, you and all your servants!"

15Then the king returned and came to the Jordan. And Judah came to Gilgal, to go to meet the king, to escort the king across the Jordan. 16And Shimei the son of Gera, a Benjamite, who *was* from Bahurim, hurried and came down with the men of Judah to meet King David. 17*There were* a thousand men of Ben-

jamin with him, and Ziba the
servant of the house of Saul,
and his fifteen sons and his
twenty servants with him;
and they went over the Jordan before the king. [18]Then a
ferryboat went across to carry
over the king's household,
and to do what he thought
good.

DAVID'S MERCY TO SHIMEI

Now Shimei the son of
Gera fell down before the king
when he had crossed the Jordan. [19]Then he said to the king,
"Do not let my lord impute
iniquity to me, or remember
what wrong your servant did
on the day that my lord the
king left Jerusalem, that the
king should take *it* to heart.
[20]For I, your servant, know
that I have sinned. Therefore
here I am, the first to come
today of all the house of Joseph to go down to meet my
lord the king."

[21]But Abishai the son of
Zeruiah answered and said,
"Shall not Shimei be put to
death for this, because he
cursed the LORD's anointed?"

[22]And David said, "What
have I to do with you, you sons
of Zeruiah, that you should
be adversaries to me today?
Shall any man be put to death
today in Israel? For do I not
know that today I *am* king
over Israel?" [23]Therefore the
king said to Shimei, "You shall
not die." And the king swore
to him.

DAVID AND MEPHIBOSHETH MEET

[24]Now Mephibosheth the
son of Saul came down to
meet the king. And he had
not cared for his feet, nor
trimmed his mustache, nor
washed his clothes, from the
day the king departed until
the day he returned in peace.
[25]So it was, when he had
come to Jerusalem to meet
the king, that the king said to
him, "Why did you not go with
me, Mephibosheth?"

[26]And he answered, "My
lord, O king, my servant deceived me. For your servant
said, 'I will saddle a donkey
for myself, that I may ride on
it and go to the king,' because
your servant *is* lame. [27]And he
has slandered your servant
to my lord the king, but my
lord the king *is* like the angel
of God. Therefore do *what is*
good in your eyes. [28]For all
my father's house were but
dead men before my lord the
king. Yet you set your servant
among those who eat at your
own table. Therefore what
right have I still to cry out
anymore to the king?"

[29]So the king said to him,
"Why do you speak anymore
of your matters? I have said,
'You and Ziba divide the
land.'"

[30]Then Mephibosheth said
to the king, "Rather, let him
take it all, inasmuch as my
lord the king has come back
in peace to his own house."

DAVID'S KINDNESS TO BARZILLAI

31And Barzillai the Gileadite
came down from Rogelim and
went across the Jordan with
the king, to escort him across
the Jordan. 32Now Barzillai
was a very aged man, eighty
years old. And he had provided the king with supplies
while he stayed at Mahanaim,
for he *was* a very rich man.
33And the king said to Barzillai, "Come across with me, and
I will provide for you while you
are with me in Jerusalem."

34But Barzillai said to the
king, "How long have I to live,
that I should go up with the
king to Jerusalem? 35I *am*
today eighty years old. Can
I discern between the good
and bad? Can your servant
taste what I eat or what I
drink? Can I hear any longer
the voice of singing men and
singing women? Why then
should your servant be a further burden to my lord the
king? 36Your servant will go
a little way across the Jordan
with the king. And why should
the king repay me *with* such a
reward? 37Please let your servant turn back again, that I
may die in my own city, near
the grave of my father and
mother. But here is your servant Chimham; let him cross
over with my lord the king,
and do for him what seems
good to you."

38And the king answered,
"Chimham shall cross over
with me, and I will do for him
what seems good to you. Now
whatever you request of me,
I will do for you." 39Then all
the people went over the Jordan. And when the king had
crossed over, the king kissed
Barzillai and blessed him, and
he returned to his own place.

THE QUARREL ABOUT THE KING

40Now the king went on to
Gilgal, and Chimham[a] went
on with him. And all the people of Judah escorted the king,
and also half the people of Israel. 41Just then all the men
of Israel came to the king,
and said to the king, "Why
have our brethren, the men
of Judah, stolen you away and
brought the king, his household, and all David's men with
him across the Jordan?"

42So all the men of Judah
answered the men of Israel,
"Because the king *is* a close
relative of ours. Why then
are you angry over this matter? Have we ever eaten at
the king's *expense?* Or has he
given us any gift?"

43And the men of Israel
answered the men of Judah,
and said, "We have ten shares
in the king; therefore we also
have more *right* to David
than you. Why then do you
despise us—were we not the

19:40 [a] Masoretic Text reads *Chimhan.*

first to advise bringing back
our king?"

Yet the words of the men
of Judah were fiercer than the
words of the men of Israel.

THE REBELLION OF SHEBA

20 And there happened
to be there a rebel,[a]
whose name *was* Sheba the
son of Bichri, a Benjamite.
And he blew a trumpet, and
said:

"We have no share
in David,
Nor do we have
inheritance in the
son of Jesse;
Every man to his
tents, O Israel!"

2So every man of Israel deserted David, *and* followed
Sheba the son of Bichri. But
the men of Judah, from the
Jordan as far as Jerusalem,
remained loyal to their king.
3Now David came to his
house at Jerusalem. And the
king took the ten women, his
concubines whom he had left
to keep the house, and put
them in seclusion and supported them, but did not go
in to them. So they were shut
up to the day of their death,
living in widowhood.
4And the king said to
Amasa, "Assemble the men
of Judah for me within three
days, and be present here
yourself." 5So Amasa went to
assemble *the men of* Judah.
But he delayed longer than
the set time which David had
appointed him. 6And David
said to Abishai, "Now Sheba
the son of Bichri will do us
more harm than Absalom.
Take your lord's servants and
pursue him, lest he find for
himself fortified cities, and
escape us." 7So Joab's men,
with the Cherethites, the Pelethites, and all the mighty
men, went out after him. And
they went out of Jerusalem
to pursue Sheba the son of
Bichri. 8When they *were* at
the large stone which *is* in
Gibeon, Amasa came before
them. Now Joab was dressed
in battle armor; on it was a
belt *with* a sword fastened
in its sheath at his hips; and
as he was going forward, it
fell out. 9Then Joab said to
Amasa, "*Are* you in health,
my brother?" And Joab took
Amasa by the beard with his
right hand to kiss him. 10But
Amasa did not notice the
sword that *was* in Joab's hand.
And he struck him with it in
the stomach, and his entrails
poured out on the ground;
and he did not *strike* him
again. Thus he died.

Then Joab and Abishai his
brother pursued Sheba the
son of Bichri. 11Meanwhile
one of Joab's men stood near
Amasa, and said, "Whoever

20:1 [a] Literally *man of Belial*

favors Joab and whoever *is*
for David—follow Joab!" 12 But
Amasa wallowed in *his* blood
in the middle of the highway.
And when the man saw that
all the people stood still, he
moved Amasa from the highway to the field and threw a
garment over him, when he
saw that everyone who came
upon him halted. 13 When he
was removed from the highway, all the people went on
after Joab to pursue Sheba the
son of Bichri.

14 And he went through all
the tribes of Israel to Abel and
Beth Maachah and all the Be-
rites. So they were gathered
together and also went after
Sheba.[a] 15 Then they came and
besieged him in Abel of Beth
Maachah; and they cast up a
siege mound against the city,
and it stood by the rampart.
And all the people who *were*
with Joab battered the wall to
throw it down.

16 Then a wise woman cried
out from the city, "Hear, hear!
Please say to Joab, 'Come
nearby, that I may speak with
you.'" 17 When he had come
near to her, the woman said,
"*Are* you Joab?"

He answered, "I *am*."

Then she said to him,
"Hear the words of your maidservant."

And he answered, "I am
listening."

18 So she spoke, saying, "They
used to talk in former times,
saying, 'They shall surely seek
guidance at Abel,' and so they
would end *disputes*. 19 I *am*
among the peaceable *and* faithful in Israel. You seek to destroy
a city and a mother in Israel.
Why would you swallow up the
inheritance of the LORD?"

20 And Joab answered and
said, "Far be it, far be it from
me, that I should swallow up
or destroy! 21 That *is* not so. But
a man from the mountains
of Ephraim, Sheba the son of
Bichri by name, has raised his
hand against the king, against
David. Deliver him only, and I
will depart from the city."

So the woman said to
Joab, "Watch, his head will be
thrown to you over the wall."
22 Then the woman in her wisdom went to all the people.
And they cut off the head of
Sheba the son of Bichri, and
threw *it* out to Joab. Then he
blew a trumpet, and they withdrew from the city, every man
to his tent. So Joab returned
to the king at Jerusalem.

DAVID'S GOVERNMENT OFFICERS

23 And Joab *was* over all
the army of Israel; Bena-
iah the son of Jehoiada *was*
over the Cherethites and the
Pelethites; 24 Adoram *was* in
charge of revenue; Jehoshaphat the son of Ahilud *was*
recorder; 25 Sheva *was* scribe;

20:14 [a] Literally *him*

Zadok and Abiathar *were* the
priests; [26]and Ira the Jairite
was a chief minister under
David.

DAVID AVENGES THE GIBEONITES

21 Now there was a famine
in the days of David for
three years, year after year; and
David inquired of the LORD.
And the LORD answered, "*It is*
because of Saul and *his* bloodthirsty house, because he killed
the Gibeonites." [2]So the king
called the Gibeonites and
spoke to them. Now the Gibeonites *were* not of the children
of Israel, but of the remnant of
the Amorites; the children of
Israel had sworn protection
to them, but Saul had sought
to kill them in his zeal for the
children of Israel and Judah.
[3]Therefore David said to
the Gibeonites, "What shall
I do for you? And with what
shall I make atonement, that
you may bless the inheritance
of the LORD?"
[4]And the Gibeonites said to
him, "We will have no silver
or gold from Saul or from his
house, nor shall you kill any
man in Israel for us."
So he said, "Whatever you
say, I will do for you."
[5]Then they answered the
king, "As for the man who
consumed us and plotted
against us, *that* we should be
destroyed from remaining in
any of the territories of Israel,
[6]let seven men of his descendants be delivered to us, and
we will hang them before the
LORD in Gibeah of Saul, *whom*
the LORD chose."
And the king said, "I will
give *them*."
[7]But the king spared Mephibosheth the son of Jonathan, the son of Saul, because
of the LORD's oath that *was*
between them, between David
and Jonathan the son of Saul.
[8]So the king took Armoni and
Mephibosheth, the two sons of
Rizpah the daughter of Aiah,
whom she bore to Saul, and
the five sons of Michal[a] the
daughter of Saul, whom she
brought up for Adriel the son
of Barzillai the Meholathite;
[9]and he delivered them into
the hands of the Gibeonites,
and they hanged them on the
hill before the LORD. So they
fell, *all* seven together, and
were put to death in the days of
harvest, in the first *days*, in the
beginning of barley harvest.
[10]Now Rizpah the daugh-
ter of Aiah took sackcloth
and spread it for herself on
the rock, from the begin-
ning of harvest until the late
rains poured on them from
heaven. And she did not allow
the birds of the air to rest on
them by day nor the beasts of
the field by night.

21:8 [a] Or *Merab* (compare 1 Samuel 18:19 and 25:44; 2 Samuel 3:14 and 6:23)

11 And David was told what
Rizpah the daughter of Aiah,
the concubine of Saul, had
done. 12 Then David went and
took the bones of Saul, and
the bones of Jonathan his son,
from the men of Jabesh Gilead
who had stolen them from the
street of Beth Shan,[a] where
the Philistines had hung them
up, after the Philistines had
struck down Saul in Gilboa.
13 So he brought up the bones
of Saul and the bones of Jonathan his son from there; and
they gathered the bones of
those who had been hanged.
14 They buried the bones of
Saul and Jonathan his son
in the country of Benjamin
in Zelah, in the tomb of Kish
his father. So they performed
all that the king commanded.
And after that God heeded the
prayer for the land.

PHILISTINE GIANTS DESTROYED

15 When the Philistines were
at war again with Israel, David
and his servants with him went
down and fought against the
Philistines; and David grew
faint. 16 Then Ishbi-Benob,
who *was* one of the sons of
the giant, the weight of whose
bronze spear *was* three hundred *shekels,* who was bearing
a new *sword,* thought he could
kill David. 17 But Abishai the
son of Zeruiah came to his aid,
and struck the Philistine and
killed him. Then the men of
David swore to him, saying,
"You shall go out no more with
us to battle, lest you quench
the lamp of Israel."

18 Now it happened after-
ward that there was again a battle with the Philistines at Gob.
Then Sibbechai the Hushathite
killed Saph,[a] who *was* one of
the sons of the giant. 19 Again
there was war at Gob with the
Philistines, where Elhanan the
son of Jaare-Oregim[a] the Bethlehemite killed *the brother of*
Goliath the Gittite, the shaft of
whose spear *was* like a weaver's beam.

20 Yet again there was war at
Gath, where there was a man
of *great* stature, who had six
fingers on each hand and six
toes on each foot, twenty-four
in number; and he also was
born to the giant. 21 So when
he defied Israel, Jonathan
the son of Shimea,[a] David's
brother, killed him.

22 These four were born to
the giant in Gath, and fell by
the hand of David and by the
hand of his servants.

PRAISE FOR GOD'S DELIVERANCE

22 Then David spoke to
the Lord the words of
this song, on the day when the

21:12 [a] Spelled *Beth Shean* in Joshua 17:11 and elsewhere 21:18 [a] Spelled *Sippai* in 1 Chronicles 20:4 21:19 [a] Spelled *Jair* in 1 Chronicles 20:5 21:21 [a] Spelled *Shammah* in 1 Samuel 16:9 and elsewhere

LORD had delivered him from
the hand of all his enemies,
and from the hand of Saul.
2And he said:[a]

"The LORD *is* my rock
and my fortress
and my deliverer;
3 The God of my strength,
in whom I will trust;
My shield and the horn
of my salvation,
My stronghold and
my refuge;
My Savior, You save
me from violence.
4 I will call upon the
LORD, *who is worthy*
to be praised;
So shall I be saved
from my enemies.

5 "When the waves of
death surrounded me,
The floods of ungodliness
made me afraid.
6 The sorrows of Sheol
surrounded me;
The snares of death
confronted me.
7 In my distress I called
upon the LORD,
And cried out to
my God;
He heard my voice
from His temple,
And my cry *entered*
His ears.

8 "Then the earth shook
and trembled;
The foundations of
heaven[a] quaked
and were shaken,
Because He was angry.
9 Smoke went up from
His nostrils,
And devouring fire
from His mouth;
Coals were kindled
by it.
10 He bowed the heavens
also, and came down
With darkness
under His feet.
11 He rode upon a
cherub, and flew;
And He was seen[a] upon
the wings of the wind.
12 He made darkness
canopies around Him,
Dark waters *and* thick
clouds of the skies.
13 From the brightness
before Him
Coals of fire were kindled.

14 "The LORD thundered
from heaven,
And the Most High
uttered His voice.
15 He sent out arrows and
scattered them;
Lightning bolts, and He
vanquished them.
16 Then the channels of
the sea were seen,

22:2 [a] Compare Psalm 18 **22:8** [a] Following Masoretic Text, Septuagint, and Targum; Syriac and Vulgate read *hills* (compare Psalm 18:7). **22:11** [a] Following Masoretic Text and Septuagint; many Hebrew manuscripts, Syriac, and Vulgate read *He flew* (compare Psalm 18:10); Targum reads *He spoke with power*.

The foundations of the
world were uncovered,
At the rebuke of the LORD,
At the blast of the breath
of His nostrils.

17 "He sent from above,
He took me,
He drew me out of
many waters.
18 He delivered me from
my strong enemy,
From those who
hated me;
For they were too
strong for me.
19 They confronted me in
the day of my calamity,
But the LORD was
my support.
20 He also brought me out
into a broad place;
He delivered me because
He delighted in me.

21 "The LORD rewarded
me according to my
righteousness;
According to the
cleanness of my hands
He has recompensed me.
22 For I have kept the
ways of the LORD,
And have not wickedly
departed from my God.
23 For all His judgments
were before me;
And *as for* His statutes,
I did not depart
from them.
24 I was also blameless
before Him,
And I kept myself
from my iniquity.
25 Therefore the LORD
has recompensed
me according to my
righteousness,
According to my
cleanness in His eyes.[a]

26 "With the merciful
You will show
Yourself merciful;
With a blameless
man You will show
Yourself blameless;
27 With the pure You will
show Yourself pure;
And with the devious
You will show
Yourself shrewd.
28 You will save the
humble people;
But Your eyes *are* on the
haughty, *that* You may
bring *them* down.

29 "For You *are* my
lamp, O LORD;
The LORD shall enlighten
my darkness.
30 For by You I can run
against a troop;
By my God I can
leap over a wall.
31 *As for* God, His way
is perfect;
The word of the
LORD *is* proven;

22:25 [a] Septuagint, Syriac, and Vulgate read *the cleanness of my hands in His sight* (compare Psalm 18:24); Targum reads *my cleanness before His word.*

He *is* a shield to all
who trust in Him.

32 "For who *is* God,
except the LORD?
And who *is* a rock,
except our God?
33 God *is* my strength
and power,[a]
And He makes my[b]
way perfect.
34 He makes my[a] feet like
the *feet* of deer,
And sets me on my
high places.
35 He teaches my hands
to make war,
So that my arms can
bend a bow of bronze.

36 "You have also given
me the shield of
Your salvation;
Your gentleness has
made me great.
37 You enlarged my
path under me;
So my feet did not slip.

38 "I have pursued
my enemies and
destroyed them;
Neither did I turn
back again till they
were destroyed.
39 And I have destroyed
them and
wounded them,
So that they could
not rise;
They have fallen
under my feet.
40 For You have armed
me with strength
for the battle;
You have subdued
under me those who
rose against me.
41 You have also given
me the necks of
my enemies,
So that I destroyed
those who hated me.
42 They looked, but *there*
was none to save;
Even to the LORD, but He
did not answer them.
43 Then I beat them as fine
as the dust of the earth;
I trod them like dirt
in the streets,
And I spread them out.

44 "You have also delivered
me from the strivings
of my people;
You have kept me as the
head of the nations.
A people I have not
known shall serve me.
45 The foreigners
submit to me;
As soon as they hear,
they obey me.
46 The foreigners fade
away,

22:33 [a] Dead Sea Scrolls, Septuagint, Syriac, and Vulgate read *It is God who arms me with strength* (compare Psalm 18:32); Targum reads *It is God who sustains me with strength.* [b] Following Qere, Septuagint, Syriac, Targum, and Vulgate (compare Psalm 18:32); Kethib reads *His.* 22:34 [a] Following Qere, Septuagint, Syriac, Targum, and Vulgate (compare Psalm 18:33); Kethib reads *His.*

And come frightened[a]
from their hideouts.

47 "The LORD lives!
Blessed *be* my Rock!
Let God be exalted,
The Rock of my salvation!
48 *It is* God who avenges me,
And subdues the
peoples under me;
49 He delivers me from
my enemies.
You also lift me up
above those who
rise against me;
You have delivered me
from the violent man.
50 Therefore I will give
thanks to You, O LORD,
among the Gentiles,
And sing praises to
Your name.

51 "*He is* the tower of
salvation to His king,
And shows mercy to
His anointed,
To David and his
descendants
forevermore."

DAVID'S LAST WORDS

23 Now these *are* the last
words of David.

Thus says David the
son of Jesse;
Thus says the man
raised up on high,
The anointed of the
God of Jacob,
And the sweet
psalmist of Israel:

2 "The Spirit of the
LORD spoke by me,
And His word *was*
on my tongue.
3 The God of Israel said,
The Rock of Israel
spoke to me:
'He who rules over
men *must be* just,
Ruling in the fear of God.
4 And *he shall be* like the
light of the morning
when the sun rises,
A morning without clouds,
Like the tender grass
springing out of
the earth,
By clear shining after rain.'

5 "Although my house
is not so with God,
Yet He has made with me
an everlasting covenant,
Ordered in all *things*
and secure.
For *this is* all my salvation
and all *my* desire;
Will He not make
it increase?
6 But *the sons* of rebellion
shall all *be* as thorns
thrust away,
Because they cannot be
taken with hands.
7 But the man *who*
touches them
Must be armed with iron
and the shaft of a spear,

22:46 [a] Following Septuagint, Targum, and Vulgate (compare Psalm 18:45); Masoretic Text reads *gird themselves.*

And they shall be
utterly burned with
fire in *their* place."

DAVID'S MIGHTY MEN

8These *are* the names of
the mighty men whom David
had: Josheb-Basshebeth[a] the
Tachmonite, chief among
the captains.[b] He was called
Adino the Eznite, because he
had killed eight hundred men
at one time. 9And after him
was Eleazar the son of Dodo,[a]
the Ahohite, *one* of the three
mighty men with David when
they defied the Philistines
who were gathered there for
battle, and the men of Israel
had retreated. 10He arose and
attacked the Philistines until
his hand was weary, and his
hand stuck to the sword. The
LORD brought about a great
victory that day; and the people returned after him only
to plunder. 11And after him
was Shammah the son of Agee
the Hararite. The Philistines
had gathered together into a
troop where there was a piece
of ground full of lentils. So
the people fled from the Philistines. 12But he stationed
himself in the middle of the
field, defended it, and killed
the Philistines. So the LORD
brought about a great victory.
13Then three of the thirty
chief men went down at harvest
time and came to David at the
cave of Adullam. And the troop
of Philistines encamped in the
Valley of Rephaim. 14David
was then in the stronghold,
and the garrison of the Philistines *was* then *in* Bethlehem.
15And David said with longing,
"Oh, that someone would give
me a drink of the water from
the well of Bethlehem, which
is by the gate!" 16So the three
mighty men broke through the
camp of the Philistines, drew
water from the well of Bethlehem that *was* by the gate,
and took it and brought *it* to
David. Nevertheless he would
not drink it, but poured it out
to the LORD. 17And he said, "Far
be it from me, O LORD, that I
should do this! Is *this not* the
blood of the men who went in
jeopardy of their lives?" Therefore he would not drink it.

These things were done by
the three mighty men.

18Now Abishai the brother
of Joab, the son of Zeruiah,
was chief of *another* three.[a] He
lifted his spear against three
hundred *men,* killed *them,*
and won a name among *these*
three. 19Was he not the most
honored of three? Therefore
he became their captain. However, he did not attain to the
first three.

23:8 [a] Literally *One Who Sits in the Seat* (compare 1 Chronicles 11:11) [b] Following Masoretic Text and Targum; Septuagint and Vulgate read *the three.* 23:9 [a] Spelled *Dodai* in 1 Chronicles 27:4 23:18 [a] Following Masoretic Text, Septuagint, and Vulgate; some Hebrew manuscripts and Syriac read *thirty;* Targum reads *the mighty men.*

20Benaiah *was* the son of Jehoiada, the son of a valiant man
from Kabzeel, who had done
many deeds. He had killed two
lion-like heroes of Moab. He
also had gone down and killed
a lion in the midst of a pit on a
snowy day. 21And he killed an
Egyptian, a spectacular man.
The Egyptian *had* a spear in
his hand; so he went down to
him with a staff, wrested the
spear out of the Egyptian's
hand, and killed him with his
own spear. 22These *things* Benaiah the son of Jehoiada did,
and won a name among three
mighty men. 23He was more
honored than the thirty, but he
did not attain to the *first* three.
And David appointed him over
his guard.

24Asahel the brother of
Joab *was* one of the thirty;
Elhanan the son of Dodo of
Bethlehem, 25Shammah the
Harodite, Elika the Harodite,
26Helez the Paltite, Ira the son
of Ikkesh the Tekoite, 27Abie-
zer the Anathothite, Mebunnai
the Hushathite, 28Zalmon the
Ahohite, Maharai the Netophathite, 29Heleb the son of Baanah (the Netophathite), Ittai
the son of Ribai from Gibeah
of the children of Benjamin,
30Benaiah a Pirathonite, Hiddai from the brooks of Gaash,
31Abi-Albon the Arbathite, Azmaveth the Barhumite, 32Eli-
ahba the Shaalbonite (of the
sons of Jashen), Jonathan,
33Shammah the Hararite,
Ahiam the son of Sharar the
Hararite, 34Eliphelet the son
of Ahasbai, the son of the
Maachathite, Eliam the son
of Ahithophel the Gilonite,
35Hezrai[a] the Carmelite, Pa-
arai the Arbite, 36Igal the son
of Nathan of Zobah, Bani the
Gadite, 37Zelek the Ammonite, Naharai the Beerothite
(armorbearer of Joab the son
of Zeruiah), 38Ira the Ithrite,
Gareb the Ithrite, 39*and* Uriah
the Hittite: thirty-seven in all.

DAVID'S CENSUS OF ISRAEL AND JUDAH

24 Again the anger of
the LORD was aroused
against Israel, and He moved
David against them to say, "Go,
number Israel and Judah."

2So the king said to Joab
the commander of the army
who *was* with him, "Now go
throughout all the tribes of
Israel, from Dan to Beersheba,
and count the people, that I
may know the number of the
people."

3And Joab said to the king,
"Now may the LORD your God
add to the people a hundred
times more than there are, and
may the eyes of my lord the
king see *it*. But why does my
lord the king desire this thing?"
4Nevertheless the king's word
prevailed against Joab and
against the captains of the
army. Therefore Joab and the

23:35 [a] Spelled *Hezro* in 1 Chronicles 11:37

captains of the army went out
from the presence of the king
to count the people of Israel.
5And they crossed over the
Jordan and camped in Aroer,
on the right side of the town
which *is* in the midst of the ravine of Gad, and toward Jazer.
6Then they came to Gilead and
to the land of Tahtim Hodshi;
they came to Dan Jaan and
around to Sidon; 7and they
came to the stronghold of Tyre
and to all the cities of the Hivites and the Canaanites. Then
they went out to South Judah
as far as Beersheba. 8So when
they had gone through all the
land, they came to Jerusalem
at the end of nine months and
twenty days. 9Then Joab gave
the sum of the number of the
people to the king. And there
were in Israel eight hundred
thousand valiant men who
drew the sword, and the men
of Judah were five hundred
thousand men.

THE JUDGMENT ON DAVID'S SIN

10And David's heart con-
demned him after he had
numbered the people. So
David said to the LORD, "I have
sinned greatly in what I have
done; but now, I pray, O LORD,
take away the iniquity of Your
servant, for I have done very
foolishly."
11Now when David arose
in the morning, the word of
the LORD came to the prophet
Gad, David's seer, saying, 12"Go
and tell David, 'Thus says the
LORD: "I offer you three *things;*
choose one of them for yourself, that I may do *it* to you." ' "
13So Gad came to David and
told him; and he said to him,
"Shall seven[a] years of famine
come to you in your land? Or
shall you flee three months
before your enemies, while
they pursue you? Or shall
there be three days' plague in
your land? Now consider and
see what answer I should take
back to Him who sent me."
14And David said to Gad, "I
am in great distress. Please
let us fall into the hand of
the LORD, for His mercies *are*
great; but do not let me fall
into the hand of man."
15So the LORD sent a plague
upon Israel from the morning
till the appointed time. From
Dan to Beersheba seventy
thousand men of the people
died. 16And when the angel[a]
stretched out His hand over
Jerusalem to destroy it, the
LORD relented from the destruction, and said to the angel
who was destroying the people, "It is enough; now restrain
your hand." And the angel of
the LORD was by the threshing
floor of Araunah[b] the Jebusite.

24:13 [a] Following Masoretic Text, Syriac, Targum, and Vulgate; Septuagint reads *three* (compare 1 Chronicles 21:12).
24:16 [a] Or *Angel* [b] Spelled *Ornan* in 1 Chronicles 21:15

[17]Then David spoke to the
LORD when he saw the angel
who was striking the people,
and said, "Surely I have sinned,
and I have done wickedly; but
these sheep, what have they
done? Let Your hand, I pray,
be against me and against my
father's house."

THE ALTAR ON THE THRESHING FLOOR

[18]And Gad came that day
to David and said to him,
"Go up, erect an altar to the
LORD on the threshing floor
of Araunah the Jebusite." [19]So
David, according to the word
of Gad, went up as the LORD
commanded. [20]Now Araunah
looked, and saw the king and
his servants coming toward
him. So Araunah went out and
bowed before the king with
his face to the ground.

[21]Then Araunah said, "Why
has my lord the king come to
his servant?"

And David said, "To buy the
threshing floor from you, to
build an altar to the LORD, that
the plague may be withdrawn
from the people."

[22]Now Araunah said to
David, "Let my lord the king
take and offer up whatever
seems good to him. Look, *here*
are oxen for burnt sacrifice,
and threshing implements and
the yokes of the oxen for wood.
[23]All these, O king, Araunah
has given to the king."

And Araunah said to the
king, "May the LORD your God
accept you."

[24]Then the king said to
Araunah, "No, but I will surely
buy *it* from you for a price; nor
will I offer burnt offerings to
the LORD my God with that
which costs me nothing." So
David bought the threshing
floor and the oxen for fifty
shekels of silver. [25]And David
built there an altar to the
LORD, and offered burnt offerings and peace offerings. So
the LORD heeded the prayers
for the land, and the plague
was withdrawn from Israel.

THE FIRST BOOK OF THE KINGS

ADONIJAH PRESUMES TO BE KING

1 Now King David was old,
advanced in years; and they
put covers on him, but he
could not get warm. [2]There-
fore his servants said to him,
"Let a young woman, a virgin, be sought for our lord
the king, and let her stand

before the king, and let her
care for him; and let her lie
in your bosom, that our lord
the king may be warm." 3So
they sought for a lovely young
woman throughout all the
territory of Israel, and found
Abishag the Shunammite,
and brought her to the king.
4The young woman *was* very
lovely; and she cared for the
king, and served him; but the
king did not know her.

5Then Adonijah the son of
Haggith exalted himself, saying, "I will be king"; and he
prepared for himself chariots
and horsemen, and fifty men
to run before him. 6(And his
father had not rebuked him
at any time by saying, "Why
have you done so?" He *was*
also very good-looking. *His
mother* had borne him after
Absalom.) 7Then he conferred
with Joab the son of Zeruiah
and with Abiathar the priest,
and they followed and helped
Adonijah. 8But Zadok the
priest, Benaiah the son of Jehoiada, Nathan the prophet,
Shimei, Rei, and the mighty
men who *belonged* to David
were not with Adonijah.

9And Adonijah sacrificed
sheep and oxen and fattened
cattle by the stone of Zoheleth,
which *is* by En Rogel; he also invited all his brothers, the king's
sons, and all the men of Judah,
the king's servants. 10But he did
not invite Nathan the prophet,
Benaiah, the mighty men, or
Solomon his brother.

11So Nathan spoke to Bathsheba the mother of Sol-
omon, saying, "Have you not
heard that Adonijah the son
of Haggith has become king,
and David our lord does not
know *it?* 12Come, please, let
me now give you advice, that
you may save your own life
and the life of your son Solomon. 13Go immediately to
King David and say to him,
'Did you not, my lord, O king,
swear to your maidservant,
saying, "Assuredly your son
Solomon shall reign after me,
and he shall sit on my throne"?
Why then has Adonijah be-
come king?' 14Then, while you
are still talking there with the
king, I also will come in after
you and confirm your words."

15So Bathsheba went into
the chamber to the king. (Now
the king was very old, and Abishag the Shunammite was
serving the king.) 16And Bathsheba bowed and did homage
to the king. Then the king said,
"What is your wish?"

17Then she said to him, "My
lord, you swore by the LORD
your God to your maidservant,
saying, 'Assuredly Solomon
your son shall reign after me,
and he shall sit on my throne.'
18So now, look! Adonijah has
become king; and now, my
lord the king, you do not know
about *it.* 19He has sacrificed
oxen and fattened cattle and
sheep in abundance, and has
invited all the sons of the king,
Abiathar the priest, and Joab

the commander of the army;
but Solomon your servant he
has not invited. 20And as for
you, my lord, O king, the eyes
of all Israel *are* on you, that
you should tell them who will
sit on the throne of my lord
the king after him. 21Otherwise
it will happen, when my lord
the king rests with his fathers,
that I and my son Solomon
will be counted as offenders."
22And just then, while she
was still talking with the king,
Nathan the prophet also came
in. 23So they told the king,
saying, "Here is Nathan the
prophet." And when he came
in before the king, he bowed
down before the king with his
face to the ground. 24And Nathan said, "My lord, O king,
have you said, 'Adonijah shall
reign after me, and he shall sit
on my throne'? 25For he has
gone down today, and has sacrificed oxen and fattened cattle and sheep in abundance,
and has invited all the king's
sons, and the commanders
of the army, and Abiathar the
priest; and look! They are eating and drinking before him;
and they say, '*Long* live King
Adonijah!' 26But he has not invited me—me your servant—
nor Zadok the priest, nor
Benaiah the son of Jehoiada,
nor your servant Solomon.
27*Has this thing* been done
by my lord the king, and you
have not told your servant
who should sit on the throne
of my lord the king after him?"

DAVID PROCLAIMS SOLOMON KING

28Then King David an-
swered and said, "Call Bathsheba to me." So she came
into the king's presence and
stood before the king. 29And
the king took an oath and said,
"*As* the LORD lives, who has
redeemed my life from every
distress, 30just as I swore to
you by the LORD God of Israel, saying, 'Assuredly Solomon your son shall be king
after me, and he shall sit on
my throne in my place,' so I
certainly will do this day."
31Then Bathsheba bowed
with *her* face to the earth, and
paid homage to the king, and
said, "Let my lord King David
live forever!"
32And King David said,
"Call to me Zadok the priest,
Nathan the prophet, and Benaiah the son of Jehoiada."
So they came before the king.
33The king also said to them,
"Take with you the servants
of your lord, and have Solomon my son ride on my own
mule, and take him down to
Gihon. 34There let Zadok the
priest and Nathan the prophet
anoint him king over Israel;
and blow the horn, and say,
'*Long* live King Solomon!'
35Then you shall come up
after him, and he shall come
and sit on my throne, and he
shall be king in my place. For
I have appointed him to be
ruler over Israel and Judah."
36Benaiah the son of Jehoi-

ada answered the king and
said, "Amen! May the LORD
God of my lord the king say
so *too.* 37As the LORD has been
with my lord the king, even so
may He be with Solomon, and
make his throne greater than
the throne of my lord King
David."

38So Zadok the priest, Nathan the prophet, Benaiah the
son of Jehoiada, the Cherethites, and the Pelethites went
down and had Solomon ride
on King David's mule, and
took him to Gihon. 39Then
Zadok the priest took a horn
of oil from the tabernacle and
anointed Solomon. And they
blew the horn, and all the people said, "*Long* live King Solomon!" 40And all the people
went up after him; and the
people played the flutes and
rejoiced with great joy, so that
the earth *seemed to* split with
their sound.

41Now Adonijah and all the
guests who *were* with him
heard *it* as they finished eating. And when Joab heard the
sound of the horn, he said,
"Why *is* the city in such a noisy
uproar?" 42While he was still
speaking, there came Jonathan, the son of Abiathar the
priest. And Adonijah said to
him, "Come in, for you *are* a
prominent man, and bring
good news."

43Then Jonathan answered
and said to Adonijah, "No! Our
lord King David has made
Solomon king. 44The king
has sent with him Zadok the
priest, Nathan the prophet,
Benaiah the son of Jehoi-
ada, the Cherethites, and the
Pelethites; and they have
made him ride on the king's
mule. 45So Zadok the priest
and Nathan the prophet
have anointed him king at
Gihon; and they have gone
up from there rejoicing, so
that the city is in an uproar.
This *is* the noise that you have
heard. 46Also Solomon sits on
the throne of the kingdom.
47And moreover the king's
servants have gone to bless
our lord King David, saying,
'May God make the name of
Solomon better than your
name, and may He make
his throne greater than your
throne.' Then the king bowed
himself on the bed. 48Also the
king said thus, 'Blessed *be* the
LORD God of Israel, who has
given *one* to sit on my throne
this day, while my eyes see *it!*'"

49So all the guests who
were with Adonijah were
afraid, and arose, and each
one went his way.

50Now Adonijah was afraid
of Solomon; so he arose, and
went and took hold of the
horns of the altar. 51And it
was told Solomon, saying,
"Indeed Adonijah is afraid of
King Solomon; for look, he
has taken hold of the horns
of the altar, saying, 'Let King
Solomon swear to me today
that he will not put his servant
to death with the sword.'"

52Then Solomon said, "If
he proves himself a worthy
man, not one hair of him shall
fall to the earth; but if wickedness is found in him, he shall
die." 53So King Solomon sent
them to bring him down from
the altar. And he came and fell
down before King Solomon;
and Solomon said to him, "Go
to your house."

DAVID'S INSTRUCTIONS TO SOLOMON

2 Now the days of David
drew near that he should
die, and he charged Solomon
his son, saying: 2"I go the way
of all the earth; be strong,
therefore, and prove yourself
a man. 3And keep the charge
of the LORD your God: to walk
in His ways, to keep His statutes, His commandments,
His judgments, and His testimonies, as it is written in the
Law of Moses, that you may
prosper in all that you do and
wherever you turn; 4that the
LORD may fulfill His word
which He spoke concerning
me, saying, 'If your sons take
heed to their way, to walk before Me in truth with all their
heart and with all their soul,'
He said, 'you shall not lack a
man on the throne of Israel.'
5"Moreover you know also
what Joab the son of Zeruiah
did to me, *and* what he did to
the two commanders of the
armies of Israel, to Abner the
son of Ner and Amasa the son
of Jether, whom he killed. And
he shed the blood of war in
peacetime, and put the blood
of war on his belt that *was*
around his waist, and on his
sandals that *were* on his feet.
6Therefore do according to
your wisdom, and do not let
his gray hair go down to the
grave in peace.
7"But show kindness to the
sons of Barzillai the Gileadite,
and let them be among those
who eat at your table, for so
they came to me when I fled
from Absalom your brother.
8"And see, *you have* with
you Shimei the son of Gera,
a Benjamite from Bahurim,
who cursed me with a mali-
cious curse in the day when
I went to Mahanaim. But he
came down to meet me at the
Jordan, and I swore to him
by the LORD, saying, 'I will
not put you to death with the
sword.' 9Now therefore, do not
hold him guiltless, for you *are*
a wise man and know what
you ought to do to him; but
bring his gray hair down to
the grave with blood."

DEATH OF DAVID

10So David rested with his
fathers, and was buried in the
City of David. 11The period
that David reigned over Israel
was forty years; seven years
he reigned in Hebron, and in
Jerusalem he reigned thirty-
three years. 12Then Solomon
sat on the throne of his father
David; and his kingdom was
firmly established.

SOLOMON EXECUTES ADONIJAH

13Now Adonijah the son of
Haggith came to Bathsheba
the mother of Solomon. So
she said, "Do you come peaceably?"

And he said, "Peaceably."
14Moreover he said, "I have
something *to say* to you."

And she said, "Say it."

15Then he said, "You know
that the kingdom was mine,
and all Israel had set their
expectations on me, that I
should reign. However, the
kingdom has been turned
over, and has become my
brother's; for it was his from
the LORD. 16Now I ask one petition
of you; do not deny me."

And she said to him, "Say it."

17Then he said, "Please
speak to King Solomon, for
he will not refuse you, that he
may give me Abishag the Shunammite
as wife."

18So Bathsheba said, "Very
well, I will speak for you to
the king."

19Bathsheba therefore went
to King Solomon, to speak to
him for Adonijah. And the
king rose up to meet her and
bowed down to her, and sat
down on his throne and had
a throne set for the king's
mother; so she sat at his right
hand. 20Then she said, "I desire
one small petition of you;
do not refuse me."

And the king said to her,
"Ask it, my mother, for I will
not refuse you."

21So she said, "Let Abishag
the Shunammite be given to
Adonijah your brother as
wife."

22And King Solomon answered
and said to his mother,
"Now why do you ask Abishag
the Shunammite for
Adonijah? Ask for him the
kingdom also—for he *is* my
older brother—for him, and
for Abiathar the priest, and
for Joab the son of Zeruiah."
23Then King Solomon swore
by the LORD, saying, "May God
do so to me, and more also,
if Adonijah has not spoken
this word against his own life!
24Now therefore, *as* the LORD
lives, who has confirmed me
and set me on the throne of
David my father, and who has
established a house[a] for me,
as He promised, Adonijah
shall be put to death today!"
25So King Solomon sent by
the hand of Benaiah the son of
Jehoiada; and he struck him
down, and he died.

ABIATHAR EXILED, JOAB EXECUTED

26And to Abiathar the priest
the king said, "Go to Anathoth,
to your own fields, for you *are*
deserving of death; but I will
not put you to death at this
time, because you carried the
ark of the Lord GOD before
my father David, and because

2:24 [a] That is, a royal dynasty

you were afflicted every time my father was afflicted." 27So Solomon removed Abiathar from being priest to the LORD, that he might fulfill the word of the LORD which He spoke concerning the house of Eli at Shiloh.

28Then news came to Joab, for Joab had defected to Adonijah, though he had not defected to Absalom. So Joab fled to the tabernacle of the LORD, and took hold of the horns of the altar. 29And King Solomon was told, "Joab has fled to the tabernacle of the LORD; there *he is,* by the altar." Then Solomon sent Benaiah the son of Jehoiada, saying, "Go, strike him down." 30So Benaiah went to the tabernacle of the LORD, and said to him, "Thus says the king, 'Come out!'"

And he said, "No, but I will die here." And Benaiah brought back word to the king, saying, "Thus said Joab, and thus he answered me."

31Then the king said to him, "Do as he has said, and strike him down and bury him, that you may take away from me and from the house of my father the innocent blood which Joab shed. 32So the LORD will return his blood on his head, because he struck down two men more righteous and better than he, and killed them with the sword—Abner the son of Ner, the commander of the army of Israel, and Amasa the son of Jether, the commander of the army of Judah—though my father David did not know *it.* 33Their blood shall therefore return upon the head of Joab and upon the head of his descendants forever. But upon David and his descendants, upon his house and his throne, there shall be peace forever from the LORD."

34So Benaiah the son of Jehoiada went up and struck and killed him; and he was buried in his own house in the wilderness. 35The king put Benaiah the son of Jehoiada in his place over the army, and the king put Zadok the priest in the place of Abiathar.

SHIMEI EXECUTED

36Then the king sent and called for Shimei, and said to him, "Build yourself a house in Jerusalem and dwell there, and do not go out from there anywhere. 37For it shall be, on the day you go out and cross the Brook Kidron, know for certain you shall surely die; your blood shall be on your own head."

38And Shimei said to the king, "The saying *is* good. As my lord the king has said, so your servant will do." So Shimei dwelt in Jerusalem many days.

39Now it happened at the end of three years, that two slaves of Shimei ran away to Achish the son of Maachah, king of Gath. And they told

Shimei, saying, "Look, your
slaves *are* in Gath!" 40So Shimei
arose, saddled his donkey, and
went to Achish at Gath to seek
his slaves. And Shimei went
and brought his slaves from
Gath. 41And Solomon was told
that Shimei had gone from
Jerusalem to Gath and had
come back. 42Then the king
sent and called for Shimei, and
said to him, "Did I not make
you swear by the LORD, and
warn you, saying, 'Know for
certain that on the day you go
out and travel anywhere, you
shall surely die'? And you said
to me, 'The word I have heard
is good.' 43Why then have you
not kept the oath of the LORD
and the commandment that
I gave you?" 44The king said
moreover to Shimei, "You
know, as your heart acknowledges, all the wickedness that
you did to my father David;
therefore the LORD will return
your wickedness on your own
head. 45But King Solomon
shall be blessed, and the throne
of David shall be established
before the LORD forever."

46So the king commanded
Benaiah the son of Jehoiada;
and he went out and struck
him down, and he died. Thus
the kingdom was established
in the hand of Solomon.

SOLOMON REQUESTS WISDOM

3 Now Solomon made
a treaty with Pharaoh
king of Egypt, and married
Pharaoh's daughter; then he
brought her to the City of
David until he had finished
building his own house, and
the house of the LORD, and
the wall all around Jerusalem. 2Meanwhile the people
sacrificed at the high places,
because there was no house
built for the name of the LORD
until those days. 3And Solomon loved the LORD, walking
in the statutes of his father
David, except that he sacrificed and burned incense at
the high places.

4Now the king went to
Gibeon to sacrifice there, for
that *was* the great high place:
Solomon offered a thousand
burnt offerings on that altar.
5At Gibeon the LORD appeared
to Solomon in a dream by
night; and God said, "Ask!
What shall I give you?"

6And Solomon said: "You
have shown great mercy to
Your servant David my father,
because he walked before You
in truth, in righteousness, and
in uprightness of heart with
You; You have continued this
great kindness for him, and
You have given him a son to
sit on his throne, as *it is* this
day. 7Now, O LORD my God,
You have made Your servant
king instead of my father
David, but I *am* a little child;
I do not know *how* to go out
or come in. 8And Your servant
is in the midst of Your people whom You have chosen,
a great people, too numerous

to be numbered or counted.
[9]Therefore give to Your servant an understanding heart
to judge Your people, that I
may discern between good
and evil. For who is able to
judge this great people of
Yours?"
[10]The speech pleased the
Lord, that Solomon had asked
this thing. [11]Then God said to
him: "Because you have asked
this thing, and have not asked
long life for yourself, nor have
asked riches for yourself, nor
have asked the life of your
enemies, but have asked for
yourself understanding to discern justice, [12]behold, I have
done according to your words;
see, I have given you a wise
and understanding heart, so
that there has not been anyone like you before you, nor
shall any like you arise after
you. [13]And I have also given
you what you have not asked:
both riches and honor, so that
there shall not be anyone like
you among the kings all your
days. [14]So if you walk in My
ways, to keep My statutes and
My commandments, as your
father David walked, then I
will lengthen your days."
[15]Then Solomon awoke;
and indeed it had been a
dream. And he came to Jerusalem and stood before the
ark of the covenant of the
LORD, offered up burnt offerings, offered peace offerings,
and made a feast for all his
servants.

SOLOMON'S WISE JUDGMENT

[16]Now two women *who*
were harlots came to the king,
and stood before him. [17]And
one woman said, "O my lord,
this woman and I dwell in the
same house; and I gave birth
while she *was* in the house.
[18]Then it happened, the third
day after I had given birth,
that this woman also gave
birth. And we *were* together;
no one *was* with us in the
house, except the two of us in
the house. [19]And this woman's
son died in the night, because
she lay on him. [20]So she arose
in the middle of the night and
took my son from my side,
while your maidservant slept,
and laid him in her bosom,
and laid her dead child in my
bosom. [21]And when I rose in
the morning to nurse my son,
there he was, dead. But when
I had examined him in the
morning, indeed, he was not
my son whom I had borne."
[22]Then the other woman
said, "No! But the living one
is my son, and the dead one
is your son."

And the first woman said, "No! But the dead one *is* your son, and the living one *is* my son."

Thus they spoke before the king.

[23]And the king said, "The
one says, 'This *is* my son, who
lives, and your son *is* the dead
one'; and the other says, 'No!
But your son *is* the dead one,

and my son *is* the living one.’” 24Then the king said, “Bring me a sword.” So they brought a sword before the king. 25And the king said, “Divide the living child in two, and give half to one, and half to the other.”

26Then the woman whose son *was* living spoke to the king, for she yearned with compassion for her son; and she said, “O my lord, give her the living child, and by no means kill him!”

But the other said, “Let him be neither mine nor yours, *but* divide *him*.”

27So the king answered and said, “Give the first woman the living child, and by no means kill him; she *is* his mother.”

28And all Israel heard of the judgment which the king had rendered; and they feared the king, for they saw that the wisdom of God *was* in him to administer justice.

SOLOMON’S ADMINISTRATION

4 So King Solomon was king over all Israel. 2And these *were* his officials: Azariah the son of Zadok, the priest; 3Elihoreph and Ahijah, the sons of Shisha, scribes; Jehoshaphat the son of Ahilud, the recorder; 4Benaiah the son of Jehoiada, over the army; Zadok and Abiathar, the priests; 5Azariah the son of Nathan, over the officers; Zabud the son of Nathan, a priest *and* the king’s friend; 6Ahishar, over the household; and Adoniram the son of Abda, over the labor force.

7And Solomon had twelve governors over all Israel, who provided food for the king and his household; each one made provision for one month of the year. 8These *are* their names: Ben-Hur,[a] in the mountains of Ephraim; 9Ben-Deker,[a] in Makaz, Shaalbim, Beth Shemesh, and Elon Beth Hanan; 10Ben-Hesed,[a] in Arubboth; to him *belonged* Sochoh and all the land of Hepher; 11Ben-Abinadab,[a] *in* all the regions of Dor; he had Taphath the daughter of Solomon as wife; 12Baana the son of Ahilud, *in* Taanach, Megiddo, and all Beth Shean, which *is* beside Zaretan below Jezreel, from Beth Shean to Abel Meholah, as far as the other side of Jokneam; 13Ben-Geber,[a] in Ramoth Gilead; to him *belonged* the towns of Jair the son of Manasseh, in Gilead; to him *also belonged* the region of Argob in Bashan—sixty large cities with walls and bronze gate-bars; 14Ahinadab the son of Iddo, *in* Mahanaim; 15Ahimaaz, in Naphtali; he also took Basemath the

4:8 [a] Literally *Son of Hur* **4:9** [a] Literally *Son of Deker* **4:10** [a] Literally *Son of Hesed* **4:11** [a] Literally *Son of Abinadab* **4:13** [a] Literally *Son of Geber*

daughter of Solomon as wife;
[16]Baanah the son of Hushai,
in Asher and Aloth; [17]Jehosh-
aphat the son of Paruah, in
Issachar; [18]Shimei the son of
Elah, in Benjamin; [19]Geber the
son of Uri, in the land of Gilead, *in* the country of Sihon
king of the Amorites, and of
Og king of Bashan. *He was* the
only governor who *was* in the
land.

PROSPERITY AND WISDOM OF SOLOMON'S REIGN

[20]Judah and Israel *were*
as numerous as the sand by
the sea in multitude, eating
and drinking and rejoicing.
[21]So Solomon reigned over all
kingdoms from the River[a] *to*
the land of the Philistines,
as far as the border of Egypt.
They brought tribute and
served Solomon all the days
of his life.

[22]Now Solomon's provision
for one day was thirty kors of
fine flour, sixty kors of meal,
[23]ten fatted oxen, twenty oxen
from the pastures, and one
hundred sheep, besides deer,
gazelles, roebucks, and fatted
fowl.

[24]For he had dominion
over all *the region* on this
side of the River[a] from Tiphsah even to Gaza, namely over
all the kings on this side of
the River; and he had peace
on every side all around him.
[25]And Judah and Israel dwelt
safely, each man under his
vine and his fig tree, from
Dan as far as Beersheba, all
the days of Solomon.

[26]Solomon had forty[a]
thousand stalls of horses
for his chariots, and twelve
thousand horsemen. [27]And
these governors, each man
in his month, provided food
for King Solomon and for
all who came to King Sol-
omon's table. There was no
lack in their supply. [28]They
also brought barley and straw
to the proper place, for the
horses and steeds, each man
according to his charge.

[29]And God gave Solomon
wisdom and exceedingly great
understanding, and largeness
of heart like the sand on the
seashore. [30]Thus Solomon's
wisdom excelled the wisdom
of all the men of the East and
all the wisdom of Egypt. [31]For
he was wiser than all men—
than Ethan the Ezrahite, and
Heman, Chalcol, and Darda,
the sons of Mahol; and his
fame was in all the surrounding nations. [32]He spoke three
thousand proverbs, and his
songs were one thousand
and five. [33]Also he spoke of
trees, from the cedar tree of
Lebanon even to the hyssop
that springs out of the wall;

4:21 [a] That is, the Euphrates 4:24 [a] That is, the Euphrates
4:26 [a] Following Masoretic Text and most other authorities; some manuscripts of the Septuagint read *four* (compare 2 Chronicles 9:25).

he spoke also of animals, of
birds, of creeping things, and
of fish. 34And men of all nations, from all the kings of
the earth who had heard of
his wisdom, came to hear the
wisdom of Solomon.

SOLOMON PREPARES TO BUILD THE TEMPLE

5 Now Hiram king of Tyre
sent his servants to Sol-
omon, because he heard that
they had anointed him king in
place of his father, for Hiram
had always loved David. 2Then
Solomon sent to Hiram, saying:

3 You know how my father
David could not build a
house for the name of
the LORD his God because
of the wars which were
fought against him on
every side, until the LORD
put *his foes*[a] under the
soles of his feet.
4 But now the LORD my
God has given me rest
on every side; *there is*
neither adversary nor evil
occurrence.
5 And behold, I propose
to build a house for the
name of the LORD my
God, as the LORD spoke to
my father David, saying,
"Your son, whom I will set
on your throne in your
place, he shall build the
house for My name."
6 Now therefore, command
that they cut down cedars
for me from Lebanon;
and my servants will be
with your servants, and
I will pay you wages for
your servants according
to whatever you say. For
you know *there is* none
among us who has skill
to cut timber like the
Sidonians.

7So it was, when Hiram
heard the words of Solomon,
that he rejoiced greatly and
said,

Blessed *be* the LORD this
day, for He has given
David a wise son over this
great people!

8Then Hiram sent to Sol-
omon, saying:

I have considered *the
message* which you sent
me, *and* I will do all you
desire concerning the
cedar and cypress logs.
9 My servants shall bring
them down from Lebanon
to the sea; I will float
them in rafts by sea to
the place you indicate to
me, and will have them
broken apart there; then
you can take *them* away.
And you shall fulfill my
desire by giving food for
my household.

5:3 [a] Literally *them*

10Then Hiram gave Sol-
omon cedar and cypress logs
according to all his desire.
11And Solomon gave Hiram
twenty thousand kors of wheat
as food for his household, and
twenty[a] kors of pressed oil.
Thus Solomon gave to Hiram
year by year.
12So the LORD gave Sol-
omon wisdom, as He had
promised him; and there
was peace between Hiram
and Solomon, and the two of
them made a treaty together.
13Then King Solomon
raised up a labor force out of
all Israel; and the labor force
was thirty thousand men.
14And he sent them to Lebanon, ten thousand a month in
shifts: they were one month
in Lebanon *and* two months
at home; Adoniram *was* in
charge of the labor force. 15Sol-
omon had seventy thousand
who carried burdens, and
eighty thousand who quarried
stone in the mountains, 16be-
sides three thousand three
hundred[a] from the chiefs
of Solomon's deputies, who
supervised the people who
labored in the work. 17And
the king commanded them
to quarry large stones, costly
stones, *and* hewn stones, to lay
the foundation of the temple.[a]
18So Solomon's builders, Hiram's builders, and the Gebalites quarried *them;* and they
prepared timber and stones
to build the temple.

SOLOMON BUILDS THE TEMPLE

6 And it came to pass in the
four hundred and eight-
ieth[a] year after the children
of Israel had come out of the
land of Egypt, in the fourth
year of Solomon's reign over
Israel, in the month of Ziv,
which *is* the second month,
that he began to build the
house of the LORD. 2Now the
house which King Solomon
built for the LORD, its length
was sixty cubits, its width
twenty, and its height thirty
cubits. 3The vestibule in front
of the sanctuary[a] of the house
was twenty cubits long across
the width of the house, *and*
the width of *the vestibule*[b]
extended ten cubits from the
front of the house. 4And he
made for the house windows
with beveled frames.
5Against the wall of the
temple he built chambers all
around, *against* the walls of the

5:11 [a] Following Masoretic Text, Targum, and Vulgate; Septuagint and Syriac read *twenty thousand.* 5:16 [a] Following Masoretic Text, Targum, and Vulgate; Septuagint reads *three thousand six hundred.* 5:17 [a] Literally *house,* and so frequently throughout this book 6:1 [a] Following Masoretic Text, Targum, and Vulgate; Septuagint reads *fortieth.* 6:3 [a] Hebrew *heykal;* here the main room of the temple, elsewhere called the holy place (compare Exodus 26:33 and Ezekiel 41:1) [b] Literally *it*

temple, all around the sanctuary and the inner sanctuary.[a]
Thus he made side chambers
all around it. 6The lowest
chamber *was* five cubits wide,
the middle *was* six cubits wide,
and the third *was* seven cubits wide; for he made narrow
ledges around the outside of
the temple, so that *the support
beams* would not be fastened
into the walls of the temple.
7And the temple, when it was
being built, was built with
stone finished at the quarry,
so that no hammer or chisel *or*
any iron tool was heard in the
temple while it was being built.
8The doorway for the middle
story[a] *was* on the right side of
the temple. They went up by
stairs to the middle *story,* and
from the middle to the third.

9So he built the temple and
finished it, and he paneled
the temple with beams and
boards of cedar. 10And he built
side chambers against the entire temple, each five cubits
high; they were attached to
the temple with cedar beams.

11Then the word of the
LORD came to Solomon, saying: 12"*Concerning* this temple
which you are building, if you
walk in My statutes, execute
My judgments, keep all My
commandments, and walk in
them, then I will perform My
word with you, which I spoke
to your father David. 13And I
will dwell among the children
of Israel, and will not forsake
My people Israel."

14So Solomon built the temple and finished it. 15And he
built the inside walls of the
temple with cedar boards;
from the floor of the temple
to the ceiling he paneled the
inside with wood; and he covered the floor of the temple
with planks of cypress. 16Then
he built the twenty-cubit room
at the rear of the temple, from
floor to ceiling, with cedar
boards; he built *it* inside as the
inner sanctuary, as the Most
Holy *Place.* 17And in front of it
the temple sanctuary was forty
cubits *long.* 18The inside of the
temple was cedar, carved with
ornamental buds and open
flowers. All *was* cedar; there
was no stone *to be* seen.

19And he prepared the inner
sanctuary inside the temple,
to set the ark of the covenant
of the LORD there. 20The inner
sanctuary *was* twenty cubits
long, twenty cubits wide, and
twenty cubits high. He overlaid it with pure gold, and
overlaid the altar of cedar.
21So Solomon overlaid the inside of the temple with pure
gold. He stretched gold chains
across the front of the inner
sanctuary, and overlaid it with
gold. 22The whole temple he

6:5 [a] Hebrew *debir;* here the inner room of the temple, elsewhere called the Most Holy Place (compare verse 16) 6:8 [a] Following Masoretic Text and Vulgate; Septuagint reads *upper story;* Targum reads *ground story.*

overlaid with gold, until he
had finished all the temple;
also he overlaid with gold the
entire altar that *was* by the
inner sanctuary.

23 Inside the inner sanctuary he made two cherubim
of olive wood, *each* ten cubits high. 24 One wing of the
cherub *was* five cubits, and
the other wing of the cherub
five cubits: ten cubits from
the tip of one wing to the tip
of the other. 25 And the other
cherub *was* ten cubits; both
cherubim *were* of the same
size and shape. 26 The height
of one cherub *was* ten cubits,
and so *was* the other cherub.
27 Then he set the cherubim
inside the inner room;[a] and
they stretched out the wings
of the cherubim so that the
wing of the one touched *one*
wall, and the wing of the other
cherub touched the other
wall. And their wings touched
each other in the middle of
the room. 28 Also he overlaid
the cherubim with gold.

29 Then he carved all the
walls of the temple all around,
both the inner and outer *sanctuaries,* with carved figures
of cherubim, palm trees, and
open flowers. 30 And the floor
of the temple he overlaid with
gold, both the inner and outer
sanctuaries.

31 For the entrance of the
inner sanctuary he made
doors *of* olive wood; the lintel
and doorposts *were* one-fifth
of the wall. 32 The two doors
were of olive wood; and he
carved on them figures of
cherubim, palm trees, and
open flowers, and overlaid
them with gold; and he spread
gold on the cherubim and on
the palm trees. 33 So for the
door of the sanctuary he also
made doorposts *of* olive wood,
one-fourth *of the wall.* 34 And
the two doors *were of* cypress
wood; two panels *comprised*
one folding door, and two panels *comprised* the other folding
door. 35 Then he carved cherubim, palm trees, and open
flowers *on them,* and overlaid
them with gold applied evenly
on the carved work.

36 And he built the inner
court with three rows of
hewn stone and a row of cedar
beams.

37 In the fourth year the
foundation of the house of the
LORD was laid, in the month
of Ziv. 38 And in the eleventh
year, in the month of Bul,
which is the eighth month,
the house was finished in all
its details and according to
all its plans. So he was seven
years in building it.

SOLOMON'S OTHER BUILDINGS

7 But Solomon took thir-
teen years to build his own
house; so he finished all his
house.

6:27 [a] Literally *house*

2He also built the House of the Forest of Lebanon; its length *was* one hundred cubits, its width fifty cubits, and its height thirty cubits, with four rows of cedar pillars, and cedar beams on the pillars. 3And *it was* paneled with cedar above the beams that *were* on forty-five pillars, fifteen *to* a row. 4*There were* windows *with beveled frames in* three rows, and window *was* opposite window *in* three tiers. 5And all the doorways and doorposts *had* rectangular frames; and window *was* opposite window *in* three tiers.

6He also made the Hall of Pillars: its length *was* fifty cubits, and its width thirty cubits; and in front of them *was* a portico with pillars, and a canopy *was* in front of them.

7Then he made a hall for the throne, the Hall of Judgment, where he might judge; and *it was* paneled with cedar from floor to ceiling.[a]

8And the house where he dwelt *had* another court inside the hall, of like workmanship. Solomon also made a house like this hall for Pharaoh's daughter, whom he had taken *as wife.*

9All these *were of* costly stones cut to size, trimmed with saws, inside and out, from the foundation to the eaves, and also on the outside to the great court. 10The foundation *was of* costly stones, large stones, some ten cubits and some eight cubits. 11And above *were* costly stones, hewn to size, and cedar wood. 12The great court *was* enclosed with three rows of hewn stones and a row of cedar beams. So were the inner court of the house of the LORD and the vestibule of the temple.

HIRAM THE CRAFTSMAN

13Now King Solomon sent and brought Huram[a] from Tyre. 14He *was* the son of a widow from the tribe of Naphtali, and his father *was* a man of Tyre, a bronze worker; he was filled with wisdom and understanding and skill in working with all kinds of bronze work. So he came to King Solomon and did all his work.

THE BRONZE PILLARS FOR THE TEMPLE

15And he cast two pillars of bronze, each one eighteen cubits high, and a line of twelve cubits measured the circumference of each. 16Then he made two capitals *of* cast bronze, to set on the tops of the pillars. The height of one capital *was* five cubits, and the height of the other capital *was* five cubits. 17*He*

7:7 [a] Literally *floor,* that is, of the upper level 7:13 [a] Hebrew *Hiram* (compare 2 Chronicles 2:13, 14)

made a lattice network, with
wreaths of chainwork, for the
capitals which *were* on top of
the pillars: seven chains for
one capital and seven for the
other capital. 18So he made
the pillars, and two rows of
pomegranates above the network all around to cover the
capitals that *were* on top; and
thus he did for the other capital.

19The capitals which *were*
on top of the pillars in the hall
were in the shape of lilies, four
cubits. 20The capitals on the
two pillars also *had pomegranates* above, by the convex
surface which *was* next to the
network; and there *were* two
hundred such pomegranates
in rows on each of the capitals
all around.

21Then he set up the pillars
by the vestibule of the temple; he set up the pillar on
the right and called its name
Jachin, and he set up the pillar on the left and called its
name Boaz. 22The tops of the
pillars were in the shape of
lilies. So the work of the pillars
was finished.

THE SEA AND THE OXEN

23And he made the Sea of
cast bronze, ten cubits from
one brim to the other; *it was*
completely round. Its height
was five cubits, and a line of
thirty cubits measured its circumference.

24Below its brim *were* ornamental buds encircling it
all around, ten to a cubit, all
the way around the Sea. The
ornamental buds *were* cast
in two rows when it was cast.
25It stood on twelve oxen:
three looking toward the
north, three looking toward
the west, three looking toward
the south, and three looking
toward the east; the Sea *was
set* upon them, and all their
back parts *pointed* inward. 26It
was a handbreadth thick; and
its brim was shaped like the
brim of a cup, *like* a lily blossom. It contained two thousand[a] baths.

THE CARTS AND THE LAVERS

27He also made ten carts
of bronze; four cubits *was*
the length of each cart, four
cubits its width, and three
cubits its height. 28And this
was the design of the carts:
They had panels, and the
panels *were* between frames;
29on the panels that *were* between the frames *were* lions,
oxen, and cherubim. And on
the frames *was* a pedestal on
top. Below the lions and oxen
were wreaths of plaited work.
30Every cart had four bronze
wheels and axles of bronze,
and its four feet had supports.
Under the laver *were* supports
of cast *bronze* beside each
wreath. 31Its opening inside

7:26 [a] Or *three thousand* (compare 2 Chronicles 4:5)

the crown at the top *was* one
cubit in diameter; and the
opening *was* round, shaped
like a pedestal, one and a
half cubits in outside diameter; and also on the opening
were engravings, but the panels were square, not round.
32Under the panels *were* the
four wheels, and the axles of
the wheels *were joined* to the
cart. The height of a wheel *was*
one and a half cubits. 33The
workmanship of the wheels
was like the workmanship
of a chariot wheel; their axle
pins, their rims, their spokes,
and their hubs *were* all of cast
bronze. 34And *there were* four
supports at the four corners
of each cart; its supports *were*
part of the cart itself. 35On the
top of the cart, at the height
of half a cubit, *it was* perfectly
round. And on the top of the
cart, its flanges and its panels
were of the same casting. 36On
the plates of its flanges and on
its panels he engraved cherubim, lions, and palm trees,
wherever there was a clear
space on each, with wreaths
all around. 37Thus he made
the ten carts. All of them were
of the same mold, one measure, *and* one shape.

38Then he made ten lavers
of bronze; each laver contained forty baths, *and* each
laver *was* four cubits. On each
of the ten carts *was* a laver.
39And he put five carts on
the right side of the house,
and five on the left side of the
house. He set the Sea on the
right side of the house, toward
the southeast.

FURNISHINGS OF THE TEMPLE

40Huram[a] made the lavers
and the shovels and the bowls.
So Huram finished doing all
the work that he was to do for
King Solomon *for* the house of
the LORD: 41the two pillars, the
two bowl-shaped capitals that
were on top of the two pillars;
the two networks covering
the two bowl-shaped capitals
which *were* on top of the pillars; 42four hundred pomegranates for the two networks
(two rows of pomegranates
for each network, to cover
the two bowl-shaped capitals
that *were* on top of the pillars);
43the ten carts, and ten lavers
on the carts; 44one Sea, and
twelve oxen under the Sea;
45the pots, the shovels, and
the bowls.

All these articles which
Huram[a] made for King Solomon *for* the house of the
LORD *were of* burnished
bronze. 46In the plain of Jordan the king had them cast in
clay molds, between Succoth
and Zaretan. 47And Solomon
did not weigh all the articles,
because *there were* so many;

7:40 [a] Hebrew *Hiram* (compare 2 Chronicles 2:13, 14)
7:45 [a] Hebrew *Hiram* (compare 2 Chronicles 2:13, 14)

the weight of the bronze was
not determined.
48Thus Solomon had all
the furnishings made for the
house of the LORD: the altar
of gold, and the table of gold
on which *was* the showbread;
49the lampstands of pure gold,
five on the right *side* and five
on the left in front of the inner
sanctuary, with the flowers
and the lamps and the wick-
trimmers of gold; 50the basins, the trimmers, the bowls,
the ladles, and the censers of
pure gold; and the hinges of
gold, *both* for the doors of the
inner room (the Most Holy
Place) *and* for the doors of the
main hall of the temple.
51So all the work that King
Solomon had done for the
house of the LORD was finished; and Solomon brought
in the things which his father
David had dedicated: the silver and the gold and the furnishings. He put them in the
treasuries of the house of the
LORD.

THE ARK BROUGHT INTO THE TEMPLE

8 Now Solomon assembled
the elders of Israel and all
the heads of the tribes, the
chief fathers of the children
of Israel, to King Solomon in
Jerusalem, that they might
bring up the ark of the covenant of the LORD from the
City of David, which *is* Zion.
2Therefore all the men of
Israel assembled with King
Solomon at the feast in the
month of Ethanim, which *is*
the seventh month. 3So all
the elders of Israel came, and
the priests took up the ark.
4Then they brought up the ark
of the LORD, the tabernacle
of meeting, and all the holy
furnishings that *were* in the
tabernacle. The priests and
the Levites brought them up.
5Also King Solomon, and all
the congregation of Israel
who were assembled with
him, *were* with him before
the ark, sacrificing sheep
and oxen that could not be
counted or numbered for
multitude. 6Then the priests
brought in the ark of the covenant of the LORD to its place,
into the inner sanctuary of
the temple, to the Most Holy
Place, under the wings of the
cherubim. 7For the cherubim
spread *their* two wings over
the place of the ark, and the
cherubim overshadowed the
ark and its poles. 8The poles
extended so that the ends of
the poles could be seen from
the holy *place,* in front of the
inner sanctuary; but they
could not be seen from outside. And they are there to this
day. 9Nothing *was* in the ark
except the two tablets of stone
which Moses put there at
Horeb, when the LORD made
a covenant with the children
of Israel, when they came out
of the land of Egypt.
10And it came to pass, when
the priests came out of the

holy *place,* that the cloud filled
the house of the LORD, 11so
that the priests could not continue ministering because of
the cloud; for the glory of the
LORD filled the house of the
LORD.
12Then Solomon spoke:

"The LORD said He
would dwell in
the dark cloud.
13 I have surely built You
an exalted house,
And a place for You to
dwell in forever."

SOLOMON'S SPEECH AT COMPLETION OF THE WORK

14Then the king turned
around and blessed the whole
assembly of Israel, while all
the assembly of Israel was
standing. 15And he said:
"Blessed *be* the LORD God of
Israel, who spoke with His
mouth to my father David,
and with His hand has fulfilled *it,* saying, 16'Since the
day that I brought My people Israel out of Egypt, I have
chosen no city from any tribe
of Israel *in which* to build a
house, that My name might be
there; but I chose David to be
over My people Israel.' 17Now
it was in the heart of my father
David to build a temple[a] for
the name of the LORD God of
Israel. 18But the LORD said to
my father David, 'Whereas it
was in your heart to build a
temple for My name, you did
well that it was in your heart.
19Nevertheless you shall not
build the temple, but your
son who will come from your
body, he shall build the temple
for My name.' 20So the LORD
has fulfilled His word which
He spoke; and I have filled the
position of my father David,
and sit on the throne of Israel,
as the LORD promised; and
I have built a temple for the
name of the LORD God of Israel. 21And there I have made
a place for the ark, in which
is the covenant of the LORD
which He made with our fathers, when He brought them
out of the land of Egypt."

SOLOMON'S PRAYER OF DEDICATION

22Then Solomon stood
before the altar of the LORD
in the presence of all the assembly of Israel, and spread
out his hands toward heaven;
23and he said: "LORD God of Israel, *there is* no God in heaven
above or on earth below like
You, who keep *Your* covenant
and mercy with Your ser-
vants who walk before You
with all their hearts. 24You
have kept what You prom-
ised Your servant David my
father; You have both spoken
with Your mouth and ful-
filled *it* with Your hand, as *it*
is this day. 25Therefore, LORD

8:17 [a] Literally *house,* and so in verses 18–20

God of Israel, now keep what
You promised Your servant
David my father, saying, 'You
shall not fail to have a man
sit before Me on the throne of
Israel, only if your sons take
heed to their way, that they
walk before Me as you have
walked before Me.' 26And now
I pray, O God of Israel, let Your
word come true, which You
have spoken to Your servant
David my father.

27"But will God indeed dwell
on the earth? Behold, heaven
and the heaven of heavens
cannot contain You. How
much less this temple which
I have built! 28Yet regard the
prayer of Your servant and
his supplication, O LORD my
God, and listen to the cry and
the prayer which Your servant
is praying before You today:
29that Your eyes may be open
toward this temple night and
day, toward the place of which
You said, 'My name shall be
there,' that You may hear the
prayer which Your servant
makes toward this place.
30And may You hear the supplication of Your servant and
of Your people Israel, when
they pray toward this place.
Hear in heaven Your dwelling place; and when You hear,
forgive.

31"When anyone sins
against his neighbor, and is
forced to take an oath, and
comes *and* takes an oath before Your altar in this temple,
32then hear in heaven, and act,
and judge Your servants, condemning the wicked, bringing his way on his head, and
justifying the righteous by
giving him according to his
righteousness.

33"When Your people Israel
are defeated before an enemy
because they have sinned
against You, and when they
turn back to You and confess
Your name, and pray and
make supplication to You in
this temple, 34then hear in
heaven, and forgive the sin of
Your people Israel, and bring
them back to the land which
You gave to their fathers.

35"When the heavens are
shut up and there is no rain
because they have sinned
against You, when they pray
toward this place and confess Your name, and turn
from their sin because You
afflict them, 36then hear in
heaven, and forgive the sin
of Your servants, Your people Israel, that You may teach
them the good way in which
they should walk; and send
rain on Your land which You
have given to Your people as
an inheritance.

37"When there is famine in
the land, pestilence *or* blight
or mildew, locusts *or* grasshoppers; when their enemy
besieges them in the land of
their cities; whatever plague
or whatever sickness *there*
is; 38whatever prayer, whatever supplication is made by
anyone, *or* by all Your people

Israel, when each one knows
the plague of his own heart,
and spreads out his hands toward this temple: 39then hear
in heaven Your dwelling place,
and forgive, and act, and give
to everyone according to all
his ways, whose heart You
know (for You alone know the
hearts of all the sons of men),
40that they may fear You all
the days that they live in the
land which You gave to our
fathers.

41"Moreover, concerning a
foreigner, who *is* not of Your
people Israel, but has come
from a far country for Your
name's sake 42(for they will
hear of Your great name and
Your strong hand and Your
outstretched arm), when he
comes and prays toward this
temple, 43hear in heaven
Your dwelling place, and do
according to all for which the
foreigner calls to You, that
all peoples of the earth may
know Your name and fear You,
as *do* Your people Israel, and
that they may know that this
temple which I have built is
called by Your name.

44"When Your people go
out to battle against their
enemy, wherever You send
them, and when they pray
to the LORD toward the city
which You have chosen and
the temple which I have built
for Your name, 45then hear in
heaven their prayer and their
supplication, and maintain
their cause.

46"When they sin against
You (for *there is* no one who
does not sin), and You become
angry with them and deliver
them to the enemy, and they
take them captive to the land
of the enemy, far or near; 47*yet*
when they come to themselves
in the land where they were
carried captive, and repent,
and make supplication to You
in the land of those who took
them captive, saying, 'We have
sinned and done wrong, we
have committed wickedness';
48and *when* they return to You
with all their heart and with
all their soul in the land of
their enemies who led them
away captive, and pray to You
toward their land which You
gave to their fathers, the city
which You have chosen and
the temple which I have built
for Your name: 49then hear in
heaven Your dwelling place
their prayer and their supplication, and maintain their
cause, 50and forgive Your people who have sinned against
You, and all their transgressions which they have transgressed against You; and grant
them compassion before
those who took them captive,
that they may have compassion on them 51(for they *are*
Your people and Your inheritance, whom You brought
out of Egypt, out of the iron
furnace), 52that Your eyes may
be open to the supplication of
Your servant and the supplication of Your people Israel,

to listen to them whenever
they call to You. [53]For You
separated them from among
all the peoples of the earth *to
be* Your inheritance, as You
spoke by Your servant Moses,
when You brought our fathers
out of Egypt, O Lord GOD."

SOLOMON BLESSES THE ASSEMBLY

[54]And so it was, when Solomon had finished praying all
this prayer and supplication to
the LORD, that he arose from
before the altar of the LORD,
from kneeling on his knees
with his hands spread up to
heaven. [55]Then he stood and
blessed all the assembly of Israel with a loud voice, saying:
[56]"Blessed *be* the LORD, who
has given rest to His people
Israel, according to all that
He promised. There has not
failed one word of all His good
promise, which He promised
through His servant Moses.
[57]May the LORD our God be
with us, as He was with our
fathers. May He not leave us
nor forsake us, [58]that He may
incline our hearts to Himself,
to walk in all His ways, and
to keep His commandments
and His statutes and His judgments, which He commanded
our fathers. [59]And may these
words of mine, with which I
have made supplication before the LORD, be near the
LORD our God day and night,
that He may maintain the
cause of His servant and the
cause of His people Israel, as
each day may require, [60]that
all the peoples of the earth
may know that the LORD *is*
God; *there is* no other. [61]Let
your heart therefore be loyal
to the LORD our God, to walk
in His statutes and keep His
commandments, as at this
day."

SOLOMON DEDICATES THE TEMPLE

[62]Then the king and all Israel with him offered sacrifices before the LORD. [63]And
Solomon offered a sacrifice
of peace offerings, which he
offered to the LORD, twenty-
two thousand bulls and one
hundred and twenty thousand
sheep. So the king and all the
children of Israel dedicated
the house of the LORD. [64]On
the same day the king consecrated the middle of the court
that *was* in front of the house
of the LORD; for there he offered burnt offerings, grain
offerings, and the fat of the
peace offerings, because the
bronze altar that *was* before
the LORD *was* too small to receive the burnt offerings, the
grain offerings, and the fat of
the peace offerings.

[65]At that time Solomon
held a feast, and all Israel with
him, a great assembly from
the entrance of Hamath to
the Brook of Egypt, before the
LORD our God, seven days and
seven *more* days—fourteen
days. [66]On the eighth day he

sent the people away; and
they blessed the king, and
went to their tents joyful and
glad of heart for all the good
that the LORD had done for
His servant David, and for Israel His people.

GOD'S SECOND APPEARANCE TO SOLOMON

9 And it came to pass,
when Solomon had fin-
ished building the house
of the LORD and the king's
house, and all Solomon's desire which he wanted to do,
2that the LORD appeared to
Solomon the second time, as
He had appeared to him at
Gibeon. 3And the LORD said
to him: "I have heard your
prayer and your supplication
that you have made before
Me; I have consecrated this
house which you have built
to put My name there forever,
and My eyes and My heart will
be there perpetually. 4Now if
you walk before Me as your father David walked, in integrity
of heart and in uprightness,
to do according to all that I
have commanded you, *and*
if you keep My statutes and
My judgments, 5then I will
establish the throne of your
kingdom over Israel forever,
as I promised David your father, saying, 'You shall not fail
to have a man on the throne
of Israel.' 6*But* if you or your
sons at all turn from following
Me, and do not keep My commandments *and* My statutes
which I have set before you,
but go and serve other gods
and worship them, 7then I will
cut off Israel from the land
which I have given them; and
this house which I have consecrated for My name I will
cast out of My sight. Israel will
be a proverb and a byword
among all peoples. 8And *as
for* this house, *which* is exalted, everyone who passes
by it will be astonished and
will hiss, and say, 'Why has the
LORD done thus to this land
and to this house?' 9Then they
will answer, 'Because they forsook the LORD their God, who
brought their fathers out of
the land of Egypt, and have
embraced other gods, and
worshiped them and served
them; therefore the LORD has
brought all this calamity on
them.'"

SOLOMON AND HIRAM EXCHANGE GIFTS

10Now it happened at the
end of twenty years, when
Solomon had built the two
houses, the house of the LORD
and the king's house 11(Hiram
the king of Tyre had supplied
Solomon with cedar and cypress and gold, as much as he
desired), *that* King Solomon
then gave Hiram twenty cities
in the land of Galilee. 12Then
Hiram went from Tyre to see
the cities which Solomon
had given him, but they did
not please him. 13So he said,

"What *kind of* cities *are* these which you have given me, my brother?" And he called them the land of Cabul,[a] as they are to this day. 14Then Hiram sent the king one hundred and twenty talents of gold.

SOLOMON'S ADDITIONAL ACHIEVEMENTS

15And this *is* the reason for the labor force which King Solomon raised: to build the house of the LORD, his own house, the Millo,[a] the wall of Jerusalem, Hazor, Megiddo, and Gezer. 16(Pharaoh king of Egypt had gone up and taken Gezer and burned it with fire, had killed the Canaanites who dwelt in the city, and had given it *as* a dowry to his daughter, Solomon's wife.) 17And Solomon built Gezer, Lower Beth Horon, 18Baalath, and Tadmor in the wilderness, in the land *of Judah,* 19all the storage cities that Solomon had, cities for his chariots and cities for his cavalry, and whatever Solomon desired to build in Jerusalem, in Lebanon, and in all the land of his dominion.

20All the people *who were* left of the Amorites, Hittites, Perizzites, Hivites, and Jebusites, who *were* not of the children of Israel— 21that is, *their descendants* who were left in the land after them, whom the children of Israel had not been able to destroy completely—from these Solomon raised forced labor, as it is to this day. 22But of the children of Israel Solomon made no forced laborers, because they *were* men of war and his servants: his officers, his captains, commanders of his chariots, and his cavalry.

23Others *were* chiefs of the officials who *were* over Solomon's work: five hundred and fifty, who ruled over the people who did the work.

24But Pharaoh's daughter came up from the City of David to her house which *Solomon*[a] had built for her. Then he built the Millo.

25Now three times a year Solomon offered burnt offerings and peace offerings on the altar which he had built for the LORD, and he burned incense with them *on the altar* that *was* before the LORD. So he finished the temple.

26King Solomon also built a fleet of ships at Ezion Geber, which *is* near Elath[a] on the shore of the Red Sea, in the land of Edom. 27Then Hiram sent his servants with the fleet, seamen who knew the sea, to work with the servants of Solomon. 28And they went to Ophir, and acquired four

9:13 [a] Literally *Good for Nothing* 9:15 [a] Literally *The Landfill* 9:24 [a] Literally *he* (compare 2 Chronicles 8:11) 9:26 [a] Hebrew *Eloth* (compare 2 Kings 14:22)

hundred and twenty talents of gold from there, and brought *it* to King Solomon.

THE QUEEN OF SHEBA'S PRAISE OF SOLOMON

10 Now when the queen of Sheba heard of the fame of Solomon concerning the name of the LORD, she came to test him with hard questions. [2]She came to Jerusalem with a very great retinue, with camels that bore spices, very much gold, and precious stones; and when she came to Solomon, she spoke with him about all that was in her heart. [3]So Solomon answered all her questions; there was nothing so difficult for the king that he could not explain *it* to her. [4]And when the queen of Sheba had seen all the wisdom of Solomon, the house that he had built, [5]the food on his table, the seating of his servants, the service of his waiters and their apparel, his cupbearers, and his entryway by which he went up to the house of the LORD, there was no more spirit in her. [6]Then she said to the king: "It was a true report which I heard in my own land about your words and your wisdom. [7]However I did not believe the words until I came and saw with my own eyes; and indeed the half was not told me. Your wisdom and prosperity exceed the fame of which I heard. [8]Happy *are* your men and happy *are* these your servants, who stand continually before you *and* hear your wisdom! [9]Blessed be the LORD your God, who delighted in you, setting you on the throne of Israel! Because the LORD has loved Israel forever, therefore He made you king, to do justice and righteousness."

[10]Then she gave the king one hundred and twenty talents of gold, spices in great quantity, and precious stones. There never again came such abundance of spices as the queen of Sheba gave to King Solomon. [11]Also, the ships of Hiram, which brought gold from Ophir, brought great quantities of almug[a] wood and precious stones from Ophir. [12]And the king made steps of the almug wood for the house of the LORD and for the king's house, also harps and stringed instruments for singers. There never again came such almug wood, nor has the like been seen to this day.

[13]Now King Solomon gave the queen of Sheba all she desired, whatever she asked, besides what Solomon had given her according to the royal generosity. So she turned and went to her own country, she and her servants.

10:11 [a] Or *algum* (compare 2 Chronicles 9:10, 11)

SOLOMON'S GREAT WEALTH

14The weight of gold that
came to Solomon yearly was
six hundred and sixty-six
talents of gold, 15besides *that*
from the traveling merchants,
from the income of traders,
from all the kings of Arabia,
and from the governors of the
country.

16And King Solomon made
two hundred large shields *of*
hammered gold; six hundred
shekels of gold went into each
shield. 17He also *made* three
hundred shields *of* hammered
gold; three minas of gold went
into each shield. The king put
them in the House of the Forest of Lebanon.

18Moreover the king made
a great throne of ivory, and
overlaid it with pure gold.
19The throne had six steps,
and the top of the throne *was*
round at the back; *there were*
armrests on either side of the
place of the seat, and two lions
stood beside the armrests.
20Twelve lions stood there,
one on each side of the six
steps; nothing like *this* had
been made for any *other* kingdom.

21All King Solomon's drinking vessels *were* gold, and all
the vessels of the House of the
Forest of Lebanon *were* pure
gold. Not *one was* silver, for
this was accounted as nothing in the days of Solomon.
22For the king had merchant
ships[a] at sea with the fleet of
Hiram. Once every three years
the merchant ships came
bringing gold, silver, ivory,
apes, and monkeys.[b] 23So
King Solomon surpassed all
the kings of the earth in riches
and wisdom.

24Now all the earth sought
the presence of Solomon to
hear his wisdom, which God
had put in his heart. 25Each
man brought his present: articles of silver and gold, garments, armor, spices, horses,
and mules, at a set rate year
by year.

26And Solomon gathered
chariots and horsemen; he
had one thousand four hundred chariots and twelve
thousand horsemen, whom
he stationed[a] in the chariot
cities and with the king at
Jerusalem. 27The king made
silver *as common* in Jerusalem as stones, and he made
cedar trees as abundant as the
sycamores which *are* in the
lowland.

28Also Solomon had horses
imported from Egypt and
Keveh; the king's merchants
bought them in Keveh at the
current price. 29Now a chariot
that was imported from Egypt
cost six hundred *shekels* of sil-

10:22 [a] Literally *ships of Tarshish,* deep-sea vessels [b] Or *peacocks* 10:26 [a] Following Septuagint, Syriac, Targum, and Vulgate (compare 2 Chronicles 9:25); Masoretic Text reads *led.*

ver, and a horse one hundred
and fifty; and thus, through
their agents,[a] they exported
them to all the kings of the
Hittites and the kings of Syria.

SOLOMON'S HEART TURNS FROM THE LORD

11 But King Solomon loved
many foreign women, as
well as the daughter of Pharaoh: women of the Moabites,
Ammonites, Edomites, Sidonians, *and* Hittites— 2from
the nations of whom the LORD
had said to the children of Israel, "You shall not intermarry
with them, nor they with you.
Surely they will turn away your
hearts after their gods." Solomon clung to these in love.
3And he had seven hundred
wives, princesses, and three
hundred concubines; and his
wives turned away his heart.
4For it was so, when Solomon
was old, that his wives turned
his heart after other gods;
and his heart was not loyal
to the LORD his God, as *was*
the heart of his father David.
5For Solomon went after Ashtoreth the goddess of the Sidonians, and after Milcom the
abomination of the Ammon-
ites. 6Solomon did evil in the
sight of the LORD, and did not
fully follow the LORD, as *did*
his father David. 7Then Solomon built a high place for
Chemosh the abomination of
Moab, on the hill that *is* east of
Jerusalem, and for Molech the
abomination of the people of
Ammon. 8And he did likewise
for all his foreign wives, who
burned incense and sacrificed
to their gods.
9So the LORD became
angry with Solomon, because
his heart had turned from
the LORD God of Israel, who
had appeared to him twice,
10and had commanded him
concerning this thing, that
he should not go after other
gods; but he did not keep what
the LORD had commanded.
11Therefore the LORD said to
Solomon, "Because you have
done this, and have not kept
My covenant and My statutes,
which I have commanded you,
I will surely tear the kingdom
away from you and give it to
your servant. 12Nevertheless I
will not do it in your days, for
the sake of your father David;
I will tear it out of the hand of
your son. 13However I will not
tear away the whole kingdom;
I will give one tribe to your
son for the sake of My servant
David, and for the sake of Jerusalem which I have chosen."

ADVERSARIES OF SOLOMON

14Now the LORD raised up
an adversary against Sol-
omon, Hadad the Edomite; he
was a descendant of the king
in Edom. 15For it happened,
when David was in Edom, and

10:29 [a] Literally *by their hands*

Joab the commander of the
army had gone up to bury the
slain, after he had killed every
male in Edom 16(because for
six months Joab remained
there with all Israel, until he
had cut down every male in
Edom), 17that Hadad fled to
go to Egypt, he and certain
Edomites of his father's servants with him. Hadad *was*
still a little child. 18Then they
arose from Midian and came
to Paran; and they took men
with them from Paran and
came to Egypt, to Pharaoh
king of Egypt, who gave him
a house, apportioned food for
him, and gave him land. 19And
Hadad found great favor in the
sight of Pharaoh, so that he
gave him as wife the sister of
his own wife, that is, the sister
of Queen Tahpenes. 20Then
the sister of Tahpenes bore
him Genubath his son, whom
Tahpenes weaned in Phar-
aoh's house. And Genubath
was in Pharaoh's household
among the sons of Pharaoh.

21So when Hadad heard in
Egypt that David rested with
his fathers, and that Joab the
commander of the army was
dead, Hadad said to Pharaoh,
"Let me depart, that I may go
to my own country."

22Then Pharaoh said to him,
"But what have you lacked with
me, that suddenly you seek to
go to your own country?"

So he answered, "Nothing,
but do let me go anyway."

23And God raised up *an-
other* adversary against him,
Rezon the son of Eliadah, who
had fled from his lord, Hadadezer king of Zobah. 24So
he gathered men to him and
became captain over a band
of raiders, when David killed
those *of Zobah.* And they went
to Damascus and dwelt there,
and reigned in Damascus.
25He was an adversary of Israel
all the days of Solomon (besides the trouble that Hadad
caused); and he abhorred Israel, and reigned over Syria.

JEROBOAM'S REBELLION

26Then Solomon's servant,
Jeroboam the son of Nebat,
an Ephraimite from Zereda,
whose mother's name *was* Ze-
ruah, a widow, also rebelled
against the king.

27And this *is* what caused
him to rebel against the king:
Solomon had built the Millo
and repaired the damages to
the City of David his father.
28The man Jeroboam *was* a
mighty man of valor; and Solomon, seeing that the young
man was industrious, made
him the officer over all the
labor force of the house of
Joseph.

29Now it happened at that
time, when Jeroboam went out
of Jerusalem, that the prophet
Ahijah the Shilonite met him
on the way; and he had clothed
himself with a new garment,
and the two *were* alone in the
field. 30Then Ahijah took hold
of the new garment that *was*

on him, and tore it *into* twelve pieces. 31And he said to Jeroboam, "Take for yourself ten pieces, for thus says the LORD, the God of Israel: 'Behold, I will tear the kingdom out of the hand of Solomon and will give ten tribes to you 32(but he shall have one tribe for the sake of My servant David, and for the sake of Jerusalem, the city which I have chosen out of all the tribes of Israel), 33because they have[a] forsaken Me, and worshiped Ashtoreth the goddess of the Sidonians, Chemosh the god of the Moabites, and Milcom the god of the people of Ammon, and have not walked in My ways to do *what is* right in My eyes and *keep* My statutes and My judgments, as *did* his father David. 34However I will not take the whole kingdom out of his hand, because I have made him ruler all the days of his life for the sake of My servant David, whom I chose because he kept My commandments and My statutes. 35But I will take the kingdom out of his son's hand and give it to you—ten tribes. 36And to his son I will give one tribe, that My servant David may always have a lamp before Me in Jerusalem, the city which I have chosen for Myself, to put My name there. 37So I will take you, and you shall reign over all your heart desires, and you shall be king over Israel. 38Then it shall be, if you heed all that I command you, walk in My ways, and do *what is* right in My sight, to keep My statutes and My commandments, as My servant David did, then I will be with you and build for you an enduring house, as I built for David, and will give Israel to you. 39And I will afflict the descendants of David because of this, but not forever.'"

40Solomon therefore sought to kill Jeroboam. But Jeroboam arose and fled to Egypt, to Shishak king of Egypt, and was in Egypt until the death of Solomon.

DEATH OF SOLOMON

41Now the rest of the acts of Solomon, all that he did, and his wisdom, *are* they not written in the book of the acts of Solomon? 42And the period that Solomon reigned in Jerusalem over all Israel *was* forty years. 43Then Solomon rested with his fathers, and was buried in the City of David his father. And Rehoboam his son reigned in his place.

THE REVOLT AGAINST REHOBOAM

12 And Rehoboam went to Shechem, for all Israel had gone to Shechem to

11:33 [a] Following Masoretic Text and Targum; Septuagint, Syriac, and Vulgate read *he has.*

make him king. 2So it happened, when Jeroboam the
son of Nebat heard *it* (he was
still in Egypt, for he had fled
from the presence of King Solomon and had been dwelling
in Egypt), 3that they sent and
called him. Then Jeroboam
and the whole assembly of
Israel came and spoke to Rehoboam, saying, 4"Your father
made our yoke heavy; now
therefore, lighten the burdensome service of your father,
and his heavy yoke which he
put on us, and we will serve
you."

5So he said to them, "De-
part *for* three days, then come
back to me." And the people
departed.

6Then King Rehoboam
consulted the elders who
stood before his father Solomon while he still lived, and
he said, "How do you advise
me to answer these people?"

7And they spoke to him,
saying, "If you will be a servant to these people today,
and serve them, and answer
them, and speak good words
to them, then they will be your
servants forever."

8But he rejected the advice
which the elders had given
him, and consulted the young
men who had grown up with
him, who stood before him.
9And he said to them, "What
advice do you give? How
should we answer this people
who have spoken to me, saying, 'Lighten the yoke which
your father put on us'?"

10Then the young men
who had grown up with him
spoke to him, saying, "Thus
you should speak to this people who have spoken to you,
saying, 'Your father made our
yoke heavy, but you make
it lighter on us'—thus you
shall say to them: 'My little
finger shall be thicker than
my father's waist! 11And now,
whereas my father put a heavy
yoke on you, I will add to your
yoke; my father chastised you
with whips, but I will chastise
you with scourges!'"[a]

12So Jeroboam and all the
people came to Rehoboam
the third day, as the king had
directed, saying, "Come back
to me the third day." 13Then
the king answered the people roughly, and rejected the
advice which the elders had
given him; 14and he spoke to
them according to the advice
of the young men, saying, "My
father made your yoke heavy,
but I will add to your yoke;
my father chastised you with
whips, but I will chastise you
with scourges!"[a] 15So the king
did not listen to the people;
for the turn *of events* was from
the LORD, that He might fulfill
His word, which the LORD had
spoken by Ahijah the Shilonite to Jeroboam the son of
Nebat.

12:11 [a] Literally *scorpions*

12:14 [a] Literally *scorpions*

16Now when all Israel saw
that the king did not listen to
them, the people answered
the king, saying:

"What share have
  we in David?
We have no inheritance
  in the son of Jesse.
To your tents, O Israel!
Now, see to your own
  house, O David!"

So Israel departed to
their tents. 17But Rehoboam
reigned over the children of
Israel who dwelt in the cities
of Judah.
18Then King Rehoboam
sent Adoram, who *was* in
charge of the revenue; but all
Israel stoned him with stones,
and he died. Therefore King
Rehoboam mounted his chariot in haste to flee to Jerusalem. 19So Israel has been in
rebellion against the house
of David to this day.
20Now it came to pass when
all Israel heard that Jeroboam
had come back, they sent
for him and called him to
the congregation, and made
him king over all Israel. There
was none who followed the
house of David, but the tribe
of Judah only.
21And when Rehoboam
came to Jerusalem, he assembled all the house of Judah
with the tribe of Benjamin,
one hundred and eighty thousand chosen *men* who were
warriors, to fight against the
house of Israel, that he might
restore the kingdom to Rehoboam the son of Solomon.
22But the word of God came
to Shemaiah the man of God,
saying, 23"Speak to Rehoboam
the son of Solomon, king of
Judah, to all the house of
Judah and Benjamin, and to
the rest of the people, saying, 24'Thus says the LORD:
"You shall not go up nor fight
against your brethren the children of Israel. Let every man
return to his house, for this
thing is from Me."'" Therefore they obeyed the word of
the LORD, and turned back,
according to the word of the
LORD.

JEROBOAM'S GOLD CALVES

25Then Jeroboam built
Shechem in the mountains
of Ephraim, and dwelt there.
Also he went out from there
and built Penuel. 26And Jeroboam said in his heart, "Now
the kingdom may return to
the house of David: 27If these
people go up to offer sacrifices in the house of the LORD
at Jerusalem, then the heart
of this people will turn back
to their lord, Rehoboam king
of Judah, and they will kill
me and go back to Rehoboam
king of Judah."
28Therefore the king asked
advice, made two calves of
gold, and said to the people,
"It is too much for you to go
up to Jerusalem. Here are
your gods, O Israel, which

brought you up from the land of Egypt!" 29And he set up one in Bethel, and the other he put in Dan. 30Now this thing became a sin, for the people went *to worship* before the one as far as Dan. 31He made shrines[a] on the high places, and made priests from every class of people, who were not of the sons of Levi.

32Jeroboam ordained a feast on the fifteenth day of the eighth month, like the feast that *was* in Judah, and offered sacrifices on the altar. So he did at Bethel, sacrificing to the calves that he had made. And at Bethel he installed the priests of the high places which he had made. 33So he made offerings on the altar which he had made at Bethel on the fifteenth day of the eighth month, in the month which he had devised in his own heart. And he ordained a feast for the children of Israel, and offered sacrifices on the altar and burned incense.

THE MESSAGE OF THE MAN OF GOD

13 And behold, a man of God went from Judah to Bethel by the word of the LORD, and Jeroboam stood by the altar to burn incense. 2Then he cried out against *the altar by the word of the* LORD, and said, "O altar, altar! Thus says the LORD: 'Behold, a child, Josiah by name, shall be born to the house of David; and on you he shall sacrifice the priests of the high places who burn incense on you, and men's bones shall be burned on you.'" 3And he gave a sign the same day, saying, "This *is* the sign which the LORD has spoken: Surely the altar shall split apart, and the ashes on it shall be poured out."

4So it came to pass when King Jeroboam heard the saying of the man of God, who cried out against the altar in Bethel, that he stretched out his hand from the altar, saying, "Arrest him!" Then his hand, which he stretched out toward him, withered, so that he could not pull it back to himself. 5The altar also was split apart, and the ashes poured out from the altar, according to the sign which the man of God had given by the word of the LORD. 6Then the king answered and said to the man of God, "Please entreat the favor of the LORD your God, and pray for me, that my hand may be restored to me."

So the man of God entreated the LORD, and the king's hand was restored to him, and became as before. 7Then the king said to the man of God, "Come home with me and refresh yourself, and I will give you a reward."

12:31 [a] Literally *a house*

[8]But the man of God said to
the king, "If you were to give
me half your house, I would
not go in with you; nor would
I eat bread nor drink water in
this place. [9]For so it was commanded me by the word of the
LORD, saying, 'You shall not
eat bread, nor drink water, nor
return by the same way you
came.'" [10]So he went another
way and did not return by the
way he came to Bethel.

DEATH OF THE MAN OF GOD

[11]Now an old prophet dwelt
in Bethel, and his sons came
and told him all the works
that the man of God had done
that day in Bethel; they also
told their father the words
which he had spoken to the
king. [12]And their father said
to them, "Which way did he
go?" For his sons had seen[a]
which way the man of God
went who came from Judah.
[13]Then he said to his sons,
"Saddle the donkey for me."
So they saddled the donkey
for him; and he rode on it,
[14]and went after the man of
God, and found him sitting
under an oak. Then he said
to him, "*Are* you the man of
God who came from Judah?"

And he said, "I *am*."

[15]Then he said to him,
"Come home with me and eat
bread."

[16]And he said, "I cannot return with you nor go in with
you; neither can I eat bread
nor drink water with you in
this place. [17]For I have been
told by the word of the LORD,
'You shall not eat bread nor
drink water there, nor return
by going the way you came.'"

[18]He said to him, "I too
am a prophet as you *are*, and
an angel spoke to me by the
word of the LORD, saying,
'Bring him back with you to
your house, that he may eat
bread and drink water.'" (He
was lying to him.)

[19]So he went back with him,
and ate bread in his house,
and drank water.

[20]Now it happened, as
they sat at the table, that the
word of the LORD came to
the prophet who had brought
him back; [21]and he cried out
to the man of God who came
from Judah, saying, "Thus
says the LORD: 'Because you
have disobeyed the word of
the LORD, and have not kept
the commandment which the
LORD your God commanded
you, [22]but you came back, ate
bread, and drank water in the
place of which *the LORD* said to
you, "Eat no bread and drink
no water," your corpse shall
not come to the tomb of your
fathers.'"

[23]So it was, after he had
eaten bread and after he had
drunk, that he saddled the
donkey for him, the prophet

13:12 [a] Septuagint, Syriac, Targum, and Vulgate read *showed him*.

whom he had brought back.
24When he was gone, a lion
met him on the road and
killed him. And his corpse
was thrown on the road, and
the donkey stood by it. The
lion also stood by the corpse.
25And there, men passed by
and saw the corpse thrown on
the road, and the lion standing by the corpse. Then they
went and told *it* in the city
where the old prophet dwelt.
26Now when the prophet
who had brought him back
from the way heard *it,* he said,
"It *is* the man of God who was
disobedient to the word of the
LORD. Therefore the LORD
has delivered him to the lion,
which has torn him and killed
him, according to the word of
the LORD which He spoke to
him." 27And he spoke to his
sons, saying, "Saddle the donkey for me." So they saddled
it. 28Then he went and found
his corpse thrown on the road,
and the donkey and the lion
standing by the corpse. The
lion had not eaten the corpse
nor torn the donkey. 29And the
prophet took up the corpse of
the man of God, laid it on the
donkey, and brought it back.
So the old prophet came to
the city to mourn, and to bury
him. 30Then he laid the corpse
in his own tomb; and they
mourned over him, *saying,*
"Alas, my brother!" 31So it was,
after he had buried him, that
he spoke to his sons, saying,
"When I am dead, then bury
me in the tomb where the
man of God *is* buried; lay my
bones beside his bones. 32For
the saying which he cried
out by the word of the LORD
against the altar in Bethel, and
against all the shrines[a] on the
high places which *are* in the
cities of Samaria, will surely
come to pass."
33After this event Jero-
boam did not turn from his
evil way, but again he made
priests from every class of
people for the high places;
whoever wished, he conse-
crated him, and he became
one of the priests of the high
places. 34And this thing was
the sin of the house of Jeroboam, so as to exterminate
and destroy *it* from the face
of the earth.

JUDGMENT ON THE HOUSE OF JEROBOAM

14 At that time Abijah the
son of Jeroboam became
sick. 2And Jeroboam said to
his wife, "Please arise, and disguise yourself, that they may
not recognize you as the wife
of Jeroboam, and go to Shiloh.
Indeed, Ahijah the prophet *is*
there, who told me that *I would*
be king over this people. 3Also
take with you ten loaves, *some*
cakes, and a jar of honey, and
go to him; he will tell you what
will become of the child." 4And

13:32 [a] Literally *houses*

Jeroboam's wife did so; she
arose and went to Shiloh, and
came to the house of Ahijah.
But Ahijah could not see, for
his eyes were glazed by reason
of his age.
5Now the LORD had said to
Ahijah, "Here is the wife of
Jeroboam, coming to ask you
something about her son, for
he *is* sick. Thus and thus you
shall say to her; for it will be,
when she comes in, that she
will pretend *to be* another
woman."
6And so it was, when Ahijah
heard the sound of her footsteps as she came through the
door, he said, "Come in, wife
of Jeroboam. Why do you pretend *to be* another *person?* For
I *have been* sent to you *with*
bad *news.* 7Go, tell Jeroboam,
'Thus says the LORD God of
Israel: "Because I exalted
you from among the people,
and made you ruler over My
people Israel, 8and tore the
kingdom away from the house
of David, and gave it to you;
and *yet* you have not been as
My servant David, who kept
My commandments and who
followed Me with all his heart,
to do only *what was* right in
My eyes; 9but you have done
more evil than all who were
before you, for you have gone
and made for yourself other
gods and molded images to
provoke Me to anger, and have
cast Me behind your back—
10therefore behold! I will bring
disaster on the house of Jeroboam, and will cut off from
Jeroboam every male in Israel, bond and free; I will take
away the remnant of the house
of Jeroboam, as one takes
away refuse until it is all gone.
11The dogs shall eat whoever
belongs to Jeroboam and dies
in the city, and the birds of the
air shall eat whoever dies in
the field; for the LORD has spoken!"' 12Arise therefore, go to
your own house. When your
feet enter the city, the child
shall die. 13And all Israel shall
mourn for him and bury him,
for he is the only one of Jeroboam who shall come to the
grave, because in him there is
found something good toward
the LORD God of Israel in the
house of Jeroboam.
14"Moreover the LORD will
raise up for Himself a king
over Israel who shall cut off
the house of Jeroboam; this is
the day. What? Even now! 15For
the LORD will strike Israel, as
a reed is shaken in the water.
He will uproot Israel from this
good land which He gave to
their fathers, and will scatter
them beyond the River,[a] because they have made their
wooden images,[b] provoking
the LORD to anger. 16And He
will give Israel up because
of the sins of Jeroboam, who
sinned and who made Israel
sin."

14:15 [a] That is, the Euphrates [b] Hebrew *Asherim,* Canaanite deities

17Then Jeroboam's wife arose and departed, and came to Tirzah. When she came to the threshold of the house, the child died. 18And they buried him; and all Israel mourned for him, according to the word of the LORD which He spoke through His servant Ahijah the prophet.

DEATH OF JEROBOAM

19Now the rest of the acts of Jeroboam, how he made war and how he reigned, indeed they *are* written in the book of the chronicles of the kings of Israel. 20The period that Jeroboam reigned *was* twenty-two years. So he rested with his fathers. Then Nadab his son reigned in his place.

REHOBOAM REIGNS IN JUDAH

21And Rehoboam the son of Solomon reigned in Judah. Rehoboam *was* forty-one years old when he became king. He reigned seventeen years in Jerusalem, the city which the LORD had chosen out of all the tribes of Israel, to put His name there. His mother's name *was* Naamah, an Ammonitess. 22Now Judah did evil in the sight of the LORD, and they provoked Him to jealousy with their sins which they committed, more than all that their fathers had done. 23For they also built for themselves high places, *sacred* pillars, and wooden images on every high hill and under every green tree. 24And there were also perverted persons[a] in the land. They did according to all the abominations of the nations which the LORD had cast out before the children of Israel.

25It happened in the fifth year of King Rehoboam *that* Shishak king of Egypt came up against Jerusalem. 26And he took away the treasures of the house of the LORD and the treasures of the king's house; he took away everything. He also took away all the gold shields which Solomon had made. 27Then King Rehoboam made bronze shields in their place, and committed *them* to the hands of the captains of the guard, who guarded the doorway of the king's house. 28And whenever the king entered the house of the LORD, the guards carried them, then brought them back into the guardroom.

29Now the rest of the acts of Rehoboam, and all that he did, *are* they not written in the book of the chronicles of the kings of Judah? 30And there was war between Rehoboam and Jeroboam all *their* days. 31So Rehoboam rested with his fathers, and was buried with his fathers in the City of David. His

14:24 [a] Hebrew *qadesh,* that is, one practicing sodomy and prostitution in religious rituals

mother's name *was* Naamah, an Ammonitess. Then Abijam[a] his son reigned in his place.

ABIJAM REIGNS IN JUDAH

15 In the eighteenth year of King Jeroboam the son of Nebat, Abijam became king over Judah. 2He reigned three years in Jerusalem. His mother's name *was* Maachah the granddaughter of Abishalom. 3And he walked in all the sins of his father, which he had done before him; his heart was not loyal to the LORD his God, as was the heart of his father David. 4Nevertheless for David's sake the LORD his God gave him a lamp in Jerusalem, by setting up his son after him and by establishing Jerusalem; 5because David did *what was* right in the eyes of the LORD, and had not turned aside from anything that He commanded him all the days of his life, except in the matter of Uriah the Hittite. 6And there was war between Rehoboam[a] and Jeroboam all the days of his life. 7Now the rest of the acts of Abijam, and all that he did, *are* they not written in the book of the chronicles of the kings of Judah? And there was war between Abijam and Jeroboam.

8So Abijam rested with his fathers, and they buried him in the City of David. Then Asa his son reigned in his place.

ASA REIGNS IN JUDAH

9In the twentieth year of Jeroboam king of Israel, Asa became king over Judah. 10And he reigned forty-one years in Jerusalem. His grandmother's name *was* Maachah the granddaughter of Abishalom. 11Asa did *what was* right in the eyes of the LORD, as *did* his father David. 12And he banished the perverted persons[a] from the land, and removed all the idols that his fathers had made. 13Also he removed Maachah his grandmother from *being* queen mother, because she had made an obscene image of Asherah.[a] And Asa cut down her obscene image and burned *it* by the Brook Kidron. 14But the high places were not removed. Nevertheless Asa's heart was loyal to the LORD all his days. 15He also brought into the house of the LORD the things which his father had dedicated, and the things which he himself had dedicated: silver and gold and utensils.

16Now there was war between Asa and Baasha king of Israel all their days. 17And Baasha king of Israel came up against Judah, and built Ramah, that he might let none

14:31 [a] Spelled *Abijah* in 2 Chronicles 12:16ff 15:6 [a] Following Masoretic Text, Septuagint, Targum, and Vulgate; some Hebrew manuscripts and Syriac read *Abijam*. 15:12 [a] Hebrew *qedeshim,* that is, those practicing sodomy and prostitution in religious rituals 15:13 [a] A Canaanite goddess

go out or come in to Asa king
of Judah. 18Then Asa took all
the silver and gold *that was* left
in the treasuries of the house
of the LORD and the treasuries
of the king's house, and delivered them into the hand of his
servants. And King Asa sent
them to Ben-Hadad the son
of Tabrimmon, the son of He-
zion, king of Syria, who dwelt
in Damascus, saying, 19"*Let*
there be a treaty between you
and me, as there was between
my father and your father.
See, I have sent you a present
of silver and gold. Come and
break your treaty with Baasha
king of Israel, so that he will
withdraw from me."

20So Ben-Hadad heeded
King Asa, and sent the captains
of his armies against the cities
of Israel. He attacked Ijon, Dan,
Abel Beth Maachah, and all
Chinneroth, with all the land of
Naphtali. 21Now it happened,
when Baasha heard *it,* that he
stopped building Ramah, and
remained in Tirzah.

22Then King Asa made a
proclamation throughout all
Judah; none *was* exempted.
And they took away the stones
and timber of Ramah, which
Baasha had used for building;
and with them King Asa built
Geba of Benjamin, and Mizpah.

23The rest of all the acts
of Asa, all his might, all that
he did, and the cities which
he built, *are* they not written
in the book of the chronicles
of the kings of Judah? But in
the time of his old age he was
diseased in his feet. 24So Asa
rested with his fathers, and
was buried with his fathers
in the City of David his father.
Then Jehoshaphat his son
reigned in his place.

NADAB REIGNS IN ISRAEL

25Now Nadab the son of Jeroboam became king over Israel in the second year of Asa
king of Judah, and he reigned
over Israel two years. 26And
he did evil in the sight of the
LORD, and walked in the way
of his father, and in his sin by
which he had made Israel sin.

27Then Baasha the son of
Ahijah, of the house of Issachar, conspired against him.
And Baasha killed him at Gibbethon, which *belonged* to
the Philistines, while Nadab
and all Israel laid siege to
Gibbethon. 28Baasha killed
him in the third year of Asa
king of Judah, and reigned
in his place. 29And it was so,
when he became king, *that* he
killed all the house of Jeroboam. He did not leave to Jeroboam anyone that breathed,
until he had destroyed him,
according to the word of the
LORD which He had spoken
by His servant Ahijah the Shilonite, 30because of the sins
of Jeroboam, which he had
sinned and by which he had
made Israel sin, because of
his provocation with which he
had provoked the LORD God
of Israel to anger.

[31]Now the rest of the acts of
Nadab, and all that he did, *are*
they not written in the book
of the chronicles of the kings
of Israel? [32]And there was war
between Asa and Baasha king
of Israel all their days.

BAASHA REIGNS IN ISRAEL

[33]In the third year of Asa
king of Judah, Baasha the son
of Ahijah became king over all
Israel in Tirzah, and *reigned*
twenty-four years. [34]He did
evil in the sight of the LORD,
and walked in the way of Jeroboam, and in his sin by which
he had made Israel sin.

16 Then the word of the
LORD came to Jehu the
son of Hanani, against Baasha,
saying: [2]"Inasmuch as I lifted
you out of the dust and made
you ruler over My people Israel, and you have walked in
the way of Jeroboam, and have
made My people Israel sin, to
provoke Me to anger with their
sins, [3]surely I will take away
the posterity of Baasha and
the posterity of his house, and
I will make your house like the
house of Jeroboam the son
of Nebat. [4]The dogs shall eat
whoever belongs to Baasha
and dies in the city, and the
birds of the air shall eat whoever dies in the fields."

[5]Now the rest of the acts of
Baasha, what he did, and his
might, *are* they not written in
the book of the chronicles of
the kings of Israel? [6]So Baasha
rested with his fathers and was
buried in Tirzah. Then Elah his
son reigned in his place.

[7]And also the word of the
LORD came by the prophet
Jehu the son of Hanani against
Baasha and his house, because
of all the evil that he did in the
sight of the LORD in provoking
Him to anger with the work
of his hands, in being like the
house of Jeroboam, and because he killed them.

ELAH REIGNS IN ISRAEL

[8]In the twenty-sixth year
of Asa king of Judah, Elah the
son of Baasha became king
over Israel, *and reigned* two
years in Tirzah. [9]Now his servant Zimri, commander of
half *his* chariots, conspired
against him as he was in Tirzah drinking himself drunk
in the house of Arza, steward
of *his* house in Tirzah. [10]And
Zimri went in and struck him
and killed him in the twenty-
seventh year of Asa king of
Judah, and reigned in his
place.

[11]Then it came to pass,
when he began to reign, as
soon as he was seated on
his throne, *that* he killed all
the household of Baasha; he
did not leave him one male,
neither of his relatives nor
of his friends. [12]Thus Zimri
destroyed all the household
of Baasha, according to the
word of the LORD, which He
spoke against Baasha by Jehu
the prophet, [13]for all the sins
of Baasha and the sins of Elah

his son, by which they had
sinned and by which they had
made Israel sin, in provoking the LORD God of Israel to
anger with their idols.
14Now the rest of the acts of
Elah, and all that he did, *are*
they not written in the book
of the chronicles of the kings
of Israel?

ZIMRI REIGNS IN ISRAEL

15In the twenty-seventh
year of Asa king of Judah,
Zimri had reigned in Tirzah
seven days. And the people
were encamped against Gibbethon, which *belonged* to the
Philistines. 16Now the people
who were encamped heard
it said, "Zimri has conspired
and also has killed the king."
So all Israel made Omri, the
commander of the army,
king over Israel that day in
the camp. 17Then Omri and all
Israel with him went up from
Gibbethon, and they besieged
Tirzah. 18And it happened,
when Zimri saw that the city
was taken, that he went into
the citadel of the king's house
and burned the king's house
down upon himself with fire,
and died, 19because of the sins
which he had committed in
doing evil in the sight of the
LORD, in walking in the way
of Jeroboam, and in his sin
which he had committed to
make Israel sin.
20Now the rest of the acts
of Zimri, and the treason he
committed, *are* they not written in the book of the chronicles of the kings of Israel?

OMRI REIGNS IN ISRAEL

21Then the people of Israel
were divided into two parts:
half of the people followed
Tibni the son of Ginath, to
make him king, and half followed Omri. 22But the people
who followed Omri prevailed
over the people who followed
Tibni the son of Ginath. So
Tibni died and Omri reigned.
23In the thirty-first year of Asa
king of Judah, Omri became
king over Israel, *and reigned*
twelve years. Six years he
reigned in Tirzah. 24And he
bought the hill of Samaria
from Shemer for two talents of
silver; then he built on the hill,
and called the name of the city
which he built, Samaria, after
the name of Shemer, owner
of the hill. 25Omri did evil in
the eyes of the LORD, and did
worse than all who *were* before him. 26For he walked in
all the ways of Jeroboam the
son of Nebat, and in his sin by
which he had made Israel sin,
provoking the LORD God of Israel to anger with their idols.
27Now the rest of the acts
of Omri which he did, and
the might that he showed, *are*
they not written in the book
of the chronicles of the kings
of Israel?
28So Omri rested with his
fathers and was buried in
Samaria. Then Ahab his son
reigned in his place.

AHAB REIGNS IN ISRAEL

29In the thirty-eighth year of
Asa king of Judah, Ahab the son
of Omri became king over Israel; and Ahab the son of Omri
reigned over Israel in Samaria
twenty-two years. 30Now Ahab
the son of Omri did evil in the
sight of the LORD, more than
all who *were* before him. 31And
it came to pass, as though it
had been a trivial thing for him
to walk in the sins of Jeroboam
the son of Nebat, that he took
as wife Jezebel the daughter of
Ethbaal, king of the Sidonians;
and he went and served Baal
and worshiped him. 32Then he
set up an altar for Baal in the
temple of Baal, which he had
built in Samaria. 33And Ahab
made a wooden image.[a] Ahab
did more to provoke the LORD
God of Israel to anger than all
the kings of Israel who were
before him. 34In his days Hiel
of Bethel built Jericho. He laid
its foundation with Abiram his
firstborn, and with his youngest *son* Segub he set up its
gates, according to the word
of the LORD, which He had spoken through Joshua the son
of Nun.[a]

ELIJAH PROCLAIMS A DROUGHT

17 And Elijah the Tish-
bite, of the inhabitants
of Gilead, said to Ahab, "*As*
the LORD God of Israel lives,
before whom I stand, there
shall not be dew nor rain these
years, except at my word."

2Then the word of the LORD
came to him, saying, 3"Get
away from here and turn eastward, and hide by the Brook
Cherith, which flows into the
Jordan. 4And it will be *that* you
shall drink from the brook,
and I have commanded the
ravens to feed you there."

5So he went and did according to the word of the LORD,
for he went and stayed by the
Brook Cherith, which flows
into the Jordan. 6The ravens
brought him bread and meat
in the morning, and bread and
meat in the evening; and he
drank from the brook. 7And it
happened after a while that the
brook dried up, because there
had been no rain in the land.

ELIJAH AND THE WIDOW

8Then the word of the LORD
came to him, saying, 9"Arise,
go to Zarephath, which *belongs*
to Sidon, and dwell there. See,
I have commanded a widow
there to provide for you." 10So
he arose and went to Zarephath. And when he came to
the gate of the city, indeed a
widow *was* there gathering
sticks. And he called to her
and said, "Please bring me
a little water in a cup, that I
may drink." 11And as she was
going to get *it*, he called to her

16:33 [a] Hebrew *Asherah*, a Canaanite goddess **16:34** [a] Compare Joshua 6:26

and said, “Please bring me a
morsel of bread in your hand.”
12So she said, “As the LORD
your God lives, I do not have
bread, only a handful of flour
in a bin, and a little oil in a
jar; and see, I *am* gathering a
couple of sticks that I may go
in and prepare it for myself
and my son, that we may eat
it, and die.”
13And Elijah said to her,
“Do not fear; go *and* do as
you have said, but make me
a small cake from it first, and
bring *it* to me; and afterward
make *some* for yourself and
your son. 14For thus says the
LORD God of Israel: ‘The bin
of flour shall not be used up,
nor shall the jar of oil run dry,
until the day the LORD sends
rain on the earth.’”
15So she went away and did
according to the word of Elijah; and she and he and her
household ate for *many* days.
16The bin of flour was not used
up, nor did the jar of oil run
dry, according to the word of
the LORD which He spoke by
Elijah.

ELIJAH REVIVES THE WIDOW’S SON

17Now it happened after
these things *that* the son of the
woman who owned the house
became sick. And his sickness
was so serious that there was
no breath left in him. 18So she
said to Elijah, “What have I to
do with you, O man of God?
Have you come to me to bring
my sin to remembrance, and
to kill my son?”
19And he said to her, “Give
me your son.” So he took him
out of her arms and carried
him to the upper room where
he was staying, and laid him
on his own bed. 20Then he
cried out to the LORD and
said, “O LORD my God, have
You also brought tragedy on
the widow with whom I lodge,
by killing her son?” 21And he
stretched himself out on the
child three times, and cried
out to the LORD and said,
“O LORD my God, I pray, let
this child’s soul come back to
him.” 22Then the LORD heard
the voice of Elijah; and the
soul of the child came back
to him, and he revived.
23And Elijah took the child
and brought him down from
the upper room into the
house, and gave him to his
mother. And Elijah said, “See,
your son lives!”
24Then the woman said to
Elijah, “Now by this I know
that you *are* a man of God, *and*
that the word of the LORD in
your mouth *is* the truth.”

ELIJAH’S MESSAGE TO AHAB

18 And it came to pass *after*
many days that the word
of the LORD came to Elijah,
in the third year, saying, “Go,
present yourself to Ahab, and
I will send rain on the earth.”
2So Elijah went to present
himself to Ahab; and *there was*
a severe famine in Samaria.

3And Ahab had called Obadiah,
who *was* in charge of *his* house.
(Now Obadiah feared the LORD
greatly. 4For so it was, while
Jezebel massacred the prophets of the LORD, that Obadiah
had taken one hundred prophets and hidden them, fifty to
a cave, and had fed them with
bread and water.) 5And Ahab
had said to Obadiah, "Go into
the land to all the springs of
water and to all the brooks;
perhaps we may find grass
to keep the horses and mules
alive, so that we will not have
to kill any livestock." 6So they
divided the land between them
to explore it; Ahab went one
way by himself, and Obadiah
went another way by himself.

7Now as Obadiah was on
his way, suddenly Elijah met
him; and he recognized him,
and fell on his face, and said,
"*Is* that you, my lord Elijah?"

8And he answered him, "*It
is* I. Go, tell your master, 'Elijah
is here.'"

9So he said, "How have I
sinned, that you are delivering
your servant into the hand of
Ahab, to kill me? 10*As* the LORD
your God lives, there is no
nation or kingdom where my
master has not sent someone
to hunt for you; and when they
said, '*He is* not *here,*' he took
an oath from the kingdom
or nation that they could not
find you. 11And now you say,
'Go, tell your master, "Elijah
is here"'! 12And it shall come
to pass, *as soon as* I am gone
from you, that the Spirit of the
LORD will carry you to a place
I do not know; so when I go
and tell Ahab, and he cannot
find you, he will kill me. But I
your servant have feared the
LORD from my youth. 13Was it
not reported to my lord what
I did when Jezebel killed the
prophets of the LORD, how I
hid one hundred men of the
LORD's prophets, fifty to a
cave, and fed them with bread
and water? 14And now you say,
'Go, tell your master, "Elijah *is
here.*"' He will kill me!"

15Then Elijah said, "*As* the
LORD of hosts lives, before
whom I stand, I will surely
present myself to him today."

16So Obadiah went to meet
Ahab, and told him; and Ahab
went to meet Elijah.

17Then it happened, when
Ahab saw Elijah, that Ahab
said to him, "*Is that* you,
O troubler of Israel?"

18And he answered, "I have
not troubled Israel, but you
and your father's house *have,*
in that you have forsaken
the commandments of the
LORD and have followed the
Baals. 19Now therefore, send
and gather all Israel to me
on Mount Carmel, the four
hundred and fifty prophets
of Baal, and the four hundred
prophets of Asherah,[a] who eat
at Jezebel's table."

18:19 [a] A Canaanite goddess

ELIJAH'S MOUNT CARMEL VICTORY

20 So Ahab sent for all the children of Israel, and gathered the prophets together on Mount Carmel. 21 And Elijah came to all the people, and said, "How long will you falter between two opinions? If the LORD *is* God, follow Him; but if Baal, follow him." But the people answered him not a word. 22 Then Elijah said to the people, "I alone am left a prophet of the LORD; but Baal's prophets *are* four hundred and fifty men. 23 Therefore let them give us two bulls; and let them choose one bull for themselves, cut it in pieces, and lay *it* on the wood, but put no fire *under it;* and I will prepare the other bull, and lay *it* on the wood, but put no fire *under it.* 24 Then you call on the name of your gods, and I will call on the name of the LORD; and the God who answers by fire, He is God."

So all the people answered and said, "It is well spoken."

25 Now Elijah said to the prophets of Baal, "Choose one bull for yourselves and prepare *it* first, for you *are* many; and call on the name of your god, but put no fire *under it.*"

26 So they took the bull which was given them, and they prepared *it,* and called on the name of Baal from morning even till noon, saying, "O Baal, hear us!" But *there was* no voice; no one answered. Then they leaped about the altar which they had made.

27 And so it was, at noon, that Elijah mocked them and said, "Cry aloud, for he *is* a god; either he is meditating, or he is busy, or he is on a journey, *or* perhaps he is sleeping and must be awakened." 28 So they cried aloud, and cut themselves, as was their custom, with knives and lances, until the blood gushed out on them. 29 And when midday was past, they prophesied until the *time* of the offering of the *evening* sacrifice. But *there was* no voice; no one answered, no one paid attention.

30 Then Elijah said to all the people, "Come near to me." So all the people came near to him. And he repaired the altar of the LORD *that was* broken down. 31 And Elijah took twelve stones, according to the number of the tribes of the sons of Jacob, to whom the word of the LORD had come, saying, "Israel shall be your name."[a] 32 Then with the stones he built an altar in the name of the LORD; and he made a trench around the altar large enough to hold two seahs of seed. 33 And he put the wood in order, cut the bull in pieces, and laid *it* on the wood, and said, "Fill four waterpots with water, and pour *it* on the burnt sacrifice and

18:31 [a] Genesis 32:28

on the wood." 34Then he said,
"Do *it* a second time," and they
did *it* a second time; and he
said, "Do *it* a third time," and
they did *it* a third time. 35So the
water ran all around the altar;
and he also filled the trench
with water.

36And it came to pass, at *the*
time of the offering of the *eve-*
ning sacrifice, that Elijah the
prophet came near and said,
"LORD God of Abraham, Isaac,
and Israel, let it be known
this day that You *are* God in
Israel and I *am* Your servant,
and *that* I have done all these
things at Your word. 37Hear
me, O LORD, hear me, that this
people may know that You *are*
the LORD God, and *that* You
have turned their hearts back
to You again."

38Then the fire of the LORD
fell and consumed the burnt
sacrifice, and the wood and
the stones and the dust, and
it licked up the water that *was*
in the trench. 39Now when all
the people saw *it,* they fell on
their faces; and they said, "The
LORD, He *is* God! The LORD,
He *is* God!"

40And Elijah said to them,
"Seize the prophets of Baal! Do
not let one of them escape!"
So they seized them; and Elijah brought them down to the
Brook Kishon and executed
them there.

THE DROUGHT ENDS

41Then Elijah said to Ahab,
"Go up, eat and drink; for *there*
is the sound of abundance of
rain." 42So Ahab went up to eat
and drink. And Elijah went up
to the top of Carmel; then he
bowed down on the ground,
and put his face between his
knees, 43and said to his servant, "Go up now, look toward
the sea."

So he went up and looked,
and said, "*There is* nothing."
And seven times he said, "Go
again."

44Then it came to pass the
seventh *time,* that he said,
"There is a cloud, as small as
a man's hand, rising out of the
sea!" So he said, "Go up, say to
Ahab, 'Prepare *your chariot,*
and go down before the rain
stops you.'"

45Now it happened in the
meantime that the sky be-
came black with clouds and
wind, and there was a heavy
rain. So Ahab rode away and
went to Jezreel. 46Then the
hand of the LORD came upon
Elijah; and he girded up his
loins and ran ahead of Ahab
to the entrance of Jezreel.

ELIJAH ESCAPES FROM JEZEBEL

19 And Ahab told Jezebel all
that Elijah had done, also
how he had executed all the
prophets with the sword. 2Then
Jezebel sent a messenger to
Elijah, saying, "So let the gods
do *to me,* and more also, if I do
not make your life as the life
of one of them by tomorrow
about this time." 3And when he

saw *that,* he arose and ran for
his life, and went to Beersheba,
which *belongs* to Judah, and
left his servant there.
4But he himself went a
day's journey into the wilderness, and came and sat down
under a broom tree. And he
prayed that he might die, and
said, "It is enough! Now, LORD,
take my life, for I *am* no better
than my fathers!"
5Then as he lay and slept
under a broom tree, suddenly
an angel[a] touched him, and
said to him, "Arise *and* eat."
6Then he looked, and there by
his head *was* a cake baked on
coals, and a jar of water. So he
ate and drank, and lay down
again. 7And the angel[a] of the
LORD came back the second
time, and touched him, and
said, "Arise *and* eat, because
the journey *is* too great for
you." 8So he arose, and ate
and drank; and he went in
the strength of that food forty
days and forty nights as far as
Horeb, the mountain of God.
9And there he went into a
cave, and spent the night in
that place; and behold, the
word of the LORD *came* to him,
and He said to him, "What are
you doing here, Elijah?"
10So he said, "I have been
very zealous for the LORD God
of hosts; for the children of
Israel have forsaken Your covenant, torn down Your altars,
and killed Your prophets with
the sword. I alone am left; and
they seek to take my life."

GOD'S REVELATION TO ELIJAH

11Then He said, "Go out, and
stand on the mountain before
the LORD." And behold, the
LORD passed by, and a great
and strong wind tore into
the mountains and broke
the rocks in pieces before the
LORD, *but* the LORD *was* not in
the wind; and after the wind
an earthquake, *but* the LORD
was not in the earthquake;
12and after the earthquake a
fire, *but* the LORD *was* not in
the fire; and after the fire a
still small voice.
13So it was, when Elijah
heard *it,* that he wrapped his
face in his mantle and went
out and stood in the entrance
of the cave. Suddenly a voice
came to him, and said, "What
are you doing here, Elijah?"
14And he said, "I have been
very zealous for the LORD God
of hosts; because the children
of Israel have forsaken Your
covenant, torn down Your altars, and killed Your prophets
with the sword. I alone am left;
and they seek to take my life."
15Then the LORD said to
him: "Go, return on your way to
the Wilderness of Damascus;
and when you arrive, anoint
Hazael *as* king over Syria.
16Also you shall anoint Jehu
the son of Nimshi *as* king over

19:5 [a] Or *Angel*

19:7 [a] Or *Angel*

Israel. And Elisha the son of
Shaphat of Abel Meholah you
shall anoint *as* prophet in your
place. 17It shall be *that* whoever
escapes the sword of Hazael,
Jehu will kill; and whoever escapes the sword of Jehu, Elisha
will kill. 18Yet I have reserved
seven thousand in Israel, all
whose knees have not bowed
to Baal, and every mouth that
has not kissed him."

ELISHA FOLLOWS ELIJAH

19So he departed from
there, and found Elisha the
son of Shaphat, who *was*
plowing *with* twelve yoke *of*
oxen before him, and he was
with the twelfth. Then Elijah
passed by him and threw his
mantle on him. 20And he left
the oxen and ran after Elijah,
and said, "Please let me kiss
my father and my mother, and
then I will follow you."

And he said to him, "Go
back again, for what have I
done to you?"

21So *Elisha* turned back
from him, and took a yoke of
oxen and slaughtered them
and boiled their flesh, using
the oxen's equipment, and
gave it to the people, and
they ate. Then he arose and
followed Elijah, and became
his servant.

AHAB DEFEATS THE SYRIANS

20 Now Ben-Hadad the
king of Syria gathered
all his forces together; thirty-
two kings *were* with him, with
horses and chariots. And he
went up and besieged Sa-
maria, and made war against
it. 2Then he sent messengers
into the city to Ahab king of
Israel, and said to him, "Thus
says Ben-Hadad: 3'Your silver
and your gold *are* mine; your
loveliest wives and children
are mine.'"

4And the king of Israel answered and said, "My lord,
O king, just as you say, I and
all that I have *are* yours."

5Then the messengers
came back and said, "Thus
speaks Ben-Hadad, saying,
'Indeed I have sent to you,
saying, "You shall deliver to
me your silver and your gold,
your wives and your children";
6but I will send my servants
to you tomorrow about this
time, and they shall search
your house and the houses
of your servants. And it shall
be, *that* whatever is pleasant
in your eyes, they will put *it* in
their hands and take *it*.'"

7So the king of Israel called
all the elders of the land, and
said, "Notice, please, and see
how this *man* seeks trouble,
for he sent to me for my wives,
my children, my silver, and
my gold; and I did not deny
him."

8And all the elders and all
the people said to him, "Do
not listen or consent."

9Therefore he said to the
messengers of Ben-Hadad,
"Tell my lord the king, 'All that

you sent for to your servant the first time I will do, but this thing I cannot do.'"

And the messengers departed and brought back word to him.

10 Then Ben-Hadad sent to him and said, "The gods do so to me, and more also, if enough dust is left of Samaria for a handful for each of the people who follow me."

11 So the king of Israel answered and said, "Tell *him*, 'Let not the one who puts on *his armor* boast like the one who takes *it off*.'"

12 And it happened when *Ben-Hadad* heard this message, as he and the kings *were* drinking at the command post, that he said to his servants, "Get ready." And they got ready to attack the city.

13 Suddenly a prophet approached Ahab king of Israel, saying, "Thus says the LORD: 'Have you seen all this great multitude? Behold, I will deliver it into your hand today, and you shall know that I *am* the LORD.'"

14 So Ahab said, "By whom?"

And he said, "Thus says the LORD: 'By the young leaders of the provinces.'"

Then he said, "Who will set the battle in order?"

And he answered, "You."

15 *Then he mustered the* young leaders of the provinces, and there were two hundred and thirty-two; and after them he mustered all the people, all the children of Israel—seven thousand.

16 So they went out at noon. Meanwhile Ben-Hadad and the thirty-two kings helping him were getting drunk at the command post. 17 The young leaders of the provinces went out first. And Ben-Hadad sent out *a patrol*, and they told him, saying, "Men are coming out of Samaria!" 18 So he said, "If they have come out for peace, take them alive; and if they have come out for war, take them alive."

19 Then these young leaders of the provinces went out of the city with the army which followed them. 20 And each one killed his man; so the Syrians fled, and Israel pursued them; and Ben-Hadad the king of Syria escaped on a horse with the cavalry. 21 Then the king of Israel went out and attacked the horses and chariots, and killed the Syrians with a great slaughter.

22 And the prophet came to the king of Israel and said to him, "Go, strengthen yourself; take note, and see what you should do, for in the spring of the year the king of Syria will come up against you."

THE SYRIANS AGAIN DEFEATED

23 Then the servants of the king of Syria said to him, "Their gods *are* gods of the hills. Therefore they were stronger than we; but if we

fight against them in the plain,
surely we will be stronger than
they. 24So do this thing: Dismiss the kings, each from his
position, and put captains in
their places; 25and you shall
muster an army like the army
that you have lost, horse for
horse and chariot for chariot. Then we will fight against
them in the plain; surely we
will be stronger than they."

And he listened to their
voice and did so.

26So it was, in the spring of
the year, that Ben-Hadad mustered the Syrians and went
up to Aphek to fight against
Israel. 27And the children of
Israel were mustered and
given provisions, and they
went against them. Now the
children of Israel encamped
before them like two little
flocks of goats, while the Syrians filled the countryside.

28Then a man of God came
and spoke to the king of Israel, and said, "Thus says the
LORD: 'Because the Syrians
have said, "The LORD *is* God
of the hills, but He *is* not God
of the valleys," therefore I will
deliver all this great multitude
into your hand, and you shall
know that I *am* the LORD.'"
29And they encamped oppo-
site each other for seven days.
So it was that on the seventh
day the battle was joined; and
the children of Israel killed
one hundred thousand foot
soldiers *of* the Syrians in
one day. 30But the rest fled
to Aphek, into the city; then
a wall fell on twenty-seven
thousand of the men *who
were* left.

And Ben-Hadad fled and
went into the city, into an
inner chamber.

AHAB'S TREATY WITH BEN-HADAD

31Then his servants said to
him, "Look now, we have heard
that the kings of the house
of Israel *are* merciful kings.
Please, let us put sackcloth
around our waists and ropes
around our heads, and go out
to the king of Israel; perhaps
he will spare your life." 32So
they wore sackcloth around
their waists and *put* ropes
around their heads, and came
to the king of Israel and said,
"Your servant Ben-Hadad says,
'Please let me live.'"

And he said, "*Is* he still
alive? He *is* my brother."

33Now the men were watch-
ing closely to see whether *any
sign of mercy would come* from
him; and they quickly grasped
at this word and said, "Your
brother Ben-Hadad."

So he said, "Go, bring him."
Then Ben-Hadad came out to
him; and he had him come up
into the chariot.

34So *Ben-Hadad* said to
him, "The cities which my father took from your father I
will restore; and you may set
up marketplaces for yourself
in Damascus, as my father did
in Samaria."

Then *Ahab said,* "I will send
you away with this treaty." So
he made a treaty with him and
sent him away.

AHAB CONDEMNED

[35]Now a certain man of the
sons of the prophets said to
his neighbor by the word of
the LORD, "Strike me, please."
And the man refused to strike
him. [36]Then he said to him,
"Because you have not obeyed
the voice of the LORD, surely,
as soon as you depart from
me, a lion shall kill you." And
as soon as he left him, a lion
found him and killed him.
[37]And he found another
man, and said, "Strike me,
please." So the man struck
him, inflicting a wound.
[38]Then the prophet departed
and waited for the king by the
road, and disguised himself
with a bandage over his eyes.
[39]Now as the king passed by,
he cried out to the king and
said, "Your servant went out
into the midst of the battle;
and there, a man came over
and brought a man to me, and
said, 'Guard this man; if by
any means he is missing, your
life shall be for his life, or else
you shall pay a talent of silver.' [40]While your servant was
busy here and there, he was
gone."
Then the king of Israel said
to him, "So *shall* your judgment *be;* you yourself have
decided *it.*"
[41]And he hastened to take
the bandage away from his
eyes; and the king of Israel
recognized him as one of the
prophets. [42]Then he said to
him, "Thus says the LORD: 'Because you have let slip out of
your hand a man whom I appointed to utter destruction,
therefore your life shall go for
his life, and your people for
his people.'"
[43]So the king of Israel went
to his house sullen and displeased, and came to Samaria.

NABOTH IS MURDERED FOR HIS VINEYARD

21 And it came to pass after
these things *that* Naboth
the Jezreelite had a vineyard
which *was* in Jezreel, next to
the palace of Ahab king of Samaria. [2]So Ahab spoke to Naboth, saying, "Give me your
vineyard, that I may have it for
a vegetable garden, because it
is near, next to my house; and
for it I will give you a vineyard
better than it. *Or,* if it seems
good to you, I will give you its
worth in money."
[3]But Naboth said to Ahab,
"The LORD forbid that I should
give the inheritance of my fathers to you!"
[4]So Ahab went into his
house sullen and displeased
because of the word which Naboth the Jezreelite had spoken
to him; for he had said, "I will
not give you the inheritance
of my fathers." And he lay
down on his bed, and turned
away his face, and would eat

no food. 5But Jezebel his wife
came to him, and said to him,
"Why is your spirit so sullen
that you eat no food?"
6He said to her, "Because
I spoke to Naboth the Jezreelite, and said to him, 'Give
me your vineyard for money;
or else, if it pleases you, I will
give you *another* vineyard for
it.' And he answered, 'I will not
give you my vineyard.'"
7Then Jezebel his wife said
to him, "You now exercise authority over Israel! Arise, eat
food, and let your heart be
cheerful; I will give you the
vineyard of Naboth the Jezreelite."
8And she wrote letters in
Ahab's name, sealed *them* with
his seal, and sent the letters to
the elders and the nobles who
were dwelling in the city with
Naboth. 9She wrote in the letters, saying,

Proclaim a fast, and
seat Naboth with high
honor among the people;
10and seat two men,
scoundrels, before him
to bear witness against
him, saying, "You have
blasphemed God and the
king." *Then* take him out,
and stone him, that he
may die.

11So the men of his city, the
elders and nobles who were
inhabitants of his city, did as
Jezebel had sent to them, as
it *was* written in the letters
which she had sent to them.
12They proclaimed a fast,
and seated Naboth with high
honor among the people.
13And two men, scoundrels,
came in and sat before him;
and the scoundrels witnessed
against him, against Naboth,
in the presence of the people, saying, "Naboth has blasphemed God and the king!"
Then they took him outside
the city and stoned him with
stones, so that he died. 14Then
they sent to Jezebel, saying,
"Naboth has been stoned and
is dead."
15And it came to pass, when
Jezebel heard that Naboth had
been stoned and was dead,
that Jezebel said to Ahab,
"Arise, take possession of the
vineyard of Naboth the Jezreelite, which he refused to give
you for money; for Naboth is
not alive, but dead." 16So it
was, when Ahab heard that
Naboth was dead, that Ahab
got up and went down to take
possession of the vineyard of
Naboth the Jezreelite.

THE LORD CONDEMNS AHAB

17Then the word of the
LORD came to Elijah the Tishbite, saying, 18"Arise, go down
to meet Ahab king of Israel,
who *lives* in Samaria. There
he is, in the vineyard of Naboth, where he has gone down
to take possession of it. 19You
shall speak to him, saying,
'Thus says the LORD: "Have

you murdered and also taken
possession?"' And you shall
speak to him, saying, 'Thus
says the LORD: "In the place
where dogs licked the blood
of Naboth, dogs shall lick your
blood, even yours."'"
20 So Ahab said to Elijah,
"Have you found me, O my
enemy?"
And he answered, "I have
found *you,* because you have
sold yourself to do evil in the
sight of the LORD: 21 'Behold,
I will bring calamity on you.
I will take away your posterity, and will cut off from Ahab
every male in Israel, both
bond and free. 22 I will make
your house like the house of
Jeroboam the son of Nebat,
and like the house of Baasha
the son of Ahijah, because of
the provocation with which
you have provoked *Me* to
anger, and made Israel sin.'
23 And concerning Jezebel the
LORD also spoke, saying, 'The
dogs shall eat Jezebel by the
wall[a] of Jezreel.' 24 The dogs
shall eat whoever belongs to
Ahab and dies in the city, and
the birds of the air shall eat
whoever dies in the field."
25 But there was no one like
Ahab who sold himself to do
wickedness in the sight of the
LORD, because Jezebel his wife
stirred him up. 26 And he behaved very abominably in following idols, according to all
that the Amorites had done,
whom the LORD had cast out
before the children of Israel.
27 So it was, when Ahab
heard those words, that he
tore his clothes and put sackcloth on his body, and fasted
and lay in sackcloth, and went
about mourning.
28 And the word of the LORD
came to Elijah the Tishbite,
saying, 29 "See how Ahab has
humbled himself before Me?
Because he has humbled himself before Me, I will not bring
the calamity in his days. In the
days of his son I will bring the
calamity on his house."

MICAIAH WARNS AHAB

22 Now three years passed
without war between
Syria and Israel. 2 Then it came
to pass, in the third year, that
Jehoshaphat the king of Judah
went down to *visit* the king of
Israel.
3 And the king of Israel said
to his servants, "Do you know
that Ramoth in Gilead *is* ours,
but we hesitate to take it out of
the hand of the king of Syria?"
4 So he said to Jehoshaphat,
"Will you go with me to fight
at Ramoth Gilead?"
Jehoshaphat said to the
king of Israel, "I *am* as you *are,*
my people as your people, my
horses as your horses." 5 Also

21:23 [a] Following Masoretic Text and Septuagint; some Hebrew manuscripts, Syriac, Targum, and Vulgate read *plot of ground* (compare 2 Kings 9:36).

Jehoshaphat said to the king
of Israel, "Please inquire for
the word of the LORD today."
6Then the king of Israel
gathered the prophets to-
gether, about four hundred
men, and said to them, "Shall
I go against Ramoth Gilead to
fight, or shall I refrain?"
So they said, "Go up, for
the Lord will deliver *it* into
the hand of the king."
7And Jehoshaphat said, "*Is*
there not still a prophet of the
LORD here, that we may inquire of Him?"[a]
8So the king of Israel said
to Jehoshaphat, "*There is* still
one man, Micaiah the son of
Imlah, by whom we may in-
quire of the LORD; but I hate
him, because he does not
prophesy good concerning
me, but evil."
And Jehoshaphat said, "Let
not the king say such things!"
9Then the king of Israel
called an officer and said,
"Bring Micaiah the son of
Imlah quickly!"
10The king of Israel and Jehoshaphat the king of Judah,
having put on *their* robes,
sat each on his throne, at a
threshing floor at the entrance of the gate of Samaria;
and all the prophets prophesied before them. 11Now Zedekiah the son of Chenaanah
had made horns of iron for
himself; and he said, "Thus
says the LORD: 'With these you
shall gore the Syrians until
they are destroyed.'" 12And all
the prophets prophesied so,
saying, "Go up to Ramoth Gilead and prosper, for the LORD
will deliver *it* into the king's
hand."
13Then the messenger who
had gone to call Micaiah spoke
to him, saying, "Now listen,
the words of the prophets with
one accord encourage the
king. Please, let your word be
like the word of one of them,
and speak encouragement."
14And Micaiah said, "*As* the
LORD lives, whatever the LORD
says to me, that I will speak."
15Then he came to the king;
and the king said to him,
"Micaiah, shall we go to war
against Ramoth Gilead, or
shall we refrain?"
And he answered him, "Go
and prosper, for the LORD will
deliver *it* into the hand of the
king!"
16So the king said to him,
"How many times shall I make
you swear that you tell me
nothing but the truth in the
name of the LORD?"
17Then he said, "I saw all
Israel scattered on the mountains, as sheep that have no
shepherd. And the LORD said,
'These have no master. Let
each return to his house in
peace.'"
18And the king of Israel
said to Jehoshaphat, "Did
I not tell you he would not

22:7 [a] Or *him*

prophesy good concerning
me, but evil?"
19Then *Micaiah* said,
"Therefore hear the word of
the LORD: I saw the LORD sitting on His throne, and all
the host of heaven standing
by, on His right hand and on
His left. 20And the LORD said,
'Who will persuade Ahab to go
up, that he may fall at Ramoth
Gilead?' So one spoke in this
manner, and another spoke in
that manner. 21Then a spirit
came forward and stood before the LORD, and said, 'I will
persuade him.' 22The LORD
said to him, 'In what way?' So
he said, 'I will go out and be a
lying spirit in the mouth of all
his prophets.' And the LORD
said, 'You shall persuade *him,*
and also prevail. Go out and
do so.' 23Therefore look! The
LORD has put a lying spirit in
the mouth of all these prophets of yours, and the LORD has
declared disaster against you."
24Now Zedekiah the son
of Chenaanah went near and
struck Micaiah on the cheek,
and said, "Which way did the
spirit from the LORD go from
me to speak to you?"
25And Micaiah said, "In-
deed, you shall see on that
day when you go into an inner
chamber to hide!"
26So the king of Israel said,
"Take Micaiah, and return him
to Amon the governor of the
city and to Joash the king's
son; 27and say, 'Thus says the
king: "Put this *fellow* in prison,
and feed him with bread of affliction and water of affliction,
until I come in peace."'"
28But Micaiah said, "If you
ever return in peace, the LORD
has not spoken by me." And
he said, "Take heed, all you
people!"

AHAB DIES IN BATTLE

29So the king of Israel
and Jehoshaphat the king of
Judah went up to Ramoth Gilead. 30And the king of Israel
said to Jehoshaphat, "I will
disguise myself and go into
battle; but you put on your
robes." So the king of Israel
disguised himself and went
into battle.
31Now the king of Syria had
commanded the thirty-two
captains of his chariots, saying, "Fight with no one small
or great, but only with the king
of Israel." 32So it was, when
the captains of the chariots
saw Jehoshaphat, that they
said, "Surely it *is* the king of
Israel!" Therefore they turned
aside to fight against him, and
Jehoshaphat cried out. 33And
it happened, when the captains of the chariots saw that
it *was* not the king of Israel,
that they turned back from
pursuing him. 34Now a *certain*
man drew a bow at random,
and struck the king of Israel between the joints of his
armor. So he said to the driver
of his chariot, "Turn around
and take me out of the battle,
for I am wounded."

35The battle increased that
day; and the king was propped
up in his chariot, facing the
Syrians, and died at evening.
The blood ran out from the
wound onto the floor of the
chariot. 36Then, as the sun
was going down, a shout went
throughout the army, saying,
"Every man to his city, and
every man to his own country!"
37So the king died, and was
brought to Samaria. And they
buried the king in Samaria.
38Then *someone* washed
the chariot at a pool in Samaria, and the dogs licked
up his blood while the harlots bathed,[a] according to the
word of the LORD which He
had spoken.
39Now the rest of the acts
of Ahab, and all that he did,
the ivory house which he
built and all the cities that he
built, *are* they not written in
the book of the chronicles of
the kings of Israel? 40So Ahab
rested with his fathers. Then
Ahaziah his son reigned in his
place.

JEHOSHAPHAT REIGNS IN JUDAH

41Jehoshaphat the son of
Asa had become king over
Judah in the fourth year of
Ahab king of Israel. 42Jehoshaphat *was* thirty-five years old
when he became king, and
he reigned twenty-five years
in Jerusalem. His mother's
name *was* Azubah the daughter of Shilhi. 43And he walked
in all the ways of his father
Asa. He did not turn aside
from them, doing *what was*
right in the eyes of the LORD.
Nevertheless the high places
were not taken away, *for* the
people offered sacrifices and
burned incense on the high
places. 44Also Jehoshaphat
made peace with the king of
Israel.
45Now the rest of the acts of
Jehoshaphat, the might that
he showed, and how he made
war, *are* they not written in
the book of the chronicles of
the kings of Judah? 46And the
rest of the perverted persons,[a]
who remained in the days of
his father Asa, he banished
from the land. 47*There was*
then no king in Edom, only a
deputy of the king.
48Jehoshaphat made merchant ships[a] to go to Ophir for
gold; but they never sailed,
for the ships were wrecked
at Ezion Geber. 49Then Ahaziah the son of Ahab said to
Jehoshaphat, "Let my servants go with your servants
in the ships." But Jehoshaphat
would not.
50And Jehoshaphat rested
with his fathers, and was buried with his fathers in the City

22:38 [a] Syriac and Targum read *they washed his armor.*
22:46 [a] Hebrew *qadesh,* that is, one practicing sodomy and prostitution in religious rituals 22:48 [a] Or *ships of Tarshish*

of David his father. Then Jehoram his son reigned in his
place.

AHAZIAH REIGNS IN ISRAEL

51Ahaziah the son of Ahab
became king over Israel in
Samaria in the seventeenth
year of Jehoshaphat king of
Judah, and reigned two years
over Israel. 52He did evil in the
sight of the LORD, and walked
in the way of his father and in
the way of his mother and in
the way of Jeroboam the son
of Nebat, who had made Israel sin; 53for he served Baal
and worshiped him, and provoked the LORD God of Israel
to anger, according to all that
his father had done.

THE SECOND BOOK OF THE KINGS

GOD JUDGES AHAZIAH

1 Moab rebelled against Israel after the death of Ahab.
2Now Ahaziah fell through
the lattice of his upper room
in Samaria, and was injured;
so he sent messengers and
said to them, "Go, inquire of
Baal-Zebub, the god of Ekron,
whether I shall recover from
this injury." 3But the angel[a]
of the LORD said to Elijah the
Tishbite, "Arise, go up to meet
the messengers of the king
of Samaria, and say to them,
'*Is it* because *there is* no God
in Israel *that* you are going
to inquire of Baal-Zebub, the
god of Ekron?' 4Now therefore,
thus says the LORD: 'You shall
not come down from the bed
to which you have gone up,
but you shall surely die.'" So
Elijah departed.
5And when the messengers
returned to him, he said to
them, "Why have you come
back?"
6So they said to him, "A
man came up to meet us, and
said to us, 'Go, return to the
king who sent you, and say
to him, "Thus says the LORD:
'*Is it* because *there is* no God
in Israel *that* you are sending
to inquire of Baal-Zebub, the
god of Ekron? Therefore you
shall not come down from the
bed to which you have gone
up, but you shall surely die.'"'"
7Then he said to them,
"What kind of man *was it* who
came up to meet you and told
you these words?"

1:3 [a] Or *Angel*

8So they answered him, "A
hairy man wearing a leather
belt around his waist."
And he said, "It *is* Elijah the
Tishbite."
9Then the king sent to him
a captain of fifty with his fifty
men. So he went up to him;
and there he was, sitting on
the top of a hill. And he spoke
to him: "Man of God, the king
has said, 'Come down!'"
10So Elijah answered and
said to the captain of fifty, "If I
am a man of God, then let fire
come down from heaven and
consume you and your fifty
men." And fire came down
from heaven and consumed
him and his fifty. 11Then he
sent to him another captain
of fifty with his fifty men.
And he answered and said
to him: "Man of God, thus has
the king said, 'Come down
quickly!'"
12So Elijah answered and
said to them, "If I *am* a man of
God, let fire come down from
heaven and consume you and
your fifty men." And the fire of
God came down from heaven
and consumed him and his
fifty.
13Again, he sent a third captain of fifty with his fifty men.
And the third captain of fifty
went up, and came and fell on
his knees before Elijah, and
pleaded with him, and said to
him: "Man of God, please let
my life and the life of these
fifty servants of yours be precious in your sight. 14Look, fire
has come down from heaven
and burned up the first two
captains of fifties with their
fifties. But let my life now be
precious in your sight."
15And the angel[a] of the
LORD said to Elijah, "Go down
with him; do not be afraid of
him." So he arose and went
down with him to the king.
16Then he said to him, "Thus
says the LORD: 'Because you
have sent messengers to inquire of Baal-Zebub, the god
of Ekron, *is it* because *there is*
no God in Israel to inquire of
His word? Therefore you shall
not come down from the bed
to which you have gone up,
but you shall surely die.'"
17So *Ahaziah* died according to the word of the LORD
which Elijah had spoken.
Because he had no son, Jehoram[a] became king in his
place, in the second year of
Jehoram the son of Jehoshaphat, king of Judah.
18Now the rest of the acts
of Ahaziah which he did, *are*
they not written in the book
of the chronicles of the kings
of Israel?

ELIJAH ASCENDS TO HEAVEN

2 And it came to pass, when
the LORD was about to
take up Elijah into heaven by
a whirlwind, that Elijah went

1:15 [a] Or *Angel* 1:17 [a] The son of Ahab king of Israel (compare 3:1)

with Elisha from Gilgal. 2Then
Elijah said to Elisha, "Stay
here, please, for the LORD has
sent me on to Bethel."

But Elisha said, "*As* the
LORD lives, and *as* your soul
lives, I will not leave you!" So
they went down to Bethel.

3Now the sons of the prophets who *were* at Bethel came
out to Elisha, and said to him,
"Do you know that the LORD
will take away your master
from over you today?"

And he said, "Yes, I know;
keep silent!"

4Then Elijah said to him,
"Elisha, stay here, please, for
the LORD has sent me on to
Jericho."

But he said, "*As* the LORD
lives, and *as* your soul lives,
I will not leave you!" So they
came to Jericho.

5Now the sons of the prophets who *were* at Jericho came
to Elisha and said to him, "Do
you know that the LORD will
take away your master from
over you today?"

So he answered, "Yes, I
know; keep silent!"

6Then Elijah said to him,
"Stay here, please, for the LORD
has sent me on to the Jordan."

But he said, "*As* the LORD
lives, and *as* your soul lives,
I will not leave you!" So the
two of them went on. 7And
fifty men of the sons of the
prophets went and stood facing *them* at a distance, while
the two of them stood by the
Jordan. 8Now Elijah took
his mantle, rolled *it* up, and
struck the water; and it was
divided this way and that, so
that the two of them crossed
over on dry ground.

9And so it was, when they
had crossed over, that Elijah
said to Elisha, "Ask! What may
I do for you, before I am taken
away from you?"

Elisha said, "Please let a
double portion of your spirit
be upon me."

10So he said, "You have
asked a hard thing. *Nevertheless,* if you see me *when I am*
taken from you, it shall be so
for you; but if not, it shall not
be *so.*" 11Then it happened, as
they continued on and talked,
that suddenly a chariot of fire
appeared with horses of fire,
and separated the two of
them; and Elijah went up by
a whirlwind into heaven.

12And Elisha saw *it,* and he
cried out, "My father, my father, the chariot of Israel and
its horsemen!" So he saw him
no more. And he took hold of
his own clothes and tore them
into two pieces. 13He also took
up the mantle of Elijah that
had fallen from him, and went
back and stood by the bank
of the Jordan. 14Then he took
the mantle of Elijah that had
fallen from him, and struck
the water, and said, "Where *is*
the LORD God of Elijah?" And
when he also had struck the
water, it was divided this way
and that; and Elisha crossed
over.

15 Now when the sons of the
prophets who *were* from Jericho saw him, they said, "The
spirit of Elijah rests on Elisha." And they came to meet
him, and bowed to the ground
before him. 16 Then they said
to him, "Look now, there are
fifty strong men with your servants. Please let them go and
search for your master, lest
perhaps the Spirit of the LORD
has taken him up and cast him
upon some mountain or into
some valley."

And he said, "You shall not
send anyone."

17 But when they urged
him till he was ashamed, he
said, "Send *them!*" Therefore
they sent fifty men, and they
searched for three days but
did not find him. 18 And when
they came back to him, for he
had stayed in Jericho, he said
to them, "Did I not say to you,
'Do not go'?"

ELISHA PERFORMS MIRACLES

19 Then the men of the city
said to Elisha, "Please notice, the situation of this city
is pleasant, as my lord sees;
but the water *is* bad, and the
ground barren."

20 And he said, "Bring me a
new bowl, and put salt in it." So
they brought *it* to him. 21 Then
he went out to the source of
the water, and cast in the salt
there, and said, "Thus says
the LORD: 'I have healed this
water; from it there shall be
no more death or barren-
ness.'" 22 So the water remains
healed to this day, according
to the word of Elisha which
he spoke.

23 Then he went up from
there to Bethel; and as he
was going up the road, some
youths came from the city and
mocked him, and said to him,
"Go up, you baldhead! Go up,
you baldhead!"

24 So he turned around
and looked at them, and pronounced a curse on them in
the name of the LORD. And
two female bears came out of
the woods and mauled forty-
two of the youths.

25 Then he went from there
to Mount Carmel, and from
there he returned to Samaria.

MOAB REBELS AGAINST ISRAEL

3 Now Jehoram the son of
Ahab became king over
Israel at Samaria in the eighteenth year of Jehoshaphat
king of Judah, and reigned
twelve years. 2 And he did evil
in the sight of the LORD, but
not like his father and mother;
for he put away the *sacred*
pillar of Baal that his father
had made. 3 Nevertheless he
persisted in the sins of Jeroboam the son of Nebat, who
had made Israel sin; he did
not depart from them.

4 Now Mesha king of Moab
was a sheepbreeder, and he
regularly paid the king of Israel one hundred thousand

lambs and the wool of one
hundred thousand rams. 5But
it happened, when Ahab died,
that the king of Moab rebelled
against the king of Israel.

6So King Jehoram went out
of Samaria at that time and
mustered all Israel. 7Then he
went and sent to Jehoshaphat
king of Judah, saying, "The
king of Moab has rebelled
against me. Will you go with
me to fight against Moab?"

And he said, "I will go up;
I *am* as you *are,* my people
as your people, my horses as
your horses." 8Then he said,
"Which way shall we go up?"

And he answered, "By way
of the Wilderness of Edom."

9So the king of Israel went
with the king of Judah and
the king of Edom, and they
marched on that roundabout
route seven days; and there
was no water for the army, nor
for the animals that followed
them. 10And the king of Israel said, "Alas! For the LORD
has called these three kings
together to deliver them into
the hand of Moab."

11But Jehoshaphat said, "*Is
there* no prophet of the LORD
here, that we may inquire of
the LORD by him?"

So one of the servants of
the king of Israel answered
and said, "Elisha the son of
Shaphat *is* here, who poured
water on the hands of Elijah."

12And Jehoshaphat said,
"The word of the LORD is with
him." So the king of Israel and
Jehoshaphat and the king of
Edom went down to him.

13Then Elisha said to the
king of Israel, "What have
I to do with you? Go to the
prophets of your father and
the prophets of your mother."

But the king of Israel said
to him, "No, for the LORD has
called these three kings *together* to deliver them into
the hand of Moab."

14And Elisha said, "*As* the
LORD of hosts lives, before
whom I stand, surely were it
not that I regard the presence
of Jehoshaphat king of Judah,
I would not look at you, nor
see you. 15But now bring me
a musician."

Then it happened, when
the musician played, that the
hand of the LORD came upon
him. 16And he said, "Thus says
the LORD: 'Make this valley
full of ditches.' 17For thus says
the LORD: 'You shall not see
wind, nor shall you see rain;
yet that valley shall be filled
with water, so that you, your
cattle, and your animals may
drink.' 18And this is a simple matter in the sight of the
LORD; He will also deliver
the Moabites into your hand.
19Also you shall attack every
fortified city and every choice
city, and shall cut down every
good tree, and stop up every
spring of water, and ruin
every good piece of land with
stones."

20Now it happened in the
morning, when the grain of-

fering was offered, that suddenly water came by way of
Edom, and the land was filled
with water.
21And when all the Mo-
abites heard that the kings
had come up to fight against
them, all who were able to
bear arms and older were
gathered; and they stood at
the border. 22Then they rose
up early in the morning, and
the sun was shining on the
water; and the Moabites saw
the water on the other side
as red as blood. 23And they
said, "This is blood; the kings
have surely struck swords and
have killed one another; now
therefore, Moab, to the spoil!"
24So when they came to the
camp of Israel, Israel rose up
and attacked the Moabites, so
that they fled before them;
and they entered *their* land,
killing the Moabites. 25Then
they destroyed the cities, and
each man threw a stone on
every good piece of land and
filled it; and they stopped up
all the springs of water and
cut down all the good trees.
But they left the stones of Kir
Haraseth *intact*. However the
slingers surrounded and attacked it.
26And when the king of
Moab saw that the battle was
too fierce for him, he took
with him seven hundred men
who drew swords, to break
through to the king of Edom,
but they could not. 27Then he
took his eldest son who would
have reigned in his place, and
offered him *as* a burnt offering upon the wall; and there
was great indignation against
Israel. So they departed from
him and returned to *their own*
land.

ELISHA AND THE WIDOW'S OIL

4 A certain woman of the
wives of the sons of the
prophets cried out to Elisha,
saying, "Your servant my husband is dead, and you know
that your servant feared the
LORD. And the creditor is
coming to take my two sons
to be his slaves."
2So Elisha said to her,
"What shall I do for you? Tell
me, what do you have in the
house?" And she said, "Your
maidservant has nothing in
the house but a jar of oil."
3Then he said, "Go, bor-
row vessels from everywhere,
from all your neighbors—
empty vessels; do not gather
just a few. 4And when you have
come in, you shall shut the
door behind you and your
sons; then pour it into all
those vessels, and set aside
the full ones."
5So she went from him and
shut the door behind her and
her sons, who brought *the vessels* to her; and she poured
it out. 6Now it came to pass,
when the vessels were full,
that she said to her son, "Bring
me another vessel."
And he said to her, "*There is*

not another vessel." So the oil
ceased. 7Then she came and
told the man of God. And he
said, "Go, sell the oil and pay
your debt; and you *and* your
sons live on the rest."

ELISHA RAISES THE SHUNAMMITE'S SON

8Now it happened one day
that Elisha went to Shunem,
where there *was* a notable
woman, and she persuaded
him to eat some food. So it
was, as often as he passed by,
he would turn in there to eat
some food. 9And she said to
her husband, "Look now, I
know that this *is* a holy man
of God, who passes by us regularly. 10Please, let us make a
small upper room on the wall;
and let us put a bed for him
there, and a table and a chair
and a lampstand; so it will be,
whenever he comes to us, he
can turn in there."

11And it happened one day
that he came there, and he
turned in to the upper room
and lay down there. 12Then
he said to Gehazi his servant, "Call this Shunammite
woman." When he had called
her, she stood before him.
13And he said to him, "Say now
to her, 'Look, you have been
concerned for us with all this
care. What *can I* do for you?
Do you want me to speak on
your behalf to the king or to
the commander of the army?'"

She answered, "I dwell
among my own people."

14So he said, "What then *is*
to be done for her?"

And Gehazi answered, "Ac-
tually, she has no son, and her
husband is old."

15So he said, "Call her."
When he had called her, she
stood in the doorway. 16Then
he said, "About this time next
year you shall embrace a son."

And she said, "No, my lord.
Man of God, do not lie to your
maidservant!"

17But the woman con-
ceived, and bore a son when
the appointed time had come,
of which Elisha had told her.

18And the child grew. Now
it happened one day that he
went out to his father, to the
reapers. 19And he said to his
father, "My head, my head!"

So he said to a servant,
"Carry him to his mother."
20When he had taken him and
brought him to his mother,
he sat on her knees till noon,
and *then* died. 21And she went
up and laid him on the bed
of the man of God, shut *the
door* upon him, and went out.
22Then she called to her husband, and said, "Please send
me one of the young men and
one of the donkeys, that I may
run to the man of God and
come back."

23So he said, "Why are you
going to him today? *It is* neither the New Moon nor the
Sabbath."

And she said, "*It is* well."
24Then she saddled a don-
key, and said to her servant,

"Drive, and go forward; do
not slacken the pace for me
unless I tell you." 25And so she
departed, and went to the man
of God at Mount Carmel.

So it was, when the man
of God saw her afar off, that
he said to his servant Gehazi, "Look, the Shunammite
woman! 26Please run now to
meet her, and say to her, '*Is it*
well with you? *Is it* well with
your husband? *Is it* well with
the child?'"

And she answered, "*It is*
well." 27Now when she came
to the man of God at the hill,
she caught him by the feet,
but Gehazi came near to push
her away. But the man of God
said, "Let her alone; for her
soul *is* in deep distress, and
the LORD has hidden *it* from
me, and has not told me."

28So she said, "Did I ask a
son of my lord? Did I not say,
'Do not deceive me'?"

29Then he said to Gehazi,
"Get yourself ready, and take
my staff in your hand, and
be on your way. If you meet
anyone, do not greet him; and
if anyone greets you, do not
answer him; but lay my staff
on the face of the child."

30And the mother of the
child said, "*As* the LORD lives,
and *as* your soul lives, I will
not leave you." So he arose and
followed her. 31Now Gehazi
went on ahead of them, and
laid the staff on the face of the
child; but *there was* neither
voice nor hearing. Therefore
he went back to meet him, and
told him, saying, "The child
has not awakened."

32When Elisha came into
the house, there was the child,
lying dead on his bed. 33He
went in therefore, shut the
door behind the two of them,
and prayed to the LORD. 34And
he went up and lay on the
child, and put his mouth on
his mouth, his eyes on his eyes,
and his hands on his hands;
and he stretched himself out
on the child, and the flesh of
the child became warm. 35He
returned and walked back and
forth in the house, and again
went up and stretched himself out on him; then the child
sneezed seven times, and the
child opened his eyes. 36And
he called Gehazi and said, "Call
this Shunammite woman." So
he called her. And when she
came in to him, he said, "Pick
up your son." 37So she went in,
fell at his feet, and bowed to
the ground; then she picked
up her son and went out.

ELISHA PURIFIES THE POT OF STEW

38And Elisha returned to
Gilgal, and *there was* a famine in the land. Now the sons
of the prophets *were* sitting
before him; and he said to his
servant, "Put on the large pot,
and boil stew for the sons of
the prophets." 39So one went
out into the field to gather
herbs, and found a wild vine,
and gathered from it a lapful

of wild gourds, and came
and sliced *them* into the pot
of stew, though they did not
know *what they were.* 40Then
they served it to the men to
eat. Now it happened, as they
were eating the stew, that they
cried out and said, "Man of
God, *there is* death in the pot!"
And they could not eat *it.*

41So he said, "Then bring
some flour." And he put *it* into
the pot, and said, "Serve *it* to
the people, that they may eat."
And there was nothing harmful in the pot.

ELISHA FEEDS ONE HUNDRED MEN

42Then a man came from
Baal Shalisha, and brought
the man of God bread of the
firstfruits, twenty loaves of
barley bread, and newly ripened grain in his knapsack.
And he said, "Give *it* to the
people, that they may eat."

43But his servant said,
"What? Shall I set this before
one hundred men?"

He said again, "Give it to
the people, that they may eat;
for thus says the LORD: 'They
shall eat and have *some* left
over.'" 44So he set *it* before
them; and they ate and had
some left over, according to
the word of the LORD.

NAAMAN'S LEPROSY HEALED

5 Now Naaman, commander
of the army of the king of
Syria, was a great and honorable man in the eyes of his
master, because by him the
LORD had given victory to
Syria. He was also a mighty
man of valor, *but* a leper. 2And
the Syrians had gone out on
raids, and had brought back
captive a young girl from the
land of Israel. She waited on
Naaman's wife. 3Then she
said to her mistress, "If only
my master *were* with the
prophet who *is* in Samaria!
For he would heal him of his
leprosy." 4And *Naaman* went
in and told his master, saying,
"Thus and thus said the girl
who *is* from the land of Israel."

5Then the king of Syria
said, "Go now, and I will send
a letter to the king of Israel."

So he departed and took
with him ten talents of silver,
six thousand *shekels* of gold,
and ten changes of clothing.
6Then he brought the letter to
the king of Israel, which said,

> Now be advised, when
> this letter comes to you,
> that I have sent Naaman
> my servant to you, that
> you may heal him of his
> leprosy.

7And it happened, when the
king of Israel read the letter,
that he tore his clothes and
said, "*Am* I God, to kill and
make alive, that this man
sends a man to me to heal
him of his leprosy? Therefore
please consider, and see how
he seeks a quarrel with me."

8So it was, when Elisha the
man of God heard that the king
of Israel had torn his clothes,
that he sent to the king, saying, "Why have you torn your
clothes? Please let him come
to me, and he shall know that
there is a prophet in Israel."
9Then Naaman went with
his horses and chariot, and he
stood at the door of Elisha's
house. 10And Elisha sent a
messenger to him, saying, "Go
and wash in the Jordan seven
times, and your flesh shall be
restored to you, and *you shall*
be clean." 11But Naaman became furious, and went away
and said, "Indeed, I said to myself, 'He will surely come out *to*
me, and stand and call on the
name of the LORD his God, and
wave his hand over the place,
and heal the leprosy.' 12*Are* not
the Abanah[a] and the Pharpar,
the rivers of Damascus, better
than all the waters of Israel?
Could I not wash in them and
be clean?" So he turned and
went away in a rage. 13And his
servants came near and spoke
to him, and said, "My father, *if*
the prophet had told you *to do*
something great, would you
not have done *it?* How much
more then, when he says to
you, 'Wash, and be clean'?"
14So he went down and dipped
seven times in the Jordan, according to the saying of the
man of God; and his flesh was
restored like the flesh of a little
child, and he was clean.
15And he returned to the
man of God, he and all his
aides, and came and stood before him; and he said, "Indeed,
now I know that *there is* no
God in all the earth, except in
Israel; now therefore, please
take a gift from your servant."
16But he said, "*As* the LORD
lives, before whom I stand, I
will receive nothing." And he
urged him to take *it,* but he
refused.
17So Naaman said, "Then, if
not, please let your servant be
given two mule-loads of earth;
for your servant will no longer
offer either burnt offering or
sacrifice to other gods, but to
the LORD. 18Yet in this thing
may the LORD pardon your
servant: when my master goes
into the temple of Rimmon to
worship there, and he leans
on my hand, and I bow down
in the temple of Rimmon—
when I bow down in the temple of Rimmon, may the LORD
please pardon your servant in
this thing."
19Then he said to him, "Go
in peace." So he departed from
him a short distance.

GEHAZI'S GREED

20But Gehazi, the servant
of Elisha the man of God, said,
"Look, my master has spared
Naaman this Syrian, while not

5:12 [a] Following Kethib, Septuagint, and Vulgate; Qere, Syriac, and Targum read *Amanah*.

receiving from his hands what he brought; but *as* the LORD lives, I will run after him and take something from him." 21So Gehazi pursued Naaman. When Naaman saw *him* running after him, he got down from the chariot to meet him, and said, "*Is* all well?"

22And he said, "All *is* well. My master has sent me, saying, 'Indeed, just now two young men of the sons of the prophets have come to me from the mountains of Ephraim. Please give them a talent of silver and two changes of garments.'"

23So Naaman said, "Please, take two talents." And he urged him, and bound two talents of silver in two bags, with two changes of garments, and handed *them* to two of his servants; and they carried *them* on ahead of him. 24When he came to the citadel, he took *them* from their hand, and stored *them* away in the house; then he let the men go, and they departed. 25Now he went in and stood before his master. Elisha said to him, "Where *did you go,* Gehazi?"

And he said, "Your servant did not go anywhere."

26Then he said to him, "Did not my heart go *with you* when the man turned back from his chariot to meet you? *Is it* time to receive money and to receive clothing, olive groves and vineyards, sheep and oxen, male and female servants? 27Therefore the leprosy of Naaman shall cling to you and your descendants forever." And he went out from his presence leprous, *as white* as snow.

THE FLOATING AX HEAD

6 And the sons of the prophets said to Elisha, "See now, the place where we dwell with you is too small for us. 2Please, let us go to the Jordan, and let every man take a beam from there, and let us make there a place where we may dwell."

So he answered, "Go."

3Then one said, "Please consent to go with your servants."

And he answered, "I will go." 4So he went with them. And when they came to the Jordan, they cut down trees. 5But as one was cutting down a tree, the iron *ax head* fell into the water; and he cried out and said, "Alas, master! For it was borrowed."

6So the man of God said, "Where did it fall?" And he showed him the place. So he cut off a stick, and threw *it* in there; and he made the iron float. 7Therefore he said, "Pick *it* up for yourself." So he reached out his hand and took it.

THE BLINDED SYRIANS CAPTURED

8Now the king of Syria was making war against Israel; and he consulted with his servants, saying, "My camp

will be in such and such a
place." 9And the man of God
sent to the king of Israel, saying, "Beware that you do not
pass this place, for the Syrians are coming down there."
10Then the king of Israel sent
someone to the place of which
the man of God had told him.
Thus he warned him, and he
was watchful there, not just
once or twice.

11Therefore the heart of
the king of Syria was greatly
troubled by this thing; and he
called his servants and said to
them, "Will you not show me
which of us *is* for the king of
Israel?"

12And one of his servants
said, "None, my lord, O king;
but Elisha, the prophet who *is*
in Israel, tells the king of Israel the words that you speak
in your bedroom."

13So he said, "Go and see
where he *is,* that I may send
and get him."

And it was told him, saying,
"Surely *he is* in Dothan."

14Therefore he sent horses
and chariots and a great army
there, and they came by night
and surrounded the city. 15And
when the servant of the man
of God arose early and went
out, there was an army, surrounding the city with horses
and chariots. And his servant
said to him, "Alas, my master!
What shall we do?"

16So he answered, "Do not
fear, for those who *are* with
us *are* more than those who
are with them." 17And Elisha
prayed, and said, "LORD, I
pray, open his eyes that he
may see." Then the LORD
opened the eyes of the young
man, and he saw. And be-
hold, the mountain *was* full
of horses and chariots of fire
all around Elisha. 18So when
the Syrians came down to him,
Elisha prayed to the LORD,
and said, "Strike this people,
I pray, with blindness." And
He struck them with blindness according to the word
of Elisha.

19Now Elisha said to them,
"This *is* not the way, nor *is* this
the city. Follow me, and I will
bring you to the man whom
you seek." But he led them to
Samaria.

20So it was, when they had
come to Samaria, that Elisha
said, "LORD, open the eyes of
these *men,* that they may see."
And the LORD opened their
eyes, and they saw; and there
they were, inside Samaria!

21Now when the king of
Israel saw them, he said to
Elisha, "My father, shall I kill
them? Shall I kill *them?*"

22But he answered, "You
shall not kill *them.* Would you
kill those whom you have
taken captive with your sword
and your bow? Set food and
water before them, that they
may eat and drink and go to
their master." 23Then he prepared a great feast for them;
and after they ate and drank,
he sent them away and they

went to their master. So the bands of Syrian *raiders* came no more into the land of Israel.

SYRIA BESIEGES SAMARIA IN FAMINE

24And it happened after this that Ben-Hadad king of Syria gathered all his army, and went up and besieged Samaria. 25And there was a great famine in Samaria; and indeed they besieged it until a donkey's head was *sold* for eighty *shekels* of silver, and one-fourth of a kab of dove droppings for five *shekels* of silver.

26Then, as the king of Israel was passing by on the wall, a woman cried out to him, saying, "Help, my lord, O king!"

27And he said, "If the LORD does not help you, where can I find help for you? From the threshing floor or from the winepress?" 28Then the king said to her, "What is troubling you?"

And she answered, "This woman said to me, 'Give your son, that we may eat him today, and we will eat my son tomorrow.' 29So we boiled my son, and ate him. And I said to her on the next day, 'Give your son, that we may eat him'; but she has hidden her son."

30Now it happened, when the king heard the words of the woman, that he tore his clothes; and as he passed by on the wall, the people looked, and there underneath *he had* sackcloth on his body. 31Then he said, "God do so to me and more also, if the head of Elisha the son of Shaphat remains on him today!"

32But Elisha was sitting in his house, and the elders were sitting with him. And *the king* sent a man ahead of him, but before the messenger came to him, he said to the elders, "Do you see how this son of a murderer has sent someone to take away my head? Look, when the messenger comes, shut the door, and hold him fast at the door. *Is* not the sound of his master's feet behind him?" 33And while he was still talking with them, there was the messenger, coming down to him; and then *the king* said, "Surely this calamity *is* from the LORD; why should I wait for the LORD any longer?"

7 Then Elisha said, "Hear the word of the LORD. Thus says the LORD: 'Tomorrow about this time a seah of fine flour *shall be sold* for a shekel, and two seahs of barley for a shekel, at the gate of Samaria.'"

2So an officer on whose hand the king leaned answered the man of God and said, "Look, *if* the LORD would make windows in heaven, could this thing be?"

And he said, "In fact, you shall see *it* with your eyes, but you shall not eat of it."

THE SYRIANS FLEE

3Now there were four leprous men at the entrance of

the gate; and they said to one
another, "Why are we sitting
here until we die? 4If we say,
'We will enter the city,' the
famine *is* in the city, and we
shall die there. And if we sit
here, we die also. Now therefore, come, let us surrender to
the army of the Syrians. If they
keep us alive, we shall live; and
if they kill us, we shall only
die." 5And they rose at twilight
to go to the camp of the Syrians; and when they had come
to the outskirts of the Syrian
camp, to their surprise no one
was there. 6For the Lord had
caused the army of the Syrians
to hear the noise of chariots
and the noise of horses—the
noise of a great army; so they
said to one another, "Look, the
king of Israel has hired against
us the kings of the Hittites and
the kings of the Egyptians to
attack us!" 7Therefore they
arose and fled at twilight, and
left the camp intact—their
tents, their horses, and their
donkeys—and they fled for
their lives. 8And when these
lepers came to the outskirts
of the camp, they went into
one tent and ate and drank,
and carried from it silver and
gold and clothing, and went
and hid *them;* then they came
back and entered another tent,
and carried *some* from there
also, and went and hid *it.*

9Then they said to one
another, "We are not doing
right. This day *is* a day of good
news, and we remain silent. If
we wait until morning light,
some punishment will come
upon us. Now therefore, come,
let us go and tell the king's
household." 10So they went
and called to the gatekeepers
of the city, and told them, saying, "We went to the Syrian
camp, and surprisingly no
one *was* there, not a human
sound—only horses and donkeys tied, and the tents intact."
11And the gatekeepers called
out, and they told *it* to the
king's household inside.

12So the king arose in the
night and said to his servants, "Let me now tell you
what the Syrians have done
to us. They know that we *are*
hungry; therefore they have
gone out of the camp to hide
themselves in the field, saying, 'When they come out of
the city, we shall catch them
alive, and get into the city.' "

13And one of his servants
answered and said, "Please, let
several *men* take five of the
remaining horses which are
left in the city. Look, they *may*
either become like all the multitude of Israel that are left in it;
or indeed, *I say,* they *may be-*
come like all the multitude of
Israel left from those who are
consumed; so let us send them
and see." 14Therefore they took
two chariots with horses; and
the king sent them in the direction of the Syrian army, saying,
"Go and see." 15And they went
after them to the Jordan; and
indeed all the road *was* full of

garments and weapons which
the Syrians had thrown away
in their haste. So the messengers returned and told the
king. 16Then the people went
out and plundered the tents of
the Syrians. So a seah of fine
flour was *sold* for a shekel, and
two seahs of barley for a shekel, according to the word of
the LORD.

17Now the king had ap-
pointed the officer on whose
hand he leaned to have charge
of the gate. But the people
trampled him in the gate, and
he died, just as the man of God
had said, who spoke when the
king came down to him. 18So
it happened just as the man of
God had spoken to the king,
saying, "Two seahs of barley
for a shekel, and a seah of fine
flour for a shekel, shall be *sold*
tomorrow about this time in
the gate of Samaria."

19Then that officer had answered the man of God, and
said, "Now look, *if* the LORD
would make windows in
heaven, could such a thing be?"

And he had said, "In fact,
you shall see *it* with your
eyes, but you shall not eat of
it." 20And so it happened to
him, for the people trampled
him in the gate, and he died.

THE KING RESTORES THE SHUNAMMITE'S LAND

8 Then Elisha spoke to the
woman whose son he had
restored to life, saying, "Arise
and go, you and your household, and stay wherever you
can; for the LORD has called
for a famine, and furthermore, it will come upon the
land for seven years." 2So the
woman arose and did according to the saying of the man
of God, and she went with her
household and dwelt in the
land of the Philistines seven
years.

3It came to pass, at the end
of seven years, that the woman
returned from the land of the
Philistines; and she went to
make an appeal to the king
for her house and for her land.
4Then the king talked with Gehazi, the servant of the man of
God, saying, "Tell me, please,
all the great things Elisha has
done." 5Now it happened, as
he was telling the king how
he had restored the dead to
life, that there was the woman
whose son he had restored to
life, appealing to the king for
her house and for her land.
And Gehazi said, "My lord,
O king, this *is* the woman, and
this *is* her son whom Elisha
restored to life." 6And when
the king asked the woman, she
told him.

So the king appointed a
certain officer for her, saying,
"Restore all that *was* hers, and
all the proceeds of the field
from the day that she left the
land until now."

DEATH OF BEN-HADAD

7Then Elisha went to Da-
mascus, and Ben-Hadad king

of Syria was sick; and it was
told him, saying, "The man
of God has come here." [8]And
the king said to Hazael, "Take
a present in your hand, and
go to meet the man of God,
and inquire of the LORD by
him, saying, 'Shall I recover
from this disease?'" [9]So Hazael went to meet him and took
a present with him, of every
good thing of Damascus, forty
camel-loads; and he came and
stood before him, and said,
"Your son Ben-Hadad king
of Syria has sent me to you,
saying, 'Shall I recover from
this disease?'"
[10]And Elisha said to him,
"Go, say to him, 'You shall certainly recover.' However the
LORD has shown me that he
will really die." [11]Then he set his
countenance in a stare until he
was ashamed; and the man of
God wept. [12]And Hazael said,
"Why is my lord weeping?"
He answered, "Because I
know the evil that you will do
to the children of Israel: Their
strongholds you will set on
fire, and their young men you
will kill with the sword; and
you will dash their children,
and rip open their women
with child."
[13]So Hazael said, "But what
is your servant—a dog, that he
should do this gross thing?"
And Elisha answered, "The
LORD has shown me that you
will become king over Syria."
[14]Then he departed from
Elisha, and came to his master, who said to him, "What
did Elisha say to you?" And
he answered, "He told me you
would surely recover." [15]But
it happened on the next day
that he took a thick cloth
and dipped *it* in water, and
spread *it* over his face so that
he died; and Hazael reigned
in his place.

JEHORAM REIGNS IN JUDAH

[16]Now in the fifth year of
Joram the son of Ahab, king
of Israel, Jehoshaphat *having
been* king of Judah, Jehoram
the son of Jehoshaphat began
to reign as king of Judah.
[17]He was thirty-two years old
when he became king, and
he reigned eight years in Jerusalem. [18]And he walked in
the way of the kings of Israel,
just as the house of Ahab had
done, for the daughter of Ahab
was his wife; and he did evil
in the sight of the LORD. [19]Yet
the LORD would not destroy
Judah, for the sake of His servant David, as He promised
him to give a lamp to him *and*
his sons forever.
[20]In his days Edom revolted
against Judah's authority,
and made a king over themselves. [21]So Joram[a] went to
Zair, and all his chariots with
him. Then he rose by night
and attacked the Edomites

8:21 [a] Spelled *Jehoram* in verse 16

who had surrounded him and
the captains of the chariots;
and the troops fled to their
tents. 22Thus Edom has been
in revolt against Judah's authority to this day. And Libnah
revolted at that time.
23Now the rest of the acts of
Joram, and all that he did, *are*
they not written in the book of
the chronicles of the kings of
Judah? 24So Joram rested with
his fathers, and was buried
with his fathers in the City of
David. Then Ahaziah his son
reigned in his place.

AHAZIAH REIGNS IN JUDAH

25In the twelfth year of
Joram the son of Ahab, king
of Israel, Ahaziah the son
of Jehoram, king of Judah,
began to reign. 26Ahaziah
was twenty-two years old
when he became king, and
he reigned one year in Jerusalem. His mother's name *was*
Athaliah the granddaughter
of Omri, king of Israel. 27And
he walked in the way of the
house of Ahab, and did evil
in the sight of the LORD, like
the house of Ahab, for he *was*
the son-in-law of the house
of Ahab.
28Now he went with Joram
the son of Ahab to war against
Hazael king of Syria at Ramoth Gilead; and the Syrians wounded Joram. 29Then
King Joram went back to
Jezreel to recover from the
wounds which the Syrians had
inflicted on him at Ramah,
when he fought against Hazael king of Syria. And Ahaziah the son of Jehoram, king
of Judah, went down to see
Joram the son of Ahab in Jezreel, because he was sick.

JEHU ANOINTED KING OF ISRAEL

9 And Elisha the prophet
called one of the sons of
the prophets, and said to him,
"Get yourself ready, take this
flask of oil in your hand, and
go to Ramoth Gilead. 2Now
when you arrive at that place,
look there for Jehu the son
of Jehoshaphat, the son of
Nimshi, and go in and make
him rise up from among his
associates, and take him to an
inner room. 3Then take the
flask of oil, and pour *it* on his
head, and say, 'Thus says the
LORD: "I have anointed you
king over Israel."' Then open
the door and flee, and do not
delay."
4So the young man, the servant of the prophet, went to
Ramoth Gilead. 5And when
he arrived, there *were* the captains of the army sitting; and
he said, "I have a message for
you, Commander."

Jehu said, "For which *one*
of us?"

And he said, "For you, Commander." 6Then he arose and
went into the house. And he
poured the oil on his head,
and said to him, "Thus says
the LORD God of Israel: 'I have

anointed you king over the
people of the LORD, over Israel. 7You shall strike down
the house of Ahab your master, that I may avenge the
blood of My servants the
prophets, and the blood of
all the servants of the LORD,
at the hand of Jezebel. 8For
the whole house of Ahab shall
perish; and I will cut off from
Ahab all the males in Israel,
both bond and free. 9So I will
make the house of Ahab like
the house of Jeroboam the
son of Nebat, and like the
house of Baasha the son of
Ahijah. 10The dogs shall eat
Jezebel on the plot *of ground*
at Jezreel, and *there shall be*
none to bury *her.*'" And he
opened the door and fled.

11Then Jehu came out to
the servants of his master, and
one said to him, "*Is* all well?
Why did this madman come
to you?"

And he said to them, "You
know the man and his babble."

12And they said, "A lie! Tell
us now."

So he said, "Thus and thus
he spoke to me, saying, 'Thus
says the LORD: "I have anointed
you king over Israel."'"

13Then each man hastened
to take his garment and put *it*
under him on the top of the
steps; and they blew trumpets,
saying, "Jehu is king!"

JORAM OF ISRAEL KILLED

14So Jehu the son of Je-
hoshaphat, the son of Nimshi, conspired against Joram.
(Now Joram had been defending Ramoth Gilead, he and all
Israel, against Hazael king of
Syria. 15But King Joram had
returned to Jezreel to recover
from the wounds which the
Syrians had inflicted on him
when he fought with Hazael
king of Syria.) And Jehu said,
"If you are so minded, let no
one leave *or* escape from the
city to go and tell *it* in Jezreel."
16So Jehu rode in a chariot and
went to Jezreel, for Joram was
laid up there; and Ahaziah
king of Judah had come down
to see Joram.

17Now a watchman stood
on the tower in Jezreel, and
he saw the company of Jehu
as he came, and said, "I see a
company of men."

And Joram said, "Get a
horseman and send him to
meet them, and let him say,
'*Is it* peace?'"

18So the horseman went
to meet him, and said, "Thus
says the king: '*Is it* peace?'"

And Jehu said, "What have
you to do with peace? Turn
around and follow me."

So the watchman reported,
saying, "The messenger went
to them, but is not coming
back."

19Then he sent out a second
horseman who came to them,
and said, "Thus says the king:
'*Is it* peace?'"

And Jehu answered, "What
have you to do with peace?
Turn around and follow me."

20So the watchman reported, saying, "He went up to them and is not coming back; and the driving *is* like the driving of Jehu the son of Nimshi, for he drives furiously!"

21Then Joram said, "Make ready." And his chariot was made ready. Then Joram king of Israel and Ahaziah king of Judah went out, each in his chariot; and they went out to meet Jehu, and met him on the property of Naboth the Jezreelite. 22Now it happened, when Joram saw Jehu, that he said, "*Is it* peace, Jehu?"

So he answered, "What peace, as long as the harlotries of your mother Jezebel and her witchcraft *are so* many?"

23Then Joram turned around and fled, and said to Ahaziah, "Treachery, Ahaziah!" 24Now Jehu drew his bow with full strength and shot Jehoram between his arms; and the arrow came out at his heart, and he sank down in his chariot. 25Then *Jehu* said to Bidkar his captain, "Pick *him* up, *and* throw him into the tract of the field of Naboth the Jezreelite; for remember, when you and I were riding together behind Ahab his father, that the LORD laid this burden upon him: 26'Surely I saw yesterday the blood of Naboth and the blood of his sons,' says the LORD, 'and I will repay you in this plot,' says the LORD. Now therefore, take *and* throw him on the plot *of ground,* according to the word of the LORD."

AHAZIAH OF JUDAH KILLED

27But when Ahaziah king of Judah saw *this,* he fled by the road to Beth Haggan.[a] So Jehu pursued him, and said, "Shoot him also in the chariot." *And they shot him* at the Ascent of Gur, which is by Ibleam. Then he fled to Megiddo, and died there. 28And his servants carried him in the chariot to Jerusalem, and buried him in his tomb with his fathers in the City of David. 29In the eleventh year of Joram the son of Ahab, Ahaziah had become king over Judah.

JEZEBEL'S VIOLENT DEATH

30Now when Jehu had come to Jezreel, Jezebel heard *of it;* and she put paint on her eyes and adorned her head, and looked through a window. 31Then, as Jehu entered at the gate, she said, "*Is it* peace, Zimri, murderer of your master?"

32And he looked up at the window, and said, "Who *is* on my side? Who?" So two *or* three eunuchs looked out at him. 33Then he said, "Throw her down." So they threw her down, and *some* of her blood spattered on the wall and on the horses; and he trampled

9:27 [a] Literally *The Garden House*

her underfoot. 34And when he
had gone in, he ate and drank.
Then he said, "Go now, see to
this accursed *woman,* and
bury her, for she was a king's
daughter." 35So they went to
bury her, but they found no
more of her than the skull
and the feet and the palms
of *her* hands. 36Therefore they
came back and told him. And
he said, "This *is* the word of
the LORD, which He spoke by
His servant Elijah the Tishbite, saying, 'On the plot *of*
ground at Jezreel dogs shall
eat the flesh of Jezebel;[a] 37and
the corpse of Jezebel shall be
as refuse on the surface of the
field, in the plot at Jezreel, so
that they shall not say, "Here
lies Jezebel." ' "

AHAB'S SEVENTY SONS KILLED

10 Now Ahab had seventy
sons in Samaria. And
Jehu wrote and sent letters
to Samaria, to the rulers of
Jezreel,[a] to the elders, and to
those who reared Ahab's *sons,*
saying:

2 Now as soon as this letter
comes to you, since
your master's sons *are*
with you, and you have
chariots and horses, a
fortified city also, and
weapons, 3choose the
best qualified of your
master's sons, set *him* on
his father's throne, and
fight for your master's
house.

4But they were exceedingly
afraid, and said, "Look, two
kings could not stand up to
him; how then can we stand?"
5And he who *was* in charge of
the house, and he who *was* in
charge of the city, the elders
also, and those who reared *the*
sons, sent to Jehu, saying, "We
are your servants, we will do
all you tell us; but we will not
make anyone king. Do *what is*
good in your sight." 6Then he
wrote a second letter to them,
saying:

If you *are* for me and will
obey my voice, take the
heads of the men, your
master's sons, and come
to me at Jezreel by this
time tomorrow.

Now the king's sons, sev-
enty persons, *were* with the
great men of the city, *who* were
rearing them. 7So it was, when
the letter came to them, that
they took the king's sons and
slaughtered seventy persons,
put their heads in baskets and
sent *them* to him at Jezreel.
8Then a messenger came
and told him, saying, "They
have brought the heads of the
king's sons."

9:36 [a] 1 Kings 21:23 10:1 [a] Following Masoretic Text, Syriac, and Targum; Septuagint reads *Samaria;* Vulgate reads *city.*

And he said, "Lay them in two heaps at the entrance of the gate until morning."

[9]So it was, in the morning, that he went out and stood, and said to all the people, "You *are* righteous. Indeed I conspired against my master and killed him; but who killed all these? [10]Know now that nothing shall fall to the earth of the word of the LORD which the LORD spoke concerning the house of Ahab; for the LORD has done what He spoke by His servant Elijah."
[11]So Jehu killed all who remained of the house of Ahab in Jezreel, and all his great men and his close acquaintances and his priests, until he left him none remaining.

AHAZIAH'S FORTY-TWO BROTHERS KILLED

[12]And he arose and departed and went to Samaria. On the way, at Beth Eked[a] of the Shepherds, [13]Jehu met with the brothers of Ahaziah king of Judah, and said, "Who *are* you?"

So they answered, "We *are* the brothers of Ahaziah; we have come down to greet the sons of the king and the sons of the queen mother."

[14]And he said, "Take them alive!" So they took them alive, and killed them at the well of Beth Eked, forty-two men; and he left none of them.

THE REST OF AHAB'S FAMILY KILLED

[15]Now when he departed from there, he met Jehonadab the son of Rechab, *coming* to meet him; and he greeted him and said to him, "Is your heart right, as my heart *is* toward your heart?"

And Jehonadab answered, "It is."

Jehu said, "If it is, give *me* your hand." So he gave *him* his hand, and he took him up to him into the chariot.
[16]Then he said, "Come with me, and see my zeal for the LORD." So they had him ride in his chariot. [17]And when he came to Samaria, he killed all who remained to Ahab in Samaria, till he had destroyed them, according to the word of the LORD which He spoke to Elijah.

WORSHIPERS OF BAAL KILLED

[18]Then Jehu gathered all the people together, and said to them, "Ahab served Baal a little, Jehu will serve him much. [19]Now therefore, call to me all the prophets of Baal, all his servants, and all his priests. Let no one be missing, for I have a great sacrifice for Baal. Whoever is missing shall not live." But Jehu acted deceptively, with the intent of destroying the worshipers of Baal. [20]And Jehu said, "Pro-

10:12 [a] Or *The Shearing House*

claim a solemn assembly for
Baal." So they proclaimed *it.*
21Then Jehu sent throughout
all Israel; and all the worshipers of Baal came, so that there
was not a man left who did
not come. So they came into
the temple[a] of Baal, and the
temple of Baal was full from
one end to the other. 22And
he said to the one in charge
of the wardrobe, "Bring out
vestments for all the worshipers of Baal." So he brought out
vestments for them. 23Then
Jehu and Jehonadab the son
of Rechab went into the temple of Baal, and said to the
worshipers of Baal, "Search
and see that no servants of the
LORD are here with you, but
only the worshipers of Baal."
24So they went in to offer sacrifices and burnt offerings.
Now Jehu had appointed
for himself eighty men on
the outside, and had said, "*If*
any of the men whom I have
brought into your hands escapes, *whoever lets him escape,*
it shall be his life for the life of
the other."

25Now it happened, as soon
as he had made an end of offering the burnt offering, that
Jehu said to the guard and to
the captains, "Go in *and* kill
them; let no one come out!"
And they killed them with the
edge of the sword; then the
guards and the officers threw
them out, and went into the
inner room of the temple of
Baal. 26And they brought the
sacred pillars out of the temple of Baal and burned them.
27Then they broke down the
sacred pillar of Baal, and tore
down the temple of Baal and
made it a refuse dump to this
day. 28Thus Jehu destroyed
Baal from Israel.

29However Jehu did not
turn away from the sins of
Jeroboam the son of Nebat,
who had made Israel sin, *that*
is, from the golden calves
that *were* at Bethel and Dan.
30And the LORD said to Jehu,
"Because you have done well
in doing *what is* right in My
sight, *and* have done to the
house of Ahab all that *was* in
My heart, your sons shall sit
on the throne of Israel to the
fourth *generation.*" 31But Jehu
took no heed to walk in the
law of the LORD God of Israel
with all his heart; for he did
not depart from the sins of
Jeroboam, who had made Israel sin.

DEATH OF JEHU

32In those days the LORD
began to cut off *parts* of Israel;
and Hazael conquered them
in all the territory of Israel
33from the Jordan eastward:
all the land of Gilead—Gad,
Reuben, and Manasseh—from
Aroer, which *is* by the River
Arnon, including Gilead and
Bashan.

10:21 [a] Literally *house,* and so elsewhere in this chapter

34Now the rest of the acts
of Jehu, all that he did, and all
his might, *are* they not written
in the book of the chronicles
of the kings of Israel? 35So
Jehu rested with his fathers,
and they buried him in Samaria. Then Jehoahaz his son
reigned in his place. 36And the
period that Jehu reigned over
Israel in Samaria *was* twenty-
eight years.

ATHALIAH REIGNS IN JUDAH

11 When Athaliah the
mother of Ahaziah saw
that her son was dead, she
arose and destroyed all the
royal heirs. 2But Jehosheba,
the daughter of King Joram,
sister of Ahaziah, took Joash
the son of Ahaziah, and stole
him away from among the
king's sons *who were* being
murdered; and they hid him
and his nurse in the bedroom,
from Athaliah, so that he was
not killed. 3So he was hidden
with her in the house of the
LORD for six years, while Athaliah reigned over the land.

JOASH CROWNED KING OF JUDAH

4In the seventh year Je-
hoiada sent and brought the
captains of hundreds—of the
bodyguards and the escorts—
and brought them into the
house of the LORD to him. And
he made a covenant with them
and took an oath from them
in the house of the LORD, and
showed them the king's son.
5Then he commanded them,
saying, "This *is* what you shall
do: One-third of you who
come on duty on the Sabbath
shall be keeping watch over
the king's house, 6one-third
shall be at the gate of Sur, and
one-third at the gate behind
the escorts. You shall keep
the watch of the house, lest
it be broken down. 7The two
contingents of you who go
off duty on the Sabbath shall
keep the watch of the house
of the LORD for the king. 8But
you shall surround the king
on all sides, every man with
his weapons in his hand; and
whoever comes within range,
let him be put to death. You
are to be with the king as he
goes out and as he comes in."

9So the captains of the
hundreds did according to
all that Jehoiada the priest
commanded. Each of them
took his men who were to be
on duty on the Sabbath, with
those who were going off duty
on the Sabbath, and came to
Jehoiada the priest. 10And
the priest gave the captains
of hundreds the spears and
shields which *had belonged* to
King David, that were in the
temple of the LORD. 11Then
the escorts stood, every man
with his weapons in his hand,
all around the king, from the
right side of the temple to
the left side of the temple, by
the altar and the house. 12And
he brought out the king's son,

put the crown on him, and
gave him the Testimony;[a] they
made him king and anointed
him, and they clapped their
hands and said, "Long live the
king!"

DEATH OF ATHALIAH

13Now when Athaliah heard
the noise of the escorts *and*
the people, she came to the
people *in* the temple of the
LORD. 14When she looked,
there was the king standing
by a pillar according to custom; and the leaders and the
trumpeters were by the king.
All the people of the land
were rejoicing and blowing
trumpets. So Athaliah tore
her clothes and cried out,
"Treason! Treason!"

15And Jehoiada the priest
commanded the captains of
the hundreds, the officers of
the army, and said to them,
"Take her outside under
guard, and slay with the sword
whoever follows her." For the
priest had said, "Do not let
her be killed in the house of
the LORD." 16So they seized
her; and she went by way of
the horses' entrance *into* the
king's house, and there she
was killed.

17Then Jehoiada made a
covenant between the LORD,
the king, and the people, that
they should be the LORD's
people, and *also* between the
king and the people. 18And all
the people of the land went to
the temple of Baal, and tore it
down. They thoroughly broke
in pieces its altars and images,
and killed Mattan the priest
of Baal before the altars. And
the priest appointed officers
over the house of the LORD.
19Then he took the captains
of hundreds, the bodyguards,
the escorts, and all the people
of the land; and they brought
the king down from the house
of the LORD, and went by way
of the gate of the escorts to the
king's house. Then he sat on
the throne of the kings. 20So
all the people of the land rejoiced; and the city was quiet,
for they had slain Athaliah
with the sword *in* the king's
house. 21Jehoash *was* seven
years old when he became
king.

JEHOASH REPAIRS THE TEMPLE

12 In the seventh year
of Jehu, Jehoash[a] be-
came king, and he reigned
forty years in Jerusalem. His
mother's name *was* Zibiah of
Beersheba. 2Jehoash did *what*
was right in the sight of the
LORD all the days in which Jehoiada the priest instructed
him. 3But the high places were
not taken away; the people
still sacrificed and burned incense on the high places.

11:12 [a] That is, the Law (compare Exodus 25:16, 21 and Deuteronomy 31:9) 12:1 [a] Spelled *Joash* in 11:2ff

4And Jehoash said to the
priests, "All the money of
the dedicated gifts that are
brought into the house of
the LORD—each man's cen-
sus money, each man's assessment money[a]—*and* all the
money that a man purposes
in his heart to bring into the
house of the LORD, 5let the
priests take *it* themselves,
each from his constituency;
and let them repair the damages of the temple, wherever
any dilapidation is found."

6Now it was so, by the
twenty-third year of King Jehoash, *that* the priests had
not repaired the damages of
the temple. 7So King Jehoash called Jehoiada the priest
and the *other* priests, and said
to them, "Why have you not
repaired the damages of the
temple? Now therefore, do
not take *more* money from
your constituency, but deliver it for repairing the damages of the temple." 8And
the priests agreed that they
would neither receive *more*
money from the people, nor
repair the damages of the
temple.

9Then Jehoiada the priest
took a chest, bored a hole in
its lid, and set it beside the
altar, on the right side as
one comes into the house
of the LORD; and the priests
who kept the door put there
all the money brought into
the house of the LORD. 10So
it was, whenever they saw
that *there was* much money
in the chest, that the king's
scribe and the high priest
came up and put it in bags,
and counted the money that
was found in the house of the
LORD. 11Then they gave the
money, which had been ap-
portioned, into the hands of
those who did the work, who
had the oversight of the house
of the LORD; and they paid
it out to the carpenters and
builders who worked on the
house of the LORD, 12and to
masons and stonecutters, and
for buying timber and hewn
stone, to repair the damage
of the house of the LORD, and
for all that was paid out to repair the temple. 13However
there were not made for the
house of the LORD basins of
silver, trimmers, sprinkling-
bowls, trumpets, any articles
of gold or articles of silver,
from the money brought into
the house of the LORD. 14But
they gave that to the workmen, and they repaired the
house of the LORD with it.
15Moreover they did not require an account from the
men into whose hand they
delivered the money to be
paid to workmen, for they
dealt faithfully. 16The money
from the trespass offerings
and the money from the sin
offerings was not brought

12:4 [a] Compare Leviticus 27:2ff

into the house of the LORD. It belonged to the priests.

HAZAEL THREATENS JERUSALEM

17Hazael king of Syria went
up and fought against Gath,
and took it; then Hazael set
his face to go up to Jerusalem.
18And Jehoash king of Judah
took all the sacred things that his fathers, Jehoshaphat and Jehoram and Ahaziah, kings of Judah, had dedicated, and his own sacred things, and all the gold found in the treasuries of the house of the LORD and in the king's house, and sent *them* to Hazael king of Syria. Then he went away from Jerusalem.

DEATH OF JOASH

19Now the rest of the acts of Joash,[a] and all that he did, *are* they not written in the book of the chronicles of the kings of Judah?

20And his servants arose
and formed a conspiracy, and
killed Joash in the house of
the Millo,[a] which goes down to
Silla. 21For Jozachar[a] the son
of Shimeath and Jehozabad the son of Shomer,[b] his servants, struck him. So he died, and they buried him with his fathers in the City of David. Then Amaziah his son reigned in his place.

JEHOAHAZ REIGNS IN ISRAEL

13 In the twenty-third year
of Joash[a] the son of Ahaziah, king of Judah, Jehoahaz
the son of Jehu became king
over Israel in Samaria, *and*
reigned seventeen years. 2And
he did evil in the sight of the LORD, and followed the sins of Jeroboam the son of Nebat, who had made Israel sin. He did not depart from them.

3Then the anger of the
LORD was aroused against Israel, and He delivered them
into the hand of Hazael king
of Syria, and into the hand of
Ben-Hadad the son of Hazael,
all *their* days. 4So Jehoahaz
pleaded with the LORD, and the LORD listened to him; for He saw the oppression of Israel, because the king of Syria
oppressed them. 5Then the
LORD gave Israel a deliverer, so that they escaped from under the hand of the Syrians; and the children of Israel
dwelt in their tents as before.
6Nevertheless they did not de-
part from the sins of the house of Jeroboam, who had made Israel sin, *but* walked in them; and the wooden image[a] also
remained in Samaria. 7For
He left of the army of Jehoahaz only fifty horsemen, ten chariots, and ten thousand foot soldiers; for the king of

12:19 [a] Spelled *Jehoash* in 12:1ff 12:20 [a] Literally *The Landfill* 12:21 [a] Called *Zabad* in 2 Chronicles 24:26 [b] Called *Shimrith* in 2 Chronicles 24:26 13:1 [a] Spelled *Jehoash* in 12:1ff 13:6 [a] Hebrew *Asherah,* a Canaanite goddess

Syria had destroyed them and made them like the dust at threshing.

[8]Now the rest of the acts of Jehoahaz, all that he did, and his might, *are* they not written in the book of the chronicles of the kings of Israel? [9]So Jehoahaz rested with his fathers, and they buried him in Samaria. Then Joash his son reigned in his place.

JEHOASH REIGNS IN ISRAEL

[10]In the thirty-seventh year of Joash king of Judah, Jehoash[a] the son of Jehoahaz became king over Israel in Samaria, *and reigned* sixteen years. [11]And he did evil in the sight of the LORD. He did not depart from all the sins of Jeroboam the son of Nebat, who made Israel sin, *but* walked in them.

[12]Now the rest of the acts of Joash, all that he did, and his might with which he fought against Amaziah king of Judah, *are* they not written in the book of the chronicles of the kings of Israel? [13]So Joash rested with his fathers. Then Jeroboam sat on his throne. And Joash was buried in Samaria with the kings of Israel.

DEATH OF ELISHA

[14]Elisha had become sick with the illness of which he would die. Then Joash the king of Israel came down to him, and wept over his face, and said, "O my father, my father, the chariots of Israel and their horsemen!"

[15]And Elisha said to him, "Take a bow and some arrows." So he took himself a bow and some arrows. [16]Then he said to the king of Israel, "Put your hand on the bow." So he put his hand *on it,* and Elisha put his hands on the king's hands. [17]And he said, "Open the east window"; and he opened *it.* Then Elisha said, "Shoot"; and he shot. And he said, "The arrow of the LORD's deliverance and the arrow of deliverance from Syria; for you must strike the Syrians at Aphek till you have destroyed *them.*" [18]Then he said, "Take the arrows"; so he took *them.* And he said to the king of Israel, "Strike the ground"; so he struck three times, and stopped. [19]And the man of God was angry with him, and said, "You should have struck five or six times; then you would have struck Syria till you had destroyed *it!* But now you will strike Syria *only* three times."

[20]Then Elisha died, and they buried him. And the *raiding* bands from Moab invaded the land in the spring of the year. [21]So it was, as they were burying a man, that suddenly they spied a band *of raiders;*

13:10 [a] Spelled *Joash* in verse 9

and they put the man in the tomb of Elisha; and when the man was let down and touched the bones of Elisha, he revived and stood on his feet.

ISRAEL RECAPTURES CITIES FROM SYRIA

22And Hazael king of Syria oppressed Israel all the days of Jehoahaz. 23But the LORD was gracious to them, had compassion on them, and regarded them, because of His covenant with Abraham, Isaac, and Jacob, and would not yet destroy them or cast them from His presence.

24Now Hazael king of Syria died. Then Ben-Hadad his son reigned in his place. 25And Jehoash[a] the son of Jehoahaz recaptured from the hand of Ben-Hadad, the son of Hazael, the cities which he had taken out of the hand of Jehoahaz his father by war. Three times Joash defeated him and recaptured the cities of Israel.

AMAZIAH REIGNS IN JUDAH

14 In the second year of Joash the son of Jehoahaz, king of Israel, Amaziah the son of Joash, king of Judah, became king. 2He was twenty-five years old when he became king, and he reigned twenty-nine years in Jerusalem. His mother's name was Jehoaddan of Jerusalem. 3And he did *what was* right in the sight of the LORD, yet not like his father David; he did everything as his father Joash had done. 4However the high places were not taken away, and the people still sacrificed and burned incense on the high places.

5Now it happened, as soon as the kingdom was established in his hand, that he executed his servants who had murdered his father the king. 6But the children of the murderers he did not execute, according to what is written in the Book of the Law of Moses, in which the LORD commanded, saying, "Fathers shall not be put to death for their children, nor shall children be put to death for their fathers; but a person shall be put to death for his own sin."[a]

7He killed ten thousand Edomites in the Valley of Salt, and took Sela by war, and called its name Joktheel to this day.

8Then Amaziah sent messengers to Jehoash[a] the son of Jehoahaz, the son of Jehu, king of Israel, saying, "Come, let us face one another *in battle.*" 9And Jehoash king of Israel sent to Amaziah king of Judah, saying, "The thistle that *was* in Lebanon sent to

13:25 [a] Spelled *Joash* in verses 12–14, 25 14:6 [a] Deuteronomy 24:16 14:8 [a] Spelled *Joash* in 13:12ff and 2 Chronicles 25:17ff

the cedar that *was* in Lebanon,
saying, 'Give your daughter
to my son as wife'; and a wild
beast that *was* in Lebanon
passed by and trampled the
thistle. [10]You have indeed defeated Edom, and your heart
has lifted you up. Glory *in
that,* and stay at home; for
why should you meddle with
trouble so that you fall—you
and Judah with you?"

[11]But Amaziah would not
heed. Therefore Jehoash king
of Israel went out; so he and
Amaziah king of Judah faced
one another at Beth Shemesh,
which *belongs* to Judah. [12]And
Judah was defeated by Israel,
and every man fled to his tent.
[13]Then Jehoash king of Israel
captured Amaziah king of
Judah, the son of Jehoash, the
son of Ahaziah, at Beth Shemesh; and he went to Jerusalem, and broke down the wall
of Jerusalem from the Gate of
Ephraim to the Corner Gate—
four hundred cubits. [14]And he
took all the gold and silver, all
the articles that were found
in the house of the LORD and
in the treasuries of the king's
house, and hostages, and returned to Samaria.

[15]Now the rest of the acts
of Jehoash which he did—his
might, and how he fought with
Amaziah king of Judah—*are*
they not written in the book
of the chronicles of the kings
of Israel? [16]So Jehoash rested
with his fathers, and was buried in Samaria with the kings
of Israel. Then Jeroboam his
son reigned in his place.

[17]Amaziah the son of Joash,
king of Judah, lived fifteen
years after the death of Jehoash the son of Jehoahaz,
king of Israel. [18]Now the rest
of the acts of Amaziah, *are*
they not written in the book
of the chronicles of the kings
of Judah? [19]And they formed
a conspiracy against him in
Jerusalem, and he fled to
Lachish; but they sent after
him to Lachish and killed him
there. [20]Then they brought
him on horses, and he was
buried at Jerusalem with his
fathers in the City of David.

[21]And all the people of
Judah took Azariah,[a] who *was*
sixteen years old, and made
him king instead of his father
Amaziah. [22]He built Elath and
restored it to Judah, after the
king rested with his fathers.

JEROBOAM II REIGNS IN ISRAEL

[23]In the fifteenth year of
Amaziah the son of Joash, king
of Judah, Jeroboam the son of
Joash, king of Israel, became
king in Samaria, *and reigned*
forty-one years. [24]And he did
evil in the sight of the LORD;
he did not depart from all the
sins of Jeroboam the son of
Nebat, who had made Israel
sin. [25]He restored the territory

14:21 [a] Called *Uzziah* in 2 Chronicles 26:1ff, Isaiah 6:1, and elsewhere

of Israel from the entrance of Hamath to the Sea of the Arabah, according to the word of the LORD God of Israel, which He had spoken through His servant Jonah the son of Amittai, the prophet who *was* from Gath Hepher. 26For the LORD saw *that* the affliction of Israel *was* very bitter; and whether bond or free, there was no helper for Israel. 27And the LORD did not say that He would blot out the name of Israel from under heaven; but He saved them by the hand of Jeroboam the son of Joash.

28Now the rest of the acts of Jeroboam, and all that he did—his might, how he made war, and how he recaptured for Israel, from Damascus and Hamath, *what had belonged* to Judah—*are* they not written in the book of the chronicles of the kings of Israel? 29So Jeroboam rested with his fathers, the kings of Israel. Then Zechariah his son reigned in his place.

AZARIAH REIGNS IN JUDAH

15 In the twenty-seventh year of Jeroboam king of Israel, Azariah the son of Amaziah, king of Judah, became king. 2He was sixteen years old when he became king, and he reigned fifty-two years in Jerusalem. His mother's name *was* Jecholiah of Jerusalem. 3And he did *what was* right in the sight of the LORD, according to all that his father Amaziah had done, 4except that the high places were not removed; the people still sacrificed and burned incense on the high places. 5Then the LORD struck the king, so that he was a leper until the day of his death; so he dwelt in an isolated house. And Jotham the king's son *was* over the *royal* house, judging the people of the land.

6Now the rest of the acts of Azariah, and all that he did, *are* they not written in the book of the chronicles of the kings of Judah? 7So Azariah rested with his fathers, and they buried him with his fathers in the City of David. Then Jotham his son reigned in his place.

ZECHARIAH REIGNS IN ISRAEL

8In the thirty-eighth year of Azariah king of Judah, Zechariah the son of Jeroboam reigned over Israel in Samaria six months. 9And he did evil in the sight of the LORD, as his fathers had done; he did not depart from the sins of Jeroboam the son of Nebat, who had made Israel sin. 10Then Shallum the son of Jabesh conspired against him, and struck and killed him in front of the people; and he reigned in his place.

11Now the rest of the acts of Zechariah, indeed they *are* written in the book of the chronicles of the kings of Israel.

12 This *was* the word of the
LORD which He spoke to Jehu,
saying, "Your sons shall sit
on the throne of Israel to the
fourth *generation.*"[a] And so
it was.

SHALLUM REIGNS IN ISRAEL

13 Shallum the son of Jabesh
became king in the thirty-
ninth year of Uzziah[a] king of
Judah; and he reigned a full
month in Samaria. 14 For Menahem the son of Gadi went up
from Tirzah, came to Samaria,
and struck Shallum the son of
Jabesh in Samaria and killed
him; and he reigned in his
place.
15 Now the rest of the acts
of Shallum, and the conspiracy which he led, indeed they
are written in the book of the
chronicles of the kings of
Israel. 16 Then from Tirzah,
Menahem attacked Tiphsah,
all who *were* there, and its
territory. Because they did
not surrender, therefore he
attacked *it.* All the women
there who were with child he
ripped open.

MENAHEM REIGNS IN ISRAEL

17 In the thirty-ninth year of
Azariah king of Judah, Menahem the son of Gadi became
king over Israel, *and reigned*
ten years in Samaria. 18 And
he did evil in the sight of the
LORD; he did not depart all
his days from the sins of Jeroboam the son of Nebat, who
had made Israel sin. 19 Pul[a]
king of Assyria came against
the land; and Menahem gave
Pul a thousand talents of silver,
that his hand might be with
him to strengthen the kingdom under his control. 20 And
Menahem exacted the money
from Israel, from all the very
wealthy, from each man fifty
shekels of silver, to give to the
king of Assyria. So the king of
Assyria turned back, and did
not stay there in the land.
21 Now the rest of the acts
of Menahem, and all that he
did, *are* they not written in the
book of the chronicles of the
kings of Israel? 22 So Menahem
rested with his fathers. Then
Pekahiah his son reigned in
his place.

PEKAHIAH REIGNS IN ISRAEL

23 In the fiftieth year of Azariah king of Judah, Pekahiah
the son of Menahem became
king over Israel in Samaria,
and reigned two years. 24 And
he did evil in the sight of the
LORD; he did not depart from
the sins of Jeroboam the son
of Nebat, who had made Israel
sin. 25 Then Pekah the son of
Remaliah, an officer of his,
conspired against him and

15:12 [a] 2 Kings 10:30 15:13 [a] Called *Azariah* in 14:21ff and 15:1ff 15:19 [a] That is, Tiglath-Pileser III (compare verse 29)

killed him in Samaria, in the citadel of the king's house, along with Argob and Arieh; and with him were fifty men of Gilead. He killed him and reigned in his place.

26Now the rest of the acts of Pekahiah, and all that he did, indeed they *are* written in the book of the chronicles of the kings of Israel.

PEKAH REIGNS IN ISRAEL

27In the fifty-second year of Azariah king of Judah, Pekah the son of Remaliah became king over Israel in Samaria, *and reigned* twenty
years. 28And he did evil in the sight of the LORD; he did not depart from the sins of Jeroboam the son of Nebat, who
had made Israel sin. 29In the days of Pekah king of Israel, Tiglath-Pileser king of Assyria came and took Ijon, Abel Beth Maachah, Janoah, Kedesh, Hazor, Gilead, and Galilee, all the land of Naphtali; and he carried them captive to
Assyria. 30Then Hoshea the son of Elah led a conspiracy against Pekah the son of Remaliah, and struck and killed him; so he reigned in his place in the twentieth year of Jotham the son of Uzziah.

31Now the rest of the acts of Pekah, and all that he did, indeed they *are* written in the book of the chronicles of the kings of Israel.

JOTHAM REIGNS IN JUDAH

32In the second year of Pekah the son of Remaliah, king of Israel, Jotham the son of Uzziah, king of Judah,
began to reign. 33He was twenty-five years old when he became king, and he reigned sixteen years in Jerusalem. His mother's name *was* Jerusha[a] the daughter of Zadok.
34And he did *what was* right in the sight of the LORD; he did according to all that his father
Uzziah had done. 35However the high places were not removed; the people still sacrificed and burned incense on the high places. He built the Upper Gate of the house of the LORD.

36Now the rest of the acts of Jotham, and all that he did, *are* they not written in the book of the chronicles of
the kings of Judah? 37In those days the LORD began to send Rezin king of Syria and Pekah the son of Remaliah against
Judah. 38So Jotham rested with his fathers, and was buried with his fathers in the City of David his father. Then Ahaz his son reigned in his place.

AHAZ REIGNS IN JUDAH

16 In the seventeenth year of Pekah the son of Remaliah, Ahaz the son of Jotham, king of Judah, began
to reign. 2Ahaz *was* twenty years old when he became

15:33 [a] Spelled *Jerushah* in 2 Chronicles 27:1

king, and he reigned sixteen
years in Jerusalem; and he
did not do *what was* right in
the sight of the LORD his God,
as his father David *had done.*
3 But he walked in the way of
the kings of Israel; indeed he
made his son pass through
the fire, according to the
abominations of the nations
whom the LORD had cast out
from before the children of
Israel. 4 And he sacrificed and
burned incense on the high
places, on the hills, and under
every green tree.

5 Then Rezin king of Syria
and Pekah the son of Remaliah, king of Israel, came up
to Jerusalem to *make* war;
and they besieged Ahaz but
could not overcome *him.* 6 At
that time Rezin king of Syria
captured Elath for Syria, and
drove the men of Judah from
Elath. Then the Edomites[a]
went to Elath, and dwell there
to this day.

7 So Ahaz sent messengers
to Tiglath-Pileser king of Assyria, saying, "I *am* your servant and your son. Come up
and save me from the hand
of the king of Syria and from
the hand of the king of Israel,
who rise up against me." 8 And
Ahaz took the silver and gold
that was found in the house
of the LORD, and in the trea-
suries of the king's house, and
sent *it as* a present to the king
of Assyria. 9 So the king of Assyria heeded him; for the king
of Assyria went up against Damascus and took it, carried
its people captive to Kir, and
killed Rezin.

10 Now King Ahaz went to
Damascus to meet Tiglath-
Pileser king of Assyria, and
saw an altar that *was* at Damascus; and King Ahaz sent
to Urijah the priest the design
of the altar and its pattern,
according to all its workmanship. 11 Then Urijah the priest
built an altar according to
all that King Ahaz had sent
from Damascus. So Urijah
the priest made *it* before King
Ahaz came back from Damascus. 12 And when the king came
back from Damascus, the king
saw the altar; and the king approached the altar and made
offerings on it. 13 So he burned
his burnt offering and his
grain offering; and he poured
his drink offering and sprinkled the blood of his peace
offerings on the altar. 14 He
also brought the bronze altar
which *was* before the LORD,
from the front of the temple—
from between the *new* altar
and the house of the LORD—
and put it on the north side
of the *new* altar. 15 Then King
Ahaz commanded Urijah the
priest, saying, "On the great
new altar burn the morning
burnt offering, the evening
grain offering, the king's
burnt sacrifice, and his grain

16:6 [a] Some ancient authorities read *Syrians.*

offering, with the burnt offering of all the people of
the land, their grain offering,
and their drink offerings; and
sprinkle on it all the blood of
the burnt offering and all the
blood of the sacrifice. And the
bronze altar shall be for me to
inquire *by*." [16]Thus did Urijah
the priest, according to all that
King Ahaz commanded.

[17]And King Ahaz cut off
the panels of the carts, and
removed the lavers from
them; and he took down the
Sea from the bronze oxen that
were under it, and put it on
a pavement of stones. [18]Also
he removed the Sabbath pavilion which they had built
in the temple, and he removed
the king's outer entrance from
the house of the LORD, on account of the king of Assyria.

[19]Now the rest of the acts
of Ahaz which he did, *are* they
not written in the book of
the chronicles of the kings of
Judah? [20]So Ahaz rested with
his fathers, and was buried
with his fathers in the City of
David. Then Hezekiah his son
reigned in his place.

HOSHEA REIGNS IN ISRAEL

17 In the twelfth year of
Ahaz king of Judah, Ho-
shea the son of Elah became
king of Israel in Samaria, *and
he reigned* nine years. [2]And
he did evil in the sight of the
LORD, but not as the kings of
Israel who were before him.
[3]Shalmaneser king of Assyria
came up against him; and Hoshea became his vassal, and
paid him tribute money. [4]And
the king of Assyria uncovered
a conspiracy by Hoshea; for
he had sent messengers to So,
king of Egypt, and brought no
tribute to the king of Assyria,
as *he had done* year by year.
Therefore the king of Assyria
shut him up, and bound him
in prison.

ISRAEL CARRIED CAPTIVE TO ASSYRIA

[5]Now the king of Assyria
went throughout all the land,
and went up to Samaria and
besieged it for three years.
[6]In the ninth year of Hoshea,
the king of Assyria took Samaria and carried Israel away
to Assyria, and placed them
in Halah and by the Habor,
the River of Gozan, and in the
cities of the Medes.

[7]For so it was that the
children of Israel had sinned
against the LORD their God,
who had brought them up
out of the land of Egypt, from
under the hand of Pharaoh
king of Egypt; and they had
feared other gods, [8]and had
walked in the statutes of
the nations whom the LORD
had cast out from before the
children of Israel, and of the
kings of Israel, which they had
made. [9]Also the children of
Israel secretly did against the
LORD their God things that
were not right, and they built
for themselves high places in

all their cities, from watchtower to fortified city. [10]They
set up for themselves *sacred*
pillars and wooden images[a]
on every high hill and under
every green tree. [11]There they
burned incense on all the
high places, like the nations
whom the LORD had carried
away before them; and they
did wicked things to provoke
the LORD to anger, [12]for they
served idols, of which the
LORD had said to them, "You
shall not do this thing."

[13]Yet the LORD testified
against Israel and against
Judah, by all of His prophets,
every seer, saying, "Turn from
your evil ways, and keep My
commandments *and* My statutes, according to all the law
which I commanded your fathers, and which I sent to you
by My servants the prophets."
[14]Nevertheless they would
not hear, but stiffened their
necks, like the necks of their
fathers, who did not believe
in the LORD their God. [15]And
they rejected His statutes
and His covenant that He
had made with their fathers,
and His testimonies which He
had testified against them;
they followed idols, became
idolaters, and *went* after the
nations who *were* all around
them, *concerning* whom the
LORD had charged them
that they should not do like
them. [16]So they left all the
commandments of the LORD
their God, made for them-
selves a molded image *and*
two calves, made a wooden
image and worshiped all the
host of heaven, and served
Baal. [17]And they caused their
sons and daughters to pass
through the fire, practiced
witchcraft and soothsaying,
and sold themselves to do
evil in the sight of the LORD,
to provoke Him to anger.
[18]Therefore the LORD was
very angry with Israel, and removed them from His sight;
there was none left but the
tribe of Judah alone.

[19]Also Judah did not keep
the commandments of the
LORD their God, but walked
in the statutes of Israel which
they made. [20]And the LORD
rejected all the descendants of
Israel, afflicted them, and delivered them into the hand of
plunderers, until He had cast
them from His sight. [21]For He
tore Israel from the house of
David, and they made Jeroboam the son of Nebat king.
Then Jeroboam drove Israel
from following the LORD, and
made them commit a great
sin. [22]For the children of Israel walked in all the sins of
Jeroboam which he did; they
did not depart from them,
[23]until the LORD removed Israel out of His sight, as He had
said by all His servants the
prophets. So Israel was car-

17:10 [a] Hebrew *Asherim,* Canaanite deities

ried away from their own land
to Assyria, *as it is* to this day.

ASSYRIA RESETTLES SAMARIA

24Then the king of Assyria
brought *people* from Babylon,
Cuthah, Ava, Hamath, and
from Sepharvaim, and placed
them in the cities of Samaria
instead of the children of Israel; and they took possession
of Samaria and dwelt in its
cities. 25And it was so, at the
beginning of their dwelling
there, *that* they did not fear
the LORD; therefore the LORD
sent lions among them, which
killed *some* of them. 26So they
spoke to the king of Assyria,
saying, "The nations whom
you have removed and placed
in the cities of Samaria do not
know the rituals of the God
of the land; therefore He has
sent lions among them, and
indeed, they are killing them
because they do not know the
rituals of the God of the land."
27Then the king of Assyria
commanded, saying, "Send
there one of the priests whom
you brought from there; let
him go and dwell there, and
let him teach them the rituals
of the God of the land." 28Then
one of the priests whom
they had carried away from
Samaria came and dwelt in
Bethel, and taught them how
they should fear the LORD.

29However every nation
continued to make gods of
its own, and put *them* in the
shrines on the high places
which the Samaritans had
made, *every* nation in the cities where they dwelt. 30The
men of Babylon made Suc-
coth Benoth, the men of Cuth
made Nergal, the men of Hamath made Ashima, 31and
the Avites made Nibhaz and
Tartak; and the Sepharvites
burned their children in fire to
Adrammelech and Anamme-
lech, the gods of Sepharvaim.
32So they feared the LORD,
and from every class they appointed for themselves priests
of the high places, who sacrificed for them in the shrines
of the high places. 33They
feared the LORD, yet served
their own gods—according
to the rituals of the nations
from among whom they were
carried away.

34To this day they continue
practicing the former rituals;
they do not fear the LORD, nor
do they follow their statutes
or their ordinances, or the law
and commandment which the
LORD had commanded the
children of Jacob, whom He
named Israel, 35with whom
the LORD had made a cov-
enant and charged them, saying: "You shall not fear other
gods, nor bow down to them
nor serve them nor sacrifice
to them; 36but the LORD, who
brought you up from the land
of Egypt with great power
and an outstretched arm,
Him you shall fear, Him you
shall worship, and to Him you

shall offer sacrifice. 37And the statutes, the ordinances, the law, and the commandment which He wrote for you, you shall be careful to observe forever; you shall not fear other gods. 38And the covenant that I have made with you, you shall not forget, nor shall you fear other gods. 39But the LORD your God you shall fear; and He will deliver you from the hand of all your enemies." 40However they did not obey, but they followed their former rituals. 41So these nations feared the LORD, yet served their carved images; also their children and their children's children have continued doing as their fathers did, even to this day.

HEZEKIAH REIGNS IN JUDAH

18 Now it came to pass in the third year of Hoshea the son of Elah, king of Israel, *that* Hezekiah the son of Ahaz, king of Judah, began to reign. 2He was twenty-five years old when he became king, and he reigned twenty-nine years in Jerusalem. His mother's name *was* Abi[a] the daughter of Zechariah. 3And he did *what was* right in the sight of the LORD, according to all that his father David had done.

4He removed the high places and broke the *sacred* pillars, cut down the wooden image[a] and broke in pieces the bronze serpent that Moses had made; for until those days the children of Israel burned incense to it, and called it Nehushtan.[b] 5He trusted in the LORD God of Israel, so that after him was none like him among all the kings of Judah, nor who were before him. 6For he held fast to the LORD; he did not depart from following Him, but kept His commandments, which the LORD had commanded Moses. 7The LORD was with him; he prospered wherever he went. And he rebelled against the king of Assyria and did not serve him. 8He subdued the Philistines, as far as Gaza and its territory, from watchtower to fortified city.

9Now it came to pass in the fourth year of King Hezekiah, which *was* the seventh year of Hoshea the son of Elah, king of Israel, *that* Shalmaneser king of Assyria came up against Samaria and besieged it. 10And at the end of three years they took it. In the sixth year of Hezekiah, that *is,* the ninth year of Hoshea king of Israel, Samaria was taken. 11Then the king of Assyria carried Israel away captive to Assyria, and put them in Halah and by the Habor, the River of Gozan, and in the cities of

18:2 [a] Called *Abijah* in 2 Chronicles 29:1ff 18:4 [a] Hebrew *Asherah,* a Canaanite goddess [b] Literally *Bronze Thing*

the Medes, 12because they did not obey the voice of the LORD their God, but transgressed His covenant *and* all that Moses the servant of the LORD had commanded; and they would neither hear nor do *them.*

13And in the fourteenth year of King Hezekiah, Sennacherib king of Assyria came up against all the fortified cities of Judah and took them. 14Then Hezekiah king of Judah sent to the king of Assyria at Lachish, saying, "I have done wrong; turn away from me; whatever you impose on me I will pay." And the king of Assyria assessed Hezekiah king of Judah three hundred talents of silver and thirty talents of gold. 15So Hezekiah gave *him* all the silver that was found in the house of the LORD and in the treasuries of the king's house. 16At that time Hezekiah stripped *the gold from* the doors of the temple of the LORD, and *from* the pillars which Hezekiah king of Judah had overlaid, and gave it to the king of Assyria.

SENNACHERIB BOASTS AGAINST THE LORD

17Then the king of Assyria sent *the* Tartan,[a] *the* Rabsaris,[b] *and the* Rabshakeh[c] from Lachish, with a great army against Jerusalem, to King Hezekiah. And they went up and came to Jerusalem. When they had come up, they went and stood by the aqueduct from the upper pool, which *was* on the highway to the Fuller's Field. 18And when they had called to the king, Eliakim the son of Hilkiah, who *was* over the household, Shebna the scribe, and Joah the son of Asaph, the recorder, came out to them. 19Then *the* Rabshakeh said to them, "Say now to Hezekiah, 'Thus says the great king, the king of Assyria: "What confidence *is* this in which you trust? 20You speak of *having* plans and power for war; but *they are* mere words. And in whom do you trust, that you rebel against me? 21Now look! You are trusting in the staff of this broken reed, Egypt, on which if a man leans, it will go into his hand and pierce it. So *is* Pharaoh king of Egypt to all who trust in him. 22But if you say to me, 'We trust in the LORD our God,' *is* it not He whose high places and whose altars Hezekiah has taken away, and said to Judah and Jerusalem, 'You shall worship before this altar in Jerusalem'?"' 23Now therefore, I urge you, give a pledge to my master the king of Assyria, and I will give you two thousand horses—if you

18:17 [a] A title, probably *Commander in Chief* [b] A title, probably *Chief Officer* [c] A title, probably *Chief of Staff* or *Governor*

are able on your part to put
riders on them! 24How then
will you repel one captain of
the least of my master's servants, and put your trust in
Egypt for chariots and horsemen? 25Have I now come up
without the Lord against this
place to destroy it? The Lord
said to me, 'Go up against this
land, and destroy it.'"

26Then Eliakim the son of
Hilkiah, Shebna, and Joah
said to *the* Rabshakeh, "Please
speak to your servants in Aramaic, for we understand *it;*
and do not speak to us in Hebrew[a] in the hearing of the
people who *are* on the wall."

27But *the* Rabshakeh said
to them, "Has my master sent
me to your master and to you
to speak these words, and not
to the men who sit on the wall,
who will eat and drink their
own waste with you?"

28Then *the* Rabshakeh
stood and called out with a
loud voice in Hebrew, and
spoke, saying, "Hear the word
of the great king, the king of
Assyria! 29Thus says the king:
'Do not let Hezekiah deceive
you, for he shall not be able
to deliver you from his hand;
30nor let Hezekiah make you
trust in the Lord, saying, "The
Lord will surely deliver us;
this city shall not be given into
the hand of the king of Assyria."' 31Do not listen to Hezekiah; for thus says the king of
Assyria: 'Make *peace* with me
by a present and come out to
me; and every one of you eat
from his own vine and every
one from his own fig tree,
and every one of you drink
the waters of his own cistern;
32until I come and take you
away to a land like your own
land, a land of grain and new
wine, a land of bread and vineyards, a land of olive groves
and honey, that you may live
and not die. But do not listen
to Hezekiah, lest he persuade
you, saying, "The Lord will
deliver us." 33Has any of the
gods of the nations at all delivered its land from the hand of
the king of Assyria? 34Where
are the gods of Hamath and
Arpad? Where *are* the gods
of Sepharvaim and Hena and
Ivah? Indeed, have they delivered Samaria from my hand?
35Who among all the gods of
the lands have delivered their
countries from my hand, that
the Lord should deliver Jerusalem from my hand?'"

36But the people held their
peace and answered him not
a word; for the king's commandment was, "Do not an-
swer him." 37Then Eliakim
the son of Hilkiah, who *was*
over the household, Shebna
the scribe, and Joah the son
of Asaph, the recorder, came
to Hezekiah with *their* clothes
torn, and told him the words
of *the* Rabshakeh.

18:26 [a] Literally *Judean*

ISAIAH ASSURES DELIVERANCE

19 And so it was, when King
Hezekiah heard *it,* that
he tore his clothes, covered
himself with sackcloth, and
went into the house of the
LORD. 2Then he sent Eliakim,
who *was* over the household,
Shebna the scribe, and the elders of the priests, covered
with sackcloth, to Isaiah the
prophet, the son of Amoz.
3And they said to him, "Thus
says Hezekiah: 'This day *is* a
day of trouble, and rebuke,
and blasphemy; for the children have come to birth, but
there is no strength to bring
them forth. 4It may be that the
LORD your God will hear all
the words of *the* Rabshakeh,
whom his master the king of
Assyria has sent to reproach
the living God, and will rebuke
the words which the LORD
your God has heard. Therefore lift up *your* prayer for the
remnant that is left.' "

5So the servants of King
Hezekiah came to Isaiah.
6And Isaiah said to them,
"Thus you shall say to your
master, 'Thus says the LORD:
"Do not be afraid of the words
which you have heard, with
which the servants of the king
of Assyria have blasphemed
Me. 7Surely I will send a spirit
upon him, and he shall hear a
rumor and return to his own
land; and I will cause him to
fall by the sword in his own
land." ' "

SENNACHERIB'S THREAT AND HEZEKIAH'S PRAYER

8Then *the* Rabshakeh re-
turned and found the king of
Assyria warring against Libnah, for he heard that he had
departed from Lachish. 9And
the king heard concerning Tir-
hakah king of Ethiopia, "Look,
he has come out to make war
with you." So he again sent
messengers to Hezekiah, saying, 10"Thus you shall speak
to Hezekiah king of Judah,
saying: 'Do not let your God
in whom you trust deceive you,
saying, "Jerusalem shall not be
given into the hand of the king
of Assyria." 11Look! You have
heard what the kings of Assyria have done to all lands by
utterly destroying them; and
shall you be delivered? 12Have
the gods of the nations delivered those whom my fathers
have destroyed, Gozan and
Haran and Rezeph, and the
people of Eden who *were* in
Telassar? 13Where *is* the king
of Hamath, the king of Arpad,
and the king of the city of
Sepharvaim, Hena, and Ivah?' "

14And Hezekiah received
the letter from the hand of
the messengers, and read it;
and Hezekiah went up to the
house of the LORD, and spread
it before the LORD. 15Then
Hezekiah prayed before the
LORD, and said: "O LORD God
of Israel, *the One* who dwells
between the cherubim, You
are God, You alone, of all the
kingdoms of the earth. You

have made heaven and earth.
[16]Incline Your ear, O LORD, and
hear; open Your eyes, O LORD,
and see; and hear the words
of Sennacherib, which he has
sent to reproach the living
God. [17]Truly, LORD, the kings
of Assyria have laid waste the
nations and their lands, [18]and
have cast their gods into the
fire; for they *were* not gods,
but the work of men's hands—
wood and stone. Therefore
they destroyed them. [19]Now
therefore, O LORD our God, I
pray, save us from his hand,
that all the kingdoms of the
earth may know that You *are*
the LORD God, You alone."

THE WORD OF THE LORD CONCERNING SENNACHERIB

[20]Then Isaiah the son of
Amoz sent to Hezekiah, saying,
"Thus says the LORD God of Israel: 'Because you have prayed
to Me against Sennacherib king
of Assyria, I have heard.' [21]This
is the word which the LORD has
spoken concerning him:

'The virgin, the
daughter of Zion,
Has despised you,
laughed you to scorn;
The daughter of
Jerusalem
Has shaken *her* head
behind your back!

22 'Whom have you
reproached and
blasphemed?
Against whom have you
raised *your* voice,
And lifted up your
eyes on high?
Against the Holy
One of Israel.
23 By your messengers
you have reproached
the Lord,
And said: "By the
multitude of
my chariots
I have come up to
the height of the
mountains,
To the limits of Lebanon;
I will cut down its
tall cedars
And its choice
cypress trees;
I will enter the extremity
of its borders,
To its fruitful forest.
24 I have dug and drunk
strange water,
And with the soles of my
feet I have dried up
All the brooks of defense."

25 'Did you not hear long ago
How I made it,
From ancient times
that I formed it?
Now I have brought
it to pass,
That you should be
For crushing fortified
cities *into* heaps
of ruins.
26 Therefore their
inhabitants had
little power;
They were dismayed
and confounded;

They were *as* the
grass of the field
And the green herb,
As the grass on the
housetops
And *grain* blighted
before it is grown.

27 'But I know your
dwelling place,
Your going out and
your coming in,
And your rage against Me.
28 Because your rage against
Me and your tumult
Have come up to My ears,
Therefore I will put My
hook in your nose
And My bridle in
your lips,
And I will turn you back
By the way which
you came.

29"This *shall be* a sign to
you:

'You shall eat this year
such as grows of itself,
And in the second
year what springs
from the same;
Also in the third year
sow and reap,
Plant vineyards and eat
the fruit of them.
30 And the remnant who
have escaped of the
house of Judah
Shall again take root
downward,
And bear fruit upward.
31 For out of Jerusalem
shall go a remnant,
And those who escape
from Mount Zion.
The zeal of the LORD of
hosts[a] will do this.'

32"Therefore thus says the
LORD concerning the king of
Assyria:

'He shall not come
into this city,
Nor shoot an arrow there,
Nor come before it
with shield,
Nor build a siege
mound against it.
33 By the way that he came,
By the same shall
he return;
And he shall not come
into this city,'
Says the LORD.
34 'For I will defend this
city, to save it
For My own sake
and for My servant
David's sake.'"

SENNACHERIB'S DEFEAT AND DEATH

35And it came to pass on a
certain night that the angel[a] of
the LORD went out, and killed
in the camp of the Assyrians
one hundred and eighty-five
thousand; and when *people*
arose early in the morning,
there were the corpses—all

19:31 [a] Following many Hebrew manuscripts and ancient versions (compare Isaiah 37:32); Masoretic Text omits *of hosts*. 19:35 [a] Or *Angel*

dead. [36]So Sennacherib king
of Assyria departed and went
away, returned *home,* and remained at Nineveh. [37]Now
it came to pass, as he was
worshiping in the temple
of Nisroch his god, that his
sons Adrammelech and Sha-
rezer struck him down with
the sword; and they escaped
into the land of Ararat. Then
Esarhaddon his son reigned
in his place.

HEZEKIAH'S LIFE EXTENDED

20 In those days Hezekiah was sick and near
death. And Isaiah the prophet,
the son of Amoz, went to him
and said to him, "Thus says
the LORD: 'Set your house in
order, for you shall die, and
not live.'"

[2]Then he turned his face
toward the wall, and prayed to
the LORD, saying, [3]"Remember now, O LORD, I pray, how
I have walked before You in
truth and with a loyal heart,
and have done *what was* good
in Your sight." And Hezekiah
wept bitterly.

[4]And it happened, before
Isaiah had gone out into the
middle court, that the word of
the LORD came to him, saying, [5]"Return and tell Hezekiah the leader of My people,
'Thus says the LORD, the God
of David your father: "I have
heard your prayer, I have seen
your tears; surely I will heal
you. On the third day you
shall go up to the house of the
LORD. [6]And I will add to your
days fifteen years. I will deliver you and this city from the
hand of the king of Assyria;
and I will defend this city for
My own sake, and for the sake
of My servant David."'"

[7]Then Isaiah said, "Take
a lump of figs." So they took
and laid *it* on the boil, and he
recovered.

[8]And Hezekiah said to Isaiah, "What *is* the sign that the
LORD will heal me, and that I
shall go up to the house of the
LORD the third day?"

[9]Then Isaiah said, "This is
the sign to you from the LORD,
that the LORD will do the thing
which He has spoken: *shall* the
shadow go forward ten degrees
or go backward ten degrees?"

[10]And Hezekiah answered,
"It is an easy thing for the
shadow to go down ten de-
grees; no, but let the shadow
go backward ten degrees."

[11]So Isaiah the prophet
cried out to the LORD, and
He brought the shadow ten
degrees backward, by which it
had gone down on the sundial
of Ahaz.

THE BABYLONIAN ENVOYS

[12]At that time Berodach-
Baladan[a] the son of Baladan,
king of Babylon, sent letters
and a present to Hezekiah, for
he heard that Hezekiah had

20:12 [a] Spelled *Merodach-Baladan* in Isaiah 39:1

been sick. 13And Hezekiah
was attentive to them, and
showed them all the house
of his treasures—the silver
and gold, the spices and precious ointment, and all[a] his
armory—all that was found
among his treasures. There
was nothing in his house or
in all his dominion that Hezekiah did not show them.
14Then Isaiah the prophet
went to King Hezekiah, and
said to him, "What did these
men say, and from where did
they come to you?"
So Hezekiah said, "They
came from a far country, from
Babylon."
15And he said, "What have
they seen in your house?"
So Hezekiah answered,
"They have seen all that *is* in
my house; there is nothing
among my treasures that I
have not shown them."
16Then Isaiah said to Hezekiah, "Hear the word of the
LORD: 17'Behold, the days are
coming when all that *is* in your
house, and what your fathers
have accumulated until this
day, shall be carried to Babylon; nothing shall be left,'
says the LORD. 18'And they
shall take away some of your
sons who will descend from
you, whom you will beget; and
they shall be eunuchs in the
palace of the king of Babylon.'"
19So Hezekiah said to Isaiah, "The word of the LORD
which you have spoken *is*
good!" For he said, "Will there
not be peace and truth at least
in my days?"

DEATH OF HEZEKIAH

20Now the rest of the acts
of Hezekiah—all his might,
and how he made a pool and a
tunnel and brought water into
the city—*are* they not written
in the book of the chronicles
of the kings of Judah? 21So
Hezekiah rested with his fathers. Then Manasseh his son
reigned in his place.

MANASSEH REIGNS IN JUDAH

21 Manasseh *was* twelve
years old when he be-
came king, and he reigned
fifty-five years in Jerusalem.
His mother's name *was* Hephzibah. 2And he did evil in the
sight of the LORD, according
to the abominations of the
nations whom the LORD had
cast out before the children
of Israel. 3For he rebuilt the
high places which Hezekiah
his father had destroyed; he
raised up altars for Baal, and
made a wooden image,[a] as
Ahab king of Israel had done;
and he worshiped all the host
of heaven[b] and served them.
4He also built altars in the

20:13 [a] Following many Hebrew manuscripts, Syriac, and Targum; Masoretic Text omits *all*. 21:3 [a] Hebrew *Asherah*, a Canaanite goddess [b] The gods of the Assyrians

house of the LORD, of which
the LORD had said, "In Jerusalem I will put My name." 5And
he built altars for all the host
of heaven in the two courts of
the house of the LORD. 6Also
he made his son pass through
the fire, practiced soothsaying, used witchcraft, and
consulted spiritists and mediums. He did much evil in the
sight of the LORD, to provoke
Him to anger. 7He even set a
carved image of Asherah[a] that
he had made, in the house of
which the LORD had said to
David and to Solomon his
son, "In this house and in Jerusalem, which I have chosen
out of all the tribes of Israel,
I will put My name forever;
8and I will not make the feet
of Israel wander anymore
from the land which I gave
their fathers—only if they are
careful to do according to all
that I have commanded them,
and according to all the law
that My servant Moses commanded them." 9But they paid
no attention, and Manasseh
seduced them to do more evil
than the nations whom the
LORD had destroyed before
the children of Israel.

10And the LORD spoke by
His servants the prophets,
saying, 11"Because Manas-
seh king of Judah has done
these abominations (he has
acted more wickedly than all
the Amorites who *were* before
him, and has also made Judah
sin with his idols), 12therefore
thus says the LORD God of Israel: 'Behold, *I* am bringing
such calamity upon Jerusalem
and Judah, that whoever hears
of it, both his ears will tingle.
13And I will stretch over Jerusalem the measuring line of
Samaria and the plummet of
the house of Ahab; I will wipe
Jerusalem as *one* wipes a dish,
wiping *it* and turning *it* upside
down. 14So I will forsake the
remnant of My inheritance
and deliver them into the
hand of their enemies; and
they shall become victims of
plunder to all their enemies,
15because they have done evil
in My sight, and have provoked Me to anger since the
day their fathers came out of
Egypt, even to this day.'"

16Moreover Manasseh shed
very much innocent blood,
till he had filled Jerusalem
from one end to another, besides his sin by which he made
Judah sin, in doing evil in the
sight of the LORD.

17Now the rest of the acts of
Manasseh—all that he did, and
the sin that he committed—
are they not written in the
book of the chronicles of the
kings of Judah? 18So Manasseh rested with his fathers,
and was buried in the garden of his own house, in the
garden of Uzza. Then his son
Amon reigned in his place.

21:7 [a] A Canaanite goddess

AMON'S REIGN AND DEATH

19Amon *was* twenty-two
years old when he became
king, and he reigned two years
in Jerusalem. His mother's
name *was* Meshullemeth the
daughter of Haruz of Jotbah.
20And he did evil in the sight
of the LORD, as his father
Manasseh had done. 21So he
walked in all the ways that
his father had walked; and
he served the idols that his
father had served, and worshiped them. 22He forsook
the LORD God of his fathers,
and did not walk in the way
of the LORD.

23Then the servants of
Amon conspired against him,
and killed the king in his own
house. 24But the people of the
land executed all those who
had conspired against King
Amon. Then the people of the
land made his son Josiah king
in his place.

25Now the rest of the acts
of Amon which he did, *are*
they not written in the book
of the chronicles of the kings
of Judah? 26And he was buried in his tomb in the garden
of Uzza. Then Josiah his son
reigned in his place.

JOSIAH REIGNS IN JUDAH

22 Josiah *was* eight years
old when he became
king, and he reigned thirty-
one years in Jerusalem. His
mother's name *was* Jedidah
the daughter of Adaiah of Bozkath. 2And he did *what was*
right in the sight of the LORD,
and walked in all the ways of
his father David; he did not
turn aside to the right hand
or to the left.

HILKIAH FINDS THE BOOK OF THE LAW

3Now it came to pass, in
the eighteenth year of King
Josiah, *that* the king sent
Shaphan the scribe, the son
of Azaliah, the son of Meshullam, to the house of the LORD,
saying: 4"Go up to Hilkiah
the high priest, that he may
count the money which has
been brought into the house
of the LORD, which the doorkeepers have gathered from
the people. 5And let them deliver it into the hand of those
doing the work, who are the
overseers in the house of
the LORD; let them give it to
those who *are* in the house
of the LORD doing the work,
to repair the damages of the
house— 6to carpenters and
builders and masons—and to
buy timber and hewn stone to
repair the house. 7However
there need be no accounting
made with them of the money
delivered into their hand, because they deal faithfully."

8Then Hilkiah the high
priest said to Shaphan the
scribe, "I have found the Book
of the Law in the house of the
LORD." And Hilkiah gave the
book to Shaphan, and he read
it. 9So Shaphan the scribe

went to the king, bringing
the king word, saying, "Your
servants have gathered the
money that was found in the
house, and have delivered it
into the hand of those who
do the work, who oversee the
house of the LORD." 10Then
Shaphan the scribe showed
the king, saying, "Hilkiah the
priest has given me a book."
And Shaphan read it before
the king.
11Now it happened, when
the king heard the words of
the Book of the Law, that he
tore his clothes. 12Then the
king commanded Hilkiah
the priest, Ahikam the son of
Shaphan, Achbor[a] the son of
Michaiah, Shaphan the scribe,
and Asaiah a servant of the
king, saying, 13"Go, inquire
of the LORD for me, for the
people and for all Judah, concerning the words of this book
that has been found; for great
is the wrath of the LORD that
is aroused against us, because
our fathers have not obeyed
the words of this book, to do
according to all that is written
concerning us."
14So Hilkiah the priest,
Ahikam, Achbor, Shaphan,
and Asaiah went to Huldah
the prophetess, the wife of
Shallum the son of Tikvah,
the son of Harhas, keeper
of the wardrobe. (She dwelt
in Jerusalem in the Second
Quarter.) And they spoke
with her. 15Then she said to
them, "Thus says the LORD
God of Israel, 'Tell the man
who sent you to Me, 16"Thus
says the LORD: 'Behold, I will
bring calamity on this place
and on its inhabitants—all
the words of the book which
the king of Judah has read—
17because they have forsaken
Me and burned incense to
other gods, that they might
provoke Me to anger with
all the works of their hands.
Therefore My wrath shall be
aroused against this place
and shall not be quenched.'"'
18But as for the king of Judah,
who sent you to inquire of the
LORD, in this manner you
shall speak to him, 'Thus says
the LORD God of Israel: "*Concerning* the words which you
have heard— 19because your
heart was tender, and you
humbled yourself before the
LORD when you heard what I
spoke against this place and
against its inhabitants, that
they would become a deso-
lation and a curse, and you
tore your clothes and wept
before Me, I also have heard
you," says the LORD. 20"Surely,
therefore, I will gather you to
your fathers, and you shall
be gathered to your grave in
peace; and your eyes shall not
see all the calamity which I
will bring on this place."'" So
they brought back word to the
king.

22:12 [a] *Abdon the son of Micah* in 2 Chronicles 34:20

JOSIAH RESTORES TRUE WORSHIP

23 Now the king sent them to gather all the elders of Judah and Jerusalem to him. [2]The king went up to the house of the LORD with all the men of Judah, and with him all the inhabitants of Jerusalem—the priests and the prophets and all the people, both small and great. And he read in their hearing all the words of the Book of the Covenant which had been found in the house of the LORD.

[3]Then the king stood by a pillar and made a covenant before the LORD, to follow the LORD and to keep His commandments and His testimonies and His statutes, with all *his* heart and all *his* soul, to perform the words of this covenant that were written in this book. And all the people took a stand for the covenant.
[4]And the king commanded Hilkiah the high priest, the priests of the second order, and the doorkeepers, to bring out of the temple of the LORD all the articles that were made for Baal, for Asherah,[a] and for all the host of heaven;[b] and he burned them outside Jerusalem in the fields of Kidron, and carried their ashes to Bethel. [5]Then he removed the idolatrous priests whom the kings of Judah had ordained to burn incense on the high places in the cities of Judah and in the places all around Jerusalem, and those who burned incense to Baal, to the sun, to the moon, to the constellations, and to all the host of heaven. [6]And he brought out the wooden image[a] from the house of the LORD, to the Brook Kidron outside Jerusalem, burned it at the Brook Kidron and ground *it* to ashes, and threw its ashes on the graves of the common people.
[7]Then he tore down the *ritual* booths of the perverted persons[a] that *were* in the house of the LORD, where the women wove hangings for the wooden image. [8]And he brought all the priests from the cities of Judah, and defiled the high places where the priests had burned incense, from Geba to Beersheba; also he broke down the high places at the gates which *were* at the entrance of the Gate of Joshua the governor of the city, which *were* to the left of the city gate.
[9]Nevertheless the priests of the high places did not come up to the altar of the LORD in Jerusalem, but they ate unleavened bread among their brethren.

[10]And he defiled Topheth, which *is* in the Valley of the

23:4 [a] A Canaanite goddess [b] The gods of the Assyrians **23:6** [a] Hebrew *Asherah,* a Canaanite goddess **23:7** [a] Hebrew *qedeshim,* that is, those practicing sodomy and prostitution in religious rituals

Son[a] of Hinnom, that no
man might make his son or
his daughter pass through
the fire to Molech. 11Then he
removed the horses that the
kings of Judah had dedicated
to the sun, at the entrance to
the house of the LORD, by the
chamber of Nathan-Melech,
the officer who *was* in the
court; and he burned the chariots of the sun with fire. 12The
altars that *were* on the roof,
the upper chamber of Ahaz,
which the kings of Judah had
made, and the altars which
Manasseh had made in the
two courts of the house of
the LORD, the king broke
down and pulverized there,
and threw their dust into the
Brook Kidron. 13Then the
king defiled the high places
that *were* east of Jerusalem,
which *were* on the south of the
Mount of Corruption, which
Solomon king of Israel had
built for Ashtoreth the abomination of the Sidonians, for
Chemosh the abomination of
the Moabites, and for Milcom
the abomination of the people
of Ammon. 14And he broke in
pieces the *sacred* pillars and
cut down the wooden images,
and filled their places with the
bones of men.

15Moreover the altar that
was at Bethel, *and* the high
place which Jeroboam the
son of Nebat, who made Israel
sin, had made, both that altar
and the high place he broke
down; and he burned the high
place *and* crushed *it* to powder, and burned the wooden
image. 16As Josiah turned, he
saw the tombs that *were* there
on the mountain. And he sent
and took the bones out of the
tombs and burned *them* on the
altar, and defiled it according
to the word of the LORD which
the man of God proclaimed,
who proclaimed these words.
17Then he said, "What grave-
stone *is* this that I see?"

So the men of the city told
him, "*It is* the tomb of the man
of God who came from Judah
and proclaimed these things
which you have done against
the altar of Bethel."

18And he said, "Let him
alone; let no one move his
bones." So they let his bones
alone, with the bones of the
prophet who came from Sa-
maria.

19Now Josiah also took
away all the shrines of the
high places that *were* in the
cities of Samaria, which the
kings of Israel had made to
provoke the LORD[a] to anger;
and he did to them according
to all the deeds he had done in
Bethel. 20He executed all the
priests of the high places who
were there, on the altars, and
burned men's bones on them;
and he returned to Jerusalem.

23:10 [a] Kethib reads *Sons.* 23:19 [a] Following Septuagint, Syriac, and Vulgate; Masoretic Text and Targum omit *the LORD.*

21Then the king com-
manded all the people, saying, "Keep the Passover to the
LORD your God, as *it is* written
in this Book of the Covenant."
22Such a Passover surely had
never been held since the days
of the judges who judged Israel, nor in all the days of the
kings of Israel and the kings
of Judah. 23But in the eighteenth year of King Josiah this
Passover was held before the
LORD in Jerusalem. 24More-
over Josiah put away those
who consulted mediums
and spiritists, the household
gods and idols, all the abominations that were seen in the
land of Judah and in Jerusalem, that he might perform
the words of the law which
were written in the book that
Hilkiah the priest found in the
house of the LORD. 25Now before him there was no king
like him, who turned to the
LORD with all his heart, with
all his soul, and with all his
might, according to all the
Law of Moses; nor after him
did *any* arise like him.

IMPENDING JUDGMENT ON JUDAH

26Nevertheless the LORD
did not turn from the fierceness of His great wrath, with
which His anger was aroused
against Judah, because of all
the provocations with which
Manasseh had provoked Him.
27And the LORD said, "I will
also remove Judah from My
sight, as I have removed Israel,
and will cast off this city Jerusalem which I have chosen,
and the house of which I said,
'My name shall be there.'"[a]

JOSIAH DIES IN BATTLE

28Now the rest of the acts of
Josiah, and all that he did, *are*
they not written in the book of
the chronicles of the kings of
Judah? 29In his days Pharaoh
Necho king of Egypt went to
the aid of the king of Assyria, to
the River Euphrates; and King
Josiah went against him. And
Pharaoh Necho killed him at
Megiddo when he confronted
him. 30Then his servants
moved his body in a chariot
from Megiddo, brought him to
Jerusalem, and buried him in
his own tomb. And the people
of the land took Jehoahaz the
son of Josiah, anointed him,
and made him king in his father's place.

THE REIGN AND CAPTIVITY OF JEHOAHAZ

31Jehoahaz *was* twenty-
three years old when he became king, and he reigned
three months in Jerusalem.
His mother's name *was* Ha-
mutal the daughter of Jeremiah of Libnah. 32And he
did evil in the sight of the
LORD, according to all that
his fathers had done. 33Now

23:27 [a] 1 Kings 8:29

Pharaoh Necho put him in prison at Riblah in the land of Hamath, that he might not reign in Jerusalem; and he imposed on the land a tribute of one hundred talents of silver and a talent of gold. 34 Then Pharaoh Necho made Eliakim the son of Josiah king in place of his father Josiah, and changed his name to Jehoiakim. And *Pharaoh* took Jehoahaz and went to Egypt, and he[a] died there.

JEHOIAKIM REIGNS IN JUDAH

35 So Jehoiakim gave the silver and gold to Pharaoh; but he taxed the land to give money according to the command of Pharaoh; he exacted the silver and gold from the people of the land, from every one according to his assessment, to give *it* to Pharaoh Necho. 36 Jehoiakim *was* twenty-five years old when he became king, and he reigned eleven years in Jerusalem. His mother's name *was* Zebudah the daughter of Pedaiah of Rumah. 37 And he did evil in the sight of the LORD, according to all that his fathers had done.

JUDAH OVERRUN BY ENEMIES

24 In his days Nebuchadnezzar king of Babylon came up, and Jehoiakim became his vassal *for* three years. Then he turned and rebelled against him. 2 And the LORD sent against him *raiding* bands of Chaldeans, bands of Syrians, bands of Moabites, and bands of the people of Ammon; He sent them against Judah to destroy it, according to the word of the LORD which He had spoken by His servants the prophets. 3 Surely at the commandment of the LORD *this* came upon Judah, to remove *them* from His sight because of the sins of Manasseh, according to all that he had done, 4 and also because of the innocent blood that he had shed; for he had filled Jerusalem with innocent blood, which the LORD would not pardon.

5 Now the rest of the acts of Jehoiakim, and all that he did, *are* they not written in the book of the chronicles of the kings of Judah? 6 So Jehoiakim rested with his fathers. Then Jehoiachin his son reigned in his place.

7 And the king of Egypt did not come out of his land anymore, for the king of Babylon had taken all that belonged to the king of Egypt from the Brook of Egypt to the River Euphrates.

THE REIGN AND CAPTIVITY OF JEHOIACHIN

8 Jehoiachin *was* eighteen years old when he became king, and he reigned in Je-

23:34 [a] That is, Jehoahaz

rusalem three months. His
mother's name *was* Nehushta
the daughter of Elnathan of
Jerusalem. 9And he did evil
in the sight of the LORD, according to all that his father
had done.

10At that time the servants
of Nebuchadnezzar king of
Babylon came up against
Jerusalem, and the city was
besieged. 11And Nebuchad-
nezzar king of Babylon came
against the city, as his servants
were besieging it. 12Then Jehoiachin king of Judah, his
mother, his servants, his
princes, and his officers went
out to the king of Babylon;
and the king of Babylon, in
the eighth year of his reign,
took him prisoner.

THE CAPTIVITY OF JERUSALEM

13And he carried out from
there all the treasures of the
house of the LORD and the
treasures of the king's house,
and he cut in pieces all the articles of gold which Solomon
king of Israel had made in
the temple of the LORD, as
the LORD had said. 14Also he
carried into captivity all Jerusalem: all the captains and all
the mighty men of valor, ten
thousand captives, and all the
craftsmen and smiths. None
remained except the poorest
people of the land. 15And he
carried Jehoiachin captive to
Babylon. The king's mother,
the king's wives, his officers,
and the mighty of the land he
carried into captivity from Jerusalem to Babylon. 16All the
valiant men, seven thousand,
and craftsmen and smiths,
one thousand, all *who were*
strong *and* fit for war, these
the king of Babylon brought
captive to Babylon.

ZEDEKIAH REIGNS IN JUDAH

17Then the king of Babylon
made Mattaniah, *Jehoiachin's*[a]
uncle, king in his place, and
changed his name to Zede-
kiah.

18Zedekiah *was* twenty-
one years old when he be-
came king, and he reigned
eleven years in Jerusalem.
His mother's name *was* Ha-
mutal the daughter of Jeremiah of Libnah. 19He also did
evil in the sight of the LORD,
according to all that Jehoiakim had done. 20For because
of the anger of the LORD *this*
happened in Jerusalem and
Judah, that He finally cast
them out from His presence.
Then Zedekiah rebelled
against the king of Babylon.

THE FALL AND CAPTIVITY OF JUDAH

25 Now it came to pass in
the ninth year of his
reign, in the tenth month, on
the tenth *day* of the month,

24:17 [a] Literally *his*

that Nebuchadnezzar king of Babylon and all his army came against Jerusalem and encamped against it; and they built a siege wall against it all around. 2So the city was besieged until the eleventh year of King Zedekiah. 3By the ninth *day* of the *fourth* month the famine had become so severe in the city that there was no food for the people of the land.

4Then the city wall was broken through, and all the men of war *fled* at night by way of the gate between two walls, which was by the king's garden, even though the Chaldeans *were* still encamped all around against the city. And *the king*[a] went by way of the plain.[b] 5But the army of the Chaldeans pursued the king, and they overtook him in the plains of Jericho. All his army was scattered from him. 6So they took the king and brought him up to the king of Babylon at Riblah, and they pronounced judgment on him. 7Then they killed the sons of Zedekiah before his eyes, put out the eyes of Zedekiah, bound him with bronze fetters, and took him to Babylon.

8And in the fifth month, on the seventh *day* of the month (which *was* the nineteenth year of King Nebuchadnezzar king of Babylon), Nebuzaradan the captain of the guard, a servant of the king of Babylon, came to Jerusalem. 9He burned the house of the LORD and the king's house; all the houses of Jerusalem, that is, all the houses of the great, he burned with fire. 10And all the army of the Chaldeans who *were with* the captain of the guard broke down the walls of Jerusalem all around.

11Then Nebuzaradan the captain of the guard carried away captive the rest of the people *who* remained in the city and the defectors who had deserted to the king of Babylon, with the rest of the multitude. 12But the captain of the guard left *some* of the poor of the land as vinedressers and farmers. 13The bronze pillars that *were* in the house of the LORD, and the carts and the bronze Sea that *were* in the house of the LORD, the Chaldeans broke in pieces, and carried their bronze to Babylon. 14They also took away the pots, the shovels, the trimmers, the spoons, and all the bronze utensils with which the priests ministered. 15The firepans and the basins, the things of solid gold and solid silver, the captain of the guard took away. 16The two pillars, one Sea, and the carts, which Solomon had made for the house of the LORD, the bronze of all these articles was beyond measure. 17The height of one pillar *was* eighteen cubits,

25:4 [a] Literally *he* [b] Or *Arabah,* that is, the Jordan Valley

and the capital on it *was* of bronze. The height of the capital was three cubits, and the network and pomegranates all around the capital were all of bronze. The second pillar was the same, with a network.

18And the captain of the guard took Seraiah the chief priest, Zephaniah the second priest, and the three doorkeepers. 19He also took out of the city an officer who had charge of the men of war, five men of the king's close associates who were found in the city, the chief recruiting officer of the army, who mustered the people of the land, and sixty men of the people of the land *who were* found in the city. 20So Nebuzaradan, captain of the guard, took these and brought them to the king of Babylon at Riblah. 21Then the king of Babylon struck them and put them to death at Riblah in the land of Hamath. Thus Judah was carried away captive from its own land.

GEDALIAH MADE GOVERNOR OF JUDAH

22Then he made Gedaliah the son of Ahikam, the son of Shaphan, governor over the people who remained in the land of Judah, whom Nebuchadnezzar king of Babylon had left. 23Now when all the captains of the armies, they and *their* men, heard that the king of Babylon had made Gedaliah governor, they came to Gedaliah at Mizpah—Ishmael the son of Nethaniah, Johanan the son of Careah, Seraiah the son of Tanhumeth the Netophathite, and Jaazaniah[a] the son of a Maachathite, they and their men. 24And Gedaliah took an oath before them and their men, and said to them, "Do not be afraid of the servants of the Chaldeans. Dwell in the land and serve the king of Babylon, and it shall be well with you."

25But it happened in the seventh month that Ishmael the son of Nethaniah, the son of Elishama, of the royal family, came with ten men and struck and killed Gedaliah, the Jews, as well as the Chaldeans who were with him at Mizpah. 26And all the people, small and great, and the captains of the armies, arose and went to Egypt; for they were afraid of the Chaldeans.

JEHOIACHIN RELEASED FROM PRISON

27Now it came to pass in the thirty-seventh year of the captivity of Jehoiachin king of Judah, in the twelfth month, on the twenty-seventh *day* of the month, *that* Evil-Merodach[a] king of Babylon, in the year that he began to reign,

25:23 [a] Spelled *Jezaniah* in Jeremiah 40:8 **25:27** [a] Literally *Man of Marduk*

released Jehoiachin king of
Judah from prison. [28]He spoke
kindly to him, and gave him
a more prominent seat than
those of the kings who *were*
with him in Babylon. [29]So Jehoiachin changed from his
prison garments, and he ate
bread regularly before the king
all the days of his life. [30]And as
for his provisions, *there was* a
regular ration given him by the
king, a portion for each day, all
the days of his life.

THE FIRST BOOK OF THE CHRONICLES

THE FAMILY OF ADAM— SETH TO ABRAHAM

1 Adam, Seth, Enosh, [2]Ca-
inan,[a] Mahalalel, Jared,
[3]Enoch, Methuselah, Lamech,
[4]Noah,[a] Shem, Ham, and Japheth.
[5]The sons of Japheth *were*
Gomer, Magog, Madai, Javan,
Tubal, Meshech, and Tiras.
[6]The sons of Gomer *were* Ashkenaz, Diphath,[a] and Togarmah. [7]The sons of Javan *were*
Elishah, Tarshishah,[a] Kittim,
and Rodanim.[b]
[8]The sons of Ham *were*
Cush, Mizraim, Put, and Canaan. [9]The sons of Cush
were Seba, Havilah, Sabta,[a]
Raama,[b] and Sabtecha. The
sons of Raama *were* Sheba
and Dedan. [10]Cush begot Nimrod; he began to be a mighty
one on the earth. [11]Mizraim
begot Ludim, Anamim, Le-
habim, Naphtuhim, [12]Path-
rusim, Casluhim (from whom
came the Philistines and the
Caphtorim). [13]Canaan begot
Sidon, his firstborn, and Heth;
[14]the Jebusite, the Amorite,
and the Girgashite; [15]the Hivite, the Arkite, and the Sinite;
[16]the Arvadite, the Zemarite,
and the Hamathite.
[17]The sons of Shem *were*
Elam, Asshur, Arphaxad, Lud,
Aram, Uz, Hul, Gether, and
Meshech.[a] [18]Arphaxad begot
Shelah, and Shelah begot Eber.
[19]To Eber were born two sons:
the name of one *was* Peleg,[a]
for in his days the earth was
divided; and his brother's
name *was* Joktan. [20]Joktan
begot Almodad, Sheleph, Ha-

1:2 [a] Hebrew *Qenan* 1:4 [a] Following Masoretic Text and Vulgate; Septuagint adds *the sons of Noah.* 1:6 [a] Spelled *Riphath* in Genesis 10:3 1:7 [a] Spelled *Tarshish* in Genesis 10:4 [b] Spelled *Dodanim* in Genesis 10:4 1:9 [a] Spelled *Sabtah* in Genesis 10:7 [b] Spelled *Raamah* in Genesis 10:7 1:17 [a] Spelled *Mash* in Genesis 10:23 1:19 [a] Literally *Division*

zarmaveth, Jerah, 21Hadoram,
Uzal, Diklah, 22Ebal,[a] Abimael,
Sheba, 23Ophir, Havilah, and
Jobab. All these *were* the sons
of Joktan.
24Shem, Arphaxad, Shelah,
25Eber, Peleg, Reu, 26Serug,
Nahor, Terah, 27and Abram,
who *is* Abraham. 28The sons
of Abraham *were* Isaac and
Ishmael.

THE FAMILY OF ISHMAEL

29These *are* their genealogies: The firstborn of Ishmael
was Nebajoth; then Kedar,
Adbeel, Mibsam, 30Mishma,
Dumah, Massa, Hadad,[a] Tema,
31Jetur, Naphish, and Kedemah. These *were* the sons of
Ishmael.

THE FAMILY OF KETURAH

32Now the sons born to Ke-
turah, Abraham's concubine,
were Zimran, Jokshan, Medan,
Midian, Ishbak, and Shuah.
The sons of Jokshan *were*
Sheba and Dedan. 33The sons
of Midian *were* Ephah, Epher,
Hanoch, Abida, and Eldaah.
All these were the children of
Keturah.

THE FAMILY OF ISAAC

34And Abraham begot
Isaac. The sons of Isaac *were*
Esau and Israel. 35The sons
of Esau *were* Eliphaz, Reuel,
Jeush, Jaalam, and Korah.
36And the sons of Eliphaz
were Teman, Omar, Zephi,[a]
Gatam, *and* Kenaz; and *by*
Timna,[b] Amalek. 37The sons
of Reuel *were* Nahath, Zerah,
Shammah, and Mizzah.

THE FAMILY OF SEIR

38The sons of Seir *were*
Lotan, Shobal, Zibeon, Anah,
Dishon, Ezer, and Dishan.
39And the sons of Lotan *were*
Hori and Homam; Lotan's sis-
ter *was* Timna. 40The sons of
Shobal *were* Alian,[a] Manahath,
Ebal, Shephi,[b] and Onam. The
sons of Zibeon *were* Ajah and
Anah. 41The son of Anah *was*
Dishon. The sons of Dishon
were Hamran,[a] Eshban, Ith-
ran, and Cheran. 42The sons of
Ezer *were* Bilhan, Zaavan, *and*
Jaakan.[a] The sons of Dishan
were Uz and Aran.

THE KINGS OF EDOM

43Now these *were* the kings
who reigned in the land of
Edom before a king reigned
over the children of Israel:
Bela the son of Beor, and the
name of his city was Dinhabah.
44And when Bela died, Jobab
the son of Zerah of Bozrah
reigned in his place. 45When
Jobab died, Husham of the

1:22 [a] Spelled *Obal* in Genesis 10:28 1:30 [a] Spelled *Hadar* in Genesis 25:15 1:36 [a] Spelled *Zepho* in Genesis 36:11 [b] Compare Genesis 36:12 1:40 [a] Spelled *Alvan* in Genesis 36:23 [b] Spelled *Shepho* in Genesis 36:23 1:41 [a] Spelled *Hemdan* in Genesis 36:26 1:42 [a] Spelled *Akan* in Genesis 36:27

land of the Temanites reigned in his place. 46And when Husham died, Hadad the son of Bedad, who attacked Midian in the field of Moab, reigned in his place. The name of his city *was* Avith. 47When Hadad died, Samlah of Masrekah reigned in his place. 48And when Samlah died, Saul of Rehoboth-by-the-River reigned in his place. 49When Saul died, Baal-Hanan the son of Achbor reigned in his place. 50And when Baal-Hanan died, Hadad[a] reigned in his place; and the name of his city was Pai.[b] His wife's name was Mehetabel the daughter of Matred, the daughter of Mezahab. 51Hadad died also. And the chiefs of Edom were Chief Timnah, Chief Aliah,[a] Chief Jetheth, 52Chief Aholibamah, Chief Elah, Chief Pinon, 53Chief Kenaz, Chief Teman, Chief Mibzar, 54Chief Magdiel, and Chief Iram. These *were* the chiefs of Edom.

THE FAMILY OF ISRAEL

2 These *were* the sons of Israel: Reuben, Simeon, Levi, Judah, Issachar, Zebulun, 2Dan, Joseph, Benjamin, Naphtali, Gad, and Asher.

FROM JUDAH TO DAVID

3The sons of Judah *were* Er, Onan, and Shelah. *These* three were born to him by the daughter of Shua, the Canaanitess. Er, the firstborn of Judah, was wicked in the sight of the LORD; so He killed him. 4And Tamar, his daughter-in-law, bore him Perez and Zerah. All the sons of Judah *were* five.

5The sons of Perez *were* Hezron and Hamul. 6The sons of Zerah *were* Zimri, Ethan, Heman, Calcol, and Dara—five of them in all.

7The son of Carmi *was* Achar,[a] the troubler of Israel, who transgressed in the accursed thing.

8The son of Ethan *was* Azariah.

9Also the sons of Hezron who were born to him *were* Jerahmeel, Ram, and Chelubai.[a] 10Ram begot Amminadab, and Amminadab begot Nahshon, leader of the children of Judah; 11Nahshon begot Salma,[a] and Salma begot Boaz; 12Boaz begot Obed, and Obed begot Jesse; 13Jesse begot Eliab his firstborn, Abinadab the second, Shimea[a] the third, 14Nethanel the fourth, Raddai the fifth, 15Ozem the sixth, *and* David the seventh.

16Now their sisters *were* Zeruiah and Abigail. And the sons of Zeruiah *were* Abishai, Joab, and Asahel—three. 17Ab-

1:50 [a] Spelled *Hadar* in Genesis 36:39 [b] Spelled *Pau* in Genesis 36:39 1:51 [a] Spelled *Alvah* in Genesis 36:40 2:7 [a] Spelled *Achan* in Joshua 7:1 and elsewhere 2:9 [a] Spelled *Caleb* in 2:18, 42 2:11 [a] Spelled *Salmon* in Ruth 4:21 and Luke 3:32 2:13 [a] Spelled *Shammah* in 1 Samuel 16:9 and elsewhere

igail bore Amasa; and the father of Amasa *was* Jether the
Ishmaelite.[a]

THE FAMILY OF HEZRON

18Caleb the son of Hez-
ron had children by Azubah,
his wife, and by Jerioth. Now
these were her sons: Jesher,
Shobab, and Ardon. 19When
Azubah died, Caleb took Ephrath[a] as his wife, who bore
him Hur. 20And Hur begot Uri,
and Uri begot Bezalel.

21Now afterward Hezron
went in to the daughter of
Machir the father of Gilead,
whom he married when he
was sixty years old; and she
bore him Segub. 22Segub begot
Jair, who had twenty-three
cities in the land of Gilead.
23(Geshur and Syria took from
them the towns of Jair, with
Kenath and its towns—sixty
towns.) All these *belonged to*
the sons of Machir the father
of Gilead. 24After Hezron died
in Caleb Ephrathah, Hezron's
wife Abijah bore him Ashhur
the father of Tekoa.

THE FAMILY OF JERAHMEEL

25The sons of Jerahmeel,
the firstborn of Hezron, *were*
Ram, the firstborn, and Bunah,
Oren, Ozem, *and* Ahijah. 26Je-
rahmeel had another wife,
whose name was Atarah; she
was the mother of Onam. 27The
sons of Ram, the firstborn of
Jerahmeel, were Maaz, Jamin,
and Eker. 28The sons of Onam
were Shammai and Jada. The
sons of Shammai *were* Nadab
and Abishur.

29And the name of the wife
of Abishur *was* Abihail, and she
bore him Ahban and Molid.
30The sons of Nadab *were* Seled
and Appaim; Seled died without children. 31The son of Appaim *was* Ishi, the son of Ishi
was Sheshan, and Sheshan's
son *was* Ahlai. 32The sons of
Jada, the brother of Shammai,
were Jether and Jonathan; Jether died without children.
33The sons of Jonathan *were*
Peleth and Zaza. These were
the sons of Jerahmeel.

34Now Sheshan had no
sons, only daughters. And
Sheshan had an Egyptian servant whose name *was* Jarha.
35Sheshan gave his daughter
to Jarha his servant as wife,
and she bore him Attai. 36Attai
begot Nathan, and Nathan
begot Zabad; 37Zabad begot
Ephlal, and Ephlal begot Obed;
38Obed begot Jehu, and Jehu
begot Azariah; 39Azariah begot
Helez, and Helez begot Eleasah; 40Eleasah begot Sismai,
and Sismai begot Shallum;
41Shallum begot Jekamiah,
and Jekamiah begot Elishama.

THE FAMILY OF CALEB

42The descendants of Caleb
the brother of Jerahmeel *were*
Mesha, his firstborn, who was
the father of Ziph, and the

2:17 [a] Compare 2 Samuel 17:25 2:19 [a] Spelled *Ephrathah* elsewhere

sons of Mareshah the father of
Hebron. 43The sons of Hebron
were Korah, Tappuah, Rekem,
and Shema. 44Shema begot
Raham the father of Jorkoam,
and Rekem begot Shammai.
45And the son of Shammai
was Maon, and Maon *was* the
father of Beth Zur.

46Ephah, Caleb's concu-
bine, bore Haran, Moza, and
Gazez; and Haran begot Gazez.
47And the sons of Jahdai *were*
Regem, Jotham, Geshan, Pelet,
Ephah, and Shaaph.

48Maachah, Caleb's concu-
bine, bore Sheber and Tirha-
nah. 49She also bore Shaaph
the father of Madmannah,
Sheva the father of Mach-
benah and the father of Gibea.
And the daughter of Caleb *was*
Achsah.

50These were the descen-
dants of Caleb: The sons of
Hur, the firstborn of Ephrathah, *were* Shobal the father
of Kirjath Jearim, 51Salma the
father of Bethlehem, *and* Ha-
reph the father of Beth Gader.

52And Shobal the father of
Kirjath Jearim had descendants: Haroeh, *and* half of the
families of Manuhoth.[a] 53The
families of Kirjath Jearim *were*
the Ithrites, the Puthites, the
Shumathites, and the Mish-
raites. From these came the
Zorathites and the Eshtaolites.

54The sons of Salma *were*
Bethlehem, the Netopha-
thites, Atroth Beth Joab, half
of the Manahethites, and the
Zorites.

55And the families of the
scribes who dwelt at Jabez
were the Tirathites, the Shim-
eathites, *and* the Suchathites.
These *were* the Kenites who
came from Hammath, the father of the house of Rechab.

THE FAMILY OF DAVID

3 Now these were the sons
of David who were born to
him in Hebron: The firstborn
was Amnon, by Ahinoam the
Jezreelitess; the second, Daniel,[a] by Abigail the Carmelitess; 2the third, Absalom the
son of Maacah, the daughter
of Talmai, king of Geshur; the
fourth, Adonijah the son of
Haggith; 3the fifth, Shephatiah, by Abital; the sixth, Ithream, by his wife Eglah.

4*These* six were born to him
in Hebron. There he reigned
seven years and six months,
and in Jerusalem he reigned
thirty-three years. 5And these
were born to him in Jerusalem: Shimea,[a] Shobab, Nathan, and Solomon—four by
Bathshua[b] the daughter of
Ammiel.[c] 6Also *there* were
Ibhar, Elishama,[a] Eliphelet,[b] 7Nogah, Nepheg, Japhia,

2:52 [a] Same as *the Manahethites,* verse 54 3:1 [a] Called *Chileab* in 2 Samuel 3:3 3:5 [a] Spelled *Shammua* in 14:4 and 2 Samuel 5:14 [b] Spelled *Bathsheba* in 2 Samuel 11:3 [c] Called *Eliam* in 2 Samuel 11:3 3:6 [a] Spelled *Elishua* in 14:5 and 2 Samuel 5:15 [b] Spelled *Elpelet* in 14:5

8 Elishama, Eliada,[a] and Eliphelet—nine *in all.* 9 *These were* all the sons of David, besides the sons of the concubines, and Tamar their sister.

THE FAMILY OF SOLOMON

10 Solomon's son *was* Rehoboam; Abijah[a] *was* his son, Asa his son, Jehoshaphat his son, 11 Joram[a] his son, Ahaziah his son, Joash[b] his son, 12 Amaziah his son, Azariah[a] his son, Jotham his son, 13 Ahaz his son, Hezekiah his son, Manasseh his son, 14 Amon his son, *and* Josiah his son. 15 The sons of Josiah *were* Johanan the firstborn, the second Jehoiakim, the third Zedekiah, and the fourth Shallum.[a] 16 The sons of Jehoiakim *were* Jeconiah his son *and* Zedekiah[a] his son.

THE FAMILY OF JECONIAH

17 And the sons of Jeconiah[a] *were* Assir,[b] Shealtiel his son, 18 *and* Malchiram, Pedaiah, Shenazzar, Jecamiah, Hoshama, and Nedabiah. 19 The sons of Pedaiah *were* Zerubbabel and Shimei. The sons of Zerubbabel *were* Meshullam, Hananiah, Shelomith their sister, 20 and Hashubah, Ohel, Berechiah, Hasadiah, and Jushab-Hesed—five *in all.*

21 The sons of Hananiah *were* Pelatiah and Jeshaiah, the sons of Rephaiah, the sons of Arnan, the sons of Obadiah, and the sons of Shechaniah. 22 The son of Shechaniah was Shemaiah. The sons of Shemaiah *were* Hattush, Igal, Bariah, Neariah, and Shaphat—six *in all.* 23 The sons of Neariah *were* Elioenai, Hezekiah, and Azrikam—three *in all.* 24 The sons of Elioenai *were* Hodaviah, Eliashib, Pelaiah, Akkub, Johanan, Delaiah, and Anani—seven *in all.*

THE FAMILY OF JUDAH

4 The sons of Judah *were* Perez, Hezron, Carmi, Hur, and Shobal. 2 And Reaiah the son of Shobal begot Jahath, and Jahath begot Ahumai and Lahad. These *were* the families of the Zorathites. 3 These *were the sons of* the father of Etam: Jezreel, Ishma, and Idbash; and the name of their sister *was* Hazelelponi; 4 and Penuel *was* the father of Gedor, and Ezer *was the* father of Hushah.

These *were* the sons of Hur, the firstborn of Ephrathah the father of Bethlehem.

5 And Ashhur the father of Tekoa had two wives, Helah and Naarah. 6 Naarah bore him Ahuzzam, Hepher, Temeni, and Haahashtari. These

3:8 [a] Spelled *Beeliada* in 14:7 **3:10** [a] Spelled *Abijam* in 1 Kings 15:1 **3:11** [a] Spelled *Jehoram* in 2 Kings 1:17 and 8:16 [b] Spelled *Jehoash* in 2 Kings 12:1 **3:12** [a] Called *Uzziah* in Isaiah 6:1 **3:15** [a] Called *Jehoahaz* in 2 Kings 23:31 **3:16** [a] Compare 2 Kings 24:17 **3:17** [a] Also called *Coniah* in Jeremiah 22:24 and *Jehoiachin* in 2 Kings 24:8 [b] Or *Jeconiah the captive were*

were the sons of Naarah. 7The sons of Helah *were* Zereth, Zohar, and Ethnan; 8and Koz begot Anub, Zobebah, and the families of Aharhel the son of Harum.

9Now Jabez was more honorable than his brothers, and his mother called his name Jabez,[a] saying, "Because I bore *him* in pain." 10And Jabez called on the God of Israel saying, "Oh, that You would bless me indeed, and enlarge my territory, that Your hand would be with me, and that You would keep *me* from evil, that I may not cause pain!" So God granted him what he requested.

11Chelub the brother of Shuhah begot Mehir, who *was* the father of Eshton. 12And Eshton begot Beth-Rapha, Paseah, and Tehinnah the father of Ir-Nahash. These *were* the men of Rechah.

13The sons of Kenaz *were* Othniel and Seraiah. The sons of Othniel *were* Hathath,[a] 14and Meonothai *who* begot Ophrah. Seraiah begot Joab the father of Ge Harashim,[a] for they were craftsmen. 15The sons of Caleb the son of Jephunneh *were* Iru, Elah, and Naam. The son of Elah *was* Kenaz. 16The sons of Jehallelel *were* Ziph, Ziphah, Tiria, and Asarel. 17The sons of Ezrah *were* Jether, Mered, Epher, and Jalon. And *Mered's wife*[a] bore Miriam, Shammai, and Ishbah the father of Eshtemoa. 18(His wife Jehudijah[a] bore Jered the father of Gedor, Heber the father of Sochoh, and Jekuthiel the father of Zanoah.) And these were the sons of Bithiah the daughter of Pharaoh, whom Mered took.

19The sons of Hodiah's wife, the sister of Naham, *were* the fathers of Keilah the Garmite and of Eshtemoa the Maachathite. 20And the sons of Shimon *were* Amnon, Rinnah, Ben-Hanan, and Tilon. And the sons of Ishi *were* Zoheth and Ben-Zoheth.

21The sons of Shelah the son of Judah *were* Er the father of Lecah, Laadah the father of Mareshah, and the families of the house of the linen workers of the house of Ashbea; 22also Jokim, the men of Chozeba, and Joash; Saraph, who ruled in Moab, and Jashubi-Lehem. Now the records are ancient. 23These *were* the potters and those who dwell at Netaim[a] and Gederah;[b] there they dwelt with the king for his work.

THE FAMILY OF SIMEON

24The sons of Simeon *were* Nemuel, Jamin, Jarib,[a] Zerah,[b] *and* Shaul, 25Shallum his son,

4:9 [a] Literally *He Will Cause Pain* 4:13 [a] Septuagint and Vulgate add *and Meonothai.* 4:14 [a] Literally *Valley of Craftsmen* 4:17 [a] Literally *she* 4:18 [a] Or *His Judean wife* 4:23 [a] Literally *Plants* [b] Literally *Hedges* 4:24 [a] Called *Jachin* in Genesis 46:10 [b] Called *Zohar* in Genesis 46:10

Mibsam his son, and Mishma his son. 26And the sons of Mishma *were* Hamuel his son, Zacchur his son, and Shimei his son. 27Shimei had sixteen sons and six daughters; but his brothers did not have many children, nor did any of their families multiply as much as the children of Judah.

28They dwelt at Beersheba, Moladah, Hazar Shual, 29Bilhah, Ezem, Tolad, 30Bethuel, Hormah, Ziklag, 31Beth Marcaboth, Hazar Susim, Beth Biri, and at Shaaraim. These *were* their cities until the reign of David. 32And their villages *were* Etam, Ain, Rimmon, Tochen, and Ashan—five cities— 33and all the villages that *were* around these cities as far as Baal.[a] These *were* their dwelling places, and they maintained their genealogy: 34Meshobab, Jamlech, and Joshah the son of Amaziah; 35Joel, and Jehu the son of Joshibiah, the son of Seraiah, the son of Asiel; 36Elioenai, Jaakobah, Jeshohaiah, Asaiah, Adiel, Jesimiel, and Benaiah; 37Ziza the son of Shiphi, the son of Allon, the son of Jedaiah, the son of Shimri, the son of Shemaiah— 38these mentioned by name *were* leaders in their families, and their father's house increased greatly.

39So they went to the entrance of Gedor, as far as the east side of the valley, to seek pasture for their flocks. 40And they found rich, good pasture, and the land *was* broad, quiet, and peaceful; for some Hamites formerly lived there.

41These recorded by name came in the days of Hezekiah king of Judah; and they attacked their tents and the Meunites who were found there, and utterly destroyed them, as it is to this day. So they dwelt in their place, because *there was* pasture for their flocks there. 42Now *some* of them, five hundred men of the sons of Simeon, went to Mount Seir, having as their captains Pelatiah, Neariah, Rephaiah, and Uzziel, the sons of Ishi. 43And they defeated the rest of the Amalekites who had escaped. They have dwelt there to this day.

THE FAMILY OF REUBEN

5 Now the sons of Reuben the firstborn of Israel—he *was* indeed the firstborn, but because he defiled his father's bed, his birthright was given to the sons of Joseph, the son of Israel, so that the genealogy is not listed according to the birthright; 2yet Judah prevailed over his brothers, and from him *came* a ruler, although the birthright was Joseph's— 3the sons of Reuben the firstborn of Israel were Hanoch, Pallu, Hezron, and Carmi.

4:33 [a] Or *Baalath Beer* (compare Joshua 19:8)

[4]The sons of Joel *were* Shemaiah his son, Gog his son, Shimei his son, [5]Micah his son, Reaiah his son, Baal his son, [6]and Beerah his son, whom Tiglath-Pileser[a] king of Assyria carried into captivity. He *was* leader of the Reubenites. [7]And his brethren by their families, when the genealogy of their generations was registered: the chief, Jeiel, and Zechariah, [8]and Bela the son of Azaz, the son of Shema, the son of Joel, who dwelt in Aroer, as far as Nebo and Baal Meon. [9]Eastward they settled as far as the entrance of the wilderness this side of the River Euphrates, because their cattle had multiplied in the land of Gilead.

[10]Now in the days of Saul they made war with the Hagrites, who fell by their hand; and they dwelt in their tents throughout the entire *area* east of Gilead.

THE FAMILY OF GAD

[11]And the children of Gad dwelt next to them in the land of Bashan as far as Salcah: [12]Joel *was* the chief, Shapham the next, then Jaanai and Shaphat in Bashan, [13]and their brethren of their father's house: Michael, Meshullam, Sheba, Jorai, Jachan, Zia, and Eber—seven *in all.* [14]These *were* the children of Abihail the son of Huri, the son of Jaroah, the son of Gilead, the son of Michael, the son of Jeshishai, the son of Jahdo, the son of Buz; [15]Ahi the son of Abdiel, the son of Guni, *was* chief of their father's house. [16]And *the Gadites* dwelt in Gilead, in Bashan and in its villages, and in all the common-lands of Sharon within their borders. [17]All these were registered by genealogies in the days of Jotham king of Judah, and in the days of Jeroboam king of Israel.

[18]The sons of Reuben, the Gadites, and half the tribe of Manasseh *had* forty-four thousand seven hundred and sixty valiant men, men able to bear shield and sword, to shoot with the bow, and skillful in war, who went to war. [19]They made war with the Hagrites, Jetur, Naphish, and Nodab. [20]And they were helped against them, and the Hagrites were delivered into their hand, and all who *were* with them, for they cried out to God in the battle. He heeded their prayer, because they put their trust in Him. [21]Then they took away their livestock—fifty thousand of their camels, two hundred and fifty thousand of their sheep, and two thousand of their donkeys—also one hundred thousand of their men; [22]for many fell dead, because the war *was* God's. And they dwelt in their place until the captivity.

5:6 [a] Hebrew *Tilgath-Pilneser*

THE FAMILY OF MANASSEH (EAST)

23So the children of the half-tribe of Manasseh dwelt in the land. Their *numbers* increased from Bashan to Baal Hermon, that is, to Senir, or Mount Hermon. 24These *were* the heads of their fathers' houses: Epher, Ishi, Eliel, Azriel, Jeremiah, Hodaviah, and Jahdiel. They were mighty men of valor, famous men, *and* heads of their fathers' houses.

25And they were unfaithful to the God of their fathers, and played the harlot after the gods of the peoples of the land, whom God had destroyed before them. 26So the God of Israel stirred up the spirit of Pul king of Assyria, that is, Tiglath-Pileser[a] king of Assyria. He carried the Reubenites, the Gadites, and the half-tribe of Manasseh into captivity. He took them to Halah, Habor, Hara, and the river of Gozan to this day.

THE FAMILY OF LEVI

6 The sons of Levi *were* Gershon, Kohath, and Merari. 2The sons of Kohath *were* Amram, Izhar, Hebron, and Uzziel. 3The children of Amram *were* Aaron, Moses, and Miriam. And the sons of Aaron *were* Nadab, Abihu, Eleazar, and Ithamar. 4Eleazar begot Phinehas, *and* Phinehas begot Abishua; 5Abishua begot Bukki, and Bukki begot Uzzi; 6Uzzi begot Zerahiah, and Zerahiah begot Meraioth; 7Meraioth begot Amariah, and Amariah begot Ahitub; 8Ahitub begot Zadok, and Zadok begot Ahimaaz; 9Ahimaaz begot Azariah, and Azariah begot Johanan; 10Johanan begot Azariah (it was he who ministered as priest in the temple that Solomon built in Jerusalem); 11Azariah begot Amariah, and Amariah begot Ahitub; 12Ahitub begot Zadok, and Zadok begot Shallum; 13Shallum begot Hilkiah, and Hilkiah begot Azariah; 14Azariah begot Seraiah, and Seraiah begot Jehozadak. 15Jehozadak went *into captivity* when the LORD carried Judah and Jerusalem into captivity by the hand of Nebuchadnezzar.

16The sons of Levi *were* Gershon,[a] Kohath, and Merari. 17These are the names of the sons of Gershon: Libni and Shimei. 18The sons of Kohath *were* Amram, Izhar, Hebron, and Uzziel. 19The sons of Merari *were* Mahli and Mushi. Now these *are* the families of the Levites according to their fathers: 20Of Gershon *were* Libni his son, Jahath his son, Zimmah his son, 21Joah his son, Iddo his son, Zerah his

5:26 [a] Hebrew *Tilgath-Pilneser* **6:16** [a] Hebrew *Gershom* (alternate spelling of *Gershon*, as in verses 1, 17, 20, 43, 62, and 71)

son, *and* Jeatherai his son. [22]The sons of Kohath *were* Amminadab his son, Korah his son, Assir his son, [23]Elkanah his son, Ebiasaph his son, Assir his son, [24]Tahath his son, Uriel his son, Uzziah his son, and Shaul his son. [25]The sons of Elkanah *were* Amasai and Ahimoth. [26]*As for* Elkanah,[a] the sons of Elkanah *were* Zophai[b] his son, Nahath[c] his son, [27]Eliab[a] his son, Jeroham his son, *and* Elkanah his son. [28]The sons of Samuel *were* *Joel*[a] the firstborn, and Abijah the second.[b] [29]The sons of Merari *were* Mahli, Libni his son, Shimei his son, Uzzah his son, [30]Shimea his son, Haggiah his son, *and* Asaiah his son.

MUSICIANS IN THE HOUSE OF THE LORD

[31]Now these are the men whom David appointed over the service of song in the house of the LORD, after the ark came to rest. [32]They were ministering with music before the dwelling place of the tabernacle of meeting, until Solomon had built the house of the LORD in Jerusalem, and they served in their office according to their order.

[33]And these *are* the ones who ministered with their sons: Of the sons of the Kohathites *were* Heman the singer, the son of Joel, the son of Samuel, [34]the son of Elkanah, the son of Jeroham, the son of Eliel,[a] the son of Toah,[b] [35]the son of Zuph, the son of Elkanah, the son of Mahath, the son of Amasai, [36]the son of Elkanah, the son of Joel, the son of Azariah, the son of Zephaniah, [37]the son of Tahath, the son of Assir, the son of Ebiasaph, the son of Korah, [38]the son of Izhar, the son of Kohath, the son of Levi, the son of Israel. [39]And his brother Asaph, who stood at his right hand, *was* Asaph the son of Berachiah, the son of Shimea, [40]the son of Michael, the son of Baaseiah, the son of Malchijah, [41]the son of Ethni, the son of Zerah, the son of Adaiah, [42]the son of Ethan, the son of Zimmah, the son of Shimei, [43]the son of Jahath, the son of Gershon, the son of Levi.

[44]Their brethren, the sons of Merari, on the left hand, *were* Ethan the son of Kishi, the son of Abdi, the son of Malluch, [45]the son of Hashabiah, the son of Amaziah, the son of Hilkiah, [46]the son of Amzi, the son of Bani, the son of Shamer, [47]the son of Mahli, the son of Mushi, the son of Merari, the son of Levi.

6:26 [a] Compare verse 35 [b] Spelled *Zuph* in verse 35 and 1 Samuel 1:1 [c] Compare verse 34 **6:27** [a] Compare verse 34 **6:28** [a] Following Septuagint, Syriac, and Arabic (compare verse 33 and 1 Samuel 8:2) [b] Hebrew *Vasheni* **6:34** [a] Spelled *Elihu* in 1 Samuel 1:1 [b] Spelled *Tohu* in 1 Samuel 1:1

48And their brethren, the
Levites, *were* appointed to
every kind of service of the
tabernacle of the house of
God.

THE FAMILY OF AARON

49But Aaron and his sons
offered sacrifices on the altar
of burnt offering and on the
altar of incense, for all the
work of the Most Holy *Place,*
and to make atonement for
Israel, according to all that
Moses the servant of God had
commanded. 50Now these
are the sons of Aaron: Eleazar his son, Phinehas his son,
Abishua his son, 51Bukki his
son, Uzzi his son, Zerahiah his
son, 52Meraioth his son, Amariah his son, Ahitub his son,
53Zadok his son, *and* Ahimaaz
his son.

DWELLING PLACES OF THE LEVITES

54Now these *are* their dwelling places throughout their
settlements in their territory,
for they were *given* by lot to
the sons of Aaron, of the family of the Kohathites: 55They
gave them Hebron in the land
of Judah, with its surrounding common-lands. 56But the
fields of the city and its villages they gave to Caleb the
son of Jephunneh. 57And to
the sons of Aaron they gave
one of the cities of refuge,
Hebron; also Libnah with its
common-lands, Jattir, Eshtemoa with its common-lands,
58Hilen[a] with its common-
lands, Debir with its common-
lands, 59Ashan[a] with its
common-lands, and Beth
Shemesh with its common-
lands. 60And from the tribe
of Benjamin: Geba with its
common-lands, Alemeth[a]
with its common-lands, and
Anathoth with its common-
lands. All their cities among
their families *were* thirteen.

61To the rest of the family
of the tribe of the Kohathites
they gave by lot ten cities from
half the tribe of Manasseh.
62And to the sons of Gershon,
throughout their families,
they gave thirteen cities from
the tribe of Issachar, from the
tribe of Asher, from the tribe
of Naphtali, and from the tribe
of Manasseh in Bashan. 63To
the sons of Merari, throughout their families, *they gave*
twelve cities from the tribe
of Reuben, from the tribe of
Gad, and from the tribe of Zebulun. 64So the children of Israel gave *these* cities with their
common-lands to the Levites.
65And they gave by lot from
the tribe of the children of
Judah, from the tribe of the
children of Simeon, and from
the tribe of the children of
Benjamin these cities which
are called by *their* names.

6:58 [a] Spelled *Holon* in Joshua 21:15 **6:59** [a] Spelled *Ain* in Joshua 21:16 **6:60** [a] Spelled *Almon* in Joshua 21:18

[66]Now some of the families of the sons of Kohath *were given* cities as their territory from the tribe of Ephraim. [67]And they gave them *one of* the cities of refuge, Shechem with its common-lands, in the mountains of Ephraim, also Gezer with its common-lands, [68]Jokmeam with its common-lands, Beth Horon with its common-lands, [69]Aijalon with its common-lands, and Gath Rimmon with its common-lands. [70]And from the half-tribe of Manasseh: Aner with its common-lands and Bileam with its common-lands, for the rest of the family of the sons of Kohath.

[71]From the family of the half-tribe of Manasseh the sons of Gershon *were given* Golan in Bashan with its common-lands and Ashtaroth with its common-lands. [72]And from the tribe of Issachar: Kedesh with its common-lands, Daberath with its common-lands, [73]Ramoth with its common-lands, and Anem with its common-lands. [74]And from the tribe of Asher: Mashal with its common-lands, Abdon with its common-lands, [75]Hukok with its common-lands, and Rehob with its common-lands. [76]And from the tribe of Naphtali: Kedesh in Galilee with its common-lands, Hammon with its common-lands, and Kirjathaim with its common-lands.

[77]From the tribe of Zebulun the rest of the children of Merari *were given* Rimmon[a] with its common-lands and Tabor with its common-lands. [78]And on the other side of the Jordan, across from Jericho, on the east side of the Jordan, *they were given* from the tribe of Reuben: Bezer in the wilderness with its common-lands, Jahzah with its common-lands, [79]Kedemoth with its common-lands, and Mephaath with its common-lands. [80]And from the tribe of Gad: Ramoth in Gilead with its common-lands, Mahanaim with its common-lands, [81]Heshbon with its common-lands, and Jazer with its common-lands.

THE FAMILY OF ISSACHAR

7 The sons of Issachar *were* Tola, Puah,[a] Jashub, and Shimron—four *in all.* [2]The sons of Tola *were* Uzzi, Rephaiah, Jeriel, Jahmai, Jibsam, and Shemuel, heads of their father's house. *The sons* of Tola *were* mighty men of valor in their generations; their number in the days of David *was* twenty-two thousand six hundred. [3]The son of Uzzi *was* Izrahiah, and the sons of Izrahiah *were* Michael,

6:77 [a] Hebrew *Rimmono,* alternate spelling of *Rimmon;* see 4:32 7:1 [a] Spelled *Puvah* in Genesis 46:13

Obadiah, Joel, and Ishiah. All
five of them *were* chief men.
4And with them, by their generations, according to their
fathers' houses, *were* thirty-
six thousand troops ready for
war; for they had many wives
and sons.

5Now their brethren among
all the families of Issachar
were mighty men of valor,
listed by their genealogies,
eighty-seven thousand in all.

THE FAMILY OF BENJAMIN

6*The sons* of Benjamin *were*
Bela, Becher, and Jediael—
three *in all.* 7The sons of Bela
were Ezbon, Uzzi, Uzziel, Jerimoth, and Iri—five *in all.* They
were heads of *their* fathers'
houses, and they were listed
by their genealogies, twenty-
two thousand and thirty-four
mighty men of valor.

8The sons of Becher *were*
Zemirah, Joash, Eliezer, Elioenai, Omri, Jerimoth, Abijah,
Anathoth, and Alemeth. All
these *are* the sons of Becher.
9And they were recorded by
genealogy according to their
generations, heads of their
fathers' houses, twenty thousand two hundred mighty men
of valor. 10The son of Jediael
was Bilhan, and the sons of
Bilhan *were* Jeush, Benjamin,
Ehud, Chenaanah, Zethan,
Tharshish, and Ahishahar.

11All these sons of Jediael
were heads of their fathers'
houses; *there were* seventeen thousand two hundred
mighty men of valor fit to go
out for war *and* battle. 12Shup-
pim and Huppim[a] *were* the
sons of Ir, *and* Hushim *was*
the son of Aher.

THE FAMILY OF NAPHTALI

13The sons of Naphtali *were*
Jahziel,[a] Guni, Jezer, and Shallum,[b] the sons of Bilhah.

THE FAMILY OF MANASSEH (WEST)

14The descendants of Ma-
nasseh: his Syrian concubine
bore him Machir the father
of Gilead, the father of Asriel.[a] 15Machir took as his wife
the sister of Huppim and
Shuppim,[a] whose name *was*
Maachah. The name of *Gilead's*
grandson[b] *was* Zelophehad,[c]
but Zelophehad begot only
daughters. 16(Maachah the
wife of Machir bore a son, and
she called his name Peresh.
The name of his brother *was*
Sheresh, and his sons *were*
Ulam and Rakem. 17The son
of Ulam *was* Bedan.) These
were the descendants of Gilead the son of Machir, the son
of Manasseh.

18His sister Hammoleketh
bore Ishhod, Abiezer, and
Mahlah.

7:12 [a] Called *Hupham* in Numbers 26:39 7:13 [a] Spelled *Jahzeel* in Genesis 46:24 [b] Spelled *Shillem* in Genesis 46:24 7:14 [a] The son of Gilead (compare Numbers 26:30, 31) 7:15 [a] Compare verse 12 [b] Literally *the second* [c] Compare Numbers 26:30–33

19And the sons of Shemida were Ahian, Shechem, Likhi, and Aniam.

THE FAMILY OF EPHRAIM

20The sons of Ephraim *were* Shuthelah, Bered his son, Tahath his son, Eladah his son, Tahath his son, 21Zabad his son, Shuthelah his son, and Ezer and Elead. The men of Gath who were born in *that* land killed *them* because they came down to take away their cattle. 22Then Ephraim their father mourned many days, and his brethren came to comfort him.

23And when he went in to his wife, she conceived and bore a son; and he called his name Beriah,[a] because tragedy had come upon his house. 24Now his daughter *was* Sheerah, who built Lower and Upper Beth Horon and Uzzen Sheerah; 25and Rephah *was* his son, *as well* as Resheph, and Telah his son, Tahan his son, 26Laadan his son, Ammihud his son, Elishama his son, 27Nun[a] his son, and Joshua his son.

28Now their possessions and dwelling places *were* Bethel and its towns: to the east Naaran, to the west Gezer and its towns, and Shechem and its towns, as far as Ayyah[a] and its towns; 29and by the borders of the children of Manasseh *were* Beth Shean and its towns, Taanach and its towns, Megiddo and its towns, Dor and its towns. In these dwelt the children of Joseph, the son of Israel.

THE FAMILY OF ASHER

30The sons of Asher *were* Imnah, Ishvah, Ishvi, Beriah, and their sister Serah. 31The sons of Beriah *were* Heber and Malchiel, who was the father of Birzaith.[a] 32And Heber begot Japhlet, Shomer,[a] Hotham,[b] and their sister Shua. 33The sons of Japhlet *were* Pasach, Bimhal, and Ashvath. These *were* the children of Japhlet. 34The sons of Shemer *were* Ahi, Rohgah, Jehubbah, and Aram. 35And the sons of his brother Helem *were* Zophah, Imna, Shelesh, and Amal. 36The sons of Zophah *were* Suah, Harnepher, Shual, Beri, Imrah, 37Bezer, Hod, Shamma, Shilshah, Jithran,[a] and Beera. 38The sons of Jether *were* Jephunneh, Pispah, and Ara. 39The sons of Ulla *were* Arah, Haniel, and Rizia.

40All these *were* the children of Asher, heads of *their* fathers' houses, choice men, mighty men of valor, chief leaders. And they were recorded by genealogies among the army fit for battle; their number *was* twenty-six thousand.

7:23 [a] Literally *In Tragedy* 7:27 [a] Hebrew *Non* 7:28 [a] Many Hebrew manuscripts, Bomberg, Septuagint, Targum, and Vulgate read *Gazza.* 7:31 [a] Or *Birzavith* or *Birzoth* 7:32 [a] Spelled *Shemer* in verse 34 [b] Spelled *Helem* in verse 35 7:37 [a] Spelled *Jether* in verse 38

THE FAMILY TREE OF KING SAUL OF BENJAMIN

8 Now Benjamin begot
Bela his firstborn, Ash-
bel the second, Aharah[a] the
third, 2Nohah the fourth, and
Rapha the fifth. 3The sons
of Bela *were* Addar,[a] Gera,
Abihud, 4Abishua, Naaman,
Ahoah, 5Gera, Shephuphan,
and Huram.

6These *are* the sons of
Ehud, who were the heads
of the fathers' *houses* of the
inhabitants of Geba, and
who forced them to move to
Manahath: 7Naaman, Ahijah,
and Gera who forced them
to move. He begot Uzza and
Ahihud.

8Also Shaharaim had chil-
dren in the country of Moab,
after he had sent away Hushim and Baara his wives.
9By Hodesh his wife he begot
Jobab, Zibia, Mesha, Malcam,
10Jeuz, Sachiah, and Mirmah.
These *were* his sons, heads of
their fathers' *houses*.

11And by Hushim he begot
Abitub and Elpaal. 12The sons
of Elpaal *were* Eber, Misham,
and Shemed, who built Ono
and Lod with its towns; 13and
Beriah and Shema, who *were*
heads of their fathers' *houses*
of the inhabitants of Aijalon,
who drove out the inhabitants
of Gath. 14Ahio, Shashak, Jeremoth, 15Zebadiah, Arad,
Eder, 16Michael, Ispah, and
Joha *were* the sons of Beriah.
17Zebadiah, Meshullam, Hizki,
Heber, 18Ishmerai, Jizliah, and
Jobab *were* the sons of Elpaal.
19Jakim, Zichri, Zabdi, 20Elie-
nai, Zillethai, Eliel, 21Adaiah,
Beraiah, and Shimrath *were*
the sons of Shimei. 22Ishpan,
Eber, Eliel, 23Abdon, Zichri,
Hanan, 24Hananiah, Elam,
Antothijah, 25Iphdeiah, and
Penuel *were* the sons of Shashak. 26Shamsherai, Sheha-
riah, Athaliah, 27Jaareshiah,
Elijah, and Zichri *were* the
sons of Jeroham.

28These *were* heads of the
fathers' *houses* by their generations, chief men. These dwelt
in Jerusalem.

29Now the father of Gibeon,
whose wife's name *was* Maacah, dwelt at Gibeon. 30And his
firstborn son *was* Abdon, then
Zur, Kish, Baal, Nadab, 31Gedor,
Ahio, Zecher, 32and Mikloth,
who begot Shimeah.[a] They
also dwelt alongside their
relatives in Jerusalem, with
their brethren. 33Ner[a] begot
Kish, Kish begot Saul, and Saul
begot Jonathan, Malchishua,
Abinadab,[b] and Esh-Baal.[c]
34The son of Jonathan *was*
Merib-Baal,[a] and Merib-Baal
begot Micah. 35The sons of
Micah *were* Pithon, Melech,

8:1 [a] Spelled *Ahiram* in Numbers 26:38 8:3 [a] Called *Ard* in Numbers 26:40 8:32 [a] Spelled *Shimeam* in 9:38 8:33 [a] Also the son of Gibeon (compare 9:36, 39) [b] Called *Jishui* in 1 Samuel 14:49 [c] Called *Ishbosheth* in 2 Samuel 2:8 and elsewhere 8:34 [a] Called *Mephibosheth* in 2 Samuel 4:4

Tarea, and Ahaz. 36And Ahaz
begot Jehoaddah;[a] Jehoaddah
begot Alemeth, Azmaveth, and
Zimri; and Zimri begot Moza.
37Moza begot Binea, Raphah[a]
his son, Eleasah his son, *and*
Azel his son.

38Azel had six sons whose
names *were* these: Azrikam,
Bocheru, Ishmael, Sheariah,
Obadiah, and Hanan. All these
were the sons of Azel. 39And
the sons of Eshek his brother
were Ulam his firstborn, Jeush
the second, and Eliphelet the
third.

40The sons of Ulam were
mighty men of valor—archers.
They had many sons and
grandsons, one hundred and
fifty *in all.* These *were* all sons
of Benjamin.

9 So all Israel was recorded
by genealogies, and in-
deed, they *were* inscribed in
the book of the kings of Israel.
But Judah was carried away
captive to Babylon because
of their unfaithfulness. 2And
the first inhabitants who *dwelt*
in their possessions in their
cities *were* Israelites, priests,
Levites, and the Nethinim.

DWELLERS IN JERUSALEM

3Now in Jerusalem the children of Judah dwelt, and some
of the children of Benjamin,
and of the children of Ephraim
and Manasseh: 4Uthai the
son of Ammihud, the son of
Omri, the son of Imri, the son
of Bani, of the descendants
of Perez, the son of Judah.
5Of the Shilonites: Asaiah the
firstborn and his sons. 6Of
the sons of Zerah: Jeuel, and
their brethren—six hundred
and ninety. 7Of the sons of
Benjamin: Sallu the son of
Meshullam, the son of Hodaviah, the son of Hassenuah;
8Ibneiah the son of Jeroham;
Elah the son of Uzzi, the son of
Michri; Meshullam the son of
Shephatiah, the son of Reuel,
the son of Ibnijah; 9and their
brethren, according to their
generations—nine hundred
and fifty-six. All these men
were heads of a father's *house*
in their fathers' houses.

THE PRIESTS AT JERUSALEM

10Of the priests: Jedaiah, Jehoiarib, and Jachin; 11Azariah
the son of Hilkiah, the son of
Meshullam, the son of Zadok,
the son of Meraioth, the son
of Ahitub, the officer over
the house of God; 12Adaiah
the son of Jeroham, the son
of Pashur, the son of Malchijah; Maasai the son of Adiel,
the son of Jahzerah, the son
of Meshullam, the son of Me-
shillemith, the son of Immer;
13and their brethren, heads
of their fathers' houses—one
thousand seven hundred and
sixty. *They were* very able men
for the work of the service of
the house of God.

8:36 [a] Spelled *Jarah* in 9:42 8:37 [a] Spelled *Rephaiah* in 9:43

THE LEVITES AT JERUSALEM

14Of the Levites: Shemaiah
the son of Hasshub, the son
of Azrikam, the son of Hashabiah, of the sons of Merari;
15Bakbakkar, Heresh, Galal,
and Mattaniah the son of
Micah, the son of Zichri, the
son of Asaph; 16Obadiah the
son of Shemaiah, the son of
Galal, the son of Jeduthun;
and Berechiah the son of Asa,
the son of Elkanah, who lived
in the villages of the Netophathites.

THE LEVITE GATEKEEPERS

17And the gatekeepers *were*
Shallum, Akkub, Talmon, Ahiman, and their brethren. Shallum *was* the chief. 18Until then
they had been gatekeepers for
the camps of the children of
Levi at the King's Gate on the
east.

19Shallum the son of Kore,
the son of Ebiasaph, the son of
Korah, and his brethren, from
his father's house, the Korahites, *were* in charge of the work
of the service, gatekeepers of
the tabernacle. Their fathers
had been keepers of the entrance to the camp of the
LORD. 20And Phinehas the son
of Eleazar had been the officer
over them in time past; the
LORD *was* with him. 21Zecha-
riah the son of Meshelemiah
was keeper of the door of the
tabernacle of meeting.

22All those chosen as gatekeepers *were* two hundred
and twelve. They were re-
corded by their genealogy, in
their villages. David and Samuel the seer had appointed
them to their trusted office.
23So they and their children
were in charge of the gates
of the house of the LORD,
the house of the tabernacle,
by assignment. 24The gatekeepers were assigned to the
four directions: the east, west,
north, and south. 25And their
brethren in their villages *had*
to come with them from time
to time for seven days. 26For
in this trusted office *were* four
chief gatekeepers; they were
Levites. And they had charge
over the chambers and treasuries of the house of God.
27And they lodged *all* around
the house of God because they
had the responsibility, and
they *were* in charge of opening *it* every morning.

OTHER LEVITE RESPONSIBILITIES

28Now *some* of them were
in charge of the serving vessels, for they brought them in
and took them out by count.
29*Some* of them *were* appointed over the furnishings
and over all the implements
of the sanctuary, and over the
fine flour and the wine and
the oil and the incense and
the spices. 30And *some* of the
sons of the priests made the
ointment of the spices.

31Mattithiah of the Levites,
the firstborn of Shallum the
Korahite, had the trusted

office over the things that
were baked in the pans. [32]And
some of their brethren of the
sons of the Kohathites *were* in
charge of preparing the showbread for every Sabbath.

[33]These are the singers,
heads of the fathers' *houses* of
the Levites, *who lodged* in the
chambers, *and were* free *from
other duties;* for they were employed in *that* work day and
night. [34]These heads of the
fathers' *houses* of the Levites
were heads throughout their
generations. They dwelt at Jerusalem.

THE FAMILY OF KING SAUL

[35]Jeiel the father of Gibeon,
whose wife's name *was* Maacah, dwelt at Gibeon. [36]His
firstborn son *was* Abdon, then
Zur, Kish, Baal, Ner, Nadab, [37]
Gedor, Ahio, Zechariah,[a] and
Mikloth. [38]And Mikloth begot
Shimeam.[a] They also dwelt
alongside their relatives in Jerusalem, with their brethren.
[39]Ner begot Kish, Kish begot
Saul, and Saul begot Jonathan,
Malchishua, Abinadab, and
Esh-Baal. [40]The son of Jonathan *was* Merib-Baal, and
Merib-Baal begot Micah. [41]The
sons of Micah *were* Pithon,
Melech, Tahrea,[a] and Ahaz.[b]
[42]And Ahaz begot Jarah;[a]
Jarah begot Alemeth, Azma-
veth, and Zimri; and Zimri
begot Moza; [43]Moza begot
Binea, Rephaiah[a] his son, Eleasah his son, and Azel his son.

[44]And Azel had six sons
whose names *were* these: Azrikam, Bocheru, Ishmael, Sheariah, Obadiah, and Hanan;
these *were* the sons of Azel.

TRAGIC END OF SAUL AND HIS SONS

10 Now the Philistines
fought against Israel;
and the men of Israel fled
from before the Philistines,
and fell slain on Mount Gilboa.
[2]Then the Philistines followed
hard after Saul and his sons.
And the Philistines killed Jonathan, Abinadab, and Malchishua, Saul's sons. [3]The battle
became fierce against Saul.
The archers hit him, and he
was wounded by the archers.
[4]Then Saul said to his armorbearer, "Draw your sword, and
thrust me through with it, lest
these uncircumcised men
come and abuse me." But his
armorbearer would not, for
he was greatly afraid. Therefore Saul took a sword and fell
on it. [5]And when his armorbearer saw that Saul was dead,
he also fell on his sword and
died. [6]So Saul and his three
sons died, and all his house
died together. [7]And when all

9:37 [a] Called *Zecher* in 8:31 9:38 [a] Spelled *Shimeah* in 8:32 9:41 [a] Spelled *Tarea* in 8:35 [b] Following Arabic, Syriac, Targum, and Vulgate (compare 8:35); Masoretic Text and Septuagint omit *and Ahaz.* 9:42 [a] Spelled *Jehoaddah* in 8:36 9:43 [a] Spelled *Raphah* in 8:37

the men of Israel who *were* in
the valley saw that they had
fled and that Saul and his sons
were dead, they forsook their
cities and fled; then the Philistines came and dwelt in them.
8So it happened the next
day, when the Philistines
came to strip the slain, that
they found Saul and his sons
fallen on Mount Gilboa. 9And
they stripped him and took
his head and his armor, and
sent word throughout the
land of the Philistines to proclaim the news *in the temple*
of their idols and among the
people. 10Then they put his
armor in the temple of their
gods, and fastened his head
in the temple of Dagon.
11And when all Jabesh Gilead heard all that the Philistines had done to Saul, 12all
the valiant men arose and
took the body of Saul and the
bodies of his sons; and they
brought them to Jabesh, and
buried their bones under the
tamarisk tree at Jabesh, and
fasted seven days.
13So Saul died for his unfaithfulness which he had
committed against the LORD,
because he did not keep the
word of the LORD, and also
because he consulted a medium for guidance. 14But *he*
did not inquire of the LORD;
therefore He killed him, and
turned the kingdom over to
David the son of Jesse.

DAVID MADE KING OVER ALL ISRAEL

11 Then all Israel came together to David at He-
bron, saying, "Indeed we *are*
your bone and your flesh.
2Also, in time past, even when
Saul was king, you *were* the
one who led Israel out and
brought them in; and the
LORD your God said to you,
'You shall shepherd My people
Israel, and be ruler over My
people Israel.'" 3Therefore all
the elders of Israel came to
the king at Hebron, and David
made a covenant with them at
Hebron before the LORD. And
they anointed David king over
Israel, according to the word
of the LORD by Samuel.

THE CITY OF DAVID

4And David and all Israel
went to Jerusalem, which is
Jebus, where the Jebusites
were, the inhabitants of the
land. 5But the inhabitants of
Jebus said to David, "You shall
not come in here!" Nevertheless David took the stronghold of Zion (that is, the City
of David). 6Now David said,
"Whoever attacks the Jebusites first shall be chief and
captain." And Joab the son of
Zeruiah went up first, and became chief. 7Then David dwelt
in the stronghold; therefore
they called it the City of
David. 8And he built the city
around it, from the Millo[a] to

11:8 [a] Literally *The Landfill*

the surrounding area. Joab repaired the rest of the city. 9So David went on and became great, and the LORD of hosts *was* with him.

THE MIGHTY MEN OF DAVID

10Now these *were* the heads of the mighty men whom David had, who strengthened themselves with him in his kingdom, with all Israel, to make him king, according to the word of the LORD concerning Israel.

11And this *is* the number of the mighty men whom David had: Jashobeam the son of a Hachmonite, chief of the captains;[a] he had lifted up his spear against three hundred, killed *by him* at one time.

12After him *was* Eleazar the son of Dodo, the Ahohite, who *was one* of the three mighty men. 13He was with David at Pasdammim. Now there the Philistines were gathered for battle, and there was a piece of ground full of barley. So the people fled from the Philistines. 14But they stationed themselves in the middle of *that* field, defended it, and killed the Philistines. So the LORD brought about a great victory.

15Now three of the thirty *chief men went down* to the rock to David, into the cave of Adullam; and the army of the Philistines encamped in the Valley of Rephaim. 16David *was* then in the stronghold, and the garrison of the Philistines *was* then in Bethlehem. 17And David said with longing, “Oh, that someone would give me a drink of water from the well of Bethlehem, which is by the gate!” 18So the three broke through the camp of the Philistines, drew water from the well of Bethlehem that *was* by the gate, and took *it* and brought *it* to David. Nevertheless David would not drink it, but poured it out to the LORD. 19And he said, “Far be it from me, O my God, that I should do this! Shall I drink the blood of these men *who have put* their lives *in jeopardy?* For at the risk of their lives they brought it.” Therefore he would not drink it. These things were done by the three mighty men.

20Abishai the brother of Joab was chief of *another* three.[a] He had lifted up his spear against three hundred *men,* killed *them,* and won a name among *these* three. 21Of the three he was more honored than the other two men. Therefore he became their captain. However he did not attain to the *first* three.

11:11 [a] Following Qere; Kethib, Septuagint, and Vulgate read *the thirty* (compare 2 Samuel 23:8). 11:20 [a] Following Masoretic Text, Septuagint, and Vulgate; Syriac reads *thirty*.

22Benaiah was the son of
Jehoiada, the son of a valiant
man from Kabzeel, who had
done many deeds. He had
killed two lion-like heroes
of Moab. He also had gone
down and killed a lion in the
midst of a pit on a snowy day.
23And he killed an Egyptian,
a man of *great* height, five
cubits tall. In the Egyptian's
hand *there was* a spear like
a weaver's beam; and he
went down to him with a
staff, wrested the spear out
of the Egyptian's hand, and
killed him with his own spear.
24These *things* Benaiah the
son of Jehoiada did, and won
a name among three mighty
men. 25Indeed he was more
honored than the thirty, but
he did not attain to the *first*
three. And David appointed
him over his guard.

26Also the mighty war-
riors *were* Asahel the brother
of Joab, Elhanan the son of
Dodo of Bethlehem, 27Sham-
moth the Harorite,[a] Helez
the Pelonite,[b] 28Ira the son
of Ikkesh the Tekoite, Abiezer the Anathothite, 29Sibbe-
chai the Hushathite, Ilai the
Ahohite, 30Maharai the Netophathite, Heled[a] the son
of Baanah the Netophathite,
31Ithai[a] the son of Ribai of
Gibeah, of the sons of Benjamin, Benaiah the Pirathonite, 32Hurai[a] of the brooks of
Gaash, Abiel[b] the Arbathite,
33Azmaveth the Baharumite,[a]
Eliahba the Shaalbonite, 34the
sons of Hashem the Gizonite,
Jonathan the son of Shageh
the Hararite, 35Ahiam the son
of Sacar the Hararite, Eliphal
the son of Ur, 36Hepher the
Mecherathite, Ahijah the Pelonite, 37Hezro the Carmelite,
Naarai the son of Ezbai, 38Joel
the brother of Nathan, Mibhar
the son of Hagri, 39Zelek the
Ammonite, Naharai the Be-
rothite[a] (the armorbearer of
Joab the son of Zeruiah), 40Ira
the Ithrite, Gareb the Ithrite,
41Uriah the Hittite, Zabad the
son of Ahlai, 42Adina the son
of Shiza the Reubenite (a chief
of the Reubenites) and thirty
with him, 43Hanan the son of
Maachah, Joshaphat the Mith-
nite, 44Uzzia the Ashterathite,
Shama and Jeiel the sons of
Hotham the Aroerite, 45Je-
diael the son of Shimri, and
Joha his brother, the Tizite,
46Eliel the Mahavite, Jeribai
and Joshaviah the sons of El-
naam, Ithmah the Moabite,
47Eliel, Obed, and Jaasiel the
Mezobaite.

11:27 [a] Spelled *Harodite* in 2 Samuel 23:25 [b] Called *Paltite* in 2 Samuel 23:26 **11:30** [a] Spelled *Heleb* in 2 Samuel 23:29 and *Heldai* in 1 Chronicles 27:15 **11:31** [a] Spelled *Ittai* in 2 Samuel 23:29 **11:32** [a] Spelled *Hiddai* in 2 Samuel 23:30 [b] Spelled *Abi-Albon* in 2 Samuel 23:31 **11:33** [a] Spelled *Barhumite* in 2 Samuel 23:31 **11:39** [a] Spelled *Beerothite* in 2 Samuel 23:37

THE GROWTH OF DAVID'S ARMY

12 Now these *were* the men
who came to David at
Ziklag while he was still a fugitive from Saul the son of
Kish; and they *were* among
the mighty men, helpers in
the war, 2armed with bows,
using both the right hand and
the left in *hurling* stones and
shooting arrows with the bow.
They were of Benjamin, Saul's
brethren.
3The chief *was* Ahiezer, then
Joash, the sons of Shemaah
the Gibeathite; Jeziel and
Pelet the sons of Azmaveth;
Berachah, and Jehu the Anathothite; 4Ishmaiah the Gibeonite, a mighty man among
the thirty, and over the thirty;
Jeremiah, Jahaziel, Johanan,
and Jozabad the Gederathite;
5Eluzai, Jerimoth, Bealiah,
Shemariah, and Shephatiah
the Haruphite; 6Elkanah, Jis-
shiah, Azarel, Joezer, and Jashobeam, the Korahites; 7and
Joelah and Zebadiah the sons
of Jeroham of Gedor.
8*Some* Gadites joined David
at the stronghold in the wilderness, mighty men of valor,
men trained for battle, who
could handle shield and spear,
whose faces *were like* the faces
of lions, and *were* as swift as gazelles on the mountains: 9Ezer
the first, Obadiah the second,
Eliab the third, 10Mishman-
nah the fourth, Jeremiah the
fifth, 11Attai the sixth, Eliel the
seventh, 12Johanan the eighth,
Elzabad the ninth, 13Jeremiah
the tenth, and Machbanai the
eleventh. 14These *were* from
the sons of Gad, captains of
the army; the least was over a
hundred, and the greatest was
over a thousand. 15These *are*
the ones who crossed the Jordan in the first month, when it
had overflowed all its banks;
and they put to flight all *those*
in the valleys, to the east and
to the west.
16Then some of the sons of
Benjamin and Judah came to
David at the stronghold. 17And
David went out to meet them,
and answered and said to them,
"If you have come peaceably to
me to help me, my heart will be
united with you; but if to betray
me to my enemies, since *there
is* no wrong in my hands, may
the God of our fathers look and
bring judgment." 18Then the
Spirit came upon Amasai, chief
of the captains, *and he said:*

"*We are* yours, O David;
We *are* on your side,
  O son of Jesse!
Peace, peace to you,
And peace to your
  helpers!
For your God helps you."

So David received them, and
made them captains of the
troop.
19And *some* from Manas-
seh defected to David when
he was going with the Philistines to battle against Saul;
but they did not help them,

for the lords of the Philistines
sent him away by agreement,
saying, "He may defect to his
master Saul *and endanger* our
heads." 20When he went to
Ziklag, those of Manasseh who
defected to him were Adnah,
Jozabad, Jediael, Michael,
Jozabad, Elihu, and Zillethai,
captains of the thousands who
were from Manasseh. 21And
they helped David against
the bands *of raiders,* for they
were all mighty men of valor,
and they were captains in the
army. 22For at *that* time they
came to David day by day to
help him, until *it was* a great
army, like the army of God.

DAVID'S ARMY AT HEBRON

23Now these *were* the numbers of the divisions *that were*
equipped for war, *and* came to
David at Hebron to turn *over*
the kingdom of Saul to him,
according to the word of the
LORD: 24of the sons of Judah
bearing shield and spear,
six thousand eight hundred
armed for war; 25of the sons
of Simeon, mighty men of
valor fit for war, seven thousand one hundred; 26of the
sons of Levi four thousand
six hundred; 27Jehoiada, the
leader of the Aaronites, and
with him three thousand
seven hundred; 28Zadok, a
young man, a valiant warrior,
and from his father's house
twenty-two captains; 29of the
sons of Benjamin, relatives
of Saul, three thousand (until
then the greatest part of them
had remained loyal to the
house of Saul); 30of the sons
of Ephraim twenty thousand
eight hundred, mighty men of
valor, famous men throughout their father's house; 31of
the half-tribe of Manasseh
eighteen thousand, who were
designated by name to come
and make David king; 32of
the sons of Issachar who had
understanding of the times, to
know what Israel ought to do,
their chiefs were two hundred;
and all their brethren were at
their command; 33of Zebulun
there were fifty thousand who
went out to battle, expert in
war with all weapons of war,
stouthearted men who could
keep ranks; 34of Naphtali one
thousand captains, and with
them thirty-seven thousand
with shield and spear; 35of the
Danites who could keep battle formation, twenty-eight
thousand six hundred; 36of
Asher, those who could go out
to war, able to keep battle formation, forty thousand; 37of
the Reubenites and the Gadites and the half-tribe of Manasseh, from the other side
of the Jordan, one hundred
and twenty thousand armed
for battle with every *kind* of
weapon of war.

38All these men of war,
who could keep ranks, came
to Hebron with a loyal heart,
to make David king over all
Israel; and all the rest of Israel *were* of one mind to

make David king. 39And they
were there with David three
days, eating and drinking, for
their brethren had prepared
for them. 40Moreover those
who were near to them, from
as far away as Issachar and
Zebulun and Naphtali, were
bringing food on donkeys and
camels, on mules and oxen—
provisions of flour and cakes
of figs and cakes of raisins,
wine and oil and oxen and
sheep abundantly, for *there*
was joy in Israel.

THE ARK BROUGHT FROM KIRJATH JEARIM

13 Then David consulted
with the captains of
thousands and hundreds, *and*
with every leader. 2And David
said to all the assembly of Israel, "If *it seems* good to you,
and if it is of the LORD our God,
let us send out to our brethren everywhere *who are* left
in all the land of Israel, and
with them to the priests and
Levites *who are* in their cities
and their common-lands, that
they may gather together to
us; 3and let us bring the ark
of our God back to us, for we
have not inquired at it since
the days of Saul." 4Then all the
assembly said that they would
do so, for the thing was right
in the eyes of all the people.

5So David gathered all Israel together, from Shihor in
Egypt to as far as the entrance
of Hamath, to bring the ark
of God from Kirjath Jearim.
6And David and all Israel went
up to Baalah,[a] to Kirjath Jearim, which belonged to Judah,
to bring up from there the ark
of God the LORD, who dwells
between the cherubim, where
His name is proclaimed. 7So
they carried the ark of God
on a new cart from the house
of Abinadab, and Uzza and
Ahio drove the cart. 8Then
David and all Israel played
music before God with all *their*
might, with singing, on harps,
on stringed instruments, on
tambourines, on cymbals, and
with trumpets.

9And when they came to
Chidon's[a] threshing floor,
Uzza put out his hand to hold
the ark, for the oxen stumbled.
10Then the anger of the LORD
was aroused against Uzza, and
He struck him because he put
his hand to the ark; and he
died there before God. 11And
David became angry because
of the LORD's outbreak against
Uzza; therefore that place is
called Perez Uzza[a] to this day.
12David was afraid of God that
day, saying, "How can I bring
the ark of God to me?"

13So David would not
move the ark with him into
the City of David, but took it
aside into the house of Obed-
Edom the Gittite. 14The ark of

13:6 [a] Called *Baale Judah* in 2 Samuel 6:2 13:9 [a] Called *Nachon* in 2 Samuel 6:6 13:11 [a] Literally *Outburst Against Uzza*

God remained with the family
of Obed-Edom in his house
three months. And the LORD
blessed the house of Obed-
Edom and all that he had.

DAVID ESTABLISHED AT JERUSALEM

14 Now Hiram king of Tyre
sent messengers to
David, and cedar trees, with
masons and carpenters, to
build him a house. 2So David
knew that the LORD had established him as king over
Israel, for his kingdom was
highly exalted for the sake of
His people Israel.

3Then David took more
wives in Jerusalem, and David
begot more sons and daughters. 4And these are the names
of his children whom he had in
Jerusalem: Shammua,[a] Shobab, Nathan, Solomon, 5Ibhar,
Elishua,[a] Elpelet,[b] 6Nogah, Nepheg, Japhia, 7Elishama, Beeliada,[a] and Eliphelet.

THE PHILISTINES DEFEATED

8Now when the Philistines
heard that David had been
anointed king over all Israel, all the Philistines went
up to search for David. And
David heard *of it* and went
out against them. 9Then the
Philistines went and made a
raid on the Valley of Rephaim.
10And David inquired of God,
saying, "Shall I go up against
the Philistines? Will You deliver them into my hand?"

The LORD said to him, "Go
up, for I will deliver them into
your hand."

11So they went up to Baal
Perazim, and David defeated
them there. Then David said,
"God has broken through
my enemies by my hand like
a breakthrough of water."
Therefore they called the
name of that place Baal Perazim.[a] 12And when they left
their gods there, David gave
a commandment, and they
were burned with fire.

13Then the Philistines once
again made a raid on the
valley. 14Therefore David inquired again of God, and God
said to him, "You shall not go
up after them; circle around
them, and come upon them
in front of the mulberry trees.
15And it shall be, when you
hear a sound of marching in
the tops of the mulberry trees,
then you shall go out to battle,
for God has gone out before
you to strike the camp of the
Philistines." 16So David did as
God commanded him, and
they drove back the army of
the Philistines from Gibeon as
far as Gezer. 17Then the fame of
David went out into all lands,
and the LORD brought the fear
of him upon all nations.

14:4 [a] Spelled *Shimea* in 3:5 14:5 [a] Spelled *Elishama* in 3:6 [b] Spelled *Eliphelet* in 3:6 14:7 [a] Spelled *Eliada* in 3:8 14:11 [a] Literally *Master of Breakthroughs*

THE ARK BROUGHT TO JERUSALEM

15 *David* built houses for himself in the City of David; and he prepared a place for the ark of God, and pitched a tent for it. 2Then David said, "No one may carry the ark of God but the Levites, for the LORD has chosen them to carry the ark of God and to minister before Him forever." 3And David gathered all Israel together at Jerusalem, to bring up the ark of the LORD to its place, which he had prepared for it. 4Then David assembled the children of Aaron and the Levites: 5of the sons of Kohath, Uriel the chief, and one hundred and twenty of his brethren; 6of the sons of Merari, Asaiah the chief, and two hundred and twenty of his brethren; 7of the sons of Gershom, Joel the chief, and one hundred and thirty of his brethren; 8of the sons of Elizaphan, Shemaiah the chief, and two hundred of his brethren; 9of the sons of Hebron, Eliel the chief, and eighty of his brethren; 10of the sons of Uzziel, Amminadab the chief, and one hundred and twelve of his brethren.

11And David called for Zadok and Abiathar the priests, and for the Levites: for Uriel, Asaiah, Joel, Shemaiah, Eliel, and Amminadab. 12He said to them, "You *are* the heads of the fathers' *houses* of the Levites; sanctify yourselves, you and your brethren, that you may bring up the ark of the LORD God of Israel to *the place* I have prepared for it. 13For because you *did* not *do it* the first *time,* the LORD our God broke out against us, because we did not consult Him about the proper order."

14So the priests and the Levites sanctified themselves to bring up the ark of the LORD God of Israel. 15And the children of the Levites bore the ark of God on their shoulders, by its poles, as Moses had commanded according to the word of the LORD.

16Then David spoke to the leaders of the Levites to appoint their brethren *to be* the singers accompanied by instruments of music, stringed instruments, harps, and cymbals, by raising the voice with resounding joy. 17So the Levites appointed Heman the son of Joel; and of his brethren, Asaph the son of Berechiah; and of their brethren, the sons of Merari, Ethan the son of Kushaiah; 18and with them their brethren of the second *rank:* Zechariah, Ben,[a] Jaaziel, Shemiramoth, Jehiel, Unni, Eliab, Benaiah, Maaseiah, Mattithiah, Elipheleh, Mikneiah, Obed-Edom, and Jeiel, the gatekeepers; 19the singers, Heman, Asaph,

15:18 [a] Following Masoretic Text and Vulgate; Septuagint omits *Ben.*

and Ethan, *were* to sound the
cymbals of bronze; 20Zecha-
riah, Aziel, Shemiramoth, Jehiel, Unni, Eliab, Maaseiah,
and Benaiah, with strings according to Alamoth; 21Matti-
thiah, Elipheleh, Mikneiah,
Obed-Edom, Jeiel, and Azaziah, to direct with harps on
the Sheminith; 22Chenaniah,
leader of the Levites, was
instructor *in charge of* the
music, because he *was* skillful; 23Berechiah and Elkanah
were doorkeepers for the ark;
24Shebaniah, Joshaphat, Nethanel, Amasai, Zechariah, Benaiah, and Eliezer, the priests,
were to blow the trumpets
before the ark of God; and
Obed-Edom and Jehiah, doorkeepers for the ark.

25So David, the elders of
Israel, and the captains over
thousands went to bring up
the ark of the covenant of
the LORD from the house of
Obed-Edom with joy. 26And
so it was, when God helped
the Levites who bore the ark
of the covenant of the LORD,
that they offered seven bulls
and seven rams. 27David
was clothed with a robe of
fine linen, as were all the Levites who bore the ark, the
singers, and Chenaniah the
music master *with* the singers.
David also wore a linen ephod.
28Thus all Israel brought up
the ark of the covenant of the
LORD with shouting and with
the sound of the horn, with
trumpets and with cymbals,
making music with stringed
instruments and harps.

29And it happened, *as*
the ark of the covenant of
the LORD came to the City
of David, that Michal, Saul's
daughter, looked through a
window and saw King David
whirling and playing music;
and she despised him in her
heart.

THE ARK PLACED IN THE TABERNACLE

16 So they brought the ark
of God, and set it in the
midst of the tabernacle that
David had erected for it. Then
they offered burnt offerings
and peace offerings before
God. 2And when David had
finished offering the burnt
offerings and the peace offerings, he blessed the people in
the name of the LORD. 3Then
he distributed to everyone of
Israel, both man and woman,
to everyone a loaf of bread, a
piece *of meat,* and a cake of
raisins.

4And he appointed some
of the Levites to minister before the ark of the LORD, to
commemorate, to thank, and
to praise the LORD God of Israel: 5Asaph the chief, and
next to him Zechariah, *then*
Jeiel, Shemiramoth, Jehiel,
Mattithiah, Eliab, Benaiah,
and Obed-Edom: Jeiel with
stringed instruments and
harps, but Asaph made music
with cymbals; 6Benaiah and
Jahaziel the priests regularly

blew the trumpets before the ark of the covenant of God.

DAVID'S SONG OF THANKSGIVING

7On that day David first
delivered *this psalm* into the
hand of Asaph and his brethren, to thank the LORD:

8 Oh, give thanks
to the LORD!
Call upon His name;
Make known His deeds
among the peoples!
9 Sing to Him, sing
psalms to Him;
Talk of all His
wondrous works!
10 Glory in His holy name;
Let the hearts of
those rejoice who
seek the LORD!
11 Seek the LORD and
His strength;
Seek His face evermore!
12 Remember His
marvelous works
which He has done,
His wonders, and
the judgments
of His mouth,
13 O seed of Israel
His servant,
You children of Jacob,
His chosen ones!

14 He *is* the LORD our God;
His judgments *are*
in all the earth.
15 Remember His
covenant forever,
The word which He
commanded, for a
thousand generations,
16 *The covenant which*
He made with
Abraham,
And His oath to Isaac,
17 And confirmed it to
Jacob for a statute,
To Israel *for* an
everlasting covenant,
18 Saying, "To you I will give
the land of Canaan
As the allotment of
your inheritance,"
19 When you were few
in number,
Indeed very few, and
strangers in it.

20 When they went from
one nation to another,
And from *one* kingdom
to another people,
21 He permitted no man
to do them wrong;
Yes, He rebuked kings
for their sakes,
22 *Saying,* "Do not touch
My anointed ones,
And do My prophets
no harm."[a]

23 Sing to the LORD,
all the earth;
Proclaim the good
news of His salvation
from day to day.
24 Declare His glory
among the nations,
His wonders among
all peoples.

16:22 [a] Compare verses 8–22 with Psalm 105:1–15

25 For the LORD *is* great
and greatly to
be praised;
He *is* also to be feared
above all gods.
26 For all the gods of the
peoples *are* idols,
But the LORD made
the heavens.
27 Honor and majesty
are before Him;
Strength and gladness
are in His place.

28 Give to the LORD,
O families of
the peoples,
Give to the LORD glory
and strength.
29 Give to the LORD the
glory *due* His name;
Bring an offering, and
come before Him.
Oh, worship the LORD
in the beauty
of holiness!
30 Tremble before Him,
all the earth.
The world also is
firmly established,
It shall not be moved.

31 Let the heavens
rejoice, and let the
earth be glad;
And let them say
among the nations,
"The LORD reigns."
32 Let the sea roar, and
all its fullness;
Let the field rejoice,
and all that *is* in it.
33 Then the trees of the
woods shall rejoice
before the LORD,
For He is coming to
judge the earth.[a]

34 Oh, give thanks to
the LORD, for
He is good!
For His mercy
endures forever.[a]
35 And say, "Save us, O God
of our salvation;
Gather us together,
and deliver us from
the Gentiles,
To give thanks to
Your holy name,
To triumph in
Your praise."

36 Blessed *be* the LORD
God of Israel
From everlasting to
everlasting![a]

And all the people said, "Amen!" and praised the LORD.

REGULAR WORSHIP MAINTAINED

37So he left Asaph and his
brothers there before the ark
of the covenant of the LORD
to minister before the ark
regularly, as every day's work
required; 38and Obed-Edom

16:33 [a] Compare verses 23–33 with Psalm 96:1–13 16:34 [a] Compare verse 34 with Psalm 106:1 16:36 [a] Compare verses 35, 36 with Psalm 106:47, 48

with his sixty-eight brethren, including Obed-Edom the son of Jeduthun, and Hosah, *to be* gatekeepers; 39and Zadok the priest and his brethren the priests, before the tabernacle of the LORD at the high place that *was* at Gibeon, 40to offer burnt offerings to the LORD on the altar of burnt offering regularly morning and evening, and *to do* according to all that is written in the Law of the LORD which He commanded Israel; 41and with them Heman and Jeduthun and the rest who were chosen, who were designated by name, to give thanks to the LORD, because His mercy *endures* forever; 42and with them Heman and Jeduthun, to sound aloud with trumpets and cymbals and the musical instruments of God. Now the sons of Jeduthun *were* gatekeepers.

43Then all the people departed, every man to his house; and David returned to bless his house.

GOD'S COVENANT WITH DAVID

17 Now it came to pass, when David was dwelling in his house, that David said to Nathan the prophet, "See now, I dwell in a house of cedar, but the ark of the covenant of the LORD *is* under tent curtains."

2Then Nathan said to David, "Do all that *is* in your heart, for God *is* with you."

3But it happened that night that the word of God came to Nathan, saying, 4"Go and tell My servant David, 'Thus says the LORD: "You shall not build Me a house to dwell in. 5For I have not dwelt in a house since the time that I brought up Israel, even to this day, but have gone from tent to tent, and from *one* tabernacle *to another.* 6Wherever I have moved about with all Israel, have I ever spoken a word to any of the judges of Israel, whom I commanded to shepherd My people, saying, 'Why have you not built Me a house of cedar?'"' 7Now therefore, thus shall you say to My servant David, 'Thus says the LORD of hosts: "I took you from the sheepfold, from following the sheep, to be ruler over My people Israel. 8And I have been with you wherever you have gone, and have cut off all your enemies from before you, and have made you a name like the name of the great men who *are* on the earth. 9Moreover I will appoint a place for My people Israel, and will plant them, that they may dwell in a place of their own and move no more; nor shall the sons of wickedness oppress them anymore, as previously, 10since the time that I commanded judges *to be* over My people Israel. Also I will subdue all your enemies. Furthermore I tell you that the LORD will build

you a house.[a] 11And it shall be, when your days are fulfilled, when you must go *to be* with your fathers, that I will set up your seed after you, who will be of your sons; and I will establish his kingdom. 12He shall build Me a house, and I will establish his throne forever. 13I will be his Father, and he shall be My son; and I will not take My mercy away from him, as I took *it* from *him* who was before you. 14And I will establish him in My house and in My kingdom forever; and his throne shall be established forever.""'

15According to all these words and according to all this vision, so Nathan spoke to David.

16Then King David went in and sat before the LORD; and he said: "Who *am* I, O LORD God? And what is my house, that You have brought me this far? 17And *yet* this was a small thing in Your sight, O God; and You have *also* spoken of Your servant's house for a great while to come, and have regarded me according to the rank of a man of high degree, O LORD God. 18What more can David *say* to You for the honor of Your servant? For You know Your servant. 19O LORD, for Your servant's sake, and according to Your own heart, You have done all this greatness, in making known all these great things. 20O LORD, *there is* none like You, nor *is there any* God besides You, according to all that we have heard with our ears. 21And who *is* like Your people Israel, the one nation on the earth whom God went to redeem for Himself *as* a people—to make for Yourself a name by great and awesome deeds, by driving out nations from before Your people whom You redeemed from Egypt? 22For You have made Your people Israel Your very own people forever; and You, LORD, have become their God.

23"And now, O LORD, the word which You have spoken concerning Your servant and concerning his house, *let it* be established forever, and do as You have said. 24So let it be established, that Your name may be magnified forever, saying, 'The LORD of hosts, the God of Israel, *is* Israel's God.' And let the house of Your servant David be established before You. 25For You, O my God, have revealed to Your servant that You will build him a house. Therefore Your servant has found it *in his heart* to pray before You. 26And now, LORD, You are God, and have promised this goodness to Your servant. 27Now You have been pleased to bless the house of Your servant, that it may continue

17:10 [a] That is, a royal dynasty

before You forever; for You have blessed it, O LORD, and *it shall be* blessed forever."

DAVID'S FURTHER CONQUESTS

18 After this it came to pass that David attacked the Philistines, subdued them, and took Gath and its towns from the hand of the Philistines. 2 Then he defeated Moab, and the Moabites became David's servants, *and* brought tribute.

3 And David defeated Hadadezer[a] king of Zobah *as far as* Hamath, as he went to establish his power by the River Euphrates. 4 David took from him one thousand chariots, seven thousand[a] horsemen, and twenty thousand foot soldiers. Also David hamstrung all the chariot *horses,* except that he spared enough of them for one hundred chariots.

5 When the Syrians of Damascus came to help Hadadezer king of Zobah, David killed twenty-two thousand of the Syrians. 6 Then David put *garrisons* in Syria of Damascus; and the Syrians became David's servants, *and* brought tribute. So the LORD preserved David wherever he went. 7 And David took the shields of gold that were on the servants of Hadadezer, and brought them to Jerusalem. 8 Also from Tibhath[a] and from Chun, cities of Hadadezer, David brought a large amount of bronze, with which Solomon made the bronze Sea, the pillars, and the articles of bronze.

9 Now when Tou[a] king of Hamath heard that David had defeated all the army of Hadadezer king of Zobah, 10 he sent Hadoram[a] his son to King David, to greet him and bless him, because he had fought against Hadadezer and defeated him (for Hadadezer had been at war with Tou); and *Hadoram brought with him* all kinds of articles of gold, silver, and bronze. 11 King David also dedicated these to the LORD, along with the silver and gold that he had brought from all *these* nations—from Edom, from Moab, from the people of Ammon, from the Philistines, and from Amalek.

12 Moreover Abishai the son of Zeruiah killed eighteen thousand Edomites[a] in the Valley of Salt. 13 He also put garrisons in Edom, and all the Edomites became David's servants. And the LORD preserved David wherever he went.

DAVID'S ADMINISTRATION

14 So David reigned over all Israel, and administered judgment and justice to all

18:3 [a] Hebrew *Hadarezer,* and so throughout chapters 18 and 19
18:4 [a] Or *seven hundred* (compare 2 Samuel 8:4) 18:8 [a] Spelled *Betah* in 2 Samuel 8:8 18:9 [a] Spelled *Toi* in 2 Samuel 8:9, 10 18:10 [a] Spelled *Joram* in 2 Samuel 8:10 18:12 [a] Or *Syrians* (compare 2 Samuel 8:13)

his people. 15Joab the son of Zeruiah *was* over the army; Jehoshaphat the son of Ahilud *was* recorder; 16Zadok the son of Ahitub and Abimelech the son of Abiathar *were* the priests; Shavsha[a] *was* the scribe; 17Benaiah the son of Jehoiada *was* over the Cherethites and the Pelethites; and David's sons *were* chief ministers at the king's side.

THE AMMONITES AND SYRIANS DEFEATED

19 It happened after this that Nahash the king of the people of Ammon died, and his son reigned in his place. 2Then David said, "I will show kindness to Hanun the son of Nahash, because his father showed kindness to me." So David sent messengers to comfort him concerning his father. And David's servants came to Hanun in the land of the people of Ammon to comfort him.

3And the princes of the people of Ammon said to Hanun, "Do you think that David really honors your father because he has sent comforters to you? Did his servants not come to you to search and to overthrow and to spy out the land?"

4Therefore Hanun took David's servants, shaved them, and cut off their garments in the middle, at their buttocks, and sent them away. 5Then *some* went and told David about the men; and he sent to meet them, because the men were greatly ashamed. And the king said, "Wait at Jericho until your beards have grown, and *then* return."

6When the people of Ammon saw that they had made themselves repulsive to David, Hanun and the people of Ammon sent a thousand talents of silver to hire for themselves chariots and horsemen from Mesopotamia,[a] from Syrian Maacah, and from Zobah.[b] 7So they hired for themselves thirty-two thousand chariots, with the king of Maacah and his people, who came and encamped before Medeba. Also the people of Ammon gathered together from their cities, and came to battle.

8Now when David heard *of it,* he sent Joab and all the army of the mighty men. 9Then the people of Ammon came out and put themselves in battle array before the gate of the city, and the kings who had come *were* by themselves in the field.

10When Joab saw that the battle line was against him before and behind, he chose some of Israel's best and put *them* in battle array against

18:16 [a] Spelled *Seraiah* in 2 Samuel 8:17 19:6 [a] Hebrew *Aram Naharaim* [b] Spelled *Zoba* in 2 Samuel 10:6

the Syrians. 11And the rest
of the people he put under
the command of Abishai his
brother, and they set *them-*
selves in battle array against
the people of Ammon. 12Then
he said, "If the Syrians are too
strong for me, then you shall
help me; but if the people of
Ammon are too strong for
you, then I will help you. 13Be
of good courage, and let us be
strong for our people and for
the cities of our God. And may
the LORD do *what is* good in
His sight."

14So Joab and the people
who *were* with him drew near
for the battle against the Syrians, and they fled before him.
15When the people of Ammon
saw that the Syrians were
fleeing, they also fled before
Abishai his brother, and entered the city. So Joab went
to Jerusalem.

16Now when the Syrians saw
that they had been defeated by
Israel, they sent messengers
and brought the Syrians who
were beyond the River,[a] and
Shophach[b] the commander
of Hadadezer's army *went* before them. 17When it was told
David, he gathered all Israel,
crossed over the Jordan and
came upon them, and set up
in battle array against them.
So when David had set up in
battle array against the Syrians, they fought with him.
18Then the Syrians fled before
Israel; and David killed seven
thousand[a] charioteers and
forty thousand foot soldiers[b]
of the Syrians, and killed Shophach the commander of the
army. 19And when the ser-
vants of Hadadezer saw that
they were defeated by Israel,
they made peace with David
and became his servants. So
the Syrians were not willing
to help the people of Ammon
anymore.

RABBAH IS CONQUERED

20 It happened in the
spring of the year,
at the time kings go out *to*
battle, that Joab led out the
armed forces and ravaged
the country of the people of
Ammon, and came and be-
sieged Rabbah. But David
stayed at Jerusalem. And Joab
defeated Rabbah and over-
threw it. 2Then David took
their king's crown from his
head, and found it to weigh a
talent of gold, and *there were*
precious stones in it. And it
was set on David's head. Also
he brought out the spoil of the
city in great abundance. 3And
he brought out the people
who *were* in it, and put *them*
to work[a] with saws, with iron
picks, and with axes. So David
did to all the cities of the peo-

19:16 [a] That is, the Euphrates [b] Spelled *Shobach* in 2 Samuel 10:16
19:18 [a] Or *seven hundred* (compare 2 Samuel 10:18) [b] Or *horsemen* (compare 2 Samuel 10:18) 20:3 [a] Septuagint reads *cut them.*

ple of Ammon. Then David and all the people returned *to* Jerusalem.

PHILISTINE GIANTS DESTROYED

4 Now it happened afterward that war broke out at Gezer with the Philistines, at which time Sibbechai the Hushathite killed Sippai,[a] *who was one* of the sons of the giant. And they were subdued.

5 Again there was war with the Philistines, and Elhanan the son of Jair[a] killed Lahmi the brother of Goliath the Gittite, the shaft of whose spear *was* like a weaver's beam.

6 Yet again there was war at Gath, where there was a man of *great* stature, with twenty-four fingers and toes, six *on each hand* and six *on each foot;* and he also was born to the giant. 7 So when he defied Israel, Jonathan the son of Shimea,[a] David's brother, killed him.

8 These were born to the giant in Gath, and they fell by the hand of David and by the hand of his servants.

THE CENSUS OF ISRAEL AND JUDAH

21 Now Satan stood up against Israel, and moved David to number Israel. 2 So David said to Joab and to the leaders of the people, "Go, number Israel from Beersheba to Dan, and bring the number of them to me that I may know *it.*"

3 And Joab answered, "May the LORD make His people a hundred times more than they are. But, my lord the king, *are* they not all my lord's servants? Why then does my lord require this thing? Why should he be a cause of guilt in Israel?"

4 Nevertheless the king's word prevailed against Joab. Therefore Joab departed and went throughout all Israel and came to Jerusalem. 5 Then Joab gave the sum of the number of the people to David. All Israel *had* one million one hundred thousand men who drew the sword, and Judah *had* four hundred and seventy thousand men who drew the sword. 6 But he did not count Levi and Benjamin among them, for the king's word was abominable to Joab.

7 And God was displeased with this thing; therefore He struck Israel. 8 So David said to God, "I have sinned greatly, because I have done this thing; but now, I pray, take away the iniquity of Your servant, for I have done very foolishly."

9 Then the LORD spoke to

20:4 [a] Spelled *Saph* in 2 Samuel 21:18 **20:5** [a] Spelled *Jaare-Oregim* in 2 Samuel 21:19 **20:7** [a] Spelled *Shimeah* in 2 Samuel 21:21 and *Shammah* in 1 Samuel 16:9

Gad, David's seer, saying, 10"Go
and tell David, saying, 'Thus
says the LORD: "I offer you
three *things;* choose one of
them for yourself, that I may
do *it* to you."'"
11So Gad came to David
and said to him, "Thus says
the LORD: 'Choose for yourself, 12either three[a] years of
famine, or three months to be
defeated by your foes with the
sword of your enemies over-
taking *you,* or else for three
days the sword of the LORD—
the plague in the land, with the
angel[b] of the LORD destroying
throughout all the territory
of Israel.' Now consider what
answer I should take back to
Him who sent me."
13And David said to Gad, "I
am in great distress. Please let
me fall into the hand of the
LORD, for His mercies *are* very
great; but do not let me fall
into the hand of man."
14So the LORD sent a plague
upon Israel, and seventy thousand men of Israel fell. 15And
God sent an angel to Jerusalem to destroy it. As he[a] was
destroying, the LORD looked
and relented of the disaster,
and said to the angel who was
destroying, "It is enough; now
restrain your[b] hand." And the
angel of the LORD stood by the
threshing floor of Ornan[c] the
Jebusite.
16Then David lifted his eyes
and saw the angel of the LORD
standing between earth and
heaven, having in his hand
a drawn sword stretched out
over Jerusalem. So David
and the elders, clothed in
sackcloth, fell on their faces.
17And David said to God, "Was
it not I who commanded the
people to be numbered? I am
the one who has sinned and
done evil indeed; but these
sheep, what have they done?
Let Your hand, I pray, O LORD
my God, be against me and my
father's house, but not against
Your people that they should
be plagued."
18Therefore, the angel of
the LORD commanded Gad to
say to David that David should
go and erect an altar to the
LORD on the threshing floor
of Ornan the Jebusite. 19So
David went up at the word of
Gad, which he had spoken in
the name of the LORD. 20Now
Ornan turned and saw the
angel; and his four sons *who
were* with him hid themselves,
but Ornan continued threshing wheat. 21So David came
to Ornan, and Ornan looked
and saw David. And he went
out from the threshing floor,
and bowed before David with
his face to the ground. 22Then
David said to Ornan, "Grant
me the place of *this* thresh-

21:12 [a] Or *seven* (compare 2 Samuel 24:13) [b] Or *Angel*, and so elsewhere in this chapter 21:15 [a] Or *He* [b] Or *Your* [c] Spelled *Araunah* in 2 Samuel 24:16

ing floor, that I may build an
altar on it to the LORD. You
shall grant it to me at the full
price, that the plague may be
withdrawn from the people."
23But Ornan said to David,
"Take *it* to yourself, and let
my lord the king do *what is*
good in his eyes. Look, I *also*
give *you* the oxen for burnt
offerings, the threshing implements for wood, and the
wheat for the grain offering;
I give *it* all."
24Then King David said to
Ornan, "No, but I will surely
buy *it* for the full price, for I
will not take what is yours for
the LORD, nor offer burnt offerings with *that which* costs
me nothing." 25So David gave
Ornan six hundred shekels of
gold by weight for the place.
26And David built there an
altar to the LORD, and offered
burnt offerings and peace
offerings, and called on the
LORD; and He answered him
from heaven by fire on the
altar of burnt offering.
27So the LORD commanded
the angel, and he returned his
sword to its sheath.
28At that time, when David
saw that the LORD had an-
swered him on the threshing
floor of Ornan the Jebusite,
he sacrificed there. 29For the
tabernacle of the LORD and
the altar of the burnt offering,
which Moses had made in the
wilderness, *were* at that time
at the high place in Gibeon.
30But David could not go before it to inquire of God, for
he was afraid of the sword of
the angel of the LORD.

DAVID PREPARES TO BUILD THE TEMPLE

22 Then David said,
"This *is* the house of
the LORD God, and this *is*
the altar of burnt offering
for Israel." 2So David commanded to gather the aliens
who *were* in the land of Israel;
and he appointed masons to
cut hewn stones to build the
house of God. 3And David prepared iron in abundance for
the nails of the doors of the
gates and for the joints, and
bronze in abundance beyond
measure, 4and cedar trees in
abundance; for the Sidonians
and those from Tyre brought
much cedar wood to David.
5Now David said, "Solomon
my son *is* young and inexperienced, and the house to be
built for the LORD *must be*
exceedingly magnificent, famous and glorious throughout all countries. I will now
make preparation for it." So
David made abundant preparations before his death.
6Then he called for his son
Solomon, and charged him
to build a house for the LORD
God of Israel. 7And David
said to Solomon: "My son, as
for me, it was in my mind to
build a house to the name of
the LORD my God; 8but the
word of the LORD came to me,
saying, 'You have shed much

blood and have made great
wars; you shall not build a
house for My name, because
you have shed much blood on
the earth in My sight. 9Behold,
a son shall be born to you,
who shall be a man of rest;
and I will give him rest from
all his enemies all around.
His name shall be Solomon,[a]
for I will give peace and quietness to Israel in his days.
10He shall build a house for
My name, and he shall be My
son, and I *will be* his Father;
and I will establish the throne
of his kingdom over Israel
forever.' 11Now, my son, may
the LORD be with you; and
may you prosper, and build
the house of the LORD your
God, as He has said to you.
12Only may the LORD give you
wisdom and understanding,
and give you charge concerning Israel, that you may keep
the law of the LORD your God.
13Then you will prosper, if you
take care to fulfill the statutes
and judgments with which
the LORD charged Moses concerning Israel. Be strong and
of good courage; do not fear
nor be dismayed. 14Indeed
I have taken much trouble
to prepare for the house of
the LORD one hundred thousand talents of gold and one
million talents of silver, and
*bronze and iron beyond mea-
sure,* for it is so abundant. I
have prepared timber and
stone also, and you may add
to them. 15Moreover *there
are* workmen with you in
abundance: woodsmen and
stonecutters, and all types of
skillful men for every kind
of work. 16Of gold and silver
and bronze and iron *there
is* no limit. Arise and begin
working, and the LORD be
with you."

17David also commanded
all the leaders of Israel to help
Solomon his son, *saying,* 18"Is
not the LORD your God with
you? And has He *not* given
you rest on every side? For
He has given the inhabitants
of the land into my hand, and
the land is subdued before the
LORD and before His people.
19Now set your heart and your
soul to seek the LORD your
God. Therefore arise and build
the sanctuary of the LORD
God, to bring the ark of the
covenant of the LORD and
the holy articles of God into
the house that is to be built for
the name of the LORD."

THE DIVISIONS OF THE LEVITES

23 So when David was
old and full of days, he
made his son Solomon king
over Israel.

2And he gathered together
all the leaders of Israel, with
the priests and the Levites.
3Now the Levites were numbered from the age of thirty

22:9 [a] Literally *Peaceful*

years and above; and the number of individual males was thirty-eight thousand. 4Of these, twenty-four thousand *were* to look after the work of the house of the LORD, six thousand *were* officers and judges, 5four thousand *were* gatekeepers, and four thousand praised the LORD with *musical* instruments, "which I made," *said David,* "for giving praise."

6Also David separated them into divisions among the sons of Levi: Gershon, Kohath, and Merari.

7Of the Gershonites: Laadan[a] and Shimei. 8The sons of Laadan: the first Jehiel, then Zetham and Joel—three *in all.* 9The sons of Shimei: Shelomith, Haziel, and Haran—three *in all.* These were the heads of the fathers' *houses* of Laadan. 10And the sons of Shimei: Jahath, Zina,[a] Jeush, and Beriah. These *were* the four sons of Shimei. 11Jahath was the first and Zizah the second. But Jeush and Beriah did not have many sons; therefore they were assigned as one father's house.

12The sons of Kohath: Amram, Izhar, Hebron, and Uzziel—four *in all.* 13The sons of Amram: Aaron and Moses; and Aaron was set apart, he and his sons forever, that he should sanctify the most holy things, to burn incense before the LORD, to minister to Him, and to give the blessing in His name forever. 14Now the sons of Moses the man of God were reckoned to the tribe of Levi. 15The sons of Moses *were* Gershon[a] and Eliezer. 16Of the sons of Gershon, Shebuel[a] *was* the first. 17Of the descendants of Eliezer, Rehabiah was the first. And Eliezer had no other sons, but the sons of Rehabiah were very many. 18Of the sons of Izhar, Shelomith *was* the first. 19Of the sons of Hebron, Jeriah *was* the first, Amariah the second, Jahaziel the third, and Jekameam the fourth. 20Of the sons of Uzziel, Michah *was* the first and Jesshiah the second.

21The sons of Merari *were* Mahli and Mushi. The sons of Mahli *were* Eleazar and Kish. 22And Eleazar died, and had no sons, but only daughters; and their brethren, the sons of Kish, took them *as wives.* 23The sons of Mushi *were* Mahli, Eder, and Jeremoth—three *in all.*

24These *were* the sons of Levi by their fathers' houses—the heads of the fathers' *houses* as they were counted individually by the number of their names, who did the work for the service of the house

23:7 [a] Spelled *Libni* in Exodus 6:17 **23:10** [a] Septuagint and Vulgate read *Zizah* (compare verse 11). **23:15** [a] Hebrew *Gershom* (compare 6:16) **23:16** [a] Spelled *Shubael* in 24:20

of the LORD, from the age of twenty years and above.

25For David said, "The LORD God of Israel has given rest to His people, that they may dwell in Jerusalem forever"; 26and also to the Levites, "They shall no longer carry the tabernacle, or any of the articles for its service." 27For by the last words of David the Levites *were* numbered from twenty years old and above; 28because their duty *was* to help the sons of Aaron in the service of the house of the LORD, in the courts and in the chambers, in the purifying of all holy things and the work of the service of the house of God, 29both with the showbread and the fine flour for the grain offering, with the unleavened cakes and *what is baked in* the pan, with what is mixed and with all kinds of measures and sizes; 30to stand every morning to thank and praise the LORD, and likewise at evening; 31and at every presentation of a burnt offering to the LORD on the Sabbaths and on the New Moons and on the set feasts, by number according to the ordinance governing them, regularly before the LORD; 32and that they should attend to the needs of the tabernacle of meeting, the needs of the holy *place,* and the needs of the sons of Aaron their brethren in the work of the house of the LORD.

THE DIVISIONS OF THE PRIESTS

24 Now *these are* the divisions of the sons of Aaron. The sons of Aaron *were* Nadab, Abihu, Eleazar, and Ithamar. 2And Nadab and Abihu died before their father, and had no children; therefore Eleazar and Ithamar ministered as priests. 3Then David with Zadok of the sons of Eleazar, and Ahimelech of the sons of Ithamar, divided them according to the schedule of their service.

4There were more leaders found of the sons of Eleazar than of the sons of Ithamar, and *thus* they were divided. Among the sons of Eleazar *were* sixteen heads of *their* fathers' houses, and eight heads of their fathers' houses among the sons of Ithamar. 5Thus they were divided by lot, one group as another, for there were officials of the sanctuary and officials *of the house* of God, from the sons of Eleazar and from the sons of Ithamar. 6And the scribe, Shemaiah the son of Nethanel, *one of* the Levites, wrote them down before the king, the leaders, Zadok the priest, Ahimelech the son of Abiathar, and the heads of the fathers' *houses* of the priests and Levites, one father's house taken for Eleazar and *one* for Ithamar.

7Now the first lot fell to Jehoiarib, the second to Jedaiah, 8the third to Harim, the fourth

to Seorim, [9]the fifth to Malchijah, the sixth to Mijamin,
[10]the seventh to Hakkoz, the
eighth to Abijah, [11]the ninth
to Jeshua, the tenth to Shecaniah, [12]the eleventh to Eliashib, the twelfth to Jakim,
[13]the thirteenth to Huppah,
the fourteenth to Jeshebeab,
[14]the fifteenth to Bilgah, the
sixteenth to Immer, [15]the seventeenth to Hezir, the eighteenth to Happizzez,[a] [16]the
nineteenth to Pethahiah,
the twentieth to Jehezekel,[a]
[17]the twenty-first to Jachin,
the twenty-second to Gamul,
[18]the twenty-third to Delaiah,
the twenty-fourth to Maaziah.

[19]This *was* the schedule of
their service for coming into
the house of the LORD according to their ordinance by the
hand of Aaron their father, as
the LORD God of Israel had
commanded him.

OTHER LEVITES

[20]And the rest of the sons
of Levi: of the sons of Amram,
Shubael;[a] of the sons of Shubael, Jehdeiah. [21]Concerning
Rehabiah, of the sons of Rehabiah, the first *was* Isshiah.
[22]Of the Izharites, Shelo-
moth;[a] of the sons of Shelo-
moth, Jahath. [23]Of the sons *of*
Hebron,[a] Jeriah *was the first*,[b]
Amariah the second, Jahaziel
the third, *and* Jekameam the
fourth. [24]*Of* the sons of Uzziel, Michah; of the sons of Michah, Shamir. [25]The brother of
Michah, Isshiah; of the sons
of Isshiah, Zechariah. [26]The
sons of Merari *were* Mahli
and Mushi; the son of Jaaziah,
Beno. [27]The sons of Merari by
Jaaziah *were* Beno, Shoham,
Zaccur, and Ibri. [28]Of Mahli:
Eleazar, who had no sons. [29]Of
Kish: the son of Kish, Jerahmeel.

[30]Also the sons of Mushi
were Mahli, Eder, and Jerimoth. These *were* the sons of
the Levites according to their
fathers' houses.

[31]These also cast lots just
as their brothers the sons of
Aaron did, in the presence of
King David, Zadok, Ahime-
lech, and the heads of the fathers' *houses* of the priests and
Levites. The chief fathers *did*
just as their younger brethren.

THE MUSICIANS

25 Moreover David and
the captains of the
army separated for the service
some of the sons of Asaph, of
Heman, and of Jeduthun, who
should prophesy with harps,
stringed instruments, and
cymbals. And the number

24:15 [a] Septuagint and Vulgate read *Aphses*. 24:16 [a] Masoretic Text reads *Jehezkel*. 24:20 [a] Spelled *Shebuel* in 23:16 24:22 [a] Spelled *Shelomith* in 23:18 24:23 [a] Supplied from 23:19 (following some Hebrew manuscripts and Septuagint manuscripts) [b] Supplied from 23:19 (following some Hebrew manuscripts and Septuagint manuscripts)

of the skilled men performing their service was: 2Of the
sons of Asaph: Zaccur, Joseph,
Nethaniah, and Asharelah;[a]
the sons of Asaph *were* under
the direction of Asaph, who
prophesied according to the
order of the king. 3Of Jeduthun, the sons of Jeduthun:
Gedaliah, Zeri,[a] Jeshaiah,
Shimei, Hashabiah, and Mattithiah, six,[b] under the direction of their father Jeduthun,
who prophesied with a harp to
give thanks and to praise the
LORD. 4Of Heman, the sons of
Heman: Bukkiah, Mattaniah,
Uzziel,[a] Shebuel,[b] Jerimoth,[c]
Hananiah, Hanani, Eliathah,
Giddalti, Romamti-Ezer, Joshbekashah, Mallothi, Hothir,
and Mahazioth. 5All these
were the sons of Heman the
king's seer in the words of
God, to exalt his horn.[a] For
God gave Heman fourteen
sons and three daughters.

6All these *were* under the
direction of their father for
the music *in* the house of the
LORD, with cymbals, stringed
instruments, and harps, for
the service of the house of
God. Asaph, Jeduthun, and
Heman *were* under the authority of the king. 7So the
number of them, with their
brethren who were instructed
in the songs of the LORD, all
who were skillful, *was* two
hundred and eighty-eight.

8And they cast lots for their
duty, the small as well as the
great, the teacher with the
student.

9Now the first lot for Asaph
came out for Joseph; the second for Gedaliah, him with his
brethren and sons, twelve;
10the third for Zaccur, his sons
and his brethren, twelve; 11the
fourth for Jizri,[a] his sons and
his brethren, twelve; 12the
fifth for Nethaniah, his sons
and his brethren, twelve; 13the
sixth for Bukkiah, his sons
and his brethren, twelve; 14the
seventh for Jesharelah,[a] his
sons and his brethren, twelve;
15the eighth for Jeshaiah, his
sons and his brethren, twelve;
16the ninth for Mattaniah, his
sons and his brethren, twelve;
17the tenth for Shimei, his
sons and his brethren, twelve;
18the eleventh for Azarel,[a] his
sons and his brethren, twelve;
19the twelfth for Hashabiah,
his sons and his brethren,
twelve; 20the thirteenth for
Shubael,[a] his sons and his
brethren, twelve; 21the four-

25:2 [a] Spelled *Jesharelah* in verse 14 **25:3** [a] Spelled *Jizri* in verse 11 [b] *Shimei*, appearing in one Hebrew and several Septuagint manuscripts, completes the total of six sons (compare verse 17). **25:4** [a] Spelled *Azarel* in verse 18 [b] Spelled *Shubael* in verse 20 [c] Spelled *Jeremoth* in verse 22 **25:5** [a] That is, to increase his power or influence **25:11** [a] Spelled *Zeri* in verse 3 **25:14** [a] Spelled *Asharelah* in verse 2 **25:18** [a] Spelled *Uzziel* in verse 4 **25:20** [a] Spelled *Shebuel* in verse 4

teenth for Mattithiah, his sons
and his brethren, twelve; 22the
fifteenth for Jeremoth,[a] his
sons and his brethren, twelve;
23the sixteenth for Hananiah,
his sons and his brethren,
twelve; 24the seventeenth for
Joshbekashah, his sons and
his brethren, twelve; 25the
eighteenth for Hanani, his
sons and his brethren, twelve;
26the nineteenth for Mallothi, his sons and his brethren,
twelve; 27the twentieth for Eliathah, his sons and his brethren, twelve; 28the twenty-first
for Hothir, his sons and his
brethren, twelve; 29the twenty-
second for Giddalti, his sons
and his brethren, twelve; 30the
twenty-third for Mahazioth,
his sons and his brethren,
twelve; 31the twenty-fourth
for Romamti-Ezer, his sons
and his brethren, twelve.

THE GATEKEEPERS

26 Concerning the di-
visions of the gate-
keepers: of the Korahites,
Meshelemiah the son of Kore,
of the sons of Asaph. 2And the
sons of Meshelemiah *were*
Zechariah the firstborn, Jediael the second, Zebadiah
the third, Jathniel the fourth,
3Elam the fifth, Jehohanan the
sixth, Eliehoenai the seventh.
4Moreover the sons of
Obed-Edom *were* Shemaiah
the firstborn, Jehozabad the
second, Joah the third, Sacar
the fourth, Nethanel the fifth,
5Ammiel the sixth, Issachar
the seventh, Peulthai the
eighth; for God blessed him.
6Also to Shemaiah his son
were sons born who governed
their fathers' houses, because
they *were* men of great ability. 7The sons of Shemaiah
were Othni, Rephael, Obed,
and Elzabad, whose brothers
Elihu and Semachiah *were*
able men.
8All these *were* of the sons
of Obed-Edom, they and their
sons and their brethren, able
men with strength for the
work: sixty-two of Obed-
Edom.
9And Meshelemiah had
sons and brethren, eighteen
able men.
10Also Hosah, of the children of Merari, had sons:
Shimri the first (for *though* he
was not the firstborn, his father made him the first), 11Hil-
kiah the second, Tebaliah the
third, Zechariah the fourth;
all the sons and brethren of
Hosah *were* thirteen.
12Among these *were* the
divisions of the gatekeepers,
among the chief men, *having*
duties just like their brethren,
to serve in the house of the
LORD. 13And they cast lots for
each gate, the small as well as
the great, according to their
father's house. 14The lot for
the East *Gate* fell to Shelemiah.
Then they cast lots *for* his son

25:22 [a] Spelled *Jerimoth* in verse 4

Zechariah, a wise counselor, and his lot came out for the North Gate; [15]to Obed-Edom the South Gate, and to his sons the storehouse.[a] [16]To Shuppim and Hosah *the lot came out* for the West Gate, with the Shallecheth Gate on the ascending highway—watchman opposite watchman. [17]On the east *were* six Levites, on the north four each day, on the south four each day, and for the storehouse[a] two by two. [18]As for the Parbar[a] on the west, *there were* four on the highway *and* two at the Parbar. [19]These were the divisions of the gatekeepers among the sons of Korah and among the sons of Merari.

THE TREASURIES AND OTHER DUTIES

[20]Of the Levites, Ahijah *was* over the treasuries of the house of God and over the treasuries of the dedicated things. [21]The sons of Laadan, the descendants of the Gershonites of Laadan, heads of their fathers' *houses,* of Laadan the Gershonite: Jehieli. [22]The sons of Jehieli, Zetham and Joel his brother, *were* over the treasuries of the house of the LORD. [23]Of the Amramites, the Izharites, the Hebronites, and the Uzzielites: [24]Shebuel the son of Gershom, the son of Moses, *was* overseer of the treasuries. [25]And his brethren by Eliezer *were* Rehabiah his son, Jeshaiah his son, Joram his son, Zichri his son, and Shelomith his son.

[26]This Shelomith and his brethren *were* over all the treasuries of the dedicated things which King David and the heads of fathers' *houses,* the captains over thousands and hundreds, and the captains of the army, had dedicated. [27]Some of the spoils won in battles they dedicated to maintain the house of the LORD. [28]And all that Samuel the seer, Saul the son of Kish, Abner the son of Ner, and Joab the son of Zeruiah had dedicated, every dedicated *thing,* was under the hand of Shelomith and his brethren.

[29]Of the Izharites, Chenaniah and his sons *performed* duties as officials and judges over Israel outside Jerusalem.

[30]Of the Hebronites, Hashabiah and his brethren, one thousand seven hundred able men, had the oversight of Israel on the west side of the Jordan for all the business of the LORD, and in the service of the king. [31]Among the Hebronites, Jerijah *was* head of the Hebronites according to his genealogy of the fathers. In the fortieth year of the reign of David they were sought, and there

26:15 [a] Hebrew *asuppim* **26:17** [a] Hebrew *asuppim*
26:18 [a] Probably a court or colonnade extending west of the temple

were found among them ca-
pable men at Jazer of Gilead.
32And his brethren *were* two
thousand seven hundred able
men, heads of fathers' *houses,*
whom King David made officials over the Reubenites, the
Gadites, and the half-tribe of
Manasseh, for every matter
pertaining to God and the affairs of the king.

THE MILITARY DIVISIONS

27 And the children of Israel, according to their
number, the heads of fathers'
houses, the captains of thousands and hundreds and their
officers, served the king in
every matter of the *military*
divisions. *These divisions*
came in and went out month
by month throughout all the
months of the year, each division *having* twenty-four
thousand.

2Over the first division for
the first month *was* Jashobeam the son of Zabdiel, and
in his division *were* twenty-
four thousand; 3*he was* of the
children of Perez, and the chief
of all the captains of the army
for the first month. 4Over the
division of the second month
was Dodai[a] an Ahohite, and of
his division Mikloth also *was*
the leader; in his division *were*
twenty-four thousand. 5The
third captain of the army for
the third month *was* Benaiah,
the son of Jehoiada the priest,
who was chief; in his division
were twenty-four thousand.
6This was the Benaiah *who*
was mighty *among* the thirty,
and was over the thirty; in his
division *was* Ammizabad his
son. 7The fourth *captain* for
the fourth month *was* Asahel the brother of Joab, and
Zebadiah his son after him;
in his division *were* twenty-
four thousand. 8The fifth captain for the fifth month *was*
Shamhuth[a] the Izrahite; in
his division were twenty-four
thousand. 9The sixth *captain*
for the sixth month *was* Ira
the son of Ikkesh the Tekoite;
in his division *were* twenty-
four thousand. 10The seventh
captain for the seventh month
was Helez the Pelonite, of the
children of Ephraim; in his division *were* twenty-four thousand. 11The eighth *captain* for
the eighth month *was* Sibbechai the Hushathite, of the
Zarhites; in his division *were*
twenty-four thousand. 12The
ninth *captain* for the ninth
month *was* Abiezer the Anathothite, of the Benjamites; in
his division *were* twenty-four
thousand. 13The tenth *captain*
for the tenth month *was* Maharai the Netophathite, of the
Zarhites; in his division *were*
twenty-four thousand. 14The
eleventh *captain* for the eleventh month *was* Benaiah the

27:4 [a] Hebrew *Dodai,* usually spelled *Dodo* (compare 2 Samuel 23:9)
27:8 [a] Spelled *Shammoth* in 11:27 and *Shammah* in 2 Samuel 23:11

Pirathonite, of the children
of Ephraim; in his division
were twenty-four thousand.
15 The twelfth *captain* for the
twelfth month *was* Heldai[a]
the Netophathite, of Othniel;
in his division *were* twenty-
four thousand.

LEADERS OF TRIBES

16 Furthermore, over the
tribes of Israel: the officer
over the Reubenites *was* Eliezer the son of Zichri; over
the Simeonites, Shephatiah
the son of Maachah; 17 *over* the
Levites, Hashabiah the son of
Kemuel; over the Aaronites,
Zadok; 18 *over* Judah, Elihu,
one of David's brothers; *over*
Issachar, Omri the son of Michael; 19 *over* Zebulun, Ishma-
iah the son of Obadiah; *over*
Naphtali, Jerimoth the son
of Azriel; 20 *over* the children
of Ephraim, Hoshea the son of
Azaziah; *over* the half-tribe of
Manasseh, Joel the son of Pedaiah; 21 *over* the half-*tribe* of
Manasseh in Gilead, Iddo the
son of Zechariah; *over* Benjamin, Jaasiel the son of Abner;
22 *over* Dan, Azarel the son of
Jeroham. These *were* the leaders of the tribes of Israel.

23 But David did not take
the number of those twenty
years old and under, because
the LORD had said He would
multiply Israel like the stars
of the heavens. 24 Joab the son
of Zeruiah began a census, but
he did not finish, for wrath
came upon Israel because of
this census; nor was the number recorded in the account of
the chronicles of King David.

OTHER STATE OFFICIALS

25 And Azmaveth the son
of Adiel *was* over the king's
treasuries; and Jehonathan
the son of Uzziah was over
the storehouses in the field,
in the cities, in the villages,
and in the fortresses. 26 Ezri
the son of Chelub was over
those who did the work of the
field for tilling the ground.
27 And Shimei the Ramathite
was over the vineyards, and
Zabdi the Shiphmite was over
the produce of the vineyards
for the supply of wine. 28 Baal-
Hanan the Gederite was over
the olive trees and the sycamore trees that *were* in the
lowlands, and Joash *was* over
the store of oil. 29 And Shitrai
the Sharonite *was* over the
herds that fed in Sharon, and
Shaphat the son of Adlai was
over the herds *that were* in the
valleys. 30 Obil the Ishmaelite
was over the camels, Jehdeiah
the Meronothite *was* over the
donkeys, 31 and Jaziz the Hag-
rite *was* over the flocks. All
these *were* the officials over
King David's property.

32 Also Jehonathan, David's
uncle, *was* a counselor, a wise
man, and a scribe; and Jehiel
the son of Hachmoni *was* with

27:15 [a] Spelled *Heled* in 11:30 and *Heleb* in 2 Samuel 23:29

the king's sons. 33Ahithophel
was the king's counselor, and
Hushai the Archite *was* the
king's companion. 34After
Ahithophel *was* Jehoiada the
son of Benaiah, then Abiathar.
And the general of the king's
army *was* Joab.

SOLOMON INSTRUCTED TO BUILD THE TEMPLE

28 Now David assembled
at Jerusalem all the
leaders of Israel: the officers
of the tribes and the captains
of the divisions who served
the king, the captains over
thousands and captains over
hundreds, and the stewards
over all the substance and
possessions of the king and
of his sons, with the officials,
the valiant men, and all the
mighty men of valor.

2Then King David rose to
his feet and said, "Hear me, my
brethren and my people: I *had*
it in my heart to build a house
of rest for the ark of the covenant of the LORD, and for the
footstool of our God, and had
made preparations to build
it. 3But God said to me, 'You
shall not build a house for My
name, because you *have been*
a man of war and have shed
blood.' 4However the LORD
God of Israel chose me above
all the house of my father to
be king over Israel forever,
for He has chosen Judah *to be*
the ruler. And of the house of
Judah, the house of my father,
and among the sons of my father, He was pleased with me
to make *me* king over all Israel. 5And of all my sons (for
the LORD has given me many
sons) He has chosen my son
Solomon to sit on the throne
of the kingdom of the LORD
over Israel. 6Now He said to
me, 'It is your son Solomon
who shall build My house and
My courts; for I have chosen
him *to be* My son, and I will
be his Father. 7Moreover I will
establish his kingdom forever,
if he is steadfast to observe
My commandments and My
judgments, as it is this day.'
8Now therefore, in the sight
of all Israel, the assembly of
the LORD, and in the hearing
of our God, be careful to seek
out all the commandments of
the LORD your God, that you
may possess this good land,
and leave *it* as an inheritance
for your children after you forever.

9"As for you, my son Sol-
omon, know the God of your
father, and serve Him with a
loyal heart and with a willing
mind; for the LORD searches
all hearts and understands
all the intent of the thoughts.
If you seek Him, He will be
found by you; but if you forsake Him, He will cast you off
forever. 10Consider now, for
the LORD has chosen you to
build a house for the sanctuary; be strong, and do it."

11Then David gave his son
Solomon the plans for the vestibule, its houses, its treasuries,

its upper chambers, its inner
chambers, and the place of the
mercy seat; 12and the plans for
all that he had by the Spirit,
of the courts of the house of
the LORD, of all the chambers
all around, of the treasuries of
the house of God, and of the
treasuries for the dedicated
things; 13also for the division
of the priests and the Levites,
for all the work of the service
of the house of the LORD, and
for all the articles of service
in the house of the LORD. 14*He*
gave gold by weight for *things*
of gold, for all articles used
in every kind of service; also
silver for all articles of silver
by weight, for all articles used
in every kind of service; 15the
weight for the lampstands of
gold, and their lamps of gold,
by weight for each lampstand
and its lamps; for the lampstands of silver by weight, for
the lampstand and its lamps,
according to the use of each
lampstand. 16And by weight *he*
gave gold for the tables of the
showbread, for each table, and
silver for the tables of silver;
17also pure gold for the forks,
the basins, the pitchers of pure
gold, and the golden bowls—*he*
gave gold by weight for every
bowl; and for the silver bowls,
silver by weight for every bowl;
18and refined gold by weight
for the altar of incense, and for
the construction of the chariot,
that is, the gold cherubim that
spread *their wings* and overshadowed the ark of the covenant of the LORD. 19"All *this,*"
said David, "the LORD made me
understand in writing, by *His*
hand upon me, all the works
of these plans."

20And David said to his son
Solomon, "Be strong and of
good courage, and do *it;* do
not fear nor be dismayed, for
the LORD God—my God—*will*
be with you. He will not leave
you nor forsake you, until you
have finished all the work for
the service of the house of the
LORD. 21*Here are* the divisions
of the priests and the Levites
for all the service of the house
of God; and every willing
craftsman *will be* with you for
all manner of workmanship,
for every kind of service; also
the leaders and all the people *will be* completely at your
command."

OFFERINGS FOR BUILDING THE TEMPLE

29 Furthermore King
David said to all the
assembly: "My son Solomon,
whom alone God has chosen,
is young and inexperienced;
and the work *is* great, because
the temple[a] *is* not for man but
for the LORD God. 2Now for
the house of my God I have
prepared with all my might:
gold for *things to be made* of
gold, silver for *things of* silver,
bronze for *things of* bronze,

29:1 [a] Literally *palace*

iron for *things of* iron, wood for
things of wood, onyx stones,
stones to be set, glistening
stones of various colors, all
kinds of precious stones, and
marble slabs in abundance.
3Moreover, because I have set
my affection on the house of
my God, I have given to the
house of my God, over and
above all that I have prepared
for the holy house, my own
special treasure of gold and
silver: 4three thousand talents
of gold, of the gold of Ophir,
and seven thousand talents of
refined silver, to overlay the
walls of the houses; 5the gold
for *things of* gold and the silver
for *things of* silver, and for all
kinds of work *to be done* by
the hands of craftsmen. Who
then is willing to consecrate
himself this day to the LORD?"
6Then the leaders of the
fathers' *houses,* leaders of the
tribes of Israel, the captains of
thousands and of hundreds,
with the officers over the king's
work, offered willingly. 7They
gave for the work of the house
of God five thousand talents
and ten thousand darics of
gold, ten thousand talents of
silver, eighteen thousand talents of bronze, and one hundred thousand talents of iron.
8And whoever had *precious*
stones gave *them* to the treasury of the house of the LORD,
into the hand of Jehiel[a] the
Gershonite. 9Then the people
rejoiced, for they had offered
willingly, because with a loyal
heart they had offered willingly to the LORD; and King
David also rejoiced greatly.

DAVID'S PRAISE TO GOD

10Therefore David blessed
the LORD before all the assembly; and David said:

"Blessed are You,
LORD God of
Israel, our Father,
forever and ever.
11 Yours, O LORD, *is*
the greatness,
The power and the glory,
The victory and
the majesty;
For all *that is* in heaven
and in earth *is Yours;*
Yours *is* the kingdom,
O LORD,
And You are exalted
as head over all.
12 Both riches and honor
come from You,
And You reign over all.
In Your hand *is* power
and might;
In Your hand *it is*
to make great
And to give
strength to all.

13 "Now therefore, our God,
We thank You
And praise Your
glorious name.
14 But who *am* I, and who
are my people,

29:8 [a] Possibly the same as *Jehieli* (compare 26:21, 22)

That we should be
able to offer so
willingly as this?
For all things *come*
from You,
And of Your own we
have given You.
15 For we *are* aliens and
pilgrims before You,
As *were* all our fathers;
Our days on earth
are as a shadow,
And without hope.

16"O LORD our God, all this
abundance that we have prepared to build You a house for
Your holy name is from Your
hand, and *is* all Your own. 17I
know also, my God, that You
test the heart and have pleasure in uprightness. As for
me, in the uprightness of my
heart I have willingly offered
all these *things;* and now with
joy I have seen Your people,
who are present here to offer
willingly to You. 18O LORD God
of Abraham, Isaac, and Israel,
our fathers, keep this forever
in the intent of the thoughts
of the heart of Your people,
and fix their heart toward You.
19And give my son Solomon a
loyal heart to keep Your commandments and Your testi-
monies and Your statutes, to
do all *these things,* and to build
the temple[a] for which I have
made provision."

20Then David said to all the
assembly, "Now bless the LORD
your God." So all the assembly
blessed the LORD God of their
fathers, and bowed their heads
and prostrated themselves before the LORD and the king.

SOLOMON ANOINTED KING

21And they made sacrifices
to the LORD and offered burnt
offerings to the LORD on the
next day: a thousand bulls,
a thousand rams, a thou-
sand lambs, with their drink
offerings, and sacrifices in
abundance for all Israel. 22So
they ate and drank before the
LORD with great gladness on
that day. And they made Solomon the son of David king
the second time, and anointed
him before the LORD *to be* the
leader, and Zadok *to be* priest.
23Then Solomon sat on the
throne of the LORD as king
instead of David his father,
and prospered; and all Israel
obeyed him. 24All the leaders and the mighty men, and
also all the sons of King David,
submitted themselves to King
Solomon. 25So the LORD exalted Solomon exceedingly
in the sight of all Israel, and
bestowed on him *such* royal
majesty as had not been on
any king before him in Israel.

THE CLOSE OF DAVID'S REIGN

26Thus David the son of
Jesse reigned over all Israel.

29:19 [a] Literally *palace*

27And the period that he
reigned over Israel *was* forty
years; seven years he reigned in
Hebron, and thirty-three *years*
he reigned in Jerusalem. 28So
he died in a good old age, full of
days and riches and honor; and
Solomon his son reigned in his
place. 29Now the acts of King
David, first and last, indeed
they *are* written in the book
of Samuel the seer, in the book
of Nathan the prophet, and in
the book of Gad the seer, 30with
all his reign and his might, and
the events that happened to
him, to Israel, and to all the
kingdoms of the lands.

THE SECOND BOOK OF THE CHRONICLES

SOLOMON REQUESTS WISDOM

1 Now Solomon the son of
David was strengthened in
his kingdom, and the LORD
his God *was* with him and exalted him exceedingly.

2And Solomon spoke to all
Israel, to the captains of thousands and of hundreds, to the
judges, and to every leader in
all Israel, the heads of the fathers' *houses.* 3Then Solomon,
and all the assembly with
him, went to the high place
that *was* at Gibeon; for the
tabernacle of meeting with
God was there, which Moses
the servant of the LORD had
made in the wilderness. 4But
David had brought up the ark
of God from Kirjath Jearim to
the place David had prepared
for it, for he had pitched a tent
for it at Jerusalem. 5Now the
bronze altar that Bezalel the
son of Uri, the son of Hur, had
made, he put[a] before the tabernacle of the LORD; Solomon
and the assembly sought Him
there. 6And Solomon went up
there to the bronze altar before the LORD, which *was* at
the tabernacle of meeting,
and offered a thousand burnt
offerings on it.

7On that night God ap-
peared to Solomon, and said
to him, "Ask! What shall I give
you?"

8And Solomon said to God:
"You have shown great mercy
to David my father, and have
made me king in his place.
9Now, O LORD God, let Your
promise to David my father
be established, for You have
made me king over a people

1:5 [a] Some authorities read *it was there.*

like the dust of the earth in
multitude. [10]Now give me
wisdom and knowledge, that
I may go out and come in
before this people; for who
can judge this great people
of Yours?"
[11]Then God said to Sol-
omon: "Because this was in
your heart, and you have not
asked riches or wealth or
honor or the life of your enemies, nor have you asked long
life—but have asked wisdom
and knowledge for yourself,
that you may judge My people
over whom I have made you
king— [12]wisdom and knowledge *are* granted to you; and I
will give you riches and wealth
and honor, such as none of
the kings have had who *were*
before you, nor shall any after
you have the like."

SOLOMON'S MILITARY AND ECONOMIC POWER

[13]So Solomon came to Jerusalem from the high place
that *was* at Gibeon, from before the tabernacle of meeting, and reigned over Israel.
[14]And Solomon gathered
chariots and horsemen; he
had one thousand four hundred chariots and twelve
thousand horsemen, whom
he stationed in the chariot cities and with the king in Jerusalem. [15]Also the king made
silver and gold as common
in Jerusalem as stones, and
he made cedars as abundant
as the sycamores which *are* in
the lowland. [16]And Solomon
had horses imported from
Egypt and Keveh; the king's
merchants bought them in
Keveh at the *current* price.
[17]They also acquired and imported from Egypt a chariot
for six hundred *shekels* of silver, and a horse for one hundred and fifty; thus, through
their agents,[a] they exported
them to all the kings of the
Hittites and the kings of Syria.

SOLOMON PREPARES TO BUILD THE TEMPLE

2 Then Solomon deter-
mined to build a temple
for the name of the LORD, and
a royal house for himself. [2]Sol-
omon selected seventy thousand men to bear burdens,
eighty thousand to quarry
stone in the mountains, and
three thousand six hundred
to oversee them.
[3]Then Solomon sent to
Hiram[a] king of Tyre, saying:

As you have dealt with
David my father, and
sent him cedars to build
himself a house to dwell
in, *so deal with me.*
[4]Behold, I am building
a temple for the name
of the LORD my God, to
dedicate *it* to Him, to

1:17 [a] Literally *by their hands* 2:3 [a] Hebrew *Huram* (compare 1 Kings 5:1)

burn before Him sweet
incense, for the continual
showbread, for the burnt
offerings morning and
evening, on the Sabbaths,
on the New Moons, and
on the set feasts of the
LORD our God. This *is*
an ordinance forever to
Israel.

5 And the temple which I
build *will be* great, for our
God is greater than all
gods. 6But who is able to
build Him a temple, since
heaven and the heaven of
heavens cannot contain
Him? Who *am* I then,
that I should build Him
a temple, except to burn
sacrifice before Him?

7 Therefore send me at
once a man skillful to
work in gold and silver,
in bronze and iron, in
purple and crimson and
blue, who has skill to
engrave with the skillful
men who are with me in
Judah and Jerusalem,
whom David my father
provided. 8Also send
me cedar and cypress
and algum logs from
Lebanon, for I know that
your servants have skill
to cut timber in Lebanon;
and indeed my servants
will be with your servants,
9to prepare timber for
me in abundance, for the
temple which I am about
to build *shall be* great and
wonderful.

10 And indeed I will give
to your servants, the
woodsmen who cut
timber, twenty thousand
kors of ground wheat,
twenty thousand kors of
barley, twenty thousand
baths of wine, and twenty
thousand baths of oil.

11Then Hiram king of Tyre
answered in writing, which he
sent to Solomon:

Because the LORD loves
His people, He has made
you king over them.

12Hiram[a] also said:

Blessed *be* the LORD
God of Israel, who made
heaven and earth, for
He has given King David
a wise son, endowed
with prudence and
understanding, who will
build a temple for the
LORD and a royal house
for himself!

13 And now I have sent a
skillful man, endowed
with understanding,
Huram[a] my master[b]

2:12 [a] Hebrew *Huram* (compare 1 Kings 5:1) 2:13 [a] Spelled *Hiram* in 1 Kings 7:13 [b] Literally *father* (compare 1 Kings 7:13, 14)

craftsman 14(the son of a
woman of the daughters
of Dan, and his father
was a man of Tyre),
skilled to work in gold
and silver, bronze and
iron, stone and wood,
purple and blue, fine
linen and crimson, and
to make any engraving
and to accomplish any
plan which may be given
to him, with your skillful
men and with the skillful
men of my lord David
your father.

15 Now therefore, the wheat,
the barley, the oil, and the
wine which my lord has
spoken of, let him send
to his servants. 16And
we will cut wood from
Lebanon, as much as
you need; we will bring it
to you in rafts by sea to
Joppa, and you will carry
it up to Jerusalem.

17Then Solomon numbered
all the aliens who *were* in the
land of Israel, after the census
in which David his father had
numbered them; and there
were found to be one hun-
dred and fifty-three thousand
six hundred. 18And he made
seventy thousand of them
bearers of burdens, eighty
thousand stonecutters in the
mountain, and three thou-
sand six hundred overseers
to make the people work.

SOLOMON BUILDS THE TEMPLE

3 Now Solomon began to
build the house of the
LORD at Jerusalem on Mount
Moriah, where *the LORD*[a] had
appeared to his father David,
at the place that David had
prepared on the threshing
floor of Ornan[b] the Jebusite.
2And he began to build on
the second *day* of the second
month in the fourth year of
his reign.

3This is the foundation
which Solomon laid for building the house of God: The
length *was* sixty cubits (by
cubits according to the former measure) and the width
twenty cubits. 4And the vestibule that *was* in front *of the
sanctuary*[a] was twenty cubits
long across the width of the
house, and the height *was*
one hundred and[b] twenty. He
overlaid the inside with pure
gold. 5The larger room[a] he
paneled with cypress which
he overlaid with fine gold,
and he carved palm trees and
chainwork on it. 6And he deco-

3:1 [a] Literally *He,* following Masoretic Text and Vulgate; Septuagint reads *the LORD;* Targum reads *the Angel of the LORD.* [b] Spelled *Araunah* in 2 Samuel 24:16ff 3:4 [a] The main room of the temple; elsewhere called the holy place (compare 1 Kings 6:3) [b] Following Masoretic Text, Septuagint, and Vulgate; Arabic, some manuscripts of the Septuagint, and Syriac omit *one hundred and.* 3:5 [a] Literally *house*

rated the house with precious
stones for beauty, and the gold
was gold from Parvaim. 7He
also overlaid the house—the
beams and doorposts, its walls
and doors—with gold; and he
carved cherubim on the walls.
8And he made the Most
Holy Place. Its length was according to the width of the
house, twenty cubits, and its
width twenty cubits. He overlaid it with six hundred talents of fine gold. 9The weight
of the nails *was* fifty shekels
of gold; and he overlaid the
upper area with gold. 10In
the Most Holy Place he made
two cherubim, fashioned by
carving, and overlaid them
with gold. 11The wings of the
cherubim *were* twenty cubits
in *overall* length: one wing *of
the one cherub was* five cubits,
touching the wall of the room,
and the other wing *was* five
cubits, touching the wing of
the other cherub; 12*one* wing
of the other cherub *was* five
cubits, touching the wall of
the room, and the other wing
also was five cubits, touching
the wing of the other cherub.
13The wings of these cherubim
spanned twenty cubits overall. They stood on their feet,
and they faced inward. 14And
he made the veil of blue, purple, crimson, and fine linen,
and wove cherubim into it.
15Also he made in front of
the temple[a] two pillars thirty-
five[b] cubits high, and the capital that *was* on the top of each
of *them* was five cubits. 16He
made wreaths of chainwork,
as in the inner sanctuary, and
put *them* on top of the pillars;
and he made one hundred
pomegranates, and put *them*
on the wreaths of chainwork.
17Then he set up the pillars
before the temple, one on the
right hand and the other on
the left; he called the name
of the one on the right hand
Jachin, and the name of the
one on the left Boaz.

FURNISHINGS OF THE TEMPLE

4 Moreover he made a
bronze altar: twenty cubits
was its length, twenty cubits
its width, and ten cubits its
height.
2Then he made the Sea of
cast *bronze,* ten cubits from
one brim to the other; *it was*
completely round. Its height
was five cubits, and a line of
thirty cubits measured its
circumference. 3And under
it *was* the likeness of oxen
encircling it all around, ten
to a cubit, all the way around
the Sea. The oxen *were* cast in
two rows, when it was cast. 4It
stood on twelve oxen: three
looking toward the north,
three looking toward the
west, three looking toward

3:15 [a] Literally *house* [b] Or *eighteen* (compare 1 Kings 7:15; 2 Kings 25:17; and Jeremiah 52:21)

the south, and three looking toward the east; the Sea *was set* upon them, and all their back parts *pointed* inward. 5It *was* a handbreadth thick; and its brim was shaped like the brim of a cup, *like* a lily blossom. It contained three thousand[a] baths.

6He also made ten lavers, and put five on the right side and five on the left, to wash in them; such things as they offered for the burnt offering they would wash in them, but the Sea *was* for the priests to wash in. 7And he made ten lampstands of gold according to their design, and set *them* in the temple, five on the right side and five on the left. 8He also made ten tables, and placed *them* in the temple, five on the right side and five on the left. And he made one hundred bowls of gold.

9Furthermore he made the court of the priests, and the great court and doors for the court; and he overlaid these doors with bronze. 10He set the Sea on the right side, toward the southeast.

11Then Huram made the pots and the shovels and the bowls. So Huram finished doing the work that he was to do for King Solomon for the house of God: 12the two *pillars and the bowl-shaped* capitals *that were* on top of the two pillars; the two networks covering the two bowl-shaped capitals which *were* on top of the pillars; 13four hundred pomegranates for the two networks (two rows of pomegranates for each network, to cover the two bowl-shaped capitals that *were* on the pillars); 14he also made carts and the lavers on the carts; 15one Sea and twelve oxen under it; 16also the pots, the shovels, the forks—and all their articles Huram his master[a] *craftsman* made of burnished bronze for King Solomon for the house of the LORD.

17In the plain of Jordan the king had them cast in clay molds, between Succoth and Zeredah.[a] 18And Solomon had all these articles made in such great abundance that the weight of the bronze was not determined.

19Thus Solomon had all the furnishings made for the house of God: the altar of gold and the tables on which *was* the showbread; 20the lampstands with their lamps of pure gold, to burn in the prescribed manner in front of the inner sanctuary, 21with the flowers and the lamps and the wick-trimmers of gold, of purest gold; 22the trimmers, the bowls, the ladles, and the censers of pure gold. As for the entry of the sanctuary, its inner

4:5 [a] Or *two thousand* (compare 1 Kings 7:26) 4:16 [a] Literally *father* 4:17 [a] Spelled *Zaretan* in 1 Kings 7:46

doors to the Most Holy *Place,*
and the doors of the main hall
of the temple, *were* gold.

5 So all the work that Solomon had done for the
house of the LORD was finished; and Solomon brought
in the things which his father
David had dedicated: the silver and the gold and all the
furnishings. And he put *them*
in the treasuries of the house
of God.

THE ARK BROUGHT INTO THE TEMPLE

2Now Solomon assembled
the elders of Israel and all the
heads of the tribes, the chief
fathers of the children of Israel, in Jerusalem, that they
might bring the ark of the covenant of the LORD up from the
City of David, which *is* Zion.
3Therefore all the men of Israel assembled with the king
at the feast, which *was* in the
seventh month. 4So all the elders of Israel came, and the
Levites took up the ark. 5Then
they brought up the ark, the
tabernacle of meeting, and all
the holy furnishings that *were*
in the tabernacle. The priests
and the Levites brought them
up. 6Also King Solomon, and
all the congregation of Israel
who were assembled with him
before the ark, were sacrificing
sheep and oxen that could not
be counted or numbered for
multitude. 7Then the priests
brought in the ark of the covenant of the LORD to its place,
into the inner sanctuary of
the temple,[a] to the Most Holy
Place, under the wings of the
cherubim. 8For the cherubim
spread *their* wings over the
place of the ark, and the cherubim overshadowed the ark and
its poles. 9The poles extended
so that the ends of the poles of
the ark could be seen from *the*
holy place, in front of the inner
sanctuary; but they could not
be seen from outside. And they
are there to this day. 10Nothing
was in the ark except the two
tablets which Moses put *there*
at Horeb, when the LORD made
a covenant with the children
of Israel, when they had come
out of Egypt.

11And it came to pass when
the priests came out of the
Most Holy *Place* (for all the
priests who *were* present had
sanctified themselves, without keeping to their divisions),
12and the Levites *who were* the
singers, all those of Asaph and
Heman and Jeduthun, with
their sons and their brethren,
stood at the east end of the
altar, clothed in white linen,
having cymbals, stringed
instruments and harps, and
with them one hundred and
twenty priests sounding with
trumpets— 13indeed it came
to pass, when the trumpeters
and singers *were* as one, to
make one sound to be heard

5:7 [a] Literally *house*

in praising and thanking the
LORD, and when they lifted
up their voice with the trumpets and cymbals and instruments of music, and praised
the LORD, *saying:*

"*For He is* good,
For His mercy *endures*
forever,"[a]

that the house, the house
of the LORD, was filled with
a cloud, 14so that the priests
could not continue ministering because of the cloud; for
the glory of the LORD filled
the house of God.

6 Then Solomon spoke:

"The LORD said He
would dwell in
the dark cloud.
2 I have surely built You
an exalted house,
And a place for You to
dwell in forever."

SOLOMON'S SPEECH UPON COMPLETION OF THE WORK

3Then the king turned
around and blessed the whole
assembly of Israel, while all the
assembly of Israel was standing. 4And he said: "Blessed *be*
the LORD God of Israel, who
has fulfilled with His hands
what He spoke with His mouth
to my father David, saying,
5'Since the day that I brought
My people out of the land of
Egypt, I have chosen no city
from any tribe of Israel *in
which* to build a house, that
My name might be there, nor
did I choose any man to be a
ruler over My people Israel.
6Yet I have chosen Jerusalem,
that My name may be there,
and I have chosen David to be
over My people Israel.' 7Now
it was in the heart of my father David to build a temple[a]
for the name of the LORD God
of Israel. 8But the LORD said
to my father David, 'Whereas
it was in your heart to build
a temple for My name, you
did well in that it was in your
heart. 9Nevertheless you shall
not build the temple, but your
son who will come from your
body, he shall build the temple
for My name.' 10So the LORD
has fulfilled His word which
He spoke, and I have filled the
position of my father David,
and sit on the throne of Israel,
as the LORD promised; and I
have built the temple for the
name of the LORD God of Israel. 11And there I have put the
ark, in which *is* the covenant of
the LORD which He made with
the children of Israel."

SOLOMON'S PRAYER OF DEDICATION

12Then *Solomon*[a] stood before the altar of the LORD in
the presence of all the assem-

5:13 [a] Compare Psalm 106:1 **6:7** [a] Literally *house,* and so in verses 8–10 **6:12** [a] Literally *he* (compare 1 Kings 8:22)

bly of Israel, and spread out
his hands [13](for Solomon had
made a bronze platform five
cubits long, five cubits wide,
and three cubits high, and
had set it in the midst of the
court; and he stood on it, knelt
down on his knees before all
the assembly of Israel, and
spread out his hands toward
heaven); [14]and he said: "LORD
God of Israel, *there is* no God
in heaven or on earth like You,
who keep *Your* covenant and
mercy with Your servants who
walk before You with all their
hearts. [15]You have kept what
You promised Your servant
David my father; You have
both spoken with Your mouth
and fulfilled *it* with Your hand,
as *it is* this day. [16]Therefore,
LORD God of Israel, now keep
what You promised Your servant David my father, saying,
'You shall not fail to have a
man sit before Me on the
throne of Israel, only if your
sons take heed to their way,
that they walk in My law as you
have walked before Me.' [17]And
now, O LORD God of Israel, let
Your word come true, which
You have spoken to Your servant David.

[18]"But will God indeed dwell
with men on the earth? Behold, heaven and the heaven
of heavens cannot contain
You. How much less this
temple[a] which I have built!
[19]Yet regard the prayer of Your
servant and his supplication,
O LORD my God, and listen to
the cry and the prayer which
Your servant is praying before
You: [20]that Your eyes may be
open toward this temple day
and night, toward the place
where *You* said *You would* put
Your name, that You may hear
the prayer which Your servant makes toward this place.
[21]And may You hear the supplications of Your servant and
of Your people Israel, when
they pray toward this place.
Hear from heaven Your dwelling place, and when You hear,
forgive.

[22]"If anyone sins against
his neighbor, and is forced to
take an oath, and comes *and*
takes an oath before Your altar
in this temple, [23]then hear
from heaven, and act, and
judge Your servants, bringing
retribution on the wicked by
bringing his way on his own
head, and justifying the righteous by giving him according
to his righteousness.

[24]"Or if Your people Israel
are defeated before an enemy
because they have sinned
against You, and return and
confess Your name, and pray
and make supplication before
You in this temple, [25]then hear
from heaven and forgive the
sin of Your people Israel, and
bring them back to the land
which You gave to them and
their fathers.

6:18 [a] Literally *house*

[26]"When the heavens are
shut up and there is no rain
because they have sinned
against You, when they pray
toward this place and confess Your name, and turn
from their sin because You
afflict them, [27]then hear *in*
heaven, and forgive the sin
of Your servants, Your people Israel, that You may teach
them the good way in which
they should walk; and send
rain on Your land which You
have given to Your people as
an inheritance.

[28]"When there is famine in
the land, pestilence or blight
or mildew, locusts or grasshoppers; when their enemies
besiege them in the land of
their cities; whatever plague
or whatever sickness *there is;*
[29]whatever prayer, whatever
supplication is *made* by anyone, or by all Your people Israel, when each one knows his
own burden and his own grief,
and spreads out his hands to
this temple: [30]then hear from
heaven Your dwelling place,
and forgive, and give to everyone according to all his ways,
whose heart You know (for
You alone know the hearts of
the sons of men), [31]that they
may fear You, to walk in Your
ways as long as they live in
the land which You gave to
our fathers.

[32]"Moreover, concerning a
foreigner, who is not of Your
people Israel, but has come
from a far country for the
sake of Your great name and
Your mighty hand and Your
outstretched arm, when they
come and pray in this temple; [33]then hear from heaven
Your dwelling place, and do
according to all for which the
foreigner calls to You, that
all peoples of the earth may
know Your name and fear You,
as *do* Your people Israel, and
that they may know that this
temple which I have built is
called by Your name.

[34]"When Your people go
out to battle against their
enemies, wherever You send
them, and when they pray to
You toward this city which
You have chosen and the
temple which I have built for
Your name, [35]then hear from
heaven their prayer and their
supplication, and maintain
their cause.

[36]"When they sin against
You (for *there is* no one who
does not sin), and You become
angry with them and deliver
them to the enemy, and they
take them captive to a land
far or near; [37]*yet* when they
come to themselves in the
land where they were carried
captive, and repent, and make
supplication to You in the land
of their captivity, saying, 'We
have sinned, we have done
wrong, and have committed
wickedness'; [38]and *when* they
return to You with all their
heart and with all their soul
in the land of their captivity,
where they have been carried

captive, and pray toward their
land which You gave to their
fathers, the city which You
have chosen, and toward the
temple which I have built for
Your name: 39 then hear from
heaven Your dwelling place
their prayer and their supplications, and maintain their
cause, and forgive Your people who have sinned against
You. 40 Now, my God, I pray, let
Your eyes be open and *let* Your
ears *be* attentive to the prayer
made in this place.

41 "Now therefore,
Arise, O LORD God, to
Your resting place,
You and the ark of
Your strength.
Let Your priests, O LORD
God, be clothed
with salvation,
And let Your saints
rejoice in goodness.

42 "O LORD God, do not
turn away the face
of Your Anointed;
Remember the mercies of
Your servant David."[a]

SOLOMON DEDICATES THE TEMPLE

7 When Solomon had finished praying, *fire came*
down from heaven and con-
sumed the burnt offering and
the sacrifices; and the glory
of the LORD filled the temple.[a] 2 *And the priests could*
not enter the house of the
LORD, because the glory of
the LORD had filled the LORD's
house. 3 When all the children
of Israel saw how the fire
came down, and the glory
of the LORD on the temple,
they bowed their faces to the
ground on the pavement, and
worshiped and praised the
LORD, *saying:*

"For *He is* good,
For His mercy *endures*
forever."[a]

4 Then the king and all the
people offered sacrifices before the LORD. 5 King Solomon
offered a sacrifice of twenty-
two thousand bulls and one
hundred and twenty thousand
sheep. So the king and all the
people dedicated the house of
God. 6 And the priests attended
to their services; the Levites
also with instruments of the
music of the LORD, which King
David had made to praise the
LORD, saying, "For His mercy
endures forever,"[a] whenever
David offered praise by their
ministry. The priests sounded
trumpets opposite them,
while all Israel stood.
7 *Furthermore* Solomon
consecrated the middle of the
court that *was* in front of the
house of the LORD; for there
he offered burnt offerings

6:42 [a] Compare Psalm 132:8–10 7:1 [a] Literally *house*
7:3 [a] Compare Psalm 106:1 7:6 [a] Compare Psalm 106:1

and the fat of the peace offerings, because the bronze altar
which Solomon had made was
not able to receive the burnt
offerings, the grain offerings,
and the fat.
8At that time Solomon kept
the feast seven days, and all
Israel with him, a very great
assembly from the entrance
of Hamath to the Brook of
Egypt.[a] 9And on the eighth
day they held a sacred assembly, for they observed the
dedication of the altar seven
days, and the feast seven days.
10On the twenty-third day of
the seventh month he sent
the people away to their tents,
joyful and glad of heart for the
good that the LORD had done
for David, for Solomon, and
for His people Israel. 11Thus
Solomon finished the house
of the LORD and the king's
house; and Solomon successfully accomplished all that
came into his heart to make
in the house of the LORD and
in his own house.

GOD'S SECOND APPEARANCE TO SOLOMON

12Then the LORD appeared
to Solomon by night, and said
to him: "I have heard your
prayer, and have chosen this
place for Myself as a house
of sacrifice. 13*When I shut up*
heaven and there is no rain, or
command the locusts to de-
vour the land, or send pesti-
lence among My people, 14*if My*
people who are called by My
name will humble themselves,
and pray and seek My face, and
turn from their wicked ways,
then I will hear from heaven,
and will forgive their sin and
heal their land. 15Now My eyes
will be open and My ears attentive to prayer *made* in this
place. 16For now I have chosen
and sanctified this house, that
My name may be there forever;
and My eyes and My heart will
be there perpetually. 17As for
you, if you walk before Me as
your father David walked, and
do according to all that I have
commanded you, and if you
keep My statutes and My judgments, 18then I will establish
the throne of your kingdom, as
I covenanted with David your
father, saying, 'You shall not
fail *to have* a man as ruler in
Israel.'
19"But if you turn away and
forsake My statutes and My
commandments which I have
set before you, and go and
serve other gods, and worship them, 20then I will uproot them from My land which
I have given them; and this
house which I have sanctified
for My name I will cast out of
My sight, and will make it a
proverb and a byword among
all peoples.
21"And *as for* this house,
which is exalted, everyone

7:8 [a] That is, the Shihor (compare 1 Chronicles 13:5)

who passes by it will be astonished and say, 'Why has the
LORD done thus to this land
and this house?' [22]Then they
will answer, 'Because they forsook the LORD God of their fathers, who brought them out
of the land of Egypt, and embraced other gods, and worshiped them and served them;
therefore He has brought all
this calamity on them.'"

SOLOMON'S ADDITIONAL ACHIEVEMENTS

8 It came to pass at the end
of twenty years, when Solomon had built the house of
the LORD and his own house,
[2]that the cities which Hiram[a]
had given to Solomon, Solomon built them; and he
settled the children of Israel
there. [3]And Solomon went
to Hamath Zobah and seized
it. [4]He also built Tadmor in
the wilderness, and all the
storage cities which he built
in Hamath. [5]He built Upper
Beth Horon and Lower Beth
Horon, fortified cities *with*
walls, gates, and bars, [6]also
Baalath and all the storage cities that Solomon had, and all
the chariot cities and the cities of the cavalry, and all that
Solomon desired to build in
Jerusalem, in Lebanon, and in
all the land of his dominion.

[7]All the people *who were*
left of the Hittites, Amorites,
Perizzites, Hivites, and Jebusites, who *were* not of Israel—
[8]that is, their descendants
who were left in the land after
them, whom the children of
Israel did not destroy—from
these Solomon raised forced
labor, as it is to this day. [9]But
Solomon did not make the
children of Israel servants for
his work. Some *were* men of
war, captains of his officers,
captains of his chariots, and
his cavalry. [10]And others *were*
chiefs of the officials of King
Solomon: two hundred and
fifty, who ruled over the people.

[11]Now Solomon brought
the daughter of Pharaoh up
from the City of David to the
house he had built for her,
for he said, "My wife shall not
dwell in the house of David
king of Israel, because *the
places* to which the ark of the
LORD has come are holy."

[12]Then Solomon offered
burnt offerings to the LORD
on the altar of the LORD which
he had built before the vestibule, [13]according to the daily
rate, offering according to the
commandment of Moses, for
the Sabbaths, the New Moons,
and the three appointed
yearly feasts—the Feast of
Unleavened Bread, the Feast
of Weeks, and the Feast of Tabernacles. [14]And, according to
the order of David his father,
he appointed the divisions of
the priests for their service,

8:2 [a] Hebrew *Huram* (compare 2 Chronicles 2:3)

the Levites for their duties (to praise and serve before the priests) as the duty of each day required, and the gatekeepers by their divisions at each gate; for so David the man of God
had commanded. 15They did not depart from the command of the king to the priests and Levites concerning any matter or concerning the treasuries.

16Now all the work of Solomon was well-ordered from[a] the day of the foundation of the house of the LORD until it was finished. So the house of the LORD was completed.

17Then Solomon went to Ezion Geber and Elath[a] on the seacoast, in the land of Edom.
18And Hiram sent him ships by the hand of his servants, and servants who knew the sea. They went with the servants of Solomon to Ophir, and acquired four hundred and fifty talents of gold from there, and brought it to King Solomon.

THE QUEEN OF SHEBA'S PRAISE OF SOLOMON

9 Now when the queen of Sheba heard of the fame of Solomon, she came to Jerusalem to test Solomon with hard questions, *having* a very great retinue, camels that bore spices, gold in abun*dance, and precious stones;* and when she came to Solomon, she spoke with him about all that was in her heart.
2So Solomon answered all her questions; there was nothing so difficult for Solomon that he could not explain it to her.
3And when the queen of Sheba had seen the wisdom of Solomon, the house that he had
built, 4the food on his table, the seating of his servants, the service of his waiters and their apparel, his cupbearers and their apparel, and his entryway by which he went up to the house of the LORD, there was no more spirit in her.

5Then she said to the king: "*It was* a true report which I heard in my own land about your words and your wisdom.
6However I did not believe their words until I came and saw with my own eyes; and indeed the half of the greatness of your wisdom was not told me. You exceed the fame
of which I heard. 7Happy *are* your men and happy *are* these your servants, who stand continually before you and
hear your wisdom! 8Blessed be the LORD your God, who delighted in you, setting you on His throne *to be* king for the LORD your God! Because your God has loved Israel, to establish them forever, therefore He made you king over them, to do justice and righteousness."

8:16 [a] Following Septuagint, Syriac, and Vulgate; Masoretic Text reads *as far as.* 8:17 [a] Hebrew *Eloth* (compare 2 Kings 14:22)

9And she gave the king one
hundred and twenty talents
of gold, spices in great abundance, and precious stones;
there never were any spices
such as those the queen of
Sheba gave to King Solomon.

10Also, the servants of
Hiram and the servants of
Solomon, who brought gold
from Ophir, brought algum[a]
wood and precious stones.
11And the king made walk-
ways *of* the algum[a] wood for
the house of the LORD and for
the king's house, also harps
and stringed instruments for
singers; and there were none
such *as these* seen before in
the land of Judah.

12Now King Solomon gave
to the queen of Sheba all she
desired, whatever she asked,
much more than she had
brought to the king. So she
turned and went to her own
country, she and her servants.

SOLOMON'S GREAT WEALTH

13The weight of gold that
came to Solomon yearly was
six hundred and sixty-six talents of gold, 14besides *what* the
traveling merchants and traders brought. And all the kings
of Arabia and governors of the
country brought gold and silver to Solomon. 15And King
Solomon made two hundred
large shields of hammered
gold; six hundred *shekels* of
hammered gold went into each
shield. 16*He* also *made* three
hundred shields of hammered
gold; three hundred *shekels*[a] of
gold went into each shield. The
king put them in the House of
the Forest of Lebanon.

17Moreover the king made
a great throne of ivory, and
overlaid it with pure gold.
18The throne *had* six steps,
with a footstool of gold, *which*
were fastened to the throne;
there were armrests on either
side of the place of the seat,
and two lions stood beside
the armrests. 19Twelve lions
stood there, one on each side
of the six steps; nothing like
this had been made for any
other kingdom.

20All King Solomon's drinking vessels *were* gold, and all
the vessels of the House of the
Forest of Lebanon *were* pure
gold. Not *one was* silver, for
this was accounted as nothing in the days of Solomon.
21For the king's ships went to
Tarshish with the servants
of Hiram.[a] Once every three
years the merchant ships[b]
came, bringing gold, silver,
ivory, apes, and monkeys.[c]

22So King Solomon sur-
passed all the kings of the
earth in riches and wisdom.
23And all the kings of the

9:10 [a] Or *almug* (compare 1 Kings 10:11, 12) **9:11** [a] Or *almug* (compare 1 Kings 10:11, 12) **9:16** [a] Or *three minas* (compare 1 Kings 10:17) **9:21** [a] Hebrew *Huram* (compare 1 Kings 10:22) [b] Literally *ships of Tarshish* (deep-sea vessels) [c] Or *peacocks*

earth sought the presence
of Solomon to hear his wisdom, which God had put in
his heart. 24Each man brought
his present: articles of silver
and gold, garments, armor,
spices, horses, and mules, at
a set rate year by year.
25Solomon had four thou-
sand stalls for horses and
chariots, and twelve thousand
horsemen whom he stationed
in the chariot cities and with
the king at Jerusalem.
26So he reigned over all the
kings from the River[a] to the
land of the Philistines, as far
as the border of Egypt. 27The
king made silver *as common*
in Jerusalem as stones, and
he made cedar trees as abundant as the sycamores which
are in the lowland. 28And they
brought horses to Solomon
from Egypt and from all lands.

DEATH OF SOLOMON

29Now the rest of the acts
of Solomon, first and last, *are*
they not written in the book
of Nathan the prophet, in the
prophecy of Ahijah the Shilonite, and in the visions of Iddo
the seer concerning Jeroboam
the son of Nebat? 30Solomon
reigned in Jerusalem over all
Israel forty years. 31Then Solomon rested with his fathers,
and was buried in the City of
David his father. And Rehoboam his son reigned in his
place.

THE REVOLT AGAINST REHOBOAM

10 And Rehoboam went
to Shechem, for all Is-
rael had gone to Shechem to
make him king. 2So it happened, when Jeroboam the
son of Nebat heard *it* (he was
in Egypt, where he had fled
from the presence of King
Solomon), that Jeroboam
returned from Egypt. 3Then
they sent for him and called
him. And Jeroboam and all
Israel came and spoke to Rehoboam, saying, 4"Your father
made our yoke heavy; now
therefore, lighten the burdensome service of your father
and his heavy yoke which he
put on us, and we will serve
you."
5So he said to them, "Come
back to me after three days."
And the people departed.
6Then King Rehoboam
consulted the elders who
stood before his father Solomon while he still lived, saying, "How do you advise *me* to
answer these people?"
7And they spoke to him,
saying, "If you are kind to
these people, and please
them, and speak good words
to them, they will be your servants forever."
8But he rejected the advice
which the elders had given
him, and consulted the young
men who had grown up with
him, who stood before him.

9:26 [a] That is, the Euphrates

9And he said to them, "What
advice do you give? How
should we answer this people
who have spoken to me, saying, 'Lighten the yoke which
your father put on us'?"
10Then the young men
who had grown up with him
spoke to him, saying, "Thus
you should speak to the people who have spoken to you,
saying, 'Your father made our
yoke heavy, but you make
it lighter on us'—thus you
shall say to them: 'My little
finger shall be thicker than
my father's waist! 11And now,
whereas my father put a heavy
yoke on you, I will add to your
yoke; my father chastised you
with whips, but I *will chastise*
you with scourges!'"[a]
12So Jeroboam and all the
people came to Rehoboam on
the third day, as the king had
directed, saying, "Come back
to me the third day." 13Then the
king answered them roughly.
King Rehoboam rejected the
advice of the elders, 14and he
spoke to them according to
the advice of the young men,
saying, "My father[a] made your
yoke heavy, but I will add to it;
my father chastised you with
whips, but I *will chastise you*
with scourges!"[b] 15So the king
did not listen to the people;
for the turn *of events* was from
God, that the LORD might fulfill His word, which He had
spoken by the hand of Ahijah
the Shilonite to Jeroboam the
son of Nebat.
16Now when all Israel *saw*
that the king did not listen to
them, the people answered
the king, saying:

"What share have
we in David?
We have no inheritance
in the son of Jesse.
Every man to your
tents, O Israel!
Now see to your own
house, O David!"

So all Israel departed to
their tents. 17But Rehoboam
reigned over the children of
Israel who dwelt in the cities
of Judah.
18Then King Rehoboam
sent Hadoram, who *was* in
charge of revenue; but the
children of Israel stoned him
with stones, and he died.
Therefore King Rehoboam
mounted *his* chariot in haste
to flee to Jerusalem. 19So Israel
has been in rebellion against
the house of David to this day.

11 Now when Rehoboam
came to Jerusalem, he
assembled from the house of
Judah and Benjamin one hundred and eighty thousand chosen *men* who were warriors,
to fight against Israel, that he

10:11 [a] Literally *scorpions* 10:14 [a] Following many Hebrew manuscripts, Septuagint, Syriac, and Vulgate (compare verse 10 and 1 Kings 12:14); Masoretic Text reads *I*. [b] Literally *scorpions*

might restore the kingdom to
Rehoboam.
[2]But the word of the LORD
came to Shemaiah the man
of God, saying, [3]"Speak to Rehoboam the son of Solomon,
king of Judah, and to all Israel
in Judah and Benjamin, saying, [4]'Thus says the LORD: "You
shall not go up or fight against
your brethren! Let every man
return to his house, for this
thing is from Me."'" Therefore
they obeyed the words of the
LORD, and turned back from
attacking Jeroboam.

REHOBOAM FORTIFIES THE CITIES

[5]So Rehoboam dwelt in Jerusalem, and built cities for defense in Judah. [6]And he built
Bethlehem, Etam, Tekoa, [7]Beth
Zur, Sochoh, Adullam, [8]Gath,
Mareshah, Ziph, [9]Adoraim, Lachish, Azekah, [10]Zorah, Aijalon, and Hebron, which are in
Judah and Benjamin, fortified
cities. [11]And he fortified the
strongholds, and put captains
in them, and stores of food,
oil, and wine. [12]Also in every
city *he put* shields and spears,
and made them very strong,
having Judah and Benjamin
on his side.

PRIESTS AND LEVITES MOVE TO JUDAH

[13]And from all their territories the priests and the Levites
who *were* in all Israel took
their stand with him. [14]For
the Levites left their common-
lands and their possessions
and came to Judah and Jerusalem, for Jeroboam and his
sons had rejected them from
serving as priests to the LORD.
[15]Then he appointed for himself priests for the high places,
for the demons, and the calf
idols which he had made.
[16]And after *the* Levites *left*,[a]
those from all the tribes of Israel, such as set their heart to
seek the LORD God of Israel,
came to Jerusalem to sacrifice to the LORD God of their
fathers. [17]So they strengthened the kingdom of Judah,
and made Rehoboam the son
of Solomon strong for three
years, because they walked in
the way of David and Solomon
for three years.

THE FAMILY OF REHOBOAM

[18]Then Rehoboam took for
himself as wife Mahalath the
daughter of Jerimoth the son
of David, *and of* Abihail the
daughter of Eliah the son of
Jesse. [19]And she bore him children: Jeush, Shamariah, and
Zaham. [20]After her he took
Maachah the granddaughter[a]
of Absalom; and she bore him
Abijah, Attai, Ziza, and Shelomith. [21]Now Rehoboam loved
Maachah the granddaughter
of Absalom more than all his

11:16 [a] Literally *after them* 11:20 [a] Literally *daughter,* but in the broader sense of granddaughter (compare 2 Chronicles 13:2)

wives and his concubines; for
he took eighteen wives and
sixty concubines, and begot
twenty-eight sons and sixty
daughters. 22And Rehoboam
appointed Abijah the son of
Maachah as chief, *to be* leader
among his brothers; for he *in-*
tended to make him king. 23He
dealt wisely, and dispersed
some of his sons throughout
all the territories of Judah and
Benjamin, to every fortified
city; and he gave them provisions in abundance. He also
sought many wives *for them.*

EGYPT ATTACKS JUDAH

12 Now it came to pass,
when Rehoboam had
established the kingdom and
had strengthened himself,
that he forsook the law of the
LORD, and all Israel along with
him. 2And it happened in the
fifth year of King Rehoboam
that Shishak king of Egypt
came up against Jerusalem,
because they had transgressed
against the LORD, 3with twelve
hundred chariots, sixty thousand horsemen, and people
without number who came
with him out of Egypt—the
Lubim and the Sukkiim and
the Ethiopians. 4And he took
the fortified cities of Judah
and came to Jerusalem.

5Then Shemaiah the
prophet came to Rehoboam
and the leaders of Judah, who
were gathered together in Jerusalem because of Shishak,
and said to them, "Thus says
the LORD: 'You have forsaken
Me, and therefore I also have
left you in the hand of Shishak.'"

6So the leaders of Israel
and the king humbled themselves; and they said, "The
LORD *is* righteous."

7Now when the LORD saw
that they humbled them-
selves, the word of the LORD
came to Shemaiah, saying,
"They have humbled them-
selves; *therefore* I will not destroy them, but I will grant
them some deliverance. My
wrath shall not be poured out
on Jerusalem by the hand of
Shishak. 8Nevertheless they
will be his servants, that they
may distinguish My service
from the service of the kingdoms of the nations."

9So Shishak king of Egypt
came up against Jerusalem,
and took away the treasures of
the house of the LORD and the
treasures of the king's house;
he took everything. He also
carried away the gold shields
which Solomon had made.
10Then King Rehoboam made
bronze shields in their place,
and committed *them* to the
hands of the captains of the
guard, who guarded the doorway of the king's house. 11And
whenever the king entered the
house of the LORD, the guard
would go and bring them out;
then they would take them
back into the guardroom.
12When he humbled himself,
the wrath of the LORD turned

from him, so as not to destroy
him completely; and things
also went well in Judah.

THE END OF REHOBOAM'S REIGN

13Thus King Rehoboam
strengthened himself in Jerusalem and reigned. Now Rehoboam *was* forty-one years
old when he became king; and
he reigned seventeen years
in Jerusalem, the city which
the LORD had chosen out of
all the tribes of Israel, to put
His name there. His mother's
name *was* Naamah, an Am-
monitess.
14And he did evil,
because he did not prepare his
heart to seek the LORD.

15The acts of Rehoboam,
first and last, *are* they not
written in the book of Shemaiah the prophet, and of
Iddo the seer concerning
genealogies? And *there were*
wars between Rehoboam and
Jeroboam all their days.
16So
Rehoboam rested with his fathers, and was buried in the
City of David. Then Abijah[a]
his son reigned in his place.

ABIJAH REIGNS IN JUDAH

13 In the eighteenth year
of King Jeroboam, Abi-
jah became king over Judah.
2He reigned three years in Jerusalem. His mother's name
was Michaiah[a] the daughter
of Uriel of Gibeah.

And there was war between
Abijah and Jeroboam.
3Abijah
set the battle in order with an
army of valiant warriors, four
hundred thousand choice
men. Jeroboam also drew up
in battle formation against
him with eight hundred thousand choice men, mighty men
of valor.

4Then Abijah stood on
Mount Zemaraim, which *is* in
the mountains of Ephraim,
and said, "Hear me, Jeroboam
and all Israel:
5Should you not
know that the LORD God of Israel gave the dominion over
Israel to David forever, to him
and his sons, by a covenant of
salt?
6Yet Jeroboam the son
of Nebat, the servant of Solomon the son of David, rose
up and rebelled against his
lord.
7Then worthless rogues
gathered to him, and strengthened themselves against Rehoboam the son of Solomon,
when Rehoboam was young
and inexperienced and could
not withstand them.
8And now
you think to withstand the
kingdom of the LORD, which
is in the hand of the sons of
David; and you *are* a great
multitude, and with you are
the gold calves which Jeroboam made for you as gods.
9Have you not cast out the
priests of the LORD, the sons
of Aaron, and the Levites, and
made for yourselves priests,

12:16 [a] Spelled *Abijam* in 1 Kings 14:31 13:2 [a] Spelled *Maachah* in 11:20, 21 and 1 Kings 15:2

like the peoples of *other* lands,
so that whoever comes to consecrate himself with a young
bull and seven rams may be
a priest of *things that are* not
gods? 10But as for us, the LORD
is our God, and we have not
forsaken Him; and the priests
who minister to the LORD *are*
the sons of Aaron, and the
Levites *attend* to *their* duties.
11And they burn to the LORD
every morning and every
evening burnt sacrifices and
sweet incense; *they* also *set*
the showbread *in order on* the
pure *gold* table, and the lampstand of gold with its lamps
to burn every evening; for
we keep the command of the
LORD our God, but you have
forsaken Him. 12Now look, God
Himself is with us as *our* head,
and His priests with sounding
trumpets to sound the alarm
against you. O children of Israel, do not fight against the
LORD God of your fathers, for
you shall not prosper!"

13But Jeroboam caused an
ambush to go around behind
them; so they were in front of
Judah, and the ambush *was*
behind them. 14And when
Judah looked around, to their
surprise the battle line *was* at
both front and rear; and they
cried out to the LORD, and the
priests sounded the trumpets.
15Then the men of Judah gave
a shout; and as the men of
Judah shouted, it happened
that God struck Jeroboam and
all Israel before Abijah and
Judah. 16And the children of
Israel fled before Judah, and
God delivered them into their
hand. 17Then Abijah and his
people struck them with a
great slaughter; so five hundred thousand choice men
of Israel fell slain. 18Thus the
children of Israel were subdued at that time; and the
children of Judah prevailed,
because they relied on the
LORD God of their fathers.

19And Abijah pursued Jer-
oboam and took cities from
him: Bethel with its villages,
Jeshanah with its villages, and
Ephrain[a] with its villages. 20So
Jeroboam did not recover
strength again in the days of
Abijah; and the LORD struck
him, and he died.

21But Abijah grew mighty,
married fourteen wives, and
begot twenty-two sons and
sixteen daughters. 22Now
the rest of the acts of Abijah,
his ways, and his sayings *are*
written in the annals of the
prophet Iddo.

14 So Abijah rested with his
fathers, and they bur-
ied him in the City of David.
Then Asa his son reigned in
his place. In his days the land
was quiet for ten years.

ASA REIGNS IN JUDAH

2Asa did *what was* good
and right in the eyes of the

13:19 [a] Or *Ephron*

LORD his God, 3for he removed
the altars of the foreign *gods*
and the high places, and broke
down the *sacred* pillars and
cut down the wooden images.
4He commanded Judah to
seek the LORD God of their
fathers, and to observe the
law and the commandment.
5He also removed the high
places and the incense altars
from all the cities of Judah,
and the kingdom was quiet
under him. 6And he built fortified cities in Judah, for the
land had rest; he had no war in
those years, because the LORD
had given him rest. 7There-
fore he said to Judah, "Let us
build these cities and make
walls around *them,* and towers, gates, and bars, *while* the
land *is* yet before us, because
we have sought the LORD our
God; we have sought *Him,*
and He has given us rest on
every side." So they built and
prospered. 8And Asa had an
army of three hundred thousand from Judah who carried
shields and spears, and from
Benjamin two hundred and
eighty thousand men who
carried shields and drew
bows; all these *were* mighty
men of valor.

9Then Zerah the Ethiopian
came out against them with
an army of a million men and
three hundred chariots, and
he came to Mareshah. 10So
Asa went out against him, and
they set the troops in battle
array in the Valley of Zepha-
thah at Mareshah. 11And Asa
cried out to the LORD his God,
and said, "LORD, *it is* nothing
for You to help, whether with
many or with those who have
no power; help us, O LORD our
God, for we rest on You, and
in Your name we go against
this multitude. O LORD, You
are our God; do not let man
prevail against You!"

12So the LORD struck the
Ethiopians before Asa and
Judah, and the Ethiopians
fled. 13And Asa and the people
who *were* with him pursued
them to Gerar. So the Ethiopians were overthrown, and
they could not recover, for
they were broken before the
LORD and His army. And they
carried away very much spoil.
14Then they defeated all the
cities around Gerar, for the
fear of the LORD came upon
them; and they plundered
all the cities, for there was
exceedingly much spoil in
them. 15They also attacked
the livestock enclosures, and
carried off sheep and camels
in abundance, and returned
to Jerusalem.

THE REFORMS OF ASA

15 Now the Spirit of God
came upon Azariah the
son of Oded. 2And he went out
to meet Asa, and said to him:
"Hear me, Asa, and all Judah
and Benjamin. The LORD *is*
with you while you are with
Him. If you seek Him, He will
be found by you; but if you

forsake Him, He will forsake
you. 3For a long time Israel
has been without the true God,
without a teaching priest, and
without law; 4but when in
their trouble they turned to
the LORD God of Israel, and
sought Him, He was found
by them. 5And in those times
there was no peace to the one
who went out, nor to the one
who came in, but great turmoil *was* on all the inhabitants of the lands. 6So nation
was destroyed by nation, and
city by city, for God troubled
them with every adversity.
7But you, be strong and do not
let your hands be weak, for
your work shall be rewarded!"

8And when Asa heard these
words and the prophecy of
Oded[a] the prophet, he took
courage, and removed the
abominable idols from all the
land of Judah and Benjamin
and from the cities which he
had taken in the mountains
of Ephraim; and he restored
the altar of the LORD that
was before the vestibule of
the LORD. 9Then he gathered
all Judah and Benjamin, and
those who dwelt with them
from Ephraim, Manasseh,
and Simeon, for they came
over to him in great num-
bers from Israel when they
saw that the LORD his God was
with him.

10So they gathered together
at Jerusalem in the third
month, in the fifteenth year
of the reign of Asa. 11And they
offered to the LORD at that
time seven hundred bulls and
seven thousand sheep from
the spoil they had brought.
12Then they entered into a covenant to seek the LORD God
of their fathers with all their
heart and with all their soul;
13and whoever would not seek
the LORD God of Israel was
to be put to death, whether
small or great, whether man
or woman. 14Then they took
an oath before the LORD with a
loud voice, with shouting and
trumpets and rams' horns.
15And all Judah rejoiced at the
oath, for they had sworn with
all their heart and sought Him
with all their soul; and He was
found by them, and the LORD
gave them rest all around.

16Also he removed
Maachah, the mother of Asa
the king, from *being* queen
mother, because she had
made an obscene image of
Asherah;[a] and Asa cut down
her obscene image, then
crushed and burned *it* by the
Brook Kidron. 17But the high
places were not removed from
Israel. Nevertheless the heart
of Asa was loyal all his days.

18He also brought into the
house of God the things that

15:8 [a] Following Masoretic Text and Septuagint; Syriac and Vulgate read *Azariah the son of Oded* (compare verse 1). 15:16 [a] A Canaanite deity

his father had dedicated and
that he himself had dedicated:
silver and gold and utensils.
19And there was no war until
the thirty-fifth year of the
reign of Asa.

ASA'S TREATY WITH SYRIA

16 In the thirty-sixth year of
the reign of Asa, Baasha
king of Israel came up against
Judah and built Ramah, that
he might let none go out or
come in to Asa king of Judah.
2Then Asa brought silver and
gold from the treasuries of
the house of the LORD and of
the king's house, and sent to
Ben-Hadad king of Syria, who
dwelt in Damascus, saying,
3"*Let there be* a treaty between
you and me, as there was between my father and your father. See, I have sent you silver
and gold; come, break your
treaty with Baasha king of Israel, so that he will withdraw
from me."

4So Ben-Hadad heeded
King Asa, and sent the captains of his armies against
the cities of Israel. They attacked Ijon, Dan, Abel Maim,
and all the storage cities of
Naphtali. 5Now it happened,
when Baasha heard *it,* that he
stopped building Ramah and
ceased his work. 6Then King
Asa took all Judah, and they
carried away the stones and
timber of Ramah, which Baasha had used for building;
and with them he built Geba
and Mizpah.

HANANI'S MESSAGE TO ASA

7And at that time Hanani
the seer came to Asa king of
Judah, and said to him: "Because you have relied on the
king of Syria, and have not
relied on the LORD your God,
therefore the army of the king
of Syria has escaped from
your hand. 8Were the Ethiopians and the Lubim not a huge
army with very many chariots
and horsemen? Yet, because
you relied on the LORD, He delivered them into your hand.
9For the eyes of the LORD run
to and fro throughout the
whole earth, to show Himself strong on behalf of *those*
whose heart *is* loyal to Him. In
this you have done foolishly;
therefore from now on you
shall have wars." 10Then Asa
was angry with the seer, and
put him in prison, for *he was*
enraged at him because of
this. And Asa oppressed *some*
of the people at that time.

ILLNESS AND DEATH OF ASA

11Note that the acts of Asa,
first and last, are indeed written in the book of the kings
of Judah and Israel. 12And in
the thirty-ninth year of his
reign, Asa became diseased
in his feet, and his malady was
severe; yet in his disease he
did not seek the LORD, but the
physicians.

13So Asa rested with his
fathers; he died in the forty-

first year of his reign. 14They buried him in his own tomb, which he had made for himself in the City of David; and they laid him in the bed which was filled with spices and various ingredients prepared in a mixture of ointments. They made a very great burning for him.

JEHOSHAPHAT REIGNS IN JUDAH

17 Then Jehoshaphat his son reigned in his place, and strengthened himself against Israel. 2And he placed troops in all the fortified cities of Judah, and set garrisons in the land of Judah and in the cities of Ephraim which Asa his father had taken. 3Now the LORD was with Jehoshaphat, because he walked in the former ways of his father David; he did not seek the Baals, 4but sought the God[a] of his father, and walked in His commandments and not according to the acts of Israel. 5Therefore the LORD established the kingdom in his hand; and all Judah gave presents to Jehoshaphat, and he had riches and honor in abundance. 6And his heart took delight in the ways of the LORD; moreover he removed the high places and wooden images from Judah.

7Also in the third year of his reign he sent his leaders, Ben-Hail, Obadiah, Zechariah, Nethanel, and Michaiah, to teach in the cities of Judah. 8And with them *he sent* Levites: Shemaiah, Nethaniah, Zebadiah, Asahel, Shemiramoth, Jehonathan, Adonijah, Tobijah, and Tobadonijah—the Levites; and with them Elishama and Jehoram, the priests. 9So they taught in Judah, and *had* the Book of the Law of the LORD with them; they went throughout all the cities of Judah and taught the people.

10And the fear of the LORD fell on all the kingdoms of the lands that *were* around Judah, so that they did not make war against Jehoshaphat. 11Also *some* of the Philistines brought Jehoshaphat presents and silver as tribute; and the Arabians brought him flocks, seven thousand seven hundred rams and seven thousand seven hundred male goats.

12So Jehoshaphat became increasingly powerful, and he built fortresses and storage cities in Judah. 13He had much property in the cities of Judah; and the men of war, mighty men of valor, *were* in Jerusalem.

14These *are* their numbers, according to their fathers' houses. Of Judah, the captains of thousands: Adnah the captain, and with him three hundred thousand mighty men of

17:4 [a] Septuagint reads *LORD God*.

valor; 15and next to him *was* Jehohanan the captain, and with him two hundred and eighty thousand; 16and next to him *was* Amasiah the son of Zichri, who willingly offered himself to the LORD, and with him two hundred thousand mighty men of valor. 17Of Benjamin: Eliada a mighty man of valor, and with him two hundred thousand men armed with bow and shield; 18and next to him *was* Jehozabad, and with him one hundred and eighty thousand prepared for war. 19These served the king, besides those the king put in the fortified cities throughout all Judah.

MICAIAH WARNS AHAB

18 Jehoshaphat had riches and honor in abundance; and by marriage he allied himself with Ahab. 2After some years he went down to *visit* Ahab in Samaria; and Ahab killed sheep and oxen in abundance for him and the people who were with him, and persuaded him to go up *with him* to Ramoth Gilead. 3So Ahab king of Israel said to Jehoshaphat king of Judah, "Will you go with me *against* Ramoth Gilead?"

And he answered him, "I *am* as you *are,* and my people as your people; *we will be* with you in the war."

4Also Jehoshaphat said to the king of Israel, "Please inquire for the word of the LORD today."

5Then the king of Israel gathered the prophets together, four hundred men, and said to them, "Shall we go to war against Ramoth Gilead, or shall I refrain?"

So they said, "Go up, for God will deliver it into the king's hand."

6But Jehoshaphat said, "*Is there* not still a prophet of the LORD here, that we may inquire of Him?"[a]

7So the king of Israel said to Jehoshaphat, "*There is* still one man by whom we may inquire of the LORD; but I hate him, because he never prophesies good concerning me, but always evil. He *is* Micaiah the son of Imla."

And Jehoshaphat said, "Let not the king say such things!"

8Then the king of Israel called one *of his* officers and said, "Bring Micaiah the son of Imla quickly!"

9The king of Israel and Jehoshaphat king of Judah, clothed in *their* robes, sat each on his throne; and they sat at a threshing floor at the entrance of the gate of Samaria; and all the prophets prophesied before them. 10Now Zedekiah the son of Chenaanah had made horns of iron for himself; and he said, "Thus says the LORD: 'With these you

18:6 [a] Or *him*

shall gore the Syrians until
they are destroyed.'"
11And all the prophets
prophesied so, saying, "Go up
to Ramoth Gilead and prosper, for the LORD will deliver
it into the king's hand."
12Then the messenger
who had gone to call Micaiah
spoke to him, saying, "Now listen, the words of the prophets
with one accord encourage
the king. Therefore please let
your word be like *the word of*
one of them, and speak encouragement."
13And Micaiah said, "*As* the
LORD lives, whatever my God
says, that I will speak."
14Then he came to the king;
and the king said to him,
"Micaiah, shall we go to war
against Ramoth Gilead, or
shall I refrain?"
And he said, "Go and prosper, and they shall be delivered into your hand!"
15So the king said to him,
"How many times shall I make
you swear that you tell me
nothing but the truth in the
name of the LORD?"
16Then he said, "I saw all
Israel scattered on the mountains, as sheep that have no
shepherd. And the LORD said,
'These have no master. Let
each return to his house in
peace.'"
17And the king of Israel said
to Jehoshaphat, "Did I not tell
you he would not prophesy
good concerning me, but
evil?"
18Then *Micaiah* said,
"Therefore hear the word of
the LORD: I saw the LORD sitting on His throne, and all the
host of heaven standing on
His right hand and His left.
19And the LORD said, 'Who
will persuade Ahab king of
Israel to go up, that he may
fall at Ramoth Gilead?' So one
spoke in this manner, and another spoke in that manner.
20Then a spirit came forward
and stood before the LORD,
and said, 'I will persuade him.'
The LORD said to him, 'In what
way?' 21So he said, 'I will go
out and be a lying spirit in
the mouth of all his prophets.'
And *the LORD* said, 'You shall
persuade *him* and also prevail;
go out and do so.' 22Therefore
look! The LORD has put a lying
spirit in the mouth of these
prophets of yours, and the
LORD has declared disaster
against you."
23Then Zedekiah the son
of Chenaanah went near and
struck Micaiah on the cheek,
and said, "Which way did the
spirit from the LORD go from
me to speak to you?"
24And Micaiah said, "In-
deed you shall see on that
day when you go into an inner
chamber to hide!"
25Then the king of Israel
said, "Take Micaiah, and return
him to Amon the governor of
the city and to Joash the king's
son; 26and say, 'Thus says the
king: "Put this *fellow* in prison,
and feed him with bread of

affliction and water of affliction, until I return in peace."'"
27But Micaiah said, "If you
ever return in peace, the LORD
has not spoken by me." And
he said, "Take heed, all you
people!"

AHAB DIES IN BATTLE

28So the king of Israel
and Jehoshaphat the king of
Judah went up to Ramoth Gilead. 29And the king of Israel
said to Jehoshaphat, "I will
disguise myself and go into
battle; but you put on your
robes." So the king of Israel
disguised himself, and they
went into battle.
30Now the king of Syria had
commanded the captains of
the chariots who *were* with
him, saying, "Fight with no
one small or great, but only
with the king of Israel."
31So it was, when the captains of the chariots saw Jehoshaphat, that they said, "It
is the king of Israel!" Therefore they surrounded him to
attack; but Jehoshaphat cried
out, and the LORD helped him,
and God diverted them from
him. 32For so it was, when the
captains of the chariots saw
that it was not the king of Israel, that they turned back
from pursuing him. 33Now
a certain man drew a bow at
random, and struck the king of
Israel between the joints of his
armor. So he said to the driver
of his chariot, "Turn around
and take me out of the battle,
for I am wounded." 34The battle increased that day, and the
king of Israel propped *himself*
up in *his* chariot facing the Syrians until evening; and about
the time of sunset he died.

19 Then Jehoshaphat the
king of Judah returned
safely to his house in Jerusalem. 2And Jehu the son of
Hanani the seer went out to
meet him, and said to King Jehoshaphat, "Should you help
the wicked and love those who
hate the LORD? Therefore the
wrath of the LORD *is* upon you.
3Nevertheless good things are
found in you, in that you have
removed the wooden images
from the land, and have prepared your heart to seek God."

THE REFORMS OF JEHOSHAPHAT

4So Jehoshaphat dwelt at
Jerusalem; and he went out
again among the people from
Beersheba to the mountains
of Ephraim, and brought
them back to the LORD God
of their fathers. 5Then he set
judges in the land throughout all the fortified cities of
Judah, city by city, 6and said
to the judges, "Take heed to
what you are doing, for you do
not judge for man but for the
LORD, who *is* with you in the
judgment. 7Now therefore, let
the fear of the LORD be upon
you; take care and do *it*, for
there is no iniquity with the
LORD our God, no partiality,
nor taking of bribes."

8Moreover in Jerusalem,
for the judgment of the LORD
and for controversies, Jehoshaphat appointed some of the
Levites and priests, and some
of the chief fathers of Israel,
when they returned to Jerusalem.[a] 9And he commanded
them, saying, "Thus you shall
act in the fear of the LORD,
faithfully and with a loyal
heart: 10Whatever case comes
to you from your brethren who
dwell in their cities, whether of
bloodshed or offenses against
law or commandment, against
statutes or ordinances, you
shall warn them, lest they
trespass against the LORD
and wrath come upon you and
your brethren. Do this, and
you will not be guilty. 11And
take notice: Amariah the chief
priest *is* over you in all matters
of the LORD; and Zebadiah the
son of Ishmael, the ruler of
the house of Judah, for all the
king's matters; also the Levites
will be officials before you. Behave courageously, and the
LORD will be with the good."

AMMON, MOAB, AND MOUNT SEIR DEFEATED

20 It happened after
this *that* the people
of Moab with the people of
Ammon, and *others* with them
besides the Ammonites,[a]
came to battle against Jehoshaphat. 2Then some came and
told Jehoshaphat, saying, "A
great multitude is coming
against you from beyond the
sea, from Syria;[a] and they are
in Hazazon Tamar" (which *is*
En Gedi). 3And Jehoshaphat
feared, and set himself to seek
the LORD, and proclaimed a
fast throughout all Judah. 4So
Judah gathered together to
ask *help* from the LORD; and
from all the cities of Judah
they came to seek the LORD.

5Then Jehoshaphat stood
in the assembly of Judah and
Jerusalem, in the house of the
LORD, before the new court,
6and said: "O LORD God of
our fathers, *are* You not God
in heaven, and do You *not* rule
over all the kingdoms of the
nations, and in Your hand *is*
there not power and might,
so that no one is able to withstand You? 7*Are* You not our
God, *who* drove out the inhabitants of this land before Your
people Israel, and gave it to
the descendants of Abraham
Your friend forever? 8And they
dwell in it, and have built You a
sanctuary in it for Your name,
saying, 9'If disaster comes
upon us—sword, judgment,
pestilence, or famine—we
will stand before this temple
and in Your presence (for Your
name *is* in this temple), and

19:8 [a] Septuagint and Vulgate read *for the inhabitants of Jerusalem.*
20:1 [a] Following Masoretic Text and Vulgate; Septuagint reads *Meunites* (compare 26:7). 20:2 [a] Following Masoretic Text, Septuagint, and Vulgate; some Hebrew manuscripts and Old Latin read *Edom.*

cry out to You in our affliction,
and You will hear and save.'
10And now, here are the people
of Ammon, Moab, and Mount
Seir—whom You would not let
Israel invade when they came
out of the land of Egypt, but
they turned from them and
did not destroy them— 11here
they are, rewarding us by coming to throw us out of Your
possession which You have
given us to inherit. 12O our
God, will You not judge them?
For we have no power against
this great multitude that is
coming against us; nor do we
know what to do, but our eyes
are upon You."

13Now all Judah, with their
little ones, their wives, and
their children, stood before
the LORD.

14Then the Spirit of the
LORD came upon Jahaziel
the son of Zechariah, the son
of Benaiah, the son of Jeiel,
the son of Mattaniah, a Levite of the sons of Asaph, in
the midst of the assembly.
15And he said, "Listen, all
you of Judah and you inhabitants of Jerusalem, and you,
King Jehoshaphat! Thus says
the LORD to you: 'Do not be
afraid nor dismayed because
of this great multitude, for the
battle *is* not yours, but God's.
16Tomorrow go down against
them. They will surely come
up by the Ascent of Ziz, and
you will find them at the end
of the brook before the Wilderness of Jeruel. 17You will
not *need* to fight in this *battle.* Position yourselves, stand
still and see the salvation of
the LORD, who is with you,
O Judah and Jerusalem!' Do
not fear or be dismayed; tomorrow go out against them,
for the LORD *is* with you."

18And Jehoshaphat bowed
his head with *his* face to the
ground, and all Judah and
the inhabitants of Jerusalem
bowed before the LORD, worshiping the LORD. 19Then the
Levites of the children of the
Kohathites and of the children
of the Korahites stood up to
praise the LORD God of Israel
with voices loud and high.

20So they rose early in the
morning and went out into
the Wilderness of Tekoa; and
as they went out, Jehoshaphat stood and said, "Hear
me, O Judah and you inhabitants of Jerusalem: Believe
in the LORD your God, and you
shall be established; believe
His prophets, and you shall
prosper." 21And when he had
consulted with the people, he
appointed those who should
sing to the LORD, and who
should praise the beauty of
holiness, as they went out before the army and were saying:

"Praise the LORD,
For His mercy *endures*
forever."[a]

20:21 [a] Compare Psalm 106:1

22Now when they began to sing and to praise, the LORD set ambushes against the people of Ammon, Moab, and Mount Seir, who had come against Judah; and they were defeated. 23For the people of Ammon and Moab stood up against the inhabitants of Mount Seir to utterly kill and destroy *them.* And when they had made an end of the inhabitants of Seir, they helped to destroy one another.

24So when Judah came to a place overlooking the wilderness, they looked toward the multitude; and there *were* their dead bodies, fallen on the earth. No one had escaped.

25When Jehoshaphat and his people came to take away their spoil, they found among them an abundance of valuables on the dead bodies,[a] and precious jewelry, which they stripped off for themselves, more than they could carry away; and they were three days gathering the spoil because there was so much. 26And on the fourth day they assembled in the Valley of Berachah, for there they blessed the LORD; therefore the name of that place was called The Valley of Berachah[a] until this day. 27Then they returned, every man of Judah and Jerusalem, with Jehoshaphat in front of them, to go back to Jerusalem with joy, for the LORD had made them rejoice over their enemies. 28So they came to Jerusalem, with stringed instruments and harps and trumpets, to the house of the LORD. 29And the fear of God was on all the kingdoms of *those* countries when they heard that the LORD had fought against the enemies of Israel. 30Then the realm of Jehoshaphat was quiet, for his God gave him rest all around.

THE END OF JEHOSHAPHAT'S REIGN

31So Jehoshaphat was king over Judah. *He was* thirty-five years old when he became king, and he reigned twenty-five years in Jerusalem. His mother's name *was* Azubah the daughter of Shilhi. 32And he walked in the way of his father Asa, and did not turn aside from it, doing *what was* right in the sight of the LORD. 33Nevertheless the high places were not taken away, for as yet the people had not directed their hearts to the God of their fathers.

34Now the rest of the acts of Jehoshaphat, first and last, indeed they *are* written in the book of Jehu the son of Hanani, which *is* mentioned in the book of the kings of Israel.

35After this Jehoshaphat king of Judah allied himself

20:25 [a] A few Hebrew manuscripts, Old Latin, and Vulgate read *garments;* Septuagint reads *armor.* **20:26** [a] Literally *Blessing*

with Ahaziah king of Israel,
who acted very wickedly.
36And he allied himself with
him to make ships to go to
Tarshish, and they made the
ships in Ezion Geber. 37But Eliezer the son of Dodavah of
Mareshah prophesied against
Jehoshaphat, saying, "Be-
cause you have allied yourself
with Ahaziah, the LORD has
destroyed your works." Then
the ships were wrecked, so
that they were not able to go
to Tarshish.

JEHORAM REIGNS IN JUDAH

21 And Jehoshaphat rested
with his fathers, and was
buried with his fathers in the
City of David. Then Jehoram
his son reigned in his place.
2He had brothers, the sons of
Jehoshaphat: Azariah, Jehiel,
Zechariah, Azaryahu, Michael,
and Shephatiah; all these *were*
the sons of Jehoshaphat king
of Israel. 3Their father gave
them great gifts of silver and
gold and precious things, with
fortified cities in Judah; but
he gave the kingdom to Jehoram, because he *was* the
firstborn.

4Now when Jehoram was
established over the kingdom
of his father, he strengthened
himself and killed all his
brothers with the sword, and
also *others* of the princes of
Israel.

5Jehoram *was* thirty-two
years old when he became
king, and he reigned eight
years in Jerusalem. 6And
he walked in the way of the
kings of Israel, just as the
house of Ahab had done, for
he had the daughter of Ahab
as a wife; and he did evil in
the sight of the LORD. 7Yet the
LORD would not destroy the
house of David, because of the
covenant that He had made
with David, and since He had
promised to give a lamp to
him and to his sons forever.

8In his days Edom revolted
against Judah's authority, and
made a king over themselves.
9So Jehoram went out with
his officers, and all his chariots with him. And he rose by
night and attacked the Edomites who had surrounded him
and the captains of the chariots. 10Thus Edom has been
in revolt against Judah's authority to this day. At that time
Libnah revolted against his
rule, because he had forsaken
the LORD God of his fathers.
11Moreover he made high
places in the mountains of
Judah, and caused the inhabitants of Jerusalem to commit
harlotry, and led Judah astray.

12And a letter came to him
from Elijah the prophet, saying,

Thus says the LORD God
of your father David:
Because you have not
walked in the ways of
Jehoshaphat your father,
or in the ways of Asa

king of Judah, [13]but
have walked in the way
of the kings of Israel,
and have made Judah
and the inhabitants of
Jerusalem to play the
harlot like the harlotry
of the house of Ahab,
and also have killed your
brothers, those of your
father's household, *who*
were better than yourself,
[14]behold, the LORD will
strike your people with a
serious affliction—your
children, your wives, and
all your possessions;
[15]and you *will become*
very sick with a disease
of your intestines, until
your intestines come out
by reason of the sickness,
day by day.

[16]Moreover the LORD
stirred up against Jehoram
the spirit of the Philistines
and the Arabians who *were*
near the Ethiopians. [17]And
they came up into Judah and
invaded it, and carried away
all the possessions that were
found in the king's house, and
also his sons and his wives, so
that there was not a son left
to him except Jehoahaz,[a] the
youngest of his sons.

[18]After all this the LORD
struck him in his intestines
with an incurable disease.
[19]Then it happened in the
course of time, after the end
of two years, that his intestines came out because of his
sickness; so he died in severe
pain. And his people made
no burning for him, like the
burning for his fathers.

[20]He was thirty-two years
old when he became king. He
reigned in Jerusalem eight
years and, to no one's sorrow,
departed. However they buried him in the City of David,
but not in the tombs of the
kings.

AHAZIAH REIGNS IN JUDAH

22 Then the inhabitants of
Jerusalem made Aha-
ziah his youngest son king
in his place, for the raiders
who came with the Arabians
into the camp had killed all
the older *sons.* So Ahaziah
the son of Jehoram, king of
Judah, reigned. [2]Ahaziah *was*
forty-two[a] years old when he
became king, and he reigned
one year in Jerusalem. His
mother's name *was* Athaliah
the granddaughter of Omri.
[3]He also walked in the ways
of the house of Ahab, for his
mother advised him to do
wickedly. [4]Therefore he did
evil in the sight of the LORD,
like the house of Ahab; for
they were his counselors after
the death of his father, to his
destruction. [5]He also followed

21:17 [a] Elsewhere called *Ahaziah* (compare 2 Chronicles 22:1) 22:2 [a] Or *twenty-two* (compare 2 Kings 8:26)

their advice, and went with Jehoram[a] the son of Ahab king
of Israel to war against Hazael
king of Syria at Ramoth Gilead; and the Syrians wounded
Joram. 6Then he returned to
Jezreel to recover from the
wounds which he had re-
ceived at Ramah, when he
fought against Hazael king of
Syria. And Azariah[a] the son of
Jehoram, king of Judah, went
down to see Jehoram the son
of Ahab in Jezreel, because he
was sick.

7His going to Joram was
God's occasion for Ahaziah's
downfall; for when he arrived,
he went out with Jehoram
against Jehu the son of Nimshi,
whom the LORD had anointed
to cut off the house of Ahab.
8And it happened, when Jehu
was executing judgment on
the house of Ahab, and found
the princes of Judah and the
sons of Ahaziah's brothers who
served Ahaziah, that he killed
them. 9Then he searched for
Ahaziah; and they caught him
(he was hiding in Samaria), and
brought him to Jehu. When
they had killed him, they buried him, "because," they said,
"he is the son of Jehoshaphat,
who sought the LORD with all
his heart."

So the house of Ahaziah
had no one to assume power
over the kingdom.

ATHALIAH REIGNS IN JUDAH

10Now when Athaliah the
mother of Ahaziah saw that
her son was dead, she arose
and destroyed all the royal
heirs of the house of Judah.
11But Jehoshabeath,[a] the
daughter of the king, took
Joash the son of Ahaziah,
and stole him away from
among the king's sons who
were being murdered, and put
him and his nurse in a bedroom. So Jehoshabeath, the
daughter of King Jehoram, the
wife of Jehoiada the priest (for
she was the sister of Ahaziah),
hid him from Athaliah so that
she did not kill him. 12And he
was hidden with them in the
house of God for six years,
while Athaliah reigned over
the land.

JOASH CROWNED KING OF JUDAH

23 In the seventh year Jehoiada strengthened
himself, *and made a* covenant
with the captains of hun-
dreds: Azariah the son of Jeroham, Ishmael the son of
Jehohanan, Azariah the son
of Obed, Maaseiah the son of
Adaiah, and Elishaphat the
son of Zichri. 2And they went
throughout Judah and gathered the Levites from all the
cities of Judah, and the chief

22:5 [a] Also spelled *Joram* (compare verses 5 and 7; 2 Kings 8:28; and elsewhere) 22:6 [a] Some Hebrew manuscripts, Septuagint, Syriac, Vulgate, and 2 Kings 8:29 read *Ahaziah*. 22:11 [a] Spelled *Jehosheba* in 2 Kings 11:2

fathers of Israel, and they
came to Jerusalem.
3Then all the assembly
made a covenant with the
king in the house of God. And
he said to them, "Behold, the
king's son shall reign, as the
LORD has said of the sons of
David. 4This *is* what you shall
do: One-third of you entering
on the Sabbath, of the priests
and the Levites, *shall be* keeping watch over the doors;
5one-third *shall be* at the
king's house; and one-third
at the Gate of the Foundation.
All the people *shall be* in the
courts of the house of the
LORD. 6But let no one come
into the house of the LORD
except the priests and those
of the Levites who serve. They
may go in, for they *are* holy;
but all the people shall keep
the watch of the LORD. 7And
the Levites shall surround the
king on all sides, every man
with his weapons in his hand;
and whoever comes into the
house, let him be put to death.
You are to be with the king
when he comes in and when
he goes out."
8So the Levites and all
Judah did according to all
that Jehoiada the priest commanded. And each man took
his men who were to be on
duty on the Sabbath, with
those who were going *off duty*
on the Sabbath; for Jehoiada
the priest had not dismissed
the divisions. 9And Jehoiada
the priest gave to the captains
of hundreds the spears and
the large and small shields
which *had belonged* to King
David, that *were* in the temple of God. 10Then he set all
the people, every man with
his weapon in his hand, from
the right side of the temple
to the left side of the temple,
along by the altar and by the
temple, all around the king.
11And they brought out the
king's son, put the crown on
him, *gave him* the Testimony,[a]
and made him king. Then Jehoiada and his sons anointed
him, and said, "*Long* live the
king!"

DEATH OF ATHALIAH

12Now when Athaliah heard
the noise of the people running and praising the king,
she came to the people *in* the
temple of the LORD. 13*When*
she looked, there was the king
standing by his pillar at the
entrance; and the leaders and
the trumpeters *were* by the
king. All the people of the land
were rejoicing and blowing
trumpets, also the singers
with musical instruments,
and those who led in praise.
So Athaliah tore her clothes
and said, "Treason! Treason!"
14And Jehoiada the priest
brought out the captains of
hundreds who were set over
the army, and said to them,

23:11 [a] That is, the Law (compare Exodus 25:16, 21; 31:18)

"Take her outside under
guard, and slay with the sword
whoever follows her." For the
priest had said, "Do not kill
her in the house of the LORD."
15So they seized her; and
she went by way of the entrance of the Horse Gate *into*
the king's house, and they
killed her there.
16Then Jehoiada made a
covenant between himself,
the people, and the king, that
they should be the LORD's
people. 17And all the people
went to the temple[a] of Baal,
and tore it down. They broke
in pieces its altars and images,
and killed Mattan the priest of
Baal before the altars. 18Also
Jehoiada appointed the oversight of the house of the LORD
to the hand of the priests, the
Levites, whom David had assigned in the house of the
LORD, to offer the burnt offerings of the LORD, as *it is*
written in the Law of Moses,
with rejoicing and with singing, *as it was established* by
David. 19And he set the gatekeepers at the gates of the
house of the LORD, so that
no one *who was* in any way
unclean should enter.
20Then he took the captains
of hundreds, the nobles, the
governors of the people, and
all the people of the land, and
brought the king down from
the house of the LORD; and
they went through the Upper
Gate to the king's house, and
set the king on the throne of
the kingdom. 21So all the people of the land rejoiced; and
the city was quiet, for they had
slain Athaliah with the sword.

JOASH REPAIRS THE TEMPLE

24 Joash *was* seven years
old when he became
king, and he reigned forty
years in Jerusalem. His
mother's name *was* Zibiah of
Beersheba. 2Joash did *what*
was right in the sight of the
LORD all the days of Jehoiada
the priest. 3And Jehoiada took
two wives for him, and he had
sons and daughters.
4Now it happened after this
that Joash set his heart on repairing the house of the LORD.
5Then he gathered the priests
and the Levites, and said to
them, "Go out to the cities of
Judah, and gather from all
Israel money to repair the
house of your God from year
to year, and see that you do it
quickly."
However the Levites did
not do it quickly. 6So the
king called Jehoiada the
chief *priest*, and said to him,
"Why have you not required
the Levites to bring in from
Judah and from Jerusalem
the collection, *according to*
the commandment of Moses
the servant of the LORD and
of the assembly of Israel, for

23:17 [a] Literally *house*

the tabernacle of witness?"
7For the sons of Athaliah, that
wicked woman, had broken
into the house of God, and had
also presented all the dedicated things of the house of
the LORD to the Baals.

8Then at the king's com-
mand they made a chest, and
set it outside at the gate of
the house of the LORD. 9And
they made a proclamation
throughout Judah and Jerusalem to bring to the LORD
the collection *that* Moses the
servant of God *had imposed*
on Israel in the wilderness.
10Then all the leaders and all
the people rejoiced, brought
their contributions, and put
them into the chest until all
had given. 11So it was, at that
time, when the chest was
brought to the king's official
by the hand of the Levites, and
when they saw that *there was*
much money, that the king's
scribe and the high priest's
officer came and emptied
the chest, and took it and
returned it to its place. Thus
they did day by day, and gathered money in abundance.

12The king and Jehoiada
gave it to those who did the
work of the service of the
house of the LORD; and they
hired masons and carpen-
ters to repair the house of
the LORD, and also those who
worked in iron and bronze to
restore the house of the LORD.
13So the workmen labored,
and the work was completed
by them; they restored the
house of God to its original
condition and reinforced it.
14When they had finished,
they brought the rest of the
money before the king and
Jehoiada; they made from it
articles for the house of the
LORD, articles for serving and
offering, spoons and vessels
of gold and silver. And they
offered burnt offerings in the
house of the LORD continually
all the days of Jehoiada.

APOSTASY OF JOASH

15But Jehoiada grew old
and was full of days, and he
died; *he was* one hundred and
thirty years old when he died.
16And they buried him in the
City of David among the kings,
because he had done good in
Israel, both toward God and
His house.

17Now after the death of Jehoiada the leaders of Judah
came and bowed down to the
king. And the king listened to
them. 18Therefore they left the
house of the LORD God of their
fathers, and served wooden
images and idols; and wrath
came upon Judah and Jeru-
salem because of their trespass. 19Yet He sent prophets
to them, to bring them back
to the LORD; and they testified
against them, but they would
not listen.

20Then the Spirit of God
came upon Zechariah the
son of Jehoiada the priest,
who stood above the people,

and said to them, "Thus says
God: 'Why do you transgress
the commandments of the
LORD, so that you cannot
prosper? Because you have
forsaken the LORD, He also
has forsaken you.'" 21So they
conspired against him, and
at the command of the king
they stoned him with stones
in the court of the house of
the LORD. 22Thus Joash the
king did not remember the
kindness which Jehoiada his
father had done to him, but
killed his son; and as he died,
he said, "The LORD look on *it,*
and repay!"

DEATH OF JOASH

23So it happened in the
spring of the year *that* the
army of Syria came up against
him; and they came to Judah
and Jerusalem, and destroyed
all the leaders of the people
from among the people, and
sent all their spoil to the king
of Damascus. 24For the army of
the Syrians came with a small
company of men; but the
LORD delivered a very great
army into their hand, because
they had forsaken the LORD
God of their fathers. So they
executed judgment against
Joash. 25And when they had
withdrawn from him (for they
left him severely wounded),
his own servants conspired
against him because of the
blood of the sons[a] of Jehoiada the priest, and killed him
on his bed. So he died. And
they buried him in the City of
David, but they did not bury
him in the tombs of the kings.

26These are the ones
who conspired against him:
Zabad[a] the son of Shimeath
the Ammonitess, and Jehozabad the son of Shimrith[b] the
Moabitess. 27Now *concerning*
his sons, and the many oracles
about him, and the repairing
of the house of God, indeed
they *are* written in the annals
of the book of the kings. Then
Amaziah his son reigned in
his place.

AMAZIAH REIGNS IN JUDAH

25 Amaziah *was* twenty-
five years old *when* he
became king, and he reigned
twenty-nine years in Jerusalem. His mother's name *was*
Jehoaddan of Jerusalem. 2And
he did *what was* right in the
sight of the LORD, but not with
a loyal heart.

3Now it happened, as soon
as the kingdom was estab-
lished for him, that he executed his servants who had
murdered his father the king.
4However he did not execute
their children, but *did* as *it is*
written in the Law in the Book

24:25 [a] Septuagint and Vulgate read *son* (compare verses 20–22). 24:26 [a] Or *Jozachar* (compare 2 Kings 12:21) [b] Or *Shomer* (compare 2 Kings 12:21)

of Moses, where the LORD
commanded, saying, "The fathers shall not be put to death
for their children, nor shall
the children be put to death
for their fathers; but a person
shall die for his own sin."[a]

THE WAR AGAINST EDOM

5Moreover Amaziah gath-
ered Judah together and set
over them captains of thousands and captains of hundreds, according to *their*
fathers' houses, throughout
all Judah and Benjamin; and
he numbered them from
twenty years old and above,
and found them to be three
hundred thousand choice
men, able to go to war, who
could handle spear and shield.
6He also hired one hundred
thousand mighty men of valor
from Israel for one hundred
talents of silver. 7But a man
of God came to him, saying,
"O king, do not let the army
of Israel go with you, for the
LORD *is* not with Israel—*not*
with any of the children of
Ephraim. 8But if you go, be
gone! Be strong in battle! *Even*
so, God shall make you fall before the enemy; for God has
power to help and to overthrow."

9Then Amaziah said to the
man of God, "But what *shall*
we do about the hundred talents which I have given to the
troops of Israel?"

And the man of God an-
swered, "The LORD is able
to give you much more than
this." 10So Amaziah discharged
the troops that had come to
him from Ephraim, to go back
home. Therefore their anger
was greatly aroused against
Judah, and they returned
home in great anger.

11Then Amaziah strength-
ened himself, and leading his
people, he went to the Valley
of Salt and killed ten thousand
of the people of Seir. 12Also
the children of Judah took
captive ten thousand alive,
brought them to the top of
the rock, and cast them down
from the top of the rock, so
that they all were dashed in
pieces.

13But as for the soldiers
of the army which Amaziah
had discharged, so that they
would not go with him to battle, they raided the cities of
Judah from Samaria to Beth
Horon, killed three thousand
in them, and took much spoil.

14Now it was so, after Amaziah came from the slaughter of the Edomites, that he
brought the gods of the people of Seir, set them up *to be*
his gods, and bowed down
before them and burned incense to them. 15Therefore
the anger of the LORD was
aroused against Amaziah, and
He sent him a prophet who
said to him, "Why have you

25:4 [a] Deuteronomy 24:16

sought the gods of the people,
which could not rescue their
own people from your hand?"
16So it was, as he talked
with him, that *the king* said
to him, "Have we made you
the king's counselor? Cease!
Why should you be killed?"

Then the prophet ceased,
and said, "I know that God has
determined to destroy you,
because you have done this
and have not heeded my advice."

ISRAEL DEFEATS JUDAH

17Now Amaziah king of
Judah asked advice and sent
to Joash[a] the son of Jehoahaz,
the son of Jehu, king of Israel,
saying, "Come, let us face one
another *in battle.*"
18And Joash king of Israel
sent to Amaziah king of
Judah, saying, "The thistle
that *was* in Lebanon sent to
the cedar that was in Lebanon,
saying, 'Give your daughter
to my son as wife'; and a wild
beast that *was* in Lebanon
passed by and trampled the
thistle. 19Indeed you say that
you have defeated the Edomites,
and your heart is lifted up
to boast. Stay at home now;
why should you meddle with
trouble, that you should fall—
you and Judah with you?"
20But Amaziah would not
heed, for it *came* from God,
that He might give them into
the hand *of their enemies,* because
they sought the gods
of Edom. 21So Joash king of
Israel went out; and he and
Amaziah king of Judah faced
one another at Beth Shemesh,
which *belongs* to Judah. 22And
Judah was defeated by Israel,
and every man fled to his tent.
23Then Joash the king of Israel
captured Amaziah king
of Judah, the son of Joash, the
son of Jehoahaz, at Beth Shemesh;
and he brought him to
Jerusalem, and broke down
the wall of Jerusalem from
the Gate of Ephraim to the
Corner Gate—four hundred
cubits. 24And *he took* all the
gold and silver, all the articles
that were found in the house
of God with Obed-Edom, the
treasures of the king's house,
and hostages, and returned to
Samaria.

DEATH OF AMAZIAH

25Amaziah the son of Joash,
king of Judah, lived fifteen
years after the death of Joash
the son of Jehoahaz, king of
Israel. 26Now the rest of the
acts of Amaziah, from first to
last, indeed *are* they not written
in the book of the kings
of Judah and Israel? 27After
the time that Amaziah turned
away from following the
LORD, they made a conspiracy
against him in Jerusalem, and
he fled to Lachish; but they
sent after him to Lachish and
killed him there. 28Then they

25:17 [a] Spelled *Jehoash* in 2 Kings 14:8ff

brought him on horses and
buried him with his fathers
in the City of Judah.

UZZIAH REIGNS IN JUDAH

26 Now all the people of
Judah took Uzziah,[a]
who *was* sixteen years old,
and made him king instead
of his father Amaziah. 2He
built Elath[a] and restored it to
Judah, after the king rested
with his fathers.

3Uzziah *was* sixteen years
old when he became king, and
he reigned fifty-two years in
Jerusalem. His mother's name
was Jecholiah of Jerusalem.
4And he did *what was* right in
the sight of the LORD, according to all that his father Amaziah had done. 5He sought
God in the days of Zechariah,
who had understanding in the
visions[a] of God; and as long
as he sought the LORD, God
made him prosper.

6Now he went out and
made war against the Philistines, and broke down the wall
of Gath, the wall of Jabneh,
and the wall of Ashdod; and
he built cities *around* Ashdod
and among the Philistines.
7God helped him against the
Philistines, against the Arabians who lived in Gur Baal, and
against the Meunites. 8Also
the Ammonites brought tribute to Uzziah. His fame spread
as far as the entrance of Egypt,
for he became exceedingly
strong.

9And Uzziah built towers
in Jerusalem at the Corner
Gate, at the Valley Gate, and
at the corner buttress of the
wall; then he fortified them.
10Also he built towers in the
desert. He dug many wells,
for he had much livestock,
both in the lowlands and in
the plains; *he also had* farmers and vinedressers in the
mountains and in Carmel, for
he loved the soil.

11Moreover Uzziah had an
army of fighting men who
went out to war by compa-
nies, according to the number
on their roll as prepared by
Jeiel the scribe and Maaseiah
the officer, under the hand of
Hananiah, *one* of the king's
captains. 12The total number of chief officers[a] of the
mighty men of valor *was* two
thousand six hundred. 13And
under their authority *was* an
army of three hundred and
seven thousand five hundred,
that made war with mighty
power, to help the king against
the enemy. 14Then Uzziah
prepared for them, for the
entire army, shields, spears,
helmets, body armor, bows,
and slings *to cast* stones.
15And he made devices in Jerusalem, invented by skillful

26:1 [a] Called *Azariah* in 2 Kings 14:21ff 26:2 [a] Hebrew *Eloth* 26:5 [a] Several Hebrew manuscripts, Septuagint, Syriac, Targum, and Arabic read *fear.* 26:12 [a] Literally *chief fathers*

men, to be on the towers and
the corners, to shoot arrows
and large stones. So his fame
spread far and wide, for he
was marvelously helped till
he became strong.

THE PENALTY FOR UZZIAH'S PRIDE

16But when he was strong
his heart was lifted up, to *his*
destruction, for he transgressed against the LORD his
God by entering the temple
of the LORD to burn incense
on the altar of incense. 17So
Azariah the priest went in
after him, and with him were
eighty priests of the LORD—
valiant men. 18And they withstood King Uzziah, and said to
him, "*It is* not for you, Uzziah,
to burn incense to the LORD,
but for the priests, the sons of
Aaron, who are consecrated
to burn incense. Get out of
the sanctuary, for you have
trespassed! You *shall have* no
honor from the LORD God."

19Then Uzziah became fu-
rious; and he *had* a censer
in his hand to burn incense.
And while he was angry with
the priests, leprosy broke out
on his forehead, before the
priests in the house of the
LORD, beside the incense altar.
20And Azariah the chief priest
and all the priests looked at
him, and there, on his forehead, he *was* leprous; so they
thrust him out of that place.
Indeed he also hurried to get
out, because the LORD had
struck him.

21King Uzziah was a leper
until the day of his death. He
dwelt in an isolated house,
because he was a leper; for
he was cut off from the house
of the LORD. Then Jotham his
son *was* over the king's house,
judging the people of the land.

22Now the rest of the acts
of Uzziah, from first to last,
the prophet Isaiah the son
of Amoz wrote. 23So Uzziah
rested with his fathers, and
they buried him with his fathers in the field of burial
which *belonged* to the kings,
for they said, "He is a leper."
Then Jotham his son reigned
in his place.

JOTHAM REIGNS IN JUDAH

27 Jotham *was* twenty-five
years old when he be-
came king, and he reigned sixteen years in Jerusalem. His
mother's name *was* Jerushah[a]
the daughter of Zadok. 2And
he did *what was* right in the
sight of the LORD, according
to all that his father Uzziah
had done (although he did not
enter the temple of the LORD).
But still the people acted corruptly.

3He built the Upper Gate
of the house of the LORD, and
he built extensively on the
wall of Ophel. 4Moreover he
built cities in the mountains

27:1 [a] Spelled *Jerusha* in 2 Kings 15:33

of Judah, and in the forests
he built fortresses and towers. 5He also fought with the
king of the Ammonites and
defeated them. And the people of Ammon gave him in
that year one hundred talents
of silver, ten thousand kors of
wheat, and ten thousand of
barley. The people of Ammon
paid this to him in the second
and third years also. 6So Jotham became mighty, because
he prepared his ways before
the LORD his God.
7Now the rest of the acts of
Jotham, and all his wars and
his ways, indeed they *are* written in the book of the kings
of Israel and Judah. 8He was
twenty-five years old when he
became king, and he reigned
sixteen years in Jerusalem.
9So Jotham rested with his fathers, and they buried him in
the City of David. Then Ahaz
his son reigned in his place.

AHAZ REIGNS IN JUDAH

28 Ahaz *was* twenty years
old when he became
king, and he reigned sixteen
years in Jerusalem; and he
did not do *what was* right
in the sight of the LORD, as
his father David *had done.*
2For he walked in the ways
of the kings of Israel, and
made molded images for the
Baals. 3He burned incense in
the Valley of the Son of Hinnom, and burned his children
in the fire, according to the
abominations of the nations
whom the LORD had cast out
before the children of Israel.
4And he sacrificed and burned
incense on the high places,
on the hills, and under every
green tree.

SYRIA AND ISRAEL DEFEAT JUDAH

5Therefore the LORD his
God delivered him into the
hand of the king of Syria.
They defeated him, and carried away a great multitude
of them as captives, and
brought *them* to Damascus.
Then he was also delivered
into the hand of the king of
Israel, who defeated him with
a great slaughter. 6For Pekah
the son of Remaliah killed one
hundred and twenty thousand
in Judah in one day, all valiant
men, because they had forsaken the LORD God of their
fathers. 7Zichri, a mighty man
of Ephraim, killed Maaseiah
the king's son, Azrikam the
officer over the house, and
Elkanah *who was* second to
the king. 8And the children
of Israel carried away captive
of their brethren two hundred
thousand women, sons, and
daughters; and they also took
away much spoil from them,
and brought the spoil to Samaria.

ISRAEL RETURNS THE CAPTIVES

9But a prophet of the LORD
was there, whose name *was*
Oded; and he went out before

the army that came to Samaria,
and said to them: "Look, because the LORD God of your
fathers was angry with Judah,
He has delivered them into
your hand; but you have killed
them in a rage *that* reaches
up to heaven. [10]And now you
propose to force the children
of Judah and Jerusalem to be
your male and female slaves;
but are you not also guilty before the LORD your God? [11]Now
hear me, therefore, and return the captives, whom you
have taken captive from your
brethren, for the fierce wrath
of the LORD *is* upon you."
[12]Then some of the heads
of the children of Ephraim,
Azariah the son of Johanan,
Berechiah the son of Meshillemoth, Jehizkiah the son of
Shallum, and Amasa the son
of Hadlai, stood up against
those who came from the war,
[13]and said to them, "You shall
not bring the captives here,
for we *already* have offended
the LORD. You intend to add
to our sins and to our guilt; for
our guilt is great, and *there is*
fierce wrath against Israel."
[14]So the armed men left the
captives and the spoil before
the leaders and all the assembly. [15]Then the men who were
designated by name rose up
and took the captives, and
from the spoil they clothed all
who were naked among them,
dressed them and gave them
sandals, gave them food and
drink, and anointed them;
and they let all the feeble
ones ride on donkeys. So they
brought them to their brethren at Jericho, the city of palm
trees. Then they returned to
Samaria.

ASSYRIA REFUSES TO HELP JUDAH

[16]At the same time King
Ahaz sent to the kings[a] of Assyria to help him. [17]For again
the Edomites had come, attacked Judah, and carried
away captives. [18]The Philistines also had invaded the
cities of the lowland and of
the South of Judah, and had
taken Beth Shemesh, Aijalon,
Gederoth, Sochoh with its villages, Timnah with its villages,
and Gimzo with its villages;
and they dwelt there. [19]For the
LORD brought Judah low because of Ahaz king of Israel,
for he had encouraged moral
decline in Judah and had been
continually unfaithful to the
LORD. [20]Also Tiglath-Pileser[a]
king of Assyria came to him
and distressed him, and did
not assist him. [21]For Ahaz took
part *of the treasures* from the
house of the LORD, from the
house of the king, and from
the leaders, and he gave *it* to
the king of Assyria; but he did
not help him.

28:16 [a] Septuagint, Syriac, and Vulgate read *king* (compare verse 20). **28:20** [a] Hebrew *Tilgath-Pilneser*

APOSTASY AND DEATH OF AHAZ

22Now in the time of his
distress King Ahaz became
increasingly unfaithful to the
LORD. This *is that* King Ahaz.
23For he sacrificed to the gods
of Damascus which had de-
feated him, saying, "Because
the gods of the kings of Syria
help them, I will sacrifice to
them that they may help me."
But they were the ruin of him
and of all Israel. 24So Ahaz
gathered the articles of the
house of God, cut in pieces the
articles of the house of God,
shut up the doors of the house
of the LORD, and made for himself altars in every corner of
Jerusalem. 25And in every single city of Judah he made high
places to burn incense to other
gods, and provoked to anger
the LORD God of his fathers.

26Now the rest of his acts
and all his ways, from first to
last, indeed they *are* written in
the book of the kings of Judah
and Israel. 27So Ahaz rested
with his fathers, and they buried him in the city, in Jerusalem; but they did not bring him
into the tombs of the kings of
Israel. Then Hezekiah his son
reigned in his place.

HEZEKIAH REIGNS IN JUDAH

29 Hezekiah became king
when he was twenty-
five years old, and he reigned
twenty-nine years in Jerusalem. His mother's name *was*
Abijah[a] the daughter of Zechariah. 2And he did *what was*
right in the sight of the LORD,
according to all that his father
David had done.

HEZEKIAH CLEANSES THE TEMPLE

3In the first year of his
reign, in the first month, he
opened the doors of the house
of the LORD and repaired
them. 4Then he brought in
the priests and the Levites,
and gathered them in the East
Square, 5and said to them:
"Hear me, Levites! Now sanctify yourselves, sanctify the
house of the LORD God of your
fathers, and carry out the rubbish from the holy *place.* 6For
our fathers have trespassed
and done evil in the eyes of the
LORD our God; they have forsaken Him, have turned their
faces away from the dwelling
place of the LORD, and turned
their backs *on Him.* 7They have
also shut up the doors of the
vestibule, put out the lamps,
and have not burned incense
or offered burnt offerings in
the holy *place* to the God of
Israel. 8Therefore the wrath of
the LORD fell upon Judah and
Jerusalem, and He has given
them up to trouble, to desolation, and to jeering, as you see
with your eyes. 9For indeed,
because of this our fathers

29:1 [a] Spelled *Abi* in 2 Kings 18:2

have fallen by the sword; and
our sons, our daughters, and
our wives *are* in captivity.
10"Now *it is* in my heart
to make a covenant with the
LORD God of Israel, that His
fierce wrath may turn away
from us. 11My sons, do not be
negligent now, for the LORD
has chosen you to stand before Him, to serve Him, and
that you should minister to
Him and burn incense."
12Then these Levites arose:
Mahath the son of Amasai and
Joel the son of Azariah, of the
sons of the Kohathites; of the
sons of Merari, Kish the son of
Abdi and Azariah the son of
Jehallelel; of the Gershonites,
Joah the son of Zimmah and
Eden the son of Joah; 13of the
sons of Elizaphan, Shimri and
Jeiel; of the sons of Asaph,
Zechariah and Mattaniah; 14of
the sons of Heman, Jehiel and
Shimei; and of the sons of Jeduthun, Shemaiah and Uzziel.
15And they gathered their
brethren, sanctified themselves, and went according
to the commandment of
the king, at the words of the
LORD, to cleanse the house of
the LORD. 16Then the priests
went into the inner part of
the house of the LORD to
cleanse *it*, and brought out
all the debris that they found
in the temple of the LORD to
the court of the house of the
LORD. And the Levites took *it*
out and carried *it* to the Brook
Kidron.
17Now they began to sanc-
tify on the first *day* of the first
month, and on the eighth day
of the month they came to the
vestibule of the LORD. So they
sanctified the house of the
LORD in eight days, and on
the sixteenth day of the first
month they finished.
18Then they went in to King
Hezekiah and said, "We have
cleansed all the house of the
LORD, the altar of burnt offerings with all its articles, and
the table of the showbread
with all its articles. 19Moreover
all the articles which King
Ahaz in his reign had cast
aside in his transgression we
have prepared and sanctified;
and there they *are*, before the
altar of the LORD."

HEZEKIAH RESTORES TEMPLE WORSHIP

20Then King Hezekiah rose
early, gathered the rulers of
the city, and went up to the
house of the LORD. 21And
they brought seven bulls,
seven rams, seven lambs,
and seven male goats for a
sin offering for the kingdom,
for the sanctuary, and for
Judah. Then he commanded
the priests, the sons of Aaron,
to offer *them* on the altar of
the LORD. 22So they killed the
bulls, and the priests received
the blood and sprinkled *it* on
the altar. Likewise they killed
the rams and sprinkled the
blood on the altar. They also
killed the lambs and sprin-

kled the blood on the altar.
[23]Then they brought out the
male goats *for* the sin offering before the king and the
assembly, and they laid their
hands on them. [24]And the
priests killed them; and they
presented their blood on the
altar as a sin offering to make
an atonement for all Israel,
for the king commanded *that*
the burnt offering and the sin
offering *be made* for all Israel.

[25]And he stationed the Levites in the house of the LORD
with cymbals, with stringed
instruments, and with harps,
according to the command-
ment of David, of Gad the
king's seer, and of Nathan
the prophet; for thus *was* the
commandment of the LORD
by His prophets. [26]The Levites
stood with the instruments of
David, and the priests with the
trumpets. [27]Then Hezekiah
commanded *them* to offer the
burnt offering on the altar.
And when the burnt offering
began, the song of the LORD
also began, with the trumpets
and with the instruments of
David king of Israel. [28]So all
the assembly worshiped, the
singers sang, and the trumpeters sounded; all *this continued* until the burnt offering
was finished. [29]And when they
had finished offering, the king
and all who were present with
him bowed and worshiped.
[30]Moreover King Hezekiah
and the leaders commanded
the Levites to sing praise to
the LORD with the words of
David and of Asaph the seer.
So they sang praises with
gladness, and they bowed
their heads and worshiped.

[31]Then Hezekiah answered
and said, "Now *that* you have
consecrated yourselves to the
LORD, come near, and bring
sacrifices and thank offerings
into the house of the LORD." So
the assembly brought in sacrifices and thank offerings, and
as many as were of a willing
heart *brought* burnt offerings.
[32]And the number of the burnt
offerings which the assembly
brought was seventy bulls, one
hundred rams, *and* two hundred lambs; all these *were* for
a burnt offering to the LORD.
[33]The consecrated things *were*
six hundred bulls and three
thousand sheep. [34]But the
priests were too few, so that
they could not skin all the
burnt offerings; therefore their
brethren the Levites helped
them until the work was ended
and until the *other* priests had
sanctified themselves, for the
Levites were more diligent in
sanctifying themselves than
the priests. [35]Also the burnt
offerings *were* in abundance,
with the fat of the peace offerings and *with* the drink offerings for *every* burnt offering.

So the service of the house
of the LORD was set in order.
[36]Then Hezekiah and all the
people rejoiced that God had
prepared the people, since the
events took place so suddenly.

HEZEKIAH KEEPS THE PASSOVER

30 And Hezekiah sent to
all Israel and Judah,
and also wrote letters to
Ephraim and Manasseh,
that they should come to the
house of the LORD at Jerusalem, to keep the Passover to
the LORD God of Israel. 2For
the king and his leaders and
all the assembly in Jerusalem
had agreed to keep the Passover in the second month.
3For they could not keep it at
the regular time,[a] because a
sufficient number of priests
had not consecrated them-
selves, nor had the people
gathered together at Jerusalem. 4And the matter pleased
the king and all the assembly.
5So they resolved to make a
proclamation throughout all
Israel, from Beersheba to Dan,
that they should come to keep
the Passover to the LORD God
of Israel at Jerusalem, since
they had not done *it* for a long
time in the *prescribed* manner.
6Then the runners went
throughout all Israel and
Judah with the letters from
the king and his leaders, and
spoke according to the command of the king: "Children of
Israel, return to the LORD God
of Abraham, Isaac, and Israel;
then He will return to the remnant of you who have escaped
from the hand of the kings of
Assyria. 7And do not be like
your fathers and your brethren, who trespassed against
the LORD God of their fathers,
so that He gave them up to
desolation, as you see. 8Now
do not be stiff-necked, as your
fathers *were, but* yield yourselves to the LORD; and enter
His sanctuary, which He has
sanctified forever, and serve
the LORD your God, that the
fierceness of His wrath may
turn away from you. 9For if you
return to the LORD, your brethren and your children *will be*
treated with compassion by
those who lead them captive,
so that they may come back
to this land; for the LORD your
God *is* gracious and merciful,
and will not turn *His* face from
you if you return to Him."
10So the runners passed
from city to city through the
country of Ephraim and Manasseh, as far as Zebulun; but
they laughed at them and
mocked them. 11Nevertheless
some from Asher, Manasseh,
and Zebulun humbled them-
selves and came to Jerusalem.
12Also the hand of God was on
Judah to give them singleness
of heart to obey the command
of the king and the leaders, at
the word of the LORD.
13Now many people, a very
great assembly, gathered at
Jerusalem to keep the Feast of
Unleavened Bread in the sec-

30:3 [a] That is, the first month (compare Leviticus 23:5); literally *at that time*

ond month. 14They arose and took away the altars that *were* in Jerusalem, and they took away all the incense altars and cast *them* into the Brook Kidron. 15Then they slaughtered the Passover *lambs* on the fourteenth *day* of the second month. The priests and the Levites were ashamed, and sanctified themselves, and brought the burnt offerings to the house of the LORD. 16They stood in their place according to their custom, according to the Law of Moses the man of God; the priests sprinkled the blood *received* from the hand of the Levites. 17For *there were* many in the assembly who had not sanctified themselves; therefore the Levites had charge of the slaughter of the Passover *lambs* for everyone *who was* not clean, to sanctify *them* to the LORD. 18For a multitude of the people, many from Ephraim, Manasseh, Issachar, and Zebulun, had not cleansed themselves, yet they ate the Passover contrary to what was written. But Hezekiah prayed for them, saying, "May the good LORD provide atonement for everyone 19*who* prepares his heart to seek God, the LORD God of his fathers, though *he is* not *cleansed* according to the purification of the sanctuary." 20And the LORD listened to Hezekiah and healed the people.

21So the children of Israel who were present at Jerusalem kept the Feast of Unleavened Bread seven days with great gladness; and the Levites and the priests praised the LORD day by day, *singing* to the LORD, accompanied by loud instruments. 22And Hezekiah gave encouragement to all the Levites who taught the good knowledge of the LORD; and they ate throughout the feast seven days, offering peace offerings and making confession to the LORD God of their fathers.

23Then the whole assembly agreed to keep *the feast* another seven days, and they kept it *another* seven days with gladness. 24For Hezekiah king of Judah gave to the assembly a thousand bulls and seven thousand sheep, and the leaders gave to the assembly a thousand bulls and ten thousand sheep; and a great number of priests sanctified themselves. 25The whole assembly of Judah rejoiced, also the priests and Levites, all the assembly that came from Israel, the sojourners who came from the land of Israel, and those who dwelt in Judah. 26So there was great joy in Jerusalem, for since the time of Solomon the son of David, king of Israel, *there had* been nothing like this in Jerusalem. 27Then the priests, the Levites, arose and blessed the people, and their voice was heard; and their prayer came *up* to His holy dwelling place, to heaven.

THE REFORMS OF HEZEKIAH

31 Now when all this was
finished, all Israel who
were present went out to the
cities of Judah and broke the
sacred pillars in pieces, cut
down the wooden images,
and threw down the high
places and the altars—from
all Judah, Benjamin, Ephraim,
and Manasseh—until they
had utterly destroyed them
all. Then all the children of
Israel returned to their own
cities, every man to his possession.
2And Hezekiah appointed
the divisions of the priests
and the Levites according
to their divisions, each man
according to his service, the
priests and Levites for burnt
offerings and peace offerings,
to serve, to give thanks, and
to praise in the gates of the
camp[a] of the LORD. 3The king
also *appointed* a portion of his
possessions for the burnt offerings: for the morning and
evening burnt offerings, the
burnt offerings for the Sabbaths and the New Moons and
the set feasts, as *it is* written
in the Law of the LORD.
4Moreover he commanded
the people who dwelt in Jerusalem to contribute support
for the priests and the Levites,
that they might devote themselves to the Law of the LORD.
5As soon as the command-
ment was circulated, the
children of Israel brought in
abundance the firstfruits of
grain and wine, oil and honey,
and of all the produce of the
field; and they brought in
abundantly the tithe of everything. 6And the children of
Israel and Judah, who dwelt
in the cities of Judah, brought
the tithe of oxen and sheep;
also the tithe of holy things
which were consecrated to
the LORD their God they laid
in heaps.
7In the third month they
began laying them in heaps,
and they finished in the seventh month. 8And when Hezekiah and the leaders came and
saw the heaps, they blessed
the LORD and His people Israel. 9Then Hezekiah questioned the priests and the
Levites concerning the heaps.
10And Azariah the chief priest,
from the house of Zadok, answered him and said, "Since
the people began to bring the
offerings into the house of the
LORD, we have had enough
to eat and have plenty left,
for the LORD has blessed His
people; and what is left *is* this
great abundance."
11Now Hezekiah com-
manded *them* to prepare
rooms in the house of the
LORD, and they prepared
them. 12Then they faithfully
brought in the offerings, the
tithes, and the dedicated

31:2 [a] That is, the temple

things; Cononiah the Levite had charge of them, and Shimei his brother *was* the next. [13]Jehiel, Azaziah, Nahath, Asahel, Jerimoth, Jozabad, Eliel, Ismachiah, Mahath, and Benaiah *were* overseers under the hand of Cononiah and Shimei his brother, at the commandment of Hezekiah the king and Azariah the ruler of the house of God. [14]Kore the son of Imnah the Levite, the keeper of the East Gate, *was* over the freewill offerings to God, to distribute the offerings of the LORD and the most holy things. [15]And under him *were* Eden, Miniamin, Jeshua, Shemaiah, Amariah, and Shecaniah, *his* faithful assistants in the cities of the priests, to distribute allotments to their brethren by divisions, to the great as well as the small.

[16]Besides those males from three years old and up who were written in the genealogy, they distributed to everyone who entered the house of the LORD his daily portion for the work of his service, by his division, [17]and to the priests who were written in the genealogy according to their father's house, and to the Levites from twenty years old and up according to their work, by their divisions, [18]and to all who were written in the genealogy—their little ones and their wives, their sons and daughters, the whole company of them—for in their faithfulness they sanctified themselves in holiness.

[19]Also for the sons of Aaron the priests, *who were* in the fields of the common-lands of their cities, in every single city, *there were* men who were designated by name to distribute portions to all the males among the priests and to all who were listed by genealogies among the Levites.

[20]Thus Hezekiah did throughout all Judah, and he did what *was* good and right and true before the LORD his God. [21]And in every work that he began in the service of the house of God, in the law and in the commandment, to seek his God, he did *it* with all his heart. So he prospered.

SENNACHERIB BOASTS AGAINST THE LORD

32 After these deeds of faithfulness, Sennacherib king of Assyria came and entered Judah; he encamped against the fortified cities, thinking to win them over to himself. [2]And when Hezekiah saw that Sennacherib had come, and that his purpose was to make war against Jerusalem, [3]he consulted with his leaders and commanders[a] to stop the water from the springs which *were* outside the city; and they helped him.

32:3 [a] Literally *mighty men*

4Thus many people gathered
together who stopped all the
springs and the brook that
ran through the land, saying,
"Why should the kings[a] of
Assyria come and find much
water?" 5And he strengthened
himself, built up all the wall
that was broken, raised *it* up
to the towers, and *built* another wall outside; also he repaired the Millo[a] *in* the City of
David, and made weapons and
shields in abundance. 6Then
he set military captains over
the people, gathered them
together to him in the open
square of the city gate, and
gave them encouragement,
saying, 7"Be strong and courageous; do not be afraid nor
dismayed before the king of
Assyria, nor before all the
multitude that *is* with him;
for *there are* more with us
than with him. 8With him *is*
an arm of flesh; but with us *is*
the LORD our God, to help us
and to fight our battles." And
the people were strengthened
by the words of Hezekiah king
of Judah.

9After this Sennacherib
king of Assyria sent his servants to Jerusalem (but he
and all the forces with him *laid
siege* against Lachish), to Hezekiah king of Judah, and to all
Judah who *were* in Jerusalem,
saying, 10"Thus says Sennacherib king of Assyria: 'In what
do you trust, that you remain
under siege in Jerusalem?
11Does not Hezekiah persuade
you to give yourselves over to
die by famine and by thirst,
saying, "The LORD our God
will deliver us from the hand
of the king of Assyria"? 12Has
not the same Hezekiah taken
away His high places and His
altars, and commanded Judah
and Jerusalem, saying, "You
shall worship before one altar
and burn incense on it"? 13Do
you not know what I and my
fathers have done to all the
peoples of *other* lands? Were
the gods of the nations of
those lands in any way able
to deliver their lands out of
my hand? 14Who *was there*
among all the gods of those
nations that my fathers utterly destroyed that could
deliver his people from my
hand, that your God should
be able to deliver you from
my hand? 15Now therefore, do
not let Hezekiah deceive you
or persuade you like this, and
do not believe him; for no god
of any nation or kingdom was
able to deliver his people from
my hand or the hand of my
fathers. How much less will
your God deliver you from my
hand?'"

16Furthermore, his ser-
vants spoke against the LORD
God and against His servant
Hezekiah.

32:4 [a] Following Masoretic Text and Vulgate; Arabic, Septuagint, and Syriac read *king*. 32:5 [a] Literally *The Landfill*

17He also wrote letters to revile the LORD God of Israel, and to speak against Him, saying, "As the gods of the nations of *other* lands have not delivered their people from my hand, so the God of Hezekiah will not deliver His people from my hand." 18Then they called out with a loud voice in Hebrew[a] to the people of Jerusalem who *were* on the wall, to frighten them and trouble them, that they might take the city. 19And they spoke against the God of Jerusalem, as against the gods of the people of the earth—the work of men's hands.

SENNACHERIB'S DEFEAT AND DEATH

20Now because of this King Hezekiah and the prophet Isaiah, the son of Amoz, prayed and cried out to heaven. 21Then the LORD sent an angel who cut down every mighty man of valor, leader, and captain in the camp of the king of Assyria. So he returned shamefaced to his own land. And when he had gone into the temple of his god, some of his own offspring struck him down with the sword there.

22Thus the LORD saved Hezekiah and the inhabitants of Jerusalem from the hand of Sennacherib the king of Assyria, and from the hand of all *others,* and guided them[a] on every side. 23And many brought gifts to the LORD at Jerusalem, and presents to Hezekiah king of Judah, so that he was exalted in the sight of all nations thereafter.

HEZEKIAH HUMBLES HIMSELF

24In those days Hezekiah was sick and near death, and he prayed to the LORD; and He spoke to him and gave him a sign. 25But Hezekiah did not repay according to the favor *shown* him, for his heart was lifted up; therefore wrath was looming over him and over Judah and Jerusalem. 26Then Hezekiah humbled himself for the pride of his heart, he and the inhabitants of Jerusalem, so that the wrath of the LORD did not come upon them in the days of Hezekiah.

HEZEKIAH'S WEALTH AND HONOR

27Hezekiah had very great riches and honor. And he made himself treasuries for silver, for gold, for precious stones, for spices, for shields, and for all kinds of desirable items; 28storehouses for the harvest of grain, wine, and oil; and stalls for all kinds of livestock, and folds for flocks.[a] 29Moreover he provided cities

32:18 [a] Literally *Judean* **32:22** [a] Septuagint reads *gave them rest;* Vulgate reads *gave them treasures.* **32:28** [a] Following Septuagint and Vulgate; Arabic and Syriac omit *folds for flocks;* Masoretic Text reads *flocks for sheepfolds.*

for himself, and possessions
of flocks and herds in abundance; for God had given him
very much property. 30This
same Hezekiah also stopped
the water outlet of Upper
Gihon, and brought the water
by tunnel[a] to the west side of
the City of David. Hezekiah
prospered in all his works.
31However, *regarding* the
ambassadors of the princes
of Babylon, whom they sent
to him to inquire about the
wonder that was *done* in the
land, God withdrew from him,
in order to test him, that He
might know all *that was* in his
heart.

DEATH OF HEZEKIAH

32Now the rest of the acts of
Hezekiah, and his goodness,
indeed they *are* written in the
vision of Isaiah the prophet,
the son of Amoz, *and* in the
book of the kings of Judah and
Israel. 33So Hezekiah rested
with his fathers, and they buried him in the upper tombs
of the sons of David; and all
Judah and the inhabitants of
Jerusalem honored him at his
death. Then Manasseh his son
reigned in his place.

MANASSEH REIGNS IN JUDAH

33 Manasseh *was* twelve
years old when he be-
came king, and he reigned
fifty-five years in Jerusalem.
2But he did evil in the sight
of the LORD, according to the
abominations of the nations
whom the LORD had cast out
before the children of Israel.
3For he rebuilt the high places
which Hezekiah his father had
broken down; he raised up altars for the Baals, and made
wooden images; and he worshiped all the host of heaven[a]
and served them. 4He also
built altars in the house of
the LORD, of which the LORD
had said, "In Jerusalem shall
My name be forever." 5And he
built altars for all the host of
heaven in the two courts of
the house of the LORD. 6Also
he caused his sons to pass
through the fire in the Valley of the Son of Hinnom; he
practiced soothsaying, used
witchcraft and sorcery, and
consulted mediums and spiritists. He did much evil in the
sight of the LORD, to provoke
Him to anger. 7He even set a
carved image, the idol which
he had made, in the house of
God, of which God had said to
David and to Solomon his son,
"In this house and in Jerusalem, which I have chosen out
of all the tribes of Israel, I will
put My name forever; 8and
I will not again remove the
foot of Israel from the land
which I have appointed for
your fathers—only if they are

32:30 [a] Literally *brought it straight* (compare 2 Kings 20:20) 33:3 [a] The gods of the Assyrians

careful to do all that I have
commanded them, accord-
ing to the whole law and the
statutes and the ordinances
by the hand of Moses." [9]So
Manasseh seduced Judah
and the inhabitants of Jerusalem to do more evil than the
nations whom the LORD had
destroyed before the children
of Israel.

MANASSEH RESTORED AFTER REPENTANCE

[10]And the LORD spoke to
Manasseh and his people, but
they would not listen. [11]There-
fore the LORD brought upon
them the captains of the army
of the king of Assyria, who
took Manasseh with hooks,[a]
bound him with bronze *fetters*, and carried him off to
Babylon. [12]Now when he was
in affliction, he implored the
LORD his God, and humbled
himself greatly before the God
of his fathers, [13]and prayed
to Him; and He received his
entreaty, heard his supplication, and brought him back to
Jerusalem into his kingdom.
Then Manasseh knew that the
LORD *was* God.

[14]After this he built a wall
outside the City of David on
the west side of Gihon, in the
valley, as far as the entrance
of the Fish Gate; and *it* enclosed Ophel, and he raised
it to a very great height. Then
he put military captains in all
the fortified cities of Judah.
[15]He took away the foreign
gods and the idol from the
house of the LORD, and all
the altars that he had built in
the mount of the house of the
LORD and in Jerusalem; and
he cast *them* out of the city.
[16]He also repaired the altar
of the LORD, sacrificed peace
offerings and thank offerings
on it, and commanded Judah
to serve the LORD God of Israel. [17]Nevertheless the people still sacrificed on the high
places, *but* only to the LORD
their God.

DEATH OF MANASSEH

[18]Now the rest of the acts
of Manasseh, his prayer to
his God, and the words of the
seers who spoke to him in the
name of the LORD God of Israel, indeed they *are written*
in the book[a] of the kings of
Israel. [19]Also his prayer and
how God received his entreaty, and all his sin and trespass, and the sites where he
built high places and set up
wooden images and carved
images, before he was humbled, indeed they *are* written
among the sayings of Hozai.[a]
[20]So Manasseh rested with
his fathers, and they buried
him in his own house. Then
his son Amon reigned in his
place.

33:11 [a] That is, nose hooks (compare 2 Kings 19:28)
33:18 [a] Literally *words* 33:19 [a] Septuagint reads *the seers*.

AMON'S REIGN AND DEATH

21 Amon *was* twenty-two years old when he became king, and he reigned two years in Jerusalem. 22 But he did evil in the sight of the LORD, as his father Manasseh had done; for Amon sacrificed to all the carved images which his father Manasseh had made, and served them. 23 And he did not humble himself before the LORD, as his father Manasseh had humbled himself; but Amon trespassed more and more.

24 Then his servants conspired against him, and killed him in his own house. 25 But the people of the land executed all those who had conspired against King Amon. Then the people of the land made his son Josiah king in his place.

JOSIAH REIGNS IN JUDAH

34 Josiah *was* eight years old when he became king, and he reigned thirty-one years in Jerusalem. 2 And he did *what was* right in the sight of the LORD, and walked in the ways of his father David; *he* did *not* turn aside to the right hand or to the left.

3 For in the eighth year of his reign, while he was still young, he began to seek the God of his father David; and in the twelfth year he began to purge Judah and Jerusalem of the high places, the wooden images, the carved images, and the molded images. 4 They broke down the altars of the Baals in his presence, and the incense altars which *were* above them he cut down; and the wooden images, the carved images, and the molded images he broke in pieces, and made dust of them and scattered *it* on the graves of those who had sacrificed to them. 5 He also burned the bones of the priests on their altars, and cleansed Judah and Jerusalem. 6 And *so he did* in the cities of Manasseh, Ephraim, and Simeon, as far as Naphtali and all around, with axes.[a] 7 When he had broken down the altars and the wooden images, had beaten the carved images into powder, and cut down all the incense altars throughout all the land of Israel, he returned to Jerusalem.

HILKIAH FINDS THE BOOK OF THE LAW

8 In the eighteenth year of his reign, when he had purged the land and the temple,[a] he sent Shaphan the son of Azaliah, Maaseiah the governor of the city, and Joah the son of Joahaz the recorder, to repair the house of the LORD his God. 9 When they came to Hilkiah the high priest, they delivered the money that was brought into the house of God, which

34:6 [a] Literally *swords* 34:8 [a] Literally *house*

the Levites who kept the doors
had gathered from the hand of
Manasseh and Ephraim, from
all the remnant of Israel, from
all Judah and Benjamin, and
which they had brought back
to Jerusalem. [10]Then they put
it in the hand of the foremen
who had the oversight of the
house of the LORD; and they
gave it to the workmen who
worked in the house of the
LORD, to repair and restore
the house. [11]They gave *it* to
the craftsmen and builders to
buy hewn stone and timber for
beams, and to floor the houses
which the kings of Judah had
destroyed. [12]And the men did
the work faithfully. Their overseers *were* Jahath and Obadiah the Levites, of the sons
of Merari, and Zechariah and
Meshullam, of the sons of the
Kohathites, to supervise. *Others of* the Levites, all of whom
were skillful with instruments
of music, [13]*were* over the burden bearers and *were* overseers of all who did work in
any kind of service. And *some*
of the Levites *were* scribes, officers, and gatekeepers.

[14]Now when they brought
out the money that was
brought into the house of the
LORD, Hilkiah the priest found
the Book of the Law of the
LORD *given* by Moses. [15]Then
Hilkiah answered and said to
Shaphan the scribe, "I have
found the Book of the Law in
the house of the LORD." And
Hilkiah gave the book to Shaphan. [16]So Shaphan carried
the book to the king, bringing the king word, saying, "All
that was committed to your
servants they are doing. [17]And
they have gathered the money
that was found in the house of
the LORD, and have delivered it
into the hand of the overseers
and the workmen." [18]Then Shaphan the scribe told the king,
saying, "Hilkiah the priest has
given me a book." And Shaphan read it before the king.

[19]Thus it happened, when
the king heard the words of the
Law, that he tore his clothes.
[20]Then the king commanded
Hilkiah, Ahikam the son of
Shaphan, Abdon[a] the son of
Micah, Shaphan the scribe,
and Asaiah a servant of the
king, saying, [21]"Go, inquire
of the LORD for me, and for
those who are left in Israel
and Judah, concerning the
words of the book that is
found; for great *is* the wrath of
the LORD that is poured out on
us, because our fathers have
not kept the word of the LORD,
to do according to all that is
written in this book."

[22]So Hilkiah and those the
king *had appointed* went to
Huldah the prophetess, the
wife of Shallum the son of
Tokhath,[a] the son of Hasrah,[b]

34:20 [a] *Achbor the son of Michaiah* in 2 Kings 22:12 34:22 [a] Spelled *Tikvah* in 2 Kings 22:14 [b] Spelled *Harhas* in 2 Kings 22:14

keeper of the wardrobe. (She
dwelt in Jerusalem in the Second Quarter.) And they spoke
to her to that *effect.*
23Then she answered them,
"Thus says the LORD God of
Israel, 'Tell the man who sent
you to Me, 24"Thus says the
LORD: 'Behold, I will bring calamity on this place and on its
inhabitants, all the curses that
are written in the book which
they have read before the king
of Judah, 25because they have
forsaken Me and burned incense to other gods, that they
might provoke Me to anger
with all the works of their
hands. Therefore My wrath
will be poured out on this
place, and not be quenched.'"'
26But as for the king of Judah,
who sent you to inquire of the
LORD, in this manner you shall
speak to him, 'Thus says the
LORD God of Israel: "*Concerning* the words which you have
heard— 27because your heart
was tender, and you humbled
yourself before God when you
heard His words against this
place and against its inhabitants, and you humbled yourself before Me, and you tore
your clothes and wept before
Me, I also have heard *you,*"
says the LORD. 28"Surely I will
gather you to your fathers, and
you shall be gathered to your
grave in peace; and your eyes
shall not see all the calamity
which I will bring on this place
and its inhabitants."'" So they
brought back word to the king.

JOSIAH RESTORES TRUE WORSHIP

29Then the king sent and
gathered all the elders of Judah
and Jerusalem. 30The king
went up to the house of the
LORD, with all the men of Judah
and the inhabitants of Jerusalem—the priests and the Levites, and all the people, great
and small. And he read in their
hearing all the words of the
Book of the Covenant which
had been found in the house
of the LORD. 31Then the king
stood in his place and made a
covenant before the LORD, to
follow the LORD, and to keep
His commandments and His
testimonies and His statutes
with all his heart and all his
soul, to perform the words of
the covenant that were written
in this book. 32And he made all
who were present in Jerusalem
and Benjamin take a stand. So
the inhabitants of Jerusalem
did according to the covenant
of God, the God of their fathers.
33Thus Josiah removed all the
abominations from all the
country that *belonged* to the
children of Israel, and made
all who were present in Israel diligently serve the LORD
their God. All his days they did
not depart from following the
LORD God of their fathers.

JOSIAH KEEPS THE PASSOVER

35 Now Josiah kept a Passover to the LORD in
Jerusalem, and they slaugh-

tered the Passover *lambs* on
the fourteenth *day* of the first
month. 2And he set the priests
in their duties and encouraged
them for the service of the
house of the LORD. 3Then he
said to the Levites who taught
all Israel, who were holy to the
LORD: "Put the holy ark in the
house which Solomon the son
of David, king of Israel, built. *It
shall* no longer *be* a burden on
your shoulders. Now serve the
LORD your God and His people
Israel. 4Prepare *yourselves* according to your fathers' houses,
according to your divisions,
following the written instruction of David king of Israel
and the written instruction of
Solomon his son. 5And stand
in the holy *place* according to
the divisions of the fathers'
houses of your brethren the *lay*
people, and *according to* the
division of the father's house
of the Levites. 6So slaughter
the Passover *offerings,* consecrate yourselves, and prepare
them for your brethren, that
they may do according to the
word of the LORD by the hand
of Moses."

7Then Josiah gave the *lay*
people lambs and young goats
from the flock, all for Passover
offerings for all who were present, to the number of thirty
thousand, as well as three
thousand cattle; these *were*
from the king's possessions.
8And his leaders gave willingly
to the people, to the priests,
and to the Levites. Hilkiah,
Zechariah, and Jehiel, rulers
of the house of God, gave to
the priests for the Passover *offerings* two thousand six hundred *from the flock,* and three
hundred cattle. 9Also Cona-
niah, his brothers Shemaiah
and Nethanel, and Hashabiah
and Jeiel and Jozabad, chief
of the Levites, gave to the Levites for Passover *offerings* five
thousand *from the flock* and
five hundred cattle.

10So the service was pre-
pared, and the priests stood
in their places, and the Levites
in their divisions, according
to the king's command. 11And
they slaughtered the Passover
offerings; and the priests sprinkled *the blood* with their hands,
while the Levites skinned *the
animals.* 12Then they removed
the burnt offerings that *they*
might give them to the divisions of the fathers' houses
of the *lay* people, to offer to
the LORD, as *it is* written in the
Book of Moses. And so *they
did* with the cattle. 13Also they
roasted the Passover *offerings*
with fire according to the ordinance; but the *other* holy
offerings they boiled in pots,
in caldrons, and in pans, and
divided *them* quickly among
all the *lay* people. 14Then afterward they prepared portions
for themselves and for the
priests, because the priests,
the sons of Aaron, *were busy*
in offering burnt offerings and
fat until night; therefore the
Levites prepared portions for

themselves and for the priests, the sons of Aaron. 15And the singers, the sons of Asaph, *were* in their places, according to the command of David, Asaph, Heman, and Jeduthun the king's seer. Also the gatekeepers were at each gate; they did not have to leave their position, because their brethren the Levites prepared portions for them.

16So all the service of the LORD was prepared the same day, to keep the Passover and to offer burnt offerings on the altar of the LORD, according to the command of King Josiah. 17And the children of Israel who were present kept the Passover at that time, and the Feast of Unleavened Bread for seven days. 18There had been no Passover kept in Israel like that since the days of Samuel the prophet; and none of the kings of Israel had kept such a Passover as Josiah kept, with the priests and the Levites, all Judah and Israel who were present, and the inhabitants of Jerusalem. 19In the eighteenth year of the reign of Josiah this Passover was kept.

JOSIAH DIES IN BATTLE

20After all this, when Josiah had prepared the temple, Necho king of Egypt came up to fight against Carchemish by the Euphrates; and Josiah went out against him. 21But he sent messengers to him, saying, "What have I to do with you, king of Judah? *I have* not *come* against you this day, but against the house with which I have war; for God commanded me to make haste. Refrain *from meddling with* God, who *is* with me, lest He destroy you." 22Nevertheless Josiah would not turn his face from him, but disguised himself so that he might fight with him, and did not heed the words of Necho from the mouth of God. So he came to fight in the Valley of Megiddo.

23And the archers shot King Josiah; and the king said to his servants, "Take me away, for I am severely wounded." 24His servants therefore took him out of that chariot and put him in the second chariot that he had, and they brought him to Jerusalem. So he died, and was buried in *one of* the tombs of his fathers. And all Judah and Jerusalem mourned for Josiah.

25Jeremiah also lamented for Josiah. And to this day all the singing men and the singing women speak of Josiah in their lamentations. They made it a custom in Israel; and indeed they *are* written in the Laments.

26Now the rest of the acts of Josiah and his goodness, according to *what was* written in the Law of the LORD, 27and his deeds from first to last, indeed they *are* written in the book of the kings of Israel and Judah.

THE REIGN AND CAPTIVITY OF JEHOAHAZ

36 Then the people of the
land took Jehoahaz the
son of Josiah, and made him
king in his father's place in
Jerusalem. 2Jehoahaz[a] *was*
twenty-three years old when
he became king, and he
reigned three months in Jerusalem. 3Now the king of Egypt
deposed him at Jerusalem;
and he imposed on the land a
tribute of one hundred talents
of silver and a talent of gold.
4Then the king of Egypt made
Jehoahaz's[a] brother Eliakim
king over Judah and Jerusalem, and changed his name to
Jehoiakim. And Necho took
Jehoahaz[b] his brother and
carried him off to Egypt.

THE REIGN AND CAPTIVITY OF JEHOIAKIM

5Jehoiakim *was* twenty-five
years old when he became
king, and he reigned eleven
years in Jerusalem. And he
did evil in the sight of the
LORD his God. 6Nebuchad-
nezzar king of Babylon came
up against him, and bound
him in bronze *fetters* to carry
him off to Babylon. 7Nebu-
chadnezzar also carried off
some of the articles from the
house of the LORD to Babylon,
and put them in his temple at
Babylon. 8Now the rest of the
acts of Jehoiakim, the abominations which he did, and
what was found against him,
indeed they *are* written in the
book of the kings of Israel and
Judah. Then Jehoiachin his
son reigned in his place.

THE REIGN AND CAPTIVITY OF JEHOIACHIN

9Jehoiachin *was* eight[a]
years old when he became
king, and he reigned in Jerusalem three months and ten
days. And he did evil in the
sight of the LORD. 10At the
turn of the year King Nebuchadnezzar summoned *him*
and took him to Babylon,
with the costly articles from
the house of the LORD, and
made Zedekiah, *Jehoiakim's*[a]
brother, king over Judah and
Jerusalem.

ZEDEKIAH REIGNS IN JUDAH

11Zedekiah *was* twenty-one
years old when he became
king, and he reigned eleven
years in Jerusalem. 12He did
evil in the sight of the LORD
his God, *and* did not humble
himself before Jeremiah the
prophet, *who spoke* from the
mouth of the LORD. 13And he
also rebelled against King
Nebuchadnezzar, who had
made him swear *an oath*
by God; but he stiffened his

36:2 [a] Masoretic Text reads *Joahaz.* **36:4** [a] Literally *his* [b] Masoretic Text reads *Joahaz.* **36:9** [a] Some Hebrew manuscripts, Septuagint, Syriac, and 2 Kings 24:8 read *eighteen.* **36:10** [a] Literally *his* (compare 2 Kings 24:17)

neck and hardened his heart against turning to the LORD God of Israel. 14Moreover all the leaders of the priests and the people transgressed more and more, *according* to all the abominations of the nations, and defiled the house of the LORD which He had consecrated in Jerusalem.

THE FALL OF JERUSALEM

15And the LORD God of their fathers sent *warnings* to them by His messengers, rising up early and sending *them,* because He had compassion on His people and on His dwelling place. 16But they mocked the messengers of God, despised His words, and scoffed at His prophets, until the wrath of the LORD arose against His people, till *there was* no remedy.

17Therefore He brought against them the king of the Chaldeans, who killed their young men with the sword in the house of their sanctuary, and had no compassion on young man or virgin, on the aged or the weak; He gave *them* all into his hand. 18And all the articles from the house of God, great and small, the treasures of the house of the LORD, and the treasures of the king and of his leaders, all *these* he took to Babylon. 19Then they burned the house of God, broke down the wall of Jerusalem, burned all its palaces with fire, and destroyed all its precious possessions. 20And those who escaped from the sword he carried away to Babylon, where they became servants to him and his sons until the rule of the kingdom of Persia, 21to fulfill the word of the LORD by the mouth of Jeremiah, until the land had enjoyed her Sabbaths. As long as she lay desolate she kept Sabbath, to fulfill seventy years.

THE PROCLAMATION OF CYRUS

22Now in the first year of Cyrus king of Persia, that the word of the LORD by the mouth of Jeremiah might be fulfilled, the LORD stirred up the spirit of Cyrus king of Persia, so that he made a proclamation throughout all his kingdom, and also *put it* in writing, saying,

23 Thus says Cyrus king of
Persia:
All the kingdoms of the
earth the LORD God of
heaven has given me.
And He has commanded
me to build Him a house
at Jerusalem which is in
Judah. Who *is* among you
of all His people? May
the LORD his God *be* with
him, and let him go up!

THE BOOK OF EZRA

END OF THE BABYLONIAN CAPTIVITY

1 Now in the first year of
Cyrus king of Persia, that
the word of the LORD by the
mouth of Jeremiah might be
fulfilled, the LORD stirred up
the spirit of Cyrus king of Persia, so that he made a proclamation throughout all his
kingdom, and also *put it* in
writing, saying,

2 Thus says Cyrus king of
Persia:
All the kingdoms of the
earth the LORD God of
heaven has given me.
And He has commanded
me to build Him a house
at Jerusalem which *is* in
Judah. 3Who *is* among
you of all His people?
May his God be with
him, and let him go up
to Jerusalem which *is*
in Judah, and build the
house of the LORD God of
Israel (He *is* God), which
is in Jerusalem. 4And
whoever is left in any
place where he dwells, let
the men of his place help
him with silver and gold,
with goods and livestock,
besides the freewill
offerings for the house of
God which *is* in Jerusalem.

5Then the heads of the fathers' *houses* of Judah and
Benjamin, and the priests
and the Levites, with all whose
spirits God had moved, arose
to go up and build the house
of the LORD which *is* in Jerusalem. 6And all those who
were around them encouraged them with articles of
silver and gold, with goods
and livestock, and with precious things, besides all *that*
was willingly offered.

7King Cyrus also brought
out the articles of the house
of the LORD, which Nebuchadnezzar had taken from Jerusalem and put in the temple
of his gods; 8and Cyrus king
of Persia brought them out
by the hand of Mithredath
the treasurer, and counted
them out to Sheshbazzar the
prince of Judah. 9This *is* the
number of them: thirty gold
platters, one thousand silver
platters, twenty-nine knives,
10thirty gold basins, four
hundred and ten silver basins of a similar *kind, and* one
thousand other articles. 11All
the articles of gold and silver
were five thousand four hundred. All *these* Sheshbazzar
took with the captives who
were brought from Babylon
to Jerusalem.

THE CAPTIVES WHO RETURNED TO JERUSALEM

2 Now[a] these *are* the people of the province who
came back from the captivity,
of those who had been carried
away, whom Nebuchadnez-
zar the king of Babylon had
carried away to Babylon, and
who returned to Jerusalem
and Judah, everyone to his
own city.

2 *Those* who came with Zerubbabel *were* Jeshua, Nehemiah, Seraiah, Reelaiah,
Mordecai, Bilshan, Mispar,[a]
Bigvai, Rehum,[b] *and* Baanah.
The number of the men of the
people of Israel: 3 the people
of Parosh, two thousand one
hundred and seventy-two;
4 the people of Shephatiah,
three hundred and seventy-
two; 5 the people of Arah,
seven hundred and seventy-
five; 6 the people of Pahath-
Moab, of the people of Jeshua
and Joab, two thousand eight
hundred and twelve; 7 the people of Elam, one thousand two
hundred and fifty-four; 8 the
people of Zattu, nine hundred
and forty-five; 9 the people of
Zaccai, seven hundred and
sixty; 10 the people of Bani,[a] six
hundred and forty-two; 11 the
people of Bebai, six hundred
and twenty-three; 12 the people of Azgad, one thousand
two hundred and twenty-two;
13 the people of Adonikam, six
hundred and sixty-six; 14 the
people of Bigvai, two thousand
and fifty-six; 15 the people of
Adin, four hundred and fifty-
four; 16 the people of Ater of
Hezekiah, ninety-eight; 17 the
people of Bezai, three hundred and twenty-three; 18 the
people of Jorah,[a] one hundred
and twelve; 19 the people of
Hashum, two hundred and
twenty-three; 20 the people of
Gibbar,[a] ninety-five; 21 the people of Bethlehem, one hundred and twenty-three; 22 the
men of Netophah, fifty-six;
23 the men of Anathoth, one
hundred and twenty-eight;
24 the people of Azmaveth,[a]
forty-two; 25 the people of
Kirjath Arim,[a] Chephirah, and
Beeroth, seven hundred and
forty-three; 26 the people of
Ramah and Geba, six hundred
and twenty-one; 27 the men of
Michmas, one hundred and
twenty-two; 28 the men of
Bethel and Ai, two hundred
and twenty-three; 29 the people of Nebo, fifty-two; 30 the
people of Magbish, one hundred and fifty-six; 31 the people
of the other Elam, one thousand two hundred and fifty-
four; 32 the people of Harim,

2:1 [a] Compare this chapter with Nehemiah 7:6–73. 2:2 [a] Spelled *Mispereth* in Nehemiah 7:7 [b] Spelled *Nehum* in Nehemiah 7:7 2:10 [a] Spelled *Binnui* in Nehemiah 7:15 2:18 [a] Called *Hariph* in Nehemiah 7:24 2:20 [a] Called *Gibeon* in Nehemiah 7:25 2:24 [a] Called *Beth Azmaveth* in Nehemiah 7:28 2:25 [a] Called *Kirjath Jearim* in Nehemiah 7:29

three hundred and twenty;
33the people of Lod, Hadid,
and Ono, seven hundred and
twenty-five; 34the people of
Jericho, three hundred and
forty-five; 35the people of Senaah, three thousand six hundred and thirty.

36The priests: the sons
of Jedaiah, of the house of
Jeshua, nine hundred and
seventy-three; 37the sons of
Immer, one thousand and
fifty-two; 38the sons of Pashhur, one thousand two hundred and forty-seven; 39the
sons of Harim, one thousand
and seventeen.

40The Levites: the sons of
Jeshua and Kadmiel, of the
sons of Hodaviah,[a] seventy-
four.

41The singers: the sons
of Asaph, one hundred and
twenty-eight.

42The sons of the gate-
keepers: the sons of Shallum,
the sons of Ater, the sons of
Talmon, the sons of Akkub,
the sons of Hatita, and the
sons of Shobai, one hundred
and thirty-nine *in* all.

43The Nethinim: the sons of
Ziha, the sons of Hasupha, the
sons of Tabbaoth, 44the sons
of Keros, the sons of Siaha,[a]
the sons of Padon, 45the sons
of Lebanah, the sons of Hag-
abah, the sons of Akkub, 46the
sons of Hagab, the sons of
Shalmai, the sons of Hanan,
47the sons of Giddel, the sons
of Gahar, the sons of Reaiah,
48the sons of Rezin, the sons
of Nekoda, the sons of Gazzam, 49the sons of Uzza, the
sons of Paseah, the sons of
Besai, 50the sons of Asnah, the
sons of Meunim, the sons of
Nephusim,[a] 51the sons of Bakbuk, the sons of Hakupha, the
sons of Harhur, 52the sons of
Bazluth,[a] the sons of Mehida,
the sons of Harsha, 53the sons
of Barkos, the sons of Sisera,
the sons of Tamah, 54the sons
of Neziah, and the sons of Hatipha.

55The sons of Solomon's
servants: the sons of Sotai, the
sons of Sophereth, the sons of
Peruda,[a] 56the sons of Jaala,
the sons of Darkon, the sons
of Giddel, 57the sons of Shephatiah, the sons of Hattil, the
sons of Pochereth of Zebaim,
and the sons of Ami.[a] 58All the
Nethinim and the children of
Solomon's servants were three
hundred and ninety-two.

59And these *were* the ones
who came up from Tel Melah,
Tel Harsha, Cherub, Addan,[a]
and Immer; but they could not
identify their father's house or
their genealogy,[b] whether they
were of Israel: 60the sons of
Delaiah, the sons of Tobiah,

2:40 [a] Spelled *Hodevah* in Nehemiah 7:43 **2:44** [a] Spelled *Sia* in Nehemiah 7:47 **2:50** [a] Spelled *Nephishesim* in Nehemiah 7:52 **2:52** [a] Spelled *Bazlith* in Nehemiah 7:54 **2:55** [a] Spelled *Perida* in Nehemiah 7:57 **2:57** [a] Spelled *Amon* in Nehemiah 7:59 **2:59** [a] Spelled *Addon* in Nehemiah 7:61 [b] Literally *seed*

and the sons of Nekoda, six
hundred and fifty-two; [61]and
of the sons of the priests: the
sons of Habaiah, the sons of
Koz,[a] and the sons of Barzillai,
who took a wife of the daughters of Barzillai the Gileadite,
and was called by their name.
[62]These sought their listing
among those who were registered by genealogy, but they
were not found; therefore
they *were excluded* from the
priesthood as defiled. [63]And
the governor[a] said to them
that they should not eat of the
most holy things till a priest
could consult with the Urim
and Thummim.

[64]The whole assembly together *was* forty-two thousand
three hundred *and* sixty, [65]be-
sides their male and female
servants, of whom *there were*
seven thousand three hun-
dred and thirty-seven; and
they had two hundred men
and women singers. [66]Their
horses *were* seven hundred
and thirty-six, their mules two
hundred and forty-five, [67]their
camels four hundred and
thirty-five, and *their* donkeys
six thousand seven hundred
and twenty.

[68]*Some* of the heads of the
fathers' *houses,* when they
came to the house of the
LORD which *is* in Jerusalem,
offered freely for the house
of God, to erect it in its place:
[69]According to their ability,
they gave to the treasury for
the work sixty-one thousand
gold drachmas, five thousand
minas of silver, and one hundred priestly garments.

[70]So the priests and the Levites, *some* of the people, the
singers, the gatekeepers, and
the Nethinim, dwelt in their
cities, and all Israel in their
cities.

WORSHIP RESTORED AT JERUSALEM

3 And when the seventh
month had come, and the
children of Israel *were* in the
cities, the people gathered
together as one man to Jerusalem. [2]Then Jeshua the son
of Jozadak[a] and his brethren
the priests, and Zerubbabel
the son of Shealtiel and his
brethren, arose and built the
altar of the God of Israel, to
offer burnt offerings on it, as *it
is* written in the Law of Moses
the man of God. [3]Though fear
had come upon them because
of the people of those countries, they set the altar on its
bases; and they offered burnt
offerings on it to the LORD,
both the morning and evening burnt offerings. [4]They
also kept the Feast of Tabernacles, as *it is* written, and *offered* the daily burnt offerings
in the number required by ordinance for each day. [5]After-

2:61 [a] Or *Hakkoz* 2:63 [a] Hebrew *Tirshatha*
3:2 [a] Spelled *Jehozadak* in 1 Chronicles 6:14

wards *they offered* the regular burnt offering, and *those* for New Moons and for all the appointed feasts of the LORD that were consecrated, and *those* of everyone who willingly offered a freewill offering to the LORD. 6From the first day of the seventh month they began to offer burnt offerings to the LORD, although the foundation of the temple of the LORD had not been laid. 7They also gave money to the masons and the carpenters, and food, drink, and oil to the people of Sidon and Tyre to bring cedar logs from Lebanon to the sea, to Joppa, according to the permission which they had from Cyrus king of Persia.

RESTORATION OF THE TEMPLE BEGINS

8Now in the second month of the second year of their coming to the house of God at Jerusalem, Zerubbabel the son of Shealtiel, Jeshua the son of Jozadak,[a] and the rest of their brethren the priests and the Levites, and all those who had come out of the captivity to Jerusalem, began *work* and appointed the Levites from twenty years old and above to oversee the work of the house of the LORD. 9Then Jeshua *with* his sons and brothers, Kadmiel *with* his sons, and the sons of Judah,[a] arose as one to oversee those working on the house of God: the sons of Henadad *with* their sons and their brethren the Levites.

10When the builders laid the foundation of the temple of the LORD, the priests stood[a] in their apparel with trumpets, and the Levites, the sons of Asaph, with cymbals, to praise the LORD, according to the ordinance of David king of Israel. 11And they sang responsively, praising and giving thanks to the LORD:

"For *He is* good,
For His mercy *endures*
forever toward Israel."[a]

Then all the people shouted with a great shout, when they praised the LORD, because the foundation of the house of the LORD was laid.

12But many of the priests and Levites and heads of the fathers' *houses,* old men who had seen the first temple, wept with a loud voice when the foundation of this temple was laid before their eyes. Yet many shouted aloud for joy, 13so that the people could not discern the noise of the shout of joy from the noise of the weeping of the people, for the people shouted with a loud shout, and the sound was heard afar off.

3:8 [a] Spelled *Jehozadak* in 1 Chronicles 6:14 3:9 [a] Or *Hodaviah* (compare 2:40) 3:10 [a] Following Septuagint, Syriac, and Vulgate; Masoretic Text reads *they stationed the priests.* 3:11 [a] Compare Psalm 136:1

RESISTANCE TO REBUILDING THE TEMPLE

4 Now when the adversaries
of Judah and Benjamin
heard that the descendants of
the captivity were building the
temple of the LORD God of Israel, 2they came to Zerubbabel
and the heads of the fathers'
houses, and said to them, "Let
us build with you, for we seek
your God as you *do;* and we
have sacrificed to Him since
the days of Esarhaddon king of
Assyria, who brought us here."
3But Zerubbabel and Jeshua
and the rest of the heads of the
fathers' *houses* of Israel said to
them, "You may do nothing
with us to build a house for our
God; but we alone will build
to the LORD God of Israel, as
King Cyrus the king of Persia
has commanded us." 4Then the
people of the land tried to discourage the people of Judah.
They troubled them in building, 5and hired counselors
against them to frustrate their
purpose all the days of Cyrus
king of Persia, even until the
reign of Darius king of Persia.

REBUILDING OF JERUSALEM OPPOSED

6In the reign of Ahasue-
rus, in the beginning of his
reign, they wrote an accusation against the inhabitants
of Judah and Jerusalem.

7In the days of Artaxerxes
also, Bishlam, Mithredath,
Tabel, and the rest of their
companions wrote to Arta-
xerxes king of Persia; and the
letter *was* written in Aramaic
script, and translated into the
Aramaic language. 8Rehum[a]
the commander and Shim-
shai the scribe wrote a letter
against Jerusalem to King Artaxerxes in this fashion:

9 From[a] Rehum the
commander, Shimshai
the scribe, and the rest
of their companions—
representatives of
the Dinaites, the
Apharsathchites, the
Tarpelites, the people
of Persia and Erech and
Babylon and Shushan,[b]
the Dehavites, the
Elamites, 10and the rest
of the nations whom the
great and noble Osnapper
took captive and settled
in the cities of Samaria
and the remainder
beyond the River[a]—and
so forth.[b]

11(This *is* a copy of the letter
that they sent him.)

To King Artaxerxes from
your servants, the men
of the region beyond the
River, and so forth:[a]

4:8 [a] The original language of Ezra 4:8 through 6:18 is Aramaic.
4:9 [a] Literally *Then* [b] Or *Susa* 4:10 [a] That is, the Euphrates
[b] Literally *and now* 4:11 [a] Literally *and now*

12 Let it be known to the
king that the Jews who
came up from you have
come to us at Jerusalem,
and are building the
rebellious and evil city,
and are finishing *its*
walls and repairing the
foundations. 13Let it now
be known to the king
that, if this city is built
and the walls completed,
they will not pay tax,
tribute, or custom, and
the king's treasury will
be diminished. 14Now
because we receive
support from the palace,
it was not proper for us to
see the king's dishonor;
therefore we have sent
and informed the king,
15that search may be
made in the book of the
records of your fathers.
And you will find in the
book of the records and
know that this city *is* a
rebellious city, harmful
to kings and provinces,
and that they have incited
sedition within the city
in former times, for
which cause this city was
destroyed.

16 We inform the king that
if this city is rebuilt and
its walls are completed,
the result will be that you
will have no dominion
beyond the River.

17The king sent an answer:

To Rehum the
commander, *to* Shimshai
the scribe, *to* the rest of
their companions who
dwell in Samaria, and *to*
the remainder beyond
the River:

Peace, and so forth.[a]

18 The letter which you sent
to us has been clearly
read before me. 19And I
gave the command, and
a search has been made,
and it was found that
this city in former times
has revolted against
kings, and rebellion
and sedition have been
fostered in it. 20There
have also been mighty
kings over Jerusalem,
who have ruled over all
the region beyond the
River; and tax, tribute,
and custom were paid
to them. 21Now give the
command to make these
men cease, that this city
may not be built until the
command is given by me.

22 Take heed now that you
do not fail to do this. Why
should damage increase
to the hurt of the kings?

23Now when the copy of
King Artaxerxes' letter *was*

4:17 [a] Literally *and now*

read before Rehum, Shimshai
the scribe, and their companions, they went up in haste to
Jerusalem against the Jews,
and by force of arms made
them cease. 24 Thus the work
of the house of God which *is*
at Jerusalem ceased, and it
was discontinued until the
second year of the reign of
Darius king of Persia.

RESTORATION OF THE TEMPLE RESUMED

5 Then the prophet Haggai
and Zechariah the son of
Iddo, prophets, prophesied to
the Jews who *were* in Judah
and Jerusalem, in the name
of the God of Israel, *who was*
over them. 2 So Zerubbabel the
son of Shealtiel and Jeshua
the son of Jozadak[a] rose up
and began to build the house
of God which *is* in Jerusalem;
and the prophets of God *were*
with them, helping them.
3 At the same time Tatte-
nai the governor of *the region* beyond the River[a] and
Shethar-Boznai and their
companions came to them
and spoke thus to them: "Who
has commanded you to build
this temple and finish this
wall?" 4 Then, accordingly, we
told them the names of the
men who were constructing
this building. 5 But the eye of
their God was upon the elders
of the Jews, so that they could
not make them cease till a report could go to Darius. Then
a written answer was returned
concerning this *matter.* 6 This
is a copy of the letter that Tattenai sent:

> The governor of *the region* beyond the River, and Shethar-Boznai, and his companions, the Persians who *were in the region* beyond the River, to Darius the king.

7 (They sent a letter to him, in
which was written thus.)

> To Darius the king:
>
> All peace.
>
> 8 Let it be known to the king that we went into the province of Judea, to the temple of the great God, which is being built with heavy stones, and timber is being laid in the walls; and this work goes on diligently and prospers in their hands.
>
> 9 Then we asked those elders, *and* spoke thus to them: "Who commanded you to build this temple and to finish these walls?"
> 10 We also asked them their names to inform you, that we might write

5:2 [a] Spelled *Jehozadak* in 1 Chronicles 6:14 5:3 [a] That is, the Euphrates

the names of the men
who *were* chief among
them.

11 And thus they returned us
an answer, saying: "We are
the servants of the God of
heaven and earth, and we
are rebuilding the temple
that was built many
years ago, which a great
king of Israel built and
completed. 12But because
our fathers provoked the
God of heaven to wrath,
He gave them into the
hand of Nebuchadnezzar
king of Babylon, the
Chaldean, *who* destroyed
this temple and carried
the people away to
Babylon. 13However, in
the first year of Cyrus king
of Babylon, King Cyrus
issued a decree to build
this house of God. 14Also,
the gold and silver articles
of the house of God, which
Nebuchadnezzar had
taken from the temple
that *was* in Jerusalem and
carried into the temple
of Babylon—those King
Cyrus took from the
temple of Babylon, and
they were given to one
named Sheshbazzar,
whom he had made
governor. 15And he
said to him, 'Take these
articles; go, carry them
to the temple *site* that *is*
in Jerusalem, and let the
house of God be rebuilt on
its former site.' 16Then the
same Sheshbazzar came
and laid the foundation
of the house of God which
is in Jerusalem; but from
that time even until
now it has been under
construction, and it is not
finished."

17 Now therefore, if *it seems*
good to the king, let a
search be made in the
king's treasure house,
which *is* there in Babylon,
whether it is *so* that a
decree was issued by King
Cyrus to build this house
of God at Jerusalem, and
let the king send us his
pleasure concerning this
matter.

THE DECREE OF DARIUS

6 Then King Darius issued a
decree, and a search was
made in the archives,[a] where
the treasures were stored in
Babylon. 2And at Achmetha,[a]
in the palace that *is* in the
province of Media, a scroll
was found, and in it a record
was written thus:

3 In the first year of King
Cyrus, King Cyrus issued
a decree *concerning*
the house of God at

6:1 [a] Literally *house of the scrolls* 6:2 [a] Probably *Ecbatana,* the ancient capital of Media

Jerusalem: "Let the house
be rebuilt, the place where
they offered sacrifices;
and let the foundations of
it be firmly laid, its height
sixty cubits *and* its width
sixty cubits, 4*with* three
rows of heavy stones
and one row of new
timber. Let the expenses
be paid from the king's
treasury. 5Also let the
gold and silver articles
of the house of God,
which Nebuchadnezzar
took from the temple
which *is* in Jerusalem and
brought to Babylon, be
restored and taken back
to the temple which *is*
in Jerusalem, *each* to its
place; and deposit *them* in
the house of God"—

6 Now *therefore,* Tattenai,
governor of *the region*
beyond the River, and
Shethar-Boznai, and your
companions the Persians
who *are* beyond the River,
keep yourselves far from
there. 7Let the work of
this house of God alone;
let the governor of the
Jews and the elders of the
Jews build this house of
God on its site.

8 Moreover I issue a decree
as to what you shall do
for the elders of these
Jews, for the building of
this house of God: Let the
cost be paid at the king's
expense from taxes *on*
the region beyond the
River; this is to be given
immediately to these
men, so that they are not
hindered. 9And whatever
they need—young
bulls, rams, and lambs
for the burnt offerings
of the God of heaven,
wheat, salt, wine, and oil,
according to the request
of the priests who *are* in
Jerusalem—let it be given
them day by day without
fail, 10that they may offer
sacrifices of sweet aroma
to the God of heaven, and
pray for the life of the
king and his sons.

11 Also I issue a decree
that whoever alters this
edict, let a timber be
pulled from his house
and erected, and let him
be hanged on it; and
let his house be made a
refuse heap because of
this. 12And may the God
who causes His name to
dwell there destroy any
king or people who put
their hand to alter it, or to
destroy this house of God
which is in Jerusalem. I
Darius issue a decree; let
it be done diligently.

THE TEMPLE COMPLETED AND DEDICATED

13Then Tattenai, governor
of *the region* beyond the River,
Shethar-Boznai, and their

companions diligently did according to what King Darius
had sent. 14So the elders of the
Jews built, and they prospered
through the prophesying of
Haggai the prophet and Zechariah the son of Iddo. And they
built and finished *it*, according
to the commandment of the
God of Israel, and according
to the command of Cyrus, Darius, and Artaxerxes king of
Persia. 15Now the temple was
finished on the third day of the
month of Adar, which was in
the sixth year of the reign of
King Darius. 16Then the children of Israel, the priests and
the Levites and the rest of the
descendants of the captivity,
celebrated the dedication of
this house of God with joy.
17And they offered sacrifices
at the dedication of this house
of God, one hundred bulls, two
hundred rams, four hundred
lambs, and as a sin offering for
all Israel twelve male goats,
according to the number of
the tribes of Israel. 18They assigned the priests to their divisions and the Levites to their
divisions, over the service of
God in Jerusalem, as it is written in the Book of Moses.

THE PASSOVER CELEBRATED

19And the descendants of
the captivity kept the Passover on the fourteenth *day*
of the first month. 20For the
priests and the Levites had
purified themselves; all of
them *were ritually* clean. And
they slaughtered the Passover
lambs for all the descendants
of the captivity, for their brethren the priests, and for themselves. 21Then the children of
Israel who had returned from
the captivity ate together with
all who had separated themselves from the filth of the nations of the land in order to
seek the LORD God of Israel.
22And they kept the Feast of
Unleavened Bread seven days
with joy; for the LORD made
them joyful, and turned the
heart of the king of Assyria toward them, to strengthen their
hands in the work of the house
of God, the God of Israel.

THE ARRIVAL OF EZRA

7 Now after these things, in
the reign of Artaxerxes
king of Persia, Ezra the son
of Seraiah, the son of Azariah,
the son of Hilkiah, 2the son
of Shallum, the son of Zadok,
the son of Ahitub, 3the son of
Amariah, the son of Azariah,
the son of Meraioth, 4the son
of Zerahiah, the son of Uzzi,
the son of Bukki, 5the son of
Abishua, the son of Phinehas,
the son of Eleazar, the son of
Aaron the chief priest— 6this
Ezra came up from Babylon;
and he *was* a skilled scribe in
the Law of Moses, which the
LORD God of Israel had given.
The king granted him all his
request, according to the hand
of the LORD his God upon him.
7*Some* of the children of Israel,

the priests, the Levites, the
singers, the gatekeepers, and
the Nethinim came up to Jerusalem in the seventh year
of King Artaxerxes. 8 And Ezra
came to Jerusalem in the fifth
month, which *was* in the seventh year of the king. 9 On the
first *day* of the first month he
began *his* journey from Babylon, and on the first *day* of
the fifth month he came to
Jerusalem, according to the
good hand of his God upon
him. 10 For Ezra had prepared
his heart to seek the Law of
the LORD, and to do *it,* and to
teach statutes and ordinances
in Israel.

THE LETTER OF ARTAXERXES TO EZRA

11 This *is* a copy of the letter that King Artaxerxes gave
Ezra the priest, the scribe, expert in the words of the commandments of the LORD, and
of His statutes to Israel:

12 Artaxerxes,[a] king of
kings,

To Ezra the priest, a
scribe of the Law of the
God of heaven:

Perfect *peace,* and so
forth.[b]

13 I issue a decree that all
those of the people of
Israel and the priests
and Levites in my realm,
who volunteer to go up to
Jerusalem, may go with
you. 14 And whereas you
are being sent by the king
and his seven counselors
to inquire concerning
Judah and Jerusalem,
with regard to the Law
of your God which *is* in
your hand; 15 and *whereas
you are* to carry the silver
and gold which the king
and his counselors have
freely offered to the God
of Israel, whose dwelling
is in Jerusalem; 16 and
whereas all the silver and
gold that you may find
in all the province of
Babylon, along with the
freewill offering of the
people and the priests,
are to be freely offered
for the house of their God
in Jerusalem— 17 now
therefore, be careful to
buy with this money
bulls, rams, and lambs,
with their grain offerings
and their drink offerings,
and offer them on the
altar of the house of your
God in Jerusalem.

18 And whatever seems good
to you and your brethren
to do with the rest of the
silver and the gold, do
it according to the will

7:12 [a] The original language of Ezra 7:12–26 is Aramaic. [b] Literally *and now*

of your God. 19Also the
articles that are given
to you for the service of
the house of your God,
deliver in full before the
God of Jerusalem. 20And
whatever more may be
needed for the house of
your God, which you may
have occasion to provide,
pay *for it* from the king's
treasury.

21 And I, *even* I, Artaxerxes
the king, issue a decree
to all the treasurers
who *are in the region*
beyond the River, that
whatever Ezra the priest,
the scribe of the Law of
the God of heaven, may
require of you, let it be
done diligently, 22up to
one hundred talents of
silver, one hundred kors
of wheat, one hundred
baths of wine, one
hundred baths of oil, and
salt without prescribed
limit. 23Whatever is
commanded by the God
of heaven, let it diligently
be done for the house
of the God of heaven.
For why should there be
wrath against the realm
of the king and his sons?

24 Also we inform you that
it shall not be lawful to
impose tax, tribute, or
custom on any of the
priests, Levites, singers,
gatekeepers, Nethinim,
or servants of this house
of God. 25And you,
Ezra, according to your
God-given wisdom, set
magistrates and judges
who may judge all the
people who *are in the*
region beyond the River,
all such as know the laws
of your God; and teach
those who do not know
them. 26Whoever will
not observe the law of
your God and the law of
the king, let judgment
be executed speedily
on him, whether *it be*
death, or banishment, or
confiscation of goods, or
imprisonment.

27Blessed *be* the LORD God
of our fathers, who has put
such a thing as this in the
king's heart, to beautify the
house of the LORD which *is*
in Jerusalem, 28and has extended mercy to me before
the king and his counsel-
ors, and before all the king's
mighty princes.

So I was encouraged, as
the hand of the LORD my God
was upon me; and I gathered
leading men of Israel to go up
with me.

HEADS OF FAMILIES WHO RETURNED WITH EZRA

8 These *are* the heads of
their fathers' *houses,* and
this is the genealogy of those
who went up with me from
Babylon, in the reign of King

Artaxerxes: 2of the sons of
Phinehas, Gershom; of the
sons of Ithamar, Daniel; of
the sons of David, Hattush;
3of the sons of Shecaniah, of
the sons of Parosh, Zechariah;
and registered with him *were*
one hundred and fifty males;
4of the sons of Pahath-Moab,
Eliehoenai the son of Zerahiah, and with him two hundred males; 5of the sons of
Shechaniah,[a] Ben-Jahaziel,
and with him three hundred
males; 6of the sons of Adin,
Ebed the son of Jonathan,
and with him fifty males;
7of the sons of Elam, Jeshaiah the son of Athaliah, and
with him seventy males; 8of
the sons of Shephatiah, Zebadiah the son of Michael, and
with him eighty males; 9of the
sons of Joab, Obadiah the son
of Jehiel, and with him two
hundred and eighteen males;
10of the sons of Shelomith,[a]
Ben-Josiphiah, and with him
one hundred and sixty males;
11of the sons of Bebai, Zechariah the son of Bebai, and
with him twenty-eight males;
12of the sons of Azgad, Johanan the son of Hakkatan, and
with him one hundred and
ten males; 13of the last sons of
Adonikam, whose names *are*
these—Eliphelet, Jeiel, and
Shemaiah—and with them
sixty males; 14also of the sons
of Bigvai, Uthai and Zabbud,
and with them seventy males.

SERVANTS FOR THE TEMPLE

15Now I gathered them by
the river that flows to Ahava,
and we camped there three
days. And I looked among the
people and the priests, and
found none of the sons of Levi
there. 16Then I sent for Eliezer, Ariel, Shemaiah, Elnathan,
Jarib, Elnathan, Nathan, Zechariah, and Meshullam, leaders;
also for Joiarib and Elnathan,
men of understanding. 17And
I gave them a command for
Iddo the chief man at the place
Casiphia, and I told them what
they should say to Iddo *and*
his brethren[a] the Nethinim at
the place Casiphia—that they
should bring us servants for
the house of our God. 18Then,
by the good hand of our God
upon us, they brought us a
man of understanding, of
the sons of Mahli the son of
Levi, the son of Israel, namely
Sherebiah, with his sons and
brothers, eighteen men; 19and
Hashabiah, and with him Jeshaiah of the sons of Merari,
his brothers and their sons,
twenty men; 20also of the Nethinim, whom David and the
leaders had appointed for the

8:5 [a] Following Masoretic Text and Vulgate; Septuagint reads *the sons of Zatho, Shechaniah.* 8:10 [a] Following Masoretic Text and Vulgate; Septuagint reads *the sons of Banni, Shelomith.* 8:17 [a] Following Vulgate; Masoretic Text reads *to Iddo his brother;* Septuagint reads *to their brethren.*

service of the Levites, two
hundred and twenty Nethi-
nim. All of them were designated by name.

FASTING AND PRAYER FOR PROTECTION

21 Then I proclaimed a fast
there at the river of Ahava, that
we might humble ourselves
before our God, to seek from
Him the right way for us and
our little ones and all our possessions. 22 For I was ashamed
to request of the king an escort
of soldiers and horsemen to
help us against the enemy on
the road, because we had spoken to the king, saying, "The
hand of our God *is* upon all
those for good who seek Him,
but His power and His wrath
are against all those who forsake Him." 23 So we fasted and
entreated our God for this, and
He answered our prayer.

GIFTS FOR THE TEMPLE

24 And I separated twelve
of the leaders of the priests—
Sherebiah, Hashabiah, and ten
of their brethren with them—
25 and weighed out to them the
silver, the gold, and the articles, the offering for the house
of our God which the king and
his counselors and his princes,
and all Israel *who were* present, had offered. 26 I weighed
into their hand six hundred
and fifty talents of silver, silver
articles *weighing* one hundred
talents, one hundred talents
of gold, 27 twenty gold basins
worth a thousand drachmas,
and two vessels of fine polished bronze, precious as gold.
28 And I said to them, "You *are*
holy to the LORD; the articles
are holy also; and the silver
and the gold *are* a freewill
offering to the LORD God of
your fathers. 29 Watch and keep
them until you weigh *them* before the leaders of the priests
and the Levites and heads of
the fathers' *houses* of Israel in
Jerusalem, *in* the chambers of
the house of the LORD." 30 So
the priests and the Levites received the silver and the gold
and the articles by weight, to
bring *them* to Jerusalem to the
house of our God.

THE RETURN TO JERUSALEM

31 Then we departed from
the river of Ahava on the
twelfth *day* of the first month,
to go to Jerusalem. And the
hand of our God was upon us,
and He delivered us from the
hand of the enemy and from
ambush along the road. 32 So
we came to Jerusalem, and
stayed there three days.

33 Now on the fourth day
the silver and the gold and the
articles were weighed in the
house of our God by the hand
of Meremoth the son of Uriah
the priest, and with him *was*
Eleazar the son of Phinehas;
with them *were* the Levites,
Jozabad the son of Jeshua and
Noadiah the son of Binnui,
34 with the number *and* weight

of everything. All the weight
was written down at that time.
35The children of those who
had been carried away captive,
who had come from the captivity, offered burnt offerings
to the God of Israel: twelve
bulls for all Israel, ninety-six
rams, seventy-seven lambs,
and twelve male goats *as* a sin
offering. All *this was* a burnt
offering to the LORD.
36And they delivered the
king's orders to the king's
satraps and the governors *in
the region* beyond the River.
So they gave support to the
people and the house of God.

INTERMARRIAGE WITH PAGANS

9 When these things were
done, the leaders came
to me, saying, "The people of
Israel and the priests and the
Levites have not separated
themselves from the peoples
of the lands, with respect to the
abominations of the Canaanites, the Hittites, the Perizzites,
the Jebusites, the Ammon-
ites, the Moabites, the Egyptians, and the Amorites. 2For
they have taken some of their
daughters *as wives* for themselves and their sons, so that
the holy seed is mixed with
the peoples of *those* lands. Indeed, the hand of the leaders
and rulers has been foremost
in this trespass." 3So when I
heard this thing, I tore my
garment and my robe, and
plucked out some of the hair
of my head and beard, and
sat down astonished. 4Then
everyone who trembled at
the words of the God of Israel
assembled to me, because of
the transgression of those who
had been carried away captive,
and I sat astonished until the
evening sacrifice.
5At the evening sacrifice
I arose from my fasting; and
having torn my garment and
my robe, I fell on my knees
and spread out my hands to
the LORD my God. 6And I said:
"O my God, I am too ashamed
and humiliated to lift up my
face to You, my God; for our
iniquities have risen higher
than *our* heads, and our guilt
has grown up to the heavens.
7Since the days of our fathers
to this day we *have been* very
guilty, and for our iniquities
we, our kings, *and* our priests
have been delivered into the
hand of the kings of the lands,
to the sword, to captivity, to
plunder, and to humiliation,
as *it is* this day. 8And now for
a little while grace has been
shown from the LORD our God,
to leave us a remnant to escape, and to give us a peg in
His holy place, that our God
may enlighten our eyes and
give us a measure of revival
in our bondage. 9For we *were*
slaves. Yet our God did not forsake us in our bondage; but
He extended mercy to us in
the sight of the kings of Persia, to revive us, to repair the
house of our God, to rebuild its

ruins, and to give us a wall in
Judah and Jerusalem. 10And
now, O our God, what shall we
say after this? For we have forsaken Your commandments,
11which You commanded by
Your servants the prophets,
saying, 'The land which you
are entering to possess is an
unclean land, with the uncleanness of the peoples of
the lands, with their abominations which have filled it from
one end to another with their
impurity. 12Now therefore, do
not give your daughters as
wives for their sons, nor take
their daughters to your sons;
and never seek their peace or
prosperity, that you may be
strong and eat the good of the
land, and leave *it* as an inheritance to your children forever.'
13And after all that has come
upon us for our evil deeds and
for our great guilt, since You
our God have punished us less
than our iniquities *deserve*,
and have given us *such* deliverance as this, 14should we
again break Your commandments, and join in marriage
with the people *committing*
these abominations? Would
You not be angry with us until
You had consumed *us*, so that
there would be no remnant or
survivor? 15O LORD God of Israel, You *are* righteous, for we
are left as a remnant, as *it is*
this day. Here we *are* before
You, in our guilt, though no
one can stand before You because of this!"

CONFESSION OF IMPROPER MARRIAGES

10 Now while Ezra was
praying, and while he
was confessing, weeping, and
bowing down before the house
of God, a very large assembly
of men, women, and children
gathered to him from Israel;
for the people wept very bitterly. 2And Shechaniah the
son of Jehiel, *one* of the sons
of Elam, spoke up and said
to Ezra, "We have trespassed
against our God, and have
taken pagan wives from the
peoples of the land; yet now
there is hope in Israel in spite
of this. 3Now therefore, let us
make a covenant with our God
to put away all these wives and
those who have been born to
them, according to the advice
of my master and of those who
tremble at the commandment
of our God; and let it be done
according to the law. 4Arise,
for *this* matter *is* your *responsibility*. We also *are* with you.
Be of good courage, and do *it*."

5Then Ezra arose, and made
the leaders of the priests, the
Levites, and all Israel swear
an oath that they would do
according to this word. So
they swore an oath. 6Then
Ezra rose up from before the
house of God, and went into
the chamber of Jehohanan
the son of Eliashib; and *when*
he came there, he ate no bread
and drank no water, for he
mourned because of the guilt
of those from the captivity.

7And they issued a proclamation throughout Judah and
Jerusalem to all the descendants of the captivity, that
they must gather at Jerusalem, 8and that whoever would
not come within three days,
according to the instructions
of the leaders and elders, all
his property would be confis-
cated, and he himself would
be separated from the assembly of those from the captivity.
9So all the men of Judah
and Benjamin gathered at Jerusalem within three days. It
was the ninth month, on the
twentieth of the month; and
all the people sat in the open
square of the house of God,
trembling because of *this* matter and because of heavy rain.
10Then Ezra the priest stood
up and said to them, "You have
transgressed and have taken
pagan wives, adding to the
guilt of Israel. 11Now therefore,
make confession to the Lord
God of your fathers, and do
His will; separate yourselves
from the peoples of the land,
and from the pagan wives."
12Then all the assembly answered and said with a loud
voice, "Yes! As you have said,
so we must do. 13But *there are*
many people; *it is* the season
for heavy rain, and we are not
able to stand outside. Nor *is this*
the work of one or two days, for
there are many of us who have
transgressed in this matter.
14Please, let the leaders of our
entire assembly stand; and let
all those in our cities who have
taken pagan wives come at appointed times, together with
the elders and judges of their
cities, until the fierce wrath of
our God is turned away from
us in this matter." 15Only Jonathan the son of Asahel and
Jahaziah the son of Tikvah
opposed this, and Meshullam
and Shabbethai the Levite gave
them support.
16Then the descendants
of the captivity did so. And
Ezra the priest, *with* certain
heads of the fathers' *house-*
holds, were set apart by the
fathers' households, each of
them by name; and they sat
down on the first day of the
tenth month to examine the
matter. 17By the first day of
the first month they finished
questioning all the men who
had taken pagan wives.

PAGAN WIVES PUT AWAY

18And among the sons of
the priests who had taken
pagan wives *the following* were
found of the sons of Jeshua
the son of Jozadak,[a] and his
brothers: Maaseiah, Eliezer,
Jarib, and Gedaliah. 19And
they gave their promise that
they would put away their
wives; and *being* guilty, *they*
presented a ram of the flock
as their trespass offering.
20Also of the sons of Immer:

10:18 [a] Spelled *Jehozadak* in 1 Chronicles 6:14

Hanani and Zebadiah; [21]of the
sons of Harim: Maaseiah, Elijah, Shemaiah, Jehiel, and Uzziah; [22]of the sons of Pashhur:
Elioenai, Maaseiah, Ishmael,
Nethanel, Jozabad, and Elasah.
[23]Also of the Levites: Jozabad, Shimei, Kelaiah (the
same *is* Kelita), Pethahiah,
Judah, and Eliezer.
[24]Also of the singers: Eliashib; and of the gatekeepers:
Shallum, Telem, and Uri.
[25]And others of Israel: of
the sons of Parosh: Ramiah,
Jeziah, Malchiah, Mijamin,
Eleazar, Malchijah, and Benaiah; [26]of the sons of Elam:
Mattaniah, Zechariah, Jehiel,
Abdi, Jeremoth, and Eliah;
[27]of the sons of Zattu: Elioenai, Eliashib, Mattaniah, Jeremoth, Zabad, and Aziza; [28]of
the sons of Bebai: Jehohanan,
Hananiah, Zabbai, *and* Athlai;
[29]of the sons of Bani: Meshullam, Malluch, Adaiah, Jashub,
Sheal, *and* Ramoth;[a] [30]of the
sons of Pahath-Moab: Adna,
Chelal, Benaiah, Maaseiah,
Mattaniah, Bezalel, Binnui,
and Manasseh; [31]*of* the sons
of Harim: Eliezer, Ishijah,
Malchijah, Shemaiah, Shim-
eon, [32]Benjamin, Malluch, *and*
Shemariah; [33]of the sons of
Hashum: Mattenai, Mattat-
tah, Zabad, Eliphelet, Jere-
mai, Manasseh, *and* Shimei;
[34]of the sons of Bani: Maadai,
Amram, Uel, [35]Benaiah, Bede-
iah, Cheluh,[a] [36]Vaniah, Meremoth, Eliashib, [37]Mattaniah,
Mattenai, Jaasai,[a] [38]Bani, Binnui, Shimei, [39]Shelemiah, Nathan, Adaiah, [40]Machnadebai,
Shashai, Sharai, [41]Azarel, Shelemiah, Shemariah, [42]Shallum,
Amariah, *and* Joseph; [43]of the
sons of Nebo: Jeiel, Mattithiah, Zabad, Zebina, Jaddai,[a]
Joel, *and* Benaiah.
[44]All these had taken pagan
wives, and *some* of them had
wives *by whom* they had children.

THE BOOK OF

NEHEMIAH

NEHEMIAH PRAYS FOR HIS PEOPLE

1 The words of Nehemiah the
son of Hachaliah.
It came to pass in the
month of Chislev, *in* the twentieth year, as I was in Shushan[a]
the citadel, [2]that Hanani
one of my brethren came
with men from Judah; and I

10:29 [a] Or *Jeremoth* 10:35 [a] Or *Cheluhi,* or *Cheluhu*
10:37 [a] Or *Jaasu* 10:43 [a] Or *Jaddu* 1:1 [a] Or *Susa*

asked them concerning the
Jews who had escaped, who
had survived the captivity,
and concerning Jerusalem.
3And they said to me, "The
survivors who are left from
the captivity in the province
are there in great distress and
reproach. The wall of Jerusalem *is* also broken down, and
its gates are burned with fire."

4So it was, when I heard
these words, that I sat down
and wept, and mourned *for*
many days; I was fasting and
praying before the God of
heaven.

5And I said: "I pray, LORD
God of heaven, O great and
awesome God, *You* who keep
Your covenant and mercy with
those who love You[a] and observe Your[b] commandments,
6please let Your ear be attentive and Your eyes open, that
You may hear the prayer of
Your servant which I pray before You now, day and night,
for the children of Israel Your
servants, and confess the sins
of the children of Israel which
we have sinned against You.
Both my father's house and I
have sinned. 7We have acted
very corruptly against You,
and have not kept the commandments, the statutes, nor
the ordinances which You
commanded Your servant
Moses. 8*Remember, I pray,* the
word that You commanded
Your servant Moses, saying, '*If*
you are unfaithful, I will scatter you among the nations;[a]
9but *if* you return to Me, and
keep My commandments and
do them, though some of you
were cast out to the farthest
part of the heavens, *yet* I will
gather them from there, and
bring them to the place which
I have chosen as a dwelling for
My name.'[a] 10Now these *are*
Your servants and Your people, whom You have redeemed
by Your great power, and by
Your strong hand. 11O Lord,
I pray, please let Your ear be
attentive to the prayer of Your
servant, and to the prayer of
Your servants who desire to
fear Your name; and let Your
servant prosper this day, I
pray, and grant him mercy in
the sight of this man."

For I was the king's cup-
bearer.

NEHEMIAH SENT TO JUDAH

2 And it came to pass in the
month of Nisan, in the
twentieth year of King Artaxerxes, *when* wine *was* before him,
that I took the wine and gave
it to the king. Now I had never
been sad in his presence before. 2Therefore the king said
to me, "Why *is* your face sad,
since you *are* not sick? This *is*
nothing but sorrow of heart."

So I became dreadfully
afraid, 3and said to the king,

1:5 [a] Literally *Him* [b] Literally *His* 1:8 [a] Leviticus 26:33 1:9 [a] Deuteronomy 30:2–5

"May the king live forever!
Why should my face not be
sad, when the city, the place of
my fathers' tombs, *lies* waste,
and its gates are burned with
fire?"
4Then the king said to me,
"What do you request?"
So I prayed to the God of
heaven. 5And I said to the
king, "If it pleases the king,
and if your servant has found
favor in your sight, I ask that
you send me to Judah, to the
city of my fathers' tombs, that
I may rebuild it."
6Then the king said to
me (the queen also sitting
beside him), "How long will
your journey be? And when
will you return?" So it pleased
the king to send me; and I set
him a time.
7Furthermore I said to the
king, "If it pleases the king, let
letters be given to me for the
governors *of the region* beyond
the River,[a] that they must permit me to pass through till I
come to Judah, 8and a letter to
Asaph the keeper of the king's
forest, that he must give me
timber to make beams for the
gates of the citadel which *pertains* to the temple,[a] for the
city wall, and for the house
that I will occupy." And the
king granted *them* to me according to the good hand of
my God upon me.
9Then I went to the gov-
ernors *in the region* beyond
the River, and gave them the
king's letters. Now the king had
sent captains of the army and
horsemen with me. 10When
Sanballat the Horonite and Tobiah the Ammonite official[a]
heard *of it,* they were deeply
disturbed that a man had
come to seek the well-being
of the children of Israel.

NEHEMIAH VIEWS THE WALL OF JERUSALEM

11So I came to Jerusalem
and was there three days.
12Then I arose in the night,
I and a few men with me; I
told no one what my God had
put in my heart to do at Jerusalem; nor was there any
animal with me, except the
one on which I rode. 13And
I went out by night through
the Valley Gate to the Serpent
Well and the Refuse Gate, and
viewed the walls of Jerusalem
which were broken down and
its gates which were burned
with fire. 14Then I went on to
the Fountain Gate and to the
King's Pool, but *there was* no
room for the animal under
me to pass. 15So I went up in
the night by the valley, and
viewed the wall; then I turned
back and entered by the Valley
Gate, and so returned. 16And
the officials did not know

2:7 [a] That is, the Euphrates, and so elsewhere in this book 2:8 [a] Literally *house* 2:10 [a] Literally *servant,* and so elsewhere in this book

where I had gone or what I
had done; I had not yet told
the Jews, the priests, the nobles, the officials, or the others who did the work.
17Then I said to them, "You
see the distress that we *are*
in, how Jerusalem *lies* waste,
and its gates are burned with
fire. Come and let us build
the wall of Jerusalem, that we
may no longer be a reproach."
18And I told them of the hand
of my God which had been
good upon me, and also of
the king's words that he had
spoken to me.
So they said, "Let us rise up
and build." Then they set their
hands to *this* good *work.*
19But when Sanballat the
Horonite, Tobiah the Ammonite official, and Geshem the
Arab heard *of it,* they laughed
at us and despised us, and
said, "What *is* this thing that
you are doing? Will you rebel
against the king?"
20So I answered them, and
said to them, "The God of
heaven Himself will prosper
us; therefore we His servants
will arise and build, but you
have no heritage or right or
memorial in Jerusalem."

REBUILDING THE WALL

3 Then Eliashib the high
priest rose up with his
brethren the priests and built
the Sheep Gate; they consecrated it and hung its doors.
They built as far as the Tower
of the Hundred,[a] *and* consecrated it, then as far as the
Tower of Hananel. 2Next to
Eliashib[a] the men of Jericho
built. And next to them Zaccur
the son of Imri built.
3Also the sons of Hassenaah
built the Fish Gate; they laid
its beams and hung its doors
with its bolts and bars. 4And
next to them Meremoth the
son of Urijah, the son of Koz,[a]
made repairs. Next to them
Meshullam the son of Berechiah, the son of Meshezabel,
made repairs. Next to them
Zadok the son of Baana made
repairs. 5Next to them the Te-
koites made repairs; but their
nobles did not put their shoulders[a] to the work of their Lord.
6Moreover Jehoiada the
son of Paseah and Meshul-
lam the son of Besodeiah
repaired the Old Gate; they
laid its beams and hung its
doors, with its bolts and bars.
7And next to them Melatiah
the Gibeonite, Jadon the Meronothite, the men of Gibeon
and Mizpah, repaired the residence[a] of the governor *of the
region* beyond the River. 8Next
to him Uzziel the son of Har-
haiah, one of the goldsmiths,
made repairs. Also next to
him Hananiah, one[a] of the

3:1 [a] Hebrew *Hammeah,* also at 12:39 3:2 [a] Literally *On his hand* 3:4 [a] Or *Hakkoz* 3:5 [a] Literally *necks* 3:7 [a] Literally *throne* 3:8 [a] Literally *the son*

perfumers, made repairs; and
they fortified Jerusalem as far
as the Broad Wall. 9And next
to them Rephaiah the son of
Hur, leader of half the district
of Jerusalem, made repairs.
10Next to them Jedaiah the
son of Harumaph made re-
pairs in front of his house.
And next to him Hattush the
son of Hashabniah made repairs.

11Malchijah the son of
Harim and Hashub the son
of Pahath-Moab repaired another section, as well as the
Tower of the Ovens. 12And
next to him was Shallum the
son of Hallohesh, leader of
half the district of Jerusalem;
he and his daughters made
repairs.

13Hanun and the inhab-
itants of Zanoah repaired
the Valley Gate. They built it,
hung its doors with its bolts
and bars, and *repaired* a thousand cubits of the wall as far
as the Refuse Gate.

14Malchijah the son of
Rechab, leader of the district
of Beth Haccerem, repaired
the Refuse Gate; he built it and
hung its doors with its bolts
and bars.

15Shallun the son of Col-
Hozeh, leader of the district
of Mizpah, repaired the Fountain Gate; he built it, covered
it, hung its doors with its bolts
and bars, and repaired the
wall of the Pool of Shelah by
the King's Garden, as far as
the stairs that go down from
the City of David. 16After him
Nehemiah the son of Azbuk,
leader of half the district of
Beth Zur, made repairs as far
as *the place* in front of the
tombs[a] of David, to the man-
made pool, and as far as the
House of the Mighty.

17After him the Levites,
under Rehum the son of
Bani, made repairs. Next to
him Hashabiah, leader of half
the district of Keilah, made
repairs for his district. 18After
him their brethren, *under*
Bavai[a] the son of Henadad,
leader of the *other* half of the
district of Keilah, made repairs. 19And next to him Ezer
the son of Jeshua, the leader
of Mizpah, repaired another
section in front of the Ascent
to the Armory at the buttress.
20After him Baruch the son of
Zabbai[a] carefully repaired the
other section, from the buttress to the door of the house
of Eliashib the high priest.
21After him Meremoth the son
of Urijah, the son of Koz,[a] repaired another section, from
the door of the house of Eliashib to the end of the house
of Eliashib.

22And after him the priests,
the men of the plain, made

3:16 [a] Septuagint, Syriac, and Vulgate read *tomb*. 3:18 [a] Following Masoretic Text and Vulgate; some Hebrew manuscripts, Septuagint, and Syriac read *Binnui* (compare verse 24). 3:20 [a] A few Hebrew manuscripts, Syriac, and Vulgate read *Zaccai*. 3:21 [a] Or *Hakkoz*

repairs. [23]After him Benjamin
and Hasshub made repairs
opposite their house. After
them Azariah the son of Maaseiah, the son of Ananiah,
made repairs by his house.
[24]After him Binnui the son
of Henadad repaired another
section, from the house of
Azariah to the buttress, even
as far as the corner. [25]Palal
the son of Uzai *made repairs*
opposite the buttress, and on
the tower which projects from
the king's upper house that
was by the court of the prison.
After him Pedaiah the son of
Parosh *made repairs.*

[26]Moreover the Nethinim
who dwelt in Ophel *made repairs* as far as *the place* in front
of the Water Gate toward the
east, and on the projecting
tower. [27]After them the Teko-
ites repaired another section,
next to the great projecting
tower, and as far as the wall
of Ophel.

[28]Beyond the Horse Gate
the priests made repairs, each
in front of his *own* house.
[29]After them Zadok the son of
Immer made repairs in front
of his *own* house. After him
Shemaiah the son of Shechaniah, the keeper of the East
Gate, made repairs. [30]After
him Hananiah the son of
Shelemiah, and Hanun, the
sixth son of Zalaph, repaired
another section. After him
Meshullam the son of Berechiah made repairs in front
of his dwelling. [31]After him
Malchijah, one of the goldsmiths, made repairs as far
as the house of the Nethinim
and of the merchants, in
front of the Miphkad[a] Gate,
and as far as the upper room
at the corner. [32]And between
the upper room at the corner, as far as the Sheep Gate,
the goldsmiths and the merchants made repairs.

THE WALL DEFENDED AGAINST ENEMIES

4 But it so happened, when
Sanballat heard that we
were rebuilding the wall,
that he was furious and very
indignant, and mocked the
Jews. [2]And he spoke before
his brethren and the army
of Samaria, and said, "What
are these feeble Jews doing?
Will they fortify themselves?
Will they offer sacrifices? Will
they complete it in a day? Will
they revive the stones from
the heaps of rubbish—*stones*
that are burned?"

[3]Now Tobiah the Ammon-
ite *was* beside him, and he
said, "Whatever they build, if
even a fox goes up *on it,* he will
break down their stone wall."

[4]Hear, O our God, for we are
despised; turn their reproach
on their own heads, and give
them as plunder to a land of
captivity! [5]Do not cover their
iniquity, and do not let their

3:31 [a] Literally *Inspection* or *Recruiting*

sin be blotted out from before
You; for they have provoked
You to anger before the builders.
6So we built the wall, and
the entire wall was joined together up to half its *height,*
for the people had a mind to
work.
7Now it happened, when
Sanballat, Tobiah, the Arabs,
the Ammonites, and the Ashdodites heard that the walls
of Jerusalem were being restored and the gaps were beginning to be closed, that they
became very angry, 8and all of
them conspired together to
come *and* attack Jerusalem
and create confusion. 9Never-
theless we made our prayer to
our God, and because of them
we set a watch against them
day and night.
10Then Judah said, "The
strength of the laborers is
failing, and *there is* so much
rubbish that we are not able
to build the wall."
11And our adversaries said,
"They will neither know nor
see anything, till we come into
their midst and kill them and
cause the work to cease."
12So it was, when the Jews
who dwelt near them came,
that they told us ten times,
"From whatever place you
turn, *they will be* upon us."
13Therefore I positioned
men behind the lower parts
of the wall, at the openings;
and I set the people according to their families, with their
swords, their spears, and their
bows. 14And I looked, and
arose and said to the nobles, to
the leaders, and to the rest of
the people, "Do not be afraid
of them. Remember the Lord,
great and awesome, and fight
for your brethren, your sons,
your daughters, your wives,
and your houses."
15And it happened, when
our enemies heard that it
was known to us, and *that*
God had brought their plot
to nothing, that all of us returned to the wall, everyone
to his work. 16So it was, from
that time on, *that* half of my
servants worked at construction, while the other half held
the spears, the shields, the
bows, and *wore* armor; and
the leaders *were* behind all the
house of Judah. 17Those who
built on the wall, and those
who carried burdens, loaded
themselves so that with one
hand they worked at construction, and with the other held
a weapon. 18Every one of the
builders had his sword girded
at his side as he built. And the
one who sounded the trumpet
was beside me.
19Then I said to the nobles,
the rulers, and the rest of the
people, "The work *is* great and
extensive, and we are separated far from one another
on the wall. 20Wherever you
hear the sound of the trumpet, rally to us there. Our God
will fight for us."
21So we labored in the work,

and half of *the men*[a] held the
spears from daybreak until
the stars appeared. 22At the
same time I also said to the
people, "Let each man and his
servant stay at night in Jerusalem, that they may be our
guard by night and a working
party by day." 23So neither I,
my brethren, my servants, nor
the men of the guard who followed me took off our clothes,
except that everyone took
them off for washing.

NEHEMIAH DEALS WITH OPPRESSION

5 And there was a great
outcry of the people and
their wives against their Jewish brethren. 2For there were
those who said, "We, our sons,
and our daughters *are* many;
therefore let us get grain, that
we may eat and live."

3There were also *some* who
said, "We have mortgaged
our lands and vineyards and
houses, that we might buy
grain because of the famine."

4There were also those
who said, "We have borrowed
money for the king's tax *on*
our lands and vineyards. 5Yet
now our flesh *is* as the flesh of
our brethren, our children as
their children; and indeed we
are forcing our sons and our
daughters to be slaves, and
some of our daughters have
been brought into slavery. *It*
is not in our power *to redeem*
them, for other men have our
lands and vineyards."

6And I became very angry
when I heard their outcry and
these words. 7After serious
thought, I rebuked the nobles
and rulers, and said to them,
"Each of you is exacting usury
from his brother." So I called a
great assembly against them.
8And I said to them, "According to our ability we have redeemed our Jewish brethren
who were sold to the nations.
Now indeed, will you even sell
your brethren? Or should they
be sold to us?"

Then they were silenced
and found nothing *to say.*
9Then I said, "What you are
doing *is* not good. Should you
not walk in the fear of our God
because of the reproach of
the nations, our enemies? 10I
also, *with* my brethren and
my servants, am lending them
money and grain. Please, let
us stop this usury! 11Restore
now to them, even this day,
their lands, their vineyards,
their olive groves, and their
houses, also a hundredth of
the money and the grain, the
new wine and the oil, that you
have charged them."

12So they said, "We will restore *it,* and will require nothing from them; we will do as
you say."

Then I called the priests,
and required an oath from
them that they would do ac-

4:21 [a] Literally *them*

cording to this promise. 13 Then
I shook out the fold of my garment[a] and said, "So may God
shake out each man from his
house, and from his property,
who does not perform this
promise. Even thus may he
be shaken out and emptied."
And all the assembly said,
"Amen!" and praised the
LORD. Then the people did
according to this promise.

THE GENEROSITY OF NEHEMIAH

14 Moreover, from the time
that I was appointed to be their
governor in the land of Judah,
from the twentieth year until
the thirty-second year of King
Artaxerxes, twelve years, neither I nor my brothers ate the
governor's provisions. 15 But
the former governors who
were before me laid burdens
on the people, and took from
them bread and wine, besides
forty shekels of silver. Yes,
even their servants bore rule
over the people, but I did not
do so, because of the fear of
God. 16 Indeed, I also continued the work on this wall, and
we[a] did not buy any land. All
my servants *were* gathered
there for the work.
17 And at my table *were* one
hundred and fifty Jews and
rulers, besides those who
came to us from the nations
around us. 18 Now *that* which
was prepared daily *was* one
ox *and* six choice sheep. Also
fowl were prepared for me,
and once every ten days an
abundance of all kinds of
wine. Yet in spite of this I did
not demand the governor's
provisions, because the bondage was heavy on this people.
19 Remember me, my God,
for good, *according to* all that
I have done for this people.

CONSPIRACY AGAINST NEHEMIAH

6 Now it happened when
Sanballat, Tobiah, Ge-
shem the Arab, and the rest
of our enemies heard that I
had rebuilt the wall, and *that*
there were no breaks left in it
(though at that time I had not
hung the doors in the gates),
2 that Sanballat and Geshem
sent to me, saying, "Come, let
us meet together among the
villages in the plain of Ono."
But they thought to do me
harm.
3 So I sent messengers to
them, saying, "I *am* doing a
great work, so that I cannot
come down. Why should the
work cease while I leave it and
go down to you?"
4 But they sent me this
message four times, and I
answered them in the same
manner.
5 Then Sanballat sent his
servant to me as before, the

5:13 [a] Literally *my lap* 5:16 [a] Following Masoretic Text; Septuagint, Syriac, and Vulgate read *I*.

fifth time, with an open letter
in his hand. 6In it *was* written:

> It is reported among the
> nations, and Geshem[a]
> says, *that* you and the
> Jews plan to rebel;
> therefore, according
> to these rumors, you
> are rebuilding the wall,
> that you may be their
> king. 7And you have also
> appointed prophets to
> proclaim concerning
> you at Jerusalem, saying,
> "*There is* a king in Judah!"
> Now these matters will be
> reported to the king. So
> come, therefore, and let
> us consult together.

8Then I sent to him, saying,
"No such things as you say are
being done, but you invent
them in your own heart."

9For they all *were trying to*
make us afraid, saying, "Their
hands will be weakened in the
work, and it will not be done."

Now therefore, *O God,*
strengthen my hands.

10Afterward I came to the
house of Shemaiah the son of
Delaiah, the son of Mehetabel,
who *was* a secret informer;
and he said, "Let us meet together in the house of God,
within the temple, and let us
close the doors of the temple, for they are coming to kill
you; indeed, at night they will
come to kill you."

11And I said, "Should such
a man as I flee? And who *is
there* such as I who would go
into the temple to save his
life? I will not go in!" 12Then
I perceived that God had not
sent him at all, but that he pronounced *this* prophecy against
me because Tobiah and Sanballat had hired him. 13For
this reason he *was* hired, that
I should be afraid and act that
way and sin, so *that* they might
have *cause* for an evil report,
that they might reproach me.

14My God, remember To-
biah and Sanballat, according to these their works, and
the prophetess Noadiah and
the rest of the prophets who
would have made me afraid.

THE WALL COMPLETED

15So the wall was finished
on the twenty-fifth *day* of Elul,
in fifty-two days. 16And it happened, when all our enemies
heard *of it,* and all the nations
around us saw *these things,*
that they were very disheart-
ened in their own eyes; for
they perceived that this work
was done by our God.

17Also in those days the nobles of Judah sent many letters
to Tobiah, and *the letters of* Tobiah came to them. 18For many
in Judah were pledged to him,
because he was the son-in-law
of Shechaniah the son of Arah,
and his son Jehohanan had
married the daughter of Me-

6:6 [a] Hebrew *Gashmu*

shullam the son of Berechiah.
19Also they reported his good
deeds before me, and reported
my words to him. Tobiah sent
letters to frighten me.

7 Then it was, when the wall
was built and I had hung
the doors, when the gate-
keepers, the singers, and the
Levites had been appointed,
2that I gave the charge of Jerusalem to my brother Hanani,
and Hananiah the leader of
the citadel, for he *was* a faithful man and feared God more
than many.

3And I said to them, "Do
not let the gates of Jerusalem be opened until the sun
is hot; and while they stand
guard, let them shut and bar
the doors; and appoint guards
from among the inhabitants
of Jerusalem, one at his watch
station and another in front
of his own house."

THE CAPTIVES WHO RETURNED TO JERUSALEM

4Now the city *was* large and
spacious, but the people in it
were few, and the houses *were*
not rebuilt. 5Then my God
put it into my heart to gather
the nobles, the rulers, and
the people, that they might
be registered by genealogy.
And I found a register of the
genealogy of those who had
come up in the first *return,*
and found written in it:

6 These[a] *are* the people of
the province who came
back from the captivity,
of those who had been
carried away, whom
Nebuchadnezzar the king
of Babylon had carried
away, and who returned
to Jerusalem and Judah,
everyone to his city.

7 Those who came with
Zerubbabel *were* Jeshua,
Nehemiah, Azariah,
Raamiah, Nahamani,
Mordecai, Bilshan,
Mispereth,[a] Bigvai,
Nehum, and Baanah.

The number of the men
of the people of Israel:
8the sons of Parosh, two
thousand one hundred
and seventy-two;
9the sons of Shephatiah,
three hundred and
seventy-two;
10the sons of Arah, six
hundred and fifty-two;
11the sons of
Pahath-Moab, of the sons
of Jeshua and Joab, two
thousand eight hundred
and eighteen;
12the sons of Elam, one
thousand two hundred
and fifty-four;
13the sons of Zattu, eight
hundred and forty-five;
14the sons of Zaccai, seven
hundred and sixty;

7:6 [a] Compare verses 6–72 with Ezra 2:1–70 **7:7** [a] Spelled *Mispar* in Ezra 2:2

[15]the sons of Binnui,[a] six
hundred and forty-eight;
[16]the sons of Bebai,
six hundred and
twenty-eight;
[17]the sons of Azgad, two
thousand three hundred
and twenty-two;
[18]the sons of Adonikam,
six hundred and
sixty-seven;
[19]the sons of Bigvai, two
thousand and sixty-seven;
[20]the sons of Adin, six
hundred and fifty-five;
[21]the sons of Ater of
Hezekiah, ninety-eight;
[22]the sons of Hashum,
three hundred and
twenty-eight;
[23]the sons of Bezai, three
hundred and twenty-four;
[24]the sons of Hariph,[a]
one hundred and twelve;
[25]the sons of Gibeon,[a]
ninety-five;
[26]the men of Bethlehem
and Netophah,
one hundred and
eighty-eight;
[27]the men of Anathoth,
one hundred and
twenty-eight;
[28]the men of Beth
Azmaveth,[a] forty-two;
[29]the men of Kirjath
Jearim, Chephirah, and
Beeroth, seven hundred
and forty-three;
[30]the men of Ramah and
Geba, six hundred and
twenty-one;
[31]the men of Michmas,
one hundred and
twenty-two;
[32]the men of Bethel and
Ai, one hundred and
twenty-three;
[33]the men of the other
Nebo, fifty-two;
[34]the sons of the other
Elam, one thousand two
hundred and fifty-four;
[35]the sons of Harim,
three hundred and
twenty;
[36]the sons of Jericho,
three hundred and
forty-five;
[37]the sons of Lod, Hadid,
and Ono, seven hundred
and twenty-one;
[38]the sons of Senaah,
three thousand nine
hundred and thirty.

39 The priests: the sons of
Jedaiah, of the house of
Jeshua, nine hundred
and seventy-three;
[40]the sons of Immer, one
thousand and fifty-two;
[41]the sons of Pashhur, one
thousand two hundred
and forty-seven;
[42]the sons of Harim, one
thousand and seventeen.

43 The Levites: the sons of
Jeshua, of Kadmiel,

7:15 [a] Spelled *Bani* in Ezra 2:10 **7:24** [a] Called *Jorah* in Ezra 2:18 **7:25** [a] Called *Gibbar* in Ezra 2:20 **7:28** [a] Called *Azmaveth* in Ezra 2:24

and of the sons of
Hodevah,[a] seventy-four.

44 The singers: the sons of
Asaph, one hundred and
forty-eight.

45 The gatekeepers: the sons
of Shallum,
the sons of Ater,
the sons of Talmon,
the sons of Akkub,
the sons of Hatita,
the sons of Shobai, one
hundred and thirty-eight.

46 The Nethinim: the sons of
Ziha,
the sons of Hasupha,
the sons of Tabbaoth,
47the sons of Keros,
the sons of Sia,[a]
the sons of Padon,
48the sons of Lebana,[a]
the sons of Hagaba,[b]
the sons of Salmai,[c]
49the sons of Hanan,
the sons of Giddel,
the sons of Gahar,
50the sons of Reaiah,
the sons of Rezin,
the sons of Nekoda,
51the sons of Gazzam,
the sons of Uzza,
the sons of Paseah,
52the sons of Besai,
the sons of Meunim,
the sons of Nephishesim,[a]
53the sons of Bakbuk,
the sons of Hakupha,
the sons of Harhur,
54the sons of Bazlith,[a]
the sons of Mehida,
the sons of Harsha,
55the sons of Barkos,
the sons of Sisera,
the sons of Tamah,
56the sons of Neziah,
and the sons of Hatipha.

57 The sons of Solomon's
servants: the sons of
Sotai,
the sons of Sophereth,
the sons of Perida,[a]
58the sons of Jaala,
the sons of Darkon,
the sons of Giddel,
59the sons of Shephatiah,
the sons of Hattil,
the sons of Pochereth of
Zebaim,
and the sons of Amon.[a]
60All the Nethinim, and
the sons of Solomon's
servants, *were* three
hundred and ninety-two.

61 And these *were* the
ones who came up from
Tel Melah, Tel Harsha,
Cherub, Addon,[a] and
Immer, but they could
not identify their father's
house nor their lineage,
whether they *were* of

7:43 [a] Spelled *Hodaviah* in Ezra 2:40 **7:47** [a] Spelled *Siaha* in Ezra 2:44 **7:48** [a] Masoretic Text reads *Lebanah.* [b] Masoretic Text reads *Hogabah.* [c] Or *Shalmai,* or *Shamlai* **7:52** [a] Spelled *Nephusim* in Ezra 2:50 **7:54** [a] Spelled *Bazluth* in Ezra 2:52 **7:57** [a] Spelled *Peruda* in Ezra 2:55 **7:59** [a] Spelled *Ami* in Ezra 2:57 **7:61** [a] Spelled *Addan* in Ezra 2:59

Israel: 62the sons of
Delaiah,
the sons of Tobiah,
the sons of Nekoda, six
hundred and forty-two;
63and of the priests: the
sons of Habaiah,
the sons of Koz,[a]
the sons of Barzillai,
who took a wife of the
daughters of Barzillai the
Gileadite, and was called
by their name.
64These sought their
listing *among* those
who were registered by
genealogy, but it was not
found; therefore they
were excluded from the
priesthood as defiled.
65And the governor[a] said
to them that they should
not eat of the most holy
things till a priest could
consult with the Urim
and Thummim.

66 Altogether the whole
assembly *was* forty-two
thousand three hundred
and sixty, 67besides
their male and female
servants, of whom *there
were* seven thousand
three hundred and
thirty-seven; and they
had two hundred and
forty-five men and
women singers. 68Their
horses were seven
hundred and thirty-six,
their mules two hundred
and forty-five, 69*their*
camels four hundred and
thirty-five, *and* donkeys
six thousand seven
hundred and twenty.

70 And some of the heads of
the fathers' *houses* gave to
the work. The governor[a]
gave to the treasury
one thousand gold
drachmas, fifty basins,
and five hundred and
thirty priestly garments.
71Some of the heads of
the fathers' *houses* gave
to the treasury of the
work twenty thousand
gold drachmas, and two
thousand two hundred
silver minas. 72And that
which the rest of the
people gave *was* twenty
thousand gold drachmas,
two thousand silver
minas, and sixty-seven
priestly garments.

73So the priests, the Levites,
the gatekeepers, the singers,
some of the people, the Nethinim, and all Israel dwelt in
their cities.

EZRA READS THE LAW

When the seventh month
came, the children of Israel
were in their cities.

8 Now all the people gathered together as one man
in the open square that *was*
in front of the Water Gate;

7:63 [a] Or *Hakkoz* 7:65 [a] Hebrew *Tirshatha* 7:70 [a] Hebrew *Tirshatha*

and they told Ezra the scribe
to bring the Book of the Law
of Moses, which the LORD had
commanded Israel. 2So Ezra
the priest brought the Law
before the assembly of men
and women and all who *could*
hear with understanding on
the first day of the seventh
month. 3Then he read from
it in the open square that *was*
in front of the Water Gate from
morning until midday, before
the men and women and those
who could understand; and the
ears of all the people *were attentive*
to the Book of the Law.

4So Ezra the scribe stood on
a platform of wood which they
had made for the purpose; and
beside him, at his right hand,
stood Mattithiah, Shema,
Anaiah, Urijah, Hilkiah, and
Maaseiah; and at his left hand
Pedaiah, Mishael, Malchijah,
Hashum, Hashbadana, Zechariah,
and Meshullam. 5And
Ezra opened the book in the
sight of all the people, for he
was *standing* above all the
people; and when he opened
it, all the people stood up.
6And Ezra blessed the LORD,
the great God.

Then all the people answered,
"Amen, Amen!" while
lifting up their hands. And
they bowed their heads and
worshiped the LORD with *their*
faces to the ground.

7Also Jeshua, Bani, Sherebiah,
Jamin, Akkub, Shabbethai,
Hodijah, Maaseiah, Kelita,
Azariah, Jozabad, Hanan, Pelaiah,
and the Levites, helped
the people to understand the
Law; and the people *stood*
in their place. 8So they read
distinctly from the book, in
the Law of God; and they gave
the sense, and helped *them* to
understand the reading.

9And Nehemiah, who *was*
the governor,[a] Ezra the priest
and scribe, and the Levites
who taught the people said
to all the people, "This day *is*
holy to the LORD your God; do
not mourn nor weep." For all
the people wept, when they
heard the words of the Law.

10Then he said to them, "Go
your way, eat the fat, drink the
sweet, and send portions to
those for whom nothing is
prepared; for *this* day *is* holy
to our Lord. Do not sorrow,
for the joy of the LORD is your
strength."

11So the Levites quieted all
the people, saying, "Be still,
for the day *is* holy; do not be
grieved." 12And all the people
went their way to eat and
drink, to send portions and
rejoice greatly, because they
understood the words that
were declared to them.

THE FEAST OF TABERNACLES

13Now on the second day
the heads of the fathers'
houses of all the people, with

8:9 [a] Hebrew *Tirshatha*

the priests and Levites, were
gathered to Ezra the scribe, in
order to understand the words
of the Law. 14And they found
written in the Law, which the
LORD had commanded by
Moses, that the children of
Israel should dwell in booths
during the feast of the seventh
month, 15and that they should
announce and proclaim in all
their cities and in Jerusalem,
saying, "Go out to the mountain, and bring olive branches,
branches of oil trees, myrtle
branches, palm branches,
and branches of leafy trees, to
make booths, as *it is* written."

16Then the people went out
and brought *them* and made
themselves booths, each one
on the roof of his house, or in
their courtyards or the courts
of the house of God, and in
the open square of the Water
Gate and in the open square of
the Gate of Ephraim. 17So the
whole assembly of those who
had returned from the captivity made booths and sat under
the booths; for since the days
of Joshua the son of Nun until
that day the children of Israel
had not done so. And there was
very great gladness. 18Also day
by day, from the first day until
the last day, he read from the
Book of the Law of God. And
they kept the feast seven days;
and on the eighth day *there*
was a sacred assembly, according to the *prescribed* manner.

THE PEOPLE CONFESS THEIR SINS

9 Now on the twenty-fourth
day of this month the children of Israel were assembled
with fasting, in sackcloth, and
with dust on their heads.[a]
2Then those of Israelite lineage separated themselves
from all foreigners; and they
stood and confessed their sins
and the iniquities of their fathers. 3And they stood up in
their place and read from the
Book of the Law of the LORD
their God *for one*-fourth of the
day; and *for another* fourth
they confessed and worshiped
the LORD their God.

4Then Jeshua, Bani, Kad-
miel, Shebaniah, Bunni, Sherebiah, Bani, *and* Chenani
stood on the stairs of the
Levites and cried out with a
loud voice to the LORD their
God. 5And the Levites, Jeshua,
Kadmiel, Bani, Hashabniah,
Sherebiah, Hodijah, Shebaniah, *and* Pethahiah, said:

"Stand up *and* bless the
LORD your God
Forever and ever!

"Blessed be Your
glorious name,
Which is exalted above
all blessing and praise!
6 You alone *are* the LORD;
You have made heaven,
The heaven of heavens,
with all their host,

9:1 [a] Literally *earth on them*

The earth and
everything on it,
The seas and all
that is in them,
And You preserve
them all.
The host of heaven
worships You.

7 "You *are* the LORD God,
Who chose Abram,
And brought him out of
Ur of the Chaldeans,
And gave him the
name Abraham;
8 You found his heart
faithful before You,
And made a covenant
with him
To give the land of
the Canaanites,
The Hittites, the Amorites,
The Perizzites, the
Jebusites,
And the Girgashites—
To give *it* to his
descendants.
You have performed
Your words,
For You *are* righteous.

9 "You saw the affliction
of our fathers in Egypt,
And heard their cry
by the Red Sea.
10 You showed signs
and wonders
against Pharaoh,
Against all his servants,
And against all the
people of his land.
For You knew that
they acted proudly
against them.
So You made a name for
Yourself, as *it is* this day.
11 And You divided the
sea before them,
So that they went through
the midst of the sea
on the dry land;
And their persecutors You
threw into the deep,
As a stone into the
mighty waters.
12 Moreover You led them by
day with a cloudy pillar,
And by night with
a pillar of fire,
To give them light
on the road
Which they should travel.

13 "You came down also
on Mount Sinai,
And spoke with them
from heaven,
And gave them
just ordinances
and true laws,
Good statutes and
commandments.
14 You made known to them
Your holy Sabbath,
And commanded
them precepts,
statutes and laws,
By the hand of Moses
Your servant.
15 You gave them bread from
heaven for their hunger,
And brought them
water out of the rock
for their thirst,
And told them to go in
to possess the land
Which You had sworn
to give them.

16 "But they and our fathers
acted proudly,
Hardened their necks,
And did not heed Your
commandments.
17 They refused to obey,
And they were not mindful
of Your wonders
That You did among them.
But they hardened
their necks,
And in their rebellion[a]
They appointed a leader
To return to their bondage.
But You *are* God,
Ready to pardon,
Gracious and merciful,
Slow to anger,
Abundant in kindness,
And did not forsake them.

18 "Even when they made
a molded calf for
themselves,
And said, 'This *is* your god
That brought you up
out of Egypt,'
And worked great
provocations,
19 Yet in Your manifold
mercies
You did not forsake them
in the wilderness.
The pillar of the cloud
did not depart from
them by day,
To lead them on the road;
Nor the pillar of
fire by night,
To show them light,
And the way they
should go.
20 You also gave Your good
Spirit to instruct them,
And did not withhold
Your manna from
their mouth,
And gave them water
for their thirst.
21 Forty years You sustained
them in the wilderness;
They lacked nothing;
Their clothes did
not wear out[a]
And their feet did
not swell.

22 "Moreover You gave them
kingdoms and nations,
And divided them
into districts.[a]
So they took possession
of the land of Sihon,
The land of[b] the king
of Heshbon,
And the land of Og
king of Bashan.
23 You also multiplied
their children as the
stars of heaven,
And brought them
into the land
Which You had told
their fathers
To go in and possess.
24 So the people went in
And possessed the land;
You subdued before
them the inhabitants
of the land,

9:17 [a] Following Masoretic Text and Vulgate; Septuagint reads *in Egypt.* **9:21** [a] Compare Deuteronomy 29:5 **9:22** [a] Literally *corners* [b] Following Masoretic Text and Vulgate; Septuagint omits *The land of.*

The Canaanites,
And gave them into
their hands,
With their kings
And the people
of the land,
That they might do with
them as they wished.
25 And they took strong
cities and a rich land,
And possessed houses
full of all goods,
Cisterns *already* dug,
vineyards, olive groves,
And fruit trees in
abundance.
So they ate and were
filled and grew fat,
And delighted themselves
in Your great goodness.

26 "Nevertheless they
were disobedient
And rebelled against You,
Cast Your law behind
their backs
And killed Your
prophets, who testified
against them
To turn them to Yourself;
And they worked great
provocations.
27 Therefore You delivered
them into the hand
of their enemies,
Who oppressed them;
And in the time of
their trouble,
When they cried to You,
You heard from heaven;
And according to Your
abundant mercies
You gave them deliverers
who saved them
From the hand of
their enemies.

28 "But after they had rest,
They again did evil
before You.
Therefore You left
them in the hand
of their enemies,
So that they had
dominion over them;
Yet when they returned
and cried out to You,
You heard from heaven;
And many times
You delivered
them according to
Your mercies,
29 And testified
against them,
That You might bring
them back to Your law.
Yet they acted proudly,
And did not heed Your
commandments,
But sinned against
Your judgments,
'Which if a man does,
he shall live by them.'[a]
And they shrugged
their shoulders,
Stiffened their necks,
And would not hear.
30 Yet for many years You
had patience with them,
And testified against
them by Your Spirit
in Your prophets.
Yet they would not
listen;

9:29 [a] Leviticus 18:5

Therefore You gave them
into the hand of the
peoples of the lands.
31 Nevertheless in Your
great mercy
You did not utterly
consume them nor
forsake them;
For You *are* God, gracious
and merciful.

32 "Now therefore, our God,
The great, the mighty,
and awesome God,
Who keeps covenant
and mercy:
Do not let all the trouble
seem small before You
That has come upon us,
Our kings and our princes,
Our priests and
our prophets,
Our fathers and on
all Your people,
From the days of the kings
of Assyria until this day.
33 However You *are* just in
all that has befallen us;
For You have dealt
faithfully,
But we have done
wickedly.
34 Neither our kings
nor our princes,
Our priests nor
our fathers,
Have kept Your law,
Nor heeded Your
commandments and
Your testimonies,
With which You testified
against them.
35 For they have not served
You in their kingdom,
Or in the many good
things that You
gave them,
Or in the large and
rich land which You
set before them;
Nor did they turn from
their wicked works.

36 "Here we *are*,
servants today!
And the land that You
gave to our fathers,
To eat its fruit and
its bounty,
Here we *are*, servants in it!
37 And it yields much
increase to the kings
You have set over us,
Because of our sins;
Also they have dominion
over our bodies
and our cattle
At their pleasure;
And we *are* in great
distress.

38 "And because of all this,
We make a sure *covenant*
and write *it*;
Our leaders, our Levites,
and our priests seal *it*."

THE PEOPLE WHO SEALED THE COVENANT

10 Now those who placed
their seal on *the docu-*
ment were:
Nehemiah the governor, the
son of Hacaliah, and Zedekiah,
2 Seraiah, Azariah, Jeremiah,
3 Pashhur, Amariah, Malchijah,
4 Hattush, Shebaniah, Malluch,
5 Harim, Meremoth, Obadiah,

6 Daniel, Ginnethon, Baruch,
7 Meshullam, Abijah, Mijamin,
8 Maaziah, Bilgai, *and* Shemaiah. These *were* the priests.
9 The Levites: Jeshua the son
of Azaniah, Binnui of the sons
of Henadad, *and* Kadmiel.
10 Their brethren: Sheba-
niah, Hodijah, Kelita, Pelaiah,
Hanan, 11 Micha, Rehob, Hashabiah, 12 Zaccur, Sherebiah,
Shebaniah, 13 Hodijah, Bani,
and Beninu.
14 The leaders of the people:
Parosh, Pahath-Moab, Elam,
Zattu, Bani, 15 Bunni, Azgad,
Bebai, 16 Adonijah, Bigvai,
Adin, 17 Ater, Hezekiah, Azzur,
18 Hodijah, Hashum, Bezai,
19 Hariph, Anathoth, Nebai,
20 Magpiash, Meshullam, Hezir,
21 Meshezabel, Zadok, Jaddua,
22 Pelatiah, Hanan, Anaiah,
23 Hoshea, Hananiah, Hasshub,
24 Hallohesh, Pilha, Shobek, 25-
Rehum, Hashabnah, Maase-
iah, 26 Ahijah, Hanan, Anan,
27 Malluch, Harim, *and* Baanah.

THE COVENANT THAT WAS SEALED

28 Now the rest of the
people—the priests, the Levites, the gatekeepers, the singers, the Nethinim, and all those
who had separated themselves
from the peoples of the lands
to the Law of God, their wives,
their sons, and their daughters,
everyone who had knowledge
and understanding— 29 these
joined with their brethren,
their nobles, and entered into
a curse and an oath to walk in
God's Law, which was given by
Moses the servant of God, and
to observe and do all the commandments of the LORD our
Lord, and His ordinances and
His statutes: 30 We would not
give our daughters as wives
to the peoples of the land,
nor take their daughters for
our sons; 31 *if* the peoples of
the land brought wares or any
grain to sell on the Sabbath
day, we would not buy it from
them on the Sabbath, or on a
holy day; and we would forego
the seventh year's *produce* and
the exacting of every debt.
32 Also we made ordinances
for ourselves, to exact from
ourselves yearly one-third of
a shekel for the service of the
house of our God: 33 for the
showbread, for the regular
grain offering, for the regular burnt offering of the Sabbaths, the New Moons, and the
set feasts; for the holy things,
for the sin offerings to make
atonement for Israel, and all
the work of the house of our
God. 34 We cast lots among the
priests, the Levites, and the
people, for bringing the wood
offering into the house of our
God, according to our fathers'
houses, at the appointed
times year by year, to burn
on the altar of the LORD our
God as *it is* written in the Law.
35 And *we made ordinances*
to bring the firstfruits of our
ground and the firstfruits of all
fruit of all trees, year by year,
to the house of the LORD; 36 to

bring the firstborn of our sons
and our cattle, as *it is* written in
the Law, and the firstborn of
our herds and our flocks, to the
house of our God, to the priests
who minister in the house of
our God; 37to bring the firstfruits of our dough, our offerings, the fruit from all kinds of
trees, *the* new wine and oil, to
the priests, to the storerooms
of the house of our God; and
to bring the tithes of our land
to the Levites, for the Levites
should receive the tithes in
all our farming communities.
38And the priest, the descendant of Aaron, shall be with
the Levites when the Levites
receive tithes; and the Levites
shall bring up a tenth of the
tithes to the house of our God,
to the rooms of the storehouse.

39For the children of Israel
and the children of Levi shall
bring the offering of the grain,
of the new wine and the oil,
to the storerooms where the
articles of the sanctuary *are,*
where the priests who minister
and the gatekeepers and the
singers *are;* and we will not
neglect the house of our God.

THE PEOPLE DWELLING IN JERUSALEM

11 Now the leaders of the
people dwelt at Jerusa-
lem; the rest of the people cast
lots to bring one out of ten to
dwell in Jerusalem, the holy
city, and nine-tenths *were to*
dwell in *other* cities. 2And the
people blessed all the men
who willingly offered themselves to dwell at Jerusalem.

3These *are* the heads of
the province who dwelt in
Jerusalem. (But in the cities
of Judah everyone dwelt in
his own possession in their
cities—Israelites, priests, Levites, Nethinim, and descendants of Solomon's servants.)
4Also in Jerusalem dwelt *some*
of the children of Judah and
of the children of Benjamin.

The children of Judah:
Athaiah the son of Uzziah, the
son of Zechariah, the son of
Amariah, the son of Shephatiah, the son of Mahalalel, of
the children of Perez; 5and Maaseiah the son of Baruch, the
son of Col-Hozeh, the son of
Hazaiah, the son of Adaiah, the
son of Joiarib, the son of Zechariah, the son of Shiloni. 6All
the sons of Perez who dwelt at
Jerusalem *were* four hundred
and sixty-eight valiant men.

7And these are the sons of
Benjamin: Sallu the son of
Meshullam, the son of Joed,
the son of Pedaiah, the son of
Kolaiah, the son of Maaseiah,
the son of Ithiel, the son of Jeshaiah; 8and after him Gabbai
and Sallai, nine hundred and
twenty-eight. 9Joel the son of
Zichri *was* their overseer, and
Judah the son of Senuah[a] *was*
second over the city.

10Of the priests: Jedaiah

11:9 [a] Or *Hassenuah*

the son of Joiarib, and Jachin;
11Seraiah the son of Hilkiah,
the son of Meshullam, the
son of Zadok, the son of Meraioth, the son of Ahitub, *was*
the leader of the house of God.
12Their brethren who did the
work of the house *were* eight
hundred and twenty-two; and
Adaiah the son of Jeroham,
the son of Pelaliah, the son
of Amzi, the son of Zechariah,
the son of Pashhur, the son of
Malchijah, 13and his brethren,
heads of the fathers' *houses,*
were two hundred and forty-
two; and Amashai the son
of Azarel, the son of Ahzai,
the son of Meshillemoth, the
son of Immer, 14and their
brethren, mighty men of
valor, *were* one hundred and
twenty-eight. Their overseer
was Zabdiel the son of *one of*
the great men.[a]

15Also of the Levites: Shemaiah the son of Hasshub,
the son of Azrikam, the son of
Hashabiah, the son of Bunni;
16Shabbethai and Jozabad, of
the heads of the Levites, *had*
the oversight of the business
outside of the house of God;
17Mattaniah the son of Micha,[a]
the son of Zabdi, the son of
Asaph, the leader *who* began
the thanksgiving with prayer;
Bakbukiah, the second among
his brethren; and Abda the
son of Shammua, the son of
Galal, the son of Jeduthun.
18All the Levites in the holy
city *were* two hundred and
eighty-four.

19Moreover the gate-
keepers, Akkub, Talmon, and
their brethren who kept the
gates, *were* one hundred and
seventy-two.

20And the rest of Israel, of
the priests *and* Levites, *were*
in all the cities of Judah,
everyone in his inheritance.
21But the Nethinim dwelt in
Ophel. And Ziha and Gishpa
were over the Nethinim.

22Also the overseer of the
Levites at Jerusalem *was* Uzzi
the son of Bani, the son of
Hashabiah, the son of Mattaniah, the son of Micha, of the
sons of Asaph, the singers in
charge of the service of the
house of God. 23For *it was* the
king's command concerning
them that a certain portion
should be for the singers, a
quota day by day. 24Pethahiah
the son of Meshezabel, of the
children of Zerah the son of
Judah, *was* the king's deputy[a]
in all matters concerning the
people.

THE PEOPLE DWELLING OUTSIDE JERUSALEM

25And as for the villages
with their fields, some of the
children of Judah dwelt in
Kirjath Arba and its villages,
Dibon and its villages, Je-
kabzeel and its villages; 26in

11:14 [a] Or *the son of Haggedolim* 11:17 [a] Or *Michah* 11:24 [a] Literally *at the king's hand*

Jeshua, Moladah, Beth Pelet,
27Hazar Shual, and Beersheba
and its villages; 28in Ziklag
and Meconah and its villages;
29in En Rimmon, Zorah, Jarmuth, 30Zanoah, Adullam, and
their villages; in Lachish and
its fields; in Azekah and its
villages. They dwelt from Beersheba to the Valley of Hinnom.

31Also the children of Benjamin from Geba *dwelt* in
Michmash, Aija, and Bethel,
and their villages; 32in Anathoth, Nob, Ananiah; 33in
Hazor, Ramah, Gittaim; 34in
Hadid, Zeboim, Neballat;
35in Lod, Ono, *and* the Valley
of Craftsmen. 36Some of the
Judean divisions of Levites
were in Benjamin.

THE PRIESTS AND LEVITES

12 Now these *are* the
priests and the Levites
who came up with Zerubba-
bel the son of Shealtiel, and
Jeshua: Seraiah, Jeremiah,
Ezra, 2Amariah, Malluch, Hattush, 3Shechaniah, Rehum,
Meremoth, 4Iddo, Ginnethoi,[a]
Abijah, 5Mijamin, Maadiah,
Bilgah, 6Shemaiah, Joiarib, Jedaiah, 7Sallu, Amok, Hilkiah,
and Jedaiah.

These *were* the heads of the
priests and their brethren in
the days of Jeshua.

8Moreover the Levites *were*
Jeshua, Binnui, Kadmiel,
Sherebiah, Judah, *and* Mattaniah *who led* the thanksgiving
psalms, he and his brethren.
9Also Bakbukiah and Unni,
their brethren, *stood* across
from them in *their* duties.

10Jeshua begot Joiakim,
Joiakim begot Eliashib, Eliashib begot Joiada, 11Joiada
begot Jonathan, and Jonathan
begot Jaddua.

12Now in the days of Joi-
akim, the priests, the heads
of the fathers' *houses were:* of
Seraiah, Meraiah; of Jeremiah,
Hananiah; 13of Ezra, Meshullam; of Amariah, Jehohanan;
14of Melichu,[a] Jonathan; of
Shebaniah,[b] Joseph; 15of
Harim,[a] Adna; of Meraioth,[b]
Helkai; 16of Iddo, Zechariah;
of Ginnethon, Meshullam; 17of
Abijah, Zichri; *the son* of Minjamin;[a] of Moadiah,[b] Piltai;
18of Bilgah, Shammua; of Shemaiah, Jehonathan; 19of Joiarib, Mattenai; of Jedaiah, Uzzi;
20of Sallai,[a] Kallai; of Amok,
Eber; 21of Hilkiah, Hashabiah;
and of Jedaiah, Nethanel.

22During the reign of Da-
rius the Persian, a record *was
also kept* of the Levites and
priests *who had been* heads
of their fathers' *houses* in the
days of Eliashib, Joiada, Johanan, and Jaddua. 23The sons

12:4 [a] Or *Ginnethon* (compare verse 16) **12:14** [a] Or Malluch (compare verse 2) [b] Or *Shechaniah* (compare verse 3) **12:15** [a] Or *Rehum* (compare verse 3) [b] Or *Meremoth* (compare verse 3) **12:17** [a] Or *Mijamin* (compare verse 5) [b] Or *Maadiah* (compare verse 5) **12:20** [a] Or *Sallu* (compare verse 7)

of Levi, the heads of the fathers' *houses* until the days of
Johanan the son of Eliashib,
were written in the book of the
chronicles.
[24]And the heads of the Levites *were* Hashabiah, Sherebiah, and Jeshua the son of
Kadmiel, with their brothers
across from them, to praise
and give thanks, group alter-
nating with group, according
to the command of David the
man of God. [25]Mattaniah, Bakbukiah, Obadiah, Meshullam,
Talmon, and Akkub *were* gatekeepers keeping the watch at
the storerooms of the gates.
[26]These *lived* in the days of
Joiakim the son of Jeshua, the
son of Jozadak,[a] and in the
days of Nehemiah the governor, and of Ezra the priest, the
scribe.

NEHEMIAH DEDICATES THE WALL

[27]Now at the dedication
of the wall of Jerusalem they
sought out the Levites in all
their places, to bring them
to Jerusalem to celebrate the
dedication with gladness,
both with thanksgivings
and singing, *with* cymbals
and stringed instruments and
harps. [28]And the sons of the
singers gathered together
from the countryside around
Jerusalem, from the villages
of the Netophathites, [29]from
the house of Gilgal, and from
the fields of Geba and Azmaveth; for the singers had
built themselves villages all
around Jerusalem. [30]Then the
priests and Levites purified
themselves, and purified the
people, the gates, and the wall.
[31]So I brought the leaders
of Judah up on the wall, and
appointed two large thanksgiving choirs. *One* went to the
right hand on the wall toward
the Refuse Gate. [32]After them
went Hoshaiah and half of
the leaders of Judah, [33]and
Azariah, Ezra, Meshullam,
[34]Judah, Benjamin, Shemaiah, Jeremiah, [35]and some
of the priests' sons with
trumpets—Zechariah the son
of Jonathan, the son of Shemaiah, the son of Mattaniah,
the son of Michaiah, the son
of Zaccur, the son of Asaph,
[36]and his brethren, Shemaiah,
Azarel, Milalai, Gilalai, Maai,
Nethanel, Judah, *and* Hanani,
with the musical instruments
of David the man of God. And
Ezra the scribe *went* before
them. [37]By the Fountain Gate,
in front of them, they went up
the stairs of the City of David,
on the stairway of the wall,
beyond the house of David, as
far as the Water Gate eastward.
[38]The other thanksgiving
choir went the opposite *way,*
and I *was* behind them with
half of the people on the wall,
going past the Tower of the
Ovens as far as the Broad

12:26 [a] Spelled *Jehozadak* in 1 Chronicles 6:14

Wall, 39and above the Gate of
Ephraim, above the Old Gate,
above the Fish Gate, the Tower
of Hananel, the Tower of the
Hundred, as far as the Sheep
Gate; and they stopped by the
Gate of the Prison.
40So the two thanksgiving
choirs stood in the house of
God, likewise I and the half
of the rulers with me; 41and
the priests, Eliakim, Maaseiah, Minjamin,[a] Michaiah,
Elioenai, Zechariah, *and* Hananiah, with trumpets; 42also
Maaseiah, Shemaiah, Eleazar,
Uzzi, Jehohanan, Malchijah,
Elam, and Ezer. The singers
sang loudly with Jezrahiah the
director.
43Also that day they of-
fered great sacrifices, and
rejoiced, for God had made
them rejoice with great joy;
the women and the children
also rejoiced, so that the joy of
Jerusalem was heard afar off.

TEMPLE RESPONSIBILITIES

44And at the same time
some were appointed over the
rooms of the storehouse for
the offerings, the firstfruits,
and the tithes, to gather into
them from the fields of the
cities the portions specified
by the Law for the priests and
Levites; for Judah rejoiced
over the priests and Levites
who ministered. 45Both the
singers and the gatekeepers
kept the charge of their God
and the charge of the purification, according to the command of David *and* Solomon
his son. 46For in the days of
David and Asaph of old *there
were* chiefs of the singers, and
songs of praise and thanksgiving to God. 47In the days
of Zerubbabel and in the days
of Nehemiah all Israel gave
the portions for the singers
and the gatekeepers, a portion for each day. They also
consecrated *holy things* for the
Levites, and the Levites consecrated *them* for the children
of Aaron.

PRINCIPLES OF SEPARATION

13 On that day they read
from the Book of Moses
in the hearing of the people,
and in it was found written
that no Ammonite or Moabite
should ever come into the assembly of God, 2because they
had not met the children of Israel with bread and water, but
hired Balaam against them
to curse them. However, our
God turned the curse into a
blessing. 3So it was, when they
had heard the Law, that they
separated all the mixed multitude from Israel.

THE REFORMS OF NEHEMIAH

4Now before this, Eliashib
the priest, having authority
over the storerooms of the

12:41 [a] Or *Mijamin* (compare verse 5)

house of our God, *was* allied
with Tobiah. 5And he had prepared for him a large room,
where previously they had
stored the grain offerings,
the frankincense, the articles, the tithes of grain, the
new wine and oil, which were
commanded *to be given* to
the Levites and singers and
gatekeepers, and the offerings
for the priests. 6But during
all this I was not in Jerusalem, for in the thirty-second
year of Artaxerxes king of
Babylon I had returned to
the king. Then after certain
days I obtained leave from
the king, 7and I came to Jerusalem and discovered the
evil that Eliashib had done for
Tobiah, in preparing a room
for him in the courts of the
house of God. 8And it grieved
me bitterly; therefore I threw
all the household goods of Tobiah out of the room. 9Then I
commanded them to cleanse
the rooms; and I brought back
into them the articles of the
house of God, with the grain
offering and the frankincense.

10I also realized that the
portions for the Levites had
not been given *them;* for each
of the Levites and the singers
who did the work had gone
back to his field. 11So I contended with the rulers, and
said, "Why is the house of God
forsaken?" And I gathered
them together and set them
in their place. 12Then all Judah
brought the tithe of the grain
and the new wine and the oil
to the storehouse. 13And I
appointed as treasurers over
the storehouse Shelemiah the
priest and Zadok the scribe,
and of the Levites, Pedaiah;
and next to them *was* Hanan
the son of Zaccur, the son
of Mattaniah; for they were
considered faithful, and their
task *was* to distribute to their
brethren.

14Remember me, O my God,
concerning this, and do not
wipe out my good deeds that
I have done for the house of
my God, and for its services!

15In those days I saw *people*
in Judah treading winepresses
on the Sabbath, and bringing in sheaves, and loading
donkeys with wine, grapes,
figs, and all *kinds of* burdens,
which they brought into Jerusalem on the Sabbath day.
And I warned *them* about the
day on which they were selling provisions. 16Men of Tyre
dwelt there also, who brought
in fish and all kinds of goods,
and sold *them* on the Sabbath
to the children of Judah, and
in Jerusalem.

17Then I contended with
the nobles of Judah, and said
to them, "What evil thing *is*
this that you do, by which
you profane the Sabbath day?
18Did not your fathers do thus,
and did not our God bring all
this disaster on us and on
this city? Yet you bring added
wrath on Israel by profaning
the Sabbath."

19So it was, at the gates of
Jerusalem, as it began to be
dark before the Sabbath, that
I commanded the gates to be
shut, and charged that they
must not be opened till after
the Sabbath. Then I posted
some of my servants at the
gates, *so that* no burdens
would be brought in on the
Sabbath day. 20Now the merchants and sellers of all kinds
of wares lodged outside Jerusalem once or twice.

21Then I warned them, and
said to them, "Why do you
spend the night around the
wall? If you do *so* again, I will
lay hands on you!" From that
time on they came no *more*
on the Sabbath. 22And I commanded the Levites that they
should cleanse themselves,
and that they should go and
guard the gates, to sanctify
the Sabbath day.

Remember me, O my God,
concerning this also, and spare
me according to the greatness
of Your mercy!

23In those days I also
saw Jews *who* had married
women of Ashdod, Ammon,
and Moab. 24And half of their
children spoke the language
of Ashdod, and could not
speak the language of Judah,
but spoke according to the
language of one or the other
people.

25So I contended with them
and cursed them, struck some
of them and pulled out their
hair, and made them swear
by God, *saying,* "You shall not
give your daughters as wives
to their sons, nor take their
daughters for your sons or
yourselves. 26Did not Solomon king of Israel sin by
these things? Yet among many
nations there was no king
like him, who was beloved of
his God; and God made him
king over all Israel. Nevertheless pagan women caused
even him to sin. 27Should we
then hear of your doing all
this great evil, transgressing
against our God by marrying
pagan women?"

28And *one* of the sons of
Joiada, the son of Eliashib the
high priest, *was* a son-in-law of
Sanballat the Horonite; therefore I drove him from me.

29Remember them, O my
God, because they have defiled the priesthood and the
covenant of the priesthood
and the Levites.

30Thus I cleansed them of
everything pagan. I also assigned duties to the priests
and the Levites, each to his
service, 31and *to bringing* the
wood offering and the firstfruits at appointed times.

Remember me, O my God,
for good!

THE BOOK OF ESTHER

THE KING DETHRONES QUEEN VASHTI

1 Now it came to pass in the days of Ahasuerus[a] (this *was* the Ahasuerus who reigned over one hundred and twenty-seven provinces, from India to Ethiopia), 2in those days when King Ahasuerus sat on the throne of his kingdom, which *was* in Shushan[a] the citadel, 3*that* in the third year of his reign he made a feast for all his officials and servants—the powers of Persia and Media, the nobles, and the princes of the provinces *being* before him— 4when he showed the riches of his glorious kingdom and the splendor of his excellent majesty for many days, one hundred and eighty days *in all.*

5And when these days were completed, the king made a feast lasting seven days for all the people who were present in Shushan the citadel, from great to small, in the court of the garden of the king's palace. 6*There were* white and blue linen *curtains* fastened with cords of fine linen and purple on silver rods and marble pillars; *and the* couches *were* of gold and silver on a *mosaic* pavement of alabaster, turquoise, and white and black marble. 7And they served drinks in golden vessels, each vessel being different from the other, with royal wine in abundance, according to the generosity of the king. 8In accordance with the law, the drinking was not compulsory; for so the king had ordered all the officers of his household, that they should do according to each man's pleasure.

9Queen Vashti also made a feast for the women *in* the royal palace which *belonged* to King Ahasuerus.

10On the seventh day, when the heart of the king was merry with wine, he commanded Mehuman, Biztha, Harbona, Bigtha, Abagtha, Zethar, and Carcas, seven eunuchs who served in the presence of King Ahasuerus, 11to bring Queen Vashti before the king, *wearing* her royal crown, in order to show her beauty to the people and the officials, for she *was* beautiful to behold. 12But Queen Vashti refused to come at the king's

1:1 [a] Generally identified with Xerxes I (485–464 BC) 1:2 [a] Or *Susa,* and so throughout this book

command *brought* by *his* eunuchs; therefore the king was
furious, and his anger burned
within him.
13 Then the king said to the
wise men who understood the
times (for this *was* the king's
manner toward all who knew
law and justice, 14 those closest to him *being* Carshena,
Shethar, Admatha, Tarshish,
Meres, Marsena, and Memu-
can, the seven princes of Persia and Media, who had access
to the king's presence, *and*
who ranked highest in the
kingdom): 15 "What *shall we* do
to Queen Vashti, according to
law, because she did not obey
the command of King Ahas-
uerus *brought to her* by the
eunuchs?"
16 And Memucan answered
before the king and the
princes: "Queen Vashti has
not only wronged the king,
but also all the princes, and all
the people who *are* in all the
provinces of King Ahasuerus.
17 For the queen's behavior will
become known to all women,
so that they will despise their
husbands in their eyes, when
they report, 'King Ahasuerus
commanded Queen Vashti to
be brought in before him, but
she did not come.' 18 This very
day the *noble* ladies of Persia
and Media will say to all the
king's officials that they have
heard of the behavior of the
queen. Thus *there will be* ex-
cessive contempt and wrath.
19 If it pleases the king, let a
royal decree go out from him,
and let it be recorded in the
laws of the Persians and the
Medes, so that it will not be
altered, that Vashti shall come
no more before King Ahasuerus; and let the king give her
royal position to another who
is better than she. 20 When the
king's decree which he will
make is proclaimed throughout all his empire (for it is
great), all wives will honor
their husbands, both great
and small."
21 And the reply pleased the
king and the princes, and the
king did according to the word
of Memucan. 22 Then he sent
letters to all the king's provinces, to each province in its
own script, and to every people in their own language, that
each man should be master
in his own house, and speak
in the language of his own
people.

ESTHER BECOMES QUEEN

2 After these things, when
the wrath of King Ahasue-
rus subsided, he remembered
Vashti, what she had done,
and what had been decreed
against her. 2 Then the king's
servants who attended him
said: "Let beautiful young virgins be sought for the king;
3 and let the king appoint officers *in* all the provinces of
his kingdom, that they may
gather all the beautiful young
virgins to Shushan the citadel,
into the women's quarters,

under the custody of Hegai[a]
the king's eunuch, custodian
of the women. And let beauty
preparations be given *them.*
4Then let the young woman
who pleases the king be queen
instead of Vashti."

This thing pleased the king,
and he did so.

5In Shushan the citadel
there was a certain Jew whose
name *was* Mordecai the son
of Jair, the son of Shimei,
the son of Kish, a Benjamite.
6*Kish*[a] had been carried away
from Jerusalem with the captives who had been captured
with Jeconiah[b] king of Judah,
whom Nebuchadnezzar the
king of Babylon had carried
away. 7And *Mordecai* had
brought up Hadassah, that *is,*
Esther, his uncle's daughter,
for she had neither father nor
mother. The young woman
was lovely and beautiful.
When her father and mother
died, Mordecai took her as his
own daughter.

8So it was, when the king's
command and decree were
heard, and when many young
women were gathered at
Shushan the citadel, *under*
the custody of Hegai, that
Esther also was taken to the
king's palace, into the care
of Hegai the custodian of
the women. 9Now the young
woman pleased him, and
she obtained his favor; so he
readily gave beauty preparations to her, besides her al-
lowance. Then seven choice
maidservants were provided
for her from the king's palace, and he moved her and her
maidservants to the best *place*
in the house of the women.

10Esther had not revealed
her people or family, for Mordecai had charged her not
to reveal *it.* 11And every day
Mordecai paced in front of the
court of the women's quarters,
to learn of Esther's welfare
and what was happening to
her.

12Each young woman's turn
came to go in to King Ahasuerus after she had completed
twelve months' preparation,
according to the regulations
for the women, for thus were
the days of their preparation
apportioned: six months with
oil of myrrh, and six months
with perfumes and preparations for beautifying women.
13Thus *prepared, each* young
woman went to the king, and
she was given whatever she
desired to take with her from
the women's quarters to the
king's palace. 14In the evening
she went, and in the morning she returned to the second house of the women, to
the custody of Shaashgaz, the
king's eunuch who kept the
concubines. She would not
go in to the king again unless

2:3 [a] Hebrew *Hege* 2:6 [a] Literally *Who* [b] Same as *Jehoiachin,* 2 Kings 24:6 and elsewhere

the king delighted in her and
called for her by name.
15Now when the turn came
for Esther the daughter of
Abihail the uncle of Mordecai, who had taken her as his
daughter, to go in to the king,
she requested nothing but
what Hegai the king's eunuch,
the custodian of the women,
advised. And Esther obtained
favor in the sight of all who saw
her. 16So Esther was taken to
King Ahasuerus, into his royal
palace, in the tenth month,
which *is* the month of Tebeth,
in the seventh year of his reign.
17The king loved Esther more
than all the *other* women, and
she obtained grace and favor
in his sight more than all the
virgins; so he set the royal
crown upon her head and
made her queen instead of
Vashti. 18Then the king made
a great feast, the Feast of Esther, for all his officials and
servants; and he proclaimed
a holiday in the provinces and
gave gifts according to the generosity of a king.

MORDECAI DISCOVERS A PLOT

19When virgins were gath-
ered together a second time,
Mordecai sat within the king's
gate. 20*Now* Esther had not
revealed her family and her
people, just as Mordecai had
charged her, for Esther obeyed
the command of Mordecai as
when she was brought up by
him.
21In those days, while Mordecai sat within the king's gate,
two of the king's eunuchs,
Bigthan and Teresh, door-
keepers, became furious and
sought to lay hands on King
Ahasuerus. 22So the matter
became known to Mordecai,
who told Queen Esther, and
Esther informed the king in
Mordecai's name. 23And when
an inquiry was made into the
matter, it was confirmed, and
both were hanged on a gallows; and it was written in the
book of the chronicles in the
presence of the king.

HAMAN'S CONSPIRACY AGAINST THE JEWS

3 After these things King
Ahasuerus promoted
Haman, the son of Hamme-
datha the Agagite, and advanced him and set his seat
above all the princes who *were*
with him. 2And all the king's
servants who *were* within the
king's gate bowed and paid
homage to Haman, for so the
king had commanded con-
cerning him. But Mordecai
would not bow or pay homage.
3Then the king's servants who
were within the king's gate
said to Mordecai, "Why do
you transgress the king's command?" 4Now it happened,
when they spoke to him
daily and he would not listen
to them, that they told *it* to
Haman, to see whether Mordecai's words would stand; for
Mordecai had told them that

he *was* a Jew. [5]When Haman
saw that Mordecai did not bow
or pay him homage, Haman
was filled with wrath. [6]But
he disdained to lay hands on
Mordecai alone, for they had
told him of the people of Mordecai. Instead, Haman sought
to destroy all the Jews who
were throughout the whole
kingdom of Ahasuerus—the
people of Mordecai.

[7]In the first month, which
is the month of Nisan, in the
twelfth year of King Ahasuerus, they cast Pur (that *is,* the
lot), before Haman to determine the day and the month,[a]
until *it fell on the* twelfth
month,[b] which *is* the month
of Adar.

[8]Then Haman said to King
Ahasuerus, "There is a certain people scattered and dispersed among the people in
all the provinces of your kingdom; their laws *are* different
from all *other* people's, and
they do not keep the king's
laws. Therefore it *is* not fitting for the king to let them
remain. [9]If it pleases the king,
let *a decree* be written that
they be destroyed, and I will
pay ten thousand talents of
silver into the hands of those
who do the work, to bring *it*
into the king's treasuries."

[10]So the king took his signet ring from his hand and
gave it to Haman, the son of
Hammedatha the Agagite,
the enemy of the Jews. [11]And
the king said to Haman, "The
money and the people *are*
given to you, to do with them
as seems good to you."

[12]Then the king's scribes
were called on the thirteenth
day of the first month, and *a*
decree was written according
to all that Haman commanded—to the king's satraps, to
the governors who *were* over
each province, to the officials
of all people, to every province according to its script,
and to every people in their
language. In the name of King
Ahasuerus it was written, and
sealed with the king's signet
ring. [13]And the letters were
sent by couriers into all the
king's provinces, to destroy,
to kill, and to annihilate all
the Jews, both young and old,
little children and women, in
one day, on the thirteenth *day*
of the twelfth month, which
is the month of Adar, and to
plunder their possessions.[a]
[14]A copy of the document was
to be issued as law in every
province, being published for
all people, that they should
be ready for that day. [15]The
couriers went out, hastened
by the king's command; and

3:7 [a] Septuagint adds *to destroy the people of Mordecai in one day;* Vulgate adds *the nation of the Jews should be destroyed.* [b] Following Masoretic Text and Vulgate; Septuagint reads *and the lot fell on the fourteenth of the month.* 3:13 [a] Septuagint adds the text of the letter here.

the decree was proclaimed in
Shushan the citadel. So the
king and Haman sat down to
drink, but the city of Shushan
was perplexed.

ESTHER AGREES TO HELP THE JEWS

4 When Mordecai learned
all that had happened, he
tore his clothes and put on
sackcloth and ashes, and went
out into the midst of the city.
He cried out with a loud and
bitter cry. 2He went as far as
the front of the king's gate,
for no one *might* enter the
king's gate clothed with sackcloth. 3And in every province
where the king's command
and decree arrived, *there was*
great mourning among the
Jews, with fasting, weeping,
and wailing; and many lay in
sackcloth and ashes.

4So Esther's maids and
eunuchs came and told her,
and the queen was deeply
distressed. Then she sent garments to clothe Mordecai and
take his sackcloth away from
him, but he would not accept
them. 5Then Esther called Hathach, *one* of the king's eunuchs whom he had appointed
to attend her, and she gave
him a command concerning
Mordecai, to learn what and
why this *was.* 6So Hathach
went out to Mordecai in the
city square that *was* in front of
the king's gate. 7And Mordecai
told him all that had happened
to him, and the sum of money
that Haman had promised to
pay into the king's treasuries
to destroy the Jews. 8He also
gave him a copy of the written
decree for their destruction,
which was given at Shushan,
that he might show it to Esther and explain it to her, and
that he might command her
to go in to the king to make
supplication to him and plead
before him for her people. 9So
Hathach returned and told Esther the words of Mordecai.

10Then Esther spoke to Hathach, and gave him a command for Mordecai: 11"All the
king's servants and the people
of the king's provinces know
that any man or woman who
goes into the inner court to
the king, who has not been
called, *he has* but one law: put
all to death, except the one to
whom the king holds out the
golden scepter, that he may
live. Yet I myself have not
been called to go in to the king
these thirty days." 12So they
told Mordecai Esther's words.

13And Mordecai told *them* to
answer Esther: "Do not think in
your heart that you will escape
in the king's palace any more
than all the other Jews. 14For if
you remain completely silent
at this time, relief and deliverance will arise for the Jews
from another place, but you
and your father's house will
perish. Yet who knows whether
you have come to the kingdom
for *such* a time as this?"

15Then Esther told *them*

to reply to Mordecai: 16“Go,
gather all the Jews who are
present in Shushan, and fast
for me; neither eat nor drink
for three days, night or day.
My maids and I will fast likewise. And so I will go to the
king, which *is* against the law;
and if I perish, I perish!”

17So Mordecai went his way
and did according to all that
Esther commanded him.[a]

ESTHER'S BANQUET

5 Now it happened on the
third day that Esther put
on *her* royal *robes* and stood
in the inner court of the king's
palace, across from the king's
house, while the king sat on
his royal throne in the royal
house, facing the entrance of
the house.[a] 2So it was, when
the king saw Queen Esther
standing in the court, *that* she
found favor in his sight, and
the king held out to Esther
the golden scepter that *was*
in his hand. Then Esther went
near and touched the top of
the scepter.

3And the king said to her,
“What do you wish, Queen Esther? What *is* your request? It
shall be given to you—up to
half the kingdom!”

4So Esther answered, “If it
pleases the king, let the king
and Haman come today to the
banquet that I have prepared
for him.”

5Then the king said, “Bring
Haman quickly, that he may
do as Esther has said.” So the
king and Haman went to the
banquet that Esther had prepared.

6At the banquet of wine the
king said to Esther, “What *is*
your petition? It shall be
granted you. What *is* your request, up to half the kingdom?
It shall be done!”

7Then Esther answered and
said, “My petition and request
is this: 8If I have found favor
in the sight of the king, and if
it pleases the king to grant my
petition and fulfill my request,
then let the king and Haman
come to the banquet which
I will prepare for them, and
tomorrow I will do as the king
has said.”

HAMAN'S PLOT AGAINST MORDECAI

9So Haman went out that
day joyful and with a glad
heart; but when Haman saw
Mordecai in the king's gate,
and that he did not stand or
tremble before him, he was
filled with indignation against
Mordecai. 10Nevertheless
Haman restrained himself
and went home, and he sent
and called for his friends and
his wife Zeresh. 11Then Haman
told them of his great riches,
the multitude of his children,
everything in which the king

4:17 [a] Septuagint adds a prayer of Mordecai here.
5:1 [a] Septuagint adds many extra details in verses 1 and 2.

had promoted him, and how
he had advanced him above
the officials and servants of
the king.
12Moreover Haman said,
"Besides, Queen Esther invited no one but me to come
in with the king to the banquet that she prepared; and
tomorrow I am again invited
by her, along with the king.
13Yet all this avails me nothing, so long as I see Mordecai
the Jew sitting at the king's
gate."
14Then his wife Zeresh and
all his friends said to him, "Let
a gallows be made, fifty cubits
high, and in the morning suggest to the king that Mordecai be hanged on it; then go
merrily with the king to the
banquet."
And the thing pleased
Haman; so he had the gallows
made.

THE KING HONORS MORDECAI

6 That night the king could
not sleep. So one was commanded to bring the book of
the records of the chronicles;
and they were read before the
king. 2And it was found written that Mordecai had told of
Bigthana and Teresh, two of
the king's eunuchs, the doorkeepers who had sought to lay
hands on King Ahasuerus.
3Then the king said, "What
honor or dignity has been bestowed on Mordecai for this?"
And the king's servants
who attended him said, "Nothing has been done for him."
4So the king said, "Who *is* in
the court?" Now Haman had
just entered the outer court
of the king's palace to suggest
that the king hang Mordecai
on the gallows that he had
prepared for him.
5The king's servants said to
him, "Haman is there, standing in the court."
And the king said, "Let him
come in."
6So Haman came in, and
the king asked him, "What
shall be done for the man
whom the king delights to
honor?"
Now Haman thought in his
heart, "Whom would the king
delight to honor more than
me?" 7And Haman answered
the king, "*For* the man whom
the king delights to honor,
8let a royal robe be brought
which the king has worn, and
a horse on which the king has
ridden, which has a royal crest
placed on its head. 9Then let
this robe and horse be delivered to the hand of one of the
king's most noble princes,
that he may array the man
whom the king delights to
honor. Then parade him on
horseback through the city
square, and proclaim before
him: 'Thus shall it be done to
the man whom the king delights to honor!'"
10Then the king said to
Haman, "Hurry, take the robe
and the horse, as you have

suggested, and do so for Mordecai the Jew who sits within
the king's gate! Leave nothing
undone of all that you have
spoken."
11So Haman took the robe
and the horse, arrayed Mordecai and led him on horseback through the city square,
and proclaimed before him,
"Thus shall it be done to the
man whom the king delights
to honor!"
12Afterward Mordecai went
back to the king's gate. But
Haman hurried to his house,
mourning and with his head
covered. 13When Haman told
his wife Zeresh and all his
friends everything that had
happened to him, his wise
men and his wife Zeresh said
to him, "If Mordecai, before
whom you have begun to fall,
is of Jewish descent, you will
not prevail against him but
will surely fall before him."
14While they *were* still
talking with him, the king's
eunuchs came, and hastened
to bring Haman to the banquet which Esther had prepared.

HAMAN HANGED INSTEAD OF MORDECAI

7 So the king and Haman
went to dine with Queen
Esther. 2And on the second
day, at the banquet of wine,
the king again said to Esther,
"What *is* your petition, Queen
Esther? It shall be granted you.
And what *is* your request, up
to half the kingdom? It shall
be done!"
3Then Queen Esther an-
swered and said, "If I have
found favor in your sight,
O king, and if it pleases the
king, let my life be given me
at my petition, and my people
at my request. 4For we have
been sold, my people and I,
to be destroyed, to be killed,
and to be annihilated. Had we
been sold as male and female
slaves, I would have held my
tongue, although the enemy
could never compensate for
the king's loss."
5So King Ahasuerus an-
swered and said to Queen Esther, "Who is he, and where
is he, who would dare pre-
sume in his heart to do such
a thing?"
6And Esther said, "The
adversary and enemy *is* this
wicked Haman!"
So Haman was terrified before the king and queen.
7Then the king arose in
his wrath from the banquet
of wine *and went* into the palace garden; but Haman stood
before Queen Esther, pleading for his life, for he saw that
evil was determined against
him by the king. 8When the
king returned from the palace garden to the place of
the banquet of wine, Haman
had fallen across the couch
where Esther *was*. Then the
king said, "Will he also assault
the queen while I *am* in the
house?"

As the word left the king's
mouth, they covered Haman's
face. 9 Now Harbonah, one of
the eunuchs, said to the king,
"Look! The gallows, fifty cubits
high, which Haman made for
Mordecai, who spoke good on
the king's behalf, is standing
at the house of Haman."
Then the king said, "Hang
him on it!"
10 So they hanged Haman
on the gallows that he had
prepared for Mordecai. Then
the king's wrath subsided.

ESTHER SAVES THE JEWS

8 On that day King Ahasuerus gave Queen Esther the
house of Haman, the enemy of
the Jews. And Mordecai came
before the king, for Esther had
told how he *was related* to her.
2 So the king took off his signet
ring, which he had taken from
Haman, and gave it to Mordecai; and Esther appointed
Mordecai over the house of
Haman.
3 Now Esther spoke again
to the king, fell down at his
feet, and implored him with
tears to counteract the evil
of Haman the Agagite, and
the scheme which he had devised against the Jews. 4 And
the king held out the golden
scepter toward Esther. So
Esther arose and stood before the king, 5 and said, "If it
pleases the king, and if I have
found favor in his sight and
the thing *seems* right to the
king and I am pleasing in his
eyes, let it be written to revoke
the letters devised by Haman,
the son of Hammedatha the
Agagite, which he wrote to
annihilate the Jews who *are*
in all the king's provinces.
6 For how can I endure to see
the evil that will come to my
people? Or how can I endure
to see the destruction of my
countrymen?"
7 Then King Ahasuerus said
to Queen Esther and Mordecai
the Jew, "Indeed, I have given
Esther the house of Haman,
and they have hanged him on
the gallows because he *tried
to* lay his hand on the Jews.
8 You yourselves write *a decree*
concerning the Jews, as you
please, in the king's name, and
seal *it* with the king's signet
ring; for whatever is written
in the king's name and sealed
with the king's signet ring no
one can revoke."
9 So the king's scribes were
called at that time, in the third
month, which *is* the month
of Sivan, on the twenty-third
day; and it was written, according to all that Mordecai
commanded, to the Jews, the
satraps, the governors, and
the princes of the provinces
from India to Ethiopia, one
hundred and twenty-seven
provinces *in all,* to every province in its own script, to every
people in their own language,
and to the Jews in their own
script and language. 10 And
he wrote in the name of King
Ahasuerus, sealed *it* with the

king's signet ring, and sent letters by couriers on horseback,
riding on royal horses bred
from swift steeds.[a]

11By these letters the king
permitted the Jews who *were*
in every city to gather together
and protect their lives—to destroy, kill, and annihilate all
the forces of any people or
province that would assault
them, *both* little children and
women, and to plunder their
possessions, 12on one day in
all the provinces of King Ahasuerus, on the thirteenth *day*
of the twelfth month, which *is*
the month of Adar.[a] 13A copy
of the document was to be
issued as a decree in every
province and published for
all people, so that the Jews
would be ready on that day
to avenge themselves on their
enemies. 14The couriers who
rode on royal horses went out,
hastened and pressed on by
the king's command. And the
decree was issued in Shushan
the citadel.

15So Mordecai went out
from the presence of the king
in royal apparel of blue and
white, with a great crown of
gold and a garment of fine
linen and purple; and the
city of Shushan rejoiced and
was glad. 16The Jews had light
and gladness, joy and honor.
17And in every province and
city, wherever the king's command and decree came, the
Jews had joy and gladness,
a feast and a holiday. Then
many of the people of the land
became Jews, because fear of
the Jews fell upon them.

THE JEWS DESTROY THEIR TORMENTORS

9 Now in the twelfth month,
that *is,* the month of
Adar, on the thirteenth day,
the time came for the king's
command and his decree to
be executed. On the day that
the enemies of the Jews had
hoped to overpower them, the
opposite occurred, in that the
Jews themselves overpow-
ered those who hated them.
2The Jews gathered together
in their cities throughout all
the provinces of King Ahasuerus to lay hands on those
who sought their harm. And
no one could withstand them,
because fear of them fell upon
all people. 3And all the officials of the provinces, the satraps, the governors, and all
those doing the king's work,
helped the Jews, because the
fear of Mordecai fell upon
them. 4For Mordecai *was* great
in the king's palace, and his
fame spread throughout all
the provinces; for this man
Mordecai became increas-
ingly prominent. 5Thus the
Jews defeated all their enemies with the stroke of the

8:10 [a] Literally *sons of the swift horses* 8:12 [a] Septuagint adds the text of the letter here.

sword, with slaughter and destruction, and did what they
pleased with those who hated
them.
6And in Shushan the citadel
the Jews killed and destroyed
five hundred men. 7Also Par-
shandatha, Dalphon, Aspatha,
8Poratha, Adalia, Aridatha,
9Parmashta, Arisai, Aridai, and
Vajezatha— 10the ten sons of
Haman the son of Hammeda-
tha, the enemy of the Jews—
they killed; but they did not lay
a hand on the plunder.
11On that day the num-
ber of those who were killed
in Shushan the citadel was
brought to the king. 12And
the king said to Queen Esther, "The Jews have killed
and destroyed five hundred
men in Shushan the citadel,
and the ten sons of Haman.
What have they done in the
rest of the king's provinces?
Now what *is* your petition?
It shall be granted to you. Or
what *is* your further request?
It shall be done."
13Then Esther said, "If
it pleases the king, let it be
granted to the Jews who *are*
in Shushan to do again tomorrow according to today's decree, and let Haman's ten sons
be hanged on the gallows."
14So the king commanded
this to be done; the decree was
issued in Shushan, and they
hanged Haman's ten sons.
15And the Jews who *were*
in Shushan gathered together
again on the fourteenth day
of the month of Adar and
killed three hundred men at
Shushan; but they did not lay
a hand on the plunder.
16The remainder of the
Jews in the king's provinces
gathered together and protected their lives, had rest
from their enemies, and killed
seventy-five thousand of their
enemies; but they did not lay
a hand on the plunder. 17*This*
was on the thirteenth day of
the month of Adar. And on
the fourteenth of *the month*[a]
they rested and made it a day
of feasting and gladness.

THE FEAST OF PURIM

18But the Jews who *were* at
Shushan assembled together
on the thirteenth *day,* as well
as on the fourteenth; and on
the fifteenth of *the month*[a]
they rested, and made it a
day of feasting and gladness.
19Therefore the Jews of the
villages who dwelt in the unwalled towns celebrated the
fourteenth day of the month of
Adar *with* gladness and feasting, as a holiday, and for sending presents to one another.
20And Mordecai wrote
these things and sent letters
to all the Jews, near and far,
who *were* in all the provinces
of King Ahasuerus, 21to establish among them that they
should celebrate yearly the

9:17 [a] Literally *it* 9:18 [a] Literally *it*

fourteenth and fifteenth days
of the month of Adar, 22as the
days on which the Jews had
rest from their enemies, as
the month which was turned
from sorrow to joy for them,
and from mourning to a holiday; that they should make
them days of feasting and joy,
of sending presents to one
another and gifts to the poor.
23So the Jews accepted the custom which they had begun, as
Mordecai had written to them,
24because Haman, the son of
Hammedatha the Agagite, the
enemy of all the Jews, had plotted against the Jews to annihilate them, and had cast Pur
(that *is,* the lot), to consume
them and destroy them; 25but
when *Esther*[a] came before the
king, he commanded by letter
that this[b] wicked plot which
Haman had devised against
the Jews should return on his
own head, and that he and his
sons should be hanged on the
gallows.

26So they called these days
Purim, after the name Pur.
Therefore, because of all the
words of this letter, what they
had seen concerning this matter, and what had happened to
them, 27the Jews established
and imposed it upon them-
selves and their descendants
and all who would join them,
that without fail they should
celebrate these two days every
year, according to the written
instructions and according to
the *prescribed* time, 28*that*
these days *should be* remembered and kept throughout
every generation, every family, every province, and every
city, that these days of Purim
should not fail *to be observed*
among the Jews, and *that* the
memory of them should not
perish among their descendants.

29Then Queen Esther, the
daughter of Abihail, with Mordecai the Jew, wrote with full
authority to confirm this second letter about Purim. 30And
Mordecai sent letters to all the
Jews, to the one hundred and
twenty-seven provinces of the
kingdom of Ahasuerus, *with*
words of peace and truth, 31to
confirm these days of Purim at
their *appointed* time, as Mordecai the Jew and Queen Esther had prescribed for them,
and as they had decreed for
themselves and their descendants concerning matters of
their fasting and lamenting.
32So the decree of Esther confirmed these matters of Purim,
and it was written in the book.

MORDECAI'S ADVANCEMENT

10 And King Ahasuerus
imposed tribute on the
land and *on* the islands of the
sea. 2Now all the acts of his
power and his might, and the
account of the greatness of

9:25 [a] Literally *she* or *it* [b] Literally *his*

Mordecai, to which the king
advanced him, *are* they not
written in the book of the
chronicles of the kings of
Media and Persia? 3For Mordecai the Jew *was* second
to King Ahasuerus, and was
great among the Jews and well
received by the multitude of
his brethren, seeking the good
of his people and speaking
peace to all his countrymen.[a]

THE BOOK OF JOB

JOB AND HIS FAMILY IN UZ

1 There was a man in the land
of Uz, whose name *was* Job;
and that man was blameless
and upright, and one who
feared God and shunned evil.
2And seven sons and three
daughters were born to him.
3Also, his possessions were
seven thousand sheep, three
thousand camels, five hundred yoke of oxen, five hundred female donkeys, and a
very large household, so that
this man was the greatest of
all the people of the East.

4And his sons would go and
feast *in their* houses, each on
his *appointed* day, and would
send and invite their three sisters to eat and drink with them.
5So it was, when the days of
feasting had run their course,
that Job would send and sanctify them, and he would rise
early in the morning and offer
burnt offerings *according to*
the number of them all. For
Job said, "It may be that my
sons have sinned and cursed[a]
God in their hearts." Thus Job
did regularly.

SATAN ATTACKS JOB'S CHARACTER

6Now there was a day when
the sons of God came to present themselves before the
LORD, and Satan[a] also came
among them. 7And the LORD
said to Satan, "From where do
you come?"

So Satan answered the
LORD and said, "From going
to and fro on the earth, and
from walking back and forth
on it."

8Then the LORD said to
Satan, "Have you considered
My servant Job, that *there is*

10:3 [a] Literally *seed.* Septuagint and Vulgate add a dream of Mordecai here; Vulgate adds six more chapters. 1:5 [a] Literally *blessed,* but used here in the evil sense, and so in verse 11 and 2:5, 9 1:6 [a] Literally *the Adversary,* and so throughout this book

none like him on the earth, a
blameless and upright man,
one who fears God and shuns
evil?"
9So Satan answered the
LORD and said, "Does Job
fear God for nothing? 10Have
You not made a hedge around
him, around his household,
and around all that he has on
every side? You have blessed
the work of his hands, and his
possessions have increased
in the land. 11But now, stretch
out Your hand and touch all
that he has, and he will surely
curse You to Your face!"
12And the LORD said to
Satan, "Behold, all that he has
is in your power; only do not
lay a hand on his *person.*"
So Satan went out from the
presence of the LORD.

JOB LOSES HIS PROPERTY AND CHILDREN

13Now there was a day when
his sons and daughters *were*
eating and drinking wine in
their oldest brother's house;
14and a messenger came to
Job and said, "The oxen were
plowing and the donkeys
feeding beside them, 15when
the Sabeans[a] raided *them* and
took them away—indeed they
have killed the servants with
the edge of the sword; and
I alone have escaped to tell
you!"
16While he *was* still speaking, another also came and
said, "The fire of God fell from
heaven and burned up the
sheep and the servants, and
consumed them; and I alone
have escaped to tell you!"
17While he *was* still speaking, another also came and
said, "The Chaldeans formed
three bands, raided the camels and took them away, yes,
and killed the servants with
the edge of the sword; and
I alone have escaped to tell
you!"
18While he *was* still speaking, another also came and
said, "Your sons and daughters *were* eating and drinking
wine in their oldest brother's
house, 19and suddenly a great
wind came from across[a] the
wilderness and struck the four
corners of the house, and it
fell on the young people, and
they are dead; and I alone
have escaped to tell you!"
20Then Job arose, tore his
robe, and shaved his head;
and he fell to the ground and
worshiped. 21And he said:

"Naked I came from my
  mother's womb,
And naked shall I
  return there.
The LORD gave, and the
  LORD has taken away;
Blessed be the name
  of the LORD."

22In all this Job did not sin
nor charge God with wrong.

1:15 [a] Literally *Sheba* (compare 6:19) 1:19 [a] Septuagint omits *across.*

SATAN ATTACKS JOB'S HEALTH

2 Again there was a day when
the sons of God came to
present themselves before
the LORD, and Satan came
also among them to present
himself before the LORD. 2And
the LORD said to Satan, "From
where do you come?"
Satan answered the LORD
and said, "From going to and
fro on the earth, and from
walking back and forth on it."
3Then the LORD said to
Satan, "Have you considered
My servant Job, that *there is*
none like him on the earth, a
blameless and upright man,
one who fears God and shuns
evil? And still he holds fast
to his integrity, although you
incited Me against him, to destroy him without cause."
4So Satan answered the
LORD and said, "Skin for skin!
Yes, all that a man has he will
give for his life. 5But stretch out
Your hand now, and touch his
bone and his flesh, and he will
surely curse You to Your face!"
6And the LORD said to
Satan, "Behold, he *is* in your
hand, but spare his life."
7So Satan went out from
the presence of the LORD, and
struck Job with painful boils
from the sole of his foot to the
crown of his head. 8And he
took for himself *a potsherd*
with which to scrape himself
while he sat in the midst of
the ashes.
9Then his wife said to him,
"Do you still hold fast to your
integrity? Curse God and die!"
10But he said to her, "You
speak as one of the foolish
women speaks. Shall we indeed accept good from God,
and shall we not accept adversity?" In all this Job did not
sin with his lips.

JOB'S THREE FRIENDS

11Now when Job's three
friends heard of all this adversity that had come upon
him, each one came from his
own place—Eliphaz the Te-
manite, Bildad the Shuhite,
and Zophar the Naamathite.
For they had made an ap-
pointment together to come
and mourn with him, and to
comfort him. 12And when they
raised their eyes from afar,
and did not recognize him,
they lifted their voices and
wept; and each one tore his
robe and sprinkled dust on
his head toward heaven. 13So
they sat down with him on the
ground seven days and seven
nights, and no one spoke a
word to him, for they saw that
his grief was very great.

JOB DEPLORES HIS BIRTH

3 After this Job opened his
mouth and cursed the day
of his *birth.* 2And Job spoke,
and said:

3 "May the day perish on
which I was born,
And the night *in*
which it was said,

'A male child is conceived.'
4 May that day be darkness;
May God above
not seek it,
Nor the light shine
upon it.
5 May darkness and
the shadow of
death claim it;
May a cloud settle on it;
May the blackness of
the day terrify it.
6 *As for* that night, may
darkness seize it;
May it not rejoice[a] among
the days of the year,
May it not come into the
number of the months.
7 Oh, may that night
be barren!
May no joyful shout
come into it!
8 May those curse it
who curse the day,
Those who are ready to
arouse Leviathan.
9 May the stars of its
morning be dark;
May it look for light,
but *have* none,
And not see the
dawning of the day;
10 Because it did not shut
up the doors of my
mother's womb,
Nor hide sorrow
from my eyes.

11 "Why did I not
die at birth?
Why did I *not* perish when
I came from the womb?
12 Why did the knees
receive me?
Or why the breasts, that
I should nurse?
13 For now I would have lain
still and been quiet,
I would have been asleep;
Then I would have
been at rest
14 With kings and
counselors of the earth,
Who built ruins for
themselves,
15 Or with princes
who had gold,
Who filled their
houses *with* silver;
16 Or *why* was I not hidden
like a stillborn child,
Like infants who
never saw light?
17 There the wicked cease
from troubling,
And there the weary
are at rest.
18 *There* the prisoners
rest together;
They do not hear the
voice of the oppressor.
19 The small and great
are there,
And the servant *is* free
from his master.

20 "Why is light given to
him who is in misery,
And life to the
bitter of soul,
21 Who long for death, but
it does not *come,*
And search for it more
than hidden treasures;

3:6 [a] Septuagint, Syriac, Targum, and Vulgate read *be joined.*

22 Who rejoice exceedingly,
And are glad when they
can find the grave?
23 *Why is light given*
to a man whose
way is hidden,
And whom God has
hedged in?
24 For my sighing comes
before I eat,[a]
And my groanings
pour out like water.
25 For the thing I
greatly feared has
come upon me,
And what I dreaded has
happened to me.
26 I am not at ease,
nor am I quiet;
I have no rest, for
trouble comes."

ELIPHAZ: JOB HAS SINNED

4 Then Eliphaz the Temanite answered and said:

2 "*If* one attempts a word
with you, will you
become weary?
But who can withhold
himself from speaking?
3 Surely you have
instructed many,
And you have
strengthened
weak hands.
4 Your words have
upheld him who
was stumbling,
And you have
strengthened the
feeble knees;
5 But now it comes upon
you, and you are weary;
It touches you, and
you are troubled.
6 *Is* not your reverence
your confidence?
And the integrity of your
ways your hope?

7 "Remember now,
who *ever* perished
being innocent?
Or where were the
upright *ever* cut off?
8 Even as I have seen,
Those who plow iniquity
And sow trouble
reap the same.
9 By the blast of God
they perish,
And by the breath
of His anger they
are consumed.
10 The roaring of the lion,
The voice of the
fierce lion,
And the teeth of the
young lions are broken.
11 The old lion perishes
for lack of prey,
And the cubs of the
lioness are scattered.

12 "Now a word was secretly
brought to me,
And my ear received
a whisper of it.
13 In disquieting thoughts
from the visions
of the night,
When deep sleep
falls on men,

3:24 [a] Literally *my bread*

14 Fear came upon me,
and trembling,
Which made all my
bones shake.
15 Then a spirit passed
before my face;
The hair on my
body stood up.
16 It stood still,
But I could not discern
its appearance.
A form *was* before
my eyes;
There was silence;
Then I heard a
voice *saying:*
17 'Can a mortal be more
righteous than God?
Can a man be more pure
than his Maker?
18 If He puts no trust
in His servants,
If He charges His
angels with error,
19 How much more
those who dwell in
houses of clay,
Whose foundation
is in the dust,
Who are crushed
before a moth?
20 They are broken in
pieces from morning
till evening;
They perish forever, with
no one regarding.
21 Does not their own
excellence go away?
They die, even
without wisdom.'

ELIPHAZ: JOB IS CHASTENED BY GOD

5 "Call out now;
Is there anyone who
will answer you?
And to which of the holy
ones will you turn?
2 For wrath kills a
foolish man,
And envy slays a
simple one.
3 I have seen the foolish
taking root,
But suddenly I cursed
his dwelling place.
4 His sons are far
from safety,
They are crushed
in the gate,
And *there is* no deliverer.
5 Because the hungry
eat up his harvest,
Taking it even from
the thorns,[a]
And a snare snatches
their substance.[b]
6 For affliction does not
come from the dust,
Nor does trouble spring
from the ground;
7 Yet man is born
to trouble,
As the sparks fly upward.

8 "But as for me, I
would seek God,
And to God I would
commit my cause—
9 Who does great things,
and unsearchable,

5:5 [a] Septuagint reads *They shall not be taken from evil men;* Vulgate reads *And the armed man shall take him by violence.* [b] Septuagint reads *The might shall draw them off;* Vulgate reads *And the thirsty shall drink up their riches.*

Marvelous things
without number.
10 He gives rain on
the earth,
And sends waters
on the fields.
11 He sets on high those
who are lowly,
And those who mourn
are lifted to safety.
12 He frustrates the
devices of the crafty,
So that their hands
cannot carry out
their plans.
13 He catches the wise in
their own craftiness,
And the counsel of
the cunning comes
quickly upon them.
14 They meet with darkness
in the daytime,
And grope at noontime
as in the night.
15 But He saves the needy
from the sword,
From the mouth
of the mighty,
And from their hand.
16 So the poor have hope,
And injustice shuts
her mouth.

17 "Behold, happy *is* the man
whom God corrects;
Therefore do not despise
the chastening of
the Almighty.
18 For He bruises, but
He binds up;
He wounds, but His
hands make whole.
19 He shall deliver you
in six troubles,
Yes, in seven no evil
shall touch you.
20 In famine He shall
redeem you from
death,
And in war from the
power of the sword.
21 You shall be hidden
from the scourge
of the tongue,
And you shall not be
afraid of destruction
when it comes.
22 You shall laugh at
destruction and
famine,
And you shall not be
afraid of the beasts
of the earth.
23 For you shall have a
covenant with the
stones of the field,
And the beasts of
the field shall be at
peace with you.
24 You shall know that
your tent *is* in peace;
You shall visit your
dwelling and find
nothing amiss.
25 You shall also know
that your descendants
shall be many,
And your offspring like
the grass of the earth.
26 You shall come to the
grave at a full age,
As a sheaf of grain
ripens in its season.
27 Behold, this we have
searched out;
It *is* true.
Hear it, and know
for yourself."

JOB: MY COMPLAINT IS JUST

6 Then Job answered and said:

2 "Oh, that my grief were fully weighed,
And my calamity laid with it on the scales!
3 For then it would be heavier than the sand of the sea—
Therefore my words have been rash.
4 For the arrows of the Almighty *are* within me;
My spirit drinks in their poison;
The terrors of God are arrayed against me.
5 Does the wild donkey bray when it has grass,
Or does the ox low over its fodder?
6 Can flavorless food be eaten without salt?
Or is there *any* taste in the white of an egg?
7 My soul refuses to touch them;
They *are* as loathsome food to me.

8 "Oh, that I might have my request,
That God would grant *me* the thing that I long for!
9 That it would please God to crush me,
That He would loose His hand and cut me off!
10 Then I would still have comfort;
Though in anguish I would exult,
He will not spare;
For I have not concealed the words of the Holy One.

11 "What strength do I have, that I should hope?
And what *is* my end, that I should prolong my life?
12 *Is* my strength the strength of stones?
Or is my flesh bronze?
13 *Is* my help not within me?
And is success driven from me?

14 "To him who is afflicted, kindness *should be shown* by his friend,
Even though he forsakes the fear of the Almighty.
15 My brothers have dealt deceitfully like a brook,
Like the streams of the brooks that pass away,
16 Which are dark because of the ice,
And into which the snow vanishes.
17 When it is warm, they cease to flow;
When it is hot, they vanish from their place.
18 The paths of their way turn aside,
They go nowhere and perish.
19 The caravans of Tema look,
The travelers of Sheba hope for them.

20 They are disappointed
because they were
confident;
They come there and
are confused.
21 For now you are
nothing,
You see terror and
are afraid.
22 Did I ever say, 'Bring
something to me'?
Or, 'Offer a bribe for me
from your wealth'?
23 Or, 'Deliver me from
the enemy's hand'?
Or, 'Redeem me from the
hand of oppressors'?

24 "Teach me, and I will
hold my tongue;
Cause me to understand
wherein I have erred.
25 How forceful are
right words!
But what does your
arguing prove?
26 Do you intend to
rebuke *my* words,
And the speeches of
a desperate one,
which are as wind?
27 Yes, you overwhelm
the fatherless,
And you undermine
your friend.
28 Now therefore, be
pleased to look at me;
For I would never
lie to your face.
29 Yield now, let there
be no injustice!
Yes, concede, my
righteousness
still stands!
30 Is there injustice
on my tongue?
Cannot my taste discern
the unsavory?

JOB: MY SUFFERING IS COMFORTLESS

7 "*Is there* not a time
of hard service for
man on earth?
Are not his days also
like the days of
a hired man?
2 Like a servant who
earnestly desires
the shade,
And like a hired man
who eagerly looks
for his wages,
3 So I have been allotted
months of futility,
And wearisome
nights have been
appointed to me.
4 When I lie down, I say,
'When shall I arise,
And the night be
ended?'
For I have had my fill
of tossing till dawn.
5 My flesh is caked with
worms and dust,
My skin is cracked and
breaks out afresh.

6 "My days are swifter
than a weaver's
shuttle,
And are spent
without hope.
7 Oh, remember that
my life *is* a breath!
My eye will never
again see good.

8 The eye of him who sees
me will see me no *more;*
While your eyes *are* upon
me, I shall no longer *be.*
9 *As* the cloud disappears
and vanishes away,
So he who goes down
to the grave does
not come up.
10 He shall never return
to his house,
Nor shall his place
know him anymore.

11 "Therefore I will not
restrain my mouth;
I will speak in the
anguish of my spirit;
I will complain in the
bitterness of my soul.
12 *Am* I a sea, or a
sea serpent,
That You set a guard
over me?
13 When I say, 'My bed
will comfort me,
My couch will ease
my complaint,'
14 Then You scare me
with dreams
And terrify me
with visions,
15 So that my soul
chooses strangling
And death rather
than my body.[a]
16 I loathe *my life;*
I would not live forever.
Let me alone,
For my days *are*
but a breath.
17 "What *is* man, that You
should exalt him,
That You should set
Your heart on him,
18 That You should visit
him every morning,
And test him every
moment?
19 How long?
Will You not look
away from me,
And let me alone till I
swallow my saliva?
20 Have I sinned?
What have I done to You,
O watcher of men?
Why have You set me
as Your target,
So that I am a burden
to myself?[a]
21 Why then do You
not pardon my
transgression,
And take away my
iniquity?
For now I will lie
down in the dust,
And You will seek
me diligently,
But I *will* no longer *be.*"

BILDAD: JOB SHOULD REPENT

8 Then Bildad the Shuhite answered and said:

2 "How long will you
speak these *things,*
And the words of
your mouth *be like*
a strong wind?

7:15 [a] Literally *my bones* 7:20 [a] Following Masoretic Text, Targum, and Vulgate; Septuagint and Jewish tradition read *to You.*

3 Does God subvert
judgment?
Or does the Almighty
pervert justice?
4 If your sons have
sinned against Him,
He has cast them
away for their
transgression.
5 If you would earnestly
seek God
And make your
supplication to
the Almighty,
6 If you *were* pure
and upright,
Surely now He would
awake for you,
And prosper your rightful
dwelling place.
7 Though your beginning
was small,
Yet your latter end would
increase abundantly.

8 "For inquire, please, of
the former age,
And consider the
things discovered
by their fathers;
9 For we *were born*
yesterday, and
know nothing,
Because our days on
earth *are* a shadow.
10 Will they not teach
you and tell you,
And utter words from
their heart?

11 "Can the papyrus grow
up without a marsh?
Can the reeds flourish
without water?
12 While it *is* yet green
and not cut down,
It withers before
any *other* plant.
13 So *are* the paths of all
who forget God;
And the hope of the
hypocrite shall perish,
14 Whose confidence
shall be cut off,
And whose trust *is*
a spider's web.
15 He leans on his house,
but it does not stand.
He holds it fast, but it
does not endure.
16 He grows green
in the sun,
And his branches spread
out in his garden.
17 His roots wrap around
the rock heap,
And look for a place
in the stones.
18 If he is destroyed
from his place,
Then *it* will deny
him, *saying,* 'I have
not seen you.'

19 "Behold, this is the
joy of His way,
And out of the earth
others will grow.
20 Behold, God will not cast
away the blameless,
Nor will He uphold
the evildoers.
21 He will yet fill your
mouth with laughing,
And your lips with
rejoicing.
22 Those who hate you will
be clothed with shame,

And the dwelling place
of the wicked will
come to nothing."[a]

JOB: THERE IS NO MEDIATOR

9 Then Job answered and
said:

2 "Truly I know *it is* so,
But how can a man
be righteous
before God?
3 If one wished to
contend with Him,
He could not answer
Him one time out
of a thousand.
4 *God is* wise in heart and
mighty in strength.
Who has hardened
himself against Him
and prospered?
5 He removes the
mountains, and
they do not know
When He overturns
them in His anger;
6 He shakes the earth
out of its place,
And its pillars tremble;
7 He commands the sun,
and it does not rise;
He seals off the stars;
8 He alone spreads
out the heavens,
And treads on the
waves of the sea;
9 He made the Bear, Orion,
and the Pleiades,
And the chambers
of the south;
10 He does great things
past finding out,
Yes, wonders without
number.
11 If He goes by me, I
do not see *Him;*
If He moves past, I do
not perceive Him;
12 If He takes away, who
can hinder Him?
Who can say to Him,
'What are You doing?'
13 God will not withdraw
His anger,
The allies of the proud[a] lie
prostrate beneath Him.

14 "How then can I
answer Him,
And choose my words
to reason with Him?
15 For though I were
righteous, I could
not answer Him;
I would beg mercy
of my Judge.
16 If I called and He
answered me,
I would not believe
that He was listening
to my voice.
17 For He crushes me
with a tempest,
And multiplies my
wounds without cause.
18 He will not allow me
to catch my breath,
But fills me with
bitterness.
19 If *it is a matter* of
strength, indeed
He is strong;

8:22 [a] Literally *will not be* 9:13 [a] Hebrew *rahab*

And if of justice, who
will appoint my
day *in court?*
20 Though I were righteous,
my own mouth would
condemn me;
Though I *were*
blameless, it would
prove me perverse.

21 "I am blameless, yet I do
not know myself;
I despise my life.
22 It *is* all one *thing;*
Therefore I say, 'He
destroys the blameless
and the wicked.'
23 If the scourge slays
suddenly,
He laughs at the plight
of the innocent.
24 The earth is given into
the hand of the wicked.
He covers the faces
of its judges.
If it is not *He,* who
else could it be?

25 "Now my days are swifter
than a runner;
They flee away, they
see no good.
26 They pass by like
swift ships,
Like an eagle swooping
on its prey.
27 If I say, 'I will forget
my complaint,
I will put off my sad face
and wear a smile,'
28 I am afraid of all
my sufferings;
I know that You will not
hold me innocent.
29 *If* I am condemned,
Why then do I
labor in vain?
30 If I wash myself with
snow water,
And cleanse my
hands with soap,
31 Yet You will plunge
me into the pit,
And my own clothes
will abhor me.

32 "For *He is* not a
man, as I *am,*
That I may answer Him,
And that we should go
to court together.
33 Nor is there any
mediator between us,
Who may lay his
hand on us both.
34 Let Him take His rod
away from me,
And do not let dread
of Him terrify me.
35 *Then* I would speak
and not fear Him,
But it is not so with me.

JOB: I WOULD PLEAD WITH GOD

10 "My soul loathes
my life;
I will give free course
to my complaint,
I will speak in the
bitterness of my soul.
2 I will say to God, 'Do
not condemn me;
Show me why You
contend with me.
3 *Does it* seem good
to You that You
should oppress,

That You should despise
the work of Your hands,
And smile on the counsel
of the wicked?
4 Do You have eyes of flesh?
Or do You see as
man sees?
5 *Are* Your days like the
days of a mortal man?
Are Your years like the
days of a mighty man,
6 That You should seek
for my iniquity
And search out my sin,
7 Although You know that
I am not wicked,
And *there is* no one
who can deliver
from Your hand?

8 'Your hands have made
me and fashioned me,
An intricate unity;
Yet You would destroy me.
9 Remember, I pray,
that You have made
me like clay.
And will You turn me
into dust again?
10 Did You not pour me
out like milk,
And curdle me like cheese,
11 Clothe me with
skin and flesh,
And knit me together
with bones and sinews?
12 You have granted me
life and favor,
And Your care has
preserved my spirit.

13 'And these *things*
You have hidden
in Your heart;
I know that this
was with You:
14 If I sin, then You mark me,
And will not acquit
me of my iniquity.
15 If I am wicked, woe to me;
Even *if* I am righteous, I
cannot lift up my head.
I am full of disgrace;
See my misery!
16 If *my head* is exalted,
You hunt me like
a fierce lion,
And again You show
Yourself awesome
against me.
17 You renew Your
witnesses against me,
And increase Your
indignation toward me;
Changes and war are
ever with me.

18 'Why then have You
brought me out
of the womb?
Oh, that I had
perished and no
eye had seen me!
19 I would have been as
though I had not been.
I would have been
carried from the
womb to the grave.
20 Are not my days few?
Cease! Leave me alone,
that I may take a
little comfort,
21 Before I go *to the
place from which* I
shall not return,
To the land of
darkness and the
shadow of death,

22 A land as dark as
darkness *itself,*
As the shadow of death,
without any order,
Where even the light
is like darkness.'"

ZOPHAR URGES JOB TO REPENT

11 Then Zophar the Naamathite answered and said:

2 "Should not the
multitude of words
be answered?
And should a man full
of talk be vindicated?
3 Should your empty
talk make men
hold their peace?
And when you mock,
should no one
rebuke you?
4 For you have said,
'My doctrine *is* pure,
And I am clean in
your eyes.'
5 But oh, that God
would speak,
And open His lips
against you,
6 That He would show you
the secrets of wisdom!
For *they would* double
your prudence.
Know therefore that
God exacts from you
Less than your
iniquity *deserves.*

7 "Can you search out the
deep things of God?
Can you find out the
limits of the Almighty?
8 *They are* higher than
heaven—what
can you do?
Deeper than Sheol—what
can you know?
9 Their measure *is* longer
than the earth
And broader than the sea.

10 "If He passes by,
imprisons, and
gathers *to judgment,*
Then who can
hinder Him?
11 For He knows
deceitful men;
He sees wickedness also.
Will He not then
consider *it?*
12 For an empty-headed
man will be wise,
When a wild donkey's
colt is born a man.

13 "If you would prepare
your heart,
And stretch out your
hands toward Him;
14 If iniquity *were* in
your hand, *and you*
put it far away,
And would not let
wickedness dwell
in your tents;
15 Then surely you could
lift up your face
without spot;
Yes, you could be
steadfast, and not fear;
16 Because you would
forget *your* misery,
And remember *it* as
waters *that have*
passed away,

17 And *your* life would be
brighter than noonday.
Though you were dark,
you would be like
the morning.
18 And you would be secure,
because there is hope;
Yes, you would dig
around you, and take
your rest in safety.
19 You would also lie down,
and no one would
make *you* afraid;
Yes, many would
court your favor.
20 But the eyes of the
wicked will fail,
And they shall not escape,
And their hope—loss
of life!"

JOB ANSWERS HIS CRITICS

12 Then Job answered and
said:

2 "No doubt you *are*
the people,
And wisdom will
die with you!
3 But I have understanding
as well as you;
I *am* not inferior to you.
Indeed, who does
not *know* such
things as these?

4 "I am one mocked
by his friends,
Who called on God, and
He answered him,
The just and blameless
who is ridiculed.
5 A lamp[a] is despised in
the thought of one
who is at ease;
It is made ready for
those whose feet slip.
6 The tents of robbers
prosper,
And those who provoke
God are secure—
In what God provides
by His hand.

7 "But now ask the
beasts, and they
will teach you;
And the birds of the air,
and they will tell you;
8 Or speak to the earth,
and it will teach you;
And the fish of the sea
will explain to you.
9 Who among all these
does not know
That the hand of the
LORD has done this,
10 In whose hand *is* the life
of every living thing,
And the breath of
all mankind?
11 Does not the ear
test words
And the mouth
taste its food?
12 Wisdom *is* with
aged men,
And with length of days,
understanding.

13 "With Him *are* wisdom
and strength,
He has counsel and
understanding.

12:5 [a] Or *disaster*

14 If He breaks *a thing* down,
it cannot be rebuilt;
If He imprisons a man,
there can be no release.
15 If He withholds the
waters, they dry up;
If He sends them out,
they overwhelm
the earth.
16 With Him *are* strength
and prudence.
The deceived and the
deceiver *are* His.
17 He leads counselors
away plundered,
And makes fools
of the judges.
18 He loosens the
bonds of kings,
And binds their waist
with a belt.
19 He leads princes[a]
away plundered,
And overthrows
the mighty.
20 He deprives the trusted
ones of speech,
And takes away the
discernment of
the elders.
21 He pours contempt
on princes,
And disarms the mighty.
22 He uncovers deep things
out of darkness,
And brings the shadow
of death to light.
23 He makes nations great,
and destroys them;
He enlarges nations,
and guides them.
24 He takes away the
understanding[a] of
the chiefs of the
people of the earth,
And makes them
wander in a pathless
wilderness.
25 They grope in the dark
without light,
And He makes them
stagger like a
drunken *man*.

13 "Behold, my eye has
seen all *this*,
My ear has heard and
understood it.
2 What you know, I
also know;
I *am* not inferior to you.
3 But I would speak to
the Almighty,
And I desire to
reason with God.
4 But you forgers of lies,
You *are* all worthless
physicians.
5 Oh, that you would
be silent,
And it would be
your wisdom!
6 Now hear my reasoning,
And heed the pleadings
of my lips.
7 Will you speak
wickedly for God,
And talk deceitfully
for Him?
8 Will you show
partiality for Him?
Will you contend for God?

12:19 [a] Literally *priests,* but not in a technical sense **12:24** [a] Literally *heart*

9 Will it be well when He
searches you out?
Or can you mock Him
as one mocks a man?
10 He will surely rebuke you
If you secretly show
partiality.
11 Will not His excellence
make you afraid,
And the dread of Him
fall upon you?
12 Your platitudes *are*
proverbs of ashes,
Your defenses are
defenses of clay.

13 "Hold your peace with
me, and let me speak,
Then let come on
me what *may!*
14 Why do I take my
flesh in my teeth,
And put my life in
my hands?
15 Though He slay me,
yet will I trust Him.
Even so, I will defend my
own ways before Him.
16 He also *shall* be
my salvation,
For a hypocrite could
not come before Him.
17 Listen carefully to
my speech,
And to my declaration
with your ears.
18 See now, I have
prepared *my* case,
I know that I shall
be vindicated.
19 Who *is* he *who* will
contend with me?
If now I hold my
tongue, I perish.

JOB'S DESPONDENT PRAYER

20 "Only two *things* do
not do to me,
Then I will not hide
myself from You:
21 Withdraw Your hand
far from me,
And let not the dread of
You make me afraid.
22 Then call, and I
will answer;
Or let me speak, then
You respond to me.
23 How many *are* my
iniquities and sins?
Make me know my
transgression
and my sin.
24 Why do You hide
Your face,
And regard me as
Your enemy?
25 Will You frighten a leaf
driven to and fro?
And will You pursue
dry stubble?
26 For You write bitter
things against me,
And make me inherit the
iniquities of my youth.
27 You put my feet in
the stocks,
And watch closely
all my paths.
You set a limit[a] for the
soles of my feet.

28 "*Man*[a] decays like a
rotten thing,

13:27 [a] Literally *inscribe a print* 13:28 [a] Literally *He*

Like a garment that
is moth-eaten.

14 "Man *who is* born
of woman
Is of few days and
full of trouble.
2 He comes forth like
a flower and
fades away;
He flees like a shadow
and does not continue.
3 And do You open Your
eyes on such a one,
And bring me[a] to
judgment with
Yourself?
4 Who can bring a clean
thing out of an unclean?
No one!
5 Since his days *are*
determined,
The number of his
months *is* with You;
You have appointed
his limits, so that
he cannot pass.
6 Look away from him
that he may rest,
Till like a hired man
he finishes his day.

7 "For there is hope
for a tree,
If it is cut down, that it
will sprout again,
And that its tender
shoots will not cease.
8 Though its root may
grow old in the earth,
And its stump may
die in the ground,
9 *Yet* at the scent of
water it will bud
And bring forth
branches like a plant.
10 But man dies and
is laid away;
Indeed he breathes
his last
And where *is* he?
11 *As* water disappears
from the sea,
And a river becomes
parched and dries up,
12 So man lies down and
does not rise.
Till the heavens
are no more,
They will not awake
Nor be roused from
their sleep.

13 "Oh, that You would hide
me in the grave,
That You would
conceal me until
Your wrath is past,
That You would appoint
me a set time, and
remember me!
14 If a man dies, shall
he live *again?*
All the days of my hard
service I will wait,
Till my change comes.
15 You shall call, and I
will answer You;
You shall desire the
work of Your hands.
16 For now You number
my steps,
But do not watch
over my sin.

14:3 [a] Septuagint, Syriac, and Vulgate read *him.*

17 My transgression *is*
sealed up in a bag,
And You cover[a]
my iniquity.

18 "But *as* a mountain falls
and crumbles away,
And *as* a rock is moved
from its place;
19 *As* water wears
away stones,
And as torrents
wash away the soil
of the earth;
So You destroy the
hope of man.
20 You prevail forever
against him, and
he passes on;
You change his
countenance and
send him away.
21 His sons come to
honor, and he does
not know *it;*
They are brought low, and
he does not perceive *it.*
22 But his flesh will be
in pain over it,
And his soul will
mourn over it."

ELIPHAZ ACCUSES JOB OF FOLLY

15 Then Eliphaz the Temanite answered and said:

2 "Should a wise man
answer with empty
knowledge,
And fill himself with
the east wind?
3 Should he reason with
unprofitable talk,
Or by speeches with
which he can
do no good?
4 Yes, you cast off fear,
And restrain prayer
before God.
5 For your iniquity
teaches your mouth,
And you choose the
tongue of the crafty.
6 Your own mouth
condemns you,
and not I;
Yes, your own lips
testify against you.

7 "*Are* you the first man
who was born?
Or were you made
before the hills?
8 Have you heard the
counsel of God?
Do you limit wisdom
to yourself?
9 What do you know that
we do not know?
What do you understand
that *is* not in us?
10 Both the gray-haired and
the aged *are* among us,
Much older than
your father.
11 *Are* the consolations of
God too small for you,
And the word *spoken*
gently[a] with you?
12 Why does your heart
carry you away,
And what do your
eyes wink at,

14:17 [a] Literally *plaster over* 15:11 [a] Septuagint reads *a secret thing.*

13 That you turn your
spirit against God,
And let *such* words go
out of your mouth?

14 "What *is* man, that
he could be pure?
And *he who is* born of
a woman, that he
could be righteous?
15 If *God* puts no trust
in His saints,
And the heavens are not
pure in His sight,
16 How much less man,
who is abominable
and filthy,
Who drinks iniquity
like water!

17 "I will tell you, hear me;
What I have seen I
will declare,
18 What wise men have told,
Not hiding *anything*
received from
their fathers,
19 To whom alone the
land was given,
And no alien passed
among them:
20 The wicked man writhes
with pain all *his* days,
And the number of
years is hidden from
the oppressor.
21 Dreadful sounds
are in his ears;
In prosperity the
destroyer comes
upon him.
22 He does not believe
that he will return
from darkness,
For a sword is
waiting for him.
23 He wanders about
for bread, *saying,*
'Where *is it?*'
He knows that a day
of darkness is ready
at his hand.
24 Trouble and anguish
make him afraid;
They overpower him,
like a king ready
for battle.
25 For he stretches out his
hand against God,
And acts defiantly
against the Almighty,
26 Running stubbornly
against Him
With his strong,
embossed shield.

27 "Though he has covered
his face with his
fatness,
And made *his* waist
heavy with fat,
28 He dwells in
desolate cities,
In houses which no
one inhabits,
Which are destined
to become ruins.
29 He will not be rich,
Nor will his wealth
continue,
Nor will his possessions
overspread the earth.
30 He will not depart
from darkness;
The flame will dry
out his branches,
And by the breath of His
mouth he will go away.

31 Let him not trust
in futile *things,*
deceiving himself,
For futility will be
his reward.
32 It will be accomplished
before his time,
And his branch will
not be green.
33 He will shake off his
unripe grape like a vine,
And cast off his blossom
like an olive tree.
34 For the company
of hypocrites *will*
be barren,
And fire will consume
the tents of bribery.
35 They conceive trouble
and bring forth futility;
Their womb prepares
deceit."

JOB REPROACHES HIS PITILESS FRIENDS

16 Then Job answered and said:

2 "I have heard many
such things;
Miserable comforters
are you all!
3 Shall words of wind
have an end?
Or what provokes you
that you answer?
4 I also could speak
as you *do,*
If your soul were in
my soul's place.
I could heap up words
against you,
And shake my
head at you;
5 *But* I would strengthen
you with my mouth,
And the comfort
of my lips would
relieve *your grief.*

6 "Though I speak, my
grief is not relieved;
And *if* I remain silent,
how am I eased?
7 But now He has
worn me out;
You have made desolate
all my company.
8 You have shriveled
me up,
And it is a witness
against me;
My leanness rises
up against me
And bears witness
to my face.
9 He tears *me* in His
wrath, and hates me;
He gnashes at me
with His teeth;
My adversary sharpens
His gaze on me.
10 They gape at me with
their mouth,
They strike me
reproachfully
on the cheek,
They gather together
against me.
11 God has delivered me
to the ungodly,
And turned me over to
the hands of the wicked.
12 I was at ease, but He
has shattered me;
He also has taken *me*
by my neck, and
shaken me to pieces;

He has set me up
for His target,
13 His archers surround me.
He pierces my heart[a]
and does not pity;
He pours out my gall
on the ground.
14 He breaks me with
wound upon wound;
He runs at me like
a warrior.[a]

15 "I have sewn sackcloth
over my skin,
And laid my head[a]
in the dust.
16 My face is flushed
from weeping,
And on my eyelids *is*
the shadow of death;
17 Although no violence
is in my hands,
And my prayer *is* pure.

18 "O earth, do not cover
my blood,
And let my cry have
no *resting* place!
19 Surely even now my
witness *is* in heaven,
And my evidence
is on high.
20 My friends scorn me;
My eyes pour out
tears to God.
21 Oh, that one might plead
for a man with God,
As a man *pleads* for
his neighbor!
22 *For when* a few years
are finished,
I shall go the way
of no return.

JOB PRAYS FOR RELIEF

17 "My spirit is broken,
My days are
extinguished,
The grave *is ready* for me.
2 *Are* not mockers with me?
And does not my
eye dwell on their
provocation?

3 "Now put down a pledge
for me with Yourself.
Who *is* he *who* will shake
hands with me?
4 For You have hidden
their heart from
understanding;
Therefore You will
not exalt *them.*
5 He who speaks flattery
to *his* friends,
Even the eyes of his
children will fail.

6 "But He has made me
a byword of the
people,
And I have become one
in whose face men spit.
7 My eye has also grown
dim because of sorrow,
And all my members
are like shadows.
8 Upright *men* are
astonished at this,
And the innocent stirs
himself up against
the hypocrite.

16:13 [a] Literally *kidneys* 16:14 [a] Vulgate reads *giant.* 16:15 [a] Literally *horn*

9 Yet the righteous will
hold to his way,
And he who has clean
hands will be stronger
and stronger.

10 "But please, come back
again, all of you,[a]
For I shall not find *one*
wise *man* among you.
11 My days are past,
My purposes are
broken off,
Even the thoughts
of my heart.
12 They change the
night into day;
'The light *is* near,'
they say, in the
face of darkness.
13 If I wait *for* the grave
as my house,
If I make my bed in
the darkness,
14 If I say to corruption,
'You *are* my father,'
And to the worm,
'You *are* my mother
and my sister,'
15 Where then *is* my hope?
As for my hope,
who can see it?
16 *Will* they go down to
the gates of Sheol?
Shall *we have* rest
together in the dust?"

BILDAD: THE WICKED ARE PUNISHED

18 Then Bildad the Shuhite
answered and said:

2 "How long *till* you put
an end to words?
Gain understanding, and
afterward we will speak.
3 Why are we counted
as beasts,
And regarded as stupid
in your sight?
4 You who tear yourself
in anger,
Shall the earth be
forsaken for you?
Or shall the rock be
removed from its place?

5 "The light of the wicked
indeed goes out,
And the flame of his
fire does not shine.
6 The light is dark
in his tent,
And his lamp beside
him is put out.
7 The steps of his strength
are shortened,
And his own counsel
casts him down.
8 For he is cast into a net
by his own feet,
And he walks into a snare.
9 The net takes *him*
by the heel,
And a snare lays
hold of him.
10 A noose *is* hidden for
him on the ground,
And a trap for him
in the road.
11 Terrors frighten him
on every side,
And drive him to his feet.

17:10 [a] Following some Hebrew manuscripts, Septuagint, Syriac, and Vulgate; Masoretic Text and Targum read *all of them.*

12 His strength is starved,
And destruction *is*
ready at his side.
13 It devours patches
of his skin;
The firstborn of death
devours his limbs.
14 He is uprooted from the
shelter of his tent,
And they parade
him before the
king of terrors.
15 They dwell in his tent
who are none of his;
Brimstone is scattered
on his dwelling.
16 His roots are dried
out below,
And his branch
withers above.
17 The memory of him
perishes from the earth,
And he has no name
among the renowned.[a]
18 He is driven from light
into darkness,
And chased out
of the world.
19 He has neither son
nor posterity among
his people,
Nor any remaining
in his dwellings.
20 Those in the west are
astonished at his day,
As those in the east
are frightened.
21 Surely such *are* the
dwellings of the wicked,
And this *is* the place *of him*
who does not know God."

JOB TRUSTS IN HIS REDEEMER

19 Then Job answered and
said:

2 "How long will you
torment my soul,
And break me in
pieces with words?
3 These ten times you
have reproached me;
You are not ashamed *that*
you have wronged me.[a]
4 And if indeed I have erred,
My error remains with me.
5 If indeed you exalt
yourselves against me,
And plead my disgrace
against me,
6 Know then that God
has wronged me,
And has surrounded
me with His net.

7 "If I cry out concerning
wrong, I am not heard.
If I cry aloud, *there*
is no justice.
8 He has fenced up my way,
so that I cannot pass;
And He has set darkness
in my paths.
9 He has stripped me
of my glory,
And taken the crown
from my head.
10 He breaks me down
on every side,
And I am gone;
My hope He has
uprooted like a tree.

18:17 [a] Literally *before the outside,* meaning distinguished, famous
19:3 [a] A Jewish tradition reads *make yourselves strange to me.*

11 He has also kindled His
wrath against me,
And He counts me as
one of His enemies.
12 His troops come together
And build up their
road against me;
They encamp all
around my tent.

13 "He has removed my
brothers far from me,
And my acquaintances
are completely
estranged from me.
14 My relatives have failed,
And my close friends
have forgotten me.
15 Those who dwell in
my house, and my
maidservants,
Count me as a stranger;
I am an alien in
their sight.
16 I call my servant, but
he gives no answer;
I beg him with my mouth.
17 My breath is offensive
to my wife,
And I am repulsive
to the children of
my own body.
18 Even young children
despise me;
I arise, and they speak
against me.
19 All my close friends
abhor me,
And those whom I love
have turned against me.
20 My bone clings to my
skin and to my flesh,
And I have escaped by
the skin of my teeth.

21 "Have pity on me,
have pity on me,
O you my friends,
For the hand of God
has struck me!
22 Why do you persecute
me as God *does,*
And are not satisfied
with my flesh?

23 "Oh, that my words
were written!
Oh, that they were
inscribed in a book!
24 That they were
engraved on a rock
With an iron pen and
lead, forever!
25 For I know *that* my
Redeemer lives,
And He shall stand at
last on the earth;
26 And after my skin is
destroyed, this *I know,*
That in my flesh I
shall see God,
27 Whom I shall see
for myself,
And my eyes shall behold,
and not another.
How my heart yearns
within me!
28 If you should say,
'How shall we
persecute him?'—
Since the root of the
matter is found in me,
29 Be afraid of the sword
for yourselves;
For wrath *brings*
the punishment
of the sword,
That you may know
there is a judgment."

ZOPHAR'S SERMON ON THE WICKED MAN

20 Then Zophar the Naamathite answered and said:

2 "Therefore my anxious thoughts make me answer,
Because of the turmoil within me.
3 I have heard the rebuke that reproaches me,
And the spirit of my understanding causes me to answer.

4 "Do you *not* know this of old,
Since man was placed on earth,
5 That the triumphing of the wicked is short,
And the joy of the hypocrite is *but* for a moment?
6 Though his haughtiness mounts up to the heavens,
And his head reaches to the clouds,
7 *Yet* he will perish forever like his own refuse;
Those who have seen him will say, 'Where is he?'
8 He will fly away like a dream, and not be found;
Yes, he will be chased away like a vision of the night.
9 The eye *that* saw him will *see him* no more,
Nor will his place behold him anymore.
10 His children will seek the favor of the poor,
And his hands will restore his wealth.
11 His bones are full of his youthful vigor,
But it will lie down with him in the dust.

12 "Though evil is sweet in his mouth,
And he hides it under his tongue,
13 *Though* he spares it and does not forsake it,
But still keeps it in his mouth,
14 *Yet* his food in his stomach turns sour;
It becomes cobra venom within him.
15 He swallows down riches
And vomits them up again;
God casts them out of his belly.
16 He will suck the poison of cobras;
The viper's tongue will slay him.
17 He will not see the streams,
The rivers flowing with honey and cream.
18 He will restore that for which he labored,
And will not swallow *it* down;
From the proceeds of business
He will get no enjoyment.
19 For he has oppressed *and* forsaken the poor,

He has violently seized
a house which he
did not build.

20 "Because he knows
no quietness in
his heart,[a]
He will not save
anything he desires.
21 Nothing is left for
him to eat;
Therefore his well-being
will not last.
22 In his self-sufficiency
he will be in distress;
Every hand of misery
will come against him.
23 *When* he is about to
fill his stomach,
God will cast on him the
fury of His wrath,
And will rain *it* on him
while he is eating.
24 He will flee from the
iron weapon;
A bronze bow will
pierce him through.
25 It is drawn, and comes
out of the body;
Yes, the glittering *point*
comes out of his gall.
Terrors *come* upon him;
26 Total darkness *is* reserved
for his treasures.
An unfanned fire will
consume him;
It shall go ill with him
who is left in his tent.
27 The heavens will
reveal his iniquity,
And the earth will rise
up against him.
28 The increase of his
house will depart,
And his goods will
flow away in the
day of His wrath.
29 This *is* the portion from
God for a wicked man,
The heritage appointed
to him by God."

JOB'S DISCOURSE ON THE WICKED

21 Then Job answered and
said:

2 "Listen carefully to
my speech,
And let this be your
consolation.
3 Bear with me that
I may speak,
And after I have spoken,
keep mocking.

4 "As for me, *is* my
complaint against
man?
And if *it were,* why
should I not be
impatient?
5 Look at me and be
astonished;
Put *your* hand over
your mouth.
6 Even when I remember
I am terrified,
And trembling takes
hold of my flesh.
7 Why do the wicked live
and become old,
Yes, become mighty
in power?

20:20 [a] Literally *belly*

8 Their descendants
are established with
them in their sight,
And their offspring
before their eyes.
9 Their houses *are*
safe from fear,
Neither *is* the rod of
God upon them.
10 Their bull breeds
without failure;
Their cow calves without
miscarriage.
11 They send forth their
little ones like a flock,
And their children dance.
12 They sing to the
tambourine and harp,
And rejoice to the
sound of the flute.
13 They spend their
days in wealth,
And in a moment go
down to the grave.[a]
14 Yet they say to God,
'Depart from us,
For we do not desire
the knowledge
of Your ways.
15 Who *is* the Almighty,
that we should
serve Him?
And what profit do we
have if we pray to Him?'
16 Indeed their prosperity
is not in their hand;
The counsel of the
wicked is far from me.

17 "How often is the lamp of
the wicked put out?
How often does their
destruction come
upon them,
The sorrows *God*
distributes in
His anger?
18 They are like straw
before the wind,
And like chaff that a
storm carries away.
19 *They say,* 'God lays
up one's[a] iniquity
for his children';
Let Him recompense
him, that he
may know *it.*
20 Let his eyes see his
destruction,
And let him drink of the
wrath of the Almighty.
21 For what does he care
about his household
after him,
When the number of his
months is cut in half?

22 "Can *anyone* teach
God knowledge,
Since He judges
those on high?
23 One dies in his
full strength,
Being wholly at ease
and secure;
24 His pails[a] are full of milk,
And the marrow of his
bones is moist.
25 Another man dies in the
bitterness of his soul,
Never having eaten
with pleasure.

21:13 [a] Or *Sheol* 21:19 [a] Literally *his* 21:24 [a] Septuagint and Vulgate read *bowels;* Syriac reads *sides;* Targum reads *breasts.*

26 They lie down alike
in the dust,
And worms cover them.

27 "Look, I know your
thoughts,
And the schemes
with which you
would wrong me.
28 For you say,
'Where *is* the house
of the prince?
And where *is* the tent,[a]
The dwelling place
of the wicked?'
29 Have you not asked those
who travel the road?
And do you not know
their signs?
30 For the wicked are
reserved for the
day of doom;
They shall be brought out
on the day of wrath.
31 Who condemns his
way to his face?
And who repays him *for
what* he has done?
32 Yet he shall be brought
to the grave,
And a vigil kept
over the tomb.
33 The clods of the valley
shall be sweet to him;
Everyone shall follow him,
As countless *have
gone* before him.
34 How then can you
comfort me with
empty words,
Since falsehood remains
in your answers?"

ELIPHAZ ACCUSES JOB OF WICKEDNESS

22 Then Eliphaz the Temanite answered and
said:

2 "Can a man be
profitable to God,
Though he who is wise
may be profitable
to himself?
3 *Is it* any pleasure to
the Almighty that
you are righteous?
Or *is it* gain *to Him*
that you make your
ways blameless?

4 "Is it because of your
fear of Him that
He corrects you,
And enters into
judgment with you?
5 *Is* not your wickedness
great,
And your iniquity
without end?
6 For you have taken
pledges from your
brother for no reason,
And stripped the naked
of their clothing.
7 You have not given the
weary water to drink,
And you have withheld
bread from the hungry.
8 But the mighty man
possessed the land,
And the honorable
man dwelt in it.
9 You have sent widows
away empty,

21:28 [a] Vulgate omits *the tent.*

And the strength of the
fatherless was crushed.
10 Therefore snares *are*
all around you,
And sudden fear
troubles you,
11 Or darkness *so that*
you cannot see;
And an abundance of
water covers you.

12 "Is not God in the
height of heaven?
And see the highest
stars, how lofty
they are!
13 And you say, 'What
does God know?
Can He judge through
the deep darkness?
14 Thick clouds cover Him,
so that He cannot see,
And He walks above the
circle of heaven.'
15 Will you keep to
the old way
Which wicked men
have trod,
16 Who were cut down
before their time,
Whose foundations were
swept away by a flood?
17 They said to God,
'Depart from us!
What can the Almighty
do to them?'[a]
18 Yet He filled their houses
with good *things;*
But the counsel of the
wicked is far from me.

19 "The righteous see
it and are glad,
And the innocent
laugh at them:
20 'Surely our adversaries[a]
are cut down,
And the fire consumes
their remnant.'

21 "Now acquaint yourself
with Him, and
be at peace;
Thereby good will
come to you.
22 Receive, please,
instruction from
His mouth,
And lay up His words
in your heart.
23 If you return to the
Almighty, you will
be built up;
You will remove iniquity
far from your tents.
24 Then you will lay your
gold in the dust,
And the *gold* of Ophir
among the stones
of the brooks.
25 Yes, the Almighty will
be your gold[a]
And your precious silver;
26 For then you will
have your delight
in the Almighty,
And lift up your
face to God.
27 You will make your
prayer to Him,
He will hear you,

22:17 [a] Septuagint and Syriac read *us.* **22:20** [a] Septuagint reads *substance.* **22:25** [a] The ancient versions suggest *defense;* Hebrew reads *gold* as in verse 24.

And you will pay
your vows.
28 You will also declare
a thing,
And it will be
established for you;
So light will shine
on your ways.
29 When they cast *you*
down, and you say,
'Exaltation *will come!*'
Then He will save the
humble *person.*
30 He will *even* deliver one
who is not innocent;
Yes, he will be delivered
by the purity of
your hands."

JOB PROCLAIMS GOD'S RIGHTEOUS JUDGMENTS

23 Then Job answered and said:

2 "Even today my
complaint is bitter;
My[a] hand is listless
because of my groaning.
3 Oh, that I knew where
I might find Him,
That I might come
to His seat!
4 I would present *my*
case before Him,
And fill my mouth
with arguments.
5 I would know the
words *which* He
would answer me,
And understand what
He would say to me.
6 Would He contend with
me in His great power?
No! But He would
take *note* of me.
7 There the upright could
reason with Him,
And I would be delivered
forever from my Judge.

8 "Look, I go forward,
but He is not *there,*
And backward, but I
cannot perceive Him;
9 When He works on the
left hand, I cannot
behold *Him;*
When He turns to
the right hand, I
cannot see *Him.*
10 But He knows the
way that I take;
When He has tested me, I
shall come forth as gold.
11 My foot has held fast
to His steps;
I have kept His way and
not turned aside.
12 I have not departed from
the commandment
of His lips;
I have treasured the
words of His mouth
More than my
necessary *food.*

13 "But He *is* unique, and who
can make Him change?
And *whatever* His soul
desires, *that* He does.
14 For He performs *what*
is appointed for me,

23:2 [a] Following Masoretic Text, Targum, and Vulgate; Septuagint and Syriac read *His.*

And many such *things*
are with Him.
15 Therefore I am terrified
at His presence;
When I consider *this,* I
am afraid of Him.
16 For God made my
heart weak,
And the Almighty
terrifies me;
17 Because I was not cut
off from the presence
of darkness,
And He did *not* hide deep
darkness from my face.

JOB COMPLAINS OF VIOLENCE ON THE EARTH

24 "*Since* times are
not hidden from
the Almighty,
Why do those who know
Him see not His days?

2 "*Some* remove landmarks;
They seize flocks violently
and feed *on them;*
3 They drive away
the donkey of the
fatherless;
They take the widow's
ox as a pledge.
4 They push the needy
off the road;
All the poor of the land
are forced to hide.
5 Indeed, *like* wild donkeys
in the desert,
They go out to their work,
searching for food.
The wilderness *yields*
food for them *and*
for *their* children.
6 They gather their
fodder in the field
And glean in the vineyard
of the wicked.
7 They spend the night
naked, without clothing,
And have no covering
in the cold.
8 They are wet with
the showers of
the mountains,
And huddle around the
rock for want of shelter.

9 "*Some* snatch the
fatherless from
the breast,
And take a pledge
from the poor.
10 They cause *the*
poor to go naked,
without clothing;
And they take away
the sheaves from
the hungry.
11 They press out oil
within their walls,
And tread winepresses,
yet suffer thirst.
12 The dying groan
in the city,
And the souls of the
wounded cry out;
Yet God does not charge
them with wrong.

13 "There are those who
rebel against the light;
They do not know its ways
Nor abide in its paths.
14 The murderer rises
with the light;
He kills the poor
and needy;

And in the night he
is like a thief.
15 The eye of the adulterer
waits for the twilight,
Saying, 'No eye
will see me';
And he disguises *his* face.
16 In the dark they break
into houses
Which they marked
for themselves in
the daytime;
They do not know
the light.
17 For the morning is the
same to them as the
shadow of death;
If *someone* recognizes
them,
They are in the terrors of
the shadow of death.

18 "They *should be* swift on
the face of the waters,
Their portion *should be*
cursed in the earth,
So that no *one would*
turn into the way of
their vineyards.
19 As drought and
heat consume the
snow waters,
So the grave[a] *consumes*
those who have sinned.
20 The womb *should*
forget him,
The worm *should* feed
sweetly on him;
He *should* be
remembered no more,
And wickedness *should*
be broken like a tree.
21 For he preys on the
barren *who* do not bear,
And does no good
for the widow.

22 "But *God* draws the mighty
away with His power;
He rises up, but no
man is sure of life.
23 He gives them security,
and they rely *on it;*
Yet His eyes *are* on
their ways.
24 They are exalted for
a little while,
Then they are gone.
They are brought low;
They are taken out of the
way like all *others;*
They dry out like the
heads of grain.

25 "Now if *it is* not *so,* who
will prove me a liar,
And make my speech
worth nothing?"

BILDAD: HOW CAN MAN BE RIGHTEOUS?

25 Then Bildad the Shuhite answered and said:

2 "Dominion and fear
belong to Him;
He makes peace in
His high places.
3 Is there any number
to His armies?
Upon whom does His
light not rise?
4 How then can man be
righteous before God?

24:19 [a] Or *Sheol*

Or how can he be
pure *who is* born
of a woman?
5 If even the moon
does not shine,
And the stars are not
pure in His sight,
6 How much less man,
who is a maggot,
And a son of man,
who is a worm?"

JOB: MAN'S FRAILTY AND GOD'S MAJESTY

26 But Job answered and said:

2 "How have you helped *him*
who is without power?
How have you saved
the arm *that has*
no strength?
3 How have you
counseled *one who*
has no wisdom?
And *how* have you
declared sound
advice to many?
4 To whom have you
uttered words?
And whose spirit
came from you?

5 "The dead tremble,
Those under the
waters and those
inhabiting them.
6 Sheol *is* naked
before Him,
And Destruction has
no covering.
7 He stretches out
the north over
empty space;
He hangs the earth
on nothing.
8 He binds up the water
in His thick clouds,
Yet the clouds are not
broken under it.
9 He covers the face
of *His* throne,
And spreads His
cloud over it.
10 He drew a circular
horizon on the face
of the waters,
At the boundary of
light and darkness.
11 The pillars of heaven
tremble,
And are astonished
at His rebuke.
12 He stirs up the sea
with His power,
And by His
understanding He
breaks up the storm.
13 By His Spirit He adorned
the heavens;
His hand pierced the
fleeing serpent.
14 Indeed these *are* the
mere edges of His ways,
And how small a whisper
we hear of Him!
But the thunder of
His power who can
understand?"

JOB MAINTAINS HIS INTEGRITY

27 Moreover Job continued his discourse, and said:

2 "*As* God lives, *who* has
taken away my justice,

And the Almighty,
who has made
my soul bitter,
3 As long as my
breath *is* in me,
And the breath of God
in my nostrils,
4 My lips will not speak
wickedness,
Nor my tongue
utter deceit.
5 Far be it from me
That I should say
you are right;
Till I die I will not put
away my integrity
from me.
6 My righteousness I
hold fast, and will
not let it go;
My heart shall not
reproach *me* as
long as I live.

7 "May my enemy be
like the wicked,
And he who rises up
against me like the
unrighteous.
8 For what is the hope
of the hypocrite,
Though he may
gain *much,*
If God takes away his
life?
9 Will God hear his cry
When trouble comes
upon him?
10 Will he delight himself
in the Almighty?
Will he always
call on God?

11 "I will teach you about
the hand of God;
What *is* with the Almighty
I will not conceal.
12 Surely all of you
have seen *it;*
Why then do you
behave with complete
nonsense?

13 "This is the portion of a
wicked man with God,
And the heritage of
oppressors, received
from the Almighty:
14 If his children are
multiplied, *it is*
for the sword;
And his offspring
shall not be satisfied
with bread.
15 Those who survive him
shall be buried in death,
And their[a] widows
shall not weep,
16 Though he heaps up
silver like dust,
And piles up clothing
like clay—
17 He may pile *it* up, but
the just will wear *it,*
And the innocent will
divide the silver.
18 He builds his house
like a moth,[a]
Like a booth *which* a
watchman makes.

27:15 [a] Literally *his* **27:18** [a] Following Masoretic Text and Vulgate; Septuagint and Syriac read *spider* (compare 8:14); Targum reads *decay.*

19 The rich man will
lie down,
But not be gathered *up;*[a]
He opens his eyes,
And he *is* no more.
20 Terrors overtake
him like a flood;
A tempest steals him
away in the night.
21 The east wind carries him
away, and he is gone;
It sweeps him out
of his place.
22 It hurls against him
and does not spare;
He flees desperately
from its power.
23 *Men* shall clap their
hands at him,
And shall hiss him
out of his place.

JOB'S DISCOURSE ON WISDOM

28 "Surely there is a
mine for silver,
And a place *where*
gold is refined.
2 Iron is taken from
the earth,
And copper *is* smelted
from ore.
3 *Man* puts an end
to darkness,
And searches every recess
For ore in the
darkness and the
shadow of death.
4 He breaks open a shaft
away from people;
In places forgotten by feet
They hang far away
from men;
They swing to and fro.
5 *As for* the earth, from
it comes bread,
But underneath it is
turned up as by fire;
6 Its stones *are* the
source of sapphires,
And it contains gold dust.
7 *That* path no bird knows,
Nor has the falcon's
eye seen it.
8 The proud lions[a] have
not trodden it,
Nor has the fierce lion
passed over it.
9 He puts his hand
on the flint;
He overturns the
mountains at the
roots.
10 He cuts out channels
in the rocks,
And his eye sees every
precious thing.
11 He dams up the streams
from trickling;
What is hidden he
brings forth to light.

12 "But where can wisdom
be found?
And where *is* the place
of understanding?
13 Man does not know
its value,
Nor is it found in the
land of the living.

27:19 [a] Following Masoretic Text and Targum; Septuagint and Syriac read *But shall not add* (that is, do it again); Vulgate reads *But take away nothing.* **28:8** [a] Literally *sons of pride,* figurative of the great lions

14 The deep says, '*It*
is not in me';
And the sea says, '*It*
is not with me.'
15 It cannot be purchased
for gold,
Nor can silver be
weighed *for* its price.
16 It cannot be valued in
the gold of Ophir,
In precious onyx
or sapphire.
17 Neither gold nor
crystal can equal it,
Nor can it be exchanged
for jewelry of fine gold.
18 No mention shall be
made of coral or quartz,
For the price of wisdom
is above rubies.
19 The topaz of Ethiopia
cannot equal it,
Nor can it be valued
in pure gold.

20 "From where then does
wisdom come?
And where *is* the place
of understanding?
21 It is hidden from the
eyes of all living,
And concealed from
the birds of the air.
22 Destruction and
Death say,
'We have heard a
report about it
with our ears.'
23 God understands its way,
And He knows its place.
24 For He looks to the
ends of the earth,
And sees under the
whole heavens,
25 To establish a weight
for the wind,
And apportion the
waters by measure.
26 When He made a
law for the rain,
And a path for the
thunderbolt,
27 Then He saw *wisdom*[a]
and declared it;
He prepared it, indeed,
He searched it out.
28 And to man He said,
'Behold, the fear of the
Lord, that *is* wisdom,
And to depart from evil
is understanding.'"

JOB'S SUMMARY DEFENSE

29 Job further continued his discourse, and said:

2 "Oh, that I were as *in*
months past,
As *in* the days *when* God
watched over me;
3 When His lamp shone
upon my head,
And when by His light
I walked *through*
darkness;
4 Just as I was in the
days of my prime,
When the friendly
counsel of God *was*
over my tent;
5 When the Almighty
was yet with me,
When my children
were around me;

28:27 [a] Literally *it*

6 When my steps were
bathed with cream,[a]
And the rock poured out
rivers of oil for me!

7 "When I went out to
the gate by the city,
When I took my seat in
the open square,
8 The young men saw
me and hid,
And the aged arose
and stood;
9 The princes refrained
from talking,
And put *their* hand
on their mouth;
10 The voice of nobles
was hushed,
And their tongue stuck to
the roof of their mouth.
11 When the ear heard,
then it blessed me,
And when the eye saw,
then it approved me;
12 Because I delivered the
poor who cried out,
The fatherless and *the
one who* had no helper.
13 The blessing of a
perishing *man*
came upon me,
And I caused the widow's
heart to sing for joy.
14 I put on righteousness,
and it clothed me;
My justice *was* like a
robe and a turban.
15 I *was* eyes to the blind,
And I *was* feet to
the lame.
16 I *was* a father to the poor,
And I searched out the
case *that* I did not know.
17 I broke the fangs
of the wicked,
And plucked the victim
from his teeth.

18 "Then I said, 'I shall
die in my nest,
And multiply *my*
days as the sand.
19 My root *is* spread out
to the waters,
And the dew lies all
night on my branch.
20 My glory *is* fresh
within me,
And my bow is renewed
in my hand.'

21 "*Men* listened to me
and waited,
And kept silence for
my counsel.
22 After my words they
did not speak again,
And my speech settled
on them *as dew*.
23 They waited for me
as for the rain,
And they opened their
mouth wide *as* for
the spring rain.
24 *If* I mocked at them, they
did not believe *it*,
And the light of my
countenance they
did not cast down.
25 I chose the way for them,
and sat as chief;

29:6 [a] Masoretic Text reads *wrath;* ancient versions and some Hebrew manuscripts read *cream* (compare 20:17).

So I dwelt as a king
in the army,
As one *who* comforts
mourners.

30 "But now they
mock at me, *men*
younger than I,
Whose fathers I
disdained to put with
the dogs of my flock.
2 Indeed, what *profit*
is the strength of
their hands to me?
Their vigor has
perished.
3 *They are* gaunt from
want and famine,
Fleeing late to the
wilderness, desolate
and waste,
4 Who pluck mallow
by the bushes,
And broom tree roots
for their food.
5 They were driven out
from among *men*,
They shouted at them
as *at* a thief.
6 *They had* to live in the
clefts of the valleys,
In caves of the earth
and the rocks.
7 Among the bushes
they brayed,
Under the nettles
they nestled.
8 *They were* sons of fools,
Yes, sons of vile men;
They were scourged
from the land.
9 "And now I am their
taunting song;
Yes, I am their byword.
10 They abhor me, they
keep far from me;
They do not hesitate
to spit in my face.
11 Because He has loosed
my[a] bowstring and
afflicted me,
They have cast off
restraint before me.
12 At *my* right *hand* the
rabble arises;
They push away my
feet,
And they raise against
me their ways of
destruction.
13 They break up my path,
They promote my
calamity;
They have no helper.
14 They come as broad
breakers;
Under the ruinous storm
they roll along.
15 Terrors are turned
upon me;
They pursue my honor
as the wind,
And my prosperity has
passed like a cloud.

16 "And now my soul is
poured out because
of my *plight*;
The days of affliction
take hold of me.
17 My bones are pierced
in me at night,

30:11 [a] Following Masoretic Text, Syriac, and Targum; Septuagint and Vulgate read *His*.

And my gnawing
pains take no rest.
18 By great force my
garment is disfigured;
It binds me about as the
collar of my coat.
19 He has cast me
into the mire,
And I have become
like dust and ashes.

20 "I cry out to You, but You
do not answer me;
I stand up, and You
regard me.
21 *But* You have become
cruel to me;
With the strength of Your
hand You oppose me.
22 You lift me up to the
wind and cause
me to ride *on it;*
You spoil my success.
23 For I know *that* You will
bring me *to* death,
And *to* the house
appointed for all living.

24 "Surely He would not
stretch out *His* hand
against a heap of ruins,
If they cry out when
He destroys *it.*
25 Have I not wept for him
who was in trouble?
Has *not* my soul grieved
for the poor?
26 But when I looked for
good, evil came *to me;*
And when I waited
for light, then
came darkness.
27 My heart is in turmoil
and cannot rest;
Days of affliction
confront me.
28 I go about mourning,
but not in the sun;
I stand up in the assembly
and cry out for help.
29 I am a brother of jackals,
And a companion
of ostriches.
30 My skin grows black
and falls from me;
My bones burn with fever.
31 My harp is *turned*
to mourning,
And my flute to the voice
of those who weep.

31

"I have made a
covenant with
my eyes;
Why then should I look
upon a young woman?
2 For what *is* the allotment
of God from above,
And the inheritance
of the Almighty
from on high?
3 *Is* it not destruction
for the wicked,
And disaster for the
workers of iniquity?
4 Does He not see my ways,
And count all my steps?

5 "If I have walked
with falsehood,
Or if my foot has
hastened to deceit,
6 Let me be weighed
on honest scales,
That God may know
my integrity.
7 If my step has turned
from the way,

Or my heart walked
after my eyes,
Or if any spot adheres
to my hands,
8 *Then* let me sow, and
another eat;
Yes, let my harvest
be rooted out.

9 "If my heart has been
enticed by a woman,
Or *if* I have lurked at
my neighbor's door,
10 *Then* let my wife grind
for another,
And let others bow
down over her.
11 For that *would be*
wickedness;
Yes, it *would be* iniquity
deserving of judgment.
12 For that *would be* a
fire *that* consumes
to destruction,
And would root out
all my increase.

13 "If I have despised the
cause of my male
or female servant
When they complained
against me,
14 What then shall I do
when God rises up?
When He punishes, how
shall I answer Him?
15 Did not He who made
me in the womb
make them?
Did not the same
One fashion us
in the womb?

16 "If I have kept the poor
from *their* desire,
Or caused the eyes of
the widow to fail,
17 Or eaten my morsel
by myself,
So that the fatherless
could not eat of it
18 (But from my youth I
reared him as a father,
And from my mother's
womb I guided
the widow[a]);
19 If I have seen anyone
perish for lack
of clothing,
Or any poor *man*
without covering;
20 If his heart[a] has not
blessed me,
And *if* he was *not*
warmed with the
fleece of my sheep;
21 If I have raised my
hand against the
fatherless,
When I saw I had
help in the gate;
22 *Then* let my arm fall
from my shoulder,
Let my arm be torn
from the socket.
23 For destruction *from*
God *is* a terror to me,
And because of His
magnificence I
cannot endure.

24 "If I have made gold
my hope,
Or said to fine gold, '*You
are* my confidence';

31:18 [a] Literally *her* (compare verse 16) 31:20 [a] Literally *loins*

25 If I have rejoiced because
my wealth *was* great,
And because my hand
had gained much;
26 If I have observed the
sun[a] when it shines,
Or the moon moving
in brightness,
27 So that my heart has
been secretly enticed,
And my mouth has
kissed my hand;
28 This also *would be* an
iniquity *deserving*
of judgment,
For I would have denied
God *who is* above.

29"If I have rejoiced at
the destruction of
him who hated me,
Or lifted myself up
when evil found him
30 (Indeed I have
not allowed my
mouth to sin
By asking for a curse
on his soul);
31 If the men of my tent
have not said,
'Who is there that has
not been satisfied
with his meat?'
32 (*But* no sojourner had
to lodge in the street,
For I have opened my
doors to the traveler[a]);
33 If I have covered
my transgressions
as Adam,
By hiding my iniquity
in my bosom,
34 Because I feared the
great multitude,
And dreaded the
contempt of families,
So that I kept silence
And did not go out
of the door—
35 Oh, that I had one
to hear me!
Here is my mark.
Oh, that the Almighty
would answer me,
That my Prosecutor
had written a book!
36 Surely I would carry
it on my shoulder,
And bind it on me
like a crown;
37 I would declare to
Him the number
of my steps;
Like a prince I would
approach Him.

38"If my land cries out
against me,
And its furrows
weep together;
39 If I have eaten its fruit[a]
without money,
Or caused its owners
to lose their lives;
40 *Then* let thistles grow
instead of wheat,
And weeds instead
of barley."

The words of Job are ended.

31:26 [a] Literally *light* **31:32** [a] Following Septuagint, Syriac, Targum, and Vulgate; Masoretic Text reads *road.* **31:39** [a] Literally *its strength*

ELIHU CONTRADICTS JOB'S FRIENDS

32 So these three men ceased answering Job,
because he *was* righteous in
his own eyes. 2Then the wrath
of Elihu, the son of Barachel
the Buzite, of the family of
Ram, was aroused against
Job; his wrath was aroused
because he justified himself
rather than God. 3Also against
his three friends his wrath was
aroused, because they had
found no answer, and *yet* had
condemned Job.
4Now because they *were*
years older than he, Elihu
had waited to speak to Job.[a]
5When Elihu saw that *there*
was no answer in the mouth
of these three men, his wrath
was aroused.
6So Elihu, the son of Barachel the Buzite, answered and
said:

"I *am* young in years,
 and you *are* very old;
Therefore I was afraid,
And dared not declare
 my opinion to you.
7 I said, 'Age[a] should speak,
And multitude of years
 should teach wisdom.'
8 But *there is* a spirit in man,
And the breath of the
 Almighty gives him
 understanding.
9 Great men[a] are not
 always wise,
Nor do the aged *always*
 understand justice.

10 "Therefore I say,
 'Listen to me,
I also will declare
 my opinion.'
11 Indeed I waited for
 your words,
I listened to your
 reasonings, while
 you searched out
 what to say.
12 I paid close attention
 to you;
And surely not one of
 you convinced Job,
Or answered his words—
13 Lest you say,
'We have found wisdom';
God will vanquish
 him, not man.
14 Now he has not directed
 his words against me;
So I will not answer him
 with your words.

15 "They are dismayed
 and answer no more;
Words escape them.
16 And I have waited,
 because they did
 not speak,
Because they stood still
 and answered no more.
17 I also will answer my part,
I too will declare
 my opinion.
18 For I am full of words;
The spirit within me
 compels me.

32:4 [a] Vulgate reads *till Job had spoken.* 32:7 [a] Literally *Days,* that is, years 32:9 [a] Or *Men of many years*

19 Indeed my belly *is* like
wine *that* has no vent;
It is ready to burst like
new wineskins.
20 I will speak, that I
may find relief;
I must open my lips
and answer.
21 Let me not, I pray, show
partiality to anyone;
Nor let me flatter
any man.
22 For I do not know
how to flatter,
Else my Maker would
soon take me away.

ELIHU CONTRADICTS JOB

33 "But please, Job,
hear my speech,
And listen to all
my words.
2 Now, I open my mouth;
My tongue speaks
in my mouth.
3 My words *come* from
my upright heart;
My lips utter pure
knowledge.
4 The Spirit of God
has made me,
And the breath of the
Almighty gives me life.
5 If you can answer me,
Set *your words* in
order before me;
Take your stand.
6 Truly I *am* as your
spokesman[a]
before God;
I also have been
formed out of clay.
7 Surely no fear of me
will terrify you,
Nor will my hand be
heavy on you.
8 "Surely you have spoken
in my hearing,
And I have heard
the sound of *your*
words, *saying,*
9 'I *am* pure, without
transgression;
I *am* innocent, and *there*
is no iniquity in me.
10 Yet He finds occasions
against me,
He counts me as
His enemy;
11 He puts my feet in
the stocks,
He watches all my paths.'

12 "Look, *in* this you are
not righteous.
I will answer you,
For God is greater
than man.
13 Why do you contend
with Him?
For He does not give
an accounting of
any of His words.
14 For God may speak in
one way, or in another,
Yet man does not
perceive it.
15 In a dream, in a vision
of the night,
When deep sleep
falls upon men,
While slumbering
on their beds,

33:6 [a] Literally *as your mouth*

16 Then He opens the
ears of men,
And seals their
instruction.
17 In order to turn man
from his deed,
And conceal pride
from man,
18 He keeps back his
soul from the Pit,
And his life from
perishing by the sword.

19 "*Man* is also chastened
with pain on his bed,
And with strong *pain* in
many of his bones,
20 So that his life
abhors bread,
And his soul
succulent food.
21 His flesh wastes
away from sight,
And his bones stick
out *which once*
were not seen.
22 Yes, his soul draws
near the Pit,
And his life to the
executioners.

23 "If there is a messenger
for him,
A mediator, one among
a thousand,
To show man His
uprightness,
24 Then He is gracious
to him, and says,
'Deliver him from going
down to the Pit;
I have found a ransom';
25 His flesh shall be
young like a child's,
He shall return to the
days of his youth.
26 He shall pray to God, and
He will delight in him,
He shall see His
face with joy,
For He restores to man
His righteousness.
27 Then he looks at
men and says,
'I have sinned, and
perverted *what*
was right,
And it did not profit me.'
28 He will redeem his[a]
soul from going
down to the Pit,
And his[b] life shall
see the light.

29 "Behold, God works
all these *things*,
Twice, *in fact*, three
times with a man,
30 To bring back his
soul from the Pit,
That he may be
enlightened with
the light of life.

31 "Give ear, Job, listen to me;
Hold your peace,
and I will speak.
32 If you have anything
to say, answer me;
Speak, for I desire
to justify you.
33 If not, listen to me;
Hold your peace, and I
will teach you wisdom."

33:28 [a] Or *my* (Kethib) [b] Or *my* (Kethib)

ELIHU PROCLAIMS GOD'S JUSTICE

34 Elihu further answered and said:

2 "Hear my words,
you wise *men;*
Give ear to me, you who
have knowledge.
3 For the ear tests words
As the palate tastes food.
4 Let us choose justice
for ourselves;
Let us know among
ourselves what *is* good.

5 "For Job has said, 'I
am righteous,
But God has taken
away my justice;
6 Should I lie concerning
my right?
My wound *is* incurable,
though I am without
transgression.'
7 What man *is* like Job,
Who drinks scorn
like water,
8 Who goes in company with
the workers of iniquity,
And walks with
wicked men?
9 For he has said, 'It profits
a man nothing
That he should
delight in God.'

10 "Therefore listen
to me, you men of
understanding:
Far be it from God *to
do* wickedness,
And *from* the Almighty
to *commit* iniquity.
11 For He repays man
according to his work,
And makes man
to find a reward
according to *his* way.
12 Surely God will never
do wickedly,
Nor will the Almighty
pervert justice.
13 Who gave Him charge
over the earth?
Or who appointed *Him
over* the whole world?
14 If He should set His
heart on it,
If He should gather to
Himself His Spirit
and His breath,
15 All flesh would
perish together,
And man would
return to dust.

16 "If *you have*
understanding,
hear this;
Listen to the sound
of my words:
17 Should one who hates
justice govern?
Will you condemn *Him
who is* most just?
18 *Is it fitting* to say to a king,
'*You are* worthless,'
And to nobles, '*You
are* wicked'?
19 Yet He is not partial
to princes,
Nor does He regard the
rich more than the poor;
For they *are* all the
work of His hands.
20 In a moment they die, in
the middle of the night;

The people are shaken
and pass away;
The mighty are taken
away without a hand.

21 "For His eyes *are* on
the ways of man,
And He sees all his steps.
22 There is no darkness
nor shadow of death
Where the workers
of iniquity may
hide themselves.
23 For He need not further
consider a man,
That he should go before
God in judgment.
24 He breaks in pieces mighty
men without inquiry,
And sets others in
their place.
25 Therefore He knows
their works;
He overthrows *them*
in the night,
And they are crushed.
26 He strikes them as
wicked *men*
In the open sight of others,
27 Because they turned
back from Him,
And would not consider
any of His ways,
28 So that they caused
the cry of the poor
to come to Him;
For He hears the cry
of the afflicted.
29 When He gives
quietness, who then
can make trouble?
And when He hides
His face, who then
can see Him,
Whether *it is* against
a nation or a
man alone?—
30 That the hypocrite
should not reign,
Lest the people be
ensnared.

31 "For has *anyone*
said to God,
'I have borne *chastening;*
I will offend no more;
32 Teach me *what* I
do not see;
If I have done iniquity,
I will do no more'?
33 Should He repay *it*
according to your *terms,*
Just because you
disavow it?
You must choose,
and not I;
Therefore speak
what you know.

34 "Men of understanding
say to me,
Wise men who
listen to me:
35 'Job speaks without
knowledge,
His words *are* without
wisdom.'
36 Oh, that Job were tried
to the utmost,
Because *his* answers
are like those of
wicked men!
37 For he adds rebellion
to his sin;
He claps *his hands*
among us,
And multiplies his
words against God."

ELIHU CONDEMNS SELF-RIGHTEOUSNESS

35 Moreover Elihu answered and said:

2 "Do you think this is right?
Do you say,
'My righteousness is
more than God's'?
3 For you say,
'What advantage
will it be to You?
What profit shall I
have, more than *if*
I had sinned?'

4 "I will answer you,
And your companions
with you.
5 Look to the heavens
and see;
And behold the clouds—
They are higher than you.
6 If you sin, what do
you accomplish
against Him?
Or, *if* your transgressions
are multiplied, what
do you do to Him?
7 If you are righteous, what
do you give Him?
Or what does He receive
from your hand?
8 Your wickedness affects
a man such as you,
And your righteousness
a son of man.

9 "Because of the multitude
of oppressions
they cry out;
They cry out for help
because of the arm
of the mighty.
10 But no one says, 'Where
is God my Maker,
Who gives songs
in the night,
11 Who teaches us more
than the beasts
of the earth,
And makes us wiser than
the birds of heaven?'
12 There they cry out, but
He does not answer,
Because of the pride
of evil men.
13 Surely God will not
listen to empty *talk*,
Nor will the Almighty
regard it.
14 Although you say you
do not see Him,
Yet justice *is* before
Him, and you must
wait for Him.
15 And now, because He
has not punished
in His anger,
Nor taken much
notice of folly,
16 Therefore Job opens
his mouth in vain;
He multiplies words
without knowledge."

ELIHU PROCLAIMS GOD'S GOODNESS

36 Elihu also proceeded and said:

2 "Bear with me a little,
and I will show you
That *there are* yet
words to speak on
God's behalf.
3 I will fetch my knowledge
from afar;

I will ascribe
righteousness
to my Maker.
4 For truly my words
are not false;
One who is perfect in
knowledge *is* with you.

5 "Behold, God *is* mighty,
but despises *no one;*
He is mighty in strength
of understanding.
6 He does not preserve
the life of the wicked,
But gives justice to
the oppressed.
7 He does not withdraw His
eyes from the righteous;
But *they are* on the
throne with kings,
For He has seated
them forever,
And they are exalted.
8 And if *they are*
bound in fetters,
Held in the cords
of affliction,
9 Then He tells them
their work and their
transgressions—
That they have
acted defiantly.
10 He also opens their
ear to instruction,
And commands that they
turn from iniquity.
11 If they obey and
serve *Him,*
They shall spend their
days in prosperity,
And their years in
pleasures.
12 But if they do not obey,
They shall perish
by the sword,
And they shall die
without knowledge.[a]

13 "But the hypocrites in
heart store up wrath;
They do not cry for help
when He binds them.
14 They die in youth,
And their life *ends* among
the perverted persons.[a]
15 He delivers the poor
in their affliction,
And opens their ears
in oppression.

16 "Indeed He would have
brought you out
of dire distress,
Into a broad place where
there is no restraint;
And what is set on
your table *would be*
full of richness.
17 But you are filled
with the judgment
due the wicked;
Judgment and justice
take hold *of you.*
18 Because *there is* wrath,
beware lest He take you
away with *one* blow;
For a large ransom would
not help you avoid *it.*
19 Will your riches,
Or all the mighty forces,

36:12 [a] Masoretic Text reads *as one without knowledge.*
36:14 [a] Hebrew *qedeshim,* that is, those practicing sodomy and prostitution in religious rituals

Keep you from distress?
20 Do not desire the night,
When people are cut
off in their place.
21 Take heed, do not
turn to iniquity,
For you have chosen this
rather than affliction.

22 "Behold, God is exalted
by His power;
Who teaches like Him?
23 Who has assigned
Him His way,
Or who has said, 'You
have done wrong'?

ELIHU PROCLAIMS GOD'S MAJESTY

24 "Remember to magnify
His work,
Of which men have sung.
25 Everyone has seen it;
Man looks on *it* from afar.

26 "Behold, God *is* great, and
we do not know *Him;*
Nor can the number of
His years *be* discovered.
27 For He draws up
drops of water,
Which distill as rain
from the mist,
28 Which the clouds
drop down
And pour abundantly
on man.
29 Indeed, can *anyone*
understand the
spreading of clouds,
The thunder from
His canopy?
30 Look, He scatters His
light upon it,
And covers the
depths of the sea.
31 For by these He judges
the peoples;
He gives food in
abundance.
32 He covers *His* hands
with lightning,
And commands
it to strike.
33 His thunder declares it,
The cattle also, concerning
the rising *storm.*

37 "At this also my
heart trembles,
And leaps from its place.
2 Hear attentively the
thunder of His voice,
And the rumbling *that*
comes from His mouth.
3 He sends it forth under
the whole heaven,
His lightning to the
ends of the earth.
4 After it a voice roars;
He thunders with His
majestic voice,
And He does not
restrain them when
His voice is heard.
5 God thunders
marvelously with
His voice;
He does great things
which we cannot
comprehend.
6 For He says to the snow,
'Fall *on* the earth';
Likewise to the gentle
rain and the heavy
rain of His strength.
7 He seals the hand
of every man,

That all men may
know His work.
8 The beasts go into dens,
And remain in their lairs.
9 From the chamber
of the south comes
the whirlwind,
And cold from the
scattering winds
of the north.
10 By the breath of God
ice is given,
And the broad waters
are frozen.
11 Also with moisture
He saturates the
thick clouds;
He scatters His
bright clouds.
12 And they swirl about,
being turned by
His guidance,
That they may do
whatever He
commands them
On the face of the
whole earth.[a]
13 He causes it to come,
Whether for correction,
Or for His land,
Or for mercy.

14 "Listen to this, O Job;
Stand still and consider
the wondrous
works of God.
15 Do you know when God
dispatches them,
And causes the light of
His cloud to shine?
16 Do you know how the
clouds are balanced,
Those wondrous works
of Him who is perfect
in knowledge?
17 Why *are* your
garments hot,
When He quiets the earth
by the south *wind?*
18 With Him, have you
spread out the skies,
Strong as a cast
metal mirror?

19 "Teach us what we
should say to Him,
For we can prepare
nothing because
of the darkness.
20 Should He be told that
I *wish to* speak?
If a man were to speak,
surely he would be
swallowed up.
21 Even now *men* cannot
look at the light *when
it is* bright in the skies,
When the wind
has passed and
cleared them.
22 He comes from the north
as golden *splendor;*
With God *is* awesome
majesty.
23 *As for* the Almighty, we
cannot find Him;
He is excellent in power,
In judgment and
abundant justice;
He does not oppress.
24 Therefore men fear Him;
He shows no partiality
to any *who are*
wise of heart."

37:12 [a] Literally *the world of the earth*

THE LORD REVEALS HIS OMNIPOTENCE TO JOB

38 Then the LORD answered Job out of the whirlwind, and said:

2 "Who *is* this who
darkens counsel
By words without
knowledge?
3 Now prepare yourself
like a man;
I will question you, and
you shall answer Me.

4 "Where were you when
I laid the foundations
of the earth?
Tell *Me,* if you have
understanding.
5 Who determined its
measurements?
Surely you know!
Or who stretched the
line upon it?
6 To what were its
foundations fastened?
Or who laid its
cornerstone,
7 When the morning
stars sang together,
And all the sons of God
shouted for joy?

8 "Or *who* shut in the
sea with doors,
When it burst forth *and*
issued from the womb;
9 When I made the
clouds its garment,
And thick darkness its
swaddling band;
10 When I fixed My
limit for it,
And set bars and doors;
11 When I said,
'This far you may
come, but no farther,
And here your proud
waves must stop!'

12 "Have you commanded
the morning since
your days *began,*
And caused the dawn
to know its place,
13 That it might take hold of
the ends of the earth,
And the wicked be
shaken out of it?
14 It takes on form like
clay *under* a seal,
And stands out like
a garment.
15 From the wicked their
light is withheld,
And the upraised
arm is broken.

16 "Have you entered the
springs of the sea?
Or have you walked in
search of the depths?
17 Have the gates of death
been revealed to you?
Or have you seen
the doors of the
shadow of death?
18 Have you comprehended
the breadth of
the earth?
Tell *Me,* if you
know all this.

19 "Where *is* the way *to*
the dwelling of light?
And darkness, where
is its place,

20 That you may take it
to its territory,
That you may know the
paths *to* its home?
21 Do you know *it,* because
you were born then,
Or *because* the number
of your days *is* great?

22 "Have you entered the
treasury of snow,
Or have you seen the
treasury of hail,
23 Which I have reserved
for the time of trouble,
For the day of battle
and war?
24 By what way is
light diffused,
Or the east wind scattered
over the earth?

25 "Who has divided
a channel for the
overflowing *water,*
Or a path for the
thunderbolt,
26 To cause it to rain
on a land *where*
there is no one,
A wilderness in which
there is no man;
27 To satisfy the
desolate waste,
And cause to spring
forth the growth
of tender grass?
28 Has the rain a father?
Or who has begotten
the drops of dew?
29 From whose womb
comes the ice?
And the frost of heaven,
who gives it birth?
30 The waters harden
like stone,
And the surface of the
deep is frozen.

31 "Can you bind the cluster
of the Pleiades,
Or loose the belt of Orion?
32 Can you bring out
Mazzaroth[a] in
its season?
Or can you guide the
Great Bear with its cubs?
33 Do you know the
ordinances of
the heavens?
Can you set their
dominion over
the earth?

34 "Can you lift up your
voice to the clouds,
That an abundance of
water may cover you?
35 Can you send out
lightnings, that
they may go,
And say to you,
'Here we *are!*'?
36 Who has put wisdom
in the mind?[a]
Or who has given
understanding
to the heart?
37 Who can number the
clouds by wisdom?
Or who can pour out the
bottles of heaven,
38 When the dust hardens
in clumps,

38:32 [a] Literally *Constellations* **38:36** [a] Literally *inward parts*

And the clods cling
together?

39 "Can you hunt the
prey for the lion,
Or satisfy the appetite
of the young lions,
40 When they crouch
in *their* dens,
Or lurk in their lairs
to lie in wait?
41 Who provides food
for the raven,
When its young
ones cry to God,
And wander about
for lack of food?

39

"Do you know the
time when the
wild mountain
goats bear young?
Or can you mark when
the deer gives birth?
2 Can you number the
months *that* they fulfill?
Or do you know the time
when they bear young?
3 They bow down,
They bring forth
their young,
They deliver their
offspring.[a]
4 Their young ones
are healthy,
They grow strong
with grain;
They depart and do
not return to them.

5 "Who set the wild
donkey free?
Who loosed the bonds
of the onager,
6 Whose home I have
made the wilderness,
And the barren land
his dwelling?
7 He scorns the tumult
of the city;
He does not heed the
shouts of the driver.
8 The range of the
mountains *is*
his pasture,
And he searches after
every green thing.

9 "Will the wild ox be
willing to serve you?
Will he bed by your
manger?
10 Can you bind the wild
ox in the furrow
with ropes?
Or will he plow the
valleys behind you?
11 Will you trust
him because his
strength *is* great?
Or will you leave your
labor to him?
12 Will you trust him to
bring home your grain,
And gather it to your
threshing floor?

13 "The wings of the
ostrich wave proudly,
But are her wings
and pinions *like the*
kindly stork's?
14 For she leaves her eggs
on the ground,

39:3 [a] Literally *pangs,* figurative of offspring

And warms them
in the dust;
15 She forgets that a foot
may crush them,
Or that a wild beast
may break them.
16 She treats her young
harshly, as though
they were not hers;
Her labor is in vain,
without concern,
17 Because God deprived
her of wisdom,
And did not endow her
with understanding.
18 When she lifts
herself on high,
She scorns the horse
and its rider.

19 "Have you given the
horse strength?
Have you clothed his
neck with thunder?[a]
20 Can you frighten him
like a locust?
His majestic snorting
strikes terror.
21 He paws in the valley, and
rejoices in *his* strength;
He gallops into the
clash of arms.
22 He mocks at fear, and
is not frightened;
Nor does he turn back
from the sword.
23 The quiver rattles
against him,
The glittering spear
and javelin.
24 He devours the distance
with fierceness and rage;
Nor does he come to
a halt because the
trumpet *has* sounded.
25 At *the blast of* the trumpet
he says, 'Aha!'
He smells the battle
from afar,
The thunder of captains
and shouting.

26 "Does the hawk fly by
your wisdom,
And spread its wings
toward the south?
27 Does the eagle mount
up at your command,
And make its nest
on high?
28 On the rock it dwells
and resides,
On the crag of the rock
and the stronghold.
29 From there it spies
out the prey;
Its eyes observe from afar.
30 Its young ones suck
up blood;
And where the slain
are, there it *is.*"

40 Moreover the LORD answered Job, and said:

2 "Shall the one who
contends with the
Almighty correct *Him?*
He who rebukes God,
let him answer it."

JOB'S RESPONSE TO GOD

3 Then Job answered the
LORD and said:

39:19 [a] Or *a mane*

4 "Behold, I am vile;
What shall I answer You?
I lay my hand over
my mouth.
5 Once I have spoken, but
I will not answer;
Yes, twice, but I will
proceed no further."

GOD'S CHALLENGE TO JOB

6Then the LORD answered
Job out of the whirlwind, and
said:

7 "Now prepare yourself
like a man;
I will question you, and
you shall answer Me:

8 "Would you indeed
annul My judgment?
Would you condemn
Me that you may
be justified?
9 Have you an arm
like God?
Or can you thunder
with a voice like His?
10 Then adorn yourself *with*
majesty and splendor,
And array yourself with
glory and beauty.
11 Disperse the rage
of your wrath;
Look on everyone
who is proud, and
humble him.
12 Look on everyone
who is proud, *and*
bring him low;
Tread down the wicked
in their place.
13 Hide them in the
dust together,
Bind their faces in
hidden *darkness.*
14 Then I will also
confess to you
That your own right
hand can save you.

15 "Look now at the
behemoth,[a] which I
made *along* with you;
He eats grass like an ox.
16 See now, his strength
is in his hips,
And his power *is* in his
stomach muscles.
17 He moves his tail
like a cedar;
The sinews of his thighs
are tightly knit.
18 His bones *are like*
beams of bronze,
His ribs like bars of iron.
19 He *is* the first of the
ways of God;
Only He who made
him can bring
near His sword.
20 Surely the mountains
yield food for him,
And all the beasts of
the field play there.
21 He lies under the
lotus trees,
In a covert of reeds
and marsh.
22 The lotus trees cover
him *with* their shade;
The willows by the
brook surround him.
23 Indeed the river may rage,

40:15 [a] A large animal, exact identity unknown

Yet he is not disturbed;
He is confident, though
the Jordan gushes
into his mouth,
24 *Though* he takes it
in his eyes,
Or one pierces *his*
nose with a snare.

41 "Can you draw
out Leviathan[a]
with a hook,
Or *snare* his tongue with
a line *which* you lower?
2 Can you put a reed
through his nose,
Or pierce his jaw
with a hook?
3 Will he make many
supplications to you?
Will he speak softly to you?
4 Will he make a
covenant with you?
Will you take him as
a servant forever?
5 Will you play with him
as *with* a bird,
Or will you leash him
for your maidens?
6 Will *your* companions
make a banquet[a]
of him?
Will they apportion him
among the merchants?
7 Can you fill his skin
with harpoons,
Or his head with
fishing spears?
8 Lay your hand on him;
Remember the battle—
Never do it again!
9 Indeed, *any* hope of
overcoming him is false;
Shall *one not* be
overwhelmed at
the sight of him?
10 No one *is so* fierce that he
would dare stir him up.
Who then is able to
stand against Me?
11 Who has preceded Me,
that I should pay *him?*
Everything under
heaven is Mine.

12 "I will not conceal[a]
his limbs,
His mighty power, or his
graceful proportions.
13 Who can remove
his outer coat?
Who can approach *him*
with a double bridle?
14 Who can open the
doors of his face,
With his terrible
teeth all around?
15 *His* rows of scales
are *his* pride,
Shut up tightly *as*
with a seal;
16 One is so near another
That no air can come
between them;
17 They are joined one
to another,
They stick together and
cannot be parted.
18 His sneezings flash
forth light,
And his eyes *are* like the
eyelids of the morning.

41:1 [a] A large sea creature, exact identity unknown **41:6** [a] Or *bargain over him* **41:12** [a] Literally *keep silent about*

19 Out of his mouth go
burning lights;
Sparks of fire shoot out.
20 Smoke goes out of
his nostrils,
As *from* a boiling pot
and burning rushes.
21 His breath kindles coals,
And a flame goes out
of his mouth.
22 Strength dwells
in his neck,
And sorrow dances
before him.
23 The folds of his flesh
are joined together;
They are firm on him
and cannot be moved.
24 His heart is as hard
as stone,
Even as hard as the
lower *millstone.*
25 When he raises
himself up, the
mighty are afraid;
Because of his crashings
they are beside[a]
themselves.
26 *Though* the sword
reaches him, it
cannot avail;
Nor does spear,
dart, or javelin.
27 He regards iron as straw,
And bronze as
rotten wood.
28 The arrow cannot
make him flee;
Slingstones become
like stubble to *him.*
29 Darts are regarded
as straw;
He laughs at the
threat of javelins.
30 His undersides *are* like
sharp potsherds;
He spreads pointed
marks in the mire.
31 He makes the deep
boil like a pot;
He makes the sea like
a pot of ointment.
32 He leaves a shining
wake behind him;
One would think the
deep had white hair.
33 On earth there is
nothing like him,
Which is made
without fear.
34 He beholds every
high *thing;*
He *is* king over all the
children of pride."

JOB'S REPENTANCE AND RESTORATION

42 Then Job answered the
LORD and said:

2 "I know that You can
do everything,
And that no purpose
of Yours can be
withheld from You.
3 *You asked,* 'Who *is* this
who hides counsel
without knowledge?'
Therefore I have
uttered what I did
not understand,
Things too wonderful
for me, which I
did not know.

41:25 [a] Or *purify themselves*

4 Listen, please, and
let me speak;
You said, 'I will question
you, and you shall
answer Me.'

5 "I have heard of You by
the hearing of the ear,
But now my eye sees You.
6 Therefore I abhor *myself,*
And repent in dust
and ashes."

7And so it was, after the
LORD had spoken these words
to Job, that the LORD said to
Eliphaz the Temanite, "My
wrath is aroused against you
and your two friends, for you
have not spoken of Me *what*
is right, as My servant Job *has.*
8Now therefore, take for yourselves seven bulls and seven
rams, go to My servant Job,
and offer up for yourselves a
burnt offering; and My servant Job shall pray for you.
For I will accept him, lest I
deal with you *according to*
your folly; because you have
not spoken of Me *what is* right,
as My servant Job *has.*"
9So Eliphaz the Temanite
and Bildad the Shuhite *and* Zophar the Naamathite went and
did as the LORD commanded
them; for the LORD had accepted Job. 10And the LORD
restored Job's losses[a] when he
prayed for his friends. Indeed
the LORD gave Job twice as
much as he had before. 11Then
all his brothers, all his sisters,
and all those who had been his
acquaintances before, came to
him and ate food with him in
his house; and they consoled
him and comforted him for
all the adversity that the LORD
had brought upon him. Each
one gave him a piece of silver
and each a ring of gold.
12Now the LORD blessed the
latter *days* of Job more than
his beginning; for he had
fourteen thousand sheep, six
thousand camels, one thousand yoke of oxen, and one
thousand female donkeys.
13He also had seven sons and
three daughters. 14And he
called the name of the first
Jemimah, the name of the
second Keziah, and the name
of the third Keren-Happuch.
15In all the land were found
no women *so* beautiful as the
daughters of Job; and their father gave them an inheritance
among their brothers.
16After this Job lived one
hundred and forty years, and
saw his children and grandchildren *for* four generations.
17So Job died, old and full of
days.

42:10 [a] Literally *Job's captivity,* that is, what was captured from Job

THE BOOK OF PSALMS

BOOK ONE

PSALMS 1–41

PSALM 1

THE WAY OF THE RIGHTEOUS AND THE END OF THE UNGODLY

1 Blessed *is* the man
Who walks not in the
counsel of the ungodly,
Nor stands in the
path of sinners,
Nor sits in the seat
of the scornful;
2 But his delight *is* in the
law of the LORD,
And in His law he
meditates day
and night.
3 He shall be like a tree
Planted by the
rivers of water,
That brings forth its
fruit in its season,
Whose leaf also
shall not wither;
And whatever he does
shall prosper.

4 The ungodly *are* not so,
But *are* like the chaff which
the wind drives away.
5 Therefore the ungodly
shall not *stand in*
the judgment,
Nor sinners in the
congregation of
the righteous.
6 For the LORD knows the
way of the righteous,
But the way of the
ungodly shall perish.

PSALM 2

THE MESSIAH'S TRIUMPH AND KINGDOM

1 Why do the nations rage,
And the people plot
a vain thing?
2 The kings of the earth
set themselves,
And the rulers take
counsel together,
Against the LORD
and against His
Anointed, *saying,*
3 "Let us break Their
bonds in pieces
And cast away Their
cords from us."

4 He who sits in the
heavens shall laugh;
The Lord shall hold
them in derision.
5 Then He shall speak to
them in His wrath,
And distress them in
His deep displeasure:
6 "Yet I have set My King
On My holy hill of Zion."

7 "I will declare the decree:
The LORD has said to Me,
'You *are* My Son,

Today I have
begotten You.
8 Ask of Me, and I
will give *You*
The nations *for* Your
inheritance,
And the ends of the earth
for Your possession.
9 You shall break[a] them
with a rod of iron;
You shall dash them
to pieces like a
potter's vessel.'"

10 Now therefore, be
wise, O kings;
Be instructed, you
judges of the earth.
11 Serve the LORD with fear,
And rejoice with
trembling.
12 Kiss the Son,[a] lest
He[b] be angry,
And you perish
in the way,
When His wrath is
kindled but a little.
Blessed *are* all those who
put their trust in Him.

PSALM 3

THE LORD HELPS HIS TROUBLED PEOPLE

A Psalm of David when he fled from Absalom his son.

1 LORD, how they have
increased who
trouble me!
Many *are* they who
rise up against me.
2 Many *are* they who
say of me,
"*There is* no help for him
in God." *Selah*

3 But You, O LORD, *are*
a shield for me,
My glory and the
One who lifts
up my head.
4 I cried to the LORD
with my voice,
And He heard me
from His holy
hill. *Selah*

5 I lay down and slept;
I awoke, for the LORD
sustained me.
6 I will not be afraid of
ten thousands of
people
Who have set *themselves*
against me all around.

7 Arise, O LORD;
Save me, O my God!
For You have struck
all my enemies on
the cheekbone;
You have broken
the teeth of the
ungodly.
8 Salvation *belongs*
to the LORD.
Your blessing *is* upon
Your people. *Selah*

2:9 [a] Following Masoretic Text and Targum; Septuagint, Syriac, and Vulgate read *rule* (compare Revelation 2:27).
2:12 [a] Septuagint and Vulgate read *Embrace discipline;* Targum reads *Receive instruction.* [b] Septuagint reads *the LORD.*

PSALM 4
THE SAFETY OF THE FAITHFUL

To the Chief Musician.
With stringed instruments.
A Psalm of David.

1 Hear me when I
call, O God of my
righteousness!
You have relieved me
in *my* distress;
Have mercy on me,
and hear my prayer.

2 How long, O you
sons of men,
Will you turn my
glory to shame?
How long will you love
worthlessness
And seek
falsehood? *Selah*
3 But know that the
LORD has set apart[a]
for Himself him
who is godly;
The LORD will hear
when I call to Him.

4 Be angry, and do not sin.
Meditate within your
heart on your bed, and
be still. *Selah*
5 Offer the sacrifices of
righteousness,
And put your trust
in the LORD.

6 *There are* many who say,
"Who will show
us *any* good?"
LORD, lift up the light
of Your countenance
upon us.
7 You have put gladness
in my heart,
More than in the season
that their grain and
wine increased.
8 I will both lie down in
peace, and sleep;
For You alone,
O LORD, make me
dwell in safety.

PSALM 5
A PRAYER FOR GUIDANCE

To the Chief Musician. With
flutes.[a] A Psalm of David.

1 Give ear to my
words, O LORD,
Consider my meditation.
2 Give heed to the
voice of my cry,
My King and my God,
For to You I will pray.
3 My voice You shall hear in
the morning, O LORD;
In the morning I will
direct *it* to You,
And I will look up.

4 For You *are* not a God
who takes pleasure
in wickedness,
Nor shall evil dwell
with You.
5 The boastful shall not
stand in Your sight;
You hate all workers
of iniquity.

4:3 [a] Many Hebrew manuscripts, Septuagint, Targum, and Vulgate read *made wonderful*. 5:title [a] Hebrew *nehiloth*

6 You shall destroy those
who speak falsehood;
The LORD abhors the
bloodthirsty and
deceitful man.

7 But as for me, I will
come into Your house
in the multitude
of Your mercy;
In fear of You I will
worship toward
Your holy temple.
8 Lead me, O LORD, in Your
righteousness because
of my
enemies;
Make Your way straight
before my face.

9 For *there is* no
faithfulness in
their mouth;
Their inward part
is destruction;
Their throat *is* an
open tomb;
They flatter with
their tongue.
10 Pronounce them
guilty, O God!
Let them fall by their
own counsels;
Cast them out in the
multitude of their
transgressions,
For they have rebelled
against You.

11 But let all those
rejoice who put
their trust in You;
Let them ever shout
for joy, because You
defend them;
Let those also who
love Your name
Be joyful in You.
12 For You, O LORD, will
bless the righteous;
With favor You will
surround him as
with a shield.

PSALM 6

A PRAYER OF FAITH IN TIME OF DISTRESS

To the Chief Musician.
With stringed instruments.
On an eight-stringed harp.[a]
A Psalm of David.

1 O LORD, do not rebuke
me in Your anger,
Nor chasten me in Your
hot displeasure.
2 Have mercy on me,
O LORD, for I *am* weak;
O LORD, heal me, for my
bones are troubled.
3 My soul also is
greatly troubled;
But You, O LORD—how
long?

4 Return, O LORD,
deliver me!
Oh, save me for Your
mercies' sake!
5 For in death *there is*
no remembrance
of You;
In the grave who will
give You thanks?

6:title [a] Hebrew *Sheminith*

6 I am weary with
my groaning;
All night I make
my bed swim;
I drench my couch
with my tears.
7 My eye wastes away
because of grief;
It grows old because
of all my enemies.

8 Depart from me, all you
workers of iniquity;
For the LORD has
heard the voice of
my weeping.
9 The LORD has heard
my supplication;
The LORD will receive
my prayer.
10 Let all my enemies
be ashamed and
greatly troubled;
Let them turn back *and*
be ashamed suddenly.

PSALM 7

PRAYER AND PRAISE FOR DELIVERANCE FROM ENEMIES

A Meditation[a] of David, which he sang to the LORD concerning the words of Cush, a Benjamite.

1 O LORD my God, in
You I put my trust;
Save me from all those
who persecute me;
And deliver me,
2 Lest they tear me
like a lion,
Rending *me* in pieces,
while *there is* none
to deliver.

3 O LORD my God, if I
have done this:
If there is iniquity
in my hands,
4 If I have repaid evil
to him who was at
peace with me,
Or have plundered
my enemy
without cause,
5 Let the enemy pursue
me and overtake *me;*
Yes, let him trample
my life to the earth,
And lay my honor in the
dust. *Selah*

6 Arise, O LORD, in
Your anger;
Lift Yourself up
because of the rage
of my enemies;
Rise up for me[a] *to* the
judgment You have
commanded!
7 So the congregation
of the peoples shall
surround You;
For their sakes, therefore,
return on high.
8 The LORD shall judge
the peoples;
Judge me, O LORD,
according to my
righteousness,
And according to my
integrity within me.

7:title [a] Hebrew *Shiggaion* 7:6 [a] Following Masoretic Text, Targum, and Vulgate; Septuagint reads *O LORD my God.*

9 Oh, let the wickedness
of the wicked
come to an end,
But establish the just;
For the righteous God tests
the hearts and minds.
10 My defense *is* of God,
Who saves the
upright in heart.

11 God *is* a just judge,
And God is angry *with
the wicked* every day.
12 If he does not turn back,
He will sharpen His sword;
He bends His bow and
makes it ready.
13 He also prepares for
Himself instruments
of death;
He makes His arrows
into fiery shafts.

14 Behold, *the wicked*
brings forth iniquity;
Yes, he conceives
trouble and brings
forth falsehood.
15 He made a pit and
dug it out,
And has fallen into the
ditch *which* he made.
16 His trouble shall return
upon his own head,
And his violent dealing
shall come down on
his own crown.

17 I will praise the LORD
according to His
righteousness,
And will sing praise
to the name of the
LORD Most High.

PSALM 8

THE GLORY OF THE LORD IN CREATION

To the Chief Musician.
On the instrument of Gath.[a]
A Psalm of David.

1 O LORD, our Lord,
How excellent *is* Your
name in all the earth,
Who have set Your glory
above the heavens!

2 Out of the mouth of babes
and nursing infants
You have ordained
strength,
Because of Your enemies,
That You may silence the
enemy and the avenger.

3 When I consider Your
heavens, the work
of Your fingers,
The moon and the
stars, which You
have ordained,
4 What is man that You
are mindful of him,[a]
And the son of man
that You visit him?
5 For You have made
him a little lower
than the angels,[a]
And You have crowned
him with glory
and honor.

8:title [a] Hebrew *Al Gittith* 8:5 [a] Hebrew *Elohim, God;* Septuagint, Syriac, Targum, and Jewish tradition translate as *angels.*

6 You have made him
to have dominion
over the works of
Your hands;
You have put all *things*
under his feet,
7 All sheep and oxen—
Even the beasts
of the field,
8 The birds of the air,
And the fish of the sea
That pass through the
paths of the seas.

9 O LORD, our Lord,
How excellent *is* Your
name in all the earth!

PSALM 9

PRAYER AND THANKSGIVING FOR THE LORD'S RIGHTEOUS JUDGMENTS

To the Chief Musician.
To *the tune of* "Death
of the Son."[a] A Psalm of David.

1 I will praise *You,* O LORD,
with my whole heart;
I will tell of all Your
marvelous works.
2 I will be glad and
rejoice in You;
I will sing praise to
Your name,
O Most High.

3 When my enemies
turn back,
They shall fall and perish
at Your presence.
4 For You have maintained
my right and my cause;
You sat on the
throne judging in
righteousness.
5 You have rebuked
the nations,
You have destroyed
the wicked;
You have blotted out their
name forever and ever.

6 O enemy, destructions
are finished forever!
And you have
destroyed cities;
Even their memory
has perished.
7 But the LORD shall
endure forever;
He has prepared His
throne for judgment.
8 He shall judge the world
in righteousness,
And He shall administer
judgment for the
peoples in uprightness.

9 The LORD also will
be a refuge for
the oppressed,
A refuge in times
of trouble.
10 And those who know
Your name will put
their trust in You;
For You, LORD, have
not forsaken those
who seek You.

11 Sing praises to the LORD,
who dwells in Zion!
Declare His deeds
among the people.

9:title [a] Hebrew *Muth Labben*

12 When He avenges blood,
He remembers them;
He does not forget the
cry of the humble.

13 Have mercy on
me, O LORD!
Consider my trouble from
those who hate me,
You who lift me up from
the gates of death,
14 That I may tell of
all Your praise
In the gates of the
daughter of Zion.
I will rejoice in
Your salvation.

15 The nations have
sunk down in the pit
which they made;
In the net which they hid,
their own foot is caught.
16 The LORD is known *by* the
judgment He executes;
The wicked is snared
in the work of his
own hands.
Meditation.[a] *Selah*

17 The wicked shall be
turned into hell,
And all the nations
that forget God.
18 For the needy shall not
always be forgotten;
The expectation of
the poor shall *not*
perish forever.

19 Arise, O LORD,
Do not let man prevail;
Let the nations be
judged in Your sight.
20 Put them in fear, O LORD,
That the nations may
know themselves
to be but men. *Selah*

PSALM 10

A SONG OF CONFIDENCE IN GOD'S TRIUMPH OVER EVIL

1 Why do You stand
afar off, O LORD?
Why do You hide in
times of trouble?
2 The wicked in *his* pride
persecutes the poor;
Let them be caught
in the plots which
they have devised.

3 For the wicked boasts
of his heart's desire;
He blesses the greedy
and renounces
the LORD.
4 The wicked in his
proud countenance
does not seek *God;*
God *is* in none of
his thoughts.

5 His ways are always
prospering;
Your judgments *are* far
above, out of his sight;
As for all his enemies,
he sneers at them.
6 He has said in his heart,
"I shall not be moved;
I shall never be in
adversity."

9:16 [a] Hebrew *Higgaion*

7 His mouth is full of
cursing and deceit
and oppression;
Under his tongue *is*
trouble and iniquity.

8 He sits in the lurking
places of the villages;
In the secret places he
murders the innocent;
His eyes are secretly
fixed on the helpless.
9 He lies in wait secretly,
as a lion in his den;
He lies in wait to
catch the poor;
He catches the poor
when he draws
him into his net.
10 So he crouches,
he lies low,
That the helpless may
fall by his strength.
11 He has said in his heart,
"God has forgotten;
He hides His face;
He will never see."

12 Arise, O LORD!
O God, lift up Your hand!
Do not forget the
humble.
13 Why do the wicked
renounce God?
He has said in his heart,
"You will not require
an account."

14 But You have seen,
for You observe
trouble and grief,
To repay *it* by Your hand.
The helpless commits
himself to You;
You are the helper of
the fatherless.
15 Break the arm of
the wicked and
the evil *man;*
Seek out his wickedness
until You find none.

16 The LORD *is* King
forever and ever;
The nations have
perished out of
His land.
17 LORD, You have heard the
desire of the humble;
You will prepare
their heart;
You will cause Your
ear to hear,
18 To do justice to the
fatherless and
the oppressed,
That the man of the earth
may oppress no more.

PSALM 11

FAITH IN THE LORD'S RIGHTEOUSNESS

To the Chief Musician.
A Psalm of David.

1 In the LORD I put
my trust;
How can you say
to my soul,
"Flee *as* a bird to your
mountain"?
2 For look! The wicked
bend *their* bow,
They make ready their
arrow on the string,
That they may shoot
secretly at the
upright in heart.

3 If the foundations
are destroyed,
What can the
righteous do?

4 The LORD *is* in His
holy temple,
The LORD's throne
is in heaven;
His eyes behold,
His eyelids test the
sons of men.
5 The LORD tests the
righteous,
But the wicked and the
one who loves violence
His soul hates.
6 Upon the wicked He
will rain coals;
Fire and brimstone
and a burning wind
Shall be the portion
of their cup.

7 For the LORD *is* righteous,
He loves righteousness;
His countenance
beholds the upright.[a]

PSALM 12

MAN'S TREACHERY AND GOD'S CONSTANCY

To the Chief Musician.
On an eight-stringed harp.[a]
A Psalm of David.

1 Help, LORD, for the
godly man ceases!
For the faithful disappear
from among the
sons of men.
2 They speak idly everyone
with his neighbor;
With flattering lips
and a double heart
they speak.

3 May the LORD cut off
all flattering lips,
And the tongue that
speaks proud things,
4 Who have said,
"With our tongue
we will prevail;
Our lips *are* our own;
Who *is* lord over us?"

5 "For the oppression
of the poor, for the
sighing of the needy,
Now I will arise,"
says the LORD;
"I will set *him* in the
safety for which
he yearns."

6 The words of the LORD
are pure words,
Like silver tried in a
furnace of earth,
Purified seven times.
7 You shall keep
them, O LORD,
You shall preserve
them from this
generation forever.

8 The wicked prowl
on every side,
When vileness is
exalted among the
sons of men.

11:7 [a] Or *The upright beholds His countenance*
12:title [a] Hebrew *Sheminith*

PSALM 13

TRUST IN THE SALVATION OF THE LORD

To the Chief Musician.
A Psalm of David.

1 How long, O LORD? Will
You forget me forever?
How long will You hide
Your face from me?
2 How long shall I take
counsel in my soul,
Having sorrow in
my heart daily?
How long will my enemy
be exalted over me?

3 Consider *and* hear me,
O LORD my God;
Enlighten my eyes,
Lest I sleep the
sleep of death;
4 Lest my enemy say,
"I have prevailed
against him";
Lest those who trouble
me rejoice when
I am moved.

5 But I have trusted
in Your mercy;
My heart shall rejoice
in Your salvation.
6 I will sing to the LORD,
Because He has dealt
bountifully with me.

PSALM 14

FOLLY OF THE GODLESS, AND GOD'S FINAL TRIUMPH

To the Chief Musician.
A Psalm of David.

1 The fool has said
in his heart,
"*There is* no God."
They are corrupt,
They have done
abominable works,
There is none who
does good.

2 The LORD looks down
from heaven upon
the children of men,
To see if there are any
who understand,
who seek God.
3 They have all
turned aside,
They have together
become corrupt;
There is none who
does good,
No, not one.

4 Have all the workers of
iniquity no knowledge,
Who eat up my people
as they eat bread,
And do not call on
the LORD?
5 There they are in
great fear,
For God *is* with the
generation of
the righteous.
6 You shame the counsel
of the poor,
But the LORD *is* his refuge.

7 Oh, that the salvation
of Israel *would*
come out of Zion!
When the LORD brings
back the captivity
of His people,
Let Jacob rejoice *and*
Israel be glad.

PSALM 15

THE CHARACTER OF THOSE WHO MAY DWELL WITH THE LORD

A Psalm of David.

1 LORD, who may abide
in Your tabernacle?
Who may dwell in
Your holy hill?

2 He who walks uprightly,
And works
righteousness,
And speaks the truth
in his heart;
3 He *who* does not backbite
with his tongue,
Nor does evil to
his neighbor,
Nor does he take up
a reproach against
his friend;
4 In whose eyes a vile
person is despised,
But he honors those
who fear the LORD;
He *who* swears to
his own hurt and
does not change;
5 He *who* does not put out
his money at usury,
Nor does he take a bribe
against the innocent.

He who does these *things*
shall never be moved.

PSALM 16

THE HOPE OF THE FAITHFUL, AND THE MESSIAH'S VICTORY

A Michtam of David.

1 Preserve me, O God, for
in You I put my trust.

2 *O my soul,* you have
said to the LORD,
"You *are* my Lord,
My goodness is nothing
apart from You."
3 As for the saints who
are on the earth,
"They are the excellent
ones, in whom is
all my delight."

4 Their sorrows shall be
multiplied who hasten
after another *god;*
Their drink offerings of
blood I will not offer,
Nor take up their
names on my lips.

5 O LORD, *You are*
the portion of
my inheritance
and my cup;
You maintain my lot.
6 The lines have fallen to
me in pleasant *places;*
Yes, I have a good
inheritance.

7 I will bless the LORD who
has given me counsel;
My heart also instructs
me in the night seasons.
8 I have set the LORD
always before me;
Because *He is* at my
right hand I shall
not be moved.

9 Therefore my heart
is glad, and my
glory rejoices;
My flesh also will
rest in hope.

10 For You will not leave
my soul in Sheol,
Nor will You allow
Your Holy One to
see corruption.
11 You will show me
the path of life;
In Your presence *is*
fullness of joy;
At Your right hand *are*
pleasures forevermore.

PSALM 17

PRAYER WITH CONFIDENCE IN FINAL SALVATION

A Prayer of David.

1 Hear a just cause, O LORD,
Attend to my cry;
Give ear to my prayer
which is not from
deceitful lips.
2 Let my vindication come
from Your presence;
Let Your eyes look on the
things that are upright.

3 You have tested my heart;
You have visited *me*
in the night;
You have tried me and
have found nothing;
I have purposed that
my mouth shall
not transgress.
4 Concerning the
works of men,
By the word of Your lips,
I have kept away from the
paths of the destroyer.
5 Uphold my steps
in Your paths,
That my footsteps
may not slip.
6 I have called upon
You, for You will
hear me, O God;
Incline Your ear to me,
and hear my speech.
7 Show Your marvelous
lovingkindness by
Your right hand,
O You who save those
who trust *in You*
From those who rise
up *against them.*
8 Keep me as the apple
of Your eye;
Hide me under the
shadow of Your wings,
9 From the wicked
who oppress me,
From my deadly enemies
who surround me.

10 They have closed up
their fat *hearts;*
With their mouths
they speak proudly.
11 They have now
surrounded us
in our steps;
They have set their
eyes, crouching
down to the earth,
12 As a lion is eager to
tear his prey,
And like a young lion
lurking in secret places.

13 Arise, O LORD,
Confront him, cast
him down;
Deliver my life from
the wicked with
Your sword,
14 With Your hand from
men, O LORD,

From men of the
world *who have* their
portion in *this* life,
And whose belly
You fill with Your
hidden treasure.
They are satisfied
with children,
And leave the rest
of their *possession*
for their babes.

15 As for me, I will see Your
face in righteousness;
I shall be satisfied when
I awake in Your
likeness.

PSALM 18

GOD THE SOVEREIGN SAVIOR

To the Chief Musician.
A *Psalm* of David the servant
of the LORD, who spoke
to the LORD the words of this
song on the day that the LORD
delivered him from the hand
of all his enemies and from
the hand of Saul. And he said:

1 I will love You, O LORD,
my strength.
2 The LORD is my rock
and my fortress
and my deliverer;
My God, my strength,
in whom I will trust;
My shield and the horn
of my salvation,
my stronghold.
3 I will call upon the
LORD, *who is worthy*
to be praised;
So shall I be saved
from my enemies.
4 The pangs of death
surrounded me,
And the floods of
ungodliness made
me afraid.
5 The sorrows of Sheol
surrounded me;
The snares of death
confronted me.
6 In my distress I called
upon the LORD,
And cried out to my God;
He heard my voice
from His temple,
And my cry came before
Him, *even* to His ears.

7 Then the earth shook
and trembled;
The foundations of
the hills also quaked
and were shaken,
Because He was angry.
8 Smoke went up from
His nostrils,
And devouring fire
from His mouth;
Coals were kindled by it.
9 He bowed the heavens
also, and came down
With darkness
under His feet.
10 And He rode upon a
cherub, and flew;
He flew upon the
wings of the wind.
11 He made darkness
His secret place;
His canopy around Him
was dark waters
And thick clouds
of the skies.
12 From the brightness
before Him,

His thick clouds passed
with hailstones
and coals of fire.

13 The LORD thundered
from heaven,
And the Most High
uttered His voice,
Hailstones and
coals of fire.[a]
14 He sent out His arrows
and scattered the foe,
Lightnings in
abundance, and He
vanquished them.
15 Then the channels of
the sea were seen,
The foundations of the
world were uncovered
At Your rebuke, O LORD,
At the blast of the breath
of Your nostrils.

16 He sent from above,
He took me;
He drew me out of
many waters.
17 He delivered me from
my strong enemy,
From those who
hated me,
For they were too
strong for me.
18 They confronted me in
the day of my calamity,
But the LORD was
my support.
19 He also brought me out
into a broad place;
He delivered me because
He delighted in me.

20 The LORD rewarded
me according to my
righteousness;
According to the
cleanness of my hands
He has recompensed me.
21 For I have kept the
ways of the LORD,
And have not wickedly
departed from my God.
22 For all His judgments
were before me,
And I did not put away
His statutes from me.
23 I was also blameless
before Him,
And I kept myself
from my iniquity.
24 Therefore the LORD
has recompensed
me according to my
righteousness,
According to the
cleanness of my
hands in His sight.

25 With the merciful You
will show Yourself
merciful;
With a blameless
man You will show
Yourself blameless;
26 With the pure You will
show Yourself pure;
And with the devious
You will show
Yourself shrewd.
27 For You will save the
humble people,
But will bring down
haughty looks.

18:13 [a] Following Masoretic Text, Targum, and Vulgate; a few Hebrew manuscripts and Septuagint omit *Hailstones and coals of fire*.

28 For You will light
my lamp;
The LORD my God
will enlighten
my darkness.
29 For by You I can run
against a troop,
By my God I can
leap over a wall.
30 *As for* God, His way
is perfect;
The word of the
LORD is proven;
He *is* a shield to all
who trust in Him.

31 For who *is* God,
except the LORD?
And who *is* a rock,
except our God?
32 *It is* God who arms
me with strength,
And makes my
way perfect.
33 He makes my feet like
the *feet of* deer,
And sets me on my
high places.
34 He teaches my hands
to make war,
So that my arms
can bend a bow
of bronze.

35 You have also given
me the shield of
Your salvation;
Your right hand has
held me up,
Your gentleness has
made me great.
36 You enlarged my
path under me,
So my feet did not slip.
37 I have pursued
my enemies and
overtaken them;
Neither did I turn
back again till they
were destroyed.
38 I have wounded them,
So that they could
not rise;
They have fallen
under my feet.
39 For You have armed
me with strength
for the battle;
You have subdued
under me those who
rose up against me.
40 You have also given
me the necks of
my enemies,
So that I destroyed
those who hated me.
41 They cried out, but *there*
was none to save;
Even to the LORD, but He
did not answer them.
42 Then I beat them
as fine as the dust
before the wind;
I cast them out like
dirt in the streets.

43 You have delivered me
from the strivings
of the people;
You have made me the
head of the nations;
A people I have not
known shall serve me.
44 As soon as they hear of
me they obey me;
The foreigners
submit to me.
45 The foreigners fade away,

And come frightened
from their hideouts.

46 The LORD lives!
Blessed *be* my Rock!
Let the God of my
salvation be exalted.
47 *It is* God who avenges me,
And subdues the
peoples under me;
48 He delivers me from
my enemies.
You also lift me up
above those who
rise against me;
You have delivered me
from the violent man.
49 Therefore I will give
thanks to You, O LORD,
among the Gentiles,
And sing praises to
Your name.

50 Great deliverance He
gives to His king,
And shows mercy to
His anointed,
To David and his
descendants
forevermore.

PSALM 19

THE PERFECT REVELATION OF THE LORD

To the Chief Musician.
A Psalm of David.

1 The heavens declare
the glory of God;
And the firmament
shows His handiwork.
2 Day unto day
utters speech,
And night unto night
reveals knowledge.
3 *There is* no speech
nor language
Where their voice
is not heard.
4 Their line[a] has gone out
through all the earth,
And their words to the
end of the world.

In them He has set a
tabernacle for the sun,
5 Which *is* like a
bridegroom coming
out of his chamber,
And rejoices like a strong
man to run its race.
6 Its rising *is* from one
end of heaven,
And its circuit to
the other end;
And there is nothing
hidden from its heat.

7 The law of the LORD *is*
perfect, converting
the soul;
The testimony of the
LORD *is* sure, making
wise the simple;
8 The statutes of the
LORD *are* right,
rejoicing the heart;
The commandment
of the LORD *is* pure,
enlightening the eyes;
9 The fear of the LORD *is*
clean, enduring forever;

19:4 [a] Septuagint, Syriac, and Vulgate read *sound;* Targum reads *business.*

The judgments of the
LORD *are* true *and*
righteous altogether.
10 More to be desired *are*
they than gold,
Yea, than much fine
gold;
Sweeter also than honey
and the honeycomb.
11 Moreover by them Your
servant is warned,
And in keeping them
there is great reward.

12 Who can understand
his errors?
Cleanse me from
secret *faults.*
13 Keep back Your
servant also from
presumptuous *sins;*
Let them not have
dominion over me.
Then I shall be blameless,
And I shall be innocent
of great transgression.

14 Let the words of my
mouth and the
meditation of my heart
Be acceptable in
Your sight,
O LORD, my strength
and my Redeemer.

PSALM 20

THE ASSURANCE OF GOD'S SAVING WORK

To the Chief Musician.
A Psalm of David.

1 May the LORD answer
you in the day
of trouble;
May the name of the God
of Jacob defend you;
2 May He send you help
from the sanctuary,
And strengthen you
out of Zion;
3 May He remember all
your offerings,
And accept your burnt
sacrifice. *Selah*

4 May He grant you
according to your
heart's *desire,*
And fulfill all your
purpose.
5 We will rejoice in
your salvation,
And in the name of
our God we will set
up *our* banners!
May the LORD fulfill
all your petitions.

6 Now I know that the LORD
saves His anointed;
He will answer him from
His holy heaven
With the saving strength
of His right hand.

7 Some *trust* in chariots,
and some in horses;
But we will remember
the name of the
LORD our God.
8 They have bowed
down and fallen;
But we have risen and
stand upright.

9 Save, LORD!
May the King answer
us when we call.

PSALM 21

JOY IN THE SALVATION OF THE LORD

To the Chief Musician.
A Psalm of David.

1 The king shall have joy in
Your strength, O LORD;
And in Your salvation how
greatly shall he rejoice!
2 You have given him
his heart's desire,
And have not withheld
the request of his
lips. *Selah*

3 For You meet him
with the blessings
of goodness;
You set a crown of pure
gold upon his head.
4 He asked life from
You, *and* You gave
it to him—
Length of days
forever and ever.
5 His glory *is* great in
Your salvation;
Honor and majesty You
have placed upon him.
6 For You have made him
most blessed forever;
You have made him
exceedingly glad with
Your presence.
7 For the king trusts
in the LORD,
And through the mercy
of the Most High he
shall not be moved.

8 Your hand will find
all Your enemies;
Your right hand will find
those who hate You.
9 You shall make them
as a fiery oven in the
time of Your anger;
The LORD shall swallow
them up in His wrath,
And the fire shall
devour them.
10 Their offspring You shall
destroy from the earth,
And their descendants
from among the
sons of men.
11 For they intended
evil against You;
They devised a plot
which they are not
able *to perform.*
12 Therefore You will make
them turn their back;
You will make ready *Your
arrows* on Your string
toward their faces.

13 Be exalted, O LORD, in
Your own strength!
We will sing and praise
Your power.

PSALM 22

THE SUFFERING, PRAISE, AND POSTERITY OF THE MESSIAH

To the Chief Musician. Set
to "The Deer of the Dawn."[a]
A Psalm of David.

1 My God, My God, why
have You forsaken Me?
Why are You so far
from helping Me,

22:title [a] Hebrew *Aijeleth Hashahar*

And from the words
of My groaning?
2 O My God, I cry in
the daytime, but
You do not hear;
And in the night season,
and am not silent.

3 But You *are* holy,
Enthroned in the
praises of Israel.
4 Our fathers trusted in You;
They trusted, and You
delivered them.
5 They cried to You, and
were delivered;
They trusted in You, and
were not ashamed.

6 But I *am* a worm,
and no man;
A reproach of men, and
despised by the people.
7 All those who see
Me ridicule Me;
They shoot out the lip, they
shake the head, *saying*,
8 "He trusted[a] in the LORD,
let Him rescue Him;
Let Him deliver Him, since
He delights in Him!"

9 But You *are* He who took
Me out of the womb;
You made Me trust *while*
on My mother's breasts.
10 I was cast upon You
from birth.
From My mother's womb
You *have been* My God.

11 Be not far from Me,
For trouble *is* near;
For *there is* none to help.

12 Many bulls have
surrounded Me;
Strong *bulls* of Bashan
have encircled Me.
13 They gape at Me *with*
their mouths,
Like a raging and
roaring lion.

14 I am poured out like water,
And all My bones
are out of joint;
My heart is like wax;
It has melted within Me.
15 My strength is dried
up like a potsherd,
And My tongue clings
to My jaws;
You have brought Me
to the dust of death.

16 For dogs have
surrounded Me;
The congregation of the
wicked has enclosed Me.
They pierced[a] My
hands and My feet;
17 I can count all My bones.
They look *and* stare at Me.
18 They divide My garments
among them,
And for My clothing
they cast lots.

19 But You, O LORD, do
not be far from Me;

22:8 [a] Septuagint, Syriac, and Vulgate read *hoped;* Targum reads *praised.* **22:16** [a] Following some Hebrew manuscripts, Septuagint, Syriac, Vulgate; Masoretic Text reads *Like a lion.*

O My Strength, hasten
to help Me!
20 Deliver Me from the sword,
My precious *life* from
the power of the dog.
21 Save Me from the
lion's mouth
And from the horns
of the wild oxen!

You have answered Me.

22 I will declare Your name
to My brethren;
In the midst of the
assembly I will
praise You.
23 You who fear the
LORD, praise Him!
All you descendants of
Jacob, glorify Him,
And fear Him, all you
offspring of Israel!
24 For He has not despised
nor abhorred the
affliction of the afflicted;
Nor has He hidden His
face from Him;
But when He cried to
Him, He heard.

25 My praise *shall be* of You
in the great assembly;
I will pay My vows before
those who fear Him.
26 The poor shall eat
and be satisfied;
Those who seek Him
will praise the LORD.
Let your heart
live forever!

27 All the ends of the world
Shall remember and
turn to the LORD,
And all the families
of the nations
Shall worship before You.[a]
28 For the kingdom
is the LORD's,
And He rules over
the nations.

29 All the prosperous
of the earth
Shall eat and worship;
All those who go
down to the dust
Shall bow before Him,
Even he who cannot
keep himself alive.

30 A posterity shall
serve Him.
It will be recounted
of the Lord to the
next generation,
31 They will come
and declare His
righteousness
to a people who
will be born,
That He has done *this*.

PSALM 23

THE LORD THE SHEPHERD OF HIS PEOPLE

A Psalm of David.

1 The LORD *is* my shepherd;
I shall not want.
2 He makes me to lie down
in green pastures;

22:27 [a] Following Masoretic Text, Septuagint, and Targum; Arabic, Syriac, and Vulgate read *Him*.

He leads me beside
the still waters.
3 He restores my soul;
He leads me in the paths
of righteousness
For His name's sake.

4 Yea, though I walk
through the valley of
the shadow of death,
I will fear no evil;
For You *are* with me;
Your rod and Your staff,
they comfort me.

5 You prepare a table before
me in the presence
of my enemies;
You anoint my
head with oil;
My cup runs over.
6 Surely goodness and
mercy shall follow me
All the days of my life;
And I will dwell[a] in the
house of the LORD
Forever.

PSALM 24

THE KING OF GLORY AND HIS KINGDOM

A Psalm of David.

1 The earth *is* the LORD's,
and all its fullness,
The world and those
who dwell therein.
2 For He has founded
it upon the seas,
And established it
upon the waters.

3 Who may ascend into
the hill of the LORD?
Or who may stand in
His holy place?
4 He who has clean hands
and a pure heart,
Who has not lifted up
his soul to an idol,
Nor sworn deceitfully.
5 He shall receive blessing
from the LORD,
And righteousness
from the God of
his salvation.
6 This *is* Jacob, the
generation of those
who seek Him,
Who seek Your
face. *Selah*

7 Lift up your heads,
O you gates!
And be lifted up, you
everlasting doors!
And the King of glory
shall come in.
8 Who *is* this King of glory?
The LORD strong
and mighty,
The LORD mighty
in battle.
9 Lift up your heads,
O you gates!
Lift up, you everlasting
doors!
And the King of glory
shall come in.
10 Who is this King of glory?
The LORD of hosts,
He *is* the King of
glory. *Selah*

23:6 [a] Following Septuagint, Syriac, Targum, and Vulgate; Masoretic Text reads *return*.

PSALM 25

A PLEA FOR DELIVERANCE AND FORGIVENESS

A Psalm of David.

1 To You, O LORD, I
lift up my soul.
2 O my God, I trust in You;
Let me not be ashamed;
Let not my enemies
triumph over me.
3 Indeed, let no one
who waits on You
be ashamed;
Let those be ashamed
who deal treacherously
without cause.

4 Show me Your
ways, O LORD;
Teach me Your paths.
5 Lead me in Your truth
and teach me,
For You *are* the God
of my salvation;
On You I wait all the day.

6 Remember, O LORD, Your
tender mercies and
Your lovingkindnesses,
For they *are* from of old.
7 Do not remember the
sins of my youth, nor
my transgressions;
According to Your mercy
remember me,
For Your goodness'
sake, O LORD.

8 Good and upright
is the LORD;
Therefore He teaches
sinners in the way.
9 The humble He
guides in justice,
And the humble He
teaches His way.
10 All the paths of the LORD
are mercy and truth,
To such as keep His
covenant and His
testimonies.
11 For Your name's
sake, O LORD,
Pardon my iniquity,
for it *is* great.

12 Who *is* the man that
fears the LORD?
Him shall He[a] teach in
the way He[b] chooses.
13 He himself shall dwell
in prosperity,
And his descendants
shall inherit the earth.
14 The secret of the
LORD *is* with those
who fear Him,
And He will show them
His covenant.
15 My eyes *are* ever
toward the LORD,
For He shall pluck my
feet out of the net.

16 Turn Yourself to me, and
have mercy on me,
For I *am* desolate
and afflicted.
17 The troubles of my
heart have enlarged;
Bring me out of
my distresses!
18 Look on my affliction
and my pain,

25:12 [a] Or *he* [b] Or *he*

And forgive all my sins.
19 Consider my enemies,
for they are many;
And they hate me
with cruel hatred.
20 Keep my soul, and
deliver me;
Let me not be ashamed,
for I put my trust in You.
21 Let integrity and
uprightness
preserve me,
For I wait for You.

22 Redeem Israel, O God,
Out of all their troubles!

PSALM 26

A PRAYER FOR DIVINE SCRUTINY AND REDEMPTION

A Psalm of David.

1 Vindicate me, O LORD,
For I have walked
in my integrity.
I have also trusted
in the LORD;
I shall not slip.
2 Examine me, O LORD,
and prove me;
Try my mind and
my heart.
3 For Your lovingkindness
is before my eyes,
And I have walked
in Your truth.
4 I have not sat with
idolatrous mortals,
Nor will I go in with
hypocrites.
5 I have hated the assembly
of evildoers,
And will not sit with
the wicked.
6 I will wash my hands
in innocence;
So I will go about Your
altar, O LORD,
7 That I may proclaim
with the voice of
thanksgiving,
And tell of all Your
wondrous works.
8 LORD, I have loved
the habitation of
Your house,
And the place where
Your glory dwells.

9 Do not gather my
soul with sinners,
Nor my life with
bloodthirsty men,
10 In whose hands *is* a
sinister scheme,
And whose right hand
is full of bribes.

11 But as for me, I will
walk in my integrity;
Redeem me and be
merciful to me.
12 My foot stands in
an even place;
In the congregations I
will bless the LORD.

PSALM 27

AN EXUBERANT DECLARATION OF FAITH

A Psalm of David.

1 The LORD *is* my light
and my salvation;
Whom shall I fear?
The LORD *is* the
strength of my life;
Of whom shall I be afraid?

2 When the wicked
came against me
To eat up my flesh,
My enemies and foes,
They stumbled and fell.
3 Though an army may
encamp against me,
My heart shall not fear;
Though war may
rise against me,
In this I *will be* confident.

4 One *thing* I have desired
of the LORD,
That will I seek:
That I may dwell in the
house of the LORD
All the days of my life,
To behold the beauty
of the LORD,
And to inquire in
His temple.
5 For in the time of
trouble
He shall hide me in
His pavilion;
In the secret place of
His tabernacle
He shall hide me;
He shall set me high
upon a rock.

6 And now my head
shall be lifted up
above my enemies
all around me;
Therefore I will offer
sacrifices of joy in
His tabernacle;
I will sing, yes, I will sing
praises to the LORD.

7 Hear, O LORD, *when* I
cry with my voice!
Have mercy also upon
me, and answer me.
8 *When You said,*
"Seek My face,"
My heart said to You,
"Your face, LORD,
I will seek."
9 Do not hide Your
face from me;
Do not turn Your servant
away in anger;
You have been my help;
Do not leave me nor
forsake me,
O God of my salvation.
10 When my father and my
mother forsake me,
Then the LORD will
take care of me.

11 Teach me Your
way, O LORD,
And lead me in a
smooth path, because
of my enemies.
12 Do not deliver me to
the will of my
adversaries;
For false witnesses have
risen against me,
And such as breathe
out violence.
13 *I would have lost*
heart, unless I
had believed
That I would see the
goodness of the LORD
In the land of the living.

14 Wait on the LORD;
Be of good courage,
And He shall strengthen
your heart;
Wait, I say, on the LORD!

PSALM 28

REJOICING IN ANSWERED PRAYER

A Psalm of David.

1 To You I will cry,
O LORD my Rock:
Do not be silent to me,
Lest, if You *are*
silent to me,
I become like those who
go down to the pit.
2 Hear the voice of my
supplications
When I cry to You,
When I lift up my
hands toward Your
holy sanctuary.

3 Do not take me away
with the wicked
And with the workers
of iniquity,
Who speak peace to
their neighbors,
But evil *is* in their hearts.
4 Give them according
to their deeds,
And according to
the wickedness of
their endeavors;
Give them according to
the work of their hands;
Render to them what
they deserve.
5 Because they do not
regard the works
of the LORD,
Nor the operation
of His hands,
He shall destroy them
And not build them up.

6 Blessed *be* the LORD,
Because He has heard
the voice of my
supplications!
7 The LORD *is* my strength
and my shield;
My heart trusted in Him,
and I am helped;
Therefore my heart
greatly rejoices,
And with my song I
will praise Him.

8 The LORD *is* their
strength,[a]
And He *is* the saving
refuge of His anointed.
9 Save Your people,
And bless Your
inheritance;
Shepherd them also,
And bear them
up forever.

PSALM 29

PRAISE TO GOD IN HIS HOLINESS AND MAJESTY

A Psalm of David.

1 Give unto the LORD,
O you mighty ones,
Give unto the LORD
glory and strength.
2 Give unto the LORD
the glory due to
His name;
Worship the LORD in the
beauty of holiness.

3 The voice of the LORD
is over the waters;

28:8 [a] Following Masoretic Text and Targum; Septuagint, Syriac, and Vulgate read *the strength of His people.*

The God of glory thunders;
The LORD *is* over
many waters.
4 The voice of the LORD
is powerful;
The voice of the LORD
is full of majesty.

5 The voice of the LORD
breaks the cedars,
Yes, the LORD splinters
the cedars of Lebanon.
6 He makes them also
skip like a calf,
Lebanon and Sirion
like a young wild ox.
7 The voice of the
LORD divides the
flames of fire.

8 The voice of the LORD
shakes the wilderness;
The LORD shakes the
Wilderness of Kadesh.
9 The voice of the
LORD makes the
deer give birth,
And strips the
forests bare;
And in His temple
everyone says, "Glory!"

10 The LORD sat *enthroned*
at the Flood,
And the LORD sits
as King forever.
11 The LORD will give
strength to His people;
The LORD will bless His
people with peace.

PSALM 30
THE BLESSEDNESS OF ANSWERED PRAYER

A Psalm. A Song
at the dedication
of the house of David.

1 I will extol You,
O LORD, for You
have lifted me up,
And have not let my
foes rejoice over me.
2 O LORD my God, I
cried out to You,
And You healed me.
3 O LORD, You brought
my soul up from
the grave;
You have kept me alive,
that I should not go
down to the pit.[a]

4 Sing praise to the LORD,
you saints of His,
And give thanks at the
remembrance of
His holy name.[a]
5 For His anger *is but*
for a moment,
His favor *is for* life;
Weeping may endure
for a night,
But joy *comes* in
the morning.

6 Now in my prosperity
I said,
"I shall never be moved."
7 LORD, by Your favor
You have made my
mountain stand strong;

30:3 [a] Following Qere and Targum; Kethib, Septuagint, Syriac, and Vulgate read *from those who descend to the pit.* **30:4** [a] Or *His holiness*

You hid Your face, *and*
I was troubled.

8 I cried out to You, O LORD;
And to the LORD I
made supplication:
9 "What profit *is there*
in my blood,
When I go down
to the pit?
Will the dust praise You?
Will it declare Your truth?
10 Hear, O LORD, and
have mercy on me;
LORD, be my helper!"

11 You have turned for
me my mourning
into dancing;
You have put off my
sackcloth and clothed
me with gladness,
12 To the end that *my* glory
may sing praise to You
and not be silent.
O LORD my God, I will give
thanks to You forever.

PSALM 31

THE LORD A FORTRESS IN ADVERSITY

To the Chief Musician.
A Psalm of David.

1 In You, O LORD, I
put my trust;
Let me never be ashamed;
Deliver me in Your
righteousness.
2 Bow down Your ear to me,
Deliver me speedily;
Be my rock of refuge,
A fortress of defense
to save me.
3 For You *are* my rock
and my fortress;
Therefore, for Your
name's sake,
Lead me and guide me.
4 Pull me out of the net
which they have
secretly laid for me,
For You *are* my strength.
5 Into Your hand I
commit my spirit;
You have redeemed me,
O LORD God of truth.

6 I have hated those who
regard useless idols;
But I trust in the LORD.
7 I will be glad and rejoice
in Your mercy,
For You have considered
my trouble;
You have known my
soul in adversities,
8 And have not shut me
up into the hand
of the enemy;
You have set my feet
in a wide place.

9 Have mercy on me,
O LORD, for I am
in trouble;
My eye wastes away
with grief,
Yes, my soul and
my body!
10 For my life is spent
with grief,
And my years
with sighing;
My strength fails because
of my iniquity,
And my bones
waste away.

11 I am a reproach among
all my enemies,
But especially among
my neighbors,
And *am* repulsive to
my acquaintances;
Those who see me
outside flee from me.
12 I am forgotten like a dead
man, out of mind;
I am like a broken vessel.
13 For I hear the slander
of many;
Fear *is* on every side;
While they take counsel
together against me,
They scheme to take
away my life.

14 But as for me, I trust
in You, O LORD;
I say, "You *are* my God."
15 My times *are* in Your hand;
Deliver me from the
hand of my enemies,
And from those who
persecute me.
16 Make Your face shine
upon Your servant;
Save me for Your
mercies' sake.
17 Do not let me be
ashamed, O LORD, for I
have called upon You;
Let the wicked be
ashamed;
Let them be silent
in the grave.
18 Let the lying lips be
put to silence,
Which speak insolent
things proudly and
contemptuously
against the righteous.
19 Oh, how great *is*
Your goodness,
Which You have laid
up for those who
fear You,
Which You have
prepared for those
who trust in You
In the presence of
the sons of men!
20 You shall hide them
in the secret place
of Your presence
From the plots of
man;
You shall keep them
secretly in a pavilion
From the strife
of tongues.

21 Blessed *be* the LORD,
For He has shown
me His marvelous
kindness in a
strong city!
22 For I said in my haste,
"I am cut off from
before Your eyes";
Nevertheless You
heard the voice of
my supplications
When I cried out to You.

23 Oh, love the LORD, all
you His saints!
For the LORD preserves
the faithful,
And fully repays the
proud person.
24 Be of good courage,
And He shall strengthen
your heart,
All you who hope
in the LORD.

PSALM 32

THE JOY OF FORGIVENESS

A *Psalm* of David.
A Contemplation.[a]

1 Blessed *is he whose*
transgression
is forgiven,
Whose sin *is* covered.
2 Blessed *is* the man to
whom the LORD does
not impute iniquity,
And in whose spirit
there is no deceit.

3 When I kept silent, my
bones grew old
Through my groaning
all the day long.
4 For day and night
Your hand was
heavy upon me;
My vitality was turned
into the drought of
summer. *Selah*
5 I acknowledged
my sin to You,
And my iniquity I
have not hidden.
I said, "I will confess
my transgressions
to the LORD,"
And You forgave
the iniquity of my
sin. *Selah*

6 For this cause everyone
who is godly shall
pray to You
In a time when You
may be found;
Surely in a flood of
great waters
They shall not come
near him.
7 You *are* my hiding place;
You shall preserve
me from trouble;
You shall surround
me with songs of
deliverance. *Selah*

8 I will instruct you and
teach you in the way
you should go;
I will guide you
with My eye.
9 Do not be like the horse
or like the mule,
Which have no
understanding,
Which must be harnessed
with bit and bridle,
Else they will not
come near you.

10 Many sorrows *shall*
be to the wicked;
But he who trusts in
the LORD, mercy
shall surround him.
11 Be glad in the LORD and
rejoice, you righteous;
And shout for joy, all
you upright in heart!

PSALM 33

THE SOVEREIGNTY OF THE LORD IN CREATION AND HISTORY

1 Rejoice in the LORD,
O you righteous!
For praise from the
upright is beautiful.

32:title [a] Hebrew *Maschil*

2 Praise the LORD
with the harp;
Make melody to Him
with an instrument
of ten strings.
3 Sing to Him a new song;
Play skillfully with
a shout of joy.

4 For the word of the
LORD *is* right,
And all His work *is*
done in truth.
5 He loves righteousness
and justice;
The earth is full of the
goodness of the LORD.

6 By the word of the LORD
the heavens were made,
And all the host of
them by the breath
of His mouth.
7 He gathers the waters
of the sea together
as a heap;[a]
He lays up the deep
in storehouses.

8 Let all the earth
fear the LORD;
Let all the inhabitants
of the world stand
in awe of Him.
9 For He spoke, and
it was *done;*
He commanded, and
it stood fast.

10 *The LORD brings*
the counsel of the
nations to nothing;
He makes the plans of the
peoples of no effect.
11 The counsel of the LORD
stands forever,
The plans of His heart
to all generations.
12 Blessed *is* the nation
whose God *is* the LORD,
The people He has
chosen as His own
inheritance.

13 The LORD looks
from heaven;
He sees all the
sons of men.
14 From the place of His
dwelling He looks
On all the inhabitants
of the earth;
15 He fashions their
hearts individually;
He considers all
their works.

16 No king *is* saved by
the multitude
of an army;
A mighty man is
not delivered by
great strength.
17 A horse *is* a vain
hope for safety;
Neither shall it
deliver *any* by its
great strength.

18 Behold, the eye of the
LORD *is* on those
who fear Him,
On those who hope
in His mercy,

33:7 [a] Septuagint, Targum, and Vulgate read *in a vessel.*

19 To deliver their soul
from death,
And to keep them
alive in famine.

20 Our soul waits for
the LORD;
He *is* our help and
our shield.
21 For our heart shall
rejoice in Him,
Because we have
trusted in His
holy name.
22 Let Your mercy, O LORD,
be upon us,
Just as we hope in You.

PSALM 34

THE HAPPINESS OF THOSE WHO TRUST IN GOD

A *Psalm* of David when he pretended madness before Abimelech, who drove him away, and he departed.

1 I will bless the LORD
at all times;
His praise *shall*
continually *be* in
my mouth.
2 My soul shall make its
boast in the LORD;
The humble shall hear
of it and be glad.
3 Oh, magnify the
LORD with me,
And let us exalt His
name together.

4 I sought the LORD,
and He heard me,
And delivered me
from all my fears.
5 They looked to Him
and were radiant,
And their faces were
not ashamed.
6 This poor man cried
out, and the LORD
heard *him*,
And saved him out of
all his troubles.
7 The angel[a] of the LORD
encamps all around
those who fear Him,
And delivers them.

8 Oh, taste and see that
the LORD *is* good;
Blessed *is* the man
who trusts in Him!
9 Oh, fear the LORD,
you His saints!
There is no want to
those who fear Him.
10 The young lions lack
and suffer hunger;
But those who seek the
LORD shall not lack
any good *thing*.

11 Come, you children,
listen to me;
I will teach you the
fear of the LORD.
12 Who *is* the man *who*
desires life,
And loves *many* days,
that he may see good?
13 Keep your tongue
from evil,
And your lips from
speaking deceit.

34:7 [a] Or *Angel*

14 Depart from evil
and do good;
Seek peace and pursue it.

15 The eyes of the LORD
are on the righteous,
And His ears *are*
open to their cry.
16 The face of the LORD
is against those
who do evil,
To cut off the
remembrance of them
from the earth.

17 *The righteous* cry out,
and the LORD hears,
And delivers them out
of all their troubles.
18 The LORD *is* near to
those who have a
broken heart,
And saves such as have
a contrite spirit.

19 Many *are* the afflictions
of the righteous,
But the LORD delivers
him out of them all.
20 He guards all his bones;
Not one of them
is broken.
21 Evil shall slay the
wicked,
And those who hate
the righteous shall
be condemned.
22 The LORD redeems the
soul of His servants,
And none of those who
trust in Him shall
be condemned.

PSALM 35

THE LORD THE AVENGER OF HIS PEOPLE

A Psalm of David.

1 Plead *my cause,* O LORD,
with those who
strive with me;
Fight against those who
fight against me.
2 Take hold of shield
and buckler,
And stand up for
my help.
3 Also draw out the
spear,
And stop those who
pursue me.
Say to my soul,
"I *am* your salvation."

4 Let those be put to
shame and brought
to dishonor
Who seek after my life;
Let those be turned
back and brought
to confusion
Who plot my hurt.
5 Let them be like chaff
before the wind,
And let the angel[a] of the
LORD chase *them.*
6 Let their way be dark
and slippery,
And let the angel of the
LORD pursue them.
7 For without cause they
have hidden their
net for me *in* a pit,
Which they have
dug without cause
for my life.

35:5 [a] Or *Angel*

8 Let destruction
come upon him
unexpectedly,
And let his net that he has
hidden catch himself;
Into that very destruction
let him fall.

9 And my soul shall be
joyful in the LORD;
It shall rejoice in
His salvation.
10 All my bones shall say,
"LORD, who *is* like You,
Delivering the poor
from him who is too
strong for him,
Yes, the poor and the
needy from him who
plunders him?"

11 Fierce witnesses rise up;
They ask me *things*
that I do not know.
12 They reward me
evil for good,
To the sorrow of my soul.
13 But as for me, when
they were sick,
My clothing *was*
sackcloth;
I humbled myself
with fasting;
And my prayer would
return to my own heart.
14 I paced about as
though *he were* my
friend *or* brother;
I bowed down heavily,
as one who mourns
for his mother.

15 But in my adversity
they rejoiced
And gathered together;
Attackers gathered
against me,
And I did not know *it;*
They tore *at me* and
did not cease;
16 With ungodly
mockers at feasts
They gnashed at me
with their teeth.

17 Lord, how long will
You look on?
Rescue me from their
destructions,
My precious *life*
from the lions.
18 I will give You thanks in
the great assembly;
I will praise You among
many people.

19 Let them not rejoice over
me who are wrongfully
my enemies;
Nor let them wink with
the eye who hate me
without a cause.
20 For they do not
speak peace,
But they devise
deceitful matters
Against *the* quiet
ones in the land.
21 They also opened their
mouth wide against me,
And said, "Aha, aha!
Our eyes have seen *it*."

22 *This* You have seen,
O LORD;
Do not keep silence.
O Lord, do not be
far from me.

23 Stir up Yourself,
and awake to my vindication,
To my cause, my God and my Lord.
24 Vindicate me, O LORD my God, according to Your righteousness;
And let them not rejoice over me.
25 Let them not say in their hearts, "Ah, so we would have it!"
Let them not say, "We have swallowed him up."

26 Let them be ashamed and brought to mutual confusion
Who rejoice at my hurt;
Let them be clothed with shame and dishonor
Who exalt themselves against me.

27 Let them shout for joy and be glad,
Who favor my righteous cause;
And let them say continually,
"Let the LORD be magnified,
Who has pleasure in the prosperity of His servant."
28 And my tongue shall speak of Your righteousness
And of Your praise all the day long.

PSALM 36

MAN'S WICKEDNESS AND GOD'S PERFECTIONS

To the Chief Musician. *A Psalm* of David the servant of the LORD.

1 An oracle within my heart concerning the transgression of the wicked:
There is no fear of God before his eyes.
2 For he flatters himself in his own eyes,
When he finds out his iniquity *and* when he hates.
3 The words of his mouth *are* wickedness and deceit;
He has ceased to be wise *and* to do good.
4 He devises wickedness on his bed;
He sets himself in a way *that is* not good;
He does not abhor evil.

5 Your mercy, O LORD, *is* in the heavens;
Your faithfulness *reaches* to the clouds.
6 Your righteousness *is* like the great mountains;
Your judgments *are* a great deep;
O LORD, You preserve man and beast.

7 How precious *is* Your lovingkindness, O God!
Therefore the children of men put their trust under the shadow of Your wings.

8 They are abundantly
satisfied with the
fullness of Your house,
And You give them
drink from the river
of Your pleasures.
9 For with You *is* the
fountain of life;
In Your light we see light.

10 Oh, continue Your
lovingkindness to
those who know You,
And Your righteousness
to the upright in heart.
11 Let not the foot of pride
come against me,
And let not the hand
of the wicked
drive me away.
12 There the workers of
iniquity have fallen;
They have been cast
down and are not
able to rise.

PSALM 37

THE HERITAGE OF THE RIGHTEOUS AND THE CALAMITY OF THE WICKED

A Psalm of David.

1 Do not fret because
of evildoers,
Nor be envious of the
workers of iniquity.
2 For they shall soon be cut
down like the grass,
And wither as the
green herb.

3 Trust in the LORD,
and do good;
Dwell in the land,
and feed on His
faithfulness.
4 Delight yourself also
in the LORD,
And He shall give you the
desires of your heart.

5 Commit your way
to the LORD,
Trust also in Him,
And He shall bring
it to pass.
6 He shall bring forth
your righteousness
as the light,
And your justice as
the noonday.

7 Rest in the LORD, and
wait patiently for Him;
Do not fret because of
him who prospers
in his way,
Because of the man
who brings wicked
schemes to pass.
8 Cease from anger, and
forsake wrath;
Do not fret—*it* only
causes harm.

9 For evildoers shall
be cut off;
But those who wait
on the LORD,
They shall inherit
the earth.
10 For yet a little while
and the wicked
shall be no *more;*
Indeed, you will look
carefully for his place,
But it *shall be* no *more.*

11 But the meek shall
inherit the earth,
And shall delight
themselves in the
abundance of peace.

12 The wicked plots
against the just,
And gnashes at him
with his teeth.
13 The Lord laughs at him,
For He sees that his
day is coming.
14 The wicked have
drawn the sword
And have bent their bow,
To cast down the
poor and needy,
To slay those who are
of upright conduct.
15 Their sword shall enter
their own heart,
And their bows shall
be broken.

16 A little that a righteous
man has
Is better than the riches
of many wicked.
17 For the arms of the
wicked shall be broken,
But the LORD upholds
the righteous.

18 The LORD knows the
days of the upright,
And their inheritance
shall be forever.
19 They shall not be ashamed
in the evil time,
And in the days of famine
they shall be satisfied.
20 But the wicked
shall perish;
And the enemies
of the LORD,
Like the splendor of the
meadows, shall vanish.
Into smoke they shall
vanish away.

21 The wicked borrows
and does not repay,
But the righteous shows
mercy and gives.
22 For *those* blessed by Him
shall inherit the earth,
But *those* cursed by
Him shall be cut off.

23 The steps of a *good*
man are ordered
by the LORD,
And He delights
in his way.
24 Though he fall, he
shall not be utterly
cast down;
For the LORD upholds
him with His hand.

25 I have been young,
and *now* am old;
Yet I have not seen the
righteous forsaken,
Nor his descendants
begging bread.
26 *He is* ever merciful,
and lends;
And his descendants
are blessed.

27 Depart from evil,
and do good;
And dwell forevermore.
28 For the LORD loves justice,
And does not forsake
His saints;

They are preserved
forever,
But the descendants
of the wicked
shall be cut off.
29 The righteous shall
inherit the land,
And dwell in it forever.

30 The mouth of the
righteous speaks
wisdom,
And his tongue
talks of justice.
31 The law of his God
is in his heart;
None of his steps
shall slide.

32 The wicked watches
the righteous,
And seeks to slay him.
33 The LORD will not leave
him in his hand,
Nor condemn him
when he is judged.

34 Wait on the LORD,
And keep His way,
And He shall exalt you
to inherit the land;
When the wicked are cut
off, you shall see *it*.
35 I have seen the wicked
in great power,
And spreading himself
like a native green tree.
36 Yet he passed away,[a] and
behold, he *was* no *more;*
Indeed I sought him, but
he could not be found.

37 Mark the blameless *man,*
and observe the upright;
For the future of *that*
man *is* peace.
38 But the transgressors
shall be destroyed
together;
The future of the wicked
shall be cut off.

39 But the salvation of
the righteous *is*
from the LORD;
He is their strength in
the time of trouble.
40 And the LORD shall help
them and deliver them;
He shall deliver them
from the wicked,
And save them,
Because they trust
in Him.

PSALM 38

PRAYER IN TIME OF CHASTENING

A Psalm of David. To bring to remembrance.

1 O LORD, do not rebuke
me in Your wrath,
Nor chasten me in Your
hot displeasure!
2 For Your arrows
pierce me deeply,
And Your hand
presses me down.

3 *There is* no soundness
in my flesh
Because of Your anger,

37:36 [a] Following Masoretic Text, Septuagint, and Targum; Syriac and Vulgate read *I passed by*.

Nor *any* health in
my bones
Because of my sin.
4 For my iniquities have
gone over my head;
Like a heavy burden they
are too heavy for me.
5 My wounds are foul
and festering
Because of my
foolishness.

6 I am troubled, I am
bowed down greatly;
I go mourning all
the day long.
7 For my loins are full
of inflammation,
And *there is* no
soundness in my flesh.
8 I am feeble and
severely broken;
I groan because of the
turmoil of my heart.

9 Lord, all my desire
is before You;
And my sighing is not
hidden from You.
10 My heart pants, my
strength fails me;
As for the light of
my eyes, it also has
gone from me.

11 My loved ones and my
friends stand aloof
from my plague,
And my relatives
stand afar off.
12 Those also who seek my
life lay snares *for me;*
Those who seek my hurt
speak of destruction,
And plan deception
all the day long.

13 But I, like a deaf *man,*
do not hear;
And *I am* like a mute
who does not open
his mouth.
14 Thus I am like a man
who does not hear,
And in whose mouth
is no response.

15 For in You, O LORD,
I hope;
You will hear, O Lord
my God.
16 For I said, "*Hear me,* lest
they rejoice over me,
Lest, when my foot slips,
they exalt *themselves*
against me."

17 For I *am* ready to fall,
And my sorrow *is*
continually before me.
18 For I will declare
my iniquity;
I will be in anguish
over my sin.
19 But my enemies
are vigorous, *and*
they are strong;
And those who hate
me wrongfully
have multiplied.
20 Those also who render
evil for good,
They are my adversaries,
because I follow
what is good.

21 Do not forsake
me, O LORD;

O my God, be not
far from me!
22 Make haste to help me,
O Lord, my salvation!

PSALM 39

PRAYER FOR WISDOM AND FORGIVENESS

To the Chief Musician.
To Jeduthun. A Psalm of David.

1 I said, "I will guard
my ways,
Lest I sin with my tongue;
I will restrain my mouth
with a muzzle,
While the wicked
are before me."
2 I was mute with silence,
I held my peace *even*
from good;
And my sorrow was
stirred up.
3 My heart was hot
within me;
While I was musing,
the fire burned.
Then I spoke with
my tongue:

4 "LORD, make me to
know my end,
And what *is* the measure
of my days,
That I may know
how frail I *am*.
5 Indeed, You have
made my days *as*
handbreadths,
And my age *is* as
nothing before You;
Certainly every man at
his best state *is* but
vapor. *Selah*

6 Surely every man walks
about like a shadow;
Surely they busy
themselves in vain;
He heaps up *riches,*
And does not know who
will gather them.

7 "And now, Lord, what
do I wait for?
My hope *is* in You.
8 Deliver me from all
my transgressions;
Do not make me the
reproach of the foolish.
9 I was mute, I did not
open my mouth,
Because it was You
who did *it*.
10 Remove Your plague
from me;
I am consumed by the
blow of Your hand.
11 When with rebukes
You correct man
for iniquity,
You make his beauty
melt away like a moth;
Surely every man *is*
vapor. *Selah*

12 "Hear my prayer, O LORD,
And give ear to my cry;
Do not be silent
at my tears;
For I *am* a stranger
with You,
A sojourner, as all
my fathers *were*.
13 Remove Your gaze
from me, that I may
regain strength,
Before I go away and
am no more."

PSALM 40

FAITH PERSEVERING IN TRIAL

To the Chief Musician.
A Psalm of David.

1 I waited patiently
for the LORD;
And He inclined to me,
And heard my cry.
2 He also brought me up
out of a horrible pit,
Out of the miry clay,
And set my feet
upon a rock,
And established my steps.
3 He has put a new song
in my mouth—
Praise to our God;
Many will see *it* and fear,
And will trust in the LORD.

4 Blessed *is* that man
who makes the
LORD his trust,
And does not respect
the proud, nor such
as turn aside to lies.
5 Many, O LORD my God, *are*
Your wonderful works
Which You have done;
And Your thoughts
toward us
Cannot be recounted
to You in order;
If I would declare and
speak *of them,*
They are more than
can be numbered.

6 Sacrifice and offering
You did not desire;
My ears You have opened.
Burnt offering and
sin offering You
did not require.
7 Then I said, "Behold,
I come;
In the scroll of the book
it is written of me.
8 I delight to do Your
will, O my God,
And Your law *is*
within my heart."

9 I have proclaimed
the good news of
righteousness
In the great assembly;
Indeed, I do not
restrain my lips,
O LORD, You
Yourself know.
10 I have not hidden
Your righteousness
within my heart;
I have declared Your
faithfulness and
Your salvation;
I have not concealed
Your lovingkindness
and Your truth
From the great assembly.

11 Do not withhold Your
tender mercies
from me, O LORD;
Let Your lovingkindness
and Your truth
continually
preserve me.
12 For innumerable evils
have surrounded me;
My iniquities have
overtaken me, so that I
am not able to look up;
They are more than the
hairs of my head;
Therefore my heart
fails me.

13 Be pleased, O LORD,
to deliver me;
O LORD, make haste
to help me!
14 Let them be ashamed
and brought to
mutual confusion
Who seek to destroy
my life;
Let them be driven
backward and
brought to dishonor
Who wish me evil.
15 Let them be confounded
because of their shame,
Who say to me, "Aha, aha!"

16 Let all those who seek
You rejoice and
be glad in You;
Let such as love Your
salvation say continually,
"The LORD be magnified!"
17 But I *am* poor and needy;
Yet the LORD thinks
upon me.
You *are* my help and
my deliverer;
Do not delay, O my God.

PSALM 41

THE BLESSING AND SUFFERING OF THE GODLY

To the Chief Musician.
A Psalm of David.

1 Blessed *is* he who
considers the poor;
The LORD will deliver
him in time of trouble.
2 The LORD will preserve
him and keep him alive,
And he will be blessed
on the earth;
You will not deliver him to
the will of his enemies.
3 The LORD will strengthen
him on his bed of illness;
You will sustain him
on his sickbed.

4 I said, "LORD, be
merciful to me;
Heal my soul, for I have
sinned against You."
5 My enemies speak
evil of me:
"When will he die, and
his name perish?"
6 And if he comes to see
me, he speaks lies;
His heart gathers
iniquity to itself;
When he goes out,
he tells *it.*

7 All who hate me whisper
together against me;
Against me they
devise my hurt.
8 "An evil disease," *they
say,* "clings to him.
And *now* that he lies down,
he will rise up no more."
9 Even my own familiar
friend in whom
I trusted,
Who ate my bread,
Has lifted up *his* heel
against me.

10 But You, O LORD, be
merciful to me,
and raise me up,
That I may repay them.
11 By this I know
that You are well
pleased with me,

Because my enemy does
not triumph over me.
12 As for me, You uphold
me in my integrity,
And set me before
Your face forever.

13 Blessed *be* the LORD
God of Israel
From everlasting
to everlasting!
Amen and Amen.

BOOK TWO

PSALMS 42–72

PSALM 42

YEARNING FOR GOD IN THE MIDST OF DISTRESSES

To the Chief Musician.
A Contemplation[a]
of the sons of Korah.

1 As the deer pants for
the water brooks,
So pants my soul
for You, O God.
2 My soul thirsts for God,
for the living God.
When shall I come and
appear before God?[a]
3 My tears have been my
food day and night,
While they continually
say to me,
"Where *is* your God?"
4 When I remember
these *things*,
I pour out my soul
within me.
For I used to go with
the multitude;
I went with them to
the house of God,
With the voice of
joy and praise,
With a multitude that
kept a pilgrim feast.

5 Why are you cast
down, O my soul?
And *why* are you
disquieted within me?
Hope in God, for I shall
yet praise Him
For the help of His
countenance.[a]

6 O my God,[a] my soul is
cast down within me;
Therefore I will
remember You from
the land of the Jordan,
And from the heights
of Hermon,
From the Hill Mizar.
7 Deep calls unto deep at the
noise of Your waterfalls;
All Your waves and billows
have gone over me.
8 The LORD will command
His lovingkindness
in the daytime,

42:title [a] Hebrew *Maschil* **42:2** [a] Following Masoretic Text and Vulgate; some Hebrew manuscripts, Septuagint, Syriac, and Targum read *I see the face of God.* **42:5** [a] Following Masoretic Text and Targum; a few Hebrew manuscripts, Septuagint, Syriac, and Vulgate read *The help of my countenance, my God.* **42:6** [a] Following Masoretic Text and Targum; a few Hebrew manuscripts, Septuagint, Syriac, and Vulgate put *my God* at the end of verse 5.

And in the night His song
shall be with me—
A prayer to the God
of my life.

9 I will say to God my Rock,
"Why have You
forgotten me?
Why do I go mourning
because of the
oppression of
the enemy?"
10 *As* with a breaking
of my bones,
My enemies reproach me,
While they say to
me all day long,
"Where *is* your God?"

11 Why are you cast
down, O my soul?
And why are you
disquieted within me?
Hope in God;
For I shall yet praise Him,
The help of my
countenance
and my God.

PSALM 43

PRAYER TO GOD IN TIME OF TROUBLE

1 Vindicate me, O God,
And plead my
cause against an
ungodly nation;
Oh, deliver me from
the deceitful and
unjust man!
2 For You *are* the God
of my strength;
Why do You cast me off?
Why do I go mourning
because of the
oppression of
the enemy?

3 Oh, send out Your light
and Your truth!
Let them lead me;
Let them bring me
to Your holy hill
And to Your tabernacle.
4 Then I will go to the
altar of God,
To God my exceeding joy;
And on the harp I
will praise You,
O God, my God.

5 Why are you cast
down, O my soul?
And why are you
disquieted within me?
Hope in God;
For I shall yet praise Him,
The help of my
countenance
and my God.

PSALM 44

REDEMPTION REMEMBERED IN PRESENT DISHONOR

To the Chief Musician.
A Contemplation[a]
of the sons of Korah.

1 We have heard with
our ears, O God,
Our fathers have told us,
The deeds You did
in their days,
In days of old:

44:title [a] Hebrew *Maschil*

2 You drove out the nations
with Your hand,
But them You planted;
You afflicted the peoples,
and cast them out.
3 For they did not gain
possession of the land
by their own sword,
Nor did their own
arm save them;
But it was Your right
hand, Your arm, and
the light of Your
countenance,
Because You
favored them.

4 You are my King, O God;[a]
Command[b] victories
for Jacob.
5 Through You we will push
down our enemies;
Through Your name we
will trample those who
rise up against us.
6 For I will not trust
in my bow,
Nor shall my sword
save me.
7 But You have saved us
from our enemies,
And have put to shame
those who hated us.
8 In God we boast
all day long,
And praise Your name
forever. *Selah*

9 But You have cast *us* off
and put us to shame,
And You do not go out
with our armies.
10 You make us turn back
from the enemy,
And those who hate
us have taken spoil
for themselves.
11 You have given us up like
sheep *intended* for food,
And have scattered us
among the nations.
12 You sell Your people
for *next to* nothing,
And are not enriched
by selling them.

13 You make us a reproach
to our neighbors,
A scorn and a derision to
those all around us.
14 You make us a byword
among the nations,
A shaking of the head
among the peoples.
15 My dishonor *is*
continually before me,
And the shame of my
face has covered me,
16 Because of the voice of
him who reproaches
and reviles,
Because of the enemy
and the avenger.

17 All this has come
upon us;
But we have not
forgotten You,
Nor have we dealt falsely
with Your covenant.

44:4 [a] Following Masoretic Text and Targum; Septuagint and Vulgate read *and my God*. [b] Following Masoretic Text and Targum; Septuagint, Syriac, and Vulgate read *Who commands*.

18 Our heart has not
turned back,
Nor have our steps
departed from
Your way;
19 But You have severely
broken us in the
place of jackals,
And covered us with
the shadow of death.

20 If we had forgotten
the name of our
God,
Or stretched out our
hands to a foreign
god,
21 Would not God
search this out?
For He knows the
secrets of the heart.
22 Yet for Your sake we are
killed all day long;
We are accounted
as sheep for the
slaughter.

23 Awake! Why do You
sleep, O Lord?
Arise! Do not cast
us off forever.
24 Why do You hide
Your face,
And forget our affliction
and our oppression?
25 For our soul is bowed
down to the dust;
Our body clings to
the ground.
26 Arise for our help,
And redeem us for
Your mercies' sake.

PSALM 45

THE GLORIES OF THE MESSIAH AND HIS BRIDE

To the Chief Musician.
Set to "The Lilies."[a]
A Contemplation[b] of the sons
of Korah. A Song of Love.

1 My heart is overflowing
with a good theme;
I recite my composition
concerning the King;
My tongue *is* the pen
of a ready writer.

2 You are fairer than
the sons of men;
Grace is poured
upon Your lips;
Therefore God has
blessed You forever.
3 Gird Your sword
upon *Your* thigh,
O Mighty One,
With Your glory and
Your majesty.
4 And in Your majesty
ride prosperously
because of truth,
humility, *and*
righteousness;
And Your right hand
shall teach You
awesome things.
5 Your arrows *are* sharp
in the heart of the
King's enemies;
The peoples fall
under You.

6 Your throne, O God, *is*
forever and ever;

45:title [a] Hebrew *Shoshannim* [b] Hebrew *Maschil*

A scepter of righteousness
is the scepter of
Your kingdom.
7 You love righteousness
and hate wickedness;
Therefore God, Your God,
has anointed You
With the oil of gladness
more than Your
companions.
8 All Your garments *are*
scented with myrrh
and aloes *and* cassia,
Out of the ivory palaces,
by which they have
made You glad.
9 Kings' daughters
are among Your
honorable women;
At Your right hand
stands the queen in
gold from Ophir.

10 Listen, O daughter,
Consider and incline
your ear;
Forget your own
people also, and your
father's house;
11 So the King will greatly
desire your beauty;
Because He *is* your
Lord, worship Him.
12 And the daughter of Tyre
will come with a gift;
The rich among the
people will seek
your favor.

13 The royal daughter *is*
all glorious within
the palace;
Her clothing *is* woven
with gold.
14 She shall be brought
to the King in robes
of many colors;
The virgins, her
companions who
follow her, shall be
brought to You.
15 With gladness and
rejoicing they shall
be brought;
They shall enter the
King's palace.

16 Instead of Your fathers
shall be Your sons,
Whom You shall make
princes in all the earth.
17 I will make Your name
to be remembered
in all generations;
Therefore the people
shall praise You
forever and ever.

PSALM 46

GOD THE REFUGE OF HIS PEOPLE AND CONQUEROR OF THE NATIONS

To the Chief Musician.
A Psalm of the sons of Korah.
A Song for Alamoth.

1 God *is* our refuge
and strength,
A very present help
in trouble.
2 Therefore we will not fear,
Even though the earth
be removed,
And though the
mountains be carried
into the midst of the sea;
3 *Though* its waters roar
and be troubled,

Though the mountains
shake with its swelling.
Selah

4 *There is* a river whose
streams shall make
glad the city of God,
The holy *place* of
the tabernacle of
the Most High.
5 God *is* in the midst
of her, she shall
not be moved;
God shall help her, just
at the break of dawn.
6 The nations raged,
the kingdoms
were moved;
He uttered His voice,
the earth melted.

7 The LORD of hosts
is with us;
The God of Jacob *is* our
refuge. *Selah*

8 Come, behold the
works of the LORD,
Who has made
desolations in
the earth.
9 He makes wars cease to
the end of the earth;
He breaks the bow and
cuts the spear in two;
He burns the chariot
in the fire.

10 Be still, and know
that I *am* God;
I will be exalted among
the nations,
I will be exalted
in the earth!
11 The LORD of hosts
is with us;
The God of Jacob *is*
our refuge. *Selah*

PSALM 47

PRAISE TO GOD, THE RULER OF THE EARTH

To the Chief Musician. A Psalm of the sons of Korah.

1 Oh, clap your hands,
all you peoples!
Shout to God with the
voice of triumph!
2 For the LORD Most
High *is* awesome;
He is a great King
over all the earth.
3 He will subdue the
peoples under us,
And the nations
under our feet.
4 He will choose our
inheritance for us,
The excellence of
Jacob whom He
loves. *Selah*

5 God has gone up
with a shout,
The LORD with the
sound of a trumpet.
6 Sing praises to God,
sing praises!
Sing praises to our
King, sing praises!
7 For God *is* the King
of all the earth;
Sing praises with
understanding.

8 God reigns over
the nations;

God sits on His
holy throne.
9 The princes of the
people have
gathered together,
The people of the
God of Abraham.
For the shields of the
earth *belong* to God;
He is greatly exalted.

PSALM 48

THE GLORY OF GOD IN ZION

A Song. A Psalm
of the sons of Korah.

1 Great *is* the LORD, and
greatly to be praised
In the city of our God,
In His holy mountain.
2 Beautiful in elevation,
The joy of the
whole earth,
Is Mount Zion *on* the
sides of the north,
The city of the great King.
3 God *is* in her palaces;
He is known as
her refuge.

4 For behold, the kings
assembled,
They passed by together.
5 They saw *it, and* so
they marveled;
They were troubled,
they hastened away.
6 Fear took hold of
them there,
And pain, as of a woman
in birth pangs,
7 *As when* You break the
ships of Tarshish
With an east wind.

8 As we have heard,
So we have seen
In the city of the
LORD of hosts,
In the city of our God:
God will establish it
forever. *Selah*

9 We have thought,
O God, on Your
lovingkindness,
In the midst of
Your temple.
10 According to Your
name, O God,
So *is* Your praise to the
ends of the earth;
Your right hand is full
of righteousness.
11 Let Mount Zion rejoice,
Let the daughters of
Judah be glad,
Because of Your
judgments.

12 Walk about Zion,
And go all around her.
Count her towers;
13 Mark well her bulwarks;
Consider her palaces;
That you may tell *it* to
the generation
following.
14 For this *is* God,
Our God forever and ever;
He will be our guide
Even to death.[a]

48:14 [a] Following Masoretic Text and Syriac; Septuagint and Vulgate read *Forever*.

PSALM 49
THE CONFIDENCE OF THE FOOLISH

To the Chief Musician. A Psalm of the sons of Korah.

1 Hear this, all peoples;
Give ear, all inhabitants of the world,
2 Both low and high,
Rich and poor together.
3 My mouth shall speak wisdom,
And the meditation of my heart *shall give* understanding.
4 I will incline my ear to a proverb;
I will disclose my dark saying on the harp.

5 Why should I fear in the days of evil,
When the iniquity at my heels surrounds me?
6 Those who trust in their wealth
And boast in the multitude of their riches,
7 None *of them* can by any means redeem *his* brother,
Nor give to God a ransom for him—
8 For the redemption of their souls *is* costly,
And it shall cease forever—
9 That he should continue to live eternally,
And not see the Pit.
10 For he sees wise men die;
Likewise the fool and the senseless person perish,
And leave their wealth to others.
11 Their inner thought *is that* their houses *will last* forever,[a]
Their dwelling places to all generations;
They call *their* lands after their own names.
12 Nevertheless man, *though* in honor, does not remain;[a]
He is like the beasts *that* perish.

13 This is the way of those who *are* foolish,
And of their posterity who approve their sayings. *Selah*
14 Like sheep they are laid in the grave;
Death shall feed on them;
The upright shall have dominion over them in the morning;
And their beauty shall be consumed in the grave, far from their dwelling.
15 But God will redeem my soul from the power of the grave,
For He shall receive me. *Selah*

49:11 [a] Septuagint, Syriac, Targum, and Vulgate read *Their graves shall be their houses forever.* 49:12 [a] Following Masoretic Text and Targum; Septuagint, Syriac, and Vulgate read *understand* (compare verse 20).

16 Do not be afraid when
one becomes rich,
When the glory of his
house is increased;
17 For when he dies he shall
carry nothing away;
His glory shall not
descend after him.
18 Though while he lives
he blesses himself
(For *men* will praise
you when you do
well for yourself),
19 He shall go to the
generation of
his fathers;
They shall never see light.
20 A man *who is* in
honor, yet does
not understand,
Is like the beasts
that perish.

PSALM 50

GOD THE RIGHTEOUS JUDGE

A Psalm of Asaph.

1 The Mighty One,
God the LORD,
Has spoken and
called the earth
From the rising of the
sun to its going down.
2 Out of Zion, the
perfection of beauty,
God will shine forth.
3 Our God shall come,
and shall not
keep silent;
A fire shall devour
before Him,
And it shall be very
tempestuous all
around Him.
4 He shall call to the
heavens from above,
And to the earth, that
He may judge
His people:
5 "Gather My saints
together to Me,
Those who have made
a covenant with
Me by sacrifice."
6 Let the heavens declare
His righteousness,
For God Himself *is*
Judge. *Selah*

7 "Hear, O My people,
and I will speak,
O Israel, and I will
testify against you;
I *am* God, your God!
8 I will not rebuke you
for your sacrifices
Or your burnt offerings,
Which are continually
before Me.
9 I will not take a bull
from your house,
Nor goats out of
your folds.
10 For every beast of the
forest *is* Mine,
And the cattle on a
thousand hills.
11 I know all the birds of
the mountains,
And the wild beasts of
the field *are* Mine.

12 "If I were hungry, I
would not tell you;
For the world *is* Mine,
and all its fullness.
13 Will I eat the flesh
of bulls,

Or drink the blood
of goats?
14 Offer to God
thanksgiving,
And pay your vows to
the Most High.
15 Call upon Me in the
day of trouble;
I will deliver you, and
you shall glorify Me."

16 But to the wicked
God says:
"What *right* have you to
declare My statutes,
Or take My covenant
in your mouth,
17 Seeing you hate
instruction
And cast My words
behind you?
18 When you saw a thief,
you consented[a]
with him,
And have been a partaker
with adulterers.
19 You give your
mouth to evil,
And your tongue
frames deceit.
20 You sit *and* speak
against your brother;
You slander your own
mother's son.
21 These *things* you
have done, and
I kept silent;
You thought that I was
altogether like you;
But I will rebuke you,
And set *them* in order
before your eyes.

22 "Now consider this, you
who forget God,
Lest I tear *you* in pieces,
And *there be* none
to deliver:
23 Whoever offers praise
glorifies Me;
And to him who orders
his conduct *aright*
I will show the
salvation of God."

PSALM 51

A PRAYER OF REPENTANCE

To the Chief Musician.
A Psalm of David when Nathan
the prophet went to him,
after he had gone
in to Bathsheba.

1 Have mercy upon
me, O God,
According to Your
lovingkindness;
According to the
multitude of Your
tender mercies,
Blot out my
transgressions.
2 Wash me thoroughly
from my iniquity,
And cleanse me
from my sin.

3 For I acknowledge my
transgressions,
And my sin *is* always
before me.
4 Against You, You only,
have I sinned,
And done *this* evil
in Your sight—

50:18 [a] Septuagint, Syriac, Targum, and Vulgate read *ran*.

That You may be found
just when You speak,[a]
And blameless when
You judge.

5 Behold, I was brought
forth in iniquity,
And in sin my mother
conceived me.
6 Behold, You desire
truth in the
inward parts,
And in the hidden *part*
You will make me
to know wisdom.

7 Purge me with hyssop,
and I shall be clean;
Wash me, and I shall be
whiter than snow.
8 Make me hear joy
and gladness,
That the bones You have
broken may rejoice.
9 Hide Your face
from my sins,
And blot out all
my iniquities.

10 Create in me a clean
heart, O God,
And renew a steadfast
spirit within me.
11 Do not cast me away
from Your presence,
And do not take Your
Holy Spirit from me.

12 Restore to me the joy
of Your salvation,
And uphold me *by Your*
generous Spirit.
13 *Then* I will teach
transgressors
Your ways,
And sinners shall be
converted to You.

14 Deliver me from the
guilt of bloodshed,
O God,
The God of my salvation,
And my tongue shall
sing aloud of Your
righteousness.
15 O Lord, open my lips,
And my mouth shall
show forth Your
praise.
16 For You do not desire
sacrifice, or else I
would give *it;*
You do not delight in
burnt offering.
17 The sacrifices of God
are a broken spirit,
A broken and a
contrite heart—
These, O God, You
will not despise.

18 Do good in Your good
pleasure to Zion;
Build the walls of
Jerusalem.
19 Then You shall be
pleased with
the sacrifices of
righteousness,
With burnt offering
and whole burnt
offering;
Then they shall offer
bulls on Your altar.

51:4 [a] Septuagint, Targum, and Vulgate read *in Your words.*

PSALM 52

THE END OF THE WICKED AND THE PEACE OF THE GODLY

To the Chief Musician.
A Contemplation[a] of David when Doeg the Edomite went and told Saul, and said to him, "David has gone to the house of Ahimelech."

1 Why do you boast in
evil, O mighty man?
The goodness of God
endures continually.
2 Your tongue devises
destruction,
Like a sharp razor,
working deceitfully.
3 You love evil more
than good,
Lying rather than speaking
righteousness. *Selah*
4 You love all devouring
words,
You deceitful tongue.

5 God shall likewise
destroy you forever;
He shall take you away,
and pluck you out of
your dwelling place,
And uproot you from the
land of the living. *Selah*
6 The righteous also
shall see and fear,
And shall laugh at
him, *saying,*
7 "Here is the man *who*
did not make God
his strength,
But trusted in the
abundance of
his riches,
And strengthened himself
in his wickedness."

8 But I *am* like a green
olive tree in the
house of God;
I trust in the mercy of
God forever and ever.
9 I will praise You forever,
Because You have done *it;*
And in the presence
of Your saints
I will wait on Your
name, for *it is* good.

PSALM 53

FOLLY OF THE GODLESS, AND THE RESTORATION OF ISRAEL

To the Chief Musician.
Set to "Mahalath."
A Contemplation[a] of David.

1 The fool has said
in his heart,
"*There is* no God."
They are corrupt,
and have done
abominable iniquity;
There is none who
does good.

2 God looks down from
heaven upon the
children of men,
To see if there are *any*
who understand,
who seek God.
3 Every one of them
has turned aside;
They have together
become corrupt;

52:title [a] Hebrew *Maschil* 53:title [a] Hebrew *Maschil*

There is none who
does good,
No, not one.

4 Have the workers of
iniquity no knowledge,
Who eat up my people
as they eat bread,
And do not call
upon God?
5 There they are in
great fear
Where no fear was,
For God has scattered
the bones of him who
encamps against you;
You have put *them*
to shame,
Because God has
despised them.

6 Oh, that the salvation
of Israel would
come out of Zion!
When God brings back the
captivity of His people,
Let Jacob rejoice *and*
Israel be glad.

PSALM 54

ANSWERED PRAYER FOR DELIVERANCE FROM ADVERSARIES

To the Chief Musician. With stringed instruments.[a]
A Contemplation[b] of David when the Ziphites went and said to Saul, "Is David not hiding with us?"

1 *Save me, O God, by*
Your name,
And vindicate me by
Your strength.
2 Hear my prayer, O God;
Give ear to the words
of my mouth.
3 For strangers have
risen up against me,
And oppressors have
sought after my life;
They have not set God
before them. *Selah*

4 Behold, God *is* my helper;
The Lord *is* with those
who uphold my life.
5 He will repay my
enemies for their evil.
Cut them off in
Your truth.

6 I will freely sacrifice
to You;
I will praise Your name,
O LORD, for *it is* good.
7 For He has delivered me
out of all trouble;
And my eye has seen
its desire upon
my enemies.

PSALM 55

TRUST IN GOD CONCERNING THE TREACHERY OF FRIENDS

To the Chief Musician. With stringed instruments.[a]
A Contemplation[b] of David.

1 Give ear to my
prayer, O God,
And do not hide Yourself
from my supplication.

54:title [a] Hebrew *neginoth* [b] Hebrew *Maschil*
55:title [a] Hebrew *neginoth* [b] Hebrew *Maschil*

2 Attend to me, and
hear me;
I am restless in my
complaint, and
moan noisily,
3 Because of the voice
of the enemy,
Because of the
oppression of
the wicked;
For they bring down
trouble upon me,
And in wrath they
hate me.

4 My heart is severely
pained within me,
And the terrors of death
have fallen upon me.
5 Fearfulness and
trembling have
come upon me,
And horror has
overwhelmed me.
6 So I said, "Oh, that I had
wings like a dove!
I would fly away
and be at rest.
7 Indeed, I would
wander far off,
And remain in the
wilderness. *Selah*
8 I would hasten my
escape
From the windy storm
and tempest."

9 Destroy, O Lord, *and*
divide their tongues,
For I have seen violence
and strife in the city.
10 Day and night they
go around it on
its walls;
Iniquity and trouble *are*
also in the midst of it.
11 Destruction *is* in
its midst;
Oppression and
deceit do not depart
from its streets.

12 For *it is* not an enemy
who reproaches me;
Then I could bear *it.*
Nor *is it* one *who* hates
me who has exalted
himself against me;
Then I could hide
from him.
13 But *it was* you, a
man my equal,
My companion and
my acquaintance.
14 We took sweet
counsel together,
And walked to the house
of God in the throng.

15 Let death seize them;
Let them go down
alive into hell,
For wickedness *is* in
their dwellings *and*
among them.

16 As for me, I will
call upon God,
And the LORD shall
save me.
17 Evening and morning
and at noon
I will pray, and cry aloud,
And He shall hear
my voice.
18 He has redeemed my soul
in peace from the battle
that was against me,

For there were many
against me.
19 God will hear, and
afflict them,
Even He who abides
from of old. *Selah*
Because they do
not change,
Therefore they do
not fear God.

20 He has put forth
his hands against
those who were at
peace with him;
He has broken his
covenant.
21 *The words* of his mouth
were smoother
than butter,
But war *was* in his heart;
His words were
softer than oil,
Yet they *were*
drawn swords.

22 Cast your burden
on the LORD,
And He shall sustain
you;
He shall never permit
the righteous to
be moved.

23 But You, O God, shall
bring them down to
the pit of destruction;
Bloodthirsty and
deceitful men shall
not live out half
their days;
But I will trust in You.

PSALM 56

PRAYER FOR RELIEF FROM TORMENTORS

To the Chief Musician.
Set to "The Silent Dove
in Distant Lands."[a] A Michtam
of David when the Philistines
captured him in Gath.

1 Be merciful to me,
O God, for man would
swallow me up;
Fighting all day he
oppresses me.
2 My enemies would
hound *me* all day,
For *there are* many
who fight against
me, O Most High.

3 Whenever I am afraid,
I will trust in You.
4 In God (I will praise
His word),
In God I have put
my trust;
I will not fear.
What can flesh do
to me?

5 All day they twist
my words;
All their thoughts *are*
against me for evil.
6 They gather together,
They hide, they
mark my steps,
When they lie in
wait for my life.
7 Shall they escape
by iniquity?
In anger cast down the
peoples, O God!

56:title [a] Hebrew *Jonath Elem Rechokim*

8 You number my
wanderings;
Put my tears into
Your bottle;
Are they not in Your book?
9 When I cry out *to You,*
Then my enemies
will turn back;
This I know, because
God *is* for me.
10 In God (I will praise
His word),
In the LORD (I will
praise *His* word),
11 In God I have put
my trust;
I will not be afraid.
What can man do to me?

12 Vows *made* to You
are binding upon
me, O God;
I will render praises
to You,
13 For You have delivered
my soul from death.
Have You not *kept* my
feet from falling,
That I may walk
before God
In the light of the living?

PSALM 57

PRAYER FOR SAFETY FROM ENEMIES

To the Chief Musician.
Set to "Do Not Destroy."[a]
A Michtam of David when he
fled from Saul into the cave.

1 Be merciful to me, O God,
be merciful to me!
For my soul trusts
in You;
And in the shadow
of Your wings I will
make my refuge,
Until *these* calamities
have passed by.

2 I will cry out to God
Most High,
To God who performs
all things for me.
3 He shall send from
heaven and save me;
He reproaches the one
who would swallow
me up. *Selah*
God shall send forth
His mercy and
His truth.

4 My soul *is* among lions;
I lie *among* the
sons of men
Who are set on fire,
Whose teeth *are*
spears and arrows,
And their tongue a
sharp sword.
5 Be exalted, O God,
above the heavens;
Let Your glory *be* above
all the earth.

6 They have prepared a
net for my steps;
My soul is bowed down;
They have dug a
pit before me;
Into the midst of it
they *themselves* have
fallen. *Selah*

57:title [a] Hebrew *Al Tashcheth*

7 My heart is steadfast,
O God, my heart
is steadfast;
I will sing and give praise.
8 Awake, my glory!
Awake, lute and harp!
I will awaken the dawn.

9 I will praise You, O Lord,
among the peoples;
I will sing to You
among the nations.
10 For Your mercy reaches
unto the heavens,
And Your truth unto
the clouds.

11 Be exalted, O God,
above the heavens;
Let Your glory *be* above
all the earth.

PSALM 58

THE JUST JUDGMENT OF THE WICKED

To the Chief Musician.
Set to "Do Not Destroy."[a]
A Michtam of David.

1 Do you indeed speak
righteousness,
you silent ones?
Do you judge uprightly,
you sons of men?
2 No, in heart you work
wickedness;
You weigh out the
violence of your
hands in the earth.

3 The wicked are estranged
from the womb;
They go astray as soon
as they are born,
speaking lies.
4 Their poison *is* like
the poison of a
serpent;
They are like the deaf
cobra *that* stops
its ear,
5 Which will not heed the
voice of charmers,
Charming ever
so skillfully.

6 Break their teeth in
their mouth, O God!
Break out the fangs
of the young
lions, O LORD!
7 Let them flow away
as waters *which*
run continually;
When he bends *his bow,*
Let his arrows be as
if cut in pieces.
8 *Let them be* like a
snail which melts
away as it goes,
Like a stillborn child of
a woman, that they
may not see the sun.

9 Before your pots can
feel *the burning*
thorns,
He shall take them away
as with a whirlwind,
As in His living and
burning wrath.
10 The righteous shall
rejoice when he sees
the vengeance;

58:title [a] Hebrew *Al Tashcheth*

He shall wash his feet in
the blood of the wicked,
11 So that men will say,
"Surely *there is* a reward
for the righteous;
Surely He is God who
judges in the earth."

PSALM 59

THE ASSURED JUDGMENT OF THE WICKED

To the Chief Musician.
Set to "Do Not Destroy."[a]
A Michtam of David when Saul
sent men, and they watched
the house in order to kill him.

1 Deliver me from my
enemies, O my God;
Defend me from those
who rise up against me.
2 Deliver me from the
workers of iniquity,
And save me from
bloodthirsty men.

3 For look, they lie in
wait for my life;
The mighty gather
against me,
Not *for* my transgression
nor *for* my sin, O LORD.
4 They run and prepare
themselves through
no fault *of mine.*

Awake to help me,
and behold!
5 You therefore, O LORD
God of hosts, the
God of Israel,
Awake to punish all
the nations;
Do not be merciful
to any wicked
transgressors. *Selah*

6 At evening they return,
They growl like a dog,
And go all around
the city.
7 Indeed, they belch
with their mouth;
Swords *are* in their
lips;
For *they say,* "Who
hears?"

8 But You, O LORD, shall
laugh at them;
You shall have all the
nations in derision.
9 I will wait for You,
O You his Strength;[a]
For God *is* my defense.
10 My God of mercy[a] shall
come to meet me;
God shall let me see
my desire on my
enemies.

11 Do not slay them, lest
my people forget;
Scatter them by
Your power,
And bring them down,

59:title [a] Hebrew *Al Tashcheth* **59:9** [a] Following Masoretic Text and Syriac; some Hebrew manuscripts, Septuagint, Targum, and Vulgate read *my Strength.* **59:10** [a] Following Qere; some Hebrew manuscripts, Septuagint, and Vulgate read *My God, His mercy;* Kethib, some Hebrew manuscripts and Targum read *O God, my mercy;* Syriac reads *O God, Your mercy.*

O Lord our shield.
12 *For* the sin of their mouth *and* the words of their lips,
Let them even be taken in their pride,
And for the cursing and lying *which* they speak.
13 Consume *them* in wrath, consume *them,*
That they *may* not *be;*
And let them know that God rules in Jacob
To the ends of the earth. *Selah*

14 And at evening they return,
They growl like a dog,
And go all around the city.
15 They wander up and down for food,
And howl[a] if they are not satisfied.

16 But I will sing of Your power;
Yes, I will sing aloud of Your mercy in the morning;
For You have been my defense
And refuge in the day of my trouble.
17 To You, O my Strength, I will sing praises;
For God *is* my defense,
My God of mercy.

PSALM 60

URGENT PRAYER FOR THE RESTORED FAVOR OF GOD

To the Chief Musician. Set to "Lily of the Testimony."[a] A Michtam of David. For teaching. When he fought against Mesopotamia and Syria of Zobah, and Joab returned and killed twelve thousand Edomites in the Valley of Salt.

1 O God, You have cast us off;
You have broken us down;
You have been displeased;
Oh, restore us again!
2 You have made the earth tremble;
You have broken it;
Heal its breaches, for it is shaking.
3 You have shown Your people hard things;
You have made us drink the wine of confusion.

4 You have given a banner to those who fear You,
That it may be displayed because of the truth. *Selah*
5 That Your beloved may be delivered,
Save *with* Your right hand, and hear me.

6 God has spoken in His holiness:
"I will rejoice;
I will divide Shechem

59:15 [a] Following Septuagint and Vulgate; Masoretic Text, Syriac, and Targum read *spend the night.* 60:title [a] Hebrew *Shushan Eduth*

And measure out the
Valley of Succoth.
7 Gilead *is* Mine, and
Manasseh *is* Mine;
Ephraim also *is* the
helmet for My head;
Judah *is* My lawgiver.
8 Moab *is* My washpot;
Over Edom I will
cast My shoe;
Philistia, shout in
triumph because of Me."

9 Who will bring me *to*
the strong city?
Who will lead me
to Edom?
10 *Is it* not You, O God,
who cast us off?
And You, O God, *who*
did not go out with
our armies?
11 Give us help from trouble,
For the help of man
is useless.
12 Through God we will
do valiantly,
For *it is* He *who*
shall tread down
our enemies.[a]

PSALM 61

ASSURANCE OF GOD'S ETERNAL PROTECTION

To the Chief Musician.
On a stringed instrument.[a]
A Psalm of David.

1 Hear my cry, O God;
Attend to my prayer.
2 From the end of the
earth I will cry to You,
When my heart is
overwhelmed;
Lead me to the rock
that is higher than I.

3 For You have been a
shelter for me,
A strong tower from
the enemy.
4 I will abide in Your
tabernacle forever;
I will trust in the shelter
of Your wings. *Selah*

5 For You, O God, have
heard my vows;
You have given *me* the
heritage of those who
fear Your name.
6 You will prolong
the king's life,
His years as many
generations.
7 He shall abide before
God forever.
Oh, prepare mercy
and truth, *which*
may preserve him!

8 So I will sing praise to
Your name forever,
That I may daily
perform my vows.

PSALM 62

A CALM RESOLVE TO WAIT FOR THE SALVATION OF GOD

To the Chief Musician.
To Jeduthun. A Psalm of David.

1 Truly my soul silently
waits for God;

60:12 [a] Compare verses 5–12 with 108:6–13 61:title [a] Hebrew *neginah*

From Him *comes*
my salvation.
2 He only *is* my rock
and my salvation;
He is my defense;
I shall not be
greatly moved.

3 How long will you
attack a man?
You shall be slain,
all of you,
Like a leaning wall and
a tottering fence.
4 They only consult to
cast *him* down from
his high position;
They delight in lies;
They bless with
their mouth,
But they curse
inwardly. *Selah*

5 My soul, wait silently
for God alone,
For my expectation
is from Him.
6 He only *is* my rock
and my salvation;
He is my defense;
I shall not be moved.
7 In God *is* my salvation
and my glory;
The rock of my
strength,
And my refuge, *is*
in God.

8 Trust in Him at all
times, you people;
Pour out your heart
before Him;
God *is* a refuge for
us. *Selah*

9 Surely men of low
degree *are* a vapor,
Men of high degree
are a lie;
If they are weighed
on the scales,
They *are* altogether
lighter than vapor.
10 Do not trust in
oppression,
Nor vainly hope
in robbery;
If riches increase,
Do not set *your*
heart *on them.*

11 God has spoken once,
Twice I have heard
this:
That power *belongs*
to God.
12 Also to You, O Lord,
belongs mercy;
For You render to
each one according
to his work.

PSALM 63

JOY IN THE FELLOWSHIP OF GOD

A Psalm of David when he was in the wilderness of Judah.

1 O God, You *are* my God;
Early will I seek You;
My soul thirsts for You;
My flesh longs for You
In a dry and thirsty
land
Where there is no water.
2 So I have looked for You
in the sanctuary,
To see Your power
and Your glory.

3 Because Your
lovingkindness *is*
better than life,
My lips shall praise
You.
4 Thus I will bless You
while I live;
I will lift up my hands
in Your name.
5 My soul shall be
satisfied as with
marrow and fatness,
And my mouth
shall praise *You*
with joyful lips.

6 When I remember
You on my bed,
I meditate on You in
the *night* watches.
7 Because You have
been my help,
Therefore in the
shadow of Your
wings I will rejoice.
8 My soul follows close
behind You;
Your right hand
upholds me.

9 But those *who* seek my
life, to destroy *it*,
Shall go into the
lower parts of the
earth.
10 They shall fall by
the sword;
They shall be a portion
for jackals.

11 But the king shall
rejoice in God;
Everyone who swears
by Him shall glory;
But the mouth of
those who speak lies
shall be stopped.

PSALM 64

OPPRESSED BY THE WICKED BUT REJOICING IN THE LORD

To the Chief Musician.
A Psalm of David.

1 Hear my voice, O God,
in my meditation;
Preserve my life from
fear of the enemy.
2 Hide me from the secret
plots of the wicked,
From the rebellion of the
workers of iniquity,
3 Who sharpen their
tongue like a sword,
And bend *their bows*
to shoot their
arrows—bitter words,
4 That they may shoot in
secret at the blameless;
Suddenly they shoot at
him and do not fear.

5 They encourage
themselves *in* an
evil matter;
They talk of laying
snares secretly;
They say, "Who will
see them?"
6 They devise iniquities:
"We have perfected a
shrewd scheme."
Both the inward thought
and the heart of
man are deep.

7 But God shall shoot at
them *with* an arrow;

Suddenly they shall
be wounded.
8 So He will make them
stumble over their
own tongue;
All who see them
shall flee away.
9 All men shall fear,
And shall declare
the work of God;
For they shall wisely
consider His doing.

10 The righteous shall
be glad in the LORD,
and trust in Him.
And all the upright in
heart shall glory.

PSALM 65

PRAISE TO GOD FOR HIS SALVATION AND PROVIDENCE

To the Chief Musician.
A Psalm of David. A Song.

1 Praise is awaiting You,
O God, in Zion;
And to You the vow
shall be performed.
2 O You who hear prayer,
To You all flesh will come.
3 Iniquities prevail
against me;
As for our transgressions,
You will provide
atonement for them.

4 Blessed *is the man*
You choose,
And cause to
approach *You,*
That he may dwell
in Your courts.
We shall be satisfied
with the goodness
of Your house,
Of Your holy temple.

5 *By* awesome deeds in
righteousness You
will answer us,
O God of our salvation,
You who are the
confidence of all the
ends of the earth,
And of the far-off seas;
6 Who established
the mountains by
His strength,
Being clothed with
power;
7 You who still the
noise of the seas,
The noise of their waves,
And the tumult of
the peoples.
8 They also who dwell in
the farthest parts are
afraid of Your signs;
You make the outgoings
of the morning and
evening rejoice.

9 You visit the earth
and water it,
You greatly enrich it;
The river of God is
full of water;
You provide their grain,
For so You have
prepared it.
10 You water its ridges
abundantly,
You settle its furrows;
You make it soft
with showers,
You bless its growth.

11 You crown the year
with Your goodness,
And Your paths drip
with abundance.
12 They drop *on* the pastures
of the wilderness,
And the little hills
rejoice on every side.
13 The pastures are
clothed with flocks;
The valleys also are
covered with grain;
They shout for joy,
they also sing.

PSALM 66

PRAISE TO GOD FOR HIS AWESOME WORKS

To the Chief Musician.
A Song. A Psalm.

1 Make a joyful shout to
God, all the earth!
2 Sing out the honor
of His name;
Make His praise glorious.
3 Say to God,
"How awesome are
Your works!
Through the greatness
of Your power
Your enemies shall submit
themselves to You.
4 All the earth shall
worship You
And sing praises to You;
They shall sing praises *to*
Your name." *Selah*

5 Come and see the
works of God;
He is awesome *in His*
doing toward the
sons of men.
6 He turned the sea
into dry *land;*
They went through
the river on foot.
There we will
rejoice in Him.
7 He rules by His
power forever;
His eyes observe
the nations;
Do not let the rebellious
exalt themselves. *Selah*

8 Oh, bless our God,
you peoples!
And make the voice of
His praise to be heard,
9 Who keeps our soul
among the living,
And does not allow our
feet to be moved.
10 For You, O God,
have tested us;
You have refined us as
silver is refined.
11 You brought us
into the net;
You laid affliction
on our backs.
12 You have caused men to
ride over our heads;
We went through fire
and through water;
But You brought us out
to rich *fulfillment.*

13 I will go into Your house
with burnt offerings;
I will pay You my vows,
14 Which my lips
have uttered
And my mouth has
spoken when I
was in trouble.

15 I will offer You burnt
sacrifices of fat animals,
With the sweet
aroma of rams;
I will offer bulls with
goats. *Selah*

16 Come *and* hear, all
you who fear God,
And I will declare
what He has done
for my soul.
17 I cried to Him with
my mouth,
And He was extolled
with my tongue.
18 If I regard iniquity
in my heart,
The Lord will not hear.
19 *But* certainly God
has heard *me;*
He has attended to the
voice of my prayer.

20 Blessed *be* God,
Who has not turned
away my prayer,
Nor His mercy from me!

PSALM 67

AN INVOCATION AND A DOXOLOGY

To the Chief Musician.
On stringed instruments.[a]
A Psalm. A Song.

1 God be merciful to
us and bless us,
And cause His face to
shine upon us, *Selah*
2 That Your way may be
known on earth,
Your salvation among
all nations.

3 Let the peoples praise
You, O God;
Let all the peoples
praise You.
4 Oh, let the nations be
glad and sing for joy!
For You shall judge the
people righteously,
And govern the nations
on earth. *Selah*

5 Let the peoples praise
You, O God;
Let all the peoples
praise You.
6 *Then* the earth shall
yield her increase;
God, our own God,
shall bless us.
7 God shall bless us,
And all the ends of the
earth shall fear Him.

PSALM 68

THE GLORY OF GOD IN HIS GOODNESS TO ISRAEL

To the Chief Musician.
A Psalm of David. A Song.

1 Let God arise,
Let His enemies
be scattered;
Let those also who hate
Him flee before Him.
2 As smoke is driven
away,
So drive *them* away;
As wax melts before
the fire,

67:title [a] Hebrew *neginoth*

So let the wicked perish
at the presence of God.
3 But let the righteous
be glad;
Let them rejoice
before God;
Yes, let them rejoice
exceedingly.

4 Sing to God, sing praises
to His name;
Extol Him who rides
on the clouds,[a]
By His name YAH,
And rejoice before Him.

5 A father of the fatherless,
a defender of widows,
Is God in His holy
habitation.
6 God sets the solitary
in families;
He brings out those
who are bound
into prosperity;
But the rebellious
dwell in a dry *land.*

7 O God, when You went
out before Your
people,
When You marched
through the
wilderness, *Selah*
8 The earth shook;
The heavens also
dropped *rain* at the
presence of God;
Sinai itself *was moved* at
the presence of God,
the God of Israel.
9 You, O God, sent a
plentiful rain,
Whereby You confirmed
Your inheritance,
When it was weary.
10 Your congregation
dwelt in it;
You, O God, provided
from Your goodness
for the poor.

11 The Lord gave the word;
Great *was* the company of
those who proclaimed *it:*
12 "Kings of armies
flee, they flee,
And she who remains at
home divides the spoil.
13 Though you lie down
among the sheepfolds,
You will be like the
wings of a dove
covered with silver,
And her feathers with
yellow gold."
14 When the Almighty
scattered kings in it,
It was *white* as snow
in Zalmon.

15 A mountain of God *is* the
mountain of Bashan;
A mountain *of many*
peaks *is* the mountain
of Bashan.
16 Why do you fume with
envy, you mountains
of *many* peaks?
This is the mountain
which God desires
to dwell in;

68:4 [a] Masoretic Text reads *deserts;* Targum reads *heavens* (compare verse 34 and Isaiah 19:1).

Yes, the LORD will
dwell *in it* forever.

17 The chariots of God *are*
twenty thousand,
Even thousands of
thousands;
The Lord is among
them *as in* Sinai, in
the Holy *Place.*
18 You have ascended
on high,
You have led captivity
captive;
You have received
gifts among men,
Even *from* the rebellious,
That the LORD God
might dwell *there.*

19 Blessed *be* the Lord,
Who daily loads us
with benefits,
The God of our
salvation! *Selah*
20 Our God *is* the God
of salvation;
And to GOD the Lord
belong escapes
from death.

21 But God will wound
the head of His
enemies,
The hairy scalp of the
one who still goes on
in his trespasses.
22 The Lord said, "I
will bring back
from Bashan,
I will bring *them* back
from the depths
of the sea,
23 That your foot may
crush *them*[a] in blood,
And the tongues of
your dogs *may have*
their portion from
your enemies."

24 They have seen Your
procession, O God,
The procession of my
God, my King, into
the sanctuary.
25 The singers went
before, the players
on instruments
followed after;
Among *them were*
the maidens
playing timbrels.
26 Bless God in the
congregations,
The Lord, from the
fountain of Israel.
27 There *is* little Benjamin,
their leader,
The princes of Judah
and their company,
The princes of Zebulun
and the princes
of Naphtali.

28 Your God has
commanded[a]
your strength;
Strengthen, O God,
what You have
done for us.

68:23 [a] Septuagint, Syriac, Targum, and Vulgate read *you may dip your foot.* **68:28** [a] Septuagint, Syriac, Targum, and Vulgate read *Command, O God.*

29 Because of Your temple
at Jerusalem,
Kings will bring
presents to You.
30 Rebuke the beasts
of the reeds,
The herd of bulls with
the calves of
the peoples,
Till everyone submits
himself with
pieces of silver.
Scatter the peoples
who delight in war.
31 Envoys will come
out of Egypt;
Ethiopia will quickly
stretch out her
hands to God.

32 Sing to God, you
kingdoms of the earth;
Oh, sing praises to the
Lord, *Selah*
33 To Him who rides on the
heaven of heavens,
which were of old!
Indeed, He sends out His
voice, a mighty voice.
34 Ascribe strength to God;
His excellence *is*
over Israel,
And His strength *is*
in the clouds.
35 O God, *You are* more
awesome than
Your holy places.
The God of Israel *is* He
who gives strength and
power to *His* people.

Blessed *be* God!

PSALM 69

AN URGENT PLEA FOR HELP IN TROUBLE

To the Chief Musician.
Set to "The Lilies."[a]
A Psalm of David.

1 Save me, O God!
For the waters have
come up to *my* neck.
2 I sink in deep mire,
Where *there is* no
standing;
I have come into
deep waters,
Where the floods
overflow me.
3 I am weary with
my crying;
My throat is dry;
My eyes fail while I
wait for my God.

4 Those who hate me
without a cause
Are more than the
hairs of my head;
They are mighty who
would destroy me,
Being my enemies
wrongfully;
Though I have
stolen nothing,
I *still* must restore *it.*

5 O God, You know
my foolishness;
And my sins are not
hidden from You.
6 Let not those who wait
for You, O Lord GOD
of hosts, be ashamed
because of me;

69:title [a] Hebrew *Shoshannim*

Let not those who seek
You be confounded
because of me,
O God of Israel.
7 Because for Your sake I
have borne reproach;
Shame has covered
my face.
8 I have become a stranger
to my brothers,
And an alien to my
mother's children;
9 Because zeal for Your
house has eaten me up,
And the reproaches of
those who reproach
You have fallen on me.
10 When I wept *and*
chastened my soul
with fasting,
That became my reproach.
11 I also made sackcloth
my garment;
I became a byword
to them.
12 Those who sit in the gate
speak against me,
And I *am* the song of
the drunkards.

13 But as for me, my
prayer *is* to You,
O LORD, *in* the
acceptable time;
O God, in the multitude
of Your mercy,
Hear me in the truth
of Your salvation.
14 Deliver me out of the mire,
And let me not sink;
Let me be delivered from
those who hate me,
And out of the
deep waters.
15 Let not the floodwater
overflow me,
Nor let the deep
swallow me up;
And let not the pit shut
its mouth on me.

16 Hear me, O LORD, for Your
lovingkindness *is* good;
Turn to me according
to the multitude of
Your tender mercies.
17 And do not hide Your face
from Your servant,
For I am in trouble;
Hear me speedily.
18 Draw near to my soul,
and redeem it;
Deliver me because
of my enemies.

19 You know my reproach,
my shame, and
my dishonor;
My adversaries *are*
all before You.
20 Reproach has broken
my heart,
And I am full of heaviness;
I looked *for someone*
to take pity, but
there was none;
And for comforters,
but I found none.
21 They also gave me
gall for my food,
And for my thirst
they gave me
vinegar to drink.

22 Let their table become
a snare before them,
And their well-being
a trap.

23 Let their eyes be
darkened, so that
they do not see;
And make their loins
shake continually.
24 Pour out Your
indignation upon them,
And let Your wrathful
anger take hold of them.
25 Let their dwelling
place be desolate;
Let no one live in
their tents.
26 For they persecute the
ones You have struck,
And talk of the grief
of those You have
wounded.
27 Add iniquity to
their iniquity,
And let them not
come into Your
righteousness.
28 Let them be blotted out of
the book of the living,
And not be written
with the righteous.

29 But I *am* poor and
sorrowful;
Let Your salvation, O God,
set me up on high.
30 I will praise the name
of God with a song,
And will magnify Him
with thanksgiving.
31 *This* also shall please
the LORD better
than an ox *or* bull,
Which has horns
and hooves.
32 The humble shall see
this and be glad;
And you who seek God,
your hearts shall live.
33 For the LORD hears
the poor,
And does not despise
His prisoners.

34 Let heaven and earth
praise Him,
The seas and everything
that moves in them.
35 For God will save Zion
And build the cities
of Judah,
That they may dwell
there and possess it.
36 Also, the descendants
of His servants
shall inherit it,
And those who love His
name shall dwell in it.

PSALM 70

PRAYER FOR RELIEF FROM ADVERSARIES

To the Chief Musician.
A Psalm of David. To bring
to remembrance.

1 *Make haste*, O God,
to deliver me!
Make haste to help
me, O LORD!

2 Let them be ashamed
and confounded
Who seek my life;
Let them be turned
back[a] and confused

70:2 [a] Following Masoretic Text, Septuagint, Targum, and Vulgate; some Hebrew manuscripts and Syriac read *be appalled* (compare 40:15).

Who desire my hurt.
3 Let them be turned back
because of their shame,
Who say, "Aha, aha!"

4 Let all those who seek
You rejoice and
be glad in You;
And let those who
love Your salvation
say continually,
"Let God be magnified!"

5 But I *am* poor and needy;
Make haste to me, O God!
You *are* my help and
my deliverer;
O LORD, do not delay.

PSALM 71

GOD THE ROCK OF SALVATION

1 In You, O LORD, I
put my trust;
Let me never be
put to shame.
2 Deliver me in Your
righteousness, and
cause me to escape;
Incline Your ear to
me, and save me.
3 Be my strong refuge,
To which I may resort
continually;
You have given the
commandment
to save me,
For You *are* my rock
and my fortress.

4 Deliver me, O my God,
out of the hand
of the wicked,
Out of the hand of
the unrighteous
and cruel man.
5 For You are my hope,
O Lord GOD;
You are my trust
from my youth.
6 By You I have been
upheld from birth;
You are He who
took me out of my
mother's womb.
My praise *shall be*
continually of You.

7 I have become as a
wonder to many,
But You *are* my
strong refuge.
8 Let my mouth be filled
with Your praise
And with Your glory
all the day.

9 Do not cast me off in
the time of old age;
Do not forsake me
when my strength
fails.
10 For my enemies speak
against me;
And those who lie in
wait for my life take
counsel together,
11 Saying, "God has
forsaken him;
Pursue and take him,
for *there is* none
to deliver *him*."

12 O God, do not be
far from me;
O my God, make
haste to help me!

13 Let them be confounded
and consumed
Who are adversaries
of my life;
Let them be covered *with*
reproach and dishonor
Who seek my hurt.

14 But I will hope continually,
And will praise You yet
more and more.
15 My mouth shall tell of
Your righteousness
And Your salvation
all the day,
For I do not know
their limits.
16 I will go in the strength
of the Lord GOD;
I will make mention of
Your righteousness,
of Yours only.

17 O God, You have taught
me from my youth;
And to this *day* I declare
Your wondrous works.
18 Now also when *I am* old
and grayheaded,
O God, do not forsake me,
Until I declare Your
strength to *this*
generation,
Your power to everyone
who is to come.

19 Also Your righteousness,
O God, *is* very high,
You who have done
great things;
O God, who *is* like You?
20 *You,* who have shown
me great and
severe troubles,
Shall revive me again,
And bring me up again
from the depths
of the earth.
21 You shall increase
my greatness,
And comfort me
on every side.

22 Also with the lute I
will praise You—
And Your faithfulness,
O my God!
To You I will sing
with the harp,
O Holy One of Israel.
23 My lips shall greatly
rejoice when I
sing to You,
And my soul, which
You have redeemed.
24 My tongue also shall talk
of Your righteousness
all the day long;
For they are confounded,
For they are brought
to shame
Who seek my hurt.

PSALM 72

GLORY AND UNIVERSALITY OF THE MESSIAH'S REIGN

A Psalm of Solomon.

1 Give the king Your
judgments, O God,
And Your righteousness
to the king's Son.
2 He will judge Your people
with righteousness,
And Your poor
with justice.
3 The mountains will bring
peace to the people,

And the little hills, by
righteousness.
4 He will bring justice to
the poor of the people;
He will save the children
of the needy,
And will break in pieces
the oppressor.

5 They shall fear You[a]
As long as the sun and
moon endure,
Throughout all
generations.
6 He shall come down like
rain upon the grass
before mowing,
Like showers *that*
water the earth.
7 In His days the righteous
shall flourish,
And abundance of peace,
Until the moon is no more.

8 He shall have dominion
also from sea to sea,
And from the River to
the ends of the earth.
9 Those who dwell in
the wilderness will
bow before Him,
And His enemies will
lick the dust.
10 The kings of Tarshish
and of the isles
Will bring presents;
The kings of Sheba
and Seba
Will offer gifts.
11 Yes, all kings shall fall
down before Him;
All nations shall
serve Him.

12 For He will deliver the
needy when he cries,
The poor also, and *him*
who has no helper.
13 He will spare the
poor and needy,
And will save the souls
of the needy.
14 He will redeem their
life from oppression
and violence;
And precious shall
be their blood
in His sight.

15 And He shall live;
And the gold of Sheba
will be given to Him;
Prayer also will be made
for Him continually,
And daily He shall
be praised.

16 There will be an
abundance of grain
in the earth,
On the top of the
mountains;
Its fruit shall wave
like Lebanon;
And *those* of the city
shall flourish like
grass of the earth.

17 His name shall
endure forever;
His name shall continue
as long as the sun.

72:5 [a] Following Masoretic Text and Targum; Septuagint and Vulgate read *They shall continue*.

And *men* shall be
blessed in Him;
All nations shall call
Him blessed.

18 Blessed *be* the LORD God,
the God of Israel,
Who only does
wondrous things!
19 And blessed *be* His
glorious name forever!
And let the whole earth
be filled *with* His glory.
Amen and Amen.

20 The prayers of David the
son of Jesse are ended.

BOOK THREE

PSALMS 73–89

PSALM 73

THE TRAGEDY OF THE WICKED, AND THE BLESSEDNESS OF TRUST IN GOD

A Psalm of Asaph.

1 Truly God *is* good to Israel,
To such as are
pure in heart.
2 But as for me, my feet
had almost stumbled;
My steps had nearly
slipped.
3 For I *was* envious
of the boastful,
When I saw the prosperity
of the wicked.

4 For *there are* no pangs
in their death,
But their strength
is firm.
5 They *are* not in trouble
as other men,
Nor are they plagued
like *other* men.
6 Therefore pride serves
as their necklace;
Violence covers them
like a garment.
7 Their eyes bulge[a]
with abundance;
They have more than
heart could wish.
8 They scoff and speak
wickedly *concerning*
oppression;
They speak loftily.
9 They set their mouth
against the heavens,
And their tongue walks
through the earth.

10 Therefore his people
return here,
And waters of a full *cup*
are drained by them.
11 And they say, "How
does God know?
And is there knowledge
in the Most High?"
12 Behold, these *are*
the ungodly,
Who are always at ease;
They increase *in* riches.
13 Surely I have cleansed
my heart *in* vain,
And washed my hands
in innocence.
14 For all day long I have
been plagued,

73:7 [a] Targum reads *face bulges;* Septuagint, Syriac, and Vulgate read *iniquity bulges.*

And chastened
every morning.

15 If I had said, "I will
speak thus,"
Behold, I would have been
untrue to the generation
of Your children.
16 When I thought *how*
to understand this,
It *was* too painful
for me—
17 Until I went into the
sanctuary of God;
Then I understood
their end.

18 Surely You set them
in slippery places;
You cast them down
to destruction.
19 Oh, how they are
brought to desolation,
as in a moment!
They are utterly
consumed with terrors.
20 As a dream when
one awakes,
So, Lord, when You awake,
You shall despise
their image.

21 Thus my heart
was grieved,
And I was vexed
in my mind.
22 I *was* so foolish
and ignorant;
I was *like* a beast
before You.
23 Nevertheless I *am*
continually with You;
You hold *me* by my
right hand.
24 You will guide me
with Your counsel,
And afterward receive
me *to* glory.

25 Whom have I in
heaven *but You?*
And *there is* none
upon earth *that* I
desire besides You.
26 My flesh and my
heart fail;
But God *is* the strength
of my heart and my
portion forever.

27 For indeed, those
who are far from
You shall perish;
You have destroyed
all those who desert
You for harlotry.
28 But *it is* good for me to
draw near to God;
I have put my trust
in the Lord GOD,
That I may declare
all Your works.

PSALM 74

A PLEA FOR RELIEF FROM OPPRESSORS

A Contemplation[a] of Asaph.

1 O God, why have You
cast *us* off forever?
Why does Your anger
smoke against
the sheep of
Your pasture?

74:title [a] Hebrew *Maschil*

2 Remember Your congregation,
which You have purchased of old,
The tribe of Your inheritance, *which* You have redeemed—
This Mount Zion where You have dwelt.
3 Lift up Your feet to the perpetual desolations.
The enemy has damaged everything in the sanctuary.
4 Your enemies roar in the midst of Your meeting place;
They set up their banners *for* signs.
5 They seem like men who lift up
Axes among the thick trees.
6 And now they break down its carved work, all at once,
With axes and hammers.
7 They have set fire to Your sanctuary;
They have defiled the dwelling place of Your name to the ground.
8 They said in their hearts,
"Let us destroy them altogether."
They have burned up all the meeting places of God in the land.

9 We do not see our signs;
There is no longer any prophet;
Nor *is there* any among us who knows how long.
10 O God, how long will the adversary reproach?
Will the enemy blaspheme Your name forever?
11 Why do You withdraw Your hand, even Your right hand?
Take it out of Your bosom and destroy *them.*
12 For God *is* my King from of old,
Working salvation in the midst of the earth.
13 You divided the sea by Your strength;
You broke the heads of the sea serpents in the waters.
14 You broke the heads of Leviathan in pieces,
And gave him *as* food to the people inhabiting the wilderness.
15 You broke open the fountain and the flood;
You dried up mighty rivers.
16 The day *is* Yours, the night also *is* Yours;
You have prepared the light and the sun.
17 You have set all the borders of the earth;
You have made summer and winter.

18 Remember this, *that* the enemy has reproached, O LORD,
And *that* a foolish people has blasphemed Your name.

19 Oh, do not deliver the
life of Your turtledove
to the wild beast!
Do not forget the life of
Your poor forever.
20 Have respect to
the covenant;
For the dark places of
the earth are full of
the haunts of cruelty.
21 Oh, do not let the
oppressed return
ashamed!
Let the poor and needy
praise Your name.

22 Arise, O God, plead
Your own cause;
Remember how
the foolish man
reproaches You daily.
23 Do not forget the voice
of Your enemies;
The tumult of those who
rise up against You
increases continually.

PSALM 75

THANKSGIVING FOR GOD'S RIGHTEOUS JUDGMENT

To the Chief Musician.
Set to "Do Not Destroy."[a]
A Psalm of Asaph. A Song.

1 We give thanks to You,
O God, we give thanks!
For Your wondrous
works declare *that*
Your name is near.

2 "When I choose the
proper time,
I will judge uprightly.
3 The earth and all
its inhabitants
are dissolved;
I set up its pillars
firmly. *Selah*

4 "I said to the boastful, 'Do
not deal boastfully,'
And to the wicked, 'Do
not lift up the horn.
5 Do not lift up your
horn on high;
Do *not* speak with
a stiff neck.'"

6 For exaltation *comes*
neither from the east
Nor from the west nor
from the south.
7 But God *is* the Judge:
He puts down one,
And exalts another.
8 For in the hand of the
LORD *there is* a cup,
And the wine is red;
It is fully mixed, and
He pours it out;
Surely its dregs shall all
the wicked of the earth
Drain *and* drink down.

9 But I will declare forever,
I will sing praises to
the God of Jacob.

10 "All the horns of
the wicked I will
also cut off,
But the horns of the
righteous shall
be exalted."

75:title [a] Hebrew *Al Tashcheth*

PSALM 76

THE MAJESTY OF GOD IN JUDGMENT

To the Chief Musician.
On stringed instruments.[a]
A Psalm of Asaph. A Song.

1 In Judah God *is* known;
His name *is* great in Israel.
2 In Salem[a] also is
His tabernacle,
And His dwelling
place in Zion.
3 There He broke the
arrows of the bow,
The shield and sword of
battle. *Selah*

4 You *are* more glorious
and excellent
Than the mountains
of prey.
5 The stouthearted
were plundered;
They have sunk into
their sleep;
And none of the mighty
men have found the
use of their hands.
6 At Your rebuke,
O God of Jacob,
Both the chariot and
horse were cast
into a dead sleep.

7 You, Yourself, *are*
to be feared;
And who may stand
in Your presence
When once You
are angry?
8 You caused judgment to
be heard from heaven;
The earth feared
and was still,
9 When God arose
to judgment,
To deliver all the
oppressed of the
earth. *Selah*

10 Surely the wrath of man
shall praise You;
With the remainder
of wrath You shall
gird Yourself.

11 Make vows to the
LORD your God,
and pay *them;*
Let all who are around
Him bring presents
to Him who ought
to be feared.
12 He shall cut off the
spirit of princes;
He is awesome to the
kings of the earth.

PSALM 77

THE CONSOLING MEMORY OF GOD'S REDEMPTIVE WORKS

To the Chief Musician.
To Jeduthun. A Psalm of Asaph.

1 I cried out to God
with my voice—
To God with my voice;
And He gave ear to me.
2 In the day of my trouble
I sought the Lord;
My hand was stretched
out in the night
without ceasing;

76:title [a] Hebrew *neginoth* 76:2 [a] That is, Jerusalem

My soul refused to
be comforted.
3 I remembered God,
and was troubled;
I complained, and
my spirit was
overwhelmed. *Selah*

4 You hold my eyelids *open;*
I am so troubled that
I cannot speak.
5 I have considered
the days of old,
The years of ancient times.
6 I call to remembrance
my song in the night;
I meditate within
my heart,
And my spirit makes
diligent search.

7 Will the Lord cast
off forever?
And will He be
favorable no more?
8 Has His mercy
ceased forever?
Has *His* promise failed
forevermore?
9 Has God forgotten
to be gracious?
Has He in anger
shut up His tender
mercies? *Selah*

10 And I said, "This *is*
my anguish;
But I will remember the
years of the right hand
of the Most High."
11 I will remember the
works of the LORD;
Surely I will remember
Your wonders of old.
12 I will also meditate
on all Your work,
And talk of Your deeds.
13 Your way, O God, *is*
in the sanctuary;
Who *is* so great a
God as *our* God?
14 You *are* the God who
does wonders;
You have declared
Your strength among
the peoples.
15 You have with *Your* arm
redeemed Your people,
The sons of Jacob and
Joseph. *Selah*

16 The waters saw
You, O God;
The waters saw You,
they were afraid;
The depths also trembled.
17 The clouds poured
out water;
The skies sent out
a sound;
Your arrows also
flashed about.
18 The voice of Your
thunder *was* in
the whirlwind;
The lightnings lit
up the world;
The earth trembled
and shook.
19 Your way *was* in the sea,
Your path in the
great waters,
And Your footsteps
were not known.
20 You led Your people
like a flock
By the hand of Moses
and Aaron.

PSALM 78
GOD'S KINDNESS TO REBELLIOUS ISRAEL

A Contemplation[a] of Asaph.

1 Give ear, O my people,
to my law;
Incline your ears to the
words of my mouth.
2 I will open my mouth
in a parable;
I will utter dark
sayings of old,
3 Which we have heard
and known,
And our fathers
have told us.
4 We will not hide *them*
from their children,
Telling to the generation
to come the praises
of the LORD,
And His strength and
His wonderful works
that He has done.

5 For He established a
testimony in Jacob,
And appointed a
law in Israel,
Which He commanded
our fathers,
That they should
make them known
to their children;
6 That the generation
to come might
know *them*,
The children *who*
would be born,
That they may arise
and declare *them*
to their children,
7 That they may set
their hope in God,
And not forget the
works of God,
But keep His
commandments;
8 And may not be like
their fathers,
A stubborn and
rebellious generation,
A generation *that* did not
set its heart aright,
And whose spirit was
not faithful to God.

9 The children of Ephraim,
being armed *and*
carrying bows,
Turned back in the
day of battle.
10 They did not keep the
covenant of God;
They refused to
walk in His law,
11 And forgot His works
And His wonders that
He had shown them.

12 Marvelous things He
did in the sight of
their fathers,
In the land of Egypt, *in*
the field of Zoan.
13 He divided the sea
and caused them
to pass through;
And He made the waters
stand up like a heap.
14 In the daytime also He
led them with the cloud,
And all the night with
a light of fire.

78:title [a] Hebrew *Maschil*

15 He split the rocks in
the wilderness,
And gave *them* drink
in abundance like
the depths.
16 He also brought streams
out of the rock,
And caused waters to
run down like rivers.

17 But they sinned even
more against Him
By rebelling against
the Most High in
the wilderness.
18 And they tested God
in their heart
By asking for the food
of their fancy.
19 Yes, they spoke
against God:
They said, "Can God
prepare a table in
the wilderness?
20 Behold, He struck
the rock,
So that the waters
gushed out,
And the streams
overflowed.
Can He give bread also?
Can He provide meat
for His people?"

21 Therefore the LORD heard
this and was furious;
So a fire was kindled
against Jacob,
And anger also came
up against Israel,
22 Because they did not
believe in God,
And did not trust in
His salvation.
23 Yet He had commanded
the clouds above,
And opened the
doors of heaven,
24 Had rained down manna
on them to eat,
And given them of the
bread of heaven.
25 Men ate angels' food;
He sent them food
to the full.

26 He caused an east wind
to blow in the heavens;
And by His power
He brought in the
south wind.
27 He also rained meat on
them like the dust,
Feathered fowl like the
sand of the seas;
28 And He let *them* fall in
the midst of their camp,
All around their
dwellings.
29 So they ate and were
well filled,
For He gave them
their own desire.
30 They were not deprived
of their craving;
But while their food *was*
still in their mouths,
31 The wrath of God came
against them,
And slew the stoutest
of them,
And struck down the
choice *men* of Israel.

32 In spite of this they
still sinned,
And did not believe in
His wondrous works.

33 Therefore their days He
consumed in futility,
And their years in fear.

34 When He slew them,
then they sought Him;
And they returned
and sought
earnestly for God.
35 Then they remembered
that God *was* their rock,
And the Most High God
their Redeemer.
36 Nevertheless they
flattered Him with
their mouth,
And they lied to Him
with their tongue;
37 For their heart was not
steadfast with Him,
Nor were they faithful
in His covenant.
38 But He, *being* full of
compassion, forgave
their iniquity,
And did not destroy *them.*
Yes, many a time He
turned His anger away,
And did not stir up
all His wrath;
39 For He remembered that
they *were but* flesh,
A breath that passes
away and does not
come again.

40 How often they provoked
Him in the wilderness,
And grieved Him
in the desert!
41 Yes, again and again
they tempted God,
And limited the Holy
One of Israel.
42 They did not remember
His power:
The day when He
redeemed them
from the enemy,
43 When He worked His
signs in Egypt,
And His wonders in
the field of Zoan;
44 Turned their rivers
into blood,
And their streams, that
they could not drink.
45 He sent swarms of flies
among them, which
devoured them,
And frogs, which
destroyed them.
46 He also gave their crops
to the caterpillar,
And their labor to
the locust.
47 He destroyed their
vines with hail,
And their sycamore
trees with frost.
48 He also gave up their
cattle to the hail,
And their flocks to
fiery lightning.
49 He cast on them
the fierceness
of His anger,
Wrath, indignation,
and trouble,
By sending angels
of destruction
among them.
50 He made a path
for His anger;
He did not spare their
soul from death,
But gave their life over
to the plague,

51 And destroyed all the
firstborn in Egypt,
The first of *their* strength
in the tents of Ham.
52 But He made His
own people go
forth like sheep,
And guided them in the
wilderness like a flock;
53 And He led them on safely,
so that they did not fear;
But the sea overwhelmed
their enemies.
54 And He brought them
to His holy border,
This mountain *which*
His right hand
had acquired.
55 He also drove out the
nations before them,
Allotted them an
inheritance by survey,
And made the tribes
of Israel dwell in
their tents.

56 Yet they tested and
provoked the
Most High God,
And did not keep
His testimonies,
57 But turned back and
acted unfaithfully
like their fathers;
They were turned aside
like a deceitful bow.
58 For they provoked
Him to anger with
their high places,
And moved Him to
jealousy with their
carved images.
59 When God heard *this,*
He was furious,
And greatly abhorred
Israel,
60 So that He forsook the
tabernacle of Shiloh,
The tent He had placed
among men,
61 And delivered His
strength into captivity,
And His glory into the
enemy's hand.
62 He also gave His people
over to the sword,
And was furious with
His inheritance.
63 The fire consumed
their young men,
And their maidens were
not given in marriage.
64 Their priests fell
by the sword,
And their widows made
no lamentation.

65 Then the Lord awoke
as *from* sleep,
Like a mighty man
who shouts
because of wine.
66 And He beat back
His enemies;
He put them to a
perpetual reproach.

67 Moreover He rejected
the tent of Joseph,
And did not choose the
tribe of Ephraim,
68 But chose the tribe
of Judah,
Mount Zion which
He loved.
69 And He built His
sanctuary like
the heights,

Like the earth which He
has established forever.
70 He also chose David
His servant,
And took him from
the sheepfolds;
71 From following the
ewes that had young
He brought him,
To shepherd Jacob
His people,
And Israel His
inheritance.
72 So he shepherded them
according to the
integrity of his heart,
And guided them by the
skillfulness of his hands.

PSALM 79

A DIRGE AND A PRAYER FOR ISRAEL, DESTROYED BY ENEMIES

A Psalm of Asaph.

1 O God, the nations
have come into
Your inheritance;
Your holy temple
they have defiled;
They have laid
Jerusalem in heaps.
2 The dead bodies of
Your servants
They have given *as*
food for the birds
of the heavens,
The flesh of Your saints to
the beasts of the earth.
3 Their blood they have
shed like water all
around Jerusalem,
And *there was* no one
to bury *them*.
4 We have become a
reproach to our
neighbors,
A scorn and derision
to those who are
around us.

5 How long, LORD?
Will You be angry forever?
Will Your jealousy
burn like fire?
6 Pour out Your wrath
on the nations that
do not know You,
And on the kingdoms
that do not call
on Your name.
7 For they have
devoured Jacob,
And laid waste his
dwelling place.

8 Oh, do not remember
former iniquities
against us!
Let Your tender mercies
come speedily
to meet us,
For we have been
brought very low.
9 Help us, O God of
our salvation,
For the glory of
Your name;
And deliver us, and
provide atonement
for our sins,
For Your name's sake!
10 Why should the
nations say,
"Where *is* their God?"
Let there be known
among the nations
in our sight

The avenging of the
blood of Your servants
which has been shed.

11 Let the groaning of
the prisoner come
before You;
According to the
greatness of Your power
Preserve those who are
appointed to die;
12 And return to our
neighbors sevenfold
into their bosom
Their reproach with
which they have
reproached You, O Lord.

13 So we, Your people and
sheep of Your pasture,
Will give You thanks
forever;
We will show forth Your
praise to all generations.

PSALM 80

PRAYER FOR ISRAEL'S RESTORATION

To the Chief Musician. Set
to "The Lilies."[a] A Testimony[b]
of Asaph. A Psalm.

1 Give ear, O Shepherd
of Israel,
You who lead Joseph
like a flock;
You who dwell *between* the
cherubim, shine forth!
2 Before Ephraim,
Benjamin, and
Manasseh,
Stir up Your strength,
And come *and* save us!

3 Restore us, O God;
Cause Your face to shine,
And we shall be saved!

4 O LORD God of hosts,
How long will You
be angry
Against the prayer
of Your people?
5 You have fed them with
the bread of tears,
And given them tears
to drink in great
measure.
6 You have made us a strife
to our neighbors,
And our enemies laugh
among themselves.

7 Restore us, O God
of hosts;
Cause Your face to shine,
And we shall be saved!

8 You have brought a
vine out of Egypt;
You have cast out the
nations, and planted it.
9 You prepared *room* for it,
And caused it to
take deep root,
And it filled the land.
10 The hills were covered
with its shadow,
And the mighty cedars
with its boughs.
11 She sent out her
boughs to the Sea,[a]

80:title [a] Hebrew *Shoshannim* [b] Hebrew *Eduth* 80:11 [a] That is, the Mediterranean

And her branches
to the River.[b]

12 Why have You broken
down her hedges,
So that all who pass by
the way pluck her *fruit?*
13 The boar out of the
woods uproots it,
And the wild beast of
the field devours it.

14 Return, we beseech
You, O God of hosts;
Look down from
heaven and see,
And visit this vine
15 And the vineyard
which Your right
hand has planted,
And the branch *that*
You made strong
for Yourself.
16 *It is* burned with fire,
it is cut down;
They perish at the rebuke
of Your countenance.
17 Let Your hand be
upon the man of
Your right hand,
Upon the son of man
whom You made
strong for Yourself.
18 Then we will not turn
back from You;
Revive us, and we will
call upon Your name.

19 Restore us, O LORD
God of hosts;
Cause Your face to shine,
And we shall be saved!

PSALM 81

AN APPEAL FOR ISRAEL'S REPENTANCE

To the Chief Musician.
On an instrument of Gath.[a]
A *Psalm* of Asaph.

1 Sing aloud to God
our strength;
Make a joyful shout to
the God of Jacob.
2 Raise a song and
strike the timbrel,
The pleasant harp
with the lute.

3 Blow the trumpet at the
time of the New Moon,
At the full moon, on our
solemn feast day.
4 For this *is* a statute
for Israel,
A law of the God of Jacob.
5 This He established in
Joseph *as* a testimony,
When He went throughout
the land of Egypt,
Where I heard a language
I did not understand.

6 "I removed his shoulder
from the burden;
His hands were freed
from the baskets.
7 You called in trouble,
and I delivered you;
I answered you in the
secret place of thunder;
I tested you at the waters
of Meribah. *Selah*

8 "Hear, O My people, and
I will admonish you!

80:11 [b] That is, the Euphrates 81:title [a] Hebrew *Al Gittith*

O Israel, if you will
listen to Me!
9 There shall be no foreign
god among you;
Nor shall you worship
any foreign god.
10 I *am* the LORD your God,
Who brought you out
of the land of Egypt;
Open your mouth wide,
and I will fill it.

11 "But My people would
not heed My voice,
And Israel would
have none of Me.
12 So I gave them
over to their own
stubborn heart,
To walk in their
own counsels.

13 "Oh, that My people
would listen to Me,
That Israel would
walk in My ways!
14 I would soon subdue
their enemies,
And turn My hand against
their adversaries.
15 The haters of the
LORD would pretend
submission to Him,
But their fate would
endure forever.
16 He would have fed
them also with the
finest of wheat;
And with honey from
the rock I would
have satisfied you."

PSALM 82

A PLEA FOR JUSTICE

A Psalm of Asaph.

1 God stands in the
congregation of
the mighty;
He judges among
the gods.[a]
2 How long will you
judge unjustly,
And show partiality to the
wicked? *Selah*
3 Defend the poor
and fatherless;
Do justice to the
afflicted and needy.
4 Deliver the poor
and needy;
Free *them* from the
hand of the wicked.

5 They do not know, nor
do they understand;
They walk about
in darkness;
All the foundations of
the earth are unstable.

6 I said, "You *are* gods,[a]
And all of you *are*
children of the
Most High.
7 But you shall die
like men,
And fall like one of
the princes."

8 Arise, O God, judge
the earth;
For You shall inherit
all nations.

82:1 [a] Hebrew *elohim, mighty ones;* that is, the judges
82:6 [a] Hebrew *elohim, mighty ones;* that is, the judges

PSALM 83

PRAYER TO FRUSTRATE CONSPIRACY AGAINST ISRAEL

A Song. A Psalm of Asaph.

1 Do not keep silent, O God!
Do not hold Your peace,
And do not be still, O God!
2 For behold, Your enemies
make a tumult;
And those who hate
You have lifted
up their head.
3 They have taken crafty
counsel against
Your people,
And consulted
together against Your
sheltered ones.
4 They have said, "Come,
and let us cut them off
from *being* a nation,
That the name of Israel
may be remembered
no more."

5 For they have consulted
together with
one consent;
They form a confederacy
against You:
6 The tents of Edom and
the Ishmaelites;
Moab and the Hagrites;
7 Gebal, Ammon,
and Amalek;
Philistia with the
inhabitants of Tyre;
8 Assyria also has
joined with them;
They have helped the
children of Lot. *Selah*

9 Deal with them as
with Midian,
As *with* Sisera,
As *with* Jabin at the
Brook Kishon,
10 Who perished at
En Dor,
Who became *as* refuse
on the earth.
11 Make their nobles like
Oreb and like Zeeb,
Yes, all their princes
like Zebah and
Zalmunna,
12 Who said, "Let us take
for ourselves
The pastures of God
for a possession."

13 O my God, make
them like the
whirling dust,
Like the chaff before
the wind!
14 As the fire burns
the woods,
And as the flame sets
the mountains
on fire,
15 So pursue them with
Your tempest,
And frighten them
with Your storm.
16 Fill their faces
with shame,
That they may seek
Your name, O LORD.
17 Let them be confounded
and dismayed forever;
Yes, let them be put to
shame and perish,
18 That they may know
that You, whose name
alone *is* the LORD,
Are the Most High
over all the earth.

PSALM 84

THE BLESSEDNESS OF DWELLING IN THE HOUSE OF GOD

To the Chief Musician.
On an instrument of Gath.[a]
A Psalm of the sons of Korah.

1 How lovely *is* Your
tabernacle,
O LORD of hosts!
2 My soul longs, yes,
even faints
For the courts of the LORD;
My heart and my flesh cry
out for the living God.

3 Even the sparrow has
found a home,
And the swallow a
nest for herself,
Where she may lay
her young—
Even Your altars,
O LORD of hosts,
My King and my God.
4 Blessed *are* those who
dwell in Your house;
They will still be praising
You. *Selah*

5 Blessed *is* the man whose
strength *is* in You,
Whose heart *is* set
on pilgrimage.
6 *As they* pass through
the Valley of Baca,
They make it a spring;
The rain also covers
it with pools.
7 *They go from* strength
to strength;
Each one appears
before God in Zion.[a]

8 O LORD God of hosts,
hear my prayer;
Give ear, O God of
Jacob! *Selah*
9 O God, behold our shield,
And look upon the face
of Your anointed.

10 For a day in Your courts *is*
better than a thousand.
I would rather be a
doorkeeper in the
house of my God
Than dwell in the tents
of wickedness.
11 For the LORD God *is*
a sun and shield;
The LORD will give
grace and glory;
No good *thing* will
He withhold
From those who
walk uprightly.

12 O LORD of hosts,
Blessed *is* the man
who trusts in You!

PSALM 85

PRAYER THAT THE LORD WILL RESTORE FAVOR TO THE LAND

To the Chief Musician. A Psalm
of the sons of Korah.

1 LORD, You have been
favorable to Your land;
You have brought back
the captivity of Jacob.

84:title [a] Hebrew *Al Gittith* 84:7 [a] Septuagint, Syriac, and Vulgate read *The God of gods shall be seen.*

2 You have forgiven the
iniquity of Your people;
You have covered all their
sin. *Selah*
3 You have taken away
all Your wrath;
You have turned from the
fierceness of Your anger.

4 Restore us, O God of
our salvation,
And cause Your anger
toward us to cease.
5 Will You be angry
with us forever?
Will You prolong
Your anger to all
generations?
6 Will You not revive
us again,
That Your people may
rejoice in You?
7 Show us Your
mercy, LORD,
And grant us Your
salvation.

8 I will hear what God the
LORD will speak,
For He will speak peace
To His people and
to His saints;
But let them not turn
back to folly.
9 Surely His salvation
is near to those
who fear Him,
That glory may dwell
in our land.

10 Mercy and truth have
met together;
Righteousness and
peace have kissed.
11 Truth shall spring
out of the earth,
And righteousness shall
look down from heaven.
12 Yes, the LORD will
give *what is* good;
And our land will
yield its increase.
13 Righteousness will
go before Him,
And shall make His
footsteps *our* pathway.

PSALM 86

PRAYER FOR MERCY, WITH MEDITATION ON THE EXCELLENCIES OF THE LORD

A Prayer of David.

1 Bow down Your ear,
O LORD, hear me;
For I *am* poor and needy.
2 Preserve my life,
for I *am* holy;
You are my God;
Save Your servant
who trusts in You!
3 Be merciful to
me, O Lord,
For I cry to You
all day long.
4 Rejoice the soul of
Your servant,
For to You, O Lord, I
lift up my soul.
5 For You, Lord, *are* good,
and ready to forgive,
And abundant in
mercy to all those
who call upon You.

6 Give ear, O LORD,
to my prayer;

And attend to the
voice of my
supplications.
7 In the day of my
trouble I will call
upon You,
For You will answer me.

8 Among the gods *there is*
none like You, O Lord;
Nor *are there any works*
like Your works.
9 All nations whom
You have made
Shall come and worship
before You, O Lord,
And shall glorify
Your name.
10 For You *are* great, and
do wondrous things;
You alone *are* God.

11 Teach me Your
way, O LORD;
I will walk in Your truth;
Unite my heart to
fear Your name.
12 I will praise You,
O Lord my God,
with all my heart,
And I will glorify Your
name forevermore.
13 For great *is* Your
mercy toward me,
And You have delivered
my soul from the
depths of Sheol.

14 O God, the proud have
risen against me,
And a mob of violent *men*
have sought my life,
And have not set You
before them.
15 But You, O Lord, *are* a
God full of compassion,
and gracious,
Longsuffering and
abundant in mercy
and truth.

16 Oh, turn to me, and
have mercy on me!
Give Your strength
to Your servant,
And save the son of
Your maidservant.
17 Show me a sign for good,
That those who hate
me may see *it* and
be ashamed,
Because You, LORD,
have helped me and
comforted me.

PSALM 87

THE GLORIES OF THE CITY OF GOD

A Psalm of the sons
of Korah. A Song.

1 His foundation *is* in the
holy mountains.
2 The LORD loves the
gates of Zion
More than all the
dwellings of Jacob.
3 Glorious things are
spoken of you,
O city of God! *Selah*

4 "I will make mention of
Rahab and Babylon to
those who know Me;
Behold, O Philistia and
Tyre, with Ethiopia:
'This *one* was
born there.'"

5 And of Zion it will be said,
"This *one* and that *one*
were born in her;
And the Most High
Himself shall
establish her."
6 The LORD will record,
When He registers
the peoples:
"This *one* was born
there." *Selah*

7 Both the singers
and the players on
instruments *say,*
"All my springs
are in you."

PSALM 88

A PRAYER FOR HELP IN DESPONDENCY

A Song. A Psalm of the sons of Korah. To the Chief Musician. Set to "Mahalath Leannoth." A Contemplation[a] of Heman the Ezrahite.

1 O LORD, God of my
salvation,
I have cried out day and
night before You.
2 Let my prayer come
before You;
Incline Your ear
to my cry.

3 For my soul is full
of troubles,
And my life draws
near to the grave.
4 I am counted with those
who go down to the pit;
I am like a man *who*
has no strength,
5 Adrift among the dead,
Like the slain who
lie in the grave,
Whom You remember
no more,
And who are cut off
from Your hand.

6 You have laid me in
the lowest pit,
In darkness, in the depths.
7 Your wrath lies
heavy upon me,
And You have afflicted
me with all Your
waves. *Selah*
8 You have put away
my acquaintances
far from me;
You have made me an
abomination to them;
I am shut up, and I
cannot get out;
9 My eye wastes away
because of affliction.

LORD, I have called
daily upon You;
I have stretched out
my hands to You.
10 Will You work wonders
for the dead?
Shall the dead arise *and*
praise You? *Selah*
11 Shall Your lovingkindness
be declared in the grave?
Or Your faithfulness in the
place of destruction?
12 Shall Your wonders be
known in the dark?

88:title [a] Hebrew *Maschil*

And Your righteousness
in the land of
forgetfulness?

13 But to You I have
cried out, O LORD,
And in the morning
my prayer comes
before You.
14 LORD, why do You
cast off my soul?
Why do You hide Your
face from me?
15 I *have been* afflicted
and ready to die
from *my* youth;
I suffer Your terrors;
I am distraught.
16 Your fierce wrath has
gone over me;
Your terrors have
cut me off.
17 They came around me
all day long like water;
They engulfed me
altogether.
18 Loved one and friend
You have put
far from me,
And my acquaintances
into darkness.

PSALM 89

REMEMBERING THE COVENANT WITH DAVID, AND SORROW FOR LOST BLESSINGS

A Contemplation[a]
of Ethan the Ezrahite.

1 I will sing of the mercies
of the LORD forever;
With my mouth will I
make known Your
faithfulness to all
generations.
2 For I have said,
"Mercy shall be
built up forever;
Your faithfulness You
shall establish in
the very heavens."

3 "I have made a covenant
with My chosen,
I have sworn to My
servant David:
4 'Your seed I will
establish forever,
And build up your
throne to all
generations.'" *Selah*

5 And the heavens
will praise Your
wonders, O LORD;
Your faithfulness also
in the assembly
of the saints.
6 For who in the heavens
can be compared
to the LORD?
Who among the sons
of the mighty can be
likened to the LORD?
7 God is greatly to be
feared in the assembly
of the saints,
And to be held in
reverence by all
those around Him.
8 O LORD God of hosts,
Who *is* mighty like
You, O LORD?

89:title [a] Hebrew *Maschil*

Your faithfulness also
surrounds You.
9 You rule the raging
of the sea;
When its waves rise,
You still them.
10 You have broken
Rahab in pieces, as
one who is slain;
You have scattered
Your enemies with
Your mighty arm.

11 The heavens *are* Yours,
the earth also *is*
Yours;
The world and all its
fullness, You have
founded them.
12 The north and the
south, You have
created them;
Tabor and Hermon
rejoice in Your name.
13 You have a mighty arm;
Strong is Your hand,
and high is Your
right hand.
14 Righteousness and justice
are the foundation
of Your throne;
Mercy and truth go
before Your face.
15 Blessed *are* the
people who know
the joyful sound!
They walk, O LORD,
in the light of Your
countenance.
16 In Your name they
rejoice all day long,
And in Your
righteousness they
are exalted.
17 For You *are* the glory
of their strength,
And in Your favor our
horn is exalted.
18 For our shield *belongs*
to the LORD,
And our king to the
Holy One of Israel.

19 Then You spoke in
a vision to Your
holy one,[a]
And said: "I have
given help to *one*
who is mighty;
I have exalted one
chosen from
the people.
20 I have found My
servant David;
With My holy oil I have
anointed him,
21 With whom My hand
shall be established;
Also My arm shall
strengthen him.
22 The enemy shall not
outwit him,
Nor the son of
wickedness afflict him.
23 I will beat down his
foes before his face,
And plague those
who hate him.

24 "But My faithfulness
and My mercy *shall*
be with him,

89:19 [a] Following many Hebrew manuscripts; Masoretic Text, Septuagint, Targum, and Vulgate read *holy ones*.

And in My name his
horn shall be exalted.
25 Also I will set his
hand over the sea,
And his right hand
over the rivers.
26 He shall cry to Me,
'You *are* my Father,
My God, and the rock
of my salvation.'
27 Also I will make him
My firstborn,
The highest of the
kings of the earth.
28 My mercy I will keep
for him forever,
And My covenant
shall stand firm
with him.
29 His seed also I will make
to endure forever,
And his throne as the
days of heaven.

30 "If his sons forsake
My law
And do not walk in
My judgments,
31 If they break My statutes
And do not keep My
commandments,
32 Then I will punish
their transgression
with the rod,
And their iniquity
with stripes.
33 Nevertheless My
lovingkindness
I will not utterly
take from him,
Nor allow My
faithfulness to fail.
34 My covenant I will
not break,
Nor alter the word that
has gone out of My lips.
35 Once I have sworn
by My holiness;
I will not lie to David:
36 His seed shall
endure forever,
And his throne as the
sun before Me;
37 It shall be established
forever like the moon,
Even *like* the faithful
witness in the
sky." *Selah*

38 But You have cast off
and abhorred,
You have been furious
with Your anointed.
39 You have renounced
the covenant of
Your servant;
You have profaned
his crown *by casting*
it to the ground.
40 You have broken down
all his hedges;
You have brought his
strongholds to ruin.
41 All who pass by the
way plunder him;
He is a reproach to
his neighbors.
42 You have exalted the right
hand of his adversaries;
You have made all his
enemies rejoice.
43 You have also turned
back the edge
of his sword,
And have not sustained
him in the battle.
44 You have made his
glory cease,

And cast his throne
down to the ground.
45 The days of his
youth You have
shortened;
You have covered him
with shame. *Selah*

46 How long, LORD?
Will You hide
Yourself forever?
Will Your wrath
burn like fire?
47 Remember how
short my time is;
For what futility have
You created all the
children of men?
48 What man can live
and not see death?
Can he deliver his life
from the power of the
grave? *Selah*

49 Lord, where *are*
Your former
lovingkindnesses,
Which You swore to
David in Your truth?
50 Remember, Lord,
the reproach of
Your servants—
How I bear in my bosom
the reproach of all
the many peoples,
51 With which Your
enemies have
reproached, O LORD,
With which they
have reproached
the footsteps of
Your anointed.

52 Blessed *be* the LORD
forevermore!
Amen and Amen.

BOOK FOUR

PSALMS 90–106

PSALM 90

THE ETERNITY OF GOD, AND MAN'S FRAILTY

A Prayer of Moses
the man of God.

1 Lord, You have been
our dwelling place[a]
in all generations.
2 Before the mountains
were brought forth,
Or ever You had formed
the earth and the world,
Even from everlasting to
everlasting, You *are* God.

3 You turn man to
destruction,
And say, "Return,
O children of men."
4 For a thousand years
in Your sight
Are like yesterday
when it is past,
And *like* a watch
in the night.
5 You carry them away
like a flood;
They are like a sleep.
In the morning
they are like grass
which grows up:
6 In the morning it
flourishes and
grows up;

90:1 [a] Septuagint, Targum, and Vulgate read *refuge*.

In the evening it is cut
down and withers.

7 For we have been
consumed by
Your anger,
And by Your wrath
we are terrified.
8 You have set our
iniquities before You,
Our secret *sins* in the
light of Your
countenance.
9 For all our days have
passed away in
Your wrath;
We finish our years
like a sigh.
10 The days of our lives
are seventy years;
And if by reason of
strength *they are*
eighty years,
Yet their boast *is* only
labor and sorrow;
For it is soon cut off,
and we fly away.
11 Who knows the power
of Your anger?
For as the fear of You,
so is Your wrath.
12 So teach *us* to number
our days,
That we may gain a
heart of wisdom.

13 Return, O LORD!
How long?
And have compassion
on Your servants.
14 Oh, satisfy us early
with Your mercy,
That we may rejoice
and be glad all
our days!
15 Make us glad according
to the days *in which*
You have afflicted us,
The years *in which* we
have seen evil.
16 Let Your work appear
to Your servants,
And Your glory to
their children.
17 And let the beauty
of the LORD our
God be upon us,
And establish the work
of our hands for us;
Yes, establish the work
of our hands.

PSALM 91

SAFETY OF ABIDING IN THE PRESENCE OF GOD

1 He who dwells in
the secret place of
the Most High
Shall abide under the
shadow of the Almighty.
2 I will say of the LORD,
"*He is* my refuge
and my fortress;
My God, in Him I
will trust."

3 Surely He shall deliver
you from the snare
of the fowler[a]
And from the perilous
pestilence.
4 He shall cover you
with His feathers,

91:3 [a] That is, one who catches birds in a trap or snare

And under His wings
you shall take refuge;
His truth *shall be your*
shield and buckler.
5 You shall not be afraid
of the terror by night,
Nor of the arrow *that*
flies by day,
6 *Nor* of the pestilence *that*
walks in darkness,
Nor of the destruction
that lays waste
at noonday.

7 A thousand may fall
at your side,
And ten thousand at
your right hand;
But it shall not
come near you.
8 Only with your eyes
shall you look,
And see the reward
of the wicked.

9 Because you have
made the LORD,
who is my refuge,
Even the Most High,
your dwelling place,
10 No evil shall befall you,
Nor shall any plague
come near your
dwelling;
11 For He shall give His
angels charge over you,
To keep you in all
your ways.
12 In *their* hands they
shall bear you up,
Lest you dash your foot
against a stone.
13 You shall tread upon the
lion and the cobra,
The young lion and
the serpent you shall
trample underfoot.

14 "Because he has set his
love upon Me, therefore
I will deliver him;
I will set him on high,
because he has
known My name.
15 He shall call upon Me,
and I will answer him;
I *will be* with him
in trouble;
I will deliver him
and honor him.
16 With long life I will
satisfy him,
And show him My
salvation."

PSALM 92

PRAISE TO THE LORD FOR HIS LOVE AND FAITHFULNESS

A Psalm. A Song
for the Sabbath day.

1 *It is* good to give thanks
to the LORD,
And to sing praises to Your
name, O Most High;
2 To declare Your
lovingkindness in
the morning,
And Your faithfulness
every night,
3 On an instrument
of ten strings,
On the lute,
And on the harp,
With harmonious sound.
4 For You, LORD, have
made me glad
through Your work;

I will triumph in the
works of Your hands.

5 O LORD, how great
are Your works!
Your thoughts are
very deep.
6 A senseless man
does not know,
Nor does a fool
understand this.
7 When the wicked
spring up like grass,
And when all the workers
of iniquity flourish,
It is that they may be
destroyed forever.

8 But You, LORD, *are* on
high forevermore.
9 For behold, Your
enemies, O LORD,
For behold, Your
enemies shall perish;
All the workers of iniquity
shall be scattered.

10 But my horn You have
exalted like a wild ox;
I have been anointed
with fresh oil.
11 My eye also has seen *my
desire* on my enemies;
My ears hear *my desire*
on the wicked
Who rise up against me.

12 The righteous shall
flourish like a
palm tree,
He shall grow like a
cedar in Lebanon.
13 Those who are planted in
the house of the LORD
Shall flourish in the
courts of our God.
14 They shall still bear
fruit in old age;
They shall be fresh
and flourishing,
15 To declare that the
LORD is upright;
He is my rock, and *there
is* no unrighteousness
in Him.

PSALM 93

THE ETERNAL REIGN OF THE LORD

1 The LORD reigns, He
is clothed with
majesty;
The LORD is clothed,
He has girded Himself
with strength.
Surely the world is
established, so that it
cannot be moved.
2 Your throne *is* established
from of old;
You *are* from everlasting.

3 The floods have lifted
up, O LORD,
The floods have lifted
up their voice;
The floods lift up
their waves.
4 The LORD on high
is mightier
Than the noise of
many waters,
Than the mighty
waves of the sea.

5 Your testimonies
are very sure;

Holiness adorns
Your house,
O LORD, forever.

PSALM 94

GOD THE REFUGE OF THE RIGHTEOUS

1 O LORD God, to whom
vengeance belongs—
O God, to whom
vengeance belongs,
shine forth!
2 Rise up, O Judge
of the earth;
Render punishment
to the proud.
3 LORD, how long will
the wicked,
How long will the
wicked triumph?

4 They utter speech, *and*
speak insolent things;
All the workers of
iniquity boast in
themselves.
5 They break in pieces
Your people, O LORD,
And afflict Your heritage.
6 They slay the widow
and the stranger,
And murder the
fatherless.
7 Yet they say, "The
LORD does not see,
Nor does the God of
Jacob understand."

8 Understand, you
senseless among
the people;
And *you* fools, when
will you be wise?
9 He who planted the ear,
shall He not hear?
He who formed the eye,
shall He not see?
10 He who instructs
the nations, shall
He not correct,
He who teaches man
knowledge?
11 The LORD knows the
thoughts of man,
That they *are* futile.

12 Blessed *is* the man whom
You instruct, O LORD,
And teach out of Your law,
13 That You may give
him rest from the
days of adversity,
Until the pit is dug
for the wicked.
14 For the LORD will not
cast off His people,
Nor will He forsake
His inheritance.
15 But judgment will return
to righteousness,
And all the upright in
heart will follow it.

16 Who will rise up for me
against the evildoers?
Who will stand up
for me against the
workers of iniquity?
17 Unless the LORD *had*
been my help,
My soul would soon have
settled in silence.
18 If I say, "My foot slips,"
Your mercy, O LORD,
will hold me up.
19 In the multitude of my
anxieties within me,

Your comforts
delight my soul.

20 Shall the throne of
iniquity, which
devises evil by law,
Have fellowship
with You?
21 They gather together
against the life of
the righteous,
And condemn
innocent blood.
22 But the LORD has
been my defense,
And my God the rock
of my refuge.
23 He has brought on them
their own iniquity,
And shall cut them off in
their own wickedness;
The LORD our God
shall cut them off.

PSALM 95

A CALL TO WORSHIP AND OBEDIENCE

1 Oh come, let us sing
to the LORD!
Let us shout joyfully
to the Rock of
our salvation.
2 Let us come before
His presence with
thanksgiving;
Let us shout joyfully to
Him with psalms.
3 For the LORD *is* the
great God,
And the great King
above all gods.
4 In His hand *are* the
deep places of
the earth;
The heights of the
hills *are* His also.
5 The sea *is* His, for
He made it;
And His hands formed
the dry *land.*

6 Oh come, let us worship
and bow down;
Let us kneel before the
LORD our Maker.
7 For He *is* our God,
And we *are* the people
of His pasture,
And the sheep of
His hand.

Today, if you will
hear His voice:
8 "Do not harden your
hearts, as in the
rebellion,[a]
As *in* the day of trial[b]
in the wilderness,
9 When your fathers
tested Me;
They tried Me, though
they saw My work.
10 For forty years I was
grieved with *that*
generation,
And said, 'It *is* a people
who go astray in
their hearts,
And they do not
know My ways.'
11 So I swore in My wrath,
'They shall not
enter My rest.'"

95:8 [a] Or *Meribah* [b] Or *Massah*

PSALM 96

A SONG OF PRAISE TO GOD COMING IN JUDGMENT

1 Oh, sing to the LORD
a new song!
Sing to the LORD,
all the earth.
2 Sing to the LORD,
bless His name;
Proclaim the good
news of His salvation
from day to day.
3 Declare His glory
among the nations,
His wonders among
all peoples.

4 For the LORD *is* great
and greatly to
be praised;
He *is* to be feared
above all gods.
5 For all the gods of the
peoples *are* idols,
But the LORD made
the heavens.
6 Honor and majesty
are before Him;
Strength and beauty
are in His sanctuary.

7 Give to the LORD,
O families of
the peoples,
Give to the LORD glory
and strength.
8 Give to the LORD the
glory *due* His name;
Bring an offering, and
come into His courts.
9 Oh, worship the LORD in
the beauty of holiness!
Tremble before Him,
all the earth.
10 Say among the nations,
"The LORD reigns;
The world also is
firmly established,
It shall not be moved;
He shall judge the
peoples righteously."

11 Let the heavens rejoice,
and let the earth be glad;
Let the sea roar, and
all its fullness;
12 Let the field be joyful,
and all that *is* in it.
Then all the trees of the
woods will rejoice
13 before the LORD.
For He is coming, for
He is coming to
judge the earth.
He shall judge the world
with righteousness,
And the peoples
with His truth.

PSALM 97

A SONG OF PRAISE TO THE SOVEREIGN LORD

1 The LORD reigns;
Let the earth rejoice;
Let the multitude
of isles be glad!

2 Clouds and darkness
surround Him;
Righteousness and justice
are the foundation
of His throne.
3 A fire goes before Him,
And burns up His
enemies round about.
4 His lightnings light
the world;

The earth sees and
trembles.
5 The mountains melt like
wax at the presence
of the LORD,
At the presence of the
Lord of the whole earth.
6 The heavens declare
His righteousness,
And all the peoples
see His glory.

7 Let all be put to
shame who serve
carved images,
Who boast of idols.
Worship Him, all *you* gods.
8 Zion hears and is glad,
And the daughters
of Judah rejoice
Because of Your
judgments, O LORD.
9 For You, LORD, *are* most
high above all the earth;
You are exalted far
above all gods.

10 You who love the
LORD, hate evil!
He preserves the souls
of His saints;
He delivers them out of
the hand of the wicked.
11 Light is sown for
the righteous,
And gladness for the
upright in heart.
12 Rejoice in the LORD,
you righteous,
And give thanks at the
remembrance of
His holy name.[a]

PSALM 98

A SONG OF PRAISE TO THE LORD FOR HIS SALVATION AND JUDGMENT

A Psalm.

1 Oh, sing to the LORD
a new song!
For He has done
marvelous things;
His right hand and
His holy arm have
gained Him the
victory.
2 The LORD has made
known His salvation;
His righteousness He
has revealed in the
sight of the nations.
3 He has remembered
His mercy and His
faithfulness to the
house of Israel;
All the ends of the
earth have seen the
salvation of our God.

4 Shout joyfully to the
LORD, all the earth;
Break forth in
song, rejoice, and
sing praises.
5 Sing to the LORD
with the harp,
With the harp and the
sound of a psalm,
6 With trumpets and the
sound of a horn;
Shout joyfully before
the LORD, the King.

7 Let the sea roar, and
all its fullness,

97:12 [a] Or *His holiness*

The world and those
who dwell in it;
8 Let the rivers clap
their hands;
Let the hills be
joyful together
9 before the LORD,
For He is coming to
judge the earth.
With righteousness He
shall judge the world,
And the peoples
with equity.

PSALM 99

PRAISE TO THE LORD FOR HIS HOLINESS

1 The LORD reigns;
Let the peoples tremble!
He dwells *between*
the cherubim;
Let the earth be moved!
2 The LORD *is* great
in Zion,
And He *is* high above
all the peoples.
3 Let them praise
Your great and
awesome name—
He *is* holy.

4 The King's strength
also loves justice;
You have established
equity;
You have executed
justice and
righteousness in
Jacob.
5 Exalt the LORD our God,
And worship at His
footstool—
He *is* holy.

6 Moses and Aaron
were among His
priests,
And Samuel was among
those who called
upon His name;
They called upon
the LORD, and He
answered them.
7 He spoke to them in
the cloudy pillar;
They kept His testimonies
and the ordinance
He gave them.

8 You answered them,
O LORD our God;
You were to them
God-Who-Forgives,
Though You took
vengeance on
their deeds.
9 Exalt the LORD our God,
And worship at
His holy hill;
For the LORD our
God *is* holy.

PSALM 100

A SONG OF PRAISE FOR THE LORD'S FAITHFULNESS TO HIS PEOPLE

A Psalm of Thanksgiving.

1 Make a joyful shout
to the LORD, all
you lands!
2 Serve the LORD
with gladness;
Come before His
presence with singing.
3 Know that the LORD,
He *is* God;

It is He *who* has made us,
and not we ourselves;[a]
We are His people and the
sheep of His pasture.

4 Enter into His gates
with thanksgiving,
And into His courts
with praise.
Be thankful to Him,
and bless His name.
5 For the LORD *is* good;
His mercy *is* everlasting,
And His truth *endures*
to all generations.

PSALM 101

PROMISED FAITHFULNESS TO THE LORD

A Psalm of David.

1 I will sing of mercy
and justice;
To You, O LORD, I
will sing praises.

2 I will behave wisely
in a perfect way.
Oh, when will You
come to me?
I will walk within
my house with a
perfect heart.

3 I will set nothing wicked
before my eyes;
I hate the work of those
who fall away;
It shall not cling to me.
4 *A perverse heart shall*
depart from me;
I will not know
wickedness.

5 Whoever secretly
slanders his neighbor,
Him I will destroy;
The one who has a
haughty look and
a proud heart,
Him I will not endure.

6 My eyes *shall be* on the
faithful of the land,
That they may
dwell with me;
He who walks in a
perfect way,
He shall serve me.
7 He who works deceit
shall not dwell
within my house;
He who tells lies shall
not continue in
my presence.
8 Early I will destroy all
the wicked of the
land,
That I may cut off all
the evildoers from
the city of the LORD.

PSALM 102

THE LORD'S ETERNAL LOVE

A Prayer of the afflicted,
when he is overwhelmed
and pours out his complaint
before the LORD.

1 Hear my prayer, O LORD,
And let my cry
come to You.

100:3 [a] Following Kethib, Septuagint, and Vulgate; Qere, many Hebrew manuscripts, and Targum read *we are His.*

2 Do not hide Your face
from me in the day
of my trouble;
Incline Your ear to me;
In the day that I call,
answer me speedily.

3 For my days are
consumed like smoke,
And my bones are
burned like a hearth.
4 My heart is stricken and
withered like grass,
So that I forget to
eat my bread.
5 Because of the sound
of my groaning
My bones cling to my skin.
6 I am like a pelican of
the wilderness;
I am like an owl of
the desert.
7 I lie awake,
And am like a sparrow
alone on the housetop.

8 My enemies reproach
me all day long;
Those who deride
me swear an oath
against me.
9 For I have eaten
ashes like bread,
And mingled my drink
with weeping,
10 Because of Your
indignation and
Your wrath;
For You have lifted me
up and cast me away.
11 My days *are* like a shadow
that lengthens,
And I wither away
like grass.

12 But You, O LORD, shall
endure forever,
And the remembrance
of Your name to
all generations.
13 You will arise *and* have
mercy on Zion;
For the time to favor her,
Yes, the set time,
has come.
14 For Your servants take
pleasure in her stones,
And show favor
to her dust.
15 So the nations shall fear
the name of the LORD,
And all the kings of the
earth Your glory.
16 For the LORD shall
build up Zion;
He shall appear
in His glory.
17 He shall regard the
prayer of the destitute,
And shall not despise
their prayer.

18 This will be written
for the generation
to come,
That a people yet to
be created may
praise the LORD.
19 For He looked down
from the height of
His sanctuary;
From heaven the LORD
viewed the earth,
20 To hear the groaning
of the prisoner,
To release those
appointed to death,
21 To declare the name of
the LORD in Zion,

And His praise in
Jerusalem,
22 When the peoples are
gathered together,
And the kingdoms, to
serve the LORD.

23 He weakened my
strength in the way;
He shortened my days.
24 I said, "O my God,
Do not take me away in
the midst of my days;
Your years *are*
throughout all
generations.
25 Of old You laid the
foundation of the earth,
And the heavens *are* the
work of Your hands.
26 They will perish, but
You will endure;
Yes, they will all grow
old like a garment;
Like a cloak You will
change them,
And they will be changed.
27 But You *are* the same,
And Your years will
have no end.
28 The children of Your
servants will continue,
And their descendants
will be established
before You."

PSALM 103

PRAISE FOR THE LORD'S MERCIES

A Psalm of David.

1 Bless the LORD, O my soul;
And all that is within me,
bless His holy name!
2 Bless the LORD, O my soul,
And forget not all
His benefits:
3 Who forgives all
your iniquities,
Who heals all your
diseases,
4 Who redeems your life
from destruction,
Who crowns you with
lovingkindness and
tender mercies,
5 Who satisfies your mouth
with good *things*,
So that your youth is
renewed like the eagle's.

6 The LORD executes
righteousness
And justice for all who
are oppressed.
7 He made known His
ways to Moses,
His acts to the
children of Israel.
8 The LORD *is* merciful
and gracious,
Slow to anger, and
abounding in mercy.
9 He will not always
strive *with us*,
Nor will He keep *His*
anger forever.
10 He has not dealt with us
according to our sins,
Nor punished us
according to our
iniquities.

11 For as the heavens are
high above the earth,
So great is His mercy
toward those
who fear Him;

12 As far as the east is
from the west,
So far has He removed
our transgressions
from us.
13 As a father pities
his children,
So the LORD pities those
who fear Him.
14 For He knows our frame;
He remembers that
we *are* dust.

15 *As for* man, his days
are like grass;
As a flower of the field,
so he flourishes.
16 For the wind passes over
it, and it is gone,
And its place remembers
it no more.[a]
17 But the mercy of
the LORD *is* from
everlasting to
everlasting
On those who fear Him,
And His righteousness
to children's children,
18 To such as keep
His covenant,
And to those who
remember His
commandments
to do them.

19 The LORD has established
His throne in heaven,
And His kingdom
rules over all.

20 Bless the LORD, you
His angels,
Who excel in strength,
who do His word,
Heeding the voice
of His word.
21 Bless the LORD, all
you His hosts,
You ministers of His,
who do His pleasure.
22 Bless the LORD, all
His works,
In all places of His
dominion.

Bless the LORD, O my soul!

PSALM 104

PRAISE TO THE SOVEREIGN LORD FOR HIS CREATION AND PROVIDENCE

1 Bless the LORD, O my soul!

O LORD my God, You
are very great:
You are clothed with
honor and majesty,
2 Who cover *Yourself* with
light as *with* a garment,
Who stretch out the
heavens like a curtain.

3 He lays the beams of
His upper chambers
in the waters,
Who makes the clouds
His chariot,
Who walks on the
wings of the wind,
4 Who makes His
angels spirits,
His ministers a
flame of fire.

103:16 [a] Compare Job 7:10

5 *You who* laid the
foundations of
the earth,
So *that* it should not
be moved forever,
6 You covered it with the
deep as *with* a garment;
The waters stood above
the mountains.
7 At Your rebuke they fled;
At the voice of Your
thunder they
hastened away.
8 They went up over
the mountains;
They went down
into the valleys,
To the place which You
founded for them.
9 You have set a
boundary that they
may not pass over,
That they may not return
to cover the earth.

10 He sends the springs
into the valleys;
They flow among
the hills.
11 They give drink to every
beast of the field;
The wild donkeys
quench their thirst.
12 By them the birds of
the heavens have
their home;
They sing among
the branches.
13 He waters the hills from
His upper chambers;
The earth is satisfied with
the fruit of Your works.
14 He causes the grass to
grow for the cattle,
And vegetation for the
service of man,
That he may bring forth
food from the earth,
15 And wine *that* makes
glad the heart of man,
Oil to make *his* face shine,
And bread *which*
strengthens
man's heart.
16 The trees of the LORD
are full *of sap,*
The cedars of Lebanon
which He planted,
17 Where the birds
make their nests;
The stork has her home
in the fir trees.
18 The high hills *are* for
the wild goats;
The cliffs are a refuge
for the rock badgers.[a]

19 He appointed the
moon for seasons;
The sun knows its
going down.
20 You make darkness,
and it is night,
In which all the beasts of
the forest creep about.
21 The young lions roar
after their prey,
And seek their food
from God.
22 *When* the sun rises,
they gather together
And lie down in
their dens.
23 Man goes out to his work

104:18 [a] Or *rock hyrax* (compare Leviticus 11:5)

And to his labor until
the evening.

24 O LORD, how manifold
are Your works!
In wisdom You have
made them all.
The earth is full of
Your possessions—
25 This great and wide sea,
In which *are* innumerable
teeming things,
Living things both
small and great.
26 There the ships
sail about;
There is that Leviathan
Which You have made
to play there.

27 These all wait for You,
That You may give
them their food
in due season.
28 *What* You give them
they gather in;
You open Your hand, they
are filled with good.
29 You hide Your face,
they are troubled;
You take away their
breath, they die and
return to their dust.
30 You send forth Your
Spirit, they are created;
And You renew the
face of the earth.

31 May the glory of the
LORD endure forever;
May the LORD rejoice
in His works.
32 He looks on the earth,
and it trembles;
He touches the hills,
and they smoke.

33 I will sing to the LORD
as long as I live;
I will sing praise to
my God while I
have my being.
34 May my meditation
be sweet to Him;
I will be glad in the LORD.
35 May sinners be consumed
from the earth,
And the wicked
be no more.

Bless the LORD,
O my soul!
Praise the LORD!

PSALM 105

THE ETERNAL FAITHFULNESS OF THE LORD

1 Oh, give thanks
to the LORD!
Call upon His name;
Make known His deeds
among the peoples!
2 Sing to Him, sing
psalms to Him;
Talk of all His
wondrous works!
3 Glory in His holy
name;
Let the hearts of
those rejoice who
seek the LORD!
4 Seek the LORD and
His strength;
Seek His face evermore!
5 Remember His
marvelous works
which He has done,

His wonders, and
the judgments
of His mouth,
6 O seed of Abraham
His servant,
You children of Jacob,
His chosen ones!

7 He *is* the LORD our God;
His judgments *are*
in all the earth.
8 He remembers His
covenant forever,
The word *which* He
commanded, for a
thousand generations,
9 *The covenant* which He
made with Abraham,
And His oath to Isaac,
10 And confirmed it to
Jacob for a statute,
To Israel *as* an
everlasting covenant,
11 Saying, "To you I will give
the land of Canaan
As the allotment of
your inheritance,"
12 When they were
few in number,
Indeed very few, and
strangers in it.

13 When they went from
one nation to another,
From *one* kingdom to
another people,
14 He permitted no one
to do them wrong;
Yes, He rebuked kings
for their sakes,
15 *Saying,* "Do not touch
My anointed ones,
And do My prophets
no harm."

16 Moreover He called for
a famine in the land;
He destroyed all the
provision of bread.
17 He sent a man
before them—
Joseph—*who* was
sold as a slave.
18 They hurt his feet
with fetters,
He was laid in irons.
19 Until the time that his
word came to pass,
The word of the LORD
tested him.
20 The king sent and
released him,
The ruler of the people
let him go free.
21 He made him lord
of his house,
And ruler of all his
possessions,
22 To bind his princes
at his pleasure,
And teach his elders
wisdom.

23 Israel also came
into Egypt,
And Jacob dwelt in
the land of Ham.
24 He increased His
people greatly,
And made them stronger
than their enemies.
25 He turned their heart
to hate His people,
To deal craftily with
His servants.

26 He sent Moses His servant,
And Aaron whom
He had chosen.

27 They performed His
signs among them,
And wonders in the
land of Ham.
28 He sent darkness,
and made *it* dark;
And they did not rebel
against His word.
29 He turned their
waters into blood,
And killed their fish.
30 Their land abounded
with frogs,
Even in the chambers
of their kings.
31 He spoke, and there
came swarms of flies,
And lice in all their
territory.
32 He gave them hail
for rain,
And flaming fire
in their land.
33 He struck their vines also,
and their fig trees,
And splintered the trees
of their territory.
34 He spoke, and
locusts came,
Young locusts
without number,
35 And ate up all the
vegetation in their land,
And devoured the fruit
of their ground.
36 He also destroyed all the
firstborn in their land,
The first of all their
strength.

37 He also brought them out
with silver and gold,
And *there was* none feeble
among His tribes.
38 Egypt was glad when
they departed,
For the fear of them had
fallen upon them.
39 He spread a cloud
for a covering,
And fire to give light
in the night.
40 *The people* asked, and
He brought quail,
And satisfied them with
the bread of heaven.
41 He opened the rock, and
water gushed out;
It ran in the dry
places *like* a river.

42 For He remembered
His holy promise,
And Abraham His servant.
43 He brought out His
people with joy,
His chosen ones
with gladness.
44 He gave them the lands
of the Gentiles,
And they inherited the
labor of the nations,
45 That they might
observe His statutes
And keep His laws.

Praise the LORD!

PSALM 106

JOY IN FORGIVENESS OF ISRAEL'S SINS

1 Praise the LORD!

Oh, give thanks to the
LORD, for *He is* good!
For His mercy
endures forever.

2 Who can utter the mighty
acts of the LORD?
Who can declare
all His praise?
3 Blessed *are* those
who keep justice,
And he who does[a]
righteousness
at all times!

4 Remember me, O LORD,
with the favor *You have*
toward Your people.
Oh, visit me with
Your salvation,
5 That I may see the benefit
of Your chosen ones,
That I may rejoice in
the gladness of
Your nation,
That I may glory with
Your inheritance.

6 We have sinned with
our fathers,
We have committed
iniquity,
We have done wickedly.
7 Our fathers in Egypt
did not understand
Your wonders;
They did not remember
the multitude of
Your mercies,
But rebelled by the
sea—the Red Sea.

8 Nevertheless He
saved them for His
name's sake,
That He might make His
mighty power known.
9 He rebuked the Red Sea
also, and it dried up;
So He led them through
the depths,
As through the
wilderness.
10 He saved them from
the hand of him
who hated *them,*
And redeemed them from
the hand of the enemy.
11 The waters covered
their enemies;
There was not one
of them left.
12 Then they believed
His words;
They sang His praise.

13 They soon forgot
His works;
They did not wait
for His counsel,
14 But lusted exceedingly
in the wilderness,
And tested God in
the desert.
15 And He gave them
their request,
But sent leanness
into their soul.

16 When they envied
Moses in the camp,
And Aaron the saint
of the LORD,
17 The earth opened up and
swallowed Dathan,
And covered the
faction of Abiram.
18 A fire was kindled in
their company;

106:3 [a] Septuagint, Syriac, Targum, and Vulgate read *those who do.*

The flame burned
up the wicked.

19 They made a calf
in Horeb,
And worshiped the
molded image.
20 Thus they changed
their glory
Into the image of an
ox that eats grass.
21 They forgot God
their Savior,
Who had done great
things in Egypt,
22 Wondrous works in
the land of Ham,
Awesome things by
the Red Sea.
23 Therefore He said that
He would destroy
them,
Had not Moses His
chosen one stood
before Him in
the breach,
To turn away His wrath,
lest He destroy *them.*

24 Then they despised
the pleasant land;
They did not believe
His word,
25 But complained in
their tents,
And did not heed the
voice of the LORD.
26 Therefore He raised
His hand *in an oath*
against them,
To overthrow them
in the wilderness,
27 To overthrow their
descendants among
the nations,
And to scatter them
in the lands.

28 They joined themselves
also to Baal of Peor,
And ate sacrifices
made to the dead.
29 Thus they provoked
Him to anger with
their deeds,
And the plague broke
out among them.
30 Then Phinehas stood
up and intervened,
And the plague
was stopped.
31 And that was accounted to
him for righteousness
To all generations
forevermore.

32 They angered *Him* also
at the waters of strife,[a]
So that it went ill
with Moses on
account of them;
33 Because they rebelled
against His Spirit,
So that he spoke rashly
with his lips.

34 They did not destroy
the peoples,
Concerning whom
the LORD had
commanded them,
35 But they mingled
with the Gentiles
And learned their works;

106:32 [a] Or *Meribah*

36 They served their idols,
Which became a
snare to them.
37 They even sacrificed
their sons
And their daughters
to demons,
38 And shed innocent blood,
The blood of their sons
and daughters,
Whom they sacrificed to
the idols of Canaan;
And the land was
polluted with blood.
39 Thus they were defiled
by their own works,
And played the harlot
by their own deeds.

40 Therefore the wrath of
the LORD was kindled
against His people,
So that He abhorred His
own inheritance.
41 And He gave them
into the hand of
the Gentiles,
And those who hated
them ruled over them.
42 Their enemies also
oppressed them,
And they were brought
into subjection
under their hand.
43 Many times He
delivered them;
But they rebelled in
their counsel,
And were brought low
for their iniquity.

44 Nevertheless He regarded
their affliction,
When He heard their cry;
45 And for their sake
He remembered
His covenant,
And relented according
to the multitude
of His mercies.
46 He also made them
to be pitied
By all those who carried
them away captive.

47 Save us, O LORD our God,
And gather us from
among the Gentiles,
To give thanks to
Your holy name,
To triumph in Your praise.

48 Blessed *be* the LORD
God of Israel
From everlasting
to everlasting!
And let all the people
say, "Amen!"

Praise the LORD!

BOOK FIVE

PSALMS 107–150

PSALM 107

THANKSGIVING TO THE LORD FOR HIS GREAT WORKS OF DELIVERANCE

1 Oh, give thanks to the
LORD, for *He is* good!
For His mercy
endures forever.
2 Let the redeemed of
the LORD say *so,*
Whom He has redeemed
from the hand
of the enemy,

3 And gathered out
of the lands,
From the east and
from the west,
From the north and
from the south.

4 They wandered in
the wilderness in
a desolate way;
They found no city
to dwell in.
5 Hungry and thirsty,
Their soul fainted
in them.
6 Then they cried out to the
LORD in their trouble,
And He delivered them
out of their distresses.
7 And He led them forth
by the right way,
That they might go to a
city for a dwelling place.
8 Oh, that *men* would give
thanks to the LORD
for His goodness,
And *for* His wonderful
works to the
children of men!
9 For He satisfies the
longing soul,
And fills the hungry
soul with goodness.

10 Those who sat in
darkness and in the
shadow of death,
Bound in affliction
and irons—
11 Because they
rebelled against the
words of God,
And despised the counsel
of the Most High,
12 Therefore He brought
down their heart
with labor;
They fell down, and *there
was* none to help.
13 Then they cried out to the
LORD in their trouble,
And He saved them out
of their distresses.
14 He brought them out
of darkness and the
shadow of death,
And broke their
chains in pieces.
15 Oh, that *men* would give
thanks to the LORD
for His goodness,
And *for* His wonderful
works to the
children of men!
16 For He has broken the
gates of bronze,
And cut the bars of
iron in two.

17 Fools, because of their
transgression,
And because of their
iniquities, were afflicted.
18 Their soul abhorred
all manner of food,
And they drew near to
the gates of death.
19 Then they cried out to the
LORD in their trouble,
And He saved them out
of their distresses.
20 He sent His word and
healed them,
And delivered *them* from
their destructions.
21 Oh, that *men* would give
thanks to the LORD
for His goodness,

And *for* His wonderful
works to the
children of men!
22 Let them sacrifice
the sacrifices of
thanksgiving,
And declare His works
with rejoicing.

23 Those who go down
to the sea in ships,
Who do business on
great waters,
24 They see the works
of the LORD,
And His wonders
in the deep.
25 For He commands and
raises the stormy wind,
Which lifts up the
waves of the sea.
26 They mount up to
the heavens,
They go down again
to the depths;
Their soul melts
because of trouble.
27 They reel to and fro,
and stagger like a
drunken man,
And are at their wits' end.
28 Then they cry out to the
LORD in their trouble,
And He brings them out
of their distresses.
29 He calms the storm,
So that its waves are still.
30 Then they are glad
because they are quiet;
So He guides them to
their desired haven.
31 Oh, that *men* would give
thanks to the LORD
for His goodness,
And *for* His wonderful
works to the
children of men!
32 Let them exalt Him
also in the assembly
of the people,
And praise Him in
the company of
the elders.

33 He turns rivers into
a wilderness,
And the watersprings
into dry ground;
34 A fruitful land into
barrenness,
For the wickedness of
those who dwell in it.
35 He turns a wilderness
into pools of water,
And dry land into
watersprings.
36 There He makes the
hungry dwell,
That they may establish
a city for a
dwelling place,
37 And sow fields and
plant vineyards,
That they may yield a
fruitful harvest.
38 He also blesses them,
and they multiply
greatly;
And He does not let
their cattle decrease.

39 When they are
diminished and
brought low
Through oppression,
affliction, and sorrow,
40 He pours contempt
on princes,

And causes them
to wander in the
wilderness *where*
there is no way;
41 Yet He sets the poor
on high, far from
affliction,
And makes *their*
families like a flock.
42 The righteous see
it and rejoice,
And all iniquity
stops its mouth.

43 Whoever *is* wise will
observe these *things,*
And they will understand
the lovingkindness
of the LORD.

PSALM 108

ASSURANCE OF GOD'S VICTORY OVER ENEMIES

A Song. A Psalm of David.

1 O God, my heart
is steadfast;
I will sing and give praise,
even with my glory.
2 Awake, lute and harp!
I will awaken the dawn.
3 I will praise You, O LORD,
among the peoples,
And I will sing praises to
You among the nations.
4 For Your mercy *is* great
above the heavens,
And Your truth *reaches*
to the clouds.

5 Be exalted, O God,
above the heavens,
And Your glory above
all the earth;
6 That Your beloved
may be delivered,
Save *with* Your right
hand, and hear me.

7 God has spoken in
His holiness:
"I will rejoice;
I will divide Shechem
And measure out the
Valley of Succoth.
8 Gilead *is* Mine;
Manasseh *is* Mine;
Ephraim also *is* the
helmet for My head;
Judah *is* My lawgiver.
9 Moab *is* My washpot;
Over Edom I will
cast My shoe;
Over Philistia I will
triumph."

10 Who will bring me *into*
the strong city?
Who will lead me
to Edom?
11 *Is it* not *You,* O God,
who cast us off?
And *You,* O God, *who*
did not go out with
our armies?
12 Give us help from
trouble,
For the help of man
is useless.
13 Through God we will
do valiantly,
For *it is* He *who*
shall tread down
our enemies.[a]

108:13 [a] Compare verses 6–13 with 60:5–12

PSALM 109

PLEA FOR JUDGMENT OF FALSE ACCUSERS

To the Chief Musician.
A Psalm of David.

1 Do not keep silent,
O God of my praise!
2 For the mouth of the
wicked and the mouth
of the deceitful
Have opened against me;
They have spoken against
me with a lying tongue.
3 They have also surrounded
me with words of hatred,
And fought against me
without a cause.
4 In return for my love
they are my accusers,
But I *give myself to* prayer.
5 Thus they have rewarded
me evil for good,
And hatred for my love.

6 Set a wicked man
over him,
And let an accuser[a] stand
at his right hand.
7 When he is judged, let
him be found guilty,
And let his prayer
become sin.
8 Let his days be few,
And let another
take his office.
9 Let his children be
fatherless,
And his wife a widow.
10 Let his children
continually be
vagabonds, and beg;
Let them seek *their
bread*[a] also from their
desolate places.
11 Let the creditor seize
all that he has,
And let strangers
plunder his labor.
12 Let there be none to
extend mercy to him,
Nor let there be
any to favor his
fatherless children.
13 Let his posterity
be cut off,
And in the generation
following let their
name be blotted out.

14 Let the iniquity of his
fathers be remembered
before the LORD,
And let not the sin of
his mother be
blotted out.
15 Let them be continually
before the LORD,
That He may cut off
the memory of them
from the earth;
16 Because he did not
remember to
show mercy,
But persecuted the poor
and needy man,
That he might even slay
the broken in heart.
17 As he loved cursing, so
let it come to him;
As he did not delight
in blessing, so let it
be far from him.

109:6 [a] Hebrew *satan* 109:10 [a] Following Masoretic Text and Targum; Septuagint and Vulgate read *be cast out*.

18 As he clothed himself
with cursing as
with his garment,
So let it enter his
body like water,
And like oil into
his bones.
19 Let it be to him like
the garment which
covers him,
And for a belt with
which he girds
himself continually.
20 *Let* this *be* the LORD's
reward to my accusers,
And to those who speak
evil against my person.

21 But You, O GOD the Lord,
Deal with me for Your
name's sake;
Because Your mercy *is*
good, deliver me.
22 For I *am* poor and needy,
And my heart is
wounded within me.
23 I am gone like a shadow
when it lengthens;
I am shaken off
like a locust.
24 My knees are weak
through fasting,
And my flesh is feeble
from lack of fatness.
25 I also have become a
reproach to them;
When they look at me,
they shake their heads.

26 Help me, O LORD my God!
Oh, save me according
to Your mercy,
27 That they may know that
this *is* Your hand—
That You, LORD,
have done it!
28 Let them curse,
but You bless;
When they arise, let
them be ashamed,
But let Your servant
rejoice.
29 Let my accusers be
clothed with shame,
And let them cover
themselves with
their own disgrace
as with a mantle.

30 I will greatly praise the
LORD with my mouth;
Yes, I will praise Him
among the multitude.
31 For He shall stand at
the right hand
of the poor,
To save *him* from those
who condemn him.

PSALM 110

ANNOUNCEMENT OF THE MESSIAH'S REIGN

A Psalm of David.

1 The LORD said to
my Lord,
"Sit at My right hand,
Till I make Your enemies
Your footstool."
2 The LORD shall send
the rod of Your
strength out of Zion.
Rule in the midst of
Your enemies!

3 Your people *shall*
be volunteers
In the day of Your power;

In the beauties of
holiness, from the
womb of the morning,
You have the dew
of Your youth.
4 The LORD has sworn
And will not relent,
"You *are* a priest forever
According to the order
of Melchizedek."

5 The Lord *is* at Your
right hand;
He shall execute kings
in the day of His
wrath.
6 He shall judge among
the nations,
He shall fill *the places*
with dead bodies,
He shall execute the
heads of many
countries.
7 He shall drink of the
brook by the wayside;
Therefore He shall
lift up the head.

PSALM 111

PRAISE TO GOD FOR HIS FAITHFULNESS AND JUSTICE

1 Praise the LORD!

I will praise the LORD
with *my* whole heart,
In the assembly of
the upright and *in*
the congregation.

2 The works of the
LORD *are* great,
Studied by all who have
pleasure in them.
3 His work *is* honorable
and glorious,
And His righteousness
endures forever.
4 He has made His
wonderful works to
be remembered;
The LORD *is* gracious and
full of compassion.
5 He has given food to
those who fear Him;
He will ever be mindful
of His covenant.
6 He has declared to His
people the power
of His works,
In giving them the
heritage of the nations.

7 The works of His
hands *are* verity
and justice;
All His precepts *are*
sure.
8 They stand fast
forever and ever,
And are done in truth
and uprightness.
9 He has sent redemption
to His people;
He has commanded His
covenant forever:
Holy and awesome
is His name.

10 The fear of the LORD
is the beginning
of wisdom;
A good understanding
have all those
who do *His*
commandments.
His praise endures
forever.

PSALM 112
THE BLESSED STATE OF THE RIGHTEOUS

1 Praise the LORD!

Blessed *is* the man *who*
fears the LORD,
Who delights greatly in
His commandments.

2 His descendants will
be mighty on earth;
The generation of the
upright will be blessed.
3 Wealth and riches *will*
be in his house,
And his righteousness
endures forever.
4 Unto the upright
there arises light
in the darkness;
He is gracious, and
full of compassion,
and righteous.
5 A good man deals
graciously and lends;
He will guide his affairs
with discretion.
6 Surely he will never
be shaken;
The righteous will
be in everlasting
remembrance.
7 He will not be afraid
of evil tidings;
His heart is steadfast,
trusting in the LORD.
8 His heart *is* established;
He will not be afraid,
Until he sees *his desire*
upon his enemies.

9 He has dispersed abroad,
He has given to the poor;
His righteousness
endures forever;
His horn will be exalted
with honor.
10 The wicked will see *it*
and be grieved;
He will gnash his teeth
and melt away;
The desire of the
wicked shall perish.

PSALM 113
THE MAJESTY AND CONDESCENSION OF GOD

1 Praise the LORD!

Praise, O servants
of the LORD,
Praise the name
of the LORD!
2 Blessed be the name
of the LORD
From this time forth
and forevermore!
3 From the rising of
the sun to its
going down
The LORD's name *is*
to be praised.

4 The LORD *is* high
above all nations,
His glory above
the heavens.
5 Who *is* like the
LORD our God,
Who dwells on high,
6 Who humbles Himself
to behold
The things that are in
the heavens and
in the earth?

7 He raises the poor
out of the dust,
And lifts the needy out
of the ash heap,
8 That He may seat *him*
with princes—
With the princes
of His people.
9 He grants the barren
woman a home,
Like a joyful mother
of children.

Praise the LORD!

PSALM 114

THE POWER OF GOD IN HIS DELIVERANCE OF ISRAEL

1 When Israel went
out of Egypt,
The house of Jacob
from a people of
strange language,
2 Judah became His
sanctuary,
And Israel His dominion.

3 The sea saw *it* and fled;
Jordan turned back.
4 The mountains
skipped like rams,
The little hills like lambs.
5 What ails you, O sea,
that you fled?
O Jordan, *that* you
turned back?
6 O mountains, *that* you
skipped like rams?
O little hills, like lambs?

7 Tremble, O earth, at
the presence of
the Lord,
At the presence of
the God of Jacob,
8 Who turned the rock
into a pool of water,
The flint into a
fountain of waters.

PSALM 115

THE FUTILITY OF IDOLS AND THE TRUSTWORTHINESS OF GOD

1 Not unto us, O LORD,
not unto us,
But to Your name
give glory,
Because of Your mercy,
Because of Your truth.
2 Why should the
Gentiles say,
"So where *is* their God?"

3 But our God *is* in heaven;
He does whatever
He pleases.
4 Their idols *are* silver
and gold,
The work of men's hands.
5 They have mouths, but
they do not speak;
Eyes they have, but
they do not see;
6 They have ears, but
they do not hear;
Noses they have, but
they do not smell;
7 They have hands, but
they do not handle;
Feet they have, but
they do not walk;
Nor do they mutter
through their throat.
8 Those who make them
are like them;

So is everyone who
trusts in them.

9 O Israel, trust in the LORD;
He *is* their help and
their shield.
10 O house of Aaron,
trust in the LORD;
He *is* their help and
their shield.
11 You who fear the LORD,
trust in the LORD;
He *is* their help and
their shield.

12 The LORD has been
mindful of *us;*
He will bless us;
He will bless the
house of Israel;
He will bless the
house of Aaron.
13 He will bless those
who fear the LORD,
Both small and great.

14 May the LORD give
you increase more
and more,
You and your children.
15 *May* you *be* blessed
by the LORD,
Who made heaven
and earth.

16 The heaven, *even* the
heavens, *are* the LORD's;
But the earth He has given
to the children of men.
17 The dead do not
praise the LORD,
Nor any who go down
into silence.
18 But we will bless the LORD
From this time forth
and forevermore.

Praise the LORD!

PSALM 116

THANKSGIVING FOR DELIVERANCE FROM DEATH

1 I love the LORD, because
He has heard
My voice *and* my
supplications.
2 Because He has inclined
His ear to me,
Therefore I will call *upon
Him* as long as I live.

3 The pains of death
surrounded me,
And the pangs of Sheol
laid hold of me;
I found trouble
and sorrow.
4 Then I called upon the
name of the LORD:
"O LORD, I implore You,
deliver my soul!"

5 Gracious *is* the LORD,
and righteous;
Yes, our God *is* merciful.
6 The LORD preserves
the simple;
I was brought low,
and He saved me.
7 Return to your rest,
O my soul,
For the LORD has dealt
bountifully with you.

8 For You have delivered
my soul from death,

My eyes from tears,
And my feet from falling.
9 I will walk before
the LORD
In the land of the living.
10 I believed, therefore
I spoke,
"I am greatly afflicted."
11 I said in my haste,
"All men *are* liars."

12 What shall I render
to the LORD
For all His benefits
toward me?
13 I will take up the cup
of salvation,
And call upon the
name of the LORD.
14 I will pay my vows
to the LORD
Now in the presence
of all His people.

15 Precious in the sight
of the LORD
Is the death of His saints.

16 O LORD, truly I *am*
Your servant;
I *am* Your servant, the son
of Your maidservant;
You have loosed
my bonds.
17 I will offer to You
the sacrifice of
thanksgiving,
And will call upon the
name of the LORD.

18 I will pay my vows
to the LORD
Now in the presence
of all His people,
19 In the courts of the
LORD's house,
In the midst of you,
O Jerusalem.

Praise the LORD!

PSALM 117

LET ALL PEOPLES PRAISE THE LORD

1 Praise the LORD, all
you Gentiles!
Laud Him, all you peoples!
2 For His merciful kindness
is great toward us,
And the truth of the
LORD *endures* forever.

Praise the LORD!

PSALM 118

PRAISE TO GOD FOR HIS EVERLASTING MERCY

1 Oh, give thanks to the
LORD, for *He is* good!
For His mercy
endures forever.

2 Let Israel now say,
"His mercy *endures*
forever."
3 Let the house of
Aaron now say,
"His mercy *endures*
forever."
4 Let those who fear the
LORD now say,
"His mercy *endures*
forever."

5 I called on the LORD
in distress;

The LORD answered
me *and set me* in
a broad place.
6 The LORD *is* on my side;
I will not fear.
What can man do to me?
7 The LORD is for me among
those who help me;
Therefore I shall see
my desire on those
who hate me.
8 *It is* better to trust
in the LORD
Than to put confidence
in man.
9 *It is* better to trust
in the LORD
Than to put confidence
in princes.

10 All nations
surrounded me,
But in the name of
the LORD I will
destroy them.
11 They surrounded me,
Yes, they surrounded me;
But in the name of
the LORD I will
destroy them.
12 They surrounded
me like bees;
They were quenched
like a fire of thorns;
For in the name of
the LORD I will
destroy them.
13 You pushed me violently,
that I might fall,
But the LORD helped me.
14 The LORD *is* my
strength and song,
And He has become
my salvation.[a]
15 The voice of rejoicing
and salvation
Is in the tents of
the righteous;
The right hand of the
LORD does valiantly.
16 The right hand of the
LORD is exalted;
The right hand of the
LORD does valiantly.
17 I shall not die, but live,
And declare the works
of the LORD.
18 The LORD has chastened
me severely,
But He has not given
me over to death.

19 Open to me the gates
of righteousness;
I will go through them,
And I will praise the LORD.
20 This is the gate of
the LORD,
Through which the
righteous shall enter.

21 I will praise You,
For You have
answered me,
And have become
my salvation.

22 The stone *which* the
builders rejected
Has become the chief
cornerstone.
23 This was the LORD's doing;
It *is* marvelous in our eyes.

118:14 [a] Compare Exodus 15:2

24 This *is* the day the
LORD has made;
We will rejoice and
be glad in it.

25 Save now, I pray, O LORD;
O LORD, I pray, send
now prosperity.
26 Blessed *is* he who comes
in the name of the LORD!
We have blessed you from
the house of the LORD.
27 God *is* the LORD,
And He has given us light;
Bind the sacrifice
with cords to the
horns of the altar.
28 You *are* my God, and
I will praise You;
You are my God, I
will exalt You.

29 Oh, give thanks to the
LORD, for *He is* good!
For His mercy
endures forever.

PSALM 119

MEDITATIONS ON THE EXCELLENCIES OF THE WORD OF GOD

א ALEPH

1 Blessed *are* the
undefiled in the way,
Who walk in the law
of the LORD!
2 Blessed *are* those who
keep His testimonies,
Who seek Him with
the whole heart!
3 They also do no iniquity;
They walk in His ways.
4 You have commanded *us*
To keep Your precepts
diligently.
5 Oh, that my ways
were directed
To keep Your statutes!
6 Then I would not
be ashamed,
When I look into all Your
commandments.
7 I will praise You with
uprightness of heart,
When I learn Your
righteous judgments.
8 I will keep Your statutes;
Oh, do not forsake
me utterly!

ב BETH

9 How can a young man
cleanse his way?
By taking heed according
to Your word.
10 With my whole heart
I have sought You;
Oh, let me not
wander from Your
commandments!
11 Your word I have
hidden in my heart,
That I might not sin
against You.
12 Blessed *are* You, O LORD!
Teach me Your statutes.
13 With my lips I have
declared
All the judgments
of Your mouth.
14 I have rejoiced in the way
of Your testimonies,
As *much as* in all riches.
15 I will meditate on
Your precepts,
And contemplate
Your ways.

16 I will delight myself
in Your statutes;
I will not forget
Your word.

ג GIMEL

17 Deal bountifully with
Your servant,
That I may live and
keep Your word.
18 Open my eyes, that
I may see
Wondrous things
from Your law.
19 I *am* a stranger in
the earth;
Do not hide Your
commandments
from me.
20 My soul breaks
with longing
For Your judgments
at all times.
21 You rebuke the
proud—the cursed,
Who stray from Your
commandments.
22 Remove from me
reproach and contempt,
For I have kept Your
testimonies.
23 Princes also sit *and*
speak against me,
But Your servant
meditates on
Your statutes.
24 Your testimonies also
are my delight
And my counselors.

ד DALETH

25 My soul clings to the dust;
Revive me according
to Your word.
26 I have declared my ways,
and You answered me;
Teach me Your statutes.
27 Make me understand the
way of Your precepts;
So shall I meditate on
Your wonderful works.
28 My soul melts from
heaviness;
Strengthen me according
to Your word.
29 Remove from me
the way of lying,
And grant me Your
law graciously.
30 I have chosen the
way of truth;
Your judgments I have
laid *before me.*
31 I cling to Your testimonies;
O LORD, do not put
me to shame!
32 I will run the course of
Your commandments,
For You shall enlarge
my heart.

ה HE

33 Teach me, O LORD, the
way of Your statutes,
And I shall keep
it *to* the end.
34 Give me understanding,
and I shall keep
Your law;
Indeed, I shall observe it
with *my* whole heart.
35 Make me walk in
the path of Your
commandments,
For I delight in it.
36 Incline my heart to
Your testimonies,
And not to covetousness.

37 Turn away my eyes
from looking at
worthless things,
And revive me in
Your way.[a]
38 Establish Your word
to Your servant,
Who *is devoted* to
fearing You.
39 Turn away my reproach
which I dread,
For Your judgments
are good.
40 Behold, I long for
Your precepts;
Revive me in Your
righteousness.

ו WAW

41 Let Your mercies come
also to me, O LORD—
Your salvation according
to Your word.
42 So shall I have an
answer for him who
reproaches me,
For I trust in Your word.
43 And take not the word
of truth utterly out
of my mouth,
For I have hoped in
Your ordinances.
44 So shall I keep Your
law continually,
Forever and ever.
45 And I will walk at liberty,
For I seek Your precepts.
46 I will speak of Your
testimonies also
before kings,
And will not be ashamed.
47 And I will delight
myself in Your
commandments,
Which I love.
48 My hands also I
will lift up to Your
commandments,
Which I love,
And I will meditate
on Your statutes.

ז ZAYIN

49 Remember the word
to Your servant,
Upon which You have
caused me to hope.
50 This *is* my comfort
in my affliction,
For Your word has
given me life.
51 The proud have me
in great derision,
Yet I do not turn aside
from Your law.
52 I remembered Your
judgments of
old, O LORD,
And have comforted
myself.
53 Indignation has
taken hold of me
Because of the wicked,
who forsake Your law.
54 Your statutes have
been my songs
In the house of my
pilgrimage.
55 I remember Your
name in the
night, O LORD,
And I keep Your law.

119:37 [a] Following Masoretic Text, Septuagint, and Vulgate; Targum reads *Your words.*

56 This has become mine,
Because I kept
Your precepts.

ח HETH

57 *You are* my portion,
O LORD;
I have said that I would
keep Your words.
58 I entreated Your favor
with *my* whole heart;
Be merciful to me
according to Your
word.
59 I thought about my ways,
And turned my feet to
Your testimonies.
60 I made haste, and
did not delay
To keep Your
commandments.
61 The cords of the wicked
have bound me,
But I have not
forgotten Your law.
62 At midnight I will rise
to give thanks to You,
Because of Your
righteous judgments.
63 I *am* a companion of
all who fear You,
And of those who keep
Your precepts.
64 The earth, O LORD, is
full of Your mercy;
Teach me Your statutes.

ט TETH

65 You have dealt well
with Your servant,
O LORD, according
to Your word.
66 Teach me good judgment
and knowledge,
For I believe Your
commandments.
67 Before I was afflicted
I went astray,
But now I keep
Your word.
68 You *are* good, and
do good;
Teach me Your statutes.
69 The proud have forged
a lie against me,
But I will keep Your
precepts with *my*
whole heart.
70 Their heart is as
fat as grease,
But I delight in Your law.
71 *It is* good for me that I
have been afflicted,
That I may learn
Your statutes.
72 The law of Your mouth
is better to me
Than thousands of *coins
of* gold and silver.

י YOD

73 Your hands have made
me and fashioned me;
Give me understanding,
that I may learn Your
commandments.
74 Those who fear You
will be glad when
they see me,
Because I have hoped
in Your word.
75 I know, O LORD, that Your
judgments *are* right,
And *that* in faithfulness
You have afflicted me.
76 Let, I pray, Your
merciful kindness
be for my comfort,

According to Your word
to Your servant.
77 Let Your tender
mercies come to me,
that I may live;
For Your law *is*
my delight.
78 Let the proud be
ashamed,
For they treated me
wrongfully with
falsehood;
But I will meditate on
Your precepts.
79 Let those who fear
You turn to me,
Those who know Your
testimonies.
80 Let my heart be blameless
regarding Your statutes,
That I may not be
ashamed.

כ KAPH

81 My soul faints for
Your salvation,
But I hope in Your word.
82 My eyes fail *from*
searching Your word,
Saying, "When will
You comfort me?"
83 For I have become like
a wineskin in smoke,
Yet I do not forget
Your statutes.
84 How many *are* the days
of Your servant?
When will You execute
judgment on those
who persecute me?
85 The proud have dug
pits for me,
Which *is* not according
to Your law.
86 All Your commandments
are faithful;
They persecute me
wrongfully;
Help me!
87 They almost made an
end of me on earth,
But I did not forsake
Your precepts.
88 Revive me according to
Your lovingkindness,
So that I may keep
the testimony of
Your mouth.

ל LAMED

89 Forever, O LORD,
Your word is settled
in heaven.
90 Your faithfulness
endures to all
generations;
You established the
earth, and it abides.
91 They continue this
day according to
Your ordinances,
For all *are* Your servants.
92 Unless Your law *had*
been my delight,
I would then have
perished in my
affliction.
93 I will never forget
Your precepts,
For by them You have
given me life.
94 I *am* Yours, save me;
For I have sought
Your precepts.
95 The wicked wait for
me to destroy me,
But I will consider
Your testimonies.

96 I have seen the
consummation of
all perfection,
But Your commandment
is exceedingly broad.

מ MEM

97 Oh, how I love Your law!
It *is* my meditation
all the day.
98 You, through Your
commandments,
make me wiser than
my enemies;
For they *are* ever with me.
99 I have more understanding
than all my teachers,
For Your testimonies
are my meditation.
100 I understand more
than the ancients,
Because I keep
Your precepts.
101 I have restrained my feet
from every evil way,
That I may keep
Your word.
102 I have not departed from
Your judgments,
For You Yourself
have taught me.
103 How sweet are Your
words to my taste,
Sweeter than honey
to my mouth!
104 Through Your precepts
I get understanding;
Therefore I hate
every false way.

נ NUN

105 Your word *is* a lamp
to my feet
And a light to my path.
106 I have sworn and
confirmed
That I will keep Your
righteous judgments.
107 I am afflicted very much;
Revive me, O LORD,
according to Your word.
108 Accept, I pray, the
freewill offerings of
my mouth, O LORD,
And teach me Your
judgments.
109 My life *is* continually
in my hand,
Yet I do not forget
Your law.
110 The wicked have laid
a snare for me,
Yet I have not strayed
from Your precepts.
111 Your testimonies I
have taken as a
heritage forever,
For they *are* the rejoicing
of my heart.
112 I have inclined my
heart to perform
Your statutes
Forever, to the very end.

ס SAMEK

113 I hate the double-minded,
But I love Your law.
114 You *are* my hiding place
and my shield;
I hope in Your word.
115 Depart from me,
you evildoers,
For I will keep the
commandments
of my God!
116 Uphold me according
to Your word, that
I may live;

And do not let me be
ashamed of my hope.
117 Hold me up, and I
shall be safe,
And I shall observe Your
statutes continually.
118 You reject all those
who stray from
Your statutes,
For their deceit *is*
falsehood.
119 You put away all
the wicked of the
earth *like* dross;
Therefore I love Your
testimonies.
120 My flesh trembles
for fear of You,
And I am afraid of
Your judgments.

ע AYIN

121 I have done justice
and righteousness;
Do not leave me to
my oppressors.
122 Be surety for Your
servant for good;
Do not let the proud
oppress me.
123 My eyes fail *from seeking*
Your salvation
And Your righteous word.
124 Deal with Your
servant according
to Your mercy,
And teach me Your
statutes.
125 I *am* Your servant;
Give me understanding,
That I may know Your
testimonies.
126 *It is* time for *You* to
act, O LORD,
For they have regarded
Your law as void.
127 Therefore I love Your
commandments
More than gold, yes,
than fine gold!
128 Therefore all *Your*
precepts *concerning*
all *things*
I consider *to be* right;
I hate every false way.

פ PE

129 Your testimonies
are wonderful;
Therefore my soul
keeps them.
130 The entrance of Your
words gives light;
It gives understanding
to the simple.
131 I opened my mouth
and panted,
For I longed for Your
commandments.
132 Look upon me and be
merciful to me,
As Your custom *is*
toward those who
love Your name.
133 Direct my steps by
Your word,
And let no iniquity have
dominion over me.
134 Redeem me from the
oppression of man,
That I may keep
Your precepts.
135 Make Your face shine
upon Your servant,
And teach me Your
statutes.
136 Rivers of water run
down from my eyes,

Because *men* do not
keep Your law.

 צ TSADDE

137 Righteous *are*
You, O LORD,
And upright *are* Your
judgments.
138 Your testimonies, *which*
You have commanded,
Are righteous and
very faithful.
139 My zeal has
consumed me,
Because my enemies have
forgotten Your words.
140 Your word *is* very pure;
Therefore Your
servant loves it.
141 I *am* small and despised,
Yet I do not forget
Your precepts.
142 Your righteousness
is an everlasting
righteousness,
And Your law *is* truth.
143 Trouble and anguish
have overtaken me,
Yet Your commandments
are my delights.
144 The righteousness of
Your testimonies
is everlasting;
Give me understanding,
and I shall live.

ק QOPH

145 I cry out with *my*
whole heart;
Hear me, O LORD!
I will keep Your statutes.
146 I cry out to You;
Save me, and I will keep
Your testimonies.
147 I rise before the dawning
of the morning,
And cry for help;
I hope in Your word.
148 My eyes are awake
through the *night*
watches,
That I may meditate
on Your word.
149 Hear my voice
according to Your
lovingkindness;
O LORD, revive
me according to
Your justice.
150 They draw near who
follow after wickedness;
They are far from
Your law.
151 You *are* near, O LORD,
And all Your
commandments
are truth.
152 Concerning Your
testimonies,
I have known of old that
You have founded
them forever.

ר RESH

153 Consider my affliction
and deliver me,
For I do not forget
Your law.
154 Plead my cause and
redeem me;
Revive me according
to Your word.
155 Salvation *is* far from
the wicked,
For they do not seek
Your statutes.
156 Great *are* Your tender
mercies, O LORD;

Revive me according
to Your judgments.
157 Many *are* my persecutors
and my enemies,
Yet I do not turn from
Your testimonies.
158 I see the treacherous,
and am disgusted,
Because they do not
keep Your word.
159 Consider how I love
Your precepts;
Revive me, O LORD,
according to Your
lovingkindness.
160 The entirety of Your
word *is* truth,
And every one of Your
righteous judgments
endures forever.

ש SHIN

161 Princes persecute me
without a cause,
But my heart stands in
awe of Your word.
162 I rejoice at Your word
As one who finds
great treasure.
163 I hate and abhor lying,
But I love Your law.
164 Seven times a day
I praise You,
Because of Your
righteous judgments.
165 Great peace have
those who love
Your law,
And nothing causes
them to stumble.
166 LORD, I hope for
Your salvation,
And I do Your
commandments.
167 My soul keeps Your
testimonies,
And I love them
exceedingly.
168 I keep Your precepts and
Your testimonies,
For all my ways *are*
before You.

ת TAU

169 Let my cry come before
You, O LORD;
Give me understanding
according to Your word.
170 Let my supplication
come before You;
Deliver me according
to Your word.
171 My lips shall utter
praise,
For You teach me
Your statutes.
172 My tongue shall speak
of Your word,
For all Your
commandments *are*
righteousness.
173 Let Your hand
become my help,
For I have chosen
Your precepts.
174 I long for Your
salvation, O LORD,
And Your law *is*
my delight.
175 Let my soul live, and
it shall praise You;
And let Your judgments
help me.
176 I have gone astray
like a lost sheep;
Seek Your servant,
For I do not forget Your
commandments.

PSALM 120

PLEA FOR RELIEF FROM BITTER FOES

A Song of Ascents.

1 In my distress I cried
to the LORD,
And He heard me.
2 Deliver my soul, O LORD,
from lying lips
And from a deceitful
tongue.

3 What shall be given to you,
Or what shall be
done to you,
You false tongue?
4 Sharp arrows of
the warrior,
With coals of the
broom tree!

5 Woe is me, that I
dwell in Meshech,
That I dwell among
the tents of Kedar!
6 My soul has dwelt
too long
With one who
hates peace.
7 I *am for* peace;
But when I speak,
they *are* for war.

PSALM 121

GOD THE HELP OF THOSE WHO SEEK HIM

A Song of Ascents.

1 I will lift up my eyes
to the hills—
From whence comes
my help?
2 My help *comes* from
the LORD,
Who made heaven
and earth.

3 He will not allow your
foot to be moved;
He who keeps you
will not slumber.
4 Behold, He who
keeps Israel
Shall neither slumber
nor sleep.

5 The LORD *is* your
keeper;
The LORD *is* your
shade at your
right hand.
6 The sun shall not
strike you by day,
Nor the moon by night.

7 The LORD shall preserve
you from all evil;
He shall preserve
your soul.
8 The LORD shall preserve
your going out and
your coming in
From this time forth, and
even forevermore.

PSALM 122

THE JOY OF GOING TO THE HOUSE OF THE LORD

A Song of Ascents. Of David.

1 I was glad when
they said to me,
"Let us go into the
house of the LORD."
2 Our feet have been
standing
Within your gates,
O Jerusalem!

3 Jerusalem is built
As a city that is
compact together,
4 Where the tribes go up,
The tribes of the LORD,
To the Testimony
of Israel,
To give thanks to the
name of the LORD.
5 For thrones are set
there for judgment,
The thrones of the
house of David.

6 Pray for the peace
of Jerusalem:
"May they prosper
who love you.
7 Peace be within
your walls,
Prosperity within
your palaces."
8 For the sake of my
brethren and
companions,
I will now say, "Peace
be within you."
9 Because of the house
of the LORD our God
I will seek your good.

PSALM 123

PRAYER FOR RELIEF FROM CONTEMPT

A Song of Ascents.

1 Unto You I lift up
my eyes,
O You who dwell in
the *heavens.*
2 Behold, as the eyes
of servants *look* to
the hand of their
masters,
As the eyes of a
maid to the hand
of her mistress,
So our eyes *look* to the
LORD our God,
Until He has mercy on us.

3 Have mercy on us,
O LORD, have
mercy on us!
For we are exceedingly
filled with contempt.
4 Our soul is
exceedingly filled
With the scorn of those
who are at ease,
With the contempt
of the proud.

PSALM 124

THE LORD THE DEFENSE OF HIS PEOPLE

A Song of Ascents. Of David.

1 "If it had not been
the LORD who was
on our side,"
Let Israel now say—
2 "If it had not been
the LORD who was
on our side,
When men rose up
against us,
3 Then they would have
swallowed us alive,
When their wrath was
kindled against us;
4 Then the waters would
have overwhelmed us,
The stream would have
gone over our soul;
5 Then the swollen waters
Would have gone
over our soul."

6 Blessed *be* the LORD,
Who has not given
us *as* prey to their
teeth.
7 Our soul has escaped
as a bird from the
snare of the fowlers;[a]
The snare is broken, and
we have escaped.
8 Our help *is* in the
name of the LORD,
Who made heaven
and earth.

PSALM 125

THE LORD THE STRENGTH OF HIS PEOPLE

A Song of Ascents.

1 Those who trust
in the LORD
Are like Mount Zion,
Which cannot be moved,
but abides forever.
2 As the mountains
surround Jerusalem,
So the LORD surrounds
His people
From this time forth
and forever.

3 For the scepter
of wickedness
shall not rest
On the land allotted
to the righteous,
Lest the righteous
reach out their
hands to iniquity.

4 Do good, O LORD, to
those who are good,
And to *those who are*
upright in their hearts.

5 As for such as turn aside
to their crooked ways,
The LORD shall lead
them away
With the workers
of iniquity.

Peace *be* upon Israel!

PSALM 126

A JOYFUL RETURN TO ZION

A Song of Ascents.

1 When the LORD
brought back the
captivity of Zion,
We were like those
who dream.
2 Then our mouth was
filled with laughter,
And our tongue
with singing.
Then they said among
the nations,
"The LORD has done
great things for them."
3 The LORD has done
great things for us,
And we are glad.

4 Bring back our
captivity, O LORD,
As the streams in
the South.

5 Those who sow in tears
Shall reap in joy.
6 He who continually
goes forth weeping,

124:7 [a] That is, persons who catch birds in a trap or snare

Bearing seed for sowing,
Shall doubtless come
again with rejoicing,
Bringing his sheaves
with him.

PSALM 127

LABORING AND PROSPERING WITH THE LORD

A Song of Ascents. Of Solomon.

1 Unless the LORD
builds the house,
They labor in vain
who build it;
Unless the LORD
guards the city,
The watchman stays
awake in vain.
2 *It is* vain for you to
rise up early,
To sit up late,
To eat the bread
of sorrows;
For so He gives His
beloved sleep.

3 Behold, children *are*
a heritage from
the LORD,
The fruit of the womb
is a reward.
4 Like arrows in the
hand of a warrior,
So *are* the children
of one's youth.
5 Happy *is* the man
who has his quiver
full of them;
They *shall not be*
ashamed,
But shall speak with
their enemies
in the gate.

PSALM 128

BLESSINGS OF THOSE WHO FEAR THE LORD

A Song of Ascents.

1 Blessed *is* every one
who fears the LORD,
Who walks in His ways.

2 When you eat the labor
of your hands,
You *shall be* happy,
and *it shall be*
well with you.
3 Your wife *shall be* like
a fruitful vine
In the very heart of
your house,
Your children like
olive plants
All around your table.
4 Behold, thus shall the
man be blessed
Who fears the LORD.

5 The LORD bless you
out of Zion,
And may you see the
good of Jerusalem
All the days of your
life.
6 Yes, may you see your
children's children.

Peace *be* upon Israel!

PSALM 129

SONG OF VICTORY OVER ZION'S ENEMIES

A Song of Ascents.

1 "Many a time they
have afflicted me
from my youth,"
Let Israel now say—

2 "Many a time they
have afflicted me
from my youth;
Yet they have not
prevailed against me.
3 The plowers plowed
on my back;
They made their
furrows long."
4 The LORD *is* righteous;
He has cut in pieces the
cords of the wicked.

5 Let all those who
hate Zion
Be put to shame and
turned back.
6 Let them be as the grass
on the housetops,
Which withers before
it grows up,
7 With which the reaper
does not fill his hand,
Nor he who binds
sheaves, his arms.
8 Neither let those who
pass by them say,
"The blessing of the
LORD *be* upon you;
We bless you in the
name of the LORD!"

PSALM 130

WAITING FOR THE REDEMPTION OF THE LORD

A Song of Ascents.

1 Out of the depths I have
cried to You, O LORD;
2 Lord, hear my voice!
Let Your ears be attentive
To the voice of my
supplications.
3 If You, LORD, should
mark iniquities,
O Lord, who could stand?
4 But *there is* forgiveness
with You,
That You may be feared.

5 I wait for the LORD,
my soul waits,
And in His word I do hope.
6 My soul *waits* for the Lord
More than those
who watch for the
morning—
Yes, more than those who
watch for the morning.

7 O Israel, hope in
the LORD;
For with the LORD
there is mercy,
And with Him *is*
abundant redemption.
8 And He shall
redeem Israel
From all his iniquities.

PSALM 131

SIMPLE TRUST IN THE LORD

A Song of Ascents. Of David.

1 LORD, my heart is
not haughty,
Nor my eyes lofty.
Neither do I concern
myself with great
matters,
Nor with things too
profound for me.

2 Surely I have calmed
and quieted my soul,
Like a weaned child
with his mother;

Like a weaned child *is*
my soul within me.

3 O Israel, hope in
the LORD
From this time forth
and forever.

PSALM 132
THE ETERNAL DWELLING OF GOD IN ZION

A Song of Ascents.

1 LORD, remember David
And all his afflictions;
2 How he swore to
the LORD,
And vowed to the Mighty
One of Jacob:
3 "Surely I will not go
into the chamber
of my house,
Or go up to the comfort
of my bed;
4 I will not give sleep
to my eyes
Or slumber to my eyelids,
5 Until I find a place
for the LORD,
A dwelling place for the
Mighty One of Jacob."

6 Behold, we heard of
it in Ephrathah;
We found it in the fields
of the woods.[a]
7 Let us go into His
tabernacle;
Let us worship at
His footstool.
8 Arise, O LORD, to Your
resting place,
You and the ark of
Your strength.
9 Let Your priests be clothed
with righteousness,
And let Your saints
shout for joy.

10 For Your servant
David's sake,
Do not turn away the
face of Your Anointed.

11 The LORD has sworn
in truth to David;
He will not turn from it:
"I will set upon your
throne the fruit
of your body.
12 If your sons will keep
My covenant
And My testimony which
I shall teach them,
Their sons also shall
sit upon your throne
forevermore."

13 For the LORD has
chosen Zion;
He has desired *it* for
His dwelling place:
14 "This *is* My resting
place forever;
Here I will dwell, for
I have desired it.
15 I will abundantly bless
her provision;
I will satisfy her poor
with bread.
16 I will also clothe her
priests with salvation,
And her saints shall
shout aloud for joy.

132:6 [a] Hebrew *Jaar*

17 There I will make the
horn of David grow;
I will prepare a lamp
for My Anointed.
18 His enemies I will
clothe with shame,
But upon Himself His
crown shall flourish."

PSALM 133
BLESSED UNITY OF THE PEOPLE OF GOD

A Song of Ascents. Of David.

1 Behold, how good and
how pleasant *it is*
For brethren to dwell
together in unity!

2 *It is* like the precious
oil upon the head,
Running down on
the beard,
The beard of Aaron,
Running down on
the edge of his
garments.
3 *It is* like the dew
of Hermon,
Descending upon the
mountains of Zion;
For there the LORD
commanded the
blessing—
Life forevermore.

PSALM 134
PRAISING THE LORD IN HIS HOUSE AT NIGHT

A Song of Ascents.

1 Behold, bless the LORD,
All *you* servants
of the LORD,
Who by night stand
in the house of
the LORD!
2 Lift up your hands *in*
the sanctuary,
And bless the LORD.

3 The LORD who made
heaven and earth
Bless you from Zion!

PSALM 135
PRAISE TO GOD IN CREATION AND REDEMPTION

1 Praise the LORD!

Praise the name
of the LORD;
Praise *Him,* O you
servants of the LORD!
2 You who stand in the
house of the LORD,
In the courts of the
house of our God,
3 Praise the LORD, for
the LORD *is* good;
Sing praises to His name,
for *it is* pleasant.
4 For the LORD has
chosen Jacob
for Himself,
Israel for His special
treasure.

5 For I know that the
LORD *is* great,
And our Lord *is*
above all gods.
6 Whatever the LORD
pleases He does,
In heaven and in earth,
In the seas and in
all deep places.

7 He causes the vapors
to ascend from the
ends of the earth;
He makes lightning
for the rain;
He brings the wind out
of His treasuries.

8 He destroyed the
firstborn of Egypt,
Both of man and beast.
9 He sent signs and
wonders into the midst
of you, O Egypt,
Upon Pharaoh and
all his servants.
10 He defeated many nations
And slew mighty kings—
11 Sihon king of the
Amorites,
Og king of Bashan,
And all the kingdoms
of Canaan—
12 And gave their land
as a heritage,
A heritage to Israel
His people.

13 Your name, O LORD,
endures forever,
Your fame, O LORD,
throughout all
generations.
14 For the LORD will
judge His people,
And He will have
compassion on
His servants.

15 The idols of the nations
are silver and gold,
The work of men's hands.
16 They have mouths, but
they do not speak;
Eyes they have, but
they do not see;
17 They have ears, but
they do not hear;
Nor is there *any* breath
in their mouths.
18 Those who make them
are like them;
So is everyone who
trusts in them.

19 Bless the LORD,
O house of Israel!
Bless the LORD,
O house of Aaron!
20 Bless the LORD,
O house of Levi!
You who fear the LORD,
bless the LORD!
21 Blessed be the LORD
out of Zion,
Who dwells in Jerusalem!

Praise the LORD!

PSALM 136

THANKSGIVING TO GOD FOR HIS ENDURING MERCY

1 Oh, give thanks to the
LORD, for *He is* good!
For His mercy
endures forever.
2 Oh, give thanks to
the God of gods!
For His mercy
endures forever.
3 Oh, give thanks to
the Lord of lords!
For His mercy
endures forever:

4 To Him who alone does
great wonders,

For His mercy
endures forever;
5 To Him who by wisdom
made the heavens,
For His mercy
endures forever;
6 To Him who laid out
the earth above
the waters,
For His mercy
endures forever;
7 To Him who made
great lights,
For His mercy
endures forever—
8 The sun to rule by day,
For His mercy
endures forever;
9 The moon and stars
to rule by night,
For His mercy
endures forever.

10 To Him who struck Egypt
in their firstborn,
For His mercy
endures forever;
11 And brought out Israel
from among them,
For His mercy
endures forever;
12 With a strong hand,
and with an
outstretched arm,
For His mercy
endures forever;
13 To Him who divided
the Red Sea in two,
For His mercy
endures forever;
14 And made Israel pass
through the midst of it,
For His mercy
endures forever;
15 But overthrew Pharaoh
and his army in
the Red Sea,
For His mercy
endures forever;
16 To Him who led His
people through
the wilderness,
For His mercy
endures forever;
17 To Him who struck
down great kings,
For His mercy
endures forever;
18 And slew famous kings,
For His mercy
endures forever—
19 Sihon king of the
Amorites,
For His mercy
endures forever;
20 And Og king of Bashan,
For His mercy
endures forever—
21 And gave their land
as a heritage,
For His mercy
endures forever;
22 A heritage to Israel
His servant,
For His mercy
endures forever.

23 Who remembered us
in our lowly state,
For His mercy
endures forever;
24 And rescued us from
our enemies,
For His mercy
endures forever;
25 Who gives food to all flesh,
For His mercy
endures forever.

26 Oh, give thanks to the
God of heaven!
For His mercy
endures forever.

PSALM 137

LONGING FOR ZION IN A FOREIGN LAND

1 By the rivers of Babylon,
There we sat down,
yea, we wept
When we remembered
Zion.
2 We hung our harps
Upon the willows in
the midst of it.
3 For there those who
carried us away captive
asked of us a song,
And those who plundered
us *requested* mirth,
Saying, "Sing us *one* of
the songs of Zion!"

4 How shall we sing
the LORD's song
In a foreign land?
5 If I forget you,
O Jerusalem,
Let my right hand
forget *its skill!*
6 If I do not remember you,
Let my tongue cling to
the roof of my mouth—
If I do not exalt Jerusalem
Above my chief joy.

7 Remember, O LORD,
against the sons
of Edom
The day of Jerusalem,
Who said, "Raze *it,* raze *it,*
To its very foundation!"
8 O daughter of Babylon,
who are to be destroyed,
Happy the one who
repays you as you
have served us!
9 Happy the one who
takes and dashes
Your little ones
against the rock!

PSALM 138

THE LORD'S GOODNESS TO THE FAITHFUL

A Psalm of David.

1 I will praise You with
my whole heart;
Before the gods I will
sing praises to You.
2 I will worship toward
Your holy temple,
And praise Your name
For Your lovingkindness
and Your truth;
For You have magnified
Your word above
all Your name.
3 In the day when I cried
out, You answered me,
And made me bold *with*
strength in my soul.

4 All the kings of the
earth shall praise
You, O LORD,
When they hear the
words of Your mouth.
5 Yes, they shall sing of
the ways of the LORD,
For great *is* the glory
of the LORD.
6 Though the LORD
is on high,
Yet He regards the lowly;

But the proud He
knows from afar.

7 Though I walk in the
midst of trouble,
You will revive me;
You will stretch out
Your hand
Against the wrath
of my enemies,
And Your right hand
will save me.
8 The LORD will perfect *that*
which concerns me;
Your mercy, O LORD,
endures forever;
Do not forsake the
works of Your hands.

PSALM 139

GOD'S PERFECT KNOWLEDGE OF MAN

For the Chief Musician.
A Psalm of David.

1 O LORD, You have
searched me and
known *me.*
2 You know my sitting
down and my rising up;
You understand my
thought afar off.
3 You comprehend my path
and my lying down,
And are acquainted
with all my ways.
4 For *there is* not a word
on my tongue,
But behold, O LORD, You
know it altogether.
5 You have hedged me
behind and before,
And laid Your hand
upon me.
6 *Such* knowledge *is* too
wonderful for me;
It is high, I cannot
attain it.

7 Where can I go from
Your Spirit?
Or where can I flee from
Your presence?
8 If I ascend into heaven,
You *are* there;
If I make my bed in hell,
behold, You *are there.*
9 *If* I take the wings of
the morning,
And dwell in the
uttermost parts
of the sea,
10 Even there Your hand
shall lead me,
And Your right hand
shall hold me.
11 If I say, "Surely the
darkness shall
fall[a] on me,"
Even the night shall
be light about me;
12 Indeed, the darkness
shall not hide
from You,
But the night shines
as the day;
The darkness and
the light *are* both
alike *to You.*

13 For You formed my
inward parts;
You covered me in my
mother's womb.

139:11 [a] Vulgate and Symmachus read *cover.*

14 I will praise You, for
I am fearfully *and*
wonderfully made;[a]
Marvelous are
Your works,
And *that* my soul
knows very well.
15 My frame was not
hidden from You,
When I was made
in secret,
And skillfully wrought
in the lowest parts
of the earth.
16 Your eyes saw my
substance, being
yet unformed.
And in Your book they
all were written,
The days fashioned
for me,
When *as yet there were*
none of them.

17 How precious also
are Your thoughts
to me, O God!
How great is the
sum of them!
18 *If* I should count them,
they would be more in
number than the sand;
When I awake, I am
still with You.

19 Oh, that You would slay
the wicked, O God!
Depart from me,
therefore, you
bloodthirsty *men.*
20 For they speak against
You wickedly;
Your enemies take
Your name in vain.[a]
21 Do I not hate them,
O LORD, who hate You?
And do I not loathe those
who rise up against You?
22 I hate them with
perfect hatred;
I count them my
enemies.

23 Search me, O God, and
know my heart;
Try me, and know
my anxieties;
24 And see if *there is any*
wicked way in me,
And lead me in the
way everlasting.

PSALM 140

PRAYER FOR DELIVERANCE FROM EVIL MEN

To the Chief Musician.
A Psalm of David.

1 Deliver me, O LORD,
from evil men;
Preserve me from
violent men,
2 Who plan evil things
in *their* hearts;
They continually gather
together *for* war.
3 They sharpen their
tongues like a serpent;
The poison of asps *is*
under their lips. *Selah*

139:14 [a] Following Masoretic Text and Targum; Septuagint, Syriac, and Vulgate read *You are fearfully wonderful.* 139:20 [a] Septuagint and Vulgate read *They take Your cities in vain.*

4 Keep me, O LORD,
from the hands
of the wicked;
Preserve me from
violent men,
Who have purposed
to make my steps
stumble.
5 The proud have hidden
a snare for me,
and cords;
They have spread a
net by the wayside;
They have set traps for
me. *Selah*

6 I said to the LORD:
"You *are* my God;
Hear the voice of my
supplications, O LORD.
7 O GOD the Lord,
the strength of
my salvation,
You have covered
my head in the
day of battle.
8 Do not grant, O LORD,
the desires of
the wicked;
Do not further his
wicked scheme,
Lest they be
exalted. *Selah*

9 "*As for* the head of those
who surround me,
Let the evil of their
lips cover them;
10 Let burning coals
fall upon them;
Let them be cast
into the fire,
Into deep pits, that they
rise not up again.
11 Let not a slanderer be
established in the earth;
Let evil hunt the violent
man to overthrow *him*."

12 I know that the LORD
will maintain
The cause of the afflicted,
And justice for the poor.
13 Surely the righteous
shall give thanks
to Your name;
The upright shall dwell
in Your presence.

PSALM 141

PRAYER FOR SAFEKEEPING FROM WICKEDNESS

A Psalm of David.

1 LORD, I cry out to You;
Make haste to me!
Give ear to my voice
when I cry out to You.
2 Let my prayer be set
before You *as* incense,
The lifting up of
my hands *as* the
evening sacrifice.

3 Set a guard, O LORD,
over my mouth;
Keep watch over the
door of my lips.
4 Do not incline my heart
to any evil thing,
To practice wicked works
With men who
work iniquity;
And do not let me eat
of their delicacies.

5 Let the righteous
strike me;

It shall be a kindness.
And let him rebuke me;
It shall be as excellent oil;
Let my head not refuse it.

For still my prayer *is*
against the deeds
of the wicked.
6 Their judges are
overthrown by the
sides of the cliff,
And they hear my words,
for they are sweet.
7 Our bones are scattered
at the mouth of
the grave,
As when one plows and
breaks up the earth.

8 But my eyes *are* upon
You, O GOD the Lord;
In You I take refuge;
Do not leave my
soul destitute.
9 Keep me from the
snares they have
laid for me,
And from the traps of the
workers of iniquity.
10 Let the wicked fall into
their own nets,
While I escape safely.

PSALM 142

A PLEA FOR RELIEF FROM PERSECUTORS

A Contemplation[a] of David. A Prayer when he was in the cave.

1 I cry out to the LORD
with my voice;
With my voice to the
LORD I make my
supplication.
2 I pour out my complaint
before Him;
I declare before Him
my trouble.

3 When my spirit was
overwhelmed
within me,
Then You knew my
path.
In the way in which
I walk
They have secretly set
a snare for me.
4 Look on *my* right
hand and see,
For *there is* no one who
acknowledges me;
Refuge has failed me;
No one cares for my soul.

5 I cried out to You,
O LORD:
I said, "You *are* my refuge,
My portion in the
land of the living.
6 Attend to my cry,
For I am brought
very low;
Deliver me from my
persecutors,
For they are stronger
than I.
7 Bring my soul out
of prison,
That I may praise
Your name;
The righteous shall
surround me,

142:title [a] Hebrew *Maschil*

For You shall deal
bountifully with me."

PSALM 143

AN EARNEST APPEAL FOR GUIDANCE AND DELIVERANCE

A Psalm of David.

1 Hear my prayer, O LORD,
Give ear to my
supplications!
In Your faithfulness
answer me,
And in Your
righteousness.
2 Do not enter into
judgment with
Your servant,
For in Your sight no one
living is righteous.

3 For the enemy has
persecuted my soul;
He has crushed my
life to the ground;
He has made me
dwell in darkness,
Like those who have
long been dead.
4 Therefore my spirit
is overwhelmed
within me;
My heart within me
is distressed.

5 I remember the
days of old;
I meditate on all
Your works;
I muse on the work
of Your hands.
6 I spread out my
hands to You;
My soul *longs* for You
like a thirsty land.
Selah

7 Answer me speedily,
O LORD;
My spirit fails!
Do not hide Your
face from me,
Lest I be like those who
go down into the pit.
8 Cause me to hear Your
lovingkindness in
the morning,
For in You do I trust;
Cause me to know
the way in which
I should walk,
For I lift up my
soul to You.

9 Deliver me, O LORD,
from my enemies;
In You I take shelter.[a]
10 Teach me to do Your will,
For You *are* my God;
Your Spirit *is* good.
Lead me in the land
of uprightness.

11 Revive me, O LORD, for
Your name's sake!
For Your righteousness'
sake bring my soul
out of trouble.
12 In Your mercy cut
off my enemies,
And destroy all those
who afflict my soul;
For I *am* Your servant.

143:9 [a] Septuagint and Vulgate read *To You I flee.*

PSALM 144

A SONG TO THE LORD WHO PRESERVES AND PROSPERS HIS PEOPLE

A Psalm of David.

1 Blessed *be* the LORD
my Rock,
Who trains my
hands for war,
And my fingers
for battle—
2 My lovingkindness
and my fortress,
My high tower and
my deliverer,
My shield and *the One* in
whom I take refuge,
Who subdues my
people[a] under me.

3 LORD, what *is* man,
that You take
knowledge of him?
Or the son of man,
that You are
mindful of him?
4 Man is like a breath;
His days *are* like a
passing shadow.

5 Bow down Your
heavens, O LORD,
and come down;
Touch the mountains,
and they shall smoke.
6 Flash forth lightning
and scatter them;
Shoot out Your arrows
and destroy them.
7 Stretch out Your hand
from above;
Rescue me and deliver
me out of great
waters,
From the hand of
foreigners,
8 Whose mouth speaks
lying words,
And whose right hand
is a right hand
of falsehood.

9 I will sing a new song
to You, O God;
On a harp of ten strings
I will sing praises
to You,
10 *The One* who gives
salvation to kings,
Who delivers David
His servant
From the deadly sword.

11 Rescue me and deliver
me from the hand
of foreigners,
Whose mouth speaks
lying words,
And whose right hand
is a right hand of
falsehood—
12 That our sons *may be*
as plants grown up
in their youth;
That our daughters
may be as pillars,
Sculptured in
palace style;
13 *That* our barns
may be full,
Supplying all kinds
of produce;

144:2 [a] Following Masoretic Text, Septuagint, and Vulgate; Syriac and Targum read *the peoples* (compare 18:47).

That our sheep may
bring forth thousands
And ten thousands
in our fields;
14 *That* our oxen *may*
be well laden;
That there be no breaking
in or going out;
That there be no outcry
in our streets.
15 Happy *are* the people
who are in such
a state;
Happy *are* the people
whose God *is* the LORD!

PSALM 145

A SONG OF GOD'S MAJESTY AND LOVE

A Praise of David.

1 I will extol You, my
God, O King;
And I will bless Your
name forever and
ever.
2 Every day I will bless You,
And I will praise Your
name forever and
ever.
3 Great *is* the LORD, and
greatly to be praised;
And His greatness *is*
unsearchable.

4 One generation shall
praise Your works
to another,
And shall declare
Your mighty acts.
5 I[a] will meditate on the
glorious splendor
of Your majesty,
And on Your
wondrous works.[b]
6 *Men* shall speak of
the might of Your
awesome acts,
And I will declare
Your greatness.
7 They shall utter the
memory of Your
great goodness,
And shall sing of Your
righteousness.

8 The LORD *is* gracious and
full of compassion,
Slow to anger and
great in mercy.
9 The LORD *is* good to all,
And His tender
mercies *are* over
all His works.

10 All Your works shall
praise You, O LORD,
And Your saints
shall bless You.
11 They shall speak of
the glory of Your
kingdom,
And talk of Your power,
12 To make known to
the sons of men
His mighty acts,
And the glorious majesty
of His kingdom.
13 Your kingdom *is* an
everlasting kingdom,

145:5 [a] Following Masoretic Text and Targum; Dead Sea Scrolls, Septuagint, Syriac, and Vulgate read *They*. [b] Literally *on the words of Your wondrous works*

And Your dominion
endures throughout
all generations.[a]

14 The LORD upholds
all who fall,
And raises up all *who*
are bowed down.
15 The eyes of all look
expectantly to You,
And You give them
their food in
due season.
16 You open Your hand
And satisfy the desire
of every living thing.

17 The LORD *is* righteous
in all His ways,
Gracious in all His
works.
18 The LORD *is* near to all
who call upon Him,
To all who call upon
Him in truth.
19 He will fulfill the
desire of those
who fear Him;
He also will hear their
cry and save them.
20 The LORD preserves
all who love Him,
But all the wicked
He will destroy.
21 My mouth shall
speak the praise
of the LORD,
And all flesh shall bless
His holy name
Forever and ever.

PSALM 146

THE HAPPINESS OF THOSE WHOSE HELP IS THE LORD

1 Praise the LORD!

Praise the LORD,
O my soul!
2 While I live I will
praise the LORD;
I will sing praises
to my God while I
have my being.

3 Do not put your
trust in princes,
Nor in a son of man,
in whom *there*
is no help.
4 His spirit departs, he
returns to his earth;
In that very day his
plans perish.

5 Happy *is he* who *has*
the God of Jacob
for his help,
Whose hope *is* in the
LORD his God,
6 Who made heaven
and earth,
The sea, and all that
is in them;
Who keeps truth forever,
7 Who executes justice
for the oppressed,
Who gives food to
the hungry.
The LORD gives freedom
to the prisoners.

145:13 [a] Following Masoretic Text and Targum; Dead Sea Scrolls, Septuagint, Syriac, and Vulgate add *The LORD is faithful in all His words, And holy in all His works.*

8 The LORD opens *the eyes of* the blind;
The LORD raises those who are bowed down;
The LORD loves the righteous.
9 The LORD watches over the strangers;
He relieves the fatherless and widow;
But the way of the wicked He turns upside down.

10 The LORD shall reign forever—
Your God, O Zion, to all generations.

Praise the LORD!

PSALM 147

PRAISE TO GOD FOR HIS WORD AND PROVIDENCE

1 Praise the LORD!
For *it is* good to sing praises to our God;
For *it is* pleasant, *and* praise is beautiful.

2 The LORD builds up Jerusalem;
He gathers together the outcasts of Israel.
3 He heals the brokenhearted
And binds up their wounds.
4 He counts the number of the stars;
He calls them all by name.
5 Great *is* our Lord, and mighty in power;
His understanding *is* infinite.
6 The LORD lifts up the humble;
He casts the wicked down to the ground.

7 Sing to the LORD with thanksgiving;
Sing praises on the harp to our God,
8 Who covers the heavens with clouds,
Who prepares rain for the earth,
Who makes grass to grow on the mountains.
9 He gives to the beast its food,
And to the young ravens that cry.

10 He does not delight in the strength of the horse;
He takes no pleasure in the legs of a man.
11 The LORD takes pleasure in those who fear Him,
In those who hope in His mercy.

12 Praise the LORD, O Jerusalem!
Praise your God, O Zion!
13 For He has strengthened the bars of your gates;
He has blessed your children within you.
14 He makes peace *in* your borders,
And fills you with the finest wheat.

15 He sends out His
command *to the* earth;
His word runs
very swiftly.
16 He gives snow like wool;
He scatters the frost
like ashes;
17 He casts out His hail
like morsels;
Who can stand
before His cold?
18 He sends out His word
and melts them;
He causes His wind
to blow, *and* the
waters flow.

19 He declares His
word to Jacob,
His statutes and His
judgments to Israel.
20 He has not dealt thus
with any nation;
And *as for His*
judgments, they have
not known them.

Praise the LORD!

PSALM 148

PRAISE TO THE LORD FROM CREATION

1 Praise the LORD!

Praise the LORD from
the heavens;
Praise Him in the heights!
2 Praise Him, all His angels;
Praise Him, all His hosts!
3 Praise Him, sun
and moon;
Praise Him, all you
stars of light!
4 Praise Him, you
heavens of heavens,
And you waters above
the heavens!

5 Let them praise the
name of the LORD,
For He commanded and
they were created.
6 He also established them
forever and ever;
He made a decree which
shall not pass away.

7 Praise the LORD
from the earth,
You great sea creatures
and all the depths;
8 Fire and hail, snow
and clouds;
Stormy wind, fulfilling
His word;
9 Mountains and all hills;
Fruitful trees and
all cedars;
10 Beasts and all cattle;
Creeping things and
flying fowl;
11 Kings of the earth
and all peoples;
Princes and all judges
of the earth;
12 Both young men
and maidens;
Old men and children.

13 Let them praise the
name of the LORD,
For His name alone
is exalted;
His glory *is* above the
earth and heaven.
14 And He has exalted the
horn of His people,

The praise of all
His saints—
Of the children of Israel,
A people near to Him.

Praise the LORD!

PSALM 149

PRAISE TO GOD FOR HIS SALVATION AND JUDGMENT

1 Praise the LORD!

Sing to the LORD
a new song,
And His praise in the
assembly of saints.

2 Let Israel rejoice in
their Maker;
Let the children of Zion
be joyful in their King.
3 Let them praise His
name with the dance;
Let them sing praises
to Him with the
timbrel and harp.
4 For the LORD takes
pleasure in His people;
He will beautify the
humble with salvation.

5 Let the saints be
joyful in glory;
Let them sing aloud
on their beds.
6 *Let* the high praises of
God *be* in their mouth,
And a two-edged sword
in their hand,
7 To execute vengeance
on the nations,
And punishments
on the peoples;
8 To bind their kings
with chains,
And their nobles with
fetters of iron;
9 To execute on them the
written judgment—
This honor have
all His saints.

Praise the LORD!

PSALM 150

LET ALL THINGS PRAISE THE LORD

1 Praise the LORD!

Praise God in His
sanctuary;
Praise Him in His
mighty firmament!

2 Praise Him for His
mighty acts;
Praise Him according to
His excellent greatness!

3 Praise Him with the
sound of the trumpet;
Praise Him with the
lute and harp!
4 Praise Him with the
timbrel and dance;
Praise Him with stringed
instruments and flutes!
5 Praise Him with
loud cymbals;
Praise Him with
clashing cymbals!

6 Let everything that has
breath praise the LORD.

Praise the LORD!

THE BOOK OF PROVERBS

THE BEGINNING OF KNOWLEDGE

1 The proverbs of Solomon the son of David, king of Israel:

2 To know wisdom
and instruction,
To perceive the words
of understanding,
3 To receive the instruction
of wisdom,
Justice, judgment,
and equity;
4 To give prudence
to the simple,
To the young man
knowledge and
discretion—
5 A wise *man* will hear and
increase learning,
And a man of
understanding
will attain wise
counsel,
6 To understand a proverb
and an enigma,
The words of the wise
and their riddles.

7 The fear of the LORD
is the beginning
of knowledge,
But fools despise wisdom
and instruction.

SHUN EVIL COUNSEL

8 My son, hear the
instruction of
your father,
And do not forsake the
law of your mother;
9 For they *will be* a graceful
ornament on your head,
And chains about
your neck.

10 My son, if sinners
entice you,
Do not consent.
11 If they say, "Come with us,
Let us lie in wait to
shed blood;
Let us lurk secretly for the
innocent without cause;
12 Let us swallow them
alive like Sheol,[a]
And whole, like those
who go down to the Pit;
13 We shall find all *kinds* of
precious possessions,
We shall fill our
houses with spoil;
14 Cast in your lot among us,
Let us all have one
purse"—
15 My son, do not walk in
the way with them,
Keep your foot from
their path;
16 For their feet run to evil,

1:12 [a] Or *the grave*

And they make haste
to shed blood.
17 Surely, in vain the
net is spread
In the sight of any bird;
18 But they lie in wait for
their *own* blood,
They lurk secretly for
their *own* lives.
19 So *are* the ways of
everyone who is
greedy for gain;
It takes away the life
of its owners.

THE CALL OF WISDOM

20 Wisdom calls aloud
outside;
She raises her voice in
the open squares.
21 She cries out in the
chief concourses,[a]
At the openings of the
gates in the city
She speaks her words:
22 "How long, you simple
ones, will you love
simplicity?
For scorners delight
in their scorning,
And fools hate knowledge.
23 Turn at my rebuke;
Surely I will pour out
my spirit on you;
I will make my words
known to you.
24 Because I have called
and you refused,
I have stretched out
my hand and no
one regarded,
25 Because you disdained
all my counsel,
And would have none
of my rebuke,
26 I also will laugh at
your calamity;
I will mock when your
terror comes,
27 When your terror
comes like a storm,
And your destruction
comes like a whirlwind,
When distress and
anguish come upon you.

28 "Then they will call
on me, but I will
not answer;
They will seek me
diligently, but they
will not find me.
29 Because they hated
knowledge
And did not choose the
fear of the LORD,
30 They would have none
of my counsel
And despised my
every rebuke.
31 Therefore they shall
eat the fruit of
their own way,
And be filled to the full
with their own fancies.
32 For the turning
away of the simple
will slay them,
And the complacency of
fools will destroy them;
33 But whoever listens to
me will dwell safely,

1:21 [a] Septuagint, Syriac, and Targum read *top of the walls;* Vulgate reads *the head of multitudes.*

And will be secure,
without fear of evil."

THE VALUE OF WISDOM

2 My son, if you receive
my words,
And treasure my
commands within you,
2 So that you incline
your ear to wisdom,
And apply your heart
to understanding;
3 Yes, if you cry out for
discernment,
And lift up your voice
for understanding,
4 If you seek her as silver,
And search for her as
for hidden treasures;
5 Then you will understand
the fear of the LORD,
And find the
knowledge of God.
6 For the LORD gives
wisdom;
From His mouth *come*
knowledge and
understanding;
7 He stores up sound
wisdom for the upright;
He is a shield to those
who walk uprightly;
8 He guards the paths
of justice,
And preserves the
way of His saints.
9 Then you will understand
righteousness
and justice,
Equity *and* every
good path.

10 When wisdom enters
your heart,
And knowledge is
pleasant to your soul,
11 Discretion will
preserve you;
Understanding
will keep you,
12 To deliver you from
the way of evil,
From the man who
speaks perverse things,
13 From those who leave the
paths of uprightness
To walk in the ways
of darkness;
14 Who rejoice in doing evil,
And delight in the
perversity of
the wicked;
15 Whose ways *are* crooked,
And *who are* devious
in their paths;
16 To deliver you from the
immoral woman,
From the seductress *who*
flatters with her words,
17 Who forsakes the
companion of
her youth,
And forgets the
covenant of her God.
18 For her house leads
down to death,
And her paths to
the dead;
19 None who go to
her return,
Nor do they regain
the paths of life—
20 So you may walk in the
way of goodness,
And keep *to* the paths
of righteousness.
21 For the upright will
dwell in the land,

And the blameless
will remain in it;
22 But the wicked will be
cut off from the earth,
And the unfaithful will
be uprooted from it.

GUIDANCE FOR THE YOUNG

3 My son, do not
forget my law,
But let your heart keep
my commands;
2 For length of days
and long life
And peace they will
add to you.

3 Let not mercy and
truth forsake you;
Bind them around
your neck,
Write them on the
tablet of your heart,
4 *And* so find favor
and high esteem
In the sight of God
and man.

5 Trust in the LORD with
all your heart,
And lean not on your
own understanding;
6 In all your ways
acknowledge Him,
And He shall direct[a]
your paths.

7 Do not be wise in
your own eyes;
Fear the LORD and
depart from evil.
8 It will be health to
your flesh,[a]
And strength[b] to
your bones.

9 Honor the LORD with
your possessions,
And with the firstfruits
of all your increase;
10 So your barns will be
filled with plenty,
And your vats will
overflow with new wine.

11 My son, do not despise
the chastening
of the LORD,
Nor detest His correction;
12 For whom the LORD
loves He corrects,
Just as a father the son
in whom he delights.

13 Happy *is* the man *who*
finds wisdom,
And the man *who* gains
understanding;
14 For her proceeds
are better than the
profits of silver,
And her gain than
fine gold.
15 She *is* more precious
than rubies,
And all the things you
may desire cannot
compare with her.
16 Length of days *is* in
her right hand,
In her left hand
riches and honor.

3:6 [a] Or *make smooth* or *straight* 3:8 [a] Literally *navel,* figurative of the body [b] Literally *drink* or *refreshment*

17 Her ways *are* ways
of pleasantness,
And all her paths
are peace.
18 She *is* a tree of life
to those who take
hold of her,
And happy *are all*
who retain her.

19 The LORD by wisdom
founded the earth;
By understanding
He established
the heavens;
20 By His knowledge the
depths were broken up,
And clouds drop
down the dew.

21 My son, let them
not depart from
your eyes—
Keep sound wisdom
and discretion;
22 So they will be life
to your soul
And grace to your neck.
23 Then you will walk
safely in your way,
And your foot will
not stumble.
24 When you lie down, you
will not be afraid;
Yes, you will lie down and
your sleep will be sweet.
25 Do not be afraid of
sudden terror,
Nor of trouble from the
wicked when it comes;
26 For the LORD will be
your confidence,
And will keep your foot
from being caught.

27 Do not withhold
good from those to
whom it is due,
When it is in the
power of your
hand to do *so.*
28 Do not say to your
neighbor,
"Go, and come back,
And tomorrow I
will give *it,*"
When you have
it with you.
29 Do not devise evil against
your neighbor,
For he dwells by you
for safety's sake.
30 Do not strive with a
man without cause,
If he has done you
no harm.

31 Do not envy the
oppressor,
And choose none
of his ways;
32 For the perverse *person*
is an abomination
to the LORD,
But His secret counsel
is with the upright.
33 The curse of the LORD
is on the house
of the wicked,
But He blesses the
home of the just.
34 Surely He scorns
the scornful,
But gives grace to
the humble.
35 The wise shall
inherit glory,
But shame shall be
the legacy of fools.

SECURITY IN WISDOM

4 Hear, *my* children, the
instruction of a father,
And give attention to
know understanding;
2 For I give you good
doctrine:
Do not forsake my law.
3 When I was my
father's son,
Tender and the only
one in the sight
of my mother,
4 He also taught me,
and said to me:
"Let your heart retain
my words;
Keep my commands,
and live.
5 Get wisdom! Get
understanding!
Do not forget, nor
turn away from the
words of my mouth.
6 Do not forsake her, and
she will preserve you;
Love her, and she
will keep you.
7 Wisdom *is* the
principal thing;
Therefore get wisdom.
And in all your getting,
get understanding.
8 Exalt her, and she will
promote you;
She will bring you honor,
when you embrace her.
9 She will place on your
head an ornament
of grace;
A crown of glory she
will deliver to you."
10 Hear, my son, and
receive my sayings,
And the years of your
life will be many.
11 I have taught you in
the way of wisdom;
I have led you in
right paths.
12 When you walk, your steps
will not be hindered,
And when you run, you
will not stumble.
13 Take firm hold of
instruction, do
not let go;
Keep her, for she
is your life.

14 Do not enter the path
of the wicked,
And do not walk in
the way of evil.
15 Avoid it, do not travel on it;
Turn away from it
and pass on.
16 For they do not
sleep unless they
have done evil;
And their sleep is taken
away unless they
make *someone* fall.
17 For they eat the bread
of wickedness,
And drink the wine
of violence.

18 But the path of the just *is*
like the shining sun,[a]
That shines ever brighter
unto the perfect day.
19 The way of the wicked
is like darkness;

4:18 [a] Literally *light*

They do not know
what makes them
stumble.

20 My son, give attention
to my words;
Incline your ear to
my sayings.
21 Do not let them depart
from your eyes;
Keep them in the midst
of your heart;
22 For they *are* life to those
who find them,
And health to all
their flesh.
23 Keep your heart with
all diligence,
For out of it *spring*
the issues of life.
24 Put away from you a
deceitful mouth,
And put perverse lips
far from you.
25 Let your eyes look
straight ahead,
And your eyelids look
right before you.
26 Ponder the path
of your feet,
And let all your ways
be established.
27 Do not turn to the
right or the left;
Remove your foot
from evil.

THE PERIL OF ADULTERY

5 My son, pay attention
to my wisdom;
Lend your ear to my
understanding,
2 That you may preserve
discretion,
And your lips may
keep knowledge.
3 For the lips of an immoral
woman drip honey,
And her mouth *is*
smoother than oil;
4 But in the end she is
bitter as wormwood,
Sharp as a two-edged
sword.
5 Her feet go down
to death,
Her steps lay hold of hell.[a]
6 Lest you ponder *her*
path of life—
Her ways are unstable;
You do not know *them.*

7 Therefore hear me
now, *my* children,
And do not depart
from the words
of my mouth.
8 Remove your way
far from her,
And do not go near the
door of her house,
9 Lest you give your
honor to others,
And your years to
the cruel *one;*
10 Lest aliens be filled
with your wealth,
And your labors *go* to the
house of a foreigner;
11 And you mourn at last,
When your flesh and
your body are
consumed,
12 And say:

5:5 [a] Or *Sheol*

"How I have hated
instruction,
And my heart despised
correction!
13 I have not obeyed the
voice of my teachers,
Nor inclined my
ear to those who
instructed me!
14 I was on the verge
of total ruin,
In the midst of the
assembly and
congregation."

15 Drink water from
your own cistern,
And running water
from your own well.
16 Should your fountains
be dispersed abroad,
Streams of water
in the streets?
17 Let them be only
your own,
And not for strangers
with you.
18 Let your fountain
be blessed,
And rejoice with the
wife of your youth.
19 *As a* loving deer and
a graceful doe,
Let her breasts satisfy
you at all times;
And always be enraptured
with her love.
20 For why should you, my
son, be enraptured by
an immoral woman,
And be embraced in the
arms of a seductress?
21 For the ways of man
are before the eyes
of the LORD,
And He ponders
all his paths.
22 His own iniquities entrap
the wicked *man,*
And he is caught in the
cords of his sin.
23 He shall die for lack
of instruction,
And in the greatness of his
folly he shall go astray.

DANGEROUS PROMISES

6 My son, if you become
surety for your friend,
If you have shaken hands
in pledge for a stranger,
2 You are snared by the
words of your mouth;
You are taken by the
words of your mouth.
3 So do this, my son, and
deliver yourself;
For you have come into
the hand of your friend:
Go and humble yourself;
Plead with your friend.
4 Give no sleep to
your eyes,
Nor slumber to
your eyelids.
5 Deliver yourself like
a gazelle from the
hand *of the hunter,*
And like a bird from the
hand of the fowler.[a]

THE FOLLY OF INDOLENCE

6 Go to the ant, you
sluggard!

6:5 [a] That is, one who catches birds in a trap or snare

Consider her ways
and be wise,
7 Which, having no captain,
Overseer or ruler,
8 Provides her supplies
in the summer,
And gathers her food
in the harvest.
9 How long will you
slumber, O sluggard?
When will you rise
from your sleep?
10 A little sleep, a
little slumber,
A little folding of the
hands to sleep—
11 So shall your poverty
come on you like
a prowler,
And your need like
an armed man.

THE WICKED MAN

12 A worthless person,
a wicked man,
Walks with a perverse
mouth;
13 He winks with his eyes,
He shuffles his feet,
He points with
his fingers;
14 Perversity *is* in his heart,
He devises evil
continually,
He sows discord.
15 Therefore his calamity
shall come suddenly;
Suddenly he shall be
broken without remedy.

16 These six *things* the
LORD hates,
Yes, seven *are* an
abomination to Him:
17 A proud look,
A lying tongue,
Hands that shed
innocent blood,
18 A heart that devises
wicked plans,
Feet that are swift in
running to evil,
19 A false witness *who*
speaks lies,
And one who sows
discord among
brethren.

BEWARE OF ADULTERY

20 My son, keep your
father's command,
And do not forsake the
law of your mother.
21 Bind them continually
upon your heart;
Tie them around
your neck.
22 When you roam, they[a]
will lead you;
When you sleep, they
will keep you;
And *when* you awake, they
will speak with you.
23 For the commandment
is a lamp,
And the law a light;
Reproofs of instruction
are the way of life,
24 To keep you from
the evil woman,
From the flattering
tongue of a seductress.
25 Do not lust after her
beauty in your heart,

6:22 [a] Literally *it*

Nor let her allure you
with her eyelids.
26 For by means of a harlot
A man is reduced to
a crust of bread;
And an adulteress[a]
will prey upon his
precious life.
27 Can a man take fire
to his bosom,
And his clothes not
be burned?
28 Can one walk on
hot coals,
And his feet not
be seared?
29 So *is* he who goes in to
his neighbor's wife;
Whoever touches her
shall not be innocent.

30 *People* do not
despise a thief
If he steals to satisfy
himself when he
is starving.
31 Yet *when* he is found, he
must restore sevenfold;
He may have to give
up all the substance
of his house.
32 Whoever commits
adultery with a woman
lacks understanding;
He *who* does so destroys
his own soul.
33 Wounds and dishonor
he will get,
And his reproach will
not be wiped away.
34 For jealousy *is* a
husband's fury;
Therefore he will not spare
in the day of vengeance.
35 He will accept no
recompense,
Nor will he be appeased
though you give
many gifts.

7 My son, keep my words,
And treasure my
commands within you.
2 Keep my commands
and live,
And my law as the
apple of your eye.
3 Bind them on
your fingers;
Write them on the
tablet of your heart.
4 Say to wisdom, "You
are my sister,"
And call understanding
your nearest kin,
5 That they may keep
you from the
immoral woman,
From the seductress *who*
flatters with her words.

THE CRAFTY HARLOT

6 For at the window
of my house
I looked through
my lattice,
7 And saw among
the simple,
I perceived among
the youths,
A young man devoid
of understanding,
8 Passing along the street
near her corner;

6:26 [a] Literally *a man's wife,* that is, of another

And he took the path
to her house
9 In the twilight, in
the evening,
In the black and
dark night.

10 And there a woman
met him,
With the attire of a harlot,
and a crafty heart.
11 She *was* loud and
rebellious,
Her feet would not
stay at home.
12 At times *she was*
outside, at times in
the open square,
Lurking at every corner.
13 So she caught him
and kissed him;
With an impudent face
she said to him:
14 "*I have* peace offerings
with me;
Today I have paid
my vows.
15 So I came out to
meet you,
Diligently to seek
your face,
And I have found you.
16 I have spread my bed
with tapestry,
Colored coverings of
Egyptian linen.
17 I have perfumed my bed
With myrrh, aloes,
and cinnamon.
18 Come, let us take our fill
of love until morning;
Let us delight ourselves
with love.
19 For my husband *is*
not at home;
He has gone on a
long journey;
20 He has taken a bag of
money with him,
And will come home on
the appointed day."

21 With her enticing
speech she caused
him to yield,
With her flattering lips
she seduced him.
22 Immediately he went
after her, as an ox goes
to the slaughter,
Or as a fool to the
correction of
the stocks,[a]
23 Till an arrow struck
his liver.
As a bird hastens
to the snare,
He did not know it
would cost his life.

24 Now therefore, listen
to me, *my* children;
Pay attention to the
words of my mouth:
25 Do not let your heart
turn aside to her ways,
Do not stray into
her paths;
26 For she has cast down
many wounded,
And all who were slain by
her were strong *men*.

7:22 [a] Septuagint, Syriac, and Targum read *as a dog to bonds;* Vulgate reads *as a lamb . . . to bonds.*

27 Her house *is* the
way to hell,[a]
Descending to the
chambers of death.

THE EXCELLENCE OF WISDOM

8 Does not wisdom
cry out,
And understanding
lift up her voice?
2 She takes her stand on
the top of the high hill,
Beside the way, where
the paths meet.
3 She cries out by the gates,
at the entry of the city,
At the entrance of
the doors:
4 "To you, O men, I call,
And my voice *is* to
the sons of men.
5 O you simple ones,
understand prudence,
And you fools, be of an
understanding heart.
6 Listen, for I will speak
of excellent things,
And from the opening
of my lips *will come*
right things;
7 For my mouth will
speak truth;
Wickedness *is* an
abomination to my lips.
8 All the words of my
mouth *are* with
righteousness;
Nothing crooked or
perverse *is* in them.
9 They *are* all plain to him
who understands,
And right to those who
find knowledge.
10 Receive my instruction,
and not silver,
And knowledge rather
than choice gold;
11 For wisdom *is* better
than rubies,
And all the things one
may desire cannot be
compared with her.

12 "I, wisdom, dwell
with prudence,
And find out knowledge
and discretion.
13 The fear of the LORD
is to hate evil;
Pride and arrogance
and the evil way
And the perverse
mouth I hate.
14 Counsel *is* mine, and
sound wisdom;
I *am* understanding,
I have strength.
15 By me kings reign,
And rulers decree justice.
16 By me princes rule,
and nobles,
All the judges of
the earth.[a]
17 I love those who love me,
And those who seek
me diligently
will find me.
18 Riches and honor
are with me,

7:27 [a] Or *Sheol* 8:16 [a] Masoretic Text, Syriac, Targum, and Vulgate read *righteousness;* Septuagint, Bomberg, and some manuscripts and editions read *earth.*

Enduring riches and
righteousness.
19 My fruit *is* better than
gold, yes, than fine gold,
And my revenue than
choice silver.
20 I traverse the way of
righteousness,
In the midst of the
paths of justice,
21 That I may cause
those who love me
to inherit wealth,
That I may fill their
treasuries.

22 "The LORD possessed
me at the beginning
of His way,
Before His works of old.
23 I have been established
from everlasting,
From the beginning,
before there was
ever an earth.
24 When *there were*
no depths I was
brought forth,
When *there were* no
fountains abounding
with water.
25 Before the mountains
were settled,
Before the hills, I was
brought forth;
26 While as yet He had
not made the earth
or the fields,
Or the primal dust
of the world.
27 When He prepared the
heavens, I *was* there,
When He drew a circle on
the face of the deep,
28 When He established
the clouds above,
When He strengthened
the fountains
of the deep,
29 When He assigned to
the sea its limit,
So that the waters
would not transgress
His command,
When He marked out
the foundations
of the earth,
30 Then I was beside
Him *as* a master
craftsman;[a]
And I was daily
His delight,
Rejoicing always
before Him,
31 Rejoicing in His
inhabited world,
And my delight *was* with
the sons of men.

32 "Now therefore, listen
to me, *my* children,
For blessed *are those*
who keep my ways.
33 Hear instruction
and be wise,
And do not disdain *it.*
34 Blessed is the man
who listens to me,
Watching daily at
my gates,
Waiting at the posts
of my doors.
35 For whoever finds
me finds life,

8:30 [a] A Jewish tradition reads *one brought up.*

And obtains favor
from the LORD;
36 But he who sins
against me wrongs
his own soul;
All those who hate
me love death."

THE WAY OF WISDOM

9 Wisdom has built
her house,
She has hewn out her
seven pillars;
2 She has slaughtered
her meat,
She has mixed her wine,
She has also furnished
her table.
3 She has sent out
her maidens,
She cries out from
the highest places
of the city,
4 "Whoever *is* simple, let
him turn in here!"
As for him who lacks
understanding,
she says to him,
5 "Come, eat of my bread
And drink of the wine
I have mixed.
6 Forsake foolishness
and live,
And go in the way of
understanding.

7 "He who corrects a
scoffer gets shame
for himself,
And he who rebukes
a wicked *man only*
harms himself.
8 Do not correct a scoffer,
lest he hate you;
Rebuke a wise *man,* and
he will love you.
9 Give *instruction* to a
wise *man,* and he
will be still wiser;
Teach a just *man,* and he
will increase in learning.

10 "The fear of the LORD
is the beginning
of wisdom,
And the knowledge
of the Holy One *is*
understanding.
11 For by me your days
will be multiplied,
And years of life will
be added to you.
12 If you are wise, you are
wise for yourself,
And *if* you scoff, you
will bear *it* alone."

THE WAY OF FOLLY

13 A foolish woman
is clamorous;
She is simple, and
knows nothing.
14 For she sits at the
door of her house,
On a seat *by* the highest
places of the city,
15 To call to those
who pass by,
Who go straight
on their way:
16 "Whoever *is* simple, let
him turn in here";
And *as for* him who
lacks understanding,
she says to him,
17 "Stolen water is sweet,
And bread *eaten* in
secret is pleasant."

18 But he does not know
that the dead *are* there,
That her guests *are* in
the depths of hell.[a]

WISE SAYINGS OF SOLOMON

10 The proverbs of Solomon:

A wise son makes
a glad father,
But a foolish son *is* the
grief of his mother.

2 Treasures of wickedness
profit nothing,
But righteousness
delivers from death.
3 The LORD will not
allow the righteous
soul to famish,
But He casts away the
desire of the wicked.

4 He who has a slack
hand becomes poor,
But the hand of the
diligent makes rich.
5 He who gathers in
summer *is* a wise son;
He who sleeps in harvest *is*
a son who causes shame.

6 Blessings *are* on the
head of the righteous,
But violence covers the
mouth of the wicked.
7 The memory of the
righteous *is* blessed,
But the name of the
wicked will rot.

8 The wise in heart will
receive commands,
But a prating fool will fall.

9 He who walks with
integrity walks securely,
But he who perverts
his ways will
become known.

10 He who winks with the
eye causes trouble,
But a prating fool will fall.

11 The mouth of the
righteous *is* a well of life,
But violence covers the
mouth of the wicked.

12 Hatred stirs up strife,
But love covers all sins.

13 Wisdom is found on
the lips of him who
has understanding,
But a rod *is* for the back
of him who is devoid
of understanding.

14 Wise *people* store
up knowledge,
But the mouth of
the foolish *is* near
destruction.

15 The rich man's wealth
is his strong city;
The destruction of the
poor *is* their poverty.

16 The labor of the
righteous *leads* to life,

9:18 [a] Or *Sheol*

The wages of the
wicked to sin.

17 He who keeps instruction
is in the way of life,
But he who refuses
correction goes astray.

18 Whoever hides hatred
has lying lips,
And whoever spreads
slander *is* a fool.

19 In the multitude of words
sin is not lacking,
But he who restrains
his lips *is* wise.
20 The tongue of
the righteous *is*
choice silver;
The heart of the wicked
is worth little.
21 The lips of the righteous
feed many,
But fools die for lack
of wisdom.[a]

22 The blessing of the LORD
makes *one* rich,
And He adds no
sorrow with it.

23 To do evil *is* like
sport to a fool,
But a man of
understanding
has wisdom.
24 The fear of the wicked
will come upon him,
And the desire of
the righteous will
be granted.

25 When the whirlwind
passes by, the
wicked *is* no *more*,
But the righteous *has* an
everlasting foundation.

26 As vinegar to the teeth
and smoke to the eyes,
So *is* the lazy *man* to
those who send him.

27 The fear of the LORD
prolongs days,
But the years of
the wicked will
be shortened.
28 The hope of the righteous
will be gladness,
But the expectation of
the wicked will perish.
29 The way of the LORD
is strength for
the upright,
But destruction *will*
come to the workers
of iniquity.

30 The righteous will
never be removed,
But the wicked will not
inhabit the earth.
31 The mouth of the
righteous brings
forth wisdom,
But the perverse tongue
will be cut out.
32 The lips of the
righteous know
what is acceptable,
But the mouth of
the wicked *what*
is perverse.

10:21 [a] Literally *heart*

11 Dishonest scales *are*
an abomination
to the LORD,
But a just weight *is*
His delight.

2 When pride comes,
then comes shame;
But with the humble
is wisdom.

3 The integrity of the
upright will guide
them,
But the perversity of
the unfaithful will
destroy them.
4 Riches do not profit in
the day of wrath,
But righteousness
delivers from death.
5 The righteousness of
the blameless will
direct[a] his way aright,
But the wicked will
fall by his own
wickedness.
6 The righteousness
of the upright will
deliver them,
But the unfaithful will be
caught by *their* lust.

7 When a wicked man
dies, *his* expectation
will perish,
And the hope of the
unjust perishes.
8 The righteous is delivered
from trouble,
And it comes to the
wicked instead.

9 The hypocrite with
his mouth destroys
his neighbor,
But through knowledge
the righteous will
be delivered.
10 When it goes well
with the righteous,
the city rejoices;
And when the wicked
perish, *there is*
jubilation.
11 By the blessing of
the upright the
city is exalted,
But it is overthrown
by the mouth of
the wicked.

12 He who is devoid of
wisdom despises
his neighbor,
But a man of
understanding
holds his peace.

13 A talebearer reveals
secrets,
But he who is of a
faithful spirit
conceals a matter.

14 Where *there is* no
counsel, the people fall;
But in the multitude
of counselors
there is safety.

15 He who is surety for a
stranger will suffer,
But one who hates being
surety is secure.

11:5 [a] Or *make smooth* or *straight*

16 A gracious woman
retains honor,
But ruthless *men*
retain riches.
17 The merciful man
does good for
his own soul,
But *he who is* cruel
troubles his own flesh.
18 The wicked *man* does
deceptive work,
But he who sows
righteousness *will
have* a sure reward.
19 As righteousness
leads to life,
So he who pursues
evil *pursues it* to
his own death.
20 Those who are of a
perverse heart *are*
an abomination
to the LORD,
But *the* blameless in
their ways *are*
His delight.
21 *Though they join* forces,[a]
the wicked will not
go unpunished;
But the posterity of
the righteous will
be delivered.

22 *As* a ring of gold in
a swine's snout,
So is a lovely woman
who lacks discretion.

23 The desire of the
righteous *is* only good,
But the expectation of
the wicked *is* wrath.

24 There is *one* who scatters,
yet increases more;
And there is *one* who
withholds more
than is right,
But it *leads* to poverty.
25 The generous soul
will be made rich,
And he who waters will
also be watered himself.
26 The people will curse him
who withholds grain,
But blessing *will be* on the
head of him who sells *it*.

27 He who earnestly seeks
good finds favor,
But trouble will come to
him who seeks *evil*.

28 He who trusts in his
riches will fall,
But the righteous will
flourish like foliage.

29 He who troubles his
own house will
inherit the wind,
And the fool *will
be* servant to the
wise of heart.

30 The fruit of the righteous
is a tree of life,
And he who wins
souls *is* wise.

31 If the righteous will
be recompensed
on the earth,
How much more the
ungodly and the sinner.

11:21 [a] Literally *hand to hand*

12 Whoever loves
instruction loves
knowledge,
But he who hates
correction *is* stupid.

2 A good *man* obtains
favor from the LORD,
But a man of wicked
intentions He
will condemn.

3 A man is not established
by wickedness,
But the root of the
righteous cannot
be moved.

4 An excellent[a] wife *is*
the crown of her
husband,
But she who causes
shame *is* like
rottenness in his
bones.

5 The thoughts of the
righteous *are* right,
But the counsels of the
wicked *are* deceitful.
6 The words of the
wicked *are,* "Lie in
wait for blood,"
But the mouth of
the upright will
deliver them.

7 The wicked are
overthrown and
are no more,
But the house of the
righteous will stand.

8 A man will be
commended according
to his wisdom,
But he who is of a
perverse heart will
be despised.

9 Better *is the one* who
is slighted but
has a servant,
Than he who honors
himself but lacks bread.

10 A righteous *man* regards
the life of his animal,
But the tender mercies of
the wicked *are* cruel.

11 He who tills his land will
be satisfied with bread,
But he who follows
frivolity *is* devoid of
understanding.[a]

12 The wicked covet the
catch of evil *men,*
But the root of the
righteous yields *fruit.*
13 The wicked is ensnared
by the transgression
of *his* lips,
But the righteous will
come through trouble.
14 A man will be satisfied
with good by the
fruit of *his* mouth,
And the recompense
of a man's hands will
be rendered to him.

15 The way of a fool *is* right
in his own eyes,

12:4 [a] Literally *A wife of valor* 12:11 [a] Literally *heart*

But he who heeds
counsel *is* wise.
16 A fool's wrath is
known at once,
But a prudent *man*
covers shame.

17 He *who* speaks truth
declares righteousness,
But a false witness, deceit.
18 There is one who speaks
like the piercings
of a sword,
But the tongue of the
wise *promotes* health.
19 The truthful lip shall be
established forever,
But a lying tongue *is*
but for a moment.
20 Deceit is in the heart
of those who
devise evil,
But counselors of
peace have joy.
21 No grave trouble will
overtake the righteous,
But the wicked shall
be filled with evil.
22 Lying lips *are* an
abomination to
the LORD,
But those who deal
truthfully *are*
His delight.

23 A prudent man conceals
knowledge,
But the heart of fools
proclaims foolishness.

24 The hand of the
diligent will rule,
But the lazy *man* will be
put to forced labor.

25 Anxiety in the heart of
man causes depression,
But a good word
makes it glad.

26 The righteous should
choose his friends
carefully,
For the way of the wicked
leads them astray.

27 The lazy *man* does
not roast what he
took in hunting,
But diligence *is* man's
precious possession.

28 In the way of
righteousness *is* life,
And in *its* pathway
there is no death.

13 A wise son *heeds* his
father's instruction,
But a scoffer does not
listen to rebuke.

2 A man shall eat well by
the fruit of *his* mouth,
But the soul of the
unfaithful feeds
on violence.
3 He who guards his mouth
preserves his life,
But he who opens
wide his lips shall
have destruction.

4 The soul of a lazy
man desires, and
has nothing;
But the soul of the
diligent shall be
made rich.

5 A righteous *man*
hates lying,
But a wicked *man*
is loathsome and
comes to shame.
6 Righteousness guards
him whose way
is blameless,
But wickedness
overthrows the sinner.

7 There is one who
makes himself rich,
yet *has* nothing;
And one who makes
himself poor, yet
has great riches.

8 The ransom of a man's
life *is* his riches,
But the poor does
not hear rebuke.
9 The light of the
righteous rejoices,
But the lamp of the
wicked will be put out.

10 By pride comes
nothing but strife,
But with the well-advised
is wisdom.

11 Wealth *gained by*
dishonesty will
be diminished,
But he who gathers by
labor will increase.

12 Hope deferred makes
the heart sick,
But *when* the desire
comes, *it is* a tree
of life.

13 He who despises the word
will be destroyed,
But he who fears the
commandment
will be rewarded.
14 The law of the wise *is*
a fountain of life,
To turn *one* away from
the snares of death.

15 Good understanding
gains favor,
But the way of the
unfaithful *is* hard.
16 Every prudent *man* acts
with knowledge,
But a fool lays
open *his* folly.

17 A wicked messenger
falls into trouble,
But a faithful ambassador
brings health.

18 Poverty and shame
will come to him who
disdains correction,
But he who regards a
rebuke will be honored.

19 A desire accomplished
is sweet to the soul,
But *it is* an abomination
to fools to depart
from evil.

20 He who walks with wise
men will be wise,
But the companion of
fools will be destroyed.

21 Evil pursues sinners,
But to the righteous,
good shall be repaid.

22 A good *man* leaves an
inheritance to his
children's children,
But the wealth of the
sinner is stored up
for the righteous.

23 Much food *is in* the fallow
ground of the poor,
And for lack of justice
there is waste.[a]

24 He who spares his
rod hates his son,
But he who loves
him disciplines
him promptly.

25 The righteous eats to the
satisfying of his soul,
But the stomach of the
wicked shall be in want.

14

The wise woman
builds her house,
But the foolish pulls it
down with her hands.

2 He who walks in
his uprightness
fears the LORD,
But *he who is* perverse
in his ways
despises Him.

3 In the mouth of a fool
is a rod of pride,
But the lips of the wise
will preserve them.

4 Where no oxen *are,*
the trough *is* clean;
But much increase *comes*
by the strength of an ox.

5 A faithful witness
does not lie,
But a false witness
will utter lies.

6 A scoffer seeks wisdom
and does not *find it,*
But knowledge *is* easy
to him who
understands.

7 Go from the presence
of a foolish man,
When you do not
perceive *in him* the
lips of knowledge.

8 The wisdom of
the prudent *is* to
understand his way,
But the folly of
fools *is* deceit.

9 Fools mock at sin,
But among the upright
there is favor.

10 The heart knows its
own bitterness,
And a stranger does
not share its joy.

11 The house of the wicked
will be overthrown,
But the tent of the
upright will flourish.

12 There is a way *that*
seems right to a man,
But its end *is* the
way of death.

13:23 [a] Literally *what is swept away*

13 Even in laughter the
heart may sorrow,
And the end of mirth
may be grief.

14 The backslider in heart
will be filled with
his own ways,
But a good man *will be*
satisfied from above.[a]

15 The simple believes
every word,
But the prudent
considers well his steps.
16 A wise *man* fears and
departs from evil,
But a fool rages and
is self-confident.
17 A quick-tempered
man acts foolishly,
And a man of wicked
intentions is hated.
18 The simple inherit folly,
But the prudent
are crowned with
knowledge.
19 The evil will bow
before the good,
And the wicked at the
gates of the righteous.

20 The poor *man* is
hated even by his
own neighbor,
But the rich *has*
many friends.
21 He who despises his
neighbor sins;
But he who has mercy on
the poor, happy *is* he.

22 Do they not go astray
who devise evil?
But mercy and truth
belong to those who
devise good.

23 In all labor there is profit,
But idle chatter[a] *leads*
only to poverty.

24 The crown of the wise
is their riches,
But the foolishness
of fools *is* folly.

25 A true witness
delivers souls,
But a deceitful *witness*
speaks lies.

26 In the fear of the
Lord *there is* strong
confidence,
And His children will
have a place of refuge.
27 The fear of the Lord *is*
a fountain of life,
To turn *one* away from
the snares of death.

28 In a multitude of people
is a king's honor,
But in the lack of
people *is* the downfall
of a prince.

29 *He who is* slow to
wrath has great
understanding,
But *he who is* impulsive[a]
exalts folly.

14:14 [a] Literally *from above himself* 14:23 [a] Literally *talk of the lips* 14:29 [a] Literally *short of spirit*

30 A sound heart *is* life
to the body,
But envy *is* rottenness
to the bones.

31 He who oppresses the
poor reproaches
his Maker,
But he who honors
Him has mercy
on the needy.

32 The wicked is banished
in his wickedness,
But the righteous has a
refuge in his death.

33 Wisdom rests in the
heart of him who has
understanding,
But *what is* in the heart of
fools is made known.

34 Righteousness
exalts a nation,
But sin *is* a reproach
to *any* people.

35 The king's favor *is* toward
a wise servant,
But his wrath *is against*
him who causes shame.

15 A soft answer turns
away wrath,
But a harsh word
stirs up anger.
2 The tongue of the wise
uses knowledge rightly,
But the mouth of fools
pours forth foolishness.

3 The eyes of the LORD
are in every place,
Keeping watch on the
evil and the good.

4 A wholesome tongue
is a tree of life,
But perverseness in it
breaks the spirit.

5 A fool despises his
father's instruction,
But he who receives
correction is prudent.

6 *In* the house of the
righteous *there is*
much treasure,
But in the revenue
of the wicked is
trouble.

7 The lips of the wise
disperse knowledge,
But the heart of the
fool *does* not *do* so.

8 The sacrifice of
the wicked *is* an
abomination to
the LORD,
But the prayer of
the upright *is*
His delight.
9 The way of the wicked
is an abomination
to the LORD,
But He loves him
who follows
righteousness.

10 Harsh discipline
is for him who
forsakes the way,
And he who hates
correction will die.

11 Hell[a] and Destruction[b]
are before the LORD;
So how much more
the hearts of the
sons of men.

12 A scoffer does not love
one who corrects him,
Nor will he go to the wise.

13 A merry heart makes a
cheerful countenance,
But by sorrow of the
heart the spirit
is broken.

14 The heart of him who
has understanding
seeks knowledge,
But the mouth of fools
feeds on foolishness.

15 All the days of the
afflicted *are* evil,
But he who is of a
merry heart *has* a
continual feast.

16 Better *is* a little with the
fear of the LORD,
Than great treasure
with trouble.
17 Better *is* a dinner of
herbs[a] where love is,
Than a fatted calf
with hatred.

18 A wrathful man
stirs up strife,
But *he who is* slow to
anger allays contention.

19 The way of the lazy *man is*
like a hedge of thorns,
But the way of the
upright *is* a highway.

20 A wise son makes
a father glad,
But a foolish man
despises his mother.

21 Folly *is* joy *to him*
who is destitute of
discernment,
But a man of
understanding
walks uprightly.

22 Without counsel,
plans go awry,
But in the multitude
of counselors they
are established.

23 A man has joy by the
answer of his mouth,
And a word *spoken* in due
season, how good *it is!*

24 The way of life *winds*
upward for the wise,
That he may turn away
from hell[a] below.

25 The LORD will destroy the
house of the proud,
But He will establish the
boundary of the widow.

26 The thoughts of the wicked
are an abomination
to the LORD,

15:11 [a] Or *Sheol* [b] Hebrew *Abaddon* 15:17 [a] Or *vegetables* 15:24 [a] Or *Sheol*

But the words of the
pure *are* pleasant.

27 He who is greedy for gain
troubles his own house,
But he who hates
bribes will live.

28 The heart of the righteous
studies how to answer,
But the mouth of the
wicked pours forth evil.

29 The LORD *is* far from
the wicked,
But He hears the prayer
of the righteous.

30 The light of the eyes
rejoices the heart,
And a good report makes
the bones healthy.[a]

31 The ear that hears the
rebukes of life
Will abide among the wise.
32 He who disdains
instruction despises
his own soul,
But he who heeds rebuke
gets understanding.
33 The fear of the LORD *is* the
instruction of wisdom,
And before honor
is humility.

16 The preparations
of the heart
belong to man,
But the answer
of the tongue *is*
from the LORD.

2 All the ways of a man *are*
pure in his own eyes,
But the LORD weighs
the spirits.

3 Commit your works
to the LORD,
And your thoughts
will be established.

4 The LORD has made
all for Himself,
Yes, even the wicked
for the day of doom.

5 Everyone proud in heart
is an abomination
to the LORD;
Though they join
forces,[a] none will
go unpunished.

6 In mercy and truth
Atonement is provided
for iniquity;
And by the fear of the
LORD *one* departs
from evil.

7 When a man's ways
please the LORD,
He makes even his
enemies to be at
peace with him.

8 Better *is* a little with
righteousness,
Than vast revenues
without justice.

9 A man's heart
plans his way,

15:30 [a] Literally *fat* 16:5 [a] Literally *hand to hand*

But the LORD directs
his steps.

10 Divination *is* on the
lips of the king;
His mouth must not
transgress in judgment.
11 Honest weights and
scales *are* the LORD's;
All the weights in the
bag *are* His work.
12 *It is* an abomination
for kings to commit
wickedness,
For a throne is
established by
righteousness.
13 Righteous lips *are* the
delight of kings,
And they love him who
speaks *what is* right.
14 As messengers of death
is the king's wrath,
But a wise man will
appease it.
15 In the light of the
king's face *is* life,
And his favor *is* like a
cloud of the latter rain.

16 How much better to get
wisdom than gold!
And to get understanding
is to be chosen
rather than silver.

17 The highway of
the upright *is* to
depart from evil;
He who keeps his way
preserves his soul.

18 Pride *goes* before
destruction,
And a haughty spirit
before a fall.
19 Better *to be* of a humble
spirit with the lowly,
Than to divide the spoil
with the proud.

20 He who heeds the
word wisely will
find good,
And whoever trusts
in the LORD,
happy *is* he.

21 The wise in heart will
be called prudent,
And sweetness of the lips
increases learning.

22 Understanding *is* a
wellspring of life to
him who has it.
But the correction
of fools *is* folly.

23 The heart of the wise
teaches his mouth,
And adds learning
to his lips.

24 Pleasant words *are*
like a honeycomb,
Sweetness to the soul and
health to the bones.

25 There is a way *that*
seems right to a man,
But its end *is* the
way of death.

26 The person who labors,
labors for himself,
For his *hungry* mouth
drives him *on.*

27 An ungodly man
digs up evil,
And *it is* on his lips
like a burning fire.
28 A perverse man
sows strife,
And a whisperer separates
the best of friends.
29 A violent man entices
his neighbor,
And leads him in a way
that is not good.
30 He winks his eye to
devise perverse things;
He purses his lips *and*
brings about evil.

31 The silver-haired head
is a crown of glory,
If it is found in the way
of righteousness.

32 *He who is* slow to anger *is*
better than the mighty,
And he who rules his spirit
than he who takes a city.

33 The lot is cast into the lap,
But its every decision
is from the LORD.

17 Better *is* a dry morsel
with quietness,
Than a house full of
feasting[a] *with* strife.

2 A wise servant will
rule over a son who
causes shame,
And will share an
inheritance among
the brothers.

3 The refining pot *is*
for silver and the
furnace for gold,
But the LORD tests
the hearts.

4 An evildoer gives
heed to false lips;
A liar listens eagerly to
a spiteful tongue.

5 He who mocks the poor
reproaches his Maker;
He who is glad at calamity
will not go unpunished.

6 Children's children *are*
the crown of old men,
And the glory of children
is their father.

7 Excellent speech is not
becoming to a fool,
Much less lying lips
to a prince.

8 A present *is* a precious
stone in the eyes
of its possessor;
Wherever he turns,
he prospers.

9 He who covers a
transgression
seeks love,
But he who repeats a
matter separates friends.

10 Rebuke is more effective
for a wise *man*
Than a hundred
blows on a fool.

17:1 [a] Or *sacrificial meals*

11 An evil *man* seeks
only rebellion;
Therefore a cruel
messenger will be
sent against him.

12 Let a man meet a bear
robbed of her cubs,
Rather than a fool
in his folly.

13 Whoever rewards
evil for good,
Evil will not depart
from his house.

14 The beginning of strife
is like releasing water;
Therefore stop
contention before
a quarrel starts.

15 He who justifies the
wicked, and he who
condemns the just,
Both of them alike
are an abomination
to the LORD.

16 Why *is there* in the hand
of a fool the purchase
price of wisdom,
Since *he has* no
heart *for it?*

17 A friend loves at all times,
And a brother is born
for adversity.

18 A man devoid of
understanding shakes
hands in a pledge,
And becomes surety
for his friend.

19 He who loves
transgression
loves strife,
And he who exalts his
gate seeks destruction.

20 He who has a deceitful
heart finds no good,
And he who has a
perverse tongue
falls into evil.

21 He who begets a scoffer
does so to his sorrow,
And the father of a
fool has no joy.

22 A merry heart does
good, *like* medicine,[a]
But a broken spirit
dries the bones.

23 A wicked *man* accepts
a bribe behind
the back[a]
To pervert the ways
of justice.

24 Wisdom *is* in the sight
of him who has
understanding,
But the eyes of a fool
are on the ends
of the earth.

25 A foolish son *is* a grief
to his father,
And bitterness to her
who bore him.

17:22 [a] Or *makes medicine even better*   17:23 [a] Literally *from the bosom*

26 Also, to punish the
righteous *is* not good,
Nor to strike princes for
their uprightness.

27 He who has knowledge
spares his words,
And a man of
understanding is
of a calm spirit.
28 Even a fool is counted
wise when he
holds his peace;
When he shuts his lips,
he is considered
perceptive.

18 A man who isolates
himself seeks his
own desire;
He rages against all
wise judgment.

2 A fool has no delight
in understanding,
But in expressing
his own heart.

3 When the wicked comes,
contempt comes also;
And with dishonor
comes reproach.

4 The words of a man's
mouth *are* deep waters;
The wellspring of wisdom
is a flowing brook.

5 *It is* not good to show
partiality to the wicked,
Or to overthrow the
righteous in judgment.

6 A fool's lips enter
into contention,
And his mouth
calls for blows.
7 A fool's mouth *is* his
destruction,
And his lips *are* the
snare of his soul.
8 The words of a talebearer
are like tasty trifles,[a]
And they go down into
the inmost body.

9 He who is slothful
in his work
Is a brother to him who
is a great destroyer.

10 The name of the LORD
is a strong tower;
The righteous run to
it and are safe.
11 The rich man's wealth
is his strong city,
And like a high wall in
his own esteem.

12 Before destruction
the heart of a man
is haughty,
And before honor
is humility.

13 He who answers a matter
before he hears *it*,
It *is* folly and
shame to him.

14 The spirit of a man will
sustain him in sickness,
But who can bear a
broken spirit?

18:8 [a] A Jewish tradition reads *wounds*.

15 The heart of the prudent
acquires knowledge,
And the ear of the wise
seeks knowledge.

16 A man's gift makes
room for him,
And brings him
before great men.

17 The first *one* to plead his
cause *seems* right,
Until his neighbor comes
and examines him.

18 Casting lots causes
contentions to cease,
And keeps the
mighty apart.

19 A brother offended *is*
harder to win than
a strong city,
And contentions *are* like
the bars of a castle.

20 A man's stomach shall
be satisfied from the
fruit of his mouth;
From the produce of his
lips he shall be filled.

21 Death and life *are* in the
power of the tongue,
And those who love it
will eat its fruit.

22 *He who* finds a wife
finds a good *thing,*
And obtains favor
from the LORD.

23 The poor *man* uses
entreaties,
But the rich answers
roughly.

24 A man *who has* friends
must himself
be friendly,[a]
But there is a friend
who sticks closer
than a brother.

19 Better *is* the poor
who walks in
his integrity
Than *one who is* perverse
in his lips, and is a fool.

2 Also it is not good *for*
a soul *to be* without
knowledge,
And he sins who hastens
with *his* feet.

3 The foolishness of a
man twists his way,
And his heart frets
against the LORD.

4 Wealth makes
many friends,
But the poor is separated
from his friend.

5 A false witness will not
go unpunished,
And *he who* speaks lies
will not escape.

6 Many entreat the favor
of the nobility,

18:24 [a] Following Greek manuscripts, Syriac, Targum, and Vulgate; Masoretic Text reads *may come to ruin.*

And every man *is* a friend
to one who gives gifts.
7 All the brothers of the
poor hate him;
How much more do his
friends go far from him!
He may pursue *them*
with words, *yet* they
abandon *him.*

8 He who gets wisdom
loves his own soul;
He who keeps
understanding
will find good.

9 A false witness will not
go unpunished,
And *he who* speaks
lies shall perish.

10 Luxury is not fitting
for a fool,
Much less for a servant
to rule over princes.

11 The discretion of a
man makes him
slow to anger,
And his glory *is*
to overlook a
transgression.

12 The king's wrath *is* like
the roaring of a lion,
But his favor *is* like
dew on the grass.

13 A foolish son *is* the
ruin of his father,
And the contentions
of a wife *are* a
continual dripping.

14 Houses and riches
are an inheritance
from fathers,
But a prudent wife *is*
from the LORD.

15 Laziness casts *one*
into a deep sleep,
And an idle person
will suffer hunger.

16 He who keeps the
commandment
keeps his soul,
But he who is careless[a]
of his ways will die.

17 He who has pity on the
poor lends to the LORD,
And He will pay back
what he has given.

18 Chasten your son while
there is hope,
And do not set your heart
on his destruction.[a]

19 *A man of* great wrath will
suffer punishment;
For if you rescue *him,* you
will have to do it again.

20 Listen to counsel and
receive instruction,
That you may be wise
in your latter days.

19:16 [a] Literally *despises,* figurative of recklessness or carelessness 19:18 [a] Literally *to put him to death;* a Jewish tradition reads *on his crying.*

21 There are many plans
in a man's heart,
Nevertheless the
LORD's counsel—that
will stand.

22 What is desired in a
man is kindness,
And a poor man is
better than a liar.

23 The fear of the LORD
leads to life,
And *he who has it* will
abide in satisfaction;
He will not be visited
with evil.

24 A lazy *man* buries his
hand in the bowl,[a]
And will not so much
as bring it to his
mouth again.

25 Strike a scoffer, and
the simple will
become wary;
Rebuke one who has
understanding, *and* he
will discern knowledge.

26 He who mistreats *his*
father *and* chases
away *his* mother
Is a son who causes
shame and brings
reproach.

27 Cease listening to
instruction, my son,
And you will stray from
the words of knowledge.

28 A disreputable witness
scorns justice,
And the mouth
of the wicked
devours iniquity.

29 Judgments are prepared
for scoffers,
And beatings for the
backs of fools.

20 Wine *is* a mocker,
Strong drink *is*
a brawler,
And whoever is led astray
by it is not wise.

2 The wrath[a] of a king
is like the roaring
of a lion;
Whoever provokes
him to anger sins
against his own life.

3 *It is* honorable for a
man to stop striving,
Since any fool can
start a quarrel.

4 The lazy *man* will not
plow because of winter;
He will beg during
harvest and *have*
nothing.

5 Counsel in the heart of
man *is like* deep water,

19:24 [a] Septuagint and Syriac read *bosom;* Targum and Vulgate read *armpit.* 20:2 [a] Literally *fear* or *terror* which is produced by the king's wrath

But a man of
understanding
will draw it out.

6 Most men will proclaim
each his own goodness,
But who can find a
faithful man?

7 The righteous *man*
walks in his integrity;
His children *are*
blessed after him.

8 A king who sits on the
throne of judgment
Scatters all evil
with his eyes.

9 Who can say, "I have
made my heart
clean,
I am pure from my sin"?

10 Diverse weights *and*
diverse measures,
They *are* both alike,
an abomination
to the LORD.

11 Even a child is known
by his deeds,
Whether what he does
is pure and right.

12 The hearing ear and
the seeing eye,
The LORD has made
them both.

13 Do not love sleep, lest
you come to poverty;
Open your eyes, *and*
you will be satisfied
with bread.

14 "*It is* good for nothing,"[a]
cries the buyer;
But when he has gone his
way, then he boasts.

15 There is gold and a
multitude of rubies,
But the lips of knowledge
are a precious jewel.

16 Take the garment of
one who is surety
for a stranger,
And hold it as a
pledge *when it* is
for a seductress.

17 Bread gained by deceit
is sweet to a man,
But afterward his
mouth will be filled
with gravel.

18 Plans are established
by counsel;
By wise counsel wage war.

19 He who goes about
as a talebearer
reveals secrets;
Therefore do not
associate with one who
flatters with his lips.

20 Whoever curses his
father or his mother,
His lamp will be put out
in deep darkness.

20:14 [a] Literally *evil, evil*

21 An inheritance gained
hastily at the beginning
Will not be blessed
at the end.

22 Do not say, "I will
recompense evil";
Wait for the LORD, and
He will save you.

23 Diverse weights *are*
an abomination
to the LORD,
And dishonest scales
are not good.

24 A man's steps *are*
of the LORD;
How then can a
man understand
his own way?

25 *It is* a snare for a man
to devote rashly
something as holy,
And afterward to
reconsider *his* vows.

26 A wise king sifts out
the wicked,
And brings the threshing
wheel over them.

27 The spirit of a man
is the lamp of the
LORD,
Searching all the inner
depths of his heart.[a]

28 Mercy and truth
preserve the king,
And by lovingkindness
he upholds his throne.

29 The glory of young men
is their strength,
And the splendor of old
men *is* their gray head.

30 Blows that hurt
cleanse away evil,
As *do* stripes the inner
depths of the heart.[a]

21 The king's heart
is in the hand
of the LORD,
Like the rivers of water;
He turns it wherever
He wishes.

2 Every way of a man *is*
right in his own eyes,
But the LORD weighs
the hearts.

3 To do righteousness
and justice
Is more acceptable
to the LORD than
sacrifice.

4 A haughty look, a
proud heart,
And the plowing[a] of
the wicked *are* sin.

5 The plans of the diligent
lead surely to plenty,
But *those of* everyone
who is hasty, surely
to poverty.

20:27 [a] Literally *the rooms of the belly* 20:30 [a] Literally *the rooms of the belly* 21:4 [a] Or *lamp*

6 Getting treasures by
a lying tongue
Is the fleeting fantasy of
those who seek death.[a]

7 The violence of
the wicked will
destroy them,[a]
Because they refuse
to do justice.

8 The way of a guilty
man *is* perverse;[a]
But *as for* the pure,
his work *is* right.

9 Better to dwell in a
corner of a housetop,
Than in a house shared
with a contentious
woman.

10 The soul of the wicked
desires evil;
His neighbor finds no
favor in his eyes.

11 When the scoffer is
punished, the simple
is made wise;
But when the wise
is instructed, he
receives knowledge.

12 The righteous *God*
wisely considers the
house of the wicked,
Overthrowing the wicked
for *their* wickedness.

13 Whoever shuts his
ears to the cry
of the poor
Will also cry himself
and not be heard.

14 A gift in secret
pacifies anger,
And a bribe behind the
back,[a] strong wrath.

15 *It is* a joy for the just
to do justice,
But destruction *will
come* to the workers
of iniquity.

16 A man who wanders
from the way of
understanding
Will rest in the assembly
of the dead.

17 He who loves pleasure
will be a poor man;
He who loves wine
and oil will not be
rich.

18 The wicked *shall
be* a ransom for
the righteous,
And the unfaithful
for the upright.

19 Better to dwell in
the wilderness,
Than with a contentious
and angry woman.

21:6 [a] Septuagint reads *Pursue vanity on the snares of death;* Vulgate reads *Is vain and foolish, and shall stumble on the snares of death;* Targum reads *They shall be destroyed, and they shall fall who seek death.* 21:7 [a] Literally *drag them away* 21:8 [a] Or *The way of a man is perverse and strange* 21:14 [a] Literally *in the bosom*

20 *There is* desirable treasure,
And oil in the dwelling
of the wise,
But a foolish man
squanders it.

21 He who follows
righteousness
and mercy
Finds life, righteousness,
and honor.

22 A wise *man* scales the
city of the mighty,
And brings down the
trusted stronghold.

23 Whoever guards his
mouth and tongue
Keeps his soul
from troubles.

24 A proud *and* haughty
man—"Scoffer"
is his name;
He acts with
arrogant pride.

25 The desire of the lazy
man kills him,
For his hands refuse
to labor.
26 He covets greedily
all day long,
But the righteous gives
and does not spare.

27 The sacrifice of the wicked
is an abomination;
How much more *when*
he brings it with
wicked intent!

28 A false witness
shall perish,
But the man who
hears *him* will
speak endlessly.

29 A wicked man
hardens his face,
But *as for* the upright,
he establishes[a]
his way.

30 *There is* no wisdom
or understanding
Or counsel against
the LORD.

31 The horse *is* prepared
for the day of battle,
But deliverance *is*
of the LORD.

22 A *good* name is to
be chosen rather
than great riches,
Loving favor rather
than silver and gold.

2 The rich and the poor
have this in common,
The LORD *is* the maker
of them all.

3 A prudent *man* foresees
evil and hides himself,
But the simple pass on
and are punished.

4 By humility *and* the
fear of the LORD
Are riches and
honor and life.

21:29 [a] Qere and Septuagint read *understands.*

5 Thorns *and* snares *are* in
the way of the perverse;
He who guards his soul
will be far from them.

6 Train up a child in the
way he should go,
And when he is old he
will not depart from it.

7 The rich rules over
the poor,
And the borrower *is*
servant to the lender.

8 He who sows iniquity
will reap sorrow,
And the rod of his
anger will fail.

9 He who has a generous
eye will be blessed,
For he gives of his
bread to the poor.

10 Cast out the scoffer, and
contention will leave;
Yes, strife and reproach
will cease.

11 He who loves purity
of heart
And has grace on his lips,
The king *will be* his friend.

12 The eyes of the LORD
preserve knowledge,
But He overthrows the
words of the faithless.

13 The lazy *man* says, "*There
is* a lion outside!
I shall be slain in
the streets!"

14 The mouth of an immoral
woman *is* a deep pit;
He who is abhorred by
the LORD will fall there.

15 Foolishness *is* bound up
in the heart of a child;
The rod of correction will
drive it far from him.

16 He who oppresses the
poor to increase
his *riches,*
And he who gives to
the rich, *will* surely
come to poverty.

SAYINGS OF THE WISE

17 Incline your ear and hear
the words of the wise,
And apply your heart
to my knowledge;
18 For *it is* a pleasant
thing if you keep
them within you;
Let them all be fixed
upon your lips,
19 So that your trust may
be in the LORD;
I have instructed you
today, even you.
20 Have I not written to
you excellent things
Of counsels and
knowledge,
21 That I may make you
know the certainty of
the words of truth,
That you may answer
words of truth
To those who send to you?

22 Do not rob the poor
because he *is* poor,

Nor oppress the
afflicted at the gate;
23 For the LORD will
plead their cause,
And plunder the
soul of those who
plunder them.

24 Make no friendship
with an angry man,
And with a furious
man do not go,
25 Lest you learn his ways
And set a snare for
your soul.

26 Do not be one of
those who shakes
hands in a pledge,
One of those who is
surety for debts;
27 If you have nothing
with which to pay,
Why should he take
away your bed
from under you?

28 Do not remove the
ancient landmark
Which your fathers
have set.

29 Do you see a man *who*
excels in his work?
He will stand before kings;
He will not stand before
unknown *men*.

23

When you sit down
to eat with a ruler,
Consider carefully
what *is* before you;
2 And put a knife to
your throat
If you *are* a man
given to appetite.
3 Do not desire his
delicacies,
For they *are*
deceptive food.

4 Do not overwork
to be rich;
Because of your own
understanding, cease!
5 Will you set your eyes
on that which is not?
For *riches* certainly make
themselves wings;
They fly away like an
eagle *toward* heaven.

6 Do not eat the bread
of a miser,[a]
Nor desire his delicacies;
7 For as he thinks in
his heart, so *is* he.
"Eat and drink!" he
says to you,
But his heart is
not with you.
8 The morsel you
have eaten, you
will vomit up,
And waste your
pleasant words.

9 Do not speak in the
hearing of a fool,
For he will despise the
wisdom of your words.

10 Do not remove the
ancient landmark,

23:6 [a] Literally *one who has an evil eye*

Nor enter the fields
of the fatherless;
11 For their Redeemer
is mighty;
He will plead their
cause against you.

12 Apply your heart
to instruction,
And your ears to words
of knowledge.

13 Do not withhold
correction from a child,
For *if* you beat him with
a rod, he will not die.
14 You shall beat him
with a rod,
And deliver his soul
from hell.[a]

15 My son, if your
heart is wise,
My heart will
rejoice—indeed,
I myself;
16 Yes, my inmost being
will rejoice
When your lips speak
right things.

17 Do not let your heart
envy sinners,
But *be zealous* for the fear
of the LORD all the day;
18 For surely there is
a hereafter,
And your hope will
not be cut off.

19 Hear, my son, and
be wise;
And guide your
heart in the way.
20 Do not mix with
winebibbers,
Or with gluttonous
eaters of meat;
21 For the drunkard
and the glutton will
come to poverty,
And drowsiness will
clothe *a man* with rags.

22 Listen to your father
who begot you,
And do not despise your
mother when she is old.

23 Buy the truth, and
do not sell *it,*
Also wisdom and
instruction and
understanding.

24 The father of the
righteous will
greatly rejoice,
And he who begets a wise
child will delight in him.
25 Let your father and your
mother be glad,
And let her who bore
you rejoice.

26 My son, give me
your heart,
And let your eyes
observe my ways.
27 For a harlot *is* a deep pit,
And a seductress *is*
a narrow well.
28 She also lies in wait
as *for* a victim,

23:14 [a] Or *Sheol*

And increases the
unfaithful among men.

29 Who has woe?
Who has sorrow?
Who has contentions?
Who has complaints?
Who has wounds
without cause?
Who has redness of eyes?
30 Those who linger
long at the wine,
Those who go in search
of mixed wine.
31 Do not look on the
wine when it is red,
When it sparkles
in the cup,
When it swirls around
smoothly;
32 At the last it bites
like a serpent,
And stings like a viper.
33 Your eyes will see
strange things,
And your heart will utter
perverse things.
34 Yes, you will be like one
who lies down in the
midst of the sea,
Or like one who lies at the
top of the mast, *saying:*
35 "They have struck me,
but I was not hurt;
They have beaten me,
but I did not feel *it.*
When shall I awake,
that I may seek
another *drink?*"

24 Do not be envious
of evil men,
Nor desire to be
with them;
2 For their heart
devises violence,
And their lips talk of
troublemaking.

3 Through wisdom a
house is built,
And by understanding
it is established;
4 By knowledge the
rooms are filled
With all precious and
pleasant riches.

5 A wise man *is* strong,
Yes, a man of knowledge
increases strength;
6 For by wise counsel you
will wage your own war,
And in a multitude
of counselors
there is safety.

7 Wisdom *is* too lofty
for a fool;
He does not open his
mouth in the gate.

8 He who plots to do evil
Will be called a schemer.
9 The devising of
foolishness *is* sin,
And the scoffer *is* an
abomination to men.

10 *If* you faint in the
day of adversity,
Your strength *is* small.

11 Deliver *those who* are
drawn toward death,
And hold back *those*
stumbling to the
slaughter.

12 If you say, "Surely we
did not know this,"
Does not He who weighs
the hearts consider *it?*
He who keeps your soul,
does He *not* know *it?*
And will He *not* render
to *each* man according
to his deeds?

13 My son, eat honey
because *it is* good,
And the honeycomb
which is sweet to
your taste;
14 So *shall* the knowledge
of wisdom *be* to
your soul;
If you have found *it,*
there is a prospect,
And your hope will
not be cut off.

15 Do not lie in wait,
O wicked *man,*
against the dwelling
of the righteous;
Do not plunder his
resting place;
16 For a righteous *man*
may fall seven times
And rise again,
But the wicked shall
fall by calamity.

17 Do not rejoice when
your enemy falls,
And do not let your
heart be glad when
he stumbles;
18 Lest the LORD see *it,* and
it displease Him,
And He turn away His
wrath from him.

19 Do not fret because
of evildoers,
Nor be envious of
the wicked;
20 For there will be
no prospect for
the evil *man;*
The lamp of the wicked
will be put out.

21 My son, fear the LORD
and the king;
Do not associate with
those given to change;
22 For their calamity will
rise suddenly,
And who knows the ruin
those two can bring?

FURTHER SAYINGS OF THE WISE

23These *things* also *belong*
to the wise:

It is not good to show
partiality in judgment.
24 He who says to the wicked,
"You *are* righteous,"
Him the people will curse;
Nations will abhor him.
25 But those who rebuke *the
wicked* will have delight,
And a good blessing will
come upon them.

26 He who gives a right
answer kisses the lips.

27 Prepare your
outside work,
Make it fit for yourself
in the field;
And afterward build
your house.

28 Do not be a witness
against your neighbor
without cause,
For would you deceive[a]
with your lips?
29 Do not say, "I will do
to him just as he
has done to me;
I will render to the man
according to his work."

30 I went by the field
of the lazy *man*,
And by the vineyard
of the man devoid
of understanding;
31 And there it was, all
overgrown with
thorns;
Its surface was covered
with nettles;
Its stone wall was
broken down.
32 When I saw *it*, I
considered *it* well;
I looked on *it and*
received instruction:
33 A little sleep, a
little slumber,
A little folding of the
hands to rest;
34 So shall your poverty
come *like* a prowler,
And your need like
an armed man.

FURTHER WISE SAYINGS OF SOLOMON

25 These also *are* proverbs of Solomon *which* the men of Hezekiah king of Judah copied:

2 *It is* the glory of God to
conceal a matter,
But the glory of kings *is*
to search out a matter.

3 *As* the heavens for height
and the earth for depth,
So the heart of kings
is unsearchable.

4 Take away the dross
from silver,
And it will go to the
silversmith *for* jewelry.
5 Take away the wicked
from before the king,
And his throne will
be established in
righteousness.

6 Do not exalt yourself in
the presence of the king,
And do not stand in the
place of the great;
7 For *it is* better that
he say to you,
"Come up here,"
Than that you should
be put lower in the
presence of the prince,
Whom your eyes
have seen.

8 Do not go hastily to court;
For what will you
do in the end,
When your neighbor has
put you to shame?
9 Debate your case with
your neighbor,
And do not disclose the
secret to another;

24:28 [a] Septuagint and Vulgate read *Do not deceive*.

10 Lest he who hears *it*
expose your shame,
And your reputation
be ruined.

11 A word fitly spoken *is*
like apples of gold
In settings of silver.
12 *Like* an earring of gold and
an ornament of fine gold
Is a wise rebuker to
an obedient ear.

13 Like the cold of snow
in time of harvest
Is a faithful messenger to
those who send him,
For he refreshes the
soul of his masters.

14 Whoever falsely
boasts of giving
Is like clouds and wind
without rain.

15 By long forbearance a
ruler is persuaded,
And a gentle tongue
breaks a bone.

16 Have you found honey?
Eat only as much
as you need,
Lest you be filled with
it and vomit.

17 Seldom set foot in your
neighbor's house,
Lest he become weary
of you and hate you.

18 A man who bears false
witness against
his neighbor
Is like a club, a sword,
and a sharp arrow.

19 Confidence in an
unfaithful *man* in
time of trouble
Is like a bad tooth and
a foot out of joint.

20 *Like* one who takes away a
garment in cold weather,
And like vinegar on soda,
Is one who sings songs
to a heavy heart.

21 If your enemy is hungry,
give him bread to eat;
And if he is thirsty, give
him water to drink;
22 For *so* you will heap coals
of fire on his head,
And the LORD will
reward you.

23 The north wind
brings forth rain,
And a backbiting tongue
an angry countenance.

24 *It is* better to dwell in a
corner of a housetop,
Than in a house shared
with a contentious
woman.

25 *As* cold water to a
weary soul,
So *is* good news from
a far country.

26 A righteous *man* who
falters before the wicked
Is like a murky spring
and a polluted well.

27 *It is* not good to eat
much honey;
So to seek one's own
glory *is not* glory.

28 Whoever *has* no rule
over his own spirit
Is like a city broken
down, without walls.

26 As snow in summer
and rain in harvest,
So honor is not
fitting for a fool.

2 Like a flitting sparrow,
like a flying swallow,
So a curse without cause
shall not alight.

3 A whip for the horse,
A bridle for the donkey,
And a rod for the
fool's back.
4 Do not answer a fool
according to his folly,
Lest you also be like him.
5 Answer a fool according
to his folly,
Lest he be wise in
his own eyes.
6 He who sends a message
by the hand of a fool
Cuts off *his own* feet
and drinks violence.
7 *Like* the legs of the lame
that hang limp
Is a proverb in the
mouth of fools.
8 Like one who binds
a stone in a sling
Is he who gives
honor to a fool.
9 *Like* a thorn *that* goes into
the hand of a drunkard
Is a proverb in the
mouth of fools.
10 The great *God* who
formed everything
Gives the fool *his* hire
and the transgressor
his wages.[a]
11 As a dog returns to
his own vomit,
So a fool repeats his folly.
12 Do you see a man wise
in his own eyes?
There is more hope for
a fool than for him.

13 The lazy *man* says, "*There*
is a lion in the road!
A fierce lion *is* in
the streets!"
14 *As* a door turns on
its hinges,
So *does* the lazy *man*
on his bed.
15 The lazy *man* buries his
hand in the bowl;[a]
It wearies him to bring
it back to his mouth.
16 The lazy *man is* wiser
in his own eyes
Than seven men who
can answer sensibly.

17 He who passes by
and meddles in a
quarrel not his own
Is like one who takes
a dog by the ears.

26:10 [a] The Hebrew is difficult; ancient and modern translators differ greatly. 26:15 [a] Compare 19:24

18 Like a madman who
throws firebrands,
arrows, and death,
19 *Is* the man *who* deceives
his neighbor,
And says, "I was
only joking!"

20 Where *there is* no wood,
the fire goes out;
And where *there is* no
talebearer, strife ceases.
21 *As* charcoal *is* to burning
coals, and wood to fire,
So *is* a contentious man
to kindle strife.
22 The words of a talebearer
are like tasty trifles,
And they go down into
the inmost body.

23 Fervent lips with a
wicked heart
Are like earthenware
covered with
silver dross.

24 He who hates, disguises
it with his lips,
And lays up deceit
within himself;
25 When he speaks kindly,
do not believe him,
For *there are* seven
abominations
in his heart;
26 *Though his* hatred is
covered by deceit,
His wickedness will
be revealed before
the assembly.

27 Whoever digs a pit
will fall into it,
And he who rolls a
stone will have it
roll back on him.

28 A lying tongue hates *those*
who are crushed by it,
And a flattering mouth
works ruin.

27 Do not boast about
tomorrow,
For you do not know what
a day may bring forth.

2 Let another man
praise you, and not
your own mouth;
A stranger, and not
your own lips.

3 A stone *is* heavy and
sand *is* weighty,
But a fool's wrath
is heavier than
both of them.

4 Wrath *is* cruel and
anger a torrent,
But who *is* able to stand
before jealousy?

5 Open rebuke *is* better
Than love carefully
concealed.

6 Faithful *are* the
wounds of a friend,
But the kisses of an
enemy *are* deceitful.

7 A satisfied soul loathes
the honeycomb,
But to a hungry soul every
bitter thing *is* sweet.

8 Like a bird that wanders
from its nest
Is a man who wanders
from his place.

9 Ointment and perfume
delight the heart,
And the sweetness
of a man's friend
gives delight by
hearty counsel.

10 Do not forsake your
own friend or your
father's friend,
Nor go to your brother's
house in the day of
your calamity;
Better *is* a neighbor
nearby than a
brother far away.

11 My son, be wise, and
make my heart glad,
That I may answer him
who reproaches me.

12 A prudent *man* foresees
evil *and* hides himself;
The simple pass on
and are punished.

13 Take the garment of
him who is surety
for a stranger,
And hold it in pledge
when he is surety
for a seductress.

14 He who blesses his friend
with a loud voice, rising
early in the morning,
It will be counted a
curse to him.

15 A continual dripping
on a very rainy day
And a contentious
woman are alike;
16 Whoever restrains her
restrains the wind,
And grasps oil with
his right hand.

17 *As* iron sharpens iron,
So a man sharpens
the countenance
of his friend.

18 Whoever keeps the fig
tree will eat its fruit;
So he who waits on his
master will be honored.

19 As in water face
reflects face,
So a man's heart
reveals the man.

20 Hell[a] and Destruction[b]
are never full;
So the eyes of man are
never satisfied.

21 The refining pot *is*
for silver and the
furnace for gold,
And a man *is valued* by
what others say of him.

22 Though you grind a
fool in a mortar with
a pestle along with
crushed grain,

27:20 [a] Or *Sheol* [b] Hebrew *Abaddon*

Yet his foolishness will
not depart from him.

23 Be diligent to know the
state of your flocks,
And attend to your herds;
24 For riches *are* not forever,
Nor does a crown *endure*
to all generations.
25 *When* the hay is removed,
and the tender grass
shows itself,
And the herbs of
the mountains are
gathered in,
26 The lambs *will provide*
your clothing,
And the goats the
price of a field;
27 *You shall have* enough
goats' milk for
your food,
For the food of your
household,
And the nourishment of
your maidservants.

28 The wicked flee when
no one pursues,
But the righteous are
bold as a lion.

2 Because of the
transgression of a land,
many *are* its princes;
But by a man of
understanding
and knowledge
Right will be prolonged.

3 A poor man who
oppresses the poor
Is like a driving rain
which leaves no food.

4 Those who forsake the
law praise the wicked,
But such as keep the law
contend with them.

5 Evil men do not
understand justice,
But those who seek the
LORD understand all.

6 Better *is* the poor who
walks in his integrity
Than one perverse *in
his* ways, though
he *be* rich.

7 Whoever keeps the law
is a discerning son,
But a companion of
gluttons shames
his father.

8 One who increases
his possessions by
usury and extortion
Gathers it for him who
will pity the poor.

9 One who turns
away his ear from
hearing the law,
Even his prayer *is* an
abomination.

10 Whoever causes the
upright to go astray
in an evil way,
He himself will fall
into his own pit;
But the blameless
will inherit good.

11 The rich man *is* wise
in his own eyes,

But the poor who
has understanding
searches him out.

12 When the righteous
rejoice, *there is*
great glory;
But when the wicked
arise, men hide
themselves.

13 He who covers his sins
will not prosper,
But whoever confesses
and forsakes *them*
will have mercy.

14 Happy *is* the man
who is always
reverent,
But he who hardens
his heart will fall
into calamity.

15 *Like* a roaring lion and
a charging bear
Is a wicked ruler over
poor people.

16 A ruler who lacks
understanding *is* a
great oppressor,
But he who hates
covetousness will
prolong *his* days.

17 A man burdened
with bloodshed will
flee into a pit;
Let no one help him.

18 Whoever walks
blamelessly will
be saved,
But *he who is* perverse
in his ways will
suddenly fall.

19 He who tills his land
will have plenty
of bread,
But he who follows
frivolity will have
poverty enough!

20 A faithful man will
abound with blessings,
But he who hastens
to be rich will not
go unpunished.

21 To show partiality
is not good,
Because for a piece
of bread a man
will transgress.

22 A man with an evil eye
hastens after riches,
And does not consider
that poverty will
come upon him.

23 He who rebukes a
man will find more
favor afterward
Than he who flatters
with the tongue.

24 Whoever robs his father
or his mother,
And says, "*It is* no
transgression,"
The same is companion
to a destroyer.

25 He who is of a proud
heart stirs up strife,

But he who trusts in the
LORD will be prospered.

26 He who trusts in his
own heart is a fool,
But whoever walks wisely
will be delivered.

27 He who gives to the
poor will not lack,
But he who hides his eyes
will have many curses.

28 When the wicked arise,
men hide themselves;
But when they perish, the
righteous increase.

29 He who is often
rebuked, *and*
hardens *his* neck,
Will suddenly be
destroyed, and that
without remedy.

2 When the righteous
are in authority, the
people rejoice;
But when a wicked *man*
rules, the people groan.

3 Whoever loves
wisdom makes his
father rejoice,
But a companion
of harlots wastes
his wealth.

4 The king establishes
the land by justice,
But he who receives
bribes overthrows it.

5 A man who flatters
his neighbor
Spreads a net for his feet.

6 By transgression an
evil man is snared,
But the righteous
sings and rejoices.

7 The righteous considers
the cause of the poor,
But the wicked does
not understand
such knowledge.

8 Scoffers set a city aflame,
But wise *men* turn
away wrath.

9 *If* a wise man contends
with a foolish man,
Whether *the fool* rages or
laughs, *there is* no peace.

10 The bloodthirsty hate
the blameless,
But the upright seek
his well-being.[a]

11 A fool vents all his
feelings,[a]
But a wise *man* holds
them back.

12 If a ruler pays
attention to lies,
All his servants
become wicked.

13 The poor *man* and
the oppressor have
this in common:

29:10 [a] Literally *soul* 29:11 [a] Literally *spirit*

The LORD gives light
to the eyes of both.

14 The king who judges
the poor with truth,
His throne will be
established forever.

15 The rod and rebuke
give wisdom,
But a child left *to*
himself brings shame
to his mother.

16 When the wicked
are multiplied,
transgression increases;
But the righteous
will see their fall.

17 Correct your son, and
he will give you rest;
Yes, he will give delight
to your soul.

18 Where *there is* no
revelation,[a] the people
cast off restraint;
But happy *is* he who
keeps the law.

19 A servant will not
be corrected by
mere words;
For though he
understands, he
will not respond.

20 Do you see a man
hasty in his *words?*
There is more hope for
a fool than for him.

21 He who pampers
his servant from
childhood
Will have him as a
son in the end.

22 An angry man stirs
up strife,
And a furious
man abounds in
transgression.

23 A man's pride will
bring him low,
But the humble in spirit
will retain honor.

24 Whoever is a partner
with a thief hates
his own life;
He swears to tell
the truth,[a] but
reveals nothing.

25 The fear of man
brings a snare,
But whoever trusts
in the LORD
shall be safe.

26 Many seek the
ruler's favor,
But justice for man
comes from the LORD.

27 An unjust man *is* an
abomination to
the righteous,
And *he who is* upright
in the way *is* an
abomination to
the wicked.

29:18 [a] Or *prophetic vision* 29:24 [a] Literally *hears the adjuration*

THE WISDOM OF AGUR

30 The words of Agur the son of Jakeh, *his* utterance. This man declared to Ithiel—to Ithiel and Ucal:

2 Surely I *am* more stupid
than *any* man,
And do not have the
understanding
of a man.
3 I neither learned wisdom
Nor have knowledge
of the Holy One.

4 Who has ascended into
heaven, or descended?
Who has gathered the
wind in His fists?
Who has bound the
waters in a garment?
Who has established all
the ends of the earth?
What *is* His name, and
what *is* His Son's name,
If you know?

5 Every word of
God *is* pure;
He *is* a shield to
those who put their
trust in Him.
6 Do not add to His words,
Lest He rebuke you, and
you be found a liar.

7 Two *things* I
request of You
(Deprive me not
before I die):
8 Remove falsehood and
lies far from me;
Give me neither poverty
nor riches—
Feed me with the food
allotted to me;
9 Lest I be full and
deny *You*,
And say, "Who *is*
the LORD?"
Or lest I be poor and steal,
And profane the
name of my God.

10 Do not malign a servant
to his master,
Lest he curse you, and
you be found guilty.

11 *There is* a generation
that curses its father,
And does not bless
its mother.
12 *There is* a generation *that*
is pure in its own eyes,
Yet is not washed
from its filthiness.
13 *There is* a generation—oh,
how lofty are their eyes!
And their eyelids
are lifted up.
14 *There is* a generation
whose teeth *are*
like swords,
And whose fangs
are like knives,
To devour the poor
from off the earth,
And the needy from
among men.

15 The leech has two
daughters—
Give *and* Give!

There are three *things*
that are never satisfied,
Four never say, "Enough!":

16 The grave,[a]
The barren womb,
The earth *that* is not
satisfied with water—
And the fire never
says, "Enough!"

17 The eye *that* mocks
his father,
And scorns obedience
to *his* mother,
The ravens of the valley
will pick it out,
And the young
eagles will eat it.

18 There are three
things which are too
wonderful for me,
Yes, four *which* I do
not understand:
19 The way of an eagle
in the air,
The way of a serpent
on a rock,
The way of a ship in the
midst of the sea,
And the way of a man
with a virgin.

20 This *is* the way of an
adulterous woman:
She eats and wipes
her mouth,
And says, "I have done
no wickedness."

21 For three *things* the
earth is perturbed,
Yes, for four it
cannot bear up:
22 For a servant when
he reigns,
A fool when he is
filled with food,
23 A hateful *woman* when
she is married,
And a maidservant who
succeeds her mistress.

24 There are four *things*
which are little
on the earth,
But they *are*
exceedingly wise:
25 The ants *are* a people
not strong,
Yet they prepare their
food in the summer;
26 The rock badgers[a]
are a feeble folk,
Yet they make their
homes in the crags;
27 The locusts have no
king,
Yet they all advance
in ranks;
28 The spider[a] skillfully
grasps with its hands,
And it is in kings' palaces.

29 There are three
things which are
majestic in pace,
Yes, four *which* are
stately in walk:
30 A lion, *which is* mighty
among beasts
And does not turn
away from any;
31 A greyhound,[a]
A male goat also,

30:16 [a] Or *Sheol* 30:26 [a] Or *hyraxes* 30:28 [a] Or *lizard* 30:31 [a] Exact identity unknown

And a king *whose* troops
are with him.[b]

32 If you have been foolish
in exalting yourself,
Or if you have devised
evil, *put your* hand
on *your* mouth.
33 For *as* the churning of
milk produces butter,
And wringing the nose
produces blood,
So the forcing of wrath
produces strife.

THE WORDS OF KING LEMUEL'S MOTHER

31 The words of King Lemuel, the utterance which his mother taught him:

2 What, my son?
And what, son of
my womb?
And what, son of
my vows?
3 Do not give your
strength to women,
Nor your ways to that
which destroys kings.

4 *It is* not for kings,
O Lemuel,
It is not for kings
to drink wine,
Nor for princes
intoxicating drink;
5 Lest they drink and
forget the law,
And pervert the justice
of all the afflicted.
6 Give strong drink to him
who is perishing,
And wine to those who
are bitter of heart.
7 Let him drink and
forget his poverty,
And remember his
misery no more.

8 Open your mouth for
the speechless,
In the cause of all *who
are* appointed to die.[a]
9 Open your mouth,
judge righteously,
And plead the cause of
the poor and needy.

THE VIRTUOUS WIFE

10 Who[a] can find a
virtuous[b] wife?
For her worth *is* far
above rubies.
11 The heart of her husband
safely trusts her;
So he will have no
lack of gain.
12 She does him good
and not evil
All the days of her life.
13 She seeks wool and flax,
And willingly works
with her hands.
14 She is like the
merchant ships,
She brings her food
from afar.

30:31 [b] A Jewish tradition reads *a king against whom there is no uprising.* 31:8 [a] Literally *sons of passing away* 31:10 [a] Verses 10 through 31 are an alphabetic acrostic in Hebrew (compare Psalm 119). [b] Literally *a wife of valor,* in the sense of all forms of excellence

15 She also rises while
it is yet night,
And provides food for
her household,
And a portion for her
maidservants.
16 She considers a field
and buys it;
From her profits she
plants a vineyard.
17 She girds herself
with strength,
And strengthens
her arms.
18 She perceives that her
merchandise *is* good,
And her lamp does not
go out by night.
19 She stretches out her
hands to the distaff,
And her hand holds
the spindle.
20 She extends her hand
to the poor,
Yes, she reaches out her
hands to the needy.
21 She is not afraid of snow
for her household,
For all her household *is*
clothed with scarlet.
22 She makes tapestry
for herself;
Her clothing *is* fine
linen and purple.
23 Her husband is known
in the gates,
When he sits among the
elders of the land.
24 She makes linen
garments and
sells *them,*
And supplies sashes
for the merchants.
25 Strength and honor
are her clothing;
She shall rejoice in
time to come.
26 She opens her mouth
with wisdom,
And on her tongue *is*
the law of kindness.
27 She watches over the
ways of her household,
And does not eat the
bread of idleness.
28 Her children rise up
and call her blessed;
Her husband *also,* and
he praises her:
29 "Many daughters
have done well,
But you excel them all."
30 Charm *is* deceitful and
beauty *is* passing,
But a woman *who*
fears the LORD, she
shall be praised.
31 Give her of the fruit
of her hands,
And let her own
works praise her
in the gates.

THE BOOK OF ECCLESIASTES

THE VANITY OF LIFE

1 The words of the Preacher, the son of David, king in Jerusalem.

2 "Vanity[a] of vanities,"
says the Preacher;
"Vanity of vanities,
all *is* vanity."

3 What profit has a man
from all his labor
In which he toils
under the sun?
4 *One* generation passes
away, and *another*
generation comes;
But the earth abides
forever.
5 The sun also rises,
and the sun goes
down,
And hastens to the
place where it arose.
6 The wind goes toward
the south,
And turns around
to the north;
The wind whirls about
continually,
And comes again
on its circuit.
7 All the rivers run
into the sea,
Yet the sea *is* not full;
To the place from which
the rivers come,
There they return again.
8 All things *are* full
of labor;
Man cannot express *it.*
The eye is not satisfied
with seeing,
Nor the ear filled
with hearing.

9 That which has been
is what will be,
That which *is* done is
what will be done,
And *there is* nothing
new under the sun.
10 Is there anything of
which it may be said,
"See, this *is* new"?
It has already been in
ancient times before us.
11 *There is* no remembrance
of former *things,*
Nor will there be any
remembrance of *things*
that are to come
By *those* who will
come after.

THE GRIEF OF WISDOM

12I, the Preacher, was king
over Israel in Jerusalem.
13And I set my heart to seek
and search out by wisdom

1:2 [a] Or *Absurdity, Frustration, Futility, Nonsense;* and so throughout this book

concerning all that is done
under heaven; this burdensome task God has given to
the sons of man, by which
they may be exercised. 14 I
have seen all the works that
are done under the sun; and
indeed, all *is* vanity and grasping for the wind.

15 *What is* crooked cannot
  be made straight,
And what is lacking
  cannot be numbered.

16 I communed with my
heart, saying, "Look, I have
attained greatness, and have
gained more wisdom than all
who were before me in Jerusalem. My heart has understood great wisdom and
knowledge." 17 And I set my
heart to know wisdom and
to know madness and folly.
I perceived that this also is
grasping for the wind.

18 For in much wisdom
  is much grief,
And he who increases
  knowledge
  increases sorrow.

THE VANITY OF PLEASURE

2 I said in my heart, "Come
now, I will test you with
mirth; therefore enjoy pleasure"; but surely, this also *was*
vanity. 2 I said of laughter—
"Madness!"; and of mirth,
"What does it accomplish?"
3 I searched in my heart *how*
to gratify my flesh with wine,
while guiding my heart with
wisdom, and how to lay hold
on folly, till I might see what
was good for the sons of men
to do under heaven all the
days of their lives.
4 I made my works great,
I built myself houses, and
planted myself vineyards. 5 I
made myself gardens and or-
chards, and I planted all *kinds*
of fruit trees in them. 6 I made
myself water pools from which
to water the growing trees of
the grove. 7 I acquired male
and female servants, and had
servants born in my house.
Yes, I had greater possessions
of herds and flocks than all
who were in Jerusalem before
me. 8 I also gathered for myself silver and gold and the
special treasures of kings and
of the provinces. I acquired
male and female singers, the
delights of the sons of men,
and musical instruments[a] of
all kinds.
9 So I became great and
excelled more than all who
were before me in Jerusalem.
Also my wisdom remained
with me.

10 Whatever my eyes
  desired I did not
  keep from them.
I did not withhold
  my heart from
  any pleasure,

2:8 [a] Exact meaning unknown

For my heart rejoiced
in all my labor;
And this was my reward
from all my labor.
11 Then I looked on all
the works that my
hands had done
And on the labor in
which I had toiled;
And indeed all *was*
vanity and grasping
for the wind.
There was no profit
under the sun.

THE END OF THE WISE AND THE FOOL

12 Then I turned myself to
consider wisdom and
madness and folly;
For what *can* the man
do who succeeds
the king?—
Only what he has
already done.
13 Then I saw that wisdom
excels folly
As light excels darkness.
14 The wise man's eyes
are in his head,
But the fool walks
in darkness.
Yet I myself perceived
That the same event
happens to them all.

15 So I said in my heart,
"As it happens
to the fool,
It also happens to me,
And why was I then
more wise?"
Then I said in my heart,
"This also *is* vanity."
16 For *there is* no more
remembrance of
the wise than of
the fool forever,
Since all that now *is*
will be forgotten in
the days to come.
And how does a
wise *man* die?
As the fool!

17Therefore I hated life because the work that was done
under the sun *was* distressing to me, for all *is* vanity and
grasping for the wind.
18Then I hated all my labor
in which I had toiled under
the sun, because I must leave
it to the man who will come
after me. 19And who knows
whether he will be wise or a
fool? Yet he will rule over all
my labor in which I toiled and
in which I have shown myself
wise under the sun. This also
is vanity. 20Therefore I turned
my heart and despaired of all
the labor in which I had toiled
under the sun. 21For there is a
man whose labor *is* with wisdom, knowledge, and skill; yet
he must leave his heritage to
a man who has not labored
for it. This also *is* vanity and
a great evil. 22For what has
man for all his labor, and for
the striving of his heart with
which he has toiled under the
sun? 23For all his days *are* sorrowful, and his work burdensome; even in the night his
heart takes no rest. This also
is vanity.

24 Nothing *is* better for a
man *than* that he should eat
and drink, and *that* his soul
should enjoy good in his labor.
This also, I saw, was from the
hand of God. 25 For who can
eat, or who can have enjoyment, more than I?[a] 26 For *God*
gives wisdom and knowledge
and joy to a man who *is* good
in His sight; but to the sinner
He gives the work of gathering
and collecting, that he may
give to *him who is* good before
God. This also *is* vanity and
grasping for the wind.

EVERYTHING HAS ITS TIME

3 To everything *there*
is a season,
A time for every purpose
under heaven:

2 A time to be born,
And a time to die;
A time to plant,
And a time to pluck
what is planted;
3 A time to kill,
And a time to heal;
A time to break down,
And a time to build up;
4 A time to weep,
And a time to laugh;
A time to mourn,
And a time to dance;
5 A time to cast
away stones,
And a time to
gather stones;
A *time* to embrace,
And a time to refrain
from embracing;
6 A time to gain,
And a time to lose;
A time to keep,
And a time to
throw away;
7 A time to tear,
And a time to sew;
A time to keep silence,
And a time to speak;
8 A time to love,
And a time to hate;
A time of war,
And a time of peace.

THE GOD-GIVEN TASK

9 What profit has the worker
from that in which he labors?
10 I have seen the God-given
task with which the sons of
men are to be occupied. 11 He
has made everything beau-
tiful in its time. Also He has
put eternity in their hearts,
except that no one can find
out the work that God does
from beginning to end.

12 I know that nothing *is*
better for them than to rejoice, and to do good in their
lives, 13 and also that every
man should eat and drink
and enjoy the good of all his
labor—it *is* the gift of God.

14 I know that whatever
God does,
It shall be forever.
Nothing can be
added to it,

2:25 [a] Following Masoretic Text, Targum, and Vulgate; some Hebrew manuscripts, Septuagint, and Syriac read *without Him*.

And nothing taken
from it.
God does *it,* that men
should fear before Him.
15 That which is has
already been,
And what is to be has
already been;
And God requires an
account of what is past.

INJUSTICE SEEMS TO PREVAIL

16Moreover I saw under the
sun:

In the place of judgment,
Wickedness *was* there;
And *in* the place of
righteousness,
Iniquity *was* there.

17I said in my heart,

"God shall judge the
righteous and
the wicked,
For *there is* a time there
for every purpose
and for every work."

18I said in my heart, "Concerning the condition of the sons
of men, God tests them, that
they may see that they themselves are *like* animals." 19For
what happens to the sons of
men also happens to animals;
one thing befalls them: as one
dies, so dies the other. Surely,
they all have one breath; man
has no advantage over animals, for all *is* vanity. 20All go
to one place: all are from the
dust, and all return to dust.
21Who knows the spirit of
the sons of men, which goes
upward, and the spirit of the
animal, which goes down to
the earth?[a] 22So I perceived
that nothing *is* better than
that a man should rejoice in
his own works, for that *is* his
heritage. For who can bring
him to see what will happen
after him?

4 Then I returned and considered all the oppression
that is done under the sun:

And look! The tears
of the oppressed,
But they have no
comforter—
On the side of their
oppressors *there*
is power,
But they have no
comforter.
2 Therefore I praised
the dead who were
already dead,
More than the living
who are still alive.
3 Yet, better than both
is he who has
never existed,
Who has not seen the
evil work that is done
under the sun.

3:21 [a] Septuagint, Syriac, Targum, and Vulgate read *Who knows whether the spirit . . . goes upward, and whether . . . goes downward to the earth?*

THE VANITY OF SELFISH TOIL

4Again, I saw that for all toil and every skillful work a man is envied by his neighbor. This also *is* vanity and grasping for the wind.

5 The fool folds his hands
And consumes his
own flesh.
6 Better a handful
with quietness
Than both hands full,
together with toil and
grasping for the wind.

7Then I returned, and I saw vanity under the sun:

8 There is one alone,
without companion:
He has neither son
nor brother.
Yet *there is* no end
to all his labors,
Nor is his eye satisfied
with riches.
But he never asks,
"For whom do I toil and
deprive myself of good?"
This also *is* vanity and
a grave misfortune.

THE VALUE OF A FRIEND

9 Two *are* better than one,
Because they have a good
reward for their labor.
10 For if they fall, one will
lift up his compan*ion.*
But woe to him *who is*
alone when he falls,
For *he has* no one to
help him up.
11 Again, if two lie down
together, they will
keep warm;
But how can one be
warm *alone?*
12 Though one may be
overpowered by another,
two can withstand him.
And a threefold cord is
not quickly broken.

POPULARITY PASSES AWAY

13 Better a poor and
wise youth
Than an old and foolish
king who will be
admonished no more.
14 For he comes out of
prison to be king,
Although he was born
poor in his kingdom.
15 I saw all the living who
walk under the sun;
They were with the
second youth who
stands in his place.
16 *There was* no end of all
the people over whom
he was made king;
Yet those who come
afterward will not
rejoice in him.
Surely this also *is*
vanity and grasping
for the wind.

FEAR GOD, KEEP YOUR VOWS

5 Walk prudently when you *go to the house of God;* and draw near to hear rather than to give the sacrifice of fools, for they do not know that they do evil.

2 Do not be rash with
your mouth,
And let not your
heart utter anything
hastily before God.
For God *is* in heaven,
and you on earth;
Therefore let your
words be few.
3 For a dream comes
through much activity,
And a fool's voice
is known by *his*
many words.

4 When you make a
vow to God, do not
delay to pay it;
For *He has* no
pleasure in fools.
Pay what you have
vowed—
5 Better not to vow than
to vow and not pay.

6Do not let your mouth cause
your flesh to sin, nor say before the messenger *of God* that
it *was* an error. Why should
God be angry at your excuse[a]
and destroy the work of your
hands? 7For in the multitude
of dreams and many words
there is also vanity. But fear
God.

THE VANITY OF GAIN AND HONOR

8If you see the oppression
of the poor, and the violent
perversion of justice and righteousness in a province, do
not marvel at the matter; for
high official watches over high
official, and higher officials
are over them.
9Moreover the profit of the
land is for all; *even* the king is
served from the field.

10 He who loves silver
will not be satisfied
with silver;
Nor he who loves
abundance, with
increase.
This also *is* vanity.

11 When goods increase,
They increase who
eat them;
So what profit have
the owners
Except to see *them*
with their eyes?

12 The sleep of a laboring
man *is* sweet,
Whether he eats
little or much;
But the abundance
of the rich will not
permit him to sleep.

13 There is a severe evil
which I have seen
under the sun:
Riches kept for their
owner to his hurt.
14 But those riches perish
through misfortune;
When he begets a
son, *there is* nothing
in his hand.

5:6 [a] Literally *voice*

15 As he came from his
mother's womb, naked
shall he return,
To go as he came;
And he shall take nothing
from his labor
Which he may carry
away in his hand.

16 And this also *is* a
severe evil—
Just exactly as he came,
so shall he go.
And what profit has
he who has labored
for the wind?
17 All his days he also
eats in darkness,
And *he has* much sorrow
and sickness and anger.

18Here is what I have seen:
It is good and fitting *for one*
to eat and drink, and to enjoy
the good of all his labor in
which he toils under the sun
all the days of his life which
God gives him; for it *is* his heritage. 19As for every man to
whom God has given riches
and wealth, and given him
power to eat of it, to receive
his heritage and rejoice in his
labor—this *is* the gift of God.
20For he will not dwell unduly
on the days of his life, because
God keeps *him* busy with the
joy of his heart.

6 There is an evil which I
have seen under *the sun*,
and it *is* common among
men: 2A man to whom God
has given riches and wealth
and honor, so that he lacks
nothing for himself of all he
desires; yet God does not give
him power to eat of it, but a
foreigner consumes it. This
is vanity, and it *is* an evil affliction.
3If a man begets a hundred
children and lives many years,
so that the days of his years
are many, but his soul is not
satisfied with goodness, or indeed he has no burial, I say
that a stillborn child *is* better
than he— 4for it comes in vanity and departs in darkness,
and its name is covered with
darkness. 5Though it has not
seen the sun or known *anything*, this has more rest than
that man, 6even if he lives a
thousand years twice—but
has not seen goodness. Do
not all go to one place?

7 All the labor of man
is for his mouth,
And yet the soul is
not satisfied.
8 For what more has the
wise *man* than the fool?
What does the poor
man have,
Who knows *how* to walk
before the living?
9 Better *is* the sight of
the eyes than the
wandering of desire.
This also *is* vanity and
grasping for the wind.

10 Whatever one is, he has
been named already,
For it is known that
he *is* man;

And he cannot contend
with Him who is
mightier than he.
11 Since there are
many things that
increase vanity,
How *is* man the better?

12For who knows what *is*
good for man in life, all the
days of his vain life which he
passes like a shadow? Who can
tell a man what will happen
after him under the sun?

THE VALUE OF PRACTICAL WISDOM

7 A good name *is* better
than precious
ointment,
And the day of death than
the day of one's birth;
2 Better to go to the
house of mourning
Than to go to the
house of feasting,
For that *is* the end
of all men;
And the living will
take *it* to heart.
3 Sorrow *is* better
than laughter,
For by a sad countenance
the heart is
made better.
4 The heart of the wise *is* in
the house of mourning,
But the heart of fools *is*
in the house of mirth.

5 *It is* better to hear the
rebuke of the wise
Than for a man to hear
the song of fools.
6 For like the crackling of
thorns under a pot,
So *is* the laughter
of the fool.
This also is vanity.
7 Surely oppression
destroys a wise
man's reason,
And a bribe debases
the heart.

8 The end of a thing
is better than its
beginning;
The patient in spirit
is better than the
proud in spirit.
9 Do not hasten in your
spirit to be angry,
For anger rests in the
bosom of fools.
10 Do not say,
"Why were the former
days better than these?"
For you do not inquire
wisely concerning this.

11 Wisdom *is* good with
an inheritance,
And profitable to those
who see the sun.
12 For wisdom *is* a defense
as money *is* a defense,
But the excellence of
knowledge *is that*
wisdom gives life to
those who have it.

13 Consider the work of God;
For who can make
straight what He has
made crooked?
14 In the day of prosperity
be joyful,

But in the day of
adversity consider:
Surely God has
appointed the one as
well as the other,
So that man can find
out nothing *that will
come* after him.

15 I have seen everything in
my days of vanity:

There is a just *man*
who perishes in his
righteousness,
And there is a wicked
man who prolongs *life*
in his wickedness.

16 Do not be overly
righteous,
Nor be overly wise:
Why should you
destroy yourself?
17 Do not be overly wicked,
Nor be foolish:
Why should you die
before your time?
18 *It is* good that you
grasp this,
And also not remove your
hand from the other;
For he who fears God
will escape them all.

19 Wisdom strengthens
the wise
More than ten rulers
of the city.

20 For *there is* not a just
man on earth
who does good
And does not sin.

21 Also do not take to heart
everything people say,
Lest you hear your
servant cursing you.
22 For many times, also,
your own heart
has known
That even you have
cursed others.

23 All this I have proved
by wisdom.
I said, "I will be wise";
But it *was* far from me.
24 As for that which is far off
and exceedingly deep,
Who can find it out?
25 I applied my heart
to know,
To search and seek
out wisdom and the
reason *of things,*
To know the wickedness
of folly,
Even of foolishness
and madness.
26 And I find more
bitter than death
The woman whose heart
is snares and nets,
Whose hands *are* fetters.
He who pleases God
shall escape from her,
But the sinner shall
be trapped by her.

27 "Here is what I have
found," says the
Preacher,
"*Adding* one thing
to the other to find
out the reason,
28 Which my soul still seeks
but I cannot find:

One man among a
thousand I have found,
But a woman among all
these I have not found.
29 Truly, this only I
have found:
That God made
man upright,
But they have sought
out many schemes."

8 Who *is* like a wise *man?*
And who knows the
interpretation
of a thing?
A man's wisdom makes
his face shine,
And the sternness of
his face is changed.

OBEY AUTHORITIES FOR GOD'S SAKE

2I *say,* "Keep the king's
commandment for the sake
of your oath to God. 3Do not
be hasty to go from his presence. Do not take your stand
for an evil thing, for he does
whatever pleases him."

4 Where the word of a king
is, there is power;
And who may say to him,
"What are you doing?"
5 He who keeps his
command will
experience nothing
harmful;
And a wise man's heart
discerns both time
and judgment,
6 Because for every
matter there is a time
and judgment,
Though the misery of
man increases greatly.
7 For he does not know
what will happen;
So who can tell him
when it will occur?
8 No one has power
over the spirit to
retain the spirit,
And no one has power
in the day of death.
There is no release
from that war,
And wickedness will
not deliver those
who are given to it.

9All this I have seen, and
applied my heart to every
work that is done under the
sun: *There is* a time in which
one man rules over another
to his own hurt.

DEATH COMES TO ALL

10Then I saw the wicked
buried, who had come and
gone from the place of holiness, and they were forgotten[a]
in the city where they had so
done. This also *is* vanity. 11Be-
cause the sentence against
an evil work is not executed
speedily, therefore the heart
of the sons of men is fully set
in them to do evil. 12Though
a sinner does evil a hun-
dred *times,* and his *days* are

8:10 [a] Some Hebrew manuscripts, Septuagint, and Vulgate read *praised.*

prolonged, yet I surely know
that it will be well with those
who fear God, who fear before
Him. 13But it will not be well
with the wicked; nor will he
prolong *his* days, *which are*
as a shadow, because he does
not fear before God.

14There is a vanity which
occurs on earth, that there
are just *men* to whom it happens according to the work of
the wicked; again, there are
wicked *men* to whom it happens according to the work of
the righteous. I said that this
also *is* vanity.

15So I commended enjoy-
ment, because a man has
nothing better under the sun
than to eat, drink, and be
merry; for this will remain
with him in his labor *all* the
days of his life which God
gives him under the sun.

16When I applied my heart
to know wisdom and to see
the business that is done on
earth, even though one sees
no sleep day or night, 17then I
saw all the work of God, that a
man cannot find out the work
that is done under the sun.
For though a man labors to
discover *it*, yet he will not find
it; moreover, though a wise
man attempts to know *it*, he
will not be able to find *it*.

9 For I considered all this in
my heart, so that I could
declare it all: that the righteous and the wise and their
works *are* in the hand of God.
People know neither love nor
hatred *by* anything *they see*
before them. 2All things *come*
alike to all:

One event *happens*
to the righteous
and the wicked;
To the good,[a] the clean,
and the unclean;
To him who sacrifices
and him who does
not sacrifice.
As is the good, so
is the sinner;
He who takes an oath as
he who fears an oath.

3This *is* an evil in all that is
done under the sun: that one
thing *happens* to all. Truly the
hearts of the sons of men are
full of evil; madness *is* in their
hearts while they live, and
after that *they go* to the dead.
4But for him who is joined to
all the living there is hope, for
a living dog is better than a
dead lion.

5 For the living know
that they will die;
But the dead know
nothing,
And they have no
more reward,
For the memory of
them is forgotten.
6 Also their love, their
hatred, and their envy
have now perished;

9:2 [a] Septuagint, Syriac, and Vulgate read *good and bad*.

Nevermore will they
have a share
In anything done
under the sun.

7 Go, eat your bread
with joy,
And drink your wine
with a merry heart;
For God has already
accepted your works.
8 Let your garments
always be white,
And let your head
lack no oil.

9Live joyfully with the wife
whom you love all the days of
your vain life which He has
given you under the sun, all
your days of vanity; for that
is your portion in life, and in
the labor which you perform
under the sun.
10Whatever your hand finds
to do, do *it* with your might;
for *there is* no work or device
or knowledge or wisdom in
the grave where you are going.
11I returned and saw under
the sun that—

The race *is* not to
the swift,
Nor the battle to
the strong,
Nor bread to the wise,
Nor riches to men of
understanding,
Nor favor to men of skill;
But time and chance
happen to them all.

12 For man also does not
know his time:
Like fish taken in
a cruel net,
Like birds caught
in a snare,
So the sons of men *are*
snared in an evil time,
When it falls suddenly
upon them.

WISDOM SUPERIOR TO FOLLY

13This wisdom I have also
seen under the sun, and it
seemed great to me: 14*There
was* a little city with few men
in it; and a great king came
against it, besieged it, and
built great snares[a] around it.
15Now there was found in it
a poor wise man, and he by
his wisdom delivered the city.
Yet no one remembered that
same poor man.
16Then I said:

"Wisdom *is* better
than strength.
Nevertheless the
poor man's wisdom
is despised,
And his words are
not heard.
17 Words of the wise, *spoken*
quietly, *should be* heard
Rather than the shout
of a ruler of fools.
18 Wisdom *is* better than
weapons of war;
But one sinner destroys
much good."

9:14 [a] Septuagint, Syriac, and Vulgate read *bulwarks*.

10 Dead flies putrefy[a] the
perfumer's ointment,
And cause it to give
off a foul odor;
So does a little folly to
one respected for
wisdom *and* honor.
2 A wise man's heart *is*
at his right hand,
But a fool's heart
at his left.
3 Even when a fool walks
along the way,
He lacks wisdom,
And he shows everyone
that he *is* a fool.
4 If the spirit of the ruler
rises against you,
Do not leave your post;
For conciliation pacifies
great offenses.

5 There is an evil I have
seen under the sun,
As an error proceeding
from the ruler:
6 Folly is set in great
dignity,
While the rich sit in
a lowly place.
7 I have seen servants
on horses,
While princes walk on the
ground like servants.

8 He who digs a pit
will fall into it,
And whoever breaks
through a wall will be
bitten by a serpent.
9 He who quarries stones
may be hurt by them,
And he who splits wood
may be endangered by it.
10 If the ax is dull,
And one does not
sharpen the edge,
Then he must use
more strength;
But wisdom brings
success.

11 A serpent may bite when
it is not charmed;
The babbler is no different.
12 The words of a wise man's
mouth *are* gracious,
But the lips of a fool
shall swallow him up;
13 The words of his mouth
begin with foolishness,
And the end of his talk
is raving madness.
14 A fool also multiplies
words.
No man knows
what is to be;
Who can tell him what
will be after him?
15 The labor of fools
wearies them,
For they do not even
know how to go
to the city!

16 Woe to you, O land, when
your king *is* a child,
And your princes feast
in the morning!
17 Blessed *are* you, O land,
when your king *is*
the son of nobles,
And your princes feast
at the proper time—

10:1 [a] Targum and Vulgate omit *putrefy*.

For strength and not
for drunkenness!
18 Because of laziness the
building decays,
And through idleness of
hands the house leaks.
19 A feast is made
for laughter,
And wine makes merry;
But money answers
everything.

20 Do not curse the king,
even in your thought;
Do not curse the rich,
even in your bedroom;
For a bird of the air may
carry your voice,
And a bird in flight
may tell the matter.

THE VALUE OF DILIGENCE

11 Cast your bread
upon the waters,
For you will find it
after many days.
2 Give a serving to seven,
and also to eight,
For you do not know what
evil will be on the earth.

3 If the clouds are
full of rain,
They empty *themselves*
upon the earth;
And if a tree falls to the
south or the north,
In the place where
the tree falls, there
it shall lie.
4 He who observes the
wind will not sow,
And he who regards the
clouds will not reap.

5 As you do not know what
is the way of the wind,[a]
Or how the bones *grow*
in the womb of her
who is with child,
So you do not know the
works of God who
makes everything.
6 In the morning sow
your seed,
And in the evening do not
withhold your hand;
For you do not know
which will prosper,
Either this or that,
Or whether both alike
will be good.

7 Truly the light is sweet,
And *it is* pleasant for the
eyes to behold the sun;
8 But if a man lives
many years
And rejoices in them all,
Yet let him remember
the days of darkness,
For they will be many.
All that is coming *is* vanity.

SEEK GOD IN EARLY LIFE

9 Rejoice, O young man,
in your youth,
And let your heart
cheer you in the days
of your youth;
Walk in the ways
of your heart,
And in the sight
of your eyes;

11:5 [a] Or *spirit*

But know that for all these
God will bring you
into judgment.
10 Therefore remove sorrow
from your heart,
And put away evil
from your flesh,
For childhood and
youth *are* vanity.

12 Remember now your
Creator in the days
of your youth,
Before the difficult
days come,
And the years draw
near when you say,
"I have no pleasure
in them":
2 While the sun and
the light,
The moon and the stars,
Are not darkened,
And the clouds do not
return after the rain;
3 In the day when
the keepers of the
house tremble,
And the strong men
bow down;
When the grinders cease
because they are few,
And those that look
through the windows
grow dim;
4 When the doors are
shut in the streets,
And the sound of
grinding is low;
When one rises up at
the sound of a bird,
And all the daughters of
music are brought low.
5 Also they are afraid
of height,
And of terrors in the way;
When the almond
tree blossoms,
The grasshopper
is a burden,
And desire fails.
For man goes to his
eternal home,
And the mourners go
about the streets.

6 *Remember your Creator*
before the silver
cord is loosed,[a]
Or the golden bowl
is broken,
Or the pitcher shattered
at the fountain,
Or the wheel broken
at the well.
7 Then the dust will return
to the earth as it was,
And the spirit will return
to God who gave it.

8 "Vanity of vanities,"
says the Preacher,
"All *is* vanity."

THE WHOLE DUTY OF MAN

9And moreover, because
the Preacher was wise, he still
taught the people knowledge;
yes, he pondered and sought
out *and* set in order many
proverbs. 10The Preacher
sought to find acceptable

12:6 [a] Following Qere and Targum; Kethib reads *removed;* Septuagint and Vulgate read *broken.*

words; and *what was* written
was upright—words of truth.
11The words of the wise are
like goads, and the words of
scholars[a] are like well-driven
nails, given by one Shepherd.
12And further, my son, be admonished by these. Of making
many books *there is* no end,
and much study *is* wearisome
to the flesh.

13Let us hear the conclu-
sion of the whole matter:

Fear God and keep His
commandments,
For this is man's all.
14 For God will bring every
work into judgment,
Including every
secret thing,
Whether good or evil.

THE SONG OF SOLOMON

1 The song of songs, which *is*
Solomon's.

THE BANQUET

THE SHULAMITE[a]

2 Let him kiss me with the
kisses of his mouth—
For your[b] love *is*
better than wine.
3 Because of the fragrance
of your good ointments,
Your name *is* ointment
poured forth;
Therefore the virgins
love you.
4 Draw me away!

THE DAUGHTERS OF JERUSALEM

We will run after you.[a]

THE SHULAMITE

The king has brought me
into his chambers.

THE DAUGHTERS OF JERUSALEM

We will be glad and
rejoice in you.[b]

We will remember your[c]
love more than wine.

12:11 [a] Literally *masters of the assemblies* 1:2 [a] A young woman from the town of Shulam or Shunem (compare 6:13). The speaker and audience are identified according to the number, gender, and person of the Hebrew words. Occasionally the identity is not certain. [b] Masculine singular, that is, the Beloved 1:4 [a] Masculine singular, that is, the Beloved [b] Feminine singular, that is, the Shulamite [c] Masculine singular, that is, the Beloved

THE SHULAMITE

Rightly do they love you.[d]

5 I *am* dark, but lovely,
O daughters of Jerusalem,
Like the tents of Kedar,
Like the curtains
of Solomon.
6 Do not look upon me,
because I *am* dark,
Because the sun has
tanned me.
My mother's sons were
angry with me;
They made me the keeper
of the vineyards,
But my own vineyard
I have not kept.

(TO HER BELOVED)

7 Tell me, O you
whom I love,
Where you feed
your flock,
Where you make *it*
rest at noon.
For why should I be as
one who veils herself[a]
By the flocks of your
companions?

THE BELOVED

8 If you do not know,
O fairest among
women,
Follow in the footsteps
of the flock,
And feed your little goats
Beside the shepherds'
tents.

9 I have compared
you, my love,
To my filly among
Pharaoh's chariots.
10 Your cheeks are lovely
with ornaments,
Your neck with
chains *of gold.*

THE DAUGHTERS OF JERUSALEM

11 We will make you[a]
ornaments of gold
With studs of silver.

THE SHULAMITE

12 While the king *is*
at his table,
My spikenard sends
forth its fragrance.
13 A bundle of myrrh *is*
my beloved to me,
That lies all night
between my breasts.
14 My beloved *is* to me
a cluster of
henna *blooms*
In the vineyards
of En Gedi.

THE BELOVED

15 Behold, you *are*
fair, my love!
Behold, you *are* fair!
You *have* dove's eyes.

THE SHULAMITE

16 Behold, you *are*
handsome, my beloved!
Yes, pleasant!
Also our bed *is* green.

1:4 [d] Masculine singular, that is, the Beloved
1:7 [a] Septuagint, Syriac, and Vulgate read *wanders*.
1:11 [a] Feminine singular, that is, the Shulamite

17 The beams of our
houses *are* cedar,
And our rafters of fir.

2 I *am* the rose of Sharon,
And the lily of the valleys.

THE BELOVED

2 Like a lily among thorns,
So is my love among
the daughters.

THE SHULAMITE

3 Like an apple tree among
the trees of the woods,
So *is* my beloved
among the sons.
I sat down in his shade
with great delight,
And his fruit *was*
sweet to my taste.

THE SHULAMITE
TO THE DAUGHTERS
OF JERUSALEM

4 He brought me to the
banqueting house,
And his banner over
me *was* love.
5 Sustain me with
cakes of raisins,
Refresh me with apples,
For I *am* lovesick.

6 His left hand *is*
under my head,
And his right hand
embraces me.
7 I charge you, O daughters
of Jerusalem,
By the gazelles or by
the does of the field,
Do not stir up nor
awaken love
Until it pleases.

THE BELOVED'S REQUEST

THE SHULAMITE

8 The voice of my beloved!
Behold, he comes
Leaping upon the
mountains,
Skipping upon the hills.
9 My beloved is like a
gazelle or a young stag.
Behold, he stands
behind our wall;
He is looking through
the windows,
Gazing through
the lattice.

10 My beloved spoke,
and said to me:
"Rise up, my love,
my fair one,
And come away.
11 For lo, the winter is past,
The rain is over *and* gone.
12 The flowers appear
on the earth;
The time of singing
has come,
And the voice of
the turtledove
Is heard in our land.
13 The fig tree puts forth
her green figs,
And the vines *with*
the tender grapes
Give a *good* smell.
Rise up, my love,
my fair one,
And come away!

14 "O my dove, in the
clefts of the rock,
In the secret *places*
of the cliff,
Let me see your face,

Let me hear your voice;
For your voice *is* sweet,
And your face *is* lovely."

HER BROTHERS

15 Catch us the foxes,
The little foxes that
spoil the vines,
For our vines *have*
tender grapes.

THE SHULAMITE

16 My beloved *is* mine,
and I *am* his.
He feeds *his flock*
among the lilies.

(TO HER BELOVED)

17 Until the day breaks
And the shadows flee away,
Turn, my beloved,
And be like a gazelle
Or a young stag
Upon the mountains
of Bether.[a]

A TROUBLED NIGHT

THE SHULAMITE

3 By night on my bed I
sought the one I love;
I sought him, but I
did not find him.
2 "I will rise now," *I said,*
"And go about the city;
In the streets and
in the squares
I will seek the one I love."
I sought him, but I
did not find him.
3 The watchmen who go
about the city found me;
I said,
"Have you seen the
one I love?"
4 Scarcely had I
passed by them,
When I found the
one I love.
I held him and would
not let him go,
Until I had brought him to
the house of my mother,
And into the chamber of
her who conceived me.
5 I charge you, O daughters
of Jerusalem,
By the gazelles or by
the does of the field,
Do not stir up nor
awaken love
Until it pleases.

THE COMING OF SOLOMON

THE SHULAMITE

6 Who *is* this coming out
of the wilderness
Like pillars of smoke,
Perfumed with myrrh
and frankincense,
With all the merchant's
fragrant powders?
7 Behold, it *is* Solomon's
couch,
With sixty valiant
men around it,
Of the valiant of Israel.
8 They all hold swords,
Being expert in war.
Every man *has* his
sword on his thigh
Because of fear in
the night.

2:17 [a] Literally *Separation*

9 Of the wood of Lebanon
Solomon the King
Made himself a
palanquin:[a]
10 He made its pillars
of silver,
Its support *of* gold,
Its seat *of* purple,
Its interior paved
with love
By the daughters
of Jerusalem.
11 Go forth, O daughters
of Zion,
And see King Solomon
with the crown
With which his mother
crowned him
On the day of his wedding,
The day of the gladness
of his heart.

THE BRIDEGROOM PRAISES THE BRIDE

THE BELOVED

4 Behold, you *are*
fair, my love!
Behold, you *are* fair!
You *have* dove's eyes
behind your veil.
Your hair *is* like a
flock of goats,
Going down from
Mount Gilead.
2 Your teeth *are* like a
flock of shorn *sheep*
Which have come up
from the washing,
Every one of which
bears twins,
And none *is* barren
among them.
3 Your lips *are* like a
strand of scarlet,
And your mouth is lovely.
Your temples behind
your veil
Are like a piece of
pomegranate.
4 Your neck *is* like the
tower of David,
Built for an armory,
On which hang a
thousand bucklers,
All shields of mighty men.
5 Your two breasts *are*
like two fawns,
Twins of a gazelle,
Which feed among
the lilies.

6 Until the day breaks
And the shadows flee away,
I will go my way to the
mountain of myrrh
And to the hill of
frankincense.

7 You *are* all fair, my love,
And *there is* no spot in you.
8 Come with me from
Lebanon, *my* spouse,
With me from Lebanon.
Look from the top
of Amana,
From the top of Senir
and Hermon,
From the lions' dens,
From the mountains
of the leopards.

9 You have ravished
my heart,
My sister, *my* spouse;

3:9 [a] A portable enclosed chair

You have ravished
my heart
With one *look* of your eyes,
With one link of
your necklace.
10 How fair is your love,
My sister, *my* spouse!
How much better than
wine is your love,
And the scent of
your perfumes
Than all spices!
11 Your lips, O *my* spouse,
Drip as the honeycomb;
Honey and milk *are*
under your tongue;
And the fragrance of
your garments
Is like the fragrance
of Lebanon.

12 A garden enclosed
Is my sister, *my* spouse,
A spring shut up,
A fountain sealed.
13 Your plants *are* an orchard
of pomegranates
With pleasant fruits,
Fragrant henna
with spikenard,
14 Spikenard and saffron,
Calamus and cinnamon,
With all trees of
frankincense,
Myrrh and aloes,
With all the chief spices—
15 A fountain of gardens,
A well of living waters,
And streams from
Lebanon.

THE SHULAMITE

16 Awake, O north *wind*,
And come, O south!
Blow upon my garden,
That its spices may
flow out.
Let my beloved come
to his garden
And eat its pleasant fruits.

THE BELOVED

5 I have come to my
garden, my sister,
my spouse;
I have gathered my
myrrh with my spice;
I have eaten my
honeycomb with
my honey;
I have drunk my wine
with my milk.

(TO HIS FRIENDS)

Eat, O friends!
Drink, yes, drink deeply,
O beloved ones!

THE SHULAMITE'S TROUBLED EVENING

THE SHULAMITE

2 I sleep, but my
heart is awake;
It is the voice of
my beloved!
He knocks, *saying*,
"Open for me, my
sister, my love,
My dove, my perfect one;
For my head is
covered with dew,
My locks with the
drops of the night."

3 I have taken off my robe;
How can I put it on *again?*
I have washed my feet;
How can I defile them?

4 My beloved put his hand
By the latch *of the door,*
And my heart
yearned for him.
5 I arose to open for
my beloved,
And my hands dripped
with myrrh,
My fingers with
liquid myrrh,
On the handles of the lock.

6 I opened for my beloved,
But my beloved
had turned away
and was gone.
My heart leaped up
when he spoke.
I sought him, but I
could not find him;
I called him, but he
gave me no answer.
7 The watchmen who went
about the city found me.
They struck me, they
wounded me;
The keepers of the walls
Took my veil away
from me.
8 I charge you, O daughters
of Jerusalem,
If you find my beloved,
That you tell him I
am lovesick!

THE DAUGHTERS OF JERUSALEM

9 What *is* your beloved
More than *another*
beloved,
O fairest among women?
What *is* your beloved
More than *another*
beloved,
That you so charge us?

THE SHULAMITE

10 My beloved *is* white
and ruddy,
Chief among ten
thousand.
11 His head *is like* the
finest gold;
His locks *are* wavy,
And black as a raven.
12 His eyes *are* like doves
By the rivers of waters,
Washed with milk,
And fitly set.
13 His cheeks *are* like
a bed of spices,
Banks of scented herbs.
His lips *are* lilies,
Dripping liquid myrrh.

14 His hands *are* rods of gold
Set with beryl.
His body *is* carved ivory
Inlaid *with* sapphires.
15 His legs *are* pillars
of marble
Set on bases of fine gold.
His countenance *is*
like Lebanon,
Excellent as the cedars.
16 His mouth *is* most sweet,
Yes, he *is* altogether
lovely.
This *is* my beloved,
And this *is* my friend,
O daughters of Jerusalem!

THE DAUGHTERS OF JERUSALEM

6 Where has your
beloved gone,
O fairest among women?
Where has your beloved
turned aside,
That we may seek
him with you?

THE SHULAMITE

2 My beloved has gone
to his garden,
To the beds of spices,
To feed *his flock* in
the gardens,
And to gather lilies.
3 I *am* my beloved's,
And my beloved *is* mine.
He feeds *his flock*
among the lilies.

PRAISE OF THE SHULAMITE'S BEAUTY

THE BELOVED

4 O my love, you *are as*
beautiful as Tirzah,
Lovely as Jerusalem,
Awesome as *an army*
with banners!
5 Turn your eyes
away from me,
For they have
overcome me.
Your hair *is* like a
flock of goats
Going down from Gilead.
6 Your teeth *are* like a
flock of sheep
Which have come up
from the washing;
Every one bears twins,
And none *is* barren
among them.
7 Like a piece of
pomegranate
Are your temples
behind your veil.

8 There are sixty queens
And eighty concubines,
And virgins without
number.
9 My dove, my perfect one,
Is the only one,
The only one of
her mother,
The favorite of the
one who bore her.
The daughters saw her
And called her blessed,
The queens and the
concubines,
And they praised her.

10 Who is she who
looks forth as
the morning,
Fair as the moon,
Clear as the sun,
Awesome as *an army*
with banners?

THE SHULAMITE

11 I went down to the
garden of nuts
To see the verdure
of the valley,
To see whether the
vine had budded
And the pomegranates
had bloomed.
12 Before I was even
aware,
My soul had made me
As the chariots of my
noble people.[a]

THE BELOVED AND HIS FRIENDS

13 Return, return,
O Shulamite;
Return, return, that we
may look upon you!

6:12 [a] Hebrew *Ammi Nadib*

THE SHULAMITE

What would you see in
the Shulamite—
As it were, the dance
of the two camps?[a]

EXPRESSIONS OF PRAISE

THE BELOVED

7 How beautiful are your
feet in sandals,
O prince's daughter!
The curves of your
thighs *are* like jewels,
The work of the hands
of a skillful workman.
2 Your navel *is* a
rounded goblet;
It lacks no blended
beverage.
Your waist *is* a
heap of wheat
Set about with lilies.
3 Your two breasts *are*
like two fawns,
Twins of a gazelle.
4 Your neck *is* like an
ivory tower,
Your eyes *like* the
pools in Heshbon
By the gate of Bath
Rabbim.
Your nose *is* like the
tower of Lebanon
Which looks toward
Damascus.
5 Your head *crowns* you
like *Mount* Carmel,
And the hair of your
head *is* like purple;
A king *is* held captive
by *your* tresses.

6 How fair and how
pleasant you are,
O love, with your delights!
7 This stature of yours
is like a palm tree,
And your breasts
like its clusters.
8 I said, "I will go up
to the palm tree,
I will take hold of
its branches."
Let now your breasts be
like clusters of the vine,
The fragrance of your
breath like apples,
9 And the roof of
your mouth like
the best wine.

THE SHULAMITE

The wine goes *down*
smoothly for
my beloved,
Moving gently the
lips of sleepers.[a]
10 I *am* my beloved's,
And his desire *is*
toward me.

11 Come, my beloved,
Let us go forth to the field;
Let us lodge in
the villages.
12 Let us get up early to
the vineyards;
Let us see if the vine
has budded,
Whether the grape
blossoms are open,
And the pomegranates
are in bloom.

6:13 [a] Hebrew *Mahanaim* 7:9 [a] Septuagint, Syriac, and Vulgate read *lips and teeth*.

There I will give
you my love.
13 The mandrakes give
off a fragrance,
And at our gates *are*
pleasant *fruits*,
All manner, new
and old,
Which I have laid up
for you, my beloved.

8 Oh, that you were
like my brother,
Who nursed at my
mother's breasts!
If I should find
you outside,
I would kiss you;
I would not be despised.
2 I would lead you
and bring you
Into the house of
my mother,
She *who* used to
instruct me.
I would cause you to
drink of spiced wine,
Of the juice of my
pomegranate.

(TO THE DAUGHTERS OF JERUSALEM)

3 His left hand *is*
under my head,
And his right hand
embraces me.
4 I charge you, O daughters
of Jerusalem,
Do not stir up nor
awaken love
Until it pleases.

LOVE RENEWED IN LEBANON

A RELATIVE

5 Who *is* this coming up
from the wilderness,
Leaning upon her beloved?

I awakened you under
the apple tree.
There your mother
brought you forth;
There she *who* bore you
brought *you* forth.

THE SHULAMITE TO HER BELOVED

6 Set me as a seal upon
your heart,
As a seal upon your arm;
For love *is as* strong
as death,
Jealousy *as* cruel
as the grave;[a]
Its flames *are*
flames of fire,
A most vehement flame.[b]

7 Many waters cannot
quench love,
Nor can the floods
drown it.
If a man would
give for love
All the wealth of his house,
It would be utterly
despised.

THE SHULAMITE'S BROTHERS

8 We have a little sister,
And she has no breasts.
What shall we do
for our sister

8:6 [a] Or *Sheol* [b] Literally *A flame of* YAH (a poetic form of *YHWH, the* LORD)

In the day when she
  is spoken for?
9 If she *is* a wall,
We will build upon her
A battlement of silver;
And if she *is* a door,
We will enclose her
With boards of cedar.

THE SHULAMITE

10 I *am* a wall,
And my breasts
  like towers;
Then I became in his eyes
As one who found peace.
11 Solomon had a vineyard
  at Baal Hamon;
He leased the vineyard
  to keepers;
Everyone was to
  bring for its fruit
A thousand silver *coins*.

(TO SOLOMON)

12 My own vineyard
  is before me.
You, O Solomon, *may
  have* a thousand,
And those who
  tend its fruit two
  hundred.

THE BELOVED

13 You who dwell in
  the gardens,
The companions listen
  for your voice—
Let me hear it!

THE SHULAMITE

14 Make haste, my beloved,
And be like a gazelle
Or a young stag
On the mountains
  of spices.

THE BOOK OF ISAIAH

1 The vision of Isaiah the son
of Amoz, which he saw concerning Judah and Jerusalem
in the days of Uzziah, Jotham,
Ahaz, *and* Hezekiah, kings of
Judah.

THE WICKEDNESS OF JUDAH

2 Hear, O heavens, and
  give ear, O earth!
For the LORD has spoken:
"I have nourished and
  brought up children,
And they have rebelled
  against Me;
3 The ox knows its owner
And the donkey its
  master's crib;
But Israel does not know,
My people do not
  consider."

4 Alas, sinful nation,
A people laden
  with iniquity,
A brood of evildoers,

Children who are
corrupters!
They have forsaken
the LORD,
They have provoked
to anger
The Holy One of Israel,
They have turned
away backward.

5 Why should you be
stricken again?
You will revolt more
and more.
The whole head is sick,
And the whole
heart faints.
6 From the sole of the foot
even to the head,
There is no
soundness in it,
But wounds and bruises
and putrefying sores;
They have not been
closed or bound up,
Or soothed with
ointment.

7 Your country *is* desolate,
Your cities *are*
burned with fire;
Strangers devour your
land in your presence;
And *it is* desolate,
as overthrown
by strangers.
8 So the daughter of
Zion is left as a booth
in a vineyard,
As a hut in a garden
of cucumbers,
As a besieged city.
9 Unless the LORD
of hosts
Had left to us a very
small remnant,
We would have become
like Sodom,
We would have been
made like Gomorrah.

10 Hear the word of
the LORD,
You rulers of Sodom;
Give ear to the law
of our God,
You people of Gomorrah:
11 "To what purpose *is*
the multitude of your
sacrifices to Me?"
Says the LORD.
"I have had enough of
burnt offerings of rams
And the fat of fed cattle.
I do not delight in the
blood of bulls,
Or of lambs or goats.

12 "When you come to
appear before Me,
Who has required this
from your hand,
To trample My courts?
13 Bring no more futile
sacrifices;
Incense is an
abomination to Me.
The New Moons, the
Sabbaths, and the
calling of assemblies—
I cannot endure iniquity
and the sacred meeting.
14 Your New Moons and
your appointed feasts
My soul hates;
They are a trouble to Me,
I am weary of
bearing *them.*

15 When you spread
out your hands,
I will hide My eyes
from you;
Even though you make
many prayers,
I will not hear.
Your hands are
full of blood.

16 "Wash yourselves, make
yourselves clean;
Put away the evil of
your doings from
before My eyes.
Cease to do evil,
17 Learn to do good;
Seek justice,
Rebuke the oppressor;[a]
Defend the fatherless,
Plead for the widow.

18 "Come now, and let us
reason together,"
Says the LORD,
"Though your sins
are like scarlet,
They shall be as
white as snow;
Though they are red
like crimson,
They shall be as wool.
19 If you are willing
and obedient,
You shall eat the
good of the land;
20 But if you refuse
and rebel,
You shall be devoured
by the sword";
For the mouth of the
LORD has spoken.

THE DEGENERATE CITY

21 How the faithful city
has become a harlot!
It was full of justice;
Righteousness
lodged in it,
But now murderers.
22 Your silver has
become dross,
Your wine mixed
with water.
23 Your princes *are*
rebellious,
And companions
of thieves;
Everyone loves bribes,
And follows after
rewards.
They do not defend
the fatherless,
Nor does the cause
of the widow come
before them.

24 Therefore the Lord says,
The LORD of hosts,
the Mighty One
of Israel,
"Ah, I will rid Myself
of My adversaries,
And take vengeance
on My enemies.
25 I will turn My hand
against you,
And thoroughly purge
away your dross,
And take away all
your alloy.
26 I will restore your
judges as at the first,
And your counselors
as at the beginning.

1:17 [a] Some ancient versions read *the oppressed.*

Afterward you shall
be called the city
of righteousness,
the faithful city."

27 Zion shall be redeemed
with justice,
And her penitents with
righteousness.
28 The destruction of
transgressors and of
sinners *shall be* together,
And those who forsake
the LORD shall
be consumed.
29 For they[a] shall be
ashamed of the
terebinth trees
Which you have desired;
And you shall be
embarrassed because
of the gardens
Which you have chosen.
30 For you shall be as
a terebinth whose
leaf fades,
And as a garden that
has no water.
31 The strong shall
be as tinder,
And the work of
it as a spark;
Both will burn together,
And no one shall
quench *them*.

THE FUTURE HOUSE OF GOD

2 The word that Isaiah the
son of Amoz saw concern-
ing Judah and Jerusalem.

2 Now it shall come to
pass in the latter days
That the mountain of
the LORD's house
Shall be established
on the top of the
mountains,
And shall be exalted
above the hills;
And all nations
shall flow to it.
3 Many people shall
come and say,
"Come, and let us go
up to the mountain
of the LORD,
To the house of the
God of Jacob;
He will teach us His ways,
And we shall walk
in His paths."
For out of Zion shall
go forth the law,
And the word of the
LORD from Jerusalem.
4 He shall judge between
the nations,
And rebuke many people;
They shall beat their
swords into plowshares,
And their spears into
pruning hooks;
Nation shall not lift up
sword against nation,
Neither shall they learn
war anymore.

THE DAY OF THE LORD

5 O house of Jacob, come
and let us walk
In the light of the LORD.

1:29 [a] Following Masoretic Text, Septuagint, and Vulgate; some Hebrew manuscripts and Targum read *you*.

6 For You have forsaken
Your people, the
house of Jacob,
Because they are filled
with eastern ways;
They *are* soothsayers
like the Philistines,
And they are pleased
with the children
of foreigners.
7 Their land is also full
of silver and gold,
And there is no end
to their treasures;
Their land is also
full of horses,
And there is no end
to their chariots.
8 Their land is also
full of idols;
They worship the work
of their own hands,
That which their own
fingers have made.
9 People bow down,
And each man
humbles himself;
Therefore do not
forgive them.

10 Enter into the rock, and
hide in the dust,
From the terror
of the LORD
And the glory of
His majesty.
11 The lofty looks of man
shall be humbled,
The haughtiness of
men shall be
bowed down,
And the LORD alone
shall be exalted
in that day.

12 For the day of the
LORD of hosts
Shall come upon
everything proud
and lofty,
Upon everything
lifted up—
And it shall be
brought low—
13 Upon all the cedars
of Lebanon *that are*
high and lifted up,
And upon all the
oaks of Bashan;
14 Upon all the high
mountains,
And upon all the hills
that are lifted up;
15 Upon every high tower,
And upon every
fortified wall;
16 Upon all the ships
of Tarshish,
And upon all the
beautiful sloops.
17 The loftiness of
man shall be
bowed down,
And the haughtiness
of men shall be
brought low;
The LORD alone will be
exalted in that day,
18 But the idols He shall
utterly abolish.

19 They shall go into the
holes of the rocks,
And into the caves
of the earth,
From the terror
of the LORD
And the glory of
His majesty,

When He arises to shake
the earth mightily.

20 In that day a man
will cast away his
idols of silver
And his idols of gold,
Which they made, *each*
for himself to worship,
To the moles and bats,
21 To go into the clefts
of the rocks,
And into the crags of
the rugged rocks,
From the terror
of the LORD
And the glory of
His majesty,
When He arises to shake
the earth mightily.

22 Sever yourselves
from such a man,
Whose breath *is* in
his nostrils;
For of what account is he?

JUDGMENT ON JUDAH AND JERUSALEM

3 For behold, the Lord,
the LORD of hosts,
Takes away from
Jerusalem and
from Judah
The stock and the store,
The whole supply of
bread and the whole
supply of water;
2 The mighty man and
the man of war,
The judge and the
prophet,
And the diviner
and the elder;
3 The captain of fifty and
the honorable man,
The counselor and the
skillful artisan,
And the expert enchanter.

4 "I will give children *to*
be their princes,
And babes shall
rule over them.
5 The people will be
oppressed,
Every one by another
and every one by
his neighbor;
The child will be insolent
toward the elder,
And the base toward
the honorable."

6 When a man takes
hold of his brother
In the house of his
father, *saying,*
"You have clothing;
You be our ruler,
And *let* these ruins *be*
under your power,"[a]
7 In that day he will
protest, saying,
"I cannot cure *your* ills,
For in my house *is* neither
food nor clothing;
Do not make me a ruler
of the people."

8 For Jerusalem stumbled,
And Judah is fallen,
Because their tongue
and their doings

3:6 [a] Literally *hand*

Are against the LORD,
To provoke the eyes
of His glory.
9 The look on their
countenance witnesses
against them,
And they declare their
sin as Sodom;
They do not hide *it*.
Woe to their soul!
For they have brought
evil upon themselves.

10 "Say to the righteous
that *it shall be*
well *with them*,
For they shall eat the
fruit of their doings.
11 Woe to the wicked! *It
shall be* ill *with him*,
For the reward of
his hands shall
be given him.
12 *As for* My people, children
are their oppressors,
And women rule
over them.
O My people! Those
who lead you
cause *you* to err,
And destroy the way
of your paths."

OPPRESSION AND LUXURY CONDEMNED

13 The LORD stands
up to plead,
And stands to judge
the people.
14 The LORD will enter
into judgment
With the elders of
His people
And His princes:
"For you have eaten
up the vineyard;
The plunder of the poor
is in your houses.
15 What do you mean by
crushing My people
And grinding the
faces of the poor?"
Says the Lord GOD
of hosts.

16 Moreover the LORD says:

"Because the daughters
of Zion are haughty,
And walk with
outstretched necks
And wanton eyes,
Walking and mincing
as they go,
Making a jingling
with their feet,
17 Therefore the Lord will
strike with a scab
The crown of the head of
the daughters of Zion,
And the LORD will
uncover their
secret parts."

18 In that day the Lord will
take away the finery:
The jingling anklets,
the scarves, and
the crescents;
19 The pendants, the
bracelets, and the veils;
20 The headdresses, the
leg ornaments, and
the headbands;
The perfume boxes,
the charms,
21 and the rings;
The nose jewels,

22 the festal apparel,
and the mantles;
The outer garments,
the purses,
23 and the mirrors;
The fine linen, the
turbans, and the robes.

24And so it shall be:

Instead of a sweet smell
there will be a stench;
Instead of a sash, a rope;
Instead of well-set
hair, baldness;
Instead of a rich robe, a
girding of sackcloth;
And branding instead
of beauty.
25 Your men shall fall
by the sword,
And your mighty
in the war.

26 Her gates shall lament
and mourn,
And she *being* desolate
shall sit on the ground.

4 And in that day seven
women shall take hold
of one man, saying,
"We will eat our own
food and wear our
own apparel;
Only let us be called
by your name,
To take away our
reproach."

THE RENEWAL OF ZION

2 In that day the Branch
of the LORD shall be
beautiful and glorious;
And the fruit of the
earth *shall be* excellent
and appealing
For those of Israel
who have escaped.

3And it shall come to pass
that *he who is* left in Zion and
remains in Jerusalem will be
called holy—everyone who is
recorded among the living in
Jerusalem. 4When the Lord
has washed away the filth of
the daughters of Zion, and
purged the blood of Jerusalem
from her midst, by the spirit of
judgment and by the spirit of
burning, 5then the LORD will
create above every dwelling
place of Mount Zion, and above
her assemblies, a cloud and
smoke by day and the shining
of a flaming fire by night. For
over all the glory there *will be*
a covering. 6And there will be
a tabernacle for shade in the
daytime from the heat, for a
place of refuge, and for a shelter from storm and rain.

GOD'S DISAPPOINTING VINEYARD

5 Now let me sing to
my Well-beloved
A song of my Beloved
regarding His vineyard:

My Well-beloved
has a vineyard
On a very fruitful hill.
2 He dug it up and cleared
out its stones,
And planted it with
the choicest vine.

He built a tower
in its midst,
And also made a
winepress in it;
So He expected *it* to bring
forth *good* grapes,
But it brought forth
wild grapes.

3 "And now, O inhabitants
of Jerusalem and
men of Judah,
Judge, please, between
Me and My vineyard.
4 What more could
have been done
to My vineyard
That I have not done in it?
Why then, when I
expected *it* to bring
forth *good* grapes,
Did it bring forth
wild grapes?
5 And now, please let Me
tell you what I will
do to My vineyard:
I will take away its hedge,
and it shall be burned;
And break down its
wall, and it shall be
trampled down.
6 I will lay it waste;
It shall not be
pruned or dug,
But there shall come up
briers and thorns.
I will also command
the clouds
That they rain no
rain on it."

7 For the vineyard of the
LORD of hosts *is* the
house of Israel,
And the men of Judah
are His pleasant plant.
He looked for justice, but
behold, oppression;
For righteousness, but
behold, a cry *for help.*

IMPENDING JUDGMENT ON EXCESSES

8 Woe to those who join
house to house;
They add field to field,
Till *there is* no place
Where they may
dwell alone in the
midst of the land!
9 In my hearing the
LORD of hosts *said,*
"Truly, many houses
shall be desolate,
Great and beautiful
ones, without
inhabitant.
10 For ten acres of vineyard
shall yield one bath,
And a homer of seed
shall yield one ephah."

11 Woe to those who rise
early in the morning,
That they may follow
intoxicating drink;
Who continue until
night, *till* wine
inflames them!
12 The harp and the strings,
The tambourine
and flute,
And wine are in
their feasts;
But they do not regard
the work of the LORD,
Nor consider the
operation of His hands.

13 Therefore my people have
gone into captivity,
Because *they have*
no knowledge;
Their honorable men
are famished,
And their multitude
dried up with thirst.
14 Therefore Sheol has
enlarged itself
And opened its mouth
beyond measure;
Their glory and their
multitude and
their pomp,
And he who is jubilant,
shall descend into it.
15 People shall be
brought down,
Each man shall
be humbled,
And the eyes of the lofty
shall be humbled.
16 But the LORD of hosts
shall be exalted
in judgment,
And God who is holy
shall be hallowed
in righteousness.
17 Then the lambs shall
feed in their pasture,
And in the waste
places of the fat ones
strangers shall eat.

18 Woe to those who
draw iniquity with
cords of vanity,
And sin as if with
a cart rope;
19 That say, "Let Him
make speed *and*
hasten His work,
That we may see *it;*
And let the counsel of
the Holy One of Israel
draw near and come,
That we may know *it.*"

20 Woe to those who call evil
good, and good evil;
Who put darkness
for light, and light
for darkness;
Who put bitter for sweet,
and sweet for bitter!

21 Woe to *those who are*
wise in their own eyes,
And prudent in
their own sight!

22 Woe to men mighty
at drinking wine,
Woe to men valiant
for mixing
intoxicating drink,
23 Who justify the wicked
for a bribe,
And take away justice
from the righteous man!

24 Therefore, as the fire
devours the stubble,
And the flame
consumes the chaff,
So their root will be
as rottenness,
And their blossom will
ascend like dust;
Because they have
rejected the law of
the LORD of hosts,
And despised the word of
the Holy One of Israel.
25 Therefore the anger of
the LORD is aroused
against His people;

He has stretched out His
hand against them
And stricken them,
And the hills trembled.
Their carcasses *were* as
refuse in the midst
of the streets.

For all this His anger
is not turned away,
But His hand *is*
stretched out still.

26 He will lift up a banner
to the nations
from afar,
And will whistle to
them from the end
of the earth;
Surely they shall come
with speed, swiftly.
27 No one will be weary or
stumble among them,
No one will slumber
or sleep;
Nor will the belt on their
loins be loosed,
Nor the strap of their
sandals be broken;
28 Whose arrows *are* sharp,
And all their bows bent;
Their horses' hooves
will seem like flint,
And their wheels like
a whirlwind.
29 Their roaring *will*
be like a lion,
They will roar like
young lions;
Yes, they will roar
And lay hold of the prey;
They will carry *it*
away safely,
And no one will deliver.
30 In that day they will
roar against them
Like the roaring of the sea.
And if *one* looks
to the land,
Behold, darkness
and sorrow;
And the light is darkened
by the clouds.

ISAIAH CALLED TO BE A PROPHET

6 In the year that King Uzziah died, I saw the Lord
sitting on a throne, high and
lifted up, and the train of His
robe filled the temple. 2Above
it stood seraphim; each one
had six wings: with two he
covered his face, with two he
covered his feet, and with two
he flew. 3And one cried to another and said:

"Holy, holy, holy *is* the
LORD of hosts;
The whole earth *is*
full of His glory!"

4And the posts of the door
were shaken by the voice of
him who cried out, and the
house was filled with smoke.
5So I said:

"Woe *is* me, for I
am undone!
Because I *am* a man
of unclean lips,
And I dwell in the midst of
a people of unclean lips;
For my eyes have
seen the King,
The LORD of hosts."

6Then one of the seraphim
flew to me, having in his hand
a live coal *which* he had taken
with the tongs from the altar.
7And he touched my mouth
with it, and said:

"Behold, this has
touched your lips;
Your iniquity is
taken away,
And your sin purged."

8Also I heard the voice of
the Lord, saying:

"Whom shall I send,
And who will go for Us?"

Then I said, "Here *am* I!
Send me."
9And He said, "Go, and tell
this people:

'Keep on hearing, but
do not understand;
Keep on seeing, but
do not perceive.'

10"Make the heart of
this people dull,
And their ears heavy,
And shut their eyes;
Lest they see with
their eyes,
And hear with their
ears,
And understand
with their heart,
And return and
be healed."

11Then I said, "Lord, how
long?"

And He answered:

"Until the cities are laid
waste and without
inhabitant,
The houses are
without a man,
The land is utterly
desolate,
12 The LORD has removed
men far away,
And the forsaken places
are many in the
midst of the land.
13 But yet a tenth
will be in it,
And will return and
be for consuming,
As a terebinth tree
or as an oak,
Whose stump *remains*
when it is cut down.
So the holy seed *shall*
be its stump."

ISAIAH SENT TO KING AHAZ

7 Now it came to pass in the
days of Ahaz the son of Jotham, the son of Uzziah, king
of Judah, *that* Rezin king of
Syria and Pekah the son of
Remaliah, king of Israel, went
up to Jerusalem to *make* war
against it, but could not prevail against it. 2And it was told
to the house of David, saying,
"Syria's forces are deployed in
Ephraim." So his heart and the
heart of his people were moved
as the trees of the woods are
moved with the wind.
3Then the LORD said to Isaiah, "Go out now to meet Ahaz,

you and Shear-Jashub[a] your
son, at the end of the aqueduct
from the upper pool, on the
highway to the Fuller's Field,
4and say to him: 'Take heed,
and be quiet; do not fear or
be fainthearted for these two
stubs of smoking firebrands,
for the fierce anger of Rezin
and Syria, and the son of Remaliah. 5Because Syria, Ephraim,
and the son of Remaliah have
plotted evil against you, saying, 6"Let us go up against
Judah and trouble it, and let
us make a gap in its wall for
ourselves, and set a king over
them, the son of Tabel"— 7thus
says the Lord GOD:

"It shall not stand,
Nor shall it come to pass.
8 For the head of Syria
is Damascus,
And the head of
Damascus *is* Rezin.
Within sixty-five years
Ephraim will be broken,
So that it will not
be a people.
9 The head of Ephraim
is Samaria,
And the head of Samaria
is Remaliah's son.
If you will not believe,
Surely you shall not
be established." ' "

THE IMMANUEL PROPHECY

10Moreover the LORD spoke
again to Ahaz, saying, 11"Ask
a sign for yourself from the
LORD your God; ask it either
in the depth or in the height
above."

12But Ahaz said, "I will not
ask, nor will I test the LORD!"

13Then he said, "Hear now,
O house of David! *Is it* a small
thing for you to weary men, but
will you weary my God also?
14Therefore the Lord Himself
will give you a sign: Behold, the
virgin shall conceive and bear
a Son, and shall call His name
Immanuel.[a] 15Curds and honey
He shall eat, that He may know
to refuse the evil and choose
the good. 16For before the Child
shall know to refuse the evil
and choose the good, the land
that you dread will be forsaken
by both her kings. 17The LORD
will bring the king of Assyria
upon you and your people and
your father's house—days that
have not come since the day
that Ephraim departed from
Judah."

18 And it shall come to
pass in that day
That the LORD will
whistle for the fly
That *is* in the farthest part
of the rivers of Egypt,
And for the bee that *is* in
the land of Assyria.
19 They will come, and all
of them will rest
In the desolate valleys and
in the clefts of the rocks,
And on all thorns and
in all pastures.

7:3 [a] Literally *A Remnant Shall Return*

7:14 [a] Literally *God-With-Us*

20 In the same day the
Lord will shave with
a hired razor,
With those from beyond
the River,[a] with the
king of Assyria,
The head and the
hair of the legs,
And will also remove
the beard.

21 It shall be in that day
That a man will keep
alive a young cow
and two sheep;
22 So it shall be, from
the abundance of
milk they give,
That he will eat curds;
For curds and honey
everyone will eat who
is left in the land.

23 It shall happen
in that day,
That wherever
there could be a
thousand vines
Worth a thousand
shekels of silver,
It will be for briers
and thorns.
24 With arrows and bows
men will come there,
Because all the land
will become briers
and thorns.

25 And to any hill which
could be dug
with the hoe,
You will not go there for
fear of briers and thorns;
But it will become a
range for oxen
And a place for
sheep to roam.

ASSYRIA WILL INVADE THE LAND

8 Moreover the LORD said
to me, "Take a large
scroll, and write on it with
a man's pen concerning
Maher-Shalal-Hash-Baz.[a]
2And I will take for Myself
faithful witnesses to record,
Uriah the priest and Zechariah the son of Jeberechiah."
3Then I went to the prophetess, and she conceived and
bore a son. Then the LORD
said to me, "Call his name
Maher-Shalal-Hash-Baz; 4for
before the child shall have
knowledge to cry 'My father'
and 'My mother,' the riches
of Damascus and the spoil of
Samaria will be taken away
before the king of Assyria."
5The LORD also spoke to me
again, saying:

6 "Inasmuch as these
people refused
The waters of Shiloah
that flow softly,
And rejoice in Rezin and
in Remaliah's son;
7 Now therefore, behold,
the Lord brings
up over them

7:20 [a] That is, the Euphrates 8:1 [a] Literally *Speed the Spoil, Hasten the Booty*

The waters of the River,[a]
strong and mighty—
The king of Assyria
and all his glory;
He will go up over
all his channels
And go over all his banks.
8 He will pass through
Judah,
He will overflow
and pass over,
He will reach up
to the neck;
And the stretching
out of his wings
Will fill the breadth
of Your land,
O Immanuel.[a]

9 "Be shattered, O you
peoples, and be
broken in pieces!
Give ear, all you from
far countries.
Gird yourselves, but be
broken in pieces;
Gird yourselves, but be
broken in pieces.
10 Take counsel together,
but it will come
to nothing;
Speak the word, but
it will not stand,
For God *is* with us."[a]

FEAR GOD, HEED HIS WORD

11For the LORD spoke thus
to me with a strong hand, and
instructed me that I should
not walk in the way of this
people, saying:

12"Do not say, 'A conspiracy,'
Concerning all that
this people call
a conspiracy,
Nor be afraid of their
threats, nor be troubled.
13 The LORD of hosts, Him
you shall hallow;
Let Him *be* your fear,
And *let* Him *be*
your dread.
14 He will be as a sanctuary,
But a stone of stumbling
and a rock of offense
To both the houses
of Israel,
As a trap and a snare
to the inhabitants
of Jerusalem.
15 And many among them
shall stumble;
They shall fall and
be broken,
Be snared and taken."

16 Bind up the testimony,
Seal the law among
my disciples.
17 And I will wait on
the LORD,
Who hides His face from
the house of Jacob;
And I will hope in Him.
18 Here am I and the
children whom the
LORD has given me!
We are for signs and
wonders in Israel
From the LORD of hosts,
Who dwells in
Mount Zion.

8:7 [a] That is, the Euphrates 8:8 [a] Literally *God-With-Us* 8:10 [a] Hebrew *Immanuel*

19And when they say to you,
"Seek those who are mediums
and wizards, who whisper and
mutter," should not a people
seek their God? *Should they
seek* the dead on behalf of
the living? 20To the law and
to the testimony! If they do
not speak according to this
word, *it is* because *there is* no
light in them.

21They will pass through
it hard-pressed and hungry;
and it shall happen, when they
are hungry, that they will be
enraged and curse their king
and their God, and look upward. 22Then they will look to
the earth, and see trouble and
darkness, gloom of anguish;
and *they will be* driven into
darkness.

THE GOVERNMENT OF THE PROMISED SON

9 Nevertheless the gloom
will not *be* upon her
who *is* distressed,
As when at first He
lightly esteemed
The land of Zebulun and
the land of Naphtali,
And afterward more
heavily oppressed *her*,
By the way of the sea,
beyond the Jordan,
In Galilee of the Gentiles.
2 The people who walked
in darkness
Have seen a great light;
Those who dwelt
in the land of the
shadow of death,
Upon them a light
has shined.

3 You have multiplied
the nation
And increased its joy;[a]
They rejoice before You
According to the
joy of harvest,
As *men* rejoice when
they divide the spoil.
4 For You have broken the
yoke of his burden
And the staff of
his shoulder,
The rod of his oppressor,
As in the day of Midian.
5 For every warrior's sandal
from the noisy battle,
And garments
rolled in blood,
Will be used for burning
and fuel of fire.

6 For unto us a Child
is born,
Unto us a Son is given;
And the government will
be upon His shoulder.
And His name
will be called
Wonderful, Counselor,
Mighty God,
Everlasting Father,
Prince of Peace.
7 Of the increase of *His*
government and peace

9:3 [a] Following Qere and Targum; Kethib and Vulgate read *not increased joy;* Septuagint reads *Most of the people You brought down in Your joy.*

There will be no end,
Upon the throne of David
and over His kingdom,
To order it and establish
it with judgment
and justice
From that time forward,
even forever.
The zeal of the LORD of
hosts will perform this.

THE PUNISHMENT OF SAMARIA

8 The Lord sent a word
against Jacob,
And it has fallen
on Israel.
9 All the people
will know—
Ephraim and the
inhabitant of Samaria—
Who say in pride and
arrogance of heart:
10 "The bricks have
fallen down,
But we will rebuild
with hewn stones;
The sycamores are
cut down,
But we will replace
them with cedars."
11 Therefore the LORD
shall set up
The adversaries of
Rezin against him,
And spur his enemies on,
12 The Syrians before and
the Philistines behind;
And they shall devour
Israel with an
open mouth.

For all this His anger
is not turned away,
But His hand *is*
stretched out still.

13 For the people do not
turn to Him who
strikes them,
Nor do they seek the
LORD of hosts.
14 Therefore the LORD
will cut off head and
tail from Israel,
Palm branch and
bulrush in one day.
15 The elder and honorable,
he *is* the head;
The prophet who teaches
lies, he *is* the tail.
16 For the leaders of
this people cause
them to err,
And *those who are* led by
them are destroyed.
17 Therefore the Lord
will have no joy in
their young men,
Nor have mercy on their
fatherless and widows;
For everyone *is* a
hypocrite and
an evildoer,
And every mouth
speaks folly.

For all this His anger
is not turned away,
But His hand *is*
stretched out still.

18 For wickedness burns
as the fire;
It shall devour the
briers and thorns,
And kindle in the
thickets of the forest;

They shall mount up
like rising smoke.
19 Through the wrath of
the LORD of hosts
The land is burned up,
And the people shall be
as fuel for the fire;
No man shall spare
his brother.
20 And he shall snatch
on the right hand
And be hungry;
He shall devour on
the left hand
And not be satisfied;
Every man shall eat the
flesh of his own arm.
21 Manasseh *shall devour*
Ephraim, and
Ephraim Manasseh;
Together they *shall*
be against Judah.

For all this His anger
is not turned away,
But His hand *is*
stretched out still.

10 "Woe to those who
decree unrighteous
decrees,
Who write misfortune,
Which they have
prescribed
2 To rob the needy of justice,
And to take what is
right from the poor
of My people,
That widows may
be their prey,
And *that* they may
rob the fatherless.
3 What will you do in the
day of punishment,
And in the desolation
which will come
from afar?
To whom will you
flee for help?
And where will you
leave your glory?
4 Without Me they shall
bow down among
the prisoners,
And they shall fall
among the slain."

For all this His anger
is not turned away,
But His hand *is*
stretched out still.

ARROGANT ASSYRIA ALSO JUDGED

5 "Woe to Assyria, the
rod of My anger
And the staff in whose
hand is My indignation.
6 I will send him against
an ungodly nation,
And against the people
of My wrath
I will give him charge,
To seize the spoil, to
take the prey,
And to tread them
down like the mire
of the streets.
7 Yet he does not mean so,
Nor does his heart
think so;
But *it is* in his heart
to destroy,
And cut off not a
few nations.
8 For he says,
'*Are* not my princes
altogether kings?

9 *Is* not Calno like
Carchemish?
Is not Hamath like Arpad?
Is not Samaria like
Damascus?
10 As my hand has found the
kingdoms of the idols,
Whose carved images
excelled those of
Jerusalem and Samaria,
11 As I have done to
Samaria and her idols,
Shall I not do also
to Jerusalem and
her idols?' "

12Therefore it shall come to
pass, when the Lord has performed all His work on Mount
Zion and on Jerusalem, *that
He will say,* "I will punish the
fruit of the arrogant heart of
the king of Assyria, and the
glory of his haughty looks."
13For he says:

"By the strength of my
hand I have done *it,*
And by my wisdom,
for I am prudent;
Also I have removed
the boundaries
of the people,
And have robbed
their treasuries;
So I have put down
the inhabitants like
a valiant *man.*
14 My hand has found
like a nest the riches
of the people,
And as one gathers
eggs *that are* left,
I have gathered
all the earth;
And there was no one
who moved *his* wing,
Nor opened *his* mouth
with even a peep."

15 Shall the ax boast
itself against him
who chops with it?
Or shall the saw exalt
itself against him
who saws with it?
As if a rod could wield
itself against those
who lift it up,
Or as if a staff could
lift up, *as if it were*
not wood!
16 Therefore the Lord,
the Lord[a] of hosts,
Will send leanness
among his fat ones;
And under his glory
He will kindle a burning
Like the burning of a fire.
17 So the Light of Israel
will be for a fire,
And his Holy One
for a flame;
It will burn and devour
His thorns and his
briers in one day.
18 And it will consume the
glory of his forest and
of his fruitful field,
Both soul and body;
And they will be as when
a sick man wastes away.

10:16 [a] Following Bomberg; Masoretic Text and Dead Sea Scrolls read *YHWH* (*the* LORD).

19 Then the rest of the
trees of his forest
Will be so few in number
That a child may
write them.

THE RETURNING REMNANT OF ISRAEL

20 And it shall come to
pass in that day
That the remnant
of Israel,
And such as have escaped
of the house of Jacob,
Will never again
depend on him who
defeated them,
But will depend on the
LORD, the Holy One
of Israel, in truth.
21 The remnant will return,
the remnant of Jacob,
To the Mighty God.
22 For though your people,
O Israel, be as the
sand of the sea,
A remnant of them
will return;
The destruction decreed
shall overflow with
righteousness.
23 For the Lord GOD of hosts
Will make a
determined end
In the midst of
all the land.

24Therefore thus says the
Lord GOD of hosts: "O My people, who dwell in Zion, *do not*
be afraid of the Assyrian. He
shall strike you with a rod and
lift up his staff against you, in
the manner of Egypt. 25For
yet a very little while and the
indignation will cease, as will
My anger in their destruction."
26And the LORD of hosts will
stir up a scourge for him like
the slaughter of Midian at the
rock of Oreb; *as* His rod was
on the sea, so will He lift it up
in the manner of Egypt.

27 It shall come to pass
in that day
That his burden will
be taken away from
your shoulder,
And his yoke from
your neck,
And the yoke will be
destroyed because of
the anointing oil.

28 He has come to Aiath,
He has passed Migron;
At Michmash he
has attended to
his equipment.
29 They have gone
along the ridge,
They have taken up
lodging at Geba.
Ramah is afraid,
Gibeah of Saul has fled.
30 Lift up your voice,
O daughter of Gallim!
Cause it to be heard
as far as Laish—
O poor Anathoth![a]
31 Madmenah has fled,

10:30 [a] Following Masoretic Text, Targum, and Vulgate; Septuagint and Syriac read *Listen to her, O Anathoth*.

The inhabitants of
Gebim seek refuge.
32 As yet he will remain
at Nob that day;
He will shake his fist
at the mount of the
daughter of Zion,
The hill of Jerusalem.

33 Behold, the Lord,
The LORD of hosts,
Will lop off the bough
with terror;
Those of high stature
will be hewn down,
And the haughty will
be humbled.
34 He will cut down
the thickets of the
forest with iron,
And Lebanon will fall
by the Mighty One.

THE REIGN OF JESSE'S OFFSPRING

11 There shall come
forth a Rod from
the stem of Jesse,
And a Branch shall grow
out of his roots.
2 The Spirit of the LORD
shall rest upon Him,
The Spirit of wisdom
and understanding,
The Spirit of counsel
and might,
The Spirit of knowledge
and of the fear
of the LORD.

3 His delight *is* in the
fear of the LORD,
And He shall not judge by
the sight of His eyes,
Nor decide by the
hearing of His ears;
4 But with righteousness
He shall judge the
poor,
And decide with
equity for the meek
of the earth;
He shall strike the
earth with the rod
of His mouth,
And with the breath
of His lips He shall
slay the wicked.
5 Righteousness shall be
the belt of His loins,
And faithfulness the
belt of His waist.

6 "The wolf also shall
dwell with the lamb,
The leopard shall
lie down with the
young goat,
The calf and the
young lion and the
fatling together;
And a little child
shall lead them.
7 The cow and the
bear shall graze;
Their young ones shall
lie down together;
And the lion shall eat
straw like the ox.
8 The nursing child
shall play by the
cobra's hole,
And the weaned child
shall put his hand
in the viper's den.
9 They shall not hurt
nor destroy in all My
holy mountain,

For the earth shall be
full of the knowledge
of the LORD
As the waters
cover the sea.

10 "And in that day there
shall be a Root of Jesse,
Who shall stand as a
banner to the people;
For the Gentiles
shall seek Him,
And His resting place
shall be glorious."

11 It shall come to pass
in that day
That the Lord shall
set His hand again
the second time
To recover the remnant
of His people
who are left,
From Assyria and Egypt,
From Pathros and Cush,
From Elam and Shinar,
From Hamath and the
islands of the sea.

12 He will set up a banner
for the nations,
And will assemble the
outcasts of Israel,
And gather together the
dispersed of Judah
From the four corners
of the earth.
13 Also the envy of Ephraim
shall depart,
And the adversaries of
Judah shall be cut off;
Ephraim shall not
envy Judah,
And Judah shall not
harass Ephraim.
14 But they shall fly down
upon the shoulder
of the Philistines
toward the west;
Together they shall
plunder the people
of the East;
They shall lay their hand
on Edom and Moab;
And the people of Ammon
shall obey them.
15 The LORD will utterly
destroy[a] the tongue
of the Sea of Egypt;
With His mighty wind
He will shake His fist
over the River,[b]
And strike it in the
seven streams,
And make *men* cross
over dry-shod.
16 There will be a highway
for the remnant
of His people
Who will be left
from Assyria,
As it was for Israel
In the day that he came up
from the land of Egypt.

A HYMN OF PRAISE

12 And in that day you will
say:

"O LORD, I will praise You;
Though You were
angry with me,

11:15 [a] Following Masoretic Text and Vulgate; Septuagint, Syriac, and Targum read *dry up*. [b] That is, the Euphrates

Your anger is turned
away, and You
comfort me.
2 Behold, God *is* my
salvation,
I will trust and not
be afraid;
'For YAH, the LORD, *is* my
strength and song;
He also has become
my salvation.'"[a]

3 Therefore with joy you
will draw water
From the wells of
salvation.

4And in that day you will
say:

"Praise the LORD, call
upon His name;
Declare His deeds
among the peoples,
Make mention that His
name is exalted.
5 Sing to the LORD,
For He has done
excellent things;
This *is* known in
all the earth.
6 Cry out and shout,
O inhabitant of Zion,
For great *is* the
Holy One of Israel
in your midst!"

PROCLAMATION AGAINST BABYLON

13 The burden against Babylon which Isaiah the
son of Amoz saw.

2 "Lift up a banner on the
high mountain,
Raise your voice to them;
Wave your hand, that
they may enter the
gates of the nobles.
3 I have commanded My
sanctified ones;
I have also called
My mighty ones
for My anger—
Those who rejoice in
My exaltation."

4 The noise of a multitude
in the mountains,
Like that of many people!
A tumultuous noise of the
kingdoms of nations
gathered together!
The LORD of hosts
musters
The army for battle.
5 They come from a
far country,
From the end of
heaven—
The LORD and His
weapons of indignation,
To destroy the
whole land.

6 Wail, for the day of the
LORD *is* at hand!
It will come as
destruction from
the Almighty.
7 Therefore all hands
will be limp,
Every man's heart
will melt,
8 And they will be afraid.

12:2 [a] Exodus 15:2

Pangs and sorrows will
take hold of *them;*
They will be in pain as a
woman in childbirth;
They will be amazed
at one another;
Their faces *will be*
like flames.

9 Behold, the day of
the LORD comes,
Cruel, with both wrath
and fierce anger,
To lay the land desolate;
And He will destroy
its sinners from it.
10 For the stars of heaven
and their constellations
Will not give their light;
The sun will be darkened
in its going forth,
And the moon will not
cause its light to shine.

11 "I will punish the
world for *its* evil,
And the wicked for
their iniquity;
I will halt the arrogance
of the proud,
And will lay low the
haughtiness of
the terrible.
12 I will make a mortal
more rare than
fine gold,
A man more than the
golden wedge of Ophir.
13 Therefore I will shake
the heavens,
And the earth will move
out of her place,
In the wrath of the
LORD of hosts
And in the day of
His fierce anger.
14 It shall be as the
hunted gazelle,
And as a sheep that
no man takes up;
Every man will turn
to his own people,
And everyone will flee
to his own land.
15 Everyone who is found
will be thrust through,
And everyone who
is captured will fall
by the sword.
16 Their children also will
be dashed to pieces
before their eyes;
Their houses will
be plundered
And their wives ravished.

17 "Behold, I will stir up the
Medes against them,
Who will not regard silver;
And *as for* gold, they
will not delight in it.
18 Also *their* bows will dash
the young men to pieces,
And they will have no pity
on the fruit of the womb;
Their eye will not
spare children.
19 And Babylon, the glory
of kingdoms,
The beauty of the
Chaldeans' pride,
Will be as when God
overthrew Sodom
and Gomorrah.
20 It will never be inhabited,
Nor will it be settled
from generation
to generation;

Nor will the Arabian
pitch tents there,
Nor will the shepherds
make their
sheepfolds there.
21 But wild beasts of the
desert will lie there,
And their houses will
be full of owls;
Ostriches will dwell there,
And wild goats will
caper there.
22 The hyenas will howl
in their citadels,
And jackals in their
pleasant palaces.
Her time *is* near to come,
And her days will not
be prolonged."

MERCY ON JACOB

14 For the LORD will have
mercy on Jacob, and will
still choose Israel, and settle
them in their own land. The
strangers will be joined with
them, and they will cling to
the house of Jacob. 2Then people will take them and bring
them to their place, and the
house of Israel will possess
them for servants and maids
in the land of the LORD; they
will take them captive whose
captives they were, and rule
over their oppressors.

FALL OF THE KING OF BABYLON

3It shall come to pass in the
day the LORD gives you rest
from your sorrow, and from
your fear and the hard bondage in which you were made
to serve, 4that you will take up
this proverb against the king
of Babylon, and say:

"How the oppressor
has ceased,
The golden[a] city ceased!
5 The LORD has broken the
staff of the wicked,
The scepter of the rulers;
6 He who struck the
people in wrath with
a continual stroke,
He who ruled the
nations in anger,
Is persecuted *and*
no one hinders.
7 The whole earth is at
rest *and* quiet;
They break forth
into singing.
8 Indeed the cypress trees
rejoice over you,
And the cedars of
Lebanon,
Saying, 'Since you
were cut down,
No woodsman has
come up against us.'

9 "Hell from beneath is
excited about you,
To meet *you* at
your coming;
It stirs up the dead
for you,
All the chief ones
of the earth;
It has raised up from
their thrones

14:4 [a] Or *insolent*

All the kings of
the nations.
10 They all shall speak
and say to you:
'Have you also become
as weak as we?
Have you become like us?
11 Your pomp is brought
down to Sheol,
And the sound of your
stringed instruments;
The maggot is spread
under you,
And worms cover you.'

THE FALL OF LUCIFER

12 "How you are fallen
from heaven,
O Lucifer,[a] son of
the morning!
How you are cut down
to the ground,
You who weakened
the nations!
13 For you have said
in your heart:
'I will ascend into heaven,
I will exalt my throne
above the stars of God;
I will also sit on
the mount of the
congregation
On the farthest sides
of the north;
14 I will ascend above the
heights of the clouds,
I will be like the
Most High.'
15 Yet you shall be brought
down to Sheol,
To the lowest depths
of the Pit.

16 "Those who see you
will gaze at you,
And consider you, *saying:*
'*Is* this the man who made
the earth tremble,
Who shook kingdoms,
17 Who made the world
as a wilderness
And destroyed its cities,
Who did not open the
house of his prisoners?'

18 "All the kings of
the nations,
All of them, sleep in glory,
Everyone in his
own house;
19 But you are cast out
of your grave
Like an abominable
branch,
Like the garment of
those who are slain,
Thrust through
with a sword,
Who go down to the
stones of the pit,
Like a corpse trodden
underfoot.
20 You will not be joined
with them in burial,
Because you have
destroyed your land
And slain your people.
The brood of evildoers
shall never be named.
21 Prepare slaughter
for his children
Because of the iniquity
of their fathers,
Lest they rise up and
possess the land,

14:12 [a] Literally *Day Star*

And fill the face of the
world with cities."

BABYLON DESTROYED

22"For I will rise up
against them," says
the LORD of hosts,
"And cut off from
Babylon the name
and remnant,
And offspring and
posterity," says
the LORD.
23"I will also make it
a possession for
the porcupine,
And marshes of
muddy water;
I will sweep it with the
broom of destruction,"
says the LORD of hosts.

ASSYRIA DESTROYED

24 The LORD of hosts has
sworn, saying,
"Surely, as I have
thought, so it shall
come to pass,
And as I have purposed,
so it shall stand:
25 That I will break the
Assyrian in My land,
And on My mountains
tread him underfoot.
Then his yoke shall be
removed from them,
And his burden removed
from their shoulders.
26 This *is* the purpose that
is purposed against
the whole earth,
And this *is* the hand
that is stretched out
over all the nations.
27 For the LORD of hosts
has purposed,
And who will annul *it?*
His hand *is* stretched out,
And who will turn it back?"

PHILISTIA DESTROYED

28This is the burden which
came in the year that King
Ahaz died.

29"Do not rejoice, all
you of Philistia,
Because the rod that
struck you is broken;
For out of the serpent's
roots will come
forth a viper,
And its offspring *will be*
a fiery flying serpent.
30 The firstborn of the
poor will feed,
And the needy will lie
down in safety;
I will kill your roots
with famine,
And it will slay
your remnant.
31 Wail, O gate! Cry, O city!
All you of Philistia
are dissolved;
For smoke will come
from the north,
And no one *will be* alone
in his appointed times."

32 What will they answer
the messengers
of the nation?
That the LORD has
founded Zion,
And the poor of His
people shall take
refuge in it.

PROCLAMATION AGAINST MOAB

15 The burden against Moab.

Because in the night Ar
of Moab is laid waste
And destroyed,
Because in the night Kir
of Moab is laid waste
And destroyed,
2 He has gone up to the
temple[a] and Dibon,
To the high places
to weep.
Moab will wail over Nebo
and over Medeba;
On all their heads
will be baldness,
And every beard cut off.
3 In their streets they will
clothe themselves
with sackcloth;
On the tops of
their houses
And in their streets
Everyone will wail,
weeping bitterly.
4 Heshbon and Elealeh
will cry out,
Their voice shall be
heard as far as Jahaz;
Therefore the armed
soldiers[a] of Moab
will cry out;
His life will be
burdensome to him.

5 "My heart will cry
out for Moab;
His fugitives *shall*
flee to Zoar,
Like a three-year-old
heifer.[a]
For by the Ascent of Luhith
They will go up
with weeping;
For in the way of
Horonaim
They will raise up a
cry of destruction,
6 For the waters of Nimrim
will be desolate,
For the green grass
has withered away;
The grass fails, there
is nothing green.
7 Therefore the abundance
they have gained,
And what they
have laid up,
They will carry away to the
Brook of the Willows.
8 For the cry has gone
all around the
borders of Moab,
Its wailing to Eglaim
And its wailing to
Beer Elim.
9 For the waters of Dimon[a]
will be full of blood;
Because I will bring
more upon Dimon,[b]
Lions upon him who
escapes from Moab,

15:2 [a] Hebrew *bayith,* literally *house* 15:4 [a] Following Masoretic Text, Targum, and Vulgate; *Septuagint* and Syriac read *loins.* 15:5 [a] Or *The Third Eglath,* an unknown city (compare Jeremiah 48:34) 15:9 [a] Following Masoretic Text and Targum; Dead Sea Scrolls and Vulgate read *Dibon;* Septuagint reads *Rimon.* [b] Following Masoretic Text and Targum; Dead Sea Scrolls and Vulgate read *Dibon;* Septuagint reads *Rimon.*

And on the remnant
of the land."

MOAB DESTROYED

16 Send the lamb to the
ruler of the land,
From Sela to the
wilderness,
To the mount of the
daughter of Zion.
2 For it shall be as a
wandering bird thrown
out of the nest;
So shall be the daughters
of Moab at the fords
of the Arnon.

3 "Take counsel,
execute judgment;
Make your shadow
like the night in the
middle of the day;
Hide the outcasts,
Do not betray him
who escapes.
4 Let My outcasts dwell
with you, O Moab;
Be a shelter to them
from the face of
the spoiler.
For the extortioner
is at an end,
Devastation ceases,
The oppressors are
consumed out
of the land.
5 In mercy the throne
will be established;
And One will sit on
it in truth, in the
tabernacle of David,
Judging and seeking
justice and hastening
righteousness."

6 We have heard of the
pride of Moab—
He is very proud—
Of his haughtiness and
his pride and his wrath;
But his lies *shall* not *be* so.
7 Therefore Moab shall
wail for Moab;
Everyone shall wail.
For the foundations
of Kir Hareseth you
shall mourn;
Surely *they are* stricken.

8 For the fields of
Heshbon languish,
And the vine of Sibmah;
The lords of the nations
have broken down
its choice plants,
Which have reached
to Jazer
And wandered through
the wilderness.
Her branches are
stretched out,
They are gone
over the sea.
9 Therefore I will bewail
the vine of Sibmah,
With the weeping of Jazer;
I will drench you
with my tears,
O Heshbon and Elealeh;
For battle cries
have fallen
Over your summer fruits
and your harvest.

10 Gladness is taken away,
And joy from the
plentiful field;
In the vineyards there
will be no singing,

Nor will there be
shouting;
No treaders will tread out
wine in the presses;
I have made their
shouting cease.
11 Therefore my heart
shall resound like
a harp for Moab,
And my inner being
for Kir Heres.

12 And it shall come to pass,
When it is seen that
Moab is weary on
the high place,
That he will come to his
sanctuary to pray;
But he will not prevail.

13This *is* the word which the
LORD has spoken concerning
Moab since that time. 14But
now the LORD has spoken,
saying, "Within three years, as
the years of a hired man, the
glory of Moab will be despised
with all that great multitude,
and the remnant *will be* very
small *and* feeble."

PROCLAMATION AGAINST SYRIA AND ISRAEL

17 The burden against Damascus.

"Behold, Damascus will
cease from *being* a city,
And it will be a
ruinous heap.
2 The cities of Aroer
are forsaken;[a]
They will be for flocks
Which lie down, and
no one will make
them afraid.
3 The fortress also will
cease from Ephraim,
The kingdom from
Damascus,
And the remnant of Syria;
They will be as the glory of
the children of Israel,"
Says the LORD of hosts.

4 "In that day it shall
come to pass
That the glory of
Jacob will wane,
And the fatness of his
flesh grow lean.
5 It shall be as when
the harvester
gathers the grain,
And reaps the heads
with his arm;
It shall be as he who
gathers heads of grain
In the Valley of Rephaim.
6 Yet gleaning grapes
will be left in it,
Like the shaking of
an olive tree,
Two *or* three olives
at the top of the
uppermost bough,
Four *or* five in its most
fruitful branches,"
Says the LORD God
of Israel.

17:2 [a] Following Masoretic Text and Vulgate; Septuagint reads *It shall be forsaken forever;* Targum reads *Its cities shall be forsaken and desolate.*

7 In that day a man will
look to his Maker,
And his eyes will have
respect for the Holy
One of Israel.
8 He will not look
to the altars,
The work of his hands;
He will not respect what
his fingers have made,
Nor the wooden images[a]
nor the incense altars.

9 In that day his strong
cities will be as a
forsaken bough[a]
And an uppermost
branch,[b]
Which they left because
of the children of Israel;
And there will be
desolation.

10 Because you have
forgotten the God
of your salvation,
And have not been
mindful of the Rock
of your stronghold,
Therefore you will plant
pleasant plants
And set out foreign
seedlings;
11 In the day you will make
your plant to grow,
And in the morning
you will make your
seed to flourish;
But the harvest *will
be* a heap of ruins
In the day of grief and
desperate sorrow.

12 Woe to the multitude
of many people
Who make a noise like
the roar of the seas,
And to the rushing
of nations
That make a rushing
like the rushing of
mighty waters!
13 The nations will rush
like the rushing of
many waters;
But *God* will rebuke
them and they will
flee far away,
And be chased like
the chaff of the
mountains before
the wind,
Like a rolling thing
before the whirlwind.
14 Then behold, at
eventide, trouble!
And before the morning,
he *is* no more.
This *is* the portion of
those who plunder us,
And the lot of those
who rob us.

PROCLAMATION AGAINST ETHIOPIA

18 Woe to the land
shadowed with
buzzing wings,
Which *is* beyond the
rivers of Ethiopia,

17:8 [a] Hebrew *Asherim,* Canaanite deities 17:9 [a] Septuagint reads *Hivites;* Targum reads *laid waste;* Vulgate reads *as the plows.* [b] Septuagint reads *Amorites;* Targum reads *in ruins;* Vulgate reads *corn.*

2 Which sends
ambassadors by sea,
Even in vessels of reed
on the waters, *saying,*
"Go, swift messengers,
to a nation tall and
smooth *of skin,*
To a people terrible
from their beginning
onward,
A nation powerful and
treading down,
Whose land the
rivers divide."

3 All inhabitants of the
world and dwellers
on the earth:
When he lifts up
a banner on the
mountains, you see *it;*
And when he blows a
trumpet, you hear *it.*
4 For so the LORD
said to me,
"I will take My rest,
And I will look from
My dwelling place
Like clear heat in
sunshine,
Like a cloud of dew in
the heat of harvest."
5 For before the harvest,
when the bud is perfect
And the sour grape is
ripening in the flower,
He will both cut off
the sprigs with
pruning hooks
And take away *and* cut
down the branches.
6 They will be left together
for the mountain
birds of prey
And for the beasts
of the earth;
The birds of prey will
summer on them,
And all the beasts
of the earth will
winter on them.

7 In that time a present
will be brought to
the LORD of hosts
From[a] a people tall
and smooth *of skin,*
And from a people
terrible from their
beginning onward,
A nation powerful and
treading down,
Whose land the
rivers divide—
To the place of the
name of the
LORD of hosts,
To Mount Zion.

PROCLAMATION AGAINST EGYPT

19 The burden against Egypt.

Behold, the LORD rides
on a swift cloud,
And will come into
Egypt;
The idols of Egypt will
totter at His presence,
And the heart of Egypt
will melt in its midst.

18:7 [a] Following Dead Sea Scrolls, Septuagint, and Vulgate; Masoretic Text omits *From;* Targum reads *To.*

2 "I will set Egyptians
against Egyptians;
Everyone will fight
against his brother,
And everyone against
his neighbor,
City against city, kingdom
against kingdom.
3 The spirit of Egypt will
fail in its midst;
I will destroy their
counsel,
And they will consult the
idols and the charmers,
The mediums and
the sorcerers.
4 And the Egyptians
I will give
Into the hand of a
cruel master,
And a fierce king will
rule over them,"
Says the Lord, the
LORD of hosts.

5 The waters will fail
from the sea,
And the river will be
wasted and dried up.
6 The rivers will turn foul;
The brooks of defense
will be emptied
and dried up;
The reeds and rushes
will wither.
7 The papyrus reeds by
the River,[a] by the
mouth of the River,
And everything sown
by the River,
Will wither, be driven
away, and be no more.
8 The fishermen also
will mourn;
All those will lament who
cast hooks into the River,
And they will languish
who spread nets
on the waters.
9 Moreover those who
work in fine flax
And those who weave fine
fabric will be ashamed;
10 And its foundations
will be broken.
All who make wages *will
be* troubled of soul.

11 Surely the princes of
Zoan *are* fools;
Pharaoh's wise counselors
give foolish counsel.
How do you say to
Pharaoh, "I *am* the
son of the wise,
The son of ancient kings?"
12 Where *are* they?
Where are your wise men?
Let them tell you now,
And let them know
what the LORD of
hosts has purposed
against Egypt.
13 The princes of Zoan
have become fools;
The princes of Noph[a]
are deceived;
They have also
deluded Egypt,
Those who are the
mainstay of its tribes.
14 The LORD has mingled
a perverse spirit
in her midst;

19:7 [a] That is, the Nile 19:13 [a] That is, ancient Memphis

And they have caused
Egypt to err in
all her work,
As a drunken man
staggers in his vomit.
15 Neither will there be
any work for Egypt,
Which the head or tail,
Palm branch or
bulrush, may do.[a]

16 In that day Egypt will be
like women, and will be afraid
and fear because of the wav-
ing of the hand of the LORD of
hosts, which He waves over it.
17 And the land of Judah will
be a terror to Egypt; everyone who makes mention of
it will be afraid in himself,
because of the counsel of the
LORD of hosts which He has
determined against it.

EGYPT, ASSYRIA, AND ISRAEL BLESSED

18 In that day five cities in the
land of Egypt will speak the language of Canaan and swear by
the LORD of hosts; one will be
called the City of Destruction.[a]
19 In that day there will be an
altar to the LORD in the midst
of the land of Egypt, and a pillar to the LORD at its border.
20 And it will be for a sign and
for a witness to the LORD of
hosts in the land of Egypt; for
they will cry to the LORD because of the oppressors, and
He will send them a Savior and
a Mighty One, and He will deliver them.
21 Then the LORD
will be known to Egypt, and the
Egyptians will know the LORD
in that day, and will make sacrifice and offering; yes, they will
make a vow to the LORD and
perform *it.*
22 And the LORD will
strike Egypt, He will strike and
heal *it;* they will return to the
LORD, and He will be entreated
by them and heal them.
23 In that day there will be a
highway from Egypt to Assyria,
and the Assyrian will come
into Egypt and the Egyptian
into Assyria, and the Egyptians
will serve with the Assyrians.
24 In that day Israel will be
one of three with Egypt and
Assyria—a blessing in the
midst of the land,
25 whom
the LORD of hosts shall bless,
saying, "Blessed *is* Egypt My
people, and Assyria the work
of My hands, and Israel My
inheritance."

THE SIGN AGAINST EGYPT AND ETHIOPIA

20 In the year that Tar-
tan[a] came to Ashdod,
when Sargon the king of Assyria sent him, and he fought
against Ashdod and took it,
2 at
the same time the LORD spoke
by Isaiah the son of Amoz,
saying, "Go, and remove the
sackcloth from your body,

19:15 [a] Compare Isaiah 9:14–16 19:18 [a] Some Hebrew manuscripts, Arabic, Dead Sea Scrolls, Targum, and Vulgate read *Sun;* Septuagint reads *Asedek* (literally *Righteousness*). 20:1 [a] Or *the Commander in Chief*

and take your sandals off your
feet." And he did so, walking
naked and barefoot.

3Then the LORD said, "Just
as My servant Isaiah has
walked naked and barefoot
three years *for* a sign and a
wonder against Egypt and
Ethiopia, 4so shall the king of
Assyria lead away the Egyptians as prisoners and the Ethiopians as captives, young and
old, naked and barefoot, with
their buttocks uncovered, to
the shame of Egypt. 5Then they
shall be afraid and ashamed
of Ethiopia their expectation
and Egypt their glory. 6And the
inhabitant of this territory will
say in that day, 'Surely such *is*
our expectation, wherever we
flee for help to be delivered
from the king of Assyria; and
how shall we escape?'"

THE FALL OF BABYLON PROCLAIMED

21 The burden against the Wilderness of the Sea.

As whirlwinds in the
South pass through,
So it comes from
the desert, from
a terrible land.
2 A distressing vision
is declared to me;
The treacherous dealer
deals treacherously,
And the plunderer
plunders.
Go up, O Elam!
Besiege, O Media!
All its sighing I have
made to cease.

3 Therefore my loins are
filled with pain;
Pangs have taken hold
of me, like the pangs
of a woman in labor.
I was distressed
when *I* heard *it;*
I was dismayed
when *I* saw *it.*
4 My heart wavered,
fearfulness
frightened me;
The night for which
I longed He turned
into fear for me.
5 Prepare the table,
Set a watchman
in the tower,
Eat and drink.
Arise, you princes,
Anoint the shield!

6 For thus has the
Lord said to me:
"Go, set a watchman,
Let him declare
what he sees."
7 And he saw a chariot *with*
a pair of horsemen,
A chariot of donkeys, *and*
a chariot of camels,
And he listened earnestly
with great care.
8 Then he cried, "A
lion,[a] my Lord!
I stand continually
on the watchtower
in the daytime;

21:8 [a] Dead Sea Scrolls read *Then the observer cried.*

I have sat at my post
every night.
9 And look, here comes a
chariot of men *with* a
pair of horsemen!"
Then he answered
and said,
"Babylon is fallen, is fallen!
And all the carved
images of her gods
He has broken to
the ground."

10 Oh, my threshing and
the grain of my floor!
That which I have heard
from the LORD of hosts,
The God of Israel,
I have declared to you.

PROCLAMATION AGAINST EDOM

11The burden against Dumah.

He calls to me out of Seir,
"Watchman, what
of the night?
Watchman, what
of the night?"
12 The watchman said,
"The morning comes,
and also the night.
If you will inquire, inquire;
Return! Come back!"

PROCLAMATION AGAINST ARABIA

13The burden against Arabia.

In the forest in Arabia
you will lodge,
O you traveling companies
of Dedanites.
14 O inhabitants of the
land of Tema,
Bring water to him
who is thirsty;
With their bread they
met him who fled.
15 For they fled from
the swords, from
the drawn sword,
From the bent bow, and
from the distress of war.

16For thus the LORD has
said to me: "Within a year, according to the year of a hired
man, all the glory of Kedar
will fail; 17and the remainder
of the number of archers, the
mighty men of the people of
Kedar, will be diminished; for
the LORD God of Israel has
spoken *it*."

PROCLAMATION AGAINST JERUSALEM

22 The burden against the Valley of Vision.

What ails you now, that
you have all gone up
to the housetops,
2 You who are full of noise,
A tumultuous city,
a joyous city?
Your slain *men are* not
slain with the sword,
Nor dead in battle.
3 All your rulers have
fled together;
They are captured
by the archers.
All who are found in you
are bound together;
They have fled from afar.

4 Therefore I said, "Look
away from me,
I will weep bitterly;
Do not labor to
comfort me
Because of the
plundering of the
daughter of my people."

5 For *it is* a day of trouble
and treading down
and perplexity
By the Lord GOD of hosts
In the Valley of Vision—
Breaking down the walls
And of crying to
the mountain.
6 Elam bore the quiver
With chariots of men
and horsemen,
And Kir uncovered
the shield.
7 It shall come to pass *that*
your choicest valleys
Shall be full of chariots,
And the horsemen
shall set themselves
in array at the gate.

8 He removed the
protection of Judah.
You looked in that day
to the armor of the
House of the Forest;
9 You also saw the damage
to the city of David,
That it was great;
And you gathered
together the waters
of the lower pool.
10 You numbered the
houses of Jerusalem,
And the houses you
broke down
To fortify the wall.
11 You also made a reservoir
between the two walls
For the water of
the old pool.
But you did not look
to its Maker,
Nor did you have
respect for Him who
fashioned it long ago.

12 And in that day the
Lord GOD of hosts
Called for weeping
and for mourning,
For baldness and for
girding with sackcloth.
13 But instead, joy
and gladness,
Slaying oxen and
killing sheep,
Eating meat and
drinking wine:
"Let us eat and drink, for
tomorrow we die!"

14 Then it was revealed
in my hearing by
the LORD of hosts,
"Surely for this iniquity
there will be no
atonement for you,
Even to your death," says
the Lord GOD of hosts.

THE JUDGMENT ON SHEBNA

15Thus says the Lord GOD of hosts:

"Go, proceed to
this steward,
To Shebna, who *is* over
the house, *and say:*

16 'What have you
here, and whom
have you here,
That you have hewn
a sepulcher here,
As he who hews himself
a sepulcher on high,
Who carves a tomb for
himself in a rock?
17 Indeed, the LORD
will throw you
away violently,
O mighty man,
And will surely seize you.
18 He will surely turn
violently and toss
you like a ball
Into a large country;
There you shall die,
and there your
glorious chariots
Shall be the shame of
your master's house.
19 So I will drive you out
of your office,
And from your position
he will pull you down.[a]

20 'Then it shall be
in that day,
That I will call My
servant Eliakim the
son of Hilkiah;
21 I will clothe him
with your robe
And strengthen him
with your belt;
I will commit your
responsibility
into his hand.
He shall be a father to the
inhabitants of Jerusalem
And to the house of Judah.
22 The key of the
house of David
I will lay on his shoulder;
So he shall open, and
no one shall shut;
And he shall shut, and
no one shall open.
23 I will fasten him *as* a
peg in a secure place,
And he will become a
glorious throne to
his father's house.

24 'They will hang on him all
the glory of his father's house,
the offspring and the posterity, all vessels of small quantity, from the cups to all the
pitchers. 25 In that day,' says
the LORD of hosts, 'the peg
that is fastened in the secure
place will be removed and be
cut down and fall, and the burden that *was* on it will be cut
off; for the LORD has spoken.'"

PROCLAMATION AGAINST TYRE

23 The burden against Tyre.

Wail, you ships of Tarshish!
For it is laid waste,
So that there is no
house, no harbor;
From the land of Cyprus[a]
it is revealed to them.

22:19 [a] Septuagint omits *he will pull you down;* Syriac, Targum, and Vulgate read *I will pull you down.* 23:1 [a] Hebrew *Kittim,* western lands, especially Cyprus

2 Be still, you inhabitants
of the coastland,
You merchants of Sidon,
Whom those who cross
the sea have filled.[a]
3 And on great waters
the grain of Shihor,
The harvest of the River,[a]
is her revenue;
And she is a marketplace
for the nations.

4 Be ashamed, O Sidon;
For the sea has spoken,
The strength of the
sea, saying,
"I do not labor, nor bring
forth children;
Neither do I rear
young men,
Nor bring up virgins."
5 When the report
reaches Egypt,
They also will be in
agony at the
report of Tyre.

6 Cross over to Tarshish;
Wail, you inhabitants
of the coastland!
7 *Is* this your joyous *city,*
Whose antiquity *is*
from ancient days,
Whose feet carried her
far off to dwell?
8 Who has taken this
counsel against Tyre,
the crowning *city,*
Whose merchants
are princes,
Whose traders *are* the
honorable of the earth?
9 The LORD of hosts
has purposed it,
To bring to dishonor
the pride of all glory,
To bring into contempt
all the honorable
of the earth.

10 Overflow through your
land like the River,[a]
O daughter of Tarshish;
There is no more strength.
11 He stretched out His
hand over the sea,
He shook the kingdoms;
The LORD has given
a commandment
against Canaan
To destroy its strongholds.
12 And He said, "You will
rejoice no more,
O you oppressed virgin
daughter of Sidon.
Arise, cross over
to Cyprus;
There also you will
have no rest."

13 Behold, the land of
the Chaldeans,
This people *which*
was not;
Assyria founded
it for wild beasts
of the desert.
They set up its towers,
They raised up its palaces,
And brought it to ruin.

23:2 [a] Following Masoretic Text and Vulgate; Septuagint and Targum read *Passing over the water;* Dead Sea Scrolls read *Your messengers passing over the sea.* 23:3 [a] That is, the Nile 23:10 [a] That is, the Nile

14 Wail, you ships of
Tarshish!
For your strength
is laid waste.

15Now it shall come to pass
in that day that Tyre will be
forgotten seventy years, according to the days of one
king. At the end of seventy
years it will happen to Tyre
as *in* the song of the harlot:

16"Take a harp, go
about the city,
You forgotten harlot;
Make sweet melody,
sing many songs,
That you may be
remembered."

17And it shall be, at the end
of seventy years, that the LORD
will deal with Tyre. She will return to her hire, and commit
fornication with all the kingdoms of the world on the face
of the earth. 18Her gain and
her pay will be set apart for the
LORD; it will not be treasured
nor laid up, for her gain will
be for those who dwell before
the LORD, to eat sufficiently,
and for fine clothing.

IMPENDING JUDGMENT ON THE EARTH

24 Behold, the LORD
makes the earth
empty *and*
makes it waste,
Distorts its surface
And scatters abroad
its inhabitants.

2 And it shall be:
As with the people, so
with the priest;
As with the servant, so
with his master;
As with the maid, so
with her mistress;
As with the buyer, so
with the seller;
As with the lender, so
with the borrower;
As with the creditor,
so with the debtor.

3 The land shall be
entirely emptied and
utterly plundered,
For the LORD has
spoken this word.

4 The earth mourns
and fades away,
The world languishes
and fades away;
The haughty people of
the earth languish.

5 The earth is also defiled
under its inhabitants,
Because they have
transgressed the laws,
Changed the ordinance,
Broken the everlasting
covenant.

6 Therefore the curse has
devoured the earth,
And those who dwell
in it are desolate.
Therefore the inhabitants
of the earth are burned,
And few men *are* left.

7 The new wine fails, the
vine languishes,
All the merry-hearted
sigh.

8 The mirth of the
tambourine ceases,
The noise of the
jubilant ends,
The joy of the
harp ceases.
9 They shall not drink
wine with a song;
Strong drink is bitter to
those who drink it.
10 The city of confusion
is broken down;
Every house is shut up, so
that none may go in.
11 *There is* a cry for wine
in the streets,
All joy is darkened,
The mirth of the
land is gone.
12 In the city desolation
is left,
And the gate is stricken
with destruction.
13 When it shall be thus in
the midst of the land
among the people,
It shall be like the shaking
of an olive tree,
Like the gleaning of
grapes when the
vintage is done.

14 They shall lift up their
voice, they shall sing;
For the majesty
of the LORD
They shall cry aloud
from the sea.
15 Therefore glorify
the LORD in the
dawning light,
The name of the LORD
God of Israel in the
coastlands of the sea.
16 From the ends of
the earth we have
heard songs:
"Glory to the righteous!"
But I said, "I am
ruined, ruined!
Woe to me!
The treacherous
dealers have dealt
treacherously,
Indeed, the treacherous
dealers have dealt
very treacherously."

17 Fear and the pit
and the snare
Are upon you,
O inhabitant of
the earth.
18 And it shall be
That he who flees from
the noise of the fear
Shall fall into the pit,
And he who comes up
from the midst of the pit
Shall be caught in
the snare;
For the windows from
on high are open,
And the foundations of
the earth are shaken.

19 The earth is violently
broken,
The earth is split open,
The earth is shaken
exceedingly.
20 The earth shall reel to
and fro like a drunkard,
And shall totter like a hut;
Its transgression shall
be heavy upon it,
And it will fall, and
not rise again.

21 It shall come to pass
in that day
That the LORD will
punish on high the
host of exalted ones,
And on the earth the
kings of the earth.
22 They will be gathered
together,
As prisoners are
gathered in the pit,
And will be shut up
in the prison;
After many days they
will be punished.
23 Then the moon will
be disgraced
And the sun ashamed;
For the LORD of
hosts will reign
On Mount Zion and
in Jerusalem
And before His elders,
gloriously.

PRAISE TO GOD

25 O LORD, You *are*
my God.
I will exalt You,
I will praise Your name,
For You have done
wonderful *things;*
Your counsels of old *are*
faithfulness *and* truth.
2 For You have made
a city a ruin,
A fortified city a ruin,
A palace of foreigners
to be a city no more;
It will never be rebuilt.
3 Therefore the strong
people will glorify You;
The city of the terrible
nations will fear You.
4 For You have been a
strength to the poor,
A strength to the needy
in his distress,
A refuge from the storm,
A shade from the heat;
For the blast of the
terrible ones *is* as a
storm *against* the wall.
5 You will reduce the
noise of aliens,
As heat in a dry place;
As heat in the shadow
of a cloud,
The song of the
terrible ones will
be diminished.

6 And in this mountain
The LORD of hosts will
make for all people
A feast of choice pieces,
A feast of wines
on the lees,
Of fat things full
of marrow,
Of well-refined wines
on the lees.
7 And He will destroy
on this mountain
The surface of the
covering cast over
all people,
And the veil that is
spread over all nations.
8 He will swallow up
death forever,
And the Lord GOD
will wipe away tears
from all faces;
The rebuke of His people
He will take away
from all the earth;
For the LORD has spoken.

9 And it will be said
in that day:
"Behold, this *is* our God;
We have waited for Him,
and He will save us.
This *is* the LORD;
We have waited for Him;
We will be glad and
rejoice in His salvation."

10 For on this mountain
the hand of the
LORD will rest,
And Moab shall be
trampled down
under Him,
As straw is trampled down
for the refuse heap.
11 And He will spread
out His hands in
their midst
As a swimmer reaches
out to swim,
And He will bring
down their pride
Together with the trickery
of their hands.
12 The fortress of the high
fort of your walls
He will bring down,
lay low,
And bring to the ground,
down to the dust.

A SONG OF SALVATION

26 In that day this song will be sung in the land of Judah:

"We have a strong city;
God will appoint salvation
for walls and bulwarks.
2 Open the gates,
That the righteous
nation which keeps the
truth may enter in.
3 You will keep *him* in
perfect peace,
Whose mind *is*
stayed *on You*,
Because he trusts in You.
4 Trust in the LORD forever,
For in YAH, the LORD, *is*
everlasting strength.[a]
5 For He brings down those
who dwell on high,
The lofty city;
He lays it low,
He lays it low to
the ground,
He brings it down
to the dust.
6 The foot shall tread
it down—
The feet of the poor
And the steps of
the needy."

7 The way of the just
is uprightness;
O Most Upright,
You weigh the path
of the just.
8 Yes, in the way of
Your judgments,
O LORD, we have
waited for You;
The desire of *our* soul
is for Your name
And for the
remembrance of You.
9 With my soul I
have desired You
in the night,

26:4 [a] Or *Rock of Ages*

Yes, by my spirit within
me I will seek You early;
For when Your judgments
are in the earth,
The inhabitants of
the world will learn
righteousness.

10 Let grace be shown
to the wicked,
Yet he will not learn
righteousness;
In the land of uprightness
he will deal unjustly,
And will not behold the
majesty of the LORD.
11 LORD, *when* Your
hand is lifted up,
they will not see.
But they will see and
be ashamed
For *their* envy of people;
Yes, the fire of Your
enemies shall
devour them.

12 LORD, You will establish
peace for us,
For You have also done
all our works in us.
13 O LORD our God,
masters besides You
Have had dominion
over us;
But by You only we
make mention of
Your name.
14 *They are* dead, they
will not live;
They are deceased,
they will not rise.
Therefore You have
punished and
destroyed them,
And made all their
memory to perish.
15 You have increased the
nation, O LORD,
You have increased
the nation;
You are glorified;
You have expanded all
the borders of the land.

16 LORD, in trouble they
have visited You,
They poured out a prayer
when Your chastening
was upon them.
17 As a woman with child
Is in pain and cries
out in her pangs,
When she draws near the
time of her delivery,
So have we been in
Your sight, O LORD.
18 We have been with child,
we have been in pain;
We have, as it were,
brought forth wind;
We have not
accomplished
any deliverance
in the earth,
Nor have the inhabitants
of the world fallen.

19 Your dead shall live;
Together with my dead
body[a] they shall arise.
Awake and sing, you
who dwell in dust;

26:19 [a] Following Masoretic Text and Vulgate; Syriac and Targum read *their dead bodies;* Septuagint reads *those in the tombs.*

For your dew *is like*
the dew of herbs,
And the earth shall
cast out the dead.

TAKE REFUGE FROM THE COMING JUDGMENT

20 Come, my people, enter
your chambers,
And shut your doors
behind you;
Hide yourself, as it were,
for a little moment,
Until the indignation
is past.
21 For behold, the LORD
comes out of His place
To punish the inhabitants
of the earth for
their iniquity;
The earth will also
disclose her blood,
And will no more
cover her slain.

27 In that day the LORD
with His severe
sword, great
and strong,
Will punish Leviathan
the fleeing serpent,
Leviathan that
twisted serpent;
And He will slay the
reptile that *is* in the sea.

THE RESTORATION OF ISRAEL

2 In that day sing to her,
"A vineyard of red wine![a]
3 I, the LORD, keep it,
I water it every moment;
Lest any hurt it,
I keep it night and day.
4 Fury *is* not in Me.
Who would set briers
and thorns
Against Me in battle?
I would go through them,
I would burn them
together.
5 Or let him take hold
of My strength,
That he may make
peace with Me;
And he shall make
peace with Me."

6 Those who come He
shall cause to take
root in Jacob;
Israel shall blossom
and bud,
And fill the face of the
world with fruit.

7 Has He struck Israel
as He struck those
who struck him?
Or has He been slain
according to the
slaughter of those who
were slain by Him?
8 In measure, by
sending it away,
You contended with it.
He removes *it* by
His rough wind
In the day of the
east wind.

27:2 [a] Following Masoretic Text (Kittel's *Biblia Hebraica*), Bomberg, and Vulgate; Masoretic Text (*Biblia Hebraica Stuttgartensia*), some Hebrew manuscripts, and Septuagint read *delight;* Targum reads *choice vineyard.*

9 Therefore by this the
iniquity of Jacob
will be covered;
And this *is* all the fruit of
taking away his sin:
When he makes all the
stones of the altar
Like chalkstones that
are beaten to dust,
Wooden images[a]
and incense altars
shall not stand.

10 Yet the fortified city
will be desolate,
The habitation
forsaken and left
like a wilderness;
There the calf will
feed, and there it
will lie down
And consume its
branches.
11 When its boughs are
withered, they will
be broken off;
The women come *and*
set them on fire.
For it *is* a people of no
understanding;
Therefore He who made
them will not have
mercy on them,
And He who formed them
will show them no favor.

12 And it shall come to
pass in that day
That the LORD will thresh,
From the channel of
the River[a] to the
Brook of Egypt;
And you will be gathered
one by one,
O you children of Israel.

13 So it shall be in that day:
The great trumpet
will be blown;
They will come, who
are about to perish in
the land of Assyria,
And they who are
outcasts in the
land of Egypt,
And shall worship the
LORD in the holy
mount at Jerusalem.

WOE TO EPHRAIM AND JERUSALEM

28 Woe to the crown
of pride, to the
drunkards of
Ephraim,
Whose glorious beauty
is a fading flower
Which *is* at the head of
the verdant valleys,
To those who are
overcome with wine!
2 Behold, the Lord has a
mighty and strong one,
Like a tempest of hail and
a destroying storm,
Like a flood of mighty
waters overflowing,
Who will bring *them*
down to the earth
with *His* hand.
3 The crown of pride, the
drunkards of Ephraim,
Will be trampled
underfoot;

27:9 [a] Hebrew *Asherim,* Canaanite deities 27:12 [a] That is, the Euphrates

4 And the glorious beauty
is a fading flower
Which *is* at the head of
the verdant valley,
Like the first fruit
before the summer,
Which an observer sees;
He eats it up while it
is still in his hand.

5 In that day the LORD
of hosts will be
For a crown of glory and
a diadem of beauty
To the remnant of
His people,
6 For a spirit of justice
to him who sits
in judgment,
And for strength to
those who turn back
the battle at the gate.

7 But they also have
erred through wine,
And through intoxicating
drink are out of the way;
The priest and the
prophet have
erred through
intoxicating drink,
They are swallowed
up by wine,
They are out of
the way through
intoxicating drink;
They err in vision, they
stumble *in* judgment.
8 For all tables are full
of vomit *and* filth;
No place *is clean.*

9 "Whom will he teach
knowledge?
And whom will he
make to understand
the message?
Those *just* weaned
from milk?
Those *just* drawn
from the breasts?
10 For precept *must be*
upon precept, precept
upon precept,
Line upon line, line
upon line,
Here a little, there a little."

11 For with stammering lips
and another tongue
He will speak to
this people,
12 To whom He said, "This
is the rest *with which*
You may cause the
weary to rest,"
And, "This *is* the
refreshing";
Yet they would not hear.
13 But the word of the
LORD was to them,
"Precept upon precept,
precept upon precept,
Line upon line, line
upon line,
Here a little, there a little,"
That they might go and fall
backward, and be broken
And snared and caught.

14 Therefore hear the
word of the LORD,
you scornful men,
Who rule this people
who *are* in Jerusalem,
15 Because you have said,
"We have made a
covenant with death,

And with Sheol we
are in agreement.
When the overflowing
scourge passes through,
It will not come to us,
For we have made
lies our refuge,
And under falsehood we
have hidden ourselves."

A CORNERSTONE IN ZION

16Therefore thus says the
Lord GOD:

"Behold, I lay in Zion a
stone for a foundation,
A tried stone, a precious
cornerstone, a sure
foundation;
Whoever believes will
not act hastily.
17 Also I will make justice
the measuring line,
And righteousness
the plummet;
The hail will sweep away
the refuge of lies,
And the waters
will overflow the
hiding place.
18 Your covenant with death
will be annulled,
And your agreement
with Sheol will
not stand;
When the overflowing
scourge passes through,
Then you will be
trampled down by it.
19 *As often as it* goes out
it will take you;
For morning by morning
it will pass over,
And by day and by night;
It will be a terror just to
understand the report."
20 For the bed is too short
to stretch out *on,*
And the covering so
narrow that one cannot
wrap himself *in it.*
21 For the LORD will rise up
as *at* Mount Perazim,
He will be angry as in the
Valley of Gibeon—
That He may do His work,
His awesome work,
And bring to pass His
act, His unusual act.
22 Now therefore, do
not be mockers,
Lest your bonds be
made strong;
For I have heard from
the Lord GOD of hosts,
A destruction determined
even upon the
whole earth.

LISTEN TO THE TEACHING OF GOD

23 Give ear and hear
my voice,
Listen and hear
my speech.
24 Does the plowman
keep plowing all
day to sow?
Does he keep turning
his soil and breaking
the clods?
25 When he has leveled
its surface,
Does he not sow the
black cummin
And scatter the cummin,
Plant the wheat in rows,

The barley in the
appointed place,
And the spelt in its place?
26 For He instructs him
in right judgment,
His God teaches him.

27 For the black cummin
is not threshed with
a threshing sledge,
Nor is a cartwheel rolled
over the cummin;
But the black cummin
is beaten out
with a stick,
And the cummin
with a rod.
28 Bread *flour* must
be ground;
Therefore he does not
thresh it forever,
Break *it with* his
cartwheel,
Or crush it *with* his
horsemen.
29 This also comes from
the LORD of hosts,
Who is wonderful in
counsel *and* excellent
in guidance.

WOE TO JERUSALEM

29 "Woe to Ariel,[a] to
Ariel, the city
where David dwelt!
Add year to year;
Let feasts come around.
2 Yet I will distress Ariel;
There shall be heaviness
and sorrow,
And it shall be to
Me as Ariel.
3 I will encamp against
you all around,
I will lay siege against
you with a mound,
And I will raise
siegeworks against you.
4 You shall be
brought down,
You shall speak out
of the ground;
Your speech shall be
low, out of the dust;
Your voice shall be
like a medium's, out
of the ground;
And your speech
shall whisper out
of the dust.

5 "Moreover the multitude
of your foes
Shall be like fine dust,
And the multitude of
the terrible ones
Like chaff that
passes away;
Yes, it shall be in an
instant, suddenly.
6 You will be punished by
the LORD of hosts
With thunder and
earthquake and
great noise,
With storm and tempest
And the flame of
devouring fire.
7 The multitude of all
the nations who
fight against Ariel,
Even all who fight against
her and her fortress,
And distress her,

29:1 [a] That is, Jerusalem

Shall be as a dream
of a night vision.
8 It shall even be as when
a hungry man dreams,
And look—he eats;
But he awakes, and his
soul is still empty;
Or as when a thirsty
man dreams,
And look—he drinks;
But he awakes, and
indeed *he is* faint,
And his soul still craves:
So the multitude of all
the nations shall be,
Who fight against
Mount Zion."

THE BLINDNESS OF DISOBEDIENCE

9 Pause and wonder!
Blind yourselves
and be blind!
They are drunk, but
not with wine;
They stagger, but not with
intoxicating drink.
10 For the LORD has
poured out on you
The spirit of deep sleep,
And has closed your eyes,
namely, the prophets;
And He has covered
your heads, *namely,*
the seers.

11The whole vision has become to you like the words of
a book that is sealed, which
men deliver to one who is
literate, saying, "Read this,
please."
And he says, "I cannot, for
it *is* sealed."
12Then the book is deliv-
ered to one who is illiterate,
saying, "Read this, please."
And he says, "I am not literate."
13Therefore the Lord said:

"Inasmuch as these
people draw near
with their mouths
And honor Me with
their lips,
But have removed their
hearts far from Me,
And their fear toward
Me is taught by the
commandment of men,
14 Therefore, behold,
I will again do a
marvelous work
Among this people,
A marvelous work
and a wonder;
For the wisdom of their
wise *men* shall perish,
And the understanding
of their prudent *men*
shall be hidden."

15 Woe to those who
seek deep to hide
their counsel far
from the LORD,
And their works are
in the dark;
They say, "Who sees us?"
and, "Who knows us?"
16 Surely you have things
turned around!
Shall the potter be
esteemed as the clay;
For shall the thing made
say of him who made it,
"He did not make me"?

Or shall the thing
formed say of him
who formed it,
"He has no
understanding"?

FUTURE RECOVERY OF WISDOM

17 *Is* it not yet a very
little while
Till Lebanon shall
be turned into a
fruitful field,
And the fruitful field be
esteemed as a forest?
18 In that day the deaf
shall hear the words
of the book,
And the eyes of the
blind shall see out
of obscurity and
out of darkness.
19 The humble also
shall increase *their*
joy in the LORD,
And the poor among
men shall rejoice
In the Holy One of Israel.
20 For the terrible one is
brought to nothing,
The scornful one
is consumed,
And all who watch for
iniquity are cut off—
21 Who make a man an
offender by a word,
And lay a snare for
him who reproves
in the gate,
And turn aside the just
by empty words.

22Therefore thus says the
LORD, who redeemed Abra-
ham, concerning the house
of Jacob:

"Jacob shall not now
be ashamed,
Nor shall his face
now grow pale;
23 But when he sees
his children,
The work of My hands,
in his midst,
They will hallow
My name,
And hallow the Holy
One of Jacob,
And fear the God
of Israel.
24 These also who erred
in spirit will come
to understanding,
And those who
complained will
learn doctrine."

FUTILE CONFIDENCE IN EGYPT

30 "Woe to the rebellious
children," says
the LORD,
"Who take counsel,
but not of Me,
And who devise plans,
but not of My Spirit,
That they may add
sin to sin;
2 Who walk to go
down to Egypt,
And have not asked
My advice,
To strengthen
themselves in the
strength of Pharaoh,
And to trust in the
shadow of Egypt!

3 Therefore the strength
of Pharaoh
Shall be your shame,
And trust in the
shadow of Egypt
Shall be *your* humiliation.
4 For his princes
were at Zoan,
And his ambassadors
came to Hanes.
5 They were all ashamed
of a people *who* could
not benefit them,
Or be help or benefit,
But a shame and
also a reproach."

6The burden against the beasts of the South.

Through a land of
trouble and anguish,
From which *came* the
lioness and lion,
The viper and fiery
flying serpent,
They will carry their
riches on the backs
of young donkeys,
And their treasures on
the humps of camels,
To a people *who*
shall not profit;
7 For the Egyptians shall
help in vain and
to no purpose.
Therefore I have called her
Rahab-Hem-Shebeth.[a]

A REBELLIOUS PEOPLE

8 Now go, write it before
them on a tablet,
And note it on a scroll,
That it may be for
time to come,
Forever and ever:
9 That this *is* a
rebellious people,
Lying children,
Children *who* will not hear
the law of the LORD;
10 Who say to the seers,
"Do not see,"
And to the prophets,
"Do not prophesy
to us right things;
Speak to us smooth
things, prophesy deceits.
11 Get out of the way,
Turn aside from the path,
Cause the Holy
One of Israel
To cease from before us."

12Therefore thus says the Holy One of Israel:

"Because you despise
this word,
And trust in oppression
and perversity,
And rely on them,
13 Therefore this iniquity
shall be to you
Like a breach ready to fall,
A bulge in a high wall,
Whose breaking comes
suddenly, in an instant.
14 And He shall break it
like the breaking of
the potter's vessel,
Which is broken
in pieces;
He shall not spare.

30:7 [a] Literally *Rahab Sits Idle*

So there shall not be found
among its fragments
A shard to take fire
from the hearth,
Or to take water from
the cistern."

15For thus says the Lord
GOD, the Holy One of Israel:

"In returning and rest
you shall be saved;
In quietness and
confidence shall be
your strength."
But you would not,
16 And you said, "No, for we
will flee on horses"—
Therefore you shall flee!
And, "We will ride on
swift *horses*"—
Therefore those
who pursue you
shall be swift!

17 One thousand *shall flee*
at the threat of one,
At the threat of five
you shall flee,
Till you are left as a pole
on top of a mountain
And as a banner on a hill.

GOD WILL BE GRACIOUS

18 Therefore the LORD
will wait, that He may
be gracious to you;
And therefore He will be
exalted, that He may
have mercy on you.
For the LORD *is* a
God of justice;
Blessed *are* all those
who wait for Him.

19 For the people shall dwell
in Zion at Jerusalem;
You shall weep no more.
He will be very gracious
to you at the sound
of your cry;
When He hears it, He
will answer you.
20 And *though* the
Lord gives you
The bread of adversity
and the water
of affliction,
Yet your teachers will
not be moved into a
corner anymore,
But your eyes shall
see your teachers.
21 Your ears shall hear
a word behind
you, saying,
"This *is* the way,
walk in it,"
Whenever you turn
to the right hand
Or whenever you
turn to the left.
22 You will also defile
the covering of your
images of silver,
And the ornament of your
molded images of gold.
You will throw them away
as an unclean thing;
You will say to them,
"Get away!"

23 Then He will give the
rain for your seed
With which you sow
the ground,
And bread of the
increase of the earth;
It will be fat and plentiful.

In that day your
cattle will feed
In large pastures.
24 Likewise the oxen and
the young donkeys
that work the ground
Will eat cured fodder,
Which has been winnowed
with the shovel and fan.
25 There will be on every
high mountain
And on every high hill
Rivers *and* streams
of waters,
In the day of the
great slaughter,
When the towers fall.
26 Moreover the light of
the moon will be as
the light of the sun,
And the light of the sun
will be sevenfold,
As the light of seven days,
In the day that the
LORD binds up the
bruise of His people
And heals the stroke
of their wound.

JUDGMENT ON ASSYRIA

27 Behold, the name of the
LORD comes from afar,
Burning *with* His anger,
And *His* burden *is* heavy;
His lips are full of
indignation,
And His tongue like
a devouring fire.
28 His breath is like an
overflowing stream,
Which reaches up
to the neck,
To sift the nations with
the sieve of futility;
And *there shall be* a
bridle in the jaws
of the people,
Causing *them* to err.

29 You shall have a song
As in the night *when* a
holy festival is kept,
And gladness of heart
as when one goes
with a flute,
To come into the
mountain of the
LORD,
To the Mighty One
of Israel.
30 The LORD will cause
His glorious voice
to be heard,
And show the descent
of His arm,
With the indignation
of *His* anger
And the flame of a
devouring fire,
With scattering, tempest,
and hailstones.
31 For through the voice
of the LORD
Assyria will be
beaten down,
As He strikes with the rod.
32 And *in* every place
where the staff of
punishment passes,
Which the LORD
lays on him,
It will be with
tambourines and harps;
And in battles of
brandishing He
will fight with it.
33 For Tophet *was*
established of old,

Yes, for the king it
is prepared.
He has made *it* deep
and large;
Its pyre *is* fire with
much wood;
The breath of the
LORD, like a stream
of brimstone,
Kindles it.

THE FOLLY OF NOT TRUSTING GOD

31 Woe to those who
go down to Egypt
for help,
And rely on horses,
Who trust in chariots
because *they are* many,
And in horsemen because
they are very strong,
But who do not look to
the Holy One of Israel,
Nor seek the LORD!
2 Yet He also *is* wise and
will bring disaster,
And will not call
back His words,
But will arise against the
house of evildoers,
And against the help of
those who work iniquity.
3 Now the Egyptians *are*
men, and not God;
And their horses are
flesh, and not spirit.
When the LORD stretches
out His hand,
Both he who helps
will fall,
And he who is helped
will fall down;
They all will perish
together.

GOD WILL DELIVER JERUSALEM

4For thus the LORD has spoken to me:

"As a lion roars,
And a young lion
over his prey
(When a multitude
of shepherds
is summoned
against him,
He will not be afraid
of their voice
Nor be disturbed
by their noise),
So the LORD of hosts
will come down
To fight for Mount Zion
and for its hill.
5 Like birds flying about,
So will the LORD of hosts
defend Jerusalem.
Defending, He will
also deliver *it;*
Passing over, He will
preserve *it.*"

6Return *to Him* against
whom the children of Israel
have deeply revolted. 7For
in that day every man shall
throw away his idols of silver
and his idols of gold—sin,
which your own hands have
made for yourselves.

8 "Then Assyria shall fall
by a sword not of man,
And a sword not
of mankind shall
devour him.
But he shall flee
from the sword,

And his young men shall
become forced labor.
9 He shall cross over to his
stronghold for fear,
And his princes shall be
afraid of the banner,"
Says the LORD,
Whose fire *is* in Zion
And whose furnace
is in Jerusalem.

A REIGN OF RIGHTEOUSNESS

32 Behold, a king
will reign in
righteousness,
And princes will rule
with justice.
2 A man will be as a hiding
place from the wind,
And a cover from
the tempest,
As rivers of water
in a dry place,
As the shadow of a great
rock in a weary land.
3 The eyes of those who
see will not be dim,
And the ears of those
who hear will listen.
4 Also the heart of the
rash will understand
knowledge,
And the tongue of the
stammerers will be
ready to speak plainly.

5 The foolish person
will no longer be
called generous,
Nor the miser said
to be bountiful;
6 For the foolish person
will speak foolishness,
And his heart will
work iniquity:
To practice ungodliness,
To utter error against
the LORD,
To keep the hungry
unsatisfied,
And he will cause
the drink of the
thirsty to fail.
7 Also the schemes of the
schemer *are* evil;
He devises wicked plans
To destroy the poor
with lying words,
Even when the needy
speaks justice.
8 But a generous man
devises generous things,
And by generosity
he shall stand.

CONSEQUENCES OF COMPLACENCY

9 Rise up, you women
who are at ease,
Hear my voice;
You complacent
daughters,
Give ear to my speech.
10 In a year and *some* days
You will be troubled, you
complacent women;
For the vintage will fail,
The gathering will
not come.
11 Tremble, you *women*
who are at ease;
Be troubled, you
complacent ones;
Strip yourselves, make
yourselves bare,
And gird *sackcloth*
on *your* waists.

12 People shall mourn
upon their breasts
For the pleasant fields,
for the fruitful vine.
13 On the land of my
people will come up
thorns *and* briers,
Yes, on all the happy
homes *in* the
joyous city;
14 Because the palaces
will be forsaken,
The bustling city will
be deserted.
The forts and towers
will become
lairs forever,
A joy of wild donkeys, a
pasture of flocks—
15 Until the Spirit is poured
upon us from on high,
And the wilderness
becomes a fruitful field,
And the fruitful field is
counted as a forest.

THE PEACE OF GOD'S REIGN

16 Then justice will dwell
in the wilderness,
And righteousness
remain in the
fruitful field.
17 The work of
righteousness
will be peace,
And the effect of
righteousness,
quietness and
assurance forever.
18 My people will dwell in
a peaceful habitation,
In secure dwellings, and
in quiet resting places,
19 Though hail comes
down on the forest,
And the city is brought
low in humiliation.

20 Blessed *are* you who sow
beside all waters,
Who send out freely
the feet of the ox
and the donkey.

A PRAYER IN DEEP DISTRESS

33 Woe to you who
plunder, though
you *have* not *been*
plundered;
And you who deal
treacherously, though
they have not dealt
treacherously with you!
When you cease
plundering,
You will be plundered;
When you make an end of
dealing treacherously,
They will deal
treacherously with you.

2 O LORD, be gracious to us;
We have waited for You.
Be their[a] arm every
morning,
Our salvation also in
the time of trouble.
3 At the noise of the tumult
the people shall flee;
When You lift Yourself
up, the nations shall
be scattered;

33:2 [a] Septuagint omits *their;* Syriac, Targum, and Vulgate read *our*.

4 And Your plunder
shall be gathered
Like the gathering of
the caterpillar;
As the running to and
fro of locusts,
He shall run upon them.

5 The LORD is exalted, for
He dwells on high;
He has filled Zion
with justice and
righteousness.
6 Wisdom and knowledge
will be the stability
of your times,
And the strength
of salvation;
The fear of the LORD
is His treasure.

7 Surely their valiant ones
shall cry outside,
The ambassadors of peace
shall weep bitterly.
8 The highways lie waste,
The traveling man ceases.
He has broken the
covenant,
He has despised
the cities,[a]
He regards no man.
9 The earth mourns
and languishes,
Lebanon is shamed
and shriveled;
Sharon is like a
wilderness,
And Bashan and Carmel
shake off *their fruits.*

IMPENDING JUDGMENT ON ZION

10 "Now I will rise,"
says the LORD;
"Now I will be exalted,
Now I will lift Myself up.
11 You shall conceive chaff,
You shall bring
forth stubble;
Your breath, *as* fire,
shall devour you.
12 And the people
shall be *like* the
burnings of lime;
Like thorns cut up
they shall be burned
in the fire.
13 Hear, you *who are* afar
off, what I have done;
And you *who are* near,
acknowledge My might."

14 The sinners in Zion
are afraid;
Fearfulness has seized
the hypocrites:
"Who among us
shall dwell with the
devouring fire?
Who among us shall
dwell with everlasting
burnings?"
15 He who walks righteously
and speaks uprightly,
He who despises the
gain of oppressions,
Who gestures with his
hands, refusing bribes,
Who stops his ears from
hearing of bloodshed,

33:8 [a] Following Masoretic Text and Vulgate; Dead Sea Scrolls read *witnesses;* Septuagint omits *cities;* Targum reads *They have been removed from their cities.*

And shuts his eyes
from seeing evil:
16 He will dwell on high;
His place of defense *will be* the fortress of rocks;
Bread will be given him,
His water *will be* sure.

THE LAND OF THE MAJESTIC KING

17 Your eyes will see the
King in His beauty;
They will see the land
that is very far off.
18 Your heart will
meditate on terror:
"Where *is* the scribe?
Where *is* he who weighs?
Where *is* he who counts
the towers?"
19 You will not see a
fierce people,
A people of obscure
speech, beyond
perception,
Of a stammering
tongue *that you*
cannot understand.

20 Look upon Zion, the city
of our appointed feasts;
Your eyes will see
Jerusalem, a
quiet home,
A tabernacle *that* will
not be taken down;
Not one of its stakes will
ever be removed,
Nor will any of its
cords be broken.
21 But there the majestic
LORD *will be* for us
A place of broad rivers
and streams,
In which no galley
with oars will sail,
Nor majestic ships pass by
22 (For the LORD *is* our Judge,
The LORD *is* our Lawgiver,
The LORD *is* our King;
He will save us);
23 Your tackle is loosed,
They could not
strengthen their mast,
They could not
spread the sail.

Then the prey of great
plunder is divided;
The lame take the prey.
24 And the inhabitant will
not say, "I am sick";
The people who dwell
in it *will be* forgiven
their iniquity.

JUDGMENT ON THE NATIONS

34 Come near, you
nations, to hear;
And heed, you people!
Let the earth hear, and
all that is in it,
The world and all things
that come forth from it.
2 For the indignation of
the LORD *is* against
all nations,
And *His* fury against
all their armies;
He has utterly
destroyed them,
He has given them over
to the slaughter.
3 Also their slain shall
be thrown out;
Their stench shall rise
from their corpses,

And the mountains
shall be melted
with their blood.
4 All the host of heaven
shall be dissolved,
And the heavens
shall be rolled up
like a scroll;
All their host shall
fall down
As the leaf falls
from the vine,
And as *fruit* falling
from a fig tree.

5 "For My sword shall be
bathed in heaven;
Indeed it shall come
down on Edom,
And on the people of My
curse, for judgment.
6 The sword of the LORD
is filled with blood,
It is made overflowing
with fatness,
With the blood of
lambs and goats,
With the fat of the
kidneys of rams.
For the LORD has a
sacrifice in Bozrah,
And a great slaughter
in the land of Edom.
7 The wild oxen shall come
down with them,
And the young bulls with
the mighty bulls;
Their land shall be
soaked with blood,
And their dust saturated
with fatness."

8 For *it is* the day of the
LORD's vengeance,
The year of recompense
for the cause of Zion.
9 Its streams shall be
turned into pitch,
And its dust into
brimstone;
Its land shall become
burning pitch.
10 It shall not be quenched
night or day;
Its smoke shall
ascend forever.
From generation
to generation it
shall lie waste;
No one shall pass through
it forever and ever.
11 But the pelican and
the porcupine
shall possess it,
Also the owl and the
raven shall dwell in it.
And He shall stretch
out over it
The line of confusion and
the stones of emptiness.
12 They shall call its nobles
to the kingdom,
But none *shall be* there,
and all its princes
shall be nothing.

13 And thorns shall come
up in its palaces,
Nettles and brambles
in its fortresses;
It shall be a habitation
of jackals,
A courtyard for ostriches.
14 The wild beasts of the
desert shall also meet
with the jackals,
And the wild goat shall
bleat to its companion;

Also the night creature
shall rest there,
And find for herself
a place of rest.
15 There the arrow snake
shall make her nest
and lay *eggs*
And hatch, and gather
them under her shadow;
There also shall the
hawks be gathered,
Every one with her mate.

16 "Search from the book of
the LORD, and read:
Not one of these shall fail;
Not one shall lack
her mate.
For My mouth has
commanded it,
and His Spirit has
gathered them.
17 He has cast the
lot for them,
And His hand has divided
it among them with
a measuring line.
They shall possess
it forever;
From generation to
generation they
shall dwell in it."

THE FUTURE GLORY OF ZION

35 The wilderness and
the wasteland shall
be glad for them,
And the desert shall
rejoice and blossom
as the rose;
2 It shall blossom
abundantly and rejoice,
Even with joy and singing.
The glory of Lebanon
shall be given to it,
The excellence of
Carmel and Sharon.
They shall see the
glory of the LORD,
The excellency of our God.

3 Strengthen the
weak hands,
And make firm the
feeble knees.
4 Say to those *who are*
fearful-hearted,
"Be strong, do not fear!
Behold, your God will
come *with* vengeance,
With the recompense
of God;
He will come and
save you."

5 Then the eyes of the
blind shall be opened,
And the ears of the deaf
shall be unstopped.
6 Then the lame shall
leap like a deer,
And the tongue of
the dumb sing.
For waters shall burst
forth in the wilderness,
And streams in the desert.
7 The parched ground
shall become a pool,
And the thirsty land
springs of water;
In the habitation of
jackals, where each lay,
There shall be grass with
reeds and rushes.

8 A highway shall be
there, and a road,

And it shall be called the
Highway of Holiness.
The unclean shall
not pass over it,
But it *shall be* for others.
Whoever walks the road,
although a fool,
Shall not go astray.
9 No lion shall be there,
Nor shall *any* ravenous
beast go up on it;
It shall not be found there.
But the redeemed
shall walk *there,*
10 And the ransomed of the
LORD shall return,
And come to Zion
with singing,
With everlasting joy
on their heads.
They shall obtain joy
and gladness,
And sorrow and sighing
shall flee away.

SENNACHERIB BOASTS AGAINST THE LORD

36 Now it came to pass in
the fourteenth year of
King Hezekiah *that* Sennacherib king of Assyria came up
against all the fortified cities of Judah and took them.
[2]Then the king of Assyria sent
the Rabshakeh[a] with a great
army from Lachish to King
Hezekiah at Jerusalem. And
he stood by the aqueduct from
the upper pool, on the high-
way to the Fuller's Field. [3]And
Eliakim the son of Hilkiah,
who was over the household,
Shebna the scribe, and Joah
the son of Asaph, the recorder,
came out to him.
[4]Then *the* Rabshakeh said
to them, "Say now to Hezekiah,
'Thus says the great king, the
king of Assyria: "What confidence is this in which you
trust? [5]I say you speak of having plans and power for war;
but *they are* mere words. Now
in whom do you trust, that you
rebel against me? [6]Look! You
are trusting in the staff of this
broken reed, Egypt, on which
if a man leans, it will go into
his hand and pierce it. So *is*
Pharaoh king of Egypt to all
who trust in him.
[7]"But if you say to me, 'We
trust in the LORD our God,' *is it*
not He whose high places and
whose altars Hezekiah has
taken away, and said to Judah
and Jerusalem, 'You shall worship before this altar'?"' [8]Now
therefore, I urge you, give a
pledge to my master the king
of Assyria, and I will give you
two thousand horses—if you
are able on your part to put
riders on them! [9]How then
will you repel one captain of
the least of my master's servants, and put your trust in
Egypt for chariots and horsemen? [10]Have I now come up
without the LORD against this
land to destroy it? The LORD
said to me, 'Go up against this
land, and destroy it.'"
[11]Then Eliakim, Shebna, and

36:2 [a] A title, probably *Chief of Staff* or *Governor*

Joah said to *the* Rabshakeh,
"Please speak to your servants
in Aramaic, for we understand
it; and do not speak to us in
Hebrew[a] in the hearing of the
people who *are* on the wall."
12But *the* Rabshakeh said,
"Has my master sent me to
your master and to you to
speak these words, and not
to the men who sit on the wall,
who will eat and drink their
own waste with you?"
13Then *the* Rabshakeh stood
and called out with a loud voice
in Hebrew, and said, "Hear the
words of the great king, the
king of Assyria! 14Thus says
the king: 'Do not let Hezekiah
deceive you, for he will not be
able to deliver you; 15nor let
Hezekiah make you trust in
the LORD, saying, "The LORD
will surely deliver us; this city
will not be given into the hand
of the king of Assyria."' 16Do
not listen to Hezekiah; for
thus says the king of Assyria:
'Make *peace* with me *by a* present and come out to me; and
every one of you eat from his
own vine and every one from
his own fig tree, and every one
of you drink the waters of his
own cistern; 17until I come
and take you away to a land
like your own land, a land of
grain and new wine, a land of
bread and vineyards. 18*Beware*
lest Hezekiah persuade you,
saying, "The LORD will deliver
us." Has any one of the gods of
the nations delivered its land
from the hand of the king of
Assyria? 19Where *are* the gods
of Hamath and Arpad? Where
are the gods of Sepharvaim?
Indeed, have they delivered
Samaria from my hand? 20Who
among all the gods of these
lands have delivered their
countries from my hand, that
the LORD should deliver Jerusalem from my hand?"'"
21But they held their peace
and answered him not a word;
for the king's commandment
was, "Do not answer him."
22Then Eliakim the son of Hilkiah, who *was* over the household, Shebna the scribe, and
Joah the son of Asaph, the recorder, came to Hezekiah with
their clothes torn, and told him
the words of *the* Rabshakeh.

ISAIAH ASSURES DELIVERANCE

37 And so it was, when King
Hezekiah heard *it,* that
he tore his clothes, covered
himself with sackcloth, and
went into the house of the
LORD. 2Then he sent Eliakim,
who *was* over the household,
Shebna the scribe, and the
elders of the priests, covered
with sackcloth, to Isaiah the
prophet, the son of Amoz.
3And they said to him, "Thus
says Hezekiah: 'This day *is* a
day of trouble and rebuke and
blasphemy; for the children
have come to birth, but *there*

36:11 [a] Literally *Judean*

is no strength to bring them
forth. 4It may be that the LORD
your God will hear the words of
the Rabshakeh, whom his master the king of Assyria has sent
to reproach the living God, and
will rebuke the words which
the LORD your God has heard.
Therefore lift up *your* prayer
for the remnant that is left.'"

5So the servants of King
Hezekiah came to Isaiah. 6And
Isaiah said to them, "Thus
you shall say to your master,
'Thus says the LORD: "Do not
be afraid of the words which
you have heard, with which the
servants of the king of Assyria
have blasphemed Me. 7Surely
I will send a spirit upon him,
and he shall hear a rumor and
return to his own land; and I
will cause him to fall by the
sword in his own land."'"

SENNACHERIB'S THREAT AND HEZEKIAH'S PRAYER

8Then *the* Rabshakeh re-
turned, and found the king of
Assyria warring against Libnah, for he heard that he had
departed from Lachish. 9And
the king heard concerning Tir-
hakah king of Ethiopia, "He
has come out to make war with
you." So when he heard *it,* he
sent messengers to Hezekiah,
saying, 10"Thus you shall speak
to Hezekiah king of Judah,
saying: 'Do not let your God
in whom you trust deceive you,
saying, "Jerusalem shall not be
given into the hand of the king
of Assyria." 11Look! You have
heard what the kings of Assyria have done to all lands by
utterly destroying them; and
shall you be delivered? 12Have
the gods of the nations delivered those whom my fathers
have destroyed, Gozan and
Haran and Rezeph, and the
people of Eden who *were* in
Telassar? 13Where *is* the king
of Hamath, the king of Arpad,
and the king of the city of
Sepharvaim, Hena, and Ivah?'"

14And Hezekiah received
the letter from the hand of
the messengers, and read it;
and Hezekiah went up to the
house of the LORD, and spread
it before the LORD. 15Then Hezekiah prayed to the LORD, saying: 16"O LORD of hosts, God
of Israel, *the One* who dwells
between the cherubim, You
are God, You alone, of all the
kingdoms of the earth. You
have made heaven and earth.
17Incline Your ear, O LORD, and
hear; open Your eyes, O LORD,
and see; and hear all the words
of Sennacherib, which he has
sent to reproach the living
God. 18Truly, LORD, the kings
of Assyria have laid waste all
the nations and their lands,
19and have cast their gods into
the fire; for they *were* not gods,
but the work of men's hands—
wood and stone. Therefore
they destroyed them. 20Now
therefore, O LORD our God,
save us from his hand, that all
the kingdoms of the earth may
know that You *are* the LORD,
You alone."

THE WORD OF THE LORD CONCERNING SENNACHERIB

21Then Isaiah the son of
Amoz sent to Hezekiah, saying, "Thus says the LORD God
of Israel, 'Because you have
prayed to Me against Sennacherib king of Assyria, 22this *is*
the word which the LORD has
spoken concerning him:

"The virgin, the
daughter of Zion,
Has despised you,
laughed you to scorn;
The daughter of Jerusalem
Has shaken *her* head
behind your back!

23"Whom have you
reproached and
blasphemed?
Against whom have you
raised *your* voice,
And lifted up your
eyes on high?
Against the Holy
One of Israel.
24 By your servants you have
reproached the Lord,
And said, 'By the
multitude of
my chariots
I have come up to
the height of the
mountains,
To the limits of Lebanon;
I will cut down its
tall cedars
And its choice
cypress trees;
I will enter its
farthest height,
To its fruitful forest.
25 I have dug and
drunk water,
And with the soles of my
feet I have dried up
All the brooks of defense.'

26"Did you not hear long ago
How I made it,
From ancient times
that I formed it?
Now I have brought
it to pass,
That you should be
For crushing fortified
cities *into* heaps
of ruins.
27 Therefore their
inhabitants *had*
little power;
They were dismayed
and confounded;
They were *as* the
grass of the field
And the green herb,
As the grass on the
housetops
And *grain* blighted
before it is grown.

28"But I know your
dwelling place,
Your going out and
your coming in,
And your rage against Me.
29 Because your rage against
Me and your tumult
Have come up to My ears,
Therefore I will put My
hook in your nose
And My bridle in your lips,
And I will turn you back
By the way which
you came."'

30"This *shall be* a sign to you:

You shall eat this year
such as grows of itself,
And the second year
what springs from
the same;
Also in the third year
sow and reap,
Plant vineyards and eat
the fruit of them.
31 And the remnant who
have escaped of the
house of Judah
Shall again take root
downward,
And bear fruit upward.
32 For out of Jerusalem
shall go a remnant,
And those who escape
from Mount Zion.
The zeal of the LORD of
hosts will do this.

33"Therefore thus says the LORD concerning the king of Assyria:

'He shall not come
into this city,
Nor shoot an arrow there,
Nor come before it
with shield,
Nor build a siege
mound against it.
34 By the way that he came,
By the same shall
he return;
And he shall not come
into this city,'
Says the LORD.
35 'For I will defend this
city, to save it
For My own sake
and for My servant
David's sake.'"

SENNACHERIB'S DEFEAT AND DEATH

36Then the angel[a] of the
LORD went out, and killed in
the camp of the Assyrians one
hundred and eighty-five thousand; and when *people* arose
early in the morning, there
were the corpses—all dead.
37So Sennacherib king of Assyria departed and went away,
returned *home,* and remained
at Nineveh. 38Now it came to
pass, as he was worshiping
in the house of Nisroch his
god, that his sons Adrammelech and Sharezer struck him
down with the sword; and they
escaped into the land of Ararat. Then Esarhaddon his son
reigned in his place.

HEZEKIAH'S LIFE EXTENDED

38 In those days Heze-
kiah was sick and near
death. And Isaiah the prophet,
the son of Amoz, went to him
and said to him, "Thus says
the LORD: 'Set your house in
order, for you shall die and
not live.'"

2Then Hezekiah turned
his face toward the wall, and
prayed to the LORD, 3and said,
"Remember now, O LORD, I
pray, how I have walked before

37:36 [a] Or *Angel*

You in truth and with a loyal
heart, and have done *what is*
good in Your sight." And Hezekiah wept bitterly.
4And the word of the LORD
came to Isaiah, saying, 5"Go
and tell Hezekiah, 'Thus says
the LORD, the God of David
your father: "I have heard your
prayer, I have seen your tears;
surely I will add to your days
fifteen years. 6I will deliver you
and this city from the hand of
the king of Assyria, and I will
defend this city."' 7And this *is*
the sign to you from the LORD,
that the LORD will do this thing
which He has spoken: 8Behold,
I will bring the shadow on the
sundial, which has gone down
with the sun on the sundial of
Ahaz, ten degrees backward."
So the sun returned ten degrees on the dial by which it
had gone down.
9This is the writing of Hezekiah king of Judah, when he
had been sick and had recovered from his sickness:

10 I said,
"In the prime of my life
I shall go to the
gates of Sheol;
I am deprived of the
remainder of my years."
11 I said,
"I shall not see YAH,
The LORD[a] in the
land of the living;
I shall observe man
no more among
the inhabitants
of the world.[b]
12 My life span is gone,
Taken from me like a
shepherd's tent;
I have cut off my life
like a weaver.
He cuts me off from
the loom;
From day until night You
make an end of me.
13 I have considered
until morning—
Like a lion,
So He breaks all
my bones;
From day until night
You make an end
of me.
14 Like a crane *or* a swallow,
so I chattered;
I mourned like a dove;
My eyes fail *from*
looking upward.
O LORD,[a] I am oppressed;
Undertake for me!

15 "What shall I say?
He has both spoken
to me,[a]
And He Himself
has done *it*.

38:11 [a] Hebrew *YAH, YAH* [b] Following some Hebrew manuscripts; Masoretic Text and Vulgate read *rest;* Septuagint omits *among the inhabitants of the world;* Targum reads *land.* **38:14** [a] Following Bomberg; Masoretic Text and Dead Sea Scrolls read *Lord.* **38:15** [a] Following Masoretic Text and Vulgate; Dead Sea Scrolls and Targum read *And shall I say to Him;* Septuagint omits first half of this verse.

I shall walk carefully
all my years
In the bitterness
of my soul.
16 O Lord, by these
things men live;
And in all these *things is*
the life of my spirit;
So You will restore me
and make me live.
17 Indeed *it was* for
my own peace
That I had great
bitterness;
But You have lovingly
delivered my soul from
the pit of corruption,
For You have cast all my
sins behind Your back.
18 For Sheol cannot
thank You,
Death cannot praise You;
Those who go down to
the pit cannot hope
for Your truth.
19 The living, the living man,
he shall praise You,
As I *do* this day;
The father shall make
known Your truth
to the children.

20 "The LORD *was*
ready to save me;
Therefore we will
sing my songs with
stringed instruments
All the days of our life, in
the house of the LORD."

21 Now Isaiah had said, "Let
them take a lump of figs, and
apply *it* as a poultice on the
boil, and he shall recover."
22 And Hezekiah had said,
"What *is* the sign that I shall
go up to the house of the
LORD?"

THE BABYLONIAN ENVOYS

39 At that time Merodach-
Baladan[a] the son of
Baladan, king of Babylon, sent
letters and a present to Hezekiah, for he heard that he had
been sick and had recovered.
2 And Hezekiah was pleased
with them, and showed them
the house of his treasures—
the silver and gold, the spices
and precious ointment, and
all his armory—all that was
found among his treasures.
There was nothing in his
house or in all his dominion
that Hezekiah did not show
them.
3 Then Isaiah the prophet
went to King Hezekiah, and
said to him, "What did these
men say, and from where did
they come to you?"
So Hezekiah said, "They
came to me from a far country, from Babylon."
4 And he said, "What have
they seen in your house?"
So Hezekiah answered,
"They have seen all that *is* in
my house; there is nothing
among my treasures that I
have not shown them."
5 Then Isaiah said to Hezekiah, "Hear the word of the

39:1 [a] Spelled *Berodach-Baladan* in 2 Kings 20:12

LORD of hosts: [6]'Behold, the
days are coming when all that
is in your house, and what
your fathers have accumu-
lated until this day, shall be
carried to Babylon; nothing
shall be left,' says the LORD.
[7]'And they shall take away
some of your sons who will
descend from you, whom you
will beget; and they shall be
eunuchs in the palace of the
king of Babylon.'"

[8]So Hezekiah said to Isaiah,
"The word of the LORD which
you have spoken *is* good!" For
he said, "At least there will be
peace and truth in my days."

GOD'S PEOPLE ARE COMFORTED

40 "Comfort, yes, comfort
My people!"
Says your God.
2 "Speak comfort to
Jerusalem, and
cry out to her,
That her warfare is ended,
That her iniquity
is pardoned;
For she has received
from the LORD's hand
Double for all her sins."

3 The voice of one crying
in the wilderness:
"Prepare the way
of the LORD;
Make straight in
the desert[a]
A highway for our God.
4 Every valley shall
be exalted
And every mountain
and hill brought low;
The crooked places shall
be made straight
And the rough
places smooth;
5 The glory of the LORD
shall be revealed,
And all flesh shall
see *it* together;
For the mouth of the
LORD has spoken."

6 The voice said, "Cry out!"
And he[a] said, "What
shall I cry?"

"All flesh *is* grass,
And all its loveliness
is like the flower
of the field.
7 The grass withers,
the flower fades,
Because the breath of the
LORD blows upon it;
Surely the people
are grass.
8 The grass withers,
the flower fades,
But the word of our
God stands forever."

9 O Zion,
You who bring
good tidings,
Get up into the high
mountain;

40:3 [a] Following Masoretic Text, Targum, and Vulgate; Septuagint omits *in the desert*. 40:6 [a] Following Masoretic Text and Targum; Dead Sea Scrolls, Septuagint, and Vulgate read *I*.

O Jerusalem,
You who bring
good tidings,
Lift up your voice
with strength,
Lift *it* up, be not afraid;
Say to the cities of Judah,
"Behold your God!"

10 Behold, the Lord GOD
shall come with
a strong *hand,*
And His arm shall
rule for Him;
Behold, His reward
is with Him,
And His work before Him.
11 He will feed His flock
like a shepherd;
He will gather the
lambs with His arm,
And carry *them* in
His bosom,
And gently lead those
who are with young.

12 Who has measured
the waters[a] in the
hollow of His hand,
Measured heaven
with a span
And calculated the dust of
the earth in a measure?
Weighed the mountains
in scales
And the hills in
a balance?
13 Who has directed the
Spirit of the LORD,
Or as His counselor
has taught Him?
14 With whom did He take
counsel, and *who*
instructed Him,
And taught Him in the
path of justice?
Who taught Him
knowledge,
And showed Him the way
of understanding?

15 Behold, the nations *are*
as a drop in a bucket,
And are counted as the
small dust on the scales;
Look, He lifts up the isles
as a very little thing.
16 And Lebanon *is* not
sufficient to burn,
Nor its beasts sufficient
for a burnt offering.
17 All nations before Him
are as nothing,
And they are counted by
Him less than nothing
and worthless.

18 To whom then will
you liken God?
Or what likeness will you
compare to Him?
19 The workman molds
an image,
The goldsmith
overspreads it with gold,
And the silversmith
casts silver chains.
20 Whoever *is* too
impoverished for
such a contribution
Chooses a tree *that*
will not rot;

40:12 [a] Following Masoretic Text, Septuagint, and Vulgate; Dead Sea Scrolls read *waters of the sea;* Targum reads *waters of the world.*

He seeks for himself a
skillful workman
To prepare a carved image
that will not totter.

21 Have you not known?
Have you not heard?
Has it not been told you
from the beginning?
Have you not understood
from the foundations
of the earth?
22 *It is* He who sits above
the circle of the earth,
And its inhabitants *are*
like grasshoppers,
Who stretches out the
heavens like a curtain,
And spreads them out
like a tent to dwell in.
23 He brings the princes
to nothing;
He makes the judges of
the earth useless.

24 Scarcely shall they
be planted,
Scarcely shall they
be sown,
Scarcely shall their stock
take root in the earth,
When He will also
blow on them,
And they will wither,
And the whirlwind
will take them away
like stubble.

25 "To whom then will
you liken Me,
Or *to whom* shall I
be equal?" says
the Holy One.
26 Lift up your eyes on high,
And see who has
created these *things,*
Who brings out their
host by number;
He calls them all by name,
By the greatness
of His might
And the strength
of *His* power;
Not one is missing.

27 Why do you say, O Jacob,
And speak, O Israel:
"My way is hidden
from the LORD,
And my just claim is
passed over by my God"?
28 Have you not known?
Have you not heard?
The everlasting
God, the LORD,
The Creator of the
ends of the earth,
Neither faints nor is weary.
His understanding
is unsearchable.
29 He gives power
to the weak,
And to *those who
have* no might He
increases strength.
30 Even the youths shall
faint and be weary,
And the young men
shall utterly fall,
31 But those who wait
on the LORD
Shall renew *their* strength;
They shall mount up
with wings like eagles,
They shall run and
not be weary,
They shall walk
and not faint.

ISRAEL ASSURED OF GOD'S HELP

41 "Keep silence before
Me, O coastlands,
And let the people
renew *their* strength!
Let them come near,
then let them speak;
Let us come near
together for judgment.

2 "Who raised up one
from the east?
Who in righteousness
called him to His feet?
Who gave the nations
before him,
And made *him* rule
over kings?
Who gave *them* as the
dust *to* his sword,
As driven stubble
to his bow?
3 Who pursued them,
and passed safely
By the way *that* he had
not gone with his feet?
4 Who has performed
and done *it*,
Calling the generations
from the beginning?
'I, the LORD, am the first;
And with the last
I *am* He.'"

5 The coastlands saw
it and feared,
The ends of the earth
were afraid;
They drew near and came.
6 Everyone helped
his neighbor,
And said to his brother,
"Be of good courage!"
7 So the craftsman
encouraged the
goldsmith;
He who smooths *with* the
hammer *inspired* him
who strikes the anvil,
Saying, "It *is* ready for
the soldering";
Then he fastened
it with pegs,
That it might not totter.

8 "But you, Israel, *are*
My servant,
Jacob whom I
have chosen,
The descendants of
Abraham My friend.
9 *You* whom I have
taken from the
ends of the earth,
And called from its
farthest regions,
And said to you,
'You *are* My servant,
I have chosen you and
have not cast you away:
10 Fear not, for I *am*
with you;
Be not dismayed, for
I *am* your God.
I will strengthen you,
Yes, I will help you,
I will uphold you with My
righteous right hand.'

11 "Behold, all those
who were incensed
against you
Shall be ashamed
and disgraced;
They shall be as nothing,
And those who strive
with you shall perish.

12 You shall seek them
and not find them—
Those who contended
with you.
Those who war
against you
Shall be as nothing,
As a nonexistent thing.
13 For I, the LORD your
God, will hold your
right hand,
Saying to you, 'Fear
not, I will help you.'

14 "Fear not, you worm
Jacob,
You men of Israel!
I will help you,"
says the LORD
And your Redeemer, the
Holy One of Israel.
15 "Behold, I will make you
into a new threshing
sledge with sharp teeth;
You shall thresh the
mountains and
beat *them* small,
And make the hills
like chaff.
16 You shall winnow
them, the wind shall
carry them away,
And the whirlwind
shall scatter them;
You shall rejoice
in the LORD,
And glory in the Holy
One of Israel.

17 "The poor and needy
seek water, but
there is none,
Their tongues fail
for thirst.
I, the LORD, will
hear them;
I, the God of Israel, will
not forsake them.
18 I will open rivers in
desolate heights,
And fountains in the
midst of the valleys;
I will make the wilderness
a pool of water,
And the dry land
springs of water.
19 I will plant in the
wilderness the cedar
and the acacia tree,
The myrtle and
the oil tree;
I will set in the desert
the cypress tree
and the pine
And the box tree together,
20 That they may see
and know,
And consider and
understand together,
That the hand of the
LORD has done this,
And the Holy One of
Israel has created it.

THE FUTILITY OF IDOLS

21 "Present your case,"
says the LORD.
"Bring forth your strong
reasons," says the
King of Jacob.
22 "Let them bring forth
and show us what
will happen;
Let them show the
former things,
what they *were,*
That we may
consider them,

And know the latter
end of them;
Or declare to us
things to come.
23 Show the things that are
to come hereafter,
That we may know
that you *are* gods;
Yes, do good or do evil,
That we may be dismayed
and see *it* together.
24 Indeed you *are* nothing,
And your work *is* nothing;
He who chooses you *is*
an abomination.

25 "I have raised up one
from the north,
And he shall come;
From the rising of
the sun he shall
call on My name;
And he shall come
against princes as
though mortar,
As the potter treads clay.
26 Who has declared from
the beginning, that
we may know?
And former times,
that we may say,
'*He is* righteous'?
Surely *there is* no
one who shows,
Surely *there is* no one
who declares,
Surely *there is* no one
who hears your words.
27 The first time *I*
said to Zion,
'Look, there they are!'
And I will give to
Jerusalem one who
brings good tidings.
28 For I looked, and *there*
was no man;
I looked among them, but
there was no counselor,
Who, when I asked
of them, could
answer a word.
29 Indeed they *are* all
worthless;[a]
Their works *are* nothing;
Their molded images *are*
wind and confusion.

THE SERVANT OF THE LORD

42 "Behold! My Servant
whom I uphold,
My Elect One *in whom*
My soul delights!
I have put My Spirit
upon Him;
He will bring forth
justice to the Gentiles.
2 He will not cry out,
nor raise *His voice,*
Nor cause His voice to
be heard in the street.
3 A bruised reed He
will not break,
And smoking flax He
will not quench;
He will bring forth
justice for truth.
4 He will not fail nor
be discouraged,
Till He has established
justice in the earth;
And the coastlands shall
wait for His law."

41:29 [a] Following Masoretic Text and Vulgate; Dead Sea Scrolls, Syriac, and Targum read *nothing;* Septuagint omits the first line.

5 Thus says God the LORD,
Who created the heavens
and stretched them out,
Who spread forth the
earth and that which
comes from it,
Who gives breath to
the people on it,
And spirit to those
who walk on it:
6 "I, the LORD, have called
You in righteousness,
And will hold Your hand;
I will keep You and give
You as a covenant
to the people,
As a light to the Gentiles,
7 To open blind eyes,
To bring out prisoners
from the prison,
Those who sit in darkness
from the prison house.
8 I *am* the LORD, that
is My name;
And My glory I will not
give to another,
Nor My praise to
carved images.
9 Behold, the former things
have come to pass,
And new things I declare;
Before they spring forth
I tell you of them."

PRAISE TO THE LORD

10 Sing to the LORD
a new song,
And His praise from the
ends of the earth,
You who go down to
the sea, and all
that is in it,
You coastlands and you
inhabitants of them!
11 Let the wilderness and
its cities lift up
their voice,
The villages *that*
Kedar inhabits.
Let the inhabitants
of Sela sing,
Let them shout from the
top of the mountains.
12 Let them give glory
to the LORD,
And declare His praise
in the coastlands.
13 The LORD shall go forth
like a mighty man;
He shall stir up *His* zeal
like a man of war.
He shall cry out, yes,
shout aloud;
He shall prevail against
His enemies.

PROMISE OF THE LORD'S HELP

14 "I have held My peace
a long time,
I have been still and
restrained Myself.
Now I will cry like a
woman in labor,
I will pant and
gasp at once.
15 I will lay waste the
mountains and hills,
And dry up all their
vegetation;
I will make the rivers
coastlands,
And I will dry up
the pools.
16 I will bring the blind by a
way they did not know;
I will lead them in paths
they have not known.

I will make darkness
light before them,
And crooked places
straight.
These things I will
do for them,
And not forsake them.
17 They shall be turned
back,
They shall be greatly
ashamed,
Who trust in carved
images,
Who say to the
molded images,
'You *are* our gods.'

18 "Hear, you deaf;
And look, you blind,
that you may see.
19 Who *is* blind but
My servant,
Or deaf as My messenger
whom I send?
Who *is* blind as *he*
who is perfect,
And blind as the
LORD's servant?
20 Seeing many things, but
you do not observe;
Opening the ears, but
he does not hear."

ISRAEL'S OBSTINATE DISOBEDIENCE

21 The LORD is well
pleased for His
righteousness' sake;
He will exalt the law and
make *it* honorable.
22 But this *is* a people
robbed and plundered;
All of them are
snared in holes,
And they are hidden
in prison houses;
They are for prey, and
no one delivers;
For plunder, and no
one says, "Restore!"

23 Who among you will
give ear to this?
Who will listen and hear
for the time to come?
24 Who gave Jacob for
plunder, and Israel
to the robbers?
Was it not the LORD,
He against whom we
have sinned?
For they would not
walk in His ways,
Nor were they obedient
to His law.
25 Therefore He has
poured on him the
fury of His anger
And the strength
of battle;
It has set him on
fire all around,
Yet he did not know;
And it burned him,
Yet he did not take
it to heart.

THE REDEEMER OF ISRAEL

43 But now, thus says the
LORD, who created
you, O Jacob,
And He who formed
you, O Israel:
"Fear not, for I have
redeemed you;
I have called *you*
by your name;
You *are* Mine.

2 When you pass through
the waters, I *will*
be with you;
And through the
rivers, they shall
not overflow you.
When you walk through
the fire, you shall
not be burned,
Nor shall the flame
scorch you.
3 For I *am* the LORD
your God,
The Holy One of Israel,
your Savior;
I gave Egypt for
your ransom,
Ethiopia and Seba
in your place.
4 Since you were precious
in My sight,
You have been honored,
And I have loved you;
Therefore I will give
men for you,
And people for your life.
5 Fear not, for I *am*
with you;
I will bring your
descendants
from the east,
And gather you
from the west;
6 I will say to the north,
'Give them up!'
And to the south, 'Do
not keep them back!'
Bring My sons from afar,
And My daughters from
the ends of the earth—
7 Everyone who is called
by My name,
Whom I have created
for My glory;
I have formed him, yes,
I have made him."

8 Bring out the blind
people who have eyes,
And the deaf who
have ears.
9 Let all the nations be
gathered together,
And let the people
be assembled.
Who among them
can declare this,
And show us former
things?
Let them bring out their
witnesses, that they
may be justified;
Or let them hear and
say, "*It is* truth."
10 "You *are* My witnesses,"
says the LORD,
"And My servant whom
I have chosen,
That you may know
and believe Me,
And understand
that I *am* He.
Before Me there was
no God formed,
Nor shall there
be after Me.
11 I, *even* I, *am* the LORD,
And besides Me *there*
is no savior.
12 I have declared
and saved,
I have proclaimed,
And *there was* no foreign
god among you;
Therefore you *are*
My witnesses,"
Says the LORD, "that
I *am* God.

13 Indeed before the
day *was,* I *am* He;
And *there is* no one
who can deliver
out of My hand;
I work, and who will
reverse it?"

14 Thus says the LORD,
your Redeemer,
The Holy One of Israel:
"For your sake I will
send to Babylon,
And bring them all
down as fugitives—
The Chaldeans, who
rejoice in their ships.
15 I *am* the LORD, your
Holy One,
The Creator of Israel,
your King."

16 Thus says the LORD,
who makes a way
in the sea
And a path through
the mighty waters,
17 Who brings forth the
chariot and horse,
The army and the power
(They shall lie down
together, they
shall not rise;
They are extinguished,
they are quenched
like a wick):
18 "Do not remember the
former things,
Nor consider the
things of old.
19 Behold, I will do
a new thing,
Now it shall spring
forth;
Shall you not know it?
I will even make a road
in the wilderness
And rivers in the desert.
20 The beast of the field
will honor Me,
The jackals and
the ostriches,
Because I give waters
in the wilderness
And rivers in the desert,
To give drink to My
people, My chosen.
21 This people I have
formed for Myself;
They shall declare
My praise.

PLEADING WITH UNFAITHFUL ISRAEL

22 "But you have not called
upon Me, O Jacob;
And you have been
weary of Me, O Israel.
23 You have not brought
Me the sheep for your
burnt offerings,
Nor have you honored Me
with your sacrifices.
I have not caused
you to serve with
grain offerings,
Nor wearied you
with incense.
24 You have bought Me
no sweet cane
with money,
Nor have you satisfied
Me with the fat of
your sacrifices;
But you have burdened
Me with your sins,
You have wearied Me
with your iniquities.

25"I, *even* I, *am* He who blots
out your transgressions
for My own sake;
And I will not remember
your sins.
26 Put Me in remembrance;
Let us contend together;
State your *case,* that you
may be acquitted.
27 Your first father sinned,
And your mediators
have transgressed
against Me.
28 Therefore I will
profane the princes
of the sanctuary;
I will give Jacob
to the curse,
And Israel to reproaches.

GOD'S BLESSING ON ISRAEL

44 "Yet hear now, O Jacob
My servant,
And Israel whom I
have chosen.
2 Thus says the LORD
who made you
And formed you from
the womb, *who*
will help you:
'Fear not, O Jacob
My servant;
And you, Jeshurun,
whom I have chosen.
3 For I will pour water on
him who is thirsty,
And floods on the
dry ground;
I will pour My Spirit on
your descendants,
And My blessing on
your offspring;
4 They will spring up
among the grass
Like willows by the
watercourses.'
5 One will say, 'I *am*
the LORD's';
Another will call *himself*
by the name of Jacob;
Another will write *with*
his hand, 'The LORD's,'
And name *himself* by
the name of Israel.

THERE IS NO OTHER GOD

6 "Thus says the LORD,
the King of Israel,
And his Redeemer,
the LORD of hosts:
'I *am* the First and
I *am* the Last;
Besides Me *there is* no God.
7 And who can
proclaim as I do?
Then let him declare
it and set it in
order for Me,
Since I appointed the
ancient people.
And the things that are
coming and shall come,
Let them show
these to them.
8 Do not fear, nor be afraid;
Have I not told you
from that time,
and declared *it?*
You *are* My witnesses.
Is there a God besides Me?
Indeed *there is* no
other Rock;
I know not *one.*'"

IDOLATRY IS FOOLISHNESS

9 Those who make an
image, all of them
are useless,

And their precious things
shall not profit;
They *are* their own
witnesses;
They neither see nor
know, that they
may be ashamed.
10 Who would form a god
or mold an image
That profits him nothing?
11 Surely all his companions
would be ashamed;
And the workmen,
they *are* mere men.
Let them all be
gathered together,
Let them stand up;
Yet they shall fear,
They shall be ashamed
together.

12 The blacksmith with
the tongs works
one in the coals,
Fashions it with hammers,
And works it with the
strength of his arms.
Even so, he is hungry,
and his strength fails;
He drinks no water
and is faint.

13 The craftsman stretches
out *his* rule,
He marks one out
with chalk;
He fashions it with a plane,
He marks it out with
the compass,
And makes it like the
figure of a man,
According to the beauty
of a man, that it may
remain in the house.
14 He cuts down cedars
for himself,
And takes the cypress
and the oak;
He secures *it* for
himself among the
trees of the forest.
He plants a pine, and
the rain nourishes *it*.

15 Then it shall be for
a man to burn,
For he will take some of
it and warm himself;
Yes, he kindles *it* and
bakes bread;
Indeed he makes a god
and worships *it;*
He makes it a carved
image, and falls
down to it.
16 He burns half of
it in the fire;
With this half he
eats meat;
He roasts a roast,
and is satisfied.
He even warms
himself and says,
"Ah! I am warm,
I have seen the fire."
17 And the rest of it he
makes into a god,
His carved image.
He falls down before
it and worships *it,*
Prays to it and says,
"Deliver me, for you
are my god!"

18 They do not know
nor understand;
For He has shut their eyes,
so that they cannot see,

And their hearts, so that
they cannot understand.
19 And no one considers
in his heart,
Nor *is there* knowledge nor
understanding to say,
"I have burned half
of it in the fire,
Yes, I have also baked
bread on its coals;
I have roasted meat
and eaten *it;*
And shall I make the rest
of it an abomination?
Shall I fall down before
a block of wood?"
20 He feeds on ashes;
A deceived heart has
turned him aside;
And he cannot
deliver his soul,
Nor say, "*Is there* not a
lie in my right hand?"

ISRAEL IS NOT FORGOTTEN

21 "Remember these, O Jacob,
And Israel, for you
are My servant;
I have formed you, you
are My servant;
O Israel, you will not
be forgotten by Me!
22 I have blotted out, like
a thick cloud, your
transgressions,
And like a cloud,
your sins.
Return to Me, for I have
redeemed you."

23 Sing, O heavens, for the
LORD has done *it!*
Shout, you lower
parts of the earth;
Break forth into singing,
you mountains,
O forest, and every
tree in it!
For the LORD has
redeemed Jacob,
And glorified Himself
in Israel.

JUDAH WILL BE RESTORED

24 Thus says the LORD,
your Redeemer,
And He who formed
you from the womb:
"I *am* the LORD, who
makes all *things,*
Who stretches out the
heavens all alone,
Who spreads abroad
the earth by Myself;
25 Who frustrates the signs
of the babblers,
And drives diviners mad;
Who turns wise
men backward,
And makes their
knowledge foolishness;
26 Who confirms the word
of His servant,
And performs the
counsel of His
messengers;
Who says to Jerusalem,
'You shall be inhabited,'
To the cities of Judah,
'You shall be built,'
And I will raise up
her waste places;
27 Who says to the
deep, 'Be dry!
And I will dry up
your rivers';
28 Who says of Cyrus, '*He*
is My shepherd,

And he shall perform
all My pleasure,
Saying to Jerusalem,
"You shall be built,"
And to the temple,
"Your foundation
shall be laid."'

CYRUS, GOD'S INSTRUMENT

45 "Thus says the LORD
to His anointed,
To Cyrus, whose right
hand I have held—
To subdue nations
before him
And loose the
armor of kings,
To open before him
the double doors,
So that the gates will
not be shut:
2 'I will go before you
And make the crooked
places[a] straight;
I will break in pieces
the gates of bronze
And cut the bars of iron.
3 I will give you the
treasures of darkness
And hidden riches
of secret places,
That you may know
that I, the LORD,
Who call *you* by
your name,
Am the God of Israel.
4 For Jacob My
servant's sake,
And Israel My elect,
I have even called you
by your name;
I have named you, though
you have not known Me.
5 I *am* the LORD, and
there is no other;
There is no God
besides Me.
I will gird you, though you
have not known Me,
6 That they may know
from the rising of the
sun to its setting
That *there is* none
besides Me.
I *am* the LORD, and
there is no other;
7 I form the light and
create darkness,
I make peace and
create calamity;
I, the LORD, do all
these *things*.'

8 "Rain down, you heavens,
from above,
And let the skies pour
down righteousness;
Let the earth open,
let them bring
forth salvation,
And let righteousness
spring up together.
I, the LORD, have created it.

9 "Woe to him who strives
with his Maker!
Let the potsherd *strive*
with the potsherds
of the earth!

45:2 [a] Dead Sea Scrolls and Septuagint read *mountains;* Targum reads *I will trample down the walls;* Vulgate reads *I will humble the great ones of the earth.*

Shall the clay say to him
who forms it, 'What
are you making?'
Or shall your handiwork
say, 'He has no hands'?
10 Woe to him who says
to *his* father, 'What
are you begetting?'
Or to the woman,
'What have you
brought forth?'"

11 Thus says the LORD,
The Holy One of Israel,
and his Maker:
"Ask Me of things to
come concerning
My sons;
And concerning the
work of My hands,
you command Me.
12 I have made the earth,
And created man on it.
I—My hands—stretched
out the heavens,
And all their host I
have commanded.
13 I have raised him up
in righteousness,
And I will direct
all his ways;
He shall build My city
And let My exiles go free,
Not for price nor reward,"
Says the LORD of hosts.

THE LORD, THE ONLY SAVIOR

14Thus says the LORD:

"The labor of Egypt and
merchandise of Cush
And of the Sabeans,
men of stature,
Shall come over to
you, and they
shall be yours;
They shall walk
behind you,
They shall come
over in chains;
And they shall bow
down to you.
They will make
supplication to
you, *saying,* 'Surely
God *is* in you,
And *there is* no other;
There is no other God.'"

15 Truly You *are* God,
who hide Yourself,
O God of Israel,
the Savior!
16 They shall be ashamed
And also disgraced,
all of them;
They shall go in
confusion together,
Who are makers of idols.
17 *But* Israel shall be
saved by the LORD
With an everlasting
salvation;
You shall not be ashamed
or disgraced
Forever and ever.

18 For thus says the LORD,
Who created the heavens,
Who is God,
Who formed the earth
and made it,
Who has established it,
Who did not create
it in vain,
Who formed it to
be inhabited:

"I *am* the LORD, and
there is no other.
19 I have not spoken
in secret,
In a dark place of
the earth;
I did not say to the
seed of Jacob,
'Seek Me in vain';
I, the LORD, speak
righteousness,
I declare things
that are right.

20 "Assemble yourselves
and come;
Draw near together,
You *who have* escaped
from the nations.
They have no knowledge,
Who carry the wood of
their carved image,
And pray to a god
that cannot save.
21 Tell and bring forth
your case;
Yes, let them take
counsel together.
Who has declared this
from ancient time?
Who has told it from
that time?
Have not I, the LORD?
And *there is* no other
God besides Me,
A just God and a Savior;
There is none besides Me.

22 "Look to Me, and be
saved,
All you ends of the earth!
For I *am* God, and
there is no other.
23 I have sworn by Myself;
The word has gone
out of My mouth *in*
righteousness,
And shall not return,
That to Me every
knee shall bow,
Every tongue shall
take an oath.
24 He shall say,
'Surely in the LORD I
have righteousness
and strength.
To Him *men* shall come,
And all shall be ashamed
Who are incensed
against Him.
25 In the LORD all the
descendants of Israel
Shall be justified,
and shall glory.'"

DEAD IDOLS AND THE LIVING GOD

46 Bel bows down,
Nebo stoops;
Their idols were on the
beasts and on the cattle.
Your carriages *were*
heavily loaded,
A burden to the
weary *beast.*
2 They stoop, they bow
down together;
They could not deliver
the burden,
But have themselves
gone into captivity.

3 "Listen to Me, O house
of Jacob,
And all the remnant of
the house of Israel,
Who have been upheld
by Me from birth,

Who have been carried
from the womb:
4 Even to *your* old
age, I *am* He,
And *even* to gray hairs
I will carry *you!*
I have made, and
I will bear;
Even I will carry, and
will deliver *you.*

5 "To whom will you
liken Me, and
make *Me* equal
And compare Me, that
we should be alike?
6 They lavish gold
out of the bag,
And weigh silver
on the scales;
They hire a goldsmith,
and he makes it a god;
They prostrate
themselves, yes,
they worship.
7 They bear it on the
shoulder, they carry it
And set it in its place,
and it stands;
From its place it
shall not move.
Though *one* cries out to
it, yet it cannot answer
Nor save him out
of his trouble.

8 "Remember this, and
show yourselves men;
Recall to mind, O you
transgressors.
9 Remember the former
things of old,
For I *am* God, and
there is no other;
I am God, and *there*
is none like Me,
10 Declaring the end from
the beginning,
And from ancient
times *things* that
are not *yet* done,
Saying, 'My counsel
shall stand,
And I will do all
My pleasure,'
11 Calling a bird of prey
from the east,
The man who executes
My counsel, from
a far country.
Indeed I have spoken *it;*
I will also bring it to pass.
I have purposed *it;*
I will also do it.

12 "Listen to Me, you
stubborn-hearted,
Who *are* far from
righteousness:
13 I bring My righteousness
near, it shall not
be far off;
My salvation shall
not linger.
And I will place
salvation in Zion,
For Israel My glory.

THE HUMILIATION OF BABYLON

47 "Come down and
sit in the dust,
O virgin daughter
of Babylon;
Sit on the ground
without a throne,
O daughter of the
Chaldeans!

For you shall no
more be called
Tender and delicate.
2 Take the millstones
and grind meal.
Remove your veil,
Take off the skirt,
Uncover the thigh,
Pass through the rivers.
3 Your nakedness shall
be uncovered,
Yes, your shame
will be seen;
I will take vengeance,
And I will not arbitrate
with a man."

4 *As for* our Redeemer,
the LORD of hosts
is His name,
The Holy One of Israel.

5 "Sit in silence, and go
into darkness,
O daughter of the
Chaldeans;
For you shall no
longer be called
The Lady of Kingdoms.
6 I was angry with
My people;
I have profaned My
inheritance,
And given them
into your hand.
You showed them
no mercy;
On the elderly you
laid your yoke
very heavily.
7 And you said, 'I shall
be a lady forever,'
So that you did not take
these *things* to heart,
Nor remember the
latter end of them.

8 "Therefore hear this
now, *you who are*
given to pleasures,
Who dwell securely,
Who say in your heart,
'I *am,* and *there is* no
one else besides me;
I shall not sit *as* a widow,
Nor shall I know the
loss of children';
9 But these two *things*
shall come to you
In a moment, in one day:
The loss of children,
and widowhood.
They shall come upon
you in their fullness
Because of the multitude
of your sorceries,
For the great abundance
of your enchantments.

10 "For you have trusted in
your wickedness;
You have said, 'No
one sees me';
Your wisdom and
your knowledge
have warped you;
And you have said
in your heart,
'I *am,* and *there is* no
one else besides me.'
11 Therefore evil shall
come upon you;
You shall not know
from where it arises.
And trouble shall
fall upon you;
You will not be able
to put it off.

And desolation
shall come upon
you suddenly,
Which you shall not know.

12 "Stand now with your
enchantments
And the multitude of
your sorceries,
In which you have
labored from
your youth—
Perhaps you will be
able to profit,
Perhaps you will prevail.
13 You are wearied in
the multitude of
your counsels;
Let now the astrologers,
the stargazers,
And the monthly
prognosticators
Stand up and save you
From what shall
come upon you.
14 Behold, they shall
be as stubble,
The fire shall burn them;
They shall not deliver
themselves
From the power
of the flame;
It shall not *be* a coal
to be warmed by,
Nor a fire to sit before!
15 Thus shall they be
to you
With whom you
have labored,
Your merchants from
your youth;
They shall wander each
one to his quarter.
No one shall save you.

ISRAEL REFINED FOR GOD'S GLORY

48 "Hear this, O house
of Jacob,
Who are called by the
name of Israel,
And have come forth
from the wellsprings
of Judah;
Who swear by the
name of the LORD,
And make mention of
the God of Israel,
But not in truth or in
righteousness;
2 For they call themselves
after the holy city,
And lean on the
God of Israel;
The LORD of hosts
is His name:

3 "I have declared the
former things from
the beginning;
They went forth from My
mouth, and I caused
them to hear it.
Suddenly I did *them,* and
they came to pass.
4 Because I knew that
you *were* obstinate,
And your neck *was*
an iron sinew,
And your brow bronze,
5 Even from the beginning I
have declared *it* to you;
Before it came to pass I
proclaimed *it* to you,
Lest you should say, 'My
idol has done them,
And my carved image
and my molded image
Have commanded them.'

6 "You have heard;
See all this.
And will you not
declare *it?*
I have made you hear new
things from this time,
Even hidden things,
and you did not
know them.
7 They are created now
and not from the
beginning;
And before this day you
have not heard them,
Lest you should say, 'Of
course I knew them.'
8 Surely you did not hear,
Surely you did not know;
Surely from long ago your
ear was not opened.
For I knew that you would
deal very treacherously,
And were called a
transgressor from
the womb.

9 "For My name's sake I
will defer My anger,
And *for* My praise I will
restrain it from you,
So that I do not
cut you off.
10 Behold, I have refined
you, but not as silver;
I have tested you in the
furnace of affliction.
11 For My own sake, for My
own sake, I will do *it;*
For how should *My*
name be profaned?
And I will not give My
glory to another.

GOD'S ANCIENT PLAN TO REDEEM ISRAEL

12 "Listen to Me, O Jacob,
And Israel, My called:
I *am* He, I *am* the First,
I *am* also the Last.
13 Indeed My hand has
laid the foundation
of the earth,
And My right hand
has stretched out
the heavens;
When I call to them,
They stand up together.

14 "All of you, assemble
yourselves, and
hear!
Who among them
has declared
these *things?*
The LORD loves him;
He shall do His pleasure
on Babylon,
And His arm *shall be*
against the Chaldeans.
15 I, *even* I, have spoken;
Yes, I have called him,
I have brought him,
and his way will
prosper.

16 "Come near to Me,
hear this:
I have not spoken
in secret from
the beginning;
From the time that it
was, I *was* there.
And now the Lord
GOD and His Spirit
Have[a] sent Me."

48:16 [a] The Hebrew verb is singular.

17 Thus says the LORD,
your Redeemer,
The Holy One of Israel:
"I *am* the LORD your God,
Who teaches you
to profit,
Who leads you by the
way you should go.
18 Oh, that you had heeded
My commandments!
Then your peace would
have been like a river,
And your righteousness
like the waves
of the sea.
19 Your descendants also
would have been
like the sand,
And the offspring of
your body like the
grains of sand;
His name would not
have been cut off
Nor destroyed from
before Me."

20 Go forth from Babylon!
Flee from the Chaldeans!
With a voice of singing,
Declare, proclaim this,
Utter it to the end
of the earth;
Say, "The LORD has
redeemed
His servant Jacob!"
21 And they did not thirst
When He led them
through the deserts;
He caused the waters
to flow from the
rock for them;
He also split the rock,
and the waters
gushed out.

22 "*There is* no peace,"
says the LORD, "for
the wicked."

THE SERVANT, THE LIGHT TO THE GENTILES

49 "Listen, O coastlands,
to Me,
And take heed, you
peoples from afar!
The LORD has called
Me from the womb;
From the matrix of My
mother He has made
mention of My name.
2 And He has made
My mouth like a
sharp sword;
In the shadow of His
hand He has hidden Me,
And made Me a
polished shaft;
In His quiver He has
hidden Me."

3 "And He said to me,
'You *are* My servant,
O Israel,
In whom I will be
glorified.'
4 Then I said, 'I have
labored in vain,
I have spent my strength
for nothing and in vain;
Yet surely my just reward
is with the LORD,
And my work with
my God.'"

5 "And now the LORD says,
Who formed Me from the
womb *to be* His Servant,
To bring Jacob
back to Him,

So that Israel is
gathered to Him[a]
(For I shall be glorious in
the eyes of the LORD,
And My God shall be
My strength),
6 Indeed He says,
'It is too small a thing
that You should
be My Servant
To raise up the
tribes of Jacob,
And to restore the
preserved ones
of Israel;
I will also give You as a
light to the Gentiles,
That You should be
My salvation to the
ends of the earth.'"

7 Thus says the LORD,
The Redeemer of Israel,
their Holy One,
To Him whom man
despises,
To Him whom the
nation abhors,
To the Servant of rulers:
"Kings shall see and arise,
Princes also shall
worship,
Because of the LORD
who is faithful,
The Holy One of Israel;
And He has chosen You."

8 Thus says the LORD:

"In an acceptable time
I have heard You,
And in the day of
salvation I have
helped You;
I will preserve You
and give You
As a covenant to
the people,
To restore the earth,
To cause them to inherit
the desolate heritages;
9 That You may say to the
prisoners, 'Go forth,'
To those who *are* in
darkness, 'Show
yourselves.'

"They shall feed
along the roads,
And their pastures *shall be*
on all desolate heights.
10 They shall neither
hunger nor thirst,
Neither heat nor sun
shall strike them;
For He who has mercy on
them will lead them,
Even by the springs
of water He will
guide them.
11 I will make each of My
mountains a road,
And My highways
shall be elevated.
12 Surely these shall
come from afar;
Look! Those from the
north and the west,
And these from the
land of Sinim."

13 Sing, O heavens!

49:5 [a] Qere, Dead Sea Scrolls, and Septuagint read *is gathered to Him;* Kethib reads *is not gathered.*

Be joyful, O earth!
And break out in singing,
O mountains!
For the LORD has
comforted His people,
And will have mercy
on His afflicted.

GOD WILL REMEMBER ZION

14 But Zion said, "The LORD
has forsaken me,
And my Lord has
forgotten me."

15 "Can a woman forget
her nursing child,
And not have
compassion on the
son of her womb?
Surely they may forget,
Yet I will not forget you.
16 See, I have inscribed
you on the palms
of My hands;
Your walls *are* continually
before Me.
17 Your sons[a] shall
make haste;
Your destroyers and those
who laid you waste
Shall go away from you.
18 Lift up your eyes, look
around and see;
All these gather together
and come to you.
As I live," says the LORD,
"You shall surely clothe
yourselves with them
all as an ornament,
And bind them *on you*
as a bride *does.*

19 "For your waste and
desolate places,
And the land of your
destruction,
Will even now be
too small for the
inhabitants;
And those who swallowed
you up will be far away.
20 The children you
will have,
After you have lost
the others,
Will say again in
your ears,
'The place *is* too
small for me;
Give me a place where
I may dwell.'
21 Then you will say
in your heart,
'Who has begotten
these for me,
Since I have lost
my children and
am desolate,
A captive, and wandering
to and fro?
And who has brought
these up?
There I was, left alone;
But these, where
were they?'"

22 Thus says the Lord GOD:

"Behold, I will lift My
hand in an oath
to the nations,
And set up My standard
for the peoples;

49:17 [a] Dead Sea Scrolls, Septuagint, Targum, and Vulgate read *builders*.

They shall bring your
sons in *their* arms,
And your daughters
shall be carried on
their shoulders;
23 Kings shall be your
foster fathers,
And their queens your
nursing mothers;
They shall bow down
to you with *their*
faces to the earth,
And lick up the dust
of your feet.
Then you will know
that I *am* the LORD,
For they shall not
be ashamed who
wait for Me."

24 Shall the prey be taken
from the mighty,
Or the captives of
the righteous[a]
be delivered?

25 But thus says the LORD:

"Even the captives of
the mighty shall
be taken away,
And the prey of the
terrible be delivered;
For I will contend
with him who
contends with you,
And I will save
your children.
26 I will feed those who
oppress you with
their own flesh,
And they shall be drunk
with their own blood
as with sweet wine.
All flesh shall know
That I, the LORD, *am*
your Savior,
And your Redeemer, the
Mighty One of Jacob."

THE SERVANT, ISRAEL'S HOPE

50 Thus says the LORD:

"Where *is* the
certificate of your
mother's divorce,
Whom I have put away?
Or which of My creditors
is it to whom I
have sold you?
For your iniquities you
have sold yourselves,
And for your
transgressions
your mother has
been put away.
2 Why, when I came,
was there no man?
Why, when I called, *was*
there none to answer?
Is My hand shortened
at all that it cannot
redeem?
Or have I no power
to deliver?
Indeed with My rebuke
I dry up the sea,
I make the rivers
a wilderness;
Their fish stink because
there is no water,

49:24 [a] Following Masoretic Text and Targum; Dead Sea Scrolls, Syriac, and Vulgate read *the mighty;* Septuagint reads *unjustly*.

And die of thirst.
3 I clothe the heavens
with blackness,
And I make sackcloth
their covering."

4 "The Lord GOD
has given Me
The tongue of the learned,
That I should know
how to speak
A word in season to
him who is weary.
He awakens Me morning
by morning,
He awakens My ear
To hear as the learned.
5 The Lord GOD has
opened My ear;
And I was not rebellious,
Nor did I turn away.
6 I gave My back to those
who struck *Me,*
And My cheeks to
those who plucked
out the beard;
I did not hide My
face from shame
and spitting.

7 "For the Lord GOD
will help Me;
Therefore I will not
be disgraced;
Therefore I have set
My face like a flint,
And I know that I will
not be ashamed.
8 *He is* near who
justifies Me;
Who will contend
with Me?
Let us stand together.
Who *is* My adversary?
Let him come near Me.
9 Surely the Lord GOD
will help Me;
Who *is* he *who* will
condemn Me?
Indeed they will all grow
old like a garment;
The moth will eat them up.

10 "Who among you
fears the LORD?
Who obeys the voice
of His Servant?
Who walks in darkness
And has no light?
Let him trust in the
name of the LORD
And rely upon his God.
11 Look, all you who
kindle a fire,
Who encircle *yourselves*
with sparks:
Walk in the light of your
fire and in the sparks
you have kindled—
This you shall have
from My hand:
You shall lie down
in torment.

THE LORD COMFORTS ZION

51 "Listen to Me, you
who follow after
righteousness,
You who seek the LORD:
Look to the rock *from
which* you were hewn,
And to the hole of
the pit *from which*
you were dug.
2 Look to Abraham
your father,
And to Sarah *who*
bore you;

For I called him alone,
And blessed him and
increased him."

3 For the LORD will
comfort Zion,
He will comfort all
her waste places;
He will make her
wilderness like Eden,
And her desert like the
garden of the LORD;
Joy and gladness will
be found in it,
Thanksgiving and the
voice of melody.

4 "Listen to Me, My people;
And give ear to Me,
O My nation:
For law will proceed
from Me,
And I will make My
justice rest
As a light of the peoples.
5 My righteousness *is* near,
My salvation has
gone forth,
And My arms will
judge the peoples;
The coastlands will
wait upon Me,
And on My arm
they will trust.
6 Lift up your eyes to
the heavens,
And look on the
earth beneath.
For the heavens will
vanish away like smoke,
The earth will grow
old like a garment,
And those who dwell in it
will die in like manner;
But My salvation
will be forever,
And My righteousness
will not be abolished.

7 "Listen to Me, you who
know righteousness,
You people in whose
heart *is* My law:
Do not fear the
reproach of men,
Nor be afraid of
their insults.
8 For the moth will eat
them up like a garment,
And the worm will eat
them like wool;
But My righteousness
will be forever,
And My salvation
from generation
to generation."

9 Awake, awake, put
on strength,
O arm of the LORD!
Awake as in the
ancient days,
In the generations of old.
Are You not *the arm* that
cut Rahab apart,
And wounded the
serpent?

10 *Are* You not *the One* who
dried up the sea,
The waters of the
great deep;
That made the depths
of the sea a road
For the redeemed
to cross over?
11 So the ransomed of the
LORD shall return,

And come to Zion
with singing,
With everlasting joy
on their heads.
They shall obtain joy
and gladness;
Sorrow and sighing
shall flee away.

12 "I, *even* I, *am* He who
comforts you.
Who *are* you that you
should be afraid
Of a man *who* will die,
And of the son of a
man *who* will be
made like grass?
13 And you forget the
LORD your Maker,
Who stretched out
the heavens
And laid the foundations
of the earth;
You have feared
continually every day
Because of the fury
of the oppressor,
When *he has* prepared
to destroy.
And where *is* the fury
of the oppressor?
14 The captive exile
hastens, that he
may be loosed,
That he should not
die in the pit,
And that his bread
should not fail.
15 But I *am* the LORD
your God,
Who divided the sea
whose waves roared—
The LORD of hosts
is His name.
16 And I have put My words
in your mouth;
I have covered you with
the shadow of My hand,
That I may plant
the heavens,
Lay the foundations
of the earth,
And say to Zion, 'You
are My people.'"

GOD'S FURY REMOVED

17 Awake, awake!
Stand up, O Jerusalem,
You who have drunk at
the hand of the LORD
The cup of His fury;
You have drunk the dregs
of the cup of trembling,
And drained *it* out.
18 *There is* no one to
guide her
Among all the sons she
has brought forth;
Nor *is there any* who
takes her by the hand
Among all the sons she
has brought up.
19 These two *things* have
come to you;
Who will be sorry
for you?—
Desolation and
destruction, famine
and sword—
By whom will I
comfort you?
20 Your sons have fainted,
They lie at the head
of all the streets,
Like an antelope in a net;
They are full of the
fury of the LORD,
The rebuke of your God.

21 Therefore please hear
this, you afflicted,
And drunk but not
with wine.
22 Thus says your Lord,
The LORD and your God,
Who pleads the cause
of His people:
"See, I have taken out
of your hand
The cup of trembling,
The dregs of the
cup of My fury;
You shall no longer
drink it.
23 But I will put it into
the hand of those
who afflict you,
Who have said to you,[a]
'Lie down, that we may
walk over you.'
And you have laid your
body like the ground,
And as the street, for
those who walk over."

GOD REDEEMS JERUSALEM

52 Awake, awake!
Put on your
strength, O Zion;
Put on your beautiful
garments,
O Jerusalem, the holy city!
For the uncircumcised
and the unclean
Shall no longer
come to you.
2 Shake yourself from
the dust, arise;
Sit down, O Jerusalem!
Loose yourself from the
bonds of your neck,
O captive daughter
of Zion!

3For thus says the LORD:

"You have sold
yourselves for nothing,
And you shall be
redeemed without
money."

4For thus says the Lord GOD:

"My people went
down at first
Into Egypt to dwell there;
Then the Assyrian
oppressed them
without cause.
5 Now therefore, what have
I here," says the LORD,
"That My people are
taken away for nothing?
Those who rule over them
Make them wail,"[a]
says the LORD,
"And My name
is blasphemed
continually every day.
6 Therefore My people
shall know My name;
Therefore *they shall
know* in that day
That I *am* He who speaks:
'Behold, *it is* I.'"

7 How beautiful upon
the mountains

51:23 [a] Literally *your soul* 52:5 [a] Dead Sea Scrolls read *Mock;* Septuagint reads *Marvel and wail;* Targum reads *Boast themselves;* Vulgate reads *Treat them unjustly.*

Are the feet of him who
brings good news,
Who proclaims peace,
Who brings glad tidings
of good *things*,
Who proclaims salvation,
Who says to Zion,
"Your God reigns!"
8 Your watchmen shall
lift up *their* voices,
With their voices they
shall sing together;
For they shall see
eye to eye
When the LORD
brings back Zion.
9 Break forth into joy,
sing together,
You waste places
of Jerusalem!
For the LORD has
comforted His people,
He has redeemed
Jerusalem.
10 The LORD has made
bare His holy arm
In the eyes of all
the nations;
And all the ends of
the earth shall see
The salvation of our God.

11 Depart! Depart! Go
out from there,
Touch no unclean *thing;*
Go out from the
midst of her,
Be clean,
You who bear the
vessels of the LORD.
12 For you shall not go
out with haste,
Nor go by flight;
For the LORD will
go before you,
And the God of Israel *will*
be your rear guard.

THE SIN-BEARING SERVANT

13 Behold, My Servant
shall deal prudently;
He shall be exalted
and extolled and
be very high.
14 Just as many were
astonished at you,
So His visage was marred
more than any man,
And His form more than
the sons of men;
15 So shall He sprinkle[a]
many nations.
Kings shall shut their
mouths at Him;
For what had not
been told them
they shall see,
And what they had
not heard they
shall consider.

53 Who has believed
our report?
And to whom has the
arm of the LORD
been revealed?
2 For He shall grow
up before Him as
a tender plant,
And as a root out
of dry ground.
He has no form or
comeliness;
And when we see Him,

52:15 [a] Or *startle*

There is no beauty that
we should desire Him.
3 He is despised and
rejected by men,
A Man of sorrows and
acquainted with grief.
And we hid, as it were,
our faces from Him;
He was despised, and we
did not esteem Him.

4 Surely He has borne
our griefs
And carried our sorrows;
Yet we esteemed
Him stricken,
Smitten by God,
and afflicted.
5 But He *was* wounded for
our transgressions,
He was bruised for
our iniquities;
The chastisement for our
peace *was* upon Him,
And by His stripes
we are healed.
6 All we like sheep have
gone astray;
We have turned, every
one, to his own way;
And the LORD has
laid on Him the
iniquity of us all.

7 He was oppressed and
He was afflicted,
Yet He opened not
His mouth;
He was led as a lamb
to the slaughter,
And as a sheep before
its shearers is silent,
So He opened not
His mouth.
8 He was taken from prison
and from judgment,
And who will declare
His generation?
For He was cut off from
the land of the living;
For the transgressions
of My people He
was stricken.
9 And they[a] made His
grave with the wicked—
But with the rich
at His death,
Because He had done
no violence,
Nor *was any* deceit
in His mouth.

10 Yet it pleased the LORD
to bruise Him;
He has put *Him* to grief.
When You make His soul
an offering for sin,
He shall see *His* seed, He
shall prolong *His* days,
And the pleasure of the
LORD shall prosper
in His hand.
11 He shall see the labor
of His soul,[a] *and*
be satisfied.
By His knowledge My
righteous Servant
shall justify many,
For He shall bear
their iniquities.

53:9 [a] Literally *he* or *He* **53:11** [a] Following Masoretic Text, Targum, and Vulgate; Dead Sea Scrolls and Septuagint read *From the labor of His soul He shall see light.*

12 Therefore I will divide
Him a portion
with the great,
And He shall divide the
spoil with the strong,
Because He poured out
His soul unto death,
And He was numbered
with the transgressors,
And He bore the
sin of many,
And made intercession
for the transgressors.

A PERPETUAL COVENANT OF PEACE

54 "Sing, O barren,
You *who* have
not borne!
Break forth into singing,
and cry aloud,
You *who* have not
labored with child!
For more *are* the children
of the desolate
Than the children of
the married woman,"
says the LORD.
2 "Enlarge the place
of your tent,
And let them stretch
out the curtains of
your dwellings;
Do not spare;
Lengthen your cords,
And strengthen
your stakes.
3 For you shall expand
to the right and
to the left,
And your descendants
will inherit the nations,
And make the desolate
cities inhabited.

4 "Do not fear, for you will
not be ashamed;
Neither be disgraced,
for you will not be
put to shame;
For you will forget the
shame of your youth,
And will not remember
the reproach of your
widowhood anymore.
5 For your Maker *is*
your husband,
The LORD of hosts
is His name;
And your Redeemer *is*
the Holy One of Israel;
He is called the God of
the whole earth.
6 For the LORD has
called you
Like a woman forsaken
and grieved in spirit,
Like a youthful wife when
you were refused,"
Says your God.
7 "For a mere moment I
have forsaken you,
But with great mercies
I will gather you.
8 With a little wrath I
hid My face from
you for a moment;
But with everlasting
kindness I will have
mercy on you,"
Says the LORD, your
Redeemer.

9 "For this *is* like the waters
of Noah to Me;
For as I have sworn
That the waters of Noah
would no longer
cover the earth,

So have I sworn
That I would not be
angry with you,
nor rebuke you.
10 For the mountains
shall depart
And the hills be removed,
But My kindness shall
not depart from you,
Nor shall My covenant
of peace be removed,"
Says the LORD, who
has mercy on you.

11 "O you afflicted one,
Tossed with tempest,
and not comforted,
Behold, I will lay
your stones with
colorful gems,
And lay your foundations
with sapphires.
12 I will make your
pinnacles of rubies,
Your gates of crystal,
And all your walls of
precious stones.
13 All your children *shall be*
taught by the LORD,
And great *shall be* the
peace of your children.
14 In righteousness you
shall be established;
You shall be far from
oppression, for you
shall not fear;
And from terror, for it
shall not come near you.
15 Indeed they shall surely
assemble, but not
because of Me.
Whoever assembles
against you shall
fall for your sake.

16 "Behold, I have created
the blacksmith
Who blows the coals
in the fire,
Who brings forth
an instrument
for his work;
And I have created the
spoiler to destroy.
17 No weapon formed
against you shall
prosper,
And every tongue
which rises against
you in judgment
You shall condemn.
This *is* the heritage of the
servants of the LORD,
And their righteousness
is from Me,"
Says the LORD.

AN INVITATION TO ABUNDANT LIFE

55 "Ho! Everyone
who thirsts,
Come to the waters;
And you who have
no money,
Come, buy and eat.
Yes, come, buy
wine and milk
Without money and
without price.
2 Why do you spend money
for *what is* not bread,
And your wages for *what*
does not satisfy?
Listen carefully to Me,
and eat *what is* good,
And let your soul delight
itself in abundance.
3 Incline your ear, and
come to Me.

Hear, and your soul
shall live;
And I will make an
everlasting covenant
with you—
The sure mercies of David.
4 Indeed I have given
him *as* a witness
to the people,
A leader and commander
for the people.
5 Surely you shall call a
nation you do not know,
And nations *who*
do not know you
shall run to you,
Because of the LORD
your God,
And the Holy One
of Israel;
For He has glorified you."

6 Seek the LORD while
He may be found,
Call upon Him while
He is near.
7 Let the wicked
forsake his way,
And the unrighteous
man his thoughts;
Let him return to
the LORD,
And He will have
mercy on him;
And to our God,
For He will abundantly
pardon.

8 "For My thoughts *are*
not your thoughts,
Nor *are* your ways My
ways," says the LORD.
9 "For *as* the heavens are
higher than the earth,
So are My ways higher
than your ways,
And My thoughts than
your thoughts.

10 "For as the rain comes
down, and the snow
from heaven,
And do not return there,
But water the earth,
And make it bring
forth and bud,
That it may give seed
to the sower
And bread to the eater,
11 So shall My word
be that goes forth
from My mouth;
It shall not return
to Me void,
But it shall accomplish
what I please,
And it shall prosper *in the
thing* for which I sent it.

12 "For you shall go
out with joy,
And be led out
with peace;
The mountains
and the hills
Shall break forth into
singing before you,
And all the trees of
the field shall clap
their hands.
13 Instead of the thorn
shall come up the
cypress tree,
And instead of the
brier shall come up
the myrtle tree;
And it shall be to the
LORD for a name,

For an everlasting
sign *that* shall
not be cut off."

SALVATION FOR THE GENTILES

56 Thus says the LORD:

"Keep justice, and do
righteousness,
For My salvation *is*
about to come,
And My righteousness
to be revealed.
2 Blessed *is* the man
who does this,
And the son of man
who lays hold on it;
Who keeps from
defiling the Sabbath,
And keeps his hand
from doing any evil."

3 Do not let the son
of the foreigner
Who has joined himself
to the LORD
Speak, saying,
"The LORD has utterly
separated me from
His people";
Nor let the eunuch say,
"Here I am, a dry tree."
4 For thus says the LORD:
"To the eunuchs who
keep My Sabbaths,
And choose what
pleases Me,
And hold fast My
covenant,
5 Even to them I will
give in My house
And within My walls a
place and a name
Better than that of sons
and daughters;
I will give them[a] an
everlasting name
That shall not be cut off.

6 "Also the sons of
the foreigner
Who join themselves to
the LORD, to serve Him,
And to love the name
of the LORD, to be
His servants—
Everyone who keeps
from defiling
the Sabbath,
And holds fast My
covenant—
7 Even them I will bring
to My holy mountain,
And make them joyful in
My house of prayer.
Their burnt offerings
and their sacrifices
Will be accepted
on My altar;
For My house shall
be called a house of
prayer for all nations."
8 The Lord GOD, who
gathers the outcasts
of Israel, says,
"Yet I will gather to him
Others besides those who
are gathered to him."

ISRAEL'S IRRESPONSIBLE LEADERS

9 All you beasts of the
field, come to devour,

56:5 [a] Literally *him*

All you beasts in
the forest.
10 His watchmen *are* blind,
They are all ignorant;
They *are* all dumb dogs,
They cannot bark;
Sleeping, lying down,
loving to slumber.
11 Yes, *they are* greedy dogs
Which never have enough.
And they *are* shepherds
Who cannot understand;
They all look to
their own way,
Every one for his
own gain,
From his *own* territory.
12 "Come," *one says*, "I
will bring wine,
And we will fill ourselves
with intoxicating drink;
Tomorrow will
be as today,
And much more
abundant."

ISRAEL'S FUTILE IDOLATRY

57 The righteous
perishes,
And no man takes
it to heart;
Merciful men *are*
taken away,
While no one considers
That the righteous is
taken away from evil.
2 He shall enter into peace;
They shall rest in
their beds,
Each one walking *in*
his uprightness.

3 "But come here,
You sons of the sorceress,
You offspring of
the adulterer and
the harlot!
4 Whom do you ridicule?
Against whom do you
make a wide mouth
And stick out the tongue?
Are you not children
of transgression,
Offspring of falsehood,
5 Inflaming yourselves
with gods under
every green tree,
Slaying the children
in the valleys,
Under the clefts
of the rocks?
6 Among the smooth
stones of the stream
Is your portion;
They, they, *are* your lot!
Even to them you have
poured a drink offering,
You have offered a
grain offering.
Should I receive
comfort in these?

7 "On a lofty and high
mountain
You have set your bed;
Even there you went up
To offer sacrifice.
8 Also behind the doors
and their posts
You have set up your
remembrance;
For you have uncovered
yourself *to those*
other than Me,
And have gone
up to them;
You have enlarged
your bed

And made *a covenant*
with them;
You have loved their bed,
Where you saw
their nudity.[a]

9 You went to the king
with ointment,
And increased your
perfumes;
You sent your
messengers far off,
And *even* descended
to Sheol.

10 You are wearied in the
length of your way;
Yet you did not say,
'There is no hope.'
You have found the
life of your hand;
Therefore you were
not grieved.

11 "And of whom have you
been afraid, or feared,
That you have lied
And not remembered Me,
Nor taken *it* to your heart?
Is it not because I
have held My peace
from of old
That you do not fear Me?

12 I will declare your
righteousness
And your works,
For they will not
profit you.

13 When you cry out,
Let your collection *of
idols* deliver you.
But the wind will carry
them all away,
A breath will take *them*.
But he who puts his
trust in Me shall
possess the land,
And shall inherit My
holy mountain."

HEALING FOR THE BACKSLIDER

14 And one shall say,
"Heap it up! Heap it up!
Prepare the way,
Take the stumbling
block out of the way
of My people."

15 For thus says the High
and Lofty One
Who inhabits eternity,
whose name *is* Holy:
"I dwell in the high
and holy *place*,
With him *who* has
a contrite and
humble spirit,
To revive the spirit
of the humble,
And to revive the
heart of the
contrite ones.

16 For I will not contend
forever,
Nor will I always
be angry;
For the spirit would
fail before Me,
And the souls *which*
I have made.

17 For the iniquity of
his covetousness
I was angry and
struck him;
I hid and was angry,

57:8 [a] Literally *hand*, a euphemism

And he went on
backsliding in the
way of his heart.
18 I have seen his ways,
and will heal him;
I will also lead him,
And restore comforts
to him
And to his mourners.

19 "I create the fruit
of the lips:
Peace, peace to *him
who is* far off and to
him who is near,"
Says the LORD,
"And I will heal him."
20 But the wicked *are* like
the troubled sea,
When it cannot rest,
Whose waters cast
up mire and dirt.

21 "*There is* no peace,"
Says my God, "for
the wicked."

FASTING THAT PLEASES GOD

58 "Cry aloud, spare not;
Lift up your voice
like a trumpet;
Tell My people their
transgression,
And the house of
Jacob their sins.
2 Yet they seek Me daily,
And delight to
know My ways,
As a nation that did
righteousness,
And did not forsake
the ordinance
of their God.
They ask of Me the
ordinances of justice;
They take delight in
approaching God.
3 'Why have we fasted,'
they say, 'and You
have not seen?
Why have we afflicted
our souls, and You
take no notice?'

"In fact, in the day
of your fast you
find pleasure,
And exploit all
your laborers.
4 Indeed you fast for
strife and debate,
And to strike with the
fist of wickedness.
You will not fast as
you do this day,
To make your voice
heard on high.
5 Is it a fast that I
have chosen,
A day for a man to
afflict his soul?
Is it to bow down his
head like a bulrush,
And to spread out
sackcloth and ashes?
Would you call this a fast,
And an acceptable
day to the LORD?

6 "*Is* this not the fast that
I have chosen:
To loose the bonds
of wickedness,
To undo the heavy
burdens,
To let the oppressed
go free,

And that you break
every yoke?
7 *Is it* not to share your
bread with the hungry,
And that you bring to
your house the poor
who are cast out;
When you see the naked,
that you cover him,
And not hide yourself
from your own flesh?
8 Then your light shall
break forth like
the morning,
Your healing shall
spring forth speedily,
And your righteousness
shall go before you;
The glory of the
LORD shall be your
rear guard.
9 Then you shall call,
and the LORD
will answer;
You shall cry, and He
will say, 'Here I *am.*'

"If you take away the yoke
from your midst,
The pointing of the
finger, and speaking
wickedness,
10 *If* you extend your
soul to the hungry
And satisfy the
afflicted soul,
Then your light shall
dawn in the darkness,
And your darkness shall
be as the noonday.
11 The LORD will guide
you continually,
And satisfy your
soul in drought,
And strengthen
your bones;
You shall be like a
watered garden,
And like a spring
of water, whose
waters do not fail.
12 Those from among you
Shall build the old
waste places;
You shall raise up
the foundations of
many generations;
And you shall be
called the Repairer
of the Breach,
The Restorer of Streets
to Dwell In.

13 "If you turn away your
foot from the Sabbath,
From doing your pleasure
on My holy day,
And call the Sabbath
a delight,
The holy *day* of the
LORD honorable,
And shall honor Him,
not doing your
own ways,
Nor finding your
own pleasure,
Nor speaking *your
own* words,
14 Then you shall delight
yourself in the LORD;
And I will cause you
to ride on the high
hills of the earth,
And feed you with the
heritage of Jacob
your father.
The mouth of the
LORD has spoken."

SEPARATED FROM GOD

59 Behold, the LORD's
hand is not
shortened,
That it cannot save;
Nor His ear heavy,
That it cannot hear.
2 But your iniquities
have separated you
from your God;
And your sins have
hidden *His* face
from you,
So that He will not hear.
3 For your hands are
defiled with blood,
And your fingers
with iniquity;
Your lips have
spoken lies,
Your tongue has
muttered perversity.

4 No one calls for justice,
Nor does *any* plead
for truth.
They trust in empty
words and speak lies;
They conceive evil and
bring forth iniquity.
5 They hatch vipers'
eggs and weave
the spider's web;
He who eats of their
eggs dies,
And *from* that which
is crushed a viper
breaks out.

6 Their webs will not
become garments,
Nor will they cover
themselves with
their works;
Their works *are* works
of iniquity,
And the act of violence
is in their hands.
7 Their feet run to evil,
And they make haste to
shed innocent blood;
Their thoughts *are*
thoughts of iniquity;
Wasting and destruction
are in their paths.
8 The way of peace they
have not known,
And *there is* no justice
in their ways;
They have made
themselves
crooked paths;
Whoever takes that
way shall not
know peace.

SIN CONFESSED

9 Therefore justice
is far from us,
Nor does righteousness
overtake us;
We look for light, but
there is darkness!
For brightness, *but* we
walk in blackness!
10 We grope for the wall
like the blind,
And we grope as if
we had no eyes;
We stumble at noonday
as at twilight;
We are as dead *men* in
desolate places.
11 We all growl like bears,
And moan sadly
like doves;
We look for justice,
but *there is* none;

For salvation, *but* it
is far from us.
12 For our transgressions are
multiplied before You,
And our sins testify
against us;
For our transgressions
are with us,
And *as for* our iniquities,
we know them:
13 In transgressing and
lying against the LORD,
And departing
from our God,
Speaking oppression
and revolt,
Conceiving and uttering
from the heart words
of falsehood.
14 Justice is turned back,
And righteousness
stands afar off;
For truth is fallen
in the street,
And equity cannot enter.
15 So truth fails,
And he *who* departs
from evil makes
himself a prey.

THE REDEEMER OF ZION

Then the LORD saw *it,*
and it displeased Him
That *there was* no justice.
16 He saw that *there*
was no man,
And wondered that *there*
was no intercessor;
Therefore His own
arm brought
salvation for Him;
And His own
righteousness, it
sustained Him.
17 For He put on
righteousness as
a breastplate,
And a helmet of salvation
on His head;
He put on the garments
of vengeance
for clothing,
And was clad with
zeal as a cloak.
18 According to *their*
deeds, accordingly
He will repay,
Fury to His adversaries,
Recompense to
His enemies;
The coastlands He
will fully repay.
19 So shall they fear
The name of the LORD
from the west,
And His glory from the
rising of the sun;
When the enemy comes
in like a flood,
The Spirit of the LORD
will lift up a standard
against him.

20 "The Redeemer will
come to Zion,
And to those who turn
from transgression
in Jacob,"
Says the LORD.

21 "As for Me," says the LORD,
"this *is* My covenant with
them: My Spirit who *is* upon
you, and My words which I
have put in your mouth, shall
not depart from your mouth,
nor from the mouth of your
descendants, nor from the

mouth of your descendants'
descendants," says the LORD,
"from this time and forevermore."

THE GENTILES BLESS ZION

60 Arise, shine;
For your light
has come!
And the glory of the LORD
is risen upon you.
2 For behold, the darkness
shall cover the earth,
And deep darkness
the people;
But the LORD will
arise over you,
And His glory will be
seen upon you.
3 The Gentiles shall
come to your light,
And kings to the
brightness of
your rising.

4 "Lift up your eyes all
around, and see:
They all gather together,
they come to you;
Your sons shall
come from afar,
And your daughters shall
be nursed at *your* side.
5 Then you shall see and
become radiant,
And your heart shall
swell with joy;
Because the abundance
of the sea shall be
turned to you,
The wealth of the Gentiles
shall come to you.
6 The multitude of camels
shall cover your *land*,
The dromedaries of
Midian and Ephah;
All those from Sheba
shall come;
They shall bring gold
and incense,
And they shall proclaim
the praises of the LORD.
7 All the flocks of Kedar
shall be gathered
together to you,
The rams of Nebaioth
shall minister to you;
They shall ascend with
acceptance on My altar,
And I will glorify the
house of My glory.

8 "Who *are* these *who*
fly like a cloud,
And like doves to
their roosts?
9 Surely the coastlands
shall wait for Me;
And the ships of Tarshish
will come first,
To bring your sons
from afar,
Their silver and their
gold with them,
To the name of the
LORD your God,
And to the Holy
One of Israel,
Because He has
glorified you.

10 "The sons of foreigners
shall build up
your walls,
And their kings shall
minister to you;
For in My wrath I
struck you,

But in My favor I have
had mercy on you.
11 Therefore your gates shall
be open continually;
They shall not be
shut day or night,
That *men* may bring
to you the wealth
of the Gentiles,
And their kings in
procession.
12 For the nation and
kingdom which will not
serve you shall perish,
And *those* nations shall
be utterly ruined.

13 "The glory of Lebanon
shall come to you,
The cypress, the pine, and
the box tree together,
To beautify the place
of My sanctuary;
And I will make the place
of My feet glorious.
14 Also the sons of those
who afflicted you
Shall come bowing
to you,
And all those who
despised you shall
fall prostrate at the
soles of your feet;
And they shall call you
The City of the Lord,
Zion of the Holy
One of Israel.

15 "Whereas you have been
forsaken and hated,
So that no one went
through *you,*
I will make you an
eternal excellence,
A joy of many generations.
16 You shall drink the
milk of the Gentiles,
And milk the breast
of kings;
You shall know that I, the
Lord, *am* your Savior
And your Redeemer, the
Mighty One of Jacob.

17 "Instead of bronze I
will bring gold,
Instead of iron I will
bring silver,
Instead of wood, bronze,
And instead of
stones, iron.
I will also make your
officers peace,
And your magistrates
righteousness.
18 Violence shall no longer
be heard in your land,
Neither wasting nor
destruction within
your borders;
But you shall call your
walls Salvation,
And your gates Praise.

GOD THE GLORY OF HIS PEOPLE

19 "The sun shall no longer
be your light by day,
Nor for brightness
shall the moon
give light to you;
But the Lord will be to
you an everlasting light,
And your God your glory.
20 Your sun shall no
longer go down,
Nor shall your moon
withdraw itself;

For the LORD will be
your everlasting light,
And the days of
your mourning
shall be ended.
21 Also your people *shall*
all *be* righteous;
They shall inherit
the land forever,
The branch of My
planting,
The work of My hands,
That I may be glorified.
22 A little one shall
become a thousand,
And a small one a
strong nation.
I, the LORD, will hasten
it in its time."

THE GOOD NEWS OF SALVATION

61 "The Spirit of the Lord
GOD *is* upon Me,
Because the LORD
has anointed Me
To preach good tidings
to the poor;
He has sent Me to heal
the brokenhearted,
To proclaim liberty
to the captives,
And the opening of
the prison to *those*
who are bound;
2 To proclaim the
acceptable year
of the LORD,
And the day of vengeance
of our God;
To comfort all
who mourn,
3 To console those who
mourn in Zion,
To give them beauty
for ashes,
The oil of joy for
mourning,
The garment of praise for
the spirit of heaviness;
That they may be called
trees of righteousness,
The planting of the
LORD, that He may
be glorified."

4 And they shall rebuild
the old ruins,
They shall raise up the
former desolations,
And they shall repair
the ruined cities,
The desolations of
many generations.
5 Strangers shall stand
and feed your flocks,
And the sons of
the foreigner
Shall be your plowmen
and your vinedressers.
6 But you shall be named
the priests of the LORD,
They shall call you the
servants of our God.
You shall eat the riches
of the Gentiles,
And in their glory
you shall boast.
7 Instead of your shame *you*
shall have double *honor,*
And *instead of* confusion
they shall rejoice
in their portion.
Therefore in their
land they shall
possess double;
Everlasting joy
shall be theirs.

8 "For I, the LORD,
love justice;
I hate robbery for
burnt offering;
I will direct their
work in truth,
And will make with them
an everlasting covenant.
9 Their descendants shall
be known among
the Gentiles,
And their offspring
among the people.
All who see them shall
acknowledge them,
That they *are* the
posterity *whom* the
LORD has blessed."

10 I will greatly rejoice
in the LORD,
My soul shall be
joyful in my God;
For He has clothed me
with the garments
of salvation,
He has covered me
with the robe of
righteousness,
As a bridegroom decks
himself with ornaments,
And as a bride adorns
herself with her jewels.
11 For as the earth brings
forth its bud,
As the garden causes the
things that are sown
in it to spring forth,
So the Lord GOD will cause
righteousness and
praise to spring forth
before all the nations.

ASSURANCE OF ZION'S SALVATION

62 For Zion's sake I will
not hold My peace,
And for Jerusalem's
sake I will not rest,
Until her righteousness
goes forth as brightness,
And her salvation as
a lamp *that* burns.
2 The Gentiles shall see
your righteousness,
And all kings your glory.
You shall be called
by a new name,
Which the mouth of
the LORD will name.
3 You shall also be a
crown of glory
In the hand of the LORD,
And a royal diadem
In the hand of your God.
4 You shall no longer be
termed Forsaken,
Nor shall your land
any more be
termed Desolate;
But you shall be called
Hephzibah,[a] and
your land Beulah;[b]
For the LORD
delights in you,
And your land shall
be married.
5 For *as* a young man
marries a virgin,
So shall your sons
marry you;
And *as* the bridegroom
rejoices over the bride,
So shall your God
rejoice over you.

62:4 [a] Literally *My Delight Is in Her* [b] Literally *Married*

6 I have set watchmen on
your walls, O Jerusalem;
They shall never hold
their peace day or night.
You who make mention
of the LORD, do
not keep silent,
7 And give Him no rest
till He establishes
And till He makes
Jerusalem a praise
in the earth.

8 The LORD has sworn
by His right hand
And by the arm of
His strength:
"Surely I will no longer
give your grain
As food for your enemies;
And the sons of the
foreigner shall not
drink your new wine,
For which you
have labored.
9 But those who have
gathered it shall eat it,
And praise the LORD;
Those who have brought
it together shall drink
it in My holy courts."

10 Go through,
Go through the gates!
Prepare the way for
the people;
Build up,
Build up the highway!
Take out the stones,
Lift up a banner for
the peoples!

11 Indeed the LORD
has proclaimed
To the end of the world:
"Say to the daughter
of Zion,
'Surely your salvation
is coming;
Behold, His reward
is with Him,
And His work
before Him.'"
12 And they shall call them
The Holy People,
The Redeemed of
the LORD;
And you shall be
called Sought Out,
A City Not Forsaken.

THE LORD IN JUDGMENT AND SALVATION

63 Who *is* this who
comes from
Edom,
With dyed garments
from Bozrah,
This *One who is* glorious
in His apparel,
Traveling in the greatness
of His strength?—

"I who speak in
righteousness,
mighty to save."

2 Why *is* Your apparel red,
And Your garments
like one who treads
in the winepress?

3 "I have trodden the
winepress alone,
And from the peoples
no one *was* with Me.
For I have trodden
them in My anger,

And trampled them
in My fury;
Their blood is sprinkled
upon My garments,
And I have stained
all My robes.
4 For the day of vengeance
is in My heart,
And the year of My
redeemed has come.
5 I looked, but *there was*
no one to help,
And I wondered
That *there was* no
one to uphold;
Therefore My own
arm brought
salvation for Me;
And My own fury, it
sustained Me.
6 I have trodden down the
peoples in My anger,
Made them drunk
in My fury,
And brought down
their strength to
the earth."

GOD'S MERCY REMEMBERED

7 I will mention the
lovingkindnesses
of the LORD
And the praises
of the LORD,
According to all
that the LORD has
bestowed on us,
And the great
goodness toward the
house of Israel,
Which He has bestowed
on them according
to His mercies,
According to the
multitude of His
lovingkindnesses.
8 For He said, "Surely
they *are* My people,
Children *who* will not lie."
So He became
their Savior.
9 In all their affliction
He was afflicted,
And the Angel of His
Presence saved them;
In His love and in His pity
He redeemed them;
And He bore them
and carried them
All the days of old.
10 But they rebelled and
grieved His Holy Spirit;
So He turned Himself
against them as
an enemy,
And He fought
against them.

11 Then he remembered
the days of old,
Moses *and* his
people, *saying:*
"Where *is* He who
brought them up
out of the sea
With the shepherd
of His flock?
Where *is* He who put
His Holy Spirit
within them,
12 Who led *them* by the
right hand of Moses,
With His glorious arm,
Dividing the water
before them
To make for Himself an
everlasting name,

24 "It shall come to pass
That before they call,
I will answer;
And while they are still
speaking, I will hear.
25 The wolf and the lamb
shall feed together,
The lion shall eat
straw like the ox,
And dust *shall be* the
serpent's food.
They shall not hurt
nor destroy in all My
holy mountain,"
Says the LORD.

TRUE WORSHIP AND FALSE

66 Thus says the LORD:

"Heaven *is* My throne,
And earth *is* My footstool.
Where *is* the house that
you will build Me?
And where *is* the
place of My rest?
2 For all those *things* My
hand has made,
And all those
things exist,"
Says the LORD.
"But on this *one* will I look:
On *him who is* poor and
of a contrite spirit,
And who trembles
at My word.

3 "He who kills a bull *is as
if* he slays a man;
He who sacrifices a
lamb, *as if* he breaks
a dog's neck;
He who offers a grain
offering, *as if he offers*
swine's blood;
He who burns incense,
as if he blesses an idol.
Just as they have chosen
their own ways,
And their soul delights
in their abominations,
4 So will I choose
their delusions,
And bring their
fears on them;
Because, when I called,
no one answered,
When I spoke they
did not hear;
But they did evil
before My eyes,
And chose *that* in which
I do not delight."

THE LORD VINDICATES ZION

5 Hear the word of
the LORD,
You who tremble
at His word:
"Your brethren
who hated you,
Who cast you out for My
name's sake, said,
'Let the LORD be glorified,
That we may see your joy.'
But they shall be
ashamed."

6 The sound of noise
from the city!
A voice from the temple!
The voice of the LORD,
Who fully repays
His enemies!

7 "Before she was in labor,
she gave birth;
Before her pain came,

She delivered a male child.
8 Who has heard
such a thing?
Who has seen such things?
Shall the earth be made
to give birth in one day?
Or shall a nation be
born at once?
For as soon as Zion
was in labor,
She gave birth to
her children.
9 Shall I bring to the time
of birth, and not cause
delivery?" says the LORD.
"Shall I who cause delivery
shut up *the womb?*"
says your God.
10 "Rejoice with Jerusalem,
And be glad with her,
all you who love her;
Rejoice for joy with her, all
you who mourn for her;
11 That you may feed
and be satisfied
With the consolation
of her bosom,
That you may drink
deeply and be delighted
With the abundance
of her glory."

12 For thus says the LORD:

"Behold, I will extend
peace to her like a river,
And the glory of
the Gentiles like a
flowing stream.
Then you shall feed;
On *her* sides shall
you be carried,
And be dandled
on *her* knees.
13 As one whom his
mother comforts,
So I will comfort you;
And you shall be
comforted in
Jerusalem."

THE REIGN AND INDIGNATION OF GOD

14 When you see *this,* your
heart shall rejoice,
And your bones shall
flourish like grass;
The hand of the LORD
shall be known to
His servants,
And *His* indignation
to His enemies.
15 For behold, the LORD
will come with fire
And with His chariots,
like a whirlwind,
To render His anger
with fury,
And His rebuke with
flames of fire.
16 For by fire and by
His sword
The LORD will judge
all flesh;
And the slain of the
LORD shall be many.

17 "Those who sanctify
themselves and
purify themselves,
To go to the gardens
After an *idol* in the midst,
Eating swine's flesh
and the abomination
and the mouse,
Shall be consumed
together," says
the LORD.

18"For I *know* their works
and their thoughts. It shall be
that I will gather all nations
and tongues; and they shall
come and see My glory. 19I
will set a sign among them;
and those among them who
escape I will send to the nations: *to* Tarshish and Pul[a]
and Lud, who draw the bow,
and Tubal and Javan, *to* the
coastlands afar off who have
not heard My fame nor seen
My glory. And they shall declare My glory among the
Gentiles. 20Then they shall
bring all your brethren for
an offering to the LORD out
of all nations, on horses and
in chariots and in litters, on
mules and on camels, to My
holy mountain Jerusalem,"
says the LORD, "as the children
of Israel bring an offering in
a clean vessel into the house
of the LORD. 21And I will also
take some of them for priests
and Levites," says the LORD.

22"For as the new heavens
and the new earth
Which I will make shall
remain before Me,"
says the LORD,
"So shall your descendants
and your name remain.
23 And it shall come to pass
That from one New
Moon to another,
And from one Sabbath
to another,
All flesh shall come to
worship before Me,"
says the LORD.

24"And they shall go
forth and look
Upon the corpses
of the men
Who have transgressed
against Me.
For their worm
does not die,
And their fire is
not quenched.
They shall be an
abhorrence to all flesh."

THE BOOK OF JEREMIAH

1 The words of Jeremiah the
son of Hilkiah, of the priests
who *were* in Anathoth in the
land of Benjamin, 2to whom
the word of the LORD came in
the days of Josiah the son of
Amon, king of Judah, in the
thirteenth year of his reign.

66:19 [a] Following Masoretic Text and Targum; Septuagint reads *Put* (compare Jeremiah 46:9).

3It came also in the days of
Jehoiakim the son of Josiah,
king of Judah, until the end
of the eleventh year of Zedekiah the son of Josiah, king
of Judah, until the carrying
away of Jerusalem captive in
the fifth month.

THE PROPHET IS CALLED

4Then the word of the LORD
came to me, saying:

5 "Before I formed you in
the womb I knew you;
Before you were born
I sanctified you;
I ordained you a prophet
to the nations."

6Then said I:

"Ah, Lord GOD!
Behold, I cannot speak,
for I *am* a youth."

7But the LORD said to me:

"Do not say, 'I *am*
a youth,'
For you shall go to all
to whom I send you,
And whatever I command
you, you shall speak.
8 Do not be afraid
of their faces,
For I *am* with you
to deliver you,"
says the LORD.

9Then the LORD put forth
His hand and touched my
mouth, and the LORD said to
me:

"Behold, I have put My
words in your mouth.
10 See, I have this day set
you over the nations
and over the kingdoms,
To root out and to
pull down,
To destroy and to
throw down,
To build and to plant."

11Moreover the word of the
LORD came to me, saying,
"Jeremiah, what do you see?"
And I said, "I see a branch
of an almond tree."
12Then the LORD said to me,
"You have seen well, for I am
ready to perform My word."
13And the word of the LORD
came to me the second time,
saying, "What do you see?"
And I said, "I see a boiling
pot, and it is facing away from
the north."
14Then the LORD said to
me:

"Out of the north calamity
shall break forth
On all the inhabitants
of the land.
15 For behold, I am calling
All the families of the
kingdoms of the
north," says the LORD;
"They shall come and
each one set his throne
At the entrance of the
gates of Jerusalem,
Against all its walls
all around,
And against all the
cities of Judah.

16 I will utter My judgments
Against them concerning
all their wickedness,
Because they have
forsaken Me,
Burned incense to
other gods,
And worshiped the works
of their own hands.

17 "Therefore prepare
yourself and arise,
And speak to them all
that I command you.
Do not be dismayed
before their faces,
Lest I dismay you
before them.
18 For behold, I have
made you this day
A fortified city and
an iron pillar,
And bronze walls against
the whole land—
Against the kings
of Judah,
Against its princes,
Against its priests,
And against the
people of the land.
19 They will fight against you,
But they shall not
prevail against you.
For I *am* with you,"
says the LORD, "to
deliver you."

GOD'S CASE AGAINST ISRAEL

2 Moreover the word of the
LORD came to me, saying,
2"Go and cry in the hearing of
Jerusalem, saying, 'Thus says
the LORD:

"I remember you,
The kindness of
your youth,
The love of your
betrothal,
When you went after Me
in the wilderness,
In a land not sown.
3 Israel *was* holiness
to the LORD,
The firstfruits of
His increase.
All that devour him
will offend;
Disaster will come upon
them," says the LORD.'"

4Hear the word of the LORD,
O house of Jacob and all the
families of the house of Israel.
5Thus says the LORD:

"What injustice
have your fathers
found in Me,
That they have gone
far from Me,
Have followed idols,
And have become
idolaters?
6 Neither did they say,
'Where *is* the LORD,
Who brought us up out
of the land of Egypt,
Who led us through
the wilderness,
Through a land of
deserts and pits,
Through a land of
drought and the
shadow of death,
Through a land that
no one crossed
And where no one dwelt?'

7 I brought you into a
bountiful country,
To eat its fruit and
its goodness.
But when you entered,
you defiled My land
And made My heritage
an abomination.
8 The priests did not say,
'Where *is* the LORD?'
And those who
handle the law did
not know Me;
The rulers also
transgressed
against Me;
The prophets
prophesied by Baal,
And walked after *things*
that do not profit.

9 "Therefore I will yet
bring charges against
you," says the LORD,
"And against your
children's children I
will bring charges.
10 For pass beyond the
coasts of Cyprus[a]
and see,
Send to Kedar[b] and
consider diligently,
And see if there has
been such *a thing.*
11 Has a nation changed
its gods,
Which *are* not gods?
But My people have
changed their Glory
For *what* does not profit.
12 Be astonished,
O heavens, at this,
And be horribly afraid;
Be very desolate,"
says the LORD.
13 "For My people have
committed two evils:
They have forsaken
Me, the fountain
of living waters,
And hewn themselves
cisterns—broken
cisterns that can
hold no water.

14 "*Is* Israel a servant?
Is he a homeborn *slave?*
Why is he plundered?
15 The young lions roared
at him, *and* growled;
They made his
land waste;
His cities are burned,
without inhabitant.
16 Also the people of Noph[a]
and Tahpanhes
Have broken the crown
of your head.
17 Have you not brought
this on yourself,
In that you have forsaken
the LORD your God
When He led you
in the way?
18 And now why take the
road to Egypt,
To drink the waters
of Sihor?
Or why take the
road to Assyria,

2:10 [a] Hebrew *Kittim,* western lands, especially Cyprus [b] In the northern Arabian desert, representative of the eastern cultures 2:16 [a] That is, Memphis in ancient Egypt

To drink the waters
of the River?[a]
19 Your own wickedness
will correct you,
And your backslidings
will rebuke you.
Know therefore and
see that *it is* an evil
and bitter *thing*
That you have forsaken
the LORD your God,
And the fear of Me
is not in you,"
Says the Lord GOD
of hosts.

20 "For of old I have broken
your yoke *and* burst
your bonds;
And you said, 'I will
not transgress,'
When on every high
hill and under
every green tree
You lay down, playing
the harlot.
21 Yet I had planted you
a noble vine, a seed
of highest quality.
How then have you
turned before Me
Into the degenerate
plant of an alien vine?
22 For though you wash
yourself with lye, and
use much soap,
Yet your iniquity is
marked before Me,"
says the Lord GOD.

23 "How can you say, 'I
am not polluted,
I have not gone after
the Baals'?
See your way in the valley;
Know what you have done:
You are a swift
dromedary breaking
loose in her ways,
24 A wild donkey used
to the wilderness,
That sniffs at the wind
in her desire;
In her time of mating,
who can turn her away?
All those who seek her will
not weary themselves;
In her month they
will find her.
25 Withhold your foot from
being unshod, and your
throat from thirst.
But you said, 'There
is no hope.
No! For I have loved aliens,
and after them I will go.'

26 "As the thief is ashamed
when he is found out,
So is the house of
Israel ashamed;
They and their kings
and their princes,
and their priests and
their prophets,
27 Saying to a tree, 'You
are my father,'
And to a stone, 'You
gave birth to me.'
For they have turned
their back to Me,
and not *their* face.
But in the time of
their trouble

2:18 [a] That is, the Euphrates

They will say, 'Arise
and save us.'
28 But where *are* your gods
that you have made
for yourselves?
Let them arise,
If they can save you
in the time of
your trouble;
For *according to* the
number of your cities
Are your gods, O Judah.

29 "Why will you
plead with Me?
You all have transgressed
against Me," says
the LORD.
30 "In vain I have chastened
your children;
They received no
correction.
Your sword has devoured
your prophets
Like a destroying lion.

31 "O generation, see the
word of the LORD!
Have I been a
wilderness to Israel,
Or a land of darkness?
Why do My people
say, 'We are lords;
We will come no
more to You'?
32 Can a virgin forget
her ornaments,
Or a bride her attire?
Yet My people have
forgotten Me days
without number.

33 "Why do you beautify
your way to seek love?
Therefore you have
also taught
The wicked women
your ways.
34 Also on your skirts
is found
The blood of the lives of
the poor innocents.
I have not found it
by secret search,
But plainly on all
these things.
35 Yet you say, 'Because
I am innocent,
Surely His anger shall
turn from me.'
Behold, I will plead My
case against you,
Because you say, 'I
have not sinned.'
36 Why do you gad
about so much to
change your way?
Also you shall be
ashamed of Egypt as
you were ashamed
of Assyria.
37 Indeed you will go
forth from him
With your hands
on your head;
For the LORD has rejected
your trusted allies,
And you will not
prosper by them.

ISRAEL IS SHAMELESS

3 "They say, 'If a man
divorces his wife,
And she goes from him
And becomes
another man's,
May he return to
her again?'

Would not that land be
greatly polluted?
But you have played the
harlot with many lovers;
Yet return to Me,"
says the LORD.

2 "Lift up your eyes
to the desolate
heights and see:
Where have you not
lain *with men?*
By the road you have
sat for them
Like an Arabian in
the wilderness;
And you have
polluted the land
With your harlotries and
your wickedness.
3 Therefore the showers
have been withheld,
And there has been
no latter rain.
You have had a
harlot's forehead;
You refuse to be ashamed.
4 Will you not from this
time cry to Me,
'My Father, You *are* the
guide of my youth?
5 Will He remain
angry forever?
Will He keep it to
the end?'
Behold, you have spoken
and done evil things,
As you were able."

A CALL TO REPENTANCE

6The LORD said also to me
in the days of Josiah the king:
"Have you seen what back-
sliding Israel has done? She
has gone up on every high
mountain and under every
green tree, and there played
the harlot. 7And I said, after
she had done all these *things*,
'Return to Me.' But she did not
return. And her treacherous
sister Judah saw it. 8Then I
saw that for all the causes for
which backsliding Israel had
committed adultery, I had
put her away and given her a
certificate of divorce; yet her
treacherous sister Judah did
not fear, but went and played
the harlot also. 9So it came
to pass, through her casual
harlotry, that she defiled the
land and committed adultery
with stones and trees. 10And
yet for all this her treacherous
sister Judah has not turned to
Me with her whole heart, but
in pretense," says the LORD.
11Then the LORD said to me,
"Backsliding Israel has shown
herself more righteous than
treacherous Judah. 12Go and
proclaim these words toward
the north, and say:

'Return, backsliding
Israel,' says the LORD;
'I will not cause My
anger to fall on you.
For I *am* merciful,'
says the LORD;
'I will not remain
angry forever.
13 Only acknowledge
your iniquity,
That you have
transgressed against
the LORD your God,

And have scattered
your charms
To alien deities under
every green tree,
And you have not
obeyed My voice,'
says the LORD.

14"Return, O backsliding
children," says the LORD; "for I
am married to you. I will take
you, one from a city and two
from a family, and I will bring
you to Zion. 15And I will give
you shepherds according to
My heart, who will feed you
with knowledge and understanding.
16"Then it shall come to
pass, when you are multiplied
and increased in the land in
those days," says the LORD,
"that they will say no more,
'The ark of the covenant of
the LORD.' It shall not come to
mind, nor shall they remember it, nor shall they visit *it*,
nor shall it be made anymore.
17"At that time Jerusalem
shall be called The Throne of
the LORD, and all the nations
shall be gathered to it, to the
name of the LORD, to Jerusalem. No more shall they follow the dictates of their evil
hearts.
18"In those days the house
of Judah shall walk with the
house of Israel, and they shall
come together out of the land
of the north to the land that I
have given as an inheritance
to your fathers.
19"But I said:

'How can I put you
among the children
And give you a
pleasant land,
A beautiful heritage of
the hosts of nations?'

"And I said:

'You shall call Me,
"My Father,"
And not turn away
from Me.'
20 Surely, *as* a wife
treacherously departs
from her husband,
So have you dealt
treacherously with Me,
O house of Israel,"
says the LORD.

21 A voice was heard on
the desolate heights,
Weeping *and*
supplications of the
children of Israel.
For they have perverted
their way;
They have forgotten
the LORD their God.

22"Return, you backsliding
children,
And I will heal your
backslidings."

"Indeed we do
come to You,
For You are the
LORD our God.
23 Truly, in vain *is salvation*
hoped for from the hills,
And from the multitude
of mountains;

Truly, in the LORD
our God
Is the salvation of Israel.
24 For shame has devoured
The labor of our fathers
from our youth—
Their flocks and
their herds,
Their sons and their
daughters.
25 We lie down in our shame,
And our reproach
covers us.
For we have sinned
against the LORD
our God,
We and our fathers,
From our youth
even to this day,
And have not obeyed
the voice of the
LORD our God."

4 "If you will return,
O Israel," says
the LORD,
"Return to Me;
And if you will put away
your abominations
out of My sight,
Then you shall not
be moved.
2 And you shall swear,
'The LORD lives,'
In truth, in judgment,
and in righteousness;
The nations shall bless
themselves in Him,
And in Him they
shall glory."

3For thus says the LORD to
the men of Judah and Jerusalem:

"Break up your
fallow ground,
And do not sow
among thorns.
4 Circumcise yourselves
to the LORD,
And take away the
foreskins of your hearts,
You men of Judah
and inhabitants
of Jerusalem,
Lest My fury come
forth like fire,
And burn so that no
one can quench *it,*
Because of the evil
of your doings."

AN IMMINENT INVASION

5Declare in Judah and proclaim in Jerusalem, and say:

"Blow the trumpet
in the land;
Cry, 'Gather together,'
And say, 'Assemble
yourselves,
And let us go into the
fortified cities.'
6 Set up the standard
toward Zion.
Take refuge! Do not delay!
For I will bring disaster
from the north,
And great destruction."

7 The lion has come up
from his thicket,
And the destroyer of
nations is on his way.
He has gone forth
from his place
To make your land
desolate.

Your cities will be
laid waste,
Without inhabitant.
8 For this, clothe yourself
with sackcloth,
Lament and wail.
For the fierce anger
of the LORD
Has not turned
back from us.

9 "And it shall come
to pass in that day,"
says the LORD,
"*That* the heart of the
king shall perish,
And the heart of
the princes;
The priests shall be
astonished,
And the prophets
shall wonder."

10 Then I said, "Ah,
Lord GOD!
Surely You have greatly
deceived this people
and Jerusalem,
Saying, 'You shall
have peace,'
Whereas the sword
reaches to the heart."

11 At that time it will be said
To this people and
to Jerusalem,
"A dry wind of the
desolate heights *blows*
in the wilderness
Toward the daughter
of My people—
Not to fan or to cleanse—
12 A wind too strong for
these will come for Me;
Now I will also
speak judgment
against them."

13 "Behold, he shall come
up like clouds,
And his chariots like
a whirlwind.
His horses are swifter
than eagles.
Woe to us, for we
are plundered!"

14 O Jerusalem, wash your
heart from wickedness,
That you may be saved.
How long shall your
evil thoughts lodge
within you?
15 For a voice declares
from Dan
And proclaims affliction
from Mount Ephraim:
16 "Make mention to
the nations,
Yes, proclaim against
Jerusalem,
That watchers come
from a far country
And raise their
voice against the
cities of Judah.
17 Like keepers of a field
they are against
her all around,
Because she has been
rebellious against
Me," says the LORD.
18 "Your ways and
your doings
Have procured these
things for you.
This *is* your wickedness,
Because it is bitter,

Because it reaches
to your heart."

SORROW FOR THE DOOMED NATION

19 O my soul, my soul!
I am pained in my
very heart!
My heart makes a
noise in me;
I cannot hold my peace,
Because you have
heard, O my soul,
The sound of the
trumpet,
The alarm of war.
20 Destruction upon
destruction is cried,
For the whole land
is plundered.
Suddenly my tents
are plundered,
And my curtains
in a moment.
21 How long will I see
the standard,
And hear the sound
of the trumpet?

22 "For My people *are* foolish,
They have not
known Me.
They *are* silly children,
And they have no
understanding.
They *are* wise to do evil,
But to do good they
have no knowledge."

23 I beheld the earth, and
indeed *it was* without
form, and void;
And the heavens,
they *had* no light.
24 I beheld the mountains,
and indeed they
trembled,
And all the hills moved
back and forth.
25 I beheld, and indeed
there was no man,
And all the birds of the
heavens had fled.
26 I beheld, and indeed
the fruitful land
was a wilderness,
And all its cities were
broken down
At the presence
of the LORD,
By His fierce anger.

27 For thus says the LORD:

"The whole land
shall be desolate;
Yet I will not make
a full end.
28 For this shall the
earth mourn,
And the heavens
above be black,
Because I have spoken.
I have purposed and
will not relent,
Nor will I turn
back from it.
29 The whole city shall
flee from the noise
of the horsemen
and bowmen.
They shall go into
thickets and climb
up on the rocks.
Every city *shall*
be forsaken,
And not a man shall
dwell in it.

30 "And *when* you
are plundered,
What will you do?
Though you clothe
yourself with crimson,
Though you adorn
yourself with
ornaments of gold,
Though you enlarge
your eyes with paint,
In vain you will make
yourself fair;
Your lovers will
despise you;
They will seek your life.

31 "For I have heard a
voice as of a
woman in labor,
The anguish as of her
who brings forth
her first child,
The voice of the
daughter of Zion
bewailing herself;
She spreads her
hands, *saying,*
'Woe *is* me now, for
my soul is weary
Because of murderers!'

THE JUSTICE OF GOD'S JUDGMENT

5 "Run to and fro
through the streets
of Jerusalem;
See now and know;
And seek in her
open places
If you can find a man,
If there is *anyone* who
executes judgment,
Who seeks the truth,
And I will pardon her.

2 Though they say, '*As*
the LORD lives,'
Surely they swear falsely."

3 O LORD, *are* not Your
eyes on the truth?
You have stricken them,
But they have not
grieved;
You have consumed
them,
But they have refused
to receive correction.
They have made their
faces harder than rock;
They have refused
to return.

4 Therefore I said, "Surely
these *are* poor.
They are foolish;
For they do not know
the way of the LORD,
The judgment of
their God.
5 I will go to the great men
and speak to them,
For they have known
the way of the LORD,
The judgment of
their God."

But these have altogether
broken the yoke
And burst the bonds.
6 Therefore a lion from the
forest shall slay them,
A wolf of the deserts
shall destroy them;
A leopard will watch
over their cities.
Everyone who goes
out from there shall
be torn in pieces,

Because their
transgressions
are many;
Their backslidings
have increased.

7 "How shall I pardon
you for this?
Your children have
forsaken Me
And sworn by *those*
that are not gods.
When I had fed
them to the full,
Then they committed
adultery
And assembled
themselves by
troops in the
harlots' houses.
8 They were *like* well-fed
lusty stallions;
Every one neighed after
his neighbor's wife.
9 Shall I not punish *them*
for these *things?*"
says the LORD.
"And shall I not avenge
Myself on such a
nation as this?

10 "Go up on her walls
and destroy,
But do not make a
complete end.
Take away her branches,
For they *are* not
the LORD's.
11 For the house of
Israel and the
house of Judah
Have dealt very
treacherously with
Me," says the LORD.
12 They have lied about
the LORD,
And said, "*It is* not He.
Neither will evil
come upon us,
Nor shall we see
sword or famine.
13 And the prophets
become wind,
For the word *is*
not in them.
Thus shall it be
done to them."

14 Therefore thus says the
LORD God of hosts:

"Because you speak
this word,
Behold, I will make
My words in your
mouth fire,
And this people wood,
And it shall devour them.
15 Behold, I will bring
a nation against
you from afar,
O house of Israel,"
says the LORD.
"It *is* a mighty nation,
It *is* an ancient nation,
A nation whose language
you do not know,
Nor can you understand
what they say.
16 Their quiver *is* like
an open tomb;
They *are* all mighty men.
17 And they shall eat up your
harvest and your bread,
Which your sons and
daughters should eat.
They shall eat up your
flocks and your herds;

They shall eat up your
vines and your fig trees;
They shall destroy your
fortified cities,
In which you trust,
with the sword.

18"Nevertheless in those
days," says the LORD, "I will not
make a complete end of you.
19And it will be when you say,
'Why does the LORD our God
do all these *things* to us?' then
you shall answer them, 'Just
as you have forsaken Me and
served foreign gods in your
land, so you shall serve aliens
in a land *that is* not yours.'

20"Declare this in the
house of Jacob
And proclaim it in
Judah, saying,
21 'Hear this now,
O foolish people,
Without understanding,
Who have eyes
and see not,
And who have ears
and hear not:
22 Do you not fear Me?'
says the LORD.
'Will you not tremble
at My presence,
Who have placed the sand
as the bound of the sea,
By a perpetual decree,
that it cannot
pass beyond it?
And though its waves
toss to and fro,
Yet they cannot prevail;
Though they roar, yet
they cannot pass over it.
23 But this people
has a defiant and
rebellious heart;
They have revolted
and departed.
24 They do not say in
their heart,
"Let us now fear the
LORD our God,
Who gives rain, both
the former and the
latter, in its season.
He reserves for us the
appointed weeks
of the harvest."
25 Your iniquities
have turned these
things away,
And your sins have
withheld good from you.

26 'For among My people
are found wicked *men;*
They lie in wait as one
who sets snares;
They set a trap;
They catch men.
27 As a cage is full of birds,
So their houses *are*
full of deceit.
Therefore they have
become great and
grown rich.
28 They have grown fat,
they are sleek;
Yes, they surpass the
deeds of the wicked;
They do not plead
the cause,
The cause of the
fatherless;
Yet they prosper,
And the right of the needy
they do not defend.

29 Shall I not punish *them*
for these *things?'*
says the LORD.
'Shall I not avenge
Myself on such a
nation as this?'

30 "An astonishing and
horrible thing
Has been committed
in the land:
31 The prophets
prophesy falsely,
And the priests rule by
their *own* power;
And My people love
to have it so.
But what will you
do in the end?

IMPENDING DESTRUCTION FROM THE NORTH

6 "O you children of
Benjamin,
Gather yourselves to
flee from the midst
of Jerusalem!
Blow the trumpet
in Tekoa,
And set up a signal-fire
in Beth Haccerem;
For disaster appears
out of the north,
And great destruction.
2 I have likened the
daughter of Zion
To a lovely and
delicate woman.
3 The shepherds with their
flocks shall come to her.
They shall pitch *their* tents
against her all around.
Each one shall pasture
in his own place."
4 "Prepare war against her;
Arise, and let us go
up at noon.
Woe to us, for the
day goes away,
For the shadows of
the evening are
lengthening.
5 Arise, and let us
go by night,
And let us destroy
her palaces."

6 For thus has the LORD of
hosts said:

"Cut down trees,
And build a mound
against Jerusalem.
This *is* the city to
be punished.
She *is* full of oppression
in her midst.
7 As a fountain wells
up with water,
So she wells up with
her wickedness.
Violence and plundering
are heard in her.
Before Me continually
are grief and wounds.
8 Be instructed,
O Jerusalem,
Lest My soul depart
from you;
Lest I make you desolate,
A land not inhabited."

9 Thus says the LORD of
hosts:

"They shall thoroughly
glean as a vine the
remnant of Israel;

As a grape-gatherer,
put your hand back
into the branches."

10 To whom shall I speak
and give warning,
That they may hear?
Indeed their ear *is*
uncircumcised,
And they cannot
give heed.
Behold, the word
of the LORD is a
reproach to them;
They have no delight in it.
11 Therefore I am full of
the fury of the LORD.
I am weary of
holding *it* in.
"I will pour it out on the
children outside,
And on the assembly of
young men together;
For even the husband
shall be taken
with the wife,
The aged with *him*
who is full of days.
12 And their houses shall be
turned over to others,
Fields and wives together;
For I will stretch
out My hand
Against the inhabitants
of the land," says
the LORD.
13 "Because from the least
of them even to the
greatest of them,
Everyone *is* given to
covetousness;
And from the prophet
even to the priest,
Everyone deals falsely.
14 They have also healed
the hurt of My
people slightly,
Saying, 'Peace, peace!'
When *there is* no peace.
15 Were they ashamed when
they had committed
abomination?
No! They were not
at all ashamed;
Nor did they know
how to blush.
Therefore they shall fall
among those who fall;
At the time I
punish them,
They shall be cast down,"
says the LORD.

16 Thus says the LORD:

"Stand in the ways and see,
And ask for the old paths,
where the good way *is*,
And walk in it;
Then you will find rest
for your souls.
But they said, 'We will
not walk *in it*.'
17 Also, I set watchmen
over you, *saying*,
'Listen to the sound
of the trumpet!'
But they said, 'We
will not listen.'
18 Therefore hear,
you nations,
And know,
O congregation, what
is among them.
19 Hear, O earth!
Behold, I will certainly
bring calamity on
this people—

The fruit of their
thoughts,
Because they have not
heeded My words
Nor My law, but rejected it.
20 For what purpose to Me
Comes frankincense
from Sheba,
And sweet cane from
a far country?
Your burnt offerings
are not acceptable,
Nor your sacrifices
sweet to Me."

21Therefore thus says the
LORD:

"Behold, I will lay
stumbling blocks
before this people,
And the fathers and
the sons together
shall fall on them.
The neighbor and his
friend shall perish."

22Thus says the LORD:

"Behold, a people comes
from the north country,
And a great nation will be
raised from the farthest
parts of the earth.
23 They will lay hold on
bow and spear;
They *are* cruel and
have no mercy;
Their voice roars
like the sea;
And they ride on horses,
As men of war set in
array against you,
O daughter of Zion."
24 We have heard the
report of it;
Our hands grow feeble.
Anguish has taken
hold of us,
Pain as of a woman
in labor.
25 Do not go out into
the field,
Nor walk by the way.
Because of the sword
of the enemy,
Fear *is* on every side.
26 O daughter of my people,
Dress in sackcloth
And roll about in ashes!
Make mourning *as for*
an only son, most
bitter lamentation;
For the plunderer
will suddenly
come upon us.

27"I have set you *as* an
assayer *and* a fortress
among My people,
That you may know
and test their way.
28 They *are* all stubborn
rebels, walking
as slanderers.
They are bronze and iron,
They *are* all corrupters;
29 The bellows blow fiercely,
The lead is consumed
by the fire;
The smelter refines
in vain,
For the wicked are
not drawn off.
30 *People* will call them
rejected silver,
Because the LORD has
rejected them."

TRUSTING IN LYING WORDS

7 The word that came to Jeremiah from the LORD, say-
ing, 2“Stand in the gate of the
LORD’s house, and proclaim
there this word, and say, ‘Hear
the word of the LORD, all *you*
of Judah who enter in at these
gates to worship the LORD!’”
3Thus says the LORD of hosts,
the God of Israel: “Amend
your ways and your doings,
and I will cause you to dwell
in this place. 4Do not trust in
these lying words, saying, ‘The
temple of the LORD, the temple of the LORD, the temple of
the LORD *are* these.’

5“For if you thoroughly
amend your ways and your
doings, if you thoroughly execute judgment between a man
and his neighbor, 6*if* you do
not oppress the stranger, the
fatherless, and the widow, and
do not shed innocent blood
in this place, or walk after
other gods to your hurt, 7then
I will cause you to dwell in this
place, in the land that I gave to
your fathers forever and ever.

8“Behold, you trust in lying
words that cannot profit. 9Will
you steal, murder, commit
adultery, swear falsely, burn
incense to Baal, and walk after
other gods whom you do not
know, 10and *then* come and
stand before Me in this house
which is called by My name,
and say, ‘We are delivered to
do all these abominations’?
11Has this house, which is
called by My name, become
a den of thieves in your eyes?
Behold, I, even I, have seen *it*,”
says the LORD.

12“But go now to My place
which *was* in Shiloh, where I
set My name at the first, and
see what I did to it because of
the wickedness of My people
Israel. 13And now, because you
have done all these works,”
says the LORD, “and I spoke
to you, rising up early and
speaking, but you did not
hear, and I called you, but you
did not answer, 14therefore I
will do to the house which is
called by My name, in which
you trust, and to this place
which I gave to you and your
fathers, as I have done to Shiloh. 15And I will cast you out
of My sight, as I have cast out
all your brethren—the whole
posterity of Ephraim.

16“Therefore do not pray
for this people, nor lift up a
cry or prayer for them, nor
make intercession to Me; for
I will not hear you. 17Do you
not see what they do in the cities of Judah and in the streets
of Jerusalem? 18The children
gather wood, the fathers kindle the fire, and the women
knead dough, to make cakes
for the queen of heaven; and
they pour out drink offerings
to other gods, that they may
provoke Me to anger. 19Do
they provoke Me to anger?”
says the LORD. “*Do they* not
provoke themselves, to the
shame of their own faces?”

20Therefore thus says the
Lord GOD: "Behold, My anger
and My fury will be poured out
on this place—on man and
on beast, on the trees of the
field and on the fruit of the
ground. And it will burn and
not be quenched."

21Thus says the LORD of
hosts, the God of Israel: "Add
your burnt offerings to your
sacrifices and eat meat. 22For
I did not speak to your fathers, or command them in
the day that I brought them
out of the land of Egypt, concerning burnt offerings or
sacrifices. 23But this is what
I commanded them, saying,
'Obey My voice, and I will be
your God, and you shall be My
people. And walk in all the
ways that I have commanded
you, that it may be well with
you.' 24Yet they did not obey
or incline their ear, but followed the counsels *and* the
dictates of their evil hearts,
and went backward and not
forward. 25Since the day that
your fathers came out of the
land of Egypt until this day, I
have even sent to you all My
servants the prophets, daily
rising up early and sending
them. 26Yet they did not obey
Me or incline their ear, but
stiffened their neck. They did
worse than their fathers.

27"Therefore you shall
speak all these words to them,
but they will not obey you.
You shall also call to them,
but they will not answer you.

JUDGMENT ON OBSCENE RELIGION

28"So you shall say to them,
'This *is* a nation that does not
obey the voice of the LORD
their God nor receive correction. Truth has perished and
has been cut off from their
mouth. 29Cut off your hair
and cast *it* away, and take up
a lamentation on the desolate
heights; for the LORD has rejected and forsaken the generation of His wrath.' 30For
the children of Judah have
done evil in My sight," says
the LORD. "They have set their
abominations in the house
which is called by My name,
to pollute it. 31And they have
built the high places of Tophet, which *is* in the Valley of
the Son of Hinnom, to burn
their sons and their daughters in the fire, which I did not
command, nor did it come
into My heart.

32"Therefore behold, the
days are coming," says the
LORD, "when it will no more
be called Tophet, or the Valley
of the Son of Hinnom, but the
Valley of Slaughter; for they
will bury in Tophet until there
is no room. 33The corpses of
this people will be food for the
birds of the heaven and for the
beasts of the earth. And no
one will frighten *them away.*
34Then I will cause to cease
from the cities of Judah and
from the streets of Jerusalem
the voice of mirth and the
voice of gladness, the voice of

the bridegroom and the voice
of the bride. For the land shall
be desolate.

8 "At that time," says the
LORD, "they shall bring
out the bones of the kings of
Judah, and the bones of its
princes, and the bones of the
priests, and the bones of the
prophets, and the bones of
the inhabitants of Jerusalem,
out of their graves. 2They shall
spread them before the sun
and the moon and all the host
of heaven, which they have
loved and which they have
served and after which they
have walked, which they have
sought and which they have
worshiped. They shall not be
gathered nor buried; they shall
be like refuse on the face of
the earth. 3Then death shall
be chosen rather than life by
all the residue of those who
remain of this evil family, who
remain in all the places where
I have driven them," says the
LORD of hosts.

THE PERIL OF FALSE TEACHING

4"Moreover you shall say
to them, 'Thus says the LORD:

"Will they fall
and not rise?
Will one turn away
and not return?
5 Why has this people
slidden back,
Jerusalem, in a perpetual
backsliding?
They hold fast to deceit,
They refuse to return.
6 I listened and heard,
But they do not
speak aright.
No man repented of
his wickedness,
Saying, 'What
have I done?'
Everyone turned to
his own course,
As the horse rushes
into the battle.

7 "Even the stork in
the heavens
Knows her appointed
times;
And the turtledove, the
swift, and the swallow
Observe the time of
their coming.
But My people do not
know the judgment
of the LORD.

8 "How can you say,
'We *are* wise,
And the law of the
LORD *is* with us'?
Look, the false pen of
the scribe certainly
works falsehood.
9 The wise men are
ashamed,
They are dismayed
and taken.
Behold, they have rejected
the word of the LORD;
So what wisdom
do they have?
10 Therefore I will give
their wives to others,
And their fields to those
who will inherit *them;*

Because from the least
even to the greatest
Everyone is given to
covetousness;
From the prophet
even to the priest
Everyone deals falsely.
11 For they have healed the
hurt of the daughter
of My people slightly,
Saying, 'Peace, peace!'
When *there is* no peace.
12 Were they ashamed when
they had committed
abomination?
No! They were not
at all ashamed,
Nor did they know
how to blush.
Therefore they shall fall
among those who fall;
In the time of their
punishment
They shall be cast down,"
says the LORD.

13 "I will surely consume
them," says the LORD.
"No grapes *shall be*
on the vine,
Nor figs on the fig tree,
And the leaf shall fade;
And *the things* I have
given them shall pass
away from them." ' "

14 "Why do we sit still?
Assemble yourselves,
And let us enter the
fortified cities,
And let us be silent
there.
For the LORD our God
has put us to silence
And given us water
of gall to drink,
Because we have sinned
against the LORD.

15 "*We* looked for peace,
but no good *came;*
And for a time of health,
and there was trouble!
16 The snorting of His horses
was heard from Dan.
The whole land
trembled at the sound
of the neighing of
His strong ones;
For they have come and
devoured the land
and all that is in it,
The city and those
who dwell in it."

17 "For behold, I will send
serpents among you,
Vipers which cannot
be charmed,
And they shall bite
you," says the LORD.

THE PROPHET MOURNS FOR THE PEOPLE

18 I would comfort
myself in sorrow;
My heart *is* faint in me.
19 Listen! The voice,
The cry of the daughter
of my people
From a far country:
"*Is* not the LORD in Zion?
Is not her King in her?"

"Why have they
provoked Me to anger
With their carved images—
With foreign idols?"

20 "The harvest is past,
The summer is ended,
And we are not saved!"

21 For the hurt of the
daughter of my
people I am hurt.
I am mourning;
Astonishment has
taken hold of me.
22 *Is there* no balm in Gilead,
Is there no physician
there?
Why then is there
no recovery
For the health of the
daughter of my people?

9

Oh, that my head
were waters,
And my eyes a
fountain of tears,
That I might weep
day and night
For the slain of the
daughter of my people!
2 Oh, that I had in
the wilderness
A lodging place
for travelers;
That I might leave
my people,
And go from them!
For they *are* all adulterers,
An assembly of
treacherous men.

3 "And *like* their bow
they have bent their
tongues *for* lies.
They are not valiant for
the truth on the earth.
For they proceed
from evil to evil,
And they do not know
Me," says the LORD.
4 "Everyone take heed
to his neighbor,
And do not trust
any brother;
For every brother will
utterly supplant,
And every neighbor
will walk with
slanderers.
5 Everyone will deceive
his neighbor,
And will not speak
the truth;
They have taught their
tongue to speak lies;
They weary themselves
to commit iniquity.
6 Your dwelling place *is* in
the midst of deceit;
Through deceit they
refuse to know Me,"
says the LORD.

7 Therefore thus says the
LORD of hosts:

"Behold, I will refine
them and try them;
For how shall I deal
with the daughter
of My people?
8 Their tongue *is* an
arrow shot out;
It speaks deceit;
One speaks peaceably
to his neighbor
with his mouth,
But in his heart he
lies in wait.
9 Shall I not punish them
for these *things*?"
says the LORD.

"Shall I not avenge
Myself on such a
nation as this?"

10 I will take up a weeping
and wailing for
the mountains,
And for the dwelling
places of the wilderness
a lamentation,
Because they are
burned up,
So that no one can
pass through;
Nor can *men* hear the
voice of the cattle.
Both the birds of the
heavens and the
beasts have fled;
They are gone.

11 "I will make Jerusalem
a heap of ruins, a
den of jackals.
I will make the cities
of Judah desolate,
without an inhabitant."

12Who *is* the wise man who
may understand this? And
who is he to whom the mouth
of the LORD has spoken, that
he may declare it? Why does
the land perish *and* burn up
like a wilderness, so that no
one can pass through?
13And the LORD said, "Be-
cause they have forsaken My
law which I set before them,
and have not obeyed My
voice, nor walked according
to it, 14but they have walked
according to the dictates of
their own hearts and after
the Baals, which their fathers
taught them," 15therefore thus
says the LORD of hosts, the God
of Israel: "Behold, I will feed
them, this people, with wormwood, and give them water of
gall to drink. 16I will scatter
them also among the Gentiles,
whom neither they nor their
fathers have known. And I will
send a sword after them until
I have consumed them."

THE PEOPLE MOURN IN JUDGMENT

17Thus says the LORD of
hosts:

"Consider and call for the
mourning women,
That they may come;
And send for skillful
wailing women,
That they may come.
18 Let them make haste
And take up a
wailing for us,
That our eyes may
run with tears,
And our eyelids gush
with water.
19 For a voice of wailing
is heard from Zion:
'How we are plundered!
We are greatly ashamed,
Because we have
forsaken the land,
Because we have been cast
out of our dwellings.'"

20 Yet hear the word of
the LORD, O women,
And let your ear receive
the word of His mouth;

Teach your daughters
wailing,
And everyone her
neighbor a lamentation.
21 For death has come
through our windows,
Has entered our palaces,
To kill off the
children—*no longer*
to be outside!
And the young men—*no*
longer on the streets!

22Speak, "Thus says the LORD:

'Even the carcasses of
men shall fall as refuse
on the open field,
Like cuttings after
the harvester,
And no one shall
gather *them.*'"

23Thus says the LORD:

"Let not the wise *man*
glory in his wisdom,
Let not the mighty *man*
glory in his might,
Nor let the rich *man*
glory in his riches;
24 But let him who glories
glory in this,
That he understands
and knows Me,
That I *am* the
LORD, exercising
lovingkindness,
judgment, and
*right*eousness
in the earth.
For in these I delight,"
says the LORD.

25"Behold, the days are
coming," says the LORD, "that
I will punish all *who are* circumcised with the uncircumcised— 26Egypt, Judah, Edom,
the people of Ammon, Moab,
and all *who are* in the farthest
corners, who dwell in the wilderness. For all *these* nations
are uncircumcised, and all the
house of Israel *are* uncircumcised in the heart."

IDOLS AND THE TRUE GOD

10 Hear the word which
the LORD speaks to you,
O house of Israel.
2Thus says the LORD:

"Do not learn the way
of the Gentiles;
Do not be dismayed at
the signs of heaven,
For the Gentiles are
dismayed at them.
3 For the customs of the
peoples *are* futile;
For *one* cuts a tree
from the forest,
The work of the hands
of the workman,
with the ax.
4 They decorate it with
silver and gold;
They fasten it with
nails and hammers
So that it will not topple.
5 They *are* upright,
like a palm tree,
And they cannot speak;
They must be carried,
Because they cannot
go *by themselves.*
Do not be afraid of them,

For they cannot do evil,
Nor can they do
any good."

6 Inasmuch as *there is*
none like You, O LORD
(You *are* great, and Your
name *is* great in might),
7 Who would not fear You,
O King of the nations?
For this is Your
rightful due.
For among all the wise
men of the nations,
And in all their kingdoms,
There is none like You.
8 But they are altogether
dull-hearted
and foolish;
A wooden idol *is* a
worthless doctrine.
9 Silver is beaten
into plates;
It is brought from
Tarshish,
And gold from Uphaz,
The work of the craftsman
And of the hands of
the metalsmith;
Blue and purple *are*
their clothing;
They *are* all the work
of skillful *men*.
10 But the LORD *is*
the true God;
He *is* the living God and
the everlasting King.
At His wrath the earth
will tremble,
And the nations will
not be able to endure
His indignation.

11 Thus you shall say to
them: "The gods that have
not made the heavens and the
earth shall perish from the
earth and from under these
heavens."

12 He has made the earth
by His power,
He has established the
world by His wisdom,
And has stretched
out the heavens at
His discretion.
13 When He utters His voice,
There is a multitude of
waters in the heavens:
"And He causes the
vapors to ascend from
the ends of the earth.
He makes lightning
for the rain,
He brings the wind out
of His treasuries."[a]

14 Everyone is dull-hearted,
without knowledge;
Every metalsmith is put
to shame by an image;
For his molded image
is falsehood,
And *there is* no
breath in them.
15 They *are* futile, a
work of errors;
In the time of their
punishment they
shall perish.
16 The Portion of Jacob
is not like them,
For He *is* the Maker
of all *things*,

10:13 [a] Psalm 135:7

And Israel *is* the tribe
of His inheritance;
The LORD of hosts
is His name.

THE COMING CAPTIVITY OF JUDAH

17 Gather up your wares
from the land,
O inhabitant of
the fortress!

18For thus says the LORD:

"Behold, I will throw
out at this time
The inhabitants
of the land,
And will distress them,
That they may find *it so.*"

19 Woe is me for my hurt!
My wound is severe.
But I say, "Truly this
is an infirmity,
And I must bear it."
20 My tent is plundered,
And all my cords
are broken;
My children have
gone from me,
And they *are* no more.
There is no one to pitch
my tent anymore,
Or set up my curtains.

21 For the shepherds have
become dull-hearted,
And have not sought
the LORD;
Therefore they shall
not prosper,
And all their flocks
shall be scattered.
22 Behold, the noise of the
report has come,
And a great commotion
out of the north
country,
To make the cities of
Judah desolate, a
den of jackals.

23 O LORD, I know the way of
man *is* not in himself;
It is not in man who walks
to direct his own steps.
24 O LORD, correct me,
but with justice;
Not in Your anger,
lest You bring me
to nothing.
25 Pour out Your fury on
the Gentiles, who
do not know You,
And on the families
who do not call
on Your name;
For they have eaten
up Jacob,
Devoured him and
consumed him,
And made his dwelling
place desolate.

THE BROKEN COVENANT

11 The word that came to
Jeremiah from the LORD,
saying, 2"Hear the words of
this covenant, and speak to the
men of Judah and to the inhabitants of Jerusalem; 3and say
to them, 'Thus says the LORD
God of Israel: "Cursed *is* the
man who does not obey the
words of this covenant 4which
I commanded your fathers in
the day I brought them out of

the land of Egypt, from the
iron furnace, saying, 'Obey My
voice, and do according to all
that I command you; so shall
you be My people, and I will
be your God,' 5that I may establish the oath which I have
sworn to your fathers, to give
them 'a land flowing with milk
and honey,'[a] as *it is* this day."'"

And I answered and said,
"So be it, LORD."

6Then the LORD said to me,
"Proclaim all these words in
the cities of Judah and in the
streets of Jerusalem, saying:
'Hear the words of this covenant and do them. 7For I earnestly exhorted your fathers
in the day I brought them
up out of the land of Egypt,
until this day, rising early and
exhorting, saying, "Obey My
voice." 8Yet they did not obey
or incline their ear, but everyone followed the dictates of
his evil heart; therefore I will
bring upon them all the words
of this covenant, which I commanded *them* to do, but *which*
they have not done.'"

9And the LORD said to me,
"A conspiracy has been found
among the men of Judah and
among the inhabitants of Jerusalem. 10They have turned
back to the iniquities of their
forefathers who refused to
hear My words, and they have
gone after other gods to serve
them; the house of Israel
and the house of Judah have
broken My covenant which I
made with their fathers."

11Therefore thus says the
LORD: "Behold, I will surely
bring calamity on them which
they will not be able to escape;
and though they cry out to
Me, I will not listen to them.
12Then the cities of Judah and
the inhabitants of Jerusalem
will go and cry out to the gods
to whom they offer incense,
but they will not save them at
all in the time of their trouble.
13For *according to* the number
of your cities were your gods,
O Judah; and *according to* the
number of the streets of Jerusalem you have set up altars
to *that* shameful thing, altars
to burn incense to Baal.

14"So do not pray for this
people, or lift up a cry or
prayer for them; for I will
not hear *them* in the time that
they cry out to Me because of
their trouble.

15 "What has My beloved
  to do in My house,
Having done lewd
  deeds with many?
And the holy flesh has
  passed from you.
When you do evil,
  then you rejoice.
16 The LORD called
  your name,
Green Olive Tree, Lovely
  and of Good Fruit.
With the noise of a
  great tumult

11:5 [a] Exodus 3:8

He has kindled fire on it,
And its branches
are broken.

17"For the LORD of hosts,
who planted you, has pro-
nounced doom against you
for the evil of the house of Israel and of the house of Judah,
which they have done against
themselves to provoke Me to
anger in offering incense to
Baal."

JEREMIAH'S LIFE THREATENED

18Now the LORD gave me
knowledge *of it,* and I know *it;*
for You showed me their doings. 19But I *was* like a docile
lamb brought to the slaughter;
and I did not know that they
had devised schemes against
me, *saying,* "Let us destroy the
tree with its fruit, and let us
cut him off from the land of
the living, that his name may
be remembered no more."

20 But, O LORD of hosts,
You who judge
righteously,
Testing the mind
and the heart,
Let me see Your
vengeance on them,
For to You I have
revealed my cause.

21"Therefore thus says the
LORD concerning the men of
Anathoth who seek your life,
saying, 'Do not prophesy in
the name of the LORD, lest you
die by our hand'— 22therefore
thus says the LORD of hosts:
'Behold, I will punish them.
The young men shall die by
the sword, their sons and their
daughters shall die by famine;
23and there shall be no remnant of them, for I will bring
catastrophe on the men of Anathoth, *even* the year of their
punishment.'"

JEREMIAH'S QUESTION

12 Righteous *are* You,
O LORD, when I
plead with You;
Yet let me talk with You
about *Your* judgments.
Why does the way of
the wicked prosper?
Why are those happy who
deal so treacherously?
2 You have planted
them, yes, they
have taken root;
They grow, yes, they
bear fruit.
You *are* near in
their mouth
But far from their mind.

3 But You, O LORD,
know me;
You have seen me,
And You have tested my
heart toward You.
Pull them out like sheep
for the slaughter,
And prepare them for
the day of slaughter.
4 How long will the
land mourn,
And the herbs of every
field wither?

The beasts and birds
are consumed,
For the wickedness of
those who dwell there,
Because they said, "He will
not see our final end."

THE LORD ANSWERS JEREMIAH

5 "If you have run with the
footmen, and they
have wearied you,
Then how can you
contend with horses?
And *if* in the land
of peace,
In which you trusted,
they wearied you,
Then how will you do
in the floodplain[a]
of the Jordan?
6 For even your
brothers, the house
of your father,
Even they have dealt
treacherously with you;
Yes, they have called a
multitude after you.
Do not believe them,
Even though they speak
smooth words to you.

7 "I have forsaken My house,
I have left My heritage;
I have given the dearly
beloved of My soul
into the hand of
her enemies.
8 My heritage is to Me like
a lion in the forest;
It cries out against Me;
Therefore I have hated it.
9 My heritage *is* to Me *like*
a speckled vulture;
The vultures all around
are against her.
Come, assemble all the
beasts of the field,
Bring them to devour!

10 "Many rulers[a] have
destroyed My vineyard,
They have trodden My
portion underfoot;
They have made My
pleasant portion a
desolate wilderness.
11 They have made
it desolate;
Desolate, it mourns to Me;
The whole land is
made desolate,
Because no one
takes *it* to heart.
12 The plunderers
have come
On all the desolate
heights in the
wilderness,
For the sword of the
LORD shall devour
From *one* end of the
land to the *other*
end of the land;
No flesh shall have peace.
13 They have sown wheat
but reaped thorns;
They have put
themselves to pain
but do not profit.
But be ashamed of
your harvest
Because of the fierce
anger of the LORD."

12:5 [a] Or *thicket* **12:10** [a] Literally *shepherds* or *pastors*

14Thus says the LORD:
"Against all My evil neighbors
who touch the inheritance
which I have caused My people Israel to inherit—behold,
I will pluck them out of their
land and pluck out the house
of Judah from among them.
15Then it shall be, after I have
plucked them out, that I will
return and have compassion
on them and bring them back,
everyone to his heritage and
everyone to his land. 16And it
shall be, if they will learn carefully the ways of My people,
to swear by My name, 'As the
LORD lives,' as they taught My
people to swear by Baal, then
they shall be established in
the midst of My people. 17But
if they do not obey, I will utterly pluck up and destroy
that nation," says the LORD.

SYMBOL OF THE LINEN SASH

13 Thus the LORD said to
me: "Go and get yourself
a linen sash, and put it around
your waist, but do not put it in
water." 2So I got a sash according to the word of the LORD,
and put *it* around my waist.

3And the word of the LORD
came to me the second time,
saying, 4"Take the sash that
you acquired, which *is* around
your waist, and arise, go to
the Euphrates,[a] and hide it
there in a hole in the rock."
5So I went and hid it by the
Euphrates, as the LORD commanded me.

6Now it came to pass after
many days that the LORD said
to me, "Arise, go to the Euphrates, and take from there the
sash which I commanded you
to hide there." 7Then I went to
the Euphrates and dug, and I
took the sash from the place
where I had hidden it; and
there was the sash, ruined. It
was profitable for nothing.

8Then the word of the LORD
came to me, saying, 9"Thus
says the LORD: 'In this manner
I will ruin the pride of Judah
and the great pride of Jerusalem. 10This evil people, who
refuse to hear My words, who
follow the dictates of their
hearts, and walk after other
gods to serve them and worship them, shall be just like
this sash which is profitable
for nothing. 11For as the sash
clings to the waist of a man, so
I have caused the whole house
of Israel and the whole house
of Judah to cling to Me,' says
the LORD, 'that they may become My people, for renown,
for praise, and for glory; but
they would not hear.'

SYMBOL OF THE WINE BOTTLES

12"Therefore you shall
speak to them this word: 'Thus
says the LORD God of Israel:
"Every bottle shall be filled
with wine."'

13:4 [a] Hebrew *Perath*

"And they will say to you,
'Do we not certainly know that
every bottle will be filled with
wine?'
13"Then you shall say to
them, 'Thus says the LORD:
"Behold, I will fill all the
inhabitants of this land—even
the kings who sit on David's
throne, the priests, the prophets, and all the inhabitants of
Jerusalem—with drunken-
ness! 14And I will dash them
one against another, even the
fathers and the sons together,"
says the LORD. "I will not pity
nor spare nor have mercy, but
will destroy them."'"

PRIDE PRECEDES CAPTIVITY

15 Hear and give ear:
Do not be proud,
For the LORD has spoken.
16 Give glory to the
LORD your God
Before He causes
darkness,
And before your
feet stumble
On the dark mountains,
And while you are
looking for light,
He turns it into the
shadow of death
And makes *it* dense
darkness.
17 But if you will not hear it,
My soul will weep in
secret for *your* pride;
My eyes will weep bitterly
And run down with tears,
Because the LORD's flock
has been taken captive.

18 Say to the king and to
the queen mother,
"Humble yourselves;
Sit down,
For your rule shall
collapse, the crown
of your glory."
19 The cities of the South
shall be shut up,
And no one shall
open *them;*
Judah shall be carried
away captive, all of it;
It shall be wholly carried
away captive.

20 Lift up your eyes and see
Those who come
from the north.
Where *is* the flock *that*
was given to you,
Your beautiful sheep?
21 What will you say when
He punishes you?
For you have taught them
To be chieftains, to be
head over you.
Will not pangs seize you,
Like a woman in labor?
22 And if you say in
your heart,
"Why have these things
come upon me?"
For the greatness of
your iniquity
Your skirts have
been uncovered,
Your heels made bare.
23 Can the Ethiopian
change his skin or the
leopard its spots?
Then may you also
do good who are
accustomed to do evil.

24"Therefore I will scatter
them like stubble
That passes away by the
wind of the wilderness.
25 This is your lot,
The portion of your
measures from Me,"
says the LORD,
"Because you have
forgotten Me
And trusted in falsehood.
26 Therefore I will
uncover your skirts
over your face,
That your shame
may appear.
27 I have seen your adulteries
And your *lustful*
neighings,
The lewdness of
your harlotry,
Your abominations on
the hills in the fields.
Woe to you, O Jerusalem!
Will you still not be
made clean?"

SWORD, FAMINE, AND PESTILENCE

14 The word of the LORD that came to Jeremiah concerning the droughts.

2 "Judah mourns,
And her gates languish;
They mourn for the land,
And the cry of Jerusalem
has gone up.
3 Their nobles have sent
their lads for water;
They went to the cisterns
and found no water.
They returned with
their vessels empty;
They were ashamed
and confounded
And covered their heads.
4 Because the ground
is parched,
For there was no
rain in the land,
The plowmen were
ashamed;
They covered their heads.
5 Yes, the deer also gave
birth in the field,
But left because there
was no grass.
6 And the wild donkeys
stood in the
desolate heights;
They sniffed at the
wind like jackals;
Their eyes failed because
there was no grass."

7 O LORD, though our
iniquities testify
against us,
Do it for Your name's sake;
For our backslidings
are many,
We have sinned
against You.
8 O the Hope of Israel,
his Savior in time
of trouble,
Why should You be like
a stranger in the land,
And like a traveler
who turns aside to
tarry for a night?
9 Why should You be like
a man astonished,
Like a mighty one
who cannot save?
Yet You, O LORD, *are*
in our midst,

And we are called
by Your name;
Do not leave us!

10Thus says the LORD to
this people:

"Thus they have
loved to wander;
They have not
restrained their feet.
Therefore the LORD does
not accept them;
He will remember
their iniquity now,
And punish their sins."

11Then the LORD said to me,
"Do not pray for this people,
for *their* good. 12When they
fast, I will not hear their cry;
and when they offer burnt
offering and grain offering,
I will not accept them. But
I will consume them by the
sword, by the famine, and by
the pestilence."
13Then I said, "Ah, Lord
GOD! Behold, the prophets
say to them, 'You shall not see
the sword, nor shall you have
famine, but I will give you assured peace in this place.'"
14And the LORD said to
me, "The prophets proph-
esy lies in My name. I have
not sent them, commanded
them, nor spoken to them;
they prophesy to you a false
vision, divination, a worthless thing, and the deceit of
their heart. 15Therefore thus
says the LORD concerning the
prophets who prophesy in My
name, whom I did not send,
and who say, 'Sword and famine shall not be in this land'—
'By sword and famine those
prophets shall be consumed!
16And the people to whom
they prophesy shall be cast
out in the streets of Jerusalem
because of the famine and the
sword; they will have no one
to bury them—them nor their
wives, their sons nor their
daughters—for I will pour
their wickedness on them.'
17"Therefore you shall say
this word to them:

'Let my eyes flow with
tears night and day,
And let them not cease;
For the virgin daughter
of my people
Has been broken with
a mighty stroke, with
a very severe blow.
18 If I go out to the field,
Then behold, those
slain with the sword!
And if I enter the city,
Then behold, those
sick from famine!
Yes, both prophet and
priest go about in a
land they do not know.'"

THE PEOPLE PLEAD FOR MERCY

19 Have You utterly
rejected Judah?
Has Your soul
loathed Zion?
Why have You stricken
us so that *there is*
no healing for us?

We looked for peace, but
there was no good;
And for the time of
healing, and there
was trouble.
20 We acknowledge, O LORD,
our wickedness
And the iniquity of
our fathers,
For we have sinned
against You.
21 Do not abhor *us*, for
Your name's sake;
Do not disgrace the
throne of Your glory.
Remember, do not break
Your covenant with us.
22 Are there any among the
idols of the nations
that can cause rain?
Or can the heavens
give showers?
Are You not He,
O LORD our God?
Therefore we will
wait for You,
Since You have
made all these.

THE LORD WILL NOT RELENT

15 Then the LORD said to
me, "*Even* if Moses and
Samuel stood before Me, My
mind *would* not *be* favorable
toward this people. Cast *them*
out of My sight, and let them
go forth. 2And it shall be, if
they say to you, 'Where should
we go?' then you shall tell
them, 'Thus says the LORD:

"Such as *are* for
death, to death;
And such as *are* for the
sword, to the sword;
And such as *are* for the
famine, to the famine;
And such as *are* for
the captivity, to
the captivity."'

3"And I will appoint over
them four forms *of destruc-*
tion," says the LORD: "the
sword to slay, the dogs to
drag, the birds of the heavens and the beasts of the earth
to devour and destroy. 4I will
hand them over to trouble,
to all kingdoms of the earth,
because of Manasseh the son
of Hezekiah, king of Judah,
for what he did in Jerusalem.

5 "For who will have pity
on you, O Jerusalem?
Or who will bemoan you?
Or who will turn
aside to ask how
you are doing?
6 You have forsaken
Me," says the LORD,
"You have gone
backward.
Therefore I will stretch
out My hand against
you and destroy you;
I am weary of relenting!
7 And I will winnow them
with a winnowing
fan in the gates
of the land;
I will bereave *them*
of children;
I will destroy My people,
Since they do not return
from their ways.

8 Their widows will
be increased to
Me more than the
sand of the seas;
I will bring against them,
Against the mother of
the young men,
A plunderer at noonday;
I will cause anguish
and terror to fall on
them suddenly.

9 "She languishes who
has borne seven;
She has breathed her last;
Her sun has gone down
While *it was* yet day;
She has been ashamed
and confounded.
And the remnant of them I
will deliver to the sword
Before their enemies,"
says the LORD.

JEREMIAH'S DEJECTION

10 Woe is me, my mother,
That you have borne me,
A man of strife and a
man of contention
to the whole earth!
I have neither lent
for interest,
Nor have men lent to
me for interest.
Every one of them
curses me.

11 The LORD said:

"Surely it will be well
with your remnant;
Surely I will cause
the enemy to
intercede with you
In the time of adversity
and in the time
of affliction.
12 Can anyone break iron,
The northern iron
and the bronze?
13 Your wealth and
your treasures
I will give as plunder
without price,
Because of all your sins,
Throughout your
territories.
14 And I will make *you*
cross over with[a]
your enemies
Into a land *which* you
do not know;
For a fire is kindled
in My anger,
Which shall burn
upon you."

15 O LORD, You know;
Remember me
and visit me,
And take vengeance for
me on my persecutors.
In Your enduring
patience, do not
take me away.
Know that for Your sake I
have suffered rebuke.
16 Your words were found,
and I ate them,
And Your word was
to me the joy and
rejoicing of my heart;

15:14 [a] Following Masoretic Text and Vulgate; Septuagint, Syriac, and Targum read *cause you to serve* (compare 17:4).

For I am called by
Your name,
O LORD God of hosts.
17 I did not sit in the
assembly of the
mockers,
Nor did I rejoice;
I sat alone because
of Your hand,
For You have filled me
with indignation.
18 Why is my pain perpetual
And my wound incurable,
Which refuses to
be healed?
Will You surely
be to me like an
unreliable stream,
As waters *that* fail?

THE LORD REASSURES JEREMIAH

19Therefore thus says the
LORD:

"If you return,
Then I will bring
you back;
You shall stand before Me;
If you take out the
precious from the vile,
You shall be as My mouth.
Let them return to you,
But you must not
return to them.
20 And I will make you
to this people a
fortified bronze wall;
And they will fight
against you,
But they shall not
prevail against you;
For I *am* with you
to save you
And deliver you,"
says the LORD.
21"I will deliver you from
the hand of the wicked,
And I will redeem
you from the grip
of the terrible."

JEREMIAH'S LIFESTYLE AND MESSAGE

16 The word of the LORD
also came to me, saying,
2"You shall not take a wife, nor
shall you have sons or daughters in this place." 3For thus
says the LORD concerning
the sons and daughters who
are born in this place, and
concerning their mothers
who bore them and their fathers who begot them in this
land: 4"They shall die grue-
some deaths; they shall not
be lamented nor shall they be
buried, *but* they shall be like
refuse on the face of the earth.
They shall be consumed by
the sword and by famine, and
their corpses shall be meat for
the birds of heaven and for the
beasts of the earth."

5For thus says the LORD:
"Do not enter the house of
mourning, nor go to lament or
bemoan them; for I have taken
away My peace from this people," says the LORD, "lovingkindness and mercies. 6Both
the great and the small shall
die in this land. They shall not
be buried; neither shall men
lament for them, cut themselves, nor make themselves
bald for them. 7Nor shall *men*

break *bread* in mourning for
them, to comfort them for
the dead; nor shall *men* give
them the cup of consolation to
drink for their father or their
mother. 8Also you shall not go
into the house of feasting to sit
with them, to eat and drink."

9For thus says the LORD of
hosts, the God of Israel: "Behold, I will cause to cease from
this place, before your eyes and
in your days, the voice of mirth
and the voice of gladness, the
voice of the bridegroom and
the voice of the bride.

10"And it shall be, when
you show this people all
these words, and they say to
you, 'Why has the LORD pronounced all this great disaster
against us? Or what *is* our iniquity? Or what *is* our sin that
we have committed against
the LORD our God?' 11then you
shall say to them, 'Because
your fathers have forsaken
Me,' says the LORD; 'they have
walked after other gods and
have served them and wor-
shiped them, and have forsaken Me and not kept My law.
12And you have done worse
than your fathers, for behold,
each one follows the dictates
of his own evil heart, so that
no one listens to Me. 13There-
fore I will cast you out of this
land into a land that you do
not know, neither you nor
your fathers; and there you
shall serve other gods day and
night, where I will not show
you favor.'

GOD WILL RESTORE ISRAEL

14"Therefore behold, the
days are coming," says the
LORD, "that it shall no more
be said, 'The LORD lives who
brought up the children of Israel from the land of Egypt,'
15but, 'The LORD lives who
brought up the children of Israel from the land of the north
and from all the lands where
He had driven them.' For I will
bring them back into their land
which I gave to their fathers.

16"Behold, I will send for
many fishermen," says the
LORD, "and they shall fish
them; and afterward I will
send for many hunters, and
they shall hunt them from
every mountain and every
hill, and out of the holes of
the rocks. 17For My eyes *are*
on all their ways; they are not
hidden from My face, nor is
their iniquity hidden from My
eyes. 18And first I will repay
double for their iniquity and
their sin, because they have
defiled My land; they have
filled My inheritance with the
carcasses of their detestable
and abominable idols."

19 O LORD, my strength
and my fortress,
My refuge in the day
of affliction,
The Gentiles shall
come to You
From the ends of the
earth and say,
"Surely our fathers
have inherited lies,

Worthlessness and
unprofitable *things.*"
20 Will a man make
gods for himself,
Which *are* not gods?

21 "Therefore behold, I
will this once cause
them to know,
I will cause them to know
My hand and My might;
And they shall know
that My name
is the LORD.

JUDAH'S SIN AND PUNISHMENT

17 "The sin of Judah
is written with
a pen of iron;
With the point of a
diamond *it is* engraved
On the tablet of
their heart,
And on the horns
of your altars,
2 While their children
remember
Their altars and their
wooden images[a]
By the green trees on
the high hills.
3 O My mountain
in the field,
I will give as plunder
your wealth, all
your treasures,
And your high places
of sin within all
your borders.
4 And you, even yourself,
Shall let go of your
heritage which
I gave you;
And I will cause you to
serve your enemies
In the land which
you do not know;
For you have kindled a
fire in My anger *which*
shall burn forever."

5 Thus says the LORD:

"Cursed *is* the man
who trusts in man
And makes flesh
his strength,
Whose heart departs
from the LORD.
6 For he shall be like a
shrub in the desert,
And shall not see
when good comes,
But shall inhabit the
parched places in
the wilderness,
In a salt land *which*
is not inhabited.

7 "Blessed *is* the man who
trusts in the LORD,
And whose hope
is the LORD.
8 For he shall be like
a tree planted by
the waters,
Which spreads out its
roots by the river,
And will not fear[a]
when heat comes;
But its leaf will be green,

17:2 [a] Hebrew *Asherim,* Canaanite deities
17:8 [a] Qere and Targum read *see.*

And will not be anxious
in the year of drought,
Nor will cease from
yielding fruit.

9 "The heart *is* deceitful
above all *things*,
And desperately wicked;
Who can know it?
10 I, the LORD, search
the heart,
I test the mind,
Even to give every man
according to his ways,
According to the fruit
of his doings.

11 "*As* a partridge
that broods but
does not hatch,
So is he who gets riches,
but not by right;
It will leave him in the
midst of his days,
And at his end he
will be a fool."

12 A glorious high throne
from the beginning
Is the place of our
sanctuary.
13 O LORD, the hope
of Israel,
All who forsake You
shall be ashamed.

"Those who depart
from Me
Shall be written
in the earth,
Because they have
forsaken the LORD,
The fountain of
living waters."

JEREMIAH PRAYS FOR DELIVERANCE

14 Heal me, O LORD, and
I shall be healed;
Save me, and I
shall be saved,
For You *are* my praise.
15 Indeed they say to me,
"Where *is* the word
of the LORD?
Let it come now!"
16 As for me, I have not
hurried away from
being a shepherd
who follows You,
Nor have I desired
the woeful day;
You know what came
out of my lips;
It was right there
before You.
17 Do not be a terror to me;
You *are* my hope in
the day of doom.
18 Let them be ashamed
who persecute me,
But do not let me be
put to shame;
Let them be dismayed,
But do not let me
be dismayed.
Bring on them the
day of doom,
And destroy them with
double destruction!

HALLOW THE SABBATH DAY

19Thus the LORD said to me:
"Go and stand in the gate of
the children of the people,
by which the kings of Judah
come in and by which they
go out, and in all the gates of
Jerusalem; 20and say to them,

'Hear the word of the LORD,
you kings of Judah, and all
Judah, and all the inhabitants
of Jerusalem, who enter by
these gates. 21Thus says the
LORD: "Take heed to your-
selves, and bear no burden
on the Sabbath day, nor bring
it in by the gates of Jerusalem;
22nor carry a burden out of
your houses on the Sabbath
day, nor do any work, but hallow the Sabbath day, as I commanded your fathers. 23But
they did not obey nor incline
their ear, but made their neck
stiff, that they might not hear
nor receive instruction.

24"And it shall be, if you
heed Me carefully," says the
LORD, "to bring no burden
through the gates of this city
on the Sabbath day, but hallow the Sabbath day, to do no
work in it, 25then shall enter
the gates of this city kings and
princes sitting on the throne
of David, riding in chariots
and on horses, they and their
princes, accompanied by the
men of Judah and the inhabitants of Jerusalem; and this
city shall remain forever.
26And they shall come from
the cities of Judah and from
the places around Jerusalem,
from the land of Benjamin
and from the lowland, from
the mountains and from the
South, bringing burnt of-
ferings and sacrifices, grain
offerings and incense, bringing sacrifices of praise to the
house of the LORD.

27"But if you will not heed
Me to hallow the Sabbath day,
such as not carrying a burden
when entering the gates of Jerusalem on the Sabbath day,
then I will kindle a fire in its
gates, and it shall devour the
palaces of Jerusalem, and it
shall not be quenched." ' "

THE POTTER AND THE CLAY

18 The word which came to
Jeremiah from the LORD,
saying: 2"Arise and go down to
the potter's house, and there
I will cause you to hear My
words." 3Then I went down to
the potter's house, and there
he was, making something at
the wheel. 4And the vessel that
he made of clay was marred
in the hand of the potter; so
he made it again into another
vessel, as it seemed good to
the potter to make.

5Then the word of the LORD
came to me, saying: 6"O house
of Israel, can I not do with
you as this potter?" says the
LORD. "Look, as the clay *is* in
the potter's hand, so *are* you
in My hand, O house of Israel!
7The instant I speak concerning a nation and concerning a
kingdom, to pluck up, to pull
down, and to destroy *it*, 8if that
nation against whom I have
spoken turns from its evil, I
will relent of the disaster that I
thought to bring upon it. 9And
the instant I speak concerning a nation and concerning a
kingdom, to build and to plant
it, 10if it does evil in My sight so

that it does not obey My voice, then I will relent concerning the good with which I said I would benefit it.
11"Now therefore, speak to the men of Judah and to the inhabitants of Jerusalem, saying, 'Thus says the LORD: "Behold, I am fashioning a disaster and devising a plan against you. Return now every one from his evil way, and make your ways and your doings good."'"

GOD'S WARNING REJECTED

12And they said, "That is hopeless! So we will walk according to our own plans, and we will every one obey the dictates of his evil heart."
13Therefore thus says the LORD:

"Ask now among
the Gentiles,
Who has heard
such things?
The virgin of Israel
has done a very
horrible thing.
14 Will *a man* leave the snow
water of Lebanon,
Which comes from the
rock of the field?
Will the cold flowing
waters be forsaken
for strange waters?

15 "Because My people
have forgotten Me,
They have burned incense
to worthless idols.
And they have caused
themselves to stumble
in their ways,
From the ancient paths,
To walk in pathways and
not on a highway,
16 To make their land
desolate *and* a
perpetual hissing;
Everyone who passes by
it will be astonished
And shake his head.
17 I will scatter them as
with an east wind
before the enemy;
I will show them[a] the
back and not the face
In the day of their
calamity."

JEREMIAH PERSECUTED

18Then they said, "Come and let us devise plans against Jeremiah; for the law shall not perish from the priest, nor counsel from the wise, nor the word from the prophet. Come and let us attack him with the tongue, and let us not give heed to any of his words."

19 Give heed to me, O LORD,
And listen to the
voice of those who
contend with me!
20 Shall evil be repaid
for good?
For they have dug a
pit for my life.

18:17 [a] Following Septuagint, Syriac, Targum, and Vulgate; Masoretic Text reads *look them in*.

Remember that I
stood before You
To speak good for them,
To turn away Your
wrath from them.
21 Therefore deliver up their
children to the famine,
And pour out their *blood*
By the force of the sword;
Let their wives
become widows
And bereaved of
their children.
Let their men be
put to death,
Their young men *be* slain
By the sword in battle.
22 Let a cry be heard
from their houses,
When You bring a troop
suddenly upon them;
For they have dug a
pit to take me,
And hidden snares
for my feet.
23 Yet, LORD, You know
all their counsel
Which is against
me, to slay *me.*
Provide no atonement
for their iniquity,
Nor blot out their sin
from Your sight;
But let them be
overthrown before You.
Deal *thus* with them
In the time of Your anger.

THE SIGN OF THE BROKEN FLASK

19 Thus says the LORD:
"Go and get a potter's
earthen flask, and *take* some
of the elders of the people
and some of the elders of the
priests. 2And go out to the
Valley of the Son of Hinnom,
which *is* by the entry of the
Potsherd Gate; and proclaim
there the words that I will tell
you, 3and say, 'Hear the word
of the LORD, O kings of Judah
and inhabitants of Jerusalem.
Thus says the LORD of hosts,
the God of Israel: "Behold, I
will bring such a catastrophe
on this place, that whoever
hears of it, his ears will tingle.
4"Because they have for-
saken Me and made this an
alien place, because they have
burned incense in it to other
gods whom neither they, their
fathers, nor the kings of Judah
have known, and have filled
this place with the blood of
the innocents 5(they have also
built the high places of Baal,
to burn their sons with fire *for*
burnt offerings to Baal, which
I did not command or speak,
nor did it come into My mind),
6therefore behold, the days
are coming," says the LORD,
"that this place shall no more
be called Tophet or the Valley of the Son of Hinnom, but
the Valley of Slaughter. 7And
I will make void the counsel
of Judah and Jerusalem in
this place, and I will cause
them to fall by the sword before their enemies and by the
hands of those who seek their
lives; their corpses I will give
as meat for the birds of the
heaven and for the beasts of
the earth. 8I will make this city

desolate and a hissing; everyone who passes by it will be
astonished and hiss because
of all its plagues. 9And I will
cause them to eat the flesh
of their sons and the flesh of
their daughters, and everyone shall eat the flesh of his
friend in the siege and in the
desperation with which their
enemies and those who seek
their lives shall drive them to
despair."'

10"Then you shall break the
flask in the sight of the men
who go with you, 11and say to
them, 'Thus says the LORD of
hosts: "Even so I will break
this people and this city, as *one*
breaks a potter's vessel, which
cannot be made whole again;
and they shall bury *them* in
Tophet till *there is* no place to
bury. 12Thus I will do to this
place," says the LORD, "and
to its inhabitants, and make
this city like Tophet. 13And the
houses of Jerusalem and the
houses of the kings of Judah
shall be defiled like the place
of Tophet, because of all the
houses on whose roofs they
have burned incense to all the
host of heaven, and poured
out drink offerings to other
gods."'"

14Then Jeremiah came
from Tophet, where the LORD
had sent him to prophesy; and
he stood in the court of the
LORD's house and said to all
the people, 15"Thus says the
LORD of hosts, the God of Israel: 'Behold, I will bring on
this city and on all her towns
all the doom that I have pronounced against it, because
they have stiffened their necks
that they might not hear My
words.'"

THE WORD OF GOD TO PASHHUR

20 Now Pashhur the son of
Immer, the priest who
was also chief governor in the
house of the LORD, heard that
Jeremiah prophesied these
things. 2Then Pashhur struck
Jeremiah the prophet, and put
him in the stocks that *were*
in the high gate of Benjamin,
which *was* by the house of the
LORD.

3And it happened on
the next day that Pashhur
brought Jeremiah out of the
stocks. Then Jeremiah said
to him, "The LORD has not
called your name Pashhur,
but Magor-Missabib.[a] 4For thus
says the LORD: 'Behold, I will
make you a terror to yourself
and to all your friends; and
they shall fall by the sword of
their enemies, and your eyes
shall see *it*. I will give all Judah
into the hand of the king of
Babylon, and he shall carry
them captive to Babylon and
slay them with the sword.
5Moreover I will deliver all
the wealth of this city, all its
produce, and all its precious

20:3 [a] Literally *Fear on Every Side*

things; all the treasures of the kings of Judah I will give into the hand of their enemies, who will plunder them, seize them, and carry them to Babylon.
6And you, Pashhur, and all who dwell in your house, shall go into captivity. You shall go to Babylon, and there you shall die, and be buried there, you and all your friends, to whom you have prophesied lies.'"

JEREMIAH'S UNPOPULAR MINISTRY

7 O LORD, You induced me,
and I was persuaded;
You are stronger than I,
and have prevailed.
I am in derision daily;
Everyone mocks me.
8 For when I spoke,
I cried out;
I shouted, "Violence
and plunder!"
Because the word of the
LORD was made to me
A reproach and a
derision daily.
9 Then I said, "I will not
make mention of Him,
Nor speak anymore
in His name."
But *His word* was in my
heart like a burning fire
Shut up in my bones;
I was weary of
holding *it* back,
And I could not.
10 For I heard many
mocking:
"Fear on every side!"
"Report," *they say,* "and
we will report it!"
All my acquaintances
watched for my
stumbling, *saying,*
"Perhaps he can
be induced;
Then we will prevail
against him,
And we will take our
revenge on him."

11 But the LORD *is* with me as
a mighty, awesome One.
Therefore my persecutors
will stumble, and
will not prevail.
They will be greatly
ashamed, for they
will not prosper.
Their everlasting
confusion will never
be forgotten.
12 But, O LORD of hosts,
You who test the
righteous,
And see the mind
and heart,
Let me see Your
vengeance on them;
For I have pleaded my
cause before You.

13 Sing to the LORD!
Praise the LORD!
For He has delivered
the life of the poor
From the hand of
evildoers.

14 Cursed *be* the day in
which I was born!
Let the day not be
blessed in which my
mother bore me!
15 Let the man *be* cursed

Who brought news to
my father, saying,
"A male child has
been born to you!"
Making him very glad.
16 And let that man be
like the cities
Which the LORD
overthrew, and
did not relent;
Let him hear the cry
in the morning
And the shouting at noon,
17 Because he did not kill
me from the womb,
That my mother might
have been my grave,
And her womb always
enlarged *with me.*
18 Why did I come forth
from the womb to see
labor and sorrow,
That my days should be
consumed with shame?

JERUSALEM'S DOOM IS SEALED

21 The word which came
to Jeremiah from the
LORD when King Zedekiah
sent to him Pashhur the son of
Melchiah, and Zephaniah the
son of Maaseiah, the priest,
saying, 2"Please inquire of
the LORD for us, for Nebuchadnezzar[a] king of Babylon
makes war against us. Perhaps
the LORD will deal with us according to all His wonderful
works, that *the king* may go
away from us."

3Then Jeremiah said to
them, "Thus you shall say to
Zedekiah, 4'Thus says the LORD
God of Israel: "Behold, I will
turn back the weapons of war
that *are* in your hands, with
which you fight against the king
of Babylon and the Chaldeans[a]
who besiege you outside the
walls; and I will assemble them
in the midst of this city. 5I Myself will fight against you with
an outstretched hand and with
a strong arm, even in anger
and fury and great wrath. 6I
will strike the inhabitants of
this city, both man and beast;
they shall die of a great pestilence. 7And afterward," says the
LORD, "I will deliver Zedekiah
king of Judah, his servants and
the people, and such as are left
in this city from the pestilence
and the sword and the famine,
into the hand of Nebuchadnezzar king of Babylon, into
the hand of their enemies, and
into the hand of those who
seek their life; and he shall
strike them with the edge of
the sword. He shall not spare
them, or have pity or mercy."'

8"Now you shall say to this
people, 'Thus says the LORD:
"Behold, I set before you the
way of life and the way of
death. 9He who remains in this
city shall die by the sword, by
famine, and by pestilence; but
he who goes out and defects
to the Chaldeans who besiege

21:2 [a] Hebrew *Nebuchadrezzar,* and so elsewhere 21:4 [a] Or *Babylonians*

you, he shall live, and his life
shall be as a prize to him. 10For
I have set My face against this
city for adversity and not for
good," says the LORD. "It shall
be given into the hand of the
king of Babylon, and he shall
burn it with fire."'

MESSAGE TO THE HOUSE OF DAVID

11"And concerning the
house of the king of Judah,
say, 'Hear the word of the
LORD, 12O house of David!
Thus says the LORD:

"Execute judgment
in the morning;
And deliver *him who*
is plundered
Out of the hand of
the oppressor,
Lest My fury go
forth like fire
And burn so that no
one can quench *it,*
Because of the evil
of your doings.

13"Behold, I *am* against
you, O inhabitant
of the valley,
And rock of the plain,"
says the LORD,
"Who say, 'Who
shall come down
against us?
Or who shall enter
our dwellings?'
14 *But I will* punish you
according to the
fruit of your doings,"
says the LORD;
"I will kindle a fire
in its forest,
And it shall devour all
things around it."'"

22 Thus says the LORD:
"Go down to the house
of the king of Judah, and there
speak this word, 2and say,
'Hear the word of the LORD,
O king of Judah, you who sit
on the throne of David, you
and your servants and your
people who enter these gates!
3Thus says the LORD: "Execute
judgment and righteousness,
and deliver the plundered out
of the hand of the oppressor.
Do no wrong and do no vi-
olence to the stranger, the
fatherless, or the widow, nor
shed innocent blood in this
place. 4For if you indeed do
this thing, then shall enter
the gates of this house, riding on horses and in chariots,
accompanied by servants and
people, kings who sit on the
throne of David. 5But if you
will not hear these words, I
swear by Myself," says the
LORD, "that this house shall
become a desolation."'"
6For thus says the LORD to
the house of the king of Judah:

"You *are* Gilead to Me,
The head of Lebanon;
Yet I surely will make
you a wilderness,
Cities *which* are
not inhabited.
7 I will prepare destroyers
against you,

Everyone with his
weapons;
They shall cut down
your choice cedars
And cast *them*
into the fire.

8And many nations will pass
by this city; and everyone will
say to his neighbor, 'Why has
the LORD done so to this great
city?' 9Then they will answer,
'Because they have forsaken
the covenant of the LORD their
God, and worshiped other
gods and served them.'"

10 Weep not for the dead,
nor bemoan him;
Weep bitterly for him
who goes away,
For he shall return
no more,
Nor see his native
country.

MESSAGE TO THE SONS OF JOSIAH

11For thus says the LORD
concerning Shallum[a] the son
of Josiah, king of Judah, who
reigned instead of Josiah his
father, who went from this
place: "He shall not return
here anymore, 12but he shall
die in the place where they
have led him captive, and
shall see this land no more.

13 "Woe to him who
builds his house by
unrighteousness
And his chambers
by injustice,
Who uses his neighbor's
service without wages
And gives him nothing
for his work,
14 Who says, 'I will
build myself a wide
house with spacious
chambers,
And cut out
windows for it,
Paneling *it* with cedar
And painting *it* with
vermilion.'

15 "Shall you reign
because you enclose
yourself in cedar?
Did not your father
eat and drink,
And do justice and
righteousness?
Then *it was* well with him.
16 He judged the cause of
the poor and needy;
Then *it was* well.
Was not this knowing
Me?" says the LORD.
17 "Yet your eyes and your
heart *are* for nothing
but your covetousness,
For shedding
innocent blood,
And practicing
oppression and
violence."

18Therefore thus says the
LORD concerning Jehoiakim
the son of Josiah, king of
Judah:

22:11 [a] Also called *Jehoahaz*

"They shall not
lament for him,
Saying, 'Alas, my brother!'
or 'Alas, my sister!'

"They shall not
lament for him,
Saying, 'Alas, master!'
or 'Alas, his glory!'
19 He shall be buried with
the burial of a donkey,
Dragged and cast out
beyond the gates
of Jerusalem.

20"Go up to Lebanon,
and cry out,
And lift up your
voice in Bashan;
Cry from Abarim,
For all your lovers
are destroyed.
21 I spoke to you in
your prosperity,
But you said, 'I
will not hear.'
This *has been* your
manner from
your youth,
That you did not
obey My voice.
22 The wind shall eat up
all your rulers,
And your lovers shall
go into captivity;
Surely then you will
be ashamed and
humiliated
For all your wickedness.
23 O inhabitant of Lebanon,
Making your nest
in the cedars,
How gracious will
you be when pangs
come upon you,
Like the pain of a
woman in labor?

MESSAGE TO CONIAH

24"*As* I live," says the LORD,
"though Coniah[a] the son of
Jehoiakim, king of Judah,
were the signet on My right
hand, yet I would pluck you
off; 25and I will give you into
the hand of those who seek
your life, and into the hand
of those whose face you fear—
the hand of Nebuchadnezzar
king of Babylon and the hand
of the Chaldeans. 26So I will
cast you out, and your mother
who bore you, into another
country where you were not
born; and there you shall die.
27But to the land to which they
desire to return, there they
shall not return.

28"Is this man Coniah a
despised, broken idol—
A vessel in which *is*
no pleasure?
Why are they cast out, he
and his descendants,
And cast into a
land which they
do not know?
29 O earth, earth, earth,
Hear the word of
the LORD!
30 *Thus* says the LORD:
'Write this man
down as childless,

22:24 [a] Also called *Jeconiah* and *Jehoiachin*

A man *who* shall not
prosper in his days;
For none of his
descendants
shall prosper,
Sitting on the throne
of David,
And ruling anymore
in Judah.'"

THE BRANCH OF RIGHTEOUSNESS

23 "Woe to the shepherds
who destroy and scatter
the sheep of My pasture!" says
the LORD. 2Therefore thus says
the LORD God of Israel against
the shepherds who feed My
people: "You have scattered My
flock, driven them away, and
not attended to them. Behold,
I will attend to you for the evil
of your doings," says the LORD.
3"But I will gather the remnant
of My flock out of all countries
where I have driven them, and
bring them back to their folds;
and they shall be fruitful and
increase. 4I will set up shepherds over them who will feed
them; and they shall fear no
more, nor be dismayed, nor
shall they be lacking," says the
LORD.

5 "Behold, *the* days are
coming," says the LORD,
"That I will raise to
David a Branch of
righteousness;
A King shall reign
and prosper,
And execute judgment
and righteousness
in the earth.
6 In His days Judah
will be saved,
And Israel will
dwell safely;
Now this *is* His name by
which He will be called:

THE LORD OUR
RIGHTEOUSNESS.[a]

7"Therefore, behold, *the*
days are coming," says the
LORD, "that they shall no longer say, 'As the LORD lives who
brought up the children of Israel from the land of Egypt,'
8but, 'As the LORD lives who
brought up and led the descendants of the house of Israel from the north country
and from all the countries
where I had driven them.' And
they shall dwell in their own
land."

FALSE PROPHETS AND EMPTY ORACLES

9 My heart within
me is broken
Because of the prophets;
All my bones shake.
I am like a drunken man,
And like a man whom
wine has overcome,
Because of the LORD,
And because of His
holy words.
10 For the land is full
of adulterers;

23:6 [a] Hebrew *YHWH Tsidkenu*

For because of a curse
the land mourns.
The pleasant places of the
wilderness are dried up.
Their course of life is evil,
And their might
is not right.

11 "For both prophet and
priest are profane;
Yes, in My house I
have found their
wickedness," says
the LORD.
12 "Therefore their way
shall be to them
Like slippery *ways;*
In the darkness they
shall be driven on
And fall in them;
For I will bring
disaster on them,
The year of their
punishment,"
says the LORD.
13 "And I have seen
folly in the prophets
of Samaria:
They prophesied by Baal
And caused My people
Israel to err.
14 Also I have seen a
horrible thing in the
prophets of Jerusalem:
They commit adultery
and walk in lies;
They also strengthen the
hands of evildoers,
So that no one turns back
from his wickedness.
All of them are like
Sodom to Me,
And her inhabitants
like Gomorrah.

15 "Therefore thus says the
LORD of hosts concerning the
prophets:

'Behold, I will feed them
with wormwood,
And make them drink
the water of gall;
For from the prophets
of Jerusalem
Profaneness has gone
out into all the land.'"

16 Thus says the LORD of
hosts:

"Do not listen to the
words of the prophets
who prophesy to you.
They make you worthless;
They speak a vision of
their own heart,
Not from the mouth
of the LORD.
17 They continually say to
those who despise Me,
'The LORD has said,
"You shall have peace"';
And *to* everyone who
walks according to
the dictates of his
own heart, they say,
'No evil shall come
upon you.'"

18 For who has stood in the
counsel of the LORD,
And has perceived and
heard His word?
Who has marked His
word and heard *it?*
19 Behold, a whirlwind of
the LORD has gone
forth in fury—

A violent whirlwind!
It will fall violently on the
head of the wicked.
20 The anger of the LORD
will not turn back
Until He has executed
and performed the
thoughts of His heart.
In the latter days you will
understand it perfectly.

21 "I have not sent these
prophets, yet they ran.
I have not spoken
to them, yet they
prophesied.
22 But if they had stood
in My counsel,
And had caused My
people to hear
My words,
Then they would have
turned them from
their evil way
And from the evil
of their doings.

23 "*Am* I a God near at
hand," says the LORD,
"And not a God afar off?
24 Can anyone hide himself
in secret places,
So I shall not see him?"
says the LORD;
"Do I not fill heaven and
earth?" says the LORD.

25 "I have heard what the
prophets have said who
prophesy lies in My name,
saying, 'I have dreamed, I
have dreamed!'
26 How long
will *this* be in the heart of the
prophets who prophesy lies?
Indeed *they are* prophets of
the deceit of their own heart,
27 who try to make My people forget My name by their
dreams which everyone tells
his neighbor, as their fathers
forgot My name for Baal.

28 "The prophet who
has a dream, let
him tell a dream;
And he who has My
word, let him speak
My word faithfully.
What *is* the chaff to the
wheat?" says the LORD.
29 "*Is* not My word like a
fire?" says the LORD,
"And like a hammer
that breaks the
rock in pieces?

30 "Therefore behold, I *am*
against the prophets," says the
LORD, "who steal My words
every one from his neighbor.
31 Behold, I *am* against the
prophets," says the LORD,
"who use their tongues and
say, 'He says.'
32 Behold, I *am*
against those who prophesy
false dreams," says the LORD,
"and tell them, and cause My
people to err by their lies and
by their recklessness. Yet I did
not send them or command
them; therefore they shall not
profit this people at all," says
the LORD.
33 "So when these people
or the prophet or the priest
ask you, saying, 'What is
the oracle of the LORD?' you
shall then say to them, 'What

oracle?'[a] I will even forsake you," says the LORD. 34"And *as for* the prophet and the priest and the people who say, 'The oracle of the LORD!' I will even punish that man and his house. 35Thus every one of you shall say to his neighbor, and every one to his brother, 'What has the LORD answered?' and, 'What has the LORD spoken?' 36And the oracle of the LORD you shall mention no more. For every man's word will be his oracle, for you have perverted the words of the living God, the LORD of hosts, our God. 37Thus you shall say to the prophet, 'What has the LORD answered you?' and, 'What has the LORD spoken?' 38But since you say, 'The oracle of the LORD!' therefore thus says the LORD: 'Because you say this word, "The oracle of the LORD!" and I have sent to you, saying, "Do not say, 'The oracle of the LORD!'" 39therefore behold, I, even I, will utterly forget you and forsake you, and the city that I gave you and your fathers, and *will cast you* out of My presence. 40And I will bring an everlasting reproach upon you, and a perpetual shame, which shall not be forgotten.'"

THE SIGN OF TWO BASKETS OF FIGS

24 The LORD showed me, and there were two baskets of figs set before the temple of the LORD, after Nebuchadnezzar king of Babylon had carried away captive Jeconiah the son of Jehoiakim, king of Judah, and the princes of Judah with the craftsmen and smiths, from Jerusalem, and had brought them to Babylon. 2One basket *had* very good figs, like the figs *that are* first ripe; and the other basket *had* very bad figs which could not be eaten, they were so bad. 3Then the LORD said to me, "What do you see, Jeremiah?"

And I said, "Figs, the good figs, very good; and the bad, very bad, which cannot be eaten, they are so bad."

4Again the word of the LORD came to me, saying, 5"Thus says the LORD, the God of Israel: 'Like these good figs, so will I acknowledge those who are carried away captive from Judah, whom I have sent out of this place for *their own* good, into the land of the Chaldeans. 6For I will set My eyes on them for good, and I will bring them back to this land; I will build them and not pull *them* down, and I will plant them and not pluck *them* up. 7Then I will give them a heart to know Me, that I *am* the LORD; and they shall be My people, and I will be their God, for they *shall return* to Me with their whole heart.

8'And as the bad figs which

23:33 [a] Septuagint, Targum, and Vulgate read '*You are the burden.*'

cannot be eaten, they are so
bad'—surely thus says the
LORD—'so will I give up Zedekiah the king of Judah, his
princes, the residue of Jerusalem who remain in this land,
and those who dwell in the
land of Egypt. 9I will deliver
them to trouble into all the
kingdoms of the earth, for
their harm, *to be* a reproach
and a byword, a taunt and a
curse, in all places where I
shall drive them. 10And I will
send the sword, the famine,
and the pestilence among
them, till they are consumed
from the land that I gave to
them and their fathers.'"

SEVENTY YEARS OF DESOLATION

25 The word that came
to Jeremiah concern-
ing all the people of Judah,
in the fourth year of Jehoiakim the son of Josiah, king
of Judah (which *was* the first
year of Nebuchadnezzar king
of Babylon), 2which Jeremiah
the prophet spoke to all the
people of Judah and to all
the inhabitants of Jerusalem, saying: 3"From the thirteenth year of Josiah the son
of Amon, king of Judah, even
to this day, this *is* the twenty-
third year in which the word of
the LORD has come to me; and
I have spoken to you, rising
early and speaking, but you
have not listened. 4And the
LORD has sent to you all His
servants the prophets, rising
early and sending *them,* but
you have not listened nor inclined your ear to hear. 5They
said, 'Repent now everyone of
his evil way and his evil doings, and dwell in the land that
the LORD has given to you and
your fathers forever and ever.
6Do not go after other gods
to serve them and worship
them, and do not provoke
Me to anger with the works
of your hands; and I will not
harm you.' 7Yet you have not
listened to Me," says the LORD,
"that you might provoke Me to
anger with the works of your
hands to your own hurt.

8"Therefore thus says the
LORD of hosts: 'Because you
have not heard My words, 9be-
hold, I will send and take all
the families of the north,' says
the LORD, 'and Nebuchadnezzar the king of Babylon, My
servant, and will bring them
against this land, against its
inhabitants, and against these
nations all around, and will
utterly destroy them, and
make them an astonishment,
a hissing, and perpetual desolations. 10Moreover I will take
from them the voice of mirth
and the voice of gladness, the
voice of the bridegroom and
the voice of the bride, the
sound of the millstones and
the light of the lamp. 11And
this whole land shall be a desolation *and* an astonishment,
and these nations shall serve
the king of Babylon seventy
years.

12'Then it will come to
pass, when seventy years are
completed, *that* I will punish
the king of Babylon and that
nation, the land of the Chaldeans, for their iniquity,' says
the LORD; 'and I will make it
a perpetual desolation. 13So
I will bring on that land all
My words which I have pronounced against it, all that is
written in this book, which
Jeremiah has prophesied concerning all the nations. 14(For
many nations and great kings
shall be served by them also;
and I will repay them according to their deeds and according to the works of their own
hands.)' "

JUDGMENT ON THE NATIONS

15For thus says the LORD
God of Israel to me: "Take
this wine cup of fury from My
hand, and cause all the nations, to whom I send you, to
drink it. 16And they will drink
and stagger and go mad because of the sword that I will
send among them."

17Then I took the cup from
the LORD's hand, and made
all the nations drink, to whom
the LORD had sent me: 18Jeru-
salem and the cities of Judah,
its kings and its princes, to
make them a desolation, an
astonishment, a hissing, and a
curse, as *it is* this day; 19Phar-
aoh king of Egypt, his servants,
his princes, and all his people;
20all the mixed multitude, all
the kings of the land of Uz, all
the kings of the land of the
Philistines (namely, Ashkelon,
Gaza, Ekron, and the remnant
of Ashdod); 21Edom, Moab,
and the people of Ammon;
22all the kings of Tyre, all the
kings of Sidon, and the kings
of the coastlands which *are*
across the sea; 23Dedan, Tema,
Buz, and all *who are* in the farthest corners; 24all the kings of
Arabia and all the kings of the
mixed multitude who dwell in
the desert; 25all the kings of
Zimri, all the kings of Elam,
and all the kings of the Medes;
26all the kings of the north, far
and near, one with another;
and all the kingdoms of the
world which *are* on the face of
the earth. Also the king of Sheshach[a] shall drink after them.

27"Therefore you shall say
to them, 'Thus says the LORD
of hosts, the God of Israel:
"Drink, be drunk, and vomit!
Fall and rise no more, because
of the sword which I will send
among you." ' 28And it shall be,
if they refuse to take the cup
from your hand to drink, then
you shall say to them, 'Thus
says the LORD of hosts: "You
shall certainly drink! 29For behold, I begin to bring calamity on the city which is called
by My name, and should you
be utterly unpunished? You
shall not be unpunished, for I

25:26 [a] A code word for Babylon (compare 51:41)

will call for a sword on all the
inhabitants of the earth," says
the LORD of hosts.'
30"Therefore prophesy
against them all these words,
and say to them:

'The LORD will roar
from on high,
And utter His voice from
His holy habitation;
He will roar mightily
against His fold.
He will give a shout,
as those who tread
the grapes,
Against all the
inhabitants of the earth.
31 A noise will come to the
ends of the earth—
For the LORD has a
controversy with
the nations;
He will plead His case
with all flesh.
He will give those *who*
are wicked to the
sword,' says the LORD."

32Thus says the LORD of
hosts:

"Behold, disaster
shall go forth
From nation to nation,
And a great whirlwind
shall be raised up
From the farthest
parts of the earth.

33And at that day the slain of
the LORD shall be from *one*
end of the earth even to the
other end of the earth. They
shall not be lamented, or gathered, or buried; they shall become refuse on the ground.

34"Wail, shepherds,
and cry!
Roll about *in the ashes,*
You leaders of the flock!
For the days of your
slaughter and
your dispersions
are fulfilled;
You shall fall like a
precious vessel.
35 And the shepherds will
have no way to flee,
Nor the leaders of the
flock to escape.
36 A voice of the cry of
the shepherds,
And a wailing of the
leaders to the flock
will be heard.
For the LORD has
plundered their
pasture,
37 And the peaceful
dwellings are cut down
Because of the fierce
anger of the LORD.
38 He has left His lair
like the lion;
For their land is desolate
Because of the fierceness
of the Oppressor,
And because of His
fierce anger."

JEREMIAH SAVED FROM DEATH

26 In the beginning of
the reign of Jehoia-
kim the son of Josiah, king of
Judah, this word came from

the LORD, saying, 2“Thus says
the LORD: ‘Stand in the court
of the LORD’s house, and speak
to all the cities of Judah, which
come to worship *in* the LORD’s
house, all the words that I
command you to speak to
them. Do not diminish a word.
3Perhaps everyone will listen
and turn from his evil way,
that I may relent concerning
the calamity which I purpose
to bring on them because of
the evil of their doings.’ 4And
you shall say to them, ‘Thus
says the LORD: “If you will not
listen to Me, to walk in My law
which I have set before you, 5to
heed the words of My servants
the prophets whom I sent to
you, both rising up early and
sending *them* (but you have
not heeded), 6then I will make
this house like Shiloh, and will
make this city a curse to all the
nations of the earth.” ’ ”

7So the priests and the
prophets and all the people
heard Jeremiah speaking
these words in the house of
the LORD. 8Now it happened,
when Jeremiah had made an
end of speaking all that the
LORD had commanded *him*
to speak to all the people, that
the priests and the prophets
and all the people seized him,
saying, “You will surely die!
9Why have you prophesied in
the name of the LORD, saying,
‘This house shall be like Shiloh, and this city shall be desolate, without an inhabitant’?”
And all the people were gathered against Jeremiah in the
house of the LORD.

10When the princes of
Judah heard these things, they
came up from the king’s house
to the house of the LORD and
sat down in the entry of the
New Gate of the LORD’s *house.*
11And the priests and the
prophets spoke to the princes
and all the people, saying,
“This man deserves to die! For
he has prophesied against this
city, as you have heard with
your ears.”

12Then Jeremiah spoke to
all the princes and all the people, saying: “The LORD sent
me to prophesy against this
house and against this city
with all the words that you
have heard. 13Now therefore,
amend your ways and your
doings, and obey the voice of
the LORD your God; then the
LORD will relent concerning
the doom that He has pro-
nounced against you. 14As for
me, here I am, in your hand;
do with me as seems good and
proper to you. 15But know for
certain that if you put me to
death, you will surely bring
innocent blood on yourselves,
on this city, and on its inhabitants; for truly the LORD has
sent me to you to speak all
these words in your hearing.”

16So the princes and all the
people said to the priests and
the prophets, “This man does
not deserve to die. For he has
spoken to us in the name of
the LORD our God.”

17Then certain of the el-
ders of the land rose up and
spoke to all the assembly of
the people, saying: 18"Micah
of Moresheth prophesied in
the days of Hezekiah king of
Judah, and spoke to all the
people of Judah, saying, 'Thus
says the LORD of hosts:

"Zion shall be plowed
  like a field,
Jerusalem shall become
  heaps of ruins,
And the mountain
  of the temple[a]
Like the bare hills
  of the forest."'[b]

19Did Hezekiah king of Judah
and all Judah ever put him
to death? Did he not fear the
LORD and seek the LORD's
favor? And the LORD relented
concerning the doom which
He had pronounced against
them. But we are doing great
evil against ourselves."
20Now there was also a man
who prophesied in the name
of the LORD, Urijah the son of
Shemaiah of Kirjath Jearim,
who prophesied against this
city and against this land according to all the words of Jeremiah. 21And when Jehoiakim
the king, with all his mighty
men and all the princes,
heard his words, the king
sought to put him to death;
but when Urijah heard *it,* he
was afraid and fled, and went
to Egypt. 22Then Jehoiakim
the king sent men to Egypt:
Elnathan the son of Achbor,
and *other* men *who went* with
him to Egypt. 23And they
brought Urijah from Egypt
and brought him to Jehoiakim the king, who killed him
with the sword and cast his
dead body into the graves of
the common people.
24Nevertheless the hand of
Ahikam the son of Shaphan
was with Jeremiah, so that
they should not give him into
the hand of the people to put
him to death.

SYMBOL OF THE BONDS AND YOKES

27 In the beginning of the
reign of Jehoiakim[a] the
son of Josiah, king of Judah,
this word came to Jeremiah
from the LORD, saying,[b] 2"Thus
says the LORD to me: 'Make for
yourselves bonds and yokes,
and put them on your neck,
3and send them to the king of
Edom, the king of Moab, the
king of the Ammonites, the
king of Tyre, and the king of
Sidon, by the hand of the messengers who come to Jerusalem to Zedekiah king of Judah.
4And command them to say
to their masters, "Thus says
the LORD of hosts, the God of

26:18 [a] Literally *house* [b] Compare Micah 3:12 27:1 [a] Following Masoretic Text, Targum, and Vulgate; some Hebrew manuscripts, Arabic, and Syriac read *Zedekiah* (compare 27:3, 12; 28:1). [b] Septuagint omits verse 1.

Israel—thus you shall say to your masters: 5‘I have made the earth, the man and the beast that *are* on the ground, by My great power and by My outstretched arm, and have given it to whom it seemed proper to Me. 6And now I have given all these lands into the hand of Nebuchadnezzar the king of Babylon, My servant; and the beasts of the field I have also given him to serve him. 7So all nations shall serve him and his son and his son’s son, until the time of his land comes; and then many nations and great kings shall make him serve them. 8And it shall be, *that* the nation and kingdom which will not serve Nebuchadnezzar the king of Babylon, and which will not put its neck under the yoke of the king of Babylon, that nation I will punish,’ says the LORD, ‘with the sword, the famine, and the pestilence, until I have consumed them by his hand. 9Therefore do not listen to your prophets, your diviners, your dreamers, your soothsayers, or your sorcerers, who speak to you, saying, “You shall not serve the king of Babylon.” 10For they prophesy a lie to you, to remove you far from your land; and I will drive you out, and you will perish. 11But the nations that bring their necks under the yoke of the king of Babylon and serve him, I will let them remain in their own land,’ says the LORD, ‘and they shall till it and dwell in it.’ ” ’ ”

12I also spoke to Zedekiah king of Judah according to all these words, saying, “Bring your necks under the yoke of the king of Babylon, and serve him and his people, and live! 13Why will you die, you and your people, by the sword, by the famine, and by the pestilence, as the LORD has spoken against the nation that will not serve the king of Babylon? 14Therefore do not listen to the words of the prophets who speak to you, saying, ‘You shall not serve the king of Babylon,’ for they prophesy a lie to you; 15for I have not sent them,” says the LORD, “yet they prophesy a lie in My name, that I may drive you out, and that you may perish, you and the prophets who prophesy to you.”

16Also I spoke to the priests and to all this people, saying, “Thus says the LORD: ‘Do not listen to the words of your prophets who prophesy to you, saying, “Behold, the vessels of the LORD’s house will now shortly be brought back from Babylon”; for they prophesy a lie to you. 17Do not listen to them; serve the king of Babylon, and live! Why should this city be laid waste? 18But if they *are* prophets, and if the word of the LORD is with them, let them now make intercession to the LORD of hosts, that the vessels which

are left in the house of the
LORD, *in* the house of the king
of Judah, and at Jerusalem, do
not go to Babylon.’
19“For thus says the LORD of
hosts concerning the pillars,
concerning the Sea, concerning the carts, and concerning
the remainder of the ves-
sels that remain in this city,
20which Nebuchadnezzar king
of Babylon did not take, when
he carried away captive Jeconiah the son of Jehoiakim, king
of Judah, from Jerusalem to
Babylon, and all the nobles of
Judah and Jerusalem— 21yes,
thus says the LORD of hosts,
the God of Israel, concerning
the vessels that remain in the
house of the LORD, and in the
house of the king of Judah and
of Jerusalem: 22‘They shall be
carried to Babylon, and there
they shall be until the day that
I visit them,’ says the LORD.
‘Then I will bring them up and
restore them to this place.’ ”

HANANIAH’S FALSEHOOD AND DOOM

28 And it happened in
the same year, at the
beginning of the reign of Zedekiah king of Judah, in the
fourth year *and* in the fifth
month, *that* Hananiah the son
of Azur the prophet, who *was*
from Gibeon, spoke to me in
the house of the LORD in the
presence of the priests and of
all the people, saying, 2“Thus
speaks the LORD of hosts,
the God of Israel, saying: ‘I
have broken the yoke of the
king of Babylon. 3Within two
full years I will bring back to
this place all the vessels of
the LORD’s house, that Nebuchadnezzar king of Babylon
took away from this place and
carried to Babylon. 4And I will
bring back to this place Jeconiah the son of Jehoiakim,
king of Judah, with all the
captives of Judah who went to
Babylon,’ says the LORD, ‘for I
will break the yoke of the king
of Babylon.’ ”
5Then the prophet Jere-
miah spoke to the prophet
Hananiah in the presence of
the priests and in the presence of all the people who
stood in the house of the
LORD, 6and the prophet Jeremiah said, “Amen! The LORD
do so; the LORD perform
your words which you have
prophesied, to bring back the
vessels of the LORD’s house
and all who were carried away
captive, from Babylon to this
place. 7Nevertheless hear now
this word that I speak in your
hearing and in the hearing of
all the people: 8The prophets
who have been before me and
before you of old prophesied
against many countries and
great kingdoms—of war and
disaster and pestilence. 9As
for the prophet who prophesies of peace, when the word
of the prophet comes to pass,
the prophet will be known *as*
one whom the LORD has truly
sent.”

10 Then Hananiah the
prophet took the yoke off
the prophet Jeremiah's neck
and broke it. 11 And Hananiah
spoke in the presence of all the
people, saying, "Thus says the
LORD: 'Even so I will break the
yoke of Nebuchadnezzar king
of Babylon from the neck of all
nations within the space of two
full years.'" And the prophet
Jeremiah went his way.

12 Now the word of the LORD
came to Jeremiah, after Hananiah the prophet had broken the yoke from the neck
of the prophet Jeremiah, saying, 13 "Go and tell Hananiah,
saying, 'Thus says the LORD:
"You have broken the yokes of
wood, but you have made in
their place yokes of iron." 14 For
thus says the LORD of hosts,
the God of Israel: "I have put a
yoke of iron on the neck of all
these nations, that they may
serve Nebuchadnezzar king
of Babylon; and they shall
serve him. I have given him
the beasts of the field also."'"

15 Then the prophet Jere-
miah said to Hananiah the
prophet, "Hear now, Hana-
niah, the LORD has not sent
you, but you make this people trust in a lie. 16 Therefore
thus says the LORD: 'Behold, I
will cast you from the face of
the earth. This year you shall
die, because you have taught
rebellion against the LORD.'"

17 So Hananiah the prophet
died the same year in the seventh month.

JEREMIAH'S LETTER TO THE CAPTIVES

29 Now these *are* the words
of the letter that Jere-
miah the prophet sent from
Jerusalem to the remainder
of the elders who were carried
away captive—to the priests,
the prophets, and all the people whom Nebuchadnezzar
had carried away captive from
Jerusalem to Babylon. 2 (This
happened after Jeconiah the
king, the queen mother, the
eunuchs, the princes of Judah
and Jerusalem, the craftsmen,
and the smiths had departed
from Jerusalem.) 3 *The letter
was sent* by the hand of Elasah
the son of Shaphan, and Gemariah the son of Hilkiah, whom
Zedekiah king of Judah sent to
Babylon, to Nebuchadnezzar
king of Babylon, saying,

4 Thus says the LORD of
hosts, the God of Israel,
to all who were carried
away captive, whom I
have caused to be carried
away from Jerusalem to
Babylon:

5 Build houses and dwell
in them; plant gardens
and eat their fruit. 6 Take
wives and beget sons
and daughters; and take
wives for your sons and
give your daughters
to husbands, so that
they may bear sons and
daughters—that you may
be increased there, and

not diminished. 7And
seek the peace of the
city where I have caused
you to be carried away
captive, and pray to the
LORD for it; for in its
peace you will have peace.
8For thus says the LORD
of hosts, the God of Israel:
Do not let your prophets
and your diviners who
are in your midst deceive
you, nor listen to your
dreams which you cause
to be dreamed. 9For they
prophesy falsely to you in
My name; I have not sent
them, says the LORD.

10 For thus says the LORD:
After seventy years are
completed at Babylon, I
will visit you and perform
My good word toward
you, and cause you to
return to this place. 11For
I know the thoughts that
I think toward you, says
the LORD, thoughts of
peace and not of evil, to
give you a future and a
hope. 12Then you will call
upon Me and go and pray
to Me, and I will listen to
you. 13And you will seek
Me and find *Me,* when
you search for Me with
all your heart. 14I will be
found by you, says the
LORD, and I will bring you
back from your captivity;
I will gather you from
all the nations and from
all the places where I
have driven you, says the
LORD, and I will bring you
to the place from which
I cause you to be carried
away captive.

15 Because you have said,
"The LORD has raised
up prophets for us in
Babylon"— 16therefore
thus says the LORD
concerning the king who
sits on the throne of
David, concerning all the
people who dwell in this
city, and concerning your
brethren who have not
gone out with you into
captivity— 17thus says the
LORD of hosts: Behold,
I will send on them the
sword, the famine, and
the pestilence, and will
make them like rotten
figs that cannot be eaten,
they are so bad. 18And I
will pursue them with
the sword, with famine,
and with pestilence;
and I will deliver them
to trouble among all
the kingdoms of the
earth—to be a curse, an
astonishment, a hissing,
and a reproach among all
the nations where I have
driven them, 19because
they have not heeded My
words, says the LORD,
which I sent to them by
My servants the prophets,
rising up early and
sending *them;* neither
would you heed, says the

LORD. 20Therefore hear
the word of the LORD,
all you of the captivity,
whom I have sent from
Jerusalem to Babylon.

21 Thus says the LORD of
hosts, the God of Israel,
concerning Ahab the son
of Kolaiah, and Zedekiah
the son of Maaseiah, who
prophesy a lie to you in
My name: Behold, I will
deliver them into the
hand of Nebuchadnezzar
king of Babylon, and
he shall slay them
before your eyes. 22And
because of them a curse
shall be taken up by all
the captivity of Judah
who *are* in Babylon,
saying, "The LORD make
you like Zedekiah and
Ahab, whom the king of
Babylon roasted in the
fire"; 23because they have
done disgraceful things
in Israel, have committed
adultery with their
neighbors' wives, and
have spoken lying words
in My name, which I have
not commanded them.
Indeed I know, and *am* a
witness, says the LORD.

24 You shall also speak
to Shemaiah the
Nehelamite, saying,
25Thus speaks the LORD
of hosts, the God of Israel,
saying: You have sent
letters in your name to
all the people who *are* at
Jerusalem, to Zephaniah
the son of Maaseiah
the priest, and to all the
priests, saying, 26"The
LORD has made you
priest instead of Jehoiada
the priest, so that there
should be officers *in*
the house of the LORD
over every man *who* is
demented and considers
himself a prophet, that
you should put him in
prison and in the stocks.
27Now therefore, why have
you not rebuked Jeremiah
of Anathoth who makes
himself a prophet to you?
28For he has sent to us
in Babylon, saying, 'This
captivity is long; build
houses and dwell *in them,*
and plant gardens and eat
their fruit.'"

29Now Zephaniah the priest
read this letter in the hearing of Jeremiah the prophet.
30Then the word of the LORD
came to Jeremiah, saying:
31Send to all those in captivity, saying, Thus says the LORD
concerning Shemaiah the Nehelamite: Because Shemaiah
has prophesied to you, and
I have not sent him, and he
has caused you to trust in a
lie— 32therefore thus says the
LORD: Behold, I will punish
Shemaiah the Nehelamite and
his family: he shall not have
anyone to dwell among this
people, nor shall he see the

good that I will do for My people, says the LORD, because he
has taught rebellion against
the LORD.

RESTORATION OF ISRAEL AND JUDAH

30 The word that came
to Jeremiah from the
LORD, saying, 2"Thus speaks
the LORD God of Israel, saying: 'Write in a book for yourself all the words that I have
spoken to you. 3For behold,
the days are coming,' says the
LORD, 'that I will bring back
from captivity My people Israel and Judah,' says the LORD.
'And I will cause them to return to the land that I gave to
their fathers, and they shall
possess it.'"

4Now these *are* the words
that the LORD spoke concerning Israel and Judah.

5"For thus says the LORD:

'We have heard a
voice of trembling,
Of fear, and not of peace.
6 Ask now, and see,
Whether a man is ever
in labor with child?
So why do I see every
man *with* his hands
on his loins
Like a woman in labor,
And all faces turned pale?
7 Alas! For that day *is* great,
So that none *is* like it;
And it *is* the time of
Jacob's trouble,
But he shall be
saved out of it.

8 'For it shall come to
pass in that day,'
Says the LORD of hosts,
'*That* I will break his
yoke from your neck,
And will burst
your bonds;
Foreigners shall no
more enslave them.
9 But they shall serve
the LORD their God,
And David their king,
Whom I will raise
up for them.

10 'Therefore do not fear,
O My servant Jacob,'
says the LORD,
'Nor be dismayed, O Israel;
For behold, I will save
you from afar,
And your seed from the
land of their captivity.
Jacob shall return, have
rest and be quiet,
And no one shall
make *him* afraid.
11 For I *am* with you,' says
the LORD, 'to save you;
Though I make a full end
of all nations where I
have scattered you,
Yet I will not make a
complete end of you.
But I will correct
you in justice,
And will not let you go
altogether unpunished.'

12"For thus says the LORD:

'Your affliction
is incurable,
Your wound *is* severe.

13 *There is* no one to
plead your cause,
That you may be
bound up;
You have no healing
medicines.
14 All your lovers have
forgotten you;
They do not seek you;
For I have wounded
you with the wound
of an enemy,
With the chastisement
of a cruel one,
For the multitude of
your iniquities,
Because your sins
have increased.
15 Why do you cry about
your affliction?
Your sorrow *is* incurable.
Because of the multitude
of your iniquities,
Because your sins
have increased,
I have done these
things to you.

16 'Therefore all those
who devour you
shall be devoured;
And all your adversaries,
every one of them,
shall go into captivity;
Those who plunder you
shall become plunder,
And all who prey upon
you I will make a prey.
17 For I will restore
health to you
And heal you of your
wounds,' says the LORD,
'Because they called you
an outcast *saying:*
"This *is* Zion;
No one seeks her." '

18 "Thus says the LORD:

'Behold, I will bring
back the captivity
of Jacob's tents,
And have mercy on his
dwelling places;
The city shall be built
upon its own mound,
And the palace shall
remain according
to its own plan.
19 Then out of them shall
proceed thanksgiving
And the voice of those
who make merry;
I will multiply them, and
they shall not diminish;
I will also glorify
them, and they shall
not be small.
20 Their children also
shall be as before,
And their congregation
shall be established
before Me;
And I will punish all
who oppress them.
21 Their nobles shall be
from among them,
And their governor shall
come from their midst;
Then I will cause him
to draw near,
And he shall approach Me;
For who *is* this who
pledged his heart
to approach Me?'
says the LORD.
22 'You shall be My people,
And I will be your God.' "

23 Behold, the whirlwind
of the LORD
Goes forth with fury,
A continuing whirlwind;
It will fall violently on the
head of the wicked.
24 The fierce anger of the
LORD will not return
until He has done it,
And until He has
performed the
intents of His heart.

In the latter days you
will consider it.

THE REMNANT OF ISRAEL SAVED

31 "At the same time," says
the LORD, "I will be the
God of all the families of Israel,
and they shall be My people."
2Thus says the LORD:

"The people who
survived the sword
Found grace in the
wilderness—
Israel, when I went
to give him rest."

3 The LORD has appeared
of old to me, *saying:*
"Yes, I have loved you
with an everlasting love;
Therefore with
lovingkindness I
have drawn you.
4 Again I will build you,
and you shall be rebuilt,
O virgin of Israel!
You shall again be
adorned with your
tambourines,
And shall go forth in
the dances of those
who rejoice.
5 You shall yet plant vines
on the mountains
of Samaria;
The planters shall
plant and eat *them*
as ordinary food.
6 For there shall be a day
When the watchmen will
cry on Mount Ephraim,
'Arise, and let us
go up *to* Zion,
To the LORD our God.'"

7For thus says the LORD:

"Sing with gladness
for Jacob,
And shout among the
chief of the nations;
Proclaim, give
praise, and say,
'O LORD, save Your people,
The remnant of Israel!'
8 Behold, I will bring
them from the
north country,
And gather them from
the ends of the earth,
Among them the blind
and the lame,
The woman with child
And the one who labors
with child, together;
A great throng shall
return there.
9 They shall come
with weeping,
And with supplications
I will lead them.
I will cause them to walk
by the rivers of waters,

In a straight way in
which they shall
not stumble;
For I am a Father
to Israel,
And Ephraim *is*
My firstborn.

10 "Hear the word of the
LORD, O nations,
And declare *it* in the
isles afar off, and say,
'He who scattered Israel
will gather him,
And keep him as a
shepherd *does* his flock.'
11 For the LORD has
redeemed Jacob,
And ransomed him
from the hand of one
stronger than he.
12 Therefore they shall
come and sing in
the height of Zion,
Streaming to the
goodness of the LORD—
For wheat and new
wine and oil,
For the young of the
flock and the herd;
Their souls shall be like a
well-watered garden,
And they shall sorrow
no more at all.

13 "Then shall the virgin
rejoice in the dance,
And the young men and
the old, together;
For I will turn their
mourning to joy,
Will comfort them,
And make them rejoice
rather than sorrow.
14 I will satiate the soul
of the priests with
abundance,
And My people shall
be satisfied with
My goodness, says
the LORD."

MERCY ON EPHRAIM

15 Thus says the LORD:

"A voice was heard
in Ramah,
Lamentation *and*
bitter weeping,
Rachel weeping for
her children,
Refusing to be comforted
for her children,
Because they *are*
no more."

16 Thus says the LORD:

"Refrain your voice
from weeping,
And your eyes from tears;
For your work shall
be rewarded, says
the LORD,
And they shall come
back from the land
of the enemy.
17 There is hope in your
future, says the LORD,
That *your* children
shall come back to
their own border.

18 "I have surely heard
Ephraim bemoaning
himself:
'You have chastised me,
and I was chastised,

Like an untrained bull;
Restore me, and I
will return,
For You *are* the
LORD my God.
19 Surely, after my
turning, I repented;
And after I was
instructed, I struck
myself on the thigh;
I was ashamed, yes,
even humiliated,
Because I bore the
reproach of my youth.'
20 *Is* Ephraim My dear son?
Is he a pleasant child?
For though I spoke
against him,
I earnestly remember
him still;
Therefore My heart
yearns for him;
I will surely have mercy
on him, says the LORD.

21 "Set up signposts,
Make landmarks;
Set your heart toward
the highway,
The way in *which*
you went.
Turn back, O virgin
of Israel,
Turn back to these
your cities.
22 How long will you
gad about,
O you backsliding
daughter?
For the LORD has
created a new thing
in the earth—
A woman shall
encompass a man."

FUTURE PROSPERITY OF JUDAH

23 Thus says the LORD of
hosts, the God of Israel: "They
shall again use this speech in
the land of Judah and in its
cities, when I bring back their
captivity: 'The LORD bless you,
O home of justice, *and* mountain of holiness!' 24 And there
shall dwell in Judah itself, and
in all its cities together, farmers and those going out with
flocks. 25 For I have satiated
the weary soul, and I have
replenished every sorrowful
soul."

26 After this I awoke and
looked around, and my sleep
was sweet to me.

27 "Behold, the days are
coming, says the LORD, that
I will sow the house of Israel
and the house of Judah with
the seed of man and the seed
of beast. 28 And it shall come
to pass, *that* as I have watched
over them to pluck up, to
break down, to throw down,
to destroy, and to afflict, so I
will watch over them to build
and to plant, says the LORD.
29 In those days they shall say
no more:

'The fathers have
eaten sour grapes,
And the children's teeth
are set on edge.'

30 But every one shall die for
his own iniquity; every man
who eats the sour grapes, his
teeth shall be set on edge.

A NEW COVENANT

31“Behold, the days are
coming, says the LORD, when
I will make a new covenant
with the house of Israel and
with the house of Judah—
32not according to the covenant that I made with their
fathers in the day *that* I took
them by the hand to lead them
out of the land of Egypt, My
covenant which they broke,
though I was a husband to
them,[a] says the LORD. 33But
this *is* the covenant that I
will make with the house of
Israel after those days, says
the LORD: I will put My law
in their minds, and write it
on their hearts; and I will be
their God, and they shall be
My people. 34No more shall
every man teach his neighbor,
and every man his brother,
saying, ‘Know the LORD,’ for
they all shall know Me, from
the least of them to the greatest of them, says the LORD.
For I will forgive their iniquity, and their sin I will remember no more.”

35 Thus says the LORD,
Who gives the sun
for a light by day,
The ordinances of
the moon and the
stars for a light
by night,
Who disturbs the sea,
And its waves roar
(The LORD of hosts
is His name):

36“If those ordinances
depart
From before Me,
says the LORD,
Then the seed of Israel
shall also cease
From being a nation
before Me forever.”

37Thus says the LORD:

“If heaven above can
be measured,
And the foundations
of the earth searched
out beneath,
I will also cast off all
the seed of Israel
For all that they have
done, says the LORD.

38“Behold, the days are
coming, says the LORD, that
the city shall be built for the
LORD from the Tower of Hananel to the Corner Gate. 39The
surveyor’s line shall again extend straight forward over the
hill Gareb; then it shall turn toward Goath. 40And the whole
valley of the dead bodies and
of the ashes, and all the fields
as far as the Brook Kidron, to
the corner of the Horse Gate
toward the east, *shall be* holy
to the LORD. It shall not be
plucked up or thrown down
anymore forever.”

31:32 [a] Following Masoretic Text, Targum, and Vulgate; Septuagint and Syriac read *and I turned away from them.*

JEREMIAH BUYS A FIELD

32 The word that came
to Jeremiah from the
LORD in the tenth year of Zedekiah king of Judah, which
was the eighteenth year of
Nebuchadnezzar. 2For then
the king of Babylon's army
besieged Jerusalem, and Jeremiah the prophet was shut
up in the court of the prison,
which *was in* the king of Judah's house. 3For Zedekiah
king of Judah had shut him
up, saying, "Why do you
prophesy and say, 'Thus says
the LORD: "Behold, I will give
this city into the hand of the
king of Babylon, and he shall
take it; 4and Zedekiah king of
Judah shall not escape from
the hand of the Chaldeans, but
shall surely be delivered into
the hand of the king of Babylon, and shall speak with him
face to face,[a] and see him eye
to eye; 5then he shall lead Zedekiah to Babylon, and there he
shall be until I visit him," says
the LORD; "though you fight
with the Chaldeans, you shall
not succeed"'?"

6And Jeremiah said, "The
word of the LORD came to
me, saying, 7'Behold, Hanamel the son of Shallum your
uncle will come to you, saying, "Buy my field which *is* in
Anathoth, for the right of redemption *is* yours to buy *it*."'
8Then Hanamel my uncle's
son came to me in the court
of the prison according to the
word of the LORD, and said to
me, 'Please buy my field that
is in Anathoth, which *is* in the
country of Benjamin; for the
right of inheritance *is* yours,
and the redemption yours;
buy *it* for yourself.' Then I
knew that this was the word
of the LORD. 9So I bought the
field from Hanamel, the son
of my uncle who *was* in Anathoth, and weighed *out to* him
the money—seventeen shek-
els of silver. 10And I signed
the deed and sealed *it,* took
witnesses, and weighed the
money on the scales. 11So I
took the purchase deed, *both*
that which was sealed *according* to the law and custom, and
that which was open; 12and
I gave the purchase deed to
Baruch the son of Neriah,
son of Mahseiah, in the presence of Hanamel my uncle's
son, and in the presence of
the witnesses who signed the
purchase deed, before all the
Jews who sat in the court of
the prison.

13"Then I charged Baruch
before them, saying, 14'Thus
says the LORD of hosts, the
God of Israel: "Take these
deeds, both this purchase
deed which is sealed and
this deed which is open, and
put them in an earthen vessel, that they may last many
days." 15For thus says the LORD
of hosts, the God of Israel:

32:4 [a] Literally *mouth to mouth*

"Houses and fields and vineyards shall be possessed again
in this land."'

JEREMIAH PRAYS FOR UNDERSTANDING

[16]"Now when I had delivered the purchase deed to
Baruch the son of Neriah, I
prayed to the LORD, saying:
[17]'Ah, Lord GOD! Behold, You
have made the heavens and
the earth by Your great power
and outstretched arm. There
is nothing too hard for You.
[18]*You* show lovingkindness
to thousands, and repay the
iniquity of the fathers into the
bosom of their children after
them—the Great, the Mighty
God, whose name *is* the LORD
of hosts. [19]*You are* great in
counsel and mighty in work,
for Your eyes *are* open to all
the ways of the sons of men,
to give everyone according
to his ways and according to
the fruit of his doings. [20]You
have set signs and wonders in
the land of Egypt, to this day,
and in Israel and among *other*
men; and You have made
Yourself a name, as it is this
day. [21]You have brought Your
people Israel out of the land
of Egypt with signs and wonders, with a strong hand and
an outstretched arm, and with
great terror; [22]You have given
them this land, of which You
swore to their fathers to give
them—"a land flowing with
milk and honey."[a] [23]And they
came in and took possession
of it, but they have not obeyed
Your voice or walked in Your
law. They have done nothing
of all that You commanded
them to do; therefore You
have caused all this calamity
to come upon them.

[24]'Look, the siege mounds!
They have come to the city to
take it; and the city has been
given into the hand of the
Chaldeans who fight against
it, because of the sword and
famine and pestilence. What
You have spoken has hap-
pened; there You see *it!* [25]And
You have said to me, O Lord
GOD, "Buy the field for money,
and take witnesses"!—yet the
city has been given into the
hand of the Chaldeans.'"

GOD'S ASSURANCE OF THE PEOPLE'S RETURN

[26]Then the word of the
LORD came to Jeremiah, saying, [27]"Behold, I *am* the LORD,
the God of all flesh. Is there
anything too hard for Me?
[28]Therefore thus says the
LORD: 'Behold, I will give this
city into the hand of the Chaldeans, into the hand of Nebuchadnezzar king of Babylon,
and he shall take it. [29]And the
Chaldeans who fight against
this city shall come and set fire
to this city and burn it, with
the houses on whose roofs
they have offered incense to

32:22 [a] Exodus 3:8

Baal and poured out drink offerings to other gods, to provoke Me to anger; 30because
the children of Israel and the
children of Judah have done
only evil before Me from their
youth. For the children of Israel have provoked Me only to
anger with the work of their
hands,' says the LORD. 31'For
this city has been to Me *a provocation of* My anger and My
fury from the day that they
built it, even to this day; so I
will remove it from before My
face 32because of all the evil of
the children of Israel and the
children of Judah, which they
have done to provoke Me to
anger—they, their kings, their
princes, their priests, their
prophets, the men of Judah,
and the inhabitants of Jerusalem. 33And they have turned to
Me the back, and not the face;
though I taught them, rising
up early and teaching *them,*
yet they have not listened to
receive instruction. 34But they
set their abominations in the
house which is called by My
name, to defile it. 35And they
built the high places of Baal
which *are* in the Valley of the
Son of Hinnom, to cause their
sons and their daughters to
pass through *the fire* to Molech, which I did not command
them, nor did it come into My
mind that they should do this
abomination, to cause Judah
to sin.'

36"Now therefore, thus says
the LORD, the God of Israel,
concerning this city of which
you say, 'It shall be delivered
into the hand of the king of
Babylon by the sword, by the
famine, and by the pestilence:
37Behold, I will gather them
out of all countries where I
have driven them in My anger,
in My fury, and in great wrath;
I will bring them back to this
place, and I will cause them
to dwell safely. 38They shall be
My people, and I will be their
God; 39then I will give them
one heart and one way, that
they may fear Me forever, for
the good of them and their
children after them. 40And I
will make an everlasting covenant with them, that I will
not turn away from doing
them good; but I will put My
fear in their hearts so that
they will not depart from Me.
41Yes, I will rejoice over them
to do them good, and I will
assuredly plant them in this
land, with all My heart and
with all My soul.'

42"For thus says the LORD:
'Just as I have brought all this
great calamity on this people, so I will bring on them
all the good that I have promised them. 43And fields will be
bought in this land of which
you say, "*It is* desolate, without
man or beast; it has been given
into the hand of the Chaldeans." 44Men will buy fields for
money, sign deeds and seal
them, and take witnesses, in
the land of Benjamin, in the
places around Jerusalem, in

the cities of Judah, in the cities of the mountains, in the
cities of the lowland, and in
the cities of the South; for I
will cause their captives to
return,' says the LORD."

EXCELLENCE OF THE RESTORED NATION

33 Moreover the word of
the LORD came to Jere-
miah a second time, while he
was still shut up in the court of
the prison, saying, 2"Thus says
the LORD who made it, the
LORD who formed it to establish it (the LORD *is* His name):
3'Call to Me, and I will answer
you, and show you great and
mighty things, which you do
not know.'

4"For thus says the LORD,
the God of Israel, concerning
the houses of this city and the
houses of the kings of Judah,
which have been pulled down
to fortify[a] against the siege
mounds and the sword: 5'They
come to fight with the Chaldeans, but *only* to fill their
places[a] with the dead bodies of men whom I will slay
in My anger and My fury, all
for whose wickedness I have
hidden My face from this city.
6Behold, I will bring it health
and healing; I will heal them
and reveal to them the abundance of peace and truth.
7And I will cause the captives
of Judah and the captives of
Israel to return, and will rebuild those places as at the
first. 8I will cleanse them from
all their iniquity by which they
have sinned against Me, and
I will pardon all their iniquities by which they have sinned
and by which they have transgressed against Me. 9Then it
shall be to Me a name of joy,
a praise, and an honor before
all nations of the earth, who
shall hear all the good that I
do to them; they shall fear and
tremble for all the goodness
and all the prosperity that I
provide for it.'

10"Thus says the LORD:
'Again there shall be heard in
this place—of which you say,
"It *is* desolate, without man
and without beast"—in the
cities of Judah, in the streets
of Jerusalem that are desolate, without man and without
inhabitant and without beast,
11the voice of joy and the voice
of gladness, the voice of the
bridegroom and the voice of
the bride, the voice of those
who will say:

"Praise the LORD of hosts,
For the LORD *is* good,
For His mercy *endures*
forever"—

and of those *who will* bring
the sacrifice of praise into the
house of the LORD. For I will
cause the captives of the land
to return as at the first,' says
the LORD.

33:4 [a] Compare Isaiah 22:10 33:5 [a] Compare 2 Kings 23:14

12“Thus says the LORD of
hosts: ‘In this place which is
desolate, without man and
without beast, and in all its cities, there shall again be a dwelling place of shepherds causing
their flocks to lie down. 13In
the cities of the mountains,
in the cities of the lowland, in
the cities of the South, in the
land of Benjamin, in the places
around Jerusalem, and in the
cities of Judah, the flocks shall
again pass under the hands of
him who counts *them*,’ says
the LORD.

14‘Behold, the days are
coming,’ says the LORD, ‘that
I will perform that good thing
which I have promised to the
house of Israel and to the
house of Judah:

15 ‘In those days and
at that time
I will cause to grow
up to David
A Branch of
righteousness;
He shall execute
judgment and
righteousness
in the earth.
16 In those days Judah
will be saved,
And Jerusalem will
dwell safely.
And this *is the name* by
which she will be called:

THE LORD OUR
RIGHTEOUSNESS.’[a]

17“For thus says the LORD:
‘David shall never lack a man
to sit on the throne of the
house of Israel; 18nor shall the
priests, the Levites, lack a man
to offer burnt offerings before
Me, to kindle grain offerings,
and to sacrifice continually.’ ”

THE PERMANENCE OF GOD’S COVENANT

19And the word of the LORD
came to Jeremiah, saying,
20“Thus says the LORD: ‘If you
can break My covenant with
the day and My covenant with
the night, so that there will
not be day and night in their
season, 21then My covenant
may also be broken with David
My servant, so that he shall
not have a son to reign on his
throne, and with the Levites,
the priests, My ministers. 22As
the host of heaven cannot be
numbered, nor the sand of the
sea measured, so will I multiply the descendants of David
My servant and the Levites
who minister to Me.’ ”

23Moreover the word of
the LORD came to Jeremiah,
saying, 24“Have you not considered what these people
have spoken, saying, ‘The two
families which the LORD has
chosen, He has also cast them
off’? Thus they have despised
My people, as if they should no
more be a nation before them.

25“Thus says the LORD: ‘If
My covenant *is* not with day

33:16 [a] Compare 23:5, 6

and night, *and if* I have not appointed the ordinances of heaven and earth, 26then I will cast away the descendants of Jacob and David My servant, *so* that I will not take *any* of his descendants *to be* rulers over the descendants of Abraham, Isaac, and Jacob. For I will cause their captives to return, and will have mercy on them.'"

ZEDEKIAH WARNED BY GOD

34 The word which came to Jeremiah from the LORD, when Nebuchadnezzar king of Babylon and all his army, all the kingdoms of the earth under his dominion, and all the people, fought against Jerusalem and all its cities, saying, 2"Thus says the LORD, the God of Israel: 'Go and speak to Zedekiah king of Judah and tell him, "Thus says the LORD: 'Behold, I will give this city into the hand of the king of Babylon, and he shall burn it with fire. 3And you shall not escape from his hand, but shall surely be taken and delivered into his hand; your eyes shall see the eyes of the king of Babylon, he shall speak with you face to face,[a] and you shall go to Babylon.'"' 4Yet hear the word of the LORD, O Zedekiah king of Judah! Thus says the LORD concerning you: 'You shall not die by the sword. 5You shall die in peace; as in the ceremonies of your fathers, the former kings who were before you, so they shall burn *incense* for you and lament for you, *saying,* "Alas, lord!" For I have pronounced the word, says the LORD.'"

6Then Jeremiah the prophet spoke all these words to Zedekiah king of Judah in Jerusalem, 7when the king of Babylon's army fought against Jerusalem and all the cities of Judah that were left, against Lachish and Azekah; for *only* these fortified cities remained of the cities of Judah.

TREACHEROUS TREATMENT OF SLAVES

8*This is* the word that came to Jeremiah from the LORD, after King Zedekiah had made a covenant with all the people who *were* at Jerusalem to proclaim liberty to them: 9that every man should set free his male and female slave—a Hebrew man or woman—that no one should keep a Jewish brother in bondage. 10Now when all the princes and all the people, who had entered into the covenant, heard that everyone should set free his male and female slaves, that no one should keep them in bondage anymore, they obeyed and let *them* go. 11But afterward they changed their

34:3 [a] Literally *mouth to mouth*

minds and made the male and
female slaves return, whom
they had set free, and brought
them into subjection as male
and female slaves.
12Therefore the word of the
LORD came to Jeremiah from
the LORD, saying, 13"Thus says
the LORD, the God of Israel: 'I
made a covenant with your fathers in the day that I brought
them out of the land of Egypt,
out of the house of bondage,
saying, 14"At the end of seven
years let every man set free
his Hebrew brother, who has
been sold to him; and when
he has served you six years,
you shall let him go free from
you." But your fathers did not
obey Me nor incline their ear.
15Then you recently turned
and did what was right in My
sight—every man proclaim-
ing liberty to his neighbor;
and you made a covenant before Me in the house which
is called by My name. 16Then
you turned around and profaned My name, and every
one of you brought back his
male and female slaves, whom
you had set at liberty, at their
pleasure, and brought them
back into subjection, to be
your male and female slaves.'
17"Therefore thus says the
LORD: 'You have not obeyed
Me in proclaiming liberty,
every one to his brother and
every one to his neighbor.
Behold, I proclaim liberty to
you,' says the LORD—'to the
sword, to pestilence, and to
famine! And I will deliver
you to trouble among all the
kingdoms of the earth. 18And
I will give the men who have
transgressed My covenant,
who have not performed the
words of the covenant which
they made before Me, when
they cut the calf in two and
passed between the parts of
it— 19the princes of Judah,
the princes of Jerusalem, the
eunuchs, the priests, and all
the people of the land who
passed between the parts of
the calf— 20I will give them
into the hand of their enemies
and into the hand of those
who seek their life. Their dead
bodies shall be for meat for
the birds of the heaven and
the beasts of the earth. 21And
I will give Zedekiah king of
Judah and his princes into the
hand of their enemies, into
the hand of those who seek
their life, and into the hand
of the king of Babylon's army
which has gone back from
you. 22Behold, I will command,' says the LORD, 'and
cause them to return to this
city. They will fight against it
and take it and burn it with
fire; and I will make the cities
of Judah a desolation without
inhabitant.'"

THE OBEDIENT RECHABITES

35 The word which came
to Jeremiah from the
LORD in the days of Jehoiakim the son of Josiah, king

of Judah, saying, 2"Go to the
house of the Rechabites, speak
to them, and bring them into
the house of the LORD, into
one of the chambers, and give
them wine to drink."

3Then I took Jaazaniah
the son of Jeremiah, the son
of Habazziniah, his brothers
and all his sons, and the whole
house of the Rechabites,
4and I brought them into
the house of the LORD, into
the chamber of the sons of
Hanan the son of Igdaliah, a
man of God, which *was* by the
chamber of the princes, above
the chamber of Maaseiah the
son of Shallum, the keeper of
the door. 5Then I set before
the sons of the house of the
Rechabites bowls full of wine,
and cups; and I said to them,
"Drink wine."

6But they said, "We will
drink no wine, for Jonadab
the son of Rechab, our father,
commanded us, saying, 'You
shall drink no wine, you nor
your sons, forever. 7You shall
not build a house, sow seed,
plant a vineyard, nor have *any
of these;* but all your days you
shall dwell in tents, that you
may live many days in the
land where you are sojourners.' 8Thus we have obeyed
the voice of Jonadab the son
of Rechab, our father, in all
that he charged us, to drink
no wine all our days, we, our
wives, our sons, or our daughters, 9nor to build ourselves
houses to dwell in; nor do we
have vineyard, field, or seed.
10But we have dwelt in tents,
and have obeyed and done according to all that Jonadab our
father commanded us. 11But
it came to pass, when Nebuchadnezzar king of Babylon
came up into the land, that we
said, 'Come, let us go to Jerusalem for fear of the army of
the Chaldeans and for fear of
the army of the Syrians.' So we
dwell at Jerusalem."

12Then came the word of
the LORD to Jeremiah, saying, 13"Thus says the LORD of
hosts, the God of Israel: 'Go
and tell the men of Judah and
the inhabitants of Jerusalem,
"Will you not receive instruction to obey My words?" says
the LORD. 14"The words of
Jonadab the son of Rechab,
which he commanded his
sons, not to drink wine, are
performed; for to this day
they drink none, and obey
their father's commandment.
But although I have spoken to
you, rising early and speaking, you did not obey Me. 15I
have also sent to you all My
servants the prophets, rising
up early and sending *them,*
saying, 'Turn now everyone
from his evil way, amend your
doings, and do not go after
other gods to serve them;
then you will dwell in the land
which I have given you and
your fathers.' But you have not
inclined your ear, nor obeyed
Me. 16Surely the sons of Jonadab the son of Rechab have

performed the commandment of their father, which he commanded them, but this people has not obeyed Me."'

17"Therefore thus says the LORD God of hosts, the God of Israel: 'Behold, I will bring on Judah and on all the inhabitants of Jerusalem all the doom that I have pronounced against them; because I have spoken to them but they have not heard, and I have called to them but they have not answered.'"

18And Jeremiah said to the house of the Rechabites, "Thus says the LORD of hosts, the God of Israel: 'Because you have obeyed the commandment of Jonadab your father, and kept all his precepts and done according to all that he commanded you, 19therefore thus says the LORD of hosts, the God of Israel: "Jonadab the son of Rechab shall not lack a man to stand before Me forever."'"

THE SCROLL READ IN THE TEMPLE

36 Now it came to pass in the fourth year of Jehoiakim the son of Josiah, king of Judah, *that* this word came to Jeremiah from the LORD, saying: 2"Take a scroll of a book and write on it all the words that I have spoken to you against Israel, against Judah, and against all the nations, from the day I spoke to you, from the days of Josiah even to this day. 3It may be that the house of Judah will hear all the adversities which I purpose to bring upon them, that everyone may turn from his evil way, that I may forgive their iniquity and their sin."

4Then Jeremiah called Baruch the son of Neriah; and Baruch wrote on a scroll of a book, at the instruction of Jeremiah,[a] all the words of the LORD which He had spoken to him. 5And Jeremiah commanded Baruch, saying, "I *am* confined, I cannot go into the house of the LORD. 6You go, therefore, and read from the scroll which you have written at my instruction,[a] the words of the LORD, in the hearing of the people in the LORD's house on the day of fasting. And you shall also read them in the hearing of all Judah who come from their cities. 7It may be that they will present their supplication before the LORD, and everyone will turn from his evil way. For great *is* the anger and the fury that the LORD has pronounced against this people." 8And Baruch the son of Neriah did according to all that Jeremiah the prophet commanded him, reading from the book the words of the LORD in the LORD's house.

36:4 [a] Literally *from Jeremiah's mouth*
36:6 [a] Literally *from my mouth*

9 Now it came to pass in the
fifth year of Jehoiakim the son
of Josiah, king of Judah, in the
ninth month, *that* they proclaimed a fast before the LORD
to all the people in Jerusalem,
and to all the people who came
from the cities of Judah to Jerusalem. 10 Then Baruch read
from the book the words of
Jeremiah in the house of the
LORD, in the chamber of Gemariah the son of Shaphan the
scribe, in the upper court at
the entry of the New Gate of
the LORD's house, in the hearing of all the people.

THE SCROLL READ IN THE PALACE

11 When Michaiah the son
of Gemariah, the son of Shaphan, heard all the words of
the LORD from the book, 12 he
then went down to the king's
house, into the scribe's chamber; and there all the princes
were sitting—Elishama the
scribe, Delaiah the son of
Shemaiah, Elnathan the son
of Achbor, Gemariah the son of
Shaphan, Zedekiah the son of
Hananiah, and all the princes.
13 Then Michaiah declared to
them all the words that he had
heard when Baruch read the
book in the hearing of the people. 14 Therefore all the princes
sent Jehudi the son of Nethaniah, the son of Shelemiah, the
son of Cushi, to Baruch, saying,
"Take in your hand the scroll
from which you have read in
the hearing of the people, and
come." So Baruch the son of
Neriah took the scroll in his
hand and came to them. 15 And
they said to him, "Sit down
now, and read it in our hearing." So Baruch read *it* in their
hearing.

16 Now it happened, when
they had heard all the words,
that they looked in fear from
one to another, and said to
Baruch, "We will surely tell
the king of all these words."
17 And they asked Baruch, saying, "Tell us now, how did you
write all these words—at his
instruction?"[a]

18 So Baruch answered
them, "He proclaimed with
his mouth all these words to
me, and I wrote *them* with ink
in the book."

19 Then the princes said to
Baruch, "Go and hide, you
and Jeremiah; and let no one
know where you are."

THE KING DESTROYS JEREMIAH'S SCROLL

20 And they went to the king,
into the court; but they stored
the scroll in the chamber of
Elishama the scribe, and told
all the words in the hearing
of the king. 21 So the king sent
Jehudi to bring the scroll, and
he took it from Elishama the
scribe's chamber. And Jehudi
read it in the hearing of the
king and in the hearing of all

36:17 [a] Literally *with his mouth*

the princes who stood beside
the king. 22Now the king was
sitting in the winter house in
the ninth month, with *a fire*
burning on the hearth before
him. 23And it happened, when
Jehudi had read three or four
columns, *that the king* cut it
with the scribe's knife and
cast *it* into the fire that *was* on
the hearth, until all the scroll
was consumed in the fire that
was on the hearth. 24Yet they
were not afraid, nor did they
tear their garments, the king
nor any of his servants who
heard all these words. 25Nevertheless Elnathan, Delaiah,
and Gemariah implored the
king not to burn the scroll; but
he would not listen to them.
26And the king commanded
Jerahmeel the king's[a] son, Seraiah the son of Azriel, and
Shelemiah the son of Abdeel,
to seize Baruch the scribe and
Jeremiah the prophet, but the
LORD hid them.

JEREMIAH REWRITES THE SCROLL

27Now after the king had
burned the scroll with the
words which Baruch had
written at the instruction of
Jeremiah,[a] the word of the
LORD came to Jeremiah, saying: 28"Take yet another scroll,
and write on it all the former
words that were in the first
scroll which Jehoiakim the
king of Judah has burned.
29And you shall say to Jehoiakim king of Judah, 'Thus says
the LORD: "You have burned
this scroll, saying, 'Why have
you written in it that the king
of Babylon will certainly come
and destroy this land, and
cause man and beast to cease
from here?'" 30Therefore thus
says the LORD concerning Jehoiakim king of Judah: "He
shall have no one to sit on the
throne of David, and his dead
body shall be cast out to the
heat of the day and the frost of
the night. 31I will punish him,
his family, and his servants for
their iniquity; and I will bring
on them, on the inhabitants of
Jerusalem, and on the men of
Judah all the doom that I have
pronounced against them; but
they did not heed."'"

32Then Jeremiah took another scroll and gave it to
Baruch the scribe, the son of
Neriah, who wrote on it at the
instruction of Jeremiah[a] all
the words of the book which
Jehoiakim king of Judah had
burned in the fire. And besides, there were added to
them many similar words.

ZEDEKIAH'S VAIN HOPE

37 Now King Zedekiah the
son of Josiah reigned
instead of Coniah the son of
Jehoiakim, whom Nebuchadnezzar king of Babylon made

36:26 [a] Hebrew *Hammelech* 36:27 [a] Literally *from Jeremiah's mouth* 36:32 [a] Literally *from Jeremiah's mouth*

king in the land of Judah. 2But
neither he nor his servants
nor the people of the land
gave heed to the words of the
LORD which He spoke by the
prophet Jeremiah.
3And Zedekiah the king
sent Jehucal the son of Shelemiah, and Zephaniah the
son of Maaseiah, the priest,
to the prophet Jeremiah, saying, "Pray now to the LORD
our God for us." 4Now Jeremiah was coming and going
among the people, for they
had not *yet* put him in prison.
5Then Pharaoh's army came
up from Egypt; and when the
Chaldeans who were besieging Jerusalem heard news of
them, they departed from Jerusalem.
6Then the word of the
LORD came to the prophet
Jeremiah, saying, 7"Thus says
the LORD, the God of Israel,
'Thus you shall say to the
king of Judah, who sent you
to Me to inquire of Me: "Behold, Pharaoh's army which
has come up to help you will
return to Egypt, to their own
land. 8And the Chaldeans
shall come back and fight
against this city, and take it
and burn it with fire."' 9Thus
says the LORD: 'Do not deceive yourselves, saying, "The
Chaldeans will surely depart
from us," for they will not depart. 10For though you had defeated the whole army of the
Chaldeans who fight against
you, and there remained *only*
wounded men among them,
they would rise up, every man
in his tent, and burn the city
with fire.'"

JEREMIAH IMPRISONED

11And it happened, when
the army of the Chaldeans
left *the siege* of Jerusalem for
fear of Pharaoh's army, 12that
Jeremiah went out of Jerusalem to go into the land of
Benjamin to claim his property there among the people.
13And when he was in the Gate
of Benjamin, a captain of the
guard *was* there whose name
was Irijah the son of Shelemiah, the son of Hananiah;
and he seized Jeremiah the
prophet, saying, "You are defecting to the Chaldeans!"
14Then Jeremiah said,
"False! I am not defecting to
the Chaldeans." But he did not
listen to him.
So Irijah seized Jere-
miah and brought him to
the princes. 15Therefore the
princes were angry with Jeremiah, and they struck him
and put him in prison in the
house of Jonathan the scribe.
For they had made that the
prison.
16When Jeremiah entered
the dungeon and the cells,
and Jeremiah had remained
there many days, 17then Zedekiah the king sent and took
him *out*. The king asked him
secretly in his house, and said,
"Is there *any* word from the
LORD?"

And Jeremiah said, "There is." Then he said, "You shall be delivered into the hand of the king of Babylon!"

18 Moreover Jeremiah said to King Zedekiah, "What offense have I committed against you, against your servants, or against this people, that you have put me in prison? 19 Where now *are* your prophets who prophesied to you, saying, 'The king of Babylon will not come against you or against this land'? 20 Therefore please hear now, O my lord the king. Please, let my petition be accepted before you, and do not make me return to the house of Jonathan the scribe, lest I die there."

21 Then Zedekiah the king commanded that they should commit Jeremiah to the court of the prison, and that they should give him daily a piece of bread from the bakers' street, until all the bread in the city was gone. Thus Jeremiah remained in the court of the prison.

JEREMIAH IN THE DUNGEON

38 Now Shephatiah the son of Mattan, Gedaliah the son of Pashhur, Jucal[a] the son of Shelemiah, and Pashhur the son of Malchiah heard the words that Jeremiah had spoken to all the people, saying, 2 "Thus says the LORD: 'He who remains in this city shall die by the sword, by famine, and by pestilence; but he who goes over to the Chaldeans shall live; his life shall be as a prize to him, and he shall live.'[a] 3 Thus says the LORD: 'This city shall surely be given into the hand of the king of Babylon's army, which shall take it.'"

4 Therefore the princes said to the king, "Please, let this man be put to death, for thus he weakens the hands of the men of war who remain in this city, and the hands of all the people, by speaking such words to them. For this man does not seek the welfare of this people, but their harm."

5 Then Zedekiah the king said, "Look, he *is* in your hand. For the king can *do* nothing against you." 6 So they took Jeremiah and cast him into the dungeon of Malchiah the king's[a] son, which *was* in the court of the prison, and they let Jeremiah down with ropes. And in the dungeon *there was* no water, but mire. So Jeremiah sank in the mire.

7 Now Ebed-Melech the Ethiopian, one of the eunuchs, who was in the king's house, heard that they had put Jeremiah in the dungeon. When the king was sitting at the Gate of Benjamin, 8 Ebed-Melech

38:1 [a] Same as *Jehucal* (compare 37:3) 38:2 [a] Compare 21:9 38:6 [a] Hebrew *Hammelech*

went out of the king's house
and spoke to the king, saying: [9]"My lord the king, these
men have done evil in all that
they have done to Jeremiah
the prophet, whom they have
cast into the dungeon, and he
is likely to die from hunger in
the place where he is. For *there
is* no more bread in the city."
[10]Then the king commanded
Ebed-Melech the Ethiopian,
saying, "Take from here thirty
men with you, and lift Jeremiah the prophet out of the
dungeon before he dies." [11]So
Ebed-Melech took the men
with him and went into the
house of the king under the
treasury, and took from there
old clothes and old rags, and
let them down by ropes into
the dungeon to Jeremiah.
[12]Then Ebed-Melech the
Ethiopian said to Jeremiah,
"Please put these old clothes
and rags under your armpits,
under the ropes." And Jeremiah did so. [13]So they pulled
Jeremiah up with ropes and
lifted him out of the dungeon.
And Jeremiah remained in
the court of the prison.

ZEDEKIAH'S FEARS AND JEREMIAH'S ADVICE

[14]Then Zedekiah the king
sent and had Jeremiah the
prophet brought to him at the
third entrance of the house
of the LORD. And the king
said to Jeremiah, "I will ask
you something. Hide nothing
from me."

[15]Jeremiah said to Zedekiah, "If I declare *it* to you,
will you not surely put me to
death? And if I give you advice, you will not listen to me."

[16]So Zedekiah the king
swore secretly to Jeremiah,
saying, "*As* the LORD lives,
who made our very souls, I
will not put you to death, nor
will I give you into the hand of
these men who seek your life."

[17]Then Jeremiah said to
Zedekiah, "Thus says the
LORD, the God of hosts, the
God of Israel: 'If you surely
surrender to the king of Babylon's princes, then your soul
shall live; this city shall not be
burned with fire, and you and
your house shall live. [18]But if
you do not surrender to the
king of Babylon's princes,
then this city shall be given
into the hand of the Chaldeans; they shall burn it with
fire, and you shall not escape
from their hand.'"

[19]And Zedekiah the king
said to Jeremiah, "I am afraid
of the Jews who have defected
to the Chaldeans, lest they deliver me into their hand, and
they abuse me."

[20]But Jeremiah said, "They
shall not deliver *you*. Please,
obey the voice of the LORD
which I speak to you. So it
shall be well with you, and
your soul shall live. [21]But if
you refuse to surrender, this
is the word that the LORD has
shown me: [22]'Now behold, all
the women who are left in the

king of Judah's house *shall be* surrendered to the king of Babylon's princes, and those *women* shall say:

"Your close friends
have set upon you
And prevailed
against you;
Your feet have sunk
in the mire,
And they have turned
away again."

23'So they shall surrender all your wives and children to the Chaldeans. You shall not escape from their hand, but shall be taken by the hand of the king of Babylon. And you shall cause this city to be burned with fire.'"

24Then Zedekiah said to Jeremiah, "Let no one know of these words, and you shall not die. 25But if the princes hear that I have talked with you, and they come to you and say to you, 'Declare to us now what you have said to the king, and also what the king said to you; do not hide *it* from us, and we will not put you to death,' 26then you shall say to them, 'I presented my request before the king, that he would not make me return to Jonathan's house to die there.'"

27Then all the princes came to Jeremiah and asked him. And he told them according to all these words that the king had commanded. So they stopped speaking with him, for the conversation had not been heard. 28Now Jeremiah remained in the court of the prison until the day that Jerusalem was taken. And he was *there* when Jerusalem was taken.

THE FALL OF JERUSALEM

39 In the ninth year of Zedekiah king of Judah, in the tenth month, Nebuchadnezzar king of Babylon and all his army came against Jerusalem, and besieged it. 2In the eleventh year of Zedekiah, in the fourth month, on the ninth *day* of the month, the city was penetrated.

3Then all the princes of the king of Babylon came in and sat in the Middle Gate: Nergal-Sharezer, Samgar-Nebo, Sarsechim, Rabsaris,[a] Nergal-Sarezer, Rabmag,[b] with the rest of the princes of the king of Babylon.

4So it was, when Zedekiah the king of Judah and all the men of war saw them, that they fled and went out of the city by night, by way of the king's garden, by the gate between the two walls. And he went out by way of the plain.[a] 5But the Chaldean

39:3 [a] A title, probably *Chief Officer;* also verse 13 [b] A title, probably *Troop Commander;* also verse 13 **39:4** [a] Or *the Arabah,* that is, the Jordan Valley

army pursued them and overtook Zedekiah in the plains of
Jericho. And when they had
captured him, they brought
him up to Nebuchadnezzar
king of Babylon, to Riblah in
the land of Hamath, where
he pronounced judgment on
him. 6Then the king of Babylon killed the sons of Zedekiah before his eyes in Riblah;
the king of Babylon also killed
all the nobles of Judah. 7More-
over he put out Zedekiah's
eyes, and bound him with
bronze fetters to carry him
off to Babylon. 8And the Chaldeans burned the king's house
and the houses of the people
with fire, and broke down the
walls of Jerusalem. 9Then
Nebuzaradan the captain of
the guard carried away captive to Babylon the remnant
of the people who remained
in the city and those who defected to him, with the rest
of the people who remained.
10But Nebuzaradan the captain of the guard left in the
land of Judah the poor people,
who had nothing, and gave
them vineyards and fields at
the same time.

JEREMIAH GOES FREE

11Now Nebuchadnezzar
king of Babylon gave charge
concerning Jeremiah to Nebuzaradan the captain of the
guard, saying, 12"Take him
and look after him, and do
him no harm; but do to him
just as he says to you." 13So
Nebuzaradan the captain of
the guard sent Nebushasban,
Rabsaris, Nergal-Sharezer,
Rabmag, and all the king of
Babylon's chief officers; 14then
they sent *someone* to take Jeremiah from the court of the
prison, and committed him to
Gedaliah the son of Ahikam,
the son of Shaphan, that he
should take him home. So he
dwelt among the people.

15Meanwhile the word of
the LORD had come to Jeremiah while he was shut up in
the court of the prison, saying, 16"Go and speak to Ebed-
Melech the Ethiopian, saying,
'Thus says the LORD of hosts,
the God of Israel: "Behold, I
will bring My words upon this
city for adversity and not for
good, and they shall be *performed* in that day before you.
17But I will deliver you in that
day," says the LORD, "and you
shall not be given into the
hand of the men of whom you
are afraid. 18For I will surely
deliver you, and you shall not
fall by the sword; but your life
shall be as a prize to you, because you have put your trust
in Me," says the LORD.'"

JEREMIAH WITH GEDALIAH THE GOVERNOR

40 The word that came
to Jeremiah from the
LORD after Nebuzaradan the
captain of the guard had let
him go from Ramah, when
he had taken him bound in
chains among all who were

carried away captive from Jerusalem and Judah, who were carried away captive to Babylon.

2And the captain of the guard took Jeremiah and said to him: "The LORD your God has pronounced this doom on this place. 3Now the LORD has brought *it,* and has done just as He said. Because you *people* have sinned against the LORD, and not obeyed His voice, therefore this thing has come upon you. 4And now look, I free you this day from the chains that *were* on your hand. If it seems good to you to come with me to Babylon, come, and I will look after you. But if it seems wrong for you to come with me to Babylon, remain here. See, all the land *is* before you; wherever it seems good and convenient for you to go, go there."

5Now while Jeremiah had not yet gone back, *Nebuzaradan said,* "Go back to Gedaliah the son of Ahikam, the son of Shaphan, whom the king of Babylon has made governor over the cities of Judah, and dwell with him among the people. Or go wherever it seems convenient for you to go." So the captain of the guard gave him rations and a gift and let him go. 6Then Jeremiah went to Gedaliah the son of Ahikam, to Mizpah, and dwelt with him among the people who were left in the land.

7And when all the captains of the armies who *were* in the fields, they and their men, heard that the king of Babylon had made Gedaliah the son of Ahikam governor in the land, and had committed to him men, women, children, and the poorest of the land who had not been carried away captive to Babylon, 8then they came to Gedaliah at Mizpah—Ishmael the son of Nethaniah, Johanan and Jonathan the sons of Kareah, Seraiah the son of Tanhumeth, the sons of Ephai the Netophathite, and Jezaniah[a] the son of a Maachathite, they and their men. 9And Gedaliah the son of Ahikam, the son of Shaphan, took an oath before them and their men, saying, "Do not be afraid to serve the Chaldeans. Dwell in the land and serve the king of Babylon, and it shall be well with you. 10As for me, I will indeed dwell at Mizpah and serve the Chaldeans who come to us. But you, gather wine and summer fruit and oil, put *them* in your vessels, and dwell in your cities that you have taken." 11Likewise, when all the Jews who *were* in Moab, among the Ammonites, in Edom, and who *were* in all the countries, heard that the king of Babylon had left

40:8 [a] Spelled *Jaazaniah* in 2 Kings 25:23

a remnant of Judah, and that
he had set over them Gedaliah the son of Ahikam, the
son of Shaphan, 12then all
the Jews returned out of all
places where they had been
driven, and came to the land
of Judah, to Gedaliah at Mizpah, and gathered wine and
summer fruit in abundance.
13Moreover Johanan the
son of Kareah and all the captains of the forces that *were* in
the fields came to Gedaliah at
Mizpah, 14and said to him, "Do
you certainly know that Baalis
the king of the Ammonites
has sent Ishmael the son of
Nethaniah to murder you?"
But Gedaliah the son of Ahikam did not believe them.
15Then Johanan the son of
Kareah spoke secretly to Gedaliah in Mizpah, saying, "Let
me go, please, and I will kill
Ishmael the son of Nethaniah,
and no one will know *it*. Why
should he murder you, so that
all the Jews who are gathered
to you would be scattered, and
the remnant in Judah perish?"
16But Gedaliah the son of
Ahikam said to Johanan the
son of Kareah, "You shall not
do this thing, for you speak
falsely concerning Ishmael."

INSURRECTION AGAINST GEDALIAH

41 *Now it came to pass in*
the seventh month *that*
Ishmael the son of Nethaniah,
the son of Elishama, of the
royal family and of the officers of the king, came with
ten men to Gedaliah the son
of Ahikam, at Mizpah. And
there they ate bread together
in Mizpah. 2Then Ishmael the
son of Nethaniah, and the ten
men who were with him, arose
and struck Gedaliah the son of
Ahikam, the son of Shaphan,
with the sword, and killed him
whom the king of Babylon had
made governor over the land.
3Ishmael also struck down all
the Jews who were with him,
that is, with Gedaliah at Mizpah, and the Chaldeans who
were found there, the men of
war.
4And it happened, on the
second day after he had killed
Gedaliah, when as yet no one
knew *it,* 5that certain men
came from Shechem, from
Shiloh, and from Samaria,
eighty men with their beards
shaved and their clothes
torn, having cut themselves,
with offerings and incense in
their hand, to bring *them* to
the house of the LORD. 6Now
Ishmael the son of Nethaniah
went out from Mizpah to meet
them, weeping as he went
along; and it happened as he
met them that he said to them,
"Come to Gedaliah the son of
Ahikam!" 7So it was, when
they came into the midst of
the city, that Ishmael the son
of Nethaniah killed them *and*
cast them into the midst of a
pit, he and the men who were
with him. 8But ten men were
found among them who said

to Ishmael, "Do not kill us, for
we have treasures of wheat,
barley, oil, and honey in the
field." So he desisted and did
not kill them among their
brethren. 9Now the pit into
which Ishmael had cast all the
dead bodies of the men whom
he had slain, because of Gedaliah, *was* the same one Asa
the king had made for fear of
Baasha king of Israel. Ishmael
the son of Nethaniah filled it
with *the* slain. 10Then Ishmael
carried away captive all the
rest of the people who *were*
in Mizpah, the king's daughters and all the people who
remained in Mizpah, whom
Nebuzaradan the captain of
the guard had committed to
Gedaliah the son of Ahikam.
And Ishmael the son of Nethaniah carried them away captive and departed to go over
to the Ammonites.

11But when Johanan the
son of Kareah and all the captains of the forces that *were*
with him heard of all the evil
that Ishmael the son of Nethaniah had done, 12they took
all the men and went to fight
with Ishmael the son of Nethaniah; and they found him by
the great pool that *is* in Gibeon. 13So it was, when all the
people who *were* with Ishmael
saw Johanan the son of Kareah, and all the captains of
the forces who *were* with him,
that they were glad. 14Then all
the people whom Ishmael had
carried away captive from
Mizpah turned around and
came back, and went to Johanan the son of Kareah. 15But
Ishmael the son of Nethaniah
escaped from Johanan with
eight men and went to the
Ammonites.

16Then Johanan the son of
Kareah, and all the captains of
the forces that were with him,
took from Mizpah all the rest
of the people whom he had
recovered from Ishmael the
son of Nethaniah after he had
murdered Gedaliah the son of
Ahikam—the mighty men of
war and the women and the
children and the eunuchs,
whom he had brought back
from Gibeon. 17And they departed and dwelt in the habitation of Chimham, which
is near Bethlehem, as they
went on their way to Egypt,
18because of the Chaldeans;
for they were afraid of them,
because Ishmael the son of
Nethaniah had murdered
Gedaliah the son of Ahikam,
whom the king of Babylon had
made governor in the land.

THE FLIGHT TO EGYPT FORBIDDEN

42 Now all the captains
of the forces, Johanan
the son of Kareah, Jezaniah
the son of Hoshaiah, and all
the people, from the least to
the greatest, came near 2and
said to Jeremiah the prophet,
"Please, let our petition be acceptable to you, and pray for
us to the LORD your God, for

all this remnant (since we are
left *but* a few of many, as you
can see), 3that the LORD your
God may show us the way in
which we should walk and the
thing we should do."
4Then Jeremiah the
prophet said to them, "I have
heard. Indeed, I will pray to
the LORD your God according
to your words, and it shall be,
that whatever the LORD answers you, I will declare *it* to
you. I will keep nothing back
from you."
5So they said to Jeremiah,
"Let the LORD be a true and
faithful witness between us,
if we do not do according to
everything which the LORD
your God sends us by you.
6Whether *it is* pleasing or
displeasing, we will obey the
voice of the LORD our God to
whom we send you, that it
may be well with us when we
obey the voice of the LORD our
God."
7And it happened after ten
days that the word of the LORD
came to Jeremiah. 8Then he
called Johanan the son of Kareah, all the captains of the
forces which *were* with him,
and all the people from the
least even to the greatest, 9and
said to them, "Thus says the
LORD, the God of Israel, to
whom you sent me to pres-
ent your petition before Him:
10'If you will still remain in
this land, then I will build you
and not pull *you* down, and I
will plant you and not pluck
you up. For I relent concerning the disaster that I have
brought upon you. 11Do not be
afraid of the king of Babylon,
of whom you are afraid; do
not be afraid of him,' says the
LORD, 'for I *am* with you, to
save you and deliver you from
his hand. 12And I will show
you mercy, that he may have
mercy on you and cause you
to return to your own land.'
13"But if you say, 'We will
not dwell in this land,' dis-
obeying the voice of the
LORD your God, 14saying, 'No,
but we will go to the land of
Egypt where we shall see no
war, nor hear the sound of
the trumpet, nor be hungry
for bread, and there we will
dwell'— 15Then hear now the
word of the LORD, O remnant
of Judah! Thus says the LORD
of hosts, the God of Israel: 'If
you wholly set your faces to
enter Egypt, and go to dwell
there, 16then it shall be *that*
the sword which you feared
shall overtake you there in the
land of Egypt; the famine of
which you were afraid shall
follow close after you there
in Egypt; and there you shall
die. 17So shall it be with all the
men who set their faces to go
to Egypt to dwell there. They
shall die by the sword, by famine, and by pestilence. And
none of them shall remain or
escape from the disaster that
I will bring upon them.'
18"For thus says the LORD of
hosts, the God of Israel: 'As My

anger and My fury have been
poured out on the inhabitants
of Jerusalem, so will My fury
be poured out on you when
you enter Egypt. And you shall
be an oath, an astonishment, a
curse, and a reproach; and you
shall see this place no more.'

19"The LORD has said con-
cerning you, O remnant of
Judah, 'Do not go to Egypt!'
Know certainly that I have admonished you this day. 20For
you were hypocrites in your
hearts when you sent me to
the LORD your God, saying,
'Pray for us to the LORD our
God, and according to all that
the LORD your God says, so
declare to us and we will do *it*.'
21And I have this day declared
it to you, but you have not
obeyed the voice of the LORD
your God, or anything which
He has sent you by me. 22Now
therefore, know certainly that
you shall die by the sword, by
famine, and by pestilence in
the place where you desire to
go to dwell."

JEREMIAH TAKEN TO EGYPT

43 Now it happened, when
Jeremiah had stopped
speaking to all the people all
the words of the LORD their
God, for which the LORD their
God had sent him to them, all
these words, 2that Azariah
the son of Hoshaiah, Johanan the son of Kareah, and
all the proud men spoke, saying to Jeremiah, "You speak
falsely! The LORD our God has
not sent you to say, 'Do not go
to Egypt to dwell there.' 3But
Baruch the son of Neriah has
set you against us, to deliver
us into the hand of the Chaldeans, that they may put us to
death or carry us away captive
to Babylon." 4So Johanan the
son of Kareah, all the captains
of the forces, and all the people would not obey the voice
of the LORD, to remain in the
land of Judah. 5But Johanan
the son of Kareah and all the
captains of the forces took all
the remnant of Judah who had
returned to dwell in the land
of Judah, from all nations
where they had been driven—
6men, women, children, the
king's daughters, and every
person whom Nebuzaradan
the captain of the guard had
left with Gedaliah the son of
Ahikam, the son of Shaphan,
and Jeremiah the prophet and
Baruch the son of Neriah. 7So
they went to the land of Egypt,
for they did not obey the voice
of the LORD. And they went as
far as Tahpanhes.

8Then the word of the
LORD came to Jeremiah in
Tahpanhes, saying, 9"Take
large stones in your hand, and
hide them in the sight of the
men of Judah, in the clay in
the brick courtyard which *is*
at the entrance to Pharaoh's
house in Tahpanhes; 10and say
to them, 'Thus says the LORD
of hosts, the God of Israel:
"Behold, I will send and bring

Nebuchadnezzar the king of
Babylon, My servant, and will
set his throne above these
stones that I have hidden.
And he will spread his royal
pavilion over them. 11When he
comes, he shall strike the land
of Egypt *and deliver* to death
those appointed for death, and
to captivity *those appointed*
for captivity, and to the sword
those appointed for the sword.
12I[a] will kindle a fire in the
houses of the gods of Egypt,
and he shall burn them and
carry them away captive. And
he shall array himself with the
land of Egypt, as a shepherd
puts on his garment, and he
shall go out from there in
peace. 13He shall also break
the *sacred* pillars of Beth Shemesh[a] that *are* in the land of
Egypt; and the houses of the
gods of the Egyptians he shall
burn with fire." ' "

ISRAELITES WILL BE PUNISHED IN EGYPT

44 The word that came
to Jeremiah concern-
ing all the Jews who dwell in
the land of Egypt, who dwell
at Migdol, at Tahpanhes, at
Noph,[a] and in the country of
Pathros, saying, 2"Thus says
the LORD of hosts, the God of
Israel: 'You have seen all the
calamity that I have brought
on Jerusalem and on all the
cities of Judah; and behold,
this day they *are* a desolation,
and no one dwells in them,
3because of their wickedness
which they have committed to
provoke Me to anger, in that
they went to burn incense *and*
to serve other gods whom they
did not know, they nor you nor
your fathers. 4However I have
sent to you all My servants the
prophets, rising early and
sending *them,* saying, "Oh, do
not do this abominable thing
that I hate!" 5But they did not
listen or incline their ear to
turn from their wickedness, to
burn no incense to other gods.
6So My fury and My anger
were poured out and kindled
in the cities of Judah and in
the streets of Jerusalem; and
they are wasted *and* desolate,
as it is this day.'

7"Now therefore, thus says
the LORD, the God of hosts,
the God of Israel: 'Why do you
commit *this* great evil against
yourselves, to cut off from you
man and woman, child and
infant, out of Judah, leaving
none to remain, 8in that you
provoke Me to wrath with the
works of your hands, burning
incense to other gods in the
land of Egypt where you have
gone to dwell, that you may
cut yourselves off and be a
curse and a reproach among
all the nations of the earth?

43:12 [a] Following Masoretic Text and Targum; Septuagint, Syriac, and Vulgate read *He.* 43:13 [a] Literally *House of the Sun,* ancient On; later called Heliopolis 44:1 [a] That is, ancient Memphis

9Have you forgotten the wickedness of your fathers, the
wickedness of the kings of
Judah, the wickedness of their
wives, your own wickedness,
and the wickedness of your
wives, which they committed
in the land of Judah and in the
streets of Jerusalem? 10They
have not been humbled, to
this day, nor have they feared;
they have not walked in My
law or in My statutes that I set
before you and your fathers.'

11"Therefore thus says the
LORD of hosts, the God of Israel: 'Behold, I will set My face
against you for catastrophe
and for cutting off all Judah.
12And I will take the remnant
of Judah who have set their
faces to go into the land of
Egypt to dwell there, and they
shall all be consumed *and* fall
in the land of Egypt. They shall
be consumed by the sword *and*
by famine. They shall die, from
the least to the greatest, by the
sword and by famine; and they
shall be an oath, an astonishment, a curse and a reproach!
13For I will punish those who
dwell in the land of Egypt, as I
have punished Jerusalem, by
the sword, by famine, and by
pestilence, 14so that none of the
remnant of Judah who have
gone into the land of Egypt
to dwell there shall escape or
survive, lest they return to the
land of Judah, to which they
desire to return and dwell. For
none shall return except those
who escape.'"

15Then all the men who knew
that their wives had burned
incense to other gods, with
all the women who stood by,
a great multitude, and all the
people who dwelt in the land
of Egypt, in Pathros, answered
Jeremiah, saying: 16"*As for* the
word that you have spoken to
us in the name of the LORD, we
will not listen to you! 17But we
will certainly do whatever has
gone out of our own mouth, to
burn incense to the queen of
heaven and pour out drink offerings to her, as we have done,
we and our fathers, our kings
and our princes, in the cities
of Judah and in the streets of
Jerusalem. For *then* we had
plenty of food, were well-off,
and saw no trouble. 18But since
we stopped burning incense to
the queen of heaven and pouring out drink offerings to her,
we have lacked everything and
have been consumed by the
sword and by famine."

19*The women also said,* "And
when we burned incense to
the queen of heaven and
poured out drink offerings to
her, did we make cakes for her,
to worship her, and pour out
drink offerings to her without
our husbands' *permission?*"

20Then Jeremiah spoke to
all the people—the men, the
women, and all the people who
had given him *that* answer—
saying: 21"The incense that
you burned in the cities of
Judah and in the streets of Jerusalem, you and your fathers,

your kings and your princes, and the people of the land, did not the LORD remember them, and did it *not* come into His mind? 22So the LORD could no longer bear *it,* because of the evil of your doings *and* because of the abominations which you committed. Therefore your land is a desolation, an astonishment, a curse, and without an inhabitant, as *it is* this day. 23Because you have burned incense and because you have sinned against the LORD, and have not obeyed the voice of the LORD or walked in His law, in His statutes or in His testimonies, therefore this calamity has happened to you, as *at* this day."

24Moreover Jeremiah said to all the people and to all the women, "Hear the word of the LORD, all Judah who *are* in the land of Egypt! 25Thus says the LORD of hosts, the God of Israel, saying: 'You and your wives have spoken with your mouths and fulfilled with your hands, saying, "We will surely keep our vows that we have made, to burn incense to the queen of heaven and pour out drink offerings to her." You will surely keep your vows and perform your vows!' 26Therefore hear the word of the LORD, all Judah who dwell in the land of Egypt: 'Behold, I have sworn by My great name,' says the LORD, 'that My name shall no more be named in the mouth of any man of Judah in all the land of Egypt, saying, "The Lord GOD lives." 27Behold, I will watch over them for adversity and not for good. And all the men of Judah who *are* in the land of Egypt shall be consumed by the sword and by famine, until there is an end to them. 28Yet a small number who escape the sword shall return from the land of Egypt to the land of Judah; and all the remnant of Judah, who have gone to the land of Egypt to dwell there, shall know whose words will stand, Mine or theirs. 29And this *shall be* a sign to you,' says the LORD, 'that I will punish you in this place, that you may know that My words will surely stand against you for adversity.'

30"Thus says the LORD: 'Behold, I will give Pharaoh Hophra king of Egypt into the hand of his enemies and into the hand of those who seek his life, as I gave Zedekiah king of Judah into the hand of Nebuchadnezzar king of Babylon, his enemy who sought his life.'"

ASSURANCE TO BARUCH

45 The word that Jeremiah the prophet spoke to Baruch the son of Neriah, when he had written *these words* in a book at the instruction of Jeremiah,[a] in the fourth year of Jehoia-

45:1 [a] Literally *from Jeremiah's mouth*

kim the son of Josiah, king
of Judah, saying, 2"Thus says
the LORD, the God of Israel,
to you, O Baruch: 3'You said,
"Woe is me now! For the LORD
has added grief to my sorrow.
I fainted in my sighing, and I
find no rest."'

4"Thus you shall say to him,
'Thus says the LORD: "Be-
hold, what I have built I will
break down, and what I have
planted I will pluck up, that is,
this whole land. 5And do you
seek great things for yourself?
Do not seek *them;* for behold,
I will bring adversity on all
flesh," says the LORD. "But I
will give your life to you as a
prize in all places, wherever
you go."'"

JUDGMENT ON EGYPT

46 The word of the LORD
which came to Jere-
miah the prophet against the
nations. 2Against Egypt.

Concerning the army of
Pharaoh Necho, king of Egypt,
which was by the River Euphrates in Carchemish, and
which Nebuchadnezzar king
of Babylon defeated in the
fourth year of Jehoiakim the
son of Josiah, king of Judah:

3 "Order the buckler
and shield,
And draw near to battle!
4 Harness the horses,
And mount up, you
horsemen!
Stand forth with
your helmets,
Polish the spears,
Put on the armor!
5 Why have I seen
them dismayed
and turned back?
Their mighty ones
are beaten down;
They have speedily fled,
And did not look back,
For fear *was* all around,"
says the LORD.
6 "Do not let the swift
flee away,
Nor the mighty
man escape;
They will stumble and fall
Toward the north, by
the River Euphrates.

7 "Who *is* this coming
up like a flood,
Whose waters move
like the rivers?
8 Egypt rises up
like a flood,
And *its* waters move
like the rivers;
And he says, 'I will go up
and cover the earth,
I will destroy the city
and its inhabitants.'
9 Come up, O horses, and
rage, O chariots!
And let the mighty
men come forth:
The Ethiopians and
the Libyans who
handle the shield,
And the Lydians
who handle *and*
bend the bow.
10 For this *is* the day of the
Lord GOD of hosts,
A day of vengeance,

That He may avenge
Himself on His
adversaries.
The sword shall devour;
It shall be satiated
and made drunk
with their blood;
For the Lord GOD of
hosts has a sacrifice
In the north country by
the River Euphrates.

11 "Go up to Gilead and
take balm,
O virgin, the daughter
of Egypt;
In vain you will use
many medicines;
You shall not be cured.
12 The nations have heard
of your shame,
And your cry has
filled the land;
For the mighty man
has stumbled against
the mighty;
They both have
fallen together."

BABYLONIA WILL STRIKE EGYPT

13 The word that the LORD
spoke to Jeremiah the
prophet, how Nebuchadnez-
zar king of Babylon would
come *and* strike the land of
Egypt.

14 "Declare in Egypt, and
proclaim in Migdol;
Proclaim in Noph[a]
and in Tahpanhes;
Say, 'Stand fast and
prepare yourselves,
For the sword devours
all around you.'
15 Why are your valiant
men swept away?
They did not stand
Because the LORD
drove them away.
16 He made many fall;
Yes, one fell upon
another.
And they said, 'Arise!
Let us go back to
our own people
And to the land of
our nativity
From the oppressing
sword.'
17 They cried there,
'Pharaoh, king of Egypt,
is but a noise.
He has passed by the
appointed time!'

18 "*As* I live," says the King,
Whose name *is* the
LORD of hosts,
"Surely as Tabor *is* among
the mountains
And as Carmel by the
sea, *so* he shall come.
19 O you daughter
dwelling in Egypt,
Prepare yourself to
go into captivity!
For Noph[a] shall be
waste and desolate,
without inhabitant.

20 "Egypt *is* a very
pretty heifer,

46:14 [a] That is, ancient Memphis

46:19 [a] That is, ancient Memphis

But destruction comes, it
comes from the north.
21 Also her mercenaries
are in her midst
like fat bulls,
For they also are
turned back,
They have fled
away together.
They did not stand,
For the day of their
calamity had come
upon them,
The time of their
punishment.
22 Her noise shall go
like a serpent,
For they shall march
with an army
And come against
her with axes,
Like those who
chop wood.

23 "They shall cut down her
forest," says the LORD,
"Though it cannot
be searched,
Because they *are*
innumerable,
And more numerous
than grasshoppers.
24 The daughter of Egypt
shall be ashamed;
She shall be delivered
into the hand
Of the people of
the north."

25 The LORD of hosts, the
God of Israel, says: "Behold,
I will bring punishment on
Amon[a] of No,[b] and Pharaoh
and Egypt, with their gods
and their kings—Pharaoh and
those who trust in him. 26 And
I will deliver them into the
hand of those who seek their
lives, into the hand of Nebuchadnezzar king of Babylon
and the hand of his servants.
Afterward it shall be inhabited
as in the days of old," says the
LORD.

GOD WILL PRESERVE ISRAEL

27 "But do not fear, O My
servant Jacob,
And do not be
dismayed, O Israel!
For behold, I will save
you from afar,
And your offspring
from the land of
their captivity;
Jacob shall return, have
rest and be at ease;
No one shall make
him afraid.
28 Do not fear, O Jacob
My servant," says
the LORD,
"For I *am* with you;
For I will make a
complete end of
all the nations
To which I have
driven you,
But I will not make a
complete end of you.
I will rightly correct you,
For I will not leave you
wholly unpunished."

46:25 [a] A sun god [b] That is, ancient Thebes

JUDGMENT ON PHILISTIA

47 The word of the LORD that came to Jeremiah the prophet against the Philistines, before Pharaoh attacked Gaza.

2Thus says the LORD:

"Behold, waters rise
out of the north,
And shall be an
overflowing flood;
They shall overflow the
land and all that is in it,
The city and those
who dwell within;
Then the men shall cry,
And all the inhabitants
of the land shall wail.
3 At the noise of the
stamping hooves of
his strong horses,
At the rushing of
his chariots,
At the rumbling of
his wheels,
The fathers will not look
back for *their* children,
Lacking courage,
4 Because of the day that
comes to plunder
all the Philistines,
To cut off from Tyre
and Sidon every
helper who remains;
For the LORD shall
plunder the Philistines,
The remnant of the
country of Caphtor.
5 *Baldness has come*
upon Gaza,
Ashkelon is cut off
With the remnant
of their valley.
How long will you
cut yourself?

6 "O you sword of the LORD,
How long until you
are quiet?
Put yourself up into
your scabbard,
Rest and be still!
7 How can it be quiet,
Seeing the LORD has
given it a charge
Against Ashkelon and
against the seashore?
There He has
appointed it."

JUDGMENT ON MOAB

48 Against Moab.
Thus says the LORD of hosts, the God of Israel:

"Woe to Nebo!
For it is plundered,
Kirjathaim is shamed
and taken;
The high stronghold[a]
is shamed and
dismayed—
2 No more praise of Moab.
In Heshbon they have
devised evil against her:
'Come, and let us cut
her off as a nation.'
You also shall be cut
down, O Madmen![a]
The sword shall
pursue you;
3 A voice of crying *shall*
be from Horonaim:

48:1 [a] Hebrew *Misgab* 48:2 [a] A city of Moab

'Plundering and great
destruction!'

4 "Moab is destroyed;
Her little ones have
caused a cry to
be heard;[a]
5 For in the Ascent of
Luhith they ascend with
continual weeping;
For in the descent
of Horonaim the
enemies have heard
a cry of destruction.

6 "Flee, save your lives!
And be like the juniper[a]
in the wilderness.
7 For because you have
trusted in your works
and your treasures,
You also shall be taken.
And Chemosh shall go
forth into captivity,
His priests and his
princes together.
8 And the plunderer shall
come against every city;
No one shall escape.
The valley also
shall perish,
And the plain shall
be destroyed,
As the LORD has spoken.

9 "Give wings to Moab,
That she may flee
and get away;
For her cities shall
be desolate,
Without any to
dwell in them.
10 Cursed *is* he who does
the work of the
LORD deceitfully,
And cursed *is* he
who keeps back his
sword from blood.

11 "Moab has been at ease
from his[a] youth;
He has settled on
his dregs,
And has not been
emptied from
vessel to vessel,
Nor has he gone
into captivity.
Therefore his taste
remained in him,
And his scent has
not changed.

12 "Therefore behold,
the days are coming,"
says the LORD,
"That I shall send
him wine-workers
Who will tip him over
And empty his vessels
And break the bottles.
13 Moab shall be ashamed
of Chemosh,
As the house of Israel
was ashamed of Bethel,
their confidence.

14 "How can you say,
'We *are* mighty

48:4 [a] Following Masoretic Text, Targum, and Vulgate; Septuagint reads *Proclaim it in Zoar*. 48:6 [a] Or *Aroer*, a city of Moab 48:11 [a] The Hebrew uses masculine and feminine pronouns interchangeably in this chapter.

And strong men
for the war'?
15 Moab is plundered and
gone up *from* her cities;
Her chosen young
men have gone down
to the slaughter,"
says the King,
Whose name *is* the
LORD of hosts.

16 "The calamity of Moab
is near at hand,
And his affliction
comes quickly.
17 Bemoan him, all you
who are around him;
And all you who
know his name,
Say, 'How the strong
staff is broken,
The beautiful rod!'

18 "O daughter inhabiting
Dibon,
Come down from
your glory,
And sit in thirst;
For the plunderer
of Moab has come
against you,
He has destroyed
your strongholds.
19 O inhabitant of Aroer,
Stand by the way
and watch;
Ask him who flees
And her who escapes;
Say, 'What has happened?'
20 *Moab is shamed, for*
he is broken down.
Wail and cry!
Tell it in Arnon, that
Moab is plundered.

21 "And judgment
has come on the
plain country:
On Holon and Jahzah
and Mephaath,
22 On Dibon and Nebo and
Beth Diblathaim,
23 On Kirjathaim and Beth
Gamul and Beth Meon,
24 On Kerioth and Bozrah,
On all the cities of
the land of Moab,
Far or near.
25 The horn of Moab
is cut off,
And his arm is broken,"
says the LORD.

26 "Make him drunk,
Because he exalted
himself against
the LORD.
Moab shall wallow
in his vomit,
And he shall also
be in derision.
27 For was not Israel a
derision to you?
Was he found
among thieves?
For whenever you
speak of him,
You shake *your*
head in scorn.
28 You who dwell in Moab,
Leave the cities and
dwell in the rock,
And be like the dove
which makes her nest
In the sides of the
cave's mouth.

29 "We have heard the
pride of Moab

(He *is* exceedingly proud),
Of his loftiness and
arrogance and pride,
And of the haughtiness
of his heart."

30 "I know his wrath,"
says the LORD,
"But it *is* not right;
His lies have made
nothing right.
31 Therefore I will
wail for Moab,
And I will cry out
for all Moab;
I[a] will mourn for the
men of Kir Heres.
32 O vine of Sibmah! I will
weep for you with the
weeping of Jazer.
Your plants have gone
over the sea,
They reach to the
sea of Jazer.
The plunderer has fallen
on your summer fruit
and your vintage.
33 Joy and gladness
are taken
From the plentiful field
And from the land
of Moab;
I have caused wine to fail
from the winepresses;
No one will tread with
joyous shouting—
Not joyous shouting!

34 "From the cry of Heshbon
to Elealeh and to Jahaz
They have uttered
their voice,
From Zoar to Horonaim,
Like a three-year-old
heifer;[a]
For the waters of Nimrim
also shall be desolate.

35 "Moreover," says the LORD,
"I will cause to
cease in Moab
The one who offers
sacrifices in the
high places
And burns incense
to his gods.
36 Therefore My heart
shall wail like
flutes for Moab,
And like flutes My
heart shall wail
For the men of Kir Heres.
Therefore the riches
they have acquired
have perished.

37 "For every head *shall
be* bald, and every
beard clipped;
On all the hands *shall
be* cuts, and on the
loins sackcloth—
38 A general lamentation
On all the housetops
of Moab,
And in its streets;
For I have broken
Moab like a vessel in
which *is* no pleasure,"
says the LORD.

48:31 [a] Following Dead Sea Scrolls, Septuagint, and Vulgate; Masoretic Text reads *He*. 48:34 [a] Or *The Third Eglath*, an unknown city (compare Isaiah 15:5)

39 "They shall wail:
'How she is broken
down!
How Moab has turned
her back with shame!'
So Moab shall be
a derision
And a dismay to all
those about her."

40 For thus says the LORD:

"Behold, one shall fly
like an eagle,
And spread his wings
over Moab.
41 Kerioth is taken,
And the strongholds
are surprised;
The mighty men's
hearts in Moab on
that day shall be
Like the heart of a woman
in birth pangs.
42 And Moab shall be
destroyed as a people,
Because he exalted
himself against
the LORD.
43 Fear and the pit and the
snare *shall be* upon you,
O inhabitant of Moab,"
says the LORD.
44 "He who flees from
the fear shall fall
into the pit,
And he who gets out
of the pit shall be
caught in the snare.
For upon Moab, upon
it I will bring
The year of their
punishment,"
says the LORD.

45 "Those who fled stood
under the shadow
of Heshbon
Because of exhaustion.
But a fire shall come
out of Heshbon,
A flame from the
midst of Sihon,
And shall devour the
brow of Moab,
The crown of the head
of the sons of tumult.
46 Woe to you, O Moab!
The people of
Chemosh perish;
For your sons have
been taken captive,
And your daughters
captive.

47 "Yet I will bring back
the captives of Moab
In the latter days,"
says the LORD.

Thus far *is* the judgment of Moab.

JUDGMENT ON AMMON

49 Against the Ammonites.
Thus says the LORD:

"Has Israel no sons?
Has he no heir?
Why *then* does Milcom[a]
inherit Gad,

49:1 [a] Hebrew *Malcam,* literally *their king,* a god of the Ammonites; also called *Molech* (compare verse 3)

And his people dwell
in its cities?
2 Therefore behold, the
days are coming,"
says the LORD,
"That I will cause to be
heard an alarm of war
In Rabbah of the
Ammonites;
It shall be a desolate
mound,
And her villages shall
be burned with fire.
Then Israel shall
take possession of
his inheritance,"
says the LORD.

3 "Wail, O Heshbon, for
Ai is plundered!
Cry, you daughters
of Rabbah,
Gird yourselves
with sackcloth!
Lament and run to and
fro by the walls;
For Milcom shall go
into captivity
With his priests and his
princes together.
4 Why do you boast
in the valleys,
Your flowing valley,
O backsliding daughter?
Who trusted in her
treasures, *saying,*
'Who will come
against me?'
5 Behold, I will bring
fear upon you,"
Says the Lord GOD
of hosts,
"From all those who
are around you;
You shall be driven out,
everyone headlong,
And no one will gather
those who wander off.
6 But afterward I will
bring back
The captives of the
people of Ammon,"
says the LORD.

JUDGMENT ON EDOM

7 Against Edom.
Thus says the LORD of hosts:

"*Is* wisdom no more
in Teman?
Has counsel perished
from the prudent?
Has their wisdom
vanished?
8 Flee, turn back, dwell
in the depths,
O inhabitants of Dedan!
For I will bring the
calamity of Esau
upon him,
The time *that* I will
punish him.
9 If grape-gatherers
came to you,
Would they not leave
some gleaning grapes?
If thieves by night,
Would they not destroy
until they have enough?
10 But I have made
Esau bare;
I have uncovered his
secret places,[a]

49:10 [a] Compare Obadiah 5, 6

And he shall not be
able to hide himself.
His descendants
are plundered,
His brethren and
his neighbors,
And he *is* no more.
11 Leave your fatherless
children,
I will preserve *them* alive;
And let your widows
trust in Me."

12For thus says the LORD:
"Behold, those whose judgment *was* not to drink of the
cup have assuredly drunk.
And *are* you the one who will
altogether go unpunished?
You shall not go unpunished,
but you shall surely drink *of it.*
13For I have sworn by Myself,"
says the LORD, "that Bozrah
shall become a desolation, a
reproach, a waste, and a curse.
And all its cities shall be perpetual wastes."

14 I have heard a message
from the LORD,
And an ambassador
has been sent to
the nations:
"Gather together,
come against her,
And rise up to battle!

15 "For indeed, I will
make you small
among nations,
Despised among men.
16 Your fierceness has
deceived you,
The pride of your heart,
O you who dwell in the
clefts of the rock,
Who hold the height
of the hill!
Though you make
your nest as high
as the eagle,
I will bring you down
from there," says
the LORD.[a]

17 "Edom also shall be
an astonishment;
Everyone who goes by
it will be astonished
And will hiss at all
its plagues.
18 As in the overthrow of
Sodom and Gomorrah
And their neighbors,"
says the LORD,
"No one shall
remain there,
Nor shall a son of
man dwell in it.

19 "Behold, he shall come
up like a lion from
the floodplain[a]
of the Jordan
Against the dwelling
place of the strong;
But I will suddenly make
him run away from her.
And who *is* a chosen
man that I may
appoint over her?
For who *is* like Me?

49:16 [a] Compare Obadiah 3, 4 49:19 [a] Or *thicket* 49:27 [a] Compare Amos 1:4

Who will arraign Me?
And who *is* that shepherd
Who will withstand Me?"

20 Therefore hear the
counsel of the LORD
that He has taken
against Edom,
And His purposes that
He has proposed
against the inhabitants
of Teman:
Surely the least of
the flock shall
draw them out;
Surely He shall make
their dwelling places
desolate with them.
21 The earth shakes at the
noise of their fall;
At the cry its noise is
heard at the Red Sea.
22 Behold, He shall come up
and fly like the eagle,
And spread His wings
over Bozrah;
The heart of the mighty
men of Edom in
that day shall be
Like the heart of a woman
in birth pangs.

JUDGMENT ON DAMASCUS

23 Against Damascus.

"Hamath and Arpad
are shamed,
For they have heard
bad news.
They are fainthearted;
There is trouble on the sea;
It cannot be quiet.
24 Damascus has
grown feeble;
She turns to flee,
And fear has seized *her.*
Anguish and sorrows
have taken her like
a woman in labor.
25 Why is the city of
praise not deserted,
the city of My joy?
26 Therefore her young men
shall fall in her streets,
And all the men of
war shall be cut off
in that day," says the
LORD of hosts.
27 "I will kindle a fire in the
wall of Damascus,
And it shall consume the
palaces of Ben-Hadad."[a]

JUDGMENT ON KEDAR AND HAZOR

28 Against Kedar and
against the kingdoms of
Hazor, which Nebuchadnezzar
king of Babylon shall strike.
Thus says the LORD:

"Arise, go up to Kedar,
And devastate the
men of the East!
29 Their tents and
their flocks they
shall take away.
They shall take
for themselves
their curtains,
All their vessels and
their camels;
And they shall cry
out to them,
'Fear *is* on every side!'

30 "Flee, get far away!
Dwell in the depths,

O inhabitants of Hazor!"
says the LORD.
"For Nebuchadnezzar king
of Babylon has taken
counsel against you,
And has conceived a
plan against you.

31 "Arise, go up to the
wealthy nation that
dwells securely,"
says the LORD,
"Which has neither
gates nor bars,
Dwelling alone.
32 Their camels shall
be for booty,
And the multitude of
their cattle for plunder.
I will scatter to all
winds those in the
farthest corners,
And I will bring their
calamity from all its
sides," says the LORD.
33 "Hazor shall be a
dwelling for jackals, a
desolation forever;
No one shall reside there,
Nor son of man
dwell in it."

JUDGMENT ON ELAM

34 The word of the LORD that
came to Jeremiah the prophet
against Elam, in the beginning of the reign of Zedekiah
king of Judah, saying, 35 "Thus
says the LORD of hosts:

'Behold, I will break
the bow of Elam,
The foremost of
their might.
36 Against Elam I will
bring the four winds
From the four quarters
of heaven,
And scatter them toward
all those winds;
There shall be no nations
where the outcasts
of Elam will not go.
37 For I will cause Elam to
be dismayed before
their enemies
And before those who
seek their life.
I will bring disaster
upon them,
My fierce anger,'
says the LORD;
'And I will send the
sword after them
Until I have
consumed them.
38 I will set My throne
in Elam,
And will destroy from
there the king and the
princes,' says the LORD.

39 'But it shall come to pass
in the latter days:
I will bring back the
captives of Elam,'
says the LORD."

JUDGMENT ON BABYLON AND BABYLONIA

50 The word that the LORD
spoke against Babylon
and against the land of the
Chaldeans by Jeremiah the
prophet.

2 "Declare among
the nations,

Proclaim, and set
up a standard;
Proclaim—do not
conceal *it*—
Say, 'Babylon is taken,
Bel is shamed.
Merodach[a] is broken
in pieces;
Her idols are humiliated,
Her images are
broken in pieces.'
3 For out of the north
a nation comes
up against her,
Which shall make her
land desolate,
And no one shall
dwell therein.
They shall move, they
shall depart,
Both man and beast.

4 "In those days and in that
time," says the LORD,
"The children of
Israel shall come,
They and the children
of Judah together;
With continual weeping
they shall come,
And seek the LORD
their God.
5 They shall ask the
way to Zion,
With their faces
toward it, *saying,*
'Come and let us join
ourselves to the LORD
In a perpetual covenant
That will not be forgotten.'

6 "My people have
been lost sheep.
Their shepherds have
led them astray;
They have turned them
away *on* the mountains.
They have gone from
mountain to hill;
They have forgotten
their resting place.
7 All who found them
have devoured them;
And their adversaries said,
'We have not offended,
Because they have sinned
against the LORD, the
habitation of justice,
The LORD, the hope
of their fathers.'

8 "Move from the midst
of Babylon,
Go out of the land of
the Chaldeans;
And be like the rams
before the flocks.
9 For behold, I will raise
and cause to come
up against Babylon
An assembly of great
nations from the
north country,
And they shall array
themselves against her;
From there she shall
be captured.
Their arrows *shall*
be like *those* of an
expert warrior;[a]
None shall return in vain.

50:2 [a] A Babylonian god; sometimes spelled *Marduk* 50:9 [a] Following some Hebrew manuscripts, Septuagint, and Syriac; Masoretic Text, Targum, and Vulgate read *a warrior who makes childless.*

10 And Chaldea shall
become plunder;
All who plunder her
shall be satisfied,"
says the Lord.

11 "Because you were glad,
because you rejoiced,
You destroyers of
My heritage,
Because you have
grown fat like a heifer
threshing grain,
And you bellow like bulls,
12 Your mother shall be
deeply ashamed;
She who bore you
shall be ashamed.
Behold, the least of
the nations *shall*
be a wilderness,
A dry land and a desert.
13 Because of the wrath
of the Lord
She shall not be
inhabited,
But she shall be
wholly desolate.
Everyone who goes
by Babylon shall
be horrified
And hiss at all
her plagues.

14 "Put yourselves in array
against Babylon
all around,
All you who bend the bow;
Shoot at her, spare
no arrows,
For she has sinned
against the Lord.
15 Shout against her
all around;
She has given her hand,
Her foundations
have fallen,
Her walls are
thrown down;
For it *is* the vengeance
of the Lord.
Take vengeance on her.
As she has done,
so do to her.
16 Cut off the sower
from Babylon,
And him who handles
the sickle at
harvest time.
For fear of the
oppressing sword
Everyone shall turn
to his own people,
And everyone shall flee
to his own land.

17 "Israel *is* like scattered
sheep;
The lions have driven
him away.
First the king of Assyria
devoured him;
Now at last this
Nebuchadnezzar
king of Babylon has
broken his bones."

18 Therefore thus says the Lord of hosts, the God of Israel:

"Behold, I will punish
the king of Babylon
and his land,
As I have punished the
king of Assyria.
19 But I will bring back
Israel to his home,

And he shall feed on
Carmel and Bashan;
His soul shall be
satisfied on Mount
Ephraim and Gilead.
20 In those days and in that
time," says the LORD,
"The iniquity of Israel
shall be sought, but
there shall be none;
And the sins of Judah,
but they shall
not be found;
For I will pardon those
whom I preserve.

21 "Go up against the land of
Merathaim, against it,
And against the
inhabitants of Pekod.
Waste and utterly destroy
them," says the LORD,
"And do according
to all that I have
commanded you.
22 A sound of battle
is in the land,
And of great destruction.
23 How the hammer of the
whole earth has been
cut apart and broken!
How Babylon has
become a desolation
among the nations!
24 I have laid a snare
for you;
You have indeed been
trapped, O Babylon,
And you were not aware;
You have been found
and also caught,
Because you have
contended against
the LORD.
25 The LORD has opened
His armory,
And has brought out
the weapons of His
indignation;
For this *is* the work of
the Lord GOD of hosts
In the land of the
Chaldeans.
26 Come against her from
the farthest border;
Open her storehouses;
Cast her up as
heaps of ruins,
And destroy her utterly;
Let nothing of her be left.
27 Slay all her bulls,
Let them go down to
the slaughter.
Woe to them!
For their day has
come, the time of
their punishment.
28 The voice of those who
flee and escape from
the land of Babylon
Declares in Zion the
vengeance of the
LORD our God,
The vengeance of
His temple.

29 "Call together the archers
against Babylon.
All you who bend the
bow, encamp against
it all around;
Let none of them escape.[a]

50:29 [a] Qere, some Hebrew manuscripts, Septuagint, and Targum add *to her*.

Repay her according
to her work;
According to all she
has done, do to her;
For she has been proud
against the LORD,
Against the Holy
One of Israel.
30 Therefore her young men
shall fall in the streets,
And all her men of war
shall be cut off in that
day," says the LORD.
31 "Behold, I *am* against you,
O most haughty
one!" says the Lord
GOD of hosts;
"For your day has come,
The time *that* I will
punish you.[a]
32 The most proud shall
stumble and fall,
And no one will
raise him up;
I will kindle a fire
in his cities,
And it will devour
all around him."

33 Thus says the LORD of hosts:

"The children of Israel
were oppressed,
Along with the
children of Judah;
All who took them captive
have held them fast;
They have refused
to let them go.
34 Their Redeemer *is* strong;
The LORD of hosts
is His name.
He will thoroughly
plead their case,
That He may give
rest to the land,
And disquiet the
inhabitants of
Babylon.

35 "A sword *is* against
the Chaldeans,"
says the LORD,
"Against the inhabitants
of Babylon,
And against her princes
and her wise men.
36 A sword *is* against the
soothsayers, and
they will be fools.
A sword *is* against her
mighty men, and they
will be dismayed.
37 A sword *is* against
their horses,
Against their chariots,
And against all the
mixed peoples who
are in her midst;
And they will become
like women.
A sword *is* against her
treasures, and they
will be robbed.
38 A drought[a] *is* against
her waters, and they
will be dried up.
For it *is* the land of
carved images,

50:31 [a] Following Masoretic Text and Targum; Septuagint and Vulgate read *The time of your punishment*.
50:38 [a] Following Masoretic Text, Targum, and Vulgate; Syriac reads *sword;* Septuagint omits *A drought is*.

And they are insane
with *their* idols.

39 "Therefore the wild
desert beasts shall dwell
there with the jackals,
And the ostriches
shall dwell in it.
It shall be inhabited
no more forever,
Nor shall it be dwelt
in from generation
to generation.
40 As God overthrew Sodom
and Gomorrah
And their neighbors,"
says the LORD,
"*So* no one shall
reside there,
Nor son of man dwell in it.

41 "Behold, a people shall
come from the north,
And a great nation
and many kings
Shall be raised up from
the ends of the earth.
42 They shall hold the
bow and the lance;
They *are* cruel and shall
not show mercy.
Their voice shall roar
like the sea;
They shall ride on horses,
Set in array, like a man
for the battle,
Against you, O daughter
of Babylon.

43 "The king of Babylon
has heard the report
about them,
And his hands grow feeble;
Anguish has taken
hold of him,
Pangs as of a woman
in childbirth.

44 "Behold, he shall come
up like a lion from
the floodplain[a]
of the Jordan
Against the dwelling
place of the strong;
But I will make them
suddenly run
away from her.
And who *is* a chosen
man that I may
appoint over her?
For who *is* like Me?
Who will arraign Me?
And who *is* that shepherd
Who will withstand Me?"

45 Therefore hear the
counsel of the LORD
that He has taken
against Babylon,
And His purposes that
He has proposed
against the land of
the Chaldeans:
Surely the least of
the flock shall
draw them out;
Surely He will make
their dwelling place
desolate with them.
46 At the noise of the
taking of Babylon
The earth trembles,
And the cry is heard
among the nations.

50:44 [a] Or *thicket*

THE UTTER DESTRUCTION OF BABYLON

51 Thus says the LORD:

"Behold, I will raise up
against Babylon,
Against those who
dwell in Leb Kamai,[a]
A destroying wind.
2 And I will send
winnowers to
Babylon,
Who shall winnow her
and empty her land.
For in the day of doom
They shall be against
her all around.
3 Against *her* let the
archer bend his bow,
And lift himself
up against *her*
in his armor.
Do not spare her
young men;
Utterly destroy all
her army.
4 Thus the slain shall
fall in the land of
the Chaldeans,
And *those* thrust through
in her streets.
5 For Israel is not
forsaken, nor Judah,
By his God, the
LORD of hosts,
Though their land was
filled with sin against
the Holy One of Israel."

6 *Flee from the midst*
of Babylon,
And every one
save his life!
Do not be cut off in
her iniquity,
For this *is* the time of the
LORD's vengeance;
He shall recompense her.
7 Babylon *was* a golden cup
in the LORD's hand,
That made all the
earth drunk.
The nations drank
her wine;
Therefore the nations
are deranged.
8 Babylon has suddenly
fallen and been
destroyed.
Wail for her!
Take balm for her pain;
Perhaps she may
be healed.

9 We would have
healed Babylon,
But she is not healed.
Forsake her, and let
us go everyone to
his own country;
For her judgment
reaches to heaven
and is lifted up
to the skies.
10 The LORD has revealed
our righteousness.
Come and let us declare
in Zion the work of
the LORD our God.

11 *Make the arrows bright!*
Gather the shields!

51:1 [a] A code word for Chaldea (Babylonia); may be translated *The Midst of Those Who Rise Up Against Me*

The LORD has raised
up the spirit of the
kings of the Medes.
For His plan *is* against
Babylon to destroy it,
Because it *is* the
vengeance of
the LORD,
The vengeance for
His temple.
12 Set up the standard on
the walls of Babylon;
Make the guard strong,
Set up the watchmen,
Prepare the ambushes.
For the LORD has both
devised and done
What He spoke against
the inhabitants
of Babylon.
13 O you who dwell by
many waters,
Abundant in treasures,
Your end has come,
The measure of your
covetousness.
14 The LORD of hosts has
sworn by Himself:
"Surely I will fill you with
men, as with locusts,
And they shall lift up a
shout against you."

15 He has made the earth
by His power;
He has established the
world by His wisdom,
And stretched out
the heaven by His
understanding.
16 When He utters
His voice—
There is a multitude of
waters in the heavens:
"He causes the vapors
to ascend from the
ends of the earth;
He makes lightnings
for the rain;
He brings the wind out
of His treasuries."[a]

17 Everyone is dull-hearted,
without knowledge;
Every metalsmith is
put to shame by the
carved image;
For his molded image
is falsehood,
And *there is* no
breath in them.
18 They *are* futile, a
work of errors;
In the time of their
punishment they
shall perish.
19 The Portion of Jacob
is not like them,
For He *is* the Maker
of all things;
And *Israel is* the tribe
of His inheritance.
The LORD of hosts
is His name.

20 "You *are* My battle-ax
and weapons of war:
For with you I will break
the nation in pieces;
With you I will destroy
kingdoms;
21 With you I will break
in pieces the horse
and its rider;

51:16 [a] Psalm 135:7

With you I will break
in pieces the chariot
and its rider;
22 With you also I will
break in pieces
man and woman;
With you I will break in
pieces old and young;
With you I will break in
pieces the young man
and the maiden;
23 With you also I will
break in pieces the
shepherd and his flock;
With you I will break
in pieces the farmer
and his yoke of oxen;
And with you I will
break in pieces
governors and rulers.

24 "And I will repay
Babylon
And all the inhabitants
of Chaldea
For all the evil they
have done
In Zion in your sight,"
says the LORD.

25 "Behold, I *am* against you,
O destroying mountain,
Who destroys all the
earth," says the LORD.
"And I will stretch out
My hand against you,
Roll you down from
the rocks,
And make you a
burnt *mountain.*
26 They shall not take from
you a stone for a corner
Nor a stone for a
foundation,
But you shall be desolate
forever," says the LORD.

27 Set up a banner
in the land,
Blow the trumpet
among the nations!
Prepare the nations
against her,
Call the kingdoms
together against her:
Ararat, Minni, and
Ashkenaz.
Appoint a general
against her;
Cause the horses to
come up like the
bristling locusts.
28 Prepare against her
the nations,
With the kings of
the Medes,
Its governors and
all its rulers,
All the land of his
dominion.
29 And the land will
tremble and sorrow;
For every purpose
of the LORD shall
be performed
against Babylon,
To make the land of
Babylon a desolation
without inhabitant.
30 The mighty men
of Babylon have
ceased fighting,
They have remained in
their strongholds;
Their might has failed,
They became *like* women;
They have burned her
dwelling places,

The bars of her *gate*
are broken.
31 One runner will run
to meet another,
And one messenger
to meet another,
To show the king of
Babylon that his city
is taken on *all* sides;
32 The passages are blocked,
The reeds they have
burned with fire,
And the men of war
are terrified.

33For thus says the LORD of
hosts, the God of Israel:

"The daughter of Babylon
is like a threshing floor
When it is time to
thresh her;
Yet a little while
And the time of her
harvest will come."

34"Nebuchadnezzar the
king of Babylon
Has devoured me, he
has crushed me;
He has made me an
empty vessel,
He has swallowed me
up like a monster;
He has filled his stomach
with my delicacies,
He has spit me out.
35 Let the violence *done*
to me and my flesh
be upon Babylon,"
The inhabitant of
Zion will say;
"And my blood be
upon the inhabitants
of Chaldea!"
Jerusalem will say.

36Therefore thus says the
LORD:

"Behold, I will plead
your case and take
vengeance for you.
I will dry up her sea and
make her springs dry.
37 Babylon shall
become a heap,
A dwelling place
for jackals,
An astonishment
and a hissing,
Without an inhabitant.
38 They shall roar
together like lions,
They shall growl like
lions' whelps.
39 In their excitement I will
prepare their feasts;
I will make them drunk,
That they may rejoice,
And sleep a
perpetual sleep
And not awake,"
says the LORD.
40"I will bring them down
Like lambs to the
slaughter,
Like rams with
male goats.

41"Oh, how Sheshach[a]
is taken!
Oh, how the praise of the
whole earth is seized!

51:41 [a] A code word for Babylon (compare Jeremiah 25:26)

How Babylon has
become desolate
among the nations!
42 The sea has come up
over Babylon;
She is covered with the
multitude of its waves.
43 Her cities are a
desolation,
A dry land and a
wilderness,
A land where no
one dwells,
Through which no son
of man passes.
44 I will punish Bel
in Babylon,
And I will bring out
of his mouth what
he has swallowed;
And the nations
shall not stream to
him anymore.
Yes, the wall of
Babylon shall fall.

45 "My people, go out of
the midst of her!
And let everyone deliver
himself from the fierce
anger of the LORD.
46 And lest your heart faint,
And you fear for the
rumor that *will be*
heard in the land
(A *rumor* will come
one year,
And after that, in
another year
A rumor *will come,*
And violence in the land,
Ruler against ruler),
47 Therefore behold, the
days are coming
That I will bring
judgment on the carved
images of Babylon;
Her whole land shall
be ashamed,
And all her slain shall
fall in her midst.
48 Then the heavens
and the earth and
all that *is* in them
Shall sing joyously
over Babylon;
For the plunderers shall
come to her from the
north," says the LORD.

49 As Babylon *has caused*
the slain of Israel to fall,
So at Babylon the slain of
all the earth shall fall.
50 You who have escaped
the sword,
Get away! Do not
stand still!
Remember the
LORD afar off,
And let Jerusalem
come to your mind.

51 We are ashamed
because we have
heard reproach.
Shame has covered
our faces,
For strangers have come
into the sanctuaries
of the LORD's house.

52 "Therefore behold,
the days are coming,"
says the LORD,
"That I will bring
judgment on her
carved images,

And throughout all her
land the wounded
shall groan.
53 Though Babylon were to
mount up to heaven,
And though she were
to fortify the height
of her strength,
Yet from Me plunderers
would come to her,"
says the LORD.

54 The sound of a cry
comes from Babylon,
And great destruction
from the land of
the Chaldeans,
55 Because the LORD is
plundering Babylon
And silencing her
loud voice,
Though her waves roar
like great waters,
And the noise of their
voice is uttered,
56 Because the plunderer
comes against her,
against Babylon,
And her mighty
men are taken.
Every one of their
bows is broken;
For the LORD *is* the God
of recompense,
He will surely repay.

57 "And I will make drunk
Her princes and
wise men,
Her governors, her
deputies, and her
mighty men.
And they shall sleep
a perpetual sleep
And not awake,"
says the King,
Whose name *is* the
LORD of hosts.

58Thus says the LORD of
hosts:

"The broad walls of
Babylon shall be
utterly broken,
And her high gates shall
be burned with fire;
The people will
labor in vain,
And the nations,
because of the fire;
And they shall be weary."

JEREMIAH'S COMMAND TO SERAIAH

59The word which Jeremiah
the prophet commanded Se-
raiah the son of Neriah, the
son of Mahseiah, when he
went with Zedekiah the king of
Judah to Babylon in the fourth
year of his reign. And Seraiah
was the quartermaster. 60So
Jeremiah wrote in a book all
the evil that would come upon
Babylon, all these words that
are written against Babylon.
61And Jeremiah said to Seraiah, "When you arrive in Babylon and see it, and read all
these words, 62then you shall
say, 'O LORD, You have spoken
against this place to cut it off,
so that none shall remain in
it, neither man nor beast, but
it shall be desolate forever.'
63Now it shall be, when you
have finished reading this

book, *that* you shall tie a stone
to it and throw it out into the
Euphrates. 64Then you shall
say, 'Thus Babylon shall sink
and not rise from the catastrophe that I will bring upon her.
And they shall be weary.'"

Thus far *are* the words of
Jeremiah.

THE FALL OF JERUSALEM REVIEWED

52 Zedekiah *was* twenty-
one years old when he
became king, and he reigned
eleven years in Jerusalem.
His mother's name *was* Ha-
mutal the daughter of Jeremiah of Libnah. 2He also did
evil in the sight of the LORD,
according to all that Jehoiakim had done. 3For because
of the anger of the LORD *this*
happened in Jerusalem and
Judah, till He finally cast them
out from His presence. Then
Zedekiah rebelled against the
king of Babylon.

4Now it came to pass in the
ninth year of his reign, in the
tenth month, on the tenth *day*
of the month, *that* Nebuchadnezzar king of Babylon and all
his army came against Jerusalem and encamped against
it; and *they* built a siege wall
against it all around. 5So the
city was besieged until the
eleventh year of King Zedekiah. 6By the fourth month, on
the ninth day of the month, the
famine had become so severe
in the city that there was no
food for the people of the land.
7Then the city *wall* was broken
through, and all the men of
war fled and went out of the
city at night by way of the gate
between the two walls, which
was by the king's garden, even
though the Chaldeans *were*
near the city all around. And
they went by way of the plain.[a]

8But the army of the Chaldeans pursued the king, and
they overtook Zedekiah in
the plains of Jericho. All his
army was scattered from him.
9So they took the king and
brought him up to the king
of Babylon at Riblah in the
land of Hamath, and he pronounced judgment on him.
10Then the king of Babylon
killed the sons of Zedekiah before his eyes. And he killed all
the princes of Judah in Riblah. 11He also put out the eyes
of Zedekiah; and the king of
Babylon bound him in bronze
fetters, took him to Babylon,
and put him in prison till the
day of his death.

THE TEMPLE AND CITY PLUNDERED AND BURNED

12Now in the fifth month,
on the tenth *day* of the month
(which *was* the nineteenth
year of King Nebuchadnezzar
king of Babylon), Nebuzaradan, the captain of the guard,
who served the king of Babylon, came to Jerusalem. 13He

52:7 [a] Or *the Arabah,* that is, the Jordan Valley

burned the house of the LORD
and the king's house; all the
houses of Jerusalem, that is,
all the houses of the great,
he burned with fire. 14And all
the army of the Chaldeans
who *were* with the captain of
the guard broke down all the
walls of Jerusalem all around.
15Then Nebuzaradan the captain of the guard carried away
captive *some* of the poor people, the rest of the people who
remained in the city, the defectors who had deserted to the
king of Babylon, and the rest of
the craftsmen. 16But Nebuzaradan the captain of the guard
left *some* of the poor of the land
as vinedressers and farmers.

17The bronze pillars that
were in the house of the LORD,
and the carts and the bronze
Sea that *were* in the house of
the LORD, the Chaldeans broke
in pieces, and carried all their
bronze to Babylon. 18They also
took away the pots, the shovels, the trimmers, the bowls,
the spoons, and all the bronze
utensils with which the *priests*
ministered. 19The basins, the
firepans, the bowls, the pots,
the lampstands, the spoons,
and the cups, whatever *was*
solid gold and whatever *was*
solid silver, the captain of the
guard took away. 20The two pillars, one Sea, the twelve bronze
bulls which *were* under *it, and*
the carts, which King Solomon
had made for the house of the
LORD—the bronze of all these
articles was beyond measure.
21Now *concerning* the pillars:
the height of one pillar *was*
eighteen cubits, a measuring
line of twelve cubits could
measure its circumference,
and its thickness *was* four fingers; *it was* hollow. 22A capital
of bronze *was* on it; and the
height of one capital *was* five
cubits, with a network and
pomegranates all around the
capital, all of bronze. The second pillar, with pomegranates
was the same. 23There were
ninety-six pomegranates on
the sides; all the pomegranates, all around on the network, *were* one hundred.

THE PEOPLE TAKEN CAPTIVE TO BABYLONIA

24The captain of the guard
took Seraiah the chief priest,
Zephaniah the second priest,
and the three doorkeepers.
25He also took out of the city
an officer who had charge of
the men of war, seven men
of the king's close associates
who were found in the city, the
principal scribe of the army
who mustered the people of
the land, and sixty men of the
people of the land who were
found in the midst of the city.
26And Nebuzaradan the captain of the guard took these
and brought them to the king
of Babylon at Riblah. 27Then
the king of Babylon struck
them and put them to death at
Riblah in the land of Hamath.
Thus Judah was carried away
captive from its own land.

28These *are* the people
whom Nebuchadnezzar car-
ried away captive: in the seventh year, three thousand
and twenty-three Jews; 29in
the eighteenth year of Nebuchadnezzar he carried away
captive from Jerusalem eight
hundred and thirty-two persons; 30in the twenty-third
year of Nebuchadnezzar, Nebuzaradan the captain of the
guard carried away captive of
the Jews seven hundred and
forty-five persons. All the persons *were* four thousand six
hundred.

JEHOIACHIN RELEASED FROM PRISON

31Now it came to pass in
the thirty-seventh year of the
captivity of Jehoiachin king of
Judah, in the twelfth month,
on the twenty-fifth *day* of the
month, *that* Evil-Merodach[a]
king of Babylon, in the *first*
year of his reign, lifted up the
head of Jehoiachin king of
Judah and brought him out of
prison. 32And he spoke kindly
to him and gave him a more
prominent seat than those of
the kings who *were* with him
in Babylon. 33So Jehoiachin
changed from his prison garments, and he ate bread regularly before the *king* all the
days of his life. 34And as for his
provisions, there was a regular
ration given him by the king
of Babylon, a portion for each
day until the day of his death,
all the days of his life.

THE BOOK OF LAMENTATIONS

JERUSALEM IN AFFLICTION

1 How lonely sits the city
That was full of people!
How like a widow is she,
Who *was* great among
the nations!
The princess among
the provinces
Has become a slave!

2 She weeps bitterly
in the night,
Her tears *are* on
her cheeks;
Among all her lovers
She has none to
comfort *her*.
All her friends have dealt
treacherously with her;
They have become
her enemies.

3 Judah has gone
into captivity,

52:31 [a] Or *Awil-Marduk*

Under affliction and
hard servitude;
She dwells among
the nations,
She finds no rest;
All her persecutors
overtake her in
dire straits.

4 The roads to Zion mourn
Because no one comes
to the set feasts.
All her gates are desolate;
Her priests sigh,
Her virgins are afflicted,
And she *is* in bitterness.

5 Her adversaries have
become the master,
Her enemies prosper;
For the LORD has
afflicted her
Because of the multitude
of her transgressions.
Her children have
gone into captivity
before the enemy.

6 And from the
daughter of Zion
All her splendor
has departed.
Her princes have
become like deer
That find no pasture,
That flee without
strength
Before the pursuer.

7 In the days of her
affliction and roaming,
Jerusalem remembers
all her pleasant things
That she had in the
days of old.
When her people fell
into the hand of
the enemy,
With no one to help her,
The adversaries saw her
And mocked at her
downfall.[a]

8 Jerusalem has
sinned gravely,
Therefore she has
become vile.[a]
All who honored
her despise her
Because they have seen
her nakedness;
Yes, she sighs and
turns away.

9 Her uncleanness *is*
in her skirts;
She did not consider
her destiny;
Therefore her collapse
was awesome;
She had no comforter.
"O LORD, behold
my affliction,
For *the* enemy is exalted!"

10 The adversary has
spread his hand
Over all her pleasant
things;
For she has seen
the nations enter
her sanctuary,

1:7 [a] Vulgate reads *her Sabbaths.* 1:8 [a] Septuagint and Vulgate read *moved* or *removed.*

Those whom You
commanded
Not to enter Your
assembly.

11 All her people sigh,
They seek bread;
They have given their
valuables for food
to restore life.
"See, O LORD, and
consider,
For I am scorned."

12 "*Is it* nothing to you, all
you who pass by?
Behold and see
If there is any sorrow
like my sorrow,
Which has been
brought on me,
Which the LORD
has inflicted
In the day of His
fierce anger.

13 "From above He has sent
fire into my bones,
And it overpowered
them;
He has spread a net
for my feet
And turned me back;
He has made me desolate
And faint all the day.

14 "The yoke of my
transgressions
was bound;[a]
They were woven
together by His hands,
And thrust upon my neck.
He made my strength fail;
The Lord delivered me
into the hands of
those whom I am not
able to withstand.

15 "The Lord has
trampled underfoot
all my mighty *men*
in my midst;
He has called an
assembly against me
To crush my young men;
The Lord trampled
as in a winepress
The virgin daughter
of Judah.

16 "For these *things* I weep;
My eye, my eye overflows
with water;
Because the comforter,
who should
restore my life,
Is far from me.
My children are desolate
Because the enemy
prevailed."

17 Zion spreads out
her hands,
But no one comforts her;
The LORD has
commanded
concerning Jacob
That those around him
become his adversaries;
Jerusalem has become
an unclean thing
among them.

1:14 [a] Following Masoretic Text and Targum; Septuagint, Syriac, and Vulgate read *watched over.*

18 "The LORD is righteous,
For I rebelled against
His commandment.
Hear now, all peoples,
And behold my sorrow;
My virgins and my
young men
Have gone into captivity.

19 "I called for my lovers,
But they deceived me;
My priests and my elders
Breathed their last
in the city,
While they sought food
To restore their life.

20 "See, O LORD, that I
am in distress;
My soul is troubled;
My heart is overturned
within me,
For I have been very
rebellious.
Outside the sword
bereaves,
At home *it is* like death.

21 "They have heard
that I sigh,
But no one comforts me.
All my enemies have
heard of my trouble;
They are glad that
You have done *it*.
Bring on the day You
have announced,
That they may
become like me.

22 "Let all their wickedness
come before You,
And do to them as You
have done to me
For all my transgressions;
For my sighs *are* many,
And my heart *is* faint."

GOD'S ANGER WITH JERUSALEM

2 How the Lord has
covered the
daughter of Zion
With a cloud in His anger!
He cast down from
heaven to the earth
The beauty of Israel,
And did not remember
His footstool
In the day of His anger.

2 The Lord has swallowed
up and has not pitied
All the dwelling
places of Jacob.
He has thrown down
in His wrath
The strongholds of the
daughter of Judah;
He has brought *them*
down to the ground;
He has profaned the
kingdom and its princes.

3 He has cut off in
fierce anger
Every horn of Israel;
He has drawn back
His right hand
From before the enemy.
He has blazed against
Jacob like a flaming fire
Devouring all around.

4 Standing like an enemy,
He has bent His bow;
With His right hand,
like an adversary,

He has slain all *who were*
pleasing to His eye;
On the tent of the
daughter of Zion,
He has poured out
His fury like fire.

5 The Lord was like
an enemy.
He has swallowed
up Israel,
He has swallowed up
all her palaces;
He has destroyed
her strongholds,
And has increased
mourning and
lamentation
In the daughter of Judah.

6 He has done violence
to His tabernacle,
As if it were a garden;
He has destroyed His
place of assembly;
The LORD has caused
The appointed feasts
and Sabbaths to be
forgotten in Zion.
In His burning indignation
He has spurned the
king and the priest.

7 The Lord has spurned
His altar,
He has abandoned
His sanctuary;
He has given up the
walls of her palaces
Into the hand of
the enemy.
They have made a noise in
the house of the LORD
As on the day of a set feast.

8 The LORD has purposed
to destroy
The wall of the
daughter of Zion.
He has stretched
out a line;
He has not withdrawn His
hand from destroying;
Therefore He has
caused the rampart
and wall to lament;
They languished together.

9 Her gates have sunk
into the ground;
He has destroyed and
broken her bars.
Her king and her princes
are among the nations;
The Law *is* no *more,*
And her prophets find no
vision from the LORD.

10 The elders of the
daughter of Zion
Sit on the ground
and keep silence;
They throw dust on
their heads
And gird themselves
with sackcloth.
The virgins of Jerusalem
Bow their heads to
the ground.

11 My eyes fail with tears,
My heart is troubled;
My bile is poured
on the ground
Because of the
destruction of the
daughter of my people,
Because the children
and the infants

Faint in the streets
of the city.

12 They say to their mothers,
"Where *is* grain
and wine?"
As they swoon like
the wounded
In the streets of the city,
As their life is poured out
In their mothers' bosom.

13 How shall I console you?
To what shall I liken you,
O daughter of Jerusalem?
What shall I compare
with you, that I may
comfort you,
O virgin daughter of Zion?
For your ruin *is* spread
wide as the sea;
Who can heal you?

14 Your prophets have
seen for you
False and deceptive
visions;
They have not uncovered
your iniquity,
To bring back your
captives,
But have envisioned for
you false prophecies
and delusions.

15 All who pass by clap
their hands at you;
They hiss and shake
their heads
At the daughter of
Jerusalem:
"*Is* this the city
that is called
'The perfection of beauty,
The joy of the
whole earth'?"

16 All your enemies
have opened their
mouth against you;
They hiss and gnash
their teeth.
They say, "We have
swallowed *her* up!
Surely this *is* the day
we have waited for;
We have found *it*, we
have seen *it!*"

17 The LORD has done
what He purposed;
He has fulfilled His word
Which He commanded
in days of old.
He has thrown down
and has not pitied,
And He has caused
an enemy to
rejoice over you;
He has exalted the horn
of your adversaries.

18 Their heart cried
out to the Lord,
"O wall of the daughter
of Zion,
Let tears run down like
a river day and night;
Give yourself no relief;
Give your eyes no rest.

19 "Arise, cry out
in the night,
At the beginning of
the watches;
Pour out your heart
like water before the
face of the Lord.

Lift your hands
toward Him
For the life of your
young children,
Who faint from
hunger at the head
of every street."

20"See, O LORD, and
consider!
To whom have You
done this?
Should the women eat
their offspring,
The children they
have cuddled?[a]
Should the priest and
prophet be slain
In the sanctuary
of the Lord?

21"Young and old lie
On the ground in
the streets;
My virgins and my
young men
Have fallen by the sword;
You have slain *them* in
the day of Your anger,
You have slaughtered
and not pitied.

22"You have invited
as to a feast day
The terrors that
surround me.
In the day of the
LORD's anger
There was no refugee
or survivor.
Those whom I have
borne and brought up
My enemies have
destroyed."

THE PROPHET'S ANGUISH AND HOPE

3 I *am* the man *who* has
seen affliction by the
rod of His wrath.
2 He has led me and
made *me* walk
In darkness and
not *in* light.
3 Surely He has turned
His hand against me
Time and time again
throughout the day.

4 He has aged my flesh
and my skin,
And broken my bones.
5 He has besieged me
And surrounded *me* with
bitterness and woe.
6 He has set me in
dark places
Like the dead of long ago.

7 He has hedged me in so
that I cannot get out;
He has made my
chain heavy.
8 Even when I cry
and shout,
He shuts out my prayer.
9 He has blocked my ways
with hewn stone;
He has made my
paths crooked.

10 He *has been* to me a
bear lying in wait,
Like a lion in ambush.

2:20 [a] Vulgate reads *a span long.*

11 He has turned aside
my ways and torn
me in pieces;
He has made me desolate.
12 He has bent His bow
And set me up as a
target for the arrow.

13 He has caused the
arrows of His quiver
To pierce my loins.[a]
14 I have become the
ridicule of all
my people—
Their taunting song
all the day.
15 He has filled me
with bitterness,
He has made me
drink wormwood.

16 He has also broken my
teeth with gravel,
And covered me
with ashes.
17 You have moved my
soul far from peace;
I have forgotten
prosperity.
18 And I said, "My strength
and my hope
Have perished from
the LORD."

19 Remember my affliction
and roaming,
The wormwood
and the gall.
20 My soul still remembers
And sinks within me.
21 This I recall to my mind,
Therefore I have hope.

22 *Through* the LORD's
mercies we are
not consumed,
Because His compassions
fail not.
23 *They are* new every
morning;
Great *is* Your faithfulness.
24 "The LORD *is* my
portion," says my soul,
"Therefore I hope
in Him!"

25 The LORD *is* good to those
who wait for Him,
To the soul *who*
seeks Him.
26 *It is* good that *one* should
hope and wait quietly
For the salvation
of the LORD.
27 *It is* good for a
man to bear
The yoke in his youth.

28 Let him sit alone
and keep silent,
Because *God* has
laid *it* on him;
29 Let him put his mouth
in the dust—
There may yet be hope.
30 Let him give *his*
cheek to the one
who strikes him,
And be full of reproach.

31 For the Lord will not
cast off forever.
32 Though He causes grief,
Yet He will show
compassion

3:13 [a] Literally *kidneys*

According to the
multitude of
His mercies.
33 For He does not
afflict willingly,
Nor grieve the
children of men.

34 To crush under one's feet
All the prisoners
of the earth,
35 To turn aside the
justice *due* a man
Before the face of
the Most High,
36 Or subvert a man
in his cause—
The Lord does not
approve.

37 Who *is* he *who* speaks
and it comes to pass,
When the Lord has not
commanded *it?*
38 *Is it* not from the mouth
of the Most High
That woe and well-being
proceed?
39 Why should a living
man complain,
A man for the
punishment of his sins?

40 Let us search out and
examine our ways,
And turn back to the LORD;
41 Let us lift our hearts
and hands
To God in heaven.
42 We have transgressed
and rebelled;
You have not pardoned.

43 You have covered
Yourself with anger
And pursued us;
You have slain *and*
not pitied.
44 You have covered
Yourself with a cloud,
That prayer should
not pass through.
45 You have made us an
offscouring and refuse
In the midst of
the peoples.

46 All our enemies
Have opened their
mouths against us.
47 Fear and a snare have
come upon us,
Desolation and
destruction.
48 My eyes overflow with
rivers of water
For the destruction of the
daughter of my people.

49 My eyes flow and
do not cease,
Without interruption,
50 Till the LORD from heaven
Looks down and sees.
51 My eyes bring suffering
to my soul
Because of all the
daughters of my city.

52 My enemies without cause
Hunted me down
like a bird.
53 They silenced[a] my
life in the pit
And threw stones at me.

3:53 [a] Septuagint reads *put to death.*

54 The waters flowed
over my head;
I said, "I am cut off!"

55 I called on Your
name, O LORD,
From the lowest pit.
56 You have heard my voice:
"Do not hide Your ear
From my sighing, from
my cry for help."
57 You drew near on the
day I called on You,
And said, "Do not fear!"

58 O Lord, You have pleaded
the case for my soul;
You have redeemed
my life.
59 O LORD, You have seen
how I am wronged;
Judge my case.
60 You have seen all
their vengeance,
All their schemes
against me.

61 You have heard their
reproach, O LORD,
All their schemes
against me,
62 The lips of my enemies
And their whispering
against me all the day.
63 Look at their sitting
down and their
rising up;
I *am* their taunting song.

64 Repay them, O LORD,
According to the work
of their hands.
65 Give them a veiled[a] heart;
Your curse *be* upon them!
66 In Your anger,
Pursue and destroy them
From under the heavens
of the LORD.

THE DEGRADATION OF ZION

4 How the gold has
become dim!
How changed the
fine gold!
The stones of the
sanctuary are scattered
At the head of
every street.

2 The precious sons
of Zion,
Valuable as fine gold,
How they are regarded
as clay pots,
The work of the hands
of the potter!

3 Even the jackals present
their breasts
To nurse their young;
But the daughter of
my people *is* cruel,
Like ostriches in
the wilderness.

4 The tongue of the
infant clings
To the roof of its
mouth for thirst;
The young children
ask for bread,
But no one breaks
it for them.

3:65 [a] A Jewish tradition reads *sorrow of*.

5 Those who ate delicacies
Are desolate in
the streets;
Those who were brought
up in scarlet
Embrace ash heaps.

6 The punishment of
the iniquity of the
daughter of my people
Is greater than the
punishment of the
sin of Sodom,
Which was overthrown
in a moment,
With no hand to
help her!

7 Her Nazirites[a] were
brighter than snow
And whiter than milk;
They were more ruddy
in body than rubies,
Like sapphire in their
appearance.

8 *Now* their appearance
is blacker than soot;
They go unrecognized
in the streets;
Their skin clings to
their bones,
It has become as
dry as wood.

9 *Those* slain by the
sword are better off
Than *those* who die
of hunger;
For these *pine away,*
Stricken *for lack* of the
fruits of the field.

10 The hands of the
compassionate women
Have cooked their
own children;
They became food
for them
In the destruction of
the daughter of
my people.

11 The LORD has
fulfilled His fury,
He has poured out
His fierce anger.
He kindled a fire
in Zion,
And it has devoured
its foundations.

12 The kings of the earth,
And all inhabitants
of the world,
Would not have believed
That the adversary
and the enemy
Could enter the gates
of Jerusalem—

13 Because of the sins
of her prophets
And the iniquities
of her priests,
Who shed in her midst
The blood of the just.

14 They wandered blind
in the streets;
They have defiled
themselves with
blood,
So that no one would
touch their garments.

4:7 [a] Or *nobles*

15 They cried out to them,
"Go away, unclean!
Go away, go away,
Do not touch us!"
When they fled and
wandered,
Those among the
nations said,
"They shall no longer
dwell *here.*"

16 The face[a] of the LORD
scattered them;
He no longer
regards them.
The people do not
respect the priests
Nor show favor to
the elders.

17 Still our eyes failed us,
Watching vainly
for our help;
In our watching
we watched
For a nation *that*
could not save *us.*

18 They tracked our steps
So that we could not
walk in our streets.
Our end was near;
Our days were over,
For our end had come.

19 Our pursuers were swifter
Than the eagles of
the heavens.
They pursued us on
the mountains
And lay in wait for us
in the wilderness.

20 The breath of our
nostrils, the anointed
of the LORD,
Was caught in their pits,
Of whom we said,
"Under his shadow
We shall live among
the nations."

21 Rejoice and be glad,
O daughter of Edom,
You who dwell in
the land of Uz!
The cup shall also
pass over to you
And you shall become
drunk and make
yourself naked.

22 *The punishment of*
your iniquity is
accomplished,
O daughter of Zion;
He will no longer send
you into captivity.
He will punish
your iniquity,
O daughter of Edom;
He will uncover your sins!

PRAYER FOR RESTORATION

5 Remember, O LORD,
what has come
upon us;
Look, and behold
our reproach!
2 Our inheritance has been
turned over to aliens,
And our houses to
foreigners.
3 We have become
orphans and waifs,

4:16 [a] Targum reads *anger.*

Our mothers *are*
like widows.

4 We pay for the water
we drink,
And our wood comes
at a price.
5 *They* pursue at our
heels;[a]
We labor *and* have
no rest.
6 We have given our hand
to the Egyptians
And the Assyrians, to be
satisfied with bread.

7 Our fathers sinned
and are no more,
But we bear their
iniquities.
8 Servants rule over us;
There is none to deliver
us from their hand.
9 We get our bread *at the
risk* of our lives,
Because of the sword
in the wilderness.

10 Our skin is hot
as an oven,
Because of the fever
of famine.
11 They ravished the
women in Zion,
The maidens in the
cities of Judah.
12 Princes were hung up
by their hands,
And elders were
not respected.
13 Young men ground
at the millstones;
Boys staggered under
loads of wood.
14 The elders have ceased
gathering at the gate,
And the young men
from their music.

15 The joy of our heart
has ceased;
Our dance has turned
into mourning.
16 The crown has fallen
from our head.
Woe to us, for we
have sinned!
17 Because of this our
heart is faint;
Because of these
things our eyes
grow dim;
18 Because of Mount Zion
which is desolate,
With foxes walking
about on it.

19 You, O LORD, remain
forever;
Your throne from
generation to
generation.
20 Why do You forget
us forever,
And forsake us for
so long a time?
21 Turn us back to You,
O LORD, and we
will be restored;
Renew our days as of old,
22 Unless You have
utterly rejected us,
And are very angry
with us!

5:5 [a] Literally *necks*

THE BOOK OF EZEKIEL

EZEKIEL'S VISION OF GOD

1 Now it came to pass in the
thirtieth year, in the fourth
month, on the fifth *day* of the
month, as I *was* among the
captives by the River Chebar,
that the heavens were opened
and I saw visions[a] of God. 2On
the fifth *day* of the month,
which *was* in the fifth year of
King Jehoiachin's captivity,
3the word of the LORD came
expressly to Ezekiel the priest,
the son of Buzi, in the land of
the Chaldeans[a] by the River
Chebar; and the hand of the
LORD was upon him there.

4Then I looked, and behold,
a whirlwind was coming out
of the north, a great cloud
with raging fire engulfing itself; and brightness *was* all
around it and radiating out
of its midst like the color of
amber, out of the midst of
the fire. 5Also from within it
came the likeness of four living creatures. And this *was*
their appearance: they had the
likeness of a man. 6Each one
had four faces, and each one
had four wings. 7Their legs
were straight, and the soles
of their feet *were* like the soles
of calves' feet. They sparkled
like the color of burnished
bronze. 8The hands of a man
were under their wings on
their four sides; and each of
the four had faces and wings.
9Their wings touched one another. *The creatures* did not
turn when they went, but each
one went straight forward.

10As for the likeness of their
faces, *each* had the face of a
man; each of the four had the
face of a lion on the right side,
each of the four had the face
of an ox on the left side, and
each of the four had the face
of an eagle. 11Thus *were* their
faces. Their wings stretched
upward; two *wings* of each
one touched one another,
and two covered their bodies.
12And each one went straight
forward; they went wherever
the spirit wanted to go, and
they did not turn when they
went.

13As for the likeness of the
living creatures, their appearance *was* like burning coals
of fire, like the appearance of
torches going back and forth
among the living creatures.
The fire was bright, and out of

1:1 [a] Following Masoretic Text, Septuagint, and Vulgate; Syriac and Targum read *a vision.* 1:3 [c] Or *Babylonians,* and so elsewhere in this book

the fire went lightning. 14And
the living creatures ran back
and forth, in appearance like
a flash of lightning.

15Now as I looked at the living creatures, behold, a wheel
was on the earth beside each
living creature with its four
faces. 16The appearance of the
wheels and their workings *was*
like the color of beryl, and all
four had the same likeness.
The appearance of their workings *was,* as it were, a wheel in
the middle of a wheel. 17When
they moved, they went to-
ward any one of four directions; they did not turn aside
when they went. 18As for their
rims, they were so high they
were awesome; and their rims
were full of eyes, all around the
four of them. 19When the living creatures went, the wheels
went beside them; and when
the living creatures were lifted
up from the earth, the wheels
were lifted up. 20Wherever the
spirit wanted to go, they went,
because there the spirit went;
and the wheels were lifted together with them, for the spirit
of the living creatures[a] *was*
in the wheels. 21When those
went, *these* went; when those
stood, *these* stood; and when
those were lifted up from the
earth, the wheels were lifted
up together with them, for the
spirit of the living creatures[a]
was in the wheels.

22The likeness of the firmament above the heads of the
living creatures[a] *was* like the
color of an awesome crystal,
stretched out over their heads.
23And under the firmament
their wings *spread out* straight,
one toward another. Each one
had two which covered one
side, and each one had two
which covered the other side of
the body. 24When they went, I
heard the noise of their wings,
like the noise of many waters,
like the voice of the Almighty,
a tumult like the noise of an
army; and when they stood
still, they let down their wings.
25A voice came from above the
firmament that *was* over their
heads; whenever they stood,
they let down their wings.

26And above the firmament
over their heads *was* the likeness of a throne, in appearance like a sapphire stone; on
the likeness of the throne *was*
a likeness with the appearance
of a man high above it. 27Also
from the appearance of His
waist and upward I saw, as it
were, the color of amber with
the appearance of fire all
around within it; and from the
appearance of His waist and
downward I saw, as it were,
the appearance of fire with

1:20 [a] Literally *living creature;* Septuagint and Vulgate read *spirit of life;* Targum reads *creatures.* 1:21 [a] Literally *living creature;* Septuagint and Vulgate read *spirit of life;* Targum reads *creatures.* 1:22 [a] Following Septuagint, Targum, and Vulgate; Masoretic Text reads *living creature.*

brightness all around. 28Like
the appearance of a rainbow in
a cloud on a rainy day, so *was*
the appearance of the brightness all around it. This *was* the
appearance of the likeness of
the glory of the LORD.

EZEKIEL SENT TO REBELLIOUS ISRAEL

So when I saw *it,* I fell on
my face, and I heard a voice
of One speaking.

2 And He said to me, "Son of
man, stand on your feet,
and I will speak to you." 2Then
the Spirit entered me when He
spoke to me, and set me on
my feet; and I heard Him who
spoke to me. 3And He said to
me: "Son of man, I am sending you to the children of Israel, to a rebellious nation that
has rebelled against Me; they
and their fathers have transgressed against Me to this very
day. 4For *they are* impudent
and stubborn children. I am
sending you to them, and you
shall say to them, 'Thus says
the Lord GOD.' 5As for them,
whether they hear or whether
they refuse—for they *are* a rebellious house—yet they will
know that a prophet has been
among them.

6"And you, son of man, do
not be afraid of them nor be
afraid of their words, though
briers and thorns *are* with you
and you dwell among scorpions; do not be afraid of their
words or dismayed by their
looks, though they *are* a rebellious house. 7You shall speak
My words to them, whether
they hear or whether they refuse, for they *are* rebellious.
8But you, son of man, hear
what I say to you. Do not be
rebellious like that rebellious
house; open your mouth and
eat what I give you."

9Now when I looked, there
was a hand stretched out to
me; and behold, a scroll of
a book *was* in it. 10Then He
spread it before me; and *there
was* writing on the inside and
on the outside, and written
on it *were* lamentations and
mourning and woe.

3 Moreover He said to me,
"Son of man, eat what you
find; eat this scroll, and go,
speak to the house of Israel."
2So I opened my mouth, and
He caused me to eat that scroll.

3And He said to me, "Son of
man, feed your belly, and fill
your stomach with this scroll
that I give you." So I ate, and
it was in my mouth like honey
in sweetness.

4Then He said to me: "Son
of man, go to the house of
Israel and speak with My
words to them. 5For you *are*
not sent to a people of unfamiliar speech and of hard
language, *but* to the house of
Israel, 6not to many people of
unfamiliar speech and of hard
language, whose words you
cannot understand. Surely,
had I sent you to them, they
would have listened to you.
7But the house of Israel will

not listen to you, because they
will not listen to Me; for all the
house of Israel *are* impudent
and hard-hearted. 8Behold, I
have made your face strong
against their faces, and your
forehead strong against their
foreheads. 9Like adamant
stone, harder than flint, I have
made your forehead; do not
be afraid of them, nor be dismayed at their looks, though
they *are* a rebellious house."

10Moreover He said to me:
"Son of man, receive into your
heart all My words that I speak
to you, and hear with your
ears. 11And go, get to the captives, to the children of your
people, and speak to them and
tell them, 'Thus says the Lord
GOD,' whether they hear, or
whether they refuse."

12Then the Spirit lifted me
up, and I heard behind me
a great thunderous voice:
"Blessed *is* the glory of the
LORD from His place!" 13*I* also
heard the noise of the wings
of the living creatures that
touched one another, and
the noise of the wheels beside
them, and a great thunderous
noise. 14So the Spirit lifted me
up and took me away, and I
went in bitterness, in the heat
of my spirit; but the hand of
the LORD was strong upon
me. 15Then I came to the captives at Tel Abib, *who dwelt*
by the River Chebar; and I sat
where they sat, and remained
there astonished among them
seven days.

EZEKIEL IS A WATCHMAN

16Now it came to pass at
the end of seven days that the
word of the LORD came to me,
saying, 17"Son of man, I have
made you a watchman for the
house of Israel; therefore hear
a word from My mouth, and
give them warning from Me:
18When I say to the wicked,
'You shall surely die,' and you
give him no warning, nor
speak to warn the wicked from
his wicked way, to save his life,
that same wicked *man* shall die
in his iniquity; but his blood I
will require at your hand. 19Yet,
if you warn the wicked, and he
does not turn from his wickedness, nor from his wicked way,
he shall die in his iniquity; but
you have delivered your soul.

20"Again, when a righteous
man turns from his righteousness and commits iniquity,
and I lay a stumbling block
before him, he shall die; because you did not give him
warning, he shall die in his sin,
and his righteousness which
he has done shall not be remembered; but his blood I will
require at your hand. 21Never-
theless if you warn the righteous *man* that the righteous
should not sin, and he does not
sin, he shall surely live because
he took warning; also you will
have delivered your soul."

22*Then* the hand of the
LORD was upon me there,
and He said to me, "Arise, go
out into the plain, and there
I shall talk with you."

23So I arose and went out into the plain, and behold, the glory of the LORD stood there, like the glory which I saw by the River Chebar; and I fell on my face. 24Then the Spirit entered me and set me on my feet, and spoke with me and said to me: "Go, shut yourself inside your house. 25And you, O son of man, surely they will put ropes on you and bind you with them, so that you cannot go out among them. 26I will make your tongue cling to the roof of your mouth, so that you shall be mute and not be one to rebuke them, for they *are* a rebellious house. 27But when I speak with you, I will open your mouth, and you shall say to them, 'Thus says the Lord GOD.' He who hears, let him hear; and he who refuses, let him refuse; for they *are* a rebellious house.

THE SIEGE OF JERUSALEM PORTRAYED

4 "You also, son of man, take a clay tablet and lay it before you, and portray on it a city, Jerusalem. 2Lay siege against it, build a siege wall against it, and heap up a mound against it; set camps against it also, and place battering rams against it all around. 3Moreover take for yourself an iron plate, and set it *as* an iron wall between you and the city. Set your face against it, and it shall be besieged, and you shall lay siege against it. This *will be* a sign to the house of Israel.

4"Lie also on your left side, and lay the iniquity of the house of Israel upon it. *According* to the number of the days that you lie on it, you shall bear their iniquity. 5For I have laid on you the years of their iniquity, according to the number of the days, three hundred and ninety days; so you shall bear the iniquity of the house of Israel. 6And when you have completed them, lie again on your right side; then you shall bear the iniquity of the house of Judah forty days. I have laid on you a day for each year.

7"Therefore you shall set your face toward the siege of Jerusalem; your arm *shall be* uncovered, and you shall prophesy against it. 8And surely I will restrain you so that you cannot turn from one side to another till you have ended the days of your siege.

9"Also take for yourself wheat, barley, beans, lentils, millet, and spelt; put them into one vessel, and make bread of them for yourself. *During* the number of days that you lie on your side, three hundred and ninety days, you shall eat it. 10And your food which you eat *shall be* by weight, twenty shekels a day; from time to time you shall eat it. 11You shall also drink water by measure, one-sixth of a hin; from time to time you

shall drink. 12And you shall
eat it *as* barley cakes; and bake
it using fuel of human waste
in their sight."
13Then the LORD said, "So
shall the children of Israel eat
their defiled bread among the
Gentiles, where I will drive
them."
14So I said, "Ah, Lord GOD!
Indeed I have never defiled
myself from my youth till now;
I have never eaten what died
of itself or was torn by beasts,
nor has abominable flesh ever
come into my mouth."
15Then He said to me, "See,
I am giving you cow dung instead of human waste, and
you shall prepare your bread
over it."
16Moreover He said to me,
"Son of man, surely I will cut
off the supply of bread in Jerusalem; they shall eat bread
by weight and with anxiety,
and shall drink water by measure and with dread, 17that
they may lack bread and
water, and be dismayed with
one another, and waste away
because of their iniquity.

A SWORD AGAINST JERUSALEM

5 "And you, son of man,
take a sharp sword, take
it as a barber's razor, and
pass *it* over your head and
your beard; *then take scales*
to weigh and divide the *hair.*
2You shall burn with fire one-
third in the midst of the city,
when the days of the siege are
finished; then you shall take
one-third and strike around *it*
with the sword, and one-third
you shall scatter in the wind:
I will draw out a sword after
them. 3You shall also take a
small number of them and
bind them in the edge of your
garment. 4Then take some of
them again and throw them
into the midst of the fire, and
burn them in the fire. From
there a fire will go out into all
the house of Israel.
5"Thus says the Lord GOD:
'This *is* Jerusalem; I have set
her in the midst of the nations
and the countries all around
her. 6She has rebelled against
My judgments by doing wickedness more than the nations,
and against My statutes more
than the countries that *are*
all around her; for they have
refused My judgments, and
they have not walked in My
statutes.' 7Therefore thus says
the Lord GOD: 'Because you
have multiplied *disobedience*
more than the nations that
are all around you, have not
walked in My statutes nor
kept My judgments, nor even
done[a] according to the judgments of the nations that *are*
all around you'— 8therefore

5:7 [a] Following Masoretic Text, Septuagint, Targum, and Vulgate; many Hebrew manuscripts and Syriac read *but have done* (compare 11:12).

thus says the Lord GOD: 'Indeed I, even I, *am* against you
and will execute judgments in
your midst in the sight of the
nations. 9And I will do among
you what I have never done,
and the like of which I will
never do again, because of all
your abominations. 10There-
fore fathers shall eat *their* sons
in your midst, and sons shall
eat their fathers; and I will execute judgments among you,
and all of you who remain I
will scatter to all the winds.

11'Therefore, *as* I live,' says
the Lord GOD, 'surely, because
you have defiled My sanctuary
with all your detestable things
and with all your abominations, therefore I will also diminish *you;* My eye will not
spare, nor will I have any pity.
12One-third of you shall die
of the pestilence, and be consumed with famine in your
midst; and one-third shall fall
by the sword all around you;
and I will scatter another third
to all the winds, and I will
draw out a sword after them.

13'Thus shall My anger be
spent, and I will cause My fury
to rest upon them, and I will be
avenged; and they shall know
that I, the LORD, have spoken
it in My zeal, when I have spent
My fury upon them. 14More-
over I will make you a waste
and a reproach among the nations that *are* all around you,
in the sight of all who pass by.

15'So it[a] shall be a reproach,
a taunt, a lesson, and an astonishment to the nations
that *are* all around you, when
I execute judgments among
you in anger and in fury and
in furious rebukes. I, the
LORD, have spoken. 16When
I send against them the terrible arrows of famine which
shall be for destruction, which
I will send to destroy you, I
will increase the famine upon
you and cut off your supply of
bread. 17So I will send against
you famine and wild beasts,
and they will bereave you. Pestilence and blood shall pass
through you, and I will bring
the sword against you. I, the
LORD, have spoken.'"

JUDGMENT ON IDOLATROUS ISRAEL

6 Now the word of the LORD
came to me, saying: 2"Son
of man, set your face toward
the mountains of Israel, and
prophesy against them, 3and
say, 'O mountains of Israel,
hear the word of the Lord
GOD! Thus says the Lord GOD
to the mountains, to the hills,
to the ravines, and to the valleys: "Indeed I, *even* I, will
bring a sword against you,
and I will destroy your high
places. 4Then your altars shall
be desolate, your incense altars shall be broken, and I
will cast down your slain
men before your idols. 5And

5:15 [a] Septuagint, Syriac, Targum, and Vulgate read *you*.

I will lay the corpses of the
children of Israel before their
idols, and I will scatter your
bones all around your altars.
6In all your dwelling places
the cities shall be laid waste,
and the high places shall be
desolate, so that your altars
may be laid waste and made
desolate, your idols may be
broken and made to cease,
your incense altars may be cut
down, and your works may be
abolished. 7The slain shall fall
in your midst, and you shall
know that I *am* the LORD.

8"Yet I will leave a rem-
nant, so that you may have
some who escape the sword
among the nations, when
you are scattered through
the countries. 9Then those of
you who escape will remember Me among the nations
where they are carried captive, because I was crushed by
their adulterous heart which
has departed from Me, and
by their eyes which play the
harlot after their idols; they
will loathe themselves for the
evils which they committed in
all their abominations. 10And
they shall know that I *am* the
LORD; I have not said in vain
that I would bring this calamity upon them."

11'Thus says the Lord GOD:
"Pound your fists and stamp
your feet, and say, 'Alas, for
all the evil abominations of
the house of Israel! For they
shall fall by the sword, by
famine, and by pestilence.
12He who is far off shall die
by the pestilence, he who is
near shall fall by the sword,
and he who remains and is
besieged shall die by the famine. Thus will I spend My fury
upon them. 13Then you shall
know that I *am* the LORD,
when their slain are among
their idols all around their
altars, on every high hill, on
all the mountaintops, under
every green tree, and under
every thick oak, wherever they
offered sweet incense to all
their idols. 14So I will stretch
out My hand against them
and make the land desolate,
yes, more desolate than the
wilderness toward Diblah, in
all their dwelling places. Then
they shall know that I *am* the
LORD.' " ' "

JUDGMENT ON ISRAEL IS NEAR

7 Moreover the word of the
LORD came to me, saying,
2"And you, son of man, thus
says the Lord GOD to the land
of Israel:

'An end! The end has
come upon the four
corners of the land.
3 Now the end *has*
come upon you,
And I will send My
anger against you;
I will judge you according
to your ways,
And I will repay you for
all your abominations.
4 My eye will not spare you,

Nor will I have pity;
But I will repay your ways,
And your abominations
will be in your midst;
Then you shall know
that I *am* the LORD!'

5 "Thus says the Lord GOD:

'A disaster, a singular
disaster;
Behold, it has come!
6 An end has come,
The end has come;
It has dawned for you;
Behold, it has come!
7 Doom has come to
you, you who dwell
in the land;
The time has come,
A day of trouble *is* near,
And not of rejoicing
in the mountains.
8 Now upon you I will soon
pour out My fury,
And spend My anger
upon you;
I will judge you according
to your ways,
And I will repay you for
all your abominations.

9 'My eye will not spare,
Nor will I have pity;
I will repay you according
to your ways,
And your abominations
will be in your midst.
Then you shall know
that I *am* the LORD
who strikes.

10 'Behold, the day!
Behold, it has come!
Doom has gone out;
The rod has blossomed,
Pride has budded.
11 Violence has risen up into
a rod of wickedness;
None of them
shall remain,
None of their multitude,
None of them;
Nor *shall there be*
wailing for them.
12 The time has come,
The day draws near.

'Let not the buyer rejoice,
Nor the seller mourn,
For wrath *is* on their
whole multitude.
13 For the seller shall
not return to what
has been sold,
Though he may
still be alive;
For the vision concerns
the whole multitude,
And it shall not turn back;
No one will strengthen
himself
Who lives in iniquity.

14 'They have blown the
trumpet and made
everyone ready,
But no one goes to battle;
For My wrath *is* on all
their multitude.
15 The sword *is* outside,
And the pestilence
and famine within.
Whoever *is* in the field
Will die by the sword;
And whoever *is* in the city,
Famine and pestilence
will devour him.

16 'Those who survive
will escape and be
on the mountains
Like doves of the valleys,
All of them mourning,
Each for his iniquity.
17 Every hand will be
feeble,
And every knee will be
as weak *as* water.
18 They will also be girded
with sackcloth;
Horror will cover them;
Shame *will be* on
every face,
Baldness on all
their heads.

19 'They will throw their
silver into the streets,
And their gold will
be like refuse;
Their silver and their
gold will not be able
to deliver them
In the day of the wrath
of the LORD;
They will not satisfy
their souls,
Nor fill their stomachs,
Because it became
their stumbling
block of iniquity.

20 'As for the beauty of
his ornaments,
He set it in majesty;
But they made from it
The images of their
abominations—
Their detestable things;
Therefore I have made it
Like refuse to them.
21 I will give it as plunder
Into the hands of
strangers,
And to the wicked of
the earth as spoil;
And they shall defile it.
22 I will turn My face
from them,
And they will defile
My secret place;
For robbers shall enter
it and defile it.

23 'Make a chain,
For the land is filled
with crimes of blood,
And the city is full
of violence.
24 Therefore I will bring
the worst of the
Gentiles,
And they will possess
their houses;
I will cause the pomp of
the strong to cease,
And their holy places
shall be defiled.
25 Destruction comes;
They will seek peace, but
there shall be none.
26 Disaster will come
upon disaster,
And rumor will be
upon rumor.
Then they will seek
a vision from a
prophet;
But the law will perish
from the priest,
And counsel from
the elders.

27 'The king will mourn,
The prince will be clothed
with desolation,

And the hands of the
common people
will tremble.
I will do to them
according to their way,
And according to
what they deserve I
will judge them;
Then they shall know
that I *am* the LORD!'"

ABOMINATIONS IN THE TEMPLE

8 And it came to pass in
the sixth year, in the sixth
month, on the fifth *day* of the
month, as I sat in my house
with the elders of Judah sitting
before me, that the hand of the
Lord GOD fell upon me there.
2Then I looked, and there was
a likeness, like the appearance
of fire—from the appearance
of His waist and downward,
fire; and from His waist and
upward, like the appearance
of brightness, like the color
of amber. 3He stretched out
the form of a hand, and took
me by a lock of my hair; and
the Spirit lifted me up between earth and heaven, and
brought me in visions of God
to Jerusalem, to the door of
the north gate of the inner
court, where the seat of the
image of jealousy *was,* which
provokes to jealousy. 4And behold, the glory of the God of
Israel *was* there, like the vision
that I saw in the plain.

5Then He said to me, "Son
of man, lift your eyes now
toward the north." So I lifted
my eyes toward the north, and
there, north of the altar gate,
was this image of jealousy in
the entrance.

6Furthermore He said to
me, "Son of man, do you see
what they are doing, the great
abominations that the house
of Israel commits here, to
make Me go far away from My
sanctuary? Now turn again,
you will see greater abominations." 7So He brought me
to the door of the court; and
when I looked, there was a
hole in the wall. 8Then He said
to me, "Son of man, dig into
the wall"; and when I dug into
the wall, there was a door.

9And He said to me, "Go
in, and see the wicked abominations which they are doing
there." 10So I went in and saw,
and there—every sort of creeping thing, abominable beasts,
and all the idols of the house
of Israel, portrayed all around
on the walls. 11And there stood
before them seventy men of
the elders of the house of Israel, and in their midst stood
Jaazaniah the son of Shaphan.
Each man had a censer in his
hand, and a thick cloud of incense went up. 12Then He said
to me, "Son of man, have you
seen what the elders of the
house of Israel do in the dark,
every man in the room of his
idols? For they say, 'The LORD
does not see us, the LORD has
forsaken the land.'"

13And He said to me, "Turn
again, *and* you will see greater

abominations that they are
doing." 14So He brought me to
the door of the north gate of
the LORD's house; and to my
dismay, women were sitting
there weeping for Tammuz.
15Then He said to me,
"Have you seen *this,* O son of
man? Turn again, you will see
greater abominations than
these." 16So He brought me
into the inner court of the
LORD's house; and there, at
the door of the temple of the
LORD, between the porch and
the altar, *were* about twenty-
five men with their backs toward the temple of the LORD
and their faces toward the
east, and they were worshiping the sun toward the east.
17And He said to me, "Have
you seen *this,* O son of man? Is
it a trivial thing to the house
of Judah to commit the abominations which they commit
here? For they have filled the
land with violence; then they
have returned to provoke Me
to anger. Indeed they put the
branch to their nose. 18There-
fore I also will act in fury. My
eye will not spare nor will I
have pity; and though they cry
in My ears with a loud voice, I
will not hear them."

THE WICKED ARE SLAIN

9 Then He called out in my
hearing with a loud voice,
saying, "Let those who have
charge over the city draw near,
each *with* a deadly weapon in
his hand." 2And suddenly six
men came from the direction
of the upper gate, which faces
north, each with his battle-ax
in his hand. One man among
them *was* clothed with linen
and had a writer's inkhorn
at his side. They went in and
stood beside the bronze altar.
3Now the glory of the God
of Israel had gone up from
the cherub, where it had been,
to the threshold of the temple.[a] And He called to the man
clothed with linen, who *had*
the writer's inkhorn at his
side; 4and the LORD said to
him, "Go through the midst
of the city, through the midst
of Jerusalem, and put a mark
on the foreheads of the men
who sigh and cry over all the
abominations that are done
within it."
5To the others He said in
my hearing, "Go after him
through the city and kill; do
not let your eye spare, nor
have any pity. 6Utterly slay
old *and* young men, maidens and little children and
women; but do not come near
anyone on whom *is* the mark;
and begin at My sanctuary."
So they began with the elders
who *were* before the temple.
7Then He said to them, "Defile
the temple, and fill the courts
with the slain. Go out!" And
they went out and killed in
the city.

9:3 [a] Literally *house*

8So it was, that while they
were killing them, I was left
alone; and I fell on my face
and cried out, and said, "Ah,
Lord GOD! Will You destroy
all the remnant of Israel in
pouring out Your fury on Jerusalem?"

9Then He said to me, "The
iniquity of the house of Israel and Judah *is* exceedingly
great, and the land is full of
bloodshed, and the city full of
perversity; for they say, 'The
LORD has forsaken the land,
and the LORD does not see!'
10And as for Me also, My eye
will neither spare, nor will I
have pity, *but* I will recompense their deeds on their
own head."

11Just then, the man clothed
with linen, who *had* the inkhorn at his side, reported back
and said, "I have done as You
commanded me."

THE GLORY DEPARTS FROM THE TEMPLE

10 And I looked, and there
in the firmament that
was above the head of the
cherubim, there appeared
something like a sapphire
stone, having the appearance
of the likeness of a throne.
2Then He spoke to the man
clothed with linen, and said,
"Go in among the wheels,
under the cherub, fill your
hands with coals of fire from
among the cherubim, and
scatter *them* over the city."
And he went in as I watched.

3Now the cherubim were
standing on the south side
of the temple[a] when the man
went in, and the cloud filled
the inner court. 4Then the
glory of the LORD went up
from the cherub, *and paused*
over the threshold of the temple; and the house was filled
with the cloud, and the court
was full of the brightness of
the LORD's glory. 5And the
sound of the wings of the
cherubim was heard *even* in
the outer court, like the voice
of Almighty God when He
speaks.

6Then it happened, when
He commanded the man
clothed in linen, saying, "Take
fire from among the wheels,
from among the cherubim,"
that he went in and stood
beside the wheels. 7And the
cherub stretched out his hand
from among the cherubim to
the fire that *was* among the
cherubim, and took *some of*
it and put *it* into the hands of
the *man* clothed with linen,
who took *it* and went out.
8The cherubim appeared to
have the form of a man's hand
under their wings.

9And when I looked, there
were four wheels by the
cherubim, one wheel by one
cherub and another wheel by
each other cherub; the wheels
appeared *to have* the color of

10:3 [a] Literally *house,* also in verses 4 and 18

a beryl stone. 10*As for* their
appearance, all four looked
alike—as it were, a wheel in
the middle of a wheel. 11When
they went, they went toward
any of their four directions;
they did not turn aside when
they went, but followed in the
direction the head was facing.
They did not turn aside when
they went. 12And their whole
body, with their back, their
hands, their wings, and the
wheels that the four had, *were*
full of eyes all around. 13As for
the wheels, they were called in
my hearing, "Wheel."

14Each one had four faces:
the first face *was* the face of
a cherub, the second face the
face of a man, the third the
face of a lion, and the fourth
the face of an eagle. 15And
the cherubim were lifted up.
This *was* the living creature
I saw by the River Chebar.
16When the cherubim went,
the wheels went beside them;
and when the cherubim lifted
their wings to mount up from
the earth, the same wheels
also did not turn from beside
them. 17When *the cherubim*[a]
stood still, *the wheels* stood
still, and when *one*[b] was lifted
up, *the other*[c] lifted itself up,
for the spirit of the living creature *was* in them.

18Then the glory of the LORD
departed from the threshold
of the temple and stood over
the cherubim. 19And the cherubim lifted their wings and
mounted up from the earth
in my sight. When they went
out, the wheels *were* beside
them; and they stood at the
door of the east gate of the
LORD's house, and the glory
of the God of Israel *was* above
them.

20This *is* the living creature I saw under the God of
Israel by the River Chebar, and
I knew they *were* cherubim.
21Each one had four faces and
each one four wings, and the
likeness of the hands of a man
was under their wings. 22And
the likeness of their faces *was*
the same *as* the faces which
I had seen by the River Chebar, their appearance and
their persons. They each went
straight forward.

JUDGMENT ON WICKED COUNSELORS

11 Then the Spirit lifted me
up and brought me to
the East Gate of the LORD's
house, which faces eastward;
and there at the door of the
gate were twenty-five men,
among whom I saw Jaazaniah
the son of Azzur, and Pelatiah
the son of Benaiah, princes
of the people. 2And He said to
me: "Son of man, these *are* the
men who devise iniquity and
give wicked counsel in this
city, 3who say, '*The time is* not
near to build houses; this *city*
is the caldron, and we *are* the

10:17 [a] Literally *they* [b] Literally *they* [c] Literally *they*

meat.' [4]Therefore prophesy
against them, prophesy, O son
of man!"

[5]Then the Spirit of the
LORD fell upon me, and said
to me, "Speak! 'Thus says the
LORD: "Thus you have said,
O house of Israel; for I know
the things that come into your
mind. [6]You have multiplied
your slain in this city, and you
have filled its streets with the
slain." [7]Therefore thus says the
Lord GOD: "Your slain whom
you have laid in its midst, they
are the meat, and this *city is*
the caldron; but I shall bring
you out of the midst of it. [8]You
have feared the sword; and I
will bring a sword upon you,"
says the Lord GOD. [9]"And I will
bring you out of its midst, and
deliver you into the hands of
strangers, and execute judgments on you. [10]You shall fall
by the sword. I will judge you
at the border of Israel. Then
you shall know that I *am* the
LORD. [11]This *city* shall not be
your caldron, nor shall you
be the meat in its midst. I
will judge you at the border
of Israel. [12]And you shall know
that I *am* the LORD; for you
have not walked in My statutes
nor executed My judgments,
but have done according to
the customs of the Gentiles
which *are* all around you."'"

[13]Now it happened, while
I was prophesying, that Pelatiah the son of Benaiah died.
Then I fell on my face and
cried with a loud voice, and
said, "Ah, Lord GOD! Will You
make a complete end of the
remnant of Israel?"

GOD WILL RESTORE ISRAEL

[14]Again the word of the
LORD came to me, saying,
[15]"Son of man, your brethren,
your relatives, your countrymen, and all the house of Israel in its entirety, *are* those
about whom the inhabitants
of Jerusalem have said, 'Get
far away from the LORD; this
land has been given to us as
a possession.' [16]Therefore say,
'Thus says the Lord GOD: "Although I have cast them far off
among the Gentiles, and although I have scattered them
among the countries, yet I
shall be a little sanctuary for
them in the countries where
they have gone."' [17]Therefore
say, 'Thus says the Lord GOD:
"I will gather you from the
peoples, assemble you from
the countries where you have
been scattered, and I will give
you the land of Israel."' [18]And
they will go there, and they
will take away all its detestable
things and all its abominations from there. [19]Then I will
give them one heart, and I will
put a new spirit within them,[a]
and take the stony heart out
of their flesh, and give them a
heart of flesh, [20]that they may
walk in My statutes and keep

11:19 [a] Literally *you*

My judgments and do them;
and they shall be My people,
and I will be their God. [21]But *as
for those* whose hearts follow
the desire for their detestable
things and their abomina-
tions, I will recompense their
deeds on their own heads,"
says the Lord GOD.
[22]So the cherubim lifted up
their wings, with the wheels
beside them, and the glory
of the God of Israel *was* high
above them. [23]And the glory
of the LORD went up from the
midst of the city and stood on
the mountain, which *is* on the
east side of the city.
[24]Then the Spirit took me
up and brought me in a vision by the Spirit of God into
Chaldea,[a] to those in captivity. And the vision that I had
seen went up from me. [25]So I
spoke to those in captivity of
all the things the LORD had
shown me.

JUDAH'S CAPTIVITY PORTRAYED

12 Now the word of the
LORD came to me, say-
ing: [2]"Son of man, you dwell
in the midst of a rebellious
house, which has eyes to see
but does not see, and ears to
hear but does not hear; for
they *are* a rebellious house.
[3]"Therefore, son of man,
prepare your belongings for
captivity, and go into captivity
by day in their sight. You shall
go from your place into captivity to another place in their
sight. It may be that they will
consider, though they *are* a
rebellious house. [4]By day you
shall bring out your belongings in their sight, as though
going into captivity; and at
evening you shall go in their
sight, like those who go into
captivity. [5]Dig through the
wall in their sight, and carry
your belongings out through it.
[6]In their sight you shall bear
them on *your* shoulders *and*
carry *them* out at twilight; you
shall cover your face, so that
you cannot see the ground,
for I have made you a sign to
the house of Israel."
[7]So I did as I was com-
manded. I brought out my
belongings by day, as though
going into captivity, and at
evening I dug through the
wall with my hand. I brought
them out at twilight, *and* I
bore *them* on *my* shoulder in
their sight.
[8]And in the morning the
word of the LORD came to me,
saying, [9]"Son of man, has not
the house of Israel, the rebellious house, said to you, 'What
are you doing?' [10]Say to them,
'Thus says the Lord GOD: "This
burden *concerns* the prince in
Jerusalem and all the house of
Israel who are among them."'
[11]Say, 'I *am* a sign to you. As I
have done, so shall it be done
to them; they shall be carried

11:24 [a] Or *Babylon,* and so elsewhere in this book

away into captivity.' 12And the
prince who *is* among them
shall bear *his belongings* on
his shoulder at twilight and
go out. They shall dig through
the wall to carry *them* out
through it. He shall cover his
face, so that he cannot see the
ground with *his* eyes. 13I will
also spread My net over him,
and he shall be caught in My
snare. I will bring him to Babylon, *to* the land of the Chaldeans; yet he shall not see it,
though he shall die there. 14I
will scatter to every wind all
who *are* around him to help
him, and all his troops; and I
will draw out the sword after
them.

15"Then they shall know that
I *am* the LORD, when I scatter
them among the nations and
disperse them throughout the
countries. 16But I will spare
a few of their men from the
sword, from famine, and from
pestilence, that they may declare all their abominations
among the Gentiles wherever
they go. Then they shall know
that I *am* the LORD."

JUDGMENT NOT POSTPONED

17Moreover the word of
the LORD came to me, say-
ing, 18"Son of man, eat your
bread with quaking, and drink
your water with trembling and
anxiety. 19And say to the people of the land, 'Thus says the
Lord GOD to the inhabitants
of Jerusalem *and* to the land
of Israel: "They shall eat their
bread with anxiety, and drink
their water with dread, so that
her land may be emptied of
all who are in it, because of
the violence of all those who
dwell in it. 20Then the cities
that are inhabited shall be laid
waste, and the land shall become desolate; and you shall
know that I *am* the LORD."'"

21And the word of the LORD
came to me, saying, 22"Son
of man, what *is* this proverb
that you *people* have about
the land of Israel, which says,
'The days are prolonged, and
every vision fails'? 23Tell them
therefore, 'Thus says the Lord
GOD: "I will lay this proverb to
rest, and they shall no more
use it as a proverb in Israel."'
But say to them, '"The days
are at hand, and the fulfillment of every vision. 24For
no more shall there be any
false vision or flattering divination within the house of
Israel. 25For I *am* the LORD. I
speak, and the word which I
speak will come to pass; it will
no more be postponed; for in
your days, O rebellious house,
I will say the word and perform it," says the Lord GOD.'"

26Again the word of the
LORD came to me, saying,
27"Son of man, look, the house
of Israel is saying, 'The vision
that he sees *is* for many days
from now, and he prophesies
of times far off.' 28Therefore
say to them, 'Thus says the
Lord GOD: "None of My words

will be postponed any more,
but the word which I speak will
be done," says the Lord GOD.'"

WOE TO FOOLISH PROPHETS

13 And the word of the
LORD came to me, say-
ing, 2"Son of man, prophesy
against the prophets of Israel who prophesy, and say
to those who prophesy out
of their own heart, 'Hear the
word of the LORD!'"

3Thus says the Lord GOD:
"Woe to the foolish prophets,
who follow their own spirit
and have seen nothing! 4O Israel, your prophets are like
foxes in the deserts. 5You have
not gone up into the gaps to
build a wall for the house of
Israel to stand in battle on the
day of the LORD. 6They have
envisioned futility and false
divination, saying, 'Thus says
the LORD!' But the LORD has
not sent them; yet they hope
that the word may be con-
firmed. 7Have you not seen
a futile vision, and have you
not spoken false divination?
You say, 'The LORD says,' but
I have not spoken."

8Therefore thus says the
Lord GOD: "Because you have
spoken nonsense and envi-
sioned lies, therefore I *am*
indeed against you," says the
Lord GOD. 9"My hand will be
against the prophets who envision futility and who divine
lies; they shall not be in the
assembly of My people, nor
be written in the record of the
house of Israel, nor shall they
enter into the land of Israel.
Then you shall know that I *am*
the Lord GOD.

10"Because, indeed, be-
cause they have seduced
My people, saying, 'Peace!'
when *there is* no peace—and
one builds a wall, and they
plaster it with untempered
mortar— 11say to those who
plaster *it* with untempered
mortar, that it will fall. There
will be flooding rain, and you,
O great hailstones, shall fall;
and a stormy wind shall tear *it*
down. 12Surely, when the wall
has fallen, will it not be said
to you, 'Where *is* the mortar
with which you plastered *it?*'"

13Therefore thus says the
Lord GOD: "I will cause a
stormy wind to break forth
in My fury; and there shall be
a flooding rain in My anger,
and great hailstones in fury
to consume *it.* 14So I will break
down the wall you have plastered with untempered *mor-*
tar, and bring it down to the
ground, so that its foundation
will be uncovered; it will fall,
and you shall be consumed in
the midst of it. Then you shall
know that I *am* the LORD.

15"Thus will I accomplish
My wrath on the wall and on
those who have plastered it
with untempered *mortar;* and
I will say to you, 'The wall *is*
no *more,* nor those who plastered it, 16*that is,* the prophets
of Israel who prophesy con-

cerning Jerusalem, and who
see visions of peace for her
when *there is* no peace,’” says
the Lord GOD.
17“Likewise, son of man, set
your face against the daughters of your people, who
prophesy out of their own
heart; prophesy against them,
18and say, ‘Thus says the Lord
GOD: “Woe to the *women* who
sew *magic* charms on their
sleeves[a] and make veils for
the heads of people of every
height to hunt souls! Will you
hunt the souls of My people,
and keep yourselves alive?
19And will you profane Me
among My people for hand-
fuls of barley and for pieces
of bread, killing people who
should not die, and keeping
people alive who should not
live, by your lying to My people who listen to lies?”
20‘Therefore thus says
the Lord GOD: “Behold, I *am*
against your *magic* charms by
which you hunt souls there
like birds. I will tear them
from your arms, and let the
souls go, the souls you hunt
like birds. 21I will also tear
off your veils and deliver My
people out of your hand, and
they shall no longer be as prey
in your hand. Then you shall
know that I *am* the LORD.
22“Because with lies you
have made the heart of the
righteous sad, whom I have
not made sad; and you have
strengthened the hands of the
wicked, so that he does not
turn from his wicked way to
save his life. 23Therefore you
shall no longer envision futility nor practice divination; for
I will deliver My people out of
your hand, and you shall know
that I *am* the LORD.”’”

IDOLATRY WILL BE PUNISHED

14 Now some of the elders
of Israel came to me and
sat before me. 2And the word
of the LORD came to me, saying, 3“Son of man, these men
have set up their idols in their
hearts, and put before them
that which causes them to
stumble into iniquity. Should
I let Myself be inquired of at
all by them?
4“Therefore speak to them,
and say to them, ‘Thus says
the Lord GOD: “Everyone of
the house of Israel who sets up
his idols in his heart, and puts
before him what causes him
to stumble into iniquity, and
then comes to the prophet,
I the LORD will answer him
who comes, according to the
multitude of his idols, 5that I
may seize the house of Israel
by their heart, because they
are all estranged from Me by
their idols.”’
6“Therefore say to the house
of Israel, ‘Thus says the Lord

13:18 [a] Literally *over all the joints of My hands;* Vulgate reads *under every elbow;* Septuagint and Targum read *on all elbows of the hands.*

GOD: "Repent, turn away from
your idols, and turn your faces
away from all your abominations. 7For anyone of the house
of Israel, or of the strangers
who dwell in Israel, who separates himself from Me and sets
up his idols in his heart and
puts before him what causes
him to stumble into iniquity,
then comes to a prophet to inquire of him concerning Me,
I the LORD will answer him
by Myself. 8I will set My face
against that man and make
him a sign and a proverb, and I
will cut him off from the midst
of My people. Then you shall
know that I *am* the LORD.

9"And if the prophet is induced to speak anything, I
the LORD have induced that
prophet, and I will stretch
out My hand against him and
destroy him from among My
people Israel. 10And they shall
bear their iniquity; the punishment of the prophet shall
be the same as the punishment of the one who inquired,
11that the house of Israel may
no longer stray from Me, nor
be profaned anymore with all
their transgressions, but that
they may be My people and I
may be their God," says the
Lord GOD.'"

JUDGMENT ON PERSISTENT UNFAITHFULNESS

12The word of the LORD
came again to me, saying:
13"Son of man, when a land
sins against Me by persistent
unfaithfulness, I will stretch
out My hand against it; I will
cut off its supply of bread,
send famine on it, and cut off
man and beast from it. 14Even
if these three men, Noah, Daniel, and Job, were in it, they
would deliver *only* themselves
by their righteousness," says
the Lord GOD.

15"If I cause wild beasts
to pass through the land,
and they empty it, and make
it so desolate that no man
may pass through because
of the beasts, 16*even though*
these three men *were* in it,
as I live," says the Lord GOD,
"they would deliver neither
sons nor daughters; only they
would be delivered, and the
land would be desolate.

17"Or *if* I bring a sword on
that land, and say, 'Sword, go
through the land,' and I cut off
man and beast from it, 18even
though these three men *were*
in it, *as* I live," says the Lord
GOD, "they would deliver neither sons nor daughters, but
only they themselves would
be delivered.

19"Or *if* I send a pestilence
into that land and pour out My
fury on it in blood, and cut off
from it man and beast, 20even
though Noah, Daniel, and Job
were in it, *as* I live," says the
Lord GOD, "they would deliver
neither son nor daughter; they
would deliver *only* themselves
by their righteousness."

21For thus says the Lord
GOD: "How much more it shall

be when I send My four severe judgments on Jerusalem—the sword and famine and wild beasts and pestilence—to cut off man and beast from it? 22Yet behold, there shall be left in it a remnant who will be brought out, *both* sons and daughters; surely they will come out to you, and you will see their ways and their doings. Then you will be comforted concerning the disaster that I have brought upon Jerusalem, all that I have brought upon it. 23And they will comfort you, when you see their ways and their doings; and you shall know that I have done nothing without cause that I have done in it," says the Lord GOD.

THE OUTCAST VINE

15 Then the word of the LORD came to me, saying: 2"Son of man, how is the wood of the vine *better* than any other wood, the vine branch which is among the trees of the forest? 3Is wood taken from it to make any object? Or can *men* make a peg from it to hang any vessel on? 4Instead, it is thrown into the fire for fuel; the fire devours both ends of it, and its middle is burned. Is it useful for *any* work? 5Indeed, when it was whole, no object could be made from it. How much less will it be useful for *any* work when the fire has devoured it, and it is burned?

6"Therefore thus says the Lord GOD: 'Like the wood of the vine among the trees of the forest, which I have given to the fire for fuel, so I will give up the inhabitants of Jerusalem; 7and I will set My face against them. They will go out from *one* fire, but *another* fire shall devour them. Then you shall know that I *am* the LORD, when I set My face against them. 8Thus I will make the land desolate, because they have persisted in unfaithfulness,' says the Lord GOD."

GOD'S LOVE FOR JERUSALEM

16 Again the word of the LORD came to me, saying, 2"Son of man, cause Jerusalem to know her abominations, 3and say, 'Thus says the Lord GOD to Jerusalem: "Your birth and your nativity *are* from the land of Canaan; your father *was* an Amorite and your mother a Hittite. 4*As for* your nativity, on the day you were born your navel cord was not cut, nor were you washed in water to cleanse *you;* you were not rubbed with salt nor wrapped in swaddling cloths. 5No eye pitied you, to do any of these things for you, to have compassion on you; but you were thrown out into the open field, when you yourself were loathed on the day you were born.

6"And when I passed by you and saw you struggling in your own blood, I said to you in your blood, 'Live!' Yes,

I said to you in your blood,
'Live!' 7I made you thrive like
a plant in the field; and you
grew, matured, and became
very beautiful. *Your* breasts
were formed, your hair grew,
but you *were* naked and bare.
8"When I passed by you
again and looked upon you,
indeed your time *was* the
time of love; so I spread My
wing over you and covered
your nakedness. Yes, I swore
an oath to you and entered
into a covenant with you, and
you became Mine," says the
Lord GOD.
9"Then I washed you in
water; yes, I thoroughly
washed off your blood, and
I anointed you with oil. 10I
clothed you in embroidered
cloth and gave you sandals
of badger skin; I clothed you
with fine linen and covered
you with silk. 11I adorned you
with ornaments, put bracelets
on your wrists, and a chain on
your neck. 12And I put a jewel
in your nose, earrings in your
ears, and a beautiful crown on
your head. 13Thus you were
adorned with gold and silver,
and your clothing *was of* fine
linen, silk, and embroidered
cloth. You ate *pastry of* fine
flour, honey, and oil. You were
exceedingly beautiful, and succeeded to royalty. 14Your fame
went out among the nations
because of your beauty, for it
was perfect through My splendor which I had bestowed on
you," says the Lord GOD.

JERUSALEM'S HARLOTRY

15"But you trusted in your
own beauty, played the harlot because of your fame, and
poured out your harlotry on
everyone passing by who
would have it. 16You took some
of your garments and adorned
multicolored high places for
yourself, and played the harlot
on them. *Such* things should
not happen, nor be. 17You
have also taken your beautiful jewelry from My gold and
My silver, which I had given
you, and made for yourself
male images and played the
harlot with them. 18You took
your embroidered garments
and covered them, and you set
My oil and My incense before
them. 19Also My food which I
gave you—the pastry of fine
flour, oil, and honey *which*
I fed you—you set it before
them as sweet incense; and
so it was," says the Lord GOD.
20"Moreover you took
your sons and your daugh-
ters, whom you bore to Me,
and these you sacrificed to
them to be devoured. *Were*
your *acts* of harlotry a small
matter, 21that you have slain
My children and offered them
up to them by causing them
to pass through *the fire?* 22And
in all your abominations and
acts of harlotry you did not
remember the days of your
youth, when you were naked
and bare, struggling in your
blood.
23"Then it was so, after all

your wickedness—'Woe, woe
to you!' says the Lord GOD—
24*that* you also built for yourself a shrine, and made a high
place for yourself in every
street. 25You built your high
places at the head of every
road, and made your beauty to
be abhorred. You offered yourself to everyone who passed
by, and multiplied your acts of
harlotry. 26You also committed
harlotry with the Egyptians,
your very fleshly neighbors,
and increased your acts of harlotry to provoke Me to anger.
27"Behold, therefore, I
stretched out My hand against
you, diminished your allotment, and gave you up to the
will of those who hate you,
the daughters of the Philistines, who were ashamed of
your lewd behavior. 28You
also played the harlot with the
Assyrians, because you were
insatiable; indeed you played
the harlot with them and still
were not satisfied. 29Moreover
you multiplied your acts of
harlotry as far as the land of
the trader, Chaldea; and even
then you were not satisfied.
30"How degenerate is your
heart!" says the Lord GOD,
"seeing you do all these *things*,
the deeds of a brazen harlot.

JERUSALEM'S ADULTERY

31"You erected your shrine
at the head of every road, and
built your high place in every
street. Yet you were not like a
harlot, because you scorned
payment. 32*You are* an adulterous wife, *who* takes strangers instead of her husband.
33Men make payment to all
harlots, but you made your
payments to all your lovers,
and hired them to come to
you from all around for your
harlotry. 34You are the opposite of *other* women in your
harlotry, because no one solic-
ited you to be a harlot. In that
you gave payment but no payment was given you, therefore
you are the opposite."

JERUSALEM'S LOVERS WILL ABUSE HER

35'Now then, O harlot, hear
the word of the LORD! 36Thus
says the Lord GOD: "Because
your filthiness was poured
out and your nakedness
uncovered in your harlotry
with your lovers, and with all
your abominable idols, and
because of the blood of your
children which you gave to
them, 37surely, therefore, I
will gather all your lovers with
whom you took pleasure, all
those you loved, *and* all those
you hated; I will gather them
from all around against you
and will uncover your nakedness to them, that they may
see all your nakedness. 38And
I will judge you as women who
break wedlock or shed blood
are judged; I will bring blood
upon you in fury and jealousy.
39I will also give you into their
hand, and they shall throw
down your shrines and break

down your high places. They
shall also strip you of your
clothes, take your beautiful
jewelry, and leave you naked
and bare.
40“They shall also bring
up an assembly against you,
and they shall stone you with
stones and thrust you through
with their swords. 41They
shall burn your houses with
fire, and execute judgments
on you in the sight of many
women; and I will make you
cease playing the harlot, and
you shall no longer hire lovers. 42So I will lay to rest My
fury toward you, and My jealousy shall depart from you. I
will be quiet, and be angry no
more. 43Because you did not
remember the days of your
youth, but agitated Me[a] with
all these *things,* surely I will
also recompense your deeds
on *your own* head,” says the
Lord GOD. “And you shall not
commit lewdness in addition
to all your abominations.

MORE WICKED THAN SAMARIA AND SODOM

44“Indeed everyone who
quotes proverbs will use *this*
proverb against you: ‘Like
mother, like daughter!’ 45You
are your mother’s daughter,
loathing husband and children; and you *are* the sister
of your sisters, who loathed
their husbands and children;
your mother *was* a Hittite and
your father an Amorite.
46“Your elder sister *is* Samaria, who dwells with her
daughters to the north of you;
and your younger sister, who
dwells to the south of you, *is*
Sodom and her daughters.
47You did not walk in their
ways nor act according to
their abominations; but, as
if that were too little, you became more corrupt than they
in all your ways.
48“*As* I live,” says the Lord
GOD, “neither your sister
Sodom nor her daughters
have done as you and your
daughters have done. 49Look,
this was the iniquity of your
sister Sodom: She and her
daughter had pride, fullness
of food, and abundance of
idleness; neither did she
strengthen the hand of the
poor and needy. 50And they
were haughty and commit-
ted abomination before Me;
therefore I took them away
as I saw *fit.*[a]
51“Samaria did not commit
half of your sins; but you have
multiplied your abominations
more than they, and have justified your sisters by all the
abominations which you
have done. 52You who judged
your sisters, bear your own
shame also, because the sins

16:43 [a] Following Septuagint, Syriac, Targum, and Vulgate; Masoretic Text reads *were agitated with Me.* 16:50 [a] Vulgate reads *you saw;* Septuagint reads *he saw;* Targum reads *as was revealed to Me.*

which you committed were more abominable than theirs; they are more righteous than you. Yes, be disgraced also, and bear your own shame, because you justified your sisters.

53“When I bring back their captives, the captives of Sodom and her daughters, and the captives of Samaria and her daughters, then *I will also bring back* the captives of your captivity among them, 54that you may bear your own shame and be disgraced by all that you did when you comforted them. 55When your sisters, Sodom and her daughters, return to their former state, and Samaria and her daughters return to their former state, then you and your daughters will return to your former state. 56For your sister Sodom was not a byword in your mouth in the days of your pride, 57before your wickedness was uncovered. It was like the time of the reproach of the daughters of Syria[a] and all *those* around her, and of the daughters of the Philistines, who despise you everywhere. 58You have paid for your lewdness and your abominations,” says the LORD. 59For thus says the Lord GOD: “I will deal with you as you have done, who despised the oath by breaking the covenant.

AN EVERLASTING COVENANT

60“Nevertheless I will remember My covenant with you in the days of your youth, and I will establish an everlasting covenant with you. 61Then you will remember your ways and be ashamed, when you receive your older and your younger sisters; for I will give them to you for daughters, but not because of My covenant with you. 62And I will establish My covenant with you. Then you shall know that I *am* the LORD, 63that you may remember and be ashamed, and never open your mouth anymore because of your shame, when I provide you an atonement for all you have done,” says the Lord GOD.’”

THE EAGLES AND THE VINE

17 And the word of the LORD came to me, saying, 2“Son of man, pose a riddle, and speak a parable to the house of Israel, 3and say, ‘Thus says the Lord GOD:

“A great eagle with large
 wings and long pinions,
Full of feathers of
 various colors,
Came to Lebanon
And took from the cedar
 the highest branch.
4 He cropped off its
 topmost young twig

16:57 [a] Following Masoretic Text, Septuagint, Targum, and Vulgate; many Hebrew manuscripts and Syriac read *Edom*.

And carried it to a
land of trade;
He set it in a city
of merchants.
5 Then he took some of
the seed of the land
And planted it in
a fertile field;
He placed *it* by
abundant waters
And set it like a
willow tree.
6 And it grew and became
a spreading vine
of low stature;
Its branches turned
toward him,
But its roots were
under it.
So it became a vine,
Brought forth branches,
And put forth shoots.

7 "But there was another[a]
great eagle with
large wings and
many feathers;
And behold, this vine bent
its roots toward him,
And stretched its
branches toward him,
From the garden
terrace where it had
been planted,
That he might water it.
8 It was planted in good
soil by many waters,
To bring forth branches,
bear fruit,
And become a
majestic vine."'

9"Say, 'Thus says the Lord
GOD:

"Will it thrive?
Will he not pull
up its roots,
Cut off its fruit,
And leave it to wither?
All of its spring leaves
will wither,
And no great power
or many people
Will be needed to pluck
it up by its roots.
10 Behold, *it is* planted,
Will it thrive?
Will it not utterly
wither when the east
wind touches it?
It will wither in the garden
terrace where it grew."'"

11Moreover the word of the
LORD came to me, saying,
12"Say now to the rebellious
house: 'Do you not know what
these *things mean?*' Tell *them,*
'Indeed the king of Babylon
went to Jerusalem and took
its king and princes, and led
them with him to Babylon.
13And he took the king's offspring, made a covenant with
him, and put him under oath.
He also took away the mighty
of the land, 14that the kingdom
might be brought low and not
lift itself up, *but* that by keeping
his covenant it might stand.
15But he rebelled against him
by sending his ambassadors

17:7 [a] Following Septuagint, Syriac, and Vulgate; Masoretic Text and Targum read *one*.

to Egypt, that they might give
him horses and many people.
Will he prosper? Will he who
does such *things* escape? Can
he break a covenant and still
be delivered?
16'*As* I live,' says the Lord
GOD, 'surely in the place *where*
the king *dwells* who made
him king, whose oath he despised and whose covenant he
broke—with him in the midst
of Babylon he shall die. 17Nor
will Pharaoh with *his* mighty
army and great company do
anything in the war, when
they heap up a siege mound
and build a wall to cut off
many persons. 18Since he despised the oath by breaking
the covenant, and in fact gave
his hand and still did all these
things, he shall not escape.'"
19Therefore thus says the
Lord GOD: "*As* I live, surely
My oath which he despised,
and My covenant which he
broke, I will recompense on
his own head. 20I will spread
My net over him, and he shall
be taken in My snare. I will
bring him to Babylon and
try him there for the treason
which he committed against
Me. 21All his fugitives[a] with
all his troops shall fall by the
sword, and those who remain
shall be scattered to every
wind; and you shall know that
I, the LORD, have spoken."

ISRAEL EXALTED AT LAST

22Thus says the Lord GOD:
"I will take also *one* of the
highest branches of the high
cedar and set *it* out. I will
crop off from the topmost of
its young twigs a tender one,
and will plant *it* on a high and
prominent mountain. 23On
the mountain height of Israel
I will plant it; and it will bring
forth boughs, and bear fruit,
and be a majestic cedar. Under
it will dwell birds of every sort;
in the shadow of its branches
they will dwell. 24And all the
trees of the field shall know
that I, the LORD, have brought
down the high tree and exalted the low tree, dried up the
green tree and made the dry
tree flourish; I, the LORD, have
spoken and have done *it.*"

A FALSE PROVERB REFUTED

18 The word of the LORD
came to me again, say-
ing, 2"What do you mean
when you use this proverb
concerning the land of Israel,
saying:

'The fathers have
eaten sour grapes,
And the children's teeth
are set on edge'?

3"*As* I live," says the Lord
GOD, "you shall no longer use
this proverb in Israel.

17:21 [a] Following Masoretic Text and Vulgate; many Hebrew manuscripts and Syriac read *choice men;* Targum reads *mighty men;* Septuagint omits *All his fugitives.*

4 "Behold, all souls
are Mine;
The soul of the father
As well as the soul of
the son is Mine;
The soul who sins
shall die.
5 But if a man is just
And does what is
lawful and right;
6 If he has not eaten on
the mountains,
Nor lifted up his eyes
to the idols of the
house of Israel,
Nor defiled his
neighbor's wife,
Nor approached a woman
during her impurity;
7 If he has not oppressed
anyone,
But has restored to the
debtor his pledge;
Has robbed no one
by violence,
But has given his bread
to the hungry
And covered the naked
with clothing;
8 If he has not
exacted usury
Nor taken any increase,
But has withdrawn his
hand from iniquity
And executed true
judgment between
man and man;
9 *If* he has walked in
My statutes
And kept My judgments
faithfully—
He *is* just;
He shall surely live!"
Says the Lord GOD.

10 "If he begets a son
who is a robber
Or a shedder of blood,
Who does any of
these *things*
11 And does none of
those *duties,*
But has eaten on
the mountains
Or defiled his
neighbor's wife;
12 If he has oppressed the
poor and needy,
Robbed by violence,
Not restored the pledge,
Lifted his eyes to the idols,
Or committed
abomination;
13 If he has exacted usury
Or taken increase—
Shall he then live?
He shall not live!
If he has done any of
these abominations,
He shall surely die;
His blood shall be
upon him.

14 "*If,* however, he
begets a son
Who sees all the
sins which his
father has done,
And considers but does
not do likewise;
15 *Who* has not eaten on
the mountains,
Nor lifted his eyes
to the idols of the
house of Israel,
Nor defiled his
neighbor's wife;
16 Has not oppressed
anyone,

Nor withheld a pledge,
Nor robbed by violence,
But has given his bread
to the hungry
And covered the naked
with clothing;
17 *Who* has withdrawn his
hand from the poor[a]
And not received
usury or increase,
But has executed
My judgments
And walked in My
statutes—
He shall not die for the
iniquity of his father;
He shall surely live!

18 "*As for* his father,
Because he cruelly
oppressed,
Robbed his brother
by violence,
And did what *is* not good
among his people,
Behold, he shall die
for his iniquity.

TURN AND LIVE

19"Yet you say, 'Why should
the son not bear the guilt of
the father?' Because the son
has done what is lawful and
right, and has kept all My statutes and observed them, he
shall surely live. 20The soul
who sins shall die. The son
shall not bear the guilt of the
father, nor the father bear
the guilt of the son. The righteousness of the righteous
shall be upon himself, and
the wickedness of the wicked
shall be upon himself.
21"But if a wicked man
turns from all his sins which
he has committed, keeps all
My statutes, and does what
is lawful and right, he shall
surely live; he shall not die.
22None of the transgressions
which he has committed shall
be remembered against him;
because of the righteousness
which he has done, he shall
live. 23Do I have any pleasure
at all that the wicked should
die?" says the Lord GOD, "*and*
not that he should turn from
his ways and live?
24"But when a righteous
man turns away from his
righteousness and commits
iniquity, and does according
to all the abominations that
the wicked *man* does, shall
he live? All the righteousness
which he has done shall not
be remembered; because of
the unfaithfulness of which
he is guilty and the sin which
he has committed, because of
them he shall die.
25"Yet you say, 'The way
of the Lord is not fair.' Hear
now, O house of Israel, is it
not My way which is fair, and
your ways which are not fair?
26When a righteous *man* turns
away from his righteousness,
commits iniquity, and dies in
it, it is because of the iniquity

18:17 [a] Following Masoretic Text, Targum, and Vulgate; Septuagint reads *iniquity* (compare verse 8).

which he has done that he dies.
27 Again, when a wicked *man*
turns away from the wickedness which he committed, and
does what is lawful and right,
he preserves himself alive.
28 Because he considers and
turns away from all the transgressions which he committed,
he shall surely live; he shall not
die. 29 Yet the house of Israel
says, 'The way of the Lord is
not fair.' O house of Israel, is it
not My ways which are fair, and
your ways which are not fair?
30 "Therefore I will judge
you, O house of Israel, every
one according to his ways,"
says the Lord GOD. "Repent,
and turn from all your transgressions, so that iniquity will
not be your ruin. 31 Cast away
from you all the transgressions which you have committed, and get yourselves a new
heart and a new spirit. For why
should you die, O house of Israel? 32 For I have no pleasure
in the death of one who dies,"
says the Lord GOD. "Therefore
turn and live!"

ISRAEL DEGRADED

19 "Moreover take up a
lamentation for the
princes of Israel, 2 and say:

'What *is* your
mother? A lioness:
She lay down among
the lions;
Among the young lions
she nourished her cubs.
3 She brought up one
of her cubs,
And he became a
young lion;
He learned to catch prey,
And he devoured men.
4 The nations also
heard of him;
He was trapped
in their pit,
And they brought him
with chains to the
land of Egypt.

5 'When she saw that
she waited, *that* her
hope was lost,
She took another of
her cubs *and* made
him a young lion.
6 He roved among the lions,
And became a young lion;
He learned to catch prey;
He devoured men.
7 He knew their
desolate places,[a]
And laid waste
their cities;
The land with its fullness
was desolated
By the noise of
his roaring.
8 Then the nations set
against him from the
provinces on every side,
And spread their
net over him;
He was trapped
in their pit.

19:7 [a] Septuagint reads *He stood in insolence;* Targum reads *He destroyed its palaces;* Vulgate reads *He learned to make widows.*

9 They put him in a
cage with chains,
And brought him to
the king of Babylon;
They brought him in nets,
That his voice should no
longer be heard on the
mountains of Israel.

10 'Your mother *was* like a
vine in your bloodline,[a]
Planted by the waters,
Fruitful and full
of branches
Because of many waters.
11 She had strong branches
for scepters of rulers.
She towered in
stature above the
thick branches,
And was seen in her height
amid the dense foliage.
12 But she was plucked
up in fury,
She was cast down
to the ground,
And the east wind
dried her fruit.
Her strong branches were
broken and withered;
The fire consumed them.
13 And now she *is* planted
in the wilderness,
In a dry and thirsty land.
14 Fire has come out from
a rod of her branches
And devoured her fruit,
So that she has no
strong branch—a
scepter for ruling.'"

This *is* a lamentation, and has become a lamentation.

THE REBELLIONS OF ISRAEL

20 It came to pass in the
seventh year, in the
fifth *month,* on the tenth *day*
of the month, *that* certain of
the elders of Israel came to
inquire of the LORD, and sat
before me. 2Then the word
of the LORD came to me, saying, 3"Son of man, speak to
the elders of Israel, and say
to them, 'Thus says the Lord
GOD: "Have you come to inquire of Me? *As* I live," says
the Lord GOD, "I will not be
inquired of by you."' 4Will you
judge them, son of man, will
you judge *them?* Then make
known to them the abominations of their fathers.
5"Say to them, 'Thus says
the Lord GOD: "On the day
when I chose Israel and raised
My hand in an oath to the descendants of the house of Jacob, and made Myself known
to them in the land of Egypt,
I raised My hand in an oath
to them, saying, 'I *am* the
LORD your God.' 6On that day
I raised My hand in an oath
to them, to bring them out of
the land of Egypt into a land
that I had searched out for
them, 'flowing with milk and
honey,'[a] the glory of all lands.
7Then I said to them, 'Each of

19:10 [a] Literally *blood,* following Masoretic Text, Syriac, and Vulgate; Septuagint reads *like a flower on a pomegranate tree;* Targum reads *in your likeness.* 20:6 [a] Exodus 3:8

you, throw away the abominations which are before his eyes, and do not defile yourselves with the idols of Egypt. I *am* the LORD your God.' 8But they rebelled against Me and would not obey Me. They did not all cast away the abominations which were before their eyes, nor did they forsake the idols of Egypt. Then I said, 'I will pour out My fury on them and fulfill My anger against them in the midst of the land of Egypt.' 9But I acted for My name's sake, that it should not be profaned before the Gentiles among whom they *were,* in whose sight I had made Myself known to them, to bring them out of the land of Egypt.

10"Therefore I made them go out of the land of Egypt and brought them into the wilderness. 11And I gave them My statutes and showed them My judgments, 'which, *if* a man does, he shall live by them.'[a] 12Moreover I also gave them My Sabbaths, to be a sign between them and Me, that they might know that I *am* the LORD who sanctifies them. 13Yet the house of Israel rebelled against Me in the wilderness; they did not walk in My statutes; they despised My judgments, 'which, *if* a man does, he shall live by them';[a] and they greatly defiled My Sabbaths. Then I said I would pour out My fury on them in the wilderness, to consume them. 14But I acted for My name's sake, that it should not be profaned before the Gentiles, in whose sight I had brought them out. 15So I also raised My hand in an oath to them in the wilderness, that I would not bring them into the land which I had given *them,* 'flowing with milk and honey,'[a] the glory of all lands, 16because they despised My judgments and did not walk in My statutes, but profaned My Sabbaths; for their heart went after their idols. 17Nevertheless My eye spared them from destruction. I did not make an end of them in the wilderness.

18"But I said to their children in the wilderness, 'Do not walk in the statutes of your fathers, nor observe their judgments, nor defile yourselves with their idols. 19I *am* the LORD your God: Walk in My statutes, keep My judgments, and do them; 20hallow My Sabbaths, and they will be a sign between Me and you, that you may know that I *am* the LORD your God.'

21"Notwithstanding, the children rebelled against Me; they did not walk in My statutes, and were not careful to observe My judgments, 'which, *if* a man does, he shall live by them';[a] but they pro-

20:11 [a] Leviticus 18:5 20:13 [a] Leviticus 18:5
20:15 [a] Exodus 3:8 20:21 [a] Leviticus 18:5

faned My Sabbaths. Then I
said I would pour out My fury
on them and fulfill My anger
against them in the wilderness. 22Nevertheless I withdrew My hand and acted for
My name's sake, that it should
not be profaned in the sight of
the Gentiles, in whose sight I
had brought them out. 23Also
I raised My hand in an oath to
those in the wilderness, that
I would scatter them among
the Gentiles and disperse
them throughout the coun-
tries, 24because they had not
executed My judgments, but
had despised My statutes,
profaned My Sabbaths, and
their eyes were fixed on their
fathers' idols.

25"Therefore I also gave
them up to statutes *that were*
not good, and judgments by
which they could not live;
26and I pronounced them
unclean because of their ritual gifts, in that they caused
all their firstborn to pass
through *the fire,* that I might
make them desolate and that
they might know that I am the
LORD."'

27"Therefore, son of man,
speak to the house of Israel,
and say to them, 'Thus says
the Lord GOD: "In this too
your fathers have blasphemed
Me, by being unfaithful to Me.
28When I brought them into
the land *concerning* which
I had raised My hand in an
oath to give them, and they
saw all the high hills and all
the thick trees, there they offered their sacrifices and provoked Me with their offerings.
There they also sent up their
sweet aroma and poured out
their drink offerings. 29Then
I said to them, 'What *is* this
high place to which you go?'
So its name is called Bamah[a]
to this day."' 30Therefore say
to the house of Israel, 'Thus
says the Lord GOD: "Are you
defiling yourselves in the
manner of your fathers, and
committing harlotry according to their abominations?
31For when you offer your
gifts and make your sons pass
through the fire, you defile
yourselves with all your idols,
even to this day. So shall I be
inquired of by you, O house of
Israel? *As* I live," says the Lord
GOD, "I will not be inquired
of by you. 32What you have
in your mind shall never be,
when you say, 'We will be like
the Gentiles, like the families
in other countries, serving
wood and stone.'

GOD WILL RESTORE ISRAEL

33"*As* I live," says the Lord
GOD, "surely with a mighty
hand, with an outstretched
arm, and with fury poured
out, I will rule over you. 34I
will bring you out from the
peoples and gather you out of
the countries where you are

20:29 [a] Literally *High Place*

scattered, with a mighty hand,
with an outstretched arm, and
with fury poured out. 35And
I will bring you into the wilderness of the peoples, and
there I will plead My case with
you face to face. 36Just as I
pleaded My case with your fathers in the wilderness of the
land of Egypt, so I will plead
My case with you," says the
Lord GOD.
37"I will make you pass
under the rod, and I will bring
you into the bond of the covenant; 38I will purge the rebels
from among you, and those
who transgress against Me;
I will bring them out of the
country where they dwell, but
they shall not enter the land
of Israel. Then you will know
that I *am* the LORD.
39"As for you, O house of Israel," thus says the Lord GOD:
"Go, serve every one of you his
idols—and hereafter—if you
will not obey Me; but profane
My holy name no more with
your gifts and your idols. 40For
on My holy mountain, on the
mountain height of Israel,"
says the Lord GOD, "there all
the house of Israel, all of them
in the land, shall serve Me;
there I will accept them, and
there I will require your offerings and the firstfruits of
your sacrifices, together with
all your holy things. 41I will
accept you as a sweet aroma
when I bring you out from the
peoples and gather you out
of the countries where you
have been scattered; and I
will be hallowed in you before the Gentiles. 42Then you
shall know that I *am* the LORD,
when I bring you into the land
of Israel, into the country *for*
which I raised My hand in an
oath to give to your fathers.
43And there you shall remember your ways and all your
doings with which you were
defiled; and you shall loathe
yourselves in your own sight
because of all the evils that
you have committed. 44Then
you shall know that I *am* the
LORD, when I have dealt with
you for My name's sake, not
according to your wicked ways
nor according to your corrupt
doings, O house of Israel,"
says the Lord GOD.'"

FIRE IN THE FOREST

45Furthermore the word
of the LORD came to me, saying, 46"Son of man, set your
face toward the south; preach
against the south and prophesy against the forest land, the
South,[a] 47and say to the forest
of the South, 'Hear the word of
the LORD! Thus says the Lord
GOD: "Behold, I will kindle a
fire in you, and it shall devour
every green tree and every dry
tree in you; the blazing flame
shall not be quenched, and all
faces from the south to the
north shall be scorched by it.

20:46 [a] Hebrew *Negev*

[48]All flesh shall see that I, the
LORD, have kindled it; it shall
not be quenched."'"
[49]Then I said, "Ah, Lord
GOD! They say of me, 'Does
he not speak parables?'"

BABYLON, THE SWORD OF GOD

21 And the word of the
LORD came to me, say-
ing, [2]"Son of man, set your
face toward Jerusalem, preach
against the holy places, and
prophesy against the land of
Israel; [3]and say to the land of
Israel, 'Thus says the LORD:
"Behold, I *am* against you, and
I will draw My sword out of its
sheath and cut off both righteous and wicked from you.
[4]Because I will cut off both
righteous and wicked from
you, therefore My sword shall
go out of its sheath against
all flesh from south *to* north,
[5]that all flesh may know that
I, the LORD, have drawn My
sword out of its sheath; it shall
not return anymore."' [6]Sigh
therefore, son of man, with
a breaking heart, and sigh
with bitterness before their
eyes. [7]And it shall be when
they say to you, 'Why are you
sighing?' that you shall answer, 'Because of the news;
when it comes, every heart
will melt, all hands will be feeble, every spirit will faint, and
all knees will be weak *as* water.
Behold, it is coming and shall
be brought to pass,' says the
Lord GOD."

[8]Again the word of the
LORD came to me, saying,
[9]"Son of man, prophesy and
say, 'Thus says the LORD!' Say:

'A sword, a sword
is sharpened
And also polished!
[10] Sharpened to make a
dreadful slaughter,
Polished to flash
like lightning!
Should we then
make mirth?
It despises the scepter
of My son,
As it does all wood.
[11] And He has given it
to be polished,
That it may be handled;
This sword is sharpened,
and it is polished
To be given into the
hand of the slayer.'

[12]"Cry and wail, son of man;
For it will be against
My people,
Against all the
princes of Israel.
Terrors including
the sword will be
against My people;
Therefore strike
your thigh.

[13]"Because *it is* a testing,
And what if *the sword*
despises even
the scepter?
The scepter shall
be no *more*,"

says the Lord GOD.

14 "You therefore, son
of man, prophesy,
And strike *your*
hands together.
The third time let
the sword do
double *damage.*
It *is* the sword *that* slays,
The sword that slays
the great *men,*
That enters their
private chambers.
15 I have set the point of
the sword against
all their gates,
That the heart may melt
and many may stumble.
Ah! *It is* made bright;
It is grasped for slaughter:

16 "Swords at the ready!
Thrust right!
Set your blade!
Thrust left—
Wherever your edge
is ordered!

17 "I also will beat My
fists together,
And I will cause My
fury to rest;
I, the LORD, have spoken."

18 The word of the LORD
came to me again, saying:
19 "And son of man, appoint
for yourself two ways for the
sword of the king of Babylon to
go; both of them shall go from
the same land. Make a sign;
put *it* at the head of the road
to the city. 20 Appoint a road for
the sword to go to Rabbah of
the Ammonites, and to Judah,
into fortified Jerusalem. 21 For
the king of Babylon stands at
the parting of the road, at the
fork of the two roads, to use
divination: he shakes the arrows, he consults the images,
he looks at the liver. 22 In his
right hand is the divination for
Jerusalem: to set up battering
rams, to call for a slaughter,
to lift the voice with shouting,
to set battering rams against
the gates, to heap up a *siege*
mound, and to build a wall.
23 And it will be to them like a
false divination in the eyes of
those who have sworn oaths
with them; but he will bring
their iniquity to remembrance,
that they may be taken.

24 "Therefore thus says the
Lord GOD: 'Because you have
made your iniquity to be remembered, in that your transgressions are uncovered, so
that in all your doings your
sins appear—because you
have come to remembrance,
you shall be taken in hand.

25 'Now to you, O profane,
wicked prince of Israel, whose
day has come, whose iniquity
shall end, 26 thus says the Lord
GOD:

"Remove the turban, and
take off the crown;
Nothing *shall remain*
the same.
Exalt the humble, and
humble the exalted.
27 Overthrown, overthrown,
I will make it overthrown!
It shall be no *longer,*

Until He comes
whose right it is,
And I will give it *to Him*."'

A SWORD AGAINST THE AMMONITES

28"And you, son of man,
prophesy and say, 'Thus says
the Lord GOD concerning the
Ammonites and concerning
their reproach,' and say:

'A sword, a sword *is* drawn,
Polished for slaughter,
For consuming,
for flashing—
29 While they see false
visions for you,
While they divine
a lie to you,
To bring you on the necks
of the wicked, the slain
Whose day has come,
Whose iniquity *shall* end.

30 'Return *it* to its sheath.
I will judge you
In the place where
you were created,
In the land of your
nativity.
31 I will pour out My
indignation on you;
I will blow against
you with the fire
of My wrath,
And deliver you
into the hands of
brutal men *who are*
skillful to destroy.
32 You shall be fuel
for the fire;
Your blood shall be in
the midst of the land.
You shall not be
remembered,
For I the LORD
have spoken.'"

SINS OF JERUSALEM

22 Moreover the word of
the LORD came to me,
saying, 2"Now, son of man,
will you judge, will you judge
the bloody city? Yes, show her
all her abominations! 3Then
say, 'Thus says the Lord GOD:
"The city sheds blood in her
own midst, that her time may
come; and she makes idols
within herself to defile herself. 4You have become guilty
by the blood which you have
shed, and have defiled yourself with the idols which you
have made. You have caused
your days to draw near, and
have come to *the end of* your
years; therefore I have made
you a reproach to the nations,
and a mockery to all countries. 5*Those* near and *those*
far from you will mock you as
infamous *and* full of tumult.
6"Look, the princes of Israel:
each one has used his power
to shed blood in you. 7In you
they have made light of father
and mother; in your midst they
have oppressed the stranger;
in you they have mistreated
the fatherless and the widow.
8You have despised My holy
things and profaned My Sabbaths. 9In you are men who
slander to cause bloodshed;
in you are those who eat on
the mountains; in your midst

they commit lewdness. 10In you men uncover their fathers' nakedness; in you they violate women who are set apart during their impurity. 11One commits abomination with his neighbor's wife; another lewdly defiles his daughter-in-law; and another in you violates his sister, his father's daughter. 12In you they take bribes to shed blood; you take usury and increase; you have made profit from your neighbors by extortion, and have forgotten Me," says the Lord GOD.

13"Behold, therefore, I beat My fists at the dishonest profit which you have made, and at the bloodshed which has been in your midst. 14Can your heart endure, or can your hands remain strong, in the days when I shall deal with you? I, the LORD, have spoken, and will do *it.* 15I will scatter you among the nations, disperse you throughout the countries, and remove your filthiness completely from you. 16You shall defile yourself in the sight of the nations; then you shall know that I *am* the LORD."'"

ISRAEL IN THE FURNACE

17The word of the LORD came to me, saying, 18"Son of man, the house of Israel has become dross to Me; they *are* all bronze, tin, iron, and lead, in the midst of a furnace; they have become dross from silver. 19Therefore thus says the Lord GOD: 'Because you have all become dross, therefore behold, I will gather you into the midst of Jerusalem. 20*As men* gather silver, bronze, iron, lead, and tin into the midst of a furnace, to blow fire on it, to melt *it;* so I will gather *you* in My anger and in My fury, and I will leave *you there* and melt you. 21Yes, I will gather you and blow on you with the fire of My wrath, and you shall be melted in its midst. 22As silver is melted in the midst of a furnace, so shall you be melted in its midst; then you shall know that I, the LORD, have poured out My fury on you.'"

ISRAEL'S WICKED LEADERS

23And the word of the LORD came to me, saying, 24"Son of man, say to her: 'You *are* a land that is not cleansed[a] or rained on in the day of indignation.' 25The conspiracy of her prophets[a] in her midst is like a roaring lion tearing the prey; they have devoured people; they have taken treasure and precious things; they have made many widows in her midst. 26Her priests have violated My law and profaned My holy things; they have not distin-

22:24 [a] Following Masoretic Text, Syriac, and Vulgate; Septuagint reads *showered upon.* 22:25 [a] Following Masoretic Text and Vulgate; Septuagint reads *princes;* Targum reads *scribes.*

guished between the holy and
unholy, nor have they made
known *the difference* between
the unclean and the clean; and
they have hidden their eyes
from My Sabbaths, so that I
am profaned among them.
27Her princes in her midst *are*
like wolves tearing the prey,
to shed blood, to destroy people, and to get dishonest gain.
28Her prophets plastered them
with untempered *mortar*, seeing false visions, and divining
lies for them, saying, 'Thus says
the Lord GOD,' when the LORD
had not spoken. 29The people
of the land have used oppressions, committed robbery,
and mistreated the poor and
needy; and they wrongfully
oppress the stranger. 30So I
sought for a man among them
who would make a wall, and
stand in the gap before Me on
behalf of the land, that I should
not destroy it; but I found no
one. 31Therefore I have poured
out My indignation on them; I
have consumed them with the
fire of My wrath; and I have
recompensed their deeds on
their own heads," says the Lord
GOD.

TWO HARLOT SISTERS

23 The word of the LORD came again to me, saying:

2 "Son of man, there
were two women,
The daughters of
one mother.
3 They committed
harlotry in Egypt,
They committed harlotry
in their youth;
Their breasts were
there embraced,
Their virgin bosom
was there pressed.
4 Their names: Oholah[a]
the elder and
Oholibah[b] her sister;
They were Mine,
And they bore sons
and daughters.
As for their names,
Samaria *is* Oholah, and
Jerusalem *is* Oholibah.

THE OLDER SISTER, SAMARIA

5 "Oholah played the
harlot even though
she was Mine;
And she lusted for her
lovers, the neighboring
Assyrians,
6 *Who were* clothed
in purple,
Captains and rulers,
All of them desirable
young men,
Horsemen riding
on horses.
7 Thus she committed
her harlotry with
them,
All of them choice
men of Assyria;
And with all for
whom she lusted,

23:4 [a] Literally *Her Own Tabernacle* [b] Literally *My Tabernacle Is in Her*

With all their idols,
she defiled herself.
8 She has never given
up her harlotry
brought from Egypt,
For in her youth they
had lain with her,
Pressed her virgin bosom,
And poured out their
immorality upon her.

9 "Therefore I have
delivered her
Into the hand of
her lovers,
Into the hand of
the Assyrians,
For whom she lusted.
10 They uncovered her
nakedness,
Took away her sons
and daughters,
And slew her with
the sword;
She became a byword
among women,
For they had executed
judgment on her.

THE YOUNGER SISTER, JERUSALEM

11 "Now although her sister
Oholibah saw *this,* she became
more corrupt in her lust than
she, and in her harlotry more
corrupt than her sister's harlotry.

12 "She lusted for the
neighboring Assyrians,
Captains and rulers,
Clothed most gorgeously,
Horsemen riding
on horses,
All of them desirable
young men.
13 Then I saw that she
was defiled;
Both *took* the same way.
14 But she increased
her harlotry;
She looked at men
portrayed on the wall,
Images of Chaldeans
portrayed in vermilion,
15 Girded with belts
around their waists,
Flowing turbans on
their heads,
All of them looking
like captains,
In the manner of the
Babylonians of Chaldea,
The land of their nativity.
16 As soon as her eyes
saw them,
She lusted for them
And sent messengers
to them in Chaldea.

17 "Then the Babylonians
came to her, into
the bed of love,
And they defiled her with
their immorality;
So she was defiled by
them, and alienated
herself from them.
18 She revealed her harlotry
and uncovered
her nakedness.
Then I alienated
Myself from her,
As I had alienated Myself
from her sister.

19 "Yet she multiplied
her harlotry

In calling to
remembrance the
days of her youth,
When she had played
the harlot in the
land of Egypt.
20 For she lusted for
her paramours,
Whose flesh *is like* the
flesh of donkeys,
And whose issue *is like*
the issue of horses.
21 Thus you called to
remembrance the
lewdness of your
youth,
When the Egyptians
pressed your bosom
Because of your
youthful breasts.

JUDGMENT ON JERUSALEM

22"Therefore, Oholibah,
thus says the Lord GOD:

'Behold, I will stir up your
lovers against you,
From whom you have
alienated yourself,
And I will bring
them against you
from every side:
23 The Babylonians,
All the Chaldeans,
Pekod, Shoa, Koa,
All the Assyrians
with them,
All of them desirable
young men,
Governors and rulers,
Captains and men
of renown,
All of them riding
on horses.
24 And they shall come
against you
With chariots, wagons,
and war-horses,
With a horde of people.
They shall array
against you
Buckler, shield, and
helmet all around.

'I will delegate
judgment to them,
And they shall judge
you according to
their judgments.
25 I will set My jealousy
against you,
And they shall deal
furiously with you;
They shall remove your
nose and your ears,
And your remnant shall
fall by the sword;
They shall take your sons
and your daughters,
And your remnant shall
be devoured by fire.
26 They shall also strip
you of your clothes
And take away your
beautiful jewelry.

27 'Thus I will make you
cease your lewdness
and your harlotry
Brought from the
land of Egypt,
So that you will not lift
your eyes to them,
Nor remember Egypt
anymore.'

28"For thus says the Lord
GOD: 'Surely I will deliver you

into the hand of those you
hate, into the hand *of those*
from whom you alienated
yourself. 29They will deal hate-
fully with you, take away all
you have worked for, and leave
you naked and bare. The nakedness of your harlotry shall
be uncovered, both your lewdness and your harlotry. 30I will
do these *things* to you because
you have gone as a harlot after
the Gentiles, because you have
become defiled by their idols.
31You have walked in the way
of your sister; therefore I will
put her cup in your hand.'
32"Thus says the Lord GOD:

'You shall drink of
your sister's cup,
The deep and wide one;
You shall be laughed
to scorn
And held in derision;
It contains much.
33 You will be filled
with drunkenness
and sorrow,
The cup of horror
and desolation,
The cup of your
sister Samaria.
34 You shall drink
and drain it,
You shall break its
shards,
And tear at your
own breasts;
For I *have spoken,'*
Says the Lord GOD.

35"Therefore thus says the
Lord GOD:

'Because you have
forgotten Me and cast
Me behind your back,
Therefore you shall
bear the *penalty*
Of your lewdness and
your harlotry.'"

BOTH SISTERS JUDGED

36The LORD also said to me:
"Son of man, will you judge
Oholah and Oholibah? Then
declare to them their abominations. 37For they have committed adultery, and blood *is*
on their hands. They have
committed adultery with their
idols, and even *sacrificed* their
sons whom they bore to Me,
passing them through *the*
fire, to devour *them.* 38More-
over they have done this to
Me: They have defiled My
sanctuary on the same day
and profaned My Sabbaths.
39For after they had slain their
children for their idols, on the
same day they came into My
sanctuary to profane it; and
indeed thus they have done
in the midst of My house.

40"Furthermore you sent
for men to come from afar,
to whom a messenger *was*
sent; and there they came.
And you washed yourself for
them, painted your eyes, and
adorned yourself with ornaments. 41You sat on a stately
couch, with a table prepared
before it, on which you had set
My incense and My oil. 42The
sound of a carefree multitude
was with her, and Sabeans

were brought from the wilderness with men of the common sort, who put bracelets
on their wrists and beautiful
crowns on their heads. 43Then
I said concerning *her who had*
grown old in adulteries, 'Will
they commit harlotry with her
now, and she *with them?*' 44Yet
they went in to her, as men
go in to a woman who plays
the harlot; thus they went in
to Oholah and Oholibah, the
lewd women. 45But righteous
men will judge them after the
manner of adulteresses, and
after the manner of women
who shed blood, because they
are adulteresses, and blood *is*
on their hands.

46"For thus says the Lord
GOD: 'Bring up an assembly
against them, give them up to
trouble and plunder. 47The assembly shall stone them with
stones and execute them with
their swords; they shall slay
their sons and their daughters, and burn their houses
with fire. 48Thus I will cause
lewdness to cease from the
land, that all women may be
taught not to practice your
lewdness. 49They shall repay
you for your lewdness, and
you shall pay for your idolatrous sins. Then you shall
know that I *am* the Lord GOD.'"

SYMBOL OF THE COOKING POT

24 Again, in the ninth year,
in the tenth month, on
the tenth *day* of the month,
the word of the LORD came to
me, saying, 2"Son of man, write
down the name of the day, this
very day—the king of Babylon
started his siege against Jerusalem this very day. 3And utter
a parable to the rebellious
house, and say to them, 'Thus
says the Lord GOD:

"Put on a pot, set *it* on,
And also pour
water into it.
4 Gather pieces *of meat* in it,
Every good piece,
The thigh and the
shoulder.
Fill *it* with choice cuts;
5 Take the choice
of the flock.
Also pile *fuel* bones
under it,
Make it boil well,
And let the cuts
simmer in it."

6'Therefore thus says the
Lord GOD:

"Woe to the bloody city,
To the pot whose
scum *is* in it,
And whose scum is
not gone from it!
Bring it out piece
by piece,
On which no lot
has fallen.
7 For her blood is in
her midst;
She set it on top of a rock;
She did not pour it
on the ground,
To cover it with dust.

8 That it may raise up fury
and take vengeance,
I have set her blood
on top of a rock,
That it may not
be covered."

9'Therefore thus says the
Lord GOD:

"Woe to the bloody city!
I too will make the
pyre great.
10 Heap on the wood,
Kindle the fire;
Cook the meat well,
Mix in the spices,
And let the cuts be
burned up.

11 "Then set the pot
empty on the coals,
That it may become
hot and its bronze
may burn,
That its filthiness may
be melted in it,
That its scum may
be consumed.
12 She has grown
weary with lies,
And her great scum has
not gone from her.
Let her scum *be* in the fire!
13 In your filthiness
is lewdness.
Because I have cleansed
you, and you were
not cleansed,
You will not be
cleansed of your
filthiness anymore,
Till I have caused My
fury to rest upon you.
14 I, the LORD, have
spoken *it;*
It shall come to pass,
and I will do *it;*
I will not hold back,
Nor will I spare,
Nor will I relent;
According to your ways
And according to
your deeds
They[a] will judge you,"
Says the Lord GOD.'"

THE PROPHET'S WIFE DIES

15Also the word of the LORD
came to me, saying, 16"Son
of man, behold, I take away
from you the desire of your
eyes with one stroke; yet you
shall neither mourn nor weep,
nor shall your tears run down.
17Sigh in silence, make no
mourning for the dead; bind
your turban on your head, and
put your sandals on your feet;
do not cover *your* lips, and do
not eat man's bread *of sorrow.*"
18So I spoke to the people
in the morning, and at evening my wife died; and the
next morning I did as I was
commanded.
19And the people said to
me, "Will you not tell us what
these *things signify* to us, that
you behave so?"
20Then I answered them,
"The word of the LORD came
to me, saying, 21'Speak to the
house of Israel, "Thus says the

24:14 [a] Septuagint, Syriac, Targum, and Vulgate read *I.*

Lord GOD: 'Behold, I will profane My sanctuary, your arrogant boast, the desire of your
eyes, the delight of your soul;
and your sons and daughters
whom you left behind shall
fall by the sword. 22And you
shall do as I have done; you
shall not cover *your* lips nor
eat man's bread *of sorrow.*
23Your turbans shall be on
your heads and your sandals
on your feet; you shall neither
mourn nor weep, but you shall
pine away in your iniquities
and mourn with one another.
24Thus Ezekiel is a sign to you;
according to all that he has
done you shall do; and when
this comes, you shall know
that I *am* the Lord GOD.'"

25'And you, son of man—
will it not *be* in the day when
I take from them their stronghold, their joy and their glory,
the desire of their eyes, and
that on which they set their
minds, their sons and their
daughters: 26*that* on that day
one who escapes will come
to you to let *you* hear *it* with
your ears? 27On that day
your mouth will be opened
to him who has escaped; you
shall speak and no longer be
mute. Thus you will be a sign
to them, and they shall know
that I *am* the LORD.'"

PROCLAMATION AGAINST AMMON

25 The word of the LORD
came to me, saying,
2"Son of man, set your face
against the Ammonites, and
prophesy against them. 3Say
to the Ammonites, 'Hear the
word of the Lord GOD! Thus
says the Lord GOD: "Because
you said, 'Aha!' against My
sanctuary when it was profaned, and against the land
of Israel when it was desolate, and against the house of
Judah when they went into
captivity, 4indeed, therefore,
I will deliver you as a possession to the men of the East,
and they shall set their en-
campments among you and
make their dwellings among
you; they shall eat your fruit,
and they shall drink your
milk. 5And I will make Rabbah a stable for camels and
Ammon a resting place for
flocks. Then you shall know
that I *am* the LORD."

6'For thus says the Lord
GOD: "Because you clapped
your hands, stamped your
feet, and rejoiced in heart
with all your disdain for the
land of Israel, 7indeed, therefore, I will stretch out My hand
against you, and give you as
plunder to the nations; I will
cut you off from the peoples,
and I will cause you to perish
from the countries; I will destroy you, and you shall know
that I *am* the LORD."

PROCLAMATION AGAINST MOAB

8'Thus says the Lord GOD:
"Because Moab and Seir say,
'Look! The house of Judah *is*

like all the nations,' [9]there-
fore, behold, I will clear the
territory of Moab of cities, of
the cities on its frontier, the
glory of the country, Beth
Jeshimoth, Baal Meon, and
Kirjathaim. [10]To the men of
the East I will give it as a possession, together with the
Ammonites, that the Ammonites may not be remembered
among the nations. [11]And I
will execute judgments upon
Moab, and they shall know
that I *am* the LORD."

PROCLAMATION AGAINST EDOM

[12]"Thus says the Lord GOD:
"Because of what Edom did
against the house of Judah
by taking vengeance, and has
greatly offended by avenging
itself on them," [13]therefore
thus says the Lord GOD: "I
will also stretch out My hand
against Edom, cut off man
and beast from it, and make it
desolate from Teman; Dedan
shall fall by the sword. [14]I will
lay My vengeance on Edom by
the hand of My people Israel,
that they may do in Edom according to My anger and according to My fury; and they
shall know My vengeance,"
says the Lord GOD.

PROCLAMATION AGAINST PHILISTIA

[15]"Thus says the Lord GOD:
"Because the Philistines dealt
vengefully and took ven-
geance with a spiteful heart,
to destroy because of the old
hatred," [16]therefore thus says
the Lord GOD: "I will stretch
out My hand against the Philistines, and I will cut off the
Cherethites and destroy the
remnant of the seacoast. [17]I
will execute great vengeance
on them with furious rebukes;
and they shall know that I *am*
the LORD, when I lay My vengeance upon them." ' "

PROCLAMATION AGAINST TYRE

26 And it came to pass in
the eleventh year, on
the first *day* of the month, *that*
the word of the LORD came
to me, saying, [2]"Son of man,
because Tyre has said against
Jerusalem, 'Aha! She is broken
who *was* the gateway of the
peoples; now she is turned
over to me; I shall be filled;
she is laid waste.'

[3]"Therefore thus says
the Lord GOD: 'Behold, I *am*
against you, O Tyre, and will
cause many nations to come
up against you, as the sea
causes its waves to come up.
[4]And they shall destroy the
walls of Tyre and break down
her towers; I will also scrape
her dust from her, and make
her like the top of a rock. [5]It
shall be *a place for* spreading
nets in the midst of the sea,
for I have spoken,' says the
Lord GOD; 'it shall become
plunder for the nations. [6]Also
her daughter *villages* which
are in the fields shall be slain

by the sword. Then they shall
know that I am the LORD.'
7"For thus says the Lord
GOD: 'Behold, I will bring
against Tyre from the north
Nebuchadnezzar[a] king of
Babylon, king of kings, with
horses, with chariots, and with
horsemen, and an army with
many people. 8He will slay
with the sword your daughter
villages in the fields; he will
heap up a siege mound against
you, build a wall against you,
and raise a defense against
you. 9He will direct his battering rams against your
walls, and with his axes he
will break down your towers.
10Because of the abundance of
his horses, their dust will cover
you; your walls will shake at
the noise of the horsemen,
the wagons, and the chariots,
when he enters your gates, as
men enter a city that has been
breached. 11With the hooves of
his horses he will trample all
your streets; he will slay your
people by the sword, and your
strong pillars will fall to the
ground. 12They will plunder
your riches and pillage your
merchandise; they will break
down your walls and destroy
your pleasant houses; they will
lay your stones, your timber,
and your soil in the midst of
the water. 13I will put an end
to the sound of your songs,
and the sound of your harps
shall be heard no more. 14I will
make you like the top of a rock;
you shall be *a place for* spreading nets, and you shall never
be rebuilt, for I the LORD have
spoken,' says the Lord GOD.
15"Thus says the Lord GOD
to Tyre: 'Will the coastlands
not shake at the sound of your
fall, when the wounded cry,
when slaughter is made in the
midst of you? 16Then all the
princes of the sea will come
down from their thrones, lay
aside their robes, and take off
their embroidered garments;
they will clothe themselves
with trembling; they will sit
on the ground, tremble *every*
moment, and be astonished at
you. 17And they will take up a
lamentation for you, and say
to you:

"How you have perished,
O one inhabited by
seafaring men,
O renowned city,
Who was strong at sea,
She and her inhabitants,
Who caused their
terror *to be* on all
her inhabitants!
18 Now the coastlands
tremble on the
day of your fall;
Yes, the coastlands by
the sea are troubled
at your departure."'

19"For thus says the Lord
GOD: 'When I make you a desolate city, like cities that are

26:7 [a] Hebrew *Nebuchadrezzar,* and so elsewhere in this book

not inhabited, when I bring
the deep upon you, and great
waters cover you, 20then I will
bring you down with those
who descend into the Pit, to
the people of old, and I will
make you dwell in the lowest
part of the earth, in places
desolate from antiquity, with
those who go down to the Pit,
so that you may never be inhabited; and I shall establish
glory in the land of the living.
21I will make you a terror, and
you *shall be* no *more;* though
you are sought for, you will
never be found again,' says
the Lord GOD."

LAMENTATION FOR TYRE

27 The word of the LORD
came again to me, say-
ing, 2"Now, son of man, take
up a lamentation for Tyre,
3and say to Tyre, 'You who are
situated at the entrance of the
sea, merchant of the peoples
on many coastlands, thus says
the Lord GOD:

"O Tyre, you have said,
'I *am* perfect in beauty.'
4 Your borders *are* in the
midst of the seas.
Your builders have
perfected your beauty.
5 They made all *your* planks
of fir trees from Senir;
They took a cedar
from Lebanon to
make you a mast.
6 *Of* oaks from Bashan
they made your oars;
The company of Ashurites
have inlaid your planks
With ivory from the
coasts of Cyprus.[a]
7 Fine embroidered linen
from Egypt was what
you spread for your sail;
Blue and purple from
the coasts of Elishah
was what covered you.

8 "Inhabitants of Sidon
and Arvad were
your oarsmen;
Your wise men, O Tyre,
were in you;
They became your pilots.
9 Elders of Gebal and
its wise men
Were in you to caulk
your seams;
All the ships of the sea
And their oarsmen
were in you
To market your
merchandise.

10 "Those from Persia,
Lydia,[a] and Libya[b]
Were in your army
as men of war;
They hung shield and
helmet in you;
They gave splendor to you.
11 Men of Arvad with your
army *were* on your
walls *all* around,
And the men of Gammad
were in your towers;

27:6 [a] Hebrew *Kittim,* western lands, especially Cyprus 27:10 [a] Hebrew *Lud* [b] Hebrew *Put*

They hung their
shields on your
walls *all* around;
They made your
beauty perfect.

12“Tarshish *was* your merchant because of your many
luxury goods. They gave you
silver, iron, tin, and lead for
your goods. 13Javan, Tubal,
and Meshech *were* your traders. They bartered human lives
and vessels of bronze for your
merchandise. 14Those from the
house of Togarmah traded for
your wares with horses, steeds,
and mules. 15The men of Dedan
were your traders; many isles
were the market of your hand.
They brought you ivory tusks
and ebony as payment. 16Syria
was your merchant because of
the abundance of goods you
made. They gave you for your
wares emeralds, purple, embroidery, fine linen, corals, and
rubies. 17Judah and the land
of Israel *were* your traders.
They traded for your merchandise wheat of Minnith, millet,
honey, oil, and balm. 18Da-
mascus *was* your merchant
because of the abundance of
goods you made, because of
your many luxury items, with
the wine of Helbon and with
white wool. 19Dan and Javan
paid for your wares, travers-
ing back and forth. Wrought
iron, cassia, and cane were
among your merchandise.
20Dedan *was* your merchant
in saddlecloths for riding.
21Arabia and all the princes
of Kedar *were* your regular
merchants. They traded with
you in lambs, rams, and goats.
22The merchants of Sheba
and Raamah *were* your merchants. They traded for your
wares the choicest spices, all
kinds of precious stones, and
gold. 23Haran, Canneh, Eden,
the merchants of Sheba, Assyria, *and* Chilmad *were* your
merchants. 24These *were* your
merchants in choice items—in
purple clothes, in embroidered
garments, in chests of multicolored apparel, in sturdy
woven cords, which were in
your marketplace.

25“The ships of Tarshish
were carriers of your
merchandise.
You were filled and
very glorious in the
midst of the seas.
26 Your oarsmen brought
you into many waters,
But the east wind
broke you in the
midst of the seas.

27“Your riches, wares,
and merchandise,
Your mariners and pilots,
Your caulkers and
merchandisers,
All your men of war
who *are* in you,
And the entire company
which *is* in your midst,
Will fall into the midst
of the seas on the
day of your ruin.

28 The common-land will
shake at the sound of
the cry of your pilots.

29 "All who handle the oar,
The mariners,
All the pilots of the sea
Will come down from
their ships *and* stand
on the shore.
30 They will make their voice
heard because of you;
They will cry bitterly and
cast dust on their heads;
They will roll about
in ashes;
31 They will shave
themselves completely
bald because of you,
Gird themselves
with sackcloth,
And weep for you
With bitterness of heart
and bitter wailing.
32 In their wailing for you
They will take up a
lamentation,
And lament for you:
'What *city is* like Tyre,
Destroyed in the
midst of the sea?

33 'When your wares
went out by sea,
You satisfied many
people;
You enriched the
kings of the earth
With your many luxury
goods and your
merchandise.
34 But you are broken
by the seas in the
depths of the waters;
Your merchandise and
the entire company
will fall in your midst.
35 All the inhabitants
of the isles will be
astonished at you;
Their kings will be
greatly afraid,
And *their* countenance
will be troubled.
36 The merchants among the
peoples will hiss at you;
You will become a
horror, and *be* no
more forever.'""

PROCLAMATION AGAINST THE KING OF TYRE

28 The word of the LORD
came to me again, say-
ing, 2 "Son of man, say to the
prince of Tyre, 'Thus says the
Lord GOD:

"Because your heart
is lifted up,
And you say, 'I *am* a god,
I sit *in* the seat of gods,
In the midst of the seas,'
Yet you *are* a man,
and not a god,
Though you set your heart
as the heart of a god
3 (Behold, you *are* wiser
than Daniel!
There is no secret that can
be hidden from you!
4 With your wisdom and
your understanding
You have gained
riches for yourself,
And gathered gold
and silver into
your treasuries;

5 By your great wisdom
in trade you have
increased your riches,
And your heart is lifted up
because of your riches),"

6'Therefore thus says the
Lord GOD:

"Because you have set
your heart as the
heart of a god,
7 Behold, therefore, I
will bring strangers
against you,
The most terrible
of the nations;
And they shall draw their
swords against the
beauty of your wisdom,
And defile your splendor.
8 They shall throw you
down into the Pit,
And you shall die the
death of the slain
In the midst of the seas.

9 "Will you still say before
him who slays you,
'I *am* a god'?
But you *shall be* a man,
and not a god,
In the hand of him
who slays you.
10 You shall die the death
of the uncircumcised
By the hand of aliens;
For I have spoken,"
says the Lord GOD.'"

LAMENTATION FOR THE KING OF TYRE

11Moreover the word of the
LORD came to me, saying,
12"Son of man, take up a lamentation for the king of Tyre,
and say to him, 'Thus says the
Lord GOD:

"You *were* the seal
of perfection,
Full of wisdom and
perfect in beauty.
13 You were in Eden, the
garden of God;
Every precious stone
was your covering:
The sardius, topaz,
and diamond,
Beryl, onyx, and jasper,
Sapphire, turquoise, and
emerald with gold.
The workmanship
of your timbrels
and pipes
Was prepared for
you on the day you
were created.

14"You *were* the anointed
cherub who covers;
I established you;
You were on the holy
mountain of God;
You walked back and
forth in the midst
of fiery stones.
15 You *were* perfect in your
ways from the day
you were created,
Till iniquity was
found in you.

16"By the abundance
of your trading
You became filled with
violence within,
And you sinned;

Therefore I cast you
as a profane thing
Out of the mountain
of God;
And I destroyed you,
O covering cherub,
From the midst of
the fiery stones.

17 "Your heart was lifted up
because of your beauty;
You corrupted your
wisdom for the sake
of your splendor;
I cast you to the ground,
I laid you before kings,
That they might
gaze at you.

18 "You defiled your
sanctuaries
By the multitude of
your iniquities,
By the iniquity of
your trading;
Therefore I brought fire
from your midst;
It devoured you,
And I turned you to
ashes upon the earth
In the sight of all
who saw you.
19 All who knew you
among the peoples are
astonished at you;
You have become a horror,
And *shall be* no
more forever." ' "

PROCLAMATION AGAINST SIDON

20 Then the word of the
LORD came to me, saying,
21 "Son of man, set your face
toward Sidon, and prophesy
against her, 22 and say, 'Thus
says the Lord GOD:

"Behold, I *am* against
you, O Sidon;
I will be glorified
in your midst;
And they shall know
that I *am* the LORD,
When I execute
judgments in her and
am hallowed in her.
23 For I will send
pestilence upon her,
And blood in her streets;
The wounded shall be
judged in her midst
By the sword against
her on every side;
Then they shall know
that I *am* the LORD.

24 "And there shall no longer be a pricking brier or a
painful thorn for the house
of Israel from among all *who*
are around them, who despise
them. Then they shall know
that I *am* the Lord GOD."

ISRAEL'S FUTURE BLESSING

25 'Thus says the Lord GOD:
"When I have gathered the
house of Israel from the peoples among whom they are
scattered, and am hallowed in
them in the sight of the Gentiles, then they will dwell in
their own land which I gave to
My servant Jacob. 26 And they
will dwell safely there, build
houses, and plant vineyards;
yes, they will dwell securely,

when I execute judgments on all those around them who despise them. Then they shall know that I *am* the LORD their God."'"

PROCLAMATION AGAINST EGYPT

29 In the tenth year, in the tenth *month,* on the twelfth *day* of the month, the word of the LORD came to me, saying, 2"Son of man, set your face against Pharaoh king of Egypt, and prophesy against him, and against all Egypt. 3Speak, and say, 'Thus says the Lord GOD:

"Behold, I *am* against you,
O Pharaoh king of Egypt,
O great monster who
lies in the midst
of his rivers,
Who has said, 'My
River[a] *is* my own;
I have made *it* for myself.'
4 But I will put hooks
in your jaws,
And cause the fish of
your rivers to stick
to your scales;
I will bring you up out of
the midst of your rivers,
And all the fish in
your rivers will stick
to your scales.
5 I will leave you in
the wilderness,
You and all the fish
of your rivers;
You shall fall on
the open field;
You shall not be picked
up or gathered.[a]
I have given you as food
To the beasts of the field
And to the birds of
the heavens.

6 "Then all the
inhabitants of Egypt
Shall know that I
am the LORD,
Because they have been
a staff of reed to the
house of Israel.
7 When they took hold of
you with the hand,
You broke and tore all
their shoulders;[a]
When they leaned on you,
You broke and made all
their backs quiver."

8'Therefore thus says the
Lord GOD: "Surely I will bring
a sword upon you and cut
off from you man and beast.
9And the land of Egypt shall
become desolate and waste;
then they will know that I *am*
the LORD, because he said,
'The River *is* mine, and I have
made *it.*' 10Indeed, therefore,
I *am* against you and against
your rivers, and I will make
the land of Egypt utterly waste
and desolate, from Migdol[a]

29:3 [a] That is, the Nile 29:5 [a] Following Masoretic Text, Septuagint, and Vulgate; some Hebrew manuscripts and Targum read *buried.* 29:7 [a] Following Masoretic Text and Vulgate; Septuagint and Syriac read *hand.* 29:10 [a] Or *tower*

to Syene, as far as the border
of Ethiopia. 11Neither foot of
man shall pass through it nor
foot of beast pass through it,
and it shall be uninhabited
forty years. 12I will make the
land of Egypt desolate in the
midst of the countries *that are*
desolate; and among the cities
that are laid waste, her cities
shall be desolate forty years;
and I will scatter the Egyptians among the nations and
disperse them throughout the
countries."

13'Yet, thus says the Lord
GOD: "At the end of forty years I
will gather the Egyptians from
the peoples among whom they
were scattered. 14I will bring
back the captives of Egypt and
cause them to return to the
land of Pathros, to the land
of their origin, and there they
shall be a lowly kingdom. 15It
shall be the lowliest of kingdoms; it shall never again exalt
itself above the nations, for I
will diminish them so that they
will not rule over the nations
anymore. 16No longer shall it
be the confidence of the house
of Israel, but will remind them
of *their* iniquity when they
turned to follow them. Then
they shall know that I *am* the
Lord GOD."'"

BABYLONIA WILL PLUNDER EGYPT

17And it came to pass in the
twenty-seventh year, in the
first *month,* on the first *day*
of the month, *that* the word of
the LORD came to me, saying,
18"Son of man, Nebuchadnezzar king of Babylon caused
his army to labor strenuously
against Tyre; every head *was*
made bald, and every shoulder rubbed raw; yet neither he
nor his army received wages
from Tyre, for the labor which
they expended on it. 19There-
fore thus says the Lord GOD:
'Surely I will give the land
of Egypt to Nebuchadnezzar
king of Babylon; he shall take
away her wealth, carry off her
spoil, and remove her pillage;
and that will be the wages for
his army. 20I have given him
the land of Egypt *for* his labor,
because they worked for Me,'
says the Lord GOD.

21'In that day I will cause
the horn of the house of Israel
to spring forth, and I will open
your mouth to speak in their
midst. Then they shall know
that I *am* the LORD.'"

EGYPT AND HER ALLIES WILL FALL

30 The word of the LORD
came to me again, say-
ing, 2"Son of man, prophesy
and say, 'Thus says the Lord
GOD:

"Wail, 'Woe to the day!'
3 For the day *is* near,
Even the day of the
LORD *is* near;
It will be a day of clouds,
the time of the Gentiles.
4 The sword shall come
upon Egypt,

And great anguish
shall be in Ethiopia,
When the slain
fall in Egypt,
And they take away
her wealth,
And her foundations
are broken down.

5"Ethiopia, Libya,[a] Lydia,[b]
all the mingled people, Chub,
and the men of the lands who
are allied, shall fall with them
by the sword."
6'Thus says the LORD:

"Those who uphold
Egypt shall fall,
And the pride of her
power shall come down.
From Migdol *to* Syene
Those within her shall
fall by the sword,"
Says the Lord GOD.

7 "They shall be desolate
in the midst of the
desolate countries,
And her cities shall be in
the midst of the cities
that are laid waste.
8 Then they will know
that I *am* the LORD,
When I have set a
fire in Egypt
And all her helpers
are destroyed.
9 On that day messengers
shall go forth from
Me in ships
To make the careless
Ethiopians afraid,
And great anguish shall
come upon them,
As on the day of Egypt;
For indeed it is coming!"

10'Thus says the Lord GOD:

"I will also make
a multitude of
Egypt to cease
By the hand of
Nebuchadnezzar
king of Babylon.
11 He and his people with
him, the most terrible
of the nations,
Shall be brought to
destroy the land;
They shall draw their
swords against Egypt,
And fill the land
with the slain.
12 I will make the rivers dry,
And sell the land into the
hand of the wicked;
I will make the land
waste, and all
that is in it,
By the hand of aliens.
I, the LORD, have spoken."

13'Thus says the Lord GOD:

"I will also destroy
the idols,
And cause the images
to cease from Noph;[a]
There shall no longer
be princes from the
land of Egypt;
I will put fear in the
land of Egypt.

30:5 [a] Hebrew *Put* [b] Hebrew *Lud* 30:13 [a] That is, ancient Memphis

14 I will make Pathros
desolate,
Set fire to Zoan,
And execute
judgments in No.[a]
15 I will pour My fury on
Sin,[a] the strength
of Egypt;
I will cut off the
multitude of No,
16 And set a fire in Egypt;
Sin shall have great pain,
No shall be split open,
And Noph *shall be in*
distress daily.
17 The young men of Aven[a]
and Pi Beseth shall
fall by the sword,
And these *cities* shall
go into captivity.
18 At Tehaphnehes[a] the day
shall also be darkened,[b]
When I break the yokes
of Egypt there.
And her arrogant strength
shall cease in her;
As for her, a cloud
shall cover her,
And her daughters shall
go into captivity.
19 Thus I will execute
judgments on Egypt,
Then they shall know
that I *am* the LORD."'"

PROCLAMATION AGAINST PHARAOH

20And it came to pass in
the eleventh year, in the first
month, on the seventh *day* of
the month, *that* the word of
the LORD came to me, saying,
21"Son of man, I have broken the arm of Pharaoh king
of Egypt; and see, it has not
been bandaged for healing,
nor a splint put on to bind it,
to make it strong enough to
hold a sword. 22Therefore thus
says the Lord GOD: 'Surely I
am against Pharaoh king of
Egypt, and will break his arms,
both the strong one and the
one that was broken; and I will
make the sword fall out of his
hand. 23I will scatter the Egyptians among the nations, and
disperse them throughout the
countries. 24I will strengthen
the arms of the king of Babylon and put My sword in his
hand; but I will break Pharaoh's arms, and he will groan
before him with the groanings
of a mortally wounded *man.*
25Thus I will strengthen the
arms of the king of Babylon,
but the arms of Pharaoh shall
fall down; they shall know that
I *am* the LORD, when I put My
sword into the hand of the king
of Babylon and he stretches it
out against the land of Egypt.
26I will scatter the Egyptians among the nations and
disperse them throughout
the countries. Then they shall
know that I *am* the LORD.'"

30:14 [a] That is, ancient Thebes **30:15** [a] That is, ancient Pelusium **30:17** [a] That is, ancient On (Heliopolis) **30:18** [a] Spelled *Tahpanhes* in Jeremiah 43:7 and elsewhere [b] Following many Hebrew manuscripts, Bomberg, Septuagint, Syriac, Targum, and Vulgate; Masoretic Text reads *refrained.*

EGYPT CUT DOWN LIKE A GREAT TREE

31 Now it came to pass in
the eleventh year, in the
third *month,* on the first *day*
of the month, *that* the word of
the LORD came to me, saying,
2"Son of man, say to Pharaoh
king of Egypt and to his multitude:

'Whom are you like
in your greatness?
3 Indeed Assyria *was* a
cedar in Lebanon,
With fine branches that
shaded the forest,
And of high stature;
And its top was among
the thick boughs.
4 The waters made it grow;
Underground waters
gave it height,
With their rivers running
around the place
where it was planted,
And sent out rivulets
to all the trees
of the field.

5 'Therefore its height
was exalted above all
the trees of the field;
Its boughs were
multiplied,
And its branches became
long because of the
abundance of water,
As it sent them out.
6 All the birds of the
heavens made their
nests in its boughs;
Under its branches
all the beasts of
the field brought
forth their young;
And in its shadow
all great nations
made their home.

7 'Thus it was beautiful
in greatness and in the
length of its branches,
Because its roots reached
to abundant waters.
8 The cedars in the garden
of God could not hide it;
The fir trees were not
like its boughs,
And the chestnut[a]
trees were not like
its branches;
No tree in the garden of
God was like it in beauty.
9 I made it beautiful with a
multitude of branches,
So that all the trees
of Eden envied it,
That *were* in the
garden of God.'

10"Therefore thus says the
Lord GOD: 'Because you have
increased in height, and it set
its top among the thick boughs,
and its heart was lifted up in its
height, 11therefore I will deliver
it into the hand of the mighty
one of the nations, and he
shall surely deal with it; I have
driven it out for its wickedness.
12And aliens, the most terrible
of the nations, have cut it down
and left it; its branches have

31:8 [a] Hebrew *armon*

fallen on the mountains and in all the valleys; its boughs lie broken by all the rivers of the land; and all the peoples of the earth have gone from under its shadow and left it.

13 'On its ruin will remain all
the birds of the heavens,
And all the beasts of
the field will come
to its branches—

14So that no trees by the waters may ever again exalt themselves for their height, nor set their tops among the thick boughs, that no tree which drinks water may ever be high enough to reach up to them.

'For they have all been
delivered to death,
To the depths of the earth,
Among the children
of men who go
down to the Pit.'

15"Thus says the Lord GOD:
'In the day when it went down to hell, I caused mourning. I covered the deep because of it. I restrained its rivers, and the great waters were held back. I caused Lebanon to mourn for it, and all the trees of the
field wilted because of it. 16I
made the nations shake at the sound of its fall, when I cast it down to hell together with those who descend into the Pit; and all the trees of Eden, the choice and best of Lebanon, all that drink water, were comforted in the depths of the
earth. 17They also went down
to hell with it, with those slain by the sword; and *those who were* its *strong* arm dwelt in its shadows among the nations.

18'To which of the trees in Eden will you then be likened in glory and greatness? Yet you shall be brought down with the trees of Eden to the depths of the earth; you shall lie in the midst of the uncircumcised, with *those* slain by the sword. This *is* Pharaoh and all his multitude,' says the Lord GOD."

LAMENTATION FOR PHARAOH AND EGYPT

32 And it came to pass in the twelfth year, in the twelfth *month,* on the first *day* of the month, *that* the word of the LORD came to me, saying,
2"Son of man, take up a lamentation for Pharaoh king of Egypt, and say to him:

'You are like a young
lion among the nations,
And you *are* like a
monster in the seas,
Bursting forth in
your rivers,
Troubling the waters
with your feet,
And fouling their rivers.

3'Thus says the Lord GOD:

"I will therefore spread
My net over you
with a company of
many people,

And they will draw
you up in My net.
4 Then I will leave you
on the land;
I will cast you out on
the open fields,
And cause to settle
on you all the birds
of the heavens.
And with you I will
fill the beasts of
the whole earth.
5 I will lay your flesh on
the mountains,
And fill the valleys
with your carcass.

6 "I will also water the
land with the flow
of your blood,
Even to the mountains;
And the riverbeds
will be full of you.
7 When *I* put out your light,
I will cover the
heavens, and make
its stars dark;
I will cover the sun
with a cloud,
And the moon shall
not give her light.
8 All the bright lights
of the heavens I will
make dark over you,
And bring darkness
upon your land,"
Says the Lord GOD.

9'I will also trouble the
hearts of many peoples,
when I bring your destruction among the nations, into
the countries which you have
not known. 10Yes, I will make
many peoples astonished at
you, and their kings shall be
horribly afraid of you when
I brandish My sword before
them; and they shall tremble
every moment, every man for
his own life, in the day of your
fall.

11"For thus says the Lord
GOD: 'The sword of the king of
Babylon shall come upon you.
12By the swords of the mighty
warriors, all of them the most
terrible of the nations, I will
cause your multitude to fall.

'They shall plunder
the pomp of Egypt,
And all its multitude
shall be destroyed.
13 Also I will destroy
all its animals
From beside its
great waters;
The foot of man shall
muddy them no more,
Nor shall the hooves
of animals
muddy them.
14 Then I will make their
waters clear,
And make their rivers
run like oil,'
Says the Lord GOD.

15 'When I make the land
of Egypt desolate,
And the country is
destitute of all that
once filled it,
When I strike all
who dwell in it,
Then they shall know
that I *am* the LORD.

16 'This *is* the lamentation
With which they shall
lament her;
The daughters of
the nations shall
lament her;
They shall lament for
her, for Egypt,
And for all her multitude,'
Says the Lord GOD."

EGYPT AND OTHERS CONSIGNED TO THE PIT

17It came to pass also in the
twelfth year, on the fifteenth
day of the month, *that* the
word of the LORD came to me,
saying:

18"Son of man, wail over the
multitude of Egypt,
And cast them down to
the depths of the earth,
Her and the daughters of
the famous nations,
With those who go
down to the Pit:
19 'Whom do you
surpass in beauty?
Go down, be placed with
the uncircumcised.'

20"They shall fall in
the midst of *those*
slain by the sword;
She is delivered to
the sword,
Drawing her and all
her multitudes.
21 The strong among
the mighty
Shall speak to him out
of the midst of hell
With those who help him:
'They have gone down,
They lie with the
uncircumcised, slain
by the sword.'

22"Assyria *is* there, and
all her company,
With their graves
all around her,
All of them slain, fallen
by the sword.
23 Her graves are set in the
recesses of the Pit,
And her company is all
around her grave,
All of them slain, fallen
by the sword,
Who caused terror in
the land of the living.

24"There *is* Elam and
all her multitude,
All around her grave,
All of them slain, fallen
by the sword,
Who have gone down
uncircumcised to the
lower parts of the earth,
Who caused their terror
in the land of the living;
Now they bear their
shame with those who
go down to the Pit.
25 They have set her bed in
the midst of the slain,
With all her multitude,
With her graves
all around it,
All of them
uncircumcised, slain
by the sword;
Though their terror
was caused
In the land of the living,

Yet they bear their shame
With those who go
down to the Pit;
It was put in the midst
of the slain.

26 "There *are* Meshech
and Tubal and all
their multitudes,
With all their graves
around it,
All of them
uncircumcised, slain
by the sword,
Though they caused
their terror in the
land of the living.
27 They do not lie with
the mighty
Who are fallen of the
uncircumcised,
Who have gone down
to hell with their
weapons of war;
They have laid their
swords under
their heads,
But their iniquities will
be on their bones,
Because of the terror
of the mighty in the
land of the living.
28 Yes, you shall be broken
in the midst of the
uncircumcised,
And lie with *those*
slain by the sword.

29 "There *is* Edom,
Her kings and all
her princes,
Who despite their might
Are laid beside *those*
slain by the sword;
They shall lie with the
uncircumcised,
And with those who
go down to the Pit.
30 There *are* the princes
of the north,
All of them, and all
the Sidonians,
Who have gone down
with the slain
In shame at the terror
which they caused
by their might;
They lie uncircumcised
with *those* slain
by the sword,
And bear their shame
with those who go
down to the Pit.

31 "Pharaoh will see them
And be comforted over
all his multitude,
Pharaoh and all his army,
Slain by the sword,"
Says the Lord GOD.

32 "For I have caused My
terror in the land
of the living;
And he shall be placed
in the midst of the
uncircumcised
With *those* slain
by the sword,
Pharaoh and all his
multitude,"
Says the Lord GOD.

THE WATCHMAN AND HIS MESSAGE

33 Again the word of the
LORD came to me, say-
ing, 2 "Son of man, speak to the

children of your people, and say to them: 'When I bring the sword upon a land, and the people of the land take a man from their territory and make him their watchman, 3when he sees the sword coming upon the land, if he blows the trumpet and warns the people, 4then whoever hears the sound of the trumpet and does not take warning, if the sword comes and takes him away, his blood shall be on his *own* head. 5He heard the sound of the trumpet, but did not take warning; his blood shall be upon himself. But he who takes warning will save his life. 6But if the watchman sees the sword coming and does not blow the trumpet, and the people are not warned, and the sword comes and takes *any* person from among them, he is taken away in his iniquity; but his blood I will require at the watchman's hand.'

7"So you, son of man: I have made you a watchman for the house of Israel; therefore you shall hear a word from My mouth and warn them for Me. 8When I say to the wicked, 'O wicked *man,* you shall surely die!' and you do not speak to warn the wicked from his way, that wicked *man* shall die in his iniquity; but his blood I will require at your hand. 9Nevertheless if you warn the wicked to turn from his way, and he does not turn from his way, he shall die in his iniquity; but you have delivered your soul.

10"Therefore you, O son of man, say to the house of Israel: 'Thus you say, "If our transgressions and our sins *lie* upon us, and we pine away in them, how can we then live?"' 11Say to them: '*As* I live,' says the Lord GOD, 'I have no pleasure in the death of the wicked, but that the wicked turn from his way and live. Turn, turn from your evil ways! For why should you die, O house of Israel?'

THE FAIRNESS OF GOD'S JUDGMENT

12"Therefore you, O son of man, say to the children of your people: 'The righteousness of the righteous man shall not deliver him in the day of his transgression; as for the wickedness of the wicked, he shall not fall because of it in the day that he turns from his wickedness; nor shall the righteous be able to live because of *his righteousness* in the day that he sins.' 13When I say to the righteous *that* he shall surely live, but he trusts in his own righteousness and commits iniquity, none of his righteous works shall be remembered; but because of the iniquity that he has committed, he shall die. 14Again, when I say to the wicked, 'You shall surely die,' if he turns from

his sin and does what is lawful and right, 15*if* the wicked restores the pledge, gives back what he has stolen, and walks in the statutes of life without committing iniquity, he shall surely live; he shall not die. 16None of his sins which he has committed shall be remembered against him; he has done what is lawful and right; he shall surely live.

17"Yet the children of your people say, 'The way of the Lord is not fair.' But it is their way which is not fair! 18When the righteous turns from his righteousness and commits iniquity, he shall die because of it. 19But when the wicked turns from his wickedness and does what is lawful and right, he shall live because of it. 20Yet you say, 'The way of the Lord is not fair.' O house of Israel, I will judge every one of you according to his own ways."

THE FALL OF JERUSALEM

21And it came to pass in the twelfth year of our captivity, in the tenth *month,* on the fifth *day* of the month, *that* one who had escaped from Jerusalem came to me and said, "The city has been captured!"

22Now the hand of the LORD had been upon me the evening before the man came who had escaped. And He had opened my mouth; so when he came to me in the morning, my mouth was opened, and I was no longer mute.

THE CAUSE OF JUDAH'S RUIN

23Then the word of the LORD came to me, saying: 24"Son of man, they who inhabit those ruins in the land of Israel are saying, 'Abraham was only one, and he inherited the land. But we *are* many; the land has been given to us as a possession.'

25"Therefore say to them, 'Thus says the Lord GOD: "You eat *meat* with blood, you lift up your eyes toward your idols, and shed blood. Should you then possess the land? 26You rely on your sword, you commit abominations, and you defile one another's wives. Should you then possess the land?"'

27"Say thus to them, 'Thus says the Lord GOD: "*As* I live, surely those who *are* in the ruins shall fall by the sword, and the one who *is* in the open field I will give to the beasts to be devoured, and those who *are* in the strongholds and caves shall die of the pestilence. 28For I will make the land most desolate, her arrogant strength shall cease, and the mountains of Israel shall be so desolate that no one will pass through. 29Then they shall know that I *am* the LORD, when I have made the land most desolate because of all their abominations which they have committed."'

HEARING AND NOT DOING

30“As for you, son of man,
the children of your people
are talking about you beside
the walls and in the doors of
the houses; and they speak to
one another, everyone saying
to his brother, ‘Please come
and hear what the word is that
comes from the LORD.’ 31So
they come to you as people
do, they sit before you *as* My
people, and they hear your
words, but they do not do
them; for with their mouth
they show much love, *but* their
hearts pursue their *own* gain.
32Indeed you *are* to them as a
very lovely song of one who
has a pleasant voice and can
play well on an instrument;
for they hear your words, but
they do not do them. 33And
when this comes to pass—
surely it will come—then they
will know that a prophet has
been among them.”

IRRESPONSIBLE SHEPHERDS

34 And the word of the
LORD came to me, say-
ing, 2“Son of man, prophesy
against the shepherds of Israel, prophesy and say to them,
‘Thus says the Lord GOD to
the shepherds: “Woe to the
shepherds of Israel who feed
themselves! Should not the
shepherds feed the flocks?
3You eat the fat and clothe
yourselves with the wool; you
slaughter the fatlings, *but* you
do not feed the flock. 4The weak
you have not strengthened,
nor have you healed those who
were sick, nor bound up the
broken, nor brought back what
was driven away, nor sought
what was lost; but with force
and cruelty you have ruled
them. 5So they were scattered
because *there was* no shepherd; and they became food
for all the beasts of the field
when they were scattered. 6My
sheep wandered through all
the mountains, and on every
high hill; yes, My flock was
scattered over the whole face
of the earth, and no one was
seeking or searching *for them.*”

7‘Therefore, you shepherds,
hear the word of the LORD:
8“*As* I live,” says the Lord GOD,
“surely because My flock became a prey, and My flock became food for every beast of
the field, because *there was* no
shepherd, nor did My shepherds search for My flock, but
the shepherds fed themselves
and did not feed My flock”—
9therefore, O shepherds, hear
the word of the LORD! 10Thus
says the Lord GOD: “Behold,
I *am* against the shepherds,
and I will require My flock at
their hand; I will cause them
to cease feeding the sheep,
and the shepherds shall feed
themselves no more; for I
will deliver My flock from
their mouths, that they may
no longer be food for them.”

GOD, THE TRUE SHEPHERD

11‘For thus says the Lord
GOD: “Indeed I Myself will

search for My sheep and
seek them out. 12As a shepherd seeks out his flock on the
day he is among his scattered
sheep, so will I seek out My
sheep and deliver them from
all the places where they were
scattered on a cloudy and dark
day. 13And I will bring them
out from the peoples and
gather them from the countries, and will bring them to
their own land; I will feed
them on the mountains of
Israel, in the valleys and in
all the inhabited places of the
country. 14I will feed them in
good pasture, and their fold
shall be on the high mountains of Israel. There they
shall lie down in a good fold
and feed in rich pasture on
the mountains of Israel. 15I
will feed My flock, and I will
make them lie down," says the
Lord GOD. 16"I will seek what
was lost and bring back what
was driven away, bind up the
broken and strengthen what
was sick; but I will destroy the
fat and the strong, and feed
them in judgment."

17'And *as for* you, O My
flock, thus says the Lord GOD:
"Behold, I shall judge between
sheep and sheep, between
rams and goats. 18*Is it* too little
for you to have eaten up the
good pasture, that you must
tread down with your feet the
residue of your pasture—and
to have drunk of the clear waters, that you must foul the
residue with your feet? 19And
as for My flock, they eat what
you have trampled with your
feet, and they drink what you
have fouled with your feet."

20'Therefore thus says the
Lord GOD to them: "Behold,
I Myself will judge between
the fat and the lean sheep.
21Because you have pushed
with side and shoulder, butted
all the weak ones with your
horns, and scattered them
abroad, 22therefore I will save
My flock, and they shall no
longer be a prey; and I will
judge between sheep and
sheep. 23I will establish one
shepherd over them, and he
shall feed them—My servant
David. He shall feed them and
be their shepherd. 24And I, the
LORD, will be their God, and
My servant David a prince
among them; I, the LORD,
have spoken.

25"I will make a covenant
of peace with them, and cause
wild beasts to cease from the
land; and they will dwell safely
in the wilderness and sleep in
the woods. 26I will make them
and the places all around My
hill a blessing; and I will cause
showers to come down in their
season; there shall be showers
of blessing. 27Then the trees of
the field shall yield their fruit,
and the earth shall yield her
increase. They shall be safe in
their land; and they shall know
that I *am* the LORD, when
I have broken the bands of
their yoke and delivered them
from the hand of those who

enslaved them. 28And they
shall no longer be a prey for
the nations, nor shall beasts
of the land devour them; but
they shall dwell safely, and no
one shall make *them* afraid.
29I will raise up for them a
garden of renown, and they
shall no longer be consumed
with hunger in the land, nor
bear the shame of the Gentiles
anymore. 30Thus they shall
know that I, the LORD their
God, *am* with them, and they,
the house of Israel, *are* My
people," says the Lord GOD.'
31"You are My flock, the
flock of My pasture; you *are*
men, *and* I *am* your God," says
the Lord GOD.

JUDGMENT ON MOUNT SEIR

35 Moreover the word of
the LORD came to me,
saying, 2"Son of man, set your
face against Mount Seir and
prophesy against it, 3and say
to it, 'Thus says the Lord GOD:

"Behold, O Mount Seir,
I *am* against you;
I will stretch out My
hand against you,
And make you
most desolate;
4 I shall lay your
cities waste,
And you shall be desolate.
Then you shall know
that I *am* the LORD.

5"Because you have had an
ancient hatred, and have shed
the blood of the children of Israel by the power of the sword
at the time of their calamity,
when their iniquity *came to an*
end, 6therefore, *as* I live," says
the Lord GOD, "I will prepare
you for blood, and blood shall
pursue you; since you have
not hated blood, therefore
blood shall pursue you. 7Thus
I will make Mount Seir most
desolate, and cut off from it
the one who leaves and the
one who returns. 8And I will
fill its mountains with the
slain; on your hills and in
your valleys and in all your
ravines those who are slain
by the sword shall fall. 9I will
make you perpetually desolate, and your cities shall be
uninhabited; then you shall
know that I *am* the LORD.
10"Because you have said,
'These two nations and these
two countries shall be mine,
and we will possess them,' although the LORD was there,
11therefore, *as* I live," says the
Lord GOD, "I will do according
to your anger and according
to the envy which you showed
in your hatred against them;
and I will make Myself known
among them when I judge you.
12Then you shall know that I
am the LORD. I have heard
all your blasphemies which
you have spoken against the
mountains of Israel, say-
ing, 'They are desolate; they
are given to us to consume.'
13Thus with your mouth you
have boasted against Me and

multiplied your words against
Me; I have heard *them*."
14"Thus says the Lord GOD:
"The whole earth will rejoice
when I make you desolate.
15As you rejoiced because the
inheritance of the house of
Israel was desolate, so I will
do to you; you shall be desolate, O Mount Seir, as well as
all of Edom—all of it! Then
they shall know that I *am* the
LORD."'

BLESSING ON ISRAEL

36 "And you, son of
man, prophesy to the
mountains of Israel, and say,
'O mountains of Israel, hear
the word of the LORD! 2Thus
says the Lord GOD: "Because
the enemy has said of you,
'Aha! The ancient heights have
become our possession,'"'
3therefore prophesy, and say,
'Thus says the Lord GOD: "Because they made *you* desolate and swallowed you up on
every side, so that you became
the possession of the rest of
the nations, and you are taken
up by the lips of talkers and
slandered by the people"—
4therefore, O mountains of
Israel, hear the word of the
Lord GOD! Thus says the Lord
GOD to the mountains, the
hills, the rivers, the valleys,
the desolate wastes, and the
cities that have been forsaken,
which became plunder and
mockery to the rest of the
nations all around— 5there-
fore thus says the Lord GOD:
"Surely I have spoken in My
burning jealousy against the
rest of the nations and against
all Edom, who gave My land
to themselves as a possession, with wholehearted joy
and spiteful minds, in order
to plunder its open country."'
6"Therefore prophesy con-
cerning the land of Israel,
and say to the mountains,
the hills, the rivers, and the
valleys, 'Thus says the Lord
GOD: "Behold, I have spoken
in My jealousy and My fury,
because you have borne the
shame of the nations." 7There-
fore thus says the Lord GOD:
"I have raised My hand in an
oath that surely the nations
that *are* around you shall
bear their own shame. 8But
you, O mountains of Israel,
you shall shoot forth your
branches and yield your fruit
to My people Israel, for they
are about to come. 9For indeed
I *am* for you, and I will turn to
you, and you shall be tilled
and sown. 10I will multiply
men upon you, all the house
of Israel, all of it; and the cities shall be inhabited and the
ruins rebuilt. 11I will multiply
upon you man and beast; and
they shall increase and bear
young; I will make you inhabited as in former times, and do
better *for you* than at your beginnings. Then you shall know
that I *am* the LORD. 12Yes, I will
cause men to walk on you, My
people Israel; they shall take
possession of you, and you

shall be their inheritance; no
more shall you bereave them
of children.”
13‘Thus says the Lord GOD:
“Because they say to you, ‘You
devour men and bereave your
nation *of children,*’ 14therefore
you shall devour men no
more, nor bereave your nation anymore,” says the Lord
GOD. 15“Nor will I let you hear
the taunts of the nations anymore, nor bear the reproach
of the peoples anymore, nor
shall you cause your nation to
stumble anymore,” says the
Lord GOD.’”

THE RENEWAL OF ISRAEL

16Moreover the word of
the LORD came to me, say-
ing: 17“Son of man, when the
house of Israel dwelt in their
own land, they defiled it by
their own ways and deeds; to
Me their way was like the uncleanness of a woman in her
customary impurity. 18There-
fore I poured out My fury on
them for the blood they had
shed on the land, and for their
idols *with which* they had defiled it. 19So I scattered them
among the nations, and they
were dispersed throughout
the countries; I judged them
according to their ways and
their deeds. 20When they
came to the nations, wherever
they went, they profaned My
holy name—when they said
of them, ‘These *are* the people
of the LORD, *and* yet they have
gone out of His land.’ 21But
I had concern for My holy
name, which the house of Israel had profaned among the
nations wherever they went.
22“Therefore say to the
house of Israel, ‘Thus says the
Lord GOD: “I do not do *this* for
your sake, O house of Israel,
but for My holy name’s sake,
which you have profaned
among the nations wherever
you went. 23And I will sanctify My great name, which
has been profaned among
the nations, which you have
profaned in their midst; and
the nations shall know that I
am the LORD,” says the Lord
GOD, “when I am hallowed in
you before their eyes. 24For I
will take you from among the
nations, gather you out of all
countries, and bring you into
your own land. 25Then I will
sprinkle clean water on you,
and you shall be clean; I will
cleanse you from all your filthiness and from all your idols.
26I will give you a new heart
and put a new spirit within
you; I will take the heart of
stone out of your flesh and
give you a heart of flesh. 27I
will put My Spirit within you
and cause you to walk in My
statutes, and you will keep
My judgments and do *them.*
28Then you shall dwell in the
land that I gave to your fathers; you shall be My people, and I will be your God. 29I
will deliver you from all your
uncleannesses. I will call for
the grain and multiply it, and

bring no famine upon you.
30And I will multiply the fruit
of your trees and the increase
of your fields, so that you need
never again bear the reproach
of famine among the nations.
31Then you will remember
your evil ways and your deeds
that *were* not good; and you
will loathe yourselves in your
own sight, for your iniquities
and your abominations. 32Not
for your sake do I do *this,*" says
the Lord GOD, "let it be known
to you. Be ashamed and confounded for your own ways,
O house of Israel!"

33'Thus says the Lord GOD:
"On the day that I cleanse you
from all your iniquities, I will
also enable *you* to dwell in the
cities, and the ruins shall be
rebuilt. 34The desolate land
shall be tilled instead of lying
desolate in the sight of all who
pass by. 35So they will say,
'This land that was desolate
has become like the garden
of Eden; and the wasted, desolate, and ruined cities *are*
now fortified *and* inhabited.'
36Then the nations which
are left all around you shall
know that I, the LORD, have
rebuilt the ruined places *and*
planted what was desolate. I,
the LORD, have spoken *it,* and
I will do *it.*"

37'Thus says the Lord GOD:
"I will also let the house of Israel inquire of Me to do this
for them: I will increase their
men like a flock. 38Like a flock
offered as holy *sacrifices,* like
the flock at Jerusalem on its
feast days, so shall the ruined
cities be filled with flocks of
men. Then they shall know
that I *am* the LORD."'"

THE DRY BONES LIVE

37 The hand of the LORD
came upon me and
brought me out in the Spirit
of the LORD, and set me down
in the midst of the valley; and
it *was* full of bones. 2Then He
caused me to pass by them all
around, and behold, *there were*
very many in the open valley;
and indeed *they were* very dry.
3And He said to me, "Son of
man, can these bones live?"

So I answered, "O Lord
GOD, You know."

4Again He said to me,
"Prophesy to these bones, and
say to them, 'O dry bones, hear
the word of the LORD! 5Thus
says the Lord GOD to these
bones: "Surely I will cause
breath to enter into you, and
you shall live. 6I will put sinews on you and bring flesh
upon you, cover you with skin
and put breath in you; and you
shall live. Then you shall know
that I *am* the LORD."'"

7So I prophesied as I was
commanded; and as I prophesied, there was a noise, and
suddenly a rattling; and the
bones came together, bone
to bone. 8Indeed, as I looked,
the sinews and the flesh came
upon them, and the skin covered them over; but *there was*
no breath in them.

9Also He said to me,
"Prophesy to the breath,
prophesy, son of man, and
say to the breath, 'Thus says
the Lord GOD: "Come from
the four winds, O breath, and
breathe on these slain, that
they may live."'" 10So I prophesied as He commanded me,
and breath came into them,
and they lived, and stood
upon their feet, an exceedingly great army.

11Then He said to me, "Son
of man, these bones are the
whole house of Israel. They
indeed say, 'Our bones are dry,
our hope is lost, and we ourselves are cut off!' 12Therefore
prophesy and say to them,
'Thus says the Lord GOD: "Behold, O My people, I will open
your graves and cause you to
come up from your graves,
and bring you into the land of
Israel. 13Then you shall know
that I *am* the LORD, when I
have opened your graves,
O My people, and brought
you up from your graves.
14I will put My Spirit in you,
and you shall live, and I will
place you in your own land.
Then you shall know that I,
the LORD, have spoken *it* and
performed *it*," says the LORD.'"

ONE KINGDOM, ONE KING

15Again the word of the
LORD came to me, saying,
16"As for you, son of man, take
a stick for yourself and write
on it: 'For Judah and for the
children of Israel, his companions.' Then take another
stick and write on it, 'For Joseph, the stick of Ephraim,
and *for* all the house of Israel,
his companions.' 17Then join
them one to another for yourself into one stick, and they
will become one in your hand.

18"And when the children
of your people speak to you,
saying, 'Will you not show us
what you *mean* by these?'—
19say to them, 'Thus says the
Lord GOD: "Surely I will take
the stick of Joseph, which *is*
in the hand of Ephraim, and
the tribes of Israel, his companions; and I will join them
with it, with the stick of Judah,
and make them one stick, and
they will be one in My hand."'
20And the sticks on which you
write will be in your hand before their eyes.

21"Then say to them, 'Thus
says the Lord GOD: "Surely I
will take the children of Israel from among the nations,
wherever they have gone, and
will gather them from every
side and bring them into their
own land; 22and I will make
them one nation in the land,
on the mountains of Israel;
and one king shall be king
over them all; they shall no
longer be two nations, nor
shall they ever be divided into
two kingdoms again. 23They
shall not defile themselves
anymore with their idols, nor
with their detestable things,
nor with any of their transgressions; but I will deliver

them from all their dwelling
places in which they have
sinned, and will cleanse them.
Then they shall be My people,
and I will be their God.
[24]"David My servant *shall
be* king over them, and they
shall all have one shepherd;
they shall also walk in My
judgments and observe My
statutes, and do them. [25]Then
they shall dwell in the land
that I have given to Jacob My
servant, where your fathers
dwelt; and they shall dwell
there, they, their children,
and their children's children,
forever; and My servant David
shall be their prince forever.
[26]Moreover I will make a covenant of peace with them, and
it shall be an everlasting covenant with them; I will establish them and multiply them,
and I will set My sanctuary in
their midst forevermore. [27]My
tabernacle also shall be with
them; indeed I will be their
God, and they shall be My
people. [28]The nations also will
know that I, the LORD, sanctify
Israel, when My sanctuary is
in their midst forevermore.""

GOG AND ALLIES ATTACK ISRAEL

38 Now the word of the
LORD came to me, say-
ing, [2]"Son of man, set your
face against Gog, of the land
of Magog, the prince of Rosh,[a] Meshech, and Tubal, and
prophesy against him, [3]and
say, 'Thus says the Lord GOD:
"Behold, I *am* against you,
O Gog, the prince of Rosh, Meshech, and Tubal. [4]I will turn
you around, put hooks into
your jaws, and lead you out,
with all your army, horses,
and horsemen, all splendidly
clothed, a great company *with*
bucklers and shields, all of
them handling swords. [5]Per-
sia, Ethiopia,[a] and Libya[b] are
with them, all of them *with*
shield and helmet; [6]Gomer
and all its troops; the house of
Togarmah *from* the far north
and all its troops—many people *are* with you.
[7]"Prepare yourself and
be ready, you and all your
companies that are gathered
about you; and be a guard for
them. [8]After many days you
will be visited. In the latter
years you will come into the
land of those brought back
from the sword *and* gathered
from many people on the
mountains of Israel, which
had long been desolate; they
were brought out of the nations, and now all of them
dwell safely. [9]You will ascend,
coming like a storm, covering
the land like a cloud, you and
all your troops and many peoples with you."
[10]'Thus says the Lord GOD:
"On that day it shall come to

38:2 [a] Targum, Vulgate, and Aquila read *chief prince of* (also verse 3). 38:5 [a] Hebrew *Cush* [b] Hebrew *Put*

pass *that* thoughts will arise in
your mind, and you will make
an evil plan: 11You will say, 'I
will go up against a land of
unwalled villages; I will go to
a peaceful people, who dwell
safely, all of them dwelling
without walls, and having neither bars nor gates'— 12to take
plunder and to take booty, to
stretch out your hand against
the waste places *that are again*
inhabited, and against a people gathered from the nations,
who have acquired livestock
and goods, who dwell in the
midst of the land. 13Sheba,
Dedan, the merchants of
Tarshish, and all their young
lions will say to you, 'Have
you come to take plunder?
Have you gathered your army
to take booty, to carry away
silver and gold, to take away
livestock and goods, to take
great plunder?' "'

14"Therefore, son of man,
prophesy and say to Gog,
'Thus says the Lord GOD: "On
that day when My people Israel dwell safely, will you not
know *it?* 15Then you will come
from your place out of the far
north, you and many peoples
with you, all of them riding
on horses, a great company
and a mighty army. 16You will
come up against My people
Israel like a cloud, to cover
the land. It will be in the lat-
ter days that I will bring you
against My land, so that the
nations may know Me, when
I am hallowed in you, O Gog,
before their eyes." 17Thus says
the Lord GOD: "Are *you* he of
whom I have spoken in former days by My servants the
prophets of Israel, who prophesied for years in those days
that I would bring you against
them?

JUDGMENT ON GOG

18"And it will come to pass
at the same time, when Gog
comes against the land of Israel," says the Lord GOD, "*that*
My fury will show in My face.
19For in My jealousy *and* in
the fire of My wrath I have
spoken: 'Surely in that day
there shall be a great earthquake in the land of Israel,
20so that the fish of the sea,
the birds of the heavens, the
beasts of the field, all creeping things that creep on the
earth, and all men who *are*
on the face of the earth shall
shake at My presence. The
mountains shall be thrown
down, the steep places shall
fall, and every wall shall fall to
the ground.' 21I will call for a
sword against Gog throughout
all My mountains," says the
Lord GOD. "Every man's sword
will be against his brother.
22And I will bring him to
judgment with pestilence and
bloodshed; I will rain down on
him, on his troops, and on the
many peoples who *are* with
him, flooding rain, great hailstones, fire, and brimstone.
23Thus I will magnify Myself
and sanctify Myself, and I will

be known in the eyes of many
nations. Then they shall know
that I *am* the LORD."'

GOG'S ARMIES DESTROYED

39 "And you, son of man,
prophesy against Gog,
and say, 'Thus says the Lord
GOD: "Behold, I *am* against
you, O Gog, the prince of
Rosh,[a] Meshech, and Tubal;
2and I will turn you around
and lead you on, bringing
you up from the far north,
and bring you against the
mountains of Israel. 3Then I
will knock the bow out of your
left hand, and cause the arrows
to fall out of your right
hand. 4You shall fall upon the
mountains of Israel, you and
all your troops and the peoples
who *are* with you; I will
give you to birds of prey of
every sort and *to* the beasts of
the field to be devoured. 5You
shall fall on the open field; for
I have spoken," says the Lord
GOD. 6"And I will send fire on
Magog and on those who live
in security in the coastlands.
Then they shall know that I
am the LORD. 7So I will make
My holy name known in the
midst of My people Israel, and
I will not *let them* profane My
holy name anymore. Then the
nations shall know that *I am*
the LORD, the Holy One in Israel.
8Surely it is coming, and
it shall be done," says the Lord
GOD. "This *is* the day of which
I have spoken.
9"Then those who dwell
in the cities of Israel will go
out and set on fire and burn
the weapons, both the shields
and bucklers, the bows and arrows,
the javelins and spears;
and they will make fires with
them for seven years. 10They
will not take wood from the
field nor cut down *any* from
the forests, because they will
make fires with the weapons;
and they will plunder those
who plundered them, and pillage
those who pillaged them,"
says the Lord GOD.

THE BURIAL OF GOG

11"It will come to pass in
that day *that* I will give Gog
a burial place there in Israel,
the valley of those who pass by
east of the sea; and it will obstruct
travelers, because there
they will bury Gog and all his
multitude. Therefore they will
call *it* the Valley of Hamon
Gog.[a] 12For seven months the
house of Israel will be burying
them, in order to cleanse the
land. 13Indeed all the people of
the land will be burying, and
they will gain renown for it on
the day that I am glorified,"
says the Lord GOD. 14"They
will set apart men regularly
employed, with the help of a
search party,[a] to pass through
the land and bury those bodies

39:1 [a] Targum, Vulgate and Aquila read *chief prince of.* 39:11 [a] Literally *The Multitude of Gog* 39:14 [a] Literally *those who pass through*

remaining on the ground, in
order to cleanse it. At the end
of seven months they will
make a search. 15The search
party will pass through the
land; and *when anyone* sees
a man's bone, he shall set up
a marker by it, till the buriers
have buried it in the Valley
of Hamon Gog. 16*The* name
of *the* city *will* also *be* Hamo-
nah. Thus they shall cleanse
the land."'

A TRIUMPHANT FESTIVAL

17"And as for you, son of
man, thus says the Lord GOD,
'Speak to every sort of bird
and to every beast of the field:

"Assemble yourselves
  and come;
Gather together from
  all sides to My
  sacrificial meal
Which I am sacrificing
  for you,
A great sacrificial meal on
  the mountains of Israel,
That you may eat flesh
  and drink blood.
18 You shall eat the flesh
  of the mighty,
Drink the blood of the
  princes of the earth,
Of rams and lambs,
Of goats and bulls,
All of them fatlings
  of Bashan.
19 You shall eat fat till
  you are full,
And drink blood till
  you are drunk,
At My sacrificial meal
Which I am sacrificing
  for you.
20 You shall be filled
  at My table
With horses and riders,
With mighty men
And with all the men of
  war," says the Lord GOD.

ISRAEL RESTORED TO THE LAND

21"I will set My glory among
the nations; all the nations
shall see My judgment which
I have executed, and My hand
which I have laid on them.
22So the house of Israel shall
know that I *am* the LORD their
God from that day forward.
23The Gentiles shall know that
the house of Israel went into
captivity for their iniquity;
because they were unfaithful to Me, therefore I hid My
face from them. I gave them
into the hand of their enemies, and they all fell by the
sword. 24According to their
uncleanness and according
to their transgressions I have
dealt with them, and hidden
My face from them."'

25"Therefore thus says the
Lord GOD: 'Now I will bring
back the captives of Jacob,
and have mercy on the whole
house of Israel; and I will be
jealous for My holy name—
26after they have borne their
shame, and all their unfaithfulness in which they were
unfaithful to Me, when they
dwelt safely in their *own*
land and no one made *them*

afraid. 27When I have brought
them back from the peoples
and gathered them out of
their enemies' lands, and I
am hallowed in them in the
sight of many nations, 28then
they shall know that I *am* the
LORD their God, who sent
them into captivity among
the nations, but also brought
them back to their land, and
left none of them captive any
longer. 29And I will not hide
My face from them anymore;
for I shall have poured out My
Spirit on the house of Israel,'
says the Lord GOD."

A NEW CITY, A NEW TEMPLE

40 In the twenty-fifth year
of our captivity, at the
beginning of the year, on
the tenth *day* of the month,
in the fourteenth year after
the city was captured, on the
very same day the hand of
the LORD was upon me; and
He took me there. 2In the visions of God He took me into
the land of Israel and set me
on a very high mountain;
on it toward the south *was*
something like the structure
of a city. 3He took me there,
and behold, *there was* a man
whose appearance *was* like
the appearance of bronze. He
had a line of flax and a measuring rod in his hand, and he
stood in the gateway.

4And the man said to me,
"Son of man, look with your
eyes and hear with your ears,
and fix your mind on everything I show you; for you *were*
brought here so that I might
show *them* to you. Declare
to the house of Israel everything you see." 5Now there was
a wall all around the outside
of the temple.[a] In the man's
hand was a measuring rod
six cubits *long, each being a*
cubit and a handbreadth; and
he measured the width of the
wall structure, one rod; and
the height, one rod.

THE EASTERN GATEWAY OF THE TEMPLE

6Then he went to the gateway which faced east; and he
went up its stairs and measured the threshold of the
gateway, *which was* one rod
wide, and the other threshold
was one rod wide. 7Each gate
chamber *was* one rod long
and one rod wide; between the
gate chambers *was a space of*
five cubits; and the threshold
of the gateway by the vestibule
of the inside gate *was* one rod.
8He also measured the vestibule of the inside gate, one
rod. 9Then he measured the
vestibule of the gateway, eight
cubits; and the gateposts, two
cubits. The vestibule of the
gate *was* on the inside. 10In
the eastern gateway *were*
three gate chambers on one
side and three on the other;

40:5 [a] Literally *house,* and so elsewhere in this book

the three *were* all the same
size; also the gateposts were
of the same size on this side
and that side.
11He measured the width
of the entrance to the gateway, ten cubits; *and* the length
of the gate, thirteen cubits.
12*There was* a space in front of
the gate chambers, one cubit
on this side and one cubit on
that side; the gate chambers
were six cubits on this side and
six cubits on that side. 13Then
he measured the gateway from
the roof of *one* gate chamber
to the roof of the other; the
width *was* twenty-five cubits, as door faces door. 14He
measured the gateposts, sixty
cubits high, and the court all
around the gateway *extended*
to the gatepost. 15*From* the
front of the entrance gate to
the front of the vestibule of
the inner gate *was* fifty cubits.
16*There were* beveled window
frames in the gate chambers
and in their intervening archways on the inside of the gateway all around, and likewise
in the vestibules. *There were*
windows all around on the
inside. And on each gatepost
were palm trees.

THE OUTER COURT

17Then he brought me into
the outer court; and *there were*
chambers and a pavement
made all around the court;
thirty chambers faced the
pavement. 18The pavement
was by the side of the gateways,
corresponding to the length
of the gateways; *this was* the
lower pavement. 19Then he
measured the width from the
front of the lower gateway to
the front of the inner court
exterior, one hundred cubits
toward the east and the north.

THE NORTHERN GATEWAY

20On the outer court was
also a gateway facing north,
and he measured its length
and its width. 21Its gate chambers, three on this side and
three on that side, its gateposts and its archways, had the
same measurements as the
first gate; its length *was* fifty
cubits and its width twenty-
five cubits. 22Its windows and
those of its archways, and also
its palm trees, *had* the same
measurements as the gateway
facing east; it was ascended
by seven steps, and its archway *was* in front of it. 23A gate
of the inner court was opposite the northern gateway, just
as the eastern *gateway;* and
he measured from gateway to
gateway, one hundred cubits.

THE SOUTHERN GATEWAY

24After that he brought me
toward the south, and there a
gateway was facing south; and
he measured its gateposts and
archways according to these
same measurements. 25*There
were* windows in it and in its
archways all around like those
windows; its length *was* fifty
cubits and its width twenty-

five cubits. 26Seven steps led up to it, and its archway *was* in front of them; and it had palm trees on its gateposts, one on this side and one on that side. 27*There was* also a gateway on the inner court, facing south; and he measured from gateway to gateway toward the south, one hundred cubits.

GATEWAYS OF THE INNER COURT

28Then he brought me to the inner court through the southern gateway; he measured the southern gateway according to these same measurements. 29Also its gate chambers, its gateposts, and its archways *were* according to these same measurements; *there were* windows in it and in its archways all around; *it was* fifty cubits long and twenty-five cubits wide. 30*There were* archways all around, twenty-five cubits long and five cubits wide. 31Its archways faced the outer court, palm trees *were* on its gateposts, and going up to it *were* eight steps.

32And he brought me into the inner court facing east; he measured the gateway according to these same measurements. 33Also its gate chambers, its gateposts, and its archways *were* according to these same measurements; and *there were* windows in it and in its archways all around; *it was* fifty cubits long and twenty-five cubits wide. 34Its archways faced the outer court, and palm trees *were* on its gateposts on this side and on that side; and going up to it *were* eight steps.

35Then he brought me to the north gateway and measured *it* according to these same measurements— 36also its gate chambers, its gateposts, and its archways. It had windows all around; its length *was* fifty cubits and its width twenty-five cubits. 37Its gateposts faced the outer court, palm trees *were* on its gateposts on this side and on that side, and going up to it *were* eight steps.

WHERE SACRIFICES WERE PREPARED

38*There was* a chamber and its entrance by the gateposts of the gateway, where they washed the burnt offering. 39In the vestibule of the gateway *were* two tables on this side and two tables on that side, on which to slay the burnt offering, the sin offering, and the trespass offering. 40At the outer side of the *vestibule*, as one goes up to the entrance of the northern gateway, *were* two tables; and on the other side of the vestibule of the gateway *were* two tables. 41Four tables *were* on this side and four tables on that side, by the side of the gateway, eight tables on which they slaughtered *the sacrifices.* 42*There were* also four tables

of hewn stone for the burnt offering, one cubit and a half long, one cubit and a half wide, and one cubit high; on these they laid the instruments with which they slaughtered the burnt offering and the sacrifice. 43Inside *were* hooks, a handbreadth wide, fastened all around; and the flesh of the sacrifices *was* on the tables.

CHAMBERS FOR SINGERS AND PRIESTS

44Outside the inner gate *were* the chambers for the singers in the inner court, one facing south at the side of the northern gateway, and the other facing north at the side of the southern[a] gateway. 45Then he said to me, "This chamber which faces south *is* for the priests who have charge of the temple. 46The chamber which faces north *is* for the priests who have charge of the altar; these *are* the sons of Zadok, from the sons of Levi, who come near the LORD to minister to Him."

DIMENSIONS OF THE INNER COURT AND VESTIBULE

47And he measured the court, one hundred cubits long and one hundred cubits wide, foursquare. The altar *was* in front of the temple. 48Then he brought me to the vestibule of the temple and measured the doorposts of the vestibule, five cubits on this side and five cubits on that side; and the width of the gateway was three cubits on this side and three cubits on that side. 49The length of the vestibule *was* twenty cubits, and the width eleven cubits; and by the steps which led up to it *there were* pillars by the doorposts, one on this side and another on that side.

DIMENSIONS OF THE SANCTUARY

41 Then he brought me into the sanctuary[a] and measured the doorposts, six cubits wide on one side and six cubits wide on the other side—the width of the tabernacle. 2The width of the entryway *was* ten cubits, and the side walls of the entrance *were* five cubits on this side and five cubits on the other side; and he measured its length, forty cubits, and its width, twenty cubits.

3Also he went inside and measured the doorposts, two cubits; and the entrance, six cubits *high;* and the width of the entrance, seven cubits. 4He measured the length, twenty cubits; and the width, twenty cubits, beyond the sanctuary; and he said to me, "This *is* the Most Holy *Place.*"

40:44 [a] Following Septuagint; Masoretic Text and Vulgate read *eastern.* 41:1 [a] Hebrew *heykal,* here the main room of the temple, sometimes called the *holy place* (compare Exodus 26:33)

THE SIDE CHAMBERS ON THE WALL

[5]Next, he measured the
wall of the temple, six cubits.
The width of each side chamber all around the temple *was*
four cubits on every side. [6]The
side chambers *were* in three
stories, one above the other,
thirty chambers in each story;
they rested on ledges which
were for the side chambers
all around, that they might be
supported, but not fastened to
the wall of the temple. [7]As one
went up from story to story,
the side chambers became
wider all around, because
their supporting ledges in the
wall of the temple ascended
like steps; therefore the width
of the structure increased as
one went up *from* the lowest
story to the highest by way of
the middle one. [8]I also saw
an elevation all around the
temple; it was the foundation
of the side chambers, a full
rod, *that is,* six cubits *high.*
[9]The thickness of the outer
wall of the side chambers *was*
five cubits, and so also the remaining terrace by the place
of the side chambers of the
temple. [10]And between *it and*
the *wall* chambers was a width
of twenty cubits all around the
temple on every side. [11]The
doors of the side chambers
opened on the terrace, one
door toward the north and another toward the south; and
the width of the terrace *was*
five cubits all around.

THE BUILDING AT THE WESTERN END

[12]The building that faced
the separating courtyard at its
western end *was* seventy cubits wide; the wall of the building *was* five cubits thick all
around, and its length ninety
cubits.

DIMENSIONS AND DESIGN OF THE TEMPLE AREA

[13]So he measured the temple, one hundred cubits long;
and the separating courtyard
with the building and its walls
was one hundred cubits long;
[14]also the width of the eastern
face of the temple, including
the separating courtyard,
was one hundred cubits.
[15]He measured the length of
the building behind it, facing the separating courtyard,
with its galleries on the one
side and on the other side,
one hundred cubits, as well
as the inner temple and the
porches of the court, [16]their
doorposts and the beveled
window frames. And the galleries all around their three
stories opposite the threshold
were paneled with wood from
the ground to the windows—
the windows were covered—
[17]from the space above the
door, even to the inner room,[a]
as well as outside, and on

41:17 [a] Literally *house,* here *the Most Holy Place*

every wall all around, inside
and outside, by measure.
18And *it was* made with
cherubim and palm trees, a
palm tree between cherub and
cherub. *Each* cherub had two
faces, 19so that the face of a
man *was* toward a palm tree
on one side, and the face of a
young lion toward a palm tree
on the other side; thus *it was*
made throughout the temple
all around. 20From the floor to
the space above the door, and
on the wall of the sanctuary,
cherubim and palm trees *were*
carved.
21The doorposts of the temple *were* square, *as was* the
front of the sanctuary; their
appearance was similar. 22The
altar *was* of wood, three cubits
high, and its length two cubits.
Its corners, its length, and its
sides *were* of wood; and he
said to me, "This *is* the table
that *is* before the LORD."
23The temple and the sanctuary had two doors. 24The
doors had two panels *apiece,*
two folding panels: two *panels*
for one door and two panels
for the other *door.* 25Cherubim
and palm trees *were* carved on
the doors of the temple just as
they *were* carved on the walls.
A wooden canopy *was* on the
front of the vestibule outside.
26*There were* beveled window
frames and palm trees on one
side and on the other, on the
sides of the vestibule—also
on the side chambers of the
temple and on the canopies.

THE CHAMBERS FOR THE PRIESTS

42 Then he brought me
out into the outer
court, by the way toward the
north; and he brought me into
the chamber which *was* opposite the separating courtyard,
and which *was* opposite the
building toward the north.
2Facing the length, *which*
was one hundred cubits (the
width was fifty cubits), was
the north door. 3Opposite the
inner court of twenty *cubits,*
and opposite the pavement
of the outer court, *was* gallery
against gallery in three *stories.*
4In front of the chambers, toward the inside, *was* a walk
ten cubits wide, at a distance
of one cubit; and their doors
faced north. 5Now the upper
chambers *were* shorter, because the galleries took away
space from them more than
from the lower and middle
stories of the building. 6For
they *were* in three *stories* and
did not have pillars like the
pillars of the courts; therefore
the upper level was shortened
more than the lower and middle levels from the ground up.
7And a wall which *was* outside
ran parallel to the chambers,
at the front of the chambers,
toward the outer court; its
length *was* fifty cubits. 8The
length of the chambers toward the outer court *was* fifty
cubits, whereas that facing the
temple *was* one hundred cubits. 9At the lower chambers

was the entrance on the east side, as one goes into them from the outer court.

10Also *there were* chambers in the thickness of the wall of the court toward the east, opposite the separating courtyard and opposite the building. 11*There was* a walk in front of them also, and their appearance *was* like the chambers which *were* toward the north; they *were* as long and as wide as the others, and all their exits and entrances *were* according to plan. 12And corresponding to the doors of the chambers that *were* facing south, as one enters them, *there was* a door in front of the walk, the way directly in front of the wall toward the east.

13Then he said to me, "The north chambers *and* the south chambers, which *are* opposite the separating courtyard, *are* the holy chambers where the priests who approach the LORD shall eat the most holy offerings. There they shall lay the most holy offerings—the grain offering, the sin offering, and the trespass offering—for the place *is* holy. 14When the priests enter them, they shall not go out of *the holy chamber* into the outer court; but there they shall leave their garments in which they minister, for they *are* holy. They shall put on other garments; then they may approach *that* which *is* for the people."

OUTER DIMENSIONS OF THE TEMPLE

15Now when he had finished measuring the inner temple, he brought me out through the gateway that faces toward the east, and measured it all around. 16He measured the east side with the measuring rod,[a] five hundred rods by the measuring rod all around. 17He measured the north side, five hundred rods by the measuring rod all around. 18He measured the south side, five hundred rods by the measuring rod. 19He came around to the west side *and* measured five hundred rods by the measuring rod. 20He measured it on the four sides; it had a wall all around, five hundred *cubits* long and five hundred wide, to separate the holy areas from the common.

THE TEMPLE, THE LORD'S DWELLING PLACE

43 Afterward he brought me to the gate, the gate that faces toward the east. 2And behold, the glory of the God of Israel came from the way of the east. His voice *was* like the sound of many waters; and the earth shone with His glory. 3*It was* like the appearance of the vision which

42:16 [a] Compare 40:5

I saw—like the vision which I
saw when I[a] came to destroy
the city. The visions *were* like
the vision which I saw by the
River Chebar; and I fell on
my face. 4And the glory of the
LORD came into the temple by
way of the gate which faces
toward the east. 5The Spirit
lifted me up and brought me
into the inner court; and behold, the glory of the LORD
filled the temple.

6Then I heard *Him* speaking to me from the temple,
while a man stood beside me.
7And He said to me, "Son of
man, *this is* the place of My
throne and the place of the
soles of My feet, where I will
dwell in the midst of the
children of Israel forever. No
more shall the house of Israel
defile My holy name, they nor
their kings, by their harlotry
or with the carcasses of their
kings on their high places.
8When they set their threshold by My threshold, and their
doorpost by My doorpost,
with a wall between them and
Me, they defiled My holy name
by the abominations which
they committed; therefore I
have consumed them in My
anger. 9Now let them put their
harlotry and the carcasses of
their kings far away from Me,
and I will dwell in their midst
forever.

10"Son of man, describe the
temple to the house of Israel,
that they may be ashamed of
their iniquities; and let them
measure the pattern. 11And if
they are ashamed of all that
they have done, make known
to them the design of the temple and its arrangement, its
exits and its entrances, its
entire design and all its ordinances, all its forms and all
its laws. Write *it* down in their
sight, so that they may keep
its whole design and all its ordinances, and perform them.
12This *is* the law of the temple:
The whole area surrounding
the mountaintop *is* most holy.
Behold, this *is* the law of the
temple.

DIMENSIONS OF THE ALTAR

13"These are the measure-
ments of the altar in cubits
(the cubit *is* one cubit and a
handbreadth): the base one
cubit high and one cubit
wide, with a rim all around
its edge of one span. This *is*
the height of the altar: 14from
the base on the ground to the
lower ledge, two cubits; the
width of the ledge, one cubit;
from the smaller ledge to
the larger ledge, four cubits;
and the width of the ledge,
one cubit. 15The altar hearth
is four cubits high, with four
horns extending upward from
the hearth. 16The altar hearth
is twelve cubits long, twelve
wide, square at its four cor-

43:3 [a] Some Hebrew manuscripts and Vulgate read *He*.

ners; 17the ledge, fourteen *cu-*
bits long and fourteen wide
on its four sides, with a rim of
half a cubit around it; its base,
one cubit all around; and its
steps face toward the east."

CONSECRATING THE ALTAR

18And He said to me, "Son
of man, thus says the Lord
GOD: 'These *are* the ordinances for the altar on the day
when it is made, for sacrificing
burnt offerings on it, and for
sprinkling blood on it. 19You
shall give a young bull for a
sin offering to the priests, the
Levites, who are of the seed
of Zadok, who approach Me
to minister to Me,' says the
Lord GOD. 20'You shall take
some of its blood and put *it* on
the four horns of the altar, on
the four corners of the ledge,
and on the rim around it; thus
you shall cleanse it and make
atonement for it. 21Then you
shall also take the bull of the
sin offering, and burn it in the
appointed place of the temple, outside the sanctuary.
22On the second day you shall
offer a kid of the goats without
blemish for a sin offering; and
they shall cleanse the altar, as
they cleansed *it* with the bull.
23When you have finished
cleansing *it,* you shall offer
a young bull without blemish, and a ram from the flock
without blemish. 24When you
offer them before the LORD,
the priests shall throw salt
on them, and they will offer
them up *as* a burnt offering
to the LORD. 25Every day for
seven days you shall prepare
a goat *for* a sin offering; they
shall also prepare a young bull
and a ram from the flock, both
without blemish. 26Seven days
they shall make atonement
for the altar and purify it, and
so consecrate *it.* 27When these
days are over it shall be, on
the eighth day and thereafter,
that the priests shall offer
your burnt offerings and your
peace offerings on the altar;
and I will accept you,' says the
Lord GOD."

THE EAST GATE AND THE PRINCE

44 Then He brought me
back to the outer gate
of the sanctuary which faces
toward the east, but it *was*
shut. 2And the LORD said to
me, "This gate shall be shut;
it shall not be opened, and no
man shall enter by it, because
the LORD God of Israel has entered by it; therefore it shall
be shut. 3*As for* the prince, *be-*
cause he *is* the prince, he may
sit in it to eat bread before the
LORD; he shall enter by way of
the vestibule of the gateway,
and go out the same way."

THOSE ADMITTED TO THE TEMPLE

4Also He brought me
by way of the north gate to
the front of the temple; so I
looked, and behold, the glory
of the LORD filled the house

of the LORD; and I fell on my face. 5And the LORD said to me, "Son of man, mark well, see with your eyes and hear with your ears, all that I say to you concerning all the ordinances of the house of the LORD and all its laws. Mark well who may enter the house and all who go out from the sanctuary.

6"Now say to the rebellious, to the house of Israel, 'Thus says the Lord GOD: "O house of Israel, let Us have no more of all your abominations. 7When you brought in foreigners, uncircumcised in heart and uncircumcised in flesh, to be in My sanctuary to defile it—My house—and when you offered My food, the fat and the blood, then they broke My covenant because of all your abominations. 8And you have not kept charge of My holy things, but you have set *others* to keep charge of My sanctuary for you." 9Thus says the Lord GOD: "No foreigner, uncircumcised in heart or uncircumcised in flesh, shall enter My sanctuary, including any foreigner who *is* among the children of Israel.

LAWS GOVERNING PRIESTS

10"And the Levites who went far from Me, when Israel went astray, who strayed *away* from Me after their idols, they shall bear their iniquity. 11Yet they shall be ministers in My sanctuary, *as* gatekeepers of the house and ministers of the house; they shall slay the burnt offering and the sacrifice for the people, and they shall stand before them to minister to them. 12Because they ministered to them before their idols and caused the house of Israel to fall into iniquity, therefore I have raised My hand in an oath against them," says the Lord GOD, "that they shall bear their iniquity. 13And they shall not come near Me to minister to Me as priest, nor come near any of My holy things, nor into the Most Holy *Place;* but they shall bear their shame and their abominations which they have committed. 14Nevertheless I will make them keep charge of the temple, for all its work, and for all that has to be done in it.

15"But the priests, the Levites, the sons of Zadok, who kept charge of My sanctuary when the children of Israel went astray from Me, they shall come near Me to minister to Me; and they shall stand before Me to offer to Me the fat and the blood," says the Lord GOD. 16"They shall enter My sanctuary, and they shall come near My table to minister to Me, and they shall keep My charge. 17And *it shall be,* whenever they enter the gates of the inner court, that they shall put on linen garments; no wool shall come upon them while they

minister within the gates
of the inner court or within
the house. [18]They shall have
linen turbans on their heads
and linen trousers on their
bodies; they shall not clothe
themselves with *anything that
causes* sweat. [19]When they go
out to the outer court, to the
outer court to the people, they
shall take off their garments
in which they have minis-
tered, leave them in the holy
chambers, and put on other
garments; and in their holy
garments they shall not sanctify the people.

[20]"They shall neither shave
their heads nor let their hair
grow long, but they shall keep
their hair well trimmed. [21]No
priest shall drink wine when
he enters the inner court.
[22]They shall not take as wife
a widow or a divorced woman,
but take virgins of the descendants of the house of Israel, or
widows of priests.

[23]"And they shall teach My
people *the difference* between
the holy and the unholy, and
cause them to discern be-
tween the unclean and the
clean. [24]In controversy they
shall stand as judges, *and*
judge it according to My
judgments. They shall keep
My laws and My statutes in all
My appointed meetings, and
they shall hallow My Sabbaths.

[25]"They shall not defile
themselves by coming near a
dead person. Only for father
or mother, for son or daughter, for brother or unmarried
sister may they defile themselves. [26]After he is cleansed,
they shall count seven days
for him. [27]And on the day that
he goes to the sanctuary to
minister in the sanctuary, he
must offer his sin offering in
the inner court," says the Lord
GOD.

[28]"It shall be, in regard to
their inheritance, *that* I *am*
their inheritance. You shall
give them no possession in
Israel, for I *am* their possession. [29]They shall eat the grain
offering, the sin offering, and
the trespass offering; every
dedicated thing in Israel
shall be theirs. [30]The best of
all firstfruits of any kind, and
every sacrifice of any kind
from all your sacrifices, shall
be the priest's; also you shall
give to the priest the first of
your ground meal, to cause a
blessing to rest on your house.
[31]The priests shall not eat anything, bird or beast, that died
naturally or was torn *by wild
beasts*.

THE HOLY DISTRICT

45 "Moreover, when you
divide the land by lot
into inheritance, you shall set
apart a district for the LORD,
a holy section of the land;
its length *shall be* twenty-
five thousand *cubits*, and the
width ten thousand. It *shall
be* holy throughout its territory all around. [2]Of this there
shall be a square plot for the

sanctuary, five hundred by
five hundred *rods,* with fifty
cubits around it for an open
space. 3So this is the district
you shall measure: twenty-
five thousand *cubits* long and
ten thousand wide; in it shall
be the sanctuary, the Most
Holy *Place.* 4It shall be a holy
section of the land, belonging to the priests, the ministers of the sanctuary, who
come near to minister to the
LORD; it shall be a place for
their houses and a holy place
for the sanctuary. 5*An area*
twenty-five thousand *cubits*
long and ten thousand wide
shall belong to the Levites, the
ministers of the temple; they
shall have twenty chambers
as a possession.[a]

PROPERTIES OF THE CITY AND THE PRINCE

6"You shall appoint as the
property of the city *an area*
five thousand *cubits* wide and
twenty-five thousand long,
adjacent to the district of the
holy *section;* it shall belong
to the whole house of Israel.

7"The prince shall have *a*
section on one side and the
other of the holy district and
the city's property; and bor-
dering on the holy district and
the city's property, extending
westward on the west side and
eastward on the east *side,* the
length *shall be* side by side
with one of the *tribal* portions,
from the west border to the
east border. 8The land shall
be his possession in Israel;
and My princes shall no more
oppress My people, but they
shall give *the rest of* the land to
the house of Israel, according
to their tribes."

LAWS GOVERNING THE PRINCE

9"Thus says the Lord GOD:
"Enough, O princes of Israel!
Remove violence and plun-
dering, execute justice and
righteousness, and stop dis-
possessing My people," says
the Lord GOD. 10"You shall
have honest scales, an honest
ephah, and an honest bath.
11The ephah and the bath shall
be of the same measure, so
that the bath contains one-
tenth of a homer, and the
ephah one-tenth of a homer;
their measure shall be according to the homer. 12The shekel
shall be twenty gerahs; twenty
shekels, twenty-five shekels,
and fifteen shekels shall be
your mina.

13"This *is* the offering which
you shall offer: you shall give
one-sixth of an ephah from
a homer of wheat, and one-
sixth of an ephah from a
homer of barley. 14The ordinance concerning oil, the bath
of oil, is one-tenth of a bath
from a kor. *A kor is* a homer or

45:5 [a] Following Masoretic Text, Targum, and Vulgate; Septuagint reads *a possession, cities of dwelling.*

ten baths, for ten baths *are* a
homer. 15And one lamb shall
be given from a flock of two
hundred, from the rich pastures of Israel. These shall be
for grain offerings, burnt offerings, and peace offerings,
to make atonement for them,"
says the Lord God. 16"All the
people of the land shall give
this offering for the prince in
Israel. 17Then it shall be the
prince's part *to give* burnt offerings, grain offerings, and
drink offerings, at the feasts,
the New Moons, the Sabbaths,
and at all the appointed seasons of the house of Israel. He
shall prepare the sin offering,
the grain offering, the burnt
offering, and the peace offerings to make atonement for
the house of Israel."

KEEPING THE FEASTS

18"Thus says the Lord God:
"In the first *month,* on the
first *day* of the month, you
shall take a young bull without blemish and cleanse the
sanctuary. 19The priest shall
take some of the blood of the
sin offering and put *it* on the
doorposts of the temple, on
the four corners of the ledge of
the altar, and on the gateposts
of the gate of the inner court.
20And so you shall do on the
seventh *day* of the month for
everyone who has sinned unintentionally or in ignorance.
Thus you shall make atonement for the temple.

21"In the first *month,* on the
fourteenth day of the month,
you shall observe the Passover, a feast of seven days; unleavened bread shall be eaten.
22And on that day the prince
shall prepare for himself and
for all the people of the land
a bull *for* a sin offering. 23On
the seven days of the feast he
shall prepare a burnt offering
to the Lord, seven bulls and
seven rams without blemish,
daily for seven days, and a kid
of the goats daily *for* a sin offering. 24And he shall prepare
a grain offering of one ephah
for each bull and one ephah
for each ram, together with a
hin of oil for each ephah.

25"In the seventh *month,*
on the fifteenth day of the
month, at the feast, he shall
do likewise for seven days,
according to the sin offering,
the burnt offering, the grain
offering, and the oil."

THE MANNER OF WORSHIP

46 "Thus says the Lord
God: "The gateway of
the inner court that faces toward the east shall be shut the
six working days; but on the
Sabbath it shall be opened,
and on the day of the New
Moon it shall be opened. 2The
prince shall enter by way of
the vestibule of the gateway
from the outside, and stand by
the gatepost. The priests shall
prepare his burnt offering and
his peace offerings. He shall
worship at the threshold of
the gate. Then he shall go out,

but the gate shall not be shut until evening. 3Likewise the people of the land shall worship at the entrance to this gateway before the LORD on the Sabbaths and the New Moons. 4The burnt offering that the prince offers to the LORD on the Sabbath day *shall be* six lambs without blemish, and a ram without blemish; 5and the grain offering *shall be one* ephah for a ram, and the grain offering for the lambs, as much as he wants to give, as well as a hin of oil with every ephah. 6On the day of the New Moon *it shall be* a young bull without blemish, six lambs, and a ram; they shall be without blemish. 7He shall prepare a grain offering of an ephah for a bull, an ephah for a ram, as much as he wants to give for the lambs, and a hin of oil with every ephah. 8When the prince enters, he shall go in by way of the vestibule of the gateway, and go out the same way.

9"But when the people of the land come before the LORD on the appointed feast days, whoever enters by way of the north gate to worship shall go out by way of the south gate; and whoever enters by way of the south gate shall go out by way of the north gate. He shall not return by way of the gate through which he came, but shall go out through the opposite gate. 10The prince shall then be in their midst. When they go in, he shall go in; and when they go out, he shall go out. 11At the festivals and the appointed feast days the grain offering shall be an ephah for a bull, an ephah for a ram, as much as he wants to give for the lambs, and a hin of oil with every ephah.

12"Now when the prince makes a voluntary burnt offering or voluntary peace offering to the LORD, the gate that faces toward the east shall then be opened for him; and he shall prepare his burnt offering and his peace offerings as he did on the Sabbath day. Then he shall go out, and after he goes out the gate shall be shut.

13"You shall daily make a burnt offering to the LORD *of* a lamb of the first year without blemish; you shall prepare it every morning. 14And you shall prepare a grain offering with it every morning, a sixth of an ephah, and a third of a hin of oil to moisten the fine flour. This grain offering is a perpetual ordinance, to be made regularly to the LORD. 15Thus they shall prepare the lamb, the grain offering, and the oil, *as* a regular burnt offering every morning."

THE PRINCE AND INHERITANCE LAWS

16'Thus says the Lord GOD: "If the prince gives a gift *of some* of his inheritance to any of his sons, it shall belong to

his sons; it is their possession by inheritance. 17But if
he gives a gift of some of his
inheritance to one of his servants, it shall be his until the
year of liberty, after which it
shall return to the prince. But
his inheritance shall belong
to his sons; it shall become
theirs. 18Moreover the prince
shall not take any of the people's inheritance by evicting
them from their property; he
shall provide an inheritance
for his sons from his own
property, so that none of My
people may be scattered from
his property." ' "

HOW THE OFFERINGS WERE PREPARED

19Now he brought me
through the entrance, which
was at the side of the gate,
into the holy chambers of the
priests which face toward the
north; and there a place *was*
situated at their extreme western end. 20And he said to me,
"This *is* the place where the
priests shall boil the trespass
offering and the sin offering,
and where they shall bake the
grain offering, so that they do
not bring *them* out into the
outer court to sanctify the
people."

21Then he brought me
out into the outer court and
caused me to pass by the four
corners of the court; and in
fact, in every corner of the
court *there was another* court.
22In the four corners of the
court *were* enclosed courts,
forty *cubits* long and thirty
wide; all four corners *were* the
same size. 23*There was* a row
of building stones all around
in them, all around the four
of them; and cooking hearths
were made under the rows of
stones all around. 24And he
said to me, "These *are* the
kitchens where the ministers
of the temple shall boil the
sacrifices of the people."

THE HEALING WATERS AND TREES

47 Then he brought me
back to the door of
the temple; and there was
water, flowing from under
the threshold of the temple
toward the east, for the front
of the temple faced east; the
water was flowing from under
the right side of the temple,
south of the altar. 2He brought
me out by way of the north
gate, and led me around on
the outside to the outer gateway that faces east; and there
was water, running out on the
right side.

3And when the man went
out to the east with the line
in his hand, he measured
one thousand cubits, and he
brought me through the waters; the water *came up to my*
ankles. 4Again he measured
one thousand and brought me
through the waters; the water
came up to my knees. Again
he measured one thousand
and brought me through; the

water *came up to my* waist.
5 Again he measured one thousand, *and it was* a river that I
could not cross; for the water
was too deep, water in which
one must swim, a river that
could not be crossed. 6 He said
to me, "Son of man, have you
seen *this?*" Then he brought
me and returned me to the
bank of the river.

7 When I returned, there,
along the bank of the river,
were very many trees on one
side and the other. 8 Then he
said to me: "This water flows
toward the eastern region,
goes down into the valley, and
enters the sea. *When it* reaches
the sea, *its* waters are healed.
9 And it shall be *that* every living thing that moves, wherever the rivers go, will live.
There will be a very great multitude of fish, because these
waters go there; for they will
be healed, and everything will
live wherever the river goes.
10 It shall be *that* fishermen
will stand by it from En Gedi to
En Eglaim; they will be *places*
for spreading their nets. Their
fish will be of the same kinds
as the fish of the Great Sea,
exceedingly many. 11 But its
swamps and marshes will not
be healed; they will be given
over to salt. 12 Along the bank
of the river, on this side and
that, will grow all *kinds of* trees
used for food; their leaves will
not wither, and their fruit will
not fail. They will bear fruit
every month, because their
water flows from the sanctuary. Their fruit will be for food,
and their leaves for medicine."

BORDERS OF THE LAND

13 Thus says the Lord GOD:
"These *are* the borders by
which you shall divide the land
as an inheritance among the
twelve tribes of Israel. Joseph
shall have two portions. 14 You
shall inherit it equally with one
another; for I raised My hand
in an oath to give it to your fathers, and this land shall fall to
you as your inheritance.

15 "This *shall be* the border
of the land on the north: from
the Great Sea, *by* the road to
Hethlon, as one goes to Zedad,
16 Hamath, Berothah, Sibraim
(which *is* between the border
of Damascus and the border
of Hamath), to Hazar Hatti-
con (which *is* on the border
of Hauran). 17 Thus the boundary shall be from the Sea to
Hazar Enan, the border of Damascus; and as for the north,
northward, it is the border of
Hamath. *This is* the north side.

18 "On the east side you shall
mark out the border from between Hauran and Damascus,
and between Gilead and the
land of Israel, along the Jordan, and along the eastern side
of the sea. *This is* the east side.

19 "The south side, toward
the South,[a] *shall be* from Tamar

47:19 [a] Hebrew *Negev*

to the waters of Meribah by Kadesh, along the brook to the
Great Sea. *This is* the south
side, toward the South.
20"The west side *shall be* the
Great Sea, from the *southern*
boundary until one comes to
a point opposite Hamath. This
is the west side.
21"Thus you shall divide
this land among yourselves
according to the tribes of
Israel. 22It shall be that you
will divide it by lot as an inheritance for yourselves, and
for the strangers who dwell
among you and who bear children among you. They shall be
to you as native-born among
the children of Israel; they
shall have an inheritance with
you among the tribes of Israel.
23And it shall be *that* in whatever tribe the stranger dwells,
there you shall give *him* his inheritance," says the Lord GOD.

DIVISION OF THE LAND

48 "Now these *are* the
names of the tribes:
From the northern border
along the road to Hethlon
at the entrance of Hamath,
to Hazar Enan, the border of
Damascus northward, in the
direction of Hamath, *there
shall be* one *section for* Dan
from its east to its west side;
2by the border of Dan, from
the east side to the west, one
section for Asher; 3by the border of Asher, from the east
side to the west, one *section
for* Naphtali; 4by the border
of Naphtali, from the east
side to the west, one *section
for* Manasseh; 5by the border
of Manasseh, from the east
side to the west, one *section
for* Ephraim; 6by the border of
Ephraim, from the east side to
the west, one *section for* Reuben; 7by the border of Reuben,
from the east side to the west,
one *section for* Judah; 8by the
border of Judah, from the east
side to the west, shall be the
district which you shall set
apart, twenty-five thousand
cubits in width, and *in* length
the same as one of the *other*
portions, from the east side to
the west, with the sanctuary in
the center.
9"The district that you shall
set apart for the LORD *shall be*
twenty-five thousand *cubits*
in length and ten thousand
in width. 10To these—to the
priests—the holy district shall
belong: on the north twenty-
five thousand *cubits in length,*
on the west ten thousand in
width, on the east ten thousand in width, and on the
south twenty-five thousand
in length. The sanctuary of
the LORD shall be in the center. 11*It shall be* for the priests
of the sons of Zadok, who are
sanctified, who have kept My
charge, who did not go astray
when the children of Israel
went astray, as the Levites
went astray. 12And *this* district
of land that is set apart shall
be to them a thing most holy
by the border of the Levites.

[13]"Opposite the border of
the priests, the Levites *shall
have an area* twenty-five thousand *cubits* in length and ten
thousand in width; its entire
length *shall be* twenty-five
thousand and its width ten
thousand. [14]And they shall
not sell or exchange any of
it; they may not alienate this
best *part* of the land, for *it is*
holy to the LORD.

[15]"The five thousand *cubits*
in width that remain, along the
edge of the twenty-five thousand, shall be for general use
by the city, for dwellings and
common-land; and the city
shall be in the center. [16]These
shall be its measurements: the
north side four thousand five
hundred *cubits,* the south side
four thousand five hundred,
the east side four thousand
five hundred, and the west
side four thousand five hundred. [17]The common-land of
the city shall be: to the north
two hundred and fifty *cubits,*
to the south two hundred and
fifty, to the east two hundred
and fifty, and to the west two
hundred and fifty. [18]The rest of
the length, alongside the district of the holy *section, shall
be* ten thousand *cubits* to the
east and ten thousand to the
west. It shall be adjacent to the
district of the holy *section,* and
its produce shall be food for
the workers of the city. [19]The
workers of the city, from all
the tribes of Israel, shall cul-
tivate it. [20]The entire district
shall be twenty-five thousand
cubits by twenty-five thousand
cubits, foursquare. You shall
set apart the holy district with
the property of the city.

[21]"The rest *shall belong* to
the prince, on one side and on
the other of the holy district
and of the city's property, next
to the twenty-five thousand
cubits of the *holy* district as
far as the eastern border, and
westward next to the twenty-
five thousand as far as the
western border, adjacent to the
tribal portions; *it shall belong*
to the prince. It shall be the
holy district, and the sanctuary
of the temple *shall be* in the
center. [22]Moreover, apart from
the possession of the Levites
and the possession of the city
which are in the midst of what
belongs to the prince, *the area*
between the border of Judah
and the border of Benjamin
shall belong to the prince.

[23]"As for the rest of the
tribes, from the east side to
the west, Benjamin *shall have*
one *section;* [24]by the border of
Benjamin, from the east side
to the west, Simeon *shall have*
one *section;* [25]by the border of
Simeon, from the east side to
the west, Issachar *shall have*
one *section;* [26]by the border
of Issachar, from the east side
to the west, Zebulun *shall have*
one *section;* [27]by the border of
Zebulun, from the east side to
the west, Gad *shall have* one
section; [28]by the border of Gad,
on the south side, toward the

South,[a] the border shall be
from Tamar *to* the waters of
Meribah *by* Kadesh, along the
brook to the Great Sea. 29This
is the land which you shall divide by lot as an inheritance
among the tribes of Israel,
and these *are* their portions,"
says the Lord GOD.

THE GATES OF THE CITY AND ITS NAME

30"These *are* the exits of
the city. On the north side,
measuring four thousand five
hundred *cubits* 31(the gates of
the city *shall be* named after
the tribes of Israel), the three
gates northward: one gate for
Reuben, one gate for Judah,
and one gate for Levi; 32on the
east side, four thousand five
hundred *cubits,* three gates:
one gate for Joseph, one gate
for Benjamin, and one gate
for Dan; 33on the south side,
measuring four thousand five
hundred *cubits,* three gates:
one gate for Simeon, one gate
for Issachar, and one gate for
Zebulun; 34on the west side,
four thousand five hundred
cubits with their three gates:
one gate for Gad, one gate for
Asher, and one gate for Naphtali. 35All the way around *shall
be* eighteen thousand *cubits;*
and the name of the city from
that day *shall be:* THE LORD *IS*
THERE."[a]

THE BOOK OF DANIEL

DANIEL AND HIS FRIENDS OBEY GOD

1 In the third year of the
reign of Jehoiakim king of
Judah, Nebuchadnezzar king
of Babylon came to Jerusalem
and besieged it. 2And the Lord
gave Jehoiakim king of Judah
into his hand, with some of
the articles of the house of
God, which he carried into the
land of Shinar to the house
of his god; and he brought
the articles into the treasure
house of his god.

3Then the king instructed
Ashpenaz, the master of his
eunuchs, to bring some of the
children of Israel and some
of the king's descendants and
some of the nobles, 4young
men in whom *there was* no
blemish, but good-looking,
gifted in all wisdom, possessing knowledge and quick to
understand, who *had* ability

48:28 [a] Hebrew *Negev* 48:35 [a] Hebrew *YHWH Shammah*

to serve in the king's palace,
and whom they might teach
the language and literature of
the Chaldeans. 5And the king
appointed for them a daily
provision of the king's delicacies and of the wine which
he drank, and three years
of training for them, so that
at the end of *that time* they
might serve before the king.
6Now from among those of
the sons of Judah were Daniel,
Hananiah, Mishael, and Azariah. 7To them the chief of the
eunuchs gave names: he gave
Daniel *the name* Belteshazzar; to Hananiah, Shadrach;
to Mishael, Meshach; and to
Azariah, Abed-Nego.

8But Daniel purposed in
his heart that he would not
defile himself with the portion of the king's delicacies,
nor with the wine which he
drank; therefore he requested
of the chief of the eunuchs
that he might not defile himself. 9Now God had brought
Daniel into the favor and
goodwill of the chief of the
eunuchs. 10And the chief of
the eunuchs said to Daniel,
"I fear my lord the king, who
has appointed your food and
drink. For why should he see
your faces looking worse than
the young men who *are* your
age? Then you would endanger my head before the king."

11So Daniel said to the steward[a] whom the chief of the
eunuchs had set over Dan-
iel, Hananiah, Mishael, and
Azariah, 12"Please test your
servants for ten days, and let
them give us vegetables to eat
and water to drink. 13Then let
our appearance be examined
before you, and the appearance of the young men who
eat the portion of the king's
delicacies; and as you see fit,
so deal with your servants."
14So he consented with them
in this matter, and tested
them ten days.

15And at the end of ten days
their features appeared better and fatter in flesh than all
the young men who ate the
portion of the king's delicacies. 16Thus the steward took
away their portion of delicacies and the wine that they
were to drink, and gave them
vegetables.

17As for these four young
men, God gave them knowl-
edge and skill in all literature
and wisdom; and Daniel had
understanding in all visions
and dreams.

18Now at the end of the
days, when the king had said
that they should be brought
in, the chief of the eunuchs
brought them in before Nebuchadnezzar. 19Then the
king interviewed[a] them, and
among them all none was
found like Daniel, Hananiah,
Mishael, and Azariah; therefore they served before the

1:11 [a] Hebrew *Melzar,* also in verse 16 1:19 [a] Literally *talked with them*

king. [20]And in all matters of wisdom *and* understanding about which the king examined them, he found them ten times better than all the magicians *and* astrologers who *were* in all his realm. [21]Thus Daniel continued until the first year of King Cyrus.

NEBUCHADNEZZAR'S DREAM

2 Now in the second year of Nebuchadnezzar's reign, Nebuchadnezzar had dreams; and his spirit was *so* troubled that his sleep left him. [2]Then the king gave the command to call the magicians, the astrologers, the sorcerers, and the Chaldeans to tell the king his dreams. So they came and stood before the king. [3]And the king said to them, "I have had a dream, and my spirit is anxious to know the dream."

[4]Then the Chaldeans spoke to the king in Aramaic,[a] "O king, live forever! Tell your servants the dream, and we will give the interpretation."

[5]The king answered and said to the Chaldeans, "My decision is firm: if you do not make known the dream to me, and its interpretation, you shall be cut in pieces, and your houses shall be made an ash heap. [6]However, if you tell the dream and its interpretation, you shall receive from me gifts, rewards, and great honor. Therefore tell me the dream and its interpretation."

[7]They answered again and said, "Let the king tell his servants the dream, and we will give its interpretation."

[8]The king answered and said, "I know for certain that you would gain time, because you see that my decision is firm: [9]if you do not make known the dream to me, *there is only* one decree for you! For you have agreed to speak lying and corrupt words before me till the time has changed. Therefore tell me the dream, and I shall know that you can give me its interpretation."

[10]The Chaldeans answered the king, and said, "There is not a man on earth who can tell the king's matter; therefore no king, lord, or ruler has *ever* asked such things of any magician, astrologer, or Chaldean. [11]*It is* a difficult thing that the king requests, and there is no other who can tell it to the king except the gods, whose dwelling is not with flesh."

[12]For this reason the king was angry and very furious, and gave the command to destroy all the wise *men* of Babylon. [13]So the decree went out, and they began killing the wise *men;* and they sought Daniel and his companions, to kill *them.*

2:4 [a] The original language of Daniel 2:4b through 7:28 is Aramaic.

GOD REVEALS NEBUCHADNEZZAR'S DREAM

14Then with counsel and
wisdom Daniel answered Arioch, the captain of the king's
guard, who had gone out to
kill the wise *men* of Babylon;
15he answered and said to Arioch the king's captain, "Why
is the decree from the king so
urgent?" Then Arioch made
the decision known to Daniel.
16So Daniel went in and
asked the king to give him
time, that he might tell the
king the interpretation. 17Then
Daniel went to his house, and
made the decision known to
Hananiah, Mishael, and Azariah, his companions, 18that
they might seek mercies from
the God of heaven concerning
this secret, so that Daniel and
his companions might not
perish with the rest of the wise
men of Babylon. 19Then the
secret was revealed to Daniel
in a night vision. So Daniel
blessed the God of heaven.
20Daniel answered and said:

"Blessed be the name of
God forever and ever,
For wisdom and
might are His.
21 And He changes the
times and the seasons;
He removes kings and
raises up kings;
He gives wisdom
to the wise
And knowledge to
those who have
understanding.
22 He reveals deep and
secret things;
He knows what *is* in
the darkness,
And light dwells
with Him.

23"I thank You and
praise You,
O God of my fathers;
You have given me
wisdom and might,
And have now made
known to me what
we asked of You,
For You have made
known to us the
king's demand."

DANIEL EXPLAINS THE DREAM

24Therefore Daniel went to
Arioch, whom the king had
appointed to destroy the wise
men of Babylon. He went and
said thus to him: "Do not destroy the wise *men* of Babylon;
take me before the king, and
I will tell the king the interpretation."
25Then Arioch quickly
brought Daniel before the
king, and said thus to him,
"I have found a man of the
captives[a] of Judah, who will
make known to the king the
interpretation."
26The king answered and
said to Daniel, whose name

2:25 [a] Literally *of the sons of the captivity*

was Belteshazzar, "Are you able to make known to me the dream which I have seen, and its interpretation?"

27Daniel answered in the presence of the king, and said, "The secret which the king has demanded, the wise *men*, the astrologers, the magicians, and the soothsayers cannot declare to the king. 28But there is a God in heaven who reveals secrets, and He has made known to King Nebuchadnezzar what will be in the latter days. Your dream, and the visions of your head upon your bed, were these: 29As for you, O king, thoughts came *to* your *mind while* on your bed, *about* what would come to pass after this; and He who reveals secrets has made known to you what will be. 30But as for me, this secret has not been revealed to me because I have more wisdom than anyone living, but for *our* sakes who make known the interpretation to the king, and that you may know the thoughts of your heart.

31"You, O king, were watching; and behold, a great image! This great image, whose splendor *was* excellent, stood before you; and its form *was* awesome. 32This image's head *was* of fine gold, its chest and arms of silver, its belly and thighs[a] of bronze, 33its legs of iron, its feet partly of iron and partly of clay.[a] 34You watched while a stone was cut out without hands, which struck the image on its feet of iron and clay, and broke them in pieces. 35Then the iron, the clay, the bronze, the silver, and the gold were crushed together, and became like chaff from the summer threshing floors; the wind carried them away so that no trace of them was found. And the stone that struck the image became a great mountain and filled the whole earth.

36"This *is* the dream. Now we will tell the interpretation of it before the king. 37You, O king, *are* a king of kings. For the God of heaven has given you a kingdom, power, strength, and glory; 38and wherever the children of men dwell, or the beasts of the field and the birds of the heaven, He has given *them* into your hand, and has made you ruler over them all—you *are* this head of gold. 39But after you shall arise another kingdom inferior to yours; then another, a third kingdom of bronze, which shall rule over all the earth. 40And the fourth kingdom shall be as strong as iron, inasmuch as iron breaks in pieces and shatters everything; and like iron that crushes, *that kingdom* will break in pieces and crush all the others. 41Whereas you

2:32 [a] Or *sides* 2:33 [a] Or *baked clay,* and so in verses 34, 35, and 42

saw the feet and toes, partly
of potter's clay and partly of
iron, the kingdom shall be
divided; yet the strength of
the iron shall be in it, just as
you saw the iron mixed with
ceramic clay. 42And *as* the toes
of the feet *were* partly of iron
and partly of clay, *so* the kingdom shall be partly strong
and partly fragile. 43As you
saw iron mixed with ceramic
clay, they will mingle with the
seed of men; but they will not
adhere to one another, just as
iron does not mix with clay.
44And in the days of these
kings the God of heaven will
set up a kingdom which shall
never be destroyed; and the
kingdom shall not be left to
other people; it shall break in
pieces and consume all these
kingdoms, and it shall stand
forever. 45Inasmuch as you
saw that the stone was cut
out of the mountain without
hands, and that it broke in
pieces the iron, the bronze,
the clay, the silver, and the
gold—the great God has made
known to the king what will
come to pass after this. The
dream is certain, and its interpretation is sure."

DANIEL AND HIS FRIENDS PROMOTED

46Then King Nebuchadnez-
zar fell on his face, prostrate before Daniel, and commanded
that they should present an
offering and incense to him.
47The king answered Daniel,
and said, "Truly your God *is*
the God of gods, the Lord of
kings, and a revealer of secrets, since you could reveal
this secret." 48Then the king
promoted Daniel and gave
him many great gifts; and he
made him ruler over the whole
province of Babylon, and chief
administrator over all the wise
men of Babylon. 49Also Daniel petitioned the king, and he
set Shadrach, Meshach, and
Abed-Nego over the affairs of
the province of Babylon; but
Daniel *sat* in the gate[a] of the
king.

THE IMAGE OF GOLD

3 Nebuchadnezzar the king
made an image of gold,
whose height *was* sixty cubits
and its width six cubits. He
set it up in the plain of Dura,
in the province of Babylon.
2And King Nebuchadnezzar
sent *word* to gather together
the satraps, the administrators, the governors, the counselors, the treasurers, the
judges, the magistrates, and
all the officials of the provinces, to come to the dedication of the image which King
Nebuchadnezzar had set up.
3So the satraps, the administrators, the governors, the
counselors, the treasurers, the
judges, the magistrates, and
all the officials of the prov-

2:49 [a] That is, the king's court

inces gathered together for
the dedication of the image
that King Nebuchadnezzar
had set up; and they stood
before the image that Nebuchadnezzar had set up. 4Then
a herald cried aloud: "To you
it is commanded, O peoples,
nations, and languages, 5*that*
at the time you hear the sound
of the horn, flute, harp, lyre,
and psaltery, in symphony
with all kinds of music, you
shall fall down and worship
the gold image that King Nebuchadnezzar has set up; 6and
whoever does not fall down
and worship shall be cast immediately into the midst of a
burning fiery furnace."

7So at that time, when all
the people heard the sound of
the horn, flute, harp, *and* lyre,
in symphony with all kinds of
music, all the people, nations,
and languages fell down *and*
worshiped the gold image
which King Nebuchadnezzar
had set up.

DANIEL'S FRIENDS DISOBEY THE KING

8Therefore at that time certain Chaldeans came forward
and accused the Jews. 9They
spoke and said to King Nebuchadnezzar, "O king, live forever! 10You, O king, have made
a decree that everyone who
hears the sound of the horn,
flute, harp, lyre, *and* psaltery,
in symphony with all kinds
of music, shall fall down and
worship the gold image; 11and
whoever does not fall down
and worship shall be cast into
the midst of a burning fiery
furnace. 12There are certain
Jews whom you have set over
the affairs of the province of
Babylon: Shadrach, Meshach,
and Abed-Nego; these men,
O king, have not paid due regard to you. They do not serve
your gods or worship the gold
image which you have set up."

13Then Nebuchadnezzar, in
rage and fury, gave the command to bring Shadrach, Meshach, and Abed-Nego. So they
brought these men before
the king. 14Nebuchadnezzar
spoke, saying to them, "*Is it*
true, Shadrach, Meshach, and
Abed-Nego, *that* you do not
serve my gods or worship the
gold image which I have set
up? 15Now if you are ready at
the time you hear the sound of
the horn, flute, harp, lyre, *and*
psaltery, in symphony with all
kinds of music, and you fall
down and worship the image
which I have made, *good!* But
if you do not worship, you
shall be cast immediately into
the midst of a burning fiery
furnace. And who *is* the god
who will deliver you from my
hands?"

16Shadrach, Meshach, and
Abed-Nego answered and said
to the king, "O Nebuchadnezzar, we have no need to answer
you in this matter. 17If that *is*
the case, our God whom we
serve is able to deliver us from
the burning fiery furnace, and

He will deliver *us* from your
hand, O king. 18But if not, let it
be known to you, O king, that
we do not serve your gods,
nor will we worship the gold
image which you have set up."

SAVED IN FIERY TRIAL

19Then Nebuchadnezzar
was full of fury, and the ex-
pression on his face changed
toward Shadrach, Meshach,
and Abed-Nego. He spoke and
commanded that they heat
the furnace seven times more
than it was usually heated.
20And he commanded cer-
tain mighty men of valor who
were in his army to bind Shadrach, Meshach, and Abed-
Nego, *and* cast *them* into the
burning fiery furnace. 21Then
these men were bound in
their coats, their trousers,
their turbans, and their *other*
garments, and were cast into
the midst of the burning fiery
furnace. 22Therefore, because
the king's command was urgent, and the furnace exceedingly hot, the flame of the fire
killed those men who took
up Shadrach, Meshach, and
Abed-Nego. 23And these three
men, Shadrach, Meshach, and
Abed-Nego, fell down bound
into the midst of the burning
fiery furnace.

24Then King Nebuchad-
nezzar was astonished; *and*
he rose in haste *and* spoke,
saying to his counselors, "Did
we not cast three men bound
into the midst of the fire?"

They answered and said to
the king, "True, O king."

25"Look!" he answered, "I
see four men loose, walking in
the midst of the fire; and they
are not hurt, and the form of
the fourth is like the Son of
God."[a]

NEBUCHADNEZZAR PRAISES GOD

26Then Nebuchadnezzar
went near the mouth of the
burning fiery furnace *and*
spoke, saying, "Shadrach, Meshach, and Abed-Nego, servants of the Most High God,
come out, and come *here.*"
Then Shadrach, Meshach,
and Abed-Nego came from
the midst of the fire. 27And
the satraps, administrators,
governors, and the king's
counselors gathered together,
and they saw these men on
whose bodies the fire had no
power; the hair of their head
was not singed nor were their
garments affected, and the
smell of fire was not on them.

28Nebuchadnezzar spoke,
saying, "Blessed be the God
of Shadrach, Meshach, and
Abed-Nego, who sent His
Angel[a] and delivered His servants who trusted in Him, and
they have frustrated the king's
word, and yielded their bodies, that they should not serve
nor worship any god except

3:25 [a] Or *a son of the gods* 3:28 [a] Or *angel*

their own God! 29Therefore I
make a decree that any people, nation, or language which
speaks anything amiss against
the God of Shadrach, Meshach,
and Abed-Nego shall be cut in
pieces, and their houses shall
be made an ash heap; because
there is no other God who can
deliver like this."
30Then the king promoted
Shadrach, Meshach, and Abed-
Nego in the province of Babylon.

NEBUCHADNEZZAR'S SECOND DREAM

4 Nebuchadnezzar the
king,

To all peoples, nations,
and languages that dwell
in all the earth:

Peace be multiplied to
you.

2 I thought it good to
declare the signs and
wonders that the Most
High God has worked
for me.

3 How great *are* His signs,
And how mighty
His wonders!
His kingdom *is* an
everlasting kingdom,
And His dominion
is from generation
to generation.

4 I, Nebuchadnezzar, was
at rest in my house, and
flourishing in my palace.
5I saw a dream which
made me afraid, and the
thoughts on my bed and
the visions of my head
troubled me. 6Therefore
I issued a decree to bring
in all the wise *men* of
Babylon before me, that
they might make known
to me the interpretation
of the dream. 7Then
the magicians, the
astrologers, the
Chaldeans, and the
soothsayers came in,
and I told them the
dream; but they did
not make known to me
its interpretation. 8But
at last Daniel came
before me (his name *is*
Belteshazzar, according
to the name of my god;
in him *is* the Spirit of
the Holy God), and I told
the dream before him,
saying: 9"Belteshazzar,
chief of the magicians,
because I know that the
Spirit of the Holy God
is in you, and no secret
troubles you, explain
to me the visions of my
dream that I have seen,
and its interpretation.

10 "These *were* the visions of
my head *while* on my bed:

I was looking, and behold,
A tree in the midst
of the earth,
And its height was great.

11 The tree grew and
became strong;
Its height reached
to the heavens,
And it could be seen to
the ends of all the earth.
12 Its leaves *were* lovely,
Its fruit abundant,
And in it *was* food for all.
The beasts of the field
found shade under it,
The birds of the heavens
dwelt in its branches,
And all flesh was
fed from it.

13 "I saw in the visions of
my head *while* on my bed,
and there was a watcher,
a holy one, coming down
from heaven. 14He cried
aloud and said thus:

'Chop down the tree and
cut off its branches,
Strip off its leaves and
scatter its fruit.
Let the beasts get out
from under it,
And the birds from
its branches.
15 Nevertheless leave
the stump and roots
in the earth,
Bound with a band of
iron and bronze,
In the tender grass
of the field.
Let it be wet with the
dew of heaven,
And *let* him graze
with the beasts
On the grass of the earth.
16 Let his heart be changed
from *that of* a man,
Let him be given the
heart of a beast,
And let seven times[a]
pass over him.

17 'This decision *is* by
the decree of the
watchers,
And the sentence by the
word of the holy ones,
In order that the
living may know
That the Most High rules
in the kingdom of men,
Gives it to whomever
He will,
And sets over it the
lowest of men.'

18 "This dream I, King
Nebuchadnezzar,
have seen. Now you,
Belteshazzar, declare
its interpretation, since
all the wise *men* of my
kingdom are not able to
make known to me the
interpretation; but you
are able, for the Spirit of
the Holy God *is* in you."

DANIEL EXPLAINS THE SECOND DREAM

19 Then Daniel, whose name
was Belteshazzar, was
astonished for a time,
and his thoughts troubled
him. *So* the king spoke,
and said, "Belteshazzar,

4:16 [a] Possibly *seven years,* and so in verses 23, 25, and 32

do not let the dream or
its interpretation trouble
you."

Belteshazzar answered
and said, "My lord, *may*
the dream concern those
who hate you, and its
interpretation concern
your enemies!

20 "The tree that you saw,
which grew and became
strong, whose height
reached to the heavens
and which *could be* seen
by all the earth, [21]whose
leaves *were* lovely and its
fruit abundant, in which
was food for all, under
which the beasts of the
field dwelt, and in whose
branches the birds of the
heaven had their home—
[22]it *is* you, O king, who
have grown and become
strong; for your greatness
has grown and reaches
to the heavens, and your
dominion to the end of
the earth.

23 "And inasmuch as the
king saw a watcher, a
holy one, coming down
from heaven and saying,
'Chop down the tree and
destroy it, but leave its
stump and roots in the
earth, *bound* with a band
of iron and bronze in the
tender grass of the field;
let it be wet with the dew
of heaven, and let him
graze with the beasts of
the field, till seven times
pass over him'; [24]this is
the interpretation, O king,
and this is the decree of
the Most High, which
has come upon my lord
the king: [25]They shall
drive you from men, your
dwelling shall be with the
beasts of the field, and
they shall make you eat
grass like oxen. They shall
wet you with the dew of
heaven, and seven times
shall pass over you, till
you know that the Most
High rules in the kingdom
of men, and gives it to
whomever He chooses.

26 "And inasmuch as they
gave the command to
leave the stump *and*
roots of the tree, your
kingdom shall be assured
to you, after you come to
know that Heaven rules.
[27]Therefore, O king, let
my advice be acceptable
to you; break off your
sins by *being* righteous,
and your iniquities by
showing mercy to *the*
poor. Perhaps there may
be a lengthening of your
prosperity."

NEBUCHADNEZZAR'S HUMILIATION

28 All *this* came upon King
Nebuchadnezzar. [29]At the
end of the twelve months
he was walking about the
royal palace of Babylon.
[30]The king spoke, saying,
"Is not this great Babylon,

that I have built for a
royal dwelling by my
mighty power and for the
honor of my majesty?"
31 While the word *was still* in
the king's mouth, a voice
fell from heaven: "King
Nebuchadnezzar, to you
it is spoken: the kingdom
has departed from you!
32And they shall drive
you from men, and your
dwelling *shall be* with the
beasts of the field. They
shall make you eat grass
like oxen; and seven times
shall pass over you, until
you know that the Most
High rules in the kingdom
of men, and gives it to
whomever He chooses."
33 That very hour the word
was fulfilled concerning
Nebuchadnezzar; he was
driven from men and ate
grass like oxen; his body
was wet with the dew of
heaven till his hair had
grown like eagles' *feathers*
and his nails like birds'
claws.

NEBUCHADNEZZAR PRAISES GOD

34 And at the end of the
time[a] I, Nebuchadnezzar,
lifted my eyes to heaven,
and my understanding
returned to me; and I
blessed the Most High
and praised and honored
Him who lives forever:

For His dominion *is* an
everlasting dominion,
And His kingdom *is*
from generation
to generation.
35 All the inhabitants
of the earth *are*
reputed as nothing;
He does according
to His will in the
army of heaven
And *among* the
inhabitants of the earth.
No one can restrain
His hand
Or say to Him, "What
have You done?"

36 At the same time my
reason returned to me,
and for the glory of my
kingdom, my honor and
splendor returned to me.
My counselors and nobles
resorted to me, I was
restored to my kingdom,
and excellent majesty
was added to me. 37Now I,
Nebuchadnezzar, praise
and extol and honor the
King of heaven, all of
whose works *are* truth,
and His ways justice. And
those who walk in pride
He is able to put down.

BELSHAZZAR'S FEAST

5 Belshazzar the king made
a great feast for a thousand
of his lords, and drank wine in
the presence of the thousand.
2While he tasted the wine, Bel-

4:34 [a] Literally *days*

shazzar gave the command
to bring the gold and silver
vessels which his father Nebuchadnezzar had taken from
the temple which *had been* in
Jerusalem, that the king and
his lords, his wives, and his
concubines might drink from
them. 3Then they brought the
gold vessels that had been
taken from the temple of the
house of God which *had been*
in Jerusalem; and the king
and his lords, his wives, and
his concubines drank from
them. 4They drank wine, and
praised the gods of gold and
silver, bronze and iron, wood
and stone.

5In the same hour the fingers of a man's hand appeared
and wrote opposite the lampstand on the plaster of the wall
of the king's palace; and the
king saw the part of the hand
that wrote. 6Then the king's
countenance changed, and
his thoughts troubled him,
so that the joints of his hips
were loosened and his knees
knocked against each other.
7The king cried aloud to bring
in the astrologers, the Chaldeans, and the soothsayers. The
king spoke, saying to the wise
men of Babylon, "Whoever
reads this writing, and tells
me its interpretation, shall
be clothed with purple and
have a chain of gold around
his neck; and he shall be the
third ruler in the kingdom."
8Now all the king's wise *men*
came, but they could not read
the writing, or make known
to the king its interpretation.
9Then King Belshazzar was
greatly troubled, his countenance was changed, and his
lords were astonished.

10The queen, because of
the words of the king and his
lords, came to the banquet
hall. The queen spoke, saying, "O king, live forever! Do
not let your thoughts trouble
you, nor let your countenance
change. 11There is a man in
your kingdom in whom *is* the
Spirit of the Holy God. And
in the days of your father,
light and understanding and
wisdom, like the wisdom of
the gods, were found in him;
and King Nebuchadnezzar
your father—your father the
king—made him chief of the
magicians, astrologers, Chaldeans, *and* soothsayers. 12In-
asmuch as an excellent spirit,
knowledge, understanding,
interpreting dreams, solv-
ing riddles, and explaining
enigmas[a] were found in this
Daniel, whom the king named
Belteshazzar, now let Daniel
be called, and he will give the
interpretation."

THE WRITING ON THE WALL EXPLAINED

13Then Daniel was brought
in before the king. The king
spoke, and said to Daniel, "*Are*

5:12 [a] Literally *untying knots,* and so in verse 16

you that Daniel who is one
of the captives[a] from Judah,
whom my father the king
brought from Judah? 14 I have
heard of you, that the Spirit of
God *is* in you, and *that* light
and understanding and excellent wisdom are found in you.
15 Now the wise *men,* the astrologers, have been brought
in before me, that they should
read this writing and make
known to me its interpretation, but they could not give
the interpretation of the thing.
16 And I have heard of you, that
you can give interpretations
and explain enigmas. Now if
you can read the writing and
make known to me its interpretation, you shall be clothed
with purple and *have* a chain
of gold around your neck, and
shall be the third ruler in the
kingdom."

17 Then Daniel answered,
and said before the king, "Let
your gifts be for yourself, and
give your rewards to another;
yet I will read the writing to
the king, and make known
to him the interpretation.
18 O king, the Most High God
gave Nebuchadnezzar your
father a kingdom and maj-
esty, glory and honor. 19 And
because of the majesty that He
gave him, all peoples, nations,
and languages trembled and
feared before him. Whom-
ever he wished, he executed;
whomever he wished, he kept
alive; whomever he wished,
he set up; and whomever he
wished, he put down. 20 But
when his heart was lifted up,
and his spirit was hardened in
pride, he was deposed from his
kingly throne, and they took
his glory from him. 21 Then he
was driven from the sons of
men, his heart was made like
the beasts, and his dwelling
was with the wild donkeys.
They fed him with grass like
oxen, and his body was wet
with the dew of heaven, till he
knew that the Most High God
rules in the kingdom of men,
and appoints over it whomever He chooses.

22 "But you his son, Belshazzar, have not humbled your
heart, although you knew all
this. 23 And you have lifted
yourself up against the Lord
of heaven. They have brought
the vessels of His house before you, and you and your
lords, your wives and your
concubines, have drunk wine
from them. And you have
praised the gods of silver and
gold, bronze and iron, wood
and stone, which do not see
or hear or know; and the God
who *holds* your breath in His
hand and owns all your ways,
you have not glorified. 24 Then
the fingers[a] of the hand were
sent from Him, and this writ-
ing was written.

25 "And this is the inscription that was written:

5:13 [a] Literally *of the sons of the captivity* 5:24 [a] Literally *palm*

MENE,[a] MENE, TEKEL,[b]
UPHARSIN.[c]

26This *is* the interpretation
of *each* word. MENE: God has
numbered your kingdom, and
finished it; 27TEKEL: You have
been weighed in the balances,
and found wanting; 28PERES:
Your kingdom has been di-
vided, and given to the Medes
and Persians."[a] 29Then Belshazzar gave the command,
and they clothed Daniel with
purple and *put* a chain of gold
around his neck, and made a
proclamation concerning him
that he should be the third
ruler in the kingdom.

BELSHAZZAR'S FALL

30That very night Belshazzar, king of the Chaldeans, was
slain. 31And Darius the Mede
received the kingdom, *being*
about sixty-two years old.

THE PLOT AGAINST DANIEL

6 It pleased Darius to set
over the kingdom one hun-
dred and twenty satraps, to be
over the whole kingdom; 2and
over these, three governors, of
whom Daniel *was* one, that the
satraps might give account to
them, so that the king would
suffer no loss. 3Then this Daniel distinguished himself above
the governors and satraps,
because an excellent spirit
was in him; and the king gave
thought to setting him over
the whole realm. 4So the governors and satraps sought to
find *some* charge against Daniel concerning the kingdom;
but they could find no charge
or fault, because he *was* faithful; nor was there any error or
fault found in him. 5Then these
men said, "We shall not find
any charge against this Daniel
unless we find *it* against him
concerning the law of his God."

6So these governors and satraps thronged before the king,
and said thus to him: "King Darius, live forever! 7All the governors of the kingdom, the
administrators and satraps, the
counselors and advisors, have
consulted together to establish
a royal statute and to make a
firm decree, that whoever petitions any god or man for thirty
days, except you, O king, shall
be cast into the den of lions.
8Now, O king, establish the decree and sign the writing, so
that it cannot be changed, according to the law of the Medes
and Persians, which does not
alter." 9Therefore King Darius
signed the written decree.

DANIEL IN THE LIONS' DEN

10Now when Daniel knew
that the writing was signed, he
went home. And in his upper
room, with his windows open

5:25 [a] Literally *a mina* (50 shekels) from the verb "to number" [b] Literally *a shekel* from the verb "to weigh" [c] Literally *and half-shekels* from the verb "to divide" 5:28 [a] Aramaic *Paras,* consonant with *Peres*

toward Jerusalem, he knelt
down on his knees three times
that day, and prayed and gave
thanks before his God, as was
his custom since early days.
11Then these men assem-
bled and found Daniel praying
and making supplication before his God. 12And they went
before the king, and spoke
concerning the king's decree:
"Have you not signed a decree
that every man who petitions
any god or man within thirty
days, except you, O king, shall
be cast into the den of lions?"
The king answered and said,
"The thing *is* true, according to
the law of the Medes and Persians, which does not alter."
13So they answered and said
before the king, "That Daniel,
who is one of the captives[a]
from Judah, does not show
due regard for you, O king, or
for the decree that you have
signed, but makes his petition
three times a day."
14And the king, when he
heard *these* words, was greatly
displeased with himself, and
set *his* heart on Daniel to deliver him; and he labored till
the going down of the sun to
deliver him. 15Then these men
approached the king, and said
to the king, "Know, O king,
that *it is* the law of the Medes
and Persians that no decree
or *statute which the king establishes* may be changed."
16So the king gave the command, and they brought Daniel
and cast *him* into the den of
lions. *But* the king spoke, saying to Daniel, "Your God, whom
you serve continually, He will
deliver you." 17Then a stone was
brought and laid on the mouth
of the den, and the king sealed
it with his own signet ring and
with the signets of his lords,
that the purpose concerning
Daniel might not be changed.

DANIEL SAVED FROM THE LIONS

18Now the king went to his
palace and spent the night
fasting; and no musicians[a]
were brought before him.
Also his sleep went from
him. 19Then the king arose
very early in the morning and
went in haste to the den of
lions. 20And when he came
to the den, he cried out with a
lamenting voice to Daniel. The
king spoke, saying to Daniel,
"Daniel, servant of the living
God, has your God, whom you
serve continually, been able to
deliver you from the lions?"
21Then Daniel said to the
king, "O king, live forever! 22My
God sent His angel and shut
the lions' mouths, so that they
have not hurt me, because I
was found innocent before
Him; and also, O king, I have
done no wrong before you."
23Now the king was exceed-

6:13 [a] Literally *of the sons of the captivity*
6:18 [a] Exact meaning unknown

ingly glad for him, and commanded that they should take Daniel up out of the den. So Daniel was taken up out of the den, and no injury whatever was found on him, because he believed in his God.

DARIUS HONORS GOD

24And the king gave the command, and they brought those men who had accused Daniel, and they cast *them* into the den of lions—them, their children, and their wives; and the lions overpowered them, and broke all their bones in pieces before they ever came to the bottom of the den.

25Then King Darius wrote:

To all peoples, nations,
and languages that dwell
in all the earth:

Peace be multiplied to
you.

26 I make a decree that
in every dominion of
my kingdom *men must*
tremble and fear before
the God of Daniel.

For He *is* the living God,
And steadfast forever;
His kingdom *is the*
one which shall not
be destroyed,
And His dominion *shall*
endure to the end.
27 He delivers and rescues,
And He works signs
and wonders
In heaven and on earth,
Who has delivered
Daniel from the
power of the lions.

28So this Daniel prospered in the reign of Darius and in the reign of Cyrus the Persian.

VISION OF THE FOUR BEASTS

7 In the first year of Belshazzar king of Babylon, Daniel had a dream and visions of his head *while* on his bed. Then he wrote down the dream, telling the main facts.[a]

2Daniel spoke, saying, "I saw in my vision by night, and behold, the four winds of heaven were stirring up
the Great Sea. 3And four great beasts came up from the sea, each different from the other.
4The first *was* like a lion, and had eagle's wings. I watched till its wings were plucked off; and it was lifted up from the earth and made to stand on two feet like a man, and a man's heart was given to it.

5"And suddenly another beast, a second, like a bear. It was raised up on one side, and *had* three ribs in its mouth between its teeth. And they said thus to it: 'Arise, devour much flesh!'

6"After this I looked, and there was another, like a

7:1 [a] Literally *the head* (or *chief*) *of the words*

leopard, which had on its back
four wings of a bird. The beast
also had four heads, and dominion was given to it.

7"After this I saw in the
night visions, and behold, a
fourth beast, dreadful and
terrible, exceedingly strong.
It had huge iron teeth; it was
devouring, breaking in pieces,
and trampling the residue
with its feet. It *was* different
from all the beasts that *were*
before it, and it had ten horns.
8I was considering the horns,
and there was another horn, a
little one, coming up among
them, before whom three of
the first horns were plucked
out by the roots. And there, in
this horn, *were* eyes like the
eyes of a man, and a mouth
speaking pompous words.

VISION OF THE ANCIENT OF DAYS

9 "I watched till thrones
were put in place,
And the Ancient of
Days was seated;
His garment *was*
white as snow,
And the hair of His head
was like pure wool.
His throne *was* a
fiery flame,
Its wheels a burning fire;
10 A fiery stream issued
And came forth from
before Him.
A thousand thousands
ministered to Him;
Ten thousand times
ten thousand stood
before Him.
The court[a] was seated,
And the books
were opened.

11"I watched then because
of the sound of the pompous
words which the horn was
speaking; I watched till the
beast was slain, and its body
destroyed and given to the
burning flame. 12As for the
rest of the beasts, they had
their dominion taken away,
yet their lives were prolonged
for a season and a time.

13 "I was watching in the
night visions,
And behold, *One* like
the Son of Man,
Coming with the
clouds of heaven!
He came to the
Ancient of Days,
And they brought Him
near before Him.
14 Then to Him was given
dominion and glory
and a kingdom,
That all peoples, nations,
and languages
should serve Him.
His dominion *is* an
everlasting dominion,
Which shall not
pass away,
And His kingdom *the one*
Which shall not be
destroyed.

7:10 [a] Or *judgment*

DANIEL'S VISIONS INTERPRETED

15"I, Daniel, was grieved in
my spirit within *my* body, and
the visions of my head troubled me. 16I came near to one of
those who stood by, and asked
him the truth of all this. So he
told me and made known to
me the interpretation of these
things: 17'Those great beasts,
which are four, *are* four kings[a]
which arise out of the earth.
18But the saints of the Most
High shall receive the kingdom, and possess the kingdom
forever, even forever and ever.'

19"Then I wished to know
the truth about the fourth
beast, which was different
from all the others, exceedingly dreadful, *with* its teeth
of iron and its nails of bronze,
which devoured, broke in
pieces, and trampled the residue with its feet; 20and the ten
horns that *were* on its head,
and the other *horn* which
came up, before which three
fell, namely, that horn which
had eyes and a mouth which
spoke pompous words, whose
appearance *was* greater than
his fellows.

21"I was watching; and the
same horn was making war
against the saints, and pre-
vailing against them, 22until
the Ancient of Days came, and
a judgment was made *in favor*
of the saints of the Most High,
and the time came for the
saints to possess the kingdom.

23"Thus he said:

'The fourth beast shall be
A fourth kingdom
on earth,
Which shall be different
from all *other* kingdoms,
And shall devour the
whole earth,
Trample it and break
it in pieces.
24 The ten horns *are*
ten kings
Who shall arise from
this kingdom.
And another shall
rise after them;
He shall be different
from the first *ones,*
And shall subdue
three kings.
25 He shall speak *pompous*
words against the
Most High,
Shall persecute[a] the
saints of the Most High,
And shall intend to
change times and law.
Then *the saints* shall be
given into his hand
For a time and times
and half a time.

26 'But the court shall
be seated,
And they shall take
away his dominion,
To consume and
destroy *it* forever.

7:17 [a] Representing their kingdoms (compare verse 23) **7:25** [a] Literally *wear out*

27 Then the kingdom
and dominion,
And the greatness of
the kingdoms under
the whole heaven,
Shall be given to the
people, the saints
of the Most High.
His kingdom *is* an
everlasting kingdom,
And all dominions shall
serve and obey Him.'

28"This *is* the end of the
account.[a] As for me, Daniel,
my thoughts greatly troubled
me, and my countenance
changed; but I kept the matter in my heart."

VISION OF A RAM AND A GOAT

8 In the third year of the
reign of King Belshazzar
a vision appeared *to* me—to
me, Daniel—after the one that
appeared to me the first time.
2I saw in the vision, and it so
happened while I was looking,
that I *was* in Shushan, the citadel, which *is* in the province
of Elam; and I saw in the vision that I was by the River
Ulai. 3Then I lifted my eyes
and saw, and there, standing
beside the river, was a ram
which had two horns, and the
two horns *were* high; but one
was higher than the other, and
the higher *one* came up last.
4I saw the ram pushing westward, northward, and southward, so that no animal could
withstand him; nor *was there*
any that could deliver from
his hand, but he did according
to his will and became great.
5And as I was considering,
suddenly a male goat came
from the west, across the surface of the whole earth, without touching the ground; and
the goat *had* a notable horn
between his eyes. 6Then he
came to the ram that had
two horns, which I had seen
standing beside the river, and
ran at him with furious power.
7And I saw him confronting
the ram; he was moved with
rage against him, attacked the
ram, and broke his two horns.
There was no power in the
ram to withstand him, but he
cast him down to the ground
and trampled him; and there
was no one that could deliver
the ram from his hand.
8Therefore the male goat
grew very great; but when he
became strong, the large horn
was broken, and in place of it
four notable ones came up toward the four winds of heaven.
9And out of one of them came
a little horn which grew exceedingly great toward the
south, toward the east, and
toward the Glorious *Land*.
10And it grew up to the host of
heaven; and it cast down *some*
of the host and *some* of the
stars to the ground, and trampled them. 11He even exalted

7:28 [a] Literally *the word*

himself as high as the Prince of
the host; and by him the daily
sacrifices were taken away, and
the place of His sanctuary was
cast down. 12Because of transgression, an army was given
over *to the horn* to oppose the
daily *sacrifices;* and he cast
truth down to the ground. He
did *all this* and prospered.

13Then I heard a holy one
speaking; and *another* holy
one said to that certain *one*
who was speaking, "How long
will the vision *be, concerning*
the daily *sacrifices* and the
transgression of desolation,
the giving of both the sanctuary and the host to be trampled underfoot?"

14And he said to me, "For
two thousand three hundred
days;[a] then the sanctuary
shall be cleansed."

GABRIEL INTERPRETS THE VISION

15Then it happened, when I,
Daniel, had seen the vision and
was seeking the meaning, that
suddenly there stood before
me one having the appearance
of a man. 16And I heard a man's
voice between *the banks of* the
Ulai, who called, and said, "Gabriel, make this *man* understand the vision." 17So he came
near where I stood, and when
he came I was afraid and fell
on my face; but he said to me,
"Understand, son of man, that
the vision *refers* to the time of
the end."

18Now, as he was speaking
with me, I was in a deep sleep
with my face to the ground; but
he touched me, and stood me
upright. 19And he said, "Look, I
am making known to you what
shall happen in the latter time
of the indignation; for at the
appointed time the end *shall
be.* 20The ram which you saw,
having the two horns—*they are*
the kings of Media and Persia.
21And the male goat *is* the kingdom[a] of Greece. The large horn
that *is* between its eyes *is* the
first king. 22As for the broken
horn and the four that stood
up in its place, four kingdoms
shall arise out of that nation,
but not with its power.

23 "And in the latter time
 of their kingdom,
When the transgressors
 have reached
 their fullness,
A king shall arise,
Having fierce features,
Who understands
 sinister schemes.
24 His power shall be
 mighty, but not by
 his own power;
He shall destroy fearfully,
And shall prosper
 and thrive;
He shall destroy the
 mighty, and *also*
 the holy people.

8:14 [a] Literally *evening-mornings* 8:21 [a] Literally *king,* representing his kingdom (compare 7:17, 23)

25 “Through his cunning
He shall cause deceit to
prosper under his rule;[a]
And he shall exalt
himself in his heart.
He shall destroy many
in *their* prosperity.
He shall even rise against
the Prince of princes;
But he shall be broken
without *human* means.[b]

26 “And the vision of the
evenings and mornings
Which was told is true;
Therefore seal up
the vision,
For *it refers* to many
days *in the future.*”

27 And I, Daniel, fainted and
was sick for days; afterward
I arose and went about the
king's business. I was astonished by the vision, but no one
understood it.

DANIEL'S PRAYER FOR THE PEOPLE

9 In the first year of Darius
the son of Ahasuerus,
of the lineage of the Medes,
who was made king over the
realm of the Chaldeans— 2 in
the first year of his reign I,
Daniel, understood by the
books the number of the
years *specified* by the word of
the LORD through Jeremiah
the prophet, that He would
accomplish seventy years in
the desolations of Jerusalem.

3 Then I set my face toward
the Lord God to make request
by prayer and supplications,
with fasting, sackcloth, and
ashes. 4 And I prayed to the
LORD my God, and made confession, and said, “O Lord, great
and awesome God, who keeps
His covenant and mercy with
those who love Him, and with
those who keep His commandments, 5 we have sinned and
committed iniquity, we have
done wickedly and rebelled,
even by departing from Your
precepts and Your judgments.
6 Neither have we heeded Your
servants the prophets, who
spoke in Your name to our
kings and our princes, to our
fathers and all the people of
the land. 7 O Lord, righteousness *belongs* to You, but to
us shame of face, as *it is* this
day—to the men of Judah, to
the inhabitants of Jerusalem
and all Israel, those near and
those far off in all the countries to which You have driven
them, because of the unfaithfulness which they have committed against You.

8 “O Lord, to us *belongs*
shame of face, to our kings,
our princes, and our fathers,
because we have sinned
against You. 9 To the Lord our
God *belong* mercy and forgiveness, though we have rebelled
against Him. 10 We have not
obeyed the voice of the LORD
our God, to walk in His laws,

8:25 [a] Literally *hand* [b] Literally *hand*

which He set before us by His
servants the prophets. 11Yes, all
Israel has transgressed Your
law, and has departed so as not
to obey Your voice; therefore
the curse and the oath written
in the Law of Moses the servant of God have been poured
out on us, because we have
sinned against Him. 12And
He has confirmed His words,
which He spoke against us and
against our judges who judged
us, by bringing upon us a great
disaster; for under the whole
heaven such has never been
done as what has been done
to Jerusalem.

13"As *it is* written in the Law
of Moses, all this disaster has
come upon us; yet we have
not made our prayer before
the LORD our God, that we
might turn from our iniq-
uities and understand Your
truth. 14Therefore the LORD
has kept the disaster in mind,
and brought it upon us; for
the LORD our God *is* righteous in all the works which
He does, though we have not
obeyed His voice. 15And now,
O Lord our God, who brought
Your people out of the land of
Egypt with a mighty hand, and
made Yourself a name, as *it is*
this day—we have sinned, we
have done wickedly!

16"O Lord, according to all
Your righteousness, I pray, let
Your anger and Your fury be
turned away from Your city
Jerusalem, Your holy mountain; because for our sins,
and for the iniquities of our
fathers, Jerusalem and Your
people *are* a reproach to all
those around us. 17Now therefore, our God, hear the prayer
of Your servant, and his supplications, and for the Lord's
sake cause Your face to shine
on Your sanctuary, which is
desolate. 18O my God, incline
Your ear and hear; open Your
eyes and see our desolations,
and the city which is called
by Your name; for we do not
present our supplications before You because of our righteous deeds, but because of
Your great mercies. 19O Lord,
hear! O Lord, forgive! O Lord,
listen and act! Do not delay for
Your own sake, my God, for
Your city and Your people are
called by Your name."

THE SEVENTY-WEEKS PROPHECY

20Now while I *was* speaking, praying, and confessing
my sin and the sin of my people Israel, and presenting my
supplication before the LORD
my God for the holy mountain
of my God, 21yes, while I *was*
speaking in prayer, the man
Gabriel, whom I had seen in
the vision at the beginning,
being caused to fly swiftly,
reached me about the time of
the evening offering. 22And he
informed *me,* and talked with
me, and said, "O Daniel, I have
now come forth to give you
skill to understand. 23At the beginning of your supplications

the command went out, and I have come to tell *you,* for you *are* greatly beloved; therefore consider the matter, and understand the vision:

24 "Seventy weeks[a] are
determined
For your people and
for your holy city,
To finish the
transgression,
To make an end of[b] sins,
To make reconciliation
for iniquity,
To bring in everlasting
righteousness,
To seal up vision
and prophecy,
And to anoint the
Most Holy.

25 "Know therefore and
understand,
That from the going
forth of the command
To restore and build
Jerusalem
Until Messiah the Prince,
There shall be seven weeks
and sixty-two weeks;
The street[a] shall be built
again, and the wall,[b]
Even in troublesome
times.

26 "And after the
sixty-two weeks
Messiah shall be cut off,
but not for Himself;
And the people of the
prince who is to come
Shall destroy the city
and the sanctuary.
The end of it *shall*
be with a flood,
And till the end of
the war desolations
are determined.
27 Then he shall confirm
a covenant with
many for one week;
But in the middle
of the week
He shall bring an end to
sacrifice and offering.
And on the wing of
abominations shall be
one who makes desolate,
Even until the
consummation, which
is determined,
Is poured out on
the desolate."

VISION OF THE GLORIOUS MAN

10 In the third year of Cyrus
king of Persia a message
was revealed to Daniel, whose
name was called Belteshazzar. The message *was* true, but
the appointed time *was* long;[a]
and he understood the message, and had understanding
of the vision. 2 In those days I,
Daniel, was mourning three
full weeks. 3 I ate no pleasant
food, no meat or wine came
into my mouth, nor did I

9:24 [a] Literally *sevens,* and so throughout the chapter [b] Following Qere, Septuagint, Syriac, and Vulgate; Kethib and Theodotion read *To seal up.* 9:25 [a] Or *open square* [b] Or *moat* 10:1 [a] Or *and of great conflict*

anoint myself at all, till three
whole weeks were fulfilled.
4Now on the twenty-fourth
day of the first month, as I was
by the side of the great river,
that *is,* the Tigris,[a] 5I lifted my
eyes and looked, and behold, a
certain man clothed in linen,
whose waist *was* girded with
gold of Uphaz! 6His body *was*
like beryl, his face like the
appearance of lightning, his
eyes like torches of fire, his
arms and feet like burnished
bronze in color, and the sound
of his words like the voice of
a multitude.
7And I, Daniel, alone saw
the vision, for the men who
were with me did not see the
vision; but a great terror fell
upon them, so that they fled to
hide themselves. 8Therefore I
was left alone when I saw this
great vision, and no strength
remained in me; for my vigor
was turned to frailty in me,
and I retained no strength.
9Yet I heard the sound of his
words; and while I heard the
sound of his words I was in a
deep sleep on my face, with
my face to the ground.

PROPHECIES CONCERNING PERSIA AND GREECE

10Suddenly, a hand touched
me, which made me tremble
on my knees and *on* the palms
of my hands. 11And he said to
me, "O Daniel, man greatly beloved, understand the words
that I speak to you, and stand
upright, for I have now been
sent to you." While he was
speaking this word to me, I
stood trembling.
12Then he said to me, "Do
not fear, Daniel, for from the
first day that you set your
heart to understand, and to
humble yourself before your
God, your words were heard;
and I have come because of
your words. 13But the prince
of the kingdom of Persia withstood me twenty-one days;
and behold, Michael, one of
the chief princes, came to help
me, for I had been left alone
there with the kings of Persia.
14Now I have come to make
you understand what will happen to your people in the latter days, for the vision *refers*
to *many* days yet *to come.*"
15When he had spoken such
words to me, I turned my face
toward the ground and became
speechless. 16And suddenly,
one having the likeness of the
sons[a] of men touched my lips;
then I opened my mouth and
spoke, saying to him who stood
before me, "My lord, because
of the vision my sorrows have
overwhelmed me, and I have
retained no strength. 17For how
can this servant of my lord talk
with you, my lord? As for me,
no strength remains in me now,
nor is any breath left in me."

10:4 [a] Hebrew *Hiddekel* 10:16 [a] Theodotion and Vulgate read *the son;* Septuagint reads *a hand.*

18Then again, *the one* having the likeness of a man
touched me and strengthened
me. 19And he said, “O man
greatly beloved, fear not!
Peace *be* to you; be strong,
yes, be strong!”
So when he spoke to me I
was strengthened, and said,
“Let my lord speak, for you
have strengthened me.”
20Then he said, “Do you
know why I have come to
you? And now I must return to
fight with the prince of Persia;
and when I have gone forth,
indeed the prince of Greece
will come. 21But I will tell you
what is noted in the Scripture
of Truth. (No one upholds me
against these, except Michael
your prince.
11 “Also in the first year of
Darius the Mede, I, *even*
I, stood up to confirm and
strengthen him.) 2And now
I will tell you the truth: Behold, three more kings will
arise in Persia, and the fourth
shall be far richer than *them*
all; by his strength, through
his riches, he shall stir up all
against the realm of Greece.
3Then a mighty king shall
arise, who shall rule with great
dominion, and do according
to his will. 4And when he has
arisen, his kingdom shall be
broken up and divided toward
the four winds of heaven, but
not among his posterity nor
according to his dominion
with which he ruled; for his
kingdom shall be uprooted,
even for others besides these.

WARRING KINGS OF NORTH AND SOUTH

5“Also the king of the South
shall become strong, as well as
one of his princes; and he shall
gain power over him and have
dominion. His dominion *shall*
be a great dominion. 6And at
the end of *some* years they shall
join forces, for the daughter of
the king of the South shall go to
the king of the North to make
an agreement; but she shall
not retain the power of her authority,[a] and neither he nor his
authority[b] shall stand; but she
shall be given up, with those
who brought her, and with
him who begot her, and with
him who strengthened her in
those times. 7But from a branch
of her roots *one* shall arise in
his place, who shall come with
an army, enter the fortress of
the king of the North, and deal
with them and prevail. 8And
he shall also carry their gods
captive to Egypt, with their
princes[a] *and* their precious articles of silver and gold; and he
shall continue *more* years than
the king of the North.
9“Also *the king of the North*
shall come to the kingdom
of the king of the South, but
shall return to his own land.
10However his sons shall stir
up strife, and assemble a mul-

11:6 [a] Literally *arm* [b] Literally *arm* 11:8 [a] Or *molded images*

titude of great forces; and *one*
shall certainly come and overwhelm and pass through; then
he shall return to his fortress
and stir up strife.
11"And the king of the South
shall be moved with rage, and
go out and fight with him,
with the king of the North,
who shall muster a great multitude; but the multitude shall
be given into the hand of his
enemy. 12When he has taken
away the multitude, his heart
will be lifted up; and he will
cast down tens of thousands,
but he will not prevail. 13For
the king of the North will return and muster a multitude
greater than the former, and
shall certainly come at the
end of some years with a great
army and much equipment.
14"Now in those times many
shall rise up against the king
of the South. Also, violent
men[a] of your people shall
exalt themselves in fulfillment of the vision, but they
shall fall. 15So the king of the
North shall come and build a
siege mound, and take a fortified city; and the forces[a] of
the South shall not withstand
him. Even his choice troops
shall have no strength to resist.
16But he who comes against
him shall do according to his
own will, and no one shall
stand against him. He shall
stand in the Glorious Land
with destruction in his power.[a]
17"He shall also set his face
to enter with the strength of his
whole kingdom, and upright
ones[a] with him; thus shall he
do. And he shall give him the
daughter of women to destroy
it; but she shall not stand *with
him,* or be for him. 18After this
he shall turn his face to the
coastlands, and shall take
many. But a ruler shall bring
the reproach against them to
an end; and with the reproach
removed, he shall turn back on
him. 19Then he shall turn his
face toward the fortress of his
own land; but he shall stumble
and fall, and not be found.
20"There shall arise in his
place one who imposes taxes
on the glorious kingdom; but
within a few days he shall be
destroyed, but not in anger
or in battle. 21And in his place
shall arise a vile person, to
whom they will not give the
honor of royalty; but he shall
come in peaceably, and seize
the kingdom by intrigue.
22With the force[a] of a flood
they shall be swept away from
before him and be broken,
and also the prince of the covenant. 23And after the league
is made with him he shall act
deceitfully, for he shall come
up and become strong with
a small *number of* people.

11:14 [a] Or *robbers,* literally *sons of breakage* **11:15** [a] Literally *arms* **11:16** [a] Literally *hand* **11:17** [a] Or *bring equitable terms* **11:22** [a] Literally *arms*

24 He shall enter peaceably,
even into the richest places
of the province; and he shall
do *what* his fathers have not
done, nor his forefathers: he
shall disperse among them
the plunder, spoil, and riches;
and he shall devise his plans
against the strongholds, but
only for a time.

25 "He shall stir up his
power and his courage against
the king of the South with a
great army. And the king of
the South shall be stirred up
to battle with a very great and
mighty army; but he shall
not stand, for they shall devise plans against him. 26 Yes,
those who eat of the portion
of his delicacies shall destroy him; his army shall be
swept away, and many shall
fall down slain. 27 Both these
kings' hearts *shall be* bent on
evil, and they shall speak lies
at the same table; but it shall
not prosper, for the end *will*
still *be* at the appointed time.
28 While returning to his land
with great riches, his heart
shall be *moved* against the
holy covenant; so he shall do
damage and return to his own
land.

THE NORTHERN KING'S BLASPHEMIES

29 "At the appointed time
he shall return *and go toward*
the south; but it shall not be
like the former or the latter.
30 For ships from Cyprus[a] shall
come against him; therefore
he shall be grieved, and return
in rage against the holy covenant, and do *damage.*

"So he shall return and
show regard for those who
forsake the holy covenant.
31 And forces[a] shall be mustered by him, and they shall
defile the sanctuary fortress;
then they shall take away the
daily *sacrifices,* and place *there*
the abomination of desola-
tion. 32 Those who do wickedly
against the covenant he shall
corrupt with flattery; but the
people who know their God
shall be strong, and carry out
great exploits. 33 And those of
the people who understand
shall instruct many; yet *for
many* days they shall fall by
sword and flame, by captivity
and plundering. 34 Now when
they fall, they shall be aided
with a little help; but many
shall join with them by intrigue. 35 And *some* of those
of understanding shall fall,
to refine them, purify *them,*
and make *them* white, *until*
the time of the end; because *it
is* still for the appointed time.

36 "Then the king shall do
according to his own will: he
shall exalt and magnify himself above every god, shall
speak blasphemies against the
God of gods, and shall prosper

11:30 [a] Hebrew *Kittim,* western lands, especially Cyprus 11:31 [a] Literally *arms*

till the wrath has been accomplished; for what has been determined shall be done. 37He
shall regard neither the God[a]
of his fathers nor the desire of
women, nor regard any god;
for he shall exalt himself above
them all. 38But in their place he
shall honor a god of fortresses;
and a god which his fathers did
not know he shall honor with
gold and silver, with precious
stones and pleasant things.
39Thus he shall act against
the strongest fortresses with
a foreign god, which he shall
acknowledge, *and* advance *its*
glory; and he shall cause them
to rule over many, and divide
the land for gain.

THE NORTHERN KING'S CONQUESTS

40"At the time of the end
the king of the South shall attack him; and the king of the
North shall come against him
like a whirlwind, with chariots, horsemen, and with many
ships; and he shall enter the
countries, overwhelm *them,*
and pass through. 41He shall
also enter the Glorious Land,
and many *countries* shall be
overthrown; but these shall
escape from his hand: Edom,
Moab, and the prominent
people of Ammon. 42He shall
stretch out his hand against
the countries, and the land of
Egypt shall not escape. 43He
shall have power over the treasures of gold and silver, and
over all the precious things of
Egypt; also the Libyans and
Ethiopians *shall follow* at his
heels. 44But news from the
east and the north shall trouble him; therefore he shall go
out with great fury to destroy
and annihilate many. 45And
he shall plant the tents of his
palace between the seas and
the glorious holy mountain;
yet he shall come to his end,
and no one will help him.

PROPHECY OF THE END TIME

12 "At that time Michael
shall stand up,
The great prince who
stands *watch* over the
sons of your people;
And there shall be a
time of trouble,
Such as never was since
there was a nation,
Even to that time.
And at that time
your people shall
be delivered,
Every one who is found
written in the book.
2 And many of those who
sleep in the dust of the
earth shall awake,
Some to everlasting life,
Some to shame *and*
everlasting contempt.
3 Those who are wise
shall shine
Like the brightness of
the firmament,

11:37 [a] Or *gods*

And those who turn
many to righteousness
Like the stars forever
and ever.

4 “But you, Daniel, shut up
the words, and seal the book
until the time of the end;
many shall run to and fro, and
knowledge shall increase.”
5 Then I, Daniel, looked; and
there stood two others, one on
this riverbank and the other on
that riverbank. 6 And *one* said to
the man clothed in linen, who
was above the waters of the
river, “How long shall the fulfillment of these wonders *be?*”
7 Then I heard the man
clothed in linen, who *was*
above the waters of the river,
when he held up his right hand
and his left hand to heaven,
and swore by Him who lives
forever, that *it shall be* for a
time, times, and half *a time;*
and when the power of the
holy people has been com-
pletely shattered, all these
things shall be finished.
8 Although I heard, I did not
understand. Then I said, “My
lord, what *shall be* the end of
these *things?*”
9 And he said, “Go *your*
way, Daniel, for the words *are*
closed up and sealed till the
time of the end. 10 Many shall
be purified, made white, and
refined, but the wicked shall
do wickedly; and none of the
wicked shall understand, but
the wise shall understand.
11 “And from the time *that*
the daily *sacrifice* is taken
away, and the abomination of
desolation is set up, *there shall*
be one thousand two hundred
and ninety days. 12 Blessed *is*
he who waits, and comes to
the one thousand three hundred and thirty-five days.
13 “But you, go *your way* till
the end; for you shall rest, and
will arise to your inheritance
at the end of the days.”

THE BOOK OF HOSEA

1 The word of the LORD that
came to Hosea the son of
Beeri, in the days of Uzziah,
Jotham, Ahaz, *and* Hezekiah,
kings of Judah, and in the
days of Jeroboam the son of
Joash, king of Israel.

THE FAMILY OF HOSEA

2 When the LORD began to
speak by Hosea, the LORD said
to Hosea:

“Go, take yourself a
wife of harlotry

And children of harlotry,
For the land has
committed great
harlotry
By departing from
the LORD."

[3]So he went and took Gomer
the daughter of Diblaim, and
she conceived and bore him
a son. [4]Then the LORD said
to him:

"Call his name Jezreel,
For in a little *while*
I will avenge the
bloodshed of Jezreel
on the house of Jehu,
And bring an end to
the kingdom of the
house of Israel.
5 It shall come to pass
in that day
That I will break the
bow of Israel in the
Valley of Jezreel."

[6]And she conceived again
and bore a daughter. Then *God*
said to him:

"Call her name
Lo-Ruhamah,[a]
For I will no longer
have mercy on the
house of Israel,
But I will utterly take
them away.[b]
7 Yet I will have mercy on
the house of Judah,
Will save them by the
LORD their God,
And will not save
them by bow,
Nor by sword or battle,
By horses or horsemen."

[8]Now when she had weaned
Lo-Ruhamah, she conceived
and bore a son. [9]Then *God*
said:

"Call his name Lo-Ammi,[a]
For you *are* not
My people,
And I will not be your *God*.

THE RESTORATION OF ISRAEL

10 "Yet the number of the
children of Israel
Shall be as the sand
of the sea,
Which cannot be
measured or numbered.
And it shall come to pass
In the place where it
was said to them,
'You *are* not My people,'[a]
There it shall be
said to them,
'*You are* sons of the
living God.'
11 Then the children
of Judah and the
children of Israel
Shall be gathered
together,
And appoint for
themselves one head;

1:6 [a] Literally *No-Mercy* [b] Or *That I may forgive them at all* 1:9 [a] Literally *Not-My-People*
1:10 [a] Hebrew *lo-ammi* (compare verse 9)

And they shall come
up out of the land,
For great *will be* the
day of Jezreel!

2 Say to your brethren,
'My people,'[a]
And to your sisters,
'Mercy[b] *is shown.*'

GOD'S UNFAITHFUL PEOPLE

2 "Bring charges against
your mother,
bring charges;
For she *is* not My wife,
nor *am* I her Husband!
Let her put away
her harlotries
from her sight,
And her adulteries from
between her breasts;
3 Lest I strip her naked
And expose her, as in
the day she was born,
And make her like
a wilderness,
And set her like
a dry land,
And slay her with thirst.

4 "I will not have mercy
on her children,
For they *are* the
children of harlotry.
5 For their mother has
played the harlot;
She who conceived
them has behaved
shamefully.
For she said, 'I will go
after my lovers,
Who give *me* my bread
and my water,
My wool and my linen,
My oil and my drink.'

6 "Therefore, behold,
I will hedge up your
way with thorns,
And wall her in,
So that she cannot
find her paths.
7 She will chase her lovers,
But not overtake them;
Yes, she will seek them,
but not find *them.*
Then she will say,
'I will go and return to
my first husband,
For then *it was* better
for me than now.'
8 For she did not know
That I gave her grain,
new wine, and oil,
And multiplied her
silver and gold—
Which they prepared
for Baal.

9 "Therefore I will return
and take away
My grain in its time
And My new wine
in its season,
And will take back My
wool and My linen,
Given to cover her
nakedness.
10 Now I will uncover
her lewdness in the
sight of her lovers,
And no one shall deliver
her from My hand.
11 I will also cause all her
mirth to cease,

2:1 [a] Hebrew *Ammi* (compare 1:9, 10) [b] Hebrew *Ruhamah* (compare 1:6)

Her feast days,
Her New Moons,
Her Sabbaths—
All her appointed feasts.

12 "And I will destroy her
vines and her fig trees,
Of which she has said,
'These *are* my wages
that my lovers
have given me.'
So I will make
them a forest,
And the beasts of the
field shall eat them.
13 I will punish her
For the days of the
Baals to which she
burned incense.
She decked herself with
her earrings and jewelry,
And went after her lovers;
But Me she forgot,"
says the LORD.

GOD'S MERCY ON HIS PEOPLE

14 "Therefore, behold,
I will allure her,
Will bring her into
the wilderness,
And speak comfort to her.
15 I will give her her
vineyards from there,
And the Valley of Achor
as a door of hope;
She shall sing there,
As in the days of
her youth,
As in the day when
she came up from
the land of Egypt.

16 "And it shall be,
in that day,"
Says the LORD,
"*That* you will call Me
'My Husband,'[a]
And no longer call
Me 'My Master,'[b]
17 For I will take from her
mouth the names
of the Baals,
And they shall be
remembered by their
name no more.
18 In that day I will make
a covenant for them
With the beasts
of the field,
With the birds of
the air,
And *with* the creeping
things of the ground.
Bow and sword of
battle I will shatter
from the earth,
To make them lie
down safely.

19 "I will betroth you
to Me forever;
Yes, I will betroth
you to Me
In righteousness
and justice,
In lovingkindness
and mercy;
20 I will betroth you to
Me in faithfulness,
And you shall know
the LORD.

21 "It shall come to pass
in that day

2:16 [a] Hebrew *Ishi* [b] Hebrew *Baali*

That I will answer,"
says the LORD;
"I will answer the heavens,
And they shall answer
the earth.
22 The earth shall answer
With grain,
With new wine,
And with oil;
They shall answer
Jezreel.[a]
23 Then I will sow her for
Myself in the earth,
And I will have mercy
on *her who had* not
obtained mercy;[a]
Then I will say to
those who were
not My people,[b]
'You *are* My people!'
And they shall say,
'*You are* my God!'"

ISRAEL WILL RETURN TO GOD

3 Then the LORD said to me,
"Go again, love a woman
who is loved by a lover[a] and is
committing adultery, just like
the love of the LORD for the
children of Israel, who look to
other gods and love *the* raisin
cakes *of the pagans*."
2So I bought her for myself
for fifteen *shekels* of silver, and
one and one-half homers of
barley. 3And I said to her, "You
shall stay with me many days;
you shall not play the harlot,
nor shall you have a *man*—so,
too, *will* I *be* toward you."
4For the children of Is-
rael shall abide many days
without king or prince, without sacrifice or *sacred* pillar,
without ephod or teraphim.
5Afterward the children of
Israel shall return and seek
the LORD their God and David
their king. They shall fear the
LORD and His goodness in the
latter days.

GOD'S CHARGE AGAINST ISRAEL

4 Hear the word of
the LORD,
You children of Israel,
For the LORD *brings* a
charge against the
inhabitants of the land:

"There is no truth
or mercy
Or knowledge of
God in the land.
2 *By* swearing and lying,
Killing and stealing
and committing
adultery,
They break all restraint,
With bloodshed
upon bloodshed.
3 Therefore the land
will mourn;
And everyone who dwells
there will waste away
With the beasts
of the field
And the birds of the air;
Even the fish of the sea
will be taken away.

2:22 [a] Literally *God Will Sow* 2:23 [a] Hebrew *lo-ruhamah*
[b] Hebrew *lo-ammi* 3:1 [a] Literally *friend* or *husband*

4 "Now let no man contend,
or rebuke another;
For your people *are* like
those who contend
with the priest.
5 Therefore you shall
stumble in the day;
The prophet also
shall stumble with
you in the night;
And I will destroy
your mother.
6 My people are destroyed
for lack of knowledge.
Because you have
rejected knowledge,
I also will reject you from
being priest for Me;
Because you have
forgotten the law
of your God,
I also will forget
your children.

7 "The more they
increased,
The more they sinned
against Me;
I will change[a] their
glory[b] into shame.
8 They eat up the sin
of My people;
They set their heart
on their iniquity.
9 And it shall be: like
people, like priest.
So I will punish them
for their ways,
And reward them
for their deeds.
10 For they shall eat, but
not have enough;
They shall commit
harlotry, but not
increase;
Because they have ceased
obeying the LORD.

THE IDOLATRY OF ISRAEL

11 "Harlotry, wine, and new
wine enslave the heart.
12 My people ask counsel
from their wooden *idols,*
And their staff
informs them.
For the spirit of
harlotry has caused
them to stray,
And they have played the
harlot against their God.
13 They offer sacrifices on
the mountaintops,
And burn incense
on the hills,
Under oaks, poplars,
and terebinths,
Because their
shade *is* good.
Therefore your daughters
commit harlotry,
And your brides
commit adultery.

14 "I will not punish your
daughters when they
commit harlotry,
Nor your brides when
they commit adultery;
For *the men* themselves
go apart with harlots,

4:7 [a] Following Masoretic Text, Septuagint, and Vulgate; scribal tradition, Syriac, and Targum read *They will change.* [b] Following Masoretic Text, Septuagint, Syriac, Targum, and Vulgate; scribal tradition reads *My glory*.

And offer sacrifices
with a ritual harlot.[a]
Therefore people *who*
do not understand
will be trampled.

15 "Though you, Israel,
play the harlot,
Let not Judah offend.
Do not come up to Gilgal,
Nor go up to Beth Aven,
Nor swear an oath, *saying,*
'As the LORD lives'—

16 "For Israel is stubborn
Like a stubborn calf;
Now the LORD will
let them forage
Like a lamb in
open country.

17 "Ephraim *is* joined to idols,
Let him alone.
18 Their drink is rebellion,
They commit harlotry
continually.
Her rulers dearly[a]
love dishonor.
19 The wind has wrapped
her up in its wings,
And they shall be
ashamed because
of their sacrifices.

IMPENDING JUDGMENT ON ISRAEL AND JUDAH

5 "Hear this, O priests!
Take heed, O house
of Israel!
Give ear, O house
of the king!
For yours *is* the judgment,
Because you have been
a snare to Mizpah
And a net spread
on Tabor.
2 The revolters are deeply
involved in slaughter,
Though I rebuke them all.
3 I know Ephraim,
And Israel is not
hidden from Me;
For now, O Ephraim, you
commit harlotry;
Israel is defiled.

4 "They do not direct
their deeds
Toward turning
to their God,
For the spirit of harlotry
is in their midst,
And they do not
know the LORD.
5 The pride of Israel
testifies to his face;
Therefore Israel and
Ephraim stumble
in their iniquity;
Judah also stumbles
with them.

6 "With their flocks
and herds
They shall go to
seek the LORD,
But they will not find *Him;*
He has withdrawn
Himself from them.
7 They have dealt
treacherously
with the LORD,

4:14 [a] Compare Deuteronomy 23:18 4:18 [a] Hebrew is difficult; a Jewish tradition reads *Her rulers shamefully love, 'Give!'*

For they have begotten
pagan children.
Now a New Moon shall
devour them and
their heritage.

8 "Blow the ram's horn
in Gibeah,
The trumpet in Ramah!
Cry aloud *at* Beth Aven,
'*Look* behind you,
O Benjamin!'
9 Ephraim shall be desolate
in the day of rebuke;
Among the tribes of
Israel I make known
what is sure.

10 "The princes of Judah
are like those who
remove a landmark;
I will pour out My wrath
on them like water.
11 Ephraim is oppressed *and*
broken in judgment,
Because he willingly
walked by *human*
precept.
12 Therefore I *will be* to
Ephraim like a moth,
And to the house of
Judah like rottenness.

13 "When Ephraim
saw his sickness,
And Judah *saw* his wound,
Then Ephraim went
to Assyria
And sent to King Jareb;
Yet he cannot cure you,
Nor heal you of
your wound.
14 For I *will be* like a
lion to Ephraim,
And like a young lion to
the house of Judah.
I, *even* I, will tear *them*
and go away;
I will take *them* away, and
no one shall rescue.
15 I will return again
to My place
Till they acknowledge
their offense.
Then they will
seek My face;
In their affliction
they will earnestly
seek Me."

A CALL TO REPENTANCE

6 Come, and let us
return to the LORD;
For He has torn, but
He will heal us;
He has stricken, but
He will bind us up.
2 After two days He
will revive us;
On the third day He
will raise us up,
That we may live
in His sight.
3 Let us know,
Let us pursue the
knowledge of the LORD.
His going forth is
established as
the morning;
He will come to us
like the rain,
Like the latter *and* former
rain to the earth.

IMPENITENCE OF ISRAEL AND JUDAH

4 "O Ephraim, what
shall I do to you?

O Judah, what shall
I do to you?
For your faithfulness is
like a morning cloud,
And like the early
dew it goes away.
5 Therefore I have hewn
them by the prophets,
I have slain them by the
words of My mouth;
And your judgments
are like light *that*
goes forth.
6 For I desire mercy
and not sacrifice,
And the knowledge
of God more than
burnt offerings.

7 "But like men[a] they
transgressed the
covenant;
There they dealt
treacherously with Me.
8 Gilead *is* a city of
evildoers
And defiled with blood.
9 As bands of robbers lie
in wait for a man,
So the company of
priests murder on the
way to Shechem;
Surely they commit
lewdness.
10 I have seen a horrible
thing in the house
of Israel:
There *is* the harlotry
of Ephraim;
Israel is defiled.
11 Also, O Judah, a harvest
is appointed for you,
When I return the
captives of My people.

7 "When I would have
healed Israel,
Then the iniquity
of Ephraim was
uncovered,
And the wickedness
of Samaria.
For they have
committed fraud;
A thief comes in;
A band of robbers
takes spoil outside.
2 They do not consider
in their hearts
That I remember all
their wickedness;
Now their own deeds
have surrounded them;
They are before My face.
3 They make a king glad
with their wickedness,
And princes with
their lies.

4 "They *are* all adulterers.
Like an oven heated
by a baker—
He ceases stirring *the*
fire after kneading
the dough,
Until it is leavened.
5 In the day of our king
Princes have made
him sick, inflamed
with wine;
He stretched out his
hand with scoffers.
6 They prepare their
heart like an oven,

6:7 [a] Or *like Adam*

While they lie in wait;
Their baker[a] sleeps
all night;
In the morning it burns
like a flaming fire.
7 They are all hot,
like an oven,
And have devoured
their judges;
All their kings have fallen.
None among them
calls upon Me.

8 "Ephraim has mixed
himself among
the peoples;
Ephraim is a cake
unturned.
9 Aliens have devoured
his strength,
But he does not know *it;*
Yes, gray hairs are here
and there on him,
Yet he does not know *it.*
10 And the pride of Israel
testifies to his face,
But they do not return
to the LORD their God,
Nor seek Him for all this.

FUTILE RELIANCE ON THE NATIONS

11 "Ephraim also is like a silly
dove, without sense—
They call to Egypt,
They go to Assyria.
12 Wherever they go, I will
spread My net on them;
I will bring them down
like birds of the air;
I will chastise them
According to what their
congregation has heard.

13 "Woe to them, for they
have fled from Me!
Destruction to them,
Because they have
transgressed
against Me!
Though I redeemed
them,
Yet they have spoken
lies against Me.
14 They did not cry out to
Me with their heart
When they wailed
upon their beds.

"They assemble
together for[a] grain
and new wine,
They rebel against Me;[b]
15 Though I disciplined
and strengthened
their arms,
Yet they devise evil
against Me;
16 They return, *but* not
to the Most High;[a]
They are like a
treacherous bow.
Their princes shall
fall by the sword
For the cursings of
their tongue.

7:6 [a] Following Masoretic Text and Vulgate; Syriac and Targum read *Their anger;* Septuagint reads *Ephraim.* 7:14 [a] Following Masoretic Text and Targum; Vulgate reads *thought upon;* Septuagint reads *slashed themselves for* (compare 1 Kings 18:28). [b] Following Masoretic Text, Syriac, and Targum; Septuagint omits *They rebel against Me;* Vulgate reads *They departed from Me.* 7:16 [a] Or *upward*

This *shall be* their derision
in the land of Egypt.

THE APOSTASY OF ISRAEL

8 "*Set* the trumpet[a] to
your mouth!
He shall come like an
eagle against the
house of the LORD,
Because they have
transgressed My
covenant
And rebelled
against My law.
2 Israel will cry to Me,
'My God, we know You!'
3 Israel has rejected
the good;
The enemy will
pursue him.

4 "They set up kings,
but not by Me;
They made princes,
but I did not
acknowledge *them*.
From their silver and gold
They made idols for
themselves—
That they might
be cut off.
5 Your calf is rejected,
O Samaria!
My anger is aroused
against them—
How long until they
attain to innocence?
6 For from Israel *is*
even this:
A workman made it,
and it *is* not God;
But the calf of
Samaria shall be
broken to pieces.

7 "They sow the wind,
And reap the whirlwind.
The stalk has no bud;
It shall never
produce meal.
If it should produce,
Aliens would
swallow it up.
8 Israel is swallowed up;
Now they are among
the Gentiles
Like a vessel in which
is no pleasure.
9 For they have gone
up to Assyria,
Like a wild donkey
alone by itself;
Ephraim has hired lovers.
10 Yes, though they
have hired among
the nations,
Now I will gather them;
And they shall
sorrow a little,[a]
Because of the burden[b]
of the king of princes.

11 "Because Ephraim
has made many
altars for sin,
They have become for
him altars for sinning.
12 I have written for him
the great things
of My law,
But they were considered
a strange thing.

8:1 [a] Hebrew *shophar*, ram's horn **8:10** [a] Or *begin to diminish* [b] Or *oracle*

13 *For* the sacrifices of My
offerings they sacrifice
flesh and eat *it,*
But the LORD does
not accept them.
Now He will remember
their iniquity and
punish their sins.
They shall return
to Egypt.

14 "For Israel has forgotten
his Maker,
And has built temples;[a]
Judah also has multiplied
fortified cities;
But I will send fire
upon his cities,
And it shall devour
his palaces."

JUDGMENT OF ISRAEL'S SIN

9 Do not rejoice,
O Israel, with joy
like *other* peoples,
For you have played the
harlot against your God.
You have made love
for hire on every
threshing floor.
2 The threshing floor
and the winepress
Shall not feed them,
And the new wine
shall fail in her.

3 They shall not dwell
in the LORD's land,
But Ephraim shall
return to Egypt,
And shall eat unclean
things in Assyria.
4 They shall not offer wine
offerings to the LORD,
Nor shall their sacrifices
be pleasing to Him.
It shall be like bread of
mourners to them;
All who eat it shall
be defiled.
For their bread *shall be*
for their *own* life;
It shall not come into the
house of the LORD.

5 What will you do in
the appointed day,
And in the day of the
feast of the LORD?
6 For indeed they are gone
because of destruction.
Egypt shall gather
them up;
Memphis shall
bury them.
Nettles shall possess their
valuables of silver;
Thorns *shall be* in
their tents.

7 The days of punishment
have come;
The days of recompense
have come.
Israel knows!
The prophet *is* a fool,
The spiritual man
is insane,
Because of the greatness
of your iniquity and
great enmity.
8 The watchman
of Ephraim *is*
with my God;

8:14 [a] Or *palaces*

But the prophet *is* a
fowler's[a] snare in
all his ways—
Enmity in the house
of his God.
9 They are deeply
corrupted,
As in the days of Gibeah.
He will remember
their iniquity;
He will punish their sins.

10 "I found Israel
Like grapes in the
wilderness;
I saw your fathers
As the firstfruits on the fig
tree in its first season.
But they went to Baal Peor,
And separated
themselves *to*
that shame;
They became an
abomination like the
thing they loved.
11 *As for* Ephraim, their
glory shall fly away
like a bird—
No birth, no pregnancy,
and no conception!
12 Though they bring
up their children,
Yet I will bereave them
to the last man.
Yes, woe to them when
I depart from them!
13 Just as I saw Ephraim
like Tyre, planted in
a pleasant place,
So Ephraim will bring
out his children to
the murderer."

14 Give them, O LORD—
What will You give?
Give them a
miscarrying womb
And dry breasts!

15 "All their wickedness
is in Gilgal,
For there I hated them.
Because of the evil
of their deeds
I will drive them
from My house;
I will love them no more.
All their princes
are rebellious.
16 Ephraim is stricken,
Their root is dried up;
They shall bear no fruit.
Yes, were they to
bear children,
I would kill the darlings
of their womb."

17 My God will cast
them away,
Because they did
not obey Him;
And they shall be
wanderers among
the nations.

ISRAEL'S SIN AND CAPTIVITY

10 Israel empties *his*
vine;
He brings forth fruit
for himself.
According to the
multitude of his fruit
He has increased
the altars;

9:8 [a] That is, one who catches birds in a trap or snare

According to the
bounty of his land
They have embellished
his sacred pillars.
2 Their heart is divided;
Now they are held guilty.
He will break down
their altars;
He will ruin their
sacred pillars.

3 For now they say,
"We have no king,
Because we did not
fear the LORD.
And as for a king, what
would he do for us?"
4 They have spoken words,
Swearing falsely in
making a covenant.
Thus judgment springs
up like hemlock in the
furrows of the field.

5 The inhabitants of
Samaria fear
Because of the calf[a]
of Beth Aven.
For its people
mourn for it,
And its priests
shriek for it—
Because its glory has
departed from it.
6 *The idol* also shall be
carried to Assyria
As a present for
King Jareb.
Ephraim shall
receive shame,
And Israel shall be
ashamed of his
own counsel.

7 *As for* Samaria, her
king is cut off
Like a twig on the water.
8 Also the high places of
Aven, the sin of Israel,
Shall be destroyed.
The thorn and
thistle shall grow
on their altars;
They shall say to the
mountains, "Cover us!"
And to the hills,
"Fall on us!"

9 "O Israel, you have
sinned from the
days of Gibeah;
There they stood.
The battle in Gibeah
against the children
of iniquity[a]
Did not overtake them.
10 When *it is* My desire, I
will chasten them.
Peoples shall be gathered
against them
When I bind them
for their two
transgressions.[a]
11 Ephraim *is* a
trained heifer
That loves to thresh *grain;*
But I harnessed
her fair neck,
I will make Ephraim
pull *a plow.*

10:5 [a] Literally *calves* 10:9 [a] So read many Hebrew manuscripts, Septuagint, and Vulgate; Masoretic Text reads *unruliness.* 10:10 [a] Or *in their two habitations*

Judah shall plow;
Jacob shall break
his clods."

12 Sow for yourselves
righteousness;
Reap in mercy;
Break up your
fallow ground,
For *it is* time to
seek the LORD,
Till He comes and rains
righteousness on you.

13 You have plowed
wickedness;
You have reaped iniquity.
You have eaten the
fruit of lies,
Because you trusted
in your own way,
In the multitude of
your mighty men.
14 Therefore tumult
shall arise among
your people,
And all your fortresses
shall be plundered
As Shalman plundered
Beth Arbel in the
day of battle—
A mother dashed
in pieces upon
her children.
15 Thus it shall be done
to you, O Bethel,
Because of your great
wickedness.
At dawn the king of Israel
Shall be cut off utterly.

GOD'S CONTINUING LOVE FOR ISRAEL

11 "When Israel *was* a
child, I loved him,
And out of Egypt I
called My son.
2 *As* they called them,[a]
So they went from them;[b]
They sacrificed to
the Baals,
And burned incense
to carved images.

3 "I taught Ephraim to walk,
Taking them by
their arms;[a]
But they did not know
that I healed them.
4 I drew them with
gentle cords,[a]
With bands of love,
And I was to them as
those who take the
yoke from their neck.[b]
I stooped *and* fed them.

5 "He shall not return to
the land of Egypt;
But the Assyrian
shall be his king,
Because they refused
to repent.
6 And the sword shall
slash in his cities,
Devour his districts,

11:2 [a] Following Masoretic Text and Vulgate; Septuagint reads *Just as I called them*; Targum interprets as *I sent prophets to a thousand of them.* [b] Following Masoretic Text, Targum, and Vulgate; Septuagint reads *from My face.* 11:3 [a] Some Hebrew manuscripts, Septuagint, Syriac, and Vulgate read *My arms.* 11:4 [a] Literally *cords of a man* [b] Literally *jaws*

And consume *them,*
Because of their
own counsels.
7 My people are bent on
backsliding from Me.
Though they call to
the Most High,[a]
None at all exalt *Him.*

8 "How can I give you
up, Ephraim?
How can I hand you
over, Israel?
How can I make you
like Admah?
How can I set you
like Zeboiim?
My heart churns
within Me;
My sympathy is stirred.
9 I will not execute the
fierceness of My anger;
I will not again
destroy Ephraim.
For I *am* God, and
not man,
The Holy One in
your midst;
And I will not come
with terror.[a]

10 "They shall walk
after the LORD.
He will roar like a lion.
When He roars,
Then *His* sons shall
come trembling
from the west;
11 They shall come
trembling like a
bird from Egypt,
Like a dove from the
land of Assyria.
And I will let them dwell
in their houses,"
Says the LORD.

GOD'S CHARGE AGAINST EPHRAIM

12 "Ephraim has encircled
Me with lies,
And the house of
Israel with deceit;
But Judah still walks
with God,
Even with the Holy
One[a] *who is* faithful.

12 "Ephraim feeds
on the wind,
And pursues the
east wind;
He daily increases lies
and desolation.
Also they make a
covenant with
the Assyrians,
And oil is carried
to Egypt.

2 "The LORD also *brings* a
charge against Judah,
And will punish Jacob
according to his ways;
According to his deeds He
will recompense him.
3 He took his brother by
the heel in the womb,
And in his strength he
struggled with God.[a]
4 Yes, he struggled with the
Angel and prevailed;

11:7 [a] Or *upward* 11:9 [a] Or *I will not enter a city* 11:12 [a] Or *holy ones* 12:3 [a] Compare Genesis 32:28

He wept, and sought
favor from Him.
He found Him *in* Bethel,
And there He
spoke to us—
5 That is, the LORD
God of hosts.
The LORD *is* His
memorable name.
6 So you, by *the help of*
your God, return;
Observe mercy
and justice,
And wait on your
God continually.

7 "A cunning Canaanite!
Deceitful scales *are*
in his hand;
He loves to oppress.
8 And Ephraim said,
'Surely I have
become rich,
I have found wealth
for myself;
In all my labors
They shall find in me no
iniquity that *is* sin.'

9 "But I *am* the LORD
your God,
Ever since the land
of Egypt;
I will again make you
dwell in tents,
As in the days of the
appointed feast.
10 I have also spoken
by the prophets,
And have multiplied
visions;
I have given symbols
through the witness
of the prophets."

11 Though Gilead
has idols—
Surely they are vanity—
Though they sacrifice
bulls in Gilgal,
Indeed their altars
shall be heaps in the
furrows of the field.

12 Jacob fled to the
country of Syria;
Israel served for a spouse,
And for a wife he
tended *sheep*.
13 By a prophet the
LORD brought Israel
out of Egypt,
And by a prophet he
was preserved.
14 Ephraim provoked *Him*
to anger most bitterly;
Therefore his Lord will
leave the guilt of his
bloodshed upon him,
And return his reproach
upon him.

RELENTLESS JUDGMENT ON ISRAEL

13 When Ephraim
spoke, trembling,
He exalted *himself*
in Israel;
But when he offended
through Baal
worship, he died.
2 Now they sin more
and more,
And have made
for themselves
molded images,
Idols of their silver,
according to
their skill;

All of it *is* the work
of craftsmen.
They say of them,
"Let the men who
sacrifice[a] kiss
the calves!"
3 Therefore they shall be
like the morning cloud
And like the early dew
that passes away,
Like chaff blown off from
a threshing floor
And like smoke from
a chimney.

4 "Yet I *am* the LORD
your God
Ever since the land
of Egypt,
And you shall know
no God but Me;
For *there is* no savior
besides Me.
5 I knew you in the
wilderness,
In the land of great
drought.
6 When they had pasture,
they were filled;
They were filled and their
heart was exalted;
Therefore they forgot Me.

7 "So I will be to them
like a lion;
Like a leopard by the
road I will lurk;
8 I will meet them like
a bear deprived
of her cubs;
I will tear open
their rib cage,
And there I will devour
them like a lion.
The wild beast shall
tear them.

9 "O Israel, you are
destroyed,[a]
But your help[b] *is*
from Me.
10 I will be your King;[a]
Where *is any other,*
That he may save you
in all your cities?
And your judges to
whom you said,
'Give me a king
and princes'?
11 I gave you a king
in My anger,
And took *him* away
in My wrath.

12 "The iniquity of
Ephraim *is* bound up;
His sin *is* stored up.
13 The sorrows of a woman
in childbirth shall
come upon him.
He *is* an unwise son,
For he should not
stay long where
children are born.

14 "I will ransom them
from the power
of the grave;[a]
I will redeem them
from death.

13:2 [a] Or *those who offer human sacrifice* 13:9 [a] Literally *it* or *he destroyed you* [b] Literally *in your help* 13:10 [a] Septuagint, Syriac, Targum, and Vulgate read *Where is your king?* 13:14 [a] Or *Sheol*

O Death, I will be
your plagues![b]
O Grave,[c] I will be
your destruction![d]
Pity is hidden from
My eyes."

15 Though he is fruitful
among *his* brethren,
An east wind shall come;
The wind of the LORD
shall come up from
the wilderness.
Then his spring shall
become dry,
And his fountain
shall be dried up.
He shall plunder the
treasury of every
desirable prize.
16 Samaria is held guilty,[a]
For she has rebelled
against her God.
They shall fall by
the sword,
Their infants shall be
dashed in pieces,
And their women with
child ripped open.

ISRAEL RESTORED AT LAST

14 O Israel, return to the
LORD your God,
For you have stumbled
because of your
iniquity;
2 Take words with you,
And return to the LORD.
Say to Him,
"Take away all iniquity;
Receive *us* graciously,
For we will offer the
sacrifices[a] of our lips.
3 Assyria shall not save us,
We will not ride on horses,
Nor will we say
anymore to the
work of our hands,
'*You are* our gods.'
For in You the fatherless
finds mercy."

4 "I will heal their
backsliding,
I will love them freely,
For My anger has turned
away from him.
5 I will be like the
dew to Israel;
He shall grow like the lily,
And lengthen his roots
like Lebanon.
6 His branches shall spread;
His beauty shall be
like an olive tree,
And his fragrance
like Lebanon.
7 Those who dwell under
his shadow shall return;
They shall be revived
like grain,
And grow like a vine.
Their scent[a] *shall be* like
the wine of Lebanon.

8 "Ephraim *shall say,*
'What have I to do
anymore with idols?'
I have heard and
observed him.

13:14 [b] Septuagint reads *where is your punishment?* [c] Or *Sheol* [d] Septuagint reads *where is your sting?* 13:16 [a] Septuagint reads *shall be disfigured* 14:2 [a] Literally *bull calves;* Septuagint reads *fruit.* 14:7 [a] Literally *remembrance*

I *am* like a green
cypress tree;
Your fruit is found
in Me."

9 Who *is* wise?
Let him understand
these things.
Who is prudent?
Let him know them.
For the ways of the
LORD *are* right;
The righteous
walk in them,
But transgressors
stumble in them.

THE BOOK OF JOEL

1 The word of the LORD that
came to Joel the son of Pe-
thuel.

THE LAND LAID WASTE

2 Hear this, you elders,
And give ear, all you
inhabitants of the land!
Has *anything like* this
happened in your days,
Or even in the days
of your fathers?
3 Tell your children
about it,
Let your children *tell*
their children,
And their children
another generation.

4 What the chewing locust[a]
left, the swarming
locust has eaten;
What the swarming
locust left, the crawling
locust has eaten;
And what the crawling
locust left, the
consuming locust
has eaten.

5 Awake, you drunkards,
and weep;
And wail, all you
drinkers of wine,
Because of the new wine,
For it has been cut off
from your mouth.
6 For a nation has come
up against My land,
Strong, and without
number;
His teeth *are* the
teeth of a lion,
And he has the fangs
of a fierce lion.
7 He has laid waste
My vine,
And ruined My fig tree;
He has stripped it bare
and thrown *it* away;

1:4 [a] Exact identity of these locusts is unknown.

Its branches are
made white.

8 Lament like a virgin
girded with sackcloth
For the husband
of her youth.
9 The grain offering and
the drink offering
Have been cut off from
the house of the LORD;
The priests mourn, who
minister to the LORD.
10 The field is wasted,
The land mourns;
For the grain is ruined,
The new wine is dried up,
The oil fails.

11 Be ashamed, you farmers,
Wail, you vinedressers,
For the wheat and
the barley;
Because the harvest of
the field has perished.
12 The vine has dried up,
And the fig tree
has withered;
The pomegranate tree,
The palm tree also,
And the apple tree—
All the trees of the
field are withered;
Surely joy has withered
away from the
sons of men.

MOURNING FOR THE LAND

13 Gird yourselves and
lament, you priests;
Wail, you who minister
before the altar;
Come, lie all night
in sackcloth,
You who minister
to my God;
For the grain offering
and the drink offering
Are withheld from the
house of your God.
14 Consecrate a fast,
Call a sacred assembly;
Gather the elders
And all the inhabitants
of the land
Into the house of the
LORD your God,
And cry out to the LORD.

15 Alas for the day!
For the day of the
LORD *is* at hand;
It shall come as
destruction from
the Almighty.
16 Is not the food cut off
before our eyes,
Joy and gladness from
the house of our God?
17 The seed shrivels
under the clods,
Storehouses are
in shambles;
Barns are broken down,
For the grain has
withered.
18 How the animals groan!
The herds of cattle
are restless,
Because they have
no pasture;
Even the flocks of
sheep suffer
punishment.[a]

1:18 [a] Septuagint and Vulgate read *are made desolate.*

19 O LORD, to You I cry out;
For fire has devoured
the open pastures,
And a flame has burned
all the trees of the field.
20 The beasts of the field
also cry out to You,
For the water brooks
are dried up,
And fire has devoured
the open pastures.

THE DAY OF THE LORD

2 Blow the trumpet in Zion,
And sound an alarm in
My holy mountain!
Let all the inhabitants
of the land tremble;
For the day of the
LORD is coming,
For it is at hand:
2 A day of darkness
and gloominess,
A day of clouds and
thick darkness,
Like the morning
clouds spread over
the mountains.
A people *come,* great
and strong,
The like of whom
has never been;
Nor will there ever be
any *such* after them,
Even for many successive
generations.

3 A fire devours
before them,
And behind them
a flame burns;
The land *is* like the Garden
of Eden before them,
And behind them a
desolate wilderness;
Surely nothing shall
escape them.
4 Their appearance is
like the appearance
of horses;
And like swift steeds,
so they run.
5 With a noise like chariots
Over mountaintops
they leap,
Like the noise of a
flaming fire that
devours the stubble,
Like a strong people
set in battle array.

6 Before them the people
writhe in pain;
All faces are drained
of color.[a]
7 They run like
mighty men,
They climb the wall
like men of war;
Every one marches
in formation,
And they do not
break ranks.
8 They do not push
one another;
Every one marches in
his own column.[a]
Though they lunge
between the weapons,
They are not cut down.[b]
9 They run to and
fro in the city,

2:6 [a] Septuagint, Targum, and Vulgate read *gather blackness.*
2:8 [a] Literally *his own highway* [b] That is, they are not halted by losses

They run on the wall;
They climb into
the houses,
They enter at the
windows like a thief.

10 The earth quakes
before them,
The heavens tremble;
The sun and moon
grow dark,
And the stars diminish
their brightness.
11 The LORD gives voice
before His army,
For His camp is
very great;
For strong *is the One* who
executes His word.
For the day of the LORD
is great and very
terrible;
Who can endure it?

A CALL TO REPENTANCE

12 "Now, therefore,"
says the LORD,
"Turn to Me with
all your heart,
With fasting, with
weeping, and with
mourning."
13 So rend your heart, and
not your garments;
Return to the LORD
your God,
For He *is* gracious
and merciful,
Slow to anger, and of
great kindness;
And He relents from
doing harm.
14 Who knows *if* He will
turn and relent,
And leave a blessing
behind Him—
A grain offering and
a drink offering
For the LORD your God?

15 Blow the trumpet in Zion,
Consecrate a fast,
Call a sacred assembly;
16 Gather the people,
Sanctify the
congregation,
Assemble the elders,
Gather the children
and nursing babes;
Let the bridegroom go
out from his chamber,
And the bride from
her dressing room.
17 Let the priests, who
minister to the LORD,
Weep between the
porch and the altar;
Let them say, "Spare
Your people, O LORD,
And do not give Your
heritage to reproach,
That the nations should
rule over them.
Why should they say
among the peoples,
'Where *is* their God?'"

THE LAND REFRESHED

18 Then the LORD will be
zealous for His land,
And pity His people.
19 The LORD will answer
and say to His people,
"Behold, I will send
you grain and new
wine and oil,
And you will be
satisfied by them;

I will no longer make
you a reproach
among the nations.

20 "But I will remove far
from you the
northern *army,*
And will drive him
away into a barren
and desolate land,
With his face toward
the eastern sea
And his back toward
the western sea;
His stench will come up,
And his foul odor
will rise,
Because he has done
monstrous things."

21 Fear not, O land;
Be glad and rejoice,
For the LORD has done
marvelous things!
22 Do not be afraid, you
beasts of the field;
For the open pastures
are springing up,
And the tree bears
its fruit;
The fig tree and the vine
yield their strength.
23 Be glad then, you
children of Zion,
And rejoice in the
LORD your God;
For He has given you the
former rain faithfully,[a]
And He will cause
the rain to come
down for you—
The former rain,
And the latter rain in
the first *month.*
24 The threshing floors
shall be full of wheat,
And the vats shall
overflow with new
wine and oil.

25 "So I will restore to you the
years that the swarming
locust has eaten,
The crawling locust,
The consuming locust,
And the chewing locust,[a]
My great army which
I sent among you.
26 You shall eat in plenty
and be satisfied,
And praise the name of
the LORD your God,
Who has dealt
wondrously with you;
And My people shall
never be put to shame.
27 Then you shall know
that I *am* in the
midst of Israel:
I *am* the LORD your God
And there is no other.
My people shall never
be put to shame.

GOD'S SPIRIT POURED OUT

28 "And it shall come
to pass afterward
That I will pour out My
Spirit on all flesh;
Your sons and your
daughters shall
prophesy,
Your old men shall
dream dreams,

2:23 [a] Or *the teacher of righteousness* 2:25 [a] Compare 1:4

Your young men
shall see visions.
29 And also on *My*
menservants and on
My maidservants
I will pour out My
Spirit in those days.

30 "And I will show
wonders in the heavens
and in the earth:
Blood and fire and
pillars of smoke.
31 The sun shall be turned
into darkness,
And the moon into blood,
Before the coming of the
great and awesome
day of the LORD.
32 And it shall come to pass
That whoever calls on
the name of the LORD
Shall be saved.
For in Mount Zion and
in Jerusalem there
shall be deliverance,
As the LORD has said,
Among the remnant
whom the LORD calls.

GOD JUDGES THE NATIONS

3 "For behold, in those
days and at that time,
When I bring back the
captives of Judah
and Jerusalem,
2 I will also gather
all nations,
And bring them
down to the Valley
of Jehoshaphat;
And I will enter into
judgment with
them there
On account of My people,
My heritage Israel,
Whom they have
scattered among
the nations;
They have also divided
up My land.
3 They have cast lots
for My people,
Have given a boy *as*
payment for a harlot,
And sold a girl for wine,
that they may drink.

4 "Indeed, what have
you to do with Me,
O Tyre and Sidon, and
all the coasts of
Philistia?
Will you retaliate
against Me?
But if you retaliate
against Me,
Swiftly and speedily I
will return your
retaliation upon
your own head;
5 Because you have taken
My silver and My gold,
And have carried into
your temples My
prized possessions.
6 Also the people of
Judah and the people
of Jerusalem
You have sold to
the Greeks,
That you may remove
them far from
their borders.

7 "Behold, I will raise them
Out of the place to which
you have sold them,

5 I will also break the *gate*
bar of Damascus,
And cut off the inhabitant
from the Valley of Aven,
And the one who
holds the scepter
from Beth Eden.
The people of Syria shall
go captive to Kir,"
Says the LORD.

6Thus says the LORD:

"For three transgressions
of Gaza, and for four,
I will not turn away
its *punishment,*
Because they took captive
the whole captivity
To deliver *them*
up to Edom.
7 But I will send a fire
upon the wall of Gaza,
Which shall devour
its palaces.
8 I will cut off the inhabitant
from Ashdod,
And the one who holds the
scepter from Ashkelon;
I will turn My hand
against Ekron,
And the remnant of the
Philistines shall perish,"
Says the Lord GOD.

9Thus says the LORD:

"For three transgressions
of Tyre, and for four,
I will not turn away
its *punishment,*
Because they delivered
up the whole
captivity to Edom,
And did not remember
the covenant of
brotherhood.
10 But I will send a fire
upon the wall of Tyre,
Which shall devour
its palaces."

11Thus says the LORD:

"For three transgressions
of Edom, and for four,
I will not turn away
its *punishment,*
Because he pursued his
brother with the sword,
And cast off all pity;
His anger tore
perpetually,
And he kept his
wrath forever.
12 But I will send a fire
upon Teman,
Which shall devour the
palaces of Bozrah."

13Thus says the LORD:

"For three transgressions
of the people of
Ammon, and for four,
I will not turn away
its *punishment,*
Because they ripped
open the women
with child in Gilead,
That they might enlarge
their territory.
14 But I will kindle a fire in
the wall of Rabbah,
And it shall devour
its palaces,
Amid shouting in
the day of battle,

And a tempest in the
day of the whirlwind.
15 Their king shall go
into captivity,
He and his princes
together,"
Says the LORD.

2 Thus says the LORD:

"For three transgressions
of Moab, and for four,
I will not turn away
its *punishment,*
Because he burned the
bones of the king
of Edom to lime.
2 But I will send a fire
upon Moab,
And it shall devour the
palaces of Kerioth;
Moab shall die with tumult,
With shouting *and*
trumpet sound.
3 And I will cut off the
judge from its midst,
And slay all its princes
with him,"
Says the LORD.

JUDGMENT ON JUDAH

4 Thus says the LORD:

"For three transgressions
of Judah, and for four,
I will not turn away
its *punishment,*
Because they have
despised the law
of the LORD,
And have not kept His
commandments.
Their lies lead
them astray,
Lies which their
fathers followed.
5 But I will send a fire
upon Judah,
And it shall devour the
palaces of Jerusalem."

JUDGMENT ON ISRAEL

6 Thus says the LORD:

"For three transgressions
of Israel, and for four,
I will not turn away
its *punishment,*
Because they sell the
righteous for silver,
And the poor for a
pair of sandals.
7 They pant after[a] the dust
of the earth *which is* on
the head of the poor,
And pervert the way
of the humble.
A man and his father go
in to the *same* girl,
To defile My holy name.
8 They lie down by every
altar on clothes
taken in pledge,
And drink the wine of
the condemned *in* the
house of their god.

9 "Yet *it was* I *who*
destroyed the Amorite
before them,
Whose height *was* like
the height of the cedars,
And he *was as* strong
as the oaks;

2:7 [a] Or *trample on*

Yet I destroyed his
fruit above
And his roots beneath.
10 Also *it was* I *who*
brought you up from
the land of Egypt,
And led you forty years
through the wilderness,
To possess the land
of the Amorite.
11 I raised up some of your
sons as prophets,
And some of your young
men as Nazirites.
Is it not so, O you
children of Israel?"
Says the LORD.
12 "But you gave the Nazirites
wine to drink,
And commanded the
prophets saying,
'Do not prophesy!'

13 "Behold, I am weighed
down by you,
As a cart full of sheaves
is weighed down.
14 Therefore flight shall
perish from the swift,
The strong shall not
strengthen his power,
Nor shall the mighty
deliver himself;
15 He shall not stand who
handles the bow,
The swift of foot
shall not escape,
Nor shall he who rides a
horse deliver himself.
16 The most courageous
men of might
Shall flee naked
in that day,"
Says the LORD.

AUTHORITY OF THE PROPHET'S MESSAGE

3 Hear this word that the
LORD has spoken against
you, O children of Israel,
against the whole family
which I brought up from the
land of Egypt, saying:

2 "You only have I
known of all the
families of the earth;
Therefore I will
punish you for all
your iniquities."

3 Can two walk together,
unless they are agreed?
4 Will a lion roar in
the forest, when
he has no prey?
Will a young lion cry
out of his den, if he
has caught nothing?
5 Will a bird fall into
a snare on the
earth, where there
is no trap for it?
Will a snare spring up
from the earth, if it has
caught nothing at all?
6 If a trumpet is blown
in a city, will not the
people be afraid?
If there is calamity in
a city, will not the
LORD have done *it?*

7 Surely the Lord GOD
does nothing,
Unless He reveals His
secret to His servants
the prophets.

8 A lion has roared!
Who will not fear?
The Lord GOD
has spoken!
Who can but prophesy?

PUNISHMENT OF ISRAEL'S SINS

9 "Proclaim in the palaces
at Ashdod,[a]
And in the palaces in the
land of Egypt, and say:
'Assemble on the
mountains of Samaria;
See great tumults
in her midst,
And the oppressed
within her.
10 For they do not know
to do right,'
Says the LORD,
'Who store up violence
and robbery in
their palaces.'"

11Therefore thus says the
Lord GOD:

"An adversary *shall be*
all around the land;
He shall sap your
strength from you,
And your palaces shall
be plundered."

12Thus says the LORD:

"As a shepherd takes
from the mouth of a lion
Two legs or a piece
of an ear,
So shall the children of
Israel be taken out
Who dwell in Samaria—
In the corner of a bed and
on the edge[a] of a couch!
13 Hear and testify against
the house of Jacob,"
Says the Lord GOD,
the God of hosts,
14 "That in the day I
punish Israel for their
transgressions,
I will also visit *destruction*
on the altars of Bethel;
And the horns of the
altar shall be cut off
And fall to the ground.
15 I will destroy the winter
house along with the
summer house;
The houses of ivory
shall perish,
And the great houses
shall have an end,"
Says the LORD.

4 Hear this word, you
cows of Bashan, who
are on the mountain
of Samaria,
Who oppress the poor,
Who crush the needy,
Who say to your
husbands,[a] "Bring
wine, let us drink!"
2 The Lord GOD has sworn
by His holiness:
"Behold, the days shall
come upon you
When He will take you
away with fishhooks,

3:9 [a] Following Masoretic Text; Septuagint reads *Assyria.* 3:12 [a] The Hebrew is uncertain. 4:1 [a] Literally *their lords* or *their masters*

And your posterity
with fishhooks.
3 You will go out *through*
broken *walls*,
Each one straight
ahead of her,
And you will be cast
into Harmon,"
Says the LORD.

4 "Come to Bethel and
transgress,
At Gilgal multiply
transgression;
Bring your sacrifices
every morning,
Your tithes every
three days.[a]
5 Offer a sacrifice
of thanksgiving
with leaven,
Proclaim *and* announce
the freewill offerings;
For this you love,
You children of Israel!"
Says the Lord GOD.

ISRAEL DID NOT ACCEPT CORRECTION

6 "Also I gave you
cleanness of teeth
in all your cities,
And lack of bread in
all your places;
Yet you have not
returned to Me,"
Says the LORD.

7 "I also withheld rain
from you,
When *there were* still three
months to the harvest.
I made it rain on one city,
I withheld rain from
another city.
One part was
rained upon,
And where it did not rain
the part withered.
8 So two *or* three cities
wandered to another
city to drink water,
But they were not
satisfied;
Yet you have not
returned to Me,"
Says the LORD.

9 "I blasted you with
blight and mildew.
When your gardens
increased,
Your vineyards,
Your fig trees,
And your olive trees,
The locust devoured
them;
Yet you have not
returned to Me,"
Says the LORD.

10 "I sent among you a
plague after the
manner of Egypt;
Your young men I
killed with a sword,
Along with your
captive horses;
I made the stench of
your camps come up
into your nostrils;
Yet you have not
returned to Me,"
Says the LORD.

4:4 [a] Or *years* (compare Deuteronomy 14:28)

11 "I overthrew *some* of you,
As God overthrew Sodom
and Gomorrah,
And you were like a
firebrand plucked
from the burning;
Yet you have not
returned to Me,"
Says the LORD.

12 "Therefore thus will I
do to you, O Israel;
Because I will do
this to you,
Prepare to meet your
God, O Israel!"

13 For behold,
He who forms
mountains,
And creates the wind,
Who declares to man
what his[a] thought *is*,
And makes the
morning darkness,
Who treads the high
places of the earth—
The LORD God of
hosts *is* His name.

A LAMENT FOR ISRAEL

5 Hear this word which I
take up against you, a lamentation, O house of Israel:

2 The virgin of Israel
has fallen;
She will rise no more.
She lies forsaken
on her land;
There is no one to
raise her up.

3For thus says the Lord
GOD:

"The city that goes
out by a thousand
Shall have a hundred left,
And that which goes
out by a hundred
Shall have ten left to
the house of Israel."

A CALL TO REPENTANCE

4For thus says the LORD to
the house of Israel:

"Seek Me and live;
5 But do not seek Bethel,
Nor enter Gilgal,
Nor pass over to
Beersheba;
For Gilgal shall surely
go into captivity,
And Bethel shall
come to nothing.
6 Seek the LORD and live,
Lest He break out like
fire *in* the house
of Joseph,
And devour *it*,
With no one to quench
it in Bethel—
7 You who turn justice
to wormwood,
And lay righteousness
to rest in the earth!"

8 He made the Pleiades
and Orion;
He turns the shadow of
death into morning
And makes the day
dark as night;

4:13 [a] Or *His*

He calls for the
waters of the sea
And pours them out on
the face of the earth;
The LORD *is* His name.
9 He rains ruin upon
the strong,
So that fury comes
upon the fortress.

10 They hate the one who
rebukes in the gate,
And they abhor the
one who speaks
uprightly.
11 Therefore, because you
tread down the poor
And take grain taxes
from him,
Though you have built
houses of hewn stone,
Yet you shall not
dwell in them;
You have planted
pleasant vineyards,
But you shall not drink
wine from them.
12 For I know your manifold
transgressions
And your mighty sins:
Afflicting the just *and*
taking bribes;
Diverting the poor *from*
justice at the gate.
13 Therefore the prudent
keep silent at that time,
For it *is* an evil time.

14 Seek good and not evil,
That you may live;
So the LORD God of hosts
will be with you,
As you have spoken.
15 Hate evil, love good;
Establish justice
in the gate.
It may be that the
LORD God of hosts
Will be gracious to the
remnant of Joseph.

THE DAY OF THE LORD

16Therefore the LORD God
of hosts, the Lord, says this:

"*There shall be* wailing
in all streets,
And they shall say in
all the highways,
'Alas! Alas!'
They shall call the
farmer to mourning,
And skillful lamenters
to wailing.
17 In all vineyards *there*
shall be wailing,
For I will pass
through you,"
Says the LORD.

18 Woe to you who desire
the day of the LORD!
For what good *is* the day
of the LORD to you?
It *will be* darkness,
and not light.
19 It *will be* as though a
man fled from a lion,
And a bear met him!
Or *as though* he went
into the house,
Leaned his hand
on the wall,
And a serpent bit him!
20 *Is* not the day of the LORD
darkness, and not light?
Is it not very dark, with
no brightness in it?

21"I hate, I despise
your feast days,
And I do not savor your
sacred assemblies.
22 Though you offer Me
burnt offerings and
your grain offerings,
I will not accept *them,*
Nor will I regard your
fattened peace offerings.
23 Take away from Me the
noise of your songs,
For I will not hear
the melody of your
stringed instruments.
24 But let justice run
down like water,
And righteousness like
a mighty stream.

25"Did you offer Me
sacrifices and offerings
In the wilderness forty
years, O house of Israel?
26 You also carried
Sikkuth[a] your king[b]
And Chiun,[c] your idols,
The star of your gods,
Which you made
for yourselves.
27 Therefore I will send
you into captivity
beyond Damascus,"
Says the LORD,
whose name *is* the
God of hosts.

WARNINGS TO ZION AND SAMARIA

6 Woe to you *who are*
at ease in Zion,
And trust in Mount
Samaria,
Notable persons in
the chief nation,
To whom the house
of Israel comes!
2 Go over to Calneh and see;
And from there go to
Hamath the great;
Then go down to Gath
of the Philistines.
Are you better than
these kingdoms?
Or is their territory greater
than your territory?
3 *Woe to* you who put far
off the day of doom,
Who cause the seat of
violence to come near;
4 Who lie on beds of ivory,
Stretch out on
your couches,
Eat lambs from the flock
And calves from the
midst of the stall;
5 Who sing idly to the
sound of stringed
instruments,
And invent for yourselves
musical instruments
like David;
6 Who drink wine
from bowls,
And anoint yourselves
with the best ointments,
But are not grieved for
the affliction of Joseph.
7 Therefore they shall
now go captive as the
first of the captives,

5:26 [a] A pagan deity [b] Septuagint and Vulgate read *tabernacle of Moloch.* [c] A pagan deity

And those who recline
at banquets shall
be removed.

8 The Lord GOD has
sworn by Himself,
The LORD God of
hosts says:
"I abhor the pride of
Jacob,
And hate his palaces;
Therefore I will
deliver up *the* city
And all that is in it."

9Then it shall come to pass,
that if ten men remain in one
house, they shall die. 10And
when a relative *of the dead,*
with one who will burn *the*
bodies, picks up the bodies[a]
to take them out of the house,
he will say to one inside the
house, "*Are there* any more
with you?"

Then someone will say,
"None."

And he will say, "Hold your
tongue! For we dare not mention the name of the LORD."

11 For behold, the LORD
gives a command:
He will break the great
house into bits,
And the little house
into pieces.

12 Do horses run on rocks?
Does *one* plow *there*
with oxen?
Yet you have turned
justice into gall,
And the fruit of
righteousness into
wormwood,
13 You who rejoice
over Lo Debar,[a]
Who say, "Have we
not taken Karnaim[b]
for ourselves
By our own strength?"

14 "But, behold, I will raise
up a nation against you,
O house of Israel,"
Says the LORD
God of hosts;
"And they will afflict
you from the entrance
of Hamath
To the Valley of
the Arabah."

VISION OF THE LOCUSTS

7 Thus the Lord GOD showed
me: Behold, He formed lo-
cust swarms at the beginning
of the late crop; indeed *it was*
the late crop after the king's
mowings. 2And so it was, when
they had finished eating the
grass of the land, that I said:

"O Lord GOD, forgive,
I pray!
Oh, that Jacob may stand,
For he *is* small!"
3 *So* the LORD relented
concerning this.
"It shall not be,"
said the LORD.

6:10 [a] Literally *bones* 6:13 [a] Literally *Nothing*
[b] Literally *Horns,* symbol of strength

VISION OF THE FIRE

4Thus the Lord GOD showed me: Behold, the Lord GOD called for conflict by fire, and it consumed the great deep and devoured the territory.
5Then I said:

"O Lord GOD, cease,
I pray!
Oh, that Jacob may
stand,
For he *is* small!"
6 *So* the LORD relented
concerning this.
"This also shall not be,"
said the Lord GOD.

VISION OF THE PLUMB LINE

7Thus He showed me: Behold, the Lord stood on a wall *made* with a plumb line, with a plumb line in His hand.
8And the LORD said to me, "Amos, what do you see?"

And I said, "A plumb line."
Then the Lord said:

"Behold, I am setting
a plumb line
In the midst of My
people Israel;
I will not pass by
them anymore.
9 The high places of Isaac
shall be desolate,
And the sanctuaries
of Israel shall be
laid waste.
I will rise with the
sword against the
house of Jeroboam."

AMAZIAH'S COMPLAINT

10Then Amaziah the priest of Bethel sent to Jeroboam king of Israel, saying, "Amos has conspired against you in the midst of the house of Israel. The land is not able to bear all his words.
11For thus Amos has said:

'Jeroboam shall die
by the sword,
And Israel shall surely
be led away captive
From their own land.'"

12Then Amaziah said to Amos:

"Go, you seer!
Flee to the land of Judah.
There eat bread,
And there prophesy.
13 But never again
prophesy at Bethel,
For it *is* the king's
sanctuary,
And it *is* the royal
residence."

14Then Amos answered, and said to Amaziah:

"I *was* no prophet,
Nor *was* I a son of
a prophet,
But I *was* a sheepbreeder[a]
And a tender of
sycamore fruit.
15 Then the LORD took me
as I followed the flock,
And the LORD said to me,

7:14 [a] Compare 2 Kings 3:4

'Go, prophesy to My
people Israel.'
16 Now therefore, hear the
word of the LORD:
You say, 'Do not prophesy
against Israel,
And do not spout against
the house of Isaac.'

17"Therefore thus says the
LORD:

'Your wife shall be a
harlot in the city;
Your sons and daughters
shall fall by the sword;
Your land shall be
divided by *survey* line;
You shall die in a
defiled land;
And Israel shall surely
be led away captive
From his own land.'"

VISION OF THE SUMMER FRUIT

8 Thus the Lord GOD showed
me: Behold, a basket of
summer fruit. 2And He said,
"Amos, what do you see?"
So I said, "A basket of summer fruit."
Then the LORD said to me:

"The end has come upon
My people Israel;
I will not pass by
them anymore.
3 And the songs of
the temple
Shall be wailing
in that day,"
Says the Lord GOD—
"Many dead bodies
everywhere,
They shall be thrown
out in silence."

4 Hear this, you who
swallow up[a] the needy,
And make the poor
of the land fail,

5Saying:

"When will the New
Moon be past,
That we may sell grain?
And the Sabbath,
That we may trade wheat?
Making the ephah small
and the shekel large,
Falsifying the scales
by deceit,
6 That we may buy the
poor for silver,
And the needy for a
pair of sandals—
Even sell the bad wheat?"

7 The LORD has sworn by
the pride of Jacob:
"Surely I will never forget
any of their works.
8 Shall the land not
tremble for this,
And everyone mourn
who dwells in it?
All of it shall swell
like the River,[a]

8:4 [a] Or *trample on* (compare 2:7) 8:8 [a] That is, the Nile; some Hebrew manuscripts, Septuagint, Syriac, Targum, and Vulgate read *River;* Masoretic Text reads *the light.*

Heave and subside
Like the River of Egypt.

9 "And it shall come
to pass in that day,"
says the Lord GOD,
"That I will make the
sun go down at noon,
And I will darken the
earth in broad daylight;
10 I will turn your feasts
into mourning,
And all your songs
into lamentation;
I will bring sackcloth
on every waist,
And baldness on
every head;
I will make it like
mourning for
an only *son,*
And its end like
a bitter day.

11 "Behold, the days
are coming," says
the Lord GOD,
"That I will send a
famine on the land,
Not a famine of bread,
Nor a thirst for water,
But of hearing the
words of the LORD.
12 They shall wander
from sea to sea,
And from north to east;
They shall run to and
fro, seeking the
word of the LORD,
But shall not find *it.*

13 "In that day the fair virgins
And strong young men
Shall faint from thirst.
14 Those who swear by
the sin[a] of Samaria,
Who say,
'As your god lives, O Dan!'
And, 'As the way of
Beersheba lives!'
They shall fall and
never rise again."

THE DESTRUCTION OF ISRAEL

9 I saw the Lord standing by the altar, and He said:

"Strike the doorposts,
that the thresholds
may shake,
And break them on the
heads of them all.
I will slay the last of
them with the sword.
He who flees from them
shall not get away,
And he who escapes
from them shall
not be delivered.

2 "Though they dig
into hell,[a]
From there My hand
shall take them;
Though they climb
up to heaven,
From there I will
bring them down;
3 And though they
hide themselves on
top of Carmel,
From there I will search
and take them;

8:14 [a] Or *Ashima,* a Syrian goddess 9:2 [a] Or *Sheol*

Though they hide
from My sight at the
bottom of the sea,
From there I will
command the serpent,
and it shall bite them;
4 Though they go into
captivity before
their enemies,
From there I will
command the sword,
And it shall slay them.
I will set My eyes on
them for harm and
not for good."

5 The Lord GOD of hosts,
He who touches the
earth and it melts,
And all who dwell
there mourn;
All of it shall swell
like the River,[a]
And subside like the
River of Egypt.
6 He who builds His
layers in the sky,
And has founded His
strata in the earth;
Who calls for the
waters of the sea,
And pours them out on
the face of the earth—
The LORD *is* His name.

7 "*Are* you not like the
people of Ethiopia to Me,
O children of Israel?"
says the LORD.
"Did I not bring up Israel
from the land of Egypt,
The Philistines
from Caphtor,
And the Syrians from Kir?

8 "Behold, the eyes of the
Lord GOD *are* on the
sinful kingdom,
And I will destroy it from
the face of the earth;
Yet I will not utterly
destroy the house
of Jacob,"
Says the LORD.

9 "For surely I will
command,
And will sift the house of
Israel among all nations,
As *grain* is sifted
in a sieve;
Yet not the smallest grain
shall fall to the ground.
10 All the sinners of My
people shall die
by the sword,
Who say, 'The calamity
shall not overtake
nor confront us.'

ISRAEL WILL BE RESTORED

11 "On that day I will raise up
The tabernacle[a] of David,
which has fallen down,
And repair its damages;
I will raise up its ruins,
And rebuild it as in
the days of old;
12 That they may possess
the remnant of Edom,[a]
And all the Gentiles who
are called by My name,"

9:5 [a] That is, the Nile 9:11 [a] Literally *booth,* figure of a deposed dynasty 9:12 [a] Septuagint reads *mankind.*

Says the LORD who
does this thing.

13 "Behold, the days are
coming," says the LORD,
"When the plowman shall
overtake the reaper,
And the treader of grapes
him who sows seed;
The mountains shall
drip with sweet wine,
And all the hills shall
flow *with it.*
14 I will bring back the
captives of My
people Israel;
They shall build the
waste cities and
inhabit *them;*
They shall plant
vineyards and drink
wine from them;
They shall also make
gardens and eat
fruit from them.
15 I will plant them
in their land,
And no longer shall
they be pulled up
From the land I have
given them,"
Says the LORD your God.

THE BOOK OF OBADIAH

THE COMING JUDGMENT ON EDOM

The vision of Obadiah.

Thus says the Lord GOD
concerning Edom
(We have heard a report
from the LORD,
And a messenger has
been sent among the
nations, *saying,*
"Arise, and let us rise up
against her for battle"):

2 "*Behold, I will make*
you small among
the nations;
You shall be greatly
despised.
3 The pride of your heart
has deceived you,
You who dwell in the
clefts of the rock,
Whose habitation is high;
You who say in your heart,
'Who will bring me
down to the ground?'
4 Though you ascend *as*
high as the eagle,
And though you set your
nest among the stars,
From there I will
bring you down,"
says the LORD.

5 "If thieves had
come to you,
If robbers by night—

Oh, how you will
be cut off!—
Would they not have
stolen till they
had enough?
If grape-gatherers
had come to you,
Would they not have
left *some* gleanings?

6 "Oh, how Esau shall
be searched out!
How his hidden treasures
shall be sought after!
7 All the men in your
confederacy
Shall force you to
the border;
The men at peace
with you
Shall deceive you *and*
prevail against you.
Those who eat your
bread shall lay a
trap[a] for you.
No one is aware of it.

8 "Will I not in that
day," says the LORD,
"Even destroy the wise
men from Edom,
And understanding
from the mountains
of Esau?
9 Then your mighty
men, O Teman, shall
be dismayed,
To the end that
everyone from the
mountains of Esau
May be cut off by
slaughter.

EDOM MISTREATED HIS BROTHER

10 "For violence against
your brother Jacob,
Shame shall cover you,
And you shall be
cut off forever.
11 In the day that you
stood on the
other side—
In the day that
strangers carried
captive his forces,
When foreigners
entered his gates
And cast lots for
Jerusalem—
Even you *were* as
one of them.

12 "But you should not
have gazed on the
day of your brother
In the day of his captivity;[a]
Nor should you have
rejoiced over the
children of Judah
In the day of their
destruction;
Nor should you have
spoken proudly
In the day of distress.
13 You should not have
entered the gate
of My people
In the day of their
calamity.
Indeed, you should
not have gazed on
their affliction
In the day of their
calamity,

7 [a] Or *wound,* or *plot* 12 [a] Literally *On the day he became a foreigner*

Nor laid *hands* on
their substance
In the day of their
calamity.
14 You should not have
stood at the crossroads
To cut off those among
them who escaped;
Nor should you
have delivered up
those among them
who remained
In the day of distress.

15 "For the day of the
LORD upon all the
nations *is* near;
As you have done, it
shall be done to you;
Your reprisal shall return
upon your own head.
16 For as you drank on
My holy mountain,
So shall all the nations
drink continually;
Yes, they shall drink,
and swallow,
And they shall be as
though they had
never been.

ISRAEL'S FINAL TRIUMPH

17 "But on Mount Zion there
shall be deliverance,
And there shall
be holiness;
The house of Jacob
shall possess their
possessions.
18 The house of Jacob
shall be a fire,
And the house of
Joseph a flame;
But the house of Esau
shall be stubble;
They shall kindle them
and devour them,
And no survivor
shall *remain* of the
house of Esau,"
For the LORD has spoken.

19 The South[a] shall possess
the mountains of Esau,
And the Lowland shall
possess Philistia.
They shall possess the
fields of Ephraim
And the fields of Samaria.
Benjamin *shall*
possess Gilead.
20 And the captives of
this host of the
children of Israel
Shall possess the land
of the Canaanites
As far as Zarephath.
The captives of
Jerusalem who
are in Sepharad
Shall possess the cities
of the South.[a]
21 Then saviors[a] shall
come to Mount Zion
To judge the mountains
of Esau,
And the kingdom shall
be the LORD's.

19 [a] Hebrew *Negev* 20 [a] Hebrew *Negev* 21 [a] Or *deliverers*

THE BOOK OF
JONAH

JONAH'S DISOBEDIENCE

1 Now the word of the LORD
came to Jonah the son of
Amittai, saying, 2“Arise, go to
Nineveh, that great city, and cry
out against it; for their wickedness has come up before
Me.” 3But Jonah arose to flee
to Tarshish from the presence
of the LORD. He went down to
Joppa, and found a ship going
to Tarshish; so he paid the fare,
and went down into it, to go
with them to Tarshish from the
presence of the LORD.

THE STORM AT SEA

4But the LORD sent out a
great wind on the sea, and
there was a mighty tempest
on the sea, so that the ship was
about to be broken up.

5Then the mariners were
afraid; and every man cried out
to his god, and threw the cargo
that *was* in the ship into the
sea, to lighten the load.[a] But
Jonah had gone down into the
lowest parts of the ship, had
lain down, and was fast asleep.

6So the captain came to
him, and said to him, “What
do you mean, sleeper? Arise,
call on your God; perhaps
your God will consider us, so
that we may not perish.”

7And they said to one an-
other, “Come, let us cast lots,
that we may know for whose
cause this trouble *has come*
upon us.” So they cast lots,
and the lot fell on Jonah. 8Then
they said to him, “Please tell us!
For whose cause *is* this trouble
upon us? What is your occupation? And where do you come
from? What is your country?
And of what people are you?”

9So he said to them, “I *am* a
Hebrew; and I fear the LORD,
the God of heaven, who made
the sea and the dry *land*.”

JONAH THROWN INTO THE SEA

10Then the men were ex-
ceedingly afraid, and said to
him, “Why have you done
this?” For the men knew that
he fled from the presence of
the LORD, because he had told
them. 11Then they said to him,
“What shall we do to you that
the sea may be calm for us?”—
for the sea was growing more
tempestuous.

12And he said to them, “Pick
me up and throw me into the
sea; then the sea will become
calm for you. For I know that
this great tempest *is* because
of me.”

1:5 [a] Literally *from upon them*

13Nevertheless the men
rowed hard to return to land,
but they could not, for the
sea continued to grow more
tempestuous against them.
14Therefore they cried out to
the LORD and said, "We pray,
O LORD, please do not let us
perish for this man's life, and
do not charge us with innocent blood; for You, O LORD,
have done as it pleased You."
15So they picked up Jonah and
threw him into the sea, and
the sea ceased from its raging. 16Then the men feared the
LORD exceedingly, and offered
a sacrifice to the LORD and
took vows.

JONAH'S PRAYER AND DELIVERANCE

17Now the LORD had pre-
pared a great fish to swallow
Jonah. And Jonah was in the
belly of the fish three days and
three nights.

2 Then Jonah prayed to the
LORD his God from the
fish's belly. 2And he said:

"I cried out to the
LORD because of
my affliction,
And He answered me.

"Out of the belly of
Sheol I cried,
And You heard my voice.
3 For You cast me
into the deep,
Into the heart of the seas,
And the floods
surrounded me;
All Your billows and
Your waves passed
over me.
4 Then I said, 'I have been
cast out of Your sight;
Yet I will look again
toward Your
holy temple.'
5 The waters surrounded
me, *even* to my soul;
The deep closed
around me;
Weeds were wrapped
around my head.
6 I went down to the
moorings of the
mountains;
The earth with its
bars *closed* behind
me forever;
Yet You have brought up
my life from the pit,
O LORD, my God.

7 "When my soul
fainted within me,
I remembered the LORD;
And my prayer went
up to You,
Into Your holy temple.

8 "Those who regard
worthless idols
Forsake their own Mercy.
9 But I will sacrifice to You
With the voice of
thanksgiving;
I will pay what I
have vowed.
Salvation *is* of the LORD."

10So the LORD spoke to the
fish, and it vomited Jonah
onto dry *land*.

JONAH PREACHES AT NINEVEH

3 Now the word of the LORD came to Jonah the second time, saying, 2“Arise, go to Nineveh, that great city, and preach to it the message that I tell you.” 3So Jonah arose and went to Nineveh, according to the word of the LORD. Now Nineveh was an exceedingly great city, a three-day journey[a] *in extent.* 4And Jonah began to enter the city on the first day's walk. Then he cried out and said, “Yet forty days, and Nineveh shall be overthrown!”

THE PEOPLE OF NINEVEH BELIEVE

5So the people of Nineveh believed God, proclaimed a fast, and put on sackcloth, from the greatest to the least of them. 6Then word came to the king of Nineveh; and he arose from his throne and laid aside his robe, covered *himself* with sackcloth and sat in ashes. 7And he caused *it* to be proclaimed and published throughout Nineveh by the decree of the king and his nobles, saying,

Let neither man nor
beast, herd nor flock,
taste anything; do not let
them eat, or drink water.
8But let man and beast be
covered with sackcloth,
and cry mightily to God;
yes, let every one turn
from his evil way and
from the violence that is
in his hands. 9Who can
tell *if* God will turn and
relent, and turn away
from His fierce anger, so
that we may not perish?

10Then God saw their works, that they turned from their evil way; and God relented from the disaster that He had said He would bring upon them, and He did not do it.

JONAH'S ANGER AND GOD'S KINDNESS

4 But it displeased Jonah exceedingly, and he became angry. 2So he prayed to the LORD, and said, “Ah, LORD, was not this what I said when I was still in my country? Therefore I fled previously to Tarshish; for I know that You *are* a gracious and merciful God, slow to anger and abundant in lovingkindness, One who relents from doing harm. 3Therefore now, O LORD, please take my life from me, for *it is* better for me to die than to live!”

4Then the LORD said, “*Is it* right for you to be angry?”

5So Jonah went out of the city and sat on the east side of the city. There he made himself a shelter and sat under it in the shade, till he might see

3:3 [a] Exact meaning unknown

what would become of the city.
6 And the LORD God prepared
a plant[a] and made it come up
over Jonah, that it might be
shade for his head to deliver
him from his misery. So Jonah
was very grateful for the plant.
7 But as morning dawned the
next day God prepared a
worm, and it *so* damaged the
plant that it withered. 8 And
it happened, when the sun
arose, that God prepared a
vehement east wind; and the
sun beat on Jonah's head, so
that he grew faint. Then he
wished death for himself, and
said, "*It is* better for me to die
than to live."
9 Then God said to Jonah,
"*Is it* right for you to be angry
about the plant?"
And he said, "*It is* right
for me to be angry, even to
death!"
10 But the LORD said, "You
have had pity on the plant for
which you have not labored,
nor made it grow, which came
up in a night and perished in
a night. 11 And should I not
pity Nineveh, that great city,
in which are more than one
hundred and twenty thousand
persons who cannot discern
between their right hand and
their left—and much live-
stock?"

THE BOOK OF MICAH

1 The word of the LORD that came to Micah of Moresheth in the days of Jotham, Ahaz, *and* Hezekiah, kings of Judah, which he saw concerning Samaria and Jerusalem.

THE COMING JUDGMENT ON ISRAEL

2 Hear, all you peoples!
Listen, O earth, and
all that is in it!
Let the Lord GOD be a
witness against you,
The Lord from His
holy temple.

3 For behold, the LORD
is coming out
of His place;
He will come down
And tread on the
high places of the
earth.
4 The mountains will
melt under Him,
And the valleys will split
Like wax before the fire,

4:6 [a] Hebrew *kikayon,* exact identity unknown

Like waters poured
down a steep place.
5 All this is for the
transgression of Jacob
And for the sins of the
house of Israel.
What *is* the transgression
of Jacob?
Is it not Samaria?
And what *are* the high
places of Judah?
Are they not Jerusalem?

6 "Therefore I will make
Samaria a heap of
ruins in the field,
Places for planting
a vineyard;
I will pour down her
stones into the valley,
And I will uncover
her foundations.
7 All her carved images
shall be beaten
to pieces,
And all her pay as a
harlot shall be burned
with the fire;
All her idols I will
lay desolate,
For she gathered *it* from
the pay of a harlot,
And they shall return to
the pay of a harlot."

MOURNING FOR ISRAEL AND JUDAH

8 Therefore I will
wail and howl,
I will go stripped
and naked;
I will make a wailing
like the jackals
And a mourning like
the ostriches,
9 For her wounds
are incurable.
For it has come to Judah;
It has come to the gate
of My people—
To Jerusalem.

10 Tell *it* not in Gath,
Weep not at all;
In Beth Aphrah[a]
Roll yourself in the dust.
11 Pass by in naked shame,
you inhabitant
of Shaphir;
The inhabitant of Zaanan[a]
does not go out.
Beth Ezel mourns;
Its place to stand is
taken away from you.

12 For the inhabitant of
Maroth pined[a] for good,
But disaster came down
from the LORD
To the gate of Jerusalem.
13 O inhabitant of Lachish,
Harness the chariot
to the swift steeds
(She *was* the beginning
of sin to the
daughter of Zion),
For the transgressions of
Israel were found in you.

14 Therefore you shall
give presents to
Moresheth Gath;[a]

1:10 [a] Literally *House of Dust* 1:11 [a] Literally *Going Out*
1:12 [a] Literally *was sick* 1:14 [a] Literally *Possession of Gath*

The houses of Achzib[b]
shall be a lie to the
kings of Israel.
15 I will yet bring an heir
to you, O inhabitant
of Mareshah;[a]
The glory of Israel shall
come to Adullam.
16 Make yourself bald and
cut off your hair,
Because of your
precious children;
Enlarge your baldness
like an eagle,
For they shall go from
you into captivity.

WOE TO EVILDOERS

2 Woe to those who
devise iniquity,
And work out evil
on their beds!
At morning light
they practice it,
Because it is in the
power of their hand.
2 They covet fields and
take *them* by violence,
Also houses, and
seize *them*.
So they oppress a man
and his house,
A man and his inheritance.

3Therefore thus says the
LORD:

"Behold, against
this family I am
devising disaster,
From which you cannot
remove your necks;
Nor shall you walk
haughtily,
For this *is* an evil time.
4 In that day *one* shall
take up a proverb
against you,
And lament with a bitter
lamentation, saying:
'We are utterly
destroyed!
He has changed the
heritage of my people;
How He has removed
it from me!
To a turncoat He has
divided our fields.'"

5 Therefore you will have
no one to determine
boundaries[a] by lot
In the assembly
of the LORD.

LYING PROPHETS

6 "Do not prattle," *you say*
to those who prophesy.
So they shall not
prophesy to you;[a]
They shall not return
insult for insult.[b]
7 *You who are* named
the house of Jacob:
"Is the Spirit of the
LORD restricted?
Are these His doings?
Do not My words do good
To him who walks
uprightly?

1:14 [b] Literally *Lie* 1:15 [a] Literally *Inheritance* 2:5 [a] Literally *one casting a surveyor's line* 2:6 [a] Literally *to these* [b] Vulgate reads *He shall not take shame.*

8 "Lately My people have
risen up as an enemy—
You pull off the robe
with the garment
From those who trust
you, as they pass by,
Like men returned
from war.
9 The women of My
people you cast out
From their pleasant
houses;
From their children
You have taken away
My glory forever.

10 "Arise and depart,
For this *is* not *your* rest;
Because it is defiled,
it shall destroy,
Yes, with utter
destruction.
11 If a man should walk
in a false spirit
And speak a lie, *saying,*
'I will prophesy to you
of wine and drink,'
Even he would be the
prattler of this people.

ISRAEL RESTORED

12 "I will surely assemble
all of you, O Jacob,
I will surely gather the
remnant of Israel;
I will put them together
like sheep of the fold,[a]
Like a flock in the midst
of their pasture;
They shall make a loud
noise because of
so many people.
13 The one who breaks
open will come up
before them;
They will break out,
Pass through the gate,
And go out by it;
Their king will pass
before them,
With the LORD at
their head."

WICKED RULERS AND PROPHETS

3 And I said:

"Hear now, O heads
of Jacob,
And you rulers of the
house of Israel:
Is it not for you to
know justice?
2 You who hate good
and love evil;
Who strip the skin
from My people,[a]
And the flesh from
their bones;
3 Who also eat the flesh
of My people,
Flay their skin from them,
Break their bones,
And chop *them* in pieces
Like *meat* for the pot,
Like flesh in the caldron."

4 Then they will cry
to the LORD,
But He will not hear them;
He will even hide His face
from them at that time,
Because they have been
evil in their deeds.

2:12 [a] Hebrew *Bozrah* 3:2 [a] Literally *them*

5 Thus says the LORD
concerning the
prophets
Who make my
people stray;
Who chant "Peace"
While they chew
with their teeth,
But who prepare
war against him
Who puts nothing
into their mouths:
6 "Therefore you shall have
night without vision,
And you shall have
darkness without
divination;
The sun shall go down
on the prophets,
And the day shall be
dark for them.
7 So the seers shall
be ashamed,
And the diviners abashed;
Indeed they shall all
cover their lips;
For *there is* no answer
from God."

8 But truly I am full of
power by the Spirit
of the LORD,
And of justice and might,
To declare to Jacob
his transgression
And to Israel his sin.
9 Now hear this,
You heads of the
house of Jacob
And rulers of the
house of Israel,
Who abhor justice
And pervert all equity,
10 Who build up Zion
with bloodshed
And Jerusalem
with iniquity:
11 Her heads judge
for a bribe,
Her priests teach for pay,
And her prophets
divine for money.
Yet they lean on the
LORD, and say,
"Is not the LORD
among us?
No harm can come
upon us."
12 Therefore because of you
Zion shall be plowed
like a field,
Jerusalem shall become
heaps of ruins,
And the mountain
of the temple[a]
Like the bare hills
of the forest.

THE LORD'S REIGN IN ZION

4 Now it shall come to
pass in the latter days
That the mountain of
the LORD's house
Shall be established on the
top of the mountains,
And shall be exalted
above the hills;
And peoples shall
flow to it.
2 Many nations shall
come and say,
"Come, and let us go
up to the mountain
of the LORD,

3:12 [a] Literally *house*

To the house of the
God of Jacob;
He will teach us His ways,
And we shall walk
in His paths."
For out of Zion the
law shall go forth,
And the word of the
LORD from Jerusalem.
3 He shall judge between
many peoples,
And rebuke strong
nations afar off;
They shall beat their
swords into plowshares,
And their spears into
pruning hooks;
Nation shall not lift up
sword against nation,
Neither shall they learn
war anymore.[a]

4 But everyone shall sit
under his vine and
under his fig tree,
And no one shall
make *them* afraid;
For the mouth of
the LORD of hosts
has spoken.
5 For all people walk
each in the name
of his god,
But we will walk in
the name of the
LORD our God
Forever and ever.

ZION'S FUTURE TRIUMPH

6 "In that day," says
the LORD,
"I will assemble the lame,
I will gather the outcast
And those whom I
have afflicted;
7 I will make the lame
a remnant,
And the outcast a
strong nation;
So the LORD will
reign over them
in Mount Zion
From now on,
even forever.
8 And you, O tower
of the flock,
The stronghold of the
daughter of Zion,
To you shall it come,
Even the former
dominion shall come,
The kingdom of the
daughter of Jerusalem."

9 Now why do you
cry aloud?
Is there no king in
your midst?
Has your counselor
perished?
For pangs have seized
you like a woman
in labor.
10 Be in pain, and labor
to bring forth,
O daughter of Zion,
Like a woman in
birth pangs.
For now you shall go
forth from the city,
You shall dwell
in the field,
And to Babylon
you shall go.

4:3 [a] Compare Isaiah 2:2–4

There you shall be
delivered;
There the LORD will
redeem you
From the hand of
your enemies.

11 Now also many nations
have gathered
against you,
Who say, "Let her
be defiled,
And let our eye look
upon Zion."
12 But they do not know the
thoughts of the LORD,
Nor do they understand
His counsel;
For He will gather them
like sheaves to the
threshing floor.

13 "Arise and thresh,
O daughter of Zion;
For I will make your
horn iron,
And I will make your
hooves bronze;
You shall beat in pieces
many peoples;
I will consecrate their
gain to the LORD,
And their substance
to the Lord of the
whole earth."

5 Now gather yourself
in troops,
O daughter of troops;
He has laid siege
against us;
They will strike the
judge of Israel with
a rod on the cheek.

THE COMING MESSIAH

2 "But you, Bethlehem
Ephrathah,
Though you are
little among the
thousands of Judah,
Yet out of you shall
come forth to Me
The One to be Ruler
in Israel,
Whose goings forth
are from of old,
From everlasting."

3 Therefore He shall
give them up,
Until the time *that*
she who is in labor
has given birth;
Then the remnant
of His brethren
Shall return to the
children of Israel.
4 And He shall stand
and feed *His flock*
In the strength of
the LORD,
In the majesty of
the name of the
LORD His God;
And they shall abide,
For now He shall be great
To the ends of the earth;
5 And this *One* shall
be peace.

JUDGMENT ON ISRAEL'S ENEMIES

When the Assyrian
comes into our land,
And when he treads
in our palaces,
Then we will raise
against him

Seven shepherds and
eight princely men.
6 They shall waste
with the sword the
land of Assyria,
And the land of Nimrod
at its entrances;
Thus He shall deliver *us*
from the Assyrian,
When he comes
into our land
And when he treads
within our borders.

7 Then the remnant of Jacob
Shall be in the midst
of many peoples,
Like dew from the LORD,
Like showers on the grass,
That tarry for no man
Nor wait for the
sons of men.
8 And the remnant of Jacob
Shall be among
the Gentiles,
In the midst of
many peoples,
Like a lion among the
beasts of the forest,
Like a young lion among
flocks of sheep,
Who, if he passes through,
Both treads down and
tears in pieces,
And none can deliver.
9 Your hand shall be lifted
against your adversaries,
And all your enemies
shall be cut off.

10 "And it shall be in that
day," says the LORD,
"That I will cut off your
horses from your midst
And destroy your chariots.
11 I will cut off the cities
of your land
And throw down all
your strongholds.
12 I will cut off sorceries
from your hand,
And you shall have
no soothsayers.
13 Your carved images I
will also cut off,
And your *sacred* pillars
from your midst;
You shall no more
worship the work
of your hands;
14 I will pluck your
wooden images[a]
from your midst;
Thus I will destroy
your cities.
15 And I will execute
vengeance in
anger and fury
On the nations that
have not heard."[a]

GOD PLEADS WITH ISRAEL

6 Hear now what the LORD
says:

"Arise, plead your case
before the mountains,
And let the hills hear
your voice.
2 Hear, O you mountains,
the LORD's complaint,
And you strong
foundations of
the earth;

5:14 [a] Hebrew *Asherim,* Canaanite deities 5:15 [a] Or *obeyed*

For the LORD has a
complaint against
His people,
And He will contend
with Israel.

3 "O My people, what
have I done to you?
And how have I
wearied you?
Testify against Me.
4 For I brought you up
from the land of Egypt,
I redeemed you from the
house of bondage;
And I sent before
you Moses, Aaron,
and Miriam.
5 O My people,
remember now
What Balak king of
Moab counseled,
And what Balaam the son
of Beor answered him,
From Acacia Grove[a]
to Gilgal,
That you may know
the righteousness
of the LORD."

6 With what shall I come
before the LORD,
And bow myself before
the High God?
Shall I come before Him
with burnt offerings,
With calves a year old?
7 Will the LORD be pleased
with thousands of rams,
Ten thousand rivers of oil?
Shall I give my firstborn
for my transgression,
The fruit of my body *for*
the sin of my soul?

8 He has shown you,
O man, what *is* good;
And what does the
LORD require of you
But to do justly,
To love mercy,
And to walk humbly
with your God?

PUNISHMENT OF ISRAEL'S INJUSTICE

9 The LORD's voice
cries to the city—
Wisdom shall see
Your name:

"Hear the rod!
Who has appointed it?
10 Are there yet the
treasures of wickedness
In the house of the wicked,
And the short measure
that is an abomination?
11 Shall I count pure *those*
with the wicked scales,
And with the bag of
deceitful weights?
12 For her rich men are
full of violence,
Her inhabitants have
spoken lies,
And their tongue is
deceitful in their mouth.

13 "Therefore I will
also make *you* sick
by striking you,
By making *you* desolate
because of your sins.

6:5 [a] Hebrew *Shittim* (compare Numbers 25:1; Joshua 2:1; 3:1)

14 You shall eat, but
not be satisfied;
Hunger[a] *shall be* in
your midst.
You may carry *some* away,[b]
but shall not save *them;*
And what you do
rescue I will give
over to the sword.

15 "You shall sow,
but not reap;
You shall tread the
olives, but not anoint
yourselves with oil;
And *make* sweet wine,
but not drink wine.
16 For the statutes of
Omri are kept;
All the works of Ahab's
house *are done;*
And you walk in
their counsels,
That I may make you
a desolation,
And your inhabitants
a hissing.
Therefore you shall
bear the reproach
of My people."[a]

SORROW FOR ISRAEL'S SINS

7 Woe is me!
For I am like those who
gather summer fruits,
Like those who glean
vintage grapes;
There is no cluster to eat
Of the first-ripe fruit
which my soul desires.
2 The faithful *man*
has perished from
the earth,
And *there is* no one
upright among men.
They all lie in wait
for blood;
Every man hunts his
brother with a net.

3 That they may
successfully do evil
with both hands—
The prince asks *for gifts,*
The judge *seeks* a bribe,
And the great *man*
utters his evil desire;
So they scheme together.
4 The best of them
is like a brier;
The most upright
is sharper than a
thorn hedge;
The day of your
watchman and your
punishment comes;
Now shall be their
perplexity.

5 Do not trust in a friend;
Do not put your
confidence in a
companion;
Guard the doors of
your mouth
From her who lies
in your bosom.
6 For son dishonors father,
Daughter rises against
her mother,

6:14 [a] Or *Emptiness* or *Humiliation* [b] Targum and Vulgate read *You shall take hold.* 6:16 [a] Following Masoretic Text, Targum, and Vulgate; Septuagint reads *of nations.*

Daughter-in-law against
her mother-in-law;
A man's enemies
are the men of his
own household.

7 Therefore I will look
to the LORD;
I will wait for the God
of my salvation;
My God will hear me.

ISRAEL'S CONFESSION AND COMFORT

8 Do not rejoice over
me, my enemy;
When I fall, I will arise;
When I sit in darkness,
The LORD *will be* a
light to me.
9 I will bear the indignation
of the LORD,
Because I have sinned
against Him,
Until He pleads my case
And executes
justice for me.
He will bring me
forth to the light;
I will see His
righteousness.
10 Then *she who is* my
enemy will see,
And shame will cover
her who said to me,
"Where is the LORD
your God?"
My eyes will see her;
Now she will be
trampled down
Like mud in the streets.
11 *In* the day when your
walls are to be built,
In that day the decree
shall go far and wide.[a]
12 *In* that day they[a] shall
come to you
From Assyria and the
fortified cities,[b]
From the fortress[c]
to the River,[d]
From sea to sea,
And mountain *to*
mountain.
13 Yet the land shall
be desolate
Because of those
who dwell in it,
And for the fruit of
their deeds.

GOD WILL FORGIVE ISRAEL

14 Shepherd Your people
with Your staff,
The flock of Your heritage,
Who dwell solitarily
in a woodland,
In the midst of Carmel;
Let them feed *in*
Bashan and Gilead,
As in days of old.

15 "As in the days when
you came out of the
land of Egypt,
I will show them[a]
wonders."

16 The nations shall see
and be ashamed of
all their might;

7:11 [a] Or *the boundary shall be extended* 7:12 [a] Literally *he,* collective of the captives [b] Hebrew *arey mazor,* possibly *cities of Egypt* [c] Hebrew *mazor,* possibly *Egypt* [d] That is, the Euphrates 7:15 [a] Literally *him,* collective for the captives

They shall put *their* hand
over *their* mouth;
Their ears shall be deaf.
17 They shall lick the
dust like a serpent;
They shall crawl from
their holes like
snakes of the earth.
They shall be afraid of
the LORD our God,
And shall fear
because of You.
18 Who *is* a God like You,
Pardoning iniquity
And passing over the
transgression of the
remnant of His heritage?
He does not retain
His anger forever,
Because He delights
in mercy.
19 He will again have
compassion on us,
And will subdue
our iniquities.

You will cast all our[a] sins
Into the depths of the sea.
20 You will give truth
to Jacob
And mercy to Abraham,
Which You have sworn
to our fathers
From days of old.

THE BOOK OF NAHUM

1 The burden[a] against Nineveh. The book of the vision
of Nahum the Elkoshite.

GOD'S WRATH ON HIS ENEMIES

2 God *is* jealous, and the
LORD avenges;
The LORD avenges
and *is* furious.
The LORD will take
vengeance on His
adversaries,
And He reserves *wrath*
for His enemies;
3 The LORD *is* slow to anger
and great in power,
And will not at all
acquit *the wicked.*

The LORD has His way
In the whirlwind and
in the storm,
And the clouds *are* the
dust of His feet.
4 He rebukes the sea
and makes it dry,
And dries up all
the rivers.
Bashan and Carmel wither,
And the flower of
Lebanon wilts.
5 The mountains quake
before Him,

7:19 [a] Literally *their* 1:1 [a] Or *oracle*

The hills melt,
And the earth heaves[a]
at His presence,
Yes, the world and all
who dwell in it.

6 Who can stand before
His indignation?
And who can endure
the fierceness of
His anger?
His fury is poured
out like fire,
And the rocks are thrown
down by Him.

7 The LORD *is* good,
A stronghold in the
day of trouble;
And He knows those
who trust in Him.
8 But with an
overflowing flood
He will make an utter
end of its place,
And darkness will
pursue His enemies.

9 What do you conspire
against the LORD?
He will make an
utter end *of it.*
Affliction will not rise
up a second time.
10 For while tangled
like thorns,
And while drunken
like drunkards,
They shall be devoured
like stubble fully dried.
11 From you comes
forth *one*
Who plots evil against
the LORD,
A wicked counselor.

12 Thus says the LORD:

"Though *they are* safe,
and likewise many,
Yet in this manner they
will be cut down
When he passes through.
Though I have
afflicted you,
I will afflict you no more;
13 For now I will break off
his yoke from you,
And burst your
bonds apart."

14 The LORD has given
a command
concerning you:
"Your name shall be
perpetuated no longer.
Out of the house
of your gods
I will cut off the carved
image and the
molded image.
I will dig your grave,
For you are vile."

15 Behold, on the mountains
The feet of him who
brings good tidings,
Who proclaims peace!
O Judah, keep your
appointed feasts,
Perform your vows.
For the wicked one shall no
more pass through you;
He is utterly cut off.

1:5 [a] Targum reads *burns.*

THE DESTRUCTION OF NINEVEH

2 He who scatters[a] has
come up before
your face.
Man the fort!
Watch the road!
Strengthen *your* flanks!
Fortify *your* power
mightily.

2 For the LORD will restore
the excellence of Jacob
Like the excellence
of Israel,
For the emptiers have
emptied them out
And ruined their
vine branches.

3 The shields of his mighty
men *are* made red,
The valiant men
are in scarlet.
The chariots *come* with
flaming torches
In the day of his
preparation,
And the spears are
brandished.[a]
4 The chariots rage
in the streets,
They jostle one another
in the broad roads;
They seem like torches,
They run like lightning.

5 He remembers his nobles;
They stumble in
their walk;
They make haste
to her walls,
And the defense
is prepared.
6 The gates of the rivers
are opened,
And the palace is
dissolved.
7 It is decreed:[a]
She shall be led
away captive,
She shall be brought up;
And her maidservants
shall lead *her* as with
the voice of doves,
Beating their breasts.

8 Though Nineveh of old
was like a pool of water,
Now they flee away.
"Halt! Halt!" *they cry;*
But no one turns back.
9 Take spoil of silver!
Take spoil of gold!
There is no end
of treasure,
Or wealth of every
desirable prize.
10 She is empty, desolate,
and waste!
The heart melts, and
the knees shake;
Much pain *is* in every side,
And all their faces are
drained of color.[a]

11 Where *is* the dwelling
of the lions,
And the feeding place
of the young lions,

2:1 [a] Vulgate reads *He who destroys.* 2:3 [a] Literally *the cypresses are shaken;* Septuagint and Syriac read *the horses rush about;* Vulgate reads *the drivers are stupefied.* 2:7 [a] Hebrew *Huzzab* 2:10 [a] Compare Joel 2:6

Where the lion
walked, the lioness
and lion's cub,
And no one made
them afraid?
12 The lion tore in pieces
enough for his cubs,
Killed for his lionesses,
Filled his caves with prey,
And his dens with flesh.

13"Behold, I *am* against
you," says the LORD of hosts,
"I will burn your[a] chariots in
smoke, and the sword shall
devour your young lions; I
will cut off your prey from the
earth, and the voice of your
messengers shall be heard no
more."

THE WOE OF NINEVEH

3 Woe to the bloody city!
It *is* all full of lies
and robbery.
Its victim never departs.
2 The noise of a whip
And the noise of
rattling wheels,
Of galloping horses,
Of clattering chariots!
3 Horsemen charge with
bright sword and
glittering spear.
There is a multitude
of slain,
A great number of bodies,
Countless corpses—
They stumble over
the corpses—
4 Because of the multitude
of harlotries of the
seductive harlot,
The mistress of sorceries,
Who sells nations
through her harlotries,
And families through
her sorceries.

5 "Behold, I *am* against you,"
says the LORD of hosts;
"I will lift your skirts
over your face,
I will show the nations
your nakedness,
And the kingdoms
your shame.
6 I will cast abominable
filth upon you,
Make you vile,
And make you a
spectacle.
7 It shall come to pass *that*
all who look upon you
Will flee from
you, and say,
'Nineveh is laid waste!
Who will bemoan her?'
Where shall I seek
comforters for you?"

8 Are you better than
No Amon[a]
That was situated
by the River,[b]
That had the waters
around her,
Whose rampart
was the sea,
Whose wall *was* the sea?

2:13 [a] Literally *her* **3:8** [a] That is, ancient Thebes; Targum and Vulgate read *populous Alexandria.* [b] Literally *rivers,* that is, the Nile and the surrounding canals

9 Ethiopia and Egypt
were her strength,
And *it was* boundless;
Put and Lubim were
your[a] helpers.
10 Yet she *was* carried away,
She went into captivity;
Her young children also
were dashed to pieces
At the head of
every street;
They cast lots for her
honorable men,
And all her great men
were bound in chains.
11 You also will be drunk;
You will be hidden;
You also will seek refuge
from the enemy.

12 All your strongholds
are fig trees with
ripened figs:
If they are shaken,
They fall into the
mouth of the eater.
13 Surely, your people in
your midst *are* women!
The gates of your land
are wide open for
your enemies;
Fire shall devour the
bars of your *gates.*

14 Draw your water
for the siege!
Fortify your strongholds!
Go into the clay and
tread the mortar!
Make strong the brick kiln!
15 There the fire will
devour you,
The sword will
cut you off;
It will eat you up
like a locust.

Make yourself
many—like the locust!
Make yourself many—like
the *swarming* locusts!
16 You have multiplied your
merchants more than
the stars of heaven.
The locust plunders
and flies away.
17 Your commanders
are like *swarming*
locusts,
And your generals like
great grasshoppers,
Which camp in the
hedges on a cold day;
When the sun rises
they flee away,
And the place where
they *are* is not known.

18 Your shepherds slumber,
O king of Assyria;
Your nobles rest
in the dust.
Your people are scattered
on the mountains,
And no one gathers them.
19 Your injury *has*
no healing,
Your wound is severe.
All who hear news of you
Will clap *their* hands
over you,
For upon whom has
not your wickedness
passed continually?

3:9 [a] Septuagint reads *her.*

THE BOOK OF HABAKKUK

1 The burden[a] which the prophet Habakkuk saw.

THE PROPHET'S QUESTION

2 O LORD, how long
shall I cry,
And You will not hear?
Even cry out to You,
"Violence!"
And You will not save.
3 Why do You show
me iniquity,
And cause *me* to
see trouble?
For plundering and
violence *are* before me;
There is strife, and
contention arises.
4 Therefore the law
is powerless,
And justice never
goes forth.
For the wicked surround
the righteous;
Therefore perverse
judgment proceeds.

THE LORD'S REPLY

5 "Look among the nations
and watch—
Be utterly astounded!
For *I will* work a work
in your days
Which you would not
believe, though it
were told *you.*
6 For indeed I am raising
up the Chaldeans,
A bitter and hasty nation
Which marches
through the breadth
of the earth,
To possess dwelling
places *that are*
not theirs.
7 They are terrible
and dreadful;
Their judgment and
their dignity proceed
from themselves.
8 Their horses also are
swifter than leopards,
And more fierce than
evening wolves.
Their chargers
charge ahead;
Their cavalry comes
from afar;
They fly as the eagle
that hastens to eat.

9 "They all come
for violence;
Their faces are set
like the east wind.
They gather captives
like sand.
10 They scoff at kings,
And princes are
scorned by them.
They deride every
stronghold,

1:1 [a] Or *oracle*

For they heap up earthen
mounds and seize it.
11 Then *his* mind[a] changes,
and he transgresses;
He commits offense,
Ascribing this power
to his god."

THE PROPHET'S SECOND QUESTION

12 Are You not from
everlasting,
O LORD my God,
my Holy One?
We shall not die.
O LORD, You have
appointed them
for judgment;
O Rock, You have marked
them for correction.
13 *You are* of purer eyes
than to behold evil,
And cannot look on
wickedness.
Why do You look on
those who deal
treacherously,
And hold Your
tongue when the
wicked devours
A *person* more
righteous than he?
14 *Why* do You make men
like fish of the sea,
Like creeping things
that have no ruler
over them?

15 They take up all of
them with a hook,
They catch them
in their net,
And gather them in
their dragnet.
Therefore they rejoice
and are glad.
16 Therefore they sacrifice
to their net,
And burn incense to
their dragnet;
Because by them their
share *is* sumptuous
And their food plentiful.
17 Shall they therefore
empty their net,
And continue to slay
nations without pity?

2 I will stand my watch
And set myself on
the rampart,
And watch to see what
He will say to me,
And what I will answer
when I am corrected.

THE JUST LIVE BY FAITH

2Then the LORD answered
me and said:

"Write the vision
And make *it* plain
on tablets,
That he may run
who reads it.
3 For the vision *is* yet for
an appointed time;
But at the end it will
speak, and it will not lie.
Though it tarries,
wait for it;
Because it will
surely come,
It will not tarry.

1:11 [a] Literally *spirit* or *wind*

4 "Behold the proud,
His soul is not
upright in him;
But the just shall
live by his faith.

WOE TO THE WICKED

5 "Indeed, because he
transgresses by wine,
He is a proud man,
And he does not
stay at home.
Because he enlarges
his desire as hell,[a]
And he *is* like death, and
cannot be satisfied,
He gathers to himself
all nations
And heaps up for
himself all peoples.

6 "Will not all these take up
a proverb against him,
And a taunting riddle
against him, and say,
'Woe to him who
increases
What is not his—how long?
And to him who
loads himself with
many pledges'?[a]
7 Will not your creditors[a]
rise up suddenly?
Will they not awaken
who oppress you?
And you will become
their booty.
8 Because you have
plundered many
nations,
All the remnant of
the people shall
plunder you,
Because of men's blood
And the violence of the
land *and* the city,
And of all who dwell in it.

9 "Woe to him who covets
evil gain for his house,
That he may set his
nest on high,
That he may be
delivered from the
power of disaster!
10 You give shameful
counsel to your house,
Cutting off many
peoples,
And sin *against* your soul.
11 For the stone will cry
out from the wall,
And the beam from the
timbers will answer it.

12 "Woe to him who builds
a town with bloodshed,
Who establishes a
city by iniquity!
13 Behold, *is it* not of
the LORD of hosts
That the peoples labor
to feed the fire,[a]
And nations weary
themselves in vain?
14 For the earth will be filled
With the knowledge of
the glory of the LORD,
As the waters
cover the sea.

2:5 [a] Or *Sheol* **2:6** [a] Syriac and Vulgate read *thick clay.* **2:7** [a] Literally *those who bite you* **2:13** [a] Literally *for what satisfies fire,* that is, for what is of no lasting value

15 "Woe to him who gives
drink to his neighbor,
Pressing[a] *him to*
your bottle,
Even to make *him* drunk,
That you may look on
his nakedness!
16 You are filled with shame
instead of glory.
You also—drink!
And be exposed as
uncircumcised![a]
The cup of the LORD's
right hand *will be*
turned against you,
And utter shame will
be on your glory.
17 For the violence *done to*
Lebanon will cover you,
And the plunder of beasts
which made them afraid,
Because of men's blood
And the violence of the
land *and* the city,
And of all who dwell in it.

18 "What profit is the
image, that its maker
should carve it,
The molded image,
a teacher of lies,
That the maker of its
mold should trust in it,
To make mute idols?
19 Woe to him who says
to wood, 'Awake!'
To silent stone, 'Arise!
It shall teach!'
Behold, it is overlaid
with gold and silver,
Yet in it there is no
breath at all.

20 "But the LORD is in
His holy temple.
Let all the earth keep
silence before Him."

THE PROPHET'S PRAYER

3 A prayer of Habakkuk the
prophet, on Shigionoth.[a]

2 O LORD, I have heard Your
speech *and* was afraid;
O LORD, revive Your
work in the midst
of the years!
In the midst of the years
make *it* known;
In wrath remember
mercy.

3 God came from Teman,
The Holy One from
Mount Paran. *Selah*

His glory covered
the heavens,
And the earth was
full of His praise.
4 *His* brightness was
like the light;
He had rays *flashing*
from His hand,
And there His power
was hidden.
5 Before Him went
pestilence,
And fever followed
at His feet.

2:15 [a] Literally *Attaching* or *Joining* **2:16** [a] Dead Sea Scrolls and Septuagint read *And reel!;* Syriac and Vulgate read *And fall fast asleep!* **3:1** [a] Exact meaning unknown

6 He stood and measured
the earth;
He looked and startled
the nations.
And the everlasting
mountains were
scattered,
The perpetual
hills bowed.
His ways *are* everlasting.
7 I saw the tents of
Cushan in affliction;
The curtains of the land
of Midian trembled.

8 O LORD, were *You*
displeased with
the rivers,
Was Your anger
against the rivers,
Was Your wrath
against the sea,
That You rode on
Your horses,
Your chariots of
salvation?
9 Your bow was made
quite ready;
Oaths were sworn over
Your arrows.[a] *Selah*

You divided the earth
with rivers.
10 The mountains saw
You *and* trembled;
The overflowing of the
water passed by.
The deep uttered its voice,
And lifted its hands
on high.
11 The sun and moon stood
still in their habitation;
At the light of Your
arrows they went,
At the shining of Your
glittering spear.

12 You marched through the
land in indignation;
You trampled the
nations in anger.
13 You went forth for
the salvation of
Your people,
For salvation with
Your Anointed.
You struck the head from
the house of the wicked,
By laying bare from
foundation to
neck. *Selah*

14 You thrust through
with his own arrows
The head of his villages.
They came out like a
whirlwind to scatter me;
Their rejoicing was
like feasting on the
poor in secret.
15 You walked through the
sea with Your horses,
Through the heap
of great waters.

16 When I heard, my
body trembled;
My lips quivered
at *the* voice;
Rottenness entered
my bones;
And I trembled in myself,
That I might rest in
the day of trouble.

3:9 [a] Literally *rods* or *tribes* (compare verse 14)

When he comes up
to the people,
He will invade them
with his troops.

A HYMN OF FAITH

17 Though the fig tree
may not blossom,
Nor fruit be on the
vines;
Though the labor of
the olive may fail,
And the fields
yield no food;
Though the flock may be
cut off from the fold,
And there be no herd
in the stalls—
18 Yet I will rejoice
in the LORD,
I will joy in the God
of my salvation.

19 The LORD God[a] is
my strength;
He will make my feet
like deer's *feet*,
And He will make me
walk on my high hills.

To the Chief Musician. With my stringed instruments.

THE BOOK OF

ZEPHANIAH

1 The word of the LORD which
came to Zephaniah the son
of Cushi, the son of Gedaliah,
the son of Amariah, the son
of Hezekiah, in the days of Josiah the son of Amon, king of
Judah.

THE GREAT DAY OF THE LORD

2 "I will utterly consume
everything
From the face of
the land,"
Says the LORD;
3 "I will consume man
and beast;
I will consume the birds
of the heavens,
The fish of the sea,
And the stumbling
blocks[a] along with
the wicked.
I will cut off man from
the face of the land,"
Says the LORD.

4 "I will stretch out My
hand against Judah,
And against all the
inhabitants of
Jerusalem.
I will cut off every trace
of Baal from this place,

3:19 [a] Hebrew *YHWH Adonai* 1:3 [a] Figurative of idols

The names of the
idolatrous priests[a] with
the *pagan* priests—
5 Those who worship
the host of heaven
on the housetops;
Those who worship and
swear *oaths* by the LORD,
But who *also* swear
by Milcom;[a]
6 Those who have
turned back from
following the LORD,
And have not sought
the LORD, nor
inquired of Him."

7 Be silent in the presence
of the Lord GOD;
For the day of the
LORD *is* at hand,
For the LORD has
prepared a sacrifice;
He has invited[a]
His guests.

8 "And it shall be,
In the day of the
LORD's sacrifice,
That I will punish
the princes and the
king's children,
And all such as
are clothed with
foreign apparel.
9 In the same day I
will punish
All those who leap over
the threshold,[a]
Who fill their masters'
houses with violence
and deceit.

10 "And there shall be on
that day," says the LORD,
"The sound of a mournful
cry from the Fish Gate,
A wailing from the
Second Quarter,
And a loud crashing
from the hills.
11 Wail, you inhabitants
of Maktesh![a]
For all the merchant
people are cut down;
All those who handle
money are cut off.

12 "And it shall come to
pass at that time
That I will search
Jerusalem with lamps,
And punish the men
Who are settled in
complacency,[a]
Who say in their heart,
'The LORD will
not do good,
Nor will He do evil.'
13 Therefore their goods
shall become booty,
And their houses
a desolation;
They shall build houses,
but not inhabit *them;*
They shall plant
vineyards, but not
drink their wine."

1:4 [a] Hebrew *chemarim* 1:5 [a] Or *Malcam,* an Ammonite god, also called *Molech* (compare Leviticus 18:21) 1:7 [a] Literally *set apart, consecrated* 1:9 [a] Compare 1 Samuel 5:5 1:11 [a] Literally *Mortar,* a market district of Jerusalem 1:12 [a] Literally *on their lees,* that is, settled like the dregs of wine

14 The great day of the
LORD *is* near;
It is near and
hastens quickly.
The noise of the day of
the LORD is bitter;
There the mighty
men shall cry out.
15 That day *is* a day of wrath,
A day of trouble
and distress,
A day of devastation
and desolation,
A day of darkness
and gloominess,
A day of clouds and
thick darkness,
16 A day of trumpet
and alarm
Against the fortified cities
And against the
high towers.

17 "I will bring distress
upon men,
And they shall walk
like blind men,
Because they have sinned
against the LORD;
Their blood shall be
poured out like dust,
And their flesh
like refuse."

18 Neither their silver
nor their gold
Shall be able to
deliver them
In the day of the
LORD's wrath;
But the whole land
shall be devoured
By the fire of His jealousy,
For He will make
speedy riddance
Of all those who
dwell in the land.

A CALL TO REPENTANCE

2 Gather yourselves
together, yes,
gather together,
O undesirable[a] nation,
2 Before the decree
is issued,
Or the day passes
like chaff,
Before the LORD's fierce
anger comes upon you,
Before the day of
the LORD's anger
comes upon you!
3 Seek the LORD, all you
meek of the earth,
Who have upheld
His justice.
Seek righteousness,
seek humility.
It may be that you
will be hidden
In the day of the
LORD's anger.

JUDGMENT ON NATIONS

4 For Gaza shall be forsaken,
And Ashkelon desolate;
They shall drive out
Ashdod at noonday,
And Ekron shall
be uprooted.
5 Woe to the inhabitants
of the seacoast,
The nation of the
Cherethites!

2:1 [a] Or *shameless*

The word of the LORD
is against you,
O Canaan, land of
the Philistines:
"I will destroy you;
So there shall be no
inhabitant."

6 The seacoast shall
be pastures,
With shelters[a] for
shepherds and
folds for flocks.
7 The coast shall be for
the remnant of the
house of Judah;
They shall feed *their*
flocks there;
In the houses of
Ashkelon they shall
lie down at evening.
For the LORD their God
will intervene for them,
And return their captives.

8 "I have heard the
reproach of Moab,
And the insults of the
people of Ammon,
With which they have
reproached My people,
And made arrogant
threats against
their borders.
9 Therefore, as I live,"
Says the LORD of hosts,
the God of Israel,
"Surely Moab shall
be like Sodom,
And the people
of Ammon like
Gomorrah—
Overrun with weeds
and saltpits,
And a perpetual
desolation.
The residue of My people
shall plunder them,
And the remnant of
My people shall
possess them."

10 This they shall have
for their pride,
Because they have
reproached and made
arrogant threats
Against the people of
the LORD of hosts.
11 The LORD *will be*
awesome to them,
For He will reduce
to nothing all the
gods of the earth;
People shall worship Him,
Each one from
his place,
Indeed all the shores
of the nations.

12 "You Ethiopians also,
You shall be slain
by My sword."

13 And He will stretch
out His hand
against the north,
Destroy Assyria,
And make Nineveh
a desolation,
As dry as the wilderness.
14 The herds shall lie
down in her midst,
Every beast of the nation.

2:6 [a] Literally *excavations,* either underground huts or cisterns

Both the pelican
and the bittern
Shall lodge on the
capitals *of* her *pillars;*
Their voice shall sing
in the windows;
Desolation *shall be*
at the threshold;
For He will lay bare
the cedar work.
15 This is the rejoicing
city
That dwelt securely,
That said in her heart,
"I *am it,* and *there is*
none besides me."
How has she become
a desolation,
A place for beasts
to lie down!
Everyone who
passes by her
Shall hiss and
shake his fist.

THE WICKEDNESS OF JERUSALEM

3 Woe to her who is
rebellious and
polluted,
To the oppressing city!
2 She has not obeyed
His voice,
She has not received
correction;
She has not trusted
in the LORD,
She has not drawn
near to her God.

3 Her princes in her midst
are roaring lions;
Her judges *are*
evening wolves
That leave not a bone
till morning.
4 Her prophets are
insolent, treacherous
people;
Her priests have polluted
the sanctuary,
They have done
violence to the law.
5 The LORD *is* righteous
in her midst,
He will do no
unrighteousness.
Every morning He brings
His justice to light;
He never fails,
But the unjust knows
no shame.

6 "I have cut off nations,
Their fortresses are
devastated;
I have made their
streets desolate,
With none passing by.
Their cities are destroyed;
There is no one, no
inhabitant.
7 I said, 'Surely you
will fear Me,
You will receive
instruction'—
So that her dwelling
would not be cut off,
Despite everything
for which I
punished her.
But they rose early
and corrupted all
their deeds.

A FAITHFUL REMNANT

8 "Therefore wait for
Me," says the LORD,

"Until the day I rise
up for plunder;[a]
My determination *is* to
gather the nations
To My assembly of
kingdoms,
To pour on them My
indignation,
All My fierce anger;
All the earth shall
be devoured
With the fire of
My jealousy.

9 "For then I will restore
to the peoples a
pure language,
That they all may
call on the name
of the LORD,
To serve Him with
one accord.
10 From beyond the
rivers of Ethiopia
My worshipers,
The daughter of My
dispersed ones,
Shall bring My offering.
11 In that day you shall
not be shamed for
any of your deeds
In which you transgress
against Me;
For then I will take away
from your midst
Those who rejoice
in your pride,
And you shall no
longer be haughty
In My holy mountain.
12 I will leave in your
midst
A meek and humble
people,
And they shall trust
in the name of
the LORD.
13 The remnant of
Israel shall do no
unrighteousness
And speak no lies,
Nor shall a deceitful
tongue be found
in their mouth;
For they shall feed *their*
flocks and lie down,
And no one shall
make *them* afraid."

JOY IN GOD'S FAITHFULNESS

14 Sing, O daughter of Zion!
Shout, O Israel!
Be glad and rejoice
with all *your* heart,
O daughter of Jerusalem!
15 The LORD has taken
away your judgments,
He has cast out
your enemy.
The King of Israel,
the LORD, *is* in
your midst;
You shall see[a] disaster
no more.

16 In that day it shall be
said to Jerusalem:

3:8 [a] Septuagint and Syriac read *for witness;* Targum reads *for the day of My revelation for judgment;* Vulgate reads *for the day of My resurrection that is to come.* 3:15 [a] Some Hebrew manuscripts, Septuagint, and Bomberg read *see;* Masoretic Text and Vulgate read *fear.*

"Do not fear;
Zion, let not your
hands be weak.
17 The LORD your God
in your midst,
The Mighty One, will
save;
He will rejoice over
you with gladness,
He will quiet *you*
with His love,
He will rejoice over
you with singing."

18 "I will gather those
who sorrow over the
appointed assembly,
Who are among you,
To whom its reproach
is a burden.
19 Behold, at that time
I will deal with all
who afflict you;
I will save the lame,
And gather those who
were driven out;
I will appoint them for
praise and fame
In every land where they
were put to shame.
20 At that time I will
bring you back,
Even at the time I
gather you;
For I will give you
fame and praise
Among all the peoples
of the earth,
When I return your
captives before
your eyes,"
Says the LORD.

THE BOOK OF HAGGAI

THE COMMAND TO BUILD GOD'S HOUSE

1 In the second year of King Darius, in the sixth month, on the first day of the month, the word of the LORD came by Haggai the prophet to Zerubbabel the son of Shealtiel, governor of Judah, and to Joshua the son of Jehozadak, the high priest, saying, 2"Thus speaks the LORD of hosts, saying: 'This people says, "The time has not come, the time that the LORD's house should be built."'"

3Then the word of the LORD came by Haggai the prophet, saying, 4"*Is it* time for you yourselves to dwell in your paneled houses, and this temple[a] *to lie* in ruins?" 5Now therefore, thus says the LORD of hosts: "Consider your ways!

1:4 [a] Literally *house,* and so in verse 8

6 "You have sown much,
and bring in little;
You eat, but do not
have enough;
You drink, but you are
not filled with drink;
You clothe yourselves,
but no one is warm;
And he who earns wages,
Earns wages *to put* into
a bag with holes."

7Thus says the LORD of
hosts: "Consider your ways!
8Go up to the mountains and
bring wood and build the temple, that I may take pleasure
in it and be glorified," says the
LORD. 9"*You* looked for much,
but indeed *it came to* little; and
when you brought it home, I
blew it away. Why?" says the
LORD of hosts. "Because of My
house that *is in* ruins, while
every one of you runs to his
own house. 10Therefore the
heavens above you withhold
the dew, and the earth withholds its fruit. 11For I called for
a drought on the land and the
mountains, on the grain and
the new wine and the oil, on
whatever the ground brings
forth, on men and livestock,
and on all the labor of *your*
hands."

THE PEOPLE'S OBEDIENCE

12Then Zerubbabel the son
of Shealtiel, and Joshua the
son of Jehozadak, the high
priest, with all the remnant
of the people, obeyed the voice
of the LORD their God, and the
words of Haggai the prophet,
as the LORD their God had sent
him; and the people feared the
presence of the LORD. 13Then
Haggai, the LORD's messenger,
spoke the LORD's message to
the people, saying, "I *am* with
you, says the LORD." 14So the
LORD stirred up the spirit of
Zerubbabel the son of Shealtiel, governor of Judah, and
the spirit of Joshua the son
of Jehozadak, the high priest,
and the spirit of all the remnant of the people; and they
came and worked on the house
of the LORD of hosts, their God,
15on the twenty-fourth day of
the sixth month, in the second
year of King Darius.

THE COMING GLORY OF GOD'S HOUSE

2 In the seventh *month,*
on the twenty-first of the
month, the word of the LORD
came by Haggai the prophet,
saying: 2"Speak now to Zerubbabel the son of Shealtiel, governor of Judah, and to Joshua
the son of Jehozadak, the high
priest, and to the remnant of
the people, saying: 3'Who is
left among you who saw this
temple[a] in its former glory?
And how do you see it now?
In comparison with it, *is this*
not in your eyes as nothing?
4Yet now be strong, Zerubbabel,' says the LORD; 'and be

2:3 [a] Literally *house,* and so in verses 7 and 9

strong, Joshua, son of Jehozadak, the high priest; and
be strong, all you people of
the land,’ says the LORD, ‘and
work; for I *am* with you,’ says
the LORD of hosts. 5‘*According
to* the word that I covenanted
with you when you came out
of Egypt, so My Spirit remains
among you; do not fear!’
6“For thus says the LORD of
hosts: ‘Once more (it *is* a little
while) I will shake heaven and
earth, the sea and dry land;
7and I will shake all nations,
and they shall come to the Desire of All Nations,[a] and I will
fill this temple with glory,’ says
the LORD of hosts. 8‘The silver
is Mine, and the gold *is* Mine,’
says the LORD of hosts. 9‘The
glory of this latter temple shall
be greater than the former,’
says the LORD of hosts. ‘And
in this place I will give peace,’
says the LORD of hosts.”

THE PEOPLE ARE DEFILED

10On the twenty-fourth *day*
of the ninth *month,* in the second year of Darius, the word of
the LORD came by Haggai the
prophet, saying, 11“Thus says
the LORD of hosts: ‘Now, ask the
priests *concerning the* law, saying, 12“If one carries holy meat
in the fold of his garment, and
with the edge he touches bread
or stew, wine or oil, or any food,
will it become holy?” ’ ”
Then the priests answered
and said, “No.”
13And Haggai said, “If *one
who is* unclean *because* of a
dead body touches any of
these, will it be unclean?”
So the priests answered
and said, “It shall be unclean.”
14Then Haggai answered
and said, “ ‘So is this people,
and so is this nation before
Me,’ says the LORD, ‘and so
is every work of their hands;
and what they offer there is
unclean.

PROMISED BLESSING

15‘And now, carefully consider from this day forward:
from before stone was laid
upon stone in the temple
of the LORD— 16since those
days, when *one* came to a
heap of twenty ephahs, there
were *but* ten; when *one* came
to the wine vat to draw out
fifty baths from the press,
there were *but* twenty. 17I
struck you with blight and
mildew and hail in all the labors of your hands; yet you
did not *turn* to Me,’ says the
LORD. 18‘Consider now from
this day forward, from the
twenty-fourth day of the
ninth month, from the day
that the foundation of the
LORD’s temple was laid—
consider it: 19Is the seed still
in the barn? As yet the vine,
the fig tree, the pomegranate,
and the olive tree have not
yielded *fruit. But* from this
day I will bless *you.*’ ”

2:7 [a] Or *the desire of all nations*

ZERUBBABEL CHOSEN AS A SIGNET

20And again the word of
the LORD came to Haggai on
the twenty-fourth day of the
month, saying, 21"Speak to Zerubbabel, governor of Judah,
saying:

'I will shake heaven
and earth.
22 I will overthrow the
throne of kingdoms;
I will destroy the
strength of the
Gentile kingdoms.
I will overthrow
the chariots
And those who
ride in them;
The horses and their
riders shall come down,
Every one by the sword
of his brother.

23'In that day,' says the
LORD of hosts, 'I will take
you, Zerubbabel My servant,
the son of Shealtiel,' says the
LORD, 'and will make you like
a signet *ring;* for I have chosen
you,' says the LORD of hosts."

THE BOOK OF ZECHARIAH

A CALL TO REPENTANCE

1 In the eighth month of
the second year of Darius,
the word of the LORD came
to Zechariah the son of Berechiah, the son of Iddo the
prophet, saying, 2"The LORD
has been very angry with
your fathers. 3Therefore say
to them, 'Thus says the LORD
of hosts: "Return to Me," says
the LORD of hosts, "and I will
return to you," says the LORD
of hosts. 4"Do not be like your
fathers, to whom the former
prophets preached, saying,
'Thus says the LORD of hosts:
"Turn now from your evil
ways and your evil deeds."'
But they did not hear nor heed
Me," says the LORD.

5 "Your fathers,
where *are* they?
And the prophets, do
they live forever?
6 Yet surely My words
and My statutes,
Which I commanded My
servants the prophets,
Did they not overtake
your fathers?

"So they returned and said:

'Just as the LORD of
hosts determined
to do to us,

According to our
ways and according
to our deeds,
So He has dealt
with us.'"'"

VISION OF THE HORSES

7On the twenty-fourth
day of the eleventh month,
which is the month Shebat,
in the second year of Darius,
the word of the LORD came
to Zechariah the son of Berechiah, the son of Iddo the
prophet: 8I saw by night, and
behold, a man riding on a red
horse, and it stood among the
myrtle trees in the hollow; and
behind him *were* horses: red,
sorrel, and white. 9Then I said,
"My lord, what *are* these?" So
the angel who talked with me
said to me, "I will show you
what they *are*."

10And the man who stood
among the myrtle trees answered and said, "These *are
the ones* whom the LORD
has sent to walk to and fro
throughout the earth."

11So they answered the
Angel of the LORD, who stood
among the myrtle trees, and
said, "We have walked to and
fro throughout the earth,
and behold, all the earth is
resting quietly."

THE LORD WILL COMFORT ZION

12Then the Angel of the
LORD answered and said,
"O LORD of hosts, how long
will You not have mercy on
Jerusalem and on the cities of
Judah, against which You were
angry these seventy years?"

13And the LORD answered
the angel who talked to me,
with good *and* comforting
words. 14So the angel who
spoke with me said to me,
"Proclaim, saying, 'Thus says
the LORD of hosts:

"I am zealous for
Jerusalem
And for Zion with
great zeal.
15 I am exceedingly
angry with the
nations at ease;
For I was a little angry,
And they helped—*but*
with evil *intent*."

16'Therefore thus says the
LORD:

"I am returning to
Jerusalem with mercy;
My house shall be
built in it," says the
LORD of hosts,
"And a *surveyor's* line
shall be stretched out
over Jerusalem."'

17"Again proclaim, saying,
'Thus says the LORD of hosts:

"My cities shall again
spread out through
prosperity;
The LORD will again
comfort Zion,
And will again choose
Jerusalem."'"

VISION OF THE HORNS

18Then I raised my eyes
and looked, and there *were*
four horns. 19And I said to
the angel who talked with me,
"What *are* these?"

So he answered me, "These
are the horns that have scattered Judah, Israel, and Jerusalem."

20Then the LORD showed
me four craftsmen. 21And I
said, "What are these coming
to do?"

So he said, "These *are* the
horns that scattered Judah,
so that no one could lift up
his head; but the craftsmen[a]
are coming to terrify them, to
cast out the horns of the nations that lifted up *their* horn
against the land of Judah to
scatter it."

VISION OF THE MEASURING LINE

2 Then I raised my eyes and
looked, and behold, a man
with a measuring line in his
hand. 2So I said, "Where are
you going?"

And he said to me, "To
measure Jerusalem, to see
what *is* its width and what *is*
its length."

3And there *was* the angel
who talked with me, going
out; and another angel was
coming out to meet him, 4who
said to him, "Run, speak to
this young man, saying: 'Jerusalem shall be inhabited *as*
towns without walls, because
of the multitude of men and
livestock in it. 5For I,' says the
LORD, 'will be a wall of fire all
around her, and I will be the
glory in her midst.'"

FUTURE JOY OF ZION AND MANY NATIONS

6"Up, up! Flee from the
land of the north," says the
LORD; "for I have spread you
abroad like the four winds of
heaven," says the LORD. 7"Up,
Zion! Escape, you who dwell
with the daughter of Babylon."

8For thus says the LORD of
hosts: "He sent Me after glory,
to the nations which plunder
you; for he who touches you
touches the apple of His eye.
9For surely I will shake My
hand against them, and they
shall become spoil for their
servants. Then you will know
that the LORD of hosts has
sent Me.

10"Sing and rejoice,
O daughter of Zion! For behold, I am coming and I will
dwell in your midst," says the
LORD. 11"Many nations shall
be joined to the LORD in that
day, and they shall become
My people. And I will dwell
in your midst. Then you will
know that the LORD of hosts
has sent Me to you. 12And the
LORD will take possession of
Judah as His inheritance in
the Holy Land, and will again
choose Jerusalem. 13Be silent,

1:21 [a] Literally *these*

all flesh, before the LORD, for
He is aroused from His holy
habitation!"

VISION OF THE HIGH PRIEST

3 Then he showed me
Joshua the high priest
standing before the Angel of
the LORD, and Satan standing
at his right hand to oppose
him. 2And the LORD said to
Satan, "The LORD rebuke you,
Satan! The LORD who has chosen Jerusalem rebuke you! *Is*
this not a brand plucked from
the fire?"

3Now Joshua was clothed
with filthy garments, and was
standing before the Angel.

4Then He answered and
spoke to those who stood before Him, saying, "Take away
the filthy garments from him."
And to him He said, "See, I
have removed your iniquity
from you, and I will clothe you
with rich robes."

5And I said, "Let them put
a clean turban on his head."
So they put a clean turban
on his head, and they put the
clothes on him. And the Angel
of the LORD stood by.

THE COMING BRANCH

6Then the Angel of the
LORD admonished Joshua,
saying, 7"Thus says the LORD
of hosts:

'If you will walk
in My ways,
And if you will keep
My command,
Then you shall also
judge My house,
And likewise have
charge of My courts;
I will give you
places to walk
Among these who
stand here.

8 'Hear, O Joshua, the
high priest,
You and your companions
who sit before you,
For they are a
wondrous sign;
For behold, I am bringing
forth My Servant
the BRANCH.
9 For behold, the stone
That I have laid
before Joshua:
Upon the stone *are*
seven eyes.
Behold, I will engrave
its inscription,'
Says the LORD of hosts,
'And I will remove
the iniquity of that
land in one day.
10 In that day,' says the
LORD of hosts,
'Everyone will invite
his neighbor
Under his vine and
under his fig tree.'"

VISION OF THE LAMPSTAND AND OLIVE TREES

4 Now the angel who talked
with me came back and
wakened me, as a man who
is wakened out of his sleep.
2And he said to me, "What do
you see?"

So I said, "I am looking, and there *is* a lampstand of solid gold with a bowl on top of it, and on the *stand* seven lamps with seven pipes to the
seven lamps. 3Two olive trees
are by it, one at the right of the bowl and the other at its
left." 4So I answered and spoke to the angel who talked with me, saying, "What *are* these, my lord?"

5Then the angel who talked with me answered and said to me, "Do you not know what these are?"

And I said, "No, my lord."

6So he answered and said to me:

"This *is* the word of the
LORD to Zerubbabel:
'Not by might nor by
power, but by My Spirit,'
Says the LORD of hosts.
7 'Who *are* you, O great
mountain?
Before Zerubbabel *you*
shall become a plain!
And he shall bring
forth the capstone
With shouts of "Grace,
grace to it!"'"

8Moreover the word of the LORD came to me, saying:

9 "The hands of Zerubbabel
Have laid the foundation
of this temple;[a]
His hands shall
also finish *it*.
Then you will know
That the LORD of hosts
has sent Me to you.
10 For who has despised the
day of small things?
For these seven
rejoice to see
The plumb line in the
hand of Zerubbabel.
They are the eyes
of the LORD,
Which scan to and
fro throughout the
whole earth."

11Then I answered and said to him, "What *are* these two olive trees—at the right of the lampstand and at its left?"
12And I further answered and said to him, "What *are these* two olive branches that *drip* into the receptacles[a] of the two gold pipes from which the golden *oil* drains?"

13Then he answered me and said, "Do you not know what these *are?*"

And I said, "No, my lord."

14So he said, "These *are* the two anointed ones, who stand beside the Lord of the whole earth."

VISION OF THE FLYING SCROLL

5 Then I turned and raised my eyes, and saw there a flying scroll.

2And he said to me, "What do you see?"

So I answered, "I see a fly-

4:9 [a] Literally *house* 4:12 [a] Literally *into the hands of*

ing scroll. Its length *is* twenty
cubits and its width ten cubits."
3Then he said to me, "This
is the curse that goes out over
the face of the whole earth:
'Every thief shall be expelled,'
according *to* this side of *the*
scroll; and, 'Every perjurer
shall be expelled,' according
to that side of it."

4 "I will send out *the curse*,"
says the LORD of hosts;
"It shall enter the
house of the thief
And the house of the
one who swears
falsely by My name.
It shall remain in the
midst of his house
And consume it, with its
timber and stones."

VISION OF THE WOMAN IN A BASKET

5Then the angel who talked
with me came out and said
to me, "Lift your eyes now,
and see what this *is* that goes
forth."
6So I asked, "What *is* it?"
And he said, "It *is* a basket[a]
that is going forth."
He also said, "This *is* their
resemblance throughout the
earth: 7Here *is* a lead disc lifted
up, and this *is* a woman sitting
inside the basket"; 8then he
said, "This *is* Wickedness!"
And he thrust her down into
the basket, and threw the lead
cover[a] over its mouth. 9Then
I raised my eyes and looked,
and there *were* two women,
coming with the wind in their
wings; for they had wings like
the wings of a stork, and they
lifted up the basket between
earth and heaven.
10So I said to the angel who
talked with me, "Where are
they carrying the basket?"
11And he said to me, "To
build a house for it in the land
of Shinar;[a] when it is ready,
the basket will be set there on
its base."

VISION OF THE FOUR CHARIOTS

6 Then I turned and raised
my eyes and looked, and
behold, four chariots *were*
coming from between two
mountains, and the moun-
tains *were* mountains of
bronze. 2With the first chariot *were* red horses, with the
second chariot black horses,
3with the third chariot white
horses, and with the fourth
chariot dappled horses—
strong *steeds*. 4Then I answered and said to the angel
who talked with me, "What *are*
these, my lord?"
5And the angel answered
and said to me, "These *are* four
spirits of heaven, who go out
from *their* station before the
Lord of all the earth. 6The one

5:6 [a] Hebrew *ephah*, a measuring container, and so elsewhere 5:8 [a] Literally *stone* 5:11 [a] That is, Babylon

with the black horses is going
to the north country, the white
are going after them, and the
dappled are going toward
the south country." 7Then
the strong *steeds* went out,
eager to go, that they might
walk to and fro throughout
the earth. And He said, "Go,
walk to and fro throughout the
earth." So they walked to and
fro throughout the earth. 8And
He called to me, and spoke to
me, saying, "See, those who
go toward the north country
have given rest to My Spirit in
the north country."

THE COMMAND TO CROWN JOSHUA

9Then the word of the
LORD came to me, saying:
10"Receive *the gift* from the
captives—from Heldai, To-
bijah, and Jedaiah, who have
come from Babylon—and go
the same day and enter the
house of Josiah the son of
Zephaniah. 11Take the silver
and gold, make an elaborate
crown, and set *it* on the head
of Joshua the son of Jehozadak, the high priest. 12Then
speak to him, saying, 'Thus
says the LORD of hosts, saying:

"Behold, the Man whose
name *is* the BRANCH!
From His place He
shall branch out,
And He shall build the
temple of the LORD;
13 Yes, He shall build the
temple of the LORD.
He shall bear the glory,
And shall sit and rule
on His throne;
So He shall be a priest
on His throne,
And the counsel of
peace shall be between
them both."'

14"Now the elaborate crown
shall be for a memorial in
the temple of the LORD for
Helem,[a] Tobijah, Jedaiah, and
Hen the son of Zephaniah.
15Even those from afar shall
come and build the temple
of the LORD. Then you shall
know that the LORD of hosts
has sent Me to you. And *this*
shall come to pass if you diligently obey the voice of the
LORD your God."

OBEDIENCE BETTER THAN FASTING

7 Now in the fourth year
of King Darius it came
to pass *that* the word of the
LORD came to Zechariah, on
the fourth *day* of the ninth
month, Chislev, 2when *the*
people[a] sent Sherezer,[b] with
Regem-Melech and his men,
to the house of God,[c] to pray
before the LORD, 3*and* to ask
the priests who *were* in the

6:14 [a] Following Masoretic Text, Targum, and Vulgate; Syriac reads *for Heldai* (compare verse 10); Septuagint reads *for the patient ones*.
7:2 [a] Literally *they* (compare verse 5) [b] Or *Sar-Ezer* [c] Hebrew *Bethel*

house of the LORD of hosts,
and the prophets, saying,
"Should I weep in the fifth
month and fast as I have done
for so many years?"

[4]Then the word of the LORD
of hosts came to me, saying,
[5]"Say to all the people of the
land, and to the priests: 'When
you fasted and mourned in
the fifth and seventh *months*
during those seventy years,
did you really fast for Me—for
Me? [6]When you eat and when
you drink, do you not eat and
drink *for yourselves?* [7]*Should
you* not *have obeyed* the words
which the LORD proclaimed
through the former prophets
when Jerusalem and the cities
around it were inhabited and
prosperous, and the South[a]
and the Lowland were inhabited?'"

DISOBEDIENCE RESULTED IN CAPTIVITY

[8]Then the word of the
LORD came to Zechariah, saying, [9]"Thus says the LORD of
hosts:

'Execute true justice,
Show mercy and
compassion
Everyone to his brother.
10 Do not oppress the widow
or the fatherless,
The alien or the poor.
Let none of you plan
evil in his heart
Against his brother.'

[11]"But they refused to heed,
shrugged their shoulders, and
stopped their ears so that they
could not hear. [12]Yes, they
made their hearts like flint,
refusing to hear the law and
the words which the LORD of
hosts had sent by His Spirit
through the former prophets.
Thus great wrath came from
the LORD of hosts. [13]Therefore
it happened, *that* just as He
proclaimed and they would
not hear, so they called out
and I would not listen," says
the LORD of hosts. [14]"But I
scattered them with a whirlwind among all the nations
which they had not known.
Thus the land became desolate after them, so that no one
passed through or returned;
for they made the pleasant
land desolate."

JERUSALEM, HOLY CITY OF THE FUTURE

8 Again the word of the
LORD of hosts came, say-
ing, [2]"Thus says the LORD of
hosts:

'I am zealous for Zion
with great zeal;
With great fervor I am
zealous for her.'

[3]"Thus says the LORD:

'I will return to Zion,
And dwell in the midst
of Jerusalem.

7:7 [a] Hebrew *Negev*

Jerusalem shall be called
the City of Truth,
The Mountain of the
LORD of hosts,
The Holy Mountain.'

4"Thus says the LORD of
hosts:

'Old men and old women
shall again sit
In the streets of
Jerusalem,
Each one with his
staff in his hand
Because of great age.
5 The streets of the city
Shall be full of
boys and girls
Playing in its streets.'

6"Thus says the LORD of
hosts:

'If it is marvelous in the
eyes of the remnant
of this people in
these days,
Will it also be marvelous
in My eyes?'
Says the LORD of hosts.

7"Thus says the LORD of
hosts:

'Behold, I will save My
people from the
land of the east
And from the land
of the west;
8 I will bring them *back*,
And they shall dwell in
the midst of Jerusalem.
They shall be My people
And I will be their God,
In truth and
righteousness.'

9"Thus says the LORD of
hosts:

'Let your hands be strong,
You who have been
hearing in these days
These words by the
mouth of the prophets,
Who *spoke* in the day the
foundation was laid
For the house of the
LORD of hosts,
That the temple
might be built.
10 For before these days
There were no wages
for man nor any
hire for beast;
There was no peace from
the enemy for whoever
went out or came in;
For I set all men,
everyone, against
his neighbor.

11But now I *will* not *treat* the
remnant of this people as
in the former days,' says the
LORD of hosts.

12 'For the seed *shall
be* prosperous,
The vine shall
give its fruit,
The ground shall give
her increase,
And the heavens shall
give their dew—
I will cause the remnant
of this people

To possess all these.
13 And it shall come to pass
That just as you were
a curse among
the nations,
O house of Judah and
house of Israel,
So I will save you, and
you shall be a blessing.
Do not fear,
Let your hands be strong.'

14"For thus says the LORD
of hosts:

'Just as I determined
to punish you
When your fathers
provoked Me to wrath,'
Says the LORD of hosts,
'And I would not relent,
15 So again in these days
I am determined
to do good
To Jerusalem and to
the house of Judah.
Do not fear.
16 These *are* the things
you shall do:
Speak each man the
truth to his neighbor;
Give judgment in
your gates for truth,
justice, and peace;
17 Let none of you think
evil in your[a] heart
against your neighbor;
And do not love
a false oath.
For all these *are*
things that I hate,'
Says the LORD."

18Then the word of the
LORD of hosts came to me,
saying, 19"Thus says the LORD
of hosts:

'The fast of the
fourth *month*,
The fast of the fifth,
The fast of the seventh,
And the fast of the tenth,
Shall be joy and gladness
and cheerful feasts
For the house of Judah.
Therefore love truth
and peace.'

20"Thus says the LORD of
hosts:

'Peoples shall yet come,
Inhabitants of
many cities;
21 The inhabitants of
one *city* shall go to
another, saying,
"Let us continue to go and
pray before the LORD,
And seek the LORD
of hosts.
I myself will go also."
22 Yes, many peoples and
strong nations
Shall come to seek
the LORD of hosts
in Jerusalem,
And to pray before
the LORD.'

23"Thus says the LORD of
hosts: 'In those days ten men
from every language of the
nations shall grasp the sleeve

8:17 [a] Literally *his*

of a Jewish man, saying, "Let us go with you, for we have heard *that* God *is* with you." ' "

ISRAEL DEFENDED AGAINST ENEMIES

9 The burden[a] of the
word of the LORD
Against the land
of Hadrach,
And Damascus its
resting place
(For the eyes of men
And all the tribes of Israel
Are on the LORD);
2 Also *against* Hamath,
which borders on it,
And *against* Tyre and
Sidon, though they
are very wise.

3 For Tyre built
herself a tower,
Heaped up silver
like the dust,
And gold like the mire
of the streets.
4 Behold, the Lord will
cast her out;
He will destroy her
power in the sea,
And she will be
devoured by fire.

5 Ashkelon shall see
it and fear;
Gaza also shall be
very sorrowful;
And Ekron, for He dried
up her expectation.
The king shall perish
from Gaza,
And Ashkelon shall
not be inhabited.

6 "A mixed race shall
settle in Ashdod,
And I will cut off the
pride of the Philistines.
7 I will take away the blood
from his mouth,
And the abominations
from between his teeth.
But he who remains,
even he *shall be*
for our God,
And shall be like a
leader in Judah,
And Ekron like a Jebusite.
8 I will camp around
My house
Because of the army,
Because of him who
passes by and him
who returns.
No more shall an
oppressor pass
through them,
For now I have seen
with My eyes.

THE COMING KING

9 "Rejoice greatly,
O daughter of Zion!
Shout, O daughter
of Jerusalem!
Behold, your King is
coming to you;
He *is* just and having
salvation,
Lowly and riding
on a donkey,
A colt, the foal of
a donkey.

9:1 [a] Or *oracle*

10 I will cut off the chariot
from Ephraim
And the horse from
Jerusalem;
The battle bow shall
be cut off.
He shall speak peace
to the nations;
His dominion *shall be*
'from sea to sea,
And from the River to
the ends of the earth.'[a]

GOD WILL SAVE HIS PEOPLE

11 "As for you also,
Because of the blood
of your covenant,
I will set your prisoners
free from the
waterless pit.
12 Return to the
stronghold,
You prisoners of hope.
Even today I declare
That I will restore
double to you.
13 For I have bent
Judah, My *bow,*
Fitted the bow with
Ephraim,
And raised up your
sons, O Zion,
Against your sons,
O Greece,
And made you like
the sword of a
mighty man."

14 Then the LORD will be
seen over them,
And His arrow will go
forth like lightning.
The Lord GOD will
blow the trumpet,
And go with whirlwinds
from the south.
15 The LORD of hosts
will defend them;
They shall devour
and subdue with
slingstones.
They shall drink *and*
roar as if with wine;
They shall be filled *with*
blood like basins,
Like the corners
of the altar.
16 The LORD their God will
save them in that day,
As the flock of His people.
For they *shall be like* the
jewels of a crown,
Lifted like a banner
over His land—
17 For how great is
its[a] goodness
And how great
its[b] beauty!
Grain shall make the
young men thrive,
And new wine the
young women.

RESTORATION OF JUDAH AND ISRAEL

10 Ask the LORD for rain
In the time of the
latter rain.[a]
The LORD will make
flashing clouds;
He will give them
showers of rain,
Grass in the field
for everyone.

9:10 [a] Psalm 72:8 9:17 [a] Or *His* [b] Or *His* 10:1 [a] That is, spring rain

2 For the idols[a] speak
delusion;
The diviners envision lies,
And tell false dreams;
They comfort in vain.
Therefore *the people* wend
their way like sheep;
They are in trouble
because *there is*
no shepherd.

3 "My anger is kindled
against the shepherds,
And I will punish
the goatherds.
For the LORD of hosts
will visit His flock,
The house of Judah,
And will make them as His
royal horse in the battle.
4 From him comes the
cornerstone,
From him the tent peg,
From him the battle bow,
From him every
ruler[a] together.
5 They shall be like
mighty men,
Who tread down
their enemies
In the mire of the
streets in the battle.
They shall fight because
the LORD is with them,
And the riders on horses
shall be put to shame.

6 "I will strengthen the
house of Judah,
And I will save the
house of Joseph.
I will bring them back,
Because I have
mercy on them.
They shall be as though I
had not cast them aside;
For I *am* the LORD
their God,
And I will hear them.
7 *Those of* Ephraim shall
be like a mighty man,
And their heart shall
rejoice as if with wine.
Yes, their children shall
see *it* and be glad;
Their heart shall
rejoice in the LORD.
8 I will whistle for them
and gather them,
For I will redeem them;
And they shall increase
as they once increased.

9 "I will sow them among
the peoples,
And they shall remember
Me in far countries;
They shall live, together
with their children,
And they shall return.
10 I will also bring them
back from the
land of Egypt,
And gather them
from Assyria.
I will bring them into
the land of Gilead
and Lebanon,
Until no *more room* is
found for them.
11 He shall pass through
the sea with affliction,
And strike the waves
of the sea:

10:2 [a] Hebrew *teraphim* 10:4 [a] Or *despot*

All the depths of the
River[a] shall dry up.
Then the pride of Assyria
shall be brought down,
And the scepter of
Egypt shall depart.

12 "So I will strengthen
them in the LORD,
And they shall walk up
and down in His name,"
Says the LORD.

DESOLATION OF ISRAEL

11 Open your doors,
O Lebanon,
That fire may devour
your cedars.
2 Wail, O cypress, for the
cedar has fallen,
Because the mighty
trees are ruined.
Wail, O oaks of Bashan,
For the thick forest
has come down.
3 *There is* the sound of
wailing shepherds!
For their glory is in ruins.
There is the sound
of roaring lions!
For the pride[a] of the
Jordan is in ruins.

PROPHECY OF THE SHEPHERDS

4 Thus says the LORD my
God, "Feed the flock for slaughter, 5 whose owners slaughter
them and feel no guilt; those
who sell them say, 'Blessed be
the LORD, for I am rich'; and
their shepherds do not pity
them. 6 For I will no longer pity
the inhabitants of the land,"
says the LORD. "But indeed
I will give everyone into his
neighbor's hand and into the
hand of his king. They shall
attack the land, and I will not
deliver *them* from their hand."
7 So I fed the flock for
slaughter, in particular the
poor of the flock.[a] I took for
myself two staffs: the one I
called Beauty,[b] and the other
I called Bonds;[c] and I fed the
flock. 8 I dismissed the three
shepherds in one month. My
soul loathed them, and their
soul also abhorred me. 9 Then
I said, "I will not feed you. Let
what is dying die, and what
is perishing perish. Let those
that are left eat each other's
flesh." 10 And I took my staff,
Beauty, and cut it in two, that
I might break the covenant
which I had made with all the
peoples. 11 So it was broken on
that day. Thus the poor[a] of
the flock, who were watching
me, knew that it *was* the word
of the LORD. 12 Then I said to
them, "If it is agreeable to you,
give *me* my wages; and if not,
refrain." So they weighed out
for my wages thirty *pieces* of
silver.

10:11 [a] That is, the Nile 11:3 [a] Or *floodplain, thicket* 11:7 [a] Following Masoretic Text, Targum, and Vulgate; Septuagint reads *for the Canaanites.* [b] Or *Grace,* and so in verse 10 [c] Or *Unity,* and so in verse 14 11:11 [a] Following Masoretic Text, Targum, and Vulgate; Septuagint reads *the Canaanites.*

13And the LORD said to me,
"Throw it to the potter"—that
princely price they set on me.
So I took the thirty *pieces* of
silver and threw them into
the house of the LORD for
the potter. 14Then I cut in two
my other staff, Bonds, that I
might break the brotherhood
between Judah and Israel.

15And the LORD said to me,
"Next, take for yourself the
implements of a foolish shepherd. 16For indeed I will raise
up a shepherd in the land *who*
will not care for those who are
cut off, nor seek the young, nor
heal those that are broken, nor
feed those that still stand. But
he will eat the flesh of the fat
and tear their hooves in pieces.

17"Woe to the worthless
shepherd,
Who leaves the flock!
A sword *shall be*
against his arm
And against his right eye;
His arm shall
completely wither,
And his right eye shall
be totally blinded."

THE COMING DELIVERANCE OF JUDAH

12 The burden[a] of the word
of the LORD against Is-
rael. Thus says the LORD, who
stretches out the heavens,
lays the foundation of the
earth, and forms the spirit of
man within him: 2"Behold, I
will make Jerusalem a cup of
drunkenness to all the surrounding peoples, when they
lay siege against Judah and
Jerusalem. 3And it shall happen in that day that I will make
Jerusalem a very heavy stone
for all peoples; all who would
heave it away will surely be cut
in pieces, though all nations of
the earth are gathered against
it. 4In that day," says the LORD,
"I will strike every horse with
confusion, and its rider with
madness; I will open My eyes
on the house of Judah, and will
strike every horse of the peoples with blindness. 5And the
governors of Judah shall say in
their heart, 'The inhabitants of
Jerusalem *are* my strength in
the LORD of hosts, their God.'
6In that day I will make the
governors of Judah like a fire-
pan in the woodpile, and like a
fiery torch in the sheaves; they
shall devour all the surrounding peoples on the right hand
and on the left, but Jerusalem
shall be inhabited again in her
own place—Jerusalem.

7"The LORD will save the
tents of Judah first, so that the
glory of the house of David
and the glory of the inhabitants of Jerusalem shall not
become greater than that of
Judah. 8In that day the LORD
will defend the inhabitants
of Jerusalem; the one who is
feeble among them in that
day shall be like David, and

12:1 [a] Or *oracle*

the house of David *shall be*
like God, like the Angel of the
LORD before them. 9It shall
be in that day *that* I will seek
to destroy all the nations that
come against Jerusalem.

MOURNING FOR THE PIERCED ONE

10"And I will pour on the
house of David and on the
inhabitants of Jerusalem the
Spirit of grace and supplication; then they will look on Me
whom they pierced. Yes, they
will mourn for Him as one
mourns for *his* only *son,* and
grieve for Him as one grieves
for a firstborn. 11In that day
there shall be a great mourning in Jerusalem, like the
mourning at Hadad Rimmon
in the plain of Megiddo.[a] 12And
the land shall mourn, every
family by itself: the family of
the house of David by itself,
and their wives by themselves;
the family of the house of Nathan by itself, and their wives
by themselves; 13the family
of the house of Levi by itself,
and their wives by themselves;
the family of Shimei by itself,
and their wives by themselves;
14all the families that remain,
every family by itself, and their
wives by themselves.

IDOLATRY CUT OFF

13 "In that day a fountain
shall be opened for the
house of David and for the
inhabitants of Jerusalem, for
sin and for uncleanness.
2"It shall be in that day,"
says the LORD of hosts, "*that*
I will cut off the names of the
idols from the land, and they
shall no longer be remem-
bered. I will also cause the
prophets and the unclean
spirit to depart from the land.
3It shall come to pass *that* if
anyone still prophesies, then
his father and mother who
begot him will say to him,
'You shall not live, because
you have spoken lies in the
name of the LORD.' And his
father and mother who begot
him shall thrust him through
when he prophesies.
4"And it shall be in that
day *that* every prophet will be
ashamed of his vision when
he prophesies; they will not
wear a robe of coarse hair to
deceive. 5But he will say, 'I *am*
no prophet, I *am* a farmer; for
a man taught me to keep cattle
from my youth.' 6And *one* will
say to him, 'What are these
wounds between your arms?'[a]
Then he will answer, '*Those*
with which I was wounded in
the house of my friends.'

THE SHEPHERD SAVIOR

7 "Awake, O sword,
against My Shepherd,
Against the Man who
is My Companion,"
Says the LORD of hosts.
"Strike the Shepherd,

12:11 [a] Hebrew *Megiddon* 13:6 [a] Or *hands*

And the sheep will
be scattered;
Then I will turn My
hand against the
little ones.
8 And it shall come to
pass in all the land,"
Says the LORD,
"*That* two-thirds in it shall
be cut off *and* die,
But *one*-third shall
be left in it:
9 I will bring the *one*-third
through the fire,
Will refine them as
silver is refined,
And test them as
gold is tested.
They will call on
My name,
And I will answer them.
I will say, 'This *is*
My people';
And each one will say,
'The LORD *is* my God.'"

THE DAY OF THE LORD

14 Behold, the day of the
LORD is coming,
And your spoil will be
divided in your midst.
2 For I will gather all
the nations to battle
against Jerusalem;
The city shall be taken,
The houses rifled,
And the women ravished.
Half of the city shall
go into captivity,
But the remnant of the
people shall not be
cut off from the city.
3 Then the LORD
will go forth
And fight against
those nations,
As He fights in the
day of battle.
4 And in that day His
feet will stand on the
Mount of Olives,
Which faces Jerusalem
on the east.
And the Mount of Olives
shall be split in two,
From east to west,
Making a very
large valley;
Half of the mountain
shall move toward
the north
And half of it toward
the south.

5 Then you shall
flee *through* My
mountain valley,
For the mountain valley
shall reach to Azal.
Yes, you shall flee
As you fled from
the earthquake
In the days of Uzziah
king of Judah.

Thus the LORD my
God will come,
And all the saints
with You.[a]

6 It shall come to pass
in that day
That there will
be no light;

14:5 [a] Or *you;* Septuagint, Targum, and Vulgate read *Him.*

The lights will diminish.
7 It shall be one day
Which is known to
the LORD—
Neither day nor night.
But at evening time
it shall happen
That it will be light.

8 And in that day it
shall be
That living waters shall
flow from Jerusalem,
Half of them toward
the eastern sea
And half of them toward
the western sea;
In both summer and
winter it shall occur.
9 And the LORD shall be
King over all the earth.
In that day it shall be—
"The LORD *is* one,"[a]
And His name one.

10All the land shall be
turned into a plain from
Geba to Rimmon south of
Jerusalem. *Jerusalem*[a] shall
be raised up and inhabited
in her place from Benjamin's
Gate to the place of the First
Gate and the Corner Gate, and
from the Tower of Hananel to
the king's winepresses.

11 *The people* shall
dwell in it;
And no longer shall there
be utter destruction,
But Jerusalem shall be
safely inhabited.

12And this shall be the
plague with which the LORD
will strike all the people who
fought against Jerusalem:

Their flesh shall
dissolve while they
stand on their feet,
Their eyes shall dissolve
in their sockets,
And their tongues
shall dissolve in
their mouths.

13 It shall come to pass
in that day
That a great panic
from the LORD will
be among them.
Everyone will seize the
hand of his neighbor,
And raise his
hand against his
neighbor's hand;
14 Judah also will fight
at Jerusalem.
And the wealth of all the
surrounding nations
Shall be gathered
together:
Gold, silver, and apparel
in great abundance.

15 Such also shall be
the plague
On the horse *and*
the mule,
On the camel and
the donkey,
And on all the cattle that
will be in those camps.
So *shall* this plague *be.*

14:9 [a] Compare Deuteronomy 6:4 14:10 [a] Literally *She*

THE NATIONS WORSHIP THE KING

16 And it shall come to pass
that everyone who is left of
all the nations which came
against Jerusalem shall go up
from year to year to worship
the King, the LORD of hosts,
and to keep the Feast of Tabernacles. 17 And it shall be *that*
whichever of the families of
the earth do not come up to
Jerusalem to worship the King,
the LORD of hosts, on them
there will be no rain. 18 If the
family of Egypt will not come
up and enter in, they *shall have*
no *rain;* they shall receive the
plague with which the LORD
strikes the nations who do not
come up to keep the Feast of
Tabernacles. 19 This shall be the
punishment of Egypt and the
punishment of all the nations
that do not come up to keep
the Feast of Tabernacles.

20 In that day "HOLINESS
TO THE LORD" shall be *engraved* on the bells of the
horses. The pots in the LORD's
house shall be like the bowls
before the altar. 21 Yes, every
pot in Jerusalem and Judah
shall be holiness to the LORD
of hosts.[a] Everyone who sacrifices shall come and take
them and cook in them. In
that day there shall no longer
be a Canaanite in the house of
the LORD of hosts.

THE BOOK OF MALACHI

1 The burden[a] of the word of
the LORD to Israel by Malachi.

ISRAEL BELOVED OF GOD

2 "I have loved you,"
says the LORD.
"Yet you say, 'In what
way have You loved us?'
Was not Esau Jacob's
brother?"
Says the LORD.
"Yet Jacob I have loved;
3 But Esau I have hated,
And laid waste his
mountains and
his heritage
For the jackals of
the wilderness."
4 Even though Edom
has said,

14:21 [a] Or *on every pot . . . shall be (engraved) "HOLINESS TO THE LORD OF HOSTS"* 1:1 [a] Or *oracle*

"We have been
impoverished,
But we will return
and build the
desolate places,"

Thus says the LORD of hosts:

"They may build, but
I will throw down;
They shall be called the
Territory of Wickedness,
And the people
against whom the
LORD will have
indignation forever.
5 Your eyes shall see,
And you shall say,
'The LORD is
magnified beyond
the border of Israel.'

POLLUTED OFFERINGS

6 "A son honors *his* father,
And a servant *his* master.
If then I am the Father,
Where *is* My honor?
And if I *am* a Master,
Where *is* My reverence?
Says the LORD of hosts
To you priests who
despise My name.
Yet you say, 'In what
way have we despised
Your name?'

7 "You offer defiled
food on My altar,
But say,
'In what way have we
defiled You?'
By saying,
'The table of the LORD
is contemptible.'
8 And when you offer the
blind as a sacrifice,
Is it not evil?
And when you offer
the lame and sick,
Is it not evil?
Offer it then to your
governor!
Would he be pleased
with you?
Would he accept
you favorably?"
Says the LORD of hosts.

9 "But now entreat
God's favor,
That He may be
gracious to us.
While this is being *done*
by your hands,
Will He accept you
favorably?"
Says the LORD of hosts.
10 "Who *is there* even
among you who would
shut the doors,
So that you would
not kindle fire *on*
My altar in vain?
I have no pleasure
in you,"
Says the LORD of hosts,
"Nor will I accept
an offering from
your hands.
11 For from the rising
of the sun, even to
its going down,
My name *shall be* great
among the Gentiles;
In every place incense
shall be offered
to My name,
And a pure offering;

For My name shall
be great among
the nations,"
Says the LORD of hosts.

12 "But you profane it,
In that you say,
'The table of the
LORD[a] is defiled;
And its fruit, its food,
is contemptible.'
13 You also say,
'Oh, what a weariness!'
And you sneer at it,"
Says the LORD of hosts.
"And you bring the
stolen, the lame,
and the sick;
Thus you bring
an offering!
Should I accept this
from your hand?"
Says the LORD.
14 "But cursed *be* the
deceiver
Who has in his
flock a male,
And takes a vow,
But sacrifices to the Lord
what is blemished—
For I *am* a great King,"
Says the LORD of hosts,
"And My name *is to*
be feared among
the nations.

CORRUPT PRIESTS

2 "And now, O priests,
this commandment
is for you.
2 If you will not hear,
And if you will not
take *it* to heart,
To give glory to My name,"
Says the LORD of hosts,
"I will send a curse
upon you,
And I will curse
your blessings.
Yes, I have cursed
them already,
Because you do not
take *it* to heart.

3 "Behold, I will rebuke
your descendants
And spread refuse
on your faces,
The refuse of your
solemn feasts;
And *one* will take
you away with it.
4 Then you shall know
that I have sent this
commandment to you,
That My covenant with
Levi may continue,"
Says the LORD of hosts.
5 "My covenant was
with him, *one* of
life and peace,
And I gave them to him
that he might fear *Me;*
So he feared Me
And was reverent
before My name.
6 The law of truth[a] was
in his mouth,
And injustice was not
found on his lips.
He walked with Me in
peace and equity,

1:12 [a] Following Bomberg; Masoretic Text reads *Lord.* 2:6 [a] Or *true instruction*

And turned many away
from iniquity.

7 "For the lips of a priest
should keep knowledge,
And *people* should
seek the law from
his mouth;
For he is the messenger
of the LORD of hosts.
8 But you have departed
from the way;
You have caused many
to stumble at the law.
You have corrupted the
covenant of Levi,"
Says the LORD of hosts.
9 "Therefore I also
have made you
contemptible and base
Before all the people,
Because you have
not kept My ways
But have shown
partiality in the law."

TREACHERY OF INFIDELITY

10 Have we not all
one Father?
Has not one God
created us?
Why do we deal
treacherously with
one another
By profaning the
covenant of the fathers?
11 Judah has dealt
treacherously,
And an abomination has
been committed in
Israel and in Jerusalem,
For Judah has profaned
The LORD's holy *institution*
which He loves:
He has married
the daughter of
a foreign god.
12 May the LORD cut off
from the tents of Jacob
The man who does
this, being awake
and aware,[a]
Yet who brings an
offering to the
LORD of hosts!

13 And this is the second
thing you do:
You cover the altar of
the LORD with tears,
With weeping and crying;
So He does not regard
the offering anymore,
Nor receive *it* with
goodwill from
your hands.
14 Yet you say, "For
what reason?"
Because the LORD
has been witness
Between you and the
wife of your youth,
With whom you have
dealt treacherously;
Yet she is your
companion
And your wife by
covenant.
15 But did He not make
them one,
Having a remnant
of the Spirit?
And why one?
He seeks godly offspring.

2:12 [a] Talmud and Vulgate read *teacher and student.*

Therefore take heed
to your spirit,
And let none deal
treacherously with
the wife of his youth.

16 "For the LORD God
of Israel says
That He hates divorce,
For it covers one's
garment with violence,"
Says the LORD of hosts.
"Therefore take heed
to your spirit,
That you do not deal
treacherously."

17 You have wearied the
LORD with your words;
Yet you say,
"In what way have we
wearied *Him?*"
In that you say,
"Everyone who does evil
Is good in the sight
of the LORD,
And He delights in them,"
Or, "Where *is* the
God of justice?"

THE COMING MESSENGER

3 "Behold, I send My
messenger,
And he will prepare
the way before Me.
And the Lord, whom
you seek,
Will suddenly come
to His temple,
Even the Messenger
of the covenant,
In whom you delight.
Behold, He is coming,"
Says the LORD of hosts.

2 "But who can endure the
day of His coming?
And who can stand
when He appears?
For He *is* like a
refiner's fire
And like launderers' soap.
3 He will sit as a refiner
and a purifier of silver;
He will purify the
sons of Levi,
And purge them as
gold and silver,
That they may offer
to the LORD
An offering in
righteousness.

4 "Then the offering of
Judah and Jerusalem
Will be pleasant
to the LORD,
As in the days of old,
As in former years.
5 And I will come near
you for judgment;
I will be a swift witness
Against sorcerers,
Against adulterers,
Against perjurers,
Against those who exploit
wage earners and
widows and orphans,
And against those who
turn away an alien—
Because they do
not fear Me,"
Says the LORD of hosts.

6 "For I *am* the LORD, I
do not change;
Therefore you are
not consumed,
O sons of Jacob.

7 Yet from the days
of your fathers
You have gone away
from My ordinances
And have not kept *them*.
Return to Me, and I
will return to you,"
Says the LORD of hosts.
"But you said,
'In what way shall
we return?'

DO NOT ROB GOD

8 "Will a man rob God?
Yet you have robbed Me!
But you say,
'In what way have we
robbed You?'
In tithes and offerings.
9 You are cursed
with a curse,
For you have robbed Me,
Even this whole nation.
10 Bring all the tithes into
the storehouse,
That there may be
food in My house,
And try Me now in this,"
Says the LORD of hosts,
"If I will not open for you
the windows of heaven
And pour out for you
such blessing
That *there will* not *be room*
enough *to receive it*.

11 "And I will rebuke the
devourer for your sakes,
So that he will not destroy
the fruit of your ground,
Nor shall the vine
fail to bear fruit for
you in the field,"
Says the LORD of hosts;
12 "And all nations will
call you blessed,
For you will be a
delightful land,"
Says the LORD of hosts.

THE PEOPLE COMPLAIN HARSHLY

13 "Your words have been
harsh against Me,"
Says the LORD,
"Yet you say,
'What have we spoken
against You?'
14 You have said,
'It is useless to serve God;
What profit *is it* that
we have kept His
ordinance,
And that we have
walked as mourners
Before the LORD of hosts?
15 So now we call the
proud blessed,
For those who do
wickedness are
raised up;
They even tempt God
and go free.'"

A BOOK OF REMEMBRANCE

16 Then those who feared
the LORD spoke
to one another,
And the LORD listened
and heard *them;*
So a book of
remembrance was
written before Him
For those who fear
the LORD
And who meditate
on His name.

17 "They shall be Mine,"
says the LORD of hosts,
"On the day that I make
them My jewels.[a]
And I will spare them
As a man spares his own
son who serves him."
18 Then you shall
again discern
Between the righteous
and the wicked,
Between one who
serves God
And one who does
not serve Him.

THE GREAT DAY OF GOD

4 "For behold, the
day is coming,
Burning like an oven,
And all the proud, yes,
all who do wickedly
will be stubble.
And the day which
is coming shall
burn them up,"
Says the LORD of hosts,
"That will leave them
neither root nor branch.
2 But to you who
fear My name
The Sun of Righteousness
shall arise
With healing in
His wings;
And you shall go out
And grow fat like
stall-fed calves.
3 You shall trample
the wicked,
For they shall be
ashes under the
soles of your feet
On the day that I do *this,*"
Says the LORD of hosts.

4 "Remember the Law of
Moses, My servant,
Which I commanded
him in Horeb
for all Israel,
With the statutes
and judgments.
5 Behold, I will send you
Elijah the prophet
Before the coming of
the great and dreadful
day of the LORD.
6 And he will turn
The hearts of the fathers
to the children,
And the hearts of
the children to
their fathers,
Lest I come and strike
the earth with a curse."

3:17 [a] Literally *special treasure*

THE NEW TESTAMENT

THE GOSPEL ACCORDING TO MATTHEW

THE GENEALOGY OF JESUS CHRIST

1 The book of the genealogy of Jesus Christ, the Son of David, the Son of Abraham:

2 Abraham begot Isaac, Isaac begot Jacob, and Jacob begot Judah and his brothers. 3 Judah begot Perez and Zerah by Tamar, Perez begot Hezron, and Hezron begot Ram. 4 Ram begot Amminadab, Amminadab begot Nahshon, and Nahshon begot Salmon. 5 Salmon begot Boaz by Rahab, Boaz begot Obed by Ruth, Obed begot Jesse, 6 and Jesse begot David the king.

David the king begot Solomon by her *who had been the wife*[a] of Uriah. 7 Solomon begot Rehoboam, Rehoboam begot Abijah, and Abijah begot Asa.[a] 8 Asa begot Jehoshaphat, Jehoshaphat begot Joram, and Joram begot Uzziah. 9 Uzziah begot Jotham, Jotham begot Ahaz, and Ahaz begot Hezekiah. 10 Hezekiah begot Manasseh, Manasseh begot Amon,[a] and Amon begot Josiah. 11 Josiah begot Jeconiah and his brothers about the time they were carried away to Babylon.

12 And after they were brought to Babylon, Jeconiah begot Shealtiel, and Shealtiel begot Zerubbabel. 13 Zerubbabel begot Abiud, Abiud begot Eliakim, and Eliakim begot Azor. 14 Azor begot Zadok, Zadok begot Achim, and Achim begot Eliud. 15 Eliud begot Eleazar, Eleazar begot Matthan, and Matthan begot Jacob. 16 And Jacob begot Joseph the husband of Mary, of whom was born Jesus who is called Christ.

17 So all the generations from Abraham to David *are* fourteen generations, from David until the captivity in Babylon *are* fourteen generations, and from the captivity in Babylon until the Christ *are* fourteen generations.

CHRIST BORN OF MARY

18 Now the birth of Jesus Christ was as follows: After His mother Mary was betrothed to Joseph, before they came together, she was found with child of the Holy Spirit. 19 Then Joseph her husband, being a just *man*, and not wanting to make her a public example, was minded to put her

1:6 [a] Words in italic type have been added for clarity. They are not found in the original Greek. 1:7 [a] NU-Text reads *Asaph*. 1:10 [a] NU-Text reads *Amos*.

away secretly. 20 But while he
thought about these things,
behold, an angel of the Lord
appeared to him in a dream,
saying, "Joseph, son of David,
do not be afraid to take to
you Mary your wife, for that
which is conceived in her is
of the Holy Spirit. 21 And she
will bring forth a Son, and you
shall call His name JESUS, for
He will save His people from
their sins."

22 So all this was done that
it might be fulfilled which was
spoken by the Lord through
the prophet, saying: 23 "Behold, the virgin shall be with
child, and bear a Son, and
they shall call His name Immanuel,"[a] which is translated,
"God with us."

24 Then Joseph, being
aroused from sleep, did as the
angel of the Lord commanded
him and took to him his wife,
25 and did not know her till she
had brought forth her firstborn Son.[a] And he called His
name JESUS.

WISE MEN FROM THE EAST

2 Now after Jesus was born
in Bethlehem of Judea in
the days of Herod the king, behold, wise men from the East
came to Jerusalem, 2 saying,
"Where is He who has been
born King of the Jews? For
we have seen His star in the
East and have come to worship Him."

3 When Herod the king
heard *this,* he was troubled,
and all Jerusalem with him.
4 And when he had gath-
ered all the chief priests and
scribes of the people together,
he inquired of them where the
Christ was to be born.

5 So they said to him, "In
Bethlehem of Judea, for thus
it is written by the prophet:

6 'But you, Bethlehem, *in*
the land of Judah,
Are not the least among
the rulers of Judah;
For out of you shall
come a Ruler
Who will shepherd My
people Israel.'"[a]

7 Then Herod, when he had
secretly called the wise men,
determined from them what
time the star appeared. 8 And
he sent them to Bethlehem
and said, "Go and search carefully for the young Child, and
when you have found *Him,*
bring back word to me, that I
may come and worship Him
also."

9 When they heard the
king, they departed; and behold, the star which they had
seen in the East went before
them, till it came and stood
over where the young Child
was. 10 When they saw the star,
they rejoiced with exceedingly
great joy. 11 And when they had
come into the house, they saw

1:23 [a] Isaiah 7:14 1:25 [a] NU-Text reads *a Son.* 2:6 [a] Micah 5:2

the young Child with Mary His
mother, and fell down and
worshiped Him. And when
they had opened their treasures, they presented gifts to
Him: gold, frankincense, and
myrrh.
12Then, being divinely
warned in a dream that they
should not return to Herod,
they departed for their own
country another way.

THE FLIGHT INTO EGYPT

13Now when they had de-
parted, behold, an angel of
the Lord appeared to Joseph
in a dream, saying, "Arise,
take the young Child and His
mother, flee to Egypt, and stay
there until I bring you word;
for Herod will seek the young
Child to destroy Him."
14When he arose, he took
the young Child and His
mother by night and departed
for Egypt, 15and was there
until the death of Herod, that
it might be fulfilled which was
spoken by the Lord through
the prophet, saying, "Out of
Egypt I called My Son."[a]

MASSACRE OF THE INNOCENTS

16Then Herod, when he saw
that he was deceived by the
wise men, was exceedingly
angry; and he sent forth and
put to death all the male children who were in Bethlehem
and in all its districts, from
two years old and under, according to the time which he
had determined from the wise
men. 17Then was fulfilled what
was spoken by Jeremiah the
prophet, saying:

18 "A voice was heard
in Ramah,
Lamentation, weeping,
and great mourning,
Rachel weeping *for*
her children,
Refusing to be comforted,
Because they are
no more."[a]

THE HOME IN NAZARETH

19Now when Herod was
dead, behold, an angel of the
Lord appeared in a dream to
Joseph in Egypt, 20saying,
"Arise, take the young Child
and His mother, and go to the
land of Israel, for those who
sought the young Child's life
are dead." 21Then he arose,
took the young Child and His
mother, and came into the
land of Israel.
22But when he heard that
Archelaus was reigning over
Judea instead of his father
Herod, he was afraid to go
there. And being warned by
God in a dream, he turned
aside into the region of Galilee. 23And he came and dwelt
in a city called Nazareth, that
it might be fulfilled which was
spoken by the prophets, "He
shall be called a Nazarene."

2:15 [a] Hosea 11:1 2:18 [a] Jeremiah 31:15

JOHN THE BAPTIST PREPARES THE WAY

3 In those days John the
Baptist came preaching in
the wilderness of Judea, 2and
saying, "Repent, for the kingdom of heaven is at hand!"
3For this is he who was spoken of by the prophet Isaiah,
saying:

"The voice of one
crying in the
wilderness:
'Prepare the way
of the LORD;
Make His paths
straight.'"[a]

4Now John himself was
clothed in camel's hair, with a
leather belt around his waist;
and his food was locusts and
wild honey. 5Then Jerusalem,
all Judea, and all the region
around the Jordan went out
to him 6and were baptized by
him in the Jordan, confessing
their sins.
7But when he saw many of
the Pharisees and Sadducees
coming to his baptism, he
said to them, "Brood of vipers!
Who warned you to flee from
the wrath to come? 8Therefore
bear fruits worthy of repentance, 9and do not think to
say to yourselves, 'We have
Abraham as *our* father.' For I
say to you that God is able to
raise up children to Abraham
from these stones. 10And even
now the ax is laid to the root of
the trees. Therefore every tree
which does not bear good fruit
is cut down and thrown into
the fire. 11I indeed baptize you
with water unto repentance,
but He who is coming after
me is mightier than I, whose
sandals I am not worthy to
carry. He will baptize you with
the Holy Spirit and fire.[a] 12His
winnowing fan *is* in His hand,
and He will thoroughly clean
out His threshing floor, and
gather His wheat into the
barn; but He will burn up the
chaff with unquenchable fire."

JOHN BAPTIZES JESUS

13Then Jesus came from
Galilee to John at the Jordan
to be baptized by him. 14And
John *tried to* prevent Him,
saying, "I need to be baptized
by You, and are You coming
to me?"
15But Jesus answered and
said to him, "Permit *it to be
so* now, for thus it is fitting for
us to fulfill all righteousness."
Then he allowed Him.
16When He had been bap-
tized, Jesus came up immediately from the water; and
behold, the heavens were
opened to Him, and He[a] saw
the Spirit of God descending
like a dove and alighting upon
Him. 17And suddenly a voice
came from heaven, saying,
"This is My beloved Son, in
whom I am well pleased."

3:3 [a] Isaiah 40:3 3:11 [a] M-Text omits *and fire.* 3:16 [a] Or *he*

SATAN TEMPTS JESUS

4 Then Jesus was led up
by the Spirit into the wilderness to be tempted by
the devil. 2And when He had
fasted forty days and forty
nights, afterward He was hungry. 3Now when the tempter
came to Him, he said, "If You
are the Son of God, command
that these stones become
bread."
4But He answered and
said, "It is written, 'Man shall
not live by bread alone, but
by every word that proceeds
from the mouth of God.'"[a]
5Then the devil took Him
up into the holy city, set Him
on the pinnacle of the temple,
6and said to Him, "If You are
the Son of God, throw Yourself
down. For it is written:

'He shall give His angels
charge over you,'

and,

'In *their* hands they
shall bear you up,
Lest you dash your foot
against a stone.'"[a]

7Jesus said to him, "It is
written again, 'You shall not
tempt the LORD your God.'"[a]
8Again, the devil took Him
up on an exceedingly high
mountain, and showed Him
all the kingdoms of the world
and their glory. 9And he said
to Him, "All these things I will
give You if You will fall down
and worship me."
10Then Jesus said to him,
"Away with you,[a] Satan! For it
is written, 'You shall worship
the LORD your God, and Him
only you shall serve.'"[b]
11Then the devil left Him,
and behold, angels came and
ministered to Him.

JESUS BEGINS HIS GALILEAN MINISTRY

12Now when Jesus heard
that John had been put in
prison, He departed to Galilee. 13And leaving Nazareth,
He came and dwelt in Capernaum, which is by the sea, in
the regions of Zebulun and
Naphtali, 14that it might be
fulfilled which was spoken
by Isaiah the prophet, saying:

15 "The land of Zebulun
and the land of
Naphtali,
By the way of the sea,
beyond the Jordan,
Galilee of the Gentiles:
16 The people who sat
in darkness have
seen a great light,
And upon those who
sat in the region and
shadow of death
Light has dawned."[a]

4:4 [a] Deuteronomy 8:3 4:6 [a] Psalm 91:11, 12
4:7 [a] Deuteronomy 6:16 4:10 [a] M-Text reads *Get behind Me.*
[b] Deuteronomy 6:13 4:16 [a] Isaiah 9:1, 2

17From that time Jesus
began to preach and to say,
"Repent, for the kingdom of
heaven is at hand."

FOUR FISHERMEN CALLED AS DISCIPLES

18And Jesus, walking by
the Sea of Galilee, saw two
brothers, Simon called Peter,
and Andrew his brother,
casting a net into the sea; for
they were fishermen. 19Then
He said to them, "Follow Me,
and I will make you fishers of
men." 20They immediately left
their nets and followed Him.
21Going on from there, He
saw two other brothers, James
the son of Zebedee, and John
his brother, in the boat with
Zebedee their father, mending their nets. He called them,
22and immediately they left
the boat and their father, and
followed Him.

JESUS HEALS A GREAT MULTITUDE

23And Jesus went about
all Galilee, teaching in their
synagogues, preaching the
gospel of the kingdom, and
healing all kinds of sickness and all kinds of disease
among the people. 24Then
His fame went throughout
all Syria; and they brought to
Him all sick people who were
afflicted with various diseases
and torments, and those who
were demon-possessed, ep-
ileptics, and paralytics; and
He healed them. 25Great multitudes followed Him—from
Galilee, and *from* Decapolis,
Jerusalem, Judea, and be-
yond the Jordan.

THE BEATITUDES

5 And seeing the multitudes,
He went up on a moun-
tain, and when He was seated
His disciples came to Him.
2Then He opened His mouth
and taught them, saying:

3 "Blessed *are* the
poor in spirit,
For theirs is the
kingdom of heaven.
4 Blessed *are* those
who mourn,
For they shall be
comforted.
5 Blessed *are* the meek,
For they shall inherit
the earth.
6 Blessed *are* those who
hunger and thirst
for righteousness,
For they shall be filled.
7 Blessed *are* the
merciful,
For they shall
obtain mercy.
8 Blessed *are* the
pure in heart,
For they shall see God.
9 Blessed *are* the
peacemakers,
For they shall be
called sons of God.
10 Blessed *are* those who
are persecuted for
righteousness' sake,
For theirs is the
kingdom of heaven.

11Blessed are you when they
revile and persecute you, and
say all kinds of evil against
you falsely for My sake. 12Re-
joice and be exceedingly
glad, for great *is* your reward
in heaven, for so they persecuted the prophets who were
before you.

BELIEVERS ARE SALT AND LIGHT

13"You are the salt of the
earth; but if the salt loses its
flavor, how shall it be seasoned? It is then good for
nothing but to be thrown out
and trampled underfoot by
men.

14"You are the light of the
world. A city that is set on a
hill cannot be hidden. 15Nor
do they light a lamp and put
it under a basket, but on a
lampstand, and it gives light
to all *who are* in the house.
16Let your light so shine before men, that they may see
your good works and glorify
your Father in heaven.

CHRIST FULFILLS THE LAW

17"Do not think that I
came to destroy the Law or
the Prophets. I did not come
to destroy but to fulfill. 18For
assuredly, I say to you, till
heaven and earth pass away,
one jot or one tittle will by no
means pass from the law till all
is fulfilled. 19Whoever therefore breaks one of the least
of these commandments,
and teaches men so, shall be
called least in the kingdom
of heaven; but whoever does
and teaches *them*, he shall be
called great in the kingdom
of heaven. 20For I say to you,
that unless your righteousness exceeds *the righteousness*
of the scribes and Pharisees,
you will by no means enter the
kingdom of heaven.

MURDER BEGINS IN THE HEART

21"You have heard that it
was said to those of old, 'You
shall not murder,[a] and whoever murders will be in danger
of the judgment.' 22But I say
to you that whoever is angry
with his brother without a
cause[a] shall be in danger of
the judgment. And whoever
says to his brother, 'Raca!'
shall be in danger of the council. But whoever says, 'You
fool!' shall be in danger of hell
fire. 23Therefore if you bring
your gift to the altar, and there
remember that your brother
has something against you,
24leave your gift there before
the altar, and go your way.
First be reconciled to your
brother, and then come and
offer your gift. 25Agree with
your adversary quickly, while
you are on the way with him,
lest your adversary deliver

5:21 [a] Exodus 20:13; Deuteronomy 5:17
5:22 [a] NU-Text omits *without a cause.*

you to the judge, the judge
hand you over to the officer, and you be thrown into
prison. 26Assuredly, I say to
you, you will by no means get
out of there till you have paid
the last penny.

ADULTERY IN THE HEART

27"You have heard that it
was said to those of old,[a] 'You
shall not commit adultery.'[b]
28But I say to you that whoever looks at a woman to lust
for her has already committed
adultery with her in his heart.
29If your right eye causes you
to sin, pluck it out and cast
it from you; for it is more
profitable for you that one of
your members perish, than
for your whole body to be cast
into hell. 30And if your right
hand causes you to sin, cut it
off and cast *it* from you; for it
is more profitable for you that
one of your members perish,
than for your whole body to
be cast into hell.

MARRIAGE IS SACRED AND BINDING

31"Furthermore it has been
said, 'Whoever divorces his
wife, let him give her a certificate of divorce.' 32But I say
to you that whoever divorces
his wife for any reason except
sexual immorality[a] causes
her to commit adultery; and
whoever marries a woman
who is divorced commits
adultery.

JESUS FORBIDS OATHS

33"Again you have heard
that it was said to those of old,
'You shall not swear falsely,
but shall perform your oaths
to the Lord.' 34But I say to you,
do not swear at all: neither by
heaven, for it is God's throne;
35nor by the earth, for it is His
footstool; nor by Jerusalem,
for it is the city of the great
King. 36Nor shall you swear by
your head, because you cannot make one hair white or
black. 37But let your 'Yes' be
'Yes,' and your 'No,' 'No.' For
whatever is more than these
is from the evil one.

GO THE SECOND MILE

38"You have heard that it
was said, 'An eye for an eye
and a tooth for a tooth.'[a] 39But
I tell you not to resist an evil
person. But whoever slaps you
on your right cheek, turn the
other to him also. 40If anyone wants to sue you and
take away your tunic, let him
have *your* cloak also. 41And
whoever compels you to go
one mile, go with him two.
42Give to him who asks you,
and from him who wants to
borrow from you do not turn
away.

5:27 [a] NU-Text and M-Text omit *to those of old.* [b] Exodus 20:14; Deuteronomy 5:18 **5:32** [a] Or *fornication* **5:38** [a] Exodus 21:24; Leviticus 24:20; Deuteronomy 19:21

LOVE YOUR ENEMIES

43"You have heard that it
was said, 'You shall love your
neighbor[a] and hate your
enemy.' 44But I say to you, love
your enemies, bless those who
curse you, do good to those
who hate you, and pray for
those who spitefully use you
and persecute you,[a] 45that you
may be sons of your Father
in heaven; for He makes His
sun rise on the evil and on the
good, and sends rain on the
just and on the unjust. 46For if
you love those who love you,
what reward have you? Do not
even the tax collectors do the
same? 47And if you greet your
brethren[a] only, what do you
do more *than others?* Do not
even the tax collectors[b] do
so? 48Therefore you shall be
perfect, just as your Father in
heaven is perfect.

DO GOOD TO PLEASE GOD

6 "Take heed that you do
not do your charitable
deeds before men, to be seen
by them. Otherwise you have
no reward from your Father
in heaven. 2Therefore, when
you do a charitable deed, do
not sound a trumpet before
you as the hypocrites do in
the synagogues and in the
streets, that they may have
glory from men. Assuredly,
I say to you, they have their
reward. 3But when you do a
charitable deed, do not let
your left hand know what your
right hand is doing, 4that your
charitable deed may be in secret; and your Father who sees
in secret will Himself reward
you openly.[a]

THE MODEL PRAYER

5"And when you pray, you
shall not be like the hypocrites. For they love to pray
standing in the synagogues
and on the corners of the
streets, that they may be seen
by men. Assuredly, I say to
you, they have their reward.
6But you, when you pray, go
into your room, and when you
have shut your door, pray to
your Father who *is* in the secret *place;* and your Father
who sees in secret will reward
you openly.[a] 7And when you
pray, do not use vain repeti-
tions as the heathen *do.* For
they think that they will be
heard for their many words.

8"Therefore do not be like
them. For your Father knows
the things you have need of
before you ask Him. 9In this
manner, therefore, pray:

Our Father in heaven,
Hallowed be Your name.
10 Your kingdom come.

5:43 [a] Compare Leviticus 19:18 5:44 [a] NU-Text omits three clauses from this verse, leaving, *"But I say to you, love your enemies and pray for those who persecute you."* 5:47 [a] M-Text reads *friends.* [b] NU-Text reads *Gentiles.* 6:4 [a] NU-Text omits *openly.* 6:6 [a] NU-Text omits *openly.*

Your will be done
On earth as *it is*
in heaven.
11 Give us this day our
daily bread.
12 And forgive us our debts,
As we forgive our debtors.
13 And do not lead us
into temptation,
But deliver us from
the evil one.
For Yours is the kingdom
and the power and
the glory forever.
Amen.[a]

14“For if you forgive men
their trespasses, your heavenly Father will also forgive
you. 15But if you do not forgive
men their trespasses, neither
will your Father forgive your
trespasses.

FASTING TO BE SEEN ONLY BY GOD

16“Moreover, when you fast,
do not be like the hypocrites,
with a sad countenance. For
they disfigure their faces that
they may appear to men to be
fasting. Assuredly, I say to you,
they have their reward. 17But
you, when you fast, anoint
your head and wash your face,
18so that you do not appear to
men to be fasting, but to your
Father who *is* in the secret
place; and your Father who
sees in secret will reward you
openly.[a]

LAY UP TREASURES IN HEAVEN

19“Do not lay up for yourselves treasures on earth,
where moth and rust destroy
and where thieves break in and
steal; 20but lay up for yourselves treasures in heaven,
where neither moth nor rust
destroys and where thieves do
not break in and steal. 21For
where your treasure is, there
your heart will be also.

THE LAMP OF THE BODY

22“The lamp of the body
is the eye. If therefore your
eye is good, your whole body
will be full of light. 23But if
your eye is bad, your whole
body will be full of darkness.
If therefore the light that is in
you is darkness, how great *is*
that darkness!

YOU CANNOT SERVE GOD AND RICHES

24“No one can serve two
masters; for either he will hate
the one and love the other, or
else he will be loyal to the one
and despise the other. You cannot serve God and mammon.

DO NOT WORRY

25“Therefore I say to you,
do not worry about your life,
what you will eat or what you
will drink; nor about your
body, what you will put on. Is
not life more than food and

6:13 [a] NU-Text omits *For Yours* through *Amen.*
6:18 [a] NU-Text and M-Text omit *openly.*

the body more than clothing?
[26]Look at the birds of the air,
for they neither sow nor reap
nor gather into barns; yet your
heavenly Father feeds them.
Are you not of more value
than they? [27]Which of you by
worrying can add one cubit
to his stature?
[28]"So why do you worry
about clothing? Consider the
lilies of the field, how they
grow: they neither toil nor
spin; [29]and yet I say to you
that even Solomon in all his
glory was not arrayed like
one of these. [30]Now if God so
clothes the grass of the field,
which today is, and tomorrow
is thrown into the oven, *will
He* not much more *clothe* you,
O you of little faith?
[31]"Therefore do not worry,
saying, 'What shall we eat?'
or 'What shall we drink?' or
'What shall we wear?' [32]For
after all these things the Gentiles seek. For your heavenly
Father knows that you need
all these things. [33]But seek
first the kingdom of God and
His righteousness, and all
these things shall be added to
you. [34]Therefore do not worry
about tomorrow, for tomorrow will worry about its own
things. Sufficient for the day
is its own trouble.

DO NOT JUDGE

7 "Judge not, that you be
not judged. [2]For with
what judgment you judge,
you will be judged; and with
the measure you use, it will
be measured back to you.
[3]And why do you look at the
speck in your brother's eye,
but do not consider the plank
in your own eye? [4]Or how can
you say to your brother, 'Let
me remove the speck from
your eye'; and look, a plank *is*
in your own eye? [5]Hypocrite!
First remove the plank from
your own eye, and then you
will see clearly to remove the
speck from your brother's eye.
[6]"Do not give what is holy
to the dogs; nor cast your
pearls before swine, lest they
trample them under their
feet, and turn and tear you in
pieces.

KEEP ASKING, SEEKING, KNOCKING

[7]"Ask, and it will be given
to you; seek, and you will
find; knock, and it will be
opened to you. [8]For everyone
who asks receives, and he who
seeks finds, and to him who
knocks it will be opened. [9]Or
what man is there among you
who, if his son asks for bread,
will give him a stone? [10]Or if
he asks for a fish, will he give
him a serpent? [11]If you then,
being evil, know how to give
good gifts to your children,
how much more will your
Father who is in heaven give
good things to those who ask
Him! [12]Therefore, whatever
you want men to do to you,
do also to them, for this is the
Law and the Prophets.

THE NARROW WAY

13“Enter by the narrow
gate; for wide *is* the gate and
broad *is* the way that leads
to destruction, and there are
many who go in by it. 14Be-
cause[a] narrow *is* the gate and
difficult *is* the way which leads
to life, and there are few who
find it.

YOU WILL KNOW THEM BY THEIR FRUITS

15“Beware of false prophets,
who come to you in sheep’s
clothing, but inwardly they
are ravenous wolves. 16You
will know them by their fruits.
Do men gather grapes from
thornbushes or figs from thistles? 17Even so, every good
tree bears good fruit, but a
bad tree bears bad fruit. 18A
good tree cannot bear bad
fruit, nor *can* a bad tree bear
good fruit. 19Every tree that
does not bear good fruit is cut
down and thrown into the fire.
20Therefore by their fruits you
will know them.

I NEVER KNEW YOU

21“Not everyone who says
to Me, ‘Lord, Lord,’ shall enter
the kingdom of heaven, but
he who does the will of My Father in heaven. 22Many will
say to Me in that day, ‘Lord,
Lord, have we not prophe-
sied in Your name, cast out
demons in Your name, and
done many wonders in Your
name?’ 23And then I will declare to them, ‘I never knew
you; depart from Me, you who
practice lawlessness!’

BUILD ON THE ROCK

24“Therefore whoever
hears these sayings of Mine,
and does them, I will liken
him to a wise man who built
his house on the rock: 25and
the rain descended, the floods
came, and the winds blew and
beat on that house; and it did
not fall, for it was founded on
the rock.
26“But everyone who hears
these sayings of Mine, and
does not do them, will be like
a foolish man who built his
house on the sand: 27and the
rain descended, the floods
came, and the winds blew and
beat on that house; and it fell.
And great was its fall.”
28And so it was, when Jesus
had ended these sayings, that
the people were astonished at
His teaching, 29for He taught
them as one having authority,
and not as the scribes.

JESUS CLEANSES A LEPER

8 When He had come down
from the mountain, great
multitudes followed Him.
2And behold, a leper came
and worshiped Him, saying,
“Lord, if You are willing, You
can make me clean.”
3Then Jesus put out *His*
hand and touched him, saying,

7:14 [a] NU-Text and M-Text read *How . . . !*

"I am willing; be cleansed."
Immediately his leprosy was
cleansed.
4And Jesus said to him,
"See that you tell no one; but
go your way, show yourself to
the priest, and offer the gift
that Moses commanded, as a
testimony to them."

JESUS HEALS A CENTURION'S SERVANT

5Now when Jesus had en-
tered Capernaum, a centurion
came to Him, pleading with
Him, 6saying, "Lord, my servant is lying at home paralyzed, dreadfully tormented."
7And Jesus said to him, "I
will come and heal him."
8The centurion answered
and said, "Lord, I am not worthy that You should come
under my roof. But only speak
a word, and my servant will
be healed. 9For I also am a
man under authority, having
soldiers under me. And I say
to this *one,* 'Go,' and he goes;
and to another, 'Come,' and he
comes; and to my servant, 'Do
this,' and he does *it.*"
10When Jesus heard *it,* He
marveled, and said to those
who followed, "Assuredly, I say
to you, I have not found such
great faith, not even in Israel!
11And I say to you that many
will come from east and west,
and sit down with Abraham,
Isaac, and Jacob in the kingdom of heaven. 12But the sons
of the kingdom will be cast out
into outer darkness. There will
be weeping and gnashing of
teeth." 13Then Jesus said to the
centurion, "Go your way; and
as you have believed, *so* let it be
done for you." And his servant
was healed that same hour.

PETER'S MOTHER-IN-LAW HEALED

14Now when Jesus had
come into Peter's house, He
saw his wife's mother lying
sick with a fever. 15So He
touched her hand, and the
fever left her. And she arose
and served them.[a]

MANY HEALED IN THE EVENING

16When evening had come,
they brought to Him many
who were demon-possessed.
And He cast out the spirits
with a word, and healed all
who were sick, 17that it might
be fulfilled which was spoken
by Isaiah the prophet, saying:

"He Himself took
our infirmities
And bore *our* sicknesses."[a]

THE COST OF DISCIPLESHIP

18And when Jesus saw great
multitudes about Him, He
gave a command to depart to
the other side. 19Then a certain scribe came and said to
Him, "Teacher, I will follow
You wherever You go."

8:15 [a] NU-Text and M-Text read *Him.* 8:17 [a] Isaiah 53:4

20And Jesus said to him,
"Foxes have holes and birds
of the air *have* nests, but the
Son of Man has nowhere to
lay *His* head."
21Then another of His disciples said to Him, "Lord, let me
first go and bury my father."
22But Jesus said to him,
"Follow Me, and let the dead
bury their own dead."

WIND AND WAVE OBEY JESUS

23Now when He got into a
boat, His disciples followed
Him. 24And suddenly a great
tempest arose on the sea, so
that the boat was covered with
the waves. But He was asleep.
25Then His disciples came to
Him and awoke Him, saying,
"Lord, save us! We are perishing!"
26But He said to them,
"Why are you fearful, O you
of little faith?" Then He arose
and rebuked the winds and
the sea, and there was a great
calm. 27So the men marveled,
saying, "Who can this be, that
even the winds and the sea
obey Him?"

TWO DEMON-POSSESSED MEN HEALED

28When He had come to
the other side, to the country
of the Gergesenes,[a] there met
Him two demon-possessed
men, coming out of the tombs,
exceedingly fierce, so that
no one could pass that way.
29And suddenly they cried
out, saying, "What have we to
do with You, Jesus, You Son of
God? Have You come here to
torment us before the time?"
30Now a good way off from
them there was a herd of many
swine feeding. 31So the demons begged Him, saying, "If
You cast us out, permit us to go
away[a] into the herd of swine."
32And He said to them,
"Go." So when they had come
out, they went into the herd
of swine. And suddenly the
whole herd of swine ran violently down the steep place
into the sea, and perished in
the water.
33Then those who kept *them*
fled; and they went away into
the city and told everything,
including what *had happened*
to the demon-possessed *men.*
34And behold, the whole city
came out to meet Jesus. And
when they saw Him, they
begged *Him* to depart from
their region.

JESUS FORGIVES AND HEALS A PARALYTIC

9 So He got into a boat,
crossed over, and came to
His own city. 2Then behold,
they brought to Him a paralytic lying on a bed. When
Jesus saw their faith, He said
to the paralytic, "Son, be of
good cheer; your sins are forgiven you."

8:28 [a] NU-Text reads *Gadarenes.* 8:31 [a] NU-Text reads *send us.*

3And at once some of the
scribes said within themselves,
"This Man blasphemes!"
4But Jesus, knowing their
thoughts, said, "Why do you
think evil in your hearts? 5For
which is easier, to say, '*Your*
sins are forgiven you,' or to
say, 'Arise and walk'? 6But that
you may know that the Son
of Man has power on earth to
forgive sins"—then He said
to the paralytic, "Arise, take
up your bed, and go to your
house." 7And he arose and departed to his house.
8Now when the multitudes
saw *it,* they marveled[a] and
glorified God, who had given
such power to men.

MATTHEW THE TAX COLLECTOR

9As Jesus passed on from
there, He saw a man named
Matthew sitting at the tax
office. And He said to him,
"Follow Me." So he arose and
followed Him.
10Now it happened, as
Jesus sat at the table in the
house, *that* behold, many tax
collectors and sinners came
and sat down with Him and
His disciples. 11And when the
Pharisees saw *it,* they said to
His disciples, "Why does your
Teacher eat with tax collectors
and sinners?"
12When Jesus heard *that,*
He said to them, "Those who
are well have no need of a physician, but those who are sick.
13But go and learn what *this*
means: 'I desire mercy and
not sacrifice.'[a] For I did not
come to call the righteous, but
sinners, to repentance."[b]

JESUS IS QUESTIONED ABOUT FASTING

14Then the disciples of John
came to Him, saying, "Why
do we and the Pharisees fast
often,[a] but Your disciples do
not fast?"
15And Jesus said to them,
"Can the friends of the bridegroom mourn as long as the
bridegroom is with them?
But the days will come when
the bridegroom will be taken
away from them, and then
they will fast. 16No one puts
a piece of unshrunk cloth on
an old garment; for the patch
pulls away from the garment,
and the tear is made worse.
17Nor do they put new wine
into old wineskins, or else the
wineskins break, the wine is
spilled, and the wineskins are
ruined. But they put new wine
into new wineskins, and both
are preserved."

A GIRL RESTORED TO LIFE AND A WOMAN HEALED

18While He spoke these
things to them, behold, a ruler
came and worshiped Him,
saying, "My daughter has just

9:8 [a] NU-Text reads *were afraid.* 9:13 [a] Hosea 6:6 [b] NU-Text omits *to repentance.* 9:14 [a] NU-Text brackets *often* as disputed.

died, but come and lay Your
hand on her and she will live."
19So Jesus arose and followed
him, and so *did* His disciples.
20And suddenly, a woman
who had a flow of blood for
twelve years came from behind and touched the hem of
His garment. 21For she said to
herself, "If only I may touch
His garment, I shall be made
well." 22But Jesus turned
around, and when He saw her
He said, "Be of good cheer,
daughter; your faith has made
you well." And the woman was
made well from that hour.
23When Jesus came into
the ruler's house, and saw
the flute players and the noisy
crowd wailing, 24He said to
them, "Make room, for the
girl is not dead, but sleeping." And they ridiculed Him.
25But when the crowd was put
outside, He went in and took
her by the hand, and the girl
arose. 26And the report of this
went out into all that land.

TWO BLIND MEN HEALED

27When Jesus departed
from there, two blind men
followed Him, crying out and
saying, "Son of David, have
mercy on us!"
28And when He had come
into the house, the blind men
came to Him. And Jesus said
to them, "Do you believe that
I am able to do this?"
They said to Him, "Yes,
Lord."
29Then He touched their
eyes, saying, "According to
your faith let it be to you."
30And their eyes were opened.
And Jesus sternly warned
them, saying, "See *that* no
one knows *it*." 31But when they
had departed, they spread the
news about Him in all that
country.

A MUTE MAN SPEAKS

32As they went out, behold,
they brought to Him a man,
mute and demon-possessed.
33And when the demon was
cast out, the mute spoke. And
the multitudes marveled, saying, "It was never seen like this
in Israel!"
34But the Pharisees said,
"He casts out demons by the
ruler of the demons."

THE COMPASSION OF JESUS

35Then Jesus went about
all the cities and villages,
teaching in their synagogues,
preaching the gospel of the
kingdom, and healing every
sickness and every disease
among the people.[a] 36But
when He saw the multitudes,
He was moved with compas-
sion for them, because they
were weary[a] and scattered,
like sheep having no shepherd. 37Then He said to His

9:35 [a] NU-Text omits *among the people.*
9:36 [a] NU-Text and M-Text read *harassed.*

disciples, "The harvest truly
is plentiful, but the laborers
are few. 38Therefore pray the
Lord of the harvest to send
out laborers into His harvest."

THE TWELVE APOSTLES

10 And when He had
called His twelve dis-
ciples to *Him,* He gave them
power *over* unclean spirits,
to cast them out, and to heal
all kinds of sickness and all
kinds of disease. 2Now the
names of the twelve apostles
are these: first, Simon, who is
called Peter, and Andrew his
brother; James the *son* of Zebedee, and John his brother;
3Philip and Bartholomew;
Thomas and Matthew the
tax collector; James the *son*
of Alphaeus, and Lebbaeus,
whose surname was[a] Thaddaeus; 4Simon the Cananite,[a]
and Judas Iscariot, who also
betrayed Him.

SENDING OUT THE TWELVE

5These twelve Jesus sent
out and commanded them,
saying: "Do not go into the
way of the Gentiles, and do not
enter a city of the Samaritans.
6But go rather to the lost sheep
of the house of Israel. 7And as
you go, preach, saying, 'The
kingdom of heaven is at hand.'
8Heal the sick, cleanse the lepers, raise the dead,[a] cast out
demons. Freely you have received, freely give. 9Provide
neither gold nor silver nor
copper in your money belts,
10nor bag for *your* journey, nor
two tunics, nor sandals, nor
staffs; for a worker is worthy
of his food.

11"Now whatever city or
town you enter, inquire who in
it is worthy, and stay there till
you go out. 12And when you
go into a household, greet it.
13If the household is worthy,
let your peace come upon it.
But if it is not worthy, let your
peace return to you. 14And
whoever will not receive you
nor hear your words, when
you depart from that house
or city, shake off the dust from
your feet. 15Assuredly, I say
to you, it will be more tolerable for the land of Sodom
and Gomorrah in the day of
judgment than for that city!

PERSECUTIONS ARE COMING

16"Behold, I send you out as
sheep in the midst of wolves.
Therefore be wise as serpents
and harmless as doves. 17But
beware of men, for they will
deliver you up to councils
and scourge you in their synagogues. 18You will be brought
before governors and kings
for My sake, as a testimony
to them and to the Gentiles.

10:3 [a] NU-Text omits *Lebbaeus, whose surname was.*
10:4 [a] NU-Text reads *Cananaean.* 10:8 [a] NU-Text reads *raise the dead, cleanse the lepers;* M-Text omits *raise the dead.*

19But when they deliver you
up, do not worry about how
or what you should speak. For
it will be given to you in that
hour what you should speak;
20for it is not you who speak,
but the Spirit of your Father
who speaks in you.
21"Now brother will deliver
up brother to death, and a father *his* child; and children
will rise up against parents
and cause them to be put to
death. 22And you will be hated
by all for My name's sake. But
he who endures to the end will
be saved. 23When they persecute you in this city, flee to
another. For assuredly, I say
to you, you will not have gone
through the cities of Israel before the Son of Man comes.
24"A disciple is not above
his teacher, nor a servant
above his master. 25It is
enough for a disciple that he
be like his teacher, and a servant like his master. If they
have called the master of the
house Beelzebub,[a] how much
more *will they call* those of
his household! 26Therefore
do not fear them. For there is
nothing covered that will not
be revealed, and hidden that
will not be known.

JESUS TEACHES THE FEAR OF GOD

27"Whatever I tell you in
the dark, speak in the light;
and what you hear in the ear,
preach on the housetops.
28And do not fear those who
kill the body but cannot kill
the soul. But rather fear Him
who is able to destroy both
soul and body in hell. 29Are
not two sparrows sold for a
copper coin? And not one of
them falls to the ground apart
from your Father's will. 30But
the very hairs of your head are
all numbered. 31Do not fear
therefore; you are of more
value than many sparrows.

CONFESS CHRIST BEFORE MEN

32"Therefore whoever con-
fesses Me before men, him I
will also confess before My
Father who is in heaven. 33But
whoever denies Me before
men, him I will also deny
before My Father who is in
heaven.

CHRIST BRINGS DIVISION

34"Do not think that I came
to bring peace on earth. I did
not come to bring peace but
a sword. 35For I have come to
'set a man against his father, a
daughter against her mother,
and a daughter-in-law against
her mother-in-law'; 36and 'a
man's enemies *will be* those
of his *own* household.'[a] 37He
who loves father or mother
more than Me is not worthy of
Me. And he who loves son or
daughter more than Me is not
worthy of Me. 38And he who

10:25 [a] NU-Text and M-Text read *Beelzebul*. 10:36 [a] Micah 7:6

does not take his cross and
follow after Me is not worthy
of Me. 39He who finds his life
will lose it, and he who loses
his life for My sake will find it.

A CUP OF COLD WATER

40"He who receives you receives Me, and he who receives
Me receives Him who sent Me.
41He who receives a prophet in
the name of a prophet shall
receive a prophet's reward.
And he who receives a righteous man in the name of a
righteous man shall receive a
righteous man's reward. 42And
whoever gives one of these
little ones only a cup of cold
water in the name of a disciple,
assuredly, I say to you, he shall
by no means lose his reward."

JOHN THE BAPTIST SENDS MESSENGERS TO JESUS

11 Now it came to pass, when
Jesus finished command-
ing His twelve disciples, that
He departed from there to
teach and to preach in their
cities.

2And when John had heard
in prison about the works of
Christ, he sent two of[a] his disciples 3and said to Him, "Are
You the Coming One, or do we
look for another?"

4Jesus answered and said
to them, "Go and tell John the
things which you hear and see:
5*The* blind see and *the* lame
walk; *the* lepers are cleansed
and *the* deaf hear; *the* dead are
raised up and *the* poor have
the gospel preached to them.
6And blessed is he who is not
offended because of Me."

7As they departed, Jesus
began to say to the multitudes
concerning John: "What did
you go out into the wilderness
to see? A reed shaken by the
wind? 8But what did you go
out to see? A man clothed in
soft garments? Indeed, those
who wear soft *clothing* are in
kings' houses. 9But what did
you go out to see? A prophet?
Yes, I say to you, and more
than a prophet. 10For this is
he of whom it is written:

'Behold, I send My
messenger before
Your face,
Who will prepare Your
way before You.'[a]

11"Assuredly, I say to you,
among those born of women
there has not risen one greater
than John the Baptist; but he
who is least in the kingdom
of heaven is greater than he.
12And from the days of John
the Baptist until now the kingdom of heaven suffers violence, and the violent take it
by force. 13For all the prophets
and the law prophesied until
John. 14And if you are willing
to receive *it,* he is Elijah who
is to come. 15He who has ears
to hear, let him hear!

11:2 [a] NU-Text reads *by* for *two of.* 11:10 [a] Malachi 3:1

16"But to what shall I liken
this generation? It is like
children sitting in the marketplaces and calling to their
companions, 17and saying:

'We played the
flute for you,
And you did not dance;
We mourned to you,
And you did not lament.'

18For John came neither eating nor drinking, and they
say, 'He has a demon.' 19The
Son of Man came eating and
drinking, and they say, 'Look,
a glutton and a winebibber, a
friend of tax collectors and
sinners!' But wisdom is justified by her children."[a]

WOE TO THE IMPENITENT CITIES

20Then He began to rebuke
the cities in which most of His
mighty works had been done,
because they did not repent:
21"Woe to you, Chorazin! Woe
to you, Bethsaida! For if the
mighty works which were
done in you had been done
in Tyre and Sidon, they would
have repented long ago in
sackcloth and ashes. 22But I
say to you, it will be more tolerable for Tyre and Sidon in
the day of judgment than for
you. 23And you, Capernaum,
who are exalted to heaven,
will be[a] brought down to
Hades; for if the mighty works
which were done in you had
been done in Sodom, it would
have remained until this day.
24But I say to you that it shall
be more tolerable for the land
of Sodom in the day of judgment than for you."

JESUS GIVES TRUE REST

25At that time Jesus an-
swered and said, "I thank You,
Father, Lord of heaven and
earth, that You have hidden
these things from *the* wise and
prudent and have revealed
them to babes. 26Even so, Father, for so it seemed good in
Your sight. 27All things have
been delivered to Me by My
Father, and no one knows the
Son except the Father. Nor
does anyone know the Fa-
ther except the Son, and *the
one* to whom the Son wills to
reveal *Him.* 28Come to Me, all
you who labor and are heavy
laden, and I will give you rest.
29Take My yoke upon you and
learn from Me, for I am gentle
and lowly in heart, and you
will find rest for your souls.
30For My yoke *is* easy and My
burden is light."

JESUS IS LORD OF THE SABBATH

12 At that time Jesus went
through the grainfields
on the Sabbath. And His disciples were hungry, and began

11:19 [a] NU-Text reads *works.* 11:23 [a] NU-Text reads *will you be exalted to heaven? No, you will be.*

to pluck heads of grain and to
eat. 2And when the Pharisees
saw *it,* they said to Him, "Look,
Your disciples are doing what
is not lawful to do on the Sabbath!"

3But He said to them, "Have
you not read what David did
when he was hungry, he and
those who were with him:
4how he entered the house of
God and ate the showbread
which was not lawful for him
to eat, nor for those who were
with him, but only for the
priests? 5Or have you not read
in the law that on the Sabbath
the priests in the temple profane the Sabbath, and are
blameless? 6Yet I say to you
that in this place there is *One*
greater than the temple. 7But
if you had known what *this*
means, 'I desire mercy and
not sacrifice,'[a] you would not
have condemned the guiltless.
8For the Son of Man is Lord
even[a] of the Sabbath."

HEALING ON THE SABBATH

9Now when He had de-
parted from there, He went
into their synagogue. 10And
behold, there was a man who
had a withered hand. And they
asked Him, saying, "Is it lawful to heal on the Sabbath?"—
that they might accuse Him.

11Then He said to them,
"What man is there among
you who has one sheep, and
if it falls into a pit on the Sabbath, will not lay hold of it
and lift *it* out? 12Of how much
more value then is a man than
a sheep? Therefore it is lawful
to do good on the Sabbath."
13Then He said to the man,
"Stretch out your hand." And
he stretched *it* out, and it was
restored as whole as the other.
14Then the Pharisees went out
and plotted against Him, how
they might destroy Him.

BEHOLD, MY SERVANT

15But when Jesus knew *it,*
He withdrew from there. And
great multitudes[a] followed
Him, and He healed them all.
16Yet He warned them not to
make Him known, 17that it
might be fulfilled which was
spoken by Isaiah the prophet,
saying:

18"Behold! My Servant
whom I have chosen,
My Beloved in whom My
soul is well pleased!
I will put My Spirit
upon Him,
And He will declare
justice to the Gentiles.
19 He will not quarrel
nor cry out,
Nor will anyone hear His
voice in the streets.
20 A bruised reed He
will not break,
And smoking flax He
will not quench,

12:7 [a] Hosea 6:6 12:8 [a] NU-Text and M-Text omit *even.*
12:15 [a] NU-Text brackets *multitudes* as disputed.

Till He sends forth
justice to victory;
21 And in His name
Gentiles will trust."[a]

A HOUSE DIVIDED CANNOT STAND

22Then one was brought
to Him who was demon-
possessed, blind and mute;
and He healed him, so that
the blind and[a] mute man both
spoke and saw. 23And all the
multitudes were amazed and
said, "Could this be the Son of
David?"
24Now when the Pharisees
heard *it* they said, "This *fellow*
does not cast out demons except by Beelzebub,[a] the ruler
of the demons."
25But Jesus knew their
thoughts, and said to them:
"Every kingdom divided
against itself is brought to
desolation, and every city
or house divided against itself will not stand. 26If Satan
casts out Satan, he is divided
against himself. How then will
his kingdom stand? 27And if
I cast out demons by Beelzebub, by whom do your sons
cast *them* out? Therefore they
shall be your judges. 28But if I
cast out demons by the Spirit
of God, surely the kingdom of
God has come upon you. 29Or
how can one enter a strong
man's house and plunder his
goods, unless he first binds
the strong man? And then
he will plunder his house.
30He who is not with Me is
against Me, and he who does
not gather with Me scatters
abroad.

THE UNPARDONABLE SIN

31"Therefore I say to you,
every sin and blasphemy
will be forgiven men, but the
blasphemy *against* the Spirit
will not be forgiven men.
32Anyone who speaks a word
against the Son of Man, it will
be forgiven him; but whoever
speaks against the Holy Spirit,
it will not be forgiven him, either in this age or in the *age*
to come.

A TREE KNOWN BY ITS FRUIT

33"Either make the tree
good and its fruit good, or
else make the tree bad and its
fruit bad; for a tree is known
by *its* fruit. 34Brood of vipers!
How can you, being evil, speak
good things? For out of the
abundance of the heart the
mouth speaks. 35A good man
out of the good treasure of
his heart[a] brings forth good
things, and an evil man out of
the evil treasure brings forth
evil things. 36But I say to you
that for every idle word men
may speak, they will give ac-

12:21 [a] Isaiah 42:1–4 12:22 [a] NU-Text omits *blind and.* 12:24 [a] NU-Text and M-Text read *Beelzebul.* 12:35 [a] NU-Text and M-Text omit *of his heart.*

count of it in the day of judgment. 37For by your words
you will be justified, and by
your words you will be condemned."

THE SCRIBES AND PHARISEES ASK FOR A SIGN

38Then some of the scribes
and Pharisees answered, saying, "Teacher, we want to see
a sign from You."
39But He answered and
said to them, "An evil and
adulterous generation seeks
after a sign, and no sign will
be given to it except the sign
of the prophet Jonah. 40For
as Jonah was three days and
three nights in the belly of the
great fish, so will the Son of
Man be three days and three
nights in the heart of the earth.
41The men of Nineveh will rise
up in the judgment with this
generation and condemn it,
because they repented at the
preaching of Jonah; and indeed a greater than Jonah *is*
here. 42The queen of the South
will rise up in the judgment
with this generation and condemn it, for she came from
the ends of the earth to hear
the wisdom of Solomon; and
indeed a greater than Solomon *is* here.

AN UNCLEAN SPIRIT RETURNS

43"When an unclean spirit
goes out of a man, he goes
through dry places, seeking
rest, and finds none. 44Then
he says, 'I will return to my
house from which I came.'
And when he comes, he finds
it empty, swept, and put in
order. 45Then he goes and
takes with him seven other
spirits more wicked than himself, and they enter and dwell
there; and the last *state* of that
man is worse than the first.
So shall it also be with this
wicked generation."

JESUS' MOTHER AND BROTHERS SEND FOR HIM

46While He was still talking
to the multitudes, behold, His
mother and brothers stood
outside, seeking to speak with
Him. 47Then one said to Him,
"Look, Your mother and Your
brothers are standing outside,
seeking to speak with You."
48But He answered and
said to the one who told Him,
"Who is My mother and who
are My brothers?" 49And He
stretched out His hand toward His disciples and said,
"Here are My mother and My
brothers! 50For whoever does
the will of My Father in heaven
is My brother and sister and
mother."

THE PARABLE OF THE SOWER

13 On the same day Jesus
went out of the house
and sat by the sea. 2And great
multitudes were gathered together to Him, so that He got

into a boat and sat; and the
whole multitude stood on the
shore.
3 Then He spoke many
things to them in parables,
saying: "Behold, a sower went
out to sow. 4 And as he sowed,
some *seed* fell by the wayside;
and the birds came and devoured them. 5 Some fell on
stony places, where they did
not have much earth; and they
immediately sprang up be-
cause they had no depth of
earth. 6 But when the sun was
up they were scorched, and
because they had no root they
withered away. 7 And some
fell among thorns, and the
thorns sprang up and choked
them. 8 But others fell on good
ground and yielded a crop:
some a hundredfold, some
sixty, some thirty. 9 He who
has ears to hear, let him hear!"

THE PURPOSE OF PARABLES

10 And the disciples came
and said to Him, "Why do You
speak to them in parables?"
11 He answered and said to
them, "Because it has been
given to you to know the
mysteries of the kingdom of
heaven, but to them it has not
been given. 12 For whoever has,
to him more will be given, and
he will have abundance; but
whoever does not have, even
what he has will be taken away
from him. 13 Therefore I speak
to them in parables, because
seeing they do not see, and
hearing they do not hear, nor
do they understand. 14 And in
them the prophecy of Isaiah
is fulfilled, which says:

'Hearing you will hear
and shall not
understand,
And seeing you will see
and not perceive;
15 For the hearts of this
people have grown dull.
Their ears are hard
of hearing,
And their eyes they
have closed,
Lest they should see
with *their* eyes and
hear with *their* ears,
Lest they should
understand with *their*
hearts and turn,
So that I should[a]
heal them.'[b]

16 But blessed *are* your eyes
for they see, and your ears for
they hear; 17 for assuredly, I
say to you that many prophets
and righteous *men* desired to
see what you see, and did not
see *it*, and to hear what you
hear, and did not hear *it*.

THE PARABLE OF THE SOWER EXPLAINED

18 "Therefore hear the parable of the sower: 19 When
anyone hears the word of
the kingdom, and does not

13:15 [a] NU-Text and M-Text read *would*. [b] Isaiah 6:9, 10

understand *it,* then the wicked
one comes and snatches away
what was sown in his heart.
This is he who received seed
by the wayside. 20But he who
received the seed on stony
places, this is he who hears
the word and immediately
receives it with joy; 21yet he
has no root in himself, but
endures only for a while. For
when tribulation or persecution arises because of the
word, immediately he stumbles. 22Now he who received
seed among the thorns is he
who hears the word, and the
cares of this world and the
deceitfulness of riches choke
the word, and he becomes unfruitful. 23But he who received
seed on the good ground is
he who hears the word and
understands *it,* who indeed
bears fruit and produces:
some a hundredfold, some
sixty, some thirty."

THE PARABLE OF THE WHEAT AND THE TARES

24Another parable He put
forth to them, saying: "The
kingdom of heaven is like a
man who sowed good seed
in his field; 25but while men
slept, his enemy came and
sowed tares among the wheat
and went his way. 26But when
the grain had sprouted and
produced a crop, then the
tares also appeared. 27So the
servants of the owner came
and said to him, 'Sir, did you
not sow good seed in your
field? How then does it have
tares?' 28He said to them, 'An
enemy has done this.' The
servants said to him, 'Do you
want us then to go and gather
them up?' 29But he said, 'No,
lest while you gather up the
tares you also uproot the
wheat with them. 30Let both
grow together until the harvest, and at the time of harvest
I will say to the reapers, "First
gather together the tares and
bind them in bundles to burn
them, but gather the wheat
into my barn." ' "

THE PARABLE OF THE MUSTARD SEED

31Another parable He put
forth to them, saying: "The
kingdom of heaven is like a
mustard seed, which a man
took and sowed in his field,
32which indeed is the least of
all the seeds; but when it is
grown it is greater than the
herbs and becomes a tree, so
that the birds of the air come
and nest in its branches."

THE PARABLE OF THE LEAVEN

33Another parable He
spoke to them: "The kingdom
of heaven is like leaven, which
a woman took and hid in three
measures[a] of meal till it was
all leavened."

13:33 [a] Greek *sata,* approximately two pecks in all

PROPHECY AND THE PARABLES

34 All these things Jesus spoke to the multitude in parables; and without a parable He did not speak to them, 35 that it might be fulfilled which was spoken by the prophet, saying:

"I will open My mouth
in parables;
I will utter things
kept secret from
the foundation
of the world."[a]

THE PARABLE OF THE TARES EXPLAINED

36 Then Jesus sent the multitude away and went into the house. And His disciples came to Him, saying, "Explain to us the parable of the tares of the field."

37 He answered and said to them: "He who sows the good seed is the Son of Man. 38 The field is the world, the good seeds are the sons of the kingdom, but the tares are the sons of the wicked *one.* 39 The enemy who sowed them is the devil, the harvest is the end of the age, and the reapers are the angels. 40 Therefore as the tares are gathered and burned in the fire, so it will be at the end of this age. 41 The Son of Man will send out His angels, and they will gather out of His kingdom all things that offend, and those who practice lawlessness, 42 and will cast them into the furnace of fire. There will be wailing and gnashing of teeth. 43 Then the righteous will shine forth as the sun in the kingdom of their Father. He who has ears to hear, let him hear!

THE PARABLE OF THE HIDDEN TREASURE

44 "Again, the kingdom of heaven is like treasure hidden in a field, which a man found and hid; and for joy over it he goes and sells all that he has and buys that field.

THE PARABLE OF THE PEARL OF GREAT PRICE

45 "Again, the kingdom of heaven is like a merchant seeking beautiful pearls, 46 who, when he had found one pearl of great price, went and sold all that he had and bought it.

THE PARABLE OF THE DRAGNET

47 "Again, the kingdom of heaven is like a dragnet that was cast into the sea and gathered some of every kind, 48 which, when it was full, they drew to shore; and they sat down and gathered the good into vessels, but threw the bad away. 49 So it will be at the end of the age. The angels

13:35 [a] Psalm 78:2

will come forth, separate the
wicked from among the just,
50and cast them into the furnace of fire. There will be wailing and gnashing of teeth."
51Jesus said to them,[a]
"Have you understood all
these things?"
They said to Him, "Yes,
Lord."[b]
52Then He said to them,
"Therefore every scribe instructed concerning[a] the
kingdom of heaven is like a
householder who brings out
of his treasure *things* new and
old."

JESUS REJECTED AT NAZARETH

53Now it came to pass,
when Jesus had finished these
parables, that He departed
from there. 54When He had
come to His own country, He
taught them in their synagogue, so that they were astonished and said, "Where did
this *Man* get this wisdom and
these mighty works? 55Is this
not the carpenter's son? Is not
His mother called Mary? And
His brothers James, Joses,[a]
Simon, and Judas? 56And His
sisters, are they not all with
us? Where then did this *Man*
get all these things?" 57So they
were offended at Him.
But Jesus said to them, "A
prophet is not without honor
except in his own country and
in his own house." 58Now He
did not do many mighty works
there because of their unbelief.

JOHN THE BAPTIST BEHEADED

14 At that time Herod the
tetrarch heard the re-
port about Jesus 2and said
to his servants, "This is John
the Baptist; he is risen from
the dead, and therefore these
powers are at work in him."
3For Herod had laid hold of
John and bound him, and put
him in prison for the sake of
Herodias, his brother Philip's
wife. 4Because John had said
to him, "It is not lawful for you
to have her." 5And although he
wanted to put him to death,
he feared the multitude, because they counted him as a
prophet.
6But when Herod's birthday
was celebrated, the daughter
of Herodias danced before
them and pleased Herod.
7Therefore he promised with
an oath to give her whatever
she might ask.
8So she, having been
prompted by her mother, said,
"Give me John the Baptist's
head here on a platter."
9And the king was sorry;
nevertheless, because of the
oaths and because of those
who sat with him, he com-
manded *it* to be given to *her*.

13:51 [a] NU-Text omits *Jesus said to them.* [b] NU-Text omits *Lord.* 13:52 [a] Or *for* 13:55 [a] NU-Text reads *Joseph.*

10So he sent and had John beheaded in prison. 11And his
head was brought on a platter and given to the girl, and
she brought *it* to her mother.
12Then his disciples came and
took away the body and buried it, and went and told Jesus.

FEEDING THE FIVE THOUSAND

13When Jesus heard *it,* He
departed from there by boat
to a deserted place by Himself. But when the multitudes
heard it, they followed Him
on foot from the cities. 14And
when Jesus went out He saw a
great multitude; and He was
moved with compassion for
them, and healed their sick.
15When it was evening, His
disciples came to Him, saying,
"This is a deserted place, and
the hour is already late. Send
the multitudes away, that they
may go into the villages and
buy themselves food."

16But Jesus said to them,
"They do not need to go away.
You give them something to
eat."

17And they said to Him, "We
have here only five loaves and
two fish."

18He said, "Bring them here
to Me." 19Then He commanded
the multitudes to sit down on
the grass. And He took the
five loaves and the two fish,
and looking up to heaven, He
blessed and broke and gave
the loaves to the disciples; and
the disciples gave to the multitudes. 20So they all ate and
were filled, and they took up
twelve baskets full of the fragments that remained. 21Now
those who had eaten were
about five thousand men,
besides women and children.

JESUS WALKS ON THE SEA

22Immediately Jesus made
His disciples get into the
boat and go before Him to
the other side, while He sent
the multitudes away. 23And
when He had sent the multitudes away, He went up on the
mountain by Himself to pray.
Now when evening came, He
was alone there. 24But the
boat was now in the middle of
the sea,[a] tossed by the waves,
for the wind was contrary.

25Now in the fourth watch of
the night Jesus went to them,
walking on the sea. 26And
when the disciples saw Him
walking on the sea, they were
troubled, saying, "It is a ghost!"
And they cried out for fear.

27But immediately Jesus
spoke to them, saying, "Be of
good cheer! It is I; do not be
afraid."

28And Peter answered Him
and said, "Lord, if it is You,
command me to come to You
on the water."

29So He said, "Come." And
when Peter had come down
out of the boat, he walked on

14:24 [a] NU-Text reads *many furlongs away from the land.*

the water to go to Jesus. 30But
when he saw that the wind *was*
boisterous,[a] he was afraid; and
beginning to sink he cried out,
saying, "Lord, save me!"
31And immediately Jesus
stretched out *His* hand and
caught him, and said to him,
"O you of little faith, why did
you doubt?" 32And when they
got into the boat, the wind
ceased.
33Then those who were in
the boat came and[a] worshiped
Him, saying, "Truly You are
the Son of God."

MANY TOUCH HIM AND ARE MADE WELL

34When they had crossed
over, they came to the land
of[a] Gennesaret. 35And when
the men of that place recognized Him, they sent out into
all that surrounding region,
brought to Him all who were
sick, 36and begged Him that
they might only touch the
hem of His garment. And as
many as touched *it* were made
perfectly well.

DEFILEMENT COMES FROM WITHIN

15 Then the scribes and
Pharisees who were from
Jerusalem came to Jesus, saying, 2"Why do Your disciples
transgress the tradition of the
elders? For they do not wash
their hands when they eat
bread."
3He answered and said to
them, "Why do you also transgress the commandment of
God because of your tradition?
4For God commanded, saying,
'Honor your father and your
mother';[a] and, 'He who curses
father or mother, let him be
put to death.'[b] 5But you say,
'Whoever says to his father
or mother, "Whatever profit
you might have received from
me *is* a gift *to God*"— 6then he
need not honor his father or
mother.'[a] Thus you have made
the commandment[b] of God
of no effect by your tradition.
7Hypocrites! Well did Isaiah
prophesy about you, saying:

8 'These people draw near
to Me with their mouth,
And[a] honor Me
with *their* lips,
But their heart is
far from Me.
9 And in vain they
worship Me,
Teaching *as* doctrines
the commandments
of men.'"[a]

10When He had called the
multitude to *Himself,* He said
to them, "Hear and under-
stand: 11Not what goes into

14:30 [a] NU-Text brackets *that* and *boisterous* as disputed.
14:33 [a] NU-Text omits *came and.* 14:34 [a] NU-Text reads *came to land at.* 15:4 [a] Exodus 20:12; Deuteronomy 5:16 [b] Exodus 21:17
15:6 [a] NU-Text omits *or mother.* [b] NU-Text reads *word.* 15:8 [a] NU-Text omits *draw near to Me with their mouth, And.* 15:9 [a] Isaiah 29:13

the mouth defiles a man; but what comes out of the mouth, this defiles a man."

12Then His disciples came and said to Him, "Do You know that the Pharisees were offended when they heard this saying?"

13But He answered and said, "Every plant which My heavenly Father has not planted will be uprooted. 14Let them alone. They are blind leaders of the blind. And if the blind leads the blind, both will fall into a ditch."

15Then Peter answered and said to Him, "Explain this parable to us."

16So Jesus said, "Are you also still without understanding? 17Do you not yet understand that whatever enters the mouth goes into the stomach and is eliminated? 18But those things which proceed out of the mouth come from the heart, and they defile a man. 19For out of the heart proceed evil thoughts, murders, adulteries, fornications, thefts, false witness, blasphemies. 20These are *the things* which defile a man, but to eat with unwashed hands does not defile a man."

A GENTILE SHOWS HER FAITH

21Then Jesus went out *from there and departed* to the region of Tyre and Sidon. 22And behold, a woman of Canaan came from that region and cried out to Him, saying, "Have mercy on me, O Lord, Son of David! My daughter is severely demon-possessed."

23But He answered her not a word.

And His disciples came and urged Him, saying, "Send her away, for she cries out after us."

24But He answered and said, "I was not sent except to the lost sheep of the house of Israel."

25Then she came and worshiped Him, saying, "Lord, help me!"

26But He answered and said, "It is not good to take the children's bread and throw *it* to the little dogs."

27And she said, "Yes, Lord, yet even the little dogs eat the crumbs which fall from their masters' table."

28Then Jesus answered and said to her, "O woman, great *is* your faith! Let it be to you as you desire." And her daughter was healed from that very hour.

JESUS HEALS GREAT MULTITUDES

29Jesus departed from there, skirted the Sea of Galilee, and went up on the mountain and sat down there. 30Then great multitudes came to Him, having with them *the* lame, blind, mute, maimed, *and many* others; and they laid them down at Jesus' feet, and He healed them. 31So the multitude marveled when they saw *the* mute speaking, *the* maimed

made whole, *the* lame walking,
and *the* blind seeing; and they
glorified the God of Israel.

FEEDING THE FOUR THOUSAND

32Now Jesus called His disciples to *Himself* and said, "I
have compassion on the multitude, because they have now
continued with Me three days
and have nothing to eat. And
I do not want to send them
away hungry, lest they faint
on the way."

33Then His disciples said
to Him, "Where could we get
enough bread in the wilderness to fill such a great multitude?"

34Jesus said to them, "How
many loaves do you have?"

And they said, "Seven, and
a few little fish."

35So He commanded the
multitude to sit down on the
ground. 36And He took the
seven loaves and the fish
and gave thanks, broke *them*
and gave *them* to His disciples; and the disciples *gave*
to the multitude. 37So they all
ate and were filled, and they
took up seven large baskets
full of the fragments that were
left. 38Now those who ate were
four thousand men, besides
women and children. 39And
He sent away the multitude,
got into the boat, and came to
the region of Magdala.[a]

THE PHARISEES AND SADDUCEES SEEK A SIGN

16 Then the Pharisees and
Sadducees came, and
testing Him asked that He
would show them a sign
from heaven. 2He answered
and said to them, "When it
is evening you say, '*It will be*
fair weather, for the sky is red';
3and in the morning, '*It will*
be foul weather today, for the
sky is red and threatening.'
Hypocrites![a] You know how to
discern the face of the sky, but
you cannot *discern* the signs
of the times. 4A wicked and
adulterous generation seeks
after a sign, and no sign shall
be given to it except the sign
of the prophet[a] Jonah." And
He left them and departed.

THE LEAVEN OF THE PHARISEES AND SADDUCEES

5Now when His disciples
had come to the other side,
they had forgotten to take
bread. 6Then Jesus said to
them, "Take heed and beware
of the leaven of the Pharisees
and the Sadducees."

7And they reasoned among
themselves, saying, "*It is* because we have taken no bread."

8But Jesus, being aware of
it, said to them, "O you of little faith, why do you reason
among yourselves because

15:39 [a] NU-Text reads *Magadan.* 16:3 [a] NU-Text omits *Hypocrites.* 16:4 [a] NU-Text omits *the prophet.*

you have brought no bread?[a]
9 Do you not yet understand,
or remember the five loaves
of the five thousand and how
many baskets you took up?
10 Nor the seven loaves of the
four thousand and how many
large baskets you took up?
11 How is it you do not understand that I did not speak to
you concerning bread?—*but*
to beware of the leaven of the
Pharisees and Sadducees."
12 Then they understood that
He did not tell *them* to beware
of the leaven of bread, but of
the doctrine of the Pharisees
and Sadducees.

PETER CONFESSES JESUS AS THE CHRIST

13 When Jesus came into the
region of Caesarea Philippi,
He asked His disciples, saying,
"Who do men say that I, the
Son of Man, am?"
14 So they said, "Some *say*
John the Baptist, some Elijah,
and others Jeremiah or one of
the prophets."
15 He said to them, "But who
do you say that I am?"
16 Simon Peter answered
and said, "You are the Christ,
the Son of the living God."
17 Jesus answered and said
to him, "Blessed are you,
Simon Bar-Jonah, for flesh and
blood has not revealed *this* to
you, but My Father who is in
heaven. 18 And I also say to you
that you are Peter, and on this
rock I will build My church,
and the gates of Hades shall
not prevail against it. 19 And
I will give you the keys of the
kingdom of heaven, and whatever you bind on earth will be
bound in heaven, and whatever you loose on earth will
be loosed[a] in heaven."
20 Then He commanded His
disciples that they should tell
no one that He was Jesus the
Christ.

JESUS PREDICTS HIS DEATH AND RESURRECTION

21 From that time Jesus
began to show to His disciples
that He must go to Jerusalem,
and suffer many things from
the elders and chief priests
and scribes, and be killed, and
be raised the third day.
22 Then Peter took Him
aside and began to rebuke
Him, saying, "Far be it from
You, Lord; this shall not happen to You!"
23 But He turned and said to
Peter, "Get behind Me, Satan!
You are an offense to Me, for
you are not mindful of the
things of God, but the things
of men."

TAKE UP THE CROSS AND FOLLOW HIM

24 Then Jesus said to His
disciples, "If anyone desires
to come after Me, let him deny

16:8 [a] NU-Text reads *you have no bread.* 16:19 [a] Or *will have been bound . . . will have been loosed*

himself, and take up his cross,
and follow Me. 25For whoever
desires to save his life will lose
it, but whoever loses his life for
My sake will find it. 26For what
profit is it to a man if he gains
the whole world, and loses his
own soul? Or what will a man
give in exchange for his soul?
27For the Son of Man will come
in the glory of His Father with
His angels, and then He will
reward each according to his
works. 28Assuredly, I say to
you, there are some standing
here who shall not taste death
till they see the Son of Man
coming in His kingdom."

JESUS TRANSFIGURED ON THE MOUNT

17 Now after six days Jesus
took Peter, James, and
John his brother, led them up
on a high mountain by themselves; 2and He was transfig-
ured before them. His face
shone like the sun, and His
clothes became as white as
the light. 3And behold, Moses
and Elijah appeared to them,
talking with Him. 4Then Peter
answered and said to Jesus,
"Lord, it is good for us to be
here; if You wish, let us[a] make
here three tabernacles: one
for You, one for Moses, and
one for Elijah."

5While he was still speaking,
behold, a bright cloud overshadowed them; and suddenly
a voice came out of the cloud,
saying, "This is My beloved Son,
in whom I am well pleased.
Hear Him!" 6And when the disciples heard *it,* they fell on their
faces and were greatly afraid.
7But Jesus came and touched
them and said, "Arise, and do
not be afraid." 8When they had
lifted up their eyes, they saw no
one but Jesus only.

9Now as they came down
from the mountain, Jesus
commanded them, saying,
"Tell the vision to no one until
the Son of Man is risen from
the dead."

10And His disciples asked
Him, saying, "Why then do the
scribes say that Elijah must
come first?"

11Jesus answered and said
to them, "Indeed, Elijah is
coming first[a] and will restore
all things. 12But I say to you
that Elijah has come already,
and they did not know him
but did to him whatever they
wished. Likewise the Son of
Man is also about to suffer at
their hands." 13Then the disciples understood that He spoke
to them of John the Baptist.

A BOY IS HEALED

14And when they had come
to the multitude, a *man* came
to Him, kneeling down to
Him and saying, 15"Lord,
have mercy on my son, for
he is an epileptic[a] and suffers

17:4 [a] NU-Text reads *I will.* 17:11 [a] NU-Text omits *first.* 17:15 [a] Literally *moonstruck*

severely; for he often falls into
the fire and often into the
water. 16So I brought him to
Your disciples, but they could
not cure him."
17Then Jesus answered and
said, "O faithless and perverse
generation, how long shall I
be with you? How long shall I
bear with you? Bring him here
to Me." 18And Jesus rebuked
the demon, and it came out of
him; and the child was cured
from that very hour.
19Then the disciples came
to Jesus privately and said,
"Why could we not cast it out?"
20So Jesus said to them,
"Because of your unbelief;[a]
for assuredly, I say to you,
if you have faith as a mustard seed, you will say to this
mountain, 'Move from here to
there,' and it will move; and
nothing will be impossible for
you. 21However, this kind does
not go out except by prayer
and fasting."[a]

JESUS AGAIN PREDICTS HIS DEATH AND RESURRECTION

22Now while they were
staying[a] in Galilee, Jesus said
to them, "The Son of Man is
about to be betrayed into the
hands of men, 23and they will
kill Him, and the third day He
will be raised up." And they
were exceedingly sorrowful.

PETER AND HIS MASTER PAY THEIR TAXES

24When they had come to
Capernaum,[a] those who received the *temple* tax came
to Peter and said, "Does your
Teacher not pay the *temple*
tax?"
25He said, "Yes."
And when he had come into
the house, Jesus anticipated
him, saying, "What do you
think, Simon? From whom
do the kings of the earth take
customs or taxes, from their
sons or from strangers?"
26Peter said to Him, "From
strangers."
Jesus said to him, "Then the
sons are free. 27Nevertheless,
lest we offend them, go to the
sea, cast in a hook, and take
the fish that comes up first.
And when you have opened its
mouth, you will find a piece of
money;[a] take that and give it
to them for Me and you."

WHO IS THE GREATEST?

18 At that time the disciples
came to Jesus, saying,
"Who then is greatest in the
kingdom of heaven?"
2Then Jesus called a little
child to Him, set him in the
midst of them, 3and said, "Assuredly, I say to you, unless
you are converted and become
as little children, you will by no
means enter the kingdom of

17:20 [a] NU-Text reads *little faith.* 17:21 [a] NU-Text omits this verse. 17:22 [a] NU-Text reads *gathering together.* 17:24 [a] NU-Text reads *Capharnaum* (here and elsewhere). 17:27 [a] Greek *stater,* the exact amount to pay the temple tax (didrachma) for two

heaven. [4]Therefore whoever
humbles himself as this little child is the greatest in the
kingdom of heaven. [5]Whoever
receives one little child like
this in My name receives Me.

JESUS WARNS OF OFFENSES

[6]"But whoever causes one
of these little ones who believe in Me to sin, it would be
better for him if a millstone
were hung around his neck,
and he were drowned in the
depth of the sea. [7]Woe to the
world because of offenses! For
offenses must come, but woe
to that man by whom the offense comes!

[8]"If your hand or foot
causes you to sin, cut it off and
cast *it* from you. It is better for
you to enter into life lame or
maimed, rather than having
two hands or two feet, to be
cast into the everlasting fire.
[9]And if your eye causes you
to sin, pluck it out and cast *it*
from you. It is better for you
to enter into life with one eye,
rather than having two eyes,
to be cast into hell fire.

THE PARABLE OF THE LOST SHEEP

[10]"Take heed that you do
not despise one of these little
ones, for I say to you that in
heaven their angels always see
the face of My Father who is in
heaven. [11]For the Son of Man
has come to save that which
was lost.[a]

[12]"What do you think? If
a man has a hundred sheep,
and one of them goes astray,
does he not leave the ninety-
nine and go to the mountains
to seek the one that is stray-
ing? [13]And if he should find
it, assuredly, I say to you, he
rejoices more over that *sheep*
than over the ninety-nine that
did not go astray. [14]Even so it
is not the will of your Father
who is in heaven that one of
these little ones should perish.

DEALING WITH A SINNING BROTHER

[15]"Moreover if your brother
sins against you, go and tell
him his fault between you and
him alone. If he hears you,
you have gained your brother.
[16]But if he will not hear, take
with you one or two more,
that 'by the mouth of two or
three witnesses every word
may be established.'[a] [17]And if
he refuses to hear them, tell *it*
to the church. But if he refuses
even to hear the church, let
him be to you like a heathen
and a tax collector.

[18]"Assuredly, I say to you,
whatever you bind on earth
will be bound in heaven,
and whatever you loose on
earth will be loosed in heaven.

[19]"Again I say[a] to you that if

18:11 [a] NU-Text omits this verse. 18:16 [a] Deuteronomy 19:15
18:19 [a] NU-Text and M-Text read *Again, assuredly, I say.*

two of you agree on earth concerning anything that they ask,
it will be done for them by My
Father in heaven. 20For where
two or three are gathered together in My name, I am there
in the midst of them."

THE PARABLE OF THE UNFORGIVING SERVANT

21Then Peter came to Him
and said, "Lord, how often
shall my brother sin against
me, and I forgive him? Up to
seven times?"

22Jesus said to him, "I do
not say to you, up to seven
times, but up to seventy times
seven. 23Therefore the kingdom of heaven is like a certain king who wanted to settle
accounts with his servants.
24And when he had begun
to settle accounts, one was
brought to him who owed him
ten thousand talents. 25But
as he was not able to pay, his
master commanded that he be
sold, with his wife and children
and all that he had, and that
payment be made. 26The servant therefore fell down before
him, saying, 'Master, have patience with me, and I will pay
you all.' 27Then the master of
that servant was moved with
compassion, released him, and
forgave him the debt.

28"*But that servant went*
out and found one of his fellow servants who owed him a
hundred denarii; and he laid
hands on him and took *him*
by the throat, saying, 'Pay me
what you owe!' 29So his fellow
servant fell down at his feet[a]
and begged him, saying, 'Have
patience with me, and I will
pay you all.'[b] 30And he would
not, but went and threw him
into prison till he should pay
the debt. 31So when his fellow
servants saw what had been
done, they were very grieved,
and came and told their master
all that had been done. 32Then
his master, after he had called
him, said to him, 'You wicked
servant! I forgave you all that
debt because you begged me.
33Should you not also have
had compassion on your fellow servant, just as I had pity
on you?' 34And his master was
angry, and delivered him to the
torturers until he should pay
all that was due to him.

35"So My heavenly Father
also will do to you if each of
you, from his heart, does not
forgive his brother his trespasses."[a]

MARRIAGE AND DIVORCE

19 Now it came to pass,
when Jesus had fin-
ished these sayings, *that* He
departed from Galilee and
came to the region of Judea

18:29 [a] NU-Text omits *at his feet*. [b] NU-Text and M-Text omit *all*. 18:35 [a] NU-Text omits *his trespasses*.

beyond the Jordan. 2And great
multitudes followed Him, and
He healed them there.
3The Pharisees also came
to Him, testing Him, and saying to Him, "Is it lawful for a
man to divorce his wife for
just any reason?"
4And He answered and said
to them, "Have you not read
that He who made[a] *them* at the
beginning 'made them male
and female,'[b] 5and said, 'For
this reason a man shall leave
his father and mother and be
joined to his wife, and the two
shall become one flesh'?[a] 6So
then, they are no longer two
but one flesh. Therefore what
God has joined together, let
not man separate."
7They said to Him, "Why
then did Moses command to
give a certificate of divorce,
and to put her away?"
8He said to them, "Moses,
because of the hardness of
your hearts, permitted you to
divorce your wives, but from
the beginning it was not so.
9And I say to you, whoever divorces his wife, except for sexual immorality,[a] and marries
another, commits adultery;
and whoever marries her who
is divorced commits adultery."
10His disciples said to Him,
"If such is the case of the man
with *his* wife, it is better not
to marry."

JESUS TEACHES ON CELIBACY

11But He said to them, "All
cannot accept this saying, but
only *those* to whom it has been
given: 12For there are eunuchs
who were born thus from
their mother's womb, and
there are eunuchs who were
made eunuchs by men, and
there are eunuchs who have
made themselves eunuchs for
the kingdom of heaven's sake.
He who is able to accept *it,* let
him accept *it.*"

JESUS BLESSES LITTLE CHILDREN

13Then little children were
brought to Him that He might
put *His* hands on them and
pray, but the disciples rebuked
them. 14But Jesus said, "Let
the little children come to
Me, and do not forbid them;
for of such is the kingdom of
heaven." 15And He laid *His*
hands on them and departed
from there.

JESUS COUNSELS THE RICH YOUNG RULER

16Now behold, one came
and said to Him, "Good[a]
Teacher, what good thing shall
I do that I may have eternal
life?"
17So He said to him, "Why
do you call Me good?[a] No
one *is* good but One, *that is,*

19:4 [a] NU-Text reads *created.* [b] Genesis 1:27; 5:2 19:5 [a] Genesis 2:24 19:9 [a] Or *fornication* 19:16 [a] NU-Text omits *Good.* 19:17 [a] NU-Text reads *Why do you ask Me about what is good?*

God.[b] But if you want to enter
into life, keep the commandments."
18 He said to Him, "Which
ones?"
Jesus said, "'You shall not
murder,' 'You shall not commit adultery,' 'You shall not
steal,' 'You shall not bear false
witness,' 19 'Honor your father
and *your* mother,'[a] and, 'You
shall love your neighbor as
yourself.'"[b]
20 The young man said to
Him, "All these things I have
kept from my youth.[a] What do
I still lack?"
21 Jesus said to him, "If
you want to be perfect, go,
sell what you have and give
to the poor, and you will have
treasure in heaven; and come,
follow Me."
22 But when the young man
heard that saying, he went
away sorrowful, for he had
great possessions.

WITH GOD ALL THINGS ARE POSSIBLE

23 Then Jesus said to His
disciples, "Assuredly, I say to
you that it is hard for a rich
man to enter the kingdom of
heaven. 24 And again I say to
you, it is easier for a camel to
go through the eye of a needle
than for a rich man to enter
the kingdom of God."
25 When His disciples heard
it, they were greatly astonished, saying, "Who then can
be saved?"
26 But Jesus looked at *them*
and said to them, "With men
this is impossible, but with
God all things are possible."
27 Then Peter answered and
said to Him, "See, we have left
all and followed You. Therefore what shall we have?"
28 So Jesus said to them,
"Assuredly I say to you, that
in the regeneration, when the
Son of Man sits on the throne
of His glory, you who have followed Me will also sit on twelve
thrones, judging the twelve
tribes of Israel. 29 And everyone who has left houses or
brothers or sisters or father or
mother or wife[a] or children
or lands, for My name's sake,
shall receive a hundredfold,
and inherit eternal life. 30 But
many *who are* first will be last,
and the last first.

THE PARABLE OF THE WORKERS IN THE VINEYARD

20 "For the kingdom of
heaven is like a land-
owner who went out early in
the morning to hire laborers
for his vineyard. 2 Now when he
had agreed with the laborers
for a denarius a day, he sent
them into his vineyard. 3 And
he went out about the third

19:17 [b] NU-Text reads *There is One who is good.* 19:19 [a] Exodus 20:12–16; Deuteronomy 5:16–20 [b] Leviticus 19:18 19:20 [a] NU-Text omits *from my youth.* 19:29 [a] NU-Text omits *or wife.*

hour and saw others standing
idle in the marketplace, [4]and
said to them, 'You also go into
the vineyard, and whatever is
right I will give you.' So they
went. [5]Again he went out about
the sixth and the ninth hour,
and did likewise. [6]And about
the eleventh hour he went out
and found others standing
idle,[a] and said to them, 'Why
have you been standing here
idle all day?' [7]They said to him,
'Because no one hired us.' He
said to them, 'You also go into
the vineyard, and whatever is
right you will receive.'[a]

[8]"So when evening had
come, the owner of the vineyard said to his steward, 'Call
the laborers and give them *their*
wages, beginning with the last
to the first.' [9]And when those
came who *were hired* about the
eleventh hour, they each received a denarius. [10]But when
the first came, they supposed
that they would receive more;
and they likewise received
each a denarius. [11]And when
they had received *it,* they complained against the landowner,
[12]saying, 'These last *men* have
worked *only* one hour, and
you made them equal to us
who have borne the burden
and the heat of the day.' [13]But
he answered one of them and
said, 'Friend, I am doing you
no wrong. Did you not agree
with me for a denarius? [14]Take
what is yours and go your way.
I wish to give to this last man
the same as to you. [15]Is it not
lawful for me to do what I wish
with my own things? Or is your
eye evil because I am good?'
[16]So the last will be first, and
the first last. For many are
called, but few chosen."[a]

JESUS A THIRD TIME PREDICTS HIS DEATH AND RESURRECTION

[17]Now Jesus, going up to
Jerusalem, took the twelve
disciples aside on the road
and said to them, [18]"Behold,
we are going up to Jerusalem,
and the Son of Man will be betrayed to the chief priests and
to the scribes; and they will
condemn Him to death, [19]and
deliver Him to the Gentiles to
mock and to scourge and to
crucify. And the third day He
will rise again."

GREATNESS IS SERVING

[20]Then the mother of Zebedee's sons came to Him with
her sons, kneeling down and
asking something from Him.

[21]And He said to her, "What
do you wish?"

She said to Him, "Grant that these two sons of mine may sit, one on Your right hand and the other on the left, in Your kingdom."

[22]But Jesus answered and
said, "You do not know what

20:6 [a] NU-Text omits *idle.* 20:7 [a] NU-Text omits the last clause of this verse. 20:16 [a] NU-Text omits the last sentence of this verse.

you ask. Are you able to drink
the cup that I am about to
drink, and be baptized with
the baptism that I am baptized with?"[a]
They said to Him, "We are
able."
23So He said to them, "You
will indeed drink My cup, and
be baptized with the baptism
that I am baptized with;[a] but
to sit on My right hand and
on My left is not Mine to give,
but *it is for those* for whom it is
prepared by My Father."
24And when the ten heard
it, they were greatly displeased
with the two brothers. 25But
Jesus called them to *Himself*
and said, "You know that the
rulers of the Gentiles lord it
over them, and those who are
great exercise authority over
them. 26Yet it shall not be so
among you; but whoever desires to become great among
you, let him be your servant.
27And whoever desires to be
first among you, let him be
your slave— 28just as the
Son of Man did not come to
be served, but to serve, and
to give His life a ransom for
many."

TWO BLIND MEN RECEIVE THEIR SIGHT

29Now as they went out of
Jericho, a great multitude
followed Him. 30And behold,
two blind men sitting by the
road, when they heard that
Jesus was passing by, cried
out, saying, "Have mercy on
us, O Lord, Son of David!"
31Then the multitude
warned them that they should
be quiet; but they cried out all
the more, saying, "Have mercy
on us, O Lord, Son of David!"
32So Jesus stood still and
called them, and said, "What
do you want Me to do for you?"
33They said to Him, "Lord,
that our eyes may be opened."
34So Jesus had compassion
and touched their eyes. And
immediately their eyes received sight, and they followed Him.

THE TRIUMPHAL ENTRY

21 Now when they drew
near Jerusalem, and
came to Bethphage,[a] at the
Mount of Olives, then Jesus
sent two disciples, 2saying
to them, "Go into the village
opposite you, and immedi-
ately you will find a donkey
tied, and a colt with her. Loose
them and bring *them* to Me.
3And if anyone says anything
to you, you shall say, 'The Lord
has need of them,' and immediately he will send them."
4All[a] this was done that it
might be fulfilled which was
spoken by the prophet, saying:

20:22 [a] NU-Text omits *and be baptized with the baptism that I am baptized with.* 20:23 [a] NU-Text omits *and be baptized with the baptism that I am baptized with.* 21:1 [a] M-Text reads *Bethsphage.* 21:4 [a] NU-Text omits *All.*

5 "Tell the daughter of Zion,
'Behold, your King is
coming to you,
Lowly, and sitting
on a donkey,
A colt, the foal of
a donkey.'"[a]

6 So the disciples went and
did as Jesus commanded
them. 7 They brought the
donkey and the colt, laid their
clothes on them, and set *Him*[a]
on them. 8 And a very great
multitude spread their clothes
on the road; others cut down
branches from the trees and
spread *them* on the road.
9 Then the multitudes who
went before and those who
followed cried out, saying:

"Hosanna to the
Son of David!
'Blessed *is* He who
comes in the name
of the LORD!'[a]
Hosanna in the highest!"

10 And when He had come
into Jerusalem, all the city was
moved, saying, "Who is this?"
11 So the multitudes said,
"This is Jesus, the prophet
from Nazareth of Galilee."

JESUS CLEANSES THE TEMPLE

12 Then Jesus went into the
temple of God[a] and drove out
all those who bought and sold
in the temple, and overturned
the tables of the money changers and the seats of those who
sold doves. 13 And He said to
them, "It is written, 'My house
shall be called a house of
prayer,'[a] but you have made
it a 'den of thieves.'"[b]
14 Then *the* blind and *the*
lame came to Him in the
temple, and He healed them.
15 But when the chief priests
and scribes saw the wonderful
things that He did, and the
children crying out in the
temple and saying, "Hosanna
to the Son of David!" they were
indignant 16 and said to Him,
"Do You hear what these are
saying?"
And Jesus said to them,
"Yes. Have you never read,

'Out of the mouth of babes
and nursing infants
You have perfected
praise'?"[a]

17 Then He left them and
went out of the city to Bethany, and He lodged there.

THE FIG TREE WITHERED

18 Now in the morning, as
He returned to the city, He
was hungry. 19 And seeing a
fig tree by the road, He came
to it and found nothing on
it but leaves, and said to it,

21:5 [a] Zechariah 9:9 21:7 [a] NU-Text reads *and He sat.* 21:9 [a] Psalm 118:26 21:12 [a] NU-Text omits *of God.* 21:13 [a] Isaiah 56:7 [b] Jeremiah 7:11 21:16 [a] Psalm 8:2

"Let no fruit grow on you ever
again." Immediately the fig
tree withered away.

THE LESSON OF THE WITHERED FIG TREE

20 And when the disciples
saw *it,* they marveled, saying,
"How did the fig tree wither
away so soon?"
21 So Jesus answered and
said to them, "Assuredly, I say
to you, if you have faith and do
not doubt, you will not only
do what was done to the fig
tree, but also if you say to this
mountain, 'Be removed and
be cast into the sea,' it will be
done. 22 And whatever things
you ask in prayer, believing,
you will receive."

JESUS' AUTHORITY QUESTIONED

23 Now when He came into
the temple, the chief priests
and the elders of the people
confronted Him as He was
teaching, and said, "By what
authority are You doing these
things? And who gave You this
authority?"
24 But Jesus answered and
said to them, "I also will ask
you one thing, which if you
tell Me, I likewise will tell
you by what authority I do
these things: 25 The baptism
of John—where was it from?
From heaven or from men?"
And they reasoned among
themselves, saying, "If we say,
'From heaven,' He will say to us,
'Why then did you not believe
him?' 26 But if we say, 'From
men,' we fear the multitude, for
all count John as a prophet."
27 So they answered Jesus and
said, "We do not know."
And He said to them, "Neither will I tell you by what authority I do these things.

THE PARABLE OF THE TWO SONS

28 "But what do you think?
A man had two sons, and he
came to the first and said, 'Son,
go, work today in my vineyard.'
29 He answered and said, 'I will
not,' but afterward he regretted it and went. 30 Then he
came to the second and said
likewise. And he answered and
said, 'I *go,* sir,' but he did not
go. 31 Which of the two did the
will of *his* father?"
They said to Him, "The
first."
Jesus said to them, "As-
suredly, I say to you that tax
collectors and harlots enter
the kingdom of God before
you. 32 For John came to you
in the way of righteousness,
and you did not believe him;
but tax collectors and harlots
believed him; and when you
saw *it,* you did not afterward
relent and believe him.

THE PARABLE OF THE WICKED VINEDRESSERS

33 "Hear another parable:
There was a certain land-
owner who planted a vineyard

and set a hedge around it, dug
a winepress in it and built a
tower. And he leased it to vinedressers and went into a far
country. 34Now when vintage-
time drew near, he sent his
servants to the vinedressers,
that they might receive its
fruit. 35And the vinedressers
took his servants, beat one,
killed one, and stoned another. 36Again he sent other
servants, more than the first,
and they did likewise to them.
37Then last of all he sent his
son to them, saying, 'They will
respect my son.' 38But when
the vinedressers saw the son,
they said among themselves,
'This is the heir. Come, let us
kill him and seize his inheritance.' 39So they took him and
cast *him* out of the vineyard
and killed *him*.

40"Therefore, when the
owner of the vineyard comes,
what will he do to those vinedressers?"

41They said to Him, "He
will destroy those wicked men
miserably, and lease *his* vineyard to other vinedressers
who will render to him the
fruits in their seasons."

42Jesus said to them, "Have
you never read in the Scriptures:

'The stone which the
builders rejected
Has become the chief
cornerstone.
This was the
LORD's doing,
And it is marvelous
in our eyes'?[a]

43"Therefore I say to you,
the kingdom of God will be
taken from you and given to
a nation bearing the fruits of
it. 44And whoever falls on this
stone will be broken; but on
whomever it falls, it will grind
him to powder."

45Now when the chief
priests and Pharisees heard
His parables, they perceived
that He was speaking of them.
46But when they sought to lay
hands on Him, they feared the
multitudes, because they took
Him for a prophet.

THE PARABLE OF THE WEDDING FEAST

22 And Jesus answered
and spoke to them
again by parables and said:
2"The kingdom of heaven is
like a certain king who arranged a marriage for his son,
3and sent out his servants to
call those who were invited to
the wedding; and they were
not willing to come. 4Again,
he sent out other servants,
saying, 'Tell those who are
invited, "See, I have prepared
my dinner; my oxen and fatted cattle *are* killed, and all
things *are* ready. Come to the
wedding."' 5But they made
light of it and went their

21:42 [a] Psalm 118:22, 23

ways, one to his own farm,
another to his business. 6And
the rest seized his servants,
treated *them* spitefully, and
killed *them.* 7But when the
king heard *about it,* he was
furious. And he sent out his
armies, destroyed those murderers, and burned up their
city. 8Then he said to his servants, 'The wedding is ready,
but those who were invited
were not worthy. 9Therefore
go into the highways, and as
many as you find, invite to the
wedding.' 10So those servants
went out into the highways
and gathered together all
whom they found, both bad
and good. And the wedding
hall was filled with guests.

11"But when the king came
in to see the guests, he saw a
man there who did not have
on a wedding garment. 12So
he said to him, 'Friend, how
did you come in here without
a wedding garment?' And he
was speechless. 13Then the
king said to the servants, 'Bind
him hand and foot, take him
away, and[a] cast *him* into outer
darkness; there will be weeping and gnashing of teeth.'

14"For many are called, but
few *are* chosen."

THE PHARISEES: IS IT LAWFUL TO PAY *TAXES TO CAESAR?*

15Then the Pharisees went
and plotted how they might
entangle Him in *His* talk.
16And they sent to Him their
disciples with the Herodians,
saying, "Teacher, we know that
You are true, and teach the
way of God in truth; nor do
You care about anyone, for
You do not regard the person
of men. 17Tell us, therefore,
what do You think? Is it lawful
to pay taxes to Caesar, or not?"

18But Jesus perceived their
wickedness, and said, "Why do
you test Me, *you* hypocrites?
19Show Me the tax money."

So they brought Him a de-
narius.

20And He said to them,
"Whose image and inscrip-
tion *is* this?"

21They said to Him, "Cae-
sar's."

And He said to them, "Render therefore to Caesar the
things that are Caesar's, and to
God the things that are God's."
22When they had heard *these*
words, they marveled, and left
Him and went their way.

THE SADDUCEES: WHAT ABOUT THE RESURRECTION?

23The same day the Sad-
ducees, who say there is no
resurrection, came to Him
and asked Him, 24saying:
"Teacher, Moses said that if a
man dies, having no children,
his brother shall marry his
wife and raise up offspring for
his brother. 25Now there were

22:13 [a] NU-Text omits *take him away, and.*

with us seven brothers. The
first died after he had married, and having no offspring,
left his wife to his brother.
26Likewise the second also,
and the third, even to the seventh. 27Last of all the woman
died also. 28Therefore, in the
resurrection, whose wife of
the seven will she be? For they
all had her."

29Jesus answered and said
to them, "You are mistaken,
not knowing the Scriptures
nor the power of God. 30For
in the resurrection they neither marry nor are given in
marriage, but are like angels
of God[a] in heaven. 31But concerning the resurrection of
the dead, have you not read
what was spoken to you by
God, saying, 32'I am the God
of Abraham, the God of Isaac,
and the God of Jacob'?[a] God is
not the God of the dead, but
of the living." 33And when
the multitudes heard *this*,
they were astonished at His
teaching.

THE SCRIBES: WHICH IS THE FIRST COMMANDMENT OF ALL?

34But when the Pharisees
heard that He had silenced
the Sadducees, they gathered
together. 35Then one of them,
a lawyer, asked *Him a question,* testing Him, and saying,
36"Teacher, which *is* the great
commandment in the law?"

37Jesus said to him, "'You
shall love the LORD your God
with all your heart, with all
your soul, and with all your
mind.'[a] 38This is *the* first and
great commandment. 39And
the second *is* like it: 'You shall
love your neighbor as yourself.'[a] 40On these two commandments hang all the Law
and the Prophets."

JESUS: HOW CAN DAVID CALL HIS DESCENDANT "LORD"?

41While the Pharisees were
gathered together, Jesus asked
them, 42saying, "What do you
think about the Christ? Whose
Son is He?"

They said to Him, "*The Son*
of David."

43He said to them, "How
then does David in the Spirit
call Him 'Lord,' saying:

44 'The LORD said
to my Lord,
"Sit at My right hand,
Till I make Your enemies
Your footstool"'?[a]

45If David then calls Him
'Lord,' how is He his Son?"
46And no one was able to answer Him a word, nor from
that day on did anyone dare
question Him anymore.

22:30 [a] NU-Text omits *of God.* 22:32 [a] Exodus 3:6, 15 22:37 [a] Deuteronomy 6:5 22:39 [a] Leviticus 19:18 22:44 [a] Psalm 110:1

WOE TO THE SCRIBES AND PHARISEES

23 Then Jesus spoke to the multitudes and to His disciples, 2saying: "The scribes and the Pharisees sit in Moses' seat. 3Therefore whatever they tell you to observe,[a] *that* observe and do, but do not do according to their works; for they say, and do not do. 4For they bind heavy burdens, hard to bear, and lay *them* on men's shoulders; but they *themselves* will not move them with one of their fingers. 5But all their works they do to be seen by men. They make their phylacteries broad and enlarge the borders of their garments. 6They love the best places at feasts, the best seats in the synagogues, 7greetings in the marketplaces, and to be called by men, 'Rabbi, Rabbi.' 8But you, do not be called 'Rabbi'; for One is your Teacher, the Christ,[a] and you are all brethren. 9Do not call anyone on earth your father; for One is your Father, He who is in heaven. 10And do not be called teachers; for One is your Teacher, the Christ. 11But he who is greatest among you shall be your servant. 12And whoever exalts himself will be humbled, and he who humbles himself will be exalted.

13"But woe to you, scribes and Pharisees, hypocrites! For you shut up the kingdom of heaven against men; for you neither go in *yourselves,* nor do you allow those who are entering to go in. 14Woe to you, scribes and Pharisees, hypocrites! For you devour widows' houses, and for a pretense make long prayers. Therefore you will receive greater condemnation.[a]

15"Woe to you, scribes and Pharisees, hypocrites! For you travel land and sea to win one proselyte, and when he is won, you make him twice as much a son of hell as yourselves.

16"Woe to you, blind guides, who say, 'Whoever swears by the temple, it is nothing; but whoever swears by the gold of the temple, he is obliged *to perform it.*' 17Fools and blind! For which is greater, the gold or the temple that sanctifies[a] the gold? 18And, 'Whoever swears by the altar, it is nothing; but whoever swears by the gift that is on it, he is obliged *to perform it.*' 19Fools and blind! For which is greater, the gift or the altar that sanctifies the gift? 20Therefore he who swears by the altar, swears by it and by all things on it. 21He who swears by the temple, swears by it and by Him who *dwells*[a] *in it.* 22And he who

23:3 [a] NU-Text omits *to observe.* 23:8 [a] NU-Text omits *the Christ.* 23:14 [a] NU-Text omits this verse. 23:17 [a] NU-Text reads *sanctified.* 23:21 [a] M-Text reads *dwelt.*

swears by heaven, swears by
the throne of God and by Him
who sits on it.
23"Woe to you, scribes and
Pharisees, hypocrites! For you
pay tithe of mint and anise
and cummin, and have ne-
glected the weightier *matters*
of the law: justice and mercy
and faith. These you ought to
have done, without leaving
the others undone. 24Blind
guides, who strain out a gnat
and swallow a camel!
25"Woe to you, scribes and
Pharisees, hypocrites! For
you cleanse the outside of the
cup and dish, but inside they
are full of extortion and self-
indulgence.[a] 26Blind Pharisee,
first cleanse the inside of the
cup and dish, that the outside
of them may be clean also.
27"Woe to you, scribes and
Pharisees, hypocrites! For you
are like whitewashed tombs
which indeed appear beau-
tiful outwardly, but inside
are full of dead *men's* bones
and all uncleanness. 28Even
so you also outwardly appear
righteous to men, but inside
you are full of hypocrisy and
lawlessness.
29"Woe to you, scribes and
Pharisees, hypocrites! Because you build the tombs of
the prophets and adorn the
monuments of the righteous,
30and say, 'If we had lived in
the days of our fathers, we
would not have been partakers with them in the blood of
the prophets.'
31"Therefore you are wit-
nesses against yourselves
that you are sons of those
who murdered the prophets.
32Fill up, then, the measure of
your fathers' *guilt.* 33Serpents,
brood of vipers! How can you
escape the condemnation of
hell? 34Therefore, indeed, I
send you prophets, wise men,
and scribes: *some* of them you
will kill and crucify, and *some*
of them you will scourge in
your synagogues and persecute from city to city, 35that
on you may come all the righteous blood shed on the earth,
from the blood of righteous
Abel to the blood of Zechariah,
son of Berechiah, whom you
murdered between the temple
and the altar. 36Assuredly, I
say to you, all these things will
come upon this generation.

JESUS LAMENTS OVER JERUSALEM

37"O Jerusalem, Jerusalem,
the one who kills the prophets
and stones those who are sent
to her! How often I wanted to
gather your children together,
as a hen gathers her chicks
under *her* wings, but you were
not willing! 38See! Your house
is left to you desolate; 39for I
say to you, you shall see Me
no more till you say, 'Blessed
is He who comes in the name
of the LORD!'"[a]

23:25 [a] M-Text reads *unrighteousness.* 23:39 [a] Psalm 118:26

JESUS PREDICTS THE DESTRUCTION OF THE TEMPLE

24 Then Jesus went out
and departed from
the temple, and His disciples came up to show Him
the buildings of the temple.
2And Jesus said to them, "Do
you not see all these things?
Assuredly, I say to you, not
one stone shall be left here
upon another, that shall not
be thrown down."

THE SIGNS OF THE TIMES AND THE END OF THE AGE

3Now as He sat on the
Mount of Olives, the disciples
came to Him privately, saying, "Tell us, when will these
things be? And what *will be*
the sign of Your coming, and
of the end of the age?"
4And Jesus answered and
said to them: "Take heed that
no one deceives you. 5For
many will come in My name,
saying, 'I am the Christ,' and
will deceive many. 6And you
will hear of wars and rumors
of wars. See that you are not
troubled; for all[a] *these things*
must come to pass, but the
end is not yet. 7For nation will
rise against nation, and kingdom against kingdom. And
there will be famines, pestilences,[a] and earthquakes in
various places. 8All these *are*
the beginning of sorrows.
9"Then they will deliver
you up to tribulation and kill
you, and you will be hated
by all nations for My name's
sake. 10And then many will
be offended, will betray one
another, and will hate one
another. 11Then many false
prophets will rise up and deceive many. 12And because
lawlessness will abound, the
love of many will grow cold.
13But he who endures to the
end shall be saved. 14And this
gospel of the kingdom will be
preached in all the world as a
witness to all the nations, and
then the end will come.

THE GREAT TRIBULATION

15"Therefore when you
see the 'abomination of desolation,'[a] spoken of by Daniel
the prophet, standing in the
holy place" (whoever reads,
let him understand), 16"then
let those who are in Judea flee
to the mountains. 17Let him
who is on the housetop not go
down to take anything out of
his house. 18And let him who
is in the field not go back to
get his clothes. 19But woe to
those who are pregnant and
to those who are nursing babies in those days! 20And pray
that your flight may not be
in winter or on the Sabbath.
21For then there will be great
tribulation, such as has not
been since the beginning of

24:6 [a] NU-Text omits *all*. 24:7 [a] NU-Text omits *pestilences*. 24:15 [a] Daniel 11:31; 12:11

the world until this time, no, nor ever shall be. 22And unless those days were shortened, no flesh would be saved; but for the elect's sake those days will be shortened.

23"Then if anyone says to you, 'Look, here *is* the Christ!' or 'There!' do not believe *it.* 24For false christs and false prophets will rise and show great signs and wonders to deceive, if possible, even the elect. 25See, I have told you beforehand.

26"Therefore if they say to you, 'Look, He is in the desert!' do not go out; *or* 'Look, *He is* in the inner rooms!' do not believe *it.* 27For as the lightning comes from the east and flashes to the west, so also will the coming of the Son of Man be. 28For wherever the carcass is, there the eagles will be gathered together.

THE COMING OF THE SON OF MAN

29"Immediately after the tribulation of those days the sun will be darkened, and the moon will not give its light; the stars will fall from heaven, and the powers of the heavens will be shaken. 30Then the sign of the Son of Man will appear in heaven, and then all the tribes of the earth will mourn, and they will see the Son of Man coming on the clouds of heaven with power and great glory. 31And He will send His angels with a great sound of a trumpet, and they will gather together His elect from the four winds, from one end of heaven to the other.

THE PARABLE OF THE FIG TREE

32"Now learn this parable from the fig tree: When its branch has already become tender and puts forth leaves, you know that summer *is* near. 33So you also, when you see all these things, know that it[a] is near—at the doors! 34Assuredly, I say to you, this generation will by no means pass away till all these things take place. 35Heaven and earth will pass away, but My words will by no means pass away.

NO ONE KNOWS THE DAY OR HOUR

36"But of that day and hour no one knows, not even the angels of heaven,[a] but My Father only. 37But as the days of Noah *were,* so also will the coming of the Son of Man be. 38For as in the days before the flood, they were eating and drinking, marrying and giving in marriage, until the day that Noah entered the ark, 39and did not know until the flood came and took them all away, so also will the coming of the Son of Man be. 40Then two *men* will be in the field:

24:33 [a] Or *He* 24:36 [a] NU-Text adds *nor the Son.*

one will be taken and the
other left. 41 Two *women will*
be grinding at the mill: one
will be taken and the other
left. 42 Watch therefore, for
you do not know what hour[a]
your Lord is coming. 43 But
know this, that if the master
of the house had known what
hour the thief would come,
he would have watched and
not allowed his house to be
broken into. 44 Therefore you
also be ready, for the Son of
Man is coming at an hour you
do not expect.

THE FAITHFUL SERVANT AND THE EVIL SERVANT

45 "Who then is a faithful
and wise servant, whom his
master made ruler over his
household, to give them food
in due season? 46 Blessed *is*
that servant whom his master, when he comes, will find
so doing. 47 Assuredly, I say
to you that he will make him
ruler over all his goods. 48 But
if that evil servant says in his
heart, 'My master is delaying
his coming,'[a] 49 and begins to
beat *his* fellow servants, and to
eat and drink with the drunkards, 50 the master of that servant will come on a day when
he is not looking for *him* and
at an hour that he is not aware
of, 51 and will cut him in two
and appoint *him* his portion
with the hypocrites. There
shall be weeping and gnashing of teeth.

THE PARABLE OF THE WISE AND FOOLISH VIRGINS

25 "Then the kingdom of
heaven shall be likened
to ten virgins who took their
lamps and went out to meet
the bridegroom. 2 Now five
of them were wise, and five
were foolish. 3 Those who *were*
foolish took their lamps and
took no oil with them, 4 but the
wise took oil in their vessels
with their lamps. 5 But while
the bridegroom was delayed,
they all slumbered and slept.

6 "And at midnight a cry
was *heard:* 'Behold, the bridegroom is coming;[a] go out to
meet him!' 7 Then all those virgins arose and trimmed their
lamps. 8 And the foolish said to
the wise, 'Give us *some* of your
oil, for our lamps are going
out.' 9 But the wise answered,
saying, '*No,* lest there should
not be enough for us and you;
but go rather to those who sell,
and buy for yourselves.' 10 And
while they went to buy, the
bridegroom came, and those
who were ready went in with
him to the wedding; and the
door was shut.

11 "Afterward the other virgins came also, saying, 'Lord,
Lord, open to us!' 12 But he answered and said, 'Assuredly, I
say to you, I do not know you.'

24:42 [a] NU-Text reads *day.* 24:48 [a] NU-Text omits *his coming.* 25:6 [a] NU-Text omits *is coming.*

13"Watch therefore, for you know neither the day nor the hour[a] in which the Son of Man is coming.

THE PARABLE OF THE TALENTS

14"For *the kingdom of heaven is* like a man traveling to a far country, *who* called his own servants and delivered his goods to them. 15And to one he gave five talents, to another two, and to another one, to each according to his own ability; and immediately he went on a journey. 16Then he who had received the five talents went and traded with them, and made another five talents. 17And likewise he who *had received* two gained two more also. 18But he who had received one went and dug in the ground, and hid his lord's money. 19After a long time the lord of those servants came and settled accounts with them.

20"So he who had received five talents came and brought five other talents, saying, 'Lord, you delivered to me five talents; look, I have gained five more talents besides them.' 21His lord said to him, 'Well *done,* good and faithful servant; you were faithful over a few things, I will make you ruler over many things. Enter into the joy of your lord.' 22He also who had received two talents came and said, 'Lord, you delivered to me two talents; look, I have gained two more talents besides them.' 23His lord said to him, 'Well *done,* good and faithful servant; you have been faithful over a few things, I will make you ruler over many things. Enter into the joy of your lord.'

24"Then he who had received the one talent came and said, 'Lord, I knew you to be a hard man, reaping where you have not sown, and gathering where you have not scattered seed. 25And I was afraid, and went and hid your talent in the ground. Look, *there* you have *what is* yours.'

26"But his lord answered and said to him, 'You wicked and lazy servant, you knew that I reap where I have not sown, and gather where I have not scattered seed. 27So you ought to have deposited my money with the bankers, and at my coming I would have received back my own with interest. 28So take the talent from him, and give *it* to him who has ten talents.

29'For to everyone who has, more will be given, and he will have abundance; but from him who does not have, even what he has will be taken away. 30And cast the unprofitable servant into the outer darkness. There will be weeping and gnashing of teeth.'

25:13 [a] NU-Text omits the rest of this verse.

THE SON OF MAN WILL JUDGE THE NATIONS

31 "When the Son of Man
comes in His glory, and all the
holy[a] angels with Him, then
He will sit on the throne of
His glory. 32 All the nations
will be gathered before Him,
and He will separate them one
from another, as a shepherd
divides *his* sheep from the
goats. 33 And He will set the
sheep on His right hand, but
the goats on the left. 34 Then
the King will say to those on
His right hand, 'Come, you
blessed of My Father, inherit
the kingdom prepared for
you from the foundation of
the world: 35 for I was hungry
and you gave Me food; I was
thirsty and you gave Me drink;
I was a stranger and you took
Me in; 36 I *was* naked and you
clothed Me; I was sick and you
visited Me; I was in prison and
you came to Me.'

37 "Then the righteous will
answer Him, saying, 'Lord,
when did we see You hungry
and feed *You,* or thirsty and
give *You* drink? 38 When did we
see You a stranger and take *You*
in, or naked and clothe *You?*
39 Or when did we see You sick,
or in prison, and come to You?'
40 And the King will answer and
say to them, 'Assuredly, I say
to you, inasmuch as you did
it to one of the least of these
My brethren, you did *it* to Me.'

41 "Then He will also say to
those on the left hand, 'Depart
from Me, you cursed, into the
everlasting fire prepared for
the devil and his angels: 42 for
I was hungry and you gave Me
no food; I was thirsty and you
gave Me no drink; 43 I was a
stranger and you did not take
Me in, naked and you did not
clothe Me, sick and in prison
and you did not visit Me.'

44 "Then they also will answer Him,[a] saying, 'Lord,
when did we see You hun-
gry or thirsty or a stranger
or naked or sick or in prison,
and did not minister to You?'
45 Then He will answer them,
saying, 'Assuredly, I say to you,
inasmuch as you did not do
it to one of the least of these,
you did not do *it* to Me.' 46 And
these will go away into everlasting punishment, but the
righteous into eternal life."

THE PLOT TO KILL JESUS

26 Now it came to pass,
when Jesus had fin-
ished all these sayings, *that*
He said to His disciples, 2 "You
know that after two days is the
Passover, and the Son of Man
will be delivered up to be crucified."

3 Then the chief priests, the
scribes,[a] and the elders of the
people assembled at the palace of the high priest, who was
called Caiaphas, 4 and plotted

25:31 [a] NU-Text omits *holy.* 25:44 [a] NU-Text and M-Text omit *Him.* 26:3 [a] NU-Text omits *the scribes.*

to take Jesus by trickery and
kill *Him.* 5But they said, "Not
during the feast, lest there be
an uproar among the people."

THE ANOINTING AT BETHANY

6And when Jesus was in
Bethany at the house of Simon
the leper, 7a woman came to
Him having an alabaster flask
of very costly fragrant oil, and
she poured *it* on His head as
He sat *at the table.* 8But when
His disciples saw *it,* they were
indignant, saying, "Why this
waste? 9For this fragrant oil
might have been sold for
much and given to *the* poor."
10But when Jesus was aware
of *it,* He said to them, "Why do
you trouble the woman? For
she has done a good work for
Me. 11For you have the poor
with you always, but Me you
do not have always. 12For in
pouring this fragrant oil on
My body, she did *it* for My
burial. 13Assuredly, I say to
you, wherever this gospel is
preached in the whole world,
what this woman has done
will also be told as a memorial to her."

JUDAS AGREES TO BETRAY JESUS

14Then one of the twelve,
called Judas Iscariot, went to
the chief priests 15and said,
"What are you willing to give
me if I deliver Him to you?"
And they counted out to him
thirty pieces of silver. 16So
from that time he sought opportunity to betray Him.

JESUS CELEBRATES PASSOVER WITH HIS DISCIPLES

17Now on the first *day of the*
Feast of the Unleavened Bread
the disciples came to Jesus,
saying to Him, "Where do You
want us to prepare for You to
eat the Passover?"
18And He said, "Go into the
city to a certain man, and say
to him, 'The Teacher says, "My
time is at hand; I will keep the
Passover at your house with
My disciples."'"
19So the disciples did as
Jesus had directed them; and
they prepared the Passover.
20When evening had come,
He sat down with the twelve.
21Now as they were eating, He
said, "Assuredly, I say to you,
one of you will betray Me."
22And they were exceed-
ingly sorrowful, and each of
them began to say to Him,
"Lord, is it I?"
23He answered and said,
"He who dipped *his* hand with
Me in the dish will betray Me.
24The Son of Man indeed goes
just as it is written of Him, but
woe to that man by whom
the Son of Man is betrayed! It
would have been good for that
man if he had not been born."
25Then Judas, who was be-
traying Him, answered and
said, "Rabbi, is it I?"
He said to him, "You have
said it."

JESUS INSTITUTES THE LORD'S SUPPER

26And as they were eating,
Jesus took bread, blessed[a] and
broke *it,* and gave *it* to the disciples and said, "Take, eat; this
is My body."
27Then He took the cup,
and gave thanks, and gave *it*
to them, saying, "Drink from
it, all of you. 28For this is My
blood of the new[a] covenant,
which is shed for many for the
remission of sins. 29But I say
to you, I will not drink of this
fruit of the vine from now on
until that day when I drink it
new with you in My Father's
kingdom."
30And when they had sung
a hymn, they went out to the
Mount of Olives.

JESUS PREDICTS PETER'S DENIAL

31Then Jesus said to them,
"All of you will be made to
stumble because of Me this
night, for it is written:

'I will strike the Shepherd,
And the sheep of the
flock will be scattered.'[a]

32But after I have been raised,
I will go before you to Galilee."
33Peter answered and said
to Him, "Even if all are made
to stumble because of You, I
will never be made to stumble."
34Jesus said to him, "As-
suredly, I say to you that
this night, before the rooster
crows, you will deny Me three
times."
35Peter said to Him, "Even
if I have to die with You, I will
not deny You!"
And so said all the disciples.

THE PRAYER IN THE GARDEN

36Then Jesus came with
them to a place called Geth-
semane, and said to the disciples, "Sit here while I go and
pray over there." 37And He
took with Him Peter and the
two sons of Zebedee, and He
began to be sorrowful and
deeply distressed. 38Then He
said to them, "My soul is exceedingly sorrowful, even to
death. Stay here and watch
with Me."
39He went a little farther
and fell on His face, and
prayed, saying, "O My Father,
if it is possible, let this cup
pass from Me; nevertheless,
not as I will, but as You *will.*"
40Then He came to the disciples and found them sleeping, and said to Peter, "What!
Could you not watch with Me
one hour? 41Watch and pray,
lest you enter into temptation.
The spirit indeed *is* willing,
but the flesh *is* weak."
42Again, a second time, He

26:26 [a] M-Text reads *gave thanks for.* **26:28** [a] NU-Text omits *new.* **26:31** [a] Zechariah 13:7

went away and prayed, saying, "O My Father, if this cup cannot pass away from Me unless[a] I drink it, Your will be done." 43And He came and found them asleep again, for their eyes were heavy.

44So He left them, went away again, and prayed the third time, saying the same words. 45Then He came to His disciples and said to them, "Are *you* still sleeping and resting? Behold, the hour is at hand, and the Son of Man is being betrayed into the hands of sinners. 46Rise, let us be going. See, My betrayer is at hand."

BETRAYAL AND ARREST IN GETHSEMANE

47And while He was still speaking, behold, Judas, one of the twelve, with a great multitude with swords and clubs, came from the chief priests and elders of the people.

48Now His betrayer had given them a sign, saying, "Whomever I kiss, He is the One; seize Him." 49Immediately he went up to Jesus and said, "Greetings, Rabbi!" and kissed Him.

50But Jesus said to him, "Friend, why have you come?"

Then they came and laid hands on Jesus and took Him. 51And suddenly, one of those *who were* with Jesus stretched out *his* hand and drew his sword, struck the servant of the high priest, and cut off his ear.

52But Jesus said to him, "Put your sword in its place, for all who take the sword will perish[a] by the sword. 53Or do you think that I cannot now pray to My Father, and He will provide Me with more than twelve legions of angels? 54How then could the Scriptures be fulfilled, that it must happen thus?"

55In that hour Jesus said to the multitudes, "Have you come out, as against a robber, with swords and clubs to take Me? I sat daily with you, teaching in the temple, and you did not seize Me. 56But all this was done that the Scriptures of the prophets might be fulfilled."

Then all the disciples forsook Him and fled.

JESUS FACES THE SANHEDRIN

57And those who had laid hold of Jesus led *Him* away to Caiaphas the high priest, where the scribes and the elders were assembled. 58But Peter followed Him at a distance to the high priest's courtyard. And he went in and sat with the servants to see the end.

26:42 [a] NU-Text reads *if this may not pass away unless.* 26:52 [a] M-Text reads *die.*

59Now the chief priests,
the elders,[a] and all the council sought false testimony
against Jesus to put Him to
death, 60but found none. Even
though many false witnesses
came forward, they found
none.[a] But at last two false
witnesses[b] came forward
61and said, "This *fellow* said, 'I
am able to destroy the temple
of God and to build it in three
days.'"
62And the high priest arose
and said to Him, "Do You answer nothing? What *is it* these
men testify against You?"
63But Jesus kept silent. And
the high priest answered and
said to Him, "I put You under
oath by the living God: Tell us
if You are the Christ, the Son
of God!"
64Jesus said to him, "It is
as you said. Nevertheless, I
say to you, hereafter you will
see the Son of Man sitting at
the right hand of the Power,
and coming on the clouds of
heaven."
65Then the high priest tore
his clothes, saying, "He has
spoken blasphemy! What further need do we have of witnesses? Look, now you have
heard His blasphemy! 66What
do you think?"
They answered and said,
"He is deserving of death."
67*Then they spat* in His
face and beat Him; and others
struck *Him* with the palms of
their hands, 68saying, "Prophesy to us, Christ! Who is the
one who struck You?"

PETER DENIES JESUS, AND WEEPS BITTERLY

69Now Peter sat outside in
the courtyard. And a servant
girl came to him, saying, "You
also were with Jesus of Galilee."
70But he denied it before
them all, saying, "I do not
know what you are saying."
71And when he had gone
out to the gateway, another
girl saw him and said to those
who were there, "This *fellow*
also was with Jesus of Nazareth."
72But again he denied with
an oath, "I do not know the
Man!"
73And a little later those
who stood by came up and
said to Peter, "Surely you
also are *one* of them, for your
speech betrays you."
74Then he began to curse
and swear, *saying,* "I do not
know the Man!"
Immediately a rooster
crowed. 75And Peter remembered the word of Jesus who
had said to him, "Before the
rooster crows, you will deny
Me three times." So he went
out and wept bitterly.

26:59 [a] NU-Text omits *the elders.* **26:60** [a] NU-Text puts a comma after *but found none,* does not capitalize *Even,* and omits *they found none.* [b] NU-Text omits *false witnesses.*

JESUS HANDED OVER TO PONTIUS PILATE

27 When morning came,
all the chief priests and
elders of the people plotted
against Jesus to put Him to
death. 2And when they had
bound Him, they led Him
away and delivered Him to
Pontius[a] Pilate the governor.

JUDAS HANGS HIMSELF

3Then Judas, His betrayer,
seeing that He had been condemned, was remorseful and
brought back the thirty pieces
of silver to the chief priests
and elders, 4saying, "I have
sinned by betraying innocent
blood."

And they said, "What *is that*
to us? You see *to it!*"

5Then he threw down the
pieces of silver in the temple
and departed, and went and
hanged himself.

6But the chief priests took
the silver pieces and said, "It
is not lawful to put them into
the treasury, because they
are the price of blood." 7And
they consulted together and
bought with them the pot-
ter's field, to bury strangers
in. 8Therefore that field has
been called the Field of Blood
to this day.

9Then was fulfilled what
was spoken by Jeremiah the
prophet, saying, "And they
took the thirty pieces of silver, the value of Him who
was priced, whom they of
the children of Israel priced,
10and gave them for the potter's field, as the LORD directed me."[a]

JESUS FACES PILATE

11Now Jesus stood before
the governor. And the governor asked Him, saying, "Are
You the King of the Jews?"

Jesus said to him, "It is as
you say." 12And while He was
being accused by the chief
priests and elders, He answered nothing.

13Then Pilate said to Him,
"Do You not hear how many
things they testify against
You?" 14But He answered him
not one word, so that the governor marveled greatly.

TAKING THE PLACE OF BARABBAS

15Now at the feast the governor was accustomed to releasing to the multitude one
prisoner whom they wished.
16And at that time they had
a notorious prisoner called
Barabbas.[a] 17Therefore, when
they had gathered together,
Pilate said to them, "Whom
do you want me to release to
you? Barabbas, or Jesus who is
called Christ?" 18For he knew
that they had handed Him
over because of envy.

19While he was sitting on

27:2 [a] NU-Text omits *Pontius.* 27:10 [a] Jeremiah 32:6–9 27:16 [a] NU-Text reads *Jesus Barabbas.*

the judgment seat, his wife
sent to him, saying, "Have
nothing to do with that just
Man, for I have suffered many
things today in a dream because of Him."
20But the chief priests and
elders persuaded the multitudes that they should ask for
Barabbas and destroy Jesus.
21The governor answered and
said to them, "Which of the
two do you want me to release
to you?"
They said, "Barabbas!"
22Pilate said to them, "What
then shall I do with Jesus who
is called Christ?"
They all said to him, "Let
Him be crucified!"
23Then the governor said,
"Why, what evil has He done?"
But they cried out all the
more, saying, "Let Him be
crucified!"
24When Pilate saw that he
could not prevail at all, but
rather *that* a tumult was rising, he took water and washed
his hands before the multitude, saying, "I am innocent
of the blood of this just Person.[a] You see *to it.*"
25And all the people an-
swered and said, "His blood
be on us and on our children."
26Then he released Barab-
bas to them; and when he had
scourged Jesus, he delivered
Him to be crucified.

THE SOLDIERS MOCK JESUS

27Then the soldiers of the
governor took Jesus into the
Praetorium and gathered
the whole garrison around
Him. 28And they stripped
Him and put a scarlet robe
on Him. 29When they had
twisted a crown of thorns,
they put *it* on His head, and
a reed in His right hand. And
they bowed the knee before
Him and mocked Him, say-
ing, "Hail, King of the Jews!"
30Then they spat on Him, and
took the reed and struck Him
on the head. 31And when they
had mocked Him, they took
the robe off Him, put His *own*
clothes on Him, and led Him
away to be crucified.

THE KING ON A CROSS

32Now as they came out,
they found a man of Cyrene,
Simon by name. Him they
compelled to bear His cross.
33And when they had come to
a place called Golgotha, that is
to say, Place of a Skull, 34they
gave Him sour[a] wine mingled
with gall to drink. But when
He had tasted *it,* He would not
drink.
35Then they crucified Him,
and divided His garments,
casting lots,[a] that it might be
fulfilled which was spoken by
the prophet:

27:24 [a] NU-Text omits *just.* **27:34** [a] NU-Text omits *sour.* **27:35** [a] NU-Text and M-Text omit the rest of this verse.

"They divided My
garments among them,
And for My clothing
they cast lots."[b]

36Sitting down, they kept
watch over Him there. 37And
they put up over His head the
accusation written against
Him:

THIS IS JESUS THE
KING OF THE JEWS.

38Then two robbers were crucified with Him, one on the
right and another on the left.
39And those who passed
by blasphemed Him, wagging
their heads 40and saying, "You
who destroy the temple and
build *it* in three days, save
Yourself! If You are the Son
of God, come down from the
cross."
41Likewise the chief priests
also, mocking with the scribes
and elders,[a] said, 42"He saved
others; Himself He cannot
save. If He is the King of Israel,[a] let Him now come down
from the cross, and we will
believe Him.[b] 43He trusted in
God; let Him deliver Him now
if He will have Him; for He
said, 'I am the Son of God.'"
44Even the robbers who
were crucified with Him reviled Him with the same
thing.

JESUS DIES ON THE CROSS

45Now from the sixth hour
until the ninth hour there was
darkness over all the land.
46And about the ninth hour
Jesus cried out with a loud
voice, saying, "Eli, Eli, lama
sabachthani?" that is, "My
God, My God, why have You
forsaken Me?"[a]
47Some of those who stood
there, when they heard *that,*
said, "This Man is calling for
Elijah!" 48Immediately one of
them ran and took a sponge,
filled *it* with sour wine and put
it on a reed, and offered it to
Him to drink.
49The rest said, "Let Him
alone; let us see if Elijah will
come to save Him."
50And Jesus cried out again
with a loud voice, and yielded
up His spirit.
51Then, behold, the veil of
the temple was torn in two
from top to bottom; and the
earth quaked, and the rocks
were split, 52and the graves
were opened; and many bodies of the saints who had fallen
asleep were raised; 53and coming out of the graves after His
resurrection, they went into
the holy city and appeared to
many.
54So when the centurion
and those with him, who were
guarding Jesus, saw the earthquake and the things that had

27:35 [b] Psalm 22:18 **27:41** [a] M-Text reads *with the scribes, the Pharisees, and the elders.* **27:42** [a] NU-Text reads *He is the King of Israel!* [b] NU-Text and M-Text read *we will believe in Him.* **27:46** [a] Psalm 22:1

happened, they feared greatly,
saying, "Truly this was the Son
of God!"
55And many women who
followed Jesus from Galilee,
ministering to Him, were
there looking on from afar,
56among whom were Mary
Magdalene, Mary the mother
of James and Joses,[a] and the
mother of Zebedee's sons.

JESUS BURIED IN JOSEPH'S TOMB

57Now when evening had
come, there came a rich man
from Arimathea, named Jo-
seph, who himself had also
become a disciple of Jesus.
58This man went to Pilate and
asked for the body of Jesus.
Then Pilate commanded
the body to be given to him.
59When Joseph had taken the
body, he wrapped it in a clean
linen cloth, 60and laid it in his
new tomb which he had hewn
out of the rock; and he rolled a
large stone against the door of
the tomb, and departed. 61And
Mary Magdalene was there,
and the other Mary, sitting
opposite the tomb.

PILATE SETS A GUARD

62On the next day, which
followed the Day of Preparation, the chief priests and
Pharisees gathered together
to Pilate, 63saying, "Sir, we
remember, while He was still
alive, how that deceiver said,
'After three days I will rise.'
64Therefore command that
the tomb be made secure until
the third day, lest His disciples
come by night[a] and steal Him
away, and say to the people,
'He has risen from the dead.'
So the last deception will be
worse than the first."
65Pilate said to them,
"You have a guard; go your
way, make *it* as secure as you
know how." 66So they went
and made the tomb secure,
sealing the stone and setting
the guard.

HE IS RISEN

28 Now after the Sabbath,
as the first *day* of the
week began to dawn, Mary
Magdalene and the other
Mary came to see the tomb.
2And behold, there was a
great earthquake; for an angel
of the Lord descended from
heaven, and came and rolled
back the stone from the door,[a]
and sat on it. 3His countenance was like lightning,
and his clothing as white as
snow. 4And the guards shook
for fear of him, and became
like dead *men*.
5But the angel answered
and said to the women, "Do
not be afraid, for I know that
you seek Jesus who was crucified. 6He is not here; for He
is risen, as He said. Come,

27:56 [a] NU-Text reads *Joseph*. 27:64 [a] NU-Text omits *by night*.
28:2 [a] NU-Text omits *from the door*.

see the place where the Lord
lay. 7And go quickly and tell
His disciples that He is risen
from the dead, and indeed He
is going before you into Galilee; there you will see Him.
Behold, I have told you."
8So they went out quickly
from the tomb with fear and
great joy, and ran to bring His
disciples word.

THE WOMEN WORSHIP THE RISEN LORD

9And as they went to tell
His disciples,[a] behold, Jesus
met them, saying, "Rejoice!"
So they came and held Him by
the feet and worshiped Him.
10Then Jesus said to them, "Do
not be afraid. Go *and* tell My
brethren to go to Galilee, and
there they will see Me."

THE SOLDIERS ARE BRIBED

11Now while they were
going, behold, some of the
guard came into the city and
reported to the chief priests
all the things that had happened. 12When they had assembled with the elders and
consulted together, they gave
a large sum of money to the
soldiers, 13saying, "Tell them,
'His disciples came at night
and stole Him *away* while we
slept.' 14And if this comes to
the governor's ears, we will
appease him and make you
secure." 15So they took the
money and did as they were
instructed; and this saying is
commonly reported among
the Jews until this day.

THE GREAT COMMISSION

16Then the eleven disciples
went away into Galilee, to the
mountain which Jesus had
appointed for them. 17When
they saw Him, they worshiped
Him; but some doubted.
18And Jesus came and
spoke to them, saying, "All
authority has been given to
Me in heaven and on earth.
19Go therefore[a] and make disciples of all the nations, baptizing them in the name of
the Father and of the Son and
of the Holy Spirit, 20teaching
them to observe all things that
I have commanded you; and
lo, I am with you always, *even*
to the end of the age." Amen.[a]

28:9 [a] NU-Text omits the first clause of this verse. 28:19 [a] M-Text omits *therefore*. 28:20 [a] NU-Text omits *Amen*.

THE GOSPEL ACCORDING TO
MARK

JOHN THE BAPTIST PREPARES THE WAY

1 The beginning of the gospel
of Jesus Christ, the Son of
God. 2As it is written in the
Prophets:[a]

> "Behold, I send My
> messenger before
> Your face,
> Who will prepare Your
> way before You."[b]
> 3 "The voice of one crying
> in the wilderness:
> 'Prepare the way
> of the LORD;
> Make His paths
> straight.'"[a]

4John came baptizing in
the wilderness and preaching a baptism of repentance
for the remission of sins.
5Then all the land of Judea,
and those from Jerusalem,
went out to him and were all
baptized by him in the Jordan
River, confessing their sins.

6Now John was clothed
with camel's hair and with a
leather belt around his waist,
and he ate locusts and wild
honey. 7And he preached, saying, "There comes One after
me who is mightier than I,
whose sandal strap I am not
worthy to stoop down and
loose. 8I indeed baptized you
with water, but He will baptize
you with the Holy Spirit."

JOHN BAPTIZES JESUS

9It came to pass in those
days *that* Jesus came from
Nazareth of Galilee, and was
baptized by John in the Jordan. 10And immediately, coming up from[a] the water, He saw
the heavens parting and the
Spirit descending upon Him
like a dove. 11Then a voice
came from heaven, "You are
My beloved Son, in whom I
am well pleased."

SATAN TEMPTS JESUS

12Immediately the Spirit
drove Him into the wilderness. 13And He was there in
the wilderness forty days,
tempted by Satan, and was
with the wild beasts; and the
angels ministered to Him.

JESUS BEGINS HIS GALILEAN MINISTRY

14Now after John was put
in prison, Jesus came to Galilee, preaching the gospel of
the kingdom[a] of God, 15and

1:2 [a] NU-Text reads *Isaiah the prophet.* [b] Malachi 3:1 1:3 [a] Isaiah 40:3
1:10 [a] NU-Text reads *out of.* 1:14 [a] NU-Text omits *of the kingdom.*

saying, "The time is fulfilled,
and the kingdom of God is at
hand. Repent, and believe in
the gospel."

FOUR FISHERMEN CALLED AS DISCIPLES

16And as He walked by the
Sea of Galilee, He saw Simon
and Andrew his brother casting a net into the sea; for they
were fishermen. 17Then Jesus
said to them, "Follow Me, and I
will make you become fishers
of men." 18They immediately
left their nets and followed
Him.

19When He had gone a
little farther from there, He
saw James the *son* of Zebedee, and John his brother, who
also *were* in the boat mending
their nets. 20And immediately
He called them, and they left
their father Zebedee in the
boat with the hired servants,
and went after Him.

JESUS CASTS OUT AN UNCLEAN SPIRIT

21Then they went into Ca-
pernaum, and immediately
on the Sabbath He entered the
synagogue and taught. 22And
they were astonished at His
teaching, for He taught them
as one having authority, and
not as the scribes.

23Now there was a man in
their synagogue with an unclean spirit. And he cried out,
24saying, "Let *us* alone! What
have we to do with You, Jesus
of Nazareth? Did You come to
destroy us? I know who You
are—the Holy One of God!"

25But Jesus rebuked him,
saying, "Be quiet, and come
out of him!" 26And when the
unclean spirit had convulsed
him and cried out with a loud
voice, he came out of him.
27Then they were all amazed,
so that they questioned among
themselves, saying, "What is
this? What new doctrine *is*
this? For with authority[a] He
commands even the unclean
spirits, and they obey Him."
28And immediately His fame
spread throughout all the region around Galilee.

PETER'S MOTHER-IN-LAW HEALED

29Now as soon as they had
come out of the synagogue,
they entered the house of
Simon and Andrew, with
James and John. 30But Si-
mon's wife's mother lay sick
with a fever, and they told
Him about her at once. 31So
He came and took her by the
hand and lifted her up, and
immediately the fever left her.
And she served them.

MANY HEALED AFTER SABBATH SUNSET

32At evening, when the sun
had set, they brought to Him
all who were sick and those
who were demon-possessed.

1:27 [a] NU-Text reads *What is this? A new doctrine with authority.*

33 And the whole city was gathered together at the door. 34 Then He healed many who were sick with various diseases, and cast out many demons; and He did not allow the demons to speak, because they knew Him.

PREACHING IN GALILEE

35 Now in the morning, having risen a long while before daylight, He went out and departed to a solitary place; and there He prayed. 36 And Simon and those *who were* with Him searched for Him. 37 When they found Him, they said to Him, "Everyone is looking for You."

38 But He said to them, "Let us go into the next towns, that I may preach there also, because for this purpose I have come forth."

39 And He was preaching in their synagogues throughout all Galilee, and casting out demons.

JESUS CLEANSES A LEPER

40 Now a leper came to Him, imploring Him, kneeling down to Him and saying to Him, "If You are willing, You can make me clean."

41 Then Jesus, moved with compassion, stretched out *His* hand and touched him, *and said to him,* "I am willing; be cleansed." 42 As soon as He had spoken, immediately the leprosy left him, and he was cleansed. 43 And He strictly warned him and sent him away at once, 44 and said to him, "See that you say nothing to anyone; but go your way, show yourself to the priest, and offer for your cleansing those things which Moses commanded, as a testimony to them."

45 However, he went out and began to proclaim *it* freely, and to spread the matter, so that Jesus could no longer openly enter the city, but was outside in deserted places; and they came to Him from every direction.

JESUS FORGIVES AND HEALS A PARALYTIC

2 And again He entered Capernaum after *some* days, and it was heard that He was in the house. 2 Immediately[a] many gathered together, so that there was no longer room to receive *them,* not even near the door. And He preached the word to them. 3 Then they came to Him, bringing a paralytic who was carried by four *men.* 4 And when they could not come near Him because of the crowd, they uncovered the roof where He was. So when they had broken through, they let down the bed on which the paralytic was lying.

5 When Jesus saw their

2:2 [a] NU-Text omits *Immediately.*

faith, He said to the paralytic,
"Son, your sins are forgiven
you."
6And some of the scribes
were sitting there and reasoning in their hearts, 7"Why does
this *Man* speak blasphemies
like this? Who can forgive sins
but God alone?"
8But immediately, when
Jesus perceived in His spirit
that they reasoned thus within
themselves, He said to them,
"Why do you reason about
these things in your hearts?
9Which is easier, to say to the
paralytic, '*Your* sins are forgiven you,' or to say, 'Arise,
take up your bed and walk'?
10But that you may know that
the Son of Man has power on
earth to forgive sins"—He
said to the paralytic, 11"I say
to you, arise, take up your bed,
and go to your house." 12Im-
mediately he arose, took up
the bed, and went out in the
presence of them all, so that
all were amazed and glorified
God, saying, "We never saw
anything like this!"

MATTHEW THE TAX COLLECTOR

13Then He went out again by
the sea; and all the multitude
came to Him, and He taught
them. 14As He passed by, He
saw Levi the *son* of Alphaeus
sitting at the tax office. And He
said to him, "Follow Me." So he
arose and followed Him.
15Now it happened, as He
was dining in *Levi's* house,
that many tax collectors and
sinners also sat together with
Jesus and His disciples; for
there were many, and they
followed Him. 16And when
the scribes and[a] Pharisees
saw Him eating with the tax
collectors and sinners, they
said to His disciples, "How *is*
it that He eats and drinks with
tax collectors and sinners?"
17When Jesus heard *it,* He
said to them, "Those who are
well have no need of a physician, but those who are sick. I
did not come to call *the* righteous, but sinners, to repentance."[a]

JESUS IS QUESTIONED ABOUT FASTING

18The disciples of John and
of the Pharisees were fasting.
Then they came and said to
Him, "Why do the disciples
of John and of the Pharisees
fast, but Your disciples do not
fast?"
19And Jesus said to them,
"Can the friends of the bridegroom fast while the bridegroom is with them? As long
as they have the bridegroom
with them they cannot fast.
20But the days will come
when the bridegroom will
be taken away from them,
and then they will fast in
those days. 21No one sews a
piece of unshrunk cloth on

2:16 [a] NU-Text reads *of the.* 2:17 [a] NU-Text omits *to repentance.*

an old garment; or else the
new piece pulls away from
the old, and the tear is made
worse. 22And no one puts new
wine into old wineskins; or
else the new wine bursts the
wineskins, the wine is spilled,
and the wineskins are ruined.
But new wine must be put into
new wineskins."

JESUS IS LORD OF THE SABBATH

23Now it happened that
He went through the grainfields on the Sabbath; and as
they went His disciples began
to pluck the heads of grain.
24And the Pharisees said to
Him, "Look, why do they do
what is not lawful on the Sabbath?"

25But He said to them,
"Have you never read what
David did when he was in need
and hungry, he and those with
him: 26how he went into the
house of God *in the days* of
Abiathar the high priest, and
ate the showbread, which is
not lawful to eat except for the
priests, and also gave some
to those who were with him?"

27And He said to them, "The
Sabbath was made for man,
and not man for the Sabbath.
28Therefore the Son of Man is
also Lord of the Sabbath."

HEALING ON THE SABBATH

3 And He entered the syn-
agogue again, and a man
was there who had a withered
hand. 2So they watched Him
closely, whether He would
heal him on the Sabbath, so
that they might accuse Him.
3And He said to the man who
had the withered hand, "Step
forward." 4Then He said to
them, "Is it lawful on the
Sabbath to do good or to do
evil, to save life or to kill?"
But they kept silent. 5And
when He had looked around
at them with anger, being
grieved by the hardness of
their hearts, He said to the
man, "Stretch out your hand."
And he stretched *it* out, and
his hand was restored as
whole as the other.[a] 6Then
the Pharisees went out and
immediately plotted with the
Herodians against Him, how
they might destroy Him.

A GREAT MULTITUDE FOLLOWS JESUS

7But Jesus withdrew with
His disciples to the sea. And a
great multitude from Galilee
followed Him, and from Judea
8and Jerusalem and Idumea
and beyond the Jordan; and
those from Tyre and Sidon,
a great multitude, when they
heard how many things He
was doing, came to Him. 9So
He told His disciples that a
small boat should be kept
ready for Him because of the
multitude, lest they should
crush Him. 10For He healed

3:5 [a] NU-Text omits *as whole as the other.*

many, so that as many as had afflictions pressed about Him to touch Him. 11And the unclean spirits, whenever they saw Him, fell down before Him and cried out, saying, "You are the Son of God." 12But He sternly warned them that they should not make Him known.

THE TWELVE APOSTLES

13And He went up on the mountain and called to *Him* those He Himself wanted. And they came to Him. 14Then He appointed twelve,[a] that they might be with Him and that He might send them out to preach, 15and to have power to heal sicknesses and[a] to cast out demons: 16Simon,[a] to whom He gave the name Peter; 17James the *son* of Zebedee and John the brother of James, to whom He gave the name Boanerges, that is, "Sons of Thunder"; 18Andrew, Philip, Bartholomew, Matthew, Thomas, James the *son* of Alphaeus, Thaddaeus, Simon the Cananite; 19and Judas Iscariot, who also betrayed Him. And they went into a house.

A HOUSE DIVIDED CANNOT STAND

20Then the multitude came together again, so that they could not so much as eat bread. 21But when His own people heard *about this,* they went out to lay hold of Him, for they said, "He is out of His mind."

22And the scribes who came down from Jerusalem said, "He has Beelzebub," and, "By the ruler of the demons He casts out demons."

23So He called them to *Himself* and said to them in parables: "How can Satan cast out Satan? 24If a kingdom is divided against itself, that kingdom cannot stand. 25And if a house is divided against itself, that house cannot stand. 26And if Satan has risen up against himself, and is divided, he cannot stand, but has an end. 27No one can enter a strong man's house and plunder his goods, unless he first binds the strong man. And then he will plunder his house.

THE UNPARDONABLE SIN

28"Assuredly, I say to you, all sins will be forgiven the sons of men, and whatever blasphemies they may utter; 29but he who blasphemes against the Holy Spirit never has forgiveness, but is subject to eternal condemnation"— 30because they said, "He has an unclean spirit."

3:14 [a] NU-Text adds *whom He also named apostles.* 3:15 [a] NU-Text omits *to heal sicknesses and.* 3:16 [a] NU-Text reads *and He appointed the twelve: Simon . . . .*

JESUS' MOTHER AND BROTHERS SEND FOR HIM

31Then His brothers and His
mother came, and standing
outside they sent to Him, calling Him. 32And a multitude
was sitting around Him; and
they said to Him, "Look, Your
mother and Your brothers[a] are
outside seeking You."

33But He answered them,
saying, "Who is My mother,
or My brothers?" 34And He
looked around in a circle at
those who sat about Him, and
said, "Here are My mother
and My brothers! 35For whoever does the will of God is
My brother and My sister and
mother."

THE PARABLE OF THE SOWER

4 And again He began to
teach by the sea. And a
great multitude was gathered
to Him, so that He got into a
boat and sat *in it* on the sea;
and the whole multitude was
on the land facing the sea.
2Then He taught them many
things by parables, and said
to them in His teaching:

3"Listen! Behold, a sower
went out to sow. 4And it happened, as he sowed, *that* some
seed fell by the wayside; and the
birds of the air[a] came and devoured it. 5Some fell on stony
ground, where it did not have
much earth; and immediately
it sprang up because it had no
depth of earth. 6But when the
sun was up it was scorched,
and because it had no root
it withered away. 7And some
seed fell among thorns; and
the thorns grew up and choked
it, and it yielded no crop. 8But
other *seed* fell on good ground
and yielded a crop that sprang
up, increased and produced:
some thirtyfold, some sixty,
and some a hundred."

9And He said to them,[a] "He
who has ears to hear, let him
hear!"

THE PURPOSE OF PARABLES

10But when He was alone,
those around Him with the
twelve asked Him about the
parable. 11And He said to
them, "To you it has been
given to know the mystery
of the kingdom of God; but
to those who are outside, all
things come in parables, 12so
that

'Seeing they may see
and not perceive,
And hearing they
may hear and not
understand;
Lest they should turn,
And *their* sins be
forgiven them.'"[a]

3:32 [a] NU-Text and M-Text add *and Your sisters.*
4:4 [a] NU-Text and M-Text omit *of the air.* 4:9 [a] NU-Text and M-Text omit *to them.* 4:12 [a] Isaiah 6:9, 10

THE PARABLE OF THE SOWER EXPLAINED

13And He said to them, "Do
you not understand this parable? How then will you understand all the parables? 14The
sower sows the word. 15And
these are the ones by the wayside where the word is sown.
When they hear, Satan comes
immediately and takes away
the word that was sown in
their hearts. 16These likewise
are the ones sown on stony
ground who, when they hear
the word, immediately receive
it with gladness; 17and they
have no root in themselves,
and so endure only for a time.
Afterward, when tribulation
or persecution arises for the
word's sake, immediately they
stumble. 18Now these are the
ones sown among thorns;
they are the ones who hear
the word, 19and the cares of
this world, the deceitfulness
of riches, and the desires for
other things entering in choke
the word, and it becomes unfruitful. 20But these are the
ones sown on good ground,
those who hear the word, accept *it,* and bear fruit: some
thirtyfold, some sixty, and
some a hundred."

LIGHT UNDER A BASKET

21Also He said to them, "Is a
lamp brought to be put under
a basket or under a bed? Is it
not to be set on a lampstand?
22For there is nothing hidden
which will not be revealed,
nor has anything been kept
secret but that it should come
to light. 23If anyone has ears
to hear, let him hear."

24Then He said to them,
"Take heed what you hear.
With the same measure you
use, it will be measured to you;
and to you who hear, more will
be given. 25For whoever has,
to him more will be given; but
whoever does not have, even
what he has will be taken away
from him."

THE PARABLE OF THE GROWING SEED

26And He said, "The king-
dom of God is as if a man
should scatter seed on the
ground, 27and should sleep by
night and rise by day, and the
seed should sprout and grow,
he himself does not know how.
28For the earth yields crops by
itself: first the blade, then the
head, after that the full grain
in the head. 29But when the
grain ripens, immediately he
puts in the sickle, because the
harvest has come."

THE PARABLE OF THE MUSTARD SEED

30Then He said, "To what
shall we liken the kingdom
of God? Or with what parable
shall we picture it? 31*It is* like
a mustard seed which, when
it is sown on the ground, is
smaller than all the seeds on
earth; 32but when it is sown, it
grows up and becomes greater
than all herbs, and shoots

out large branches, so that
the birds of the air may nest
under its shade."

JESUS' USE OF PARABLES

33And with many such
parables He spoke the word
to them as they were able to
hear *it.* 34But without a parable He did not speak to them.
And when they were alone,
He explained all things to His
disciples.

WIND AND WAVE OBEY JESUS

35On the same day, when
evening had come, He said to
them, "Let us cross over to the
other side." 36Now when they
had left the multitude, they
took Him along in the boat as
He was. And other little boats
were also with Him. 37And a
great windstorm arose, and
the waves beat into the boat,
so that it was already filling.
38But He was in the stern,
asleep on a pillow. And they
awoke Him and said to Him,
"Teacher, do You not care that
we are perishing?"

39Then He arose and re-
buked the wind, and said to
the sea, "Peace, be still!" And
the wind ceased and there was
a great calm. 40But He said to
them, "Why are you so fearful? How *is it* that you have
no faith?"[a] 41And they feared
exceedingly, and said to one
another, "Who can this be,
that even the wind and the
sea obey Him!"

A DEMON-POSSESSED MAN HEALED

5 Then they came to the
other side of the sea, to
the country of the Gadarenes.[a]
2And when He had come out
of the boat, immediately there
met Him out of the tombs a
man with an unclean spirit,
3who had *his* dwelling among
the tombs; and no one could
bind him,[a] not even with
chains, 4because he had often
been bound with shackles and
chains. And the chains had
been pulled apart by him,
and the shackles broken in
pieces; neither could anyone
tame him. 5And always, night
and day, he was in the mountains and in the tombs, crying
out and cutting himself with
stones.

6When he saw Jesus from
afar, he ran and worshiped
Him. 7And he cried out with
a loud voice and said, "What
have I to do with You, Jesus,
Son of the Most High God? I
implore You by God that You
do not torment me."

8For He said to him, "Come
out of the man, unclean
spirit!" 9Then He asked him,
"What *is* your name?"

And he answered, saying,
"My name *is* Legion; for we are

4:40 [a] NU-Text reads *Have you still no faith?* 5:1 [a] NU-Text reads *Gerasenes.* 5:3 [a] NU-Text adds *anymore.*

many." 10 Also he begged Him
earnestly that He would not
send them out of the country.
11 Now a large herd of swine
was feeding there near the
mountains. 12 So all the demons begged Him, saying,
"Send us to the swine, that
we may enter them." 13 And
at once Jesus[a] gave them
permission. Then the un-
clean spirits went out and
entered the swine (there were
about two thousand); and the
herd ran violently down the
steep place into the sea, and
drowned in the sea.
14 So those who fed the
swine fled, and they told *it* in
the city and in the country.
And they went out to see what
it was that had happened.
15 Then they came to Jesus,
and saw the one *who had been*
demon-possessed and had the
legion, sitting and clothed and
in his right mind. And they
were afraid. 16 And those who
saw it told them how it happened to him *who had been*
demon-possessed, and about
the swine. 17 Then they began
to plead with Him to depart
from their region.
18 And when He got into
the boat, he who had been
demon-possessed begged
Him that he might be with
Him. 19 However, Jesus did not
permit him, but said to him,
"Go home to your friends, and
tell them what great things
the Lord has done for you, and
how He has had compassion
on you." 20 And he departed
and began to proclaim in Decapolis all that Jesus had done
for him; and all marveled.

A GIRL RESTORED TO LIFE AND A WOMAN HEALED

21 Now when Jesus had
crossed over again by boat to
the other side, a great multitude gathered to Him; and He
was by the sea. 22 And behold,
one of the rulers of the synagogue came, Jairus by name.
And when he saw Him, he
fell at His feet 23 and begged
Him earnestly, saying, "My little daughter lies at the point
of death. Come and lay Your
hands on her, that she may
be healed, and she will live."
24 So *Jesus* went with him, and
a great multitude followed
Him and thronged Him.
25 Now a certain woman
had a flow of blood for twelve
years, 26 and had suffered
many things from many physicians. She had spent all that
she had and was no better, but
rather grew worse. 27 When she
heard about Jesus, she came
behind *Him* in the crowd and
touched His garment. 28 For
she said, "If only I may touch
His clothes, I shall be made
well."
29 Immediately the foun-
tain of her blood was dried
up, and she felt in *her* body

5:13 [a] NU-Text reads *And He gave.*

that she was healed of the affliction. 30And Jesus, immediately knowing in Himself that
power had gone out of Him,
turned around in the crowd
and said, "Who touched My
clothes?"

31But His disciples said to
Him, "You see the multitude
thronging You, and You say,
'Who touched Me?'"

32And He looked around
to see her who had done this
thing. 33But the woman, fearing and trembling, knowing
what had happened to her,
came and fell down before
Him and told Him the whole
truth. 34And He said to her,
"Daughter, your faith has made
you well. Go in peace, and be
healed of your affliction."

35While He was still speaking, *some* came from the ruler
of the synagogue's *house* who
said, "Your daughter is dead.
Why trouble the Teacher any
further?"

36As soon as Jesus heard
the word that was spoken, He
said to the ruler of the synagogue, "Do not be afraid; only
believe." 37And He permitted
no one to follow Him except
Peter, James, and John the
brother of James. 38Then He
came to the house of the ruler
of the synagogue, and saw a
tumult and those who wept
and wailed loudly. 39When
He came in, He said to them,
"Why make this commotion
and weep? The child is not
dead, but sleeping."

40And they ridiculed Him.
But when He had put them
all outside, He took the father
and the mother of the child,
and those *who were* with Him,
and entered where the child
was lying. 41Then He took the
child by the hand, and said to
her, "Talitha, cumi," which is
translated, "Little girl, I say
to you, arise." 42Immediately
the girl arose and walked, for
she was twelve years *of age*.
And they were overcome with
great amazement. 43But He
commanded them strictly
that no one should know
it, and said that *something*
should be given her to eat.

JESUS REJECTED AT NAZARETH

6 Then He went out from
there and came to His
own country, and His dis-
ciples followed Him. 2And
when the Sabbath had come,
He began to teach in the synagogue. And many hearing
Him were astonished, saying,
"Where *did* this Man *get* these
things? And what wisdom *is*
this which is given to Him,
that such mighty works are
performed by His hands! 3Is
this not the carpenter, the Son
of Mary, and brother of James,
Joses, Judas, and Simon? And
are not His sisters here with
us?" So they were offended
at Him.

4But Jesus said to them, "A
prophet is not without honor
except in his own country,

among his own relatives, and in his own house." 5Now He could do no mighty work there, except that He laid His hands on a few sick people and healed *them.* 6And He marveled because of their unbelief. Then He went about the villages in a circuit, teaching.

SENDING OUT THE TWELVE

7And He called the twelve to *Himself,* and began to send them out two *by* two, and gave them power over unclean spirits. 8He commanded them to take nothing for the journey except a staff—no bag, no bread, no copper in *their* money belts— 9but to wear sandals, and not to put on two tunics.

10Also He said to them, "In whatever place you enter a house, stay there till you depart from that place. 11And whoever[a] will not receive you nor hear you, when you depart from there, shake off the dust under your feet as a testimony against them.[b] Assuredly, I say to you, it will be more tolerable for Sodom and Gomorrah in the day of judgment than for that city!"

12So they went out and preached that *people* should repent. 13And they cast out many demons, and anointed with oil many who were sick, and healed *them.*

JOHN THE BAPTIST BEHEADED

14Now King Herod heard *of Him,* for His name had become well known. And he said, "John the Baptist is risen from the dead, and therefore these powers are at work in him."

15Others said, "It is Elijah."

And others said, "It is the Prophet, or[a] like one of the prophets."

16But when Herod heard, he said, "This is John, whom I beheaded; he has been raised from the dead!" 17For Herod himself had sent and laid hold of John, and bound him in prison for the sake of Herodias, his brother Philip's wife; for he had married her. 18Because John had said to Herod, "It is not lawful for you to have your brother's wife."

19Therefore Herodias held it against him and wanted to kill him, but she could not; 20for Herod feared John, knowing that he *was* a just and holy man, and he protected him. And when he heard him, he did many things, and heard him gladly.

21Then an opportune day came when Herod on his birthday gave a feast for his nobles, the high officers, and the chief *men* of Galilee. 22And when Herodias' daughter herself came in and danced, and

6:11 [a] NU-Text reads *whatever place.* [b] NU-Text omits the rest of this verse. **6:15** [a] NU-Text and M-Text omit *or.*

pleased Herod and those who
sat with him, the king said to
the girl, "Ask me whatever you
want, and I will give *it* to you."
23He also swore to her, "Whatever you ask me, I will give
you, up to half my kingdom."
24So she went out and said
to her mother, "What shall I
ask?"

And she said, "The head of
John the Baptist!"

25Immediately she came
in with haste to the king and
asked, saying, "I want you to
give me at once the head of
John the Baptist on a platter."

26And the king was exceedingly sorry; *yet,* because of the
oaths and because of those
who sat with him, he did not
want to refuse her. 27Imme-
diately the king sent an ex-
ecutioner and commanded
his head to be brought. And
he went and beheaded him
in prison, 28brought his head
on a platter, and gave it to the
girl; and the girl gave it to her
mother. 29When his disciples
heard *of it,* they came and took
away his corpse and laid it in
a tomb.

FEEDING THE FIVE THOUSAND

30Then the apostles gath-
ered to Jesus and told Him
all things, both what they
had done and what they had
taught. 31And He said to them,
"Come aside by yourselves to
a deserted place and rest a
while." For there were many
coming and going, and they
did not even have time to
eat. 32So they departed to a
deserted place in the boat by
themselves.

33But the multitudes[a] saw
them departing, and many
knew Him and ran there on
foot from all the cities. They
arrived before them and came
together to Him. 34And Jesus,
when He came out, saw a great
multitude and was moved
with compassion for them,
because they were like sheep
not having a shepherd. So He
began to teach them many
things. 35When the day was
now far spent, His disciples
came to Him and said, "This is
a deserted place, and already
the hour *is* late. 36Send them
away, that they may go into
the surrounding country and
villages and buy themselves
bread;[a] for they have nothing
to eat."

37But He answered and
said to them, "You give them
something to eat."

And they said to Him,
"Shall we go and buy two hundred denarii worth of bread
and give them *something* to
eat?"

38But He said to them,
"How many loaves do you
have? Go and see."

6:33 [a] NU-Text and M-Text read *they.* 6:36 [a] NU-Text reads *something to eat* and omits the rest of this verse.

And when they found out they said, "Five, and two fish."

39 Then He commanded them to make them all sit down in groups on the green grass. 40 So they sat down in ranks, in hundreds and in fifties. 41 And when He had taken the five loaves and the two fish, He looked up to heaven, blessed and broke the loaves, and gave *them* to His disciples to set before them; and the two fish He divided among *them* all. 42 So they all ate and were filled. 43 And they took up twelve baskets full of fragments and of the fish. 44 Now those who had eaten the loaves were about[a] five thousand men.

JESUS WALKS ON THE SEA

45 Immediately He made His disciples get into the boat and go before Him to the other side, to Bethsaida, while He sent the multitude away. 46 And when He had sent them away, He departed to the mountain to pray. 47 Now when evening came, the boat was in the middle of the sea; and He *was* alone on the land. 48 Then He saw them straining at rowing, for the wind was against them. Now about the fourth watch of the night He came to them, walking on the sea, and would have passed them by. 49 And when they saw Him walking on the sea, they supposed it was a ghost, and cried out; 50 for they all saw Him and were troubled. But immediately He talked with them and said to them, "Be of good cheer! It is I; do not be afraid." 51 Then He went up into the boat to them, and the wind ceased. And they were greatly amazed in themselves beyond measure, and marveled. 52 For they had not understood about the loaves, because their heart was hardened.

MANY TOUCH HIM AND ARE MADE WELL

53 When they had crossed over, they came to the land of Gennesaret and anchored there. 54 And when they came out of the boat, immediately the people recognized Him, 55 ran through that whole surrounding region, and began to carry about on beds those who were sick to wherever they heard He was. 56 Wherever He entered, into villages, cities, or the country, they laid the sick in the marketplaces, and begged Him that they might just touch the hem of His garment. And as many as touched Him were made well.

DEFILEMENT COMES FROM WITHIN

7 Then the Pharisees and some of the scribes came together to Him, having come

6:44 [a] NU-Text and M-Text omit *about*.

from Jerusalem. 2Now when[a]
they saw some of His disciples
eat bread with defiled, that is,
with unwashed hands, they
found fault. 3For the Pharisees
and all the Jews do not eat unless they wash *their* hands in a
special way, holding the tradition of the elders. 4*When they*
come from the marketplace,
they do not eat unless they
wash. And there are many
other things which they have
received and hold, *like* the
washing of cups, pitchers,
copper vessels, and couches.
5Then the Pharisees and
scribes asked Him, "Why do
Your disciples not walk according to the tradition of
the elders, but eat bread with
unwashed hands?"
6He answered and said to
them, "Well did Isaiah prophesy of you hypocrites, as it is
written:

'This people honors
Me with *their* lips,
But their heart is
far from Me.
7 And in vain they
worship Me,
Teaching *as* doctrines
the commandments
of men.'[a]

8For laying aside the commandment of God, you hold
the tradition of men[a]—the
washing of pitchers and cups,
and many other such things
you do."
9He said to them, "*All too*
well you reject the commandment of God, that you may
keep your tradition. 10For
Moses said, 'Honor your
father and your mother';[a]
and, 'He who curses father
or mother, let him be put to
death.'[b] 11But you say, 'If a man
says to his father or mother,
"Whatever profit you might
have received from me *is* Cor-
ban"—' (that is, a gift *to God*),
12then you no longer let him
do anything for his father or
his mother, 13making the word
of God of no effect through
your tradition which you have
handed down. And many such
things you do."
14When He had called all
the multitude to *Himself*, He
said to them, "Hear Me, everyone, and understand: 15There
is nothing that enters a man
from outside which can defile him; but the things which
come out of him, those are the
things that defile a man. 16If
anyone has ears to hear, let
him hear!"[a]
17When He had entered a
house away from the crowd,
His disciples asked Him concerning the parable. 18So He
said to them, "Are you thus
without understanding also?

7:2 [a] NU-Text omits *when* and *they found fault.* 7:7 [a] Isaiah 29:13
7:8 [a] NU-Text omits the rest of this verse. 7:10 [a] Exodus 20:12;
Deuteronomy 5:16 [b] Exodus 21:17 7:16 [a] NU-Text omits this verse.

Do you not perceive that whatever enters a man from outside
cannot defile him, 19because it
does not enter his heart but his
stomach, and is eliminated,
thus purifying all foods?"[a]
20And He said, "What comes
out of a man, that defiles a
man. 21For from within, out
of the heart of men, proceed
evil thoughts, adulteries, fornications, murders, 22thefts,
covetousness, wickedness,
deceit, lewdness, an evil eye,
blasphemy, pride, foolishness.
23All these evil things come
from within and defile a man."

A GENTILE SHOWS HER FAITH

24From there He arose and
went to the region of Tyre
and Sidon.[a] And He entered
a house and wanted no one
to know *it*, but He could not
be hidden. 25For a woman
whose young daughter had
an unclean spirit heard about
Him, and she came and fell
at His feet. 26The woman was
a Greek, a Syro-Phoenician
by birth, and she kept asking
Him to cast the demon out
of her daughter. 27But Jesus
said to her, "Let the children
be filled first, for it is not good
to take the children's bread
and throw *it* to the little dogs."
28And she answered and
said to Him, "Yes, Lord, yet
even the little dogs under the
table eat from the children's
crumbs."
29Then He said to her, "For
this saying go your way; the
demon has gone out of your
daughter."
30And when she had come
to her house, she found the
demon gone out, and her
daughter lying on the bed.

JESUS HEALS A DEAF-MUTE

31Again, departing from
the region of Tyre and Sidon,
He came through the midst
of the region of Decapolis
to the Sea of Galilee. 32Then
they brought to Him one who
was deaf and had an impedi-
ment in his speech, and they
begged Him to put His hand
on him. 33And He took him
aside from the multitude, and
put His fingers in his ears,
and He spat and touched his
tongue. 34Then, looking up to
heaven, He sighed, and said
to him, "Ephphatha," that is,
"Be opened."
35Immediately his ears
were opened, and the im-
pediment of his tongue was
loosed, and he spoke plainly.
36Then He commanded them
that they should tell no one;
but the more He commanded
them, the more widely they
proclaimed *it*. 37And they were
astonished beyond measure,

7:19 [a] NU-Text ends quotation with *eliminated,* setting off the final clause as Mark's comment that Jesus has declared all foods clean. 7:24 [a] NU-Text omits *and Sidon.*

saying, "He has done all things
well. He makes both the deaf
to hear and the mute to speak."

FEEDING THE FOUR THOUSAND

8 In those days, the multitude being very great and
having nothing to eat, Jesus
called His disciples *to Him*
and said to them, 2 "I have
compassion on the multi-
tude, because they have now
continued with Me three days
and have nothing to eat. 3 And
if I send them away hungry
to their own houses, they will
faint on the way; for some of
them have come from afar."

4 Then His disciples an-
swered Him, "How can one
satisfy these people with
bread here in the wilderness?"

5 He asked them, "How
many loaves do you have?"

And they said, "Seven."

6 So He commanded the
multitude to sit down on the
ground. And He took the seven
loaves and gave thanks, broke
them and gave *them* to His disciples to set before *them;* and
they set *them* before the multitude. 7 They also had a few
small fish; and having blessed
them, He said to set them also
before *them.* 8 So they ate and
were filled, and they took up
seven large baskets of leftover
fragments. 9 Now those who
had eaten were about four
thousand. And He sent them
away, 10 immediately got into
the boat with His disciples,
and came to the region of Dal-
manutha.

THE PHARISEES SEEK A SIGN

11 Then the Pharisees came
out and began to dispute
with Him, seeking from Him
a sign from heaven, testing
Him. 12 But He sighed deeply
in His spirit, and said, "Why
does this generation seek a
sign? Assuredly, I say to you,
no sign shall be given to this
generation."

BEWARE OF THE LEAVEN OF THE PHARISEES AND HEROD

13 And He left them, and
getting into the boat again, departed to the other side. 14 Now
the disciples[a] had forgotten to
take bread, and they did not
have more than one loaf with
them in the boat. 15 Then He
charged them, saying, "Take
heed, beware of the leaven of
the Pharisees and the leaven
of Herod."

16 And they reasoned
among themselves, saying, "*It
is* because we have no bread."

17 But Jesus, being aware
of *it,* said to them, "Why do
you reason because you have
no bread? Do you not yet
perceive nor understand? Is
your heart still[a] hardened?
18 Having eyes, do you not see?

8:14 [a] NU-Text and M-Text read *they.* 8:17 [a] NU-Text omits *still.*

And having ears, do you not
hear? And do you not remember? 19When I broke the five
loaves for the five thousand,
how many baskets full of fragments did you take up?"

They said to Him, "Twelve."
20"Also, when I broke the
seven for the four thousand,
how many large baskets full of
fragments did you take up?"

And they said, "Seven."
21So He said to them, "How
is it you do not understand?"

A BLIND MAN HEALED AT BETHSAIDA

22Then He came to Bethsa-
ida; and they brought a blind
man to Him, and begged Him
to touch him. 23So He took the
blind man by the hand and
led him out of the town. And
when He had spit on his eyes
and put His hands on him, He
asked him if he saw anything.
24And he looked up and
said, "I see men like trees,
walking."
25Then He put *His* hands on
his eyes again and made him
look up. And he was restored
and saw everyone clearly.
26Then He sent him away to
his house, saying, "Neither go
into the town, nor tell anyone
in the town."[a]

PETER CONFESSES JESUS AS THE CHRIST

27Now Jesus and His disciples went out to the towns of
Caesarea Philippi; and on the
road He asked His disciples,
saying to them, "Who do men
say that I am?"
28So they answered, "John
the Baptist; but some *say*,
Elijah; and others, one of the
prophets."
29He said to them, "But
who do you say that I am?"

Peter answered and said to
Him, "You are the Christ."
30Then He strictly warned
them that they should tell no
one about Him.

JESUS PREDICTS HIS DEATH AND RESURRECTION

31And He began to teach
them that the Son of Man must
suffer many things, and be rejected by the elders and chief
priests and scribes, and be
killed, and after three days
rise again. 32He spoke this
word openly. Then Peter took
Him aside and began to rebuke Him. 33But when He had
turned around and looked
at His disciples, He rebuked
Peter, saying, "Get behind Me,
Satan! For you are not mindful
of the things of God, but the
things of men."

TAKE UP THE CROSS AND FOLLOW HIM

34When He had called
the people to *Himself*, with
His disciples also, He said to
them, "Whoever desires to
come after Me, let him deny

8:26 [a] NU-Text reads *"Do not even go into the town."*

himself, and take up his
cross, and follow Me. 35 For
whoever desires to save his
life will lose it, but whoever
loses his life for My sake and
the gospel's will save it. 36 For
what will it profit a man if he
gains the whole world, and
loses his own soul? 37 Or what
will a man give in exchange
for his soul? 38 For whoever is
ashamed of Me and My words
in this adulterous and sinful
generation, of him the Son
of Man also will be ashamed
when He comes in the glory
of His Father with the holy
angels."

9 And He said to them, "Assuredly, I say to you that
there are some standing here
who will not taste death till
they see the kingdom of God
present with power."

JESUS TRANSFIGURED ON THE MOUNT

2 Now after six days Jesus
took Peter, James, and John,
and led them up on a high
mountain apart by them-
selves; and He was transfig-
ured before them. 3 His clothes
became shining, exceedingly
white, like snow, such as no
launderer on earth can whiten
them. 4 And Elijah appeared
to them with Moses, and they
were talking with Jesus. 5 Then
Peter answered and said to
Jesus, "Rabbi, it is good for
us to be here; and let us make
three tabernacles: one for
You, one for Moses, and one
for Elijah"— 6 because he did
not know what to say, for they
were greatly afraid.

7 And a cloud came and
overshadowed them; and a
voice came out of the cloud,
saying, "This is My beloved
Son. Hear Him!" 8 Suddenly,
when they had looked around,
they saw no one anymore, but
only Jesus with themselves.

9 Now as they came down
from the mountain, He commanded them that they should
tell no one the things they had
seen, till the Son of Man had
risen from the dead. 10 So they
kept this word to themselves,
questioning what the rising
from the dead meant.

11 And they asked Him, saying, "Why do the scribes say
that Elijah must come first?"

12 Then He answered and
told them, "Indeed, Elijah is
coming first and restores all
things. And how is it written
concerning the Son of Man,
that He must suffer many
things and be treated with
contempt? 13 But I say to you
that Elijah has also come, and
they did to him whatever they
wished, as it is written of him."

A BOY IS HEALED

14 And when He came to
the disciples, He saw a great
multitude around them, and
scribes disputing with them.
15 Immediately, when they
saw Him, all the people were
greatly amazed, and running
to *Him*, greeted Him. 16 And He

asked the scribes, "What are
you discussing with them?"
17Then one of the crowd
answered and said, "Teacher,
I brought You my son, who
has a mute spirit. 18And wherever it seizes him, it throws
him down; he foams at the
mouth, gnashes his teeth,
and becomes rigid. So I spoke
to Your disciples, that they
should cast it out, but they
could not."
19He answered him and
said, "O faithless generation, how long shall I be with
you? How long shall I bear
with you? Bring him to Me."
20Then they brought him to
Him. And when he saw Him,
immediately the spirit convulsed him, and he fell on the
ground and wallowed, foaming at the mouth.
21So He asked his father,
"How long has this been happening to him?"

And he said, "From child-
hood. 22And often he has
thrown him both into the fire
and into the water to destroy
him. But if You can do anything, have compassion on
us and help us."
23Jesus said to him, "If you
can believe,[a] all things *are*
possible to him who believes."
24Immediately the father
of the child cried out and said
with tears, "Lord, I believe;
help my unbelief!"
25When Jesus saw that
the people came running together, He rebuked the unclean spirit, saying to it, "Deaf
and dumb spirit, I command
you, come out of him and
enter him no more!" 26Then
the spirit cried out, convulsed
him greatly, and came out of
him. And he became as one
dead, so that many said, "He
is dead." 27But Jesus took him
by the hand and lifted him up,
and he arose.
28And when He had come
into the house, His disciples
asked Him privately, "Why
could we not cast it out?"
29So He said to them, "This
kind can come out by nothing
but prayer and fasting."[a]

JESUS AGAIN PREDICTS HIS DEATH AND RESURRECTION

30Then they departed from
there and passed through Galilee, and He did not want anyone to know *it*. 31For He taught
His disciples and said to them,
"The Son of Man is being betrayed into the hands of men,
and they will kill Him. And
after He is killed, He will rise
the third day." 32But they did
not understand this saying,
and were afraid to ask Him.

WHO IS THE GREATEST?

33Then He came to Caper-
naum. And when He was in

9:23 [a] NU-Text reads "'*If You can!' All things* . . . ."
9:29 [a] NU-Text omits *and fasting.*

the house He asked them,
"What was it you disputed
among yourselves on the
road?" 34But they kept silent,
for on the road they had disputed among themselves who
would be the greatest. 35And
He sat down, called the twelve,
and said to them, "If anyone
desires to be first, he shall be
last of all and servant of all."
36Then He took a little child
and set him in the midst of
them. And when He had taken
him in His arms, He said to
them, 37"Whoever receives
one of these little children
in My name receives Me; and
whoever receives Me, receives
not Me but Him who sent Me."

JESUS FORBIDS SECTARIANISM

38Now John answered
Him, saying, "Teacher, we saw
someone who does not follow
us casting out demons in Your
name, and we forbade him because he does not follow us."
39But Jesus said, "Do not
forbid him, for no one who
works a miracle in My name
can soon afterward speak evil
of Me. 40For he who is not
against us is on our[a] side.
41For whoever gives you a cup
of water to drink in My name,
because you belong to Christ,
assuredly, I say to you, he will
by no means lose his reward.

JESUS WARNS OF OFFENSES

42"But whoever causes
one of these little ones who
believe in Me to stumble, it
would be better for him if a
millstone were hung around
his neck, and he were thrown
into the sea. 43If your hand
causes you to sin, cut it off. It
is better for you to enter into
life maimed, rather than having two hands, to go to hell,
into the fire that shall never
be quenched— 44where

'Their worm does not die,
And the fire is not
quenched.'[a]

45And if your foot causes you
to sin, cut it off. It is better for
you to enter life lame, rather
than having two feet, to be cast
into hell, into the fire that shall
never be quenched— 46where

'Their worm does not die,
And the fire is not
quenched.'[a]

47And if your eye causes you
to sin, pluck it out. It is better
for you to enter the kingdom
of God with one eye, rather
than having two eyes, to be
cast into hell fire— 48where

'Their worm does not die,
And the fire is not
quenched.'[a]

9:40 [a] M-Text reads *against you is on your side.* 9:44 [a] NU-Text omits this verse. 9:46 [a] NU-Text omits the last clause of verse 45 and all of verse 46. 9:48 [a] Isaiah 66:24

TASTELESS SALT IS WORTHLESS

49"For everyone will be seasoned with fire,[a] and every
sacrifice will be seasoned with
salt. 50Salt *is* good, but if the
salt loses its flavor, how will
you season it? Have salt in
yourselves, and have peace
with one another."

MARRIAGE AND DIVORCE

10 Then He arose from
there and came to the
region of Judea by the other
side of the Jordan. And multitudes gathered to Him again,
and as He was accustomed, He
taught them again.

2The Pharisees came and
asked Him, "Is it lawful for
a man to divorce *his* wife?"
testing Him.

3And He answered and said
to them, "What did Moses
command you?"

4They said, "Moses permitted *a man* to write a certificate
of divorce, and to dismiss *her.*"

5And Jesus answered and
said to them, "Because of the
hardness of your heart he
wrote you this precept. 6But
from the beginning of the creation, God 'made them male
and female.'[a] 7'For this reason
a man shall leave his father
and mother and be joined to
his wife, 8and the two shall
become one flesh';[a] so then
they are no longer two, but
one flesh. 9Therefore what
God has joined together, let
not man separate."

10In the house His disciples
also asked Him again about
the same *matter.* 11So He said
to them, "Whoever divorces
his wife and marries another
commits adultery against her.
12And if a woman divorces her
husband and marries another,
she commits adultery."

JESUS BLESSES LITTLE CHILDREN

13Then they brought lit-
tle children to Him, that He
might touch them; but the
disciples rebuked those who
brought *them.* 14But when
Jesus saw *it,* He was greatly
displeased and said to them,
"Let the little children come to
Me, and do not forbid them;
for of such is the kingdom
of God. 15Assuredly, I say to
you, whoever does not receive
the kingdom of God as a little
child will by no means enter
it." 16And He took them up in
His arms, laid *His* hands on
them, and blessed them.

JESUS COUNSELS THE RICH YOUNG RULER

17Now as He was going out
on the road, one came running, knelt before Him, and
asked Him, "Good Teacher,
what shall I do that I may inherit eternal life?"

9:49 [a] NU-Text omits the rest of this verse.
10:6 [a] Genesis 1:27; 5:2 10:8 [a] Genesis 2:24

18So Jesus said to him,
"Why do you call Me good?
No one *is* good but One, *that
is,* God. 19You know the com-
mandments: 'Do not commit adultery,' 'Do not murder,' 'Do not steal,' 'Do not bear false witness,' 'Do not defraud,' 'Honor your father and your mother.'"[a]

20And he answered and said to Him, "Teacher, all these things I have kept from my youth."

21Then Jesus, looking at him, loved him, and said to him, "One thing you lack: Go your way, sell whatever you have and give to the poor, and you will have treasure in heaven; and come, take up the cross, and follow Me."

22But he was sad at this word, and went away sorrowful, for he had great possessions.

WITH GOD ALL THINGS ARE POSSIBLE

23Then Jesus looked around and said to His disciples, "How hard it is for those who have riches to enter the
kingdom of God!" 24And the
disciples were astonished at His words. But Jesus answered again and said to them, "Children, how hard it is for those who trust in riches[a] *to enter the kingdom of God!*
25It is easier for a camel to go through the eye of a needle than for a rich man to enter the kingdom of God."

26And they were greatly astonished, saying among themselves, "Who then can be saved?"

27But Jesus looked at them and said, "With men *it is* impossible, but not with God; for with God all things are possible."

28Then Peter began to say to Him, "See, we have left all and followed You."

29So Jesus answered and said, "Assuredly, I say to you, there is no one who has left house or brothers or sisters or father or mother or wife[a] or children or lands, for My
sake and the gospel's, 30who
shall not receive a hundredfold now in this time—houses and brothers and sisters and mothers and children and lands, with persecutions—and in the age to come, eternal life. 31But many *who are*
first will be last, and the last first."

JESUS A THIRD TIME PREDICTS HIS DEATH AND RESURRECTION

32Now they were on the road, going up to Jerusalem, and Jesus was going before them; and they were amazed. And as they followed they were afraid. Then He took the

10:19 [a] Exodus 20:12–16; Deuteronomy 5:16–20 10:24 [a] NU-Text omits *for those who trust in riches.* 10:29 [a] NU-Text omits *or wife.*

twelve aside again and began
to tell them the things that
would happen to Him: 33“Behold, we are going up to Jerusalem, and the Son of Man
will be betrayed to the chief
priests and to the scribes;
and they will condemn Him
to death and deliver Him to
the Gentiles; 34and they will
mock Him, and scourge Him,
and spit on Him, and kill Him.
And the third day He will rise
again.”

GREATNESS IS SERVING

35Then James and John,
the sons of Zebedee, came
to Him, saying, “Teacher, we
want You to do for us whatever we ask.”
36And He said to them,
“What do you want Me to do
for you?”
37They said to Him, “Grant
us that we may sit, one on
Your right hand and the other
on Your left, in Your glory.”
38But Jesus said to them,
“You do not know what you
ask. Are you able to drink the
cup that I drink, and be baptized with the baptism that I
am baptized with?”
39They said to Him, “We are
able.”
So Jesus said to them, “You
will indeed drink the cup that
I drink, and with the baptism
I am baptized with you will be
baptized; 40but to sit on My
right hand and on My left is
not Mine to give, but *it is for
those* for whom it is prepared.”
41And when the ten heard
it, they began to be greatly
displeased with James and
John. 42But Jesus called them
to *Himself* and said to them,
“You know that those who are
considered rulers over the
Gentiles lord it over them,
and their great ones exercise
authority over them. 43Yet it
shall not be so among you; but
whoever desires to become
great among you shall be
your servant. 44And whoever
of you desires to be first shall
be slave of all. 45For even the
Son of Man did not come to
be served, but to serve, and
to give His life a ransom for
many.”

JESUS HEALS BLIND BARTIMAEUS

46Now they came to Jeri-
cho. As He went out of Jericho
with His disciples and a great
multitude, blind Bartimaeus,
the son of Timaeus, sat by the
road begging. 47And when he
heard that it was Jesus of Nazareth, he began to cry out and
say, “Jesus, Son of David, have
mercy on me!”
48Then many warned him
to be quiet; but he cried out
all the more, “Son of David,
have mercy on me!”
49So Jesus stood still and
commanded him to be called.
Then they called the blind
man, saying to him, “Be of
good cheer. Rise, He is calling you.”
50And throwing aside his

garment, he rose and came
to Jesus.
51So Jesus answered and
said to him, "What do you
want Me to do for you?"
The blind man said to Him,
"Rabboni, that I may receive
my sight."
52Then Jesus said to him,
"Go your way; your faith has
made you well." And immediately he received his sight and
followed Jesus on the road.

THE TRIUMPHAL ENTRY

11 Now when they drew near
Jerusalem, to Bethphage[a]
and Bethany, at the Mount of
Olives, He sent two of His disciples; 2and He said to them,
"Go into the village opposite
you; and as soon as you have
entered it you will find a colt
tied, on which no one has sat.
Loose it and bring *it.* 3And if
anyone says to you, 'Why are
you doing this?' say, 'The Lord
has need of it,' and immediately he will send it here."
4So they went their way,
and found the[a] colt tied by
the door outside on the street,
and they loosed it. 5But some
of those who stood there said
to them, "What are you doing,
loosing the colt?"
6And they spoke to them
just as Jesus had commanded.
So they let them go. 7Then
they brought the colt to Jesus
and threw their clothes on it,
and He sat on it. 8And many
spread their clothes on the
road, and others cut down
leafy branches from the trees
and spread *them* on the road.
9Then those who went before
and those who followed cried
out, saying:

"Hosanna!
'Blessed *is* He who
comes in the name
of the LORD!'[a]
10 Blessed *is* the kingdom
of our father David
That comes in the
name of the Lord![a]
Hosanna in the
highest!"

11And Jesus went into Jerusalem and into the temple. So
when He had looked around
at all things, as the hour was
already late, He went out to
Bethany with the twelve.

THE FIG TREE WITHERED

12Now the next day, when
they had come out from Bethany, He was hungry. 13And
seeing from afar a fig tree
having leaves, He went to
see if perhaps He would find
something on it. When He
came to it, He found nothing
but leaves, for it was not the
season for figs. 14In response
Jesus said to it, "Let no one
eat fruit from you ever again."
And His disciples heard *it.*

11:1 [a] M-Text reads *Bethsphage.* 11:4 [a] NU-Text and M-Text read *a.*
11:9 [a] Psalm 118:26 11:10 [a] NU-Text omits *in the name of the Lord.*

JESUS CLEANSES THE TEMPLE

15So they came to Jerusa-
lem. Then Jesus went into the
temple and began to drive out
those who bought and sold in
the temple, and overturned
the tables of the money
changers and the seats of
those who sold doves. 16And
He would not allow anyone to
carry wares through the temple. 17Then He taught, saying
to them, "Is it not written, 'My
house shall be called a house
of prayer for all nations'?[a]
But you have made it a 'den
of thieves.'"[b]

18And the scribes and chief
priests heard it and sought
how they might destroy Him;
for they feared Him, because
all the people were astonished
at His teaching. 19When evening had come, He went out
of the city.

THE LESSON OF THE WITHERED FIG TREE

20Now in the morning, as
they passed by, they saw the
fig tree dried up from the
roots. 21And Peter, remembering, said to Him, "Rabbi, look!
The fig tree which You cursed
has withered away."

22So Jesus answered and
said to them, "Have faith in
God. 23For assuredly, I say
to you, whoever says to this
mountain, 'Be removed and
be cast into the sea,' and does
not doubt in his heart, but
believes that those things he
says will be done, he will have
whatever he says. 24Therefore
I say to you, whatever things
you ask when you pray, believe that you receive *them,*
and you will have *them.*

FORGIVENESS AND PRAYER

25"And whenever you stand
praying, if you have anything
against anyone, forgive him,
that your Father in heaven
may also forgive you your
trespasses. 26But if you do
not forgive, neither will your
Father in heaven forgive your
trespasses."[a]

JESUS' AUTHORITY QUESTIONED

27Then they came again
to Jerusalem. And as He was
walking in the temple, the
chief priests, the scribes, and
the elders came to Him. 28And
they said to Him, "By what authority are You doing these
things? And who gave You this
authority to do these things?"

29But Jesus answered and
said to them, "I also will ask
you one question; then answer
Me, and I will tell you by what
authority I do these things:
30The baptism of John—was
it from heaven or from men?
Answer Me."

31And they reasoned
among themselves, saying,

11:17 [a] Isaiah 56:7 [b] Jeremiah 7:11

11:26 [a] NU-Text omits this verse.

"If we say, 'From heaven,' He
will say, 'Why then did you not
believe him?' 32But if we say,
'From men'"—they feared the
people, for all counted John to
have been a prophet indeed.
33So they answered and said
to Jesus, "We do not know."

And Jesus answered and
said to them, "Neither will I
tell you by what authority I
do these things."

THE PARABLE OF THE WICKED VINEDRESSERS

12 Then He began to speak
to them in parables: "A
man planted a vineyard and
set a hedge around *it,* dug *a*
place for the wine vat and built
a tower. And he leased it to
vinedressers and went into a
far country. 2Now at vintage-
time he sent a servant to the
vinedressers, that he might
receive some of the fruit of
the vineyard from the vinedressers. 3And they took *him*
and beat him and sent *him*
away empty-handed. 4Again
he sent them another ser-
vant, and at him they threw
stones,[a] wounded *him* in
the head, and sent *him* away
shamefully treated. 5And
again he sent another, and
him they killed; and many
others, beating some and
killing some. 6Therefore still
having one son, his beloved,
he also sent him to them last,
saying, 'They will respect my
son.' 7But those vinedressers
said among themselves, 'This
is the heir. Come, let us kill
him, and the inheritance will
be ours.' 8So they took him
and killed *him* and cast *him*
out of the vineyard.

9"Therefore what will the
owner of the vineyard do?
He will come and destroy the
vinedressers, and give the
vineyard to others. 10Have you
not even read this Scripture:

'The stone which the
builders rejected
Has become the chief
cornerstone.
11 This was the
LORD's doing,
And it is marvelous
in our eyes'?"[a]

12And they sought to lay hands
on Him, but feared the multitude, for they knew He had
spoken the parable against
them. So they left Him and
went away.

THE PHARISEES: IS IT LAWFUL TO PAY TAXES TO CAESAR?

13Then they sent to Him
some of the Pharisees and the
Herodians, to catch Him in *His*
words. 14When they had come,
they said to Him, "Teacher, we
know that You are true, and

12:4 [a] NU-Text omits *and at him they threw stones.* 12:11 [a] Psalm 118:22, 23

care about no one; for You do
not regard the person of men,
but teach the way of God in
truth. Is it lawful to pay taxes
to Caesar, or not? 15Shall we
pay, or shall we not pay?"

But He, knowing their hy-
pocrisy, said to them, "Why
do you test Me? Bring Me a
denarius that I may see *it*."
16So they brought *it*.

And He said to them,
"Whose image and inscrip-
tion *is* this?" They said to Him,
"Caesar's."

17And Jesus answered and
said to them, "Render to Caesar the things that are Caesar's, and to God the things
that are God's."

And they marveled at Him.

THE SADDUCEES: WHAT ABOUT THE RESURRECTION?

18Then *some* Sadducees,
who say there is no resurrection, came to Him; and they
asked Him, saying: 19"Teacher,
Moses wrote to us that if a
man's brother dies, and leaves
his wife behind, and leaves no
children, his brother should
take his wife and raise up offspring for his brother. 20Now
there were seven brothers.
The first took a wife; and
dying, he left no offspring.
21And the second took her,
and he died; nor did he leave
any offspring. And the third
likewise. 22So the seven had
her and left no offspring. Last
of all the woman died also.
23Therefore, in the resurrection, when they rise, whose
wife will she be? For all seven
had her as wife."

24Jesus answered and said
to them, "Are you not therefore mistaken, because you do
not know the Scriptures nor
the power of God? 25For when
they rise from the dead, they
neither marry nor are given in
marriage, but are like angels
in heaven. 26But concerning
the dead, that they rise, have
you not read in the book of
Moses, in the *burning* bush
passage, how God spoke to
him, saying, 'I *am* the God of
Abraham, the God of Isaac,
and the God of Jacob'?[a] 27He
is not the God of the dead, but
the God of the living. You are
therefore greatly mistaken."

THE SCRIBES: WHICH IS THE FIRST COMMANDMENT OF ALL?

28Then one of the scribes
came, and having heard them
reasoning together, perceiving[a] that He had answered
them well, asked Him, "Which
is the first commandment of
all?"

29Jesus answered him,
"The first of all the command-
ments *is:* 'Hear, O Israel, the
LORD our God, the LORD is
one. 30And you shall love the
LORD your God with all your

12:26 [a] Exodus 3:6, 15 12:28 [a] NU-Text reads *seeing*.

heart, with all your soul, with
all your mind, and with all
your strength.'[a] This *is* the
first commandment.[b] 31And
the second, like *it, is* this: 'You
shall love your neighbor as
yourself.'[a] There is no other
commandment greater than
these."
32So the scribe said to Him,
"Well *said,* Teacher. You have
spoken the truth, for there
is one God, and there is no
other but He. 33And to love
Him with all the heart, with
all the understanding, with
all the soul,[a] and with all the
strength, and to love one's
neighbor as oneself, is more
than all the whole burnt offerings and sacrifices."
34Now when Jesus saw that
he answered wisely, He said to
him, "You are not far from the
kingdom of God."

But after that no one dared
question Him.

JESUS: HOW CAN DAVID CALL HIS DESCENDANT "LORD"?

35Then Jesus answered and
said, while He taught in the
temple, "How *is it* that the
scribes say that the Christ is
the Son of David? 36For David
himself said by the Holy Spirit:

'The LORD said
to my Lord,
"Sit at My right hand,
Till I make Your enemies
Your footstool."'[a]

37Therefore David himself
calls Him 'Lord'; how is He
then his Son?"

And the common people
heard Him gladly.

BEWARE OF THE SCRIBES

38Then He said to them
in His teaching, "Beware of
the scribes, who desire to go
around in long robes, *love*
greetings in the marketplaces,
39the best seats in the synagogues, and the best places at
feasts, 40who devour widows'
houses, and for a pretense
make long prayers. These
will receive greater condemnation."

THE WIDOW'S TWO MITES

41Now Jesus sat opposite the
treasury and saw how the people put money into the treasury. And many *who were*
rich put in much. 42Then one
poor widow came and threw
in two mites,[a] which make a
quadrans. 43So He called His
disciples to *Himself* and said
to them, "Assuredly, I say to
you that this poor widow has
put in more than all those who
have given to the treasury;
44for they all put in out of their
abundance, but she out of her

12:30 [a] Deuteronomy 6:4, 5 [b] NU-Text omits this sentence. 12:31 [a] Leviticus 19:18 12:33 [a] NU-Text omits *with all the soul.* 12:36 [a] Psalm 110:1 12:42 [a] Greek *lepta,* very small copper coins worth a fraction of a penny

poverty put in all that she had, her whole livelihood."

JESUS PREDICTS THE DESTRUCTION OF THE TEMPLE

13 Then as He went out of the temple, one of His disciples said to Him, "Teacher, see what manner of stones and what buildings *are here!*"
2And Jesus answered and said to him, "Do you see these great buildings? Not *one* stone shall be left upon another, that shall not be thrown down."

THE SIGNS OF THE TIMES AND THE END OF THE AGE

3Now as He sat on the Mount of Olives opposite the temple, Peter, James, John, and Andrew asked Him privately,
4"Tell us, when will these things be? And what *will be* the sign when all these things will be fulfilled?"
5And Jesus, answering them, began to say: "Take heed that no one deceives you.
6For many will come in My name, saying, 'I am *He,*' and will deceive many.
7But when you hear of wars and rumors of wars, do not be troubled; for *such things* must happen, but the end *is* not yet.
8For nation will rise against nation, and kingdom against kingdom. And there will be earthquakes in various places, and there will be famines and troubles.[a] These *are* the beginnings of sorrows.
9"But watch out for yourselves, for they will deliver you up to councils, and you will be beaten in the synagogues. You will be brought[a] before rulers and kings for My sake, for a testimony to them.
10And the gospel must first be preached to all the nations.
11But when they arrest *you* and deliver you up, do not worry beforehand, or premeditate[a] what you will speak. But whatever is given you in that hour, speak that; for it is not you who speak, but the Holy Spirit.
12Now brother will betray brother to death, and a father *his* child; and children will rise up against parents and cause them to be put to death.
13And you will be hated by all for My name's sake. But he who endures to the end shall be saved.

THE GREAT TRIBULATION

14"So when you see the 'abomination of desolation,'[a] spoken of by Daniel the prophet,[b] standing where it ought not" (let the reader understand), "then let those who are in Judea flee to the mountains.
15Let him who is on the housetop not go down into the house, nor

13:8 [a] NU-Text omits *and troubles.* 13:9 [a] NU-Text and M-Text read *will stand.* 13:11 [a] NU-Text omits *or premeditate.* 13:14 [a] Daniel 11:31; 12:11 [b] NU-Text omits *spoken of by Daniel the prophet.*

enter to take anything out of
his house. 16And let him who
is in the field not go back to
get his clothes. 17But woe to
those who are pregnant and
to those who are nursing babies in those days! 18And pray
that your flight may not be
in winter. 19For *in* those days
there will be tribulation, such
as has not been since the beginning of the creation which
God created until this time,
nor ever shall be. 20And unless the Lord had shortened
those days, no flesh would be
saved; but for the elect's sake,
whom He chose, He short-
ened the days.

21"Then if anyone says to
you, 'Look, here *is* the Christ!'
or, 'Look, *He is* there!' do not
believe it. 22For false christs
and false prophets will rise
and show signs and wonders
to deceive, if possible, even
the elect. 23But take heed; see,
I have told you all things beforehand.

THE COMING OF THE SON OF MAN

24"But in those days, after
that tribulation, the sun will
be darkened, and the moon
will not give its light; 25the
stars of heaven will fall, and
the powers in the heavens will
be shaken. 26Then they will
see the Son of Man *coming in*
the clouds with great power
and glory. 27And then He will
send His angels, and gather
together His elect from the
four winds, from the farthest
part of earth to the farthest
part of heaven.

THE PARABLE OF THE FIG TREE

28"Now learn this parable
from the fig tree: When its
branch has already become
tender, and puts forth leaves,
you know that summer is
near. 29So you also, when you
see these things happening,
know that it[a] is near—at the
doors! 30Assuredly, I say to
you, this generation will by no
means pass away till all these
things take place. 31Heaven
and earth will pass away, but
My words will by no means
pass away.

NO ONE KNOWS THE DAY OR HOUR

32"But of that day and hour
no one knows, not even the
angels in heaven, nor the Son,
but only the Father. 33Take
heed, watch and pray; for you
do not know when the time
is. 34*It is* like a man going to
a far country, who left his
house and gave authority
to his servants, and to each
his work, and commanded
the doorkeeper to watch.
35Watch therefore, for you do
not know when the master of
the house is coming—in the
evening, at midnight, at the

13:29 [a] Or *He*

crowing of the rooster, or in
the morning— 36lest, coming
suddenly, he find you sleeping. 37And what I say to you,
I say to all: Watch!"

THE PLOT TO KILL JESUS

14 After two days it was the
Passover and *the Feast* of
Unleavened Bread. And the
chief priests and the scribes
sought how they might take
Him by trickery and put *Him*
to death. 2But they said, "Not
during the feast, lest there be
an uproar of the people."

THE ANOINTING AT BETHANY

3And being in Bethany at
the house of Simon the leper,
as He sat at the table, a woman
came having an alabaster flask
of very costly oil of spikenard.
Then she broke the flask and
poured *it* on His head. 4But
there were some who were indignant among themselves,
and said, "Why was this fragrant oil wasted? 5For it might
have been sold for more than
three hundred denarii and
given to the poor." And they
criticized her sharply.

6But Jesus said, "Let her
alone. Why do you trouble
her? She has done a good work
for Me. 7For you have the poor
with you always, and whenever you wish you may do
them good; but Me you do not
have always. 8She has done
what she could. She has come
beforehand to anoint My body
for burial. 9Assuredly, I say to
you, wherever this gospel is
preached in the whole world,
what this woman has done
will also be told as a memorial to her."

JUDAS AGREES TO BETRAY JESUS

10Then Judas Iscariot, one
of the twelve, went to the chief
priests to betray Him to them.
11And when they heard *it,* they
were glad, and promised to
give him money. So he sought
how he might conveniently
betray Him.

JESUS CELEBRATES THE PASSOVER WITH HIS DISCIPLES

12Now on the first day of
Unleavened Bread, when they
killed the Passover *lamb,* His
disciples said to Him, "Where
do You want us to go and prepare, that You may eat the
Passover?"

13And He sent out two
of His disciples and said to
them, "Go into the city, and a
man will meet you carrying a
pitcher of water; follow him.
14Wherever he goes in, say to
the master of the house, 'The
Teacher says, "Where is the
guest room in which I may
eat the Passover with My disciples?"' 15Then he will show
you a large upper room, furnished *and* prepared; there
make ready for us."

16So His disciples went out,
and came into the city, and

found it just as He had said
to them; and they prepared
the Passover.
17In the evening He came
with the twelve. 18Now as they
sat and ate, Jesus said, "Assuredly, I say to you, one of
you who eats with Me will betray Me."
19And they began to be sorrowful, and to say to Him one
by one, "*Is* it I?" And another
said, "*Is* it I?"[a]
20He answered and said to
them, "*It is* one of the twelve,
who dips with Me in the dish.
21The Son of Man indeed goes
just as it is written of Him, but
woe to that man by whom
the Son of Man is betrayed!
It would have been good for
that man if he had never been
born."

JESUS INSTITUTES THE LORD'S SUPPER

22And as they were eating,
Jesus took bread, blessed and
broke *it*, and gave *it* to them
and said, "Take, eat;[a] this is
My body."
23Then He took the cup,
and when He had given thanks
He gave *it* to them, and they
all drank from it. 24And He
said to them, "This is My blood
of the new[a] covenant, which
is shed for many. 25Assuredly,
I say to you, I will no longer
drink of the fruit of the vine
until that day when I drink it
new in the kingdom of God."
26And when they had sung
a hymn, they went out to the
Mount of Olives.

JESUS PREDICTS PETER'S DENIAL

27Then Jesus said to them,
"All of you will be made to
stumble because of Me this
night,[a] for it is written:

'I will strike the Shepherd,
And the sheep will
be scattered.'[b]

28"But after I have been
raised, I will go before you to
Galilee."
29Peter said to Him, "Even
if all are made to stumble, yet
I *will* not *be*."
30Jesus said to him, "As-
suredly, I say to you that today,
even this night, before the
rooster crows twice, you will
deny Me three times."
31But he spoke more vehe-
mently, "If I have to die with
You, I will not deny You!"
And they all said likewise.

THE PRAYER IN THE GARDEN

32Then they came to a place
which was named Gethsem-
ane; and He said to His disciples, "Sit here while I pray."
33And He took Peter, James,

14:19 [a] NU-Text omits this sentence. 14:22 [a] NU-Text omits *eat*. 14:24 [a] NU-Text omits *new*. 14:27 [a] NU-Text omits *because of Me this night*. [b] Zechariah 13:7

and John with Him, and He
began to be troubled and
deeply distressed. 34Then He
said to them, "My soul is exceedingly sorrowful, *even* to
death. Stay here and watch."

35He went a little farther,
and fell on the ground, and
prayed that if it were possible, the hour might pass from
Him. 36And He said, "Abba,
Father, all things *are* possible
for You. Take this cup away
from Me; nevertheless, not
what I will, but what You *will*."

37Then He came and found
them sleeping, and said to
Peter, "Simon, are you sleeping? Could you not watch one
hour? 38Watch and pray, lest
you enter into temptation.
The spirit indeed *is* willing,
but the flesh *is* weak."

39Again He went away and
prayed, and spoke the same
words. 40And when He re-
turned, He found them asleep
again, for their eyes were
heavy; and they did not know
what to answer Him.

41Then He came the third
time and said to them, "Are you
still sleeping and resting? It is
enough! The hour has come;
behold, the Son of Man is being
betrayed into the hands of sinners. 42Rise, let us be going.
See, My betrayer is at hand."

BETRAYAL AND ARREST IN GETHSEMANE

43And immediately, while
He was still speaking, Judas,
one of the twelve, with a great
multitude with swords and
clubs, came from the chief
priests and the scribes and
the elders. 44Now His betrayer
had given them a signal, saying, "Whomever I kiss, He is
the One; seize Him and lead
Him away safely."

45As soon as he had come,
immediately he went up to
Him and said to Him, "Rabbi,
Rabbi!" and kissed Him.

46Then they laid their
hands on Him and took Him.
47And one of those who stood
by drew his sword and struck
the servant of the high priest,
and cut off his ear.

48Then Jesus answered and
said to them, "Have you come
out, as against a robber, with
swords and clubs to take Me?
49I was daily with you in the
temple teaching, and you did
not seize Me. But the Scriptures must be fulfilled."

50Then they all forsook
Him and fled.

A YOUNG MAN FLEES NAKED

51Now a certain young
man followed Him, having a
linen cloth thrown around *his*
naked *body*. And the young
men laid hold of him, 52and
he left the linen cloth and fled
from them naked.

JESUS FACES THE SANHEDRIN

53And they led Jesus away
to the high priest; and with
him were assembled all the

chief priests, the elders, and
the scribes. 54But Peter followed Him at a distance, right
into the courtyard of the high
priest. And he sat with the servants and warmed himself at
the fire.
55Now the chief priests and
all the council sought testimony against Jesus to put
Him to death, but found none.
56For many bore false witness
against Him, but their testimonies did not agree.
57Then some rose up and
bore false witness against
Him, saying, 58"We heard Him
say, 'I will destroy this temple
made with hands, and within
three days I will build another
made without hands.'" 59But
not even then did their testimony agree.
60And the high priest stood
up in the midst and asked
Jesus, saying, "Do You answer
nothing? What *is it* these men
testify against You?" 61But
He kept silent and answered
nothing.
Again the high priest asked
Him, saying to Him, "Are
You the Christ, the Son of the
Blessed?"
62Jesus said, "I am. And
you will see the Son of Man
sitting at the right hand of the
Power, and coming with the
clouds of heaven."
63Then the high priest tore
his clothes and said, "What
further need do we have of
witnesses? 64You have heard
the blasphemy! What do you
think?"
And they all condemned
Him to be deserving of death.
65Then some began to spit
on Him, and to blindfold Him,
and to beat Him, and to say
to Him, "Prophesy!" And the
officers struck Him with the
palms of their hands.[a]

PETER DENIES JESUS, AND WEEPS

66Now as Peter was below
in the courtyard, one of the
servant girls of the high priest
came. 67And when she saw
Peter warming himself, she
looked at him and said, "You
also were with Jesus of Nazareth."
68But he denied it, saying,
"I neither know nor understand what you are saying."
And he went out on the porch,
and a rooster crowed.
69And the servant girl saw
him again, and began to say
to those who stood by, "This is
one of them." 70But he denied
it again.
And a little later those who
stood by said to Peter again,
"Surely you are *one* of them;
for you are a Galilean, and
your speech shows *it*."[a]
71Then he began to curse
and swear, "I do not know this
Man of whom you speak!"

14:65 [a] NU-Text reads *received Him with slaps.*
14:70 [a] NU-Text omits *and your speech shows it.*

72 A second time *the* rooster
crowed. Then Peter called to
mind the word that Jesus
had said to him, "Before the
rooster crows twice, you will
deny Me three times." And
when he thought about it, he
wept.

JESUS FACES PILATE

15 Immediately, in the
morning, the chief
priests held a consultation
with the elders and scribes
and the whole council; and
they bound Jesus, led *Him*
away, and delivered *Him* to
Pilate. 2 Then Pilate asked
Him, "Are You the King of the
Jews?"

He answered and said to
him, "*It is as* you say."

3 And the chief priests accused Him of many things, but
He answered nothing. 4 Then
Pilate asked Him again, saying, "Do You answer nothing?
See how many things they testify against You!"[a] 5 But Jesus
still answered nothing, so that
Pilate marveled.

TAKING THE PLACE OF BARABBAS

6 Now at the feast he was
accustomed to releasing one
prisoner to them, whomever
they requested. 7 And there
was one named Barabbas, *who
was* chained with his fellow
rebels; they had committed
murder in the rebellion. 8 Then
the multitude, crying aloud,[a]
began to ask *him to do* just as
he had always done for them.
9 But Pilate answered them,
saying, "Do you want me to
release to you the King of the
Jews?" 10 For he knew that the
chief priests had handed Him
over because of envy.

11 But the chief priests
stirred up the crowd, so that
he should rather release
Barabbas to them. 12 Pilate
answered and said to them
again, "What then do you want
me to do *with Him* whom you
call the King of the Jews?"

13 So they cried out again,
"Crucify Him!"

14 Then Pilate said to them,
"Why, what evil has He done?"

But they cried out all the
more, "Crucify Him!"

15 So Pilate, wanting to gratify the crowd, released Barabbas to them; and he delivered
Jesus, after he had scourged
Him, to be crucified.

THE SOLDIERS MOCK JESUS

16 Then the soldiers led Him
away into the hall called Praetorium, and they called together
the whole garrison. 17 And they
clothed Him with purple; and
they twisted a crown of thorns,
put it on His *head,* 18 and began
to salute Him, "Hail, King of
the Jews!" 19 Then they struck
Him on the head with a reed

15:4 [a] NU-Text reads *of which they accuse You.* 15:8 [a] NU-Text reads *going up.*

and spat on Him; and bowing
the knee, they worshiped Him.
20And when they had mocked
Him, they took the purple
off Him, put His own clothes
on Him, and led Him out to
crucify Him.

THE KING ON A CROSS

21Then they compelled a
certain man, Simon a Cyrenian, the father of Alexander
and Rufus, as he was coming
out of the country and passing
by, to bear His cross. 22And
they brought Him to the place
Golgotha, which is translated,
Place of a Skull. 23Then they
gave Him wine mingled with
myrrh to drink, but He did
not take *it.* 24And when they
crucified Him, they divided
His garments, casting lots for
them *to determine* what every
man should take.

25Now it was the third hour,
and they crucified Him. 26And
the inscription of His accusation was written above:

THE KING OF THE JEWS.

27With Him they also crucified two robbers, one on His
right and the other on His
left. 28So the Scripture was
fulfilled[a] which says, "And
He was numbered with the
transgressors."[b]

29And those who passed
by blasphemed Him, wagging
their heads and saying, "Aha!
You who destroy the temple
and build *it* in three days,
30save Yourself, and come
down from the cross!"

31Likewise the chief priests
also, mocking among them-
selves with the scribes, said,
"He saved others; Himself He
cannot save. 32Let the Christ,
the King of Israel, descend
now from the cross, that we
may see and believe."[a]

Even those who were cru-
cified with Him reviled Him.

JESUS DIES ON THE CROSS

33Now when the sixth hour
had come, there was darkness
over the whole land until the
ninth hour. 34And at the ninth
hour Jesus cried out with a
loud voice, saying, "Eloi, Eloi,
lama sabachthani?" which is
translated, "My God, My God,
why have You forsaken Me?"[a]

35Some of those who stood
by, when they heard *that,* said,
"Look, He is calling for Elijah!" 36Then someone ran
and filled a sponge full of
sour wine, put *it* on a reed,
and offered *it* to Him to drink,
saying, "Let Him alone; let us
see if Elijah will come to take
Him down."

37And Jesus cried out with
a loud voice, and breathed His
last.

38Then the veil of the temple was torn in two from top

15:28 [a] Isaiah 53:12 [b] NU-Text omits this verse.
15:32 [a] M-Text reads *believe Him.* **15:34** [a] Psalm 22:1

to bottom. 39So when the
centurion, who stood opposite Him, saw that He cried
out like this and breathed His
last,[a] he said, "Truly this Man
was the Son of God!"
40There were also women
looking on from afar, among
whom were Mary Magdalene,
Mary the mother of James the
Less and of Joses, and Salome,
41who also followed Him and
ministered to Him when He
was in Galilee, and many other
women who came up with
Him to Jerusalem.

JESUS BURIED IN JOSEPH'S TOMB

42Now when evening had
come, because it was the
Preparation Day, that is, the
day before the Sabbath, 43Jo-
seph of Arimathea, a prominent council member, who
was himself waiting for the
kingdom of God, coming and
taking courage, went in to Pilate and asked for the body of
Jesus. 44Pilate marveled that
He was already dead; and
summoning the centurion,
he asked him if He had been
dead for some time. 45So when
he found out from the centurion, he granted the body
to Joseph. 46Then he bought
fine linen, took Him down,
and wrapped Him in the linen.
And he laid Him in a tomb
which had been hewn out of
the rock, and rolled a stone
against the door of the tomb.
47And Mary Magdalene and
Mary *the mother* of Joses observed where He was laid.

HE IS RISEN

16 Now when the Sabbath
was past, Mary Mag-
dalene, Mary *the mother* of
James, and Salome bought
spices, that they might come
and anoint Him. 2Very early
in the morning, on the first
day of the week, they came to
the tomb when the sun had
risen. 3And they said among
themselves, "Who will roll
away the stone from the door
of the tomb for us?" 4But when
they looked up, they saw that
the stone had been rolled
away—for it was very large.
5And entering the tomb, they
saw a young man clothed in
a long white robe sitting on
the right side; and they were
alarmed.
6But he said to them, "Do
not be alarmed. You seek
Jesus of Nazareth, who was
crucified. He is risen! He is
not here. See the place where
they laid Him. 7But go, tell His
disciples—and Peter—that He
is going before you into Galilee; there you will see Him, as
He said to you."
8So they went out quickly[a]
and fled from the tomb, for
they trembled and were

15:39 [a] NU-Text reads *that He thus breathed His last.* 16:8 [a] NU-Text and M-Text omit *quickly.*

amazed. And they said nothing to anyone, for they were
afraid.

MARY MAGDALENE SEES THE RISEN LORD

9Now when *He* rose early on
the first *day* of the week, He
appeared first to Mary Magdalene, out of whom He had
cast seven demons. 10She went
and told those who had been
with Him, as they mourned
and wept. 11And when they
heard that He was alive and
had been seen by her, they did
not believe.

JESUS APPEARS TO TWO DISCIPLES

12After that, He appeared in
another form to two of them
as they walked and went into
the country. 13And they went
and told *it* to the rest, *but* they
did not believe them either.

THE GREAT COMMISSION

14Later He appeared to the
eleven as they sat at the table;
and He rebuked their unbelief and hardness of heart,
because they did not believe
those who had seen Him after
He had risen. 15And He said to
them, "Go into all the world
and preach the gospel to every
creature. 16He who believes
and is baptized will be saved;
but he who does not believe
will be condemned. 17And
these signs will follow those
who believe: In My name they
will cast out demons; they
will speak with new tongues;
18they[a] will take up serpents;
and if they drink anything
deadly, it will by no means
hurt them; they will lay hands
on the sick, and they will recover."

CHRIST ASCENDS TO GOD'S RIGHT HAND

19So then, after the Lord
had spoken to them, He was
received up into heaven, and
sat down at the right hand
of God. 20And they went out
and preached everywhere,
the Lord working with *them*
and confirming the word
through the accompanying
signs. Amen.[a]

16:18 [a] NU-Text reads *and in their hands they will.* 16:20 [a] Verses 9–20 are bracketed in NU-Text as not original. They are lacking in Codex Sinaiticus and Codex Vaticanus, although nearly all other manuscripts of Mark contain them.

THE GOSPEL ACCORDING TO
LUKE

DEDICATION TO THEOPHILUS

1 Inasmuch as many have
taken in hand to set in order
a narrative of those things
which have been fulfilled[a]
among us, 2just as those who
from the beginning were eyewitnesses and ministers of the
word delivered them to us, 3it
seemed good to me also, having had perfect understanding of all things from the very
first, to write to you an orderly
account, most excellent Theophilus, 4that you may know
the certainty of those things
in which you were instructed.

JOHN'S BIRTH ANNOUNCED TO ZACHARIAS

5There was in the days of
Herod, the king of Judea, a
certain priest named Zacharias, of the division of Abijah.
His wife *was* of the daughters
of Aaron, and her name *was*
Elizabeth. 6And they were
both righteous before God,
walking in all the commandments and ordinances of the
Lord blameless. 7But they had
no child, because Elizabeth
was barren, and they were
both well advanced in years.

8So it was, that while he was
serving as priest before God
in the order of his division,
9according to the custom of
the priesthood, his lot fell to
burn incense when he went
into the temple of the Lord.
10And the whole multitude of
the people was praying outside at the hour of incense.
11Then an angel of the Lord
appeared to him, standing on
the right side of the altar of incense. 12And when Zacharias
saw *him,* he was troubled, and
fear fell upon him.

13But the angel said to him,
"Do not be afraid, Zacharias,
for your prayer is heard; and
your wife Elizabeth will bear
you a son, and you shall call
his name John. 14And you will
have joy and gladness, and
many will rejoice at his birth.
15For he will be great in the
sight of the Lord, and shall
drink neither wine nor strong
drink. He will also be filled
with the Holy Spirit, even
from his mother's womb.
16And he will turn many of
the children of Israel to the
Lord their God. 17He will also
go before Him in the spirit
and power of Elijah, 'to turn
the hearts of the fathers to the

1:1 [a] Or *are most surely believed*

children,'[a] and the disobedient to the wisdom of the just,
to make ready a people prepared for the Lord."
18 And Zacharias said to
the angel, "How shall I know
this? For I am an old man, and
my wife is well advanced in
years."
19 And the angel answered
and said to him, "I am Gabriel, who stands in the presence of God, and was sent to
speak to you and bring you
these glad tidings. 20 But behold, you will be mute and
not able to speak until the
day these things take place,
because you did not believe
my words which will be fulfilled in their own time."
21 And the people waited for
Zacharias, and marveled that
he lingered so long in the temple. 22 But when he came out,
he could not speak to them;
and they perceived that he
had seen a vision in the temple, for he beckoned to them
and remained speechless.
23 So it was, as soon as the
days of his service were completed, that he departed to his
own house. 24 Now after those
days his wife Elizabeth conceived; and she hid herself
five months, saying, 25 "Thus
the Lord has dealt with me, in
the days when He looked on
me, to take away my reproach
among people."

CHRIST'S BIRTH ANNOUNCED TO MARY

26 Now in the sixth month
the angel Gabriel was sent by
God to a city of Galilee named
Nazareth, 27 to a virgin betrothed to a man whose name
was Joseph, of the house of
David. The virgin's name *was*
Mary. 28 And having come in,
the angel said to her, "Rejoice,
highly favored *one,* the Lord
is with you; blessed *are* you
among women!"[a]
29 But when she saw *him,*[a]
she was troubled at his saying,
and considered what manner
of greeting this was. 30 Then
the angel said to her, "Do not
be afraid, Mary, for you have
found favor with God. 31 And
behold, you will conceive in
your womb and bring forth a
Son, and shall call His name
JESUS. 32 He will be great, and
will be called the Son of the
Highest; and the Lord God
will give Him the throne of
His father David. 33 And He
will reign over the house of
Jacob forever, and of His
kingdom there will be no
end."
34 Then Mary said to the
angel, "How can this be, since
I do not know a man?"
35 And the angel answered
and said to her, "*The* Holy
Spirit will come upon you, and
the power of the Highest will

1:17 [a] Malachi 4:5, 6 1:28 [a] NU-Text omits *blessed are you among women.* 1:29 [a] NU-Text omits *when she saw him.*

overshadow you; therefore,
also, that Holy One who is to
be born will be called the Son
of God. 36Now indeed, Elizabeth your relative has also
conceived a son in her old
age; and this is now the sixth
month for her who was called
barren. 37For with God nothing will be impossible."
38Then Mary said, "Behold
the maidservant of the Lord!
Let it be to me according to
your word." And the angel departed from her.

MARY VISITS ELIZABETH

39Now Mary arose in those
days and went into the hill
country with haste, to a city
of Judah, 40and entered
the house of Zacharias and
greeted Elizabeth. 41And it
happened, when Elizabeth
heard the greeting of Mary,
that the babe leaped in her
womb; and Elizabeth was
filled with the Holy Spirit.
42Then she spoke out with a
loud voice and said, "Blessed
are you among women,
and blessed *is* the fruit of
your womb! 43But why *is*
this *granted* to me, that the
mother of my Lord should
come to me? 44For indeed,
as soon as the voice of your
greeting sounded in my ears,
the babe leaped in my womb
for joy. 45Blessed *is* she who
believed, for there will be a
fulfillment of those things
which were told her from the
Lord."

THE SONG OF MARY

46And Mary said:

"My soul magnifies
the Lord,
47 And my spirit has
rejoiced in God
my Savior.
48 For He has regarded
the lowly state of
His maidservant;
For behold, henceforth
all generations will
call me blessed.
49 For He who is mighty
has done great
things for me,
And holy *is* His name.
50 And His mercy *is* on
those who fear Him
From generation
to generation.
51 He has shown strength
with His arm;
He has scattered
the proud in the
imagination of
their hearts.
52 He has put down
the mighty from
their thrones,
And exalted *the* lowly.
53 He has filled *the* hungry
with good things,
And *the* rich He has
sent away empty.
54 He has helped His
servant Israel,
In remembrance
of *His* mercy,
55 As He spoke to
our fathers,
To Abraham and to
his seed forever."

56And Mary remained with
her about three months, and
returned to her house.

BIRTH OF JOHN THE BAPTIST

57Now Elizabeth's full time
came for her to be delivered,
and she brought forth a son.
58When her neighbors and
relatives heard how the Lord
had shown great mercy to her,
they rejoiced with her.

CIRCUMCISION OF JOHN THE BAPTIST

59So it was, on the eighth
day, that they came to circumcise the child; and they
would have called him by the
name of his father, Zacharias.
60His mother answered and
said, "No; he shall be called
John."

61But they said to her,
"There is no one among your
relatives who is called by this
name." 62So they made signs
to his father—what he would
have him called.

63And he asked for a writing tablet, and wrote, saying,
"His name is John." So they all
marveled. 64Immediately his
mouth was opened and his
tongue *loosed,* and he spoke,
praising God. 65Then fear
came on all who dwelt around
them; and all these sayings
were discussed throughout
all the hill country of Judea.
66And all those who heard
them kept *them* in their hearts,
saying, "What kind of child
will this be?" And the hand of
the Lord was with him.

ZACHARIAS' PROPHECY

67Now his father Zacharias
was filled with the Holy Spirit,
and prophesied, saying:

68"Blessed *is* the Lord
God of Israel,
For He has visited and
redeemed His people,
69 And has raised up a horn
of salvation for us
In the house of His
servant David,
70 As He spoke by the
mouth of His
holy prophets,
Who *have been* since
the world began,
71 That we should be saved
from our enemies
And from the hand of
all who hate us,
72 To perform the mercy
promised to our fathers
And to remember His
holy covenant,
73 The oath which He swore
to our father Abraham:
74 To grant us that we,
Being delivered from the
hand of our enemies,
Might serve Him
without fear,
75 In holiness and
righteousness
before Him all the
days of our life.

76"And you, child, will
be called the prophet
of the Highest;

For you will go before
the face of the Lord
to prepare His ways,
77 To give knowledge of
salvation to His
people
By the remission
of their sins,
78 Through the tender
mercy of our God,
With which the
Dayspring from on
high has visited[a] us;
79 To give light to those
who sit in darkness and
the shadow of death,
To guide our feet into
the way of peace."

80So the child grew and became strong in spirit, and was in the deserts till the day of his manifestation to Israel.

CHRIST BORN OF MARY

2 And it came to pass in
those days *that* a decree
went out from Caesar Augustus that all the world should
be registered. 2This census
first took place while Qui-
rinius was governing Syria.
3So all went to be registered,
everyone to his own city.
4Joseph also went up from
Galilee, out of the city of Nazareth, into Judea, to the city of
David, which is called Bethlehem, because he was of the
house and lineage of David,
5to be registered with Mary,
his betrothed wife,[a] who was
with child. 6So it was, that
while they were there, the days
were completed for her to be
delivered. 7And she brought
forth her firstborn Son, and
wrapped Him in swaddling
cloths, and laid Him in a
manger, because there was
no room for them in the inn.

GLORY IN THE HIGHEST

8Now there were in the
same country shepherds living out in the fields, keeping watch over their flock
by night. 9And behold,[a] an
angel of the Lord stood before them, and the glory of
the Lord shone around them,
and they were greatly afraid.
10Then the angel said to them,
"Do not be afraid, for behold,
I bring you good tidings of
great joy which will be to all
people. 11For there is born
to you this day in the city of
David a Savior, who is Christ
the Lord. 12And this *will be*
the sign to you: You will find
a Babe wrapped in swaddling
cloths, lying in a manger."
13And suddenly there was
with the angel a multitude of
the heavenly host praising
God and saying:

14 "Glory to God in
the highest,
And on earth peace,
goodwill toward men!"[a]

1:78 [a] NU-Text reads *shall visit.* 2:5 [a] NU-Text omits *wife.* 2:9 [a] NU-Text omits *behold.* 2:14 [a] NU-Text reads *toward men of goodwill.*

[15]So it was, when the angels
had gone away from them into
heaven, that the shepherds
said to one another, "Let us
now go to Bethlehem and see
this thing that has come to
pass, which the Lord has made
known to us." [16]And they came
with haste and found Mary and
Joseph, and the Babe lying in a
manger. [17]Now when they had
seen *Him,* they made widely[a]
known the saying which was
told them concerning this
Child. [18]And all those who
heard *it* marveled at those
things which were told them by
the shepherds. [19]But Mary kept
all these things and pondered
them in her heart. [20]Then the
shepherds returned, glorifying
and praising God for all the
things that they had heard and
seen, as it was told them.

CIRCUMCISION OF JESUS

[21]And when eight days were
completed for the circumcision of the Child,[a] His name
was called JESUS, the name
given by the angel before He
was conceived in the womb.

JESUS PRESENTED IN THE TEMPLE

[22]Now when the days of her
purification according to the
law of Moses were completed,
they brought Him to Jerusalem to present *Him* to the Lord
[23](as it is written in the law of
the Lord, "Every male who
opens the womb shall be called
holy to the LORD"),[a] [24]and to
offer a sacrifice according to
what is said in the law of the
Lord, "A pair of turtledoves or
two young pigeons."[a]

SIMEON SEES GOD'S SALVATION

[25]And behold, there was a
man in Jerusalem whose name
was Simeon, and this man *was*
just and devout, waiting for
the Consolation of Israel, and
the Holy Spirit was upon him.
[26]And it had been revealed to
him by the Holy Spirit that he
would not see death before he
had seen the Lord's Christ. [27]So
he came by the Spirit into the
temple. And when the parents
brought in the Child Jesus, to
do for Him according to the
custom of the law, [28]he took
Him up in his arms and blessed
God and said:

[29]"Lord, now You are
letting Your servant
depart in peace,
According to Your word;
[30] For my eyes have seen
Your salvation
[31] Which You have
prepared before the
face of all peoples,
[32] A light to *bring* revelation
to the Gentiles,
And the glory of Your
people Israel."

2:17 [a] NU-Text omits *widely.* 2:21 [a] NU-Text reads *for His circumcision.* 2:23 [a] Exodus 13:2, 12, 15 2:24 [a] Leviticus 12:8

33And Joseph and His
mother[a] marveled at those
things which were spoken of
Him. 34Then Simeon blessed
them, and said to Mary His
mother, "Behold, this *Child*
is destined for the fall and
rising of many in Israel, and
for a sign which will be spoken against 35(yes, a sword
will pierce through your own
soul also), that the thoughts
of many hearts may be re-
vealed."

ANNA BEARS WITNESS TO THE REDEEMER

36Now there was one, Anna,
a prophetess, the daughter of
Phanuel, of the tribe of Asher.
She was of a great age, and had
lived with a husband seven
years from her virginity; 37and
this woman *was* a widow of
about eighty-four years,[a] who
did not depart from the temple, but served *God* with fastings and prayers night and
day. 38And coming in that instant she gave thanks to the
Lord,[a] and spoke of Him to all
those who looked for redemption in Jerusalem.

THE FAMILY RETURNS TO NAZARETH

39So when they had per-
formed all things according
to the law of the Lord, they
returned to Galilee, to their
own city, Nazareth. 40And the
Child grew and became strong
in spirit,[a] filled with wisdom;
and the grace of God was upon
Him.

THE BOY JESUS AMAZES THE SCHOLARS

41His parents went to Jerusalem every year at the Feast
of the Passover. 42And when
He was twelve years old, they
went up to Jerusalem according to the custom of the feast.
43When they had finished the
days, as they returned, the Boy
Jesus lingered behind in Jerusalem. And Joseph and His
mother[a] did not know *it;* 44but
supposing Him to have been
in the company, they went
a day's journey, and sought
Him among *their* relatives
and acquaintances. 45So when
they did not find Him, they
returned to Jerusalem, seeking Him. 46Now so it was *that*
after three days they found
Him in the temple, sitting in
the midst of the teachers, both
listening to them and asking
them questions. 47And all who
heard Him were astonished
at His understanding and
answers. 48So when they saw
Him, they were amazed; and
His mother said to Him, "Son,
why have You done this to us?
Look, Your father and I have
sought You anxiously."

2:33 [a] NU-Text reads *And His father and mother.* 2:37 [a] NU-Text reads *a widow until she was eighty-four.* 2:38 [a] NU-Text reads *to God.* 2:40 [a] NU-Text omits *in spirit.* 2:43 [a] NU-Text reads *And His parents.*

49And He said to them,
"Why did you seek Me? Did
you not know that I must be
about My Father's business?"
50But they did not understand
the statement which He spoke
to them.

JESUS ADVANCES IN WISDOM AND FAVOR

51Then He went down with
them and came to Nazareth,
and was subject to them, but
His mother kept all these
things in her heart. 52And
Jesus increased in wisdom
and stature, and in favor with
God and men.

JOHN THE BAPTIST PREPARES THE WAY

3 Now in the fifteenth year
of the reign of Tiberius
Caesar, Pontius Pilate being
governor of Judea, Herod
being tetrarch of Galilee, his
brother Philip tetrarch of Itu-
rea and the region of Tracho-
nitis, and Lysanias tetrarch
of Abilene, 2while Annas and
Caiaphas were high priests,[a]
the word of God came to John
the son of Zacharias in the wilderness. 3And he went into
all the region around the Jordan, preaching a baptism of
repentance for the remission
of sins, 4as it is written in the
book of the words of Isaiah
the prophet, saying:

"The voice of one crying
in the wilderness:
'Prepare the way
of the LORD;
Make His paths
straight.
5 Every valley shall be
filled
And every mountain
and hill brought low;
The crooked places shall
be made straight
And the rough
ways smooth;
6 And all flesh shall
see the salvation
of God.'"[a]

JOHN PREACHES TO THE PEOPLE

7Then he said to the multitudes that came out to be baptized by him, "Brood of vipers!
Who warned you to flee from
the wrath to come? 8There-
fore bear fruits worthy of repentance, and do not begin
to say to yourselves, 'We have
Abraham as *our* father.' For I
say to you that God is able to
raise up children to Abraham
from these stones. 9And even
now the ax is laid to the root
of the trees. Therefore every
tree which does not bear good
fruit is cut down and thrown
into the fire."
10So the people asked him,
saying, "What shall we do
then?"
11He answered and said to

3:2 [a] NU-Text and M-Text read *in the high priesthood of Annas and Caiaphas.* 3:6 [a] Isaiah 40:3–5

them, "He who has two tunics,
let him give to him who has
none; and he who has food,
let him do likewise."

[12]Then tax collectors also
came to be baptized, and said
to him, "Teacher, what shall
we do?"

[13]And he said to them, "Collect no more than what is appointed for you."

[14]Likewise the soldiers
asked him, saying, "And what
shall we do?"

So he said to them, "Do not
intimidate anyone or accuse
falsely, and be content with
your wages."

[15]Now as the people were in
expectation, and all reasoned
in their hearts about John,
whether he was the Christ *or*
not, [16]John answered, saying
to all, "I indeed baptize you
with water; but One mightier than I is coming, whose
sandal strap I am not worthy
to loose. He will baptize you
with the Holy Spirit and fire.
[17]His winnowing fan *is* in His
hand, and He will thoroughly
clean out His threshing floor,
and gather the wheat into
His barn; but the chaff He
will burn with unquenchable
fire."

[18]And with many other
exhortations he preached to
the people. [19]But Herod the
tetrarch, being rebuked by
him concerning Herodias, his
brother Philip's wife,[a] and for
all the evils which Herod had
done, [20]also added this, above
all, that he shut John up in
prison.

JOHN BAPTIZES JESUS

[21]When all the people were
baptized, it came to pass that
Jesus also was baptized; and
while He prayed, the heaven
was opened. [22]And the Holy
Spirit descended in bodily
form like a dove upon Him,
and a voice came from heaven
which said, "You are My beloved Son; in You I am well
pleased."

THE GENEALOGY OF JESUS CHRIST

[23]Now Jesus Himself began
His ministry at about thirty
years of age, being (as was
supposed) *the* son of Joseph,
the son of Heli, [24]*the son* of
Matthat,[a] *the son* of Levi,
the son of Melchi, *the son* of
Janna, *the son* of Joseph, [25]*the
son* of Mattathiah, *the son* of
Amos, *the son* of Nahum, *the
son* of Esli, *the son* of Naggai,
[26]*the son* of Maath, *the son* of
Mattathiah, *the son* of Semei,
the son of Joseph, *the son* of
Judah, [27]*the son* of Joannas,
the son of Rhesa, *the son* of

3:19 [a] NU-Text reads *his brother's wife.* 3:24 [a] This and several other names in the genealogy are spelled somewhat differently in the NU-Text. Since the New King James Version uses the Old Testament spelling for persons mentioned in the New Testament, these variations, which come from the Greek, have not been footnoted.

Zerubbabel, *the son* of Shealtiel, *the son* of Neri, 28 *the son*
of Melchi, *the son* of Addi, *the*
son of Cosam, *the son* of Elm-
odam, *the son* of Er, 29 *the son*
of Jose, *the son* of Eliezer, *the*
son of Jorim, *the son* of Matthat, *the son* of Levi, 30 *the son*
of Simeon, *the son* of Judah,
the son of Joseph, *the son* of
Jonan, *the son* of Eliakim,
31 *the son* of Melea, *the son* of
Menan, *the son* of Mattathah,
the son of Nathan, *the son* of
David, 32 *the son* of Jesse, *the*
son of Obed, *the son* of Boaz,
the son of Salmon, *the son* of
Nahshon, 33 *the son* of Amminadab, *the son* of Ram, *the son*
of Hezron, *the son* of Perez,
the son of Judah, 34 *the son* of
Jacob, *the son* of Isaac, *the son*
of Abraham, *the son* of Terah,
the son of Nahor, 35 *the son* of
Serug, *the son* of Reu, *the son*
of Peleg, *the son* of Eber, *the*
son of Shelah, 36 *the son* of Cainan, *the son* of Arphaxad, *the*
son of Shem, *the son* of Noah,
the son of Lamech, 37 *the son* of
Methuselah, *the son* of Enoch,
the son of Jared, *the son* of
Mahalalel, *the son* of Cainan,
38 *the son* of Enosh, *the son* of
Seth, *the son* of Adam, *the son*
of God.

SATAN TEMPTS JESUS

4 Then Jesus, being filled
with the Holy Spirit, re-
turned from the Jordan and
was led by the Spirit into[a] the
wilderness, 2 being tempted
for forty days by the devil. And
in those days He ate nothing,
and afterward, when they had
ended, He was hungry.

3 And the devil said to Him,
"If You are the Son of God,
command this stone to be-
come bread."

4 But Jesus answered him,
saying,[a] "It is written, 'Man
shall not live by bread alone,
but by every word of God.'"[b]

5 Then the devil, taking
Him up on a high mountain,
showed Him[a] all the kingdoms of the world in a moment of time. 6 And the devil
said to Him, "All this authority
I will give You, and their glory;
for *this* has been delivered to
me, and I give it to whomever
I wish. 7 Therefore, if You will
worship before me, all will be
Yours."

8 And Jesus answered and
said to him, "Get behind Me,
Satan![a] For[b] it is written, 'You
shall worship the LORD your
God, and Him only you shall
serve.'"[c]

9 Then he brought Him to
Jerusalem, set Him on the
pinnacle of the temple, and
said to Him, "If You are the
Son of God, throw Yourself
down from here. 10 For it is
written:

4:1 [a] NU-Text reads *in*. 4:4 [a] Deuteronomy 8:3 [b] NU-Text omits *but by every word of God*. 4:5 [a] NU-Text reads *And taking Him up, he showed Him*. 4:8 [a] NU-Text omits *Get behind Me, Satan*. [b] NU-Text and M-Text omit *For*. [c] Deuteronomy 6:13

'He shall give His angels
charge over you,
To keep you,'

11and,

'In *their* hands they
shall bear you up,
Lest you dash your foot
against a stone.'"[a]

12And Jesus answered and
said to him, "It has been said,
'You shall not tempt the LORD
your God.'"[a]
13Now when the devil had
ended every temptation, he
departed from Him until an
opportune time.

JESUS BEGINS HIS GALILEAN MINISTRY

14Then Jesus returned in
the power of the Spirit to Galilee, and news of Him went out
through all the surrounding
region. 15And He taught in
their synagogues, being glorified by all.

JESUS REJECTED AT NAZARETH

16So He came to Nazareth,
where He had been brought
up. And as His custom was, He
went into the synagogue on
the Sabbath day, and stood *up*
to read. 17And He was handed
the book of the prophet Isaiah. And when He had opened
the book, He found the place
where it was written:

18"The Spirit of the
LORD *is* upon Me,
Because He has
anointed Me
To preach the gospel
to *the* poor;
He has sent Me to heal
the brokenhearted,[a]
To proclaim liberty
to *the* captives
And recovery of sight
to *the* blind,
To set at liberty those
who are oppressed;
19 To proclaim the
acceptable year
of the LORD."[a]

20Then He closed the book,
and gave *it* back to the at-
tendant and sat down. And
the eyes of all who were in
the synagogue were fixed on
Him. 21And He began to say
to them, "Today this Scripture
is fulfilled in your hearing."
22So all bore witness to Him,
and marveled at the gracious
words which proceeded out of
His mouth. And they said, "Is
this not Joseph's son?"
23He said to them, "You
will surely say this proverb
to Me, 'Physician, heal yourself! Whatever we have heard
done in Capernaum,[a] do also
here in Your country.'" 24Then

4:11 [a] Psalm 91:11, 12 4:12 [a] Deuteronomy 6:16 4:18 [a] NU-Text omits *to heal the brokenhearted.* 4:19 [a] Isaiah 61:1, 2 4:23 [a] Here and elsewhere the NU-Text spelling is *Capharnaum.*

He said, "Assuredly, I say to
you, no prophet is accepted
in his own country. 25But I
tell you truly, many widows
were in Israel in the days of
Elijah, when the heaven was
shut up three years and six
months, and there was a great
famine throughout all the
land; 26but to none of them
was Elijah sent except to Zarephath,[a] *in the region* of Sidon,
to a woman *who was* a widow.
27And many lepers were in Israel in the time of Elisha the
prophet, and none of them
was cleansed except Naaman
the Syrian."

28So all those in the synagogue, when they heard these
things, were filled with wrath,
29and rose up and thrust Him
out of the city; and they led
Him to the brow of the hill on
which their city was built, that
they might throw Him down
over the cliff. 30Then passing
through the midst of them,
He went His way.

JESUS CASTS OUT AN UNCLEAN SPIRIT

31Then He went down to
Capernaum, a city of Galilee,
and was teaching them on the
Sabbaths. 32And they were astonished at His teaching, for
His word was with authority.
33Now in the synagogue there
was a man who had a spirit of
an unclean demon. And he
cried out with a loud voice,
34saying, "Let *us* alone! What
have we to do with You, Jesus
of Nazareth? Did You come to
destroy us? I know who You
are—the Holy One of God!"

35But Jesus rebuked him,
saying, "Be quiet, and come
out of him!" And when the
demon had thrown him in
their midst, it came out of
him and did not hurt him.
36Then they were all amazed
and spoke among themselves,
saying, "What a word this *is!*
For with authority and power
He commands the unclean
spirits, and they come out."
37And the report about Him
went out into every place in
the surrounding region.

PETER'S MOTHER-IN-LAW HEALED

38Now He arose from the
synagogue and entered Si-
mon's house. But Simon's
wife's mother was sick with
a high fever, and they made
request of Him concerning
her. 39So He stood over her
and rebuked the fever, and it
left her. And immediately she
arose and served them.

MANY HEALED AFTER SABBATH SUNSET

40When the sun was set-
ting, all those who had any
that were sick with various
diseases brought them to
Him; and He laid His hands
on every one of them and

4:26 [a] Greek *Sarepta*

healed them. 41And demons
also came out of many, crying
out and saying, "You are the
Christ,[a] the Son of God!"
And He, rebuking *them,*
did not allow them to speak,
for they knew that He was the
Christ.

JESUS PREACHES IN GALILEE

42Now when it was day, He
departed and went into a deserted place. And the crowd
sought Him and came to Him,
and tried to keep Him from
leaving them; 43but He said
to them, "I must preach the
kingdom of God to the other
cities also, because for this
purpose I have been sent."
44And He was preaching in the
synagogues of Galilee.[a]

FOUR FISHERMEN CALLED AS DISCIPLES

5 So it was, as the multitude pressed about Him
to hear the word of God, that
He stood by the Lake of Gennesaret, 2and saw two boats
standing by the lake; but the
fishermen had gone from
them and were washing *their*
nets. 3Then He got into one of
the boats, which was Simon's,
and asked him to put out a
little from the land. And He
sat down and taught the multitudes from the boat.
4When He had stopped
speaking, He said to Simon,
"Launch out into the deep
and let down your nets for a
catch."
5But Simon answered and
said to Him, "Master, we have
toiled all night and caught
nothing; nevertheless at Your
word I will let down the net."
6And when they had done this,
they caught a great number of
fish, and their net was breaking. 7So they signaled to *their*
partners in the other boat to
come and help them. And
they came and filled both the
boats, so that they began to
sink. 8When Simon Peter saw
it, he fell down at Jesus' knees,
saying, "Depart from me, for I
am a sinful man, O Lord!"
9For he and all who were
with him were astonished at
the catch of fish which they
had taken; 10and so also *were*
James and John, the sons of
Zebedee, who were partners
with Simon. And Jesus said
to Simon, "Do not be afraid.
From now on you will catch
men." 11So when they had
brought their boats to land,
they forsook all and followed
Him.

JESUS CLEANSES A LEPER

12And it happened when
He was in a certain city, that
behold, a man who was full of
leprosy saw Jesus; and he fell
on *his* face and implored Him,
saying, "Lord, if You are willing, You can make me clean."

4:41 [a] NU-Text omits *the Christ.* 4:44 [a] NU-Text reads *Judea.*

13Then He put out *His* hand
and touched him, saying, "I
am willing; be cleansed." Immediately the leprosy left
him. 14And He charged him
to tell no one, "But go and
show yourself to the priest,
and make an offering for your
cleansing, as a testimony to
them, just as Moses com-
manded."

15However, the report went
around concerning Him all
the more; and great multitudes came together to hear,
and to be healed by Him of
their infirmities. 16So He Himself *often* withdrew into the
wilderness and prayed.

JESUS FORGIVES AND HEALS A PARALYTIC

17Now it happened on a certain day, as He was teaching,
that there were Pharisees and
teachers of the law sitting by,
who had come out of every
town of Galilee, Judea, and
Jerusalem. And the power of
the Lord was *present* to heal
them.[a] 18Then behold, men
brought on a bed a man who
was paralyzed, whom they
sought to bring in and lay before Him. 19And when they
could not find how they might
bring him in, because of the
crowd, they went up on the
housetop and let him down
with *his* bed through the tiling
into the midst before Jesus.

20When He saw their faith,
He said to him, "Man, your
sins are forgiven you."

21And the scribes and the
Pharisees began to reason,
saying, "Who is this who
speaks blasphemies? Who can
forgive sins but God alone?"

22But when Jesus perceived
their thoughts, He answered
and said to them, "Why are
you reasoning in your hearts?
23Which is easier, to say, 'Your
sins are forgiven you,' or to say,
'Rise up and walk'? 24But that
you may know that the Son
of Man has power on earth to
forgive sins"—He said to the
man who was paralyzed, "I say
to you, arise, take up your bed,
and go to your house."

25Immediately he rose up
before them, took up what he
had been lying on, and departed to his own house, glorifying God. 26And they were
all amazed, and they glorified
God and were filled with fear,
saying, "We have seen strange
things today!"

MATTHEW THE TAX COLLECTOR

27After these things He
went out and saw a tax collector named Levi, sitting at
the tax office. And He said to
him, "Follow Me." 28So he left
all, rose up, and followed Him.

29Then Levi gave Him a
great feast in his own house.
And there were a great number of tax collectors and

5:17 [a] NU-Text reads *present with Him to heal.*

others who sat down with
them. 30And their scribes and
the Pharisees[a] complained
against His disciples, saying,
"Why do You eat and drink
with tax collectors and sinners?"
31Jesus answered and said
to them, "Those who are well
have no need of a physician,
but those who are sick. 32I
have not come to call *the* righteous, but sinners, to repentance."

JESUS IS QUESTIONED ABOUT FASTING

33Then they said to Him,
"Why do[a] the disciples of John
fast often and make prayers,
and likewise those of the
Pharisees, but Yours eat and
drink?"
34And He said to them,
"Can you make the friends
of the bridegroom fast while
the bridegroom is with them?
35But the days will come when
the bridegroom will be taken
away from them; then they
will fast in those days."
36Then He spoke a parable
to them: "No one puts a piece
from a new garment on an
old one;[a] otherwise the new
makes a tear, and also the
piece that was *taken* out of
the new does not match the
old. 37And no one puts new
wine into old wineskins; or
else the new wine will burst
the wineskins and be spilled,
and the wineskins will be ruined. 38But new wine must be
put into new wineskins, and
both are preserved.[a] 39And no
one, having drunk old *wine,*
immediately[a] desires new; for
he says, 'The old is better.'"[b]

JESUS IS LORD OF THE SABBATH

6 Now it happened on the
second Sabbath after the
first[a] that He went through
the grainfields. And His disciples plucked the heads of
grain and ate *them,* rubbing
them in *their* hands. 2And
some of the Pharisees said
to them, "Why are you doing
what is not lawful to do on the
Sabbath?"
3But Jesus answering them
said, "Have you not even read
this, what David did when he
was hungry, he and those who
were with him: 4how he went
into the house of God, took
and ate the showbread, and
also gave some to those with
him, which is not lawful for
any but the priests to eat?"
5And He said to them, "The
Son of Man is also Lord of the
Sabbath."

5:30 [a] NU-Text reads *But the Pharisees and their scribes.*
5:33 [a] NU-Text omits *Why do,* making the verse a statement.
5:36 [a] NU-Text reads *No one tears a piece from a new garment and puts it on an old one.* **5:38** [a] NU-Text omits *and both are preserved.* **5:39** [a] NU-Text omits *immediately.* [b] NU-Text reads *good.* **6:1** [a] NU-Text reads *on a Sabbath.*

HEALING ON THE SABBATH

6Now it happened on an-
other Sabbath, also, that He
entered the synagogue and
taught. And a man was there
whose right hand was withered. 7So the scribes and Pharisees watched Him closely,
whether He would heal on the
Sabbath, that they might find
an accusation against Him.
8But He knew their thoughts,
and said to the man who had
the withered hand, "Arise and
stand here." And he arose
and stood. 9Then Jesus said
to them, "I will ask you one
thing: Is it lawful on the Sabbath to do good or to do evil,
to save life or to destroy?"[a]
10And when He had looked
around at them all, He said
to the man,[a] "Stretch out your
hand." And he did so, and his
hand was restored as whole
as the other.[b] 11But they were
filled with rage, and discussed
with one another what they
might do to Jesus.

THE TWELVE APOSTLES

12Now it came to pass in
those days that He went out
to the mountain to pray, and
continued all night in prayer
to God. 13And when it was day,
He called His disciples to *Himself;* and from them He chose
twelve whom He also named
apostles: 14Simon, whom He
also named Peter, and An-
drew his brother; James and
John; Philip and Bartholomew; 15Matthew and Thomas;
James the *son* of Alphaeus,
and Simon called the Zealot;
16Judas *the son* of James, and
Judas Iscariot who also became a traitor.

JESUS HEALS A GREAT MULTITUDE

17And He came down with
them and stood on a level
place with a crowd of His
disciples and a great multitude of people from all Judea
and Jerusalem, and from the
seacoast of Tyre and Sidon,
who came to hear Him and be
healed of their diseases, 18as
well as those who were tormented with unclean spirits.
And they were healed. 19And
the whole multitude sought
to touch Him, for power went
out from Him and healed
them all.

THE BEATITUDES

20Then He lifted up His
eyes toward His disciples,
and said:

"Blessed *are you* poor,
For yours is the
kingdom of God.
21 Blessed *are you* who
hunger now,
For you shall be filled.
Blessed *are you*
who weep now,

6:9 [a] M-Text reads *to kill.* 6:10 [a] NU-Text and M-Text read *to him.* [b] NU-Text omits *as whole as the other.*

For you shall laugh.
22 Blessed are you when
men hate you,
And when they
exclude you,
And revile *you*, and cast
out your name as evil,
For the Son of
Man's sake.
23 Rejoice in that day
and leap for joy!
For indeed your reward
is great in heaven,
For in like manner
their fathers did
to the prophets.

JESUS PRONOUNCES WOES

24"But woe to you
who are rich,
For you have received
your consolation.
25 Woe to you who are full,
For you shall hunger.
Woe to you who
laugh now,
For you shall mourn
and weep.
26 Woe to you[a] when all[b]
men speak well of you,
For so did their fathers
to the false prophets.

LOVE YOUR ENEMIES

27"But I say to you who
hear: Love your enemies, do
good to those who hate you,
28bless those who curse you,
and pray for those who spitefully use you. 29To him who
strikes you on the *one* cheek,
offer the other also. And from
him who takes away your
cloak, do not withhold *your*
tunic either. 30Give to everyone who asks of you. And
from him who takes away your
goods do not ask *them* back.
31And just as you want men to
do to you, you also do to them
likewise.

32"But if you love those who
love you, what credit is that
to you? For even sinners love
those who love them. 33And
if you do good to those who
do good to you, what credit is
that to you? For even sinners
do the same. 34And if you lend
to those from whom you hope
to receive back, what credit is
that to you? For even sinners
lend to sinners to receive as
much back. 35But love your
enemies, do good, and lend,
hoping for nothing in return;
and your reward will be great,
and you will be sons of the
Most High. For He is kind
to the unthankful and evil.
36Therefore be merciful, just
as your Father also is merciful.

DO NOT JUDGE

37"Judge not, and you shall
not be judged. Condemn not,
and you shall not be con-
demned. Forgive, and you will
be forgiven. 38Give, and it will
be given to you: good measure, pressed down, shaken
together, and running over
will be put into your bosom.

6:26 [a] NU-Text and M-Text omit *to you*. [b] M-Text omits *all*.

For with the same measure
that you use, it will be measured back to you."
[39]And He spoke a parable
to them: "Can the blind lead
the blind? Will they not both
fall into the ditch? [40]A disciple is not above his teacher,
but everyone who is perfectly
trained will be like his teacher.
[41]And why do you look at the
speck in your brother's eye,
but do not perceive the plank
in your own eye? [42]Or how
can you say to your brother,
'Brother, let me remove the
speck that *is* in your eye,' when
you yourself do not see the
plank that *is* in your own eye?
Hypocrite! First remove the
plank from your own eye, and
then you will see clearly to remove the speck that is in your
brother's eye.

A TREE IS KNOWN BY ITS FRUIT

[43]"For a good tree does
not bear bad fruit, nor does a
bad tree bear good fruit. [44]For
every tree is known by its own
fruit. For *men* do not gather
figs from thorns, nor do they
gather grapes from a bramble bush. [45]A good man out of
the good treasure of his heart
brings forth good; and an evil
man out of the evil treasure
of his heart[a] brings forth evil.
For out of the abundance of
the heart his mouth speaks.

BUILD ON THE ROCK

[46]"But why do you call Me
'Lord, Lord,' and not do the
things which I say? [47]Who-
ever comes to Me, and hears
My sayings and does them, I
will show you whom he is like:
[48]He is like a man building a
house, who dug deep and laid
the foundation on the rock.
And when the flood arose,
the stream beat vehemently
against that house, and
could not shake it, for it was
founded on the rock.[a] [49]But
he who heard and did nothing is like a man who built a
house on the earth without a
foundation, against which the
stream beat vehemently; and
immediately it fell.[a] And the
ruin of that house was great."

JESUS HEALS A CENTURION'S SERVANT

7 Now when He concluded all
His sayings in the hearing
of the people, He entered Capernaum. [2]And a certain centurion's servant, who was dear
to him, was sick and ready to
die. [3]So when he heard about
Jesus, he sent elders of the Jews
to Him, pleading with Him to
come and heal his servant.
[4]And when they came to Jesus,
they begged Him earnestly,
saying that the one for whom
He should do this was deserving, [5]"for he loves our nation,
and has built us a synagogue."

6:45 [a] NU-Text omits *treasure of his heart.* 6:48 [a] NU-Text reads *for it was well built.* 6:49 [a] NU-Text reads *collapsed.*

6Then Jesus went with
them. And when He was al-
ready not far from the house,
the centurion sent friends to
Him, saying to Him, "Lord, do
not trouble Yourself, for I am
not worthy that You should
enter under my roof. 7There-
fore I did not even think myself worthy to come to You.
But say the word, and my
servant will be healed. 8For I
also am a man placed under
authority, having soldiers
under me. And I say to one,
'Go,' and he goes; and to another, 'Come,' and he comes;
and to my servant, 'Do this,'
and he does *it*."
9When Jesus heard these
things, He marveled at him,
and turned around and said to
the crowd that followed Him,
"I say to you, I have not found
such great faith, not even in
Israel!" 10And those who were
sent, returning to the house,
found the servant well who
had been sick.[a]

JESUS RAISES THE SON OF THE WIDOW OF NAIN

11Now it happened, the day
after, *that* He went into a city
called Nain; and many of His
disciples went with Him, and
a large crowd. 12And when
He came near the gate of the
city, behold, a dead man was
being carried out, the only son
of his mother; and she was
a widow. And a large crowd
from the city was with her.
13When the Lord saw her, He
had compassion on her and
said to her, "Do not weep."
14Then He came and touched
the open coffin, and those
who carried *him* stood still.
And He said, "Young man, I
say to you, arise." 15So he who
was dead sat up and began to
speak. And He presented him
to his mother.
16Then fear came upon
all, and they glorified God,
saying, "A great prophet has
risen up among us"; and, "God
has visited His people." 17And
this report about Him went
throughout all Judea and all
the surrounding region.

JOHN THE BAPTIST SENDS MESSENGERS TO JESUS

18Then the disciples of John
reported to him concerning
all these things. 19And John,
calling two of his disciples to
him, sent *them* to Jesus,[a] saying, "Are You the Coming One,
or do we look for another?"
20When the men had come
to Him, they said, "John the
Baptist has sent us to You, saying, 'Are You the Coming One,
or do we look for another?'"
21And that very hour He cured
many of infirmities, afflictions, and evil spirits; and to
many blind He gave sight.
22Jesus answered and said
to them, "Go and tell John
the things you have seen

7:10 [a] NU-Text omits *who had been sick*. 7:19 [a] NU-Text reads *the Lord*.

and heard: that *the* blind see,
the lame walk, *the* lepers are
cleansed, *the* deaf hear, *the*
dead are raised, *the* poor have
the gospel preached to them.
23And blessed is *he* who is not
offended because of Me."
24When the messengers of
John had departed, He began
to speak to the multitudes
concerning John: "What did
you go out into the wilderness
to see? A reed shaken by the
wind? 25But what did you go
out to see? A man clothed in
soft garments? Indeed those
who are gorgeously appareled
and live in luxury are in kings'
courts. 26But what did you go
out to see? A prophet? Yes, I
say to you, and more than a
prophet. 27This is *he* of whom
it is written:

'Behold, I send My
messenger before
Your face,
Who will prepare Your
way before You.'[a]

28For I say to you, among
those born of women there
is not a greater prophet than
John the Baptist;[a] but he who
is least in the kingdom of God
is greater than he."
29And when all the people
heard *Him,* even the tax collectors justified God, having
been baptized with the baptism of John. 30But the Pharisees and lawyers rejected the
will of God for themselves, not
having been baptized by him.
31And the Lord said,[a] "To
what then shall I liken the
men of this generation, and
what are they like? 32They
are like children sitting in
the marketplace and calling
to one another, saying:

'We played the
flute for you,
And you did not dance;
We mourned to you,
And you did not weep.'

33For John the Baptist came
neither eating bread nor
drinking wine, and you say,
'He has a demon.' 34The Son
of Man has come eating and
drinking, and you say, 'Look,
a glutton and a winebibber, a
friend of tax collectors and
sinners!' 35But wisdom is justified by all her children."

A SINFUL WOMAN FORGIVEN

36Then one of the Phari-
sees asked Him to eat with
him. And He went to the Pharisee's house, and sat down to
eat. 37And behold, a woman
in the city who was a sinner,
when she knew that *Jesus* sat
at the table in the Pharisee's
house, brought an alabaster
flask of fragrant oil, 38and
stood at His feet behind *Him*

7:27 [a] Malachi 3:1 7:28 [a] NU-Text reads *there is none greater than John.* 7:31 [a] NU-Text and M-Text omit *And the Lord said.*

weeping; and she began to
wash His feet with her tears,
and wiped *them* with the hair
of her head; and she kissed
His feet and anointed *them*
with the fragrant oil. 39Now
when the Pharisee who had
invited Him saw *this,* he spoke
to himself, saying, "This Man,
if He were a prophet, would
know who and what manner
of woman *this is* who is touching Him, for she is a sinner."
40And Jesus answered and
said to him, "Simon, I have
something to say to you."

So he said, "Teacher, say it."
41"There was a certain
creditor who had two debtors. One owed five hundred
denarii, and the other fifty.
42And when they had nothing
with which to repay, he freely
forgave them both. Tell Me,
therefore, which of them will
love him more?"
43Simon answered and
said, "I suppose the *one* whom
he forgave more."

And He said to him, "You
have rightly judged." 44Then
He turned to the woman and
said to Simon, "Do you see this
woman? I entered your house;
you gave Me no water for My
feet, but she has washed My
feet with her tears and wiped
them with the hair of her head.
45You gave Me no kiss, but this
woman has not ceased to kiss
My feet since the time I came
in. 46You did not anoint My
head with oil, but this woman
has anointed My feet with fragrant oil. 47Therefore I say to
you, her sins, which *are* many,
are forgiven, for she loved
much. But to whom little is
forgiven, *the same* loves little."
48Then He said to her,
"Your sins are forgiven."
49And those who sat at the
table with Him began to say to
themselves, "Who is this who
even forgives sins?"
50Then He said to the
woman, "Your faith has saved
you. Go in peace."

MANY WOMEN MINISTER TO JESUS

8 Now it came to pass, afterward, that He went
through every city and village,
preaching and bringing the
glad tidings of the kingdom of
God. And the twelve *were* with
Him, 2and certain women who
had been healed of evil spirits
and infirmities—Mary called
Magdalene, out of whom had
come seven demons, 3and Joanna the wife of Chuza, Herod's steward, and Susanna,
and many others who pro-
vided for Him[a] from their
substance.

THE PARABLE OF THE SOWER

4And when a great multi-
tude had gathered, and they
had come to Him from every
city, He spoke by a parable: 5"A

8:3 [a] NU-Text and M-Text read *them.*

sower went out to sow his seed.
And as he sowed, some fell by
the wayside; and it was trampled down, and the birds of the
air devoured it. 6Some fell on
rock; and as soon as it sprang
up, it withered away because
it lacked moisture. 7And some
fell among thorns, and the
thorns sprang up with it and
choked it. 8But others fell on
good ground, sprang up, and
yielded a crop a hundredfold."
When He had said these things
He cried, "He who has ears to
hear, let him hear!"

THE PURPOSE OF PARABLES

9Then His disciples asked
Him, saying, "What does this
parable mean?"
10And He said, "To you it
has been given to know the
mysteries of the kingdom of
God, but to the rest *it is given*
in parables, that

'Seeing they may not see,
And hearing they may
not understand.'[a]

THE PARABLE OF THE SOWER EXPLAINED

11"Now the parable is this:
The seed is the word of God.
12Those by the wayside are
the ones who hear; then the
devil comes and takes away
the word out of their hearts,
lest they should believe and
be saved. 13But the ones on
the rock *are those* who, when
they hear, receive the word
with joy; and these have no
root, who believe for a while
and in time of temptation fall
away. 14Now the ones *that* fell
among thorns are those who,
when they have heard, go out
and are choked with cares,
riches, and pleasures of life,
and bring no fruit to maturity.
15But the ones *that* fell on the
good ground are those who,
having heard the word with a
noble and good heart, keep *it*
and bear fruit with patience.

THE PARABLE OF THE REVEALED LIGHT

16"No one, when he has lit
a lamp, covers it with a vessel or puts *it* under a bed, but
sets *it* on a lampstand, that
those who enter may see the
light. 17For nothing is secret
that will not be revealed, nor
anything hidden that will not
be known and come to light.
18Therefore take heed how
you hear. For whoever has, to
him *more* will be given; and
whoever does not have, even
what he seems to have will be
taken from him."

JESUS' MOTHER AND BROTHERS COME TO HIM

19Then His mother and
brothers came to Him, and
could not approach Him because of the crowd. 20And it

8:10 [a] Isaiah 6:9

was told Him *by some,* who
said, "Your mother and Your
brothers are standing outside,
desiring to see You."
21But He answered and said
to them, "My mother and My
brothers are these who hear
the word of God and do it."

WIND AND WAVE OBEY JESUS

22Now it happened, on a
certain day, that He got into
a boat with His disciples.
And He said to them, "Let us
cross over to the other side of
the lake." And they launched
out. 23But as they sailed He
fell asleep. And a windstorm
came down on the lake, and
they were filling *with water,*
and were in jeopardy. 24And
they came to Him and awoke
Him, saying, "Master, Master,
we are perishing!"
Then He arose and rebuked
the wind and the raging of the
water. And they ceased, and
there was a calm. 25But He said
to them, "Where is your faith?"
And they were afraid, and
marveled, saying to one another, "Who can this be? For
He commands even the winds
and water, and they obey
Him!"

A DEMON-POSSESSED MAN HEALED

26Then they sailed to the
country of the Gadarenes,[a]
which is opposite Galilee.
27And when He stepped out
on the land, there met Him
a certain man from the city
who had demons for a long
time. And he wore no clothes,[a]
nor did he live in a house but
in the tombs. 28When he saw
Jesus, he cried out, fell down
before Him, and with a loud
voice said, "What have I to do
with You, Jesus, Son of the
Most High God? I beg You,
do not torment me!" 29For He
had commanded the unclean
spirit to come out of the man.
For it had often seized him,
and he was kept under guard,
bound with chains and shackles; and he broke the bonds
and was driven by the demon
into the wilderness.
30Jesus asked him, saying,
"What is your name?"
And he said, "Legion," because many demons had en-
tered him. 31And they begged
Him that He would not command them to go out into the
abyss.
32Now a herd of many
swine was feeding there on
the mountain. So they begged
Him that He would permit
them to enter them. And He
permitted them. 33Then the
demons went out of the man
and entered the swine, and
the herd ran violently down
the steep place into the lake
and drowned.

8:26 [a] NU-Text reads *Gerasenes.* **8:27** [a] NU-Text reads *who had demons and for a long time wore no clothes.*

[34]When those who fed *them*
saw what had happened, they
fled and told *it* in the city and
in the country. [35]Then they
went out to see what had happened, and came to Jesus, and
found the man from whom
the demons had departed,
sitting at the feet of Jesus,
clothed and in his right mind.
And they were afraid. [36]They
also who had seen *it* told them
by what means he who had
been demon-possessed was
healed. [37]Then the whole multitude of the surrounding region of the Gadarenes[a] asked
Him to depart from them, for
they were seized with great
fear. And He got into the boat
and returned.

[38]Now the man from whom
the demons had departed
begged Him that he might
be with Him. But Jesus sent
him away, saying, [39]"Return to
your own house, and tell what
great things God has done for
you." And he went his way and
proclaimed throughout the
whole city what great things
Jesus had done for him.

A GIRL RESTORED TO LIFE AND A WOMAN HEALED

[40]So it was, when Jesus
returned, that the multitude
welcomed Him, for they were
all waiting for Him. [41]And
behold, there came a man
named Jairus, and he was a
ruler of the synagogue. And
he fell down at Jesus' feet and
begged Him to come to his
house, [42]for he had an only
daughter about twelve years
of age, and she was dying.

But as He went, the multitudes thronged Him. [43]Now
a woman, having a flow of
blood for twelve years, who
had spent all her livelihood
on physicians and could not
be healed by any, [44]came from
behind and touched the border of His garment. And immediately her flow of blood
stopped.

[45]And Jesus said, "Who
touched Me?"

When all denied it, Peter
and those with him[a] said,
"Master, the multitudes throng
and press You, and You say,
'Who touched Me?'"[b]

[46]But Jesus said, "Some-
body touched Me, for I perceived power going out from
Me." [47]Now when the woman
saw that she was not hidden,
she came trembling; and falling down before Him, she declared to Him in the presence
of all the people the reason
she had touched Him and how
she was healed immediately.

[48]And He said to her,
"Daughter, be of good cheer;[a]
your faith has made you well.
Go in peace."

8:37 [a] NU-Text reads *Gerasenes.* **8:45** [a] NU-Text omits *and those with him.* [b] NU-Text omits *and You say, 'Who touched Me?'* **8:48** [a] NU-Text omits *be of good cheer.*

49While He was still speaking, someone came from the
ruler of the synagogue's *house*,
saying to him, "Your daughter is dead. Do not trouble the
Teacher."[a]
50But when Jesus heard *it*,
He answered him, saying, "Do
not be afraid; only believe, and
she will be made well." 51When
He came into the house, He
permitted no one to go in[a] except Peter, James, and John,[b]
and the father and mother of
the girl. 52Now all wept and
mourned for her; but He said,
"Do not weep; she is not dead,
but sleeping." 53And they ridiculed Him, knowing that she
was dead.
54But He put them all outside,[a] took her by the hand
and called, saying, "Little girl,
arise." 55Then her spirit returned, and she arose immediately. And He commanded
that she be given *something*
to eat. 56And her parents were
astonished, but He charged
them to tell no one what had
happened.

SENDING OUT THE TWELVE

9 Then He called His twelve
disciples together and
gave them power and au-
thority over all demons, and
to cure diseases. 2He sent them
to preach the kingdom of God
and to heal the sick. 3And He
said to them, "Take nothing for
the journey, neither staffs nor
bag nor bread nor money; and
do not have two tunics apiece.
4"Whatever house you
enter, stay there, and from
there depart. 5And whoever
will not receive you, when you
go out of that city, shake off
the very dust from your feet
as a testimony against them."
6So they departed and went
through the towns, preaching
the gospel and healing everywhere.

HEROD SEEKS TO SEE JESUS

7Now Herod the tetrarch
heard of all that was done by
Him; and he was perplexed,
because it was said by some
that John had risen from the
dead, 8and by some that Elijah
had appeared, and by others
that one of the old prophets
had risen again. 9Herod said,
"John I have beheaded, but
who is this of whom I hear
such things?" So he sought
to see Him.

FEEDING THE FIVE THOUSAND

10And the apostles, when
they had returned, told Him
all that they had done. Then
He took them and went aside
privately into a deserted place
belonging to the city called

8:49 [a] NU-Text adds *anymore*. 8:51 [a] NU-Text adds *with Him*. [b] NU-Text and M-Text read *Peter, John, and James*. 8:54 [a] NU-Text omits *put them all outside*.

Bethsaida. [11]But when the multitudes knew *it,* they followed Him; and He received them and spoke to them about the kingdom of God, and healed those who had need of healing. [12]When the day began to wear away, the twelve came and said to Him, "Send the multitude away, that they may go into the surrounding towns and country, and lodge and get provisions; for we are in a deserted place here."

[13]But He said to them, "You give them something to eat."

And they said, "We have no more than five loaves and two fish, unless we go and buy food for all these people." [14]For there were about five thousand men.

Then He said to His disciples, "Make them sit down in groups of fifty." [15]And they did so, and made them all sit down.

[16]Then He took the five loaves and the two fish, and looking up to heaven, He blessed and broke them, and gave *them* to the disciples to set before the multitude. [17]So they all ate and were filled, and twelve baskets of the leftover fragments were taken up by them.

PETER CONFESSES JESUS AS THE CHRIST

[18]And it happened, as He was alone praying, *that* His disciples joined Him, and He asked them, saying, "Who do the crowds say that I am?"

[19]So they answered and said, "John the Baptist, but some *say* Elijah; and others *say* that one of the old prophets has risen again."

[20]He said to them, "But who do you say that I am?"

Peter answered and said, "The Christ of God."

JESUS PREDICTS HIS DEATH AND RESURRECTION

[21]And He strictly warned and commanded them to tell this to no one, [22]saying, "The Son of Man must suffer many things, and be rejected by the elders and chief priests and scribes, and be killed, and be raised the third day."

TAKE UP THE CROSS AND FOLLOW HIM

[23]Then He said to *them* all, "If anyone desires to come after Me, let him deny himself, and take up his cross daily,[a] and follow Me. [24]For whoever desires to save his life will lose it, but whoever loses his life for My sake will save it. [25]For what profit is it to a man if he gains the whole world, and is himself destroyed or lost? [26]For whoever is ashamed of Me and My words, of him the Son of Man will be ashamed when He comes in His *own* glory,

9:23 [a] M-Text omits *daily.*

and *in His* Father's, and of the holy angels. 27But I tell you truly, there are some standing here who shall not taste death till they see the kingdom of God."

JESUS TRANSFIGURED ON THE MOUNT

28Now it came to pass, about eight days after these sayings, that He took Peter, John, and James and went up on the mountain to pray. 29As He prayed, the appearance of His face was altered, and His robe *became* white *and* glistening. 30And behold, two men talked with Him, who were Moses and Elijah, 31who appeared in glory and spoke of His decease which He was about to accomplish at Jerusalem. 32But Peter and those with him were heavy with sleep; and when they were fully awake, they saw His glory and the two men who stood with Him. 33Then it happened, as they were parting from Him, *that* Peter said to Jesus, "Master, it is good for us to be here; and let us make three tabernacles: one for You, one for Moses, and one for Elijah"—not knowing what he said.

34While he was saying this, a cloud came and overshadowed them; and they were fearful as they entered the cloud. 35And a voice came out of the cloud, saying, "This is My beloved Son.[a] Hear Him!" 36When the voice had ceased, Jesus was found alone. But they kept quiet, and told no one in those days any of the things they had seen.

A BOY IS HEALED

37Now it happened on the next day, when they had come down from the mountain, that a great multitude met Him. 38Suddenly a man from the multitude cried out, saying, "Teacher, I implore You, look on my son, for he is my only child. 39And behold, a spirit seizes him, and he suddenly cries out; it convulses him so that he foams *at the mouth;* and it departs from him with great difficulty, bruising him. 40So I implored Your disciples to cast it out, but they could not."

41Then Jesus answered and said, "O faithless and perverse generation, how long shall I be with you and bear with you? Bring your son here." 42And as he was still coming, the demon threw him down and convulsed *him.* Then Jesus rebuked the unclean spirit, healed the child, and gave him back to his father.

JESUS AGAIN PREDICTS HIS DEATH

43And they were all amazed at the majesty of God.

9:35 [a] NU-Text reads *This is My Son, the Chosen One.*

But while everyone mar-
veled at all the things which
Jesus did, He said to His disciples, 44"Let these words sink
down into your ears, for the
Son of Man is about to be betrayed into the hands of men."
45But they did not understand
this saying, and it was hidden
from them so that they did
not perceive it; and they were
afraid to ask Him about this
saying.

WHO IS THE GREATEST?

46Then a dispute arose
among them as to which of
them would be greatest. 47And
Jesus, perceiving the thought
of their heart, took a little child
and set him by Him, 48and said
to them, "Whoever receives
this little child in My name
receives Me; and whoever receives Me receives Him who
sent Me. For he who is least
among you all will be great."

JESUS FORBIDS SECTARIANISM

49Now John answered and
said, "Master, we saw someone
casting out demons in Your
name, and we forbade him
because he does not follow
with us."
50But Jesus said to him,
"Do not forbid *him,* for he
who is not against us[a] is on
our[b] side."

A SAMARITAN VILLAGE REJECTS THE SAVIOR

51Now it came to pass, when
the time had come for Him
to be received up, that He
steadfastly set His face to go
to Jerusalem, 52and sent messengers before His face. And
as they went, they entered a
village of the Samaritans, to
prepare for Him. 53But they
did not receive Him, because
His face was *set* for the journey to Jerusalem. 54And when
His disciples James and John
saw *this,* they said, "Lord, do
You want us to command fire
to come down from heaven
and consume them, just as
Elijah did?"[a]
55But He turned and re-
buked them,[a] and said, "You
do not know what manner of
spirit you are of. 56For the Son
of Man did not come to destroy men's lives but to save
them."[a] And they went to another village.

THE COST OF DISCIPLESHIP

57Now it happened as they
journeyed on the road, *that*
someone said to Him, "Lord,
I will follow You wherever
You go."
58And Jesus said to him,
"Foxes have holes and birds
of the air *have* nests, but the
Son of Man has nowhere to
lay *His* head."

9:50 [a] NU-Text reads *you.* [b] NU-Text reads *your.* 9:54 [a] NU-Text omits *just as Elijah did.* 9:55 [a] NU-Text omits the rest of this verse. 9:56 [a] NU-Text omits the first sentence of this verse.

59 Then He said to another,
"Follow Me."
But he said, "Lord, let me
first go and bury my father."
60 Jesus said to him, "Let
the dead bury their own dead,
but you go and preach the
kingdom of God."
61 And another also said,
"Lord, I will follow You, but
let me first go *and* bid them
farewell who are at my house."
62 But Jesus said to him, "No
one, having put his hand to
the plow, and looking back,
is fit for the kingdom of God."

THE SEVENTY SENT OUT

10 After these things the
Lord appointed sev-
enty others also,[a] and sent
them two by two before His
face into every city and place
where He Himself was about
to go. 2 Then He said to them,
"The harvest truly *is* great, but
the laborers *are* few; therefore
pray the Lord of the harvest to
send out laborers into His harvest. 3 Go your way; behold, I
send you out as lambs among
wolves. 4 Carry neither money
bag, knapsack, nor sandals;
and greet no one along the
road. 5 But whatever house you
enter, first say, 'Peace to this
house.' 6 And if a son of peace
is there, your peace will rest
on it; if not, it will return to
you. 7 And remain in the same
house, eating and drinking
such things as they give, for
the laborer is worthy of his
wages. Do not go from house
to house. 8 Whatever city you
enter, and they receive you, eat
such things as are set before
you. 9 And heal the sick there,
and say to them, 'The kingdom
of God has come near to you.'
10 But whatever city you enter,
and they do not receive you,
go out into its streets and say,
11 'The very dust of your city
which clings to us[a] we wipe
off against you. Nevertheless
know this, that the kingdom
of God has come near you.'
12 But[a] I say to you that it will
be more tolerable in that Day
for Sodom than for that city.

WOE TO THE IMPENITENT CITIES

13 "Woe to you, Chorazin!
Woe to you, Bethsaida! For if
the mighty works which were
done in you had been done in
Tyre and Sidon, they would
have repented long ago, sitting
in sackcloth and ashes. 14 But it
will be more tolerable for Tyre
and Sidon at the judgment
than for you. 15 And you, Capernaum, who are exalted to
heaven, will be brought down
to Hades.[a] 16 He who hears you
hears Me, he who rejects you
rejects Me, and he who rejects
Me rejects Him who sent Me."

10:1 [a] NU-Text reads *seventy-two others.* 10:11 [a] NU-Text reads *our feet.* 10:12 [a] NU-Text and M-Text omit *But.* 10:15 [a] NU-Text reads *will you be exalted to heaven? You will be thrust down to Hades!*

THE SEVENTY RETURN WITH JOY

17Then the seventy[a] re-
turned with joy, saying, "Lord,
even the demons are subject
to us in Your name."

18And He said to them, "I
saw Satan fall like lightning
from heaven. 19Behold, I give
you the authority to trample
on serpents and scorpions,
and over all the power of the
enemy, and nothing shall by
any means hurt you. 20Never-
theless do not rejoice in this,
that the spirits are subject to
you, but rather[a] rejoice because your names are written
in heaven."

JESUS REJOICES IN THE SPIRIT

21In that hour Jesus re-
joiced in the Spirit and said,
"I thank You, Father, Lord of
heaven and earth, that You
have hidden these things
from *the* wise and prudent
and revealed them to babes.
Even so, Father, for so it
seemed good in Your sight.
22All[a] things have been delivered to Me by My Father, and
no one knows who the Son is
except the Father, and who
the Father is except the Son,
and *the one* to whom the Son
wills to reveal *Him*."

23Then He turned to *His*
disciples and said privately,
"Blessed *are* the eyes which
see the things you see; 24for I
tell you that many prophets
and kings have desired to see
what you see, and have not
seen *it*, and to hear what you
hear, and have not heard *it*."

THE PARABLE OF THE GOOD SAMARITAN

25And behold, a certain lawyer stood up and tested Him,
saying, "Teacher, what shall I
do to inherit eternal life?"

26He said to him, "What
is written in the law? What is
your reading *of it?*"

27So he answered and said,
"'You shall love the LORD your
God with all your heart, with
all your soul, with all your
strength, and with all your
mind,'[a] and 'your neighbor
as yourself.'"[b]

28And He said to him, "You
have answered rightly; do this
and you will live."

29But he, wanting to justify
himself, said to Jesus, "And
who is my neighbor?"

30Then Jesus answered and
said: "A certain *man* went down
from Jerusalem to Jericho,
and fell among thieves, who
stripped him of his clothing,
wounded *him*, and departed,
leaving *him* half dead. 31Now
by chance a certain priest
came down that road. And
when he saw him, he passed by

10:17 [a] NU-Text reads *seventy-two.* 10:20 [a] NU-Text and M-Text omit *rather.* 10:22 [a] M-Text reads *And turning to the disciples He said, "All . . . .* 10:27 [a] Deuteronomy 6:5 [b] Leviticus 19:18

on the other side. 32Likewise a
Levite, when he arrived at the
place, came and looked, and
passed by on the other side.
33But a certain Samaritan, as
he journeyed, came where he
was. And when he saw him,
he had compassion. 34So he
went to *him* and bandaged his
wounds, pouring on oil and
wine; and he set him on his
own animal, brought him to
an inn, and took care of him.
35On the next day, when he departed,[a] he took out two denarii, gave *them* to the innkeeper,
and said to him, 'Take care of
him; and whatever more you
spend, when I come again,
I will repay you.' 36So which
of these three do you think
was neighbor to him who fell
among the thieves?"
37And he said, "He who
showed mercy on him."

Then Jesus said to him, "Go and do likewise."

MARY AND MARTHA WORSHIP AND SERVE

38Now it happened as they
went that He entered a certain
village; and a certain woman
named Martha welcomed
Him into her house. 39And
she had a sister called Mary,
who also sat at Jesus'[a] feet and
heard His word. 40But Martha was distracted with much
serving, and she approached
Him and said, "Lord, do You not care that my sister has left me to serve alone? Therefore tell her to help me."
41And Jesus[a] answered and
said to her, "Martha, Martha,
you are worried and troubled
about many things. 42But one
thing is needed, and Mary has
chosen that good part, which
will not be taken away from
her."

THE MODEL PRAYER

11 Now it came to pass, as He was praying in a certain place, when He ceased, *that* one of His disciples said to Him, "Lord, teach us to pray, as John also taught his disciples."
2So He said to them, "When you pray, say:

Our Father in heaven,[a]
Hallowed be Your name.
Your kingdom come.[b]
Your will be done
On earth as *it is* in heaven.
3 Give us day by day our daily bread.
4 And forgive us our sins,
For we also forgive everyone who is indebted to us.
And do not lead us into temptation,
But deliver us from the evil one."[a]

10:35 [a] NU-Text omits *when he departed.* 10:39 [a] NU-Text reads *the Lord's.* 10:41 [a] NU-Text reads *the Lord.* 11:2 [a] NU-Text omits *Our* and *in heaven.* [b] NU-Text omits the rest of this verse. 11:4 [a] NU-Text omits *But deliver us from the evil one.*

A FRIEND COMES AT MIDNIGHT

5And He said to them,
"Which of you shall have a
friend, and go to him at midnight and say to him, 'Friend,
lend me three loaves; 6for a
friend of mine has come to
me on his journey, and I have
nothing to set before him';
7and he will answer from
within and say, 'Do not trouble me; the door is now shut,
and my children are with me
in bed; I cannot rise and give
to you'? 8I say to you, though
he will not rise and give to him
because he is his friend, yet
because of his persistence he
will rise and give him as many
as he needs.

KEEP ASKING, SEEKING, KNOCKING

9"So I say to you, ask, and
it will be given to you; seek,
and you will find; knock, and
it will be opened to you. 10For
everyone who asks receives,
and he who seeks finds, and
to him who knocks it will be
opened. 11If a son asks for
bread[a] from any father among
you, will he give him a stone?
Or if *he asks* for a fish, will he
give him a serpent instead of a
fish? 12Or if he asks for an egg,
will he offer him a scorpion?
13If you then, being evil, know
how to give good gifts to your
children, how much more will
your heavenly Father give the
Holy Spirit to those who ask
Him!"

A HOUSE DIVIDED CANNOT STAND

14And He was casting out
a demon, and it was mute. So
it was, when the demon had
gone out, that the mute spoke;
and the multitudes marveled.
15But some of them said, "He
casts out demons by Beelzebub,[a] the ruler of the demons."
16Others, testing *Him*,
sought from Him a sign from
heaven. 17But He, knowing
their thoughts, said to them:
"Every kingdom divided
against itself is brought to
desolation, and a house *divided* against a house falls. 18If
Satan also is divided against
himself, how will his kingdom
stand? Because you say I cast
out demons by Beelzebub.
19And if I cast out demons by
Beelzebub, by whom do your
sons cast *them* out? Therefore they will be your judges.
20But if I cast out demons with
the finger of God, surely the
kingdom of God has come
upon you. 21When a strong
man, fully armed, guards his
own palace, his goods are in
peace. 22But when a stronger
than he comes upon him and
overcomes him, he takes from
him all his armor in which he
trusted, and divides his spoils.

11:11 [a] NU-Text omits the words from *bread* through *for* in the next sentence. **11:15** [a] NU-Text and M-Text read *Beelzebul*.

23He who is not with Me is
against Me, and he who does
not gather with Me scatters.

AN UNCLEAN SPIRIT RETURNS

24"When an unclean spirit
goes out of a man, he goes
through dry places, seek-
ing rest; and finding none,
he says, 'I will return to my
house from which I came.'
25And when he comes, he
finds *it* swept and put in order.
26Then he goes and takes with
him seven other spirits more
wicked than himself, and they
enter and dwell there; and the
last *state* of that man is worse
than the first."

KEEPING THE WORD

27And it happened, as He
spoke these things, that a certain woman from the crowd
raised her voice and said to
Him, "Blessed *is* the womb
that bore You, and *the* breasts
which nursed You!"

28But He said, "More than
that, blessed *are* those who
hear the word of God and
keep it!"

SEEKING A SIGN

29And while the crowds
were thickly gathered to-
gether, He began to say, "This
is an evil generation. It seeks
a sign, and no sign will be
given to it except the sign of
Jonah the prophet.[a] 30For as
Jonah became a sign to the
Ninevites, so also the Son of
Man will be to this generation.
31The queen of the South will
rise up in the judgment with
the men of this generation and
condemn them, for she came
from the ends of the earth to
hear the wisdom of Solomon;
and indeed a greater than Solomon *is* here. 32The men of
Nineveh will rise up in the
judgment with this generation and condemn it, for they
repented at the preaching of
Jonah; and indeed a greater
than Jonah *is* here.

THE LAMP OF THE BODY

33"No one, when he has lit a
lamp, puts *it* in a secret place
or under a basket, but on a
lampstand, that those who
come in may see the light.
34The lamp of the body is the
eye. Therefore, when your eye
is good, your whole body also
is full of light. But when *your
eye* is bad, your body also *is*
full of darkness. 35Therefore
take heed that the light which
is in you is not darkness. 36If
then your whole body *is* full of
light, having no part dark, *the*
whole *body* will be full of light,
as when the bright shining of
a lamp gives you light."

WOE TO THE PHARISEES AND LAWYERS

37And as He spoke, a cer-
tain Pharisee asked Him to

11:29 [a] NU-Text omits *the prophet.*

dine with him. So He went in
and sat down to eat. 38When
the Pharisee saw *it,* he marveled that He had not first
washed before dinner.
39Then the Lord said to
him, "Now you Pharisees
make the outside of the cup
and dish clean, but your inward part is full of greed and
wickedness. 40Foolish ones!
Did not He who made the
outside make the inside also?
41But rather give alms of such
things as you have; then indeed all things are clean to
you.
42"But woe to you Phari-
sees! For you tithe mint and
rue and all manner of herbs,
and pass by justice and the
love of God. These you ought
to have done, without leaving
the others undone. 43Woe to
you Pharisees! For you love
the best seats in the synagogues and greetings in the
marketplaces. 44Woe to you,
scribes and Pharisees, hypocrites![a] For you are like graves
which are not seen, and the
men who walk over *them* are
not aware *of them.*"
45Then one of the lawyers
answered and said to Him,
"Teacher, by saying these
things You reproach us also."
46And He said, "Woe to you
also, lawyers! For you load
men with burdens hard to
bear, and you yourselves do
not touch the burdens with
one of your fingers. 47Woe to
you! For you build the tombs of
the prophets, and your fathers
killed them. 48In fact, you bear
witness that you approve the
deeds of your fathers; for they
indeed killed them, and you
build their tombs. 49There-
fore the wisdom of God also
said, 'I will send them prophets and apostles, and *some* of
them they will kill and persecute,' 50that the blood of all
the prophets which was shed
from the foundation of the
world may be required of this
generation, 51from the blood
of Abel to the blood of Zechariah who perished between
the altar and the temple. Yes, I
say to you, it shall be required
of this generation.
52"Woe to you lawyers! For
you have taken away the key
of knowledge. You did not
enter in yourselves, and those
who were entering in you hindered."
53And as He said these
things to them,[a] the scribes
and the Pharisees began to
assail *Him* vehemently, and
to cross-examine Him about
many things, 54lying in wait
for Him, and seeking to catch
Him in something He might
say, that they might accuse
Him.[a]

11:44 [a] NU-Text omits *scribes and Pharisees, hypocrites.*
11:53 [a] NU-Text reads *And when He left there.* 11:54 [a] NU-Text omits *and seeking* and *that they might accuse Him.*

BEWARE OF HYPOCRISY

12 In the meantime, when
an innumerable multi-
tude of people had gathered
together, so that they trampled
one another, He began to say to
His disciples first *of all*, "Beware
of the leaven of the Pharisees,
which is hypocrisy. 2For there is
nothing covered that will not be
revealed, nor hidden that will
not be known. 3Therefore whatever you have spoken in the
dark will be heard in the light,
and what you have spoken in
the ear in inner rooms will be
proclaimed on the housetops.

JESUS TEACHES THE FEAR OF GOD

4"And I say to you, My
friends, do not be afraid of
those who kill the body, and
after that have no more that
they can do. 5But I will show
you whom you should fear:
Fear Him who, after He has
killed, has power to cast into
hell; yes, I say to you, fear Him!
6"Are not five sparrows sold
for two copper coins?[a] And not
one of them is forgotten before
God. 7But the very hairs of your
head are all numbered. Do not
fear therefore; you are of more
value than many sparrows.

CONFESS CHRIST BEFORE MEN

8"Also I say to you, whoever
confesses Me before men, him
the Son of Man also will confess before the angels of God.
9But he who denies Me before
men will be denied before the
angels of God.
10"And anyone who speaks
a word against the Son of Man,
it will be forgiven him; but to
him who blasphemes against
the Holy Spirit, it will not be
forgiven.
11"Now when they bring you
to the synagogues and magistrates and authorities, do
not worry about how or what
you should answer, or what
you should say. 12For the Holy
Spirit will teach you in that
very hour what you ought to
say."

THE PARABLE OF THE RICH FOOL

13Then one from the crowd
said to Him, "Teacher, tell my
brother to divide the inheritance with me."
14But He said to him, "Man,
who made Me a judge or an
arbitrator over you?" 15And He
said to them, "Take heed and
beware of covetousness,[a] for
one's life does not consist in
the abundance of the things
he possesses."
16Then He spoke a parable
to them, saying: "The ground
of a certain rich man yielded
plentifully. 17And he thought
within himself, saying, 'What
shall I do, since I have no

12:6 [a] Greek *assarion,* a coin of very small value 12:15 [a] NU-Text reads *all covetousness.*

room to store my crops?' 18So
he said, 'I will do this: I will
pull down my barns and build
greater, and there I will store
all my crops and my goods.
19And I will say to my soul,
"Soul, you have many goods
laid up for many years; take
your ease; eat, drink, *and* be
merry."' 20But God said to
him, 'Fool! This night your
soul will be required of you;
then whose will those things
be which you have provided?'
21"So *is* he who lays up treasure for himself, and is not
rich toward God."

DO NOT WORRY

22Then He said to His disciples, "Therefore I say to you,
do not worry about your life,
what you will eat; nor about
the body, what you will put on.
23Life is more than food, and
the body *is more* than clothing.
24Consider the ravens, for they
neither sow nor reap, which
have neither storehouse nor
barn; and God feeds them. Of
how much more value are you
than the birds? 25And which
of you by worrying can add
one cubit to his stature? 26If
you then are not able to do *the*
least, why are you anxious for
the rest? 27Consider the lilies,
how they grow: they neither
toil nor spin; and yet I say to
you, even Solomon in all his
glory was not arrayed like
one of these. 28If then God so
clothes the grass, which today
is in the field and tomorrow
is thrown into the oven, how
much more *will He clothe* you,
O *you* of little faith?
29"And do not seek what
you should eat or what you
should drink, nor have an
anxious mind. 30For all these
things the nations of the
world seek after, and your
Father knows that you need
these things. 31But seek the
kingdom of God, and all these
things[a] shall be added to you.
32"Do not fear, little flock,
for it is your Father's good
pleasure to give you the kingdom. 33Sell what you have and
give alms; provide yourselves
money bags which do not grow
old, a treasure in the heavens
that does not fail, where no
thief approaches nor moth
destroys. 34For where your
treasure is, there your heart
will be also.

THE FAITHFUL SERVANT AND THE EVIL SERVANT

35"Let your waist be girded
and *your* lamps burning;
36and you yourselves be like
men who wait for their master,
when he will return from the
wedding, that when he comes
and knocks they may open to
him immediately. 37Blessed
are those servants whom the
master, when he comes, will
find watching. Assuredly, I say
to you that he will gird himself

12:31 [a] NU-Text reads *His kingdom, and these things.*

and have them sit down *to eat,*
and will come and serve them.
38And if he should come in
the second watch, or come
in the third watch, and find
them so, blessed are those servants. 39But know this, that if
the master of the house had
known what hour the thief
would come, he would have
watched and[a] not allowed
his house to be broken into.
40Therefore you also be ready,
for the Son of Man is coming
at an hour you do not expect."
41Then Peter said to Him,
"Lord, do You speak this parable *only* to us, or to all *people?*"
42And the Lord said, "Who
then is that faithful and wise
steward, whom *his* master will
make ruler over his household, to give *them their* portion of food in due season?
43Blessed *is* that servant
whom his master will find so
doing when he comes. 44Truly,
I say to you that he will make
him ruler over all that he has.
45But if that servant says in
his heart, 'My master is delaying his coming,' and begins
to beat the male and female
servants, and to eat and drink
and be drunk, 46the master
of that servant will come on
a day when he is not looking
for *him,* and at an hour when
he is not aware, and will cut
him in two and appoint *him*
his portion with the unbelievers. 47And that servant
who knew his master's will,
and did not prepare *himself*
or do according to his will,
shall be beaten with many
stripes. 48But he who did not
know, yet committed things
deserving of stripes, shall be
beaten with few. For everyone
to whom much is given, from
him much will be required;
and to whom much has been
committed, of him they will
ask the more.

CHRIST BRINGS DIVISION

49"I came to send fire on
the earth, and how I wish it
were already kindled! 50But I
have a baptism to be baptized
with, and how distressed I am
till it is accomplished! 51Do
you suppose that I came to
give peace on earth? I tell you,
not at all, but rather division.
52For from now on five in one
house will be divided: three
against two, and two against
three. 53Father will be divided
against son and son against father, mother against daughter
and daughter against mother,
mother-in-law against her
daughter-in-law and daughter-
in-law against her mother-
in-law."

DISCERN THE TIME

54Then He also said to the
multitudes, "Whenever you
see a cloud rising out of the
west, immediately you say, 'A
shower is coming'; and so it is.

12:39 [a] NU-Text reads *he would not have allowed.*

55And when *you see* the south
wind blow, you say, 'There will
be hot weather'; and there is.
56Hypocrites! You can discern
the face of the sky and of the
earth, but how *is it* you do not
discern this time?

MAKE PEACE WITH YOUR ADVERSARY

57"Yes, and why, even of
yourselves, do you not judge
what is right? 58When you go
with your adversary to the
magistrate, make every effort
along the way to settle with
him, lest he drag you to the
judge, the judge deliver you
to the officer, and the officer
throw you into prison. 59I tell
you, you shall not depart from
there till you have paid the
very last mite."

REPENT OR PERISH

13 There were present at
that season some who
told Him about the Galileans whose blood Pilate had
mingled with their sacrifices.
2And Jesus answered and said
to them, "Do you suppose that
these Galileans were worse
sinners than all *other* Galileans, because they suffered
such things? 3I tell you, no; but
unless you repent you will all
likewise perish. 4Or those eighteen on whom the tower in Siloam fell and killed them, do
you think that they were worse
sinners than all *other* men who
dwelt in Jerusalem? 5I tell you,
no; but unless you repent you
will all likewise perish."

THE PARABLE OF THE BARREN FIG TREE

6He also spoke this para-
ble: "A certain *man* had a fig
tree planted in his vineyard,
and he came seeking fruit on
it and found none. 7Then he
said to the keeper of his vineyard, 'Look, for three years I
have come seeking fruit on
this fig tree and find none. Cut
it down; why does it use up the
ground?' 8But he answered and
said to him, 'Sir, let it alone this
year also, until I dig around it
and fertilize *it*. 9And if it bears
fruit, *well*. But if not, after that[a]
you can cut it down.'"

A SPIRIT OF INFIRMITY

10Now He was teaching in
one of the synagogues on the
Sabbath. 11And behold, there
was a woman who had a spirit
of infirmity eighteen years,
and was bent over and could
in no way raise *herself* up.
12But when Jesus saw her, He
called *her* to *Him* and said to
her, "Woman, you are loosed
from your infirmity." 13And
He laid *His* hands on her, and
immediately she was made
straight, and glorified God.
14But the ruler of the synagogue answered with indig-

13:9 [a] NU-Text reads *And if it bears fruit after that, well. But if not, you can cut it down.*

nation, because Jesus had
healed on the Sabbath; and he
said to the crowd, "There are
six days on which men ought
to work; therefore come and
be healed on them, and not
on the Sabbath day."
15The Lord then answered
him and said, "Hypocrite![a]
Does not each one of you on
the Sabbath loose his ox or
donkey from the stall, and
lead *it* away to water it? 16So
ought not this woman, being
a daughter of Abraham, whom
Satan has bound—think of
it—for eighteen years, be
loosed from this bond on the
Sabbath?" 17And when He said
these things, all His adversaries were put to shame; and all
the multitude rejoiced for all
the glorious things that were
done by Him.

THE PARABLE OF THE MUSTARD SEED

18Then He said, "What is
the kingdom of God like? And
to what shall I compare it? 19It
is like a mustard seed, which a
man took and put in his garden; and it grew and became
a large[a] tree, and the birds of
the air nested in its branches."

THE PARABLE OF THE LEAVEN

20And again He said, "To
what shall I liken the kingdom of God? 21It is like leaven
which a woman took and hid
in three measures[a] of meal till
it was all leavened."

THE NARROW WAY

22And He went through the
cities and villages, teaching,
and journeying toward Je-
rusalem. 23Then one said to
Him, "Lord, are there few who
are saved?"
And He said to them,
24"Strive to enter through the
narrow gate, for many, I say
to you, will seek to enter and
will not be able. 25When once
the Master of the house has
risen up and shut the door,
and you begin to stand outside and knock at the door,
saying, 'Lord, Lord, open for
us,' and He will answer and
say to you, 'I do not know you,
where you are from,' 26then
you will begin to say, 'We ate
and drank in Your presence,
and You taught in our streets.'
27But He will say, 'I tell you
I do not know you, where
you are from. Depart from
Me, all you workers of iniquity.' 28There will be weeping
and gnashing of teeth, when
you see Abraham and Isaac
and Jacob and all the prophets in the kingdom of God,
and yourselves thrust out.
29They will come from the
east and the west, from the
north and the south, and sit
down in the kingdom of God.

13:15 [a] NU-Text and M-Text rd *Hypocrites.* 13:19 [a] NU-Text omits *large.* 13:21 [a] Greek sa approximately two pecks in all

30And indeed there are last
who will be first, and there are
first who will be last."

31On that very day[a] some
Pharisees came, saying to Him,
"Get out and depart from here,
for Herod wants to kill You."

32And He said to them, "Go,
tell that fox, 'Behold, I cast out
demons and perform cures
today and tomorrow, and the
third *day* I shall be perfected.'
33Nevertheless I must journey
today, tomorrow, and the *day*
following; for it cannot be that
a prophet should perish outside of Jerusalem.

JESUS LAMENTS OVER JERUSALEM

34"O Jerusalem, Jerusalem,
the one who kills the prophets
and stones those who are sent
to her! How often I wanted
to gather your children together, as a hen *gathers* her
brood under *her* wings, but
you were not willing! 35See!
Your house is left to you desolate; and assuredly,[a] I say to
you, you shall not see Me until
the time comes when you say,
'Blessed is He who comes in
the name of the LORD!'"[b]

A MAN WITH DROPSY HEALED ON THE SABBATH

14 Now it happened, as He
went into the house of
one of the rulers of the Pharisees to eat bread on the Sabbath, that they watched Him
closely. 2And behold, there
was a certain man before Him
who had dropsy. 3And Jesus,
answering, spoke to the lawyers and Pharisees, saying, "Is
it lawful to heal on the Sabbath?"[a]

4But they kept silent. And
He took *him* and healed him,
and let him go. 5Then He answered them, saying, "Which
of you, having a donkey[a] or
an ox that has fallen into a
pit, will not immediately pull
him out on the Sabbath day?"
6And they could not answer
Him regarding these things.

TAKE THE LOWLY PLACE

7So He told a parable to
those who were invited, when
He noted how they chose the
best places, saying to them:
8"When you are invited by
anyone to a wedding feast,
do not sit down in the best
place, lest one more honorable than you be invited by
him; 9and he who invited you
and him come and say to you,
'Give place to this man,' and
then you begin with shame
to take the lowest place. 10But
when you are invited, go and
sit down in the lowest place,
so that when he who invited
you comes he may say to
you, 'Friend, go up higher.'

13:31 [a] NU-Text reads *In that* ry *hour.* 13:35 [a] NU-Text and M-Text omit *assuredly.* [b] alm 118:26 14:3 [a] NU-Text adds *or not.* 14:5 [a] NU-T and M-Text read *son.*

Then you will have glory in
the presence of those who
sit at the table with you. 11For
whoever exalts himself will be
humbled, and he who hum-
bles himself will be exalted."
12Then He also said to him
who invited Him, "When you
give a dinner or a supper, do
not ask your friends, your
brothers, your relatives, nor
rich neighbors, lest they also
invite you back, and you be
repaid. 13But when you give
a feast, invite *the* poor, *the*
maimed, *the* lame, *the* blind.
14And you will be blessed, because they cannot repay you;
for you shall be repaid at the
resurrection of the just."

THE PARABLE OF THE GREAT SUPPER

15Now when one of those
who sat at the table with Him
heard these things, he said to
Him, "Blessed *is* he who shall
eat bread[a] in the kingdom of
God!"
16Then He said to him, "A
certain man gave a great supper and invited many, 17and
sent his servant at supper
time to say to those who were
invited, 'Come, for all things
are now ready.' 18But they
all with one *accord* began to
make excuses. The first said
to him, 'I have bought a piece
of ground, and I must go and
see it. I ask you to have me excused.' 19And another said, 'I
have bought five yoke of oxen,
and I am going to test them. I
ask you to have me excused.'
20Still another said, 'I have
married a wife, and therefore I cannot come.' 21So that
servant came and reported
these things to his master.
Then the master of the house,
being angry, said to his servant, 'Go out quickly into the
streets and lanes of the city,
and bring in here *the* poor and
the maimed and *the* lame and
the blind.' 22And the servant
said, 'Master, it is done as you
commanded, and still there
is room.' 23Then the master
said to the servant, 'Go out
into the highways and hedges,
and compel *them* to come in,
that my house may be filled.
24For I say to you that none of
those men who were invited
shall taste my supper.'"

LEAVING ALL TO FOLLOW CHRIST

25Now great multitudes
went with Him. And He turned
and said to them, 26"If anyone
comes to Me and does not hate
his father and mother, wife and
children, brothers and sisters,
yes, and his own life also, he
cannot be My disciple. 27And
whoever does not bear his
cross and come after Me cannot be My disciple. 28For which
of you, intending to build a
tower, does not sit down first
and count the cost, whether he

14:15 [a] M-Text reads *dinner*.

has *enough* to finish *it*— 29lest,
after he has laid the foundation, and is not able to finish,
all who see *it* begin to mock
him, 30saying, 'This man began
to build and was not able to
finish'? 31Or what king, going
to make war against another
king, does not sit down first
and consider whether he is
able with ten thousand to meet
him who comes against him
with twenty thousand? 32Or
else, while the other is still a
great way off, he sends a delegation and asks conditions of
peace. 33So likewise, whoever
of you does not forsake all that
he has cannot be My disciple.

TASTELESS SALT IS WORTHLESS

34"Salt *is* good; but if the
salt has lost its flavor, how
shall it be seasoned? 35It is
neither fit for the land nor for
the dunghill, *but* men throw it
out. He who has ears to hear,
let him hear!"

THE PARABLE OF THE LOST SHEEP

15 Then all the tax collectors and the sinners drew
near to Him to hear Him. 2And
the Pharisees and scribes complained, saying, "This Man receives sinners and eats with
them." 3So He spoke this parable to them, saying:

4"What man of you, hav-
ing a hundred sheep, if he
loses one of them, does not
leave the ninety-nine in the
wilderness, and go after the
one which is lost until he finds
it? 5And when he has found
it, he lays *it* on his shoulders, rejoicing. 6And when
he comes home, he calls together *his* friends and neighbors, saying to them, 'Rejoice
with me, for I have found my
sheep which was lost!' 7I say to
you that likewise there will be
more joy in heaven over one
sinner who repents than over
ninety-nine just persons who
need no repentance.

THE PARABLE OF THE LOST COIN

8"Or what woman, having
ten silver coins,[a] if she loses
one coin, does not light a
lamp, sweep the house, and
search carefully until she
finds *it?* 9And when she has
found *it,* she calls *her* friends
and neighbors together, saying, 'Rejoice with me, for I
have found the piece which I
lost!' 10Likewise, I say to you,
there is joy in the presence
of the angels of God over one
sinner who repents."

THE PARABLE OF THE LOST SON

11Then He said: "A certain
man had two sons. 12And the
younger of them said to *his*

15:8 [a] Greek *drachma,* a valuable coin often worn in a ten-piece garland by married women

father, 'Father, give me the
portion of goods that falls *to*
me.' So he divided to them *his*
livelihood. 13And not many
days after, the younger son
gathered all together, journeyed to a far country, and
there wasted his possessions
with prodigal living. 14But
when he had spent all, there
arose a severe famine in that
land, and he began to be in
want. 15Then he went and
joined himself to a citizen of
that country, and he sent him
into his fields to feed swine.
16And he would gladly have
filled his stomach with the
pods that the swine ate, and
no one gave him *anything.*

17"But when he came to
himself, he said, 'How many
of my father's hired servants
have bread enough and to
spare, and I perish with hunger! 18I will arise and go to my
father, and will say to him,
"Father, I have sinned against
heaven and before you, 19and
I am no longer worthy to be
called your son. Make me like
one of your hired servants."'

20"And he arose and came
to his father. But when he was
still a great way off, his father
saw him and had compassion,
and ran and fell on his neck
and kissed him. 21And the son
said to him, 'Father, I have
sinned against heaven and in
your sight, and am no longer
worthy to be called your son.'

22"But the father said to
his servants, 'Bring[a] out the
best robe and put *it* on him,
and put a ring on his hand
and sandals on *his* feet. 23And
bring the fatted calf here and
kill *it,* and let us eat and be
merry; 24for this my son was
dead and is alive again; he was
lost and is found.' And they
began to be merry.

25"Now his older son was
in the field. And as he came
and drew near to the house,
he heard music and dancing.
26So he called one of the servants and asked what these
things meant. 27And he said to
him, 'Your brother has come,
and because he has received
him safe and sound, your father has killed the fatted calf.'

28"But he was angry and
would not go in. Therefore his
father came out and pleaded
with him. 29So he answered
and said to *his* father, 'Lo,
these many years I have been
serving you; I never transgressed your commandment
at any time; and yet you never
gave me a young goat, that I
might make merry with my
friends. 30But as soon as this
son of yours came, who has
devoured your livelihood with
harlots, you killed the fatted
calf for him.'

31"And he said to him, 'Son,
you are always with me, and
all that I have is yours. 32It
was right that we should

15:22 [a] NU-Text reads *Quickly bring.*

make merry and be glad, for
your brother was dead and is
alive again, and was lost and
is found.'"

THE PARABLE OF THE UNJUST STEWARD

16 He also said to His disciples: "There was a
certain rich man who had a
steward, and an accusation
was brought to him that this
man was wasting his goods.
2So he called him and said to
him, 'What is this I hear about
you? Give an account of your
stewardship, for you can no
longer be steward.'
3"Then the steward said
within himself, 'What shall I
do? For my master is taking the
stewardship away from me.
I cannot dig; I am ashamed
to beg. 4I have resolved what
to do, that when I am put out
of the stewardship, they may
receive me into their houses.'
5"So he called every one of
his master's debtors to *him,*
and said to the first, 'How
much do you owe my mas-
ter?' 6And he said, 'A hundred
measures[a] of oil.' So he said
to him, 'Take your bill, and
sit down quickly and write
fifty.' 7Then he said to another, 'And how much do you
owe?' So he said, 'A hundred
measures[a] of wheat.' And he
said to him, 'Take your bill,
and write eighty.' 8So the
master commended the un-
just steward because he had
dealt shrewdly. For the sons
of this world are more shrewd
in their generation than the
sons of light.
9"And I say to you, make
friends for yourselves by unrighteous mammon, that
when you fail,[a] they may receive you into an everlasting
home. 10He who *is* faithful in
what is least is faithful also in
much; and he who is unjust
in *what is* least is unjust also
in much. 11Therefore if you
have not been faithful in the
unrighteous mammon, who
will commit to your trust the
true *riches?* 12And if you have
not been faithful in what is
another man's, who will give
you what is your own?
13"No servant can serve two
masters; for either he will hate
the one and love the other,
or else he will be loyal to the
one and despise the other. You
cannot serve God and mam-
mon."

THE LAW, THE PROPHETS, AND THE KINGDOM

14Now the Pharisees, who
were lovers of money, also
heard all these things, and
they derided Him. 15And He
said to them, "You are those
who justify yourselves before

16:6 [a] Greek *batos,* eight or nine gallons each (Old Testament *bath*) 16:7 [a] Greek *koros,* ten or twelve bushels each (Old Testament *kor*) 16:9 [a] NU-Text reads *it fails.*

men, but God knows your
hearts. For what is highly
esteemed among men is an
abomination in the sight of
God.
16"The law and the proph-
ets *were* until John. Since that
time the kingdom of God has
been preached, and everyone
is pressing into it. 17And it is
easier for heaven and earth to
pass away than for one tittle
of the law to fail.
18"Whoever divorces his
wife and marries another
commits adultery; and whoever marries her who is divorced from *her* husband
commits adultery.

THE RICH MAN AND LAZARUS

19"There was a certain rich
man who was clothed in purple and fine linen and fared
sumptuously every day. 20But
there was a certain beggar
named Lazarus, full of sores,
who was laid at his gate,
21desiring to be fed with the
crumbs which fell[a] from the
rich man's table. Moreover
the dogs came and licked
his sores. 22So it was that the
beggar died, and was carried
by the angels to Abraham's
bosom. The rich man also
died and was buried. 23And
being in torments in Hades,
he lifted up his eyes and saw
Abraham afar off, and Lazarus
in his bosom.
24"Then he cried and said,
'Father Abraham, have mercy
on me, and send Lazarus that
he may dip the tip of his finger
in water and cool my tongue;
for I am tormented in this
flame.' 25But Abraham said,
'Son, remember that in your
lifetime you received your
good things, and likewise
Lazarus evil things; but now
he is comforted and you are
tormented. 26And besides all
this, between us and you there
is a great gulf fixed, so that
those who want to pass from
here to you cannot, nor can
those from there pass to us.'
27"Then he said, 'I beg you
therefore, father, that you
would send him to my fa-
ther's house, 28for I have five
brothers, that he may testify
to them, lest they also come to
this place of torment.' 29Abra-
ham said to him, 'They have
Moses and the prophets; let
them hear them.' 30And he
said, 'No, father Abraham; but
if one goes to them from the
dead, they will repent.' 31But
he said to him, 'If they do not
hear Moses and the proph-
ets, neither will they be persuaded though one rise from
the dead.'"

JESUS WARNS OF OFFENSES

17 Then He said to the disciples, "It is impossible
that no offenses should come,
but woe *to him* through whom

16:21 [a] NU-Text reads *with what fell.*

they do come! 2 It would be
better for him if a millstone
were hung around his neck,
and he were thrown into the
sea, than that he should offend one of these little ones.
3 Take heed to yourselves.
If your brother sins against
you,[a] rebuke him; and if he repents, forgive him. 4 And if he
sins against you seven times
in a day, and seven times in a
day returns to you,[a] saying, 'I
repent,' you shall forgive him."

FAITH AND DUTY

5 And the apostles said to
the Lord, "Increase our faith."
6 So the Lord said, "If you
have faith as a mustard seed,
you can say to this mulberry
tree, 'Be pulled up by the roots
and be planted in the sea,'
and it would obey you. 7 And
which of you, having a servant
plowing or tending sheep,
will say to him when he has
come in from the field, 'Come
at once and sit down to eat'?
8 But will he not rather say to
him, 'Prepare something for
my supper, and gird yourself
and serve me till I have eaten
and drunk, and afterward you
will eat and drink'? 9 Does he
thank that servant because
he did the things that were
commanded him? I think
not.[a] 10 So likewise you, when
you have done all those things
which you are commanded,
say, 'We are unprofitable servants. We have done what was
our duty to do.'"

TEN LEPERS CLEANSED

11 Now it happened as He
went to Jerusalem that He
passed through the midst of
Samaria and Galilee. 12 Then as
He entered a certain village,
there met Him ten men who
were lepers, who stood afar
off. 13 And they lifted up *their*
voices and said, "Jesus, Master, have mercy on us!"
14 So when He saw *them,* He
said to them, "Go, show yourselves to the priests." And so
it was that as they went, they
were cleansed.
15 And one of them, when
he saw that he was healed, returned, and with a loud voice
glorified God, 16 and fell down
on *his* face at His feet, giving
Him thanks. And he was a Samaritan.
17 So Jesus answered and
said, "Were there not ten
cleansed? But where *are* the
nine? 18 Were there not any
found who returned to give
glory to God except this foreigner?" 19 And He said to him,
"Arise, go your way. Your faith
has made you well."

THE COMING OF THE KINGDOM

20 Now when He was asked
by the Pharisees when the

17:3 [a] NU-Text omits *against you.* 17:4 [a] M-Text omits *to you.*
17:9 [a] NU-Text ends verse with *commanded;* M-Text omits *him.*

kingdom of God would come,
He answered them and said,
"The kingdom of God does not
come with observation; 21nor
will they say, 'See here!' or 'See
there!'[a] For indeed, the kingdom of God is within you."
22Then He said to the disciples, "The days will come when
you will desire to see one of
the days of the Son of Man, and
you will not see *it.* 23And they
will say to you, 'Look here!' or
'Look there!'[a] Do not go after
them or follow *them.* 24For
as the lightning that flashes
out of one *part* under heaven
shines to the other *part* under
heaven, so also the Son of Man
will be in His day. 25But first He
must suffer many things and
be rejected by this generation.
26And as it was in the days of
Noah, so it will be also in the
days of the Son of Man: 27They
ate, they drank, they married
wives, they were given in marriage, until the day that Noah
entered the ark, and the flood
came and destroyed them
all. 28Likewise as it was also
in the days of Lot: They ate,
they drank, they bought, they
sold, they planted, they built;
29but on the day that Lot went
out of Sodom it rained fire and
brimstone from heaven and
destroyed *them* all. 30Even so
will it be in the day when the
Son of Man is revealed.
31"In that day, he who is on
the housetop, and his goods
are in the house, let him not
come down to take them away.
And likewise the one who is
in the field, let him not turn
back. 32Remember Lot's wife.
33Whoever seeks to save his
life will lose it, and whoever
loses his life will preserve
it. 34I tell you, in that night
there will be two *men* in one
bed: the one will be taken and
the other will be left. 35Two
women will be grinding together: the one will be taken
and the other left. 36Two *men*
will be in the field: the one will
be taken and the other left."[a]
37And they answered and
said to Him, "Where, Lord?"
So He said to them, "Wherever the body is, there the eagles will be gathered together."

THE PARABLE OF THE PERSISTENT WIDOW

18 Then He spoke a para-
ble to them, that men
always ought to pray and not
lose heart, 2saying: "There was
in a certain city a judge who
did not fear God nor regard
man. 3Now there was a widow
in that city; and she came to
him, saying, 'Get justice for
me from my adversary.' 4And
he would not for a while; but
afterward he said within himself, 'Though I do not fear God
nor regard man, 5yet because

17:21 [a] NU-Text reverses *here* and *there.* 17:23 [a] NU-Text reverses *here* and *there.* 17:36 [a] NU-Text and M-Text omit verse 36.

this widow troubles me I will
avenge her, lest by her continual coming she weary me.'"
[6]Then the Lord said, "Hear
what the unjust judge said.
[7]And shall God not avenge
His own elect who cry out day
and night to Him, though He
bears long with them? [8]I tell
you that He will avenge them
speedily. Nevertheless, when
the Son of Man comes, will He
really find faith on the earth?"

THE PARABLE OF THE PHARISEE AND THE TAX COLLECTOR

[9]Also He spoke this parable
to some who trusted in themselves that they were righteous,
and despised others: [10]"Two
men went up to the temple to
pray, one a Pharisee and the
other a tax collector. [11]The
Pharisee stood and prayed
thus with himself, 'God, I thank
You that I am not like other
men—extortioners, unjust,
adulterers, or even as this tax
collector. [12]I fast twice a week; I
give tithes of all that I possess.'
[13]And the tax collector, standing afar off, would not so much
as raise *his* eyes to heaven, but
beat his breast, saying, 'God, be
merciful to me a sinner!' [14]I tell
you, this man went down to his
house justified *rather* than the
other; for everyone who exalts
himself will be humbled, and
he who humbles himself will
be exalted."

JESUS BLESSES LITTLE CHILDREN

[15]Then they also brought
infants to Him that He might
touch them; but when the disciples saw *it*, they rebuked
them. [16]But Jesus called them
to *Him* and said, "Let the little
children come to Me, and do
not forbid them; for of such
is the kingdom of God. [17]As-
suredly, I say to you, whoever
does not receive the kingdom
of God as a little child will by
no means enter it."

JESUS COUNSELS THE RICH YOUNG RULER

[18]Now a certain ruler asked
Him, saying, "Good Teacher,
what shall I do to inherit eternal life?"
[19]So Jesus said to him,
"Why do you call Me good?
No one *is* good but One, *that
is,* God. [20]You know the commandments: 'Do not commit
adultery,' 'Do not murder,' 'Do
not steal,' 'Do not bear false
witness,' 'Honor your father
and your mother.'"[a]
[21]And he said, "All these
things I have kept from my
youth."
[22]So when Jesus heard
these things, He said to him,
"You still lack one thing. Sell
all that you have and distribute to the poor, and you will
have treasure in heaven; and
come, follow Me."
[23]But when he heard this,

18:20 [a] Exodus 20:12–16; Deuteronomy 5:16–20

he became very sorrowful, for
he was very rich.

WITH GOD ALL THINGS ARE POSSIBLE

24And when Jesus saw that
he became very sorrowful,
He said, "How hard it is for
those who have riches to enter
the kingdom of God! 25For
it is easier for a camel to go
through the eye of a needle
than for a rich man to enter
the kingdom of God."

26And those who heard it
said, "Who then can be saved?"

27But He said, "The things
which are impossible with
men are possible with God."

28Then Peter said, "See,
we have left all[a] and followed
You."

29So He said to them, "Assuredly,
I say to you, there is
no one who has left house or
parents or brothers or wife or
children, for the sake of the
kingdom of God, 30who shall
not receive many times more
in this present time, and in
the age to come eternal life."

JESUS A THIRD TIME PREDICTS HIS DEATH AND RESURRECTION

31Then He took the twelve
aside and said to them, "Behold,
we are going up to Jerusalem,
and all things that
are written by the prophets
concerning the Son of Man
will be accomplished. 32For
He will be delivered to the
Gentiles and will be mocked
and insulted and spit upon.
33They will scourge *Him* and
kill Him. And the third day He
will rise again."

34But they understood
none of these things; this saying
was hidden from them,
and they did not know the
things which were spoken.

A BLIND MAN RECEIVES HIS SIGHT

35Then it happened, as He
was coming near Jericho, that
a certain blind man sat by the
road begging. 36And hearing
a multitude passing by, he
asked what it meant. 37So they
told him that Jesus of Nazareth
was passing by. 38And he
cried out, saying, "Jesus, Son
of David, have mercy on me!"

39Then those who went
before warned him that he
should be quiet; but he cried
out all the more, "Son of
David, have mercy on me!"

40So Jesus stood still
and commanded him to be
brought to Him. And when he
had come near, He asked him,
41saying, "What do you want
Me to do for you?"

He said, "Lord, that I may
receive my sight."

42Then Jesus said to him,
"Receive your sight; your faith
has made you well." 43And
immediately he received
his sight, and followed Him,

18:28 [a] NU-Text reads *our own*.

glorifying God. And all the
people, when they saw *it*, gave
praise to God.

JESUS COMES TO ZACCHAEUS' HOUSE

19 Then *Jesus* entered and
passed through Jericho.
2Now behold, *there was* a man
named Zacchaeus who was a
chief tax collector, and he was
rich. 3And he sought to see
who Jesus was, but could not
because of the crowd, for he
was of short stature. 4So he ran
ahead and climbed up into a
sycamore tree to see Him, for
He was going to pass that *way*.
5And when Jesus came to the
place, He looked up and saw
him,[a] and said to him, "Zacchaeus, make haste and come
down, for today I must stay at
your house." 6So he made haste
and came down, and received
Him joyfully. 7But when they
saw *it*, they all complained, saying, "He has gone to be a guest
with a man who is a sinner."
8Then Zacchaeus stood and
said to the Lord, "Look, Lord,
I give half of my goods to the
poor; and if I have taken anything from anyone by false
accusation, I restore fourfold."
9And Jesus said to him,
"Today salvation has come to
this house, because he also is a
son of Abraham; 10for the Son
of Man has come to seek and
to save that which was lost."

THE PARABLE OF THE MINAS

11Now as they heard these
things, He spoke another parable, because He was near
Jerusalem and because they
thought the kingdom of God
would appear immediately.
12Therefore He said: "A certain nobleman went into a far
country to receive for himself
a kingdom and to return. 13So
he called ten of his servants,
delivered to them ten minas,[a]
and said to them, 'Do business
till I come.' 14But his citizens
hated him, and sent a delegation after him, saying, 'We
will not have this *man* to reign
over us.'
15"And so it was that when
he returned, having received
the kingdom, he then commanded these servants, to
whom he had given the money,
to be called to him, that he
might know how much every
man had gained by trading.
16Then came the first, saying,
'Master, your mina has earned
ten minas.' 17And he said to
him, 'Well *done*, good servant;
because you were faithful in a
very little, have authority over
ten cities.' 18And the second
came, saying, 'Master, your
mina has earned five minas.'
19Likewise he said to him, 'You
also be over five cities.'
20"Then another came, saying, 'Master, here is your mina,

19:5 [a] NU-Text omits *and saw him*. 19:13 [a] The *mina* (Greek *mna*, Hebrew *minah*) was worth about three months' salary.

which I have kept put away in
a handkerchief. 21For I feared
you, because you are an austere man. You collect what you
did not deposit, and reap what
you did not sow.' 22And he
said to him, 'Out of your own
mouth I will judge you, *you*
wicked servant. You knew that
I was an austere man, collecting what I did not deposit and
reaping what I did not sow.
23Why then did you not put
my money in the bank, that
at my coming I might have
collected it with interest?'

24"And he said to those who
stood by, 'Take the mina from
him, and give *it* to him who
has ten minas.' 25(But they
said to him, 'Master, he has
ten minas.') 26'For I say to you,
that to everyone who has will
be given; and from him who
does not have, even what he
has will be taken away from
him. 27But bring here those
enemies of mine, who did not
want me to reign over them,
and slay *them* before me.'"

THE TRIUMPHAL ENTRY

28When He had said this,
He went on ahead, going up to
Jerusalem. 29And it came to
pass, when He drew near
to Bethphage[a] and Bethany,
at the mountain called Olivet,
that He sent two of His disciples, 30saying, "Go into the
village opposite *you,* where
as you enter you will find a
colt tied, on which no one has
ever sat. Loose it and bring *it*
here. 31And if anyone asks you,
'Why are you loosing *it?*' thus
you shall say to him, 'Because
the Lord has need of it.'"

32So those who were sent
went their way and found *it*
just as He had said to them.
33But as they were loosing the
colt, the owners of it said to
them, "Why are you loosing
the colt?"

34And they said, "The Lord
has need of him." 35Then they
brought him to Jesus. And
they threw their own clothes
on the colt, and they set Jesus
on him. 36And as He went,
many spread their clothes on
the road.

37Then, as He was now
drawing near the descent of
the Mount of Olives, the whole
multitude of the disciples
began to rejoice and praise
God with a loud voice for all
the mighty works they had
seen, 38saying:

"'Blessed *is* the King
who comes in the
name of the LORD!'[a]
Peace in heaven and
glory in the highest!"

39And some of the Phari-
sees called to Him from the
crowd, "Teacher, rebuke Your
disciples."

40But He answered and said
to them, "I tell you that if these

19:29 [a] M-Text reads *Bethsphage.* 19:38 [a] Psalm 118:26

should keep silent, the stones
would immediately cry out."

JESUS WEEPS OVER JERUSALEM

41 Now as He drew near, He
saw the city and wept over it,
42 saying, "If you had known,
even you, especially in this
your day, the things *that make*
for your peace! But now they
are hidden from your eyes.
43 For days will come upon you
when your enemies will build
an embankment around you,
surround you and close you
in on every side, 44 and level
you, and your children within
you, to the ground; and they
will not leave in you one stone
upon another, because you
did not know the time of your
visitation."

JESUS CLEANSES THE TEMPLE

45 Then He went into the
temple and began to drive out
those who bought and sold
in it,[a] 46 saying to them, "It is
written, 'My house is[a] a house
of prayer,'[b] but you have made
it a 'den of thieves.'"[c]

47 And He was teaching
daily in the temple. But the
chief priests, the scribes, and
the leaders of the people
sought to destroy Him, 48 and
were unable to do anything;
for all the people were very
attentive to hear Him.

JESUS' AUTHORITY QUESTIONED

20 Now it happened on
one of those days, as
He taught the people in the
temple and preached the gospel, *that* the chief priests and
the scribes, together with the
elders, confronted *Him* 2 and
spoke to Him, saying, "Tell
us, by what authority are You
doing these things? Or who
is he who gave You this authority?"

3 But He answered and said
to them, "I also will ask you
one thing, and answer Me:
4 The baptism of John—was
it from heaven or from men?"

5 And they reasoned among
themselves, saying, "If we say,
'From heaven,' He will say,
'Why then[a] did you not believe
him?' 6 But if we say, 'From
men,' all the people will stone
us, for they are persuaded that
John was a prophet." 7 So they
answered that they did not
know where *it was* from.

8 And Jesus said to them,
"Neither will I tell you by what
authority I do these things."

THE PARABLE OF THE WICKED VINEDRESSERS

9 Then He began to tell the
people this parable: "A certain man planted a vineyard,
leased it to vinedressers, and
went into a far country for a

19:45 [a] NU-Text reads *those who were selling.* **19:46** [a] NU-Text reads *shall be.* [b] Isaiah 56:7 [c] Jeremiah 7:11 **20:5** [a] NU-Text and M-Text omit *then.*

long time. 10 Now at vintage-
time he sent a servant to the
vinedressers, that they might
give him some of the fruit of
the vineyard. But the vinedressers beat him and sent
him away empty-handed.
11 Again he sent another servant; and they beat him also,
treated *him* shamefully, and
sent *him* away empty-handed.
12 And again he sent a third;
and they wounded him also
and cast *him* out.
13 "Then the owner of the
vineyard said, 'What shall I
do? I will send my beloved
son. Probably they will respect
him when they see him.' 14 But
when the vinedressers saw
him, they reasoned among
themselves, saying, 'This is
the heir. Come, let us kill him,
that the inheritance may be
ours.' 15 So they cast him out
of the vineyard and killed *him*.
Therefore what will the owner
of the vineyard do to them?
16 He will come and destroy
those vinedressers and give
the vineyard to others."

And when they heard *it*
they said, "Certainly not!"
17 Then He looked at them
and said, "What then is this
that is written:

> 'The stone which the
> builders rejected
> Has become the chief
> cornerstone'?[a]

18 Whoever falls on that stone
will be broken; but on whomever it falls, it will grind him
to powder."
19 And the chief priests
and the scribes that very
hour sought to lay hands on
Him, but they feared the people[a]—for they knew He had
spoken this parable against
them.

THE PHARISEES: IS IT LAWFUL TO PAY TAXES TO CAESAR?

20 So they watched *Him*, and
sent spies who pretended to
be righteous, that they might
seize on His words, in order to
deliver Him to the power and
the authority of the governor.
21 Then they asked Him,
saying, "Teacher, we know that
You say and teach rightly, and
You do not show personal favoritism, but teach the way
of God in truth: 22 Is it lawful
for us to pay taxes to Caesar
or not?"
23 But He perceived their
craftiness, and said to them,
"Why do you test Me?[a] 24 Show
Me a denarius. Whose image
and inscription does it have?"

They answered and said,
"Caesar's."
25 And He said to them,
"Render therefore to Caesar
the things that are Caesar's,
and to God the things that are
God's."

20:17 [a] Psalm 118:22 20:19 [a] M-Text reads *but they were afraid.* 20:23 [a] NU-Text omits *Why do you test Me?*

26But they could not catch
Him in His words in the presence of the people. And they
marveled at His answer and
kept silent.

THE SADDUCEES: WHAT ABOUT THE RESURRECTION?

27Then some of the Saddu-
cees, who deny that there is a
resurrection, came to *Him* and
asked Him, 28saying: "Teacher,
Moses wrote to us *that* if a
man's brother dies, having a
wife, and he dies without children, his brother should take
his wife and raise up offspring
for his brother. 29Now there
were seven brothers. And the
first took a wife, and died without children. 30And the second[a] took her as wife, and he
died childless. 31Then the third
took her, and in like manner
the seven also; and they left no
children,[a] and died. 32Last of all
the woman died also. 33There-
fore, in the resurrection, whose
wife does she become? For all
seven had her as wife."
34Jesus answered and said
to them, "The sons of this age
marry and are given in marriage. 35But those who are
counted worthy to attain that
age, and the resurrection from
the dead, neither marry nor
are given in marriage; 36nor
can they die anymore, for they
are equal to the angels and
are sons of God, being sons of
the resurrection. 37But even
Moses showed in the *burning*
bush *passage* that the dead
are raised, when he called the
Lord 'the God of Abraham, the
God of Isaac, and the God of
Jacob.'[a] 38For He is not the
God of the dead but of the
living, for all live to Him."
39Then some of the scribes
answered and said, "Teacher,
You have spoken well." 40But
after that they dared not question Him anymore.

JESUS: HOW CAN DAVID CALL HIS DESCENDANT LORD?

41And He said to them,
"How can they say that the
Christ is the Son of David?
42Now David himself said in
the Book of Psalms:

'The LORD said
to my Lord,
"Sit at My right hand,
43 Till I make Your enemies
Your footstool."'[a]

44Therefore David calls Him
'Lord'; how is He then his
Son?"

BEWARE OF THE SCRIBES

45Then, in the hearing of all
the people, He said to His disciples, 46"Beware of the scribes,

20:30 [a] NU-Text ends verse 30 here. 20:31 [a] NU-Text and M-Text read *the seven also left no children.* 20:37 [a] Exodus 3:6, 15 20:43 [a] Psalm 110:1

who desire to go around in
long robes, love greetings in
the marketplaces, the best
seats in the synagogues, and
the best places at feasts, 47who
devour widows' houses, and
for a pretense make long
prayers. These will receive
greater condemnation."

THE WIDOW'S TWO MITES

21 And He looked up and
saw the rich putting
their gifts into the treasury,
2and He saw also a certain
poor widow putting in two
mites. 3So He said, "Truly I say
to you that this poor widow
has put in more than all; 4for
all these out of their abundance have put in offerings
for God,[a] but she out of her
poverty put in all the livelihood that she had."

JESUS PREDICTS THE DESTRUCTION OF THE TEMPLE

5Then, as some spoke of the
temple, how it was adorned
with beautiful stones and
donations, He said, 6"These
things which you see—the
days will come in which not
one stone shall be left upon
another that shall not be
thrown down."

THE SIGNS OF THE TIMES AND THE END OF THE AGE

7So they asked Him, saying,
"Teacher, but when will these
things be? And what sign *will
there be* when these things are
about to take place?"

8And He said: "Take heed
that you not be deceived. For
many will come in My name,
saying, 'I am *He,*' and, 'The
time has drawn near.' Therefore[a] do not go after them.
9But when you hear of wars
and commotions, do not be
terrified; for these things
must come to pass first, but
the end *will* not *come* immediately."

10Then He said to them,
"Nation will rise against nation, and kingdom against
kingdom. 11And there will
be great earthquakes in various places, and famines and
pestilences; and there will be
fearful sights and great signs
from heaven. 12But before all
these things, they will lay their
hands on you and persecute
you, delivering *you* up to the
synagogues and prisons. You
will be brought before kings
and rulers for My name's sake.
13But it will turn out for you
as an occasion for testimony.
14Therefore settle *it* in your
hearts not to meditate beforehand on what you will answer;
15for I will give you a mouth
and wisdom which all your
adversaries will not be able to
contradict or resist. 16You will
be betrayed even by parents
and brothers, relatives and
friends; and they will put *some*

21:4 [a] NU-Text omits *for God.* 21:8 [a] NU-Text omits *Therefore.*

of you to death. 17 And you will
be hated by all for My name's
sake. 18 But not a hair of your
head shall be lost. 19 By your
patience possess your souls.

THE DESTRUCTION OF JERUSALEM

20 "But when you see Jerusalem surrounded by armies,
then know that its desolation
is near. 21 Then let those who
are in Judea flee to the mountains, let those who are in the
midst of her depart, and let
not those who are in the country enter her. 22 For these are
the days of vengeance, that
all things which are written
may be fulfilled. 23 But woe to
those who are pregnant and to
those who are nursing babies
in those days! For there will
be great distress in the land
and wrath upon this people.
24 And they will fall by the edge
of the sword, and be led away
captive into all nations. And
Jerusalem will be trampled by
Gentiles until the times of the
Gentiles are fulfilled.

THE COMING OF THE SON OF MAN

25 "And there will be signs
in the sun, in the moon, and
in the stars; and on the earth
distress of nations, with perplexity, the sea and the waves
roaring; 26 men's hearts failing
them from fear and the expectation of those things which
are coming on the earth, for
the powers of the heavens will
be shaken. 27 Then they will
see the Son of Man coming
in a cloud with power and
great glory. 28 Now when these
things begin to happen, look
up and lift up your heads, because your redemption draws
near."

THE PARABLE OF THE FIG TREE

29 Then He spoke to them a
parable: "Look at the fig tree,
and all the trees. 30 When they
are already budding, you see
and know for yourselves that
summer is now near. 31 So
you also, when you see these
things happening, know that
the kingdom of God is near.
32 Assuredly, I say to you, this
generation will by no means
pass away till all things take
place. 33 Heaven and earth will
pass away, but My words will
by no means pass away.

THE IMPORTANCE OF WATCHING

34 "But take heed to yourselves, lest your hearts be
weighed down with carous-
ing, drunkenness, and cares of
this life, and that Day come on
you unexpectedly. 35 For it will
come as a snare on all those
who dwell on the face of the
whole earth. 36 Watch therefore, and pray always that you
may be counted worthy[a] to

21:36 [a] NU-Text reads *may have strength.*

escape all these things that
will come to pass, and to stand
before the Son of Man."
37And in the daytime He
was teaching in the temple,
but at night He went out and
stayed on the mountain called
Olivet. 38Then early in the
morning all the people came
to Him in the temple to hear
Him.

THE PLOT TO KILL JESUS

22 Now the Feast of Unleavened Bread drew
near, which is called Passover.
2And the chief priests and
the scribes sought how they
might kill Him, for they feared
the people.
3Then Satan entered Judas,
surnamed Iscariot, who was
numbered among the twelve.
4So he went his way and conferred with the chief priests
and captains, how he might
betray Him to them. 5And
they were glad, and agreed to
give him money. 6So he promised and sought opportunity
to betray Him to them in the
absence of the multitude.

JESUS AND HIS DISCIPLES PREPARE THE PASSOVER

7Then came the Day of
Unleavened Bread, when the
Passover must be killed. 8And
He sent Peter and John, saying, "Go and prepare the Passover for us, that we may eat."
9So they said to Him,
"Where do You want us to
prepare?"
10And He said to them, "Behold, when you have entered
the city, a man will meet you
carrying a pitcher of water;
follow him into the house
which he enters. 11Then you
shall say to the master of the
house, 'The Teacher says to
you, "Where is the guest room
where I may eat the Passover
with My disciples?"' 12Then
he will show you a large, furnished upper room; there
make ready."
13So they went and found
it just as He had said to them,
and they prepared the Passover.

JESUS INSTITUTES THE LORD'S SUPPER

14When the hour had come,
He sat down, and the twelve[a]
apostles with Him. 15Then He
said to them, "With *fervent*
desire I have desired to eat
this Passover with you before
I suffer; 16for I say to you, I
will no longer eat of it until
it is fulfilled in the kingdom
of God."
17Then He took the cup, and
gave thanks, and said, "Take
this and divide *it* among yourselves; 18for I say to you,[a] I will
not drink of the fruit of the
vine until the kingdom of God
comes."
19And He took bread, gave

22:14 [a] NU-Text omits *twelve*. 22:18 [a] NU-Text adds *from now on*.

thanks and broke *it,* and gave
it to them, saying, "This is
My body which is given for
you; do this in remembrance
of Me."
20 Likewise He also *took*
the cup after supper, saying,
"This cup *is* the new covenant
in My blood, which is shed for
you. 21 But behold, the hand of
My betrayer *is* with Me on the
table. 22 And truly the Son of
Man goes as it has been determined, but woe to that man by
whom He is betrayed!"
23 Then they began to question among themselves, which
of them it was who would do
this thing.

THE DISCIPLES ARGUE ABOUT GREATNESS

24 Now there was also a dispute among them, as to which
of them should be considered
the greatest. 25 And He said
to them, "The kings of the
Gentiles exercise lordship
over them, and those who
exercise authority over them
are called 'benefactors.' 26 But
not so *among* you; on the
contrary, he who is greatest
among you, let him be as the
younger, and he who governs
as he who serves. 27 For who
is greater, he who sits at the
table, or he who serves? *Is* it
not he who sits at the table?
Yet I am among you as the
One who serves.
28 "But you are those who
have continued with Me in My
trials. 29 And I bestow upon
you a kingdom, just as My Father bestowed *one* upon Me,
30 that you may eat and drink
at My table in My kingdom,
and sit on thrones judging the
twelve tribes of Israel."

JESUS PREDICTS PETER'S DENIAL

31 And the Lord said,[a]
"Simon, Simon! Indeed, Satan
has asked for you, that he may
sift *you* as wheat. 32 But I have
prayed for you, that your faith
should not fail; and when
you have returned to *Me,*
strengthen your brethren."
33 But he said to Him, "Lord,
I am ready to go with You,
both to prison and to death."
34 Then He said, "I tell you,
Peter, the rooster shall not
crow this day before you will
deny three times that you
know Me."

SUPPLIES FOR THE ROAD

35 And He said to them,
"When I sent you without
money bag, knapsack, and
sandals, did you lack anything?"

So they said, "Nothing."
36 Then He said to them,
"But now, he who has a money
bag, let him take *it,* and likewise a knapsack; and he who
has no sword, let him sell his
garment and buy one. 37 For I

22:31 [a] NU-Text omits *And the Lord said.*

say to you that this which is
written must still be accomplished in Me: 'And He was
numbered with the transgressors.'[a] For the things concerning Me have an end."
38So they said, "Lord, look,
here *are* two swords."

And He said to them, "It is
enough."

THE PRAYER IN THE GARDEN

39Coming out, He went to
the Mount of Olives, as He was
accustomed, and His disciples
also followed Him. 40When He
came to the place, He said to
them, "Pray that you may not
enter into temptation."
41And He was withdrawn
from them about a stone's
throw, and He knelt down and
prayed, 42saying, "Father, if it
is Your will, take this cup away
from Me; nevertheless not
My will, but Yours, be done."
43Then an angel appeared to
Him from heaven, strengthening Him. 44And being in
agony, He prayed more earnestly. Then His sweat became
like great drops of blood falling down to the ground.[a]
45When He rose up from
prayer, and had come to His
disciples, He found them
sleeping from sorrow. 46Then
He said to them, "Why do you
sleep? Rise and pray, lest you
enter into temptation."

BETRAYAL AND ARREST IN GETHSEMANE

47And while He was still
speaking, behold, a multitude;
and he who was called Judas,
one of the twelve, went before
them and drew near to Jesus
to kiss Him. 48But Jesus said
to him, "Judas, are you betraying the Son of Man with
a kiss?"
49When those around Him
saw what was going to happen,
they said to Him, "Lord, shall
we strike with the sword?"
50And one of them struck the
servant of the high priest and
cut off his right ear.
51But Jesus answered and
said, "Permit even this." And
He touched his ear and healed
him.
52Then Jesus said to the
chief priests, captains of the
temple, and the elders who
had come to Him, "Have you
come out, as against a robber, with swords and clubs?
53When I was with you daily in
the temple, you did not try to
seize Me. But this is your hour,
and the power of darkness."

PETER DENIES JESUS, AND WEEPS BITTERLY

54Having arrested Him,
they led *Him* and brought
Him into the high priest's
house. But Peter followed
at a distance. 55Now when
they had kindled a fire in the

22:37 [a] Isaiah 53:12 22:44 [a] NU-Text brackets verses 43 and 44 as not in the original text.

midst of the courtyard and sat down together, Peter sat among them. 56 And a certain servant girl, seeing him as he sat by the fire, looked intently at him and said, "This man was also with Him."

57 But he denied Him,[a] saying, "Woman, I do not know Him."

58 And after a little while another saw him and said, "You also are of them."

But Peter said, "Man, I am not!"

59 Then after about an hour had passed, another confidently affirmed, saying, "Surely this *fellow* also was with Him, for he is a Galilean."

60 But Peter said, "Man, I do not know what you are saying!"

Immediately, while he was still speaking, the rooster[a] crowed. 61 And the Lord turned and looked at Peter. Then Peter remembered the word of the Lord, how He had said to him, "Before the rooster crows,[a] you will deny Me three times." 62 So Peter went out and wept bitterly.

JESUS MOCKED AND BEATEN

63 Now the men who held Jesus mocked Him and beat Him. 64 And having blindfolded Him, they struck Him on the face and asked Him,[a] saying, "Prophesy! Who is the one who struck You?" 65 And many other things they blasphemously spoke against Him.

JESUS FACES THE SANHEDRIN

66 As soon as it was day, the elders of the people, both chief priests and scribes, came together and led Him into their council, saying, 67 "If You are the Christ, tell us."

But He said to them, "If I tell you, you will by no means believe. 68 And if I also ask *you,* you will by no means answer Me or let *Me* go.[a] 69 Hereafter the Son of Man will sit on the right hand of the power of God."

70 Then they all said, "Are You then the Son of God?"

So He said to them, "You *rightly* say that I am."

71 And they said, "What further testimony do we need? For we have heard it ourselves from His own mouth."

JESUS HANDED OVER TO PONTIUS PILATE

23

Then the whole multitude of them arose and led Him to Pilate. 2 And they began to accuse Him, saying, "We found this *fellow* perverting the[a] nation, and forbidding to pay taxes to Cae-

22:57 [a] NU-Text reads *denied it.* 22:60 [a] NU-Text and M-Text read *a rooster.* 22:61 [a] NU-Text adds *today.* 22:64 [a] NU-Text reads *And having blindfolded Him, they asked Him.* 22:68 [a] NU-Text omits *also* and *Me or let Me go.* 23:2 [a] NU-Text reads *our.*

sar, saying that He Himself is
Christ, a King."
3Then Pilate asked Him,
saying, "Are You the King of
the Jews?"
He answered him and said,
"*It is as* you say."
4So Pilate said to the chief
priests and the crowd, "I find
no fault in this Man."
5But they were the more
fierce, saying, "He stirs up the
people, teaching throughout
all Judea, beginning from Galilee to this place."

JESUS FACES HEROD

6When Pilate heard of Galilee,[a] he asked if the Man were
a Galilean. 7And as soon as
he knew that He belonged to
Herod's jurisdiction, he sent
Him to Herod, who was also in
Jerusalem at that time. 8Now
when Herod saw Jesus, he was
exceedingly glad; for he had
desired for a long *time* to see
Him, because he had heard
many things about Him, and
he hoped to see some miracle
done by Him. 9Then he questioned Him with many words,
but He answered him nothing.
10And the chief priests and
scribes stood and vehemently
accused Him. 11Then Herod,
with his men of war, treated
Him with contempt and
mocked *Him,* arrayed Him
in a gorgeous robe, and sent
Him back to Pilate. 12That very
day Pilate and Herod became
friends with each other, for
previously they had been at
enmity with each other.

TAKING THE PLACE OF BARABBAS

13Then Pilate, when he
had called together the chief
priests, the rulers, and the
people, 14said to them, "You
have brought this Man to me,
as one who misleads the people. And indeed, having examined *Him* in your presence,
I have found no fault in this
Man concerning those things
of which you accuse Him;
15no, neither did Herod, for
I sent you back to him;[a] and
indeed nothing deserving of
death has been done by Him.
16I will therefore chastise Him
and release *Him*" 17(for it was
necessary for him to release
one to them at the feast).[a]
18And they all cried out at
once, saying, "Away with this
Man, and release to us Barabbas"— 19who had been thrown
into prison for a certain rebellion made in the city, and
for murder.
20Pilate, therefore, wish-
ing to release Jesus, again
called out to them. 21But they
shouted, saying, "Crucify *Him,*
crucify Him!"
22Then he said to them the
third time, "Why, what evil
has He done? I have found

23:6 [a] NU-Text omits *of Galilee.* 23:15 [a] NU-Text reads *for he sent Him back to us.* 23:17 [a] NU-Text omits verse 17.

no reason for death in Him.
I will therefore chastise Him
and let *Him* go."

23 But they were insistent,
demanding with loud voices
that He be crucified. And the
voices of these men and of the
chief priests prevailed.[a] 24 So
Pilate gave sentence that it
should be as they requested.
25 And he released to them[a]
the one they requested, who
for rebellion and murder had
been thrown into prison; but
he delivered Jesus to their will.

THE KING ON A CROSS

26 Now as they led Him
away, they laid hold of a certain man, Simon a Cyrenian,
who was coming from the
country, and on him they laid
the cross that he might bear
it after Jesus.

27 And a great multitude of
the people followed Him, and
women who also mourned
and lamented Him. 28 But
Jesus, turning to them, said,
"Daughters of Jerusalem, do
not weep for Me, but weep for
yourselves and for your children. 29 For indeed the days
are coming in which they will
say, 'Blessed *are* the barren,
wombs that never bore, and
breasts which never nursed!'
30 Then they will begin 'to say
to the mountains, "Fall on us!"
and to the hills, "Cover us!"'[a]
31 For if they do these things
in the green wood, what will
be done in the dry?"

32 There were also two others, criminals, led with Him to
be put to death. 33 And when
they had come to the place
called Calvary, there they crucified Him, and the criminals,
one on the right hand and the
other on the left. 34 Then Jesus
said, "Father, forgive them,
for they do not know what
they do."[a]

And they divided His gar-
ments and cast lots. 35 And
the people stood looking on.
But even the rulers with them
sneered, saying, "He saved
others; let Him save Himself
if He is the Christ, the chosen
of God."

36 The soldiers also mocked
Him, coming and offering
Him sour wine, 37 and saying,
"If You are the King of the
Jews, save Yourself."

38 And an inscription also
was written over Him in letters
of Greek, Latin, and Hebrew:[a]

THIS IS THE KING
OF THE JEWS.

39 Then one of the criminals
who were hanged blasphemed
Him, saying, "If You are the
Christ,[a] save Yourself and us."

23:23 [a] *NU-Text omits and of the chief priests.* **23:25** [a] NU-Text and M-Text omit *to them.* **23:30** [a] Hosea 10:8 **23:34** [a] NU-Text brackets the first sentence as a later addition. **23:38** [a] NU-Text omits *written* and *in letters of Greek, Latin, and Hebrew.* **23:39** [a] NU-Text reads *Are You not the Christ?*

40But the other, answering,
rebuked him, saying, "Do you
not even fear God, seeing you
are under the same condemnation? 41And we indeed justly,
for we receive the due reward
of our deeds; but this Man has
done nothing wrong." 42Then
he said to Jesus, "Lord,[a] remember me when You come
into Your kingdom."
43And Jesus said to him, "Assuredly, I say to you, today you
will be with Me in Paradise."

JESUS DIES ON THE CROSS

44Now it was[a] about the
sixth hour, and there was
darkness over all the earth
until the ninth hour. 45Then
the sun was darkened,[a] and
the veil of the temple was torn
in two. 46And when Jesus had
cried out with a loud voice, He
said, "Father, 'into Your hands
I commit My spirit.'"[a] Having
said this, He breathed His last.
47So when the centurion saw
what had happened, he glorified God, saying, "Certainly this
was a righteous Man!"
48And the whole crowd who
came together to that sight,
seeing what had been done,
beat their breasts and returned. 49But all His acquaintances, and the women who
followed Him from Galilee,
stood at a distance, watching
these things.

JESUS BURIED IN JOSEPH'S TOMB

50Now behold, *there was* a
man named Joseph, a coun-
cil member, a good and just
man. 51He had not consented
to their decision and deed. *He
was* from Arimathea, a city of
the Jews, who himself was also
waiting[a] for the kingdom of
God. 52This man went to Pilate and asked for the body of
Jesus. 53Then he took it down,
wrapped it in linen, and laid it
in a tomb *that was* hewn out
of the rock, where no one had
ever lain before. 54That day
was the Preparation, and the
Sabbath drew near.
55And the women who had
come with Him from Galilee
followed after, and they observed the tomb and how His
body was laid. 56Then they returned and prepared spices
and fragrant oils. And they
rested on the Sabbath according to the commandment.

HE IS RISEN

24 Now on the first *day* of
the week, very early in
the morning, they, and certain *other women* with them,[a]
came to the tomb bringing
the spices which they had
prepared. 2But they found
the stone rolled away from
the tomb. 3Then they went in
and did not find the body of

23:42 [a] NU-Text reads *And he said, "Jesus, remember me.*
23:44 [a] NU-Text adds *already.* 23:45 [a] NU-Text reads *obscured.*
23:46 [a] Psalm 31:5 23:51 [a] NU-Text reads *who was waiting.*
24:1 [a] NU-Text omits *and certain other women with them.*

the Lord Jesus. 4And it happened, as they were greatly[a]
perplexed about this, that
behold, two men stood by
them in shining garments.
5Then, as they were afraid
and bowed *their* faces to the
earth, they said to them, "Why
do you seek the living among
the dead? 6He is not here, but
is risen! Remember how He
spoke to you when He was still
in Galilee, 7saying, 'The Son of
Man must be delivered into
the hands of sinful men, and
be crucified, and the third day
rise again.' "

8And they remembered His
words. 9Then they returned
from the tomb and told all
these things to the eleven and
to all the rest. 10It was Mary
Magdalene, Joanna, Mary *the
mother* of James, and the other
women with them, who told
these things to the apostles.
11And their words seemed to
them like idle tales, and they
did not believe them. 12But
Peter arose and ran to the
tomb; and stooping down, he
saw the linen cloths lying[a] by
themselves; and he departed,
marveling to himself at what
had happened.

THE ROAD TO EMMAUS

13Now behold, two of them
were traveling that same day
to a village called Emmaus,
which was seven miles[a] from
Jerusalem. 14And they talked
together of all these things
which had happened. 15So
it was, while they conversed
and reasoned, that Jesus Himself drew near and went with
them. 16But their eyes were
restrained, so that they did
not know Him.

17And He said to them,
"What kind of conversation
is this that you have with one
another as you walk and are
sad?"[a]

18Then the one whose
name was Cleopas answered
and said to Him, "Are You the
only stranger in Jerusalem,
and have You not known the
things which happened there
in these days?"

19And He said to them,
"What things?"

So they said to Him, "The
things concerning Jesus of
Nazareth, who was a Prophet
mighty in deed and word before God and all the people,
20and how the chief priests
and our rulers delivered Him
to be condemned to death,
and crucified Him. 21But we
were hoping that it was He
who was going to redeem Israel. Indeed, besides all this,
today is the third day since
these things happened. 22Yes,
and certain women of our
company, who arrived at the

24:4 [a] NU-Text omits *greatly*. 24:12 [a] NU-Text omits *lying*. 24:13 [a] Literally *sixty stadia* 24:17 [a] NU-Text reads *as you walk? And they stood still, looking sad.*

tomb early, astonished us.
23When they did not find His
body, they came saying that
they had also seen a vision
of angels who said He was
alive. 24And certain of those
who were with us went to the
tomb and found *it* just as the
women had said; but Him
they did not see."
25Then He said to them,
"O foolish ones, and slow of
heart to believe in all that
the prophets have spoken!
26Ought not the Christ to have
suffered these things and to
enter into His glory?" 27And
beginning at Moses and all the
Prophets, He expounded to
them in all the Scriptures the
things concerning Himself.

THE DISCIPLES' EYES OPENED

28Then they drew near to
the village where they were
going, and He indicated that
He would have gone farther.
29But they constrained Him,
saying, "Abide with us, for it is
toward evening, and the day
is far spent." And He went in
to stay with them.
30Now it came to pass, as
He sat at the table with them,
that He took bread, blessed
and broke *it,* and gave it to
them. 31Then their eyes were
opened and they knew Him;
and He vanished from their
sight.
32And they said to one
another, "Did not our heart
burn within us while He talked
with us on the road, and while
He opened the Scriptures to
us?" 33So they rose up that
very hour and returned to
Jerusalem, and found the
eleven and those *who were*
with them gathered together,
34saying, "The Lord is risen
indeed, and has appeared to
Simon!" 35And they told about
the things *that had happened*
on the road, and how He was
known to them in the breaking of bread.

JESUS APPEARS TO HIS DISCIPLES

36Now as they said these
things, Jesus Himself stood
in the midst of them, and said
to them, "Peace to you." 37But
they were terrified and frightened, and supposed they had
seen a spirit. 38And He said
to them, "Why are you troubled? And why do doubts arise
in your hearts? 39Behold My
hands and My feet, that it is
I Myself. Handle Me and see,
for a spirit does not have flesh
and bones as you see I have."
40When He had said this,
He showed them His hands
and His feet.[a] 41But while they
still did not believe for joy, and
marveled, He said to them,
"Have you any food here?"
42So they gave Him a piece

24:40 [a] Some printed New Testaments omit this verse. It is found in nearly all Greek manuscripts.

of a broiled fish and some
honeycomb.[a] 43And He took
it and ate in their presence.

THE SCRIPTURES OPENED

44Then He said to them,
"These *are* the words which I
spoke to you while I was still
with you, that all things must
be fulfilled which were written in the Law of Moses and
the Prophets and *the* Psalms
concerning Me." 45And He
opened their understanding,
that they might comprehend
the Scriptures.

46Then He said to them,
"Thus it is written, and thus
it was necessary for the Christ
to suffer and to rise[a] from the
dead the third day, 47and that
repentance and remission of
sins should be preached in
His name to all nations, beginning at Jerusalem. 48And
you are witnesses of these
things. 49Behold, I send the
Promise of My Father upon
you; but tarry in the city of
Jerusalem[a] until you are
endued with power from on
high."

THE ASCENSION

50And He led them out as
far as Bethany, and He lifted
up His hands and blessed
them. 51Now it came to pass,
while He blessed them, that
He was parted from them and
carried up into heaven. 52And
they worshiped Him, and
returned to Jerusalem with
great joy, 53and were continually in the temple praising
and[a] blessing God. Amen.[b]

THE GOSPEL ACCORDING TO JOHN

THE ETERNAL WORD

1 In the beginning was the
Word, and the Word was
with God, and the Word was
God. 2He was in the beginning with God. 3All things
were made through Him,
and without Him nothing was
made that was made. 4In Him
was life, and the life was the
light of men. 5And the light
shines in the darkness, and
the darkness did not com-
prehend[a] it.

24:42 [a] NU-Text omits *and some honeycomb.* 24:46 [a] NU-Text reads *written, that the Christ should suffer and rise.* 24:49 [a] NU-Text omits *of Jerusalem.* 24:53 [a] NU-Text omits *praising and.* [b] NU-Text omits *Amen.* 1:5 [a] Or *overcome*

JOHN'S WITNESS: THE TRUE LIGHT

6There was a man sent from
God, whose name *was* John.
7This man came for a witness,
to bear witness of the Light,
that all through him might believe. 8He was not that Light,
but *was sent* to bear witness of
that Light. 9That was the true
Light which gives light to every
man coming into the world.[a]
10He was in the world, and
the world was made through
Him, and the world did not
know Him. 11He came to His
own,[a] and His own[b] did not
receive Him. 12But as many
as received Him, to them He
gave the right to become children of God, to those who believe in His name: 13who were
born, not of blood, nor of the
will of the flesh, nor of the will
of man, but of God.

THE WORD BECOMES FLESH

14And the Word became
flesh and dwelt among us, and
we beheld His glory, the glory
as of the only begotten of the
Father, full of grace and truth.
15John bore witness of Him
and cried out, saying, "This
was He of whom I said, 'He
who comes after me is preferred before me, for He was
before me.'"
16And[a] of His fullness we
have all received, and grace
for grace. 17For the law was
given through Moses, *but*
grace and truth came through
Jesus Christ. 18No one has
seen God at any time. The only
begotten Son,[a] who is in the
bosom of the Father, He has
declared *Him.*

A VOICE IN THE WILDERNESS

19Now this is the testimony
of John, when the Jews sent
priests and Levites from Jerusalem to ask him, "Who are
you?"
20He confessed, and did
not deny, but confessed, "I
am not the Christ."
21And they asked him,
"What then? Are you Elijah?"
He said, "I am not."
"Are you the Prophet?"
And he answered, "No."
22Then they said to him,
"Who are you, that we may
give an answer to those who
sent us? What do you say
about yourself?"
23He said: "I *am*

'The voice of one crying
in the wilderness:
"Make straight the way
of the LORD,"'[a]

as the prophet Isaiah said."
24Now those who were
sent were from the Pharisees.

1:9 [a] Or *That was the true Light which, coming into the world, gives light to every man.* 1:11 [a] That is, His own things or domain [b] That is, His own people 1:16 [a] NU-Text reads *For.* 1:18 [a] NU-Text reads *only begotten God.* 1:23 [a] Isaiah 40:3

25And they asked him, saying,
"Why then do you baptize if
you are not the Christ, nor Elijah, nor the Prophet?"
26John answered them,
saying, "I baptize with water,
but there stands One among
you whom you do not know.
27It is He who, coming after
me, is preferred before me,
whose sandal strap I am not
worthy to loose."
28These things were done in
Bethabara[a] beyond the Jordan,
where John was baptizing.

THE LAMB OF GOD

29The next day John saw
Jesus coming toward him, and
said, "Behold! The Lamb of
God who takes away the sin
of the world! 30This is He of
whom I said, 'After me comes
a Man who is preferred before
me, for He was before me.' 31I
did not know Him; but that He
should be revealed to Israel,
therefore I came baptizing
with water."
32And John bore witness,
saying, "I saw the Spirit descending from heaven like a
dove, and He remained upon
Him. 33I did not know Him,
but He who sent me to baptize
with water said to me, 'Upon
whom you see the Spirit descending, and remaining on
Him, this is He who baptizes
with the Holy Spirit.' 34And I
have seen and testified that
this is the Son of God."

THE FIRST DISCIPLES

35Again, the next day, John
stood with two of his disciples.
36And looking at Jesus as He
walked, he said, "Behold the
Lamb of God!"
37The two disciples heard
him speak, and they followed
Jesus. 38Then Jesus turned,
and seeing them following,
said to them, "What do you
seek?"
They said to Him, "Rabbi"
(which is to say, when translated, Teacher), "where are
You staying?"
39He said to them, "Come
and see." They came and saw
where He was staying, and
remained with Him that day
(now it was about the tenth
hour).
40One of the two who heard
John *speak*, and followed Him,
was Andrew, Simon Peter's
brother. 41He first found his
own brother Simon, and said
to him, "We have found the
Messiah" (which is translated,
the Christ). 42And he brought
him to Jesus.
Now when Jesus looked at
him, He said, "You are Simon
the son of Jonah.[a] You shall
be called Cephas" (which is
translated, A Stone).

PHILIP AND NATHANAEL

43The following day Jesus
wanted to go to Galilee, and He
found Philip and said to him,
"Follow Me." 44Now Philip was

1:28 [a] NU-Text and M-Text read *Bethany*. 1:42 [a] NU-Text reads *John*.

from Bethsaida, the city of Andrew and Peter. 45 Philip found
Nathanael and said to him,
"We have found Him of whom
Moses in the law, and also the
prophets, wrote—Jesus of Nazareth, the son of Joseph."

46 And Nathanael said to
him, "Can anything good
come out of Nazareth?"

Philip said to him, "Come
and see."

47 Jesus saw Nathanael
coming toward Him, and said
of him, "Behold, an Israelite
indeed, in whom is no deceit!"
48 Nathanael said to Him,
"How do You know me?"

Jesus answered and said to
him, "Before Philip called you,
when you were under the fig
tree, I saw you."

49 Nathanael answered and
said to Him, "Rabbi, You are
the Son of God! You are the
King of Israel!"

50 Jesus answered and said
to him, "Because I said to you,
'I saw you under the fig tree,'
do you believe? You will see
greater things than these."
51 And He said to him, "Most
assuredly, I say to you, hereafter[a] you shall see heaven
open, and the angels of God
ascending and descending
upon the Son of Man."

WATER TURNED TO WINE

2 On the third day there
was a wedding in Cana
of Galilee, and the mother of
Jesus was there. 2 Now both
Jesus and His disciples were
invited to the wedding. 3 And
when they ran out of wine, the
mother of Jesus said to Him,
"They have no wine."

4 Jesus said to her, "Woman,
what does your concern have
to do with Me? My hour has
not yet come."

5 His mother said to the servants, "Whatever He says to
you, do *it*."

6 Now there were set there
six waterpots of stone, according to the manner of
purification of the Jews,
containing twenty or thirty
gallons apiece. 7 Jesus said to
them, "Fill the waterpots with
water." And they filled them
up to the brim. 8 And He said
to them, "Draw *some* out now,
and take *it* to the master of
the feast." And they took *it*.
9 When the master of the feast
had tasted the water that was
made wine, and did not know
where it came from (but the
servants who had drawn the
water knew), the master of the
feast called the bridegroom.
10 And he said to him, "Every
man at the beginning sets out
the good wine, and when the
guests have well drunk, then
the inferior. You have kept the
good wine until now!"

11 This beginning of signs
Jesus did in Cana of Galilee,
and manifested His glory; and
His disciples believed in Him.

1:51 [a] NU-Text omits *hereafter*.

12After this He went down to
Capernaum, He, His mother,
His brothers, and His disciples; and they did not stay
there many days.

JESUS CLEANSES THE TEMPLE

13Now the Passover of the
Jews was at hand, and Jesus
went up to Jerusalem. 14And
He found in the temple those
who sold oxen and sheep and
doves, and the money changers doing business. 15When
He had made a whip of cords,
He drove them all out of the
temple, with the sheep and
the oxen, and poured out the
changers' money and over-
turned the tables. 16And He
said to those who sold doves,
"Take these things away! Do
not make My Father's house
a house of merchandise!"
17Then His disciples remembered that it was written, "Zeal
for Your house has eaten[a] Me
up."[b]

18So the Jews answered and
said to Him, "What sign do
You show to us, since You do
these things?"

19Jesus answered and said
to them, "Destroy this temple,
and in three days I will raise
it up."

20Then the Jews said, "It
has taken forty-six years to
build this temple, and will You
raise it up in three days?"

21But He was speaking
of the temple of His body.
22Therefore, when He had
risen from the dead, His disciples remembered that He had
said this to them;[a] and they
believed the Scripture and the
word which Jesus had said.

THE DISCERNER OF HEARTS

23Now when He was in
Jerusalem at the Passover,
during the feast, many believed in His name when they
saw the signs which He did.
24But Jesus did not commit
Himself to them, because He
knew all *men,* 25and had no
need that anyone should testify of man, for He knew what
was in man.

THE NEW BIRTH

3 There was a man of the
Pharisees named Nicode-
mus, a ruler of the Jews. 2This
man came to Jesus by night
and said to Him, "Rabbi, we
know that You are a teacher
come from God; for no one
can do these signs that You
do unless God is with him."

3Jesus answered and said
to him, "Most assuredly, I say
to you, unless one is born
again, he cannot see the kingdom of God."

4Nicodemus said to Him,
"How can a man be born when
he is old? Can he enter a sec-

2:17 [a] NU-Text and M-Text read *will eat.* [b] Psalm 69:9 2:22 [a] NU-Text and M-Text omit *to them.*

ond time into his mother's
womb and be born?"
5Jesus answered, "Most assuredly, I say to you, unless
one is born of water and the
Spirit, he cannot enter the
kingdom of God. 6That which
is born of the flesh is flesh,
and that which is born of the
Spirit is spirit. 7Do not marvel
that I said to you, 'You must be
born again.' 8The wind blows
where it wishes, and you hear
the sound of it, but cannot
tell where it comes from and
where it goes. So is everyone
who is born of the Spirit."
9Nicodemus answered and
said to Him, "How can these
things be?"
10Jesus answered and said
to him, "Are you the teacher
of Israel, and do not know
these things? 11Most assuredly,
I say to you, We speak what We
know and testify what We have
seen, and you do not receive
Our witness. 12If I have told
you earthly things and you
do not believe, how will you
believe if I tell you heavenly
things? 13No one has ascended
to heaven but He who came
down from heaven, *that is,* the
Son of Man who is in heav-
en.[a] 14And as Moses lifted up
the serpent in the wilderness,
even so must the Son of Man
be lifted up, 15that whoever
believes in Him should not
perish but[a] have eternal life.
16For God so loved the world
that He gave His only begotten Son, that whoever believes
in Him should not perish but
have everlasting life. 17For God
did not send His Son into the
world to condemn the world,
but that the world through
Him might be saved.
18"He who believes in Him
is not condemned; but he who
does not believe is condemned
already, because he has not believed in the name of the only
begotten Son of God. 19And
this is the condemnation, that
the light has come into the
world, and men loved darkness rather than light, because
their deeds were evil. 20For
everyone practicing evil hates
the light and does not come to
the light, lest his deeds should
be exposed. 21But he who does
the truth comes to the light,
that his deeds may be clearly
seen, that they have been done
in God."

JOHN THE BAPTIST EXALTS CHRIST

22After these things Jesus
and His disciples came into
the land of Judea, and there
He remained with them and
baptized. 23Now John also was
baptizing in Aenon near Salim,
because there was much water
there. And they came and were
baptized. 24For John had not
yet been thrown into prison.

3:13 [a] NU-Text omits *who is in heaven.*
3:15 [a] NU-Text omits *not perish but.*

[25]Then there arose a dispute between *some* of John's
disciples and the Jews about
purification. [26]And they came
to John and said to him,
"Rabbi, He who was with you
beyond the Jordan, to whom
you have testified—behold,
He is baptizing, and all are
coming to Him!"
[27]John answered and said,
"A man can receive nothing
unless it has been given to
him from heaven. [28]You yourselves bear me witness, that I
said, 'I am not the Christ,' but,
'I have been sent before Him.'
[29]He who has the bride is the
bridegroom; but the friend of
the bridegroom, who stands
and hears him, rejoices greatly
because of the bridegroom's
voice. Therefore this joy of
mine is fulfilled. [30]He must
increase, but I *must* decrease.
[31]He who comes from above
is above all; he who is of the
earth is earthly and speaks of
the earth. He who comes from
heaven is above all. [32]And
what He has seen and heard,
that He testifies; and no one
receives His testimony. [33]He
who has received His testimony has certified that God
is true. [34]For He whom God
has sent speaks the words of
God, for God does not give
the Spirit by measure. [35]The
Father loves the Son, and has
given all things into His hand.
[36]He who believes in the Son
has everlasting life; and he
who does not believe the Son
shall not see life, but the wrath
of God abides on him."

A SAMARITAN WOMAN MEETS HER MESSIAH

4 Therefore, when the Lord
knew that the Pharisees
had heard that Jesus made and
baptized more disciples than
John [2](though Jesus Himself
did not baptize, but His disciples), [3]He left Judea and departed again to Galilee. [4]But He
needed to go through Samaria.
[5]So He came to a city of Samaria which is called Sychar,
near the plot of ground that
Jacob gave to his son Joseph.
[6]Now Jacob's well was there.
Jesus therefore, being wearied
from *His* journey, sat thus by
the well. It was about the sixth
hour.
[7]A woman of Samaria came
to draw water. Jesus said to
her, "Give Me a drink." [8]For
His disciples had gone away
into the city to buy food.
[9]Then the woman of Sa-
maria said to Him, "How is
it that You, being a Jew, ask
a drink from me, a Samaritan woman?" For Jews have
no dealings with Samaritans.
[10]Jesus answered and said
to her, "If you knew the gift of
God, and who it is who says
to you, 'Give Me a drink,' you
would have asked Him, and
He would have given you living water."
[11]The woman said to Him,
"Sir, You have nothing to draw
with, and the well is deep.

Where then do You get that
living water? 12Are You greater
than our father Jacob, who
gave us the well, and drank
from it himself, as well as his
sons and his livestock?"
13Jesus answered and said
to her, "Whoever drinks of this
water will thirst again, 14but
whoever drinks of the water
that I shall give him will never
thirst. But the water that I shall
give him will become in him
a fountain of water springing
up into everlasting life."
15The woman said to Him,
"Sir, give me this water, that I
may not thirst, nor come here
to draw."
16Jesus said to her, "Go, call
your husband, and come here."
17The woman answered and
said, "I have no husband."
Jesus said to her, "You have
well said, 'I have no husband,'
18for you have had five husbands, and the one whom you
now have is not your husband;
in that you spoke truly."
19The woman said to Him,
"Sir, I perceive that You are a
prophet. 20Our fathers worshiped on this mountain, and
you *Jews* say that in Jerusalem is the place where one
ought to worship."
21Jesus said to her, "Woman,
believe Me, the hour is coming
when you will neither on this
mountain, nor in Jerusalem,
worship the Father. 22You worship what you do not know; we
know what we worship, for salvation is of the Jews. 23But the
hour is coming, and now is,
when the true worshipers will
worship the Father in spirit
and truth; for the Father is
seeking such to worship Him.
24God *is* Spirit, and those who
worship Him must worship in
spirit and truth."
25The woman said to Him,
"I know that Messiah is coming" (who is called Christ).
"When He comes, He will tell
us all things."
26Jesus said to her, "I who
speak to you am *He*."

THE WHITENED HARVEST

27And at this *point* His disciples came, and they marveled that He talked with
a woman; yet no one said,
"What do You seek?" or, "Why
are You talking with her?"
28The woman then left her
waterpot, went her way into
the city, and said to the men,
29"Come, see a Man who told
me all things that I ever did.
Could this be the Christ?"
30Then they went out of the
city and came to Him.
31In the meantime His
disciples urged Him, saying,
"Rabbi, eat."
32But He said to them, "I
have food to eat of which you
do not know."
33Therefore the disciples
said to one another, "Has anyone brought Him *anything* to
eat?"
34Jesus said to them, "My
food is to do the will of Him
who sent Me, and to finish His

work. 35 Do you not say, 'There are still four months and *then* comes the harvest'? Behold, I say to you, lift up your eyes and look at the fields, for they are already white for harvest! 36 And he who reaps receives wages, and gathers fruit for eternal life, that both he who sows and he who reaps may rejoice together. 37 For in this the saying is true: 'One sows and another reaps.' 38 I sent you to reap that for which you have not labored; others have labored, and you have entered into their labors."

THE SAVIOR OF THE WORLD

39 And many of the Samaritans of that city believed in Him because of the word of the woman who testified, "He told me all that I *ever* did." 40 So when the Samaritans had come to Him, they urged Him to stay with them; and He stayed there two days. 41 And many more believed because of His own word.

42 Then they said to the woman, "Now we believe, not because of what you said, for we ourselves have heard *Him* and we know that this is indeed the Christ,[a] the Savior of the world."

WELCOME AT GALILEE

43 Now after the two days He departed from there and went to Galilee. 44 For Jesus Himself testified that a prophet has no honor in his own country. 45 So when He came to Galilee, the Galileans received Him, having seen all the things He did in Jerusalem at the feast; for they also had gone to the feast.

A NOBLEMAN'S SON HEALED

46 So Jesus came again to Cana of Galilee where He had made the water wine. And there was a certain nobleman whose son was sick at Capernaum. 47 When he heard that Jesus had come out of Judea into Galilee, he went to Him and implored Him to come down and heal his son, for he was at the point of death. 48 Then Jesus said to him, "Unless you *people* see signs and wonders, you will by no means believe."

49 The nobleman said to Him, "Sir, come down before my child dies!"

50 Jesus said to him, "Go your way; your son lives." So the man believed the word that Jesus spoke to him, and he went his way. 51 And as he was now going down, his servants met him and told *him*, saying, "Your son lives!"

52 Then he inquired of them *the hour when* he got better. And they said to him, "Yesterday at the seventh hour

4:42 [a] NU-Text omits *the Christ*.

the fever left him." 53So the father knew that *it was* at the same hour in which Jesus said to him, "Your son lives." And he himself believed, and his whole household.

54This again *is* the second sign Jesus did when He had come out of Judea into Galilee.

A MAN HEALED AT THE POOL OF BETHESDA

5 After this there was a feast of the Jews, and Jesus went up to Jerusalem. 2Now there is in Jerusalem by the Sheep *Gate* a pool, which is called in Hebrew, Bethesda,[a] having five porches. 3In these lay a great multitude of sick people, blind, lame, paralyzed, waiting for the moving of the water. 4For an angel went down at a certain time into the pool and stirred up the water; then whoever stepped in first, after the stirring of the water, was made well of whatever disease he had.[a] 5Now a certain man was there who had an infirmity thirty-eight years. 6When Jesus saw him lying there, and knew that he already had been *in that condition* a long time, He said to him, "Do you want to be made well?"

7The sick man answered Him, "Sir, I have no man to put me into the pool when the water is stirred up; but while I am coming, another steps down before me."

8Jesus said to him, "Rise, take up your bed and walk." 9And immediately the man was made well, took up his bed, and walked.

And that day was the Sabbath. 10The Jews therefore said to him who was cured, "It is the Sabbath; it is not lawful for you to carry your bed."

11He answered them, "He who made me well said to me, 'Take up your bed and walk.'"

12Then they asked him, "Who is the Man who said to you, 'Take up your bed and walk'?" 13But the one who was healed did not know who it was, for Jesus had withdrawn, a multitude being in *that* place. 14Afterward Jesus found him in the temple, and said to him, "See, you have been made well. Sin no more, lest a worse thing come upon you."

15The man departed and told the Jews that it was Jesus who had made him well.

HONOR THE FATHER AND THE SON

16For this reason the Jews persecuted Jesus, and sought to kill Him,[a] because He had done these things on the Sabbath. 17But Jesus answered

5:2 [a] NU-Text reads *Bethzatha*. 5:4 [a] NU-Text omits *waiting for the moving of the water* at the end of verse 3, and all of verse 4. 5:16 [a] NU-Text omits *and sought to kill Him.*

them, "My Father has been
working until now, and I have
been working."
18 Therefore the Jews
sought all the more to kill
Him, because He not only
broke the Sabbath, but also
said that God was His Father,
making Himself equal with
God. 19 Then Jesus answered
and said to them, "Most assuredly, I say to you, the Son
can do nothing of Himself,
but what He sees the Father
do; for whatever He does, the
Son also does in like manner.
20 For the Father loves the Son,
and shows Him all things that
He Himself does; and He will
show Him greater works than
these, that you may marvel.
21 For as the Father raises the
dead and gives life to *them,*
even so the Son gives life to
whom He will. 22 For the Father judges no one, but has
committed all judgment to the
Son, 23 that all should honor
the Son just as they honor
the Father. He who does not
honor the Son does not honor
the Father who sent Him.

LIFE AND JUDGMENT ARE THROUGH THE SON

24 "Most assuredly, I say to
you, he who hears My word
and believes in Him who sent
Me has everlasting life, and
shall not come into judgment,
but has passed from death
into life. 25 Most assuredly, I
say to you, the hour is coming, and now is, when the dead
will hear the voice of the Son
of God; and those who hear
will live. 26 For as the Father
has life in Himself, so He has
granted the Son to have life
in Himself, 27 and has given
Him authority to execute
judgment also, because He
is the Son of Man. 28 Do not
marvel at this; for the hour is
coming in which all who are in
the graves will hear His voice
29 and come forth—those who
have done good, to the resurrection of life, and those who
have done evil, to the resurrection of condemnation. 30 I
can of Myself do nothing. As
I hear, I judge; and My judgment is righteous, because I
do not seek My own will but
the will of the Father who
sent Me.

THE FOURFOLD WITNESS

31 "If I bear witness of Myself, My witness is not true.
32 There is another who bears
witness of Me, and I know
that the witness which He
witnesses of Me is true. 33 You
have sent to John, and he has
borne witness to the truth.
34 Yet I do not receive testimony from man, but I say
these things that you may be
saved. 35 He was the burning
and shining lamp, and you
were willing for a time to rejoice in his light. 36 But I have
a greater witness than John's;
for the works which the Father
has given Me to finish—the
very works that I do—bear

witness of Me, that the Father
has sent Me. [37]And the Father
Himself, who sent Me, has testified of Me. You have neither
heard His voice at any time,
nor seen His form. [38]But you
do not have His word abiding in you, because whom He
sent, Him you do not believe.
[39]You search the Scriptures,
for in them you think you
have eternal life; and these are
they which testify of Me. [40]But
you are not willing to come
to Me that you may have life.

[41]"I do not receive honor
from men. [42]But I know you,
that you do not have the love
of God in you. [43]I have come
in My Father's name, and you
do not receive Me; if another
comes in his own name, him
you will receive. [44]How can
you believe, who receive
honor from one another, and
do not seek the honor that
comes from the only God?
[45]Do not think that I shall accuse you to the Father; there is
one who accuses you—Moses,
in whom you trust. [46]For if you
believed Moses, you would believe Me; for he wrote about
Me. [47]But if you do not believe
his writings, how will you believe My words?"

FEEDING THE FIVE THOUSAND

6 After these things Jesus
went over the Sea of Gal-
ilee, which is *the Sea* of Tiberias. [2]Then a great multitude
followed Him, because they
saw His signs which He performed on those who were
diseased. [3]And Jesus went up
on the mountain, and there
He sat with His disciples.

[4]Now the Passover, a feast
of the Jews, was near. [5]Then
Jesus lifted up *His* eyes, and
seeing a great multitude coming toward Him, He said to
Philip, "Where shall we buy
bread, that these may eat?"
[6]But this He said to test him,
for He Himself knew what He
would do.

[7]Philip answered Him,
"Two hundred denarii worth
of bread is not sufficient for
them, that every one of them
may have a little."

[8]One of His disciples, Andrew, Simon Peter's brother,
said to Him, [9]"There is a
lad here who has five barley
loaves and two small fish,
but what are they among so
many?"

[10]Then Jesus said, "Make
the people sit down." Now
there was much grass in the
place. So the men sat down,
in number about five thousand. [11]And Jesus took the
loaves, and when He had
given thanks He distributed
them to the disciples, and
the disciples[a] to those sitting
down; and likewise of the fish,
as much as they wanted. [12]So
when they were filled, He said

6:11 [a] NU-Text omits *to the disciples, and the disciples.*

to His disciples, "Gather up
the fragments that remain, so
that nothing is lost." 13There-
fore they gathered *them* up,
and filled twelve baskets with
the fragments of the five barley loaves which were left
over by those who had eaten.
14Then those men, when they
had seen the sign that Jesus
did, said, "This is truly the
Prophet who is to come into
the world."

JESUS WALKS ON THE SEA

15Therefore when Jesus
perceived that they were
about to come and take Him
by force to make Him king, He
departed again to the mountain by Himself alone.
16Now when evening came,
His disciples went down to the
sea, 17got into the boat, and
went over the sea toward Capernaum. And it was already
dark, and Jesus had not come
to them. 18Then the sea arose
because a great wind was
blowing. 19So when they had
rowed about three or four
miles,[a] they saw Jesus walking
on the sea and drawing near
the boat; and they were afraid.
20But He said to them, "It is I;
do not be afraid." 21Then they
willingly received Him into
the boat, and immediately the
boat was at the land where
they were going.

THE BREAD FROM HEAVEN

22On the following day,
when the people who were
standing on the other side
of the sea saw that there was
no other boat there, except
that one which His disciples
had entered,[a] and that Jesus
had not entered the boat with
His disciples, but His disciples
had gone away alone— 23how-
ever, other boats came from
Tiberias, near the place where
they ate bread after the Lord
had given thanks— 24when
the people therefore saw that
Jesus was not there, nor His
disciples, they also got into
boats and came to Caper-
naum, seeking Jesus. 25And
when they found Him on the
other side of the sea, they said
to Him, "Rabbi, when did You
come here?"
26Jesus answered them
and said, "Most assuredly, I
say to you, you seek Me, not
because you saw the signs,
but because you ate of the
loaves and were filled. 27Do
not labor for the food which
perishes, but for the food
which endures to everlasting
life, which the Son of Man will
give you, because God the Father has set His seal on Him."
28Then they said to Him,
"What shall we do, that we
may work the works of God?"
29Jesus answered and said
to them, "This is the work of

6:19 [a] Literally *twenty-five or thirty stadia* 6:22 [a] NU-Text omits *that* and *which His disciples had entered.*

God, that you believe in Him
whom He sent."
30Therefore they said to
Him, "What sign will You perform then, that we may see it
and believe You? What work
will You do? 31Our fathers ate
the manna in the desert; as
it is written, 'He gave them
bread from heaven to eat.'"[a]
32Then Jesus said to them,
"Most assuredly, I say to you,
Moses did not give you the
bread from heaven, but My Father gives you the true bread
from heaven. 33For the bread
of God is He who comes down
from heaven and gives life to
the world."
34Then they said to Him,
"Lord, give us this bread always."
35And Jesus said to them, "I
am the bread of life. He who
comes to Me shall never hunger, and he who believes in
Me shall never thirst. 36But I
said to you that you have seen
Me and yet do not believe.
37All that the Father gives Me
will come to Me, and the one
who comes to Me I will by no
means cast out. 38For I have
come down from heaven, not
to do My own will, but the will
of Him who sent Me. 39This
is the will of the Father who
sent Me, that of all He has
given Me I should lose nothing, but should raise it up at
the last day. 40And this is the
will of Him who sent Me, that
everyone who sees the Son
and believes in Him may have
everlasting life; and I will raise
him up at the last day."

REJECTED BY HIS OWN

41The Jews then com-
plained about Him, because
He said, "I am the bread which
came down from heaven."
42And they said, "Is not this
Jesus, the son of Joseph,
whose father and mother we
know? How is it then that He
says, 'I have come down from
heaven'?"
43Jesus therefore answered
and said to them, "Do not
murmur among yourselves.
44No one can come to Me unless the Father who sent Me
draws him; and I will raise
him up at the last day. 45It
is written in the prophets,
'And they shall all be taught
by God.'[a] Therefore everyone
who has heard and learned[b]
from the Father comes to Me.
46Not that anyone has seen
the Father, except He who is
from God; He has seen the Father. 47Most assuredly, I say to
you, he who believes in Me[a]
has everlasting life. 48I am the
bread of life. 49Your fathers
ate the manna in the wilderness, and are dead. 50This is
the bread which comes down
from heaven, that one may
eat of it and not die. 51I am

6:31 [a] Exodus 16:4; Nehemiah 9:15; Psalm 78:24 6:45 [a] Isaiah 54:13 [b] M-Text reads *hears and has learned.* 6:47 [a] NU-Text omits *in Me.*

the living bread which came
down from heaven. If anyone
eats of this bread, he will live
forever; and the bread that I
shall give is My flesh, which
I shall give for the life of the
world."

52 The Jews therefore quarreled among themselves, saying, "How can this Man give
us *His* flesh to eat?"

53 Then Jesus said to them,
"Most assuredly, I say to you,
unless you eat the flesh of
the Son of Man and drink His
blood, you have no life in you.
54 Whoever eats My flesh and
drinks My blood has eternal
life, and I will raise him up at
the last day. 55 For My flesh is
food indeed,[a] and My blood is
drink indeed. 56 He who eats
My flesh and drinks My blood
abides in Me, and I in him.
57 As the living Father sent Me,
and I live because of the Father, so he who feeds on Me
will live because of Me. 58 This
is the bread which came down
from heaven—not as your fathers ate the manna, and are
dead. He who eats this bread
will live forever."

59 These things He said in
the synagogue as He taught
in Capernaum.

MANY DISCIPLES TURN AWAY

60 Therefore many of His
disciples, when they heard
this, said, "This is a hard saying; who can understand it?"

61 When Jesus knew in Himself that His disciples complained about this, He said to
them, "Does this offend you?
62 *What* then if you should see
the Son of Man ascend where
He was before? 63 It is the Spirit
who gives life; the flesh profits nothing. The words that I
speak to you are spirit, and
they are life. 64 But there are
some of you who do not believe." For Jesus knew from
the beginning who they were
who did not believe, and who
would betray Him. 65 And He
said, "Therefore I have said to
you that no one can come to
Me unless it has been granted
to him by My Father."

66 From that *time* many of
His disciples went back and
walked with Him no more.
67 Then Jesus said to the twelve,
"Do you also want to go away?"

68 But Simon Peter an-
swered Him, "Lord, to whom
shall we go? You have the
words of eternal life. 69 Also
we have come to believe and
know that You are the Christ,
the Son of the living God."[a]

70 Jesus answered them,
"Did I not choose you, the
twelve, and one of you is a
devil?" 71 He spoke of Judas Iscariot, *the son* of Simon, for it
was he who would betray Him,
being one of the twelve.

6:55 [a] NU-Text reads *true food* and *true drink.*
6:69 [a] NU-Text reads *You are the Holy One of God.*

JESUS' BROTHERS DISBELIEVE

7 After these things Jesus
walked in Galilee; for He
did not want to walk in Judea,
because the Jews[a] sought to
kill Him. 2Now the Jews' Feast
of Tabernacles was at hand.
3His brothers therefore said
to Him, "Depart from here
and go into Judea, that Your
disciples also may see the
works that You are doing. 4For
no one does anything in secret while he himself seeks to
be known openly. If You do
these things, show Yourself
to the world." 5For even His
brothers did not believe in
Him.

6Then Jesus said to them,
"My time has not yet come,
but your time is always ready.
7The world cannot hate you,
but it hates Me because I
testify of it that its works are
evil. 8You go up to this feast.
I am not yet[a] going up to this
feast, for My time has not yet
fully come." 9When He had
said these things to them, He
remained in Galilee.

THE HEAVENLY SCHOLAR

10But when His brothers
had gone up, then He also
went up to the feast, not
openly, but as it were in secret.
11Then the Jews sought Him
at the feast, and said, "Where
is He?" 12And there was much
complaining among the people concerning Him. Some
said, "He is good"; others said,
"No, on the contrary, He deceives the people." 13However,
no one spoke openly of Him
for fear of the Jews.

14Now about the middle of
the feast Jesus went up into
the temple and taught. 15And
the Jews marveled, saying,
"How does this Man know letters, having never studied?"

16Jesus[a] answered them
and said, "My doctrine is not
Mine, but His who sent Me.
17If anyone wills to do His will,
he shall know concerning the
doctrine, whether it is from
God or *whether* I speak on
My own *authority.* 18He who
speaks from himself seeks his
own glory; but He who seeks
the glory of the One who sent
Him is true, and no unrighteousness is in Him. 19Did not
Moses give you the law, yet
none of you keeps the law?
Why do you seek to kill Me?"

20The people answered
and said, "You have a demon.
Who is seeking to kill You?"

21Jesus answered and said
to them, "I did one work, and
you all marvel. 22Moses therefore gave you circumcision
(not that it is from Moses,
but from the fathers), and
you circumcise a man on
the Sabbath. 23If a man receives circumcision on the

7:1 [a] That is, the ruling authorities 7:8 [a] NU-Text omits *yet.* 7:16 [a] NU-Text and M-Text read *So Jesus.*

Sabbath, so that the law of
Moses should not be bro-
ken, are you angry with Me
because I made a man com-
pletely well on the Sabbath?
24 Do not judge according to
appearance, but judge with
righteous judgment."

COULD THIS BE THE CHRIST?

25 Now some of them from
Jerusalem said, "Is this not
He whom they seek to kill?
26 But look! He speaks boldly,
and they say nothing to Him.
Do the rulers know indeed
that this is truly[a] the Christ?
27 However, we know where
this Man is from; but when the
Christ comes, no one knows
where He is from."

28 Then Jesus cried out, as
He taught in the temple, saying, "You both know Me, and
you know where I am from;
and I have not come of Myself, but He who sent Me is
true, whom you do not know.
29 But[a] I know Him, for I am
from Him, and He sent Me."

30 Therefore they sought
to take Him; but no one laid
a hand on Him, because His
hour had not yet come. 31 And
many of the people believed
in Him, and said, "When the
Christ comes, will He do more
signs than these which this
Man has done?"

JESUS AND THE RELIGIOUS LEADERS

32 The Pharisees heard
the crowd murmuring these
things concerning Him, and
the Pharisees and the chief
priests sent officers to take
Him. 33 Then Jesus said to
them,[a] "I shall be with you a
little while longer, and *then* I go
to Him who sent Me. 34 You will
seek Me and not find *Me,* and
where I am you cannot come."

35 Then the Jews said among
themselves, "Where does He
intend to go that we shall not
find Him? Does He intend to
go to the Dispersion among
the Greeks and teach the
Greeks? 36 What is this thing
that He said, 'You will seek Me
and not find Me, and where I
am you cannot come'?"

THE PROMISE OF THE HOLY SPIRIT

37 On the last day, that great
day of the feast, Jesus stood
and cried out, saying, "If anyone thirsts, let him come to
Me and drink. 38 He who believes in Me, as the Scripture
has said, out of his heart will
flow rivers of living water."
39 But this He spoke concerning the Spirit, whom those believing[a] in Him would receive;
for the Holy[b] Spirit was not yet
given, because Jesus was not
yet glorified.

7:26 [a] NU-Text omits *truly.* 7:29 [a] NU-Text and M-Text omit *But.* 7:33 [a] NU-Text and M-Text omit *to them.* 7:39 [a] NU-Text reads *who believed.* [b] NU-Text omits *Holy.*

WHO IS HE?

40Therefore many[a] from
the crowd, when they heard
this saying, said, "Truly this
is the Prophet." 41Others said,
"This is the Christ."

But some said, "Will the
Christ come out of Galilee?
42Has not the Scripture said
that the Christ comes from
the seed of David and from
the town of Bethlehem, where
David was?" 43So there was a
division among the people
because of Him. 44Now some
of them wanted to take Him,
but no one laid hands on Him.

REJECTED BY THE AUTHORITIES

45Then the officers came
to the chief priests and Pharisees, who said to them, "Why
have you not brought Him?"

46The officers answered, "No
man ever spoke like this Man!"

47Then the Pharisees an-
swered them, "Are you also
deceived? 48Have any of the
rulers or the Pharisees believed in Him? 49But this
crowd that does not know the
law is accursed."

50Nicodemus (he who came
to Jesus by night,[a] being one
of them) said to them, 51"Does
our law judge a man before it
hears him and knows what he
is doing?"

52They answered and said
to him, "Are you also from
Galilee? Search and look, for
no prophet has arisen[a] out of
Galilee."

AN ADULTERESS FACES THE LIGHT OF THE WORLD

53And everyone went to his
own house.[a]

8 But Jesus went to the
Mount of Olives.

2Now early[a] in the morning He came again into the
temple, and all the people
came to Him; and He sat down
and taught them. 3Then the
scribes and Pharisees brought
to Him a woman caught in
adultery. And when they had
set her in the midst, 4they said
to Him, "Teacher, this woman
was caught[a] in adultery, in the
very act. 5Now Moses, in the
law, commanded[a] us that such
should be stoned.[b] But what
do You say?"[c] 6This they said,
testing Him, that they might
have *something* of which to accuse Him. But Jesus stooped
down and wrote on the ground
with *His* finger, as though He
did not hear.[a]

7:40 [a] NU-Text reads *some.* 7:50 [a] NU-Text reads *before.* 7:52 [a] NU-Text reads *is to rise.* 7:53 [a] The words *And everyone* through *sin no more* (8:11) are bracketed by NU-Text as not original. They are present in over 900 manuscripts. 8:2 [a] M-Text reads *very early.* 8:4 [a] M-Text reads *we found this woman.* 8:5 [a] M-Text reads *in our law Moses commanded.* [b] NU-Text and M-Text read *to stone such.* [c] M-Text adds *about her.* 8:6 [a] NU-Text and M-Text omit *as though He did not hear.*

7 So when they continued
asking Him, He raised Himself up[a] and said to them, "He
who is without sin among
you, let him throw a stone
at her first." 8 And again He
stooped down and wrote on
the ground. 9 Then those who
heard *it,* being convicted by
their conscience,[a] went out
one by one, beginning with
the oldest *even* to the last. And
Jesus was left alone, and the
woman standing in the midst.
10 When Jesus had raised Himself up and saw no one but
the woman, He said to her,[a]
"Woman, where are those accusers of yours?[b] Has no one
condemned you?"

11 She said, "No one, Lord."
And Jesus said to her, "Neither do I condemn you; go
and[a] sin no more."

12 Then Jesus spoke to them
again, saying, "I am the light
of the world. He who follows
Me shall not walk in darkness,
but have the light of life."

JESUS DEFENDS HIS SELF-WITNESS

13 The Pharisees therefore
said to Him, "You bear witness
of Yourself; Your witness is
not true."

14 Jesus answered and said
to them, "Even if I bear witness of Myself, My witness is
true, for I know where I came
from and where I am going;
but you do not know where
I come from and where I am
going. 15 You judge according
to the flesh; I judge no one.
16 And yet if I do judge, My
judgment is true; for I am
not alone, but I *am* with the
Father who sent Me. 17 It is also
written in your law that the
testimony of two men is true.
18 I am One who bears witness
of Myself, and the Father who
sent Me bears witness of Me."

19 Then they said to Him,
"Where is Your Father?"
Jesus answered, "You know
neither Me nor My Father. If
you had known Me, you would
have known My Father also."

20 These words Jesus spoke
in the treasury, as He taught
in the temple; and no one laid
hands on Him, for His hour
had not yet come.

JESUS PREDICTS HIS DEPARTURE

21 Then Jesus said to them
again, "I am going away, and
you will seek Me, and will die
in your sin. Where I go you
cannot come."

22 So the Jews said, "Will
He kill Himself, because He
says, 'Where I go you cannot
come'?"

23 And He said to them,
"You are from beneath; I am
from above. You are of this

8:7 [a] M-Text reads *He looked up.* 8:9 [a] NU-Text and M-Text omit *being convicted by their conscience.* 8:10 [a] NU-Text omits *and saw no one but the woman;* M-Text reads *He saw her and said.* [b] NU-Text and M-Text omit *of yours.* 8:11 [a] NU-Text and M-Text add *from now on.*

world; I am not of this world.
24Therefore I said to you that
you will die in your sins; for if
you do not believe that I am
He, you will die in your sins."
25Then they said to Him,
"Who are You?"
And Jesus said to them,
"Just what I have been saying
to you from the beginning.
26I have many things to say
and to judge concerning you,
but He who sent Me is true;
and I speak to the world those
things which I heard from
Him."
27They did not understand
that He spoke to them of the
Father.
28Then Jesus said to them,
"When you lift up the Son of
Man, then you will know that
I am *He,* and *that* I do nothing of Myself; but as My Father taught Me, I speak these
things. 29And He who sent Me
is with Me. The Father has not
left Me alone, for I always do
those things that please Him."
30As He spoke these words,
many believed in Him.

THE TRUTH SHALL MAKE YOU FREE

31Then Jesus said to those
Jews who believed Him, "If
you abide in My word, you are
My disciples indeed. 32And
you shall know the truth, and
the truth shall make you free."
33They answered Him, "We
are Abraham's descendants,
and have never been in bondage to anyone. How *can* You
say, 'You will be made free'?"
34Jesus answered them,
"Most assuredly, I say to you,
whoever commits sin is a
slave of sin. 35And a slave
does not abide in the house
forever, *but* a son abides forever. 36Therefore if the Son
makes you free, you shall be
free indeed.

ABRAHAM'S SEED AND SATAN'S

37"I know that you are
Abraham's descendants, but
you seek to kill Me, because
My word has no place in you.
38I speak what I have seen
with My Father, and you do
what you have seen with[a] your
father."
39They answered and said
to Him, "Abraham is our father."
Jesus said to them, "If you
were Abraham's children, you
would do the works of Abraham. 40But now you seek to
kill Me, a Man who has told
you the truth which I heard
from God. Abraham did not
do this. 41You do the deeds of
your father."
Then they said to Him, "We
were not born of fornication;
we have one Father—God."
42Jesus said to them, "If
God were your Father, you
would love Me, for I proceeded
forth and came from God; nor

8:38 [a] NU-Text reads *heard from.*

have I come of Myself, but
He sent Me. [43]Why do you
not understand My speech?
Because you are not able to
listen to My word. [44]You are
of *your* father the devil, and
the desires of your father you
want to do. He was a murderer
from the beginning, and does
not stand in the truth, because
there is no truth in him. When
he speaks a lie, he speaks from
his own *resources,* for he is a
liar and the father of it. [45]But
because I tell the truth, you
do not believe Me. [46]Which of
you convicts Me of sin? And if
I tell the truth, why do you not
believe Me? [47]He who is of God
hears God's words; therefore
you do not hear, because you
are not of God."

BEFORE ABRAHAM WAS, I AM

[48]Then the Jews answered
and said to Him, "Do we not
say rightly that You are a Samaritan and have a demon?"

[49]Jesus answered, "I do not
have a demon; but I honor My
Father, and you dishonor Me.
[50]And I do not seek My *own*
glory; there is One who seeks
and judges. [51]Most assuredly,
I say to you, if anyone keeps
My word he shall never see
death."

[52]Then the Jews said to
Him, "Now we know that You
have a demon! Abraham is
dead, and the prophets; and
You say, 'If anyone keeps My
word he shall never taste
death.' [53]Are You greater than
our father Abraham, who is
dead? And the prophets are
dead. Who do You make Yourself out to be?"

[54]Jesus answered, "If I
honor Myself, My honor is
nothing. It is My Father who
honors Me, of whom you say
that He is your[a] God. [55]Yet you
have not known Him, but I
know Him. And if I say, 'I do
not know Him,' I shall be a liar
like you; but I do know Him
and keep His word. [56]Your
father Abraham rejoiced to
see My day, and he saw *it* and
was glad."

[57]Then the Jews said to
Him, "You are not yet fifty
years old, and have You seen
Abraham?"

[58]Jesus said to them, "Most
assuredly, I say to you, before
Abraham was, I AM."

[59]Then they took up stones
to throw at Him; but Jesus
hid Himself and went out of
the temple,[a] going through
the midst of them, and so
passed by.

A MAN BORN BLIND RECEIVES SIGHT

9 Now as *Jesus* passed by,
He saw a man who was
blind from birth. [2]And His
disciples asked Him, saying,

8:54 [a] NU-Text and M-Text read *our.* 8:59 [a] NU-Text omits the rest of this verse.

"Rabbi, who sinned, this man
or his parents, that he was
born blind?"
3Jesus answered, "Neither
this man nor his parents
sinned, but that the works
of God should be revealed in
him. 4I[a] must work the works
of Him who sent Me while it is
day; *the* night is coming when
no one can work. 5As long as I
am in the world, I am the light
of the world."
6When He had said these
things, He spat on the ground
and made clay with the saliva;
and He anointed the eyes of
the blind man with the clay.
7And He said to him, "Go,
wash in the pool of Siloam"
(which is translated, Sent).
So he went and washed, and
came back seeing.
8Therefore the neighbors
and those who previously had
seen that he was blind[a] said,
"Is not this he who sat and
begged?"
9Some said, "This is he."
Others *said,* "He is like him."[a]
He said, "I am *he.*"
10Therefore they said to
him, "How were your eyes
opened?"
11He answered and said, "A
Man called Jesus made clay
and anointed my eyes and said
to me, 'Go to the pool of[a] Siloam and wash.' So I went and
washed, and I received sight."
12Then they said to him,
"Where is He?"
He said, "I do not know."

THE PHARISEES EXCOMMUNICATE THE HEALED MAN

13They brought him who
formerly was blind to the
Pharisees. 14Now it was a Sabbath when Jesus made the clay
and opened his eyes. 15Then
the Pharisees also asked him
again how he had received his
sight. He said to them, "He put
clay on my eyes, and I washed,
and I see."
16Therefore some of the
Pharisees said, "This Man is
not from God, because He
does not keep the Sabbath."
Others said, "How can a
man who is a sinner do such
signs?" And there was a division among them.
17They said to the blind
man again, "What do you
say about Him because He
opened your eyes?"
He said, "He is a prophet."
18But the Jews did not believe concerning him, that he
had been blind and received
his sight, until they called the
parents of him who had received his sight. 19And they
asked them, saying, "Is this
your son, who you say was
born blind? How then does
he now see?"

9:4 [a] NU-Text reads *We.* 9:8 [a] NU-Text reads *a beggar.* 9:9 [a] NU-Text reads *"No, but he is like him."* 9:11 [a] NU-Text omits *the pool of.*

20His parents answered
them and said, "We know
that this is our son, and that
he was born blind; 21but by
what means he now sees we
do not know, or who opened
his eyes we do not know. He
is of age; ask him. He will
speak for himself." 22His parents said these *things* because
they feared the Jews, for the
Jews had agreed already that
if anyone confessed *that* He
was Christ, he would be put
out of the synagogue. 23There-
fore his parents said, "He is of
age; ask him."

24So they again called the
man who was blind, and said
to him, "Give God the glory!
We know that this Man is a
sinner."

25He answered and said,
"Whether He is a sinner *or
not* I do not know. One thing I
know: that though I was blind,
now I see."

26Then they said to him
again, "What did He do to you?
How did He open your eyes?"

27He answered them, "I
told you already, and you did
not listen. Why do you want
to hear *it* again? Do you also
want to become His disci-
ples?"

28Then they reviled him
and said, "You are His disciple,
but we are Moses' disciples.
29We know that God spoke to
Moses; *as for* this *fellow,* we do
not know where He is from."

30The man answered and
said to them, "Why, this is a
marvelous thing, that you do
not know where He is from;
yet He has opened my eyes!
31Now we know that God does
not hear sinners; but if anyone is a worshiper of God and
does His will, He hears him.
32Since the world began it has
been unheard of that anyone
opened the eyes of one who
was born blind. 33If this Man
were not from God, He could
do nothing."

34They answered and said
to him, "You were completely
born in sins, and are you
teaching us?" And they cast
him out.

TRUE VISION AND TRUE BLINDNESS

35Jesus heard that they
had cast him out; and when
He had found him, He said
to him, "Do you believe in the
Son of God?"[a]

36He answered and said,
"Who is He, Lord, that I may
believe in Him?"

37And Jesus said to him,
"You have both seen Him
and it is He who is talking
with you."

38Then he said, "Lord, I believe!" And he worshiped Him.

39And Jesus said, "For judgment I have come into this
world, that those who do not
see may see, and that those
who see may be made blind."

9:35 [a] NU-Text reads *Son of Man.*

[40]Then *some* of the Pharisees who were with Him heard these words, and said to Him, "Are we blind also?"

[41]Jesus said to them, "If you were blind, you would have no sin; but now you say, 'We see.' Therefore your sin remains.

JESUS THE TRUE SHEPHERD

10 "Most assuredly, I say to you, he who does not enter the sheepfold by the door, but climbs up some other way, the same is a thief and a robber. [2]But he who enters by the door is the shepherd of the sheep. [3]To him the doorkeeper opens, and the sheep hear his voice; and he calls his own sheep by name and leads them out. [4]And when he brings out his own sheep, he goes before them; and the sheep follow him, for they know his voice. [5]Yet they will by no means follow a stranger, but will flee from him, for they do not know the voice of strangers." [6]Jesus used this illustration, but they did not understand the things which He spoke to them.

JESUS THE GOOD SHEPHERD

[7]Then Jesus said to them again, "Most assuredly, I say to you, I am the door of the sheep. [8]All who *ever* came before Me[a] are thieves and robbers, but the sheep did not hear them. [9]I am the door. If anyone enters by Me, he will be saved, and will go in and out and find pasture. [10]The thief does not come except to steal, and to kill, and to destroy. I have come that they may have life, and that they may have *it* more abundantly.

[11]"I am the good shepherd. The good shepherd gives His life for the sheep. [12]But a hireling, *he who is* not the shepherd, one who does not own the sheep, sees the wolf coming and leaves the sheep and flees; and the wolf catches the sheep and scatters them. [13]The hireling flees because he is a hireling and does not care about the sheep. [14]I am the good shepherd; and I know My *sheep,* and am known by My own. [15]As the Father knows Me, even so I know the Father; and I lay down My life for the sheep. [16]And other sheep I have which are not of this fold; them also I must bring, and they will hear My voice; and there will be one flock *and* one shepherd.

[17]"Therefore My Father loves Me, because I lay down My life that I may take it again. [18]No one takes it from Me, but I lay it down of Myself. I have power to lay it down, and I have power to take it again. This command I have received from My Father."

10:8 [a] M-Text omits *before Me.*

19Therefore there was a division again among the Jews because of these sayings. 20And many of them said, "He has a demon and is mad. Why do you listen to Him?"

21Others said, "These are not the words of one who has a demon. Can a demon open the eyes of the blind?"

THE SHEPHERD KNOWS HIS SHEEP

22Now it was the Feast of Dedication in Jerusalem, and it was winter. 23And Jesus walked in the temple, in Solomon's porch. 24Then the Jews surrounded Him and said to Him, "How long do You keep us in doubt? If You are the Christ, tell us plainly."

25Jesus answered them, "I told you, and you do not believe. The works that I do in My Father's name, they bear witness of Me. 26But you do not believe, because you are not of My sheep, as I said to you.[a] 27My sheep hear My voice, and I know them, and they follow Me. 28And I give them eternal life, and they shall never perish; neither shall anyone snatch them out of My hand. 29My Father, who has given *them* to Me, is greater than all; and no one is able to snatch *them* out of My Father's hand. 30I and *My* Father are one."

RENEWED EFFORTS TO STONE JESUS

31Then the Jews took up stones again to stone Him. 32Jesus answered them, "Many good works I have shown you from My Father. For which of those works do you stone Me?"

33The Jews answered Him, saying, "For a good work we do not stone You, but for blasphemy, and because You, being a Man, make Yourself God."

34Jesus answered them, "Is it not written in your law, 'I said, "You are gods"'?[a] 35If He called them gods, to whom the word of God came (and the Scripture cannot be broken), 36do you say of Him whom the Father sanctified and sent into the world, 'You are blaspheming,' because I said, 'I am the Son of God'? 37If I do not do the works of My Father, do not believe Me; 38but if I do, though you do not believe Me, believe the works, that you may know and believe[a] that the Father *is* in Me, and I in Him." 39Therefore they sought again to seize Him, but He escaped out of their hand.

THE BELIEVERS BEYOND JORDAN

40And He went away again beyond the Jordan to the place where John was baptizing at first, and there He stayed.

10:26 [a] NU-Text omits *as I said to you.* 10:34 [a] Psalm 82:6 10:38 [a] NU-Text reads *understand.*

[41]Then many came to Him
and said, "John performed no
sign, but all the things that
John spoke about this Man
were true." [42]And many believed in Him there.

THE DEATH OF LAZARUS

11 Now a certain *man* was
sick, Lazarus of Bethany,
the town of Mary and her sister Martha. [2]It was *that* Mary
who anointed the Lord with
fragrant oil and wiped His feet
with her hair, whose brother
Lazarus was sick. [3]Therefore
the sisters sent to Him, saying,
"Lord, behold, he whom You
love is sick."

[4]When Jesus heard *that,* He
said, "This sickness is not unto
death, but for the glory of God,
that the Son of God may be
glorified through it."

[5]Now Jesus loved Martha
and her sister and Lazarus.
[6]So, when He heard that he
was sick, He stayed two more
days in the place where He
was. [7]Then after this He said
to *the* disciples, "Let us go to
Judea again."

[8]*The* disciples said to Him,
"Rabbi, lately the Jews sought
to stone You, and are You
going there again?"

[9]Jesus answered, "Are there
not twelve hours in the day?
If anyone walks in the day, he
does not stumble, because he
sees the light of this world.
[10]But if one walks in the night,
he stumbles, because the light
is not in him." [11]These things
He said, and after that He said
to them, "Our friend Lazarus
sleeps, but I go that I may
wake him up."

[12]Then His disciples said,
"Lord, if he sleeps he will get
well." [13]However, Jesus spoke
of his death, but they thought
that He was speaking about
taking rest in sleep.

[14]Then Jesus said to them
plainly, "Lazarus is dead.
[15]And I am glad for your sakes
that I was not there, that you
may believe. Nevertheless let
us go to him."

[16]Then Thomas, who is
called the Twin, said to his
fellow disciples, "Let us also
go, that we may die with Him."

I AM THE RESURRECTION AND THE LIFE

[17]So when Jesus came, He
found that he had already been
in the tomb four days. [18]Now
Bethany was near Jerusalem,
about two miles[a] away. [19]And
many of the Jews had joined
the women around Martha
and Mary, to comfort them
concerning their brother.

[20]Then Martha, as soon as
she heard that Jesus was coming, went and met Him, but
Mary was sitting in the house.
[21]Now Martha said to Jesus,
"Lord, if You had been here,
my brother would not have
died. [22]But even now I know

11:18 [a] Literally *fifteen stadia*

that whatever You ask of God, God will give You."

23 Jesus said to her, "Your brother will rise again."

24 Martha said to Him, "I know that he will rise again in the resurrection at the last day."

25 Jesus said to her, "I am the resurrection and the life. He who believes in Me, though he may die, he shall live. 26 And whoever lives and believes in Me shall never die. Do you believe this?"

27 She said to Him, "Yes, Lord, I believe that You are the Christ, the Son of God, who is to come into the world."

JESUS AND DEATH, THE LAST ENEMY

28 And when she had said these things, she went her way and secretly called Mary her sister, saying, "The Teacher has come and is calling for you." 29 As soon as she heard *that,* she arose quickly and came to Him. 30 Now Jesus had not yet come into the town, but was[a] in the place where Martha met Him. 31 Then the Jews who were with her in the house, and comforting her, when they saw that Mary rose up quickly and went out, followed her, saying, "She is going to the tomb to weep there."[a]

32 Then, when Mary came where Jesus was, and saw Him, she fell down at His feet, saying to Him, "Lord, if You had been here, my brother would not have died."

33 Therefore, when Jesus saw her weeping, and the Jews who came with her weeping, He groaned in the spirit and was troubled. 34 And He said, "Where have you laid him?"

They said to Him, "Lord, come and see."

35 Jesus wept. 36 Then the Jews said, "See how He loved him!"

37 And some of them said, "Could not this Man, who opened the eyes of the blind, also have kept this man from dying?"

LAZARUS RAISED FROM THE DEAD

38 Then Jesus, again groaning in Himself, came to the tomb. It was a cave, and a stone lay against it. 39 Jesus said, "Take away the stone."

Martha, the sister of him who was dead, said to Him, "Lord, by this time there is a stench, for he has been *dead* four days."

40 Jesus said to her, "Did I not say to you that if you would believe you would see the glory of God?" 41 Then they took away the stone *from the place* where the dead man was lying.[a] And

11:30 [a] NU-Text adds *still.* 11:31 [a] NU-Text reads *supposing that she was going to the tomb to weep there.* 11:41 [a] NU-Text omits *from the place where the dead man was lying.*

Jesus lifted up *His* eyes and said, "Father, I thank You that You have heard Me. 42And I know that You always hear Me, but because of the people who are standing by I said *this,* that they may believe that You sent Me." 43Now when He had said these things, He cried with a loud voice, "Lazarus, come forth!" 44And he who had died came out bound hand and foot with graveclothes, and his face was wrapped with a cloth. Jesus said to them, "Loose him, and let him go."

THE PLOT TO KILL JESUS

45Then many of the Jews who had come to Mary, and had seen the things Jesus did, believed in Him. 46But some of them went away to the Pharisees and told them the things Jesus did. 47Then the chief priests and the Pharisees gathered a council and said, "What shall we do? For this Man works many signs. 48If we let Him alone like this, everyone will believe in Him, and the Romans will come and take away both our place and nation."

49And one of them, Caiaphas, being high priest that year, said to them, "You know nothing at all, 50nor do you consider that it is expedient for us[a] that one man should die for the people, and not that the whole nation should perish." 51Now this he did not say on his own *authority;* but being high priest that year he prophesied that Jesus would die for the nation, 52and not for that nation only, but also that He would gather together in one the children of God who were scattered abroad.

53Then, from that day on, they plotted to put Him to death. 54Therefore Jesus no longer walked openly among the Jews, but went from there into the country near the wilderness, to a city called Ephraim, and there remained with His disciples.

55And the Passover of the Jews was near, and many went from the country up to Jerusalem before the Passover, to purify themselves. 56Then they sought Jesus, and spoke among themselves as they stood in the temple, "What do you think—that He will not come to the feast?" 57Now both the chief priests and the Pharisees had given a command, that if anyone knew where He was, he should report *it,* that they might seize Him.

THE ANOINTING AT BETHANY

12 Then, six days before the Passover, Jesus came to Bethany, where Lazarus was who had been dead,[a] whom

11:50 [a] NU-Text reads *you.* 12:1 [a] NU-Text omits *who had been dead.*

He had raised from the dead.
2There they made Him a
supper; and Martha served,
but Lazarus was one of those
who sat at the table with Him.
3Then Mary took a pound of
very costly oil of spikenard,
anointed the feet of Jesus, and
wiped His feet with her hair.
And the house was filled with
the fragrance of the oil.
4But one of His disciples,
Judas Iscariot, Simon's *son,*
who would betray Him, said,
5"Why was this fragrant oil
not sold for three hundred
denarii[a] and given to the
poor?" 6This he said, not that
he cared for the poor, but because he was a thief, and had
the money box; and he used
to take what was put in it.
7But Jesus said, "Let her
alone; she has kept[a] this for
the day of My burial. 8For the
poor you have with you always, but Me you do not have
always."

THE PLOT TO KILL LAZARUS

9Now a great many of the
Jews knew that He was there;
and they came, not for Jesus'
sake only, but that they might
also see Lazarus, whom He
had raised from the dead.
10But the chief priests plotted
to put Lazarus to death also,
11because on account of him
many of the Jews went away
and believed in Jesus.

THE TRIUMPHAL ENTRY

12The next day a great multitude that had come to the
feast, when they heard that
Jesus was coming to Jerusalem, 13took branches of palm
trees and went out to meet
Him, and cried out:

"Hosanna!
'Blessed *is* He who
comes in the name
of the LORD!'[a]
The King of Israel!"

14Then Jesus, when He had
found a young donkey, sat on
it; as it is written:

15"Fear not, daughter
of Zion;
Behold, your King
is coming,
Sitting on a donkey's
colt."[a]

16His disciples did not
understand these things at
first; but when Jesus was glorified, then they remembered
that these things were written
about Him and *that* they had
done these things to Him.
17Therefore the people,
who were with Him when
He called Lazarus out of his
tomb and raised him from
the dead, bore witness. 18For
this reason the people also
met Him, because they heard
that He had done this sign.

12:5 [a] About one year's wages for a worker 12:7 [a] NU-Text reads *that she may keep.* 12:13 [a] Psalm 118:26 12:15 [a] Zechariah 9:9

19The Pharisees therefore said
among themselves, "You see
that you are accomplishing
nothing. Look, the world has
gone after Him!"

THE FRUITFUL GRAIN OF WHEAT

20Now there were certain
Greeks among those who
came up to worship at the
feast. 21Then they came to
Philip, who was from Bethsaida of Galilee, and asked
him, saying, "Sir, we wish to
see Jesus."
22Philip came and told Andrew, and in turn Andrew and
Philip told Jesus.
23But Jesus answered them,
saying, "The hour has come
that the Son of Man should be
glorified. 24Most assuredly, I
say to you, unless a grain of
wheat falls into the ground and
dies, it remains alone; but if it
dies, it produces much grain.
25He who loves his life will lose
it, and he who hates his life in
this world will keep it for eternal life. 26If anyone serves Me,
let him follow Me; and where
I am, there My servant will be
also. If anyone serves Me, him
My Father will honor.

JESUS PREDICTS HIS DEATH ON THE CROSS

27"Now My soul is troubled,
and what shall I say? 'Father,
save Me from this hour'? But
for this purpose I came to this
hour. 28Father, glorify Your
name."
Then a voice came from
heaven, *saying,* "I have both
glorified *it* and will glorify *it*
again."
29Therefore the people who
stood by and heard *it* said that
it had thundered. Others said,
"An angel has spoken to Him."
30Jesus answered and said,
"This voice did not come because of Me, but for your sake.
31Now is the judgment of this
world; now the ruler of this
world will be cast out. 32And
I, if I am lifted up from the
earth, will draw all *peoples* to
Myself." 33This He said, signifying by what death He would
die.
34The people answered
Him, "We have heard from the
law that the Christ remains
forever; and how *can* You say,
'The Son of Man must be lifted
up'? Who is this Son of Man?"
35Then Jesus said to them,
"A little while longer the light
is with you. Walk while you
have the light, lest darkness
overtake you; he who walks
in darkness does not know
where he is going. 36While you
have the light, believe in the
light, that you may become
sons of light." These things
Jesus spoke, and departed,
and was hidden from them.

WHO HAS BELIEVED OUR REPORT?

37But although He had
done so many signs before
them, they did not believe in
Him, 38that the word of Isaiah

the prophet might be fulfilled,
which he spoke:

"Lord, who has believed
our report?
And to whom has the
arm of the LORD
been revealed?"[a]

39 Therefore they could not
believe, because Isaiah said
again:

40 "He has blinded their
eyes and hardened
their hearts,
Lest they should see
with *their* eyes,
Lest they should
understand with *their*
hearts and turn,
So that I should
heal them."[a]

41 These things Isaiah said
when[a] he saw His glory and
spoke of Him.

WALK IN THE LIGHT

42 Nevertheless even among
the rulers many believed in
Him, but because of the Pharisees they did not confess *Him,*
lest they should be put out
of the synagogue; 43 for they
loved the praise of men more
than the praise of God.

44 Then Jesus cried out and
said, "He who believes in Me,
believes not in Me but in Him
who sent Me. 45 And he who
sees Me sees Him who sent
Me. 46 I have come *as* a light
into the world, that whoever
believes in Me should not
abide in darkness. 47 And if
anyone hears My words and
does not believe,[a] I do not
judge him; for I did not come
to judge the world but to save
the world. 48 He who rejects
Me, and does not receive My
words, has that which judges
him—the word that I have
spoken will judge him in the
last day. 49 For I have not spoken on My own *authority;*
but the Father who sent Me
gave Me a command, what I
should say and what I should
speak. 50 And I know that His
command is everlasting life.
Therefore, whatever I speak,
just as the Father has told Me,
so I speak."

JESUS WASHES THE DISCIPLES' FEET

13 Now before the Feast of
the Passover, when Jesus
knew that His hour had come
that He should depart from
this world to the Father, having loved His own who were
in the world, He loved them
to the end.

2 And supper being ended,[a]
the devil having already put
it into the heart of Judas Iscariot, Simon's *son,* to betray

12:38 [a] Isaiah 53:1 12:40 [a] Isaiah 6:10 12:41 [a] NU-Text reads *because.* 12:47 [a] NU-Text reads *keep them.* 13:2 [a] NU-Text reads *And during supper.*

Him, 3 Jesus, knowing that the
Father had given all things
into His hands, and that He
had come from God and was
going to God, 4 rose from
supper and laid aside His
garments, took a towel and
girded Himself. 5 After that,
He poured water into a basin
and began to wash the disciples' feet, and to wipe *them*
with the towel with which He
was girded. 6 Then He came to
Simon Peter. And *Peter* said to
Him, "Lord, are You washing
my feet?"

7 Jesus answered and said
to him, "What I am doing you
do not understand now, but
you will know after this."

8 Peter said to Him, "You
shall never wash my feet!"

Jesus answered him, "If I
do not wash you, you have no
part with Me."

9 Simon Peter said to Him,
"Lord, not my feet only, but
also *my* hands and *my* head!"

10 Jesus said to him, "He
who is bathed needs only
to wash *his* feet, but is completely clean; and you are
clean, but not all of you." 11 For
He knew who would betray
Him; therefore He said, "You
are not all clean."

12 So when He had washed
their feet, taken His garments,
and sat down again, He said
to them, "Do you know what
I have done to you? 13 You call
Me Teacher and Lord, and you
say well, for *so* I am. 14 If I then,
your Lord and Teacher, have
washed your feet, you also
ought to wash one another's
feet. 15 For I have given you an
example, that you should do
as I have done to you. 16 Most
assuredly, I say to you, a servant is not greater than his
master; nor is he who is sent
greater than he who sent him.
17 If you know these things,
blessed are you if you do
them.

JESUS IDENTIFIES HIS BETRAYER

18 "I do not speak concerning all of you. I know whom
I have chosen; but that the
Scripture may be fulfilled,
'He who eats bread with Me[a]
has lifted up his heel against
Me.'[b] 19 Now I tell you before it
comes, that when it does come
to pass, you may believe that
I am *He.* 20 Most assuredly, I
say to you, he who receives
whomever I send receives
Me; and he who receives Me
receives Him who sent Me."

21 When Jesus had said
these things, He was troubled in spirit, and testified
and said, "Most assuredly, I
say to you, one of you will betray Me." 22 Then the disciples
looked at one another, perplexed about whom He spoke.

23 Now there was leaning
on Jesus' bosom one of His
disciples, whom Jesus loved.

13:18 [a] NU-Text reads *My bread.* [b] Psalm 41:9

24Simon Peter therefore motioned to him to ask who it
was of whom He spoke.
25Then, leaning back[a] on
Jesus' breast, he said to Him,
"Lord, who is it?"
26Jesus answered, "It is he
to whom I shall give a piece of
bread when I have dipped *it*."
And having dipped the bread,
He gave *it* to Judas Iscariot,
the son of Simon. 27Now after
the piece of bread, Satan entered him. Then Jesus said to
him, "What you do, do quickly."
28But no one at the table knew
for what reason He said this
to him. 29For some thought,
because Judas had the money
box, that Jesus had said to him,
"Buy *those things* we need for
the feast," or that he should
give something to the poor.
30Having received the
piece of bread, he then went
out immediately. And it was
night.

THE NEW COMMANDMENT

31So, when he had gone
out, Jesus said, "Now the Son
of Man is glorified, and God
is glorified in Him. 32If God
is glorified in Him, God will
also glorify Him in Himself,
and glorify Him immedi-
ately. 33Little children, I shall
be with you a little while longer. You will seek Me; and as
I said to the Jews, 'Where I
am going, you cannot come,'
so now I say to you. 34A new
commandment I give to you,
that you love one another; as
I have loved you, that you also
love one another. 35By this all
will know that you are My disciples, if you have love for one
another."

JESUS PREDICTS PETER'S DENIAL

36Simon Peter said to Him,
"Lord, where are You going?"
Jesus answered him,
"Where I am going you cannot
follow Me now, but you shall
follow Me afterward."
37Peter said to Him, "Lord,
why can I not follow You now?
I will lay down my life for Your
sake."
38Jesus answered him,
"Will you lay down your life
for My sake? Most assuredly,
I say to you, the rooster shall
not crow till you have denied
Me three times.

THE WAY, THE TRUTH, AND THE LIFE

14 "Let not your heart be
troubled; you believe in
God, believe also in Me. 2In
My Father's house are many
mansions;[a] if *it were* not *so*,
I would have told you. I go
to prepare a place for you.[b]

13:25 [a] NU-Text and M-Text add *thus*. 14:2 [a] Literally *dwellings* [b] NU-Text adds a word which would cause the text to read either *if it were not so, would I have told you that I go to prepare a place for you?* or *if it were not so I would have told you; for I go to prepare a place for you.*

3 And if I go and prepare a
place for you, I will come
again and receive you to Myself; that where I am, *there*
you may be also. 4 And where
I go you know, and the way
you know."

5 Thomas said to Him,
"Lord, we do not know where
You are going, and how can
we know the way?"

6 Jesus said to him, "I am
the way, the truth, and the life.
No one comes to the Father
except through Me.

THE FATHER REVEALED

7 "If you had known Me,
you would have known My
Father also; and from now
on you know Him and have
seen Him."

8 Philip said to Him, "Lord,
show us the Father, and it is
sufficient for us."

9 Jesus said to him, "Have
I been with you so long, and
yet you have not known Me,
Philip? He who has seen Me
has seen the Father; so how
can you say, 'Show us the Father'? 10 Do you not believe
that I am in the Father, and
the Father in Me? The words
that I speak to you I do not
speak on My own *authority;*
but the Father who dwells in
Me does the works. 11 Believe
Me that I *am* in the Father
and the Father in Me, or else
believe Me for the sake of the
works themselves.

THE ANSWERED PRAYER

12 "Most assuredly, I say to
you, he who believes in Me,
the works that I do he will do
also; and greater *works* than
these he will do, because I go
to My Father. 13 And whatever
you ask in My name, that I
will do, that the Father may
be glorified in the Son. 14 If you
ask[a] anything in My name, I
will do *it.*

JESUS PROMISES ANOTHER HELPER

15 "If you love Me, keep[a]
My commandments. 16 And I
will pray the Father, and He
will give you another Helper,
that He may abide with you
forever— 17 the Spirit of truth,
whom the world cannot re-
ceive, because it neither sees
Him nor knows Him; but you
know Him, for He dwells with
you and will be in you. 18 I will
not leave you orphans; I will
come to you.

INDWELLING OF THE FATHER AND THE SON

19 "A little while longer and
the world will see Me no more,
but you will see Me. Because
I live, you will live also. 20 At
that day you will know that
I *am* in My Father, and you
in Me, and I in you. 21 He who
has My commandments and
keeps them, it is he who loves
Me. And he who loves Me will

14:14 [a] NU-Text adds *Me.* 14:15 [a] NU-Text reads *you will keep.*

be loved by My Father, and
I will love him and manifest
Myself to him."
22Judas (not Iscariot) said
to Him, "Lord, how is it that
You will manifest Yourself to
us, and not to the world?"
23Jesus answered and said
to him, "If anyone loves Me,
he will keep My word; and My
Father will love him, and We
will come to him and make
Our home with him. 24He who
does not love Me does not
keep My words; and the word
which you hear is not Mine
but the Father's who sent Me.

THE GIFT OF HIS PEACE

25"These things I have spoken to you while being present
with you. 26But the Helper, the
Holy Spirit, whom the Father
will send in My name, He
will teach you all things, and
bring to your remembrance
all things that I said to you.
27Peace I leave with you, My
peace I give to you; not as the
world gives do I give to you.
Let not your heart be troubled,
neither let it be afraid. 28You
have heard Me say to you, 'I
am going away and coming
back to you.' If you loved Me,
you would rejoice because I
said,[a] 'I am going to the Father,' for My Father is greater
than I.
29"And now I have told you
before it comes, that when it
does come to pass, you may
believe. 30I will no longer talk
much with you, for the ruler
of this world is coming, and
he has nothing in Me. 31But
that the world may know that
I love the Father, and as the
Father gave Me command-
ment, so I do. Arise, let us go
from here.

THE TRUE VINE

15 "I am the true vine, and
My Father is the vine-
dresser. 2Every branch in
Me that does not bear fruit
He takes away;[a] and every
branch that bears fruit He
prunes, that it may bear more
fruit. 3You are already clean
because of the word which I
have spoken to you. 4Abide
in Me, and I in you. As the
branch cannot bear fruit of
itself, unless it abides in the
vine, neither can you, unless
you abide in Me.
5"I am the vine, you *are* the
branches. He who abides in
Me, and I in him, bears much
fruit; for without Me you can
do nothing. 6If anyone does
not abide in Me, he is cast out
as a branch and is withered;
and they gather them and
throw *them* into the fire, and
they are burned. 7If you abide
in Me, and My words abide in
you, you will[a] ask what you
desire, and it shall be done
for you. 8By this My Father is

14:28 [a] NU-Text omits *I said.* 15:2 [a] Or *lifts up* 15:7 [a] NU-Text omits *you will.*

glorified, that you bear much
fruit; so you will be My disciples.

LOVE AND JOY PERFECTED

9"As the Father loved Me, I
also have loved you; abide in
My love. 10If you keep My commandments, you will abide in
My love, just as I have kept My
Father's commandments and
abide in His love.

11"These things I have spoken to you, that My joy may
remain in you, and *that* your
joy may be full. 12This is My
commandment, that you love
one another as I have loved
you. 13Greater love has no one
than this, than to lay down
one's life for his friends. 14You
are My friends if you do whatever I command you. 15No
longer do I call you servants,
for a servant does not know
what his master is doing; but
I have called you friends, for
all things that I heard from My
Father I have made known to
you. 16You did not choose Me,
but I chose you and appointed
you that you should go and
bear fruit, and *that* your fruit
should remain, that whatever
you ask the Father in My name
He may give you. 17These
things I command you, that
you love one another.

THE WORLD'S HATRED

18"If the world hates you,
you know that it hated Me before *it hated* you. 19If you were
of the world, the world would
love its own. Yet because you
are not of the world, but I
chose you out of the world,
therefore the world hates
you. 20Remember the word
that I said to you, 'A servant
is not greater than his master.' If they persecuted Me,
they will also persecute you.
If they kept My word, they will
keep yours also. 21But all these
things they will do to you for
My name's sake, because they
do not know Him who sent
Me. 22If I had not come and
spoken to them, they would
have no sin, but now they have
no excuse for their sin. 23He
who hates Me hates My Fa-
ther also. 24If I had not done
among them the works which
no one else did, they would
have no sin; but now they have
seen and also hated both Me
and My Father. 25But *this happened* that the word might be
fulfilled which is written in
their law, 'They hated Me without a cause.'[a]

THE COMING REJECTION

26"But when the Helper
comes, whom I shall send to
you from the Father, the Spirit
of truth who proceeds from
the Father, He will testify of
Me. 27And you also will bear
witness, because you have
been with Me from the be-
ginning.

15:25 [a] Psalm 69:4

16 "These things I have
spoken to you, that you
should not be made to stumble. 2They will put you out of
the synagogues; yes, the time
is coming that whoever kills
you will think that he offers
God service. 3And these things
they will do to you[a] because
they have not known the Father nor Me. 4But these things
I have told you, that when the[a]
time comes, you may remember that I told you of them.

"And these things I did not
say to you at the beginning,
because I was with you.

THE WORK OF THE HOLY SPIRIT

5"But now I go away to
Him who sent Me, and none
of you asks Me, 'Where are
You going?' 6But because I
have said these things to you,
sorrow has filled your heart.
7Nevertheless I tell you the
truth. It is to your advantage
that I go away; for if I do not
go away, the Helper will not
come to you; but if I depart,
I will send Him to you. 8And
when He has come, He will
convict the world of sin, and
of righteousness, and of judgment: 9of sin, because they
do not believe in Me; 10of
righteousness, because I go
to My Father and you see Me
no more; 11of judgment, because the ruler of this world
is judged.

12"I still have many things
to say to you, but you cannot
bear *them* now. 13However,
when He, the Spirit of truth,
has come, He will guide you
into all truth; for He will not
speak on His own *authority,*
but whatever He hears He
will speak; and He will tell
you things to come. 14He will
glorify Me, for He will take of
what is Mine and declare *it* to
you. 15All things that the Father has are Mine. Therefore I
said that He will take of Mine
and declare *it* to you.[a]

SORROW WILL TURN TO JOY

16"A little while, and you
will not see Me; and again a
little while, and you will see
Me, because I go to the Father."

17Then *some* of His disciples said among themselves,
"What is this that He says to
us, 'A little while, and you will
not see Me; and again a little
while, and you will see Me';
and, 'because I go to the Father'?" 18They said therefore,
"What is this that He says, 'A
little while'? We do not know
what He is saying."

19Now Jesus knew that they
desired to ask Him, and He
said to them, "Are you inquir-

16:3 [a] NU-Text and M-Text omit *to you.* 16:4 [a] NU-Text reads *their.* 16:15 [a] NU-Text and M-Text read *He takes of Mine and will declare it to you.*

ing among yourselves about
what I said, 'A little while, and
you will not see Me; and again
a little while, and you will see
Me'? 20Most assuredly, I say
to you that you will weep and
lament, but the world will rejoice; and you will be sorrowful, but your sorrow will be
turned into joy. 21A woman,
when she is in labor, has sorrow because her hour has
come; but as soon as she has
given birth to the child, she
no longer remembers the anguish, for joy that a human
being has been born into the
world. 22Therefore you now
have sorrow; but I will see you
again and your heart will rejoice, and your joy no one will
take from you.

23"And in that day you
will ask Me nothing. Most assuredly, I say to you, whatever
you ask the Father in My name
He will give you. 24Until now
you have asked nothing in
My name. Ask, and you will
receive, that your joy may be
full.

JESUS CHRIST HAS OVERCOME THE WORLD

25"These things I have spoken to you in figurative language; but the time is coming
when I will no longer speak
to you in figurative language,
but I will tell you plainly about
the Father. 26In that day you
will ask in My name, and I
do not say to you that I shall
pray the Father for you; 27for
the Father Himself loves you,
because you have loved Me,
and have believed that I came
forth from God. 28I came forth
from the Father and have
come into the world. Again, I
leave the world and go to the
Father."

29His disciples said to Him,
"See, now You are speaking
plainly, and using no figure
of speech! 30Now we are sure
that You know all things, and
have no need that anyone
should question You. By this
we believe that You came
forth from God."

31Jesus answered them,
"Do you now believe? 32In-
deed the hour is coming, yes,
has now come, that you will be
scattered, each to his own, and
will leave Me alone. And yet I
am not alone, because the Father is with Me. 33These things
I have spoken to you, that in
Me you may have peace. In
the world you will[a] have tribulation; but be of good cheer,
I have overcome the world."

JESUS PRAYS FOR HIMSELF

17 Jesus spoke these words,
lifted up His eyes to
heaven, and said: "Father, the
hour has come. Glorify Your
Son, that Your Son also may
glorify You, 2as You have given
Him authority over all flesh,
that He should[a] give eternal

16:33 [a] NU-Text and M-Text omit *will*. 17:2 [a] M-Text reads *shall*.

life to as many as You have given Him. 3 And this is eternal life, that they may know You, the only true God, and Jesus Christ whom You have sent. 4 I have glorified You on the earth. I have finished the work which You have given Me to do. 5 And now, O Father, glorify Me together with Yourself, with the glory which I had with You before the world was.

JESUS PRAYS FOR HIS DISCIPLES

6 "I have manifested Your name to the men whom You have given Me out of the world. They were Yours, You gave them to Me, and they have kept Your word. 7 Now they have known that all things which You have given Me are from You. 8 For I have given to them the words which You have given Me; and they have received *them,* and have known surely that I came forth from You; and they have believed that You sent Me.

9 "I pray for them. I do not pray for the world but for those whom You have given Me, for they are Yours. 10 And all Mine are Yours, and Yours are Mine, and I am glorified in them. 11 Now I am no longer in the world, but these are in the world, and I come to You. Holy Father, keep through Your name those whom You have given Me,[a] that they may be one as We *are.* 12 While I was with them in the world,[a] I kept them in Your name. Those whom You gave Me I have kept;[b] and none of them is lost except the son of perdition, that the Scripture might be fulfilled. 13 But now I come to You, and these things I speak in the world, that they may have My joy fulfilled in themselves. 14 I have given them Your word; and the world has hated them because they are not of the world, just as I am not of the world. 15 I do not pray that You should take them out of the world, but that You should keep them from the evil one. 16 They are not of the world, just as I am not of the world. 17 Sanctify them by Your truth. Your word is truth. 18 As You sent Me into the world, I also have sent them into the world. 19 And for their sakes I sanctify Myself, that they also may be sanctified by the truth.

JESUS PRAYS FOR ALL BELIEVERS

20 "I do not pray for these alone, but also for those who will[a] believe in Me through their word; 21 that they all may be one, as You, Father, *are* in Me, and I in You; that they

17:11 [a] NU-Text and M-Text read *keep them through Your name which You have given Me.* 17:12 [a] NU-Text omits *in the world.* [b] NU-Text reads *in Your name which You gave Me. And I guarded them;* (or *it;*). 17:20 [a] NU-Text and M-Text omit *will.*

also may be one in Us, that
the world may believe that
You sent Me. 22And the glory
which You gave Me I have
given them, that they may be
one just as We are one: 23I in
them, and You in Me; that they
may be made perfect in one,
and that the world may know
that You have sent Me, and
have loved them as You have
loved Me.

24"Father, I desire that
they also whom You gave
Me may be with Me where I
am, that they may behold My
glory which You have given
Me; for You loved Me before
the foundation of the world.
25O righteous Father! The
world has not known You, but
I have known You; and these
have known that You sent Me.
26And I have declared to them
Your name, and will declare *it,*
that the love with which You
loved Me may be in them, and
I in them."

BETRAYAL AND ARREST IN GETHSEMANE

18 When Jesus had spoken
these words, He went
out with His disciples over
the Brook Kidron, where there
was a garden, which He and
His disciples entered. 2And
Judas, who betrayed Him, also
knew the place; for Jesus often
met there with His disciples.
3Then Judas, having received
a detachment *of troops,* and
officers from the chief priests
and Pharisees, came there
with lanterns, torches, and
weapons. 4Jesus therefore,
knowing all things that would
come upon Him, went forward
and said to them, "Whom are
you seeking?"

5They answered Him,
"Jesus of Nazareth."

Jesus said to them, "I am
He." And Judas, who betrayed
Him, also stood with them.
6Now when He said to them,
"I am *He,*" they drew back and
fell to the ground.

7Then He asked them again,
"Whom are you seeking?"

And they said, "Jesus of
Nazareth."

8Jesus answered, "I have
told you that I am *He.* Therefore, if you seek Me, let these
go their way," 9that the saying
might be fulfilled which He
spoke, "Of those whom You
gave Me I have lost none."

10Then Simon Peter, having
a sword, drew it and struck the
high priest's servant, and cut
off his right ear. The servant's
name was Malchus.

11So Jesus said to Peter, "Put
your sword into the sheath.
Shall I not drink the cup which
My Father has given Me?"

BEFORE THE HIGH PRIEST

12Then the detachment *of
troops* and the captain and the
officers of the Jews arrested
Jesus and bound Him. 13And
they led Him away to Annas
first, for he was the father-
in-law of Caiaphas who was
high priest that year. 14Now

it was Caiaphas who advised
the Jews that it was expedient
that one man should die for
the people.

PETER DENIES JESUS

[15]And Simon Peter followed
Jesus, and so *did* another[a] disciple.
Now that disciple was
known to the high priest, and
went with Jesus into the courtyard
of the high priest. [16]But
Peter stood at the door outside.
Then the other disciple, who
was known to the high priest,
went out and spoke to her who
kept the door, and brought
Peter in. [17]Then the servant
girl who kept the door said to
Peter, "You are not also *one* of
this Man's disciples, are you?"

He said, "I am not."

[18]Now the servants and officers
who had made a fire of
coals stood there, for it was
cold, and they warmed themselves.
And Peter stood with
them and warmed himself.

JESUS QUESTIONED BY THE HIGH PRIEST

[19]The high priest then
asked Jesus about His disciples
and His doctrine.

[20]Jesus answered him, "I
spoke openly to the world. I
always taught in synagogues
and in the temple, where the
Jews always meet,[a] and in secret
I have said nothing. [21]Why
do you ask Me? Ask those who
have heard Me what I said to
them. Indeed they know what
I said."

[22]And when He had said
these things, one of the officers
who stood by struck Jesus
with the palm of his hand, saying,
"Do You answer the high
priest like that?"

[23]Jesus answered him, "If I
have spoken evil, bear witness
of the evil; but if well, why do
you strike Me?"

[24]Then Annas sent Him
bound to Caiaphas the high
priest.

PETER DENIES TWICE MORE

[25]Now Simon Peter stood
and warmed himself. Therefore
they said to him, "You are
not also *one* of His disciples,
are you?"

He denied *it* and said, "I
am not!"

[26]One of the servants of the
high priest, a relative *of him*
whose ear Peter cut off, said,
"Did I not see you in the garden
with Him?" [27]Peter then
denied again; and immediately
a rooster crowed.

IN PILATE'S COURT

[28]Then they led Jesus from
Caiaphas to the Praetorium,
and it was early morning. But
they themselves did not go
into the Praetorium, lest they
should be defiled, but that
they might eat the Passover.

18:15 [a] M-Text reads *the other.* 18:20 [a] NU-Text reads *where all the Jews meet.*

29Pilate then went out to them
and said, "What accusation do
you bring against this Man?"
30They answered and said
to him, "If He were not an
evildoer, we would not have
delivered Him up to you."
31Then Pilate said to them,
"You take Him and judge Him
according to your law."
Therefore the Jews said to
him, "It is not lawful for us to
put anyone to death," 32that
the saying of Jesus might
be fulfilled which He spoke,
signifying by what death He
would die.
33Then Pilate entered the
Praetorium again, called
Jesus, and said to Him, "Are
You the King of the Jews?"
34Jesus answered him, "Are
you speaking for yourself
about this, or did others tell
you this concerning Me?"
35Pilate answered, "Am I a
Jew? Your own nation and the
chief priests have delivered
You to me. What have You
done?"
36Jesus answered, "My
kingdom is not of this world.
If My kingdom were of this
world, My servants would
fight, so that I should not be
delivered to the Jews; but now
My kingdom is not from here."
37Pilate therefore said to
Him, "Are You a king then?"
Jesus answered, "You say
rightly that I am a king. For
this cause I was born, and for
this cause I have come into
the world, that I should bear
witness to the truth. Everyone
who is of the truth hears My
voice."
38Pilate said to Him, "What
is truth?" And when he had
said this, he went out again
to the Jews, and said to them,
"I find no fault in Him at all.

TAKING THE PLACE OF BARABBAS

39"But you have a custom
that I should release someone
to you at the Passover. Do you
therefore want me to release
to you the King of the Jews?"
40Then they all cried again,
saying, "Not this Man, but Barabbas!" Now Barabbas was a
robber.

THE SOLDIERS MOCK JESUS

19 So then Pilate took Jesus
and scourged *Him.* 2And
the soldiers twisted a crown of
thorns and put *it* on His head,
and they put on Him a purple
robe. 3Then they said,[a] "Hail,
King of the Jews!" And they
struck Him with their hands.
4Pilate then went out again,
and said to them, "Behold, I
am bringing Him out to you,
that you may know that I find
no fault in Him."

PILATE'S DECISION

5Then Jesus came out,
wearing the crown of thorns
and the purple robe. And

19:3 [a] NU-Text reads *And they came up to Him and said.*

Pilate said to them, "Behold
the Man!"
6Therefore, when the chief
priests and officers saw Him,
they cried out, saying, "Crucify
Him, crucify *Him!*"
Pilate said to them, "You
take Him and crucify *Him,* for
I find no fault in Him."
7The Jews answered him,
"We have a law, and according
to our[a] law He ought to die,
because He made Himself the
Son of God."
8Therefore, when Pilate
heard that saying, he was the
more afraid, 9and went again
into the Praetorium, and said
to Jesus, "Where are You
from?" But Jesus gave him
no answer.
10Then Pilate said to Him,
"Are You not speaking to me?
Do You not know that I have
power to crucify You, and
power to release You?"
11Jesus answered, "You
could have no power at all
against Me unless it had been
given you from above. Therefore the one who delivered Me
to you has the greater sin."
12From then on Pilate
sought to release Him, but
the Jews cried out, saying, "If
you let this Man go, you are
not Caesar's friend. Whoever
makes himself a king speaks
against Caesar."
13When Pilate therefore
heard that saying, he brought
Jesus out and sat down in the
judgment seat in a place that
is called *The* Pavement, but
in Hebrew, Gabbatha. 14Now
it was the Preparation Day of
the Passover, and about the
sixth hour. And he said to the
Jews, "Behold your King!"
15But they cried out, "Away
with *Him,* away with *Him!* Crucify Him!"
Pilate said to them, "Shall
I crucify your King?"
The chief priests answered,
"We have no king but Caesar!"
16Then he delivered Him
to them to be crucified. Then
they took Jesus and led *Him*
away.[a]

THE KING ON A CROSS

17And He, bearing His cross,
went out to a place called *the
Place* of a Skull, which is called
in Hebrew, Golgotha, 18where
they crucified Him, and two
others with Him, one on either side, and Jesus in the
center. 19Now Pilate wrote a
title and put *it* on the cross.
And the writing was:

JESUS OF NAZARETH,
THE KING OF THE JEWS.

20Then many of the Jews read
this title, for the place where
Jesus was crucified was near
the city; and it was written in
Hebrew, Greek, *and* Latin.
21Therefore the chief

19:7 [a] NU-Text reads *the law.* 19:16 [a] NU-Text omits *and led Him away.*

priests of the Jews said to Pilate, "Do not write, 'The King
of the Jews,' but, 'He said, "I
am the King of the Jews." ' "
22Pilate answered, "What I
have written, I have written."
23Then the soldiers, when
they had crucified Jesus, took
His garments and made four
parts, to each soldier a part,
and also the tunic. Now the
tunic was without seam,
woven from the top in one
piece. 24They said therefore
among themselves, "Let us
not tear it, but cast lots for
it, whose it shall be," that the
Scripture might be fulfilled
which says:

"They divided My
garments among them,
And for My clothing
they cast lots."[a]

Therefore the soldiers did
these things.

BEHOLD YOUR MOTHER

25Now there stood by the
cross of Jesus His mother, and
His mother's sister, Mary the
wife of Clopas, and Mary Magdalene. 26When Jesus therefore saw His mother, and the
disciple whom He loved standing by, He said to His mother,
"Woman, behold your son!"
27Then He said to the disciple,
"Behold your mother!" And
from that hour that disciple
took her to his own *home.*

IT IS FINISHED

28After this, Jesus, knowing[a] that all things were now
accomplished, that the Scripture might be fulfilled, said, "I
thirst!" 29Now a vessel full of
sour wine was sitting there;
and they filled a sponge with
sour wine, put *it* on hyssop,
and put *it* to His mouth. 30So
when Jesus had received the
sour wine, He said, "It is finished!" And bowing His head,
He gave up His spirit.

JESUS' SIDE IS PIERCED

31Therefore, because it was
the Preparation *Day,* that the
bodies should not remain
on the cross on the Sabbath
(for that Sabbath was a high
day), the Jews asked Pilate
that their legs might be broken, and *that* they might be
taken away. 32Then the soldiers came and broke the legs
of the first and of the other
who was crucified with Him.
33But when they came to Jesus
and saw that He was already
dead, they did not break His
legs. 34But one of the soldiers
pierced His side with a spear,
and immediately blood and
water came out. 35And he who
has seen has testified, and
his testimony is true; and he
knows that he is telling the
truth, so that you may believe.
36For these things were done
that the Scripture should be
fulfilled, "Not *one* of His bones

19:24 [a] Psalm 22:18 19:28 [a] M-Text reads *seeing.*

shall be broken."[a] 37And again
another Scripture says, "They
shall look on Him whom they
pierced."[a]

JESUS BURIED IN JOSEPH'S TOMB

38After this, Joseph of Arimathea, being a disciple of
Jesus, but secretly, for fear
of the Jews, asked Pilate that
he might take away the body
of Jesus; and Pilate gave *him*
permission. So he came and
took the body of Jesus. 39And
Nicodemus, who at first came
to Jesus by night, also came,
bringing a mixture of myrrh
and aloes, about a hundred
pounds. 40Then they took the
body of Jesus, and bound it in
strips of linen with the spices,
as the custom of the Jews is to
bury. 41Now in the place where
He was crucified there was a
garden, and in the garden a
new tomb in which no one
had yet been laid. 42So there
they laid Jesus, because of the
Jews' Preparation *Day,* for the
tomb was nearby.

THE EMPTY TOMB

20 Now the first *day* of the
week Mary Magdalene
went to the tomb early, while
it was still dark, and saw *that*
the stone had been taken away
from the tomb. 2Then she ran
and came to Simon Peter, and
to the other disciple, whom
Jesus loved, and said to them,
"They have taken away the
Lord out of the tomb, and we
do not know where they have
laid Him."

3Peter therefore went out,
and the other disciple, and
were going to the tomb. 4So
they both ran together, and
the other disciple outran
Peter and came to the tomb
first. 5And he, stooping down
and looking in, saw the linen
cloths lying *there;* yet he did
not go in. 6Then Simon Peter
came, following him, and
went into the tomb; and he
saw the linen cloths lying
there, 7and the handkerchief
that had been around His
head, not lying with the linen
cloths, but folded together in
a place by itself. 8Then the
other disciple, who came to
the tomb first, went in also;
and he saw and believed. 9For
as yet they did not know the
Scripture, that He must rise
again from the dead. 10Then
the disciples went away again
to their own homes.

MARY MAGDALENE SEES THE RISEN LORD

11But Mary stood outside by
the tomb weeping, and as she
wept she stooped down *and*
looked into the tomb. 12And
she saw two angels in white
sitting, one at the head and
the other at the feet, where the

19:36 [a] Exodus 12:46; Numbers 9:12; Psalm 34:20 19:37 [a] Zechariah 12:10

body of Jesus had lain. 13Then
they said to her, "Woman, why
are you weeping?"
She said to them, "Because
they have taken away my Lord,
and I do not know where they
have laid Him."
14Now when she had said
this, she turned around and
saw Jesus standing *there,* and
did not know that it was Jesus.
15Jesus said to her, "Woman,
why are you weeping? Whom
are you seeking?"
She, supposing Him to be
the gardener, said to Him, "Sir,
if You have carried Him away,
tell me where You have laid
Him, and I will take Him away."
16Jesus said to her, "Mary!"
She turned and said to
Him,[a] "Rabboni!" (which is
to say, Teacher).
17Jesus said to her, "Do not
cling to Me, for I have not yet
ascended to My Father; but
go to My brethren and say to
them, 'I am ascending to My
Father and your Father, and *to*
My God and your God.'"
18Mary Magdalene came
and told the disciples that she
had seen the Lord,[a] and *that*
He had spoken these things
to her.

THE APOSTLES COMMISSIONED

19Then, the same day at
evening, being the first *day* of
the week, when the doors were
shut where the disciples were
assembled,[a] for fear of the
Jews, Jesus came and stood
in the midst, and said to them,
"Peace *be* with you." 20When
He had said this, He showed
them *His* hands and His side.
Then the disciples were glad
when they saw the Lord.
21So Jesus said to them
again, "Peace to you! As the
Father has sent Me, I also send
you." 22And when He had said
this, He breathed on *them,* and
said to them, "Receive the
Holy Spirit. 23If you forgive
the sins of any, they are forgiven them; if you retain the
sins of any, they are retained."

SEEING AND BELIEVING

24Now Thomas, called the
Twin, one of the twelve, was
not with them when Jesus
came. 25The other disciples
therefore said to him, "We
have seen the Lord."
So he said to them, "Unless
I see in His hands the print of
the nails, and put my finger
into the print of the nails, and
put my hand into His side, I
will not believe."
26And after eight days His
disciples were again inside,
and Thomas with them. Jesus
came, the doors being shut,
and stood in the midst, and
said, "Peace to you!" 27Then
He said to Thomas, "Reach
your finger here, and look

20:16 [a] NU-Text adds *in Hebrew.* 20:18 [a] NU-Text reads *disciples, "I have seen the Lord," ....* 20:19 [a] NU-Text omits *assembled.*

at My hands; and reach your
hand *here,* and put *it* into My
side. Do not be unbelieving,
but believing."

28And Thomas answered
and said to Him, "My Lord and
my God!"

29Jesus said to him, "Thomas,[a] because you have seen Me,
you have believed. Blessed *are*
those who have not seen and
yet have believed."

THAT YOU MAY BELIEVE

30And truly Jesus did many
other signs in the presence of
His disciples, which are not
written in this book; 31but
these are written that you may
believe that Jesus is the Christ,
the Son of God, and that believing you may have life in
His name.

BREAKFAST BY THE SEA

21 After these things Jesus
showed Himself again
to the disciples at the Sea of
Tiberias, and in this way He
showed *Himself:* 2Simon Peter,
Thomas called the Twin, Nathanael of Cana in Galilee,
the *sons* of Zebedee, and two
others of His disciples were
together. 3Simon Peter said
to them, "I am going fishing."

They said to him, "We are
going with you also." They
went out and immediately[a]
got into the boat, and that
night they caught nothing.
4But when the morning had
now come, Jesus stood on the
shore; yet the disciples did not
know that it was Jesus. 5Then
Jesus said to them, "Children,
have you any food?"

They answered Him, "No."

6And He said to them, "Cast
the net on the right side of the
boat, and you will find *some.*"
So they cast, and now they
were not able to draw it in because of the multitude of fish.

7Therefore that disciple
whom Jesus loved said to
Peter, "It is the Lord!" Now
when Simon Peter heard that
it was the Lord, he put on *his*
outer garment (for he had removed it), and plunged into
the sea. 8But the other disciples came in the little boat
(for they were not far from
land, but about two hundred
cubits), dragging the net with
fish. 9Then, as soon as they
had come to land, they saw a
fire of coals there, and fish laid
on it, and bread. 10Jesus said to
them, "Bring some of the fish
which you have just caught."

11Simon Peter went up and
dragged the net to land, full of
large fish, one hundred and
fifty-three; and although there
were so many, the net was not
broken. 12Jesus said to them,
"Come *and* eat breakfast." Yet
none of the disciples dared
ask Him, "Who are You?"—
knowing that it was the Lord.

20:29 [a] NU-Text and M-Text omit *Thomas.*
21:3 [a] NU-Text omits *immediately.*

13 Jesus then came and took the bread and gave it to them, and likewise the fish.

14 This *is* now the third time Jesus showed Himself to His disciples after He was raised from the dead.

JESUS RESTORES PETER

15 So when they had eaten breakfast, Jesus said to Simon Peter, "Simon, *son* of Jonah,[a] do you love Me more than these?"

He said to Him, "Yes, Lord; You know that I love You."

He said to him, "Feed My lambs."

16 He said to him again a second time, "Simon, *son* of Jonah,[a] do you love Me?"

He said to Him, "Yes, Lord; You know that I love You."

He said to him, "Tend My sheep."

17 He said to him the third time, "Simon, *son* of Jonah,[a] do you love Me?" Peter was grieved because He said to him the third time, "Do you love Me?"

And he said to Him, "Lord, You know all things; You know that I love You."

Jesus said to him, "Feed My sheep. 18 Most assuredly, I say to you, when you were younger, you girded yourself and walked where you wished; but when you are old, you will stretch out your hands, and another will gird you and carry *you* where you do not wish." 19 This He spoke, signifying by what death he would glorify God. And when He had spoken this, He said to him, "Follow Me."

THE BELOVED DISCIPLE AND HIS BOOK

20 Then Peter, turning around, saw the disciple whom Jesus loved following, who also had leaned on His breast at the supper, and said, "Lord, who is the one who betrays You?" 21 Peter, seeing him, said to Jesus, "But Lord, what *about* this man?"

22 Jesus said to him, "If I will that he remain till I come, what *is that* to you? You follow Me."

23 Then this saying went out among the brethren that this disciple would not die. Yet Jesus did not say to him that he would not die, but, "If I will that he remain till I come, what *is that* to you?"

24 This is the disciple who testifies of these things, and wrote these things; and we know that his testimony is true.

25 And there are also many other things that Jesus did, which if they were written one by one, I suppose that even the world itself could not contain the books that would be written. Amen.

21:15 [a] NU-Text reads *John*. **21:16** [a] NU-Text reads *John*. **21:17** [a] NU-Text reads *John*.

THE ACTS OF THE APOSTLES

PROLOGUE

1 The former account I made, O Theophilus, of all that Jesus began both to do and teach, 2until the day in which He was taken up, after He through the Holy Spirit had given commandments to the apostles whom He had chosen, 3to whom He also presented Himself alive after His suffering by many infallible proofs, being seen by them during forty days and speaking of the things pertaining to the kingdom of God.

THE HOLY SPIRIT PROMISED

4And being assembled together with *them,* He commanded them not to depart from Jerusalem, but to wait for the Promise of the Father, "which," *He said,* "you have heard from Me; 5for John truly baptized with water, but you shall be baptized with the Holy Spirit not many days from now." 6Therefore, when they had come together, they asked Him, saying, "Lord, will You at this time restore the kingdom to Israel?" 7And He said to them, "It is not for you to know times or seasons which the Father has put in His own authority. 8But you shall receive power when the Holy Spirit has come upon you; and you shall be witnesses to Me[a] in Jerusalem, and in all Judea and Samaria, and to the end of the earth."

JESUS ASCENDS TO HEAVEN

9Now when He had spoken these things, while they watched, He was taken up, and a cloud received Him out of their sight. 10And while they looked steadfastly toward heaven as He went up, behold, two men stood by them in white apparel, 11who also said, "Men of Galilee, why do you stand gazing up into heaven? This *same* Jesus, who was taken up from you into heaven, will so come in like manner as you saw Him go into heaven."

THE UPPER ROOM PRAYER MEETING

12Then they returned to Jerusalem from the mount called Olivet, which is near Jerusalem, a Sabbath day's journey. 13And when they had entered, they went up into

1:8 [a] NU-Text reads *My witnesses.*

the upper room where they
were staying: Peter, James,
John, and Andrew; Philip and
Thomas; Bartholomew and
Matthew; James *the son* of Alphaeus and Simon the Zealot;
and Judas *the son* of James.
14These all continued with one
accord in prayer and supplication,[a] with the women and
Mary the mother of Jesus, and
with His brothers.

MATTHIAS CHOSEN

15And in those days Peter
stood up in the midst of the
disciples[a] (altogether the
number of names was about
a hundred and twenty), and
said, 16"Men *and* brethren,
this Scripture had to be fulfilled, which the Holy Spirit
spoke before by the mouth of
David concerning Judas, who
became a guide to those who
arrested Jesus; 17for he was
numbered with us and ob-
tained a part in this ministry."
18(Now this man purchased
a field with the wages of iniquity; and falling headlong,
he burst open in the middle
and all his entrails gushed
out. 19And it became known
to all those dwelling in Jerusalem; so that field is called
in their own language, Akel
Dama, that is, Field of Blood.)
20"For it is written in the
Book of Psalms:

'Let his dwelling place
be desolate,
And let no one live in it';[a]

and,

'Let[b] another take
his office.'[c]

21"Therefore, of these men
who have accompanied us all
the time that the Lord Jesus
went in and out among us,
22beginning from the baptism
of John to that day when He
was taken up from us, one of
these must become a witness
with us of His resurrection."
23And they proposed two:
Joseph called Barsabas, who
was surnamed Justus, and
Matthias. 24And they prayed
and said, "You, O Lord, who
know the hearts of all, show
which of these two You have
chosen 25to take part in this
ministry and apostleship from
which Judas by transgression
fell, that he might go to his
own place." 26And they cast
their lots, and the lot fell on
Matthias. And he was num-
bered with the eleven apostles.

COMING OF THE HOLY SPIRIT

2 When the Day of Pentecost
had fully come, they were
all with one accord[a] in one
place. 2And suddenly there

1:14 [a] NU-Text omits *and supplication.* 1:15 [a] NU-Text reads *brethren.* 1:20 [a] Psalm 69:25 [b] Psalm 109:8 [c] Greek *episkopen,* position of overseer 2:1 [a] NU-Text reads *together.*

came a sound from heaven,
as of a rushing mighty wind,
and it filled the whole house
where they were sitting. 3Then
there appeared to them divided tongues, as of fire, and
one sat upon each of them.
4And they were all filled with
the Holy Spirit and began to
speak with other tongues, as
the Spirit gave them utterance.

THE CROWD'S RESPONSE

5And there were dwelling
in Jerusalem Jews, devout
men, from every nation under
heaven. 6And when this sound
occurred, the multitude came
together, and were confused,
because everyone heard them
speak in his own language.
7Then they were all amazed
and marveled, saying to one
another, "Look, are not all
these who speak Galileans?
8And how *is it that* we hear,
each in our own language in
which we were born? 9Parthi-
ans and Medes and Elamites,
those dwelling in Mesopotamia, Judea and Cappadocia,
Pontus and Asia, 10Phrygia and
Pamphylia, Egypt and the parts
of Libya adjoining Cyrene, vis-
itors from Rome, both Jews
and proselytes, 11Cretans and
Arabs—we hear them speak-
ing in our own tongues the
wonderful works of God." 12So
they were all amazed and perplexed, saying to one another,
"Whatever could this mean?"
13Others mocking said,
"They are full of new wine."

PETER'S SERMON

14But Peter, standing up
with the eleven, raised his
voice and said to them, "Men
of Judea and all who dwell in
Jerusalem, let this be known
to you, and heed my words.
15For these are not drunk, as
you suppose, since it is *only*
the third hour of the day. 16But
this is what was spoken by the
prophet Joel:

17 'And it shall come
to pass in the last
days, says God,
That I will pour out of
My Spirit on all flesh;
Your sons and your
daughters shall
prophesy,
Your young men
shall see visions,
Your old men shall
dream dreams.
18 And on My menservants
and on My
maidservants
I will pour out My
Spirit in those days;
And they shall prophesy.
19 I will show wonders
in heaven above
And signs in the
earth beneath:
Blood and fire and
vapor of smoke.
20 The sun shall be turned
into darkness,
And the moon into blood,
Before the coming of the
great and awesome
day of the LORD.
21 And it shall come to pass

That whoever calls on
the name of the LORD
Shall be saved.'[a]

22"Men of Israel, hear these
words: Jesus of Nazareth, a
Man attested by God to you by
miracles, wonders, and signs
which God did through Him in
your midst, as you yourselves
also know— 23Him, being
delivered by the determined
purpose and foreknowledge
of God, you have taken[a] by
lawless hands, have crucified,
and put to death; 24whom God
raised up, having loosed the
pains of death, because it was
not possible that He should
be held by it. 25For David says
concerning Him:

'I foresaw the LORD
always before my face,
For He is at my right hand,
that I may not be shaken.
26 Therefore my heart
rejoiced, and my
tongue was glad;
Moreover my flesh also
will rest in hope.
27 For You will not leave
my soul in Hades,
Nor will You allow
Your Holy One to
see corruption.
28 You have made known
to me the ways of life;
You will make me full of
joy in Your presence.'[a]

29"Men *and* brethren, let
me speak freely to you of the
patriarch David, that he is
both dead and buried, and his
tomb is with us to this day.
30Therefore, being a prophet,
and knowing that God had
sworn with an oath to him
that of the fruit of his body, according to the flesh, He would
raise up the Christ to sit on his
throne,[a] 31he, foreseeing this,
spoke concerning the resurrection of the Christ, that His
soul was not left in Hades, nor
did His flesh see corruption.
32This Jesus God has raised
up, of which we are all witnesses. 33Therefore being
exalted to the right hand of
God, and having received
from the Father the promise
of the Holy Spirit, He poured
out this which you now see
and hear.
34"For David did not ascend
into the heavens, but he says
himself:

'The LORD said
to my Lord,
"Sit at My right hand,
35 Till I make Your enemies
Your footstool."'[a]

36"Therefore let all the
house of Israel know as-
suredly that God has made
this Jesus, whom you crucified, both Lord and Christ."

2:21 [a] Joel 2:28–32 2:23 [a] NU-Text omits *have taken.* 2:28 [a] Psalm 16:8–11 2:30 [a] NU-Text omits *according to the flesh, He would raise up the Christ* and completes the verse with *He would seat one on his throne.* 2:35 [a] Psalm 110:1

37Now when they heard
this, they were cut to the heart,
and said to Peter and the rest
of the apostles, "Men *and*
brethren, what shall we do?"
38Then Peter said to them,
"Repent, and let every one of
you be baptized in the name
of Jesus Christ for the remission of sins; and you shall
receive the gift of the Holy
Spirit. 39For the promise is to
you and to your children, and
to all who are afar off, as many
as the Lord our God will call."

A VITAL CHURCH GROWS

40And with many other
words he testified and exhorted them, saying, "Be saved
from this perverse generation." 41Then those who gladly[a]
received his word were baptized; and that day about three
thousand souls were added *to*
them. 42And they continued
steadfastly in the apostles'
doctrine and fellowship, in
the breaking of bread, and
in prayers. 43Then fear came
upon every soul, and many
wonders and signs were done
through the apostles. 44Now
all who believed were together,
and had all things in common,
45and sold their possessions
and goods, and divided them
among all, as anyone had need.
46So continuing daily with
one accord in the temple, and
breaking bread from house
to house, they ate their food
with gladness and simplicity
of heart, 47praising God and
having favor with all the people. And the Lord added to the
church[a] daily those who were
being saved.

A LAME MAN HEALED

3 Now Peter and John went
up together to the temple
at the hour of prayer, the ninth
hour. 2And a certain man lame
from his mother's womb was
carried, whom they laid daily
at the gate of the temple which
is called Beautiful, to ask alms
from those who entered the
temple; 3who, seeing Peter
and John about to go into
the temple, asked for alms.
4And fixing his eyes on him,
with John, Peter said, "Look
at us." 5So he gave them his
attention, expecting to receive
something from them. 6Then
Peter said, "Silver and gold I do
not have, but what I do have I
give you: In the name of Jesus
Christ of Nazareth, rise up and
walk." 7And he took him by the
right hand and lifted *him* up,
and immediately his feet and
ankle bones received strength.
8So he, leaping up, stood and
walked and entered the temple with them—walking, leaping, and praising God. 9And all
the people saw him walking
and praising God. 10Then they
knew that it was he who sat
begging alms at the Beautiful
Gate of the temple; and they

2:41 [a] NU-Text omits *gladly.* 2:47 [a] NU-Text omits *to the church.*

were filled with wonder and
amazement at what had happened to him.

PREACHING IN SOLOMON'S PORTICO

11Now as the lame man who
was healed held on to Peter
and John, all the people ran
together to them in the porch
which is called Solomon's,
greatly amazed. 12So when
Peter saw *it,* he responded to
the people: "Men of Israel,
why do you marvel at this? Or
why look so intently at us, as
though by our own power or
godliness we had made this
man walk? 13The God of Abraham, Isaac, and Jacob, the
God of our fathers, glorified
His Servant Jesus, whom you
delivered up and denied in
the presence of Pilate, when
he was determined to let *Him*
go. 14But you denied the Holy
One and the Just, and asked
for a murderer to be granted
to you, 15and killed the Prince
of life, whom God raised from
the dead, of which we are
witnesses. 16And His name,
through faith in His name, has
made this man strong, whom
you see and know. Yes, the faith
which *comes* through Him has
given him this perfect soundness in the presence of you all.

17"Yet now, brethren, I
know that you did *it* in ignorance, as *did* also your rulers.
18But those things which God
foretold by the mouth of all
His prophets, that the Christ
would suffer, He has thus fulfilled. 19Repent therefore and
be converted, that your sins
may be blotted out, so that
times of refreshing may come
from the presence of the Lord,
20and that He may send Jesus
Christ, who was preached to
you before,[a] 21whom heaven
must receive until the times of
restoration of all things, which
God has spoken by the mouth
of all His holy prophets since
the world began. 22For Moses
truly said to the fathers, 'The
LORD your God will raise up
for you a Prophet like me from
your brethren. Him you shall
hear in all things, whatever He
says to you. 23And it shall be
that every soul who will not
hear that Prophet shall be utterly destroyed from among
the people.'[a] 24Yes, and all the
prophets, from Samuel and
those who follow, as many as
have spoken, have also foretold[a] these days. 25You are
sons of the prophets, and of
the covenant which God made
with our fathers, saying to
Abraham, 'And in your seed
all the families of the earth
shall be blessed.'[a] 26To you
first, God, having raised up
His Servant Jesus, sent Him

3:20 [a] NU-Text and M-Text read *Christ Jesus, who was ordained for you before.* 3:23 [a] Deuteronomy 18:15, 18, 19 3:24 [a] NU-Text and M-Text read *proclaimed.* 3:25 [a] Genesis 22:18; 26:4; 28:14

to bless you, in turning away
every one *of you* from your
iniquities."

PETER AND JOHN ARRESTED

4 Now as they spoke to the
people, the priests, the
captain of the temple, and
the Sadducees came upon
them, 2being greatly disturbed
that they taught the people
and preached in Jesus the
resurrection from the dead.
3And they laid hands on them,
and put *them* in custody until
the next day, for it was already
evening. 4However, many of
those who heard the word
believed; and the number of
the men came to be about five
thousand.

ADDRESSING THE SANHEDRIN

5And it came to pass, on
the next day, that their rulers,
elders, and scribes, 6as well
as Annas the high priest, Caiaphas, John, and Alexander,
and as many as were of the
family of the high priest, were
gathered together at Jerusalem. 7And when they had set
them in the midst, they asked,
"By what power or by what
name have you done this?"
8Then Peter, filled with the
Holy Spirit, said to them, "Rul-
ers of the people and elders
of Israel: 9If we this day are
judged for a good deed *done*
to a helpless man, by what
means he has been made
well, 10let it be known to you
all, and to all the people of Israel, that by the name of Jesus
Christ of Nazareth, whom you
crucified, whom God raised
from the dead, by Him this
man stands here before you
whole. 11This is the 'stone
which was rejected by you
builders, which has become
the chief cornerstone.'[a] 12Nor
is there salvation in any other,
for there is no other name
under heaven given among
men by which we must be
saved."

THE NAME OF JESUS FORBIDDEN

13Now when they saw the
boldness of Peter and John,
and perceived that they were
uneducated and untrained
men, they marveled. And
they realized that they had
been with Jesus. 14And seeing the man who had been
healed standing with them,
they could say nothing against
it. 15But when they had commanded them to go aside out
of the council, they conferred
among themselves, 16saying,
"What shall we do to these
men? For, indeed, that a notable miracle has been done
through them *is* evident to
all who dwell in Jerusalem,
and we cannot deny *it.* 17But
so that it spreads no further

4:11 [a] Psalm 118:22

among the people, let us severely threaten them, that
from now on they speak to
no man in this name."
18So they called them and
commanded them not to
speak at all nor teach in the
name of Jesus. 19But Peter
and John answered and said
to them, "Whether it is right
in the sight of God to listen
to you more than to God, you
judge. 20For we cannot but
speak the things which we
have seen and heard." 21So
when they had further threat-
ened them, they let them go,
finding no way of punishing
them, because of the people,
since they all glorified God for
what had been done. 22For the
man was over forty years old
on whom this miracle of healing had been performed.

PRAYER FOR BOLDNESS

23And being let go, they
went to their own *companions*
and reported all that the chief
priests and elders had said to
them. 24So when they heard
that, they raised their voice to
God with one accord and said:
"Lord, You *are* God, who made
heaven and earth and the sea,
and all that is in them, 25who
by the mouth of Your servant
David[a] have said:

'Why did the
nations rage,
And the people plot
vain things?
26 The kings of the earth
took their stand,
And the rulers were
gathered together
Against the LORD and
against His Christ.'[a]

27"For truly against Your
holy Servant Jesus, whom
You anointed, both Herod and
Pontius Pilate, with the Gentiles and the people of Israel,
were gathered together 28to
do whatever Your hand and
Your purpose determined before to be done. 29Now, Lord,
look on their threats, and
grant to Your servants that
with all boldness they may
speak Your word, 30by stretching out Your hand to heal, and
that signs and wonders may
be done through the name of
Your holy Servant Jesus."
31And when they had
prayed, the place where they
were assembled together
was shaken; and they were
all filled with the Holy Spirit,
and they spoke the word of
God with boldness.

SHARING IN ALL THINGS

32Now the multitude of
those who believed were of
one heart and one soul; neither did anyone say that any
of the things he possessed
was his own, but they had

4:25 [a] NU-Text reads *who through the Holy Spirit, by the mouth of our father, Your servant David.* 4:26 [a] Psalm 2:1, 2

all things in common. 33And with great power the apostles gave witness to the resurrection of the Lord Jesus. And great grace was upon them all. 34Nor was there anyone among them who lacked; for all who were possessors of lands or houses sold them, and brought the proceeds of the things that were sold, 35and laid *them* at the apostles' feet; and they distributed to each as anyone had need.

36And Joses,[a] who was also named Barnabas by the apostles (which is translated Son of Encouragement), a Levite of the country of Cyprus, 37having land, sold *it,* and brought the money and laid *it* at the apostles' feet.

LYING TO THE HOLY SPIRIT

5 But a certain man named Ananias, with Sapphira his wife, sold a possession. 2And he kept back *part* of the proceeds, his wife also being aware *of it,* and brought a certain part and laid *it* at the apostles' feet. 3But Peter said, "Ananias, why has Satan filled your heart to lie to the Holy Spirit and keep back *part* of the price of the land for yourself? 4While it remained, was it not your own? And after it was sold, was it not in your own control? Why have you conceived this thing in your heart? You have not lied to men but to God."

5Then Ananias, hearing these words, fell down and breathed his last. So great fear came upon all those who heard these things. 6And the young men arose and wrapped him up, carried *him* out, and buried *him.*

7Now it was about three hours later when his wife came in, not knowing what had happened. 8And Peter answered her, "Tell me whether you sold the land for so much?"

She said, "Yes, for so much."

9Then Peter said to her, "How is it that you have agreed together to test the Spirit of the Lord? Look, the feet of those who have buried your husband *are* at the door, and they will carry you out." 10Then immediately she fell down at his feet and breathed her last. And the young men came in and found her dead, and carrying *her* out, buried *her* by her husband. 11So great fear came upon all the church and upon all who heard these things.

CONTINUING POWER IN THE CHURCH

12And through the hands of the apostles many signs and wonders were done among the people. And they were all with one accord in Solomon's Porch. 13Yet none of the rest dared join them, but the people esteemed them

4:36 [a] NU-Text reads *Joseph.*

highly. [14]And believers were
increasingly added to the
Lord, multitudes of both men
and women, [15]so that they
brought the sick out into the
streets and laid *them* on beds
and couches, that at least the
shadow of Peter passing by
might fall on some of them.
[16]Also a multitude gathered
from the surrounding cities
to Jerusalem, bringing sick
people and those who were
tormented by unclean spirits,
and they were all healed.

IMPRISONED APOSTLES FREED

[17]Then the high priest rose
up, and all those who *were*
with him (which is the sect
of the Sadducees), and they
were filled with indignation,
[18]and laid their hands on the
apostles and put them in
the common prison. [19]But
at night an angel of the Lord
opened the prison doors and
brought them out, and said,
[20]"Go, stand in the temple
and speak to the people all
the words of this life."

[21]And when they heard *that,*
they entered the temple early
in the morning and taught.
But the high priest and those
with him came and called the
council together, with all the
elders of the children of Israel, and sent to the prison to
have them brought.

APOSTLES ON TRIAL AGAIN

[22]But when the officers
came and did not find them in
the prison, they returned and
reported, [23]saying, "Indeed
we found the prison shut securely, and the guards standing outside[a] before the doors;
but when we opened them, we
found no one inside!" [24]Now
when the high priest,[a] the
captain of the temple, and
the chief priests heard these
things, they wondered what
the outcome would be. [25]So
one came and told them, saying,[a] "Look, the men whom
you put in prison are standing
in the temple and teaching
the people!"

[26]Then the captain went
with the officers and brought
them without violence, for
they feared the people, lest
they should be stoned. [27]And
when they had brought them,
they set *them* before the council. And the high priest asked
them, [28]saying, "Did we not
strictly command you not to
teach in this name? And look,
you have filled Jerusalem with
your doctrine, and intend to
bring this Man's blood on us!"

[29]But Peter and the *other*
apostles answered and said:
"We ought to obey God rather
than men. [30]The God of our
fathers raised up Jesus whom
you murdered by hanging on
a tree. [31]Him God has exalted

5:23 [a] NU-Text and M-Text omit *outside.* 5:24 [a] NU-Text omits *the high priest.* 5:25 [a] NU-Text and M-Text omit *saying.*

to His right hand *to be* Prince
and Savior, to give repentance
to Israel and forgiveness of
sins. 32And we are His witnesses to these things, and *so*
also *is* the Holy Spirit whom
God has given to those who
obey Him."

GAMALIEL'S ADVICE

33When they heard *this,*
they were furious and plotted to kill them. 34Then one
in the council stood up, a
Pharisee named Gamaliel, a
teacher of the law held in respect by all the people, and
commanded them to put the
apostles outside for a little
while. 35And he said to them:
"Men of Israel, take heed to
yourselves what you intend
to do regarding these men.
36For some time ago Theudas
rose up, claiming to be some-
body. A number of men, about
four hundred, joined him. He
was slain, and all who obeyed
him were scattered and came
to nothing. 37After this man,
Judas of Galilee rose up in the
days of the census, and drew
away many people after him.
He also perished, and all who
obeyed him were dispersed.
38And now I say to you, keep
away from these men and let
them alone; for if this plan
or this work is of men, it will
come to nothing; 39but if it is
of God, you cannot overthrow
it—lest you even be found to
fight against God."

40And they agreed with
him, and when they had called
for the apostles and beaten
them, they commanded that
they should not speak in the
name of Jesus, and let them
go. 41So they departed from
the presence of the council, rejoicing that they were counted
worthy to suffer shame for
His[a] name. 42And daily in the
temple, and in every house,
they did not cease teaching
and preaching Jesus *as* the
Christ.

SEVEN CHOSEN TO SERVE

6 Now in those days, when
the number of the disciples was multiplying, there
arose a complaint against the
Hebrews by the Hellenists,[a]
because their widows were
neglected in the daily distri-
bution. 2Then the twelve summoned the multitude of the
disciples and said, "It is not
desirable that we should leave
the word of God and serve
tables. 3Therefore, brethren,
seek out from among you
seven men of *good* reputation,
full of the Holy Spirit and wisdom, whom we may appoint
over this business; 4but we will
give ourselves continually to
prayer and to the ministry of
the word."

5And the saying pleased

5:41 [a] NU-Text reads *the name;* M-Text reads *the name of Jesus.* 6:1 [a] That is, Greek-speaking Jews

the whole multitude. And they
chose Stephen, a man full of
faith and the Holy Spirit, and
Philip, Prochorus, Nicanor,
Timon, Parmenas, and Nic-
olas, a proselyte from Antioch, 6whom they set before
the apostles; and when they
had prayed, they laid hands
on them.

7Then the word of God
spread, and the number of the
disciples multiplied greatly in
Jerusalem, and a great many
of the priests were obedient
to the faith.

STEPHEN ACCUSED OF BLASPHEMY

8And Stephen, full of faith[a]
and power, did great wonders
and signs among the people.
9Then there arose some from
what is called the Synagogue
of the Freedmen (Cyrenians,
Alexandrians, and those
from Cilicia and Asia), disputing with Stephen. 10And
they were not able to resist
the wisdom and the Spirit by
which he spoke. 11Then they
secretly induced men to say,
"We have heard him speak
blasphemous words against
Moses and God." 12And they
stirred up the people, the
elders, and the scribes; and
they came upon *him*, seized
him, and brought *him* to the
council. 13They also set up
false witnesses who said, "This
man does not cease to speak
blasphemous[a] words against
this holy place and the law;
14for we have heard him say
that this Jesus of Nazareth will
destroy this place and change
the customs which Moses delivered to us." 15And all who
sat in the council, looking
steadfastly at him, saw his face
as the face of an angel.

STEPHEN'S ADDRESS: THE CALL OF ABRAHAM

7 Then the high priest said,
"Are these things so?"

2And he said, "Brethren
and fathers, listen: The God of
glory appeared to our father
Abraham when he was in Mesopotamia, before he dwelt in
Haran, 3and said to him, 'Get
out of your country and from
your relatives, and come to
a land that I will show you.'[a]
4Then he came out of the land
of the Chaldeans and dwelt in
Haran. And from there, when
his father was dead, He moved
him to this land in which you
now dwell. 5And *God* gave him
no inheritance in it, not even
enough to set his foot on. But
even when *Abraham* had no
child, He promised to give it
to him for a possession, and
to his descendants after him.
6But God spoke in this way:
that his descendants would
dwell in a foreign land, and
that they would bring them

6:8 [a] NU-Text reads *grace*. 6:13 [a] NU-Text omits *blasphemous*. 7:3 [a] Genesis 12:1

into bondage and oppress
them four hundred years.
7‘And the nation to whom
they will be in bondage I will
judge,’[a] said God, ‘and after
that they shall come out and
serve Me in this place.’[b] 8Then
He gave him the covenant of
circumcision; and so *Abraham*
begot Isaac and circumcised
him on the eighth day; and
Isaac *begot* Jacob, and Jacob
begot the twelve patriarchs.

THE PATRIARCHS IN EGYPT

9“And the patriarchs, be-
coming envious, sold Joseph
into Egypt. But God was with
him 10and delivered him out
of all his troubles, and gave
him favor and wisdom in the
presence of Pharaoh, king
of Egypt; and he made him
governor over Egypt and all
his house. 11Now a famine
and great trouble came over
all the land of Egypt and Canaan, and our fathers found
no sustenance. 12But when Jacob heard that there was grain
in Egypt, he sent out our fathers first. 13And the second
time Joseph was made known
to his brothers, and Joseph's
family became known to the
Pharaoh. 14Then Joseph sent
and called his father Jacob
and all his relatives to *him,*
seventy-five[a] people. 15So Jacob *went down to Egypt; and*
he died, he and our fathers.
16And they were carried back
to Shechem and laid in the
tomb that Abraham bought
for a sum of money from the
sons of Hamor, *the father* of
Shechem.

GOD DELIVERS ISRAEL BY MOSES

17“But when the time of the
promise drew near which God
had sworn to Abraham, the
people grew and multiplied
in Egypt 18till another king
arose who did not know Joseph. 19This man dealt treacherously with our people, and
oppressed our forefathers,
making them expose their
babies, so that they might not
live. 20At this time Moses was
born, and was well pleasing to
God; and he was brought up
in his father's house for three
months. 21But when he was set
out, Pharaoh's daughter took
him away and brought him up
as her own son. 22And Moses
was learned in all the wisdom
of the Egyptians, and was
mighty in words and deeds.

23“Now when he was forty
years old, it came into his
heart to visit his brethren, the
children of Israel. 24And seeing one of *them* suffer wrong,
he defended and avenged
him who was oppressed, and
struck down the Egyptian.
25*For he supposed* that his
brethren would have under-

7:7 [a] Genesis 15:14 [b] Exodus 3:12 7:14 [a] Or *seventy* (compare Exodus 1:5)

stood that God would deliver
them by his hand, but they
did not understand. 26And the
next day he appeared to *two
of* them as they were fighting,
and *tried to* reconcile them,
saying, 'Men, you are brethren; why do you wrong one
another?' 27But he who did
his neighbor wrong pushed
him away, saying, 'Who made
you a ruler and a judge over
us? 28Do you want to kill me
as you did the Egyptian yesterday?'[a] 29Then, at this saying, Moses fled and became a
dweller in the land of Midian,
where he had two sons.

30"And when forty years
had passed, an Angel of the
Lord[a] appeared to him in a
flame of fire in a bush, in the
wilderness of Mount Sinai.
31When Moses saw *it,* he
marveled at the sight; and as
he drew near to observe, the
voice of the Lord came to him,
32*saying,* 'I *am* the God of your
fathers—the God of Abraham,
the God of Isaac, and the God
of Jacob.'[a] And Moses trembled and dared not look.
33'Then the LORD said to him,
"Take your sandals off your
feet, for the place where you
stand is holy ground. 34I have
surely seen the oppression of
My people who are in Egypt; I
have heard their groaning and
have come down to deliver
them. And now come, I will
send you to Egypt."'[a]

35"This Moses whom they
rejected, saying, 'Who made
you a ruler and a judge?'[a] is the
one God sent *to be* a ruler and
a deliverer by the hand of the
Angel who appeared to him in
the bush. 36He brought them
out, after he had shown wonders and signs in the land of
Egypt, and in the Red Sea, and
in the wilderness forty years.

ISRAEL REBELS AGAINST GOD

37"This is that Moses who
said to the children of Israel,[a]
'The LORD your God will raise
up for you a Prophet like me
from your brethren. Him you
shall hear.'[b]

38"This is he who was in
the congregation in the wilderness with the Angel who
spoke to him on Mount Sinai,
and *with* our fathers, the one
who received the living oracles to give to us, 39whom our
fathers would not obey, but rejected. And in their hearts they
turned back to Egypt, 40saying
to Aaron, 'Make us gods to go
before us; *as for* this Moses
who brought us out of the land
of Egypt, we do not know what
has become of him.'[a] 41And
they made a calf in those days,
offered sacrifices to the idol,
and rejoiced in the works of

7:28 [a] Exodus 2:14 7:30 [a] NU-Text omits *of the Lord.* 7:32 [a] Exodus 3:6, 15 7:34 [a] Exodus 3:5, 7, 8, 10 7:35 [a] Exodus 2:14 7:37 [a] Deuteronomy 18:15 [b] NU-Text and M-Text omit *Him you shall hear.* 7:40 [a] Exodus 32:1, 23

their own hands. 42Then God
turned and gave them up to
worship the host of heaven,
as it is written in the book of
the Prophets:

'Did you offer Me
slaughtered animals
and sacrifices
during forty years
in the wilderness,
O house of Israel?
43 You also took up the
tabernacle of Moloch,
And the star of your
god Remphan,
Images which you
made to worship;
And I will carry you away
beyond Babylon.'[a]

GOD'S TRUE TABERNACLE

44"Our fathers had the
tabernacle of witness in the
wilderness, as He appointed,
instructing Moses to make it
according to the pattern that
he had seen, 45which our fathers, having received it in
turn, also brought with Joshua
into the land possessed by the
Gentiles, whom God drove out
before the face of our fathers
until the days of David, 46who
found favor before God and
asked to find a dwelling for
the God of Jacob. 47But Solomon built Him a house.

48"However, the Most
High does not dwell in temples made with hands, as the
prophet says:

49 'Heaven *is* My throne,
And earth *is* My footstool.
What house will you build
for Me? says the LORD,
Or what *is* the place
of My rest?
50 Has My hand not made
all these things?'[a]

ISRAEL RESISTS THE HOLY SPIRIT

51"*You* stiff-necked and
uncircumcised in heart and
ears! You always resist the
Holy Spirit; as your fathers
did, so *do* you. 52Which of the
prophets did your fathers not
persecute? And they killed
those who foretold the coming of the Just One, of whom
you now have become the be-
trayers and murderers, 53who
have received the law by the
direction of angels and have
not kept *it*."

STEPHEN THE MARTYR

54When they heard these
things they were cut to the
heart, and they gnashed at
him with *their* teeth. 55But he,
being full of the Holy Spirit,
gazed into heaven and saw
the glory of God, and Jesus
standing at the right hand of
God, 56and said, "Look! I see
the heavens opened and the
Son of Man standing at the
right hand of God!"

57Then they cried out with
a loud voice, stopped their
ears, and ran at him with

7:43 [a] Amos 5:25–27 7:50 [a] Isaiah 66:1, 2

one accord; [58]and they cast
him out of the city and stoned
him. And the witnesses laid
down their clothes at the feet
of a young man named Saul.
[59]And they stoned Stephen as
he was calling on *God* and saying, "Lord Jesus, receive my
spirit." [60]Then he knelt down
and cried out with a loud
voice, "Lord, do not charge
them with this sin." And when
he had said this, he fell asleep.

SAUL PERSECUTES THE CHURCH

8 Now Saul was consenting
to his death.

At that time a great per-
secution arose against the
church which was at Jerusalem; and they were all scattered throughout the regions
of Judea and Samaria, except
the apostles. [2]And devout
men carried Stephen *to his*
burial, and made great lamentation over him.

[3]As for Saul, he made havoc
of the church, entering every
house, and dragging off men
and women, committing *them*
to prison.

CHRIST IS PREACHED IN SAMARIA

[4]Therefore those who were
scattered went everywhere
preaching the word. [5]Then
Philip went down to the[a] city
of Samaria and preached
Christ to them. [6]And the
multitudes with one accord
heeded the things spoken by
Philip, hearing and seeing
the miracles which he did.
[7]For unclean spirits, crying
with a loud voice, came out
of many who were possessed;
and many who were para-
lyzed and lame were healed.
[8]And there was great joy in
that city.

THE SORCERER'S PROFESSION OF FAITH

[9]But there was a certain
man called Simon, who previously practiced sorcery in
the city and astonished the
people of Samaria, claiming
that he was someone great,
[10]to whom they all gave heed,
from the least to the greatest, saying, "This man is the
great power of God." [11]And
they heeded him because he
had astonished them with his
sorceries for a long time. [12]But
when they believed Philip as
he preached the things concerning the kingdom of God
and the name of Jesus Christ,
both men and women were
baptized. [13]Then Simon himself also believed; and when
he was baptized he continued
with Philip, and was amazed,
seeing the miracles and signs
which were done.

THE SORCERER'S SIN

[14]Now when the apos-
tles who were at Jerusalem

8:5 [a] Or *a*

heard that Samaria had received the word of God, they
sent Peter and John to them,
15who, when they had come
down, prayed for them that
they might receive the Holy
Spirit. 16For as yet He had
fallen upon none of them.
They had only been baptized
in the name of the Lord Jesus.
17Then they laid hands on
them, and they received the
Holy Spirit.

18And when Simon saw that
through the laying on of the
apostles' hands the Holy Spirit
was given, he offered them
money, 19saying, "Give me this
power also, that anyone on
whom I lay hands may receive
the Holy Spirit."

20But Peter said to him,
"Your money perish with
you, because you thought
that the gift of God could
be purchased with money!
21You have neither part nor
portion in this matter, for
your heart is not right in the
sight of God. 22Repent therefore of this your wickedness,
and pray God if perhaps the
thought of your heart may
be forgiven you. 23For I see
that you are poisoned by bitterness and bound by iniquity."

24Then Simon answered
and said, "Pray to the Lord for
me, that none of the things
which you have spoken may
come upon me."

25So when they had testi-
fied and preached the word
of the Lord, they returned
to Jerusalem, preaching the
gospel in many villages of the
Samaritans.

CHRIST IS PREACHED TO AN ETHIOPIAN

26Now an angel of the Lord
spoke to Philip, saying, "Arise
and go toward the south along
the road which goes down
from Jerusalem to Gaza." This
is desert. 27So he arose and
went. And behold, a man of
Ethiopia, a eunuch of great
authority under Candace the
queen of the Ethiopians, who
had charge of all her treasury,
and had come to Jerusalem to
worship, 28was returning. And
sitting in his chariot, he was
reading Isaiah the prophet.
29Then the Spirit said to
Philip, "Go near and overtake
this chariot."

30So Philip ran to him,
and heard him reading the
prophet Isaiah, and said, "Do
you understand what you are
reading?"

31And he said, "How can I,
unless someone guides me?"
And he asked Philip to come
up and sit with him. 32The
place in the Scripture which
he read was this:

"He was led as a sheep
to the slaughter;
And as a lamb before
its shearer *is*
silent,
So He opened not
His mouth.

33 In His humiliation His
justice was taken away,
And who will declare
His generation?
For His life is taken
from the earth."[a]

34So the eunuch answered
Philip and said, "I ask you, of
whom does the prophet say
this, of himself or of some
other man?" 35Then Philip
opened his mouth, and be-
ginning at this Scripture,
preached Jesus to him. 36Now
as they went down the road,
they came to some water. And
the eunuch said, "See, *here is*
water. What hinders me from
being baptized?"
37Then Philip said, "If you
believe with all your heart,
you may."
And he answered and said,
"I believe that Jesus Christ is
the Son of God."[a]
38So he commanded the
chariot to stand still. And both
Philip and the eunuch went
down into the water, and he
baptized him. 39Now when
they came up out of the water,
the Spirit of the Lord caught
Philip away, so that the eunuch saw him no more; and
he went on his way rejoicing.
40But Philip was found at Azo-
tus. And passing through, he
preached in all the cities till
he came to Caesarea.

THE DAMASCUS ROAD: SAUL CONVERTED

9 Then Saul, still breathing threats and murder
against the disciples of the
Lord, went to the high priest
2and asked letters from him to
the synagogues of Damascus,
so that if he found any who
were of the Way, whether men
or women, he might bring
them bound to Jerusalem.
3As he journeyed he came
near Damascus, and suddenly
a light shone around him
from heaven. 4Then he fell to
the ground, and heard a voice
saying to him, "Saul, Saul, why
are you persecuting Me?"
5And he said, "Who are You,
Lord?"
Then the Lord said, "I am
Jesus, whom you are persecuting.[a] It *is* hard for you to
kick against the goads."
6So he, trembling and as-
tonished, said, "Lord, what do
You want me to do?"
Then the Lord *said* to him,
"Arise and go into the city,
and you will be told what you
must do."
7And the men who jour-
neyed with him stood speechless, hearing a voice but
seeing no one. 8Then Saul
arose from the ground, and
when his eyes were opened he
saw no one. But they led him
by the hand and brought *him*

8:33 [a] Isaiah 53:7, 8 8:37 [a] NU-Text and M-Text omit this verse. It is found in Western texts, including the Latin tradition. 9:5 [a] NU-Text and M-Text omit the last sentence of verse 5 and begin verse 6 with *But arise and go.*

into Damascus. 9And he was
three days without sight, and
neither ate nor drank.

ANANIAS BAPTIZES SAUL

10Now there was a certain
disciple at Damascus named
Ananias; and to him the Lord
said in a vision, "Ananias."

And he said, "Here I am,
Lord."

11So the Lord *said* to him,
"Arise and go to the street
called Straight, and inquire
at the house of Judas for *one*
called Saul of Tarsus, for behold, he is praying. 12And in
a vision he has seen a man
named Ananias coming in
and putting *his* hand on him,
so that he might receive his
sight."

13Then Ananias answered,
"Lord, I have heard from
many about this man, how
much harm he has done to
Your saints in Jerusalem.
14And here he has authority
from the chief priests to bind
all who call on Your name."

15But the Lord said to him,
"Go, for he is a chosen vessel
of Mine to bear My name before Gentiles, kings, and the
children of Israel. 16For I will
show him how many things
he must suffer for My name's
sake."

17And Ananias went his way
and entered the house; and
laying his hands on him he
said, "Brother Saul, the Lord
Jesus,[a] who appeared to you
on the road as you came, has
sent me that you may receive
your sight and be filled with
the Holy Spirit." 18Immedi-
ately there fell from his eyes
something like scales, and he
received his sight at once; and
he arose and was baptized.

19So when he had received
food, he was strengthened.
Then Saul spent some days
with the disciples at Damascus.

SAUL PREACHES CHRIST

20Immediately he preached
the Christ[a] in the synagogues,
that He is the Son of God.

21Then all who heard were
amazed, and said, "Is this not
he who destroyed those who
called on this name in Jerusalem, and has come here for
that purpose, so that he might
bring them bound to the chief
priests?"

22But Saul increased all the
more in strength, and confounded the Jews who dwelt
in Damascus, proving that
this *Jesus* is the Christ.

SAUL ESCAPES DEATH

23Now after many days
were past, the Jews plotted to
kill him. 24But their plot became known to Saul. And they
watched the gates day and
night, to kill him. 25Then the
disciples took him by night
and let *him* down through the
wall in a large basket.

9:17 [a] M-Text omits *Jesus*. 9:20 [a] NU-Text reads *Jesus*.

SAUL AT JERUSALEM

26And when Saul had come
to Jerusalem, he tried to join
the disciples; but they were
all afraid of him, and did not
believe that he was a disciple.
27But Barnabas took him and
brought *him* to the apostles.
And he declared to them how
he had seen the Lord on the
road, and that He had spoken to him, and how he had
preached boldly at Damascus
in the name of Jesus. 28So he
was with them at Jerusalem,
coming in and going out.
29And he spoke boldly in the
name of the Lord Jesus and
disputed against the Hellenists, but they attempted to
kill him. 30When the brethren
found out, they brought him
down to Caesarea and sent
him out to Tarsus.

THE CHURCH PROSPERS

31Then the churches[a]
throughout all Judea, Galilee, and Samaria had peace
and were edified. And walking
in the fear of the Lord and in
the comfort of the Holy Spirit,
they were multiplied.

AENEAS HEALED

32Now it came to pass, as
Peter went through all *parts of
the country,* that he also came
down to the saints who dwelt
in Lydda. 33There he found a
certain man named Aeneas,
who had been bedridden
eight years and was paralyzed.
34And Peter said to him, "Aeneas, Jesus the Christ heals
you. Arise and make your
bed." Then he arose imme-
diately. 35So all who dwelt at
Lydda and Sharon saw him
and turned to the Lord.

DORCAS RESTORED TO LIFE

36At Joppa there was a certain disciple named Tabitha,
which is translated Dorcas.
This woman was full of good
works and charitable deeds
which she did. 37But it happened in those days that she
became sick and died. When
they had washed her, they laid
her in an upper room. 38And
since Lydda was near Joppa,
and the disciples had heard
that Peter was there, they sent
two men to him, imploring
him not to delay in coming
to them. 39Then Peter arose
and went with them. When
he had come, they brought
him to the upper room. And
all the widows stood by him
weeping, showing the tunics
and garments which Dor-
cas had made while she was
with them. 40But Peter put
them all out, and knelt down
and prayed. And turning to
the body he said, "Tabitha,
arise." And she opened her
eyes, and when she saw Peter
she sat up. 41Then he gave
her *his* hand and lifted her
up; and when he had called

9:31 [a] NU-Text reads *church . . . was edified.*

the saints and widows, he
presented her alive. 42And it
became known throughout
all Joppa, and many believed
on the Lord. 43So it was that
he stayed many days in Joppa
with Simon, a tanner.

CORNELIUS SENDS A DELEGATION

10 There was a certain man
in Caesarea called Cor-
nelius, a centurion of what
was called the Italian Regiment, 2a devout *man* and one
who feared God with all his
household, who gave alms
generously to the people, and
prayed to God always. 3About
the ninth hour of the day he
saw clearly in a vision an angel
of God coming in and saying
to him, "Cornelius!"

4And when he observed
him, he was afraid, and said,
"What is it, lord?"

So he said to him, "Your
prayers and your alms have
come up for a memorial before God. 5Now send men to
Joppa, and send for Simon
whose surname is Peter. 6He
is lodging with Simon, a tanner, whose house is by the
sea.[a] He will tell you what
you must do." 7And when the
angel who spoke to him had
departed, Cornelius called two
of his household servants and
a devout soldier from among
those who waited on him
continually. 8So when he had
explained all *these* things to
them, he sent them to Joppa.

PETER'S VISION

9The next day, as they went
on their journey and drew
near the city, Peter went up
on the housetop to pray, about
the sixth hour. 10Then he became very hungry and wanted
to eat; but while they made
ready, he fell into a trance
11and saw heaven opened and
an object like a great sheet
bound at the four corners,
descending to him and let
down to the earth. 12In it were
all kinds of four-footed animals of the earth, wild beasts,
creeping things, and birds of
the air. 13And a voice came to
him, "Rise, Peter; kill and eat."

14But Peter said, "Not so,
Lord! For I have never eaten
anything common or un-
clean."

15And a voice *spoke* to him
again the second time, "What
God has cleansed you must
not call common." 16This was
done three times. And the object was taken up into heaven
again.

SUMMONED TO CAESAREA

17Now while Peter won-
dered within himself what
this vision which he had seen
meant, behold, the men who
had been sent from Cornelius
had made inquiry for Simon's
house, and stood before the

10:6 [a] NU-Text and M-Text omit the last sentence of this verse.

gate. 18And they called and
asked whether Simon, whose
surname was Peter, was lodging there.

19While Peter thought
about the vision, the Spirit
said to him, "Behold, three
men are seeking you. 20Arise
therefore, go down and go
with them, doubting nothing;
for I have sent them."

21Then Peter went down to
the men who had been sent
to him from Cornelius,[a] and
said, "Yes, I am he whom you
seek. For what reason have
you come?"

22And they said, "Cornel-
ius *the* centurion, a just man,
one who fears God and has
a good reputation among all
the nation of the Jews, was
divinely instructed by a holy
angel to summon you to his
house, and to hear words from
you." 23Then he invited them
in and lodged *them.*

On the next day Peter went
away with them, and some
brethren from Joppa accompanied him.

PETER MEETS CORNELIUS

24And the following day
they entered Caesarea. Now
Cornelius was waiting for
them, and had called together
his relatives and close friends.
25As Peter was coming in, Cornelius met him and fell down
at his feet and worshiped
him. 26But Peter lifted him
up, saying, "Stand up; I myself am also a man." 27And as
he talked with him, he went
in and found many who had
come together. 28Then he said
to them, "You know how un-
lawful it is for a Jewish man
to keep company with or go
to one of another nation.
But God has shown me that I
should not call any man common or unclean. 29Therefore
I came without objection as
soon as I was sent for. I ask,
then, for what reason have
you sent for me?"

30So Cornelius said, "Four
days ago I was fasting until
this hour; and at the ninth
hour[a] I prayed in my house,
and behold, a man stood before me in bright clothing,
31and said, 'Cornelius, your
prayer has been heard, and
your alms are remembered
in the sight of God. 32Send
therefore to Joppa and call
Simon here, whose surname
is Peter. He is lodging in the
house of Simon, a tanner, by
the sea.[a] When he comes, he
will speak to you.' 33So I sent
to you immediately, and you
have done well to come. Now
therefore, we are all present
before God, to hear all the
things commanded you by
God."

10:21 [a] NU-Text and M-Text omit *who had been sent to him from Cornelius.* 10:30 [a] NU-Text reads *Four days ago to this hour, at the ninth hour.* 10:32 [a] NU-Text omits the last sentence of this verse.

PREACHING TO CORNELIUS' HOUSEHOLD

34Then Peter opened *his*
mouth and said: "In truth
I perceive that God shows
no partiality. 35But in every
nation whoever fears Him
and works righteousness
is accepted by Him. 36The
word which *God* sent to the
children of Israel, preaching peace through Jesus
Christ—He is Lord of all—
37that word you know, which
was proclaimed throughout
all Judea, and began from
Galilee after the baptism
which John preached: 38how
God anointed Jesus of Nazareth with the Holy Spirit and
with power, who went about
doing good and healing all
who were oppressed by the
devil, for God was with Him.
39And we are witnesses of all
things which He did both in
the land of the Jews and in
Jerusalem, whom they[a] killed
by hanging on a tree. 40Him
God raised up on the third
day, and showed Him openly,
41not to all the people, but to
witnesses chosen before by
God, *even* to us who ate and
drank with Him after He arose
from the dead. 42And He commanded us to preach to the
people, and to testify that it
is He who was ordained by
God *to be* Judge of the living
and the dead. 43To Him all
the prophets witness that,
through His name, whoever
believes in Him will receive
remission of sins."

THE HOLY SPIRIT FALLS ON THE GENTILES

44While Peter was still
speaking these words, the
Holy Spirit fell upon all those
who heard the word. 45And
those of the circumcision who
believed were astonished, as
many as came with Peter,
because the gift of the Holy
Spirit had been poured out
on the Gentiles also. 46For
they heard them speak with
tongues and magnify God.

Then Peter answered,
47"Can anyone forbid water,
that these should not be baptized who have received the
Holy Spirit just as we *have?*"
48And he commanded them
to be baptized in the name
of the Lord. Then they asked
him to stay a few days.

PETER DEFENDS GOD'S GRACE

11 Now the apostles and
brethren who were in
Judea heard that the Gentiles
had also received the word of
God. 2And when Peter came
up to Jerusalem, those of the
circumcision contended with
him, 3saying, "You went in to
uncircumcised men and ate
with them!"

4But Peter explained *it* to
them in order from the be-

10:39 [a] NU-Text and M-Text add *also*.

ginning, saying: 5“I was in the
city of Joppa praying; and in a
trance I saw a vision, an object
descending like a great sheet,
let down from heaven by four
corners; and it came to me.
6When I observed it intently
and considered, I saw four-
footed animals of the earth,
wild beasts, creeping things,
and birds of the air. 7And I
heard a voice saying to me,
‘Rise, Peter; kill and eat.’ 8But
I said, ‘Not so, Lord! For nothing common or unclean has at
any time entered my mouth.’
9But the voice answered me
again from heaven, ‘What God
has cleansed you must not
call common.’ 10Now this was
done three times, and all were
drawn up again into heaven.
11At that very moment, three
men stood before the house
where I was, having been sent
to me from Caesarea. 12Then
the Spirit told me to go with
them, doubting nothing.
Moreover these six brethren
accompanied me, and we entered the man’s house. 13And
he told us how he had seen an
angel standing in his house,
who said to him, ‘Send men
to Joppa, and call for Simon
whose surname is Peter, 14who
will tell you words by which
you and all your household
will be saved.’ 15And as I began
to speak, the Holy Spirit fell
upon them, as upon us at the
beginning. 16Then I remembered the word of the Lord,
how He said, ‘John indeed
baptized with water, but you
shall be baptized with the
Holy Spirit.’ 17If therefore God
gave them the same gift as *He
gave* us when we believed on
the Lord Jesus Christ, who was
I that I could withstand God?”
18When they heard these
things they became silent;
and they glorified God, saying,
“Then God has also granted
to the Gentiles repentance to
life.”

BARNABAS AND SAUL AT ANTIOCH

19Now those who were
scattered after the persecution that arose over Stephen
traveled as far as Phoenicia,
Cyprus, and Antioch, preaching the word to no one but the
Jews only. 20But some of them
were men from Cyprus and
Cyrene, who, when they had
come to Antioch, spoke to
the Hellenists, preaching the
Lord Jesus. 21And the hand of
the Lord was with them, and
a great number believed and
turned to the Lord.

22Then news of these things
came to the ears of the church
in Jerusalem, and they sent out
Barnabas to go as far as Antioch. 23When he came and had
seen the grace of God, he was
glad, and encouraged them all
that with purpose of heart they
should continue with the Lord.
24For he was a good man, full
of the Holy Spirit and of faith.
And a great many people were
added to the Lord.

25Then Barnabas departed
for Tarsus to seek Saul. 26And
when he had found him, he
brought him to Antioch. So it
was that for a whole year they
assembled with the church
and taught a great many people. And the disciples were first
called Christians in Antioch.

RELIEF TO JUDEA

27And in these days prophets came from Jerusalem to
Antioch. 28Then one of them,
named Agabus, stood up and
showed by the Spirit that
there was going to be a great
famine throughout all the
world, which also happened
in the days of Claudius Caesar. 29Then the disciples, each
according to his ability, determined to send relief to the
brethren dwelling in Judea.
30This they also did, and sent
it to the elders by the hands
of Barnabas and Saul.

HEROD'S VIOLENCE TO THE CHURCH

12 Now about that time
Herod the king stretched
out *his* hand to harass some
from the church. 2Then he
killed James the brother of
John with the sword. 3And because he saw that it pleased
the Jews, he proceeded further to seize Peter also. Now
it was *during* the Days of Unleavened Bread. 4So when he
had arrested him, he put *him*
in prison, and delivered *him*
to four squads of soldiers to
keep him, intending to bring
him before the people after
Passover.

PETER FREED FROM PRISON

5Peter was therefore kept in
prison, but constant[a] prayer
was offered to God for him by
the church. 6And when Herod
was about to bring him out,
that night Peter was sleeping, bound with two chains
between two soldiers; and
the guards before the door
were keeping the prison.
7Now behold, an angel of the
Lord stood by *him,* and a light
shone in the prison; and he
struck Peter on the side and
raised him up, saying, "Arise
quickly!" And his chains fell
off *his* hands. 8Then the angel
said to him, "Gird yourself and
tie on your sandals"; and so he
did. And he said to him, "Put
on your garment and follow
me." 9So he went out and followed him, and did not know
that what was done by the
angel was real, but thought
he was seeing a vision. 10When
they were past the first and
the second guard posts, they
came to the iron gate that
leads to the city, which opened
to them of its own accord; and
they went out and went down
one street, and immediately
the angel departed from him.

12:5 [a] NU-Text reads *constantly* (or *earnestly*).

11And when Peter had come
to himself, he said, "Now I
know for certain that the Lord
has sent His angel, and has
delivered me from the hand of
Herod and *from* all the expectation of the Jewish people."
12So, when he had consid-
ered *this,* he came to the house
of Mary, the mother of John
whose surname was Mark,
where many were gathered
together praying. 13And as
Peter knocked at the door of
the gate, a girl named Rhoda
came to answer. 14When she
recognized Peter's voice, because of *her* gladness she did
not open the gate, but ran in
and announced that Peter
stood before the gate. 15But
they said to her, "You are beside yourself!" Yet she kept in-
sisting that it was so. So they
said, "It is his angel."
16Now Peter continued
knocking; and when they
opened *the door* and saw him,
they were astonished. 17But
motioning to them with his
hand to keep silent, he declared to them how the Lord
had brought him out of the
prison. And he said, "Go, tell
these things to James and
to the brethren." And he departed and went to another
place.
18Then, as soon as it was
day, there was no small stir
among the soldiers about what
had become of Peter. 19But
when Herod had searched
for him and not found him,
he examined the guards and
commanded that *they* should
be put to death.

And he went down from Judea to Caesarea, and stayed *there.*

HEROD'S VIOLENT DEATH

20Now Herod had been very
angry with the people of Tyre
and Sidon; but they came to
him with one accord, and having made Blastus the king's
personal aide their friend,
they asked for peace, because
their country was supplied
with food by the king's *country.*
21So on a set day Herod, arrayed in royal apparel, sat on
his throne and gave an ora-
tion to them. 22And the people
kept shouting, "The voice of a
god and not of a man!" 23Then
immediately an angel of the
Lord struck him, because he
did not give glory to God. And
he was eaten by worms and
died.
24But the word of God grew
and multiplied.

BARNABAS AND SAUL APPOINTED

25And Barnabas and Saul
returned from[a] Jerusalem
when they had fulfilled *their*
ministry, and they also took
with them John whose sur-
name was Mark.

12:25 [a] NU-Text and M-Text read *to.*

13 Now in the church that was at Antioch there were certain prophets and teachers: Barnabas, Simeon who was called Niger, Lucius of Cyrene, Manaen who had been brought up with Herod the tetrarch, and Saul. 2As they ministered to the Lord and fasted, the Holy Spirit said, "Now separate to Me Barnabas and Saul for the work to which I have called them." 3Then, having fasted and prayed, and laid hands on them, they sent *them* away.

PREACHING IN CYPRUS

4So, being sent out by the Holy Spirit, they went down to Seleucia, and from there they sailed to Cyprus. 5And when they arrived in Salamis, they preached the word of God in the synagogues of the Jews. They also had John as *their* assistant.

6Now when they had gone through the island[a] to Paphos, they found a certain sorcerer, a false prophet, a Jew whose name *was* Bar-Jesus, 7who was with the proconsul, Sergius Paulus, an intelligent man. This man called for Barnabas and Saul and sought to hear the word of God. 8But Elymas the sorcerer (for so his name is translated) withstood them, seeking to turn the proconsul away from the faith. 9Then Saul, who also *is called* Paul, filled with the Holy Spirit, looked intently at him 10and said, "O full of all deceit and all fraud, *you* son of the devil, *you* enemy of all righteousness, will you not cease perverting the straight ways of the Lord? 11And now, indeed, the hand of the Lord *is* upon you, and you shall be blind, not seeing the sun for a time."

And immediately a dark mist fell on him, and he went around seeking someone to lead him by the hand. 12Then the proconsul believed, when he saw what had been done, being astonished at the teaching of the Lord.

AT ANTIOCH IN PISIDIA

13Now when Paul and his party set sail from Paphos, they came to Perga in Pamphylia; and John, departing from them, returned to Jerusalem. 14But when they departed from Perga, they came to Antioch in Pisidia, and went into the synagogue on the Sabbath day and sat down. 15And after the reading of the Law and the Prophets, the rulers of the synagogue sent to them, saying, "Men *and* brethren, if you have any word of exhortation for the people, say on."

16Then Paul stood up, and motioning with *his* hand said, "Men of Israel, and you who fear God, listen: 17The God of this people Israel[a] chose our fathers, and exalted the

13:6 [a] NU-Text reads *the whole island*. 13:17 [a] M-Text omits *Israel*.

people when they dwelt as
strangers in the land of Egypt,
and with an uplifted arm He
brought them out of it. [18]Now
for a time of about forty years
He put up with their ways in
the wilderness. [19]And when
He had destroyed seven nations in the land of Canaan,
He distributed their land to
them by allotment.

[20]"After that He gave *them*
judges for about four hundred
and fifty years, until Samuel
the prophet. [21]And afterward
they asked for a king; so God
gave them Saul the son of
Kish, a man of the tribe of
Benjamin, for forty years.
[22]And when He had removed
him, He raised up for them
David as king, to whom also
He gave testimony and said,
'I have found David[a] the *son*
of Jesse, a man after My *own*
heart, who will do all My will.'[b]
[23]From this man's seed, according to *the* promise, God
raised up for Israel a Savior—
Jesus—[a] [24]after John had first
preached, before His coming,
the baptism of repentance to
all the people of Israel. [25]And
as John was finishing his
course, he said, 'Who do you
think I am? I am not *He.* But
behold, there comes One after
me, the sandals of whose feet
I am not worthy to loose.'

[26]"Men *and* brethren, sons
of the family of Abraham, and
those among you who fear God,
to you the word of this salvation has been sent. [27]For those
who dwell in Jerusalem, and
their rulers, because they did
not know Him, nor even the
voices of the Prophets which
are read every Sabbath, have
fulfilled *them* in condemning
Him. [28]And though they found
no cause for death *in Him,* they
asked Pilate that He should
be put to death. [29]Now when
they had fulfilled all that was
written concerning Him, they
took *Him* down from the tree
and laid *Him* in a tomb. [30]But
God raised Him from the dead.
[31]He was seen for many days by
those who came up with Him
from Galilee to Jerusalem, who
are His witnesses to the people. [32]And we declare to you
glad tidings—that promise
which was made to the fathers.
[33]God has fulfilled this for us
their children, in that He has
raised up Jesus. As it is also
written in the second Psalm:

'You are My Son,
Today I have
begotten You.'[a]

[34]And that He raised Him
from the dead, no more to
return to corruption, He has
spoken thus:

'I will give you the sure
mercies of David.'[a]

13:22 [a] Psalm 89:20 [b] 1 Samuel 13:14 13:23 [a] M-Text reads *for Israel salvation.* 13:33 [a] Psalm 2:7 13:34 [a] Isaiah 55:3

35 Therefore He also says in
another *Psalm:*

'You will not allow
Your Holy One to
see corruption.'[a]

36 "For David, after he had
served his own generation
by the will of God, fell asleep,
was buried with his fathers,
and saw corruption; 37 but
He whom God raised up
saw no corruption. 38 Therefore let it be known to you,
brethren, that through this
Man is preached to you the
forgiveness of sins; 39 and by
Him everyone who believes is
justified from all things from
which you could not be justified by the law of Moses. 40 Beware therefore, lest what has
been spoken in the prophets
come upon you:

41 'Behold, you despisers,
Marvel and perish!
For I work a work
in your days,
A work which you will
by no means believe,
Though one were to
declare it to you.'"[a]

BLESSING AND CONFLICT AT ANTIOCH

42 So when the Jews went
out of the synagogue,[a] the
Gentiles begged that these
words might be preached to
them the next Sabbath. 43 Now
when the congregation had
broken up, many of the Jews
and devout proselytes followed Paul and Barnabas,
who, speaking to them, persuaded them to continue in
the grace of God.

44 On the next Sabbath almost the whole city came
together to hear the word
of God. 45 But when the Jews
saw the multitudes, they were
filled with envy; and contra-
dicting and blaspheming, they
opposed the things spoken
by Paul. 46 Then Paul and Barnabas grew bold and said, "It
was necessary that the word of
God should be spoken to you
first; but since you reject it,
and judge yourselves unworthy of everlasting life, behold,
we turn to the Gentiles. 47 For
so the Lord has commanded
us:

'I have set you as a light
to the Gentiles,
That you should be
for salvation to the
ends of the earth.'"[a]

48 Now when the Gentiles
heard this, they were glad and
glorified the word of the Lord.
And as many as had been
appointed to eternal life believed.

13:35 [a] Psalm 16:10 13:41 [a] Habakkuk 1:5 13:42 [a] Or *And when they went out of the synagogue of the Jews;* NU-Text reads *And when they went out, they begged.* 13:47 [a] Isaiah 49:6

DIVISION OVER JOHN MARK

36Then after some days
Paul said to Barnabas, "Let
us now go back and visit our
brethren in every city where
we have preached the word of
the Lord, *and see* how they are
doing." 37Now Barnabas was
determined to take with them
John called Mark. 38But Paul
insisted that they should not
take with them the one who
had departed from them in
Pamphylia, and had not gone
with them to the work. 39Then
the contention became so
sharp that they parted from
one another. And so Barnabas took Mark and sailed to
Cyprus; 40but Paul chose Silas
and departed, being com-
mended by the brethren to the
grace of God. 41And he went
through Syria and Cilicia,
strengthening the churches.

TIMOTHY JOINS PAUL AND SILAS

16 Then he came to Derbe
and Lystra. And behold,
a certain disciple was there,
named Timothy, *the* son of a
certain Jewish woman who
believed, but his father *was*
Greek. 2He was well spoken
of by the brethren who were
at Lystra and Iconium. 3Paul
wanted to have him go on with
him. And he took *him* and circumcised him because of the
Jews who were in that region,
for they all knew that his father
was Greek. 4And as they went
through the cities, they delivered to them the decrees to
keep, which were determined
by the apostles and elders at
Jerusalem. 5So the churches
were strengthened in the faith,
and increased in number daily.

THE MACEDONIAN CALL

6Now when they had gone
through Phrygia and the region of Galatia, they were
forbidden by the Holy Spirit
to preach the word in Asia.
7After they had come to Mysia,
they tried to go into Bithynia,
but the Spirit[a] did not permit
them. 8So passing by Mysia,
they came down to Troas.
9And a vision appeared to
Paul in the night. A man of
Macedonia stood and pleaded
with him, saying, "Come over
to Macedonia and help us."
10Now after he had seen the vision, immediately we sought
to go to Macedonia, conclud-
ing that the Lord had called us
to preach the gospel to them.

LYDIA BAPTIZED AT PHILIPPI

11Therefore, sailing from
Troas, we ran a straight course
to Samothrace, and the next
day came to Neapolis, 12and
from there to Philippi, which
is the foremost city of that part
of Macedonia, a colony. And
we were staying in that city
for some days. 13And on the
Sabbath day we went out of

16:7 [a] NU-Text adds *of Jesus.*

the city to the riverside, where
prayer was customarily made;
and we sat down and spoke
to the women who met *there.*
[14]Now a certain woman named
Lydia heard *us.* She was a seller
of purple from the city of Thyatira, who worshiped God.
The Lord opened her heart
to heed the things spoken by
Paul. [15]And when she and her
household were baptized, she
begged *us,* saying, "If you have
judged me to be faithful to the
Lord, come to my house and
stay." So she persuaded us.

PAUL AND SILAS IMPRISONED

[16]Now it happened, as we
went to prayer, that a certain
slave girl possessed with a
spirit of divination met us, who
brought her masters much
profit by fortune-telling. [17]This
girl followed Paul and us, and
cried out, saying, "These men
are the servants of the Most
High God, who proclaim to us
the way of salvation." [18]And
this she did for many days.

But Paul, greatly annoyed,
turned and said to the spirit,
"I command you in the name
of Jesus Christ to come out
of her." And he came out that
very hour. [19]But when her
masters saw that their hope
of profit was gone, they seized
Paul and Silas and dragged
them into the marketplace to
the authorities.

[20]And they brought them
to the magistrates, and said,
"These men, being Jews, exceedingly trouble our city;
[21]and they teach customs
which are not lawful for us,
being Romans, to receive or
observe." [22]Then the multitude
rose up together against them;
and the magistrates tore off
their clothes and commanded
them to be beaten with rods.
[23]And when they had laid many
stripes on them, they threw
them into prison, commanding the jailer to keep them securely. [24]Having received such
a charge, he put them into the
inner prison and fastened their
feet in the stocks.

THE PHILIPPIAN JAILER SAVED

[25]But at midnight Paul
and Silas were praying and
singing hymns to God, and
the prisoners were listening
to them. [26]Suddenly there
was a great earthquake, so
that the foundations of the
prison were shaken; and immediately all the doors were
opened and everyone's chains
were loosed. [27]And the keeper
of the prison, awaking from
sleep and seeing the prison
doors open, supposing the
prisoners had fled, drew his
sword and was about to kill
himself. [28]But Paul called with
a loud voice, saying, "Do yourself no harm, for we are all
here."

[29]Then he called for a light,
ran in, and fell down trembling before Paul and Silas.

30 And he brought them out and said, "Sirs, what must I do to be saved?"

31 So they said, "Believe on the Lord Jesus Christ, and you will be saved, you and your household." 32 Then they spoke the word of the Lord to him and to all who were in his house. 33 And he took them the same hour of the night and washed *their* stripes. And immediately he and all his *family* were baptized. 34 Now when he had brought them into his house, he set food before them; and he rejoiced, having believed in God with all his household.

PAUL REFUSES TO DEPART SECRETLY

35 And when it was day, the magistrates sent the officers, saying, "Let those men go."

36 So the keeper of the prison reported these words to Paul, saying, "The magistrates have sent to let you go. Now therefore depart, and go in peace."

37 But Paul said to them, "They have beaten us openly, uncondemned Romans, *and* have thrown *us* into prison. And now do they put us out secretly? No indeed! Let them come themselves and get us out."

38 And the officers told these words to the magistrates, and they were afraid when they heard that they were Romans. 39 Then they came and pleaded with them and brought *them* out, and asked *them* to depart from the city. 40 So they went out of the prison and entered *the house of* Lydia; and when they had seen the brethren, they encouraged them and departed.

PREACHING CHRIST AT THESSALONICA

17 Now when they had passed through Amphipolis and Apollonia, they came to Thessalonica, where there was a synagogue of the Jews. 2 Then Paul, as his custom was, went in to them, and for three Sabbaths reasoned with them from the Scriptures, 3 explaining and demonstrating that the Christ had to suffer and rise again from the dead, and *saying,* "This Jesus whom I preach to you is the Christ." 4 And some of them were persuaded; and a great multitude of the devout Greeks, and not a few of the leading women, joined Paul and Silas.

ASSAULT ON JASON'S HOUSE

5 But the Jews who were not persuaded, becoming envious,[a] took some of the evil men from the marketplace, and gathering a mob, set all

17:5 [a] NU-Text omits *who were not persuaded;* M-Text omits *becoming envious.*

the city in an uproar and attacked the house of Jason, and
sought to bring them out to
the people. 6But when they did
not find them, they dragged
Jason and some brethren to
the rulers of the city, crying
out, "These who have turned
the world upside down have
come here too. 7Jason has
harbored them, and these are
all acting contrary to the decrees of Caesar, saying there
is another king—Jesus." 8And
they troubled the crowd and
the rulers of the city when
they heard these things. 9So
when they had taken security
from Jason and the rest, they
let them go.

MINISTERING AT BEREA

10Then the brethren im-
mediately sent Paul and
Silas away by night to Berea.
When they arrived, they went
into the synagogue of the
Jews. 11These were more fair-
minded than those in Thessalonica, in that they received
the word with all readiness,
and searched the Scriptures
daily *to find out* whether these
things were so. 12Therefore
many of them believed, and
also not a few of the Greeks,
prominent women as well
as men. 13But when the Jews
from Thessalonica learned
that the word of God was
preached by Paul at Berea,
they came there also and
stirred up the crowds. 14Then
immediately the brethren
sent Paul away, to go to the
sea; but both Silas and Timothy remained there. 15So those
who conducted Paul brought
him to Athens; and receiving
a command for Silas and Timothy to come to him with all
speed, they departed.

THE PHILOSOPHERS AT ATHENS

16Now while Paul waited for
them at Athens, his spirit was
provoked within him when
he saw that the city was given
over to idols. 17Therefore he
reasoned in the synagogue
with the Jews and with the
Gentile worshipers, and in
the marketplace daily with
those who happened to be
there. 18Then[a] certain Epicu-
rean and Stoic philosophers
encountered him. And some
said, "What does this babbler
want to say?"

Others said, "He seems to
be a proclaimer of foreign
gods," because he preached
to them Jesus and the resurrection.

19And they took him and
brought him to the Areop-
agus, saying, "May we know
what this new doctrine *is* of
which you speak? 20For you
are bringing some strange
things to our ears. Therefore
we want to know what these
things mean." 21For all the

17:18 [a] NU-Text and M-Text add *also*.

Athenians and the foreigners who were there spent their
time in nothing else but either
to tell or to hear some new
thing.

ADDRESSING THE AREOPAGUS

22Then Paul stood in the
midst of the Areopagus and
said, "Men of Athens, I perceive that in all things you
are very religious; 23for as I
was passing through and considering the objects of your
worship, I even found an altar
with this inscription:

TO THE UNKNOWN GOD.

Therefore, the One whom
you worship without know-
ing, Him I proclaim to you:
24God, who made the world
and everything in it, since
He is Lord of heaven and
earth, does not dwell in temples made with hands. 25Nor
is He worshiped with men's
hands, as though He needed
anything, since He gives to
all life, breath, and all things.
26And He has made from one
blood[a] every nation of men
to dwell on all the face of the
earth, and has determined
their preappointed times and
the boundaries of their dwellings, 27so that they should
seek the Lord, in the hope that
they might grope for Him and
find Him, though He is not
far from each one of us; 28for
in Him we live and move and
have our being, as also some
of your own poets have said,
'For we are also His offspring.'
29Therefore, since we are the
offspring of God, we ought not
to think that the Divine Nature
is like gold or silver or stone,
something shaped by art and
man's devising. 30Truly, these
times of ignorance God over-
looked, but now commands
all men everywhere to repent,
31because He has appointed a
day on which He will judge the
world in righteousness by the
Man whom He has ordained.
He has given assurance of this
to all by raising Him from the
dead."

32And when they heard of
the resurrection of the dead,
some mocked, while others
said, "We will hear you again
on this *matter.*" 33So Paul departed from among them.
34However, some men joined
him and believed, among
them Dionysius the Areopa-
gite, a woman named Dama-
ris, and others with them.

MINISTERING AT CORINTH

18 After these things Paul
departed from Athens
and went to Corinth. 2And he
found a certain Jew named
Aquila, born in Pontus, who
had recently come from Italy
with his wife Priscilla (because
Claudius had commanded

17:26 [a] NU-Text omits *blood.*

all the Jews to depart from
Rome); and he came to them.
3So, because he was of the
same trade, he stayed with
them and worked; for by occupation they were tentmakers.
4And he reasoned in the synagogue every Sabbath, and persuaded both Jews and Greeks.
5When Silas and Timothy
had come from Macedonia,
Paul was compelled by the
Spirit, and testified to the
Jews *that* Jesus *is* the Christ.
6But when they opposed him
and blasphemed, he shook *his*
garments and said to them,
"Your blood *be* upon your
own heads; I *am* clean. From
now on I will go to the Gentiles." 7And he departed from
there and entered the house
of a certain *man* named Justus,[a] *one* who worshiped God,
whose house was next door to
the synagogue. 8Then Crispus,
the ruler of the synagogue, believed on the Lord with all his
household. And many of the
Corinthians, hearing, believed
and were baptized.
9Now the Lord spoke to
Paul in the night by a vision,
"Do not be afraid, but speak,
and do not keep silent; 10for I
am with you, and no one will
attack you to hurt you; for I
have many people in this city."
11And he continued *there* a
year and six months, teaching
the word of God among them.
12When Gallio was procon-
sul of Achaia, the Jews with
one accord rose up against
Paul and brought him to the
judgment seat, 13saying, "This
fellow persuades men to worship God contrary to the law."
14And when Paul was about
to open *his* mouth, Gallio said
to the Jews, "If it were a matter of wrongdoing or wicked
crimes, O Jews, there would
be reason why I should bear
with you. 15But if it is a question of words and names and
your own law, look *to it* yourselves; for I do not want to
be a judge of such *matters*."
16And he drove them from the
judgment seat. 17Then all
the Greeks[a] took Sosthenes,
the ruler of the synagogue,
and beat *him* before the judgment seat. But Gallio took no
notice of these things.

PAUL RETURNS TO ANTIOCH

18So Paul still remained a
good while. Then he took leave
of the brethren and sailed for
Syria, and Priscilla and Aquila
were with him. He had *his* hair
cut off at Cenchrea, for he had
taken a vow. 19And he came to
Ephesus, and left them there;
but he himself entered the
synagogue and reasoned with
the Jews. 20When they asked
him to stay a longer time with
them, he did not consent,
21but took leave of them, saying, "I must by all means keep

18:7 [a] NU-Text reads *Titius Justus.* 18:17 [a] NU-Text reads *they all.*

this coming feast in Jerusalem;[a] but I will return again
to you, God willing." And he
sailed from Ephesus.
22And when he had landed
at Caesarea, and gone up and
greeted the church, he went
down to Antioch. 23After he
had spent some time *there,* he
departed and went over the
region of Galatia and Phrygia
in order, strengthening all the
disciples.

MINISTRY OF APOLLOS

24Now a certain Jew named
Apollos, born at Alexandria,
an eloquent man *and* mighty
in the Scriptures, came to
Ephesus. 25This man had
been instructed in the way of
the Lord; and being fervent
in spirit, he spoke and taught
accurately the things of the
Lord, though he knew only
the baptism of John. 26So he
began to speak boldly in the
synagogue. When Aquila and
Priscilla heard him, they took
him aside and explained to
him the way of God more accurately. 27And when he desired to cross to Achaia, the
brethren wrote, exhorting the
disciples to receive him; and
when he arrived, he greatly
helped those who had be-
lieved through grace; 28for he
vigorously refuted the Jews
publicly, showing from the
Scriptures that Jesus is the
Christ.

PAUL AT EPHESUS

19 And it happened, while
Apollos was at Corinth,
that Paul, having passed
through the upper regions,
came to Ephesus. And finding some disciples 2he said
to them, "Did you receive
the Holy Spirit when you believed?"
So they said to him, "We
have not so much as heard
whether there is a Holy Spirit."
3And he said to them, "Into
what then were you baptized?"
So they said, "Into John's
baptism."
4Then Paul said, "John indeed baptized with a baptism
of repentance, saying to the
people that they should believe on Him who would come
after him, that is, on Christ
Jesus."
5When they heard *this,*
they were baptized in the
name of the Lord Jesus. 6And
when Paul had laid hands on
them, the Holy Spirit came
upon them, and they spoke
with tongues and prophesied.
7Now the men were about
twelve in all.
8And he went into the synagogue and spoke boldly for
three months, reasoning and
persuading concerning the
things of the kingdom of God.
9But when some were hard-
ened and did not believe, but
spoke evil of the Way before
the multitude, he departed

18:21 [a] NU-Text omits *I must* through *Jerusalem.*

from them and withdrew the
disciples, reasoning daily in
the school of Tyrannus. 10And
this continued for two years,
so that all who dwelt in Asia
heard the word of the Lord
Jesus, both Jews and Greeks.

MIRACLES GLORIFY CHRIST

11Now God worked unusual
miracles by the hands of Paul,
12so that even handkerchiefs
or aprons were brought from
his body to the sick, and the
diseases left them and the
evil spirits went out of them.
13Then some of the itinerant
Jewish exorcists took it upon
themselves to call the name
of the Lord Jesus over those
who had evil spirits, saying,
"We[a] exorcise you by the
Jesus whom Paul preaches."
14Also there were seven sons
of Sceva, a Jewish chief priest,
who did so.

15And the evil spirit answered and said, "Jesus I
know, and Paul I know; but
who are you?"

16Then the man in whom
the evil spirit was leaped on
them, overpowered[a] them,
and prevailed against them,[b]
so that they fled out of that
house naked and wounded.
17This became known both to
all Jews and Greeks dwelling in
Ephesus; and fear fell on them
all, and the name of the Lord
Jesus was magnified. 18And
many who had believed came
confessing and telling their
deeds. 19Also, many of those
who had practiced magic
brought their books together
and burned *them* in the sight
of all. And they counted up the
value of them, and *it* totaled
fifty thousand *pieces* of silver.
20So the word of the Lord grew
mightily and prevailed.

THE RIOT AT EPHESUS

21When these things were
accomplished, Paul purposed
in the Spirit, when he had
passed through Macedonia
and Achaia, to go to Jerusalem, saying, "After I have been
there, I must also see Rome."
22So he sent into Macedonia
two of those who ministered
to him, Timothy and Erastus,
but he himself stayed in Asia
for a time.

23And about that time
there arose a great commotion about the Way. 24For
a certain man named Demetrius, a silversmith, who
made silver shrines of Diana,[a]
brought no small profit to the
craftsmen. 25He called them
together with the workers of
similar occupation, and said:
"Men, you know that we have
our prosperity by this trade.
26Moreover you see and hear
that not only at Ephesus, but
throughout almost all Asia,
this Paul has persuaded and

19:13 [a] NU-Text reads *I*. 19:16 [a] M-Text reads *and they overpowered*. [b] NU-Text reads *both of them*. 19:24 [a] Greek *Artemis*

turned away many people,
saying that they are not gods
which are made with hands.
27So not only is this trade
of ours in danger of falling
into disrepute, but also the
temple of the great goddess
Diana may be despised and
her magnificence destroyed,[a]
whom all Asia and the world
worship."
28Now when they heard
this, they were full of wrath
and cried out, saying, "Great *is*
Diana of the Ephesians!" 29So
the whole city was filled with
confusion, and rushed into
the theater with one accord,
having seized Gaius and Aristarchus, Macedonians, Paul's
travel companions. 30And
when Paul wanted to go in
to the people, the disciples
would not allow him. 31Then
some of the officials of Asia,
who were his friends, sent to
him pleading that he would
not venture into the theater.
32Some therefore cried one
thing and some another, for
the assembly was confused,
and most of them did not
know why they had come together. 33And they drew Alexander out of the multitude,
the Jews putting him forward.
And Alexander motioned
with his hand, and wanted to
make his defense to the people. 34But when they found
out that he was a Jew, all with
one voice cried out for about
two hours, "Great *is* Diana of
the Ephesians!"
35And when the city clerk
had quieted the crowd, he
said: "Men of Ephesus, what
man is there who does not
know that the city of the Ephesians is temple guardian of
the great goddess Diana, and
of the *image* which fell down
from Zeus? 36Therefore, since
these things cannot be denied, you ought to be quiet
and do nothing rashly. 37For
you have brought these men
here who are neither robbers
of temples nor blasphemers
of your[a] goddess. 38Therefore,
if Demetrius and his fellow
craftsmen have a case against
anyone, the courts are open
and there are proconsuls. Let
them bring charges against
one another. 39But if you have
any other inquiry to make, it
shall be determined in the
lawful assembly. 40For we are
in danger of being called in
question for today's uproar,
there being no reason which
we may give to account for
this disorderly gathering."
41And when he had said these
things, he dismissed the assembly.

JOURNEYS IN GREECE

20 After the uproar had
ceased, Paul called the
disciples to *himself,* embraced

19:27 [a] NU-Text reads *she be deposed from her magnificence.* 19:37 [a] NU-Text reads *our.*

them, and departed to go to
Macedonia. 2Now when he
had gone over that region and
encouraged them with many
words, he came to Greece 3and
stayed three months. And
when the Jews plotted against
him as he was about to sail
to Syria, he decided to return
through Macedonia. 4And So-
pater of Berea accompanied
him to Asia—also Aristarchus
and Secundus of the Thessalonians, and Gaius of Derbe, and
Timothy, and Tychicus and
Trophimus of Asia. 5These
men, going ahead, waited for
us at Troas. 6But we sailed
away from Philippi after the
Days of Unleavened Bread,
and in five days joined them
at Troas, where we stayed
seven days.

MINISTERING AT TROAS

7Now on the first *day* of
the week, when the disci-
ples came together to break
bread, Paul, ready to depart
the next day, spoke to them
and continued his message
until midnight. 8There were
many lamps in the upper
room where they[a] were gathered together. 9And in a window sat a certain young man
named Eutychus, who was
sinking into a deep sleep. He
was overcome by sleep; and
as Paul continued *speaking,*
he fell down from the third
story and was taken up dead.
10But Paul went down, fell on
him, and embracing *him* said,
"Do not trouble yourselves,
for his life is in him." 11Now
when he had come up, had
broken bread and eaten, and
talked a long while, even till
daybreak, he departed. 12And
they brought the young man
in alive, and they were not a
little comforted.

FROM TROAS TO MILETUS

13Then we went ahead to
the ship and sailed to Assos,
there intending to take Paul
on board; for so he had given
orders, intending himself to
go on foot. 14And when he met
us at Assos, we took him on
board and came to Mitylene.
15We sailed from there, and
the next *day* came opposite
Chios. The following *day* we
arrived at Samos and stayed
at Trogyllium. The next *day*
we came to Miletus. 16For Paul
had decided to sail past Ephesus, so that he would not have
to spend time in Asia; for he
was hurrying to be at Jerusalem, if possible, on the Day of
Pentecost.

THE EPHESIAN ELDERS EXHORTED

17From Miletus he sent to
Ephesus and called for the
elders of the church. 18And
when they had come to him,
he said to them: "You know,
from the first day that I came

20:8 [a] NU-Text and M-Text read *we.*

to Asia, in what manner I always lived among you, [19]serv-
ing the Lord with all humility,
with many tears and trials
which happened to me by the
plotting of the Jews; [20]how I
kept back nothing that was
helpful, but proclaimed it to
you, and taught you publicly
and from house to house,
[21]testifying to Jews, and also
to Greeks, repentance toward
God and faith toward our Lord
Jesus Christ. [22]And see, now
I go bound in the spirit to
Jerusalem, not knowing the
things that will happen to me
there, [23]except that the Holy
Spirit testifies in every city,
saying that chains and tribulations await me. [24]But none
of these things move me; nor
do I count my life dear to myself,[a] so that I may finish my
race with joy, and the ministry which I received from the
Lord Jesus, to testify to the
gospel of the grace of God.

[25]"And indeed, now I know
that you all, among whom I
have gone preaching the kingdom of God, will see my face
no more. [26]Therefore I testify to you this day that I *am*
innocent of the blood of all
men. [27]For I have not shunned
to declare to you the whole
counsel of God. [28]Therefore
take heed to yourselves and
to all the flock, among which
the Holy Spirit has made you
overseers, to shepherd the
church of God[a] which He purchased with His own blood.
[29]For I know this, that after
my departure savage wolves
will come in among you, not
sparing the flock. [30]Also from
among yourselves men will
rise up, speaking perverse
things, to draw away the disciples after themselves. [31]There-
fore watch, and remember
that for three years I did not
cease to warn everyone night
and day with tears.

[32]"So now, brethren, I commend you to God and to the
word of His grace, which is
able to build you up and give
you an inheritance among all
those who are sanctified. [33]I
have coveted no one's silver
or gold or apparel. [34]Yes,[a] you
yourselves know that these
hands have provided for my
necessities, and for those
who were with me. [35]I have
shown you in every way, by
laboring like this, that you
must support the weak. And
remember the words of the
Lord Jesus, that He said, 'It is
more blessed to give than to
receive.' "

[36]And when he had said
these things, he knelt down
and prayed with them all.
[37]Then they all wept freely,
and fell on Paul's neck and

20:24 [a] NU-Text reads *But I do not count my life of any value or dear to myself.* **20:28** [a] M-Text reads *of the Lord and God.* **20:34** [a] NU-Text and M-Text omit *Yes.*

kissed him, 38sorrowing most
of all for the words which he
spoke, that they would see his
face no more. And they accompanied him to the ship.

WARNINGS ON THE JOURNEY TO JERUSALEM

21 Now it came to pass, that
when we had departed
from them and set sail, running a straight course we
came to Cos, the following *day*
to Rhodes, and from there to
Patara. 2And finding a ship
sailing over to Phoenicia,
we went aboard and set sail.
3When we had sighted Cy-
prus, we passed it on the left,
sailed to Syria, and landed at
Tyre; for there the ship was
to unload her cargo. 4And
finding disciples,[a] we stayed
there seven days. They told
Paul through the Spirit not
to go up to Jerusalem. 5When
we had come to the end of
those days, we departed and
went on our way; and they
all accompanied us, with
wives and children, till *we
were* out of the city. And we
knelt down on the shore and
prayed. 6When we had taken
our leave of one another, we
boarded the ship, and they
returned home.

7And when we had fin-
ished *our* voyage from Tyre,
we came to Ptolemais, greeted
the brethren, and stayed with
them one day. 8On the next
day we who were Paul's companions[a] departed and came
to Caesarea, and entered the
house of Philip the evangelist,
who was *one* of the seven, and
stayed with him. 9Now this
man had four virgin daughters who prophesied. 10And
as we stayed many days, a
certain prophet named Agabus came down from Judea.
11When he had come to us,
he took Paul's belt, bound his
own hands and feet, and said,
"Thus says the Holy Spirit, 'So
shall the Jews at Jerusalem
bind the man who owns this
belt, and deliver *him* into the
hands of the Gentiles.'"

12Now when we heard these
things, both we and those
from that place pleaded with
him not to go up to Jerusalem. 13Then Paul answered,
"What do you mean by weeping and breaking my heart?
For I am ready not only to be
bound, but also to die at Jerusalem for the name of the
Lord Jesus."

14So when he would not be
persuaded, we ceased, saying,
"The will of the Lord be done."

PAUL URGED TO MAKE PEACE

15And after those days we
packed and went up to Jerusalem. 16Also some of the disci-

21:4 [a] NU-Text reads *the disciples.* 21:8 [a] NU-Text omits *who were Paul's companions.*

ples from Caesarea went with
us and brought with them a
certain Mnason of Cyprus, an
early disciple, with whom we
were to lodge.
17And when we had come
to Jerusalem, the brethren
received us gladly. 18On the
following *day* Paul went in
with us to James, and all the
elders were present. 19When
he had greeted them, he told
in detail those things which
God had done among the
Gentiles through his ministry.
20And when they heard *it,* they
glorified the Lord. And they
said to him, "You see, brother,
how many myriads of Jews
there are who have believed,
and they are all zealous for
the law; 21but they have been
informed about you that you
teach all the Jews who are
among the Gentiles to forsake
Moses, saying that they ought
not to circumcise *their* children
nor to walk according
to the customs. 22What then?
The assembly must certainly
meet, for they will[a] hear that
you have come. 23Therefore
do what we tell you: We have
four men who have taken
a vow. 24Take them and be
purified with them, and pay
their expenses so that they
may shave *their* heads, and
that all may know that those
things of which they were informed
concerning you are
nothing, but *that* you yourself
also walk orderly and
keep the law. 25But concerning
the Gentiles who believe,
we have written *and* decided
that they should observe no
such thing, except[a] that they
should keep themselves from
things offered to idols, from
blood, from things strangled,
and from sexual immorality."

ARRESTED IN THE TEMPLE

26Then Paul took the men,
and the next day, having been
purified with them, entered
the temple to announce the
expiration of the days of purification,
at which time an
offering should be made for
each one of them.

27Now when the seven
days were almost ended, the
Jews from Asia, seeing him
in the temple, stirred up the
whole crowd and laid hands
on him, 28crying out, "Men of
Israel, help! This is the man
who teaches all *men* everywhere
against the people,
the law, and this place; and
furthermore he also brought
Greeks into the temple and
has defiled this holy place."
29(For they had previously[a]
seen Trophimus the Ephesian
with him in the city, whom
they supposed that Paul had
brought into the temple.)

21:22 [a] NU-Text reads *What then is to be done? They will certainly.* 21:25 [a] NU-Text omits *that they should observe no such thing, except.* 21:29 [a] M-Text omits *previously.*

30And all the city was disturbed; and the people ran together, seized Paul, and dragged him out of the temple; and immediately the doors were shut. 31Now as they were seeking to kill him, news came to the commander of the garrison that all Jerusalem was in an uproar. 32He immediately took soldiers and centurions, and ran down to them. And when they saw the commander and the soldiers, they stopped beating Paul. 33Then the commander came near and took him, and commanded *him* to be bound with two chains; and he asked who he was and what he had done. 34And some among the multitude cried one thing and some another.

So when he could not ascertain the truth because of the tumult, he commanded him to be taken into the barracks. 35When he reached the stairs, he had to be carried by the soldiers because of the violence of the mob. 36For the multitude of the people followed after, crying out, "Away with him!"

ADDRESSING THE JERUSALEM MOB

37Then as Paul was about to be led into the barracks, he said to the commander, "May I speak to you?"

He replied, "Can you speak Greek? 38Are you not the Egyptian who some time ago stirred up a rebellion and led the four thousand assassins out into the wilderness?"

39But Paul said, "I am a Jew from Tarsus, in Cilicia, a citizen of no mean city; and I implore you, permit me to speak to the people."

40So when he had given him permission, Paul stood on the stairs and motioned with his hand to the people. And when there was a great silence, he spoke to *them* in the Hebrew language, saying,

22 "Brethren and fathers, hear my defense before you now." 2And when they heard that he spoke to them in the Hebrew language, they kept all the more silent.

Then he said: 3"I am indeed a Jew, born in Tarsus of Cilicia, but brought up in this city at the feet of Gamaliel, taught according to the strictness of our fathers' law, and was zealous toward God as you all are today. 4I persecuted this Way to the death, binding and delivering into prisons both men and women, 5as also the high priest bears me witness, and all the council of the elders, from whom I also received letters to the brethren, and went to Damascus to bring in chains even those who were there to Jerusalem to be punished.

6"Now it happened, as I *journeyed* and came near Damascus at about noon, suddenly a great light from heaven shone around me. 7And I fell to the ground and heard a voice

saying to me, 'Saul, Saul, why
are you persecuting Me?' 8So I
answered, 'Who are You, Lord?'
And He said to me, 'I am Jesus
of Nazareth, whom you are
persecuting.'

9"And those who were with
me indeed saw the light and
were afraid,[a] but they did not
hear the voice of Him who
spoke to me. 10So I said, 'What
shall I do, Lord?' And the Lord
said to me, 'Arise and go into
Damascus, and there you will
be told all things which are
appointed for you to do.' 11And
since I could not see for the
glory of that light, being led
by the hand of those who were
with me, I came into Damascus.

12"Then a certain Ananias,
a devout man according to the
law, having a good testimony
with all the Jews who dwelt
there, 13came to me; and he
stood and said to me, 'Brother
Saul, receive your sight.' And
at that same hour I looked up
at him. 14Then he said, 'The
God of our fathers has chosen
you that you should know His
will, and see the Just One, and
hear the voice of His mouth.
15For you will be His witness
to all men of what you have
seen and heard. 16And now
why are you waiting? Arise
and be baptized, and wash
away your sins, calling on the
name of the Lord.'

17"Now it happened, when
I returned to Jerusalem and
was praying in the temple,
that I was in a trance 18and
saw Him saying to me, 'Make
haste and get out of Jerusalem
quickly, for they will not receive
your testimony concerning
Me.' 19So I said, 'Lord, they
know that in every synagogue
I imprisoned and beat those
who believe on You. 20And
when the blood of Your martyr
Stephen was shed, I also
was standing by consenting
to his death,[a] and guarding
the clothes of those who were
killing him.' 21Then He said to
me, 'Depart, for I will send you
far from here to the Gentiles.'"

PAUL'S ROMAN CITIZENSHIP

22And they listened to him
until this word, and *then* they
raised their voices and said,
"Away with such a *fellow* from
the earth, for he is not fit to
live!" 23Then, as they cried out
and tore off *their* clothes and
threw dust into the air, 24the
commander ordered him to
be brought into the barracks,
and said that he should be
examined under scourging,
so that he might know why
they shouted so against him.
25And as they bound him
with thongs, Paul said to the
centurion who stood by, "Is
it lawful for you to scourge

22:9 [a] NU-Text omits *and were afraid.*
22:20 [a] NU-Text omits *to his death.*

a man who is a Roman, and uncondemned?"

26When the centurion heard *that,* he went and told the commander, saying, "Take care what you do, for this man is a Roman."

27Then the commander came and said to him, "Tell me, are you a Roman?"

He said, "Yes."

28The commander answered, "With a large sum I obtained this citizenship."

And Paul said, "But I was born *a citizen.*"

29Then immediately those who were about to examine him withdrew from him; and the commander was also afraid after he found out that he was a Roman, and because he had bound him.

THE SANHEDRIN DIVIDED

30The next day, because he wanted to know for certain why he was accused by the Jews, he released him from *his* bonds, and commanded the chief priests and all their council to appear, and brought Paul down and set him before them.

23 Then Paul, looking earnestly at the council, said, "Men *and* brethren, I have lived in all good conscience before God until this day." 2And the high priest Ananias commanded those who stood by him to strike him on the mouth. 3Then Paul said to him, "God will strike you, *you* whitewashed wall! For you sit to judge me according to the law, and do you command me to be struck contrary to the law?"

4And those who stood by said, "Do you revile God's high priest?"

5Then Paul said, "I did not know, brethren, that he was the high priest; for it is written, 'You shall not speak evil of a ruler of your people.'"[a]

6But when Paul perceived that one part were Sadducees and the other Pharisees, he cried out in the council, "Men *and* brethren, I am a Pharisee, the son of a Pharisee; concerning the hope and resurrection of the dead I am being judged!"

7And when he had said this, a dissension arose between the Pharisees and the Sadducees; and the assembly was divided. 8For Sadducees say that there is no resurrection—and no angel or spirit; but the Pharisees confess both. 9Then there arose a loud outcry. And the scribes of the Pharisees' party arose and protested, saying, "We find no evil in this man; but if a spirit or an angel has spoken to him, let us not fight against God."[a]

10Now when there arose

23:5 [a] Exodus 22:28 **23:9** [a] NU-Text omits last clause and reads *what if a spirit or an angel has spoken to him?*

a great dissension, the commander, fearing lest Paul might
be pulled to pieces by them,
commanded the soldiers to go
down and take him by force
from among them, and bring
him into the barracks.

THE PLOT AGAINST PAUL

11But the following night
the Lord stood by him and
said, "Be of good cheer, Paul;
for as you have testified for
Me in Jerusalem, so you must
also bear witness at Rome."
12And when it was day, some
of the Jews banded together
and bound themselves under
an oath, saying that they would
neither eat nor drink till they
had killed Paul. 13Now there
were more than forty who
had formed this conspir-
acy. 14They came to the chief
priests and elders, and said,
"We have bound ourselves
under a great oath that we
will eat nothing until we have
killed Paul. 15Now you, therefore, together with the council, suggest to the commander
that he be brought down to
you tomorrow,[a] as though you
were going to make further in-
quiries concerning him; but
we are ready to kill him before
he comes near."
16So when Paul's sister's
son heard of their ambush,
he went and entered the barracks and told Paul. 17Then
Paul called one of the centurions to *him* and said, "Take
this young man to the commander, for he has something
to tell him." 18So he took him
and brought *him* to the commander and said, "Paul the
prisoner called me to *him* and
asked *me* to bring this young
man to you. He has something
to say to you."
19Then the commander
took him by the hand, went
aside, and asked privately,
"What is it that you have to
tell me?"
20And he said, "The Jews
have agreed to ask that you
bring Paul down to the council tomorrow, as though they
were going to inquire more
fully about him. 21But do not
yield to them, for more than
forty of them lie in wait for
him, men who have bound
themselves by an oath that
they will neither eat nor drink
till they have killed him; and
now they are ready, waiting for
the promise from you."
22So the commander let
the young man depart, and
commanded *him*, "Tell no one
that you have revealed these
things to me."

SENT TO FELIX

23And he called for two
centurions, saying, "Prepare
two hundred soldiers, seventy
horsemen, and two hundred
spearmen to go to Caesarea
at the third hour of the night;

23:15 [a] NU-Text omits *tomorrow*.

24and provide mounts to set
Paul on, and bring *him* safely
to Felix the governor." 25He
wrote a letter in the following
manner:

26 Claudius Lysias,

To the most excellent
governor Felix:

Greetings.

27 This man was seized by
the Jews and was about
to be killed by them.
Coming with the troops
I rescued him, having
learned that he was a
Roman. 28And when
I wanted to know the
reason they accused him,
I brought him before
their council. 29I found
out that he was accused
concerning questions
of their law, but had
nothing charged against
him deserving of death
or chains. 30And when it
was told me that the Jews
lay in wait for the man,[a]
I sent him immediately
to you, and also
commanded his accusers
to state before you the
charges against him.

Farewell.

31Then the soldiers, as they
were commanded, took Paul
and brought *him* by night to
Antipatris. 32The next day
they left the horsemen to go
on with him, and returned
to the barracks. 33When they
came to Caesarea and had delivered the letter to the governor, they also presented
Paul to him. 34And when the
governor had read *it,* he asked
what province he was from.
And when he understood that
he was from Cilicia, 35he said,
"I will hear you when your accusers also have come." And
he commanded him to be kept
in Herod's Praetorium.

ACCUSED OF SEDITION

24 Now after five days Ananias the high priest
came down with the elders
and a certain orator *named*
Tertullus. These gave evidence
to the governor against Paul.
2And when he was called
upon, Tertullus began his accusation, saying: "Seeing that
through you we enjoy great
peace, and prosperity is being
brought to this nation by your
foresight, 3we accept *it* always
and in all places, most noble
Felix, with all thankfulness.
4Nevertheless, not to be tedious to you any further, I beg
you to hear, by your courtesy,
a few words from us. 5For we
have found this man a plague,
a creator of dissension among
all the Jews throughout the
world, and a ringleader of

23:30 [a] NU-Text reads *there would be a plot against the man.*

the sect of the Nazarenes.
6He even tried to profane the
temple, and we seized him,[a]
and wanted to judge him according to our law. 7But the
commander Lysias came by
and with great violence took
him out of our hands, 8com-
manding his accusers to come
to you. By examining him
yourself you may ascertain
all these things of which we
accuse him." 9And the Jews
also assented,[a] maintaining
that these things were so.

THE DEFENSE BEFORE FELIX

10Then Paul, after the governor had nodded to him to
speak, answered: "Inasmuch
as I know that you have been
for many years a judge of this
nation, I do the more cheer-
fully answer for myself, 11be-
cause you may ascertain that
it is no more than twelve days
since I went up to Jerusalem
to worship. 12And they neither found me in the temple
disputing with anyone nor
inciting the crowd, either
in the synagogues or in the
city. 13Nor can they prove the
things of which they now accuse me. 14But this I confess
to you, that according to the
Way which they call a sect,
so I worship the God of my
fathers, believing all things
which are written in the Law
and in the Prophets. 15I have
hope in God, which they
themselves also accept, that
there will be a resurrection
of *the* dead,[a] both of *the* just
and *the* unjust. 16This *being* so,
I myself always strive to have
a conscience without offense
toward God and men.

17"Now after many years I
came to bring alms and offerings to my nation, 18in the
midst of which some Jews
from Asia found me purified
in the temple, neither with a
mob nor with tumult. 19They
ought to have been here before you to object if they had
anything against me. 20Or else
let those who are *here* themselves say if they found any
wrongdoing[a] in me while I
stood before the council, 21un-
less *it is* for this one statement
which I cried out, standing
among them, 'Concerning the
resurrection of the dead I am
being judged by you this day.'"

FELIX PROCRASTINATES

22But when Felix heard
these things, having more ac-
curate knowledge of *the* Way,
he adjourned the proceedings
and said, "When Lysias the
commander comes down, I
will make a decision on your
case." 23So he commanded the
centurion to keep Paul and to

24:6 [a] NU-Text ends the sentence here and omits the rest of verse 6, all of verse 7, and the first clause of verse 8. 24:9 [a] NU-Text and M-Text read *joined the attack.* 24:15 [a] NU-Text omits *of the dead.* 24:20 [a] NU-Text and M-Text read *say what wrongdoing they found.*

let *him* have liberty, and told
him not to forbid any of his
friends to provide for or visit
him.
24And after some days,
when Felix came with his wife
Drusilla, who was Jewish, he
sent for Paul and heard him
concerning the faith in Christ.
25Now as he reasoned about
righteousness, self-control,
and the judgment to come,
Felix was afraid and answered,
"Go away for now; when I have
a convenient time I will call
for you." 26Meanwhile he also
hoped that money would be
given him by Paul, that he
might release him.[a] Therefore
he sent for him more often
and conversed with him.
27But after two years Por-
cius Festus succeeded Felix;
and Felix, wanting to do the
Jews a favor, left Paul bound.

PAUL APPEALS TO CAESAR

25 Now when Festus had
come to the province,
after three days he went up
from Caesarea to Jerusalem.
2Then the high priest[a] and
the chief men of the Jews informed him against Paul; and
they petitioned him, 3asking
a favor against him, that he
would summon him to Jeru-
salem—while *they* lay in ambush along the road to kill him.
4But Festus answered that Paul
should be kept at Caesarea, and
that he himself was going *there*
shortly. 5"Therefore," he said,
"let those who have authority
among you go down with *me*
and accuse this man, to see if
there is any fault in him."
6And when he had re-
mained among them more
than ten days, he went down
to Caesarea. And the next day,
sitting on the judgment seat,
he commanded Paul to be
brought. 7When he had come,
the Jews who had come down
from Jerusalem stood about
and laid many serious complaints against Paul, which
they could not prove, 8while he
answered for himself, "Neither
against the law of the Jews, nor
against the temple, nor against
Caesar have I offended in anything at all."
9But Festus, wanting to do
the Jews a favor, answered Paul
and said, "Are you willing to go
up to Jerusalem and there be
judged before me concerning
these things?"
10So Paul said, "I stand at
Caesar's judgment seat, where
I ought to be judged. To the
Jews I have done no wrong,
as you very well know. 11For if
I am an offender, or have committed anything deserving of
death, I do not object to dying;
but if there is nothing in these
things of which these men ac-
cuse me, no one can deliver me
to them. I appeal to Caesar."

24:26 [a] NU-Text omits *that he might release him.* 25:2 [a] NU-Text reads *chief priests.*

12Then Festus, when he had
conferred with the council,
answered, "You have ap-
pealed to Caesar? To Caesar
you shall go!"

PAUL BEFORE AGRIPPA

13And after some days King
Agrippa and Bernice came
to Caesarea to greet Festus.
14When they had been there
many days, Festus laid Paul's
case before the king, saying:
"There is a certain man left
a prisoner by Felix, 15about
whom the chief priests and the
elders of the Jews informed
me, when I was in Jerusalem,
asking for a judgment against
him. 16To them I answered,
'It is not the custom of the
Romans to deliver any man
to destruction[a] before the
accused meets the accusers
face to face, and has opportunity to answer for himself
concerning the charge against
him.' 17Therefore when they
had come together, without
any delay, the next day I sat
on the judgment seat and
commanded the man to be
brought in. 18When the accusers stood up, they brought
no accusation against him of
such things as I supposed,
19but had some questions
against him about their own
religion and about a certain
Jesus, who had died, whom
Paul affirmed to be alive.
20And because I was uncertain of such questions, I asked
whether he was willing to go
to Jerusalem and there be
judged concerning these matters. 21But when Paul appealed
to be reserved for the decision
of Augustus, I commanded
him to be kept till I could send
him to Caesar."

22Then Agrippa said to Festus, "I also would like to hear
the man myself."

"Tomorrow," he said, "you
shall hear him."

23So the next day, when
Agrippa and Bernice had
come with great pomp, and
had entered the auditorium
with the commanders and the
prominent men of the city,
at Festus' command Paul was
brought in. 24And Festus said:
"King Agrippa and all the men
who are here present with
us, you see this man about
whom the whole assembly of
the Jews petitioned me, both
at Jerusalem and here, crying out that he was not fit to
live any longer. 25But when I
found that he had committed
nothing deserving of death,
and that he himself had appealed to Augustus, I decided
to send him. 26I have nothing certain to write to my lord
concerning him. Therefore I
have brought him out before
you, and especially before you,
King Agrippa, so that after the
examination has taken place I
may have something to write.

25:16 [a] NU-Text omits *to destruction,* although it is implied.

27For it seems to me unreasonable to send a prisoner and not to specify the charges against him."

PAUL'S EARLY LIFE

26 Then Agrippa said to Paul, "You are permitted to speak for yourself."

So Paul stretched out his hand and answered for himself: 2"I think myself happy, King Agrippa, because today I shall answer for myself before you concerning all the things of which I am accused by the Jews, 3especially because you are expert in all customs and questions which have to do with the Jews. Therefore I beg you to hear me patiently.

4"My manner of life from my youth, which was spent from the beginning among my own nation at Jerusalem, all the Jews know. 5They knew me from the first, if they were willing to testify, that according to the strictest sect of our religion I lived a Pharisee. 6And now I stand and am judged for the hope of the promise made by God to our fathers. 7To this *promise* our twelve tribes, earnestly serving *God* night and day, hope to attain. For this hope's sake, King Agrippa, I am accused by the Jews. 8Why should it be thought incredible by you that God raises the dead?

9"Indeed, I myself thought I must do many things contrary to the name of Jesus of Nazareth. 10This I also did in Jerusalem, and many of the saints I shut up in prison, having received authority from the chief priests; and when they were put to death, I cast my vote against *them.* 11And I punished them often in every synagogue and compelled *them* to blaspheme; and being exceedingly enraged against them, I persecuted *them* even to foreign cities.

PAUL RECOUNTS HIS CONVERSION

12"While thus occupied, as I journeyed to Damascus with authority and commission from the chief priests, 13at midday, O king, along the road I saw a light from heaven, brighter than the sun, shining around me and those who journeyed with me. 14And when we all had fallen to the ground, I heard a voice speaking to me and saying in the Hebrew language, 'Saul, Saul, why are you persecuting Me? *It is* hard for you to kick against the goads.' 15So I said, 'Who are You, Lord?' And He said, 'I am Jesus, whom you are persecuting. 16But rise and stand on your feet; for I have appeared to you for this purpose, to make you a minister and a witness both of the things which you have seen and of the things which I will yet reveal to you. 17I will deliver you from the *Jewish* people, as well as *from*

the Gentiles, to whom I now[a]
send you, 18to open their eyes,
in order to turn *them* from
darkness to light, and *from* the
power of Satan to God, that
they may receive forgiveness
of sins and an inheritance
among those who are sanctified by faith in Me.'

PAUL'S POST-CONVERSION LIFE

19"Therefore, King Agrippa,
I was not disobedient to the
heavenly vision, 20but declared first to those in Damascus and in Jerusalem, and
throughout all the region of
Judea, and *then* to the Gentiles, that they should repent,
turn to God, and do works be-
fitting repentance. 21For these
reasons the Jews seized me
in the temple and tried to
kill *me*. 22Therefore, having
obtained help from God, to
this day I stand, witnessing
both to small and great, saying no other things than those
which the prophets and Moses
said would come— 23that the
Christ would suffer, that He
would be the first to rise from
the dead, and would proclaim
light to the *Jewish* people and
to the Gentiles."

AGRIPPA PARRIES PAUL'S CHALLENGE

24Now as he thus made his
defense, Festus said with a
loud voice, "Paul, you are beside yourself! Much learning
is driving you mad!"
25But he said, "I am not
mad, most noble Festus, but
speak the words of truth and
reason. 26For the king, before
whom I also speak freely,
knows these things; for I am
convinced that none of these
things escapes his attention,
since this thing was not done
in a corner. 27King Agrippa,
do you believe the prophets?
I know that you do believe."
28Then Agrippa said to
Paul, "You almost persuade
me to become a Christian."
29And Paul said, "I would
to God that not only you, but
also all who hear me today,
might become both almost
and altogether such as I am,
except for these chains."
30When he had said these
things, the king stood up, as
well as the governor and Bernice and those who sat with
them; 31and when they had
gone aside, they talked among
themselves, saying, "This man
is doing nothing deserving of
death or chains."
32Then Agrippa said to
Festus, "This man might have
been set free if he had not appealed to Caesar."

THE VOYAGE TO ROME BEGINS

27 And when it was de-
cided that we should
sail to Italy, they delivered

26:17 [a] NU-Text and M-Text omit *now*.

Paul and some other pris-
oners to *one* named Julius,
a centurion of the Augustan
Regiment. 2So, entering a ship
of Adramyttium, we put to
sea, meaning to sail along the
coasts of Asia. Aristarchus, a
Macedonian of Thessalonica,
was with us. 3And the next *day*
we landed at Sidon. And Julius
treated Paul kindly and gave
him liberty to go to his friends
and receive care. 4When we
had put to sea from there, we
sailed under *the shelter of* Cyprus, because the winds were
contrary. 5And when we had
sailed over the sea which is
off Cilicia and Pamphylia, we
came to Myra, *a city* of Lycia.
6There the centurion found
an Alexandrian ship sailing to
Italy, and he put us on board.

7When we had sailed slowly
many days, and arrived with
difficulty off Cnidus, the wind
not permitting us to proceed,
we sailed under *the shelter of*
Crete off Salmone. 8Passing it
with difficulty, we came to a
place called Fair Havens, near
the city *of* Lasea.

PAUL'S WARNING IGNORED

9Now when much time had
been spent, and sailing was
now dangerous because the
Fast was already over, Paul advised them, 10saying, "Men, I
perceive that this voyage will
end with disaster and much
loss, not only of the cargo
and ship, but also our lives."
11Nevertheless the centurion
was more persuaded by the
helmsman and the owner of
the ship than by the things
spoken by Paul. 12And because
the harbor was not suitable
to winter in, the majority advised to set sail from there
also, if by any means they
could reach Phoenix, a harbor of Crete opening toward
the southwest and northwest,
and winter *there.*

IN THE TEMPEST

13When the south wind
blew softly, supposing that
they had obtained *their* desire,
putting out to sea, they sailed
close by Crete. 14But not long
after, a tempestuous head
wind arose, called Eurocly-
don.[a] 15So when the ship was
caught, and could not head
into the wind, we let *her* drive.
16And running under *the shelter of* an island called Clauda,[a]
we secured the skiff with difficulty. 17When they had taken
it on board, they used cables
to undergird the ship; and
fearing lest they should run
aground on the Syrtis[a] *Sands,*
they struck sail and so were
driven. 18And because we were
exceedingly tempest-tossed,
the next *day* they lightened
the ship. 19On the third *day* we
threw the ship's tackle over-

27:14 [a] NU-Text reads *Euraquilon.* 27:16 [a] NU-Text reads *Cauda.* 27:17 [a] M-Text reads *Syrtes.*

board with our own hands.
20Now when neither sun nor
stars appeared for many days,
and no small tempest beat on
us, all hope that we would be
saved was finally given up.
21But after long absti-
nence from food, then Paul
stood in the midst of them
and said, "Men, you should
have listened to me, and not
have sailed from Crete and in-
curred this disaster and loss.
22And now I urge you to take
heart, for there will be no loss
of life among you, but only
of the ship. 23For there stood
by me this night an angel of
the God to whom I belong and
whom I serve, 24saying, 'Do
not be afraid, Paul; you must
be brought before Caesar; and
indeed God has granted you
all those who sail with you.'
25Therefore take heart, men,
for I believe God that it will be
just as it was told me. 26How-
ever, we must run aground on
a certain island."
27Now when the fourteenth
night had come, as we were
driven up and down in the
Adriatic *Sea,* about midnight
the sailors sensed that they
were drawing near some land.
28And they took soundings
and found *it* to be twenty
fathoms; and when they had
gone a little farther, they took
soundings again and found *it*
to be fifteen fathoms. 29Then,
fearing lest we should run
aground on the rocks, they
dropped four anchors from
the stern, and prayed for day
to come. 30And as the sailors
were seeking to escape from
the ship, when they had let
down the skiff into the sea,
under pretense of putting out
anchors from the prow, 31Paul
said to the centurion and the
soldiers, "Unless these men
stay in the ship, you cannot
be saved." 32Then the soldiers
cut away the ropes of the skiff
and let it fall off.
33And as day was about to
dawn, Paul implored *them* all
to take food, saying, "Today is
the fourteenth day you have
waited and continued without food, and eaten nothing.
34Therefore I urge you to
take nourishment, for this is
for your survival, since not
a hair will fall from the head
of any of you." 35And when
he had said these things, he
took bread and gave thanks to
God in the presence of them
all; and when he had broken
it he began to eat. 36Then they
were all encouraged, and also
took food themselves. 37And
in all we were two hundred
and seventy-six persons on
the ship. 38So when they had
eaten enough, they lightened
the ship and threw out the
wheat into the sea.

SHIPWRECKED ON MALTA

39When it was day, they
did not recognize the land;
but they observed a bay with
a beach, onto which they
planned to run the ship if

possible. [40]And they let go the
anchors and left *them* in the
sea, meanwhile loosing the
rudder ropes; and they hoisted
the mainsail to the wind and
made for shore. [41]But striking
a place where two seas met,
they ran the ship aground;
and the prow stuck fast and
remained immovable, but the
stern was being broken up by
the violence of the waves.

[42]And the soldiers' plan
was to kill the prisoners, lest
any of them should swim
away and escape. [43]But the
centurion, wanting to save
Paul, kept them from *their*
purpose, and commanded
that those who could swim
should jump *overboard* first
and get to land, [44]and the rest,
some on boards and some on
parts of the ship. And so it was
that they all escaped safely
to land.

PAUL'S MINISTRY ON MALTA

28 Now when they had
escaped, they then
found out that the island was
called Malta. [2]And the natives
showed us unusual kindness;
for they kindled a fire and
made us all welcome, because
of the rain that was falling and
because of the cold. [3]But when
Paul had gathered a bundle
of sticks and laid *them on the
fire,* a viper came out because
of the heat, and fastened on
his hand. [4]So when the natives
saw the creature hanging from
his hand, they said to one another,
"No doubt this man is
a murderer, whom, though
he has escaped the sea, yet
justice does not allow to live."
[5]But he shook off the creature
into the fire and suffered no
harm. [6]However, they were expecting
that he would swell up
or suddenly fall down dead.
But after they had looked for
a long time and saw no harm
come to him, they changed
their minds and said that he
was a god.

[7]In that region there was an
estate of the leading citizen of
the island, whose name was
Publius, who received us and
entertained us courteously for
three days. [8]And it happened
that the father of Publius lay
sick of a fever and dysentery.
Paul went in to him and
prayed, and he laid his hands
on him and healed him. [9]So
when this was done, the rest
of those on the island who had
diseases also came and were
healed. [10]They also honored
us in many ways; and when
we departed, they provided
such things as were necessary.

ARRIVAL AT ROME

[11]After three months we
sailed in an Alexandrian
ship whose figurehead was
the Twin Brothers, which had
wintered at the island. [12]And
landing at Syracuse, we stayed
three days. [13]From there we
circled round and reached
Rhegium. And after one day

the south wind blew; and the
next day we came to Puteoli,
14where we found brethren,
and were invited to stay with
them seven days. And so we
went toward Rome. 15And
from there, when the brethren
heard about us, they came to
meet us as far as Appii Forum
and Three Inns. When Paul
saw them, he thanked God and
took courage.

16Now when we came to
Rome, the centurion delivered the prisoners to the captain of the guard; but Paul was
permitted to dwell by himself
with the soldier who guarded
him.

PAUL'S MINISTRY AT ROME

17And it came to pass after
three days that Paul called the
leaders of the Jews together.
So when they had come to-
gether, he said to them: "Men
and brethren, though I have
done nothing against our
people or the customs of our
fathers, yet I was delivered
as a prisoner from Jerusalem into the hands of the Romans, 18who, when they had
examined me, wanted to let
me go, because there was no
cause for putting me to death.
19But when the Jews[a] spoke
against *it*, I was compelled
to appeal to Caesar, not that
I had anything of which to
accuse my nation. 20For this
reason therefore I have called
for you, to see *you* and speak
with *you*, because for the hope
of Israel I am bound with this
chain."

21Then they said to him,
"We neither received letters
from Judea concerning you,
nor have any of the brethren
who came reported or spo-
ken any evil of you. 22But we
desire to hear from you what
you think; for concerning this
sect, we know that it is spoken
against everywhere."

23So when they had ap-
pointed him a day, many
came to him at *his* lodging,
to whom he explained and
solemnly testified of the
kingdom of God, persuading
them concerning Jesus from
both the Law of Moses and
the Prophets, from morning
till evening. 24And some were
persuaded by the things which
were spoken, and some disbe-
lieved. 25So when they did not
agree among themselves, they
departed after Paul had said
one word: "The Holy Spirit
spoke rightly through Isaiah
the prophet to our[a] fathers,
26saying,

'Go to this people and say:
"Hearing you will
hear, and shall not
understand;
And seeing you will see,
and not perceive;
27 For the hearts of this
people have grown dull.

28:19 [a] That is, the ruling authorities 28:25 [a] NU-Text reads *your*.

Their ears are hard
of hearing,
And their eyes they
have closed,
Lest they should see
with *their* eyes and
hear with *their* ears,
Lest they should
understand with *their*
hearts and turn,
So that I should
heal them."'[a]

28"Therefore let it be
known to you that the salvation of God has been sent
to the Gentiles, and they will
hear it!" 29And when he had
said these words, the Jews departed and had a great dispute
among themselves.[a]

30Then Paul dwelt two
whole years in his own rented
house, and received all who
came to him, 31preaching the
kingdom of God and teach-
ing the things which concern
the Lord Jesus Christ with all
confidence, no one forbidding
him.

THE EPISTLE OF PAUL THE APOSTLE TO THE

ROMANS

GREETING

1 Paul, a bondservant of Jesus
Christ, called *to be* an apostle, separated to the gospel
of God 2which He promised
before through His prophets
in the Holy Scriptures, 3con-
cerning His Son Jesus Christ
our Lord, who was born of
the seed of David according
to the flesh, 4*and* declared *to*
be the Son of God with power
according to the Spirit of holiness, by the resurrection from
the dead. 5Through Him we
have received grace and apostleship for obedience to the
faith among all nations for His
name, 6among whom you also
are the called of Jesus Christ;

7To all who are in Rome,
beloved of God, called *to be*
saints:

Grace to you and peace
from God our Father and the
Lord Jesus Christ.

DESIRE TO VISIT ROME

8First, I thank my God
through Jesus Christ for you
all, that your faith is spoken of
throughout the whole world.
9For God is my witness, whom
I serve with my spirit in the

28:27 [a] Isaiah 6:9, 10 28:29 [a] NU-Text omits this verse.

gospel of His Son, that without ceasing I make mention
of you always in my prayers,
10making request if, by some
means, now at last I may find a
way in the will of God to come
to you. 11For I long to see you,
that I may impart to you some
spiritual gift, so that you may
be established— 12that is, that
I may be encouraged together
with you by the mutual faith
both of you and me.

13Now I do not want you
to be unaware, brethren, that
I often planned to come to
you (but was hindered until
now), that I might have some
fruit among you also, just as
among the other Gentiles. 14I
am a debtor both to Greeks
and to barbarians, both to
wise and to unwise. 15So, as
much as is in me, *I am* ready
to preach the gospel to you
who are in Rome also.

THE JUST LIVE BY FAITH

16For I am not ashamed of
the gospel of Christ,[a] for it is
the power of God to salvation
for everyone who believes, for
the Jew first and also for the
Greek. 17For in it the righteousness of God is revealed from
faith to faith; as it is written,
"The just shall live by faith."[a]

GOD'S WRATH ON UNRIGHTEOUSNESS

18For the wrath of God is revealed from heaven against all
ungodliness and unrighteousness of men, who suppress
the truth in unrighteousness,
19because what may be known
of God is manifest in them,
for God has shown *it* to them.
20For since the creation of the
world His invisible *attributes*
are clearly seen, being understood by the things that are
made, *even* His eternal power
and Godhead, so that they are
without excuse, 21because, although they knew God, they
did not glorify *Him* as God,
nor were thankful, but became futile in their thoughts,
and their foolish hearts were
darkened. 22Professing to be
wise, they became fools, 23and
changed the glory of the incorruptible God into an image
made like corruptible man—
and birds and four-footed animals and creeping things.

24Therefore God also gave
them up to uncleanness, in
the lusts of their hearts, to
dishonor their bodies among
themselves, 25who exchanged
the truth of God for the lie,
and worshiped and served the
creature rather than the Creator, who is blessed forever.
Amen.

26For this reason God gave
them up to vile passions. For
even their women exchanged
the natural use for what is
against nature. 27Likewise also
the men, leaving the natural
use of the woman, burned

1:16 [a] NU-Text omits *of Christ*. 1:17 [a] Habakkuk 2:4

in their lust for one another,
men with men committing
what is shameful, and receiving in themselves the penalty
of their error which was due.
28And even as they did
not like to retain God in *their*
knowledge, God gave them
over to a debased mind, to
do those things which are not
fitting; 29being filled with all
unrighteousness, sexual immorality,[a] wickedness, covetousness, maliciousness;
full of envy, murder, strife,
deceit, evil-mindedness;
they are whisperers, 30back-
biters, haters of God, violent,
proud, boasters, inventors
of evil things, disobedient to
parents, 31undiscerning, un-
trustworthy, unloving, unforgiving,[a] unmerciful; 32who,
knowing the righteous judgment of God, that those who
practice such things are deserving of death, not only do
the same but also approve of
those who practice them.

GOD'S RIGHTEOUS JUDGMENT

2 Therefore you are inex-
cusable, O man, whoever
you are who judge, for in whatever you judge another you
condemn yourself; for you
who judge practice the same
things. 2But we know that the
judgment of God is according
to truth against those who
practice such things. 3And
do you think this, O man, you
who judge those practicing
such things, and doing the
same, that you will escape
the judgment of God? 4Or do
you despise the riches of His
goodness, forbearance, and
longsuffering, not knowing
that the goodness of God leads
you to repentance? 5But in accordance with your hardness
and your impenitent heart you
are treasuring up for yourself
wrath in the day of wrath and
revelation of the righteous
judgment of God, 6who "will
render to each one according
to his deeds":[a] 7eternal life to
those who by patient contin-
uance in doing good seek for
glory, honor, and immortality; 8but to those who are self-
seeking and do not obey the
truth, but obey unrighteousness—indignation and wrath,
9tribulation and anguish, on
every soul of man who does
evil, of the Jew first and also of
the Greek; 10but glory, honor,
and peace to everyone who
works what is good, to the Jew
first and also to the Greek. 11For
there is no partiality with God.
12For as many as have
sinned without law will also
perish without law, and as
many as have sinned in the
law will be judged by the law
13(*for not* the hearers of the
law *are* just in the sight of God,

1:29 [a] NU-Text omits *sexual immorality.* 1:31 [a] NU-Text omits *unforgiving.* 2:6 [a] Psalm 62:12; Proverbs 24:12

but the doers of the law will be justified; 14for when Gentiles, who do not have the law, by nature do the things in the law, these, although not having the law, are a law to themselves, 15who show the work of the law written in their hearts, their conscience also bearing witness, and between themselves *their* thoughts accusing or else excusing *them*) 16in the day when God will judge the secrets of men by Jesus Christ, according to my gospel.

THE JEWS GUILTY AS THE GENTILES

17Indeed[a] you are called a Jew, and rest on the law, and make your boast in God, 18and know *His* will, and approve the things that are excellent, being instructed out of the law, 19and are confident that you yourself are a guide to the blind, a light to those who are in darkness, 20an instructor of the foolish, a teacher of babes, having the form of knowledge and truth in the law. 21You, therefore, who teach another, do you not teach yourself? You who preach that a man should not steal, do you steal? 22You who say, "Do not commit adultery," do you commit adultery? You who abhor idols, do you rob temples? 23You who make your boast in the law, do you dishonor God through breaking the law? 24For "the name of God is blasphemed among the Gentiles because of you,"[a] as it is written.

CIRCUMCISION OF NO AVAIL

25For circumcision is indeed profitable if you keep the law; but if you are a breaker of the law, your circumcision has become uncircumcision. 26Therefore, if an uncircumcised man keeps the righteous requirements of the law, will not his uncircumcision be counted as circumcision? 27And will not the physically uncircumcised, if he fulfills the law, judge you who, *even* with *your* written *code* and circumcision, *are* a transgressor of the law? 28For he is not a Jew who *is one* outwardly, nor *is* circumcision that which *is* outward in the flesh; 29but *he is* a Jew who *is one* inwardly; and circumcision *is that* of the heart, in the Spirit, not in the letter; whose praise *is* not from men but from God.

GOD'S JUDGMENT DEFENDED

3 What advantage then has the Jew, or what *is* the profit of circumcision? 2Much in every way! Chiefly because to them were committed the oracles of God. 3For what if some did not believe? Will their unbelief make the faithfulness of God without effect?

2:17 [a] NU-Text reads *But if.* 2:24 [a] Isaiah 52:5; Ezekiel 36:22

4 Certainly not! Indeed, let God
be true but every man a liar.
As it is written:

"That You may be
justified in Your words,
And may overcome when
You are judged."[a]

5 But if our unrighteous-
ness demonstrates the righteousness of God, what shall
we say? *Is* God unjust who
inflicts wrath? (I speak as a
man.) 6 Certainly not! For then
how will God judge the world?
7 For if the truth of God has
increased through my lie to
His glory, why am I also still
judged as a sinner? 8 And *why*
not *say,* "Let us do evil that
good may come"?—as we are
slanderously reported and as
some affirm that we say. Their
condemnation is just.

ALL HAVE SINNED

9 What then? Are we better
than they? Not at all. For we
have previously charged both
Jews and Greeks that they are
all under sin.
10 As it is written:

"There is none
righteous, no, not one;
11 There is none who
understands;
There is none who
seeks after God.
12 They have all
turned aside;
They have together
become unprofitable;
There is none who does
good, no, not one."[a]
13 "Their throat *is* an
open tomb;
With their tongues they
have practiced deceit";[a]
"The poison of asps *is*
under their lips";[b]
14 "Whose mouth *is*
full of cursing and
bitterness."[a]
15 "Their feet *are* swift
to shed blood;
16 Destruction and misery
are in their ways;
17 And the way of peace
they have not known."[a]
18 "There is no fear of God
before their eyes."[a]

19 Now we know that what-
ever the law says, it says to
those who are under the law,
that every mouth may be
stopped, and all the world
may become guilty before
God. 20 Therefore by the deeds
of the law no flesh will be justified in His sight, for by the
law *is* the knowledge of sin.

GOD'S RIGHTEOUSNESS THROUGH FAITH

21 But now the righteous-
ness of God apart from the law
is revealed, being witnessed

3:4 [a] Psalm 51:4 3:12 [a] Psalms 14:1–3; 53:1–3; Ecclesiastes 7:20 3:13 [a] Psalm 5:9 [b] Psalm 140:3 3:14 [a] Psalm 10:7 3:17 [a] Isaiah 59:7, 8 3:18 [a] Psalm 36:1

by the Law and the Prophets,
22even the righteousness of
God, through faith in Jesus
Christ, to all and on all[a] who
believe. For there is no difference; 23for all have sinned and
fall short of the glory of God,
24being justified freely by His
grace through the redemption
that is in Christ Jesus, 25whom
God set forth *as* a propitiation
by His blood, through faith, to
demonstrate His righteousness, because in His forbearance God had passed over
the sins that were previously
committed, 26to demonstrate
at the present time His righteousness, that He might be
just and the justifier of the one
who has faith in Jesus.

BOASTING EXCLUDED

27Where *is* boasting then?
It is excluded. By what law?
Of works? No, but by the law
of faith. 28Therefore we con-
clude that a man is justified
by faith apart from the deeds
of the law. 29Or *is He* the God
of the Jews only? *Is He* not
also the God of the Gentiles?
Yes, of the Gentiles also,
30since *there is* one God who
will justify the circumcised by
faith and the uncircumcised
through faith. 31Do we then
make void the law through
faith? Certainly not! On the
contrary, we establish the law.

ABRAHAM JUSTIFIED BY FAITH

4 What then shall we say that
Abraham our father has
found according to the flesh?[a]
2For if Abraham was justified
by works, he has *something* to
boast about, but not before
God. 3For what does the Scripture say? "Abraham believed
God, and it was accounted to
him for righteousness."[a] 4Now
to him who works, the wages
are not counted as grace but
as debt.

DAVID CELEBRATES THE SAME TRUTH

5But to him who does not
work but believes on Him who
justifies the ungodly, his faith
is accounted for righteousness,
6just as David also describes
the blessedness of the man to
whom God imputes righteousness apart from works:

7 "Blessed *are those*
whose lawless deeds
are forgiven,
And whose sins
are covered;
8 Blessed *is the* man to
whom the LORD shall
not impute sin."[a]

ABRAHAM JUSTIFIED BEFORE CIRCUMCISION

9*Does* this blessedness then
come upon the circumcised

3:22 [a] NU-Text omits *and on all.* 4:1 [a] Or *Abraham our (fore)father according to the flesh has found?* 4:3 [a] Genesis 15:6 4:8 [a] Psalm 32:1, 2

only, or upon the uncircumcised also? For we say
that faith was accounted to
Abraham for righteousness.
10How then was it accounted?
While he was circumcised,
or uncircumcised? Not while
circumcised, but while uncircumcised. 11And he received
the sign of circumcision, a
seal of the righteousness of
the faith which *he had while
still* uncircumcised, that he
might be the father of all those
who believe, though they are
uncircumcised, that righ-
teousness might be imputed
to them also, 12and the father
of circumcision to those who
not only *are* of the circumcision, but who also walk in the
steps of the faith which our
father Abraham *had while still*
uncircumcised.

THE PROMISE GRANTED THROUGH FAITH

13For the promise that he
would be the heir of the world
was not to Abraham or to his
seed through the law, but
through the righteousness of
faith. 14For if those who are
of the law *are* heirs, faith is
made void and the promise
made of no effect, 15because
the law brings about wrath;
for where there is no law *there
is* no transgression.

16Therefore *it is* of faith that
it might be according to grace,
so that the promise might be
sure to all the seed, not only
to those who are of the law,
but also to those who are of
the faith of Abraham, who is
the father of us all 17(as it is
written, "I have made you a
father of many nations"[a]) in
the presence of Him whom
he believed—God, who gives
life to the dead and calls those
things which do not exist as
though they did; 18who, contrary to hope, in hope believed, so that he became the
father of many nations, according to what was spoken,
"So shall your descendants
be."[a] 19And not being weak
in faith, he did not consider
his own body, already dead
(since he was about a hundred
years old), and the deadness
of Sarah's womb. 20He did not
waver at the promise of God
through unbelief, but was
strengthened in faith, giving
glory to God, 21and being fully
convinced that what He had
promised He was also able
to perform. 22And therefore
"it was accounted to him for
righteousness."[a]

23Now it was not written
for his sake alone that it was
imputed to him, 24but also
for us. It shall be imputed to
us who believe in Him who
raised up Jesus our Lord from
the dead, 25who was delivered
up *because* of our offenses,
and was raised because of our
justification.

4:17 [a] Genesis 17:5 4:18 [a] Genesis 15:5 4:22 [a] Genesis 15:6

FAITH TRIUMPHS IN TROUBLE

5 Therefore, having been
justified by faith, we have[a]
peace with God through our
Lord Jesus Christ, 2through
whom also we have access by
faith into this grace in which
we stand, and rejoice in hope
of the glory of God. 3And not
only *that,* but we also glory
in tribulations, knowing that
tribulation produces perseverance; 4and perseverance,
character; and character,
hope. 5Now hope does not
disappoint, because the love
of God has been poured out in
our hearts by the Holy Spirit
who was given to us.

CHRIST IN OUR PLACE

6For when we were still
without strength, in due time
Christ died for the ungodly.
7For scarcely for a righteous
man will one die; yet perhaps
for a good man someone would
even dare to die. 8But God
demonstrates His own love toward us, in that while we were
still sinners, Christ died for us.
9Much more then, having now
been justified by His blood,
we shall be saved from wrath
through Him. 10For if when we
were enemies we were reconciled to God through the death
of His Son, much more, having
been reconciled, we shall be
saved by His life. 11And not only
that, but we also rejoice in God
through our Lord Jesus Christ,
through whom we have now
received the reconciliation.

DEATH IN ADAM, LIFE IN CHRIST

12Therefore, just as through
one man sin entered the
world, and death through
sin, and thus death spread to
all men, because all sinned—
13(For until the law sin was in
the world, but sin is not imputed when there is no law.
14Nevertheless death reigned
from Adam to Moses, even
over those who had not sinned
according to the likeness of
the transgression of Adam,
who is a type of Him who was
to come. 15But the free gift *is*
not like the offense. For if by
the one man's offense many
died, much more the grace of
God and the gift by the grace
of the one Man, Jesus Christ,
abounded to many. 16And the
gift *is* not like *that which came*
through the one who sinned.
For the judgment *which came*
from one *offense resulted* in
condemnation, but the free
gift *which came* from many
offenses *resulted* in justification. 17For if by the one
man's offense death reigned
through the one, much more
those who receive abundance
of grace and of the gift of
righteousness will reign in
life through the One, Jesus
Christ.)

5:1 [a] Another ancient reading is, *let us have peace.*

18Therefore, as through one
man's offense *judgment came*
to all men, resulting in condemnation, even so through
one Man's righteous act *the*
free gift came to all men, resulting in justification of life.
19For as by one man's disobedience many were made
sinners, so also by one Man's
obedience many will be made
righteous.
20Moreover the law en-
tered that the offense might
abound. But where sin
abounded, grace abounded
much more, 21so that as sin
reigned in death, even so
grace might reign through
righteousness to eternal life
through Jesus Christ our Lord.

DEAD TO SIN, ALIVE TO GOD

6 What shall we say then?
Shall we continue in sin
that grace may abound? 2Cer-
tainly not! How shall we who
died to sin live any longer in
it? 3Or do you not know that as
many of us as were baptized
into Christ Jesus were baptized into His death? 4There-
fore we were buried with Him
through baptism into death,
that just as Christ was raised
from the dead by the glory of
the Father, even so we also
should walk in newness of life.
5For if we have been united
together *in the likeness* of His
death, certainly we also shall
be *in the likeness* of *His* resurrection, 6knowing this, that
our old man was crucified
with *Him*, that the body of
sin might be done away with,
that we should no longer be
slaves of sin. 7For he who has
died has been freed from sin.
8Now if we died with Christ,
we believe that we shall also
live with Him, 9knowing that
Christ, having been raised
from the dead, dies no more.
Death no longer has dominion over Him. 10For *the death*
that He died, He died to sin
once for all; but *the life* that He
lives, He lives to God. 11Like-
wise you also, reckon yourselves to be dead indeed to
sin, but alive to God in Christ
Jesus our Lord.
12Therefore do not let sin
reign in your mortal body,
that you should obey it in
its lusts. 13And do not present your members *as* instruments of unrighteousness to
sin, but present yourselves to
God as being alive from the
dead, and your members *as*
instruments of righteousness
to God. 14For sin shall not have
dominion over you, for you
are not under law but under
grace.

FROM SLAVES OF SIN TO SLAVES OF GOD

15What then? Shall we sin
because we are not under law
but *under* grace? Certainly
not! 16Do you not know that
to whom you present your-
selves slaves to obey, you are
that one's slaves whom you

obey, whether of sin *leading* to death, or of obedience *leading* to righteousness? 17But God be thanked that *though* you were slaves of sin, yet you obeyed from the heart that form of doctrine to which you were delivered. 18And having been set free from sin, you became slaves of righteousness. 19I speak in human *terms* because of the weakness of your flesh. For just as you presented your members *as* slaves of uncleanness, and of lawlessness *leading* to *more* lawlessness, so now present your members *as* slaves *of* righteousness for holiness.

20For when you were slaves of sin, you were free in regard to righteousness. 21What fruit did you have then in the things of which you are now ashamed? For the end of those things *is* death. 22But now having been set free from sin, and having become slaves of God, you have your fruit to holiness, and the end, everlasting life. 23For the wages of sin *is* death, but the gift of God *is* eternal life in Christ Jesus our Lord.

FREED FROM THE LAW

7 Or do you not know, brethren (for I speak to those who know the law), that the law has dominion over a man as long as he lives? 2For the woman who has a husband is bound by the law to *her* husband as long as he lives. But if the husband dies, she is released from the law of *her* husband. 3So then if, while *her* husband lives, she marries another man, she will be called an adulteress; but if her husband dies, she is free from that law, so that she is no adulteress, though she has married another man. 4Therefore, my brethren, you also have become dead to the law through the body of Christ, that you may be married to another—to Him who was raised from the dead, that we should bear fruit to God. 5For when we were in the flesh, the sinful passions which were aroused by the law were at work in our members to bear fruit to death. 6But now we have been delivered from the law, having died to what we were held by, so that we should serve in the newness of the Spirit and not *in* the oldness of the letter.

SIN'S ADVANTAGE IN THE LAW

7What shall we say then? *Is* the law sin? Certainly not! On the contrary, I would not have known sin except through the law. For I would not have known covetousness unless the law had said, "You shall not covet."[a] 8But sin, taking opportunity by the

7:7 [a] Exodus 20:17; Deuteronomy 5:21

commandment, produced in
me all *manner of evil* desire.
For apart from the law sin
was dead. 9I was alive once
without the law, but when the
commandment came, sin re-
vived and I died. 10And the
commandment, which *was*
to *bring* life, I found to *bring*
death. 11For sin, taking occasion by the commandment,
deceived me, and by it killed
me. 12Therefore the law *is* holy,
and the commandment holy
and just and good.

LAW CANNOT SAVE FROM SIN

13Has then what is good become death to me? Certainly
not! But sin, that it might appear sin, was producing death
in me through what is good,
so that sin through the commandment might become
exceedingly sinful. 14For we
know that the law is spiritual,
but I am carnal, sold under
sin. 15For what I am doing, I
do not understand. For what
I will to do, that I do not practice; but what I hate, that I do.
16If, then, I do what I will not
to do, I agree with the law
that *it is* good. 17But now, *it*
is no longer I who do it, but
sin that dwells in me. 18For I
know that in me (that is, in my
flesh) nothing good dwells; for
to will is present with me, but
how to perform what is good
I do not find. 19For the good
that I will *to do,* I do not do;
but the evil I will not *to do,*
that I practice. 20Now if I do
what I will not *to do,* it is no
longer I who do it, but sin that
dwells in me.

21I find then a law, that evil
is present with me, the one
who wills to do good. 22For I
delight in the law of God according to the inward man.
23But I see another law in my
members, warring against the
law of my mind, and bringing
me into captivity to the law
of sin which is in my members. 24O wretched man that I
am! Who will deliver me from
this body of death? 25I thank
God—through Jesus Christ
our Lord!

So then, with the mind I
myself serve the law of God,
but with the flesh the law of
sin.

FREE FROM INDWELLING SIN

8 *There is* therefore now no
condemnation to those
who are in Christ Jesus,[a]
who do not walk according
to the flesh, but according to
the Spirit. 2For the law of the
Spirit of life in Christ Jesus has
made me free from the law of
sin and death. 3For what the
law could not do in that it was
weak through the flesh, God
did by sending His own Son
in the likeness of sinful flesh,
on account of sin: He con-

8:1 [a] NU-Text omits the rest of this verse.

demned sin in the flesh, 4that
the righteous requirement of
the law might be fulfilled in
us who do not walk according to the flesh but according
to the Spirit. 5For those who
live according to the flesh set
their minds on the things of
the flesh, but those *who live*
according to the Spirit, the
things of the Spirit. 6For to
be carnally minded *is* death,
but to be spiritually minded
is life and peace. 7Because the
carnal mind *is* enmity against
God; for it is not subject to the
law of God, nor indeed can be.
8So then, those who are in the
flesh cannot please God.

9But you are not in the
flesh but in the Spirit, if indeed the Spirit of God dwells
in you. Now if anyone does
not have the Spirit of Christ,
he is not His. 10And if Christ
is in you, the body *is* dead because of sin, but the Spirit *is*
life because of righteousness.
11But if the Spirit of Him who
raised Jesus from the dead
dwells in you, He who raised
Christ from the dead will also
give life to your mortal bodies
through His Spirit who dwells
in you.

SONSHIP THROUGH THE SPIRIT

12Therefore, brethren, we
are debtors—not to the flesh,
to live according to the flesh.
13For if you live according to
the flesh you will die; but if
by the Spirit you put to death
the deeds of the body, you
will live. 14For as many as are
led by the Spirit of God, these
are sons of God. 15For you did
not receive the spirit of bondage again to fear, but you received the Spirit of adoption
by whom we cry out, "Abba,
Father." 16The Spirit Himself
bears witness with our spirit
that we are children of God,
17and if children, then heirs—
heirs of God and joint heirs
with Christ, if indeed we suffer
with *Him,* that we may also be
glorified together.

FROM SUFFERING TO GLORY

18For I consider that the
sufferings of this present time
are not worthy *to be compared*
with the glory which shall be
revealed in us. 19For the earnest expectation of the creation eagerly waits for the
revealing of the sons of God.
20For the creation was sub-
jected to futility, not willingly,
but because of Him who sub-
jected *it* in hope; 21because
the creation itself also will be
delivered from the bondage
of corruption into the glorious liberty of the children of
God. 22For we know that the
whole creation groans and labors with birth pangs together
until now. 23Not only *that,* but
we also who have the firstfruits of the Spirit, even we
ourselves groan within ourselves, eagerly waiting for the
adoption, the redemption of

our body. 24For we were saved
in this hope, but hope that
is seen is not hope; for why
does one still hope for what
he sees? 25But if we hope for
what we do not see, we eagerly
wait for *it* with perseverance.
26Likewise the Spirit also
helps in our weaknesses.
For we do not know what we
should pray for as we ought,
but the Spirit Himself makes
intercession for us[a] with
groanings which cannot be uttered. 27Now He who searches
the hearts knows what the
mind of the Spirit *is*, because
He makes intercession for the
saints according to *the will of*
God.
28And we know that all
things work together for good
to those who love God, to those
who are the called according
to *His* purpose. 29For whom
He foreknew, He also pre-
destined *to be* conformed to
the image of His Son, that He
might be the firstborn among
many brethren. 30Moreover
whom He predestined, these
He also called; whom He
called, these He also justified;
and whom He justified, these
He also glorified.

GOD'S EVERLASTING LOVE

31What then shall we say to
these things? If God *is* for us,
who *can be* against us? 32He
who did not spare His own
Son, but delivered Him up
for us all, how shall He not
with Him also freely give us
all things? 33Who shall bring
a charge against God's elect? *It*
is God who justifies. 34Who *is*
he who condemns? *It is* Christ
who died, and furthermore
is also risen, who is even at
the right hand of God, who
also makes intercession for
us. 35Who shall separate us
from the love of Christ? *Shall*
tribulation, or distress, or persecution, or famine, or nakedness, or peril, or sword? 36As
it is written:

"For Your sake we are
killed all day long;
We are accounted
as sheep for the
slaughter."[a]

37Yet in all these things we
are more than conquerors
through Him who loved us.
38For I am persuaded that neither death nor life, nor angels
nor principalities nor powers,
nor things present nor things
to come, 39nor height nor
depth, nor any other created
thing, shall be able to separate
us from the love of God which
is in Christ Jesus our Lord.

ISRAEL'S REJECTION OF CHRIST

9 I tell the truth in Christ,
I am not lying, my con-
science also bearing me witness in the Holy Spirit, 2that

8:26 [a] NU-Text omits *for us*. 8:36 [a] Psalm 44:22

I have great sorrow and continual grief in my heart. 3For I
could wish that I myself were
accursed from Christ for my
brethren, my countrymen[a]
according to the flesh, 4who
are Israelites, to whom *pertain*
the adoption, the glory, the
covenants, the giving of the
law, the service *of God,* and
the promises; 5of whom *are*
the fathers and from whom,
according to the flesh, Christ
came, who is over all, *the* eternally blessed God. Amen.

ISRAEL'S REJECTION AND GOD'S PURPOSE

6But it is not that the word
of God has taken no effect.
For they *are* not all Israel who
are of Israel, 7nor *are they* all
children because they are
the seed of Abraham; but,
"In Isaac your seed shall be
called."[a] 8That is, those who
are the children of the flesh,
these *are* not the children of
God; but the children of the
promise are counted as the
seed. 9For this *is* the word of
promise: "At this time I will
come and Sarah shall have a
son."[a]

10And not only *this,* but
when Rebecca also had conceived by one man, *even* by
our father Isaac 11(for *the*
children not yet being born,
nor having done any good or
evil, that the purpose of God
according to election might
stand, not of works but of
Him who calls), 12it was said
to her, "The older shall serve
the younger."[a] 13As it is written, "Jacob I have loved, but
Esau I have hated."[a]

ISRAEL'S REJECTION AND GOD'S JUSTICE

14What shall we say then?
Is there unrighteousness with
God? Certainly not! 15For He
says to Moses, "I will have
mercy on whomever I will
have mercy, and I will have
compassion on whomever I
will have compassion."[a] 16So
then *it is* not of him who wills,
nor of him who runs, but of
God who shows mercy. 17For
the Scripture says to the Pharaoh, "For this very purpose I
have raised you up, that I may
show My power in you, and
that My name may be declared
in all the earth."[a] 18Therefore
He has mercy on whom He
wills, and whom He wills He
hardens.

19You will say to me then,
"Why does He still find fault?
For who has resisted His will?"
20But indeed, O man, who are
you to reply against God? Will
the thing formed say to him
who formed *it,* "Why have you
made me like this?" 21Does not
the potter have power over the

9:3 [a] Or *relatives* **9:7** [a] Genesis 21:12 **9:9** [a] Genesis 18:10, 14 **9:12** [a] Genesis 25:23 **9:13** [a] Malachi 1:2, 3 **9:15** [a] Exodus 33:19 **9:17** [a] Exodus 9:16

clay, from the same lump to
make one vessel for honor
and another for dishonor?
[22]*What* if God, wanting to
show *His* wrath and to make
His power known, endured
with much longsuffering the
vessels of wrath prepared for
destruction, [23]and that He
might make known the riches
of His glory on the vessels of
mercy, which He had prepared
beforehand for glory, [24]even
us whom He called, not of
the Jews only, but also of the
Gentiles?
[25]As He says also in Hosea:

"I will call them My
people, who were
not My people,
And her beloved, who
was not beloved."[a]
[26]"And it shall come to
pass in the place where
it was said to them,
'*You are* not My people,'
There they shall be
called sons of the
living God."[a]

[27]Isaiah also cries out concerning Israel:[a]

"Though the number of
the children of Israel be
as the sand of the sea,
The remnant will
be saved.
[28] For He will finish the
work and cut *it* short
in righteousness,
Because the LORD will
make a short work
upon the earth."[a]

[29]And as Isaiah said before:

"Unless the LORD
of Sabaoth[a] had
left us a seed,
We would have become
like Sodom,
And we would have been
made like Gomorrah."[b]

PRESENT CONDITION OF ISRAEL

[30]What shall we say then?
That Gentiles, who did not
pursue righteousness, have
attained to righteousness, even
the righteousness of faith;
[31]but Israel, pursuing the law of
righteousness, has not attained
to the law of righteousness.[a]
[32]Why? Because *they did* not
seek it by faith, but as it were,
by the works of the law.[a] For
they stumbled at that stumbling stone. [33]As it is written:

"Behold, I lay in Zion a
stumbling stone and
rock of offense,
And whoever believes
on Him will not be
put to shame."[a]

9:25 [a] *Hosea 2:23* **9:26** [a] Hosea 1:10 **9:27** [a] Isaiah 10:22, 23 **9:28** [a] NU-Text reads *For the LORD will finish the work and cut it short upon the earth.* **9:29** [a] Literally, in Hebrew, *Hosts* [b] Isaiah 1:9 **9:31** [a] NU-Text omits *of righteousness.* **9:32** [a] NU-Text reads *by works.* **9:33** [a] Isaiah 8:14; 28:16

ISRAEL NEEDS THE GOSPEL

10 Brethren, my heart's desire and prayer to God
for Israel[a] is that they may
be saved. 2For I bear them
witness that they have a zeal
for God, but not according to
knowledge. 3For they being
ignorant of God's righteousness, and seeking to establish
their own righteousness, have
not submitted to the righteousness of God. 4For Christ
is the end of the law for righteousness to everyone who
believes.

5For Moses writes about the
righteousness which is of the
law, "The man who does those
things shall live by them."[a]
6But the righteousness of
faith speaks in this way, "Do
not say in your heart, 'Who
will ascend into heaven?'"[a]
(that is, to bring Christ down
from above) 7or, "'Who will descend into the abyss?'"[a] (that
is, to bring Christ up from
the dead). 8But what does it
say? "The word is near you,
in your mouth and in your
heart"[a] (that is, the word of
faith which we preach): 9that if
you confess with your mouth
the Lord Jesus and believe in
your heart that God has raised
Him from the dead, you will be
saved. 10For with the heart one
believes unto righteousness,
and with the mouth confession is made unto salvation.
11For the Scripture says, "Whoever believes on Him will not
be put to shame."[a] 12For there
is no distinction between Jew
and Greek, for the same Lord
over all is rich to all who call
upon Him. 13For "whoever
calls on the name of the LORD
shall be saved."[a]

ISRAEL REJECTS THE GOSPEL

14How then shall they call
on Him in whom they have
not believed? And how shall
they believe in Him of whom
they have not heard? And
how shall they hear without
a preacher? 15And how shall
they preach unless they are
sent? As it is written:

"How beautiful are the
feet of those who
preach the gospel
of peace,[a]
Who bring glad tidings
of good things!"[b]

16But they have not all obeyed
the gospel. For Isaiah says,
"LORD, who has believed our
report?"[a] 17So then faith *comes*
by hearing, and hearing by the
word of God.

18But I say, have they not
heard? Yes indeed:

10:1 [a] NU-Text reads *them*. 10:5 [a] Leviticus 18:5
10:6 [a] Deuteronomy 30:12 10:7 [a] Deuteronomy 30:13
10:8 [a] Deuteronomy 30:14 10:11 [a] Isaiah 28:16 10:13 [a] Joel
2:32 10:15 [a] NU-Text omits *preach the gospel of peace, Who.* [b] Isaiah 52:7; Nahum 1:15 10:16 [a] Isaiah 53:1

"Their sound has gone
out to all the earth,
And their words to the
ends of the world."[a]

19But I say, did Israel not
know? First Moses says:

"I will provoke you to
jealousy by *those who*
are not a nation,
I will move you to anger
by a foolish nation."[a]

20But Isaiah is very bold
and says:

"I was found by those
who did not seek Me;
I was made manifest
to those who did
not ask for Me."[a]

21But to Israel he says:

"All day long I have
stretched out My hands
To a disobedient and
contrary people."[a]

ISRAEL'S REJECTION NOT TOTAL

11 I say then, has God cast
away His people? Cer-
tainly not! For I also am an
Israelite, of the seed of Abraham, *of* the tribe of Benjamin.
2God has not cast away His
people whom He foreknew.
Or do you not know what the
Scripture says of Elijah, how
he pleads with God against
Israel, saying, 3"LORD, they
have killed Your prophets and
torn down Your altars, and I
alone am left, and they seek
my life"?[a] 4But what does the
divine response say to him?
"I have reserved for Myself
seven thousand men who
have not bowed the knee to
Baal."[a] 5Even so then, at this
present time there is a remnant according to the election
of grace. 6And if by grace, then
it is no longer of works; otherwise grace is no longer grace.[a]
But if *it is* of works, it is no
longer grace; otherwise work
is no longer work.
7What then? Israel has not
obtained what it seeks; but the
elect have obtained it, and the
rest were blinded. 8Just as it
is written:

"God has given them
a spirit of stupor,
Eyes that they
should not see
And ears that they
should not hear,
To this very day."[a]

9And David says:

"Let their table become
a snare and a trap,
A stumbling block and a
recompense to them.

10:18 [a] Psalm 19:4 10:19 [a] Deuteronomy 32:21 10:20 [a] Isaiah 65:1 10:21 [a] Isaiah 65:2 11:3 [a] 1 Kings 19:10, 14 11:4 [a] 1 Kings 19:18 11:6 [a] NU-Text omits the rest of this verse. 11:8 [a] Deuteronomy 29:4; Isaiah 29:10

10 Let their eyes be darkened,
so that they do not see,
And bow down their
back always."[a]

ISRAEL'S REJECTION NOT FINAL

11 I say then, have they stumbled that they should fall? Certainly not! But through their
fall, to provoke them to jealousy, salvation *has come* to the
Gentiles. 12 Now if their fall *is*
riches for the world, and their
failure riches for the Gentiles,
how much more their fullness!

13 For I speak to you Gentiles; inasmuch as I am an
apostle to the Gentiles, I magnify my ministry, 14 if by any
means I may provoke to jealousy *those who are* my flesh
and save some of them. 15 For
if their being cast away *is* the
reconciling of the world, what
will their acceptance *be* but
life from the dead?

16 For if the firstfruit *is* holy,
the lump *is* also *holy;* and if
the root *is* holy, so *are* the
branches. 17 And if some of the
branches were broken off, and
you, being a wild olive tree,
were grafted in among them,
and with them became a partaker of the root and fatness of
the olive tree, 18 do not boast
against the branches. But if
you do boast, *remember that*
you do not support the root,
but the root *supports* you.

19 You will say then,
"Branches were broken off
that I might be grafted in."
20 Well *said.* Because of unbelief they were broken off,
and you stand by faith. Do not
be haughty, but fear. 21 For if
God did not spare the natural
branches, He may not spare
you either. 22 Therefore consider the goodness and severity of God: on those who
fell, severity; but toward you,
goodness,[a] if you continue in
His goodness. Otherwise you
also will be cut off. 23 And they
also, if they do not continue
in unbelief, will be grafted in,
for God is able to graft them in
again. 24 For if you were cut out
of the olive tree which is wild
by nature, and were grafted
contrary to nature into a cultivated olive tree, how much
more will these, who *are* natural *branches,* be grafted into
their own olive tree?

25 For I do not desire, brethren, that you should be ignorant of this mystery, lest you
should be wise in your own
opinion, that blindness in part
has happened to Israel until
the fullness of the Gentiles has
come in. 26 And so all Israel
will be saved,[a] as it is written:

"The Deliverer will
come out of Zion,
And He will turn away
ungodliness from Jacob;

11:10 [a] Psalm 69:22, 23 **11:22** [a] NU-Text adds *of God.* **11:26** [a] Or *delivered*

27 For this *is* My covenant
with them,
When I take away
their sins."[a]

28Concerning the gospel
they are enemies for your
sake, but concerning the election *they are* beloved for the
sake of the fathers. 29For the
gifts and the calling of God
are irrevocable. 30For as you
were once disobedient to God,
yet have now obtained mercy
through their disobedience,
31even so these also have
now been disobedient, that
through the mercy shown you
they also may obtain mercy.
32For God has committed
them all to disobedience, that
He might have mercy on all.
33Oh, the depth of the
riches both of the wisdom and
knowledge of God! How un-
searchable *are* His judgments
and His ways past finding out!

34"For who has known the
mind of the LORD?
Or who has become
His counselor?"[a]
35"Or who has first
given to Him
And it shall be repaid
to him?"[a]

36For of Him and through
Him and to Him *are* all things,
to whom *be* glory forever.
Amen.

LIVING SACRIFICES TO GOD

12 I beseech you therefore,
brethren, by the mercies
of God, that you present your
bodies a living sacrifice, holy,
acceptable to God, *which is*
your reasonable service. 2And
do not be conformed to this
world, but be transformed by
the renewing of your mind,
that you may prove what *is*
that good and acceptable and
perfect will of God.

SERVE GOD WITH SPIRITUAL GIFTS

3For I say, through the grace
given to me, to everyone who
is among you, not to think *of*
himself more highly than he
ought to think, but to think soberly, as God has dealt to each
one a measure of faith. 4For as
we have many members in one
body, but all the members do
not have the same function,
5so we, *being* many, are one
body in Christ, and individually members of one another.
6Having then gifts differing
according to the grace that is
given to us, *let us use them:* if
prophecy, *let us prophesy* in
proportion to our faith; 7or
ministry, *let us use it* in *our*
ministering; he who teaches,
in teaching; 8he who exhorts,
in exhortation; he who gives,
with liberality; he who leads,
with diligence; he who shows
mercy, with cheerfulness.

11:27 [a] Isaiah 59:20, 21 Jeremiah 23:18
11:34 [a] Isaiah 40:13;
11:35 [a] Job 41:11

BEHAVE LIKE A CHRISTIAN

9*Let* love *be* without hypocrisy. Abhor what is evil.
Cling to what is good. 10*Be*
kindly affectionate to one
another with brotherly love,
in honor giving preference
to one another; 11not lagging
in diligence, fervent in spirit,
serving the Lord; 12rejoicing
in hope, patient in tribulation, continuing steadfastly
in prayer; 13distributing to the
needs of the saints, given to
hospitality.

14Bless those who perse-
cute you; bless and do not
curse. 15Rejoice with those
who rejoice, and weep with
those who weep. 16Be of the
same mind toward one an-
other. Do not set your mind
on high things, but associate
with the humble. Do not be
wise in your own opinion.

17Repay no one evil for evil.
Have regard for good things
in the sight of all men. 18If it is
possible, as much as depends
on you, live peaceably with
all men. 19Beloved, do not
avenge yourselves, but *rather*
give place to wrath; for it is
written, "Vengeance *is* Mine,
I will repay,"[a] says the Lord.
20Therefore

"If your enemy is
hungry, feed him;
If he is thirsty, give
him a drink;
For in so doing you
will heap coals of
fire on his head."[a]

21Do not be overcome by evil,
but overcome evil with good.

SUBMIT TO GOVERNMENT

13 Let every soul be subject
to the governing author-
ities. For there is no authority except from God, and the
authorities that exist are appointed by God. 2Therefore
whoever resists the authority
resists the ordinance of God,
and those who resist will bring
judgment on themselves. 3For
rulers are not a terror to good
works, but to evil. Do you want
to be unafraid of the authority? Do what is good, and you
will have praise from the
same. 4For he is God's minister to you for good. But if
you do evil, be afraid; for he
does not bear the sword in
vain; for he is God's minister,
an avenger to *execute* wrath
on him who practices evil.
5Therefore *you* must be subject, not only because of wrath
but also for conscience' sake.
6For because of this you also
pay taxes, for they are God's
ministers attending continually to this very thing. 7Ren-
der therefore to all their due:
taxes to whom taxes *are due,*
customs to whom customs,
fear to whom fear, honor to
whom honor.

12:19 [a] Deuteronomy 32:35

12:20 [a] Proverbs 25:21, 22

LOVE YOUR NEIGHBOR

8Owe no one anything ex-
cept to love one another, for
he who loves another has fulfilled the law. 9For the commandments, "You shall not
commit adultery," "You shall
not murder," "You shall not
steal," "You shall not bear
false witness,"[a] "You shall
not covet,"[b] and if *there is* any
other commandment, are *all*
summed up in this saying,
namely, "You shall love your
neighbor as yourself."[c] 10Love
does no harm to a neighbor;
therefore love *is* the fulfillment of the law.

PUT ON CHRIST

11And *do* this, knowing the
time, that now *it is* high time
to awake out of sleep; for now
our salvation *is* nearer than
when we *first* believed. 12The
night is far spent, the day is at
hand. Therefore let us cast off
the works of darkness, and let
us put on the armor of light.
13Let us walk properly, as in
the day, not in revelry and
drunkenness, not in lewdness
and lust, not in strife and envy.
14But put on the Lord Jesus
Christ, and make no provision
for the flesh, to *fulfill its* lusts.

THE LAW OF LIBERTY

14 Receive one who is weak
in the faith, *but* not to
disputes over doubtful things.
2For one believes he may eat
all things, but he who is weak
eats *only* vegetables. 3Let not
him who eats despise him
who does not eat, and let not
him who does not eat judge
him who eats; for God has received him. 4Who are you to
judge another's servant? To
his own master he stands or
falls. Indeed, he will be made
to stand, for God is able to
make him stand.

5One person esteems *one*
day above another; another
esteems every day *alike.* Let
each be fully convinced in
his own mind. 6He who ob-
serves the day, observes *it* to
the Lord;[a] and he who does
not observe the day, to the
Lord he does not observe *it.*
He who eats, eats to the Lord,
for he gives God thanks; and
he who does not eat, to the
Lord he does not eat, and
gives God thanks. 7For none
of us lives to himself, and no
one dies to himself. 8For if
we live, we live to the Lord;
and if we die, we die to the
Lord. Therefore, whether we
live or die, we are the Lord's.
9For to this end Christ died
and rose[a] and lived again,
that He might be Lord of
both the dead and the living.
10But why do you judge your
brother? Or why do you show

13:9 [a] NU-Text omits *"You shall not bear false witness."* [b] Exodus 20:13–15, 17; Deuteronomy 5:17–19, 21 [c] Leviticus 19:18 14:6 [a] NU-Text omits the rest of this sentence. 14:9 [a] NU-Text omits *and rose.*

contempt for your brother?
For we shall all stand before
the judgment seat of Christ.[a]
11For it is written:

"*As* I live, says the LORD,
Every knee shall
bow to Me,
And every tongue shall
confess to God."[a]

12So then each of us shall
give account of himself to God.
13Therefore let us not judge
one another anymore, but
rather resolve this, not to put
a stumbling block or a cause
to fall in *our* brother's way.

THE LAW OF LOVE

14I know and am convinced
by the Lord Jesus that *there
is* nothing unclean of itself;
but to him who considers anything to be unclean, to him *it is*
unclean. 15Yet if your brother is
grieved because of *your* food,
you are no longer walking in
love. Do not destroy with your
food the one for whom Christ
died. 16Therefore do not let
your good be spoken of as evil;
17for the kingdom of God is
not eating and drinking, but
righteousness and peace and
joy in the Holy Spirit. 18For
he who serves Christ in these
things[a] *is* acceptable to God
and approved by men.
19Therefore let us pursue
the things *which make* for
peace and the things by which
one may edify another. 20Do
not destroy the work of God for
the sake of food. All things indeed *are* pure, but *it is* evil for
the man who eats with offense.
21*It is* good neither to eat meat
nor drink wine nor *do anything* by which your brother
stumbles or is offended or is
made weak.[a] 22Do you have
faith? Have[a] *it* to yourself before God. Happy *is* he who
does not condemn himself
in what he approves. 23But he
who doubts is condemned if
he eats, because *he does* not
eat from faith; for whatever *is*
not from faith is sin.[a]

BEARING OTHERS' BURDENS

15 We then who are strong
ought to bear with the
scruples of the weak, and not
to please ourselves. 2Let each
of us please *his* neighbor for *his*
good, leading to edification.
3For even Christ did not please
Himself; but as it is written,
"The reproaches of those who
reproached You fell on Me."[a]
4For whatever things were
written before were written for
our learning, that we through
the patience and comfort of
the Scriptures might have
hope. 5Now may the God of patience and comfort grant you

14:10 [a] NU-Text reads *of God.* 14:11 [a] Isaiah 45:23 14:18 [a] NU-Text reads *this.* 14:21 [a] NU-Text omits *or is offended or is made weak.* 14:22 [a] NU-Text reads *The faith which you have—have.* 14:23 [a] M-Text puts Romans 16:25–27 here. 15:3 [a] Psalm 69:9

to be like-minded toward one
another, according to Christ
Jesus, 6that you may with one
mind *and* one mouth glorify
the God and Father of our Lord
Jesus Christ.

GLORIFY GOD TOGETHER

7Therefore receive one another, just as Christ also received us,[a] to the glory of God.
8Now I say that Jesus Christ
has become a servant to the
circumcision for the truth of
God, to confirm the promises
made to the fathers, 9and that
the Gentiles might glorify God
for *His* mercy, as it is written:

"For this reason I will
confess to You among
the Gentiles,
And sing to Your name."[a]

10And again he says:

"Rejoice, O Gentiles,
with His people!"[a]

11And again:

"Praise the LORD, all
you Gentiles!
Laud Him, all you
peoples!"[a]

12And again, Isaiah says:

"There shall be a
root of Jesse;
And He who shall rise to
reign over the Gentiles,
In Him the Gentiles
shall hope."[a]

13Now may the God of hope
fill you with all joy and peace
in believing, that you may
abound in hope by the power
of the Holy Spirit.

FROM JERUSALEM TO ILLYRICUM

14Now I myself am confident concerning you, my
brethren, that you also are
full of goodness, filled with
all knowledge, able also to admonish one another.[a] 15Nevertheless, brethren, I have
written more boldly to you
on *some* points, as reminding you, because of the grace
given to me by God, 16that I
might be a minister of Jesus
Christ to the Gentiles, ministering the gospel of God,
that the offering of the Gentiles might be acceptable,
sanctified by the Holy Spirit.
17Therefore I have reason to
glory in Christ Jesus in the
things *which pertain* to God.
18For I will not dare to speak
of any of those things which
Christ has not accomplished
through me, in word and
deed, to make the Gentiles
obedient— 19in mighty signs
and *wonders*, by the power

15:7 [a] NU-Text and M-Text read *you.* 15:9 [a] 2 Samuel 22:50; Psalm 18:49 15:10 [a] Deuteronomy 32:43 15:11 [a] Psalm 117:1 15:12 [a] Isaiah 11:10 15:14 [a] M-Text reads *others.*

of the Spirit of God, so that
from Jerusalem and round
about to Illyricum I have
fully preached the gospel of
Christ. 20And so I have made it
my aim to preach the gospel,
not where Christ was named,
lest I should build on another
man's foundation, 21but as it
is written:

"To whom He was
not announced,
they shall see;
And those who have
not heard shall
understand."[a]

PLAN TO VISIT ROME

22For this reason I also have
been much hindered from
coming to you. 23But now no
longer having a place in these
parts, and having a great desire these many years to come
to you, 24whenever I journey
to Spain, I shall come to you.[a]
For I hope to see you on my
journey, and to be helped on
my way there by you, if first I
may enjoy your *company* for a
while. 25But now I am going to
Jerusalem to minister to the
saints. 26For it pleased those
from Macedonia and Achaia
to make a certain contribution for the poor among the
saints who are in Jerusalem.
27It pleased them indeed, and
they are their debtors. For if
the Gentiles have been partakers of their spiritual things,
their duty is also to minister
to them in material things.
28Therefore, when I have performed this and have sealed
to them this fruit, I shall go
by way of you to Spain. 29But I
know that when I come to you,
I shall come in the fullness of
the blessing of the gospel[a] of
Christ.

30Now I beg you, brethren,
through the Lord Jesus Christ,
and through the love of the
Spirit, that you strive together
with me in prayers to God for
me, 31that I may be delivered
from those in Judea who do
not believe, and that my service for Jerusalem may be acceptable to the saints, 32that
I may come to you with joy
by the will of God, and may
be refreshed together with
you. 33Now the God of peace
be with you all. Amen.

SISTER PHOEBE COMMENDED

16 I commend to you Phoe-
be our sister, who is a
servant of the church in Cenchrea, 2that you may receive
her in the Lord in a manner
worthy of the saints, and assist her in whatever business
she has need of you; for indeed she has been a helper
of many and of myself also.

15:21 [a] Isaiah 52:15 15:24 [a] NU-Text omits *I shall come to you* (and joins *Spain* with the next sentence). 15:29 [a] NU-Text omits *of the gospel.*

GREETING ROMAN SAINTS

[3]Greet Priscilla and Aquila,
my fellow workers in Christ
Jesus, [4]who risked their own
necks for my life, to whom not
only I give thanks, but also all
the churches of the Gentiles.
[5]Likewise *greet* the church
that is in their house.

Greet my beloved Epaene-
tus, who is the firstfruits of
Achaia[a] to Christ. [6]Greet Mary,
who labored much for us.
[7]Greet Andronicus and Junia,
my countrymen and my fel-
low prisoners, who are of note
among the apostles, who also
were in Christ before me.

[8]Greet Amplias, my beloved
in the Lord. [9]Greet Urbanus,
our fellow worker in Christ,
and Stachys, my beloved.
[10]Greet Apelles, approved in
Christ. Greet those who are of
the *household* of Aristobulus.
[11]Greet Herodion, my country-
man.[a] Greet those who are of
the *household* of Narcissus
who are in the Lord.

[12]Greet Tryphena and Try-
phosa, who have labored in
the Lord. Greet the beloved
Persis, who labored much
in the Lord. [13]Greet Rufus,
chosen in the Lord, and his
mother and mine. [14]Greet
Asyncritus, Phlegon, Hermas,
Patrobas, Hermes, and the
brethren who are with them.
[15]Greet Philologus and Julia,
Nereus and his sister, and
Olympas, and all the saints
who are with them.

[16]Greet one another with
a holy kiss. The[a] churches of
Christ greet you.

AVOID DIVISIVE PERSONS

[17]Now I urge you, brethren,
note those who cause divisions and offenses, contrary
to the doctrine which you
learned, and avoid them. [18]For
those who are such do not
serve our Lord Jesus[a] Christ,
but their own belly, and by
smooth words and flattering
speech deceive the hearts of
the simple. [19]For your obedience has become known to all.
Therefore I am glad on your
behalf; but I want you to be
wise in what is good, and simple concerning evil. [20]And the
God of peace will crush Satan
under your feet shortly.

The grace of our Lord Jesus
Christ *be* with you. Amen.

GREETINGS FROM PAUL'S FRIENDS

[21]Timothy, my fellow
worker, and Lucius, Jason,
and Sosipater, my countrymen, greet you.

[22]I, Tertius, who wrote *this*
epistle, greet you in the Lord.

[23]Gaius, my host and *the
host* of the whole church,
greets you. Erastus, the treasurer of the city, greets you,
and Quartus, a brother. [24]The

16:5 [a] NU-Text reads *Asia.* 16:11 [a] Or *relative* 16:16 [a] NU-Text reads *All the churches.* 16:18 [a] NU-Text and M-Text omit *Jesus.*

grace of our Lord Jesus Christ
be with you all. Amen.[a]

BENEDICTION

25Now to Him who is able to
establish you according to my
gospel and the preaching of
Jesus Christ, according to the
revelation of the mystery kept
secret since the world began
26but now made manifest, and
by the prophetic Scriptures
made known to all nations, according to the commandment
of the everlasting God, for obedience to the faith— 27to God,
alone wise, *be* glory through
Jesus Christ forever. Amen.[a]

THE FIRST EPISTLE OF PAUL THE APOSTLE TO THE CORINTHIANS

GREETING

1 Paul, called *to be* an apostle
of Jesus Christ through the
will of God, and Sosthenes *our*
brother,

2To the church of God
which is at Corinth, to those
who are sanctified in Christ
Jesus, called *to be* saints, with
all who in every place call on
the name of Jesus Christ our
Lord, both theirs and ours:

3Grace to you and peace
from God our Father and the
Lord Jesus Christ.

SPIRITUAL GIFTS AT CORINTH

4I thank my God always
concerning you for the grace
of God which was given to
you by Christ Jesus, 5that you
were enriched in everything
by Him in all utterance and
all knowledge, 6even as the
testimony of Christ was confirmed in you, 7so that you
come short in no gift, eagerly
waiting for the revelation of
our Lord Jesus Christ, 8who
will also confirm you to the
end, *that you may be* blameless in the day of our Lord
Jesus Christ. 9God *is* faithful, by whom you were called
into the fellowship of His Son,
Jesus Christ our Lord.

SECTARIANISM IS SIN

10Now I plead with you,
brethren, by the name of our
Lord Jesus Christ, that you all

16:24 [a] NU-Text omits this verse. 16:27 [a] M-Text puts Romans 16:25–27 after Romans 14:23.

speak the same thing, and *that*
there be no divisions among
you, but *that* you be perfectly joined together in the
same mind and in the same
judgment. 11For it has been
declared to me concerning
you, my brethren, by those of
Chloe's *household,* that there
are contentions among you.
12Now I say this, that each of
you says, "I am of Paul," or
"I am of Apollos," or "I am of
Cephas," or "I am of Christ."
13Is Christ divided? Was Paul
crucified for you? Or were you
baptized in the name of Paul?

14I thank God that I bap-
tized none of you except Crispus and Gaius, 15lest anyone
should say that I had baptized
in my own name. 16Yes, I also
baptized the household of
Stephanas. Besides, I do not
know whether I baptized any
other. 17For Christ did not send
me to baptize, but to preach
the gospel, not with wisdom of
words, lest the cross of Christ
should be made of no effect.

CHRIST THE POWER AND WISDOM OF GOD

18For the message of the
cross is foolishness to those
who are perishing, but to us
who are being saved it is the
power of God. 19For it is written:

> *"I will destroy* the
> wisdom of the wise,
> And bring to nothing
> the understanding
> of the prudent."[a]

20Where *is* the wise? Where
is the scribe? Where *is* the
disputer of this age? Has not
God made foolish the wisdom
of this world? 21For since, in
the wisdom of God, the world
through wisdom did not know
God, it pleased God through
the foolishness of the message preached to save those
who believe. 22For Jews request a sign, and Greeks seek
after wisdom; 23but we preach
Christ crucified, to the Jews
a stumbling block and to the
Greeks[a] foolishness, 24but to
those who are called, both
Jews and Greeks, Christ the
power of God and the wisdom
of God. 25Because the foolishness of God is wiser than men,
and the weakness of God is
stronger than men.

GLORY ONLY IN THE LORD

26For you see your call-
ing, brethren, that not many
wise according to the flesh,
not many mighty, not many
noble, *are called.* 27But God has
chosen the foolish things of
the world to put to shame the
wise, and God has chosen the
weak things of the world to put
to shame the things which are
mighty; 28and the base things
of the world and the things
which are despised God has

1:19 [a] Isaiah 29:14 1:23 [a] NU-Text reads *Gentiles.*

chosen, and the things which
are not, to bring to nothing the
things that are, 29that no flesh
should glory in His presence.
30But of Him you are in Christ
Jesus, who became for us wisdom from God—and righ-
teousness and sanctification
and redemption— 31that, as
it is written, "He who glories,
let him glory in the LORD."[a]

CHRIST CRUCIFIED

2 And I, brethren, when I
came to you, did not come
with excellence of speech or
of wisdom declaring to you
the testimony[a] of God. 2For I
determined not to know anything among you except Jesus
Christ and Him crucified. 3I
was with you in weakness,
in fear, and in much trembling. 4And my speech and
my preaching *were* not with
persuasive words of human[a]
wisdom, but in demonstra-
tion of the Spirit and of power,
5that your faith should not be
in the wisdom of men but in
the power of God.

SPIRITUAL WISDOM

6However, we speak wis-
dom among those who are
mature, yet not the wisdom
of this age, nor of the rulers
of this age, who are coming
to nothing. 7But we speak the
wisdom of God in a mystery,
the hidden *wisdom* which God
ordained before the ages for
our glory, 8which none of the
rulers of this age knew; for
had they known, they would
not have crucified the Lord
of glory.

9But as it is written:

"Eye has not seen,
nor ear heard,
Nor have entered into
the heart of man
The things which God
has prepared for those
who love Him."[a]

10But God has revealed *them* to
us through His Spirit. For the
Spirit searches all things, yes,
the deep things of God. 11For
what man knows the things
of a man except the spirit of
the man which is in him? Even
so no one knows the things of
God except the Spirit of God.
12Now we have received, not
the spirit of the world, but the
Spirit who is from God, that
we might know the things that
have been freely given to us
by God.

13These things we also
speak, not in words which
man's wisdom teaches but
which the Holy[a] Spirit teaches,
comparing spiritual things
with spiritual. 14But the natural man does not receive the
things of the Spirit of God,
for they are foolishness to
him; nor can he know *them*,

1:31 [a] Jeremiah 9:24 2:1 [a] NU-Text reads *mystery*. 2:4 [a] NU-Text omits *human*. 2:9 [a] Isaiah 64:4 2:13 [a] NU-Text omits *Holy*.

because they are spiritually
discerned. 15But he who is
spiritual judges all things, yet
he himself is *rightly* judged by
no one. 16For "who has known
the mind of the LORD that he
may instruct Him?"[a] But we
have the mind of Christ.

SECTARIANISM IS CARNAL

3 And I, brethren, could not
speak to you as to spiritual
people but as to carnal, as to
babes in Christ. 2I fed you with
milk and not with solid food;
for until now you were not
able *to receive it,* and even now
you are still not able; 3for you
are still carnal. For where *there
are* envy, strife, and divisions
among you, are you not carnal
and behaving like *mere* men?
4For when one says, "I am of
Paul," and another, "I *am* of
Apollos," are you not carnal?

WATERING, WORKING, WARNING

5Who then is Paul, and
who *is* Apollos, but ministers
through whom you believed,
as the Lord gave to each one?
6I planted, Apollos watered,
but God gave the increase. 7So
then neither he who plants
is anything, nor he who waters, but God who gives the
increase. 8Now he who plants
and he who waters are one,
and each one will receive his
own reward according to his
own labor.
9For we are God's fellow
workers; you are God's field,
you are God's building. 10Ac-
cording to the grace of God
which was given to me, as a
wise master builder I have laid
the foundation, and another
builds on it. But let each one
take heed how he builds on it.
11For no other foundation can
anyone lay than that which
is laid, which is Jesus Christ.
12Now if anyone builds on this
foundation *with* gold, silver,
precious stones, wood, hay,
straw, 13each one's work will
become clear; for the Day will
declare it, because it will be
revealed by fire; and the fire
will test each one's work, of
what sort it is. 14If anyone's
work which he has built on
it endures, he will receive a
reward. 15If anyone's work is
burned, he will suffer loss; but
he himself will be saved, yet
so as through fire.
16Do you not know that you
are the temple of God and *that*
the Spirit of God dwells in you?
17If anyone defiles the temple
of God, God will destroy him.
For the temple of God is holy,
which *temple* you are.

AVOID WORLDLY WISDOM

18Let no one deceive him-
self. If anyone among you
seems to be wise in this age, let
him become a fool that he may
become wise. 19For the wisdom
of this world is foolishness

2:16 [a] Isaiah 40:13

with God. For it is written, "He
catches the wise in their *own*
craftiness";[a] 20and again, "The
LORD knows the thoughts of
the wise, that they are futile."[a]
21Therefore let no one boast in
men. For all things are yours:
22whether Paul or Apollos or
Cephas, or the world or life
or death, or things present or
things to come—all are yours.
23And you *are* Christ's, and
Christ *is* God's.

STEWARDS OF THE MYSTERIES OF GOD

4 Let a man so consider us,
as servants of Christ and
stewards of the mysteries of
God. 2Moreover it is required
in stewards that one be found
faithful. 3But with me it is a
very small thing that I should
be judged by you or by a human
court.[a] In fact, I do not even
judge myself. 4For I know of
nothing against myself, yet I
am not justified by this; but
He who judges me is the Lord.
5Therefore judge nothing before the time, until the Lord
comes, who will both bring to
light the hidden things of darkness and reveal the counsels
of the hearts. Then each one's
praise will come from God.

FOOLS FOR CHRIST'S SAKE

6Now these things, breth-
ren, I have figuratively trans-
ferred to myself and Apollos
for your sakes, that you may
learn in us not to think beyond what is written, that
none of you may be puffed
up on behalf of one against
the other. 7For who makes you
differ *from another?* And what
do you have that you did not
receive? Now if you did indeed
receive *it,* why do you boast
as if you had not received *it?*
8You are already full! You
are already rich! You have
reigned as kings without
us—and indeed I could wish
you did reign, that we also
might reign with you! 9For I
think that God has displayed
us, the apostles, last, as men
condemned to death; for we
have been made a spectacle
to the world, both to angels
and to men. 10We *are* fools for
Christ's sake, but you *are* wise
in Christ! We *are* weak, but
you *are* strong! You *are* distinguished, but we *are* dishonored! 11To the present hour we
both hunger and thirst, and we
are poorly clothed, and beaten,
and homeless. 12And we labor,
working with our own hands.
Being reviled, we bless; being
persecuted, we endure; 13being
defamed, we entreat. We have
been made as the filth of the
world, the offscouring of all
things until now.

PAUL'S PATERNAL CARE

14I do not write these things
to shame you, but as my beloved children I warn *you.*

3:19 [a] Job 5:13 3:20 [a] Psalm 94:11 4:3 [a] Literally *day*

15For though you might have
ten thousand instructors in
Christ, yet *you do* not *have*
many fathers; for in Christ
Jesus I have begotten you
through the gospel. 16There-
fore I urge you, imitate me.
17For this reason I have sent
Timothy to you, who is my beloved and faithful son in the
Lord, who will remind you of
my ways in Christ, as I teach
everywhere in every church.

18Now some are puffed up,
as though I were not coming
to you. 19But I will come to you
shortly, if the Lord wills, and
I will know, not the word of
those who are puffed up, but
the power. 20For the kingdom
of God *is* not in word but in
power. 21What do you want?
Shall I come to you with a rod,
or in love and a spirit of gentleness?

IMMORALITY DEFILES THE CHURCH

5 It is actually reported *that*
there is sexual immorality
among you, and such sexual
immorality as is not even
named[a] among the Gentiles—
that a man has his father's
wife! 2And you are puffed up,
and have not rather mourned,
that he who has done this deed
might be taken away from
among you. 3For I indeed, as
absent in body but present in
spirit, have already judged (as
though I were present) him
who has so done this deed. 4In
the name of our Lord Jesus
Christ, when you are gathered
together, along with my spirit,
with the power of our Lord
Jesus Christ, 5deliver such a
one to Satan for the destruction of the flesh, that his spirit
may be saved in the day of the
Lord Jesus.[a]

6Your glorying *is* not good.
Do you not know that a little leaven leavens the whole
lump? 7Therefore purge out
the old leaven, that you may
be a new lump, since you truly
are unleavened. For indeed
Christ, our Passover, was sacrificed for us.[a] 8Therefore let
us keep the feast, not with old
leaven, nor with the leaven of
malice and wickedness, but
with the unleavened *bread* of
sincerity and truth.

IMMORALITY MUST BE JUDGED

9I wrote to you in my epistle
not to keep company with sexually immoral people. 10Yet *I*
certainly *did* not *mean* with
the sexually immoral people
of this world, or with the covetous, or extortioners, or idolaters, since then you would
need to go out of the world.
11But now I have written to
you not to keep company
with anyone named a brother,
who is sexually immoral, or

5:1 [a] NU-Text omits *named*. 5:5 [a] NU-Text omits *Jesus*. 5:7 [a] NU-Text omits *for us*.

covetous, or an idolater, or a
reviler, or a drunkard, or an
extortioner—not even to eat
with such a person.
12For what *have* I *to do*
with judging those also who
are outside? Do you not judge
those who are inside? 13But
those who are outside God
judges. Therefore "put away
from yourselves the evil person."[a]

DO NOT SUE THE BRETHREN

6 Dare any of you, having
a matter against another,
go to law before the unrighteous, and not before the
saints? 2Do you not know
that the saints will judge the
world? And if the world will be
judged by you, are you unworthy to judge the smallest matters? 3Do you not know that
we shall judge angels? How
much more, things that pertain to this life? 4If then you
have judgments concerning
things pertaining to this life,
do you appoint those who are
least esteemed by the church
to judge? 5I say this to your
shame. Is it so, that there is
not a wise man among you,
not even one, who will be able
to judge between his brethren? 6But brother goes to law
against brother, and that before unbelievers!
7Now therefore, it is already
an utter failure for you that you
go to law against one another.
Why do you not rather accept
wrong? Why do you not rather
let yourselves be cheated? 8No,
you yourselves do wrong and
cheat, and *you do* these things
to your brethren! 9Do you not
know that the unrighteous
will not inherit the kingdom
of God? Do not be deceived.
Neither fornicators, nor idolaters, nor adulterers, nor
homosexuals,[a] nor sodomites,
10nor thieves, nor covetous,
nor drunkards, nor revilers,
nor extortioners will inherit
the kingdom of God. 11And
such were some of you. But
you were washed, but you were
sanctified, but you were justified in the name of the Lord
Jesus and by the Spirit of our
God.

GLORIFY GOD IN BODY AND SPIRIT

12All things are lawful for
me, but all things are not
helpful. All things are lawful for me, but I will not be
brought under the power of
any. 13Foods for the stomach
and the stomach for foods,
but God will destroy both it
and them. Now the body *is* not
for sexual immorality but for
the Lord, and the Lord for the
body. 14And God both raised
up the Lord and will also raise
us up by His power.
15Do you not know that
your bodies are members of

5:13 [a] Deuteronomy 17:7; 19:19; 22:21, 24; 24:7 **6:9** [a] That is, catamites

Christ? Shall I then take the
members of Christ and make
them members of a harlot?
Certainly not! 16Or do you not
know that he who is joined to
a harlot is one body *with her?*
For "the two," He says, "shall
become one flesh."[a] 17But he
who is joined to the Lord is
one spirit *with Him.*

18Flee sexual immorality.
Every sin that a man does is
outside the body, but he who
commits sexual immorality
sins against his own body. 19Or
do you not know that your
body is the temple of the Holy
Spirit *who is* in you, whom you
have from God, and you are
not your own? 20For you were
bought at a price; therefore
glorify God in your body[a] and
in your spirit, which are God's.

PRINCIPLES OF MARRIAGE

7 Now concerning the things
of which you wrote to me:
It is good for a man not to
touch a woman. 2Neverthe-
less, because of sexual immorality, let each man have his
own wife, and let each woman
have her own husband. 3Let
the husband render to his
wife the affection due her,
and likewise also the wife to
her husband. 4The wife does
not have authority over her
own body, but the husband
does. And likewise the husband does not have authority over his own body, but the
wife *does.* 5Do not deprive one
another except with consent
for a time, that you may give
yourselves to fasting and
prayer; and come together
again so that Satan does not
tempt you because of your
lack of self-control. 6But I say
this as a concession, not as a
commandment. 7For I wish
that all men were even as I
myself. But each one has his
own gift from God, one in this
manner and another in that.

8But I say to the unmarried
and to the widows: It is good
for them if they remain even
as I am; 9but if they cannot
exercise self-control, let them
marry. For it is better to marry
than to burn *with passion.*

KEEP YOUR MARRIAGE VOWS

10Now to the married I
command, *yet* not I but the
Lord: A wife is not to depart
from *her* husband. 11But even
if she does depart, let her remain unmarried or be reconciled to *her* husband. And a
husband is not to divorce *his*
wife.

12But to the rest I, not the
Lord, say: If any brother has a
wife who does not believe, and
she is willing to live with him,
let him not divorce her. 13And
a woman who has a husband
who does not believe, if he
is willing to live with her, let
her not divorce him. 14For the

6:16 [a] Genesis 2:24 6:20 [a] NU-Text ends the verse at *body.*

unbelieving husband is sanctified by the wife, and the unbelieving wife is sanctified by
the husband; otherwise your
children would be unclean,
but now they are holy. 15But
if the unbeliever departs, let
him depart; a brother or a
sister is not under bondage
in such *cases.* But God has
called us to peace. 16For how
do you know, O wife, whether
you will save *your* husband?
Or how do you know, O husband, whether you will save
your wife?

LIVE AS YOU ARE CALLED

17But as God has distrib-
uted to each one, as the Lord
has called each one, so let him
walk. And so I ordain in all the
churches. 18Was anyone called
while circumcised? Let him
not become uncircumcised.
Was anyone called while uncircumcised? Let him not be
circumcised. 19Circumcision
is nothing and uncircumcision is nothing, but keeping
the commandments of God *is*
what matters. 20Let each one
remain in the same calling in
which he was called. 21Were
you called *while* a slave? Do
not be concerned about it; but
if you can be made free, rather
use *it.* 22For he who is called
in the Lord *while* a slave is the
Lord's freedman. Likewise
he who is called *while* free
is Christ's slave. 23You were
bought at a price; do not become slaves of men. 24Breth-
ren, let each one remain with
God in that *state* in which he
was called.

TO THE UNMARRIED AND WIDOWS

25Now concerning virgins: I
have no commandment from
the Lord; yet I give judgment
as one whom the Lord in His
mercy has made trustworthy.
26I suppose therefore that this
is good because of the present distress—that *it is* good
for a man to remain as he is:
27Are you bound to a wife?
Do not seek to be loosed. Are
you loosed from a wife? Do
not seek a wife. 28But even if
you do marry, you have not
sinned; and if a virgin marries,
she has not sinned. Nevertheless such will have trouble in
the flesh, but I would spare
you.

29But this I say, brethren,
the time *is* short, so that from
now on even those who have
wives should be as though
they had none, 30those who
weep as though they did not
weep, those who rejoice as
though they did not rejoice,
those who buy as though they
did not possess, 31and those
who use this world as not mis-
using *it.* For the form of this
world is passing away.

32But I want you to be without care. He who is unmarried
cares for the things of the
Lord—how he may please the
Lord. 33But he who is married
cares about the things of the

world—how he may please *his* wife. 34There is[a] a difference between a wife and a virgin. The unmarried woman cares about the things of the Lord, that she may be holy both in body and in spirit. But she who is married cares about the things of the world—how she may please *her* husband. 35And this I say for your own profit, not that I may put a leash on you, but for what is proper, and that you may serve the Lord without distraction.

36But if any man thinks he is behaving improperly toward his virgin, if she is past the flower of youth, and thus it must be, let him do what he wishes. He does not sin; let them marry. 37Nevertheless he who stands steadfast in his heart, having no necessity, but has power over his own will, and has so determined in his heart that he will keep his virgin,[a] does well. 38So then he who gives *her*[a] in marriage does well, but he who does not give *her* in marriage does better.

39A wife is bound by law as long as her husband lives; but if her husband dies, she is at liberty to be married to whom she wishes, only in the Lord. 40But she is happier if she remains as she is, according to *my* judgment—and I think I also have the Spirit of God.

BE SENSITIVE TO CONSCIENCE

8 Now concerning things offered to idols: We know that we all have knowledge. Knowledge puffs up, but love edifies. 2And if anyone thinks that he knows anything, he knows nothing yet as he ought to know. 3But if anyone loves God, this one is known by Him.

4Therefore concerning the eating of things offered to idols, we know that an idol *is* nothing in the world, and that *there is* no other God but one. 5For even if there are so-called gods, whether in heaven or on earth (as there are many gods and many lords), 6yet for us *there is* one God, the Father, of whom *are* all things, and we for Him; and one Lord Jesus Christ, through whom *are* all things, and through whom we *live.*

7However, *there is* not in everyone that knowledge; for some, with consciousness of the idol, until now eat *it* as a thing offered to an idol; and their conscience, being weak, is defiled. 8But food does not commend us to God; for neither if we eat are we the better, nor if we do not eat are we the worse.

9But beware lest somehow this liberty of yours become a stumbling block to those who are weak. 10For if anyone sees

7:34 [a] M-Text adds *also.* 7:37 [a] Or *virgin daughter* 7:38 [a] NU-Text reads *his own virgin.*

you who have knowledge eating in an idol's temple, will
not the conscience of him
who is weak be emboldened
to eat those things offered to
idols? [11]And because of your
knowledge shall the weak
brother perish, for whom
Christ died? [12]But when you
thus sin against the brethren, and wound their weak
conscience, you sin against
Christ. [13]Therefore, if food
makes my brother stumble, I
will never again eat meat, lest
I make my brother stumble.

A PATTERN OF SELF-DENIAL

9 Am I not an apostle? Am I
not free? Have I not seen
Jesus Christ our Lord? Are you
not my work in the Lord? [2]If I
am not an apostle to others,
yet doubtless I am to you. For
you are the seal of my apostleship in the Lord.

[3]My defense to those who
examine me is this: [4]Do we
have no right to eat and drink?
[5]Do we have no right to take
along a believing wife, as *do*
also the other apostles, the
brothers of the Lord, and Cephas? [6]Or *is it* only Barnabas
and I *who* have no right to
refrain from working? [7]Who
ever goes to war at his own
expense? Who plants a vineyard and does not eat of its
fruit? Or who tends a flock and
does not drink of the milk of
the flock?

[8]Do I say these things as
a *mere* man? Or does not the
law say the same also? [9]For it
is written in the law of Moses,
"You shall not muzzle an ox
while it treads out the grain."[a]
Is it oxen God is concerned
about? [10]Or does He say *it* altogether for our sakes? For
our sakes, no doubt, *this* is
written, that he who plows
should plow in hope, and he
who threshes in hope should
be partaker of his hope. [11]If
we have sown spiritual things
for you, *is it* a great thing if
we reap your material things?
[12]If others are partakers of *this*
right over you, *are* we not even
more?

Nevertheless we have not
used this right, but endure
all things lest we hinder the
gospel of Christ. [13]Do you not
know that those who minister the holy things eat *of the*
things of the temple, and
those who serve at the altar
partake of *the offerings of* the
altar? [14]Even so the Lord has
commanded that those who
preach the gospel should live
from the gospel.

[15]But I have used none of
these things, nor have I written these things that it should
be done so to me; for it *would*
be better for me to die than
that anyone should make my
boasting void. [16]For if I preach
the gospel, I have nothing to
boast of, for necessity is laid

9:9 [a] Deuteronomy 25:4

upon me; yes, woe is me if
I do not preach the gospel!
17For if I do this willingly, I
have a reward; but if against
my will, I have been entrusted
with a stewardship. 18What is
my reward then? That when
I preach the gospel, I may
present the gospel of Christ[a]
without charge, that I may
not abuse my authority in the
gospel.

SERVING ALL MEN

19For though I am free from
all *men,* I have made myself
a servant to all, that I might
win the more; 20and to the
Jews I became as a Jew, that
I might win Jews; to those *who
are* under the law, as under the
law,[a] that I might win those
who are under the law; 21to
those *who are* without law, as
without law (not being without law toward God,[a] but
under law toward Christ[b]),
that I might win those *who
are* without law; 22to the
weak I became as[a] weak, that
I might win the weak. I have
become all things to all *men,*
that I might by all means save
some. 23Now this I do for the
gospel's sake, that I may be
partaker of it with *you.*

STRIVING FOR A CROWN

24Do you not know that
those who run in a race all
run, but one receives the
prize? Run in such a way
that you may obtain *it.* 25And
everyone who competes *for
the prize* is temperate in all
things. Now they *do it* to obtain a perishable crown, but
we *for* an imperishable *crown.*
26Therefore I run thus: not
with uncertainty. Thus I fight:
not as *one who* beats the air.
27But I discipline my body and
bring *it* into subjection, lest,
when I have preached to others, I myself should become
disqualified.

OLD TESTAMENT EXAMPLES

10 Moreover, brethren, I do
not want you to be un-
aware that all our fathers were
under the cloud, all passed
through the sea, 2all were
baptized into Moses in the
cloud and in the sea, 3all ate
the same spiritual food, 4and
all drank the same spiritual
drink. For they drank of that
spiritual Rock that followed
them, and that Rock was
Christ. 5But with most of them
God was not well pleased, for
their bodies were scattered in
the wilderness.

6Now these things became
our examples, to the intent
that we should not lust after
evil things as they also lusted.
7And do not become idola-

9:18 [a] NU-Text omits *of Christ.* 9:20 [a] NU-Text adds *though not being myself under the law.* 9:21 [a] NU-Text reads *God's law.* [b] NU-Text reads *Christ's law.* 9:22 [a] NU-Text omits *as.*

ters as *were* some of them. As
it is written, "The people sat
down to eat and drink, and
rose up to play."[a] 8Nor let us
commit sexual immorality,
as some of them did, and in
one day twenty-three thousand fell; 9nor let us tempt
Christ, as some of them also
tempted, and were destroyed
by serpents; 10nor complain,
as some of them also com-
plained, and were destroyed
by the destroyer. 11Now all[a]
these things happened to
them as examples, and they
were written for our admonition, upon whom the ends of
the ages have come.
12Therefore let him who
thinks he stands take heed
lest he fall. 13No temptation
has overtaken you except
such as is common to man;
but God *is* faithful, who will
not allow you to be tempted
beyond what you are able, but
with the temptation will also
make the way of escape, that
you may be able to bear *it*.

FLEE FROM IDOLATRY

14Therefore, my beloved,
flee from idolatry. 15I speak
as to wise men; judge for yourselves what I say. 16The cup
of blessing which we bless, is
it not the communion of the
blood of Christ? The bread
which we break, is it not the
communion of the body of
Christ? 17For we, *though* many,
are one bread *and* one body;
for we all partake of that one
bread.
18Observe Israel after the
flesh: Are not those who eat
of the sacrifices partakers of
the altar? 19What am I saying
then? That an idol is anything,
or what is offered to idols is
anything? 20Rather, that the
things which the Gentiles sacrifice they sacrifice to demons
and not to God, and I do not
want you to have fellowship
with demons. 21You cannot
drink the cup of the Lord and
the cup of demons; you cannot partake of the Lord's table
and of the table of demons.
22Or do we provoke the Lord
to jealousy? Are we stronger
than He?

ALL TO THE GLORY OF GOD

23All things are lawful for
me,[a] but not all things are
helpful; all things are lawful
for me,[b] but not all things
edify. 24Let no one seek his
own, but each one the other's
well-being.
25Eat whatever is sold in
the meat market, asking no
questions for conscience'
sake; 26for "the earth *is* the
LORD's, and all its fullness."[a]
27If any of those who do not
believe invites you *to dinner*,
and you desire to go, eat whatever is set before you, asking

10:7 [a] Exodus 32:6 10:11 [a] NU-Text omits *all*. 10:23 [a] NU-Text omits *for me*. [b] NU-Text omits *for me*. 10:26 [a] Psalm 24:1

no question for conscience'
sake. 28But if anyone says
to you, "This was offered to
idols," do not eat it for the sake
of the one who told you, and
for conscience' sake;[a] for "the
earth *is* the LORD's, and all its
fullness."[b] 29"Conscience," I
say, not your own, but that of
the other. For why is my liberty judged by another *man's*
conscience? 30But if I partake
with thanks, why am I evil
spoken of for *the food* over
which I give thanks?

31Therefore, whether you
eat or drink, or whatever you
do, do all to the glory of God.
32Give no offense, either to
the Jews or to the Greeks or
to the church of God, 33just
as I also please all *men* in all
things, not seeking my own
profit, but the *profit* of many,
that they may be saved.

11 Imitate me, just as I also
imitate Christ.

HEAD COVERINGS

2Now I praise you, breth-
ren, that you remember me in
all things and keep the traditions just as I delivered *them*
to you. 3But I want you to know
that the head of every man is
Christ, the head of woman *is*
man, and the head of Christ
is God. 4Every man praying
or prophesying, having *his*
head covered, dishonors his
head. 5But every woman who
prays or prophesies with *her*
head uncovered dishonors
her head, for that is one and
the same as if her head were
shaved. 6For if a woman is
not covered, let her also be
shorn. But if it is shameful
for a woman to be shorn or
shaved, let her be covered.
7For a man indeed ought not
to cover *his* head, since he is
the image and glory of God;
but woman is the glory of
man. 8For man is not from
woman, but woman from
man. 9Nor was man created
for the woman, but woman
for the man. 10For this reason the woman ought to have
a symbol of authority on *her*
head, because of the angels.
11Nevertheless, neither *is* man
independent of woman, nor
woman independent of man,
in the Lord. 12For as woman
came from man, even so man
also *comes* through woman;
but all things are from God.

13Judge among yourselves.
Is it proper for a woman to
pray to God with her head
uncovered? 14Does not even
nature itself teach you that if
a man has long hair, it is a dishonor to him? 15But if a woman
has long hair, it is a glory to
her; for *her* hair is given to her[a]
for a covering. 16But if anyone
seems to be contentious, we
have no such custom, nor *do*
the churches of God.

10:28 [a] NU-Text omits the rest of this verse. [b] Psalm 24:1 11:15 [a] M-Text omits *to her.*

CONDUCT AT THE LORD'S SUPPER

17Now in giving these in-
structions I do not praise
you, since you come together
not for the better but for the
worse. 18For first of all, when
you come together as a church,
I hear that there are divisions
among you, and in part I believe it. 19For there must also
be factions among you, that
those who are approved may
be recognized among you.
20Therefore when you come
together in one place, it is not
to eat the Lord's Supper. 21For
in eating, each one takes his
own supper ahead of *others;*
and one is hungry and an-
other is drunk. 22What! Do
you not have houses to eat and
drink in? Or do you despise
the church of God and shame
those who have nothing? What
shall I say to you? Shall I praise
you in this? I do not praise *you.*

INSTITUTION OF THE LORD'S SUPPER

23For I received from the
Lord that which I also delivered to you: that the Lord
Jesus on the *same* night in
which He was betrayed took
bread; 24and when He had
given thanks, He broke *it*
and said, "Take, eat;[a] this is
My body which is broken[b] for
you; do this in remembrance
of Me." 25In the same manner *He* also *took* the cup after
supper, saying, "This cup is
the new covenant in My blood.
This do, as often as you drink
it, in remembrance of Me."
26For as often as you eat
this bread and drink this cup,
you proclaim the Lord's death
till He comes.

EXAMINE YOURSELF

27Therefore whoever eats
this bread or drinks *this* cup of
the Lord in an unworthy manner will be guilty of the body
and blood[a] of the Lord. 28But
let a man examine himself, and
so let him eat of the bread and
drink of the cup. 29For he who
eats and drinks in an unworthy
manner[a] eats and drinks judgment to himself, not discerning the Lord's[b] body. 30For this
reason many *are* weak and sick
among you, and many sleep.
31For if we would judge ourselves, we would not be judged.
32But when we are judged, we
are chastened by the Lord, that
we may not be condemned
with the world.
33Therefore, my brethren,
when you come together to
eat, wait for one another.
34But if anyone is hungry,
let him eat at home, lest you
come together for judgment.
And the rest I will set in order
when I come.

11:24 [a] NU-Text omits *Take, eat.* [b] NU-Text omits *broken.*
11:27 [a] NU-Text and M-Text read *the blood.* 11:29 [a] NU-Text omits *in an unworthy manner.* [b] NU-Text omits *Lord's.*

SPIRITUAL GIFTS: UNITY IN DIVERSITY

12 Now concerning spiritual *gifts,* brethren, I do not want you to be ignorant: 2You know that[a] you were Gentiles, carried away to these dumb idols, however you were led. 3Therefore I make known to you that no one speaking by the Spirit of God calls Jesus accursed, and no one can say that Jesus is Lord except by the Holy Spirit.

4There are diversities of gifts, but the same Spirit. 5There are differences of ministries, but the same Lord. 6And there are diversities of activities, but it is the same God who works all in all. 7But the manifestation of the Spirit is given to each one for the profit *of all:* 8for to one is given the word of wisdom through the Spirit, to another the word of knowledge through the same Spirit, 9to another faith by the same Spirit, to another gifts of healings by the same[a] Spirit, 10to another the working of miracles, to another prophecy, to another discerning of spirits, to another *different* kinds of tongues, to another the interpretation of tongues. 11But one and the same Spirit works all these things, distributing to each one individually as He wills.

UNITY AND DIVERSITY IN ONE BODY

12For as the body is one and has many members, but all the members of that one body, being many, are one body, so also *is* Christ. 13For by one Spirit we were all baptized into one body—whether Jews or Greeks, whether slaves or free—and have all been made to drink into[a] one Spirit. 14For in fact the body is not one member but many.

15If the foot should say, "Because I am not a hand, I am not of the body," is it therefore not of the body? 16And if the ear should say, "Because I am not an eye, I am not of the body," is it therefore not of the body? 17If the whole body *were* an eye, where *would be* the hearing? If the whole *were* hearing, where *would be* the smelling? 18But now God has set the members, each one of them, in the body just as He pleased. 19And if they were all one member, where *would* the body *be?*

20But now indeed *there are* many members, yet one body. 21And the eye cannot say to the hand, "I have no need of you"; nor again the head to the feet, "I have no need of you." 22No, much rather, those members of the body which seem to be weaker are necessary. 23And those *members* of the body which we think to

12:2 [a] NU-Text and M-Text add *when.* 12:9 [a] NU-Text reads *one.* 12:13 [a] NU-Text omits *into.*

be less honorable, on these we bestow greater honor; and our unpresentable *parts* have greater modesty, 24but our presentable *parts* have no need. But God composed the body, having given greater honor to that *part* which lacks it, 25that there should be no schism in the body, but *that* the members should have the same care for one another. 26And if one member suffers, all the members suffer with *it;* or if one member is honored, all the members rejoice with *it.*

27Now you are the body of Christ, and members individually. 28And God has appointed these in the church: first apostles, second prophets, third teachers, after that miracles, then gifts of healings, helps, administrations, varieties of tongues. 29*Are* all apostles? *Are* all prophets? *Are* all teachers? *Are* all workers of miracles? 30Do all have gifts of healings? Do all speak with tongues? Do all interpret? 31But earnestly desire the best[a] gifts. And yet I show you a more excellent way.

THE GREATEST GIFT

13 Though I speak with the tongues of men *and of angels,* but have not love, I have become sounding brass or a clanging cymbal. 2And though I have *the gift of* prophecy, and understand all mysteries and all knowledge, and though I have all faith, so that I could remove mountains, but have not love, I am nothing. 3And though I bestow all my goods to feed *the poor,* and though I give my body to be burned,[a] but have not love, it profits me nothing.

4Love suffers long *and* is kind; love does not envy; love does not parade itself, is not puffed up; 5does not behave rudely, does not seek its own, is not provoked, thinks no evil; 6does not rejoice in iniquity, but rejoices in the truth; 7bears all things, believes all things, hopes all things, endures all things.

8Love never fails. But whether *there are* prophecies, they will fail; whether *there are* tongues, they will cease; whether *there is* knowledge, it will vanish away. 9For we know in part and we prophesy in part. 10But when that which is perfect has come, then that which is in part will be done away.

11When I was a child, I spoke as a child, I understood as a child, I thought as a child; but when I became a man, I put away childish things. 12For now we see in a mirror, dimly, but then face to face. Now I know in part, but then I shall know just as I also am known.

13And now abide faith, hope, love, these three; but the greatest of these *is* love.

12:31 [a] NU-Text reads *greater.* 13:3 [a] NU-Text reads *so I may boast.*

PROPHECY AND TONGUES

14 Pursue love, and desire
spiritual *gifts,* but especially that you may prophesy.
2For he who speaks in a tongue
does not speak to men but to
God, for no one understands
him; however, in the spirit he
speaks mysteries. 3But he who
prophesies speaks edification
and exhortation and com-
fort to men. 4He who speaks
in a tongue edifies himself,
but he who prophesies edifies the church. 5I wish you
all spoke with tongues, but
even more that you prophesied; for[a] he who prophesies
is greater than he who speaks
with tongues, unless indeed
he interprets, that the church
may receive edification.

TONGUES MUST BE INTERPRETED

6But now, brethren, if I come
to you speaking with tongues,
what shall I profit you unless I
speak to you either by revelation, by knowledge, by prophesying, or by teaching? 7Even
things without life, whether
flute or harp, when they make
a sound, unless they make a
distinction in the sounds, how
will it be known what is piped
or played? 8For if the trumpet
makes an uncertain sound,
who will prepare for battle?
9So likewise you, unless you
utter by the tongue words
easy to understand, how will
it be known what is spoken?
For you will be speaking into
the air. 10There are, it may be,
so many kinds of languages
in the world, and none of
them *is* without significance.
11Therefore, if I do not know
the meaning of the language, I
shall be a foreigner to him who
speaks, and he who speaks *will
be* a foreigner to me. 12Even so
you, since you are zealous for
spiritual *gifts, let it be* for the
edification of the church *that*
you seek to excel.

13Therefore let him who
speaks in a tongue pray that
he may interpret. 14For if I pray
in a tongue, my spirit prays,
but my understanding is unfruitful. 15What is *the conclu-
sion* then? I will pray with the
spirit, and I will also pray with
the understanding. I will sing
with the spirit, and I will also
sing with the understanding.
16Otherwise, if you bless with
the spirit, how will he who
occupies the place of the uninformed say "Amen" at your
giving of thanks, since he does
not understand what you say?
17For you indeed give thanks
well, but the other is not edified.

18I thank my God I speak
with tongues more than you
all; 19yet in the church I would
rather speak five words with
my understanding, that I may
teach others also, than ten
thousand words in a tongue.

14:5 [a] NU-Text reads *and.*

TONGUES A SIGN TO UNBELIEVERS

20Brethren, do not be children in understanding; however, in malice be babes, but
in understanding be mature.
21In the law it is written:

"With *men of* other
tongues and other lips
I will speak to this people;
And yet, for all that, they
will not hear Me,"[a]

says the Lord.

22Therefore tongues are
for a sign, not to those who
believe but to unbelievers; but
prophesying is not for unbelievers but for those who believe. 23Therefore if the whole
church comes together in
one place, and all speak with
tongues, and there come in
those who are uninformed or
unbelievers, will they not say
that you are out of your mind?
24But if all prophesy, and an
unbeliever or an uninformed
person comes in, he is convinced by all, he is convicted
by all. 25And thus[a] the secrets
of his heart are revealed; and
so, falling down on *his* face, he
will worship God and report
that God is truly among you.

ORDER IN CHURCH MEETINGS

26How is it then, brethren?
Whenever you come together,
each of you has a psalm, has a
teaching, has a tongue, has a
revelation, has an interpretation. Let all things be done for
edification. 27If anyone speaks
in a tongue, *let there be* two or
at the most three, *each* in turn,
and let one interpret. 28But if
there is no interpreter, let him
keep silent in church, and let
him speak to himself and to
God. 29Let two or three prophets speak, and let the others
judge. 30But if *anything* is revealed to another who sits by,
let the first keep silent. 31For
you can all prophesy one by
one, that all may learn and
all may be encouraged. 32And
the spirits of the prophets are
subject to the prophets. 33For
God is not *the author* of confusion but of peace, as in all the
churches of the saints.

34Let your[a] women keep silent in the churches, for they
are not permitted to speak; but
they are to be submissive, as
the law also says. 35And if they
want to learn something, let
them ask their own husbands
at home; for it is shameful for
women to speak in church.

36Or did the word of God
come *originally* from you? Or
was it you only that it reached?
37If anyone thinks himself to
be a prophet or spiritual, let
him acknowledge that the
things which I write to you
are the commandments of

14:21 [a] Isaiah 28:11, 12 14:25 [a] NU-Text omits *And thus.* 14:34 [a] NU-Text omits *your.*

the Lord. 38But if anyone is
ignorant, let him be ignorant.[a]
39Therefore, brethren, desire earnestly to prophesy,
and do not forbid to speak
with tongues. 40Let all things
be done decently and in order.

THE RISEN CHRIST, FAITH'S REALITY

15 Moreover, brethren, I
declare to you the gos-
pel which I preached to you,
which also you received and
in which you stand, 2by which
also you are saved, if you
hold fast that word which I
preached to you—unless you
believed in vain.
3For I delivered to you first
of all that which I also received:
that Christ died for our sins according to the Scriptures, 4and
that He was buried, and that
He rose again the third day
according to the Scriptures,
5and that He was seen by Cephas, then by the twelve. 6After
that He was seen by over five
hundred brethren at once, of
whom the greater part remain
to the present, but some have
fallen asleep. 7After that He
was seen by James, then by
all the apostles. 8Then last of
all He was seen by me also, as
by one born out of due time.
9For I am the least of the
apostles, who am not worthy
to be called an apostle, because I persecuted the church
of God. 10But by the grace of
God I am what I am, and His
grace toward me was not in
vain; but I labored more abundantly than they all, yet not I,
but the grace of God *which was*
with me. 11Therefore, whether
it was I or they, so we preach
and so you believed.

THE RISEN CHRIST, OUR HOPE

12Now if Christ is preached
that He has been raised from
the dead, how do some among
you say that there is no resurrection of the dead? 13But if
there is no resurrection of the
dead, then Christ is not risen.
14And if Christ is not risen, then
our preaching *is* empty and
your faith *is* also empty. 15Yes,
and we are found false witnesses of God, because we have
testified of God that He raised
up Christ, whom He did not
raise up—if in fact the dead do
not rise. 16For if *the* dead do not
rise, then Christ is not risen.
17And if Christ is not risen, your
faith *is* futile; you are still in
your sins! 18Then also those
who have fallen asleep in Christ
have perished. 19If in this life
only we have hope in Christ, we
are of all men the most pitiable.

THE LAST ENEMY DESTROYED

20But now Christ is risen
from the dead, *and* has become

14:38 [a] NU-Text reads *if anyone does not recognize this, he is not recognized.*

the firstfruits of those who
have fallen asleep. 21For since
by man *came* death, by Man
also *came* the resurrection of
the dead. 22For as in Adam all
die, even so in Christ all shall be
made alive. 23But each one in
his own order: Christ the firstfruits, afterward those *who are*
Christ's at His coming. 24Then
comes the end, when He delivers the kingdom to God the
Father, when He puts an end
to all rule and all authority and
power. 25For He must reign till
He has put all enemies under
His feet. 26The last enemy *that*
will be destroyed *is* death. 27For
"He has put all things under
His feet."[a] But when He says
"all things are put under *Him*,"
it is evident that He who put all
things under Him is excepted.
28Now when all things are
made subject to Him, then the
Son Himself will also be subject to Him who put all things
under Him, that God may be
all in all.

EFFECTS OF DENYING THE RESURRECTION

29Otherwise, what will
they do who are baptized for
the dead, if the dead do not
rise at all? Why then are they
baptized for the dead? 30And
why do we stand in jeopardy
every hour? 31I affirm, by the
boasting in you which I have
in Christ Jesus our Lord, I die
daily. 32If, in the manner of
men, I have fought with beasts
at Ephesus, what advantage
is it to me? If *the* dead do not
rise, "Let us eat and drink, for
tomorrow we die!"[a]

33Do not be deceived: "Evil
company corrupts good hab-
its." 34Awake to righteousness,
and do not sin; for some do not
have the knowledge of God. I
speak *this* to your shame.

A GLORIOUS BODY

35But someone will say,
"How are the dead raised up?
And with what body do they
come?" 36Foolish one, what
you sow is not made alive unless it dies. 37And what you
sow, you do not sow that body
that shall be, but mere grain—
perhaps wheat or some other
grain. 38But God gives it a
body as He pleases, and to
each seed its own body.

39All flesh *is* not the same
flesh, but *there is* one *kind of*
flesh[a] of men, another flesh of
animals, another of fish, *and*
another of birds.

40*There are* also celestial
bodies and terrestrial bodies;
but the glory of the celestial *is*
one, and the *glory* of the terrestrial *is* another. 41*There is*
one glory of the sun, another
glory of the moon, and another glory of the stars; for
one star differs from *another*
star in glory.

15:27 [a] Psalm 8:6 15:32 [a] Isaiah 22:13
15:39 [a] NU-Text and M-Text omit *of flesh*.

42So also *is* the resurrection
of the dead. *The body* is sown
in corruption, it is raised in
incorruption. 43It is sown in
dishonor, it is raised in glory.
It is sown in weakness, it is
raised in power. 44It is sown a
natural body, it is raised a spiritual body. There is a natural
body, and there is a spiritual
body. 45And so it is written,
"The first man Adam became
a living being."[a] The last Adam
became a life-giving spirit.

46However, the spiritual is
not first, but the natural, and
afterward the spiritual. 47The
first man *was* of the earth,
made of dust; the second Man
is the Lord[a] from heaven. 48As
was the *man* of dust, so also
are those *who are made* of
dust; and as *is* the heavenly
Man, so also *are* those *who are*
heavenly. 49And as we have
borne the image of the *man*
of dust, we shall also bear[a] the
image of the heavenly *Man.*

OUR FINAL VICTORY

50Now this I say, brethren,
that flesh and blood cannot
inherit the kingdom of God;
nor does corruption inherit
incorruption. 51Behold, I tell
you a mystery: We shall not
all sleep, but we shall all be
changed— 52in a moment, in
the twinkling of an eye, at the
last trumpet. For the trumpet
will sound, and the dead will
be raised incorruptible, and
we shall be changed. 53For this
corruptible must put on incorruption, and this mortal *must*
put on immortality. 54So when
this corruptible has put on incorruption, and this mortal
has put on immortality, then
shall be brought to pass the
saying that is written: "Death
is swallowed up in victory."[a]

55"O Death, where *is*
your sting?[a]
O Hades, where *is*
your victory?"[b]

56The sting of death *is* sin, and
the strength of sin *is* the law.
57But thanks *be* to God, who
gives us the victory through
our Lord Jesus Christ.

58Therefore, my beloved
brethren, be steadfast, immovable, always abounding in
the work of the Lord, knowing
that your labor is not in vain
in the Lord.

COLLECTION FOR THE SAINTS

16 Now concerning the
collection for the saints,
as I have given orders to the
churches of Galatia, so you
must do also: 2On the first *day*
of the week let each one of you
lay something aside, storing
up as he may prosper, that

15:45 [a] Genesis 2:7 15:47 [a] NU-Text omits *the Lord.*
15:49 [a] M-Text reads *let us also bear.* 15:54 [a] Isaiah 25:8
15:55 [a] Hosea 13:14 [b] NU-Text reads *O Death, where is your victory? O Death, where is your sting?*

there be no collections when
I come. [3]And when I come,
whomever you approve by
your letters I will send to bear
your gift to Jerusalem. [4]But if
it is fitting that I go also, they
will go with me.

PERSONAL PLANS

[5]Now I will come to you
when I pass through Macedonia (for I am passing through
Macedonia). [6]And it may be
that I will remain, or even
spend the winter with you, that
you may send me on my journey, wherever I go. [7]For I do
not wish to see you now on the
way; but I hope to stay a while
with you, if the Lord permits.
[8]But I will tarry in Ephesus
until Pentecost. [9]For a great
and effective door has opened
to me, and *there are* many adversaries.
[10]And if Timothy comes,
see that he may be with you
without fear; for he does the
work of the Lord, as I also *do.*
[11]Therefore let no one despise
him. But send him on his
journey in peace, that he may
come to me; for I am waiting
for him with the brethren.
[12]Now concerning *our*
brother Apollos, I strongly
urged him to come to you with
the brethren, but he was quite
unwilling to come at this time;
however, he will come when
he has a convenient time.

FINAL EXHORTATIONS

[13]Watch, stand fast in the
faith, be brave, be strong. [14]Let
all *that* you *do* be done with
love.
[15]I urge you, brethren—you
know the household of Stephanas, that it is the firstfruits
of Achaia, and *that* they have
devoted themselves to the
ministry of the saints— [16]that
you also submit to such, and
to everyone who works and
labors with *us.*
[17]I am glad about the coming of Stephanas, Fortunatus,
and Achaicus, for what was
lacking on your part they supplied. [18]For they refreshed my
spirit and yours. Therefore acknowledge such men.

GREETINGS AND A SOLEMN FAREWELL

[19]The churches of Asia
greet you. Aquila and Priscilla greet you heartily in the
Lord, with the church that is
in their house. [20]All the brethren greet you.
Greet one another with a
holy kiss.
[21]The salutation with my
own hand—Paul's.
[22]If anyone does not love
the Lord Jesus Christ, let him
be accursed.[a] O Lord, come![b]
[23]The grace of our Lord
Jesus Christ *be* with you. [24]My
love *be* with you all in Christ
Jesus. Amen.

16:22 [a] Greek *anathema* [b] Aramaic *Maranatha*

THE SECOND EPISTLE OF PAUL THE APOSTLE TO THE CORINTHIANS

GREETING

1 Paul, an apostle of Jesus
Christ by the will of God,
and Timothy *our* brother,

To the church of God which
is at Corinth, with all the saints
who are in all Achaia:

[2]Grace to you and peace
from God our Father and the
Lord Jesus Christ.

COMFORT IN SUFFERING

[3]Blessed *be* the God and Father of our Lord Jesus Christ,
the Father of mercies and God
of all comfort, [4]who comforts
us in all our tribulation, that
we may be able to comfort
those who are in any trouble,
with the comfort with which
we ourselves are comforted
by God. [5]For as the sufferings
of Christ abound in us, so our
consolation also abounds
through Christ. [6]Now if we are
afflicted, *it is* for your consolation and salvation, which
is effective for enduring the
same sufferings which we also
suffer. Or if we are comforted,
it is for your consolation and
salvation. [7]And our hope for
you *is* steadfast, because we
know that as you are partakers
of the sufferings, so also *you
will partake* of the consolation.

DELIVERED FROM SUFFERING

[8]For we do not want you
to be ignorant, brethren,
of our trouble which came
to us in Asia: that we were
burdened beyond measure,
above strength, so that we despaired even of life. [9]Yes, we
had the sentence of death in
ourselves, that we should not
trust in ourselves but in God
who raises the dead, [10]who
delivered us from so great a
death, and does[a] deliver us;
in whom we trust that He
will still deliver *us,* [11]you also
helping together in prayer for
us, that thanks may be given
by many persons on our[a] behalf for the gift *granted* to us
through many.

PAUL'S SINCERITY

[12]For our boasting is this:
the testimony of our con-
science that we conducted
ourselves in the world in
simplicity and godly sincerity, not with fleshly wisdom

1:10 [a] NU-Text reads *shall.* 1:11 [a] M-Text reads *your behalf.*

but by the grace of God, and
more abundantly toward you.
13For we are not writing any
other things to you than what
you read or understand. Now
I trust you will understand,
even to the end 14(as also you
have understood us in part),
that we are your boast as you
also *are* ours, in the day of the
Lord Jesus.

SPARING THE CHURCH

15And in this confidence
I intended to come to you
before, that you might have
a second benefit— 16to pass
by way of you to Macedonia,
to come again from Mace-
donia to you, and be helped
by you on my way to Judea.
17Therefore, when I was plan-
ning this, did I do it lightly?
Or the things I plan, do I plan
according to the flesh, that
with me there should be Yes,
Yes, and No, No? 18But *as* God
is faithful, our word to you was
not Yes and No. 19For the Son
of God, Jesus Christ, who was
preached among you by us—
by me, Silvanus, and Timothy—was not Yes and No, but
in Him was Yes. 20For all the
promises of God in Him *are*
Yes, and in Him Amen, to the
glory of God through us. 21Now
He who establishes us with you
in Christ and has anointed us
is God, 22who also has sealed
us and given us the Spirit in
our hearts as a guarantee.

23Moreover I call God as
witness against my soul, that
to spare you I came no more
to Corinth. 24Not that we have
dominion over your faith, but
are fellow workers for your
joy; for by faith you stand.

2 But I determined this
within myself, that I
would not come again to you
in sorrow. 2For if I make you
sorrowful, then who is he who
makes me glad but the one
who is made sorrowful by me?

FORGIVE THE OFFENDER

3And I wrote this very thing
to you, lest, when I came, I
should have sorrow over those
from whom I ought to have
joy, having confidence in you
all that my joy is *the joy* of you
all. 4For out of much affliction
and anguish of heart I wrote
to you, with many tears, not
that you should be grieved,
but that you might know the
love which I have so abundantly for you.

5But if anyone has caused
grief, he has not grieved me,
but all of you to some extent—
not to be too severe. 6This punishment which *was inflicted*
by the majority *is* sufficient
for such a man, 7so that, on
the contrary, you *ought* rather
to forgive and comfort *him*,
lest perhaps such a one be
swallowed up with too much
sorrow. 8Therefore I urge you
to reaffirm *your* love to him.
9For to this end I also wrote,
that I might put you to the
test, whether you are obedient in all things. 10Now whom

you forgive anything, I also
forgive. For if indeed I have
forgiven anything, I have forgiven that one[a] for your sakes
in the presence of Christ, 11lest
Satan should take advantage
of us; for we are not ignorant
of his devices.

TRIUMPH IN CHRIST

12Furthermore, when I
came to Troas to *preach* Christ's
gospel, and a door was opened
to me by the Lord, 13I had no
rest in my spirit, because I did
not find Titus my brother; but
taking my leave of them, I departed for Macedonia.

14Now thanks *be* to God who
always leads us in triumph in
Christ, and through us diffuses
the fragrance of His knowledge in every place. 15For we
are to God the fragrance of
Christ among those who are
being saved and among those
who are perishing. 16To the
one *we are* the aroma of death
leading to death, and to the
other the aroma of life *leading*
to life. And who *is* sufficient
for these things? 17For we are
not, as so many,[a] peddling the
word of God; but as of sincerity, but as from God, we speak
in the sight of God in Christ.

CHRIST'S EPISTLE

3 Do we begin again to commend ourselves? Or do we
need, as some *others*, epistles
of commendation to you or
letters of commendation from
you? 2You are our epistle written in our hearts, known and
read by all men; 3clearly you
are an epistle of Christ, ministered by us, written not with
ink but by the Spirit of the
living God, not on tablets of
stone but on tablets of flesh,
that is, of the heart.

THE SPIRIT, NOT THE LETTER

4And we have such trust
through Christ toward God.
5Not that we are sufficient of
ourselves to think of anything
as *being* from ourselves, but
our sufficiency *is* from God,
6who also made us sufficient
as ministers of the new covenant, not of the letter but of
the Spirit;[a] for the letter kills,
but the Spirit gives life.

GLORY OF THE NEW COVENANT

7But if the ministry of
death, written *and* engraved
on stones, was glorious, so that
the children of Israel could
not look steadily at the face of
Moses because of the glory of
his countenance, which *glory*
was passing away, 8how will
the ministry of the Spirit not
be more glorious? 9For if the
ministry of condemnation *had*
glory, the ministry of righteousness exceeds much more

2:10 [a] NU-Text reads *For indeed, what I have forgiven, if I have forgiven anything, I did it.* 2:17 [a] M-Text reads *the rest.* 3:6 [a] Or *spirit*

in glory. 10For even what was
made glorious had no glory
in this respect, because of the
glory that excels. 11For if what
is passing away *was* glorious,
what remains *is* much more
glorious.

12Therefore, since we have
such hope, we use great boldness of speech— 13unlike
Moses, *who* put a veil over his
face so that the children of Israel could not look steadily at
the end of what was passing
away. 14But their minds were
blinded. For until this day the
same veil remains unlifted in
the reading of the Old Testament, because the *veil* is taken
away in Christ. 15But even to
this day, when Moses is read,
a veil lies on their heart. 16Nev-
ertheless when one turns to
the Lord, the veil is taken away.
17Now the Lord is the Spirit;
and where the Spirit of the
Lord *is*, there *is* liberty. 18But
we all, with unveiled face,
beholding as in a mirror the
glory of the Lord, are being
transformed into the same
image from glory to glory, just
as by the Spirit of the Lord.

THE LIGHT OF CHRIST'S GOSPEL

4 *Therefore,* since we have
this ministry, as we have
received mercy, we do not
lose heart. 2But we have renounced the hidden things of
shame, not walking in craftiness nor handling the word of
God deceitfully, but by manifestation of the truth com-
mending ourselves to every
man's conscience in the sight
of God. 3But even if our gospel
is veiled, it is veiled to those
who are perishing, 4whose
minds the god of this age has
blinded, who do not believe,
lest the light of the gospel of
the glory of Christ, who is the
image of God, should shine on
them. 5For we do not preach
ourselves, but Christ Jesus
the Lord, and ourselves your
bondservants for Jesus' sake.
6For it is the God who commanded light to shine out of
darkness, who has shone in
our hearts to *give* the light of
the knowledge of the glory of
God in the face of Jesus Christ.

CAST DOWN BUT UNCONQUERED

7But we have this trea-
sure in earthen vessels, that
the excellence of the power
may be of God and not of
us. 8*We are* hard-pressed on
every side, yet not crushed;
we are perplexed, but not in
despair; 9persecuted, but not
forsaken; struck down, but not
destroyed— 10always carrying
about in the body the dying of
the Lord Jesus, that the life of
Jesus also may be manifested
in our body. 11For we who live
are always delivered to death
for Jesus' sake, that the life of
Jesus also may be manifested
in our mortal flesh. 12So then
death is working in us, but life
in you.

13And since we have the same spirit of faith, according to what is written, "I believed and therefore I spoke,"[a] we also believe and therefore speak, 14knowing that He who raised up the Lord Jesus will also raise us up with Jesus, and will present *us* with you. 15For all things *are* for your sakes, that grace, having spread through the many, may cause thanksgiving to abound to the glory of God.

SEEING THE INVISIBLE

16Therefore we do not lose heart. Even though our outward man is perishing, yet the inward *man* is being renewed day by day. 17For our light affliction, which is but for a moment, is working for us a far more exceeding *and* eternal weight of glory, 18while we do not look at the things which are seen, but at the things which are not seen. For the things which are seen *are* temporary, but the things which are not seen *are* eternal.

ASSURANCE OF THE RESURRECTION

5 For we know that if our earthly house, *this* tent, is destroyed, we have a building from God, a house not made with hands, eternal in the heavens. 2For in this we groan, earnestly desiring to be clothed with our habitation which is from heaven, 3if indeed, having been clothed, we shall not be found naked. 4For we who are in *this* tent groan, being burdened, not because we want to be unclothed, but further clothed, that mortality may be swallowed up by life. 5Now He who has prepared us for this very thing *is* God, who also has given us the Spirit as a guarantee.

6So *we are* always confident, knowing that while we are at home in the body we are absent from the Lord. 7For we walk by faith, not by sight. 8We are confident, yes, well pleased rather to be absent from the body and to be present with the Lord.

THE JUDGMENT SEAT OF CHRIST

9Therefore we make it our aim, whether present or absent, to be well pleasing to Him. 10For we must all appear before the judgment seat of Christ, that each one may receive the things *done* in the body, according to what he has done, whether good or bad. 11Knowing, therefore, the terror of the Lord, we persuade men; but we are well known to God, and I also trust are well known in your consciences.

BE RECONCILED TO GOD

12For we do not commend ourselves again to you, but

4:13 [a] Psalm 116:10

give you opportunity to boast
on our behalf, that you may
have *an answer* for those who
boast in appearance and not
in heart. 13For if we are beside
ourselves, *it is* for God; or if
we are of sound mind, *it is* for
you. 14For the love of Christ
compels us, because we judge
thus: that if One died for all,
then all died; 15and He died for
all, that those who live should
live no longer for themselves,
but for Him who died for them
and rose again.

16Therefore, from now on,
we regard no one according
to the flesh. Even though we
have known Christ according
to the flesh, yet now we know
Him thus no longer. 17There-
fore, if anyone *is* in Christ, *he*
is a new creation; old things
have passed away; behold,
all things have become new.
18Now all things *are* of God,
who has reconciled us to Himself through Jesus Christ, and
has given us the ministry of
reconciliation, 19that is, that
God was in Christ reconciling the world to Himself, not
imputing their trespasses to
them, and has committed to
us the word of reconciliation.

20Now then, we are ambas-
sadors for Christ, as though
God were pleading through
us: we implore *you* on Christ's
behalf, be reconciled to God.
21For He made Him who knew
no sin *to be* sin for us, that we
might become the righteousness of God in Him.

MARKS OF THE MINISTRY

6 We then, *as* workers together *with Him* also plead
with *you* not to receive the
grace of God in vain. 2For He
says:

"In an acceptable time
I have heard you,
And in the day of
salvation I have
helped you."[a]

Behold, now *is* the accepted
time; behold, now *is* the day
of salvation.

3We give no offense in
anything, that our ministry
may not be blamed. 4But in
all *things* we commend ourselves as ministers of God:
in much patience, in tribulations, in needs, in distresses,
5in stripes, in imprison-
ments, in tumults, in labors,
in sleeplessness, in fastings;
6by purity, by knowledge, by
longsuffering, by kindness,
by the Holy Spirit, by sincere
love, 7by the word of truth,
by the power of God, by the
armor of righteousness on the
right hand and on the left, 8by
honor and dishonor, by evil
report and good report; as deceivers, and *yet* true; 9as unknown, and *yet* well known; as
dying, and behold we live; as
chastened, and *yet* not killed;

6:2 [a] Isaiah 49:8

10as sorrowful, yet always rejoicing; as poor, yet making
many rich; as having nothing,
and *yet* possessing all things.

BE HOLY

11O Corinthians! We have
spoken openly to you, our
heart is wide open. 12You are
not restricted by us, but you
are restricted by your *own* affections. 13Now in return for
the same (I speak as to children), you also be open.

14Do not be unequally
yoked together with unbe-
lievers. For what fellowship
has righteousness with lawlessness? And what commu-
nion has light with darkness?
15And what accord has Christ
with Belial? Or what part has
a believer with an unbeliever?
16And what agreement has the
temple of God with idols? For
you[a] are the temple of the living God. As God has said:

"I will dwell in them
And walk among *them*.
I will be their God,
And they shall be
My people."[b]

17Therefore

"Come out from
among them
And be separate,
says the Lord.
Do not touch what
is unclean,
And I will receive you."[a]
18"I will be a Father to you,
And you shall be My
sons and daughters,
Says the LORD Almighty."[a]

7 Therefore, having these
promises, beloved, let us
cleanse ourselves from all
filthiness of the flesh and
spirit, perfecting holiness in
the fear of God.

THE CORINTHIANS' REPENTANCE

2Open *your hearts* to us.
We have wronged no one, we
have corrupted no one, we
have cheated no one. 3I do
not say *this* to condemn; for
I have said before that you are
in our hearts, to die together
and to live together. 4Great *is*
my boldness of speech toward
you, great *is* my boasting on
your behalf. I am filled with
comfort. I am exceedingly
joyful in all our tribulation.

5For indeed, when we came
to Macedonia, our bodies had
no rest, but we were troubled
on every side. Outside *were*
conflicts, inside *were* fears.
6Nevertheless God, who comforts the downcast, comforted
us by the coming of Titus,
7and not only by his coming,
but also by the consolation
with which he was comforted

6:16 [a] NU-Text reads *we*. [b] Leviticus 26:12; Jeremiah 32:38; Ezekiel 37:27 6:17 [a] Isaiah 52:11; Ezekiel 20:34, 41 6:18 [a] 2 Samuel 7:14

in you, when he told us of your earnest desire, your mourning, your zeal for me, so that I rejoiced even more.

8For even if I made you sorry with my letter, I do not regret it; though I did regret it. For I perceive that the same epistle made you sorry, though only for a while. 9Now I rejoice, not that you were made sorry, but that your sorrow led to repentance. For you were made sorry in a godly manner, that you might suffer loss from us in nothing. 10For godly sorrow produces repentance *leading* to salvation, not to be regretted; but the sorrow of the world produces death. 11For observe this very thing, that you sorrowed in a godly manner: What diligence it produced in you, *what* clearing *of yourselves, what* indignation, *what* fear, *what* vehement desire, *what* zeal, *what* vindication! In all *things* you proved yourselves to be clear in this matter. 12Therefore, although I wrote to you, *I did* not *do it* for the sake of him who had done the wrong, nor for the sake of him who suffered wrong, but that our care for you in the sight of God might appear to you.

THE JOY OF TITUS

13Therefore we have been comforted in your comfort. And we rejoiced exceedingly more for the joy of Titus, because his spirit has been refreshed by you all. 14For if in anything I have boasted to him about you, I am not ashamed. But as we spoke all things to you in truth, even so our boasting to Titus was found true. 15And his affections are greater for you as he remembers the obedience of you all, how with fear and trembling you received him. 16Therefore I rejoice that I have confidence in you in everything.

EXCEL IN GIVING

8 Moreover, brethren, we make known to you the grace of God bestowed on the churches of Macedonia: 2that in a great trial of affliction the abundance of their joy and their deep poverty abounded in the riches of their liberality. 3For I bear witness that according to *their* ability, yes, and beyond *their* ability, *they were* freely willing, 4imploring us with much urgency that we would receive[a] the gift and the fellowship of the ministering to the saints. 5And not *only* as we had hoped, but they first gave themselves to the Lord, and *then* to us by the will of God. 6So we urged Titus, that as he had begun, so he would also complete this

8:4 [a] NU-Text and M-Text omit *that we would receive,* thus changing text to *urgency for the favor and fellowship* . . . .

grace in you as well. 7But as
you abound in everything—in faith, in speech, in knowledge, in all diligence, and in your love for us—*see* that you abound in this grace also.

CHRIST OUR PATTERN

8I speak not by commandment, but I am testing the sincerity of your love by the diligence of others.
9For you know the grace of our Lord Jesus Christ, that though He was rich, yet for your sakes He became poor, that you through His poverty might become rich.

10And in this I give advice: It is to your advantage not only to be doing what you began and were desiring to
do a year ago; 11but now you also must complete the doing *of it;* that as *there was* a readiness to desire *it,* so *there* also *may be* a completion out of
what *you* have. 12For if there is first a willing mind, *it is* accepted according to what one has, *and* not according to what he does not have.

13For *I do* not *mean* that others should be eased and
you burdened; 14but by an equality, *that* now at this time your abundance *may supply* their lack, that their abundance also may *supply* your lack—that there may
be equality. 15As it is written, "He who *gathered* much had nothing left over, and he who *gathered* little had no lack."[a]

COLLECTION FOR THE JUDEAN SAINTS

16But thanks *be* to God who puts[a] the same earnest care for you into the heart of
Titus. 17For he not only accepted the exhortation, but being more diligent, he went to you of his own accord.
18And we have sent with him the brother whose praise *is* in the gospel throughout all
the churches, 19and not only *that,* but who was also chosen by the churches to travel with us with this gift, which is administered by us to the glory of the Lord Himself and *to show* your ready mind,
20avoiding this: that anyone should blame us in this lavish gift which is administered by
us— 21providing honorable things, not only in the sight of the Lord, but also in the sight of men.

22And we have sent with them our brother whom we have often proved diligent in many things, but now much more diligent, because of the great confidence which
we have in you. 23If *anyone inquires* about Titus, *he is* my partner and fellow worker concerning you. Or if our brethren *are inquired about, they are* messengers of the churches, the glory of Christ.

8:15 [a] Exodus 16:18 8:16 [a] NU-Text reads *has put.*

24Therefore show to them,
and[a] before the churches, the
proof of your love and of our
boasting on your behalf.

ADMINISTERING THE GIFT

9 Now concerning the min-
istering to the saints, it is
superfluous for me to write
to you; 2for I know your will-
ingness, about which I boast
of you to the Macedonians,
that Achaia was ready a year
ago; and your zeal has stirred
up the majority. 3Yet I have
sent the brethren, lest our
boasting of you should be
in vain in this respect, that,
as I said, you may be ready;
4lest if *some* Macedonians
come with me and find you
unprepared, we (not to mention you!) should be ashamed
of this confident boasting.[a]
5Therefore I thought it necessary to exhort the brethren to
go to you ahead of time, and
prepare your generous gift
beforehand, which *you had*
previously promised, that it
may be ready as *a matter of*
generosity and not as a grudg-
ing obligation.

THE CHEERFUL GIVER

6But this *I say:* He who sows
sparingly will also reap sparingly, and he who sows bountifully will also reap bountifully.
7*So let* each one *give* as he purposes in his heart, not grudg-
ingly or of necessity; for God
loves a cheerful giver. 8And
God *is* able to make all grace
abound toward you, that you,
always having all sufficiency
in all *things,* may have an
abundance for every good
work. 9As it is written:

> "He has dispersed abroad,
> He has given to the poor;
> His righteousness
> endures forever."[a]

10Now may[a] He who sup-
plies seed to the sower, and
bread for food, supply and
multiply the seed you have
sown and increase the fruits
of your righteousness, 11while
you are enriched in everything for all liberality, which
causes thanksgiving through
us to God. 12For the admin-
istration of this service not
only supplies the needs of the
saints, but also is abounding
through many thanksgivings
to God, 13while, through the
proof of this ministry, they
glorify God for the obedience
of your confession to the gospel of Christ, and for *your* lib-
eral sharing with them and all
men, 14and by their prayer for
you, who long for you because
of the exceeding grace of God
in you. 15Thanks *be* to God for
His indescribable gift!

8:24 [a] NU-Text and M-Text omit *and.* 9:4 [a] NU-Text reads *this confidence.* 9:9 [a] Psalm 112:9 9:10 [a] NU-Text reads *Now He who supplies . . . will supply . . . .*

THE SPIRITUAL WAR

10 Now I, Paul, myself am
pleading with you by the
meekness and gentleness of
Christ—who in presence *am*
lowly among you, but being
absent am bold toward you.
2But I beg *you* that when I am
present I may not be bold with
that confidence by which I intend to be bold against some,
who think of us as if we walked
according to the flesh. 3For
though we walk in the flesh,
we do not war according to
the flesh. 4For the weapons
of our warfare *are* not carnal
but mighty in God for pulling
down strongholds, 5casting
down arguments and every
high thing that exalts itself
against the knowledge of God,
bringing every thought into
captivity to the obedience of
Christ, 6and being ready to
punish all disobedience when
your obedience is fulfilled.

REALITY OF PAUL'S AUTHORITY

7Do you look at things
according to the outward
appearance? If anyone is
convinced in himself that
he is Christ's, let him again
consider this in himself, that
just as he *is* Christ's, even so
we *are* Christ's.[a] 8For even if I
should boast somewhat more
about our authority, which the
Lord gave us[a] for edification
and not for your destruction,
I shall not be ashamed— 9lest
I seem to terrify you by letters. 10"For *his* letters," they
say, "*are* weighty and powerful, but *his* bodily presence
is weak, and *his* speech contemptible." 11Let such a person
consider this, that what we are
in word by letters when we are
absent, such *we will* also *be*
in deed when we are present.

LIMITS OF PAUL'S AUTHORITY

12For we dare not class ourselves or compare ourselves
with those who commend
themselves. But they, measuring themselves by themselves,
and comparing themselves
among themselves, are not
wise. 13We, however, will not
boast beyond measure, but
within the limits of the sphere
which God appointed us—a
sphere which especially in-
cludes you. 14For we are not
overextending ourselves (as
though *our authority* did not
extend to you), for it was to
you that we came with the
gospel of Christ; 15not boasting of things beyond measure,
that is, in other men's labors,
but having hope, *that* as your
faith is increased, we shall be
greatly enlarged by you in our
sphere, 16to preach the gospel
in the *regions* beyond you, *and*
not to boast in another man's
sphere of accomplishment.
17But "he who glories, let

10:7 [a] NU-Text reads *even as we are.* 10:8 [a] NU-Text omits *us.*

him glory in the LORD."[a] 18For
not he who commends him-
self is approved, but whom
the Lord commends.

CONCERN FOR THEIR FAITHFULNESS

11 Oh, that you would bear
with me in a little folly—
and indeed you do bear with
me. 2For I am jealous for you
with godly jealousy. For I have
betrothed you to one hus-
band, that I may present *you*
as a chaste virgin to Christ.
3But I fear, lest somehow, as
the serpent deceived Eve by
his craftiness, so your minds
may be corrupted from the
simplicity[a] that is in Christ.
4For if he who comes preaches
another Jesus whom we have
not preached, or *if* you receive
a different spirit which you
have not received, or a different gospel which you have not
accepted—you may well put
up with it!

PAUL AND FALSE APOSTLES

5For I consider that I am
not at all inferior to the most
eminent apostles. 6Even
though *I am* untrained in
speech, yet *I am* not in knowledge. But we have been thor-
oughly manifested[a] among
you in all things.

7Did I commit sin in hum-
bling myself that you might
be exalted, because I preached
the gospel of God to you free
of charge? 8I robbed other
churches, taking wages *from*
them to minister to you. 9And
when I was present with you,
and in need, I was a burden
to no one, for what I lacked
the brethren who came from
Macedonia supplied. And in
everything I kept myself from
being burdensome to you, and
so I will keep *myself*. 10As the
truth of Christ is in me, no one
shall stop me from this boasting in the regions of Achaia.
11Why? Because I do not love
you? God knows!

12But what I do, I will also
continue to do, that I may cut
off the opportunity from those
who desire an opportunity to
be regarded just as we are in
the things of which they boast.
13For such *are* false apostles,
deceitful workers, transform-
ing themselves into apostles
of Christ. 14And no wonder!
For Satan himself transforms
himself into an angel of light.
15Therefore *it is* no great thing
if his ministers also transform
themselves into ministers of
righteousness, whose end will
be according to their works.

RELUCTANT BOASTING

16I say again, let no one
think me a fool. If otherwise,
at least receive me as a fool,
that I also may boast a little.
17What I speak, I speak not

10:17 [a] Jeremiah 9:24 11:3 [a] NU-Text adds *and purity.* 11:6 [a] NU-Text omits *been.*

according to the Lord, but as
it were, foolishly, in this confidence of boasting. 18Seeing
that many boast according to
the flesh, I also will boast. 19For
you put up with fools gladly,
since you *yourselves* are wise!
20For you put up with it if one
brings you into bondage, if one
devours *you*, if one takes *from*
you, if one exalts himself, if one
strikes you on the face. 21To
our shame I say that we were
too weak for that! But in whatever anyone is bold—I speak
foolishly—I am bold also.

SUFFERING FOR CHRIST

22Are they Hebrews? So *am*
I. Are they Israelites? So *am*
I. Are they the seed of Abraham? So *am* I. 23Are they ministers of Christ?—I speak as
a fool—I *am* more: in labors
more abundant, in stripes
above measure, in prisons
more frequently, in deaths
often. 24From the Jews five
times I received forty *stripes*
minus one. 25Three times I
was beaten with rods; once I
was stoned; three times I was
shipwrecked; a night and a
day I have been in the deep;
26*in* journeys often, *in* perils
of waters, *in* perils of robbers,
in perils of *my own* countrymen, *in* perils of the Gentiles,
in perils in the city, *in* perils
in the wilderness, *in* perils in
the sea, *in* perils among false
brethren; 27in weariness and
toil, in sleeplessness often, in
hunger and thirst, in fastings
often, in cold and nakedness—
28besides the other things,
what comes upon me daily:
my deep concern for all the
churches. 29Who is weak, and
I am not weak? Who is made
to stumble, and I do not burn
with indignation?

30If I must boast, I will
boast in the things which
concern my infirmity. 31The
God and Father of our Lord
Jesus Christ, who is blessed
forever, knows that I am not
lying. 32In Damascus the governor, under Aretas the king,
was guarding the city of the
Damascenes with a garrison,
desiring to arrest me; 33but
I was let down in a basket
through a window in the wall,
and escaped from his hands.

THE VISION OF PARADISE

12 It is doubtless[a] not profitable for me to boast. I
will come to visions and revelations of the Lord: 2I know
a man in Christ who four-
teen years ago—whether in
the body I do not know, or
whether out of the body I do
not know, God knows—such
a one was caught up to the
third heaven. 3And I know
such a man—whether in the
body or out of the body I do
not know, God knows— 4how
he was caught up into Paradise and heard inexpressible

12:1 [a] NU-Text reads *necessary, though not profitable, to boast.*

words, which it is not lawful for a man to utter. 5Of such a one I will boast; yet of myself I will not boast, except in my infirmities. 6For though I might desire to boast, I will not be a fool; for I will speak the truth. But I refrain, lest anyone should think of me above what he sees me *to be* or hears from me.

THE THORN IN THE FLESH

7And lest I should be exalted above measure by the abundance of the revelations, a thorn in the flesh was given to me, a messenger of Satan to buffet me, lest I be exalted above measure. 8Concerning this thing I pleaded with the Lord three times that it might depart from me. 9And He said to me, "My grace is sufficient for you, for My strength is made perfect in weakness." Therefore most gladly I will rather boast in my infirmities, that the power of Christ may rest upon me. 10Therefore I take pleasure in infirmities, in reproaches, in needs, in persecutions, in distresses, for Christ's sake. For when I am weak, then I am strong.

SIGNS OF AN APOSTLE

11I have become a fool in boasting;[a] you have compelled me. For I ought to have been commended by you; for in nothing was I behind the most eminent apostles, though I am nothing. 12Truly the signs of an apostle were accomplished among you with all perseverance, in signs and wonders and mighty deeds. 13For what is it in which you were inferior to other churches, except that I myself was not burdensome to you? Forgive me this wrong!

LOVE FOR THE CHURCH

14Now *for* the third time I am ready to come to you. And I will not be burdensome to you; for I do not seek yours, but you. For the children ought not to lay up for the parents, but the parents for the children. 15And I will very gladly spend and be spent for your souls; though the more abundantly I love you, the less I am loved.

16But be that *as it may,* I did not burden you. Nevertheless, being crafty, I caught you by cunning! 17Did I take advantage of you by any of those whom I sent to you? 18I urged Titus, and sent our brother with *him.* Did Titus take advantage of you? Did we not walk in the same spirit? Did *we* not *walk* in the same steps?

19Again, do you think[a] that we excuse ourselves to you? We speak before God in Christ. But *we do* all things, beloved,

12:11 [a] NU-Text omits *in boasting.* 12:19 [a] NU-Text reads *You have been thinking for a long time . . . .*

for your edification. [20]For I
fear lest, when I come, I shall
not find you such as I wish,
and *that* I shall be found by
you such as you do not wish;
lest *there be* contentions, jealousies, outbursts of wrath,
selfish ambitions, back-
bitings, whisperings, conceits,
tumults; [21]lest, when I come
again, my God will humble me
among you, and I shall mourn
for many who have sinned before and have not repented of
the uncleanness, fornication,
and lewdness which they have
practiced.

COMING WITH AUTHORITY

13 This *will be* the third *time*
I am coming to you. "By
the mouth of two or three witnesses every word shall be established."[a] [2]I have told you
before, and foretell as if I were
present the second time, and
now being absent I write[a] to
those who have sinned before,
and to all the rest, that if I come
again I will not spare— [3]since
you seek a proof of Christ
speaking in me, who is not
weak toward you, but mighty
in you. [4]For though He was
crucified in weakness, yet He
lives by the power of God. For
we also are weak in Him, but
we shall live with Him by the
power of God toward you.
[5]Examine yourselves *as to*
whether you are in the faith.
Test yourselves. Do you not
know yourselves, that Jesus
Christ is in you?—unless indeed you are disqualified.
[6]But I trust that you will know
that we are not disqualified.

PAUL PREFERS GENTLENESS

[7]Now I[a] pray to God that you
do no evil, not that we should
appear approved, but that you
should do what is honorable,
though we may seem disqualified. [8]For we can do nothing
against the truth, but for the
truth. [9]For we are glad when we
are weak and you are strong.
And this also we pray, that
you may be made complete.
[10]Therefore I write these things
being absent, lest being present I should use sharpness, according to the authority which
the Lord has given me for edification and not for destruction.

GREETINGS AND BENEDICTION

[11]Finally, brethren, farewell.
Become complete. Be of good
comfort, be of one mind, live
in peace; and the God of love
and peace will be with you.
[12]Greet one another with a
holy kiss.
[13]All the saints greet you.
[14]The grace of the Lord
Jesus Christ, and the love of
God, and the communion of
the Holy Spirit *be* with you all.
Amen.

13:1 [a] Deuteronomy 19:15 13:2 [a] NU-Text omits *I write.* 13:7 [a] NU-Text reads *we.*

THE EPISTLE OF PAUL THE APOSTLE TO THE

GALATIANS

GREETING

1 Paul, an apostle (not from men nor through man, but through Jesus Christ and God the Father who raised Him from the dead), 2and all the brethren who are with me,

To the churches of Galatia:

3Grace to you and peace from God the Father and our Lord Jesus Christ, 4who gave Himself for our sins, that He might deliver us from this present evil age, according to the will of our God and Father, 5to whom *be* glory forever and ever. Amen.

ONLY ONE GOSPEL

6I marvel that you are turning away so soon from Him who called you in the grace of Christ, to a different gospel, 7which is not another; but there are some who trouble you and want to pervert the gospel of Christ. 8But even if we, or an angel from heaven, *preach any other* gospel to you than what we have preached to you, let him be accursed. 9As we have said before, so now I say again, if anyone preaches any other gospel to you than what you have received, let him be accursed.

10For do I now persuade men, or God? Or do I seek to please men? For if I still pleased men, I would not be a bondservant of Christ.

CALL TO APOSTLESHIP

11But I make known to you, brethren, that the gospel which was preached by me is not according to man. 12For I neither received it from man, nor was I taught *it,* but *it came* through the revelation of Jesus Christ.

13For you have heard of my former conduct in Judaism, how I persecuted the church of God beyond measure and *tried to* destroy it. 14And I advanced in Judaism beyond many of my contemporaries in my own nation, being more exceedingly zealous for the traditions of my fathers.

15But when it pleased God, who separated me from my mother's womb and called *me* through His grace, 16to reveal His Son in me, that I might preach Him among the Gentiles, I did not immediately confer with flesh and blood, 17nor did I go up to Jerusalem to those *who were* apostles before me; but I went to Arabia, and returned again to Damascus.

CONTACTS AT JERUSALEM

18Then after three years I
went up to Jerusalem to see
Peter,[a] and remained with
him fifteen days. 19But I saw
none of the other apostles except James, the Lord's brother.
20(Now *concerning* the things
which I write to you, indeed, before God, I do not lie.)

21Afterward I went into
the regions of Syria and Cilicia. 22And I was unknown by
face to the churches of Judea
which *were* in Christ. 23But
they were hearing only, "He who formerly persecuted us now preaches the faith which he once *tried to* destroy." 24And
they glorified God in me.

DEFENDING THE GOSPEL

2 Then after fourteen years I went up again to Jerusalem with Barnabas, and also
took Titus with *me.* 2And I went
up by revelation, and communicated to them that gospel which I preach among the Gentiles, but privately to those who were of reputation, lest by any means I might run, or
had run, in vain. 3Yet not even
Titus who *was* with me, being a Greek, was compelled to be
circumcised. 4And *this occurred*
because of false brethren secretly brought in (who came in by stealth to spy out our liberty which we have in Christ Jesus, that they might bring us into
bondage), 5to whom we did not
yield submission even for an hour, that the truth of the gospel might continue with you.

6But from those who
seemed to be something—whatever they were, it makes no difference to me; God shows personal favoritism to no man—for those who seemed *to be something* added nothing to me. 7But on the contrary, when they saw that the gospel for the uncircumcised had been committed to me, as *the gospel* for the circumcised *was* to Peter 8(for He who
worked effectively in Peter for the apostleship to the circumcised also worked effectively in me toward the Gentiles),
9and when James, Cephas, and
John, who seemed to be pillars, perceived the grace that had been given to me, they gave me and Barnabas the right hand of fellowship, that we *should go* to the Gentiles and they to
the circumcised. 10*They desired*
only that we should remember the poor, the very thing which I also was eager to do.

NO RETURN TO THE LAW

11Now when Peter[a] had
come to Antioch, I withstood him to his face, because he was
to be blamed; 12for before cer-
tain men came from James, he would eat with the Gentiles; but when they came, he withdrew and separated himself, fearing those who were of the

1:18 [a] NU-Text reads *Cephas.*

2:11 [a] NU-Text reads *Cephas.*

circumcision. 13And the rest of
the Jews also played the hypocrite with him, so that even
Barnabas was carried away
with their hypocrisy.

14But when I saw that they
were not straightforward
about the truth of the gospel,
I said to Peter before *them* all,
"If you, being a Jew, live in the
manner of Gentiles and not as
the Jews, why do you[a] compel Gentiles to live as Jews?[b]
15We *who are* Jews by nature,
and not sinners of the Gentiles, 16knowing that a man is
not justified by the works of
the law but by faith in Jesus
Christ, even we have believed
in Christ Jesus, that we might
be justified by faith in Christ
and not by the works of the
law; for by the works of the
law no flesh shall be justified.

17"But if, while we seek to
be justified by Christ, we ourselves also are found sinners,
is Christ therefore a minister
of sin? Certainly not! 18For if I
build again those things which
I destroyed, I make myself a
transgressor. 19For I through
the law died to the law that
I might live to God. 20I have
been crucified with Christ; it is
no longer I who live, but Christ
lives in me; and the *life* which
I now live in the flesh I live by
faith in the Son of God, who
loved me and gave Himself
for me. 21I do not set aside the
grace of God; for if righteousness *comes* through the law,
then Christ died in vain."

JUSTIFICATION BY FAITH

3 O foolish Galatians! Who
has bewitched you that you
should not obey the truth,[a] before whose eyes Jesus Christ
was clearly portrayed among
you[b] as crucified? 2This only
I want to learn from you: Did
you receive the Spirit by the
works of the law, or by the
hearing of faith? 3Are you so
foolish? Having begun in the
Spirit, are you now being made
perfect by the flesh? 4Have you
suffered so many things in
vain—if indeed *it was* in vain?

5Therefore He who sup-
plies the Spirit to you and
works miracles among you,
does He do it by the works of
the law, or by the hearing of
faith?— 6just as Abraham
"believed God, and it was accounted to him for righteousness."[a] 7Therefore know that
only those who are of faith are
sons of Abraham. 8And the
Scripture, foreseeing that God
would justify the Gentiles by
faith, preached the gospel to
Abraham beforehand, *saying,*
"In you all the nations shall be
blessed."[a] 9So then those who
are of faith are blessed with
believing Abraham.

2:14 [a] NU-Text reads *how can you.* [b] Some interpreters stop the quotation here. 3:1 [a] NU-Text omits *that you should not obey the truth.* [b] NU-Text omits *among you.* 3:6 [a] Genesis 15:6 3:8 [a] Genesis 12:3; 18:18; 22:18; 26:4; 28:14

THE LAW BRINGS A CURSE

10For as many as are of the
works of the law are under the
curse; for it is written, "Cursed
is everyone who does not continue in all things which are
written in the book of the law,
to do them."[a] 11But that no one
is justified by the law in the
sight of God *is* evident, for
"the just shall live by faith."[a]
12Yet the law is not of faith,
but "the man who does them
shall live by them."[a]

13Christ has redeemed us
from the curse of the law, having become a curse for us (for
it is written, "Cursed *is* everyone who hangs on a tree"[a]),
14that the blessing of Abraham
might come upon the Gen-
tiles in Christ Jesus, that we
might receive the promise of
the Spirit through faith.

THE CHANGELESS PROMISE

15Brethren, I speak in the
manner of men: Though *it is*
only a man's covenant, yet *if
it is* confirmed, no one annuls
or adds to it. 16Now to Abraham and his Seed were the
promises made. He does not
say, "And to seeds," as of many,
but as of one, "And to your
Seed,"[a] who is Christ. 17And
this I say, *that* the law, which
was four hundred and thirty
years later, cannot annul the
covenant that was confirmed
before by God in Christ,[a] that
it should make the promise of
no effect. 18For if the inheritance *is* of the law, *it is* no longer of promise; but God gave *it*
to Abraham by promise.

PURPOSE OF THE LAW

19What purpose then *does*
the law *serve?* It was added because of transgressions, till the
Seed should come to whom the
promise was made; *and it was*
appointed through angels by
the hand of a mediator. 20Now
a mediator does not *mediate*
for one *only,* but God is one.

21*Is* the law then against the
promises of God? Certainly
not! For if there had been a law
given which could have given
life, truly righteousness would
have been by the law. 22But
the Scripture has confined all
under sin, that the promise by
faith in Jesus Christ might be
given to those who believe.
23But before faith came, we
were kept under guard by the
law, kept for the faith which
would afterward be revealed.
24Therefore the law was our
tutor *to bring us* to Christ, that
we might be justified by faith.
25But after faith has come, we
are no longer under a tutor.

SONS AND HEIRS

26For you are all sons of
God through faith in Christ

3:10 [a] Deuteronomy 27:26 3:11 [a] Habakkuk 2:4 3:12 [a] Leviticus
18:5 3:13 [a] Deuteronomy 21:23 3:16 [a] Genesis 12:7;
13:15; 24:7 3:17 [a] NU-Text omits *in Christ.*

Jesus. 27For as many of you
as were baptized into Christ
have put on Christ. 28There is
neither Jew nor Greek, there
is neither slave nor free,
there is neither male nor female; for you are all one in
Christ Jesus. 29And if you *are*
Christ's, then you are Abraham's seed, and heirs according to the promise.

4 Now I say *that* the heir, as
long as he is a child, does
not differ at all from a slave,
though he is master of all,
2but is under guardians and
stewards until the time appointed by the father. 3Even
so we, when we were children,
were in bondage under the
elements of the world. 4But
when the fullness of the time
had come, God sent forth His
Son, born[a] of a woman, born
under the law, 5to redeem
those who were under the
law, that we might receive the
adoption as sons.

6And because you are sons,
God has sent forth the Spirit
of His Son into your hearts,
crying out, "Abba, Father!"
7Therefore you are no longer
a slave but a son, and if a son,
then an heir of[a] God through
Christ.

FEARS FOR THE CHURCH

8But then, indeed, when
you did not know God, you
served those which by nature
are not gods. 9But now after
you have known God, or rather
are known by God, how *is it
that* you turn again to the weak
and beggarly elements, to
which you desire again to be in
bondage? 10You observe days
and months and seasons and
years. 11I am afraid for you, lest
I have labored for you in vain.

12Brethren, I urge you to
become like me, for I *became*
like you. You have not injured
me at all. 13You know that because of physical infirmity I
preached the gospel to you at
the first. 14And my trial which
was in my flesh you did not despise or reject, but you received
me as an angel of God, *even* as
Christ Jesus. 15What[a] then was
the blessing you *enjoyed?* For
I bear you witness that, if possible, you would have plucked
out your own eyes and given
them to me. 16Have I therefore
become your enemy because
I tell you the truth?

17They zealously court you,
but for no good; yes, they want
to exclude you, that you may
be zealous for them. 18But it is
good to be zealous in a good
thing always, and not only
when I am present with you.
19My little children, for whom I
labor in birth again until Christ
is formed in you, 20I would like
to be present with you now and
to change my tone; for I have
doubts about you.

4:4 [a] Or *made* 4:7 [a] NU-Text reads *through God* and omits *through Christ.* 4:15 [a] NU-Text reads *Where.*

TWO COVENANTS

[21]Tell me, you who desire
to be under the law, do you
not hear the law? [22]For it is
written that Abraham had
two sons: the one by a bondwoman, the other by a freewoman. [23]But he *who was* of
the bondwoman was born according to the flesh, and he
of the freewoman through
promise, [24]which things are
symbolic. For these are the[a]
two covenants: the one from
Mount Sinai which gives birth
to bondage, which is Hagar—
[25]for this Hagar is Mount Sinai
in Arabia, and corresponds
to Jerusalem which now is,
and is in bondage with her
children— [26]but the Jerusalem above is free, which is
the mother of us all. [27]For it
is written:

"Rejoice, O barren,
You who do not bear!
Break forth and shout,
You who are not in labor!
For the desolate has
many more children
Than she who has
a husband."[a]

[28]Now we, brethren, as Isaac
was, are children of promise.
[29]But, as he who was born according to the flesh then persecuted him *who was born*
according to the Spirit, even so
it is now. [30]Nevertheless what
does the Scripture say? "Cast
out the bondwoman and her
son, for the son of the bondwoman shall not be heir with
the son of the freewoman."[a]
[31]So then, brethren, we are not
children of the bondwoman
but of the free.

CHRISTIAN LIBERTY

5 Stand fast therefore in the
liberty by which Christ has
made us free,[a] and do not be
entangled again with a yoke
of bondage. [2]Indeed I, Paul,
say to you that if you become
circumcised, Christ will profit
you nothing. [3]And I testify
again to every man who becomes circumcised that he is
a debtor to keep the whole law.
[4]You have become estranged
from Christ, you who *attempt
to* be justified by law; you
have fallen from grace. [5]For
we through the Spirit eagerly
wait for the hope of righteousness by faith. [6]For in Christ
Jesus neither circumcision
nor uncircumcision avails
anything, but faith working
through love.

LOVE FULFILLS THE LAW

[7]You ran well. Who hin-
dered you from obeying the
truth? [8]This persuasion does
not *come* from Him who calls
you. [9]A little leaven leavens

4:24 [a] NU-Text and M-Text omit *the.* 4:27 [a] Isaiah 54:1 4:30 [a] Genesis 21:10 5:1 [a] NU-Text reads *For freedom Christ has made us free; stand fast therefore.*

the whole lump. 10I have confidence in you, in the Lord,
that you will have no other
mind; but he who troubles
you shall bear his judgment,
whoever he is.

11And I, brethren, if I still
preach circumcision, why do I
still suffer persecution? Then
the offense of the cross has
ceased. 12I could wish that
those who trouble you would
even cut themselves off!

13For you, brethren, have
been called to liberty; only do
not *use* liberty as an opportunity for the flesh, but through
love serve one another. 14For all
the law is fulfilled in one word,
even in this: "You shall love
your neighbor as yourself."[a]
15But if you bite and devour
one another, beware lest you
be consumed by one another!

WALKING IN THE SPIRIT

16I say then: Walk in the
Spirit, and you shall not fulfill
the lust of the flesh. 17For the
flesh lusts against the Spirit,
and the Spirit against the
flesh; and these are contrary
to one another, so that you
do not do the things that you
wish. 18But if you are led by
the Spirit, you are not under
the law.

19Now the works of the flesh
are evident, which are: adultery,[a] fornication, uncleanness, lewdness, 20idolatry,
sorcery, hatred, contentions,
jealousies, outbursts of wrath,
selfish ambitions, dissensions,
heresies, 21envy, murders,[a]
drunkenness, revelries, and
the like; of which I tell you beforehand, just as I also told *you*
in time past, that those who
practice such things will not
inherit the kingdom of God.

22But the fruit of the Spirit
is love, joy, peace, longsuffering, kindness, goodness,
faithfulness, 23gentleness,
self-control. Against such
there is no law. 24And those
who are Christ's have crucified the flesh with its passions
and desires. 25If we live in the
Spirit, let us also walk in the
Spirit. 26Let us not become
conceited, provoking one another, envying one another.

BEAR AND SHARE BURDENS

6 Brethren, if a man is overtaken in any trespass, you
who *are* spiritual restore such
a one in a spirit of gentleness,
considering yourself lest you
also be tempted. 2Bear one
another's burdens, and so fulfill the law of Christ. 3For if
anyone thinks himself to be
something, when he is nothing, he deceives himself. 4But
let each one examine his own
work, and then he will have
rejoicing in himself alone, and
not in another. 5For each one
shall bear his own load.

5:14 [a] Leviticus 19:18 5:19 [a] NU-Text omits *adultery.* 5:21 [a] NU-Text omits *murders.*

BE GENEROUS AND DO GOOD

[6]Let him who is taught the word share in all good things with him who teaches.

[7]Do not be deceived, God is not mocked; for whatever a man sows, that he will also
reap. [8]For he who sows to his flesh will of the flesh reap corruption, but he who sows to the Spirit will of the Spirit
reap everlasting life. [9]And let us not grow weary while doing good, for in due season we shall reap if we do not lose
heart. [10]Therefore, as we have opportunity, let us do good to all, especially to those who are of the household of faith.

GLORY ONLY IN THE CROSS

[11]See with what large letters I have written to you with my
own hand! [12]As many as desire to make a good showing in the flesh, these *would* compel you to be circumcised, only that they may not suffer persecution for the cross of Christ.
[13]For not even those who are circumcised keep the law, but they desire to have you circumcised that they may boast
in your flesh. [14]But God forbid that I should boast except in the cross of our Lord Jesus Christ, by whom[a] the world has been crucified to me, and
I to the world. [15]For in Christ Jesus neither circumcision nor uncircumcision avails anything, but a new creation.

BLESSING AND A PLEA

[16]And as many as walk according to this rule, peace and mercy *be* upon them, and upon the Israel of God.

[17]From now on let no one trouble me, for I bear in my body the marks of the Lord Jesus.

[18]Brethren, the grace of our Lord Jesus Christ *be* with your spirit. Amen.

THE EPISTLE OF PAUL THE APOSTLE TO THE

EPHESIANS

GREETING

1 Paul, an apostle of Jesus Christ by the will of God,

To the saints who are in Ephesus, and faithful in Christ Jesus:

[2]Grace to you and peace from God our Father and the Lord Jesus Christ.

REDEMPTION IN CHRIST

[3]Blessed *be* the God and Father of our Lord Jesus Christ,

6:14 [a] Or *by which* (the cross)

who has blessed us with every
spiritual blessing in the heavenly *places* in Christ, [4]just as
He chose us in Him before
the foundation of the world,
that we should be holy and
without blame before Him in
love, [5]having predestined us
to adoption as sons by Jesus
Christ to Himself, according to the good pleasure of
His will, [6]to the praise of the
glory of His grace, by which
He made us accepted in the
Beloved.

[7]In Him we have redemp-
tion through His blood, the
forgiveness of sins, according to the riches of His grace
[8]which He made to abound
toward us in all wisdom and
prudence, [9]having made
known to us the mystery of
His will, according to His good
pleasure which He purposed
in Himself, [10]that in the dispensation of the fullness of
the times He might gather
together in one all things
in Christ, both[a] which are
in heaven and which are on
earth—in Him. [11]In Him also
we have obtained an inheritance, being predestined according to the purpose of Him
who works all things accord-
ing to the counsel of His will,
[12]that we who first trusted in
Christ should be to the praise
of His glory.

[13]In Him you also *trusted,*
after you heard the word of
truth, the gospel of your salvation; in whom also, having
believed, you were sealed
with the Holy Spirit of promise, [14]who[a] is the guarantee
of our inheritance until the
redemption of the purchased
possession, to the praise of
His glory.

PRAYER FOR SPIRITUAL WISDOM

[15]Therefore I also, after
I heard of your faith in the
Lord Jesus and your love for
all the saints, [16]do not cease
to give thanks for you, making mention of you in my
prayers: [17]that the God of our
Lord Jesus Christ, the Father
of glory, may give to you the
spirit of wisdom and revelation in the knowledge of Him,
[18]the eyes of your understanding[a] being enlightened; that
you may know what is the
hope of His calling, what are
the riches of the glory of His
inheritance in the saints,
[19]and what *is* the exceeding
greatness of His power toward
us who believe, according to
the working of His mighty
power [20]which He worked in
Christ when He raised Him
from the dead and seated
Him at His right hand in the
heavenly *places,* [21]far above
all principality and power
and might and dominion, and

1:10 [a] NU-Text and M-Text omit *both.* 1:14 [a] NU-Text reads *which.* 1:18 [a] NU-Text and M-Text read *hearts.*

every name that is named, not
only in this age but also in that
which is to come.
22And He put all *things*
under His feet, and gave Him
to be head over all *things* to the
church, 23which is His body,
the fullness of Him who fills
all in all.

BY GRACE THROUGH FAITH

2 And you *He made alive,*
who were dead in tres-
passes and sins, 2in which you
once walked according to the
course of this world, according to the prince of the power
of the air, the spirit who now
works in the sons of disobedience, 3among whom also we
all once conducted ourselves
in the lusts of our flesh, fulfilling the desires of the flesh
and of the mind, and were by
nature children of wrath, just
as the others.
4But God, who is rich in
mercy, because of His great
love with which He loved us,
5even when we were dead in
trespasses, made us alive together with Christ (by grace
you have been saved), 6and
raised *us* up together, and
made *us* sit together in the
heavenly *places* in Christ
Jesus, 7that in the ages to come
He might show the exceed-
ing riches of His grace in *His*
kindness toward us in Christ
Jesus. 8For by grace you have
been saved through faith, and
that not of yourselves; *it is* the
gift of God, 9not of works, lest
anyone should boast. 10For we
are His workmanship, created
in Christ Jesus for good works,
which God prepared beforehand that we should walk in
them.

BROUGHT NEAR BY HIS BLOOD

11Therefore remember
that you, once Gentiles in the
flesh—who are called Uncircumcision by what is called
the Circumcision made in
the flesh by hands— 12that at
that time you were without
Christ, being aliens from the
commonwealth of Israel and
strangers from the covenants
of promise, having no hope
and without God in the world.
13But now in Christ Jesus you
who once were far off have
been brought near by the
blood of Christ.

CHRIST OUR PEACE

14For He Himself is our
peace, who has made both
one, and has broken down
the middle wall of separation,
15having abolished in His flesh
the enmity, *that is,* the law of
commandments *contained* in
ordinances, so as to create in
Himself one new man *from*
the two, *thus* making peace,
16and that He might reconcile
them both to God in one body
through the cross, thereby
putting to death the enmity.
17And He came and preached
peace to you who were afar off
and to those who were near.

18For through Him we both have access by one Spirit to the Father.

CHRIST OUR CORNERSTONE

19Now, therefore, you are no longer strangers and foreigners, but fellow citizens with the saints and members of the household of God, 20having been built on the foundation of the apostles and prophets, Jesus Christ Himself being the chief corner*stone,* 21in whom the whole building, being fitted together, grows into a holy temple in the Lord, 22in whom you also are being built together for a dwelling place of God in the Spirit.

THE MYSTERY REVEALED

3 For this reason I, Paul, the prisoner of Christ Jesus for you Gentiles— 2if indeed you have heard of the dispensation of the grace of God which was given to me for you, 3how that by revelation He made known to me the mystery (as I have briefly written already, 4by which, when you read, you may understand my knowledge in the mystery of Christ), 5which in other ages was not *made known* to the sons of men, as it has now been revealed by the Spirit to His holy apostles and prophets: 6that the Gentiles should be fellow heirs, of the same body, and partakers of His promise in Christ through the gospel, 7of which I became a minister according to the gift of the grace of God given to me by the effective working of His power.

PURPOSE OF THE MYSTERY

8To me, who am less than the least of all the saints, this grace was given, that I should preach among the Gentiles the unsearchable riches of Christ, 9and to make all see what *is* the fellowship[a] of the mystery, which from the beginning of the ages has been hidden in God who created all things through Jesus Christ;[b] 10to the intent that now the manifold wisdom of God might be made known by the church to the principalities and powers in the heavenly *places,* 11according to the eternal purpose which He accomplished in Christ Jesus our Lord, 12in whom we have boldness and access with confidence through faith in Him. 13Therefore I ask that you do not lose heart at my tribulations for you, which is *your glory.*

APPRECIATION OF THE MYSTERY

14For this reason I bow my knees to the Father of our Lord

3:9 [a] NU-Text and M-Text read *stewardship* (dispensation).
[b] NU-Text omits *through Jesus Christ.*

Jesus Christ,[a] 15from whom
the whole family in heaven
and earth is named, 16that He
would grant you, according
to the riches of His glory, to
be strengthened with might
through His Spirit in the inner
man, 17that Christ may dwell
in your hearts through faith;
that you, being rooted and
grounded in love, 18may be
able to comprehend with all
the saints what *is* the width
and length and depth and
height— 19to know the love
of Christ which passes knowledge; that you may be filled
with all the fullness of God.
20Now to Him who is able
to do exceedingly abundantly
above all that we ask or think,
according to the power that
works in us, 21to Him *be* glory
in the church by Christ Jesus
to all generations, forever and
ever. Amen.

WALK IN UNITY

4 I, therefore, the prisoner
of the Lord, beseech you
to walk worthy of the calling
with which you were called,
2with all lowliness and gentleness, with longsuffering,
bearing with one another in
love, 3endeavoring to keep
the unity of the Spirit in the
bond of peace. 4*There is* one
body and one Spirit, just as
you were called in one hope
of your calling; 5one Lord,
one faith, one baptism; 6one
God and Father of all, who *is*
above all, and through all, and
in you[a] all.

SPIRITUAL GIFTS

7But to each one of us
grace was given according to
the measure of Christ's gift.
8Therefore He says:

"When He ascended
on high,
He led captivity captive,
And gave gifts to men."[a]

9(Now this, "He ascended"—
what does it mean but that
He also first[a] descended into
the lower parts of the earth?
10He who descended is also
the One who ascended far
above all the heavens, that
He might fill all things.)
11And He Himself gave
some *to be* apostles, some
prophets, some evangelists,
and some pastors and teachers, 12for the equipping of the
saints for the work of ministry,
for the edifying of the body of
Christ, 13till we all come to the
unity of the faith and of the
knowledge of the Son of God,
to a perfect man, to the measure of the stature of the fullness of Christ; 14that we should
no longer be children, tossed
to and fro and carried about
with every wind of doctrine,
by the trickery of men, in the

3:14 [a] NU-Text omits *of our Lord Jesus Christ*. 4:6 [a] NU-Text omits *you*; M-Text reads *us*. 4:8 [a] Psalm 68:18 4:9 [a] NU-Text omits *first*.

cunning craftiness of deceitful plotting, 15but, speaking
the truth in love, may grow
up in all things into Him who
is the head—Christ— 16from
whom the whole body, joined
and knit together by what
every joint supplies, according to the effective working
by which every part does its
share, causes growth of the
body for the edifying of itself
in love.

THE NEW MAN

17This I say, therefore, and
testify in the Lord, that you
should no longer walk as the
rest of[a] the Gentiles walk,
in the futility of their mind,
18having their understanding darkened, being alienated
from the life of God, because
of the ignorance that is in
them, because of the blindness of their heart; 19who,
being past feeling, have given
themselves over to lewdness,
to work all uncleanness with
greediness.

20But you have not so
learned Christ, 21if indeed
you have heard Him and have
been taught by Him, as the
truth is in Jesus: 22that you put
off, concerning your former
conduct, the old man which
grows corrupt according to
the deceitful lusts, 23and be
renewed in the spirit of your
mind, 24and that you put on
the new man which was created according to God, in true
righteousness and holiness.

DO NOT GRIEVE THE SPIRIT

25Therefore, putting away
lying, "*Let* each one *of you*
speak truth with his neighbor,"[a] for we are members of
one another. 26"Be angry, and
do not sin":[a] do not let the sun
go down on your wrath, 27nor
give place to the devil. 28Let
him who stole steal no longer, but rather let him labor,
working with *his* hands what is
good, that he may have something to give him who has
need. 29Let no corrupt word
proceed out of your mouth,
but what is good for necessary edification, that it may
impart grace to the hearers.
30And do not grieve the Holy
Spirit of God, by whom you
were sealed for the day of redemption. 31Let all bitterness,
wrath, anger, clamor, and evil
speaking be put away from
you, with all malice. 32And be
kind to one another, tenderhearted, forgiving one another, even as God in Christ
forgave you.

WALK IN LOVE

5 Therefore be imitators of
God as dear children. 2And
walk in love, as Christ also has
loved us and given Himself for
us, an offering and a sacrifice
to God for a sweet-smelling
aroma.

4:17 [a] NU-Text omits *the rest of.* 4:25 [a] Zechariah 8:16 4:26 [a] Psalm 4:4

[3]But fornication and all uncleanness or covetousness, let
it not even be named among
you, as is fitting for saints;
[4]neither filthiness, nor foolish talking, nor coarse jest-
ing, which are not fitting,
but rather giving of thanks.
[5]For this you know,[a] that no
fornicator, unclean person,
nor covetous man, who is an
idolater, has any inheritance
in the kingdom of Christ and
God. [6]Let no one deceive you
with empty words, for because
of these things the wrath of
God comes upon the sons of
disobedience. [7]Therefore do
not be partakers with them.

WALK IN LIGHT

[8]For you were once darkness, but now *you are* light in
the Lord. Walk as children of
light [9](for the fruit of the Spirit[a]
is in all goodness, righteousness, and truth), [10]finding out
what is acceptable to the Lord.
[11]And have no fellowship with
the unfruitful works of darkness, but rather expose *them.*
[12]For it is shameful even to
speak of those things which are
done by them in secret. [13]But
all things that are exposed are
made manifest by the light, for
whatever makes manifest is
light. [14]Therefore He says:

"Awake, you who sleep,
Arise from *the* dead,
And Christ will give
you light."

WALK IN WISDOM

[15]See then that you walk
circumspectly, not as fools but
as wise, [16]redeeming the time,
because the days are evil.

[17]Therefore do not be unwise, but understand what
the will of the Lord *is.* [18]And
do not be drunk with wine, in
which is dissipation; but be
filled with the Spirit, [19]speak-
ing to one another in psalms
and hymns and spiritual
songs, singing and making
melody in your heart to the
Lord, [20]giving thanks always
for all things to God the Father
in the name of our Lord Jesus
Christ, [21]submitting to one another in the fear of God.[a]

MARRIAGE—CHRIST AND THE CHURCH

[22]Wives, submit to your
own husbands, as to the Lord.
[23]For the husband is head of
the wife, as also Christ is head
of the church; and He is the
Savior of the body. [24]There-
fore, just as the church is subject to Christ, so *let* the wives
be to their own husbands in
everything.

[25]Husbands, love your
wives, just as Christ also loved
the church and gave Himself
for her, [26]that He might sanctify and cleanse her with the

5:5 [a] NU-Text reads *For know this.* 5:9 [a] NU-Text reads *light.* 5:21 [a] NU-Text reads *Christ.*

washing of water by the word,
27that He might present her
to Himself a glorious church,
not having spot or wrinkle
or any such thing, but that
she should be holy and without blemish. 28So husbands
ought to love their own wives
as their own bodies; he who
loves his wife loves himself.
29For no one ever hated his
own flesh, but nourishes and
cherishes it, just as the Lord
does the church. 30For we are
members of His body,[a] of His
flesh and of His bones. 31"For
this reason a man shall leave
his father and mother and
be joined to his wife, and the
two shall become one flesh."[a]
32This is a great mystery, but I
speak concerning Christ and
the church. 33Nevertheless let
each one of you in particular
so love his own wife as himself, and let the wife *see* that
she respects *her* husband.

CHILDREN AND PARENTS

6 Children, obey your parents in the Lord, for this
is right. 2"Honor your father
and mother," which is the first
commandment with promise:
3"that it may be well with you
and you may live long on the
earth."[a]

4And you, fathers, do not
provoke your children to
wrath, but bring them up in
the training and admonition
of the Lord.

BONDSERVANTS AND MASTERS

5Bondservants, be obedient
to those who are your masters
according to the flesh, with
fear and trembling, in sincerity of heart, as to Christ;
6not with eyeservice, as men-
pleasers, but as bondservants
of Christ, doing the will of God
from the heart, 7with goodwill
doing service, as to the Lord,
and not to men, 8knowing that
whatever good anyone does,
he will receive the same from
the Lord, whether *he is* a slave
or free.

9And you, masters, do the
same things to them, giving
up threatening, knowing that
your own Master also[a] is in
heaven, and there is no partiality with Him.

THE WHOLE ARMOR OF GOD

10Finally, my brethren,
be strong in the Lord and in
the power of His might. 11Put
on the whole armor of God,
that you may be able to stand
against the wiles of the devil.
12For we do not wrestle against
flesh and blood, but against
principalities, against powers, against the rulers of the
darkness of this age,[a] against

5:30 [a] NU-Text omits the rest of this verse. 5:31 [a] Genesis 2:24
6:3 [a] Deuteronomy 5:16 6:9 [a] NU-Text reads *He who is both their Master and yours.* 6:12 [a] NU-Text reads *rulers of this darkness.*

spiritual *hosts* of wickedness in
the heavenly *places.* 13There-
fore take up the whole armor
of God, that you may be able
to withstand in the evil day,
and having done all, to stand.
14Stand therefore, having
girded your waist with truth,
having put on the breastplate
of righteousness, 15and having shod your feet with the
preparation of the gospel of
peace; 16above all, taking the
shield of faith with which you
will be able to quench all the
fiery darts of the wicked one.
17And take the helmet of salvation, and the sword of the
Spirit, which is the word of
God; 18praying always with
all prayer and supplication
in the Spirit, being watchful
to this end with all perseverance and supplication for all
the saints— 19and for me, that
utterance may be given to me,
that I may open my mouth
boldly to make known the
mystery of the gospel, 20for
which I am an ambassador in
chains; that in it I may speak
boldly, as I ought to speak.

A GRACIOUS GREETING

21But that you also may
know my affairs *and* how I
am doing, Tychicus, a beloved
brother and faithful minister in the Lord, will make all
things known to you; 22whom
I have sent to you for this very
purpose, that you may know
our affairs, and *that* he may
comfort your hearts.
23Peace to the brethren,
and love with faith, from God
the Father and the Lord Jesus
Christ. 24Grace *be* with all
those who love our Lord Jesus
Christ in sincerity. Amen.

THE EPISTLE OF PAUL THE APOSTLE TO THE

PHILIPPIANS

GREETING

1 Paul and Timothy, bond-
servants of Jesus Christ,

To all the saints in Christ
Jesus who are in Philippi, with
the bishops[a] and deacons:

2Grace to you and peace
from God our Father and the
Lord Jesus Christ.

THANKFULNESS AND PRAYER

3I thank my God upon every
remembrance of you, 4always
in every prayer of mine making request for you all with

1:1 [a] Literally *overseers*

joy, [5]for your fellowship in
the gospel from the first day
until now, [6]being confident of
this very thing, that He who
has begun a good work in you
will complete *it* until the day
of Jesus Christ; [7]just as it is
right for me to think this of
you all, because I have you in
my heart, inasmuch as both
in my chains and in the defense and confirmation of the
gospel, you all are partakers
with me of grace. [8]For God is
my witness, how greatly I long
for you all with the affection
of Jesus Christ.

[9]And this I pray, that your
love may abound still more
and more in knowledge and
all discernment, [10]that you
may approve the things that
are excellent, that you may be
sincere and without offense till
the day of Christ, [11]being filled
with the fruits of righteousness which *are* by Jesus Christ,
to the glory and praise of God.

CHRIST IS PREACHED

[12]But I want you to know,
brethren, that the things
which happened to me have
actually turned out for the
furtherance of the gospel, [13]so
that it has become evident to
the whole palace guard, and
to all the rest, that my chains
are in Christ; [14]and most of
the brethren in the Lord, having become confident by my
chains, are much more bold to
speak the word without fear.

[15]Some indeed preach
Christ even from envy and
strife, and some also from
goodwill: [16]The former[a]
preach Christ from selfish
ambition, not sincerely, supposing to add affliction to my
chains; [17]but the latter out of
love, knowing that I am appointed for the defense of
the gospel. [18]What then? Only
that in every way, whether in
pretense or in truth, Christ is
preached; and in this I rejoice,
yes, and will rejoice.

TO LIVE IS CHRIST

[19]For I know that this will
turn out for my deliverance
through your prayer and
the supply of the Spirit of
Jesus Christ, [20]according to
my earnest expectation and
hope that in nothing I shall
be ashamed, but with all boldness, as always, so now also
Christ will be magnified in
my body, whether by life or
by death. [21]For to me, to live
is Christ, and to die *is* gain.
[22]But if *I* live on in the flesh,
this *will mean* fruit from *my*
labor; yet what I shall choose
I cannot tell. [23]For[a] I am hard-
pressed between the two, having a desire to depart and be
with Christ, *which is* far better.
[24]Nevertheless to remain in
the flesh *is* more needful for

1:16 [a] NU-Text reverses the contents of verses 16 and 17. 1:23 [a] NU-Text and M-Text read *But*.

you. 25And being confident
of this, I know that I shall remain and continue with you
all for your progress and joy
of faith, 26that your rejoicing
for me may be more abundant
in Jesus Christ by my coming
to you again.

STRIVING AND SUFFERING FOR CHRIST

27Only let your conduct be
worthy of the gospel of Christ,
so that whether I come and
see you or am absent, I may
hear of your affairs, that you
stand fast in one spirit, with
one mind striving together
for the faith of the gospel,
28and not in any way terrified
by your adversaries, which is
to them a proof of perdition,
but to you of salvation,[a] and
that from God. 29For to you it
has been granted on behalf
of Christ, not only to believe
in Him, but also to suffer for
His sake, 30having the same
conflict which you saw in me
and now hear *is* in me.

UNITY THROUGH HUMILITY

2 Therefore if *there is* any
consolation in Christ, if
any comfort of love, if any
fellowship of the Spirit, if any
affection and mercy, 2fulfill
my joy by being like-minded,
having the same love, *being*
of one accord, of one mind.
3*Let* nothing *be done* through
selfish ambition or conceit,
but in lowliness of mind let
each esteem others better
than himself. 4Let each of you
look out not only for his own
interests, but also for the interests of others.

THE HUMBLED AND EXALTED CHRIST

5Let this mind be in you
which was also in Christ Jesus,
6who, being in the form of
God, did not consider it robbery to be equal with God,
7but made Himself of no
reputation, taking the form
of a bondservant, *and* coming
in the likeness of men. 8And
being found in appearance
as a man, He humbled Him-
self and became obedient to
the point of death, even the
death of the cross. 9Therefore
God also has highly exalted
Him and given Him the name
which is above every name,
10that at the name of Jesus
every knee should bow, of
those in heaven, and of those
on earth, and of those under
the earth, 11and *that* every
tongue should confess that
Jesus Christ *is* Lord, to the
glory of God the Father.

LIGHT BEARERS

12Therefore, my beloved,
as you have always obeyed,
not as in my presence only,
but now much more in my
absence, work out your own
salvation with fear and trem-

1:28 [a] NU-Text reads *of your salvation.*

bling; 13for it is God who works
in you both to will and to do
for *His* good pleasure.
14Do all things without
complaining and disputing,
15that you may become blameless and harmless, children of
God without fault in the midst
of a crooked and perverse generation, among whom you
shine as lights in the world,
16holding fast the word of life,
so that I may rejoice in the day
of Christ that I have not run in
vain or labored in vain.
17Yes, and if I am being
poured out *as a drink offering*
on the sacrifice and service
of your faith, I am glad and
rejoice with you all. 18For the
same reason you also be glad
and rejoice with me.

TIMOTHY COMMENDED

19But I trust in the Lord
Jesus to send Timothy to you
shortly, that I also may be encouraged when I know your
state. 20For I have no one like-
minded, who will sincerely
care for your state. 21For all
seek their own, not the things
which are of Christ Jesus.
22But you know his proven
character, that as a son with
his father he served with me
in the gospel. 23Therefore I
hope to send him at once, as
soon as I see how it goes with
me. 24But I trust in the Lord
that I myself shall also come
shortly.

EPAPHRODITUS PRAISED

25Yet I considered it necessary to send to you Epaphroditus, my brother, fellow
worker, and fellow soldier,
but your messenger and the
one who ministered to my
need; 26since he was longing
for you all, and was distressed
because you had heard that he
was sick. 27For indeed he was
sick almost unto death; but
God had mercy on him, and
not only on him but on me
also, lest I should have sorrow upon sorrow. 28Therefore
I sent him the more eagerly,
that when you see him again
you may rejoice, and I may be
less sorrowful. 29Receive him
therefore in the Lord with all
gladness, and hold such men
in esteem; 30because for the
work of Christ he came close
to death, not regarding his
life, to supply what was lacking in your service toward me.

ALL FOR CHRIST

3 Finally, my brethren, rejoice in the Lord. For me
to write the same things to
you *is* not tedious, but for you
it is safe.
2Beware of dogs, beware
of evil workers, beware of the
mutilation! 3For we are the
circumcision, who worship
God in the Spirit,[a] rejoice in
Christ Jesus, and have no confidence in the flesh, 4though
I also might have confidence

3:3 [a] NU-Text and M-Text read *who worship in the Spirit of God.*

in the flesh. If anyone else
thinks he may have confi-
dence in the flesh, I more so:
[5]circumcised the eighth day,
of the stock of Israel, *of* the
tribe of Benjamin, a Hebrew of
the Hebrews; concerning the
law, a Pharisee; [6]concerning
zeal, persecuting the church;
concerning the righteousness
which is in the law, blameless.
[7]But what things were gain
to me, these I have counted
loss for Christ. [8]Yet indeed I
also count all things loss for
the excellence of the knowledge of Christ Jesus my Lord,
for whom I have suffered the
loss of all things, and count
them as rubbish, that I may
gain Christ [9]and be found in
Him, not having my own righteousness, which *is* from the
law, but that which *is* through
faith in Christ, the righteousness which is from God by
faith; [10]that I may know Him
and the power of His resurrection, and the fellowship
of His sufferings, being conformed to His death, [11]if, by
any means, I may attain to the
resurrection from the dead.

PRESSING TOWARD THE GOAL

[12]Not that I have already
attained, or am already perfected; but I press on, that I
may lay hold of that for which
Christ Jesus has also laid hold
of me. [13]Brethren, I do not
count myself to have appre-
hended; but one thing *I do,*
forgetting those things which
are behind and reaching forward to those things which are
ahead, [14]I press toward the goal
for the prize of the upward call
of God in Christ Jesus.
[15]Therefore let us, as many
as are mature, have this mind;
and if in anything you think
otherwise, God will reveal
even this to you. [16]Neverthe-
less, to *the degree* that we have
already attained, let us walk by
the same rule,[a] let us be of the
same mind.

OUR CITIZENSHIP IN HEAVEN

[17]Brethren, join in following
my example, and note those
who so walk, as you have us
for a pattern. [18]For many walk,
of whom I have told you often,
and now tell you even weeping, *that they are* the enemies
of the cross of Christ: [19]whose
end *is* destruction, whose god
is their belly, and *whose* glory
is in their shame—who set
their mind on earthly things.
[20]For our citizenship is in
heaven, from which we also
eagerly wait for the Savior,
the Lord Jesus Christ, [21]who
will transform our lowly body
that it may be conformed to
His glorious body, according
to the working by which He is
able even to subdue all things
to Himself.

3:16 [a] NU-Text omits *rule* and the rest of the verse.

4 Therefore, my beloved and
longed-for brethren, my
joy and crown, so stand fast
in the Lord, beloved.

BE UNITED, JOYFUL, AND IN PRAYER

2I implore Euodia and I implore Syntyche to be of the
same mind in the Lord. 3And[a]
I urge you also, true companion, help these women who
labored with me in the gospel, with Clement also, and
the rest of my fellow workers,
whose names *are* in the Book
of Life.
4Rejoice in the Lord always.
Again I will say, rejoice!
5Let your gentleness be
known to all men. The Lord
is at hand.
6Be anxious for nothing,
but in everything by prayer
and supplication, with thanksgiving, let your requests be
made known to God; 7and
the peace of God, which sur-
passes all understanding, will
guard your hearts and minds
through Christ Jesus.

MEDITATE ON THESE THINGS

8Finally, brethren, what-
ever things are true, whatever
things *are* noble, whatever
things *are* just, whatever things
are pure, whatever things *are*
lovely, whatever things *are*
of good report, if *there is* any
virtue and if *there is* anything
praiseworthy—meditate on
these things. 9The things which
you learned and received and
heard and saw in me, these do,
and the God of peace will be
with you.

PHILIPPIAN GENEROSITY

10But I rejoiced in the Lord
greatly that now at last your
care for me has flourished
again; though you surely did
care, but you lacked opportunity. 11Not that I speak in
regard to need, for I have
learned in whatever state I am,
to be content: 12I know how to
be abased, and I know how to
abound. Everywhere and in all
things I have learned both to
be full and to be hungry, both
to abound and to suffer need.
13I can do all things through
Christ[a] who strengthens me.
14Nevertheless you have
done well that you shared in
my distress. 15Now you Phi-
lippians know also that in
the beginning of the gospel,
when I departed from Mac-
edonia, no church shared
with me concerning giving
and receiving but you only.
16For even in Thessalonica
you sent *aid* once and again
for my necessities. 17Not that
I seek the gift, but I seek the
fruit that abounds to your
account. 18Indeed I have all
and abound. I am full, having

4:3 [a] NU-Text and M-Text read *Yes.* 4:13 [a] NU-Text reads *Him who.*

received from Epaphroditus
the things *sent* from you, a
sweet-smelling aroma, an acceptable sacrifice, well pleasing to God. 19And my God shall
supply all your need according to His riches in glory by
Christ Jesus. 20Now to our God
and Father *be* glory forever
and ever. Amen.

GREETING AND BLESSING

21Greet every saint in Christ
Jesus. The brethren who are
with me greet you. 22All the
saints greet you, but especially those who are of Caesar's household.

23The grace of our Lord
Jesus Christ be with you all.[a]
Amen.

THE EPISTLE OF PAUL THE APOSTLE TO THE COLOSSIANS

GREETING

1 Paul, an apostle of Jesus
Christ by the will of God,
and Timothy our brother,

2To the saints and faithful
brethren in Christ *who are* in
Colosse:

Grace to you and peace
from God our Father and the
Lord Jesus Christ.[a]

THEIR FAITH IN CHRIST

3We give thanks to the God
and Father of our Lord Jesus
Christ, praying always for you,
4since we heard of your faith in
Christ Jesus and of your love
for all the saints; 5because of
the hope which is laid up for
you in heaven, of which you
heard before in the word of the
truth of the gospel, 6which has
come to you, as *it has* also in
all the world, and is bringing
forth fruit,[a] as *it is* also among
you since the day you heard
and knew the grace of God
in truth; 7as you also learned
from Epaphras, our dear fellow servant, who is a faithful
minister of Christ on your behalf, 8who also declared to us
your love in the Spirit.

PREEMINENCE OF CHRIST

9For this reason we also,
since the day we heard it, do
not cease to pray for you, and
to ask that you may be filled
with the knowledge of His
will in all wisdom and spiritual understanding; 10that you

4:23 [a] NU-Text reads *your spirit.* 1:2 [a] NU-Text omits *and the Lord Jesus Christ.* 1:6 [a] NU-Text and M-Text add *and growing.*

may walk worthy of the Lord,
fully pleasing *Him*, being fruitful in every good work and in-
creasing in the knowledge of
God; 11strengthened with all
might, according to His glorious power, for all patience
and longsuffering with joy;
12giving thanks to the Father
who has qualified us to be partakers of the inheritance of
the saints in the light. 13He has
delivered us from the power of
darkness and conveyed *us* into
the kingdom of the Son of His
love, 14in whom we have redemption through His blood,[a]
the forgiveness of sins.

15He is the image of the invisible God, the firstborn over
all creation. 16For by Him all
things were created that are in
heaven and that are on earth,
visible and invisible, whether
thrones or dominions or principalities or powers. All things
were created through Him and
for Him. 17And He is before all
things, and in Him all things
consist. 18And He is the head
of the body, the church, who
is the beginning, the firstborn
from the dead, that in all things
He may have the preeminence.

RECONCILED IN CHRIST

19For *it pleased the Father
that* in Him all the fullness
should dwell, 20and by Him
to reconcile all things to Himself, by Him, whether things
on earth or things in heaven,
having made peace through
the blood of His cross.

21And you, who once were
alienated and enemies in your
mind by wicked works, yet
now He has reconciled 22in
the body of His flesh through
death, to present you holy,
and blameless, and above reproach in His sight— 23if indeed you continue in the faith,
grounded and steadfast, and
are not moved away from the
hope of the gospel which you
heard, which was preached to
every creature under heaven,
of which I, Paul, became a
minister.

SACRIFICIAL SERVICE FOR CHRIST

24I now rejoice in my sufferings for you, and fill up in
my flesh what is lacking in
the afflictions of Christ, for
the sake of His body, which
is the church, 25of which I
became a minister accord-
ing to the stewardship from
God which was given to me for
you, to fulfill the word of God,
26the mystery which has been
hidden from ages and from
generations, but now has
been revealed to His saints.
27To them God willed to make
known what are the riches
of the glory of this mystery
among the Gentiles: which[a]
is Christ in you, the hope of

1:14 [a] NU-Text and M-Text omit *through His blood.* 1:27 [a] M-Text reads *who.*

glory. 28Him we preach, warning every man and teaching
every man in all wisdom, that
we may present every man
perfect in Christ Jesus. 29To
this *end* I also labor, striving
according to His working
which works in me mightily.

NOT PHILOSOPHY BUT CHRIST

2 For I want you to know
what a great conflict I
have for you and those in Laodicea, and *for* as many as
have not seen my face in the
flesh, 2that their hearts may
be encouraged, being knit together in love, and *attaining*
to all riches of the full assurance of understanding, to the
knowledge of the mystery of
God, both of the Father and[a]
of Christ, 3in whom are hidden all the treasures of wisdom and knowledge.

4Now this I say lest anyone
should deceive you with persuasive words. 5For though I
am absent in the flesh, yet I
am with you in spirit, rejoicing to see your *good* order and
the steadfastness of your faith
in Christ.

6As you therefore have received Christ Jesus the Lord,
so walk in Him, 7rooted and
built up in Him and established in the faith, as you have
been taught, abounding in it[a]
with thanksgiving.

8Beware lest anyone cheat
you through philosophy and
empty deceit, according to the
tradition of men, according
to the basic principles of the
world, and not according to
Christ. 9For in Him dwells all
the fullness of the Godhead
bodily; 10and you are complete in Him, who is the head
of all principality and power.

NOT LEGALISM BUT CHRIST

11In Him you were also circumcised with the circum-
cision made without hands,
by putting off the body of the
sins[a] of the flesh, by the circumcision of Christ, 12buried
with Him in baptism, in which
you also were raised with *Him*
through faith in the working of
God, who raised Him from the
dead. 13And you, being dead in
your trespasses and the uncircumcision of your flesh, He
has made alive together with
Him, having forgiven you all
trespasses, 14having wiped out
the handwriting of requirements that was against us,
which was contrary to us. And
He has taken it out of the way,
having nailed it to the cross.
15Having disarmed principalities and powers, He made a
public spectacle of them, triumphing over them in it.

16So let no one judge you in
food or in drink, or regarding a
festival or a new moon or sab-

2:2 [a] NU-Text omits *both of the Father and.* 2:7 [a] NU-Text omits *in it.* 2:11 [a] NU-Text omits *of the sins.*

baths, 17which are a shadow of
things to come, but the substance is of Christ. 18Let no
one cheat you of your reward,
taking delight in *false* humility
and worship of angels, intrud-
ing into those things which he
has not[a] seen, vainly puffed up
by his fleshly mind, 19and not
holding fast to the Head, from
whom all the body, nourished
and knit together by joints and
ligaments, grows with the increase *that is* from God.

20Therefore,[a] if you died
with Christ from the basic
principles of the world, why,
as *though* living in the world,
do you subject yourselves to
regulations— 21"Do not touch,
do not taste, do not handle,"
22which all concern things
which perish with the using—
according to the command-
ments and doctrines of men?
23These things indeed have an
appearance of wisdom in self-
imposed religion, *false* humility, and neglect of the body,
but are of no value against the
indulgence of the flesh.

NOT CARNALITY BUT CHRIST

3 If then you were raised
with Christ, seek those
things which are above, where
Christ is, sitting at the right
hand of God. 2Set your mind
on things above, not on things
on the earth. 3For you died,
and your life is hidden with
Christ in God. 4When Christ
who is our life appears, then
you also will appear with Him
in glory.

5Therefore put to death
your members which are on
the earth: fornication, uncleanness, passion, evil desire, and covetousness, which
is idolatry. 6Because of these
things the wrath of God is
coming upon the sons of
disobedience, 7in which you
yourselves once walked when
you lived in them.

8But now you yourselves
are to put off all these: anger,
wrath, malice, blasphemy,
filthy language out of your
mouth. 9Do not lie to one another, since you have put off
the old man with his deeds,
10and have put on the new *man*
who is renewed in knowledge
according to the image of Him
who created him, 11where there
is neither Greek nor Jew, circumcised nor uncircumcised,
barbarian, Scythian, slave *nor*
free, but Christ *is* all and in all.

CHARACTER OF THE NEW MAN

12Therefore, as *the* elect of
God, holy and beloved, put
on tender *mercies*, kindness,
humility, meekness, long-
suffering; 13bearing with one
another, and forgiving one
another, if anyone has a complaint against another; even as
Christ forgave you, so you also

2:18 [a] NU-Text omits *not*. 2:20 [a] NU-Text and M-Text omit *Therefore*.

must do. 14But above all these
things put on love, which is
the bond of perfection. 15And
let the peace of God rule in
your hearts, to which also you
were called in one body; and
be thankful. 16Let the word of
Christ dwell in you richly in all
wisdom, teaching and admon-
ishing one another in psalms
and hymns and spiritual
songs, singing with grace in
your hearts to the Lord. 17And
whatever you do in word or
deed, *do* all in the name of the
Lord Jesus, giving thanks to
God the Father through Him.

THE CHRISTIAN HOME

18Wives, submit to your
own husbands, as is fitting
in the Lord.

19Husbands, love your
wives and do not be bitter toward them.

20Children, obey your parents in all things, for this is
well pleasing to the Lord.

21Fathers, do not provoke
your children, lest they become discouraged.

22Bondservants, obey in all
things your masters according to the flesh, not with eyeservice, as men-pleasers, but in
sincerity of heart, fearing God.
23And whatever you do, do it
heartily, as to the Lord and not
to men, 24knowing that from
the Lord you will receive the
reward of the *inheritance;* for[a]
you serve the Lord Christ. 25But
he who does wrong will be repaid for what he has done, and
there is no partiality.

4 Masters, give your bondservants what is just and
fair, knowing that you also
have a Master in heaven.

CHRISTIAN GRACES

2Continue earnestly in
prayer, being vigilant in it with
thanksgiving; 3meanwhile
praying also for us, that God
would open to us a door for
the word, to speak the mystery
of Christ, for which I am also
in chains, 4that I may make it
manifest, as I ought to speak.

5Walk in wisdom toward
those *who are* outside, redeeming the time. 6*Let* your
speech always *be* with grace,
seasoned with salt, that you
may know how you ought to
answer each one.

FINAL GREETINGS

7Tychicus, a beloved
brother, faithful minister, and
fellow servant in the Lord, will
tell you all the news about me.
8I am sending him to you for
this very purpose, that he[a]
may know your circumstances
and comfort your hearts,
9with Onesimus, a faithful and
beloved brother, who is *one* of
you. They will make known to
you all things which *are happening* here.

3:24 [a] NU-Text omits *for.* 4:8 [a] NU-Text reads *you may know our circumstances and he may.*

10Aristarchus my fellow
prisoner greets you, with
Mark the cousin of Barnabas
(about whom you received instructions: if he comes to you,
welcome him), 11and Jesus
who is called Justus. These *are*
my only fellow workers for the
kingdom of God who are of
the circumcision; they have
proved to be a comfort to me.
12Epaphras, who is *one* of
you, a bondservant of Christ,
greets you, always laboring
fervently for you in prayers,
that you may stand perfect and
complete[a] in all the will of God.
13For I bear him witness that
he has a great zeal[a] for you,
and those who are in Laodicea, and those in Hierapolis.
14Luke the beloved physician
and Demas greet you. 15Greet
the brethren who are in Laodicea, and Nymphas and the
church that *is* in his[a] house.

CLOSING EXHORTATIONS AND BLESSING

16Now when this epistle is
read among you, see that it
is read also in the church of
the Laodiceans, and that you
likewise read the *epistle* from
Laodicea. 17And say to Archip-
pus, "Take heed to the ministry
which you have received in the
Lord, that you may fulfill it."
18This salutation by my
own hand—Paul. Remember
my chains. Grace *be* with you.
Amen.

THE FIRST EPISTLE OF PAUL THE APOSTLE TO THE THESSALONIANS

GREETING

1 Paul, Silvanus, and Timothy,

To the church of the Thessalonians in God the Father and the Lord Jesus Christ:

Grace to you and peace from God our Father and the Lord Jesus Christ.[a]

THEIR GOOD EXAMPLE

2We give thanks to God
always for you all, making
mention of you in our prayers,
3remembering without ceasing your work of faith, labor
of love, and patience of hope
in our Lord Jesus Christ in the
sight of our God and Father,
4knowing, beloved brethren,

4:12 [a] NU-Text reads *fully assured.* 4:13 [a] NU-Text reads *concern.* 4:15 [a] NU-Text reads *Nympha . . . her house.* 1:1 [a] NU-Text omits *from God our Father and the Lord Jesus Christ.*

your election by God. 5For our gospel did not come to you in word only, but also in power, and in the Holy Spirit and in much assurance, as you know what kind of men we were among you for your sake.

6And you became followers of us and of the Lord, having received the word in much affliction, with joy of the Holy Spirit, 7so that you became examples to all in Macedonia and Achaia who believe. 8For from you the word of the Lord has sounded forth, not only in Macedonia and Achaia, but also in every place. Your faith toward God has gone out, so that we do not need to say anything. 9For they themselves declare concerning us what manner of entry we had to you, and how you turned to God from idols to serve the living and true God, 10and to wait for His Son from heaven, whom He raised from the dead, *even* Jesus who delivers us from the wrath to come.

PAUL'S CONDUCT

2 For you yourselves know, brethren, that our coming to you was not in vain. 2But even[a] after we had suffered before and were spitefully treated at Philippi, as you know, we were bold in our God to speak to you the gospel of God in much conflict. 3For our exhortation *did* not *come* from error or uncleanness, nor *was it* in deceit.

4But as we have been approved by God to be entrusted with the gospel, even so we speak, not as pleasing men, but God who tests our hearts. 5For neither at any time did we use flattering words, as you know, nor a cloak for covetousness—God *is* witness. 6Nor did we seek glory from men, either from you or from others, when we might have made demands as apostles of Christ. 7But we were gentle among you, just as a nursing *mother* cherishes her own children. 8So, affectionately longing for you, we were well pleased to impart to you not only the gospel of God, but also our own lives, because you had become dear to us. 9For you remember, brethren, our labor and toil; for laboring night and day, that we might not be a burden to any of you, we preached to you the gospel of God.

10You *are* witnesses, and God *also*, how devoutly and justly and blamelessly we behaved ourselves among you who believe; 11as you know how we exhorted, and comforted, and charged[a] every one of you, as a father *does* his own children, 12that you would walk worthy of God who

2:2 [a] NU-Text and M-Text omit *even*. 2:11 [a] NU-Text and M-Text read *implored*.

calls you into His own kingdom and glory.

THEIR CONVERSION

[13]For this reason we also
thank God without ceasing,
because when you received
the word of God which you
heard from us, you welcomed
it not *as* the word of men, but
as it is in truth, the word of
God, which also effectively
works in you who believe.
[14]For you, brethren, became
imitators of the churches of
God which are in Judea in
Christ Jesus. For you also suffered the same things from
your own countrymen, just
as they *did* from the Judeans,
[15]who killed both the Lord
Jesus and their own prophets, and have persecuted us;
and they do not please God
and are contrary to all men,
[16]forbidding us to speak to
the Gentiles that they may be
saved, so as always to fill up
the measure of their sins; but
wrath has come upon them
to the uttermost.

LONGING TO SEE THEM

[17]But we, brethren, having
been taken away from you for
a short time in presence, not
in heart, endeavored more
eagerly to see your face with
great desire. [18]Therefore we
wanted to come to you—even
I, Paul, time and again—but
Satan hindered us. [19]For what
is our hope, or joy, or crown of
rejoicing? *Is it* not even you in
the presence of our Lord Jesus
Christ at His coming? [20]For
you are our glory and joy.

CONCERN FOR THEIR FAITH

3 Therefore, when we could
no longer endure it, we
thought it good to be left in
Athens alone, [2]and sent Timothy, our brother and minister of God, and our fellow
laborer in the gospel of Christ,
to establish you and encourage you concerning your
faith, [3]that no one should be
shaken by these afflictions;
for you yourselves know that
we are appointed to this. [4]For,
in fact, we told you before
when we were with you that
we would suffer tribulation,
just as it happened, and you
know. [5]For this reason, when
I could no longer endure it, I
sent to know your faith, lest by
some means the tempter had
tempted you, and our labor
might be in vain.

ENCOURAGED BY TIMOTHY

[6]But now that Timothy
has come to us from you,
and brought us good news
of your faith and love, and
that you always have good
remembrance of us, greatly
desiring to see us, as we also
to see you— [7]therefore, brethren, in all our affliction and
distress we were comforted
concerning you by your faith.
[8]For now we live, if you stand
fast in the Lord.

9For what thanks can we
render to God for you, for all
the joy with which we rejoice
for your sake before our God,
10night and day praying exceedingly that we may see
your face and perfect what is
lacking in your faith?

PRAYER FOR THE CHURCH

11Now may our God and Fa-
ther Himself, and our Lord
Jesus Christ, direct our way to
you. 12And may the Lord make
you increase and abound in
love to one another and to
all, just as we *do* to you, 13so
that He may establish your
hearts blameless in holiness
before our God and Father at
the coming of our Lord Jesus
Christ with all His saints.

PLEA FOR PURITY

4 Finally then, brethren, we
urge and exhort in the
Lord Jesus that you should
abound more and more,
just as you received from us
how you ought to walk and
to please God; 2for you know
what commandments we gave
you through the Lord Jesus.
3For this is the will of God,
your sanctification: that you
should abstain from sexual
immorality; 4that each of you
should know how to possess
his own vessel in sanctification and honor, 5not in passion of lust, like the Gentiles
who do not know God; 6that
no one should take advantage
of and defraud his brother in
this matter, because the Lord
is the avenger of all such, as
we also forewarned you and
testified. 7For God did not call
us to uncleanness, but in holiness. 8Therefore he who rejects *this* does not reject man,
but God, who has also given[a]
us His Holy Spirit.

A BROTHERLY AND ORDERLY LIFE

9But concerning brotherly
love you have no need that I
should write to you, for you
yourselves are taught by God
to love one another; 10and
indeed you do so toward all
the brethren who are in all
Macedonia. But we urge you,
brethren, that you increase
more and more; 11that you
also aspire to lead a quiet life,
to mind your own business,
and to work with your own
hands, as we commanded
you, 12that you may walk
properly toward those who
are outside, and *that* you may
lack nothing.

THE COMFORT OF CHRIST'S COMING

13But I do not want you to
be ignorant, brethren, concerning those who have fallen
asleep, lest you sorrow as others who have no hope. 14For
if we believe that Jesus died
and rose again, even so God

4:8 [a] NU-Text reads *who also gives*.

will bring with Him those who
sleep in Jesus.[a]

15For this we say to you by
the word of the Lord, that we
who are alive *and* remain until
the coming of the Lord will by
no means precede those who
are asleep. 16For the Lord Himself will descend from heaven
with a shout, with the voice
of an archangel, and with the
trumpet of God. And the dead
in Christ will rise first. 17Then
we who are alive *and* remain
shall be caught up together
with them in the clouds to
meet the Lord in the air. And
thus we shall always be with
the Lord. 18Therefore comfort
one another with these words.

THE DAY OF THE LORD

5 But concerning the times
and the seasons, breth-
ren, you have no need that I
should write to you. 2For you
yourselves know perfectly
that the day of the Lord so
comes as a thief in the night.
3For when they say, "Peace and
safety!" then sudden destruction comes upon them, as
labor pains upon a pregnant
woman. And they shall not escape. 4But you, brethren, are
not in darkness, so that this
Day should overtake you as a
thief. 5You are all sons of light
and sons of the day. We are not
of the night nor of darkness.
6Therefore let us not sleep,
as others *do,* but let us watch
and be sober. 7For those who
sleep, sleep at night, and those
who get drunk are drunk at
night. 8But let us who are of
the day be sober, putting on
the breastplate of faith and
love, and *as* a helmet the hope
of salvation. 9For God did
not appoint us to wrath, but
to obtain salvation through
our Lord Jesus Christ, 10who
died for us, that whether we
wake or sleep, we should live
together with Him.

11Therefore comfort each
other and edify one another,
just as you also are doing.

VARIOUS EXHORTATIONS

12And we urge you, breth-
ren, to recognize those who
labor among you, and are
over you in the Lord and admonish you, 13and to esteem
them very highly in love for
their work's sake. Be at peace
among yourselves.

14Now we exhort you, brethren, warn those who are unruly, comfort the fainthearted,
uphold the weak, be patient
with all. 15See that no one
renders evil for evil to anyone, but always pursue what
is good both for yourselves
and for all.

16Rejoice always, 17pray
without ceasing, 18in everything give thanks; for this is
the will of God in Christ Jesus
for you.

19Do not quench the Spirit.

4:14 [a] Or *those who through Jesus sleep*

[20]Do not despise prophecies.
[21]Test all things; hold fast what
is good. [22]Abstain from every
form of evil.

BLESSING AND ADMONITION

[23]Now may the God of
peace Himself sanctify you
completely; and may your
whole spirit, soul, and body
be preserved blameless at
the coming of our Lord Jesus
Christ. [24]He who calls you *is*
faithful, who also will do *it*.

[25]Brethren, pray for us.

[26]Greet all the brethren
with a holy kiss.

[27]I charge you by the Lord
that this epistle be read to all
the holy[a] brethren.

[28]The grace of our Lord
Jesus Christ *be* with you.
Amen.

THE SECOND EPISTLE OF PAUL THE APOSTLE TO THE THESSALONIANS

GREETING

1 Paul, Silvanus, and Timothy,

To the church of the
Thessalonians in God our Father and the Lord Jesus Christ:

[2]Grace to you and peace
from God our Father and the
Lord Jesus Christ.

GOD'S FINAL JUDGMENT AND GLORY

[3]We are bound to thank
God always for you, brethren,
as it is fitting, because your
faith grows exceedingly, and
the love of every one of you all
abounds toward each other,
[4]so that we ourselves boast
of you among the churches
of God for your patience and
faith in all your persecutions
and tribulations that you
endure, [5]*which is* manifest
evidence of the righteous
judgment of God, that you
may be counted worthy of the
kingdom of God, for which
you also suffer; [6]since *it is* a
righteous thing with God to
repay with tribulation those
who trouble you, [7]and to *give*
you who are troubled rest
with us when the Lord Jesus
is revealed from heaven with
His mighty angels, [8]in flaming fire taking vengeance on
those who do not know God,
and on those who do not

5:27 [a] NU-Text omits *holy*.

obey the gospel of our Lord
Jesus Christ. 9These shall be
punished with everlasting
destruction from the presence of the Lord and from the
glory of His power, 10when
He comes, in that Day, to be
glorified in His saints and to
be admired among all those
who believe,[a] because our
testimony among you was
believed.

11Therefore we also pray
always for you that our God
would count you worthy of
this calling, and fulfill all the
good pleasure of *His* goodness and the work of faith with
power, 12that the name of our
Lord Jesus Christ may be glorified in you, and you in Him,
according to the grace of our
God and the Lord Jesus Christ.

THE GREAT APOSTASY

2 Now, brethren, concerning
the coming of our Lord
Jesus Christ and our gathering together to Him, we ask
you, 2not to be soon shaken
in mind or troubled, either by
spirit or by word or by letter,
as if from us, as though the
day of Christ[a] had come. 3Let
no one deceive you by any
means; for *that Day will not
come* unless the falling away
comes first, and the man of
sin[a] is revealed, the son of
perdition, 4who opposes and
exalts himself above all that
is called God or that is worshiped, so that he sits as God[a]
in the temple of God, showing
himself that he is God.

5Do you not remember that
when I was still with you I told
you these things? 6And now
you know what is restraining,
that he may be revealed in his
own time. 7For the mystery of
lawlessness is already at work;
only He[a] who now restrains
will do so until He[b] is taken
out of the way. 8And then the
lawless one will be revealed,
whom the Lord will consume
with the breath of His mouth
and destroy with the brightness of His coming. 9The
coming of the *lawless one* is
according to the working of
Satan, with all power, signs,
and lying wonders, 10and
with all unrighteous deception among those who perish,
because they did not receive
the love of the truth, that they
might be saved. 11And for this
reason God will send them
strong delusion, that they
should believe the lie, 12that
they all may be condemned
who did not believe the truth
but had pleasure in unrighteousness.

STAND FAST

13But we are bound to give
thanks to God always for you,

1:10 [a] NU-Text and M-Text read *have believed.* 2:2 [a] NU-Text reads *the Lord.* 2:3 [a] NU-Text reads *lawlessness.* 2:4 [a] NU-Text omits *as God.* 2:7 [a] Or *he* [b] Or *he*

brethren beloved by the Lord,
because God from the beginning chose you for salvation
through sanctification by the
Spirit and belief in the truth,
14to which He called you by
our gospel, for the obtaining
of the glory of our Lord Jesus
Christ. 15Therefore, brethren,
stand fast and hold the traditions which you were taught,
whether by word or our epistle.

16Now may our Lord Jesus
Christ Himself, and our God
and Father, who has loved
us and given *us* everlasting
consolation and good hope by
grace, 17comfort your hearts
and establish you in every
good word and work.

PRAY FOR US

3 Finally, brethren, pray for
us, that the word of the
Lord may run *swiftly* and be
glorified, just as *it is* with you,
2and that we may be delivered from unreasonable and
wicked men; for not all have
faith.

3But the Lord is faithful,
who will establish you and
guard *you* from the evil one.
4And we have confidence in
the Lord concerning you, both
that you do and will do the
things we command you.

5Now may the Lord direct
your hearts into the love of
God and into the patience of
Christ.

WARNING AGAINST IDLENESS

6But we command you,
brethren, in the name of our
Lord Jesus Christ, that you
withdraw from every brother
who walks disorderly and not
according to the tradition
which he[a] received from us.
7For you yourselves know how
you ought to follow us, for we
were not disorderly among you;
8nor did we eat anyone's bread
free of charge, but worked with
labor and toil night and day,
that we might not be a burden
to any of you, 9not because we
do not have authority, but to
make ourselves an example of
how you should follow us.

10For even when we were
with you, we commanded you
this: If anyone will not work,
neither shall he eat. 11For we
hear that there are some who
walk among you in a disorderly manner, not working at
all, but are busybodies. 12Now
those who are such we command and exhort through our
Lord Jesus Christ that they
work in quietness and eat their
own bread.

13But *as for* you, brethren,
do not grow weary *in* doing
good. 14And if anyone does not
obey our word in this epistle,
note that person and do not
keep company with him, that
he may be ashamed. 15Yet do
not count *him* as an enemy, but
admonish *him* as a brother.

3:6 [a] NU-Text and M-Text read *they.*

BENEDICTION

16 Now may the Lord of peace Himself give you peace always in every way. The Lord *be* with you all.

17 The salutation of Paul with my own hand, which is a sign in every epistle; so I write.

18 The grace of our Lord Jesus Christ *be* with you all. Amen.

THE FIRST EPISTLE OF PAUL THE APOSTLE TO TIMOTHY

GREETING

1 Paul, an apostle of Jesus Christ, by the commandment of God our Savior and the Lord Jesus Christ, our hope,

2 To Timothy, a true son in the faith:

Grace, mercy, *and* peace from God our Father and Jesus Christ our Lord.

NO OTHER DOCTRINE

3 As I urged you when I went into Macedonia—remain in Ephesus that you may charge some that they teach no other doctrine, 4 nor give heed to fables and endless genealogies, which cause disputes rather than godly edification which is in faith. 5 Now the purpose of the commandment is love from a pure heart, *from* a good conscience, and *from* sincere faith, 6 from which some, having strayed, have turned aside to idle talk, 7 desiring to be teachers of the law, understanding neither what they say nor the things which they affirm.

8 But we know that the law *is* good if one uses it lawfully, 9 knowing this: that the law is not made for a righteous person, but for *the* lawless and insubordinate, for *the* ungodly and for sinners, for *the* unholy and profane, for murderers of fathers and murderers of mothers, for manslayers, 10 for fornicators, for sodomites, for kidnappers, for liars, for perjurers, and if there is any other thing that is contrary to sound doctrine, 11 according to the glorious gospel of the blessed God which was committed to my trust.

GLORY TO GOD FOR HIS GRACE

12 And I thank Christ Jesus our Lord who has enabled

me, because He counted me
faithful, putting *me* into the
ministry, [13]although I was formerly a blasphemer, a perse-
cutor, and an insolent man;
but I obtained mercy because
I did *it* ignorantly in unbelief.
[14]And the grace of our Lord
was exceedingly abundant,
with faith and love which
are in Christ Jesus. [15]This *is*
a faithful saying and worthy
of all acceptance, that Christ
Jesus came into the world to
save sinners, of whom I am
chief. [16]However, for this reason I obtained mercy, that in
me first Jesus Christ might
show all longsuffering, as a
pattern to those who are going
to believe on Him for everlasting life. [17]Now to the King
eternal, immortal, invisible,
to God who alone is wise,[a] *be*
honor and glory forever and
ever. Amen.

FIGHT THE GOOD FIGHT

[18]This charge I commit to
you, son Timothy, according
to the prophecies previously
made concerning you, that by
them you may wage the good
warfare, [19]having faith and a
good conscience, which some
having rejected, concerning
the faith have suffered ship-
wreck, [20]of whom are Hymenaeus and Alexander, whom
I delivered to Satan that they
may learn not to blaspheme.

PRAY FOR ALL MEN

2 Therefore I exhort first
of all that supplications,
prayers, intercessions, *and*
giving of thanks be made for
all men, [2]for kings and all
who are in authority, that we
may lead a quiet and peaceable life in all godliness and
reverence. [3]For this *is* good
and acceptable in the sight
of God our Savior, [4]who desires all men to be saved and
to come to the knowledge of
the truth. [5]For *there is* one God
and one Mediator between
God and men, *the* Man Christ
Jesus, [6]who gave Himself a
ransom for all, to be testified
in due time, [7]for which I was
appointed a preacher and an
apostle—I am speaking the
truth in Christ[a] *and* not lying—a teacher of the Gentiles
in faith and truth.

MEN AND WOMEN IN THE CHURCH

[8]I desire therefore that
the men pray everywhere,
lifting up holy hands, without wrath and doubting; [9]in
like manner also, that the
women adorn themselves in
modest apparel, with propri-
ety and moderation, not with
braided hair or gold or pearls
or costly clothing, [10]but, which
is proper for women pro-
fessing godliness, with good
works. [11]Let a woman learn
in silence with all submis-

1:17 [a] NU-Text reads *to the only God.* 2:7 [a] NU-Text omits *in Christ.*

sion. 12And I do not permit
a woman to teach or to have
authority over a man, but to
be in silence. 13For Adam was
formed first, then Eve. 14And
Adam was not deceived, but
the woman being deceived,
fell into transgression. 15Nev-
ertheless she will be saved in
childbearing if they continue
in faith, love, and holiness,
with self-control.

QUALIFICATIONS OF OVERSEERS

3 This *is* a faithful saying:
If a man desires the position of a bishop,[a] he desires
a good work. 2A bishop then
must be blameless, the husband of one wife, temperate,
sober-minded, of good behavior, hospitable, able to teach;
3not given to wine, not violent, not greedy for money,[a]
but gentle, not quarrelsome,
not covetous; 4one who rules
his own house well, having
his children in submission
with all reverence 5(for if a
man does not know how to
rule his own house, how will
he take care of the church of
God?); 6not a novice, lest being
puffed up with pride he fall
into the *same* condemnation
as the devil. 7Moreover he
must have a good testimony
among those who are outside,
lest he fall into reproach and
the snare of the devil.

QUALIFICATIONS OF DEACONS

8Likewise deacons *must be*
reverent, not double-tongued,
not given to much wine, not
greedy for money, 9holding
the mystery of the faith with
a pure conscience. 10But let
these also first be tested;
then let them serve as deacons, being *found* blameless.
11Likewise, *their* wives *must*
be reverent, not slanderers,
temperate, faithful in all
things. 12Let deacons be the
husbands of one wife, ruling
their children and their own
houses well. 13For those who
have served well as deacons
obtain for themselves a good
standing and great boldness
in the faith which is in Christ
Jesus.

THE GREAT MYSTERY

14These things I write to
you, though I hope to come
to you shortly; 15but if I am
delayed, *I write* so that you
may know how you ought to
conduct yourself in the house
of God, which is the church
of the living God, the pillar
and ground of the truth. 16And
without controversy great is
the mystery of godliness:

God[a] was manifested
in the flesh,
Justified in the Spirit,
Seen by angels,

3:1 [a] Literally *overseer* 3:3 [a] NU-Text omits *not greedy for money.* 3:16 [a] NU-Text reads *Who.*

Preached among
the Gentiles,
Believed on in the world,
Received up in glory.

THE GREAT APOSTASY

4 Now the Spirit expressly
says that in latter times
some will depart from the
faith, giving heed to deceiving spirits and doctrines of
demons, 2speaking lies in
hypocrisy, having their own
conscience seared with a hot
iron, 3forbidding to marry,
and commanding to abstain
from foods which God created
to be received with thanksgiving by those who believe
and know the truth. 4For every
creature of God *is* good, and
nothing is to be refused if it
is received with thanksgiving;
5for it is sanctified by the word
of God and prayer.

A GOOD SERVANT OF JESUS CHRIST

6If you instruct the brethren in these things, you will be
a good minister of Jesus Christ,
nourished in the words of faith
and of the good doctrine which
you have carefully followed.
7But reject profane and old
wives' fables, and exercise
yourself toward godliness. 8For
bodily exercise profits a little,
but godliness is profitable for
all things, having promise
of the life that now is and of
that which is to come. 9This *is*
a faithful saying and worthy
of all acceptance. 10For to this
end we both labor and suffer
reproach,[a] because we trust
in the living God, who is *the*
Savior of all men, especially
of those who believe. 11These
things command and teach.

TAKE HEED TO YOUR MINISTRY

12Let no one despise your
youth, but be an example
to the believers in word, in
conduct, in love, in spirit,[a] in
faith, in purity. 13Till I come,
give attention to reading, to
exhortation, to doctrine. 14Do
not neglect the gift that is in
you, which was given to you
by prophecy with the laying
on of the hands of the el-
dership. 15Meditate on these
things; give yourself entirely
to them, that your progress
may be evident to all. 16Take
heed to yourself and to the
doctrine. Continue in them,
for in doing this you will save
both yourself and those who
hear you.

TREATMENT OF CHURCH MEMBERS

5 Do not rebuke an older
man, but exhort *him* as a father, younger men as brothers,
2older women as mothers,
younger women as sisters, with
all purity.

4:10 [a] NU-Text reads *we labor and strive.* 4:12 [a] NU-Text omits *in spirit.*

HONOR TRUE WIDOWS

3Honor widows who are re-
ally widows. 4But if any widow
has children or grandchildren,
let them first learn to show
piety at home and to repay
their parents; for this is good
and[a] acceptable before God.
5Now she who is really a widow,
and left alone, trusts in God
and continues in supplications
and prayers night and day.
6But she who lives in pleasure
is dead while she lives. 7And
these things command, that
they may be blameless. 8But
if anyone does not provide
for his own, and especially for
those of his household, he has
denied the faith and is worse
than an unbeliever.

9Do not let a widow under
sixty years old be taken into
the number, *and not unless* she
has been the wife of one man,
10well reported for good works:
if she has brought up children,
if she has lodged strangers, if
she has washed the saints' feet,
if she has relieved the afflicted,
if she has diligently followed
every good work.

11But refuse *the* younger
widows; for when they have
begun to grow wanton against
Christ, they desire to marry,
12having condemnation be-
cause they have cast off their
first faith. 13And besides they
learn *to be* idle, wandering
about from house to house,
and not only idle but also gos-
sips and busybodies, saying
things which they ought not.
14Therefore I desire that *the*
younger *widows* marry, bear
children, manage the house,
give no opportunity to the adversary to speak reproachfully.
15For some have already turned
aside after Satan. 16If any believing man or[a] woman has
widows, let them relieve them,
and do not let the church be
burdened, that it may relieve
those who are really widows.

HONOR THE ELDERS

17Let the elders who rule
well be counted worthy of
double honor, especially those
who labor in the word and doctrine. 18For the Scripture says,
"You shall not muzzle an ox
while it treads out the grain,"[a]
and, "The laborer *is* worthy of
his wages."[b] 19Do not receive
an accusation against an elder
except from two or three witnesses. 20Those who are sinning rebuke in the presence of
all, that the rest also may fear.

21I charge *you* before God
and the Lord Jesus Christ and
the elect angels that you observe these things without
prejudice, doing nothing with
partiality. 22Do not lay hands
on anyone hastily, nor share
in other people's sins; keep
yourself pure.

23No longer drink only

5:4 [a] NU-Text and M-Text omit *good and.* 5:16 [a] NU-Text omits *man or.* 5:18 [a] Deuteronomy 25:4 [b] Luke 10:7

water, but use a little wine for
your stomach's sake and your
frequent infirmities.
24Some men's sins are
clearly evident, preceding
them to judgment, but those
of some *men* follow later.
25Likewise, the good works
of some are clearly evident,
and those that are otherwise
cannot be hidden.

HONOR MASTERS

6 Let as many bondservants
as are under the yoke
count their own masters worthy of all honor, so that the
name of God and *His* doctrine
may not be blasphemed. 2And
those who have believing masters, let them not despise *them*
because they are brethren, but
rather serve *them* because
those who are benefited are
believers and beloved. Teach
and exhort these things.

ERROR AND GREED

3If anyone teaches other-
wise and does not consent to
wholesome words, *even* the
words of our Lord Jesus Christ,
and to the doctrine which accords with godliness, 4he is
proud, knowing nothing, but
is obsessed with disputes and
arguments over words, from
which come envy, strife, reviling, evil suspicions, 5useless
wranglings[a] of men of corrupt minds and destitute of
the truth, who suppose that
godliness is a *means of* gain.
From such withdraw yourself.[b]
6Now godliness with con-
tentment is great gain. 7For
we brought nothing into *this*
world, *and it is* certain[a] we can
carry nothing out. 8And having food and clothing, with
these we shall be content. 9But
those who desire to be rich fall
into temptation and a snare,
and *into* many foolish and
harmful lusts which drown
men in destruction and perdition. 10For the love of money
is a root of all *kinds of* evil,
for which some have strayed
from the faith in their greediness, and pierced themselves
through with many sorrows.

THE GOOD CONFESSION

11But you, O man of God,
flee these things and pursue
righteousness, godliness,
faith, love, patience, gentleness. 12Fight the good fight of
faith, lay hold on eternal life,
to which you were also called
and have confessed the good
confession in the presence of
many witnesses. 13I urge you
in the sight of God who gives
life to all things, and *before*
Christ Jesus who witnessed the
good confession before Pontius Pilate, 14that you keep *this*
commandment without spot,
blameless until our Lord Jesus
Christ's appearing, 15which He

6:5 [a] NU-Text and M-Text read *constant friction.* [b] NU-Text omits this sentence. 6:7 [a] NU-Text omits *and it is certain.*

will manifest in His own time, *He who is* the blessed and only Potentate, the King of kings and Lord of lords, [16]who alone has immortality, dwelling in unapproachable light, whom no man has seen or can see, to whom *be* honor and everlasting power. Amen.

INSTRUCTIONS TO THE RICH

[17]Command those who are rich in this present age not to be haughty, nor to trust in uncertain riches but in the living God, who gives us richly all things to enjoy. [18]*Let them* do good, that they be rich in good works, ready to give, willing to share, [19]storing up for themselves a good foundation for the time to come, that they may lay hold on eternal life.

GUARD THE FAITH

[20]O Timothy! Guard what was committed to your trust, avoiding the profane *and* idle babblings and contradictions of what is falsely called knowledge— [21]by professing it some have strayed concerning the faith.

Grace *be* with you. Amen.

THE SECOND EPISTLE OF PAUL THE APOSTLE TO TIMOTHY

GREETING

1 Paul, an apostle of Jesus Christ[a] by the will of God, according to the promise of life which is in Christ Jesus,

[2]To Timothy, a beloved son:

Grace, mercy, *and* peace from God the Father and Christ Jesus our Lord.

TIMOTHY'S FAITH AND HERITAGE

[3]I thank God, whom I serve with a pure conscience, as *my* forefathers *did,* as without ceasing I remember you in my prayers night and day, [4]greatly desiring to see you, being mindful of your tears, that I may be filled with joy, [5]when I call to remembrance the genuine faith that is in you, which dwelt first in your grandmother Lois and your mother Eunice, and I am persuaded is in you also. [6]Therefore I remind you to stir up the gift of God which is in you through the laying on of my hands. [7]For God has not

1:1 [a] NU-Text and M-Text read *Christ Jesus.*

given us a spirit of fear, but of power and of love and of a sound mind.

NOT ASHAMED OF THE GOSPEL

[8]Therefore do not be ashamed of the testimony of our Lord, nor of me His prisoner, but share with me in the sufferings for the gospel according to the power of God, [9]who has saved us and called *us* with a holy calling, not according to our works, but according to His own purpose and grace which was given to us in Christ Jesus before time began, [10]but has now been revealed by the appearing of our Savior Jesus Christ, *who* has abolished death and brought life and immortality to light through the gospel, [11]to which I was appointed a preacher, an apostle, and a teacher of the Gentiles.[a] [12]For this reason I also suffer these things; nevertheless I am not ashamed, for I know whom I have believed and am persuaded that He is able to keep what I have committed to Him until that Day.

BE LOYAL TO THE FAITH

[13]Hold fast the pattern of sound words which you have heard from me, in faith and *love which are in Christ Jesus.* [14]That good thing which was committed to you, keep by the Holy Spirit who dwells in us.

[15]This you know, that all those in Asia have turned away from me, among whom are Phygellus and Hermogenes. [16]The Lord grant mercy to the household of Onesiphorus, for he often refreshed me, and was not ashamed of my chain; [17]but when he arrived in Rome, he sought me out very zealously and found *me.* [18]The Lord grant to him that he may find mercy from the Lord in that Day—and you know very well how many ways he ministered *to me*[a] at Ephesus.

BE STRONG IN GRACE

2 You therefore, my son, be strong in the grace that is in Christ Jesus. [2]And the things that you have heard from me among many witnesses, commit these to faithful men who will be able to teach others also. [3]You therefore must endure[a] hardship as a good soldier of Jesus Christ. [4]No one engaged in warfare entangles himself with the affairs of *this* life, that he may please him who enlisted him as a soldier. [5]And also if anyone competes in athletics, he is not crowned unless he competes according to the rules. [6]The hardworking farmer must be first to partake of the

1:11 [a] NU-Text omits *of the Gentiles.* 1:18 [a] *To me* is from the Vulgate and a few Greek manuscripts. 2:3 [a] NU-Text reads *You must share.*

crops. 7Consider what I say,
and may[a] the Lord give you
understanding in all things.
8Remember that Jesus
Christ, of the seed of David,
was raised from the dead according to my gospel, 9for
which I suffer trouble as an
evildoer, *even* to the point of
chains; but the word of God
is not chained. 10Therefore I
endure all things for the sake
of the elect, that they also may
obtain the salvation which is in
Christ Jesus with eternal glory.
11*This is* a faithful saying:

For if we died with *Him,*
We shall also live
with *Him.*
12 If we endure,
We shall also reign
with *Him.*
If we deny *Him,*
He also will deny us.
13 If we are faithless,
He remains faithful;
He cannot deny Himself.

APPROVED AND DISAPPROVED WORKERS

14Remind *them* of these
things, charging *them* before
the Lord not to strive about
words to no profit, to the ruin
of the hearers. 15Be diligent to
present yourself approved to
God, a worker who does not
need to be ashamed, rightly dividing the word of truth. 16But
shun profane *and* idle babblings, for they will increase
to more ungodliness. 17And
their message will spread like
cancer. Hymenaeus and Phile-
tus are of this sort, 18who have
strayed concerning the truth,
saying that the resurrection is
already past; and they overthrow the faith of some. 19Nev-
ertheless the solid foundation
of God stands, having this
seal: "The Lord knows those
who are His," and, "Let everyone who names the name of
Christ[a] depart from iniquity."
20But in a great house there
are not only vessels of gold
and silver, but also of wood
and clay, some for honor and
some for dishonor. 21There-
fore if anyone cleanses himself from the latter, he will
be a vessel for honor, sanctified and useful for the Master, prepared for every good
work. 22Flee also youthful
lusts; but pursue righteousness, faith, love, peace with
those who call on the Lord out
of a pure heart. 23But avoid
foolish and ignorant disputes,
knowing that they generate
strife. 24And a servant of the
Lord must not quarrel but be
gentle to all, able to teach, patient, 25in humility correcting
those who are in opposition, if
God perhaps will grant them
repentance, so that they may
know the truth, 26and *that*

2:7 [a] NU-Text reads *the Lord will give you.*
2:19 [a] NU-Text and M-Text read *the Lord.*

they may come to their senses
and escape the snare of the
devil, having been taken captive by him to *do* his will.

PERILOUS TIMES AND PERILOUS MEN

3 But know this, that in the
last days perilous times will
come: 2For men will be lovers
of themselves, lovers of money,
boasters, proud, blasphemers, disobedient to parents,
unthankful, unholy, 3unlov-
ing, unforgiving, slanderers,
without self-control, brutal,
despisers of good, 4traitors,
headstrong, haughty, lovers
of pleasure rather than lovers
of God, 5having a form of godliness but denying its power.
And from such people turn
away! 6For of this sort are those
who creep into households
and make captives of gullible
women loaded down with sins,
led away by various lusts, 7al-
ways learning and never able
to come to the knowledge of
the truth. 8Now as Jannes and
Jambres resisted Moses, so do
these also resist the truth: men
of corrupt minds, disapproved
concerning the faith; 9but they
will progress no further, for
their folly will be manifest to
all, as theirs also was.

THE MAN OF GOD AND THE WORD OF GOD

10But you have carefully followed my doctrine, manner of
life, purpose, faith, longsuffering, love, perseverance, 11per-
secutions, afflictions, which
happened to me at Antioch, at
Iconium, at Lystra—what persecutions I endured. And out
of *them* all the Lord delivered
me. 12Yes, and all who desire to
live godly in Christ Jesus will
suffer persecution. 13But evil
men and impostors will grow
worse and worse, deceiving
and being deceived. 14But you
must continue in the things
which you have learned and
been assured of, knowing from
whom you have learned *them,*
15and that from childhood you
have known the Holy Scriptures, which are able to make
you wise for salvation through
faith which is in Christ Jesus.

16All Scripture *is* given by
inspiration of God, and *is*
profitable for doctrine, for
reproof, for correction, for
instruction in righteous-
ness, 17that the man of God
may be complete, thoroughly
equipped for every good work.

PREACH THE WORD

4 I charge *you* therefore
before God and the Lord
Jesus Christ, who will judge
the living and the dead at[a] His
appearing and His kingdom:
2Preach the word! Be ready
in season *and* out of season.
Convince, rebuke, exhort, with
all longsuffering and teaching.
3For the time will come when

4:1 [a] NU-Text omits *therefore* and reads *and by* for *at.*

they will not endure sound
doctrine, but according to their
own desires, *because* they have
itching ears, they will heap up
for themselves teachers; [4]and
they will turn *their* ears away
from the truth, and be turned
aside to fables. [5]But you be
watchful in all things, endure
afflictions, do the work of an
evangelist, fulfill your ministry.

PAUL'S VALEDICTORY

[6]For I am already being
poured out as a drink offering,
and the time of my departure
is at hand. [7]I have fought the
good fight, I have finished the
race, I have kept the faith. [8]Fi-
nally, there is laid up for me the
crown of righteousness, which
the Lord, the righteous Judge,
will give to me on that Day, and
not to me only but also to all
who have loved His appearing.

THE ABANDONED APOSTLE

[9]Be diligent to come to
me quickly; [10]for Demas has
forsaken me, having loved
this present world, and has
departed for Thessalonica—
Crescens for Galatia, Titus for
Dalmatia. [11]Only Luke is with
me. Get Mark and bring him
with you, for he is useful to me
for ministry. [12]And Tychicus I
have sent to Ephesus. [13]Bring
the cloak that I left with Car-
pus at Troas when you come—
and the books, especially the
parchments.

[14]Alexander the copper-
smith did me much harm.
May the Lord repay him according to his works. [15]You
also must beware of him, for
he has greatly resisted our
words.

[16]At my first defense no
one stood with me, but all
forsook me. May it not be
charged against them.

THE LORD IS FAITHFUL

[17]But the Lord stood with
me and strengthened me, so
that the message might be
preached fully through me,
and *that* all the Gentiles might
hear. Also I was delivered out
of the mouth of the lion. [18]And
the Lord will deliver me from
every evil work and preserve
me for His heavenly kingdom.
To Him *be* glory forever and
ever. Amen!

COME BEFORE WINTER

[19]Greet Prisca and Aquila,
and the household of On-
esiphorus. [20]Erastus stayed
in Corinth, but Trophimus I
have left in Miletus sick.

[21]Do your utmost to come
before winter.

Eubulus greets you, as well
as Pudens, Linus, Claudia, and
all the brethren.

FAREWELL

[22]The Lord Jesus Christ[a] be
with your spirit. Grace be with
you. Amen.

4:22 [a] NU-Text omits *Jesus Christ*.

THE EPISTLE OF PAUL THE APOSTLE TO TITUS

GREETING

1 Paul, a bondservant of God and an apostle of Jesus Christ, according to the faith of God's elect and the acknowledgment of the truth which accords with godliness, 2in hope of eternal life which God, who cannot lie, promised before time began, 3but has in due time manifested His word through preaching, which was committed to me according to the commandment of God our Savior;

4To Titus, a true son in *our* common faith:

Grace, mercy, *and* peace from God the Father and the Lord Jesus Christ[a] our Savior.

QUALIFIED ELDERS

5For this reason I left you in Crete, that you should set in order the things that are lacking, and appoint elders in every city as I commanded you— 6if a man is blameless, the husband of one wife, having faithful children not accused of dissipation or insubordination. 7For a bishop[a] must be blameless, as a steward of God, not self-willed, not quick-tempered, not given to wine, not violent, not greedy for money, 8but hospitable, a lover of what is good, sober-minded, just, holy, self-controlled, 9holding fast the faithful word as he has been taught, that he may be able, by sound doctrine, both to exhort and convict those who contradict.

THE ELDERS' TASK

10For there are many insubordinate, both idle talkers and deceivers, especially those of the circumcision, 11whose mouths must be stopped, who subvert whole households, teaching things which they ought not, for the sake of dishonest gain. 12One of them, a prophet of their own, said, "Cretans *are* always liars, evil beasts, lazy gluttons." 13This testimony is true. Therefore rebuke them sharply, that they may be sound in the faith, 14not giving heed to Jewish fables and commandments of men who turn from the truth. 15To the pure all things are pure, but to those who are defiled and unbelieving nothing is pure; but even their mind and conscience are defiled. 16They profess to know God, but in works

1:4 [a] NU-Text reads *and Christ Jesus.* 1:7 [a] Literally *overseer*

they deny *Him,* being abominable, disobedient, and disqualified for every good work.

QUALITIES OF A SOUND CHURCH

2 But as for you, speak the things which are proper for sound doctrine: [2]that the older men be sober, reverent, temperate, sound in faith, in love, in patience; [3]the older women likewise, that they be reverent in behavior, not slanderers, not given to much wine, teachers of good things— [4]that they admonish the young women to love their husbands, to love their children, [5]*to be* discreet, chaste, homemakers, good, obedient to their own husbands, that the word of God may not be blasphemed.

[6]Likewise, exhort the young men to be sober-minded, [7]in all things showing yourself *to be* a pattern of good works; in doctrine *showing* integrity, reverence, incorruptibility,[a] [8]sound speech that cannot be condemned, that one who is an opponent may be ashamed, having nothing evil to say of you.[a]

[9]*Exhort* bondservants to be obedient to their own masters, to be well pleasing in all *things,* not answering back, [10]not pilfering, but showing all good fidelity, that they may adorn the doctrine of God our Savior in all things.

TRAINED BY SAVING GRACE

[11]For the grace of God that brings salvation has appeared to all men, [12]teaching us that, denying ungodliness and worldly lusts, we should live soberly, righteously, and godly in the present age, [13]looking for the blessed hope and glorious appearing of our great God and Savior Jesus Christ, [14]who gave Himself for us, that He might redeem us from every lawless deed and purify for Himself *His* own special people, zealous for good works.

[15]Speak these things, exhort, and rebuke with all authority. Let no one despise you.

GRACES OF THE HEIRS OF GRACE

3 Remind them to be subject to rulers and authorities, to obey, to be ready for every good work, [2]to speak evil of no one, to be peaceable, gentle, showing all humility to all men. [3]For we ourselves were also once foolish, disobedient, deceived, serving various lusts and pleasures, living in malice and envy, hateful and hating one another. [4]But when the kindness and the love of God our Savior toward man appeared, [5]not by works of righteousness which we have done, but according to His mercy He saved us, through the washing of regeneration and renewing

2:7 [a] NU-Text omits *incorruptibility.* **2:8** [a] NU-Text and M-Text read *us.*

of the Holy Spirit, 6whom He
poured out on us abundantly
through Jesus Christ our Savior, 7that having been justified by His grace we should
become heirs according to the
hope of eternal life.
8This is a faithful saying,
and these things I want you to
affirm constantly, that those
who have believed in God
should be careful to maintain
good works. These things are
good and profitable to men.

AVOID DISSENSION

9But avoid foolish disputes,
genealogies, contentions, and
strivings about the law; for
they are unprofitable and useless. 10Reject a divisive man
after the first and second admonition, 11knowing that such
a person is warped and sinning, being self-condemned.

FINAL MESSAGES

12When I send Artemas to
you, or Tychicus, be diligent to
come to me at Nicopolis, for
I have decided to spend the
winter there. 13Send Zenas the
lawyer and Apollos on their
journey with haste, that they
may lack nothing. 14And let
our *people* also learn to maintain good works, to *meet* urgent needs, that they may not
be unfruitful.

FAREWELL

15All who *are* with me greet
you. Greet those who love us
in the faith.

Grace *be* with you all. Amen.

THE EPISTLE OF PAUL THE APOSTLE TO PHILEMON

GREETING

Paul, a prisoner of Christ
Jesus, and Timothy *our*
brother,

To Philemon our beloved
friend and fellow laborer, 2to
the beloved[a] Apphia, Archip-
pus our fellow soldier, and to
the church in your house:

3Grace to you and peace
from God our Father and the
Lord Jesus Christ.

PHILEMON'S LOVE AND FAITH

4I thank my God, making
mention of you always in my
prayers, 5hearing of your love
and faith which you have to-

2 [a] NU-Text reads *to our sister Apphia.*

ward the Lord Jesus and toward
all the saints, [6]that the sharing
of your faith may become effective by the acknowledgment
of every good thing which is in
you[a] in Christ Jesus. [7]For we
have[a] great joy[b] and consolation in your love, because the
hearts of the saints have been
refreshed by you, brother.

THE PLEA FOR ONESIMUS

[8]Therefore, though I might
be very bold in Christ to command you what is fitting, [9]*yet*
for love's sake I rather appeal
to you—being such a one as
Paul, the aged, and now also
a prisoner of Jesus Christ—
[10]I appeal to you for my son
Onesimus, whom I have be-
gotten *while* in my chains,
[11]who once was unprofitable
to you, but now is profitable
to you and to me.

[12]I am sending him back.[a]
You therefore receive him,
that is, my own heart, [13]whom
I wished to keep with me,
that on your behalf he might
minister to me in my chains
for the gospel. [14]But without
your consent I wanted to do
nothing, that your good deed
might not be by compulsion,
as it were, but voluntary.

[15]For perhaps he departed
for a while for this *purpose,*
that you might receive him
forever, [16]no longer as a slave
but more than a slave—a beloved brother, especially to
me but how much more to
you, both in the flesh and in
the Lord.

PHILEMON'S OBEDIENCE ENCOURAGED

[17]If then you count me
as a partner, receive him as
you would me. [18]But if he has
wronged you or owes any-
thing, put that on my account.
[19]I, Paul, am writing with my
own hand. I will repay—not
to mention to you that you
owe me even your own self
besides. [20]Yes, brother, let me
have joy from you in the Lord;
refresh my heart in the Lord.

[21]Having confidence in
your obedience, I write to you,
knowing that you will do even
more than I say. [22]But, meanwhile, also prepare a guest
room for me, for I trust that
through your prayers I shall
be granted to you.

FAREWELL

[23]Epaphras, my fellow prisoner in Christ Jesus, greets
you, [24]*as do* Mark, Aristarchus,
Demas, Luke, my fellow laborers.

[25]The grace of our Lord
Jesus Christ *be* with your
spirit. Amen.

6 [a] NU-Text and M-Text read *us.* 7 [a] NU-Text reads *had.* [b] M-Text reads *thanksgiving.* 12 [a] NU-Text reads *back to you in person, that is, my own heart.*

THE EPISTLE TO THE HEBREWS

GOD'S SUPREME REVELATION

1 God, who at various times
and in various ways spoke
in time past to the fathers by
the prophets, 2has in these last
days spoken to us by *His* Son,
whom He has appointed heir
of all things, through whom
also He made the worlds;
3who being the brightness
of *His* glory and the express
image of His person, and up-
holding all things by the word
of His power, when He had
by Himself[a] purged our[b] sins,
sat down at the right hand of
the Majesty on high, 4having
become so much better than
the angels, as He has by inheritance obtained a more
excellent name than they.

THE SON EXALTED ABOVE ANGELS

5For to which of the angels
did He ever say:

"You are My Son,
Today I have
begotten You"?[a]

And again:

"I will be to Him a Father,
And He shall be to
Me a Son"?[b]

6But when He again brings
the firstborn into the world,
He says:

"Let all the angels of
God worship Him."[a]

7And of the angels He says:

"Who makes His
angels spirits
And His ministers a
flame of fire."[a]

8But to the Son *He says:*

"Your throne, O God,
is forever and ever;
A scepter of
righteousness
is the scepter of
Your kingdom.
9 You have loved
righteousness and
hated lawlessness;
Therefore God, Your God,
has anointed You
With the oil of gladness
more than Your
companions."[a]

1:3 [a] NU-Text omits *by Himself.* [b] NU-Text omits *our.* 1:5 [a] Psalm 2:7 [b] 2 Samuel 7:14 1:6 [a] Deuteronomy 32:43 (Septuagint, Dead Sea Scrolls); Psalm 97:7 1:7 [a] Psalm 104:4 1:9 [a] Psalm 45:6, 7

[10]And:

"You, LORD, in the
beginning laid the
foundation of the earth,
And the heavens are the
work of Your hands.
[11] They will perish, but
You remain;
And they will all grow
old like a garment;
[12] Like a cloak You will
fold them up,
And they will be changed.
But You are the same,
And Your years
will not fail."[a]

[13]But to which of the angels
has He ever said:

"Sit at My right hand,
Till I make Your enemies
Your footstool"?[a]

[14]Are they not all ministering
spirits sent forth to minister
for those who will inherit salvation?

DO NOT NEGLECT SALVATION

2 Therefore we must give
the more earnest heed
to the things we have heard,
lest we drift away. [2]For if the
word spoken through angels
proved steadfast, and every
transgression and disobedience received a just reward,
[3]how shall we escape if we
neglect so great a salvation,
which at the first began to be
spoken by the Lord, and was
confirmed to us by those who
heard *Him,* [4]God also bearing
witness both with signs and
wonders, with various miracles, and gifts of the Holy
Spirit, according to His own
will?

THE SON MADE LOWER THAN ANGELS

[5]For He has not put the
world to come, of which we
speak, in subjection to angels.
[6]But one testified in a certain
place, saying:

"What is man that You
are mindful of him,
Or the son of man that
You take care of him?
[7] You have made him
a little lower than
the angels;
You have crowned him
with glory and honor,[a]
And set him over the
works of Your hands.
[8] You have put all
things in subjection
under his feet."[a]

For in that He put all in subjection under him, He left
nothing *that is* not put under
him. But now we do not yet
see all things put under him.
[9]But we see Jesus, who was
made a little lower than the

1:12 [a] Psalm 102:25–27 1:13 [a] Psalm 110:1 2:7 [a] NU-Text and M-Text omit the rest of verse 7. 2:8 [a] Psalm 8:4–6

angels, for the suffering of
death crowned with glory and
honor, that He, by the grace
of God, might taste death for
everyone.

BRINGING MANY SONS TO GLORY

10For it was fitting for Him,
for whom *are* all things and
by whom *are* all things, in
bringing many sons to glory,
to make the captain of their
salvation perfect through
sufferings. 11For both He who
sanctifies and those who are
being sanctified *are* all of one,
for which reason He is not
ashamed to call them brethren, 12saying:

"I will declare Your name
to My brethren;
In the midst of the
assembly I will sing
praise to You."[a]

13And again:

"I will put My trust
in Him."[a]

And again:

"Here am I and the
children whom God
has given Me."[b]

14Inasmuch then as the
children have partaken of
flesh and blood, He Himself
likewise shared in the same,
that through death He might
destroy him who had the
power of death, that is, the
devil, 15and release those who
through fear of death were all
their lifetime subject to bondage. 16For indeed He does not
give aid to angels, but He does
give aid to the seed of Abraham. 17Therefore, in all things
He had to be made like *His*
brethren, that He might be
a merciful and faithful High
Priest in things *pertaining* to
God, to make propitiation for
the sins of the people. 18For in
that He Himself has suffered,
being tempted, He is able to
aid those who are tempted.

THE SON WAS FAITHFUL

3 Therefore, holy brethren,
partakers of the heavenly
calling, consider the Apostle
and High Priest of our confession, Christ Jesus, 2who was
faithful to Him who appointed
Him, as Moses also *was faithful* in all His house. 3For this
One has been counted worthy
of more glory than Moses, inasmuch as He who built the
house has more honor than
the house. 4For every house is
built by someone, but He who
built all things *is* God. 5And
Moses indeed *was* faithful in
all His house as a servant, for
a testimony of those things
which would be spoken *afterward*, 6but Christ as a Son over
His own house, whose house

2:12 [a] Psalm 22:22 2:13 [a] 2 Samuel 22:3; Isaiah 8:17 [b] Isaiah 8:18

we are if we hold fast the confidence and the rejoicing of
the hope firm to the end.[a]

BE FAITHFUL

7 Therefore, as the Holy
Spirit says:

"Today, if you will
hear His voice,
8 Do not harden your hearts
as in the rebellion,
In the day of trial in
the wilderness,
9 Where your fathers
tested Me, tried Me,
And saw My works
forty years.
10 Therefore I was angry
with that generation,
And said, 'They always go
astray in *their* heart,
And they have not
known My ways.'
11 So I swore in My wrath,
'They shall not
enter My rest.'"[a]

12 Beware, brethren, lest
there be in any of you an evil
heart of unbelief in departing
from the living God; 13 but exhort one another daily, while
it is called "Today," lest any
of you be hardened through
the deceitfulness of sin. 14 For
we have become partakers of
Christ if we hold the beginning
of our confidence steadfast to
the end, 15 while it is said:

"Today, if you will
hear His voice,
Do not harden your
hearts as in the
rebellion."[a]

FAILURE OF THE WILDERNESS WANDERERS

16 For who, having heard,
rebelled? Indeed, *was it* not
all who came out of Egypt, *led*
by Moses? 17 Now with whom
was He angry forty years? *Was
it* not with those who sinned,
whose corpses fell in the wilderness? 18 And to whom did
He swear that they would not
enter His rest, but to those
who did not obey? 19 So we see
that they could not enter in
because of unbelief.

THE PROMISE OF REST

4 Therefore, since a promise
remains of entering His
rest, let us fear lest any of you
seem to have come short of
it. 2 For indeed the gospel was
preached to us as well as to
them; but the word which they
heard did not profit them,[a]
not being mixed with faith in
those who heard *it.* 3 For we
who have believed do enter
that rest, as He has said:

"So I swore in My wrath,
'They shall not
enter My rest,'"[a]

3:6 [a] NU-Text omits *firm to the end.* 3:11 [a] Psalm 95:7–11 3:15 [a] Psalm 95:7, 8 4:2 [a] NU-Text and M-Text read *profit them, since they were not united by faith with those who heeded it.* 4:3 [a] Psalm 95:11

although the works were finished from the foundation of
the world. 4For He has spoken in a certain place of the
seventh *day* in this way: "And
God rested on the seventh day
from all His works";[a] 5and
again in this *place:* "They shall
not enter My rest."[a]

6Since therefore it remains
that some *must* enter it, and
those to whom it was first
preached did not enter because of disobedience, 7again
He designates a certain day,
saying in David, "Today," after
such a long time, as it has
been said:

"Today, if you will
hear His voice,
Do not harden
your hearts."[a]

8For if Joshua had given
them rest, then He would
not afterward have spoken of
another day. 9There remains
therefore a rest for the people of God. 10For he who has
entered His rest has himself
also ceased from his works as
God *did* from His.

THE WORD DISCOVERS OUR CONDITION

11Let us therefore be diligent
to enter that rest, lest anyone
fall according to the same example of disobedience. 12For
the word of God *is* living and
powerful, and sharper than
any two-edged sword, pierc-
ing even to the division of soul
and spirit, and of joints and
marrow, and is a discerner of
the thoughts and intents of the
heart. 13And there is no creature hidden from His sight, but
all things *are* naked and open
to the eyes of Him to whom
we *must give* account.

OUR COMPASSIONATE HIGH PRIEST

14Seeing then that we have
a great High Priest who has
passed through the heavens,
Jesus the Son of God, let us
hold fast *our* confession. 15For
we do not have a High Priest
who cannot sympathize with
our weaknesses, but was in
all *points* tempted as *we are,*
yet without sin. 16Let us therefore come boldly to the throne
of grace, that we may obtain
mercy and find grace to help
in time of need.

QUALIFICATIONS FOR HIGH PRIESTHOOD

5 For every high priest taken
from among men is ap-
pointed for men in things
pertaining to God, that he
may offer both gifts and sacrifices for sins. 2He can have
compassion on those who are
ignorant and going astray,
since he himself is also subject to weakness. 3Because of
this he is required as for the
people, so also for himself, to

4:4 [a] Genesis 2:2 4:5 [a] Psalm 95:11 4:7 [a] Psalm 95:7, 8

offer *sacrifices* for sins. [4]And no man takes this honor to himself, but he who is called by God, just as Aaron *was.*

A PRIEST FOREVER

[5]So also Christ did not glorify Himself to become High Priest, but *it was* He who said to Him:

"You are My Son,
Today I have
begotten You."[a]

[6]As *He* also says in another *place:*

"You *are* a priest forever
According to the order
of Melchizedek";[a]

[7]who, in the days of His flesh, when He had offered up prayers and supplications, with vehement cries and tears to Him who was able to save Him from death, and was heard because of His godly fear, [8]though He was a Son, *yet* He learned obedience by the things which He suffered. [9]And having been perfected, He became the author of eternal salvation to all who obey Him, [10]called by God as High Priest "according to the order of Melchizedek," [11]of whom we have much to say, and hard to explain, since you have become dull of hearing.

SPIRITUAL IMMATURITY

[12]For though by this time you ought to be teachers, you need *someone* to teach you again the first principles of the oracles of God; and you have come to need milk and not solid food. [13]For everyone who partakes *only* of milk *is* unskilled in the word of righteousness, for he is a babe. [14]But solid food belongs to those who are of full age, *that is,* those who by reason of use have their senses exercised to discern both good and evil.

THE PERIL OF NOT PROGRESSING

6 Therefore, leaving the discussion of the elementary *principles* of Christ, let us go on to perfection, not laying again the foundation of repentance from dead works and of faith toward God, [2]of the doctrine of baptisms, of laying on of hands, of resurrection of the dead, and of eternal judgment. [3]And this we will[a] do if God permits.

[4]For *it is* impossible for those who were once enlightened, and have tasted the heavenly gift, and have become partakers of the Holy Spirit, [5]and have tasted the good word of God and the powers of the age to come, [6]if they fall away,[a] to renew them again to repentance, since

5:5 [a] Psalm 2:7 5:6 [a] Psalm 110:4 6:3 [a] M-Text reads *let us do.* 6:6 [a] Or *and have fallen away*

they crucify again for themselves the Son of God, and put *Him* to an open shame.

7For the earth which drinks in the rain that often comes upon it, and bears herbs useful for those by whom it is cultivated, receives blessing from God; 8but if it bears thorns and briers, *it is* rejected and near to being cursed, whose end *is* to be burned.

A BETTER ESTIMATE

9But, beloved, we are confident of better things concerning you, yes, things that accompany salvation, though we speak in this manner. 10For God *is* not unjust to forget your work and labor of[a] love which you have shown toward His name, *in that* you have ministered to the saints, and do minister. 11And we desire that each one of you show the same diligence to the full assurance of hope until the end, 12that you do not become sluggish, but imitate those who through faith and patience inherit the promises.

GOD'S INFALLIBLE PURPOSE IN CHRIST

13For when God made a promise to Abraham, because He could swear by no one greater, He swore by Himself, 14saying, "Surely blessing I will bless you, and multiplying I will multiply you."[a] 15And so, after he had patiently endured, he obtained the promise. 16For men indeed swear by the greater, and an oath for confirmation *is* for them an end of all dispute. 17Thus God, determining to show more abundantly to the heirs of promise the immutability of His counsel, confirmed *it* by an oath, 18that by two immutable things, in which it *is* impossible for God to lie, we might[a] have strong consolation, who have fled for refuge to lay hold of the hope set before *us.*

19This *hope* we have as an anchor of the soul, both sure and steadfast, and which enters the *Presence* behind the veil, 20where the forerunner has entered for us, *even* Jesus, having become High Priest forever according to the order of Melchizedek.

THE KING OF RIGHTEOUSNESS

7 For this Melchizedek, king of Salem, priest of the Most High God, who met Abraham returning from the slaughter of the kings and blessed him, 2to whom also Abraham gave a tenth part of all, first being translated "king of righteousness," and then also king of Salem, meaning "king of peace," 3without father, without mother, without

6:10 [a] NU-Text omits *labor of.* 6:14 [a] Genesis 22:17 6:18 [a] M-Text omits *might.*

genealogy, having neither beginning of days nor end of life,
but made like the Son of God,
remains a priest continually.
4Now consider how great
this man *was,* to whom even
the patriarch Abraham gave
a tenth of the spoils. 5And indeed those who are of the sons
of Levi, who receive the priesthood, have a commandment
to receive tithes from the people according to the law, that
is, from their brethren, though
they have come from the loins
of Abraham; 6but he whose
genealogy is not derived from
them received tithes from
Abraham and blessed him
who had the promises. 7Now
beyond all contradiction the
lesser is blessed by the better. 8Here mortal men receive
tithes, but there he *receives
them,* of whom it is witnessed
that he lives. 9Even Levi, who
receives tithes, paid tithes
through Abraham, so to speak,
10for he was still in the loins of
his father when Melchizedek
met him.

NEED FOR A NEW PRIESTHOOD

11Therefore, if perfection
were through the Levitical
priesthood (for under it the
people received the law),
what further need *was there*
that another priest should
rise according to the order
of Melchizedek, and not be
called according to the order
of Aaron? 12For the priesthood
being changed, of necessity
there is also a change of the
law. 13For He of whom these
things are spoken belongs to
another tribe, from which no
man has officiated at the altar.
14For *it is* evident that
our Lord arose from Judah,
of which tribe Moses spoke
nothing concerning priesthood.[a] 15And it is yet far more
evident if, in the likeness of
Melchizedek, there arises another priest 16who has come,
not according to the law of a
fleshly commandment, but
according to the power of an
endless life. 17For He testifies:[a]

"You *are* a priest forever
According to the order
of Melchizedek."[b]

18For on the one hand there
is an annulling of the former
commandment because of its
weakness and unprofitable-
ness, 19for the law made nothing perfect; on the other hand,
there is the bringing in of a
better hope, through which
we draw near to God.

GREATNESS OF THE NEW PRIEST

20And inasmuch as *He was*
not *made priest* without an
oath 21(for they have become

7:14 [a] NU-Text reads *priests.* 7:17 [a] NU-Text reads *it is testified.* [b] Psalm 110:4

priests without an oath, but He with an oath by Him who said to Him:

"The LORD has sworn
And will not relent,
'You *are* a priest forever[a]
According to the order
of Melchizedek'"),[b]

22by so much more Jesus has become a surety of a better covenant.
23Also there were many priests, because they were prevented by death from
continuing. 24But He, because He continues forever, has an unchangeable priesthood.
25Therefore He is also able to save to the uttermost those who come to God through Him, since He always lives to make intercession for them.
26For such a High Priest was fitting for us, *who is* holy, harmless, undefiled, separate from sinners, and has become higher than the heavens;
27who does not need daily, as those high priests, to offer up sacrifices, first for His own sins and then for the people's, for this He did once for all when He offered up Himself.
28For the law appoints as high priests men who have weakness, but the word of the oath, which came after the law, *appoints* the Son who has been perfected forever.

THE NEW PRIESTLY SERVICE

8 Now *this is* the main point of the things we are saying: We have such a High Priest, who is seated at the right hand of the throne of the Majesty in the heavens,
2a Minister of the sanctuary and of the true tabernacle which the Lord erected, and not man.
3For every high priest is appointed to offer both gifts and sacrifices. Therefore *it is* necessary that this One also have something to offer. 4For
if He were on earth, He would not be a priest, since there are priests who offer the gifts according to the law; 5who serve
the copy and shadow of the heavenly things, as Moses was divinely instructed when he was about to make the tabernacle. For He said, "See *that* you make all things according to the pattern shown you on the mountain."[a] 6But now He
has obtained a more excellent ministry, inasmuch as He is also Mediator of a better covenant, which was established on better promises.

A NEW COVENANT

7For if that first *covenant* had been faultless, then no place would have been sought for a second. 8Because finding
fault with them, He says: "Be-

7:21 [a] NU-Text ends the quotation here. [b] Psalm 110:4 8:5 [a] Exodus 25:40

hold, the days are coming, says the LORD, when I will make a new covenant with the house of Israel and with the house of Judah— 9not according to the covenant that I made with their fathers in the day when I took them by the hand to lead them out of the land of Egypt; because they did not continue in My covenant, and I disregarded them, says the LORD. 10For this *is* the covenant that I will make with the house of Israel after those days, says the LORD: I will put My laws in their mind and write them on their hearts; and I will be their God, and they shall be My people. 11None of them shall teach his neighbor, and none his brother, saying, 'Know the LORD,' for all shall know Me, from the least of them to the greatest of them. 12For I will be merciful to their unrighteousness, and their sins and their lawless deeds[a] I will remember no more."[b]

13In that He says, "A new *covenant*," He has made the first obsolete. Now what is becoming obsolete and growing old is ready to vanish away.

THE EARTHLY SANCTUARY

9 Then indeed, even the first *covenant* had ordinances of divine service and the earthly sanctuary. 2For a tabernacle was prepared: the first *part*, in which *was* the lampstand, the table, and the showbread, which is called the sanctuary; 3and behind the second veil, the part of the tabernacle which is called the Holiest of All, 4which had the golden censer and the ark of the covenant overlaid on all sides with gold, in which *were* the golden pot that had the manna, Aaron's rod that budded, and the tablets of the covenant; 5and above it were the cherubim of glory overshadowing the mercy seat. Of these things we cannot now speak in detail.

LIMITATIONS OF THE EARTHLY SERVICE

6Now when these things had been thus prepared, the priests always went into the first part of the tabernacle, performing the services. 7But into the second part the high priest *went* alone once a year, not without blood, which he offered for himself and *for* the people's sins *committed* in ignorance; 8the Holy Spirit indicating this, that the way into the Holiest of All was not yet made manifest while the first tabernacle was still standing. 9It *was* symbolic for the present time in which both gifts and sacrifices are offered which cannot make him who performed the service perfect in regard to the conscience—10*concerned*

8:12 [a] NU-Text omits *and their lawless deeds.* [b] Jeremiah 31:31–34

only with foods and drinks, various washings, and fleshly ordinances imposed until the time of reformation.

THE HEAVENLY SANCTUARY

11 But Christ came *as* High Priest of the good things to come,[a] with the greater and more perfect tabernacle not made with hands, that is, not of this creation. 12 Not with the blood of goats and calves, but with His own blood He entered the Most Holy Place once for all, having obtained eternal redemption. 13 For if the blood of bulls and goats and the ashes of a heifer, sprinkling the unclean, sanctifies for the purifying of the flesh, 14 how much more shall the blood of Christ, who through the eternal Spirit offered Himself without spot to God, cleanse your conscience from dead works to serve the living God? 15 And for this reason He is the Mediator of the new covenant, by means of death, for the redemption of the transgressions under the first covenant, that those who are called may receive the promise of the eternal inheritance.

THE MEDIATOR'S DEATH NECESSARY

16 For where there *is* a testament, there must also of necessity be the death of the testator. 17 For a testament *is* in force after men are dead, since it has no power at all while the testator lives. 18 Therefore not even the first *covenant* was dedicated without blood. 19 For when Moses had spoken every precept to all the people according to the law, he took the blood of calves and goats, with water, scarlet wool, and hyssop, and sprinkled both the book itself and all the people, 20 saying, "This *is* the blood of the covenant which God has commanded you."[a] 21 Then likewise he sprinkled with blood both the tabernacle and all the vessels of the ministry. 22 And according to the law almost all things are purified with blood, and without shedding of blood there is no remission.

GREATNESS OF CHRIST'S SACRIFICE

23 Therefore *it was* necessary that the copies of the things in the heavens should be purified with these, but the heavenly things themselves with better sacrifices than these. 24 For Christ has not entered the holy places made with hands, *which are* copies of the true, but into heaven itself, now to appear in the presence of God for us; 25 not that He should offer Himself often, as the high priest enters

9:11 [a] NU-Text reads *that have come.* 9:20 [a] Exodus 24:8

the Most Holy Place every year
with blood of another— 26He
then would have had to suffer
often since the foundation of
the world; but now, once at the
end of the ages, He has appeared to put away sin by the
sacrifice of Himself. 27And as
it is appointed for men to die
once, but after this the judgment, 28so Christ was offered
once to bear the sins of many.
To those who eagerly wait for
Him He will appear a second
time, apart from sin, for salvation.

ANIMAL SACRIFICES INSUFFICIENT

10 For the law, having a
shadow of the good
things to come, *and* not the
very image of the things, can
never with these same sacrifices, which they offer continually year by year, make
those who approach perfect.
2For then would they not have
ceased to be offered? For the
worshipers, once purified,
would have had no more
consciousness of sins. 3But
in those *sacrifices there is* a
reminder of sins every year.
4For *it is* not possible that the
blood of bulls and goats could
take away sins.

CHRIST'S DEATH FULFILLS GOD'S WILL

5Therefore, when He came
into the world, He said:

"Sacrifice and offering
You did not desire,
But a body You have
prepared for Me.
6 In burnt offerings and
sacrifices for sin
You had no pleasure.
7 Then I said, 'Behold,
I have come—
In the volume of the
book it is written
of Me—
To do Your will, O God.' "[a]

8Previously saying, "Sacrifice
and offering, burnt offerings,
and *offerings* for sin You did
not desire, nor had pleasure
in them" (which are offered
according to the law), 9then
He said, "Behold, I have come
to do Your will, O God."[a] He
takes away the first that He
may establish the second. 10By
that will we have been sanctified through the offering of
the body of Jesus Christ once
for all.

CHRIST'S DEATH PERFECTS THE SANCTIFIED

11And every priest stands
ministering daily and offering repeatedly the same sacrifices, which can never take
away sins. 12But this Man, after
He had offered one sacrifice
for sins forever, sat down at
the right hand of God, 13from
that time waiting till His enemies are made His footstool.
14For by one offering He has

10:7 [a] Psalm 40:6–8 10:9 [a] NU-Text and M-Text omit *O God.*

perfected forever those who
are being sanctified.
15But the Holy Spirit also
witnesses to us; for after He
had said before,
16"This *is* the covenant that
I will make with them after
those days, says the LORD:
I will put My laws into their
hearts, and in their minds I
will write them,"[a] 17*then He
adds,* "Their sins and their
lawless deeds I will remember
no more."[a] 18Now where there
is remission of these, *there is*
no longer an offering for sin.

HOLD FAST YOUR CONFESSION

19Therefore, brethren, having boldness to enter the Holiest by the blood of Jesus, 20by
a new and living way which He
consecrated for us, through
the veil, that is, His flesh, 21and
having a High Priest over the
house of God, 22let us draw
near with a true heart in full
assurance of faith, having our
hearts sprinkled from an evil
conscience and our bodies
washed with pure water. 23Let
us hold fast the confession
of *our* hope without waver-
ing, for He who promised *is*
faithful. 24And let us consider
one another in order to stir
up love and good works, 25not
forsaking the assembling of
ourselves together, as *is* the
manner of some, but exhorting *one another,* and so much
the more as you see the Day
approaching.

THE JUST LIVE BY FAITH

26For if we sin willfully
after we have received the
knowledge of the truth, there
no longer remains a sacrifice
for sins, 27but a certain fearful expectation of judgment,
and fiery indignation which
will devour the adversaries.
28Anyone who has rejected
Moses' law dies without
mercy on *the testimony of*
two or three witnesses. 29Of
how much worse punish-
ment, do you suppose, will
he be thought worthy who
has trampled the Son of God
underfoot, counted the blood
of the covenant by which he
was sanctified a common
thing, and insulted the Spirit
of grace? 30For we know Him
who said, "Vengeance is Mine,
I will repay,"[a] says the Lord.[b]
And again, "The LORD will
judge His people."[c] 31It is a
fearful thing to fall into the
hands of the living God.
32But recall the former
days in which, after you were
illuminated, you endured a
great struggle with sufferings: 33partly while you were
made a spectacle both by reproaches and tribulations,
and partly while you became
companions of those who

10:16 [a] Jeremiah 31:33 **10:17** [a] Jeremiah 31:34 **10:30** [a] Deuteronomy 32:35 [b] NU-Text omits *says the Lord.* [c] Deuteronomy 32:36

were so treated; 34for you had
compassion on me[a] in my
chains, and joyfully accepted
the plundering of your goods,
knowing that you have a better
and an enduring possession
for yourselves in heaven.[b]
35Therefore do not cast away
your confidence, which has
great reward. 36For you have
need of endurance, so that
after you have done the will
of God, you may receive the
promise:

37"For yet a little while,
And He[a] who is
coming will come
and will not tarry.
38 Now the[a] just shall
live by faith;
But if *anyone* draws
back,
My soul has no
pleasure in him."[b]

39But we are not of those who
draw back to perdition, but
of those who believe to the
saving of the soul.

BY FAITH WE UNDERSTAND

11 Now faith is the substance
of things hoped for, the
evidence of things not seen.
2For by it the elders obtained
a *good* testimony.
3By faith we understand
that the worlds were framed
by the word of God, so that the
things which are seen were
not made of things which are
visible.

FAITH AT THE DAWN OF HISTORY

4By faith Abel offered to
God a more excellent sacrifice than Cain, through which
he obtained witness that he
was righteous, God testifying
of his gifts; and through it he
being dead still speaks.
5By faith Enoch was taken
away so that he did not see
death, "and was not found, because God had taken him";[a]
for before he was taken he had
this testimony, that he pleased
God. 6But without faith *it is*
impossible to please *Him*, for
he who comes to God must
believe that He is, and *that* He
is a rewarder of those who diligently seek Him.
7By faith Noah, being di-
vinely warned of things not
yet seen, moved with godly
fear, prepared an ark for the
saving of his household, by
which he condemned the
world and became heir of
the righteousness which is
according to faith.

FAITHFUL ABRAHAM

8By faith Abraham obeyed
when he was called to go out
to the place which he would
receive as an inheritance.

10:34 [a] NU-Text reads *the prisoners* instead of *me in my chains.* [b] NU-Text omits *in heaven.* 10:37 [a] Or *that which* 10:38 [a] NU-Text reads *My just one.* [b] Habakkuk 2:3, 4 11:5 [a] Genesis 5:24

And he went out, not knowing
where he was going. 9By faith
he dwelt in the land of promise as *in* a foreign country,
dwelling in tents with Isaac
and Jacob, the heirs with him
of the same promise; 10for he
waited for the city which has
foundations, whose builder
and maker *is* God.
11By faith Sarah herself also
received strength to conceive
seed, and she bore a child[a]
when she was past the age, because she judged Him faithful
who had promised. 12There-
fore from one man, and him
as good as dead, were born *as*
many as the stars of the sky
in multitude—innumerable
as the sand which is by the
seashore.

THE HEAVENLY HOPE

13These all died in faith, not
having received the promises,
but having seen them afar off
were assured of them,[a] embraced *them* and confessed
that they were strangers and
pilgrims on the earth. 14For
those who say such things declare plainly that they seek a
homeland. 15And truly if they
had called to mind that *coun-*
try from which they had come
out, they would have had opportunity to return. 16But now
they desire a better, that is, a
heavenly *country.* Therefore
God is not ashamed to be
called their God, for He has
prepared a city for them.

THE FAITH OF THE PATRIARCHS

17By faith Abraham, when
he was tested, offered up Isaac,
and he who had received the
promises offered up his only
begotten *son,* 18of whom it
was said, "In Isaac your seed
shall be called,"[a] 19concluding
that God *was* able to raise *him*
up, even from the dead, from
which he also received him in
a figurative sense.
20By faith Isaac blessed
Jacob and Esau concerning
things to come.
21By faith Jacob, when he
was dying, blessed each of
the sons of Joseph, and worshiped, *leaning* on the top of
his staff.
22By faith Joseph, when he
was dying, made mention of
the departure of the children
of Israel, and gave instructions concerning his bones.

THE FAITH OF MOSES

23By faith Moses, when he
was born, was hidden three
months by his parents, because they saw *he was* a beautiful child; and they were not
afraid of the king's command.
24By faith Moses, when he
became of age, refused to be
called the son of Pharaoh's
daughter, 25choosing rather

11:11 [a] NU-Text omits *she bore a child.* **11:13** [a] NU-Text and M-Text omit *were assured of them.* **11:18** [a] Genesis 21:12

to suffer affliction with the
people of God than to enjoy
the passing pleasures of sin,
26esteeming the reproach of
Christ greater riches than the
treasures in[a] Egypt; for he
looked to the reward.

27By faith he forsook Egypt,
not fearing the wrath of the
king; for he endured as seeing Him who is invisible. 28By
faith he kept the Passover and
the sprinkling of blood, lest he
who destroyed the firstborn
should touch them.

29By faith they passed
through the Red Sea as by dry
land, whereas the Egyptians,
attempting to do so, were
drowned.

BY FAITH THEY OVERCAME

30By faith the walls of Jericho fell down after they were
encircled for seven days. 31By
faith the harlot Rahab did not
perish with those who did
not believe, when she had
received the spies with peace.

32And what more shall I
say? For the time would fail
me to tell of Gideon and Barak
and Samson and Jephthah,
also *of* David and Samuel and
the prophets: 33who through
faith subdued kingdoms,
worked righteousness, ob-
tained promises, stopped the
mouths of lions, 34quenched
the violence of fire, escaped
the edge of the sword, out of
weakness were made strong,
became valiant in battle,
turned to flight the armies of
the aliens. 35Women received
their dead raised to life again.

Others were tortured, not
accepting deliverance, that
they might obtain a better
resurrection. 36Still others
had trial of mockings and
scourgings, yes, and of chains
and imprisonment. 37They
were stoned, they were sawn
in two, were tempted,[a] were
slain with the sword. They
wandered about in sheepskins
and goatskins, being destitute, afflicted, tormented—
38of whom the world was not
worthy. They wandered in deserts and mountains, *in* dens
and caves of the earth.

39And all these, having
obtained a good testimony
through faith, did not receive
the promise, 40God having
provided something better
for us, that they should not be
made perfect apart from us.

THE RACE OF FAITH

12 Therefore we also, since
we are surrounded by
so great a cloud of witnesses,
let us lay aside every weight,
and the sin which so easily
ensnares *us,* and let us run
with endurance the race that
is set before us, 2looking unto
Jesus, the author and finisher
of *our* faith, who for the joy

11:26 [a] NU-Text and M-Text read *of.* 11:37 [a] NU-Text omits *were tempted.*

that was set before Him endured the cross, despising the
shame, and has sat down at
the right hand of the throne
of God.

THE DISCIPLINE OF GOD

3For consider Him who en-
dured such hostility from sinners against Himself, lest you
become weary and discour-
aged in your souls. 4You have
not yet resisted to bloodshed,
striving against sin. 5And you
have forgotten the exhortation which speaks to you as
to sons:

"My son, do not despise
the chastening
of the LORD,
Nor be discouraged
when you are
rebuked by Him;
6 For whom the LORD
loves He chastens,
And scourges every son
whom He receives."[a]

7If[a] you endure chastening, God deals with you as
with sons; for what son is
there whom a father does not
chasten? 8But if you are without chastening, of which all
have become partakers, then
you are illegitimate and not
sons. 9Furthermore, we have
had human fathers who corrected *us,* and we paid *them*
respect. Shall we not much
more readily be in subjection to the Father of spirits
and live? 10For they indeed
for a few days chastened *us*
as seemed *best* to them, but
He for *our* profit, that *we* may
be partakers of His holiness.
11Now no chastening seems to
be joyful for the present, but
painful; nevertheless, afterward it yields the peaceable
fruit of righteousness to those
who have been trained by it.

RENEW YOUR SPIRITUAL VITALITY

12Therefore strengthen the
hands which hang down, and
the feeble knees, 13and make
straight paths for your feet,
so that what is lame may not
be dislocated, but rather be
healed.

14Pursue peace with all
people, and holiness, without which no one will see the
Lord: 15looking carefully lest
anyone fall short of the grace
of God; lest any root of bitterness springing up cause
trouble, and by this many
become defiled; 16lest there
be any fornicator or profane
person like Esau, who for one
morsel of food sold his birthright. 17For you know that afterward, when he wanted to
inherit the blessing, he was
rejected, for he found no place
for repentance, though he
sought it diligently with tears.

12:6 [a] Proverbs 3:11, 12 12:7 [a] NU-Text and M-Text read *It is for discipline that you endure; God . . . .*

THE GLORIOUS COMPANY

18For you have not come to the mountain that[a] may be touched and that burned with fire, and to blackness and darkness[b] and tempest, 19and the sound of a trumpet and the voice of words, so that those who heard *it* begged that the word should not be spoken to them anymore. 20(For they could not endure what was commanded: "And if so much as a beast touches the mountain, it shall be stoned[a] or shot with an arrow."[b] 21And so terrifying was the sight *that* Moses said, "I am exceedingly afraid and trembling."[a])

22But you have come to Mount Zion and to the city of the living God, the heavenly Jerusalem, to an innumerable company of angels, 23to the general assembly and church of the firstborn *who are* registered in heaven, to God the Judge of all, to the spirits of just men made perfect, 24to Jesus the Mediator of the new covenant, and to the blood of sprinkling that speaks better things than *that of* Abel.

HEAR THE HEAVENLY VOICE

25See that you do not refuse Him who speaks. For if they did not escape who refused Him who spoke on earth, much more *shall we not escape* if we turn away from Him who *speaks* from heaven, 26whose voice then shook the earth; but now He has promised, saying, "Yet once more I shake[a] not only the earth, but also heaven."[b] 27Now this, "Yet once more," indicates the removal of those things that are being shaken, as of things that are made, that the things which cannot be shaken may remain.

28Therefore, since we are receiving a kingdom which cannot be shaken, let us have grace, by which we may[a] serve God acceptably with reverence and godly fear. 29For our God *is* a consuming fire.

CONCLUDING MORAL DIRECTIONS

13 Let brotherly love continue. 2Do not forget to entertain strangers, for by so *doing* some have unwittingly entertained angels. 3Remember the prisoners as if chained with them—those who are mistreated—since you yourselves are in the body also.

4Marriage *is* honorable among all, and the bed undefiled; but fornicators and adulterers God will judge.

5*Let your* conduct *be* without covetousness; *be* content with such things as you have.

12:18 [a] NU-Text reads *to that which.* [b] NU-Text reads *gloom.* 12:20 [a] NU-Text and M-Text omit the rest of this verse. [b] Exodus 19:12, 13 12:21 [a] Deuteronomy 9:19 12:26 [a] NU-Text reads *will shake.* [b] Haggai 2:6 12:28 [a] M-Text omits *may.*

For He Himself has said, "I will
never leave you nor forsake
you."[a] 6So we may boldly say:

"The LORD *is* my helper;
I will not fear.
What can man
do to me?"[a]

CONCLUDING RELIGIOUS DIRECTIONS

7Remember those who rule
over you, who have spoken
the word of God to you, whose
faith follow, considering the
outcome of *their* conduct.
8Jesus Christ *is* the same yesterday, today, and forever. 9Do
not be carried about[a] with
various and strange doctrines.
For *it is* good that the heart be
established by grace, not with
foods which have not profited
those who have been occupied
with them.

10We have an altar from
which those who serve the
tabernacle have no right to
eat. 11For the bodies of those
animals, whose blood is
brought into the sanctuary
by the high priest for sin, are
burned outside the camp.
12Therefore Jesus also, that
He might sanctify the people
with His own blood, suffered
outside the gate. 13Therefore
let us go forth to Him, outside the camp, bearing His reproach. 14For here we have no
continuing city, but we seek
the one to come. 15Therefore
by Him let us continually offer
the sacrifice of praise to God,
that is, the fruit of *our* lips,
giving thanks to His name.
16But do not forget to do good
and to share, for with such
sacrifices God is well pleased.

17Obey those who rule over
you, and be submissive, for
they watch out for your souls,
as those who must give account. Let them do so with
joy and not with grief, for that
would be unprofitable for you.

PRAYER REQUESTED

18Pray for us; for we are
confident that we have a good
conscience, in all things desiring to live honorably. 19But I
especially urge *you* to do this,
that I may be restored to you
the sooner.

BENEDICTION, FINAL EXHORTATION, FAREWELL

20Now may the God of peace
who brought up our Lord Jesus
from the dead, that great Shepherd of the sheep, through the
blood of the everlasting covenant, 21make you complete in
every good work to do His will,
working in you[a] what is well
pleasing in His sight, through
Jesus Christ, to whom *be* glory
forever and ever. Amen.

22And I appeal to you,
brethren, bear with the word
of exhortation, for I have

13:5 [a] Deuteronomy 31:6, 8; Joshua 1:5 13:6 [a] Psalm 118:6 13:9 [a] NU-Text and M-Text read *away.* 13:21 [a] NU-Text and M-Text read *us.*

written to you in few words.
23Know that *our* brother Timothy has been set free, with
whom I shall see you if he
comes shortly.
24Greet all those who rule
over you, and all the saints.
Those from Italy greet you.
25Grace *be* with you all.
Amen.

THE EPISTLE OF JAMES

GREETING TO THE TWELVE TRIBES

1 James, a bondservant of
God and of the Lord Jesus
Christ,

To the twelve tribes which
are scattered abroad:

Greetings.

PROFITING FROM TRIALS

2My brethren, count it all
joy when you fall into various trials, 3knowing that the
testing of your faith produces
patience. 4But let patience
have *its* perfect work, that you
may be perfect and complete,
lacking nothing. 5If any of you
lacks wisdom, let him ask of
God, who gives to all liberally
and without reproach, and
it will be given to him. 6But
let him ask in faith, with no
doubting, for he who doubts
is like a wave of the sea driven
and tossed by the wind. 7For
let not that man suppose
that he will receive anything
from the Lord; 8*he is* a double-
minded man, unstable in all
his ways.

THE PERSPECTIVE OF RICH AND POOR

9Let the lowly brother glory
in his exaltation, 10but the rich
in his humiliation, because
as a flower of the field he will
pass away. 11For no sooner has
the sun risen with a burning
heat than it withers the grass;
its flower falls, and its beautiful appearance perishes. So
the rich man also will fade
away in his pursuits.

LOVING GOD UNDER TRIALS

12Blessed *is* the man who
endures temptation; for when
he has been approved, he will
receive the crown of life which
the Lord has promised to
those who love Him. 13Let no
one say when he is tempted,
"I am tempted by God"; for
God cannot be tempted by
evil, nor does He Himself

tempt anyone. 14But each one
is tempted when he is drawn
away by his own desires and
enticed. 15Then, when desire
has conceived, it gives birth
to sin; and sin, when it is full-
grown, brings forth death.

16Do not be deceived, my
beloved brethren. 17Every good
gift and every perfect gift is
from above, and comes down
from the Father of lights, with
whom there is no variation or
shadow of turning. 18Of His
own will He brought us forth
by the word of truth, that we
might be a kind of firstfruits
of His creatures.

QUALITIES NEEDED IN TRIALS

19So then,[a] my beloved
brethren, let every man be
swift to hear, slow to speak,
slow to wrath; 20for the wrath
of man does not produce the
righteousness of God.

DOERS—NOT HEARERS ONLY

21Therefore lay aside all
filthiness and overflow of
wickedness, and receive with
meekness the implanted
word, which is able to save
your souls.

22But be doers of the word,
and not hearers only, deceiving yourselves. 23For if anyone
is a hearer of the word and
not a doer, he is like a man
observing his natural face in
a mirror; 24for he observes
himself, goes away, and immediately forgets what kind
of man he was. 25But he who
looks into the perfect law of
liberty and continues *in it,* and
is not a forgetful hearer but a
doer of the work, this one will
be blessed in what he does.

26If anyone among you[a]
thinks he is religious, and does
not bridle his tongue but deceives his own heart, this one's
religion *is* useless. 27Pure and
undefiled religion before God
and the Father is this: to visit
orphans and widows in their
trouble, *and* to keep oneself
unspotted from the world.

BEWARE OF PERSONAL FAVORITISM

2 My brethren, do not hold
the faith of our Lord Jesus
Christ, *the Lord* of glory, with
partiality. 2For if there should
come into your assembly a
man with gold rings, in fine
apparel, and there should also
come in a poor man in filthy
clothes, 3and you pay attention to the one wearing the
fine clothes and say to him,
"You sit here in a good place,"
and say to the poor man, "You
stand there," or, "Sit here at
my footstool," 4have you not
shown partiality among yourselves, and become judges
with evil thoughts?

1:19 [a] NU-Text reads *Know this* or *This you know.* 1:26 [a] NU-Text omits *among you.*

5Listen, my beloved brethren: Has God not chosen the
poor of this world *to be* rich in
faith and heirs of the kingdom
which He promised to those
who love Him? 6But you have
dishonored the poor man.
Do not the rich oppress you
and drag you into the courts?
7Do they not blaspheme that
noble name by which you are
called?

8If you really fulfill *the* royal
law according to the Scripture,
"You shall love your neighbor as yourself,"[a] you do well;
9but if you show partiality, you
commit sin, and are convicted
by the law as transgressors.
10For whoever shall keep the
whole law, and yet stumble
in one *point,* he is guilty of
all. 11For He who said, "Do
not commit adultery,"[a] also
said, "Do not murder."[b] Now
if you do not commit adultery, but you do murder, you
have become a transgressor
of the law. 12So speak and so
do as those who will be judged
by the law of liberty. 13For
judgment is without mercy
to the one who has shown no
mercy. Mercy triumphs over
judgment.

FAITH WITHOUT WORKS IS DEAD

14What *does it* profit, my
brethren, if someone says he
has faith but does not have
works? Can faith save him?
15If a brother or sister is naked
and destitute of daily food,
16and one of you says to them,
"Depart in peace, be warmed
and filled," but you do not
give them the things which
are needed for the body, what
does it profit? 17Thus also faith
by itself, if it does not have
works, is dead.

18But someone will say,
"You have faith, and I have
works." Show me your faith
without your[a] works, and I
will show you my faith by my[b]
works. 19You believe that there
is one God. You do well. Even
the demons believe—and
tremble! 20But do you want
to know, O foolish man, that
faith without works is dead?[a]
21Was not Abraham our father
justified by works when he
offered Isaac his son on the
altar? 22Do you see that faith
was working together with
his works, and by works faith
was made perfect? 23And the
Scripture was fulfilled which
says, "Abraham believed God,
and it was accounted to him
for righteousness."[a] And he
was called the friend of God.
24You see then that a man is
justified by works, and not by
faith only.

25Likewise, was not Rahab
the harlot also justified by

2:8 [a] Leviticus 19:18 2:11 [a] Exodus 20:14; Deuteronomy 5:18 [b] Exodus 20:13; Deuteronomy 5:17 2:18 [a] NU-Text omits *your.* [b] NU-Text omits *my.* 2:20 [a] NU-Text reads *useless.* 2:23 [a] Genesis 15:6

works when she received the messengers and sent *them* out another way?

26For as the body without the spirit is dead, so faith without works is dead also.

THE UNTAMABLE TONGUE

3 My brethren, let not many of you become teachers, knowing that we shall receive a stricter judgment. 2For we all stumble in many things. If anyone does not stumble in word, he *is* a perfect man, able also to bridle the whole body. 3Indeed,[a] we put bits in horses' mouths that they may obey us, and we turn their whole body. 4Look also at ships: although they are so large and are driven by fierce winds, they are turned by a very small rudder wherever the pilot desires. 5Even so the tongue is a little member and boasts great things.

See how great a forest a little fire kindles! 6And the tongue *is* a fire, a world of iniquity. The tongue is so set among our members that it defiles the whole body, and sets on fire the course of nature; and it is set on fire by hell. 7For every kind of beast and bird, of reptile and creature of the sea, is tamed and has been tamed by mankind. 8But no man can tame the tongue. *It is* an unruly evil, full of deadly poison. 9With it we bless our God and Father, and with it we curse men, who have been made in the similitude of God. 10Out of the same mouth proceed blessing and cursing. My brethren, these things ought not to be so. 11Does a spring send forth fresh *water* and bitter from the same opening? 12Can a fig tree, my brethren, bear olives, or a grapevine bear figs? Thus no spring yields both salt water and fresh.[a]

HEAVENLY VERSUS DEMONIC WISDOM

13Who *is* wise and understanding among you? Let him show by good conduct *that* his works *are done* in the meekness of wisdom. 14But if you have bitter envy and self-seeking in your hearts, do not boast and lie against the truth. 15This wisdom does not descend from above, but *is* earthly, sensual, demonic. 16For where envy and self-seeking *exist,* confusion and every evil thing *are* there. 17But the wisdom that is from above is first pure, then peaceable, gentle, willing to yield, full of mercy and good fruits, without partiality and without hypocrisy. 18Now the fruit of righteousness is sown in peace by those who make peace.

3:3 [a] NU-Text reads *Now if.* 3:12 [a] NU-Text reads *Neither can a salty spring produce fresh water.*

PRIDE PROMOTES STRIFE

4 Where do wars and fights *come* from among you? Do *they* not *come* from your *desires for* pleasure that war in your members? 2You lust and do not have. You murder and covet and cannot obtain. You fight and war. Yet[a] you do not have because you do not ask. 3You ask and do not receive, because you ask amiss, that you may spend *it* on your pleasures. 4Adulterers and[a] adulteresses! Do you not know that friendship with the world is enmity with God? Whoever therefore wants to be a friend of the world makes himself an enemy of God. 5Or do you think that the Scripture says in vain, "The Spirit who dwells in us yearns jealously"?

6But He gives more grace. Therefore He says:

"God resists the proud,
But gives grace to
the humble."[a]

HUMILITY CURES WORLDLINESS

7Therefore submit to God. Resist the devil and he will flee from you. 8Draw near to God and He will draw near to you. Cleanse *your* hands, *you* sinners; and purify *your* hearts, *you* double-minded. 9Lament and mourn and weep! Let your laughter be turned to mourning and *your* joy to gloom. 10Humble yourselves in the sight of the Lord, and He will lift you up.

DO NOT JUDGE A BROTHER

11Do not speak evil of one another, brethren. He who speaks evil of a brother and judges his brother, speaks evil of the law and judges the law. But if you judge the law, you are not a doer of the law but a judge. 12There is one Lawgiver,[a] who is able to save and to destroy. Who[b] are you to judge another?[c]

DO NOT BOAST ABOUT TOMORROW

13Come now, you who say, "Today or tomorrow we will[a] go to such and such a city, spend a year there, buy and sell, and make a profit"; 14whereas you do not know what *will happen* tomorrow. For what *is* your life? It is even a vapor that appears for a little time and then vanishes away. 15Instead you *ought* to say, "If the Lord wills, we shall live and do this or that." 16But now you boast in your arrogance. All such boasting is evil.

17Therefore, to him who knows to do good and does not do *it*, to him it is sin.

4:2 [a] NU-Text and M-Text omit *Yet*. 4:4 [a] NU-Text omits *Adulterers and*. 4:6 [a] Proverbs 3:34 4:12 [a] NU-Text adds *and Judge*. [b] NU-Text and M-Text read *But who*. [c] NU-Text reads *a neighbor*. 4:13 [a] M-Text reads *let us*.

RICH OPPRESSORS WILL BE JUDGED

5 Come now, *you* rich, weep and howl for your miseries that are coming upon *you!* 2Your riches are corrupted, and your garments are moth-eaten. 3Your gold and silver are corroded, and their corrosion will be a witness against you and will eat your flesh like fire. You have heaped up treasure in the last days. 4Indeed the wages of the laborers who mowed your fields, which you kept back by fraud, cry out; and the cries of the reapers have reached the ears of the Lord of Sabaoth.[a] 5You have lived on the earth in pleasure and luxury; you have fattened your hearts as[a] in a day of slaughter. 6You have condemned, you have murdered the just; he does not resist you.

BE PATIENT AND PERSEVERING

7Therefore be patient, brethren, until the coming of the Lord. See *how* the farmer waits for the precious fruit of the earth, waiting patiently for it until it receives the early and latter rain. 8You also be patient. Establish your hearts, for the coming of the Lord is at hand.

9Do not grumble against one another, brethren, lest you be condemned.[a] Behold, the Judge is standing at the door! 10My brethren, take the prophets, who spoke in the name of the Lord, as an example of suffering and patience. 11Indeed we count them blessed who endure. You have heard of the perseverance of Job and seen the end *intended by* the Lord—that the Lord is very compassionate and merciful.

12But above all, my brethren, do not swear, either by heaven or by earth or with any other oath. But let your "Yes" be "Yes," and *your* "No," "No," lest you fall into judgment.[a]

MEETING SPECIFIC NEEDS

13Is anyone among you suffering? Let him pray. Is anyone cheerful? Let him sing psalms. 14Is anyone among you sick? Let him call for the elders of the church, and let them pray over him, anointing him with oil in the name of the Lord. 15And the prayer of faith will save the sick, and the Lord will raise him up. And if he has committed sins, he will be forgiven. 16Confess *your* trespasses[a] to one another, and pray for one another, that you may be healed. The effective, fer-

5:4 [a] Literally, in Hebrew, *Hosts* 5:5 [a] NU-Text omits *as.* 5:9 [a] NU-Text and M-Text read *judged.* 5:12 [a] M-Text reads *hypocrisy.* 5:16 [a] NU-Text reads *Therefore confess your sins.*

vent prayer of a righteous man avails much. [17]Elijah was a man with a nature like ours, and he prayed earnestly that it would not rain; and it did not rain on the land for three years and six months. [18]And he prayed again, and the heaven gave rain, and the earth produced its fruit.

BRING BACK THE ERRING ONE

[19]Brethren, if anyone among you wanders from the truth, and someone turns him back, [20]let him know that he who turns a sinner from the error of his way will save a soul[a] from death and cover a multitude of sins.

THE FIRST EPISTLE OF PETER

GREETING TO THE ELECT PILGRIMS

1 Peter, an apostle of Jesus Christ,

To the pilgrims of the Dispersion in Pontus, Galatia, Cappadocia, Asia, and Bithynia, [2]elect according to the foreknowledge of God the Father, in sanctification of the Spirit, for obedience and sprinkling of the blood of Jesus Christ:

Grace to you and peace be multiplied.

A HEAVENLY INHERITANCE

[3]Blessed *be* the God and Father of our Lord Jesus Christ, who according to His abundant mercy has begotten us again to a living hope through the resurrection of Jesus Christ from the dead, [4]to an inheritance incorruptible and undefiled and that does not fade away, reserved in heaven for you, [5]who are kept by the power of God through faith for salvation ready to be revealed in the last time.

[6]In this you greatly rejoice, though now for a little while, if need be, you have been grieved by various trials, [7]that the genuineness of your faith, *being* much more precious than gold that perishes, though it is tested by fire, may be found to praise, honor, and glory at the revelation of Jesus Christ, [8]whom having not seen[a] you love. Though now you do not see *Him,* yet believing, you

5:20 [a] NU-Text reads *his soul.* 1:8 [a] M-Text reads *known.*

rejoice with joy inexpressible and full of glory, 9receiving the end of your faith—the salvation of *your* souls.

10Of this salvation the prophets have inquired and searched carefully, who prophesied of the grace *that would come* to you, 11searching what, or what manner of time, the Spirit of Christ who was in them was indicating when He testified beforehand the sufferings of Christ and the glories that would follow. 12To them it was revealed that, not to themselves, but to us[a] they were ministering the things which now have been reported to you through those who have preached the gospel to you by the Holy Spirit sent from heaven—things which angels desire to look into.

LIVING BEFORE GOD OUR FATHER

13Therefore gird up the loins of your mind, be sober, and rest *your* hope fully upon the grace that is to be brought to you at the revelation of Jesus Christ; 14as obedient children, not conforming yourselves to the former lusts, *as* in your ignorance; 15but as He who called you *is* holy, you also be holy in all *your* conduct, 16because it is written, "Be holy, for I am holy."[a]

17And if you call on the Father, who without partiality judges according to each one's work, conduct yourselves throughout the time of your stay *here* in fear; 18knowing that you were not redeemed with corruptible things, *like* silver or gold, from your aimless conduct *received* by tradition from your fathers, 19but with the precious blood of Christ, as of a lamb without blemish and without spot. 20He indeed was foreordained before the foundation of the world, but was manifest in these last times for you 21who through Him believe in God, who raised Him from the dead and gave Him glory, so that your faith and hope are in God.

THE ENDURING WORD

22Since you have purified your souls in obeying the truth through the Spirit[a] in sincere love of the brethren, love one another fervently with a pure heart, 23having been born again, not of corruptible seed but incorruptible, through the word of God which lives and abides forever,[a] 24because

"All flesh *is* as grass,
And all the glory of
man[a] as the flower
of the grass.

1:12 [a] NU-Text and M-Text read *you.* 1:16 [a] Leviticus 11:44, 45; 19:2; 20:7 1:22 [a] NU-Text omits *through the Spirit.* 1:23 [a] NU-Text omits *forever.* 1:24 [a] NU-Text reads *all its glory.*

The grass withers,
And its flower falls
away,
25 But the word of the LORD
endures forever."[a]

Now this is the word which
by the gospel was preached
to you.

2 Therefore, laying aside all
malice, all deceit, hypocrisy, envy, and all evil speaking, 2as newborn babes, desire
the pure milk of the word, that
you may grow thereby,[a] 3if indeed you have tasted that the
Lord *is* gracious.

THE CHOSEN STONE AND HIS CHOSEN PEOPLE

4Coming to Him *as to* a living stone, rejected indeed by
men, but chosen by God *and*
precious, 5you also, as living
stones, are being built up a
spiritual house, a holy priesthood, to offer up spiritual
sacrifices acceptable to God
through Jesus Christ. 6There-
fore it is also contained in the
Scripture,

"Behold, I lay in Zion
A chief cornerstone,
elect, precious,
And he who believes
on Him will by
no means be put
to shame."[a]

7Therefore, to you who believe, *He is* precious; but to
those who are disobedient,[a]

"The stone which the
builders rejected
Has become the chief
cornerstone,"[b]

8and

"A stone of stumbling
And a rock of offense."[a]

They stumble, being disobedient to the word, to which they
also were appointed.

9But you *are* a chosen generation, a royal priesthood, a
holy nation, His own special
people, that you may proclaim
the praises of Him who called
you out of darkness into His
marvelous light; 10who once
were not a people but *are* now
the people of God, who had
not obtained mercy but now
have obtained mercy.

LIVING BEFORE THE WORLD

11Beloved, I beg *you* as sojourners and pilgrims, abstain
from fleshly lusts which war
against the soul, 12having your
conduct honorable among the
Gentiles, that when they speak
against you as evildoers, they
may, by *your* good works
which they observe, glorify
God in the day of visitation.

1:25 [a] Isaiah 40:6–8 2:2 [a] NU-Text adds *up to salvation.* 2:6 [a] Isaiah 28:16 2:7 [a] NU-Text reads *to those who disbelieve.* [b] Psalm 118:22 2:8 [a] Isaiah 8:14

SUBMISSION TO GOVERNMENT

[13]Therefore submit yourselves to every ordinance of man for the Lord's sake, whether to the king as supreme, [14]or to governors, as to those who are sent by him for the punishment of evildoers and *for the* praise of those who do good. [15]For this is the will of God, that by doing good you may put to silence the ignorance of foolish men— [16]as free, yet not using liberty as a cloak for vice, but as bondservants of God. [17]Honor all *people.* Love the brotherhood. Fear God. Honor the king.

SUBMISSION TO MASTERS

[18]Servants, *be* submissive to *your* masters with all fear, not only to the good and gentle, but also to the harsh. [19]For this *is* commendable, if because of conscience toward God one endures grief, suffering wrongfully. [20]For what credit *is it* if, when you are beaten for your faults, you take it patiently? But when you do good and suffer, if you take it patiently, this *is* commendable before God. [21]For to this you were called, because Christ also suffered for us,[a] leaving us[b] an example, that you should follow His steps:

[22]"Who committed no sin,
Nor was deceit found
in His mouth";[a]

[23]who, when He was reviled, did not revile in return; when He suffered, He did not threaten, but committed *Himself* to Him who judges righteously; [24]who Himself bore our sins in His own body on the tree, that we, having died to sins, might live for righteousness—by whose stripes you were healed. [25]For you were like sheep going astray, but have now returned to the Shepherd and Overseer[a] of your souls.

SUBMISSION TO HUSBANDS

3 Wives, likewise, *be* submissive to your own husbands, that even if some do not obey the word, they, without a word, may be won by the conduct of their wives, [2]when they observe your chaste conduct *accompanied* by fear. [3]Do not let your adornment be *merely* outward—arranging the hair, wearing gold, or putting on *fine* apparel— [4]rather *let it be* the hidden person of the heart, with the incorruptible *beauty* of a gentle and quiet spirit, which is very precious in the sight of God. [5]For in this manner, in former times, the holy women who trusted in God also adorned themselves, being submissive to their own

2:21 [a] NU-Text reads *you.* [b] NU-Text and M-Text read *you.* 2:22 [a] Isaiah 53:9 2:25 [a] Greek *Episkopos*

husbands, 6as Sarah obeyed
Abraham, calling him lord,
whose daughters you are if
you do good and are not afraid
with any terror.

A WORD TO HUSBANDS

7Husbands, likewise, dwell
with *them* with understanding, giving honor to the wife,
as to the weaker vessel, and
as *being* heirs together of the
grace of life, that your prayers
may not be hindered.

CALLED TO BLESSING

8Finally, all *of you be* of one
mind, having compassion for
one another; love as brothers,
be tenderhearted, *be* courte-
ous;[a] 9not returning evil for
evil or reviling for reviling,
but on the contrary blessing,
knowing that you were called
to this, that you may inherit a
blessing. 10For

"He who would love life
And see good days,
Let him refrain his
tongue from evil,
And his lips from
speaking deceit.
11 Let him turn away from
evil and do good;
Let him seek peace
and pursue it.
12 For the eyes of the
LORD *are* on the
righteous,
And His ears *are open*
to their prayers;
But the face of the
LORD *is* against those
who do evil."[a]

SUFFERING FOR RIGHT AND WRONG

13And who *is* he who will
harm you if you become followers of what is good? 14But
even if you should suffer for
righteousness' sake, *you are*
blessed. "And do not be afraid
of their threats, nor be troubled."[a] 15But sanctify the Lord
God[a] in your hearts, and always
be ready to *give* a defense to
everyone who asks you a reason for the hope that is in you,
with meekness and fear; 16hav-
ing a good conscience, that
when they defame you as evildoers, those who revile your
good conduct in Christ may be
ashamed. 17For *it is* better, if it
is the will of God, to suffer for
doing good than for doing evil.

CHRIST'S SUFFERING AND OURS

18For Christ also suffered
once for sins, the just for the
unjust, that He might bring us[a]
to God, being put to death in
the flesh but made alive by the
Spirit, 19by whom also He went
and preached to the spirits in
prison, 20who formerly were
disobedient, when once the

3:8 [a] NU-Text reads *humble.* 3:12 [a] Psalm 34:12–16
3:14 [a] Isaiah 8:12 3:15 [a] NU-Text reads *Christ as Lord.* 3:18 [a] NU-Text and M-Text read *you.*

Divine longsuffering waited[a]
in the days of Noah, while *the*
ark was being prepared, in
which a few, that is, eight souls,
were saved through water.
21 There is also an antitype
which now saves us—baptism
(not the removal of the filth of
the flesh, but the answer of a
good conscience toward God),
through the resurrection of
Jesus Christ, 22 who has gone
into heaven and is at the right
hand of God, angels and authorities and powers having
been made subject to Him.

4 Therefore, since Christ
suffered for us[a] in the
flesh, arm yourselves also
with the same mind, for he
who has suffered in the flesh
has ceased from sin, 2 that
he no longer should live the
rest of *his* time in the flesh
for the lusts of men, but for
the will of God. 3 For we *have*
spent enough of our past lifetime[a] in doing the will of the
Gentiles—when we walked in
lewdness, lusts, drunkenness,
revelries, drinking parties,
and abominable idolatries.
4 In regard to these, they think
it strange that you do not run
with *them* in the same flood
of dissipation, speaking evil
of *you*. 5 They will give an account to Him who is ready to
judge the living and the dead.
6 For this reason the gospel
was preached also to those
who are dead, that they might
be judged according to men in
the flesh, but live according to
God in the spirit.

SERVING FOR GOD'S GLORY

7 But the end of all things is
at hand; therefore be serious
and watchful in your prayers.
8 And above all things have
fervent love for one another,
for "love will cover a multitude of sins."[a] 9 *Be* hospitable to one another without
grumbling. 10 As each one has
received a gift, minister it to
one another, as good stewards
of the manifold grace of God.
11 If anyone speaks, *let him*
speak as the oracles of God.
If anyone ministers, *let him*
do it as with the ability which
God supplies, that in all things
God may be glorified through
Jesus Christ, to whom belong
the glory and the dominion
forever and ever. Amen.

SUFFERING FOR GOD'S GLORY

12 Beloved, do not think it
strange concerning the fiery
trial which is to try you, as
though some strange thing
happened to you; 13 but rejoice
to the extent that you partake
of Christ's sufferings, that
when His glory is revealed, you
may also be glad with exceed-

3:20 [a] NU-Text and M-Text read *when the longsuffering of God waited patiently.* 4:1 [a] NU-Text omits *for us.* 4:3 [a] NU-Text reads *time.* 4:8 [a] Proverbs 10:12

ing joy. 14If you are reproached
for the name of Christ, blessed
are you, for the Spirit of glory
and of God rests upon you.[a] On
their part He is blasphemed,
but on your part He is glorified. 15But let none of you suffer as a murderer, a thief, an
evildoer, or as a busybody in
other people's matters. 16Yet
if *anyone suffers* as a Christian,
let him not be ashamed, but let
him glorify God in this matter.[a]
17For the time *has come*
for judgment to begin at the
house of God; and if *it begins*
with us first, what will *be* the
end of those who do not obey
the gospel of God? 18Now

"If the righteous one
is scarcely saved,
Where will the
ungodly and the
sinner appear?"[a]

19Therefore let those who suffer according to the will of God
commit their souls *to Him* in
doing good, as to a faithful
Creator.

SHEPHERD THE FLOCK

5 The elders who are among
you I exhort, I who am a
fellow elder and a witness of
the sufferings of Christ, and
also a partaker of the glory
that will be revealed: 2Shep-
herd the flock of God which is
among you, serving as overseers, not by compulsion but
willingly,[a] not for dishonest
gain but eagerly; 3nor as being
lords over those entrusted to
you, but being examples to
the flock; 4and when the Chief
Shepherd appears, you will
receive the crown of glory that
does not fade away.

SUBMIT TO GOD, RESIST THE DEVIL

5Likewise you younger people, submit yourselves to *your*
elders. Yes, all of *you* be submissive to one another, and
be clothed with humility, for

"God resists the proud,
But gives grace to
the humble."[a]

6Therefore humble your-
selves under the mighty hand
of God, that He may exalt you
in due time, 7casting all your
care upon Him, for He cares
for you.
8Be sober, be vigilant; because[a] your adversary the devil
walks about like a roaring lion,
seeking whom he may devour.
9Resist him, steadfast in the
faith, knowing that the same
sufferings are experienced by
your brotherhood in the world.
10But may[a] the God of all grace,

4:14 [a] NU-Text omits the rest of this verse. 4:16 [a] NU-Text reads *name.* 4:18 [a] Proverbs 11:31 5:2 [a] NU-Text adds *according to God.* 5:5 [a] Proverbs 3:34 5:8 [a] NU-Text and M-Text omit *because.* 5:10 [a] NU-Text reads *But the God of all grace . . . will perfect, establish, strengthen, and settle you.*

who called us[b] to His eternal glory by Christ Jesus, after you have suffered a while, perfect, establish, strengthen, and settle *you.* 11To Him *be* the glory and the dominion forever and ever. Amen.

FAREWELL AND PEACE

12By Silvanus, our faithful brother as I consider him, I have written to you briefly, exhorting and testifying that this is the true grace of God in which you stand.

13She who is in Babylon, elect together with *you,* greets you; and *so does* Mark my son. 14Greet one another with a kiss of love.

Peace to you all who are in Christ Jesus. Amen.

THE SECOND EPISTLE OF PETER

GREETING THE FAITHFUL

1 Simon Peter, a bondservant and apostle of Jesus Christ,

To those who have obtained like precious faith with us by the righteousness of our God and Savior Jesus Christ:

2Grace and peace be multiplied to you in the knowledge of God and of Jesus our Lord, 3as His divine power has given to us all things that *pertain* to life and godliness, through the knowledge of Him who called us by glory and virtue, 4by which have been given to us exceedingly great and precious *promises, that through* these you may be partakers of the divine nature, having escaped the corruption *that is* in the world through lust.

FRUITFUL GROWTH IN THE FAITH

5But also for this very reason, giving all diligence, add to your faith virtue, to virtue knowledge, 6to knowledge self-control, to self-control perseverance, to perseverance godliness, 7to godliness brotherly kindness, and to brotherly kindness love. 8For if these things are yours and abound, *you* will be neither barren nor unfruitful in the knowledge of our Lord Jesus Christ. 9For he who lacks these things is *shortsighted,* even to blindness, and has forgotten that he was cleansed from his old sins.

5:10 [b] NU-Text and M-Text read *you.*

10Therefore, brethren, be even more diligent to make your call and election sure, for if you do these things you will never stumble; 11for so an entrance will be supplied to you abundantly into the everlasting kingdom of our Lord and Savior Jesus Christ.

PETER'S APPROACHING DEATH

12For this reason I will not be negligent to remind you always of these things, though you know and are established in the present truth. 13Yes, I think it is right, as long as I am in this tent, to stir you up by reminding *you*, 14knowing that shortly I *must* put off my tent, just as our Lord Jesus Christ showed me. 15Moreover I will be careful to ensure that you always have a reminder of these things after my decease.

THE TRUSTWORTHY PROPHETIC WORD

16For we did not follow cunningly devised fables when we made known to you the power and coming of our Lord Jesus Christ, but were eyewitnesses of His majesty. 17For He received from God the Father honor and glory when such a voice came to Him from the Excellent Glory: "This is My beloved Son, in whom I am well pleased." 18And we heard this voice which came from heaven when we were with Him on the holy mountain.

19And so we have the prophetic word confirmed,[a] which you do well to heed as a light that shines in a dark place, until the day dawns and the morning star rises in your hearts; 20knowing this first, that no prophecy of Scripture is of any private interpretation,[a] 21for prophecy never came by the will of man, but holy men of God[a] spoke *as they were* moved by the Holy Spirit.

DESTRUCTIVE DOCTRINES

2 But there were also false prophets among the people, even as there will be false teachers among you, who will secretly bring in destructive heresies, even denying the Lord who bought them, *and* bring on themselves swift destruction. 2And many will follow their destructive ways, because of whom the way of truth will be blasphemed. 3By covetousness they will exploit you with deceptive words; for a long time their judgment has not been idle, and their destruction does[a] not slumber.

DOOM OF FALSE TEACHERS

4For if God did not spare the angels who sinned, but cast

1:19 [a] Or *We also have the more sure prophetic word.* 1:20 [a] Or *origin* 1:21 [a] NU-Text reads *but men spoke from God.* 2:3 [a] M-Text reads *will not.*

them down to hell and delivered *them* into chains of darkness, to be reserved for judgment; 5and did not spare the ancient world, but saved Noah, *one of* eight *people*, a preacher of righteousness, bringing in the flood on the world of the ungodly; 6and turning the cities of Sodom and Gomorrah into ashes, condemned *them* to destruction, making *them* an example to those who afterward would live ungodly; 7and delivered righteous Lot, *who was* oppressed by the filthy conduct of the wicked 8(for that righteous man, dwelling among them, tormented *his* righteous soul from day to day by seeing and hearing *their* lawless deeds)— 9*then* the Lord knows how to deliver the godly out of temptations and to reserve the unjust under punishment for the day of judgment, 10and especially those who walk according to the flesh in the lust of uncleanness and despise authority. *They are* presumptuous, self-willed. They are not afraid to speak evil of dignitaries, 11whereas angels, who are greater in power and might, do not bring a reviling accusation against them before the Lord.

DEPRAVITY OF FALSE TEACHERS

12But these, like natural brute beasts made to be caught and destroyed, speak evil of the things they do not understand, and will utterly perish in their own corruption, 13*and* will receive the wages of unrighteousness, *as* those who count it pleasure to carouse in the daytime. *They are* spots and blemishes, carousing in their own deceptions while they feast with you, 14having eyes full of adultery and that cannot cease from sin, enticing unstable souls. They have a heart trained in covetous practices, *and are* accursed children. 15They have forsaken the right way and gone astray, following the way of Balaam the *son* of Beor, who loved the wages of unrighteousness; 16but he was rebuked for his iniquity: a dumb donkey speaking with a man's voice restrained the madness of the prophet.

17These are wells without water, clouds[a] carried by a tempest, for whom is reserved the blackness of darkness forever.[b]

DECEPTIONS OF FALSE TEACHERS

18For when they speak great swelling *words* of emptiness, they allure through the lusts of the flesh, through lewdness, the ones who have actually escaped[a] from those who live in error. 19While they promise

2:17 [a] NU-Text reads *and mists.* [b] NU-Text omits *forever.* **2:18** [a] NU-Text reads *are barely escaping.*

them liberty, they themselves
are slaves of corruption; for by
whom a person is overcome,
by him also he is brought into
bondage. 20For if, after they
have escaped the pollutions of
the world through the knowledge of the Lord and Savior
Jesus Christ, they are again
entangled in them and overcome, the latter end is worse
for them than the beginning.
21For it would have been better
for them not to have known
the way of righteousness, than
having known *it,* to turn from
the holy commandment de-
livered to them. 22But it has
happened to them according
to the true proverb: "A dog returns to his own vomit,"[a] and,
"a sow, having washed, to her
wallowing in the mire."

GOD'S PROMISE IS NOT SLACK

3 Beloved, I now write to you
this second epistle (in *both
of* which I stir up your pure
minds by way of reminder),
2that you may be mindful of
the words which were spoken
before by the holy prophets,
and of the commandment of
us,[a] the apostles of the Lord
and Savior, 3knowing this
first: that scoffers will come in
the last days, walking according to their own lusts, 4and
saying, "Where is the promise
of His coming? For since the
fathers fell asleep, all things
continue as *they were* from
the beginning of creation."
5For this they willfully forget:
that by the word of God the
heavens were of old, and the
earth standing out of water
and in the water, 6by which
the world *that* then existed
perished, being flooded with
water. 7But the heavens and
the earth *which* are now preserved by the same word, are
reserved for fire until the day
of judgment and perdition of
ungodly men.

8But, beloved, do not forget
this one thing, that with the
Lord one day *is* as a thousand
years, and a thousand years as
one day. 9The Lord is not slack
concerning *His* promise, as
some count slackness, but is
longsuffering toward us,[a] not
willing that any should perish
but that all should come to
repentance.

THE DAY OF THE LORD

10But the day of the Lord
will come as a thief in the
night, in which the heavens
will pass away with a great
noise, and the elements will
melt with fervent heat; both
the earth and the works that
are in it will be burned up.[a]
11Therefore, since all these
things will be dissolved, what

2:22 [a] Proverbs 26:11 3:2 [a] NU-Text and M-Text read *commandment of the apostles of your Lord and Savior* or *commandment of your apostles of the Lord and Savior.* 3:9 [a] NU-Text reads *you.* 3:10 [a] NU-Text reads *laid bare* (literally *found*).

manner *of persons* ought you to be in holy conduct and godliness, 12looking for and hastening the coming of the day of God, because of which the heavens will be dissolved, being on fire, and the elements will melt with fervent heat? 13Nevertheless we, according to His promise, look for new heavens and a new earth in which righteousness dwells.

BE STEADFAST

14Therefore, beloved, looking forward to these things, be diligent to be found by Him in peace, without spot and blameless; 15and consider *that* the longsuffering of our Lord *is* salvation—as also our beloved brother Paul, according to the wisdom given to him, has written to you, 16as also in all his epistles, speaking in them of these things, in which are some things hard to understand, which untaught and unstable *people* twist to their own destruction, as *they do* also the rest of the Scriptures.

17You therefore, beloved, since you know *this* beforehand, beware lest you also fall from your own steadfastness, being led away with the error of the wicked; 18but grow in the grace and knowledge of our Lord and Savior Jesus Christ.

To Him *be* the glory both now and forever. Amen.

THE FIRST EPISTLE OF JOHN

WHAT WAS HEARD, SEEN, AND TOUCHED

1 That which was from the beginning, which we have heard, which we have seen with our eyes, which we have looked upon, and our hands have handled, concerning the Word of life— 2the life was manifested, and we have seen, and bear witness, and declare to you that eternal life which was with the Father and was manifested to us— 3that which we have seen and heard we declare to you, that you also may have fellowship with us; and truly our fellowship *is* with the Father and with His Son Jesus Christ. 4And these things we write to you that your[a] joy may be full.

1:4 [a] NU-Text and M-Text read *our*.

FELLOWSHIP WITH HIM AND ONE ANOTHER

5This is the message which
we have heard from Him and
declare to you, that God is
light and in Him is no darkness at all. 6If we say that we
have fellowship with Him, and
walk in darkness, we lie and
do not practice the truth. 7But
if we walk in the light as He is
in the light, we have fellowship with one another, and the
blood of Jesus Christ His Son
cleanses us from all sin.

8If we say that we have no
sin, we deceive ourselves, and
the truth is not in us. 9If we
confess our sins, He is faithful and just to forgive us *our*
sins and to cleanse us from
all unrighteousness. 10If we
say that we have not sinned,
we make Him a liar, and His
word is not in us.

2 My little children, these
things I write to you, so
that you may not sin. And if
anyone sins, we have an Ad-
vocate with the Father, Jesus
Christ the righteous. 2And He
Himself is the propitiation for
our sins, and not for ours only
but also for the whole world.

THE TEST OF KNOWING HIM

3Now by this we know that
we know Him, if we keep His
commandments. 4He who
says, "I know Him," and does
not keep His commandments,
is a liar, and the truth is not
in him. 5But whoever keeps
His word, truly the love of
God is perfected in him. By
this we know that we are in
Him. 6He who says he abides
in Him ought himself also to
walk just as He walked.

7Brethren,[a] I write no new
commandment to you, but an
old commandment which you
have had from the beginning.
The old commandment is the
word which you heard from
the beginning.[b] 8Again, a new
commandment I write to you,
which thing is true in Him and
in you, because the darkness
is passing away, and the true
light is already shining.

9He who says he is in the
light, and hates his brother,
is in darkness until now. 10He
who loves his brother abides
in the light, and there is no
cause for stumbling in him.
11But he who hates his brother
is in darkness and walks in
darkness, and does not know
where he is going, because the
darkness has blinded his eyes.

THEIR SPIRITUAL STATE

12 I write to you, little
children,
Because your sins
are forgiven you for
His name's sake.
13 I write to you, fathers,
Because you have
known Him *who is*
from the beginning.

2:7 [a] NU-Text reads *Beloved.* [b] NU-Text omits *from the beginning.*

I write to you, young men,
Because you have
overcome the
wicked one.
I write to you, little
children,
Because you have
known the Father.
14 I have written to
you, fathers,
Because you have
known Him *who is*
from the beginning.
I have written to you,
young men,
Because you are strong,
and the word of God
abides in you,
And you have overcome
the wicked one.

DO NOT LOVE THE WORLD

15Do not love the world or
the things in the world. If anyone loves the world, the love
of the Father is not in him.
16For all that *is* in the world—
the lust of the flesh, the lust
of the eyes, and the pride of
life—is not of the Father but is
of the world. 17And the world
is passing away, and the lust
of it; but he who does the will
of God abides forever.

DECEPTIONS OF THE LAST HOUR

18Little children, it is the
last hour; and as you have
heard that the[a] Antichrist is
coming, even now many anti-
christs have come, by which
we know that it is the last
hour. 19They went out from
us, but they were not of us;
for if they had been of us, they
would have continued with
us; but *they went out* that they
might be made manifest, that
none of them were of us.
20But you have an anoint-
ing from the Holy One, and
you know all things.[a] 21I have
not written to you because
you do not know the truth,
but because you know it, and
that no lie is of the truth.
22Who is a liar but he who
denies that Jesus is the Christ?
He is antichrist who denies the
Father and the Son. 23Who-
ever denies the Son does not
have the Father either; he who
acknowledges the Son has the
Father also.

LET TRUTH ABIDE IN YOU

24Therefore let that abide in
you which you heard from the
beginning. If what you heard
from the beginning abides in
you, you also will abide in the
Son and in the Father. 25And
this is the promise that He has
promised us—eternal life.
26These things I have written to you concerning those
who *try to* deceive you. 27But
the anointing which you have
received from Him abides in
you, and you do not need that
anyone teach you; but as the
same anointing teaches you
concerning all things, and is

2:18 [a] NU-Text omits *the.* 2:20 [a] NU-Text reads *you all know.*

true, and is not a lie, and just
as it has taught you, you will[a]
abide in Him.

THE CHILDREN OF GOD

28And now, little children,
abide in Him, that when[a] He
appears, we may have confidence and not be ashamed
before Him at His coming. 29If
you know that He is righteous,
you know that everyone who
practices righteousness is
born of Him.

3 Behold what manner of
love the Father has be-
stowed on us, that we should
be called children of God![a]
Therefore the world does not
know us,[b] because it did not
know Him. 2Beloved, now we
are children of God; and it has
not yet been revealed what
we shall be, but we know that
when He is revealed, we shall
be like Him, for we shall see
Him as He is. 3And everyone
who has this hope in Him puri-
fies himself, just as He is pure.

SIN AND THE CHILD OF GOD

4Whoever commits sin also
commits lawlessness, and
sin is lawlessness. 5And you
know that He was manifested
to take away our sins, and in
Him there is no sin. 6Whoever
abides in Him does not sin.
Whoever sins has neither seen
Him nor known Him.

7Little children, let no one
deceive you. He who practices
righteousness is righteous,
just as He is righteous. 8He
who sins is of the devil, for the
devil has sinned from the beginning. For this purpose the
Son of God was manifested,
that He might destroy the
works of the devil. 9Whoever
has been born of God does not
sin, for His seed remains in
him; and he cannot sin, because he has been born of God.

THE IMPERATIVE OF LOVE

10In this the children of
God and the children of the
devil are manifest: Whoever
does not practice righteousness is not of God, nor *is* he
who does not love his brother.
11For this is the message that
you heard from the begin-
ning, that we should love one
another, 12not as Cain *who* was
of the wicked one and murdered his brother. And why
did he murder him? Because
his works were evil and his
brother's righteous.

13Do not marvel, my
brethren, if the world hates
you. 14We know that we have
passed from death to life,
because we love the brethren. He who does not love
his brother[a] abides in death.
15Whoever hates his brother
is a murderer, and you know

2:27 [a] NU-Text reads *you abide.* 2:28 [a] NU-Text reads *if.* 3:1 [a] NU-Text adds *And we are.* [b] M-Text reads *you.* 3:14 [a] NU-Text omits *his brother.*

that no murderer has eternal
life abiding in him.

THE OUTWORKING OF LOVE

16By this we know love, because He laid down His life for
us. And we also ought to lay
down *our* lives for the brethren. 17But whoever has this
world's goods, and sees his
brother in need, and shuts up
his heart from him, how does
the love of God abide in him?
18My little children, let us
not love in word or in tongue,
but in deed and in truth. 19And
by this we know[a] that we are
of the truth, and shall assure
our hearts before Him. 20For
if our heart condemns us, God
is greater than our heart, and
knows all things. 21Beloved, if
our heart does not condemn
us, we have confidence toward
God. 22And whatever we ask
we receive from Him, because
we keep His commandments
and do those things that are
pleasing in His sight. 23And
this is His commandment:
that we should believe on the
name of His Son Jesus Christ
and love one another, as He
gave us[a] commandment.

THE SPIRIT OF TRUTH AND THE SPIRIT OF ERROR

24Now he who keeps His
commandments abides in
Him, and He *in him.* And by
this we know that He abides
in us, by the Spirit whom He
has given us.

4 Beloved, do not believe
every spirit, but test the
spirits, whether they are of
God; because many false
prophets have gone out into
the world. 2By this you know
the Spirit of God: Every spirit
that confesses that Jesus
Christ has come in the flesh
is of God, 3and every spirit that
does not confess that[a] Jesus
Christ has come in the flesh is
not of God. And this is the *spirit*
of the Antichrist, which you
have heard was coming, and
is now already in the world.
4You are of God, little children, and have overcome
them, because He who is in
you is greater than he who is
in the world. 5They are of the
world. Therefore they speak
as of the world, and the world
hears them. 6We are of God. He
who knows God hears us; he
who is not of God does not hear
us. By this we know the spirit
of truth and the spirit of error.

KNOWING GOD THROUGH LOVE

7Beloved, let us love one
another, for love is of God; and
everyone who loves is born
of God and knows God. 8He
who does not love does not
know God, for God is love. 9In
this the love of God was manifested toward us, that God has

3:19 [a] NU-Text reads *we shall know.* 3:23 [a] M-Text omits *us.*
4:3 [a] NU-Text omits *that* and *Christ has come in the flesh.*

sent His only begotten Son
into the world, that we might
live through Him. 10In this is
love, not that we loved God,
but that He loved us and sent
His Son *to be* the propitiation
for our sins. 11Beloved, if God
so loved us, we also ought to
love one another.

SEEING GOD THROUGH LOVE

12No one has seen God at
any time. If we love one another, God abides in us, and
His love has been perfected
in us. 13By this we know that
we abide in Him, and He in
us, because He has given us of
His Spirit. 14And we have seen
and testify that the Father has
sent the Son *as* Savior of the
world. 15Whoever confesses
that Jesus is the Son of God,
God abides in him, and he in
God. 16And we have known
and believed the love that God
has for us. God is love, and he
who abides in love abides in
God, and God in him.

THE CONSUMMATION OF LOVE

17Love has been perfected
among us in this: that we may
have boldness in the day of
judgment; because as He is, so
are we in this world. 18There
is no fear in love; but perfect
love casts out fear, because
fear involves torment. But he
who fears has not been made
perfect in love. 19We love Him[a]
because He first loved us.

OBEDIENCE BY FAITH

20If someone says, "I love
God," and hates his brother, he
is a liar; for he who does not
love his brother whom he has
seen, how can[a] he love God
whom he has not seen? 21And
this commandment we have
from Him: that he who loves
God *must* love his brother also.

5 Whoever believes that
Jesus is the Christ is born
of God, and everyone who
loves Him who begot also
loves him who is begotten of
Him. 2By this we know that
we love the children of God,
when we love God and keep
His commandments. 3For
this is the love of God, that
we keep His commandments.
And His commandments are
not burdensome. 4For whatever is born of God overcomes
the world. And this is the victory that has overcome the
world—our[a] faith. 5Who is he
who overcomes the world, but
he who believes that Jesus is
the Son of God?

THE CERTAINTY OF GOD'S WITNESS

6This is He who came
by water and blood—Jesus
Christ; not only by water, but
by water and blood. And it is

4:19 [a] NU-Text omits *Him.* 4:20 [a] NU-Text reads *he cannot.* 5:4 [a] M-Text reads *your.*

the Spirit who bears witness,
because the Spirit is truth.
7For there are three that bear
witness in heaven: the Father,
the Word, and the Holy Spirit;
and these three are one. 8And
there are three that bear witness on earth:[a] the Spirit,
the water, and the blood; and
these three agree as one.

9If we receive the witness
of men, the witness of God is
greater; for this is the witness
of God which[a] He has testified
of His Son. 10He who believes
in the Son of God has the witness in himself; he who does
not believe God has made Him
a liar, because he has not believed the testimony that God
has given of His Son. 11And
this is the testimony: that God
has given us eternal life, and
this life is in His Son. 12He who
has the Son has life; he who
does not have the Son of God
does not have life. 13These
things I have written to you
who believe in the name of
the Son of God, that you may
know that you have eternal
life,[a] and that you may *con-*
tinue to believe in the name
of the Son of God.

CONFIDENCE AND COMPASSION IN PRAYER

14Now this is the confidence
that we have in Him, that if
we ask anything according to
His will, He hears us. 15And
if we know that He hears us,
whatever we ask, we know that
we have the petitions that we
have asked of Him.

16If anyone sees his brother
sinning a sin *which does* not
lead to death, he will ask, and
He will give him life for those
who commit sin not *leading*
to death. There is sin *leading*
to death. I do not say that he
should pray about that. 17All
unrighteousness is sin, and
there is sin not *leading* to
death.

KNOWING THE TRUE—REJECTING THE FALSE

18We know that whoever
is born of God does not sin;
but he who has been born of
God keeps himself,[a] and the
wicked one does not touch
him.

19We know that we are of
God, and the whole world lies
under the sway of the wicked
one.

20And we know that the
Son of God has come and has
given us an understanding,
that we may know Him who is
true; and we are in Him who is
true, in His Son Jesus Christ.
This is the true God and eternal life.

21Little children, keep yourselves from idols. Amen.

5:8 [a] NU-Text and M-Text omit the words from *in heaven* (verse 7) through *on earth* (verse 8). Only four or five very late manuscripts contain these words in Greek. 5:9 [a] NU-Text reads *God, that.* 5:13 [a] NU-Text omits the rest of this verse. 5:18 [a] NU-Text reads *him.*

THE SECOND EPISTLE OF JOHN

GREETING THE ELECT LADY

The Elder,

To the elect lady and her
children, whom I love in truth,
and not only I, but also all
those who have known the
truth, 2because of the truth
which abides in us and will
be with us forever:

3Grace, mercy, *and* peace
will be with you[a] from God
the Father and from the Lord
Jesus Christ, the Son of the
Father, in truth and love.

WALK IN CHRIST'S COMMANDMENTS

4I rejoiced greatly that I
have found *some* of your children walking in truth, as we
received commandment from
the Father. 5And now I plead
with you, lady, not as though
I wrote a new commandment
to you, but that which we have
had from the beginning: that
we love one another. 6This is
love, that we walk according
to His commandments. This
is the commandment, that as
you have heard from the beginning, you should walk in it.

BEWARE OF ANTICHRIST DECEIVERS

7For many deceivers have
gone out into the world who
do not confess Jesus Christ
as coming in the flesh. This is
a deceiver and an antichrist.
8Look to yourselves, that we[a]
do not lose those things we
worked for, but *that* we[b] may
receive a full reward.

9Whoever transgresses[a]
and does not abide in the
doctrine of Christ does not
have God. He who abides in
the doctrine of Christ has
both the Father and the Son.
10If anyone comes to you and
does not bring this doctrine,
do not receive him into your
house nor greet him; 11for he
who greets him shares in his
evil deeds.

JOHN'S FAREWELL GREETING

12Having many things to
write to you, I did not wish
to do so with paper and ink;
but I hope to come to you and
speak face to face, that our joy
may be full.

13The children of your elect
sister greet you. Amen.

3 [a] NU-Text and M-Text read *us*. 8 [a] NU-Text reads *you*. [b] NU-Text reads *you*. 9 [a] NU-Text reads *goes ahead*.

THE THIRD EPISTLE OF JOHN

GREETING TO GAIUS

The Elder,

To the beloved Gaius,
whom I love in truth:

2Beloved, I pray that you
may prosper in all things
and be in health, just as your
soul prospers. 3For I rejoiced
greatly when brethren came
and testified of the truth *that*
is in you, just as you walk in
the truth. 4I have no greater
joy than to hear that my children walk in truth.[a]

GAIUS COMMENDED FOR GENEROSITY

5Beloved, you do faith-
fully whatever you do for the
brethren and[a] for strangers,
6who have borne witness of
your love before the church.
If you send them forward
on their journey in a manner worthy of God, you will
do well, 7because they went
forth for His name's sake, taking nothing from the Gen-
tiles. 8We therefore ought to
receive[a] such, that we may
become fellow workers for
the truth.

DIOTREPHES AND DEMETRIUS

9I wrote to the church, but
Diotrephes, who loves to have
the preeminence among them,
does not receive us. 10There-
fore, if I come, I will call to
mind his deeds which he does,
prating against us with mali-
cious words. And not content
with that, he himself does not
receive the brethren, and for-
bids those who wish to, putting
them out of the church.

11Beloved, do not imitate
what is evil, but what is good.
He who does good is of God,
but[a] he who does evil has not
seen God.

12Demetrius has a *good* testimony from all, and from the
truth itself. And we also bear
witness, and you know that
our testimony is true.

FAREWELL GREETING

13I had many things to
write, but I do not wish to
write to you with pen and ink;
14but I hope to see you shortly,
and we shall speak face to face.

Peace to you. Our friends
greet you. Greet the friends
by name.

4 [a] NU-Text reads *the truth.* 5 [a] NU-Text adds *especially.*
8 [a] NU-Text reads *support.* 11 [a] NU-Text and M-Text omit *but.*

THE EPISTLE OF JUDE

GREETING TO THE CALLED

Jude, a bondservant of
Jesus Christ, and brother
of James,

To those who are called,
sanctified[a] by God the Father,
and preserved in Jesus Christ:

[2]Mercy, peace, and love be
multiplied to you.

CONTEND FOR THE FAITH

[3]Beloved, while I was very
diligent to write to you concerning our common salva-
tion, I found it necessary to
write to you exhorting you to
contend earnestly for the faith
which was once for all delivered to the saints. [4]For certain
men have crept in unnoticed,
who long ago were marked out
for this condemnation, ungodly men, who turn the grace
of our God into lewdness and
deny the only Lord God[a] and
our Lord Jesus Christ.

OLD AND NEW APOSTATES

[5]But I want to remind you,
though you once knew this,
that the Lord, having saved
the people out of the land of
Egypt, afterward destroyed
those who did not believe.
[6]And the angels who did not
keep their proper domain,
but left their own abode, He
has reserved in everlasting
chains under darkness for the
judgment of the great day; [7]as
Sodom and Gomorrah, and
the cities around them in a
similar manner to these, having given themselves over to
sexual immorality and gone
after strange flesh, are set
forth as an example, suffering
the vengeance of eternal fire.
[8]Likewise also these
dreamers defile the flesh,
reject authority, and speak
evil of dignitaries. [9]Yet Michael the archangel, in con-
tending with the devil, when
he disputed about the body
of Moses, dared not bring
against him a reviling accusation, but said, "The Lord rebuke you!" [10]But these speak
evil of whatever they do not
know; and whatever they
know naturally, like brute
beasts, in these things they
corrupt themselves. [11]Woe
to them! For they have gone
in the way of Cain, have run
greedily in the error of Balaam for profit, and perished
in the rebellion of Korah.

1 [a] NU-Text reads *beloved.* 4 [a] NU-Text omits *God.*

APOSTATES DEPRAVED AND DOOMED

12 These are spots in your love feasts, while they feast with you without fear, serving *only* themselves. *They are* clouds without water, carried about[a] by the winds; late autumn trees without fruit, twice dead, pulled up by the roots; 13 raging waves of the sea, foaming up their own shame; wandering stars for whom is reserved the blackness of darkness forever.

14 Now Enoch, the seventh from Adam, prophesied about these men also, saying, "Behold, the Lord comes with ten thousands of His saints, 15 to execute judgment on all, to convict all who are ungodly among them of all their ungodly deeds which they have committed in an ungodly way, and of all the harsh things which ungodly sinners have spoken against Him."

APOSTATES PREDICTED

16 These are grumblers, complainers, walking according to their own lusts; and they mouth great swelling *words*, flattering people to gain advantage. 17 But you, beloved, remember the words which were spoken before by the apostles of our Lord Jesus Christ: 18 how they told you that there would be mockers in the last time who would walk according to their own ungodly lusts. 19 These are sensual persons, who cause divisions, not having the Spirit.

MAINTAIN YOUR LIFE WITH GOD

20 But you, beloved, building yourselves up on your most holy faith, praying in the Holy Spirit, 21 keep yourselves in the love of God, looking for the mercy of our Lord Jesus Christ unto eternal life.

22 And on some have compassion, making a distinction;[a] 23 but others save with fear, pulling *them* out of the fire,[a] hating even the garment defiled by the flesh.

GLORY TO GOD

24 Now to Him who is
able to keep you[a]
from stumbling,
And to present
you faultless
Before the presence of His
glory with exceeding joy,
25 To God our Savior,[a]
Who alone is wise,[b]
Be glory and majesty,
Dominion and power,[c]
Both now and forever.
Amen.

12 [a] NU-Text and M-Text read *along.* 22 [a] NU-Text reads *who are doubting* (or *making distinctions*). 23 [a] NU-Text adds *and on some have mercy with fear* and omits *with fear* in first clause. 24 [a] M-Text reads *them.* 25 [a] NU-Text reads *To the only God our Savior.* [b] NU-Text omits *Who . . . is wise* and adds *Through Jesus Christ our Lord.* [c] NU-Text adds *Before all time.*

THE REVELATION OF JESUS CHRIST

INTRODUCTION AND BENEDICTION

1 The Revelation of Jesus Christ, which God gave Him to show His servants—things which must shortly take place. And He sent and signified *it* by His angel to His servant John, 2who bore witness to the word of God, and to the testimony of Jesus Christ, to all things that he saw. 3Blessed *is* he who reads and those who hear the words of this prophecy, and keep those things which are written in it; for the time *is* near.

GREETING THE SEVEN CHURCHES

4John, to the seven churches which are in Asia:

Grace to you and peace from Him who is and who was and who is to come, and from the seven Spirits who are before His throne, 5and from Jesus Christ, the faithful witness, the firstborn from the dead, and the ruler over the kings of the earth.

To Him who loved us and washed[a] us from our sins in His own blood, 6and has made us kings[a] and priests to His God and Father, to Him *be* glory and dominion forever and ever. Amen.

7Behold, He is coming with clouds, and every eye will see Him, even they who pierced Him. And all the tribes of the earth will mourn because of Him. Even so, Amen.

8"I am the Alpha and the Omega, *the* Beginning and *the* End,"[a] says the Lord,[b] "who is and who was and who is to come, the Almighty."

VISION OF THE SON OF MAN

9I, John, both[a] your brother and companion in the tribulation and kingdom and patience of Jesus Christ, was on the island that is called Patmos for the word of God and for the testimony of Jesus Christ. 10I was in the Spirit on the Lord's Day, and I heard behind me a loud voice, as of a trumpet, 11saying, "I am the Alpha and the Omega, the First and the Last," and,[a]

1:5 [a] NU-Text reads *loves us and freed;* M-Text reads *loves us and washed.* 1:6 [a] NU-Text and M-Text read *a kingdom.* 1:8 [a] NU-Text and M-Text omit *the Beginning and the End.* [b] NU-Text and M-Text add *God.* 1:9 [a] NU-Text and M-Text omit *both.* 1:11 [a] NU-Text and M-Text omit *I am* through third *and.*

"What you see, write in a
book and send *it* to the seven
churches which are in Asia:[b]
to Ephesus, to Smyrna, to Pergamos, to Thyatira, to Sardis,
to Philadelphia, and to Laodicea."
12Then I turned to see the
voice that spoke with me. And
having turned I saw seven
golden lampstands, 13and in
the midst of the seven lampstands *One* like the Son of
Man, clothed with a garment
down to the feet and girded
about the chest with a golden
band. 14His head and hair *were*
white like wool, as white as
snow, and His eyes like a
flame of fire; 15His feet *were*
like fine brass, as if refined in
a furnace, and His voice as the
sound of many waters; 16He
had in His right hand seven
stars, out of His mouth went
a sharp two-edged sword, and
His countenance *was* like the
sun shining in its strength.
17And when I saw Him, I fell
at His feet as dead. But He laid
His right hand on me, saying
to me,[a] "Do not be afraid; I
am the First and the Last.
18I *am* He who lives, and was
dead, and behold, I am alive
forevermore. Amen. And I
have the keys of Hades and
of Death. 19Write[a] the things
which you have seen, and
the *things* which are, and the
things which will take place
after this. 20The mystery of
the seven stars which you
saw in My right hand, and the
seven golden lampstands: The
seven stars are the angels of
the seven churches, and the
seven lampstands which you
saw[a] are the seven churches.

THE LOVELESS CHURCH

2 "To the angel of the church
of Ephesus write,
'These things says He who
holds the seven stars in His
right hand, who walks in the
midst of the seven golden
lampstands: 2"I know your
works, your labor, your patience, and that you cannot
bear those who are evil. And
you have tested those who say
they are apostles and are not,
and have found them liars;
3and you have persevered and
have patience, and have labored for My name's sake and
have not become weary. 4Nev-
ertheless I have *this* against
you, that you have left your
first love. 5Remember therefore from where you have
fallen; repent and do the first
works, or else I will come to
you quickly and remove your
lampstand from its place—
unless you repent. 6But this
you have, that you hate the
deeds of the Nicolaitans,
which I also hate.

1:11 [b] NU-Text and M-Text omit *which are in Asia.* 1:17 [a] NU-Text and M-Text omit *to me.* 1:19 [a] NU-Text and M-Text read *Therefore, write.* 1:20 [a] NU-Text and M-Text omit *which you saw.*

7"He who has an ear, let
him hear what the Spirit says
to the churches. To him who
overcomes I will give to eat
from the tree of life, which is
in the midst of the Paradise
of God."'

THE PERSECUTED CHURCH

8"And to the angel of the
church in Smyrna write,

'These things says the First
and the Last, who was dead,
and came to life: 9"I know
your works, tribulation, and
poverty (but you are rich); and
I know the blasphemy of those
who say they are Jews and are
not, but *are* a synagogue of
Satan. 10Do not fear any of
those things which you are
about to suffer. Indeed, the
devil is about to throw *some*
of you into prison, that you
may be tested, and you will
have tribulation ten days. Be
faithful until death, and I will
give you the crown of life.

11"He who has an ear, let
him hear what the Spirit says
to the churches. He who overcomes shall not be hurt by the
second death."'

THE COMPROMISING CHURCH

12"And to the angel of the
church in Pergamos write,

'These things says He who
has the sharp two-edged
sword: 13"I know your works,
and where you dwell, where
Satan's throne *is*. And you
hold fast to My name, and
did not deny My faith even
in the days in which Antipas
was My faithful martyr, who
was killed among you, where
Satan dwells. 14But I have a
few things against you, because you have there those
who hold the doctrine of Balaam, who taught Balak to
put a stumbling block before
the children of Israel, to eat
things sacrificed to idols, and
to commit sexual immoral-
ity. 15Thus you also have those
who hold the doctrine of the
Nicolaitans, which thing I
hate.[a] 16Repent, or else I will
come to you quickly and will
fight against them with the
sword of My mouth.

17"He who has an ear, let
him hear what the Spirit says
to the churches. To him who
overcomes I will give some of
the hidden manna to eat. And
I will give him a white stone,
and on the stone a new name
written which no one knows
except him who receives *it*."'

THE CORRUPT CHURCH

18"And to the angel of the
church in Thyatira write,

'These things says the Son
of God, who has eyes like a
flame of fire, and His feet
like fine brass: 19"I know your
works, love, service, faith,[a] and

2:15 [a] NU-Text and M-Text read *likewise* for *which thing I hate*. 2:19 [a] NU-Text and M-Text read *faith, service*.

your patience; and *as* for your
works, the last *are* more than
the first. 20Nevertheless I have
a few things against you, because you allow[a] that woman[b]
Jezebel, who calls herself a
prophetess, to teach and se-
duce[c] My servants to commit sexual immorality and
eat things sacrificed to idols.
21And I gave her time to repent
of her sexual immorality, and
she did not repent.[a] 22Indeed
I will cast her into a sickbed,
and those who commit adultery with her into great tribulation, unless they repent of
their[a] deeds. 23I will kill her
children with death, and all
the churches shall know that
I am He who searches the
minds and hearts. And I will
give to each one of you according to your works.

24"Now to you I say, and[a] to
the rest in Thyatira, as many
as do not have this doctrine,
who have not known the
depths of Satan, as they say,
I will[b] put on you no other
burden. 25But hold fast what
you have till I come. 26And he
who overcomes, and keeps My
works until the end, to him I
will give power over the nations—

27 'He shall rule them
with a rod of iron;
They shall be dashed
to pieces like the
potter's vessels'[a]—

as I also have received from
My Father; 28and I will give
him the morning star.

29"He who has an ear, let
him hear what the Spirit says
to the churches."'

THE DEAD CHURCH

3 "And to the angel of the
church in Sardis write,
'These things says He who
has the seven Spirits of God
and the seven stars: "I know
your works, that you have a
name that you are alive, but
you are dead. 2Be watchful,
and strengthen the things
which remain, that are ready
to die, for I have not found
your works perfect before
God.[a] 3Remember therefore
how you have received and
heard; hold fast and repent.
Therefore if you will not
watch, I will come upon you as
a thief, and you will not know
what hour I will come upon
you. 4You[a] have a few names
even in Sardis who have not
defiled their garments; and

2:20 [a] NU-Text and M-Text read *I have against you that you tolerate.* [b] M-Text reads *your wife Jezebel.* [c] NU-Text and M-Text read *and teaches and seduces.* 2:21 [a] NU-Text and M-Text read *time to repent, and she does not want to repent of her sexual immorality.* 2:22 [a] NU-Text and M-Text read *her.* 2:24 [a] NU-Text and M-Text omit *and.* [b] NU-Text and M-Text omit *will.* 2:27 [a] Psalm 2:9 3:2 [a] NU-Text and M-Text read *My God.* 3:4 [a] NU-Text and M-Text read *Nevertheless you have a few names in Sardis.*

they shall walk with Me in
white, for they are worthy.
5He who overcomes shall be
clothed in white garments,
and I will not blot out his
name from the Book of Life;
but I will confess his name
before My Father and before
His angels.
6"He who has an ear, let
him hear what the Spirit says
to the churches."'

THE FAITHFUL CHURCH

7"And to the angel of the
church in Philadelphia write,
'These things says He who
is holy, He who is true, "He
who has the key of David, He
who opens and no one shuts,
and shuts and no one opens":[a]
8"I know your works. See, I
have set before you an open
door, and no one can shut it;[a]
for you have a little strength,
have kept My word, and have
not denied My name. 9In-
deed I will make *those* of the
synagogue of Satan, who say
they are Jews and are not, but
lie—indeed I will make them
come and worship before your
feet, and to know that I have
loved you. 10Because you have
kept My command to perse-
vere, I also will keep you from
the hour of trial which shall
come upon the whole world,
to test those who dwell on the
earth. 11Behold,[a] I am coming
quickly! Hold fast what you
have, that no one may take
your crown. 12He who overcomes, I will make him a pillar
in the temple of My God, and
he shall go out no more. I will
write on him the name of My
God and the name of the city
of My God, the New Jerusalem, which comes down out
of heaven from My God. And
I will write on him My new
name.
13"He who has an ear, let
him hear what the Spirit says
to the churches."'

THE LUKEWARM CHURCH

14"And to the angel of the
church of the Laodiceans[a]
write,
'These things says the
Amen, the Faithful and True
Witness, the Beginning of the
creation of God: 15"I know your
works, that you are neither
cold nor hot. I could wish you
were cold or hot. 16So then,
because you are lukewarm,
and neither cold nor hot,[a]
I will vomit you out of My
mouth. 17Because you say, 'I
am rich, have become wealthy,
and have need of nothing'—
and do not know that you are
wretched, miserable, poor,
blind, and naked— 18I counsel
you to buy from Me gold refined in the fire, that you may
be rich; and white garments,

3:7 [a] Isaiah 22:22 3:8 [a] NU-Text and M-Text read *which no one can shut.* 3:11 [a] NU-Text and M-Text omit *Behold.* 3:14 [a] NU-Text and M-Text read *in Laodicea.* 3:16 [a] NU-Text and M-Text read *hot nor cold.*

that you may be clothed, *that*
the shame of your nakedness
may not be revealed; and
anoint your eyes with eye
salve, that you may see. 19As
many as I love, I rebuke and
chasten. Therefore be zealous and repent. 20Behold, I
stand at the door and knock.
If anyone hears My voice and
opens the door, I will come
in to him and dine with him,
and he with Me. 21To him who
overcomes I will grant to sit
with Me on My throne, as I also
overcame and sat down with
My Father on His throne.

22"He who has an ear, let
him hear what the Spirit says
to the churches."'"

THE THRONE ROOM OF HEAVEN

4 After these things I looked,
and behold, a door *standing* open in heaven. And the
first voice which I heard *was*
like a trumpet speaking with
me, saying, "Come up here, and
I will show you things which
must take place after this."

2Immediately I was in the
Spirit; and behold, a throne
set in heaven, and *One* sat on
the throne. 3And He who sat
there was[a] like a jasper and
a sardius stone in appearance; and *there was* a rainbow
around the throne, in appearance like an emerald. 4Around
the throne *were* twenty-four
thrones, and on the thrones
I saw twenty-four elders sitting, clothed in white robes;
and they had crowns[a] of gold
on their heads. 5And from the
throne proceeded lightnings,
thunderings, and voices.[a]
Seven lamps of fire *were* burning before the throne, which
are the[b] seven Spirits of God.

6Before the throne *there
was*[a] a sea of glass, like crystal.
And in the midst of the throne,
and around the throne, *were*
four living creatures full of eyes
in front and in back. 7The first
living creature *was* like a lion,
the second living creature like
a calf, the third living creature
had a face like a man, and the
fourth living creature *was* like
a flying eagle. 8*The* four living
creatures, each having six
wings, were full of eyes around
and within. And they do not
rest day or night, saying:

"Holy, holy, holy,[a]
Lord God Almighty,
Who was and is and
is to come!"

9Whenever the living creatures give glory and honor and
thanks to Him who sits on the

4:3 [a] M-Text omits *And He who sat there was* (which *makes the description* in verse 3 modify the throne rather than God). 4:4 [a] NU-Text and M-Text read *robes, with crowns.* 4:5 [a] NU-Text and M-Text read *voices, and thunderings.* [b] M-Text omits *the.* 4:6 [a] NU-Text and M-Text add *something like.* 4:8 [a] M-Text has *holy* nine times.

throne, who lives forever and
ever, 10the twenty-four elders
fall down before Him who sits
on the throne and worship
Him who lives forever and
ever, and cast their crowns
before the throne, saying:

11 "You are worthy, O Lord,[a]
To receive glory and
honor and power;
For You created all things,
And by Your will they
exist[b] and were created."

THE LAMB TAKES THE SCROLL

5 And I saw in the right
hand of Him who sat on
the throne a scroll written inside and on the back, sealed
with seven seals. 2Then I saw
a strong angel proclaiming
with a loud voice, "Who is
worthy to open the scroll and
to loose its seals?" 3And no
one in heaven or on the earth
or under the earth was able to
open the scroll, or to look at it.
4So I wept much, because
no one was found worthy to
open and read[a] the scroll, or
to look at it. 5But one of the elders said to me, "Do not weep.
Behold, the Lion of the tribe of
Judah, the Root of David, has
prevailed to open the scroll
and to loose[a] its seven seals."
6And I looked, and behold,[a]
in the midst of the throne and
of the four living creatures,
and in the midst of the elders,
stood a Lamb as though it
had been slain, having seven
horns and seven eyes, which
are the seven Spirits of God
sent out into all the earth.
7Then He came and took the
scroll out of the right hand of
Him who sat on the throne.

WORTHY IS THE LAMB

8Now when He had taken
the scroll, the four living creatures and the twenty-four elders fell down before the Lamb,
each having a harp, and golden
bowls full of incense, which are
the prayers of the saints. 9And
they sang a new song, saying:

"You are worthy to
take the scroll,
And to open its seals;
For You were slain,
And have redeemed us
to God by Your blood
Out of every tribe and
tongue and people
and nation,
10 And have made us[a] kings[b]
and priests to our God;
And we[c] shall reign
on the earth."

11Then I looked, and I heard
the voice of many angels
around the throne, the living

4:11 [a] NU-Text and M-Text read *our Lord and God.* [b] NU-Text and M-Text read *existed.* 5:4 [a] NU-Text and M-Text omit *and read.* 5:5 [a] NU-Text and M-Text omit *to loose.* 5:6 [a] NU-Text and M-Text read *I saw in the midst . . . a Lamb standing.* 5:10 [a] NU-Text and M-Text read *them.* [b] NU-Text reads *a kingdom.* [c] NU-Text and M-Text read *they.*

creatures, and the elders; and
the number of them was ten
thousand times ten thousand,
and thousands of thousands,
12 saying with a loud voice:

"Worthy is the Lamb
who was slain
To receive power and
riches and wisdom,
And strength and honor
and glory and blessing!"

13 And every creature which
is in heaven and on the earth
and under the earth and such
as are in the sea, and all that
are in them, I heard saying:

"Blessing and honor and
glory and power
Be to Him who sits
on the throne,
And to the Lamb,
forever and ever!"[a]

14 Then the four living creatures said, "Amen!" And the
twenty-four[a] elders fell down
and worshiped Him who lives
forever and ever.[b]

FIRST SEAL: THE CONQUEROR

6 Now I saw when the Lamb
opened one of the seals;[a]
and I heard one of the four
living creatures saying with a
voice like thunder, "Come and
see." 2 And I looked, and behold,
a white horse. He who sat on it
had a bow; and a crown was
given to him, and he went out
conquering and to conquer.

SECOND SEAL: CONFLICT ON EARTH

3 When He opened the sec-
ond seal, I heard the second
living creature saying, "Come
and see."[a] 4 Another horse,
fiery red, went out. And it was
granted to the one who sat on
it to take peace from the earth,
and that *people* should kill one
another; and there was given
to him a great sword.

THIRD SEAL: SCARCITY ON EARTH

5 When He opened the third
seal, I heard the third living
creature say, "Come and see."
So I looked, and behold, a
black horse, and he who sat
on it had a pair of scales in
his hand. 6 And I heard a voice
in the midst of the four living creatures saying, "A quart[a]
of wheat for a denarius,[b] and
three quarts of barley for a
denarius; and do not harm
the oil and the wine."

FOURTH SEAL: WIDESPREAD DEATH ON EARTH

7 When He opened the
fourth seal, I heard the voice

5:13 [a] *M-Text adds Amen.* 5:14 [a] NU-Text and M-Text omit *twenty-four.* [b] NU-Text and M-Text omit *Him who lives forever and ever.* 6:1 [a] NU-Text and M-Text read *seven seals.* 6:3 [a] NU-Text and M-Text omit *and see.* 6:6 [a] Greek *choinix;* that is, approximately one quart [b] This was approximately one day's wage for a worker.

of the fourth living creature
saying, "Come and see." 8So
I looked, and behold, a pale
horse. And the name of him
who sat on it was Death, and
Hades followed with him. And
power was given to them over
a fourth of the earth, to kill
with sword, with hunger, with
death, and by the beasts of the
earth.

FIFTH SEAL: THE CRY OF THE MARTYRS

9When He opened the fifth
seal, I saw under the altar the
souls of those who had been
slain for the word of God and
for the testimony which they
held. 10And they cried with a
loud voice, saying, "How long,
O Lord, holy and true, until
You judge and avenge our
blood on those who dwell on
the earth?" 11Then a white robe
was given to each of them;
and it was said to them that
they should rest a little while
longer, until both *the number
of* their fellow servants and
their brethren, who would be
killed as they *were,* was completed.

SIXTH SEAL: COSMIC DISTURBANCES

12I looked when He opened
the sixth seal, and behold,[a]
there was a great earthquake;
and the sun became black
as sackcloth of hair, and the
moon[b] became like blood.
13And the stars of heaven fell
to the earth, as a fig tree drops
its late figs when it is shaken
by a mighty wind. 14Then the
sky receded as a scroll when it
is rolled up, and every mountain and island was moved out
of its place. 15And the kings
of the earth, the great men,
the rich men, the commanders,[a] the mighty men, every
slave and every free man, hid
themselves in the caves and in
the rocks of the mountains,
16and said to the mountains
and rocks, "Fall on us and hide
us from the face of Him who
sits on the throne and from
the wrath of the Lamb! 17For
the great day of His wrath
has come, and who is able to
stand?"

THE SEALED OF ISRAEL

7 After these things I saw
four angels standing at
the four corners of the earth,
holding the four winds of the
earth, that the wind should
not blow on the earth, on the
sea, or on any tree. 2Then I
saw another angel ascending
from the east, having the seal
of the living God. And he cried
with a loud voice to the four
angels to whom it was granted
to harm the earth and the sea,
3saying, "Do not harm the

6:12 [a] NU-Text and M-Text omit *behold.* [b] NU-Text and M-Text read *the whole moon.* 6:15 [a] NU-Text and M-Text read *the commanders, the rich men.*

earth, the sea, or the trees till
we have sealed the servants of
our God on their foreheads."
4And I heard the number of
those who were sealed. One
hundred *and* forty-four thousand of all the tribes of the
children of Israel *were* sealed:

5 of the tribe of Judah
twelve thousand
were sealed;[a]
of the tribe of Reuben
twelve thousand
were sealed;
of the tribe of Gad twelve
thousand *were* sealed;
6 of the tribe of Asher
twelve thousand
were sealed;
of the tribe of Naphtali
twelve thousand
were sealed;
of the tribe of Manasseh
twelve thousand
were sealed;
7 of the tribe of Simeon
twelve thousand
were sealed;
of the tribe of Levi twelve
thousand *were* sealed;
of the tribe of Issachar
twelve thousand
were sealed;
8 of the tribe of Zebulun
twelve thousand
were sealed;
of the tribe of Joseph
twelve thousand
were sealed;
of the tribe of Benjamin
twelve thousand
were sealed.

A MULTITUDE FROM THE GREAT TRIBULATION

9After these things I looked,
and behold, a great multitude
which no one could number,
of all nations, tribes, peoples, and tongues, standing
before the throne and before
the Lamb, clothed with white
robes, with palm branches
in their hands, 10and crying
out with a loud voice, saying,
"Salvation *belongs* to our God
who sits on the throne, and
to the Lamb!" 11All the angels
stood around the throne and
the elders and the four living
creatures, and fell on their
faces before the throne and
worshiped God, 12saying:

"Amen! Blessing and
glory and wisdom,
Thanksgiving and honor
and power and might,
Be to our God forever
and ever.
Amen."

13Then one of the elders answered, saying to me, "Who
are these arrayed in white
robes, and where did they
come from?"
14And I said to him, "Sir,[a]
you know."

7:5 [a] In NU-Text and M-Text *were sealed* is stated only in verses 5a and 8c; the words are understood in the remainder of the passage. 7:14 [a] NU-Text and M-Text read *My lord.*

So he said to me, "These are the ones who come out of the great tribulation, and washed their robes and made them white in the blood of the Lamb. 15 Therefore they are before the throne of God, and serve Him day and night in His temple. And He who sits on the throne will dwell among them. 16 They shall neither hunger anymore nor thirst anymore; the sun shall not strike them, nor any heat; 17 for the Lamb who is in the midst of the throne will shepherd them and lead them to living fountains of waters.[a] And God will wipe away every tear from their eyes."

SEVENTH SEAL: PRELUDE TO THE SEVEN TRUMPETS

8 When He opened the seventh seal, there was silence in heaven for about half an hour. 2 And I saw the seven angels who stand before God, and to them were given seven trumpets. 3 Then another angel, having a golden censer, came and stood at the altar. He was given much incense, that he should offer *it* with the prayers of all the saints upon the golden altar which was before the throne. 4 And the smoke of the incense, with the prayers of the saints, ascended before God from the angel's hand. 5 Then the angel took the censer, filled it with fire from the altar, and threw *it* to the earth. And there were noises, thunderings, lightnings, and an earthquake.

6 So the seven angels who had the seven trumpets prepared themselves to sound.

FIRST TRUMPET: VEGETATION STRUCK

7 The first angel sounded: And hail and fire followed, mingled with blood, and they were thrown to the earth.[a] And a third of the trees were burned up, and all green grass was burned up.

SECOND TRUMPET: THE SEAS STRUCK

8 Then the second angel sounded: And *something* like a great mountain burning with fire was thrown into the sea, and a third of the sea became blood. 9 And a third of the living creatures in the sea died, and a third of the ships were destroyed.

THIRD TRUMPET: THE WATERS STRUCK

10 Then the third angel sounded: And a great star fell from heaven, burning like a torch, and it fell on a third of the rivers and on the springs of water. 11 The name of the star is Wormwood. A

7:17 [a] NU-Text and M-Text read *to fountains of the waters of life.*
8:7 [a] NU-Text and M-Text add *and a third of the earth was burned up.*

third of the waters became
wormwood, and many men
died from the water, because
it was made bitter.

FOURTH TRUMPET: THE HEAVENS STRUCK

12 Then the fourth angel
sounded: And a third of the
sun was struck, a third of the
moon, and a third of the stars,
so that a third of them were
darkened. A third of the day
did not shine, and likewise
the night.
13 And I looked, and I heard
an angel[a] flying through the
midst of heaven, saying with
a loud voice, "Woe, woe, woe
to the inhabitants of the earth,
because of the remaining
blasts of the trumpet of the
three angels who are about
to sound!"

FIFTH TRUMPET: THE LOCUSTS FROM THE BOTTOMLESS PIT

9 Then the fifth angel
sounded: And I saw a
star fallen from heaven to
the earth. To him was given
the key to the bottomless pit.
2 And he opened the bottomless pit, and smoke arose out
of the pit like the smoke of a
great furnace. So the sun and
the air were darkened because
of the smoke of the pit. 3 Then
out of the smoke locusts came
upon the earth. And to them
was given power, as the scorpions of the earth have power.
4 They were commanded not
to harm the grass of the earth,
or any green thing, or any tree,
but only those men who do
not have the seal of God on
their foreheads. 5 And they
were not given *authority* to
kill them, but to torment them
for five months. Their torment
was like the torment of a scorpion when it strikes a man.
6 In those days men will seek
death and will not find it; they
will desire to die, and death
will flee from them.
7 The shape of the locusts
was like horses prepared for
battle. On their heads were
crowns of something like
gold, and their faces *were* like
the faces of men. 8 They had
hair like women's hair, and
their teeth were like lions'
teeth. 9 And they had breastplates like breastplates of
iron, and the sound of their
wings *was* like the sound of
chariots with many horses
running into battle. 10 They
had tails like scorpions, and
there were stings in their tails.
Their power *was* to hurt men
five months. 11 And they had
as king over them the angel
of the bottomless pit, whose
name in Hebrew *is* Abaddon,
but in Greek he has the name
Apollyon.
12 One woe is past. Behold,
still two more woes are coming after these things.

8:13 [a] NU-Text and M-Text read *eagle.*

SIXTH TRUMPET: THE ANGELS FROM THE EUPHRATES

13 Then the sixth angel
sounded: And I heard a voice
from the four horns of the
golden altar which is before
God, 14 saying to the sixth angel
who had the trumpet, "Re-
lease the four angels who are
bound at the great river Euphrates." 15 So the four angels,
who had been prepared for
the hour and day and month
and year, were released to kill
a third of mankind. 16 Now the
number of the army of the
horsemen *was* two hundred
million; I heard the number
of them. 17 And thus I saw the
horses in the vision: those
who sat on them had breastplates of fiery red, hyacinth
blue, and sulfur yellow; and
the heads of the horses *were*
like the heads of lions; and
out of their mouths came fire,
smoke, and brimstone. 18 By
these three *plagues* a third of
mankind was killed—by the
fire and the smoke and the
brimstone which came out
of their mouths. 19 For their
power[a] is in their mouth and
in their tails; for their tails *are*
like serpents, having heads;
and with them they do harm.

20 But the rest of mankind,
who were not killed by these
plagues, did not repent of the
works of their hands, that they
should not worship demons,
and idols of gold, silver, brass,
stone, and wood, which can
neither see nor hear nor walk.
21 And they did not repent of
their murders or their sorceries[a] or their sexual immorality or their thefts.

THE MIGHTY ANGEL WITH THE LITTLE BOOK

10 I saw still another mighty
angel coming down
from heaven, clothed with a
cloud. And a rainbow *was* on
his head, his face *was* like the
sun, and his feet like pillars
of fire. 2 He had a little book
open in his hand. And he set
his right foot on the sea and
his left *foot* on the land, 3 and
cried with a loud voice, as *when*
a lion roars. When he cried out,
seven thunders uttered their
voices. 4 Now when the seven
thunders uttered their voices,[a]
I was about to write; but I heard
a voice from heaven saying to
me,[b] "Seal up the things which
the seven thunders uttered,
and do not write them."

5 The angel whom I saw
standing on the sea and on
the land raised up his hand[a]
to heaven 6 and swore by Him
who lives forever and ever, who
created heaven and the things
that are in it, the earth and the
things that are in it, and the sea

9:19 [a] NU-Text and M-Text read *the power of the horses.*
9:21 [a] NU-Text and M-Text read *drugs.* 10:4 [a] NU-Text and M-Text read *sounded.* [b] NU-Text and M-Text omit *to me.* 10:5 [a] NU-Text and M-Text read *right hand.*

and the things that are in it,
that there should be delay no
longer, 7but in the days of the
sounding of the seventh angel,
when he is about to sound, the
mystery of God would be finished, as He declared to His
servants the prophets.

JOHN EATS THE LITTLE BOOK

8Then the voice which I
heard from heaven spoke to
me again and said, "Go, take
the little book which is open
in the hand of the angel who
stands on the sea and on the
earth."

9So I went to the angel and
said to him, "Give me the little
book."

And he said to me, "Take
and eat it; and it will make your
stomach bitter, but it will be as
sweet as honey in your mouth."

10Then I took the little book
out of the angel's hand and ate
it, and it was as sweet as honey
in my mouth. But when I had
eaten it, my stomach became
bitter. 11And he[a] said to me,
"You must prophesy again
about many peoples, nations,
tongues, and kings."

THE TWO WITNESSES

11 Then I was given a reed like
a measuring rod. And the
angel stood,[a] saying, "Rise and
measure the temple of God, the
altar, and those who worship
there. 2But leave out the court
which is outside the temple,
and do not measure it, for it
has been given to the Gentiles.
And they will tread the holy
city underfoot *for* forty-two
months. 3And I will give *power*
to my two witnesses, and they
will prophesy one thousand
two hundred and sixty days,
clothed in sackcloth."

4These are the two olive
trees and the two lampstands
standing before the God[a] of the
earth. 5And if anyone wants to
harm them, fire proceeds from
their mouth and devours their
enemies. And if anyone wants
to harm them, he must be
killed in this manner. 6These
have power to shut heaven, so
that no rain falls in the days
of their prophecy; and they
have power over waters to turn
them to blood, and to strike
the earth with all plagues, as
often as they desire.

THE WITNESSES KILLED

7When they finish their testimony, the beast that ascends
out of the bottomless pit will
make war against them, overcome them, and kill them.
8And their dead bodies *will
lie* in the street of the great
city which spiritually is called
Sodom and Egypt, where also
our[a] Lord was crucified. 9Then

10:11 [a] NU-Text and M-Text read *they*. 11:1 [a] NU-Text and M-Text omit *And the angel stood*. 11:4 [a] NU-Text and M-Text read *Lord*. 11:8 [a] NU-Text and M-Text read *their*.

those from the peoples, tribes,
tongues, and nations will see
their dead bodies three-and-a-
half days, and not allow[a] their
dead bodies to be put into
graves. 10 And those who dwell
on the earth will rejoice over
them, make merry, and send
gifts to one another, because
these two prophets tormented
those who dwell on the earth.

THE WITNESSES RESURRECTED

11 Now after the three-and-
a-half days the breath of life
from God entered them, and
they stood on their feet, and
great fear fell on those who
saw them. 12 And they[a] heard
a loud voice from heaven saying to them, "Come up here."
And they ascended to heaven
in a cloud, and their enemies
saw them. 13 In the same hour
there was a great earthquake,
and a tenth of the city fell. In
the earthquake seven thousand people were killed, and
the rest were afraid and gave
glory to the God of heaven.

14 The second woe is past.
Behold, the third woe is coming quickly.

SEVENTH TRUMPET: THE KINGDOM PROCLAIMED

15 Then the seventh angel
sounded: And there were loud
voices in heaven, saying, "The
kingdoms[a] of this world have
become *the kingdoms* of our
Lord and of His Christ, and He
shall reign forever and ever!"
16 And the twenty-four elders
who sat before God on their
thrones fell on their faces and
worshiped God, 17 saying:

"We give You thanks,
O Lord God Almighty,
The One who is and
who was and who
is to come,[a]
Because You have
taken Your great
power and reigned.
18 The nations were
angry, and Your
wrath has come,
And the time of the
dead, that they
should be judged,
And that You should
reward Your servants
the prophets and
the saints,
And those who fear Your
name, small and great,
And should destroy those
who destroy the earth."

19 Then the temple of God
was opened in heaven, and
the ark of His covenant[a] was
seen in His temple. And there
were lightnings, noises, thunderings, an earthquake, and
great hail.

11:9 [a] NU-Text and M-Text read *nations see . . . and will not allow.* 11:12 [a] M-Text reads *I.* 11:15 [a] NU-Text and M-Text read *kingdom . . . has become.* 11:17 [a] NU-Text and M-Text omit *and who is to come.* 11:19 [a] M-Text reads *the covenant of the Lord.*

THE WOMAN, THE CHILD, AND THE DRAGON

12 Now a great sign appeared in heaven: a
woman clothed with the sun,
with the moon under her feet,
and on her head a garland of
twelve stars. [2]Then being with
child, she cried out in labor
and in pain to give birth.

[3]And another sign appeared in heaven: behold, a
great, fiery red dragon having
seven heads and ten horns,
and seven diadems on his
heads. [4]His tail drew a third
of the stars of heaven and
threw them to the earth. And
the dragon stood before the
woman who was ready to give
birth, to devour her Child as
soon as it was born. [5]She bore
a male Child who was to rule
all nations with a rod of iron.
And her Child was caught up
to God and His throne. [6]Then
the woman fled into the wilderness, where she has a place
prepared by God, that they
should feed her there one
thousand two hundred and
sixty days.

SATAN THROWN OUT OF HEAVEN

[7]And war broke out in
heaven: Michael and his angels fought with the dragon;
and the dragon and his angels
fought, [8]but they did not pre-
vail, nor was a place found for
them[a] in heaven any longer.
[9]So the great dragon was cast
out, that serpent of old, called
the Devil and Satan, who deceives the whole world; he was
cast to the earth, and his angels were cast out with him.

[10]Then I heard a loud voice
saying in heaven, "Now salvation, and strength, and
the kingdom of our God, and
the power of His Christ have
come, for the accuser of our
brethren, who accused them
before our God day and night,
has been cast down. [11]And
they overcame him by the
blood of the Lamb and by the
word of their testimony, and
they did not love their lives to
the death. [12]Therefore rejoice,
O heavens, and you who dwell
in them! Woe to the inhabitants of the earth and the sea!
For the devil has come down
to you, having great wrath, because he knows that he has a
short time."

THE WOMAN PERSECUTED

[13]Now when the dragon
saw that he had been cast to
the earth, he persecuted the
woman who gave birth to the
male *Child*. [14]But the woman
was given two wings of a great
eagle, that she might fly into
the wilderness to her place,
where she is nourished for a
time and times and half a time,
from the presence of the serpent. [15]So the serpent spewed
water out of his mouth like a

12:8 [a] M-Text reads *him*.

flood after the woman, that he
might cause her to be carried
away by the flood. 16But the
earth helped the woman, and
the earth opened its mouth
and swallowed up the flood
which the dragon had spewed
out of his mouth. 17And the
dragon was enraged with the
woman, and he went to make
war with the rest of her offspring, who keep the com-
mandments of God and have
the testimony of Jesus Christ.[a]

THE BEAST FROM THE SEA

13 Then I[a] stood on the
sand of the sea. And I
saw a beast rising up out of the
sea, having seven heads and
ten horns,[b] and on his horns
ten crowns, and on his heads
a blasphemous name. 2Now
the beast which I saw was like
a leopard, his feet were like *the
feet of* a bear, and his mouth
like the mouth of a lion. The
dragon gave him his power,
his throne, and great au-
thority. 3And I saw one of his
heads as if it had been mortally wounded, and his deadly
wound was healed. And all the
world marveled and followed
the beast. 4So they worshiped
the dragon who gave authority to the beast; and they worshiped the beast, saying, "Who
is like the beast? Who is able
to make war with him?"

5And he was given a
mouth speaking great things
and blasphemies, and he
was given authority to continue[a] for forty-two months.
6Then he opened his mouth
in blasphemy against God, to
blaspheme His name, His tabernacle, and those who dwell
in heaven. 7It was granted
to him to make war with the
saints and to overcome them.
And authority was given him
over every tribe,[a] tongue, and
nation. 8All who dwell on the
earth will worship him, whose
names have not been written
in the Book of Life of the Lamb
slain from the foundation of
the world.

9If anyone has an ear, let
him hear. 10He who leads into
captivity shall go into captivity; he who kills with the
sword must be killed with the
sword. Here is the patience
and the faith of the saints.

THE BEAST FROM THE EARTH

11Then I saw another beast
coming up out of the earth,
and he had two horns like a
lamb and spoke like a dragon.
12And he exercises all the authority of the first beast in
his presence, and causes the
earth and those who dwell in
it to worship the first beast,
whose deadly wound was

12:17 [a] NU-Text and M-Text omit *Christ.* 13:1 [a] NU-Text reads *he.* [b] NU-Text and M-Text read *ten horns and seven heads.* 13:5 [a] M-Text reads *make war.* 13:7 [a] NU-Text and M-Text add *and people.*

healed. 13He performs great
signs, so that he even makes
fire come down from heaven
on the earth in the sight of
men. 14And he deceives those[a]
who dwell on the earth by
those signs which he was
granted to do in the sight of
the beast, telling those who
dwell on the earth to make an
image to the beast who was
wounded by the sword and
lived. 15He was granted *power*
to give breath to the image of
the beast, that the image of
the beast should both speak
and cause as many as would
not worship the image of the
beast to be killed. 16He causes
all, both small and great, rich
and poor, free and slave, to
receive a mark on their right
hand or on their foreheads,
17and that no one may buy or
sell except one who has the
mark or[a] the name of the
beast, or the number of his
name.

18Here is wisdom. Let him
who has understanding calcu-
late the number of the beast,
for it is the number of a man:
His number *is* 666.

THE LAMB AND THE 144,000

14 Then I looked, and be-
hold, a[a] Lamb standing
on Mount Zion, and with Him
one hundred *and* forty-four
thousand, having[b] His Father's name written on their
foreheads. 2And I heard a
voice from heaven, like the
voice of many waters, and
like the voice of loud thunder. And I heard the sound of
harpists playing their harps.
3They sang as it were a new
song before the throne, before the four living creatures,
and the elders; and no one
could learn that song except
the hundred *and* forty-four
thousand who were redeemed
from the earth. 4These are the
ones who were not defiled
with women, for they are virgins. These are the ones who
follow the Lamb wherever He
goes. These were redeemed[a]
from *among* men, *being*
firstfruits to God and to the
Lamb. 5And in their mouth
was found no deceit,[a] for they
are without fault before the
throne of God.[b]

THE PROCLAMATIONS OF THREE ANGELS

6Then I saw another angel
flying in the midst of heaven,
having the everlasting gospel
to preach to those who dwell
on the earth—to every nation,
tribe, tongue, and people—
7saying with a loud voice,
"Fear God and give glory to

13:14 [a] M-Text *reads my own people.* 13:17 [a] NU-Text and M-Text omit *or.* 14:1 [a] NU-Text and M-Text read *the.* [b] NU-Text and M-Text add *His name and.* 14:4 [a] M-Text adds *by Jesus.* 14:5 [a] NU-Text and M-Text read *falsehood.* [b] NU-Text and M-Text omit *before the throne of God.*

Him, for the hour of His judgment has come; and worship Him who made heaven and earth, the sea and springs of water."

8And another angel followed, saying, "Babylon[a] is fallen, is fallen, that great city, because she has made all nations drink of the wine of the wrath of her fornication."

9Then a third angel followed them, saying with a loud voice, "If anyone worships the beast and his image, and receives *his* mark on his forehead or on his hand,
10he himself shall also drink of the wine of the wrath of God, which is poured out full strength into the cup of His indignation. He shall be tormented with fire and brimstone in the presence of the holy angels and in the presence of the Lamb.
11And the smoke of their torment ascends forever and ever; and they have no rest day or night, who worship the beast and his image, and whoever receives the mark of his name."

12Here is the patience of the saints; here *are* those[a] who keep the commandments of God and the faith of Jesus.

13Then I heard a voice from heaven saying to me,[a] "Write: 'Blessed *are* the dead who die in the Lord from now on.'"

"Yes," says the Spirit, "that they may rest from their labors, and their works follow them."

REAPING THE EARTH'S HARVEST

14Then I looked, and behold, a white cloud, and on the cloud sat *One* like the Son of Man, having on His head a golden crown, and in His hand a sharp sickle.
15And another angel came out of the temple, crying with a loud voice to Him who sat on the cloud, "Thrust in Your sickle and reap, for the time has come for You[a] to reap, for the harvest of the earth is ripe."
16So He who sat on the cloud thrust in His sickle on the earth, and the earth was reaped.

REAPING THE GRAPES OF WRATH

17Then another angel came out of the temple which is in heaven, he also having a sharp sickle.

18And another angel came out from the altar, who had power over fire, and he cried with a loud cry to him who had the sharp sickle, saying, "Thrust in your sharp sickle and gather the clusters of the vine of the earth, for her grapes are fully ripe."
19So the angel thrust his sickle into the

14:8 [a] NU-Text reads *Babylon the great is fallen, is fallen, which has made;* M-Text reads *Babylon the great is fallen. She has made.* 14:12 [a] NU-Text and M-Text omit *here are those.* 14:13 [a] NU-Text and M-Text omit *to me.* 14:15 [a] NU-Text and M-Text omit *for You.*

earth and gathered the vine of
the earth, and threw *it* into the
great winepress of the wrath
of God. 20And the winepress
was trampled outside the city,
and blood came out of the
winepress, up to the horses'
bridles, for one thousand six
hundred furlongs.

PRELUDE TO THE BOWL JUDGMENTS

15 Then I saw another
sign in heaven, great
and marvelous: seven angels
having the seven last plagues,
for in them the wrath of God
is complete.
2And I saw *something* like
a sea of glass mingled with
fire, and those who have the
victory over the beast, over his
image and over his mark[a] *and*
over the number of his name,
standing on the sea of glass,
having harps of God. 3They
sing the song of Moses, the
servant of God, and the song
of the Lamb, saying:

"Great and marvelous
are Your works,
Lord God Almighty!
Just and true *are*
Your ways,
O King of the saints![a]
4 Who shall not fear
You, O Lord, and
glorify Your name?
For *You* alone *are* holy.
For all nations shall come
and worship before You,
For Your judgments have
been manifested."

5After these things I looked,
and behold,[a] the temple of the
tabernacle of the testimony
in heaven was opened. 6And
out of the temple came the
seven angels having the seven
plagues, clothed in pure bright
linen, and having their chests
girded with golden bands.
7Then one of the four living
creatures gave to the seven
angels seven golden bowls full
of the wrath of God who lives
forever and ever. 8The temple
was filled with smoke from
the glory of God and from His
power, and no one was able to
enter the temple till the seven
plagues of the seven angels
were completed.

16 Then I heard a loud
voice from the temple
saying to the seven angels, "Go
and pour out the bowls[a] of the
wrath of God on the earth."

FIRST BOWL: LOATHSOME SORES

2So the first went and
poured out his bowl upon
the earth, and a foul and
loathsome sore came upon
the men who had the mark
of the beast and those who
worshiped his image.

15:2 [a] NU-Text and M-Text omit *over his mark.* 15:3 [a] NU-Text and M-Text read *nations.* 15:5 [a] NU-Text and M-Text omit *behold.* 16:1 [a] NU-Text and M-Text read *seven bowls.*

SECOND BOWL: THE SEA TURNS TO BLOOD

3Then the second angel
poured out his bowl on the
sea, and it became blood as of
a dead *man;* and every living
creature in the sea died.

THIRD BOWL: THE WATERS TURN TO BLOOD

4Then the third angel
poured out his bowl on the
rivers and springs of water,
and they became blood. 5And
I heard the angel of the waters
saying:

"You are righteous,
  O Lord,[a]
The One who is and
  who was and
  who is to be,[b]
Because You have
  judged these things.
6 For they have shed
  the blood of saints
  and prophets,
And You have given
  them blood to drink.
For[a] it is their just due."

7And I heard another from[a]
the altar saying, "Even so, Lord
God Almighty, true and righteous *are* Your judgments."

FOURTH BOWL: MEN ARE SCORCHED

8Then the fourth angel
poured out his bowl on the
sun, and power was given to
him to scorch men with fire.
9And men were scorched with
great heat, and they blasphemed the name of God who
has power over these plagues;
and they did not repent and
give Him glory.

FIFTH BOWL: DARKNESS AND PAIN

10Then the fifth angel
poured out his bowl on the
throne of the beast, and his
kingdom became full of darkness; and they gnawed their
tongues because of the pain.
11They blasphemed the God of
heaven because of their pains
and their sores, and did not
repent of their deeds.

SIXTH BOWL: EUPHRATES DRIED UP

12Then the sixth angel
poured out his bowl on the
great river Euphrates, and its
water was dried up, so that
the way of the kings from the
east might be prepared. 13And
I saw three unclean spirits
like frogs *coming* out of the
mouth of the dragon, out of
the mouth of the beast, and
out of the mouth of the false
prophet. 14For they are spirits
of demons, performing signs,
which go out to the kings of
the earth and[a] of the whole
world, to gather them to the

16:5 [a] NU-Text and M-Text omit *O Lord.* [b] NU-Text and M-Text read *who was, the Holy One.* 16:6 [a] NU-Text and M-Text omit *For.* 16:7 [a] NU-Text and M-Text omit *another from.* 16:14 [a] NU-Text and M-Text omit *of the earth and.*

battle of that great day of God
Almighty.
[15]"Behold, I am coming
as a thief. Blessed *is* he who
watches, and keeps his garments, lest he walk naked and
they see his shame."
[16]And they gathered them
together to the place called in
Hebrew, Armageddon.[a]

SEVENTH BOWL: THE EARTH UTTERLY SHAKEN

[17]Then the seventh angel
poured out his bowl into the
air, and a loud voice came out
of the temple of heaven, from
the throne, saying, "It is done!"
[18]And there were noises and
thunderings and lightnings;
and there was a great earthquake, such a mighty and
great earthquake as had not
occurred since men were on
the earth. [19]Now the great city
was divided into three parts,
and the cities of the nations
fell. And great Babylon was
remembered before God, to
give her the cup of the wine
of the fierceness of His wrath.
[20]Then every island fled away,
and the mountains were not
found. [21]And great hail from
heaven fell upon men, *each
hailstone* about the weight of
a talent. Men blasphemed God
because of the plague of the
hail, since that plague was exceed*ingly great*.

THE SCARLET WOMAN AND THE SCARLET BEAST

17 Then one of the seven
angels who had the seven
bowls came and talked with
me, saying to me,[a] "Come, I
will show you the judgment
of the great harlot who sits
on many waters, [2]with whom
the kings of the earth committed fornication, and the
inhabitants of the earth were
made drunk with the wine of
her fornication."
[3]So he carried me away in
the Spirit into the wilderness.
And I saw a woman sitting
on a scarlet beast *which was*
full of names of blasphemy,
having seven heads and ten
horns. [4]The woman was arrayed in purple and scarlet,
and adorned with gold and
precious stones and pearls,
having in her hand a golden
cup full of abominations and
the filthiness of her fornication.[a] [5]And on her forehead a
name *was* written:

MYSTERY, BABYLON
THE GREAT,
THE MOTHER OF HARLOTS
AND OF THE
ABOMINATIONS
OF THE EARTH.

[6]I saw the woman, drunk with
the blood of the saints and
with the blood of the martyrs

16:16 [a] M-Text reads *Megiddo*. 17:1 [a] NU-Text and M-Text omit *to me*. 17:4 [a] M-Text reads *the filthiness of the fornication of the earth*.

of Jesus. And when I saw her,
I marveled with great amazement.

THE MEANING OF THE WOMAN AND THE BEAST

7But the angel said to me,
"Why did you marvel? I will tell
you the mystery of the woman
and of the beast that carries
her, which has the seven heads
and the ten horns. 8The beast
that you saw was, and is not,
and will ascend out of the bottomless pit and go to perdition. And those who dwell on
the earth will marvel, whose
names are not written in the
Book of Life from the foundation of the world, when they
see the beast that was, and is
not, and yet is.[a]
9"Here *is* the mind which
has wisdom: The seven heads
are seven mountains on which
the woman sits. 10There are
also seven kings. Five have
fallen, one is, *and* the other
has not yet come. And when
he comes, he must continue
a short time. 11The beast that
was, and is not, is himself also
the eighth, and is of the seven,
and is going to perdition.
12"The ten horns which you
saw are ten kings who have received no kingdom as yet, but
they receive authority for one
hour as kings with the beast.
13These are of one mind, and
they will give their power and
authority to the beast. 14These
will make war with the Lamb,
and the Lamb will overcome
them, for He is Lord of lords
and King of kings; and those
who are with Him *are* called,
chosen, and faithful."
15Then he said to me, "The
waters which you saw, where
the harlot sits, are peoples,
multitudes, nations, and
tongues. 16And the ten horns
which you saw on[a] the beast,
these will hate the harlot,
make her desolate and naked,
eat her flesh and burn her
with fire. 17For God has put it
into their hearts to fulfill His
purpose, to be of one mind,
and to give their kingdom to
the beast, until the words of
God are fulfilled. 18And the
woman whom you saw is that
great city which reigns over
the kings of the earth."

THE FALL OF BABYLON THE GREAT

18 After these things I saw
another angel coming
down from heaven, having
great authority, and the earth
was illuminated with his glory.
2And he cried mightily[a] with
a loud voice, saying, "Babylon
the great is fallen, is fallen,
and has become a dwelling
place of demons, a prison for

17:8 [a] NU-Text and M-Text read *and shall be present.* 17:16 [a] NU-Text and M-Text read *saw, and the beast.* 18:2 [a] NU-Text and M-Text omit *mightily.*

every foul spirit, and a cage
for every unclean and hated
bird! 3For all the nations have
drunk of the wine of the wrath
of her fornication, the kings
of the earth have committed
fornication with her, and the
merchants of the earth have
become rich through the
abundance of her luxury."
4And I heard another voice
from heaven saying, "Come
out of her, my people, lest you
share in her sins, and lest you
receive of her plagues. 5For her
sins have reached[a] to heaven,
and God has remembered her
iniquities. 6Render to her just
as she rendered to you,[a] and
repay her double according to
her works; in the cup which
she has mixed, mix double for
her. 7In the measure that she
glorified herself and lived luxuriously, in the same measure
give her torment and sorrow;
for she says in her heart, 'I sit
as queen, and am no widow,
and will not see sorrow.'
8Therefore her plagues will
come in one day—death and
mourning and famine. And
she will be utterly burned with
fire, for strong *is* the Lord God
who judges[a] her.

THE WORLD MOURNS BABYLON'S FALL

9"The kings of the earth
who committed fornication
and lived luxuriously with
her will weep and lament for
her, when they see the smoke
of her burning, 10standing
at a distance for fear of her
torment, saying, 'Alas, alas,
that great city Babylon, that
mighty city! For in one hour
your judgment has come.'
11"And the merchants of the
earth will weep and mourn
over her, for no one buys their
merchandise anymore: 12mer-
chandise of gold and silver,
precious stones and pearls,
fine linen and purple, silk and
scarlet, every kind of citron
wood, every kind of object of
ivory, every kind of object of
most precious wood, bronze,
iron, and marble; 13and cinnamon and incense, fragrant oil
and frankincense, wine and
oil, fine flour and wheat, cattle
and sheep, horses and chariots, and bodies and souls of
men. 14The fruit that your soul
longed for has gone from you,
and all the things which are
rich and splendid have gone
from you,[a] and you shall find
them no more at all. 15The
merchants of these things,
who became rich by her, will
stand at a distance for fear
of her torment, weeping and
wailing, 16and saying, 'Alas,
alas, that great city that was
clothed in fine linen, purple,
and scarlet, *and* adorned with

18:5 [a] NU-Text and M-Text read *have been heaped up.* 18:6 [a] NU-Text and M-Text omit *to you.* 18:8 [a] NU-Text and M-Text read *has judged.* 18:14 [a] NU-Text and M-Text read *been lost to you.*

gold and precious stones and
pearls! 17For in one hour such
great riches came to nothing.'
Every shipmaster, all who
travel by ship, sailors, and
as many as trade on the sea,
stood at a distance 18and cried
out when they saw the smoke
of her burning, saying, 'What
is like this great city?'
19"They threw dust on their
heads and cried out, weeping
and wailing, and saying, 'Alas,
alas, that great city, in which all
who had ships on the sea became rich by her wealth! For in
one hour she is made desolate.'
20"Rejoice over her,
O heaven, and *you* holy apostles[a] and prophets, for God
has avenged you on her!"

FINALITY OF BABYLON'S FALL

21Then a mighty angel took
up a stone like a great millstone and threw *it* into the sea,
saying, "Thus with violence
the great city Babylon shall be
thrown down, and shall not be
found anymore. 22The sound
of harpists, musicians, flut-
ists, and trumpeters shall not
be heard in you anymore. No
craftsman of any craft shall
be found in you anymore, and
the sound of a millstone shall
not be heard in you anymore.
23The light of a lamp shall not
shine in you anymore, and
the voice of bridegroom and
bride shall not be heard in
you anymore. For your merchants were the great men of
the earth, for by your sorcery
all the nations were deceived.
24And in her was found the
blood of prophets and saints,
and of all who were slain on
the earth."

HEAVEN EXULTS OVER BABYLON

19 After these things I
heard[a] a loud voice of
a great multitude in heaven,
saying, "Alleluia! Salvation
and glory and honor and
power *belong* to the Lord[b] our
God! 2For true and righteous
are His judgments, because
He has judged the great harlot who corrupted the earth
with her fornication; and He
has avenged on her the blood
of His servants *shed* by her."
3Again they said, "Alleluia!
Her smoke rises up forever
and ever!" 4And the twenty-
four elders and the four living creatures fell down and
worshiped God who sat on the
throne, saying, "Amen! Alleluia!" 5Then a voice came from
the throne, saying, "Praise our
God, all you His servants and
those who fear Him, both[a]
small and great!"
6And I heard, as it were, the
voice of a great multitude, as

18:20 [a] NU-Text and M-Text read *saints and apostles.*
19:1 [a] NU-Text and M-Text add *something like.* [b] NU-Text and M-Text omit *the Lord.* 19:5 [a] NU-Text and M-Text omit *both.*

the sound of many waters and
as the sound of mighty thunderings, saying, "Alleluia! For
the[a] Lord God Omnipotent
reigns! 7Let us be glad and rejoice and give Him glory, for
the marriage of the Lamb has
come, and His wife has made
herself ready." 8And to her it
was granted to be arrayed in
fine linen, clean and bright,
for the fine linen is the righteous acts of the saints.

9Then he said to me, "Write:
'Blessed *are* those who are
called to the marriage supper
of the Lamb!'" And he said to
me, "These are the true sayings of God." 10And I fell at
his feet to worship him. But
he said to me, "See *that you do*
not *do that!* I am your fellow
servant, and of your brethren
who have the testimony of
Jesus. Worship God! For the
testimony of Jesus is the spirit
of prophecy."

CHRIST ON A WHITE HORSE

11Now I saw heaven opened,
and behold, a white horse.
And He who sat on him *was*
called Faithful and True, and
in righteousness He judges
and makes war. 12His eyes
were like a flame of fire,
and on His head *were* many
crowns. He had[a] a name written that no one knew except
Himself. 13He *was* clothed
with a robe dipped in blood,
and His name is called The
Word of God. 14And the armies
in heaven, clothed in fine
linen, white and clean,[a] followed Him on white horses.
15Now out of His mouth goes
a sharp[a] sword, that with it
He should strike the nations.
And He Himself will rule them
with a rod of iron. He Himself treads the winepress of
the fierceness and wrath of
Almighty God. 16And He has
on *His* robe and on His thigh
a name written:

KING OF KINGS AND
LORD OF LORDS.

THE BEAST AND HIS ARMIES DEFEATED

17Then I saw an angel
standing in the sun; and he
cried with a loud voice, saying
to all the birds that fly in the
midst of heaven, "Come and
gather together for the supper of the great God,[a] 18that
you may eat the flesh of kings,
the flesh of captains, the flesh
of mighty men, the flesh of
horses and of those who sit
on them, and the flesh of all
people, free[a] and slave, both
small and great."

19And I saw the beast, the
kings of the earth, and their
armies, gathered together to

19:6 [a] *NU-Text and* M-Text read *our.* 19:12 [a] M-Text adds *names written, and.* 19:14 [a] NU-Text and M-Text read *pure white linen.* 19:15 [a] M-Text adds *two-edged.* 19:17 [a] NU-Text and M-Text read *the great supper of God.* 19:18 [a] NU-Text and M-Text read *both free.*

make war against Him who
sat on the horse and against
His army. [20]Then the beast
was captured, and with him
the false prophet who worked
signs in his presence, by
which he deceived those who
received the mark of the beast
and those who worshiped his
image. These two were cast
alive into the lake of fire burning with brimstone. [21]And the
rest were killed with the sword
which proceeded from the
mouth of Him who sat on the
horse. And all the birds were
filled with their flesh.

SATAN BOUND 1,000 YEARS

20 Then I saw an angel
coming down from
heaven, having the key to
the bottomless pit and a great
chain in his hand. [2]He laid
hold of the dragon, that serpent of old, who is *the* Devil
and Satan, and bound him
for a thousand years; [3]and
he cast him into the bottomless pit, and shut him up, and
set a seal on him, so that he
should deceive the nations no
more till the thousand years
were finished. But after these
things he must be released for
a little while.

THE SAINTS REIGN WITH CHRIST 1,000 YEARS

[4]And I saw thrones, and
they sat on them, and judgment was committed to them.
Then *I saw* the souls of those
who had been beheaded for
their witness to Jesus and
for the word of God, who had
not worshiped the beast or his
image, and had not received
his mark on their foreheads or
on their hands. And they lived
and reigned with Christ for a[a]
thousand years. [5]But the rest
of the dead did not live again
until the thousand years were
finished. This *is* the first resurrection. [6]Blessed and holy
is he who has part in the first
resurrection. Over such the
second death has no power,
but they shall be priests of
God and of Christ, and shall
reign with Him a thousand
years.

SATANIC REBELLION CRUSHED

[7]Now when the thousand
years have expired, Satan will
be released from his prison
[8]and will go out to deceive
the nations which are in the
four corners of the earth, Gog
and Magog, to gather them together to battle, whose number *is* as the sand of the sea.
[9]They went up on the breadth
of the earth and surrounded
the camp of the saints and the
beloved city. And fire came
down from God out of heaven
and devoured them. [10]The
devil, who deceived them, was
cast into the lake of fire and

20:4 [a] M-Text reads *the*.

brimstone where[a] the beast
and the false prophet *are.* And
they will be tormented day
and night forever and ever.

THE GREAT WHITE THRONE JUDGMENT

11Then I saw a great white
throne and Him who sat on
it, from whose face the earth
and the heaven fled away. And
there was found no place for
them. 12And I saw the dead,
small and great, standing
before God,[a] and books were
opened. And another book
was opened, which is *the Book*
of Life. And the dead were
judged according to their
works, by the things which
were written in the books.
13The sea gave up the dead
who were in it, and Death
and Hades delivered up the
dead who were in them. And
they were judged, each one
according to his works. 14Then
Death and Hades were cast
into the lake of fire. This is the
second death.[a] 15And anyone
not found written in the Book
of Life was cast into the lake
of fire.

ALL THINGS MADE NEW

21 Now I saw a new heaven
and a new earth, for the
first heaven and the first earth
had passed away. Also there
was no more sea. 2Then I,
John,[a] saw the holy city, New
Jerusalem, coming down
out of heaven from God, prepared as a bride adorned for
her husband. 3And I heard a
loud voice from heaven saying, "Behold, the tabernacle
of God *is* with men, and He
will dwell with them, and they
shall be His people. God Himself will be with them *and be*
their God. 4And God will wipe
away every tear from their
eyes; there shall be no more
death, nor sorrow, nor crying.
There shall be no more pain,
for the former things have
passed away."

5Then He who sat on the
throne said, "Behold, I make
all things new." And He said to
me,[a] "Write, for these words
are true and faithful."

6And He said to me, "It is
done![a] I am the Alpha and
the Omega, the Beginning
and the End. I will give of the
fountain of the water of life
freely to him who thirsts. 7He
who overcomes shall inherit
all things,[a] and I will be his
God and he shall be My son.
8But the cowardly, unbelieving,[a] abominable, murderers,
sexually immoral, sorcerers,
idolaters, and all liars shall

20:10 [a] NU-Text and M-Text add *also.* 20:12 [a] NU-Text and M-Text read *the throne.* 20:14 [a] NU-Text and M-Text add *the lake of fire.* 21:2 [a] NU-Text and M-Text omit *John.* 21:5 [a] NU-Text and M-Text omit *to me.* 21:6 [a] M-Text omits *It is done.* 21:7 [a] M-Text reads *overcomes, I shall give him these things.* 21:8 [a] M-Text adds *and sinners.*

have their part in the lake
which burns with fire and
brimstone, which is the second death."

THE NEW JERUSALEM

9Then one of the seven angels who had the seven bowls
filled with the seven last
plagues came to me[a] and
talked with me, saying, "Come,
I will show you the bride, the
Lamb's wife."[b] 10And he carried me away in the Spirit to
a great and high mountain,
and showed me the great city,
the holy[a] Jerusalem, descending out of heaven from God,
11having the glory of God. Her
light *was* like a most precious
stone, like a jasper stone, clear
as crystal. 12Also she had a
great and high wall with twelve
gates, and twelve angels at the
gates, and names written on
them, which are *the names* of
the twelve tribes of the children of Israel: 13three gates
on the east, three gates on the
north, three gates on the south,
and three gates on the west.

14Now the wall of the city
had twelve foundations, and
on them were the names[a]
of the twelve apostles of the
Lamb. 15And he who talked
with me had a gold reed to
measure the city, its gates, and
its wall. 16The city is laid out as
a square; its length is as great
as its breadth. And he measured the city with the reed:
twelve thousand furlongs. Its
length, breadth, and height
are equal. 17Then he measured
its wall: one hundred *and*
forty-four cubits, *according*
to the measure of a man, that
is, of an angel. 18The construction of its wall was *of* jasper;
and the city *was* pure gold,
like clear glass. 19The foundations of the wall of the city
were adorned with all kinds
of precious stones: the first
foundation *was* jasper, the
second sapphire, the third
chalcedony, the fourth emerald, 20the fifth sardonyx,
the sixth sardius, the seventh
chrysolite, the eighth beryl,
the ninth topaz, the tenth
chrysoprase, the eleventh
jacinth, and the twelfth amethyst. 21The twelve gates *were*
twelve pearls: each individual gate was of one pearl. And
the street of the city *was* pure
gold, like transparent glass.

THE GLORY OF THE NEW JERUSALEM

22But I saw no temple in
it, for the Lord God Almighty
and the Lamb are its temple.
23The city had no need of the
sun or of the moon to shine
in it,[a] for the glory[b] of God

21:9 [a] NU-Text and M-Text omit *to me.* [b] M-Text reads *I will show you the woman, the Lamb's bride.* 21:10 [a] NU-Text and M-Text omit *the great* and read *the holy city, Jerusalem.* 21:14 [a] NU-Text and M-Text read *twelve names.* 21:23 [a] NU-Text and M-Text omit *in it.* [b] M-Text reads *the very glory.*

illuminated it. The Lamb *is* its light. 24And the nations of those who are saved[a] shall walk in its light, and the kings of the earth bring their glory and honor into it.[b] 25Its gates shall not be shut at all by day (there shall be no night there). 26And they shall bring the glory and the honor of the nations into it.[a] 27But there shall by no means enter it anything that defiles, or causes[a] an abomination or a lie, but only those who are written in the Lamb's Book of Life.

THE RIVER OF LIFE

22 And he showed me a pure[a] river of water of life, clear as crystal, proceeding from the throne of God and of the Lamb. 2In the middle of its street, and on either side of the river, *was* the tree of life, which bore twelve fruits, each *tree* yielding its fruit every month. The leaves of the tree *were* for the healing of the nations. 3And there shall be no more curse, but the throne of God and of the Lamb shall be in it, and His servants shall serve Him. 4They shall see His face, and His name *shall be* on their foreheads. 5There shall be no night there: They need no lamp nor light of the sun, for the Lord God gives them light. And they shall reign forever and ever.

THE TIME IS NEAR

6Then he said to me, "These words *are* faithful and true." And the Lord God of the holy[a] prophets sent His angel to show His servants the things which must shortly take place.

7"Behold, I am coming quickly! Blessed *is* he who keeps the words of the prophecy of this book."

8Now I, John, saw and heard[a] these things. And when I heard and saw, I fell down to worship before the feet of the angel who showed me these things.

9Then he said to me, "See *that you do* not *do that.* For[a] I am your fellow servant, and of your brethren the prophets, and of those who keep the words of this book. Worship God." 10And he said to me, "Do not seal the words of the prophecy of this book, for the time is at hand. 11He who is unjust, let him be unjust still; he who is filthy, let him be filthy still; he who is righ-

21:24 [a] NU-Text and M-Text omit *of those who are saved.* [b] M-Text reads *the glory and honor of the nations to Him.* 21:26 [a] M-Text adds *that they may enter in.* 21:27 [a] NU-Text and M-Text read *anything profane, nor one who causes.* 22:1 [a] NU-Text and M-Text omit *pure.* 22:6 [a] NU-Text and M-Text read *spirits of the prophets.* 22:8 [a] NU-Text and M-Text read *am the one who heard and saw.* 22:9 [a] NU-Text and M-Text omit *For.*

teous, let him be righteous[a]
still; he who is holy, let him
be holy still."

JESUS TESTIFIES TO THE CHURCHES

12"And behold, I am com-
ing quickly, and My reward *is*
with Me, to give to every one
according to his work. 13I am
the Alpha and the Omega, *the*
Beginning and *the* End, the
First and the Last."[a]

14Blessed *are* those who do
His commandments,[a] that
they may have the right to
the tree of life, and may enter
through the gates into the
city. 15But[a] outside *are* dogs
and sorcerers and sexually
immoral and murderers and
idolaters, and whoever loves
and practices a lie.

16"I, Jesus, have sent My
angel to testify to you these
things in the churches. I am
the Root and the Offspring of
David, the Bright and Morning
Star."

17And the Spirit and the
bride say, "Come!" And let
him who hears say, "Come!"
And let him who thirsts come.
Whoever desires, let him take
the water of life freely.

A WARNING

18For[a] I testify to everyone
who hears the words of the
prophecy of this book: If anyone adds to these things, God
will add[b] to him the plagues
that are written in this book;
19and if anyone takes away
from the words of the book
of this prophecy, God shall
take away[a] his part from the
Book[b] of Life, from the holy
city, and *from* the things which
are written in this book.

I AM COMING QUICKLY

20He who testifies to these
things says, "Surely I am coming quickly."

Amen. Even so, come, Lord
Jesus!

21The grace of our Lord
Jesus Christ *be* with you all.[a]
Amen.

22:11 [a] NU-Text and M-Text read *do right.* **22:13** [a] NU-Text and M-Text read *the First and the Last, the Beginning and the End.* **22:14** [a] NU-Text reads *wash their robes.* **22:15** [a] NU-Text and M-Text omit *But.* **22:18** [a] NU-Text and M-Text omit *For.* [b] M-Text reads *may God add.* **22:19** [a] M-Text reads *may God take away.* [b] NU-Text and M-Text read *tree of life.* **22:21** [a] NU-Text reads *with all;* M-Text reads *with all the saints.*

A NOTE REGARDING THE TYPE

This Bible was set in the Thomas Nelson NKJV Typeface, commissioned by Thomas Nelson Publishers and designed in Aarhus by Klaus Krogh and Heidi Rand Sørensen of 2K/DENMARK. The letterforms take inspiration from a distinctive typeface found in an early Thomas Nelson *Novum Testamentum*, printed in 1844 in Edinburgh—which in turn reflects the Scotch Roman typefaces created by the celebrated English punchcutter Richard Austin for the type foundry of William Miller, circa 1808–1813.

Just as the NKJV translation inherits the tradition and literary beauty of the King James Bible while updating the language for today's readers, so Thomas Nelson's custom NKJV font family builds on classic letterforms of the past while reflecting cutting-edge typographical *design*. The result is a type design that is at once beautiful and efficient, traditional and modern—ideal for presenting the sacred words of ancient Scripture to readers today.

Map 1: WORLD OF THE PATRIARCHS

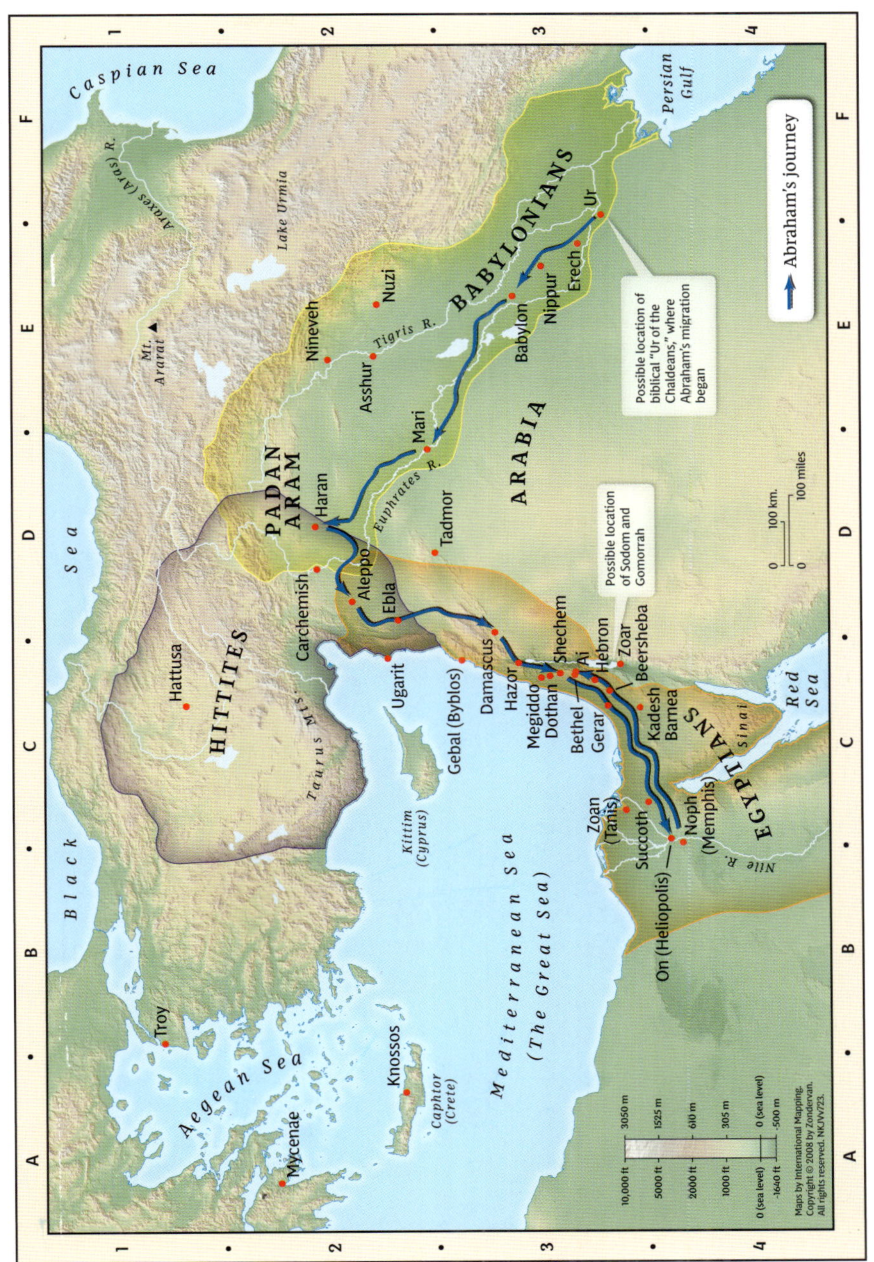

Map 2: EXODUS AND CONQUEST OF CANAAN

Map 3: LAND OF THE TWELVE TRIBES

Maps by International Mapping.

Map 4: KINGDOM OF DAVID AND SOLOMON

Map 5: JESUS' MINISTRY

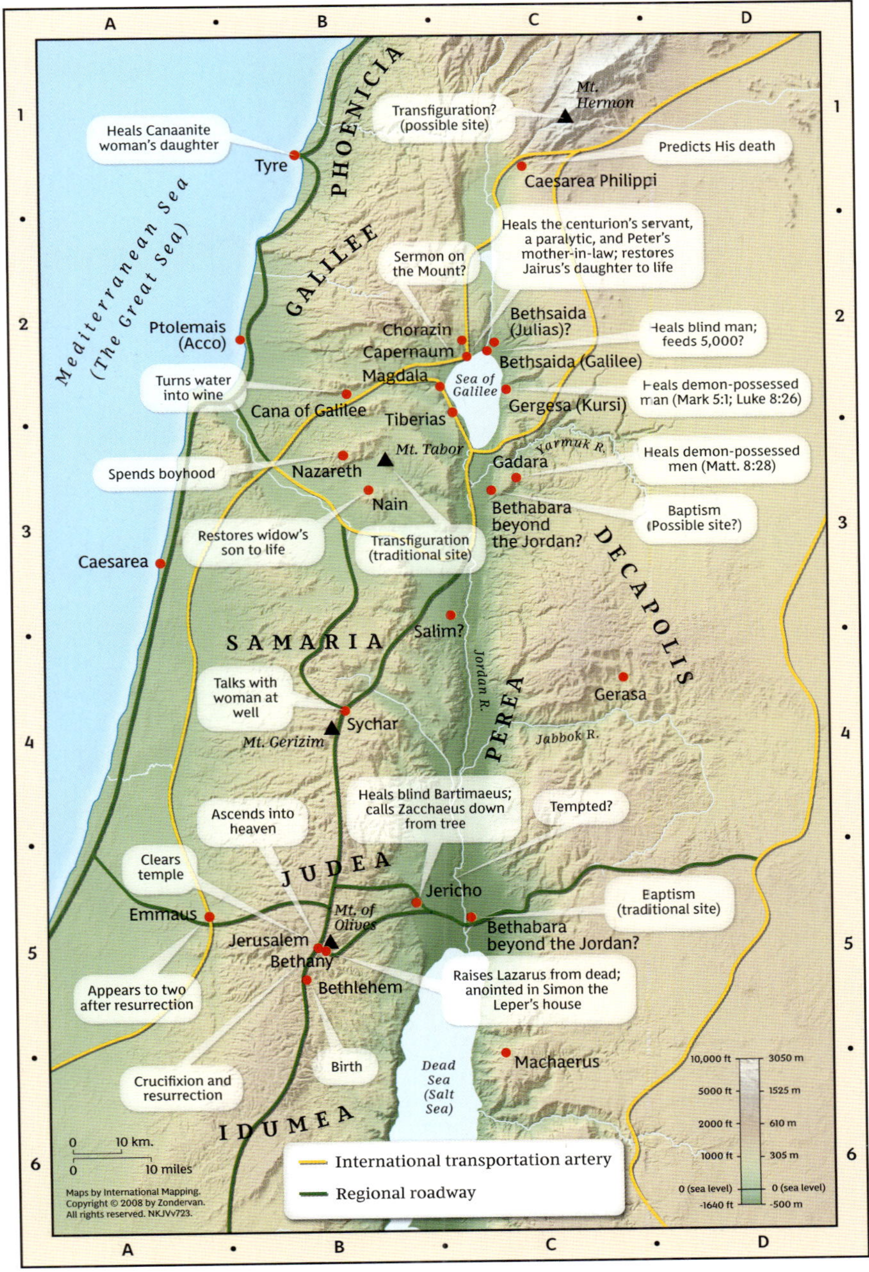

Map 6: PAUL'S MISSIONARY JOURNEYS

DACIA
MOESIA
THRACE
Black Sea
ONIA
Amphipolis
Philippi
Thessalonica
Neapolis
Samothrace
Apollonia?
BITHYNIA & PONTUS
Mt. Olympus
Troas
Assos
Mitylene
Aegean Sea
MYSIA
ASIA
Pergamos
Thyatira
Sardis
GALATIA
CAPPADOCIA
LYCAONIA
Antioch (Pisidian)
Iconium
COMMAGENE
Chios
LYDIA
Smyrna
Ephesus
Samos
Delphi
Athens
Cenchrea
Corinth
Sparta
Philadelphia
PISIDIA
PAMPHYLIA
Laodicea
Colosse
Miletus
Patmos
Lystra
Derbe
CILICIA
Euphrates R.
Tarsus
Issus
SYRIA
LYCIA
Attalia
Cos
Cnidus
Patara
Myra
Perga
Rhodes
Seleucia Pieria
Aleppo
Antioch (Syrian)
Crete
Phoenix
Salmone
Lasea
Claudа
Fair Havens
Cyprus
Salamis
Paphos
ABILENE
PHOENICIA
Sidon
Tyre
Ptolemais
Damascus
Caesarea
JUDEA
Jordan R.
Jerusalem
Dead Sea (Salt Sea)
Mediterranean Sea (The Great Sea)
ARABIA
ENAICA
EGYPT
Nile R.
Red Sea
10,000 ft
3050 m
5000 ft
1525 m
2000 ft
610 m
1000 ft
305 m
(sea level)
0 (sea level)
-1640 ft
-500 m
0
200 km.
0
200 miles
5
6
7
8
A
B
C
D
E
F

Map 7: JERUSALEM IN THE TIME OF JESUS

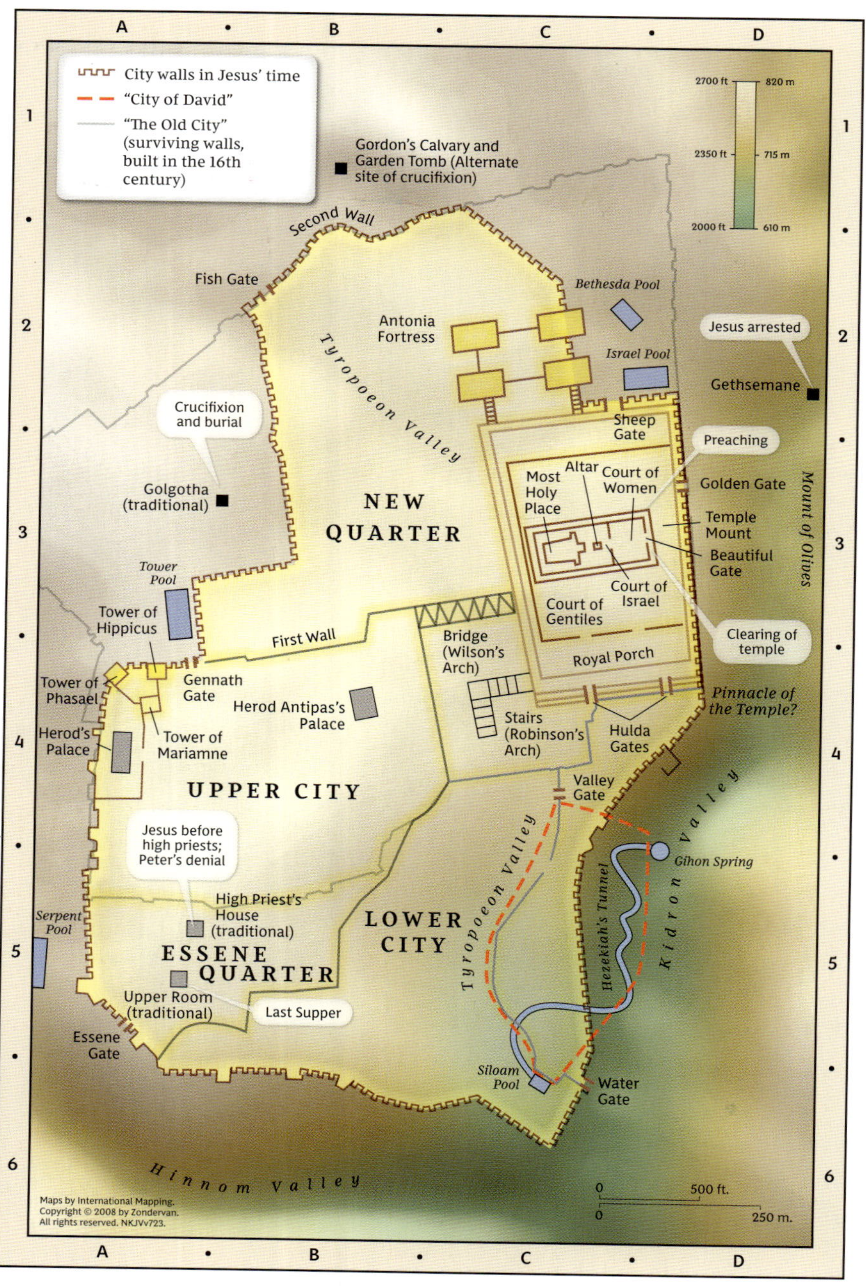